Let's Go writers travel on your budget.

"Guides that penetrate the veneer of the holiday brochures and mine the grit of real life."

—*The Economist*

"The writers seem to have experienced every rooster-packed bus and lunar-surfaced mattress about which they write."

—*The New York Times*

"All the dirt, dirt cheap."

—*People*

Great for independent travelers.

"The guides are aimed not only at young budget travelers but at the independent traveler; a sort of streetwise cookbook for traveling alone."

—*The New York Times*

"Flush with candor and irreverence, chock full of budget travel advice."

—*The Des Moines Register*

"An indispensible resource, *Let's Go*'s practical information can be used by every traveler."

—*The Chattanooga Free Press*

Let's Go is completely revised each year.

"Only *Let's Go* has the zeal to annually update every title on its list."

—*The Boston Globe*

"Unbeatable: good sightseeing advice; up-to-date info on restaurants, hotels, and inns; a commitment to money-saving travel; and a wry style that brightens nearly every page."

—*The Washington Post*

All the important information you need.

"*Let's Go* authors provide a comedic element while still providing concise information and thorough coverage of the country. Anything you need to know about budget traveling is detailed in this book."

—*The Chicago Sun-Times*

"Value-packed, unbeatable, accurate, and comprehensive."

—*Los Angeles Times*

Let's Go Publications

Let's Go: Alaska & the Pacific Northwest 2000
Let's Go: Australia 2000
Let's Go: Austria & Switzerland 2000
Let's Go: Britain & Ireland 2000
Let's Go: California 2000
Let's Go: Central America 2000
Let's Go: China 2000 **New Title!**
Let's Go: Eastern Europe 2000
Let's Go: Europe 2000
Let's Go: France 2000
Let's Go: Germany 2000
Let's Go: Greece 2000
Let's Go: India & Nepal 2000
Let's Go: Ireland 2000
Let's Go: Israel 2000 **New Title!**
Let's Go: Italy 2000
Let's Go: Mexico 2000
Let's Go: Middle East 2000 **New Title!**
Let's Go: New York City 2000
Let's Go: New Zealand 2000
Let's Go: Paris 2000
Let's Go: Perú & Ecuador 2000 **New Title!**
Let's Go: Rome 2000
Let's Go: South Africa 2000
Let's Go: Southeast Asia 2000
Let's Go: Spain & Portugal 2000
Let's Go: Turkey 2000
Let's Go: USA 2000
Let's Go: Washington, D.C. 2000

Let's Go *Map Guides*

Amsterdam
Berlin
Boston
Chicago
Florence
London
Los Angeles
Madrid
New Orleans
New York City
Paris
Prague
Rome
San Francisco
Seattle
Washington, D.C.

Coming Soon: *Sydney* and *Hong Kong*

Moscow Metro
Rechnoy Vokzal
Vodny Stadion
Voykoskaya
Sokol
Aeroport
Dinamo
Yubileynaya
Likhobori
Seligerskaya
Altufevo
Bibirevo
Otradnoye
Vladykino
Petrovsko-Razumovskaya
Chelobitevo
Medvedkovo
Babushkinskaya
Sviblovo
Botanichesky Sad
VDNKh
Alexeevskaya
Rizhskaya
Ulitsa Podbelskovo
Cherkizovskaya
Preobrazhenskaya Ploshchadz
Sokolniki
Krasnoselskaya
Planernaya
Skhodnenskaya
Tushinskaya
Shchukinskaya
Oktyabrskoye Pole
Polezhaevskaya
Begovaya
Ulitsa 1905 goda
Timiryazeskaya
Dmitrovskaya
Savelovskaya
Ostankino
Marina Roshcha
Mitino
Volokolamskoye Shosse
Strogino
Krasnopresnenskaya
Krylatskoye
Molodezhnaya
Kuntsevskaya
Pionerskaya
Filoyvsky Park
Bagrationovskaya
Fili
Kutuzovskaya
Studencheskaya
Mendeleevskaya
Dostoevskaya
Ploshchadz Suvorova
Novoslobodskaya
Belorusskaya
Prospekt Mira
Shchoylkovskaya
Pervomayskaya
Izmaylovskaya
Izmaylovskaya Park
Semenovskaya
Elektrozavodskaya
Baumanskaya
Sukharevskaya
Komsomolskaya
Barrikadnaya
Krasnoprenenskaya
Tsvetnoy Bulvar
Turgenevskaya
Chistiye Prudy
Krasnye Vorota
Sretensky Bulvar
Mayakovskaya
Pushkinskaya
Chekhovskaya
Tverskaya
Lubyanka
Kuznetsky Most
Kurskaya
Chkalovskaya
Kievskaya
Park Pobedy
Smolenskaya
Novogireevo
Perevo
Shosse Entuziastov
Aviamotornaya
Okhotny Ryad
Teatralnaya
Ploshchadz Revolyutsii
Kitay-Gorod
Arbatskaya
Smolenskaya
Alexsandrovsky Sad
Biblioteka im. Lenina
Arbatskaya
Borovitskaya
Ploshchadz Ilicha
Rimskaya
Marxistskaya
Kropotkinskaya
Tretyakovskaya
Novokuznetskaya
Taganskaya
Park Kultury
Polyanka
Frunzenskaya
Krestyanskaya Zastava
Proletarskaya
Paveletskaya
Sportivnaya
Leninskiye Gory
Universitet
Oktyabrskaya
Dobryninskaya
Serpukhovskaya
Volgogradsky Prospekt
Tekstilshchiki
Kuzminki
Ryazansky Prospekt
Avtozavodskaya
Kolomenskaya
Prospekt Vernadskovo
Yugo-Zapadnaya
Tulskaya
Nagatinskaya
Nagornaya
Nakhimovsky Prospekt
Shabolovskaya
Leninsky Prospekt
Akademicheskaya
Profsoyuznaya
Noviye Cheroymushki
Kaluzhskaya
Belyaevo
Konkovo
Toyploy Stan
Yasenevo
Bittsevsky Park
Kashirskaya
Dubrovka
Vykhino
Kozhukhovskaya
Pechatniki
Varshavskaya
Sevastopolskaya
Kakhovskaya
Volzhskaya
Lyublino
Bratislavskaya
Chertanovskaya
Yuzhnaya
Prazhskaya
Kantemiporskaya
Tsaritsyno
Orekhovo
Domodedovskaya
Marino
Brateevo
Rossoshanskaya
Anino
Kachalovo
Krasnogvardeyskaya
Borisovo
Promzona
LEGEND
1 Sokolnicheskaya
2 Zamoskvoretskaya
3 Arbatsko-Pokrovskaya
3a Filoyvskaya
4 Koltsevaya
5 Kaluzhsko-Rizhskaya
6 Taransko-Krasnopresnenskaya
7 Kalininskaya
8 Timiryazevsko-Serpukhovskaya
10 Lyublinskaya
Station
Transfer Station

Moscow

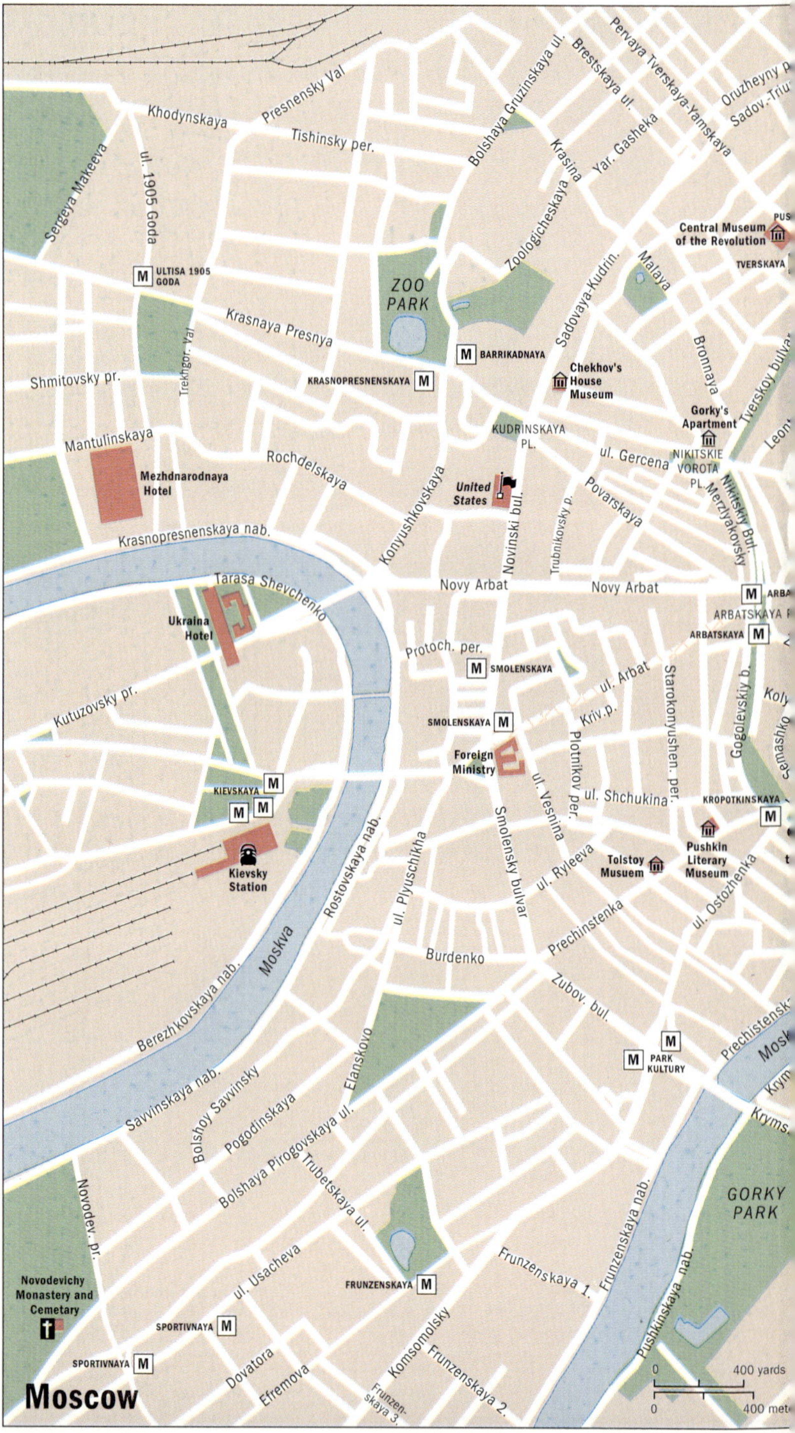
Khodynskaya
Presnensky Val
Tishinsky per.
Bolshaya Gruzinskaya ul.
Brestskaya ul.
Pervaya Tverskaya-Yamskaya
Oruzheyny p
Sadov.-Triu
Sergeya Makeeva
ul. 1905 Goda
Krasina
Yar. Gasheka
Zoologicheskaya
Central Museum of the Revolution
TVERSKAYA
ULTISA 1905 GODA
ZOO PARK
Sadovaya-Kudrin.
Malaya
Krasnaya Presnya
BARRIKADNAYA
Bronnaya
Tverskoy bulvar
Shmitovsky pr.
Trekhgor. Val
KRASNOPRESNENSKAYA
Chekhov's House Museum
Gorky's Apartment
Mantulinskaya
KUDRINSKAYA PL.
ul. Gercena
NIKITSKIE VOROTA PL.
Mezhdnarodnaya Hotel
Rochdelskaya
United States
Povarskaya
Nikitsky Bul.
Merzlyakovsky
Konyushkovskaya
Novinski bul.
Trubnikovsky p.
Krasnopresnenskaya nab.
Tarasa Shevchenko
Novy Arbat
Novy Arbat
ARBATSKAYA
ARBATSKAYA
Ukraina Hotel
Protoch. per.
SMOLENSKAYA
ul. Arbat
Starokonyushen. per.
Gogolevskiy b.
Kutuzovsky pr.
SMOLENSKAYA
Kriv.p.
Plotnikov per.
Foreign Ministry
ul. Vesnina
ul. Shchukina
KIEVSKAYA
KROPOTKINSKAYA
Smolensky bulvar
Rostovskaya nab.
ul. Plyuschikha
ul. Ryleeva
Tolstoy Museum
Pushkin Literary Museum
Kievsky Station
ul. Ostozhenka
Prechinstenka
Moskva
Burdenko
Zubov. bul.
Berezhkovskaya nab.
PARK KULTURY
Prechistensk
Elanskovo
Savvinskaya nab.
Bolshoy Savvinsky
Pogodinskaya
Bolshaya Pirogovskaya ul.
Trubetskaya ul.
Krymsk.
GORKY PARK
Novodev. pr.
Frunzenskaya nab.
Frunzenskaya 1.
ul. Usacheva
FRUNZENSKAYA
Pushkinskaya nab.
Novodevichy Monastery and Cemetary
SPORTIVNAYA
SPORTIVNAYA
Komsomolsky
Frunzenskaya 2.
Dovatora
Efremova
Frunzen-skaya 3.
Moscow
400 yards
400 met

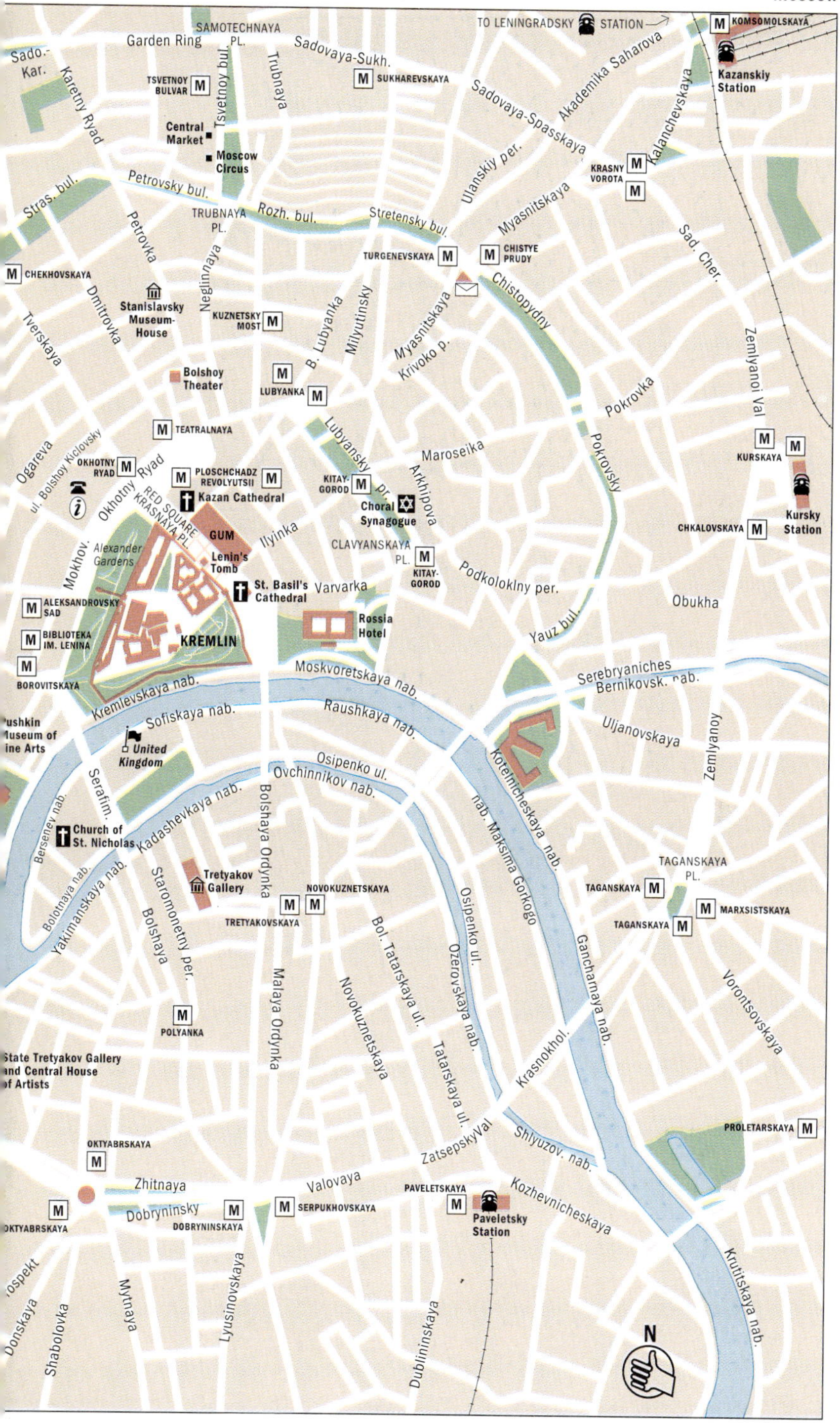
SAMOTECHNAYA PL.
Garden Ring
TO LENINGRADSKY STATION
KOMSOMOLSKAYA
Kazanskiy Station
Sado.-Kar.
Karetny Ryad
Tsvetnoy bul.
Trubnaya
Sadovaya-Sukh.
SUKHAREVSKAYA
TSVETNOY BULVAR
Central Market
Moscow Circus
Sadovaya-Spasskaya
Akademika Saharova
Kalanchevskaya
KRASNY VOROTA
Ulanskiy per.
Petrovsky bul.
Stras. bul.
TRUBNAYA PL.
Rozh. bul.
Stretensky bul.
Myasnitskaya
Petrovka
TURGENEVSKAYA
CHISTYE PRUDY
Sad. Cher.
CHEKHOVSKAYA
Dmitrovka
Stanislavsky Museum-House
Neglinnaya
KUZNETSKY MOST
B. Lubyanka
Milyutinsky
Myasnitskaya
Krivoko p.
Chistopydny
Tverskaya
Bolshoy Theater
LUBYANKA
Zemlyanoi Val
Pokrovka
TEATRALNAYA
Lubyansky pr.
Maroseika
Pokrovsky
KURSKAYA
Ogareva
ul. Bolshoy Kiclovsky
OKHOTNY RYAD
Ryad
PLOSCHCHADZ REVOLYUTSII
KITAY-GOROD
Arkhipova
Kursky Station
Okhotny
RED SQUARE
KRASNAYA PL.
Kazan Cathedral
Choral Synagogue
CHKALOVSKAYA
GUM
Ilyinka
CLAVYANSKAYA PL.
KITAY-GOROD
Mokhov.
Alexander Gardens
Lenin's Tomb
Podkoloklny per.
Obukha
St. Basil's Cathedral
Varvarka
ALEKSANDROVSKY SAD
Rossia Hotel
BIBLIOTEKA IM. LENINA
KREMLIN
Yauz bul.
BOROVITSKAYA
Moskvoretskaya nab.
Serebryaniches
Bernikovsk. nab.
Kremlevskaya nab.
Raushkaya nab.
Pushkin Museum of Fine Arts
Sofiskaya nab.
Uljanovskaya
United Kingdom
Osipenko ul.
Ovchinnikov nab.
Kotelnicheskaya nab.
Zemlyanoy
Serafim.
Bersenev nab.
Church of St. Nicholas
Kadashevkaya nab.
Bolshaya Ordynka
nab. Maksima Gorkogo
TAGANSKAYA PL.
Tretyakov Gallery
TAGANSKAYA
Bolotnaya nab.
Yakimanskaya nab.
Staromonetny per.
NOVOKUZNETSKAYA
TRETYAKOVSKAYA
Osipenko ul.
MARXSISTSKAYA
TAGANSKAYA
Bolshaya
Bol. Tatarskaya ul.
Ozerovskaya nab.
Gancharnaya nab.
Malaya Ordynka
Novokuznetskaya
Vorontsovskaya
POLYANKA
Krasnokhol.
State Tretyakov Gallery and Central House of Artists
Tatarskaya ul.
PROLETARSKAYA
Shlyuzov. nab.
OKTYABRSKAYA
Zatsepsky Val
Zhitnaya
Valovaya
PAVELETSKAYA
Kozhevnicheskaya
Dobryninsky
DOBRYNINSKAYA
SERPUKHOVSKAYA
Paveletsky Station
OKTYABRSKAYA
Prospekt
Lyusinovskaya
Mytnaya
Krutitskaya nab.
Donskaya
Shabolovka
Dubininskaya
N

Московское Метро

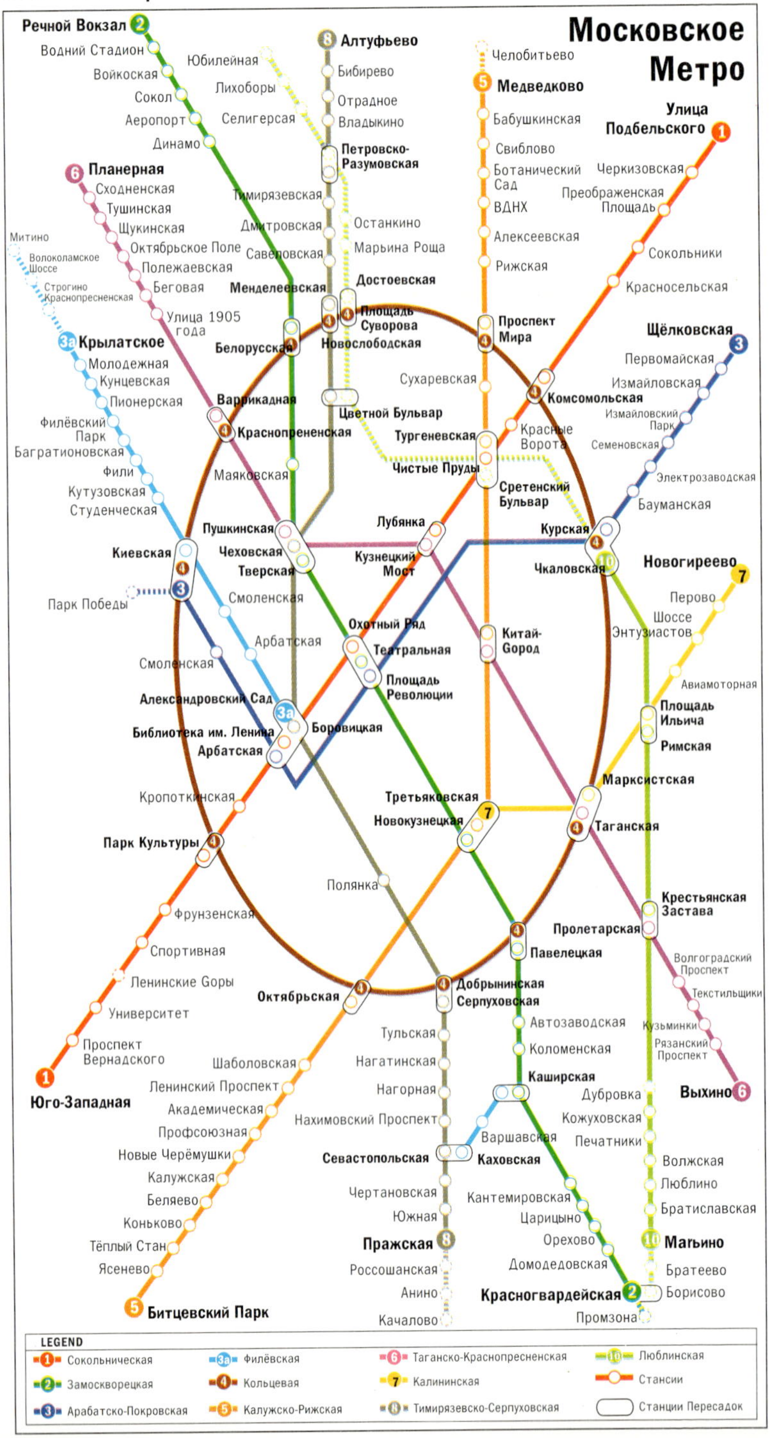

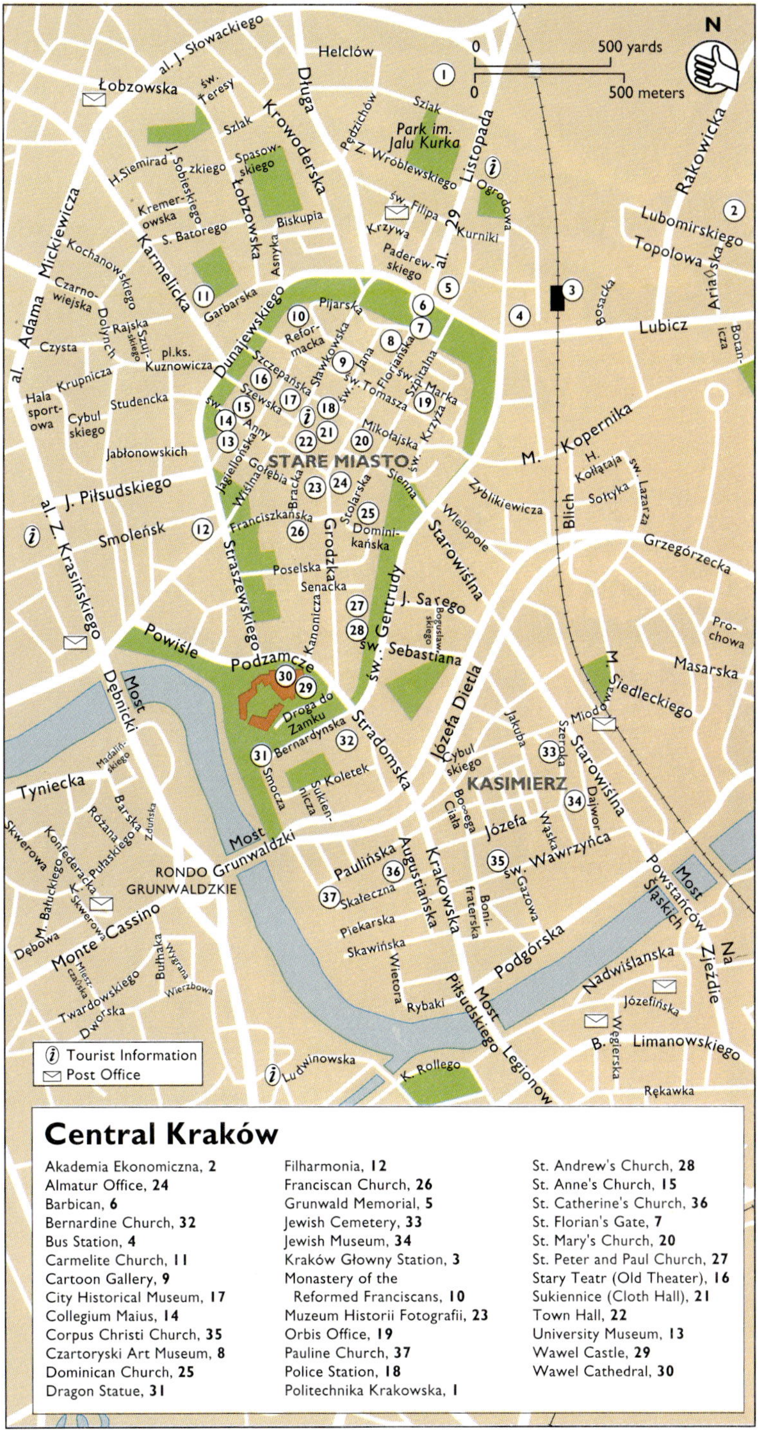

Central Kraków

Akademia Ekonomiczna, **2**
Almatur Office, **24**
Barbican, **6**
Bernardine Church, **32**
Bus Station, **4**
Carmelite Church, **11**
Cartoon Gallery, **9**
City Historical Museum, **17**
Collegium Maius, **14**
Corpus Christi Church, **35**
Czartoryski Art Museum, **8**
Dominican Church, **25**
Dragon Statue, **31**
Filharmonia, **12**
Franciscan Church, **26**
Grunwald Memorial, **5**
Jewish Cemetery, **33**
Jewish Museum, **34**
Kraków Głowny Station, **3**
Monastery of the Reformed Franciscans, **10**
Muzeum Historii Fotografii, **23**
Orbis Office, **19**
Pauline Church, **37**
Police Station, **18**
Politechnika Krakowska, **1**
St. Andrew's Church, **28**
St. Anne's Church, **15**
St. Catherine's Church, **36**
St. Florian's Gate, **7**
St. Mary's Church, **20**
St. Peter and Paul Church, **27**
Stary Teatr (Old Theater), **16**
Sukiennice (Cloth Hall), **21**
Town Hall, **22**
University Museum, **13**
Wawel Castle, **29**
Wawel Cathedral, **30**

Prague

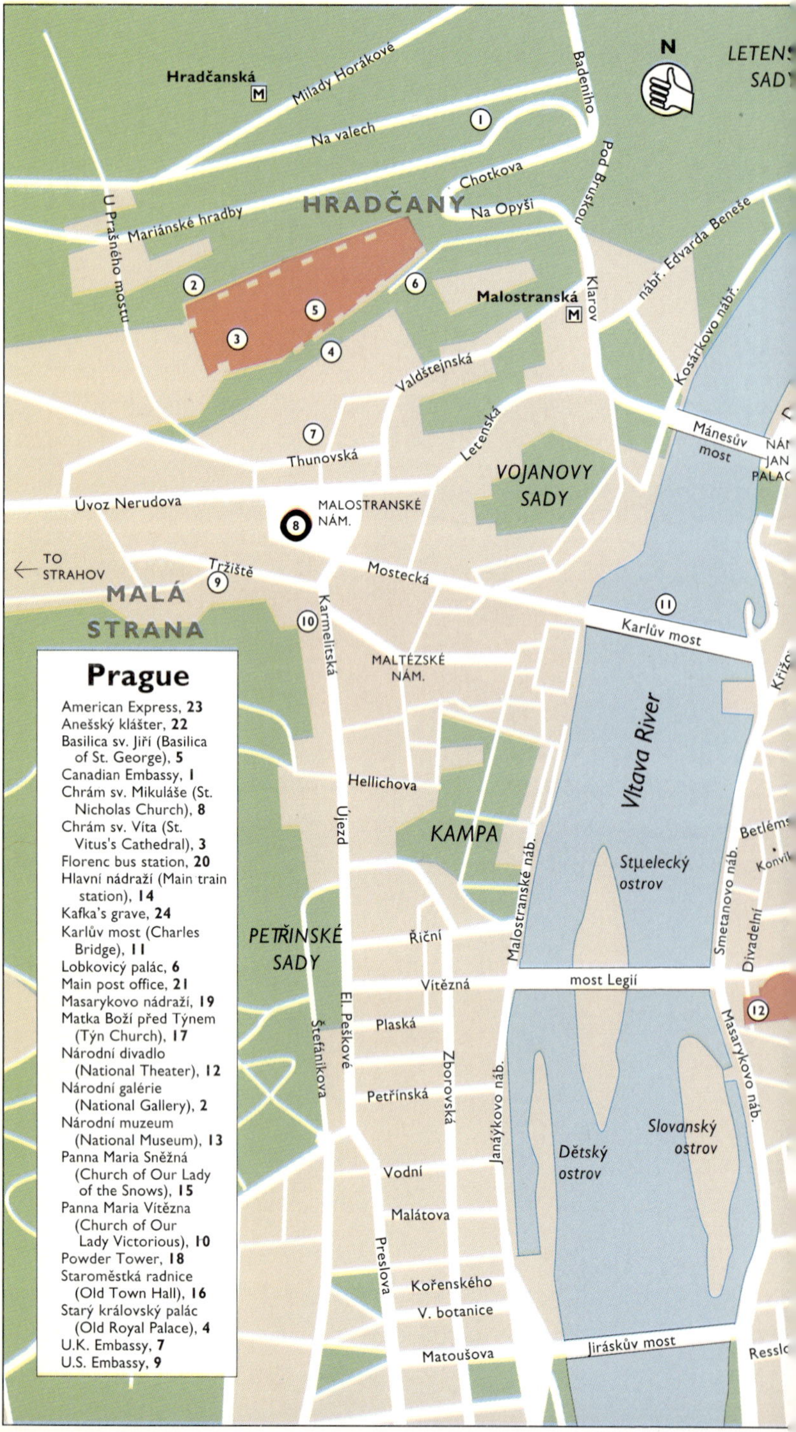
N
LETENS
SADY
Hradčanská
M
Milady Horákové
Na valech
Badeniho
Pod Bruskou
Chotkova
Na Opyši
HRADČANY
Mariánské hradby
U Prašného mostu
Malostranská
M
Klárov
nábř. Edvarda Beneše
Kosárkovo nábř.
Valdštejnská
Letenská
Thunovská
Mánesův most
NÁM
JAN
PALAC
VOJANOVY SADY
Úvoz Nerudova
MALOSTRANSKÉ NÁM.
TO STRAHOV
Tržiště
Mostecká
MALÁ STRANA
Karmelitská
Karlův most
MALTÉZSKÉ NÁM.
Křižo
Vltava River
Hellichova
Újezd
KAMPA
Malostranské nábř.
Střelecký ostrov
Smetanovo nábř.
Betléms
Konvi
Divadelní
PETŘÍNSKÉ SADY
Říční
Vítězná
most Legií
El. Peškové
Štefánikova
Plaská
Zborovská
Janáčkovo nábř.
Masarykovo nábř.
Petřínská
Slovanský ostrov
Dětský ostrov
Vodní
Malátova
Preslova
Kořenského
V. botanice
Matoušova
Jiráskův most
Ressl
Prague
American Express, 23
Anešský klášter, 22
Basilica sv. Jiří (Basilica of St. George), 5
Canadian Embassy, 1
Chrám sv. Mikuláše (St. Nicholas Church), 8
Chrám sv. Víta (St. Vitus's Cathedral), 3
Florenc bus station, 20
Hlavní nádraží (Main train station), 14
Kafka's grave, 24
Karlův most (Charles Bridge), 11
Lobkovicý palác, 6
Main post office, 21
Masarykovo nádraží, 19
Matka Boží před Týnem (Týn Church), 17
Národní divadlo (National Theater), 12
Národní galérie (National Gallery), 2
Národní muzeum (National Museum), 13
Panna Maria Sněžná (Church of Our Lady of the Snows), 15
Panna Maria Vítězna (Church of Our Lady Victorious), 10
Powder Tower, 18
Staroměstká radnice (Old Town Hall), 16
Starý královský palác (Old Royal Palace), 4
U.K. Embassy, 7
U.S. Embassy, 9

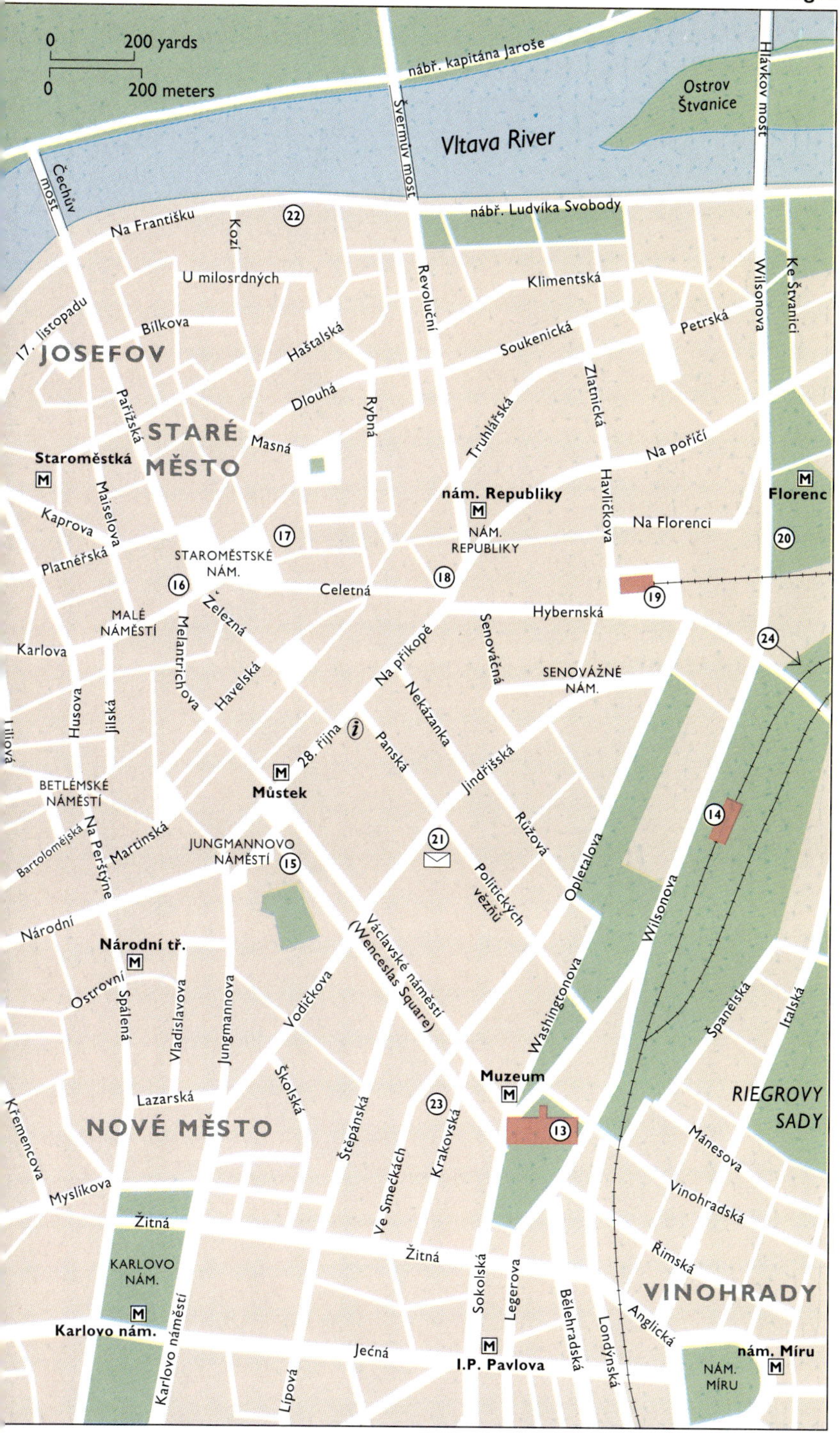
0 200 yards
0 200 meters
Vltava River
nábř. kapitána Jaroše
Ostrov Štvanice
Hlávkov most
Švermův most
Čechův most
nábř. Ludvíka Svobody
Na Františku
Kozí
U milosrdných
17. listopadu
Bílkova
JOSEFOV
Haštalská
Dlouhá
Rybná
Revoluční
Klimentská
Soukenická
Petrská
Wilsonova
Ke Štvanici
Pařížská
STARÉ MĚSTO
Masná
Staroměstská
Maiselova
Kaprova
Platnéřská
Truhlářská
Zlatnická
Na poříčí
nám. Republiky
NÁM. REPUBLIKY
Havlíčkova
Na Florenci
Florenc
STAROMĚSTSKÉ NÁM.
Celetná
Hybernská
MALÉ NÁMĚSTÍ
Železná
Melantrichova
Karlova
Husova
Jilská
Havelská
Na příkopě
Senovážná
SENOVÁŽNÉ NÁM.
Nekázanka
28. října
Panská
Jindřišská
Můstek
BETLÉMSKÉ NÁMĚSTÍ
Bartolomějská
Na Perštýne
Martinská
JUNGMANNOVO NÁMĚSTÍ
Růžová
Opletalova
Politických vězňů
Wilsonova
Národní
Národní tř.
Václavské náměstí (Wenceslas Square)
Ostrovní
Spálená
Vladislavova
Jungmannova
Vodičkova
Washingtonova
Španělská
Italská
Školská
Štěpánská
Krakovská
Muzeum
RIEGROVY SADY
Lazarská
NOVÉ MĚSTO
Křemencova
Myslíkova
Ve Smečkách
Mánesova
Vinohradská
Žitná
KARLOVO NÁM.
Karlovo nám.
Karlovo náměstí
Sokolská
Legerova
Bělehradská
Římská
VINOHRADY
Anglická
Londýnská
Ječná
I.P. Pavlova
Lípová
nám. Míru
NÁM. MÍRU

Central Budapest

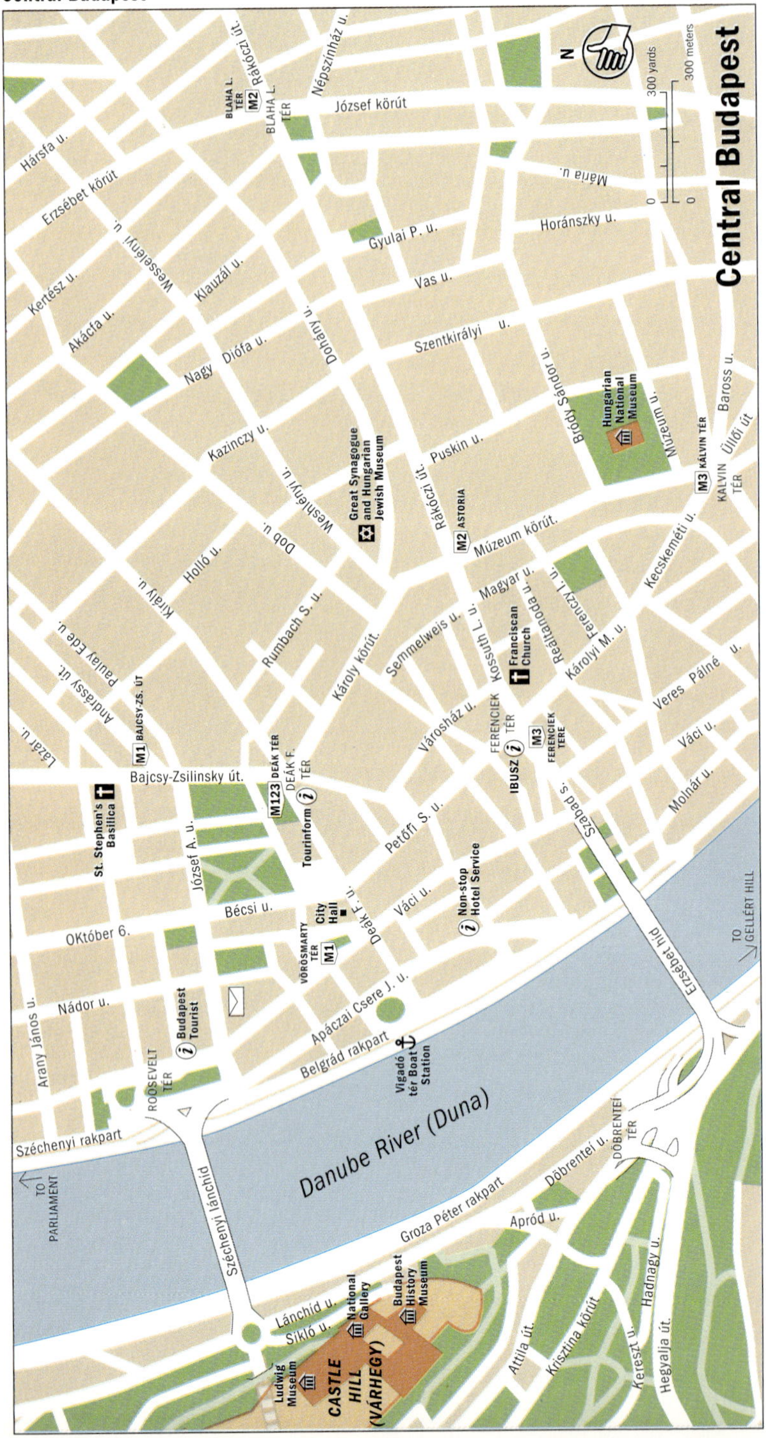
Central Budapest
N
0 300 yards
0 300 meters
Danube River (Duna)
CASTLE HILL (VÁRHEGY)
Ludwig Museum
National Gallery
Budapest History Museum
Hungarian National Museum
Great Synagogue and Hungarian Jewish Museum
St. Stephen's Basilica
Franciscan Church
Vigadó tér Boat Station
Budapest Tourist
Tourinform
IBUSZ
Non-stop Hotel Service
City Hall
TO PARLIAMENT
TO GELLÉRT HILL
ROOSEVELT TÉR
VÖRÖSMARTY TÉR
DEÁK F. TÉR
DEÁK TÉR
FERENCIEK TÉR
FERENCIEK TERE
KÁLVIN TÉR
BLAHA L. TÉR
ASTORIA
BAJCSY-ZS. ÚT
DÖBRENTEI TÉR
M1
M2
M3
M123
Széchenyi lánchíd
Erzsébet híd
Széchenyi rakpart
Belgrád rakpart
Groza Péter rakpart
Lánchíd u.
Sikló u.
Apród u.
Döbrentei u.
Attila út
Krisztina körút
Kereszt u.
Hadnagy u.
Hegyalja út
Arany János u.
Nádor u.
Október 6.
Bécsi u.
József A. u.
Bajcsy-Zsilinsky út
Apáczai Csere J. u.
Váci u.
Deák F. u.
Petőfi S. u.
Városház u.
Szabad s.
Molnár u.
Veres Pálné u.
Károlyi M. u.
Kecskeméti u.
Ferenczy I. u.
Reáltanoda u.
Kossuth L. u.
Magyar u.
Semmelweis u.
Károly körút
Múzeum körút
Múzeum u.
Bródy Sándor u.
Baross u.
Üllői út
Rákóczi út
Puskin u.
Szentkirályi u.
Vas u.
Gyulai P. u.
Horánszky u.
Mária u.
József körút
Népszínház u.
Dohány u.
Wesselényi u.
Dob u.
Rumbach S. u.
Király u.
Holló u.
Kazinczy u.
Nagy Diófa u.
Klauzál u.
Akácfa u.
Kertész u.
Erzsébet körút
Hársfa u.
Paulay Ede u.
Andrássy út
Lázár u.

Let's Go

2000 EASTERN EUROPE

Melissa Gibson
Editor

Angus Burgin
Richard Parr
Associate Editors

Researcher-Writers

Michelle Aitkin
David I. L. Beecher
Michelle Bowman
Rick Burnes
Craig Chosiad
Alicia DeSantis
Andor Meszaros
Dana Scardigli
Sarah Schauss
Gabe Struck
Andrea Volfová
Kate Wagner

Macmillan

HELPING LET'S GO If you want to share your discoveries, suggestions, or corrections, please drop us a line. We read every piece of correspondence, whether a postcard, a 10-page email, or a coconut. Please note that mail received after May 2000 may be too late for the 2001 book, but will be kept for future editions. **Address mail to:**

Let's Go: Eastern Europe
67 Mount Auburn Street
Cambridge, MA 02138
USA

Visit Let's Go at **http://www.letsgo.com,** or send email to:

feedback@letsgo.com
Subject: "Let's Go: Eastern Europe"

In addition to the invaluable travel advice our readers share with us, many are kind enough to offer their services as researchers or editors. Unfortunately, our charter enables us to employ only currently enrolled Harvard students.

Published in Great Britain 2000 by Macmillan, an imprint of Macmillan Publishers Ltd, 25 Eccleston Place, London, SW1W 9NF, Basingstoke and Oxford.
Associated companies throughout the world
www.macmillan.co.uk

Published in the United States of America by St. Martin's Press.

ISBN: 0 333 77981 9
First edition
10 9 8 7 6 5 4 3 2 1

Let's Go: Eastern Europe is written by Let's Go Publications, 67 Mount Auburn Street, Cambridge, MA 02138, USA.

HOW TO USE THIS BOOK

Budget travel does not have to mean sleeping in train stations and living solely on borscht. *Let's Go: Eastern Europe 2000* is a budget guide, but it is not a ghetto guide. Our twelve diligent researchers hauled tail across eighteen countries in summer 1999 with one goal: to find the best and to find it cheap. Day after day, our writers scoured the post-Soviet world searching for greaseless cuisine, soft beds, and stable currencies. For travelers less-than-linguistically-proficient, fear not: the **Glossary** and **Phrasebook** contain the most essential in travel-speak.

If you're unsure about the nuances of pleasing Belarussian border officials, packing for the Dalmatian Coast, or surviving Moscow as a single woman, the **Essentials** chapter at the beginning of the book includes every bit of instruction needed. Both the **History of the Region,** at the beginning of the book, and **Life & Times,** at the beginning of each country, crunch centuries of Eastern European history for your bus-time consumption. After a perusal, you'll be fully prepared to drop names like "Bogdan the One-Eyed" as you order a beer at a Moldovan pub.

Let's Go is not shy. Every city starts with a candid **introduction** telling you why you should or shouldn't visit a town. **Orientation** and **Practical Information** follows, making sure you have all the nitty-gritty you need. Here you'll also find all the transport info you'll need, with smaller attractions spoking off central transport hubs, which list connections to other big cities. Our listings of **Accommodations, Food, Sights,** and **Entertainment** come next, all indicated on our maps or given with directions from a central point. Look for our evaluation of these spots in the writing, but also in their order: the best is always the first you'll read in a section. Many have daytrips listed as **"Near" destinations,** with everything you need to know to get there and back and our candid opinion, from "must-see" to "skip-it-if-you-must."

If a club or hostel is unbeatable, it will be blessed with a nifty little thumb. Whether you're crunched for time, are picky, or just looking to get the hell out of Belarus as quickly as possible, turn head of each chapter for the **highlights** box, which details every country's must-see gems. For our final word on the best of Eastern Europe, **Let's Go Picks** lists the superb superlatives, from Best Journey and Art Collection to the Best Party Atop a Nuclear Reactor.

Even though *Let's Go: Eastern Europe* is filled to the brim with suggestions and opinions, don't be afraid to put the book down or use it to swat at those blood-thirsty Hungarian mosquitoes. After all, the only way we found any of these superb budget finds was to abandon the pavement (except in Bosnia, where all you'll find is landmines) for the cow path, *without* our trusty guide book. Eastern Europe is, after all, a place to discover without the harangue of a guidebook; eccentricities lurk around every corner.

But if all you see around the corner is yet another sausage stand, don't worry. We've scattered the bizarre, the macabre, the intriguing, and the delightful throughout these pages. Beautiful hikes, small mountain villages, and giant busts of Lenin and Frank Zappa await. But don't just rediscover our idiosyncrasies—find your own. Remember the mantra of Yogi Berra: "When you come to a fork in the road, take it."

A NOTE TO OUR READERS The information for this book was gathered by *Let's Go*'s researchers from May through August. Each listing is derived from the assigned researcher's opinion based upon his or her visit at a particular time. The opinions are expressed in a candid and forthright manner. Those traveling at a different time may have different experiences since prices, dates, hours, and conditions are always subject to change. You are urged to check beforehand to avoid inconvenience and surprises. Travel always involves a certain degree of risk, especially in low-cost areas. When traveling, especially on a budget, always take particular care to ensure your safety.

CONTENTS

MAPS

LET'S GO PICKS

MOST COMPELLING REASON TO HEAD EAST: Pilsner Urquell is cheaper than water in **Prague, CZR** (p. 183).

BEST PLACE WHERE NO ONE IS: The **Altai Republic, RUS** (p. 659).

BEST BEDS: Relive summer camp at the **Old Town Hostel,** Vilnius, LIT (p. 369). The **Krumlov House/U vodníka** complex in Český Krumlov, CZR (p. 222) are the best hostels in Eastern Europe. The *gers* at **Gana's Guest House** in Ulaanbaatar, MON (p. 668) might be the best sleep in Asia.

BEST BUSTS: While it might be the biggest in the world, the **bust of Lenin** in Ulan Ude, RUS (p. 665) can't quite compete with the massive steel statue of **Frank Zappa** in Vilnius, LIT (p. 371). Don't visit the Marzipan Museum in Szentendre, HUN (p. 295) on an empty stomach, or you might just be tempted to nibble on the life-size **Michael Jackson.** You can always pay your respects to a **noseless Stalin** at Moscow's (p. 581) graveyard of fallen statues.

BEST MONUMENTS TO FORMER SOVIET GLORY: The ironically-named **Exhibition of Soviet Economic Achievements** in Moscow, RUS (p. 579).

BEST ART COLLECTIONS: The **Hermitage** in St. Petersburg, RUS (p. 608) might have the world's largest art collection, but they've got no Warhol; you'll have to go to the **Ludwig Museum** in Budapest, HUN (p. 287) or the **Museum of Modern Art** in Medzilaborce, SLK (p. 704) to see his work. The **Egon Schiele International Cultural Center** in Český Krumlov, CZR (p. 223) has the monopoly on naked burghers' daughters. While it's not technically a museum, the **outdoor collection of Brancuși sculptures** in Târgu Jiu, ROM (p. 530) is stunning.

BEST BUILDINGS: Sure, they conjure up images of the exotic, Communist East, but hey, the brightly-colored domes of **St. Basil's Cathedral,** in Moscow, RUS (p. 575), are famous for a reason. Ceaucești's **Parliamentary Palace** in Bucharest, ROM (p. 506), nicknamed the Madman's Palace by Romanians, is the third-largest building in the world. The Legoland-like masterpiece that is **Bory Castle,** Székesfehérvár, HUN (p. 312), is a whimsical playland for the young at heart. **The Dancing House** in Prague, CZR (p. 196) is Frank Gehry's Eastern European Bilbao Guggenheim.

BEST JOURNEY: The **Trans-Siberian Railroad** (p. 655). Clearly.

MOST TERRIFYING SIGHTS IN EASTERN EUROPE: The storied waters of Croatia and Lake Baikal: beware Croatia's **fearsome aquatic hedgehogs** (p. 166) and the **nefarious siberian weasels** in Russia (p. 664). The ossuary at **Kutná Hora, CZR** (p. 210). **Dracula's Castle** in Curtea de Argeș, ROM (p. 518). **Jo's American Bar and Garáž** in Prague, CZR (p. 207).

BEST PLACE TO FORGET YOU'RE IN EUROPE: **Lake Baikal, RUS** (p. 664). It's in Asia.

BEST WAY TO INDULGE: Take a bath at the **Gellért** in Budapest, HUN (p. 290) or at a **banya** in Moscow, RUS (p. 586). Soak in a **mud bath** in Pärnu, EST (p. 248). Get a **therapeutic massage** in Karlovy Vary, CZR (p. 215).

BEST PARTIES ON TOP OF NUCLEAR REACTORS: The month-long rave in **Kazantip, UKR** (p. 753). If only Chernobyl hosted parties.

BEST MEALS THAT INCLUDE NEITHER SAUSAGE NOR SAUERKRAUT: **Smažený sýr** from a vendor on Václavské nám. or a **salad** from Universal, both in Prague, CZR (p. 193). **Mutter Paneer** from Restaurant India in Brest, BEL (p. 77). **Georgian fare** from Mama Zoya's in Moscow, RUS (p. 570).

RESEARCHER-WRITERS

Michelle Aitken *Małopolska, Slovakia*

From her first wild night in Bratislava, this fiery Kiwi took Central Europe by storm. With hiking boots on and *Diamond of Desire* in hand, Michelle revolutionized the Tatras. Whether it be by foot, raft, or hang-glider, she ensured that even the highest *chaty* and most treacherous trails were thoroughly covered for other intrepid trekkers. Just when we had her pegged for a mountain goat, she morphed into Urban Girl, storming the streets of Kraków with a pack of friends in tow. She sampled every *Żywiec* in the city, endured Polish customs, and even found time to dog-ear a few pages for us. Michelle would like to thank Suzan for "research."

David Beecher *Estonia, Latvia, Lithuania*

Nothing could stop this Baltic tiger. Not a stolen wallet, not baffling Baltic girls, not even the slipperiness of Rīga could get in the way of David's daily deconstructions of the Baltic psyche. His illustrations drew gasps from the office, and his pages of exceptional descriptions (who else could convincingly describe Rīga as a "lopsided American football?") ensured that we knew exactly what every square inch of the Baltics looked, felt, and tasted like. David elaborately revamped his countries in a way only the true iron wolf of researchers could.

Michelle Bowman *Bulgaria, Moldova*

Who knew Michelle would love Moldova? Only this hard-core goddess could've conquered Chişinău. Faced with one of the most difficult itineraries in the series, Michelle was stoic at the start and glowing at the end. In situations where other RWs would have complained or given up, Michelle always thanked us for the opportunity, and always knew that the Black Sea was waiting at the end. Sending back heaps of meticulous and thoughtful research (and Spice Girl gum), cheerful Michelle was our shining star.

Rick Burnes *Belarus, Western Ukraine, Trans-Siberian*

Rick almost got us excited about Belarus. Almost. Like the budding Muscovite journalist that he is, our intrepid reporter got us the scoop wherever he went, whether it be a scandalous transliteration of Kiev (Kyiv!), the trick to bribing border guards, or the secret that Ulaanbaatar—not Vilnius—is the "New Prague." Always diligent and always witty, we wished we could've talked to Rick more often; alas, he was off traversing seven time zones and practicing his Russian en route to Beijing. The Altai and Baikal are infinitely easier to visit, thanks to Rick.

Craig Chosiad *Romania*

Stalked by Romanian indigestion, plagued by pick-pocketing bus neighbors, and attacked by rabid dogs, Craig and danger were never far apart. The 007 of RWs, black-overcoated Craig fearlessly scouted out new cinemas, museums, and disease-infested coastal spots, then provided us with the most extensive explanations and reviews we'd seen all summer (not to mention the *best* map edit of Bucharest). By the end of his itinerary, he was sharing with us his secret-agent methods for fending off the dogs ("Just look at it and growl"), and meeting enough crazy people to keep him occupied for years. Even in California.

Alicia DeSantis *Hungary, Bosnia*

We love Alicia. We love her meticulous fact-checking and her sparkling prose (oh, the endless word-choices) and her frequent and entertaining phone calls. We love her miraculous over-haul of Budapest and her eye for historical detail. We love her appreciation for kitsch—especially of the Lake Balaton variety—and her perseverance in the face of blood-thirsty mosquitoes. We love that even after a Hungarian flasher, a stolen backpack, and a night spent sleeping in the pouring rain, she still trekked on, giggling the whole way. And just when we thought she couldn't get any better, she perfected Bosnia. Did we mention that we love Alicia?

Andor Meszaros *Kaliningrad, Poland*
Our Magyar Odysseus traveled all the way to Hel and back, and kept us laughing the whole way. Fending off swarms of Poles coveting his John Paul II phone card, steering travelers away from the thinnest of hostel mattresses, and exposing the nation's inexplicable fondness for Vietnamese food, Andor wielded his incisive, sarcastic powers on all things Polish. Even when God's love prevented beer drinking and Kaliningrad seemed utterly unconquerable, this researching warrior always remained thorough, excited, and witty.

Dana Scardigli *Czech Republic, Southwestern Poland*
Glamour-girl Dana *loved* the Czech Republic. Quickly getting through the formalities, Dana found a way to make even the smallest of towns exciting. She convinced us that Český Krumlov still is romantic and that after a few glasses of absinthe, even Prague's Lávka is fun. With video-camera in hand, she studied the *sgraffito* of Telč and revolutionized Prague's late-night scene, befriending everyone from Croatian movie stars to short Canadians along the way. She even instituted an innovative new ranking system; if only *we* could see her lip-synching routine.

Sarah Schauss *Karelia, Narva, Helsinki*
Seeking out Same north of the Arctic Circle and roachless rooms near St. Petersburg, Sarah managed to entertain herself—and us—wherever she went. Armed with nothing but patience and a personal bodyguard, she braved an overnight ride on a mailbus, the butt-numbing seats of Russian trains, and the *very* cold North (it is the Arctic Circle, after all). Through it all, she speedily delivered endless facts, found consistency in the land of post-Soviet chaos, and helped us to perfect our pronunciations of Finnish glottal stops (thanks, Mik*ko).

Gabe Struck *Caucasus, Crimea, Odessa, Volga Region*
We knew Gabe had a commando complex when we sent him off to the wilds of Southern Russia; little did we know, however, that neither run-ins with Chechnyan ruffians nor a badly twisted ankle could keep him from conquering the mighty Caucasus. By the time we finally heard from him, he'd already uncovered the nuclear party of Kazantip, spear-fishing near Yalta, and the mighty powers of *kvas*. More than anyone else, Gabe infused his chapters with endless adventure. We're just grateful he didn't try to research Dagestan.

Andrea Volfová *Croatia, Slovenia*
We sent Andrea off a Czech...and we got back a Croatian. After only one day in the capital, Andrea was dazzling the *Zagrebčani*, sneaking into local soirées, finagling tours of the city's cafes, and scoring a few marriage proposals. While she befriended everyone from Zagreb's club-kids to Kali's fisherman, Andrea not only gave us the insider's scoop on Croatian life but also updated every errant phone number, mislabeled address, and awry direction in the book. Her divine researching morphed skeletal Dalmatian coverage into the most extensive island-hopping itinerary outside Greece, infecting us with Croatian love-sickness along the way.

Kate Wagner *Moscow, St. Petersburg*
Making friends wherever she went, writing more about Russian art than we could read in a summer, and skillfully dodging the perils of Moscow nightlife, Kate was our urban warrior extraordinare. Her adventures took her from the yummiest Georgian food and salads in Moscow to the marvels of the Hermitage, stopping at all the Russian palaces and kremlined small towns in between. In the face of a sweltering Moscow summer, impossible Russian immigration officers, and copywriting while trapped in the bureaucratic black-hole of Belarus, Kate remained our unflappable, appropriately Eurotrashy, researching *tsarina*.

ACKNOWLEDGMENTS

Endless thanks to our stellar R-Ws for diligent fact-checking and tolerating the absurdity of EEUR; this book is yours. Only a little bit of Monica (and that *Diamond of Desire*) could have kept us going. Thanks to Taya for superhuman speed and wit; Ben H. for enduring the insanity; Team EUR for 3:47am laughs; Andrea for post-Croatian emergency relief; Marshall for braving nightlife; Melissa&Matt, design gurus; Map Master Lusk; Elena, editorial goddess; Christian for the damn song; Adam, Kaya, Anna, Jody, Meredith, Esti, and Lindie for making the last minute a little less painless; and all our proofers for minding our Ps&Qs, even in Cyrillic.

MELISSA THANKS: *Děkují moc* to Angus & Rich: your endurance and patience made this book. Contented sighs for 60Banks, despite the fruit flies: Alice & Peter for having fun; Olivia for late-night lamenting; Jay for velar fricatives, endless porch-sitting, and a great adventure. Hugs to Becca & Heather for transcontinental sanity, and to Jenny, Bonnie, & Lynsay for worry&food&support. Love to Mom&Jenn&Pop&Gram for forgiving my familial delinquencies. I promise to come home soon...right after Praha.

ANGUS THANKS: Rich, let's do Poznań sometime; I think we've earned it. And Melissa, thank you for always trusting us to do good work, and for always setting the example, and for the nights when you'd laugh like a crazy woman, which were the best. Sarah, Kate, and Jessica, don't you wish the summer never ended? You'll be a decent backup band. Pete, Mom, Dad, the love copy, L.L.P. Jane, and of course Jody for this summer, even if there never was a beach.

RICH THANKS: Melissa, for hiring me and astounding me every day. Angus, Poznań sounds dandy. The family, for putting me up and putting up with me. The Hubbles for showing me Big Sky. Luskin, for the maps and the tunes. Team Europe, for commiserating, entertaining, and inspiring. Jody for keeping Angus in line. Elena for mad proofing, and for the futon. Most important, thank you Joanie for wishes made on first Montana stars.

NORWAY
Oslo
Dal R.
Lake Vanern
Stockholm
Aland Island
FINLAND
Helsinki
Vyborg
Lake Ladoga
St. Petersburg
Tallinn
Novgorod
Lake Peipus
SWEDEN
ESTONIA
Pärnu
Tartu
Skagerrak
Kattegat
Lake Vattern
Gulf of Riga
Pskov
Alborg
Göteborg
Ventspils
Gotland Island
Rīga
Öland
Jelgava
LATVIA
Copenhagen
DENMARK
Malmö
Baltic Sea
LITHUANIA
Polatsk
Niemen R.
Kaunas
Kaliningrad
RUS.
Vilnius
Minsk
Sopot
Gdańsk
Mahileu
Elbe R.
Hamburg
Olsztyn
Hrodna
BELARUS
Szczecin
Białystok
Weser R.
Berlin
Baranavichy
Zhlobin
Toruń
Warta R.
Vistula R.
Luninets
Pripyat R.
Poznań
Frankfurt
Oder R.
POLAND
Warsaw
Brest
Łódź
Leipzig
Dresden
Wrocław
Kovel
Sarny
Korosten
Lublin
GERMANY
Rovno
Prague
Kraków
Przemyśl
Plžen
CARPATHIAN MOUNTAINS
Lviv
CZECH REP.
Bug R.
Danube R.
Brno
SLOVAKIA
Munich
Inn R.
Vienna
Bratislava
Balta
Salzburg
Mukacheve
Pruth R.
Tisza R.
Budapest
AUSTRIA
Satu Mare
MOLDOVA
Graz
HUNGARY
Cluj-Napoca
Chişinău
Oradea
ALPS
Lake Balaton
Bacau
ROMANIA
Szeged
Drave R.
SLOVENIA
Ljubljana
Pécs
Sighişoara
Venice
Trieste
Zagreb
Timişoara
TRANSYLVANIAN ALPS
Po R.
Braşov
Tulcea
Pula
Rijeka
Save R.
Buzău
CROATIA
BOSNIA-HERZEGOVINA
Belgrade
Tirgu Jiu
Bucharest
Constanţa
Morava R.
Zádar
Zenica
Sarajevo
Craiova
Danube R.
Ruse
Split
YUGO-SLAVIA
BALKAN MTS.
Mostar
Nis
Varna
Elbe
Tiber R.
BULGARIA
Pec
Sofia
Burgas
Dubrovnik
Stara Zagora
Rome
Shkodër
Plovdiv
Malko Turnovo
Skopje
ITALY
Tirana
F.Y.R. MACEDONIA
Durrës
ALBANIA
Naples
Thessaloniki
Korcë
Gjirokastër
GREECE
Aegean Sea

NORTH RUSSIAN PLAIN
Vologda
0
200 miles
0
200 kilometers
Izhevsk
N
Volga R.
Kazan
Yaroslavl
Nizhny Novgorod
Volga R.
Vladimir
Simbirsk
Tolyatti
Samara
Moscow
Ryazan
Penza
Tula
Smolensk
RUSSIA
Volsk
Saratov
Bryansk
Voronezh
Homel
Povorino
Kursk
KAZAKH-STAN
Konotop
Chernobyl
Volgograd
Kiev
Kharkiv
Donets R.
Volga R.
CASPIAN DEPRESSION
Dnipro R.
Don R.
Smila
Dnipropetrovsk
Astrakhan
UKRAINE
Donetsk
Rostov-na-Donu
Zaporizhya
Krivy Rih
Azov
Mariupol
CASPIAN SEA
Nikolayiv
Primorsko Akhtarsk
Sea of Azov
Odessa
Stavropol
Kerch
Yekaterinodar
Grozny
CRIMEA
CAUCASUS MOUNTAINS
Sevastopol
Simferopol
Tuapse
Yalta
Sochi
GEORGIA
BLACK SEA
Tbilisi
Batum
ARMENIA
Sinop
Yerevan
Istanbul
AZERBAIJAN
Ankara
Kizilirmak R.
Bursa
TURKEY
Eastern Europe

NORWAY
Oslo
FINLAND
Helsinki
Åland Island
Vyborg
St. Petersburg
Lake Ladoga
Stockholm
SWEDEN
Tallinn
ESTONIA
Tartu
Novgorod
Pärnu
Skagerrak
Kattegat
Göteborg
Alborg
Gulf of Rīga
Pskov
Ventspils
Gotland Island
Rīga
Öland
Liepaja
Jelgava
LATVIA
Copenhagen
Malmö
DENMARK
Baltic Sea
LITHUANIA
Polatsk
Kaunas
Kaliningrad
(RUS.)
Vilnius
Minsk
Mahileu
Sopot
Gdańsk
Olsztyn
Hamburg
Hrodna
BELARUS
Szczecin
Białystok
Berlin
Baranavichy
Zhlobin
Toruń
Poznań
Warsaw
Luninets
Frankfurt
POLAND
Brest
Łódź
Leipzig
Dresden
Wrocław
Kovel
Sarny
Lublin
Korosten
GERMANY
Rovno
Prague
Kraków
Plzeň
CZECH REP.
Przemyśl
Lviv
Brno
SLOVAKIA
Vienna
Bratislava
Uzhgorod
(Mukacheve)
Munich
Salzburg
Budapest
Satu Mare
AUSTRIA
MOLDOVA
HUNGARY
Chişinău
Graz
Cluj-Napoca
Oradea
Bacău
ROMANIA
SLOVENIA
Ljubljana
Szeged
Venice
Pécs
Sighişoara
Trieste
Zagreb
Tulcea
Braşov
Timişoara
Pula
Rijeka
Buzău
Belgrade
CROATIA
BOSNIA-HERZEGOVINA
Bucharest
Zenica
Constanta
Zádar
Sarajevo
Craiova
Ruse
Split
YUGO-SLAVIA
Varna
Nis
Pec
BULGARIA
Sofia
Burgas
Dubrovnik
Stara Zagora
Plovdiv
Malko Turnovo
Shkodër
Skopje
Rome
ITALY
Tirana
F.Y.R. MACEDONIA
Durrës
ALBANIA
Thessaloniki
Naples
Korcë
N
0
200 miles
Gjirokastër
0
200 kilometers
GREECE
Aegean Sea

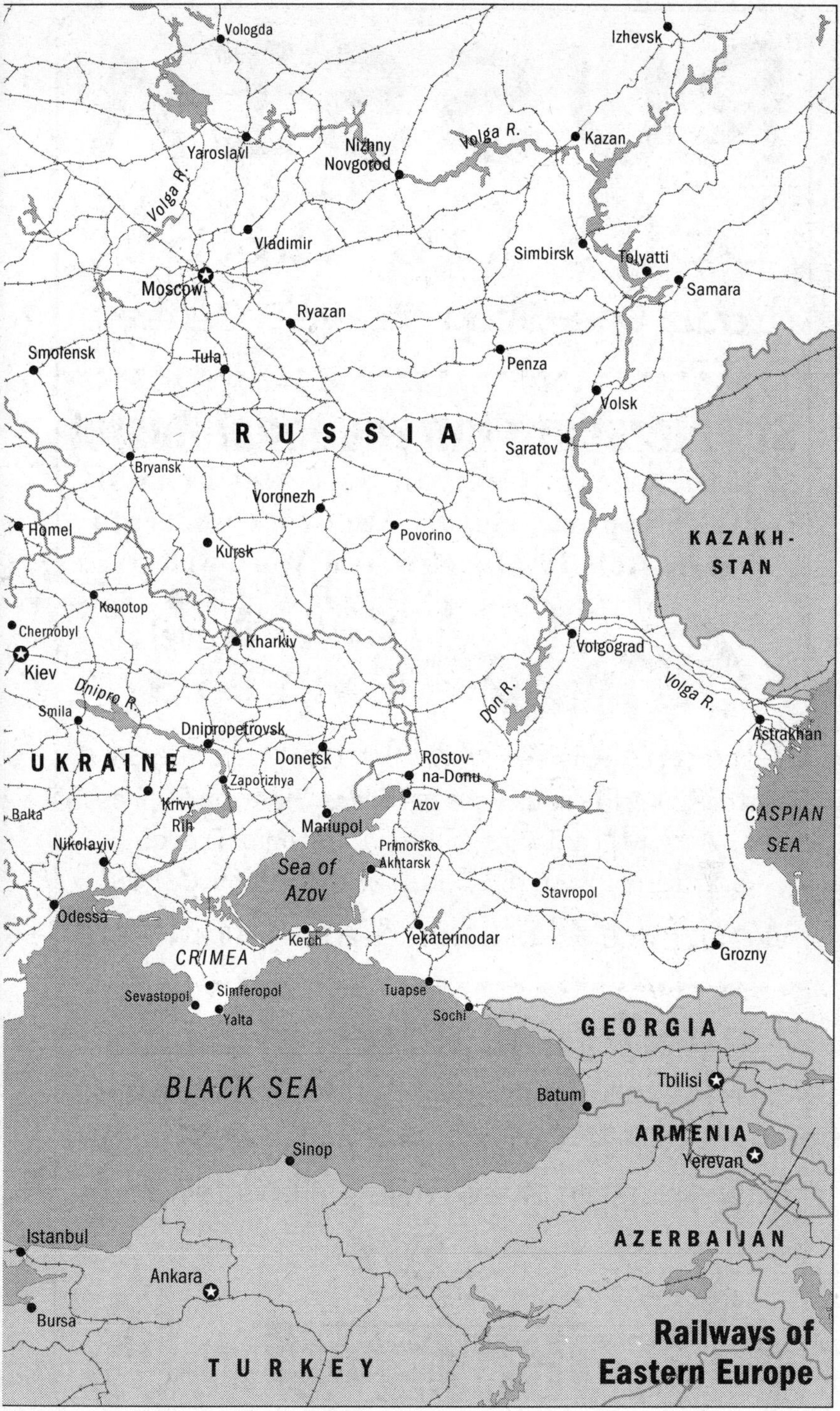

Railways of Eastern Europe

DISCOVER EASTERN EUROPE

Nearly a decade after the fall of the Iron Curtain, Eastern Europe has become the darling of budget travelers. Undiscovered cities, pristine national parks, open hostel beds, and ridiculously cheap beer are steadily luring in adventure-, culture-, and bargain-seekers. From hip, urban centers like Prague, St. Petersburg, and Budapest to the peaks of the Tatras and Caucasus, from the karst-covered shores of the Dalmatian Coast to the expanses of barren Siberia, the myriad wonders of Eastern Europe sprawl across 16 countries and two continents. While distances are great and transport connections unpredictable, it's all part of the Eastern European adventure. After all, where else in the world can a single train take you across seven time zones? Where else is a bottle of vodka a more effective visa than the visa itself? Where else is the most reliable transportation a weekly mail bus or, better yet, a yak? In the face of such dilapidated bureacracy, the most important thing to bring is flexibility; go ahead and make plans, but always be ready to scrap them.

Part of the unpredictability of the region is, of course, due to political and economic restructuring. You'll inevitably encounter frustrating delays, astronomical inflation, and mind-boggling bureaucracy. When the absurdity of the post-Soviet world is about to get you down, take a deep breath and know that for every stony border guard and badgering *babushka* (grandmotherly old women common throughout the region), there are countless locals willing to give you a bed, a shot of homemade liquor, and a ride to the next town. With a little patience and a lot of perseverence, you'll have an utterly rewarding jaunt through one of the most geographically varied, historically interesting, and culturally rich areas of the world.

THE GREAT OUTDOORS

Leave the urban bustle behind to explore the endless wonders of the Eastern European wilderness. From the rolling hills of the West to the wild expanses of Siberia, the untamed corners of Eastern Europe are a thrill-seeker's Eden. The seven-day **Trail of Eagles' Nests** (p. 454) treks through the heart of Poland's green uplands past limestone eruptions and castle ruins. Head to the **High Tatras** (p. 441, p. 693) for jagged peaks, Olympic-quality skiing, and heart-stopping hang-gliding. With Mt. Elbrus, the highest peak in Europe, at its center, the **Caucasus** (p. 646) are the kings of European mountains and boast Eastern Europe's most treacherous and rewarding hikes. Truly isolated adventure awaits along the **Trans-Siberian Railroad** (p. 655). After passing through standard Soviet cities, venture off the train-beaten-tracks to reach the **Altai Republic** (p. 659), a devastatingly beautiful, mountainous desert—with no roads and only camels to guide you—on the Mongolian border. A few more days on the train brings you to **Lake Baikal** (p. 664), the deepest, oldest, and largest freshwater lake on earth and a playground for hunters and trekkers. Other wonderlands of outdoor adventure include: **Mazury** (p. 493); **Julian Alps** (p. 719); **Southern Bohemia** (p. 217); **Białystok National Park** (p. 497); **Transylvanian Alps** (p. 527); **Lahemaa National Reserve** (p. 246); **Plitvice Lakes National Park** (p. 158); **Mljet National Park** (p. 173); and **Woliński National Park** (p. 478).

BEACH BUMMING

Most travelers don't come to Eastern Europe for its beaches, but they should: the region boasts enough surf and sand to accommodate months of lounging and sunning, provided those months are in summer. The indisputable star of the Mediterranean is Croatia's fabled **Dalmatian Coast** (p. 156). From the karst-lined cliffs near Dubrovnik to the isolated beaches of **Hvar** (p. 165) and **Vis** (p. 164), the azure waters of the Adriatic lap at the feet of this coastal god. Spear-fishing and rock-climbing are only a few of the diversions in **Crimea** (p. 750), the beauty of the Black Sea. For more relaxed Crimean days, lounge with wealthy Russians on the pebbled beaches around **Yalta** (p. 756) or dive into the dark depths near **Gurzuf** (p. 759) for warm-water frolicking. Chillier waters await to the north in the Baltic Sea, where you can bike for days along the deserted roads of the **Estonian Islands** (p. 251) to reach equally deserted beaches. Isolated from the outside world by 50 years of Soviet rule, the pristine archipelago shelters wind-swept look-outs, sandy shores, and the occasional Soviet base. If you can't make it to the coast, Hungary has the answer: **Lake Balaton** (p. 309) is like a slice of sea in the middle of the Hungarian plain, complete with tanned masses, endless water sports, and tacky discos. It's fun, we swear. You can also play Beach Blanket Bingo at: the **Romanian** (p. 545), **Bulgarian** (p. 120), and **Russian** (p. 651) **Black Sea Coasts;** on the Baltic near **Świnoujscie** (p. 477) and the **Tri-City Area** (p. 479); and along the Curonian Spit near **Kaliningrad** (p. 632) and **Klaipėda** (p. 383).

THE LEGACY OF THE 20TH CENTURY

While most of the region is successfully rebuilding after the fall of communism, the region can't quite shake off the devastating legacy of the past century. Certainly not the most uplifting of the region's highlights, the towns memorializing events of the past 100 years are some of the most powerful in Eastern Europe. The Resistance movement of Nazi-occupied **Odessa** (p. 761) hid itself underground during WWII; their headquarters are now one of Europe's most stirring war memorials. The bloodiest battle in WWII was fought in **Volgograd** (p. 761); the entire city now stands as a monument to the fallen, watched over by the immense Motherland statue. The most sobering memorials, however, are undoubtedly the numerous concentration camps; **Auschwitz-Birkenau** (p. 429) was the largest and most infamous of the Nazi death camps and today houses a sobering museum on the Holocaust. After total destruction by German bombers in WWII, re-constructed **Warsaw** (p. 402) is a testament to the region's admirable ability to regroup and rebuild, even in the face of utter ruin. **Sarajevo** (p. 85), however, is still ravaged by landmines and ethnic tensions from the recent war with Serbia, and is struggling to unravel itself from Balkan violence in order to enter the 21st century as a new city. Other cities of historical significance include: **Brest** (p. 76); **Livadia** (p. 760); **Gdańsk** (p. 480); **Cēsis** (p. 358); **Vis** (p. 164); **Schlisselburg** (p. 620); **Majdanek** (p. 435); **Terezín** (p. 209); **Sztutowo** (p. 486); **Paneriai** (p. 370); **Kaunas** (p. 375); **Dārziņi** (p. 354); **Bucharest** (p. 506); **Zadar** (p. 157); **Kaliningrad** (p. 632); and **Moscow** (p. 561).

ALCOHOLIC DELIGHTS

Mmm...beer. And vodka. Absinthe. Plum brandy. Kvas. Even wine. Eastern Europe is perhaps most loved for its endless shelves of locally produced, throat-burning liquors. Don't limit yourself to imported, far-away versions; drink these magic liquids straight from the source. The world's best hops are in the Czech Republic: the world-famous **Pilsner Urquell** is produced in **Plzeň** (p. 211) while **České Budějovice** (p. 217) brews the delectable **Budvar** (namesake of American Budweiser). The best beer in the Czech Republic, **Krušovice,** is produced right in **Prague** (p. 183); enjoy it alonside a fiery glass of **absinthe.** While it pales next to the Czechs, the Polish **Żywiec** is concocted just south of **Bielsko-Biała** (p. 447). The Ukrainian version of beer, **kvas** is sold from barrels on the streets of **Kiev** (p. 737), even in pouring rain. In **Karlovy Vary** (p. 215), imbibe on **Becherovka,** an herb liquor purported to have "curative powers." For good **vodka,** head anywhere in **Russia** (p. 550). Better yet, head to the **Latvian/Estonian** (p. 342) or **Belarussian/Polish borders** (p. 72) where vodka smuggling makes for very cheap inebriation. Hungary has the monopoly on Eastern Europe's potable wines: don't miss **Bull's Blood** in **Eger** (p. 332), **Aszú** vintages in **Tokaj** (p. 338), and the Balaton-flavored wines of **Badascony** (p. 316). The wines of twin cities **Mělník, Czech Republic** (p. 210) and **Melnik, Bulgaria** (p. 115) are so good, Churchill had them shipped to England, even during WWII.

COME FOR A WEEK, STAY FOR A YEAR

You've been on an Eastern European whirlwind tour, frantically climbing every mountain and touring every capital, determined to see it all before heading back to the real world. But then it happens: you encounter that one place, the city with the most enchanting alleys or the hostel that casts a spell over its guests, and you can't bring yourself to leave. Ever. Lucky for you, Eastern Europe is bursting with settlement-worthy towns. **Prague** (p. 183) is Eastern Europe's ex-pat capital; the number of Anglophone residents here today has elicted comparisons to 1920s Paris. If the hordes of Hemingway wannabes frequenting Prague's cafes frightens you, head south to **Český Krumlov** (p. 220), where mellower backpackers-*cum*-locals relish the tight-knit community of this medieval town. **The Backpacker's Guesthouse** (p. 279) is the home-base for **Budapest's** (p. 271) English-speaking denizens who spend their days lingering in Turkish baths and their nights dancing at Fat Mo's Speakeasy. And who can really blame **Dubrovnik's** (p. 169) recent converts? It *is* the most beautiful city on the Adriatic, after all. The most unlikely (and un-European) of the alluring locales is **Ulaanbaatar** (p. 667), the capital of Mongolia. Sure, you'll sleep in *ger* and ride yaks, but there's an *English bookstore.* Other cities that should top the lingering list include: **St. Petersburg** (p. 596), **Kraków** (p. 422), **Vilnius** (p. 365), and **Poznań** (p. 463).

SUGGESTED ITINERARIES

HABSBURG'S LAST HURRAH (40 DAYS) Start your trek in starlet **Prague** (p. 183; 4 days), the steeple-topped, tourist-filled gem of Bohemia. **Český Krumlov** (p. 220; 2 days) is the most enchanting town in Eastern Europe. **Vienna** (p. 792; 3 days) is home to world-renowned museums and chain-smoking, Freud-reading hipsters. **Ljubljana** (p. 713; 2 days) might just make you forget you're in Eastern Europe. Head down the Dalmatian Coast to **Split** (p. 159; 1-2 days) to understand why Diocletian summered here. **Hvar** (p. 165; 1-2 days) is one of the most beautiful islands in the Mediterranean. **Dubrovnik** (p. 169; 3 days), the true Dalmatian diva, delivers azure waters, endless sunshine, and a vibrant nightlife. On the way to Zagreb, stop by **Plitvice Lakes** (p. 158; 2 days) for outdoor adventures. **Zagreb** (p. 139; 2 days) offers the pleasant mix of Mediterranean idleness and modest Westernization. **Pécs** (p. 317; 1-2 days) surprises with a happening modern art scene. Relax in a radioactive thermal bath in **Keszthely** (p. 314; 2 days), a serene spot in the glam playland of Lake Balaton. **Budapest** (p. 267; 4 days) might just surpass Prague as the region's hippest city. Experience the giddiness of Bull's Blood wine in **Eger's** (p. 332; 1-2 days) Valley of the Beautiful Women. The **Tatras** (p. 693 and p. 440; 3 days) tower over Slovakia and Poland with rocky hikes and snowy skiing; **Zakopane** (p. 441) and **Tatranská Lomnica** (p. 697) are the best bases. **Kraków** (p. 422; 4 days) is Poland's answer to Prague and Budapest, backpackers included. **Auschwitz** (p. 429) is a sobering daytrip from Kraków. From here, return to **Prague.**

CENTRAL CIRCUIT (45 DAYS) Overwhelming and techno-paced, **Berlin** (p. 781; 3 days) is a city of ruins, rubble, and piercings. **Prague** (p. 183; 4 days) is a more subdued follow-up, as long as you consider beer, absinthe, and ghosts subdued. **Kutná Hora** (p. 210; 1 day) spooks with its femur-adorned church. **Karlovy Vary** (p. 215; 1-2 days), once the premier spa town of Western Bohemia, is now internationally known for its film festival. **Český Krumlov** (p. 220; 2-3 days) is a great base for exploring the surrounding virgin forest. Foray into Moravia via **Olomouc** (p. 231; 1 day), the surprisingly hip, surprisingly unpolluted gem of Moravia. Although it's often overlooked, Slovakia's capital, **Bratislava** (p. 676; 1-2 days), makes for a fascinating stop en route to the rest of the country. **Žilina** (p. 684; 2

45 days does the Central Circuit
Witness the Habsburg's Last Hurrah in 40 days
NORWAY
Oslo
Stockholm
SWEDEN
FINLAND
Helsinki
Vyborg
St. Petersburg
Tallinn
ESTONIA
Novgorod
Tartu
Saaremaa
Pärnu
Gulf of Riga
Pskov
Rīga
LATVIA
Baltic Sea
Copenhagen
DENMARK
Klaipeda
LITHUANIA
Polatsk
Nida
Kaunas
Kaliningrad
RUS.
Vilnius
Hel
Wolinski Nat'l Park
Gdańsk
Minsk
Hamburg
Hrodna
BELARUS
Berlin
Toruń
Poznań
Warsaw
Brest
POLAND
Majdanek
Lublin
Wrocław
Trail of Eagle's Nests
GERMANY
Prague
Karlovy Vary
Kutná Hora
Auschwitz
Kraków
Plżen
CZECH REP.
Lviv
Olomouc
Zakopane
CARPATHIAN MOUNTAINS
Český Krumlov
Žilnia
Tatranská Lomnica
Medzilaborce
Munich
Vienna
SLOVAKIA
Košice
Balta
Salzburg
Bratislava
Eger
AUSTRIA
Budapest
MOLDOVA
Lake Balaton
Chişinău
ALPS
Keszthely
HUNGARY
ROMANIA
Ljubljana
Pécs
Trieste
Zagreb
SLOVENIA
TRANSYLVANIAN ALPS
Venice
Rijeka
CROATIA
Tulcea
Plitvice Lakes
BOSNIA-HERZEGOVINA
Belgrade
Târgu Jiu
Curtes de Argeş
Bucharest
Constanţa
Sarajevo
ITALY
Split
YUGO-SLAVIA
Balachik
BALKAN MTS.
Varna
Hvar
BULGARIA
Dubrovnik
Sofia
Ahtopol
Shkodër
Rome
Plovdiv
Skopje
F.Y.R. MACEDONIA
Tirana
Durrës
ALBANIA
Naples
Thessaloniki
Korcë
N
Gjirokastër
GREECE
Aegean Sea

Suggested Itineraries: Eastern Europe

days) is another superb hiking base, this time in the Malá Fatra range. If the "rolling" qualities of the Malá Fatra are off-putting, head east to the jagged **Tatras** (p. 693; 2-3 days). Andy Warhol's hometown, **Medzilaborce** (p. 706; 1 day), hosts an impressive modern art museum *and* a great Warhol collection. Visas might be a hassle, but they're worth it for **Lviv** (p. 778; 2-3 days), a Kraków copy-cat in Ukraine. Follow up the copy with the original **Kraków** (p. 422; 4 days), not forgetting the haunting **Auschwitz** (p. 429). The **Trail of Eagles' Nests** (p. 454; 1-2 days) is a refreshing break from church tours and stuffy, smelly buses. **Lublin** (p. 432; 2 days) is the unofficial capital of Lesser Poland. Disturbingly close to Lublin, **Majdanek** (p. 435) was the second-largest concentration camp. **Warsaw** (p. 402; 4 days) is Poland's answer to Berlin: sprawling, hectic, and still struggling to recover from WWII. A little slower and more relaxing, **Gdánsk** (p. 480; 2 days) is the gateway to some of the Baltic's best beaches. Go to **Hel** (p. 490; 1 day), really, a sleepy village north of Gdánsk. Venture into the heart of Poland to experience **Poznań** (p. 463; 2 days), the capital of Poland's music scene. Before returning to Berlin, stop by **Woliński National Park** (p. 478; 2 days) for some bison-watchin', glacier-climbin' fun.

VIA BALTICA (30 DAYS) Although not officially Baltic, **Moscow** (p. 561; 4 days) is the post-apocalyptic Mothership of the former USSR. **St. Petersburg** (p. 596; 4 days) is Russia's alter-ego: more cultured, friendlier, and much less overwhelming. Multicultural **Helsinki** (p. 788; 3 days) is the epitome of chill. **Tallinn** (p. 239; 3 days) is surprisingly cosmopolitan. The island of **Saaremaa** (p. 251; 3-4 days) is more Estonian than Estonia itself, complete with windmills, meteor craters, and undisturbed beaches. Get muddy in **Pärnu** (p. 248; 1 day) at one of the town's infamous spas. **Tartu** (p. 258; 1 day) is the oldest city in the Baltics. **Rīga** (p. 344; 3 days) is decidedly more Soviet than its neighbors. Lithuania's third-largest city, **Klaipėda** (p. 383; 2-3 days) is the gateway to the Curonian Spit; the best beaches are at **Nida** (p. 387). On your way to Vilnius, stop by **Kaunas** (p. 375; 1 day), Lithuania's second-largest city. **Vilnius** (p. 363; 3 days), long considered the "Jerusalem of Europe," is now touted as the "New Prague."

NOT FOR THE FAINT OF HEART (30 DAYS) Start your adventure in **Istanbul** (p. 798; 4 days), the gateway to the Black Sea. Head north to **Ahtopol** (p. 126; 2 days) for Bulgaria's warmest water. Continue lounging in **Balchik** (p. 123; 2 days), without hordes of Bulgarian teeny-boppers. Experience Romania's coast in **Constanța** (p. 545; 2 days). **Bucharest** (p. 506; 4 days), once dubbed "Little Paris," now stands as a ghost of itself. Heading to the Transylvanian Alps offers the twin gems of **Târgu Jiu** (p. 530; 1-2 days)—noted for its collection of Brâncuși sculptures—and **Curtea de Argeș** (p. 518; 1-2 days), home to Dracula's castle. The journey gets rougher as you head to Moldova's capital, **Chișinău** (p. 390; 2 days), which still considers itself Soviet. Gold-domed and poplar-crowned **Kiev** (p. 731; 4 days) hasn't quite figured out how to become a thriving capitalist metropolis. **Yalta** (p. 756; 3 days) is one of the least spoiled resorts in the Black Sea. Once the party town of the USSR, **Odessa** (p. 761; 3 days) still hums, just at a lower frequency. Return to Istanbul by a 2-day ferry. *To really rough it, add a 10-day extension via* ***Rostov-na-Donu*** *(p. 646; 2 days from Simferopol) to* ***Pyatigorsk*** *(p. 647; 3-5 days) for treks on Elbrus and Dombai in the Caucasus, and to* ***Sochi*** *(p. 651; 3-5 days) for Russian-style Black Sea lounging.*

AND YOU THOUGHT YOU WERE IN EUROPE: THE TRANS-SIBERIAN RAILROAD (35 DAYS) *Times are listed as transport time between each city, not from Moscow. See the* ***Trans-Siberian Railroad*** *(p. 655) for more information.* Start your monumental journey in **Moscow** (p. 561; 4 days), stocking up on supplies and civilization. The first stop is **Yaroslavl** (p. 590; 4½hr.; 2 days), a leafy city offering the comforts of a capital. **Novosibirsk** (p. 658; 46hr.; 2 days) brings you to the heart of Central Asia and is the gateway to the **Altai Republic** (p. 659; 5-6 days). Continue on to **Irkutsk** (p. 662; 33hr.; 1-2 days), a former Siberian trading-post where you can rest up before trekking to **Lake Baikal** (p. 664; 4 days), the world's deepest freshwater lake. **Ulan Ude** (p. 665; 8hr.; 2 days), center of Russian Buddhism and home to the world's largest Lenin bust, is quite possibly Russia's most surreal city. Break up the final leg to **Beijing** (p. 804; 4 days) with a stop in **Ulaanbataar** (p. 667; 22hr., 2 days), Mongolia's sprawling desert oasis.

HISTORY OF HALF THE WORLD IN SIX PAGES

SLAVS & OTHER EARLY SETTLERS

With the exception of Hungary, Romania, and the Baltic countries, Eastern Europe is populated primarily by **Slavic** peoples who constitute the largest ethnic and linguistic group in Europe. Originally from somewhere in Central Asia, the Slavs have lived in Eastern Europe since the 2nd or 3rd century BC. However, it was not until the 6th and 7th centuries AD that they began migrating farther south and west, displacing Celts in the Czech lands and Slovakia, Illyrians in the Balkans, Turks and Avars in Bulgaria, Scandinavians in Russia and Ukraine, and Germanic tribes in Hungary. Poland was the last Eastern European nation to be settled by Slavs in the 9th century. Unlike other migrating tribes at this time, the Slavs were cultivators and settlers rather than pillagers, which contributed to their lasting presence.

After the Great Migration, Slavs were split into the three relatively distinct divisions of **west Slavs** (Czechs, Poles and Slovaks), **south Slavs** (Serbs, Croats, Slovenes and Macedonians) and **east Slavs** (Russians, Ukrainians, Belarussians and Bulgarians). Since the 6th century, there has been virtually no unity among the Slavic peoples. The cultural and political history of the west Slavs is inextricably linked to Western Europe, whereas the east and south Slavs, isolated from the West, were subjected to the rule of Mongols and Turks.

The non-Slavic nations in Eastern Europe were inhabited by a vast array of settlers and invaders. Estonia, for example, was invaded by **Vikings and Finns** in the 9th and 11th centuries, respectively, while Latvians, Lithuanians and northern Poles were all of **Baltic** descent. All of these non-Slavic nations, however, including Romania, Hungary and Bulgaria, intermingled and were strongly influenced by their Slavic neighbors and settlers. Romanians, while originally of **Roman** descent, assimilated the Slavic migrants of the 6th century while the **Magyars** who invaded Hungary in the 9th century subsumed the Slavs already settled there.

THE GREAT EMPIRES

Beginning in the eighth century, several Slavic empires emerged in Eastern Europe, from the First and Second Bulgarian Empires in the early 700s to the Empire of Great Moravia in Bohemia, Moravia, Hungary and Slovakia in 830. One of the few Eastern European empires to actually achieve longevity and greatness was the **Hungarian Kingdom.** It first came to power in the late 9th century. By the 16th century, the Kingdom extended from Silesia in Poland to Pannonia in Croatia and as far east as Wallachia and Bessarabia in Romania. The Kingdom came to an end at the **Battle of Mohács in 1526** when Louis II, king of Hungary and Bohemia, lost to the Turks. Like the Hungarian Kingdom, most of the Slavic nations of the the Middle Ages were eventually conquered by the great empires of Europe. By the nineteenth century, nearly all of Eastern Europe was controlled by either the Ottoman, Russian, or Austro-Hungarian Empire.

WHAT'S IN A NAME? When Macedonian priest Constantine and his little brother Methodius set off on a mission to the Slavs in 863, they brought with them more than their religion. To succeed where others had failed, Constantine translated liturgical text into the language of the people, using an alphabet he invented based on Greek script. The new tongue, Old Church Slavonic, was a smashing success among the people, fascilitating unions in the name of religion and language that made the great empires of the Bulgarians and the Kievan Rus possible. Rome, however, was less than thrilled to hear that the Word of God was being spread in any language less dignified than Greek or Latin. The brothers were summoned to explain themselves before Pope Nicholas I, who died before they arrived in 868. And while his successor Adrian II gave their mission his full blessing, Constantine fell ill and died before he could return to preach. Before he passed away, he adopted the name Cyril, which has been immortalized as the name of the alphabet that evolved from his work.

The **Ottoman Empire** firmly established itself in southeastern Europe when it crushed the Serb army on June 28, 1389 at the **Battle of Kosovo**. Its domain included the Balkan peninsula, including what are now Romania, Bulgaria, Macedonia, Serbia, Montenegro, Bosnia and inland Croatia. At the height of the Ottoman empire in 1699, it also indirectly controlled the Crimean Peninsula and the entire Black Sea Coast. The decline of the empire was sped along by a series of losses to Russia from the 17th to the 19th cenutry. The **1878 Congress of Berlin** marked the end of the **Russo-Turkish Wars;** only Bulgaria and Macedonia remained in the Ottoman sphere of influence. All other nations were either granted independence or ceded to the Russian and Austro-Hungarian Empires.

As the Ottoman Empire was declining, the **Russian Empire** was rapidly expanding east to the Pacific and westward into Poland and Ukraine. At the first partition of Poland in 1772, the Russians wrested the Swedish Empire's control of Estonia and Lithuania and completely dissolved the **Polish-Lithuanian Commonwealth,** one of the largest empires in Europe. By 1801, the empire controlled Lithuania, Estonia, Latvia, eastern Poland, Belarus, and Ukraine. Further expansion of the empire was halted in the 19th century. The Congress of Berlin denied Russia's vision of a large Bulgarian state and a pan-Slavic nation in Eastern Europe. Although it kept control of the entire region until the fall of Communism in 1989, Russia's empire remained influential only in far Eastern Europe after this blow from the West.

The other major empire before WWI was the Austrian Empire, known as the **Austro-Hungarian Empire** after 1867, which exercised control primarily over Central Europe. Although the Austrian Habsburgs date to the early thirteenth century, they did not dominate Central Europe until the Battle of Mohács, when the Hungarian kingdom was split between Turkish and Austrian control. The Habsburgs acquired Bohemia, Moravia, Slovakia, and parts of Croatia, including Zagreb and Rijeka. The rest of Hungary fell to the Ottomans. In 1699, however, after a series of Hungarian uprisings, the Turks relinquished the rest of Hungary to the Habsburgs. The Hungarians remained unrestful subjects, however, and in 1867, the Austrian empire entered into a **dual monarchy** with the Hungarians by which Hungary was granted full internal independence but still shared various ministries with the Austrian government. From 1867 until 1918, the Austro-Hungarian Empire controlled what is now the Czech Republic, Slovakia, Hungary, Croatia, Slovenia, Bosnia, and parts of Romania, Poland, Belarus, and Ukraine.

WORLD WAR I & THE RUSSIAN REVOLUTION

World War I started with an attempt by the Serbs to free the South Slavs from the clutches of the Austro-Hungarian Empire. Already inflamed by the First and Second Balkan Wars of the 1910s, the Serb nationalists believed that their cause would best be served by the death of **Austrian Archduke Francis Ferdinand.** On June

28, 1914, Bosnian Serb and nationalist **Gavrilo Princip** assassinated Ferdinand and his wife in Sarajevo. Exactly one month later, Austria-Hungary declared war on the Serbs. What started as an attempt to save the Empire snowballed during the ensuing month into continual war declarations that included France, Germany, Russia, Belgium, Great Britain, Montenegro, Serbia and Turkey. Because they were controlled by the Austro-Hungarian and Ottoman Empires, most Eastern European nations fought alongside the **Central Powers.** The Baltic nations, however, were controlled by both Germans and Russians and remained divided in their alliances with the Allied and Central powers. The only nations to wholeheartedly support the Allies were Serbia, Montenegro and Bosnia. Belarus and Ukraine became hotly contested battlegrounds between the Germans and the Russians and eventually fell to German war-time occupation.

As the war dragged on, Russia's participation became more tenuous. The Russians had entered the war because of their dual interests in the demise of the Ottoman and Austro-Hungarian Empires and the growth of strong, Russia-friendly, Slavic nations throughout Eastern Europe. As catastrophic losses caused the death toll to skyrocket, however, the Russian people became increasingly frustrated with an inefficient military government that seemed to be needlessly sacrificing millions of lives. Coupled with a crippled war-time economy, the tension finally erupted into the **Russian Revolution.**

Riots began over food shortages on March 8, 1917. The Tsar abdicated a week later. In November 1917, the **Bolsheviks** ascended to power, establishing Russia's first communist government. In the seven months between revolutions, Russia failed her allies and witnessed the crumbling of her empire. In all territories left unoccupied by Germany, nationalist independence movements emerged on the heels of the March 1917 revolution. By 1918, Latvia, Estonia, Poland and Ukraine had declared independence from Russia, and Lithuania had declared independence from Germany. In 1919, the Red Army attempted and (except for eastern Ukraine and Belarus) failed to reclaim Russia's former territories.

The ultimate defeat of the Central Powers in 1918 saw a similar wave of independence movements throughout former Ottoman and Austro-Hungarian states. On October 28, 1918, the Czechs and Slovaks united to declare the creation of **Czechoslovakia.** Poland, too, which had been divided as Prussia, Silesia, and Russian-occupied territory was united as a complete nation for the first time since 1772. Romania doubled its size after the war by absorbing Transylvania, Wallachia, and Bukovina. Finally, in keeping with the vision of South Slav nationalism which had sparked the war, 1918 saw the creation of the **Kingdom of Serbs, Croats and Slovenes,** later known as **Yugoslavia.** In the wake of both World War I and the Russian Revolution, the great empires in Eastern Europe came to an end as newly independent Slavic nations were born.

WORLD WAR II

World War II was essentially sparked by the continuation of many unresolved conflicts left by WWI. Eastern Europe once again became the focal point of the events leading to the war. Hitler, for example, was determined to reclaim the "Germanic" lands of Poland, Bohemia and Moravia that Germany had lost after the **Treaty of Versailles.** In May, 1938 it became clear that Hitler planned to invade the **Sudetenland** in western Czechoslovakia. He claimed that the 3,000,000 Bohemians of German descent had been treated unfairly. In an effort to avoid another war, France and Britain adopted their infamous policy of **appeasement** and signed the **Munich Agreement** with Germany on September 30, 1938, granting Germany the right to reclaim the Sudetenland without military resistance from either the West or from Czechoslovakia (without, of course, the consent of the Czechoslovak government). While France and Britain believed that peace had been achieved, Hitler ignored the stipulations of the agreement and proceeded to annex the remainder of Czechoslovakia into the **Bohemian-Moravian Protectorate** in March, 1939. In an effort to prevent retaliation from both the West and the Soviets in the case of a Polish invasion, Hitler entered into the **Molotov-Ribbentrop Nonaggression Pact** with the USSR in August which stipulated that after an invasion, Germany would control the western third of Poland and the USSR would control the eastern two-thirds. In September 1939, Hitler invaded Poland and annexed the Polish Corridor and the primarily German city of **Danzig (Gdánsk).** WWII erupted.

Hitler had no intention of maintaining the Nonaggression Pact and by 1940 had designs on invading and annexing European Russia. On June 22, 1941, Germany launched its offensive against the Soviet Union and from March to October, successfully invaded Belarus, Ukraine, Estonia, Lithuania, and Latvia. However, October 1941 saw the beginning of the end for the German army. Having underestimated the reserve power of the Soviet army, the Nazis were never able to capture Moscow and the attempted invasion actually led the Soviets to join the **Allied forces.** The **Anglo-Soviet Agreement of 1941** was a turning point in the war, as were the Allies' decisive wins in 1942. Unfortunately, the bombing campaigns of the Allies led to the utter ruin of many German-occupied Eastern European cities, among them Warsaw, Budapest, and Belgrade.

Total casualties from the war for both civilians and military personnel are estimated at 50-60,000,000. Of these, Eastern Europe suffered the most losses. The USSR lost 18,000,000 of its citizens (10% of its population), more than any other nation involved in the war. Yugoslavia also lost over 10% of its population. Poland lost nearly 6,000,000 people, a staggering 20% of its prewar population, only about 200,000 of which were military casualties. The majority of the remaining 5,500,000 were exterminated in **Nazi concentration camps;** of the 6,000,000 estimated Jews murdered by the Nazis, more than half were Polish. Before WWII, Eastern Europe had been the geographical center of the world's Jewish population but Hitler's **"final solution"** succeeded in almost entirely eliminating the Jewish communities of Poland, Slovakia, Hungary, Lithuania, Moldova, Odessa and the Czech Republic through both forced emigration and genocide.

THE IRON CURTAIN & THE COLD WAR

The incorporation of Ukraine into the USSR in September, 1939 marked the first extension of Stalin's regime beyond Russia. A pact with Germany the same year sealed the fate of the Baltic nations by granting Russia the right to occupy and annex Estonia, Latvia and Lithuania. On July 20, 1940, all three nations voted to become constituent republics in the USSR. Belarus joined the USSR at the end of WWII, when Poland ceded it to Russia. The Soviet's sphere of influence was not limited to constituent republics. The institution of communism in Czechoslovakia, Poland, Hungary, Yugoslavia, Romania and Bulgaria from 1946 to 1949 established a ring of satellite People's Democracies in Eastern Europe. This expansion was one of the primary causes of the disintegration of the uneasy alliance between the U.S., Britain and the Soviet Union at the end of World War II. The West was opposed to Russia's ideological expansion of communism but Russia claimed it necessary—especially in Eastern Europe—to prevent another German threat on Slavic nations. As the Soviet Union installed first left-wing and then outright communist governments throughout Eastern Europe, the **Cold War** began.

The **Iron Curtain** first descended with the founding of the **Council for Mutual Economic Assistance (COMECON)** in January 1949, an organization meant to facilitate and coordinate the economic growth of the Soviet Bloc and created in response to the United States' 1948 **Marshall Plan.** The only Eastern European nation not to immediately accept COMECON was Yugoslavia, which finally joined in 1964. The West reacted to this new, formal alliance in April with the creation of the **North Atlantic Treaty Organization (NATO),** a military alliance meant to "keep the Americans in, the Russians out, and the Germans down." In typical Cold War fashion, the Eastern Bloc retaliated in May 1955 with a similar military alliance, the **Warsaw Pact.** The pact was the birth of a mutual-defense organization among the communist countries that allowed for unified military units and the maintenance of Soviet military bases throughout Eastern Europe. Yugoslavia was the only communist nation not to join the pact.

The Warsaw Pact was also an attempt by the USSR to tighten its grip on satellite nations. It ushered in an era of increased repression of local governments and regimes by the Soviets. After Stalin's death in 1953, the Soviet bloc was plagued by chaos and new nationalist movements. The 1950s saw the emergence of **national communism**, or the belief that the attainment of ultimate communist goals should be dictated internally rather than by repressive orders from Moscow. The creation of a mutual-defense organization in the name of protecting communism enabled Moscow to respond to rising nationalist movements with military force. Such was the case in 1956, when the Soviets violently crushed the Hungarian Revolution and workers' strikes in Poland. The **1968 Prague Spring** was a similarly violent crushing of an emerging Czechoslovak dissidence movement which was demanding increased freedom and attention to human rights. Russia consistently used the Warsaw Pact to justify military occupation and the institution of martial law.

The Soviets squashed emerging nationalism and dissidents not merely with military force but also through the state-enforced **Russification** of various cultures. In Estonia, for example, 80,000 citizens were deported in the 1950s to make room for controlled immigration of Russians. Before the war, Estonians made up 90% of the population; by 1990, the number had fallen to 50%. In the arts, a government-enforced literary movement, **socialist realism,** claimed to objectively represent the building of socialism and a classless society. Writers throughout the Eastern Bloc who did not maintain a positive and optimistic view of socialist societies under Soviet domination were either persecuted, exiled, or sentenced to death. Eastern European literature seemed to be stunted developmentally, missing out on post-modernism and other such Western developments.

1989 & BEYOND

The Soviet Union's increasingly repressive regimes of the 1950s and 1960s did not succeed in squashing all of the nationalist and dissident movements throughout the eastern bloc. Instead, political repression coupled with the economic and political stagnancy of the Leonid Brezhnev years from 1964-1982 increased unrest and disapproval for Moscow and its policies. When **Mikhail Gorbachev** became Secretary General to the Central Committee of the Communist Party in 1985, he began to dismantle the totalitarian aspects of the Communist regime through his policies of ***glasnost*** (openness) and ***perestroika*** (restructuring). The new freedom of political expression led to a snowballing of dissidence, disapproval and revolt which finally erupted in 1989 with a series of revolutions throughout Eastern Europe. The first occurred in Poland in June when, in a contested election, the Poles voted the Soviet-supported communists out of office. In their place, the Poles elected **Lech Wałęsa** and the **Solidarity** party to create the new government. This Polish victory was swiftly followed by a new democratic constitution in Hungary in October, the crumbling of the **Berlin Wall** on November 9, the resignation of the Bulgarian communists on November 10, the **Velvet Revolution** in Czechoslovakia on November 17 and the execution of Romania's communist dictator **Nicolae Ceauşescu** on December 25. Almost all of the Warsaw Pact nations had successfully—and almost totally bloodlessly—broken away from the Soviet Union and begun the move toward democracy.

The USSR itself did not crumble until 1990. Lithuania became the first constituent republic to pull away from Moscow when, on March 11, the newly-elected Lithuanian legislature declared the nation's independence. March 30 marked Estonia's declaration of a transitional phase en route to independence. Latvia followed suit on May 4, and in June both Russia and Ukraine declared their sovereignty from the USSR. In a desperate attempt to keep the Soviet Union together, Gorbachev condoned military force against the rebellious Baltic republics. A bloody conflict between the Soviets and the Lithuanians erupted in Vilnius in January, 1991. Shortly thereafter, **Boris Yeltsin,** then President of Russia saw the communist regime and the Soviet Union finally collapse after the failure of a hard-line communist coup from August 19-22, 1991. By September 1991, the Soviet Union was dead and all of its European constituent republics and satellite nations were fully independent and rapidly moving toward democracy.

Yugoslavia was quickly disintegrating. Economic chaos had led to dissatisfaction with the communist government and in 1990, Slovenia, Croatia and Bosnia all held multi-party elections in which the Communists were defeated. Both Slovenia and Croatia declared independence on June 25, 1991, to which the Serbian-controlled government responded with military force. The conflict in Slovenia lasted only ten days; it was the first nation to successfully secede from the Yugoslav Federation. Unfortunately, Croatia's attempts to secede resulted in a war that involved Serbia, Croatia, Bosnia and Montenegro and continued until the signing of the **Dayton Peace Accords** in November, 1995. The only republics remaining in Yugoslavia were Serbia and Montenegro.

At the turn of the millennium and eighty-three years after the Russian Revolution, Eastern Europe is still grappling with its post-communist identity. In the wake of a collapsed Soviet Union, Russia established the **Commonwealth of Independent States (CIS)** on December 21, 1991, an alliance between Russia, Belarus, Ukraine, Moldova and various other Soviet republics that attempts to coordinate the foreign policies, economies and military endeavors of its members. On March 13, 1999, the CIS felt NATO move closer when Poland, Hungary and the Czech Republic joined the alliance. Lithuania, Latvia, Estonia, Slovenia and Slovakia are vying to become the next members. The economic instability of the CIS is even more disheartening for Russians, Belarussians, Moldovans, and Ukrainians when it is juxtaposed with the relative economic prosperity of other former communist states like Hungary, Poland, Estonia and Slovenia. The EU's next round of member selection in 2003 will draw these countries even further Westward. Continuing hostilities between various Caucasian republics and Russia for control of the northern Caucasus has posed yet another threat to the CIS's political staying power.

The most terrifying challenges of a post-communist Eastern Europe as the region enters a new millenium center around the former Yugoslav republics. Although the Dayton Accords brought a cease-fire to the region, another military conflict erupted in July 1999 when the ethnically Albanian **Kosovo** province attempted to declare independence from the Serb-dominated Yugoslav government. The ensuing guerilla warfare between Serbs and Kosovars resulted in NATO air attacks on Serbia and Montenegro, a volatile refugee situation in Macedonia and Albania, and growing instability in the rest of the Balkan peninsula.

ESSENTIALS

At times frustratingly bureaucratic, at times utterly lawless, the one constant of travel in Kafkaesque Eastern Europe is that it is never predictable. Start planning well in advance: begin stalking consulates for visas the moment you decide to go, faithfully follow the news, plot every detail of your itinerary—and be prepared to scrap the whole thing once you arrive. Things change quickly in Eastern Europe: exchange rates, telephone numbers, even borders. The most important thing to bring is flexibility.

WHEN TO GO

Like everywhere else in Europe, Eastern Europe's high season is summer. What high season means, however, varies for each country and region. In Prague, Kraków, and Budapest, for example, *everything* is swarmed with backpackers. On the other hand, high season in the countryside simply means that hotels might actually have guests staying in them. In Croatia and along the Baltic and Black Sea Coasts, things fill up as soon as it is warm enough to lounge on the beach, usually from June to September. In the Tatras, Julian Alps, and Transylvanian Alps, there is both a summer high season for hiking (usually only July and August) and a winter season for skiing (roughly November to March). In the low season, you'll often be the only tourist in town, aside from the occasional German family. While securing accommodations and walking down the street will be easier in low season, high season brings with it an entire sub-culture of young backpackers. You decide whether that's a good thing.

Avg Temp (hi/lo), Avg Rain	January		April		July		October	
	°C	mm	°C	mm	°C	mm	°C	mm
Bratislava, SLK	01/-4	3.9	15/6	4.5	25/15	8.4	14/7	1.3
Bucharest, ROM	01/-7	4.6	18/05	5.9	30/16	5.3	18/6	2.9
Budapest, HUN	01/-4	3.7	17/7	4.5	28/16	5.6	16/7	5.7
Kiev, UKR	-4/-10	5.8	14/5	4.5	25/15	9.1	13/6	3.3
Ljubljana, SLN	02/-4	8.8	15/4	9.8	27/14	11.3	15/6	15.1
Minsk, BEL	-4/-8	4.2	10/7	4.9	19/17	5.5	12/8	5.1
Moscow, RUS	-9/-16	3.9	10/1	3.9	23/13	8.8	09/3	4.5
Prague, CZ	0/-5	1.8	12/3	2.7	23/13	6.8	12/5	3.3
Rīga, LAT	-4/-10	3.1	10/1	3.3	22/11	5.3	11/4	6.2
Sarajevo, BOS	03/-3	4.7	18/7	5.4	28/17	6.1	18/8	5.5
Sofia, BUL	02/-3	3.6	16/5	6.1	27/16	6.8	17/8	6.5
Tallinn, EST	-4/-10	3.1	10/1	3.3	22/11	5.3	11/4	6.2
Vilnius, LIT	-4/-10	3.1	10/1	3.3	22/11	5.3	11/4	6.2
Warsaw, POL	0/-6	2.7	12/03	3.7	24/15	9.6	13/5	3.8
Zagreb, CRO	02/-4	8.8	15/4	9.8	27/14	11.3	15/6	15.1

DOCUMENTS & FORMALITIES

EMBASSIES & CONSULATES

Belarus: U.K. Embassy: 6 Kensington Ct., London, W8 5DL (tel. (0171) 937 32 88; fax 361 00 05). **U.S. Embassy:** 1619 New Hampshire Ave. NW, Washington, D.C. 20009 (tel. (202) 986-1604, for visas 986-1606; fax 986-1805).

Bosnia-Herzegovina: Australia Embassy and Consulate: 27 State Circle, Forest, Canberra ACT 2603 (tel. (0612) 623 959 55; fax 623 957 93). **U.K. Embassy:** 320 Regent St., London W1R 5AB (tel. (0171) 255 37 58; fax 255 37 60). **U.S. Embassy:** 2109 E St. NW, Washington, D.C. 20037 (tel. (202) 337-1500; fax 337-1502; email info@bosnianembassy.org).

Bulgaria: Australia Consulate: 1/4 Carlotta Rd., Double Bay, Sydney, NSW 2028 (tel. (0612) 327 7592; fax 327 8067; email lubo@tig.com.au). **Canada Embassy:** 325 Stewart St., Ottawa, ON K1N 6K5 (tel. (613) 789-3215; fax 789-3524). **South Africa Embassy:** 1071 Church St., Hatfield, PRETORIA; P.O. Box 32569, ARCADIA (tel. (012) 342 37 20; fax 342 37 21; email embulgsa@iafrica.com). **U.K. Embassy:** 186-188 Queensgate, London SW7 5HL (tel. (0171) 584 94 00; fax 584 49 48). **U.S. Embassy:** 1621 22nd St. NW, Washington, D.C. 20008 (tel. (202) 387-7969; fax 234-7973).

Croatia: Australia Embassy: 14 Jindalee Crescent, O'Malley, Canberra ACT 2606 (tel. (06) 286 69 88; fax 286 35 44). **Canada Embassy:** 130 Albert St., #1700, Ottawa, ON K1 P5 G4 (tel. (613) 230-7351; fax 230-7388). **New Zealand Consulate:** 131 Lincoln Rd., Henderson, P.O. Box 83200, Edmonton, Auckland (tel. (09) 836 55 81; fax 836 54 81). **South Africa Embassy:** 1160 Church St., Colbyn, PRETORIA; P.O. Box 11335, HATFIELD 0028 (tel. (012) 342 12 06; fax 342 18 19). **U.K. Embassy:** 21 Conway St., London W1P 5HL (tel. (0171) 387 20 22; fax 387 09 36). **U.S. Embassy:** 2343 Massachusetts Ave. NW, Washington, D.C. 20008 (tel. (202) 588-5899; fax 588-8936).

Czech Republic: Australia Embassy: 38 Culgoa Circuit, O'Malley, Canberra, ACT 2606 (tel. (612) 290 13 86; fax 290 00 06; email canberra@embassy.mzv.cz). **Canada Embassy:** 541 Sussex Dr., Ottawa, ON K1N 6Z6 (tel. (613) 562-3875; fax 562-3878; email ottowa@embassy.mzv.cz). **Ireland Embassy:** 57 Northumberland Rd., Ballsbridge, Dublin 4 (tel. (3531) 668 11 35; fax 668 16 60; email dublin@embassy.mzv.cz). **New Zealand Honorary Consul:** 48 Hair St., Wainuiomata, Wellington (tel./fax (644) 564 60 01). **South Africa Embassy:** 936 Pretorius St., Arcadia, PRETORIA; P.O. Box 3326, PRETORIA 0001 (tel. (012) 342 34 77; fax 43 20 33). **U.K. Embassy:** 26 Kensington Palace Gardens, London W8 4QY (tel. (0171) 243 11 15; fax 727 96 54; email london@embassy.mzv.cz). **U.S. Embassy:** 3900 Spring of Freedom St. NW, Washington, D.C. 20008 (tel. (202) 274-9100; fax 966-8540; www.czech.cz/washington).

Estonia: On the web: www.vm.ee. **Australia Honorary Consul:** 86 Louisa Rd., Birchgrove NSW, 2041 (tel. (612) 98 10 74 68; fax 98 18 17 79; email eestikon@ozemail.com.au). **Canada Honorary Consul:** 958 Broadview Ave., Toronto, ON M4K 2R6 (tel. (416) 461-0764; fax 461-0353; email estconsu@inforamp.net). **Ireland Embassy:** Merlyn Park 24, Ballsbridge, Dublin 4 (tel. (3531) 269 15 52; fax 260 51 19; email asjur@indigo.ie). **South Africa Honorary Consul:** 16 Hofmeyer St., Welgemoed, BELVILLE, 7530 (tel. (021)913 38 50; fax 913 25 79). **U.K. Embassy:** 16 Hyde Park Gate, London SW7 5DG (tel. (44171) 589 34 28; fax 589 34 30; email loa@estonia.gov.uk; www.estonia.gov.uk). **U.S. Embassy:** 2131 Massachusetts Ave. NW, Washington, D.C. 20008 (tel. (202) 588-0101; fax 588-0108; email info@estemb.org; www.estemb.org).

Hungary: Australia Consulate: Edgecliff Centre 203-233, #405, Head Rd., Edgecliff, Sydney, NSW 2027 (tel. (02) 93 28 78 59; fax 93 27 18 29). **Canada Embassy:** 299 Waverley St., Ottawa, ON K2P 0V9 (tel. (613) 230-2717; fax 230-7560; email huembott@docuweb.ca; www.docuweb.ca/Hungary). **Ireland Embassy:** 2 Fitzwilliam Pl., Dublin 2 (tel. (01) 661 29 03; fax 661 28 80). **South Africa Embassy:** 959 Arcadia St., Hatfield, ARCADIA; P.O. Box 27077, SUNNYSIDE 0132 (tel. (012) 43 30 20; fax 43 30 29). **New Zealand Embassy:** Wellington, 151 Orangi Kaupapa Rd. 6005 Z (tel. (644) 475 85 74; fax 475 35 55). **U.K. Embassy:** 35 Eaton Pl., London SW1X 8BY (tel. (0171) 235 52 18; fax 823 13 48). **U.S. Embassy:** 3910 Shoemaker St. NW, Washington, D.C. 20008 (tel. (202) 362-6730; fax 686-6412; email huembwash@attmail.com).

Latvia: Australia Consulate: P.O. Box 457, Strathfield NSW 2135 (tel. (02) 97 44 59 81; fax 97 47 60 55). **Canada Embassy:** 112 Kent St., Place de Ville, Tower B, #208, Ottawa, ON K1P 5P2 (tel. (613) 238-6014; fax 238-7044; email latvia-embassy@magmacom.com; www2.magmacom.com/~latemb). **U.K. Embassy:** 45 Nottingham Pl., London W1M 3FE (tel. (0171) 312 00 40; fax 312 00 42). **U.S. Embassy:** 4325 17th St. NW, Washington, D.C. 20011 (tel. (202) 726-8213; fax 726-6785; email latvia@ambergateway.com; www.latvia-usa.org).

Lithuania: Australia Honorary Consul: 40B Fiddens Wharf Rd., Killara NSW 2071 (tel. (61 2) 949 825 71). **Canada Embassy:** 130 Albert St., #204, Ottawa, ON K1P 5G4 (tel. (613) 567-5458; fax 567-5458; email ltemb@storm.ca). **New Zealand Honorary Consul:** 28 Heather St., Parnell Auckland, NEW ZEALAND (tel. (64 9) 379 66 39; fax (64 9) 307 29 11; email saul@f1rst.co.nz). **South Africa Honorary Consul:** Killarney Mall, 1st Floor, Riviera Rd., Killarney JOHANNESBURG, Postal address: P.O. Box 1737, HOUGHTON, 2041 (tel. (011) 486 36 60; fax 486 36 50; lietuvos@iafrica.com). **U.K. Embassy:** 84 Gloucester Pl., London W1H 3HN (tel. (0171) 486 64 01; fax 486 64 03). **U.S. Embassy:** 2622 16th St. NW, Washington, D.C. 20009-4202 (tel. (202) 234-5860; fax 328-0466; email admin@ltembassyus.org; www.ltembassyus.org).

Moldova: On the web: www.moldova.org. **U.S. Embassy:** 2101 S St. NW, Washington, D.C. 20008 (tel. (202) 667-1130; fax 667-1204; email moldova@dgs.dgsys.com).

Poland: On the web: www.polishworld.com/polemb. **Australia Embassy:** 7 Turrana St., Yarralumla ACT 2600 Canberra (tel. (06) 273 12 08 or 273 12 11; fax 273 31 84; email ambpol@clover.com.au). **Canada Embassy:** 443 Daly St., Ottawa, ON, K1N 6H3 (tel. (613) 789-0468; fax 789-1218; email polamb@hookup.com). **Ireland Embassy:** 5 Ailesbury Rd., Dublin 4 (tel. (01) 283 08 55; fax 283 75 62). **New Zealand Embassy:** 17 Upland Rd., Kelburn, Wellington (tel. (04) 71 24 56; fax 71 24 55; email polishembassy@xtra.co.nz). **South Africa Embassy:** 14 Amos St., Colbyn, PRETORIA 0083 (tel. (012) 43 26 31; fax 43 26 08; email amb.pol@pixie.co.za). **U.K. Embassy:** 47 Portland Pl., London W1N 4JH (tel. (0171) 580 43 24; fax 323 40 18). **U.S. Embassy:** 2640 16th St. NW, Washington, D.C. 20009 (tel. (202) 234-3800; fax 328-6271; email embpol@dgs.dgsys.com).

Romania: Canada Embassy: 655 Rideau St., Ottawa, ON K1N 6A3 (tel. (613) 789-5345; fax 789-4365). **South Africa Embassy:** 117 Charles St., Brooklyn PRETORIA; P.O. Box 11295, BROOKLYN, 0011 (tel. (012) 46 69 40; fax 46 69 47). **U.K. Embassy:** 4 Palace Green, Kensington, London W8 4QD (tel. (0171) 937 96 66; fax 937 80 69). **U.S. Embassy:** 1607 23rd St. NW, Washington, D.C. 20008 (tel. (202) 332-4848; fax 232-4748).

Russia: Australia Embassy: 78 Canberra Ave., Griffith ACT 2603 Canberra (tel. (06) 295 90 33; fax 295 18 47). **Canada Embassy:** 285 Charlotte St., Ottawa, ON K1N 8L5 (tel. (613) 235-4341; fax 236-6342). For visas call (613) 236-7220. **Ireland Embassy:** 186 Orwell Rd., Dublin 14 (tel. (01) 492 35 25; fax 269 83 09; email russiane@indigo.ie). **New Zealand Embassy:** 57 Messines Rd., Karori, Wellington (tel. (04) 476 61 13; fax 476 38 43). **South Africa Embassy:** Butano Building, 316 Brooks St., Menlo Park, PRETORIA; P.O. Box 6743, PRETORIA (tel. (012) 362 13 37; fax 362 01 16). **U.K. Embassy:** 6-7 Kensington Palace Gardens, London W84 QP (tel. (0171) 229 36 28; fax 727 86 25). **U.S. Embassy, Consular division:** 2641 Tunlaw Road, N.W., Washington, D.C. 20007 (tel. (202) 939-8907 or (202) 939-8913; fax (202) 483-7579).

Slovakia: Australia Embassy: 47 Culgoa Circuit, O'Malley, Canberra ACT 2606 (tel. (6) 290 15 16; fax 290 17 55). **Canada Embassy:** 50 Rideau Terrace, Ottawa, ON K1M 2A1 (tel. (613) 749-4442; fax 749-4989; email slovakemb@sprint.ca.) **South Africa Embassy:** 930 Arcadia St., Arcadia, PRETORIA; P.O. Box 12736, HATFIELD, 0028 (tel. (012) 342 20 51; fax 342 36 88). **U.K. Embassy:** 25 Kensington Palace Gardens, London W8 4QY (tel. (0171) 243 0803; fax 727 5824). **U.S. Embassy:** 2201 Wisconsin Ave. NW, #250, Washington, D.C. 20007 (tel. (202) 965-5160; fax 965-5166; email svkem@concentric.net; www.slovakemb.com).

Slovenia: Australia Embassy: Level 6, Advance Bank Center, 60 Marcus Clarke St. 2608, Canberra ACT 2601 (tel. (6) 243 48 30; fax 243 48 27). **Canada Embassy:** 150 Metcalfe St., #2101, Ottawa, ON K2P 1P1 (tel. (613) 565-5781; fax 565-5783). **New Zealand Honorary Consul:** Eastern Hutt Rd., Pomare, Lower Hutt, Wellington (tel. (644) 567 27; fax 567 24). **U.K. Embassy:** Cavendish Ct. 11-15, Wigmore St., London W1H 9LA (tel. (0171) 495 77 75; fax 495 77 76). **U.S. Embassy:** 1525 New Hampshire Ave. NW, Washington, D.C. 20036 (tel. (202) 667-5363; fax 667-4563).

Ukraine: Australia Honorary Consul: #3, Ground Floor, 902-912 Mt. Alexander Road, Essendon, Victoria 3040. **Canada Embassy:** 331 Metcalfe St. Ottawa., ON, K2P 0J9 (tel. (613) 230-2961; fax 230-2400; email ukremb@cyberus.ca). **South Africa Embassy:** 398 Marais Brooklyn, PRETORIA; PO Box 57291 ARCADIA, 0007 (tel. (012) 46 19 46; fax 46 19 44). **U.K. Embassy:** 60 Holand Park Rd., London W11 3SJ (tel. (0171) 727 63 12; fax 792 17 08). **U.S. Embassy:** 3350 M St. NW, Washington, D.C. 20007 (tel. (202) 333-7507; fax 333-7510; ukremb.com).

EMBASSIES & CONSULATES IN EASTERN EUROPE

American, Australian, British, Canadian, Irish, New Zealand, and South African embassies and consulates in Eastern European countries have been listed in the **Orientation & Practical Information** section for the capitals of each country.

PASSPORTS

REQUIREMENTS. Citizens of Australia, Canada, Ireland, New Zealand, South Africa, the U.K., and the U.S. need valid passports to enter any country in Eastern Europe and to re-enter their own. Many European countries will not allow you to enter if your passport expires within six months of your trip. Returning home with an expired passport is illegal and may result in a fine.

PHOTOCOPIES. It is a good idea to photocopy the page of your passport that contains your photograph and passport number, along with other important documents such as visas, travel insurance policies, airplane tickets, and traveler's check serial numbers, in case of loss or theft. Carry one set of copies in a safe place apart from the originals and leave another set at home. Consulates also recommend that you carry an expired passport or an official copy of your birth certificate in a part of your baggage separate from other documents.

LOST PASSPORTS. If you lose your passport, immediately notify the local police and the nearest embassy or consulate of your home government. To expedite its replacement, you'll need to know all information recorded and show identification and proof of citizenship. In some cases, a replacement may take weeks to process, and it may be valid only for a limited time. Any visas stamped in your old passport will be irretrievably lost. In an emergency, ask for immediate temporary traveling papers that will permit you to re-enter your home country. Your passport is a public document belonging to your nation's government. You may have to surrender it to a foreign government official, but if you don't get it back in a reasonable amount of time, inform the nearest mission of your home country.

NEW PASSPORTS. All applications for new passports or renewals should be filed several weeks before your planned departure date—remember that you're relying on government agencies. Most passport offices do offer emergency passport services for an extra charge. Citizens residing abroad who need passport services should contact the nearest embassy or consulate.

VISAS, INVITATIONS, & WORK PERMITS

VISAS. Visas can be purchased from your destination country's consulate or embassy. In most cases, you will have to send a completed visa application (also obtained from the consulate), the required fee, and your passport. You may also want to check your country for organizations offering visa services. U.S. Citizens, for example, can take advantage of the **Center for International Business and Travel (CIBT)** (tel. 800-925-2428), which will secure visas for travel to almost all countries for a variable service charge. For more information on each country's visa requirements, see the **Essentials** section at the beginning of each country chapter.

VISA REQUIREMENTS

	AUS	CAN	IRE	NZ	SA	UK	US
BELARUS	Y[3]	Y[3]	Y[3]	Y[3]	Y[3]	Y[3]	Y[3]
BOSNIA	Y	N	N	Y	Y	N	N
BULGARIA	N[1]	N[1]	N[1]	N[1]	Y	N[1]	N
CROATIA	N	N	N	N	Y	N	N
CZECH REPUBLIC	Y	N	N	N	Y	N	N[1]
ESTONIA	N	Y	N	N	Y	N	N
HUNGARY	Y	N	N	Y	N[1]	N	N
LATVIA	Y[2]	Y	N	Y[2]	Y	N	N
LITHUANIA	N	N	N	Y	Y	N	N
MOLDOVA	Y[3]	Y[3]	Y[3]	Y[3]	Y[3]	Y	Y[3]
POLAND	Y	Y	N	Y	Y	N	N
ROMANIA	Y	Y	Y	Y	Y	Y	N[1]
RUSSIA	Y[3]	Y[3]	Y[3]	Y[3]	Y[3]	Y[3]	Y[3]
SLOVAKIA	Y	N	N	Y	N[1]	N	N[1]
SLOVENIA	N	N	N	N	Y	N	N
UKRAINE	Y[3]	Y[3]	Y[3]	Y[3]	Y[3]	Y[3]	Y[3]

KEY 1 tourists can stay up to 30 days without visa; **2** tourists can stay up to 10 days without visa; **3** invitation required

INVITATIONS. Travelers heading to Belarus, Moldova, Russia, or Ukraine will need to acquire an invitation as part of the visa application process. An invitation can be from a citizen of the destination country or a travel organization in-country or in your homeland. For information on procuring an invitation, see **Russia: Essentials,** p. 551. These countries also require you to register your visa upon arrival. Failing to do so could result in heavy fines, arrest, or deportation. Most hotels will register you upon arrival; otherwise, head to the nearest visa services office.

WORK PERMITS. Admission as a visitor does not include the right to work, which is authorized only by a work permit, and entering to study requires a special visa. Many countries require both a work permit and a special "visa with work permit." The former is issued by the country's Labor Office, and the latter by the consulate, like any visa. For more information, see **Alternatives to Tourism,** p. 59, and the **Essentials** section for the country to which you're traveling.

IDENTIFICATION

When you travel, always carry two or more forms of identification with you, including at least one photo ID. A passport combined with a driver's license or birth certificate usually serves as adequate proof of your identity and citizenship. Many establishments, especially banks, require several IDs before cashing traveler's checks. Never carry all your forms of ID together.

STUDENT AND TEACHER IDENTIFICATION. The **International Student Identity Card (ISIC)** is the most widely accepted form of student identification. Flashing this card can procure you discounts for sights, theaters, museums, accommodations, meals, train, ferry, bus, and airplane transportation, and other services. Present the card wherever you go, and ask about discounts even when none are advertised. The international identification cards are preferable to institution-specific cards. For Americans traveling abroad, the ISIC also provides insurance benefits, including US$100 per day of in-hospital sickness for a maximum of 60 days, and US$3000 accident-related medical reimbursement for each accident (see **Insurance,** p. 34). In addition, cardholders have access to a toll-free 24hr. ISIC helpline (tel. 800-626-2427 in the U.S. and Canada; elsewhere call collect (181) 666 90 25).

Many student travel agencies around the world issue ISICs, including STA Travel in Australia and New Zealand; Travel CUTS in Canada; USIT in Ireland and Northern Ireland; SASTS in South Africa; Campus Travel and STA Travel in the U.K.; Council Travel, STA Travel, and via the web (www.counciltravel.com/idcards/index.htmlainw.usitcampus) in the U.S.; and any other travel agency with a student focus. When you apply for the card, request a copy of the International Student Identity Card Handbook, which lists some of the available discounts by country. You can also write to Council for a copy. The card is valid from September of one year to December of the following and costs AUS$15, CDN$15, or US$20. Applicants must be at least 12 years old and degree-seeking students of a secondary or post-secondary school. Because of the proliferation of phony ISICs, many airlines and some other services require additional proof of student identity, such as a signed letter from the registrar attesting to your student status or your school ID. The **International Teacher Identity Card (ITIC)** offers the same insurance coverage, and similar but limited discounts. The fee is AUS$13, UK£5, or US$20. For more information on these cards, contact the **International Student Travel Confederation (ISTC),** Herengracht 479, 1017 BS Amsterdam, Netherlands (tel. (20) 421 28 00; fax 421 28 10; email istcinfo@istc.org; www.istc.org).

YOUTH IDENTIFICATION. The International Student Travel Confederation also issues a discount card to travelers who are 25 years old or younger but not students. Known as the **International Youth Travel Card (IYTC)** (formerly the GO25 Card), this one-year card offers many of the same benefits as the ISIC, and most organizations that sell the ISIC also sell the IYTC. A brochure that lists discounts is free when you purchase the card. To apply, you will need either a passport, valid driver's license, or copy of a birth certificate, as well as a passport-sized photo with your name printed on the back. The fee is US$20.

CUSTOMS

Upon entering any Eastern European country, you must declare certain items from abroad and pay a duty on the value of those articles that exceed the allowance established by that country's customs service. Keeping receipts for purchases made abroad will help establish values when you return. It is wise to make a list, including serial numbers, of any valuables that you carry with you from home; if you register this list with customs before your departure and have an official stamp it, you will avoid import duty charges and ensure an easy passage upon your return. Be especially careful to document items manufactured abroad.

Upon returning home, you must declare all articles acquired abroad and pay a **duty** on the value of articles that exceed the allowance established by your country's customs service. Goods and gifts purchased at **duty-free** shops abroad are not exempt from duty or sales tax at your point of return; you must declare these items as well. "Duty-free" merely means that you need not pay a tax in the country of purchase. For more specific information on customs requirements, contact the customs information center in your country.

MONEY

The cost of your trip will vary considerably, depending on where you go, how you travel, where you stay, and what you do; fortunately, it is nearly impossible to have an extravagant experience in Eastern Europe. The biggest cost of your trip will probably be your round-trip airfare to Eastern Europe, which can be remarkably more expensive than a ticket to Western Europe (see **Getting There**, p. 45). Before you go, spend some time calculating a reasonable per-day budget that will meet your needs. To give you a general idea, a threadbare day in Eastern Europe (camping or sleeping in hostels, buying food at supermarkets) would run US$10-20; a slightly more comfortable day (sleeping in hostels and the occasional budget hotel, eating one meal a day at a restaurant, going out at night) would cost you about US$20-30; with any more than that, you'd be living like royalty. Of course, prices range throughout the region: expect to spend US$5-10 more in Slovenia and Croatia, Poland and Bulgaria are two of the least expensive countries in Eastern Europe. Don't forget to factor reserve funds (at least US$200) into your budget in case of emergency. Carrying cash with you, even in a money belt, is risky but necessary; personal checks from home are never accepted and even traveler's checks may not be accepted in some locations, particularly Russia.

CURRENCY & EXCHANGE

At the beginning of each country chapter, we list our currency abbreviation and the September 1999 exchange rates between local currency and U.S. dollars (US$), Canadian dollars (CDN$), British pounds (UK£), Irish pounds (IR£), Australian dollars (AUS$), New Zealand dollars (NZ$), South African rand (SAR), and German marks (DM). Check a large newspaper's financial pages or the web (finance.yahoo.com; www.bloomberg.com/markets/currency) for the latest rates. As a general rule, it is more expensive to buy foreign currency than domestic. In other words, Czech koruny are cheaper in the Czech Republic than in the U.K. However, it's a good idea to bring enough foreign currency to last for the first 24-72 hours of a trip to avoid being penniless after banking hours or on a holiday. Also, when accepted, using an ATM card or a credit card (see p. 21) will often get you the best possible rates.

Banks generally have the best rates. A good rule of thumb is only to go to banks or *bureaux de change* that have at most a 5% margin between their buy and sell prices. Since you lose money with every transaction, **convert large sums** (unless the currency is depreciating rapidly), **but no more than you'll need**, since it may be difficult either to change it back into your home currency or into a new one. Some countries, such as the Czech Republic, Slovakia, and Russia, may require transaction receipts to reconvert local currency. A few will not allow you to convert local currency back at all. To make matters worse, many Eastern European currencies are not exchangeable outside of their respective countries. Slovak koruny, for example, can only be exchanged in Slovakia itself; leave Slovakia with koruny and you'll have them until your next visit.

If you use traveler's checks or cash, carry some in small denominations (US$50 or less), especially for times when you are forced to exchange money at disadvantageous rates. However, it is good to carry a range of denominations since charges may be levied per check cashed. Carry your money in a variety of forms, e.g. some cash, some traveler's checks, and an ATM and/or credit card. Australians and New Zealanders should consider carrying some U.S. dollars or Deutschmarks, as some local tellers will prefer a more recognizable currency.

In some parts of Eastern Europe—particularly in countries with unstable currencies or those with a heavy German tourist industry—Deutschmarks and occasionally U.S. dollars will be preferred to local currency. Some establishments will insist that they don't accept anything else, but avoid using Western money when you can. Not only are prices quoted in dollars or marks generally more expensive than those in the local currency but Western currency may also attract thieves.

TRAVELER'S CHECKS

Traveler's checks are one of the safest and least troublesome means of carrying funds, since they can be refunded if stolen. Unfortunately, they can be a hassle—if not impossible—to cash in Russia, Belarus, and Bosnia. The general rule in Eastern Europe is the more touristed a country is by Westerners, the easier it will be to exchange traveler's checks. For country-specific information on traveler's checks, refer to the **Money and Communication** section in the **Essentials** of each chapter.

Several agencies and banks sell them, usually for face value plus a small percentage commission. (Members of the American Automobile Association, and some banks and credit unions, can get American Express checks commission-free; see **Driving Permits and Insurance,** p. 53). **American Express** and **Visa** are the most widely recognized. If you're ordering checks, do so well in advance, especially if you are requesting large sums. Each agency provides refunds if your checks are lost or stolen, and many provide additional services, such as toll-free refund hotlines in the countries you're visiting, emergency message services, and stolen credit card assistance.

In order to collect a **refund for lost or stolen checks,** keep your check receipts separate from your checks and store them in a safe place or with a traveling companion. Record check numbers when you cash them, leave a list of check numbers with someone at home, and ask for a list of refund centers when you buy your checks. Never countersign your checks until you are ready to cash them, and always bring your passport with you when you plan to use the checks.

American Express: Call (800) 25 19 02 in Australia; in New Zealand (0800) 44 10 68; in the U.K. (0800) 52 13 13; in the U.S. and Canada 800-221-7282. Elsewhere, call U.S. collect 801-964-6665; www.aexp.com. Checks can be purchased for a small fee (1-4%) at American Express Travel Service Offices, banks, and American Automobile Association offices. AAA members (see p. 53) can buy checks commission-free. American Express offices cash their checks commission-free (except where prohibited by national governments), but often at slightly worse rates than banks. The booklet *Traveler's Companion* lists travel offices and stolen check hotlines for each country.

Citicorp: Call 800-645-6556 in the U.S. and Canada; in Europe, the Middle East, or Africa, call the London office at (44 171) 508 70 07; from elsewhere, call U.S. collect 813-623-1709. Traveler's checks in 7 currencies. Commission 1-2%. Guaranteed hand-delivery of traveler's checks when a refund location is not convenient. Call 24hr.

Thomas Cook MasterCard: From the U.S., Canada, or Caribbean call 800-223-7373; from the U.K. call (0800) 62 21 01; from elsewhere, call (44) 1733 31 89 50 collect. Checks available in 13 currencies. Commission 2%. Thomas Cook offices cash checks commission-free but are much less common in Eastern Europe than American Express.

CREDIT CARDS

Where they are accepted, credit cards often offer superior exchange rates. They may also offer services like insurance or emergency help and are sometimes required to reserve hotel rooms or rental cards. Unfortunately, budget travelers will probably find that few, if any, of the establishments they frequent in Eastern Europe will accept credit cards. Aside from the occasional splurge, you will probably reserve use of your credit card for financial emergencies.

The other use to which you might put your credit card is to get a **cash advance** which allows you to extract local currency from associated banks and teller machines instantly. **MasterCard** (aka EuroCard or Access in Europe) and **Visa** (aka Carte Bleue or Barclaycard) are the most welcomed; **American Express** cards work at some ATMs, as well as at AmEx offices and major airports. However, pricey transaction fees for all credit card advances (up to US$10 per advance, plus 2-3% extra on foreign transactions after conversion to US$) typically make credit cards a more costly means of withdrawing cash than ATMs or traveler's checks. In an emergency, the transaction fee may be well worth the cost. In order to be eligible for a cash advance, request a **Personal Identification Number (PIN)** from AmEx, MasterCard, or Visa. When memorizing your PIN, be sure to remember the number code as opposed to the lettered code; key pads in Eastern Europe are not labeled with letters. If you already have a PIN, check with the company to make sure it will work in Eastern Europe; many machines require five digits.

CASH (ATM) CARDS

Cash cards—popularly called ATM (Automated Teller Machine) cards—are widespread throughout Central Europe but impossible to use in Russia. Depending on the system that your home bank uses, you can probably access your own personal bank account whenever you need money. Your home bank can provide you with a list of the countries in which your card is accepted. ATMs get the same wholesale exchange rate as credit cards. Despite these perks, do some research before relying too heavily on automation. There is often a limit on the amount of money you can withdraw per day (usually about US$500 but it can be as low as US$200, depending on the type of card and account), and computer networks sometimes fail. Additionally, both your home bank as well as the bank from which you're withdrawing money will charge you transaction fees that can be as much as US$5 per bank, per transaction. If you're traveling from the U.S. or Canada, memorize your PIN code in numeral form since machines elsewhere often don't have letters on their keys. Also, if your PIN is longer than four digits, ask your bank whether the first four digits will work, or whether you need a new, longer number.

The two major international money networks are **Cirrus** (U.S. tel. 800-4-CIRRUS (424-7787)) and **PLUS** (U.S. tel. 800-843-7587 for the "Voice Response Unit Locator"). To locate ATMs around the world, use www.visa.com/pd/atm or www.mastercard.com/atm.

GETTING MONEY FROM HOME

AMERICAN EXPRESS. Cardholders can withdraw cash from their checking accounts at any of AmEx's major offices and many of its representatives' offices, up to US$1000 every 21 days (no service charge, no interest). AmEx also offers Express Cash at any of their ATMs. Unfortunately, AmEx ATMs are few and far between in Eastern Europe. Express Cash withdrawals are automatically debited from the Cardmember's checking account or line of credit. Green card holders may withdraw up to US$1000 in a seven day period. There is a 2% transaction fee for each cash withdrawal, with a US$2.50 minimum/$20 maximum. To enroll in Express Cash, Cardmembers may call 800-CASH NOW (227-4669) in the U.S.; outside the U.S. call collect 336-668-5041.

WESTERN UNION. Travelers from the U.S., Canada, and the U.K. can wire money abroad through Western Union's international money transfer services. In the U.S., call 800-325-6000; in the U.K., call (0800) 833 833; in Canada, call 800-235-0000. The rates for sending cash are generally US$10-11 cheaper than with a credit card, and the money is usually available at the place you're sending it to within an hour. Western Union services are available only sporadically in Eastern Europe.

U.S. STATE DEPARTMENT (U.S. CITIZENS ONLY). In emergencies, U.S. citizens can have money sent via the State Department. For US$15, they will forward money within hours to the nearest consular office, which will disburse it according to instructions. The office serves only Americans in the direst of straits abroad; non-American travelers should contact their embassies for information on wiring cash. Check with the State Department or the nearest U.S. embassy or consulate for the quickest way to have the money sent. Contact the Overseas Citizens Service, American Citizens Services, Consular Affairs, Room 4811, U.S. Department of State, Washington, D.C. 20520 (tel. 202-647-5225; nights, Sundays, and holidays 647-4000; fax (on demand only) 647-3000; travel.state.gov).

SAFETY & SECURITY

Eastern Europe is generally a safe region through which to travel. In most countries, crime is restricted primarily to pickpocketing on crowded streets and public

> The US Department of State issues **Travel Warnings** against unnecessary travel to politically unstable or dangerous regions. In 1999, travel warnings were issued for Bosnia-Herzegovina, Croatia, FYR Macedonia, Moldova, Russia, and the Yugoslav provinces of Serbia and Montenegro. All of the travel warnings with the exception of Russia were at least indirectly related to the NATO bombings in Yugoslavia in the spring of 1999. Because of the bombings and at the advice of the State Department, *Let's Go* was unable to send researchers to Yugoslavia and FYR Macedonia; as a result, they are not included in this year's guide. In addition, travelers should avoid the Transdniester region of Moldova, Eastern Slavonia in Croatia, the Republika Srpska in Bosnia-Herzegovina, and the Chechnya province in Russia, due to less safe conditions. For more specific information on the travel warnings issued, consult both the country's chapter in this book as well as the State Department's web page at travel.state.gov/travel_warnings.html.

ESSENTIALS

transportation or scams by taxi drivers. Sadly, the relative safety of the region is often eclipsed by isolated political problems. While some travelers may dismiss a voyage to any part of Eastern Europe because of either economic instability in Russia or political instability in the Balkans, most Eastern Europeans will attest that there is nothing so absurd as jumping to that conclusion. The Czech Republic and Poland, for example, are as safe as—if not safer than—Western European nations and are as far removed from the situations in the Balkans and Russia as France or Italy is. With caution and common sense, a jaunt through most parts of Eastern Europe can be problem-free.

That said, a traveler to Eastern Europe does need to be more vigilant than a traveler to Western Europe. The easiest way of keeping oneself safe is by staying abreast of current events and being willing to scrap a plan or itinerary at the last minute. In addition, being aware of the dangers and taking preventative measures against them is the surest way to secure safety. In Russia, Belarus, and Ukraine, for example, organized crime is a growing problem, although primarily for locals. While a run-in with the mafia could be potentially disastrous, there are ways to prevent a disaster. Ask hostel owners and locals which restaurants and nightclubs are frequented by mafiosos and steer clear of them; restrict yourself to highly touristed nightlife and avoid any form of "adult entertainment." For almost any other potential danger, common sense and precaution are the best defenses.

> **FURTHER INFORMATION: SAFETY AND SECURITY.** *Fielding's The World's Most Dangerous Places*, edited by Kathy Knoles (US$22). Gives detailed descriptions of dangerous destinations around the world. *Don't Go!: 51 Reasons Not to Travel Abroad, But If You Must...176 Tactics for Coping With Discomforts, Distress and Danger*, by Hannah Blank (US$11). Provides great tips for taking care of oneself on the road.

BLENDING IN. Tourists are particularly vulnerable to crime because they often carry large amounts of cash and are not as street savvy as locals. To avoid unwanted attention, try to blend in as much as possible. Respecting local customs (in many cases, dressing more conservatively) may placate would-be hecklers. The gawking camera-toter is a more obvious target than the low-profile traveler. Consider dressing more like Eastern Europeans: for women, that means skirts rather than shorts, and for both men and women, avoid jeans, running shoes, sneakers, and Birkenstock or Teva sandals. Backpacks also stand out as particularly touristy; courier or shoulder bags are less likely to draw attention. Familiarize yourself with your surroundings before setting out; if you must check a map on the street, duck into a cafe or shop. Most importantly, carry yourself with confidence, as an obviously bewildered bodybuilder is more likely to be harassed than a stern and confident 98-pound weakling. If you are traveling solo, be sure that someone at home knows your itinerary and **never admit that you're traveling alone.**

Familiarity with the local language is vital to blending in. Learn at least a few phrases before you leave for any Eastern European country; "please" and "thank you" are the two most important. Always be deferential and apologetic when speaking to locals. Many Eastern Europeans simply assume that all tourists are rude and ignorant and any attempt on your part to prove them wrong will win you respect and potential friends. The more of a language you can speak, the more likely you are to gain the confidence and aid of the locals.

Follow local laws and customs. More than either dress or language, your behavior is the easiest way to peg yourself as a tourist and to draw unwanted attention. For example, women should not frequent bars by themselves; to most Eastern European men, the only women who do are prostitutes. Additionally, when entering a church, shoulders and knees must always be covered. In general, if no one is jaywalking or putting their feet on the table, you shouldn't be, either. Just as you should abide by local customs, try not to be surprised or offended by the behavior of locals. The more shocked and indignant you are when people stare or are not wearing deodorant, the more likely you are to draw attention to yourself.

EXPLORING. Extra vigilance is always wise, but there is no need for panic when exploring a new city or region. Find out about unsafe areas from tourist offices, from the manager of your hotel or hostel, or from a local you trust. You may want to carry a **whistle** to scare off attackers or attract attention; memorize the emergency number of the city or area. Whenever possible, *Let's Go* warns of unsafe neighborhoods and areas, but there are some good general tips to follow. When walking at night, stick to busy, well-lit streets and avoid dark alleyways. Do not attempt to cross through parks, parking lots or other large, deserted areas. Buildings in disrepair, vacant lots, and unpopulated areas are all bad signs. The distribution of people can reveal a great deal about the relative safety of the area; look for children playing, women walking in the open, and other signs of an active community. Keep in mind that a district can change character drastically between blocks. If you feel uncomfortable, leave as quickly and directly as you can, but don't allow fear of the unknown to turn you into a hermit. Careful, persistent exploration will build confidence and make your stay in an area that much more rewarding.

As much as you may be tempted, do not "explore" in Bosnia and Croatia; the countryside is littered with landmines and unexploded ordnance (UXO). While demining is underway, it will be years, if ever, for all of the mines to be deactivated. As long as travelers stay on paved paths and in major cities, UXOs will not be a danger. Road shoulders and abandoned buildings are particularly likely to harbor UXOs. In the Caucasus, no exploring should be done without the aid of a guide; there have been reports of mountain bandits who kidnap hikers. In addition, a guide will keep you away from dangerous borders you might otherwise unknowingly wander across.

POLITICAL INSTABILITY & TERRORISM. While most of Eastern Europe is relatively stable and safe, there are regions that are not. The most publicized of these are the Balkan Peninsula and the Caucasus region of southern Russia. Both the Caucasus and the Balkans are hotbeds of nationalism and political unrest and, as a result, periodic violence: in February 1999, a terrorist bombed a crowded market in Vladikavkaz, a border city between Russia and Chechnya. While *Let's Go* does not cover any towns which have been or are current sites of terrorist activity, travelers to the Caucasus should always exercise caution and seek out the help of locals. Under no circumstances should a traveler explore unguided.

Safety is not so easily ensured in the Balkans. NATO bombings in Yugoslavia have destabilized the region beyond its own internal tensions. The destruction of major Serbian capitals by NATO and its sympathy for other Yugoslav ethnicities is the cause of much anti-American sentiment and violence throughout the nation. And although it was not directly involved in the war, FYR Macedonia received the bulk of the Kosovar refugees; an already politically tenuous nation, FYR Macedonia is descending into further unrest. Outside of these two nations, however, much of the Balkans are in fact safe to travel. Slovenia—which doesn't even really consider itself to be Balkan—is as safe as Italy or Greece. Croatia, with the exception of Eastern Slavonia, is one of the most stable nations in the region. Sadly, the nearby war is devastating the fledgling tourist industry in both nations. Croatia, however, is the base for a few foreign terrorist organizations; although they are generally less active in Zagreb, Istria, or the Dalmatian Coast, bombings have occurred against Serbs in the contested Eastern Slavonia region. In Bosnia, travel to the Republika Srpska is unsafe; however, Sarajevo and the Bosnian Federation remain relatively stable and welcoming to tourists.

If you are traveling to Moldova, stay away from the eastern Trans-Dniester breakaway republic, particularly since the NATO bombings. Allies of Russia and Slavic sympathizers, Trans-Dniester terrorist groups have threatened retaliatory bombings against the American embassy. *Let's Go* does not cover this region of Moldova.

Terrorism and political instability are isolated problems in Eastern Europe. Aside from the threats already mentioned, the most common problem is anti-American sentiment. In general, politically stable, economically prosperous, Westernized nations are very safe; it is in economically depressed nations such as Russia, Belarus, and Ukraine where anti-American sentiment runs strong. Additionally, the recent events in Yugoslavia are aggravating anti-American sentiment; for most Eastern Europeans, NATO consists of America and no one else. The threat posed by anti-Americanism, luckily, is minimal and usually amounts to rudeness and heckling. The surest way to protect oneself is not to be American. In other words, if you are Canadian and Australian, make it clear with a flag on your backpack or by vehemently denying any American ties. Americans sometimes masquerade as different nationalities; if you can speak a language other than English, you may want to consider that option in certain situations.

In addition to anti-Americanism, neo-Nazism is on the rise in a few Eastern European nations. In February 1999, Budapest hosted a pan-European neo-Nazi conference and there has been a slow increase in hate crimes in Russia. Fortunately, neo-Nazism is still limited to isolated incidents.

GETTING AROUND. Road quality in Eastern Europe varies widely from country to country. In general, roads are poor with very few traffic signs; many are poorly lit dirt roads full of potholes. Drunk driving is common as is a general disregard for traffic laws. As with everything else though, the more Westernized the country, the better the roads: while roads in Belarus are very dangerous, Czech roads are up to Western standards. If you are using a **car,** learn local driving signals and wear a seatbelt. Children under 40 lbs. should ride only in a specially-designed carseat, available for a small fee from most car rental agencies. Study route maps before you hit the road; some roads have poor (or nonexistent) shoulders, few gas stations, and inattentive pedestrians. In many regions, road conditions necessitate driving more slowly and more cautiously than you would at home. If you plan on spending a lot of time on the road, you may want to bring spare parts. For long drives in desolate areas invest in a cellular phone and a roadside assistance program (see p. 53). Be sure to park your vehicle in a garage or well-traveled area, and use a steering wheel locking device in larger cities. **Sleeping in your car** is one of the most dangerous (and often illegal) ways to get your rest, and should be avoided.

Let's Go does not recommend **hitchhiking** under any circumstances, particularly for women—see **Getting Around,** p. 50 for more information.

SELF DEFENSE. There is no sure-fire set of precautions that will protect you from all of the situations you might encounter when you travel. A good self-defense course will give you more concrete ways to react to different types of aggression. **Impact, Prepare,** and **Model Mugging** can refer you to local self-defense courses in the United States (tel. 800-345-5425) and Vancouver, Canada (tel. 604-878-3838). Workshops (2-3 hours) start at US$50 and full courses run US$350-500. Both women and men are welcome.

FURTHER INFORMATION. The following government offices provide travel information and advisories by telephone or on their websites:

Australian Department of Foreign Affairs and Trade. Tel. (2) 6261 1111. www.dfat.gov.au.

Canadian Department of Foreign Affairs and International Trade (DFAIT). Tel. 800-267-8376 or 613-944-4000 from Ottawa. www.dfait-maeci.gc.ca. Call for their free booklet, *Bon Voyage...But.*

United Kingdom Foreign and Commonwealth Office. Tel. (0171) 238 4503. www.fco.gov.uk.

United States Department of State. Tel. 202-647-5225. travel.state.gov. For their publication *A Safe Trip Abroad,* call 202-512-1800.

FINANCIAL SECURITY

Most crimes committed in Eastern Europe are the work of con artists and pick-pockets. Muggings occur but are rare and are usually restricted to large cities. While street crime is on the rise in several economically depressed Eastern European nations such as Bulgaria and Belarus, violence and weapons are generally not used by pickpockets and thieves. Common sense, maintenance of personal space, and blending in are essential to personal safety. Obvious tourists are the primary targets of street crime.

PROTECTING YOUR VALUABLES. Carrying large sums of cash makes you an attractive target, especially when you are unfamiliar with your surroundings. The first rule of safe travel is to **bring as little with you as possible**. That means leaving expensive watches, jewelry, cameras, and electronic equipment (like your Discman) at home. Chances are you'd break it, lose it, or get sick of lugging it around anyway. Second, after you've stripped your belongings down to the bare essentials, buy a couple small combination **padlocks** to secure them either in your pack (when it's in your sight) or in a hostel locker. **Never leave your pack unattended**, especially in hostels or train stations. Third, **carry as little cash as possible** (though not so small that you go broke off of the per-withdrawal transaction fee), and carry the rest in traveler's checks and/or in the form of an ATM card. Leave your purse or wallet at home, and instead carry the bulk of your cash in a **money belt** along with your traveler's checks, your passport, and any credit/ATM/ID cards. A neck pouch is okay, but is more conspicuous (and thus less safe) than a money belt—"fanny packs" are even worse. **Don't put a wallet with money in your back pocket** and never count your money in public and carry as little as possible. Fourth, **keep at least one reserve separate from your primary stash**. This should entail about US$50 worth of cash (US dollars or German Deutchmarks are best) sewn into or stored in the depths of your pack, along with your traveler's check numbers and receipt and a photocopy of your passport. **Photocopies** of important documents allow you to recover them in case they are lost or stolen. Carry one copy separate from the documents and leave another copy at home.

CON ARTISTS AND PICKPOCKETS. Among the more colorful aspects of large cities are **con artists.** Con artists and hustlers often work in groups, and children are among the most effective. They possess an innumerable range of ruses. Be aware of certain classics: sob stories that require money, rolls of bills "found" on the street, mustard spilled (or saliva spit) onto your shoulder or babies thrown at you, both distracting you for enough time to snatch your bag. Taxi drivers are the most common con artists. Many refuse to run a meter, others drop you off and drive away before you can recover your luggage from the trunk, and many simply charge exorbitant fees. Don't ever hand over your passport to someone whose authority you question (ask to accompany them to a police station if they insist), and *never* let your passport out of your sight. Be especially suspicious in unexpected situations. Do not respond or make eye contact, walk quickly away, and keep a solid grip on your belongings. Contact the police if a hustler is particularly insistent or aggressive.

In city crowds and especially on public transportation, **pickpockets** are amazingly deft at their craft. Rush hour is no excuse for strangers to press up against you on the metro. If someone stands uncomfortably close, move to another car and hold your bags tightly. Also, be alert in public telephone booths. If you must say your calling card number, do so very quietly; if you punch it in, make sure no one can look over your shoulder.

ACCOMMODATIONS AND TRANSPORTATION. Never leave your belongings unattended; crime occurs in even the most demure-looking hostel or hotel. If you feel unsafe, look for places with either a curfew or a night attendant. *Let's Go* lists locker availability in hostels and train stations, but you'll need your own **padlock.** Lockers are useful if you plan on sleeping outdoors or don't want to lug everything with you, but don't store valuables in them. Most hotels also provide lock boxes free or for a minimal fee.

Be particularly careful on **buses,** carry your backpack in front of you where you can see it, don't check baggage on trains, and don't trust anyone to "watch your bag for a second." Thieves thrive on **trains;** professionals wait for tourists to fall asleep and then carry off everything they can. When traveling in pairs, sleep in alternating shifts; when alone, use good judgement in selecting a train compartment: never stay in an empty one, and use a lock to secure your pack to the luggage rack. Keep important documents and other valuables on your body and try to sleep on top bunks with your luggage stored above you (if not in bed with you). In Russia, however, try to sleep on bottom bunks where luggage is stored under you; the only way to lift it is by moving you. International trains between major cities (e.g., Moscow-St. Petersburg, Prague-Warsaw, or Kiev-Moscow) are generally considered to be more dangerous than countryside trains. Travelers on these trains should be especially vigilant; passengers can be drugged by criminals to prevent their waking during a robbery. Travelers are advised to secure their door with heavy wire while they sleep. Doors with chain locks can be rendered immobile by slipping hangers or shoes through the latch: it is essential that the door not budge at all even if the key-lock is broken.

If you travel by **car,** try not to leave valuable possessions—such as radios or luggage—in it while you are away. If your tape deck or radio is removable, hide it in the trunk or take it with you. If it isn't, at least conceal it under something else. Similarly, hide baggage in the trunk, although savvy thieves can tell if a car is heavily loaded by the way it sits on its tires.

DRUGS & ALCOHOL

Laws vary from country to country, but, needless to say, **illegal drugs** are best avoided altogether. Remember that you are subject to the laws of the country in which you travel, not to those of your home country, and it is your responsibility to familiarize yourself with these laws before leaving. Throughout Eastern Europe, all recreational drugs—including marijuana—are illegal. A meek "I didn't know it was illegal" will not suffice. For more specific information on the drug laws of Eastern European countries, the US State Department's Bureau for International Narcotics and Law Enforcement Affairs has a comprehensive web page detailing each country's laws (www.state.gov/www/global/narcotics_law). If you carry **prescription drugs** while you travel, it is necessary to have a copy of the prescriptions themselves and a note from a doctor, both readily accessible at country borders.

Avoid public drunkenness; it is against the law in many countries. It can also jeopardize your safety and earn the disdain of locals.

HEALTH

Common sense is the simplest prescription for good health while you travel. Travelers complain most often about their feet and their gut, so take precautionary measures: drink lots of fluids to prevent dehydration and constipation, wear sturdy, broken-in shoes and clean socks, and use talcum powder to keep your feet dry. To minimize the effects of jet lag, "reset" your body's clock by adopting the time of your destination as soon as you board the plane.

BEFORE YOU GO

Preparation can help minimize the likelihood of contracting a disease and maximize the chances of receiving effective health care in the event of an emergency.

For minor health problems, bring a compact **first-aid kit,** including bandages, aspirin or other pain killer, antibiotic cream, a thermometer, a Swiss army knife with tweezers, moleskin, decongestant for colds, motion sickness remedy, medicine for diarrhea or stomach problems (Pepto Bismol and Immodium), Ex-Lax for constipation, TUMS for heartburn, sunscreen, insect repellent, burn ointment, and anti-itch cream for rashes and insect bites (get a letter of explanation from your doctor). **Contact lens** and **glasses** wearers should bring an extra pair of glasses and a copy of the prescription. In addition, contact lens wearers should bring an extra pair of lenses, extra solution, and eyedrops. Those who use heat disinfection might consider switching to chemical cleansers for the duration of the trip.

In your **passport,** write the names of any people you wish to be contacted in case of a medical emergency and also list any **allergies** or medical conditions you would want doctors to be aware of. Allergy sufferers might want to obtain a full supply of any necessary medication before the trip. Matching a prescription to a foreign equivalent is not always easy, safe, or possible. Carry up-to-date, legible prescriptions or a statement from your doctor stating the medication's trade name, manufacturer, chemical name, and dosage. While traveling, be sure to keep all medication with you in your carry-on luggage.

> The **Centers for Disease Control and Prevention** (www.cdc.gov) in the U.S. issue current warnings particular to outbreaks of disease within Eastern Europe. A **diptheria epidemic** that began in Russia in 1990 has now spread to the remaining New Independent States of the former Soviet Union. Cases generally arise in urban areas, but incidents are increasingly reported in rural areas. The Advisory Committee on Immunization Practices recommends that travelers to these areas should be up-to-date for diptheria immunization, which is not normally required for international travel.

IMMUNIZATIONS. Take a look at your immunization records before you go. Travelers should be sure that the following vaccines are up to date: MMR (for measles, mumps, and rubella); DTaP or Td (for diptheria, tetanus, and pertussis); OPV (for polio); HbCV (for haemophilus influenza B); and HBV (for hepatitus B). Adults traveling to the Commonwealth of Independent States should consider an additional dose of **Polio** vaccine if they have not already had one during their adult years. **Hepatitis A** vaccine and/or immune globulin (IG) is recommended for all travelers to Eastern Europe. If you will be spending more than four weeks in the region, you will be required to vaccinate for **typhoid.** In addition, a **rabies** vaccine is recommended for anyone who might be exposed to domestic or wild animals. Check with a doctor for guidance through this maze of injections.

USEFUL ORGANIZATIONS. The U.S. **Centers for Disease Control and Prevention (CDC)** (tel. 888-232-3299; www.cdc.gov) is an excellent source of information for travelers around the world and maintains an international fax information service for travelers. The CDC also publishes the booklet "Health Information for International Travelers" (US$20), an annual global rundown of disease, immunization, and general health advice, including risks in particular countries. This book may be purchased by sending a check or money order to the Superintendent of Documents, U.S. Government Printing Office, P.O. Box 371954, Pittsburgh, PA, 15250-7954. Orders can be made by phone (tel. 202-512-1800) with a major credit card (Visa, MasterCard, or Discover).

The **United States State Department** (travel.state.gov) compiles Consular Information Sheets on health, entry requirements, and other issues for all countries of the world. For quick information on travel warnings, call the **Overseas Citizens' Services** (tel. 202-647-5225; after-hours 647-4000). To receive the same Consular Information Sheets by fax, dial 202-647-3000 directly from a fax machine and follow the recorded instructions. The State Department's regional passport agencies in the U.S., field offices of the U.S. Chamber of Commerce, and U.S. embassies and consulates abroad provide the same data, or send a self-addressed, stamped envelope to the Overseas Citizens' Services, Bureau of Consular Affairs, #4811, U.S. Department of State, Washington, D.C. 20520.

FURTHER READING: USEFUL ORGANIZATIONS. For detailed information and tips on travel health, including a country-by-country overview of diseases, check out the ***International Travel Health Guide,*** Stuart Rose, MD (Travel Medicine, $20). Information is also available at Travel Medicine's website (www.travmed.com).

For general health information, contact the **American Red Cross.** The ARC publishes *First-Aid and Safety Handbook* (US$5) available for purchase by calling or writing to the American Red Cross, 285 Columbus Ave., Boston, MA 02116-5114 (tel. 800-564-1234, M-F 8:30am-4:30pm).

MEDICAL ASSISTANCE ON THE ROAD. The quality and availability of medical assistance varies greatly throughout Eastern Europe. In major cities such as Prague or Budapest, there are generally English-speaking medical centers or hospitals for foreigners and ex-patriots; the care at these hospitals tends to be better than elsewhere in the region. In the countryside and in relatively untouristed countries such as Belarus or Latvia, English-speaking facilities are virtually impossible to find. Tourist offices may sometimes have names of local doctors who speak English. In general, the medical service in these regions is sporadic at best, with very few hospitals maintained at Western standards. While basic medical supplies are always available, specialized treatment is not. In these countries, private hospitals will generally have better facilities than the state-operated hospitals.

If you are concerned about being able to access medical support while traveling, contact one of these two services: **Global Emergency Medical Services (GEMS)** has products called *MedPass* that provide 24-hour international medical assistance and support coordinated through registered nurses who have online access to your medical information, your primary physician, and a worldwide network of screened, credentialed English-speaking doctors and hospitals. Subscribers also receive a personal medical record that contains vital information in case of emergencies, and GEMS will pay for medical evacuation if necessary. Prices start at about US$35 for a 30-day trip and run up to about $100 for annual services. For more information contact them at 2001 Westside Dr. #120, Alpharetta, GA 30004 (tel. 800-860-1111; fax 770-475-0058; www.globalems.com). The **International Association for Medical Assistance to Travelers (IAMAT)** has free membership and offers a directory of English-speaking doctors around the world who treat members for a set fee, and detailed charts on immunization requirements, various tropical diseases, climate, and sanitation. Chapters include: **U.S.,** 417 Center St., Lewiston, NY 14092 (tel. 716-754-4883, 8am-4pm; fax 519-836-3412; email iamat@@sentex.net; www.sentex.net/~iamat); **Canada,** 40 Regal Road, Guelph, ON, N1K 1B5 (tel. 519-

836-0102) or 1287 St. Clair Avenue West, Toronto, ON M6E 1B8 (tel. 416-652-0137; fax 519-836-3412); **New Zealand,** P.O. Box 5049, Christchurch 5 (fax (03) 352 46 30; iamat@chch.planet.org.nz).

If your regular **insurance** policy does not cover travel abroad, you may wish to purchase additional coverage. With the exception of Medicare, most health insurance plans cover members' medical emergencies during trips abroad; check with your insurance carrier to be sure. For more information, see **Insurance,** p. 34. Unfortunately, most medical facilities accept only cash payments; insurance would be used only for your own reimbursement.

MEDICAL CONDITIONS. Those with medical conditions (e.g., diabetes, allergies to antibiotics, epilepsy, heart conditions) may want to obtain a stainless steel **Medic Alert** identification tag (US$35 the first year, and $15 annually thereafter), which identifies the condition and gives a 24-hour collect-call information number. Contact the Medic Alert Foundation, 2323 Colorado Ave., Turlock, CA 95382 (tel. 800-825-3785; www.medicalert.org). Diabetics can contact the **American Diabetes Association**, 1660 Duke St., Alexandria, VA 22314 (tel. 800-232-3472), to receive copies of the article, "Travel and Diabetes," and a diabetic ID card, which carries messages in 18 languages explaining the carrier's diabetic status.

If you are **HIV** positive, contact the Bureau of Consular Affairs, #4811, Department of State, Washington, D.C. 20520 (tel. 202-647-1488; auto-fax 202-647-3000; travel.state.gov). Belarus, Moldova, and Russia all require documentation verifying that you are HIV negative in order to issue visas for more than three months.

ENVIRONMENTAL HAZARDS

Heat exhaustion and dehydration: Heat exhaustion, characterized by dehydration and salt deficiency, can lead to fatigue, headaches, and wooziness. Avoid heat exhaustion by drinking plenty of clear fluids and eating salty foods, like crackers. Always drink enough liquids to keep your urine clear. Alcoholic beverages are dehydrating, as are coffee, strong tea, and caffeinated sodas. Wear a hat, sunglasses, and a lightweight longsleeve shirt in hot sun, and take time to acclimate to a hot destination before seriously exerting yourself. Continuous heat stress can eventually lead to **heatstroke,** characterized by rising body temperature, severe headache, and cessation of sweating. Heatstroke is rare but serious, and victims must be cooled off with wet towels and taken to a doctor as soon as possible.

Sunburn: If you're prone to sunburn, bring sunscreen with you (it's often more expensive and hard to find when traveling), and apply it liberally and often to avoid burns and risk of skin cancer. If you are planning on spending time near water or in the snow, you are at risk of getting burned, even through clouds. Protect your eyes with good sunglasses, since ultraviolet rays can damage the retina of the eye after too much exposure. If you get sunburned, drink more fluids than usual and apply Calamine or an aloe-based lotion.

Hypothermia and frostbite: A rapid drop in body temperature is the clearest warning sign of overexposure to cold. Victims may also shiver, feel exhausted, have poor coordination or slurred speech, hallucinate, or suffer amnesia. Seek medical help, and *do not let hypothermia victims fall asleep*—their body temperature will continue to drop and they may die. To avoid hypothermia, keep dry, wear layers, and stay out of the wind. In wet weather, wool and synthetics such as pile retain heat. Most other fabric, especially cotton, will make you colder. When the temperature is below freezing, watch for **frostbite.** If a region of skin turns white, waxy, and cold, do not rub the area. Drink warm beverages, get dry, and slowly warm the area with dry fabric or steady body contact, until a doctor can be found.

High altitude: Travelers to high altitudes must allow their bodies a couple of days to adjust to lower oxygen levels in the air before exerting themselves. Alcohol is more potent at high elevations. High altitudes mean that ultraviolet rays are stronger, as well, and the risk of sunburn is therefore greater, even in cold weather.

PREVENTING DISEASE

INSECT-BORNE DISEASES. Many diseases are transmitted by insects—mainly mosquitoes, fleas, ticks, and lice. Be aware of insects in wet or forested areas, while hiking, and especially while camping. **Mosquitoes** are most active from dusk to dawn. Use insect repellents; only OFF is available in Eastern Europe, so if you're planning on hiking, be sure to bring along DEET. Wear long pants and long sleeves (fabric need not be thick or warm; tropic-weight cottons can keep you comfortable in the heat) as well as shoes and socks, and tuck long pants into socks. Soak or spray your gear with permethrin, which is licensed in the U.S. for use on clothing. Natural repellents can be useful supplements: taking vitamin B-12 pills regularly can eventually make you smelly to insects, as can garlic pills. Calamine lotion or topical cortisones (like Cortaid) may stop insect bites from itching, as can a bath with a half-cup of baking soda or oatmeal. **Ticks**—responsible for Lyme's and other diseases—can be particularly dangerous in rural and forested regions. Pause periodically while walking to brush off ticks using a fine-toothed comb on your neck and scalp. Do not try to remove ticks by burning them or coating them with nail polish remover or petroleum jelly.

Tick-borne encephalitis, a viral infection of the central nervous system, is transmitted during the summer by tick bites, and also by consumption of unpasteurized dairy products. The disease occurs most often in wooded areas. Symptoms can range from nothing to headaches and flu-like symptoms to swelling of the brain (encephalitis). A vaccine is available in Europe, but the immunization schedule is impractical for most tourists, and the risk of contracting the disease is relatively low, especially if you take precautions against tick bites. Encephalitis occurs primarily in Central Europe, including Poland, Slovakia, Czech Republic, and Hungary as well as in the former Soviet Union.

FOOD- AND WATER-BORNE DISEASES. If you get sick at all while in Eastern Europe, it will most likely be from something you ate or drank; food- and water-borne diseases are the most common ailments plaguing Eastern European travelers. In fact, you're more likely to suffer from **constipation** caused by high doses of meat and very little vegetables than any other ailment. With both constipation and actual diseases, prevention is the best cure: be sure that everything you eat is cooked properly and that the water you drink is clean. Since the risk of contracting traveler's diarrhea or other diseases is high throughout Eastern Europe, you should never drink unbottled water that you have not treated yourself. To purify your own water, bring it to a rolling boil or treat it with **iodine tablets,** available at any camping goods store. In risk areas, don't brush your teeth with tap water or rinse your toothbrush under the faucet, and keep your mouth closed in the shower. Ice cubes are just as dangerous as impure water in liquid form. Salads and uncooked vegetables are full of untreated water. Be particularly wary of any vegetables from Belarus and Northern Ukraine, regions still recovering from the Chernobyl disaster. Other culprits are raw shellfish, unpasteurized milk, and sauces containing raw eggs. Peel all fruits and vegetables yourself, and beware of watermelon, which is often injected with impure water. Watch out for food from markets or street vendors that may have been washed in dirty water or fried in rancid cooking oil, such as juices and peeled fruits. Always wash your hands before eating, or bring a quick-drying purifying liquid hand cleaner like Purrell. Your bowels will thank you.

Traveler's diarrhea results from drinking untreated water or eating uncooked foods. It is usually an indication of your body's temporary reaction to the bacteria in unfamiliar food ingredients. It can last three to seven days. Symptoms include nausea, bloating, urgency, and malaise. If the nasties hit you, have quick-energy, non-sugary foods with protein and carbohydrates to keep your strength up. Over-the-counter remedies (such as Pepto-Bismol or Immodium) may counteract the problems, but they can complicate serious infections. Avoid anti-diarrheals if you suspect that you are at risk for other diseases. The most dangerous side effect of diarrhea is dehydration; the simplest and most effective anti-dehydration formula is 8oz. of (clean) water with a ½ tsp. of sugar or honey and a pinch of salt. Soft drinks without caffeine or salted crackers are also good. Down several of these remedies a day, rest, and wait for the disease to run its course. If you develop a fever or your symptoms don't go away after four or five days, consult a doctor. You may have dysentery (see below). If children develop traveler's diarrhea, consult a doctor, since treatment is different.

Dysentery results from a serious intestinal infection caused by certain bacteria. The most common type is bacillary dysentery, also called shigellosis. Symptoms include bloody diarrhea or bloody stools mixed with mucus, fever, and abdominal pain and tenderness. Bacillary dysentery generally only lasts a week, but it is highly contagious. Amoebic dysentery develops more slowly. However, it is a more serious disease, and may cause long-term damage if left untreated. A stool test can determine what kind you have, so you should seek medical help immediately. In an emergency, the drugs norfloxacin or ciprofloxacin (commonly known as Cipro) can be used. If you are traveling in high-risk regions (especially rural areas) consider obtaining a prescription before you leave home.

Cholera is an intestinal disease caused by a bacteria found in contaminated food. It is a serious risk in Moldova, Russia, and Ukraine. The first severe symptoms of cholera are lots of watery diarrhea, dehydration, vomiting, and muscle cramps. Untreated cholera can cause death very quickly. See a doctor immediately. Antibiotics are available, but the most important treatment is rehydration. Consider getting a (50% effective) vaccine if you have stomach problems (e.g. ulcers), or if you will be camping a good deal or living where water is not reliable.

Hepatitis A (distinct from B and C, see below) is a moderate risk throughout Eastern Europe. Hep A is a viral infection of the liver acquired primarily through contaminated water, ice, shellfish, or unpeeled fruits, and vegetables, but also from sexual contact. Symptoms include fatigue, fever, loss of appetite, nausea, dark urine, jaundice, vomiting, aches and pains, and light stools. Ask your doctor about the vaccine called Havrix, or ask to get an injection of immuno globulin (IG; formerly called gamma globulin). Risk is highest in rural areas and the countryside, but is also present in urban areas.

Parasites such as microbes and tapeworms also hide in unsafe water and food. **Giardia,** for example, is acquired by drinking untreated water from streams or lakes all over the world. Symptoms of parasitic infections in general include swollen glands or lymph nodes, fever, rashes or itchiness, digestive problems, eye problems, and anemia. Boil your water, wear shoes, avoid bugs, and eat only cooked food.

Schistosomiasis is another parasitic disease, caused when the larvae of the flatworm penetrates unbroken skin. Swimming in fresh water, especially in rural areas, should be avoided. If your skin is exposed to untreated water, the CDC recommends immediate and vigorous rubbing with a towel and/or the application of rubbing alcohol. If infected, you may notice an itchy localized rash; later symptoms include fever, fatigue, painful urination, diarrhea, loss of appetite, night sweats, and a hive-like rash on the body. Schistosomiasis can be treated with prescription drugs once symptoms appear.

Typhoid fever occurs infrequently in villages and rural areas in Eastern Europe. While mostly transmitted through contaminated food and water, it may also be acquired by direct contact with another person. Symptoms include fever, headaches, fatigue, loss of appetite, constipation, and a rash on the abdomen or chest. Antibiotics can treat typhoid, but the CDC recommends vaccinations (70-90% effective) if you will be hiking, camping, or staying in small cities or rural areas.

OTHER INFECTIOUS DISEASES

Rabies is transmitted through the saliva of infected animals. It is fatal if untreated. Avoid contact with animals, especially strays. If you are bitten, wash the wound thoroughly and seek immediate medical care. Once you begin to show symptoms (thirst and muscle spasms), the disease is in its terminal stage. If possible, try to locate the animal that bit you to determine whether it does indeed have rabies. A rabies vaccine is available but is only semi-effective. Three shots must be administered over one year.

Hepatitis B is a viral infection of the liver transmitted through the transfer of bodily fluids, by sharing needles, or by having unprotected sex. Its incubation period varies and can be much longer than the 30-day incubation period of Hepatitis A. A person may not begin to show symptoms until many years after infection. The CDC recommends the Hepatitis B vaccination for health-care workers, sexually active travelers, and anyone planning to seek medical treatment abroad. Vaccination consists of a 3-shot series given over a period of time, and should begin 6 months before traveling.

Hepatitis C is like Hepatitis B, but the modes of transmission are different. Intravenous drug users, those with occupational exposure to blood, hemodialysis patients, or recipients of blood transfusions are at the highest risk, but the disease can also be spread through sexual contact and sharing of items like razors and toothbrushes, which may have traces of blood on them.

AIDS, HIV, STDS

Acquired Immune Deficiency Syndrome (AIDS) is a growing problem around the world. The World Health Organization estimates that there are around 30 million people infected with the HIV virus, and women now represent 40% of all new HIV infections. HIV rates in Eastern Europe are generally extremely low; the highest rate is in Ukraine, where 0.43% of the population is infected. Most nations, however, hover between 0.01% and 0.05%.

The easiest mode of HIV transmission is through direct blood-to-blood contact with an HIV-positive person; *never* share intravenous drug, tattooing, or other needles. The most common mode of transmission, however, is sexual intercourse. Health professionals recommend the use of latex condoms. Since it isn't always easy to buy condoms when traveling, take a supply with you before you depart for your trip. Belarus, Moldova, and Russia screen incoming travelers, primarily those planning extended visits for work or study, and deny entrance to HIV-positive people. Contact the consulate for information about this policy.

Council's brochure, *Travel Safe: AIDS and International Travel*, is available at all Council Travel offices and at their website (www.ciee.org/study/safety/travelsafe.htm). Other **sexually transmitted diseases** (STDs) such as gonorrhea, chlamydia, genital warts, syphilis, and herpes are easier to catch than HIV, and some can be just as deadly. **Hepatitis B** and **C** are also serious sexually-transmitted diseases (see **Other Infectious Diseases,** above). It's a wise idea to look at your partner's genitals before you have sex. Warning signs for STDs include: swelling, sores, bumps, or blisters on sex organs, rectum, or mouth; burning and pain during urination and bowel movements; itching around sex organs; swelling or redness in the throat, flu-like symptoms with fever, chills, and aches. If these symptoms develop, see a doctor immediately. When having sex, condoms may protect you from certain STDs, but oral or even tactile contact can lead to transmission.

WOMEN'S HEALTH

Women traveling in unsanitary conditions are vulnerable to **urinary tract** and **bladder infections,** common and severely uncomfortable bacterial diseases that cause a burning sensation and painful and sometimes frequent urination. To try to avoid these infections, drink plenty of vitamin-C-rich juice and clean water, and urinate frequently, especially after intercourse. Untreated, these infections can lead to kidney infections, sterility, and even death. If symptoms persist, see a doctor.

Women are also susceptible to **vaginal yeast infections,** a treatable but uncomfortable illness likely to flare up in hot and humid climates. Wearing loosely fitting trousers or a skirt and cotton underwear will help. Yeast infections can be treated with an over-the-counter remedy like Monostat or Gynelotrimin. Bring supplies from home if you are prone to infection, as they may be difficult to find on the road. Some travelers opt for a natural alternative such as plain yogurt and lemon juice douche if other remedies are unavailable.

Tampons and **pads** are sometimes hard to find when traveling, and your preferred brands may not be available, so it may be advisable to take supplies along. In Eastern Europe, only non-applicator tampons are available. **Reliable contraceptive devices** may also be difficult to find. Women on the pill should bring enough to allow for possible loss or extended stays. Bring a prescription, since forms of the pill vary a good deal. Women who use a diaphragm should bring enough contraceptive jelly. Though condoms are increasingly available, you might want to bring your favorite brand before you go, as availability and quality vary.

Women who need an **abortion** while abroad should contact the **International Planned Parenthood Federation,** European Regional Office, Regent's College Inner Circle, Regent's Park, London NW1 4NS (tel. (171) 487 7900; fax 487 7950), for more information.

INSURANCE

Travel insurance generally covers four basic areas: medical/health problems, property loss, trip cancellation/interruption, and emergency evacuation. Although your regular insurance policies may well extend to travel-related accidents, you may consider purchasing travel insurance if the cost of potential trip cancellation/interruption or emergency medical evacuation is greater than you can absorb.

Medical insurance (especially university policies) often covers costs incurred abroad; check with your provider. **Medicare does not cover foreign travel.** Canadians are protected by their home province's health insurance plan for up to 90 days after leaving the country; check with the provincial Ministry of Health or Health Plan Headquarters for details. **Homeowners' insurance** (or your family's coverage) often covers theft during travel and loss of travel documents (passport, plane ticket, railpass, etc.) up to US$500.

ISIC and **ITIC** provide basic insurance benefits, including US$100 per day of in-hospital sickness for a maximum of 60 days, US$3000 of accident-related medical reimbursement, and US$25,000 for emergency medical transport (see **Identification,** p. 17). Cardholders have access to a toll-free 24-hour helpline whose multilingual staff can provide assistance in medical, legal, and financial emergencies overseas (tel. 800-626-2427 in the U.S. and Canada; elsewhere call the U.S. collect 713-267-2525. **American Express** (tel. 800-528-4800) grants most cardholders automatic car rental insurance (collision and theft, but not liability) and ground travel accident coverage of US$100,000 on flight purchases made with the card.

Prices for travel insurance purchased separately generally run about US$50 per week for full coverage, while trip cancellation/interruption may be purchased separately at a rate of about US$5.50 per US$100 of coverage.

INSURANCE PROVIDERS. Council and **STA** (see p. 46 for complete listings) offer a range of plans that can supplement your basic insurance coverage. Other private insurance providers in the **U.S. and Canada** include: **Access America** (tel. 800-284-8300; fax 804-673-1491); **Berkely Group/Carefree Travel Insurance** (tel. 800-323-3149 or 516-294-0220; fax 516-294-1095; info@berkely.com; www.berkely.com); **Globalcare Travel Insurance** (tel. 800-821-2488; fax 781-592-7720; www.globalcare-cocco.com); and **Travel Assistance International** (tel. 800-821-2828 or 202-828-5894; fax 202-828-5896; email wassist@aol.com; www.worldwide-assistance.com). Providers in the **U.K.** include **Campus Travel** (tel. (01865) 258 000; fax (01865) 792 378) and **Columbus Travel Insurance** (tel. (0171) 375 0011; fax 375 0022). In **Australia** try **CIC Insurance** (tel. 9202 8000).

PACKING

Pack according to the extremes of climate you may experience and the type of travel you'll be doing. **Pack light:** a good rule is to lay out only what you absolutely need, then take half the clothes and twice the money. The less you have, the less you have to lose (or store, or carry on your back). Don't forget the obvious things: no matter when you're traveling, it's always a good idea to bring a rain jacket, a warm jacket or wool sweater, and sturdy shoes and thick socks. You may also want to add one outfit beyond the jeans and t-shirt uniform, and maybe a nicer pair of shoes if you have the room. Keep in mind that no one in Eastern Europe wears jeans and t-shirts, and you're bound to stand out as a tourist in it. Khakis and skirts are a less conspicuous and equally comfortable option. If you plan on exploring the nightlife in Eastern Europe, consider wearing the *de rigeur* all black clubbing uniform. Remember that wool will keep you warm even when soaked through, whereas wet cotton is colder than wearing nothing at all.

If you plan to be doing a lot of hiking, see **Outdoors,** p. 39.

LUGGAGE. If you plan to cover most of your itinerary by foot, a sturdy **frame backpack** is unbeatable. **Internal-frame packs** mold better to your back, keep a lower center of gravity, and can flex adequately on difficult hikes that require a lot of bending and maneuvering. **External-frame packs** are more comfortable for long hikes over even terrain—like city streets—since they keep the weight higher and distribute it more evenly. Look for a pack with a strong, padded hip belt to transfer weight from your shoulders to your hips. Good packs cost anywhere from US$150 to US$500. Before you leave, pack your bag, strap it on, and imagine yourself walking uphill on hot asphalt for three hours; this should give you a sense of how important it is to pack lightly. Organizations that sell packs through mail-order are listed on p. 39.

Toting a **suitcase** or **trunk** is fine if you plan to live in one or two cities and explore from there, but a very bad idea if you're going to be moving around a lot. Make sure suitcases have wheels and consider how much they weigh even when empty. Hard-sided luggage is more durable but more weighty and cumbersome. Soft-sided luggage should have a PVC frame, a strong lining to resist bad weather and rough handling, and its seams should be triple-stitched for durability.

In addition to your main vessel, a small backpack, rucksack, or courier bag may be useful as a **daypack** for sight-seeing expeditions; it doubles as an airplane **carry-on.** An empty, lightweight **duffel bag** packed inside your luggage may also be useful. Once abroad you can fill your luggage with purchases and keep your dirty clothes in the duffel.

WASHING CLOTHES. *Let's Go* attempts to provide information on laundromats in the **Practical Information** listings for larger cities, but sometimes it may be cheaper and easier to use a sink. Bring a small bar or tube of detergent soap, a small rubber ball to stop up the sink, and a travel clothes line.

ELECTRIC CURRENT. In Eastern Europe, electricity is 220 volts AC, enough to fry any 110V North American appliance. 220V electrical appliances don't like 110V current, either. Visit a hardware store for an adapter (which changes the shape of the plug) and a converter (which changes the voltage). Don't make the mistake of using only an adapter (unless appliance instructions explicitly state otherwise).

CONTACT LENSES. Machines which heat-disinfect contact lenses will require a small converter (about US$20) to 220V. Consider switching temporarily to a chemical disinfection system, but check with your lens dispenser to see if it's safe to switch; some lenses may be damaged by a chemical system. Contact lens supplies may be expensive and difficult to find; bring enough saline and cleaner for your entire vacation.

FILM. Film is one of the few expensive items in Eastern Europe, as is film developing; it makes more sense to bring film from home and develop it once you return. If you're not a serious photographer, you might want to consider bringing a **disposable camera** or two rather than an expensive permanent one. Despite disclaimers, airport security X-rays *can* fog film, so either buy a lead-lined pouch, sold at camera stores, or ask the security to hand inspect it. Always pack it in your carry-on luggage, since higher-intensity X-rays are used on checked luggage.

OTHER USEFUL ITEMS. No matter how you're traveling, it's always a good idea to carry a first-aid kit including sunscreen, insect repellent, and vitamins (see **Health,** p. 28). Other useful items include: an umbrella; sealable plastic bags (for damp clothes, soap, food, shampoo, and other spillables); alarm clock; waterproof matches; sun hat; moleskin (for blisters); needle and thread; safety pins; sunglasses; pocketknife; plastic water bottle; compass; string (makeshift clothesline and lashing material); towel; padlock; whistle; rubber bands; flashlight; cold-water soap; earplugs; electrical tape (for patching tears); tweezers; garbage bags; a small calculator for currency conversion; a pair of flip-flops for the shower; a moneybelt for carrying valuables; deodorant; razors; tampons; and condoms (see **AIDS, HIV, and STDs,** p. 33).

FURTHER READING: PACKING. *The Packing Book,* by Judith Gilford (Ten Speed Press, US$9). *Backpacking One Step at a Time,* Harvey Manning (Vintage, US$15).

ACCOMMODATIONS

HOSTELS

A HOSTELER'S BILL OF RIGHTS. There are certain standard features that we do not include in our hostel listings. Unless we state otherwise, you can expect that every hostel has: no lockout, no curfew, a kitchen, free hot showers, secure luggage storage, and no key deposit.

Hostels are generally dorm-style accommodations, often in single-sex large rooms with bunk beds, although some hostels do offer private rooms for families and couples. They sometimes have kitchens and utensils for your use, bike or moped rentals, storage areas, and laundry facilities. There can be drawbacks: some hostels close during certain daytime "lock-out" hours, have a curfew, don't accept reservations, impose a maximum stay, or, less frequently, require that you do chores. **Tourist hostels,** different from youth hostels, tend to be bare-bones establishments with no hot water, and no kitchens, but plenty of loud Eastern European school groups. Most tourist offices will be perplexed when you ask for a tourist hostel or tourist accommodation; they seem to think that only the bravest of travelers can handle the chaos and grime of a tourist hotel. In reality, they're not that bad and are usually the cheapest bed in town. Central Europe is home to a peculiar species of hostels, the **worker's hostel.** Although summer fills them up with young travelers, they are generally patronized only by locals and, you guessed it, migrant workers. In many towns, worker's hostels are the only hostels available. In Eastern Europe, a bed in any sort of hostel will range from US$5-10.

For their various services and lower rates at member hostels, hostelling associations, especially **Hostelling International (HI),** can definitely be worth joining. HI hostels are scattered throughout Eastern Europe and many accept reservations via the International Booking Network (tel. 2261 11 11 from Australia, 800-663-5777 from Canada, (171) 836 10 36 from England, 1301 766 from Ireland, 93 79 42 24 from New Zealand, 800-909-4776 from U.S.; www.hiayh.org/ushostel/reserva/ibn3.htm) for a nominal fee. HI hostels are, however, by no means as prevalent as in Western Europe. In fact, there are no HI hostels in Belarus, Bosnia, Latvia, and Ukraine and very few in Croatia, Slovenia, Estonia, Lithuania, Russia, and Slovakia. HI's umbrella organization's web page lists the web addresses and phone numbers of all national associations and can be a great place to begin researching hostelling in a specific region (www.iyhf.org). Other comprehensive hostelling websites include www.hostels.com and www.eurotrip.com/accommodation. To join HI, contact one of the following organizations in your home country:

Australian Youth Hostels Association (AYHA), 422 Kent St., Sydney NSW 2000 (tel. (02) 92 61 11 11; fax 92 61 19 69; yha@yhansw.org.au; www.yha.org.au). One-year membership AUS$44, under 18 AUS$13.50.

Hostelling International-Canada (HI-C), 400-205 Catherine St., Ottawa, ON K2P 1C3 (tel. 800-663-5777 or 613-237-7884; fax 237-7868; info@hostellingintl.ca; www.hostellingintl.ca). One-year membership CDN$25, under 18 CDN$12; 2-yr. CDN$35.

An Óige (Irish Youth Hostel Association), 61 Mountjoy St., Dublin 7 (tel. (1) 830 45 55; fax 830 58 08; anoige@iol.ie; www.irelandyha.org). One-year membership IR£10, under 18 IR£4, families IR£20.

Youth Hostels Association of New Zealand (YHANZ), P.O. Box 436, 173 Cashel St., Christchurch 1 (tel. (643) 379 99 70; fax 365 44 76; info@yha.org.nz; www.yha.org.nz). One-year membership NZ$24, ages 15-17 NZ$12, under 15 free.

Hostelling International South Africa, P.O. Box 4402, Cape Town 8000 (tel. (021) 24 25 11; fax 24 41 19; info@hisa.org.za; www.hisa.org.za). One-year membership SAR50, under 18 SAR25, lifetime SAR250.

Scottish Youth Hostels Association (SYHA), 7 Glebe Crescent, Stirling FK8 2JA (tel. (01786) 89 14 00; fax 89 13 33; info@syha.org.uk; www.syha.org.uk). Membership UK£6, under 18 UK£2.50.

Youth Hostels Association of England and Wales (YHA), 8 St. Stephen's Hill, St. Albans, Hertfordshire AL1 2DY, England (tel. (01727) 85 52 15 or 845 07; fax 84 41 26; yhacustomerservices@compuserve.com; www.yha.org.uk). One-year membership UK£11, under 18 UK£5.50, families UK£22.

Hostelling International Northern Ireland (HINI), 22-32 Donegall Rd., Belfast BT12 5JN, Northern Ireland (tel. (01232) 32 47 33 or 31 54 35; fax 43 96 99; info@hini.org.uk; www.hini.org.uk). One-year membership UK£7, under 18 UK£3, families UK£14.

Hostelling International-American Youth Hostels (HI-AYH), 733 15th St. NW, Suite 840, Washington, D.C. 20005 (tel. 202-783-6161 ext. 136; fax 783-6171; email hiayhserv@hiayh.org; www.hiayh.org). One-year membership US$25, over 54 US$15, under 18 free.

PENSIONS

After hostels, pensions are the most common budget accommodation in Eastern Europe. A cross between a hostel and a hotel, pensions are generally intimate and run by a family or out of someone's home, similar to a bed & breakfast, and usually rent by the room, although they occasionally offer dorm-style accommodations. Pensions are often the cleanest, safest, and friendliest budget accommodation available, with the owners going out of their way to arrange private excursions, and help with such daily chores as doing laundry, checking e-mail, and communicating with locals. In Eastern Europe, a single room in a pension starts at around US$10 and can range up to US$20. A night's stay usually includes breakfast and a personal key to the building.

DORMS

Many **colleges and universities** open their residence halls to travelers when school is not in session—usually only July and August. These dorms are often close to student areas—good sources for information on things to do—and tend to be very clean. Getting a room may take several frustrated phone calls and eventually require a trek to the dorm itself, but rates are low and the guests and students fun. *Let's Go* lists colleges which rent rooms among the accommodations for appropriate cities; when they're not listed, check at the tourist office for local.

PRIVATE HOMES

An increasingly popular option in nowhere-near-the-beaten-path locations is to rent a room in a private home. Differing from both pensions and home exchanges, families throughout Eastern Europe rent out spare bedrooms to weary backpackers. These are not hotels—they are private homes in which you will share the family's bathroom, kitchen, and living space. Although it may at first seem sketchy to a hyper-safety-concerned Westerner, going home with an old woman from the train station or knocking on doors with *Zimmer Frei* signs is absolutely legitimate and generally safe. In small towns, private homes often rent the only tourist rooms and offer such added perks as immaculate rooms, laundry, home-cooked meals, and a native tour guide. Prices vary greatly throughout the region but tend to hover between hostel and pension prices. *Let's Go* does not list specific homes in each town; rather, you should check with the local tourist office.

HOME EXCHANGE & RENTALS

Home exchange offers various types of homes (houses, apartments, condominiums, villas, even castles in some cases), and the opportunity to live like a native and cheaply—usually only an administration fee is paid to the matching service. Once you join or contact one of the exchange services listed below, it is then up to you to decide with whom you would like to exchange homes. Most companies have pictures of member's homes and information about the owners. A great site listing many exchange companies can be found at www.aitec.edu.au/~bwechner/Documents/Travel/Lists/Home ExchangeClubs.html. Home rentals, as opposed to exchanges, are much more expensive. However, they can be cheaper than comparably-serviced hotels. Both home exchanges and rentals are ideal for families with children, and travelers with special dietary needs; you often get your own kitchen, maid service, TV, and telephones.

HomeExchange, P.O. Box 30085, Santa Barbara, CA 93130 (tel. 805-898-9660; admin@HomeExchange.com; www.homeexchange.com.

Intervac International Home Exchange: www.intervac.com. **Intervac Czech Republic,** Antonin and Lenka Machackovi, Pod stanici 25/603, 10200 Praha 10, Czech Republic (tel. (422) 75 72 50; fax (422) 786 00 61; **Intervac Poland,** Ewa Krupska, u1.Bursztynowa 22, 31-213 Krakow, Poland (york@euro.net.pl).

The Invented City: International Home Exchange, 41 Sutter St., Suite 1090, San Francisco, CA 94104 (tel. 800-788-2489 in the U.S. or 415-252-1141 elsewhere; fax 252-1171; invented@aol.com; www.inventedcity.com). For US$75, you get your offer listed in 1 catalog and unlimited access to the club's database containing thousands of homes for exchange.

FURTHER READING: ACCOMMODATIONS. *People to People: An introduction to over a thousand Eastern Europeans who would like to meet travelers like you!*, edited by Jim Haynes (Zephyr Press, US$12).

CAMPING & THE OUTDOORS

Like so much else in Eastern Europe, the wilderness is as wild and undiscovered as they come. From the snowy Tatras bordering Slovakia and Poland to the vast expanses of the Altai Republic to the legendary Caucasus in Russia, Eastern

Europe offers myriad opportunities for hiking, mountain climbing, trekking, camping, and biking. In fact, camping is one of the most authentic ways to experience the vacation subculture of the region: not only are Eastern Europeans mountain goats who explore the outdoors for every vacation but camping is also often the only affordable accommodation for locals. Unfortunately, there is very little English-language information on Eastern European outdoor opportunities; fortunately, the lack of info means once you're in the wilderness, it'll be you, the Eastern Europeans, and the mountains with not another Anglophone tourist for miles.

As undiscovered as the Eastern European wilderness is, there is a surprising lack of opportunity for truly roughing it. In every country, it is illegal to camp within the boundaries of a national park. As a result, *chaty* dot the parks' interiors and the borders are surrounded with crowded organized campsites. **Chaty** are huts that line hiking trails, offering dorm-style rooms, running water (not always hot), and some sort of a mess hall. Beds run US$5-10 and are the more hard-core of Eastern Europe's camping options. **Organized campgrounds** offer both tent space and bungalow options. All campgrounds have running water; a few have restaurants and lounge areas. Tent sites range from US$1-10 per person with a flat tent fee of US$5-10. Bungalows hover around US$10.

USEFUL PUBLICATIONS & WEB RESOURCES

A variety of publishing companies offer hiking guidebooks to meet the educational needs of novice or expert. For information about camping, hiking, and biking, write or call the publishers listed below to receive a free catalogue.

Automobile Association, A.A. Publishing. Orders and enquiries to TBS Frating Distribution Centre, Colchester, Essex, CO7 7DW, U.K. (tel. (01206) 25 56 78; www.theaa.co.uk). Publishes *Camping and Caravanning: Europe* (UK£9). They also offer Big Road Atlases for Europe.

The Mountaineers Books, 1001 SW Klickitat Way, #201, Seattle, WA 98134 (tel. 800-553-4453 or 206-223-6303; alans@mountaineers.org; www.mountaineers.org). Over 400 titles on hiking (the *100 Hikes* series), biking, mountaineering, natural history, and conservation. Publishes *Trekking in Russia and Central Asia: A Traveler's Guide/Complete Details for 35 Treks Through These Regions* by Frith Maier (US$24.95), *On the Edge of Europe: Mountaineering in the Caucasus* by Audrey Salkeld and Jose Bermudez (US$24.95).

Bradt Publications, www.omnimap.com/catalog/guides/bradt.html. Publishes a series of hiking guides to unusual destinations including *Hiking Guide to Romania* (US$15.95) and *Hiking Guide to Poland and Ukraine* (US$15.95).

CAMPING & HIKING EQUIPMENT

Good camping equipment is both sturdy and light. Camping equipment is generally more expensive in Australia, New Zealand, and the U.K. than in North America.

Sleeping Bag: Most good sleeping bags are rated by "season," or the lowest outdoor temperature at which they will keep you warm ("summer" means 30-40°F at night and "four-season" or "winter" often means below 0°F). Sleeping bags are made either of down (warmer and lighter, but more expensive, and miserable when wet) or of synthetic material (heavier, more durable, and warmer when wet). Prices vary, but might range from US$80-210 for a summer synthetic to US$250-300 for a good down winter bag. **Sleeping bag pads,** including foam pads (US$10-20) and air mattresses (US$15-50) cushion your back and neck and insulate you from the ground. **Therm-A-Rest** brand self-inflating sleeping pads are part foam and part air-mattress and partially inflate when you unroll them, but are costly at US$45-80. Bring a **"stuff sack"** or plastic bag to store your sleeping bag and keep it dry.

Tent: The best tents are free-standing, with their own frames and suspension systems; they set up quickly and only require staking in high winds. Low-profile dome tents are the best all-around. When pitched, their internal space is almost entirely usable, which means little unnecessary bulk. Tent sizes can be somewhat misleading: two people *can* fit in a two-person tent, but will find life more pleasant in a four-person. If you're traveling by car, go for the bigger tent, but if you're hiking, stick with a smaller tent that weighs no more than 5-6 lbs (2-3kg). Good two-person tents start at US$90, four-person tents at US$300. Seal the seams of your tent with waterproofer, and make sure it has a rain fly. Other tent accessories include a **battery-operated lantern,** a **plastic groundcloth,** and a **nylon tarp.**

Backpack: If you intend to do a lot of hiking, you should have a frame backpack. **Internal-frame packs** mold better to your back, keep a lower center of gravity, and can flex adequately to allow you to hike difficult trails that require a lot of bending and maneuvering. **External-frame packs** are more comfortable for long hikes over even terrain since they keep the weight higher and distribute it more evenly. Whichever you choose, make sure your pack has a strong, padded hip belt, which transfers the weight from the shoulders to the legs. Any serious backpacking requires a pack of at least 4000 cubic inches (16,000cc). Allow an additional 500 cubic inches for your sleeping bag in internal-frame packs. Sturdy backpacks cost anywhere from US$125-420. A **waterproof backpack cover** will prove invaluable. Otherwise, plan to store all of your belongings in plastic bags inside your backpack.

Boots: Be sure to wear hiking boots with good **ankle support** which are appropriate for the terrain you plan to hike. Your boots should fit snugly and comfortably over one or two wool socks and a thin liner sock. Breaking in boots properly before setting out requires wearing them for several weeks; doing so will spare you from painful and debilitating blisters.

Other Necessities: Raingear in two pieces, a top and pants, is far superior to a poncho. **Synthetics,** like polypropylene tops, socks, and long underwear, along with a pile jacket, will keep you warm even when wet. When camping in autumn, winter, or spring, bring along a **"space blanket,"** which helps you to retain your body heat and doubles as a groundcloth (US$5-15). Plastic **canteens** or water bottles keep water cooler than metal ones do, and are virtually shatter- and leak-proof. Large, collapsible **water sacks** will significantly improve your lot in primitive campgrounds and weigh practically nothing when empty, though they are bulky and heavy when full. Bring **water-purification tablets** for when you can't boil water, unless you are willing to shell out money for a portable water-purification system. Though most campgrounds provide campfire sites, you may want to bring a small **metal grate** or **grill** of your own. For those places that forbid fires or the gathering of firewood, you'll need a **camp stove**. The classic Coleman stove starts at about US$40. You will need to purchase a **fuel bottle** and fill it with propane to operate it. A **first aid kit, swiss army knife, insect repellent, calamine lotion,** and **waterproof matches** or a **lighter** are other essential camping items.

WILDERNESS SAFETY

Stay warm, stay dry, and stay hydrated. The vast majority of life-threatening wilderness situations result from a breach of this simple dictum. On any hike, however brief, you should pack enough equipment to keep you alive should disaster befall. This includes **raingear, hat** and **mittens,** a **first-aid kit,** a **reflector,** a **whistle, high energy food,** and extra **water.** Dress in warm layers of **synthetic materials** designed for the outdoors, or **wool.** Pile fleece jackets and Gore-Tex raingear are excellent choices. Never rely on **cotton** for warmth. This "death cloth" will be absolutely useless should it get wet. Make sure to check all equipment for any defects before setting out, and see **Camping and Hiking Equipment,** above, for more information.

Check **weather forecasts** and pay attention to the skies when hiking. Weather patterns can change suddenly. Whenever possible, let someone know when and where you are going hiking, either a friend, your hostel, a park ranger, or a local hiking organization. Do not attempt a hike beyond your ability—you may be endangering your life. See **Health,** p. 28 for information about outdoor ailments such as heatstroke, hypothermia, giardia, rabies, and insects, as well as basic medical concerns and first-aid.

FURTHER READING: WILDERNESS SAFETY. *How to Stay Alive in the Woods,* Bradford Angier (Macmillan, US$8).

CAMPERS & RVS

Renting an RV will always be more expensive than tenting or hostelling, but the costs compare favorably with the price of staying in hotels and renting a car (see **Rental Cars,** p. 55), and the convenience of bringing along your own bedroom, bathroom, and kitchen makes it an attractive option, especially for older travelers and families with children.

Rates vary widely by region, season (July and August are the most expensive months), and type of RV. It always pays to contact several different companies to compare vehicles and prices. **Auto Europe** (U.S. tel. 800-223-5555; U.K. toll free tel. (0800) 899 893) rents RVs in Berlin. Weekly rates for a four-passenger RV range about US$1000-2000 high-season/US$800-1200 low-season, depending on the make of car.

FURTHER READING: CAMPING AND RVS. *Camping Your Way through Europe,* Carol Mickelsen (Affordable Press, US$15). *Exploring Europe by RV,* Dennis and Tina Jaffe (Globe Pequot, US$15). *Great Outdoor Recreation Pages,* www.gorp.com.

ORGANIZED ADVENTURE TRIPS

Organized adventure tours offer another way of exploring the wild. Activities include hiking, biking, skiing, canoeing, kayaking, rafting, climbing, photo safaris and archaeological digs. Begin by consulting tourism bureaus, which can suggest parks, trails, and outfitters. Other good sources for organized adventure options are the stores and organizations specializing in camping and outdoor equipment listed above. Sales reps at REI, EMS, or Sierra often know of a range of cheap, convenient trips. They also often offer training programs for people who want to have an independent trip. The **Specialty Travel Index,** 305 San Anselmo Ave., Suite 313, San Anselmo, CA 94960 (tel. 888-624-4030 or 415-455-1643; fax 459-4974; email spectrav@ix.netcom.com; www.specialtytravel.com) is a directory listing hundreds of tour operators worldwide. **Executive Wilderness Programs,** EWP Haulfryn, Cilycwm, SA20 0SP UK (tel. 1550-721-319; fax 1550-720-053) specializes in trips to Eastern Europe including the Russian Caucasus, the Tatras, Czech Republic, Bulgaria, and Romania. For more information on trekking in the Caucasus and the Altai Republic, see **Russia: Pyatigorsk** (p. 647) and **Russia: Altai Republic** (p. 659).

KEEPING IN TOUCH

The ease of communicating varies widely from country to country. In Central Europe, postal and telephone systems are as reliable and efficient as in Western Europe. In Russia, Ukraine, and Belarus, you'll be lucky if mail ever leaves the post office. Phone cards can also be problematic throughout the region: double-check with your carrier before assuming you'll be able to call home. Like everything else in Eastern Europe, keeping in touch can be problematic, inefficient, and downright mind boggling. Have patience: you will eventually phone home. For country-specific information, refer to the **Essentials: Communication** section at the beginning of every chapter.

ENVIRONMENTALLY RESPONSIBLE TOURISM. The idea behind responsible tourism is to leave no trace of human presence behind. A campstove is the safer (and more efficient) way to cook than using vegetation, but if you must make a fire, keep it small and use only dead branches or brush rather than cutting vegetation. Make sure your campsite is at least 150 ft. (50m) from water supplies or bodies of water. If there are no toilet facilities, bury human waste (but not paper) at least four inches (10cm) deep and above the high-water line, and 150 feet or more from any water supplies and campsites. Always pack your trash in a plastic bag and carry it with you until you reach the next trash can. For more information on these issues, contact one of the organizations listed below.

Ecotourism Society, P.O. Box 755, North Bennington, VT 05257-0755 (tel. 802-447-2121; email ecomail@ecotourism.org; www.ecotourism.org/tesinfo.html)
EcoTravel Center: www.ecotour.com.
National Audobon Society, Nature Odysseys, 700 Broadway, New York, NY 10003 (tel. 212-979-3066; email travel@audobon.org; www.audobon.org),
Tourism Concern, Stapleton House, 277-281 Holloway Rd., London N7 8HN, England (tel. (0170) 753 3330; www.gn.apc.org/tourismconcern.

MAIL

SENDING MAIL TO AND RECEIVING MAIL IN EASTERN EUROPE

Airmail letters between North America and Eastern Europe generally take 5-7 days. From the **US** (usps.gov), postcards/aerograms cost US$0.55/0.60; letters under 1 oz. cost US$1; packages under one pound cost US$7.20, while larger packages sent by parcel post cost a variable amount (around US$15). From **Canada** (www.canadapost.ca/CPC2/common/rates/ratesgen.html#international), air mail postcards and letters up to 20g cost CDN$0.95; small packages up to 0.5kg cost CDN$8.50, while larger packages up to 2kg CDN$28.30.

Allow at least 4-7 days for airmail from **Australia** (postcards and letters up to 20 grams AUS$1; packages up to 0.5kg AUS$12, up to 2kg AUS$45; www.auspost.com.au/pac), 6-12 days from **New Zealand** (postcards NZ$1, letters up to 20g NZ$1.80-6; small parcels up to 0.5kg NZ$15, up to 2kg NZ$39; www.nzpost.co.nz/nzpost/inrates), and 3-7 days from **Britain** (letters up to 20g UK£0.30; packages up to 0.5kg UK£2.22, up to 2kg UK£8.22; www.royalmail.co.uk/calculator).Envelopes should be marked "air mail" or "par avion."

There are several ways to arrange pick-up of letters sent to you by friends and relatives while you are abroad.

General Delivery: Mail can be sent to Eastern Europe through **Poste Restante** (the international phrase for General Delivery) to almost any city or town with a post office. While *Poste Restante* is reliable in most countries, the likelihood of it ever arriving in Russia, Ukraine, Belarus, and Moldova is slim. Address *Poste Restante* letters to: Jane DOE, Poste Restante, Jindřišská 14, 110 00 Prague 1, Czech Republic. Be sure to include the street address of the post office on the third line or mail may never reach the recipient. The mail will go to a special desk in the central post office. As a rule, it is best to use the largest post office in the area, and mail may be sent there regardless of what is written on the envelope. When possible, it is usually safer and quicker to send mail express or registered and is actually one of the only ways to ensure that mail gets to Russia and other postally problematic countries. When picking up your mail, bring a form of photo ID, preferably a passport. There is often no surcharge; if there is a charge, it usually does not exceed the cost of domestic postage. If the clerks insist that there is nothing for you, have them check under your first name as well. *Let's Go* lists post offices in the **Practical Information** section for each city and most towns.

American Express: AmEx's travel offices throughout the world will act as a mail service for cardholders if you contact them in advance. Under this free **Client Letter Service,** they will hold mail for up to 30 days and forward upon request. Address the letter in the same way shown above. Some offices will offer these services to non-cardholders (especially those who have purchased AmEx Travelers Cheques), but you must call ahead to make sure. Check the **Practical Information** section of the countries you plan to visit; Let's Go lists AmEx office locations for most large cities. A complete list is available free from AmEx (tel. 800-528-4800).

If regular airmail is too slow, **Federal Express** (U.S. tel. for international operator 800-247-4747;) can get a letter from New York to Moscow in two days for a whopping US$65; rates among non-U.S. locations are prohibitively expensive. By **U.S. Express Mail,** a letter from New York would arrive within four days and start at around US$20.

Surface mail is by far the cheapest and slowest way to send mail. It takes one to three months to cross the Atlantic and two to four to cross the Pacific—appropriate for sending large quantities of items you won't need to see for a while. When ordering books and materials from abroad, always include one or two **International Reply Coupons (IRCs)**—a way of providing the postage to cover delivery. IRCs should be available from your local post office and those abroad (US$1.05).

SENDING MAIL HOME FROM EASTERN EUROPE

Aerogrammes, printed sheets that fold into envelopes and travel via airmail, are available at post offices. It helps to mark "airmail" in the local language if possible, though "par avion" is universally understood. Most post offices will charge exorbitant fees or simply refuse to send aerogrammes with enclosures. Airmail from Eastern Europe averages 10-15 days, although times are more unpredictable from smaller towns. Additionally, mail from Russia, Ukraine, Belarus, and Moldova can take up to a month to reach its destination, if it arrives at all. Postage rates vary by country but are generally extremely inexpensive; for exact prices and other valuable postal information, refer to the **Essentials: Communication** sections at the beginning of each country chapter.

TELEPHONES

GMT + 1		GMT + 2		GMT + 3
Bosnia	Poland	Belarus	Lithuania	Moscow
Croatia	Slovakia	Bulgaria	Moldova	St. Petersburg
Czech Rep.	Slovenia	Estonia	Romania	most of Russia
Hungary	Yugoslavia	Latvia	W. Russia	
FYR Macedonia		Ukraine		

CALLING EASTERN EUROPE FROM HOME

To call Eastern Europe direct from home, dial:

1. The international access code of your home country. **International access codes** include: Australia 0011; Ireland 00; New Zealand 00; South Africa 09; U.K. 00; U.S. 011. Country codes and city codes are sometimes listed with a zero in front (e.g., 033), but after dialing the international access code, drop successive zeros (with an access code of 011, e.g., 011 33).
2. The country code of your Eastern European country of choice (see the phone code box on the first page of the country's chapter).
3. The city code (see the city's **Practical Information** section) and local number.

CALLING HOME FROM EASTERN EUROPE

A **calling card** is probably your best and cheapest bet. Calls are billed either collect or to your account. **MCI WorldPhone** also provides access to MCI's Traveler's Assist, which gives legal and medical advice, exchange rate information, and translation services. Other phone companies provide similar services to travelers. **To obtain a calling card** from your national telecommunications service before you leave home, contact the appropriate company below. Be warned, however, that not all calling card companies offer services in every Eastern European country. It can be particularly difficult to successfully use a calling card in Russia, Ukraine, Belarus, and—inexplicably—Slovenia.

USA: AT&T (tel. 888-288-4685); **Sprint** (tel. 800-877-4646); or **MCI** (tel. 800-444-4141; from abroad dial the country's MCI access number).

Canada: Bell Canada **Direct** (tel. 800-565-4708).

U.K.: British Telecom **BT Direct** (tel. (800) 34 51 44).

Ireland: Telecom Éireann **Ireland Direct** (tel. (800) 250 250).

Australia: Telstra **Australia Direct** (tel. 13 22 00).

New Zealand: Telecom New Zealand (tel. (0800) 000 000).

South Africa: Telkom South Africa (tel. 09 03).

To call home with a calling card, contact the Eastern European operator for your service provider by dialing the access numbers listed in the **Essentials: Communications** section at the beginning of each country chapter. Not all of these numbers are toll-free; in many countries, phones will require a coin or card deposit to call the operator, which counts as a local call.

Wherever possible, use a calling card for international phone calls. The long-distance rates for national phone services are often exorbitant. You can usually make direct international calls from pay phones, but if you aren't using a calling card you may need to drop coins as quickly as words. Where available, prepaid phone cards can be used for direct international calls, but they are still less cost-efficient. Look for pay phones in public areas, especially train stations, as private pay phones are often more expensive. In-room hotel calls invariably include an arbitrary and sky-high surcharge (as much as US$10).

If you do dial direct, you must first insert the appropriate amount of money or a prepaid card, then dial the international access code for the country you're in (listed on the opening page of every country chapter), and then dial the country code and number of your home. **Country codes** include: Australia 61; Ireland 353; New Zealand 64; South Africa 27; U.K. 44; U.S. and Canada 1.

The expensive alternative to dialing direct or using a calling card is using an international operator to place a **collect call.** An English-speaking operator from your home nation can be reached by dialing the appropriate service provider listed above, and they will typically place a collect call even if you don't possess one of their phone cards.

CALLING WITHIN EASTERN EUROPE

The simplest way to call within the country is to use a coin-operated phone or to use a **prepaid phone cards**, which are slowly phasing out coins in most Eastern European countries. Phone cards carry a certain amount of phone time depending on the card's denomination; the time is measured in minutes or impulses (e.g. one impulse/one minute). Phone cards can usually be purchased at tobacco stands, post offices, train stations, and magazine stands. Phone rates tend to be highest in the morning, lower in the evening, and lowest on Sunday and late at night.

EMAIL & INTERNET

The World Wide Web is slowly making its way into Eastern Europe. Every major city now has some sort of internet access, usually a cyber cafe, but access is also available in public libraries and in many hostels. Access is more difficult to find in smaller towns, but not impossible. Tourist offices and hotels are the best source for local internet access. Rates are extremely reasonable; one hour costs US$3 on average, although they do fluctuate from country to country. **The Cybercafe Search Engine** (cybercaptive.com) and **Cybercafe Guide** (www.cyberiacafe.net/cyberia/guide/ccafe.htm) can help you find cyber cafes in Eastern Europe.

One strategy is to befriend college students as you go and ask if you can use their email accounts. Other free, web-based email providers include Hotmail (www.hotmail.com), RocketMail (www.rocketmail.com), and Yahoo! Mail (www.yahoo.com). Many free email providers are funded by advertising and some may require subscribers to fill out a questionnaire. Almost every internet search engine has an affiliated free email service.

Travelers who have the luxury of a laptop with them can use a **modem** to call an internet service provider. Long-distance phone cards specifically intended for such calls can defray normally high phone charges. Check with your long-distance phone provider to see if they offer this option.

GETTING THERE

BY PLANE

When finding airfare to Eastern Europe, a little effort can save you a bundle. If your plans are flexible enough to deal with the restrictions, courier fares are the cheapest. Tickets bought from consolidators and standby seating are also good deals, but last-minute specials, airfare wars, and charter flights often beat these fares. Hunt around and be flexible; students, seniors, and those under 26 should never pay full price for a ticket. Your various options are outlined thoroughly in this section.

DETAILS AND TIPS

Timing: Most airfares to Eastern Europe peak between mid-June and early Sep. (the high season); mid-Dec. to early Jan. can also be expensive. The cheapest times to travel are Nov. through mid-Dec. and early Jan. through Mar. Midweek (M-Th morning) round-trip flights run US$40-50 cheaper than weekend flights, but the latter are generally less crowded and more likely to permit frequent-flier upgrades. Return-date flexibility is usually not an economical option for the budget traveler.

Route: Round-trip flights are by far the cheapest; "open-jaw" (arriving in and departing from different cities) and round-the-world (RTW) tickets are pricier but reasonable alternatives. If you are willing to make the extra effort, the least expensive route usually is to fly into London, Amsterdam, or Paris and reach your destination by train or bus; it will often be necessary to connect from one of these cities regardless.

Boarding: Pick up tickets for international flights well in advance of the departure date, and confirm by phone within 72 hours of departure. Most airlines require passengers to arrive at the airport at least two hours before departure. One carry-on item and two pieces of checked baggage is the norm for commercial flights; weight allowances vary.

Fares: Round-trip commercial tickets to the larger, more touristed cities (Prague, Budapest, Warsaw) can usually be found, with some work, for US$500-600 in the high season. Tickets to mid-range cities–including Moscow, Bucharest, Zagreb and Sofia–generally cost about US$100 more, while Bratislava, Kiev, Minsk and the Baltic capitals can cost anywhere from US$750-900. Prices drop US$100-200 the rest of the year.

BUDGET & STUDENT TRAVEL AGENCIES

A knowledgeable agent specializing in flights to Eastern Europe can make your life easy and help you save, but agents may not spend the time to find you the lowest possible fare, as they get paid on commission. Students and under-26ers holding **ISIC or IYTC cards** (see **Identification,** p. 17) can qualify for big discounts from student travel agencies. Most flights from budget agencies are on major airlines, but in peak season some may sell seats on less reliable chartered aircraft.

Council Travel (www.counciltravel.com). U.S. offices include: Emory Village, 1561 N. Decatur Rd., **Atlanta,** GA 30307 (tel. 404-377-9997); 273 Newbury St., **Boston,** MA 02116 (tel. 617-266-1926); 1160 N. State St., **Chicago,** IL 60610 (tel. 312-951-0585); 10904 Lindbrook Dr., **Los Angeles,** CA 90024 (tel. 310-208-3551); 205 E. 42nd St., **New York,** NY 10017 (tel. 212-822-2700); 530 Bush St., **San Francisco,** CA 94108 (tel. 415-421-3473); 1314 NE 43rd St. #210, **Seattle,** WA 98105 (tel. 206-632-2448); 3300 M St. NW, **Washington, D.C.** 20007 (tel. 202-337-6464). **For U.S. cities not listed,** call 800-2-COUNCIL (226-8624). Also 28A Poland St. (Oxford Circus), **London,** W1V 3DB (tel. (0171) 287 3337), **Paris** (144 41 89 89), and **Munich** (089 39 50 22).

STA Travel, 6560 Scottsdale Rd. #F100, Scottsdale, AZ 85253 (tel. 800-777-0112 fax 602-922-0793; www.sta-travel.com). A student and youth travel organization with over 150 offices worldwide. Ticket booking, travel insurance, railpasses, and more. U.S. offices include: 297 Newbury Street, **Boston,** MA 02115 (tel. 617-266-6014); 429 S. Dearborn St., **Chicago,** IL 60605 (tel. 312-786-9050); 7202 Melrose Ave., **Los Angeles,** CA 90046 (tel. 323-934-8722); 10 Downing St., **New York,** NY 10014 (tel. 212-627-3111); 4341 University Way NE, **Seattle,** WA 98105 (tel. 206-633-5000); 2401 Pennsylvania Ave., Ste. G, **Washington, D.C.** 20037 (tel. 202-887-0912); 51 Grant Ave., **San Francisco,** CA 94108 (tel. 415-391-8407). In the U.K., 6 Wrights Ln., **London** W8 6TA (tel. (0171) 938 47 11 for North American travel). In New Zealand, 10 High St., **Auckland** (tel. (09) 309 04 58). In Australia, 222 Faraday St., **Melbourne** VIC 3053 (tel. (03) 9349 2411).

Travel CUTS (Canadian Universities Travel Services Limited), 187 College St., Toronto, Ont. M5T 1P7 (tel. 416-979-2406; fax 979-8167; www.travelcuts.com). 40 offices across Canada. Also in the U.K., 295-A Regent St., **London** W1R 7YA (tel. (0171) 255 19 44).

Wasteels, Victoria Station, London, U.K. SW1V 1JT (tel. (0171) 834 70 66; fax 630 76 28; www.wasteels.dk/uk). A huge chain in Europe, with 203 locations. Sells the Wasteels BIJ tickets, which are discounted (30-45% off regular fare), 2nd class international point-to-point train tickets with unlimited stopovers (must be under 26); sold only in Europe.

COMMERCIAL AIRLINES

The commercial airlines' lowest regular offer is the **APEX** (Advance Purchase Excursion) fare, which provides confirmed reservations and allows "open-jaw" tickets. Generally, reservations must be made 7 to 21 days in advance, with 7- to 14-day minimum and up to 90-day maximum-stay limits, and hefty cancellation and change penalties (fees rise in summer). Book peak-season APEX fares early, since by May you will have a hard time getting the departure date you want.

Although APEX fares are probably not the cheapest possible fares, they will give you a sense of the average commercial price, from which to measure other bargains. Specials advertised in newspapers may be cheaper but have more restrictions and fewer available seats. Popular carriers to Eastern Europe include:

FROM NORTH AMERICA

Delta Air Lines (tel. (800) 221 1212; www.delta-air.com) flies more reliably to Eastern European cities than other US carriers, including Budapest, Moscow and Warsaw.

Continental Air Lines (tel. (800) 525 0280; www.continental.com) offers flights to a number of destinations in Eastern Europe, including Prague and Bratislava.

Lufthansa (tel. (800) 399 5838; www.lufthansa-usa.com) has a wide variety of routes covering most of Eastern Europe.

British Airways (tel. (800) 545 7644; www.british-airways.com/regional/usa/index.cgi) flies into most large cities in Eastern Europe via Heathrow.

Air France (tel. (800) 237 2747; www.airfrance.com) covers much of Eastern Europe via several Western European cities.

SAS (tel. (800) 221 2350; www.flysas.com) connects to Baltic cities from New York.

FROM THE UNITED KINGDOM

British Midland Airways (tel. (0870) 607 05 55; www.iflybritishmidland.com) flies direct to many Eastern European cities.

British Airways (tel. (0345) 22 21 11; www.british-airways.com/regional/uk/index.html) flies from Heathrow to a number of Eastern European hubs.

KLM (tel. (0870) 507 40 74; www.klmuk.com) connects to a number of cities in Eastern Europe via Amsterdam (UK£79).

Austrian Airways (tel. (0171) 434 73 00; www.aua.com) connects to many cities via Vienna.

FROM AUSTRALIA AND NEW ZEALAND

Qantas Air (tel. 13 13 13); www.qantas.com.au) flies from a variety of departure cities in Australia and New Zealand to London, from which connecting flights are easy to find.

Air New Zealand (tel. (0800) 35 22 66; www.airnz.com) has reasonable fares from Auckland to London, and often offers special sales at much lower prices. Again, it will be necessary to find connecting flights.

FROM SOUTH AFRICA

Lufthansa (tel. (011) 484 47 11; www.lufthansa.com) reliably offers flights which connect to a number of cities throughout Eastern Europe.

British Airways (tel. (011) 441 86 00; www.british-airways.com/regional/sa) has flights from Johannesburg and Cape Town to places in Europe with easy connections.

AIRCRAFT SAFETY. In general, the international carriers listed comply with safety requirements, but some of the smaller airlines in post-communist countries have been known to use unreliable equipment. They are the only carriers available for certain routes; if you have any serious concerns, region-specific safety information can be obtained from the **International Airline Passengers Association** (U.S. tel. 972-404-9980, safety office open M-F 10am-noon EST; U.K. tel. (181) 681 65 55). *The Official Airline Guide* (www.oag.com) and many travel agencies can tell you the type and age of aircraft on a particular route. The **Federal Aviation Administration** (www.faa.gov) reviews the airline authorities for countries whose airlines enter the U.S. **U.S. State Department** (tel. 202-647-5225; travel.state.gov/travel_warnings.html) travel advisories sometimes involve foreign carriers, especially when terrorist bombings may be a threat.

OTHER CHEAP ALTERNATIVES

AIR COURIER FLIGHTS. Couriers help transport cargo on international flights by guaranteeing delivery of the baggage claim slips from the company to a representative overseas. Generally, couriers must travel light (carry-ons only) and deal with complex restrictions on their flight. Most flights are round-trip only with short fixed-length stays (usually one week) and a limit of a single ticket per issue. Most operate only out of the biggest cities, like New York. Generally, you must be over 21 (in some cases 18), have a valid passport, and procure your own visa, if necessary. Groups such as the **Air Courier Association** (tel. 800-282-1202; www.aircourier.org) and the **International Association of Air Travel Couriers,** 220 South Dixie Hwy., P.O. Box 1349, Lake Worth, FL 33460 (tel. 561-582-8320; iaatc@courier.org; www.courier.org) provide their members with information on courier services worldwide for an annual fee. For more information, consult *Air Courier Bargains* by Kelly Monaghan (The Intrepid Traveler, US$15) or the *Courier Air Travel Handbook* by Mark Field (Perpetual Press, US$10).

CHARTER FLIGHTS. Charters are flights a tour operator contracts with an airline to fly extra loads of passengers during peak season. They can be cheaper than flights on scheduled airlines. Some operate nonstop, and restrictions on minimum advance-purchase and minimum stay are more lenient. However, charter flights fly less frequently than major airlines, make refunds particularly difficult, and are usually fully booked. Schedules and itineraries may also change or be cancelled at the last moment (as late as 48 hours before the trip, and without a full refund), and check-in, boarding, and baggage claim are often much slower. Pay with a credit card if you can, and consider traveler's insurance against trip interruption.

Discount clubs and **fare brokers** offer members savings on last-minute charter and tour deals. Study their contracts closely; you don't want to end up with an unwanted overnight layover. **Travelers Advantage,** Stamford, CT (tel. 800-548-1116; www.travelersadvantage.com; US$60 annual fee includes discounts, newsletters, and cheap flight directories) specializes in travel and tour packages.

STANDBY FLIGHTS. To travel standby, you will need considerable flexibility in the dates and cities of your arrival and departure. Companies that specialize in standby flights don't sell tickets but rather the promise that you will get to your destination (or near your destination) within a certain window of time (anywhere from 1-5 days). You may only receive a monetary refund if all available flights which depart within your date-range from the specified region are full, but future travel credit is always available. Carefully read agreements with any company offering standby flights, as tricky fine print can leave you in the lurch.

To check on a company's service record, call the **Better Business Bureau of New York City** (tel. 212-533-6200). It is difficult to receive refunds, and clients' vouchers will not be honored when an airline fails to receive payment in time. One reliable option is **Airhitch,** 2641 Broadway, 3rd Fl., New York, NY 10025 (tel. 800-326-2009 or 212-864-2000; fax 864-5489; www.airhitch.org) and Los Angeles, CA (tel. 310-726-5000). In Europe, the flagship office is in Paris (tel. 147 00 16 30) and the other one is in Amsterdam (tel. 312 06 26 32 20). Flights to Western Europe cost US$159 each way when departing from the Northeast, $239 from the West Coast or Northwest, $209 from the Midwest, and $189 from the Southeast, and they can help you progress from there.

TICKET CONSOLIDATORS. **Ticket consolidators,** or **"bucket shops,"** buy unsold tickets in bulk from commercial airlines and sell them at discounted rates. The best place to look is in the Sunday travel section of any major newspaper (among the best is the *New York Times*), where many bucket shops place tiny ads. Call quickly, as availability is typically extremely limited. Not all bucket shops are reliable establishments, so insist on a receipt that gives full details of restrictions, refunds, and tickets, and pay by credit card (in spite of the 2-5% fee) so you can stop payment if you never receive your tickets. For more information, check the website **Consolidators FAQ** (www.travel-library.com/air-travel/consolidators.html) or the book *Consolidators: Air Travel's Bargain Basement,* by Kelly Monaghan (Intrepid Traveler, US$8).

From **North America, Travel Avenue** (tel. (800) 333-3335; www.travelavenue.com) rebates commercial fares to or from the US (5% for over US$550) and searches for low fares for flights anywhere for a fee. Also, **NOW Voyager**, 74 Varick St. #307, New York, NY 10013 (tel. (212) 431-1616; www.nowvoyagertravel.com), acts as a consolidator and books discounted flights, mostly from New York, as well as courier flights, for an annual registration fee of US$50. Other consolidators worth calling are **Airfare Busters** (tel. (800) 232-8783; www.af.busters.com); **Interworld** (tel. (305) 443-4929; fax 443-0351); **Rebel** (tel. (800) 227-3235; email travel@rebeltours.com; www.rebeltours.com); **Cheap Tickets** (tel. 800-377-1000; www.cheaptickets.com); or **Travac** (tel. (800) 872-8800; fax (212) 714-9063; www.travac.com). In **London**, the **Air Travel Advisory Bureau** (tel. (0171) 636 50 00; www.atab.co.uk) can provide names of reliable consolidators and other discount ticket specialists.

FURTHER READING: BY PLANE. *The Worldwide Guide to Cheap Airfare,* Michael McColl (Insider Publications, US$15). *Travelocity* (www.travelocity.com) is an online database of airfares; online reservations. *SurplusTravel.com* (www.surplustravel.com) offers discounted tickets. *How to Find Cheap Airfare* (www-unix.oit.umass.edu/~kim/cheapair) has great links.

OTHER OPTIONS FROM THE U.K.

BY TRAIN. **Eurostar** (tel. (0990) 18 61 86; www.eurostar.com) runs a frequent train service from London to the continent. Eight to ten trains per day run to Paris (3hr., UK£89-145, under 26 UK£79) and Brussels (UK£89-125, under 26 UK£69). Trains can connect from Paris to destinations throughout Eastern Europe.

BY CAR. If traveling by car, **Eurotunnel** (tel. (8000) 96 99 92; www.eurotunnel.co.uk) transports travelers with their car through the Chunnel from Folkestone to Calais. Fares for a car and all passengers range from UK£104-140 depending on the season. Travelers with cars can also look into sea crossings by ferry (see below).

BY BOAT. **Seaview** (www.seaview.co.uk/Ferries.html) has a directory of ferries leaving from Britain and Ireland. **P&O Stena** (tel. (087) 06 00 06 00; www.posl.com) runs ferries between Dover and Calais (30 per day). Fares for foot passengers start at UK£24, with car UK£125. **Hoverspeed** (tel. (08705) 24 02 41; www.hoverspeed.co.uk) has frequent ferries from Dover to Calais and other destinations. Foot passengers are UK£25, with car UK£104-140.

GETTING AROUND

Fares on all modes of transportation are either "single" (one-way) or "return" (roundtrip). Unless stated otherwise *Let's Go* always lists single fares. Roundtrip fares on trains and buses in most of Europe are simply double the one-way fare.

BY TRAIN

When available, trains are often the fastest and easiest way to travel. Second-class travel is pleasant, and compartments, which seat two to six, are excellent places to meet fellow travelers. Trains, however, are not always safe; lock your compartment door and keep your valuables on you. Bring food and water; there are no on-board cafes and train water is undrinkable. For long trips make sure you are on the correct car, as trains sometimes split at crossroads. Towns listed in parentheses on Eastern European train schedules require a train switch at the town listed immediately before the parenthesis.

Many train stations have different counters for domestic and international tickets, seat reservations, and information; check before lining up. On major routes, reservations are always advisable, and often required, even with a railpass; you are not guaranteed a seat without one (US$3-5). Europeans often reserve far ahead of time; you should strongly consider reserving during peak holiday and tourist seasons (at the very latest a few hours ahead). It will be necessary to purchase a supplement (US$5-10) for trains like EuroCity, InterCity, and InterCityExpress.

You can either buy a **railpass**, which allows you unlimited travel within a particular region for a given period of time, or rely on buying individual **point-to-point** tickets as you go. Almost all countries give students or youths (under 26) direct discounts on regular domestic rail tickets, and many also sell a student or youth card that provides 20-50% off all fares for up to a year.

RAILPASSES

It may be tough to make your railpass pay for itself in Eastern Europe, where train fares are ridiculously cheap and buses usually preferable. In general, it is recommended to travel on point-to-point tickets, which are almost always a better deal.

For those dead set on purchasing a multinational railpass, there are a few options. **Eurailpass,** however, is not one of them: it covers only Hungary in Eastern Europe. The **European East Pass** covers Austria, the Czech Republic, Hungary, Poland, and Slovakia (5 days in one month US$205). The **Central Europe Pass** provides unlimited rail travel through the Czech Republic, Germany, Poland, and Slovakia for any 5 days in one month (first-class only US$199; only available in US). The **Balkan Flexipass** is valid for travel in Bulgaria, Greece, the Former Yugoslavian Republic of Macedonia, Montenegro, Romania, Serbia, and Turkey (5 days in one month US$152, under 26 US$90). Available only in the UK are the **Baltic Rail Explorer Pass**, which allows ISIC holders and/or those under 26 unlimited rail travel in Estonia, Latvia, and Lithuania for 7 days (£25), 14 days (£37), or 21 days (£49); and the **Czech Republic/Slovakia Explorer Pass**, which allows unlimited travel in those countries for 7 consecutive days in first- or second-class (for both try Campus Travel, 52 Grosvenor Gardens, London SW1W0AG, tel (0171) 730 3402).

You should purchase a pass before you arrive in Europe since most passes are available only to non-Europeans and therefore difficult to find in Europe. Contact a travel agent (see **Budget Travel Agencies,** p. 46). **Rail Europe,** 500 Mamaroneck Ave, Harrison, NY 10528 (tel. (888) 382-7245, fax (800) 432-1329 in the US; tel. (800) 361-7245, fax (905) 602-4198 in Canada; tel. (0990) 848848 in the UK; www.raileurope.com) or **DER Travel Services,** 9501 W. Devon Ave Suite #301, Rosemont, IL 60018 (tel. (888) 337-7350, fax (800) 282-7474 in the US; www.dertravel.com) provide extensive info on pass options and offers a number of passes good in Eastern European countries for various durations and prices.

For European citizens or anyone who has lived in Europe for at least six months, **InterRail Passes** are an option. Of the 8 InterRail zones, 3 service Eastern European nations: D (Croatia, Czech Republic, Hungary, Poland, and Slovakia), G (Greece, Italy, Slovenia, and Turkey, including a Greece-Italy ferry), and H (Bulgaria, Romania, Yugoslavia, and Macedonia). The pass is good for 22 days in one zone (under 26 UK£159, over 26 £229), or one month in two (£209, £279), three (£229, £309), or all (£259). If you buy a pass including the country in which you have claimed residence, you must pay 50% of all rail fares within that country. The **Under 26 InterRail Card** (UK£159-259) allows either 14 days or one month of unlimited travel within one, two, three, or all of the seven zones into which InterRail divides Europe; the cost is determined by the number of zones the pass covers. The **Over 26 InterRail Card** offers unlimited second-class travel in Bulgaria, Croatia, Czech Republic, Hungary, Poland, Romania, Slovakia, Slovenia, and Yugoslavia for 15 days or one month for UK£215 and UK£275, respectively.

Some Eastern European nations also offer national railpasses and flexipasses. Again, these tend not to be as economical as point-to-point travel, but if you're spending a significant amount of time in one country, you might be able to make the pass worthwhile. **Bulgarian Flexipass**, **Polrail Pass**, **Czech Flexipass** **Hungarian Flexipass**, and **Romanian Flexipass** are the only national passes available. Another type of regional pass covers a specific area within a country or a round-trip from any border to a particular destination and back. Examples include the **Prague Excursion Pass**, which covers travel from any Czech border to Prague and back out of the country (round-trip must be completed within 7 days; second-class US$35, under 26 US$30).

DISCOUNT RAIL TICKETS

For travelers under 26, **BIJ** tickets (Billets Internationals de Jeunesse; sold under the names **Wasteels, Eurotrain,** and **Route 26**) are a great alternative to railpasses. Available for international trips within Europe as well as most ferry services, they knock 25-40% off regular second-class fares. Tickets are good for 60 days after purchase and allow a number of stopovers along the normal direct route of the train journey. Issued for a specific international route between two points, they must be used in the direction and order of the designated route without side- or back-tracking and must be bought in Europe. They are available from European travel agents, at Wasteels or Eurotrain offices (usually in or near train stations), or occasionally at ticket counters. Contact Wasteels in Victoria Station, adjacent to Platform 2, London SW1V 1JT (tel. (0171) 834 70 66; fax 630 76 28).

FURTHER READING: TRAIN TRAVEL.

Thomas Cook European Timetable (US$28-39), includes a map of Europe highlighting all train and ferry routes. The timetable, updated annually, covers all major and most minor train routes in Europe. In Europe, find it at any Thomas Cook Money Exchange Center; elsewhere, call (44 17 33 50 35 71) or write Thomas Cook Publishing, PO Box 227, Thorpe Wood, Peterborough, PE3 6PU, UK.

Hunter Publishing, P.O. Box 7816, Edison, NJ 08818, USA (tel. 800-255-0343; fax 732-417-1744; email hunterpub@emi.net; www.hunterpublishing.com), offers a catalogue of rail atlases and travel guides. Titles include *European Rail Atlas: Scandinavia & Eastern Europe* (US$16).

BY BUS

All over Eastern Europe, short-haul buses reach rural areas inaccessible by train. In addition, long-distance bus networks may be more extensive, efficient, and occasionally even more comfortable than train services. In the Balkans, air-conditioned buses run by private companies are a godsend. **Eurolines,** 4 Cardiff Rd., Luton LU1 1PP (tel. (01582) 40 45 11; fax 40 06 94), or in London, 52 Grosvenor Gardens, Victoria (tel. (0171) 730 82 35; welcome@eurolines.uk.com; www.eurolines.uk.com), is Europe's largest operator of coach services, offering passes (UK£159-249) for unlimited 30- or 60- day travel between 20 major tourist destinations, including spots in Eastern Europe and Russia.

BY PLANE

Flying across Eastern Europe on regularly scheduled flights can devour your budget. London's **Air Travel Advisory Bureau** (tel. (0171) 636-5000; www.atab.co.uk) can point the way to discount flights. It is possible to purchase **Europe by air** passes (US$99 each, airport taxes not included, reservations recommended) to travel between cities throughout Eastern Europe (US tel. (888) 387-2479, Australia tel. (02) 9285 6811, New Zealand tel. (9) 309 8094; www.europebyair.com). **Lufthansa** (U.S. tel. (800) 399 5838; www.lufthansa-usa.com) offers "Discover Europe" to non-Europe residents, a package of three flight coupons which cost US$125-200 each depending on season and destination; up to six additional tickets cost US$105-175 each. **SAS** (US tel. (800) 221-2350) offers special airpasses for the Baltic region, ranging in price from $75-$155. Finally, **Austrian Airlines** (US tel. (800) 843 0002), **KLM/Northwest** (tel. (800) 800-1504) and **Alitalia** (tel. (800) 223-5730) all fly to many cities in Eastern Europe, and offer similarly priced package deals. Student travel agencies also sell cheap tickets. Consult budget travel agents and local newspapers and magazines for more information.

BY BOAT

Sometimes, yes, boats go to Yalta...but not today.

—Ferry ticket clerk in Odessa

Ferries serving Eastern Europe divide into two major groups. **Riverboats** acquaint you with many towns that trains can only wink at. The legendary waterways of Eastern Europe—the Danube, the Volga, the Dnieper—offer a bewitching alternative to land travel. However, the farther east you go, the more often your travel plans may be interrupted by routes canceled for political reasons and an information blockade run by the local tourist authorities. Inquire at the port.

Ferries in the **North** and **Baltic Seas** are universally reliable and go everywhere. Those content with deck passage rarely need to book ahead. You should check in at least two hours early for a prime spot and allow plenty of time for getting to the port. Bring your own food and avoid the astronomically priced and gastronomically challenging cafeteria cuisine. Fares jump sharply in July and August. Always ask for discounts; ISIC holders often get student fares, and Eurail passholders get many reductions and free trips. Advance planning and reserved tickets bought through a travel agency can spare you days of waiting in dreary ports.

For complete listings of schedules and fares for ferries, steamers, and cruises throughout Europe, find a copy of the quarterly *Official Steamship Guide International* at your travel agent. **Thomas Cook** also lists complete ferry schedules (see **By Train,** p. 50). Links to some major European ferry companies can be found at www.youra.com/ferries/intnlferries.html. For information on cruises throughout Europe and visa-free cruises to Russia contact **EuroCruises,** 303 W. 13th St., New York, NY 10014 (tel. (800) 688-3876, (212) 691-2099, or (212) 366-4747; eurocruises@compuserve.com; www.eurocruises.com).

BY CAR

DRIVING PERMITS & CAR INSURANCE

INTERNATIONAL DRIVING PERMIT (IDP). If you plan to drive a car while in Eastern Europe, you must have an International Driving Permit (IDP), though certain countries allow travelers to drive with a valid American or Canadian license for a limited number of months. It may be a good idea to get one anyway, in case you're in a situation (e.g. an accident or being stranded in a smaller town) where the police do not know English.

Your IDP, valid for one year, must be issued in your own country before you depart; AAA affiliates cannot issue IDPs valid in their own country. You must be 18 years old and have a valid driver's license from your home country to accompany the IDP. An application for an IDP usually needs to include one or two photos, a current local license, an additional form of identification, and a fee.

Australia: Contact your local Royal Automobile Club (RAC) or the National Royal Motorist Association (NRMA) if in NSW or the ACT (tel. (08) 94 21 42 98; www.rac.com.au/travel). Permits AUS$15.

Canada: Contact any Canadian Automobile Association (CAA) branch office in Canada, or write to CAA, 1145 Hunt Club Rd., Suite 200, K1V 0Y3 Canada. (tel. 613-247-0117; fax 247-0118; www.caa.ca/CAAInternet/travelservices/internationaldocumentation/idptravel.htm). Permits CDN$10.

Ireland: Contact the nearest Automobile Association (AA) office or write: The Automobile Association, International Documents, Fanum House, Erskine, Renfrewshire PA8 6BW (tel. (990) 500 600). Permits IR£4.

New Zealand: Contact your local Automobile Association (AA) or their main office at Auckland Central, 99 Albert St. (tel. (9) 377 46 60; fax 302 20 37; www.nzaa.co.nz.). Permits NZ$8.

South Africa: Contact your local Automobile Association of South Africa office or the head office at P.O. Box 596, 2000 Johannesburg (tel. (11) 799 10 00; fax 799 10 10). Permits SAR28.50.

U.K.: Visit your local AA Shop. To find the location nearest you that issues the IDP, call (0990) 50 06 00. More information available at www.theaa.co.uk/motoring/idp.asp). Permits UK£4.

U.S.: Visit any American Automobile Association (AAA) office or write to AAA Florida, Travel Related Services, 1000 AAA Drive (mail stop 100), Heathrow, FL 32746 (tel. 407-444-7000; fax 444-7380). Sells the International Driving Permit (IDP). You do not have to be a member of AAA to receive an IDP. Permits US$10.

American Automobile Association (AAA) Travel Related Services, 1000 AAA Dr. (mail stop 100), Heathrow, FL 32746 (tel. 800-222-4357). Provides road maps and many travel guides free to members. Offers emergency road services (for members), travel services, and auto insurance. The IDP is available for purchase from local AAA offices. To obtain an IDP in the U.K., contact the **Automobile Association Headquarters** (tel. (990) 44 88 66).

CAR INSURANCE. Most gold or platinum credit cards cover standard insurance. If you rent, lease, or borrow a car, you will need a **green card,** or **International Insurance Certificate,** to prove that you have liability insurance. Obtain it through the car rental agency; most include coverage in their prices. If you lease a car, you can obtain a green card from the dealer. Some travel agents offer the card; it may also be available at border crossings. Verify whether your auto insurance applies abroad; even if it does, you will still need a green card to certify this to foreign officials. If you have a collision abroad, the accident will show up on your domestic records if you report it to your insurance company. Rental agencies may require you to purchase theft insurance in countries that they consider to have a high risk of auto theft. Ask your rental agency about Eastern Europe.

BY BICYCLE

Biking is one of the key elements of the classic budget Eurovoyage. With the proliferation of mountain bikes, you can do some serious natural sightseeing. Be aware that touring involves pedaling both yourself and whatever you store in the panniers (bags that strap to your bike). Prepare by taking some reasonably challenging rides at home, and have your bike tuned up by a reputable shop. Wear visible clothing, drink plenty of water (even if you're not thirsty), and ride on the same side as the traffic. Learn and use the international signals for turns. Know how to fix a modern derailleur-equipped mount and change a tire, and practice. A few simple tools and a good bike manual will be invaluable. For information about touring routes, consult national tourist offices or the numerous books available.

Most airlines will count your bike as your second free piece of luggage (you're usually allowed two pieces of checked baggage and a carry-on). As an extra piece, it'll cost about US$60-110 each way. Bikes must be packed in a cardboard box with the pedals and front wheel detached; airlines sell bike boxes at the airport (US$10), but bring your own tools. Most ferries let you take your bike for free or for a nominal fee. You can always transport your bike on trains; the cost varies from small to substantial.

Riding a bike with a frame pack strapped on it or on your back is about as safe as pedaling blindfolded over a sheet of ice; **panniers** are essential. The first thing to buy, however, is a suitable **bike helmet.** At about US$25-50, they're a much better buy than head injury or death. U-shaped **Citadel** or **Kryptonite locks** are expensive (starting at US$30), but the companies insure against theft for one to two years.

Renting a bike beats bringing your own if your touring will be confined to one or two regions. *Let's Go* lists bike rental shops for most larger cities and towns. Some youth hostels rent bicycles for low prices.

BY THUMB

> **!** *Let's Go* strongly urges you to seriously consider the risks of hitchhiking. We do not recommend hitching as a safe means of transportation, and none of the information presented here is intended to do so.

Hitchhiking involves serious risks. Any bozo can drive a car. Hitching means entrusting your life to a random person who happens to stop next to you on the road. You risk theft, assault, sexual harassment, and unsafe driving. In spite of this, many see benefits to hitching. Favorable hitching experiences allow hitchers to meet locals and get to places where public transportation is sketchy. If you decide to hitch, consider where you are. Hitching remains common in Eastern Europe, though Westerners are a definite target for theft. In Russia, the Baltics, and some other Eastern European countries, hitchhiking can be as ordinary as hailing a taxi, and drivers will likely expect to be paid a sum at least equivalent to a bus ticket to your destination.

ADDITIONAL INFORMATION

SPECIFIC CONCERNS

WOMEN TRAVELERS

Women exploring on their own inevitably face some additional safety concerns, but it's easy to be adventurous without taking undue risks. Solo female travelers are a novel phenomenon for Eastern Europe, particularly in public places like restaurants, as Eastern European women never eat out by themselves. As a result, most women traveling alone should expect more than a few quizzical stares and hushed comments as they eat. Eating with companions is the quickest way to avoid this discomfort. Nonetheless, the attitudes that contribute to these surprised looks, when coupled with crime in urban areas, can make for dangerous situations. If you are concerned, you might consider staying in hostels which offer single rooms that lock from the inside or in religious organizations that offer rooms for women only. Communal showers in some hostels are safer than others; check them before settling in. Stick to centrally located accommodations and avoid solitary late-night treks or Metro rides.

When traveling, always carry extra money for a phone call, bus, or taxi. **Hitching** is never safe for lone women, or even for women traveling together. Choose train compartments occupied by other women or couples. Ask the conductor to put together a women-only compartment. Look as if you know where you're going (even when you don't) and consider approaching older women or couples for directions if you're lost or feel uncomfortable.

Generally, the less you look like a tourist, the better off you'll be. Dress conservatively, especially in rural areas. Shorts and t-shirts, even if unrevealing by Western standards, may identify you as a foreigner and should be avoided. Wearing the shirts, long skirts and platform shoes that are fashionable among native women will cut down on those obnoxious stares, and a *babushka*-style kerchief is like kryptonite to even the most perceptive and tenacious of cat callers. Wearing a conspicuous **wedding band** may help prevent unwanted overtures. Some travelers report that carrying pictures of a "husband" or "children" is extremely useful to help document marriage status. Even a mention of a husband waiting back at the hotel may be enough in some places to discount your potentially vulnerable, unattached appearance.

In cities, you may be harassed no matter how you're dressed. Your best answer to verbal harassment is no answer at all; feigned deafness, sitting motionless and staring straight ahead at nothing in particular will do a world of good that reactions usually don't achieve. If need be, turn to an older woman for help; her stern rebukes should usually embarrass the most persistent harrassers into silence.

Don't hesitate to seek out a police officer or a passerby if you are being harassed. *Let's Go* lists emergency numbers (including rape crisis lines) in the **Practical Information** listings of most cities. Memorize the emergency numbers in the places you visit. Carry a **whistle** or an airhorn on your keychain, and don't hesitate to use it in an emergency. An **IMPACT Model Mugging** self-defense course will not only prepare you for a potential attack, but will also raise your level of awareness of your surroundings as well as your confidence (see **Self Defense,** p. 25). Women also face some specific health concerns when traveling (see **Women's Health,** p. 33).

FURTHER READING: WOMEN TRAVELERS. *A Journey of One's Own: Uncommon Advice for the Independent Woman Traveler*, Thalia Zepatos (Eighth Mountain Press, US$17). *Active Women Vacation Guide*, Evelyn Kaye (Blue Panda Publications, US$18). *A Foxy Old Woman's Guide to Traveling Alone*, Jay Ben-Lesser (Crossing Press, US$11).

TRAVELING ALONE

There are many benefits to traveling alone, among them greater independence and challenge. As a lone traveler, you have greater opportunity to interact with the residents of the region you're visiting. Without distraction, you can write a great travelogue in the grand tradition of Mark Twain and John Steinbeck.

On the other hand, any solo traveler is a more vulnerable target of harassment and street theft. Lone travelers need to be well-organized and look confident at all times. Try not to stand out as a tourist, and be especially careful in deserted or very crowded areas. If questioned, never admit that you are traveling alone. Try to learn the basic of conversation in the local language and use them; the locals will take a liking to you much more quickly if you make even the slightest attempts at their tongue. Finally, maintain regular contact with someone at home who knows your itinerary.

A number of organizations supply information for solo travelers, and others find travel companions for those who don't want to go alone. A few are listed here.

American International Homestays, P.O. Box 1754, Nederland, CO 80466 (tel. 303-642-3088 or 800-876-2048; ash@igc.apc.org; www.commerce.com/homestays). Lodgings with English-speaking host families in Eastern Europe.

Connecting: Solo Traveler Network, P.O. Box 29088, 1996 W. Broadway, Vancouver, BC V6J 5C2, Canada (tel. 604-737-7791; info@cstn.org; www.cstn.org). Bi-monthly newsletter features going solo tips, single-friendly tips and travel companion ads. Annual directory lists holiday suppliers that avoid single supplement charges. Advice and lodging exchanges facilitated between members. Membership US$25-35.

Travel Companion Exchange, P.O. Box 833, Amityville, NY 11701 (tel. 516-454-0880 or 800-392-1256; www.travelalone.com). Publishes the pamphlet *Foiling Pickpockets & Bag Snatchers* (US$4) and *Travel Companions*, a bi-monthly newsletter for single travelers seeking a travel partner (subscription US$48).

FURTHER READING: TRAVELING ALONE. *Traveling Solo*, Eleanor Berman (Globe Pequot, US$17). *The Single Traveler Newsletter*, P.O. Box 682, Ross, CA 94957 (tel. 415-389-0227). 6 issues US$29.

OLDER TRAVELERS

Discounts for Senior Citizens in Eastern Europe are few and far between. That having been said, it never hurts to ask. Agencies for senior group travel are growing in enrollment and popularity. These are only a few:

ElderTreks, 597 Markham St., Toronto, ON, Canada, M6G 2L7 (tel. 800-741-7956 or 416-588-5000; fax 588-9839; passages@inforamp.net; www.eldertreks.com).

Elderhostel, 75 Federal St., Boston, MA 02110-1941 (tel. 617-426-7788 or 877-426-8056; registration@elderhostel.org; www.elderhostel.org). Programs at colleges, universities, and other learning centers in Western Russia on varied subjects lasting 1-4 weeks. Must be 55 or over (spouse can be of any age).

The Mature Traveler, P.O. Box 50400, Reno, NV 89513 (tel. 775-786-7419 or 800-460-6676; www.maturetraveler.com). Soft-adventure tours for seniors. Subscription US$30.

ESSENTIALS

FURTHER READING: OLDER TRAVELERS. *No Problem! Worldwise Tips for Mature Adventurers,* Janice Kenyon. (Orca Book Publishers, US$16). *A Senior's Guide to Healthy Travel,* Donald L. Sullivan (Career Press, US$15). *Unbelievably Good Deals and Great Adventures That You Absolutely Can't Get Unless You're Over 50,* Joan Rattner Heilman (Contemporary Books, US$13).

BISEXUAL, GAY, AND LESBIAN TRAVELERS

Homophobic views persist throughout much of Eastern Europe, and a degree of caution should be exercised. In Belarus, Bosnia, and Romania, homosexuality remains illegal, and in other countries laws forbidding "scandalous homosexual activity" or public displays of homosexuality can give local authorities an excuse to be troublesome. Even within major cities, gay nightclubs and social centers are often clandestine and frequently change location. Therefore, while *Let's Go* tries to list local gay and lesbian bars and clubs, word of mouth is often the best method for finding the latest hotspots. Listed below are contact organizations and publishers that offer materials addressing gay and lesbian concerns.

Gay's the Word, 66 Marchmont St., London WC1N 1AB (tel. (0171) 278 76 54; sales@gaystheword.co.uk; freespace.virgin.net/gays.theword/). The largest gay and lesbian bookshop in the U.K. Mail-order service available. No catalogue of listings, but they will provide a list of titles on a given subject.

Giovanni's Room, 345 S. 12th St., Philadelphia, PA 19107 (tel. 215-923-2960; fax 923-0813; giophilp@netaxs.com). An international feminist, lesbian, and gay bookstore with mail-order service which carries the publications listed here.

International Gay and Lesbian Travel Association, 4331 N. Federal Hwy., Suite 304, Fort Lauderdale, FL 33308 (tel. 954-776-2626 or 800-448-8550; fax 954-776-3303; IGLTA@aol.com; www.iglta.com). An organization of over 1350 companies serving gay and lesbian travelers worldwide. Call for lists of travel agents, accommodations, and events.

FURTHER READING: BISEXUAL, GAY, AND LESBIAN TRAVELERS. *Spartacus International Gay Guide,* Bruno Gmunder Verlag. (US$33). *Ferrari Guides' Gay Travel A to Z, Ferrari Guides' Men's Travel in Your Pocket, Ferrari Guides' Women's Travel in Your Pocket,* and *Ferrari Guides' Inn Places,* Ferrari Guides (US$14-16). For more information, call 602-863-2408 or 800-962-2912 or check their website (www.q-net.com). *The Gay Vacation Guide: The Best Trips and How to Plan Them,* Mark Chesnut (Citadel Press, US$15).

TRAVELERS WITH DISABILITIES

Unfortunately, compared to other travel destinations, Eastern Europe is fairly inaccessible for disabled travelers. Handicap ramps and other such amenities are all but nonexistent in most countries. As a result, some extra planning before your trip will be necessary to ensure everything gores smoothly. Contacting your destination's consulate or tourist office for information, and arranging transportation early is a good start. Those with disabilities should also inform airlines and hotels of their disabilities when making arrangements for travel; some time may be needed to prepare special accommodations. If you give notice, some major car rental agencies offer hand-controlled vehicles at select locations. Call ahead to restaurants, hotels, parks, and other facilities to find out about the existence of ramps, the widths of doors, the dimensions of elevators, etc. Guide-dog owners should inquire as to the specific quarantine policies of each destination. At the very least, they will need to provide a certificate of immunization against rabies.

The following organizations provide information or publications that might be of assistance:

Graphic Language Press, P.O. Box 270, Cardiff by the Sea, CA 92007 (tel. (760) 944-9594; niteowl@cts.com). Advice for wheelchair travelers, including accessible accommodations, transportation, and sightseeing for various European cities.

Mobility International USA (MIUSA), P.O. Box 10767, Eugene, OR 97440 (tel. 541-343-1284 voice and TDD; fax 343-6812; info@miusa.org; www.miusa.org). Sells *A World of Options: A Guide to International Educational Exchange, Community Service, and Travel for Persons with Disabilities* (US$35).

Moss Rehab Hospital Travel Information Service (tel. 215-456-9600; www.mossresourcenet.org). A telephone and internet information center on international travel accessibility and other travel-related concerns for those with disabilities.

Society for the Advancement of Travel for the Handicapped (SATH), 347 Fifth Ave., #610, New York, NY 10016 (tel. 212-447-1928; fax 725-8253; sathtravel@aol.com; www.sath.org). Advocacy group publishing a quarterly color travel magazine *OPEN WORLD* (free for members or US$13 for nonmembers). Also publishes a wide range of information sheets on disability travel facilitation and accessible destinations. Annual membership US$45, students and seniors US$30.

Directions Unlimited, 720 N. Bedford Rd., Bedford Hills, NY 10507 (tel. 800-533-5343; in NY 914-241-1700; fax 914-241-0243; cruisesusa@aol.com). Specializes in arranging individual and group vacations, tours, and cruises for the physically disabled. Group tours for blind travelers.

MINORITY TRAVELERS

The minority that encounters the most hostility in Eastern Europe is Gypsies *(Roma)*. Travelers with darker skin of any nationality might be mistaken for Gypsies and therefore face some of the same prejudice. Other minority travelers, especially those of African or Asian descent, will usually meet with more curiosity than hostility, especially outside of big cities. Travelers of Arab ethnicity may also be treated more suspiciously. The ranks of Skinheads are on the rise in Eastern Europe, and minority travelers, especially Jews and blacks, should regard them with caution. Anti-Semitism is still a problem in many countries, including Poland and the former Soviet Union; sad to say, it is generally best to be discreet about your religion.

TRAVELERS WITH CHILDREN

Family vacations often require that you slow your pace, and always require that you plan ahead. When deciding where to stay, remember the special needs of young children; when picking accommodations, call ahead and make sure it's child-friendly. If you rent a car, make sure the rental company provides a car seat for younger children. Consider using a papoose-style device to carry a baby on walking trips. Be sure that your child carries some sort of ID in case of an emergency or he or she gets lost, and arrange a reunion spot in case of separation when sight-seeing.

Virtually all museums and tourist attractions also have child or student rates. Children under two generally fly for 10% of the adult airfare on international flights (this does not necessarily include a seat). International fares are usually discounted 25% for children from two to 11. Finding a private place for **breast feeding** is often a problem while traveling, so pack accordingly. Below are resources that plan or provide information for planning a trip to Eastern Europe with kids.

Hostelling International, AYH, 733 15th St., NW, Suite 840, Washington DC 20005 (tel. (202) 783-6161; fax 783-6171; hiayhserv@hiayh.org; www.iyhf.org) Many of their hostels have family-sized rooms. Also offers some hiking and biking trips through Europe geared for families with teens.

Backroads, 801 Cedar St., Berkeley, CA 94710-1800 (tel. (800) 462-2848; fax) Biking and walking tours for families through the Czech Republic.

FURTHER READING: TRAVELERS WITH CHILDREN. *Backpacking with Babies and Small Children,* Goldie Silverman (Wilderness Press, US$10). *Take Your Kids to Europe,* Cynthia W. Harriman (Globe Pequot, US$17). *Adventuring with Children: An Inspirational Guide to World Travel and the Outdoors,* Nan Jeffrey (Avalon House Publishing, US$15).

DIETARY CONCERNS

Vegetarian and **kosher** travelers will have their work cut out for them in Eastern Europe. Most of the national cuisines tend to be meat and especially pork-heavy. Markets are always a safe bet for fresh vegetables, fruit, cheese, and bread. In Belarus, watch out for veggies and dairy products from near the Chernobyl region. Opting for more expensive imported products is worth the cost.

Travelers who keep kosher should contact synagogues in larger cities for information on kosher restaurants; your own synagogue or college Hillel should have access to lists of the abundant Jewish institutions across Eastern Europe. If you are strict in your observance, bring supplies to prepare your own food on the road.

The Jewish Travel Guide lists synagogues, kosher restaurants, and Jewish institutions in over 80 countries. Available from Vallentine-Mitchell Publishers, Newbury House 890-900, Eastern Ave., Newbury Park, Ilford, Essex, U.K. IG2 7HH (tel. (0181) 599 88 66; fax 599 09 84). It is available in the U.S. ($16) from ISBS, 5804 NE Hassallo St., Portland, OR 97213-3644 (tel. 800-944-6190).

FURTHER READING: DIETARY CONCERNS. *The Vegetarian Traveler: Where to Stay if You're Vegetarian,* Jed Civic (Larson Pub., US$16). *Europe on 10 Salads a Day,* Mary Jane (Mustang Publishing, US$10).

ALTERNATIVES TO TOURISM

STUDY

Foreign study programs have multiplied rapidly in Eastern Europe. Most American undergraduates enroll in programs sponsored by U.S. universities, and many colleges staff offices that provide advice and information on study abroad. Local libraries and bookstores are also helpful sources for current information on study abroad, or check out www.studyabroad.com or www.worldwide.edu. Take advantage of academic counselors and put in some hours at their libraries, or request the names of recent program participants and get in touch. If your language skills are decent, you may want to consider enrolling directly in a foreign university. This route is usually less expensive and more immersive than programs run through American universities. The catch is that it may be harder to get credit for your adventures abroad. Contact the nearest consulate for a list of institutions in your country of choice. There are also several international and national fellowships available (e.g. Fulbright or Rotary) to fund stays abroad.

In most Eastern European countries, studying requires a special study visa, issued for a duration longer than a tourist visa. Applying for such visa usually requires proof of admission in the University/program which you are planning to attend (for more, see **Visas**, p. 16).

Below are several independent organizations that run programs to several Eastern European countries.

American Field Service (AFS), 310 SW 4th Ave., #630, Portland, OR 97204-2608 (tel. (800) 237-4636; fax (503) 241-1653; afsinfo@afs.org;www.afs.org/). Summer, semester, and year-long homestay international exchange programs for high school students and graduating high school seniors in Czech Republic, Hungary, Latvia, Russia, Slovakia. Financial aid available.

American Institute for Foreign Study, College Division, 102 Greenwich Ave., Greenwich, CT 06830 (tel. 800-727-2437 x6084; www.aifs.com). Organizes programs for high school and college study in universities in Russia and the Czech Republic. Summer, fall, spring, and year-long programs available. Scholarships available. Contact Dana Maggio with questions at dmaggio@aifs.com.

School for International Training, College Semester Abroad, Admissions, Kipling Rd., P.O. Box 676, Brattleboro, VT 05302 (tel. 800-336-1616 or 802-258-3267; fax 258-3500; www.worldlearning.org). Runs semester- and year-long programs in Russia and the Czech Republic. Programs cost US$8200-10300, all expenses included. Financial aid available and U.S. financial aid is transferable.

Youth For Understanding International Exchange (YFU), 3501 Newark St. NW, Washington, D.C. 20016 (tel. (800) TEENAGE (833-6243) or (202) 966-6800; fax 895-1104; http://www.yfu.org). Places U.S. high school students worldwide for a year, semester, or summer in the Czech & Slovak Republics (joint program), Estonia/Latvia, Hungary, Poland, Russia, and Ukraine. US$75 application fee.

LANGUAGE SCHOOLS

Programs are run by foreign universities, independent international or local organizations, and/or American universities. Programs generally cost anywhere from US$2000 to US$5000 and include your lodging, some meals, and daytrips to cultural centers and attractions. Some of the pricier ones include airfare to and from the program.

ACTR/ACCELS, 1776 Massachusetts Ave., NW, Suite 700, Washington, DC, 20036 (tel. 202-833-7522; fax 202-833-7523; general@actr.org; www.actr.org). Offers college-level summer language study programs in Belarus, Czech and Slovak Republics (joint program), Hungary, Moldova, Russia and Ukraine. Prices range from US$2200-3400. $35 application fee.

Russian and East European Partnerships, Kenneth Fortune, President PO Box 227, Fineview, NY 14640 (tel. 888-USE-REEP; fax 800-910-1777; reep@fox.nstn.ca). Offers summer and term-time language and cultural immersion programs in Belarus, Bulgaria, Croatia, Czech Republic, Estonia, Hungary, Poland, Russia and Ukraine. Prices range from US$2995-4650.

FURTHER READING: STUDY. *Academic Year Abroad*, Institute of International Education Books (US$45). *Vacation Study Abroad*, Institute of International Education Books (US$40). *Peterson's Study Abroad Guide*, Peterson's (US$30).

WORK

Working in Eastern Europe, like studying there, forces one to jump through a whole new set of hoops involving visas in work permits. Both a work permit and a visa are required. In some countries, to make it all the more confusing, a particular visa called a "visa with work permit" is required, although, contrary to the name, this document does *not* include a work permit. Visas are issued from the nearest consulate or embassy, like any visa (see **Embassies and Consulates,** p. 13). Applying for it, however, will require that you present your work permit, which must be issued directly from the Labor Bureau in the country in question. There are often ways to make it easier. Friends living in the country can help expedite work permits or arrange work-for-accommodations swaps. In some sectors (like agricultural work) permit-less workers are rarely bothered by authorities. For more information, see **Visas**, p. 16.

TEACHING ENGLISH

Central Bureau for Educational Visits & Exchanges, 10 Spring Gardens, London SW1A 2BN (tel. (0171) 389 4419 fax 389 4426). Places British undergraduates and teachers in teaching positions in Poland and Hungary. Also arranges study abroad in Hungary, Poland, Russia, and Slovenia.

International Schools Services, Educational Staffing Program, P.O. Box 5910, Princeton, NJ 08543 (tel. 609-452-0990; fax 452-2690; edustaffing@iss.edu; www.iss.edu). Recruits teachers and administrators for American and English schools throughout Eastern Europe and the world. All instruction in English. Applicants must have a bachelor's degree and two years of relevant experience. Nonrefundable US$100 application fee. Publishes *The ISS Directory of Overseas Schools* (US$35).

Office of Overseas Schools, A/OS Room 245, SA-29, Dept. of State, Washington, D.C. 20522-2902 (tel. 703-875-7800; fax 875-7979; overseas.school@state.gov; state.gov/www/about_state/schools/). Keeps a list of schools abroad and agencies that arrange placement for Americans to teach abroad.

VOLUNTEER

Volunteer jobs are readily available throughout Eastern Europe. In some cases, you might receive room and board in exchange for your labor. You can sometimes avoid the high application fees charged by the organizations that arrange placement by contacting the individual workcamps directly; check with the organizations.

Peace Corps, 1111 20th St. NW, Washington, D.C. 20526 (tel. 800-424-8580; www.peacecorps.gov). Write for their "blue" brochure, which details application requirements. Opportunities in agriculture, business, education, the environment, and health in Bulgaria, Estonia, Latvia, Lithuania, Moldova, Poland, Romania, Russia, Slovakia, and Ukraine. Volunteers must be U.S. citizens, age 18 and over, and willing to make a 2-year commitment. A bachelor's degree is usually required.

Service Civil International Voluntary Service (SCI-VS), 814 NE 40th St., Seattle, WA 98105 (tel./fax 206-545-6585; sciivsusa@igc.apc.org). Arranges placement in workcamps in Europe for those age 18 and over, including Belarus, Bosnia, Bulgaria, Croatia, Czech Republic, Estonia, Hungary, Latvia, Lithuania, Poland, Romania, Russia, Slovakia, Slovenia, and Ukraine. Local organizations sponsor groups for physical or social work. Registration fees US$50-250, depending on the camp location.

Volunteers for Peace, 1034 Tiffany Rd., Belmont, VT 05730 (tel. 802-259-2759; fax 259-2922; vfp@vfp.org; www.vfp.org). A nonprofit organization that arranges speedy placement in 2-3 week workcamps in more than a dozen Eastern European countries comprising 10-15 people. Most complete and up-to-date listings provided in the annual *International Workcamp Directory* (US$15). Registration fee US$195. Free newsletter.

FURTHER READING: WORK AND VOLUNTEER. *Now Hiring! Jobs in Eastern Europe*, Clarke Canfield (Independent Publishers Group, US$15). *International Directory of Voluntary Work*, Victoria Pybus (Vacation Work Publications, US$16). *Teaching English Abroad*, Susan Griffin (Vacation Work, US$17). *Overseas Summer Jobs 1999*, *Work Your Way Around the World*, and *Directory of Jobs and Careers Abroad*, Peterson's (US$17-18 each).

THE WORLD WIDE WEB

Grabbing to the coattails of capitalism and democracy, internet access is asserting itself in the private sector in Eastern Europe. Cybercafes proliferate in major cities, from the heavily touristed Prague to the less well-known Zagreb, Croatia. In smaller towns, the best bets for logging on are tourist offices or hotels.

The internet is also becoming increasingly adept at handling the preparations for a trip to Eastern Europe. Many countries' embassies now maintain websites where you can check visa requirements and news related to your destination (see **Embassies and Consulates,** p. 13). Many major search engines now offer services to find and compare the lowest fares to anywhere in the world. Some highlights:

Microsoft Expedia (expedia.msn.com) has everything you'd ever need to make travel plans on the web: compare flight fares, look at maps, make reservations. FareTracker, a free service, sends you monthly mailings about the cheapest fares to any destination.

Shoestring Travel (www.stratpub.com), an alternative to Microsoft's monolithic site, is budget travel e-zine that features listings of home exchanges, links, and accommodations information.

The CIA World Factbook (www.odci.gov/cia/publications/factbook/index.html) has tons of vital statistics on East Europeans nations. Check it out for an overview of the economy, and an explanation of its system of government.

Foreign Language for Travelers (www.travlang.com) can help you brush up on your most any language in Eastern Europe.

Let's Go (www.letsgo.com) is where you can find our newsletter, information about our books, up-to-the-minute links, and more.

FURTHER READING: THE WORLD WIDE WEB. *How to Plan Your Dream Vacation Using the Web,* Elizabeth Dempsey (Coriolis Group, US$25). *Nettravel: How Travelers Use the Internet,* Michael Shapiro (O'Reilly & Associates, US$25). *Travel Planning Online for Dummies,* Noah Vadnai (IDG Books, US$25).

BELARUS (БЕЛАРУСЬ)

US$1 = 315,000BR (BELARUSSIAN RUBLES)	**100,000BR = US$0.32**
CDN$1 = 211,168BR	**100,000BR = CDN$0.47**
UK£1 = 505,291BR	**100,000BR = UK£0.20**
IR£1 = 424,285BR	**100,000BR = IR£0.24**
AUS$1 = 203,710BR	**100,000BR = AUS$0.49**
NZ$1 = 162,918BR	**100,000BR = NZ$0.61**
SAR1 = 52,408BR	**100,000BR = SAR1.90**
DM1 = 170,849BR	**100,000BR = DM0.59**

PHONE CODES Country code: **375.** International dialing prefix: **810.**

For as long as anyone can remember, Belarus has been the backwater of someone else's empire, and today it remains the black sheep of Eastern Europe. Flattened by the Germans from 1941-1945 and exploited by the Soviets from 1946-1990, the country seems to have lost its sense of self. The fall of the USSR left its people grasping for a national identity but unable to find their own way. The sum of all of these troubles is a country of sprawling urban landscapes without anything resembling conventional beauty, and tiny forest villages seemingly untouched by the centuries. For those willing to endure the difficulties inherent to travel in Belarus, the country presents a fascinated interesting case study; others should avoid its trials in favor of countries better prepared for foreign consumption.

HIGHLIGHT OF BELARUS

■ **Brest Fortress,** with its surrounding memorials and museums, gives visitors a taste of Eastern Europe at the end of WWII (p. 77).

LIFE & TIMES

HISTORY

Belarus was one of the first areas settled by the **Slavs,** and by the mid-1000s it was taken under the wing of **Kievan Rus,** the precursor of Russia and Ukraine. When the Mongols sacked Kiev in 1240, they destroyed nascent Belarussian settlements and cleared the way for the **Duchy of Lithuania,** which ruled alone until the 1386 creation of the **Polish-Lithuanian Commonwealth** (see **Poland: History,** p. 399). Under the new empire, Belarus began to develop its own language and culture; this burgeoning national identity stirred unrest among the people and eventually led to a 1648 Cossack rebellion. In the late 18th century, the **First and Second Partitions of Poland** handed the territory over to Russia. Despite new industry under Russian rule, the stagnant economy forced some 600,000 people to leave the country—for Siberia.

World War I brought heavy fighting to the region, so it was fitting that **Brest-Litovsk** (p. 76) hosted the treaty that got Russia out of the war—and ceded Belarus to Germany. The treaty lasted only a few months, but it was long enough for Belarus to declare its independence. Alas, as soon as Germany departed, the Poles and Bolsheviks came calling and divided the region. As a charter member of the USSR, the Russian portion got the full Stalinist package: more industry and fewer dissidents and intellectuals after the purges of the 1930s.

With **WWII** came another wave of German soldiers and the unification of Belarus under the Soviets. The nation bounced back quickly from the war. Industry boomed and rural Belarussians migrated to the growing cities for better job prospects. As if urbanization weren't bad enough for the environment, the 1986 explosion at **Chernobyl** spewed radioactive material across the south of the country (see p. 68). Perhaps cowed by a history of imperial domination, Belarus reluctantly declared sovereignty on July 27, 1990, and independence on August 25, 1991, amid political turmoil in Moscow. The fledgling Republic quickly found a security blanket in the **Commonwealth of Indepedent States** (see **1989 & Beyond,** p. 12) and has not strayed far from mother Russia since.

BELARUS TODAY

Of all the former Soviet republics, Belarus has the weakest national identity, is the most Russified, and has clamored the least for independence. Indeed, President **Alexander Lukashenka** publicly decreed that Belarus was to be "Slavic, Russian, and Orthodox." The Union Treaty of 1996 was supposed to move toward reunification with Russia, but Russia has grown less enthusiastic. Lukashenka's methods have included suppressing the media, arresting dissenters, and even dissolving Parliament. To the exasperation of opponents at home and in the West, Lukashenka's following among the people is almost cultish. In 1999, the two countries were continuing negotiation for a more complete merger. Ironically, the strongest dissenters were Russians, who saw no reason to assume responsibility for Belarus's economy. Meanwhile, the tragic legacy of **Chernobyl** still haunts Belarus; as much as 30% of the country was contaminated with radioactive cesium, the long-term effects of which are beginning to surface in the form of childhood thyroid cancer.

LITERATURE & ARTS

Domination by myriad rulers put off Belarus's cultural growth until the 15th century when Polatsk-born **Frantsishek Skaryna** translated the Bible into Old Church Slavonic (with original prefaces and postscripts in Belarussian), the first book printed in Eastern Europe. By the 16th century, **Andrej Rymsha** began a new genre of poetry, the **panegyric,** which served as a formal introduction in religious texts.

Polish control in the 18th century brought harsh repression of Belarussian literature and a lull in artistic activity. Resurgence came with the 1906 egalitarian journal *Our Cornfield (Nasha Niva)*, which drew contributions from 500 villages and launched the careers of **Yakub Kolas** and **Yanka Kupala,** known for their portrayal of Belarus's revolutionary struggles. Literary circles kept nationalism alive longer than the Belarussian National Republic could, but they too succumbed to state control by the end of the 1920s. Under Polish control this time, literature flowed a bit more freely; one standout is the poet **Natalla Arseneva.** After the death of Stalin, prose and poetry were finally able to flourish. Today's major figures include poets **Pimen Pachanka** and **Arkady Kalyashov** and novelists **Yanka Bryl** and **Ivan Shamyakin.**

Belarus's progress in other arts has been even more arduous than its literary history. Despite a long tradition of folk and church music, **classical composing** has only developed since WWII. Notable composers include the exile **Kulikovich Shchahlow** and **Yawhen Hlyebaw.** Architecturally, some structures dating from the 11th and 12th centuries still stand; in **Hrodna** (p. 75), one can still find **Baroque churches** from the 17th century. Unfortunately, war damage necessitated the rebuilding of **Minsk** (p. 70) in a tragically Stalinist vein.

READING LIST

For more on Belarus's fitful drive for independence, see Nicholas P. Vakar's *Belarussia: The Making of a Nation.* For samples of the poetic tradition, there's *The Images Swarm Free: A Bi-lingual Selection of Poetry* by Maksim Bahdanovic, Ales Harun, and Zmitrok Biadula.

FACTS AND FIGURES

- **Capital:** Minsk
- **Population:** 10,359,629
- **Land Area:** 207,595 km²
- **Geography:** Marshland and forest
- **Language:** Belarussian
- **Religions:** 60% Eastern Orthodox
- **GDP per capita:** US$1130
- **Major Exports:** Agricultural machinery

BELARUS ESSENTIALS

To visit Belarus, you must secure an invitation and a visa—an expensive and head-spinning process. If you have an acquaintance in Belarus who can provide you with an official invitation, you may obtain a 90-day single-entry (5-day service US$50; next-day US$100) or multiple-entry (5-day processing US$300; no rush service) visa at an embassy or consulate (see **Embassies and Consulates,** p. 13). Together with the visa application and fee (by personal check or money order), you must submit your passport and one photograph. Those without Belarussian friends can turn to **Russia House** (see **Russia Essentials,** p. 525), which will get you an invitation and visa in five business days (US$145; rush service US$215). **Host Families Association (HOFA)** provides invitations for its guests (see **Russia Essentials,** p. 526). You may also obtain an invitation by planning your trip through a **Belintourist** office. They will provide you with documentation after you have pre-paid all your hotel stays. Transit visas (US$20-30), valid for 48 hours, are issued at a consulate and theoretically at the border, but avoid the latter option anywhere other than Brest. Your train may leave while you're still outside getting your visa. At some Belarussian embassies and consulates, such as those in Daugavpils and Kiev, transit visas may be cheaper.

PRIMARY BORDER CROSSINGS. Transit visas (US$20-30; valid for 48hr.) are theoretically available at the border, but avoid this anywhere except Brest. Transit visas can also be purchased at the Belarussian embassies in Kiev and Daugavpils, Latvia. Expect to unofficially pay US$20-30 whenever you cross a Belarussian border. Allow several hours to cross a Belarussian border. The easiest way to enter or leave Belarus is by taking a direct bus or train between Minsk, Brest, or Hrodna and the capital of the neighboring country.

Latvia: Polatsk, BEL/Daugavpils, LAT (p. 357) via Druya, BEL; connects Belarus with Vidzeme and Latgale (p. 357).

Lithuania: Hrodna, BEL (p. 75)/Druskininkai, LIT (p. 380); connects Belarus with Inland Lithuania (p. 375).

Poland: Hrodna, BEL (p. 75)/Białystok, POL via Kuznica, BEL; connects Belarus with Podlasie, POL (p. 494). Brest, BEL (p. 76)/Biała Podlaska, POL via Terespol, BEL; connects Belarus with Małopolska (p. 421).

Russia: Orsha, BEL/Smolensk, RUS via Krasnol, BEL; connects Belarus with Northwest Russia (p. 596). Homel, BEL/Novozybkov, RUS; connects Belarus with the Volga Region (p. 638).

Ukraine: Brest, BEL (p. 76)/Kovel, UKR via Makrany, BEL; connects Belarus with Western Ukraine (p. 767).

GETTING THERE & GETTING AROUND

You can fly into Minsk on **Belavia,** Belarus's national airline *(if* you trust the old planes). **LOT** also flies from Warsaw, and **Lufthansa** has daily direct flights from Frankfurt. Leaving Belarus by air can be a nightmare, as customs officials are wont to rip through your bags. **Buses** and **trains** connect Brest to Warsaw, Prague, Kiev, and Lviv, and Hrodna to Warsaw, Białystok, and Vilnius. Be aware that some international train tickets must be paid partly in US dollars and partly in Belarussian rubles. All immigration and customs are done on the trains; trains between Russia and Belarus are considered domestic routes and do not stop for customs. Tickets for same-day **trains** within Belarus are purchased at the station. Information booths in the stations charge 5000BR per inquiry. It's better to ask a cashier (see p. 527 for more on post-Soviet train travel). For **city buses,** buy tickets at a kiosk (or from the driver for a surcharge) and punch them on board. **Hitchhiking** is popular outside large cities, and locals don't consider it dangerous. To catch a car, point your forefingers to the ground. *Let's Go* does not recommend hitchhiking.

TOURIST SERVICES & MONEY

INFLATION. Inflation is rampant in Belarus, meaning that the Belarussian ruble is likely to lose much of its value. Therefore, we list many prices in US$.

Belintourist (Белінтурıст) is all that's left of the once omnipotent Intourist. It varies from mostly helpful to merely rubble, but is often the only resource. The staff hands out Soviet-era brochures and sometimes books train tickets, but does not cater to budget travlers. Hotel Belarus and Hotel Yubilyenaya in Minsk have **private travel agencies.** Be sure to carry plenty of hard **cash** when not in a potential bribe situation. U.S. dollars, Deutschmarks, and Russian rubles are preferred; you'll have a great deal of trouble exchanging other currencies, even British pounds. A black currency market still exists, mostly among harmless locals who can offer you a better rate than the one sanctioned by the government. If you go this route, be careful of seedy characters eager to slip you counterfeit currency. There are no **ATMs** aside from one or two that have recently popped up in Minsk, and most bank clerks leaf through their English dictionaries at the mention of "traveler's checks." Some hotels accept **credit cards,** mostly AmEx and Visa. Cash advances on Visa and sometimes MC are available for a 4% commission at **Prior Bank** (Пріор Банк) offices in most cities, and at the occasional hotel lobby. Don't leave the country with Belarussian rubles; they're impossible to exchange abroad.

COMMUNICATION

Avoid the unreliable **mail** system at all costs; almost everything is opened and read by the authorities first. Public **telephones** have poor sound quality. **Local calls** require tokens purchased at kiosks or blue magnetic cards, available at the post office, train station, and some hotels (100,000-200,000BR). **International calls** must be placed at the post office and paid for in advance, in cash. Write down the number you're calling and say "Ya ha-tchoo po-ZVAH-neet" ("I'd like to call...") followed by the name of the country; pay with exact change. You will be told the number of a phone booth, which you then enter to make your call. Return to the kiosk to pick up any change. International access numbers include: **AT&T,** tel. 8, 80 01 01; **Australia Direct** 810; **BT Direct,** tel. 88 00 44; **Canada Direct** 8, 80 01 11; **MCI,** tel. 8, 80 01 03.

LANGUAGE

Belarussians have been more Russified than any other ethnic minority in the former Soviet Union, to the extent that most Belarussians speak mostly **Russian** and only very rarely Belarussian (see **The Cyrillic Alphabet,** p. 815, and the **Russian Glossary,** p. 827). In Hrodna and Brest, **Polish** is common. Some students will also speak **German** or **English.** Most street and place names have been converted into Belarussian since independence, but locals still use the old Russian versions, which is cause for much confusion. If you can handle substituting the Belarussian "i" for the Russian "и" and other minor spelling changes, you'll be fine. The only major difference is that the Cyrillic letter "г," which is pronounced "g" in Russian, is transliterated as "h" in Belarussian. *Let's Go* lists place names in Belarussian in deference to the official line, but in order to be understood, you'll have to replace "h" with "g" ("Hrodna" is more commonly pronounced "Grodno"). Common words in *Let's Go* include: *avtovakzal* (bus station; автовакзал), *gastsinitsa* (hotel; гасцініца), *sobor* (cathedral; собор), *vakzal* (station; вакзал), and *zamak* (castle; замак).

HEALTH & SAFETY

! EMERGENCY NUMBERS. Fire: tel. 01. **Police:** tel. 02. **Ambulance:** tel. 03.

Belarus was more affected by the 1986 **Chernobyl** accident than any other region. The faulty reactor was situated in Ukraine, just 12km south of the Belarussian border, and winds happened to blow north for the first six days after the explosion; hence, nearly 70% of the radioactive material blew into Belarus and sank into the soil of the southeast quarter of the nation. An area of approximately 1200 sq. km just north of Chernobyl has been completely evacuated because of extremely high concentrations of strontium-90, plutonium-239/240, and cesium-137. Today, more than 10 years after the tragedy, it is safe to travel through the formerly contaminated areas; experts say that a week's stay there is no worse than receiving an X-ray. None of the cities *Let's Go* covers are in affected regions. There's no need to panic, but it is important to be aware of a few safety considerations. Avoid inexpensive **dairy products,** which likely come from contaminated areas—opt instead for something German or Dutch—and stay away from **mushrooms** and **berries,** which tend to collect radioactivity. Drink only bottled water; **tap water,** especially in the southeast, may be contaminated. You will probably find plain old flat bottled water hard to come by, so get used to burping from the fizz.

Crime seems as stagnant as the rest of the country; nobody wants to go to a Belarussian jail. Nonetheless, economic hardship has brought many opportunists. Your embassy is a better bet than the police in an emergency—especially since some police have been known to deal with the mafia and may not be helpful to foreigners unless bribed. Although streets are usually safe and well lit, alcoholism in Belarus is escalating, and it is generally not a good idea to go out alone after dark. For children under 18 years old unaccompanied by an adult, there is a **mandatory 11pm curfew.** It's also a good idea to stay clear of dodgy nightclubs, which are mostly run by the mafia, especially if you aren't dressed to the nines. **Toilet paper** is available in most supermarkets, making its absence from public toilets all the more befuddling. **Condoms** and **feminine hygiene supplies** from the other side of the former Iron Curtain are becoming available.

ACCOMMODATIONS & CAMPING

There are no **hostels** in Belarus, apart from *turbazy* (tour-bases), which only Stalinist pioneers with Siberian upbringings will be able to bear. Remember to keep all receipts from hotels; you just might have to show them to the authorities to avoid fines when leaving Belarus. **Hotels** have three rates—very cheap for Belarussians, outrageous for foreigners, and in-between for CIS member countries. The desk clerks will ask where you are from and request your passport, making it impossible to pass as a native. Some **private hotels** don't accept foreigners at all, but those that do are usually much cheaper and friendlier than the Soviet dinosaurs. To find a **private room,** look around for postings at train stations, or ask taxi drivers, who may know of a lead. The *babushki* at train stations might quote high prices, but they'll be willing to feed and house you for US$10 or less.

FOOD & DRINK

Belarussian cuisine consists purely of what farmers can either grow or fatten: potatoes, bread, chicken, and pork. Thanks to Stalinist repatriations, however, many Georgian and Uzbek chefs have made Belarus their home and are sprinkling exotic spices on the cholesterol. If you guess at a menu or are a guest in a home, you'll probably receive bread, sausage, and a vegetable. Fried entities like *cheburiki* (meat wrapped in pancake; чебурікі) or puffy, divine *panchiki* (панчікі) will fill you up but will also upset your digestive system. Don't be surprised to find locals eating *morozhenoye* (ice cream; мороженое) at all hours of the day; it's one of the few edible AND tasty foods available. The favorite Belarussian drink is the godless, bread-based *kvas* (квас), which is sold at stores or from huge kegs on the street—look for the long line. (For more on *kvas*, see **"Just for the Taste,"** p. 736.)

CUSTOMS & ETIQUETTE

If invited to a Belarussian's home, bring a bottle of wine for men, or a bouquet of odd-numbered flowers for women. Nearly all shops close an hour for lunch, dinner, and breakfast. **Discrimination** exists in Belarus, especially against people with dark skin. Also, if you want to fit in, don't smile too much. **Homosexuality** is definitely frowned upon, but no one will assume you are gay unless you announce it.

SUPPLY AND DEMAND, BELARUSSIAN-STYLE

For staid westerners accustomed to price tags, Belarus's anything-goes bargaining practices can be tough to get used to. Among the most common practices is the *vzyat* (bribe). Do your best to avoid this: cross borders in the daytime, travel in train compartments with locals, and make sure your documents are in line before departing. But given enough time, even the most cautious will end up in a situation where cash is the only method of payment and receipts are not available. The uninitiated wonder how to price in such situations, but the answer is simple: supply and demand. The man with the semi-automatic weapon demands money and you supply all you have. The key is to limit the supply—as a rule, do not carry wads of cash. US$20 is usually plenty, as, after all, it's more than enough to buy a night's supply of beer.

NATIONAL HOLIDAYS

January 7, Orthodox Christmas; March 8, International Women's Day; March 15, Constitution Day; April 23, Catholic Easter; April 30, Orthodox Easter; May 1, Labor Day; May 9, Radinitsa, Victory Day (1945), and Mother's Day; July 3, Independence Day; November 2, Dzyady (Remembrance Day); November 7, October Revolution Anniversary; December 25, Catholic Christmas.

MINSK (MIHCK)

If you're looking for the supreme Soviet city, skip Moscow and head to Minsk (pop. 1,695,000), where the fall of communism has resulted in a reluctant shuffle, rather than a wanton gallop west. Most streets have been renamed, but Lenin's statue still stands. After being flattened in WWII, the city was redesigned as a showpiece of Soviet style, with wide avenues and Stalinist architecture. With imaginary political reforms and concrete everywhere, everyone is asking if Belarussian authorities are really giving Minsk a new face, or just a new facade.

GETTING THERE & GETTING AROUND

Airplanes: The main airport, **Minsk II** (tel. 279 23 33), is 40km east of the city. Take bus #300 from Avtovakzal Vostochny (40min., hourly, 56,000BR). If you don't speak Russian, a taxi will cost US$25-40. The Belarussian airline, **Belavia** (tel. 229 28 38), flies to **Moscow. LOT** (tel. 297 37 29), the Polish airline, flies to **Warsaw. Lufthansa,** F. Skaryny pr. 56 (tel. 226 66 28), flies daily to **Frankfurt.**

Trains: Tsentralni Vakzal (Центральны Вакзал; tel. 220 99 89 and 295 54 10), Privakzalnaya pl. Same-day local tickets sold on 1st floor; international tickets on 2nd floor. For info, go to window #13 on the 2nd floor with the "даведка справка" sign. The easiest way to purchase **advance tickets** is at the Intourist office next to Hotel Yubilaynaya (see **Tourist Offices,** below). Tickets through Poland must be paid for in both US$ and BR. To: **Brest** (5hr., 5 per day, *coupé* 366,000BR); **Berlin** (2 per day, US$40 and 7,000,000BR); **Kiev** (14hr., 1-3 per day, *coupé* 3,534,000BR); **Moscow** (14hr., 14-17 per day, *coupé* 4,845,000BR); **Prague** (1 per day, US$60 and 4,000,000BR); **St. Petersburg** (3 per day, *coupé* 4,173,000BR); **Vilnius** (4½hr., 5 per day, *coupé* 2,500,000BR); and **Warsaw** (12hr., 3-5 per day, US$13 and 4,000,000BR).

Buses: Avtovakzal Tsentralni (Автовакзал Центральны), vul. Babruyskaya 6 (Бабруйская; tel. 227 78 20). To the right of the train station. To **Białystok** (3 per day, 3,630,000BR) and **Vilnius** (4hr., 4 per day, 3,630,000BR).

Local Transportation: Minsk has a cookie-cutter Soviet **Metro** with two lines that efficiently cover its downtown; they cross at Kastrychniskaya (Кастрычніская). Trains run 6am-1am (6000BR). Buses, trolleys, and trams run 5:35am-12:55am (6000BR). Pick up a ticket and **map** at most kiosks around the city.

Taxis: Tel. 061 and 081. Can be found at stands throughout the city. Generally safe and somewhat reasonable. Do not pay more than US$2 for a 10min. ride.

ORIENTATION

The center of town lies in the 3km between northeast **pl. Peramohi** (Перамогі) and southwest **pl. Nezalezhnastsi** (Independence Square; Незалежнасці), with **pr. Frantsishka Skaryny** (Францішка Скарыны) running between the two. **Pr. Masherava** (Машэрава), which turns into **vul. Lenina** (Леніна), runs perpendicular to pr. F. Skaryny. The Svislac River divides the city, with most of the attractions on the southwest bank. The **train station** sits behind **Privakzalnaya pl.** (Прівакзальная)—walk up vul. Leningradskaya and go left on Svyardlova (Свярдлова) to reach pl. Nezalezhnastsi. **Jaywalking** is illegal and carries a moderate fine, so always use the underpasses to cross major streets—it's best to avoid the Minsk police.

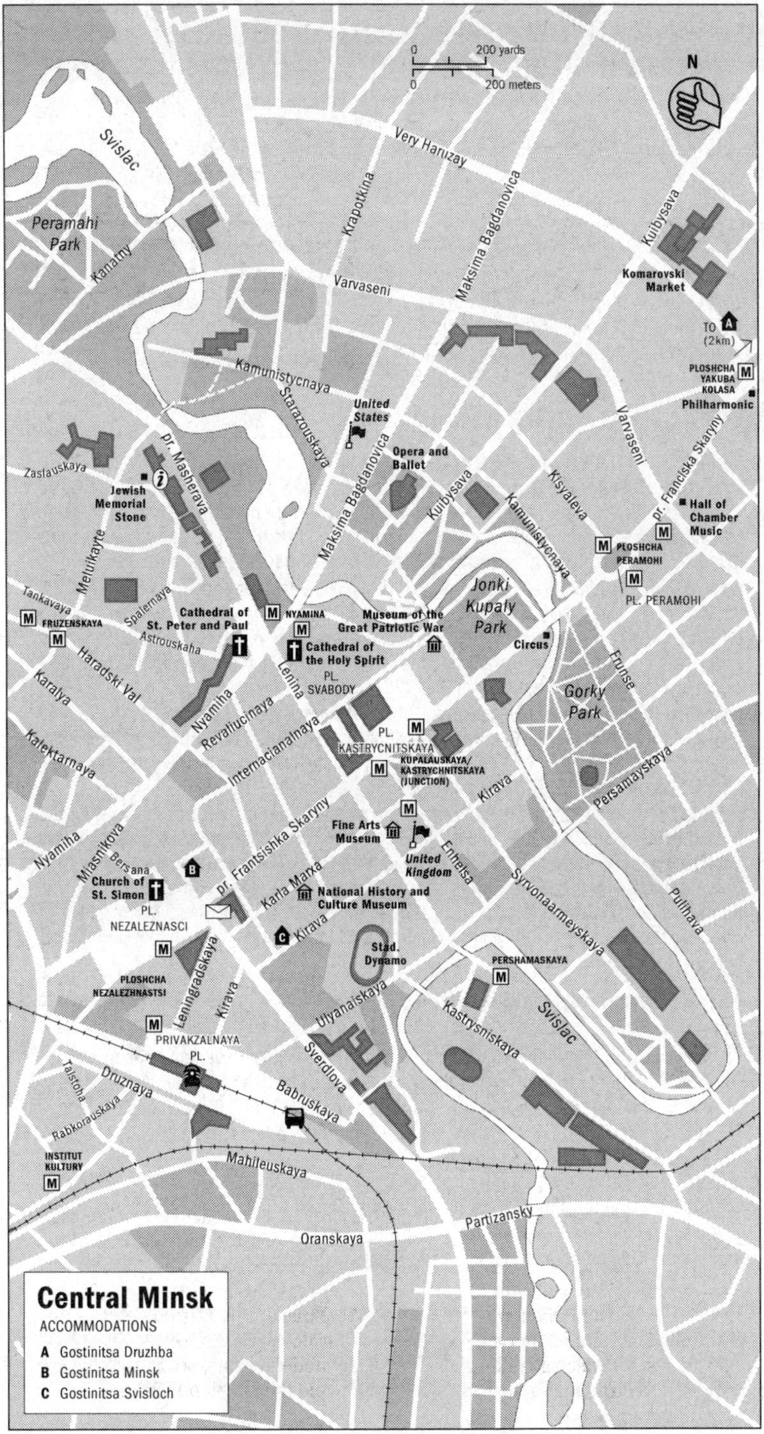
Central Minsk
ACCOMMODATIONS
A Gostinitsa Druzhba
B Gostinitsa Minsk
C Gostinitsa Svisloch
0 200 yards
0 200 meters
N
Svislac
Peramahi Park
Kanatny
Very Haruzay
Krapotkina
Maksima Bagdanovica
Kuibysava
Komarovski Market
Varvaseni
TO A (2km)
PLOSHCHA YAKUBA KOLASA
Philharmonic
Kamunistycnaya
Starazouskaya
United States
Opera and Ballet
Zaslauskaya
Jewish Memorial Stone
pr. Masherava
Varvaseni
pr. Franciska Skaryny
Kisyaleva
Hall of Chamber Music
PLOSHCHA PERAMOHI
PL. PERAMOHI
Jonki Kupaly Park
Meluikayte
Tankavaya
Spalernaya
Cathedral of St. Peter and Paul
NYAMINA
Museum of the Great Patriotic War
FRUZENSKAYA
Astrouskaha
Cathedral of the Holy Spirit
PL. SVABODY
Circus
Haradski Val
Karalya
Lenina
Nyamiha
Revalucinaya
Frunse
Gorky Park
Kalektarnaya
Internacianalnaya
PL. KASTRYCNITSKAYA
KUPALAUSKAYA/ KASTRYCHNITSKAYA (JUNCTION)
Kirava
Persamayskaya
Nyamiha
Miasnikova
Bersana
Pr. Frantsishka Skaryny
Fine Arts Museum
United Kingdom
Enhelsa
Church of St. Simon
Karla Marxa
National History and Culture Museum
Syrvonaarmeyskaya
Pulihava
PL. NEZALEZNASCI
Kirava
Stad. Dynamo
PERSHAMASKAYA
PLOSHCHA NEZALEZHNASTSI
Leningradskaya
Kirava
Ulyanaiskaya
Kastrysniskaya
Svislac
PRIVAKZALNAYA PL.
Sverdlova
Talstoha
Druznaya
Babruskaya
Rabkorauskaya
INSTITUT KULTURY
Mahileuskaya
Partizansky
Oranskaya

HOW IVAN GOT HIS HAND STUCK IN THE LIGHTING FIXTURE Because international trains are heavily taxed, the cheapest way to get from Moscow or Minsk to Warsaw is to reach Brest or Hrodna, catch an *elektrichka* across the border, and take Polish trains from there. If you choose this most budget of all routes, you will notice that as soon as the *elektrichka* embarks, quick-footed men with screwdrivers begin scaling walls and taking the train apart, hiding vodka of all shapes and sizes in the overhead compartments, the seats, and even, after unscrewing the lights, into the car ceiling. They then sit down quietly and wait. You may be asked to hold a bottle of liquor: you are allowed one duty-free liter, so it's all right to take a bottle provided you don't have your own (don't do this on international flights). At the border, guards board the train and take it apart again, impounding roughly a third of the smuggled vodka. If you don't snitch on these hard-working folk, you might get a little chocolate candy with some vodka in it.

PRACTICAL INFORMATION

TOURIST & FINANCIAL SERVICES

Tourist Office: Belintourist (Белінтурыст), pr. Masherava 19 (tel. 222 67 00). Next to Gastsinitsa Yubileynaya. Metro: Nemiga. A remnant of Intourist, but working hard to please. Visa registration and extension, sells plane and train tickets, and arranges tours of Minsk. English spoken. Open M-Sa 8am-1pm and 2-8pm, Su 9am-5pm.

Passport Office: In theory, all foreigners visiting Minsk must **register** their passport at **OVIR** (ОВИР), pr. F. Skaryny 8, room 132 (tel. 220 15 05), although some short-term visitors (under 1 week) do not need to register. Hotels will register you automatically. To extend your visa, plead with whomever provided your original invitation to apply for the extension with the **Ministry of Foreign Affairs** (tel. 222 26 74).

Embassies: Russia, vul. Staravilenskaya 48 (Старавіленская; tel. 250 36 66; fax 236 49 92). **U.K.,** vul. Karla Marxa 37 (Карла Маркса; tel. 210 59 20; fax 229 23 06). **Ukraine,** vul. Kirava 17, #306 (tel. 227 70 04; fax 227 28 61). **U.S.,** vul. Staravilenskaya 46 (tel. 210 12 83; fax 217 71 60). Open M-F 9am-5:30pm.

Currency Exchange: Follow the "Абмен Валюты" signs, but do not be deceived by the posted hours or services—they're completely random. The exchange office in **Gastsinitsa Yubileynaya** provides US$ advances on MC or Visa for a 4% commission and cashes Thomas Cook traveler's checks (open 24hr.), as does **Prior Bank** (Пріор Банк), vul. V. Kharyzhan 3a (Харыжан; tel. 269 09 64). Open M-F 9am-6pm. Cash **AmEx** traveler's checks at the exchange office in **Gastsinitsa Oktyabrskaya** (see **Accommodations,** below). Open daily 8:15am-noon and 1-7pm.

LOCAL SERVICES & COMMUNICATIONS

After years of telephone chaos, phone numbers in Minsk have finally been standardized. All numbers *should* have 7 digits and start with a "2," so if you come across a 6-digit number, add an initial "2." However, some pay phones can still only handle 6-digits; if you can't get through, drop the first "2."

Luggage Storage: In the basement of the train station, small bags can be stored for 46,000BR. Large bags must be stored alongside locals' fishing poles, potato sacks and scythes at an airplane hanger in the park 50m to the left of the station.

Laundromat: Khimchistka Taidi (Хімчістка Тайді), vul. Masherava 1 (Машерова; tel. 226 99 56). Open daily 10am-7pm.

24hr. Pharmacy: Aptetsniikiosk (Аптецнійкіоск), on the 2nd fl. of the train station.

Post Office: Pr. F. Skaryny 10 (tel. 227 15 67). To receive mail, enter on vul. Svyardlova (Свярдлова) and go to the 2nd fl. **Poste Restante** in main hall at the window marked "До Востребования." Open M-F 8am-8pm, Sa-Su 10am-5pm. **Postal code:** 220050.

Telephones: Telephones take *zhetony* (tokens; жетоны; 2400BR) and phone cards (50-100,000BR); both can be purchased at kiosks. **Central Telegraph Office,** in the hall to the left immediately upon entering the post office. Calls to the U.S. 56,000BR per min., to Western Europe 23,000BR per min. Open daily 7:30am-11pm. **Phone code:** (0)172.

ACCOMMODATIONS

Youth hostels don't exist, despite a long list of so-called hostels in the phone book (e.g., "October Revolution Tractor Plant no. 9 Tool-Makers' Association Hostel of Comrades"). **Private rooms** are the best option; taxi drivers may know about them. Ask how far the room is from the center and agree on a price (US$10) beforehand.

Gastsinitsa Svisloch (Гасцініца Свіслочь), vul. Kirava 13 (tel. 220 97 83). M-red: pl. Nezalezhnastsi (пл. Незалежнасці). Or, from the train station, walk up vul. Kirava (the road 1 block to the right of McDonald's); the hotel is three blocks up on the left. Water temperature is warm at best, but the rooms are otherwise comfortable. Bring your own toilet paper. Singles 3,005,000BR, with shower 5,200,000BR.

Gastsinitsa Druzhba (Дружба), vul. Tolbukhina 3 (tel. 266 24 81). M-red: Park Chelyuskintsev (Парк Челюскинцев). Exiting the Metro station, take a right on the road in front of you that runs perpendicular to the main road. Well-worn communal bathrooms with cold water only, but no beating the price. Bed in a triple 3,000,000BR.

Gastsinitsa Minsk (Мінск), pr. F. Skaryny 11 (tel./fax 220 07 03). M-red: pl. Nezalezhnastsi (пл. Незалежнасці). In the center. After passing thuggish characters in the lobby, you'll find rooms with TV, phone, fridge, toilet paper, and shower. Breakfast included. Singles 17,000,000BR; doubles 13,600,000BR; triples 9,900,000BR.

FOOD

The Belarussian government may well have placed restrictions on restaurants prohibiting flavor in food; such plain fare is available for a few hundred thousand rubles at any **cafe-bar** (кафе-бар) in town. If you feel the need to go local, head to **Komarovski Market.** To get there, take a left on Very Haruzay going from the city on pr. F. Skaryny, and walk a few blocks. Don't worry if nobody's at a restaurant when you show up; in Minsk, if it's still around, it must be good.

Restaran Uzbekistan (Рэстаран Узбекістан), vul. Y. Kupaly 17 (tel. 227 75 14). M-red: Kastrychnitskaya (Кастрычніцкая) or pl. Peramohi (пл. Перамогі). At the corner of pr. Skaryny. Spicy Uzbek dishes in a homey setting. Entrees 700,000-1,500,000BR. Open daily 8-11am, noon-4:30pm, and 6pm-midnight.

Patio Pizza (Патіо-Піззa), pr. Skaryny 22 (tel. 227 17 91). M-red: pl. Peramohi (пл. Перамогі). Serves up the same great thin-crust pizza as its two Moscow cousins for 900,000-1,400,000BR. Good traditional salad bar (1,495,000BR). AmEx/MC/Visa.

Restaran Novolune (Рэстаран Новолуне), vul. Zakharava 31 (Захарава; tel. 236 74 55). M-red: pl. Peramohi (пл. Перамогі). Going up pr. Skaryny, take a right on vul. Zakharova at pl. Peramohi and walk 500m. Cozy, semi-underground, and the only Czech cuisine in town. Entrees 900,-1,500,000BR. Open daily noon-midnight.

Cafe Bulbyamaya (Кафе Вульбямая), vul. Skaryny 53 (tel. 232 44 52). M-red: pl. Yakuba Kolasa (пл. Якуба Коласа). As cheap as you'll find for a restaurant where you actually sit down to eat. No fundamental change from the standard Belarussian food, but slightly fresher and tastier. Entrees 500-900,000BR. Open daily 11am-10:30pm.

SIGHTS

More than 80% of the buildings and 60% of the population—including almost all of the 300,000 Jews—were obliterated from 1941 to 1944. The city was rebuilt in grand Stalinist style, with gargantuan buildings and wide boulevards. Today, Minsk is notable for the utter Sovietness emanating from both the architecture and people.

THE OLD TOWN. Minsk's reconstructed **Old Town** sprawls between Nyamiha and pl. Nezaleshnastsi west of the Svislac river. At the southern end of the old town, **pl. Nezalezhnastsi,** formerly pl. Lenina, stands as the symbol of Belarussian independence. *(M-red: pl. Nezalezhnastsi (пл. Незалежнасцi). Just north of the train station.)* The area along Nyamiha is a nice area for a mid-afternoon stroll through shops and beer gardens. Very few of the buildings in these blocks are authentic; most of the originals were destroyed in WWII and the enormous monoliths now standing are quintessentially Soviet. There are, however, a few exceptions, including the **Church of St. Simon,** which doubled as a cinema under the Bolsheviks. *(Savetskaya 15. M-blue: Frunzenskaya (Фрунзенская). Tel. 220 44 15.)* Pl. Svobody is home to the dazzling 17th-century white **Cathedral of the Holy Spirit** (Svetadukha Kafedralni Sobor; Светадуха Кафедралнi Собор). Built in 1642 as a Bernardine convent, the building later burned down only to be rebuilt by the Russian Orthodox Church. Closed by the Soviet regime, it was reopened in 1990 and only restored to its present beauty in 1996. *(Vul. Mefodiya 3. M-blue: Nyamiha (Нямiга). Exit the Metro onto pl. Svobody (Свободы); the cathedral stands in the middle. Tel. 227 66 09.)* The yellow **Cathedral of St. Peter and St. Paul** (Petropavilsky Sobor; Петропавiлскi Совор) is the oldest church still standing in Minsk. Built in 1612, it too was closed by the Soviets, but reopened in 1992. *(Vul. Rakovskaya 4 (Раковская). M-blue: Nyamiha (Нямiга). Exit the Metro onto pr. Masherava; the cathedral is at the intersection with Nyamiha. Tel. 226 74 75.)*

WWII MEMORIALS. Standing alone on a small island in the Svislac, a quadrangled monument is dedicated to Belarussians who died fighting for the Soviet army in Afghanistan. *(M-red: pl. Nezalezhnastsi (пл. Незалежнасцi). North of pl. Nezaleshnastsi on the river, across the first small bridge.)* Farther up the river on the south bank, the vast flatness of Minsk is painfully broken by a Soviet **war memorial** spike. At the back of the memorial stands a rare preserved area of prewar Minsk, complete with park, beach, and paddle boat rental. Yet another victory obelisk pierces the cityscape from the center of pl. Peromahi. *(M-red: pl. Peramohi (пл. Перамогi).)* Before WWII, Jews comprised 52% of Minsk's population; today this figure has dwindled to 1%. The **Jewish memorial stone** commemorates the more than 5000 Jews shot and buried by the Nazis on this site in 1941. *(M-blue: Nyamiha (Нямiга). Exit the Metro onto pr. Masherava; the memorial is behind Gastsinitsa Yubileynaya, pr. Masherava 19.)*

PARKS. No tour of Soviet Minsk is complete without a visit to the city's parks, the only green within miles. Lying along the banks of the Svislac just east of the Old Town are **Gorky Park** (Park Gorkoho; Парк Горкого) and **Yanka Kupala Park** (Янка Купала Парк), where Minsk residents come to stroll hand-in-hand. *(M-red: pl. Peramohi (пл. Перамогi) or M-red: Kastrychnitskaya (Кастрычнiцкая). Between Metro stops on pr. Skaryny.)* The **Botanical Gardens** (Botanichesky Sad; Ботанiческi Сад) can transport you from urban grime to urban green. *(M-red: Park Chalyskintskaya (Парк Чалыскiнцкая). Walk toward Minsk until you reach the huge white pillars at the entrance on pr. F. Skaryny. 60,000BR.)*

MUSEUMS

Minsk's museums are on the scale of a Soviet provincial capital; it seems they exist mostly so it can be said that they exist. Still, they're dirt cheap, within five blocks of each other, and worth a peek.

Museum of the Great Patriotic War (Muzey Velikoy Otechestvennoy Voyny; Музей Велiкой Отечественной Войны), pr. Skaryny 25a (tel. 226 15 44). M-red: pl. Peramohi (пл. Перамогi). If you haven't already seen enough WWII monuments, you might appreciate the suitably grim picture painted of the war in which Belarus lost 20% of its population. Open Tu-Su 10am-6pm. 15,000BR. English tours 200,000BR.

National History and Culture Museum, vul. K. Marxa 12 (К. Маркса; tel. 227 43 22). M-red: pl. Nezalezhnastsi (пл. Незалежнасцi). Explores the history of everything Belarussian, with a particular emphasis on the glory of the Belarussian SSR. If you had doubts that Belarus was a country with true culture, this is the place to visit. Open M-Tu and Th-Su 11am-7pm. 100,000BR, students 30,000BR.

ENTERTAINMENT

Nightlife in Minsk is developing more quickly than the free-market economy. Ask a student hanging out on vul. Skaryny for the whereabouts of the latest hip club, but don't venture into a fancy **casino** without your suit, or chance a run-in with a local "beeznessmen." Otherwise, high culture abounds.

Opera and Ballet Theater, vul. E. Pashkevich 23 (Пашкевіч; tel. 234 06 66). M-blue: Nyamiha (Няміга). Exit the Metro onto Maksima Bagdanovica; the theater is in the park on your right. One of the best ballets in the former Soviet Union. Tickets (15,000-20,000BR) can be purchased in advance from the **Central Ticket Office,** pr. Skaryny 13 (tel. 220 25 70). Open M-Sa 9am-8pm, Su 11am-5pm.

Belarussian Philharmonic, pr. Skaryny 50 (tel. 284 77 66). M-red: pl. Y. Kolasa (пл. Я. Коласа). Concerts at 7pm. Open M 1:30-2pm and 2:30-7:30pm, Tu-Su 12:30-7:30pm.

Hall of Chamber Music, pr. Skaryny 44 (tel. 233 04 69). M-red: pl. Y. Kolasa (пл. Якуба Коласа). Organ music daily 7pm. *Kassa* open M-Sa 1-3pm and 3:45-7pm.

Minsk Circus, pr. Skaryny 32 (tel. 227 22 45; box office tel. 227 78 42). M-red: pl. Peramohi (пл. Перамогі). Tickets from 10,000BR. Performs Aug.-June daily at 3 and 7pm.

HRODNA (ГРОДНА)

On the road between Warsaw and Vilnius, Hrodna is a rarity in Belarus—a city where the towers to God overpower the towers to Lenin. Catholic cathedrals loom over twisting streets of Baroque buildings whose beauty remains intact because Hrodna surrendered quickly during WWII. Soviet planners had their way with the city's endless industrial outskirts, but the center is as good as it gets in Belarus.

ORIENTATION

Hrodna straddles the **Neman River,** with its downtown and sights on the north bank. The **train station** lies 2km northeast of the center at the end of **vul. Azheshka** (Ажешка). Head away from the train station on vul. Azheshka (the main road running from the far left-hand corner of the square as you leave the station) to reach **vul. Savetskaya** (Савецкая), the pedestrian thoroughfare. Take a left onto vul. Azheshka to get to the main square, recently renamed **pl. Stefana Batorya** (Стефана Баторья; formerly Sovetskaya pl.). There is no currency exchange at the train station, but you can pay for the ride into town in dollars (US$2 max.).

PRACTICAL INFORMATION

Trains: Vakzal (Вакзал), vul. Budonova (Будонова; tel. 44 85 56). Trains through Poland must be paid part in US$, part in BR. To: **Minsk** (6-9hr., 2 per day, *coupé* 370,000BR); **Białystok** (5hr., 4 per day, US$3 and 540,000BR); **Moscow** (12hr., 1 per day, *coupé* 4,900,000BR); **Vilnius** (4hr., 3 per day, 1,500,000BR); and **Warsaw** (5½hr., 4 per day, US$8 and 540,000BR). International tickets at windows #13 and 14.

Buses: Avtovakzal (Автовакзал), vul. Krasnoarmeyskaya 7a (Красноармейская; tel. 72 37 24), 1.5km from the town center. Bus #15 and vul. Budonova connect the bus and train stations, or just walk down the tracks next to the bus station with the locals. To: **Brest** (7hr., 2 per day, 538,000BR); **Minsk** (5½hr., 3 per day, 538,000,000BR); **Białystok, Poland** (3hr., 4 per day, 200,000BR); **Druskininkai, Lithuania** (1½hr., 2 per day, 35,000BR); **Kaliningrad** (10hr., 1 per day, 1,068,000BR); **Vilnius** (5hr., 1 per day, 600,000BR); and **Warsaw** (6hr., 3 per day, 2,000,000BR).

Tourist Office: Vul. Azheshka 49, 2nd Fl. (tel. 72 17 79). Offers assistance in Russian, finds rooms for free, and arranges city tours. Open M-F 9am-5pm.

Currency Exchange: In the bus station's main hall. Open M-F 9am-1pm and 2-6:30pm, Sa-Su 8am-1pm and 2-4:30pm. For MC/Visa cash advances for a 4% commission, head to **Prior Bank** (Пріор Банк), Mostovaya 37 (Мостовая; tel. 72 31 37), away from pl. Stefana Batorya and downhill toward the river. Open daily 9am-3pm.

Luggage storage: *Kamera khraneniya* (камера хранeнiя). In the train station's basement. Small bags 11,000BR; large bags 19,000BR. Open daily 8am-1pm, 2-7:30pm, and 8pm-7:30am. In the **bus station.** 10,000BR. Open daily 7am-1pm and 2-8pm.

Post Office: Vul. Karla Marksa 29 (Карла Маркса), between the bus station and pl. Stefana Batorya. Open M-F 8am-8pm, Sa-Su 10am-4pm. **Postal code:** 230025.

Telephones: Tel. 96 75 09. Next door to the post office. Brand new phones, now only 30 years behind the rest of the industrialized world. Open 24hr. **Phone code:** (0)152.

ACCOMMODATIONS & FOOD

The best deal in Hrodna is the reasonably-priced and centrally-located **Gastsinitsa Neman** (Гасцiнiца Неман), vul. Stefana Batorya 8 (tel. 72 19 36), just south of the main square and offering rooms with TV. Take bus #3 or 14 from the train station. Hot-water showers (20,000BR) and dirty toilets are down the hall; bring your own toilet paper. (Singles 1,240,000BR; doubles 1,976,000BR.) Inexpensive meat-and-potatoes entrees are available daily 11am-5pm and 6-11pm. To reach **Gastsinitsa Belarus** (Гасцiнiца Беларусь), vul. Kalinovskaya 1 (Калiновская; tel. 44 16 74), take bus #15 from the train station and get off at "Кiнотеатр Космос," the fifth stop. Turn right onto the boulevard with a median strip. Offers slightly better rooms farther from the center, all with bath. Meals are served daily 1-5pm and 6pm-1am. (Singles 1,678,000BR; doubles 2,516,000BR. MC/Visa). For typical Belarussian cafeteria food and vodka, try **Blinnaya** (Блiнная), Savetskaya 5. (Open daily 8am-8pm.)

SIGHTS & ENTERTAINMENT

Hrodna's quick capture during WWII saved most of its buildings from destruction, making it perhaps the most scenic city in Belarus. The city's best sights are its castles off vul. Zamkava (Замкава). When you come to the intersection with a tower on your right, head straight ahead on the shaded road and turn left. **Old Castle** (Stary Zamak; Стары Замак), on the right, was built in the 1570s on the ruins of a 15th-century castle. Walk up to the defensive wall for a gorgeous view of the river below. Inside, a worthwhile museum devotes 20 rooms to Hrodna's history, including, of course, WWII. (Open Tu-Su 9am-6pm; *kassa* closes at 5pm. 50,000BR.) On the opposite side of the hill, **New Castle** (Novy Zamak; Новы Замак), destroyed in WWII and rebuilt in 1951, houses the **History and Archaeology Museum,** with exhibits devoted to Hrodna's history from its first written mention in 1128. (Tel. 44 40 68. Open Tu-Su 10am-6pm; *kassa* closes at 5pm. 20,000BR.)

The awe-inspiring **Farnoy Cathedral** (Фарной), pl. Savetskaya 4 (tel. 44 26 77), was built by Jesuits during Polish rule in the 18th century. Across the square, ruins are all that remain of a red-brick Catholic cathedral, razed by the Soviets in the 1950s. Down vul. Karla Marksa toward the bus station is **Pabrihidsky Cathedral** (Pabrihidsky Sobor; Пабрiгiдскi Сабор), known in Polish as the **Holy Church of Jesus** (Najswiętsze Serce Jezusa). A former Franciscan monastery turned into a psychiatric hospital by the Russians, it was re-opened to the public in 1990. The outside, however, remains far more beautiful than the interior. Perhaps the most beautiful of the city's churches is the Russian Orthodox **Protector of the World Cathedral** (Svetopokrovsky Sobor; Светопокровскi Собор), vul. Azheshka 23 (tel. 72 29 99), built to honor the Russians who died in the 1904-05 war with Japan.

BREST (БРЕСТ)

From the windows of the trains constantly passing through, Brest is a city of nothing more than vast railroad yards. A stroll around the city's generic Soviet downtown won't change that impression, but a visit to the Brest Fortress just southwest of the city will. With its gripping images inside and eerie silence outside, the fort offers a look at Brest's history of carnage. Visitors leave with the realization that, despite its initial appearance, Brest is a city well worth getting off the train to see.

ORIENTATION & PRACTICAL INFORMATION. The **Mukhavets** and **Bug** Rivers mark the south and west boundaries of the city; at their confluence lies the **Brest-Litovsk Fortress.** The Bug also demarcates the Polish border. At the train station, head toward the main overpass and take a right over the tracks. Your first right will put you on **vul. Ardzhonikidze** (Арджонікідзе). After two blocks, you'll reach **vul. Lenina** (Леніна). Head left to reach **pl. Lenina,** the main square; **vul. Pushkinskaya** (Пушкінская) runs to the left. Farther down is **vul. Gogalya** (Гогаля), the main east-west thoroughfare. The kiosk in the train station sells **maps** (85,000BR).

The **train station** (tel. 005), just north of vul. Ardzhanikidze (Арджанікідзе), is the main border crossing for trains running between Moscow and Warsaw. Trains run to: **Minsk** (4½hr., 8-10 per day, 110,000BR); **Kiev** (16½hr., 1 per day, 550,000BR, *coupé* 850,000BR); **Moscow** (16hr., 8-10 per day, 800,000BR, *coupé* 1,200,000BR); **Prague** (18hr., 1 per day, US$96); and **Warsaw** (5 per day, US$22). No buses run to Minsk. If you're heading to Hrodna, however, take a bus. The **bus station** (tel. 225 51 36) is at the corner of vul. Kuybyshava (Куйбышава) and vul. Mitskevicha (Міцкевіча), near the central market. (Open daily 6am-11pm.) Buses run to **Hrodna** (8hr., 3 per day, 167,300BR) and **Warsaw** (6hr., 1-3 per day, 2,000,000BR). **Store luggage** in the train or bus stations. (Lockers 10,000BR.) **Gastsinitsa Intourist** (see **Accommodations & Food,** below) doesn't have maps or brochures, but the staff speaks English and the service bureau arranges **tours** of the fortress and forest if you call a week in advance. **Prior Bank** (Пріор Банк), vul. Pushkinskaya 16/1 (tel. 223 27 83), gives MC/Visa cash advances and cashes AmEx and Thomas Cook travelers' checks for a 4% commission. (Open M-F 9am-3:30pm.) The entrance is in the back of the building. The **post office** (tel. 23 29 72), with **telephones** and **fax** inside, is on vul. Pushkinskaya at pl. Lenina. (Open M-F 8:30am-8pm, Sa 8:30am-5pm, Su 8:30am-3pm.) **Postal code:** 224005. **Phone code:** (0)162.

BELARUS

> Like Minsk, Brest's phone numbers have finally been standardized. All numbers have 7 digits and start with a "2"; add a "2" to the front of old 6-digit numbers.

ACCOMMODATIONS & FOOD. **Gastsinitsa Vesta** (Веста), vul. Krupskay 16 (Крупской; tel. 223 71 69; fax 223 78 39), is the best deal in town. Walk 200m behind the Lenin statue at pl. Lenina and head a half-block down the first road you see on your left. With spotless bathrooms, TVs and fridges in the rooms, and plants in the hallways, you won't feel like you're in Belarus anymore. (Singles 3,850,000BR; doubles 7,700,000BR. Breakfast 200,000BR.) **Gastsinitsa Intourist** (Інтурiст), vul. Maskaiskaya 15 (Маскаіская; tel. 220 20 83; fax 222 19 00), is a little further from the train station, but slightly fancier. Rooms have private baths (with hot water!) and TVs. (Singles 1,165,000BR; doubles 1,990,000BR. Breakfast included.)

Diplomats in Minsk drive to Brest just to dine at the best restaurant between Warsaw and Moscow; that says more about Russian and Polish cuisine than it does about the restaurant, but you're still sure to get a quality meal. **Restaurant India** (Рестаран Індіа), vul. Gogalya 29 (Гогаля; tel. 26 63 25), at vul. K. Marxa, revives your palate with authentic, spicy Indian food. Feast on sumptuous *gosht korma* (lamb in sauce) while enjoying Belarussian music or the keyboardist's rip-off of American soft rock. (Entrees 2-4,000,000BR. Open daily noon-11pm). There's a **grocery** just past the post office. (Open M-F 7:30am-9pm, Sa 8am-8pm, Su 8am-3pm.)

SIGHTS. **Brest-Litovsk Fortress** (Krepasts Brest-Litoisk; Крэпасць Брэст-Літовск) dominates the area between the Bug and Mukhavets rivers. From the center, either take bus #17 down vul. Maskaiskaya, walk 15min., or take a cab for 400,000BR. Grassy hills and tree-lined streets were once the best-equipped fortress in tsarist Russia. After Napoleon's 1812 attack on Russia, several cities in Poland, Lithuania, and Belarus were heavily fortified; this massive fortress was intended to be the central defense point. From 1838 to 1841, the entire city was moved east to open the site for the fort. Brick walls 15m thick, moats, rivers, and encasements made this the most formidable battlement in Eastern Europe. In the 1918 **Treaty of**

Brest-Litovsk, Lenin ceded Brest to the Germans. The Poles held it between the wars, but another Russian-German agreement, this time the 1939 **German-Soviet Nonagression Pact,** brought Brest-Litovsk back into the Russian fold. Embarrassed by the associations of the old name, Stalin dropped the Litovsk just in time for Hitler's armies to attack on June 22, 1941. While the Germans swept forward to Minsk, the garrison of Brest held for six weeks. Nearly the entire fortress was reduced to rubble before the *Krepasts* finally surrendered. The defenders' courage earned Brest honor as one of the USSR's "Hero Cities." What remains of the always-open fortress is now a sometimes dramatic, sometimes dogmatic testimonial to those heroes. The monumental **Principal Entrance** (Galoiny Ivakhod; Галоіны Іваход), at the end of vul. Maskaiskaya, welcomes each visitor in grand Soviet style. Immediately to the right lies **Eastern Fort** (Uskhodni Fort; Усходны Форт), a complex where tenacious Russians, cut off from their comrades, held their ground for three weeks. Straight ahead, an immense **boulder** towers over the central island of the fortress. Around the base of the soldier-in-the-boulder monolith are **memorials** to the defenders and an eternal flame dedicated to all 13 of the "Hero Cities."

BELARUS

In front of the fortress are the foundations of **White Palace** (Bely Palats; Белы Палац), where the 1918 treaty was signed. To the right, the worthwhile **Museum of the Defense of the Brest Hero-Fortress** (Muzey Abarony Brestskay Krepastsi-Geroya; Музей Абароны Брэсцкой Крэпасці-Героя), in the reconstructed barracks, recounts the WWII siege and the perfection of Communism as demonstrated by this heroism. A display on the Molotov-Ribbentrop Pact has been added to explain why Soviet soldiers happened to be here when WWII started. (Open M and W-Su 9:30am-6pm. Free.) Walk past the museum to the right to find **Northern Gate** (Painochnaya Brama; Паіночная Брама), the only gate still fully intact. To get a sense of the fortress's former magnitude, remember that the whole place once looked like this.

Białowieża Primeval Forest (Belavezhskaya Pushcha; Белавежская Пушча), one of the only virgin forests left in Europe, spreads along the Polish border north of Brest for 80 square km. Home to the continent's largest animal—the East European bison (*zubr;* зубр)—this ocean of dark, centuries-old trees has attracted scientists since the 17th century. Today, it protects species threatened by extinction elsewhere in Europe, including the European deer, otter, golden eagle, red eagle, black stork, and black grouse. Ask the Brest Belintourist office for info on visiting this eco-labyrinth, or see **Poland: Bialowieski National Park,** p. 497, for the Polish perspective.

BOSNIA-HERZEGOVINA

US$1 = 1.85KM (CONVERTIBLE MARKS, OR KM)	**1KM = US$0.54**
CDN$1 = 1.24KM	**1KM = CDN$0.81**
UK£1 = 2.96KM	**1KM = UK£0.34**
IR£1 = 2.48KM	**1KM = IR£0.40**
AUS$1 = 1.20KM	**1KM = AUS$0.83**
NZ$1 = 0.98KM	**1KM = NZ$1.02**
SAR1 = 0.31KM	**1KM = SAR3.27**
DM1 = 1KM	**1KM = DM1**
HRV KUNA1 = 0.26KM	**1KM = KUNA3.89**

PHONE CODES	Country code: **387.** International dialing prefix: **00.**

> **!** The U.S. Department of State reiterated in August 1999 its **Travel Warning** against unnecessary travel to Bosnia, particularly the Republika Srpska. The warning cites "risks from occasional localized political violence, landmines, unexploded ordnance, and carjacking," and notes that there may be as many as one million live landmines around Sarajevo and throughout the country. Mostar and Srebrenica are among the towns considered particularly dangerous. Furthermore, a July 30, 1999 warning cites opposition to the NATO action against Serbia as another reason to avoid travel to Bosnia. Check the State Department Web page at travel.state.gov/travelwarnings.html for further updates.

The mountainous centerpiece of the former Yugoslavia, Bosnia-Herzegovina (herts-uh-goh-VIHN-ah) has defied the odds and the centuries to stand as an independent nation today. Bosnia's distinction—and its troubles—spring from its self-proclaimed role as a mixing ground for Muslims, Croats, and Serbs. In Sarajevo, its cosmopolitan capital, that ideal is at least verbally maintained, but in the countryside, ethnic problems continue. Physically, the country is marked by rolling hills and sparkling rivers, but its lush valleys are now punctuated with abandoned houses and gaping rooftops. The past decade has been brutal, a bloody war broadcast nightly to the world, and much of the population became displaced. Bosnia's future is uncertain, particularly with the imminent withdrawal of NATO troops, but its resilient people are optimistic. In this period of post-Dayton peace, rebuilding is slowly underway.

HIGHLIGHT OF BOSNIA

■ The religious and ethnic diversity of the Balkan Peninsula comes alive in **Sarajevo,** where the harmonious proximity of churches, mosques, and synagogues offers hope for the country's dream of a peaceful, multicultural society (p. 85).

LIFE & TIMES

HISTORY

Nestled in the middle of the Balkan Peninsula, Bosnia-Herzegovina has always been a hotly contested region. First fought over by the Byzantines and Goths, Bosnia's history as an embattled crossroads stems from fighting between the two Slavic tribes, the **Croats** and **Serbs,** that settled the Balkans in the 6th and 7th centuries. For the next 500 years, Bosnia bounced between Serbian and Croatian rule with occasional bouts of Hungarian and Byzantine leadership. Bosnia first became an independent nation in 1180 when, after the death of the Byzantine emperor, neither the Croatian or Serbian kingdoms could establish rule over the territory. The 13th and 14th centuries saw Bosnia expand into Herzegovina and parts of the Dalmatian Coast; for a brief period in the 14th century, Bosnia was the most powerful nation in the Balkans. The Turks invaded the Balkan Peninsula in the 1380s and by 1463 the **Ottoman Empire** had entirely conquered Bosnia, establishing it as an independent province. More Bosnians converted to **Islam** than in neighboring countries, as evidenced by the many mosques and examples of Turkish architecture in Sarajevo.

The strength of the Ottomans faded through the centuries, its decline facilitated by the increasing power of the empires that surrounded it—Orthodox Serbia to the east and Catholic Croatia to the north. In the 19th century, ethnic tensions and South Slav nationalism led to increasing unrest. Christian peasants, resentful of taxes demanded by the Ottoman rulers, rebelled in 1862 and again in 1875. The situation found an uneasy settlement when the 1878 **Congress of Berlin** (see **The Great Empires,** p. 8) allowed Austria-Hungary to occupy Bosnia.

In the early 20th century, a near-hysteric suspicion of South Slav nationalism developed in the tottering Austria-Hungarian Empire. A desire to squash morale (as well as to embarrass Russia, the South Slav "protector") motivated the Empire's **annexation** of Bosnia-Herzegovina in 1908, inflaming pan-Slavic sentiments. The anti-Austrian **Black Hand** was one of the terrorist groups that emerged.

On June 28, 1914, Gavrilo Princip, a Serb from Bosnia, assassinated **Archduke Franz Ferdinand** in Sarajevo, triggering the events that lead to **WWI.** After the war, the Kingdom of Serbs, Croats, and Slovenes was born, renamed **Yugoslavia** in 1929. Power fell to the Serb Karadjordjević dynasty. While the kingdom was a realization of the long-cherished ideal of South Slav unity, Croats quickly began to chafe under what they saw as a Serb dictatorship. During **WWII,** Yugoslavia was divided between the German-aligned Croat Ustašas, the Serb Chetniks, and the Communist Partisans, whose mountain stronghold was the site of much of the fighting.

After the war, Croatian Communist dictator **Josip Broz Tito** created a Yugoslav federation, seeking to hold the state together by decentralizing power. Tito granted Muslims status as a distinct ethnic group in the 1960s in the hopes of establishing equality with the Serbs and Croats. Under Tito, Yugoslavia experienced an economic revival, but his death in 1980 worsened ethnic tensions that eventually tore the state apart. The vacuum was filled in the late 1980s as Serbian Communist **Slobodan Milošević** rose to power, spewing forth nationalist rhetoric.

The Federal Republic of Yugoslavia began its full collapse in 1990. Within a year, two of the country's provinces, Slovenia and Croatia, had declared independence. Their **secession** was opposed both by the Serb-dominated federal government and, in the case of the Croats, by ethnic Serbs living in the self-declared independent state. In April 1992, events came to a head in Bosnia-Herzegovina, the most ethnically mixed of the former Yugoslav republics. The Bosnian government, unwilling to see the Republic remain in a Serb-dominated Yugoslavia, opted for **independence** and was soon recognized by the international community. The referendum for independence, endorsed by 99% of voters, was largely boycotted by Serbs in Bosnia. Violence broke out as the federal army and Serb militias quickly took control of 70% of Bosnian territory. Sarajevo suffered a brutal siege that lasted from May 2, 1992 to February 26, 1996. A United Nations force sent to deliver humanitarian assistance, **UNPROFOR,** had little success in stopping the ethnic cleansing undertaken principally, although not exclusively, by Serb forces.

LITERATURE & ARTS

Bosnia's literary and artistic tradition dates back to the Middle Ages, but modern works dominate the heritage. One of the nation's only writers to receive international acclaim, Bosnian Serb **Ivo Andrić** won the Nobel Prize for Literature in 1961 for the "epic force" with which he handled his subjects and the sober compassion and beauty of his works. His novels, *The Bridge on the Drina* and *The Travnik Chronicles*, exemplify his contemplative prose and his treatment of delicate political issues. Andrić's contemporary, **Mesa Selimović,** employs rich detail and folk legends in his masterpiece, *Death and the Dervish*, to grapple with the dilemmas of Bosnian Muslim identity. Bosnians celebrate **Mak Dizdar** as the nation's greatest poet. Like Selimović, Dizdar focuses on Bosnia's folk tradition and medieval history to penetrate the core of Bosnian identity. He revolutionized post-WWI Bosnian poetry with his stark modernist style and his refusal to pander to Socialist Realism. Dizdar's poems inspired the creation of the Sarajevo War Theatre in 1992, a group of playwrights and actors who performed almost 2000 productions during the four-year siege of Sarajevo. In the wake of the fighting, most Bosnian authors have turned their energies to reflecting upon the war, particularly in memoirs and diaries. *Zlata's Diary*, by **Zlata Filipović,** a teenager during the seige of Sarajevo, is considered the "Anne Frank" work of the conflict.

In 1993, several Bosnian artists organized the **Witnesses of Existence** exhibit in which language and national context were interpreted using of shrapnel, bullets as media. The exhibit toured Italy and the U.S., but its creators were trapped in Sarajevo and unable to travel with it.

READING LIST

A wealth of excellent literature is available on Bosnia and the Balkans. The long-standing classic is *Black Lamb, Grey Falcon* by Rebecca West, a lively volume of over 1000 pages detailing her impressions during a 1937 journey through Yugoslavia. A more modern—and less physically massive—travel narrative is Brian Hall's *Impossible Country*. Hall, an American, journeyed through Yugoslavia in summer 1991, just as the "Impossible Country" began to fall apart. For history of the recent war, turn to Laura Silber and Alan Little's *The Death of Yugoslavia*, a scintillating blow-by-blow account of the rise of Milošević and the tragedy of the war. Misha Glenny's *The Fall of Yugoslavia* covers similar ground; both books were updated in 1997. *Love Thy Neighbor* by Peter Maass is a more personal option, recounting stories from his days as a *Washington Post* war correspondent.

BOSNIA TODAY

Fighting in Bosnia among Serb, Bosnian, and Croatian forces continued until the 1995 **Dayton Peace Accords.** The area under dispute was divided into two loosely connected governing bodies, the **Federation of Bosnia-Herzegovina** and the **Republika Srpska (RS),** to segregate the warring ethnic groups. Today's Bosnia, however, resembles more of an international protectorate than an independent nation. High representative **Carlos Westendorp,** a diplomat appointed by foreign governments to implement the **Dayton Peace Accords,** has the power to issue legal decrees and dismiss any member of the government. By September 1998, he had implemented all the stipulations of the Accords and in March 1999, he sacked recently elected RS President and Serbian hardliner **Nikola Poplasen.** Other members of the nationalist governments elected in September 1998 remain in office. Conflicts between the Federation and RS are rising as both Bosnian Serbs and Croats shy away from moderate governments, instead favoring nationalist extremism.

The discord between international designs on Bosnia and RS desires for more power and recognition only adds to the nation's growing tensions. Especially in light of the NATO bombings in **Kosovo,** Bosnia's peace seems particularly tenuous. If Kosovo is granted independence from Yugoslavia, it is likely that secessionist Bosnian Croats (currently lobbying for a third entity in the federation) will declare—and fight for—independence from the RS. The potential for secession is aggravated by a growing refugee crisis and a strained economy: Kosovar refugees are flooding Bosnia just as Bosnian refugees themselves are beginning to return from abroad and, unfortunately, no part of Bosnia is economically equipped to deal with any them. The combination of economic instability and escalating political tensions does not bode well for Bosnia-Herzegovina's future.

FACTS AND FIGURES

- **Capital:** Sarajevo
- **Population:** 3,123,513
- **Land Area:** 51,129km^2
- **Geography:** Mountains and forests
- **Language:** Bosnian
- **Religions:** 40% Muslim, 31% Orthodox, 15% Catholic, 4% Protestant
- **GDP per capita:** US$3,208
- **Major Exports:** Manufactured goods, machinery

BOSNIA ESSENTIALS

Citizens of Ireland, the U.K., and the U.S. do not need visas; visas are required for citizens of Australia, New Zealand, and South Africa. Call your Bosnian consulate (see **Embassies & Consulates,** p. 13) for details. Applications take three to four weeks to process; send your passport, one passport-sized photo, a copy of your roundtrip ticket, a copy of your last bank statement, a completed visa application, and US$35. There are occasional police checkpoints within Bosnia; register with your embassy upon arrival, and keep your papers with you at all times.

PRIMARY BORDER CROSSINGS. The Bosnian border, with its congregation of trucks and army vehicles, is somewhat intimidating, but entering can be a fairly smooth procedure if the political climate allows. Bosnian visas are not available at the border. There is no fee for crossing a Bosnian border.

Croatia: While it's possible to take buses between smaller border cities, it's safest and most reliable to take direct buses between Sarajevo (p. 82) and Dubrovnik (p. 169), Split (p. 159), and Zagreb, CRO (p. 139).

Yugoslavia: In summer 1999, it was not possible to enter any region of Yugoslavia from Bosnia.

GETTING THERE & GETTING AROUND

Commercial **plane** service into Sarajevo is limited and expensive, but is the main recourse of the troops, journalists, and relief workers entering the country. Flights come from Zurich, Ljubljana, and Istanbul (see **Sarajevo: Airlines,** p. 86). **Croatia Airlines** (tel. in Zagreb (41) 42 77 52; in Split (21) 36 22 02) has regular service from Zagreb. Travel agencies in Sarajevo can arrange and change flights, but to buy a ticket you must pay in cash. **Railways** are barely functional and should not be considered an option. **Buses** run daily between Sarajevo and Split, Dubrovnik, and Zagreb, with the last being the most popular route into the country. Buses are reliable, clean, and not very crowded, but brace yourself for Balkan driving.

HEALTH & SAFETY

EMERGENCY NUMBERS.
Fire: tel. 93. **Police:** tel. 92. **Emergency:** tel. 94.

Outside Sarajevo, **do NOT set foot off the pavement** under any circumstances. Even in Sarajevo, de-mining experts recommend staying on paved roads and hard-covered surfaces. Do not pick up any objects on the ground. Millions of **landmines** and **unexploded ordnance** (UXOs) cover the country. Mine injuries occur daily. 15% of landmine injuries occur on **road shoulders**—partly because farmers who find unexploded ordnance in their fields occasionally bring it to the roadsides for the troops to pick up. Should your car veer off the road, carefully retrace your tracks back to the pavement; if you want to take pictures, do so from your car while the car remains firmly on pavement. If you must go to the bathroom during a road trip, stop at a gas station. **Abandoned houses** are unsafe as well; many have been rigged with booby traps by the retreating army. Absolute caution is essential at all times. Estimates are that 30 years of intensive, full-time effort would be necessary to declare Bosnia "mine-free"—and even de-mining is not 100% foolproof. See **Sarajevo: Security Information,** p. 87, for details on the Mine Action Center.

In Sarajevo, finding medical help and supplies is not a problem; your embassy is your best resource. Peacekeeping operations have brought English-speaking doctors, but not insurance; cash is the only method of payment. All drugs are sold at pharmacies, while basic hygiene products sare sold at many drugstores. Condoms are available, but inexplicably expensive. Bandages are harder to come by.

TOURIST SERVICES

Tourist services are limited, perhaps because most travelers here are journalists and relief workers with no need for them. Residents of smaller towns may regard foreigners with suspicion, but much depends on the town's political and ethnic ties. In Sarajevo, travelers are welcomed by the excellent **tourist office.** Many Bosnians speak **English** or **German.** The **U.S. Embassy** also has useful information. Several independent tourist agencies have sprung up, but most focus on arranging vacations for locals. Helpful Bosnians can often replace a tourist bureau.

MONEY

The new Bosnian currency, the **convertible mark (KM),** was introduced in summer 1998. It is fixed firmly to the **Deutschmark** at a 1:1 exchange rate. Deutschmarks can be changed directly into convertible marks for no commission at most Sarajevo banks. Beware store clerks trying to pass unsuspecting foreigners old Bosnian dinars: the dinar is no longer a valid currency. In addition, the Croatian **kuna** was named an official Bosnian currency in summer 1997. The kuna is not legal tender in Sarajevo, but it is the only valid currency in the western (Croatian) area of divided Mostar. Make sure to change your money back to Deutschmarks when you leave, as convertible marks are inconvertible outside Bosnia. The system of **banks** is improving; within Sarajevo, their number has mushroomed. **Traveler's checks** can be cashed at some Sarajevo banks. **ATMs** remain non-existent. **Western Union** in the capital has an extremely competent English-speaking staff. Most restaurants accept Visa, MC, and (to a lesser extent) AmEx, but Visa is best for getting **cash advances.** If your itinerary lies outside of Sarajevo, bring Deutschmarks with you.

COMMUNICATIONS

Bosnia's **postal** system, operative since 1996, is gaining more functions. Yellow-and-white "PTT" signs indicate post offices. Sarajevo's post office can accommodate outgoing mail, but **Poste Restante** is unavailable; the only way to receive mail is to befriend a government employee and borrow their address. Few towns outside the capital are equipped with reasonable mail service. Mail to the U.S. usually takes one to two weeks, somewhat less within Europe. **Postcards** cost KM1 to mail.

Telephone connections are troublesome and expensive; the best option is to call collect from the Sarajevo post office. To call **AT&T Direct,** dial 008 00 00 10. Calling the U.K. is roughly KM3.50 per min., the U.S. KM5. **Faxes** can be sent from the post office; the price to Australia or the U.K. is KM3 per page, to the U.S. KM5 per page.

LANGUAGE

When in Bosnia, speak Bosnian. When in Croatia, Croatian. When in Serbia, Serbian. The distinction is more in name than in substance, but never underestimate its importance, as languages in the former Yugoslavia have been co-opted by the governments as tools of nationalism. The languages do have certain distinctions. Take, for example, the translation of coffee. *Kava* is the Croatian term, *kafa* the Bosnian. So in the former Yugoslavia, mind your Ps and Qs—and Zs, Ks, Us, and Js. Foreigners who attempt to speak a little Bosnian are the exception, not the rule; an effort to pronounce even a few sentences will endear you to locals. See the **Croatian Glossary,** p. 808, for more words. **English** and **German** are widely spoken.

CUSTOMS & ETIQUETTE

Waitstaff are salaried and expect **tips** only for excellent service; 6% is generous. At restaurants and cafes, the bill is never split; instead, one person pays. The man, or the waiter, will open and pour the woman's drink. In **Muslim homes,** it is customary to remove one's shoes at the door; in mosques, watch others to pick up the proper

STICKY TERMINOLOGY Croat, Serb, and Bosnian refer to people of each ethnicity. Croatian, Serbian, and Bosnian are terms indicating the country. Thus, to say a Bosnian Serb denotes a Serb living in Bosnia (most often in the Republika Srpska (RS), the Serb-dominated entity in northeastern Bosnia). Likewise, a Bosnian Croat is a Croat living in Bosnia. Bosnian Muslims sometimes go by the term "Bosniak." Bosnians often refer to their Bosnian Serb enemies as "Četnik," or "Chetnik," a revived WWII ethnic slur. In other words, a Serb is different from a Chetnik—do not make this mistake. Another semantic caveat: the Bosnian Army is precisely that, and not the "Muslim Army."

customs. **Smoking** is popular; most Sarajevans roll their own. **Bargaining** is possible, particularly in the clothing markets. Ask a Bosnian to accompany you; the price will be miraculously lower. **Fashion** was important even during the war, so stow away your grubby t-shirt. **Foreigners** are welcomed and regarded with great interest in Sarajevo. America, particularly, is beloved among Sarajevans, who were entertained during the war by such pirated American TV as *Beverly Hills 90210.* They tend to look to America as an ideal of the diversity they seek to achieve.

BOSNIA-HERZEGOVINA

ALTERNATIVES TO TOURISM. Many visitors to Bosnia are interested not merely in tourism but rather in helping the country to rebuild after its brutal war. The following organizations gladly accept volunteers and donations.

La Benevolencija, Hamdije Kreševljakovicá 59, Sarajevo (tel. 66 34 72; fax 66 34 73; email la_bene@soros.org.ba). In the Jewish community center across the river and next to the old Sephardic synagogue. This cultural, educational, and humanitarian organization distributed free prescription medicine to the elderly during the war. In addition to its religious role, the center organizes local public service opportunities with children injured or orphaned during the conflict. Call at least one week in advance. Open M-F 9am-4pm.

UNICEF, Kolodvorska 6, Sarajevo (tel. 20 31 18 and 52 37 11; fax 64 29 70).

OXFAM, Hiseta 2, Sarajevo (tel. 66 81 33).

Save the Children, Hiseta 2, Sarajevo (66 63 43).

NATIONAL HOLIDAYS

In addition to the following holidays, Bosnia celebrates many Catholic, Orthodox, and Muslim religious holidays; we have not included them here as most are days of observance rather than public holidays. January 1, Catholic New Year's; January 7, Orthodox Christmas; January 8, Eid Al Fitr; January 14, Orthodox New Year's; March 1, Independence Day; March 17, Eid Al Adha; April 6, Islamic New Year; April 15, Day of the Army; April 23, Catholic Easter; April 30, Orthodox Easter; May 1, Labor Day; May 4, Victory Day; June 15, Prophet's Birthday; November 25, Day of the Republic; December 25, Catholic Christmas.

SARAJEVO

The posters at every bus stop in Sarajevo (pop. 360,000) read "Peace, Democracy, Prosperity and Hope are our goal," a sentiment often echoed in conversation with young Sarajevans. While it is tempting to encapsulate the city in a symbol or slogan, Sarajevo itself defies such a cliché; to define the city by its bullet-holes is to reduce it to its television presence. Although most classic tourist features of Sarajevo have been destroyed or are non-functional, the lively marketplace of the old Turkish Quarter, burgeoning arts scene, and nightlife are inspiring. Upon arrival in

Sarajevo, newcomers find themselves among warm international company, sitting at cafes next to uniformed SFOR officers, camera-wielding journalists, and foreign aid workers. Perhaps wary of CNN stereotyping, the city remains largely aloof to the short-term visitor, and tensions are on the rise with the recent influx of refugees. But it is just that sort of elusiveness that makes finding the real Sarajevo—the city loved so passionately by its residents—all the more rewarding.

> The following outlying areas of Sarajevo have served as confrontation lines and are thus at particular risk of **mines:** Grbavica, Lukavica, Illidža, and Dobrinja. The Mine Action Center (see below), however, emphasizes that all parts of the city should be considered high-risk.

GETTING THERE & GETTING AROUND

Airplanes: To: **Istanbul** (TOP Air); **Ljubljana** (Adria Air); and **Zagreb** (Croatia Air). Purchase tickets at **Centrotrans,** Ferhadija 16 (tel. 21 12 82 and 21 12 83; fax 20 54 81). Open June-Aug. M-F 8am-8pm, Sa 8am-3pm; Sept.-May M-F 8am-8pm. See **Travel Agencies,** below, for other ticket providers. Taxi service to and from the airport 15KM.

Trains: In front of the bus station (see below). Train service is extremely limited. Only 6 lines were running in summer 1999. Ticket office (tel. 61 75 84) open daily 6am-6pm.

Buses: Bus station, Kranjčevića 9 (tel. 67 01 80 and 44 54 42), behind the Holiday Inn at the corner with Halida Kajtaza. Ticket window (tel. 21 31 00) open daily 7am-7pm. **Centrotrans** (see **Airplanes,** above) services Sarajevo; purchase tickets at the Ferhadija office or at the bus station. To: **Dubrovnik** (7hr., 2 per day, 41KM); **Split** (8hr., 3 per day, 37KM); **Zagreb** (9hr., 2 per day, 65KM); and **Frankfurt** (15hr., 1 per day, 200KM). 5KM extra per bag. To reach the center from the station, walk past the taxi stands on Kranjčevića and continue straight across the first intersection and downhill for 20min., until the mosque appears at the large intersection. Cross the street to Maršala Tita, which branches at the eternal flame into Sarajevo's two central walkways.

Local Transportation: Central Sarajevo is small and simple enough to allow you to avoid public transit altogether, but if you're in a rush, an excellent **tram** network loops west along Maršala Tita and back east along Obala Kulina Bana. Regular service runs 6am-10pm or midnight, depending on the route (1KM from kiosks; 1.50KM on board). Ticket inspectors are often present and always vigilant; if you have no ticket or fail to punch it upon boarding, you risk a 15KM fine. **Buses** extend farther from the center, but operate mainly during commuter hours (M-F 6:45am-6pm or 9pm). Tickets 1KM on-board. Monthly bus pass 12KM. *Oslobodjenje,* Sarajevo's daily paper, lists a complete schedule of trams and buses (see **"Fired Up News,"** p. 90).

Taxis: Generally fair, with rates consistent among all the companies. Try **Radio Taxi** (tel. 970 and 65 21 31) or **Yello Taxicab** (tel. 66 35 55). 2KM flat rate plus 1.30KM per km. If you call, you'll be charged for pick-up. Fares 30% higher at night. Large pieces of luggage cost 2KM. Expect to pay 9KM from the bus and train station to the center.

ORIENTATION

Sarajevo's downtown is easily navigable, a series of streets running parallel to the **Milijacka** river that can be traversed end-to-end in less than 30min. **Maršala Tita** is the main street *(ulica)*, running from the yellow **Holiday Inn** to the **eternal flame,** a 1945 marker to the Bosnian state that has been less than eternal due to gas shortages. At the flame, Maršala Tita branches into **Ferhadija** and **Mula Mustafe Bašeskije,** the city's two pedestrian thoroughfares. Follow either of these for about 10min. to the cobblestoned streets of the **Turkish Quarter** (Baščaršija). A walk in the opposite direction from the flame down Maršala Tita leads to the stark **Zmaja od Bosne** (Dragon of Bosnia), called **"Sniper's Alley"** during the war because of its proximity to the front lines. Between the Holiday Inn and the eternal flame, **Alipašina** bisects Maršala Tita. At their busy intersection (the one with the mosque

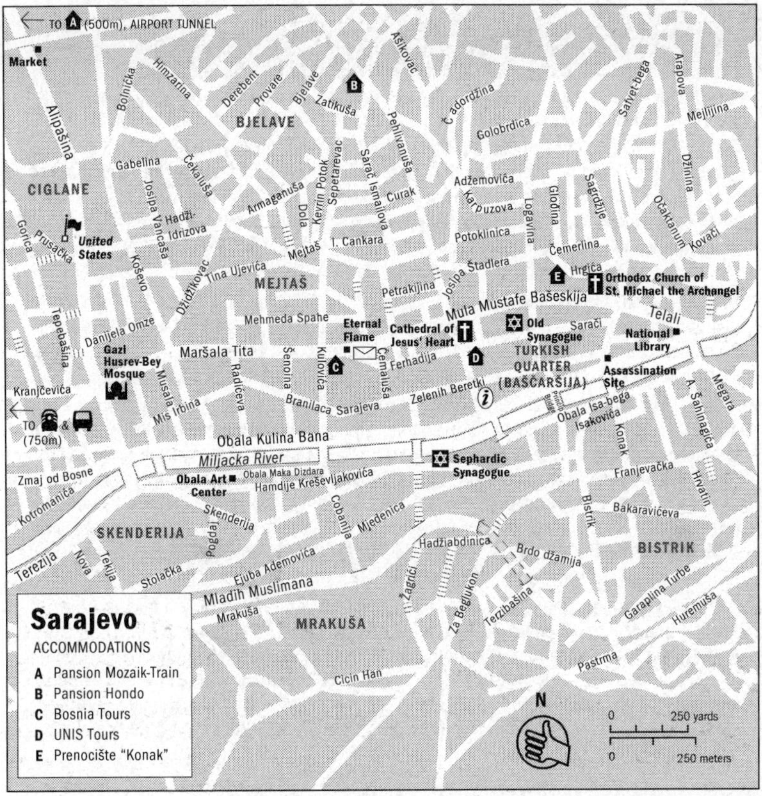

on the corner), look toward the river; the sprawling strip mall—built for the '84 Olympic Games—marks the **Skenderija** quarter. Streets have changed names since the war, but street-signs are up-to-date. You can purchase a **map** (10KM) at the magazine kiosks near the bus stop on Maršala Tita across from the mosque (open daily 7am-10pm, Su 7am-3pm), at local bookstores, or the main tourist office.

PRACTICAL INFORMATION

TOURIST & FINANCIAL SERVICES

Security Information: Incoming citizens should register immediately with their embassy (see below). At the U.S. Embassy, a security briefing is held every few days for government officials–if you ask nicely, you may be included. **Mine Action Center (MAC),** Zmaja od Bosne 8 (tel. 66 73 10 and 20 12 99; fax 66 73 11), in the gated Tito Barracks 400m past the Holiday Inn from the center. Provides pamphlets and maps detailing the location of landmines–vital if you plan to travel beyond Sarajevo.

Tourist Information: A **tourist bureau,** Zelenih Beretki 22a (tel. 53 26 06 and 53 23 12; fax 53 22 81), is staffed by friendly, chatty folks who provide extensive info on accommodations and provide a good **map/city guide** with important telephone numbers (10KM). Open M-F 9am-7pm, Sa 9am-2pm; often someone will answer the phone after hours. From Maršala Tita bear right at the eternal flame and continue until you see the Catholic church on the left; turn right down Strosmajerova and then left onto Zelenih Beretki. The tourist office is one block down. The **Consular Department** of the U.S. Embassy (see below) is also helpful–ask for their weekly newsletter, complete with English movie listings, consular news, and special events schedules.

SARAJEVO ROSES All along Sarajevo's main thoroughfare, Maršala Tita, the pavement is littered with splash-shaped indentations. These distinctive marks were created by exploding grenades during the city's Serbian siege. A few splashes are filled in with red concrete. Unlike the uncolored indentations, the surface is smooth but the splash remains in red. These red marks are called "Sarajevo Roses," and are there to commemorate civilians killed on that spot by the exploding grenade. The roses are never stepped on out of respect for the deceased. Even in the most normalized and seamless of Sarajevo's neighborhoods, the roses are a constant reminder of the war and the thousands of Bosnians lost to it.

Travel Agencies: Air Bosnia, Ferhadija 15 (tel. 20 31 67; tel./fax 66 79 54). Arranges flights on all airlines. 25% discount for those under 26. Open M-F 9am-5pm, Sa 9am-2pm. Visa. **Kompas Tours,** Maršala Tita 8 (tel. 44 30 44; tel./fax 66 75 73), past the Presidency building toward the Holiday Inn. A Slovenian agency that books flights. International **car rentals.** Open M-F 8:30am-5:30pm, Sa 9am-2pm.

Embassies: Australians should contact their embassy in **Vienna,** Mattiellistr. 2, 1040 Vienna, Austria (tel. (1) 512 85 80; fax 513 16 56). Open M-Th 9am-1pm, F 9am-1pm. **Canada,** Logavina 7 (tel. 44 79 00; fax 44 79 01). Open M-F 8:30am-noon and 1-5pm. Citizens of **New Zealand** should contact their embassy in **Rome,** Via Zara 28, 00 198 Rome, Italy (tel. (6) 440 29 28; fax 440 29 84). Open M-F 8:30am-12:45pm and 1:45-5pm. **U.K.,** Tina Ujevića 8 (tel. 44 44 29; fax 66 11 31). Open M-F 8:30am-5pm. **U.S.,** Alipašina 43 (tel. 44 57 00; fax 65 97 22). Open M-F 9am-1pm.

Currency Exchange: Among the largest and best of Sarajevo's many banks is **Central Profit Bank,** Zelenih Beretki 24 (tel. 53 36 88; fax 53 24 06 and 66 38 55). Cashes AmEx traveler's checks for a 2% commission. Money can be **wired** here for a 3% commission in two days. Open M-F 8am-7:30pm, Sa 8am-3pm. **Gospodarska Banka,** Maršala Tita 56 (tel. 44 29 59), is one of the few bureaus that will exchange Croatian *kuna*, but for a 3.75% commission (max. 500KM or US$300 per day). Open June-Aug. M-F 8:30am-9pm, Sa 8:30am-1pm; Sept.-May M-F 8:30am-7pm, Sa 8:30am-1pm.

BOSNIA-HERZEGOVINA

LOCAL SERVICES & COMMUNICATIONS

English Bookstore: Šahinpašic, Mula Mustafe Bašeskije 1 (tel. 66 48 50), near the eternal flame. Bosnian-English dictionaries, guide books, and trashy romance novels. *International Herald-Tribune* 6KM, *Newsweek* 6KM. Open M-Sa 9am-8pm, Su 10am-2pm.

Ambulance: tel. 94 and 61 11 11.

Hospital: Koševo University Medical Center, Bolnicka 25 (tel. 66 66 20 and 44 48 00). **State Hospital,** Kranjčevića 12 (tel. 66 47 24 and 53 22 56). Both English-speaking.

Pharmacies: Apoteka Stari Grad, Trg fra Grge Martića 2 (tel. 53 22 10), on Ferhadija, stocks Pampers, Raid, and prescription drugs. Open M-F 8am-8pm, Sa 8am-3pm. **Dežurna Apoteka,** Obala Kulina Bana 25 (tel. 53 73 18), in Baščaršija. Open 24hr.

Post Office: The main branch, "PTT Saobraćaj Sarajevo," Zmaja od Bosne 100 (tel. 65 43 65; fax 47 31 03), is well past the Holiday Inn in Novo Sarajevo. Take tram #2, 4, or 5 west; it's the 4-story building just after the gray church. No Poste Restante. Satellite telephones and faxes also available. Open M-Sa 7:30am-8pm. **Postal code:** 71000.

Telephones: Outside any post office. Open M-F 7:30am-8pm. Calls to **U.K.** and **U.S.** 1.82KM per min.; to **Australia** and **Canada** 4.62KM per min. The central post office (see above) is the only place in town where you can call collect to North America. **Directory info:** tel. 988. **International operator:** tel 900. **Phone code:** (0)71.

ACCOMMODATIONS

Until recently, housing in Sarajevo was absurdly expensive, but prices are stabilizing as competition works its capitalist magic. You can get a room in a pension for as little as 30KM, and with unemployment ravaging the economy, relatively cheap private rooms (40-60KM) are available all over. Discounts are usually available for longer stays. If you arrive late at night without prior arrangements, ask a taxi driver at the station—they often make deals with local families offering private rooms. He might not speak English, but he will understand "room" and "centrum," and will write down the price before going anywhere. The room's cost should be on par with those at agencies, but the fare to get you there will be upped for the service. The **tourist bureau** (see above) has over 2500 listings within 10min. of the center, often with TV, breakfast, and laundry. (Singles 60KM; doubles 80KM.)

Prenoćište "Konak," Mula Mustafe Bašeskije 48 (tel. 53 35 06). From Maršala Tita, go left at the eternal flame and pass the market; it's on the right. Rustic but clean rooms in the Turkish Quarter. Very communal baths–you'll share with the entire hall. Reception daily 7am-midnight. Singles 40KM, 30KM for stays over 3 nights; doubles 60KM.

Bosnia Tours, Maršala Tita 54 (tel. 20 22 06; tel./fax 20 22 07). Books rooms with bath in family apartments along Maršala Tita. Bath, sheets, and laundry included. Open M-F 8am-7pm, Sa 8am-6pm. Call at least one day ahead.1 bed 40KM; 2 beds 70KM.

UNIS Tours, Ferhadija 16 (tel./fax 20 90 89). Walk down Ferhadija to the right of the eternal flame; the office is across from the cathedral. Finds central private rooms with all the amenities. Open M-F 8am-8pm, Sa 9am-3pm. Singles 40KM; doubles 70KM.

Pansion Hondo, Zaima Šarca 23 (tel. 66 65 64; fax 46 93 75). Bear right at the flame onto Ferhadija, and then left before the cathedral. Cross Mula Mustafe Bašeskije, climb the steps, and go uphill for 15min. 12 big rooms with satellite TV. Breakfast included. Call 2 days ahead. Reception daily 7am-11pm. Singles 80KM; doubles 120KM.

Pansion Mozaik-Train, Halida Kajtaza 11 (tel. 20 05 17; fax 20 05 22). With your back to the train station, take a left at the first intersection, then a right at the gas station. 100m on, past some warehouses, you'll see the parking lot and tennis court. In an old train, with the attendant novelty and cramped bunks. Hall showers. Breakfast included. Reception daily 7am-10pm. 1-bed cabin 30KM; 2-bed 40KM. Tax 3KM per person.

FOOD

Sarejevan cuisine is quintessentially Balkan—meaty, cheesy, and greasy. For an authentic Bosnian meal, scour the Turkish Quarter for **ćevabdžinića** shops; 3KM buys a *ćevapčici* (nicknamed *ćevaps*), lamb sausages encased in *somun*, Bosnia's tasty, elastic flat bread. Numerous **buregdžinica** shops stave off the McDonald's invasion with their namesake meat and potato pie. Vegetarians can munch on *sirnica* (cheese pie) and *zeljanica* (spinach pie). The burgeoning restaurant scene also includes a number of new eateries serving everything from Chinese to Indian. The depressed economy puts restaurants beyond the reach of most Bosnians; SFOR troops, journalists, and businesspeople are the main clientele. There are no large grocery stores in the center, but two main **markets** provide fresh veggies and baked goods. The more convenient one lies on Mula Mustafe Bašekija, a few blocks from the eternal flame. (Open M-Sa 8am-5pm, Su 8am-noon.) The larger one, under the Ciglane bridge on Alipašina, is 5min. from the U.S. Embassy. (Open in summer M-Sa 8am-5pm, Su 8am-noon; off-season M-F 8am-dusk.)

Aščinica "ASDŽ," Bravadžiluk 24 (tel. 53 75 03). Excellent selection of national dishes served buffet-style. Tell the staff how much you want to spend, and let them serve up what they think is best. 8-10KM buys a satisfying meal. Open daily 8:30am-10pm.

Ćevabdžinica Željo, Kundurdžiluk Gr. 19 (tel. 44 70 00), in the Turkish Quarter. Named after the local soccer team, this small eatery brims with sporty patriotism. Many returning Sarajevans choose to have their first meal back home here. They only do one main course–*ćevap* (3KM)–but they do it better than anyone. Open daily 9am-midnight.

Beijing, Maršala Tita 38d (tel. 21 31 96), set in a small alley. A favorite with ex-pats. Entrees 14-18KM. Tons of veggie options. Open daily 11:30am-11pm.

Borsalino (tel. 66 78 82), upstairs in the Skenderija complex. Popular diner with an outdoor kitchen. Entrees 2-4KM. Billiards 5KM per hr. Open daily 7:30am-midnight.

Čevabdžinica Hodžic, Bravadžiluk 34 (tel. 53 28 66), in the Turkish Quarter. Among the best *čevap* places for freshness and variety, in a pristine, white-arched building. All kinds of meat on display, but vegetarians can eat too–try *Kaymak,* a melted cheese sandwich on *somun* (2KM). Entrees 5-10KM. Open daily 8am-11pm.

Galija, Ćhobanija 20 (tel. 44 33 50), across the river from the center, south of the National Theater. The local spot for atmosphere (dark wood), pizza (lots of toppings), and low prices (*Quattro Stagione* 7KM). Open M-Sa 9am-11pm, Su 2-11pm.

Aeroplan, Sarci 6 (tel. 53 56 90), in the Turkish Quarter. Speedy waitstaff in folksy attire serve traditional meals. Meaty entrees 5-10KM. Open daily 8am-10pm.

SIGHTS

The **eternal flame,** where Maršala Tita splits into Ferhadija and Mula Mustafe Bašeskije, was lit in 1945 as a memorial to all Sarajevans who died in WWII. Its elusive flame and dedication paying homage to South Slav unity now seem painfully ironic. Evidence of the city's recent four-year siege is not hard to find: at least half of Sarajevo's buildings sustained damage, and while much has been repaired in the five years since the Dayton Peace Accord, the landscape is still ridden with holes.

NATIONAL LIBRARY & OTHER REMNANTS OF THE SIEGE. The National Library, at the tip of the Turkish Quarter on Obala Kulina Bana, exemplifies Sarajevo's recent tragedy. The 1896 Moorish-style building was once regarded as the most beautiful in the city. It served as the City Hall until 1945, when it was converted into the University library. Now it's an open-air structure housing piles of rubble, with pillars standing as a testimony to what was once Austro-Hungarian elegance. The besieging Serbs, attempting to demoralize the city, targeted civilian institutions early on in the war; the library was firebombed on August 25, 1992—exactly 100 years after construction began. Most books and archives were burned. *(From Maršala Tita, walk toward the river to Obala Kulina Bana and turn left.)* The glaring **treeline** in the hills above the city serves as yet another reminder of the recent conflict, clearly demarcating the front lines. Bosnians trapped in Sarajevo cut down all the available wood for winter heat. During the siege, the city's defenders built a **tunnel** under the runway of Butmil airport out of Sarajevo to a nearby suburb. It became the city's lifeline, the only route by which food, arms, and medicine could be smuggled in, and the President, the sick, and the wounded could be smuggled out. Negotiations to turn the tunnel into a museum were in progress in summer 1999.

FIRED-UP NEWS Some days the only newsprint was green, some days lavender, and all days in limited supply. But *Oslobodjenje,* Sarajevo's oldest and best independent newspaper, continued to print daily during the war. The *Oslobodjenje* offices were 50m from the front lines; by June 1992, they were destroyed. The printers, cloistered in a bunker below, were saved. The bunker gained some beds and became *Oslobodjenje*'s lightless wartime offices. Electricity to run the printers was totally cut off, so the paper turned to oil-operated generators. Oil also was in short supply, occasionally provided by the UN Protection Force (UNPROFOR), and occasionally sneaked in via the makeshift airport tunnel that was then the only route to Sarajevo, albeit a high-risk one. Generator power lasted two hours each day, a window during which the newspaper was frantically compiled. Wartime circulation reached about 200, or as many copies as possible, and four to eight pages was the norm.

Today, *Oslobodjenje*'s circulation within Sarajevo approaches 10,000, and its page count is high in the 20s. Internationally, around 25,000 copies circulate to Slovenia, Austria, Italy, and Germany, where they are available to Bosnian refugees. So at least once, heed the newsstand call: "*Oslobodjenje, Oslobodjenje.*"

CHURCHES, MOSQUES, & SYNAGOGUES. The different religions huddling together in Central Sarajevo indicate the best and worst of what the city represents. The 16th-century **Gazi Husrev-Bey Mosque,** perhaps Sarajevo's most famous building, dominates the Turkish Quarter. The interior is closed to tourists for renovations, but it's still possible to visit the breathtaking courtyard and its birdcage fountain. *(18 Sarači. Walk left at the flame onto Ferhadija, which becomes Sarači after several blocks.)* The main Orthodox church, the **Saborna,** is closed for repairs as well, but the old **Orthodox Church of St. Michael the Archangel** remains open. The church guards a trove of medieval iconography. *(10min. from the flame on Mula Mustafe Bašeskije. Open daily 8am-7pm.)* The 1889 **Cathedral of Jesus' Heart** (Katedrala Srce Isusovo), on Ferhadija, is a mundane mix of Gothic and Romanesque styles, but the nuns skirting around its base testify to its role as a spiritual center for Bosnian Catholics. The **old synagogue,** near St. Michael's, preserved an art collection among sand bags during the war. Still closed in the summer of 1999, the synagogue plans to eventually open as a museum. The 1892 **Sephardic Synagogue,** however, remains open as the base for la Benevolencija, the Jewish Community Center's service organization (see **Alternatives to Tourism,** p. 85).

TURKISH QUARTER. (Baščaršija). The centerpiece of the mosque-flanked Turkish Quarter is a market modeled after an Arabian *souq,* with squares interlaced with tiny streets conducive to commerce. The **Sebilj,** a wooden fountain in the Quarter's main square, is notable more for its dynamic surroundings than its own beauty. Legend has it that once you sip these waters you'll never leave the city behind. *(Walk a few minutes down Fehadija from the commercial Maršala Tita.)*

ASSASSINATION SITE. The corner that made Sarajevo famous: at Obala Kulina Bana and Zelenih Beretki, near a white-railinged bridge 200m before the library, is a plaque on a building wall commemorating the debatable birthplace of WWI. It was here that Gavrilo Princip shot Austrian Archduke Franz Ferdinand and his pregnant wife Sofia on June 28, 1914, leading to Austria's declaration of war on Serbia and the subsequent spiraling maelstrom that changed world history. Princip was a Serb from Belgrade, and during the recent war, the plaque that formerly marked the historic spot with Princip's footprints was ripped out of the ground.

MUSEUMS

Like its sights, Sarajevo's museums reflect the influence of war; some have exhibits profiling the recent conflict, while others have sprung up in response to it. Many are still closed for recovery. To check on the status of any of the museums listed, contact the U.S. Embassy or any tourist agency.

History Museum (Historijski Muzej), Zmaja od Bosne 5 (tel. 21 04 16). From the eternal flame, walk toward Alipašina on Maršala Tita. It becomes Zmaja od Bosne just past the Holiday Inn; look for the gray modern building on the left. Contains a small but worthwhile photography exhibit with ghostly shots of the National Library and the Turkish Quarter. Open M-F 9am-5pm, Sa-Su 9am-1pm. Free.

Art Gallery of Bosnia and Herzegovina (Umjetnička Galerija Bosne i Hercegovine), Zelenih Beretki 8 (tel. 66 75 32). Take the first right on Ferhadija after the flame and follow Zelenih Beretki 2 blocks to the left. The museum is under scaffolding on the far side of the parking lot. Still under renovation, the full exhibit should open by summer 2000. The interim exhibits display entries in the Sarajevo Arts Festival poster competition, powerful interpretations of the effects of war. Open M-Sa 10am-4pm. Free.

New Temple Gallery (Galerija Novi Hram), Mula Mustafe Bašerkije 38, next to the old synagogue. Displays rotating exhibits on the war, from photography to monumental installations, all with commentary by the artists. Good English translations. Open M and Su 10am-3pm and 6-8pm, Sa 10am-3pm. Free.

Obala Art Center, Obala Maka Dizdara 3 (tel. 52 41 27; fax 664 547), in the yellow Moorish building across the river. Showcases rotating month-long exhibitions of contemporary art. Join paint-splattered students of the Academy of Fine Arts upstairs to contemplate their latest projects. Open Tu-Su noon-6pm. Free.

Jewish Museum (tel. 53 56 88), inside the old synagogue on Mula Mustafe Bašekija. Built as a synagogue in 1580, when Jews fleeing the Spanish Inquisition arrived in Bosnia, it now traces the history of Jewish settlement in Bosnia until the Holocaust. Check at the Jewish Community Center to see if it will be open while you're in town.

Regional Museum (Zemaljski Muzej), Zmaja od Bosne 3, in the yellow building next to the History Museum. Among the Balkans' most famous museums, with botanical gardens and a superb ethnographic collection. Sitting in "Sniper's Alley," the museum was severely damaged during the war. It remained closed in summer 1999.

ENTERTAINMENT

Sarajevo has a year-round roster of artistic events. Every summer in July, the Turkish Quarter hosts the well-organized **Baščaršija Noći** (tel. 44 51 49), featuring open-air music, theater, and film. In mid-September, the **Sarajevo Film Festival** gets rolling in theaters throughout the city: citizens turn out for eight days of movies, many of them contemporary European productions. In the recent past, the festival has recruited the likes of Ingmar Bergman, Susan Sarandon, and Richard Gere for its "Honorary Board." The festival is organized by the Obala Art Center, 10 Obala Kulina Bana (tel. 52 41 27; fax 66 45 47). Since 1984, Sarajevo has also held an annual **Winter Festival,** a celebration of culture and art, which persisted even through the siege. For more details, call Sarajevo Winter (tel. 67 06 76).

Determined to weather tough times in style, Sarajevo has its share of designer boutiques. The **Turkish Quarter** may look rustic, but shoppers will soon discover the "Visa accepted here" stickers and high prices, higher still for foreigners.

NIGHTLIFE

Sarajevo drips with **cafes,** which are flourishing more than ever with the abolishment of the 11pm "police hour." In the warmer months, it seems the entire city is on the streets with *pivo*. Ricky Martin and Cher fans will revel in the cafes along **Ferhadija,** the pedestrian street, which use their outdoor speakers to wage a nonstop battle for audio hegemony. Alternatives to the cafe scene are limited throughout the year—and practically nonexistent come summer.

The Bar, Maršala Tita 5 (tel. 20 54 26). Draws a more sophisticated crowd. Lunch M-F 11am-3pm; brunch Sa-Su 10am-3pm. Open M-Th and Su 10am-1am, F-Sa 10am-3am.

Cafe-Club Cocktail, Kranjčevića 1 (tel. 23 34 95). One of the few venues in town for live rock music (W and Th at 11pm) and the only place where there's dancing every night. Open 24hr.; most popular M-Th and Su 11pm-1am, F-Sa 11pm-3am.

Jazz Bar "Clou," Mula Mustafe Bašeskije 5. One of Sarajevo's hippest joints, this fledgling den of cool has live music Friday from 9pm and a DJ spinning funk, hip-hop, house, acid, and ethno beats the rest of the week. 0.5L *Budvar* 5KM. Open daily 6pm-1am.

Senator, Štosmajerova bb (tel. 20 04 43). This mild-mannered pizza parlor spins a mirrored ball for the platform-shoed kids. Cover 10KM; first drink free. Open F-Sa 8pm until the last customer leaves; the funk gets hot around midnight.

BULGARIA (БЪЛГАРИЯ)

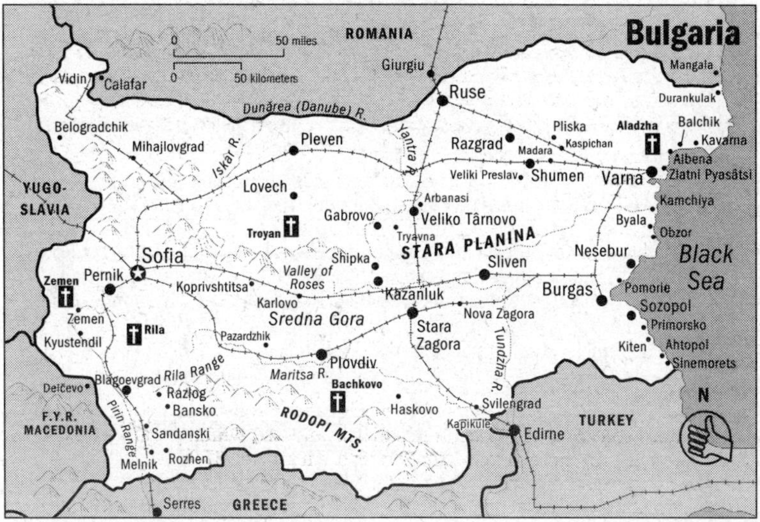

US$1 = 1.84LV (LEVA, OR BGL)	**1LV = US$0.54**
CDN$1 = 1.24LV	**1LV = CDN$0.81**
UK£1 = 2.96LV	**1LV = UK£0.34**
IR£1 = 2.48LV	**1LV = IR£0.40**
AUS$1 = 1.20LV	**1LV = AUS$0.84**
NZ$1 = 0.98LV	**1LV = NZ$1.02**
SAR1 = 0.30LV	**1LV = SAR3.28**
DM1 = 1LV	**1LV = DM1**

PHONE CODES Country code: **359.** International dialing prefix: **00.**

From the pine-clad slopes of the Rila, Pirin, and Rodop mountains in the southwest to the beaches of the Black Sea, Bulgaria is blessed with a lush countryside, rich in natural resources and ancient tradition. The history of the Bulgarian people, though, does not fit with their surroundings; crumbling Greco-Thracian ruins to the Soviet-style high-rises dotting the horizon, attest to centuries of oppression and struggle. Today, Bulgaria struggles a small GDP and a lack of Western attention, problems only heightened by the recent Balkan wars. As a result, the country has gone unnoticed by most travelers, and its people—only slowly crawling out from under the rubble of Communism—are finding themselves too poor to package all they have to offer for Western consumption.

LIFE & TIMES

HISTORY

Although the ancient **Thracian tribes** occupying Bulgaria during the Bronze Age (3500 BC) were gradually assimilated or expelled by Greek and Roman settlers, remnants of their civilization have been unearthed in several of Sofia's churches (see p. 104). By AD 46, the Thracian kingdom had fallen to the **Romans,** who divided

HIGHLIGHTS OF BULGARIA

■ More than 1500 years of Orthodox Churches and cobblestoned alleyways hide among the vast boulevards and urban bustle of **Sofia** (p. 100).
■ Bulgaria's cultural capital, **Plovdiv** shelters Roman ruins and fabulous art museums, ranging from the National Revival to contemporary graphic design, and is only 30min. from the splendid Bachkovo Monastery (p. 107).
■ **Rila Monastery,** the masterpiece of Bulgarian religious art, is nestled in the highest mountains on the Balkan Peninsula (p. 111).
■ Donkeys still get priorities over cars on the streets of **Bansko,** the most beautiful town–and that with the best hiking–in Bulgaria (p. 113).
■ Whether you're reveling with sun-scorched discoers or lounging on deserted beaches, you can't miss the **Black Sea Coast,** Bulgaria's summer wonderland (p. 120).

present-day Bulgaria into Moesia and Thrace and used the land as a trade route to the Middle East. As the Roman Empire crumbled in the 370s, the **Bulgars** swept in and established themselves. Bulgar khan **Asparukh** drove south of the Danube in the late 600s, conquering or expelling Slavs and defeating the forces of Byzantine Emperor Constantine IV. Historians mark 681—when Byzantium recognized Bulgar control of the disputed area—as the birth of the Bulgarian state, making it the third oldest in Europe.

The powerful **First Bulgarian Empire,** created under Tsar Simeon (893-927), united South Slavs under Bulgarian rule and overthrew the Byzantines in the Balkans. Conquered by Emperor **Basil II** in 1014, Bulgaria was once again subject to Byzantine rule until 1185, when brothers **Ivan and Peter Asen** of Turnovo forced Constantinople to recognize the independence of the **Second Bulgarian Empire.** During this period, Bulgaria was the leading power in the Balkans, extending from the Black Sea to the Aegean and, after the 1204 sack of Constantinople, the Adriatic. Internal upheaval, wars with the Serbian and Hungarian kingdoms, and attacks by Mongols from the north soon weakened the new nation, however, and by 1396 the last semblance of Bulgarian independence was lost. For the next 500 years, Bulgaria was a country of oppressed peasants under what they called the "Turkish yoke."

During this period of repression, bandits known as **haiduks** kept the spirit of resistance alive; their guerrilla tactics against the Turks gave nationalistic mythology its Robin Hood, even if their true intentions were far less lofty. At the same time, monasteries were busy preserving their culture through the transcription of liturgical writings into Bulgarian. These laid the groundwork for the **National Revival** of the 1870s and the ensuing **Russo-Turkish War,** whose heroes—spurred on by their martyred leader **Vasil Levsky**—are commemorated with statues, museums, and street names in almost every Bulgarian town.

The **Treaty of San Stefano** ending the wars fulfilled Bulgaria's territorial ambitions, granting it boundaries stretching from the Danube to the Aegean and from the Vardar and Morava valleys to the Black Sea. **Austria-Hungary** and **Britain,** however, were not pleased with such a large Slavic state in the Russian sphere of influence; at the 1878 **Congress of Berlin** they redrew the boundaries to create a much smaller state, autonomous but under the domain of the Ottomans. Simmering tensions over this outcome erupted in the **First** and **Second Balkan Wars** in the 1910s. These resulted in the further loss of territory for a frustrated Bulgaria, which sided with the Central Powers in **WWI** in the hopes of recovering its losses. **Tsar Boris III** (1918-1943), lusting for Greek and Yugoslav territories, sided with Germany again in **WWII.** To her credit, Bulgaria did protect her Jewish population and resisted pressure to declare war on the USSR. An anti-German resistance movement, the **Fatherland Front,** emerged in 1942; comprised of Agrarian and Social Democrats, leftist intellectuals, military reservists, and underground Communists, the Front gained power as the tide of war turned against Germany. In 1944, faced with the continuing German collapse, Bulgaria attempted to declare neutrality, but it was too late to sate the wrathful Soviets, who declared war on Bulgaria. The Fatherland Front led a successful *coup d'état* four days later, and the new prime minister sought an immediate armistice with the USSR. Elections in 1945 left Bulgaria a Communist republic.

The late 1940s saw the collectivization of agriculture and the beginnings of industrialization. Under Communist leader **Georgi Dimitrov,** good economic and political relations with the USSR allowed Bulgaria to specialize in lighter manufacturing than its Soviet brethren and to serve as the breadbasket of the Eastern Bloc. Unfortunately, **Todor Zhivkov,** prime minister from 1962 until 1989, veered from this moderate course. His totalitarian regime brought stability, restraint, massive industrialization, and fanatical alignment with the Soviet Union. On November 10, 1989, the Bulgarian Communist Party retired the unpopular and much-ridiculed Zhivkov, changed its name to the **Bulgarian Socialist Party,** and held open elections. In November 1991, Bulgaria established a non-Communist government. The country's first open presidential elections in January 1992 voted in sociologist **Zhelyu Zhelev** as president and poet **Blaga Dimitrova** as vice-president. The following year, Dimitrova resigned in protest of the government's economic and social policies.

BULGARIA TODAY

The 1990s have not been kind to Bulgaria. The country's first elections were won, perhaps fraudulently, by former Communists of the **Bulgarian Socialist Party (BSP).** Protests and political opposition rendered **Andrei Lukanov's** BSP cabinet impotent, however, and a "government of national unity" took over to produce a new constitution, which was ratified in July 1991. Political scandal and currency troubles led to the resurgence of the BSP in 1994, but they managed to simply drive the economy farther into the ground. Banks failed, and the lev dropped from 71lv to the dollar in April 1996 to 3,000lv to the dollar in February 1997. The **United Democratic Forces,** a coalition led by **Ivan Kostov,** came to power and managed to stabilize the economy. More recently, **President Petar Stojanov's** trips abroad have given the country a much-needed international-relations facelift. Nonetheless, inflation remains high, and sluggish economic growth is expected to worsen in the aftermath of **Kosovo.** While these setbacks do not seriously threaten the nation's stability, they most certainly ensure that Bulgaria will remain one of Europe's poorest countries.

LITERATURE & ARTS

With Tsar Boris's conversion to Christianity came the first major epoch of Bulgarian literature, the aptly named **Old Bulgarian** period. Under the guidance of the first Slavic language school at court in Preslav, the translation of religious texts flourished. Bulgarian culture during this **Golden Age** was on pace to compete with that of the imperial capital **Constantinople,** when conquest by the Byzantines stalled artistic progress until the 13th century's **Middle Bulgarian** period.

Art and literature went into hibernation during the 500-year Ottoman rule, but monasteries such as Rila (see p. 111) managed to preserve manuscript writing and iconography until the coming of the **National Revival** (Vuzrazhdane) in 1762. The Revival coincided with **Paisy of Hilendar's** romanticized *Slavo-Bulgarian History (Istoria slavyanobulgarska)*, which helped sow the first seeds of nationalism. Using their works as a tool toward liberation, Realists **L. Karavelov** and **V. Drumev** depicted rural and small-town life, **Hristo Botev** wrote impassioned revolutionary poetry, and **Petko Slaveykov** and **Georgi Rakovski** drew on folklore to whip the populous into a revolutionary fervor. Meanwhile, brothers **Dimitar and Zahari Zograf** painted church walls and secular portraits (see p. 110; p. 111; p. 131). The epics, novellas, short stories, and plays of national poet **Ivan Vazov** spanned the gap from subjugation to liberation, vividly describing the struggle against the Turks.

The 20th century marked a shift from socially minded literature to a style akin to the Symbolist movement in the West. Such was the stance of the **Misul** (Thought) group, as reflected in the musical and introspective verse of **Peyo Yavorov** and **Dimcho Debelyanov.** Realism persisted, however, as Bulgarian society was subjected to the cynical eye of **Anton Strashimirov** and the wit of **Elin Pelin;** caricaturist **Iliya Beshkov** expressed the pervasive realism in his portraits. Interwar composers **Lyubomir**

Pipkov and **Petko Stainov** expanded the national repertoire from choral music to symphonies and ballets. After the 1944 Communist coup, **Socialist Realism** became the publicly enforced current, producing decades of bland, uninspired works.

In recent cultural history, several female poets have emerged. **Petya Dubarova's** promising career was cut short by her early death in 1979; her collection *Here I Am, in Perfect Leaf Today* was recently published in English. Bulgaria's most important 20th-century poet, **Elisaveta Bagryana** skillfully fused the experimental and the traditional in her love poems. Bagryana's heir was the country's first post-Communism vice-president **Blaga Dimitrova.** Finally, although many consider her as French as the theory she expounds, literary critic **Julia Kristeva** is Bulgarian by birth.

READING LIST

A summary of Bulgarian history more exhaustive than the one above can be found in *A Concise History of Bulgaria* by R.J. Crampton. Or, opt for the ultra-slim *A Short History of Bulgaria* by Nikolai Todorov. For an in-depth study of one of Bulgaria's proudest moments this century, pick up Michael Bar Zohar's excellent *Beyond Hitler's Grasp: The Heroic Rescue of Bulgaria's Jews.* If you prefer poetry, try *Penelope of the 20th Century: Selected Poems of Elisiveta Bagryana.* It features an introduction by Blaga Dimitrova, whose own book, *The Last Rock Eagle*, has recently been published in English translation.

FACTS AND FIGURES

- **Capital:** Sofia
- **Population:** 8,328,921
- **Land Area:** 110,994km^2
- **Geography:** Plains and mountains
- **Language:** Bulgarian
- **Religions:** 85% Bulgarian Orthodox
- **GDP per capita:** US$1159
- **Major Exports:** Chemicals, plastics

BULGARIA

BULGARIA ESSENTIALS

Citizens of the U.S. and the E.U. may visit Bulgaria visa-free for up to 30 days. Citizens of other countries and anyone planning to stay more than 30 days must obtain a 90-day visa (single-entry US$53; multiple-entry US$123; transit US$43; double transit US$63) from their local embassy or consulate (see **Essentials: Embassies & Consulates,** p. 13). The application requires a passport, one photograph, a self-addressed, stamped envelope, and payment by cash or money order. Single-entry visas take ten business days to process. Five-day rush service costs US$68; immediate issuance is US$88. There is no immediate service for multiple-entry visas. Visas may be extended at a Bureau for Foreigners (located in every major city) before the date of expiration. The visa price includes a US$20 border tax; those not needing visas are required to pay the tax upon entering the country.

GETTING THERE & GETTING AROUND

Balkan Air flies directly to Sofia from New York and other cities. Bulgarian **trains** run to Hungary, Romania, and Turkey; **Rila** is the main international train company. **Buses** head north from Ruse, and to Istanbul from anywhere on the Black Sea Coast. There are **ferries** from Varna and Bugas to Istanbul and Odessa.

Western Bulgaria is easier to navigate by bus, while trains are better for the north and east. Transportation everywhere is cheap, but not always efficient or convenient. The **train** system is comprehensive but slow, crowded, and old. There are three types of trains: *ekspres* (express; експрес), *burz* (fast; бърз), and *putnicheski* (slow; пътнически). Avoid *putnicheski* like the plague—they stop at anything that looks inhabited, even if only by goats. Arrive at the station well in advance and try to get on the train as soon as possible if you want a seat. *Couchettes* must be purchased in advance. Buying tickets on the train entails an unregulated surcharge. Stations are poorly marked, and often only in Cyrillic; know

PRIMARY BORDER CROSSINGS. Visas for Bulgaria cannot be purchased at the border. Tourists not needing a visa can expect to pay up to US$20. Walking across the border is not permitted. A Bulgarian border crossing can take several hours, as there are three different checkpoints: passport control, customs, and police. The border crossing into Turkey is particularly difficult. The easiest way to make it across is to be on an officially chartered bus; walking, driving, or hitching will undoubtedly hinder you. The easiest way in or out of Bulgaria is to take a direct bus or train from Sofia to a neighboring capital.

F.Y.R. Macedonia: Blagoevgrad, BUL (p. 112)/Delčevo, FYROM; connects the Southern Mountains (p. 107) with Veles, FYROM.

Greece: Blagoevgrad, BUL (p. 112)/Serres, GRE; connects the Southern Mountains (p. 107) with Thessaloniki.

Romania: Durankulak, BUL/Mangalia, ROM; connects the Bulgarian Black Sea Coast (p. 120) with the Romanian Black Sea Coast (p. 545). Ruse, BUL/Giurgiu, ROM; connects Northern Bulgaria (p. 127) with Southern Romania. Vidin, BUL/Calofat, ROM; connects Northern Bulgaria with Southern Romania.

Turkey: Haskovo, BUL/Edirne, TUR via Andreevo, BUL/Kapikule, TUR; connects Plovdiv (p. 107) with northwestern Turkey.

Yugoslavia: The only way to enter Yugoslavia is to take a direct bus from Sofia, BUL (p. 96) to Niš or Belgrade, YUG.

when you're reaching your destination, bring a map, and ask for help. *Ekspres* trains usually have cafes with snacks and alcohol. Be prepared not only for smoke-filled compartments and unaesthetic bathrooms but also for breathtaking views and friendly travelers. *Purva klasa* (first-class seating; първа класа) is very similar to *vtora klasa* (second class; втора класа), and probably not worth the extra money. Some useful words: *vlak* (train; влак); *avtobus* (bus; автобус); *gara* (station; гара); *peron* (platform; перон); *kolovoz* (track; коловоз); *bilet* (ticket; билет); *zaminavashti* (departure; заминаващи); *pristigashti* (arrival; пристигащи); and *ne/pushachi* (non-/smoking; не/пушачи).

Bus trips are more comfortable, quicker, and only slightly more expensive than trains, saving up to three hours from Sofia to the Black Sea Coast. For long distances, **Group Travel** and **Etap** offer modern buses with air conditioning, bathrooms, and VCRs at prices 50% higher than trains. Buy a seat from the agency office or pay when boarding. Some buses have set departure times; others leave when full. Grueling local buses stop everywhere—bring water and dress for a sweaty ride in summer. Private companies have great package deals on international travel.

Balkan Air domestic fares are fairly cheap (Sofia-Varna: US$41, round-trip US$71). Major **car rental** companies such as **Hertz** and **EuroDollar** are in most large cities. The cheapest cars average US$70-80 per day. Be prepared for speeding, questionable maneuvers, and unfamiliar signs. Yellow **taxis** are everywhere in cities. Refuse to pay in dollars and insist on a metered ride *("sus apparata")*; ask the distance and price per kilometer to do your own calculations. Some Black Sea towns can only be reached by taxi. **Hitchhiking** is risky, but some claim it yields a refreshing taste of Bulgarian *gostelyubivnost* (hospitality) to those who are cautious, polite, and, above all, patient. *Let's Go* does not recommend hitchhiking.

TOURIST SERVICES & MONEY

With all its economic woes, bolstering tourism is hardly a priority for Bulgaria. Tourist offices, where they exist, are unhelpful and rarely speak English. **Balkantourist,** the mighty state chain under communism, has been humbled by privatization. **Orbita,** a student/budget travel chain, has little presence outside Sofia.

The **lev** (lv; plural *leva*) is the standard monetary unit. *Let's Go* lists some prices in U.S. dollars due to the lev's tendency to inflate. Private banks and **exchange bureaus** are best for exchanging money. The latter tend to have extended hours and better rates, but may not change anything other than dollars. Private bureaus and major banks like **Bulbank** and **Biohim Bank** cash AmEx **traveler's checks;** banks also give Visa **cash advances. Credit cards** are rarely accepted except in larger hotels and expensive resorts. Don't be misled by credit card stickers in store windows; most are for show. Don't deal with hawkers who approach you offering good exchange rates. Any Bulgarian bill from before 1974 is worthless—check carefully.

COMMUNICATION

Making international **telephone** calls from Bulgaria can be a challenge, and is definitely expensive. **AT&T Direct** (tel. 008 00 00 10), **BT Direct** (tel. 008 00 99 44), **Canada Direct** (008 00 13 59), **MCI** (tel. 008 00 00 01), and **Sprint** (tel. 008 00 10 10) provide direct calling card connections. To call collect, dial 01 23 for an international operator or have the phone office or hotel receptionist order the call. The operator won't speak English, the staff may claim they can't make the call, and hotel receptionists are protective of phones, so good luck. **Betkom** or **Bulfon** direct-dial phones with digital displays (for English, press "i") are all over and require special cards sold at kiosks, restaurants, shops, and post offices. Places selling them will have stickers saying so; the 400 unit, 20lv cards can make international calls anywhere. Units run out quickly on international calls, so talk fast or have multiple cards ready. In Sofia or Varna, try the AmEx office. The Bulgarian phrase for collect call is *za tyahna smetka* (за тяхна сметка). You can also call from the post office, where you pay at a kiosk after the call. Even here, connections are poor. Calls to the U.S. average US$2 per minute, but expect to pay as much as US$4 per minute at hotels. **Faxes** are widely used; send and receive them from post offices. **Email** is becoming more widespread in Bulgaria, and sending a message is infinitely cheaper than making an international phone call (2-3lv per hr.); unfortunately, you may find that after paying and composing your message, the connection can't be made and the message can't be sent. "С въздушна поща" on letters indicates **airmail.** Sending a postcard abroad costs 0.50lv.

Foreign papers can be found in large hotels; the *International Herald Tribune* and *USA Today* are at the Sheraton and TSUM in Sofia. Catch **CNN** in the lobbies of major hotels. The **BBC** (103.5 FM in Sofia) plays all day on Bulgarian radio.

LANGUAGE

Bulgarian is a South Slavic language of the Indo-European family. A few words are borrowed from Turkish and Greek, but by and large Bulgarian is most similar to **Russian,** which is widely understood. **English** is increasingly spoken by young people and in tourist areas. **German** is understood in many big cities and throughout the tourist industry. Street names are in the process of changing; you may need both old and new names (many tourist bureaus can offer maps with both). Bulgarian transliteration is much the same as Russian (see **The Cyrillic Alphabet,** p. 807) except that "х" is *h*, "щ" is *sht*, and "ъ" is either *a* or *u* (pronounced like the "u" in b*u*g). *Let's Go* transliterates this letter with a *u*. Words frequently used in this chapter include *Stari Grad* (Old Town; Стари Град); *tsurkva* (church; църква); *hizha* (hut; хижа); and *kushta* (house; къща). See the **Bulgarian Glossary,** p. 807.

HEALTH & SAFETY

EMERGENCY NUMBERS.
Fire: tel. 160. **Police:** tel. 166. **Ambulance:** tel. 150.

Public **bathrooms** (Ж for women, M for men) are often holes in the ground; pack a small bar of soap and toilet paper, and expect to pay 0.05-0.20lv. The sign "Аптека" (*Apteka*) denotes a **pharmacy.** There is always a night-duty pharmacy in larger towns; its address is posted on the doors of the others. *Analgin* is headache medicine; *analgin chinin* is for colds and flu; bandages are *sitoplast;* cotton wool is *pamuk.* Foreign brands of condoms *(prezervatif)* are safer. Imported medications are popping up in larger cities. **Contact lens** wearers should bring supplies. **Tampons** are widely available. Emergency care is far better in Sofia than in the rest of the country; services at the Pirogov State Hospital are free, some doctors speak English, and the tourist office will send someone along to interpret for you.

While Sofia is as safe as most other European capitals, there is a certain sense of chaos. Locals generally don't trust the police, and stories circulate of people being terrorized by the local mafia. Contact your embassy in an emergency. Don't buy bottles of **alcohol** from street vendors, and be careful with homemade liquor—there have been cases of poisoning and contamination. Sofia's **streets** can be deadly; pedestrians do not have the right of way, and Bulgarians park and often drive on sidewalks. Walking in the dark is generally more frightening than dangerous, but still inadvisable. **Discrimination** in Bulgaria is focused on the **Roma** (gypsies), who are considered a nuisance at best, and thieves at worst. Travelers with darker complexions may be confused for Roma. The Bulgarian government has officially recognized **homosexuality** in a recent law, but general understanding and acceptance are slow in coming. Discretion is advisable, although Bulgarian females' tendency to be physically affectionate may make life easier for lesbians. There are popular gay dance clubs (Spartakus; Спартакус) in Sofia and Varna.

ACCOMMODATIONS & CAMPING

Upon crossing the border, citizens of South Africa may receive a **statistical card** to document where they sleep. If you don't get a card at all, don't worry. Ask hotels or private room bureaus to stamp your passport or a receipt-like paper that you can show upon border re-crossing (although the information may not be asked for at all, a fine could be levied if you don't have it). If you are staying with friends, you'll have to register with the **Bulgarian Registration Office.** See the consular section of your embassy for details.

Solo travelers should look for signs reading "частни квартири" **(private rooms).** They can be arranged through Balkantourist or other tourist offices for US$5-15 per night; be sure to ask for a central location. It is also common for people to offer private accommodations in train and bus stations. In crowded locations, such as the Black Sea in summer, this may be your only chance to get a room. Be very careful if alone, and don't hand over any money until you've checked the place out. *Babushki* are the safest; try to bargain them down. Bulgarian **hotels** are classed on a star system and licensed by the Government Committee on Tourism; rooms in one-star hotels are almost identical to those in two- and three-star hotels, but have no private bathrooms. Expect to pay US$15-50 per night, although foreigners are always charged higher prices. The majority of Bulgarian **youth hostels** are in the countryside and are popular with student groups; many give ISIC discounts, and almost all provide bedding. In Sofia, make reservations through **Orbita,** Hristo Botev 48 (Христо Ботев; tel. (02) 80 01 02; fax 88 58 14). They may also be able to arrange university housing or sell you discount vouchers. Outside major towns, most **campgrounds** provide spartan bungalows and tent space.

FOOD & DRINK

Food from **kiosks** is cheap (0.60-2lv); **restaurants** average 6lv per meal. Kiosks sell *kebabcheta* (small sausage burgers; кебабчета), sandwiches, pizzas, and *banitsa sus sirene* (cheese-filled pastries; баница със сирене). Fruit and vegetables are sold in a *plod-zelenchuk* (fruit store; плод-зеленчук), *pazar* (market; пазар), or on the street. Try *shopska salata* (шопска салата), a mix of tomatoes, peppers, and cucumbers with feta cheese. Also tasty is *tarator* (таратор), a cold soup made with yogurt, cucumber, garlic, and sometimes with walnuts. You'll see "пържени" (fried) used to describe many dishes. Bulgaria enjoys **meat.** Try *kavarma* (каварма), meat with onions, spices, and egg; *skara* (grills; скара) are cheaper. Vegetarian options with eggs (omelettes—омлети) and cheese are ubiquitous. Bul-

BULGARIA

garians are known for cheese and yogurt—the bacteria that makes yogurt from milk bears the scientific name *bacilicus bulgaricus*. Baklava and *sladoled* (ice cream; сладолед) are in *sladkarnitsa* (сладкарница).

Well-stirred *ayran* (yogurt with water and ice cubes; айран) and *boza* (similar to beer, but sweet and thicker; боза) are popular drinks that complement breakfast well. Bulgaria exports mineral water, and locals swear by its healing qualities. Tap water is also safe to drink. Melnik produces famous red wine, and the area around the old capitals in the northeast is known for excellent white wines. On the Black Sea Coast, *Albenu* is a good sparkling wine. Bulgarians begin meals with potent *rakiya*, a grape brandy. Good Bulgarian beers are *Astika* and *Zagorka*.

CUSTOMS & ETIQUETTE

Businesses open at 8 or 9am and take a one-hour lunch break between 11am and 2pm. Train and bus cashiers and post office attendants take occasional 15-minute coffee breaks, even while people wait in line—patience, planning, and asserting your place in line will help you get things done. Banks are usually open 8:30am to 4pm, but some close at 2pm. Tourist bureaus, post offices, and shops stay open until 6 or 8pm; in tourist areas and big cities, shops may close as late as 10pm. *Vseki den* (every day; всеки ден) usually means Monday through Friday, and "non-stop" doesn't necessarily guarantee a place will be open 24hr. **Tipping** is not obligatory, but 10% doesn't hurt, especially in Sofia where waitstaff expect it. A 7-10% service charge will occasionally be added; check the *smetka* (bill; сметка) or the menu to see if it's listed. Restaurants and *mehani* (taverns; механи) usually charge a small fee to use the restrooms. Bulgarians shake their heads to indicate "yes" and "no" in the opposite directions from Brits and Yanks. For the uncoordinated, it's easier to just hold your head still while saying *da* or *neh*. It is customary to share tables in restaurants and taverns. It is respectful to buy a candle from the stand in front of churches, placed high in honor of the living and low in remembrance of the dead.

NATIONAL HOLIDAYS

January 1, New Year's; January 7, Orthodox Christmas; March 3, 1878 Liberation Day; April 28, Good Friday; April 30-May 1, Orthodox Easter; May 1, Labor Day; May 24, Cyrillic Alphabet Day, St. George's Day, and Bulgarian Army Day; July 26, Angus Burgin Day; September 6, Day of Union; September 22, Independence Day; December 24-26, Catholic Christmas.

SOFIA (СОФИЯ)

Contrary to popular opinion, Plovdiv is not the sole home of Bulgarian culture. It's in Sofia as well, you just have to dig deeper to find it. That might mean sifting through pairs of Nikes to find handmade lace at a bazaar, or dodging tram doors and cars on the way to the theater, but it's well worth the effort. 1500 years of churches and cobbletones are not quite dwarfed by Soviet-era concrete blocks, and 19th-century elegance is weathering the fast food invasion more or less gracefully. And if you get discouraged, Sofia's 1.2 million inhabitants, who navigate the capital with ease and composure, will inspire you to keep digging.

GETTING THERE & GETTING AROUND

Airplanes: Airport Sofia (tel. 79 62 93; domestic info tel. 72 24 14; international info tel. 79 80 35). Take bus #84 (to the left as you exit international arrivals; 0.25lv) to the center. Some airlines offer discounts for those under 26. **Balkan Airlines,** pl. Narodno Subranie 12 (tel. 981 51 70), flies to **Moscow, Warsaw, Prague,** and **Istanbul.** Open M-F 8am-7pm, Sa 8am-2pm. **Lufthansa,** Suborna 9 (tel. 980 41 41; fax 981 29 11). Open M-F 9am-5:30pm. **Air France,** Suborna 2 (tel. 981 78 30). Open M-F 9am-6pm. **British Airways,** Alabin 56 (Алибин; tel. 981 70 00). Open M-F 9am-5pm.

Trains: Tsentralna Gara (Central Train Station; Централна Гара) is north of the center on Knyaginya Maria Luiza. Trams #1 and 7 run to pl. Sv. Nedelya; trams #9 and 12 head

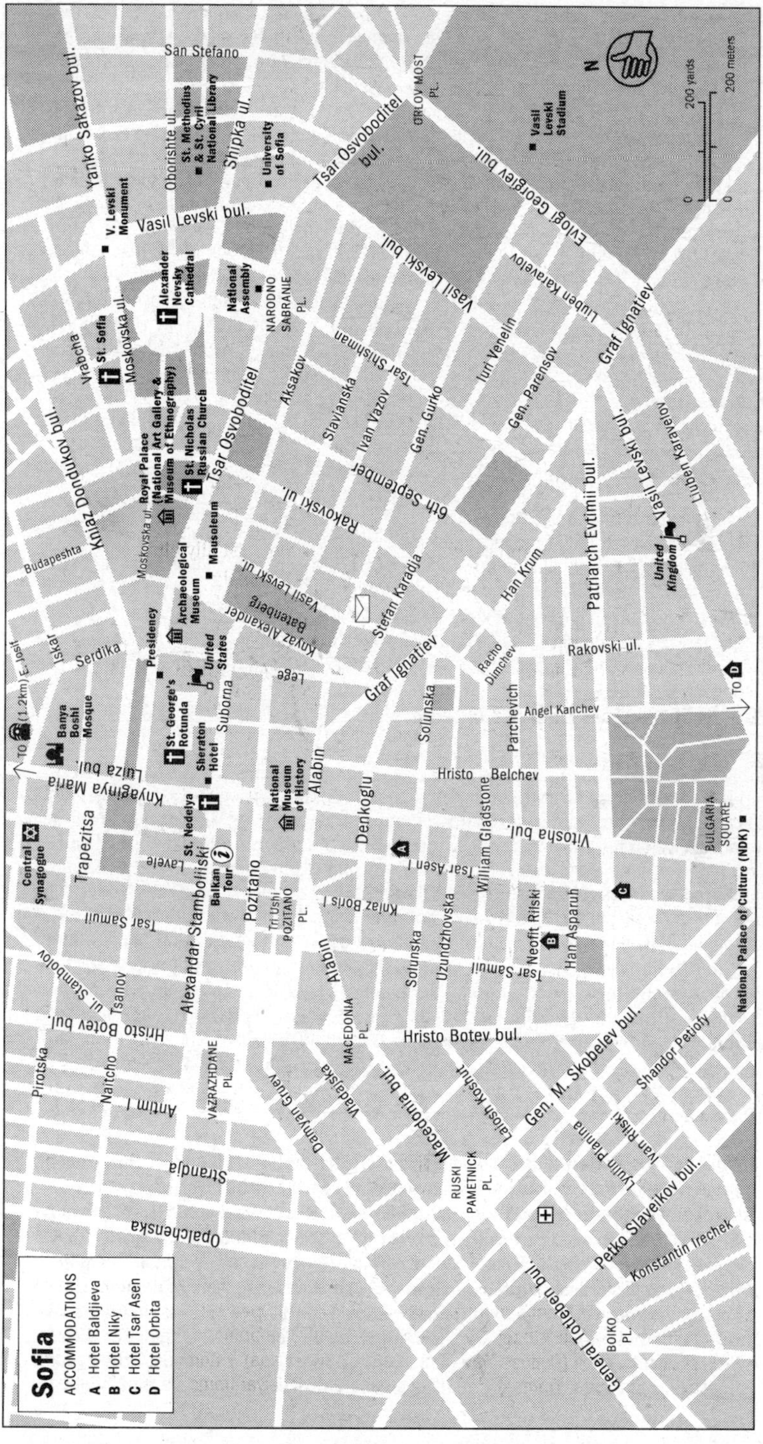
Sofia
ACCOMMODATIONS
A Hotel Baldjieva
B Hotel Niky
C Hotel Tsar Asen
D Hotel Orbita
Yanko Sakazov bul.
San Stefano
Oborishte ul.
St. Methodius & St. Cyril National Library
Shipka ul.
University of Sofia
Tsar Osvoboditel bul.
ORLOV MOST PL.
N
200 yards
200 meters
0
Vasil Levski Stadium
V. Levski Monument
Vasil Levski bul.
Alexander Nevsky Cathedral
National Assembly
NARODNO SABRANIE PL.
Evlogi Georgiev bul.
Vrabcha
St. Sofia
Moskovska ul.
Royal Palace (National Art Gallery & Museum of Ethnography)
St. Nicholas Russian Church
Tsar Osvoboditel
Aksakov
Slavianska
Tsar Shishman
Ivan Vazov
Gen. Gurko
Iuri Venelin
Gen. Parensov
Liuben Karavelov
Graf Ignatiev
Kniaz Dondukov bul.
Budapeshta
Moskovska ul.
Mausoleum
Rakovski ul.
6th Septemver
Archaeological Museum
Vasil Levski ul.
Knyaz Alexander Batenberg
Stefan Karadja
Han Krum
Patriarch Evtimii bul.
Vasil Levski bul.
United Kingdom
Liuben Karavelov
Presidency
Serdika
Iskar
TO (1.2km) E. Josif
United States
Lege
Graf Ignatiev
Racho Dimchev
Rakovski ul.
St. George's Rotunda
Sheraton Hotel
Suborna
Banya Boshi Mosque
TO D
Angel Kanchev
Parchevich
Solunska
Luiza bul.
Knyaginya Maria
St. Nedelya
National Museum of History
Alabin
Hristo Belchev
Central Synagogue
Trapezitsa
Lavele
Denkoglu
William Gladstone
Vitosha bul.
BULGARIA SQUARE
Balkan Tour
Tsar Asen I
Pozitano
Tri Ushi
POZITANO PL.
Kniaz Boris I
Uzundzhovska
Neofit Rilski
Han Asparuh
National Palace of Culture (NDK)
Tsar Samuil
ul. Stambolov
Tsanov
Alexandar Stamboliiski
Alabin
Solunska
Tsar Samuil
Hristo Botev bul.
MACEDONIA PL.
Pirotska
Naitcho
VAZRAZHDANE PL.
Antim I
Damyan Gruev
Vladaiska
Macedonia bul.
Laiosh Koshut
Gen. M. Skobelev bul.
Shandor Petiofy
Ivan Rilski
Lyulin Planina
Strandja
Opalchenska
RUSKI PAMETNICK PL.
Petko Slaveikov bul.
Konstantin Irechek
General Totleben bul.
BOIKO PL.

BULGARIA

down Hristo Botev. Buses #85, 213, 305, and 313 head to the station from different points in town. Info booth and tickets for northern Bulgaria are on the ground floor. To: **Ruse** (5 per day, 8.40lv); **Vidin** (4 per day, 5.80lv); and **Varna** (6 per day, 11lv). Southern Bulgaria and international tickets in the basement.

Rila (Рила) sells has an office on the ground floor of the station as well as across from the post office on General Garko. To: **Blagoevgrad** (7 per day, 4.10lv); **Burgas** (7 per day, 8.50lv); and **Plovdiv** (19 per day, 3.50lv). International tickets sold daily 7am-11pm.

All-purpose ticket office (tel. 843 42 80), down the stairs in front of NDK, has info and international tickets. Prices are 20lv cheaper here. One per day to: **Athens** (53lv); **Budapest** (72lv); **Istanbul** (35lv). Open M-F 7am-3pm, Sa 7am-2pm.

Buses: Ovcha Kupel (Овча Купел), on Tsar Boris III bul. (Цар Борис III), reachable by trams #5 and 19 heading away from Vitosha. Private **international** and **domestic** buses leaving from the parking lot across from the train station are cheap and fast. Get tickets at the **Billetni Tsentur kiosks** (Биллетни Център) or on the buses. Pay in lv, US$, or DM. To: **Athens** (2 per day, US$26); **Budapest** (2 per day, 80lv); and **Istanbul** (1 per day, 47lv, students 30lv). Tickets are also available through private life:

Group Travel (tel. 320 122) has a kiosk in the large parking lot near the train station. Less confusing than the train station. To: **Burgas** (2 per day, 12.50lv); **Veliko Turnovo** (1 per day, 8lv); and **Varna** (5 per day, 13.50lv). Open daily 7am-5:30pm and 6-7:30pm.

Matpu (Матпу), ul. Damyan Gruev 23 (Дамян Груев; tel. 52 50 04 and 51 92 01). To: **Athens** (1 per day, 74lv, students 60lv) and **Istanbul** (6 per week, 50lv).

Local Transportation: Trams, trolleybuses, and buses are cheap. 0.25lv per ride; day pass 1lv; 5-day pass 4.40lv. Buy tickets at kiosks with signs saying билети (tickets; *bileti*) or from the driver; punch them in the machines on board between windows to avoid a 10lv fine. Officially runs 5am-1am, but scarce after 9pm.

Taxis: A green light in the front window means the taxi is available. **Softaxi** (tel. 12 84), **OK Taxi** (tel. 21 21), and **INEX** (tel. 919 19) are three reliable options. From the airport, don't pay more than US$10 to reach the center. Fares are 0.32-0.38lv per km (and rising with gas prices), 0.45lv per km after 10pm—when it's really wise to take a cab.

Car Rental: Hertz and **Europcar,** at the airport. US$49-91 per day; 22% value-added tax.

BULGARIA

ORIENTATION

Sofia sits at the center of the Balkan peninsula, 500km southeast of Belgrade. Good **maps** of the city are sold in most hotels and tourist agencies. The city's center, **pl. Sveta Nedelya** (пл. Света Неделя), is marked by the green roof of the Tsurkva Sv. Nedelya, the wide Sheraton Hotel, and Tsentralen Universalen Magazin (TSUM). **Bul. Knyaginya Maria Luiza** (Княгиня Мария Луиза) connects pl. Sveta Nedelya to the train station. Trams #1 and 7 run from the train station through pl. Sveta Nedelya to **bul. Vitosha** (Витоша), one of the main shopping and nightlife thoroughfares. This, in turn, links pl. Sveta Nedelya to **pl. Bulgaria** and the huge, concrete **Natsionalen Dvorets Kultura** (NDK; National Palace of Culture; Национален Дворец Култура). The monthly **Sofia City Guide** (free) is a good English publication with useful phone numbers, articles, and tourist information.

PRACTICAL INFORMATION

TOURIST & FINANCIAL SERVICES

Tourist Offices: Balkan Tour, Stamboliyski bul. 27 (tel. 88 06 55; fax 88 07 95). From pl. Sveta Nedelya, walk 3 blocks up Stamboliyski. Open daily 8am-7pm.

Budget Travel: Orbita Travel, Hristo Botev 48 (tel. 986 10 63; fax 988 58 14). From pl. Sveta Nedelya, walk up Stamboliyski and go left on Hristo Botev. Books discount rooms at Hotel Orbita; US$8. Open summer M-F 8:30am-7pm; off-season M-F 9am-5:30pm.

Embassies and Cultural Centers: Australians, Canadians, and **New Zealanders** should contact the British embassy. **South Africans** should contact their embassy in **Athens** (tel. (30 01) 680 66 45). **U.K.,** bul. (*not* ul.) Vasil Levski 38 (tel. 980 12 20 and 980 12 21), 3 blocks northwest of NDK. Open M-Th 8:30am-12:30pm and 1:30-5pm, F 8:30am-1pm. Consular, visa section open M-Th 9am-noon and 2-4pm, F 9am-noon. **U.S.,** ul. Suborna

1a (Съборна; tel. 980 52 41), 3 blocks from pl. Sv. Nedelya behind the Sheraton. Consular section at Kapitan Andreev 1 (Капитан Андреев; tel. 963 00 89). Register with the consular section upon arrival in Bulgaria. Open M-F 8:30am-5pm.

Currency Exchange: Bulbank (Булбанк), pl. Sv. Nedelya 7, cashes traveler's checks for a 0.2% commission and gives Visa cash advances for a 4% commission. Open M-F 8:30am-4pm, Sa 10am-1pm. **Commercial Bank Biohim,** Sv. Nedelya 19 (tel. 986 54 45, ext. 213), next to the Sheraton, cashes traveler's checks for a 1% commission and gives MC cash advances for a 6% commission. Open M-F 8:30am-3:30pm.

ATMs: Everywhere, including at Bulbank. **Purva Investitsionna Banka** (Първа Инвестиционна Банка), Stefan Karadzha 51 (Стефан Караджа), next to the telephone office, and General Gurko 6, near the post office. All accept Cirrus/MC/Visa.

American Express: Aksakov 5 (Аксаков; tel. 986 58 37). Holds mail, cashes checks for 3.5% commission, and books hotels. Open M-F 9am-6pm, Sa 9am-2:30.

LOCAL & EMERGENCY SERVICES

Luggage Storage: Downstairs at the central train station. Look for "гардероб" *(garderob)* signs. 0.50lv per piece. Open daily 5:30am-midnight.

English Bookstore: Knizharnitsa Arbat (Книжарница Арбат), Vitosha 9 (tel. 987 18 59). Open M-F 9:30am-7:30pm, Su 10am-6pm and Su 11am-5pm. **USIS American Center,** Vitosha 18 (tel. 980 48 85), has an American library. Open Tu-F 2-5pm.

24hr. Pharmacies: Purva Chastna Apteka (Първа Частна Аптека), Tsar Asen 42, near Neofit Rilski. **Apteka #7,** Sv. Nedelya 5, near Stamboliyski and Maria Luiza.

Medical Assistance: State-owned hospitals offer foreigners free emergency aid. **Pirogov Emergency Hospital,** Gen. Totleben bul. 21 (Ген. Тотлебен; tel. 515 31), across from Hotel Rodina. Take trolley #5 or 19 from the center. Open 24hr.

Post Office: Gen. Gurko 6 (Гурко). Walk down Suborna behind Sv. Nedelya, then turn right on Knyaz Batenberg, and left on Gurko. Main entrance to the right on Vasil Levsky. **Poste Restante** for 0.20lv. Open M-F 8am-8pm. **Postal code:** 1000.

Internet: ICN (tel. 91 66 22 13), in NDK. 5lv per hr. Open daily 9am-7pm. **Internet Center,** ul. Graf Ignatiev 6 (tel. 986 59 29). 1.80lv per hr. Open daily 9am-10pm.

Telephones: Ul. Stefan Karadzha 6 (Стефан Караджа), near the post office. 1min. to: Australia, Canada, or U.S. 2.40lv; U.K. 1.80lv; New Zealand 3.60lv. Use 5lv coins for local calls. Bulgarian phone cards also sold here. Open 24hr. **Phone code:** (0)2.

ACCOMMODATIONS

Hotels are rarely worth the exorbitant price—**private rooms** are often the best option. Camping is another inexpensive choice; **Camping Varna** (tel. 78 12 13) is 10km from the center on E-80, and **Cherniya Kos** (tel. 57 11 29) is 11km away on E-79. Check with Balkan Tour (see **Budget Travel,** p. 102) for both options.

CENTRAL SOFIA

Hotel Niky, Neofit Rilski 16 (tel. 51 19 15; fax 51 60 91), off Vitosha. Shared toilets, private showers, and satellite TVs. Billiard room, cafe, and garden restaurant with 24hr. room service. Check-out noon. Singles US$22; doubles US$40.

Hotel Tsar Asen (Цар Асен), Tsar Asen 68 (tel. 54 78 01 and 70 59 20). Walk toward the NDK on Tsar Asen, cross Patr. Evtimy, and continue 40m. Ring the doorbell at the gate. White walls and wood floors contain soft beds and thermostats for each room. Cable TV and private shower. 4 doubles (US$34) also serve as singles (US$28).

Hotel Orbita, James Baucher bul. 76 (Джеймс Баучер; tel. 639 39), on the hill. Take tram #9 south past NDK to Anton Ivanov, three stops after the tunnel (30min.). A fading two-star behemoth, even bigger than Stalin's ego. Adequate rooms with private bath. Singles US$25; doubles US$30. Orbita arranges student rooms for US$8 per person.

Hotel Baldjieva (Балдиева), Tsar Asen 23 (tel. 87 29 14). From Sv. Nedelya, walk toward the NDK; Tsar Arsen is on the right, parallel to Vitosha. Excellent location, removed from the hustle of the main streets. Bright, airy rooms with direct-dial phones, mini-bars, satellite TV, and baths. Breakfast included. Doubles US$50.

DRAGALEVTSI

To avoid the expensive and sometimes unpleasant hotels in central Sofia, you can stay in the suburb Dragalevtsi (Драгалевци), which offers many private, clean, and cheap hotels. Take tram #9 or 12 to the last stop, then pick up bus #64 down the stairs and to the left. Get off in the main square after five stops.

Hotel Darling (Дарлинг), Yabulkova Gradina 14 (tel. 67 19 86). From the main square, take a left on Yabulkova. Follow it past the playground and go left onto Angel Bukoreshtliev; the hotel is in the white house. Doubles with bath, TV, and terrace US$30-40.

Hotel Orhidea (Орхидея), Angel Bukoreshtliev 9 (Ангел Букорещлиев; tel. 67 27 39), next to Hotel Darling. Rooms with cable and bath. Singles US$20; doubles US$25.

FOOD

From fast food to Bulgarian specialties, inexpensive meals are easy to find in Sofia. 24hr. supermarkets line Vitosha. An **outdoor market,** the *zhenski pazar* (women's market; женски пазар), extends for several blocks. Take Knyaginya Maria Luiza from pl. Sveta Nedelya, then make a left on Ekzarh Yosif (Екзарх Иосиф).

RESTAURANTS

Kushtata (Къщата; House), Verila 4 (Верила; tel. 52 08 30). Off Vitosha near the NDK. The menu offers a wide range of "dishes with character," including *spaghetti mafiosa* (спагети мафиоса; 5.49lv). Entrees 3.70-15lv. Open daily noon-midnight.

Borsalino (Борсалино), Chervena Stena 10 (Червена Стена; tel. 66 71 53), behind Hotel Orbita. Take a taxi (2lv from central Sofia) at night. Neighborhood hangout with fireplace and outdoor area. Tasty Bulgarian dishes like *pulneni guby* (filled mushrooms; пулнени гъби; 3.59lv). Open 24hr. Takes US$ and DM.

Eddy's Tex-Mex Diner, Vitosha 4 (tel. 981 85 58). Mosey down the stairs and break through the saloon doors into one of Sofia's hippest eateries. Buffalo wings (4900lv), nachos (3.26lv), and fajitas (6.98lv) spice up the imaginative English menu. Entrees 4.50-9lv. A different band nightly at 9:30pm. Open daily 11:30am-12:30am.

Chinese Restaurant Chen, Rakovski 86 (tel. 986 33 71), across from the Opera House. Huge portions of real Chinese food. Entrees 2.60-7.80lv. Open daily noon-11pm.

Ramayana, Hristo Belchev 32 (Христо Белчев; tel. 980 43 11), near the intersection of William Gladstone. Sofia's first and only Indian restaurant. A/C to cool you down after the curry. The chef whips up *samosas* and lots of veggie specials. Entrees 3.70-10lv. 10% service fee. Open daily noon-3pm and 6-midnight.

CAFES

Luciano, ul. Moskovska 29 (Московска; tel. 981 97 77). At the corner of Rakovski and Moskovska, just up the street from the Opera House. The decor and live piano music top off desserts so lovely you're almost inclined not to eat them (2-4lv). Deserted non-smoking section. Open daily 10:30am-11pm. Visa.

Markrit (Маркрит), Stambolijski 37 (tel. 980 60 66). Excellent fresh pastries, fruit cakes, fruit salads, and ice cream. Another branch on Patriarch Evtimy, past the NDK. Coffee, cake, and a soda for 3-8lv. Open daily 9am-10pm.

SIGHTS

ST. ALEXANDER NEVSKY CATHEDRAL. (Sv. Aleksandr Nevsky; Св. Александър Невски). The gold-domed cathedral, erected 1904-1912 in memory of the 200,000 Russians who died in the 1877-78 Russo-Turkish War, was named after the patron saint of the tsar-liberator. During the first few years of post-1989 democracy, politicians of all creeds used the cathedral steps as a podium to speak to their supporters. In a separate entrance to the left of the main church, the **crypt** houses a spectacular array of painted icons and religious artifacts from the past 1000 years. *(In the center of pl. Alexander Nevsky. Trolleybus #1 or 2 to the corner of Shipka and bul. Vasil*

Levsky. Facing the Grand Hotel Sofia, turn right on Shipka; the cathedral is on the right. Cathedral open daily 7:30am-7pm; crypt open M and W-Su 10:30am-6:30pm. Cathedral 1.50lv, English tour 4.50lv; crypt 3lv, free with ISIC card.)

ARTISTS' MARKETS. In front of St. Alexander Nevsky Cathedral, you can find antiques, Soviet paraphernalia, and handmade crafts. On the other side of the square, the market continues with Bulgarian *babushki* offering handmade lace and embroidery. In the second market in the underpass between the Sheraton and TSUM, artists of varying talent display their works in a sea of kitsch.

CATHEDRAL OF ST. NEDELYA. (Katedralen Hram Sv. Nedelya; Катедрален Храм Св. Неделя). The focal point of pl. Sveta Nedelya and all of Sofia, the Cathedral of St. Nedelya is a reconstruction of the 14th-century original, which was destroyed by a bomb in a 1925 attempt on the life of Boris III. The Tsar escaped, but the cupola buried 190 generals and politicians. The current frescoes date from 1975. *(Tram #1, 2, or 7 to pl. Sveta Nedelya. Open daily 7am-6:30pm.)*

CHURCHES OF ST. NICHOLAS AND ST. SOFIA. Down Tsar Osvoboditel from sv. Nedelya, the 1913 Russian **Church of St. Nicholas** (Sv. Nikolai; Св. Николай), named for the miracle-maker, has five traditional Russian Orthodox-style onion domes. *(Trolleybus #9 to Moskovska. Backtrack down Rakovski and turn right on bul. Tsar Osvoboditel. Open Th-Su 9am-10pm.)* Sofia's other ancient church, the 6th-century **St. Sofia's** (Sv. Sofia; Св. София), stands on pl. Alexander Nevsky. The city adopted the saint's name in the 14th century. During the 19th century, while the church was used as Sofia's main mosque, a series of earthquakes repeatedly destroyed the minarets. The Ottoman rulers interpreted the catastrophes as a warning and gave up St. Sofia as their house of prayer. Amazingly, the 5th-century floor mosaic survived intact. In summer 1999, much of the church was under renovation. *(Trolleybus #1 or 2 to the corner of Shipka and bul. Vasil Levsky. Facing the Grand Hotel Sofia, turn right on Shipka; the cathedral is on the right. South wing open daily 7am-7pm. Donation requested.)*

BULGARIA

ST. GEORGE'S ROTUNDA. (Sv. Georgi; Св. Георги). The 4th-century St. George's, one of Sofia's two most venerable churches, is accompanied by a former Roman bath. St. George's itself is a brick structure covered in 11th- to 14th-century murals. After being converted from a bath to a church in the 5th century, it served as a house of worship under Bulgarians, Byzantines, and Turks, then as a museum, and now finally as a historical monument. *(Behind padlocked doors in the Sheraton on pl. Sveta Nedelya. Tram #1, 2, or 7 to pl. Sveta Nedelya. Open daily 10:30am-1pm and 2:30-5pm.)*

CHURCH OF ST. PETYA SAMARDZHIYSKA. (Tsurkva Hram Sv. Petya Samardzhiyska; Църква Храм Св. Петя Самарджийска). The tiny, 14th-century St. Petya's contains layers of frescoes stretching across the walls and ceiling. The crypt and ruins date to Thracian times. The bones of Vasil Levsky (see **History,** p. 94), Bulgaria's national hero, are rumored to have been found inside. A museum during communist times, St. Peter's is again an operating church. *(In the underpass between pl. Sv. Nedelya and TSUM. Tram #1, 2, or 7 to pl. Sveta Nedelya. Tel. 980 78 99. Open M-Sa 9:30am-6:30pm, Su 9:30am-2:30pm. 5lv, students 2.50lv.)*

CENTRAL SYNAGOGUE. (Tsentralen Sinagog; Централен Синагог). Sofia's only synagogue opened for services in 1909. The building's foundation was built with stones from Sofia's Jewish cemetery; its six towers, six domes, and 12 stars point toward Jerusalem. The interior is currently undergoing renovation to repair damage done by a stray Allied bomb from WWII, which, miraculously, did not explode. The ceilings are now a beautiful blue once again. A museum upstairs outlines the history of Jews in Bulgaria. *(Ekzarh Yosif 16. Tram #1, 2, 3, 4, or 7; get off at the corner of bul. Maria Luiza and Ekzarh Yosif. Open Tu-Sa 10am-4:30pm. Donations accepted.)*

BUL. TSAR OSVOBODITEL. The imposing sculptures at the main entrance to the **University of Sofia** represent Evolgi and Hristo Georgiev, funders of the University's construction between 1920 and 1931. Students hang around as late as the end of July, when candidates for admission visit the "wall of tears"—the spot where acceptance results are posted after a series of rigorous exams. *(Tsar Osvoboditel 15.*

Trolleybus #9 to Moskovska. Backtrack down Rakovski and turn right on bul. Tsar Osvoboditel. On the corner of Vasil Levski and bul. Tsar Osvoboditel.) Behind the University, the **Bulgarian Artists' Union** (Suyuz na Bulgarskite Hudozhnitsi; Съюз на Българските Художници) has a four-floor gallery. *(On Shipka (Шипка). Trolleybus #1 or 2 to the corner of Shipka and bul. Vasil Levsky. Tel. 433 51, ext. 214. Open M-Sa 10am-6pm. Free.)* As you stroll down bul. Tsar Osvoboditel, keep in mind that your boots are stepping on the first paved street in Sofia, weighted down on either end by the **House of Parliament** and the **Royal Palace.** The **National Assembly,** built in 1884 and finished with materials from Vienna, provides a backdrop for a dramatic equestrian statue of the tsar *osvoboditel* (liberator) himself. Russian Tsar Alexander II towers astride his charger over the pl. Narodno Subranie (Народно Събрание), with the Declaration of the War of Liberation (the Russo-Turkish War of 1877-78) in hand. Continuing up Osvoboditel, a left on Rakovski leads to the columns of the **National Opera House,** built in 1950 to seat 1270. *(Rakovski 59; main entrance at Vrabcha 1 (Врабча). Trolleybus #9 to Moskovska. Backtrack down Rakovski. Tel. 87 13 66. Open M 9am-6pm, Tu 8:30am-7:30pm, Sa 9am-6pm. Tickets 1-15lv.)* Rakovski is Bulgaria's theater hub, with half a dozen theaters in a 1km stretch. The Neoclassical **Ivan Vazov National Theatre,** Levski 5, was built in 1907, burned down in 1923, and was restored in 1927. Many theaters shut down in summer (see **Entertainment,** below).

NATIONAL PALACE OF CULTURE. (NDK; Natsionalen Dvorets Kultura; Национален Дворец Култура). Opened in 1981 to celebrate the 13th centennial of Bulgaria, the monstrous National Palace of Culture is a barracks of culture, with restaurants, theaters, and movie halls, including the country's best cinema, which shows subtitled American films. Buy tickets (2lv) from the ticket office (биллетни център) down the outside ramp and to the left of the main entrance. Ask here about tickets for plays and concerts. *(In Yuzhen Park. From pl. Sveta Nedelya, walk down bul. Vitosha to bul. Patriarch Evtimy and enter the park. The Palace is at its far end.)*

BULGARIA

MUSEUMS

National Art Gallery (Natsionalna Hudozhestvena Galeriya; Национална Художествена Галериа). Also in the Royal Palace. Trolleybus #9 to Moskovska. Possibly the best art museum in Bulgaria. Open Tu-Su 10am-6pm. 3lv, students free; Su free.

National Museum of History (Natsionalen Istoricheski Muzey; Национален Исторически Музей), Vitosha 2 (tel. 980 22 58), off pl. Sv. Nedelya. The exhibit starts all the way back in 200,000 BC, then moves from Thracian treasures to medieval war glory. The exhibits end around 1900, not covering the tragedies that have befallen the nation since. Open M-F May-Sept. 9:30am-7:15pm; Oct.-Apr. 9:30am-4:30pm; box office closes 45min. before museum. 5lv, students 2.50lv; foreign-language tour 7.50lv.

Museum of Archaeology (Arheologicheski Muzey; Археологически), Suborna 2. Tram #1, 2, or 7 to pl. Sveta Nedelya. Houses items from Thracian, Greek, Roman, and Turkish settlements from 2000 years ago. Open Tu-Su 10am-6pm. Donations requested.

National Museum of Ethnography (Natsionalen Etnograficheski Muzey; Национален Етнографически), in the Royal Palace on pl. Knyaz Batenberg. Trolleybus #9 to Moskovska. Founded after the 1878 liberation (see **History,** p. 94), the museum covers the past 400 years. Open M and W-Su 10am-6pm. 3lv, students 1.50lv.

ENTERTAINMENT

The **opera** and **theater** seasons run from September to June; good seats are less than US$1. (Tel. 87 70 11. Box office open daily 9:30am-7pm. No performances Monday.) You can get tickets for the **Ivan Vazov National Theater** at Rakovski 98 (tel. 07 23 03). Cinemas often show subtitled **Hollywood films**—try Vitosha 62 and pl. Vasil Levski 1.

BARS & CLUBS

While nightlife in Sofia does not consume the entire city as in Plovdiv or Varna, the scene is getting wilder every year. Smartly dressed Sofians roam the main streets, filling up the outdoor bars along **Vitosha bul.** and the cafes around the NDK. Most nightlife centers around bul. Vitosha or, for the younger set, the University of Sofia at the intersection of **Vasil Levski** and **Tsar Osvoboditel.** Young people often meet at **Popa,** the irreverent nickname for Patriarh Evtimy's monument, where Patriarh Evtimy meets the intersection of Vasil Levski and **Graf Ignatiev** (Граф Игнатиев). When out on the town, be careful: the thick-necked mafia often runs the show.

Mr. Punch, 20 Stefan Karadzha, near the post office. This club extraordinaire includes several bars with themes ranging from prehistoric jungle to country-and-western. Pick up a swipe card at the door, use it at the bars downstairs, then pay when you leave. Beer 0.85lv; mixed drinks 3.50lv. Open daily noon-3pm and 6pm-late.

Frankie's Jazz Club/Piano Bar, Kurnigradska 15 (Кърниградска), right off Vitosha across from the American Center. Bulgaria's best jazz musicians play here Sept.-May, but it's just another bar in summer. Drinks 2.50lv. Cover 0.50lv. Open daily 10am-12:30am.

Yalta (Ялта; tel. 981 01 43), on the corner of Tsar Osvoboditel and Vasil Levski. *The* pilgrimage site for Sofia's disco-believers, who flock here religiously every weekend. Cover 1lv. Open daily 11pm-4am.

Biraria Luciano (Бирария Лучано), Slaveykov 9 (Славеков; tel. 980 30 50). From Vitosha heading to NDK, take a left on Alabin (Алабин), then veer right onto Graf Ignatiev. When you reach pl. Slaveykov (with McDonald's), take a left into the courtyard; the pub is in the far right-hand corner. Lively pub with international beers. Open daily noon-11pm.

Biblioteka (Библиотека), in Sts. Cyril and Methodius Library. Enter from Oborishte. Disco, bar, internet cafes, and all the 80s rock you want. Cover 3lv. Open W-Sa 11pm-5am.

Spartakus (Спартакус), in the underpass past the pl. Narodno Subranie, leading toward Vasil Levski. Keeps its gay and straight clientele happy with thumping techno. It's exclusive, though—unless you know a member, you may be out of luck. Open daily 11pm-late.

SOUTHERN MOUNTAINS

The Rila, Pirin, and Rodopi mountain ranges hid Bulgaria's cultural and political dissidents during the 500-year Turkish rule, from the manuscripts copied at Rila Monastery to the haiduk bandits that struck from the highlands. Today, a visitor will find endless attractions: hiking near Bansko, sampling vintages in Melnik, and tracing Bulgarian civilization back through the Roman ruins at Plovdiv.

PLOVDIV (ПЛОВДИВ)

Although second in size to Sofia, Plovdiv (pop. 345,000) is widely hailed as the cultural capital of Bulgaria. Founded around 600 BC as Philipopolis (for Philip II of Macedonia), the city now draws many to its trade fairs and arts festivals. A 10min. stroll through the center invariably winds thr ough its history; the cobblestoned Stari Grad—overhung with lush oaks, church crosses, and 19th-century National Revival houses—gives way to the concrete Soviet highrises and finally turning into pedestrian thoroughfares teeming with small vendors and Western ads.

ORIENTATION

With no clearly defined center and poorly-marked streets, Plovdiv is difficult to navigate; basic knowledge of the main streets and an up-to-date map are essential. Many street names have changed; most maps are updated, and streets are known by their new names. Street vendors sell good Cyrillic **maps** for 2lv. The east-west thoroughfare **bul. Hristo Botev** (Христо Ботев) marks the southern end of town, from which **bul. Ruski** (Руски) and **bul. Tsar Boris III Obedinitel** (Цар Борис III Обединител) run to the **Maritsa River** (Марица) at the northern end of **Stari Grad** (Old Town; Стари Град). In the middle of town, bul. Tsar Boris III Obedinitel runs along the east side of **pl. Tsentralen** (пл. Централен). From the northwest corner of pl. Tsentralen, **Knyaz Aleksandr** (Княз Александр), the main commercial street, runs north to **pl. Dzhumaya** (Джумая), where **bul. Suborna** (Съборна) rises to the east.

PRACTICAL INFORMATION

Trains: The **train station** is at the corner of bul. Ruski and bul. Hristo Botev. To get from the train station to pl. Tsentralen, take bus #2, 20, or 26 (buy 0.20lv tickets on the bus), or walk across bul. Hristo Botev via the underpass and take **Ivan Vazov** (Иван Вазов) to the square. To **Sofia** (2½hr., 21 per day, 3.45lv). Most trains from Sofia to **Istanbul** or **Burgas** stop in Plovdiv, and good local connections are available. Only **Rila,** bul. Hristo Botev 31a (tel. 44 61 20), sells international tickets. Open M-F 8am-7pm, Sa 8am-4pm.

Buses: Matpu (Матпу; tel./fax 63 24 42), in the underpass below bul. Tsar Boris III Obedinitel next to Hotel Trimondium (Тримондиум). Deals with all Balkan connections. To: **Istanbul** (US$20); **Athens** (US$41, under 26 US$35); and **Thessaloniki** (US$21). The buses to Greece on Wednesday and Friday connect with ferries to Italy. Open daily 8am-7pm. In addition, three separate stations serve the areas indicated by their names:

Yug (South; Юг; tel. 62 69 37), bul. Hristo Botev 45, on the other side of the street from the train station. Buses **south** and to **Sofia** (1hr., hourly, 5lv). **Traffic Express** (Трафик Экспрес), in the station (tel. 26 57 87; fax 26 51 51), services the Black Sea coast.

Rodopi (Родопи; tel. 77 76 07), for the **Rodopi Mountains,** is behind the train station and can be reached by going through the underpasses beneath the trains.

Sever (North; Север; tel. 55 37 05), north of bul. Bulgaria on Dimitur Stambolov (Димитър Стамболов) at its intersection with Pobeda (Победа). Ruski becomes Pobeda when it crosses the river. Take bus #2 from pl. Tsentralen. Sends buses **north.**

Tourist Office: Puldin Tours (Пълдин), bul. Bulgaria 106 (tel. 55 38 48), speaks English, French, and German, arranges tours of Plovdiv and the Valley of the Roses, exchanges money, and sells festival tickets. They will also find private rooms throughout Bulgaria (see **Accommodations,** below). From the train station, ride tram #2 or 102 (0.20lv) 9 stops to bul. Bulgaria and backtrack one block to the left. By foot, cross the river via bul. Tsar Boris III Obedinitel, pass Hotel Maritsa, and look for Puldin immediately after turning left on bul. Bulgaria (20min. walk). Open M-F 9am-5:30pm, until 9pm during trade fairs.

Currency Exchange: Bulbank (Булбанк), 5 Patriarch Evtimy (Патриарх Евтимий; tel. 26 02 70), off Knyaz Aleksandr in front of the large fountain. Cashes traveler's checks for US$1 per transaction. Open M-Th 9am-4:30pm, F 9am-1pm.

ATM: MC/Cirrus ATM in front of the Bulbank entrance. MC/Cirrus/AmEx ATM in the post office on pl. Tsentralen, when it works.

Luggage Storage: In the train station. Open daily 7am-6:20pm and 6:50pm-6:30am.

Police: Tel. 160.

24hr. Pharmacy: Apteka #47 The Tunnel (Аптека 47 Тунела), bul. Tsar Boris III Obedinitel 64 (tel. 27 07 93). From pl. Tsentralen, follow bul. Tsar Boris III through the tunnel; the pharmacy is on the left. Also on Knyaz Aleksandr.

Post Office: Pl. Tsentralen. **Poste Restante** in the room to the left of the west entrance. Open M-Sa 7am-7pm, Su 7-11am. **Postal code:** 4000.

Internet access: Game Zone, across from McDonald's at the corner of Knyaz Aleksandr and Patriarch Evtimy, on the third floor. 1.60lv per hr. Open daily 10am-midnight.

Telephones: In the post office. Direct international calling (to the U.K. 1.80lv per min., U.S. 2.40lv per min.). Open daily 6am-11pm. Send or receive **faxes** (fax 493 00 44) at unreliable prices. Fax open daily 8am-8pm. **Phone code:** (0)32.

ACCOMMODATIONS

Prices can triple during trade fairs during the first weeks of May and the end of September; at these times, stay in a **private room. Puldin Tours** (see above) arranges singles (US$13), doubles (US$16), and one-bedroom apartments (US$20). **Bureau Esperansa** (Буро Есперанса), Ivan Vazov 76 (English tel. 22 51 27), specializes in rooms downtown. (US$8-12 per person. Open daily 8:30am-7pm.) **Prima Vista Agency** (Прима Виста), Ivan Vazov 76 (tel. 27 27 78; fax 27 20 54), inside the red door, also finds private rooms. (Singles US$10; doubles US$16. Open daily 10am-6pm.)

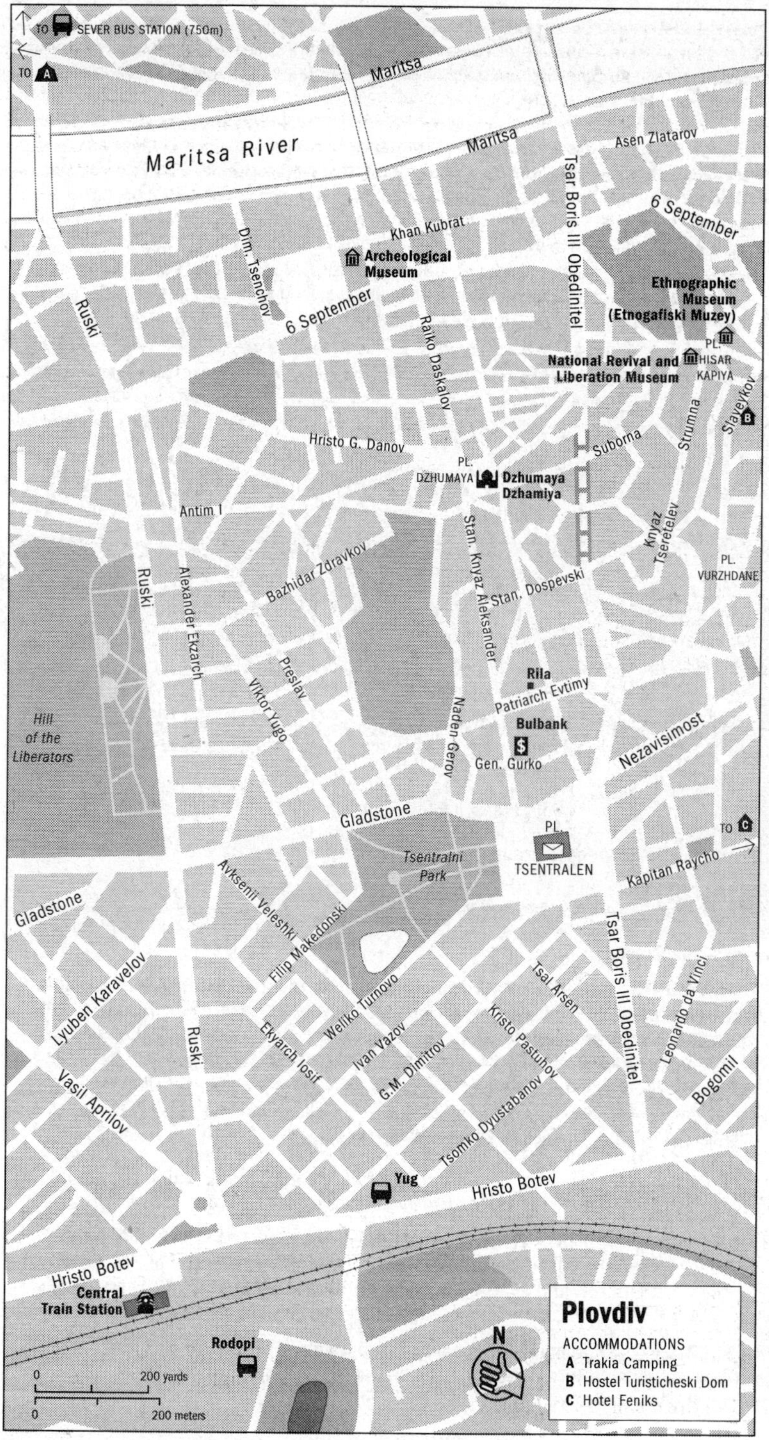
TO SEVER BUS STATION (750m)
TO A
Maritsa
Maritsa River
Maritsa
Asen Zlatarov
Tsar Boris III Obedinitel
6 September
Khan Kubrat
Dim. Tsenchov
Archeological Museum
Ethnographic Museum (Etnogafiski Muzey)
Ruski
6 September
Raiko Daskalov
PL. HISAR KAPIYA
National Revival and Liberation Museum
Slaveykov
Strumna
Hristo G. Danov
Suborna
PL. DZHUMAYA
Dzhumaya Dzhamiya
Antim I
Knyaz Tseretelev
Bazhidar Zdravkov
Stan. Knyaz Aleksander
PL. VURZHDANE
Stan. Dospevski
Ruski
Alexander Ekzarch
Preslav
Viktor Yugo
Rila
Patriarch Evtimy
Hill of the Liberators
Naden Gerov
Bulbank
Gen. Gurko
Nezavisimost
Gladstone
PL. TSENTRALEN
TO C
Tsentralni Park
Kapitan Raycho
Avkseni Veleshki
Gladstone
Filip Makedonski
Tsar Boris III Obedinitel
Lyuben Karavelov
Tsal Arsen
Leonardo da Vinci
Welko Turnovo
Kristo Pastuhov
Ruski
Ekyarch Iosif
Ivan Vazov
G.M. Dimitrov
Bogomil
Vasil Aprilov
Tsomko Dyustabanov
Yug
Hristo Botev
Hristo Botev
Central Train Station
Rodopi
N
0 200 yards
0 200 meters
Plovdiv
ACCOMMODATIONS
A Trakia Camping
B Hostel Turisticheski Dom
C Hotel Feniks

Hostel Turisticheski Dom (Туристически Дом), P.R. Slaveykov 5 (П.Р. Славейков; tel. 63 32 11), in Stari Grad. From Knyaz Aleksandr, take Patriarch Evtimy (across from McDonald's) into Stari Grad, passing under bul. Tsar Boris III Obedinitel. Take a left on Slaveykov at pl. Vuzrazhdane (Възраждане), past the fruit market. Spacious but poorly lit 1-, 2-, or 5-bed dorm rooms with sinks and shared bath in one of Plovdiv's National Revival buildings. Cafe and restaurant downstairs. Lockout 11pm. 22lv per person.

Hotel Feniks (Феникс), Kapitan Raycho 79 (Капитан Райчо; tel. 22 47 29). From pl. Tsentralen, cross bul. Tsar Boris III Obedinitel to Kapitan Raycho. After 10min., the hotel appears on the left. Reception on the 3rd floor. Nondescript rooms with shared bath and TV. Laundry available. Some English spoken. Singles US$15; doubles US$20.

Trakia Camping (Тракия Къмпинг; tel. 088 80 39 50). Take bus #222 from the train station or buses #4 or 44 from bul. Tsar Boris III Obedinitel opposite pl. Tsentralen. Go to the last stop and continue walking along highway E-80 (.5 km). 2-room bungalows are located in a woodsy—if remote—retreat from the busy city. Rooms are spacious but bare, with a toilet, shower, and (sigh) comfortable beds. 25lv per person.

FOOD

Plovdiv offers a wide array of inexpensive Bulgarian restaurants, although cafes are the cheapest option. On the way to the Hostel Turisticheski Dom, the *ponedelnik pazar* (Monday market; Понеделник Пазар) in pl. Vuzrazhdane sells fruit and veggies for 1.50-2.50lv per kilo; get there early in the day for the freshest produce.

Kambanata (Камбаната), Suborna 2B (tel. 62 06 03), up Suborna from pl. Dzhumaya. Largest veggie selection in town. Entrees 2-8lv. Open daily 10:30am-midnight.

The Grill (Грил), bul. Tsar Boris III Obedinitel 8 (tel. 62 17 18). A popular Syrian restaurant specializing in roast chicken. Entrees 2-5lv. Open daily 8am-2am.

Restaurant Gremi (Греми) ul. Parchevich 1 (Парчевич; tel. 23 30 65). Boasts a wide range of surprisingly edible Bulgarian dishes. Entrees 4-6lv.

Union Club (Юниън Клуб), Mitropolit Paisy 6 (tel. 27 05 51). Take Suborna from pl. Dzhumaya, then make a sharp right where the street branches in front of the church; head up the steps through a forboding wooden gate on the right. Features a high-walled garden where you can enjoy your brains-in-butter hors d'oeuvres. Also serves omelettes and chicken. Entrees 1.50-6lv. Open daily 11am until the last customer leaves.

SIGHTS

Most of Plovdiv's historical and cultural treasures are concentrated among Stari Grad's **Trimondium,** or three hills.

ROMAN RUINS. Reminiscent of Rome's Coliseum, the 2nd-century Roman **amphitheater** (Antichen Theater; Античен Театр) is Plovdiv's treasure (see **History,** p. 93). It currently serves as a popular venue for concerts and shows, hosting the **Festival of the Arts** in the summer and early fall (contact **Puldin Tours** for details; see p. 17) and the annual **Opera Festival** in June. *(Take a right off Knyaz Aleksandr to Stanislav Dospevski (Станислав Доспевски) after the pink art gallery, and turn right at the end of the street. Take the steep stairs to your left.)* **Philipopolis Stadium** is a less well-preserved theater where modern-day graffiti mingles with ancient architecture. The gladiator's entrance is still intact, and locals claim that lion bones were found inside when the stadium was unearthed. *(Follow Knyaz Aleksandr to the end; the stadium is underneath pl. Dzhumaya.)*

CHURCH OF ST. CONSTANTINE AND ELENA. The oldest Orthodox church in Plovdiv, dating from the 4th-century, it was renovated in 1832 to resemble a monastery, complete with murals and icons by Bulgarian artist Zahari Zograf (see **Literature and Arts,** p. 95). *(On Suborna, before the Museum of Ethnography. Open daily 8am-6:30pm. Free.)*

MUSEUMS. The **Museum of Ethnography** (Etnografski Muzey; Етнографски Музей) displays many artifacts from Bulgaria's past, including clothes, musical instruments, and tools. *(At the end of Suborna. Tel. 62 56 54. Open Tu-Su 9am-noon and 2-5pm. 3lv,* *students 0.20lv. Some signs in English.)* Each room in the **National Revival and National Liberation Museum** details a different stage in Bulgarian history through the 1800s. *(Tsanko Lavrenov 1 (Цанко Лавренов). Make a right at the end of Suborna and head through the Turkish Gate. Tel. 22 59 23. Open M-Sa 8:45am-noon and 2-5pm. 2lv, students 1lv. English brochure available.)* Gain insight into 19th- and 20th-century Bulgaria through the eyes of Plovdiv artists at **State Art Gallery** (Durzhavna Hudozhestvena Galeria; Държавна Художествена Галерия). Signs in English walk you through the extensive collection. In addition to its permanent collection at Suborna 14a, the gallery holds temporary exhibits of contemporary graphics, sculptures, and watercolors at its Knyaz Aleksandr 15 location. *(From pl. Dzhumaya turn right on Suborna and continue to the end. Tel. 26 37 90. Open Tu-Su 9-11am and 1-5pm. 2lv, students 0.30lv.)*

OTHER SIGHTS. Enjoy the beautifully patterned mosaic walls of pl. Dzhumaya's namesake, **Dzhumaya Mosque** (Dzhumaya Dzhamiya; джамия). *(Go past pl. Dzhumaya and turn right to reach the main entrance. Services daily at 6pm.)* If you grow tired of museums and relics, wander down the little **Strumna** (Стръмна) alley and watch the few remaining Plovdiv artisans pound and polish metal in the footsteps of their ancestors. The **park** in the west side of town, near the stadium, provides a welcome break from the cobblestone streets and touristed antiquity. **Swimming pools** in the park are yet another alternative, as is fishing in Bulgaria's biggest man-made **rowing canal.** On a cool evening, head to the fountainside cafe in **Tsentralni Park** (Централни Парк), near pl. Tsentralen, where strobe lights illuminate the spring. Finally, one of the **movie theaters** on Knyaz Aleksandr is bound to be showing a film in English.

NEAR PLOVDIV: BACHKOVO MONASTERY

Twenty-eight kilometers south of Plovdiv, nestled among plush green mountain slopes, is Bulgaria's second-largest monastery, Bachkovo Monastery (Bachkovski Manastir; Бачковски Манастир). Built in 1083 by Georgian brothers Grigory and Abazy Bakuriani and mostly destroyed by the Turks in the early 14th century, it was rebuilt a century later. An oasis of Bulgarian culture, history, and literature during the 500-year Turkish rule, Bachkovo today draws crowds to its phenomenal artwork. The main church is home to the **icon of the Virgin Mary and Child** (ikona Sveta Bogoroditsa; икона Света Богородица), which is said to have miraculous healing power. (Open daily 7am-dark.) The southern courtyard's **Chapel of Saint Nikola** (Hram Sveti Nikola; Храм Свети Никола) is blessed with the work of famed National Revival artist **Zahari Zograf** (see **Literature & Arts,** p. 95), and cursed with the work of some modern fans who have made their marks on the outside murals. Look carefully inside for Zograf's life-sized self-portrait. Along either of the roads leading uphill from the monastery, there are other small shrines and paths that make for great day-hiking, with picnic areas and the most gorgeous mountain vistas in Bulgaria. Below, shops and cafes flank the road leading to the monastery. If you're willing to splurge, you can eat at the **Vodapada** (waterfall; Водапада) restaurant (tel. from Plovdiv (9) 93 23 89), named for the cascade alongside its patio. It sits at the bottom of the road. (Entrees 4-10lv. Open 10am-11pm.)

GETTING THERE. Take a **train** from **Plovdiv** to **Asenovgrad** (25min., hourly, 0.80lv). Once there, catch a bus to the monastery (10min., 0.30lv). **Buses** to **Smolyan** from **Plovdiv's Rodopi bus station** (see **Plovdiv: Buses,** p. 108) also get you there (55min., 11 per day, 1lv). Get off at the second stop, after the two tunnels.

RILA MONASTERY

Holy Ivan of Rila built Rila Monastery (Rilski Manastir; Рилски Манастир) in the 10th century as a refuge from the lascivious outer world. The monastery sheltered the arts of icon painting and manuscript copying during the Byzantine and Ottoman occupations, and remained an oasis of Bulgarian culture during five of the nation's dark centuries. For the modern visitor, the Monastery, perched atop luscious Rila Mountain, offers sanctuary from crowded buses and dirty cities.

ORIENTATION & PRACTICAL INFORMATION. To get to Rila Town, first take a **bus** from **Sofia's Novotel Europa** to **Blagoevgrad** (2hr., 8-10 per day, 0.12lv), then from Blagoevgrad to Rila Town (45min., hourly, 1lv), and then catch the bus up to the monastery (45min., 4 per day, 1lv). Watch for schedules in both Rila and Blagoevgrad, but don't trust them; ask the ticket office for the correct time. On the way back, three buses leave each day from the monastery for Rila Town (9am, 2pm, and 5pm), where there are other connections back to Sofia and Blagoevgrad. **Balkantourist** arranges guided **tours** in English to the monastery (US$30 per person). There are **no currency exchanges** nearby. There is a single **telephone** behind the post office. (0.22lv per min. to Sofia; 0.36lv per min. to U.S.) Buy a phone card at Restaurant Rila (see below). **Phone code:** (0)7054.

ACCOMMODATIONS & FOOD. The three-star **Hotel Rilets** (Рилец; tel. 21 06), a 20min. walk from from the monastery (follow the signs across the river and then turn right), has clean singles with balconies and bath (hot water 8-11am and 5pm-midnight) for US$15 per person. (MC/Visa.) Inquire at room 170 in the monastery (tel. 22 08) about staying in a heated **monastery cell** (27.50lv per person), but be prepared for bare rooms, cold water, and no shower. (Reception daily 9am-noon and 2-4pm; 6-9pm in room 74. Curfew midnight.) At **Restaurant Rila** (tel. 22 90), behind the monastery, you can sit outside over the beautiful forest and rushing creek. The black-tied waitstaff will bring you anything you want, provided it's Bulgarian. (Entrees 1-9lv. 8% service fee. Open daily 7:30am-11:30pm.)

SIGHTS & HIKING. Today's monastery was built between 1834 and 1837; only a brick tower remains from the 14th-century structure. The monastery's vibrant **murals** were created by brothers Dimitar and Zahari Zograf—"Zograf" actually means "one who paints murals"—famous for their work at the Troyan and Bachkovo monasteries (see **Literature & Arts,** p. 95; **Near Plovdiv: Bachkovo Monastery,** p. 111). The 1200 **frescoes** on the central **chapel** form a brilliantly colored outdoor art gallery. Inside you can find the grave of Bulgaria's last tsar, Boris III. (Cameras and shorts not permitted.) The monastery **museum** displays religious objects, weapons, jewelry, and embroidery. The exhibit includes a wooden cross that took 12 years to carve and left its master, the monk Rafail, without his eyesight. (Open daily 8:30am-4:30pm. 5lv, students 3lv; sporadic English tours 15lv.)

Maps and suggested **hiking** routes through **Rila National Park** are on signs outside the monastery, or look in the **Manastirski Padarutsi** (Манастирски Падаръци) alcove, just outside the monastery's back entry, for a Cyrillic map of all the paths (8lv). Hiking trails in Bulgaria are marked by colored lines over a white background painted on rocks, trees, or anything else that won't walk away. Leave plenty of time to hike; these are some of the best hikes in the country. Incredible views—particularly at **Seventh Lake** (Sedemte Ezera; Седемте Езера) or from **Malyovitsa** (Мальовица)—and welcoming huts *(hizhi)* await. Follow the **yellow markings** to the Seventh Lake Hut (Hizha Sedemte Ezera; Хижа Седемте Езера; 6hr.). The **blue** trail leads to **Hizha Malyovitsa** (Мальовица; 7hr.). **Red** leads to the highest hut in the Balkans: **Ivan Vazov** (Иван Вазов; 6hr.). Expect to pay around US$2 for a spot (not necessarily a bed) to sleep. For more on hiking, see **Camping & the Outdoors,** p. 38.

BLAGOEVGRAD (БЛАГОЕВГРАД)

The epitome of Stalinist urban planning in Bulgaria, much of Blagoevgrad (blah-GOY-ehv-grahd) came into being in the 1950s, making for big, open pedestrian squares and orderly streets. The city is the transportation hub of Southwest Bulgaria, but its many parks and a vibrant cafe culture provide plenty to do if you're staying longer than it takes to get from one bus to another. The local American University of Bulgaria enlivens the downtown, one of the few in Bulgaria where Americans are not an anomaly. **Bulbank** (Булбанк), Shishman 22 (Шишман; tel. 813 32), cashes traveler's checks into *leva* for a 2% commission or into US$ for a 1.4% commission. They also give MC/Visa cash advances for a 4% commission. A Visa/MC/Cirrus/Plus **ATM** stands outside. (Open M-F 8:45am-4pm.) Spend your freshly

BULGARIA

changed money emailing home; **Internet Cafe Asta Le Vista** (tel. 583 66) is downstairs in the university. (Open 24hr. 3lv per hr.) **Alphatour** (Алфатур), Krali Marko 4 (Крали Марко; tel. 235 98), arranges private rooms for 8lv per person. (Open M-F 8am-6pm, Sa 9am-2pm.) Otherwise, stop by **Dom Narodni Armi** (Дом Народни Арми), Ivan Vazov 7 (Иван Вазов; tel. 223 87), in the Voennen Klub (Военнен Клуб), where you'll find comfortable beds, shared showers, and a less-than-thrilling toilet. (20lv per person). Fresh food (and other curiosities) can be found at the **Kooperativen Pazar** (Кооперативен Пазар), a market across the river. (Open daily dawn-dusk.) Otherwise, the restaurants and cafes on **Todor Aleksandrov** serve standard Bulgarian fare (1-4lv). At night, Anglophone students crawl out to the many cafes and bars on the squares, like **Rock House** on the south side of pl. Bulgaria. **Postal code:** 2700. **Phone code:** (0)73121.

GETTING AWAY. Blagoevgrad's **bus** and **train stations** are 50m from each other on the southwest end of town along **Sv. Dimitur Solunski** (Св. Димитър Солунски) at the end of **Sv. Kiril i Metody** (Св. Кирил и Методий). **Trains** head to **Sofia** (2hr., 6 per day, 2.94lv). **Buses** depart from the *avtogara* (автогара) to: **Sofia** (2hr., hourly, 3lv); **Melnik** (3hr., 1 per day, 2.50lv); **Rila** (50min., 4 per day, 1lv); and **Bansko** (3hr., 6 per day, 1.80lv). To get to the center from the stations, take any bus up Sv. Kiril i Metody from the bus stop across the street from the train station. Three or four stops later is the **American University of Bulgaria** (AUB), a huge building that used to be the Communist Party regional headquarters. For info, bus tickets, old **maps** (0.20lv), and private rooms (12-15lv per person), head to the **tourist office** connected to Hotel Alen Mak, Sv. Kiril i Metody 1 (tel. 232 18 and 230 31).

BANSKO (БАНСКО)

BULGARIA

At the base of the Pirin mountains, Bansko is a gateway to 180 lakes and 100 steep peaks scattered across a sea of forget-me-nots and alpine poppies. The highest peak, Vihren, reaches 2914m. The mountain range around Bansko offers hiking and skiing, while preserved stone houses and taverns line cobblestone streets below.

ORIENTATION & PRACTICAL INFORMATION

Take a **bus** from **Sofia's Ovcha Kupel station** (3½hr., 4 per day, 2800lv) or **Blagoevgrad** (1½hr., 6 per day, 1.80lv). From Bansko's **bus station** (автогара), exit the parking lot and turn left on Patriarch Evtimy (Патриарх Евтимий). Take a right at the tiny pl. Makedonia (Македония) and then veer left on **Todor Aleksandrov** (Тодор Александров), which leads to **pl. Vaptsarov** (Вапцаров). Continue on ul. Pirin (Пирин) to the second square, **pl. Vuzrazhdane** (Възраждане). You can get a **map** from a newsstand on pl. Vaptsarov (2.50lv) or from the **Tourist Information Center** (Туристически Информационен Център), to the right as you enter pl. Vaptsarov. The helpful, English-speaking staff also has bus times. (Open M-Sa 9am-noon and 1-7pm, Su 10am-noon and 2-6pm.) Near the tourist office, **Bulgarian Post Bank,** Hristo Botev 1 (Христо Ботев; tel. 21 86) exchanges currency and gives Visa advances for a 4% commission. (Open M-F 8am-noon and 1-4:30pm.) A **pharmacy** is at 57 Tsar Simeon (tel. 23 43), near the Todor Aleksandrov intersection. (Open M-F 7:30am-7:30pm, Sa-Su 8am-1pm and 2:30-7:30pm.) The **post office,** Tsar Simeon 69, has **telephones.** (Open M-F 7:30am-noon and 1-6pm.) **Postal code:** 2770. **Phone code:** (0)7443.

ACCOMMODATIONS & FOOD

Private rooms can be arranged informally with locals (US$2-5 per person), but finding cheap accommodations is not a problem. Case in point: **Hotel Mir** (Мир), Neofit Rilski 28 (Неофит Рилски; tel. 25 00 and 21 60), offers spacious rooms, spotless bathrooms, 24hr. hot water, and cable TV. From the center, take a left on Tsar Simeon and turn right on ul. Bulgaria. Continue straight and turn left on Rilski just after the playground. (Singles US$10; doubles US$15-24 per person; prices higher in off-season.) **Matsureva Kushta** (Мацурева Къща), Velyaian Ognev 7a (Веляиан

Огнев; tel. 28 14), is another excellent hotel, with five sparkling rooms, hot water, private bathrooms, and cable TV. (US$8-12 per person; US$2 more in off-season.)

With a **mehana** (tavern; механа) hiding in almost every house or courtyard, you'll never be at a loss for a meal in Bansko. **Dudo Pene** (Дъдо Пене), Aleksandr Buynov 1 (Александър Буйнов), is a rugged eatery; they grow many of their own vegetables and even have their own slaughterhouse. Live folk music pipes up after 7:30pm on weekends. (Entrees 2.20-15lv. Open daily 9am-late.) **Sireshtova Kushta** (Сирещова Къща), Yane Sandanski 12 (Яне Сандански), is in a traditional house built in 1750. The typical Bulgarian food is a bargain. (Entrees 2.60-5.70lv. Open M-Tu 6pm-midnight, W-Su noon-midnight. Live folk music weekends.)

SIGHTS

Although recent surges in tourism are pushing the town toward modernity, the 20th century has yet to destroy Bansko's traditional way of life. It's not uncommon for a car to be forced to one side by a donkey pulling a cart of hay. Well-kept museums and century-old houses make Bansko a living homage to the National Revival.

HOLY TRINITY CHURCH. (Tsurkva Sveta Troitsa; Църква Света Троица). Bulgaria's second-oldest church, the 1835 Holy Trinity is actually a product of Turkish rulers, who restricted Bulgarian Orthodox Churches to small buildings on the outskirts of town. In the early 19th century, the story goes, several of Bansko's resilient faithful hid an Orthodox icon under pl. Vuzrazhdane. Shortly thereafter, the local Turkish governor dreamt about this icon, and when the people showed him it was actually there, they convinced him it was a sign from God that an Orthodox Church should be built on the spot. When finished, the church towered above the 5m-high fence built to conceal. The villagers then worked out a deal with the Turkish officer to add an Islamic crescent to the cross on the church door, making the building a symbol of both faiths. The building later served as a shelter during attacks on the city. *(On pl. Vuzrazhdane, at the corner of Neofit Rilski. Open daily 7:30am-noon and 1-6pm.)*

NIKOLA VAPTSAROV HOUSE-MUSEUM. (Kushta-Muzey Nikola Vaptsarov; Къща-Музей Никола Вапцаров). This house-museum recalls the life and work of the 20th-century poet who gave his life in the struggle against 1940s Fascism. Connected to and included in the admission is the **House of Poetry and Art** (Dom Poezi i Iskustvo; Дом Поези и Искуство), which exhibits images of the National Revival movement, the liberation struggles of Southern Bulgaria at the outset of the century, and photographs of the region. *(On the corner of pl. Demokratsia and Vaptsarov. Tel. 30 38. Open Tu-Su 8am-noon and 2-6pm. 1lv; taped tours available in English.)*

VELIANOV HOUSE. (Velyaianova Kushta; Веляианова Къща). Named after the painter from Debur (once in Bulgaria but now in F.Y.R. Macedonia) responsible for the interior of Holy Trinity Church (see above), the house is typically Revival. Its thick walls once protected the inhabitants from *kurdzhali* brigands. *(Left on Velian Ognev from pl. Vuzrazhdane. Open M-F 9am-noon and 2-5pm. 1lv; English tour 1lv.)*

NEOFIT RILSKI HOUSE. (Kushta-Muzey Neofit Rilski; Къшта-Музей Неофит Рилски). Another National Revival structure, the house was home to one of the National Revival movement's forefathers; he eventually became father superior at Rila Monastery (see p. 111). A man of letters, collector of folklore, and founder of the Rila school of church singing, Rilski also taught Zahari Zograf. *(At the corner of Pirin and Rilski. Tel. 25 40. Open daily 9am-noon and 2-5pm. 1lv; taped English tour 1lv.)*

ICON EXHIBIT. (Ekspozitsiya na ikoni; експозиция на икони). A nunnery when it was built in 1749, the house now shelters icons from Bansko, including one initially considered sacrilegious. Why? The angels portrayed were female. *(Down Yane Sandanski from pl. Vuzrazhdane. Open M-Sa 9am-noon and 2-5pm. 1lv.)*

FESTIVALS. Bansko complements its long heritage with several cultural events. The **Annual International Jazz Festival** hits town in early August. In 2001, the biennial **Pirin Pee,** a huge folk festival, will be held in nearby Predel. For more info, contact Pirin Tourism Forum in Blagoevgrad (tel. 736 54 58; email scabrin@pop3.aubg.bg).

HIKING

Hiking routes are marked with different-colored signs. The starting point for many trails is **Vihren Hut** (hizha Vihren; Хижа Вихрен). From town, take any street leading to the Glazne (Глазне) River. When you reach the river, follow the Glazne road upstream, out of town, and up to the entrance of **Pirin National Park** (Народен Парк Пирин). Hike (5hr. each way), drive, or take a taxi (10-14lv from Bansko) up the paved road. The route is marked with a yellow line on white background, past **hizha Bunderitsa** (Бъндерица) and **baikushevata mura** (байкушевата мура), a fir tree that's as old as the Bulgarian state (1300 years). At the hut you'll find a place to sleep (US$5.50 per person) and a chef to cook your last hot meal for awhile. Four trails begin together at the hut and lead over a rocky peak. After 10min., the red and green trail branch off and cross the river. The **red** leads up Vihren peak (2914m) to hizha Yavorov (Javor's hut; Яворов; 1740m). Beware—not everyone can handle the beautiful but terrifying horse (*koncheto;* кончето) trail. The **green** trail scales Todorin peak (Тодорин) to Hizha Demyanitsa (Демяница; 6hr.). Hizha Bezbog (Безбог), which is becoming increasingly popular as a ski resort, is another 8hr. away. A **lift** connects it to Hizha Gotse Delchev (Гоце Делчев), which is 2hr. by foot from the village of Dobrinishte (Добринище). **Buses** to **Bansko** or **Razlog** can be caught there, making this an excellent route for a three-day hike. The **blue trail** goes in the other direction and is much shorter, reaching Sini vraha in only 4hr. You'll have plenty of time to turn back or to continue on the **yellow trail** to chalet Yanel Sandanski (5hr.) at the other side of the park. Mountain huts scattered throughout the park provide the barest of accommodations—floor space—for the barest of prices (US$2). Bring your own food.

MELNIK (МЕЛНИК)

Bulgaria's smallest town, tiny Melnik (pop. 300+), and its exquisitely preserved National Revival houses sit in a deep sandstone gorge where life goes on as it has for centuries. While the houses' whitewashed walls and the stones of ancient ruins outwardly attest to the town's uniqueness, Melnik is best known for what it keeps concealed in its cellars—barrels of delicious wine.

ORIENTATION & PRACTICAL INFORMATION. **Buses** come to Melnik via **Sandanski** (Sofia-Sandanski 2½hr., 1 per day, 3lv; Sandanski-Melnik 40min., 4 per day, 1.30lv) or **Blagoevgrad** (1hr., 1 per day, 0.80lv). One bus leaves Melnik for **Sandanski** (40min.), **Blagoevgrad** (2hr.), and **Sofia** (4hr.) at 6am each morning from the main street (1.30lv). The **main street** is easily recognizable and curves around a dry river bed. A **map** is not needed but is available at some restaurants and hotels (2lv). The **post office** is farther up the main street on the left of the river. (Open M-F 7:30am-noon and 1-4:30pm.) The **telephone** outside is the only phone in town; the restaurant next door sells phone cards. **Postal code:** 2820. **Phone code:** (0)997437.

ACCOMMODATIONS & FOOD. **Private rooms** run 7-14lv; signs advertising "rooms to sleep" are on houses and restaurants all over town. **Uzunova Kushta** (Узунова Къща; tel. 270) is centered around a pleasant courtyard. (Breakfast included. Doubles, triples, and quads with bath US$12 per person.) **Hotel-Vinarna MNO** (МНО; tel. 249), with a sign reading "Ресторант/Винарна" in front, is on the left past the post office. Its 30 beds are divided among large doubles and triples with private hot water baths. (US$15 per person; US$20 for two.) When it comes to culinary delights, Melnik's offerings belie its size. A **mini-market** (мини маркет) is on the right side of the main street. (Open daily 7am-10pm.) Feast on traditional Bulgarian food (1.30-9.50lv) at **Mencheva Kushta** (Менчева Къща; tel. 339). The restaurant also has three doubles (10lv per person) and a good map (1lv). It's just past the river, on the left side of the main street's right fork.

SIGHTS & HIKING. Winston Churchill had his favorite wine shipped all the way from Melnik even during WWII. Less bellicose travelers can see it in its original storage place at the 1754 **Kordopulova Kushta** (Кордопулова Къща), the biggest National Revival house in Bulgaria. It also contains the largest wine cellar in Melnik—the caves inside the sandstone hill took a full 12 years to carve and can store up to 300 tons of wine. To get there, follow the main road, take the right fork, and go left up the steep stone path. Or, follow the signs pointing to "K.K." (Open dawn to dusk. 1lv, students 0.50lv.) Mitko Manolev's **wine-tasting cellar** (Izba za Degustatsiya na Vino; Изба за Дегустация на Вино; tel. 234) is a 200-year-old establishment that offers naturally air-conditioned caverns and some of the best Melnik wine. (Open daily 8am-dusk. Glass 1lv, bottle 3-5lv.)

Melnik is an ideal base for several good day hikes. All paths are poorly marked by an orange-and-white line painted on trees and rocks. A plateau with a beautiful vista of Melnik and the surrounding hills awaits 15min. up the path behind the Sv. Nikola church. Take a right to reach the ruins of the **Despot Slav Krepost** (Деспот Слав Крепост), a fortress built by Aleksy Slav in the Middle Ages to protect the townspeople. Two rings of walls surround a central **church** whose altar still stands. Turn off the trail halfway up to Sv. Nikola (at the sign) to reach the **Tsurkva Sveta Zona** (Света Зона) where you'll find the miraculous icons of Bogoroditsa Iverksa.

A 7km hike leads to the 13th-century **Rozhen Monastery** (Rozhenski Manastir; Роженски Манастир) and its 16th-century murals, 17th-century stained glass, and magnificent views of the countryside. Either take the **one-way bus** to the monastery (1 per day, 0.70lv), or hike both ways: from the main street, take a left at the sign pointing to the monastery. It's about 1½hr. each way.

VALLEY OF ROSES (РОЗОВА ДОЛИНА)

Tourism in the Stryama and Tundzha valleys is tinted red—with roses and with the blood spilled in both the 1876 Uprising and the subsequent War of Liberation. The National Revival houses of Koprivshtitsa stand as memorials to the heroes of the fighting, while Shipka Town lies in the shadow of the famous battle fought in the pass above. Meanwhile, Kazanluk blooms with its spring rose harvest.

KOPRIVSHTITSA (КОПРИВШИЦА)

Todor Kableshkov's 1876 "letter of blood," urging rebellion against Ottoman rule, started its tour of the country in this little town, tucked away in the Sredna Gora mountains along the Topolka River. Although the subsequent rebellion was quelled violently, it brought Bulgaria's plight to the attention of Europe and eventually led to the Russo-Turkish war that liberated the country. Today, Koprivshtitsa's revolutionaries are in the tourism business, hosting such events as the Folk Days of Koprivshtitsa every August, and, in 2000, the National Folk Festival.

ORIENTATION & PRACTICAL INFORMATION. **Trains** from **Sofia** (2hr., 8 per day, 2.40lv) stop at the Koprivshtitsa train station. Other trains arrive from **Plovdiv** via **Karlovo** (3½hr., 2.34lv). A bus will take you from the train station into town (15min., 0.60lv). Get off at the Koprivshtitsa **bus station** (a dark wooden building), which posts bus and train schedules. To reach the **main square,** backtrack along the river bisecting the town. The **tourist office,** 1 Linden Karavelov (tel. 21 91; email koprivshitza@hotmail.com) is on the main square. (Open M-F 10am-1pm and 3-6pm, Sa 10am-6pm, Su 10am-3pm.) There is no place to change money in town. Continuing past the tourist office you'll find a private **pharmacy.** (Open M-Sa 9:30am-noon and 3-6pm.) The **post office** sits behind the town's other square. (Open daily 7:30am-noon and 1-4:30pm.) **Telephones** are inside. (Open M-F 8am-noon and 1-6:30pm, Sa 8am-1pm.) **Postal code:** 2077. **Phone code:** (0)7184.

ACCOMMODATIONS & FOOD. In hopeful anticipation of tourists, the town has converted many old houses into hotels; most have two to six rooms and cost US$9-15 per person. See the tourist office for a complete list, and call ahead during the festivals. **Hotel Trayanova Kushta** (Траянова Къща), ul. Gerentsloto 5 (Геренцлого; tel. 22 50), is a good walk up the steep street from the main square. (Homey rooms with shared bath and breakfast US$10 per person.) **Hotel Shuleva**

Kushta (Шулева), 37 Hadzhi Nencho Palaveev (Хаджи Ненчо Палавеев), isn't as well-kept, but features private, hot-water baths. From the bus station, walk toward the main bridge and across the river. (US$10 per person.)

Mehana Chuchura (Чучура; tel. 27 12), near the bus station on the way to the main square, serves an extensive, well-priced menu under replicas of the town's famous wood ceilings. Entrees (1.80-7lv) include a wide range of egg dishes. (Open daily 8am-midnight.) **Mehana Byaloto Konche,** next to Hotel Trayanova, serves home-cooked specialties. (Entrees 1-42lv. Open 24hr.) The **market** by the stream, past the buses, has fresh produce. (Open early morning to mid-afternoon.)

SIGHTS. If you're not here for the folk festivals, the only things to see are the wonderfully preserved **National Revival houses.** The low plank structures are the houses of the town's first settlers; the sturdy, half-timbered homes with open porches, high stone walls, and sparse ornamentation are 19th-century additions. The third, most-common type feature enclosed verandas and delicate woodwork. The houses will be interesting to architecture buffs, but may bore others. Many homes of the leaders of the 1876 Uprising have become **museums,** and all are easy to find with a map from the tourist office. (Tickets available at any one of the houses and valid for all museums 1.50lv, students 1lv.) The 1845 **Todor Kableshkov Museum-House** (Kushta-muzey Todor Kableshkov; Къща-музей Тодор Каблешков) is one of the third stage's grandest achievements, with an impressive facade, ingeniously carved ceilings, and the hero's personal possessions. (Tel. 20 54. Open Tu-Su 8am-noon and 1:30-5:30pm.) The 1831 **Georgi Benkovski Museum-House** (Георги Бенковски), away from town near the statue of Benkovski, immortalizes the life of the leader of the "Flying Troop," a more symbolic than effective calvary unit in the April Uprising. (Tel. 28 11. Open M and W-Su 8am-noon and 1:30-5:30pm.) The **Dimcho Debelyanov Museum House** (Димчо Дебелянов) is the birthplace of one of Bulgaria's best lyric poets (see **Literature & Arts,** p. 95). Debelyanov died in WWI; inside, his work is displayed and mournfully recited while a sculpture of his mother vainly awaits his return in the yard. (Tel. 20 77. Open Tu-Su 8am-noon and 1:30-5:30pm.) The houses of two merchants—**Oslekov** and **Lyutov**—are examples of the most prosperous Revival houses. (Open M and W-Su 8am-noon and 1:30-5:30pm.) Besides ornate ceiling work, the **Lyutov House** (Лютовата) houses a collection of fine carpets within the most beautiful exterior of all the museums. The **Oslekov House** (Ослековата), supported by three columns of imported Lebanese cedar, has some stunning murals and intricate wood carvings. (Open Tu-Su 8am-noon and 1:30-5:30pm.) According to legend, the blue 1817 **Assumption Church** (Uspenie Bogorodichno; Успение Богородично) was built in 11 days. Inside you can find masterpiecs by **Zahari Zograf** (see **Literature & Arts,** p. 95); ask the minister to let you in.

KAZANLUK (КАЗАНЛЪК)

A typical concrete-block skyline and heavily kiosked streets camouflage the center of Bulgaria's rose-growing world. In the first week of June, though, the city's pride blossoms forth in the annual Rose Festival, celebrated with traditional song-and-dance troupes, comedians, and soccer stars. Arrive after the festivities and you'll see nothing but a few struggling rose bushes amid the thorns of everyday life.

ORIENTATION & PRACTICAL INFORMATION

Take a **train** from: **Sofia** (3hr., 5 per day, 4.10lv); **Burgas** (3hr., 4 per day, 4.10lv); or **Plovdiv** (6 per day, 2.50lv); or a **bus** from **Plovdiv's Sever station** (1-2 per day, 2.50lv). From the train station, go left 100m then turn right on bul. Rozova Dolina (Розова Долина), which leads to the main square, **pl. Sevtopolis** (Севтополис). The main street, **23rd Pehoten Shipchenski Polk** (23ти Пехотен Шипченски Полк), creates a 'T' with ul. Rozova Dolina to constitute the square's border closest to the train station; 23rd becomes **Knyaz Aleksandr Batenberg** (Княз Александър Батенберг) to the right. **Banka Biohim** (Банка Биохим), Rozova Dolina 4 (tel. 215 20), **exchanges** all

BULGARIA

major currencies. (Open daily 8:30-11:50am and 1-4pm.) An MC/Visa **ATM** stands on 23rd Pehoten Shipchenski near the post office. **Store luggage** at the train station. (Opens only 10min. within arrival or departure of trains. 0.50lv.) **Bookstore Tezi** (Тези), 23rd Pehoten Shipchenski 16 (tel. 490 58), stocks useful **maps** of town, with street names in Roman letters. (Open M-F 10am-7pm, Sa 10am-2pm.) The **post office** is also on 23rd Pehoten Shipchenski. (Open M-F 8am-8pm, Sa 8am-1pm.) It houses **telephones** (open M-F 7am-9:30pm; 1min. to Canada and U.S. 2.40lv, U.K. 1.40lv) and **faxes** (fax 60 14 31; open M-F 8am-8pm). **Postal code:** 6100. **Phone code:** (0)431.

ACCOMMODATIONS & FOOD

Inexpensive accommodations are limited. During the Rose Festival, call at least one month in advance. The best deal in Kazanluk is **Hotel Arsenal,** (Арсенал; tel. 205 83). Head away from pl. Sevtopolis on the small road behind Hotel Kazanluk, take the first left onto Iskra (Искра), continue past the museum on the right, and take Oreshaka (Орешака) to the right when the roads splits. Arsenal is 10min. past Hotel Vesta, inside the yellow and white sports complex on the left. Take a taxi after dark. Large rooms include hot water. (30.50lv per person.) For luxurious but pricey rooms, try **Hotel Vesta** (Веста; tel. 477 40), Chavdar Voivoda 3 (Чавдар Войвода), before Hotel Arsenal on Oreshaka. Rooms include bath, huge beds, TV, and refrigerator. (Breakfast included. Singles US$40; doubles US$50.)

Budget diners can gorge at **Starata Kushta** (Старата Къща), Dr. Baev 2 (Др. Баев; tel. 212 31). From pl. Sevtopolis, take the second left onto Gen. M. Skobelev and the first right ono Gen. Gurko. Dr. Baev is on the right. (Entrees 2-5lv. Open 24hr.) **Ascent Shop,** Rozova Dolina 3 (tel. 204 89), vends groceries and lots of liquor. (Open 24hr.) A **market, Kooperativna Pazar** (Кооперативна Пазар) is on ul. L. Hilendarski (Л. Хилендарски)—follow Otets Paisy (Отец Пайсий) from pl. Sevtopolis.

SIGHTS

Kazanluk is best known for its roses, but its other attractions have been pushing up daisies for an impressive number of centuries.

ROSE MUSEUM AND GARDENS. (Muzey na Rozata; Музей на Розата). 30min. away from pl. Sevtopolis sits the Rose Museum. The museum displays centuries of rose oil production equipement, with explanations in Bulgarian. The souvenir shop sells some indispensable rose products—liquor, jam, and precious oil. To glimpse the flowers from which all this rosiness springs, head next door to the **Scientific Research Institute for Roses, Aromatic and Medicinal Plants,** home of the experimental gardens growing 250 varieties of—you guessed it—roses. *(From pl. Sevtopolis, head down Gen. Skobelev, go right at the fork and continue on bul. Osvobozhdenie (Освобождение) Gabrovo. Or, catch bus #5 across from Hotel Kazanluk (every 30min., 0.15lv) and ask to get off at "muzey." Tel. 251 70. Open May 15-Oct. 15 9am-5pm. US$1.)*

THRACIAN TOMB. (Trakiyska Grobnitsa; Тракийска Гробница). A Thracian Tomb resides in the city park, a 10min. walk from pl. Sevtopolis. The original resting place of the tomb, now sealed, dates from the 3rd century BC. The interior has been re-created 20m away. The early-Hellenistic frescoes in the corridor and dome chamber are original; those in the replica are from the more recent Soviet period. The small tomb only merits a brief visit. *(To get to the city park, head away from pl. Sevtopolis on the small road behind Hotel Kazanluk, and take the first left onto Iskra. Take a right onto Stara Reka, right in front of the cultural center. Go straight toward the steps and climb the hill. Tel. 247 50. Open Mar.-Oct. daily 8am-noon and 1:30-6pm. US$1, students US$.50.)*

KULATA. (Кулата). The oldest part of Kazanluk, Kulata is a neighborhood that preserves the architecture of the National Revival. In the enclosed courtyard, the **Ethnographic Complex of Koulata** (Etnografski Komplex Koulata; Етнографски Комплекс Кулата) displays two buildings: a village house and a city dwelling from the Revival years. During the Rose Festival, they'll treat you to a shot of genuine rose brandy. The museum's highlight is a wonderfully sculpted garden courtyard in which a distillery shows how rose oil and liquor are traditionally made. *(From the cultural center, go right on General Podetski (Генерал Подецки) and take the first right onto Knyaz Mirski (Княз Мирски). Tel. 217 33. Open daily 9am-5pm. 1.80lv, students 0.90v.)*

ISKRA ART GALLERY AND HISTORICAL MUSEUM. (Hudozhestvena Galeriya i Istoricheski Muzey Iskra; Художествена Галерия и Исторически Музей Искра). Kazanluk's foremost museum features exhibits on ancient history, Thracian culture, and roses in Kazanluk, as well as a rich permanent collection of Bulgarian masters. *(Kiril i Metody 9. Go right on the small road behind the Hotel Kazanluk from pl. Svetopolis. Take a left onto Iskra; the museum is on the right-hand corner with Kiril i Metody. Tel. 237 41. Open mid-Mar. to late Nov. daily 9am-noon and 2-5:30pm. US$1.)*

LAKE KOPRINKA. (Копринка). Ten kilometers south of Kazanluk, the man-made **Lake Koprinka** floods the remains of the Thracian city of Sevtopolis, providing a place for a cool-off swim. *(Take bus #3 across from the train station (0.12lv).)*

NEAR KAZANLUK: SHIPKA PASS (ЩИПЧЕНСКИ ПРОХОД)

At the Rose Valley's north edge looms the legendary **Shipchenski Prohod** (Shipka Pass; ship-CHEN-skee pra-HOHD), site of the bloody and pivotal battle that lasted an entire winter and ultimately liberated Bulgaria from the Turks in 1878 (see **History,** p. 93). The village at the base, Shipka, lies off the beaten path (and main highway), and offers little more than a cool breeze and a mountainous backdrop. If nothing else, visit Shipka for the gold-domed **St. Nicholas Memorial,** built in honor of the Russian soldiers who lost their lives here. (Open daily 8:30am-5:30pm. 1.50lv, English tour 2.50lv.) From the center, take the little road to the right of the grocery store, then an immediate left. Follow the cobblestone road to the steps on the right, and take them up the hill (10min.). Views of the valley are breathtaking from the top of the **Monument to Freedom** (Pametnik na Svobodata; Паметник на Свободата), 900 steps above the pass. It has stood in memory of the Russian and Bulgarian dead since August 26, 1934. Many written fragments inside the monument are from Ivan Vazov's legendary poem "Shipka" (see **Literature & Arts,** p. 95), which most Bulgarian students learn by heart. (Open daily 8:30am-5pm. 1.50lv, students 0.75lv.) A **grocery** hides under the remains of the old Hotel Shipka on the main square. (Open M-F 7:30am-9:30pm, Sa and Su 8am-9:30pm.) **Restaurant Pronto** (Пронто) conjures up a meal with soup, grills, salad, and a tall, cool one for less than US$3. (Entrees 1000-3lv. Open daily 7am-midnight.) **Postal code:** 6150. **Phone code:** (0)4324.

GETTING THERE. To get to Shipka Town from **Kazanluk**, take **city bus #6,** departing from the train station or opposite Hotel Kazanluk, heading away from the post office all the way to the last stop (25min., every 30min., 0.45lv). Buses also arrive en route from **Gabrovo** to Kazanluk. To get to Shipka Pass and the monument, either take a bus between Kazanluk and Gabrovo and get off at the pass (0.70lv), or catch one of two buses leaving from Shipka Town for Gabrovo from in front of the old Hotel Shipka (daily around 9am and 4pm, 0.50lv) and ask to get off at the pass.

NEAR KAZANLUK: ETURA (ЕТЪРА)

Midway between Kazanluk and Veliko Turnovo sits a small village where cobblers still pound at shoes and nothing is a lost art. At least, that's the way it seems at Etura's (EH-tu-rah) **Ethnographic Complex,** an outdoor museum of some 20 National Revival buildings, workshops, and mills. Climb through tiny doors and up narrow staircases into workshops, with artisans making woodcarvings, metalwork, jewelry, icons, musical instruments, and pottery just as they've done for centuries. Visit the candy store for sweet and sticky sesame-and-honey bars (0.30lv), or the bakery for fresh breads and pastries. (Open Apr.-Oct. daily 8:30am-noon, 12:30-6pm; Nov.-Mar. 8am-4:30pm. 5.30lv, students 3.50lv; English tours 5.40lv, students 3.50lv.)

GETTING THERE. Buses from **Kazanluk** (40min., 8 per day, 1.40lv) actually stop in **Gabrovo.** From the bus station, turn left and continue to the end of the street, then turn right to reach the center. Take trolley #32 or bus #1 from the center away from the bus station to the last stop, Bolshevik (20min., 0.25lv), then hop on bus #7 or 8 and ask to be dropped off at **Etura** (5min., 0.02lv). Buses are rare on weekends when it's better to approach the museum on foot (35min.). All buses stop by **Hotel/Restaurant Etura** (tel. 424 19), convenient for quick meals. (Open daily noon-midnight.) The steps leading there also go to the Ethnographic Complex.

BLACK SEA COAST (ЧЕРНО МОРЕ)

The Black Sea Coast, Bulgaria's most popular destination for foreigners and vacationers alike, is covered with centuries-old fishing villages with secluded bays, energetic seaside towns, and plastic resorts designed to suck hard currency. Warm, sandy beaches are predominant in the south, while rockier, white-cliffed shores populate the north. A true Black Sea experience will take you from generic discos in sun-scorched Varna to quiet southern Sinemorets to strolls through the cacti in Balchik. Wherever you go, however, you're bound to run into more English speakers and higher prices than in any other region of Bulgaria.

VARNA (ВАРНА)

Varna (pop. 301,000) was crawling with sunburned Greek sailors as early as 600 BC, when it was the young port city of Odessos. By the time Romans arrived in the 2nd century, Varna was already busy doing the things that cosmopolitan cultural centers do. These days, Bulgaria's sea capital is still a commercial and transport hub that draws a growing summer population to its extensive beaches.

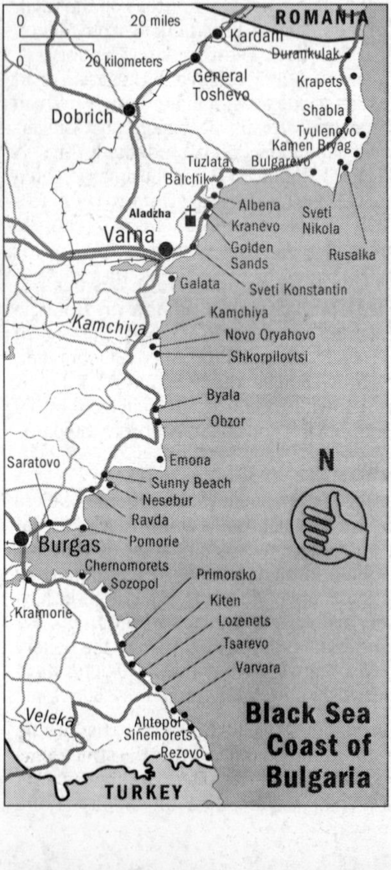

ORIENTATION

Despite Varna's sprawl, its sights are all within a 30min. walk of one another. To get to central **pl. Nezavisimost** (Независимост) from the train station, go through the underpass to **Tsar Simeon I** (Цар Симеон I). Varna's main pedestrian artery, **bul. Knyaz Boris I** (Княз Ворис I), starts at pl. Nezavisimost. Walk up Preslav from pl. Nezavisimost to the **Sv. Bogoroditsa cathedral.** From the station, go right on beachside Primorsky (Приморски—*not* Osmi Primorski Polk) for the seaside gardens.

PRACTICAL INFORMATION

Trains: Near the commercial port by the shore. To: **Sofia** (7hr., 7 per day, *couchette* 10.80lv); **Plovdiv** (5½-7hr., 3 per day, 8lv); **Burgas** (3hr., 1 per day, 4.20lv); **Ruse** (4hr., 2 per day, 5.10lv); and **Shumen** (11 per day, 2.74lv). **Rila,** ul. Preslav 13 (tel. 22 62 73), sells tickets to **Budapest** and **Istanbul.** Open M-F 8am-5:30pm, Sa 8am-3pm.

Buses: Ul. Vladislav Varenchik (Владислав Варенчик). Take city bus #22 or 41 from either the train station or the north side of the

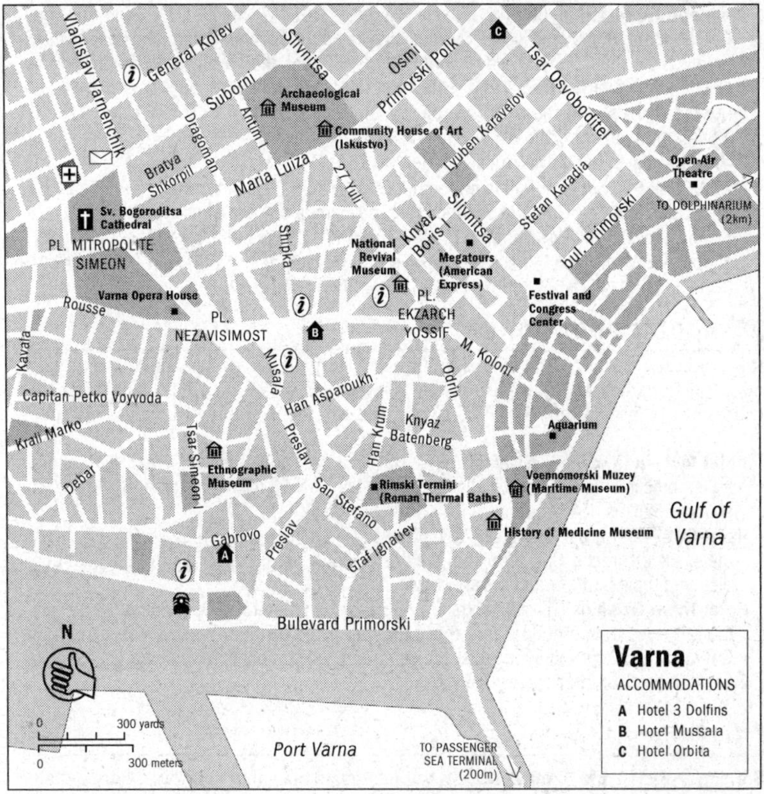

cathedral, across from the post office. Buses are the best way to and from **Burgas** (3hr., 4 per day, 5.50lv), or take a **minivan** from across from the bus station. **Group Travel,** bul. Knyaz Boris I 6 (tel. 25 67 34 and 23 04 87), hidden under a Sony sign, sends buses to: **Sofia** (6½hr., 2 per day, 11lv, students 10lv); **Budapest** (M, Tu, and F, US$40); and **Prague** (departs 10am, 85DM). Open M-F 8:30am-1pm and 2:30-5:30pm, Sa-Su 8:30am-1pm. Buy tickets in advance. **Address Elap,** operating out of Varnenski Bryag (see below), offers buses to **Sofia** (3 per day, 12lv) and **Veliko Turnovo** (3 per day, 7lv).

Ferries: At the passenger port (Морска Гора; tel. 22 23 26). Bus #48 goes here from the cathedral. Ferries sail between resorts and are a pleasant alternative to crowded buses. Cashier open 1hr. before departure. **Info kiosk** open M-F 7:30am-6:30pm. Daily **ferries** (hydro-buses) depart from Varna at 8:30am for Balchik (2½hr., 8.10lv). Wear a sweater.

Local Transportation: City **buses** cost 0.25lv; pay on the bus. Bus stops are clearly marked with small black signs listing the bus number; destinations are on the front of the bus.

Tourist Offices: Varnenski Bryag (Варненски Бряг), Musala 3 (Мусала; tel. 63 22 66 and 63 22 59; fax 25 30 83), near pl. Nezavisimost. With your back to the train station, go right on bul. Knyaz Boris I, then take the 1st right on Shipka and another right on Musala. Info, good **maps** (1.20lv), and **private rooms** arranged. Singles US$10; doubles US$14. Open daily June 8am-7pm, July-Aug. 8am-8pm, Sept.-May 8am-5pm.

Currency Exchange: Bulgarian Post Bank, Zamenhoff 1 (tel. 60 33 16 07). Cashes traveler's checks for a US$5 commission and gives Visa cash advances for a 4% commission (US$5 minimum). Open M-F 8:30am-4:30pm, Sa 8:30am-noon. There is a Cirrus/AmEx/MC **ATM** by the Valentina shopping complex.

American Express: Megatours, Slivnitsa 33 (tel. 22 00 47; fax 22 00 61), in the Hotel Cherno More. Holds mail, sells traveler's checks for a 1% commission, and cashes them for a 3.5% commission. Buy checks with your AmEx card, then receive cash for them. Also sells a **map** of Varna (US$3) and rents **cars.** Open M-F 9am-6pm, Sa 9am-2:30pm.

Luggage Storage: At the train station, by the end of track #8. 0.5lv. Open daily 6-11:30am, noon-6pm, and 6:30-11pm.

24hr. Pharmacy: Bul. Knyaz Boris I 29 (tel. 60 71 97).

Post Office: Bul. Suborni (Съборни), on the far side from the center across from the cathedral. Open M-F 7am-7pm, Sa 7:30am-7pm, Su 8am-noon. **Postal code:** 9000.

Internet Access: Bul. Knyaz Boris I 73 (tel. 23 85 22). 2lv per hr. Open 24hr.

Telephones: Around the left side of the post office. Open daily 7am-11pm. **Faxes** (fax 60 00 81) open M-F 7am-8:30pm, Sa 8am-1pm. **Phone code:** 52.

ACCOMMODATIONS

It is generally easier to find rooms in Varna or Burgas than at the smaller resorts. In addition to **Varnenski Bryag** (see above), **Solvex** (tel. 60 58 61), near track #4 at the train station, finds rooms for US$6-10 per person. (Open summer daily 6am-10pm.)

Hotel Musala (Мусала), Musala 3 (tel. 22 39 25), next to Varnenski Bryag. Neat, affordable rooms in an old building with a beautiful staircase. Plenty of hot water. Some English spoken. Singles US$14; doubles US$20; triples US$24.

Hotel Orel (Орел), bul. Primorsky 131 (Приморски; tel. 22 42 30; fax 25 92 95), along the seaside gardens. Only 50m from the beach, but far from the center. Big, spotless doubles and triples with TV and private shower. US$20 per person.

Hotel Three Dolphins (Трите Делфина), ul. Gabrovo 27 (tel. 60 09 11 and 60 09 17). Close to the train station. From the train station go up Simeon and take a right on Gabrovo. Well-kept rooms include hot water and (occassionally) TV. Some English spoken. Singles US$20; doubles US$25.

BULGARIA

FOOD

Bul. Knyaz Boris I and **Slivnitsa** swarm with cafes, kiosks, and vendors. Many restaurants along the beach have fresh seafood. **Mexican Club Rico,** at the intersection of Simeon and pl. Nezavisimost, serves decent Mexican food. Look for the fluorescent green tables and the flashing cactus at night. (Entrees 2.50-7.80lv. Open daily 11am-11pm.) Two chains, **"Happy" English Pub** and **Cafe Davidoff,** are everywhere. Happy serves Americanized Bulgarian food in a hip atmosphere. (Open 24hr.) Davidoff is equally trendy, but specializes in dessert. (Open daily 7am-11:30pm).

SIGHTS & ENTERTAINMENT

The family-dominated **beaches** are cramped in summer, but still make for an enjoyable afternoon. The sands stretch north from the train station and are separated from bul. Primorsky by the seaside gardens. The **Dolphinarium,** in the north part of the park away from the ports and train station, puts on the highest-priced 30min. show in town at 11am, 2, and 3:30pm. Take bus #8, 9, or 14 or, facing the ocean from the train station, walk left through the seaside gardens. (Tel. 30 21 99. Open Tu-Su 10am-5pm. 12lv. Box office open Tu-Su 10am-noon and 1-4pm.) Hidden among the fountains and trees on the way to the Dolphinarium sprawls a vine-covered **open-air theater,** home of international ballet festivals (May-Oct.). Buy tickets at the gate or at the festival ticket office (see below). The well-preserved **Roman Thermal Baths** (Rimski Termi; Римски Терми) stand on San Stefano in the city's old quarter, **Grutska Mahala** (Гръцка Махала; open Tu-Su 10am-5pm; 1lv).

The big red **Opera House** on the main square has a reduced summer schedule. (Tel. 22 33 88. Open M-F 10:30am-1pm and 2-7:30pm.) At ul. L. Karavelov 1 (Л. Каравелов), the tall glass building up Maria Luiza at its intersection with Slivnitsa, the **Varna Community House of Art** (Obshtina Varna Dom na Iskustvo; Община Варна Дом на Искуство), hosts chamber music concerts. In late August, Varna holds an

International Jazz Festival; for the jaded, the **"Love is Folly" film festival** takes place in the festival complex (late Aug.-early Sept.). The chamber music festival **Varna Summer** (Varnensko Lyato; Варненско Лято) runs for six weeks starting in mid-June. For tickets to everything, try the **International Advertisement office** (tel. 23 72 84), two floors below the entrance—take the elevator and go down the hall on the left.

The **Festivalen Complex,** with a cinema (4lv), pool tables, and cafes, is popular with younger crowds and is another source for tickets and cultural info. Hotel Orbita's disco, **Iguana Club,** is popular with students. (Cover 1lv. Open nightly 9pm-sunrise.) In summer, a good number of discos and bars open by the beach. **Spartakus** (Спартакус), a self-advertised "private mixed club welcoming all sexual orientations," is in the Opera House. (Cover 1lv. Open nightly after 11:30pm.)

NEAR VARNA: BALCHIK (БАЛЧИК)

If the mystical reputation of the Black Sea seems dulled by crowded boardwalks and the endless drone of Ricky Martin, **Balchik** (BAHL-chik) is the place to get reenchanted. Life in this fishing village, with houses carved into the chalky cliffs, moves at a slower pace than in Varna. The result is a postcard-perfect destination that has the conveniences of a resort without resort prices and crowds. The **public beach** is small but clean, with showers, changing rooms, bars, volleyballs, umbrellas, and paddleboat rentals (4lv per 30min.). The best sands lie sheltered by Romanian Queen Marie's **summer palace** and surrounded by restaurants. To reach the palace from pl. Ribarski (Рибарски), turn right and walk uphill along Primorska (Приморска). Once there, you can sit in her marble throne and explore the varied garden and the **largest cactus collection in the Balkans.** (Open daily 8am-8pm. 4lv.) At night, relax or dance at one of the many beachside cafes or discos.

For an epidermal treat, visit the mud baths of **Tuzlata,** 7km north. A **bus** leaves from the Balchik station (15min., 1 per day, 0.40lv), or take a **taxi** from pl. Ribarski (5lv; ask for the sanatoria). Although the spa has seen better, muddier days, you can still get a great *grazni banya* (grand bath; грязни баня). Go in the right side for women and the left for men; get naked and take a preparatory dip in the water, then rub mud all over yourself and sit in the sun while it dries. It's good for skin problems and rheumatism, supposedly—or just for fun. (Open in summer daily 8am-4pm. 1lv.) From Cherno More, work up an appetite by climbing the overgrown stairs at pl. Ribarski to **Emona** (Емона), Emona 14 (tel. 722 69). Delicious fish dishes are enhanced by an unrivaled view of the harbor. (Entrees 1-6lv. Open daily 9am-2:30pm and 5-11:30pm.) **Postal code:** 9600. **Phone code:** (0)579.

BULGARIA

GETTING THERE. Buses run from **Varna** (1hr., 4 per day, 2lv), but intermittent **minivans** waiting across the street make the trip faster for the same price (they leave when full). From Balchik's bus station, walk downhill on the main street, Cherno More (Черно Море), to pl. Nezavisimost. Continue following it to the left until pl. Ribarski. Ul. Primorska (Приморска) runs along the shore. **Bris Travel,** Zaimov 4 (tel. 764 34), on the right off Ribarski as you head down Cherno More, provides info and arranges excursions. (Open summer daily 8:30am-8pm.)

NEAR VARNA: ALADZHA MONASTERY (АЛАДЖА МАНАСТИР)

Known as the rock *(skalen)* monastery, **Aladzha Monastery** (tel. 35 54 60), 14km from Varna, was carved out of the side of a mountain during the 13th and 14th centuries. No written records of the monastery exist, and its Christian name remains a mystery ("*aladzha*" is Turkish for "patterned"). Now devoted entirely to life as a tourist attraction, the monastery rises two levels in the 40m white limestone cliff. The chapel on its second level preserves frescoes of the Madonna with child and other scenes. The view of the sea from the open cells is fantastic. (Open June-Oct. daily 9am-6pm; Nov.-May Tu-Su 10am-4pm. 2lv, students 1lv.) An **art gallery,** to the left as you enter the premises, exhibits medieval paintings and gives some background on the monastery. An excellent guidebook in English is available at the ticket office, as well as a book of legends (3lv). 800m northeast along the forest trail, the **catacombs,** a group of three-level caves once inhabited by hermits, offer a stark look into the life of 14th-century monks. Dining options at Aladzha begin and end with the fun but pricey **Lovna Sreshta** (Ловна Среща; tel. 35 51 90) at the top of the hill. *Gligan pemen* (wild boar; глиган пемен; 10.50lv) and fish (6.50-11.50lv) top the menu, while *Nestinari* dancers prance barefoot on hot coals. (Open daily 11am-2am; show 9:30-10:30pm. Call ahead to see if the show will go on.)

GETTING THERE. Bus #29 leaves **Varna** a block from the cathedral under the "НАРОДНО" sign (30min., 8am and 5:15pm, 0.25lv). Or take bus #53 to Golden Sands. It's a 15min. hike up to the left (provided landslides haven't made the road impassable). The returning bus to Varna leaves at 9am and 6pm.

BURGAS (БУРГАС)

Upon arriving in Burgas (BOOR-gahs; pop. 200,000), one notices the contrast between the black hulking freight ships and the otherwise pristine bay. The result is a city less touristed and less pleasant than Varna; Burgas is best enjoyed with a stroll along the beach as you wait for transport elsewhere (or simply as the most convenient place to sleep while exploring the wonders of the Southern Black Sea Coast). Head to bigger and better places from the Burgas **bus** and **train stations,** near the port at **Garov pl.** (Гаров). **Aleksandrovska** (Александровска), the main pedestrian drag, begins across the street. Up Aleksandrovska and to the right, pedestrian **Aleko Bogoridi** (Алеко Богориди) leads to the seaside gardens and beach. **Bulbank,** across the street from Hotel Bulgaria on Aleksandrovska, cashes **traveler's checks** for a US$1 commission and has a Cirrus/MC **ATM.** (Open M-F 8:30-11:30am and 1-4pm.) For overnight stays, **private rooms** are most convenient, running US$6-10. Secure them at **Primorets Tourist,** pl. Garov (tel. 84 27 27), a block to the right (with your back to the station) of Aleksandrovska, under the "Частни Квартири" sign. (Open M-F 6:30am-8pm, Sa-Su noon-5pm.) Otherwise, put yourself up at the **Hotel Mirage** (Мираж), Lermontov 18 (tel. 92 10 19). From the station, go up Alexsandrovska, take a right on Bogoridi, pass the Hotel Bulgaria, and take the first left onto Lermontov. (Doubles US$25, with TV US$28; triples US$33.) Grab a hot dog from a stand on the beach, or dine on Bulgarian fare at **Restaurant Odesa** (Одеса), Bogoridi 34 (tel. 84 09 91; entrees 2-8lv; open daily 10am-11:30pm). Evenings are as unexciting as the rest of the day in Burgas; try keeping yourself entertained at the open-air **Dance Club Strena,** right by Taverna Neptune, a few hundred meters north of Hotel Primorets in the Seaside Gardens. **Postal code:** 8000. **Phone code:** (0)56.

BULGARIA

GETTING AWAY. Trains run to **Varna** (4½hr., 5 per day, 4.80lv), and **Sofia** via **Plovdiv** or **Karlovo** (7hr., 13 per day, 9.20lv). **Buses** serve the **Black Sea coast,** including **Varna** (3hr., 8 per day, 5.50lv). Quicker, cheaper **minibuses** run to the resorts from the opposite end of the bus station from the train station.

RESORTS NEAR BURGAS

From the look of weedy and industrial Burgas, a visitor might never guess that resorts on the Bulgarian Black Sea Coast could be at all appealing. Although ugly, the town is an ideal base from which to explore the southern coast. Heading south from the resort-city-that-never-was reveals a surprising array of seaside beauties, from the pristine hamlets of Ahtopol, Kiten, and Sinemorets, to the thriving artistic and cultural centers of Sozopol and Nesebur. Even Bulgaria's biggest youth center lies only a short bus ride away from Burgas in Primorsko.

NESEBUR (НЕСЕБЪР)

Nesebur (neh-SEH-bur), a museum town atop the peninsula at the south end of Sunny Beach, is a break from sand and sun. Nonetheless, don't expect a respite from the summer crowds; this might be the most touristed town in Bulgaria. That said, Nesebur has done a good job of preserving a charm that its resort neighbors sacrificed at the altar of commerce long ago. A walk through the town's ancient **Stari Grad** begins with the 3rd-century stone **fortress walls.** The Byzantine **gate** and

port date from the 5th century. The **Temple of John the Baptist** (Yoan Krustitel; Йоан Кръстител), now an art gallery, has been around since the 10th century; to reach it, walk down Mitropolitska from the center and the church is on the left. (Open daily 9am-1:30pm and 3-10pm.) The 11th-century **New Metropolitan Church of St. Stephen** (Tsurkvata Sveti Stefan; Църквата Свети Стефан) is plastered in 16th-century frescoes. From the center, continue down Mesembria and take a right on Ribarska; the church is on the right. (Open daily July-Aug. 8am-8pm; May-June 9am-6pm. 1.70lv, students 0.60lv.) The 13th-century **Church of Christ the Almighty** (Hristos Pantokrator; Христос Пантократор), in the main square, doubles as an art gallery in summer. (Open daily 9am-9pm.) On Mitropolitska, the 1609 **Church of St. Spas** (Tsurkvata Sveti Spas; Свети Спас) offers an English guide about its 17th-century frescoes. (Open M-F 9:30am-1:30pm and 2-5:30pm, Sa-Su 9:30am-1:30pm. 1.20lv, children 0.60lv.) The **Archaeological Museum** (Arheologicheski Muzey; Археологически Музей), to the right of the town gate, exhibits ancient ceramics and icons. (Tel. 60 18. Open May-Oct. daily 9am-1:30pm and 2-7:30pm; Nov.-Apr. M-F 9am-5pm. 2.10lv, students 0.85lv; English tour 4lv per group.)

Along the harbor, munch on fish with fries and *shopska* salad at street **kiosks** (US$3). **Restaurant Avera,** Mitropolitska 13 (tel. 453 39), has some great ocean views. (Entrees 3lv-10lv. Open daily 10am-midnight.) **Postal code:** 8231. **Phone code:** (0)554.

GETTING THERE. Get to Nesebur by **bus** from **Burgas** (40min., every 40min., 1.60lv). Buses stop at the Old Nesebur port and the gate leading to town. **Minibuses** also make the trip (30min., 1.50lv) but only stop in new Nesebur; take a city bus from there to Stari Grad.

SOZOPOL (СОЗОПОЛ)

Thirty-four kilometers south of Burgas, Sozopol (soh-ZO-pohl)—settled in 610BC—is Bulgaria's oldest Black Sea town. It was once the resort of choice for Bulgaria's artistic community and still caters to a more creative set than its neighbors. Quieter and less expensive than Nesebur, the town still gets its share of summer visitors. Take a **boat cruise** (15lv per boat) from the seaport around Sozopol and take a peek at the two adjacent islands, St. Peter and St. Ivan. The best time to go is at sunset. One of the most popular night spots is the misleadingly named **Country Club,** right on the beach. Look out for rave nights. (Open daily 10pm-sunrise. Free.) During the first ten days of September, artists and actors take over the town for the **Arts Festival Apolonia.** For a delicious meal, walk to restaurant **Vyaturna Melnitsa** (Вятърна Мелница), Morski Skali 27a (Морски Скали; tel. 844), on the street running along the tip of the peninsula; look for the little windmill. (Entrees 3-12lv. Summer folk shows Th and Sa nights. Open daily 10am-midnight.) **Postal code:** 8130. **Phone code:** 5514.

GETTING THERE. Buses arrive from **Burgas** (45min., every 2hr. 6am-8pm, 1.20lv). Turn left on **Apolonia** (Аполония) to reach **Stari Grad.** To get to **Novi Grad,** go right through the park and turn left onto Republikanska (Републиканска). Tourist bureau **Lotos** operates at the bus station (tel./fax 282). The staff arranges private rooms (US$7 per person) and organizes trips to Istanbul. (Open daily 8am-8pm.)

PRIMORSKO (ПРИМОРСКО)

Young Bulgarians know Primorsko (pree-MOR-sko) as the site of the **International Youth Center** (Mezhdugarodni Mladezhki Tsentur; Международни Младежки Център), where the best *kosmonoltsy* and pioneers were sent to strengthen global comradeship. Today, Zhivkov would blush at this rocking, inexpensive resort and its scantily-clad youths. When open (June-Oct.), the complex and its five hotels offers everything a tourist could need or want. (July-Aug. US$12 per person; Sept.-June US$8.) At the manicured **beach,** featuring dunes and some of the cleanest water in the Black Sea, you can lay under an umbrella (2lv) or rent a paddleboat (*vodna koleva*; 15lv per hr.). In the oak forest, play tennis (US$2 per hr.), volleyball, basketball, handball, or table tennis (2lv per hr.). If you're feeling more adventurous, rent a **bike** (2lv per hr.) and explore the area. The complex also has a **medical center,** an **open-air theater,** and a **cinema.** If you still have energy come night, hit one of the five **discos.** For info on any of the activities and a free **map,** head to the **information office** (tel. 21 01) in room #1 of the building to the right of Hotel Druzhba. **Postal code:** 8290. **Phone code:** 5561.

GETTING THERE. Primorsko is on the same bus route as **Ahtopol;** buses heading there also stop in **Sozopol.** Take a southbound coastal **bus** to Primorsko from **Burgas** (1½hr., 1 per day, 2lv) and stop at the main street, **Cherno More** (Черно Море). Buses also stop here en route to Tsarevo. Minivans make the trip from Burgas faster and cheaper. To reach the ММЦ from the bus station, take a right with your back to the station and head out of town. Pass the post office, then take a left at the intersection. Cross the bridge over Dyavolka Reka (Devil's River; Дяволка Река) and continue for 15min. A cab shouldn't cost more than 3lv.

AHTOPOL (АХТОПОЛ)

Only 25km from the Turkish border, **Ahtopol** (ah-TOH-pohl) is a humble town of 1400 inhabitants. Hidden, rocky bays with crystal-clear water, the highest water temperature in all of Bulgaria's resorts, and peaceful streets with private gardens make this the best location for a truly relaxing beach experience. The public **beach** competes with several cleaner and quieter bays; try the one at the lighthouse. To get to the public beach, take Levski (the street in front of the bus station) to its end, then follow the paved path past the "жп район пловдив" sign.

Private rooms can be arranged through CREDO-OK (see below) or through the owner for US$2-6. If you prefer a hotel, try **Berlin,** Cherno More 22a (tel. 320). Take a left on Veleka (Велека) from Trakiya, then a right on Cherno More—Berlin is on the right. It offers attractive, clean doubles with veranda, fridge, shower, phone, and TV. (Breakfast included. 40lv for 1-2 people, 50lv for 3.) The town hosts a surprisingly active culinary life; vendors can be found just about everywhere. Good seafood lies along **Kraymorska** (Крайморска), which runs off Trakiya at the quay. To the right, **Restaurant Sirius** (Сириус; tel. 372), Kraymorska 17, offers cheap grills (0.70-6.50lv) and fish (2-6lv) underneath grape vines. (Open daily 5:30pm-midnight.) A cinema next to the park near the end of Trakiya shows 5th-or 6th-run U.S. flicks. Beachside **discos** grind until sunrise. **Postal code:** 8280. **Phone code:** (0)5563.

BULGARIA

GETTING THERE. Getting to Ahtopol can be difficult. There is only one **bus** per day from **Burgas** (2½hr., 3.30lv), which leaves at 5:30pm. The bus station is on the main street, **Trakiya** (Тракия), which leads to the harbor. All points of interest are within a 15min. walk. **Tourist office CREDO-OK** is at the bus station (tel. 340). A helpful staff provides **maps,** books **private rooms** (5-11lv; tax 0.50lv; 10% commission per person), and sells **bus tickets** to **Sofia** (7½hr., 2 per day, 15lv).

KITEN (КИТЕН)

Just south of Primorsko, Kiten has not yet been overwhelmed by a deluge of tourists. As more and more people discover this tiny beachside gem, though, its quiet days appear to be numbered. Since its founding in 1932, Kiten has managed to shake off concrete apartment towers, providing a rare respite from the Soviet haze that seems to hang over Bulgaria. Restaurants abound in Kiten, but the **produce market** on Strandzha is the cheapest option. A **supermarket** also lies at the turn-off to the beach. One of the more notable restaurants in town is **Mehana Kukeri** (Механа Кукери; tel. 36 50), on Altipan, whose decor resembles a pirate-themed mini-golf course. Traditional Bulgarian entrees (think fish) run 1.50-10lv. (Open daily 9am-1am.) **Postal code:** 8284. **Phone code:** (0)55 61.

GETTING THERE. Buses roll into Kiten from **Burgas** (1¾hr., 4 per day, 2.50lv) on their way to **Ahtopol** or **Tsarevo,** or from **Primorsko** (15min., 5 per day, 0.20lv). **Minivans** will get you there cheaper and faster; they leave when full. Kiosks along the street sell bus tickets to **Sofia** (at least 5 per day, 15-16lv) and **Plovdiv** (3 per day, 12lv). **Luggage storage** at the bus station (0.50lv) is open when buses arrive and depart. To reach the main beach from the **bus station,** turn left onto Strandzha and follow it 5min. Turn right after the supermarket and go down the stairs; there you'll find sand, volleyball, and paddleboats (4lv per hr.).

SINEMORETS (СИНЕМОРЕЦ)

Sinemorets, a tiny village of 400 inhabitants only 10km north of Turkey, shelters the most beautiful beach in Bulgaria—and nothing else. No post office, no pharmacy, no bank, no street names, and no tourists. Only goats and roosters and the sea and you, the intrepid budget wanderer. **Private rooms** are the best option. Unfortunately, without a central agency, you'll have to do some hunting; look for *Zimmer frei* signs. The only hotel in town is the **Hotel Bitovi Chslugi** (Битови Чслуги), with fresh rooms, terraces, and hot water. (Breakfast included. Some English spoken. US$11.) **Restaurant Shopska Creshta** is the best of this village's nine eateries. (Entrees 1400-8lv. Open daily from 8am until the last guest leaves.)

GETTING THERE. Buses run from **Ahtopol** (15min., 2 per day at 6:30am and 12:30pm, 0.20lv), which offer connections to **Burgas.** With your back to the bus stop, turn left and take the middle fork in the road. Turn right at the first street after a trio of cafes, then take the first left. This street leads to the beach; turn right at the field when you see the sand (10min.).

NORTHERN BULGARIA

From the ancient ruins of Bulgaria's first capitals at Pliska and Veliki Preslav to the war memorial in Pleven, the region between the Danube and the Balkan Mountains is most notable for its historical relics. Veliko Turnovo stands as a virtual microcosm of Bulgaria over the past 5000 years, and Madara boasts prehistoric caves. In the midst of it all, Ruse bobs along with whatever trade makes it down the Danube.

VELIKO TURNOVO (ВЕЛИКО ТЪРНОВО)

Perched on steep hills above the twisting Yantra River, Veliko Turnovo (veh-LEEK-uh TUR-nuh-vuh) has watched over Bulgaria for 5000 years. The town has blessed the country with revolutionaries, kings, and—following the overthrow of the Turks—the first Bulgarian constitution. An air of historical import hovers over Bulgaria's biggest trove of ancient ruins, but Veliko Turnovo's cozy balconies, rolling hills, and young population add levity to delight even the most jaded traveler.

ORIENTATION

Veliko Turnovo is spread along a loop in the river, with its center, **pl. Maika Bulgaria** (Майка България), on the outside bank. From the center, the main drag follows the river west, changing its name as it goes: it begins as **Nezavisimost** (Независимост), becomes **Stefan Stambolov** (Стефан Стамболов) and **Nikola Pikolo** (Никола Пиколо), and as it reaches the ruins, **Tsarevets Krepost** (Царевец Крепост). From the bus station, take bus #7 or 10 (0.20lv) five stops to the center. From the train station, go along the river toward the center and then cross the bridge, which leads to **Aleksandr Stamboliyski** (Александър Стамболийски). Turn right onto big **Hristo Botev** (Христо Ботев) to reach the center. You can also take almost any of the buses (0.20lv; timed to meet trains) from the train station; ask "*za tsentur?*" ("to the center?"). **Kingi** (Кинги), a book and paper store next to Rakovski, the small street 5min. from Hotel Trapezitsa on the way to Hotel Comfort (see **Accommodations,** below), has good **maps** (2.20lv; open daily 10am-6:30pm).

PRACTICAL INFORMATION

Trains: Trains north all have **connections** through nearby **Gorna Oryahovitsa** (Горна Оряховица), 7km northeast of town. To go direct out of Gorna, take bus #10 toward the post office from pl. Maika Bulgaria (0.70lv). To: **Sofia** (8 per day, 7.76lv); **Burgas** (5 per day, 6.20lv); **Varna** (5 per day, 6.92lv); **Gabrovo** (7 per day, 1.18lv; change in Tsareva Livada); **Ruse** (8 per day, 2.93lv); and **Pleven** (10 per day, 3.41lv).

Buses: Nikola Gabrovski. 5 stops from the center on bus #7 or 10. To: **Stara Zagora** (2hr., 1 per day, 2.10lv). **Group Travel** (tel. 62 82 92), in the Hotel Etur building, also runs bus

BULGARIA

line. To: **Sofia** (3hr., 5 per day, 7.00lv, students 5.30lv) and **Varna** (3hr., 2 per day, 6.80lv, students 6.10lv). Open M-F 8:30am-7pm, Sa-Su 10am-noon and 3:30-6:30pm.

Currency Exchange: Biohim Bank (Биохим), Rafael Mihailov 2 (Рафаел Михайлов). With your back to the post office, walk right on Nezavisimost; it's the first left. Cashes traveler's checks into US$ or *leva* for a US$2 commission per check. Open M-F 8:30am-4pm.

Luggage Storage: At the train station. 0.50lv per day.

Pharmacy: ul. Vasil Levski 23 (Васил Левски). Open daily 7:30am-7pm.

Post Office: pl. Maika Bulgaria. **Poste Restante** in the building 30m left of main entrance. Open M-F 7am-noon and 12:30-7pm, Sa 8am-noon and 1-5pm. **Postal code:** 5000.

Internet Access: At **La Scalla, Pizzeria Italiana.** From the center walk down Hristo Botev and go up the stairs to the right of the restaurant entrance. 2lv per hr. Open 24hr.

Telephones: At the post office. *Bulfon* and *Betkom* cards sold. Open daily 7am-10pm. **Fax office** (fax 62 98 77) open daily 7am-9pm. **Phone code:** (0)62.

ACCOMMODATIONS

Rooms in Veliko Turnovo are plentiful, and if you wear a backpack for more than five seconds in public you'll be approached by locals offering private rooms (US$7-12). Bargain and don't be afraid to say no; hotels are also well-equipped.

Hotel Trapezitsa (HI) (Хотел Трапезица), Stefan Stambolov 79 (tel. 220 61). From the center, walk down Nezavismost toward the post office and follow the street right (5min.). An excellent hostel with a view of the river. Clean rooms with private, hot-water bathrooms. Midnight curfew. 14,000lv per person, non-members 18,000lv.

Hotel Comfort, Panayot Tipografov 5 (Панайот Типографов; tel. 287 28). From Stambolov, walk left onto Rakovski. Turn left at the small square and continue straight; the hotel is on your left. Clean rooms, beautiful bathrooms, and amazing views of Tsarevets. Friendly owner speaks English. US$15 per person, students US$11. The top-floor apartment ($45) sleeps 4 and affords great views of the evening light shows.

FOOD

A large **outdoor market** sells fresh fruit and veggies (1.20-3lv per kg) daily from dawn to dusk at the corner of Bulgaria and Nikola Gabrovski, while multiple **taverns** (*mehana*; механа) make use of the balconies overlooking the river.

Samovodska Sresha (Самоводска Среша), 33 Rakovski, on the way to Hotel Comfort. Traditional Bulgarian food and friendly service. Break free of the *shopska salat* dependency by trying their fried pumpkin slices. Entrees 4-6lv.

Pizzeria Gustozo (Густозо), Stefan Stambolov 2. Of Veliko Turnovo's disporportionate number of pizza joints, this is by far the best. Pizzas 1.50-3.50lv. Open 24hr.

Sladkarnitsa Lotos (Сладкарница Лотос), the "Snack Bar" next to Hotel Trapezitsa. Mounds of cake: try the chocolate *garash* (гараш; 0.80lv). Open daily 8am-midnight.

SIGHTS

The ruins of **Tsarevets** (Царевец), a fortress that once housed the royal palace and a cathedral, stretch across an overgrown hilltop surveying the city. Nikola Pikolo leads to the gates. From the heights near **Baldwin's tower** (Baldvinova kula; Балдуинова кула), you'll be standing where the imprisoned Latin emperor Baldwin of Flanders spent his last days after an unsuccessful attempt in 1205AD to conquer Bulgaria. Climb uphill to the beautiful **Church of the Ascension** (Tsurkva Vuznesenegospodne; Църква Възнесениегосподне), restored in 1981 for the 1300th anniversary of Bulgaria. (Open daily in summer 8am-7pm; off-season 9am-5pm. 4lv, students 2lv.) **The National Revival Museum** (Muzey na Vuzrazhdaneto; Музей на Възраждането), proudly exhibits many relics from the National Revival, including the first Bulgarian Parliament chamber (see **History,** p. 94). From the center, follow

Nezavisimost until it becomes Nikola Pikolo, then veer right onto ul. Ivan Vazov. (Open daily 8am-noon and 1-6pm. 4lv, students 2lv.) Go down the stairs to the left and around to the back entrance to reach the **Museum of the Second Bulgarian Kingdom** (Muzey Vtoroto Bulgarsko Tsarstvo; Музей Второто Български Царство) next door, which traces the region's history from the Stone Age to the Middle Ages with Thracian pottery, medieval crafts from Turnovo, and copies of religious frescoes. (Open Tu-Su 8am-noon and 1-6pm. 4lv, students 2lv.)

ENTERTAINMENT

On summer evenings there is often a **sound and light show** above Tsarevets Hill: multi-colored lasers play out Bulgaria's history symbolically on the fortress ruins. (30min. show starts at 10pm.) Check at **Interhotel Veliko Turnovo** off Stamboliyski for dates, although they may not know if the show will go on until 2hr. before. The Interhotel's indoor **swimming pool** is open to visitors. (Open daily 1-8pm. 2.50lv per hr.) The building identifiable by the big "БАР ПОЛТАВА" (*bar poltava*) sign that shines blue above the main square houses a **disco** (dead except on weekends; cover 0.50lv) and a **movie theater.** (Th-F 0.50lv.) The **Spider Club,** one block down, pulls dancers into its web on weekends. (Cover 0.50lv.)

NEAR VELIKO TURNOVO: TRYAVNA (ТРЯВНА)

Bustling with activity, the streets of Tryavna (tr-YAHV-nah) retain much of the independent fire that made the town an important center of the National Revival (see **Literature & Arts,** p. 95). Works of the 17th-century Tryavna School of Woodworking and Icon Painting remain as a reminder of the settlement's greatest years. The 12th-century **Church of the Archangel Michael** (Tsurkvata Sv. Arhangel Mihail; Църквата Св. Архангел Михаил), Angel Kunchev 9 (Ангел Кънчев), stands across the street and a little way down from the post office. The church is unimpressive except for its treasured **Tsar's Crucifix** (Tsarskiyat Krutst; Царскяат Кръцт), a wooden relic with 12 scenes from the Gospels carved on it—ask the priest *(pop)* to remove it from its locked case for you. (Open daily 7am-noon and 3-6pm.) The **Museum of the Old School** (Muzey Shkolo; Музей Школо) stands at pl. Kapitan Dyado Nikola 7 (Капитан Дядо Никола), the only preserved National Revival square in Bulgaria. The museum displays a comprehensive collection of art, both modern and classical. (Open daily Apr.-Sept. 9am-6pm; Oct.-Mar. 8am-noon and 1-5pm. 2lv.)

From the square, cross the little arched bridge by the clocktower and turn left to find **Daskalov's House** (Daskalova Kushta; Даскалова Къща), Slaveykov 27a (Славейков), on the left past the small garden. A wood-carving museum occupies the first floor, while the second shows ceilings carved by competing masters. (Open daily Apr.-Sept. 9am-6pm; Oct.-Mar. 8am-noon and 1-5pm. 1lv.) To find the **Museum of the Tryavna School of Icon Painting** (Muzey Trevnenska Ikonopisna; Музей Тревненска Иконописна), turn off Slaveykov just after Slaveykov 18 and ascend the hill, crossing over the railroad tracks. Go left on Breza (Бреза), and after the buildings end, head up the stairs on the right. Icons, icons, and more icons, over 160 of them, and an outstanding exhibit on the making of an icon. (Open daily in summer 10am-6pm; off season 8am-4pm. 2lv, students 1lv.)

For more active recreation, **Stara Planina,** Angle Kunchez 22 (tel. 22 47), rents bikes, provides routes for daytrips, and gives info in English. After riding up an appetite, roll into local favorite **Restaurant Pri Maistora** (При Майстора; tel. 32 40). The chef's specialty is a veal and pork dish with cheese in the shape of a pyramid (3.40lv; open daily 11am-midnight). Take Chuchura (Чучура) from the old square, go straight through the intersection, and turn right on Kaleto. There's an outdoor food market on the way. **Postal code:** 5350. **Phone code:** 677.

GETTING THERE. Take a **bus** from **Gabrovo** (45min., hourly, 0.50lv) or a **train** from **Veliko Turnovo** (45min., 9 per day, 14.80lv). Cross the little square in front of the station and turn right down Angel Kunchev. Follow its turns 10min. to the center.

PLEVEN (ПЛЕВЕН)

Pleven offers an odd mix of history and modernity, drab residential neighborhoods and exciting central areas. With 150 memorials to the Battle of Pleven, it is a veritable living monument to the Russo-Turkish War of 1877-78. One of Bulgaria's most beautiful fountains fans over flower-covered parks in the lively town center, a testament to the rejuvenating waters still found in this town's stones. The staggering number of cafes shows that Pleven's current youthful image is well deserved.

ORIENTATION

The focal points of Pleven are its Siamese twin squares—**pl. Svobodata** (Свободата) and **pl. Vuzrazhdane** (Възраждане)—connected by a short stretch of the pedestrian **Vasil Levski** (Васил Левски), which continues to the train station. From the train station, go through the park in front and then walk down **Danail Popov** (Данаил Попов), which runs perpendicular to the front of the train station and turns into **Osvobozhdenie** (Освобождеине) and eventually hits pl. Svobodata (10 min. walk). **Maps** of the city aren't entirely necessary, but the kiosks on Vasil Levski sell an excellent English map of Pleven's sights (ask *"Carta na Pleven?"*).

PRACTICAL INFORMATION

Trains: To: **Sofia** (3hr., 14 per day, 3.70lv); **Ruse** (3½hr., 6 per day, 4.10lv); and the Gorna Oryahovitsa station outside **Veliko Turnovo** (1½hr., 17 per day, 2lv).

Buses: To: **Sofia** (4hr., 2 per day, 4lv) and **Ruse** (3hr., 1 per day, 3.40lv).

Luggage Storage: At the train station. 0.50lv. Closed 8:15-8:45am and 8:15-8:45pm.

Tourist Office: Orbita, Dr. Zamenhof 3 (Др. Заменхов; tel. 265 27; fax 332 88). Not too helpful as far as tourist offices go. Open M-F 9am-5pm.

Currency Exchange: Obedinena Bulgarska Banka (Обединена Българска Банка), Vasil Levski 1 (tel. 80 12 56). Charges US$5 to cash traveler's checks, has a Cirrus/MC **ATM,** and offers **Western Union** services. Open M-F 8am-4pm.

Post Office: On pl. Vuzrazhdane. **Phones** are inside. Open M-F 7am-7:30pm, Sa 8am-7pm. **Postal code:** 5800. **Phone code:** (0)64.

ACCOMMODATIONS

Rostov na Don (Ростов на Дон), Osvobozhdenie 2 (tel. 80 18 92). On the left as you enter pl. Svobodata from the train station. Central, two-star hotel with clean bathrooms. Singles US$25; doubles US$38; apartments with bath US$55. MC/Visa.

Hotel Pleven, pl. Republika 2 (Република; tel. 301 81, 363 20, or 363 22). Near the bus and train stations. Bare-bones amenities. MC/Visa. Singles US$18; doubles US$38.

Voenen Klub (Military Club; Военен Клуб), ul Doiran 77 (Дойран; tel. 298 25). Centrally located at the far right-hand corner of pl. Vuzrazhdane from the train station. Cheap shared rooms containing little more than beds. 6.20lv per person.

FOOD

Buy fresh veggies at the **produce market** on Osvobozhdenie before Rostov na Don. The famous **Peshterata** (Пещерата) is 3km from town in **Kailuka Park.** Built in a sandstone cave, the restaurant has outdoor tables and plenty of space amid cascading greenery and loud music. Take tram #3 or 7 from San Stefano (0.25lv), behind the post office and heading away from the train station. From the end of the tram line, follow the sidewalk inside the park for 15min. until you come to a circular driveway; go around to the left. (Entrees 2-4lv. Open daily 10am-late.) For a more unexpected culinary treat in the land of the bland, **Peyfon** (Пейфон), on ul. Danail Popov, serves surprisingly good Chinese food. (Entrees 4-8lv.)

SIGHTS

RUSSO-TURKISH WAR MEMORIALS. The granddaddy of Pleven's sights, the **Panorama** (Панорама) depicts the third Russo-Turkish Battle of Pleven and the liberation of Bulgaria (see **History**, p. 93). Among its attractions are a series of huge murals and one 360° panorama. *(From the center, take bus #1, 9, or 12 away from the train and bus stations (ask for the Panorama), then go left and follow the windy road to the top of the hill. Tel. 300 80. Open daily 9am-noon and 12:30-5:30pm. 3lv. Useful English tour guide 5lv.)* Built between 1903 and 1904 in late-medieval style, the **mausoleum** (Kostnitsa; Костница) was later reconstructed as a centennial memorial to Russians killed at the Battle of Pleven. Inside, Socialist Realist murals, ancient icons, and a vault of soldierly remains await. *(At the end of pl. Vuzrazhdane. Open Tu-Sa 9am-noon and 1-6pm. English tours 1lv.)* Down the path from the main entrance of the Panorama is the old battlefield, now **Park Skobelev** (Парк Скобелев). Wild greenery, guns, and an ossuary lying within make for an enjoyable walk.

MUSEUMS & GALLERIES. The nicest house in Pleven 120 years ago, the **Museum of the Liberation of Pleven** (Muzey Osvobozhdenieto na Pleven; Музей Освобождението на Плевен) was once the residence of Russian Tsar Alexander II, the Osvoboditel himself. It is now decorated to recreate his time here. *(In a fenced-in park on your right as you walk down Vasil Levski toward the train station. Open Tu-Sa 9am-noon and 1-6pm. 1lv, Bulgarian tour 2lv.)* The **Historical Museum** (Istoricheski Muzey; Исторически Музей) complex stretches across two floors in several buildings and takes you through archaeology, ethnography, and National Revival exhibits, ending with the Russo-Turkish war and early 20th-century history. *(Sv. Zaimov 3 (Св. Заимов). Minutes from the center of town; go through the park at the end of pl. Vuzrazhdane to the far right corner and cross the street. Tel. 230 69. Open Tu-Sa 9am-noon and 1-5pm. 3lv, 2.40lv with ISIC. Helpful English brochure 0.50lv.)* Named after a famous Bulgarian caricaturist, the **Iliya Beshkov Art Gallery** (Hudozhestvena Galeria "Iliya Beshkov"; Художествена Галерия "Илия Бешков") boasts a surprisingly good 5000-piece collection. Temporary exhibits have included the likes of Picasso and Rembrandt. *(bul. Skobolev 1. Across the street from the Historical Museum. Tel. 80 20 58 or 80 20 39. Open Tu-Sa 9am-5pm. Knock if door is locked. Free admission. Some English and German spoken.)* Now an **art gallery**, the **Turkish Bathhouse** (Дойран) offers a melange of Bulgarian and international painting. *(Doiran 75. Coming from the train station, it lies midway between the two main squares on the right. Tel. 383 42. Open M-F 10:30am-6pm. Free.)*

OTHER SIGHTS. Built in 1834, **St. Nicholas** (Sv. Nikolai; Св. Николай) was sunk 2m into the ground to comply with a law that no church be higher than local mosques. *(A bit farther down from the Museum of the Liberation of Pleven toward the train station. Tel. 372 08. Open daily 8:30am-6:30pm; services at 8am and 5pm.)* During the day, it is possible to rent rowboats at the small pond in **Kailuka Park,** south of the city. *(Open 10 am-6pm. 0.10lv.)* The park, with a pond and a creek surrounded by restaurants, fountains, and flowers, provides a beautiful (and cool) setting for a stroll on a hot summer evening. The myriad cafes surrounding the fountains, two main squares, and Vasil Levski are also popular venues for trying **Pleven beer**, the city's own label. When all else fails, the **movie theater** next to Rostov na Don (see **Accommodations,** p. 130) usually shows several English language films.

NEAR PLEVEN: TROYAN MONASTERY (ТРОЯНСКИ МАНАСТИР)

Perched in the picturesque Balkan mountain range near Pleven, the **Troyan Monastery** is said to have been built by a lone 14th-century monk shortly after the area came under Turkish control. The monastery attracted a large order of monks in the late 1600s, then became an active participant in the 19th-century independence movement, hiding revolutionary leader Vasil Levsky from his oppressors (see **History,** p. 93). Today, it is the largest monastery in the Balkan Range.

The monastery contains a wide range of murals by master artist **Zahari Zograf** (see **Literature and Arts,** p. 95), including some of his striking interpretations of the "Book of Revelations." Zograf's brother, **Dimitev,** contributed a number of beautifully subtle icon paintings to the monastery, most of which are in the main church. Look for the crafty, miracle-working **Three-handed Holy Virgin,** the monastery's oldest icon, traced back to the 17th century. The **iconostasis** is also noteworthy for its ornate woodcarving, featuring plumed birds and twisting grape vines. On display in the **Chapel of St. Nikolai the Miracle Worker**—the monastery's oldest, best-preserved building, a 30min. hike from the main complex—is an icon with a false-bottomed frame that once carried mail for the secret revolutionary committee.

The monastery is open daily 6am-7:30pm. You can **sleep** in a monastery cell, complete with lumpy beds and private bathrooms (10lv in the new building, 5lv in the old), and eat across the street at the **Manastirska Magernitsa Restaurant** (Манастирска Магерница; tel. 31 05). The restaurant has outdoor dining on the river and entrees range from 4-8lv. (Open daily 8am-midnight.)

GETTING THERE. The monastery is located in the tiny village of **Oreshka** (Орешка), accessible by a 30min. city bus ride from nearby Troyan. **Buses** run from Pleven to **Troyan** (1½hr., one per day, 2lv). Troyan can also be reached from Pleven through the midway town of **Lovech** (hourly, 1.60lv from each town to Lovech). In Troyan, catch the bus heading to the monastery directly in front of the station; get off when you see the monastery (25min., hourly, 0.30lv).

SHUMEN (ЩУМЕН)

Shumen is notable mainly for its proximity to archaeological sites at Preslav, Pliska, and Madara, which date from the beginning of the Bulgarian state. The city itself is mainly industrial, with little to offer tourists other than worn-down buildings well on their way to becoming archaelogical artifacts themselves.

ORIENTATION & PRACTICAL INFORMATION. Shumen can be reached by **train** from: **Varna** (1½hr., 11 per day, 2.30lv); **Ruse** (3hr., 1 per day, 3.20lv); **Sofia** (6hr., 6 per day, 8lv); and elsewhere via the rail hub of **Gorna Oryahovitsa,** just outside Veliko Turnovo. **Group Travel** (tel. 627 13), whose kiosk is next to the **bus station,** directly across from the train station, sends **buses** to: **Varna** (1hr., 1 per day, 4.70lv, students 4.20lv); **Veliko Turnovo** (2½hr., 3 per day, 5.50lv, students 4.80lv); and **Sofia** (6hr., 3 per day, 10lv, students 9lv). Shumen is centered around two main drags, both of which run from the stations to **pl. Oborishte** (Оборище), the closest thing to a town center. Take bus #4 (0.25lv) from behind the bus station and get off at Hotel Shumen. Or, walk from the station—go up the steps to the park and take any path to the far right-hand corner. You will emerge at a traffic circle, **pl. Bulgaria**—cross to the middle one of the three streets, **bul. Slavyansky** (Славянский), and follow this to the main pedestrian street which is lined with cafes, trees, and benches. Bul. Slavyansky becomes **Hristo Botev** after Hotel Madara and connects to pl. Oborishte. The **tourist office,** pl. Oborishte 6a (tel. 553 13), to the right as you face Hotel Shumen, arranges **private rooms** and provides **maps** (1lv; old street names, but useful for bus routes) and info. (Open M-F 8:30am-6pm, Sa 9am-3pm.) **Biohim Bank,** just up bul. Slavyansky from the traffic circle in pl. Bulgaria, next to Kino Herson (Кино Херсон), cashes **traveler's checks** for a 1% commission (US$2 min.; open M-F 9am-5pm). There is an **ATM** between the Halts (Халц) and the United Bulgarian Bank on Czar Osvoboditel, the cobblestoned street off Hristo Botev and near pl. Oborishte. **Store luggage** at the train station for 0.50lv. (Open 24hr.) There is a **pharmacy** at bul. Slavyansky 48 (tel. 555 14). The **post office** is at the top of bul. Slavyansky, right by Hotel Madara. (Open M-F 7:30am-noon and 1-4:15pm; **telephones** open daily 7am-9:30pm.) **Postal code:** 9700. **Email** and **internet** access are available in the cafe in the lobby of Hotel Madara (30min. 2lv, 1hr. 3lv). **Phone code:** (0)54.

ACCOMMODATIONS & FOOD. Other than **private rooms** (US$8, plus 0.50lv fee; see **tourist office,** above), options for affordable lodging are slim. **Hotel Orbita** (tel. 523 98) is in Kyoshkovete Park (Кьошковете Парк), at the western end of town near the Shumen brewery. Take bus #6 to its last stop from the train and bus stations. Enter the park and walk down the paved path; the hotel is on the right.

Sweet-smelling (no beer stench from the brewery), recently-renovated rooms boast showers, shaded terraces, and firm mattresses. (Doubles 40lv.)

Bul. Slavyansky is lined with restaurants, while fruit and vegetable stands litter Hristo Botev. **Popsheytanova Kushta** (Попшейтанова Къща; tel. 574 02), on pl. Oborishte, prepares exotic salads and not-so-exotic Bulgarian fare. (Entrees 1500-6lv. Live music after 7pm. Open daily 11am-midnight.) For a tall, cool one (0.50lv), drop by the **Shumen Brewery** restaurant, up the stairs across from the park housing Hotel Orbita. While beer is their specialty, they also do a fair job with Bulgarian cooking. (Entrees 2-6lv. Open daily 11am-midnight.)

SIGHTS & ENTERTAINMENT. Shumen's greatest treasure is its **fortress** (Shumenska krepost; Шуменска Крепост). Take the asphalt road outside the park by the last stop of bus #6 leading toward and past Hotel Orbita, and settle in for a long-but-beautiful uphill hike (30min.). Built by Thracians in the 5th century BC, the fortress was later used by Romans and Byzantines. All that remains is a maze of cobblestone walls running across the hill. (Open daily 8am-5pm. 2lv, students 1lv.) A rather poor map outside the main gate suggests some **hiking** routes in the area. One of them (1½hr.) leads to the tall hilltop structure overlooking Shumen, the **Monument to the Founders of the Bulgarian State** (Pametnik Sozdatel Bulgarski Durzhava; Паметник Създател Български Държава), erected in 1981. The exactly 1300 steps—one for each year of Bulgaria's existence—start down on bul. Slavyansky. Once—if—you reach the top, you'll find a great view as well as metallic mosaics and eerie stone figures representing scenes from medieval Bulgarian history. (Tel. 625 98. Open daily 8:30am-4:30pm. 2.70lv, students 1lv; tours 2lv.)

Dance the night away at the open-air disco **Lucky,** next to the station. (Open daily 10pm-3am.) The **Terminator 2,** Hotel Shumen, is despite the name more refined. (Open daily off-season only 10pm-5am.) Shumen also lays claim to Bulgaria's earliest theater group; the tradition of dramatic front-running is played out September to June in the **theater** on Slavyansky. (Tel. 522 43. Box office open M-F 3-7pm.)

NEAR SHUMEN: PLISKA (ПЛИСКА) AND VELIKI PRESLAV (ВЕЛИКИ ПРЕСЛАВ)

Pliska (PLEE-ska) and Veliki Preslav (Veh-LEEK-ee PRES-lav), the first and second capitals of Bulgaria (681-893 and 893-972, respectively), stand as crumbling testaments to the nation's Golden Age. They also reflect the present; their tragic neglect is a sign of a country too poor to take care of its treasures. The antithesis of a tourist trap, the tiny village of Pliska offers nothing but local hospitality. The real attraction is the huge **archaeological excavation** 3km away, which has unearthed parts of palaces and fortifications. Although the ruins are essentially unmarked, it is easy enough to let your imagination guide you through the partially reconstructed **king's palace.** Unfortunately, no public transportation services the ruins. To get there from Pliska's bus station, cross the big, white-tiled area behind the cafe, head left on Han Krum (Хан Крум), and settle in for the long haul among the sunflowers (30min.).

Preslav, 18km south of Shumen, is home to the more touristed **Veliki Preslav Archaeological Reserve.** The graffiti-embellished English map is the only one available. To get to the **Archaelogical Museum** (Arheologicheski Muzey; Археологически Музей), enter the park, walk straight past the statue, and bear right at the next intersection. Walk to the cafe, then take a sharp left onto a paved path to the museum (20min.). The museum exhibits artifacts found in the area and shows three short films in English on the town's history. (Tel. 32 43. Open daily Apr.-Sept. 8am-5pm; Oct.-May 9am-5pm. 2lv, students 1lv; films 1.50lv each. English guide free.) The ruins are down the road from the museum through a stone gate. Make sure to see the ruins of the **Golden Temple** (built in 908) and the temple's well-preserved floor mosaic. The king's palace is marked by a column, and parts of the city's **fortress wall** still stand (request a guide at the museum).

GETTING THERE. Pliska lies 23km northeast of Shumen and is accessible by **bus** (45min., 4 per day, 0.90lv). Buses returning to Shumen are few and far between, with the last one leaving around 5pm. **Preslav** can also be reached from Shumen by

BULGARIA

bus (40min., 7 per day, 0.70lv). Facing the bus station, walk to the left up the main street, then take a left on the road just before the plaza with big stone statues and a church. Pass the food market (*pazar*) to reach the Reserve and its ruins.

NEAR SHUMEN: MADARA (МАДАРА)

Madara (mah-DAH-rah), 16km east of Shumen, is home to the famous **Madara Horseman** (Мадарски Конния) stone relief. On a vertical cliff 25m above ground, the life-size figure features a horse with a rider, lion, and dog—an ensemble so legendary it graces the backs of all leva coins and the labels of *Shumen* beer. The artist and his means are unknown, but the work was created in the 8th century and supposedly symbolizes the victories of Bulgarian ruler Han Tervel over the crumbling Byzantine empire. A path leads methodically through prehistoric Stone and Copper Age caves (3500 BC). The largest one served as the **Temple of Three Thracian Nymphs** (Trakicheski Svetilishte; Тракически Светилище; 1st-4th century BC) and now houses the annual festival **Madara Music Days** (Madarski Musikalni Dni; Мадарски Музикални Дни) in June. The more than 150 cells carved into the rock stand as proof of Madara's importance as a perennial cult center. On top of the plateau sit the remains of the 4th-century **Madara Fortress,** which once—along with the Shumen Fortress—guarded the route to Pliska and Preslav. You'll have to climb nearly 400 tiring steps to reach the top. (Open daily in summer 8:30am-5:30pm; winter 8:30am-4:30pm. 1.80lv, students 0.20lv.) Apart from the Horseman, the ruins are very similar to those at Pliska, Preslav, and Shumen; the hike is only worthwhile if you're in the mood for a long trek, albeit with some beautiful vistas of the valley.

GETTING THERE. To get to Madara, take a **bus** (20min., 3 per day, 0.80lv) from Shumen or any *putnicheski* (slow train) to **Varna** (20min., 5 per day, 3 stops away, 0.50lv). With your back to the train station and facing the tracks, go left on the small path toward town. Turn left at the paved street, then veer left and follow the winding road uphill (30min.). Take the stairs on the right up to the Horseman, then take the small path to the left at the top of the stairs to the fortress.

CROATIA (HRVATSKA)

US$1 = 7.16KN (KUNA)	**1KN = US$0.14**
CDN$1 = 4.81KN	**1KN = CDN$0.21**
UK£1 = 11.51KN	**1KN = UK£0.09**
IR£1 = 9.65KN	**1KN = IR£0.10**
AUS$1 = 4.66KN	**1KN = AUS$0.21**
NZ$1 = 3.80KN	**1KN = NZ$0.26**
SAR1 = 1.18KN	**1KN = SAR0.84**
DM1 = 3.88KN	**1KN =DM0.26**

PHONE CODES Country code: **385.** International dailing prefix: **00.**

Croatia is a land of unearthly beauty. Traced with thick forests, karst, wispy plains, underground streams, and the translucent sea, it has served for centuries as a summer playground for residents of countries less scenically endowed. Positioned where the Mediterranean, the Alps, and the Pannonian plain converge, it has also been situated on dangerous divides—between the Frankish and Byzantine empires in the 9th century, the Catholic and Orthodox churches beginning in the 11th century, Christian Europe and Islamic Turkey from the 15th to the 19th centuries, and its own fractious ethnic groups in the past decade. Now, dancing in nightclubs in Dubrovnik or lounging on the beaches in Brač, it is easy to forget the tensions that have played out here in the past. Experiencing independence for the first time in 800 years, Croatians, and you, are finally free to enjoy the extraordinary landscape in peace.

HIGHLIGHTS OF CROATIA

■ Those in the know head to **Zagreb** for an alluring mix of Habsburg splendor, Mediterranean relaxation, and the hippest cafe scene in the Balkans (p. 143).

■ George Bernard Shaw called **Dubrovnik** "paradise on earth" for its stunning seascapes and walled city center; its funky nightlife is equally fab (p. 169).

■ Croatia's most impressive Roman ruins—particularly its amphitheater—stand in **Pula,** the 2000-year-old heart of Istria (p. 149).

■ Lavender-scented **Hvar** is easily the most beautiful island in the Adriatic (p. 165).

LIFE & TIMES

HISTORY

Just across the Adriatic Sea from Italy, Croatia's early history dates back to the **Roman Empire's** conquest of Dalmatia, Istria, and Pannonia from the 2nd century BC to the 4th century AD; Roman ruins still litter the country. After the fall of the Roman Empire in the 4th century, Croatia became a battlefield between the eastern **Byzantine Empire** and the western **Frankish** invaders. To this day, Croatia is marked as a crossroads between West and East, between Christianity and Islam.

The ancestors of Croatia's present inhabitants settled the region in the 6th and 7th centuries. They followed a largely unknown native religion until **Catholicism** arrived slowly over the next two centuries. The Croats successfully resisted Charlemagne's attempts to gain control of their area, and **King Tomislav** (910-28) earned his country papal recognition, consolidating Croatian independence. King Zvonimir finally expelled the Byzantines and was crowned by Pope Gregory in 1076, decisively strengthening Croatia's orientation toward Catholic Europe.

The history of Dalmatia and Istria diverged from that of Pannonia in the 12th century. The coastal regions remained under the control of various Mediterranean powers and eventually fell to the **Venetian Empire** in 1420, while inland Croatia joined politically with Central Europe in 1102 when the **Kingdom of Croatia-Slavonia** entered as a junior partner into a dynastic union with Hungary. This partnership would tie Croatia to Hungary for the next 800 years. Instability prevailed after 1241, when Mongol invaders swept through Eastern Europe, crushing the Hungarians at the Sajo River. Local rulers became more powerful at the expense of the Hungarian king until the monarchy's recovery in the late 14th to early 15th centuries. After an Ottoman victory over Hungary at the **Battle of Mohaćs** in 1526, the whole of Croatia once again became an embattled border region. In 1797, Dalmatia and Istria fell to the Austrian Empire, finally reuniting all three regions of the nation under one government. Despite centuries of Ottoman, Italian, Austrian, and Hungarian struggles for Croatian territory, there was no unified nationalist protest until Hungarian was declared the official language and minority rights were curbed in the 1830s and 40s. When Hungary revolted against Austria in 1848, the Croats sided with the Austrians, convening a diet in Zagreb to demand self-government. Josip Jelačic, chief of the **Zagreb Diet,** ordered Croatia to break with Hungary, proclaimed loyalty to the Austrian Emperor Franz Josef, and led an army toward Budapest. Although they were defeated by the Hungarians at Pákozd in 1848, the struggle continued into 1849 and Croat participation on the Habsburg side helped defeat the Magyars. With the creation of the **Austro-Hungarian Empire** in 1867, Croatia-Slavonia became part of the Hungarian kingdom while most of the coast was incorporated into the Austrian half of the kingdom.

During **WWI** Croatian troops fought with the rest of Austria-Hungary on the side of the Germans. After November 1914, however, political exiles raised the idea of political unity between the Serb, Croat, and Slovene nations as a way to further independence. On October 29, 1918, after the collapse of the Central Powers, Croatia broke with Hungary and the Dual Monarchy. Austria-Hungary sued the Allies for peace on November 3, and on December 1 the **Kingdom of the Serbs, Croats, and Slovenes** (the original name for Yugoslavia) declared its independence with two rival governments: the National Council in Zagreb and the Serb royal government in Belgrade. Croats and Slovenes demanded a federal state, but the Serbian monarch, **King Alexander,** failed to work for reconciliation and proclaimed a dictatorship in 1929. In 1934, he was assassinated by Macedonian and Croatian nationalists during a visit to Marseilles. Neutral at the outbreak of **WWII,** Yugoslavia nearly joined the Axis for protection, but British-assisted Greek triumphs over Italy provoked a pro-Allied coup in Belgrade in 1941. Hitler diverted forces into Yugoslavia, and German bombers reduced Belgrade to rubble with the help of Hungary and Bulgaria. Italy annexed Split and parts of Slovenia, while Croatia and Serbia were occupied by Germany. Savage fighting ensued between Serbs and Croats, who nearly entered into a civil war over divided sympathies for the Axis and Allied powers, with the Croats siding with the fascist Nazis. The puppet state created by Croat **Ustaše** fascists under Ante Pavelić worked to exterminate the Serbian population. While it is unclear whether historical accounts are accurate or merely nationalist propaganda, Croatia has been accused of mass genocide of Serbs, committing atrocities akin to those of the Nazis. Regardless, the majority of the Croatian population either joined or indirectly supported the anti-fascist Partisan forces led by Communists and **Josip Brož Tito,** a half-Croat, half-Slovene. Partisan resistance in Yugoslavia was fierce, and eventually led to the country's liberation. Yugoslav Croatia recovered Istria, the Adriatic islands, and Zadar from Italy after the war and became part of the **Socialist Republic of Yugoslavia.**

In 1945, Tito placed all industry and natural resources under state control. Under his unchallenged rule Yugoslavia broke with Stalin in 1948 and decentralized the administration. Ethnic rivalries aside, Yugoslavia became a relatively tolerant, prosperous communist country. In 1971, the Croatian Communists asked for greater autonomy within Yugoslavia, and Tito, under pressure from the army, dismissed the entire leadership and replaced them with more obedient Communists. Tito ruled until his death in 1980. Yugoslavia, with its volatile ethnic mix, descended into violence after communism's wholesale defeat and collapse in Europe. In April 1990, the nationalist **Franjo Tudjman** was elected president of Croatia, and on June 25, 1991, the people of Croatia, at the same time as the neighboring Slovenes, declared **independence.** Anxieties began to arise among the significant Serbian minority, which opposed Croatian independence. The Serbs, who controlled the **Yugoslav National Army,** expelled hundreds of thousands of Croatians from Eastern Slavonia and shelled Vukovar, Osijer in Slavonia, and even Zagreb.

On January 15, 1992, Croatia was recognized as an independent country by the E.U., and a U.N. military presence kept further fighting at bay. In May 1995, Croatia, frustrated with its lack of control over more than half its territory, began an operation in Western Slavonia and seized the Serb-controlled **Krajina** in August, expelling over 150,000 Serbs. Since a late-1995 agreement, there has been relative peace in Croatia, but tension has not altogether dissipated.

CROATIA

CROATIA TODAY

As Croatia copes with its burdened economy, the euphoria of independence has faded. Tensions remain high in the former Serb-held areas of the Krajina and Western Slavonia, as the Croatian government resists accommodating the returning Serbian refugees. In January 1998, fulfilling a long-delayed stipulation of the Dayton Peace Agreement, Zagreb took over Serb-held **Eastern Slavonia** after two years of U.N. control. The biggest challenge has been the exchange of refugees between Eastern Slavonia and the rest of Croatia, with violence erupting between returning refugees and the still-displaced refugees occupying their former homes. Remarkably, tensions between Croats and Serbs have not risen markedly since the outbreak of the 1999 Kosovo crisis.

Croatian politics are dominated by the **Croatian Democratic Party (HDZ),** which won the national elections in April 1997. However, as the political scene becomes increasingly bipolar, the **Social Democratic Party of Croatia (SDP)** continues to gain ground as a legitimate left-wing opposition party. **Franjo Tudjman** remains the president, although he is rumored to be dying of cancer. With elections approaching in 2000, Croatian politicians are struggling to gain widespread support, but there is little hope that any party will win a majority. Many Croatians and international powers fear that the elections will fail to produce a stable government and may instead lead to a constitutional crisis. Fear of political instability, coupled with a continual unearthing of Croatia's human rights violations toward the Serbs during both WWII and the recent wars, has inspired skepticism that Croatia is truly ready to turn toward the West. Croatia's aspirations to join the E.U. give the international community some leverage; unfortunately, the E.U. stipulates that membership is contingent upon Croatia returning some territory to Italy. The likelihood of Croatian support for such a move—even in exchange for much-desired E.U. membership—is slim.

LITERATURE & ARTS

The first Croatian texts date from the 9th century, and for the next 600 years Croatian literature consisted almost entirely of translations of Europe's greatest literary hits. **Renaissance** influences from the West made their way to the Dalmatian coast in the 1500s when the first Croatian poets, among them **Marko Marulić** and **Petar Hektorvić,** finally moved from devotional to secular writing. The 16th-century dramatist **Marin Držić** and the 17th-century poet **Ivan Gundulić** raided Italy for models (of the literary type), combining them with influences from oral traditions back home. After the 1667 Dubrovnik earthquake that devastated the city and destroyed its population, the focus of Croatian literature shifted north.

The Counter-Reformation brought the Franciscans and the Jesuits, who focused on education and established Zagreb as a cultural center. Some of Croatia's most influential 18th-century authors were the Franciscans **Filip Grabovač, Kačić Miošić,** and **Matej Reljković.** The political domination of Croatia by Austria and Hungary threatened to become a linguistic domination in the following century—**Ljudevit Gaj** led the movement to reform and codify the vernacular. With the work of the poet **Ivan Mažuranic,** the revival of Croatian literature was established at last. **August Šenoa,** Croatia's dominant 19th-century literary figure, played a key part in the formation of a literary public and in completing the work that Gaj had begun.

Poetry returned in multiple incarnations in the 20th century, first stimulated by Croatian Modernist **Anton-Gustav Matoš** and later by the interwar avant-garde writers **Anton Branko Šimić** and **Tin Ujević.** Croatian prose also sparkled in the 20th century, inspired in the 30s by the novels of **Miroslav Krleža.** It shined again in the 70s, as young prose writers dubbed the **Borgesites**—named after Argentinian author Jorge Luis Borges—wove fantastic themes into short stories and novels. Among the Borgesites were **Pavao Pavličić,** a popular author of numerous mystery and crime novels set in Zagreb, and the controversial **Dubravka Ugresić,** whose personal, reflective novels took on political overtones during the recent war, when she publicly opposed Croatian President Tudjman. Her works, which discuss nostalgia and the revision of history, are instant bestsellers in Croatia, much to the chagrin of the state media apparatus. **Slavenka Drakulić,** another novelist and feminist, is more popular abroad than at home. Her works in English include *Balkan Express: Fragments from the Other Side of War* and *Cafe Europa.*

In the 20th century, Croatian visual arts increased in importance. Characterized by the rejection of conventional and "civilized" depictions of subjects, **naive art** presides as the most popular painting style. Highly influenced by folk traditions, it eliminates perspective and uses only brilliant and vivid colors. **Ivan Meštrović** (see **Zagreb: Sights,** p. 146), Croatia's most famous modern sculptor and architect, was mentored by French sculptor Auguste Rodin and immigrated to the United States in the 1950s. Outside of Croatia, his wooden religious sculptures can be seen at London's Tate Gallery and the Metropolitan Museum of Art in New York City. **Vinko Bresan** is Croatia's recent contribution to the international film scene. His 1996 comedy, *How the War Started on My Island (Kako je poceo rat na mom otoku)*, won multiple awards at the 1996 Croatian Film Festival, including the Golden Arena for Best Director and the Golden Arc for Audience Approval.

READING LIST

The most objective book available on Croatian history is Stephen Gazi's *A History of Croatia;* unfortunately, the book only covers the country prior to 1939. It is difficult to find any book on Croatian history after the outbreak of WWII that is not rejected by either Serbs or Croats as a piece of nationalist propaganda or as media lies. The safest option, therefore, is to read the nationalist propaganda from both sides. Two opposing books about WWII and its aftermath in Yugoslavia are John Prcela and Stanko Guldescu's *Operation Slaughterhouse*, a detailed account of the persecution and murdering of Croats by Serbs, and *The Yugoslav Auschwitz and the Vatican: the Croatian Massacre of the Serbs During World War II* by Vladimir Dedijer and Harvey Kendall. Fair texts dealing with the recent wars in Croatia are as difficult to find, although Dubravka Ugresić rejects all forms of nationalist propoganda in her recent collection of controversial political essays, *The Culture of Lies: Antipolitical Essays.* A more personal perspective on the Balkan situation is offered in *The Suitcase: Refugee Voices from Bosnia and Croatia*, edited by Cornel West. If political and historical writings seem uninteresting, Francis Violich's illustrated travelogue, *The Bridge to Dalmatia: A Search for the Meaning of Place*, offers an outsider's take on the natural wonders and political horrors of the Dalmatian Coast.

FACTS AND FIGURES

- **Capital:** Zagreb
- **Population:** 4,774,000
- **Land Area:** 56,610km^2
- **Geography:** Mountainous, with farmland in the Northeast
- **Language:** Croatian
- **Religions:** 72% Catholic, 14% Eastern Orthodox, 1% Muslim
- **GDP per capita:** US$14,650
- **Major Exports:** Transport equipment

CROATIA ESSENTIALS

Citizens of Australia, Ireland, New Zealand, the U.K, and the U.S. do not need visas to enter Croatia. Visas are required of South African citizens; send your passport, a visa application, two passport-sized photos, a document proving your intent of tourism (i.e. invitation, voucher, or receipt of business arrangements) and a personal check or money order (US$29 for single-entry, US$37 for double-entry, or $59 for multiple entry) to the nearest embassy or consulate (see **Essentials: Embassies & Consulates,** p. 13). All visitors must register with the police within two days of arrival, regardless of their length of stay. Citizens of any country staying more than 90 days should fill out an "extension of stay" form at a local police station.

GETTING THERE & GETTING AROUND

Whether by plane, train, or bus, Zagreb is Croatia's main entry point. **Croatia Airlines** flies there from many cities, including Chicago, Frankfurt, London, New York, Paris, and Toronto, and often continues on to Dubrovnik and Split. Rijeka, Zadar, and Pula also have international airports. **Trains** travel to Zagreb from Budapest, Ljubljana, and Vienna, continuing on to other destinations throughout Croatia. *Odlazak* means departures, *dolazak* arrivals.

PRIMARY BORDER CROSSINGS. Only transit visas, valid for seven days, can be purchased at the border at wildly varying prices. There is no entry fee required at the border. As always, the most direct way of entering or exiting Croatia is to take a direct bus or train to or from Zagreb to a neighboring capital.

Bosnia-Herzegovina: Most travelers take a direct bus between Zagreb (p. 139) and Sarajevo (p. 82). Metkovič, CRO/Metkovič, BOS; connects Split (p. 159) and Central Dalmatian Coast with Mostar, BOS. Brgat, CRO/Trebinje, BOS; connects Dubrovnik (p. 169) and Southern Dalmatian Coast with Mostar, BOS. Ličko, CRO/Bihać, BOS via Petrovo Selo, BOS; connects Northern Dalmatia and Gulf of Kvarner (p. 153) northern Bosnia.

Hungary: Virovitica, CRO/Barcs, HUN; connects eastern Croatia (Slavonia) with Pécs, HUN (p. 317). Varižđin, CRO/Letenye, HUN; connects eastern Croatia and Zagreb (p. 139) with Lake Balaton, HUN (p. 309).

Slovenia: Sočerga, CRO/Sočerga, SLO; connects the Gulf of Kvarner, CRO (p. 153) with Slovenian Istria (p. 725). Umag, CRO/Potorož, SLN; connects Croatian Istria (p. 149) with Slovenian Istria (p. 149).

Yugoslavia: In summer 1999, borders were closed between Croatia and Montenegro and Serbia. Enter Yugoslavia through Hungary.

For domestic travel, **buses** are by far the best option, running faster than their railed counterparts for comparable prices. Tickets are actually cheaper if you buy them on board, as you bypass the 2kn "service charge" at the station kiosks. In theory, luggage must be stowed (3kn), but this is only enforced on the most crowded of lines. You can **rent a car** in larger cities, but downtown parking can be expensive, roads in the country are in atrocious condition, and those traveling through the Krajina region and other conflict areas should be wary of off-road land mines. Contact the **Croatian Automobile Association** (tel. (01) 464 08 00) for further info.

If you're on the coast, take one of the **ferries** run by **Jadrolinija.** Boats sail the Rijeka-Split-Dubrovnik route, stopping at islands along the way. Ferries also float from Split to Ancona, Italy, and from Dubrovnik to Bari, Italy. Although slower than buses and trains, they're more comfortable. A basic ticket provides only a place on the deck. Cheap beds sell out fast, so purchase tickets in advance. If the agency will only offer a basic ticket, in which case you'll need to *run* to get a bed.

TOURIST SERVICES

Most major cities have a branch of the **state-run tourist board** *(turistička zajednica)*, which speak some English and German and are quite resourceful with maps and info. Private accommodations are handled by private tourist agencies *(turistička/putnička agencija)*, the largest of which is the ubiquitous **Atlas.** Smaller local outfits are generally cheaper. Agencies also exchange money and arrange excursions, including infamous fish picnics on the coast. Tourist offices are generally open M-F 8am-6pm and Sa 9am-2pm; on the crowded coast, they may take a mid-day break and then stay open until 10pm, even on Sundays.

MONEY & COMMUNICATION

Croatia is in the process of changing its phone numbers. Although we've accounted for as many as possible, most aren't changing until the millennium. Some of the numbers listed will be wrong in summer 2000. If you call a changed number, a voice will tell you in English and Croatian what the new number is.

Most banks, tourist offices, hotels, and transportation stations exchange currency and traveler's checks. Croatia's monetary unit, the **kuna** (kn)—divided into 100 lipa—is pretty much impossible to exchange abroad, except in Hungary and Slovenia. Neither South African rand nor Irish pounds are exchangeable in Croatia. **ATMs** *(bankomat)* are widespread on the mainland and the islands. Most banks give MC/Visa **cash advances,** and most hotels and restaurants accept credit cards.

Mail from the U.S. arrives in 7 day or less; if addressed to *Poste Restante,* it will be held for 90 days at the main (not always the most central) post office. *Avionski* and *zrakoplovom* both mean "air mail" in Croatian. **Post offices** usually have **public phones;** pay after you talk. Most phones on the street require phone cards *(telekarta)*, sold at all newsstands and post offices. 50 "impulses" cost 23kn (1 impulse equals 3min. domestic, 36seconds international; 50% discount 10pm-7am and Sundays and holidays). Dial 08 00 22 01 11 for **AT&T Direct,** 0800 22 00 44 for **BT Direct,** 008 00 22 01 01 for **Canada Direct,** or 08 00 22 01 12 for **MCI World Phone.** Technically, this operator assistance is free, but some phones demand a telekarta card, and calls to the U.S. are expensive (20kn per min.). The **internet** is available in the smallest towns, making email a viable and cheap method of keeping in touch.

LANGUAGE

Croats speak a South Slavic language and write in Roman characters. Words are pronounced exactly as they are written; "č" and "ć" are both pronounced "ch" (only a Croat can tell them apart), "š" is "sh", and "ž" is a "zh" sound. The letter "r" is rolled, except when there's no vowel, then it makes an "er" sound as in "Brrrr!" The letter "j" is equivalent to "y," so *jučer* (yesterday) is pronounced "yuchur." In Zagreb and most tourist offices, some people know **English,** but the most common language on the coast is **Italian. German** is the main language of the tourist industry. Street designations on maps often differ from those on signs by "-va" or "-a" because of grammatical declensions (see p. 143). Helpful phrases include *dobar dan* (good day), *do videnja* (good bye), *hvala* (thank you), and the multi-purpose *molim* (you're welcome/please/excuse me). For more vocab, see the **Glossary,** p. 808, and **Bosnia: Language,** p. 84, for the differences between Bosnian, Croatian, and Serbian. Words that appear frequently in this chapter include: *crkva* (church); *hram* (temple); *kolodvor* (station); *ljekarna* (pharmacy); *most* (bridge); *novi grad* (new town); *stari grad* (old town); *šetalište* (promenade); and *trg* (square).

HEALTH & SAFETY

EMERGENCY NUMBERS.
Fire: tel. 93. **Police:** tel. 92. **Ambulance:** tel. 94.

The **climate** is mild and continental around Zagreb and Mediterranean along the coast. Although Croatia is no longer at war, travel to the Slavonia and Krajina regions remains dangerous due to **unexploded mines.** Travel to the coast and islands is considered safe. The **police** require foreigners to **register** within two days of entering the country. Hotels, campsites, and accommodations agencies should do this for you, but those staying with friends or in private rooms must do so themselves to avoid fines or expulsion. Police may check foreigners' passports anywhere. **Crime** is rare. **Pharmacies** are generally well-stocked with Western products, including condoms, but apart from major cities they tend to close at night.

Croatians are friendly toward foreigners and sometimes a little too friendly to female travelers; going out in public with a companion will help to ward off unwanted displays of machismo. Establishments are very receptive to travelers with young children, and discounts abound. Croatians are just beginning to accept **homosexuality,** so be discreet. The official age limit for alcohol consumption is 18, but—as far as natives are concerned—what's a couple of years between friends? Nonetheless, *Let's Go* does not recommend or condone underage drinking.

ACCOMMODATIONS & CAMPING

Two words: **private rooms.** Apart from the country's six rather shabby **youth hostels** (in Zagreb, Pula, Zadar, Šibernik, Dubrovnik, and Punat) and **camping** (bring your own tent), they are the only affordable option. Look for *sobe* signs, especially near transportation stations in small towns. Agencies generally charge 30-50% more if you stay less than three nights. All accommodations are subject to a **tourist tax** of 5-10kn (another reason the police require foreigners to register). If you opt for a hotel, calling at least a day in advance is imperative, especially during the summer on the coast when there isn't a war going on somewhere nearby. Wherever you stay, hot water is ephemeral at best. In private lodging, it is often heated in a barrel and then fed into the house's pipes. Shower fast, or shower cold.

FOOD & DRINK

After years of wartime drought, restaurants are eagerly preparing for the return of guests. *Puricas mlincima* (turkey with pasta) is the regional dish near Zagreb. The spicy *Slavonian kulen*, available everywhere, is considered one of the world's best sausages by the panel of fat German men who decide such things. Along the coast, try *lignje* (squid) or *Dalmatinski pršut* (Dalmatian smoked ham). The oysters from the Ston Bay have received a number of awards at international competitions. If your budget does not allow for such treats, *slane sardele* (salted sardines) are a tasty substitute. Vegetarians will appreciate the heavy Italian influence, especially in coastal cuisine. *Grešak varivo* (green bean stew), *tikvice va lešo* (steamed zucchini in olive oil), and *grah salata* (beans and onion salad) are meatless favorites. The eclectic nature of Croatian culture is most apparent with desserts; if you always ask for a regional specialty, you'll never eat the same sweet twice. *Zagorski štrukli* (dumplings with a cottage cheese filling) in Zagreb and *fritule* (thin baked pastry) in Dalmatia are just two examples.

Croatia offers excellent wines: the price is usually the best indicator of quality. Mix red wine with tap water to get the popular *bevanda*, and white with carbonated water to get *gemišt*. Reds famous on the coast include *Teran*, *Merlot*, and *Cabanetia Istria*. Farther south, they include *Plavac*, *Opolo*, *Dingac*, and *Postup*. Coastal white wines of renown include *Malvazija*, *Zlahtina*, *Posip*, *Kujundzusa*, and *Grk*. *Karlovačko* and *Ožujsko* are the two most popular beers.

CUSTOMS & ETIQUETTE

Tipping is not expected, but you may round up to the nearest whole figure; in some cases, the establishment will do it for you—check your change. In the beach-oriented south, beauty is most definitely skin deep; the darker your tan, the trendier you'll be with the locals. This land of skin and shorts is also predominantly Catholic, but you'll only notice the contradiction if you try to jump from the beach to the cathedral without a change of clothes. Croats have few qualms about drinking and smoking, and prove it again and again just about everywhere.

NATIONAL HOLIDAYS

January 1, New Year's; January 6, Epiphany; April 23-24, Catholic Easter; May 1, Labor Day; May 30, Statehood Day; June 22, Croatian National Uprising Day; August 5, National Thanksgiving Day; August 15, Assumption Day; November 1, All Saints' Day; and December 25-26, Catholic Christmas.

ZAGREB

Zagreb (pop. 870,000) is not a city one falls in love with instantly. It shocks at first, with layers of grime and the outmoded fashions of the older generation. But after days of strolling through its ring of flower-filled gardens, tracking down the history lurking in every street, and lounging with locals as they chain-smoke in outdoor cafes, Zagreb emerges as a rare Balkan gem. Unlike other Central European cities, it has yet to be taken over by tourists, and even in the summer it belongs solely to its residents. Zagreb somehow manages to combine its staid Austro-Hungarian past with sleepy Mediterranean idleness and its socialist roots with a modest immersion in the West; the result is a bewitching city bound to win you over.

GETTING THERE & GETTING AROUND

Airport: Buses run between the bus station and the airport (tel. 615 79 92). Buses depart hourly M-Th and Sa 3am-8pm, F 3am-9:30pm, 20kn. Taxis cost 150-200kn.

Airplanes: Croatia Airlines, Zrinjevac 17 (tel. 481 96 33; booking tel. 487 27 27). Inquire here to book flights on other airlines. Open M-F 8am-8pm, Sa 9am-noon.

Trains: All passenger trains arrive and depart from **Glavni Kolodvor** (main station), Trg kralja Tomislava 12 (domestic tel. 98 30; international tel. 457 32 38). To: **Split** (9hr., 4 per day, 90kn); **Ljubljana** (2½hr., 5 per day, 60kn); **Budapest** (7hr., 4 per day, 194kn); and **Vienna** (6½hr., 2 per day, 327kn). No trains to **Sarajevo** or **Dubrovnik**. With your back to the station, a right on Branimira leads to the bus station in 10min.

Buses: Buses depart from **Autobusni Kolodvor,** Držićeva bb (tel. 060 31 33 33; domestic info tel. 615 79 86; international info tel. 615 79 83). To reach the train station exit onto Držićeva, the main street with the tram tracks. The city center is to your left. Turn left, walk toward the railway bridge, turn left behind the bridge on Branimirova, and walk 10min. Otherwise, take tram #2, 6, or 8 and get off at the third stop. Information and tickets are on the 2nd floor. To: **Split** (6½-9hr., 30 per day, 80-100kn); **Dubrovnik** (11hr., 7 per day, 135kn); **Frankfurt** (12hr., 8 per week, 600kn); **Ljubljana** (2hr., 4 per day, 65kn); **Sarajevo** (9hr., 3 per day, 240kn); and **Vienna** (8hr., 1 daily M-F, 180kn).

Local Transportation: Trams cover the entire city. Buy tickets at any newsstand (4.50kn) or from the driver (5kn); they are valid 1½hr. from purchase. Punch them in the boxes near the doors. 100kn fine for riding ticketless. After midnight prices rise 20%.

Taxis: Rates are generally expensive but fair, averaging 15kn to start plus 6kn per km, but prices rise 20% from 10pm-5am and on Sunday. Large companies like **Radio Taxi** (tel. 970) are the most reliable. Cabs congregate at the stand on Gajeva.

ORIENTATION

Zagreb is 30km south of the Slovene border; Austria and Hungary are about 100km north. The river **Sava** separates the historical **Gornji Grad** (Upper Town)—comprised of **Kaptol** and **Gradec** hills—and the central **Donji Grad** (Lower Town) from the more residential **Novi Zagreb** (New Zagreb). To reach the main square, **Trg bana Josipa Jelačića** in Gornji Grad from the train station, cross the street with your back to the station and walk along the left side of the park on Praška for 10min.

THE NAME GAME. Many street names throughout Croatia appear differently on street signs than on maps and in addresses because of grammatical declensions. The root of the name remains the same, but the ending changes, often dramatically. For example, on a street sign, you might find ul. kralja Držislava; addresses and maps, however, will usually list the street as Držislavova. In general, the case declension from proper street name to an address or map changes the ending from -a to -ova or from -e to -ina.

PRACTICAL INFORMATION

TOURIST & FINANCIAL SERVICES

Tourist Office: Tourist Information Center (TIC), Trg b. Jelačića 11 (tel. 481 40 51, 481 40 52, and 481 40 54; fax 481 40 56; tic@zagreb-touristinfo.hr), in the southeast corner of the square. Resourceful staff distributes free **maps** and pamphlets, but doesn't arrange accommodations. Open M-F 8:30am-8pm, Sa 10am-6pm, Su 10am-2pm.

Embassies: Australia, Mihanovićeva 1 (tel./fax 457 74 33). Open M-F 10am-2pm. **Canada,** Mihanovićeva 1 (tel. 457 79 05, emergency 098 27 91 00; fax 457 79 13). Open M-F 8am-4pm. **U.K.,** Vlaška 121 (tel. 455 53 10; fax 455 16 85). Open M-Tu and Th-F 8:30am-5pm, W and Sa 9am-noon. **U.S.,** Hebrangova 2 (tel. 455 55 00, after hours 455 52 81, Citizen Services ext. 2276; fax 455 85 85). Open M-F 8am-4:45pm.

Currency Exchange: Zagrebačka Banka has branches throughout the city. The one at Trg b. Jelačića 10 is open M-F 7:30am-7pm, Sa 7:30am-noon. Traveler's checks of all kinds cashed (1.5% commission). **ATMs** *(bankomat)* are all over the center and at the bus station; the train station boasts a 24hr. AmEx ATM.

American Express: Atlas, Lastovska 23 (tel. 612 44 22). Mail held, cards replaced, and traveler's checks cashed for no commission. Open M-F 8am-7pm, Sa 8am-noon.

LOCAL SERVICES & COMMUNICATIONS

Luggage Storage: At the train station. 10kn per piece per day. Open 24hr.

Bookstores: Algoritam, Gajeva 1, in the to Hotel Dubrovnik, carries international newspapers and magazines. Excellent selection of books in English and other tongues. Major credit cards accepted. Open M-F 9am-9pm, Sa 9am-3pm.

Laundromat: PREDOM, Draškovićeva 31 (tel. 461 29 90). 2-20kn per item, next day pickup, but no English spoken. Open M-F 7am-7pm.

Police: Department for Foreign Visitors, Petrinjska 30 (tel. 456 31 11), Room 101 on the 1st floor of the police station. All foreigners staying in private accommodations must **register here within 2 days of arrival;** use Form #14. Open M-F 8am-2pm.

Pharmacy: Gradska Ljekarna Zagreb, Zrinjevac 20 (tel. 42 77 85). Open M-Sa 7am-8pm; credit cards accepted. **Night service** (8pm-7am) available at Ilica 43.

Medical assistance: Hospital REBRO, Kišpatićeva 12 (tel. 21 53 18). Open 24hr.

Post Office: Branimirova 4 (tel. 484 03 45), next to the train station. Post office exchanges cash and traveler's checks for no commission. **Poste Restante** available on the 1st floor (enter from the side), Desk #2. Mail held for one month. Open summer daily 24hr., off-season M-Sa 24hr., Su 1pm-midnight. **Postal code:** 10000.

Internet Access: Aquariusnet, ul. k. Držislava 4 (tel. 461 88 73; email kontakt@aquariusnet.hr; www.aquariusnet.hr). Super-friendly staff can connect you *and* pour beers. 16kn for 30min. or 85kn for 30hr. card. Open 24hr. For faster connections, **Sublink Cyber Cafe,** Teslina 12 (tel. 481 13 29; sublink@sublink.hr; www.sublink.hr), in the courtyard. 19kn per hr. Open M-F noon-10pm, Sa-Su 3-10pm.

Telephones: Call from inside the post office and pay afterwards. **Phone code:** (0)1.

CROATIA

ACCOMMODATIONS

Cheap accommodations are hard to come by in Zagreb. With so few young vacationers, there remains little demand for true budget accommodations. The TIC (see **Tourist Office,** p. 144) will call hotels and private agencies to see where there is a room. **Evistas,** Šenoina 28 (tel. 42 99 74 or 481 91 33; fax 43 19 87), rents apartments and rooms in private homes. They can also secure singles (175kn), doubles (240kn) or apartments (180-220kn per person; min. stay 3 days; 20% more for one night stay, 30% more during festivals; discount for those under 25). From the train station, take a right on Branimirova, walk to Petrinjska on your left and then take a right on Petrinjska to Šenoina. (Open M-F 9am-8pm, Sa 9:30am-5pm.)

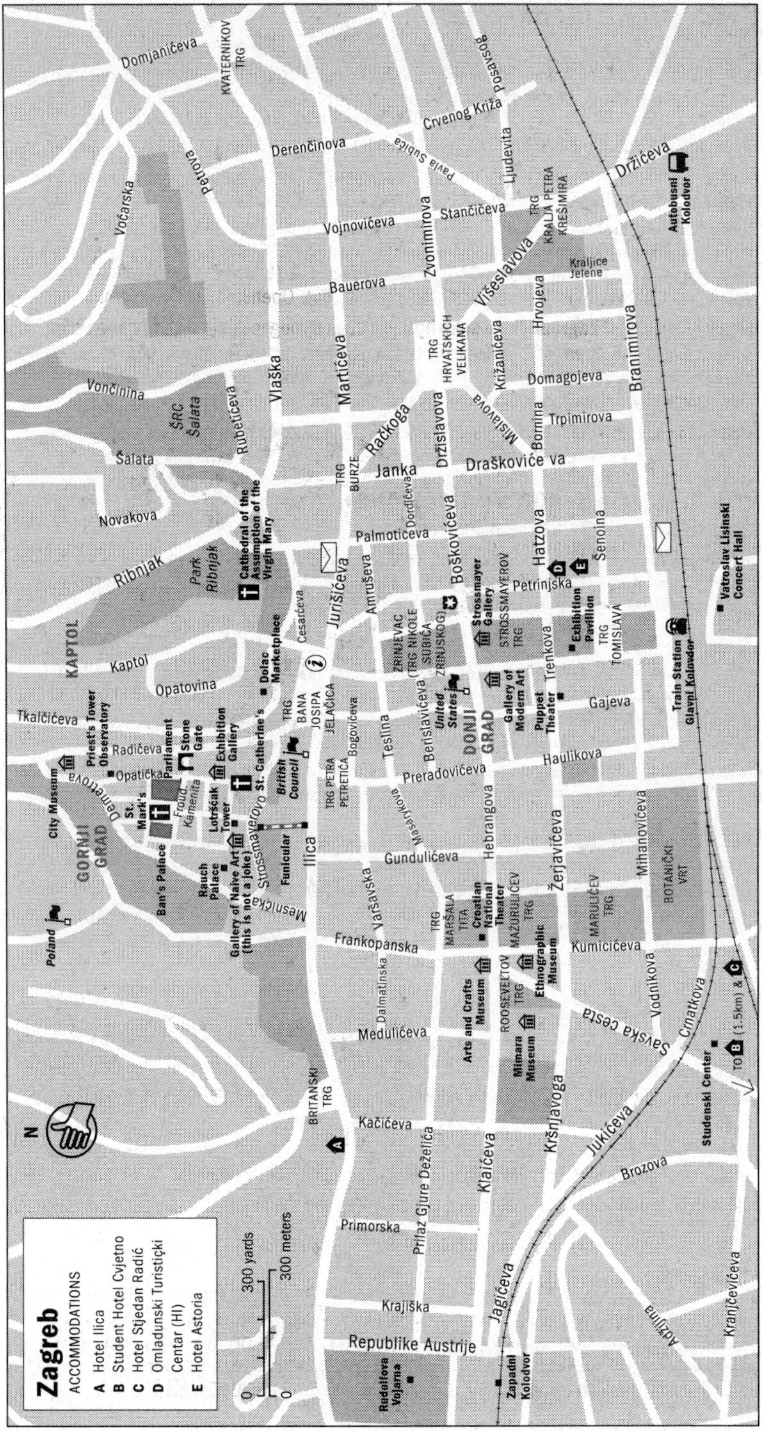
Zagreb
ACCOMMODATIONS
A Hotel Ilica
B Student Hotel Cvjetno
C Hotel Stjedan Radić
D Omladunski Turistički Centar (HI)
E Hotel Astoria
0 300 yards
0 300 meters
N
GORNJI GRAD
KAPTOL
DONJI GRAD
City Museum
St. Mark's
Parliament
Stone Gate
Priest's Tower Observatory
Lotrščak Tower
Ban's Palace
Rauch Palace
Gallery of Naive Art (this is not a joke)
Exhibition Gallery
St. Catherine's
Funicular
British Council
Dolac Marketplace
Cathedral of the Assumption of the Virgin Mary
Park Ribnjak
ŠRC Šalata
Poland
United States
Strossmayer Gallery
Gallery of Modern Art
Puppet Theater
Exhibition Pavilion
Croatian National Theater
Ethnographic Museum
Arts and Crafts Museum
Mimara Museum
Train Station Glavni Kolodvor
Autobusni Kolodvor
Vatroslav Lisinski Concert Hall
Studenski Center
Zapadni Kolodvor
Rudolfova Vojarna
BOTANIČKI VRT
TRG BANA JOSIPA JELAČIĆA
TRG PETRA PETRETIĆA
TRG BURZE
TRG HRVATSKICH VELIKANA
TRG KRALJA PETRA KREŠIMIRA
ZRINJEVAC (TRG NIKOLE SUBIĆA ZRINJSKOG)
TRG STROSSMAYEROV
TRG TOMISLAVA
MARULIĆEV TRG
TRG MARŠALA TITA
TRG MAŽURANIĆEV
ROOSEVELTOV TRG
BRITANSKI TRG
KVATERNIKOV TRG
Kraljice Jelene
TO B (1.5km) & C
Domjanićeva
Derenčinova
Crvenog Križa
Posavska
Pavla Šubića
Držićeva
Vojnovićeva
Stančićeva
Zvonimirova
Ljudevita
Bauerova
Višeslavova
Vlaška
Martićeva
Račkoga
Križanićeva
Hrvojeva
Domagojeva
Mislavova
Trpimirova
Branimirova
Vončinina
Rubetićeva
Šalata
Janka Draškovićeva
Držislavova
Bornina
Novakova
Ribnjak
Palmotićeva
Đorđićeva
Boškovićeva
Hatzova
Šenoina
Petrinjska
Cesarčeva
Jurišićeva
Amruševa
Kaptol
Opatovina
Tkalčićeva
Radićeva
Opatička
Demetrova
Mesnička
Strossmayerovo
Ilica
Bogovićeva
Teslina
Berislavićeva
Preradovićeva
Masarykova
Hebrangova
Trenkova
Gajeva
Haulikova
Gundulićeva
Varšavska
Žerjavićeva
Mihanovićeva
Frankopanska
Kumičićeva
Dalmatinska
Medulićeva
Savska cesta
Vodnikova
Crnatkova
Kačićeva
Klaićeva
Kršnjavoga
Jukićeva
Brozova
Primorska
Prilaz Gjure Deželića
Krajiška
Republike Austrije
Jagićeva
Kranjčevićeva
Vočarska
Petrova

CROATIA

Omladinski Turistički Centar (HI), Petrinjska 77 (tel. 484 12 61; fax 484 12 69). With your back to the train station, walk right on Branimirova and Petrinjska will be on your left. Perfect location makes up for a building in need of renovation. 6-bed dorm 70kn, non-members 75kn; singles 152kn, with bath 205kn; doubles 205kn, with bath 270kn.

Hotel Ilica, Ilica 102 (tel. 377 75 22 and 377 76 22; fax 377 77 22). From the train station, take tram #6 toward Črnomerec and get off at the 4th stop on Ilica. Friendly staff and modern bathrooms in a newly furnished hotel. Breakfast and parking included. Singles 299kn; doubles 399kn; apartments (for three) 639kn.

Student Hotel Cvjetno, Odranska 8 (tel. 619 12 45). From the train station, take tram #4 toward Savski most and get off at Vjesnik. Turn around and Odranska is in front of you, perpendicular to the tram tracks. A huge quiet complex of university dorms. Hall bathroom. Open July 15-Oct. 1. Singles 214kn; doubles 280kn.

Hotel Stjepan Radić, Jarunska 2 (tel. 363 42 55). From the train station, take tram #4 toward Savski most and get off at Vjesnik. Change to tram #5 or 17 and get off at Studentski dom Stjepan Radić. Walk over the crossroad toward the park. Student dorms with renovated bathrooms. Open July 15-Aug. 31. Singles 70kn; doubles 124kn.

Hotel Astoria, Petrinjska 71 (tel. 484 12 22; fax 484 12 12). With your back to the train station, walk right on Branimirova and Petrinjska will be on your left. This soon-to-be renovated hotel offers plain but clean rooms with bathrooms; for a decent view, ask for a room facing the street. Breakfast included. Singles 300kn, doubles 500kn.

FOOD

Zagrebčani adore meat, making vegetarian meals difficult to find. Along with endless bars and cafes, *slastićarne* (pastry shops)—famous for their exquisite ice cream—play an important part in the Zagreb experience. Across from the train station, an escalator leads to a huge **underground mall,** replete with inexpensive cafes, bakeries, sandwich shops, and pizzerias. Behind Trg b. Jelačića is the immaculate **Dolac** market filled with fruits and vegetables. (Open M-Sa 6am-2pm, Su 7am-noon.) There are grocery stores throughout the city, including **Konzum** at Ilica 22. (Open M-Sa 6am-9pm, Su 7am-4pm.) For a complete list of the best restaurants and pubs, pick up a free **Zagreb-Gastro** at the tourist office.

CROATIA

Boban, Gajova 9 (tel. 481 15 49). Italian eatery owned by well-known soccer player Zvonimir Boban. Cafe upstairs, restaurant downstairs, and–of course–a TV for watching soccer. Entrees 23-40kn. Cafe open daily 7am-midnight; restaurant 10am-midnight.

Bistro Kapuciner, Kaptol 6 (tel. 481 48 40), is among Zagreb's best Italian options. It serves pizza (20-60kn, depending on type and size) and pasta (20-30kn). Comfy chairs outside offer a splendid view of Kaptol. Open daily 7am-11pm.

Korčula, Teslina 17 (tel. 42 26 58), below Trg b. Jelačića. Named after the Adriatic island, Korčula brings a taste of the sea to inland Zagreb with its Dalmatian Coast specialties. Entrees 12-48kn. Buffet open daily 7am-11pm, restaurant 9am-midnight.

Grill Rubelj, Mala terasa Dolac 2/2 (tel. 481 87 77), at the Dolac market above Trg b. Jelačića. Locals laud the inexpensive grilled meat specialties. *Ćevapi* (11-20kn), *šišćevapi* (10-30kn), and burgers (12kn). Open daily 10am-11pm.

Mimice, Jurišićeva 21. Descend into this ocean-like basement restaurant and sample their buffet of seafood specialties (11-30kn). Open M-F 7am-10pm, Sa 7am-6pm.

Gostionica Tempo, Petrinjska 33a (tel. 43 11 63), near Omladinski T. Čentar. A classic Socialist cellar-restaurant. Entrees 22-25kn. Open M-F 7am-9pm.

SIGHTS

There are no regular tours of Zagreb currently available but **Zagreb Tourist Guide Association** *(Društvo Turističkih Vodića Zagreba)*, Zrinjevac 17 (tel. 481 70 22; fax 455 28 69), organizes private tours in various languages. Call in advance or stop by to arrange a time. Prices vary with the size of the group; a tour for 1-3 people runs 256kn. (Open M, W, F 10am-noon.) If you want to be your own guide, pick up the free and useful *Zagreb: City Walks* booklet at the TIC (see **Tourist Office,** p. 144). The best way to start any tour is to take the funicular (*uspinjača;* 2kn), which connects Donji Grad and Gornji Grad from Tomićeva Street. From Trg b. Jelačića, walk down Ilica, and Tomićeva is on your right. The **Strossmayerovo šetalište** on top of the funicular provides a gorgeous view of the city.

A cannon on top of **Lotrščak Tower** *(kula)* on Strossmayerovo šetalište fires daily at noon to signal time for the Zagrebčani. Named after St. Cyril and St. Methodius, ul. Cirilometodska veers off Strossmayerovo and leads to Markov trg. The colorful tiles of Gothic **St. Mark's Church** *(Crkva sv. Marka)* depict the coats of arms of Croatia, Dalmatia, and Slavonia on the left and of Zagreb on the right. The church also contains works by Ivan Meštrovič (see **Literature and Arts,** p. 138), Croatia's most famous sculptor. A ceremonial changing of the guards takes place in front of **Ban's Palace** *(Banski Dvori)* in Markov trg every Sunday at noon from April 12 to November 1. Follow ul. Kamenita to **Stone Gate** *(Kamenita Vrata)*, the only original gate left from the city wall. Legend has it that fire destroyed the entire gate except for the painting of the Blessed Virgin and Child. Many Croats still come to the gate to light candles and pray. From Kamenita, walk down Radićeva to **Blood Bridge** *(Krvavi Most)*, the main battle site between the warring clerics and craftsmen of **Kaptol** and **Gradec** hills, which were united in 1850. Medveščak brook, which once separated the two hills, was covered in 1898 and turned into ul. Tkalčićeva. The **Dolac market** takes place daily on Tkalšićeva, offering as many items as you can barter for. Kaptol hill is dominated by the **Cathedral of the Assumption of the Virgin Mary.** Its neo-Gothic bell towers blend seamlessly with the remains of the 13th-century church. (Open to the public M-Sa 10am-5pm, Su and holy days 1-5pm; services daily at 5:30pm, holy mass Sunday at 10am. Free.) **Vlaška,** the street which starts below the cathedral, is lined with tiny 19th-century houses.

MUSEUMS

Zagreb takes pride in its many well-stocked museums, which eagerly await visitors after a few years of wartime hiatus. A complete list of the museums can be found in the free *Zagreb: Events and Performances*, published monthly and available at TIC. It also lists galleries, plays, festivals, concerts, and sporting events. Many of the museums lie in Donji Grad below Ilica. A museum visit should be paired with a pleasant walk through one of Zagreb's parks, either at Trg Maršala Tita, Trg Mažuranića, or Rooseveltov trg. All museums are closed Monday.

Mimara Museum (Muzej Mimara), Rooseveltov trg 4 (tel. 482 81 00). A vast and varied collection, from Egyptian art to Raphael, Velasquez, Rubens, and Rembrandt. Open Tu-Sa 10am-5pm, Su 10am-2pm. 20kn, students 15kn.

Gallery of Modern Art (Moderna Galerija), Hebranga 1 (tel./fax 43 38 02). Fantastic collection. Open Tu-Sa 10am-6pm, Su 10am-1pm. 20kn, students 10kn.

Museum of Arts and Crafts (Muzej za Umjetnost i Obrt), Trg Maršala Tita 10 (tel. 455 41 22). Paintings, ceramics, furniture, glass, clocks, and watches from Gothic to Art Deco. Judaica collection is one of the biggest and most renowned in the world. Open Tu-F 10am-6pm, Sa-Su 10am-1pm. 20kn, students 10kn. English booklet 30kn.

Ethnographic Museum (Etnografski muzej), Trg Mažurulićev 14 (tel. 482 62 20). The best section features traditional folk robes from all parts of Croatia. Open Tu-Th 10am-6pm, F-Su 10am-1pm. 10kn, students 5kn. English booklet 50kn.

ENTERTAINMENT

Zagreb is a city of festivals. Festival season opens with a concert by the **Vienna Symphony Orchestra** on April 4, 2000, and a **week of contemporary dance** in May. The **International Garden Show FLORAART,** scheduled for June 2000, will pay tribute to Zagreb's extensive greenery. In mid-June of even-numbered years, Zagreb hosts the annual **World Festival of Animated Film,** with offerings ranging from the best of Disney to high-tech Japanese *anime*, in Vatroslav Lisinski Concert Hall at Trg S. Radića 4. **Eurokaz,** a festival of progressive European theater, takes place annually at the end of June all around Zagreb. Folklore fetishists will flock to Zagreb from July 22-26, 2000, for the **International Folklore Festival,** the premier gathering of European folk dancers and singing groups. July and August host open-air concerts and theatrical performances during the **Zagreb Summer Festival;** some of the best concerts take place in the Muzejski Prostor Atrium, Jezuitski trg 4 (tel. 27 89 57). There is also a huge, annual **International Puppet Festival** at the beginning of September. The **Zagreb Jazz Fair** at the BP Club, Teslina 7, from October 1 to 15 and **Zagreb Fest,** a pop festival, in November, round out the offerings.

NIGHTLIFE

The numerous sidewalk **cafes** along **Tkalčićeva,** in Gornji Grad, beckon an older, classier crowd while **Opatovina,** a parallel street, hosts a slightly younger and more budget-minded group. Many **discos** are empty during the week, but fill with revelers on the weekend. For a complete listing of all discos and nightclubs in Zagreb, consult the free *Zagreb: Events and Performances* available at TIC. You can fill your own bottles with homemade wine at **Vinarija Kaptol,** Kaptol 14 (tel. 481 46 75), for 7-20kn per 1L. The cellar is under the courtyard on the left side of the street. (Open M, W-Th, and Sa 8am-1pm, Tu and F 8am-1pm and 2-5pm, Su 9am-noon.)

Čvenk Caffe Bar, Radićeva 24 (tel. 42 48 51). This cellar cafe is one of the homiest spots in town. Coffee 5-10kn. Open M-Sa 8am-11pm, Su 4pm-11pm.

Kolding Club, Berislavićeva 8 (tel. 42 30 07). A romantic Rococo parlor with outdoor seating under an enormous palm. Hot chocolate with alcohol 17kn, coffee 5-8kn, 0.25L Guinness 5.50kn. Open M-Th 8am-1am, F-Su 8am-2am.

Plaza, Gajeva 12 (tel. 487 25 13). Italian-style hangout for businessfolk and students with music ranging from Eros Ramazotti to salsa. Coffee 5-8kn. Open daily 9am-2am.

Thalia, Teslina 7, next to the Hard Rock Cafe. This pub dominated by blue ashtrays is popular with locals in the winter. Coffee 5kn, beer 12-15kn. Open daily 1pm-2am.

Pivnica Medvedgrad, Savska cesta 56 (tel. 617 71 19). Take tram #13, 14, or 17 from Trg b. Jelačića to the corner of Avenija Vukovar and Savska cesta. Long wooden tables and dim lights attract crowds of students and businesspeople. Brews its own beer; try *Crna kraljica,* a dark masterpiece. Open M-Sa 10am-midnight, Su noon-midnight.

Točkica Caffe Bar, Mesnička 34 (tel. 43 32 68). Lively, young, loud, and fun. Coffee 5-6kn, 0.5L *Ožujsko* 10kn, 0.33L Guinness 18kn. Open daily 5-11pm.

Gjuro II, Medveščak 2. This self-proclaimed "arts and hearts meeting place" is a friendly, smoke-filled underground club frequented by young Croats. Open daily 10pm-4am.

BP Club, Teslina 7 (tel. 42 55 20), enter through one of the portals with a big, red circle. 0.3L beer 13kn. *The* venue for jazz in Zagreb. Open daily Sept.-July 10am-2am.

NEAR ZAGREB: HRVATSKO ZAGORJE

Nested on the hilltops surrounding Zagreb, the mysterious castles of Hrvatsko Zagorje (Croatian Ruins) are ripe for conquering—this time with Canons instead of cannons. The following three are the most popular; for a more comprehensive listing consult the free *Zagreb and Surroundings*, available at TIC in Zagreb.

MEDVEDGRAD. Officially still part of the city, Medvedgrad is a royal fortress that has guarded Mount Medvednica since the 13th century. You'll hardly get a better view of the city than from this stone beauty. It is free and open to the public except on national holidays, when the president lays flowers on the **Altar of the Homeland.** *(From Trg b. Jelačica, take tram #14 to Mihaljevac; change to #15 to Gračani. From here, follow a well-marked path up the hill to Medvedgrad (1½hr.).)*

VELIKI TABOR. This Romantic/Gothic structure is as impressive as castles get. Built in the 15th century, Veliki Tabor is home not only to several permanent art and archaeological collections, but also one **ghost.** Every year in June, a colorful fencing tournament takes place in the castle. *(From the Zagreb bus station, take a bus to Desinic (2hr., 7 per day, 30kn). Tel. (049) 34 30 52 or 34 30 53. Open daily 10am-5pm. 20kn, students 10kn.)* **Grešna Gorica,** a nearby wooden restaurant serving exclusively national specialties, should not be missed. *(Tel. 049/34 30 01; fax 049/34 32 42. Štrukli 12kn, srneči gulaš—deer goulash—25kn. Open daily 10am-10pm.)*

TRAKOŠČAN. Newly renovated and complete with original furniture, Trakošcan is likely the most beautiful castle in Croatia. This romantic 14th-century pearl belongs to the realm of fairy tales. *(From the Zagreb bus station take a bus to Varaždin (1¼ hr., 12 per day, 40kn), and change to a local bus to Trakošcan. Tel. (042) 79 62 81. Open daily 9am-6pm. 20kn, students 10kn. Guided tours in English are available. Make a reservation.)*

ISTRIA

The Istrian peninsula lies on the northern part of the Adriatic coast, where the Mediterranean Sea laps at the foot of the Alps. The region—in language, tradition, and culture—seems almost more Italian than Croatian. Perhaps this has always been the case: ancient fishing ports, countless craggy coves, and the deep blue-green hues of the sea led a Roman chronicler almost 2000 years ago to remark, "In Istria, Roman patricians feel like gods." Today, Roman Pula, UNESCO-protected Poreč, and the 19th-century resort Rovinj may worship the false idol of tourism, but the intrepid can still find two millenia of history—without a tour guide.

PULA

Originally only a single hill, ancient Pula expanded around the bay as it became an entertainment center for Roman emperors, Renaissance poets and painters, and French generals. In the heart of the town, a breathtaking Roman amphitheater has served as the center of action for 2000 years. The walls of the theater, like the town itself, have witnessed all manner of horrors, from gladiator matches to Bryan Adams concerts. In this monument, in the winding medieval streets, and in handsome Habsburg avenues, Pula's rich history resounds even today.

ORIENTATION & PRACTICAL INFORMATION. Pula is served by both train and bus. From the **train station,** Kolodvorska 5 (tel. 54 11 33), take a right and follow Kolodvorska all the way to the amphitheater, keeping the sea on your right. From there, walk up Istarska. When it becomes **Giardini,** the circular **Stari Grad** will be on your right. **Trains** make their way to: **Zagreb** (7hr., 4 per day, 192kn); **Rijeka** (2½hr., 4 per day, 33kn); and **Ljubljana** (7½hr., 1 per day, 123kn). The **bus station** (tel. 21 90 74) is downtown between Istarska and Carrarina. **Buses** run to: **Zagreb** (5-6hr., 13 per day, 100kn); **Rijeka** (2½hr., 19 per day, 40kn); **Poreč** (1½hr., 9 per day, 23kn); and **Trieste** (3¾hr., 5 per day, 90kn). For a **taxi,** call 232 28, or try the stand at Giardini and Carrarina. **Luggage storage** is available both at the bus and train stations, but the one at the former is cheaper, more accessible, and safer. (6kn. Open daily 5-9:30am, 10am-6pm, and 6:30-11pm.) The helpful staff at the **tourist office,** TIC, Istarska 11 (tel. 21 91 97; fax 21 18 55), doles out all sorts of helpful info. (Open July-Aug. daily 8am-1pm and 5-8pm; Sept.-June M-F 8am-1pm). **Zagrebačka banka,** at the corner of Giardini and Flanatička, **exchanges cash** and has a 24hr. Cirrus/MC **ATM** outside. (Open M-F 8am-noon and 6-6:30pm, Sa 8am-noon.) There is a currency exchange machine outside **Kaptol banka,** Istarska 5, next to the bus station. A **pharmacy,** Ljekarna Centar, is at Giardini 15 (tel. 225 44; open M-F 24hr., Sa 7:30am-8pm, Su 7:30am-8pm). The main **post office,** Danteov trg 4, has **telephones** and **Poste Restante** at counter #10. (Open M-F 7am-8pm, Sa 7am-5pm, Su 8am-noon.) Free **internet** is on the first floor of the **library,** Sveučilištna Knjižnica, Castropola 1. (Open M-F 7:30am-7pm.) **Postal code:** 521 00. **Phone code:** (0)52.

CROATIA

ACCOMMODATIONS & FOOD. A plethora of travel agencies help tourists find overpriced hotels, somewhat expensive apartments, and reasonably priced private rooms. **Arenaturist,** Giardini 4 (tel. 21 86 96; fax 21 22 77), may seem a bit brusque, but their rooms are in the best locations. (July-Aug. singles 65kn, doubles 53kn; June and Sept. 42-49kn; 50% more for only 1 night, 25% more for 2-3 nights. Daily tourist tax 7.60kn; registration fee 9kn. Open M-F 8am-3pm, Sa 8am-1pm, Su 9am-noon.) On the outskirts of Pula you can find the **Omladinski Hostel (HI),** Zaljev Valsaline 4 (tel. 21 00 03; fax 21 23 94), with decent but dingy rooms and its own beach. Exit the bus station onto Istarska, turn right and follow the street to a small park on Giardini where local buses stop. From the park, take bus #2 to "Veruda," exit at the last stop, and follow the signs downhill to the youth hostel. (July-Aug. 87.60kn; June and Sept. 79.60kn; May and Oct. 71.70kn; Nov. and Apr. 67.50kn. Breakfast included. Reception 9am-3pm. Call ahead.) **Stoja Camping** (tel. 241 44) lies on the tip of Pula's western peninsula. From Giardini (see directions to the hostel), take bus #1 toward Stoja to the end. (37kn. 8kn registration fee.)

Grocery Store Puljanka has several branches throughout the town, including one on Flanatička 6. (Open M-Sa 6:30am-8:30pm, Su 7am-noon.) Buffets and fast-food restaurants line the Old Town's Sergijevaca, which turns into Kandlerova after Trg Forum. **Pizzeria Orfej,** Istranina 1 (tel. 317 84), in the medieval quarter, is a standout. (Pizzas 20-25kn. Open M-Sa 8am-10pm.) **Restaurant Delfin,** Trg sv. Tome 1 (tel. 222 89), across from the 4th-century cathedral, provides cheap, excellent seafood in a heavily fish-illustrated setting. (Entrees 25-35kn. Open daily 9am-11pm.)

SIGHTS & ENTERTAINMENT. Visitors to Pula are justly enchanted by its Roman ruins. The must-see sight is the **amphitheater,** a wonder of ancient Roman architecture built in the 1st century AD and now used for concerts. From the bus station, a left on Istarska leads directly there. (Open daily 7:30am-9pm. 14kn, students 7kn.) In the opposite direction from the bus station, Istarska turns into Giardini and leads to the 29BC **Arch of the Sergians** (Slavoluk obitelji Sergi). Through the gates, stroll along narrow, shop-crammed **Sergijevaca,** a little street that comes alive in the evening. The **Forum,** at the end of Sergijevaca, holds the columned **Temple of Augustus** (Augustov hram), originally constructed between 2BC and 14AD. Pass through the **Twin Gate** (Dvojna vrata) behind the bus station and climb the hill to the **Archaeological Museum of Istria** (Arheološki Muzej Istre), Carrarina 3 (tel. 334 88). The museum offers an overview of Pula's history from prehistoric to medieval times, with an emphasis on Roman stone artifacts. (Open May-Sept. M-Sa 9am-8pm, Su 9am-3pm; Oct.-Apr. M-F 9am-2pm. 10kn, students 5kn.)

Several agencies in town offer trips to the nearby **Brijuni Archipelago,** where almighty Tito built himself a complex of mansions. The islands are accessible only by boat from **Fažana,** 15km from Pula. Only guided excursions are permitted; try **Atlas,** Starih Statuta 1 (tel. 21 41 72; fax 21 40 94), which offers a Saturday tour (220kn). Looking from Stari Grad to the shipyards, you wouldn't guess that Pula had **beaches** at all, but there are plenty of coves for private swimming. Buy a bus ticket from any kiosk (8kn) and take bus #1 to the Stoja campground.

Bistro Sirena, Trg Forum 12 (tel. 234 07), has abundant outdoor seating with an unobstructed view of the Temple of Augustus. (Coffee 4-10kn; 0.5L *Favorit* 10kn. Open daily until midnight.) Based on the unwritten rule that every city should have an Irish pub, **Bounty Pub,** Veronska 8, off Flanatička, saves Pula a lashing. (1L Guinness 50kn; *Favorit* 25kn. Open M-F 10am-11pm, Sa 7am-2pm, Su 8am-1pm.) Local love the pyramid-shaped **Piramida** and techno/rave heaven **Fort Bourguignon,** both on beaches in Zlatne Stijene, accessible by bus #3. (Cover 15kn.)

POREČ

More than 2000 years ago, Roman soldiers built a fortified colony called Parentium in Poreč (PO-retch), and the Roman character still shows today. The town is famous for the 6th-century Byzantine mosaics in St. Euphrasius's Basilica, which is complemented by the Roman churches, round towers, and Gothic and Baroque houses that huddle along the stone streets. Protected by UNESCO, the Old Town suffocates every summer under hordes of tourists in search of beautiful surf.

ORIENTATION & PRACTICAL INFORMATION. **Buses** link Poreč with the rest of Croatia, Slovenia, and Italy, including: **Zagreb** (6hr., 7 per day, 108kn); **Pula** (1hr., 12 per day, 30kn); **Rijeka** (3½hr., 8 per day, 40kn); **Ljubljana** (5hr.; July-Aug. 2 per day, off-season 1 per day; 83kn); and **Trieste** (2hr., 2 per day, 54kn). The **bus station** is on Rade Končara 1 (tel. 43 21 53); **luggage storage** is available there. (5kn, over 30kg 6.50kn. Open M-F 6-9am, 9:30am-5:30pm, and 6-8pm.) To reach the central **Trg Slobode,** turn left out of the bus station, walk down the street, and take a right onto the pedestrian Milanovića. The **tourist office,** Zagrebačka 9 (tel. 45 12 93; fax 45 16 65), won't organize accommodations but they'll tell you how to do so yourself. (Open daily in summer 8am-3:30pm and 5-9pm; off-season 9am-4pm.) **Zagrebačka banka,** Obala M. Tita bb (tel. 45 11 66), by the sea, **exchanges cash** for no commission and traveler's checks for a 1.5% commission. (Open M-F 8am-5:30pm, Sa 8am-noon.) There is a Cirrus/MC **ATM** and a currency exchange machine outside; a MC/Visa ATM is available at Negrija 2. There is a **pharmacy** at Kandlerova 1 (tel. 43 25 26), just off Trg Slobode. (Open daily 7:30am-9pm.) The **post office,** Trg Slobode 12 (tel. 43 18 08), is equipped with phone booths inside and out. (Open M-Sa 7am-9pm, Su 9am-noon.) **Postal code:** 524 41. **Phone code:** (0)52.

ACCOMMODATIONS & FOOD. For **private rooms,** try **Turizam Vits,** Zagrebačka 17 (tel./fax 43 17 38), near the tourist office. (Singles 55-77kn; doubles 77-120kn; apartments 120-180kn per person. 30% surcharge for stays less than 4 nights. Open Mar.-Oct. 8am-10pm, Nov.-Feb. 8am-1pm.) If these rooms are full, there are agencies on every corner—shop around. Encouraged by rising demand, owners often refuse to rent rooms to those staying less than three nights. Paying extra for a day or two that you won't be there may still be better than staying at a hotel (the cheapest, "Neptun" and "Poreč," are roughly 160kn per person per night). The large **Lanternacamp** (tel. 43 49 00; fax 44 30 93), often dubbed "Little Europe," is 13km to the north and has good facilities. (24kn per person; tents 50kn. Open Apr.-Oct.) The nudist camp and apartment-village **Solaris** (tel. 44 34 00) is next door. The only way to get there is by bus (15min., 12 per day, 11kn).

Riblji Restoran "Sofora," Obala M. Tita 13 (tel. 43 20 53), by the sea, has 4-course daily menus for 30kn. (Open daily noon-10pm.) **Grill Sarajevo** (tel. 43 19 04), on M. Vlačića off Dekumana, offers Bosnian and Croatian specialties like *pljeskavica* (beef patty with french fries; 30kn; open 10am-midnight). **Maša,** Kumičićova 1, at the tip of the peninsula, is a pleasant Italian eatery with pasta (20-30kn), pizza (25-35kn), and vegetarian options. (Open daily 11am-10pm.) There is a **supermarket,** Zagrebačka 2, next to the bus station. (Open M-Sa 7am-9pm, Su 7am-noon.)

SIGHTS. Stari Grad's main street is **Dekumana,** lined with shops, cafes, and restaurants. From Trg Slobode, walk past—or even climb up—the 15th-century Gothic **Pentagon Tower** (Peterokutna kula), a relic from Poreč's Venetian days. The awe-inspiring remains of the Roman **Great Temple and Temple of Neptune** (Veliki hram i Neptunov hram), from the 1st century AD, await at the end of Dekumana. **St. Euphrasius's Basilica** (Eufrazijeva bazilika) on Eufrazi jeva, one block north of Dekumana, is the city's most important monument. Composed of 6th-century foundations, late Gothic choir stalls, and a Renaissance belltower, the basilica contains a millennium of art history. The Byzantine mosaics adorning the interior—now a UNESCO heritage monument—show Jesus as a young man and (surprisingly) only female saints. (Open daily 7am-8pm.)

The best beaches are south of the Marina at the start of Obala M. Tita, near **Blue Lagoon** (Plava Laguna) and **Green Lagoon** (Zelena Laguna), 15-30 minutes down the shore. Watch out for scantily clad bodies on beaches marked "Naturists." To escape the crowds (and the nudists), find one of the small coves cut into the base of a hill, a perfect fit for two or three people. A **ferry** leaves from the Marina for the less exciting but quieter beaches on **Saint Nicholas Island** (Sveti Nikola; every 30min. 7am-midnight; round-trip 14kn). A detailed bike map is available free from the tourist office (see above). Its two marked trails take you through more than 50km of olive groves, forests, vineyards, and medieval villages.

NIGHTLIFE. Any area of the coast that has a name also has a hotel complex and disco, frequented by tourists of all ages. (Generally open nightly 10pm-4am.) If a walk down the beach sounds too strenuous, join the crowd at Capitol, Vladimira Nazora 9, in Stari Grad. (Cover 15kn. Open 10pm-4am.) Club No. 1, Marafor 10, has a higher bar-to-dance floor ratio. (0.3L *Favorit* 8kn. Open nightly 6pm-4am.) Pubs are crowded and open late. At the popular bar Casablanca, Eufrazijeva 4, Sam plays it again, and again, and again until 1am. (Open daily 9am-1am). Bar Ulixes, Dekumana 4, hides in a narrow alley off Dekumana. Drink *Favorit* (0.3L 8kn), Guinness (0.3L 18kn), and coffee (3kn) in a cool cellar or outside under a crumbly stone arch and the neighbor's drying laundry. (Open daily 9pm-1am.)

ROVINJ

At the beginning of the 19th century, a seaside sanatorium called "Maria Theresia" opened in Rovinj (ro-VEEN), and the town and island became a favorite summer resort for the Austro-Hungarian Emperor and his friends. Today, it remains oriented toward travelers with money to burn; shopkeepers and entertainment providers are as aggressive here as anywhere in the country. Some believe Rovinj has sold its soul to the tourist-pleasing Man, but if you avoid the crowds you'll still find laundry hanging from windows, roosters crowing, and crystal-clear waves breaking against the walls of buildings built long before the days of travel agencies.

ORIENTATION & PRACTICAL INFORMATION. With no train station, Rovinj depends on **buses** to reach: **Poreč** (1hr., 7 per day, 17kn); **Pula** (1hr., 18 per day, 16kn); **Rijeka** (3½hr., 7 per day, 58kn); **Zagreb** (8 per day, 122kn); and **Trieste** (2½hr., 1 per day, 82kn). The **bus station** is on Benussi Cio (tel. 81 14 53) and offers **luggage storage** (6kn). Turn left out of the bus station and walk down Nazora toward the marina, or walk up on Carera to the Old Town. Orientation can be tricky at first, as street signs are often difficult to find and some streets do not have numbers. The official **tourist office,** Turistička Zajednica Rovinj, Pino Budičina 12 (tel. 81 15 66 and 81 34 69; fax 81 60 17), doesn't do much, but offers multilingual guidance. To get there from the bus station, walk to the sea and follow the waterfront to your right for about 10min. **Istarska Banka** (tel. 81 32 33), on Aldo Negri on the way to the tourist office, has decent rates and no commission on traveler's checks and currency exchange. (Open M-F 7:30am-7pm, Sa 7:30am-noon.) There is a Cirrus/MC **ATM** at Zagrebačka Banka, Carera 21, and a Visa/AmEx ATM outside of the **Atlas** tourist agency, Trg Pignaton 1. A **pharmacy** (tel. 81 35 89) can be found on Benussi-Cio. (Open M-F 7am-8pm, Sa 7am-3pm, Su 9am-noon.) The **post office** (tel. 81 14 66) is across from the bus station and next to the pharmacy. (Open M-Sa 7am-8pm, Su 7am-7pm.) **Postal code:** 522 10. **Phone code:** (0)52.

CROATIA

ACCOMMODATIONS & FOOD. With a tourist industry that might well be on steroids, Rovinj has bulked up on accommodations. The official tourist office doesn't arrange them, but sets the prices (in DM). As a result, all agencies in town, including Atlas, Globtour, Kompas, and Generalturist, use the same prices. (July-Aug. 77kn; prices double for 1 night only; discounts off season. Tax 7kn; registration fee 15kn.) Try the agency closest to the bus station on Nello Quarantotto, **Kei Istra** (tel. 81 11 55; open daily 8am-1pm and 5-10pm). For those with tents, **Camping Polari** (tel. 81 34 41; fax 81 13 95), 2.5km east of town (buses run hourly), has a supermarket and several bars. (June-July 72-83kn. Closed Oct.-Mar.) A **grocery store** stands at Nazora 6, between the bus station and the sea. (Open M-Sa 6:30am-8pm, Su 7-11am.) There is an **open-air market** on Trg Valdibora. **Gostionica Cisterna,**

Trg Matteotti 3, in the heart of the medieval quarter, has crazy international cuisine. (Entrees 35-40kn; salads 110kn. Open daily 9am-noon and 6pm-1am.)

SIGHTS. By the 7th century, Rovinj was surrounded by town walls which were later buttressed by towers. The Old Town had seven gates, three of which still exist: **St. Benedict's Gate, Holy Cross Gate,** and **the Portico.** The Baroque archway called **Balbijer Arch** (Balbijer luk), which today serves as the threshold of the Old Town, was built on the site of the17th-cnetury outer gate. Perhaps the best view of town is from a distance: old houses packed on the tiny peninsula cascade toward **St. Euphemia's Church** (Crkva sv. Eufemije), whose Baroque-Venetian tower dominates the town. The church's sheer size and its Italian exterior are impressive, although most come to see the 6th-century Byzantine sarcophagus, containing the remains of St. Euphemia, the 3rd-century patron of Rovinj. At age 15, Euphemia refused to deny her Christian faith, and was thrown to the lions, who killed but refrained from eating her. One misty morning 500 years later, according to legend, the sarcophagus containing her remains floated into the harbor of Rovinj; it now lies behind the right-hand altar. For 5kn, you can climb the **bell tower,** 50 years older than the rest of the church. (Open daily 10am-1pm and 5-7:30pm. Services Su at 10:30am.) In the summer, the church houses many classical music performances as part of the **Rovinj Summer Festival.**

The **Museum of National Heritage,** Trg Maršala Tita 11, contains the work of local masters spanning nearly three millennia. (Open M 9am-12:30pm, Tu-Sa 9am-12:30pm and 6-9:30pm. 10kn.) Every second Sunday in August, the traditional open-air art festival **Grisia** takes place on the street of the same name, and international artists come to display their work. There are boats anchored in the harbor rearing to take off on trips around the 22 nearby **islands** (90kn) or to the **Lim Fjord,** a sea indentation that separates Rovinj from Poreč. (80kn, students 20% off. "Fish picnic" included.) You can buy tickets at the tourist offices or on the harbor.

For the prettiest **beaches** in the area, walk past the marina on the path along the shore and weigh anchor wherever you like. Or, right after the marina, cut through the park **Golden Cape** (Zlatni vrt) to reach a naturally staircase-shaped beach highly recommended by locals (30min.). Also consider renting a **bike** from the shop at Trg na Lokvi 3 (tel. 81 33 96), next to the bus station. (20kn per hr.; 70kn per day. Open M-Sa 8:30am-12:30pm and 5-8pm.) Ferries from the quay also go to beaches on **Katarina Island** (hourly, 10kn) or **Red Island** (Crveni Otok; 15 per day, 20kn).

ENTERTAINMENT. At night, Rovinj is not nearly as boisterous as nearby Poreč or Pula; check for cinema, concerts, and musicals at **Gandusio Theater,** Valdibora 17 (tel. 81 15 88; tickets around 30kn). **Bar Sax Caffe,** Rakovca 4, is a bit misleading: there is no live music, but the jazz posters covering the walls make it feel like there could be. (0.5L *Favorit* 10kn; coffee 3-7kn. Open daily 8pm-1am.) There seem to be enough tourists to supplement the local crowd and keep both **Discoteca Monte Mulini,** in the eponymous hotel near Hotel Park, and the **Monvi,** up the street from Veli Jože on Svetoga križa, hopping. (20kn cover. Both open 10pm-5am.)

GULF OF KVARNER

Blessed by long summers and gentle coastal breezes, the islands just off the coast of mainland Croatia are natural good-weather draws. Larger Krk bears the brunt of the tourist infestation. Farther south and away from the mainland, Rab is a less visited (and less disturbed) find, well worth the longer trip.

KRK ISLAND

Croatia's largest island, Krk is only a short ride across the Krk Bridge from the mainland. It is this proximity—and not its forgettable towns—that makes Krk one of the most popular Croatian beach-bumming spots. While hordes of tourists seem to think the island is the perfect Mediterranean playground (raging nightlife included), Krk is best used either as an easy island escape from Zagreb or as a starting point for a cruise down the Dalmatian Coast.

KRK TOWN

Krk's gateway to the rest of Croatia and the main intra-island transport hub, Krk Town is ideal as a base for visiting the rest of the island. The town itself is small and can be explored in a few hours; its primary attraction is the 14th-century Roman fortification, still visible today at the **South Town Gate** (Mala Vrata), the marina's entrance to the Old Town. The waters around Krk Town have more excitement to offer than the town itself. **Fun Diving Krk,** Lukobran 8 (tel./fax 22 25 63), leads a variety of underwater expeditions throughout the year. (1 dive 148kn; 2 dives and barbecue 300kn; novice dive 320kn; night dive 172kn. Equipment rental available. Open daily 9am-8pm.) The town's only **beach** is right next to the diving center on Lukobran. Better beaches are slightly farther away in Autocamp Ježevac (see below), but are still within walking distance. The town's only club, **Trezor,** Stjepana Radića bb, rages with drunk fishermen and disco music at night. (Open in summer daily 11pm-5am; off-season Sa-Su 11pm-5am.)

Autotrans, Šetalište sv. Bernardina 3 (tel. 22 26 61; fax 22 21 10), near the bus station, **exchanges cash** and traveler's checks for a 2% commission. (Open M-Sa 8am-9pm, Su 9am-1pm.) **Riječka Banka** in the center of Trg b. Josipa Jelačića has a Visa **ATM;** another stands outside of Trgovina Krk on Šetalište sv. Bernardina bb, behind the bus station (Cirrus/MC). There is a **pharmacy** at Vela pl. 3. (Open M-F 7:30am-8:30pm, Sa 7am-noon and 6-8pm, Su 9-11am.) The **post office,** Trg b. Josipa Jelačića bb, gives MC cash advances and has **telephones** outside. (Open M-F 7am-8pm, Sa 7am-2pm.) Autotrans (see above) also books **private rooms** (July-Aug. singles 105kn, doubles 140-185kn; Sept.-June 20% cheaper; 30% surcharge for less than 3days; tourist tax 7kn), but it's cheaper to look for a room yourself. *Sobe* and *apartman* signs line Slavka Nikoliča (the road to the bus station) and Plavnička. **Autocamp Ježevac,** Plavnička bb (tel./fax 22 10 81), is a 10min. walk from the bus station away from the old town. (July-Aug. 23kn per person; tent 12-16kn; car 14kn; less May-June and Sept.-Oct. Daily tax 7kn; registration 8kn. Open May-Oct.) **Galeb,** Obala hrvatske mornarice bb, serves Adriatic standards on a terrace overlooking the marina. (Entrees 20-30kn. Open daily 9am-10pm.) In the center of the Old Town, **Kantun,** Strossmayerova 38 (tel. 22 27 71), pleases with pizza (25-40kn) and sandwiches (20kn; open daily 10am-midnight). A large **supermarket** is behind the bus station. (Open daily 7am-9pm.) **Postal code:** 51500. **Phone code:** (0)51.

GETTING THERE. The **bus station,** Šetalište sv. Bernardina 1 (tel. 22 11 11), connects Krk Town to **Rijeka** (1½hr., 13 per day, 24kn) and **Baška** (1hr., 10 per day, 10kn). A short walk along the sea leads to Old Town and its main square, **Vela placa.**

BAŠKA

A narrow road winding through mountain valleys and green forests descends into the town of Baška on Krk's southern coast. Baška's famous pebbled **beach,** Vela Plaža, coils around 2km of white, coastal mountains. Packed with bodies during the day, it lights up with colored bulbs after dark to become the romantic center of the town's nightlife. The surrounding mountains host some stunning hiking trails. **St. Ivan's Church** (Crkva sv. Ivan; 2km on the blue trail) or the hill **Zakam** (3km on the yellow trail), with its vistas of the Adriatic, are particularly popular destinations. Follow the signs from the intersection of Zvonimirova and Emila Geistlicha, or grab a map from the tourist office (see below).

Across from the tourist office, Riječka Banka **exchanges cash** and **traveler's checks** for a 1% commission. (Open M-F 8am-noon and 6-8pm, Sa 8am-noon.) There is a **pharmacy** at Zvonimirova 114 (tel. 85 69 00), behind the tourist office. (Open M-Sa 7:30am-8:30pm, Su 7:30am-1pm.) The **post office,** on the corner of Prilaz Kupalištu and Zdenke Čermakove, gives MC **cash advances** and has a **tele-**

phone outside. (Open M-F 7am-7pm.) **Kompas,** Emila Geistlicha 38 (tel. 85 68 30), in Hotel Corinthia (open daily 8am-9pm), and **Primaturist,** Zvonimirova 98 (tel. 85 61 32; fax 85 69 71; open daily 8am-7pm), arrange **private rooms.** (July-Aug. singles 76-133kn; doubles 117-175kn; less Sept.-June.; 30% surcharge for stays less than 3 nights. Daily tax 9kn; registration fee 7.6kn.) If you want to search alone, *sobe* and *apartman* signs can be found on Zvonimirova. To reach **Camping Zablaće** (tel. 85 69 09 and 85 66 04; fax 85 65 04) from the bus station, walk to Zvonimirova and turn right, then take a left on Prilaz Kupalištu behind the tourist office. The campground rents the cheapest sleep in town, but only if you carry your bed on your back. (25.15kn per person; tents 16.40kn; less in the off season. Registration fee 7.80kn; daily tax 5.50kn; ecological tax 1.17kn. Open May-Sept.) On the beach just outside the campground, **Galeb,** Emila Geistlicha bb (tel. 85 66 51), cooks inexpensive Italian meals. (Entrees 25-30kn. Open daily 8am-11pm.) **Franica,** Ribarska 39, on the opposite side of the bay by the marina, serves pastas and pizzas (25-35kn) atop wooden tables. (Open daily 11:30am-2pm). There is a **grocery store** at Zvonimirova 60. (Open daily 7am-9pm.) **Postal code:** 51523. **Phone code:** (0)51.

GETTING THERE. Nine **buses** a day arrive in Baška from **Rijeka** via **Krk Town** (2¼hr., 34kn). To get to the main street, **Zvonimirova,** follow Kralja Tomislava downhill from the bus station. Jadrolinija operates a **ferry** between Baška and Lopar on the northern tip of **Rab Island** (1hr.; July-Aug. 4 per day, May-June and Sept. 2 per day; 22.30kn, car 130kn, bike 24.10kn). The **tourist office,** Turistička Zajednica Baška, Zvonimirova 114 (tel. 85 68 17; fax 85 65 44; email tz-baska@ri.tel.hr), provides transportation info. (Open M-F 8am-8pm.)

RAB ISLAND: RAB TOWN

With its whitewashed stone houses jutting like whitecaps above the sea, Rab has a way of becoming every visitor's favorite place. The town is truly ancient, having reached its zenith under the Romans when Augustus gave it the status of a municipality in the 1st century BC. If you're traveling from elsewhere on the coast, it is well worth any transportation troubles; if you're in Zagreb, it's difficult to find a more perfectly situated island.

ORIENTATION & PRACTICAL INFORMATION. Stretching along Rab's southwestern coast, Rab Town is the island's largest town. The peninsular Old Town is organized around three parallel streets: **Gornja** (Upper), **Srednja** (middle), and **Donja** (Lower). To reach them from the **bus station** on Mali Palit (tel. 72 41 89), turn left and walk downhill along the greenery until you reach the sea. **Buses** connect Rab Town to **Rijeka** (3½hr., 2 per day, 71kn) and **Zagreb** (6hr., June-Sept. 2 per day, 108kn). To head south along the coast, you can catch a Zagreb- or Rijeka-bound **bus** to **Jablanac** (20kn). Tell the driver your ultimate destination, and he'll drop you off on the *magistrala* (highway) where south-bound buses stop. (Bus station open M-Sa 5:30am-7:30pm, Su 11am-6pm.) From Baška on Krk, catch a **ferry** to **Lopar** on the northern end of the island (1hr., 2 per day, 22.30kn) and then a bus to Rab Town (20min., 9 per day, 10kn). The friendly staff at the **tourist office,** Turistička zajednica (tel. 77 11 11; fax 77 11 10), on the other side of the bus station at Mali Palit, can decipher the ferry schedules for you. (Open M-Sa 8am-10pm, Su 8am-noon and 6-8pm.) **Riječka Banka,** on Mali Palit just a few steps from the tourist office, **exchanges cash** for no commission. (Open M-F 8-11am and 5-8pm, Sa 8am-noon.) There is only one **ATM** in town, off Trg sv. Kristofora on the waterfront. A **pharmacy** (tel./fax 72 54 01) sits next to the bus station. (Open M-Sa 8am-9pm, Su 9-11:30am.) One speedy PC with **internet access** (40kn per hr.) resides at Infotel on Mali Palit (tel. 72 51 11 and 72 52 22), across the street from the tourist office. (Open M-Sa 8am-1pm and 7-9pm.) The **post office,** which also gives MC **cash advances,** is next to Infotel. **Telephones** are located inside. (Open M-Sa 7am-8pm.) **Postal code:** 51280. **Phone code:** (0)51.

ACCOMMODATIONS & FOOD. **Private rooms** are the cheapest option in Rab Town. The tourist agency **Katurbo,** Palit 491 (tel./fax 72 44 95), between the bus station to the center, arranges rooms. (July-Aug. 65kn; June and Sept. 50kn; May and Oct. 43kn; 30% surcharge for fewer than three nights. Tourist tax 4.50-7.60kn. Open daily 8am-1pm and 3-9pm.) **Camping Padova** (tel. 72 43 55; fax 72 45 39), 1km east of the bus station, is close to town without being too co-dependent. (22kn per person; tents 20kn per tent. Registration fee 7kn.) You can get there by the bus that heads to **Barbat** (10min., 7 per day, 8kn), or simply walk along the bay.

Buffet Harpun, Donja 15, is affordable and homey, serving Adriatic calamari (30kn) and spaghetti bolognese (25kn; open daily 11am-11pm). **Restaurant St. Maria,** Dinka Dokule 6 (tel. 72 41 96), on a street that is a continuation of Srednja, specializes in such Hungarian treats as *vinski gulaš* (40kn), and *punjena paprika* (stuffed bell pepper; 20kn; open daily 10am-2pm and 5-11pm). **Pizzeria Mare,** Srednja 8 (tel. 77 13 15), offers spaghetti (17-32kn), pizza (22-30kn), and beer (0.3L 6kn; open M-Sa 10am-11pm). A **supermarket** is in the basement of Merkur, Palit 71, across from the tourist office. (Open M-Sa 6:30am-9pm, Su 6:30-11am).

SIGHTS & ENTERTAINMENT. A stroll along Gornja takes you from the remains of **St. John's Church** (Crkva sv. Jvana), an outstanding Roman *bazilika,* to **St. Justine's Church** (Crkva sv. Justine), which houses a museum dedicated to Christian art. (Open M-Sa 9-11am and 8-10pm, Su 7:30-10pm. 7kn.) Sunsets from the zenith of **St. Mary's Bell Tower,** built in the beginning of the 13th century, are truly stupendous. (Open daily 10am-1pm and 7:30-10pm. 5kn.) The 12th-century **Virgin Mary Cathedral** (Katedrala Djevice Marije) and nearby 14th-century **St. Anthony's Monastery** (Samostan sv. Antuna), farther down Gornja ul., complete the tour of this history-laden quarter. **Komrčar,** one of the most beautiful parks in the Mediterranean, is at the base of the Old Town peninsula and offers thickly shaded respite as well as a beach. There are sand **beaches** around the town, but the nicest ones are scattered all over the island. To get to ones with names like "Sahara," you'll have to board a bus to Lopar, on the island's northwest corner (20min., 8 per day, 10kn). Other popular choices include **Supetarska Draga, Kampor,** or **Barbat,** all reachable by bus (inquire at the tourist office).

Cafes abound in Rab Town. The most popular spot among Rab Town's youth is the *très français* **Le Journal,** at Donja just off Kristofor trg. (Open nightly 10pm-4am.) The trendiest nightlife happens at the aptly-named **Ghetto** (tel. 72 57 00), at the Hotel Imperial. Walk from the peninsula toward the bus station and go straight on the paved path; instead of turning right at the harbor, head up the stairs. It has billiards, pinball machines, a confused attempt at exoticism (the Buddha behind the bar is draped in rosary beads), and loud music. (0.3L *Karlovačko* 10kn; 0.03L *Šljivovica*—plum brandy—6kn. Open daily 9am-2pm and 5pm-2am.)

DALMATIAN COAST

After his last visit to Dalmatia, George Bernard Shaw wrote: "The gods wanted to crown their creation and on the last day they turned tears, stars and the sea breeze into the isles of Kornati." While he was writing of specific islands, he might as well have been speaking of the entire Dalmatian Coast, a stunning seascape of hospitable locals and unfathomable beauty. With more than 1,100 islands (only 66 of which are inhabited), Dalmatia boasts not only the largest archipelago but also the cleanest and clearest waters in the Mediterranean. Resilient Zadar and its preserved envirions are an excellent starting points for exploring smaller wonders: Brač's astounding beach; Hvar, one of the most beautiful islands in the world; and UNESCO World Heritage town Trogir. Further south, the nightlife of Split and vibrant culture on Korčula are preludes to the coast's southern gem, Dubrovnik.

ZADAR

The modern center of northern Dalmatia, Zadar hides its many scars well. Allied attacks destroyed most of the city during WWII, and the Serbs ruined much of what had been rebuilt between 1991 and 1995. Its residents have rebuilt again, and today the city almost as beautiful as the shoreline road leading to it, coiling between a blue-green sea and white mountain peaks. With its extraordinary surroundings and a history deep enough to allow Roman ruins to be used as benches and playgrounds, Zadar is a quintessentially Dalmatian city.

ORIENTATION & PRACTICAL INFORMATION. Most of the city's businesses and sights are scattered along the main street of the old town, **Široka.** The **bus station** (tel. 21 19 38) and **train station** (tel. 43 05 99) are on Ante Starčevića. Avoid trains; they're more trouble than they are worth. **Buses** make their way to: **Zagreb** (5hr., 20 per day, 85kn); **Split** (3hr., 30 per day, 62kn); **Rijeka** (5hr., 14 per day, 87kn); and **Dubrovnik** (8hr., 7 per day, 125kn). To get to Široka, take a left at the large crossroad to the right of the stations, and then take another immediate left. Follow Zrinsko-Frankopanska all the way to the water, then walk along the waterfront to the gate of the Old Town. Passing through the gate, Široka shoots out of Narodni trg on the right. **Ferries** connect Zadar to the neighboring islands. They all depart from **Liburnska Obala,** where a Jadrolinija stand provides information and sells tickets. (Open M-Sa 6am-9pm, Su 7am-1pm and 3-10pm.) **Luggage storage** is available at the train station (10kn per day). Beware that Zadar's system of **public transportation** has neither schedules nor stop names; use it cautiously and ask for help whenever possible. All tourist information can be obtained at the **tourist office Liburnija,** Kotromanića 1 (tel. 21 20 39), off Narodni trg in the opposite direction from Široka. (Open in summer M-Sa 8am-noon and 2-9pm, Su 8am-noon and 3-9pm; off-season M-Sa 8am-noon and 2-6pm, Su 8am-noon and 3-9pm.) **Dalmatinska banka,** at Trg sv. Stošije 3 on Široka (tel. 31 13 11), **exchanges cash** for no commission and **traveler's checks** for a 1.5% commission. (Open M-F 8am-8pm, Sa 8am-noon.) **ATMs** are all over the city; one is situated outside of the bank and two are at the bus station. A **pharmacy** sits on Barakovića at Narodni trg. (Open M-F 7am-8pm, Sa 8am-noon.) The **post office** is on Š.K. Benje (tel. 31 21 01), off Široka, and has **telephones** inside. (Open M-F 7am-8pm, Sa 7am-2pm.) **Poste Restante** service is at the main post office, Kralja Držislava 1. The brand new Gradska Knjižnica Zadar (Zadar City Library), Stjepana Radića 116 (tel. 31 57 72; fax 31 58 57; email GKZD@zd.tel.hr), allows visitors to log onto the **internet** for free. (Open July-Aug. M-F 8am-noon and 5:30-8:30pm, Sa 8am-1pm; Sept.-June M, W, and F 8am-2pm, Tu and Th 1-8pm, Sa 8am-1pm.) **Postal code:** 23000. **Phone code:** (0)23.

ACCOMMODATIONS & FOOD. Liburnija (see above) arranges **private rooms** in homes near the city center. (July-Aug. 100kn; off-season 80kn.) You can also hunt for occasional *sobe* signs on the waterfront and along bus routes #5 and 8, but rooms tend to be pricey (100-200kn). The **Youth Hostel Zadar,** Obala kneza Trpimira 76 (tel. 33 11 45; fax 22 11 90), on the outskirts of town by the beach, has a friendly staff but claustrophobic rooms and unpleasant bathrooms. From the station, take bus #5 or 8 (6kn) heading to Diklo; plan to get off at the last stop, but ask someone to let you know when your stop comes. (July-Aug. 80kn; June and Sept. 72kn; Oct.-May 58kn. Daily tax 5kn. Breakfast included. Reception daily 7am-9pm.) To reach **Autocamp Borik,** Gustavo Matoša bb (tel. 33 20 74; fax 33 21 53), on the beach, take bus #5 or 8 to Diklo. After about 20min., look for signs to the camp on the left. (16kn per person; tents 14kn. Tourist tax 5.50kn.)

Restaurant Dva Ribara ("Two Fishermen"), Jurjeva 1 (tel. 43 37 11), has a huge selection of pasta, seafood, and mushrooms (25-40kn; open M-Sa 10am-midnight, Su 6pm-midnight). **Gostionica Zlati Vrtič,** Borelli 12, parallel with Široka, serves spaghetti, risotto, and fried squid, and all other buffet necessities for 20-30kn. (Open daily 7am-11pm.) The **supermarket** Zadranka has branches around town, including one at Široka 10 and at J. Štrossmayerova 6. (Both open daily 6:30am-10pm.)

SIGHTS & ENTERTAINMENT. The free map distributed by Liburnija (see above) contains a self-guided tour of all major sights. You can also buy a more comprehensive guide for 60kn (available in several languages). The most historically laden part of town is the ancient **Forum,** on Široka in the center of the peninsula. The city's most remarkable monument, **St. Donat's Church** (Crkva sv. Donata), dominates the square. Built at the beginning of the 9th century in early Byzantine style, the church sits on the site of an ancient Roman temple, still visible inside. (Open M-Sa 9am-noon and 5-8pm, Su 10am-noon and 6-8pm. 5kn.) **St. Mary's Church** (Sv. Marija) is just across the square from St. Donat's and houses the fabulous **Museum of Church Art** (Stalna Izložba Crkvene Umjetnosti), Trg Opatice Čike 1 (tel. 21 15 45). Buy tickets from the wandering nuns. (Open M-Sa 10am-12:30pm and 6-7:30pm, Su 10am-12:30pm. 20kn, students 10kn.) Next to St. Mary's stands the **Archeological Museum** (Arheološki Muzej), Trg Opatice Čike 1 (tel. 21 18 37 and 21 24 47), which has extensive collections documenting the history of Zadar, including a model of the town during the Roman era. (Open M-Sa 8:30am-1pm and 6-8pm. 15kn.) Although not among Croatia's best, Zadar's **beaches** are still some of the cleanest in the Mediterranean. Take bus #5 or 8 toward "Diklo" and get off where you like, or simply follow the waterfront until you find a suitable stop.

The trendiest and liveliest place to party is **Central Kavana,** Široka 1, a factory-like space that turns into a live music venue on weekends. (0.1L *Laško* 3kn, 0.33L Guinness and Corona 20kn, coffee 5-8kn. Open daily 7am-midnight.) **Caffe bar Forum,** on Široka at the Forum, has comfortable chairs and fantastic outdoor seating right on the ruins. (1L beer 20kn, coffee 5-8kn, warm sandwiches 10kn. Open daily 7am-midnight.) If you're motorized, join Zadar's youth at Saturday discos at **Saturnus** (tel. 26 44 44) in Zaton, 15km away from Zadar.

NEAR ZADAR: PLITVICE LAKES NATIONAL PARK

Plitvice Lakes National Park (Nacionalni Park Plitvička Jezera) lies in the Krajina region, where Croatia's bloody war of independence began. Throughout the conflict (1991-95), the area was held by the Serbs, who planted **landmines** in the ground. Although the park is safe and accessible, there still remain—by most estimates—over a million landmines throughout the surrounding area. **Under no circumstances should you leave the road and marked paths.** Do not let this warning stop you from visiting the natural wonder of the Plitvice lakes; just be intelligent about where you walk.

CROATIA

Few fish are fortunate enough to be born into one of Plitvice's 16 clearer-than-crystal lakes or the series of cascades and waterfalls, all of which were formed over millions of years through interaction between water and petrified vegetation. Declared a national park in 1949, the lakes were added to the UNESCO World Heritage list 30 years later. The formation is divided into Upper Lakes (Gornja Jezera) and Lower Lakes (Donja Jezera), and a complete tour of both chains (partly by bus and boat, but mostly on foot) takes approximately 4hr. Shorter 2-3hr. versions are possible. At every park entrance, there is a **tourist center** booth (tel. 75 10 15 and 75 10 14; email np-plitvice@np-plitvice.tel.hr) that provides maps and a comprehensive, colorful guide to the park, and a place to leave your **luggage** while you explore the lakes. (July-Aug. 60kn, June and Sept. 50kn., Oct.-May 40kn; students 20kn less. Open daily 8am-7pm.) **Phone code:** 053.

GETTING THERE. Buses run from **Zadar** (2½hr., every 30min., 51kn) and **Zagreb** (2½hr., every 30min., 39kn); ask the driver to drop you at the park entrance.

NEAR ZADAR: KALI

An ancient fishing village on the island of Ugljan, Kali lies a short 5km trip from Zadar. There are few—if any—tourists here, and the town remains much as it always has been: nearly every male you pass on the street is, was, or will be, a fisherman. The beaches here are far superior to those in Zadar, and virtually vacant. If possible, visit on a Sunday in order to enter and explore **Church of St. Pelegrino,** a medieval church situated atop a hill with a magnificent view of the bay.

GETTING THERE. Kali can be reached by a **ferry** running between **Zadar** and **Preko** on Ugljan (30min., 10-12 per day, 12kn). From Preko, jump on a **bus** to Kali from the ferry terminal (5min., 5kn), or turn left and walk along the sea (20min.).

SPLIT

Founded in the 7th century by Salonians fleeing a war in the Balkans, Split is a city of extraordinary culture and history. The Old Town, wedged between a high mountain range and a palm-lined waterfront, sprawls around a luxurious palace where Roman Emperor Diocletian used to summer. Split has all the advantages and disadvantages one would expect from a city much larger than Zadar or Trogir, boasting a wider variety of activities and nightlife but suffering from higher volumes of dust, noise, and traffic.

GETTING THERE & GETTING AROUND

Trains: Obala kneza Domagoja 10 (tel. 34 74 18). To: **Rijeka** (8hr., 3 per day, 107kn); **Zadar** via **Knin** (4hr., 3 per day, 52kn); **Zagreb** (9hr., 3 per day, 85kn); and **Ljubljana** (12hr.; Tu, Th, and Sa; 230kn).

Buses: Obala kneza Domagoja 12 (tel. 34 50 47and 34 28 57). Domestic and international *(međunarodni promet)* tickets are sold at ticket counters outside. To: **Dubrovnik** (4½hr., 13 per day, 77kn); **Rijeka** (8hr., 13 per day, 145kn); **Zadar** (3hr., every 30min., 55kn); **Zagreb** (7hr., 30 per day, 81-113kn); **Ljubljana** (18hr., 1 per day, 188kn); and **Sarajevo** (7hr., 8 per day, 140kn). Buses to **Trogir** (30min., 3 per hr., one-way 13.50kn, round-trip 23.50kn) leave from the **local bus station** on Domovinskog rata.

Ferries: O. kneza Domagoja bb (tel. 35 53 99). To: **Rijeka** (9hr., 1 per day, July-Aug. 128kn, Sept.-June 107kn); **Dubrovnik** (10hr., 1 per day, 86kn, 72kn); and **Ancona, Italy** (10hr., June-Sept. 5 per week, 234kn).

Local Transportation: 5kn tickets for **buses** can be purchased from the driver; punch them on board. Most buses run every 30min.

Taxis: Tel. 499 99. Many stand in front of Diocletian's Palace on Obala hrvatskog narodnog preporoda. Average fare 14kn plus 7kn per km.

ORIENTATION

The **train** and **bus stations** lie across from the ferry terminal on **Obala kneza Domagoja.** Leaving the stations, follow Obala kneza Domagoja to the waterside mouthful **Obala hrvatskog narodnog preporoda,** which runs roughly east to west. To the north lies **Stari Grad** inside the walls of **Diocletian's Palace** (Dioklecijanova Palača).

PRACTICAL INFORMATION

TOURIST & FINANCIAL SERVICES

Tourist Office: Daluma, Obala kneza Domagoja 1 (tel. 34 26 99; tel./fax 34 47 77). English-speaking staff has **maps,** exchanges currency, arranges accommodations, and sells airplane, ferry, and bus tickets. Open M-Sa 8am-8pm, Su 8am-12:30pm.

Budget Travel: Croatia Express, Obala kneza Domagoja 9 (tel. 34 26 45 and 44 44 99; fax 36 24 08). Student discounts for international bus, train, and plane fares. Also sells B.I.J. Wasteels tickets. Open daily 6:30am-10pm.

Consulates: The **British** and **Irish** consulates share a building at Obala hrvatskog narodnog preporoda 10, above the bank.

Currency Exchange: Private exchanges abound. **Zagrebačka banka,** Obala hrvatskog narodnog preporoda 10, exchanges cash and traveler's checks for a 1.5% commission. Open M-F 7:30am-12:30pm and 2:30-7pm, Sa 8-11:30am.

ATM: Cirrus/MC outside Zagrebačka banka (see above). Visa/AmEx outside Croatia Express (see above).

American Express: Atlas Travel Agency, Trg Braće Radić 7 (tel. 34 30 55). Cashes traveler's checks for a 1% commission. Open M-F 8am-1:30pm and 2-8pm, Sa 8am-1pm.

EMERGENCY & LOCAL SERVICES

Luggage Storage: At the bus station. 2.50kn per hr. Open daily 6am-10pm. At the train station. 10kn per day. Open daily 5:30-10:30am, 11am-4:30pm, and 5-10pm.

Pharmacy: Marmontova 2 (tel. 488 40). Open M-F 7am-8pm and Sa 7am-1pm.

Police: Trg hrvatske bratske zajednice 9 (tel. 30 72 81).

Hospital: Clinical Hospital Center (tel. 51 50 55), on Spinčićeva at Firule. From the Stari Grad, follow Kralja Zronimica until it runs into Pozjiča. The hospital is on the right.

English Bookstore: International Bookstore, Obala hrvatskog narodnog preporoda 21. Paltry selection of books but decent magazines. Open M-F 8am-8pm, Sa 8am-1pm.

Internet Access: Mala knjizara & Cyber Club, Kružičeva 3 (tel. 36 08 26). Three PCs for 20kn per hr. Open M-F 8am-12:30pm and 4:30-8pm, Sa 8am-1pm.

Post Office: Ul. Kralja Tomislava 9. Go in the main doors to send mail, through the left-hand doors for **telephones** and **fax,** and through the doors on the right for **Poste Restante.** Open M-F 7am-8pm, Sa 7am-3pm. **Postal code:** 21000. **Phone code:** (0)21.

ACCOMMODATIONS

For a city its size, Split has a paltry selection of budget accommodations. The tourist office (see above) can help by finding **private rooms** in the center of town. (Singles 60-100kn; doubles 100-150kn.) Other agencies also arrange rooms, but usually at higher rates. (100-150kn per person.) People at the bus station offer rooms; some may offer lower prices. **Prenoćište Slavija,** Buvinova 2 (tel./fax 59 15 58), recently renovated after a stint housing refugees, boasts 70 beds in clean rooms near the center. From the stations, follow Obala hrvatskog narodnog preporoda, then turn right onto Trg Braće Radića. Turn right onto Mihovilova širina and go up the stairs in the left-hand corner. (Singles 180kn, with shower 220kn; doubles 210kn, 260kn; triples 250kn, 300kn; quads 280kn, 360kn. Breakfast included.) There are also several medium-sized **camps** near Split; ask at the tourist office.

CROATIA

FOOD

There is a supermarket at Svačićeva 4 (open daily 7am-10pm) and a very cheap **food court** at Obala kneza Domagoja 1, right outside the train and bus stations. (Pizza 8kn; sandwiches 10kn.) At least one of the stands is always open.

Ponoćno Sunce, Teutina 15 (tel. 36 10 11). From the waterfront, follow Marmontova to Trg Gaje Bulata, then turn left onto Teutina. Pricey, but the wide array of pastas are reasonable and delicious (30-40kn). Open daily 8am-11pm.

Restaurant Libar, on the corner of Svačićeva and Manderova. As cheap as it gets: a full *menu* with soup, entree, and dessert 36kn. Open daily 7am-8pm.

Hotel Central, Narodni trg 1. From the waterfront, turn into Stari Grad at Trg Braće Radića, and from its right-hand corner follow Marunlićeva. Narodni trg is on the left. A steal before 8pm. Omelettes 15kn. Open daily 7am-11pm.

Restaurant Sarajevo, Domaldova 6 (tel. 474 54). Follow directions to Hotel Central and turn right onto Domaldova in the farthest corner of Narodni trg. Heaping portions of delicious food. Omelettes 25kn; stuffed peppers 22kn. Open daily 10am-midnight.

SIGHTS

DIOCLETIAN'S PALACE. The eastern half of Split's **Old Town** (Stari Grad) inhabits the one-time fortress and summer residence of the Roman Emperor Diocletian. In the 7th century, local residents were forced into the fortress to protect themselves from marauding Slavs, and later built their city within its walls. Today, it is a living museum of classical and medieval architecture. The **cellars** of the city are located near the entrance to the Palace; turn either direction to wander around this labyrinth. The dark stone passages originally created a flat floor for the emperor's apartments. The 1700 years of trash stored here have gained some archaeological significance. Some of the finds are displayed in hallways to the left of the entrance, which also hold a complex of dripping domes. The airier right side is used as a space for **modern art** displays. *(Under a flag just past the line of taxis on Obala hrvatskog narodnog preporoda. Cellars open M-F 10am-1pm and 6-8pm, Sa 10am-1pm. 6kn.)*

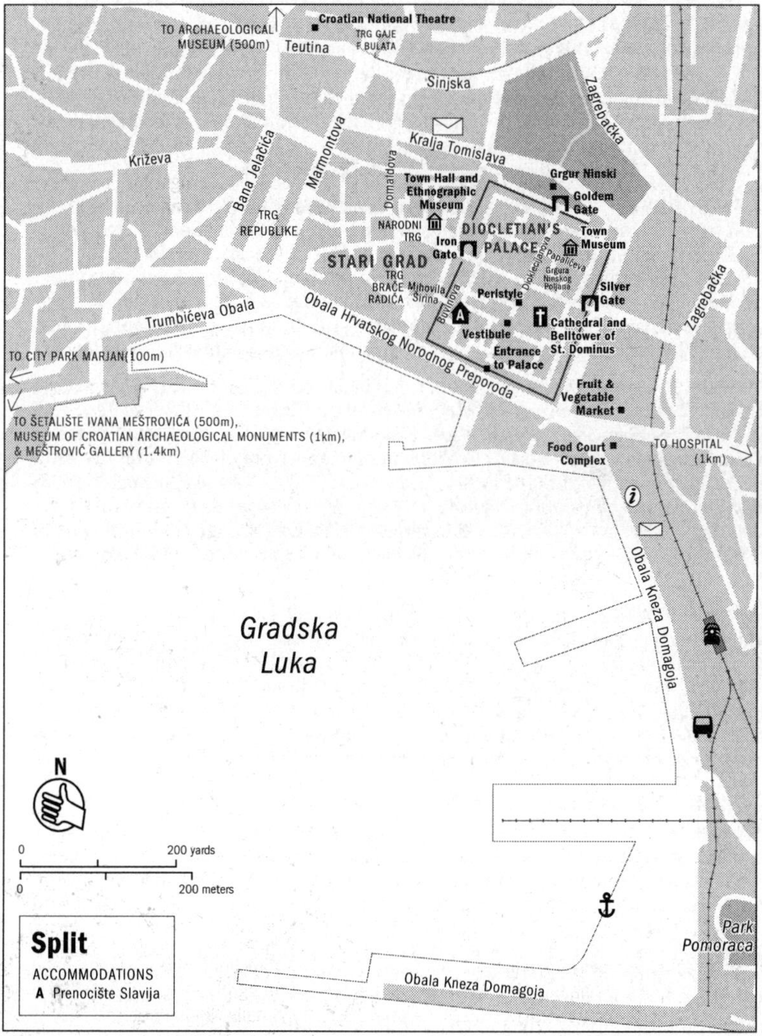

The open-air **peristyle** is a colonnaded square used for outdoor operas and ballets. The open-domed **vestibule** becomes the backstage during the **Summer Festival.** You can explore it freely during the day. *(Straight through the cellars and up the stairs.)* The **cathedral** on the right side of the peristyle is one of architecture's great ironies—it was originally the mausoleum of Diocletian, an emperor known for his violent persecution of Christians. Its later conversion to a Catholic cathedral makes it the world's oldest. The small, circular interior with intricately wrought stonework leaves almost no room for tourists who come to wonder at the magnificent inner door and altar. The adjoining **Belltower of St. Domnius** (Zvonik Sv. Duje), begun in the 13th century, took 300 years to complete. The stairs are unnerving, but the view is worth the flashes of life before you on the way up. *(Cathedral and tower open daily 7am-noon and 4-7pm. Tower 5kn.)* The collection of the **City Museum** (Muzej grada Splita) is less inspiring than the rich medieval palace in which it resides. *(Papalićeva 1. Walk from the peristyle along ul. Dioklecijana, then right on Papalićeva. Tel. 34 12 40. Open Tu-F 9am-noon and 6-9pm, Sa-Su 10am-noon. 10kn, children 5kn.)*

MEŠTROVIĆ GALLERY. Although it's quite a walk along the waterfront from the center, do not miss this gallery and its comprehensive collection of the works of Ivan Meštrović, Croatia's most famous modern sculptor (see **Literature & Arts,** p. 138). The entrance fee gets you into both the gallery—housed in a villa with fabulous ocean views that the artist built for himself—and the nearby **Kaštelet,** decorated with wood carvings. *(Šetaliste Ivana Meštrovića 46. Tel. 35 84 50. Both open Tu-Sa 10am-6pm, Su 10am-2pm. 15kn, students 10kn. Booklet in English 5kn.)*

IN STARI GRAD. The Old Town's eastern **Silver Gate** (Srebrna Vrata) leads to the main fish, fruit, and vegetable **market.** Outside the north **Golden Gate** (Zlatna Vrata) you'll find Ivan Meštrović's (see below) rendering of **Gregorius of Nin** (Grgur Ninski), the 10th-century Slavic champion of commoners' rights. The westernmost **Iron Gate** (Željezna Vrata) brings you to Narodni trg. Although this side of town lacks any excavations, medieval architecture still dominates. Browsing through the many boutiques, it's hard not to run into a centuries-old church or residence.

MUSEUMS. Headless statues meander in a beautiful garden at the **Archaeological Museum** (Arheološki muzej). *(Zrinsko Frankopanska ul. 25. North of Stari Grad. Tel. 34 45 74. Open Tu-Sa 9am-3pm, Su 10am-noon. 10kn, children 5kn.)* The **Museum of Croatian Archeological Monuments** houses Croatian monuments from the 9th and 10th centuries, many evocative of Celtic styles. *(Gunjacina ul. 1. To get there, walk down Branimirova obala and continue on Meštrovića. Tel. 34 39 83. Open M-F 9am-4pm, Sa 9am-noon. 10kn, students 5kn. English guide 10kn.)* The **Ethnographic Museum** (Etnografski muzej) rests inside the 15th-century Venetian former **town hall** in Stari Grad. *(On the north side of Narodni trg. Open daily 10am-noon and 6-9pm. 2kn.)*

PARKS & BEACHES. The rocky cliffs, green hills, and sandy beaches on the west end of Split's peninsula make up **City Park Marjan** and serve as a reminder that Diocletian once vacationed here. Paths are indicated on the tourist map; you can find your own, but watch for signs indicating that a trail leads to private lands—the dogs *do* bite.The closest **beach** to downtown Split is by the Meštrović Gallery (see above). It serves as an entertainment center for Split's youth, as well. *(Walk from the center along Branimirova obala and then Šetalište Ivana Meštrovića. 15min.)*

ENTERTAINMENT

At night, Stari Grad transforms into a teeming mass of people spilling in and out of the local bars. From mid-July to mid-August, it hosts an annual **Summer Festival;** the city's best artists join international guests in performing ballets, operas, plays, and classical concerts among the town's churches and ruins. Visit the **Croatian National Theater** (Hrvatsko Narodno Kazalište), Trg Gaje Bulata 1 (tel./fax 58 59 57 and 465 88; ticket office tel. 58 59 99, ext. 220), for an indoor version. (Box office open daily 9am-2pm and 2hr. before performances.) You can pick up a schedule at the tourist office, along with the monthly *Splitska Scena.*

NIGHTLIFE

Kavana Luxor, Kraj sv. Juana (tel. 467 68), on the peristyle in the center of Diocletian's Palace. You can't get a better view. At night, young patrons overflow into the palace itself. Awesome music, a large selection of beer (7-15kn), and *Dioklecijanova kava* (10kn)—coffee fit for an emperor. Open daily 8am-midnight.

Jazz planet, Grgura Ninskoga 3. Hidden on a tiny back street across from the City Museum, the stone interior is so mellow it draws more people than the sunny outdoor tables. Open M-Sa 8am-midnight, Su 6pm-midnight.

Obojena svjetlost (Colored Light), Uvala Zvončac. Walk along Šetalište Ivana Meštrovića to Meštrović Gallery, then go down to the beach. Hosts Croatian and international rock 'n' roll, blues, or "we-play-it-all" bands on its beachfront, open-air stage. A show goes up every night: have a beer (10kn) and bask in the colored lights. Open daily 7am-4am.

Discoteque Night Cafe, Osječka bb. From Kralja Zvonimiva, turn left onto Slobode and follow it to the mall-like Koteks center. On weekends, the guests in this high-tech disco number in the thousands. Open daily 9pm-3am.

BRAČ ISLAND: BOL

Central Dalmatia's largest island, Brač—highlighted by the town of Bol on its south coast—is a tourist's paradise. Most visitors come here for Zlatni rat, arguably the most beautiful beach in the Adriatic. Just a short walk from the town center, its white pebbles roll from the surrounding pine forest into the sea. But Brač has more to offer than location: churches, galleries, and a lively night scene will keep you busy for as long as you choose to stay.

ORIENTATION & PRACTICAL INFORMATION. The entire town is organized around the many-named waterfront: at the bus stop and marina, it is called **Obala Vladimira Nazora;** east of the bus it becomes **Riva,** then **Loža;** to the west it's called **Put Zlatnograta** and **Porad bolskich pomorca.** The ferry between **Split** and **Brač** docks at **Supetar** (1hr., July-Aug. 13 per day, Sept.-June 7 per day, 16kn).From there, take a bus to **Bol** (45min., 5 per day, 25kn). The last bus back to the ferry leaves at 6pm. Alternatively, a **catamaran** runs directly to **Bol** from **Split** (departs Bol M-Sa 7am, Split 3pm; 45kn, round-trip 70kn). The **tourist office,** Turistička zajednica općine Bol, Porad bolskich pomorca bb (tel. 63 51 22; fax 63 56 38), a 5min. walk east of the bus station, dispenses the guide *Bol.* **Zagrebačka banka,** Uz pjacu 4 (tel./fax 63 56 11), uphill from the bus station, **exchanges currency** and **traveler's checks** for no commission. (Open M-F 8am-1pm, Sa 8-11am.) **Bol Tours,** Obala Vladimira Nazora 18 (tel. 63 56 93 and 63 56 94; fax 63 56 95), exchanges currency for no commission in addition to renting cars (330kn per day, unlimited mileage) and bikes (70kn per day, 45kn per half day; open daily 8am-10pm). There's a **pharmacy** and **ambulance** (tel. 63 51 12) available on Porat bolskich pomorca bb. (Open M-F 8am-noon and 6-8pm, Sa 8am-noon.) **Hotel Elaphusa** (tel. 63 52 22), on Put zlatnog rata, boasts the first **internet cafe** on Brač. (15kn flat rate plus 30kn per hr. Open daily 6am-midnight.) The **post office,** Uz pjatu 5 (tel. 63 52 35; fax 63 52 53), shelters telephones. (Open M-Sa 7am-9pm.) **Postal code:** 21420. **Phone code:** (0)21.

ACCOMMODATIONS & FOOD. Bol Tours (see above) arranges **private rooms.** (July 17-Aug. 21 singles 92-120kn; doubles 70-97kn. July 1-17 and Aug. 21-Sept. 1 singles 80-97kn; doubles 62-85kn. April 1-July 1 and Sept. 1-Oct. 31 singles 65-80kn, doubles 50-70kn. Registration fee 10kn. 20% surcharge for stays less than 3 nights.) The tourist office's booklet *Bol* lists private rooms for rent, generally 10% cheaper than official prices. There are five camping sites around Bol; the largest is **Kito,** Bračka cesta bb (tel. 63 54 24 and 63 55 51), on the road into town. (38kn per person; tent included. Open May 1-Sept. 30.)

Tourist success has driven food prices up, but the **supermarket Vrtić,** on Uz pjatu near the post office and bank, remains affordable. (Open daily 6:30am-9pm.) **Restaurant "Plaža Borak,"** on the beach just before Zlatni rat, offers daily *menus* (soup and entree) for 40kn. (Open daily 9am-1am.) **Pizzeria Topolino,** Riva 2 (tel. 63 57 67), in the center of town, has good pizza for 30-40kn. (Open daily 8am-2am.) **Konoba Gušt,** Frane Radića 14 (tel. 63 59 11), hides on a shady street parallel to the waterfront in the center. (Pasta 30-35kn. Open daily noon-2am.)

SIGHTS & ENTERTAINMENT. The free map distributed by the tourist office (see above) shows all the town's sights, the most important of which is the **Dominican Monastery,** built in 1475. It resides on the eastern tip of Bol, and has an adjacent **museum** housing a collection of artifacts from nearby excavations. (Open daily 10am-noon and 5-7pm. 10kn.) **Dešković Gallery,** on Porat bolskih pomoraca next to the bus station, exhibits contemporary art from throughout Croatia. (Open daily 6-10pm. 5kn.) More art comes to town during **Bol Cultural Summer** (Bolsko Kulturno Ljeto; July 1-Aug. 31). Inquire at the tourist office about particular events. **Big Blue Sport,** Podan glavice 2 (tel./fax 63 56 14), organizes **scuba diving** (one dive 180kn; 5 dives 840kn; night dive 220kn; dive course 220kn) and **windsurfing** (8hr. course for beginners 640kn; rentals 260kn per day, 180kn per half-day).

Around 11pm, Bol's youth flock to the disco in **Facis Club Kaltenberg,** Bračka cesta bb (tel. 63 54 10), right by the Kito Campground (see above). Other discos pulse near the beach, including **Hotel Complex Bretanide,** on Zlatni rat. (Open daily 11pm-2am.) For a mellower time, try the **cafes** and **bars** along the waterfront.

VIS ISLAND: KOMIŽA

The island of Vis spent nearly 50 years in geographical and political isolation (it is the Dalmatian island farthest from mainland Croatia and was taken by the Yugoslav People's Army after WWII). In 1985, the inhabitants initiated the first civil action against their oppressors, signing a petition demanding that their island be opened to foreigners. But when their dreams finally came true in 1990, the islanders found themselves embroiled in the Yugoslav-Croatian war. Since the war's end in 1995, the people of Vis have been struggling to attract tourists, while fishing, growing olives, and making wine as they always have. Their location has its upside: today, Vis is by far the most pristine island in the Adriatic.

ORIENTATION & PRACTICAL INFORMATION. To reach Komiža you will need to take a ferry to Vis and then a bus into town. Jadrolinija runs a **ferry** to Vis from **Split** (2½hr., 1-2 per day, 22kn). **Buses** to Komiža are scheduled around the ferry (10min., 10kn). In the summer, a private company (SMC) runs a **catamaran** between Vis and **Split** (1½hr., 2 per day, 80kn, round-trip 120kn). Also during the summer, the ferry between **Rijeka** and **Dubrovnik** occasionally stops in Vis—inquire at any Jadrolinija office. The town of Komiža is tiny enough that you cannot get lost. The bus stops on **Hrvatskih mučenika,** and **Riva** (the waterfront) is just a few steps down. A right turn onto Riva leads to **Ribarska** and to the beach, while a left turn leads to most services and sights. The **tourist office,** Riva 2 (tel./fax 71 34 55), is on the edge of the cove. Its newly elected director, **Zoran Franičević** is an excellent source of info about Vis and Dalmatia's past, present, and future, as well as the island's hidden gems. (Open M-Sa 8am-1pm and 6-8pm, Su 9am-noon.) Closer to the bus station is the **tourist agency Darlić & Darlić,** Riva 13 (tel./fax 71 37 60; email ines.darlic@st.tel.hr; www.pl-print.tel.hr/darlic). Mother Darlić, brother Darlić, or the other brother Darlić will let you check **email** on their fast computer (free), arrange accommodations (see below), and **exchange currency** for a 1% commission. (Open daily 7:30am-10pm.) **Splitska banka,** Trg kralja Tomislava 10, on the waterfront, exchanges cash and traveler's checks for a 1% commission. (Open M-F 8-11:30am and 6-8pm, Sa 8am-noon.) There are no **ATMs.** The **pharmacy** (tel. 71 34 45) is in the middle of nowhere; from the waterfront, turn onto Hrvatskih mučenika, then take the second left. Walk straight, through the intersection, then head up the stairs to San Pedro bb. (Open M-F 8am-1pm and 7-8pm, Sa 8:30-10:30am.) The **post office,** Hrvatskih mučenika 8 (tel. 71 30 20), next to the bus, **exchanges cash** and traveler's check for a 1.5% commission, gives MC **cash advances.** (Open M-Sa 7am-9pm.) **Postal Code:** 21485. **Phone code:** (0)21.

ACCOMMODATIONS & FOOD. With no camping and only one pricey hotel, the only budget option in town is a **private room** arranged through Darlić & Darlić (see above). This family will find you a room at all costs—even in their own home. (July 11 and Aug. 19 singles 85-120kn; doubles 120-170kn. June 15- July 10 and Aug. 20-Sept. 15 singles 60-95k; doubles 85-140kn. Sept. 15-June 15 singles 50-70kn; doubles 70-100kn. Tourist tax 3.80-6kn. 30% surcharge for less than 3 nights.)

Restaurants are scarce and pricey. If you feel like splurging, though, **Riblji restoran** (Fish Restaurant; tel. 71 33 02), on Riva next to Darlić & Darlić, is one of the best seafood restaurants in Dalmatia. Cephalopods are the name of the game here, from the eminently affordable octopus (20kn) to the speciality **crno rižoto** (risotto with squid) for 40kn. (Open daily 7am-11pm.) **Konoba Bako,** Gundulićeva 1 (tel. 71 37 42), on the way to the beach, serves pasta for 20-30kn. (Open summer daily 11am-2am; off-season 6pm-midnight.) There are several small **supermarkets** in Komiža; one is right in the center on Riva. (Open M-Sa 6:30am-8:30pm.)

SIGHTS & ENTERTAINMENT. **St. Nicholas Church** (Crkva sv. Nikole), called *Muster* by the locals, overlooks Komiža. Built as part of a Benedictine monastery in the 12th century, it now holds regular services and stays open for visitors most of the day. Right on the beach sits the **Pirates' Church** (Gusarica). According to legend, pirates stole a madonna statue from this church, but were soon caught in a storm; only the Blessed Virgin made it back to shore. (Open daily 9-11am and 5-9pm.) Several agencies organize daytrips to the neighboring island; the ones by Darlić and Darlić (see above) are the cheapest. Among the sites visited are the **Green Cave** on **Ravnik Island** (daily, 85kn) and the incredible **Blue Cave** on **Biševo Island** (2 per day, 65kn). Another noteworthy nearby island is **St. Andrew,** which is inhabited by a single old woman; ask the tourist office about ways to get there. The **Fisherman's Museum** (Ribarski muzej), on Riva next to the tourist office, should not be missed. Komiža's **beach** is short and rocky, but that makes the water feel that much better. The most popular cafe-bar with the younger set is **Speed,** Škor 12. (Coffee 5-8kn; beer 10kn. Open daily 6am-midnight.)

CROATIA

HVAR ISLAND: HVAR TOWN

The scent of lavender permeates every corner of Hvar, growing fresh in the fields and sold in dried bouquets at stands throughout town. This combines with the extraordinary surroundings to make the island singular in its effect; *Traveller* magazine named Hvar one of the ten most beautiful islands in the world in 1997.

ORIENTATION & PRACTICAL INFORMATION. **Ferries** make the trip from **Split** to Hvar's **Stari Grad** (2hr., July-Aug. 7 per day, Sept.-June 5 per day, 21kn). From there, **buses** scheduled around the ferry take passengers to **Hvar Town** (15min., 11kn). Or, take a ferry from **Split** directly to Hvar Town (1½hr., 1 per day, 23kn). Inquire at the Jadrolinija terminal on the left tip of the waterfront (open M-Sa 8am-noon and 3-8pm, Su 10-11am and 3-4pm) or a tourist office about ferry schedules. During the summer, private **catamarans** between **Split** and **Vis** also stop in Hvar. **Pelegrini Tourist Agency** rents **cars** (350kn per day) and **bikes** (50kn per day) for exploring the rest of the island. Hvar Town has virtually no street names and even fewer signs, which would make navigating tricky if the town were not so small. The main square, **Trg sv. Stjepana,** directly below the bus station by the waterfront (Obala), is the one place graced with a name. Facing the sea from the main square, a left along the waterfront leads to the tourist agency, post office, bank, and ferry terminal; a right leads to the major hotels and beaches. The **tourist office,** Turistička Zajednica, Trg sv. Stjepana 21 (tel./fax 74 10 59; email tzg-hvar@st.tel.hr), is in the corner of the main square closest to the water. (Open M-Sa 8:30am-1pm and 6-9pm, Su 10am-noon and 7-9pm.) **Splitska Banka,** Obala 4 (tel. 74 19 47), **exchanges currency** for no commission and **traveler's checks** for a 2% commission. (Open M-F 7am-1pm and 2-8pm, Sa 8-11am.) There's a MC/Cirrus **ATM** on the waterfront to the right of the main square, outside Zagrebačka banka. There is a **pharmacy** in the square. (Open M-F 8am-9pm, Sa 8am-1pm and 6-8pm, Su 9am-noon.) The **post office,** Obala bb (tel. 74 24 13), has **telephones** and will hold mail for one month. (Open M-Sa 7am-9pm.) **Postal code:** 21450. **Phone code:** (0) 21.

ACCOMMODATIONS & FOOD. As in other Croatian resort towns, the only budget accommodations are **private rooms,** and even those are expensive; the tourist agency **Pelegrini,** Obala bb (tel./fax 74 22 50), can arrange them. (Singles 125 kn; doubles 85kn per person. Tourist tax 7kn. 30% surcharge for stays less than 3 nights. Open M-Sa 8:30am-12:30pm and 6-9pm, Su 6-9pm.) You may find a room on your own for a better price, particularly if not many tourists are in town. Look on the street parallel to the main square that runs up to the castle for *sobe* signs.

There is a cheap **market** between the bus station and the main square. The **supermarket,** Trg sv. Stjepana bb, is small but well-stocked. (Open M-Sa 6:30am-10pm, Su 6:30am-noon.) Overpriced restaurants line the waterfront and the square. Try the buffet-style **Alviz Crêperie,** across from the bus station, for crêpes (20-30kn) and pizza. (Open M-Sa 9am-1pm and 7pm-midnight, Su 7pm-midnight.)

SIGHTS & ENTERTAINMENT. For an overview of town, you can climb the **cathedral tower.** (Open daily 9am-noon and 5-7pm. 10kn.) The best way to see the city from above, however, is to climb the path to the 13th-century **Venetian fortress.** (Open daily 9am-8pm.) Inside, you'll find a **marine archaeological collection** *(hidroarheološka zbirka)*, consisting primarily of Greek and Byzantine amphorae collected after WWII by Hvar native Tonko Kovačić. (Open daily 10am-1pm. 10kn.) Also in the fortress you'll find a patio that plays soft dance hits in the early evening, then rages as a popular **disco** late into the night. (Disco open nightly 10pm-5am.) Any remaining museum-going thirst can be quenched at the central **Gallery Arsenal** (open daily 8am-noon), or at the **Last Supper Collection** in the **Franciscan monastery,** which includes the *other* famous *Last Supper*, painted in oil by Matteo Ignoli. (Open M-Sa 9am-noon. 7kn.) The monastery also hosts the outdoor performances of the **Hvar Summer Festival.** Indoor performances take place above the Arsenal in one of Europe's oldest **community theaters,** dating from 1612. Some of the Adriatic's clearest waters surround Hvar, but to enjoy them you'll have to brave the loud, crowded, gravel beaches and fearsome aquatic hedgehogs. You may instead choose to head out to the nearby **Hellish Islands** (Pkleni otoci), Jevolim, Stipanska, and Parmižana. Boats in the harbor run a **taxi service** between them. (Frequent boats 8am-noon. Round-trip 10-25kn, depending on which island.) The **diving center** in Hotel Amfora (tel. 74 24 90), right on the beach, offers diving (shoredives for 105-133kn; one boat dive 122kn, 2 for 245kn) and rentals (bikes 53kn per day; motorboats 200kn per day; snorkel equipment 31 kn per day; kayaks 30kn per hr.).

TROGIR

With medieval buildings packed tightly into winding streets and a surrounding sea lapping and crashing against pristine parks, Trogir is a stone beauty that seems deserved of more than its tiny island locale. The town's miniature scale has only enhanced the town's appeal, attracting Gothic and Renaissance artists to grace it with countless churches from the 13th-15th centuries and earning it a coveted place on the UNESCO World Heritage List in 1997. Best of all, its proximity to Split affords easy access to this highlight of Central Dalmatia.

ORIENTATION & PRACTICAL INFORMATION. The town spills from the mainland onto two islands, both connected by short bridges. The Old Town is on the small island of Trogir; behind it lies Čiovo Island with the town's best beaches, reachable by the Čiovski bridge. The **bus station** (tel. 88 14 05) is on the mainland. **Buses** from **Zadar** to **Split** stop in Trogir (2½hr., hourly, 54kn from Zadar). Local buses also go to **Split** (20min., 3 per hr., 23.50kn round-trip). The main street, **Kohl-Genscher,** is a short walk from the bus station across the tiny bridge and through the stone North Gate. It leads past the central square, **Trg Ivana Pavla,** to the Čiovski bridge. Catch a **taxi** across the street from the bus station or call 88 12 17. (8kn per km.) The **tourist office,** Turistička Zajednica Grada Trogir, Obala b. Berislavića 12 (tel. 88 56 28; fax 88 14 12), is at the end of Kohl-Genscher. (Open July-Aug. daily 7am-9pm; Sept.-June daily 7am-2pm.) **Zagrebačka banka,** Gradska vrata 4 (tel. 88 19 36; fax 88 51 41), just past the North Gate, **exchanges cash** for no commission and **traveler's checks** for a 1.5% commission. (Open M-F 7:30am-12:30pm and 2:30-7pm, Sa 8-11:30am.) An **ATM** stands outside the bank (Cirrus/MC). The **pharmacy** is at Kohl-Genscher 23 (tel. 88 15 35; open M-F 7am-8pm, Sa 7am-2pm). The **post office,** B. Jurjeva Trogiranina 5 (tel. 88 14 52), gives MC **cash advances** and exchanges cash for a 1.5% commission. (Open M-F 7am-8pm, Sa 7am-3pm.) **Telephones** are both inside and outside the post office. **Postal code:** 21220. **Phone code:** (0)21.

ACCOMMODATIONS & FOOD. The best deals in town are **private rooms,** arranged by **ČIPIKO,** Kohl-Genscher 41 (tel./fax 88 15 54), across from the cathedral. (July-Aug. singles 100kn, doubles 150kn; Sept.-June singles 80kn, doubles 130kn. Open daily 8am-2pm and 4-8pm.) Beachside **Hotel Saldun** (tel./fax 88 20 53), on Sv. Andrije, sprawls on Čiovo Island. Cross the Čiovski bridge and follow Gonićeva and Vicka Žiška down to the beach. It offers decent rooms with hallway bathrooms. (98kn per person. Breakfast included.) **Vila Sikaa,** Obala Kralja Zvonimira 13 (tel. 88 12 23; fax 88 51 49; email stjepan.runtic@st.tel.hr), sits on the waterfront just across the Čiovski bridge. An expensive option with gorgeous, newly furnished rooms with private bathrooms, telephones, and satellite TV. (275kn per person; off season 250kn. Breakfast included.)

The best seafood and grilled meat is at **Konoba Škrapa,** Hrvatskih mučenika 9 (tel. 88 53 13). Squid and most other dishes are only 25kn, and you can fill your own bottle with homemade wines (7.50-30kn per liter; open M-Sa 9am-2pm and 6pm-midnight). The **Big Blue,** Kohl-Genscher 27 (tel. 88 10 03), not big but definitely blue, cooks up pizza and sandwiches for 20-40kn. (Open daily 8am-midnight.) There is a large **supermarket** across the street from the bus station (open M-Sa 6am-9pm, Su 7am-noon), and a smaller one next to the North Gate on Hrvatskih Mučenika 1. (Open daily 6:30am-9pm.)

SIGHTS & ENTERTAINMENT. The entrance to the Old Town, **North Gate,** is a beautiful Renaissance arch with a statue of Trogir's patron, Sv. Ivan Orsini, on top. Most sights are at **Trg Ivana Pavla,** in the middle of the Old Town, including the **Cathedral of St. Lawrence** (Crkva sv. Lovro). Begun in 1200 as a Romanesque basilica, it was not completed until 1598. Its famous portal was chiseled by the Croatian master Radovan in 1240 and contains life-size figures of Adam and Eve. Inside the Cathedral, you can find a truly singular piece of Renaissance art, the **Chapel of St. John of Trogir.** The 47m **bell tower** *(campanile)* has four bells, once proclaimed "the most harmonious in Dalmatia," but if you climb up the scary stairs on the hour, you'll be cheated: the bells mysteriously ring without moving. (10kn, students 5kn.) Tank-tops, shorts, and gum-chewing are not permitted. (Open daily 9am-noon and 4:30-7:30pm. Mass M-Sa at 7:30am; Su at 8am, 9am, 10:30am, and 7:30pm.) The 15th-century **Kamerlengo fortress** on the tip of the island, once poised to defend its owner from rebelling commoners, now houses a summer movie theater. The **Town Museum of Trogir** (Muzej Grada Trogira), on Kohl-Genscher, exhibits the town's historical artifacts. (Open June-Sept. M-Sa 9am-noon and 6-9pm. 10kn.)

The rocky **beach** starts at Hotel Saldun and winds its way around the larger island. **Cafes** of similar atmosphere, price, and menu line Kohl-Genscher and the waterfront. One of the only stand-outs is **Radovan,** Trg Ivana Pavla 2 (tel. 88 23 80), with seating outside the cathedral and on a quiet terrace. (Coffee 5kn, cappucino 8kn, 0.33L beer 8-15kn. Open daily 7am-midnight.)

KORČULA ISLAND: KORČULA TOWN

Like Corfu, Korčula's (KOR-chu-lah) name comes from the Greek words Korkyra Melaina (black), because of the macchia thickets, woods, and preponderance of slender cypress trees cloaking the island. Directly on the water, it faces the mountains of the Croatian mainland, just a few ferry minutes away. The island's proximity to the mainland makes it an ideal trip en route from Split to Dubrovnik, and its cultural life more than makes up for its crowded beaches.

ORIENTATION & PRACTICAL INFORMATION. The town of Korčula is situated beside the sea on the northeast end of the island. The medieval part of the city was built on a small oval peninsula, its streets etched in a herring-bone pattern. A baroque suburb spreads under the old city walls, and the newer town stretches along the shore to the east and west. Street addresses are scarce, but the town is easily navigable. Korčula is one of the few islands that can be reached by **bus;** they board a short ferry to the island. Buses run to: **Zagreb** (11-13hr., 1 per day, 150kn); **Sarajevo** (8hr., 2 per week, 145kn); and **Dubrovnik** (3½hr., 1 per day, 40kn). **Ferries** run to **Dubrovnik** (3hr., 1 per day, 54kn). Ferries from other destinations arrive in **Vela Luka** on the opposite side of the island. A bus connects Vela Luka to **Korčula Town** (1hr., 6 per day, 14kn). Check the Jadrolinija office (tel. 71 54 10; fax 71 11 01) opposite the bank for info. (Open M 5am-8pm, Tu-W 7:30am-8pm, Th 7:30am-3pm, F 5:30am-8pm, Sa 5am-3pm, Su 6am-1pm.) The **tourist office** (tel. 71 57 01 and 71 58 67; fax 71 58 66) is on the opposite side of the peninsula from the bus and ferry terminals. To get there, walk along the edge of the peninsula to Hotel Korčula; the office is next door. **Splitska banka** (tel. 71 12 42), in front of the stairs leading to Stari Grad, exchanges currency for a 1% commission, cashes **traveler's checks** for a 2% commission, gives Visa cash advances, and offers Western Union services. (Open M-F 7:30am-7:30pm, Sa 7:30-11am.) There are **no ATMs.** For a **taxi** call 71 51 75. The **pharmacy,** Trg kralja Tomislava bb (tel. 71 10 57), is at the foot of the Stari Grad stairs. (Open M-F 7am-8pm, Sa 7am-noon and 6-8 pm, Su 9-11am.) You can log on to the **internet** at the **PC Centar Doom** (tel. 71 58 81), on Buculin down Hrvatske zajednica, off the main square. (25kn per hr. Open M-Sa 9am-10pm, Su 4-10pm.) The **post office** (tel. 71 12 28), hidden behind the palms next to the pharmacy on the left of the Stari Grad stairs, houses **telephones.** (Open M-F 7am-9pm, Sa 8am-1pm and 6-8pm.) **Postal code:** 20260. **Phone code:** (0)20.

ACCOMMODATIONS & FOOD. **Private rooms** are the only budget accommodations available. **Marko Polo,** Biline 5 (tel. 71 54 00; fax 71 58 00; email marko-polo-tours@du.tel.hr), will arrange one for you. (July-Aug. singles 108-136kn; doubles 144-180kn; triples 196-232kn. Sept.-June singles 76kn; doubles 100kn; triples 140kn. Tourist tax 5.50-7kn. Open daily 8am-10pm, Su 6:30-9:30pm.) **Tibo,** Biline 9 (tel./fax 71 18 94), has fewer rooms but slightly better prices. (July-Aug. singles 96-132kn; doubles 140-176kn; triples 188-232kn. Sept.-June singles 80kn; doubles 120kn; triples 164kn. Prices may be negotiable.)

Eating out in Korčula is generally expensive. For the frugal, there is a **supermarket** next to Marko Polo. (Open M-Sa 6:30am-8:30pm, Su 6:30-11am.) A **fresh fruit market** stands to the right of the stairs up to Stari Grad. **Adio Mare** (tel. 71 12 53), on the main street near St. Mark's cathedral, is probably the loveliest restaurant in the Baltics. (Entrees 30-70kn; 1L wine 25kn. Open daily 10am-11pm.) Up the double staircase by the Hotel Korčula, **Agave Pizzeria** (tel. 71 51 67), Cvit. Bokšić 6, is one of the cheapest eateries in town, serving many varieties of pizza (22-55kn; open daily 8am-midnight). **Caffe bar Kiwi** (tel. 71 57 81), Šetalište Frana Kršinića bb, has an extensive variety of ice cream and elaborate ice cream drinks. (Coffee 4kn; ice cream 3.50kn per scoop. Open M-Sa 7am-11pm, Su 3-11pm.)

SIGHTS. In the center of Stari Grad on the highest point on the peninsula, **St. Mark's Cathedral** (Katedrala Sv. Marka), named for Korčula's patron saint, is the largest church in the city. It was built to accommodate the Korčula Bishopric, founded at the beginning of the 14th century during a time of economic prosperity.

EN GARDE The Moreška sword dance, first mentioned in Korčula in the 17th century, may have started after the Turkish siege in 1571. Over the next few centuries, it was performed all over the Mediterranean, but it has been preserved only in Korčula. It is characterized by simple, fluid movements, swordsmanship, and a folk drama symbolizing a battle between Christians and Muslims. The dance is performed by two groups of young men called *moreškanti*. They are theoretically led by kings and fighting for a maiden, Bula, the Christian king's fiancée who was kidnapped by the Muslim king Moro. After a dialogue between the kings and Bula's subsequent refusal of Moro, the armies collide; the wind orchestra accompanying the dance quickens its tempo as the clashing of the swords grows more fierce. Predictably, the Christians win and Bula is returned. Today, you can catch the dance during the Sword Dance Festival (see below).

The Gothic-Renaissance cathedral is composed of large, regular rectangles of Korčula limestone. The bell tower was built before the cathedral. The **Abbey Treasury of St. Mark,** in the Abbey court on the cathedral square, contains a collection of icons of various origin, drawings by Renaissance and Baroque artists, and a hall of contemporary Croatian art. (Open Tu-Su 10am-6pm. 10kn.) The **Town Museum** sits opposite the Treasury in the Renaissance Gabrielis Palace. Its collections narrate the historical, cultural, and social life of the city, but much of its material is missing, either because it has not been preserved or is on display elsewhere. The archaeological collection contains maps of the island, indicating the most important sites of antiquity; the glass cases hold archaeological objects from those places, including 7000 year-old knives from Badija. (Open M-Sa 9am-2pm and 6:30-8:30pm. 10kn.) **Marco Polo's House,** named after the famed explorer allegedly born in Korčula in 1254, is a late-Gothic ruin on the street to the left as you face the cathedral. (Open daily 10am-noon and 4-10pm. 5kn.)

ENTERTAINMENT. Carnival celebrations, including weekly masked balls *(maškare)*, are held from mid-January to Ash Wednesday (the end of February at the latest). The **Festival of Sword Dances** (Festival Viteških Igara) takes place each July, during which the Moreška, Moštra, and Kumpanija sword dances—part of the island's unique folklore—are performed throughout the island. Tickets for the opening ceremonies are available at any major tourist agency or newsstand (35kn), but if you want to save money, the procession through town before the show is essentially the same. A **festival** every September honors Marco Polo. Korčula's nightlife is consolidated in a series of bars on Šetalište Frana Kršiniča. Apart from these, **Caffe Bar Galerija,** on Prolaz tri Sulara, is known for its great music and comfy chairs. (Coffee 5kn; beer 10kn. Open M-Sa 7am-2:30pm and 5pm-1am, Su 5pm-1am.)

DUBROVNIK

Those who seek Paradise on earth should come to Dubrovnik.

—George Bernard Shaw

Endless epithets have been given to Dubrovnik, including "the pearl of the Adriatic" and "the city made of stone and light," but words fail to grasp the majesty of this walled city wedged between the Adriatic and Dinaric Alps. Ravaged by war and Serbian shells in 1991 and 1992, Dubrovnik is miraculously almost scarless; only close inspection reveals bullet holes and crumbled buildings. Rather, as the 30,000 fiercely proud residents will attest, Dubrovnik is defined by its Mediterranean grace and its uncanny resemblance to paradise. The azure waters, copper sunsets from atop the 14th-century city walls, and glistening Italian marble of the central plaza after a rain are almost as enchanting as the cadence of the local dialect. If you make it as far south as Dubrovnik, you just might never leave.

ORIENTATION

The walled **Stari Grad** is the city's cultural, historical, and commercial center. Its main street, called both **Placa** and **Stradun,** runs from the **Pile Gate,** the official entrance of Stari Grad, to the **Old Port** at the tip of the peninsula. The main traffic roads, **Put Republike** and **Ante Starčevića,** embrace the **bus station** (from the front and behind, respectively), merge into Ante Starčevića, and end at the Pile Gate.

PRACTICAL INFORMATION

Trains: No railway connections to Dubrovnik. All trains from the north terminate in Split.

Buses: Put Republike 38 (tel. 42 30 88; fax 42 37 24). To: **Split** (4½hr., 14 per day, 65kn); **Zagreb** (11hr., 7 per day, 135-163kn); **Zadar** (8hr., 7 per day, 130kn); **Rijeka** (12hr., 3 per day, 240kn); **Sarajevo** (6hr., 1 per day, 150kn); **Mostar** (3hr. 2 per day, 80kn); and **Trieste** (15hr., 1 per day, 225kn). To get to Stari Grad, face the bus station, walk around to the other side of the building, and turn left onto Ante Starčević. Follow this road uphill; the street numbers decrease as you approach the Old Town. Ante Starčevića runs straight to the Old Town's western entrance (20min.).

Ferries: Jadrolinija, Obala S. Radića 40 (tel. 41 80 00; tel./fax 41 81 11). To: **Split** (8hr., 11 per week, off-season 2 per week, 72kn); **Zadar** (15hr., 5 per week, off-season 2 per week, 118kn); **Rijeka** (20hr., 5 per week, 144kn); and **Bari, Italy** (9hr., 2 per week, 234kn). Open M-F 8am-8pm, Sa 8am-2pm and 7-8pm, Su 8-10am and 7-8:30pm. The **ferry terminal** is across from the Jadrolinija office. To reach the terminal, face away from the bus station and head left; when the road forks, go right.

Local Transportation: All buses except #7 go to Stari Grad's gate. Tickets are 5kn in newsstands, 6kn from the driver. You must have exact change.

Taxis: Tel. 42 43 43. In front of the bus station, ferry terminal, and Pile Gate.

Tourist Office: Turistička Zajednica Grada Dubrovnika, C. Zuzorić 1/2 (tel. 42 63 03 and 42 63 04; fax 42 24 80; email tzgd@du.del.hr). Walk to the end of Placa, turn right between St. Blaise's Church and the coffee shop Gradska Kavana, and take the first right. Friendly English-speaking staff knows absolutely everything. Open M-Sa 8am-4pm. **Turistički Informativni Centar (TIC),** Placa bb (tel. 42 63 54 and 42 63 56; fax 42 63 55). Right next to the fountain at the head of Placa. Dispenses info, exchanges currency, develops photos, and sells maps, posters, and tickets. Open daily 8am-9pm.

CROATIA

Budget Travel: Atlas, Lučarica 1 (tel. 44 25 28; fax 42 02 05). Next to St. Blaise's Church at the end of Placa. Arranges private accommodations, sells airplane and ferry tickets, exchanges currency, and cashes and sells **AmEx traveler's checks.** Also organizes tours to: **Neretva River Delta** (305kn inc. lunch); **Mljet National Park** (275kn); and **Elafiti Islands** (185kn). Other branches at Sv. Durda 1, near the Pile Gate, and the ferry terminal. All open M-Sa 8am-8pm, Su 9am-1pm; off-season M-Sa 8am-7pm.

Currency Exchange: Dubrovačka Banka, Placa 1 (tel. 44 19 67 and 41 29 64). Exchanges cash and traveler's checks for no commission. Also at the bus station, Put Republike 9. Open M-F 7:30am-1:30pm and 2-8pm, Sa 7:30am-1pm.

ATM: Cirrus/MC ATMS are available at Brsalje 9, outside Croatia Airlines and on Placa 4, on the corner with Zlatarska. Visa/AmEx ATMs are at the ferry terminal and on Lučarica bb, next to Atlas and St. Blaise's Church.

Luggage Storage: At the bus station. 8kn per day. Open daily 5am-9pm.

International Bookstore: Algoritam, Placa 8 (tel./fax 42 64 31). Loads of English-language paperbacks, but a poor magazine selection. Open daily 9am-10:30pm.

Pharmacy: Ljekarna Mala Braća, Placa 2 (tel. 42 63 72), near the monastery. Open daily 8am-2pm. **Night service** (8pm-8am) alternates between **Ljekarna Gruž** (tel. 41 89 99), at the ferry terminal, and **Ljekarna Kod Zvonika** (tel. 42 86 56), Placa bb.

Post Office: Well-hidden on Put Republike. Go through the large gate at #18 next to the "ginekološka ordinacija" sign, cross the parking lot, walk upstairs, and head around the building on the left. Free **Poste Restante.** Open M-F 8am-9pm. **Postal code:** 20 000.

Internet Access: No official cyber hangout existed in summer 1999, but one was in the works at **Klub Otok,** Pobijana 8, behind the cathedral. Open M-F 10am-3pm.

Phone code: (0)20.

ACCOMMODATIONS

Dubrovnik offers accommodations in a wide range of locales: city center, beachside, or close to the ferry terminal. For two people, a **private room** is cheapest; arrange one through one of the women at the ferry and bus stations. They will ask about 70kn per person or 120-150kn for a double, but haggle to your wallet's content. There are **campgrounds** 20km from town; inquire at the tourist office (see above). **Atlas** (see above) also arranges private rooms for 80-100kn per person.

Youth Hostel (HI), B. Josipa Jelačića 15/17 (tel. 42 32 41; tel./fax 41 25 92). From the bus station, walk 10min. up ul. Ante Starčevića, turn right at the lights, and right again after 40m onto b. Josipa Jelačića. Look for a well-concealed HI sign on your left immediately before #17. Climb up 4 flights of stairs to reach the steps to the hostel. From the ferries, take bus #12 toward "Pile" and get off at the stop after the bus station, at the aforementioned traffic lights. A 15min. walk from the city center, and hands down the best hostel in Croatia. 82 beds in doubles, quads, and 6-person dorms. Hall bathrooms. July 15-Aug. 8 87kn; June 1-July 14 and Aug. 21-Sep. 15 79kn; May and Sep. 16-Oct. 30 73kn. Breakfast included. Check-out 10am. Curfew 2am.

Begović Boarding House, Primorska 17 (tel. 42 85 63). From the bus station, take bus #6 toward Dubrava and tell the driver you want to get off at Post Office Lapad. Hike up Primorska, the first street on the right, almost all the way to the top; #17 will be on your left. Call ahead and the owner will pick you up at the station. 10min. by bus to the center, but the beach is just a staircase away. A cozy villa of seven airy rooms with double beds and spectacular terrace view. Shared bath. July-Aug. 85kn, Sept.-June 70kn.

Hotel Zagreb, šetalište Kralja Zvonimira 27 (tel. 43 10 31 and 43 10 11; fax 235 81). From the bus station, take bus #6 toward Dubrava and tell the driver you want to get off at Post Office Lapad. Walk through the first intersection and proceed onto the pedestrian Šetalište Kralja Zvonimira. #27 is on the left. Beautiful location close to the beach. Modern, clean rooms with bath, TV, and phone. Singles 240kn, off-season 150kn; doubles 195kn per person, off-season 120kn. Tax 4.50-7kn. Breakfast included.

CROATIA

FOOD

If you're coming from Split, you'll be pleasantly surprised by the abundance of eateries in Dubrovnik, but disappointed by higher prices and limited offerings. Most restaurants feature meat-oriented menus of fish, squid, calamari, risotto, and some pasta. Prijeko, the first street parallel to Placa on the left when coming from the Pile Gate, is packed with cookie-cutter *konobi* (pubs), competing obnoxiously for patrons. From St. Blaise's Church, walk down Lučarica to the fruit, veggie, and cheese **market** on Gundulićeva Poljana. Right around the corner is the supermarket **Mediator,** Od puča 4. (Open M-Sa 6am-10:30pm.)

Sebastian, Prijeko bb (tel. 42 75 40), up Žudioska street. Standard fare in a pink interior; try the gnocchi with mushrooms (40kn). Open daily 8am-midnight.

Buffet Kamenice, Gundulićeva Poljana 8, behind the market. Probably the cheapest decent meals in town. Entrees 25-40kn. Open daily 7am-midnight.

Chinese Restaurant Shanghai, Ante Starčevića 25 (tel. 42 57 54). The Chinese owners cook semi-authentic Chinese food. Largest selection of vegetarian dishes in town (30-50kn). Entrees 30-70kn. Open Tu-Su noon-midnight.

Buffet Škola, Antulinska 1, just off Placa. The delicious sandwiches are the only affordable way to try *dalmatinski pršut* (12-17kn). Open daily 8:30am-midnight.

SIGHTS

The most impressive legacy of this former naval city-state are the awesome city walls *(gradske zidine)*, the entrance to which lies just inside the Pile Gate on the left. Although built primarily in the 14th century, these 25m-high walls were not finished until the 1600s. Make sure you have a camera and an hour for the 2km walk along the top. (Open daily 9am-7pm. 10kn, children 5kn.) The beautiful, Renaissance **Franciscan Monastery** (Franjevački samostan; tel. 42 63 72) is right next to the city wall entrance on Placa. It also houses the oldest working pharmacy in Croatia and a **pharmaceutical museum.** (Open daily 9am-2pm. 5kn, students 3kn.) Its church, still bearing the signs of Serbian/Montenegran aggression, holds regular services and hosts classical music during the Dubrovnik Summer Festival. Farther down Placa at Žudioska 5 is the second-oldest **Sephardic synagogue** in Europe (tel. 41 22 19), serving Dubrovnik's 47 Jews. (Open Tu and F 10am-noon.) The Renaissance **Sponza Palace** and its belltower mark the end of Placa and houses temporary exhibits of Croatian art (inquire at the tourist office). Across from the Sponza Palace stands **St. Blaise's Church** (Crkva sv. Vlaha), consecrated to the patron saint of Dubrovnik, who can be seen in statues adorning nearly every 10m of the city walls. The **Dominican Monastery** (Dominikanski samostan), Dominikanska 4 (tel. 42 64 72), between the city walls and the Old Port, is still home to monks of the order. Inside, you'll find a **museum** comprising the cloister and sacristy, as well as most of Dubrovnik's religious art. (Open M-Sa 9am-6pm. Museum 5kn.) Behind St. Blaise's Church on Drzićeva Poljana stands another Renaissance gem, the 1441 **Rector's Palace** (Knežev Dvor), which houses 16th- and 17th-century weaponry, paintings, coins, and furniture. (Open M-Sa 9am-1pm. 10kn, students 5kn.) The **cathedral** *(riznica)* dominates Držićeva Poljana. Its **treasury** contains a number of saintly relics, all in golden, jewel-encrusted containers. (Open daily 8am-noon and 3-8pm. 5kn.) There are 4,000 Bosnian Muslims in Dubrovnik who come to pray at the tiny **Bosnian Mosque,** Miha Pracata 3 (tel. 42 52 99), the eighth street right off Placa when coming from the Pile Gate. It lacks a minaret and is therefore not a real mosque, but if you are properly dressed (that is, with limbs covered), the kind staff will show you around. (Open M-W and F-Su 10am-1pm, Th 10am-1pm and 7-9pm.) Around the corner from the mosque is the 19th-century **Serbian Orthodox Church,** Od Puča 8 (tel. 42 62 60), and its **Museum of Icons** (Muzej Ikona; open M-Sa 9am-1pm; 10kn).

There aren't any beaches in the center of town, but the water is clear enough to allow bathing almost anywhere, and the smooth tops of the cliffs will even provide a place to lie down. More official beaches lie just outside the center, around Hotel Zagreb (see **Accommodations,** p. 171). The most popular option, however, is the nearby island **Lokrum,** which even features a **nude beach.** Ferries go there from the Old Port daily (10min., hourly 9am-7pm, 15kn round-trip). Once there, take a break from the sun to stroll through the **botanical garden** and look back on Dubrovnik from the fortress. If you have an entire day to spare, however, go straight to the fantastic sands of the Elafiti Archipelago (see **Lopud,** p. 173).

ENTERTAINMENT

During the summer (July 10-Aug. 15), the **Dubrovnik Summer Festival** (Dubrovački Ljetni Festival; tel. 42 88 64) transforms the city into a cultural mecca. The country's most prominent artists in theater, ballet, opera, classical music, and jazz all perform. The outdoor productions of Shakespeare (*Hamlet* is a long-standing tradition) at **Lovrjenac fortress** are a once-in-a-lifetime experience. (Tickets 35-200kn.)

NIGHTLIFE

Of Croatian cities, Dubrovnik is the liveliest at night, although just where the crowds will go defies prediction. Often, they'll overflow from Stari Grad and the cafes on **Buničeva Poljana**. Another great center of nightlife is outside the city walls on **B. Josipa Jelačića** by the Youth Hostel (see **Accommodations,** p. 171).

Trubadur, Bunićeva Poljana bb (tel. 41 21 54). This American ex-pat hangout is the place to go if you long for conversation in your native tongue. Live jazz Fridays. Draft *Tuborg* 25kn. Open daily 8am until the last guest leaves.

Galerie, Kunićera bb. The most popular bar with locals. On crowded nights, it takes over the entire neighborhood, with people sitting on pillows all over the street. Coffee 4-6kn, beer 10-15kn. Open daily 9am-2pm and 6pm-midnight.

Roxy, B. Josipa Jelačića bb. A friendly bar that plays it loud and late. Popular hangout with Dubrovnik youth and hostel-goers. Beer 10kn.

Jazz Club Bo-Bap, Kneza Damjana Jude bb. The place to go for good jazz, even if the name loses something in translation. Open daily 9am-midnight.

NEAR DUBROVNIK: LOPUD

! Beautiful as it is, parts of Lopud are still rife with **landmines.** Stick to the paved paths and beach, and at no point traipse off into the wilderness.

Less than an hour from Dubrovnik, Lopud is an enchanting island of the Elafiti Archipelago. The tiny village, dotted with white buildings, chapels, and parks, stretches along the island's waterfront *(obala)*. Currently under renovation, **Dorđič Mayneri** remains among the most beautiful parks in Croatia. Signs from Kavana Dubrava on the waterfront point to the **museum,** which is the meeting place for tours of the church, museum, and monastery. (Tours Th at 9am.) A 15min. stroll along the waterfront leads to a gazebo with a breathtaking view of the white cliffs and dark blue sea. The island's absolute highlight, however, is its **beach,** Plaza Šunj. Arguably the best beach in Croatia, it has all the qualities that most places on the Dalmatian Coast lack: sand, waves, and a secluded cove.

GETTING THERE. Lopud can be reached by the ferry from Dubrovnik to the **Elafiti islands** (50min., 2 per day, off-season daily, 25kn round-trip). The beach is on the opposite side of the island from the village. On the road between the high wall and the palm park, look for the "Konoba Barbara" sign and turn off the road onto a large path. Ignore small paths branching off; when the path forks, keep right.

NEAR DUBROVNIK: MLJET NATIONAL PARK

Mljet's relative geographical isolation and corresponding lack of population make it an ideal location for a National Park. And sure enough, the Croatian government preserved the western half of the island in 1960. Despite burgeoning tourism, the island retains its mystery, depicted in literature since the *Odyssey* and the writings of St. Paul. The saltwater **Large and Small Lake** (Veliko and Malo Jezero), created by the rising sea level 10,000 years ago, are the most unique formations on the island. They are connected to each other by a narrow passage, and to the sea by **Solin Bay.** In the center of Veliko Jezero sits the **Island of St. Maria** (Sv. Marija) with a beautiful, white-stone **Benedictine monastery,** built in the 12th century and abandoned 700 years later. Today, it also houses a restaurant and a hotel, and its **Church of St. Maria** is used for wedding ceremonies. It is nearly impossible to visit Mljet on a daytrip except on summer weekends, but *sobe* signs offering singles (80-100kn) and doubles (160-200kn) decorate all major villages.

GETTING THERE. The easiest way to visit Mljet is on an organized **Atlas tour** (see **Dubrovnik: Orientation & Practical Information,** p. 170) from **Korčula** (130kn) or **Dubrovnik** (275kn). Independent tourism is scarce, so seeing the island without such a tour is a challenge. The **Jadrolinija ferry** from Dubrovnik drops passengers in **Sobra,** on the eastern side of the island (2¼hr., 2 per day, off-season daily, 29kn).

The **bus** that meets the ferry in Sobra travels to its western end, Pomona (1hr., 12kn), stopping at villages along the way. The bus ride itself is an exciting tour of the park. Entrances to the park are in **Polače,** a coastal village showcasing decent Roman ruins and an old Christian basilica, as well as in **Pomona.** (50kn.) It's best to get off at Polače (which also has a tourist office), walk 2km to **Pristanište,** where the park's info center is located, and jump on the boat to **St. Maria** (5min., 5 per day, 10kn round-trip but included in park admission). To return, take the boat to **Mali Most** (2min.), and walk another 3km to Pomona. When you get tired, a mini-van run by park management will give you a ride to the nearest village, otherwise catch one of the Atlas-operated buses. If you want to cheat the park out of 50kn, ask the driver on the way from the ferry to drop you off at Pristanište—no park tickets are sold there but no one seems to care.

CZECH REPUBLIC

(ČESKÁ REPUBLIKA)

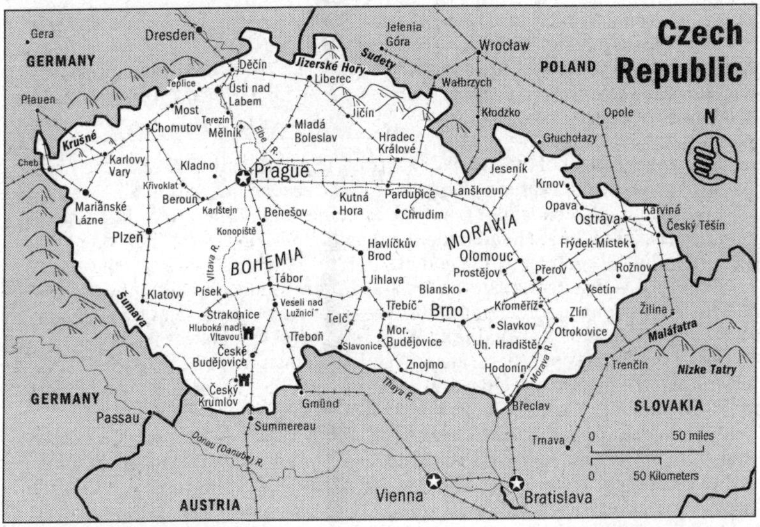

US$1 = 34.47Kč (KORUNY)	**10Kč = US$0.29**
CDN$1 = 23.15Kč	**10Kč = CDN$0.43**
UK£1 = 55.38Kč	**10Kč = UK£0.18**
IR£1 = 46.43Kč	**10Kč = IR£0.22**
AUS$1 = 22.45Kč	**10Kč = AUS$0.45**
NZ$1 = 18.31Kč	**10Kč = NZ$0.55**
SAR1 = 5.69Kč	**10Kč = SAR1.75**
DM1 = 18.68Kč	**10Kč = DM0.53**

PHONE CODES Country code: **420**. International dialing prefix: **00**.

On New Year's Day 1993, after more than 75 years of relatively calm coexistence, the Czech and Slovak Republics bloodlessly split. The notion of self-determination is relatively new to the Czech people. From the Holy Roman Empire through the Nazis and Soviets, foreigners have driven their internal affairs. The Czechs, unlike many of their neighbors, have rarely fought back as countries marched through the border, often choosing to fight with words instead of weapons; as a result, their towns and cities are among the best-preserved in Europe. Today, they are facing a different kind of invasion, as tourists sweep in to savor the magnificent capital, welcoming locals, and the world's best beer.

LIFE & TIMES

HISTORY

While the mythological inception of the Czech state is accredited to **Princess Libuše** and her founding of Prague in the 9th century, its birth is factually rooted in the

HIGHLIGHTS OF THE CZECH REPUBLIC

- Everything you've heard is true: from the medieval alleys of Staré Město and the fabulous Baroque and Art Nouveau architecture to the world's best (and cheapest) beers, **Prague** is the starlet of Central Europe (p. 183).
- Everybody's favorite town, UNESCO-protected **Český Krumlov** charms visitors with its 13th-century castle, a medieval midsummer festival, and the most rocking nightlife this side of the Vltava (p. 220).
- Femurs and crania hang from the ceilings and chandeliers of the church-cumossuary at spooky **Kutná Hora** (p. 210).
- International hipsters flock to **Karlovy Vary** every summer for its film festival and its Becherovka, a local herb liquour with "curative powers" rivaled only by those of the many local hot springs (p. 215).

first century settlement of the **Boii,** a Celtic tribe, in what is now **Bohemia.** The West Slavs arrived in the 6th century—Moravians in the east and Czechs in the west.

The Slavs of the Czech lands (Bohemia, Moravia, and Silesia) were first united under the **Empire of Great Moravia,** the dominant empire in Central Europe in the first half of the 9th century. At the end of the 10th century, however, as the Moravian Empire was disintegrating, the **Přemyslid Dynasty** quickly united the Czechs and created a strong autonomous state. The legendary patron saint of Bohemia, **Václav** (known to some as Good King Wenceslas, although he was never a king), was one of the dynasty's earliest rulers. The Holy Roman Empire invited the Czech kings to join the empire as electors in 1114. In 1140, the region became a hereditary kingdom under Vladislav II, peaking under Přemysl Otakar II (1253-1278).

Holy Roman Emperor Charles (Karel) IV (1346-1378) made Bohemia the center of Imperial power, and under his rule Prague experienced its **Golden Age.** Charles established Prague as an Archbishopric, founded the first university in Central Europe, and constructed hundreds of buildings, as well as the Charles Bridge. Charles's son Václav "the Lazy" was, as his name suggests, less productive. During Václav's reign, **Jan Hus** (1369-1415), the Rector at Charles University, spoke out against the corruption of the Catholic hierarchy and was subsequently burned to death as a heretic. The Hussite movement, a Protestant revolt throughout the Czech lands, led to the **First Defenestration of Prague,** in which Hussite protestors threw the royalist mayor and several of his councillors out of the window of the Council House. The **Second Defenestration of Prague** set off the **Thirty Years' War** (1618-1648), during which Bohemia's defeat led to forced Catholic conversion, German emigration, and the utter ruin of the country. The Czech Protestants' defeat was sealed when they suffered an early and very harsh blow in the **Battle of White Mountain** (Bílá Hora), fought outside Prague on November 8, 1620. The war led to the absorption of Czech territory into the **Austrian Empire** and three centuries of oppressive rule.

The spirit of nationalism that swept Europe from west to east, reached Bohemia in the mid-19th century. During the **1848 revolutions,** however, this new trend was crushed by imperial conservatism. While **WWI** did nothing to increase harmony among the nationalities of the Habsburg Empire, it did help unite the Czechs and Slovaks. In the post-war confusion, **Edvard Beneš** and **Tomáš Garrigue Masaryk** convinced the victorious Allies to legitimize a new state that united Bohemia, Moravia, and Slovakia into **Czechoslovakia.**

Unique in Eastern Europe, Czechoslovakia remained a parliamentary democracy between the wars, only to be torn apart as Hitler exploited the Allies' **appeasement** policy. The infamous 1938 **Munich Agreement** handed Czech territory over to Germany without consulting the Czechs themselves. The following year, Hitler brutally annexed the Sudetenland, Bohemia, and Moravia as a protectorate and turned Slovakia into an independent fascist state under Hungarian guidance. Most of Czechoslovakia's Jews were murdered by the Nazis during the five-year occupation. On May 9, 1945, Czechoslovakia was liberated by the Soviets and Americans. Immediately following, Germans were expelled from the Sudetenland and the nationalization of the Czechoslovak industry and economy began. The Communists, under **Klement Gottwald,** won 38% of the vote in the 1946 elections and instituted a hard-line communist government. Following the collapse of the Popular Front coalition in 1948, they seized power. In 1968, Communist Party Secretary **Alexander Dubček** sought to implement "socialism with a human face," dramatically reforming the country's economy and easing political oppression during the **Prague Spring.** Displeased with these developments, the Soviets violently suppressed Dubček's counter-revolution. Slovak leader **Gustáv Husák** introduced an even more repressive regime lasting for the next 21 years.

Czech artists and dissidents protested Husák's violation of human rights throughout the 70s with **Charter 77,** a nonviolent protest group. Most of its leaders were imprisoned and persecuted, but they nonetheless fostered increasing dissidence among Czechs and Slovaks. After the demise of the Communists in Hungary and Poland and the fall of the Berlin Wall in 1989, the **Velvet Revolution** rippled into Czechoslovakia, named as such for the almost entirely bloodless transition from Communism. Despite crackdowns, Czechs—united by students and the leaders of Charter 77—demonstrated and went on strike in Prague and other cities in November. Within a month the Communist government had resigned. **Václav Havel,** the long-imprisoned liberal playwright and leader of both Charter 77 and the Velvet Revolution, became president soon thereafter. After three years of debate, the Czech and Slovak nations decided to peaceably split on **January 1, 1993.**

CZECH REPUBLIC TODAY

The Czech Republic has enjoyed its status as the ex-communist pet of Western investors and politicians, but recent economic stagnancy and rising unemployment are beginning to abate Western investors' enthusiasm. In late May 1997, the poorly conceived economic policies of **Václav Klaus** resulted in a tremendous depreciation of the koruna's value. In June 1998, new elections allowed **Miloš Zeman,** leader of the **Social Democrats,** to form the first left-wing government since 1989. Unfortunately, Czechs already disapprove of Zeman and are calling for more right-wing policies. Havel was re-elected as President in 1998 by only one vote; it is unclear whether his re-election was due to public approval of his politics or because there was not a more attractive candidate.

The uncertain economic and political future of the Czech Republic sustains skepticism in the European Union, and, unlike Poland and Hungary, the Czech Republic has not been offered a 2003 membership bid. The Czechs have been successful, however, in joining the other bastion of organized Western power, NATO. In March 1999, the Czech Republic, along with Hungary and Poland, was inducted into the military organization just in time for NATO's 50th anniversary and the air raids on Yugoslavia. NATO membership has alienated disapproving Czechs and complicated economic dealings with Russia.

LITERATURE & ARTS

The Czech Republic is a literature-obsessed country in which writers hold a privileged position as social and political commentators. From the first Czechoslovak president, **T.G. Masaryk,** to current president **Václav Havel,** literary figures are revered as the nation's most powerful citizens and most subversive political figures. Indeed, for Czechs, literature takes preeminence over all other art forms.

Through the 18th century, Czech literature was marked by the Habsburgs' oppressive insistence that texts be written only in German and always praise the empire. However, the 19th century saw a nationalist literary renaissance coinciding with the 1848 revolutions against the Austrian empire. Fueled by **Josef Dobrovský** and **Josef Jungmann's** endeavors to revitalize and codify the Czech language, **Karel Hynek Mácha** penned his celebrated *May* epic (*Máj*; 1836), considered to be the lyric masterpiece of 19th century Czech literature. The founding of the literary journal *Máj* in 1856—named after Mácha's poem—marks the beginning of the **National Revival,** an explosion of nationalist literary output. One of its brightest stars was **Božena Němcová,** who introduced the novel to modern Czech literature and repopularized the folk tale with her novel *Granny* (*Babička;* 1855). Poet and fiction writer **Jan Neruda,** another prominent figure of the National Revival, inspired the Chilean poet Pablo Neruda to take on his famous pseudonym. The National Revival also filtered to Czech music. Two of the nation's most celebrated composers, **Antonín Dvořák** and **Bedřich Smetana,** are renowned for transforming Czech folk tunes and tales into 19th-century Romantic symphonies and operas.

In the 1870s, **Jaroslav Vrchlický** and the Cosmopolitan movement moved from cultural introversion to the internationalism of Western Europe. **Svatopluk Čech,** representative of the rival publication *Ruch,* wanted Czech literature to deal solely with subjects of national importance. The debate between Western internationalism and introverted nationalism continues today in both the literary and political arenas. Toward the turn of the century, political leader T.G. Masaryk followed the nationalist vein with his essays arguing for Czechoslovak independence. And while he wrote in German, **Franz Kafka's** work is pervaded by the literary traditions and dark circumstances of his native Prague under Habsburg rule.

The 20th century has proved an extraordinarily fruitful time for the Czech arts. In literature, **Jaroslav Hašek's** epic satire, *The Good Soldier Švejk* (*Dobrý voják Švejk;* 1921-23), which recounts the adventures of the bumbling Švejk during WWI, has become a classic Bohemian commentary on life under Habsburg rule. **Karel Čapek's** play *R.U.R.* (1920) is another classic of the period and presented a frightening look at a world overrun by robots (a word he coined). Jaroslav Seifert and Vítězslav Nezval explored Poetism and Surrealism, producing ecstatic and image-rich meditations on the city and nationality. In 1984, Seifert became the first Czech author to receive the Nobel Prize. In the visual arts, Čapek's brother, **Jozef Čapek,** was an important Cubist and charicaturist best known for his satirization of Hitler's ascent to power. Another prominent Cubist and post-Impressionist was **Jan Zrzavý.** Still other artists worked as expatriates, such as surrealist **Marie Čerminová Toyen** who immigrated to Paris in the 1920s and worked closely with André Breton. One of the most important Czech artists of the early 20th century, **Alfons Mucha,** also worked in Paris for most of his career and helped develop the **art nouveau** style of graphic design and painting.

After WWII, the novels of **Milan Kundera** (now in France), **Josef Škvorecký** (now in Canada), and **Bohumil Hrabal** (now dead; see p. 197) created an international following for not only Czech art and literature, but also for the support of Czechoslovakia's struggle against the Soviet bear. Although many Czech authors still write as expatriates in Western Europe and North America, Prague itself is experiencing a literary and artistic boom, both from native Czechs and American expatriates. In fact, the literary scene of 1990s Prague has been likened to Paris in the 1920s. The dramas of prisoner-turned-president **Václav Havel** remain part of the Czech Republic's daily life.

While Czechs have long been important international literary figures, they are only recently beginning to appear on the international film scene. Director **Miloš Forman** introduced Czech film to the world when he immigrated to the U.S. in 1968 and exploded into the American film industry with his critically acclaimed film *One Flew Over the Cuckoo's Nest* (1975). More recently, Jan Svěrák's film **Kolya** (1996) won the 1997 Academy Award for Best Foreign Film. Additionally, the films of **Ivan Vojnar,** particularly his 1997 *The Way Through the Bleak Woods (Cesta pustým lestém),* are celebrated for their treatment of delicate historical issues and the legacy of a rural, landlocked nation in the modern world.

READING LIST

For a comprehensive and accessible treatment of Czech history, turn to Derek Sayer's *The Coasts of Bohemia.* Peter Demetz offers a more focused historical account in *Prague in Black and Gold.* Of the many travelogues written about adventures in the Czech Republic, Douglas Lytle's *Pink Tanks and Velvet Hangovers: An American in Prague* is particularly engaging; *Kafka's Prague: A*

Travel Companion, by Klaus Wagenbach, leads the reader through the haunted streets of Kafka's life. Kundera's *The Unbearable Lightness of Being* offers an entertaining glimpse of pre-1968 Prague and the Czech psyche, while Havel's *The Art of the Impossible: Politics as Morality in Practice* meditates on the confluence of literature and politics and the role of the intellectual in Czech culture. An entirely different take on Czech cultural and political life is explored in *Allskin and Other Tales by Contemporary Czech Women*, the first collection of Czech women's fiction ever to be published or translated.

FACTS AND FIGURES

- **Capital:** Prague
- **Population:** 10,307,375
- **Land Area:** 78,886km^2
- **Geography:** Plateaus and mountains
- **Language:** Czech
- **Religions:** 39% Catholic, 4% Protestant
- **GDP per capita:** US$4624
- **Major Exports:** Machinery and transport equipment

CZECH REPUBLIC ESSENTIALS

Americans may visit the Czech Republic visa-free for up to 30 days, Irish and New Zealand citizens for up to 90 days, and Canadian and U.K. citizens for up to 180 days. Australians and South Africans must obtain 30-day tourist visas. Visas are available at some border crossings or at an embassy or consulate (see **Embassies & Consulates,** p. 13). Processing takes three days by mail, one day in person. With the application, you must submit your passport, 2 photographs glued—not stapled—to the application (for a double-entry visa send 2 applications and 4 photos; for multiple-entry, just 2 photos); a self-addressed, stamped envelope (certified or overnight mail); and a cashier's check or money order for the price of the visa plus the processing fee. Single-entry visas cost US$28 plus a US$17 processing fee for Australians; South Africans need only pay the processing fee. Two-way transit visas are also US$28, plus a US$25 fee. 90-day multiple-entry visas cost US$39 (180-day US$70), plus a US$28 processing fee.

GETTING THERE & GETTING AROUND

Air France, British Airways, ČSA, Delta, KLM, Lufthansa, and **Swissair** are among the major carriers with **flights** into Prague. The most economical way to enter the country is by **train. Eastrail** is accepted in the Czech Republic, but **Eurail** is valid only with a special supplement. The fastest trains are *EuroCity* and *InterCity* (*expresní*, marked in blue on schedules). *Rychlík* trains, also known as *zrychlený vlak*, are fast domestic trains, marked in red on schedules. Avoid slow *osobní* trains, marked in white. **ČSD,** the national transportation company, publishes the monster *Jízdní řád* train schedule (74Kč), which has a two-page English explanation. *Odjezd* (departures) are printed in train stations on yellow posters, *příjezd* (arrivals) on white. Seat reservations (*místenka;* 10Kč) are recommended on almost all express and international trains and for al' first-class seating; snag them at the counter labeled with a boxed "R."

Buses are the preferred means of domestic travel, but are inefficient for crossing borders. **ČSAD** runs national and international bus lines. Consult the timetables posted at stations or buy your own bus schedule (25Kč) from kiosks. **Hitchhikers** report that it still remains popular in the Czech Republic, especially during morning commuting hours (6-8am). *Let's Go* does not recommend hitchhiking.

TOURIST SERVICES & MONEY

CKM, junior affiliate of communist dinosaur Čedok, is helpful for the budget and student traveler, serving as a clearinghouse for youth hostel beds and issuing

PRIMARY BORDER CROSSINGS. There is no fee for crossing a Czech border by train or bus; if you're driving, there is an 800Kč entrance charge. Visas are available at three crossings: Rozvadov, Dolní Dvořiště, or Hatě for an additional US$50 fee. It is cheaper and easier to arrange visas through an embassy. If heading to Austria or Hungary, it's cheapest to buy a Czech ticket to the border; once inside the country, buy a separate ticket to your destination. When coming from Poland, it's cheapest to walk across the border at Cieszyn/Český Tešin (see p. 449). Czech border patrol is fast and efficient; border crossing delays are uncommon. It is easiest to enter or leave the Czech Republic via Prague or Brno.

Austria: Dolní Dvořiště, CZR/Rainbach, AUS; connects Český Krumlov (p. 220) with Linz. Znojmo, CZR/Hollabrunn, AUS via Hatě, CZR; connects Moravia (p. 225) with Vienna (p. 792).

Germany: Rozvadov, CZR/Waidhaus, GER; connects Plzeň (p. 211) with Nürnberg. Děčín, CZR/Dresden, GER; connects Northern Bohemia with Leipzig. Cheb, CZR/Waldsassen, GER; connects Western Bohemia (p. 211) with Jena. Vimperk, CZR/Reyung, GER; connects Southern Bohemia (p. 217) with Bavaria.

Poland: Český Těšín, CZR/Cieszyn, POL (p. 449); connects Ostrava, CZR and Moravia (p. 225) with Bielsko-Biała, POL (p. 447). Jablonec, CZR/Szklarska Poręba, POL (p. 461); connects Northern Bohemia with Jelenia Góra, POL (p. 459) and Wrocław (p. 455).

Slovakia: Břeclav, CZR/Kúty, SLK; connects Moravia (p. 225) with Bratislava (p. 676). Brumov-Bylnice, CZR/Trenčín, SLK; connects Moravia (p. 225) with Central Slovakia (p. 682).

ISICs and HI cards. **Municipal tourist offices** in major cities provide printed matter on sights and cultural events, as well as lists of hostels and hotels. If they're nice, they might even book you a room. German is most commonly spoken, but English is also common in touristed regions. Most bookstores sell a fine national hiking map, *Soubor turistických map*, with an English key.

The Czech unit of currency is the **koruna** (crown), plural *koruny* (Kč). **ATMs** are everywhere—look for the red and black "Bankomat" signs—and offer the best exchange rates available. **Traveler's checks** can be exchanged almost everywhere, if at times for an obscene commission. **Komerční banka** operates wherever a human being earns cash; its many branches accept all sorts of checks. **Česká Spořitelna** is another common chain. Banks are generally open Monday to Friday 9am to 5pm. MC and Visa are accepted at most expensive places, but rarely at hostels.

COMMUNICATION

The Czech Republic's **postal system** has embraced capitalist efficiency; letters reach the U.S. in less than 10 days. A postcard to the U.S. costs 8Kč, to Australia 7Kč. When sending by air mail, stress that you want it to go on a *plane (letecky)*. Go to the customs office to send packages heavier than 2kg abroad.

To make a call, seek out the blue cardphones (150Kč per 50 units) rather than playing Sisyphus to a coinphone's giant boulder. Calls run 31Kč per minute to the **U.K.;** 63Kč per minute to **Australia, Canada,** or the **U.S.;** and 94Kč per minute to **New Zealand.** Making calls abroad through an operator doesn't require a card—just dial one of these toll-free numbers. The international operator is at 013 15; for lower rates, try: **AT&T Direct,** tel. 00 42 00 44 01; **MCI WorldPhone,** tel. 00 42 00 01 12; **Canada Direct,** tel. 00 42 00 01 51; **BT Direct,** tel. 00 42 00 44 01; **Sprint,** tel. 00 42 08 71 87.

The **internet** has spread its spindly wires to most towns. Internet cafes are the easiest to use if you're just passing through; the computers are fast and cheap, with rates around 2Kč per minute. Most public libraries also have internet access, but computers tend to be slower and require a membership card (100-500Kč).

THE WORLD'S MOST DIFFICULT SOUND Not quite a Spanish "r" and simply not the Polish "rz" (pronounced like the second "g" in "garage"), Czech's own linguistic blue note, the letter "ř" lies excruciatingly in between. Although many of Prague's ex-pats would sacrifice a month of Saturdays at Jo's Bar to utter the elusive sound just once, few manage more than a strangely trilled whistle. Most foreigners resign themselves to using the "ž" in its place, but what we consider a subtle difference often confuses Czechs. For all those linguistic daredevils in the audience, here's a sure-fire method of tackling the randy Mr. Ř: roll your tongue and quickly follow with a "ž", then repeat. Oh, yeah—and start when you're two.

LANGUAGE

Russian *was* every student's mandatory second language, but these days, **English** will earn you more friends. A few **German** phrases go farther, especially in the western spas, but might gain you some enemies. An English-Czech dictionary is indispensable and should be on anyone's packing list. A handy phrase is *"zaplatíme"* (ZAH-plah-tee-meh—we're ready to pay; *"zaplatím"* if you're dining by yourself). Ask *"Kolik stojí?"* to find out how much something costs, and *"V kolik hodin?"* to find out when your bus is leaving. When all else fails, a polite *"Dobrý den"* ("good day"), *"prosím"* ("please," or "that's okay"), and a smile will win you more Czech friends than you'll know what to do with. If you've learned Czech abroad, beware the Prague cockney—or just allow for some imaginative "mispronunciations." For more, see the **Czech Glossary,** p. 817.

HEALTH & SAFETY

EMERGENCY NUMBERS.
Fire: tel. 150. **Police:** tel. 158. **Ambulance:** tel. 155.

The greatest risk of ill-feeling comes from food—unacclimated bodies tend to rebel against mass quantities of sausage and sauerkraut. What vegetables and fruits you do happen upon should be washed thoroughly. If you fall ill, medical services are quite good, and major foreign insurance policies are accepted. If you're not covered, pay in cash. Prague has a separate hospital for foreign patients. **Pharmacies** *(lékárna)* and supermarkets carry Western European brands of bandages *(náplast)*, tampons *(tampóny)*, and condoms *(kondomy)*. **Petty crime** has increased dramatically since 1989; beware pickpockets prowling among the crowds in Prague's main squares, on the way to the Castle, and on tram #22. In an **emergency,** notify your consulate—police may not be well versed in English.

ACCOMMODATIONS & CAMPING

Hostels, particularly in **university dorms,** are the cheapest option in July and August; two- to four-bed rooms are 200-300Kč per person. CKM's **Junior Hotels** (year-round hostels giving discounts to ISIC and HI cardholders) are comfortable but often full. Private hostels have broken the CKM monopoly, but not always surpassing its reliability. Showers and bedding are included. **Pensions** are the next most affordable option; expect to pay 600Kč, including breakfast. Reserve at least one week ahead from June to September in Prague, Český Krumlov, and Brno. If you can't keep a reservation, call to cancel so that some weary backpacker won't be sleeping on the street—at some point, that weary backpacker might be you.

Private homes are not nearly as popular (or as cheap) as in the rest of Eastern Europe. Scan train stations for *Zimmer frei* signs. Quality varies; do not pay in advance. In Prague, make sure anything you accept is easily accessible by public transport. Outside Prague, **local tourist offices** and **CKM/GTS** book rooms, with private agencies are burgeoning around train and bus stations. **Campgrounds,** strewn throughout the countryside, run 60-100Kč per person and 50-90Kč per tent. Most are only open mid-May to September. *Ubytování v ČSR*, in decodable Czech, lists all the hotels, hostels, huts, and campgrounds in Bohemia and Moravia.

FOOD & DRINK

Anyone in the mood for true Czech cuisine should start learning to pronounce *knedlíky* (KNED-lee-kee). These thick, pasty loaves of dough, feebly known in English as dumplings, serve as staples of Czech meals, soaking up *zelí* (sauerkraut) juice and other schmaltzy sauces. The Czech **national meal** is *vepřové* (roast pork), *knedlíky*, and *zelí* (known as *repřo-knedlo-zelo*), but *guláš* (stew) runs a close second. Subsidies on meat and dairy have managed to strip most meals of fruits and vegetables; the main food groups seem to be *hovězí* (beef), *sekaná pečeně* (meatloaf), *klobása* (sausage), and *brambory* (potatoes). If you're in a hurry, grab a pair of *párky* (frankfurters) or some *sýr* (cheese) at a *bufet*, *samoobsluha*, or *občerstvení*, all variations on a food stand. **Vegetarian** restaurants serve *šopský salát* (mixed salad with feta cheese) and other *bez masa* (meatless) specialties; at most restaurants, however, vegetarians will be limited to *smaženy sýr* (fried cheese). Ask for *káva espresso* rather than just *káva* to avoid the mud Czechs call coffee. *Koblihy* (doughnuts), *jablkový závin* (apple strudel), and *ovocné knedlíky* (fruit dumplings) are favorite sweets, but the most beloved is *koláč*—a tart filled with poppy-seed jam or sweet cheese. *Zmrzlina* is closer to *gelati* than American ice cream.

Moravian wines are worth a try. *Rulandské*, from Znojmo in South Moravia, is good, but the quality of *Müller-Thurgau* varies. Any *Welschriesling* or *Frankovka* is drinkable. Wine is typically drunk at a *vinárna* (wine bar) which also serve a variety of hard spirits, including *slivovice* (plum brandy) and *becherovka* (herbal bitter), the national drink. The most prominent beer is *Plzeňský Prazdroj* (Pilsner Urquell), although many Czechs are loyal to *Budvar* or *Krušovice*.

CUSTOMS & ETIQUETTE

Since Czechs rarely **discriminate** against travelers because of age, creed, race, or sexual orientation, *Let's Go* can dedicate this space to some of the finer points of etiquette and sociological curiosity. When beer is served, wait until all raise the common "*na zdraví*" ("to your health") toast, then drink. Similarly, before biting into a sauce-drowned *knedlík*, wish everyone "*dobrou chut*" ("to your health").

Another facet of Czech life governed by etiquette is public transport. *Babičky* are allowed to cut lines and evict anyone with a seat with tales of woe, hardship, and aching legs. Most younger Czechs give in to the mighty power of age, but as a result scamper over each other for seats. When it comes to public transport, there is no such thing as a line; crowds just push and lunge to get on the bus, tram, or train first, which is understandable, considering that most routes are overbooked and there's a good chance you'll have to stand for four hours. Go ahead and push, but don't push the *babičky*, because they'll clobber you with their canes.

HOW TO TIP IN CZECH The Western convention of tipping waiters a percentage (often 15%) of the meal cost makes little sense to Czechs, and it can be downright offensive. Nevertheless, waiters make little, and tipping is expected for adequate service. When it's time to pay, your waiter will tell you the cost of the meal. You should respond by rounding up; your figure will be the total cost, including the tip—learn to say your numbers. For example, if the bill comes to 322Kč, say "330Kč." Tipping is a way of saying "thank you," and you should tip more for better service, or not at all if the service is lousy. And do not just leave a few *koruny* on the table.

NATIONAL HOLIDAYS

January 1, New Year's; April 23-24, Catholic Easter; May 1, May Day; May 8, Liberation Day; July 5, Cyril and Methodius Day; July 6, Jan Hus Day; October 28, Republic Day (1918); December 24-26, Catholic Christmas.

PRAGUE (PRAHA)

No one knows for sure who cast the first spell over Prague. Some think it was Princess Libuše in the ninth century when she prophesied the founding of Praha, a "city whose glory shall touch the stars," while others hold that it was none other than Rabbi Loew and his *golem*, the mythical protector of Prague. Regardless of when or how it happened, "the city of dreams" still seems to live under this spell of fog and legend. And although no one's seen it, all Praguesters are positive that President Václav Havel rides his tricycle from office to office in the Prague Castle. Whether it's the backwards-flowing Vltava or the popularity of klobása, sauerkraut, and beer for breakfast, every aspect of Prague life teems with the inexplicable, the miraculous, and the quirky.

The magic has been well-tested in recent years. After the Iron Curtain fell, hordes of Euro-trotting foreigners flooded the Czech Republic's venerable capital. Not even the less than forty days of sunshine Prague sees per year could prevent tourists from seeking out the only Central European city left unscathed by WWII and the only city in the world where Pilsner Urquell is cheaper than water. In summer, most of Prague's citizens leave for the country, and the foreigner-to-resident ratio soars above nine-to-one; masses pack some streets so tightly that crowd-surfing could become a summer pastime. Yet somehow, Prague retains its magic. Walk a few blocks from any of the major sights and you'll be lost in a maze of cobblestone alleys, looming churches, and dark cellars. Head to an outlying Metro stop and you'll find haggling *babičky*, supermodel-esque natives, and not a backpack in sight. Even in the hyper-touristed Old Town, Prague is still majestic: the Charles Bridge—packed so tightly on a summer's day the only way off is to jump—is still breathtaking at sunrise and eerie in a fog. The spell might be fading, but if you look closely enough, there's still pleny of stardust left in the cobblestone cracks.

GETTING THERE & GETTING AROUND

Airplanes: Ruzyně Airport (tel. 20 11 11 11), 20km northwest of the city. Take bus #119 to or from Metro A: Dejvická. Punch your regular 12Kč public transport ticket (bought in kiosks or machines) and a 6Kč supplement for each large luggage item. You can't pay on the bus. If arriving or departing midnight-5am, take night tram #51 to "Divoká Šárka," then switch to night bus #510 to reach the city center. An **airport bus** (tel. 20 11 42 96) running every 30min. collects travelers at Nám. Republiky (90Kč) and Dejvická (60Kč). Taxis to the airport are extremely expensive. Many major carriers, including **Air France,** Václavské nám. 10 (tel. 24 22 71 64), **British Airways,** Ovocný trh 8 (tel. 22 11 44 44), **ČSA** (tel. 20 10 43 10), **Delta,** Národní třída 32 (tel. 24 94 73 32), **KLM,** Na Příkopě 13 (tel. 33 09 09 33), **Lufthansa,** Pařížská 28 (tel. 24 81 10 07), and **Swissair,** Pařížská 11 (tel. 24 81 21 11), all fly into Prague.

Trains: Tel. 24 22 42 00; international info tel. 24 61 52 49. Prague has four terminals—make sure you go to the right one. **Praha hlavní nádraží** (tel. 24 22 42 00; Metro C: Hlavní nádraží) is the largest, but most international service runs out of **Holešovice** (tel. 24 61 72 65; Metro C: Nádraží Holešovice). To: **Bratislava** (5hr., 9 per day, 390Kč); **Berlin** (5hr., 6 per day, 1575Kč, Wasteels 1413Kč); **Vienna** (5hr., 4 per day, 739Kč; Wasteels 574Kč); **Budapest** (8hr., 6 per day, 1282Kč, Wasteels 1040Kč); **Kraków** (6½hr., 1 per day, 1000Kč); **Munich** (9hr., 3 per day, 2025Kč); **Moscow** (30hr., 1 per day, 2000Kč); and **Warsaw** (10hr., 3 per day, 652Kč). Domestic trains go from **Masarykovo** (tel. 24 61 72 60; Metro B: Nám. Republiky), on the corner of Hybernská and Havlíčkova, or from **Smíchov** (tel. 24 61 72 55; Metro B: Smíchovské nádraží), opposite Vyšehrad. **B.I.J. Wasteels** (tel. 24 61 74 54; fax 24 22 18 72), on the 2nd fl. of Hlavní nádraží, to the right of the stairs, sells discounted international tickets to those under 26 and books *couchettes*. Open summer M-F 7:30am-8pm, Sa 8-11:30am and 12:30-3pm; off-season M-F 8:30am-6pm. Wasteels tickets are also available from the **Czech Railways Travel Agency** (tel. 800 805; fax 806 948) at Holešovice. Open daily 7-11:25am, noon-5:40pm, 6:20-9:45pm, 10:35pm-2am, and 3:15-6:35am.

Buses: ČSAD has several *autobusové nádraží*. The biggest is **Florenc,** Křižíkova 4 (tel. 24 21 49 90 and 24 21 10 60; Metro B, C: Florenc). Rarely staffed by English-speakers. Timetables can be initially confusing, but are actually self-explanatory; start by looking up bus stop numbers for your destination. Info office open M-F 6am-9pm, Sa 6am-6pm, Su 8am-8pm. Buy tickets in advance, as they often sell out. To: **Berlin** (6hr., 1 per day, 820Kč); **Vienna** (8½hr., 6 per week, 400Kč); and **Sofia** (26hr., 1 per day, 1290Kč). Students might get 10% discount. The **Tourbus** office upstairs (tel. 24 21 02 21) sells tickets for Eurolines and airport buses. Open M-F 8am-8pm, Sa-Su 9am-8pm.

Local Transportation: The **Metro, tram,** and **bus** services are excellent and share the same ticket system. Buy tickets from newsstands and *tabák* kiosks, machines in stations, or **DP** (*Dopravní Podnik;* transport authority) kiosks. From the machines, select the ticket price, then insert your coins. The basic 8Kč ticket is good for one 15min. ride (or four stops on the Metro); the 12Kč ticket is valid for 60min. (90min. 8pm-5am) anywhere in the city with unlimited connections between bus, tram, and Metro, as long as you keep heading in the same direction. Large bags 6Kč each (buy an extra 6Kč ticket and punch it as well), as are bikes and prams without babies in them (*with* babies free). Validate your ticket in the machines above the escalators, as plainclothes DP inspectors roam Prague's transport lines (most frequently the Metro) issuing 200Kč spot fines. Make sure you see their official badge and get a receipt. The Metro's three lines run daily 5am-midnight: A is green on the maps, B is yellow, C is red. **Night trams** #51-58 and **buses** run all night after the last Metro; look for the dark blue signs at bus stops. DP and the tourist office in Old Town Hall also sell **multi-day passes** valid for the entire network (24hr. 70Kč, 3 days 180Kč, 1 week 250Kč), but they should be avoided, as a Czech ID is necessary to avoid fines. A **DP office** are by the Jungmannovo nám. exit of Můstek station (tel. 24 22 51 35; open daily 7am-9pm).

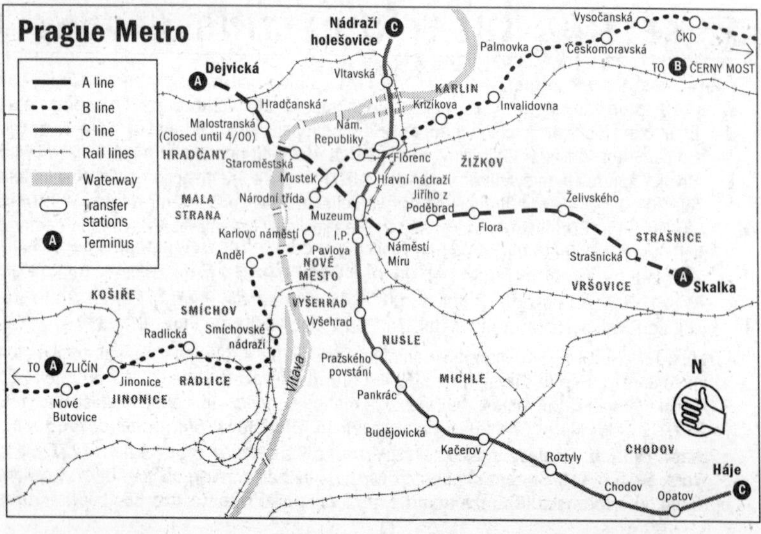

Taxis: Taxi Praha (tel. 24 91 66 66) or **AAA** (tel. 24 32 24 32). Taxi drivers are notorious scam artists. Before getting in, check that the meter is set to zero and ask the driver to start it by saying *"Zapněte taximetr."* For longer trips, agree on a price before setting off and get it in writing. Make sure the driver knows exactly where he's taking you; a common trick is to charge higher than the set price by feigning ignorance of exactly how far your destination was. Always ask for a receipt *("Prosím, dejte mi paragon")* with distance traveled, price paid, and the driver's signature. If the driver doesn't write the receipt or set the meter to zero, you don't have to pay. Prague has finally instituted set rates: 25Kč flat rate plus 17Kč per km. You're likely to get ripped off if you hail a cab on the street.

Car Rental: Hertz, at the airport (tel. 312 07 17; fax 365 998; open M-F 8am-10pm, Sa-Su 8am-8pm) and at Karlovo nám. 28 (tel. 291 851; fax 297 836; open daily 8am-8pm). Cars start at 1200Kč per day for the first 4 days with unlimited mileage. Rentals require a valid 3-year-old driver's license, a major credit card, and an over-21 renter.

ORIENTATION

Straddling the **Vltava River,** Prague is a gigantic mess of suburbs and labyrinthine medieval streets. Fortunately, nearly everything of interest lies within the compact, walkable downtown. Originally four separate towns and a Jewish ghetto, Prague's central neighborhoods have retained their distinct identities. **Staré Město** (Old Town), centered around **Staroměstské nám.** on the left bank of the Vltava, is the city's original medieval center. Its winding streets are the most confusing; it is bordered on the north and west by the river, on the south by **Národní třída** and **Na Příkopě,** and on the east by **Revoluční. Josefov,** the old Jewish ghetto, lies in the northwestern corner of Staré Město; unfortunately, all that remains are six synagogues and the Old Jewish Cemetery. Surrounding Staré Město to the south and east is **Nové Město** (New Town), the administrative and commercial center of the city. It houses **Václavské nám.** and some of the Prague's most spectacular Art Nouveau architecture. Prague's main train station, **Hlavní nádraží,** and **Florenc bus station** sit in the northeastern corner. Across the Vltava sits **Hradčany,** a sprawling hilltop neighborhood stretching into the northern suburbs, defined primarily by the giant **Prague Castle** (Pražský Hrad). At Hradčany's southern base sits the **Malá Strana** (Lesser Side), directly across from Staré Město. Hilly, cobblestoned streets lace a tiny, Baroque neighborhood clustered around St. Nicholas's Cathedral. All train and bus terminals are on or near the excellent **Metro** system. *Tabák* stands and bookstores sell the indexed *plán města* (map); this, along with the English-language weekly *The Prague Post,* will prove essential for visitors.

PRACTICAL INFORMATION

TOURIST & FINANCIAL SERVICES

Tourist Offices: The green "i"s around Prague signify the multitude of tourist agencies that book rooms and sell maps, bus tickets, postcards, and guidebooks. **Pražská Informační Služba** (Prague Info Service), in the Old Town Hall (tel. 24 48 25 62; English tel. 54 44 44). Sells **maps** (39-49Kč) and tickets to shows and public transport. Open summer M-F 9am-7pm, Sa-Su 9am-6pm; off-season M-F 9am-6pm, Sa-Su 9am-5pm. Other offices at Na příkopě 20, Hlavní nádraží, and in the tower on the Malá Strana side of the Charles Bridge (Karlův most; all have the same hours).

Budget Travel: CKM, Jindřišská 28 (tel. 24 23 02 18; fax 26 86 23; email ckmprg@mbox.vol.cz). Metro A, B: Můstek. Sells budget air tickets to those under 26. Also books accommodations in Prague from 350Kč. Open M-Th 10am-6pm, F 10am-4pm. **KMC,** Karoliny Světlé 30 (tel. 22 22 03 47). Metro B: Národní třída. Books HI hostels. Open M-Th 9am-noon and 2:30-5pm, F 9am-noon and 2:30-3:30pm.

Passport Office: Foreigner police headquarters at Olšanská 2 (tel. 683 17 39). Metro A: Flora. From the Metro, turn right onto Jičínská with the cemetery on your right, and right again onto Olšanská. Or, take tram #9 from Václavské nám. toward Spojovací and get off at Olšanská. To obtain a visa extension, get a 90Kč stamp inside, line up in front of doors #2-12, and prepare to wait up to 2hr. Little English spoken. Open M-Tu and Th 7:30-11:45am and 12:30-2:30pm, W 7:30-11:30am and 12:30-5pm, F 7:30am-noon.

Embassies: Canada, Mickiewiczova 6 (tel. 24 31 11 08). Metro A: Hradčanská. Open M-F 8am-noon and 2-4pm. **Hungary,** Badeního 1 (tel. 32 04 12). Metro A: Hradčanská. Open M-W and F 9am-noon. **Ireland,** Tržiště 13 (tel. 530 911). Metro A: Malostranská. Open M-F 9:30am-12:30pm and 2:30-4:30pm. **Poland,** Váldštejnská nám. 49 (tel. 57 32 06 78). Metro A: Malostranská. Open M-F 7am-noon. **Russia,** Pod Kaštany 1 (tel. 38 19 45). Metro A: Hradčanská. Open M, W, and F 9am-1pm. **Slovakia,** Pod Hradební 1 (tel. 32 05 07). Metro A: Dejvická. Open M-F 8:30am-noon. **South Africa,** Ruská 65 (tel. 67 31 11 14). Metro A: Flora. Open M-F 9am-noon. **U.K.,** Thunovská 14 (tel. 57 32 03 55). Metro A: Malostranská. Open M-F 9am-noon. **U.S.,** Tržiště 15 (tel. 57 53 11 62; emergency after-hours tel. 53 12 00). Metro A: Malostranská. From Malostranské nám., head down Karmelitská and take a right onto Tržiště. Open M-F 8am-1pm and 2-4:30pm. **Australia** (tel. 24 31 00 71) and **New Zealand** (tel. 25 41 98) have consuls, but citizens should contact the U.K. embassy in an emergency.

Currency Exchange: AmEx and Thomas Cook traveler's checks can be cashed commission-free at their respective offices. Exchange counters are everywhere, with wildly varying rates. Don't bother with the expensive hotels, and don't even think about changing money on the streets. **Chequepoints** are mushrooming around the center of town, but their convenient hours cost a 10% commission. **Komerční banka,** Na příkopě 33 (tel. 24 02 11 11), buys notes and checks for a 2% commission. Open M-F 8am-5pm.

ATMs: All over the place; look for the green and orange "Bankomat" signs. The one at **Krone supermarket,** Václavské nám. 21, accepts Cirrus/Plus/MC/Visa.

American Express: Václavské nám. 56 (tel. 22 80 02 51; fax 22 21 11 31). Metro A, C: Muzeum. The **ATM** outside takes AmEx cards. Address mail to "Peter Sarris, American Express, Client Letter Service, Václavské nám. 56, 113 26 Praha 1, Czech Republic." Grants MC/Visa **cash advances** for a 3% commission. Open July-Sept. M-F 9am-6pm, Sa 9am-2pm; Oct.-Apr. M-F 9am-5pm, Sa 9am-noon. Another exchange office near the Charles Bridge in Malá Strana, Mostecká 12. Open daily 9:30am-7:30pm.

Thomas Cook: Národní třída 28 (tel. 21 10 52 76; fax 24 23 60 77). Cashes Cook checks commission-free. MC/Visa cash advances. Open M-Sa 9am-7pm, Su 10am-6pm. Also Staroměstké nám. 5 (tel. 24 81 71 73). Open M-F 9am-6pm, Sa 9am-1pm.

LOCAL SERVICES

Luggage Storage: Lockers in all train and bus stations take two 5Kč coins. If you forget the locker number or combination, the station charges 20Kč. If these are full, or if you need to store your suitcase, backpack, or Maltese falcon longer than 24hr., use the luggage offices to the left in the basement of **Hlavní nádraží** (15kg and under 15Kč per day; larger bags 25Kč per day; open 24hr.) and halfway up the stairs at **Florenc** (15kg and under 10Kč per day; larger bags 20Kč per day; open daily 5am-11pm).

English Bookstores: The Globe Bookstore, Janovského 14 (tel. 66 71 26 10; www.globebookstore.cz). Metro C: Vltavská. Walk under the overpass on the right, then turn right onto Janovského. New and used books and periodicals, a big noticeboard, and a coffeehouse. A legendary (pick-up) center of Anglophone Prague. Open daily 10am-midnight. **Anagram Bookshop,** Týn 4 (tel. 24 89 57 37; fax 24 89 57 38; email anagram@terminal.cz; www.anagram.cz). Metro A: Staroměstské. Behind Týn Church in Staroměstské nám. Open M-Sa 10am-8:30pm, Su 10am-6pm. **Big Ben Bookshop,** Malá Štupartská 5 (tel. 231 80 21; fax 231 98 48; email bigben@terminal.cz). Metro A: Nám. Republiky. Turn onto U obecního domů, right behind the Powder Tower. Turn right onto Rybná, left onto Jakubská, then right onto Štupartská. Open M-F 9am-6:30pm, Sa-Su 10am-5pm. **U Knihomola International Bookshop,** Mánesova 79 (tel. 627 77 70; fax 627 77 69). Metro A: Jiřího z Poděbrad. Open M-F 11am-9pm, Sa 2-9pm.

Laundromat: Laundry Kings, Dejvická 16 (tel. 312 37 43), one block from Metro A: Hradčanská. Cross the tram *and* railroad tracks, then turn left onto Dejvická. Wash 60Kč per 6kg; dry 15Kč per 8min. (usually takes 45min.; use the spinner to save on

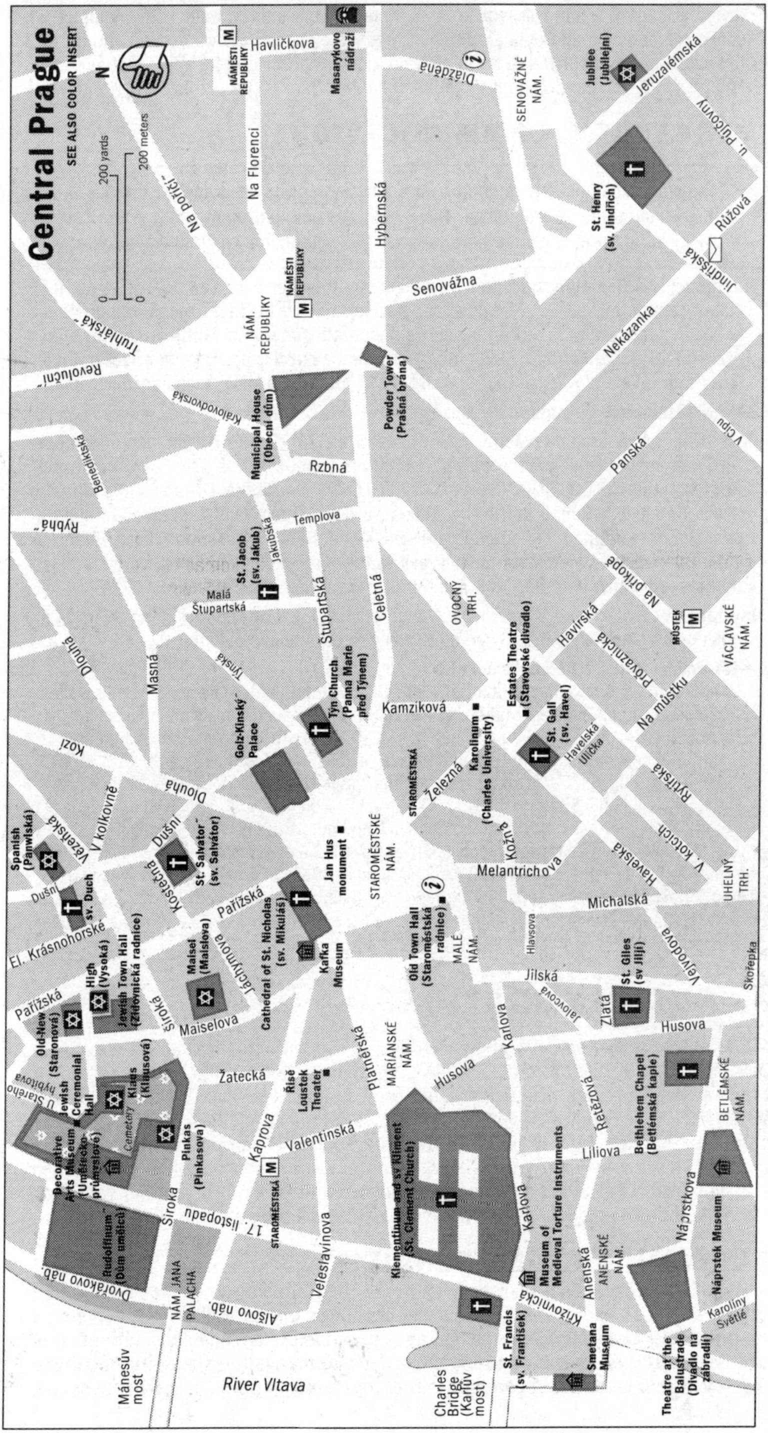

CZECH REPUBLIC

drying). Soap 10-20Kč. Full-service 30Kč more and takes 24hr. Beer 11Kč. As much a social center as a laundromat, in the evenings the place is filled with soiled and thirsty travelers who watch CNN and try to pick each other up. Bulletin for apartment seekers, English teachers, and potential "friends." Open M-F 6am-10pm, Sa-Su 8am-10pm.

EMERGENCY & COMMUNICATIONS

Prague is continuously reforming its phone system, often giving businesses no more than three weeks' notice. The 8-digit numbers provided here are the least likely to be obsolete by the time you read this—but then again, nothing's sacred.

Emergency: Na Homolce (Hospital for Foreigners), Roentgenova 2 (tel. 52 92 21 46; foreign reception tel. 52 92 21 54; after-hours tel. 57 21 11 11). Open M-F 8am-4pm. Major insurance plans and credit cards accepted. **American Medical Center,** Janovského 48 (tel. 807 756). Major foreign insurance policies accepted. **Canadian Medical Centre,** Vele Slavínska 30 (tel. 316 55 19). BUPA and MEDEX insurance accepted.

24hr. Pharmacies: U Anděla, Štefánikova 6 (tel. 57 32 09 18).

Post Office: Jindřišská 14. Metro A, B: Můstek (tel. 24 22 88 56). Stamps at window #16; letters and small parcels at #12-14; info at window #9; #17 is **Poste Restante.** Address mail to "Eve GORDON, POSTE RESTANTE, Jindřišská 14, 110 00 Praha 1, Czech Republic." Airmail to the U.S. takes 10 days. Open daily 7am-8pm. To send a package of more than 2kg abroad, go to the **Celní stanice** (Customs Office), Plzeňská 139. Take tram #4 from Metro B: I.P. Pavlova toward Sídliště Řepy to Klamovka, and go up the road. Open M-Tu and Th-F 7am-3pm, W 7am-6pm. **Postal Code:** 110 00.

Internet Access: Prague is internet nirvana. Access is everywhere: in libraries, hostels, posh cafes, and trendy bars. Národní is home to several computer-lab-like cybercafes.

Terminal Bar, see **Beerhalls & Pubs,** p. 206.

Cafe Electra, Rašínovo nábřeží 62 (tel. 297 038). Metro B: Karlovo nám. 28 computers and extensive menu. Cheapest at 80Kč per hr. Open M-F 8am-midnight, Sa-Su noon-midnight.

Internet Cafe, Národní třída 25 (tel. 21 08 52 84; email internetcafe@highland.cz; www.internetcafe.cz). Metro B: Národní třída. Across from Tesco in Pasáž paláce METRO. 10 speedy PCs and 6 Macs 120Kč per hr. and virtually no wait. Open daily 10am-11pm.

Cafe.com, Na Poříčí 36 (tel. 24 81 94 35). Metro B: Florenc. Cyber cellar with a hip blue tile bar. 50Kč per 30min.; buy 9hr. and get the 10th free. Open daily 9am-midnight.

Laundromat/Internet Cafe, Korunnil 14 (tel. 22 51 01 80). Metro A: Nám. Miru. Kill two birds with one stone. Laundry 65Kč per hr. Internet 30Kč per 15min. Open daily 8am-8pm.

Telephones: Everywhere, including at the post office. Cardphones are becoming increasingly common. Phonecards sell for 150Kč per 50 units at kiosks, post offices, and some exchange places: don't let kiosks rip you off. **Phone code:** (0)2.

ACCOMMODATIONS

While hotel prices rise beyond your wildest dreams, the hostel market is glutted; prices have stabilized around 250-350Kč per night. A few smaller hostels provide a home-away-from-home atmosphere, but rooms must be reserved at least two days in advance. The Strahov complex and other student dorms bear the brunt of the summer's backpacking crowds. Year-round hostels are popping up in both the most and least convenient places; weigh your options. A few bare-bones hotels are still cheap, and a growing number of Prague residents are renting rooms. Although everyone knows someone who's done it, sleeping on the streets is dangerous.

ACCOMMODATION AGENCIES

Many of the hawkers who besiege visitors at the train station are agents hired by other people. The going rates for apartments hover around 500-1000Kč, depending on proximity to the city center; haggling is possible. Arrangements made this way are generally safe, but if you're wary of bargaining on the street, try a private agency. Staying outside the center is fine if you're near public transport, so ask where the nearest tram, bus, or Metro stop is. Don't pay until you know what you're getting—if in doubt, ask for details in writing. You can often pay in U.S. dollars or Deutschmarks, although prices are lower if you pay in Kč.

Ave., Hlavní Nádraží (tel. 24 22 35 21, 57 31 29 85, and 57 31 29 86; fax 57 31 29 84), on the 2nd floor of the train station next to the leftmost stairs. Burgeoning firm offers hundreds of rooms (shared and private) starting at 800Kč per person. Books hostels from 300Kč. Open daily 6am-11pm. AmEx/MC/Visa.

Hello Travel Ltd., Senovážné nám. 3 (tel. 24 21 26 47), between Na příkopě and Hlavní nádraží. Arranges every sort of housing imaginable. Singles in pensions from US$23 (low season) or US$35 (high); doubles US$56; hostels US$10-13. Payment in Kč, DM, or by credit card (AmEx/MC/Visa). Open daily 10am-9pm.

HOSTELS

If you're schlepping a backpack in Hlavní nádraží or Holešovice, you *will* be bombarded by hostel runners. Many are university dorms that free up for travelers from June to August, and often you'll be offered free transport. These rooms are the easiest option for those arriving in the middle of the night without a reservation. For those who prefer hostels that offer more than just a place to sleep, there are smaller, friendlier alternatives. Unfortunately, most places no longer accept reservations. It's best to phone the night before you arrive or at 10am. Like everywhere else in Prague, the staff speaks English. Curfews are distant memories.

STARÉ MĚSTO

Traveller's Hostels (email hostel@terminal.cz; www.terminal.cz/~hostel). These summertime big-dorm specialists round up travelers at bus and train stations around the city and herd them into one of six city-center hostels for lots of beds and beer. At all hostels, breakfast is included and internet access is available.

Husova 3 (tel. 24 21 53 26). Metro B: Národní třída. Turn right onto Spálená (which turns into Na Perštýně after Národní), and then Husova. In the middle of Staré Město. Still the classiest, with dorms for 400Kč; satellite TV included.

Dlouhá 33 (tel. 24 82 66 62; fax 24 82 66 65). Metro A: Staroměstské; Metro B: Nám. Republiky. In the same building as the Roxy, but it has good soundproofing. Doubles 550Kč per person; triples 430Kč per person; 6-bed dorms 380Kč; 10-bed 350Kč.

Křížovnická 7 (tel. 232 09 87). Metro A: Staroměstská. 230Kč.

Střelecký ostrov (tel. 24 91 01 88). An island off Most Legií. Metro B: Národní třída. 300Kč.

Růžová 5 (tel. 26 01 11). Metro C: Hlavní nádraží. 220Kč.

NOVÉ MĚSTO

Libra-Q, Senovážné nám. 21 (tel. 24 23 17 54; fax 24 22 15 79). Metro B: Nám. Republiky. From Nám. Republiky, walk down Hybernská to Senovážná; the hostel is at the intersection with Jeruzalémská. Tidy, spartan dorms on the edge of Staré Město. 550Kč.

Hotel Junior, Žitná 12 (tel. 24 23 17 54; fax 24 23 17 54 and 24 22 39 11). Metro B: Karlovo nám. From the Metro, walk up Karlovo nám. toward the town hall and turn right onto Žitná before the park ends. 1970s revival decor, but rooms are neat and central. Breakfast included. Check-in 2pm. Dorms 450Kč with ISIC/HI card, otherwise 550Kč.

Hostel U Melounu (At the Watermelon), Ke Karlovu 7 (tel./fax 24 91 83 22). Metro C: I.P. Pavlova. Follow Sokolská to Na Bojišti and turn left at the street's end onto Ke Karlovu. In a historic building with great facilities 5min. from Nové Město. Breakfast included. 2- to 4-bed dorms 390-490Kč. 30Kč discount with ISIC, GO-25, or Euro-26.

Prague Lion, Na Bojišti 26 (tel./fax 96 18 00 18). Metro C: I.P. Pavlova. Follow Sokolská to Na Bojišti. Immaculate showers and rooms. Breakfast included. Internet 2Kč per min. Doubles 550Kč, with shower 725Kč; triples 775Kč, 825Kč.

Hostel SPUS, Dittrichova 15 (tel./fax 24 91 53 80). Metro B: Karlovo nám. Head down Resslova toward the river and turn left on Dittrichova. Rooms escape the institutional feel of this July-Aug. only dorm. Doubles with bath 450Kč per person; 2- to 4-bed dorms 380Kč; 6-bed dorms 320Kč. 30Kč discount with ISIC, GO-25, or Euro26.

MALÁ STRANA

Hostel Sokol, Všehrdova 10 (tel. 57 00 73 97; fax 57 00 73 40). Metro A: Malostranská. From the Metro, take tram #12 or 22 toward Hlubočepy or Nádraží Hostivař to Hellichova; walk down Újezd to Všehrdova. 10- to 12-person dorms in the Malá Strana sports club. Gets rowdy at night. Communal kitchen. Reservations accepted. 220Kč.

VINOHRADY

Domov Mládeže, Dykova 20 (tel./fax 22 51 25 97 and 22 51 17 77). From Metro A: Jiřího z Poděbrad, follow Nitranská and turn left on Dykova; it's two blocks down on your right. Possibly the most enjoyable hostel trek ever. 80 beds in the tree-lined Vinohrady district; so peaceful you might forget you're in Prague. Breakfast included. Clean 2- to 7-person dorms 350Kč; lone double 500Kč. If they're full, they might have space in a sister hostel: **Amadeus,** Slavojova 108/8. Metro C: Vyšehrad. From the Metro, descend the bridge to Čiklova, turn left, and the hostel is on the left. **Máchova,** Máchova 11. Metro A: Nám. Míru. From the Metro, walk down Ruská and turn right onto Máchova. **Košická,** Košická 12. Metro A: Nám. Míru. All hostels use the same telephone.

Clown and Bard, Bořivojova 102 (tel. 22 71 64 53). Metro A: Jiřího z Poděbrad. Follow Slavíkova to Ježkova. The hostel is on the left at the intersection with Bořivojova. New management has set this notoriously social hostel on the right track once again. Bar with nightly music, in-house salon, and summer BBQs. 6-bed loft 350Kč; 6-bed dorm 300Kč; doubles 400Kč; 36-bed dorm (not a particularly safe option), 250Kč.

SOUTH OF THE CENTER

Penzion v podzámčí, V podzámčí 27 (tel./fax 472 27 59). From Metro C: Budějovická, take bus #192 to the 3rd stop—ask the driver to stop at Nad Rybníky. Eva and Michaela make this the homiest hostel in Prague, from extraordinary laundry service (they *iron* your socks! 100Kč per 5kg) to daily clothes-folding and bed-making. They make great hot chocolate and have a communal kitchen, satellite TV, comfy beds, umbrellas, and great stories—be sure to ask about Mici the killer cat. 2- to 4-person dorms with beds and loft mattresses 250Kč; doubles 280Kč.

Hostel Boathouse, V náklích 1a (tel./fax 402 10 76). From Hlavní nádraží, Karlovo nám., Staré Město, or the Charles Bridge, take tram #3 or 17 south toward Sídliště and get off at Černý Kůň (20min.). From the tram stop, follow the yellow Boathouse signs down to the Vltava. As Věra, the owner, says, "This isn't a hostel; it's a crazy house." A young, energetic crowd, and 70 beds worth of Anglophones make this hostel the perfect fusion of nurturing home and summer camp. Also serves meals (breakfast 50Kč, dinner 70Kč) and offers board games, satellite TV, and laundry service (100Kč per load). Two night minimum. Key deposit 100Kč. Call ahead; if they're full, Vera might let you sleep in the hall. Beds in 3- to 5-bed dorms perched above a working boathouse 290Kč.

WEST OF THE CENTER

Welcome Hostel, Zíkova 13 (tel. 24 32 02 02; fax 24 32 34 89). Metro A: Dejvická. From the escalators, follow Šolinova to Zíkova. A free beer welcomes weary travelers. Good if you're arriving from the airport late at night, but very institutional. Check-in 2:30pm. Check-out 9:30am. Singles 350Kč; bed in a double 230Kč.

Strahov Complex, Vaníčkova 5. (tel. 52 7190) Take bus #217 or 143 from Metro A: Dejvická to Koleje Strahov. Known as a "hostel ghetto," Strahov is ten concrete blocks next to the enormous stadium that opens June-Aug. to accommodate the hordes. Not very convenient, but there's always space, and you can catch the Strahov concerts from the comfort of your cubicle. Singles 300Kč; doubles 220Kč; students 180Kč with ID.

HOTELS & PENSIONS

With so many tourists infiltrating Prague, hotels are upgrading service, appearance, and prices; budget hotels are now scarce. Beware that hotels may try to bill you for a more expensive room than the one you in which you stayed; arm yourself with receipts. The good, cheap ones require reservations up to a month in advance, but too many backpacker no-shows have forced many businesses to refuse reservations altogether. Call first, then confirm by fax with a credit card.

STARÉ MĚSTO

Pension Unitas/Cloister Inn, Bartolomějská 9 (tel. 232 77 00; fax 232 77 09; email cloister@cloister-inn.cz; www.cloister-inn.cz). Metro B: Národní třída. Cross Národní and head down Na Perštýně away from Tesco. Turn left on Bartolomějská. An old monastery where Beethoven once performed, and later a Communist jail where Havel was incarcerated. Breakfast included. Singles 1020Kč; doubles 1200Kč; triples 1650Kč.

Dům U krále Jiřího, Liliová 10 (tel. 22 22 09 25; fax 22 22 17 07). Metro A: Staroměstská. Exit the Metro onto Nám. Jana Palacha. Walk down Křížovnická toward the Charles Bridge and turn left onto Karlova; Liliová is the first street on the right. Gorgeous rooms with private bath. Breakfast included. Singles 1650Kč; doubles 2850Kč.

U Lilie, Liliová 15 (tel. 22 22 04 32; fax 22 22 06 41). Metro A: Staroměstská. Follow the directions to U krále Jiřího (above). Rooms include satellite TV. Breakfast included. Singles with shower 1700Kč; doubles 1700Kč, with bath 2300Kč.

Pension U Medvídků, Na Perštýně 7 (tel. 24 21 19 16; fax 24 22 09 30). Metro B: Národní třída. Above a popular pub, the renovated rooms somehow escape the noise. Breakfast included. June-Sept. 765Kč per person; Oct.-May 650Kč. Singles 50% more.

NOVÉ MĚSTO

Hotel Legie, Sokolská 33 (tel. 24 92 02 54; fax 24 91 44 41). Metro C: I.P. Pavlova. Rather grim exterior, but rooms are newly renovated with private showers, phone, and cable TV. Breakfast included. June-Sept. and Jan. doubles 2600Kč; triples 3500Kč. Feb.-May and Oct.-Dec. doubles 2200Kč; triples 3100Kč.

Hotel Junior, Senovážné nám. 21 (tel. 24 23 17 54, 22 10 55 36, or 22 10 51 18; fax 24 22 15 79). Metro B: Nám. Republiky. Singles 700Kč; 2- to 5-bed rooms 550Kč.

NORTH OF THE CENTER

Hotel Standart (HI), Přístavní 2 (tel. 875 258 and 875 674; fax 806 752). From Metro C: Vltavská, take tram #1 toward Spojavací, #3 toward Lehovec, #14 toward Vozovna Kobylisy, or #25 toward Střelničná. Continue along the street, then turn left onto Přístavní. Very quiet neighborhood. Singles 350Kč, 620Kč for non-members; doubles 700Kč, 800Kč; triples 1050Kč, 1100Kč; quads 1400Kč. Breakfast included.

Pension Sunshine, Drahobejlova 17 (tel. 66 31 52 66; reservation tel. 24 32 02 02; fax 24 32 34 89; email welcome@welcome.cz). Metro B: Českomoravská. The Welcome Hostel's foray into the budget hotel business, away from the center but near the Metro. Breakfast included. Doubles, triples and quads with bath 500Kč per person.

Hotel Kafka, Cimburkova 24 (tel. 273 101 and 22 78 04 31; fax 272 984 and 22 78 13 33), in Žižkov near the TV tower. From Metro C: Hlavní nádraží, take tram #5 toward Harfa, #9 toward Spojovací, or #26 toward Nádraží Hostivař, and get off at Husinecká. Go uphill along Seifertova three blocks and turn left onto Cimburkova. Brand-new hotel amid 19th-century buildings, near plenty of restaurants and *pivnici*. Breakfast and parking 100Kč. MC/Visa (5% commission). Mar. 15-July 31 singles 1520Kč; doubles 2000Kč; triples 2300Kč; quads 2730Kč. Aug. and New Year's 1840Kč; 2420Kč; 2730Kč; 3260Kč. Sept.-Dec. and Jan. 1-Mar. 14 890Kč; 1250Kč; 1350Kč; 1570Kč.

WEST OF THE CENTER

B&B U Oty (Ota's House), Radlická 188 (tel./fax 57 21 53 23; www.bbuoty.cz; email mb@bbuoty.cz). 400m from Metro B: Radlická, up the slope. Exit the Metro to the left and go right on the road. Ota is a charming Anglophone who strives to take the kinks out of your stay in Prague. Kitchen facilities and, after 3 nights, laundry free. Free parking, provided you're not using the car while in Prague. Singles 500Kč; doubles 770Kč; triples 950Kč; quads 1250Kč. 100Kč extra per person if staying only one night.

CAMPING

Campsites have taken over both the outskirts and the centrally located Vltava islands. Bungalows must be reserved in advance, but tent space is generally available without prior notice. Tourist offices sell a guide to sites near the city (15Kč).

Císařská louka, on a peninsula on the Vltava. Metro B: Smíchovské nádraží, then tram #12 toward Hlubočepy to Lihovar. Walk toward the river and onto the shaded path. Alternatively, take the ferry service from Smíchovské nádraží. **Caravan Park** (tel. 540 925; fax 543 305) sits near the ferry. 90-120Kč per tent, plus 110Kč per person. Singles 365Kč; doubles 630Kč; triples 945Kč. **Caravan Camping** (tel./fax 540 129) is near the tram. 90-120Kč per tent, plus 110Kč per person. 4-bed bungalows for 720Kč.

Sokol Troja, Trojská 171 (tel./fax 688 11 77). Prague's largest campground, north of the center in the Troja district. From Metro C: Nádraží Holešovice, take bus #112 to Kazanka, the fourth stop. If full (or if you're frightened by the deer heads, bear skins, and hunting apparel), at least four nearly identical places line the same road. Tents 80-160Kč plus 100Kč per person. Dorms 250Kč; bungalow 230Kč per person.

Na Vlachovce, Zenklova 217 (tel./fax 688 02 14). Take bus #102 or 175 from Nádraží Holešovice toward Okrouhlická, get off, and continue in the same direction. Great view of Prague. Breakfast included. Reserve a week ahead. If you've ever felt like crawling into a barrel of *Budvar,* this bungalow city provides romantic 2-person barrels at 250Kč per bed. The pension attached has doubles with bath for 975Kč.

FOOD

The basic rule is that the nearer you are to Staroměstské nám., Karlův most, and Václavské nám., the more you'll pay; away from the center, you can have pork, cabbage, dumplings, and a half-liter of beer for 50Kč. Check your bill carefully—you'll pay for anything the waiter brings, including ketchup and bread, and restaurants have been known to massage bills higher than they ought to. In Czech lunch spots, *hotová jídla* (prepared meals) are cheapest. Vegetarian eateries are quickly multiplying, but in most cases options are still limited to fried cheese and cabbage. Outlying Metro stops become impromptu marketplaces in the summer; look for the **daily market** at the intersection of Havelská and Melantrichova in Staré Město.

RESTAURANTS

STARÉ MĚSTO

Lotos, Platnéřská 13 (tel. 232 23 90). Metro A: Staroměstská. Exit the Metro onto the corner of Kaprova and Valentinská. Turn left down Valentinská away from the Jewish cemetery, then right onto Platnéřská. Vegetarian (and non-smoking) restaurant that deserves applause for its Czech food (soy cubes with dumplings 52Kč) and organic menu (60-140Kč). 0.5L wheat-yeast Pilsner 30Kč. Open daily 11am-10pm.

Klub architektů, Betlémské nám. 52 (tel. 24 40 12 14). Walk through the gates and descend to the right. A 12th-century cellar thrust into the 20th century with sleek table settings and copper pulley lamps. Plenty of veggie options 80-90Kč; meat dishes 100-150Kč. Chinese cabbage soup 30Kč. Open daily 11am-midnight.

U Špirků, on Kožná. Metro A: Staroměstská. With the astronomical clock to your back, go down Melantrichova and make your first left onto Kožná, which curves to the left. The restaurant is a few steps away from the armory store. Some of the city's best and cheapest food served in a spacious pub adorned with versions of the Mona Lisa and Charles Bridge. Daily specials 50-60Kč; entrees 70-90Kč. Open M-Sa 11am-midnight.

Country Life, Melantrichova 15 (tel. 24 21 33 66). Metro A, B: Můstek. The Prague link of an international chain, and the best veggie takeout in town. Sandwiches 20Kč. 25% cheaper after 5pm. Open M-Th 9am-10pm, F 9am-6pm, Su 11am-10pm.

Shalom, Maiselova 18 (tel. 24 81 09 29; fax 24 81 09 12). Metro A: Staroměstská. Walk down Kaprova away from the river and go left on Maiselova; the restaurant is in the synagogue on the right. Fine kosher lunches in Josefov. Set menu 350-500Kč. Buy tickets beforehand from Matana, the travel agent across the road (tel. 232 10 49; open M-Th and Su9am-6:30pm). Order tickets in advance for holidays. Open daily 11:30am-2pm.

NOVÉ MĚSTO

Universal, V jirchářích 6 (tel. 24 91 81 82). Metro B: Národní třída. From the Metro, turn left onto Spálená and right on Myslíkova, then right on Křemencova. A transplanted California-style eatery that prepares the biggest and freshest salads (97-135Kč) in Prague for an international crowd of hipsters. Stoplights and acid jazz make the fondue (145Kč) taste that much better. Open daily 11:30am-1am.

Velryba (The Whale), Opatovická 24 (tel. 24 91 23 91). Metro B: Národní třída. Relaxed with a bit of chic, this cafe-restaurant houses a gallery in the back. Locals, American expats, business types, and tourists enjoy inexpensive international and Czech dishes (38-115Kč) and adventurous vegetarian platters (lentils with eggs and gherkins 33Kč). Can *you* see the whale on the sea-green wall? Open daily 11am-2am.

Góvinda Vegetarian Club, Soukenická 27 (tel. 24 81 66 31). Metro B: Nám. Republiky. The restaurant is upstairs at the back of the building. Rama and Krishna gaze upon diners and delicious vegetarian stews. A plate with the works 75Kč. Daily menu. Lectures on the *Bhagavadgitá* Wednesdays at 6:30pm. Open M-Sa 11am-5pm.

Pizzeria Kmotra, V jirchářích 12 (tel. 21 91 58 09). Metro B: Národní třída Follow the directions to Universal (above), but turn right on V jirchářích. Downstairs pizza joint with pleasant ground-floor cafe. Enjoy hot cabbage salad (37Kč) and big pizzas with huge peppers (69-108Kč). Open M-Sa 11am-1am, Su 11am-midnight.

Restaurace U Pravdů, Žitná 15 (tel. 29 95 92). Metro B: Karlovo nám. A deservedly popular Czech lunch spot, where spillover from the dining room is seated in the beer garden. Entrees 80-149Kč. Open M-F 10am-11pm, Sa-Su 11am-11pm.

MALÁ STRANA

Bar bar, Všehrdova 17 (tel. 53 29 41). Metro A: Malostranská. Follow the tram tracks from the Metro station down Letenská, through Malostranské nám., and down Karmelitská. Turn left on Všehrdova after the museum. A jungle jungle of salads salads with meat meat, fish fish, cheese cheese or just veggies veggies (64-89Kč). The other choice is, shockingly, not fried pork with french fries, but pancakes pancakes–sweet sweet (22-56Kč) or savory savory (59-155Kč). The stuttering eatery has a good vibe, good music, and 40 varieties of good whiskey (from 41Kč). Open daily noon-midnight.

Bohemia Bagel, Újezd 16 (tel. 53 10 02 and 53 09 21). Metro A: Malostranská, or tram #12 or 22 to "Újezd." After New York Bagels in Budapest closed, this became the first place in Eastern Europe for bagelophiles to get their fixes. A wide variety of flavors. Bagel with cream cheese 45Kč; bagel melt 60-125Kč; Belgian waffles with Canadian syrup 60Kč. Open M-Th 7am-midnight, F 7am-2am, Sa 8am-2am, Su 8am-midnight.

Malostranská hospoda, Karmelitská 25 (tel. 53 20 76), by Malostranské nám. Metro A: Malostranská. Chairs spill out onto the street from the vaulted interior. The usual long table in the corner surrounded by beer and *Becherovka* fans is made up of women; the men are usually too drunk to notice. Good *guláš* (68Kč). Open daily 10am-midnight.

U Švejků, Újezd 22 (tel. 525 629; fax 291 476). Metro A: Malostranská. Aggressively touristy, complete with nightly accordionist, but prices are low and portions large. The place has a picture of Emperor Franz Josef on the wall–fans of Hašek's novel may wonder about its condition...Good soldiers should partake of beef in cream sauce (79Kč), dumplings (10Kč), or garlic soup (19Kč). Open daily 11am-midnight.

LATE-NIGHT EATING

4:45am. Charles Bridge. Lavka's house disco beat is still pumping ferociously, but all you can hear is your stomach growling. Rather than catching the night bus home and going to bed hungry, grab a *párek v rohlíku* (hot dog) or a *smažený sýr* (fried cheese sandwich) from a vendor on Václavské nám., or a gyros from a stand on Spálená or Vodíčkova. Or, even better, make a morning of it and uncover Prague's developing late-night eating scene.

J.J. Murphy's Breakfast Diner, Tržiště 4 (tel. 06 03 97 41 01). Metro A: Malostranská. Bar by day, night-train soul kitchen by 3am. Breakfast 80Kč. Open daily 3pm-10am.

Radost FX, Bělehradská 120. Metro C: I.P.Pavlova. The late-night veggie cafe serves spicy chili (95Kč) to sweaty, starving dancers from the club below. Open daily 8pm-5am.

Andy's Cafe, V kolkovně 3. Metro A: Staroměstská. Walk down Dlouhá and turn left on V kolkovně. In the wee hours, it's the only place on the block still open. Stay late enough sipping soup (20Kč) to catch the first Metro. Open M-F 10am-6am, Sa-Su noon-6am.

CAFES

When Prague journalists are bored, they churn out yet another "Whatever happened to cafe life?" feature. The answer: it turned into *čajovna* (teahouse) culture. Tea is all the rage, and many teahouses double as bars or clubs in the evening.

U malého Glena, Karmelitská 23 (tel. 535 81 15). From Metro A: Malostranská, take tram #12 to Malostranské nám. With their motto "Eat, Drink, Drink Some More," they've got consumption down to a science. The "light entree" menu has veggie plates (80-150Kč) and *croques-monsieur* 80Kč. Killer margaritas (80Kč). Mixed crowd of locals and foreigners descend to the Maker's Mark basement bar for nightly jazz or blues at 9pm. Cover 30-100Kč. Open M-F 10am-2am, Sa-Su 10am-3am; Su brunch 10am-4pm.

Jazz Cafe 14, Opatovická 14 (tel. 24 92 00 39). Metro B: Národní třída. Usually filled with smoke and satisfied twentysomethings. There's no live jazz music, but photos of Louis, Miles, and others line the walls. Cheap snacks (30Kč). Open daily 10am-11pm.

Unamuno Lounge, Mánesova 79 (tel. 627 77 67). Metro A: Jiřího z Poděbrad. From the Metro, walk down Slavíkova one block to Mánesova; the cafe is in the basement of the U Knihomola bookstore. The only place in Prague to get a real latté. An extended living room with comfy couches and soothing jazz. Coffee 20-40Kč; carrot cake 75Kč. Open M-Th 10am-11pm, F-Sa 10am-midnight, Su 11am-8pm.

The Globe Coffeehouse, Janovského 14 (tel. 66 71 26 10). Metro C: Vltavská. Tasty black coffee (20Kč), gazpacho (40Kč), and fresh fruit smoothies (50Kč), as well as plenty of English speakers trying to make a love connection. Open daily 10am-midnight.

Kavárna Medúza, Belgická 17 (tel. 25 85 34). Metro A: Nám. Míru. Walk down Rumunská and turn left at Belgická. Antique shop masquerading as a cafe. Fluffed-up Victorian seats and lots of coffee (19-30Kč). Open M-F 11am-1am.

Blatouch, Vězeňská 4 (tel. 232 86 43). Metro A: Staroměstská. From Staroměstské nám., walk down Dlouhá at the far northeast corner of the square and follow it as it changes into Kozí. When the street becomes U obecního dvora, turn left on Vězeňská. A scoping bar with a Europop feel. Cocktails are 50-70Kč and a pleasantly large *Bernard* beer 24Kč. Open M-Th 11am-midnight, F 11am-1am, Sa 2pm-1am, Su 2pm-midnight.

U zeleného čaje, Nerudova 19 (tel. 57 53 00 27). Metro A: Malostranská. Follow Letenská to Malostranské nám.; in the square, stay right of the church so that you walk onto Nerudova. One of the only *čajovny* that feels more like a cafe than a zen-den. Four salads (15Kč per 100g) and tons of teas (15-40Kč). Open daily 11am-10pm.

SUPERMARKETS

Go to the basement of Czech department stores for food halls and supermarkets. Small *potraviny* (delis) and vegetable stands can be found on most street corners.

Krone department store (tel. 24 23 04 77), on Václavské nám. at the intersection with Jindřišská. Metro A, B: Můstek. Open M-F 9am-8pm, Sa 9am-7pm, Su 10am-6pm.

Kotva department store (tel. 24 21 54 62), at the corner of Revoluční and Nám. Republiky. Metro B: Nám. Republiky. Open M-F 7am-8pm, Sa 8am-6pm, Su 10am-6pm.

Tesco, Národní třída 26 (tel. 24 22 79 71). Right next to Metro B: Národní třída. Open M-F 7am-8pm, Sa 8am-6pm, Su 9am-6pm.

SIGHTS

The only Central European city left unscathed by either natural disaster or WWII, central Prague is a well-preserved combination of labyrinthine alleys and Baroque buildings, and, as a result, flocks of tourists. Don't be disheartened by the hordes: you can easily leave the umbrella-following packs by venturing off Staroměstské nám., the Charles Bridge, and Václavské nám. Prague is best explored on foot; central Prague—Staré Město, Nové Město, Malá Strana, and Hradčany—is extremely compact and can be traversed in one day (but give yourself more). You can't leave Prague without wandering the back alleys of Josefov, exploring the heights of Vyšehrad, and getting lost in the maze of Malá Strana's uphill streets. With unrivaled architecture and myriad parks, you need never enter a museum or building; strolling through is enough to impress upon you the singular beauty of Prague.

NOVÉ MĚSTO

Established in 1348 by Charles IV (see **History,** p. 175) as a separate municipality, Nové Město is not exactly new. Its age, however, is not readily apparent; its wide boulevards and sprawling squares seem hundreds of years ahead of their time. Today, Nové Město has grown into the commercial core of Prague, and—with the exception of Wenceslas Square—avoids the city's infamous throngs of tourists.

WENCESLAS SQUARE (VÁCLAVSKÉ NÁMĚSTÍ)

> I've taken my grandchildren to the top of Wenceslas Square where St. Wenceslas looks over the entire square. I tell them to imagine all the things St. Wenceslas might have seen sitting there on his horse: the trading markets hundreds of years ago, Hitler's troops, the Soviet tanks, and our Velvet Revolution in 1989. I can still imagine these things; it's the boulevard where much of our history, good and bad, has passed.
>
> –Bedřich Šimáček, tram #22 driver, quoted in *The Prague Post*

Not so much a square as a broad boulevard running through the center of Nové Město, **Wenceslas Square** owes its name to the equestrian statue of Czech ruler and saint **Wenceslas** (Václav) in front of the National Museum. Kneeling beneath him in solemn prayer are smaller statues of the country's four patron saints: St. Ludmila (his grandmother), St. Agnes, St. Precopious, and St. Adalbert (Vojtěch). Wenceslas has presided over a century of turmoil and triumph, witnessing no fewer than five revolutions from his pedestal. The perfectionist sculptor Myslbek completed the statue after 25 years of deliberation; as others gasped at its 1912 unveiling, poor Myslbek just mumbled, "It could have been bigger." The inscription under St. Wenceslas declares, "Do not let us and our descendents perish." Czechs have taken this seriously: a new Czechoslovak state was proclaimed here in 1918, and Jan Palach set himself on fire here to protest the 1968 Soviet invasion. The square sweeps down from the statue and the **National Museum** (Národní muzeum) past department stores, overpriced discos, posh hotels, sausage stands, and trashy casinos. The view of the St. Wenceslas in front of the museum from Můstek's base is hypnotic at full moon. At the northern end of Wenceslas Square near the Můstek Metro station, Art Nouveau, expressed in everything from lampposts to windowsills, dominates the square. A prime example is the 1903 **Hotel Evropa** at #25.

RADIO PRAGUE BUILDING. The glass Radio Prague Building, behind the National Museum, was the scene of a tense battle during the Prague Spring as citizens tried to protect the studios from tanks with a human barricade. The station managed to transmit reports for the first 14hr. of the invasion. *(Metro A, C: Muzeum.)*

CHURCH OF OUR LADY OF THE SNOWS. (Kostel Panny Marie Sněžné). Founded by Charles IV in 1347, this church was meant to be the largest in Prague. The Gothic walls are, indeed, higher than those of any other house of worship, but the rest of the structure is still unfinished—there was only enough cash to finish the choir. *(Metro A, B: Můstek. From the bottom of Wenceslas Square, turn left onto 28. října to reach Jungmannovo nám.; the entrance will be to your back left behind the statue of Jungmann.)*

FRANCISCAN GARDENS. (Františkánská zahrada). No one is quite sure how the Franciscans who keep this rose garden have managed to maintain such a bastion of serenity in the heart of Prague's bustling commercial district. Perhaps if the friars took a break from talking to the birds, they could divulge their secrets. *(Metro A, B: Můstek. Enter through the arch at the intersection of Jungmannova and Národní. Open daily Apr. 15-Sept. 14 7am-10pm; Sept. 15-Oct. 14 7am-8pm; Oct. 15-Apr. 14 8am-7pm. Free.)*

VELVET REVOLUTION MEMORIAL. Under the arcades halfway down Národní stands a memorial to the hundreds of Prague's citizens beaten on November 17, 1989. A march, organized by FAMU students to mourn the 50th anniversary of the Nazi execution of nine Czech students, was savagely attacked by the police, sparking further mass protests against the police and the Communist regime. President Havel was one of the primary leaders of the Velvet Revolution; his Civic Forum was based at the **Magic Lantern Theater** (Laterna magika dívadlo), Národní 4.

MUNICIPAL HOUSE. (Obecní dům). By far the most impressive Art Nouveau building in the city, the Municipal House captures the opulence of Prague's 19th-century cafe culture. Originally conceived as a Czech cultural center in Habsburg-controlled Prague, the Municipal House is the National Revival's proudest architectural achievement. Appropriately, the new Czechoslovak state proclaimed its independence here on October 28, 1918. The interior was designed by celebrated Czech artist Alfons Mucha and is adorned with his posters and paintings. *(Nám. Republiky 5. Metro B: Nám. Republiky. Open daily 10am-6pm. Guided tours available.)*

THE DANCING HOUSE. (Taneční dům). Built by American architect Frank Gehry of Guggenheim-Bilbao fame, the building at the corner of Resslova and Rašínovo nábřeží—called Fred and Ginger by Anglophones and the Dancing House by Czechs—is quite possibly Prague's most controversial landmark. It opened in 1996, next to President Havel's former apartment building; he moved out when construction began. On the embankment of the Vltava amid a stretch of remarkable Art Nouveau buildings, it is considered by many to be an eyesore and an irreverent disruption of Prague's renowned architecture, while others find it a shining example of post-modern design. Its undulating glass wall and windows and its paired cone and cube evoke a dancing couple. *(Metro B: Karlovo nám.)*

STARÉ MĚSTO

Settled in the 10th century, Staré Město remains a labyrinth of narrow roads and Old World alleys. It's easy to get lost, but doing so is the best way to appreciate the neighborhood's charm. The heart of Staré Město is **Old Town Square** (Staroměstské nám.), surrounded by no less than eight magnificent towers. It is because of this region that Prague earned the nickname "city of a thousand spires." The vast stone plaza is filled with blacksmiths, carriages, and ice cream vendors in summer.

POWDER TOWER. (Prašná brána). The gothic Powder Tower looms at the edge of Nám. Republiky as the entrance to Staré Město. It is one of the only remaining of the eight original city gates. After its stint as royal fortification, it was used primarily for gunpowder storage. A small history exhibit is inside, but forego it for a climb to the top. *(Metro B: Nám. Republiky. Open daily Apr.-Sept. 10am-6pm.)*

OLD TOWN HALL. (Staroměstská radnice). Next to the grassy knoll in Old Town Square, Old Town Hall is the multi-facaded building with the bit blown off the front. The building was partially demolished by the Nazis in the final week of WWII, receiving Prague's only visible damage from the war. You can see what's left of the pink facade jutting out from the tower. Prague's town hall has long been a witness to violence—crosses on the ground mark the spot where 27 Protestant leaders were executed on June 21, 1621 for staging a rebellion against the Catholic Habsburgs. The tourist office inside offers tours of the interior. The Old Senate boasts a Baroque stove with a figure of Justice and a sculpture of Christ. The inscription reads, "Judge justly, sons of Man." Crowds gather on the hour to watch the wonderful astronomical clock *(orloj)* chime with its procession of apostles, a skeleton, and a thwarted Turk. They say the clockmaker's eyes were put out so he couldn't design another—but they say that about the man who built St. Basil's in Moscow, too. The clock's animation is turned off nightly at 9pm. *(Metro A: Staroměstská; Metro A, B: Můstek. Town hall open summer daily 9am-5:30pm. 30Kč, students 15Kč.)*

A ROOM WITHOUT A VIEW At decisive points in European history, unlucky men tend to fall from Prague's window ledges. The Hussite wars began on July 30, 1419, after Catholic councillors were thrown to the mob from the New Town Hall on Karlovo nám. The Thirty Years' War devastated Europe, starting when Habsburg officials were tossed from the windows of Prague Castle's Bohemian Chancellery into a heap of steaming manure on May 23, 1618. These first and second defenestrations echo down the ages, but two more falls this century continue the macabre tradition. On March 10, 1948, liberal foreign minister Jan Masaryk fell to his death from the top floor of his ministry just two weeks after the Communist takeover; murder was always suspected, but never proven. On February 3, 1997, Bohumil Hrabal, age 82, popular author of *I Served the King of England* and *Closely-Observed Trains*, fell from the fifth floor of his hospital window and died in his pajamas. Nothing unusual here, except that two of his books describe people committing suicide—out of fifth-floor windows.

JAN HUS STATUE. The Czech Republic's most famous martyred theologian, Jan Hus hovers over Old Town Square in bronze effigy. Anguished figures bow beneath his commanding grandeur in reverence. In summer, masses of travelers sit at the base of his robes, drinking, smoking, sucking face, and performing a hundred other deeds upon which he can only frown.

TÝN CHURCH. (Matka Boží před Týnem). Across from Old Town Hall, the spires of Týn Church rise above a mass of medieval homes. The famous astronomer Tycho de Brahe is buried inside. He overindulged at one of Emperor Rudolf's lavish dinner parties, where it was unacceptable to leave the table unless the Emporer himself did so. When poor Tycho needed to go to the bathroom, he was forced to stay seated, and his bladder burst. Although the church is under restoration, you can catch a glimpse of its gold and black interior from the entrance.

GOLTZ-KINSKÝ PALACE. The flowery 14th-century Goltz-Kinský Palace is the finest of Prague's Rococo buildings. It is also the official birthplace of Soviet Communism in the Czech Republic: on February 21, 1948, Klement Gottwald declared Communism victorious from its balcony. *(At the corner of Staroměstské nám. and Dlouhá, next to Týn Church. Open Tu-F 10am-5pm; closes early in summer for daily concerts.)*

ST. JACOB'S CHURCH. (Kostel sv. Jakuba). A thief's arm has dangled from the entrance to St. Jacob's for 500 years. Legend has it that a thief tried to pilfer a gem from the Virgin Mary of Suffering, whereupon the figure came to life, seized the thief's arm, and wrenched it off. The monks took pity on the profusely bleeding soul and invited him to join their order. He accepted and remained pious; the arm hangs as a reminder to the faithful that Mary is not averse to the occasional steel-cage maneuver. *(Metro A, B: Můstek. On Malá Štupartská, behind Týn Church.)*

BETHLEHEM CHAPEL. (Betlémská kaple). Although the current Bethlehem Chapel dates from the 1950s, it is a surprisingly accurate reconstruction of the medieval chapel made famous by Jan Hus. *(Metro A, B: Můstek. From the Metro, walk down Národní třída toward the river and turn right on Na Perštýně; the Chapel is in Betlémské nám., which will appear on your left. Open daily 9am-6pm. 30Kč, students 20Kč.)*

JAN PALACH SQUARE. (Náměstí Jana Palacha). Originally called Red Army Square in honor of the Russians who liberated Prague in 1945, the square permanently changed names in 1990. During popular unrest in 1969 and then again in

November 1989, students renamed the square in honor of the late Jan Palach, who studied at Charles University here on the square before burning himself to death to protest the 1968 Soviet invasion. A copy of Palach's death mask is mounted on the faculty building wall.

CHARLES BRIDGE. (Karlův Most). Thronged with tourists and the hawkers who prey on them, the Charles Bridge is easily Prague's most recognizable landmark. King Charles IV built this 520m bridge to replace the Judith, the only bridge crossing the Vltava, which washed away in a 1342 flood. The smaller defense tower on the Malá Strana side of the bridge dates from the 12th century as part of Judith's original fortification. Legend has it that the builder made a pact with the devil in order to complete the massive replacement. Satan was allotted the first soul to cross the completed bridge; it happened to be the builder's wife and newborn baby. The devil could not take a pure soul, so he cast a spell over the bridge instead. In the evening, one can hear the faint cry of a ghostly infant—or is it the whining of prepubescent hostel youth? When darkness falls, the street musicians emerge, but the penalty for requesting "Wish You Were Here" is being tied up in goatskin and thrown into the Vltava. This happened to St. Jan Nepomuk, although for a different reason: at the center of the bridge, the eighth statue from the right is a depiction of hapless Jan being tossed over the side of the Charles for faithfully guarding his queen's extramarital secrets from a suspicious King Wenceslas IV. Torture by hot irons and other devices failed to loosen Jan's lips, so the King ordered that he be drowned. A halo of five gold stars appeared as Jan plunged into the icy water. The right-hand rail, from which Jan was supposedly ejected, is now marked with a cross and five stars between the fifth and sixth statues. Place one finger on each star and make a wish: not only is it guaranteed to come true, but any wish made on this spot guarantees the wisher a return to Prague.

JOSEFOV

Metro A: Staroměstská. Tel. 231 71 91. Synagogues and museum open M-F and Su 9am-6pm. Closed Jewish holidays. Admission to all sights except Staronová Synagogue 450Kč, students 330Kč, children under 6 free. Staronová Synagogue 200Kč, students 140Kč, children under 6 free. Admission to museum only 250Kč, students 190Kč, children under 6 free.

Prague's historic Jewish neighborhood and the oldest Jewish settlement in Europe, Josefov is north of Starométstské nám., along Maiselova and several side streets. Its cultural wealth lies in five well-preserved synagogues. In 1179, the Pope decreed that all good Christians should avoid contact with Jews; a year later, Prague's citizens complied with a 12-foot wall. The gates were opened in 1784, and the walls came down in 1848, when the Jews were granted limited civil rights. The closed city bred exotic legends, many focusing on **Rabbi Loew ben Bezalel** (1512-1609), whose legendary *golem*—a creature made from mud that supposedly came to life to protect Prague's Jews—predates Frankenstein's monster by 200 years. Rabbi Loew lived at Široká 90, now a private residence. For the next 500 years, the city's Jews were exiled to this cramped ghetto. The century following 1848 was not a happy one for Prague's Jews. The open quarter rapidly became a disease-racked slum, and many old buildings were demolished as the area was modernized. Finally, the Nazis deported the Jewish people to Terezín and then to death camps. Hitler's decision to create a "museum of an extinct race" resulted in the preservation of Josefov's old Jewish cemetery and five of the synagogues.

MAISEL SYNAGOGU. (Maiselova synagoga). This synagogue exhibits treasures from the extensive collections of the Jewish Museum—returned to the city's Jewish community only in 1994. The introductory section serves as a good primer on the history of Czech Jews and their status in the medieval state; it makes a logical starting point for a tour of Josefov. *(On Maiselova, between Široká and Jáchymova.)*

PINKAS SYNAGOGUE. (Pinkasova synagoga). Built in the 1530s for the wealthy Pinkas family, the Pinkas Synagogue was converted in 1958 into a sobering memorial to the 77,000 Czech Jews killed in the Holocaust. After a period of Communist neglect, the synagogue reopened as a memorial in 1991, its walls once again listing the names of victims of Nazi persecution; the memorial is the longest epitaph in the world. *(On Široka, between Žatecká and 17. listopadu.)*

OLD JEWISH CEMETERY. (Starý Židovský hřbitov). This cemetery remains Josefov's most popular attraction. Between the 14th and 18th centuries, 20,000 graves were laid in 12 layers. The striking clusters of tombstones result from a process in which the older stones were lifted up from underneath. Rabbi Loew is buried by the wall directly opposite the entrance. *(At the corner of Široká and Žatecká.)*

OLD-NEW SYNAGOGUE. (Staronová synagoga). The oldest operating synagogue in Europe and the earliest Gothic structure in Prague, the 700-year-old Old-New Synagogue is still the religious center for Prague's Orthodox Jewish community. Behind the iron gates of the *bimah* flies a tattered remnant of the original Star of David flag flown by the congregation in 1357 when Charles IV allowed them to display their own municipal standard; Prague's Jews were the first to adopt the Star of David as their official symbol. *(On the corner of Maiselova and Pařížká.)*

CEREMONY HALL. (Obřadní dům). Originally a ceremonial hall for the Jewish Burial Society, Ceremony Hall now houses two permanent exhibits. The first is devoted to the themes of illness and medicine in the ghetto, Jewish cemeteries in Bohemia and Moravia, and the activities of the Prague Burial Society. The second is the world-renowned exhibit, "Children's Drawings from Terezín: 1942-44"; most of the artists died at Auschwitz. *(On Červená, just off Maiselova.)*

KLAUS SYNAGOGUE. (Klausová synagoga). Built in the 1690s in a notorious red-light district, Klaus now displays rotating exhibits on Judaica and has in-depth explanations of Jewish traditions. *(Next to Ceremony Hall on Červená, just off Maiselova.)*

JEWISH TOWN HALL. (Židovská radnice). Once the administrative control center of Josefov, the Jewish Town Hall is one of the few Jewish administrative centers in Europe to survive WWII. The Hebrew clock in the pink Rococo exterior of the town hall runs counterclockwise. On the other side of the building, a statue of Moses by František Bílek (himself a Protestant) was hidden from the Nazis during the war. *(Next to the Old-New Synagogue, on the corner of Maiselova and Červená.)*

HIGH SYNAGOGUE. (Vysoká synagoga). Now a working synagogue closed to the public, this 16th-century synagogue housed massive collections of textiles and Judaica during the war for Hitler's "museum of an extinct race." *(On Červená.)*

SPANISH SYNAGOGUE. (Španělská synagoga). The most ornate synagogue, the Moorish interior of the Spanish Synagogue was modeled after the Alhambra. It displays a history of Czech Jews since WWII. *(On the corner of Široká and Dušní.)*

MALÁ STRANA

The seedy hangout of criminals and counter-revolutionaries for nearly a century, the cobblestoned streets of Malá Strana have become the most prized real estate on either side of the Vltava. Yuppies now dream of a flat with a view of St. Nicholas' Cathedral, and affluent foreigners sip beer where Jaroslav Hašek and his bumbling soldier Švejk once guzzled suds (see **Food,** p. 193). The current trend seems to fit the plans of the original designer, King Přemysl Otakar II, who in the 13th century dreamed of creating a powerful economic quarter. This was not to occur until the 15th century, when Austrian nobility erected grand churches and palaces. As nationalism mounted, however, the quarter became known as a rat's den of surly sailors, rotten dealers, and drunken brawls. The 1989 revolution brought a new appreciation for the district's architecture, and careful restorations have made it one of the most enjoyable sections of Prague to visit.

ST. NICHOLAS' CATHEDRAL. (Chrám sv. Mikuláš). The Malá Strana is centered around **Malostranské nám.** and its centerpiece, the Baroque St. Nicholas' Cathedral, whose towering dome is one of Prague's most notable landmarks. The father-son team of Kristof and Kilian Ignaz Dienzenhofer, creators of the small Church of St. Nicholas in Staré Město and the Břevnov Monastery (see **Outer Prague,** p. 203) near Hradčany, built St. Nicholas' Cathedral as their crowning glory. Expensive and boring classical music concerts take place nightly. *(Metro A: Malostranská. Follow Letenská from the Metro to Malostranské nám. Tel. 53 69 83. Open daily 9am-4:30pm. 30Kč, students 15Kč. Concert tickets an unholy 390Kč, students 290Kč.)*

WALLENSTEIN GARDEN. (Valdštejnská zahrada). A simple wooden gate opens through a 10m wall into the Wallenstein Garden, one of Prague's best-kept secrets. This tranquil, 17th-century Baroque garden is enclosed by old buildings that glow golden on sunny afternoons. General Albert Wallenstein, owner of the palace of the same name and hero of Schiller's grim plays (the *Wallenstein* cycle), held parties here among Vredeman de Vries's classical bronze statues. When the works were plundered by Swedish troops in the waning hours of the Thirty Years' War, Wallenstein replaced the original casts with facsimiles. Frescoes inside the arcaded loggia depict episodes from Virgil's *Aeneid*. *(Letenská 10. Metro A: Malostranská. Open May-Sept. daily 9am-7pm; Mar. 21-Apr. 30 and Oct. daily 10am-6pm.)*

CHAROUSKOVÁ MEMORIAL. Across the street from the Malostranská Metro station, a plaque hidden in a lawn constitutes the Charousková Memorial, the sole monument to those slain in the 1968 Prague Spring. It commemorates **Marie Charousková,** a graduate student who was machine-gunned by a Soviet soldier for refusing to remove a black ribbon protesting the invasion.

JOHN LENNON WALL. Hidden on Hroznová, a tiny street on Kampa Island, is a 1990s version of the infamous John Lennon Wall. Until summer 1998, the mural was a crumbling memorial to John Lennon and the 1960s global peace movement. Once interesting when the authorities kept trying to suppress it, it had fallen into disarray and was plagued by unimaginative graffiti. In summer 1998, the wall was white-washed, and is now covered with a pre-fab portrait of John Lennon and even less imaginative tourist graffiti. *(Metro A: Malostranská From the Metro, walk down U Lužického semínaře to the Charles Bridge. Once on the bridge, descend the small stairs to the right.)*

CHURCH OF OUR LADY VICTORIOUS. (Kostel Panna Marie Vítězná). The modest Church of Our Lady Victorious is not notable for its exterior. Instead, the famous polished-wax statue of the **Infant Jesus of Prague,** said to bestow miracles on the faithful, resides within. The figurine has a wardrobe of more than 380 outfits; every sunrise, he's swaddled anew by the nuns of a nearby convent. The statue first arrived in town in the arms of a 16th-century Spanish noblewoman who married into the Bohemian royalty; mysteriously, the plague bypassed Prague shortly thereafter. In 1628, the Carmelite abbey gained custody of the Infant and allowed pilgrims to pray to the statue; the public has been infatuated ever since. *(Metro A: Malostranská. Follow Letecká from the Metro through Malostranské nám., and continue onto Karmelitská; the church is on your right. Open daily summer 7am-9pm; off-season 8am-8pm.)*

PETŘÍN HILL AND GARDENS. (Petřínské sady). Petřín Gardens, the largest in Prague, provide some of the most spectacular views of the city. A cable car runs to the top (8Kč; look for *lanová dráha* signs), leaving from just above the intersection of Vítězná and Újezd. It stops once along the way to deposit visitors at **Nebozízek,** Prague's most scenically endowed cafe. *(Open daily 11am-6pm and 7-11pm.)* A bag of goodies stands at the summit: a small Eiffel tower; the city's observatory; the **church of St. Lawrence;** and the wacky labyrinth of mirrors at **Bludiště.** *(Tel. 57 32 05 40. Open Tu-Su 10am-7pm. 20Kč, students and children 10Kč.)* Just east of the park is Strahov Stadium, the world's largest, covering the space of 10 soccer fields.

PRAGUE CASTLE (PRAŽSKÝ HRAD)

Metro A: Hradčanská. Tel. 24 37 11 11. Open daily Apr.-June 9am-5pm; Sept.-Mar. 9am-4pm. Ticket office across from St. Vitus' Cathedral, inside the castle walls. Ticket—valid for 3 days—good for admission to the Royal Crypt, Cathedral Tower, Old Royal Palace, Powder Tower, and Basilica of St. George. 120Kč, students 60Kč.

Founded 1000 years ago, Prague Castle has always been the seat of the Bohemian government and the center of its politics. For centuries, conflicts between medieval dynasties, Czechs and Germans, or Protestants and Catholics have played out within—sometimes plummeting down beside—its walls. This century, liberal presidents, Nazi despots, and communist apparatchiks have all held court here. The final ideological struggle saw the socialists replaced by playwright Václav Havel, who has been known to ride his scooter along the castle's corridors.

ENTERING THE CASTLE. Cross the tram tracks and turn left onto Tychonova, which leads to the glorious and newly renovated **Royal Summer Palace** (Královský letohrádek). This is the purest example of southern Renaissance architecture outside Italy. In front of the palace, leading the way to the serene and shady 1534 **Royal Garden** (Královská zahrada), is the **Singing Fountain.** Follow the hordes of schoolchildren and put your head under the fountain to hear the chiming water. Devas-

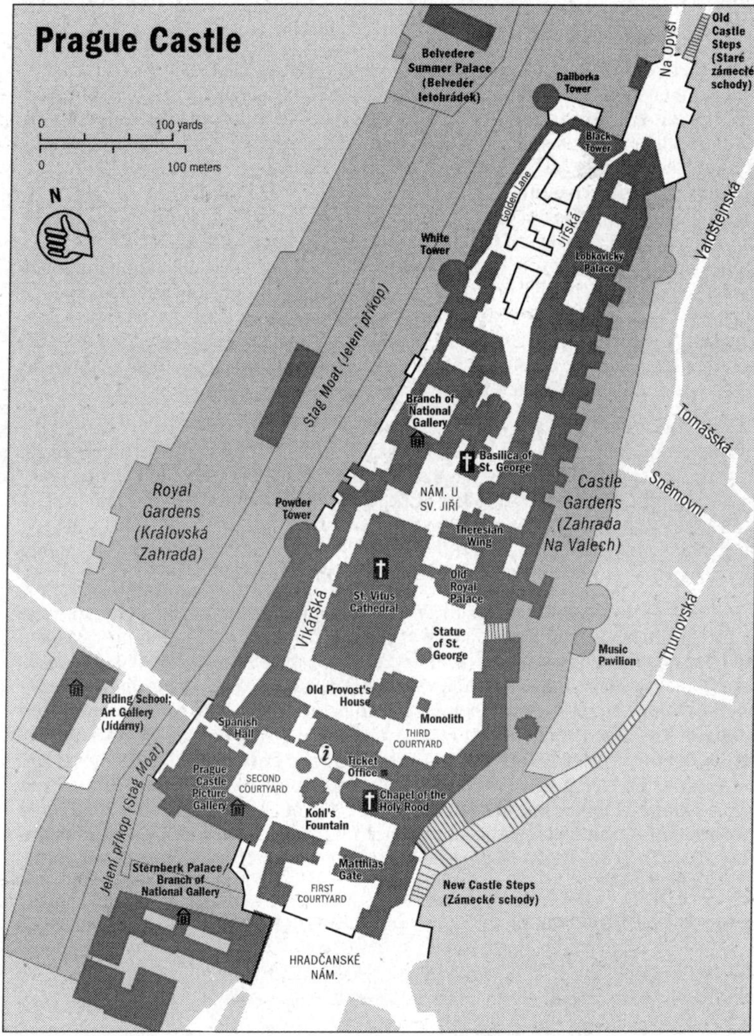

CZECH REPUBLIC

tated by Swedes and Saxons during the Thirty Years' War, the garden houses an **Orangery** and a **Fig Garden** today (both closed to the public). The **castle entrance** is at the other end of the garden across the **Powder Bridge** (Prašný most).

ŠTERNBERSKY PALACE. Before touring the castle, pass through the main gate to explore the Šternberský Palace, home of the National Gallery's European art collection. The gems include an 1815 Goya and three Rubens, including a fine *Visitation*. Willem Droost's *Annunciation* was formerly attributed to Rembrandt on the not unreasonable grounds that it bore his signature; a genuine Rembrandt is in the next room. *(Tel. 20 51 45 99. Open Tu-Su 10am-6pm. 45Kč, students 25Kč.)*

ST. VITUS' CATHEDRAL. (Katedrála sv. Víta). Inside the castle walls stands Prague Castle's centerpiece, the colossal St. Vitus' Cathedral, which may look Gothic but in fact was only finished in 1929—600 years after construction began. The cathedral's stained-glass windows were created by some of the most gifted Czech artists—Alphonse Mucha's brilliant depiction of Sts. Ludmila and Wenceslas is the most recognizable. To the right of the high altar stands the **tomb of sv. Jan Nepomuc,** 3m of solid, glistening silver, weighing in at 1800kg. Look for an angel holding a silvered tongue—Jan was allegedly tied in a goatskin and chucked into the Vltava for refusing to betray the Queen's confidences (see **Charles Bridge,** p. 198). His tongue was somehow recovered and eventually silvered. The story was declared false in 1961, but the tongue is still on display. Emperor Karel IV has his own bridge, university, and fortress (at Karlštejn)—but his tomb is in the **Royal Crypt** below the church along with a handful of other Czech kings and all four of his wives, who are tactfully buried in the same grave to his left. Back up the stairs in the main church, the walls of **St. Wenceslas's Chapel** (Svatováclavská kaple) are lined with precious stones and a painting cycle depicting the legend of this saint. In an adjoining but inaccessible room, the real crown jewels of the kings of Bohemia are stored. More superstition claims that people who try them on inappropriately meet sticky ends. The last to do so was Hitler's *Reichs-Protektor* Reinhard Heydrich, later assassinated by the Czech resistance. Finally, if you have mountain goat thighs, climb the 287 steps of the **Cathedral Tower** to the city's best view.

OLD ROYAL PALACE. (Starý královský palác).The Old Royal Palace, to the right of the cathedral behind the Old Provost's House and the statue of St. George, houses the lengthy expanse of the **Vladislav Hall,** which once hosted jousting competitions; upstairs is the **Chancellery of Bohemia,** the site of the Second Defenestration of Prague (see **A Room Without a View,** p. 197). On May 23, 1618, angry Protestants flung two Habsburg officials through the windows and into a steaming dungheap that broke their fall, triggering the Thirty Years' War.

ST. GEORGE'S BASILICA. (Bazilika sv. Jiří). Behind the cathedral and across the courtyard from the Old Royal Palace stand the Romanesque St. George's Basilica and its adjacent convent. The basilica was built in 921; in its right-hand corner you'll find the tomb of St. Ludmila, with skeleton on display. A mason who stole the thighbone supposedly activated a vicious curse that killed three before the mason's son restored the bone to the grave. The convent houses the **National Gallery of Bohemian Art,** with art ranging from Gothic to Baroque. In the medieval galleries, Master Theodorik's ecclesiastical portraits, the relief from *Matka Boží před Týnem*, and the so-called Kapucínský cycle of Christ and the apostles stand out; upstairs, paintings by Michael Leopold Willmann (1630-1706) warrant scrutiny. *(Open Tu-Su 10am-6pm. 50Kč, students and seniors 15Kč. Free 1st Friday of each month.)*

GOLDEN LANE. (Zlatá ulička).The palace street Jiřská begins to the right of the basilica. Halfway down, the tiny and colorful Golden Lane heads off to the right. Alchemists once worked here, Kafka later lived at #22, and today there is a small forest of cramped souvenir shops for tourists to squeeze in and out of. Above the souvenir shops is a hallway displaying replicas of the Bohemian court's armory; at its end, you can take three shots with a crossbow for 50Kč.

LEAVING THE CASTLE. Back on Jiřská, the **Lobkovický Palace** contains a replica of Bohemia's coronation jewels and a history of the Czech lands. *(Open Tu-Su 10am-6pm. 40Kč, students 20Kč.)* At the end of the street is the **Museum of Toys.** *(Tel. 24 37 22 94. Open daily 10am-6pm. 40Kč, students and children 15Kč.)* After passing between the two armed sentries out of the castle, peer over the battlements on the right for a fine cityscape, then descend the **Old Castle Steps** (Staré zámecké schody).

OUTER PRAGUE

If you have more than two days in Prague, explore the city's outskirts to find greenery, nifty churches, and panoramic vistas, all hidden from the tourist hordes.

BŘEVNOV MONASTERY. Bohemia's oldest Benedictine order, Břevnov Monastery was founded in 993 by King Boleslav II and St. Adalbert, each independently guided by a divine dream to create a monastery atop a bubbling stream. **St. Margaret's Church** (Kostel sv. Markéty), a Benedictine chapel, waits inside the complex. Beneath the altar rests the tomb of St. Vintíř, who, even in Bohemia, vowed to forego all forms of meat. Czechs claim that on one particular diplomatic excursion, St. Vintíř met and dined with a German king, who was a fanatical hunter; the main course was an enormous pheasant slain that morning by the monarch's own hand. The saint prayed for deliverance from the myriad *faux pas* possibilities, whereupon the main course sprang to life and flew out the window. The green belltower and red tile roof of the monastery building are all that remain of the original Romanesque construction; the complex was redesigned in high Baroque by the Dienzenhofers. During the Soviet occupation, the monastery was allegedly used to store truckloads of secret police files. *(From Mariánské hradby, the street beside the royal summer palace, take tram #22 west of the castle toward Bílá Hora to Břevnovský klášter. Guided tours set off Sa 9am, Sa-Su 10:30am, 1pm, 2:30pm, and 4pm. 40Kč.)*

TROJA. Troja is the site of French architect J. B. Mathey's masterful **château.** The pleasure palace, overlooking the Vltava from north of the U-shaped bend, includes a terraced garden, an oval staircase, and a collection of 19th-century Czech artwork. The tourist office carries schedules of **free concerts** in the château's great hall. *(Bus #112 winds from Metro C: Nádraží Holešovice. Open Tu-Su 9am-5pm.)*

VYŠEHRAD. The former haunt of Prague's 19th-century Romantics, Vyšehrad is a storehouse of nationalistic myths and imperial legends. It was here that Countess Libuše prophesied the founding of Prague and embarked on her search for the first king of Bohemia. The 20th century has passed the castle by, and Vyšehrad's elevated pathways now escape the throngs of Staré Město. Quiet walkways still wind between crumbling stone walls to a magnificent **church,** a black Romanesque rotunda, and one of the Czech Republic's most celebrated sites—**Vyšehrad Cemetery** (home to the **remains of Dvořák** and Božena Němcová of the 500Kč bill). Even the Metro C: Vyšehrad subway stop has a movie-sweep vista of Prague. *(Open 24hr.)*

VÍTKOV. For a magnificent view of Staré Město and the castle, stroll up forested Vítkov Hill, topped by the world's largest equestrian monument. One-eyed Hussite leader Jan Žižka scans the terrain for Crusaders, whom he stomped out on this spot in 1420. *(From Metro B: Křižíkova, walk down Thámova, through the tunnel, and up the hill.)*

NEW JEWISH CEMETERY. Although less a pilgrimage destination than the Old Jewish Cemetery, the New Jewish Cemetery, far to the southeast, is one of Central Europe's largest burial grounds. **Kafka** is interred here; obtain a map and, if you're male, a mandatory head covering from the attendant before you start hunting for the tombstone. *(Enter at Metro A: Želivského. Open Su-Th 9am-5pm, F 9am-1pm. Free.)*

MUSEUMS

Prague's magnificence is not harbored in her museums, which often have striking facades and mediocre collections; if the weather's good, stick to the streets. But the city is victim to many rainy days, and does have quite a few museums sheltering interesting and quirky collections. Additionally, private galleries along the side streets off Národní třída and Staroměstské nám. exhibit the works of local artists.

House of the Golden Ring (Dům u zlatého prstenu), Týnská 6 (tel. 24 82 80 04). Metro A: Staroměstská. Behind Týn Church. An astounding collection of 20th-century Czech art, curated by a refreshingly liberal gallery that emphasizes installations and technological art. Four floors, each with a separate theme; while the second floor exhibit, "In the Distorted Mirror and Behind the Mirror," might sound like the most interesting exhibit, but the basement collection of 1990s Czech art is the museum's must-see. Open Tu-Su 10am-6pm. 100Kč, students 50Kč; free first Tuesday of the month.

National Gallery (Národní galerie): Spread around nine different locations; the notable **Šternberský palác** and **Klášter sv. Jiří** are described above in the **Prague Castle** (see p. 201). The two listed below are open Tu-W and F-Su 10am-6pm, Th 10am-9pm. 70Kč, students 40Kč. All museums also carry a pamphlet describing the collections of the other galleries, which are in suburban Prague and not worth the trek.

Trade Fair Palace and the Gallery of Modern Art (Veletržní palác a Galerie moderního umění), Dukelských hrdinů 47 (tel. 24 30 11 11). Metro C: Vltavská. Displays the National Gallery's impressive collection of 20th-century Czech art. The seven-story functionalist building is almost as stunning as the art inside; even Le Corbusier approved.

St. Agnes's Cloister (Klášter sv. Anežky), U milosrdných 17 (tel. 24 81 06 28). Metro A: Staroměstská. Very much worth seeing for its collection of 19th-century Czech art.

Czech Museum of Fine Arts (České muzeum výtvarných umění), Celetná 34 (tel. 24 21 17 31). Metro A: Nám. Republiky. The building itself, the House of the Black Madonna (Dům u Černé matky boží), is one of Prague's finest examples of Cubist architecture. The collection continues with the theme, devoting two floors to a surprisingly comprehensive collection of Czech Cubism. The downstairs gallery hosts rotating exhibits of Western European Modernists. Open Tu-Su 10am-6pm. 25Kč, students 10Kč.

Museum of Medieval Torture Instruments, Karlova 2, across the street from the Charles Bridge. Metro A: Staroměstská. Not for the weak of stomach. Collection highlights include: the Head Crusher, thumbscrews, iron gag, Spanish tickle torture, and the Masks of Shame and Infamy. All accompanied by highly-detailed explanations guaranteed to nauseate. Open daily 10am-10pm. 100Kč, students 80Kč.

Mucha Museum, Panská 7. Metro A, B: Můstek. From the Metro, walk up Václavské nám. toward the St. Wenceslas statue. Turn left onto Jindřišská, then left onto Panská. Boasts the only collection devoted entirely to the work of Alfons Mucha, the Czech Republic's most celebrated artist. Collection includes his Paris works as well as his sketchbooks and furniture. Open daily 10am-6pm. 120Kč, students and children 6-15 60Kč.

Rudolfinum, Alšovo náb,. 12 (tel. 24 89 32 05). Metro A: Staroměstská. The entrance faces the river. The Czech Philharmonic shares the building with one of Prague's oldest galleries. Rotating art exhibits in a huge Art Nouveau interior. The cafe at the end seems too elegant to be self-serve. Open July-May Tu-Su 10am-6pm. 60Kč, students 30Kč.

Bertramka Mozart muzeum, Mozartova 169 (tel. 543 893). Metro B: Anděl. Take a left on Plzeňská, and look for a green sign pointing up the slope to the 3rd street on the left. Mozart, a guest at Villa Bertramka, dashed off the overture to *Don Giovanni* here the day before it opened in 1787. Open Tu-Su 9:30am-6pm; Nov-Mar. 9:30am-5pm. 50Kč, students 30Kč. Concerts W-F in summer. The gardens are free.

Municipal Museum of Prague (Muzeum hlavního města Prahy), Na poříčí 52 (tel. 24 81 67 72). Metro B, C: Florenc. In the park. Holds the original calendar board from the town hall's astronomical clock and a 1:480 scale model of old Prague, precise to the last window pane of more than 2000 houses and all of Prague's monuments. See what your hostel looked like in 1834. Borrow an English guidebook (100Kč) to walk through the fine historical galleries. Open Tu-Su 9am-6pm. 30Kč, students 15Kč.

Monument to National Literature (Památník národního písemnictví), Strahovské nádvoří 1 (tel. 816 772). Metro A: Hradčanská. From the Metro, take tram #8 toward Bílá Hora to Malovanka. Turn around, follow the tram #22 tracks, then turn right onto Strahovská. The museum is inside the monastery on the left. The star attraction here is the **Strahov**

library, with its magnificent **Theological and Philosophical Halls.** The frescoed, vaulted ceilings of the two Baroque reading rooms were intended to spur monks to the loftiest peaks of erudition. Great pagan thinkers of antiquity oversee their progress from the ceiling in the Philosophical Hall. Open Tu-Su 9am-5pm. 15Kč, students 5Kč.

ENTERTAINMENT

For a list of current concerts and performances, consult *The Prague Post*, *Threshold*, or *Do města-Downtown* (the latter two are free and distributed at many cafes and restaurants). Most performances begin at 7pm; unsold tickets are sometimes available 30min. before showtime. Most of Prague's theaters shut down in July and return in August to provide tourists with re-runs. The selection is more varied the rest of the year, peaking between mid-May and early June when the **Prague Spring Festival** draws musicians from around the world. Tickets (300-2000Kč) may sell out as far as a year in advance; try **Bohemia Ticket International,** Malé nám. 13 (tel. 24 22 78 32; fax 21 61 21 26), next to Čedok. (Open M-F 9am-6pm, Sa 9am-4pm, Su 10am-3pm.) **Národní divadlo, Stavovské divadlo,** and **Státní opera** all stage operas; while performances rarely scintillate, the staggeringly low prices do. **Cinemas** abound, showing English-language blockbusters six months to a year after release. Prices depend on the movie's popularity; ask at a tourist office for a list of current films. The **Kino Cafe-bar,** Karlovo nám. 19 (entry on Odborů; tel. 24 91 57 65), shows Czech films with English subtitles. (Tickets 50-60Kč.)

Národní divadlo (National Theater), Národní třída 2/4 (tel. 24 90 14 19). Metro B: Národní třída. Features theater, opera, and ballet. Tickets 100-1000Kč. Box office open M-F 10am-6pm, Sa-Su 10am-12:30pm and 3-6pm, and 30min. before performances.

Stavovské divadlo (Estates Theater), Ovocný trh 1 (tel. 24 91 34 37). Metro A, B: Můstek. Left from the pedestrian Na Příkopě. This is where *Don Giovanni* premiered all those years ago; it performs mostly classic theater now. Some opera and ballet. Use the Národní divadlo box office, above, or turn up 30min. before the show to try your luck.

Státní opera (State Opera), Wilsonova 4 (tel. 265 353). Metro A, C: Muzeum. Tickets 50-600Kč. Box office open M-F 10am-4pm, Sa-Su 10am-noon and 1-4pm.

Misery Loves Company, Celetná 17 (tel. 24 81 27 62). Metro B: Nám. Republiky. Walk under the Powder Tower, then left on Celetná. Inside Divadlo v Celetné. Tiny troupe puts on astonishingly good English-language productions. Tickets 50-200Kč. Call for schedule and tickets. Box office open 2-5:30pm on performance days.

Říše loutek (Marionette Theater), Žatecká 1 (tel. 232 34 29 or 232 25 36; fax 232 41 89). Metro A: Staroměstská. On the corner of Žalecká and Mariánské nám. Puppetry is taken seriously in the Czech Republic and isn't just for kids. The touristy-but-amusing version of *Don Giovanni* has become a Prague stand-by. Tickets 490Kč, students 390Kč. June performances Th-Tu 8pm; July daily 8pm. Box office open 10am-8pm.

NIGHTLIFE

The most authentic way to experience Prague at night is through an alcoholic fog. With some of the best beers in the world on tap, pubs and beer halls are understandably the city's favorite form of nighttime entertainment. These days, however, authentic pub experiences are restricted to the suburbs and outlying Metro stops; within central Prague, nearly everything has been overtaken by tourists. Irish pubs and American sports bars are cropping up everywhere, with appropriately high prices for their foreign beers (but who comes to Prague to drink Guinness?). There are a few trusty Czech pubs scattered throughout Staré Město and Malá Strana to ease the offensive sting of Jo's Bar and Garáž and T.G.I. Friday's.

Prague is not a clubbing city, although there are enough dance clubs pumping out techno to sweaty hordes to satisfy Eurotrash club scene cravings. More popular among Czechs are the city's many jazz and rock clubs, hosting excellent local

PRAGUE SCARRED ME FOR LIFE After your all-too-short stay in Prague, it's only natural to want to hold onto your memories forever. But photos fade and journals get lost. So what better way to commemorate the city of a thousand spires than putting a pointy metal implement to your body? Tattoo and piercing parlors are all the rage in the capital, and the following speak English and have very sanitary facilities: **Alien Tattoo & Piercing,** at Jilká 22 (tel. 24 23 57 66; open daily 10am-7pm.); **Tom Millhouse Tattoo & Piercing,** Spálená 31 (tel. 29 86 92; open M-Sa noon-10pm); **Primal Arts Tattoo,** Nerudova 32 (tel. 57 31 09 63).

and international acts. Otherwise, you can always retreat to the Charles Bridge to sing along with aspiring Britpop guitarists. Whichever way you indulge in Prague nightlife, swig down a few pints of *pivo*, grab some 4am snacks (see **Late Night Eating,** p. 193), and at least once, forego the night bus for the morning Metro, joining bleary-eyed Czech coeds in their scandalization of the city's hard-working adults.

BEERHALLS & WINE CELLARS

U Fleků, Křemencova 11 (tel. 24 91 51 18). Metro B: Národní třída. Turn right onto Spálená, away from Národní, then right onto Myslíkova and right again onto Křemencova; the beer hall is on the left. Founded in 1491, this is the oldest surviving brewhouse in Prague. The bands play "Roll out the Barrel" nightly. The 50Kč per 0.4L of home-brewed beer. Open daily 9am-11pm.

Vinárna U Sude, Vodičkova 10 (tel. 16 07 31 93). Metro A: Můstek. Cross over Václavské nám. to Vodičkova, and follow it as it curves left. The bar is on your left. Virtually undiscovered by tourists, this Moravian wine bar looks rather quotidian from its entrance and first floor, but beneath the veneer sprawls an infinite labyrinth of cavernous cellars, each with its own mood lighting. A liter of smooth red (100Kč) goes down frighteningly fast. Open M-F 11am-midnight, Sa-Su 2pm-midnight.

Pivnice u Sv. Tomáše, Letenská 12 (tel. 57 32 01 01). Metro A: Malostranská. The mighty dungeons echo with boisterous beer songs and slobbering toasts. The homemade brew is 30Kč. Live brass band plays nightly 7pm. Open daily 11:30am-midnight.

BARS

Kozička, Kozí 1 (tel. 24 81 83 08). Metro A: Staroměstská. Take Dlouhá from the square's northeast corner; the street becomes Kozí after veering to the right. Giant cellar bar is always packed, and you'll know why after your 1st *Krušovice* (25Kč). Twenty-something Czechs come early and stay all night. Open M-F noon-4am, Sa-Su 4pm-4am.

Terminal Bar, Soukenická 6 (tel. 21 87 11 15). Metro B: Nám. Republiky. A multimedia bar with style, this bar/cafe features superfast computers (120Kč per hr.), good coffee (20Kč), a downstairs bookstore, live music on weekends, a new sushi bar, and electronic music. You'll might even forget you came to check email. Open daily 11am-1am.

Cafe Marquis de Sade, a.k.a. **Cafe Babylon,** Templová 8 (cellular tel. (0602) 25 59 37), between Nám. Republiky and Staroměstské nám. Metro B: Nám. Republiky. A giant bar full of fresh air and red velvet couches. Although not very sadistic, mannequins, monkeys, and masks fill the walls. When the band is in full form, it plays 80s pop; on better nights, jazz. Beer 25Kč. Open M-F noon-2am, Sa-Su 3pm-2am.

Žíznivý pes (Thirsty Dog), El. Krásnohorské 1. Metro A: Staroměstská. Walk up Pařížská, the street next to St. Nicholas' Church. Go right on Široká, then left on Krásnohorské. The inspiration for the Nick Cave song, this bar is the watering hole for crazy ex-pats and a few crazy Czechs. Indie rock played *loud*. Open M-Th 11am-1am, F-Sa 11am-2am.

Újezd, Újezd 18 (tel. 53 83 62). Metro B: Národní třída. Exit the Metro onto Národní and turn left toward the river. Cross the Legií bridge, continue straight on Vítězná, and turn right onto Újezd; the bar is on your right. A mid-20s crowd smokes the night away at this mecca of mellowness—a giant mushroom chandelier hangs above the bar. DJ or live acid jazz three times a week. 0.5L *Budvar* a mere 20Kč. Open nightly 6pm-4am.

Zanzibar, on Saská. Metro A: Malostranská. From the square, head down Nostecká toward the Charles Bridge, turn right on Lázeňská, and turn left on Saská. The classiest place to see and be seen among Czech coeds. Among the most extensive (and priciest) cocktails this side of the Vltava. Huge mixed drinks 120-130Kč. Open daily 5pm-3am.

Molly Malone's, U obecního dvora 4. Metro A: Staroměstská. Turn right onto Křižonvická, away from the Charles Bridge. After Nám. Jana Palacha, turn right onto Široká, which becomes Vězeňská; at its end, turn left. The Irish prove they're the most fun at this cozy bar, where overturned beds and sewing machines double as tables. A pint of Guinness is cheaper than in Ireland at 70Kč. Open M-Th and Su noon-1am, F-Sa noon-2am.

Jáma (The Hollow), V jámě 7 (tel. 24 22 23 83). Metro A, C: Muzeum. Hidden off Vodičkova. The closest thing Prague has to a real sports bar, Jáma attracts a diverse but largely foreign crowd. Watch American sporting events live via satellite with *Staropramen* (25Kč) in hand. Happy hour 3-6pm. Open daily 11am-1am.

Jo's Bar and Garáž, Malostranské nám. 7. Metro A: Malostranská. If you can't bear the idea that the people at the next table might not speak English, all-American Jo's Bar may be for you. Other guides say this imported Long Island frat party is where the *Let's Go*-toting summer crowds come. We like to think you're more adventurous than that. Very small *Staropramen* 25Kč. Long Island iced tea 95Kč. Cuban cigars 90-490Kč.

CLUBS & DISCOS

Roxy, Dlouhá 33 (tel. 231 63 31). Metro B: Nám. Republiky. Walk up Revoluční to the river; go left on Dlouhá. Hip locals and in-the-know tourists come here for experimental DJs, theme nights, and endless dancing. Cover 50Kč. Open Tu-Su 8pm until late.

Radost FX, Bělehradská 120 (tel. 25 69 98). Metro C: I.P. Pavlova. Heavily touristed, but still plays bad-ass techno, jungle, and house music. *Staropramen* 35Kč. Cover from 50Kč. The vegetarian restaurant upstairs serves chili until 5am (95Kč) and has English poetry readings on Sunday nights. Open nightly 8pm-dawn.

Palác Akropolis, Kubelíkova 27 (tel. 697 64 11). Metro A: Jiřího z Poděbrad, then down Slavíkova and right onto Kubelíkova. Live bands several times a week; doors open at 7:30pm. Top Czech act Psí vojáci are occasional visitors.

Lávka, Novotného lávka 1 (tel. 24 21 47 97). Tourists from around the world make Prague memories under the Charles Bridge. Otherwise devoid of character. The fluorescent disco downstairs pops eyeballs. Cover from 50Kč. Open nightly 10pm-5am.

JAZZ CLUBS

U staré paní, Michalská 9 (tel. 24 23 06 71). Metro A, B: Můstek. Walk down Na můstku at the end of Václavské nám. through its name change to Melantrichova. Turn left on Havelská and right on Michalská. "The Old Lady's Place" showcases some of the finest jazz vocalists in Prague in a tiny, dark, and classy upstairs venue. Shows nightly 9pm-midnight. Cover 160Kč, includes a free drink. Open daily 7pm-4am.

ABSINTHE MAKES THE HEART GROW FOND

Shrouded in Bohemian mystique and taboo, this translucent turquoise fire water is a force to be reckoned with. Despite being banned in all but three countries this century due to allegations of opium-lacing and fatal hallucinations, Czechs have had a long love affair with absinthe. It has been the mainstay spirit of the Prague intelligentsia since Kafka's days, and during WWII every Czech adult was rationed a half-liter of it per month. Today, backpackers (who apparently will drink anything) have discovered the liquor, which at its strongest can be 160 proof. The bravest and most seasoned ex-pats sip it on the rocks, but for the most snapshot-worthy ritual douse a spoonful of sugar in the alcohol, torch it with a match until the sugar caramelizes and the alcohol burns off, and dump the residue into your glass.

U malého Glena II, Karmelitská 23 (tel. 535 81 15), the basement club of "U malého Glena" (see **Cafes,** p. 194). This small bar hosts bouncy jazz or white blues from Stan the Man nightly at 9pm. Beer 25Kč. Cover 50-70Kč. Open daily 8pm-2am.

Jazz Club Železná, Železná 16 (tel. 24 23 96 97). Metro A, B: Můstek. Walk down Na Můstku away from Václavské nám.; go right on Havelská, then left on Železná. Club is on the left at the back of the building. Dark cellar bar showcases live jazz to a student crowd. Beer 18Kč. Cover 80Kč. Shows daily 9pm-midnight. Open daily noon-1am.

Reduta, Národní 20. Metro A: Národní třída. Favorite haunt of Presidents Clinton and Havel, as the photos won't let you forget. Cover 120Kč. Open daily 9am-midnight.

Agharta, Krakovská 5 (tel. 22 21 12 75), just up Krakovská from Václavské nám. Metro B, C: Muzeum. Nightly live jazz ensembles starting at 9pm. Cover 80Kč, beer 40Kč, but the music is great and the vibe appropriately chill. Open nightly 7pm-1am.

THE FAGUE AND THE DRAGUE OF PRAGUE

If Prague had a desert, *Priscilla II* could be shot here. The scene is developing fast and in many directions: transvestite shows, stripteases, discos, bars, cafes, restaurants, and hotels aimed at gay and lesbian travelers can be found easily. At any of the places listed below, you can pick up a copy of the monthly *Amigo* (15Kč), the most thorough guide to gay life in the Czech Republic and Slovakia, with a lot in English, or *SOHO* (40Kč), a glossier piece of work mostly in Czech.

U střelce, Karolíny Světlé 12 (tel. 24 23 82 78). Metro B: Národní třída. Under the arch on the right. Gay club pulls a diverse crowd for its Friday and Saturday cabarets, when magnificent female impersonators take the stage, occasionally sitting on unprepared audience members. Cover 100Kč. Open Tu-Th 9pm-midnight, W and F-Sa 9:30pm-5am.

A Club, Milíčova 25. Metro C: Hlavní Nádraží. Take tram #5 toward Harfa, #9 toward Spojovací, or #26 toward Nádraží Hostivař, and get off at Lipanská. Walk back down Seifertova and turn right on Milíčova. A nightspot for lesbians, but men are welcome. All class, with wire sculptures, soft light, and comfy couches near the bar. Disco in the back starts at 10pm, but don't come before midnight. Beer 20Kč. Open nightly 7pm-sunrise.

L-Club, Lublaňská 48 (tel. 90 00 11 89). Metro C: I.P. Pavlova. Fun for both the guys and dolls. Black lights make the white shirts glow. Cover 75Kč. Open nightly 8pm-4am.

Drake's, Petřinská 5 (tel. 53 49 09). Tram #9 or 12. 24hr. gay complex, both adored and hated by Prague's gay community. Come here to dance, cruise, or make a love connection. Nightly strip shows and private video rooms. Very pricey.

Tom's Bar, Pernerova 4 (tel. 232 11 70). Metro B, C: Florenc. Walk down Křižíkova, pass under the tracks, and go right on Prvního pluků, which curves to the left and becomes Pernerova. Video screening rooms. Men only. Open Tu-Th 9pm-2am, F-Sa 9pm-4am.

DAYTRIPS FROM PRAGUE

Even if you're only spending a few days in the capital, take the time to explore the towns and sights in the Bohemian hills around Prague. When you're in the city, it's easy to believe that Prague is the only place worth visiting in the Czech Republic. However, one trip to the magnificent castles of Karlštejn, Konopiště, or Křivoklát; one jaunt through the wine cellars of Mělník or the motorcycles at Kámen; or one sobering day at Terezín or Kutná Hora will begin to expose the wealth of historically, aesthetically, and hedonistically significant towns in the Czech Republic.

KARLŠTEJN

Bohemia's patriotic gem, Karlštejn is a walled and turreted fortress built by Charles IV to house his crown jewels and holy relics. (Tel. (0311) 684 617. Castle open Tu-Su July-Aug. 9am-6pm; Sept.-Oct. and Apr. 9am-4pm; Mar. 9am-3pm; May-June 9am-5pm. Czech tour 70Kč, students 40Kč; foreign language tour 200Kč, students 100Kč; English tours every 2hr.) The **Chapel of the Holy Cross** is decorated with more than 2000 inlaid precious stones and 128 apocalyptic paintings by medieval artist Master Theodorik. (Open Tu-Su 9am-5pm. Mandatory tours 20Kč, in English 90Kč). Find out if they've finished restoring the chapel before setting out.

GETTING THERE. Karlštejn lies southwest of Prague; it is most easily reached by train from **Hlavní nádraží** or **Praha-Smíchov** (45min., 20Kč). The train station is a short walk from the base of the village and winding valley, at the top of which triumphantly sits the castle. Turn right out of the train station, take a left over the absurdly modern bridge, and it's only 2min. to the village.

KONOPIŠTĚ

The mighty castle Konopiště (KOH-no-peesh-tyeh; tel. (0301) 213 66; email konopiste@pusc.cz), south of Prague in Benešov, boasts more than 300,000 taxidermied animals, an eternal tribute to Archduke Franz Ferdinand's shooting prowess. His collection of ivory pistols and armor used in 16th-century Italian theater astounds, as well. (Open Tu-Su 9am-noon and 1-5pm. Tour of the public rooms 30Kč, in English 60Kč; tour of the Archduke's private rooms 120Kč, 240Kč.)

GETTING THERE. Catch a bus from **Prague's Florenc station** to **Benešov** (1hr., 1 per hr. 6am-6pm, 41Kč). From the bus station, turn left on Nádražní and go left over the bridge. Continue straight along Konopištská, then bear left at the fork.

KŘIVOKLÁT

Much less touristed (and some might argue more magnificent) than Konopiště, Křivoklát (KRZHEE-voh-klaht) is a 13th-century royal hunting lodge nestled in a UNESCO-protected nature reserve. The obligatory tour traverses the castle chapel (whose pews are adorned with malevolent animal carvings signifying "evil forces"), an amazing collection of hand-carved sleds, and the prison and starvation chambers. (Open June-Aug. Tu-Su 9am-5pm; Apr.-May and Sept. 9am-4pm; Mar. and Oct.-Dec. Tu-Su 9am-3pm. Closed noon-1pm. Last tour 1hr. before closing. Czech tours 50Kč, students 25Kč; English tours 110Kč, 55Kč.)

GETTING THERE. Take a train from **Hlavní nádraží** or **Praha-Smíchov** in Prague to **Beroun** and switch trains to Křivoklát (2hr. total, every 90min., 42Kč).

TEREZÍN (THERESIENSTADT)

The fortress town of Terezín (Theresienstadt) was built in the 1780s on Habsburg Emperor Josef II's orders to safeguard the northern frontier with the German states. In 1940, Hitler's Gestapo set up a huge prison in the Small Fortress, and in 1941 the town itself became a concentration camp for Jews—by 1942, the entire pre-war civilian population had been evacuated. 140,000 Jews were deported to the ghetto, at first just from the Bohemia-Moravia Protectorate, but later from all over the *Reich*. Twice Terezín was beautified in order to receive delegations from the Red Cross, who were wholly deceived about the true purpose of the place: Nazi propaganda films touted the area as an almost idyllic spa resort where Jews were "allowed" to educate their young, partake in arts and recreation, and live a "fulfilling" life. Terezín was one of Hitler's most successful propaganda ploys.

In reality, 35,000 died here, some of starvation and disease, others at the hands of brutal guards. 85,000 others were transported to death camps, primarily Auschwitz. More than 30,000 prisoners (mostly political) were held in the Small Fortress, and many Czech resistance fighters and Communists were shot there. After the Red Army liberated Terezín, the Czechoslovak regime used the camp to hold Sudeten Germans awaiting deportation: the Czech and German governments recently exchanged apologies for the ethnic cleansing both countries attempted during this ghastly time. Shockingly, Terezín has been repopulated, and the town's life goes on in the midst of a former concentration camp; families live in the former barracks and supermarkets occupy Nazi offices. The population, however, has never approached its pre-war levels—the last census counted less than 2,000 residents. The **Ghetto Museum,** on Komenského in the town, displays mountains of documents, helpfully setting Terezín in the wider Nazi context—all explanatory text is in English. The museum displays harrowing children's art from the ghetto alongside some staggering adult work. (Tel. (0416) 782 577. Open daily May-Sept. 9am-6pm; Oct.-Apr. 9am-5:30pm. Closed Dec. 24-26 and Jan. 1. 100Kč, students 70Kč; including Small Fortress 120Kč, 80Kč. Guided tour in English 240Kč.)

East of the town and across the river sits the **Small Fortress** (Malá pevnost). Much of the fortress is left bare and untouched for visitors to explore freely. Permanent exhibitions chart the town's development from 1780-1939, and, in the **museum,** the story of the fortress during WWII. Upon entrance to the Small Fortress, the words *"Arbeit macht frei"* ("Work makes you free") leap off the left gate leading to the first courtyard. This cruelly ironic inscription was typical of most Nazi concentration camps, but not of a Gestapo prison. Beyond the blocks of the first courtyard is the entrance to the underground passage, a dimly lit pathway with barred airholes that winds around the length of the under-camp to the excavation area. (Open daily May-Sept. 8am-6pm; Oct.-Apr. 8am-4:30pm. Closed Dec. 24-26 and Jan. 1.) You must not visit Terezín without seeing the **Jewish cemetery** and **crematorium.** The furnaces and autopsy lab are as they were 50 years ago, with the addition of flowers, cards, and photos left as tributes by the victims' descendants. Men must cover their heads. (Open Mar.-Nov. M-F and Su 10am-5pm.)

GETTING THERE. The **bus** from **Prague-Florenc** (1hr., hourly, 20Kč) stops by the central square, where the **tourist office** sells a map (25Kč). (Open daily until 6pm.)

KUTNÁ HORA

1½hr. east of Prague, the former mining town of **Kutná Hora** (Mining Mountain) has a history as morbid as the bone church that made the city famous. Founded in the latter half of the 13th century when lucky miners hit a vein, the city boomed with 100,000 gold diggers. But the Black Plague halted the fortune-seekers dead in their tracks. A few years later, a local monk sprinkled soil from the Biblical Golgotha Cemetery on Kutná Hora's cemetery; this religious infusion made the rich and superstitious quite keen to be buried there, and the graveyard quickly became over-crowded. Neighbors started to complain about the stench by the 15th century, so the Cistercian order built a chapel and started cramming in bodies. In a fit of whimsy (or possibly insanity), the monk in charge began designing flowers out of pelvi and crania. He never finished, but the artist František Rint eventually completed the project in 1870 with flying butt-bones, femur crosses, and a grotesque chandelier made from every bone in the human body. Some lucky corpse even got to spell out the artist's name, and there's an amazing rendering of the Schwarzenberg family crest. (Open daily Apr.-Sept. 8am-noon and 1-6pm; Oct. 9am-noon and 1-5pm; Nov.-Mar. 9am-noon and 1-4pm. 35Kč, students 20Kč. Cameras 30Kč).

GETTING THERE. Buses run regularly from **Prague-Florenc** (1½hr.). The chapel is 2km from the bus station: walk or take a local bus to Sedlec Tabák.

MĚLNÍK

Dramatically perched atop a hill above the confluence of the Vltava and Elbe rivers, wine-making Mělník is an ideal daytrip. In one day, you can visit the ossuary, tour the stately Renaissance *château*, sample the castle's homemade wines, and savor your favorite vintage over lunch in the old schoolhouse overlooking the Říp valley. Its vinticulture was honed about 1000 years ago, when Princess Ludmila—later St. Ludmila—planted the first vineyards for communion wine. Her grandson, St. Wenceslas, the patron saint of Bohemian wine-makers, was supposedly introduced to the secrets of wine-making in the vineyards of Mělník. Both the castle and the vineyards were abandoned during the Thirty Years' War, but recent restorations by the Lobkowicz family have unveiled the town's former glory.

The **castle** tour winds through the absurdly fancy color-themed *château* rooms and ends in the Gothic wine cellars, where you'll walk on a floor composed entirely of upside-down wine bottles. If you call in advance, you can arrange for a "big" (120Kč) or "small" (80Kč) wine tasting. (Tel. (206) 62 21 21 25. Open Mar.-Nov. Tu-Su 10am-7pm. Tours 80Kč, students 60Kč.) Directly across from the *châ-*

teau is the 15th-century **St. Peter and Paul Cathedral,** whose crypt houses the bones of 10,000 medieval plague victims. (Open Tu-Su 10am-4pm. 10Kč, students 5Kč.)

GETTING THERE. Buses run from **Prague-Florenc** (45min., hourly, 22Kč). From the bus station, make a right on Bezručova and bear left at the road split onto Kpt. Jaroše; this brings you to the town center. Head in the direction of the big clock tower; directly behind it is the onion-domed St. Peter and Paul Cathedral.

KÁMEN

If the sights closer to Prague haven't satiated you, head farther south to the **Kámen Castle and Motorcycle Museum** (tel. (036) 543 66 19) for some refreshingly different historical exhibits. Reopened to the public in 1974, the Kámen Castle is named after the stone (*kámen* in Czech) on which it was founded. Owned for 200 years by the Malovec family, it now pays homage to the Czech motorcycle industry. See a bike made out of agricultural equipment, or examine the Czech *Devil* moped. Besides the museum, the castle has a prison-turned-wedding-altar, complete with a hidden trap door leading to a torture room sure to cure even the worst case of cold feet. (Open May-Sept. Tu-Su 9am-5pm. Tours 20Kč. English guide available.)

GETTING THERE. Reach Kámen from **Prague** via **Tábor** (2hr., 6 per day, 65Kč). From the Tábor bus station, catch a local bus to Kámen (30min., 26Kč). Avoid visiting on the weekends as bus connections are infrequent.

ČESKÝ RÁJ NATIONAL PRESERVE

The sandstone **Prachov rocks** (Prachovské skály) in the Český Ráj (Czech Paradise) National Preserve are among the finest rock-climbing in the Czech Republic. Proclaimed a state nature preserve in 1931, they were formed by the sedimentation of sandstone, marl, and slate on the bottom of the Mesozoic sea. High, narrow towers and pillars separated by deep, cramped gorges make for not only stellar climbing but a series of stunning views for those who prefer not to grapple. The 588 acres of the park are interwoven by a dense network of **trails;** the longer trail is marked by green signs, the shorter by yellow. The rocks boast seventeen stunning vistas, the ruins of the 14th-century rock castle Pařez, and the rock pond Pelíšek. (Open daily 9am-5pm; swimming in rock pond May 1-Sept. 1. 20Kč, students 10Kč.)

GETTING THERE. Buses run from **Prague-Florenc** to **Jičin** (1½hr., hourly, 50Kč). From there, buses continue on to **Prachovské skály** and **Český Ráj** (30min., hourly, 17Kč). You can also walk to the park along the relatively easy 8km yellow trail, beginning at the Rumcajs Motel in Jičin. From Valdštejn nám., turn onto Palackého, go left on Jiraskova, continuing through its name change to Kollárova. When you reach the bus stop at Prachovské skály, take a right at the fork; a 10min. walk brings you to the ticket office at the base of the rocks.

WEST BOHEMIA

Bursting at the seams with curative springs, West Bohemia is the Czech mecca for those in search of a good bath. Over the centuries, emperors and intellectuals have soaked in the waters of Karlovy Vary (in German Carlsbad), but nowadays the spa-goers consist mainly of German tourists in search of cheap sulphurous draughts.

PLZEŇ

Tell a Czech you're going to Plzeň (PIL-zen; pop. 170,000), and they might say "*to je škoda*" ("what a pity"). The unfortunate pun on "Škoda" alludes to the notorious arms factory-*cum*-auto plant that made Plzeň one of Bohemia's most polluted cities. For the sightseer, however, Plzeň offers an intriguing center, thriving youth culture, and, its hometown brew, the famed *Pilsner Urquell*. If it's chic you're after, hit Prague; come here for hard rock, flowing pints, and a pinch of soot.

ORIENTATION

Nám. Republiky, the central square, lies amid a grid of streets surrounded by parks where the old city wall used to be. From the **train station,** turn right onto **Sirková,** the busy street in front of you when you exit the train station, and enter the pedestrian underpass. Veer right at the shopping center and emerge at the blue sign that says "Zastávky-Tramvaj." To get to Nám. Republiky from the bus station, hop onto tram #2 (departing from the same side of the street as the underpass), or continue on Sirková until it intersects with **Pražská,** where you'll turn left. After Pražská veers to the right, it leads straight to the square. From the bus station, turn left onto **Husova.** Follow it as it becomes **Smetanovy sady,** then turn onto **Bedřicha Smetany,** which leads to the square's southwest corner.

PRACTICAL INFORMATION

Trains: Tel. 22 20 79. On Sirková between Americká and Koterovská. To **Prague** (1¾hr., 14 per day, 60Kč). Domestic tickets on the 1st fl.; international tickets on the 2nd fl.

Buses: Husova 58 (tel. 22 37 04). Many cheap Eurolines buses pass through en route to Prague (2hr., at least 1 per hr., 60Kč) from France, Switzerland, or Germany.

Local Transportation: Tram #2 goes to the train and bus stations, Nám. Republiky, and the hostel; tram #4 runs north-south along Sady Pětatřicátníků. Get tickets from *tabáky* and punch them on board. 8Kč; backpacks (and dogs) 4Kč extra. 200Kč fine for not riding with a ticket. Identically numbered **buses** replace trams at night.

Tourist Offices: Městské informační středisko (MIS), Nám. Republiky 41 (tel. 703 27 50; fax 703 27 52; email infocenter@mmp.plzen-city.cz). Sells **maps** (50Kč) and phone cards (150Kč); also books rooms from 350Kč. English spoken. Open M-F 10am-4:30pm, Sa 9am-1pm. The town hall nearby sells the helpful *Plzeň Open Town* (33Kč).

Currency Exchange: Komerční Banka, Zbrojnická 4 (tel. 721 42 11), off Nám. Republiky's southeast corner. Cashes traveler's checks for a 2% commission (50Kč minimum). Open M-F 8am-5pm. A **currency exchange machine** sits outside **Československá obchodní banka,** Americká 60, near the train station. Open 24hr.

Luggage Storage: At the train station. 10Kč; 20Kč for over 15kg. Open 24hr.

Pharmacy: Lékárna Martinská, Martinská 4 (tel. 723 55 15). From Nám. Republiky, turn right onto Františkanská, which becomes Martinská. Open M-Sa 10am-8pm.

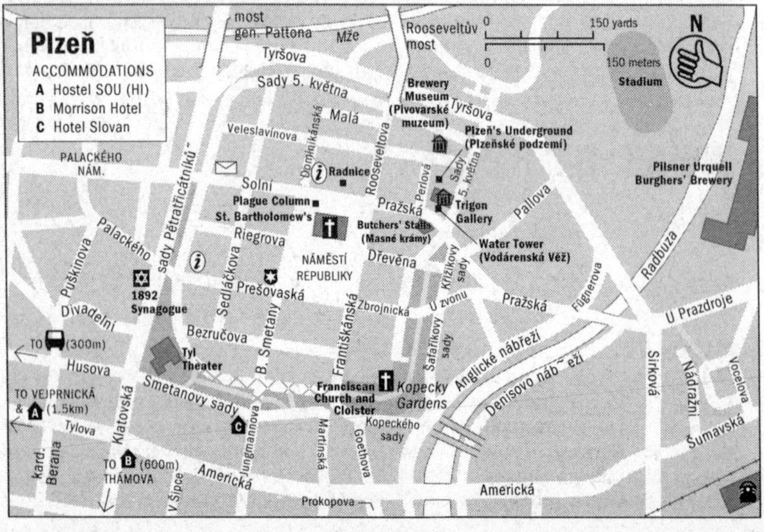

Post Office: Solní 20. Open M-F 7am-7pm, Sa-Su 8am-noon. **Postal code:** 30100.

Internet Access: Two computers at the tourist office (see above). 2Kč per min.

Phone code: (0)19.

ACCOMMODATIONS

MIS and **CKM** both book rooms; pension prices start at 350Kc and go up from there.

Hotel Slovan, Smetanovy sady 1 (tel. 722 72 56; fax 722 70 12). From the bus station, turn left onto Husova and follow it to Smetanovy sady. Clean rooms with breakfast in a Hollywood-esque building. Singles 600Kč, with bath 1400Kč; doubles 950Kč, 2000Kč.

Morrison Hotel, Thámova 9 (tel. 27 09 52; fax 27 54 80). Take tram #4 to Chodské nám. and go left on Thámova. Singles 750Kč; doubles 1100Kč; triples 1500Kč.

Hostel SOU (HI), Vejprnická 58, pavilion #8 (tel. 28 20 12). Take tram #2 to Internáty, walk back 50m, and head left into the fenced compound. This former Škoda workers' hostel is institutional and far from the center, but cheap. 210Kč.

FOOD

Every meal in Plzeň should include a glass of *Pilsner Urquell* or its dark equivalent, *Purkmistr*. If you can't decide between them, have a *řezané*, a Czech black-and-tan. For groceries, head to Rooseveltova 16a. (Open M-F 6am-6pm.)

Pizzerie, Solní 9, down the street from the tourist office. Gigantic home-cooked portions popular with students. Pizzas 30-63Kč; pasta 40-60Kč. Open M-Th 10am-10pm, F 10am-11pm, Sa 11am-11pm, and Su 11:30am-10pm.

U Salzmannu, Pražská 8 (tel. 723 54 76). Dishes out hearty Czech pub food to compliment your Pilsner. Entrees 53-98Kč. Open Tu-Th and Sa-Su 11am-11pm.

S&S Grill, Sedláčková 18 (tel. 22 66 05). From Nám. Republiky's southwest corner, take Riegrova toward Sady Petatřicátníků. Go left onto Sedláčková; S&S is on the right before Prešovská. True Bohemian fast food. Locals sit at the grill's tiny tables and eat turkey goulash (28Kc). Open M-F 9am-7pm, Sa 9am-3pm, Su 10am-2pm.

SIGHTS

NÁMĚSTÍ REPUBLIKY. Empire dwellings loom over the marketplace, Nám. Republiky, but none overshadow the belfry of the **Church of St. Bartholomew** (Kostel sv. Bartoloměje). For a vertiginous view of the town and the Škoda factory, tourists climb 60 of the 103m to the observation deck, where they can read sad stories about why the town no longer has an out-sized bell called Bartholomew (Bárta to its friends). Bárta was cracked, removed, and smelted in a fire, shot at, and cracked again before being melted down to make bullets during WWII. Now no one has the heart or the money to forge another. Inside, a rich collection of Gothic statues and altars bows to the stunning 14th-century polychrome statue **Plzeňská Madona,** recalling Bohemia's glory days under Karel IV. *(Open daily 10am-6pm. 18Kč, students 12Kč.)* The **Plague Column** (Morový sloup) seems to be working: residents may suffer from industrial diseases and liver complaints, but the plague hasn't been here for a while. Plzeň's golden-clock-topped Renaissance **town hall** connects on the inside to the 1607 **Kaiser House** (Císařský dům). *(Nám. Republiky 39.)*

PILSNER URQUELL BREWERY. (Měštanský Pivovar Plzeňský Prazdroj). The building that best epitomizes the essence of Plzeň lies outside of the city center. In 1840, over 30 independent brewers plied their trade in the beer cellars of Plzeň. Some of the suds were good, but some were awful, so the burgher brewers formed a union with the goal of creating the best beer in the world. Many would agree that the Pilsner Urquell Burghers' Brewery succeeded with its legendary *Pilsner Urquell*. A huge neo-Renaissance gate welcomes visitors to this pastel palace of the brewing arts. After the stimulating "kaleidoscope" film (with Czech, English, and German subtitles) about Prazdroj's past and present, the group divides into Czech, German, English, and French subgroups led by knowledgeable guides. *(The entrance to the complex lies 300m from Staré Město over the Radbuza river, where Pražská becomes U Prazdroje. Tel. 706 28 88. 1hr. tours M-F 12:30pm. 75Kč.)*

BREWERY MUSEUM. This labyrinthine museum exhibits beer paraphernalia from medieval taps to a coaster collection. The original malt-house room displays the top-secret Pilsner process. The last room, labeled "the room of curiosities," is the zaniest, with gigantic steins, wacky Pilsner signs, and a statue of Shakespeare's most famous drunk, Sir John Falstaff. *(Veleslavínova 6. Perlová ends at Veleslavínova. Tel. 723 55 74. Open Apr.-Dec. daily 10am-6pm; Jan.-Mar. daily 11am-2pm. 40Kč, students 10Kč.)*

WATER TOWER COMPLEX. If you bear left from the tourist office, you'll run into the **water tower** *(vodárenská věž)*, which once stored the crystal-clear water needed for fine beer. *(Pražská 19.)* The well's dried up, so the **Trigon Gallery** next door doesn't have to worry about water damage to its art. *(Tel. 22 54 71. Open M-Th 10am-6pm, F-Sa 10am-1pm. 10Kč, students 5Kč. First floor is free.)* The water tower and **Plzeň's underground** (Plzeňské podzemí) can be visited in a 40min. tour that starts inside Perlová 4 and leads through the cellars, which were used for the covert guzzling of beer. *(Tel. 722 52 14. Open W-Su 9am-5pm; last tour at 4:20pm. 30Kč, students 20Kč.)*

OTHER SIGHTS. The black iron gate of the **Franciscan Church and Cloister** (Františkánský kostel a klášter), leads through a wooden door into a quiet cloister garden with statues striking despairing Gothic poses. The church also houses the renowned **Black Madonna of Hájek,** an 18th-century sculpture protected by a gate except during services. *(Across from the corner of Františkánská and Bezručova. South of Nám. Republiky. Open daily 10am-6pm.)* People stroll and relax in the **Kopecký gardens** (Kopeckého sady) in the shade of the trees as brass bands perform polkas, waltzes, and folk tunes. *(Františkánská runs into the park south of Nám. Republiky.)* The 1892 **synagogue** is an impressive monument to Plzeň's once-large Jewish community. *(From the southern end of Nám. Republiky, walk down Prešovská to Sady Pětatřicátníků and turn left. The synagogue is on the right. Open M-F 11am-6pm. 20Kč, students 10Kč.)*

ENTERTAINMENT

For a taste of Plzeň's cultural life, **J. K. Tyl Theater** (tel. 22 25 94) offers cheap seats to Czech **plays, ballet,** and **opera.** The schedule is posted outside. Get tickets an hour before the performance (shows usually start at 7pm) in the theater or in advance at the Předprodej office, Sedláčkova 2 (tel. 722 75 48), a block southwest of the main square. (Open M-F 10am-5pm. Best seats 60Kč. Wheelchair-accessible.) To get to the theater, take tram #4 to "U synagogy," or turn right onto Přešovská from Nám. Republiky's southeast corner and turn left onto Sady pětatřicátníků.

NIGHTLIFE

Thanks to students from the University of West Bohemia, Plzeň booms with bars and late-night clubs. The young English-speaking summer staff at the tourist office eagerly gives suggestions. Things get hoppin' around 9:30pm.

U Dominika, Dominikánská 3 (tel. 22 32 26), off Nám. Republiky's northwest corner. With a bonfire in the beer garden and Pearl Jam in the bar, this boisterous pub is the ultimate student hangout. Beer (20Kč) and sludge-like coffee (13-20Kč) are the drinks of choice. Open M-Th 11am-midnight, F 11am-2am, Sa 2pm-2am, Su 2pm-midnight.

Zach's Pub, Palackého nám. 2 (tel. 723 47 93). From Nám. Republiky, turn left onto Solní, which becomes Přemyslova after intersecting with Pětatřicátníků. Palackého nám. comes right after Přemyslova's intersection with Jízdecká. The pub is on the left, acting out its role as the hottest spot in Plzeň to down a pint of Guinness (50Kč). Beer starts at 20Kč. Loud, live music on weekends. Open M-F 1pm-1am, Sa 5pm-2am, Su 5pm-midnight; garden open daily 10am-midnight.

Subway, Sady 5. května 21 (tel. 22 28 96). Descend left down the first flight of stairs on the overpass at the end of Rooseveltova off Nám. Republiky's northeast corner. Turn around, and Subway is 10m to the right. This popular underground cellar bar, newly refurbished, packs lots of people into a fairly small space then plays British classic rock at Spinal Tap-esque volumes. Dance if you can find space. Open W-F 10pm-2am.

KARLOVY VARY

From the bus station, Karlovy Vary doesn't look like much more than a dingy Bohemian town. A stroll into the spa district or up into the hills, however, reveals why this town developed into one of the great "salons" of Europe, frequented by Johann Sebastian Bach, Peter the Great, Sigmund Freud, Karl Marx. Along the Tepla, the town is peaceful and beautiful—swans, ducks, and fish populate the gurgling river while ornate pastel buildings and sweeping willows line its banks. Once a vacation spot for Holy Roman Emperor Karel IV, these days the main tourists are older Germans seeking the therapeutic powers of the springs.

ORIENTATION

To get to the center from the **bus station, Dolní nádraží,** turn left onto Západní, continue past the Becher building, and bear right onto Masaryka, which runs parallel to the other main thoroughfare, **Bechera.** From the **train station, Horní nádraží,** take bus #11 or 13 (6Kč) to the last stop. By foot, it's a 15min. walk downhill: with the station behind you, cross the street and turn right. Follow the pedestrian path that veers to the left. At its end, turn right onto the dirt road and left onto the first busy street. After passing the highway, turn right onto the bridge. This leads straight to **T.G. Masaryka,** one of the main streets. *Promenáda,* a part-English monthly, has a handy map of the town in the middle (11-25Kč; available at every kiosk).

PRACTICAL INFORMATION

Trains: Horní nádraží, on the west side of town. To **Prague** via **Chomutov** (4½hr. plus a 1-2hr. layover in Chomutov, 5 per day, 126Kč).

Buses: Dolní nádraží, on Západní. More direct than trains. To **Plzeň** (1½hr., 16 per day, 73Kč) and **Prague** (2½hr., 25 per day, 100Kč). Buy tickets at the **ČSAD office,** just before Západní runs into Nám. Republiky. Open M-F 6am-6pm, Sa 7:30am-12:30pm.

Taxi: Tel. 322 30 30.

Tourist Office: City-Info (tel. 322 33 51; fax 322 57 61), in a white booth on T.G. Masaryka across from the post office. Sells maps and books private rooms from 450Kč. Open M-F 9am-5pm, Sa 8am-5pm, Su 10am-4pm.

24hr. ATM: Outside **Komerční banka,** Tržiště 11 (tel. 322 22 05). AmEx/Cirrus/MC/Visa.

American Express: In the travel agency at Vřídelní 51 (tel. 322 18 15). Cashes AmEx traveler's checks for no commission. Open daily 9am-7pm.

Post Office: Masaryka 1 (tel. 322 49 30). Open M-F 7:30am-7pm, Sa 8am-1pm, Su 8am-noon. **Postal code:** 360 01.

Telephones: At the junction of Masaryka and Bechera. **Phone code:** (0)17.

ACCOMMODATIONS

Budget accommodations in Karlovy Vary are scarce. **Karlovarský Autorent,** the large white kiosk at Nám. Dr. Horákové 18 (tel. 322 28 33), will book you a double in a private house for 900Kč. (Open in summer M-F 9am-5pm, Sa 9am-noon; off-season M-F 9am-noon and 1-5pm, Sa 9am-noon.) **City-Info** (see above) also books rooms.

Pension Kosmos, Zahradní 39 (tel./fax 322 31 68). In the center of the spa district, down the street from the post office. Follow the directions from the bus and train stations to T.G. Masaryka, and bear right at the post office. Simply furnished rooms with giant down comforters. Singles 440Kč, with bath 750Kč; doubles 720Kč, 1340Kč.

Pension Romania, Zahradní 49 (tel. 322 28 22). Next to the post office at the corner of Zahradní and T.G. Masaryka. Luxurious singles, doubles, and triples with bath, TV, and plenty of plants. Breakfast included. 895Kč per person, students 717Kč.

FOOD

Karlovy Vary is known for its sweet *oplatky* (spa wafers) to be enjoyed with its therapeutic spa waters. You can try them at one of the many vendors on the street (8Kč). A **supermarket,** Horova 1, occupies the large building with the "Městská tržnice" sign near the local bus station; it also changes money and has a sandwich shop and bakery. (Open M-F 6am-7pm, Sa 7am-5pm, Su 10am-6pm. Visa/MC.)

Vegetarian Restaurant, I.P. Pavlova 25 (tel. 322 90 21). Combines (mostly) veggie cooking with a traditional Czech interior suitable for serious beer drinking. Fruit *kebap* 45Kč; spicy veggie (and sausage) *guláš* 40Kč. Open daily 11am-9pm.

E&T, Zeyerova 3 (tel. 322 60 22). Between Bechera and T.G. Masaryka. A more expensive eatery with faithful regulars. Meat entrees 80-130Kč; garlic soup with egg yolk 30Kč. Open M-Sa 10am-midnight, Su 11am-midnight.

SIGHTS & ENTERTAINMENT

The spa district officially begins with the Victorian **Bath 5** (Lázně 5), Smetanovy Sady 1, across the street from the post office and marked by flowers displaying the numerical date. Thermal baths (300Kč) and underwater massages (420Kč) are among the blessed services offered. (Open M-F 8am-9pm, Sa 8am-6pm, Su 10am-6pm. Massage open M-F 3-9pm, Sa and Su 10am-6pm.) Along the south rim of the **Dvořák gardens** lies the Victorian **Garden Collonade** (Sadová kolonáda). Here you can sip the curative waters of Karlovy Vary's 12th spring, **Garden Spring** (Sadový pramen), from a marble fountain shaped like a peasant woman. The pedestrian **Mlýnské nábř.** meanders alongside the Teplá under the cool protection of shady trees, peppered with folk singers and tourist-preying portrait artists. **Bath 3** lies to the right, just before **Freedom Spring** (Pramen svobody). Bring your own drinking vessel, or buy souvenir porcelain cups from the kiosks (40-180Kč). The good news for the budget traveler is that the spring waters are free to drink, although you may be able to manage only a few sips of the extremely metallic stuff—it's much stronger and warmer than the so-called mineral water you'll get in a restaurant. The bad news is water bottles are banned, as they "break the hygienic conditions of the drinking cure." Next door, the imposing **Mill Collonade** (Mlýnská kolonáda) shelters five different springs. Farther along the spa area, the former **market** (tržiště) appears with the delicate white **Market Collonade** (Tržní kolonáda), where two more springs bubble to the surface. The **Zawojski House,** now the Živnostenská Banka, a gorgeous cream-and-gold Art Nouveau building from the turn of the century, sits at Trižiště 9. Crossing the Teplá to the steps of the baroque **Church of St. Mary Magdalene** gets you a good view of the other side of the Zawojski House. Along the way, the **Vřídlo spring** (*Sprudel* to the Germans) inside the **Vřídlo Collonade** (Vřídelni kolonáda), spouts 30L of water each second at 72°...Celcius.

Follow the signs on Stará Louka to the **funicular,** which leads up to the 555m high **Diana Observatory** (Rozhledna) and a magnificent panorama of the city. (Funicular runs daily 9am-6pm, every 15min. 25Kč, round-trip 40Kč; children under 10 15Kč, round-trip 20Kč. Tower open until 6:30pm. 10Kč.) Stará Louka endsf at **Grandhotel Pupp.** Founded in 1774 by Johann Georg Pupp, the Grandhotel was the largest hotel in 19th-century Bohemia. The intricate facade is the work of the Viennese Helmer-Fellner duo. The interior features luxurious suites, a concert hall, and multiple ballrooms. Paths, with monuments to famous spa visitors, cut through the sloping woods above Stará Louka. Descend back to the town along **Petra Velikého** to see a statue of **Karl Marx** commemorating his visits to the decidedly bourgeois spa between 1874 and 1876. He apparently needed to experience the fruits of wealth before he could stir up revolution against it in good conscience.

If seeing such a monument to Comrade Marx distresses your inner Proletariat, escape for a daytrip to the 12th-century **Loket Castle,** inside an elbow in the Ohre river 12km west. Used as a prison until 1947, the castle now displays dungeons and porcelain manufactured in nearby **Loket nad Ohr.** (Open Tu-Su Apr.-Oct. 9-11:30am and 1-4:30pm; Nov.-March 10am-3pm. 50Kč.) Buses run from **Loket** to Karlovy Vary, but the **hike** here is half the fun. Follow the 17km **blue trail,** from the left side of the steps of Diana Rozhleda Observatory entrance in Karlovy Vary. Two-thirds of the way into the trail you'll find the magnificent rocks of **Svatošské skály,** a supposed source of inspiration for Goethe and the Brothers Grimm.

Promenáda (see **Orientation & Practical Information,** p. 215) lists the month's concerts and performances. Karlovy Vary's **International Film Festival,** showing independent films from all over the globe, is definitely worthwhile. Like its restaurants, Karlovy Vary's nightlife is geared toward its older tourists. Nightclubs and pubs are sparse, while expensive cafes reproduce like fruit flies. **Propaganda,** Jaltská 5 (tel. 322 22 92), off Bechera, understandably attracts Karlovy Vary's hippest and youngest crowd with live music and a trendy blue steel interior. (Drinks 20Kč. Open M-Th 5pm-3am, F-Sa 5pm-6am, Su 5pm-2am.)

SOUTHERN BOHEMIA

Truly a rustic Bohemian Eden, South Bohemia is a scenic ensemble of scattered villages, unspoiled brooks, virgin forests, and castle ruins. Low hills and plentiful attractions have made the region a favorite of Czech bicyclists, who ply the countryside wildlife-watching, castle-traipsing, and *Budvar*-guzzling.

ČESKÉ BUDĚJOVICE

No amount of beer will help you correctly pronounce České Budějovice (CHESS-kay BOOD-yeh-yoh-vee-tsay). Nestled in the heart of the Bohemian countryside, this mid-sized city's endless bus and train connections make it a great base from which to visit the region's many wonders. Mill streams, the Malše, and the Vltava wrap around the city center, a fascinating fusion of Gothic, Renaissance, and Baroque houses. While convenient, České Budějovice—unfortunately blemished by fast-food, department stores, and shampoo billboards—lacks the charm of Český Krumlov, its smaller neighbor to the south.

CZECH REPUBLIC

ORIENTATION

Staré Město (Old Town) centers around **Nám. Přemysla Otakara II.** Cheap rooms, generally beyond Staré Město's walls, are reachable by **buses** and **trolley-buses** (6Kč tickets sold at kiosks; punch them on board). The **train station** is 10min. by foot from Staré Město. From the station, turn right onto **Nádražní.** Go left at the first crosswalk, leading to the pedestrian **Lannova třída,** which becomes **Kanovnická** after the moat, and pours out into the northeast corner of the gigantic Nám. Otakara II.

PRACTICAL INFORMATION

Trains: Nádražní 12 (tel. 635 33 33). To: **Prague** (2½hr., 11 per day, 110Kč); **Plzeň** (1½hr., 9 per day, 86Kč); and **Brno** (4½hr., 2 per day, 126Kč). Info office open M-F 6:50am-6pm, Sa-Su 7:15-11:30am and noon-6:30pm.

Buses: Tel. 558 04. Across the street from the train station. To: **Prague** (2½hr., 18 per day, 96Kč); **Plzeň** (3hr., 2 per day, 96Kč); and **Brno** (4½hr., 9 per day, 123Kč).

Taxi: Tel. 477 44.

Luggage Storage: In the train station, on the far right wall of the main level. 5Kč.

Tourist Office: Turistické Informační Centrum (TIC), Nám. Otakara II 26 (tel./fax 635 25 89). English-speaking staff books private rooms (300Kč in the center, cheaper farther out) and organizes castle, museum, and brewery tours. Open May-Sept. M-F 8am-6pm, Sa 8am-3pm, Su 8am-1pm; Oct.-Apr. M-F 8am-5pm, Sa 8am-2pm, Su 8am-noon.

Currency Exchange: Komerční banka, Krajinská 15 (tel. 774 11 47). Off Nám. Otakara II. Cashes traveler's checks for a 2% commission. Open M-F 8am-5pm.

ATMs: Along Lannova and opposite the train station. Cirrus/MC.

Pharmacy: Nám. Otakara II 26 (tel. 635 30 63). Open M-F 7am-6pm, Sa 8am-noon.

Post Office: Senovážné nám. 1 (tel. 773 41 29). South of Lannova as it enters Staré Město. Open M-F 7am-7pm, Sa 8am-noon. **Postal code:** 370 01.

Internet Access: X-Files@Internet Cafe, Senovážné nám. 6 (tel. 635 04 04). M-F 40Kč per 30min.; Sa-Su 30Kč per 30min. Open M-F 10am-10pm, Sa-Su 2-10pm.

Phone code: (0)38.

ACCOMMODATIONS

Private rooms are the best option in town (check with **TIC,** above).

Penzion U Výstaviště, U Výstaviště 17 (tel. 724 01 48). Take bus #1, 14, or 17 from the bus station five stops to U parku, and continue 150m along the side street that branches off to the right behind the bus stop. If you phone from the station, the English-speaking staff may offer a free lift in their red minivan, chock full o' laundry and kids off to sports practice. This hostel-like accommodation is the friendliest sleep in town. Call ahead to reserve one of the 12 beds. 250Kč for the 1st night, 200Kč thereafter.

University of South Bohemia dorms (tel. 777 44 00), on Studentská. Take tram #1 from in front of the bus station five stops to U parku. Turn around and head back down Husova, then turn right on Studentská. Open July-Aug. Doubles 240Kč, with bath 340Kč.

FOOD

Tucked away in many of Budějovice's small streets surrounding the town center are an abundance of tiny *restaurace*, many with outdoor terraces and most with hearty Czech fare. The **Večerka** grocery sits at Palackého 10. (Entrance on Hroznova. Open M-F 7am-8pm, Sa 7am-1pm, Su 8am-8pm.)

The Petit Restaurant, Hradební 14. Right off ul. Černé věže. Wooden booths and pewter chandeliers create an atmosphere perfect for garlic soup with cheese and fried croutons. Entrees 70-130Kč. Open M-Th 11am-11pm, F 11am-midnight, Sa noon-midnight.

Vinárna u paní Emy, Široká 25 (tel. 731 28 46). Near the main square. Fine Czech cooking. Aid your digestion of Tábor steak (95Kč), large salads (60Kč), or veggie dishes (50-70Kč) with a tall *Budvar* (0.5L 20Kč). Open daily noon-9pm.

Restaurace Ameno, Riegrova 8 (tel. 636 07 33). Satisfies your pasta and chimichanga craving. Don't miss the chocolate fondue (50-70Kč). Open M-Sa 11am-midnight.

SIGHTS

Surrounded by Renaissance and Baroque architecture, cobblestoned **Nám. Otakara II** is the largest square in the Czech Republic. **Samson's fountain** (Samsonova kašna; 1726) towers over the center of the square and serves as a good orientation point for the town. Samson's right eye looks to the **Black Tower** (Černá věž). To climb the 72m tower and see all the pretty bells costs nothing, but to get to the 360° balcony after the climb costs 10Kč (children 5Kč). Beware: the stairs are treacherous even for the sober. (Tel. 635 25 08. Open July-Aug. Tu-Su 10am-7pm; Sept.-Nov. Tu-Su 9am-5pm; Mar.-June Tu-Su 10am-6pm.) The tower once served as a belfry for the

THIS BUD'S FOR E.U. Many Yankees, having tasted the malty goodness of a *Budvar* brew, return home to find that the beer from Budweis is conspicuously unavailable. The fact that *Budvar* is the Czech Republic's largest exported beer, beating out even *Pilsner Urquell* in 1995, makes its absence from American store shelves stranger still. About the only way to sip an authentic *Budvar* on a porch in New York is to sneak a few bottles in your pack and pray they don't shatter in transit.

So where's the *Budvar?* The answer lies in a tale of trademarks and town names. České Budějovice (Budweis in German) had been brewing its own style of lager for centuries when the Anheuser-Busch brewery in St. Louis, Missouri came out with its Budweiser-style beer in 1876. Not until the 1890s, however, did the Budějovice Pivovar (Brewery) begin producing a beer labeled "Budweiser." International trademark conflicts ensued, and in 1911 the companies signed a non-competition agreement: Budějovice Pivovar got markets in Europe, and Anheuser-Busch took North America. But the story continues. A few years ago, Anheuser-Busch tried to end the confusion by buying a controlling interest in the makers of *Budvar*, but the Czech government refused. Coincidentally, Anheuser-Busch didn't order its usual one-third of the Czech hop crop the following year. Anheuser-Busch then sued for trademark infringement in Finland, while Budějovice Pivovar petitioned the E.U. to make the moniker "Budweiser" as exclusive as "Champagne," meaning that any brand sold in the E.U. under that name would have to come from the Budweiser region. As long as the battle continues, there is little chance that a *Budvar* in America will be anything but an illegal alien, so fill up while you can (and take a few for the road).

neighboring 13th-century **Cathedral of St. Nicholas** (Chrám sv. Mikuláše; tel. 731 12 63), which became a cathedral when the town became a bishopric in the 18th century. The altar is from 1791; the Stations of the Cross are from the 1920s. (Open daily 7am-6pm.) Behind Samson and to the left, the square's ornate 1555 Baroque **town hall** *(radnice)* stands a full story above the other buildings on the square.

The city's most famous attraction, the **Budweiser Brewery,** Karoliny Světlé 4 (tel. 770 50 11), can be reached by bus #2 or 4 from the center. In theory, tours for groups of six or more (70Kč per person) ought to be booked weeks in advance; in practice, travelers turning up early often manage to get inside. The English leaflets available make joining non-English groups easier. Contrary to popular belief, there's no free beer at the end of this brewery tour.

NIGHTLIFE

The lakes around Budějovice host open-air disco concerts in the summer—check the posters on buses and lampposts. Later in the evening, a younger, livelier crowd—some leather, a bit of facial hair, and plenty of piercings—drinks *Budvar* (12Kč) under metal skeleton lamp shades at the **MotorCycle Legend Pub,** Radnicí 9. (Open M-Th 11am-midnight, F 11am-3am, Sa 5pm-3am, Su 5pm-midnight.) For late night munching and more *Budvar* merriment, head to the funky **Restaurant Heaven Club Zeppelin,** Nám. Otakara II 38, on the third floor. (Open M-Sa 11am-1am.) Quieter types can opt for a cup of tea at **Dobrá čajovna,** Hroznova 16, directly behind the Černá věž, where regulars take off their shoes to sip sweet herbal brews and whisper in deference to the thrumming sitar. (Open M-Sa 1-10pm, Su 3-10pm.)

NEAR ČESKÉ BUDĚJOVICE: HLUBOKÁ NAD VLTAVOU

Hluboká is an ordinary town blessed with an extraordinary castle. This structure owes its success to Eleonora Schwarzenberg, who renovated the original Renaissance-Baroque castle into a Windsor-style fairytale stronghold in the mid-19th century. The castle has 141 rooms in all, and the 45min. tour takes in 20. En route, there are more Schwarzenberg portraits than you could shake a stick at, as well as tapestries, paintings (including copies of Raphael and da Vinci), and absurdly ornate wooden furniture. A tour is compulsory, and English tours only happen once or twice per day, depending on demand and the whim of the tour guide. If there is one, it costs an exorbitant 130Kč. Czech tours are cheaper and more frequent. (Tours 60Kč, students 6-18 30Kč. English guidebooks 59-90Kč.) Tours of the armory, the second largest in Bohemia, are also available (in Czech 40Kč, students 20Kč; in a foreign language, 100Kč, students and ages 6-18 50Kč.) The castle is open May-June Tu-Su 9am-noon and 12:30-5pm, July-Aug. daily 9am-noon and 12:30-5pm, and Apr. and Sept.-Oct. Tu-Su 9am-noon and 12:30-4:30pm.

GETTING THERE. **Buses** run from České Budějovice to **Hluboká pod Kostelem** (25 min., 11Kč) frequently, although there are fewer on weekends—look for buses with Týn nad Vltavou as their final destination. The most pleasant way to daytrip here is by bike (30min.). You can also hike from České Budějovice (2hr.). From the bus stop, head left on Nad parkovištěm, the main bus route. Turn left onto Zborovská, then right onto Bezručova at the street's end. From there, hike up the hill and bear left at the fork in the path. The castle will be on the right.

NEAR ČESKÉ BUDĚJOVICE: TŘEBOŇ

Yet another Rožmberk-Schwarzenberg dream house dotting the South Bohemian hills, the **Třeboň Estate** (tel. 72 11 93) is ideally placed in a town graced by a colorful center, shady parks, and a refreshing lake. The castle itself is noted as the final home of Petr Vok, the last of the Rožmberk family. After being evicted from his Český Krumlov estate in 1602 (see **Český Krumlov: Sights,** p. 220), Vok moved his court to Třeboň, which he constantly redecorated until his death in 1611. His additions to the chateau can be seen only with a guided tour *(trasa A)* that takes you through the Rožmberk armory, the picture gallery, the women's waiting room, and the gallery of shooting targets, marked by authentic gunshot holes. *Trasa B* takes you through the 19th-century Schwarzenberg rooms. Call ahead to reserve an English-speaking guide for a group, or join a Czech tour and read along in the English pamphlets. (45min. tours daily 9-11am and 1-4pm, on the half-hour. 35Kč, students 20Kč. English tours 70Kč, students 40Kč.)

GETTING THERE. **Buses** run frequently from České Budějovice to **Třeboň** (40min., 18Kč), with fewer on weekends. From the bus station, turn left on Sportovní and right onto Svobody, which curves to the right. At Palackého nám., turn left and follow Sokolská out of the square, past the gardens and through the pedestrian underpass. Sokolská becomes Husova within the town walls; turn right onto Březanova, the first street on the right, leading to the castle courtyard. The **ticket booth** is around the corner on the right, directly under the clock.

ČESKÝ KRUMLOV

The worst part about Česky Krumlov is leaving. Maybe it's the medieval cobblestone streets that lead through stone courtyards; maybe it's the Vltava, the winding river that darts in and around the town center and on into the South Bohemian countryside; or maybe it's the 13th-century castle that hovers over it all. Whatever it is, this UNESCO-protected town lures visitors in and doesn't let them go. Weeks could (and should) be spent hiking through the surrounding hills, kayaking down the Vltava, horseback riding through the castle gardens, and exploring the meandering center. Come for a day, but you're destined to stay for forty.

ORIENTATION

16km southwest of České Budějovice, Krumlov is best reached by frequent **buses** (45min.; M-F 22 per day, Sa 8 per day, Su 12 per day; 22Kč). If you get off at the small **Špičák** stop on the northern outskirts of town, it's an easy march downhill to the medieval center. From Špičák, pass through **Budějovice gate** and follow **Latrán** past the castle and over the Vltava. The street becomes Radniční as it enters Staré Město and leads into the main **Nám. Svornosti.** The **main bus terminal,** Kaplická 439 (tel. 34 14), lies to the southeast. To get to Nám. Svornosti from here, head to the upper street where stops #20-25 are located. With the station at your back, turn right and follow the small dirt path that veers to the left and heads uphill. At the path's intersection with Kaplická, turn right. At the light, cross the highway and head straight onto Horní, which leads right into the square.

PRACTICAL INFORMATION

Trains: Nádražní 31 (tel. 71 14 77), 2km uphill from the center. Connections to **České Budějovice** are longer than buses (1hr., 9 per day, 23Kč). Bus goes to the center (5Kč).

Taxis: Tel. 71 27 12.

Tourist Office: Nám. Svornosti 1 (tel. 71 11 83), in the town hall. Books pensions (starting at 550Kč) or private rooms, which can be a bit cheaper (doubles 800Kč). Also sells maps for cycling trips (25-59Kč). Open daily 9am-6pm.

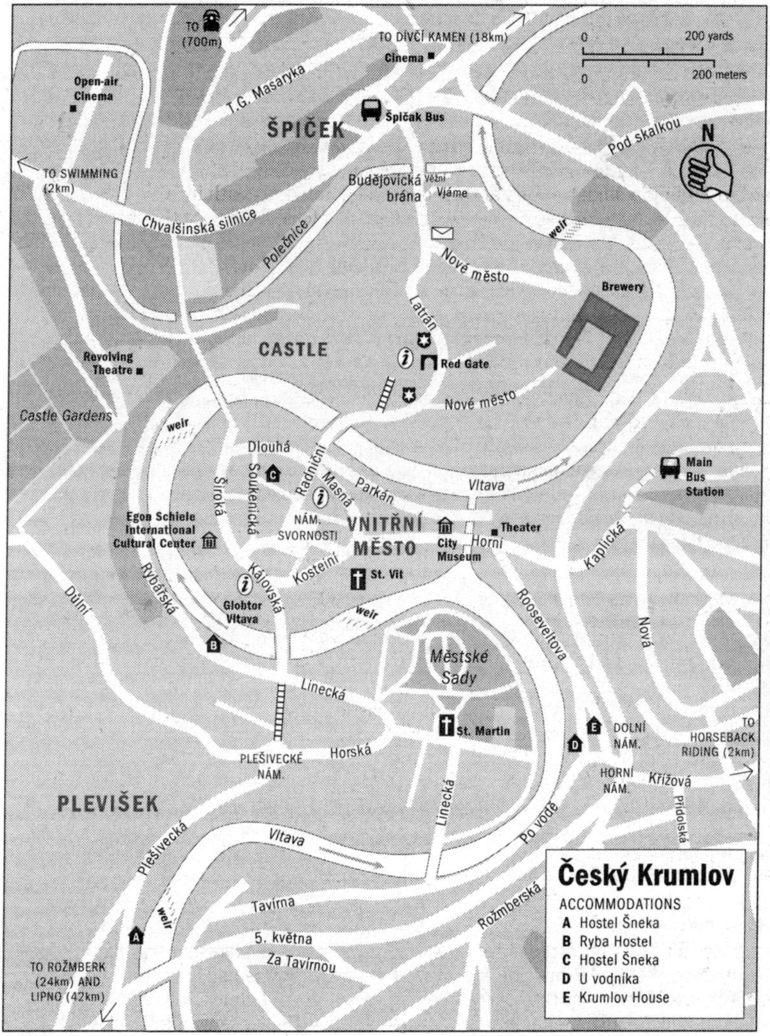

Budget Travel: Globtour Vltava, Kájovská 62 (tel./fax 71 19 78), rents boats (July-Aug. from 350Kč per day, Sept.-June from 200Kč per day) and mountain bikes (300Kč per day, outrageous 3000Kč deposit). Open daily 8am-8pm. AmEx/MC/Visa.

Currency Exchange: Moravia Bank, Soukenická 34 (tel. 71 13 77). Cashes traveler's checks for a 2% commission (min. 30Kč). Open M-F 8am-4pm. A **24hr. ATM** is available on the left side of Horní just before it merges into Nám. Svornosti.

Pharmacy: Nám. Svornosti 16 (tel. 71 17 87). Open M-F 8am-noon and 1-5pm.

Post office: Latrán 193 (tel. 71 19 98). 24hr. card-operated **phones** outside. Open M-F 7am-6pm, Sa 7-11am. **Postal code:** 381 01.

Internet: Log on for only 50Kč per hr. at **Europe Info Centrum,** Horní 155 (tel. 71 30 75). Open M-F 9am-6pm. The **Internet Café** in the castle courtyard offers better atmosphere and more computers. 30Kč for 15min., 90Kč for 1hr. Open daily 9am-10 pm.

Phone code: (0)337.

ACCOMMODATIONS

Private rooms *(Zimmer frei* or *ubytování)* abound; look for signs on ul. Parkán. Krumlov's stellar hostels, however, undoubtedly offer the best beds in town.

U vodníka, Po vodě 55 (tel. 71 19 35; email vodnik@ck.bohem-net.cz). Follow the directions to Nám. Svornosti, turn left onto Rooseveltova after the traffic light (the last street before the bridge), and follow the signs. This 13th-century hostel has a name that translates roughly to "the place of the river troll," but it is more like the place of the river god. American ex-pats Carolyn, Cal, and baby Aidan have lovingly turned their home into one of the best hostels in Europe. There's a garden out back where you can grill sausages on a spit or sit in a hand-carved seat overlooking the river. You can even borrow an innertube (free) to cruise down the Vltava. The staff will do your laundry (100Kč for 5kg), rent you a mountain bike (200Kč per day), lend you books from their fine library, and arrange boat rentals. Beds are 200Kč in the dorm and 250Kč in the 2 doubles.

Krumlov House, Rooseveltova 68 (same tel. as U vodníka), on your right before the highway, with beautiful dragon doors. Krumlov House is no less enticing than its sister hostel, U Vodnika. The same rates and services apply here, but Krumlov House hosts a livelier crowd. Sleep in hand-carved birch bunks, socialize with Australians in a huge kitchen (stereos and guitars included), and drink into the wee hours of the morning.

Hostel Skippy, Plešivecká 123 (tel. 72 83 80). Follow the directions from the main bus station to Nám. Svornosti, but at the light turn left onto the highway, which intersects with Plešivecká after it crosses the river; Hostel Skippy is on the right. Rooms are a hodge-podge mix of crazy rugs, comforters with big beds, and beautiful views of the Vltava below. Laundry 60Kč for 5kg; bike rental 180Kč per day. Manager Zdeňka (also known as 'Skippy') will serve you a made-to-order breakfast (30-50Kč). Beds 175Kč.

Ryba Hostel, Rybářská 5 (tel. 71 18 01). Overlooking the Vltava, across from the town center. Set out from the right-hand corner of Nám. Svornosti across from the tourist office, drift left onto Kájovská, then head over the bridge and down Rybářská. You'll see it from the bridge. Although it's not as hip as it used to be, this 17-bed hostel has dorm beds for 200Kč, huge comforters, and superb views of the town.

Hostel Šneka, Panská 19 (tel. 27 34 56). Follow the directions from the main bus station to Nám. Svornosti. With your back to Horní, go to the right corner of the square, then head straight down Panská; the hostel is 50m down on the right. Immaculate and centrally located, the "Snail" offers dorm beds for 190Kč and beds in a double with a gorgeous private bathroom for 250Kč. Houses a bar and rock club in its cavernous cellar.

FOOD

All of the hostels in Krumlov have kitchens. The most central supermarket in town is **SPAR,** Linecká 49. (Open M-Sa 7am-6pm, Su 9am-6pm.) For fresh produce, head to the **Cerstvé Ovoce Zelenina,** Latrán 45; the shop is on the left through the hallway.

Na louži, Kájovská 66 (tel. 71 12 80). Sizeable portions of great Czech cooking. Be prepared to wait; it's well worth it. Entrees 108-130Kč. Open daily 10am-10pm.

Cikánská jizba (Gypsy Room), Dlouhá 31 (tel. 55 85). Follow Radniční out of the main square and turn left down Dlouhá. Fire it up with spicy gypsy goulash (53Kč). The *halušky,* a gnocchi-like pasta, is not to be missed. Open M-Th 2-11pm, F-Sa 3-11pm.

Nonna Gina Pizzeria, Klášterní ul. 52 (tel. 51 87), right off Latrán. It's *amore:* pizza (65-100Kč), pasta (60-130Kč), and tiramisu (25Kč). Open daily 11am-11pm.

Vegetarian Restaurant, Parkán 105 (tel. 71 25 08). With your back to Horní from Nám. Svornosti, turn right onto Radniční. Take your second right onto Parkán; the restaurant is on the right. Find heaping portions of vegetarian dishes on a stone porch overlooking the Vltava. Entrees 60-80Kč. Open daily 11am-8:30pm. AmEx/MC/Visa.

SIGHTS

Perversely, pollution may have been Český Krumlov's biggest boon. In the early 20th century, an upstream paper mill putrefied the river, and most citizens moved to the town's outskirts. Thanks to such benign neglect, the medieval inner city escaped "development." Originally a 13th-century fortress, the **castle** was later home to a number of wealthy families. The main entrance to the castle is on Latrán. Take Radniční out of the town center, cross the river, and go up the stairs on your left. The castle gate is at the top of the stairs. The **stone courtyards** are free and open to the public. Don't miss the grizzly bears lurking in the moat. Two tours cover the castle—the first visits the older wing, taking in the **Chapel of St. George,** passing through the Baroque Schwarzenberg chambers, and emerging in the **ballroom,** adorned by frescoes of characters from Dante's *Commedia Dell'Arte.* The second tour explores the older, Renaissance-style rooms before moving into the 19th-century areas of the castle and ending with the splendid Baroque **theater.** Czech tours are only 50Kč, but to understand anything more than "Blah, blah, Schwarzenberg, blah," take the hour-long **English tour.** (Open June-Aug. Tu-Su 9am-noon and 1-5pm; May and Sept. Tu-Su 9am-noon and 1-4pm; Apr. and Oct. Tu-Su 9am-noon and 1-3pm. Enter the ticket office through the third stone courtyard. 110Kč, students 55Kč.) You can also visit the castle **tower** for a fine view of the town. (Open May-Sept. daily 9am-6pm, last entry 5:35pm; Oct. and Apr. daily 9am-5pm, last entrance 4:35pm. 25Kč, students 15Kč.) Wander the **galleries of the crypt** where local artists' works are displayed. (Open May-Oct. Tu-Su 10am-5pm. 30Kč, students 20Kč.) Or, stroll in the castle **gardens,** which house a riding school and a summer palace. (Open May-Sept. daily 8am-7pm; Apr. and Oct. daily 8am-5pm.)

The Austrian painter Egon Schiele (1890-1918) found Český Krumlov so enchanting that he decided to set up shop here in 1911. Sadly, the citizens ran him out after he started painting burghers' daughters in the nude. Decades later, the citizens realized how silly they'd been and founded the **Egon Schiele International Cultural Center,** Široká 70-72, with a wide variety of browsing material. Schiele's works, including the infamous nudes, share wall space with paintings by other 20th-century Central European artists, including Haher Fronius's excellent Kafka illustrations. The steep admission is well worth it. (Tel. 42 32; fax 28 20. Open daily 10am-6pm. 120Kč, students 80Kč.) The **city museum,** Horní 152, covers Krumlov's history with bizarre folk instruments, bone sculptures, and log barges that once plied the river. (Tel. 71 16 74). Open May-Sept. daily 10am-12:30pm and 1-5pm; Oct.-Apr. Tu-F 9am-noon and 1-5pm, Sa-Su 1-5pm. 30Kč, students 5Kč.)

ENTERTAINMENT

Hike into the hills for a pleasant afternoon of **horseback riding** at **Jezdecký klub Slupenec,** Slupenec 1. Rides take you through trails high above Český Krumlov. From the town center, take Horní to its intersection with the highway. At the second light, turn left onto Křížová and follow the red trail to Slupenec. The horses are hung over after the weekend, so there are no rides on Mondays. (Tel. 71 10 53.

Open Tu-Sa 9am-noon and 1:30-5:30pm. 220Kč per hr. Call ahead.) Summer in Krumlov gets hot; if you're not up for a swim in the Vltava, check out the town's **indoor/outdoor pool and steambaths.** For only 18Kč per hour you can plunge into icy-cold waters with the Krumlov moms and sweat off your *pivos* in a steamy sauna. From the town square, take Radniční to Latrán. Walk past the castle and the post office, take a left on the highway *Chvalšinská,* then a right on Fialková. The pool is 2min. up on the left. (Pool open Tu-Th 2:30-4pm and 7-10pm, F 1:30-4:30pm and 6-9pm, Sa 1-10pm, Su 1-9pm. Steambaths open W and F 7-9pm, Sa 6-9pm. 20Kč lock deposit.) To fully enjoy the waters of the Vltava, ask at your hostel about innertubes and spend a day lazing down the river. Jump out next to **Pepo's Pub** (or you'll float to Budějovice) and repeat the circuit. You can also traipse the river on a canoe or kayak, which can be rented from **Maleček Boat Rental,** Rooseveltova 28 (tel./fax 71 25 08; 2-person canoe and round-trip transport 600Kč).

The castle's **revolving theater** (Jihočeské divadlo) hosts opera, Shakespeare, and classic comedies. Performances are in Czech, but watching the set revolve around the audience more than makes up for it. (Open June-Sept. Tickets 60Kč. Check at the infocentrum for current showings and to purchase tickets). If you'd rather see something in English, **cinemas** abound in Český Krumlov, usually with Czech subtitles. **Kino J&K,** Highway 159 next to the Špičák bus stop, is open year-round and shows all of the latest Hollywood blockbusters. (M, W, and F 6:30pm; Sa 6pm; town film club Th 7pm. Tickets 30-40Kč.) Or, ask your hostel owner about the town's **open-air cinema** in the summer—it's like a drive-in, but without the cars. Check at the infocentrum for showings at both cinemas. The **Five-petal Rose Festival,** Krumlov's hip medieval gig the third weekend of June, is a great excuse to wear tights and joust with the locals. Krumlov also hosts two world-class music festivals—the **Early Music Festival** (the second week of July) with live appearances by basso di Gamba and other cool old instruments, and the **International Music Fest** (mid-August), which attracts hordes of major Czech acts.

NIGHTLIFE

U Hada (Snake Bar), Rybářská 37. There *is* a live snake, but that's only half the reason this place is so hip. 0.5L beer 20Kč. Open M-Th 7pm-3am, F-Sa 7pm-4am.

Rumyší díra (Mousehole, a.k.a. The Boat Bar). Continue down the steps to the river from Barbakan, for this notorious summer-only midnight spot that makes the river a little more interesting by supplying booze to canoers and kayakers who stop at the Vltava hut as they drift by. 0.5L *Eggenberg* 20Kč. Unpredictable hours.

U baby, Rooseveltova 66. An authentic Czech bar that pours hefty steins of *Eggenberg* (18Kč) in a refurbished medieval building next door to Krumlov House (see p. 222). Enjoy *horké víno* (hot wine served with lemon and cloves; 25Kč) and chat with local characters. Usually open Tu-Su 6pm-midnight, but hours vary.

Babylon, Rybářšká 6. Next to Ryba Hostel (see p. 222). Krumlov's attempt at a biker bar, with AC/DC blaring inside and men in leather dominating the river-side terrace. Occasional live music in the evening. *Budvar* 15Kč. Open Su-Th 2pm-2am, F-Sa 2pm-3am.

NEAR ČESKÝ KRUMLOV: ALONG THE VLTAVA & THROUGH THE HILLS

Local firms and hostels rent out mountain bikes (see p. 222) for the express purpose of getting you out into the South Bohemian countryside. There are also a couple of routes that begin in Český Krumlov itself. The first is a 70km loop along the banks of the Vltava, the second a much shorter, hillier trip to a couple of local sites. Check the weather before you go. (See **Camping & the Outdoors,** p. 38.)

For a ride along the Vltava, turn right onto the bridge from Globtour/Vltava Travel (where you can rent a bike for 300Kč per day). Cross the river, turn left onto Linecká, and then turn right when it crosses the river again and intersects with Po vodě. At the highway's intersection, turn right onto Května, cross the river, and follow signs to **Rožmberk** (24km), which boasts the first real sight along the way. The route leads through the towns **Vetřní** and **Zátoň.** Vetřní hosts a paper mill largely responsible for the polluted condition of the river, while Zátoň is so small it would be unnoticeable except for a lovely church perched atop a hill 200m to the left of the road. Carry on along the banks of the river until you see a pale fortress tower up on the left. Rožmberk is around the next bend. You can stop here and see the **castle** (tel. 74 98 38; fax 74 98 13), the seat of the mighty Rožmberks (Rosenbergs), but you must pay for a guided tour to get in. (Tours leave June-Aug. Tu-Su at 9am and 4:15pm; May and Sept. Tu-F at 9am and 3:15pm; Apr. and Oct. Sa-Su and holidays at 9am and 3:15pm. 30Kč, students 20Kč.)

Lipno lies another 18km upstream, and the "up" makes itself particularly evident here. Before you reach it, look for the ancient Cisterian monastery at **Vyšší Brod. Frýmburk** sits along the lake shore 8km west. Complete with a waterside church, it smacks of Swiss quaintness and is a better rest spot than Lipno. From Frymburk, a road leads back to Český Krumlov, mostly downhill for 22km, to close the 70km loop. If you can't make it this far, you must retreat the way you came: there's no alternate route. If biking up the hills seems daunting, you can take a bus to Rožmberk or Lipno—two of the best towns in southern Bohemia.

Unlike the road that curves around the Vltava, the shorter route north heads through hillside meadows. From the town center, take Horní across the river to its intersection with the highway. Turn left at the light and follow the highway as it veers left and crosses the river. Turn right at the signs toward Budějovice. Head up the giant hill and turn toward Srnín; two gas stations and a supermarket point the way. Be careful crossing railway tracks without a crossing guard. When the road splits near a factory, turn right and head up into the meadow. From here, you'll whiz through Srnín and follow the signs to **Zlatá Koruna.** The long descent ends at the gate of the 1263 monastery (tel. 74 31 26). A tour leads through the massive complex's courts, halls, library (the second largest in the Czech Republic), convent, chapel, and church. Over the course of its tumultuous history, the local order of monks was almost abolished several times and was stripped of its property by beerlord Eggenberg before finally being sent into the lay world in 1785. Since then, the building has been a pencil factory and an under-appreciated tourist attraction. (Open May-Sept. Tu-Su 8am-noon and 1-5pm; Apr. and Oct. Tu-Su 9am-noon and 1-4pm. Last tour 45min. before closing. 20Kč per person, students 10Kč. Minimum 5 people; available in English.) From here, walk your bike back uphill, and at the T-junction go straight toward Křemže (left leads back the way you came).

After entering **Třísov,** take the second right (by the village notice-board) and cross the railway line just below the tiny station. Continue down this stone path toward the river. After about 10min. you'll reach a few houses and the river bank. Here, the stone path becomes a sidewalk, passes left of an abandoned building, and comes to a metal bridge. Chain your bike and head over the bridge and to the left. Be sure not to cross the second metal bridge; trot up the steps to the right to get to the 1349 ruins of the castle **Dívčí kámen.** Climb to the top of the ruins for a gorgeous panorama of the Šumava region—it's a great spot for meditating or picnicking. Getting out of Dívčí kámen, unfortunately, is rather brutal. Once you've climbed back out of Třísov, it's downhill (almost) all the way home.

A third and easier option is to catch a train from Český Krumlov to Horní Plana (1hr., every 2-3hr., 26Kč) and enjoy the downhill 17km coast with a gorgeous vista of the South Bohemian countryside. With your back to the train station, turn right on the dirt path, left on the first road, then right at the road's intersection with the highway. There will be signs leading back to Český Krumlov.

MORAVIA

Wine-making Moravia makes up the easternmost third of the Czech Republic. Home of the country's finest folk-singing tradition and two leading universities, it's also the birthplace of a number of Central European notables: Tomáš G. Masaryk, founder and first president of Czechoslovakia; composer Leoš Janáček; and psychoanalyst Sigmund Freud. Johann Gregor Mendel founded modern genetics in his pea-garden in a Brno monastery. Brno and Olomouc are the towns most worth visiting (skip industrial Ostrava), but South Moravia also harbors the remarkable caves of the Moravský Kras and the architectural pearl Telč.

BRNO

The Czech Republic's second-largest city, Brno (berh-NO; pop. 388,900) is a mecca of business and industry, and the streets show it: scores of "erotic club" sirens call out to lonely men, while restaurant menus list prices with corporate expense accounts in mind. The city does have an upside: an extensive array of Gothic and Baroque churches, splendidly cheap opera, and amazing ice cream. While there are more exciting and beautiful places to visit in the Czech Republic, Brno lets travelers escape the tourist hordes and experience a living Czech city.

ORIENTATION

Brno's compact center makes everything in town accessible by foot. From the train station's main entrance, cross the three tram lines on **Nádražní** to **Masarykova,** which leads to the main square, **Nám. Svobody.** To get to the tourist office, turn left off Masarykova onto Květinářská just before Svobody, which leads to the smaller square, **Zelný trh.** The tourist office is across Zelný trh on **Radnická.**

PRACTICAL INFORMATION

Trains: Tel. 42 21 48 03. To: **Bratislava** (2hr., 9 per day, 99Kč); **Budapest** (4½hr., 2 per day, 768Kč); **Prague** (3hr., 12 per day, 220Kč); and **Vienna** (2hr., 1 per day, 415Kč). International booking office in the train station handles Wasteels tickets. Open 24hr.

Buses: Tel. 43 21 77 33. On Zvonařka, down Plotní from the trains. Walk over the pedestrian path at the station's far corner. Follow it to Tesco and then under the train station. To **Prague** (3hr., many, 120Kč) and **Vienna** (2½hr., 2 per day, 250Kč).

Local Transportation: Trams, trolleys, and **buses** 8Kč; luggage 4Kč; 24hr. pass 40Kč. Buy tickets at a *tabák* or kiosk. Ticket checks happen, and are accompanied by 200Kč fines. Half the tram routes run all night; the rest run 5am-8pm, 10:30pm, or 11pm.

Taxis: Radiotaxi, tel. 42 21 88 88.

Tourist Office: Kulturní a informační centrum města Brna, Radnická 8 (tel. 42 21 10 90; fax 42 21 07 58). Multilingual staff books hotels, private rooms (from 400Kč), and hostels (200Kč), and sells city **maps** (39-60Kč). Open M-F 8am-6pm, Sa-Su 9am-5pm.

Budget Travel: GTS International, Vachova 4 (tel. 42 21 31 47; fax 42 21 26 90). Books dorms July-Aug. (from 400Kč). Open M-F 9am-6pm, Sa 10am-2pm.

Currency Exchange: Komerční banka, Kobližná 3 (tel. 42 12 71 11; fax 42 21 64 76), at the northeast corner of Nám. Svobody. Gives Visa cash advances and cashes most traveler's checks for a 2% commission (minimum 50Kč), and has an AmEx/Cirrus/MC/Visa **ATM.** Open M-F 8am-5pm. **American Express,** Starobrněnská 20 (tel. 42 21 81 33). Cashes traveler's checks for no commission. Open M-F 9am-noon and 1:30-5pm.

Luggage storage: At the train station. 10Kč per bag per day.

Pharmacy: Kobližná 7 (tel. 42 21 02 22). Open M-F 7am-7pm, Sa 8am-1pm.

Post Office: Poštovská 3/5 (tel. 42 32 11 01). Open M-F 7am-10pm, Sa 8am-1pm. **Postal code:** 602 00.

Internet Access: @InternetCafe, Lidická 17 (tel. 41 24 53 44). Two levels of speedy PCs. 2Kč per min. Open M-F 10am-10pm, Sa-Su 2-10pm.

Phone code: (0)5.

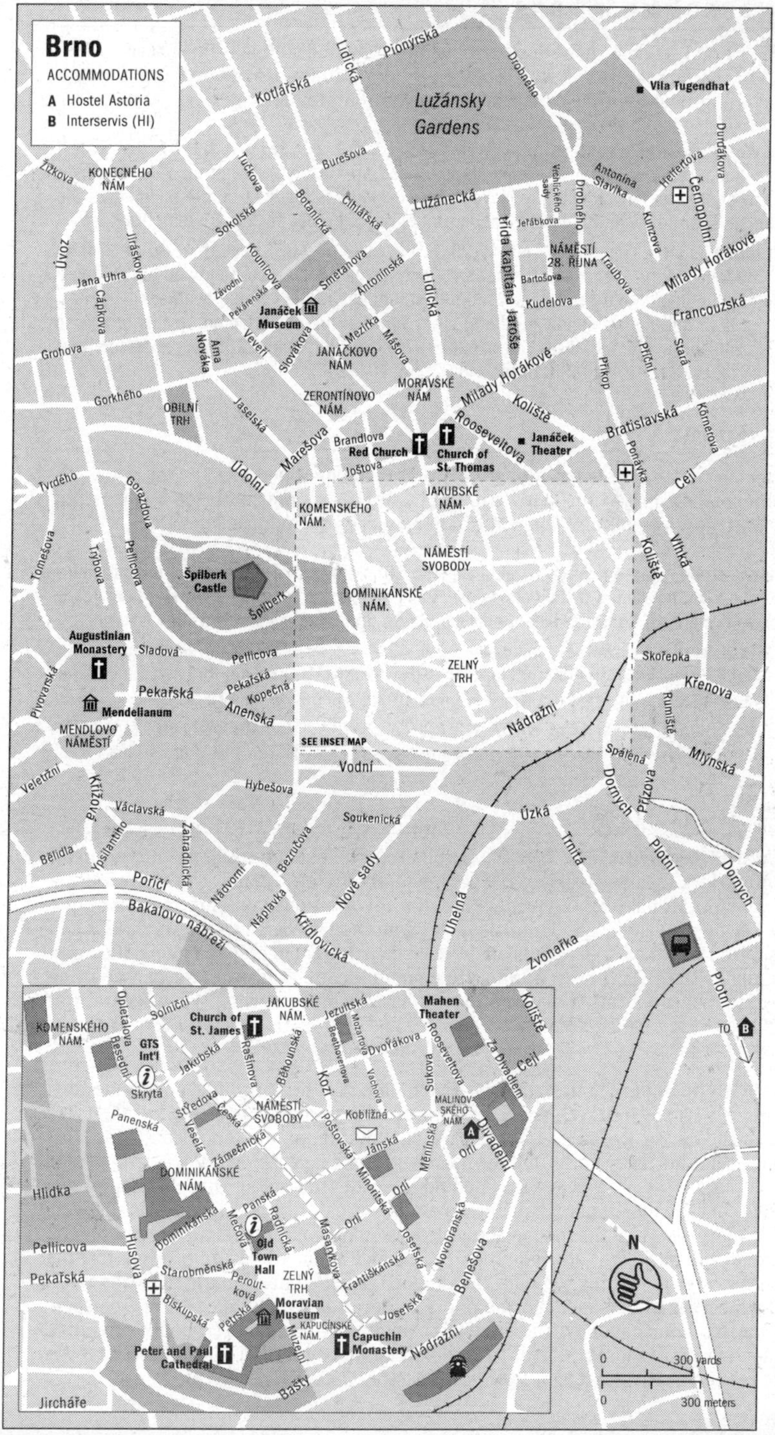

CZECH REPUBLIC

ACCOMMODATIONS

Brno's hotel scene is geared toward business visitors, so it was no surprise when one of the budget hotels was replaced by the "Moulin Rouge erotic night club disco." The tourist office can arrange private rooms in the center.

Hotel Astorka, Novobranská 3 (tel. 42 51 03 70; fax 42 51 01 06; email astorka@jamu.cz). From the train station, head up Masarykova and take the first right onto Josefská, which leads to Novobranská. Astorka is the light purple building on the right. Brand new and a great location. Doubles 200Kč per person, triples 150Kč.

Interservis (HI), Lomená 48 (tel. 45 23 31 65; fax 33 11 65). Take tram #9 or 12 from the train station to the end at Komárov. Continue along Hněvkovského and turn left onto the unmarked Pompova (the second to last turn before the railroad overpass). The hostel is on the right. Friendly staff and great views of the city brighten up this otherwise lackluster hostel. MC/Visa. Lone double 575Kč; 5-bed flatlets 265Kč per person, with breakfast 315Kč; with ISIC or HI card 230Kč, 270Kč.

FOOD

Street-side pizza joints far outnumber traditional *párek* peddlers. A fruit and vegetable **market** thrives on Zelný trh. (Open M-F 9am-6pm.) A **Tesco** awaits right behind the train station. (Open M-F 7am-8pm, Sa 7am-6pm, Su 8am-5pm.)

Livingstone, Starobrněnská 1 (tel. 42 27 51 56), across from Zelný trh. Elsa is the name of one of the animal pelts looming over this Cure-playing, angst-filled student pub/cafe. Daily menu 41Kč. Open M-F noon-1am, Sa-Su 6pm-1am; kitchen closed weekends.

Aviatik Klub a Restaurace, Jakubská 7 (tel. 42 21 45 55). From Nám. Svobody, walk up Česká past McDonald's and turn right on Jakubská. Hand-painted hot air balloon murals lead to this bistro. Czech favorites 30-75Kč. Open M-Sa 11am-11pm.

Fischer Cafe, Masarykova 8/10 (tel. 42 22 18 80). This cafe might not pull off its intended New York chic, but it serves good salads (35-77Kč). Open daily 10am-11pm.

SIGHTS

CAPUCHIN MONASTERY CRYPT. (Hrobka Kapucínského kláštera). If you liked Kutná Hora (see p. 210), you'll love this morbid resting place. The monks at the Capuchin Monastery Crypt developed a revolutionary embalming technique involving extensive ventilation, preserving more than 100 18th-century monks and assorted worthies. The results are now on display to enlighten the living: the crypt begins with the Latin inscription, "Remember death," and ends with an uplifting slogan in a room full of dead monks, "What you are, we were. What we are, you will be." *(Just to the left of Masarykova from the station. Tel. 42 21 23 32. Open M-Sa 9am-noon and 2-4:30pm, Su 11-11:45am and 2-4:30pm. 40Kč, students 20Kč.)*

OLD TOWN HALL. (Stará radnice). This building is the stuff of legends—literally. The Old Town Hall's strangely crooked Gothic portal purportedly got that way after the carver working on it blew his commission on too much good Moravian wine. Another story has it that the dismayed stone face inside is the petrified head of a burgher who met his doom behind the wall after siding with the Hussites in 1424. But the most famous tale involves the stuffed "dragon" hanging on the wall. The story goes that the medieval reptile was on the rampage. In an attempt to stop him, a valiant knight stuffed an ox carcass with quicklime and offered it to the beast. After devouring the bait, the dragon quenched his thirst in a nearby river; the lime began to slake, and the poor creature's belly exploded—thus the seam along his stomach today. The dragon is actually an Amazonian crocodile offered to the town by Archduke Matyáš to garner favor among the burghers. *(Radnická 8. Just off Zelný trh. Open Apr.-Oct. daily 9am-5pm; last tour at 4:30pm. Tower 10Kč.)*

PETER AND PAUL CATHEDRAL. (Biskupská katedrála sv. Petra a Pavla). Although destroyed by Swedes in the Thirty Years' War, the replacement Peter and Paul Cathedral was neo-Gothicized 100 years ago. You may hear the bells strike noon at eleven o'clock. Allegedly Brno was saved from the Swedish siege one day in 1645, when the besieging general gave his army until noon to capture the town; after noon, he would withdraw. When the townsfolk learned of this, they rang the bells early, and the Swedes slunk away. The bells have been striking noon at 11am ever since. *(On Petrov Hill, south of Zelný trh. Cathedral and tower open M-Su 10am-6pm; crypt open M-Su 10am-6pm. Tower 15Kč, students 7Kč; crypt 10Kč, students 7Kč.)*

NEAR NÁMĚSTÍ SVOBODY. Biskupská curves from the Peter and Paul Cathedral down Dominikanská, which flows into Dominikánské nám. From here turn right down Zámečnická to **Nám. Svobody,** Brno's largest square. The partially gold **Plague Column** (Morový sloup) has successfully warded off infections for the last 300 years (if you don't count McDonald's recent arrival). North of Nám. Svobody along Rašínova, the great **Church of St. James** (Kostel sv. Jakuba), with its strangely thin tower pointing skyward, was built for Brno's medieval Flemish and German communities. Since its construction, the church has undergone more than ten renovations. The French Huguenot Raduit de Souches, who helped save Brno from Swedish invasion in 1645, rests inside in a great stone monument. Returning to the square, go left out along Kobližná and turn left on Rooseveltova for an exercise in comparative architecture. On the left is the grand **Mahlen Theater** (Mahlenovo divadlo), built by the Viennese duo Helmer and Fellner in the 19th century; on the right stands the 1960s **Janáček Theater** (Janáčkovo divadlo), home to Brno's opera.

ŠPILBERK CASTLE. (Hrad Špilberk). Once home to Czech kings and later a mighty Habsburg fortress, Špilberk Castle has had a checkered past. Once the city's main defense against the Swedes, it was later used as a prison, first in the 1700s to hold Hungarian, Italian, Polish and Czech patriots and revolutionaries, then during WWII by the Nazis. A journey through the prison corridors is more intriguing than the rather weak collection of torture-related exhibits. *(From Nám. Svobody, take Zámečnická through Dominikánské nám. and turn right on Panĕnská to Husova, heading uphill. Tel. 42 21 41 45. Open daily June-Sept. 9am-6pm; Oct.-Mar. 9am-5pm; last tour 1hr. before closing. 20Kč, students 10Kč; English-speaking guide 200Kč.)*

MENDLOVO NÁMĚSTÍ. In the heart of Old Brno, the high Gothic **Basilica of the Assumption of the Virgin Mary** (Basilika Nanebevzetí Panny Marie) houses the 13th-century Black Madonna, the Czech Republic's oldest wooden icon, which purportedly held off—that's right—the Swedes in 1645. *(From the castle, walk downhill on Pelicova and take the stairs to Sladová. Go left onto Úvoz to Mendlovo nám. Church open daily 5-7:15pm, Su also 7am-12:15pm.)* The Augustinian monastery next door was the home of **Gregor Mendel,** the father of modern genetics. It took the scientific world 50 years to appreciate his work, but as his words now accurately predict in stone, "*Má doba přijde!*" ("My time will come!"). The **Mendelianum,** Mendlovo nám. 1a, documents Mendel's life and work, explaining his remarkable experiments with peas and bees. The Lysenkoist Communists took down his statue—it's now back in the courtyard. *(Open daily July-Aug. 9am-6pm; Sept.-June 8am-5pm. 8Kč, students 4Kč.)*

OTHER CHURCHES. The **Church of St. Thomas** (Kostel sv. Tomáše) was built in 1350 as an Augustinian monastery. Today, the church shelters the remains of its founder—the brother of Charles IV (as in the bridge)—in front of the main altar. *(From Nám. Svobody, head up Rasínova. The church is on the right.)* The **Red Church** (Červený kostel) is an 1860s medieval pastiche built by Heinrich Ferstel, who also built Vienna's neo-Gothic Votivkirche. It commemorates the 17th-century Protestant pedagogue Jan Amos Komenský (Comenius), who revolutionized the philosophy of education and was offered the presidency of the then-fledgling Harvard College, an offer he declined. *(Walk down Joštova to where it elbows with Rašínova at St. Thomas.)*

ENTERTAINMENT

The Old Town Hall hosts frequent recitals and concerts; tickets are on sale at the tourist office's **ticket agency,** Běhounská 16. (Open M-F 9am-5pm.) Get **theater and opera** tickets from the office at Dvořákova 11. **Cinemas** abound, usually showing Hollywood flicks subtitled in Czech (50-200Kč, depending on the film's age and popularity). **Kapitol Kino,** Divadelní 3 (tel. 42 21 33 51), shows American blockbusters; **Lucerna,** Minská 19 (tel. 74 70 70), shows British and American indie films.

NIGHTLIFE

Look for posters advertising **techno raves,** Brno's hottest summer entertainment. Surprisingly, it's easier to find a *pivnice* than a wine pub in the heart of wine-producing Moravia, but there is that occasional *vinárna* (bottles 80-100Kč).

Divadelní hospoda Veselá husa (Merry Goose Theatrical Pub), Zelný trh 9 (tel. 42 21 16 30). At the back of the building. An eclectic crowd gathers for impromptu performances and improv comedy. *Pilsner* 18.60Kč. Open M-F 11am-midnight, Sa-Su 3pm-midnight.

Pivnice Minipivovar Pegas, Jakubská 4 (tel. 42 21 01 04). This newfangled microbrewery has a loyal following. Pints 17Kč. Open daily 9am-midnight.

Mersey, Minská 14 (tel. 41 24 06 23). Take tram #3 or 11 from Česká to Tábor. Hosts visiting bands and DJs, sometimes from "overseas." Mostly rock, but some techno and jungle. Beer 12Kč. Open daily 2pm until dawn, but music starts at 9pm.

H46, Hybšova 46 (tel. 43 23 49 45). A 10min. walk left with your back to the train station, or a few stops on tram #1 or 2. Ring the bell if the door is locked. Inside, a mostly gay, partly lesbian, others-welcome bar. Open nightly 4pm-4am.

NEAR BRNO: MORAVSKÝ KRAS

You may spend a few hours waiting for buses to Moravský Kras (MO-rahv-skee krahs), but any amount of time spent en route is well worth it. Inside the forested hills of Southern Moravia, a network of **caves** around Skalní Mlýn has been opened to visitors. The most popular is **Punkevní,** where tour groups pass magnificent stalactites and stalagmites, many with their own silly names (like *rokoková panenká,* "rococo doll") to emerge at **Stepmother Abyss** (Propast Macocha). The story goes that a wicked stepmother from a nearby town threw her stepson into the gaping hole. When villagers found the boy suspended from a branch by his trousers, they saved him and threw in the woman instead. Over the last 20 years, 50 people have committed suicide by jumping off the abyss's 140m ledge. During the summer, spelunkers are rowed back along the underground Punkva river. Buy tickets for the tour at Skalní Mlýn's bus stop or in the entrance. Bring a sweater; it gets chilly. (July-Aug. first tour 8:20am, last 3:50pm. 70Kč, students 25Kč; Sept.-June 50Kč, students 25Kč. Photos 10Kč; video 50Kč.)

Just around the corner from Skalní Mlýn is the equally impressive but much less touristed **Catherine Cave** (Kateřinská jeskyně), named for a shepherdess who went inside looking for a stray and never reemerged. Huge halls with stunning rock formations, asthma-curing properties, and perfect acoustics await. (Open daily summer 8:20am-4pm; off-season 8:20am-2pm. 30min. tour 30Kč, students 15Kč.)

GETTING THERE. Get there early, as tours are likely to sell out. Catching a **train** from Brno to **Blansko** at 6:50am (30min., 7 per day, 17Kč) will get you to the caves before 9am. From here, either **hike** the 8km on the green trail from Blansko to Skalní Mlýn or take the **bus** (15min., 5 per day, 6Kč) from the station just up the road from the trains. The 6:50am train gets to Blansko at 7:21am. The 7:40am bus gets you to the caves by 8am, in time for the first 8:20am tour. At **Skalní Mlýn,** there's a ticket and info office (tel. (0506) 553 79; call ahead to reserve a ticket) and a shuttle to the cave. (Round-trip 40Kč, students 20Kč.) Or, walk the 1.5km along the yellow trail. The **BVV travel agency** in Brno, Starobrněnská 20 (tel. 42 21 77 45), organizes afternoon tours (640Kč per person, 4 person minimum).

NEAR BRNO: TELČ

The Italian aura of Telč (TELCH) stems from a trip **Zachariáš of Hradec,** the town's ruler, took to Genoa in 1546. He was so enamored of the new Renaissance style that he brought back a battalion of Italian artists and craftsmen to spruce up his humble Moravian castle and town. Stepping over the cobblestone footbridge into the main square makes it easy to see why UNESCO deemed the Gingerbread town of Telč a World Heritage Monument: the square is flanked by long arcades of peach-painted gables, lime-green Baroque bays, and time-worn terra cotta roofs.

While it's easy to get caught up browsing the center's porticos and watching local children in traditional Moravian costume sing and dance, don't miss a tour of Telč's castle. There are two options—*trasa A* and *trasa B* (both 45min.). Buy your ticket, wait in the courtyard, and when there are enough people and a guide is ready, a tour will begin. *Trasa A* takes you through the Renaissance hallways past tapestries, through the old chapel, and under extravagant ceilings; *trasa B* leads through the rooms decorated in later styles. Any of the guidebooks on sale around town (from 30Kč) provide useful commentary in English. (Open May-Aug. Tu-Su 9-11:30am and 1-6pm; Apr. and Sept.-Oct. Tu-Su 9am-noon and 1-5pm. Final tour leaves 45min. before the castle closes. Tours 50Kč, students 25Kč, English guide 100Kč per group.) In the arcaded courtyard, a **museum** displays examples of Telč's folklore. (Last entrance to museum 30min. before castle closes. 16Kč, students 8Kč. English leaflets available.) The **gallery** off the walled garden is a memorial to artist **Jan Zrzavý** (1890-1977), who trained as a neo-Impressionist, dabbled in Cubism, and produced some striking religious paintings. This collection of his wacky work is definitely worth a look (see **History,** p. 175). Get an English guidebook at the reception desk. (Open May-Aug. Tu-Su 8am-noon and 1-5pm; Apr. and Sept. Tu-F 9am-noon and 1-4pm, Sa 9am-1pm. 10Kč, students 5Kč.) You can also rent a **row-boat** from **Půjčovna lodí,** on the shore, to view the castle and town from the swan-filled lake. (Open June 20-Aug. 31 daily 10am-7pm. 30min. 20Kč.)

GETTING THERE. Buses running between **Brno** and **České Budějovice** stop at Telč (2hr., 7 per day, 65-75Kč). The **bus station** lies five minutes from Nám. Zachariáše z Hradce. Follow the pedestrian path and turn right on Tyršova, then left on Masarykovo. Pass under the archway on the right to enter the square.

OLOMOUC

More chic than Brno but quainter than Prague, Olomouc (OH-lo-mohts; pop. 104,800), the historic capital of North Moravia, embodies only the best aspects of the Czech Republic. The masterfully rebuilt town center offers a charming network of cobblestone paths, triangular squares, and Baroque architecture with a dose of modern sleekness. Restaurants feature tofu platters and boutiques sell only the hippest Eurofashions. Surprisingly, Olomouc remains virtually undiscovered by umbrella-toting tourists, who are far outnumbered by local scholars of Comenius and Hus, lending the squares an eerie quiet in the evenings.

ORIENTATION

All trams from the **train station** head downtown (5 stops, 6Kč per ticket). The **bus station** lies one stop beyond the trains, heading away from the center on tram #5. Take the tram to Koruna and the gigantic cement block **Prior** department store, then follow 28. října 50m to **Horní nám.,** the town's main square.

PRACTICAL INFORMATION

Trains: Jeremenkova 60 (tel. 476 21 75). To **Brno** (1½hr., 12 per day, 53-68Kč) and **Prague** (3½hr., 15 per day, 127Kč).

Buses: Sladkovského 37 (tel. 332 91). To **Brno** (1½hr., every hr. 5:30am-8pm, 70Kč) and **Prague** (4hr., 2 per day, 175-200Kč).

Local Transportation: The city's **trams** and **buses** all require 6Kč tickets, sold at kiosks marked with a big yellow arrow. Most run between the train station and Prior.

Taxis: Ekotaxi, tel. 522 06 66.

Tourist Office: Tel. 551 33 85; fax 522 08 43; email tourist@risc.upol.cz. On Horní nám., in the *radnice*. Books hotels, hostels, and private rooms (from 230Kč per person). In summer, posts student housing fliers. 10Kč trips up the town hall tower daily at 11am, 12:30pm, 3pm, and 5pm. Open daily Mar.-Nov. 9am-7pm; Dec.-Feb. 9am-5pm.

Budget Travel: CKM, Denišova 4 (tel. 522 21 48; fax 522 39 39). Books rooms (from 300Kč per person) and sells train tickets. Open M-F 9am-5pm.

Currency Exchange: Komerční banka, Svobody 14 (tel. 550 91 11) and Denišova 47 (tel. 550 91 69), cash most traveler's checks and give MC cash advances for a 2% commission. Its annex gives MC/AmEx cash advances. Both open M-F 8am-5pm.

ATMs: All over Horní nám.

Luggage storage: At the train station. 10Kč per piece per day; 24hr. lockers 5Kč.

Pharmacy: At Ostružnická and Horní nám. Open M-F 8am-6pm, Sa 8am-noon.

Post Office: Horní nám. 27. Open M-F 7am-7pm, Sa 8am-noon. **Postal code:** 771 00.

Internet Access: Ostružnická 20 (tel. 523 22 09). Open M-F 9am-8pm, Su 1-10pm.

Phone code: (0)68.

ACCOMMODATIONS

Cheap beds (100Kč) appear in July and August when **university dorms** open to tourists. Olomouc levies a 15Kč tax on all rooms, but it's usually included in the price.

Pension na Hradbách, Hrnčířská 14 (tel. 523 32 43). From Horní nám., head down Školní, go straight along Purkrabská, and turn right onto Hrnčířská. Small, friendly pension in the quiet, old streets of the town center. Not much space, so call ahead. Luxurious singles with private bath and TV a steal at 500Kč; doubles 600Kč.

Hostel Betania, Wurmova 5 (tel. 523 38 60). Take tram #2 or 4 three stops to U Domů on 1. máje; Wurmova is on the left. Spacious bedrooms and baths worthy of a 4-star hotel, 5min. from the center. Singles 290Kč; doubles 180Kč per person.

Hostel Plavecký stadion, Legionářská 11 (tel. 41 31 81; fax 541 32 56). At the swimming stadium. Take any tram from the train station to Nám. Hrdinů. Go back through the bus park, head left under the airplane, and go around the pool buildings. The hostel is part of the pool complex–airy in the morning, but with a chlorinated tang by afternoon. Swimming 30Kč. Singles 415Kč; doubles 430Kč.

FOOD

For do-it-yourselfers, a **24hr. grocery** is at Komenského 3.

U červeného volka, Dolní nám. 39 (tel. 522 60 69). Tofu pioneers in Olomouc. Delicious soy dishes (50Kč) and vegetables. Open M-Sa 10am-11pm.

Cafe Caesar, Horní nám. (tel. 522 92 87). In the town hall. Caesar was, they say, the founder of Olomouc. Garlicky pizzas (31 varieties, 48-108Kč) and cheap plates of pasta (44-67Kč). Open M-Sa 9am-1am, Su 1pm-midnight. AmEx/MC/Visa.

Restaurace U Huberta, 1. máje 7 (tel. 522 40 17). The only non-traditional thing here is the sign in the dining room requesting patrons not to smoke noon-3pm. Better-than-average Czech cuisine, with daily prepared meals (34-46Kč). Open M-Sa 10am-10pm.

SIGHTS

At the center of Staré Město sits **Horní nám.** The massive 1378 **Town Hall** *(radnice)* and its spired clock tower dominate the center. A wonderful astronomical clock is set in the town hall's north side. In 1954, communist clockmakers replaced the mechanical saints with steelworkers, who strike the hour with their glorious hammers and sickles. The black-and-gold **Trinity Column** (Sloup Nejsvětější Trojice) soars higher (35m) than all other Baroque sculptures in the Czech Republic. Farther along 28. října, next to the massive copper cube of the Prior department store, the blocky Gothic **Church of St. Maurice** (Kostel sv. Mořice) might well have been the minimalist eyesore of its day, but its rich interior more than makes up for it. One of Europe's largest Baroque organs bellows on Sunday in the church's resonant hall and stars in Olomouc's international organ festival each September.

Return to Horní nám. and take Mahlerova to the **Jan Sarkander Chapel** (Kaple sv. Jana Sarkandra) on the right, which honors the Catholic priest tortured to death by Protestants in 1620 after he refused to divulge a confessor's secret. There's an exhibit on his "three-fold torture" inside. If no regular hours are posted, ask a priest at the nearby **St. Michael's Church** (Kostel sv. Michala) to let you in.

Continue on Mahlerova to Univerzitní. Turn left and pass both the Jesuit **Chapel of God's Body** (Kaple Božího Těla) and the pretty (but closed) church to reach Nám. Republiky. (Open Tu-Su 9am-5pm. 10Kč, students 5Kč.) Seated along the northern edge of the square, the **Museum of National History and Arts** (Vlastivědné muzeum), Nám. Republiky 5, presents the history of *homo olomouciensis* from mammoth to noble, as well as the pre-Communist history of the town hall's astrological clock. (Tel. 522 84 70. Open Tu-Su 10am-6pm. 30Kč, students 15Kč.)

Leave Nám. Republiky on Mariánská to reach Biskupské nám., home of the Renaissance **Archbishop's Palace** (Arcibiskupský palác), a 17th-century palace and the place where Franz Josef ascended the Habsburg throne during the revolutionary turbulence of 1848. Turn right on Wurmova, cross 1. máje, and climb up Dómská to reach Václavské nám. Let the imposing spires of **Metropolitan Church of St. Wenceslas** (Metropolitní Kostel sv. Václava) lead the way. (Open M-Th and Sa 9am-5pm, F 1-5pm, Su 11am-5pm.) The high-vaulted church interior is in impeccable condition, having been reworked virtually every century since it caught fire in 1265. The crypt exhibits Christian paraphernalia, including the gold-encased skull of Olomouc's protectress, St. Pauline. Not much is outstanding, but the collection does give the viewer a feel for Moravian Catholicism. The **Premyslid Palace** (Přemyslovský palác) next door is a Gothic cloister with fine 15th-century frescoes and the 13th-century **Chapel of John the Baptist** (Kaple sv. Jana Křtitele). Across the square sits the **former Capitular Deaconry** (bývalé Kapitulní děkanství), where Mozart composed his Symphony in F-major.

NIGHTLIFE

Start the evening's drinking out on the terrace at the Student Center's **Kavárna Terasa,** Křížovského 14, off Nám. Republiky, where students squeeze onto silvery-gray sofas. (Cover 30Kč. Open M-Th 10am-midnight, F 10am-2am, Sa 2pm-2am.) Moving back toward Horní nám., **Depo No. 8,** Nám. Republiky 1 (tel. 522 12 73), pours *Staropramen* (20Kč) in three underground rooms with metallic decor and comfy seats. In the wee hours, the basement becomes Olomouc's most happening student dance club. (Cover 30Kč. Open M-Th 10am-4am, F-Sa 10am-6am, Su 4pm-1am.) For a quieter scene, try **OSA,** a combination bar/children's art gallery, Mahlerova 15 (tel. 522 02 97; open M-Th 4pm-midnight, F-Sa 1pm-2am).

ESTONIA (EESTI)

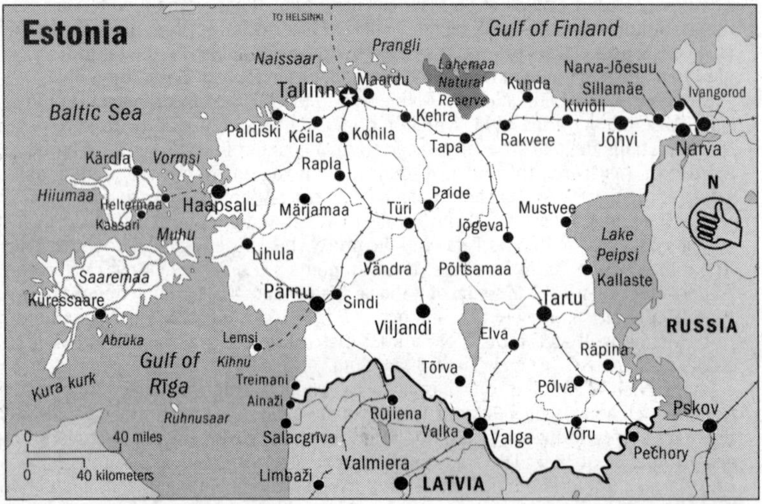

US$1 = 14.76EEK (ESTONIAN KROONS)	**10EEK = US$0.68**
CDN$1 = 9.91EEK	**10EEK = CDN$1.01**
UK£1 = 23.71EEK	**10EEK = UK£0.42**
IR£1 = 20.09EK	**10EEK = IR£0.50**
AUS$1 = 9.51EEK	**10EEK = AUS$1.04**
NZ$1 = 7.82EEK	**10EEK = NZ$1.28**
SAR1 = 2.44EEK	**10EEK = SAR4.09**
DM1 = 8.00EEK	**10EEK = DM1.25**

PHONE CODES Country code: **372.** International dialing prefix: **800.**

German cars, cellular phones, designer shops, and ever more stylish youngsters indicate that Estonia is benefitting from its transition to democracy and capitalism. Material trappings, however, mask declining living standards in the face of growing inflation. Happy to shuck its Soviet past, Estonia seems quick to revive its historical and cultural ties to its Nordic neighbors, much to the chagrin of the 35% ethnically Russian population. Having overcome successive centuries of domination by the Danes, Swedes, and Russians, the Estonians' serene, patient pragmatism has matured into a dynamic and—some would say—Scandinavian attitude.

HIGHLIGHTS OF ESTONIA

■ More Scandinavian than Eastern European, relaxed **Tallinn** lures visitors with its sleek yet intimate Old Town and trendy nightlife (p. 239).

■ University students, Estonian nationalists, and museum lovers alike congregate in **Tartu,** the oldest town in the Baltics (p. 258).

■ The 1500 **Estonian Islands** were closed to the public under Soviet rule; recently reopened, the islands are littered with deserted Soviet bases, stunning seaside cliffs, and miles of empty roads and bike paths ripe for exploration (p. 251).

LIFE & TIMES

HISTORY

Estonia's new-found freedom stands against a history of foreign domination and repression. Ninth-century **Vikings** were the first to impose themselves on the Finno-Ugric people who had settled the area long before. In 1219, **King Valdemar II** of Denmark conquered northern Estonia. Shortly thereafter, Livonia, now southern Estonia and northern Latvia, fell to the crusading German knights of the **Teutonic Order,** who purchased the rest of Estonia in 1346.

German domination continued until the emergence of Muscovite **Tsar Ivan the Terrible,** who, in 1558, crushed many of the tiny feudal states that had developed in the region. In an attempt to force Ivan out, the defeated states searched for foreign assistance: northern Estonia capitulated to Sweden, while Livonia yoked itself to the **Polish-Lithuanian Commonwealth.** By 1581, Russia had lost control of the country, and the rest of Estonia devolved to Sweden with the 1629 **Truce of Altmark.**

The **Swedish Interlude** (1629-1710), a relative improvement for the Estonian peasantry, brought an end to the worst abuses of the feudal system. During this era, Estonian-language schools and the **University of Tartu** were established. Tolerance ended in 1721 when the **Peace of Nystad,** concluding the **Great Northern War,** handed the Baltics to Peter the Great. Russian rule reinforced the power of the nobility, and serfs lost all rights until **serfdom** was finally abolished in 1819, 45 years earlier than in Mother Russia herself. Even under Russian rule, however, Estonia was a center of German culture. Benefitting from a wave of Enlightenment reforms, Estonian peasants owned two-fifths of all private land by the end of the 19th century, and the population was 97% literate. Following the coronation of **Tsar Alexander III** in 1881, however, Russia clamped down. This prompted an Estonian nationalistic backlash led by **Konstantin Päts,** which peaked in a failed bid for independence during the Russian Revolution of 1905.

At the outbreak of **World War I,** Estonians were in a difficult position; many were drafted into the Russian Army, but the Estonian-German population sympathized with Prussia. The **Russian Revolution of 1917** intensified the Estonian struggle for independence. After occupation by Germany, Estonia declared **independence** in 1918 but was subsequently taken by the Red Army. The Estonians fought off the Soviets with British and Finnish help and embarked upon **self-rule.** From 1919-33, a succession of coalition governments ruled. Although the country prospered, the Depression allowed extreme right-wing parties, led by veterans from the war for liberation, to gain public support, causing president **Konstantin Päts** to proclaim a state of emergency in 1934. Päts ruled as a benevolent dictator until calling and winning a referendum on his rule in 1938.

In 1940, as agreed to in the **German-Soviet Non-aggression Pact,** Estonia was occupied by the Soviets. Päts and other Estonian leaders, as well as a significant portion of the Estonian population, were arrested, deported, or killed. Soon after, **Hitler** reneged on the pact and Germany re-took the country, remaining from 1941 to 1944. As the Red Army slowly pushed the Nazis out, thousands of Estonians fled to Germany or Sweden; thousands more died at sea trying to escape.

The 1950s saw extreme repression and Russification under **Soviet rule,** when internal purges removed the few native Estonians in the ruling elite. *Glasnost* and *perestroika* eventually allowed enough breathing room for an Estonian political renaissance. In 1988, the **Popular Front** emerged in opposition to the Communist government, pushing a resolution on independence through the Estonian legislature. Nationalists won a legislative majority in the 1990 elections and successfully declared independence after the failed 1991 coup in the Soviet Union.

ESTONIA TODAY

One of the few Soviet republics to boast a legitimate export market, Estonia was relatively wealthy during the Soviet era. Upon independence, it quickly adopted the most radical economic reforms of any former Soviet republic, and proved itself the most vigorous of the "Baltic tigers." The youthful government eventually ran out of steam amid allegations of corruption, but Estonia continues to charge Westward. Thanks to its trading policies, Estonia has been included among the next six countries to be considered for E.U. membership, inciting some jealousy from its neighbors. These economic changes have had mixed results throughout the country, as rural life has been abandoned by city-bound youth.

After economic reforms, relations with Russia are at the top of Estonia's political agenda: the population is 30% Russian, many of whom never bothered to learn the difficult native tongue, and negotiations of the Russian-Estonian border since 1991 have been thorny. These problems have grown into significant sources of tension with Russia, but as Estonia preens itself for E.U. selection, treatment of the Russian minority has improved and claims to Russian lands have been dropped.

LITERATURE & ARTS

Anton Thor Helle's 1739 translation of the Bible created a common Estonian language based on the northern dialect. He heralded the **Estophile period** (1750-1840), built around lyric poetry rooted in national folktales and Finnish epics. Folklore provided the basis for **Friedrich Reinhold Kreutzwald's** *Kalevipoeg* (1857-61). This tale became the rallying point of Estonian national rebirth in the Romantic period, of which **Lydia Koidula's** poetry and drama, imbued with protest, marked the peak.

Deepening class barriers throughout the 1800s shifted the intelligentsia's attention from national problems to social ones. Toward the end of the century, the Neo-Romantic nationalist **Noor-Eesti** (Young Estonia) movement appeared. Its writers focused on literary form, although the stylistic experiments of **Gustav Suits,** its leader, produced poems that asked youth to revolt in the name of liberty and truth.

The interwar years saw the development of tragic poetry haunted by visions of human suffering and war. **Anton Tammsaare's** prose evolved from the Noor-Eesti approach to Realism, and his *Truth and Justice* (*Tõde ja õigus*, 1926-33) is essential to the Estonian canon. But the resurgence of Realism did not dampen the Estonian literati's interest in mysticism, as **Marie Under's** earthy love sonnets gained popularity in the 1930s. The strictures of **Socialist Realism** sent many authors into temporary exile in Siberia, although **Jaan Kross** managed to criticize the realities of Soviet life in *The Tsar's Madman* (1978). In the same year, **Aimée Beekman** addressed women's plight in *The Possibility of Choice.*

READING LIST

See **Lithuania: Reading List** (p. 363) for a good survey of Baltic history. *Estonia and the Estonians*, by Toivo U. Raun, offers a comprehensive history of the country. Jaan Kross's *The Tsar's Madman*, a historical novel about a 19th-century Baltic nobleman, is arguably the best Estonian fiction available.

ESTONIA

FACTS AND FIGURES

- **Capital:** Tallinn
- **Population:** 1,463,397
- **Land Area:** 45,227km^2
- **Geography:** Plains and rolling hills
- **Language:** Estonian
- **Religions:** 20% Orthodox, 14% Lutheran
- **GDP per capita:** US$2860
- **Major Exports:** Fossil fuels and chemicals

ESTONIA ESSENTIALS

Citizens of Australia, Ireland, New Zealand, and the U.S. can visit Estonia visa-free for up to 90 days, U.K. citizens for 180 days. Canadians and South Africans can obtain a visa at the border for 400EEK (about US$70), or use a Latvian and Lithuanian visa to enter the country. It is cheaper to apply for a visa at the closest Estonian consulate in your country, although this requires either an invitation or letter from a contact in Estonia, or copies of hotel reservations and ticket bookings from a travel agency. When arranged before departure, single-entry visas (good for 30 days) are US$14, multiple-entry (valid for 1 year, but only 90 consecutive days in Estonia) US$68. Single transit visas cost US$14, double-transit US$24; both are good for 48hr. and 96hr., respectively. To obtain a visa extension, contact the visa department of the Immigration Department, Endla 4, in Tallinn (tel. 612 69 79).

PRIMARY BORDER CROSSINGS. Although Estonian visas are available at the border, it is cheaper and more convenient to arrange them beforehand; it is also possible to use a Latvian or Lithuanian visa to enter Estonia. There is no fee for crossing an Estonian border. The easiest means of entering or exiting Estonia is to take a direct bus or train from Tallinn to St. Petersburg, Moscow, or Rīga. Estonian customs officials are quite slow; expect several hours of delay when crossing an Estonian border.

Latvia: Valga, EST/Valka, LAT; connects Tartu (p. 258) with Vidzeme and Latgale (p. 357). Treimani, EST/Ainaži, LAT; connects Pärnu (p. 248) with Vidzeme and Latgale (p. 357).

Russia: Narva, EST/Ivangorod, RUS; connects northeastern Estonia with St. Petersburg (p. 596) and the Northwest (p. 596).

GETTING THERE & GETTING AROUND

Entering Estonia by plane or boat is easiest. Either way will save you hassles with customs officials, and traveling by ferry from Finland or Sweden is extremely cheap (200-300EEK). Several **ferry lines** connect to Tallinn's harbor (tel. 631 85 50); for options, see **Tallinn: Practical Information: Ferries,** p. 240. For contact details of ferry companies across the Baltic in Helsinki, see **Gateway Cities: Helsinki,** p. 788. For more information on international **flights** into Tallinn, see **Tallinn: Practical Information,** p. 240. If you're coming from Russia or one of the other Baltic states, **trains** may be even cheaper than ferries, but expect more red tape when crossing the border. The **Baltic Express** links Tallinn to Warsaw via Kaunas, Rīga, and Tartu, mercifully by-passing Belarus (21hr., 1 per day, 477EEK, *coupé* 680EEK).

Domestically, **buses** are the best means of transport, as they are cheaper and more efficient than trains. It's even possible to ride buses direct from the mainland to island towns (via ferry) for less than the price of the ferry ride. During the school year (Sept.-June 25), students receive half-price bus tickets. On the islands, bike (100EEK per day) and car (350-900EEK) rentals are an excellent means of exploration. Those who **hitchhike** stretch out an open hand. *Let's Go* does not recommend hitchhiking as a safe form of transportation.

TOURIST SERVICES & MONEY

Unlike most of the former Soviet Union, Estonia is grasping the importance of tourist services; most small towns now offer city maps, while larger towns and cities may have well-equipped tourist offices with literature and English-speaking staff. Generally, such offices are quite knowledgeable about accommodations and the local scene, but less so about transportation. Booths marked with a green "i" sell maps and give away brochures.

The unit of currency is the **kroon** (EEK), divided into 100 **senti,** and is tied to the Deutschmark. The biggest and most stable banks in the country, Hansapank and Eesti Ühispank, cash **traveler's checks.** Many restaurants and shops take credit cards, mostly **Visa** and **MasterCard. ATMs** are common in all towns covered in *Let's Go.* When purchasing items in a shop, cash is not usually passed between hands, but is instead put in a small tray on counter tops.

COMMUNICATIONS

An airmail letter costs 5.50EEK to Europe and the CIS, and 7EEK to the rest of the world. Postcards are only 5.20EEK to Europe and the CIS or 6.70EEK everywhere else. Telephone calls are paid for with digital cards, available at any bank or newspaper kiosk. Cards come in denominations of 30, 50, and 100EEK. International access numbers include: **AT&T Direct** tel. 80 08 00 10 01; **Australia Direct** tel. 800; **BT Direct** 810 80 01 04 41; **Canada** 80 08 00 10 11. **International long-distance** calls can be made at post offices. Calls to the Baltic states and Russia cost 8.50EEK per min. (10.50EEK with a card). Phoning the U.S. is quite expensive: US$1-4 per min.

In an attempt to update and modernize telephone communication, Estonia has come up with a system that proves that, indeed, the universe tends toward chaos. There are three phone systems in Tallinn: analog, digital, and cellular. Each has its own area code. The digital system and the analog system can call each other without the area code within a given city. Calling to or from a cell phone, however, always requires an area code, with an 8 dialed first. To call within Estonia, preface the phone code with an 8. To call Tallinn from outside Estonia on the old system, dial 37 22 and then the number; on the digital system, dial 372. To call a cell phone in Estonia, dial 37 25. To call out of Estonia on the old system dial 8, wait for the second, mellower tone, then dial 00, the country code, and the rest of the number. From digital phones, dial 800 without waiting for a tone. From a cell phone, just dial 00 and the number. To call Eesti Telefon's **information** number, dial 07. If you get lost in the chaos of the Estonian phone system, call the English-speaking **Ekspress Hotline** (tel. 631 32 22 in Tallinn; elsewhere, dial 8, then 11 88). **Internet access** is becoming more widespread, and averages 30-60EEK per hour.

English-language **books** and **newspapers** are relatively easy to find in Estonia, especially in Tallinn. The English-language *City Paper—The Baltic States*, available at hotels, kiosks, and tourist info points (US$1.50), covers all three Baltic countries. The info-packed *Tallinn in Your Pocket* has detailed information and entertainment listings not only for Tallinn but also for Saaremaa and Tartu.

LANGUAGE

Estonians speak the best **English** in the Baltic states; most young people know at least a few phrases. Many also know **Finnish** or **Swedish,** but **German** is more common among the older set and in resort towns like Pärnu, Saaremaa, and Tartu. **Russian** used to be mandatory, but Estonians in secluded areas are likely to have forgotten much of it since few, if any, Russians live there. Moreover, Estonians are usually averse to using Russian. Always try English first, making it clear you're not Russian, and then switch to Russian if necessary. The clear exception to this is along the border in eastern Estonia, where many prefer it to Estonian. Estonian is a Finno-Ugric language, with 14 cases and all sorts of letters. You won't master it in a day, but basic words help: *bussijaam* (BUSS-ee-yahm; bus station); *raudteejaam* (ROWD-tee-yahm; train station); *avatud* (AH-vah-tuht; open); and *suletud* (SUH-leh-tuht; closed). Take offense if you're called a *pudru pää:* it means porridge head. For more Estonian help, see the **Estonian Glossary,** p. 811.

HEALTH & SAFETY

Public **toilets** (*tasuline*), marked by "N" or a triangle pointing up for women and "M" or a triangle pointing down for men, usually cost 3EEK and include a very limited supply of toilet paper. **Medical services** for foreigners are few and far between,

Worldwide Calling Made Easy

The MCI WorldCom Card, designed specifically to keep you in touch with the people that matter the most to you.

www.wcom.com/worldphone

Please cut out and save this reference guide for convenient U.S. and worldwide calling with the MCI WorldCom Card.

And, it's simple to call home or to other countires.

1. Dial the WorldPhone toll-free access number of the country you're calling from (listed inside).
2. Follow the easy voice instructions or hold for a WorldPhone operator. Enter or give the operator your MCI WorldCom Card number or call collect.
3. Enter or give the WorldPhone operator your home number.
4. Share your adventures with your family!

COUNTRY		WORLDPHONE TOLL-FREE ACCESS #
St. Lucia ✣		1-800-888-8000
Sweden (CC) ◆		020-795-922
Switzerland (CC) ◆		0800-89-0222
Taiwan (CC) ◆		0080-13-4567
Thailand ★		001-999-1-2001
Turkey (CC) ◆		00-8001-1177
United Kingdom	(CC) To call using BT ■	0800-89-0222
	To call using CWC ■	0500-89-0222
United States (CC)		1-800-888-8000
U.S. Virgin Islands (CC)		1-800-888-8000
Vatican City (CC)		172-1022
Venezuela (CC) ✣ ◆		800-1114-0
Vietnam ●		1201-1022

(CC)	Country-to-country calling available to/from most international locations.
✣	Limited availability.
▼	Wait for second dial tone.
▲	When calling from public phones, use phones marked LADATEL.
■	International communications carrier.
★	Not available from public pay phones.
◆	Public phones may require deposit of coin or phone card for dial tone.
●	Local service fee in U.S. currency required to complete call.
▶	Regulation does not permit Intra-Japan calls.
❖	Available from most major cities

MCI WorldCom Worldphone Access Numbers

MCI WORLDCOM℠

> **EMERGENCY NUMBERS. Fire:** tel. 01. **Police:** tel. 02. **Ambulance:** tel. 03. In Tallinn, add a leading 0 to all numbers.

and most often you'll have to pay cash. **Pharmacies** (look for the "Apteek" sign) are usually Scandinavian chains, and as a result, are well-equipped and modern. Try not to drink any unboiled tap water; **bottled water** is always a safer choice. While the petty **crime** rate is low, women should avoid going to bars and clubs alone or walking alone at night, even during white nights. As always, for English-speaking help in an emergency, contact your embassy.

ACCOMMODATIONS & CAMPING

Each **tourist office** will have listings and prices of accommodations in its town and can often arrange a bed for visitors. There is little distinction between hotels, hostels, and guesthouses; some upscale hotels still have hall toilets and showers. The word *võõrastemaja* (guesthouse) in a place's name usually implies that it's less expensive, but not always. Many hotels provide **laundry** services for an extra charge. Some hostels are part of larger hotels, so be sure to ask for the cheaper hostel rooms. **Homestays** are common and cheap, but not as cheap as the cheapest hostels. For info on HI hostels around Estonia, contact the **Estonian Youth Hostel Association,** Tatari (tel. 646 14 57; fax 646 15 95; email puhkemajad@online.ee).

FOOD & DRINK

It's hard to define Estonian food; go to any local restaurant and you'll see the same assortment of drab sausages, lifeless schnitzel, greasy bouillon, and cold fried potatoes that plague all of the former USSR. If there is a difference in Estonia, it is that there is more fish on the menu. Trout is especially popular, and often the ham-laden *soljanka* you knew as meat stew in Rīga and Moscow will undergo a seaward-change here into a deliciously thick whitefish soup. Beer (*õlu*) is the national drink in Estonia for good reason—not only is it inexpensive, but it's also delicious and high-quality. The national brand *Saku* is excellent, as is the darker *Saku Tume*. Local brews, like *Saaremaa* in Kuressaare, can be volatile.

CUSTOMS & ETIQUETTE

Businesses take hour-long **breaks** at noon, 1pm, or 2pm, and most are closed on Sunday. No one **tips** in Estonia, although a service charge might be included in the bill. Estonian fashion is currently seven or eight years behind the U.S.; think Metallica T-shirts and neon mini-skirts. **Smoking** is common, except at transport stations. **Women** traveling alone are a rarity, so expect curious glances. **Homosexuality** is legal in Estonia, but public displays are not socially accepted, even in bigger cities. Much late-night entertainment in cities and resort towns caters to *mafiosi* and the like, although not as predominately as in the rest of the former USSR.

NATIONAL HOLIDAYS

January 1, New Year's; February 24, Independence Day (1918); April 21, Good Friday; April 23-24, Catholic Easter; May 1, Spring Day; June 11, Whit Sunday; June 23, Victory Day (Battle of Võnnu, 1919); June 24, Jaanipäev (St. John's Day, Midsummer); August 20, Restoration of Independence; December 25-26, Christmas.

TALLINN

As one approaches Tallinn (pop. 430,000) by ferry, tall Germanic spires, Danish towers, and Russian minarets loom alongside the industrial cranes in the process of restoring them. The complications of combining modernity and history are felt nowhere as strongly as in Tallinn: capitalizing on tourism by restoring the past is the driving force behind the current economic boom. The modern glass structures sprouting up all over the downtown—combined with hip new shops, bars, restaurants, and cosmopolitan youth—complement the medieval serenity tourists have long been coming to see. Sadly, the ubiquitous mobile phones and BMWs of the pastel Old Town cannot efface Tallinn's drab outskirts, which remain as if frozen in Soviet rule. In regions like Kopli and Kadrioru Park, capitalism has brought nothing but increased crime. But when the sun sets over the white beaches curving around the bay and the thin church steeples piercing the pink evening sky, any doubt of the beauty and dynamism of that first view of Tallinn from the ferry fades.

GETTING THERE & GETTING AWAY

Airplanes: Bus #2 runs every 20min. from the **airport,** Lennujaama 2 (tel. 21 10 92; www.estnet.ee), to Hotel Viru.

Trains: Toompuiestee 35 (tel. 615 68 51). Trams #1 and 2 travel between the station and Hotel Viru. International trains are modern, announcements are in English, and there are no shoving crowds. International tickets are purchased on the 2nd floor, domestic tickets on the ground floor. To: **St. Petersburg** (10hr., 1 per day, 155EEK, *coupé* 246EEK); **Rīga** (7hr., 162EEK, *coupé* 293EEK); and **Warsaw** (21hr., 1 per day, 477EEK, *coupé* 680EEK). The **Baltic Express** goes to Warsaw via Rīga and Kaunas.

Buses: Lastekodu 46 (tel. 601 03 86), just south of Tartu mnt. and 1.5km southeast of Vanalinn. Trams #2, 4, and bus #22 connect the bus station to the city center. Tickets can be purchased at the station or from the driver. To: **Rīga** (7hr., 4 per day, 132EEK); **St. Petersburg** (9hr., 2 per day, 155EEK); and **Vilnius** (9hr., 2 per day, 160EEK).

Ferries: Tel. 631 85 50. At the end of Sadama, 15min. from the center. 4 different terminals, specific to each company. Boats, hydrofoils, and catamarans cross to **Helsinki.**

Eckerö Line, Terminal B (tel. 631 86 06; fax 631 86 61): 3½hr.; 3 per day; June27-Aug.16 325EEK, students 200EEK; Aug.17-June26 250EEK, students 150EEK.

Nordic Jet Line, Terminal B (tel. 613 70 00; fax 613 72 22): 1½hr.; 432-513 EEK.

Silja Line, Terminal D (tel. 631 83 31; fax 631 82 64): Daytime crossing 3½hr., nighttime 8½hr.; 2 per day; June12-Aug.9 410EEK; Aug.10-June11 Su night-F day 270EEK, F night-Su day 430EEK; cabin supplement from 540EEK.

Tallinn Express, Terminal C (tel. 640 98 77; www.tallink.ee): 1¾hr.; 3 per day; 405-460EEK.

Local Transportation: Buses, trams, and **trolley-buses** cover the entire metropolitan area; all run 6am-midnight. Tickets *(talong)* can be bought from kiosks around town (5EEK). Validate your tickets in the metal boxes on board. Tickets are checked infrequently, but getting caught brings a 410EEK fine. If you're in Tallinn for a while, buy a 10-day transit card (*kümne päeva kaart;* 70EEK) good for unlimited rides.

Taxis: Find a *Takso* stand, or call 612 00 00, 630 01 34, 655 60 00, or 55 79 05. Check the cab for a meter and expect to pay 4-6EEK per km.

Car Rental: Europcar, Magdaleena 3 (tel. 650 25 59; airport office tel. 638 80 31; fax 650 25 60), is less expensive than others. Reserve 2 days ahead. Open M-F 9am-5pm.

ORIENTATION

Tallinn's **Vanalinn** (Old Town) is an egg-shaped maze ringed by five main streets, all flowing into one another: Rannamäe tee, Mere pst., Pärnu mnt., Kaarli pst., and Toompuiestee. The best entrance to **Vanalinn** is through the 15th-century **Viru ärarad**, the main gate in the city wall. To get there from **Hotel Viru,** Tallinn's central landmark, face the post office across the street and head left toward the intersection with Virv tänav. Vanalinn peaks at the fortress-rock **Toompea,** where 13th-century streets are level with the church steeples of **All-linn** (Lower Town). To reach Vanalinn from the **ferry terminal,** walk 15min. along Sadama to Põhja pst., then go south on Pikk through the gate at **Paks Margareeta** (Fat Margaret). From the train station, cross Toom pst. and go straight through the park along Nunne; the stairway up Patkuli trepp on the right leads directly to Toompea. In Vanalinn, **Pikk tänav** (Long Street), the main artery, runs from the seaward gates of All-linn to Toompea via **Pikk Jalg. Raekoja plats** (Town Hall Square) is the scenic center of All-linn.

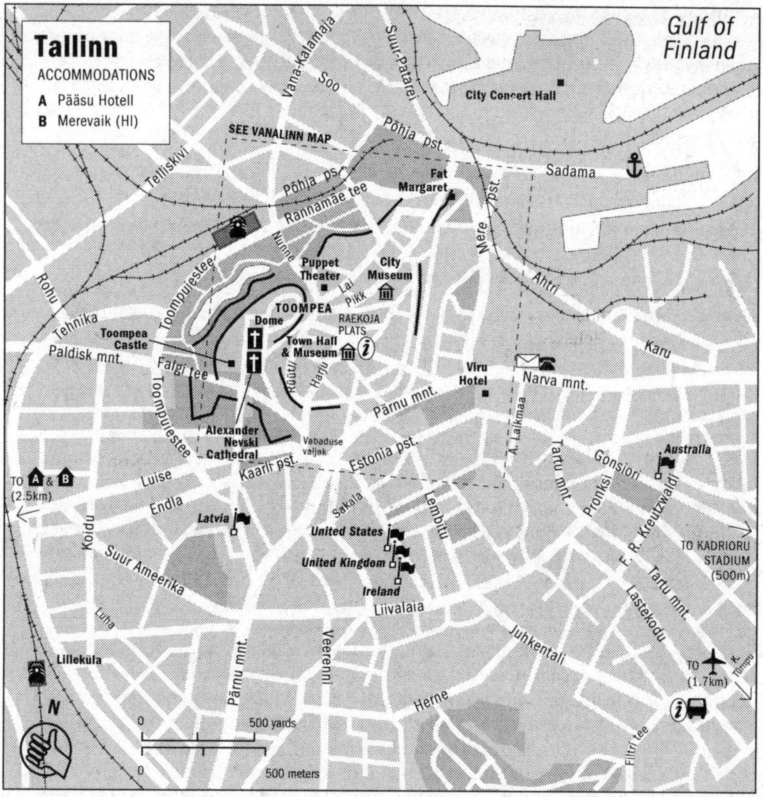

PRACTICAL INFORMATION

TOURIST & FINANCIAL SERVICES

Tourist Office: The **Tourist Information Center (TIC),** Raekoja pl. 10 (tel. 694 69 46; fax 631 39 43; email turismiinfo@tallinnlv.ee; www.tallinn.ee), across from the town hall, sells and gives out brochures and maps. Open M-F 9am-5pm, Sa-Su 10am-4pm. Another **TIC,** Sadama 25 (tel. 485 73 49; fax 485 56 72), at the harbor (Terminal A), offers info on small hotels. Open daily 9am-6pm. A **Tallinn Card,** available at either location, entitles the holder to a city tour, unlimited public transport, and entry to most museums, but at a steep price: 1 day 195EEK, 2 days 270EEK, 3 days 325EEK.

Tours: CDS Reisid, Raekoja pl. 17 (tel. 627 67 97; fax 631 36 66). Gives English walking tours of Vanalinn (1hr., May 15-Sept. 15 daily at 2pm, 60EEK). Office open M-F 10am-6pm, Sa-Su 10am-4pm. **REISI Ekspert,** Rooskirautsi 17 (tel. 610 86 00), gives tours daily at 10am, 1, and 3pm from Hotel Viru. Buy tickets (150EEK) at Hotel Viru.

Embassies: Canada, Toomkooli 13 (tel. 631 79 78; fax 631 35 73). Open M-F 9am-4:30pm. **Latvia,** Tõnismägi 10 (tel. 646 13 13; fax 631 13 66). Open M-F 10am-noon. **Russia,** Pikk 19 (tel. 646 41 69; fax 646 41 78). Open M-F 9am-noon. **U.K.,** Kentmanni 20 (tel. 631 34 61; fax 631 33 54). Open Tu-Th 10am-noon. **U.S.,** Kentmanni 20 (tel. 631 20 21; fax 631 20 25). Open M-F 8:30am-5:30pm.

Currency Exchange: Windows #11 and 47 at the central post office exchange currency, offering some of the best rates in Tallinn, although rates at the airport aren't bad either. **ATM** machines can be found on nearly every street in Vanalinn.

American Express: Suur-Karja 15, EE-090 (tel. 626 62 62; fax 631 36 56; email sales@estravel.ee). Sells and cashes traveler's checks, exchanges currency, books hotels and tours, sells airline, ferry, and rail tickets, and arranges visas to the other Baltics, Russia, and the rest of the CIS. Members can receive mail and get cash advances. Open M-F 9am-6pm, Sa 10am-5pm.

LOCAL SERVICES & COMMUNICATION

Luggage Storage: Lockers downstairs in the train station (15EEK). Luggage storage at the bus station 3-12EEK per day. Open daily 5am-noon and 12:30-11:40pm.

English Bookstore: Viruvärava Raamatu Kauplus (tel. 631 31 95), centrally located on Viru. Open M-F 10am-7pm, Sa 11am-6pm, Su 11am-4pm.

Laundry: Sauberland, Maakri 23 (tel. 646 65 81). Self-service for 55EEK per load.

Pharmacy: RAE Apteek, Pikk 47 (tel. 44 44 08). Open M-F 9am-6pm, Sa 10am-4pm.

Internet Access: Küber-kohvik, Gonsiori 4 (tel. 626 73 67), sits diagonally across from the Hotel Viru on the far side of the post office. Serves drinks to sip in the neon glow of 20 computer screens. 60EEK per hr. Open daily 10am-midnight. The **National Library of Estonia,** Tõnismägi 2, is more tranquil but has fewer computers. 40EEK per hr.

Post Office: Narva mnt. 1, 2nd Floor (tel. 625 73 00), across from Hotel Viru. Open M-F 8am-7pm, Sa 9am-5pm. **Postal code:** 0001.

Telephones: Narva mnt. 1 (tel. 640 26 66). Available all over the city; buy a phone card (30, 50, or 100EEK) from any convenience store or kiosk. **Phone code:** 22 or 2 for new digital lines; 25 for cellular phones.

ACCOMMODATIONS

Tallinn's hostels fill fast in summer; it's wise to book as far in advance as possible. In general, finding a room on weekdays is much easier than on weekends; the days surrounding **Joanipäer** (St. John's Day, June 24) are the busiest. If you find yourself in a bind, inquire at the information desk in the **bus station** about beds there (new doubles 170EEK, old 120EEK; communal bathrooms). **Bed & Breakfast,** Sadama 11 (tel./fax 641 22 91), finds rooms in private homes in Tallinn, throughout the Baltics, and St. Petersburg (from 180EEK per person). **CDS Reisid** (see **Tours,** p. 241) also arranges private rooms. Call a couple days ahead.

Hotell Küün (HI; The Barn), Väike-Karja 1, 2nd Fl. (tel. 631 32 52; fax 646 41 18), in Vanalinn. From the train station, take the underpass under Toompuis and follow Nunne through the lightly wooded park onto the streets of Vanalinn. From behind the town hall in Raekoja pl. (the main square), walk downhill, turn right up Vana turg., then take a left on Suur-Karja, and veer left. The hostel is through an arch on your left. Unbeatable cleanliness and location (there's a strip club on the third floor). Doubles with shared bath 550EEK; dorms 195EEK. 15EEK discount for HI members. Stay 10 nights and the next is free. 20EEK extra for sheets. Laundry service and towel rental available. Visa/MC.

Hotell Gasthaus Eeslitall, Dunkri 4, 2nd floor (tel. 631 37 55; fax 631 32 10). Just off Raekoja pl. Head down Dunkri around the town hall on the far side of the steeple. Colorful and clean rooms. Singles 450EEK; doubles 585EEK. Breakfast 36EEK.

Pääsu Hotell, Sõpruse pst. 182 (tel. 52 00 34; fax 654 20 13), in Mustamäe. Take bus #4 from the railway station or bus #2, 3, or 9 from the center of town to the "Linnu tee" stop. Backtrack a little, turn left on Linnu tee, then left again on Nigri and follow the white signs with the pale blue swallow icon. Comfortable rooms, all with cable TV and refrigerator. Bath shared with one other room. Single 360EEK; double 460EEK; triple 540EEK. Breakfast included. Sauna 150EEK per hr.

Merevaik (HI), Sõpruse pst. 182, 5th floor (tel. 52 96 04; fax 52 96 47). Enter from the messy stairwell behind the Pääsu Hotell (see directions above). This Russian-run hostel's sole attraction is its price. Bathroom shared with 1 other room. Beds in doubles or triples 162EEK with HI card, non-members 180EEK. Bright red bar down the hall.

FOOD

Restaurants in Vanalinn are becoming increasingly expensive as the kroon sinks and tourism surges. The city has many well-stocked **supermarkets;** the most central is **Spar,** Aia 7, near the Viru Gates. (Open daily 9am-9pm.) For the best grocery-shopping experience Estonia has to offer, follow the signs to **Stockman's,** on the corner of Livonia and A. Lauteri between Old Town and the bus station. **Open-air markets** set up most days near Lastekodu 10.

Merevaikus, Rahukohtu 5, on Patkuli vaateplats. This cafe/restaurant boasts some of the best views of medieval Tallinn and the Baltic in Toompea. An ideal place to spend a restful–or even romantic–evening, and one of the best deals in town. Crepes, salads, soups, and herring with potatoes, all 30-50EEK. Open daily 11am-11pm. MC/Visa.

Olematu Rüütel, Kiriku põik 4a (tel. 631 38 27). On Toompea, to the left of the art museum. Everything from cheap vegetarian dishes (35-45EEK) to Indonesian pork and Atlantic salmon (120EEK). Full meals from 150EEk. *Saku* 25EEK.

Padakonna Kõrts, Rüütli 28/30 (tel. 641 84 43). Behind Niguliste Kirik, nestled in a corner of the town wall. Medieval Tallinn is recreated with clay tankards of beer in this candle-lit cavern. Gorge yourself on quails in almond milk (90EEK), or just sit wide-eyed as a plate of sausages is lit afire at your table (50EEK). Open daily noon-midnight.

Eeslitall, Dunkri 4/6 (Donkey Stable; tel. 631 37 55; email donkeys@netexpress.ee). There's been a restaurant in these halls since 1362. American and Balto-Russian cuisine. Meals around 140EEK. Pint of *Tartu au Coq* 25EEK. Thronged with tourists in summer, so call ahead for dinner. Open Su-Th 11am-11pm, F-Sa 11am-1am. MC/Visa.

SIGHTS

VANALINN (OLD TOWN)

Just inside the **Viru city gate** along Müürivahe, which runs north just inside the walls, a large **sweater market** sets up in summer; in winter, it moves into the flower stalls that line Viru. On the second street to the left after passing through the gates, the **Theater and Music Museum** (Teatri-ja Muusikamuuseum; tel. 644 21 32) displays over 500 musical instruments, from rare pianos to the inventions of 19th-century Estonian farmboys. (Open W-Su 10am-5:30pm. 10EEK.) Farther up Viru lies **Town Hall Square** (Raekoja plats), where the beer flows throughout summer in its outdoor cafes and local troupes perform folk songs and dances. **Old Thomas** (Vana Toomas), the 16th-century cast-iron weather vane figurine of Tallinn's legendary defender, tops the 14th-century **Town Hall** (Raekoda; tel. 644 08 19) diagonally across the square from the TIC. Thomas has done a good job guarding so far: this is the oldest surviving town hall in Europe. (Open daily 9am-5pm. Guided tours 30EEK.) On the north side of the square, Saia kang twists onto Pühavaimu, where the 14th-century **Church of the Holy Ghost** (Pühavaimu kirik; tel. 644 14 87) houses a 15th-century bell tower and an intricate 17th-century wooden clock. The church hosts free music recitals each Monday at 6pm. (Open M-Sa 10am-4:30pm.)

For a view of the medieval city's north towers, head up Vene from Viru, take a left on Olevimägi, and right down Pikk. The history of Tallinn, from its founding in 1219 until becoming the capital of the first republic, is condensed into the **City Museum** (Linnamuuseum), Vene 17 (tel. 644 18 29). Particular attention is paid to the brief period of independence between 1918 and 1940 (see **History,** p. 235). (Open M and W-Su 10:30am-5:30pm. 5EEK.) Across the street, the **Dominican Cloister** (Dominiiklaste Klooster), Vene 16 (tel. 644 46 06), founded in 1246, comprises a Gothic limestone courtyard, two Catholic churches, a windmill, stone carvings, and a granary. (Open daily 11am-7pm. 25EEK.) At the northern end of Pikk, in the large squat tower known as **Fat Margaret** (Paks Margareeta), the **Maritime Museum** (Meremuuseum), Pikk 70 (tel. 641 41 12), houses temporary exhibits on Tallinn's port history. Visitors will find scale models of ships among the myriad nautical charts. (Open W-Su 10am-6pm, final admission 5:30pm. 7EEK, students 3EEK.)

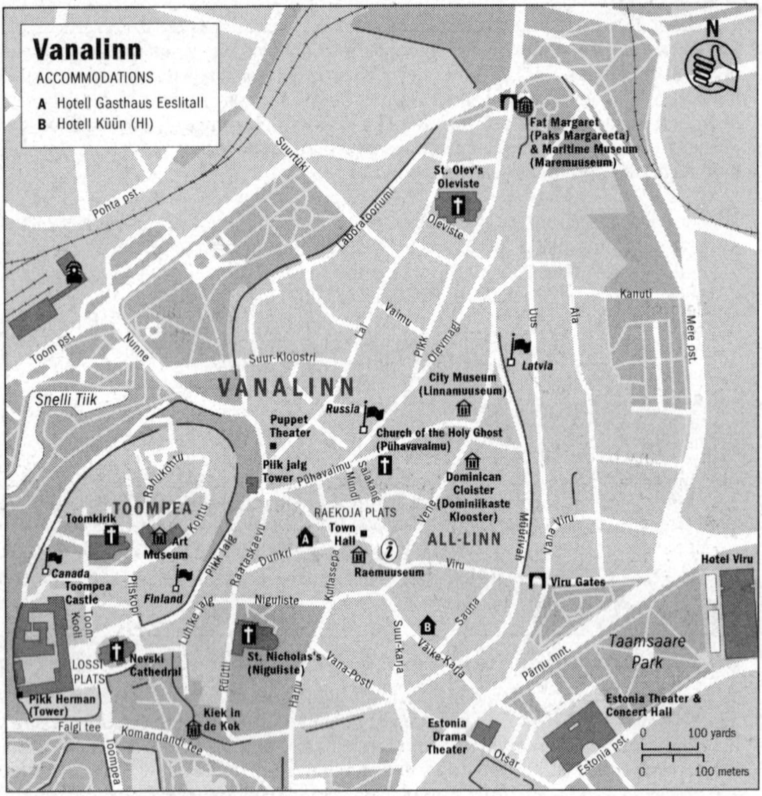

St. Olev's Church (Oleviste kirik), the tallest church in town, rises to the right on Pikk. The murals inside the adjoining chapel illustrate the architect's death: he fell from the tower. (Open M 5-9pm, Th 5-8pm, and Su 9am-noon and 5-8pm.) Go to the end of Pikk and hang a left on Rataskaevu to reach **St. Nicholas' Church** (Niguliste kirik; tel. 644 99 11) and its mighty spire. Inside, check out the ghoulish 1520 gravestone of Johannes Ballivi and the anachronistically modern stained-glass windows. The church now houses a museum of medieval art. (Open Tu 5-8pm, W 12-6pm, Th-Su 11:30am-6pm. Tu-F 12EEK, Sa-Su 15EEK, students 5EEK.) The 1475 **Peek in the Kitchen Tower** (Kiek in de Kök), Komandandi 2 (tel. 44 66 86), presents a fun and fact-filled journey through medieval Tallinn. You can find your bearings from the miniature models of the old town wall, or check out the voyeuristic panoramas of 16th-century Tallinn homes as you climb the spiral staircase to the sixth floor. The tower is shot through with history, from its museum's six floors of exhibits to the cannonballs embedded in the walls. (Open Tu-F 10:30am-5:30pm, Sa-Su 11am-4:30pm. 10EEK, students and seniors 5EEK.)

TOOMPEA

Following Lühike jalg uphill onto Toompea from Niguliste kirik leads to **Castle Square** (Lossi pl.), dominated by the Russian minarets of **Alexander Nevsky Cathedral** (tel. 644 34 84), begun under Tsar Alexander III and finished just in time for the Bolshevik Revolution. (Open daily 8am-7pm. Services 9am and 6pm.) A marble marker from 1910 recalls Peter the Great's 1710 victory over Sweden. The exterior renovations are almost complete, and are preparing to rival the rich interior, where pungent incense fills the air and gold leaf covers the vaulted ceiling. The **Toompea**

STONE-COLD Estonian folklore, as recorded by Friedrich Reinhold Kreutzwald in the national epic *Kalevipoeg*, has an interesting take on the origins of Toompea. As the story goes, the young protagonist of the title was out hunting with his brothers when a Finnish sorcerer, already jilted once by the lad's mother Linda, pounced on her and dragged her off to his make his northern fortress of solitude a little less solitary. Linda's cries for help went unheeded until the magician had lugged her nearly to the shores of the Baltic, when the forces of nature—never helpful enough in Estonian lore to be called sympathetic—intervened. In a twist of fate that can only leave feminists shaking their heads, a bolt of lightning stunned the villain but also turned his ill-gotten prize into the rocky mound where the Estonian Parliament now stands.

Castle, present seat of the Estonian parliament *(riigikogu)*, stands on the square, but its doors are shut to prying eyes. Directly behind it, a fluttering Estonian flag tops **Tall Hermann** (Pikk Hermann), Tallinn's tallest tower and most impressive medieval fortification. Walk around the castle wall and gaze up at the tower as disheartened invaders must have. The lime-green **Art Museum** (Eesti Kunstimuuseum), Kiriku plats 1 (tel. 44 93 40), across from **Toomkirik,** displays Estonian art from the 19th century to the 1940s. It provides a good opportunity to see how Estonia handled impressionism, realism, art deco, and other schools of art. (Open W-Su 11am-6pm. 10EEK, students 5EEK.) There are three excellent views of the lower town from Toompea, all framed by artists selling watercolor versions of them—the best are at the end of Kohtu and at Patkuli vaate plats.

ROCCA-AL-MARE

In **Rocca-al-mare,** a peninsula 10km west of central Tallinn, the **Estonian Open-Air Museum,** Vabaõhumuuseumi 12 (tel. 656 02 30; fax 656 02 27), preserves 18th- to 20th-century wooden mills and homesteads. Visitors duck into log cabins, climb rickety stairs, and explore stables and wells leading to dirt paths along the sea. There are 68 buildings on 207 acres, including the **Sutlepa Chapel** (kabel), where a choir sings in Estonian and Swedish during holidays. Intricately attired Estonian folk troupes perform regularly. From Tallinn's train station, take bus #21 or 21a. (Open May-Oct. daily 10am-8pm. 21EEK, students 7EEK.)

ENTERTAINMENT

Tallinn This Week, a free brochure available at the tourist office and hotels, lists performance times and locations. The premier theater in Tallinn, **Estonia Theater,** Estonia pst. 4 (tel. 626 02 15; www.oopu.ee), offers opera, ballet, musicals, and chamber music. (Ticket office open daily noon-7pm.) **Eesti Kontsert,** Estonia pst. 4 (tel. 44 31 98; fax 44 53 17; www.bcs.ee/concert), performs classical music nearly every night, with festivals dedicated to composers and singers. Stone pillars give the hall an extraordinary resonance, but obstruct most views. (Box office open M-F noon-7pm, Sa noon-5pm. Student tickets 30EEK.) The **Church of the Holy Ghost** (p. 243) holds performances by students of the Estonian Music Academy and Tallinn's conservatory. **St. Nicholas Church** (p. 244) is famous for its organ concerts and choir performances. (30min. recital Sa-Su 5pm. Tickets available Tu 3-7:30pm, W 3-5:30pm, Th 11:30am-5:30pm.) During the **Organ Festival** (Aug. 1-10), churches around town host recitals. Tickets are sold at St. Nicholas.

Tallinn loves music festivals. The **National Song Festival**, which occurs once every four to five years (next in 2004), proved instrumental to Estonia's drive to independence in the "singing revolution" of 1990-91. **Old Town Days,** June 6-10, host open-air concerts throughout Vanalinn, as well as fashion shows, singing, and skits at Raekoja pl. The first week of July provides just one more excuse (as if one were necessary) to loose the taps in Tallinn bars, as **Beersummer** celebrates all things hoppy. Check the athletic complex in Kadrioru Park for national **tennis** and **soccer** events. Tickets for international matches can be purchased at the stadium gate for 100-150EEK. On lazy Sunday afternoons, Tallinn converges on the **beach** of Pirita (buses #1, 1a, 8 or 114) on the outskirts of the city.

NIGHTLIFE

Bars have sprouted up on almost every street of Vanalinn; most have a loyal clientele, although all but the most popular empty by 11pm, as the local scene moves to the nightclubs. While young mafiosos dominate some, expats and tourists are also quickly carving out a niche. In an effort to keep their clientele suave and sophisticated, many establishments enforce an age minimum of 21-23, applied mostly to men. Barhopping with older friends should guarantee admission.

Von Krahli Teater/Baar, Rataskaevu 10 (tel. 626 90 96 and 626 90 90), on the west edge of lower Vanalinn. This day time cafe lights up with elaborate multimedia spectacles at night, including blends of Gregorian chants and techno, and performances by local jazz and rock bands. Also has a small troupe of full-time actors. Tickets for bands in the bar start at 40EEK. Theater active most nights 7-9pm (tickets from 40EEK). Cover for dance shows 60-70EEK. Open Su-Th noon-1am, F-Sa noon-3am.

Flamingo, Meriválja Str. 5 (tel. 630 01 23). Take bus #1, 1a, 8, 38, or 114 from Hotel Viru. Located on the beach at Pirita, this nightclub boasts a gorgeous view of the sea from its glass-paneled restaurant. Dancing upstairs. Attracts a cheery crowd of twenty- and thirtysomethings, locals and tourists alike. Cover up to 100EEK. Open M-Tu and Su noon-midnight, W-Th noon-3am, F-Sa noon-6am.

Nimeta Baar (The Pub with No Name), Suur-Karja 4 (tel. 44 66 66). This Scottish-owned pub draws a boisterous crowd on weekend nights, often ending in shot-drinking competitions. Open Su-Th 11am-2am, F-Sa 11am-4am. MC/Visa. Nearby **Nimega Baar** (The Pub *with* a Name), Suur-Karja 13, has the same hours but a classier crowd.

Hollywood, Vana-Posti 8 (tel. 699 78 30). Inside this gray edifice (easily mistaken for a library), the DJ drops phat beats on trendy clubbers. A casino and cinema showing the latest American imports share the same building. Cover up to 100EEK. Open Su and Tu 9pm-3am, W-Th 9pm-4am, F-Sa 9pm-6am. 21+ in theory.

COASTAL ESTONIA

Sun, sand, natural preserves...and mud. East of Tallinn, Lahemaa National Park shelters precious coastline, historic villages, and endangered species from the ravages of tourism. Hip Pärnu and quiet Haapsalu, on the other hand, welcome weary travelers with open—albeit muddy—arms. Both are famed for their spas and travelers to Haapsalu are only a ferry away from the unspoiled Estonian Islands.

LAHEMAA NATIONAL PARK (RAHVUSPARK)

Founded in 1971, Lahemaa National Park was the USSR's first national park; today it is Estonia's largest. It covers nearly 500 square kilometers, 75% of them woodland, and frames a jutting and rocky coastline. Four peninsulas stretch like stubby fingers from the mainland, sheltering quiet bays and beaches from the caprices of the Baltic Sea. Further inland, nature trails lead through forest clearings and bogs flecked with purple lupin and white tufts of grass. Lahemaa is home to 838 plant species and some striking fauna, including elk, storks, and lynx. The park serves as a cultural as well as an ecological reserve, sheltering fishing villages and 18th-century German-Baltic estates from modernity. All the same, the region has taken progressive steps to boost its tourist appeal, from renovated historical sights and improved museums to expanded lodging and dining opportunities.

ORIENTATION & PRACTICAL INFORMATION. To get to the park, take the **Rakvere** bus from Tallinn along Narva mnt. to **Viitna** (1hr., 9 per day, 13 per day return to Tallinn, 34EEK). There, check the schedule of buses to **Palmse Mõis.** Buses connect the larger of the villages, but are infrequent, and some run only on alternate days; biking and hiking are the only ways to get around if you don't want to wait. Luckily, most destinations lie within two hours of each other. For direct access to Lahemaa's coast, inquire at the Tallinn station about thrice-weekly buses to **Võsu.** These can also be used for direct transport to the Palmse manor house. Walk past the souvenir shop on your left to the English-speaking **Palmse information center** (tel. 341 96; email ekal@estpak.ee; open May-Aug. daily 9am-7pm; Sept. daily 9am-5pm; Oct.-Apr. M-F 9am-2pm). **Postal code:** 45202 (Viitna). **Phone code:** 232.

ACCOMMODATIONS & FOOD. The Palmse information center offers advice on the wide variety of accommodations in Lahemaa, and can sometimes arrange for multilingual private-room owners to pick you up by car. Situated a scenic 8km hike from Võsu in the village of Käsmu, **Lainela Puhkemajaad** (tel. 991 33), toward the end of Neema, offers small, tidy rooms within 50m of the sea. Free access to a basketball court, two tennis courts, a sauna, and the nearby Kásmús Maritime Museum (see below) are all available. (Triples 140EEK; tent space 100-120EEK.) For more luxurious, inland lodging, try the newly opened hotel/hostel/restaurant/cafe at **Sagadi Mõis** (tel. 986 47). Located about 8km from Palmse Mõis (9km from Võsu), the hostel has six rooms with a total of 17 beds. (Singles 180EEK; triples or larger rooms 100EEK per person.) Bicycles are rented to guests for 20EEK per hour or 100EEK per day. Their restaurant offers tasty meals for carnivores and a full vegetarian menu. (50-100EEK.) The most centrally located accommodation is the **campground** at Viitna, 400m past the bus stop and through the wooden arch on the right. The lakeside camping office (tel. 936 51) can set you up with tent space or singles (100EEK) and doubles (150EEK) in log cabins and also rents bikes (10EEK per hr.). Beware: while the surrounding forest protects from the wind, it also harbors hordes of blood thirsty mosquitoes. Farthest from Võsu and Viitna (16km and 25km, respectively) in the tiny fishing village Altja, a 19th-century peasant home hosts a tiny two-room **bed and breakfast** (tel. (25) 252 355; see **Sights,** below), providing spacious doubles (300EEK on weeknights, 400EEK F-Su) with central heating, shared bath and a free sauna.

In the wilds of Palmse Mõis, the **Park Hotell Restaurant** (tel. 341 67) prepares fresh salads (15-20EEK) and the obligatory schnitzel (60EEK; open daily noon-7pm). The **tavern** in Viitna (tel. 435 43), located opposite the bus stop, dishes up hearty local food. (50-100EEK. Open daily noon-midnight.) A pub on **Vergi** (tel. (25) 25 08 50) offers hearty meals (20-40EEK; open M-F noon-midnight, Sa-Su noon-2am).

SIGHTS. Palmse Manor, now a **museum** (tel. 341 91), is among the best restored and most historically significant estates in Lahemaa. From 1677, members of the von Pahlen family resided among the manor's ostentatious gazebos and swan ponds, until the government reclaimed all private land in 1923. Peter Ludwig von Pahlen was involved in the 1801 assassination of Russian Tsar Paul I, and Alexander von Pahlen initiated the building of the Tallinn-St. Petersburg railroad in 1879. The estate was the first in Estonia to be completely restored, and the eclectic furniture carted in from all overEstonia includes a 19th-century music box from St. Petersburg that makes traditional square-dance music sound suspiciously like Nine Inch Nails. (Open Apr.-Aug. M and W-Su 10am-7pm.)

Next to the Lainela Puhkemajaad, the **Kásmús Maritime Museum,** with its heavenly hours and prices (24hr., free), introduces visitors to the history of the surrounding fishing village, which once served as an Estonian ship-building center and a school for sailors. Ask the sole proprietor, old salt Aarne Vaik, for a tour. On the far side of the **Puhkemajaad Neemetee,** a dirt path through the woods opens up to a rocky beach where the **stone hill** sometimes grants wishes to those who contribute new rocks to the mound. Ice Age glaciers deposited boulders all the way from Finland, and here they remain, standing 8m tall in the sand.

The extensive grounds of **Sagodi Mõis** (see **Accommodations & Food,** above), complete with artificial pond out back, attempt to recreate the days of the German aristocracy that once presided over Lahemaa. Inside the manor itself, ornate—if slightly faded—18th- and 19th-century furniture as well as countless mirrors betray the vanity of the estate's former residents. The attic of the Baroque building, atop the spiral staircase, displays the hunting trophies of its master. Meanwhile, the **Museum of Forestry,** the first white building on the left through the gates, features exhibits on the park's plant and tree life, its historical uses, and the sobering impact of humans on the ecosystem. (Museum and manor open May 15-Sept. 30Tu-Su 11am-6pm. Joint ticket 30EEK, students 10EEK; separately 20EEK, 7EEK.)

During the 1950s, the Soviets closed much of the northern coast off with barbed wire and banned fishing; **Altja** is one of the few fishing villages remaining. The old fishing huts on the cape are part of an open-air museum. (Open 24hr.) Continuing around the cape and crossing the river, white stripes on the trees mark a short nature trail that runs through the coastal forest and loops back to town. The small island visible is **Vergi,** reachable by a land bridge 2.5km farther on the coastal road.

PÄRNU

The "summer capital" of Estonia, Pärnu (PAER-noo), long a Hanseatic center trade center, got its makeover as a resort in the early 19th century, and hasn't looked back since. Called the "Cinderella of the Baltic" by turn of the century poets, the tiny town of 50,000 has certainly made a fairy-tale comeback. After toiling long under its wicked Soviet stepmother, Pärnu, with the help of the sassy young crowds in its the beachside cafes, has gone from sooty to muddy once again. And with cultural festivals adding to the excitement, Pärnu is ready to take the ball by storm.

ORIENTATION & PRACTICAL INFORMATION

Crowds tend to congregate in two locations—**Rüütli,** the central street, and along the **beach.** The parks in between provide a measure of quiet between the party.

Trains: Tel. 226 67. 3km east of the center, by the corner of Riia and Raja; take bus #40 from the central post office to Raeküla Rdtj. (3EEK). To **Tallinn** (3½hr., 2 per day, 30EEK).

Buses: Ringi 3 (tel. 415 54). In the center. Best way to reach Pärnu. To: **Tallinn** (3hr., 36 per day, 60EEK); **Haapsalu** (3hr., 2 per day, 48EEK); **Kuressaare** (3hr., 2-3 per day, 87EEK); **Tartu** (5hr., 11 per day, 70-76EEK); **Rīga** (4hr., 5 per day, 76EEK); and **St. Petersburg** (10hr., 1 per day, 195EEK).

Taxis: Tel. 412 40 and 401 90. 5EEK per km.

Bike Rental: Rattapood, Ria 95 (tel. 440 32). 50EEK per day. Open M-F 10am-6pm, Sa 10am-2pm.

Tourist office: Rüütli 16 (tel. 730 00; fax 730 01; email info@parnu.tourism.ee; www.parnu.ee). Provides **maps** and help with lodging. Open M-F 9am-5pm.

Currency Exchange: Eeasti Ühispank, Rüütli 40a (tel. 771 11). Cashes traveler's checks, gives cash advances, and has an **ATM.** Open M-F 9am-6pm, Sa 9am-2pm. In a pinch, **Hotel Pärnu** has bad rates but is open 24hr.

Internet access: Chaplini Kunstikeskus, Esplanaadi 10. Open M-F noon-6pm.

Post office: Akadeemia 7 (tel. 711 11). At the west end of Rüütli, less than 1km from the bus station. Open M-F 8am-6pm and Sa 9am-3pm. **Postal code:** 80001.

Telephones: Rüütli 5 (tel. 707 27). Around the corner from the post office to the right. Open M-F 8am-6pm, Sa 9am-4pm. **Phone code:** 44.

ESTONIA

ACCOMMODATIONS

Now that Pärnu is popular again, many hotels are renovating and raising their prices. Places fill fast, so reserve ahead. The tourist office can also book rooms.

Kajakas Külalistemaja, Seedri 2 (tel. 789 09; email pergo@estpak.ee; www.ee/kajakas). Follow Ringi from the bus station thrgouh town and around the park to Mere past. Turn left and follow Mere pst. as it becomes Remmelga, then turn right on Seedri. Tired-looking, but rooms are comfortable. Hall bathrooms are old but clean. Singles 180EEK, with bath 300EEK; doubles 290EEK, 360EEK; triples 390EEK. Breakfast 30EEK. Sauna 80EEK.

Kalevi Pansionaat, Ranna 2 (tel. 430 08). Beach-side hotel designed for Spartans: hard beds, hall bathrooms, and not much else. Doubles and triples 200EEK. Breakast 30EEK.

Linnakämping Green, Suure-Jõe 50b (tel. 437 76). 3km from the town center along a deserted, unlit street on the river. Pärnu's cheapest and most basic accommodations. Facilities include gnome-sized cabins, a bar, a basketball court, and immaculate bathrooms. Cabin bed 95EEK; tent site 60EEK. Breakfast 30EEK. Open June-Aug.

FOOD

A **turg** (market) is at the intersection of Sepa and Karja. (Open Tu-Su 7am-1pm.)

Lehe Kohvik, Lehe 5 (tel./fax 445 67). 2min. from the Ranna Hotel and the beach. Entrees 30-80EEK. Open daily 11am-midnight.

Trahter Postipoiss, Vee 12 (tel. 402 04). In an 1834 post station. Serves great Estonian chicken salad (26EEK), and cheese schnitzel (86EEK), along with grilled dishes. Open M-Th and Su 11am-midnight, F and Sa 11am-2am.

Georg, on the corner of Rüütli and Hommiku. Cafeteria-style restaurant. Entrees under 35EEK. Open M-F 7:30am-7:30pm, Sa-Su 9am-7:30pm.

SIGHTS & ENTERTAINMENT

Adjacent to Hotell Pärnu at Rüütli 53, the **Pärnu Regional Museum** (Pärnu Rajoonide Vaheline Koduloomuuseum; tel. 434 64) displays everything from taxidermy to Stone Age tools. The final display case contains heart-wrenching letters from local children to their parents, who were deported to Siberia. (Open daily 11am-5pm. 10EEK, students 3EEK.) The **Lydia Koidula Museum,** Jannseni 37 (tel. 416 63), across Pärnu river, commemorates the 19th-century poet who revived Estonian verse and drama. (See Literature, p. 236). (Open W-Su 11am-6pm. 5EEK, students 3EEK.) South of Rüütli on Nikolai stands the 1747 Baroque rust-red **Eliisabeti kirik** named after the Russian tsarina. (Open daily 9am-6pm.) At the corner of Uus and Vee a block north of Rüütli, the Russian Orthodox **Ekateriina kirik** is a multi-spired, silver-and-green edifice built in the 1760s under the order of Catherine the Great. Rüütli ends at an **open-air theater** where music and drama performances are given in summer, starting in July. Turn left off Rüüli before you reach the open air theater to pass through the formidable **Tallinn Gate** (Tallinna värav), the only gate into the city during Swedish rule and the only surviving Baltic town gate from the 17th century.

The broad, tree-lined street stretching south from Tallinna värav leads to a long pedestrian zone just behind the white-sand **beach.** The water is clean, if a bit shallow and cold before July. Women can bathe **nude** if they wander up the beach to the right. Swings, jungle-gyms, and trampolines are set up on the sand, and there's a whirly waterslide open in summer. (Open daily 11am-7pm. 5EEK per swoosh.)_To play **tennis,** go to Ratta Sport, Ringi 14a. (Open daily 10am-10pm. 80EEK per hr. Racquets provided.) On summer evenings, drinking, partying, and sunset-watching

THE DIRTIEST BATH THIS SIDE OF THE BALTICS

Mud has never looked or felt better than at Pärnu's Neo-Classical **Mudaravila,** Ranna pst. 1 (tel. 424 61). Since 1838, when the mud baths and health resort were founded, the privilege of rolling around in gooey mud has not been limited to pigs and small children. Workers at the mud bath (and many health professionals) insist that Pärnu's sea mud has a curative effect on disorders of the bones, joints, and peripheral nervous system. There's even a special ward for patients with myocardial infarction and cardiovascular diseases. After a brief consultation, patients can choose between General Mud, Local Mud, and Electric Mud (95-120EEK). And, for those tough-to-reach areas, there's the ever-popular mud tampon (70EEK). No day at the mud bath is complete without a massage (200EEK), a "curative" bath or shower (60-75EEK), and a cup of restorative herb tea—no mud added. (Open daily 8am-3pm.)

center around the temporary bars that set up along the beach. At the low-ceilinged stone tavern **Tallinna Baar** (tel. 450 73), atop the grand gate you can get a delectable snitsel (51EEK) with you *Saku* for (20EEK). (Open daily noon-11pm.) Housed in a 1930s wooden dance hall on the beach, **La Pera Vida,** Mere 22 (tel. 432 79), spins pop and techno for a Bohemian crowd, with ocassional theme nights. (Open M-Th and Su 10am-midnight, Fand Sa 10am-2am. Ocassional 25EEK cover will get you a glass of wine.) In the heart of it all, **Diskoklub "Hamilton,"** Rüütli 1, near the outdoor theater, hosts disc-spinners from all over Estonia. (Open daily 9am-5pm. Cover 50EEK, higher when bands play.) There's a **cinema** at Mere 22, in the same building as La Pera Vida; films are usually in English (30EEK). In the first weekend of July, the **Pärnu Jazz Festival** (info tel. (06) 26 02 42) attracts artists and listeners from around the world. 1999 featured Bobby McFerrin as a special guest artist. The **David Orstrank Festival** (July 1-11) showcases classical music. Check *Pärnu in Your Pocket* for a complete calendar of events and details on times and location.

HAAPSALU

Seaside Haapsalu (HAAP-sa-loo) sprawls out from the ruins of its Bishop's Castle, the 13th-century seat of the Saare-Löäne bishopric that ruled most of western Estonia. The town was almost destroyed during the Russo-Livonian War (1558-1583), then conquered by Swedes in 1581 and Russians in 1710. In the 19th century, it was famed throughout the Russian Empire for its curative mud baths, but during Soviet times the resort image crumbled like dry mud as the town became a military airbase. Today, with the rebuilding and renovation of the sanatoriums and the sailing harbor, Haapsalu is a rapidly Westernizing tourist attraction. But the loudest noises still come from nature, as the protected caves just off the main peninsula serve as a breeding ground for thousands of squawking ducks and swans.

ORIENTATION & PRACTICAL INFORMATION. Tsar Nicholas II visited Haapsalu so often that he had a massive covered platform built to make sure none of his party would get wet while disembarking. That platform now serves as the **bus station,** Raudtee 2 (tel. 577 91), with buses to: **Tallinn** (2hr., 4 per day, 42EEK); **Kärdla** (3hr., 3 per day, pay 40EEK on the bus); and **Pärnu** (2-3hr., 2 per day direct, or via **Lihula,** 48EEK). The ticket office is open daily 5-8:30am and 9:30am-7pm. To reach the center of town, turn left after exiting the platform and then right on Jaama. It's a good idea to get your bearings at the **tourist information office** (tel. 332 48; fax 334 64; email haapsalu@tourism.eu.org; www.webs.ee/haapsalu) in the train station complex. The helpful English-speaking staff sells **maps** (25EEK). (Open May-Sept. 15 M-F 9am-6pm, Sa 10am-2pm; Sept. 16-Apr. M-F 10am-5pm.) For a **taxi,** call 333 30 (4EEK per km). Exchange money at **Hansapank,** Posti 41, or draw cash from its **ATM** outside. (Open M-F 9am-4pm.) The library, Posti 3 (tel. 451 65), has free **internet access.** The **post office** is at Nurme 2 (open M-F 7:30am-6pm, Sa 8am-4pm), and the **telephone office,** Tallinna mnt. 1 (tel. 352 57), is on the other side of the block. (Both open M-F 8am-6pm, Sa 9am-4pm). **Postal code:** 90501. **Phone code:** 247.

ESTONIA

ACCOMMODATIONS & FOOD. The **Jahtklubi** (Yacht Club), Holmi 5a (tel. 455 82; fax 455 36), is a 20min. walk to the end of the peninsula from the bus station. You can also take city bus #2 to Jahtklubi or arrange for a taxi at the tourist office. If you choose to walk, follow Posti north as it merges with Karja, then turn left on Ehte. Follow the right edge of the lake, continue on to Kaluri, and Holmi is on your right. Enter from the stairs underneath the wooden tower in the back. It sports spotless rooms with sinks, hall baths, a well-polished bar behind the front desk, and a small outdoor restaurant. (Singles 170EEK; doubles 330EEK.) The **Paralepa Puhkemaja** (tel. 25 10 67 35) is located on a gorgeous beach 10min. from the bus/train station. Look for the low wooden dorms behind the Fra Mare Sanatorium. The rooms are spartan, but clean enough. (Doubles, triples, and quads 140EEK.)

Locals frequenting **Restoran Central,** Karja 21 (tel. 446 73), hang out either in the beer cellar downstairs or in the dining room upstairs, munching away on chicken in white wine sauce (50EEK) and prawns (80EEK). The restaurant gets crowded on weekends; call ahead. (Open M-Th and Su noon-11pm, F-Sa noon-2am; bar opens 1hr. earlier.) Just outside the castle walls, **Rootsituru Kohvik,** Karja 3 (tel. 450 58), serves salads (20-30EEK) and meaty entrees (50-68EEK; open daily 10am-10pm). The **market** *(turg)* is one block from the bus station on the corner of Jürlöö and Jaama. (Open Tu-Su 7am-3pm.) There are several good **supermarkets,** including **Rema 1000,** Linula 3. (Open 9am-9pm. MC/Visa.)

SIGHTS & ENTERTAINMENT. The **Bishop's Castle** (Piiskopilinnus), where the Bishop of Saare-Lääne lived until moving to Saaremaa in 1358, is located about halfway up the peninsula. It can be reached by following **Kalda** or **Posti** from the bus/train station to the town center. There, they converge into **Karja** and flow into **Castle Square** (Lossiplats). From the square, one can enter **Lossi Park,** home of the Castle. (Open 7am-11pm.) The castle sometimes protected the bishop and townspeople from foreign invaders, and sometimes protected the bishop and foreign invaders from the townspeople. Needless to say, the bishop wasn't very popular, which may explain why the fortifications predate the chapel. Inside the park, local swallows have transformed the crumbling towers and walls into a teeming aviary. You can climb the steep and ragged steps of the tower for a view of all Haapsalu and the marshy seas that surround it (10EEK), and grab a drink at the **bar** at the base. (Hamburger 20EEK, *Saku* 15EEK. Open Tu-Su 10am-6pm.) The steeple-less **Episcopal chapel** beside the tower is accessible through the adjoining museum, which exhibits period costumes, a scale model of the complex, and informative plaques on the town's history, all in a single room. (Open Tu-Su 10am-6pm. 15EEK, students 5EEK.) The **Africa Beach** (Aafrikarand) promenade, northeast of the castle at the end of Rüütli, runs 2km to the yacht club. **Kaluri,** farther east, makes for beautiful walks amid weathered wooden houses, marsh grasses, and ducks.

FULL-MOON CAPITALIST FEVER Haapsalu's economic viability relies as much on the legend of the White Lady as it does on its famous curative mud. According to legend, the White Lady was brought into the town's cathedral by the widely disliked bishop for his not-so-holy pleasure in the 1280s (a time when only men were allowed inside), and was later walled up inside for crossing its threshold. Supposedly on the full moon each August, she makes an apparitional appearance in one of the cathedral windows to mourn her fate. The event is celebrated by a week-long festival, including dramatizations of the legend that draw people from all over the country. In order to avoid disappointment if she fails to emerge or on cloudy nights, budding Estonian capitalists set up light projectors to generate an approximate image on the chapel windows; this way, they keep the tourists flooding in, and allow the White Lady an occasional rest from her timeless woe.

ESTONIAN ISLANDS

Estonia precociously extends far out to sea, with over 1500 islands speckling the Baltic. Worried about providing an easy escape route to the West, the Soviets restricted foreigners and Estonians from visiting the islands. As a result, the islands are a preserve of all that is distinctive about Estonia: from the outdoor musems of Saaremaa to the exotic flora and fauna on Hiiumaa, to the remarkable Gothic church on Muhu. For those seeking the more eccentric, the islands also offer such curiosities as a tragically ineffective lighthouse on Hiiumaa, deserted Soviet bases, and the annual cops-versus-hooligans soccer match in Kuressaare.

SAAREMAA

The largest and most touristed of the Estonian islands, Saaremaa (SAA-reh-maa) is often reckoned to be more Estonian than Estonia itself. Silent windmills lining hilltops survey a countryside of traditional farms and stone churches. From mysterious meteorite craters and bubbling springs to the rugged coast and astounding cliffs, natural beauty abounds. Come summer, young Estonians from the mainland arrive in increasingly greater numbers to party beachside, adding a surge of energy and revelry to the otherwise subdued serenity of the island.

> At press time, Saaremaa was in the process of upgrading its telephone systems. As a result, those listed might be unreliable. Check with the tourist office in Kuressaare for the most up-to-date telephone information.

KURESSAARE

A major resort before Soviet occupation, Kuressaare (KOO-res-saa-re), on Saaremaa's south coast, is making a comeback. An abandoned 16th-century fortress attracts tourists while new bars and hotels are making the most of it.

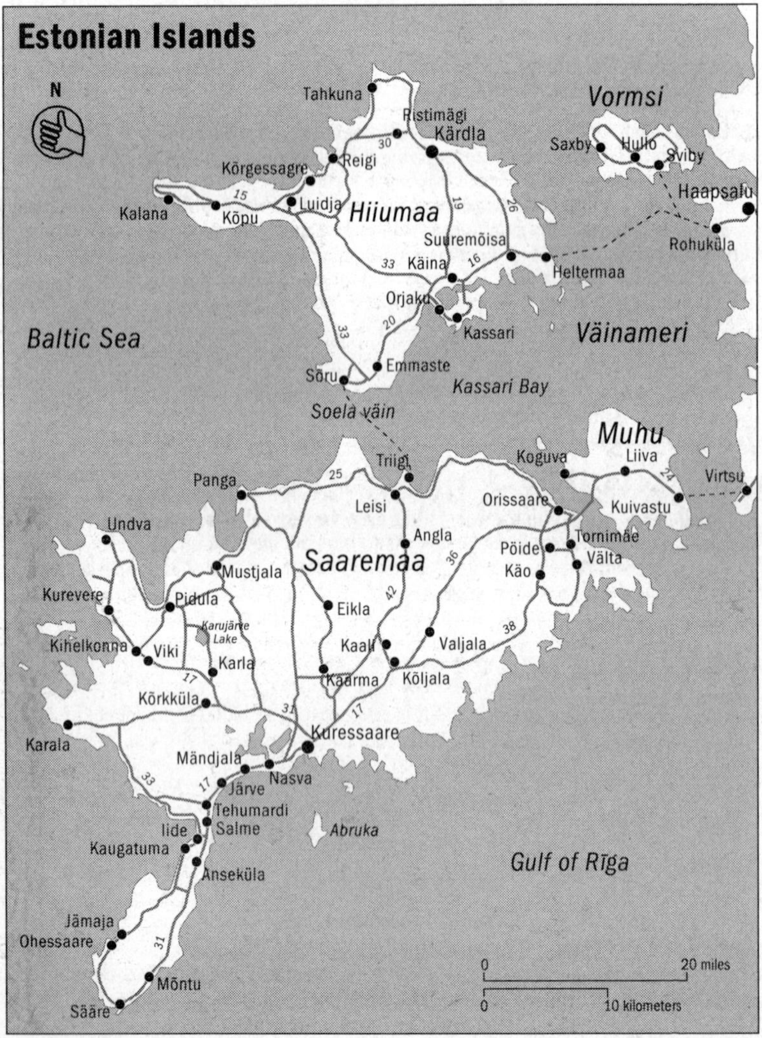

ORIENTATION & PRACTICAL INFORMATION. The town is centered around the narrow **Raekoja pl.** (Town Hall Square). **Buses,** Pihtla tee 2 (tel. 573 80), at the corner of Tallinna, head to: **Tallinn** (4hr., 9 per day, 110EEK) and **Pärnu** (3hr., 2 per day, 87EEK). Direct buses, which get priority on the ferries, are the fastest way to get to the mainland. A new **ferry** route island-hops between Saaremaa's Triigi port and **Hiiumaa's Sõru port** (65min., M-Tu and Th-Su 2 per day, 50EEK). **Taxis** (tel. 533 33) run from behind the town hall, the bus station, and Smuuli pst. (4-5EEK per km.) Saare Autex, Tallinna 21 (tel./fax 566 98) rents **bikes.** (115EEK per day.) Polar Rent, Tallinna 9 (tel. 336 60), offers **car rentals.** (490EEK-790EEK per day.) The **tourist office,** Tallinna 2 (tel./fax 331 20; email info@oesel.turism.ee; www.tourism.ee/oesel), inside the *raekoda* (town hall), sells a useful **map** (15EEK) and answers questions on food, lodging, and events. (Open May-Sept. 15 M-Sa 9am-7pm, Su 10am-3pm; Sept. 16-Apr. M-F 9am-5pm.) **Exchange currency,** cash traveler's checks, and get MC/Visa advances at Eesti Ühispank, Kohtu 1 (tel. 559 55; open M-F 9am-4pm, Sa 9am-2pm). The **post office,** Torni 1 (tel. 543 45), is on the corner of Komandandi, a block north of Tallinna. (Open M-F 8am-6pm, Sa 8:30am-3pm.) **Internet** access is available at Tolli, the multimedia room adjacent to the library. (Open M-F 11am-4pm.) The **telephone office** is to the right behind the post office. (Open M-F 8am-6pm, Sa 9am-4pm.) **Postal code:** 93 813. **Phone code:** 245.

ACCOMMODATIONS & FOOD. New pensions and B&Bs are opening all the time; check with the tourist office. Hotel management students run **Mardi Öömaja,** Vallimaa 5a (tel. 332 85; fax 332 80), which includes the cheapest hostel in town. From the south end of Raekoja plats head up Kohtu, turn right on Garnisoni, and then left on Vallimaa. Facilities are aging, but the rooms are clean and the common bathrooms modern. (Singles 150EEK; doubles 200EEK. Breakfast 50EEK.) **Hotell Pärna,** Pärna 3 (tel./fax 575 21), has eight large, homey rooms and a self-service kitchen. (Doubles 400EEK, with bath 550EEK. Breakfast included. Sauna 150EEK per hr.) **Mändjela Puhkeküla** (tel. 751 93), Kuressaare Vald, lies 11km outside Kuressaare at the "Kämping" stop on the Kuressaare-Järve bus. It offers tent space, as well as spacious, no-frills cabins along a small beach. (Dorms 145EEK. Breakfast included. Tent sites 15EEK. Open May-Sept.) Farther away from town, **Tare Motel and Camping** is reachable by the Pihta bus. Avoid the pricey doubles; stay in the bargain "motel." (110EEK, with shower 125EEK.)

New bars, restaurants, and cafes are constantly opening, and prices are rising with the town's popularity. The **supermarket** EDU, Tallina 1, is well stocked. (Open daily 9am-10pm.) **Vanalinna,** Kauba 8 (tel. 553 09), one of the best eateries in town, serves perch garnished with prawns (65EEK) and mushroom-based vegetarian dishes (from 40 EEK; open daily noon-midnight; MC/Visa). **Kodulinna Local,** Tallinna 11 (tel. 541 78), in a basement off Raekoja pl., is a cheap restaurant and bar popular with locals, who come to eat beef cutlet with egg (30EEK) and drink *Saaremaa* beer (20EEK; open daily 10am until last guest leaves). Like the adjoining hotel, **Kass Restaurant,** Vallimaa 5a (tel. 332 95), is run by hotel-school students. (Entrees 40-50EEK. Open daily noon-midnight. MC/Visa.) **Kohvik Veski,** Pärna 19 (tel. 531 61), serves up steak and seafood (55-85EEK) to four floors of eager eaters in an old windmill. (Open Su-Th noon-midnight, F and Sa noon-2am.)

SIGHTS & ENTERTAINMENT. 17th-century buildings line **Raekoja pl.,** the most notable being the 1670 Nordic Baroque **town hall** *(raekoda)*, a squarish building built by Swedish landowner Marcus Gabriel de la Gardie. Past the square's south end a **statue** commemorating the 1918-20 struggle for independence is actually a 1990 replica of the original, erected in 1928 but destroyed by the Soviets.

Heading south of Raekoja pl. along Lossi, through a sleepy park, and across a moat, lies the town's main attraction, the **Bishopric Castle** (Piiskopilinnus). Built in 1260 after the Teutonic Order conquered the island, it was renovated in the 1300s for the Bishop of Saare-Lääne, who liked it so much that in 1358 he declared it the bishopric's administrative center. The castle has changed hands several times: the Danes bought it in 1559, and it served as a Swedish and then a Russian fortress,

COPS AND ROBBERS Mention hooliganism at soccer matches to most people, and visions of pub brawls between drunk, scarved Scots come to mind. But the relation between ne'er do wells and the world's most popular sport is a global phenomenon, as evinced by the annual match between the punks and the police in Kuressaare. Someone had the bright idea a few years back to put these mortal foes together on the pitch to let out their aggressions. Since then, every June, the cops in their blue shirts and badges and the punks with their rainbow mohawks, have at each other with a flurry of slide tackles and obscenties. The quality of the footballing is usually rather poor, a fact only compounded by the keg of beer on the punks' sideline. Nonetheless, the game is a town spectacle, with almost everyone there supporting the underdogs against the long foot of the law.

until the Tsar finally retired it from military use in 1899. Most of its vaulted chambers are now empty, except those that house the **Saaremaa Regional Museum** (tel. 563 07), one of the more interesting museums in the Baltics. An eclectic collection from the island's history is on display, including intricately carved coats-of-arms, national costumes, carriages, antiques, military and maritime objects, and photographs and short biographies of Saaremaa's intellectuals and politicians. The castle's twisting passageways are enough to keep you busy for a day; pick up a much-needed map (10EEK) at the entrance. (Open May-Aug. daily 11am-7pm, last entry 6pm; Sep.-Apr. W-Su only. 30EEK, students 15EEK.) **Tornikohik,** a cafe in the castle's defense tower, serves post-castle relief (*Kuressaare* beer 20EEK) for the weary. (Open May-Aug. daily 11am-5:30pm; Sept.-Apr. W-Su only.)

At night, a mellow crowd gathers at the **Budweiser Pub,** Kauba 6 (tel. 534 24), an Irish bar popular with locals and travelers alike. (Open daily 10am-2am.) A classier crowd patronizes **Nimeta Pub** ("The Pub with No Name"), Tallinna 3, in Raekoja pl. (Open M-Th noon-1am, F-Sa 10am-4pm, Su 10am-1am.) For a livelier time, head from Nimeta Pub across Raekoja pl. to **Punane Baar,** where 20-somethings—ladies dressed to kill, men just dressed, hopefully—grind to American tunes under dark red lights. (Cover 30EEK and up. Open daily 10pm-4am.)

On weekends in July, music fills the air from the bandstand in the park around the castle; on Saturdays it's a brass band, and on Sundays it's a small symphony orchestra. The first weekend of August brings **Maritime Days,** which features sailing competitions, musical performances, and various other cultural events.

WEST SAAREMAA

Because distances are large and buses infrequent, it's necessary to rent a car to see the entire island. Those traveling by bike or bus will have to pick and choose among accessible sights. To get to unspoiled **Karujärve Lake,** take the road to Saîa just before Kaarema—which becomes unpaved—about 15km to Kärla. At the main intersection in Kärla, turn right onto a paved road. After 5km you'll see the Karujärve **campground,** Kärla vald (tel. 421 81; fax 420 34), on the left. The campground has small A-frame cabins for two with thin mattresses (250EEK) and tent places (30EEK). With swimming, horseback riding, and volleyball nearby, it seems like summer camp all over again. (Open May 15-Sept. 15.)

The main road heads toward **Kihelkonna,** with the **Mihkli Farm Museum** (Mihkli Talumuuseum) in Viki en route. 19th-century farmhouses cluster around a pretty garden. (Open daily 10am-6pm. 10EEK, students 4EEK.) Farther along the road, turn right down the hill to Kihelkonna, where the relief on the tower of the 13th-century **Kihelkonna Church** depicts archangel Michael fighting a dragon.

Continuing down the road to Silla, turn right on the unpaved road to **Pidula** to reach the bubbling **Odalästi Springs**, rumored to bring eternal youth to young ladies who splash its water on their faces, although you wouldn't know it from looking at the local matrons. Look closely for the churning earth where the water wells up from underground. Backtracking to the head of the road you'll find the **Pidula** fish farm. Here they raise 'em, release 'em, catch 'em, and fry 'em. (100EEK per kg.) Ah, the circle of life. You can stay on the lake after your meal, in one of two available rooms. (300-350EEK. Sauna 100EEK per hr.; boat rental 30EEK.) In nearby Mustjala stands **Anna's Church** (Anna Kirik), built in 1864 on the site of a medieval burial ground. Hungry travelers should follow the signs to **Käsitöösahver,** where they grill sandwiches (from 5EEK) on an open fire. (Open daily 11am-7pm.)

From Mustjala you have your choice of peninsulas—the impressive shoreline of **Tagaronna** or the even more impressive 25m drop at **Panga,** depicted on the back of the 100EEK note. If you go to Tagaronna, skirt the tip of the peninsula to reach a **Soviet training facility,** with trenches and barbed wire now overgrown with lupin. If you choose **Panga,** climb halfway up the "lighthouse," a ladder enclosed by steel scaffolding. Use caution: the steps are steep and the wind blustery. A stand at Panga sells sausages (5 for 16EEK) and beer (12EEK; open daily 10am-8pm).

SOUTHWEST SAAREMAA

Renting a bike is one of the best ways to explore the area. The first stop on the route south should be the quiet beaches of **Mändjala** and **Järve,** 8-12km west of Kuressaare. To reach Mändjala, take the first left after the "Mändjala 1" bus stop. For the beach in **Järve,** turn left after the "Ranna" bus stop. At **Tehumardi,** a giant concrete sword marks the location of a 1944 WWII battle, now remembered by rows of memorials for the dead soldiers. Farther on, the town of **Salme,** 17km out of Kuressaare, makes a good lunch stop. The restaurant **Ago & Co.** (tel. 715 34), on the main road, serves the usual Estonian fare, including fried perch with cheese (52EEK), and *seljanka* (14EEK; open daily 11am-10pm).

About 2km away from Salme, a sign points right along an unpaved road to **Iide,** cutting over to the west side of **Sõrve poolsaar** (the peninsula), where the choppy waters of the open Baltic meet rockier beaches. The "cliffs" at **Kaugatuma** are drastically overrated by locals, but you can sunbathe alongside grazing cows on the fossil-strewn, pebbly beaches. 5km farther down the road, the ruins of the **WWII defense line** are visible. At **Sõrve säär,** the very tip of Sõrve poolsaar, clear weather reveals a view of Latvia, 25km south across the Baltic. On the trip back, the road going through **Mõntu** (the opposite direction from Jämaja) passes through the **national park** (look out for foxes and deer). The ride, especially on the one-speed bikes rented in Kuressaare, may leave you with a sore rump, so bring cushioning, along with plenty of bug repellent. If you get tired, take a bus home and ask the driver to put the bike with the luggage.

EAST SAAREMAA

The East is the most rapidly developing part of Saaremaa, and it also features some of the island's more impressive religious sights. One of the island's most beautiful churches is in **Kaarma.** You can bicycle the 20km here by taking Tallinna mnt. north out of Kuressaare and turning left at the sign to Upa, then right to Kaarma. **Kaarma Church** is a 13th-century structure in need of renovation. Across the road are the earthen remains of the 12th-century **Kaarma Stronghold** (Maalinn). To leave, take the dirt road back to the paved one. Turn left and then right toward Kaali. Barely 75m from an elementary school lie several **meteorite craters,** the largest of which is big enough to necessitate steps down to the pond at its bottom. **Kalli Trahler** (tel. 911 82), across the road from the crater parking lot, serves tasty and reasonably-priced dishes (shrimp in cream sauce 84EEK) in a new building trying its hardest to look rustic. (Open daily 10am-11pm.)

To reach the easternmost parts of the island, catch a bus from Kuressaare to **Orissaare.** The **Püharisti** hotel, Ranna pst. 11 (tel. 451 49), 200m off the main road, offers comfortable rooms in its two scenic cabins by the sea. (240EEK per person. Breakfast included.) 100m away is an inexpensive **24hr. restaurant.**

South of Orrisaare lies **Pöide** and its **church.** Built as a Catholic church in the 13th century, it later became Lutheran, Russian Orthodox, and then Lutheran again. It also doubled as a fortress for the Teutonic Knights. The climb to the top of the tower is unlit and shaky, but offers a fantastic panorama. Southwest of Orissaare in the small town of **Valjala** lies **Valjala Church,** the oldest stone church in Estonia, built with buttresses for fortification.

MUHU

The island of Muhu, between Saaremaa and the mainland, has much to offer tourists. **Muhu Church** in Liiva, with no steeple and a bright asymmetrical interior, is considered one of the most remarkable early-Gothic structures in Estonia. Portions of the current building date from 1617, having withstood the ravages of the Great Northern War. While the short, modest pulpit reflects the Lutheranism still practiced here, the trapezoidal tombstones in the churchyard recall the paganism which found a refuge on these islands as the Christians converted mainland Estonia. A little east of Liiva and off the main highway, a dirt road veers right 8km to Muhu's south shore and the tall **Pädaste Manor** (Mõis), dating from the 17th century and currently in the throes of renovation. If you're looking to stay on Muhu, **Vanatoa Tunsmitalu,** Muhu vald (tel. 488 84) in Koguva, offers somewhat luxurious accommodations at very moderate prices. (250EEK per person. Breakfast included.) The restaurant **Mesimaja Trahler** (tel. 488 00), offers decent meals for 70-120EEK. (Open daily noon-midnight.)

GETTING THERE. **Buses** run from **Kuressaare** to **Kuivastu** (2hr., 11 per day, 30EEK).

HIIUMAA

By restricting access to Hiiumaa (HEE-you-ma) for 50 years, the Soviets unwittingly preserved many of the island's rare plant and animal species, as well as its unhurried way of life. Native residents tell stories of spirits, giants, trolls, and devils who inhabited Hiiumaa before them, and visitors find unadorned churches, history-laden lighthouses, and the birthplaces of legends. A woody wilderness unblemished by human habitation, Hiiumaa is a haven for peace and respite.

KÄRDLA

The Swedish settlers who first stumbled across this sleepy spot on Hiiumaa's north coast named it "Kärr-dal," meaning "lovely valley." Hardly an urban center, Kärdla contains as many meandering creeks and trees as houses. With easy access to the beach and horseback riding, it is easy to see why the 4200 residents of Hiiumaa's tiny capital receive twice as many guests in the summer.

ORIENTATION & PRACTICAL INFORMATION. The main square is named **Keskväljak.** To reach the mainland, it is cheapest and most convenient to catch a bus from Kärdla or Käina (the ticket price includes the ferry). From the **bus station,** Sadama 13 (tel. 320 77), north of Keskväljak, catch buses to: **Haapsalu** (3hr., 2-3 per day, 40EEK); **Tallinn** (4hr., 3 per day, 80EEK); and points around the island (0.40EEK per km). Local buses, however, are infrequent. **Ferries** arrive at **Heltermaa** (from **Rohuküla,** just south of Haapsalu on the mainland; for schedules tel. 316 30 in Heltermaa, tel. 24 73 36 66 in Rohuküla) and **Sõru** (from Triigi on **Saaremaa;** 1hr., 2 per day, 50EEK per person, 150EEK per car). A shuttle runs to Heltermaa's port from the Kärdla **bus station** (45min., 4 per day, 11EEK), to **Sõru** (1hr., 2 per day, 18EEK). The island's only **tourist office,** Hiiu 1 (tel. 222 33; fax 222 34; email info@hiiumaa.tourism.ee; www.hiiumaa.ee), in the main square, provides info on accommodations, and sells **maps** (35EEK) and guides to sights on Hiiumaa. (Open May-Sept. M-F 9am-6pm, Sa-Su 10am-2pm; Oct.-Apr. M-F 9am-4pm.) There's **internet access** upstairs in the yellow culture center on the main square, Rookopli 18 (tel. 963 22). At Eesti Ühispank, on Keskväljak, you can **exchange money,** get Visa **cash advances,** and find an **ATM.** (Open in summer M-F 9am-6pm, Sa 9am-2pm; off-season M-F 9am-6pm.) All **taxis** (tel. 316 95) are based in Keskväljak (5EEK per km). Rent **bikes** (100EEK per day), and **cars** (500EEK) from Kertu Sport, Vabrikuväljak 1 (tel. 963 73), just across the bridge from the bus station. (Open M-Sa 10am-6pm.) The island's main **post office** is at Posti 13 (tel. 963 18), about 200m north of the bus station, opposite the church. (Open M-F 8:30am-4:30pm, Sa 9am-1pm.) **Postal code:** 92412. **Telephones** are at Leigri väljak 9 (tel. 315 37). **Phone code:** 246.

ACCOMMODATIONS & FOOD. **Nuutri Matkamaja,** Nuutri 4 (tel. 980 23; mobile tel. 250 588 96), 7min. from the center, offers 11 beds in three rooms, with a common room, shower, sauna, two bathrooms, kitchen, fireplace, and TV. (200EEK per person.) Follow Polla past the stadium, then cross the bridge and turn right on Nuutri. The institutional but friendly **Kärdla Võõrastemaja,** Vabaduse 13 (tel. 965 81; fax 965 77), in the center of town, near the corner of Vabaduse and Valli, has 22 beds. (Singles 150EEK; doubles 240-270EEK; quads 360EEK. Breakfast included.) The grub on Hiiumaa is mediocre and remote, with most of the better meals found outside of Kärdla (see **Elsewhere on Hiiumaa,** below). EDU, in Keskväljak, is a central **supermarket.** (Open daily 9am-9pm. MC/Visa.) The big, green building in the town square houses **Kohvik** (tel. 998 43), one of Kärdla's only restaurants, serving cheap and starchy entrees. (Meals 40-80EEK. Open M-Th and Su 9am-10pm, F-Sa 9am-midnight.) By the beach at the end of Lubjaahju, **Rannapaargu** (tel. 965 09), is perfect for a drink by the sea. (Open 10am-midnight.)

SIGHTS. **Pühalepa Church,** Pikk 26 (tel. 911 20), contains the graves of the Baltic-German Count Ungeru-Stenberg's family. The Count, who came to the island in 1781, the year Catherine the Great deported all of Hiiumaa's Swedes, wanted to acquire the entire island, but his shipping and salvage business was cut short when he killed one of his ship captains in a dispute.

ELSEWHERE ON HIIUMAA

More than two-thirds of all the plant species in Estonia exist only on Hiiumaa. Due to this biodiversity, much of the island now belongs to the **West-Estonian Islands Biosphere Reserve. Hiking** and **camping** are permitted and encouraged, but be sure to pick up info at the tourist office about off-limit regions. Motor vehicles are not allowed on the seashore and certain other areas. Because of dry conditions, **campfires are prohibited.** Apart from the biosphere, the most interesting parts of the island lie on the coast. With distances so short and buses so infrequent, a bike is the best means of transportation. By bike, you can see all of the sights in two daytrips from Kärdla: one to Kõpu and one to Kassari. Heading west out of Kärdla toward Kõrgessaare the first oddity you'll encounter is the **Hill of Crosses** (Ristimägi), on your left. Further down the road, a right turn leads to **Tahkuna Lighthouse.** Built in Paris in 1874, the lighthouse was consistently ineffective in warning ships about the coast's shallow waters. This didn't hurt the economy much, though, since salvaging loot and rescuing passengers from the ships was quite profitable. Not without irony, a memorial to those lost in the 1994 sinking of ocean liner *Estonia* now stands here, alongside Soviet-era gun emplacements and bunkers.

The island's best restaurant hides in the hamlet of **Kõrgessaare** (also called **Viskoosa**), 17km west of Kärdla. The large rose-granite building that **Viinaköök** (Vodka Kitchen; tel. 933 37) inhabits was originally a 19th-century silk factory and later a vodka distillery. (Open daily 11am-2am.) Well past **Luidja,** the highway gives way to a dirt road as it approaches the most impressive sight in Western Hiiumaa, **Kõpu Lighthouse.** This pyramid-shaped tower on Hiiumaa's west peninsula was constructed in the early 1500s by the Hanseatic League. The stairwell was an afterthought, hacked out of solid rock to provide access to the top. The view from the top is a panorama of the Baltic Sea, including all of Hiiumaa and, on a sunny day, the island of Saaremaa to the south. (10EEK.)

For the journey south from Kärdla to Kassari, you could take the direct route to Käina, but the road through **Suuremõisa** is more scenic. The large rocks that make up the first sight en route to Suuremõisa, the **Contract Stones** (Põhilise leppe kivid), were placed by human hands, but their purpose is a mystery. Were they a pagan altarpiece? The burial place of a Swedish king and his gold? Or a "contract" between God and an ancient sailor bargaining for a safe voyage? The world may never know. Northeast of Käina, **Suuremõisa Palace,** a beautiful example of northern Baroque architecture, stands in disrepair. Built by the Swede Jakob de la Gardie, who purchased the entire island from the Swedes in 1624, the estate languished under Russian rule. The current building was rebuilt by Margarethe Stenbock, a relative of de la Gardie's, in 1775. (Open June 22-Aug. 15 M-F 9am-4pm and Sa-Su 9am-4pm; Aug. 16-June 21 M-F 9am-4pm. 7EEK, students 3EEK.)

With a population of 200, **Käina,** southwest of Suuremoisa, remains Hiiumaa's second-largest town. The **Käina Church** had been the focus of the Käina settlement since 1422, but a German air attack in 1941 left it in ruins. **Lilia Restoran,** Hiiu mnt. 22 (tel. 921 46), in Käina, serves cheap but good meals, such as pasta salads (17EEK), fried perch (50EEK), and fried beefsteak (42EEK).

The tiny island of **Kassari** (ka-SA-ree), south of Hiiumaa, is home to even thicker woods and wilder sights. The most beautiful of the island's sights is **Sääretirp,** a 1.3m-wide peninsula jutting 3km into the sea, lined with wild strawberry and juniper bushes. Legend holds that this is what's left of a bridge built by the giant Leiger between Hiiumaa and Saaremaa so that his brother Suur Tõll could come for a visit.

Puulaiu Matkamaja (Campground Puulaid; tel. 361 26), only a short distance from Käina (ask the bus driver to let you off at Puulaid). It could compete with some of the nicer budget hotels in Estonia, with spacious shared rooms, modern toilets, a sauna and shower, kitchen, and a splendid view. (120EEK per person; tents 20EEK. Breakfast 40EEK.) Boats (16EEK per hr.) also available for rental.

INLAND ESTONIA

The Estonian railway system makes inroads from Tallinn to the geographic, intellectual, and historic heart of the country, Tartu. Along another fork of the rails, travelers can rekindle dragon slaying fantasies of youth while climbing what's left of the medieval fortress at Viljandi.

TARTU

Tartu may be the oldest city in the Baltics—and Estonia's second largest (pop. 101,901)—but it is also a fountain of youth. It had to be to survive being razed five time since its founding in 1030. Today, that youthfulness persists at the University, long a wellspring of Estonian nationalism. Tartu may slow down a bit in summer when its budding intellectuals run off to the coast, but there's still plenty of concerts, theater, and nightlife to keep you entertained.

ORIENTATION

The **bus** and **train stations** border the center of town on opposite sides. The main artery, **Riia mnt.,** runs into the center from the southwest and ends by the bus station. Perpendicular to it near the **Emajõgi River** is **Turu pst.,** which turns into **Vabaduse pst.** and runs from the bus station along the river toward the northeast. **Raekoja plats** (Town Hall Square), the city's geographical and social center, stretches west from the Emajõgi river toward the old castle hills. **Rüütli** heads north from the square; its end at Lai marks the boundary of the historic center. Behind the town hall, **Lossi** meanders uphill between the two peaks of **Toomemägi** (Cathedral Hill) and intersects **Vallikraavi,** a crooked, cobblestone road that follows the path of the old moat circling the hills and joins **Kuperjanovi,** leading to the train station.

PRACTICAL INFORMATION

Trains: Vaksali 6 (tel. 37 32 20). At the intersection of Kuperjanovi and Vaksali, 1.5km from the city center. Info booth open daily 7am-noon and 1-7pm. To: **Tallinn** (3hr., 5 per day, 70EEK) and **Moscow** (18hr., 1 per day, 284EEK, *coupé* 416EEK).

Buses: Turu 2 (tel. 47 72 27). On the corner of Riia and Turu, 300m southeast of Raekoja plats along Vabaduse. The best way to get to and from Tartu. To: **Tallinn** (2-5hr., 40 per day, 75EEK); **Pärnu** (4hr., 13 per day, 75-88EEK); **Rīga** (5hr., 1 per day, 150EEK); and **St. Petersburg** (10hr., 2 per day, 160-178EEK). The info booth is open daily 8am-8pm.

Local Transportation: Buses cost 5EEK; tickets are available at kiosks around town. Bus #5 and 6 go from the train station to Raekoja plats and the bus station. Bus #4 travels down Võru. Buses #3, 6, 7, 11, and 21 travel down Riia.

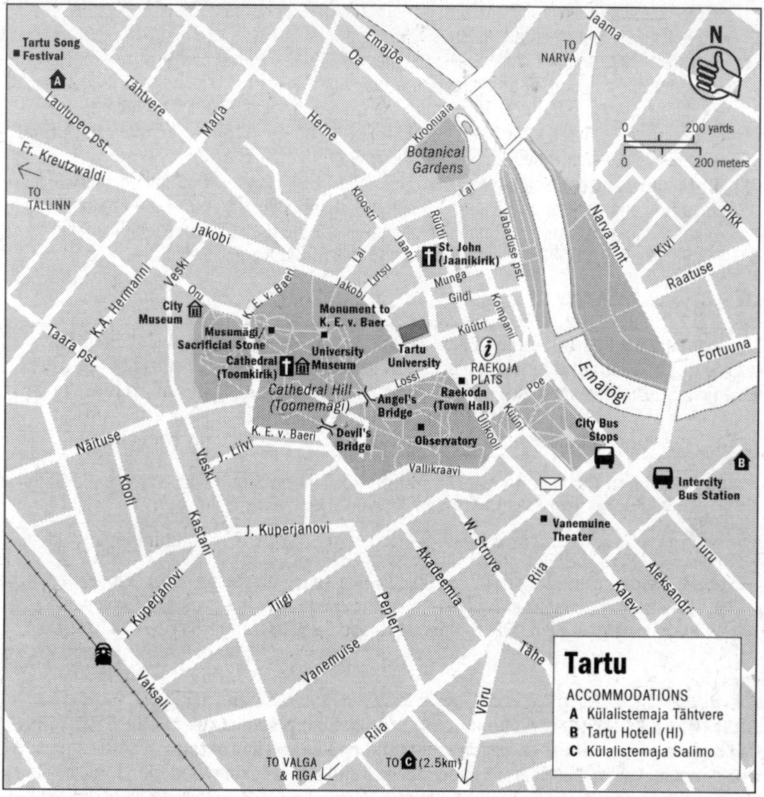

Taxis: Outside the bus and train stations (4-5EEK per km). Cross-town ride 20EEK.

Tourist Office: Raekoja plats 14 (tel./fax 43 21 41; email info@tartu.turism.ee; www.tartu.ee). Provides English info and organizes transport and tours. **Maps** 20EEK. Open M-F 10am-6pm, Sa 10am-3pm.

Currency Exchange: Best rates at banks, including **Eesti Ühispank,** Ülikooli 1, which gives cash advances, cashes AmEx traveler's checks, and has an **ATM.** Open M-F 9am-6pm.

American Express: Kompanii 2, 3rd Fl., 51003. Cashes traveler's checks and gives cash advances. Open M-F 9am-5:30pm.

Luggage Storage: Lockers in train station. Buy tokens in the room in the main lobby marked *"Vaksali Korraldaja"* (6EEK: one 3EEK token to open it and one to retrieve your stuff). Also in the bus station. 4EEK per bag. Open M-F 8am-7pm, Sa 8am-noon.

24hr. Pharmacy: Raekoja Apteek (tel. 43 35 28), on the north side of the town hall.

Post Office: Vanemuise 7 (tel. 44 06 05). Open M-F 9am-7pm, Sa 9am-3pm, Su 10am-3pm. **Postal code:** 51003.

Internet Access: Cafe Virtual, Pikk 40 (tel. 40 25 09; www.kodu.ee/virtual). 30EEK per hr. Open M-Sa 10am-9pm.

Telephones: Lai 29 (tel. 43 16 61; fax 43 39 93). At the corner of Rüütli. Cardphones and **fax** machine. Open M-F 8am-6pm, Sa-Su 9am-4pm. **Phone code:** 7.

ACCOMMODATIONS

Külalistemaja Salimo, Kopli 1 (tel./fax 47 08 88), 3km southeast of the train station off Võru. Take bus #4 from the beginning of Riia opposite the Kaubamaja to "Alasi." Walk

25m to your left, cross Võru, and turn left onto Kolpi. Unrenovated doubles 290EEK, renovated 400EEK; unrenovated triples 330EEK.

Tartu Hotell (HI), Soola 3 (tel. 43 20 91; fax 43 30 41). In the center of town directly across from bus station, in an aging yellow building. Big rooms, big beds, big TVs. A bargain for HI members but *only* HI members. Room with toilet 200EEK for members. For non-members, singles with toilet 550EEK, with shower 875EEK; doubles 640EEK, 900EEK. Breakfast included. Sauna 140EEK per hr. Check-out noon. MC/Visa.

Külalistemaja Tähtvere, Laulupeo pst. 19 (tel. 42 17 08). From the bus station, follow Riia across Turu and go right on Ülikodi. A block beyond the pink hall, turn left on Jakobi. Follow uphill and go right on Laulupeo. 16-bed hotel has the town's cheapest rooms. Singles 150EEK; doubles 250EEK; 2- and 4-person rooms 300EEK and 700EEK.

FOOD

The **supermarket,** Tartu Kaubamaja, is at Riia 2 (tel. 47 62 31; open M-F 9am-9pm, Sa 9am-8pm, Su 10am-8pm; MC/Visa). The indoor part of the **turg** (market) opposite the bus station, on the corner of Vabaduse and Vanemuise, is literally a meat market. (Open M-F 7:30am-4pm, Sa 7:30am-2pm, Su 7:30am-1pm.) For fresh produce, try the outdoor half on the far side of the bus station. (Open daily 6am-5pm.)

Central Restoran Bar (tel. 44 12 97), just off Raekoja plats on Küüni. Enjoy the best in Estonian cuisine. Full meals 60-100EEK. Open daily noon-midnight.

Rotundi Kohvik, the low wooden octagon in the park on Toomemägi near Angel's Bridge. Ample portions of Estonian favorites. Full meals 40-50EEK. Open daily 11am-8pm.

Püssirohukelder, Lossi 28 (tel. 43 42 31). Off the street, across a bridge, and inside the hill. 18th-century gunpowder cellar stays cool in even the hottest weather. Full meals 85-150EEK. Cover after 8pm 20EEK. Open M-Th and Su noon-1am, F-Sa noon-2am. Visa.

SIGHTS

TOWN HALL SQUARE. (Raekoja plats). The logical place to start is the 1775 **Town Hall Square,** the center of Tartu. The pink and white **town hall** at the top of the square was constructed in Dutch style. Since most buildings rest on wooden pylons, many are sinking slowly into the marshy ground. Near the bridge, **Raekoja plats 18,** now leans (much like the student population here) a little to the left. Inside is the **Tartu Art Museum** (Tartu Kunstimuuseum), with 19th- and 20th-century works, including those of Johann Köler and Ants Laikmaa, founders of the first studio in Tartu. *(Tel. 44 10 80. Open W-Su 11am-6pm. 5EEK, students 2EEK; Friday free.)*

TARTU UNIVERSITY. (Tartu Ülikool). The must-see sight in Tartu is, of course, **Tartu University.** The main building was built in 1809 with six imposing Corinthian columns. The university was founded to teach government officials and Protestant clergy, and was modeled on Uppsala University in Sweden. Inside the main building sits the **Museum of Classical Art,** a small collection of Roman and Greek plaster copies with a temporary exhibition of original antiquities. The only Russian university with the right to have fraternities, the school used the privilege well. The **Estonian National Awakening** began here with the founding of the **Estonian Student Association** (Eesti Üliõpilaste Selts) in 1870. The nationalists who constituted the fraternity became so central to Estonia's struggle for independence that when the country won its freedom in 1919, the frat's colors (blue, black, and white) became those of the national flag. If you arrive in early June the front hall will likely be filled with white-knuckled applicants looking for the scores of their admission exams—and the scores of the competition; only a talented 10% of the pool make the cut. *(Follow Ülikooli from behind the town hall. Art Museum is at Ülikooli 8. Tel. 46 53 84. Open M-F 11am-4:30pm. 6EEK, students 2EEK. Attic 7EEK, students 4EEK.)*

OTHER ÜLIKOOLI SIGHTS. Farther up Ülikooli (which becomes Jaani), **St. John's Church** (Jaani-kirik), completed in 1323, was unique in Gothic architecture with thousands of terra-cotta saints, martyrs, and other figures. The Russian recapture of Tartu in 1944 nearly destroyed the church, and only a few hundred figures remain in the scarcely standing edifice. Restoration began in the 80s but is still not completed. Look for the gleaming copper steeple. *(Lutsu 16/24. Tel./fax 43 38 60.)* Across the street, the **Museum of the 19th-Century Tartu Citizen** (19 saj. Tartu Linnakodaniku Majamuuseum), displays furnishings and objects that, as the name implies, deal with conceptions of citizenship in the city in the 1800s. *(Jaani 16. Follow Ülikooli past the University at is becomes Jaani. The museum will be on your left, opposite and a little past St. John's Church. Tel. 44 19 34. Open W-Su 11am-6pm. 10EEK, students 5EEK.)* Where Lai meets Toomemägi hill, a path leads up to the **Tartu Toy Museum** (Mänguasja Muuseum) which entertains with a collection of dolls and toys from around the world. *(Lai 1. Tel. 25 08 25 36. Open W-Su 11am-6am. 4EEK, children 2EEK.)*

CATHEDRAL HILL. (Toomemägi). If you're in the Old Town and find yourself moving uphill, either on a flight of stairs or a dirt path, you've probably found **Cathedral Hill.** Most of the statues here commemorate important figures affiliated with the University. At the bottom of the hill is a **statue of Nikolai Pirogov,** a pioneer in the field of anaesthesia in the 19th century who graduated from the university. On the hill itself is the **statue of Kristjan Joak Peterson,** the first Estonian to attend Tartu University and a nationalist poet. The statue of Karl Ernst von Bear (the embryologist who graces the 2EEK note) tops the hill, awaiting the annual spring ritual of biology students dousing him with champagne. The central site of the hill is its namesake, the majestic 15th-century **Cathedral of St. Peter and Paul** (Toomkirik), which served stints as a granary and university library. Today, it houses the **Tartu University Museum** (Museum Historicum Universitatis Tartuensis), which features in-depth displays of scientific instruments and a social history of the university. *(Tel. 37 56 71; www.ut.ee/REAM/museum.html. Open W-Su 11am-5pm. 10EEK, students 5EEK. English guide available.)* Near the church and two Swedish 17th-century cannons, **Kissing Hill** (Musumägi), once part of a prison tower, is now a make-out spot and the site of an ancient pagan **sacrificial stone.** Two bridges lead to the east hump of Toomemägi—the pink wooden **Angel's Bridge** (Inglisild) and the concrete **Devil's Bridge** (Kuradisild). An annual competition between the university **choirs** takes place on these bridges, women on the former, men on the latter.

OTHER MUSEUMS. The **Estonian National Museum** (Eesti Rahva Muuseum) gathers scads of ethnographic material—including folk costumes, furniture, and plenty of model houses—to discuss the 19th-century National Awakening that began in Tartu. *(J. Kuperjanov 9. Follow Riia uphill from the bus station. Turn right on Peplen and follow it around the bend on your left as it becomes Kuperjanovi. Tel. 42 13 11. Open W-Su 11am-6pm. 5EEK, students 3EEK. Temporary exhibit 8EEK, students 5EEK.)* Tartu's **City Museum** (Linnamuuseum) houses the table on which the Peace Treaty of Tartu was signed between Russia and the nascent Estonian Republic on February 2, 1920, ending the Estonian War of Independence. *(Oru 2. From Raekoja plats, follow Ülikooli past the university as it becomes Kakobi. Turn left on K.E. von Baer and head right up the hill on Oru. Tel. 42 20 22 Open W-Su 11am-6pm; closed last day of each month. 3EEK, students 2EEK.)*

ENTERTAINMENT

Tartu comes alive in the evenings with bar-hoppers roaming **Raekoja plats**. Bulletin boards in the lobby of the main university building (Ülikooli 20) advertise weekend happenings. Less frequent events include the end of May's "Rock Box" festival showcasing Estonian bands. The **Dionysia** arts festival, held from late-March to early-April, includes drama and dance performances, film screenings, and visual art exhibitions all over Tartu. The first Estonian-language theater, **Vanemuine,** Vanemuise 6 (tel. 43 29 68), founded in 1870, stages operas and classical concerts; unfortunately, it is closed in summer. (Box office open M-Sa 9am-7pm, Su noon-7pm.) **Eesti Suve Teater** (Summer Theater) picks up the slack, with swashbuckling Estonian renditions of Western classics in the medieval cloister on Cathedral Hill. (Performances run from early or mid-July through August.)

NIGHTLIFE

Wilde Bar, Vallikraavi 4 (tel. 30 97 64; fax 30 97 61). Oscar Wilde meets his Estonian Wilde counterpart Eduard on the bench outside this Wildely popular haunt. Irish and Estonian vittals served alongside corresponding national brews. 0.5L domestic beer 25EEK. Live music most nights. Open M and Su noon-midnight, Tu-Th noon-1am, F-Sa noon-2am.

Krooks, Jakobi 34 (tel. 44 15 06), at the bottom of Toomemägi. Draws in the Bohemians long after Wilde closes. 0.5L Guinness 28EEK. Live music F-Sa. Open daily noon-6am.

Atlantis, Narva mnt 2 (tel. 44 15 09), across the river. This recently renovated, enormous disco/restaurant/casino/pool hall is *the* place for the college set. Neon lights illuminate DJ Cool D, who spins for the youngsters most nights. Cover 70EEK. Open M-Th and Su 10pm-3am, F-Sa 10pm-5am. MC/Visa.

NEAR TARTU: VILJANDI

Estonia is very flat. Those with a taste for the vertical, however, will find the **Ruins of the Order's Castle** (Ordulinnuse varemed), south of Viljandi, a gratifying exception. Founded by the Knights of the Sword in the 13th century, the fortress—one of the largest in the Baltics—once spanned three hilltops with high-flying bridges. Today, the ruins afford not only a great view of **Viljandi lake** *(järv)*, but also numerous opportunities for exploration, starting with the stone archway that leads to the last remaining wall of the **keep** and now used as a backdrop for spooky summer productions. Around the back of the keep, the 1879 red-and-white **suspension footbridge** (Rippsild) leading to town was sent to Viljandi in 1931 by a German count to stop his daughter from racing her horses over it. The easiest way to the castle from the bus station is to walk down Tallinna 800m past the new shopping complex. Along the way stands the medieval **St. John's Church** (Jaani kirik) in the central castle park. The ruins of a 1466 Franciscan monastery destroyed in the 1560s are visible in the basement. (Open daily 10am-5pm.) More history lies along the longer route on **Lossi**, the main street of the Old Town. On the way you'll pass through **Laidoneri plats,** home of the former marketplace and the **Viljandi Museum,** Laidoneri plats 10 (tel. 333 16), home to taxidermy—check out the wild-eared prehistoric squirrel—and a model of the fortress in its glory days. (Open summer W-Su 11am-6pm; off-season 10am-5pm. 6EEK, students 3EEK.) When you've had enough history, head down to the **lake** for a swim or a beer from the roving bars along the water.

In a run-down building by the lake, **Kalevi Viljandi Motel,** Ranna 6 (tel. 472 70), is a hostel with simple twin rooms and quite possibly the cleanest bathrooms in Eastern Europe. (80EEK per person.) From the bus station, turn off Tallinna onto Kauba and follow it down the stairs; turn left at the statue of the hyperventilating runner. The motel is the first building on your left. Two stuffed hawks guard **Iva Restoran,** Kauba 11 (tel. 344 93), on the corner with Tallinna. (Entrees around 50EEK. Open daily 8am-9pm.) Descend the stairs opposite Iva Restoran to **Tasuja Kohvik,** Vadabuse plats 2 (tel. 331 42). Dine on snitsel or beefsteak for comparable prices. (Full meals 60-12EEK. Open M-F 9am-9pm, Sa 11am-10pm, Su 11am-9pm). **Rema 1000,** Tallinna 24, houses a huge **grocery store.** (Open daily 9am-10pm.)

GETTING THERE. The main street, **Tallinna,** runs from behind the bus station to the castle ruins. From the **bus station** (open M-F 8am-1:30pm and 3:30-6pm, Sa 8am-1:30pm), Ilmarise 1 (tel. 336 80), buses run to: **Tallinn** (2½-3hr., 20 per day, 60-70EEK); **Pärnu** (2hr., 9 per day, 38-40EEK); and **Tartu** (2hr., 14 per day, 36EEK). At the bottom of Tallinna, **Vaksali** runs to the **train station.** The **tourist office,** Tallinna 2b (tel./fax 337 55; email info@viljandi.tourism.ee; www.estonia.org/viljandi) has **maps.** (Open May-Aug. daily 9am-6pm; Sept.-Aug. M-F 10am-6pm, Sa 10am-2pm.) **Postal code:** 71008. **Phone code:** 43.

HUNGARY (MAGYARORSZÁG)

US$1 = 241 FORINTS (FT, OR HUF)	**100FT = US$0.42**
CDN$1 = 162FT	**100FT = CDN$0.62**
UK£1 = 386FT	**100FT = UK£0.26**
IR£1 = 324FT	**100FT = IR£0.31**
AUS$1 = 157FT	**100FT = AUS$0.64**
NZ$1 = 128FT	**100FT = NZ$0.78**
SAR1 = 39FT	**100FT = SAR2.51**
DM1 = 130FT	**100FT = DM0.77**

PHONE CODES Country code: **36.** International dialing prefix: **00.**

Communism was a mere blip in Hungary's 1100-year history of repression and renewal. Today, the nation appears well at ease with its new-found capitalist identity. Budapest remains Hungary's social and economic keystone, although it by no means has a monopoly on cultural attractions. Intriguing provincial capitals lie within a 3hr. train ride. Nonetheless, with luscious wine valleys nestled in the northern hills, a rough and tumble cowboy plain in the south, and a bikini-worthy beach resort in the east, the beauty of the countryside should not be forsaken for a whirlwind tour of the capital. Otherwise, you'll have seen the heart of Hungary, but missed its soul entirely.

LIFE & TIMES

HISTORY

Modern Hungary was inhabited by hunters, gatherers, Neolithic farmers, and Scythians into the Late Stone Age, as evidenced by the Istálósk cave near Budap-

HIGHLIGHTS OF HUNGARY

- Indulge yourself in **Budapest's** hedonistic Turkish baths, sinful restaurants, or opulent Habsburg Opera House (p. 267).
- Siófok's Baywatch-esque Strand, Badascony's giddy wine cellars, and Keszthely's stunning palace make **Lake Balaton** the capital of the Hungarian summer (p. 309).
- **Eger's** Bull's Blood Wine and cobblestone streets—not to mention the nearby Valley of the Beautiful Women—attract the region's most discriminating drunks (p. 332).
- With the best nightlife and contemporary art museums outside Budapest, the surprisingly cosmopolitan **Pécs** is an ideal weekend playground (p. 317).

est (see **Szilvásvárad,** p. 336). In the 3rd century BC, **Celtic tribes** forced their way onto the territory and were soon followed by the **Romans** (see **Aquincum,** p. 287), who founded the provinces of Pannonia and Dacia in the early post-Augustan period and maintained them through the 4th century BC.

The **Magyars,** mounted warrior tribes from Central Asia, arrived in AD 896. Led by **Prince Árpád,** it took them only a few years to conquer the middle basin of the Danube River. Árpád's descendant, **Stephen I,** was crowned King of Hungary with benediction from Pope Sylvester II on Christmas Day, 1000, accepting the authority of the pope and decreeing the conversion of his subjects. Canonized in 1083, Stephen is considered the founder of the modern Hungarian state.

A series of strong monarchs developed a system of imperial control over the next hundred years, generating as much revenue as its western counterpart France and uniting the country as a secular and religious whole. The nobility grew restless with the blunders of Andrew II, however, and in 1222 he was forced to sign the **Golden Bull,** granting rights to the people and restricting the powers of the monarchy. The devastating Mongolian invasion came just under two decades later, and in 1301 the Árpáds died out and were replaced by a variety of families from across Europe. As leadership changed hands in the 14th century, Hungary reached its **Golden Age,** so named for both its military stability and the gold mines controlled by its monarchs. Unfortunately, royal in-fighting gradually weakened the country and in the mid-15th century, Mátyás Hunyadi, known as **Matthias Corvinus** (1458-1490), was imprisoned in Prague by claimants to the throne after the death of his father, the legendary general **János Hunyadi**. Corvinus was freed and coronated by the nobility, and presided over Hungary's Renaissance, stressing the importance of art and science and cultivating an extensive library. Following his death, Hungary suffered a national peasant rebellion in 1514, leading to civil rights setbacks that took hundreds of years to repair. The army fell into disarray and was easily defeated by the Turks at **Mohács** in 1526.

Conflict between the Protestant nobility, the Ottomans, and the Holy Roman Empire plagued Hungary for the next 150 years, until the **Habsburgs** took over in the early 17th century. A new **war of independence** began in 1848, led spiritually by the young poet Sándor Petőfi and politically by Lajos Kossuth. Together, they convinced the Diet (parliament) to pass a series of reforms that became known as the **April Laws.** Kossuth's state held out for one year, but in the summer of 1849 Habsburg Emperor **Franz Josef I** retook Budapest with the support of **Tsar Nicholas I of Russia.** Despite a period of repression, Hungary (under the leadership of Ferenc Déak) was granted its own government coexisting with the Austrian crown by the **Compromise of 1867.** Eventually, the Habsburg Empire and Hungarian government became united as a **Dual Monarchy,** the **Austro-Hungarian Empire.** Nationalist sentiments rose, leading to linguistic and institutional policies in the Empire favoring the Magyars. In response, opposing movements emerged among Romanians, Serbs, Croats, and Slovaks. These divisions erupted during **World War I,** resulting in the permanent destruction of the empire. After the war, Hungary gave up two-thirds of its territory in the 1920 Treaty of Trianon.

The **Bourgeois Democratic Revolution** that overthrew the monarchy in 1918 was followed by the 133-day Communist Hungarian Republic of Councils under the leadership of **Béla Kun.** Counter-revolutionary forces eventually took control, though, brutally punishing those involved with the Communist administration. **Admiral Miklós Horthy** then settled in for 24 years of control (1920-44), initially overseeing a democratic government run by István Bethlen, but always ultimately maintaining dictatorial control. The depressed interwar years were followed by a tentative alliance with Hitler in **World War II,** then by a year-long Nazi occupation and the near-total destruction of Budapest during the two-month Soviet siege of 1945. Two-thirds of Hungary's Jews, whose numbers had approached one million before the war, were murdered. Nearly all survivors fled the country.

In 1949 Hungary became a People's Republic, ruled by **Mátyás Rákosi** and the Hungarian Workers Party. Under his leadership, the country became tied to the USSR economically and politically, often serving as a "workshop" to fulfill Soviet industrial needs. Rákosi lost control in the **1956 Uprising,** a violent rebellion in Budapest in which **Imre Nagy** declared a neutral, non-Warsaw Pact government. Soviet troops crushed the revolt and executed Nagy and thousands of protesters.

Over the next three decades, Nagy's replacement, **Janos Kádár,** oversaw the partial opening of borders and a rise in the national standard of living. Inflation and stagnation halted progress in the 1980s, and democratic reformers in the Communist Party pushed Kádár aside in 1988, pressing for a market economy and increased political freedom. In autumn 1989, Hungary broke away from the Soviet orbit, and the first free elections in 1990 transferred power to the Hungarian Democratic Forum. Slow progress, however, eroded its popularity, and the renamed-and-revamped Socialists returned to power in 1994, promising a moderate course.

HUNGARY TODAY

Following its rapid transition to a capitalist economy, Hungary suffered skyrocketing inflation and unemployment in the early 1990s. This led to the triumph in the 1994 elections of former prime minister **Gyula Horn** and the **Hungarian Socialist Party,** who promised easier reforms rather than a return to the past. Since then, Hungary has lowered inflation, stemmed rising unemployment, and experienced consistent GDP growth. Against the protests of former Warsaw Pact ally Russia, Hungary was offered **NATO membership** in July 1997, and E.U. accession negotiations began in March 1998.

May 1998 elections favored the conservative **Hungarian Citizen's Party,** whose leader, 36-year-old **Victor Orbán,** is the youngest prime minister in Europe. President **Árpád Göncz** is a former political prisoner who was re-elected for a second term in 1995. With increasing integration into the West, the only visible vestiges of the old regime are now benign: efficient public transportation, clean parks and streets, and a low incidence of violent crime. But change has not been easy, and Hungary's economic transition remains incomplete. Like most other budding capitalist countries, Hungary's hot political topics are wages and inflation. The 1999 conflict in Yugoslavia had little effect on Hungary, despite bombings in the politically Yugoslavian, ethnically Hungarian province of Voivodina, 10km from Szeged.

Neo-Nazism is unfortunately on the rise, particularly in Budapest and Szombathely. In early 1999, neo-Nazis staged a pan-European conference in the capital. Whether the rise in Nazi-related graffiti adorning Hungarian buildings is directly related to the high-publicity conference is unclear. What is clear, however, is that a veritable spray-paint-war is being fought on Hungarian bricks. In general, neo-Nazism does not effect tourists and is more rhetoric than action.

LITERATURE & ARTS

A Finno-Ugric tongue distantly related to Finnish and Estonian, **Magyar** occupies a strange linguistic niche. The feeling of isolation created by this unique and impenetrable language has defined the literary, social, and political history of its speakers. Magyar survives in few written records before the 11th century; the earliest extant example is a deed from 1055 founding a Benedictine Abbey (now kept at **Pannonhalma Abbey;** see p. 299). Not until Christian missionaries came to the region did the Hungarian language begin to emerge from underneath the dominant Latin culture, but Latin remained the language of the state until 1844. The history of Hungarian literature has also been affected by the problems of repression; the Ottoman occupation censored Hungarian writers for over 150 years.

During the Enlightenment, members of the Hungarian nobility, among them **Count Miklós Bethlen,** wrote memoirs in the style of Voltaire and Rousseau. **Ferenc Kazinczy** founded a language reform movement and promoted literary consciousness through his high critical standards. Furthermore, as seen in street names of post-communist Hungary, the generation of writers writing around the Revolution of 1848 played an important role in Hungary's history. Most notably, the Populist, anti-Romantic **Sándor Petőfi** (1823-1849) fueled the nationalistic rhetoric required for revolutions. This period paired changing literary ideals with the quest for social reform and political independence, but outside a few poets, such as **Arany** (1817-1882), the 19th century produced few great works. Hungarian literature matured with the founding of the *Nyugat (West)* literary journal in 1908, while the avant-garde poet and artist **Lajos Kassák,** unconnected with *Nyugat,* concerned himself with Hungarian working-class life.

László Németh was one of the most influential authors to emerge from the new Populist movements of the interwar period. He crafted stark, Realist plays depicting the battle of the individual against the world. After WWII, Communism forced Magyar writers to adopt the doctrine of **Socialist Realism,** but eventually a new generation appeared that was able to develop individual styles more freely. **György Konrád,** one of the most important Hungarian authors of the century, wrote novels that were crucial in defining the dissident movements of Central Europe. Less concerned with social issues than with the Postmodern exploration of the meaning and use of words themselves, **Péter Esterházy** began a new movement, returning Magyar literature to the world cultural scene.

Visual arts and music developed later in Hungarian history, fully maturing only at the turn of the 20th century. Lajos Kassák and **László Moholy-Nagy** were internationally significant avant-garde painters, and **Béla Bartók** is still revered for his musical compositions. In the last half of the 20th century, Hungarian film gained attention, in particular for the work of **Miklós Janscsó** and **István Szabó.**

READING LIST

A History of Modern Hungary 1867-1994, by Jorg K. Hoensch, provides a brief contextualization of Hungarian history, while *A History of Hungary,* edited by Peter Sugar, Peter Hanak, and Tibor Frank, is more exhaustive in its treatment. Recent events are covered well in dissident Gyorgy Konrad's collection of essays, *The Melancholy of Rebirth. The Bridge at Andau,* by James Michener, is a popular account of the 1956 Uprising, and Janos Nyiri's *Battlefields and Playgrounds* is a highly acclaimed recent novel on the Holocaust in Budapest. For modern fiction, anything by Peter Esterházy is outstanding, most notably *The Glance of Countess Hahn-Hahn* and (if you're willing to be seen with it) *A Little Hungarian Pornography.*

FACTS AND FIGURES

- **Capital:** Budapest
- **Population:** 9,971,000
- **Land Area:** 93,030km^2
- **Geography:** Mountains from northeast to southwest with plains on either side
- **Language:** Hungarian (Magyar)
- **Religion:** 68% Catholic, 20% Calvinist
- **GDP per capita:** US$4073
- **Major Exports:** Manufactured goods

HUNGARY ESSENTIALS

Citizens of Canada, Ireland, the U.K., and the U.S. can visit Hungary without visas for 90 days, provided their passport does not expire within six months of their journey's end. Australians, New Zealanders, and South Africans must obtain 90-day tourist visas from a Hungarian embassy or consulate. (See **Embassies & Consulates,** p. 13.) For U.S. residents, visas cost: single-entry US$40, double-entry US$75, multiple-entry US$180, and 48hr. transit US$38. Non-U.S. residents pay US$65, US$100, US$200, and US$50. Visa processing takes one day and requires proof of transportation (such as an airplane ticket), as well as a valid passport, three photographs (5 for multiple-entry visas), a money order, and a self-addressed, stamped (certified mail) envelope. You will also receive an entry-exit form to keep in your passport. Visa extensions are rare; apply at Hungarian police stations.

PRIMARY BORDER CROSSINGS. Hungarian visas are occasionally available at the border, but always priced exorbitantly; it is safer and cheaper to arrange a visa before visiting. There is no fee for crossing a Hungarian border. In general, Hungarian customs are efficient; a border crossing should add no more than 30min. to your journey. The easiest way to enter or exit Hungary is to take a direct bus or train to or from Budapest to a neighboring country's capital.

Austria: Hegyeshalom, HUN/Vienna, AUS (p. 792); connects Győr (p. 296) with Eastern Austria. Sopron, HUN (p. 301)/Eisenstadt, AUS; connects the Őrseg (p. 296) with eastern Austria. Szombathely, HUN (p. 304)/Oberwart, AUS via Bucsu, HUN; connects the Őrseg (p. 296) with eastern Austria. Rábafüzes, HUN/Graz, AUS; connects Lake Balaton (p. 309) with southeastern Austria.

Croatia: Barcs, HUN/Virovitica, CRO; connects Pécs, HUN (p. 317) with eastern Croatia (Slavonia). Letenye, HUN/Varaždin, CRO; connects Lake Balaton, HUN (p. 309) with eastern Croatia and Zagreb (p. 139).

Romania: Csenger, HUN/Satu Mare, ROM; connects Nyíregyháza, HUN and Northern Hungary (p. 332) with Northern Romania (p. 537). Ártánd, HUN/Oradea, ROM (p. 527); connects Debrecen, HUN (p. 322) and the Great Plain (p. 322) with the Western Carpathians (p. 524). Szeged, HUN (p. 325)/Arad, ROM via Nagylak, HUN; connects the Great Plain (p. 322) with Timişoara, ROM (p. 524) and the Western Carpathians (p. 524).

Slovakia: Rajka, HUN/Bratislava, SLK (p. 672); connects Győr (p. 296) with southwestern Slovakia. Komárom, HUN/Komárno, SLK; connects the Őrseg (p. 296) with southwestern Slovakia. Esztergom, HUN (p. 295)/Štúrovo, SLK; connects the Danube Bend (p. 292) with southwestern Slovakia. Salgótarján, HUN/Lučenec, SLK; connects Miskolc and Northern Hungary (p. 332) with Central Slovakia (p. 682). Tornyosnémeti, HUN/Košice, SLK (p. 699); connects Northern Hungary (p. 332) with Šariš (p. 698).

Slovenia: Őriszentpéter, HUN (p. 296)/Murska Sobota, SLN; connects the Őrseg (p. 296) and Lake Balaton (p. 309) with eastern Slovenia.

Ukraine: Nyíregyháza, HUN/Uzhorod, UKR (p. 778) via Záhony, HUN; connects Northern Hungary (p. 332) with Western Ukraine (p. 767).

Yugoslavia: Hercegszántó, HUN/Sombor, YUG; connects Pécs (p. 317) with the Voivodina region. Röszke, HUN/Subotica, YUG; connects Szeged, HUN (p. 325) with the Voivodina region.

GETTING THERE & GETTING AROUND

Hungary's national airline, **Malév,** has daily direct flights from New York to Budapest. Most **trains** pass through Budapest. Use **buses** to travel between the outer provincial centers. Hungarian **trains** *(vonat)* are reliable and inexpensive, although theft is frequent on the Vienna-Budapest line. **Eurail** and **EastRail** are valid in Hungary. Students and travelers under 26 are sometimes eligible for a 30% discount on train fares; inquire ahead and be persistent. An **ISIC** commands discounts at IBUSZ, Express, and station ticket counters. Flash your card and repeat "student," or the Hungarian, "*diák*" (DEE-ahk). Book international tickets in advance.

Személyvonat trains are excruciatingly slow; *gyorsvonat* (listed on schedules in red) cost the same and move at least twice as fast. Large provincial towns are accessible by the blue *expressz* lines. Air-conditioned *InterCity* trains are fastest. A seat reservation *(potegy)* is required on trains labeled "R." While you can board an *InterCity* train without a reservation, the fine for doing so is 1000Ft in addition to the cost of the reservation; purchasing the reservation on board will double the price of the ticket. Some basic vocabulary will help you navigate the rail system: *érkezés* (arrival), *indulás* (departure), *vágány* (track), and *állomás* or *pályaudvar* (station, abbreviated *pu.*); see the **Hungarian Glossary,** p. 824. The platform *(peron)* for arrivals and departures is rarely indicated until the train approaches the station, and then the announcement will be in Hungarian. Many train stations are not marked; ask the conductor what time the train is expected to arrive (just point at your watch and say the town's name) and watch for a stop at that time.

The cheap, clean, and crowded **bus** system links many towns that have rail connections only to Budapest. The **Erzsébet tér** bus station in Budapest posts schedules and fares. *InterCity* bus tickets are purchased on board (arrive early if you want a seat). In larger cities, tickets for **local transportation** must be bought in advance from a newsstand and punched when you get on; there's a fine if you're caught without a ticket. In smaller cities, you pay when you board (usually 60Ft).

IBUSZ and Tourinform can provide brochures about **cycling** in Hungary that include maps, suggested tours, sights, accommodations, bike rental locations, repair shops, and border-crossings. If you feel like you're moving in circles, remember that streets names change arbitrarily, and many in Budapest occur more than once. Always check the district as well as the kind of street: **út** is a major thoroughfare, **utca (u.)** a street, **körút (krt.)** a circular artery, and **tér** a square.

TOURIST SERVICES

Tourinform has branches in every county, and is generally the most useful tourist service in Hungary. They can't make reservations, but they'll check on vacancies, usually in university dorms and private *panzió*. Tourinform should be your first stop in any Hungarian town, as they always stock maps and tons of local info. **IBUSZ** offices throughout the country book private rooms, exchange money, sell train tickets, and charter tours, although they are generally better at helping with travel plans than at providing information about the actual town. Snare the pamphlet *Tourist Information: Hungary* and the monthly entertainment guides *Programme in Hungary* and *Budapest Panorama* (all free and in English). **Express,** the former national student travel bureau, handles hostels and changes money. The staff usually speaks German, and sometimes English. Regional agencies are most helpful in the outlying areas. **Tourist bureaus** are generally open in summer Monday through Saturday 8am-8pm.

MONEY

The national currency is the **forint,** divided into 100 **fillérs,** which are quickly disappearing from circulation. Make sure to keep some U.S. dollars or Deutschmarks for visas, international train tickets, and (less often) private accommodations. New Zealand and Australian dollars, as well as South African rand and Irish pounds, are not exchangeable. Rates are generally poor at exchange offices with extended hours. The maximum permissible commission for cash-to-cash exchange is 1%. Allow 30min. to exchange money, and never change money on the street. **American Express** offices in Budapest and **IBUSZ** offices around the country convert **traveler's checks** to cash for a steep 6% commission; go instead to **OTP Bank** and **Postabank** offices. **Cash advances** are available at most OTP branches, but with the already abundant and ever-increasing number of **ATMs,** many banks no longer give them. Currency exchange machines are popping up all over and have excellent rates, although they tend to be slow. Major **credit cards** are accepted at expensive hotels and many shops.

COMMUNICATION

The Hungarian **mail** system is reliable; airmail *(légiposta)* takes 5-10 days to the U.S. and the rest of Europe, and two weeks to South Africa, New Zealand, and Australia. If you're mailing to a Hungarian citizen, the family name precedes the given name, as in "DeSantis, Alicia." Internet access is increasing throughout the country, and is ubiquitous in Budapest and major provincial centers. However, be prepared to go without access at Lake Balaton or in Szombathely and Kecskemét. The Hungarian keyboard differs significantly from English-language keyboards. When you first log on, go to the bottom right-hand corner of the screen and look for the "Hu" icon; click here to switch the keyboard setting to "Angol."

Almost all phone numbers have six digits. For intercity calls, wait for the tone and dial slowly; "06" goes before the phone code. **International calls** require red phones or new, digital-display blue ones. Although the blue phones are more handsome than their red brethren, they tend to cut you off after 3-9min. Phones increasingly require **phone cards** *(telefonkártya)*, available at kiosks, train stations, and post offices in denominations of 800Ft and 1600Ft. Direct calls can also be made from Budapest's phone office. To call **collect,** dial 190 for the international operator. To reach international carriers, put in a 10Ft and a 20Ft coin (which you get back), dial 00, wait for the second tone, then dial the appropriate number: **AT&T Direct,** tel. 80 00 11 11; **BT Direct,** tel. 80 00 44 11; **Canada Direct,** tel. 80 00 12 11; **MCI WorldPhone,** tel. 80 00 14 11; **Sprint,** tel. 80 00 18 77.

English-language **press** can be found in many Budapest kiosks and large hotels, but rarely in other cities. The weekly *Budapest Sun* (280Ft) mostly includes news and business information, but its *Style* section will help navigate the capital's cultural life. English-language radio and TV programming is found in *Budapest Week*, which also has excellent listings, survival tips, and articles about life in Hungary (published Thursday; 145Ft, free at AmEx offices and larger hotels). Also published weekly, the Magyar flyer *Pesti Est* lists movies, concerts, and performances in Budapest; pick up a free copy in restaurants, theaters, and clubs. Three **radio** stations have Anglophone programming: Juventus, Radio Bridge, and Danubius. The frequencies vary from region to region, but in the Budapest area they are 89.5, 102.1, and 103.3FM, respectively.

LANGUAGE

Hungarian belongs to the Ugric branch of the Finno-Ugric language family, and is related distantly to Turkish and even more distantly to Estonian and Finnish. After Hungarian and **German, English** is the country's third language. "*Hello*" is often used as an informal greeting or farewell. "*Szia!*" (sounds like "see ya!") is another greeting—you'll often hear friends cry: "Hallo, see ya!" See the **Hungarian Glossary,** p. 813, for more.

A few starters for pronunciation: "*c*" is pronounced "ts" as in "pots"; "*cs*" is "ch" as in "which"; "*gy*" is "dy" as in "*adieu*"; "*ly*" is "y" as in "yak"; "*s*" is "sh" as in "shard"; "*sz*" is "s" as in "cell-phone"; "*zs*" is "zh" as in "fusion"; and "*a*" is "a" as in "paw." The first syllable is always stressed.

HEALTH & SAFETY

Medical assistance is most easily obtained in Budapest, where embassies carry a list of Anglophone doctors; additionally, most hospitals in the capital staff English-speaking doctors. Outside Budapest, try to bring a Hungarian speaker with you. All medical services must be paid for in cash. Tap water is usually clean and drinkable (except in the town of Tokaj, where it bears an uncanny resemblance to the neighboring Tisza River). **Bottled water** is available at every food store. Public **bathrooms** vary tremendously in cleanliness: pack soap and a towel, and be prepared to pay the attendant 30Ft. Also carry a roll of toilet paper with you, as hostels rarely have it and the single square you get in a public restroom is less than useful. Gentlemen should look for *Férfi*, and ladies for *Női* signs. **Pharmacies** *(gyógyszertar)* are well-stocked with Western brands and always carry hefty supplies of tampons and condoms. In bigger towns, there are most always 24hr. pharmacies. Violent **crime** in Hungary is low, but in larger cities, especially Budapest, foreign tourists are favorite targets of petty thieves and pickpockets.

> **EMERGENCY NUMBERS.**
> **Fire:** tel. 105. **Police:** tel. 107. **Ambulance:** tel. 104.

ACCOMMODATIONS & CAMPING

Many travelers stay in **private homes** booked through a tourist agency. Singles are scarce—it's worth finding a roommate, as solo travelers must often pay for a double room. Agencies may try to foist off their most expensive rooms on you. Outside Budapest, the best and cheapest offices are region-specific (e.g. EgerTourist in Eger). These agencies will often make advance reservations for your next stop. After staying a few nights, you can make arrangements directly with the owner, thus saving yourself the agencies' 20-30% commission. **Panzió,** run out of private homes, are the next most common option, although not necessarily the cheapest.

Hotels exist in some towns, but most have disappeared. As the industry develops and room prices rise, **hosteling** is becoming more attractive, although it is rare outside Budapest. Hostels are usually large enough to accommodate summer crowds, and **HI cards** are increasingly useful. Sheets are rarely required. Many hostels can be booked through Express, the student travel agency, or sometimes the regional tourist office. From June through August, university **dorms** become hostels. Locations change annually; inquire at Tourinform and always call ahead.

More than 300 **campgrounds** are sprinkled throughout Hungary; most sites stay open from May through September. If you rent a bungalow you must pay for unfilled spaces. Tourist offices offer the annual booklet *Camping Hungary* for free. For more info and maps, contact Tourinform in Budapest.

FOOD & DRINK

On the whole, Hungarian food is more flavorful and varied than standard Eastern European fare. **Paprika,** Hungary's chief agricultural export, colors most dishes red. In Hungarian restaurants (*vendéglő* or *étterem*), begin with *halászlé*, a deliciously spicy fish stew. Alternately, try *gyümölesleves*, a cold fruit soup topped with whipped cream. The Hungarian national dish is *bográcsgulyás*, a stew of beef, onions, green pepper, tomatoes, potatoes, dumplings, and plenty of paprika. *Borjúpaprikás* is veal with paprika and potato-dumpling pasta. Vegetarians can find recourse in the tasty *rántott sajt* (fried cheese) and *gombapörkölt* (mushroom stew) on most menus. In general Hungarian food is fried, and fresh vegetables other than peppers and cabbage are a rarity.

In a *cukrászda* (confectionery), you can satisfy your sweet tooth for dangerously few forints. Pastries in Hungary are cheap and generally delicious. *Túrós rétes* is a chewy pastry pocket filled with sweetened cottage cheese. *Somlói galuska* is a fantastically rich sponge cake of chocolate, nuts, and cream, all soaked in rum. The Austrians stole the recipe for *rétes* and called it "strudel," but this delicious concoction is as Hungarian as Zsa Zsa Gabor. *Kávé* is espresso, served in thimble-sized cups and so strong your veins will be popping before you finish your first sip.

Hungary produces a diverse array of fine wines (see **A Mini-Guide to Hungarian Wine,** p. 339). Hungarian beer *(sör)* ranges from the first-rate to the merely acceptable. *Dreher Bak* is a rich, dark brew. Good light beers include *Dreher Pils, Szalon Sör,* and licensed versions of *Steffl, Gold Fassl, Gösser,* and *Amstel.* Hungary also produces different types of *pálinka,* a liquor that resembles brandy. Among the best tasting are *barackpálinka* (similar to apricot schnapps) and *szilvapálinka* (plum brandy). *Unicum,* advertised as the national drink of Hungary, is a very fine herbal liqueur that Habsburg kings used to cure digestive ailments.

CUSTOMS & ETIQUETTE

Business hours in Hungary are Monday to Friday 9am-5pm (7am-7pm for grocers). Banks close around 3pm on Friday. **Museums** are open Tuesday to Sunday 10am-6pm, with Tuesdays an occasional free day. ISIC holders usually get discounts.

Rounding up the bill as a **tip** is standard for a job well done—especially in restaurants, but also for everyone from taxi-drivers to hairdressers. Remember in restaurants to hand the tip to the server when you pay, as it's rude to leave it on the table. Waiters usually expect foreigners to tip 15%, although locals never give more than 10%. Bathroom attendants gets 30Ft.

The frequency and extent of public displays of affection among young and old alike may be startling, or at least distracting; every bus has a couple exchanging lesser bodily fluids. Taste in **clothing,** especially for men, is casual and unpretentious; try not to laugh when you see men over 50 sweeping the streets in Speedos. Modesty is not a strong point of Hungarian women's fashions, but virtually everyone stays well-groomed, and people in small towns dress more conservatively.

Hungarians love exercise—if they're watching others do it. They are, however, serious about cigarettes; smoking is a national pastime. Dogs are family members and tend to be far bigger than the European average—no poodles here, thank you—and are spoiled rotten. **Homosexuality,** although legal, is still not fully accepted in Hungarian society; discretion is wise.

Exporting paprika is illegal. If you attempt to take it duty-free, border patrol will accost you—on trains, they check under every seat.

NATIONAL HOLIDAYS

January 1, New Year's; March 15, National Day; April 23-24, Catholic Easter; May 1, Labor Day; June 11, Whit Sunday (Pentecost); June 12, Whit Monday; August 20, Constitution Day (St. Stephen's Day); October 23, Republic Day (1956); December 25-26, Catholic Christmas.

BUDAPEST

Budapest (pop. 1,885,000) doesn't feel very Hungarian. While the rest of the country seems to linger in a slower, friendlier state, Budapest speeds along, whirling and honking through its crowded streets and frantically hopping among hip nightclubs, towering apartment buildings, and neon-bedecked Western companies, periodically pausing in a Turkish bath for a deep breath (but not too deep...oh, the pollution). Cosmopolitan and confident, Budapest is reassuming its place as a major European capital; even 40 years in a communist coma couldn't kill the spirit of this stronghold of Magyar nationalism. Originally three separate cities, Budapest was created in 1872 with the joining of Buda and Pest, and immediately went on to become the Habsburg Empire's number-two city. Endowed with an architectural majesty befitting of royalty, the noble dignity of the Hungarian capital is only enhanced by the now tattered landscape. WWII punished Budapest, but the Hungarians rebuilt it from rubble with the same pride that fomented the ill-fated 1956 Uprising, weathered the Soviet invasion, and overcame decades of subjugation.

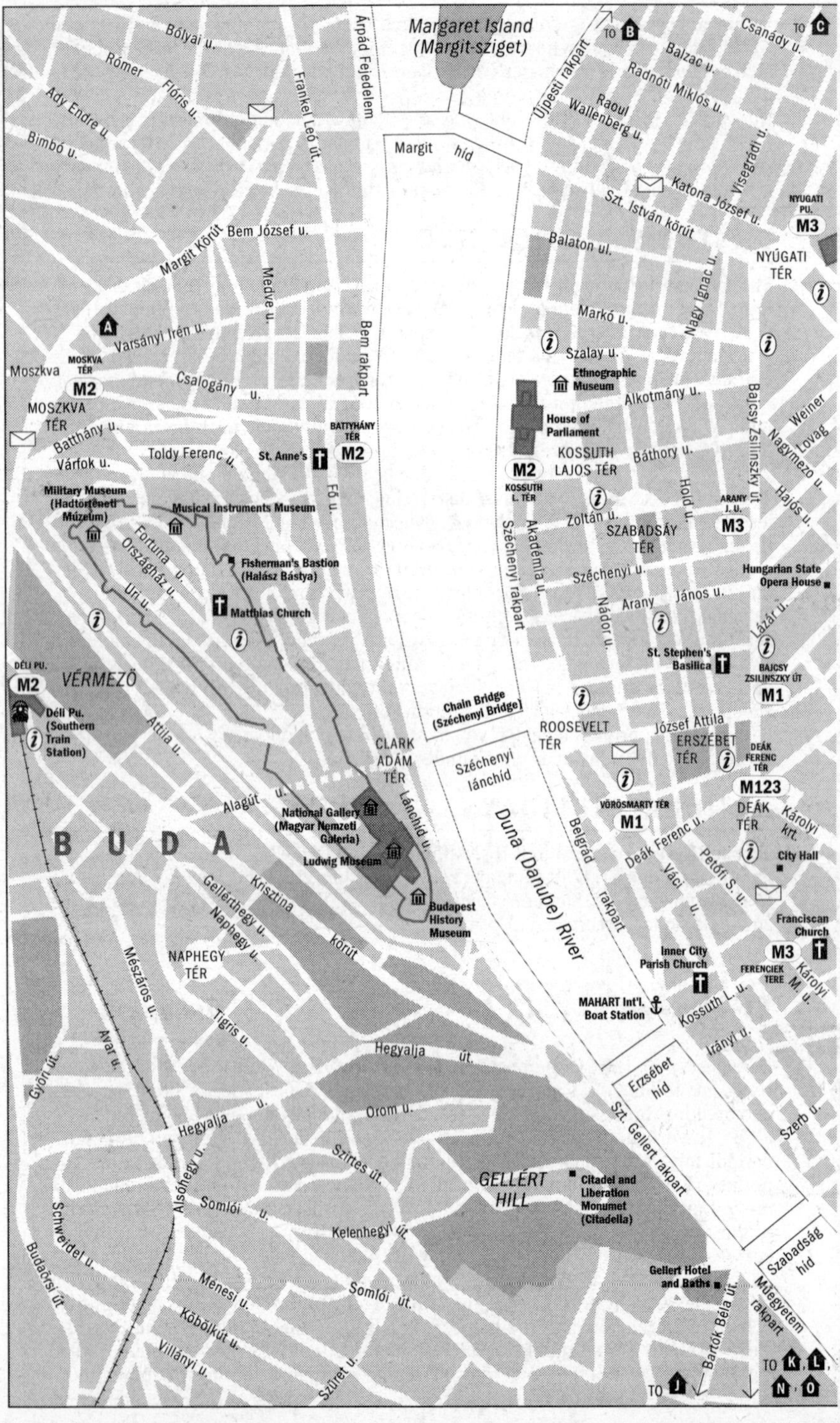
Margaret Island
(Margit-sziget)
Bólyai u.
Rómer
Flóris u.
Ady Endre u.
Bimbó u.
Frankel Leó út
Árpád Fejedelem
Margit híd
Újpesti rakpart
TO B
TO C
Csanády u.
Balzac u.
Radnóti Miklós u.
Raoul Wallenberg u.
Katona József u.
Visegrádi u.
Szt. István körút
NYUGATI PU.
M3
NYÚGATI TÉR
Balaton ul.
Bem József u.
Margit Körút
Medve u.
Bem rakpart
Nagy Ignac u.
Markó u.
A
Varsányi Irén u.
Szalay u.
MOSKVA TÉR
Moszkva
M2
Csalogány u.
Ethnographic Museum
Alkotmány u.
MOSZKVA TÉR
Bajcsy Zsilinszky út
Weiner
Lovag
Nagymezo u.
House of Parliament
Batthány u.
BATTYHÁNY TÉR
M2
Toldy Ferenc u.
St. Anne's
KOSSUTH LAJOS TÉR
Báthory u.
Várfok u.
M2
KOSSUTH L. TÉR
Military Museum (Hadtörténeti Múzeum)
Musical Instruments Museum
Fő u.
Akadémia u.
Zoltán u.
Hold u.
ARANY J. U.
M3
Hajós u.
SZABADSÁY TÉR
Fortuna u.
Országház u.
Fisherman's Bastion (Halász Bástya)
Széchenyi rakpart
Széchenyi u.
Hungarian State Opera House
Uri u.
Matthias Church
Arany János u.
Nádor u.
Lázár u.
St. Stephen's Basilica
DÉLI PU.
M2
VÉRMEZŐ
BAJCSY ZSILINSZKY ÚT
M1
Déli Pu. (Southern Train Station)
Chain Bridge (Széchenyi Bridge)
Attila u.
ROOSEVELT TÉR
József Attila
ERSZÉBET TÉR
DEÁK FERENC TÉR
CLARK ADÁM TÉR
Széchenyi lánchíd
M123
Alagút u.
National Gallery (Magyar Nemzeti Galéria)
Lánchíd u.
VÖRÖSMARTY TÉR
M1
DEÁK TÉR
Károlyi krt.
B U D A
Ludwig Museum
Duna (Danube) River
Belgrád rakpart
Deák Ferenc u.
Petőfi S. u.
City Hall
Váci u.
Gellérthegy u.
Krisztina körút
Budapest History Museum
Franciscan Church
Naphegy u.
NAPHEGY TÉR
Inner City Parish Church
M3
FERENCIEK TERE
Károlyi M. u.
Mészáros u.
MAHART Int'l. Boat Station
Kossuth L. u.
Tigris u.
Irányi u.
Avar u.
Hegyalja út
Erzsébet híd
Győri út
Orom u.
Hegyalja u.
Szt. Gellert rakpart
Szerb u.
Szirtes út
Alsóhegy u.
GELLERT HILL
Citadel and Liberation Monumet (Citadella)
Somlói u.
Schweidel u.
Kelenhegyi út
Szabadság híd
Budaörsi út
Gellert Hotel and Baths
Menesi u.
Somlói út
Bartók Béla út
Műegyetem rakpart
Köbölkút u.
Villányi u.
Szüret u.
TO J
TO K, L, N, O

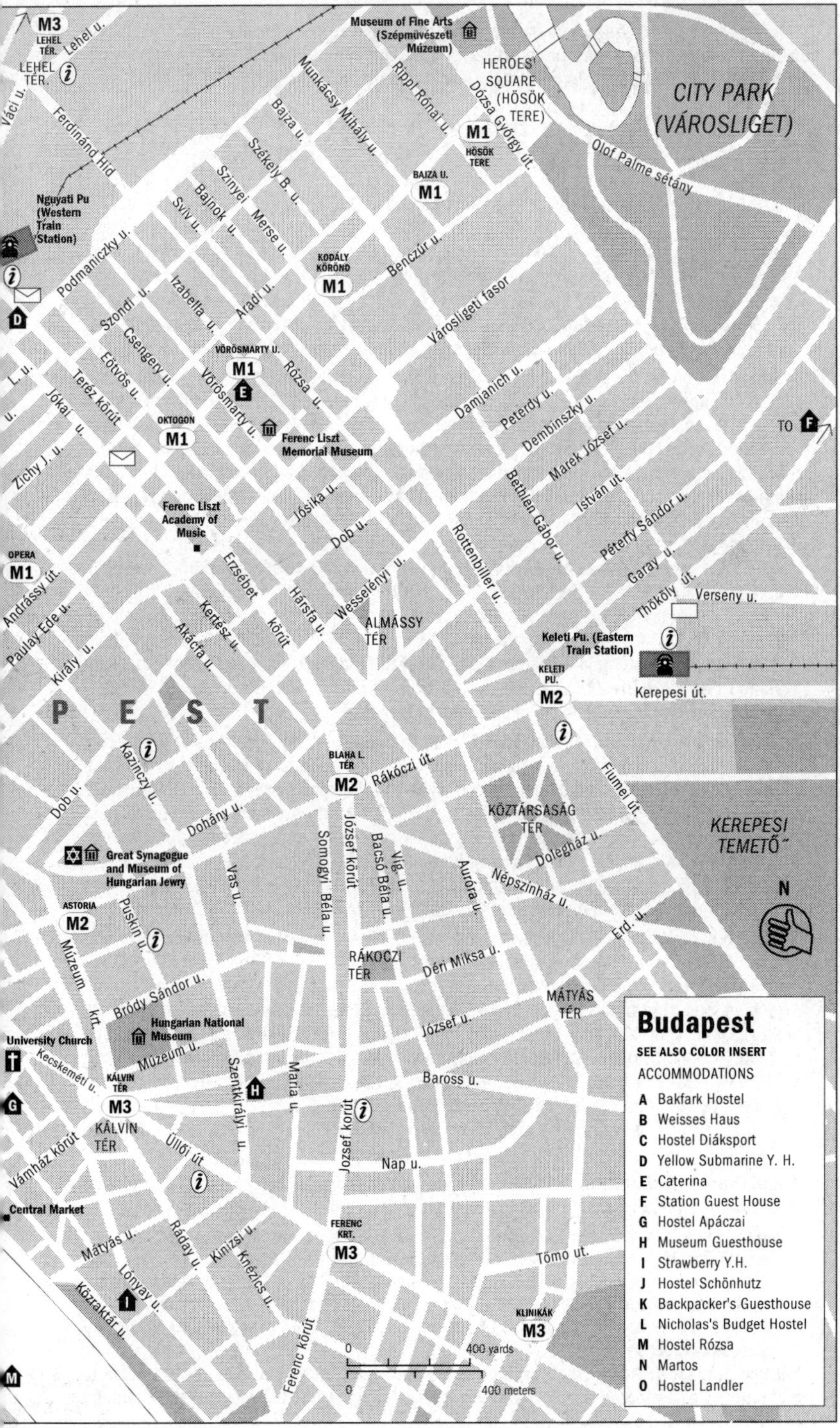
Budapest
SEE ALSO COLOR INSERT
ACCOMMODATIONS
A Bakfark Hostel
B Weisses Haus
C Hostel Diáksport
D Yellow Submarine Y. H.
E Caterina
F Station Guest House
G Hostel Apáczai
H Museum Guesthouse
I Strawberry Y.H.
J Hostel Schönhutz
K Backpacker's Guesthouse
L Nicholas's Budget Hostel
M Hostel Rózsa
N Martos
O Hostel Landler
CITY PARK (VÁROSLIGET)
HEROES' SQUARE (HŐSÖK TERE)
Museum of Fine Arts (Szépművészeti Múzeum)
Nguyati Pu (Western Train Station)
Ferenc Liszt Memorial Museum
Ferenc Liszt Academy of Music
Keleti Pu. (Eastern Train Station)
Great Synagogue and Museum of Hungarian Jewry
Hungarian National Museum
University Church
Central Market
KEREPESI TEMETŐ
PEST
ALMÁSSY TÉR
KÖZTÁRSASÁG TÉR
RÁKÓCZI TÉR
MÁTYÁS TÉR
KÁLVIN TÉR
LEHEL TÉR
Andrássy út
Rákóczi út
Kerepesi út
Városligeti fasor
Olof Palme sétány
Dózsa György út
Thököly út
Teréz körút
Erzsébet körút
József körút
Ferenc körút
Múzeum krt.
Vámház körút
Üllői út
Baross u.
József u.
Népszínház u.
Fiumei út
Ferdinánd Híd
TO F
N
0 400 yards
0 400 meters

No toyland Prague, Budapest is bigger, dirtier, and more vibrant—flashing lights and legions of tourists may have added tinsel to its tenacious streets, but beneath the kitsch, the indefatigable Budapest spirit charges on.

GETTING THERE & GETTING AROUND

Airplanes: Ferihegy Airport (tel. 267 43 33; info tel. 357 71 55; reservations tel. 357 91 23). Terminal 1 is for most foreign airlines and Malév flights to New York and Vienna. Terminal 2 is for all other Malév flights, Lufthansa, and Air France. **Volánbusz** takes 30min. to get to terminal 1 and 40min. to terminal 2 from Erzsébet tér (every 30min., 5:30am-9pm, 500Ft). The **Airport Minibus** (tel. 296 85 55) will pick you up anywhere in the city at any time, or take you anywhere in the city from the airport; call in advance. One-way 1200Ft; round-trip 2000Ft. The cheapest way to the airport is to take the M3 to Köbanya-Kispest and then follow the signs to the Ferihegy/red bus #93 (50min.).

Trains: Tel. 461 54 00 and 461 55 00. *Pályaudvar*, often abbreviated "pu.," means train station. Those under 26 are eligible for a 33% discount on international tickets; show your ISIC and your destination and tell the clerk *"diák"* (DEE-ak, student). The 3 main stations–**Keleti pu., Nyugati pu.,** and **Déli pu.**–are also Metro stops. Railway stations are favorite haunts of Budapest's infamous thieves and pickpockets, so be careful. Most international trains arrive at Keleti pu., but trains to and from a given location do not necessarily stop at the same station; trains from Prague may stop at Nyugati pu. or Keleti pu. Nyugati pu. serves eastern Hungary; Déli pu. serves western Hungary. Each station has schedules for the others. To: **Berlin** (13hr., 2 per day, 20,400Ft plus 2500Ft reservation; night train 14hr., 1 per day, 35,200Ft); **Bucharest** (14hr., 6 per day, 12,000Ft); **Prague** (3 *EuroCity* trains per day: 6hr., 13,564Ft plus 800Ft reservation; night train 9hr., 1 per day, 12,064Ft); **Vienna** (3hr., 11 per day, 7150Ft plus 700Ft reservation; round-trip if trip is completed within 4 days 10,686Ft including public transport pass for Vienna); and **Warsaw** (11hr., 2 per day, 12,857Ft plus 2000Ft reservation). The daily **Orient Express** stops on its way from Paris to **Istanbul.**

Train Ticket Agencies: International Ticket Office, Keleti pu. Open daily 7am-6pm. **IBUSZ** (see p. 276) offers generous discounts on international rail tickets. Buy several days ahead for international destinations. **MÁV Hungarian Railways,** VI, Andrássy út 35 (tel./fax 322 405), and branch offices at all train stations, sells international and domestic tickets. They offer 30-40% discounts on international fares for ISIC bearers. Open M-F 9am-6pm. MC/Visa. **Carlson Wagons-lit Travel,** V, Dorottya u. 3 (tel. 429 21 10; fax. 266 25 85), just off Vörösmarty tér. 15-20% off international fares for those under 25 or over 65. Open M-F 9am-12:45pm and 1:30-5pm. AmEx/MC/Visa.

Buses: Tel. 117 29 66. Most buses to Western Europe leave from **Volánbusz main station,** V, Erzsébet tér (international ticket office tel. 317 25 62; fax 266 54 19). M1, 2, or 3: Deák tér. The international cashier upstairs will help you with Eurail passes and reservations. Open June 1-Sept. 15 M-F 6am-7pm; Sept. 16-May 31 M-F 6am-6pm, Sa-Su 6:30am-4pm. MC/Visa. Most buses to the **Czech Republic, Poland, Romania, Slovakia, Turkey, Ukraine,** and **Eastern Hungary** depart from **Népstadion,** Hungária körút 48/52 (tel. 252 18 96). M2: Népstadion. To: **Berlin** (14½hr., 3 per week, 16,110Ft); **Prague** (8½hr., 6 per week, 9900Ft); and **Vienna** (3½hr., 5 per week, 5190Ft). Domestic buses are usually cheaper than trains, but may take longer. Buses to the **Danube Bend** leave from outside the **Árpád híd** Metro station.

Local Transportation: Built in 1896, the Budapest **Metro** is the oldest in continental Europe and yet still runs on time.

Subway, buses, and trams: The subway, buses, and trams are inexpensive, convenient, and easy to navigate–by far the best way to get around town. The Metro has 3 lines: yellow (M1), red (M2), and blue (M3). All lines converge at **Deák tér** in District V. Although most of the tourist maps include the Metro lines, if you're going to try the buses, the *Budapest közlekedési hálózata* (Network Map of Budapest Transport; 250Ft), sold at every Metro station, is indispensable.

Night Transport: Public transportation stops around midnight, but don't be surprised to find the gates locked at 11:45pm. For the city's night-owls, buses whose numbers are

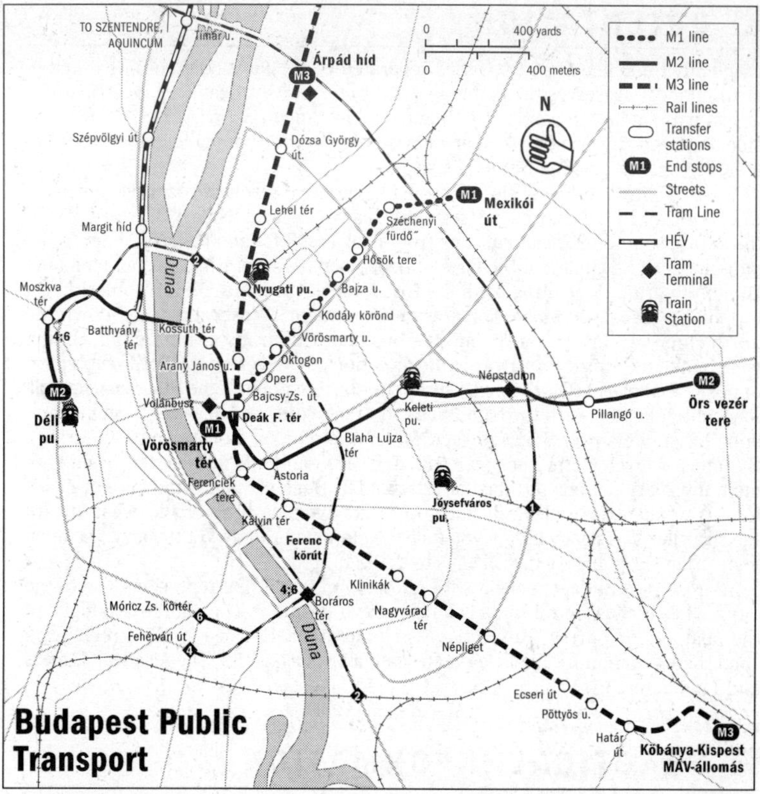

marked with an "E" run along major routes midnight-5am. Bus #7E and 78E run along the same route as M2.

Tickets: All public transport uses the same blue tickets (one-way travel on one line 90Ft), sold in Metro stations, *Trafik* shops, and by some sidewalk vendors. Punch them in the orange boxes at the gate of the Metro or on buses and trams. 10-trip tickets *(tíz jegy)* 810Ft; 20-trip packets 1500Ft. Passes are worthwhile if you're going to be in town for more than one day. 1-day 700Ft, 3-day 1400Ft, 1-week 1750Ft, 2-week 2250Ft, 1-month 3400Ft; 10-day youth passes (under 25) 1500Ft.

Fines: The fine for riding ticketless is 1000Ft, or, if you can't pay on the spot, 3000Ft. The control will also fine you for failing to punch a new ticket when switching lines and for losing the cover sheet to the 10-ticket packet.

Car Rental: There are several reliable rental agencies in Budapest, charging roughly US$35 for the cheapest cars. You'll be hard pressed to find any agency willing to rent to those under 21. **Vista** (see **Tourist Offices,** below) can help you find the most affordable option. **The Fox,** III, Obudai Hajógyári Sziget 130 (tel. 247 11 50), will pick up and drop off a car anywhere in Budapest, including the airport (small Fiats, Fords and Volvos with unlimited mileage for US$35). Open daily 8am-8pm.

Taxis: One of Budapest's most spectacular rip-offs. Check that the meter is on, and negotiate a price beforehand to make sure it hasn't been rigged against tourists. Taxis ordered by phone are considerably cheaper than those hailed on the street. **Budataxi** (tel. 233 33 33) has the best rates, at 100Ft per km on the street and 90Ft by phone. **Főtaxi** (tel. 222 22 22) and **Taxi 2000** (tel. 200 00 00) are other reliable companies with standardized rates.

ORIENTATION

Originally Buda and Pest, two cities separated by the **Duna** (Danube) River, modern Budapest preserves the distinctive character of its progenitors. **Buda** inspires artists with its hilltop citadel, trees, and cobblestoned Castle District. On the east side, **Pest,** the city's commercial engine, is home to wide shopping boulevards, theater, Parliament, and the Opera House.

Three central bridges tie Budapest together. **Széchenyi lánchíd** connects Roosevelt tér to the base of the cable car that scurries up **Várhegy** (Castle Hill). To the south, slender **Erzsébet híd** runs from near **Petőfi tér** and **Március 15 tér** to the monument of St. Gellért at the base of **Gellért-hegy** (Gellért Hill). Farther along the Duna, the green **Szabadság híd** links **Fővám tér** to the south end of Gellért-hegy, topped by **Szabadság Szobor** (Liberation Monument). **Moszkva tér,** just down the north slope of Várhegy, is Budapest's bus and tram transportation hub. On the west bank, one Metro stop away in the direction of Örs vezér tere, **Batthyány tér** lies opposite **Parliament** (Országház). This is the starting point of the **HÉV commuter railway,** which heads north through **Óbuda** to **Szentendre** (40min.; every 15min. 5am-9pm; buy tickets past Békásmeyger, Milleniumtelep, or Ilonatelep on the train). Budapest's three **Metro** lines (M1, M2, and M3) converge at **Deák tér,** beside the main international bus terminal at **Erzsébet tér.** Deák tér lies at the core of Pest's loosely concentric boulevards and spoke-like avenues. Two blocks west toward the river lies **Vörösmarty tér.** As you face the statue of Mihály Vörösmarty, the main pedestrian shopping zone, **Váci u.,** is to the right.

Addresses in Budapest begin with a Roman numeral that represents one of the city's 23 **districts.** Central Buda is I; downtown Pest is V. The middle two digits of the postal code correspond to the district number. Because many streets have shed their Communist labels, an up-to-date **map** is essential. The **American Express** and **Tourinform** offices have good free tourist maps, as does *Belváros Idegenforgalmi Térképe*, available at any Metro stop (199Ft).

PRACTICAL INFORMATION

TOURIST & FINANCIAL SERVICES

Tourist Offices: At all tourist offices you can purchase the omnipresent **Budapest Card** (Budapest Kártya), a worthwhile investment if you plan on seeing all the major sights and museums in one fell swoop. For 2450Ft, you get 2 days of public transportation, entrance to all museums, reduced rates on car rental and the airport minibus, and discounts at many shops and restaurants (3-day card 2550Ft).

Vista Travel Center, VI, Andrássy út 1 (tel. 267 86 03). MI, 2, 3: Deák tér. Exit onto Bajcsy-Zsilinszky út. Vista is a one-stop shopping center for travelers entering or leaving Budapest. The young multilingual staff arranges accommodations, books train, plane, and bus tickets, and handles car rentals with expert efficiency. Open M-F 9am-6:30pm, Sa 9am-2:30pm. 24hr. service is located at V, Apaczai u. 1. (tel. 318 48 48).

IBUSZ, V, Ferenciek tér 10 (tel. 337 09 39; fax 318 49 83). M3: Ferenciek tér. Books discounted tickets, polyglot sightseeing packages (3hr. tour 5200Ft, with Budapest Card 4000Ft), finds accommodations, and exchanges currency. Open M-F 8:15am-6pm, Sa 9am-1pm. AmEx/MC/Visa.

Tourinform, V, Sütő u. 2 (tel. 317 98 00; fax 317 95 78), off Deák tér behind McDonald's. M1, 2, 3: Deák tér. The best place to find information about events, tours, and performances in Budapest. Open M-F 9am-7pm, Sa-Su 9am-4pm.

Budget Travel: Express, V, Zoltán út 10 (tel. 311 98 98). Offers same youth discounts as the train station. 10-30% discounts on plane tickets. Open M-Th 8am-4:30pm, F 8:30am-3pm. **Malév Airlines,** V, Dorottya u. 2 (tel. 235 38 88; fax 266 27 84). M1: Vörösmarty tér. Offers 10-30% air discounts. Open in summer M-W and F 8:30am-9:30pm, Th 8:30am-6pm, Sa 8:30am-noon; off-season closed Sa. **IBUSZ** and **Vista Budget Travel** (see **Tourist Offices,** above) also sell discounted plane, train, and bus tickets.

Embassies and Consulates: Australia, XII, Királyhágo tér 8/9 (tel. 201 88 99). M2: Déli pu., then bus #21 to Királyhágo tér. Open M-F 9am-noon. **Canada,** XII, Budakeszi út 32 (tel. 275 12 00). Take bus #158 from Moszkva tér to the last stop. Open M-F 9am-noon. **South Africa,** VII, Rákóczi út 1/3 (tel. 266 21 48). **U.K.,** V, Harmincad u. 6 (tel. 266 28 88), off the corner of Vörösmarty tér. M1: Vörösmarty tér. Open M-F 9:30am-noon and 2:30-4pm. **U.S.,** V, Szabadság tér 12 (tel. 267 45 55; emergency 266 93 31). M2: Kossuth Lajos. Walk 2 blocks down Akademia and turn on Zoltán. Open M and W 8:30-11am, Tu and Th-F 8:30-10:30am. **New Zealand** and **Irish** nationals should contact the U.K. embassy.

Currency Exchange: Magyar Külkereskedelmi Bank, V, Szent István tér 11 (tel 269 09 22). M1, 2, 3: Deák tér, at the basilica's entrance. One of the few banks to give MC/Visa cash advances (no commission, Ft only; go inside the bank if you don't have a PIN code) and cash traveler's checks in US$ (2% commission, minimum $20). Outdoor Cirrus/MC/Visa **ATM.** Open M-Th 8am-4:30pm, F 8am-3pm. **Budapest Bank,** V, Váci u. 1/3 (tel. 328 31 55; fax 267 30 40). Offers credit card cash advances, **Western Union** services, cashes traveler's checks for US$ for a 3.5% commission, and has great exchange rates. Open M-F 8:30am-5pm, Sa 9am-2pm.

American Express: V, Deák Ferenc u. 10 (tel. 235 43 30; fax 267 20 28). M1: Vörösmarty tér. Next to Hotel Kempinski. Sells traveler's checks and cashes cardholders' personal checks. No commission on traveler's checks cashed in Ft, but a variable commission on those cashed in US$. They also give AmEx cash advances in Ft and replace lost or stolen cards. AmEx cardholders or traveler's check holders can receive mail sent to: "MCARTHUR, John, AmEx, Hungary Kft., Deák Ferenc u. 10, H-1052 Budapest, Hungary." AmEx **ATM.** Open June-Sept. M-F 9am-6:30pm, Sa-Su 9am-1pm; Oct.-May M-F 9am-5:30pm, Sa 9am-1pm. Currency desk open daily 9am-6:30pm.

LOCAL SERVICES

Luggage storage: At Keleti pu., large yellow lockers sit across from the international cashier (200Ft). Lockers are also available at Déli pu. and Nyugati pu. for 200Ft. Nyugati pu. has a 24hr. luggage desk in the waiting room next to the ticket windows. 140Ft per day, 280Ft for monstrous bags. The Volánbusz main bus station has smaller lockers for 90Ft per day. Open M and F-Sa 6am-8pm, Tu-Th and Su 6am-7pm. **Vista Travel Center** (see **Tourist Offices,** above) has lockers big enough to hold a pack. 100Ft per hr.

English Bookstore: Bestsellers KFT, V, Október 6 u. 11 (tel./fax 312 12 95), near the intersection with Arany János u. M1, 2, 3: Deák tér; M1: Vörösmarty tér. Small but packed with literature, pop novels, current magazines, local travel guides, and **The Phone Book,** a free English language "yellow pages," invaluable for long stays. Open M-F 9am-6:30pm, Sa 10am-6pm, Su 10am-4pm. **CEU Academic Bookshop,** V, Nador u. 9 (tel. 327 30 96), has a more erudite selection, particularly strong on all things Eastern European. Open Aug. daily 10am-4pm; Sept.-July M-Tu and Th-F 9am-6pm, W 9am-6:30pm, Sa 10am-4pm. AmEx/MC/Visa.

Gay Hotline: Gay Switchboard Budapest (tel. (0630) 32 33 34; fax 351 20 15; http://ourworld.compuserve.com/homepages/budapest) is the best resource in town. A volunteer organization providing a comprehensive gay guide on the internet and a daily Info-Hotline service to assist gay tourists in Budapest. (See also **Gay Budapest,** p. 256)

Laundromats: Irisz Szalon, V, Városház u. 3/5 (tel. 317 20 92). M3: Ferenciek tére. Wash 7kg 1100Ft, 10 kg 1400Ft; dry 450Ft per 15min. Ask what services you're getting and pay the cashier before you start. Open M-F 7am-7pm, Sa 7am-1pm.

EMERGENCY & COMMUNICATIONS

Tourist Police Station: Kulföldiket Elenörzö Osztály (KEO), VI, Városligeti Fasor 46/48 (tel. 343 00 34, ask for "KAY-o"). M1: Hősök tér. Walk 3blocks up Dósza György út and turn right on Városligeti Fasor. Staffs interpreters in summer to help deal with tourist crime and visa extensions, but don't expect them to be kind. Open Tu 8:30am-noon and 2-6pm, W 8:30am-1pm, Th 10am-6pm, F 8:30am-12:30pm.

Rape Services: Tel. 216 16 70. English spoken. Open daily 6am-10pm.

24hr. Pharmacies: II, Frankel L. út 22 (tel. 212 44 06); III, Szentendrei út 2/A (tel. 388 65 28); IV, Pozsonyi u. 19 (tel. 389 40 79); VII, Rákóczi út 39 (tel. 314 36 95); IX, Boráras tér 3 (tel. 217 07 43); X, Liget tér 3 (tel. 260 16 87); XII, Alkotás u. 1/B (tel. 355 46 91). At night, call the number on the door or ring the bell; you will be charged a slight fee for the service. Medicine (including aspirin) is sold only at state pharmacies; little is displayed but all is dispensed from behind the counter. Look for a tan-and-white motif with *Gyógyszertár, Apotheke,* or *Pharmacie* in black letters in the window.

Medical Assistance: Falck Személyi Olvosi Szolgálat KFT, II, Kapy út 40/B (tel. 200 01 00 and 275 15 35). English spoken. Ambulance service. First-aid is free for foreigners. Open 24hr. The U.S. embassy has a list of English-speaking doctors.

Post Office: V, Városház u. 18 (tel. 318 48 11). Pick up **Poste Restante** here. Open M-F 8am-8pm, Sa 8am-2pm. Branches at Nyugati pu. (tel. 312 12 00), VI, Teréz krt. 105/107; and Keleti pu. (tel. 322 14 96), VIII, Baross tér 11/C. All open M-F 8am-9pm, Sa 8am-2pm. **Postal code:** 1052.

Internet Access: Cybercafes litter the city, but computers still need to be reserved well ahead of time; 3hr. lines are not uncommon. Try to avoid afternoon peak hours. Internet access can also be found at many of Budapest's hostels.

Telefon, Petőfi Sándoru. M1, 2, 3: Deák tér. Lots of computers, but expect to wait at least 1hr. 500 Ft per hr. Open M-F 8am-8pm, Sa 9am-3pm.

Vista Travel Center (tel 269 60 32; see **Tourist Offices,** p. 276). Pricier, but lines are shorter. 11Ft. per min. Open M-F 8am-10pm, Sa-Su 10am-10pm.

Eckermann, VI, Andrássy út 24 (tel. 374 40 76). M1: Opera. Free. Call 2-3 days ahead. Open M-F 2-10pm, Sa 10am-10pm.

Center for Culture and Communication (C3), I, Orozágház u. 9 (tel. 214 68 56), inside the castle walls. Free. 2-3 day reservation required. Open M-F 9am-9pm, Su 10am-6pm.

Telephones: Local operator, tel. 01; **international operator,** tel. 09. Most phones use **phone cards,** available at newsstands, post offices, and Metro stations. 50-unit card 800Ft, 120-unit card 1800Ft. Use card phones for **international calls.** They will automatically cut you off after 20min., but it's more time than the coin phones will give you. **Telefon,** V, Petőfi Sándor u. 17. M1, 2, 3: Deák tér. Huge indoor bank of telephones. English-speaking staff will shuttle you through a series of queues for fax and internet service (500Ft per hr.). Open M-F 8am-8pm, Sa 9am-3pm. **Phone code:** 1.

ACCOMMODATIONS

In July and August, the city fills with tourists, all of whom need a place to stay. Save yourself some blisters by phoning first or stashing your pack while you seek out a bed for the night. Travelers arriving at Keleti pu. enter a feeding frenzy as hostel solicitors elbow their way to tourists in order to hawk rooms. Don't be drawn in by promises of free drinks or special discounts; the hostel-hawkers have been known to stretch the truth. Keep in mind that some of the best accommodation options are not represented at the train station.

ACCOMMODATION AGENCIES

Although Budapest is home to some of the best hostels in Europe, you may want to consider a private room. Slightly more expensive than a hostel (2000-5000Ft per person, depending on location and bathroom quality), they usually offer what hostels can't: peace, quiet, and private showers. Accommodations agencies populate nearly every square in Budapest, but don't let them overwhelm you. Arrive when they open to secure the lower-priced rooms. Haggle stubbornly and bring cash.

Budapest Tourist, V, Roosevelt tér 5 (tel. 317 35 55; fax 318 60 62), near Hotel Forum. M1, 2, 3: Deák tér. 10min. walk from Metro on the Pest end of Széchenyi lánchíd. Well-established. You can buy an "I Love Budapest" bumper sticker while you wait. Singles in Central Pest 2500-3300Ft; doubles 4000-6000Ft; triples 5000-7000Ft. Off-season prices considerably lower. Also rents flats for stays longer than 4 days. 1-bedroom with

2 beds, kitchen, and bathroom 5000Ft; 2-bedroom with 4 beds, kitchen, and bath 8000Ft. Open M-F 9am-5pm.

IBUSZ, V, Ferenciek tére 10 (tel. 337 09 39; fax 318 49 83). M3: Ferenciek tére. Rents rooms at a base price plus 1050Ft per day, but the daily charge decreases after four days. 2-beds 3500Ft; 3-beds 4500Ft; 4-beds 5000Ft. Also rents centrally located Pest apartments with kitchen and bath. 1-bedroom doubles from 5000Ft; 2-bedroom triples and quads from 6000Ft. Open M-F 8:15am-6pm, Sa 9am-1pm.

Non-Stop Hotel Service, V, Apáczai Csere J. u. 1 (tel. 318 48 48; fax 317 90 99), M1: Vörösmarty tér. As the name implies, a 24hr. tourist office and accommodation service. Private doubles in Pest from 7500Ft during the summer, off-season 6000Ft; triples and quads from 8000Ft, off-season 7000Ft.

YEAR-ROUND HOSTELS

Budapest's hostels are generally social centers, each with its own quirks. Most don't have curfews, and their common rooms—complete with beer, music and Anglophones—are often more alluring than the city's bars and clubs. Most hostel accommodations, including university dorms, are now under the aegis of the Hungarian Youth Hostel Association, which operates from a small office in Keleti pu. Their representatives are identified by Hostelling International t-shirts. Get your bearings before you accept any room, and make sure that the hostel is easily accessible by public transportation, preferably Metro. Although the hostels are generally legit, see the room before you hand over any cash. Theft is rampant in hostels. Always make sure that you keep your belongings in lockers when available, or take all valuables with you. Unless otherwise noted, all have luggage storage, kitchens, and TV in the common room.

BUDA

Backpacker's Guesthouse, XI, Takács Menyhért u. 33 (tel. 385 89 46; fax 209 84 06; email backpackguest@hotmail.com), 12min. from Central Pest. From Keleti pu. or anywhere along Rákóczi út., take bus #7 or 7A toward Buda. Get off at Tétenyi u., 5 stops past the river, walk back under the railway bridge and turn left. It's on the 3rd street on the right, in the most colorful house on the block. Budapest's quirkiest hostel. Graffitied rooms, weekly spelunking trips, and GenX slacker-guests who never leave the kitchen. Bathrooms, although tidy, are packed–10am can be brutal. The key to a good stay: bring your own sheets, get a padlock for your locker, and exploit the superb CD and video collections, internet access (15ft per min.), satellite TV, and laundry service. 5- to 8-bed dorms 1200Ft; small dorm 1500Ft; "love shack" double1800Ft.

Nicholas's Budget Hostel, XI, Takács Menyhért u. 12 (tel. 385 48 70). Follow the directions to the Backpacker's Guesthouse (see above), then continue half a block farther. Quieter and smaller than the local competition. The dorm is a musty basement room, but doubles are bright and boast an impressive collection of trashy romance novels (for inspiration, no doubt). Chirping parakeets at the gate. Reservations accepted. 12-bed dorm 1200Ft per person; doubles 4000Ft. Bedding 600Ft. Laundry 700Ft per 5kg.

PEST

Station Guest House (HI), XIV, Mexikói út 36/B (tel. 221 88 64; email station@mail.hatav.hu). From Keleti pu., take bus #7 1 stop to Hungária Körút, walk under the railway pass, and take an immediate right onto Mexikói út, walking for 2 blocks. Look for the Hostelling International logo on the building. Of the smaller hostels, this is one of the closest to the train station and among the most eccentric–they provide paints for guests to graffiti the walls. The common room rages with billiards, satellite TV, liquor at the reception, and live music twice a week. Ask for a 3rd floor room if you plan on sleeping. Well-kept rooms with private lockers. Internet access (400Ft per 30min.), laundry (350Ft per 4kg), and breakfast (250Ft). Reserve 2 days in advance or end up on a mattress in the attic (1200Ft). 2-3 bed dorms 2400Ft; 4-bed dorms 2000Ft; 6-8 bed dorms 1600Ft. 200Ft more for non-members.

Yellow Submarine Youth Hostel, VI, Teréz Körút 56, 3rd fl. (tel./fax 296 43 54). Across from Nyugati pu. Once known as the Lotus, this popular hostel changed its management and its trippy name, but kept the bright, spacious rooms and friendly staff. Sparkling bathrooms have shower curtains. Stick around for the weekly goulash fest—homemade Hungarian food and free booze. Breakfast included. Laundry 500Ft wash, 500Ft dry. Check-out 9am, but luggage stored all day. MC/Visa. 8- to 10-bed dorms 1800Ft; 4-bed dorms 2500Ft; 2-bed dorms 3000Ft. 10% HI discount.

Hostel Diáksport, XIII, Dózsa György út 152 (tel. 340 85 85 and 329 86 44; fax 320 84 25). M3: Dózsa György. Enter on Angyaföldi, 50m from the river. Huge and hugely social, Diáksport, with a 24hr. bar and live music throughout the week, has been dubbed the "party hostel." Recently-renovated and run by eager new management, the pre-fab hostel is fully loaded with all the amenities. Internet access (1100Ft per hr.), billiards, washer and dryer, cable TV, and breakfast—they'll even transport you from Keleti pu. Reserve by fax; AmEx/MC/Visa deposit required. Singles 3500Ft; doubles 2750-3300Ft, with shower 3500Ft; triples and quads 2600Ft; 6- to 12-person dorms 2500Ft. 6% HI discount.

SUMMER HOSTELS

Many university dorms reinvent themselves as hostels in July and August. Conveniently accessible by tram, the majority are clustered around Móricz Zsigmond Körtér in district XI. Although they often provide in-room refrigerators and TV rooms on each floor, they can't quite make up for the fact that most rooms have bunk beds and linoleum floors. Surprisingly enough, these multi-leveled monsters are generally quieter than their year-round counterparts. Unless otherwise noted, all have kitchens, luggage storage, and TV in the common room.

BUDA

Bakfark Hostel, I, Bakfark u. 1-3 (tel. 201 54 19 and 340 85 85). M2: Moszkva tér. From the Metro, walk along Margit krt. with Burger King to your right and take the first street after passing Mammut; the street isn't marked, but the hostel is. Some of the most comfortable hostel rooms in town, with lofts instead of bunks. The showers sparkle, but are far from the rooms. Check-out 9am. Reservations recommended. 80 beds in 4- to 6-bed dorms 2200Ft. HI discount 200Ft.

Hostel Landler, XI, Bartók Béla út 17 (tel. 463 36 21). Take bus #7 or 7A across the river and get off at Géllert. The hostel is a short walk on Bartók Béla út away from the river. Lived-in college dorms—Madonna pin-ups and all. Bring flip-flops for the shower floor. Laundry available. Some English spoken. Check-out 9am. Open July 5-Sept. 5. Singles 4100Ft; doubles 2600Ft; triples and quads 2475Ft. HI discount 10%.

Hostel Rózsa, XI, Bercsényi u. 28/30 (tel. 463 42 50). M2: Blaha Lujzatér. Continue on tram #4 and get off three stops after the river. Although it lacks accessories, it's strong on the basics with freshly painted walls and squeaky clean (but still curtainless) showers. Refrigerator in all rooms. Laundry (160Ft, wash only) requires your own detergent and the kitchen requires your own pots. Free transport from bus or train station. Open July 1-Sept. 5. Doubles 2900Ft. HI discount 10%.

Hostel Schönhutz, XI, Irinyi u. 42 (tel. 372 51 69). M2: Blaha Lujza tér. From the Metro, take tram #4 to the second stop after crossing the Danube. Cross the street and walk on the left side with your back to the river. The hostel is the blue 18-story building behind the OTP Station. This massive establishment actually fills to capacity in summer, drawing people to its in-room showers and thumping basement disco. Unfortunately, the disco closes at 1am and the personal showers are only in triples and quads, leaving everyone else to brave the curtainless co-ed showers down the hall. Laundry (wash 200Ft, dry 200Ft) and continental breakfast (300Ft). Open July 1-Aug. 31. Doubles 2600Ft; triples and quads 3200Ft.

Martos, XI, Stoczek u. 5/7 (tel. 463 37 76; tel./fax 463 36 50; email reception@hotel.martos.bme.hu). Near the Technical University. From Keleti pu., take red bus #7 to Móricz Zsigmond Körtér and trek back 300m toward the river on Bartók Béla út. When you reach the large square, make a right onto Bectalan Lajos. Stoczek u.

is the third right; the hostel is near the corner. This independent, student-run hostel is one of Buda's best deals, with truly cheap, truly clean rooms. Free laundry and internet. Satellite TV. Check-out 9am. Singles 2200Ft; doubles, triples, and quads 1800Ft.

PEST

Strawberry Youth Hostels, IX, Ráday u. 43-45 (tel. 218 47 66), and Kinizsi u. 2/6 (tel. 217 30 33). M3: Kálvin tér. With Hotel Mercure to your right, walk down Vámház krt. Ráday is 1 block toward the river on the left. Sunny, big, bunk-less rooms with fridge, drying rack, and a view of the building next door. There's a disco downstairs for those into the sticky-floor scene; ask for a 3rd floor room if you're not into heavy bass. Coin-operated laundry (360Ft wash). Free Keleti pu. pick-up. Check-out 10am. Open June 29-Sept. 1. Doubles 2600Ft; triples and quads 2300Ft. HI discount 10%.

Hostel Apáczai, V, Papnövelde u. 4-6 (tel. 267 03 11; fax 275 70 46), M3: Ferenciek tér. Follow Károlyi M. u. with the river to your right; Papnövelde u. is 3 blocks later on the right. The beds are back-breakers, but with the heart of Budapest nightlife at your doorstep, who needs a bed? Mr. Clean would approve of these convent-like accommodations; bigger rooms resemble an army barracks. Check-out 10am. Open July-Aug. Quads 2600Ft; 6-bed dorms 2500Ft; big dorms 2000Ft. HI discount 10%.

GUEST HOUSES

Guest houses and rooms in private homes lend a personal touch for about the same price as an anonymous hostel bed. These should not be confused with pensions, or *panzió*, which are larger and rarely charge less than 4000Ft per person. Although not always fluent in English, friendly owners will usually pick travelers up at the train station or the airport. Most allow guests to use their kitchens and are on hand to provide general advice or help in emergencies. Visitors receive keys to their rooms and the house; while trying not to wake a sleeping household as you tiptoe down the hall might trigger high-school flashbacks, you'll be free to come and go as you please.

Museum Guesthouse, VIII, Mikszáth Kálmán tér 4, 1st Fl. (tel. 318 95 08 and 318 21 95). M3: Kálvin tér. Take the left exit from the stop onto Baross u. Walk down Baross u. and keep to the left as it turns into Reviezky u. When you reach the open square, go to the far right corner and ring the buzzer at gate #4. In the heart of a hopping bar scene and near the Metro, the location draws a mix of young and older travelers unusual for Budapest accommodations. Somewhat of a hybrid, this guest house is run by young, hostel-style management ready to hook you up to the internet (1000Ft per hr.), do your laundry (800Ft per 5kg), or offer advice on an impulsive nose-piercing. Spacious lofts, bunks, and single beds hide its vast capacity, but the morning queue for the single shower will soon remind you. 500Ft locker and key deposit. English spoken. Reserve the morning of your stay. All beds 1800Ft.

Caterina, V, Andrássy út 47, 3rd Fl., Apt. #48 (tel. 291 95 38; mobile tel. (0620) 34 63 98). M1: Oktogon. Or, trams #4 and 6. Across from Burger King. In a century-old building on Andrássy only a few minutes from central Pest, you'll find the home of "Big" Caterina Birta and her daughter, "Little" Caterina. If you ever wondered what it would be like to stay with your doting (but stern) grandmother, this is it: an endless supply of fresh linens, a spotless kitchen and—though there's no curfew—quiet hours after 10pm. TV in all rooms. Laundry 800Ft per 5kg. Outings to Eger in the family minivan 4000Ft. Your English will be understood, but you might not understand hers. Check-out 10am. Call ahead. Double 2300Ft; 2-bed loft 2300Ft; 8- to 10-bed dorm 1500Ft.

Weisses Haus, III, Erdőalja út 11 (tel./fax 387 82 36; mobile tel. (0620) 34 36 31). M3: Árpád hid. Continue on tram #1 to the HÉV Árpád híd station. From there, take bus #137 to at Erdőalja. A family-owned villa in a classy neighborhood 30min. from the center. The details make the difference: there's a rug on the bathroom floor, doilies in the sunny bedrooms, and the price includes breakfast lovingly prepared by family matriarch Mama Zsuzsa. Four doubles with a great view of distant Pest and 2 bathrooms. Laundry 700Ft per 4kg. German and minimal English spoken. The Weisses have no curfew, but the city does: bus #137 stops at 11:30pm. 3000Ft per person.

CAMPING

For those undaunted by the commute, Budapest's two fully-loaded campgrounds by no means compromise comfort to the budget gods. More suburban than rustic, these present the perfect spot from which to escape the city's crowded streets and enjoy them at the same time. For a full listing of Hungary's campsites, pick up the pamphlet *Camping Hungary*, available at tourist offices.

Zugligeti "Niche" Camping, XII, Zugligeti út 101 (tel./fax 200 83 46). Take bus #158 from "Moszkva tér" to the last stop. An easy commute to central Budapest, located right next to the János Negyi chairlift. A grassy campsite with shady walks and friendly people. The on-site restaurant provides cheap food, but the young clientele usually spend their evenings in the big city. Communal showers and a safe. Tents 500Ft; big tents 900Ft; 850Ft per person. Cars 700Ft; electricity 500Ft. English spoken. MC/Visa.

Római Camping, III, Szentendrei út 189 (tel. 368 62 60; fax 250 04 26). M2: Batthyány tér, then take the HÉV to "Római fürdő" and walk 100m toward the river. A huge 3-star site with tip-top security, a grocery, and tons of restaurants. Enjoy the big swimming pool (300Ft) for the kids, the vast shady park for Rover, and the Roman ruins nearby for mom and dad. Communal showers and kitchen. Tents 1950Ft; bungalows with cold water 1350-2000Ft. HI discount 10%. Open mid-Apr. to mid-Oct. MC/Visa.

FOOD

Even the most expensive restaurants in Budapest may fall within your budget, but eating at family joints can be tastier and more fun. A 10% tip is generally expected; another 10% if your meal is accompanied by live music. Explore the cafeterias beneath "Önkiszolgáló Étterem" signs for something greasy and cheap. (Meat entrees 300-500Ft.) Seek out the *kifőzés* or *vendéglő* in your neighborhood for a taste of Hungarian life. For the less adventurous, the **world's largest Burger King** is on Oktogon, and McDonald's and Pizza Hut are every two blocks. For staples, Non-Stop stores and corner markets are the best options. The king of them all is the **Central Market,** V, Kőzraktár tér u. 1 (M3: Kelvin tér), near Szabadság híd, a vast indoor collection of vendors competing for the lowest prices and most alluring aromas. **Hold utca piac,** V, Hold u. 13 (tel. 332 39 76), just off Szabadság tér in central Pest, boasts two floors of fresh food. (Open M-F 6:30am-5pm, Sa 6:30am-2pm).

RESTAURANTS

BUDA

Marcello's, XI, Bartók Béla út 40 (tel. 466 62 31). Just before Móricz Zsigmond Körtér, on the river side. With imported "cigarette" bread-sticks, fresh flowers, classy high-heeled waitresses, and real tomato sauce (a rarity in Budapest), this place is pizza all-grown-up. Pizzas 480-650Ft. Reservations suggested. Open M-Sa noon-10pm.

Paksi Halászcsárda, II, Margit Körút 14 (tel. 212 55 99). Tram #4 or #6 to Margit Híd. Dimly lit, elegant restaurant where red wine and collared shirts rule the day. Well-executed Hungarian standbys with a few fun twists, like the cool peach cream soup (360Ft). Entrees 790-2900Ft. Open daily noon-midnight.

Söröző a Szent Jupáthoz, II, Dékán u. 3 (tel. 212 29 29). M2: Moszkva tér. Entrance on Retek u. The Hungarian equivalent of an American diner: huge tables, an exhaustive menu, and generous portions. Entrees 595-1709Ft. Open 24hr.

Remiz, II, Budakeszi út 8 (tel. 275 13 96). Take bus #122 from Moszkva tér 3 stops to Szépilona. Best-known for its outdoor BBQ kitchen where ribs and steak are prepared on so-called "lavastones" (i.e., hot rocks). Entrees 980-1780Ft. Open daily 9am-1am; BBQ open May-Sept. only. AmEx/Visa/MC.

Marxim, II, Kis Rókus u. 23 (tel. 316 02 31). M2: Moszkva tér. Walk along Margit krt. with your back to the castle-like building, then turn left down the industrial road. Gulag pizza,

Marxissimo pasta, and other communist-kitsch dishes served in barbed-wire-laden booths. Entrees 200-6150Ft. Open M-F noon-1am, Sa noon-2am, Su 6pm-1am.

Borpatika (Wine Pharmacy), XI, Bertalan L. u. 26 (tel. 204 26 44). Tram #47 or 49 from Deák tér to Bertalan Lajos. A bustling tavern with lively patrons, boisterous happy hours, and a dearth of expats. If the drinking songs and friendly bartender can't cure your ills, the huge jugs of *Furmint* might. Entrees start at 450Ft. Open daily 8am-midnight.

Nagyi Palacsintázója, I, Hattyú u. 16 (tel. 201 86 05). M2: Moszkva tér. For those late-night crepe cravings. A precarious ladder leads to a second floor perch. Don't worry if you drop your dinner on the ascent; with prices like this, you can afford another. *Palacsintá* from 44Ft. Open 24hr.

PEST

Fatâl Restaurant, V, Váci út 67 (tel. 266 26 07). Packs them in for large and hearty Hungarian meals. Giant, carefully garnished main courses from 980Ft. If the red velvet rope doesn't tell you this is the most exclusive restaurant in Budapest, a haughty waiter might—reservations are required. Open daily 11am-11pm.

Marquis de Salade, VI, Hajós u. 43 (tel. 302 40 86). M3: Arany János. At the corner of Bajcsy-Zsilinszky út, 2 blocks from the Metro. Chic cuisine served in an equally chic restaurant by waiters clad in head-to-toe black. Great for dinner, even better for lunch, with infinite variations on the salad (750-2500Ft) and dishes from Japan, Italy, India, Azerbaijan, France, and Hungary. Entrees 700-2200Ft. Open daily noon-midnight.

Gandhi, V, Vigyázó Ferenc u. 4 (tel. 269 16 25). From the meditation guides at the door to the trickling waterfall inside, this cellar establishment takes its customers to a higher plane. An outstanding vegetarian restaurant, with a salad bar sure to generate instant karma. New menu every day (lunar and solar), herb teas, organic wines, and wheat beers. Entrees 660-880Ft. Open M-Sa noon-10:30pm. AmEx/MC/Visa.

Korona Passage, V, Kecskeméti u. 14 (tel. 317 41 11). M3: Kálvin tér. Across from the Mercure Korona Hotel. Watch as giant Hungarian crepes (*palacsinta*) are prepared to order. Sweet and savory crepes 420-590Ft. Open daily 10am-10pm.

Alföldi Kisvendéglő, V, Kecskeméti u. 4 (tel. 267 02 24). M3: Kálvin tér. Outstanding Hungarian cuisine served in booths long enough to encourage rowdy sing-alongs and patriotic camaraderie. The spicy, sumptuous *pogácsa* (homemade bread rolls; 80Ft) are reason enough to come. Entrees 705-2300Ft. Open daily 11am-midnight.

Iguana Bar & Grill, V, Zoltán u. 16 (tel. 331 43 52). M2: Kossuth tér. Two blocks down Akadémia u. This may be the best Mexican joint this side of the Austrian Alps. American-style service, Texan-sized portions, and a few macho menu items like the "whoop-ass beef" draw crowds of homesick travelers. Entrees 1080-2580Ft. Brunch Sa-Su until 4:30pm. Open daily 11:30am-2am. AmEx/Visa/MC. Reservations recommended.

Falafel, VI, Paulay Ede u. 55 (tel. 267 95 67). M1: Opera. From the opera, cross Andrássy, head straight on Hajós u., and turn left on Paulay Ede. Fast food at its best: make-your-own-falafel with real tahini, fresh vegetables, and perfect falafel. Sandwich 310Ft; salad 360Ft. Open M-F 10am-8pm, Sa 10am-6pm.

CAFES

More than just a place to indulge in dessert and coffee, a cafe in Budapest is a living museum of a bygone era. Once the pretentious haunts of Budapest's literary, intellectual, and cultural elite, the cafes now cater to customers with simpler tastes, offering cheap and absurdly rich pastries.

Művész Kávéház, VI, Andrássy út 29 (tel. 352 13 37). M1: Opera. Diagonally across from the Opera. The name means "artist cafe", and—unlike most remaining Golden Age coffee houses—the title fits. An eclectic mix of cell-phoning Italians, Hungarian grandmothers, and even starving artists congregate here. Enjoy a fabulous *Művész torta* (170Ft) and cappuccino (180Ft) on the terrace. Open daily 9am-midnight.

Cafe New York, VII, Erzsébet krt. 9-11 (tel. 322 38 49). M2: Blaha Lujza tér. Once a center of artistic life in Budapest, this symbol of the city's *fin-de-siècle* Golden Age fell into disrepair under communism. The exterior still bears scars left by a Soviet tank, but the gorgeous interior, resplendent with exquisite velvet, gold and marble, has been restored as a tourist attraction. Ice cream and coffee delights priced accordingly (700-1200Ft). Cappucino 280Ft. Open daily 10am-midnight. AmEx/MC/Visa.

Ruszwurm, I, Szentháromság u. 7 (tel. 375 52 84). Just off the square on Várhegy in the Castle District. This cafe has been confecting since 1827, but the sweets that once attracted the Habsburgs now draw packs of tourists. Homemade ice cream 60Ft per scoop; huge slices of chocolate cake 200-280Ft. Open daily 10am-7pm.

Litea Literatura & Tea, I, Hess András tér 4 (tel. 375 69 87). In the Fortuna Passage. Choose from an immense selection of teas in this airy gardenhouse cafe. For the full literary experience, pick up some reading material in the adjoining artsy bookstore. Coffee 80Ft; cappuccino 100Ft. Open daily 10am-6pm. AmEx/Visa/MC.

Faust Wine Cellar, I, Hess András tér 1-3 (tel. 214 30 00). Enter the Hilton in the Castle District and descend into the 13th-century Dominican cloisters. Located deep under the hotel, this cellar serves nothing but wine, and features an overwhelming array of excellent Hungarian vintages. 290-5000Ft per glass. Open daily 3-11pm.

SIGHTS

In 1896, Hungary's 1000th birthday bash prompted the construction of what are today Budapest's most prominent sights. Among the works commissioned by the Habsburgs were **Heroes' Square** (Hősök tere), **Liberty Bridge** (Szbadság híd), **Vajdahunyad Castle** (Vajdahunyad vár), and continental Europe's first metro system. The domes of **Parliament** (Országház) and **St. Stephen's Basilica** (Szent István Bazilika) are both 96m high—vertical references to the historic date. Slightly grayer for wear, war, and communist occupation, these monuments still attest to the optimism of a capital on the verge of its Golden Age.

CASTLE HILL (VÁRHEGY)

Towering above the Danube, the Castle District has been razed and rebuilt three times in its 800-year history, most recently in 1945 when the Red Army left Castle Hill nearly uninhabitable. With its winding, statue-filled streets, breathtaking views and magnificent hodge-podge of architectural styles, the UNESCO-protected district now appears much as it did in Habsburg times. New additions are, of course, the ice cream stands, tour buses, and gift shops that make it a sequestered tourist haven.

THE CASTLE. (Vár). Budapest's castle was originally built in 1242, but was quickly leveled by a Mongol invasion. Centuries later, Good King Mátyás (see **History,** p. 263) made Buda the site of his Renaissance palace. The Turks, however, wouldn't have it and the castle suffered again in 1541. One hundred and forty-five years later, Habsburg forces razed the reconstruction in order to oust the Ottomans. Another reconstruction was completed just in time to be destroyed by the Germans in 1945. Determined Hungarians pasted the castle together once more, only to face the Soviet menace—bullet holes in the palace facade recall the 1956 Uprising. In the post-Soviet period, sorely needed resources have been channeled into the restoration of the castle, but nearly nothing from the good ol' days stands. Rather, the entire hill is largely a reproduction of what was once there. The WWII bombings revealed artifacts from the original 1242 version of the castle, which are now housed in the **Budapest History Museum** (Budapesti Történeti) in the **Royal Palace** (Budavári palota), at the southernmost end of the district. (For a full description of Castle Hill museums, see **Museums,** p. 287.) *(M1, 2, 3: Deák tér. From the Metro, take bus #16 across the Danube. Get off just after the river at the base of the Széchenyi Chain Bridge and take the cable car* (sikló) *up the hill. 300Ft going up, 250Ft going down. Runs daily 7:30am-10pm; closed 1st and 3rd Monday of the month. The upper lift station sits just inside the castle walls, only a few meters from the Hungarian National Gallery (Nemzeti Galéria). Or, take the Metro to M2: Moszkva tér and walk up to the hill on Várfok u., and enter the Castle at Vienna Gate (Becsi kapu).)*

MATTHIAS CHURCH. (Mátyás templom). Due to its multi-colored roof, the Neo-Gothic Matthias Church is one of the most-photographed buildings in Budapest. The church still bears the marks of Turkish rule: when Ottoman armies seized Buda on Sept. 2, 1541, it was converted into a mosque overnight. One hundred and forty-five years later, the Habsburgs defeated the Turks, sacked the city, and re-converted the church. Descend the stairway to the right of the altar to enter the **crypt** and **treasury;** explanation are unfortunately, only in Hungarian. A stunning marble bust of Habsburg Queen Sissy, sits guard at the entrance to the adjoining **St. Stephen's Chapel** (Szent István Kápelna). A second side chapel contains the **tomb of King Béla III,** the only sepulcher of the Árpád dynasty not looted by the Ottomans. *(From the cable car, turn right on Színház and veer left at Tárnok u. From Vienna Gate, walk straight down Fortuna u. High mass with full orchestra and choir Sunday 7am, 8:30am, 10am, noon, and 8:30pm; come early for a seat. Organ concerts most Fridays at 7:30pm. Call Tourinform (see* p. 276*) for info. Treasury open daily 9:30am-5:30pm. 150Ft. English guide to church 500Ft.)*

FISHERMAN'S BASTION. (Halászbástya). The **grand equestrian monument** of King Stephen bearing his trademark double cross sits in front of the Fisherman's Bastion. This arcaded stone wall supports a squat, fairy-tale **tower,** built as a romanticized reconstruction of the original. The amazing view is still the same, although now you'll have to pay to see across the Danube. *(Behind Matthias Church. M free; Tu-Su 200Ft, ages 6-18 100Ft.)*

CASTLE CAVES. (Barlangrendszer Budavárában). After seeing the sights above ground, it's worth exploring the ones below. The caverns beneath Buda Castle, formed by thermal springs and rich in stone formations, were created when Budapest's only residents were unicellular. While tours are available, the labyrinths are accessible without a guide. In fact, wannabe spelunkers can arrange a nighttime "personal labyrinth" in which thrill-seeking visitors get to grope their way alone through a pitch-dark maze. There's no minotaur in the center, but children under 14, young mothers, and people with a heart condition are advised not to participate. *(From Vienna Gate, turn right on Kard u. and left on Országház u. Entrance is at the corner with Dárda u. Tel. 214 31 22. Open Apr.-Oct. daily 9:30am-5:30pm; Nov.-Mar. 10am-4pm. 800Ft, students 650Ft. Call in advance for reservations.)*

ELSEWHERE IN BUDA

More disjointed than Pest, Buda tumbles down from Castle and Gellért Hills on the east bank of the Danube, sprawling out from their bases into Budapest's main residential areas. Buda is older and more conservative than its sister, but with the city's best parks, lush hills, and Danube islands, it is no less worth exploring.

GELLÉRT HILL. The Pope sent Bishop Gellért to the coronation of King Stephen, the first Christian Hungarian monarch, to assist in the conversion of the Magyars (see **History,** p. 263). Those unconvinced by his message hurled the good bishop to his death from atop the hill that now bears his name. Watching over the city from atop Gellért Hill (Gellért-hegy), **Liberation Monument** (Szabadság Szobor) was created to honor Soviet soldiers who died "liberating" Hungary; the Soviet star and the smaller military statues have just recently been removed. The adjoining **Citadel** was built as a symbol of Habsburg power after the foiled 1848 Revolution. The view from the top of the hill is especially spectacular at night, when the Danube and its bridges shimmer in black and gold. Only a short walk down from the Citadel through the park, the **statue of St. Gellért,** complete with colonnaded backdrop and glistening waterfall, overlooks Erzsébet híd. At the base of the hill sits the **Gellért Hotel and Baths,** Budapest's most famous Turkish Bath (see **Baths,** p. 289). The grounds are worth exploring even if you're not getting wet. *(To ascend the hill, take tram #18 or 19 to Hotel Gellért. Follow Szabó Verjték u. to Jubileumi Park, continuing on the marked paths to the summit. Or, take bus #27 to the top; get off at Búsuló Juhász and walk another 5min. to the peak.)*

MARGARET ISLAND. (Margitsziget). Off-limits to private cars but not to buses, Margaret Island offers thermal baths, garden pathways, and numerous shaded terraces, but don't expect the unexpected: the island is fairly small and fairly crowded. According to legend, the *sziget* is named after King Béla IV's daughter; he vowed to rear young Margit as a nun if the nation survived the Mongol invasion of 1241. The Mongols left Hungary decimated, but not destroyed, and Margaret was confined to the island convent. Visitors, fortunately, can come and go as they please. The outdoor **pool** is especially popular with Hungarian kids and their Speedo-clad fathers. You can **rent bikes** or the so-called **bike-carriages** to pedal around the river. A **mini-zoo** adds unpleasant odors to the eastern portion of the island, while open-air clubs to the west jockey for evening crowds. *(M3: Nyugati pu. Continue from the Metro on bus #26 or 26A; get off on Margit híd or on the island itself.)*

PÁL-VÖLGYI CAVES. The popular Pál-völgyi Caves give first-time spelunkers a taste of the real thing, with tricky paths, challenging climbs, and stalactites close enough to bring out the claustrophobe in anyone. Be sure to wear your polar fleece, even in the summer. *(Take bus #86 from Batthyány tér to Kolosyi tér, then bus #65 5 stops to the caves. Open Tu-Su 10am-4pm; last admission 3pm. 250Ft, students 150Ft.)*

CENTRAL PEST

Pest, the western half of the city, has become its animated commercial and administrative center. Although downtown Pest dates back to medieval times, its overall feel is decidedly modern. Her winding streets were constructed in the 19th century; today, they meander among European chain stores, Hungary's biggest corporations and banks, and myriad monuments. The old Inner City (Belváros), rooted in the pedestrian Váci u. and Vörösmarty tér, is a crowded tourist strip where street vendors hawk nesting dolls, embroidered linen, and over-priced postcards.

PARLIAMENT. (Országház). Filled with souvenir shops, Pest's riverbank sports a string of luxury hotels leading up to its magnificent Neo-Gothic Parliament. Hungary's Parliament building was modeled after Britain's, right down to the riverside location. The massive structure has always been too big for Hungary's government; today, the legislature uses only 12% of the building. *(M2: Kossuth Lajos tér. Tel. 268 49 04. English tours available M and W-Su at 10am. 900Ft, students 500Ft. Purchase tickets at gate #10 at the Parliament; enter at gate #12. Reservations recommended.)*

ST. STEPHEN'S BASILICA. By far the city's largest church, St. Stephen's Basilica (Sz. István Bazilika) was decimated by Allied bombs in WWII. Its Neo-Renaissance facade is under reconstruction, but the ornate interior continues to attract both tourists and worshippers. The **Panorama Tower** remains central Pest's highest vantage point, and its 360° balcony offers an amazing view. The highlight of the church, however, is the **Basilica Museum,** where St. Stephen's mummified right hand, one of Hungary's most revered religious relics, sits on public display. For the devout and the macabre, a 100Ft donation dropped in the box will light up the religious relic, allowing two minutes of closer inspection. *(M1, 2, 3: Deák tér. Basilica and museum open Apr.-Sept. M-Sa 9am-5pm, Su 1-5pm; Oct.-Mar. M-Sa 10am-4pm, Su 1-5pm. Tower open daily June-Aug. 9:30am-6pm; Sept.-Oct. 10am-5:30pm; Apr.-May 10am-4:30pm., Tower 400Ft, students 300Ft.)*

SYNAGOGUE. (Zsinagóga). Pest's other major religious sight is its synagogue, the largest active synagogue in Europe and the second largest in the world. The Moorish building was designed to hold almost 3000 worshippers. It has been under renovation since 1988, and much of the artwork is likely to be blocked from view. In the garden out back is the synagogue's **Holocaust Memorial,** an enormous metal tree that sits above a mass grave for thousands of Jews killed near the end of WWII. Each leaf bears the name of a family that perished. *(M2: Astoria. At the corner of Dohány u. and Wesselényi u. Open M-Sa 10am-2:30pm, Su 10am-1:30pm. 400Ft, students 200Ft.)*

ANDRÁSSY ÚT & HEROES' SQUARE. (Hősök tére). Hungary's grandest boulevard, Andrássy út, extends from Erzsébet tér in downtown Pest to Heroes' Square. Built in 1872 above Europe's first Metro line, the once elegant balconies and gated gardens evoke Budapest's Golden Age. Perhaps the most vivid reminder of this period is the **Hungarian National Opera House** (Magyar Állami Operaház). If you can't actually see an opera, make sure to take a tour. The 24-karat gilt interior glows on performance nights. *(Andrássy út 22. M1: Opera. Tel. 353 01 70. English tours daily 3 and 4pm. 900Ft, students 450Ft.)* Andrássy út's most majestic stretch lies near its end at Heroes' Square, where a view of the **Millennium Monument** (Millenniumi emlékmű) dominates the street. The structure, built in 1896 for the 1000-year anniversary of Hungary's history, commemorates the nation's most prominent leaders. The seven horsemen at the base of the statue represent the seven Magyar tribes who settled the Carpathian Basin, while overhead the Archangel Gabriel towers, offering St. Stephen the crown of Hungary. *(Andrássy út stretches along M1 from Bajcsy-Zsilnszky út to Hősök tere.)*

CITY PARK. (Városliget). The shady paths of City Park are perfect for an afternoon stroll. Inside, ice cream vendors, balloon men, and hot dog stands herald the presence of a permanent circus, a rather run-down amusement park, and a respectable zoo. Adding to this whimsical atmosphere, the nostalgic lake-side **Vajdahunyad Castle** (Vajdahunyad Vár) sits in the park's center. Created for the Millenary Exhibition of 1896, the facade is a collage of Romanesque, Gothic, Renaissance, and Baroque styles intended to chronicle the history of Hungarian architecture. Outside the castle broods the hooded statue of **Anonymous,** the secretive scribe to whom we owe much of our knowledge of medieval Hungary. Sit in his lap and get a picture taken (most do) or rent a **rowboat** on the lake next to the castle and explore the banks. From here you can also rent **ice skates** in the winter or **bike-trolleys** in the summer, a Flintstone-esque way to navigate the huge park's paths. *(M1: Széchenyi Fürdő. Boat and bike-trolley rental open June to mid-Sept. M-F 10am-8pm, Sa-Su 9am-8pm; ice skates rented Nov.-Mar. daily 9am-1pm and 4-8pm. Boats 400Ft per 30min.; ice skates and bike-trolleys 300Ft per 30min.)*

AQUINCUM. The ruins of the north Budapest garrison town, Aquincum, crumble in the outer regions of the third district. What look like a few fallen stones by the highway are actually the most impressive vestiges of a 400-year Roman occupation. The settlement's significance increased steadily over time; eventually, it attained the status of *colonia* and became the capital of Pannonia Inferior, a region covering most of Western Hungary. Marcus Aurelius and Constantine blessed the town with a visit. Unfortunately, the remains don't reflect the site's former grandeur. The **museum** on the grounds contains a model of the ancient city, so at least you know what you're looking at. *(Szentendrei út 139. From M2: Batthyány tér, take the HÉV to Aquincum; if you face the Danube, the site is about 100m to the right of the HÉV stop. Tel. 368 82 41. Open Apr.-Oct. Tu-Su 10am-6pm. 400Ft, students 200Ft.)*

MUSEUMS

The magnificent buildings that house Budapest's eclectic collection of museums often delight as much as their contents. Thoughtful visitors can find backroom gems and underlit masterpieces that a see-the-sights plan of attack will surely miss. Happily, most museums are small enough to invite the necessary wandering.

Buda Castle, I, Szent György tér 2 (tel. 375 75 33). M1, 2, 3: Deák tér. From the Metro, take bus #16 across the Danube to the top of Castle Hill. Leveled by the Soviets and Nazis, the reconstructed palace now houses fine museums.

Wing A (tel. 375 91 75) contains the **Museum of Contemporary Art** (Kortárs Művészeti Múzeum) and the smaller **Ludwig Museum** upstairs, devoted to Warhol, Lichtenstein, and other household names of modern art. This unassuming museum is easy to miss, but rotating special exhibits feature the best in contemporary art (exhibit calendars are at most tourist offices). The real highlight, though, is the impressive collection of works by Eastern European artists, many of whom were suppressed under Soviet rule. Open Tu-Su 10am-6pm. 200Ft, students 100Ft.

Wings B-D hold the **Hungarian National Gallery** (Magyar Nemzeti Galéria; tel. 375 79 92), a definitive collection of the best in Hungarian painting and sculpture. Its treasures include works by the Realist Mihály Munkácsy and Impressionist Pál Mersei, and Károly Markó's Classical landscapes. No, you won't recognize most of the names, but in this massive gallery you're bound to discover a new favorite. Open Tu-Su 10am-6pm. 300Ft, students 100Ft, W free; 1 ticket is valid for all 3 wings. English tour 300Ft.

Wing E houses **Budapest History Museum** (Budapesti Történéti Múzeum; tel. 355 88 49). If you've seen all the monuments and are sick of brochure history blurbs, this museum (complete with English translations) will connect the dots. Open May 16-Sept. 15 daily 10am-6pm; Sept. 16-Oct. 31 and Mar. 1-May 15 M and W-Su 10am-6pm; Nov. 1-Feb. 28 M and W-Su 10am-4pm. 100Ft, students 50Ft; W free.

Museum of Fine Arts (Szépművészeti Múzeum), XIV, Dózsa György út 41 (tel. 343 97 59). M1: Hősök tere. A simply spectacular collection of European art—from Raphael to Rembrandt, Gaugin to Goya, these are the paintings you've never seen in books, but should not miss. Highlights include an entire room devoted to El Greco, the Italian Renaissance galleries, and the range of the Impressionist collection. Open Mar. 16-Dec. 31 Tu-Su 10am-5:30pm; Jan. 1-Mar. 15 Tu-Su 10am-4pm. 500Ft, students 200Ft. Tours for up to 5 people 2000Ft.

Museum of Applied Arts (Iparművészeti Múzeum), IX, Üllői út 33-37 (tel. 217 52 22). M3: Ferenc körút. The eclectic collection of Tiffany glass, furniture, and various other *objets d'art* warrants diligent exploration. Fabergé eggs are tucked away in a small back room near the staircase. Housed in a dilapidated but breathtaking building built for the Millennial exhibition in 1896, the museum itself is as much a part of the exhibit as the pieces themselves. Open Mar. 15-Dec. 13 Tu-Su 10am-6pm; Dec. 14-Mar. 11 Tu-Su 10am-4pm. 200Ft, students 50Ft; Tu free.

Jewish Museum (Zsidó Múzeum), VII, Dohány út 2 (tel. 342 89 49). M2: Astoria. Juxtaposes a celebration of Hungary's rich Jewish past with haunting photographs and documents from the Holocaust. Open Apr.-Oct. M-F 10am-3pm, Su 10am-2pm. Tours 1200Ft.

Hungarian National Museum (Magyar Nemzeti Múzeum), VIII, Múzeum krt. 14/16 (tel. 338 21 22). M3: Kálvin tér. Two permanent exhibitions chronicle the history of Hungary. The first extends from the founding of the state to the 20th century, including the Hungarian Crown Jewels, weathered after the wear of a war-torn millenium, but intriguing nonetheless. The second exhibition covers Hungary in the 20th century—a cheery Stalin reaches out to guide you to rooms devoted to Soviet propaganda. Open Mar. 15-Oct. 15 Tu-Su 10am-6pm; Oct. 16-Mar. 14 Tu-Su 10am-5pm; cashier closes 30min. before museum. 400Ft, students 150Ft. English tour 600Ft, students 200Ft.

Museum of Ethnography (Néprajzi múzeum), V, Kossuth tér 12 (tel. 312 48 78). M2: Kossuth tér. An exhibition of international folk culture from the late 18th century to WWI, housed in a monumental gilt structure originally constructed for the Supreme Court. Open Mar.-Oct. Tu-Su 10am-6pm; Nov.-Feb. Tu-Su 10am-5pm. 300Ft, students 150Ft.

Museum of Military History (Hadtörténeti Múzeum), I, Tóth Árpád Sétány 40 (tel. 356 95 86), in the northwest corner of Várhegy. An intimidating collection of ancient and modern weapons, assembled to relate Hungary's historic moments of violence. Not a difficult task, considering the country's legacy of wars, executions, martyrs, murders, sackings, and suicides. Includes a day-by-day chronicle of the 1956 Uprising. Open Tu-Su 10am-5pm. 250Ft, students 80Ft. English guide 500Ft.

Statue Park Museum (Szoborpark Múzeum; tel. 227 74 46), XXII, on the corner of Balatoni út and Szabadkai út. Take tram #47 or 49 to its end at Kosztolányi tér, and from there take the yellow long-distance bus toward Érd (departs from terminal #6 every 15min.; the ride is about 20min. to the park). An arresting outdoor collection of communist statuary removed from Budapest's parks and squares after the collapse of Soviet rule. Open daily 10am-dusk. 150Ft, students 75Ft.

ENTERTAINMENT

Budapest's cultural life, somewhat deadened during communist rule, flourishes anew with a series of performance events throughout the year. **Óbudai island** (Óbudai sziget) hosts the week-long **Sziget Festival** in mid-August, Europe's biggest **open-air rock festival** (tel. 372 06 50; daily ticket 2000Ft, week-long ticket 9000Ft; tickets bought earlier in the summer 1500Ft). The best of all worlds come together in the last two weeks of March for the **Budapest Spring Festival** (tel. 33 23 37 or inquire at Tourinform), a showcase of Hungary's premier musicians and actors. If you miss international pop culture, many of the world's biggest shows pass through Budapest. Prices are reasonable; check the **Music Mix 33 Ticket Service,** V, Váci út 33 (tel. 266 70 70; open M-F 10am-7pm, Sa 10am-2pm). *Programme in Hungary, Budapest Panorama,* and the "Style" section of the *Budapest Sun* are the best English-language guides to entertainment, listing everything from festivals to cinemas to private art showings. All three are available at most tourist offices and hotel lobbies. Although it may take a little translating, *Pesti Est* (found at every club, pub, and McDonald's in the city) is hands-down the best local entertainment guide. It features an English section on weekly cinema; avoid films listed as *szinkronizált* or *magyarul beszélő*, which means they've been dubbed into Hungarian. (Tickets 500-600Ft.)

THEATER & MUSIC

As with any large city, Budapest hosts a world of intimate theaters, smoky club performances, and showcases of local talent, many of which merit at least as much attention as the gilt stages of Budapest's grand cultural venues. The **Central Theater Booking Office,** VI, Andrássy út 18 (tel. 312 00 00), next to the Opera House (open M-Th 9am-6pm, F 9am-5pm), and at Moszkva tér 3 (tel. 212 56 78; open M-F 10am-6pm), sells tickets to almost every performance in the city for no commission. In late summer, the Philharmonic and the Opera take a break, but Budapest's **theaters** keep up the pace. Touring companies *à la* Andrew Lloyd Webber sometimes drop into town—watch out for *Cats* on roller skates. Buy tickets at the **Madách Theater Box Office,** VII, Madách tér 6 (tel. 322 20 15; open M-Sa 2:30-7pm).

State Opera House (Magyar Allami Operaház), VI, Andrássy út 22 (tel. 332 81 97). M1: Opera. One of Europe's leading performance centers. For less than US$5 you can enjoy an opera in the splendor of Budapest's Golden Age, provided you ditch the blue-jeans. The box office (tel. 353 01 70), on the left side of the building, sells unclaimed tickets at even better prices for operas and occasional ballets 30min. before showtime. Open Tu-Sa 11am-1:45pm and 2:30-7pm, Su 10am-1pm and 4-7pm.

Philharmonic Orchestra, V, Vörösmarty tér 1 (tel. 317 62 22). The ticket office is on the side of the square farthest from the river; look for the Jegyroda sign. Equally grand music in a slightly more modest venue. Concerts almost every evening Sept.-June. Open M-F 10am-6pm, Sa-Su 10am-2pm. Tickets 1200-1700Ft, less on the day of the show.

Matthias Church (Mátyás templom), I, Szentháromság tér. M1, 2, 3: Deák tér. From the Metro, take bus #16 to the top of Castle Hill. Holds organ, orchestral, and choral recitals most Wednesdays and Fridays at 8pm. 1000Ft, occasionally free.

Margitsziget Theater (tel. 340 41 96), XIII, on Margitsziget. Tram #4 or 6 to Margitsziget. Opera and Hungarian-folk concerts on its open-air stage. Summer only.

Pesti Vigadó (Pest Concert Hall), V, Vigadó tér 2 (tel. 318 99 03; fax 375 62 22). On the Danube near Vörösmarty tér. Flashy costumes and lots of vibrato. Hosts operettas every other night. Box office open M-Sa 10am-6pm. Tickets 3200Ft.

Buda Park Theater (tel. 366 99 16), XI, Kosztolányi Dezső tér. Folk-dancers stomp across the stage at this small theater. Box office at V, Vörösmarty tér 1. Open M-F 11am-6pm. Tickets 90-350Ft.

BATHS

To soak away weeks of city grime, crowded trains, and yammering camera-clickers, sink into a **thermal bath,** the essential Budapest experience. The baths were first built in 1565 by Arslan, a Turkish ruler of Buda who feared that a siege of the city would prevent the population from bathing. Thanks to his anxiety, nothing will keep you from bathing, either: the range of services—from mud baths to massage—are cheap enough to warrant indulgence without guilt. Some baths are meeting spots for Budapest's gay community (see **Gay Budapest,** p. 292).

BUCK-NAKED IN BUDAPEST While Turkish baths might conjure up images of harems and being fanned with palm leaves, Budapest's baths—with most patrons well past 50 years old—feel more like a YMCA locker room. Nevertheless, the treatment is royally indulgent, if somewhat intimidating for the virgin bather. When you first arrive, you'll be given what is essentially a dishrag with strings: a bizarre apron no bigger and no less dingy. Modesty requires that you tie it around your waist. After depositing your belongings in a locked stall (you hold one key, the attendant keeps the other), proceed to the baths. In general, women put the apron aside as a towel while men keep theirs on. Either way, it's a good idea to do as the locals do—there's nothing more conspicuous (or embarrassing) than a Speedo-clad tourist among the naked natives. Once you've cycled through the sauna and thermal baths, repeat for good measure, and enter the massage area. If you're looking for a good scrubbing, go with the sanitary massage *(vízi);* if you're a traditionalist, stick to the medical massage *(orvosi).* In both cases, the masseuse will blithely ignore you, chattering away in Hungarian while pummeling your back. All of the baths provide a much-needed rest area once the whole process is complete. Refreshed, smiling, and somewhat sleepy, tip the attendant, lounge over mint tea, and savor your afternoon of guilt-free pampering and scrubbing.

Gellért, XI, Kelenhegyi út 4/6 (tel. 466 61 66). Bus #7 or tram #47 or 49 to Hotel Gellért, at the base of Gellért-hegy. Venerable indoor thermal baths, segregated by sex. Accustomed to slightly bewildered tourists, this is the only spa with signs in English. Boasts a rooftop sundeck and an enormous outdoor wave pool. Offers a huge range of inexpensive *à la carte* options, including mudbaths, ultrasound, and the new "Thai massage," featuring "the world famous masseuses of the Bangkok wat po": women trained to use their feet, elbows, and knees in an exhausting 1½hr. massage of strategic pressure points (6500Ft, call for reservations). Thermal bath 800Ft, under 18 750Ft; with pool privileges 1500Ft. 15min. massage 1000Ft. Open May-Sept. M-F 6am-7pm, Sa-Su 6am-4pm; Oct.-Apr. M-F 6am-7pm, Sa-Su 6am-2pm. Pools open May-Sept. daily 6am-7pm; Oct.-Apr. M-F 6am-7pm, Sa-Su 6am-6pm.

Széchenyi Fürdő, XIV, Állatkerti u. 11/14 (tel. 321 03 10). M1: Hősök tére. Indoor baths attract the city's gentry while the large **outdoor swimming pool** delights their grandchildren. Swimsuit required. 500Ft, after 5pm 400FT, under 18 500Ft. Massage 1000Ft per 15min. Open May-Sept. daily 6am-7pm; Oct.-Apr. M-F 6am-7pm, Sa-Su 6am-5pm. Baths are men-only July-Aug. M, W, and F; women-only Tu, Th, and Sa.

Király, I, Fő u. 84 (tel. 201 51 61). M2: Batthány tér. The basic bath experience, elevated by the splendor of Turkish cupolas and domes. The men's half has a reputation as a meat-market for gay men. 500Ft. Massage 750Ft per 15min. Men-only M, W, and F 6:30am-6pm; women-only Tu and Th 6:30am-6pm, Sa 6:30am-noon.

Rudas, Döbrentei tér 9 (tel. 375 83 73). Take bus #7 to the first stop in Buda. Right on the river under a dome built by Turks 400 years ago, this is the gorgeous one you see in all the brochures. Unfortunately, women will have to make do with the photographs—centuries haven't altered the dome, the bathing chamber, or the "men-only" rule. This is more of an old-boys-club than a boys' club, though—Rudas has a reputation for being one of the straightest baths in Budapest. 1½hr. bath 1000Ft. Swimming pool open to women (600Ft). Open M-F 6am-6pm, Sa-Su 6am-1pm.

NIGHTLIFE

After a few drinks in Budapest, you'll forget you're in Hungary. Global village alterna-teens wearing the usual labels and grinding to an electronic beat make the club scene in Budapest familiar to anyone who has ever partied in America or Britain. A virtually un-enforced drinking age and cheap drinks may be the only cause for culture shock. As clubs become more and more technically endowed, cover prices are rising: a night of techno may cost the same as a night at the opera, although both are cheap by Western standards. Despite the throbbing crowds in the clubs and 4am chatter in the pubs, the streets themselves—often lit only by a single dim bulb—are surprisingly empty at night, echoing pre-capitalist times. To find out what's going on where and when, pick up a copy of *Budapest Week* (126Ft).

BARS

Old Man's Pub, VII, Akácfa u. 13 (tel. 322 76 45). M2: Blaha Lujza tér. Although the name implies otherwise, the crowd is still in the larval phase of yuppie-dom. The lively atmosphere is more clean-cut hip than smoke-filled pub. For the horn-rimmed glasses set, this packed bar is pretty much the place to be on a Saturday night. Live blues and jazz. Open M-Sa 3pm-dawn.

Fat Mo's Speakeasy, V, Nyári Pal u. 11 (tel. 267 31 99). M3: Kálvin tér. "Spitting prohibited" in this Depression-era bar. Drinking, however, isn't. A large selection of tap beer (12 varieties, 0.5L 280-260Ft) and live jazz to make the booze flow quicker. Gets crowded early with the loyal patronage of "permanent tourists:" wanderers who stopped in Budapest for a few days and wound up staying indefinitely. Th-Sa DJ after 11:30pm. Open M-F noon-3am, Sa-Su 6pm-3am.

Morrison's Music Pub, VI, Révay u. 25 (tel. 269 40 60). M1: Opera. Just left of the opera. With bar overflow onto the dance floor and dance floor overflow into the bar, this jostling nightspot pulls in a crowd ready to party in any language. British telephone booth inside actually works but moonlights as a voyeuristic make-out spot. June-Aug. cover 400Ft. Open M-Sa 8:30pm-4am.

The Long Jazz Club, VII, Dohány u. 22/24 (tel. 322 00 06). While it might seem like jazz is an after-thought at this billiards-and-darts bar, this luckily isn't the case. Jazz performances grace the dueling stages nightly at 10pm. Cover M-Th and Su 300Ft, F-Sa 500Ft. Open daily 6pm-2am.

Crazy Cafe, VI, Jokai u. 30 (tel. 302 40 03). M3: Nyugati pu. A great place to start a long evening on the town. With belly-baring waitresses serving up 40 kinds of whiskey (shots 450-1190Ft), 13 kinds of tequila (350-550Ft), and 17 kinds of vodka (280-450Ft), the scene has been known to get more than a little rowdy. Live music nightly 9pm. Unless you consider Hungarians crooning in accented English entertaining, stick to the weekends–Sunday and Monday are karaoke nights. Open M-Sa 11am-1am, Su 11am-midnight.

CLUBS

Undergrass, VI, Liszt Ferenc tér 10 (tel. 322 08 30). M1: Oktogon. Or, tram #4 or 6. The hottest spot in Pest's trendiest area. The bar has only a few chairs, but most are happy to stand, kissing cheeks, waving across the room and generally expressing the life-is-grand giddiness of the young and beautiful. A glass, soundproof door allows all this to

AN OFFER YOU CAN'T REFUSE Communism may be dead in Hungary, but the mafia is alive and well in post-Soviet Budapest. But don't look for the usual Adidas-clad, gold chain-bedecked thugs; Budapest's agent extraordinaire might wear plenty of gold, but she also wears mini-skirts and high-heeled shoes. You'll meet her–an English-speaking, Hungarian hotty–at a swank bar around Váci út. Things will start off smoothly, as she suggests a new venue, down the street. Of course you join her. She asks you to buy her a drink, and of course you do. When the bill comes, it is accompanied at last by the *beezneezmen* you'd expect from the post-Soviet mafia. US$1000 for a single Sloe Gin Fizz? It's no mistake, they assure you. And what do you give a 300lb. gorilla? Anything he wants. You *will* pay, because there is no recourse for the victimized. Ask to see the menu and there it is, written in black-and-white. Just be sure to see it before you order the drinks next time. Not enough cash in your wallet? Don't worry, the mafia has learned at least a few tricks from capitalism: they now accept major credit cards. A number of establishments in the Váci út area have had complaints filed against them at the U.S. Embassy.

go on while an equally-packed disco spins out 80s hits and pop standards. Open daily 7pm-4am; disco starts at 10pm.

Fél 10 Jazz Club, VIII, Baross u. 30 (tel. 06 60 31 84 67). M3: Kálvin tér. A short walk down Baross u. A sophisticated bar and disco, "Fel TEEZ" covers 2 floors with a convoluted layout *à la* M.C. Escher. No one seems to mind, though, since the live "jams" can be heard everywhere and the drinks—once you navigate the bottleneck at the bar—are potent. Cover 400Ft. Open M-F noon-dawn, Sa-Su 6pm-dawn.

Made-Inn Music Club, VI, Andrássy út 112 (tel. 311 34 37). M1: Bajza u. With live music and a different theme every night—half-priced drinks on Wednesdays, "happy music" Fridays, and funk/soul Saturdays—the scene stays strong until closing time. The crowd looks like it just stepped off the runway. Cover 400Ft. Disco open W-Sa 10pm-5am.

Franklin Trocadero Cafe, V, Szent István körút 15 (tel. 311 46 91). The sign outside—flashing purple and green—typifies this self-consciously "Latin" dance club. The crowd, however, is far from bashful. If you're not good enough to keep up with the high-energy salsa, dance lessons on Tuesdays will bring you up to speed. Live music nightly. Cover 300Ft. Open Tu 9pm-3am, W-Th and Su 9pm-4am, F 9pm-6am, Sa 9pm-5am.

Piaf, VI, Nagymező u. 25 (tel. 312 38 23). A much-loved after-hours place and the final destination of any decent pub crawl in Budapest. Guests are admitted only after knocking on a rather inconspicuous—albeit intimidating—door and meeting the approval of the big man behind the peep-hole. The red velvet lounge demands an expensive smoke and martini. The beautiful staff tends to be icy, but that's because they can be. Cover 400Ft; includes first drink. Open daily 4pm-4am, but don't come before 1am.

GAY BUDAPEST

For decades, gay life in Budapest was completely underground; it is only just beginning to make itself visible. The city still has its share of skinheads, so it is safer to be discreet. If there are problems of any sort, call the **gay hotline** (tel. 466 92 83), open in the afternoon. The establishments below are either gay-friendly or have primarily gay clientele. Unfortunately, the gay scene in Budapest is exactly that: a *gay* scene. There are no venues other than Capella Cafe frequented by—or even welcoming to—lesbians.

Capella Cafe, V, Belgrád rakpart 23 (tel. 318 62 13). With glow-in-the-dark grafitti and an underground atmosphere, this popular spot draws a mixed crowd for a line-up that varies from transvestite lip-synchs to Wednesday night strip-teases. Nightly shows at midnight. Cover 500Ft; 500Ft minimum. Open Tu-Su 9pm-5am. Women welcome.

Angel Bar, VII, Szövetség u. 33 (tel. 351 64 90). The first gay bar in Budapest. Until a few years ago, the club moved weekly; now this huge 3-level disco, cafe, and bar is packed for its weekend programs: Friday and Sunday nights bring drag shows, while Saturday is exclusively gay night (although in reality, every night is exclusively gay night). Cover 400Ft. Open Th-Su 10pm-dawn.

Action Bar, V, Magyar u. 42 (tel. 266 91 48). M3: Kálvin tér. As the name implies, this smoky basement pub is a pick-up spot. Video-viewing room. 700Ft minimum. Open daily 9pm-4am. Men only.

THE DANUBE BEND

North of Budapest, the Danube sweeps in a dramatic arc called the Danube Bend (Dunakanyar), deservedly one of the greatest tourist attractions in Hungary. Ruins of 1st-century Roman settlements cover the countryside, Esztergom's cathedral and Visegrád's castle overlook the river as reminders of medieval glory, and an artist colony thrives amid the museums and churches of Szentendre. All this is within 2hr. of Budapest by bus, but the longer ferry ride is well worth the time, offering enough peaceful views to refresh the weariest of travelers.

SZENTENDRE

A short commute from Budapest, Szentendre (sen-TEN-dreh) appears at first to be a rural town defined by its cobblestone streets. Upon closer inspection, though, the overwhelming abundance of credit-card signs lurking in shop windows, the upscale art galleries, and the overpriced restaurants in its cheery squares betray its insidious modernity. But by maintaining its sense of humor and focusing on what it does best, Szentendre manages, against all odds, to pull the contrast off.

ORIENTATION & PRACTICAL INFORMATION. The HÉV commuter rail, train, and bus station is a 10min. walk from Fő tér; descend the stairs outside the bus station, go through the underpass, and head up Kossuth u. At the fork in the road, bear right onto Dumsta Jenő út, which leads to the **1763 Plague Cross** in the town center. **HÉV** travels to **Budapest's Batthyány tér** (45min., M-F every 20min., Sa-Su every 30min., 240Ft). Be sure to buy your ticket before boarding the commuter rail—the conductor will sell you a ticket on the train, but for 1000-3000Ft more. **Buses** run from **Budapest's Árpád híd station** (30min., every hr., 146Ft), many continuing to **Visegrád** (45min., 204Ft) and **Esztergom** (1½hr. from Szentendre, 408Ft). **MAHART boats** leave from a pier 10-15min. north of the town center; with the river on your right, walk along the water until you see the sign. In summer (May 17-Aug.), the scenic boats float to: **Budapest** (3 per day, 600Ft); **Visegrád** (3 per day, 600Ft); and **Esztergom** (2 per day, 650Ft). **Tourinform,** Dumsta Jenő u. 22 (tel. 31 79 65 and 31 79 66), between the center and the station, provides **maps** (50Ft) and brochures. (Open summer M-F 10am-1pm and 1:30-5pm, Sa-Su 10am-2pm; off-season M-F 10am-1pm and 1-5pm.) **OTP Bank,** Dumsta Jenő u. 6 (tel. 31 02 11), makes up for its sloth with great **exchange** rates, no commission on **traveler's checks,** and a **24hr. ATM.** (Open M 7:45am-6pm, Tu-F 7:45am-5pm.) **Phone code:** 26.

ACCOMMODATIONS & FOOD. Although Szentendre is most popular as a daytrip, there are a surprising number of (overpriced) lodging options. **IBUSZ,** Bogdányi u. 15 (tel. 361 81; fax 31 35 97), will hook you up with a private double for 3000Ft. (Open M-F 9am-4pm, Sa-Su 10am-3pm.) A little more expensive, **Ilona Panzió,** Rákóczi Ferenc u. 11 (tel. 31 35 99), right in the center of town, rents decent doubles with personal showers; the stalls are so small you might wind up getting personal with yourself. (3200Ft for 1 person; 4400Ft for 2. Breakfast included.) The buggy-but-beautiful **Pap-szigeti Camping** (tel. 31 06 97; fax 31 37 77) sits 1km north of the center on its very own island in the Danube. Walk along the water with the river to your right; the short bridge to the island will be obvious. This campsite rents four-bed bungalows with bath and kitchen (7200Ft), three-bed bungalows without running water (3200Ft), panzió doubles with shower (4000Ft), motel rooms with two, three, or four beds (3000, 3500, and 4000Ft respectively), and tent sites (2500Ft for 2 people, plus 900Ft per extra person; open May-Oct. 15).

The constant flow of tourists has made restaurants in town expensive by Hungarian standards—budget travelers will do best to return to Budapest or continue to Visegrád for dinner. For one of the best deals in town, walk through a beaded curtain into **Kedvac Kifőzde,** Bükköspart 21 (tel. 31 91 86). Perfect for a light lunch, this tiny corner restaurant serves up good cheap soups and delicious menus for 300Ft. (Open M-F 11:30am-8pm.) Another good value hides in the vines at **Borostyánkert,** Batthyányi u. 1 (tel. 31 08 08), right off Dumsta Jenő u. The selection is small, but huge portions of sweet or savory *palascinta* are offered for very cheap. (Crepes 180-340Ft. Open M, W-Th, and Su noon-10pm, F-Sa noon-midnight.) Of course, the most affordable food is found at the giant **grocery store** near the rail station. (Open M-F 9am-7pm, Sa-Su 10am-5pm.)

SIGHTS & ENTERTAINMENT. Start your visit by heading up **Church Hill** (Templomdomb), above the town center in Fő tér, where the 13th-century Roman Catholic church sits. Facing it, the **Czóbel Museum** houses works by Béla Czóbel, Hungary's foremost Impressionist painter, including his "Venus of Szentendre" reclining in red bikini. (Open Mar. 15-Oct. Tu-Su 10am-4pm; Nov.-Mar. 14 F-Su

10am-4pm. 150Ft, students 100Ft.) Just across Alkotmány u., the museum at the Baroque **Serbian Orthodox Church** (Szerb Ortodox Templom) displays religious art, part of Szentendre's legacy as a Serbian settlement. (Open W-Su 10am-5pm. 80Ft.) Szentendre's most frequented museum, **Margit Kovács Museum,** Vastagh György u. 1, exhibits sentimental ceramic sculptures and tiles by the popular 20th-century Hungarian artist Margit Kovács. (Open Mar. 17-Oct. Tu-Su 10am-6pm; Nov.-Mar. 14 Tu-Su 10am-4pm. 250Ft, students 150Ft.) **Szabó Marzipan Museum,** Dumtsa Jenő u. 7 (tel. 31 14 84), tests the limits of confection. The huge marzipan Parliament is impressive, but the real thriller is the larger-than-life chocolate statue of Michael Jackson. (Open daily 10am-6pm. 150Ft, students and seniors 100Ft.) Hungary's ethnological **Open Air Village Museum** (tel. 31 23 04) is a 10min. bus ride from Szentendre; take the "Skazer" bus from terminal #8 (hourly, 80Ft). The museum reconstructs traditional settlements and architecture from throughout Hungary. Craftsmen and artisans bring it to life each weekend with basket weaving, butter making, and other rustic skills. (Open Apr.-Oct. Tu-Su 9am-5pm. 350Ft, students 150Ft.) The annual **Danube Carnival** celebrates folk art with performances by dance groups from along the river. (Mid-Mar. to early Apr. Call Tourinform for details.) From mid-June to late August, **Szentendre Summer Festival** (Szentendrei Nyár Fesztivál) draws a procession of music and theater performances to the city.

VISEGRÁD

Now a sleepy rural town, Visegrád (VEE-sheh-grad) hosted the royal court in medieval times. The town's significance began to diminish after the 15th century, but was truly devastated when the Habsburgs were forced to destroy its citadel in an early 18th-century struggle against freedom fighters. Since then, Visegrád has been forced to resist communists, with their plans for power plants and modernization, as well as its continued deterioration in importance. What's left is a city caught somewhere between a recent rediscovery (the castle was only uncovered by archaeologists in 1934) and a centuries-old battle with time.

ORIENTATION & PRACTICAL INFORMATION. **Buses** from **Budapest's Árpád híd Metro station** (1½hr., 10 per day, 629Ft) and **Esztergom** (45min., hourly, 329Ft) pass through on the road along the Danube, route #11. The bus from Budapest will drop you off in front of a large parking lot—there is no station in Visegrád. To get to the center, cross the lot and turn right on Fő út, the road running parallel to the river. About 5min. later you'll reach the Catholic Church at the town center, where Mátyás Király út and Fő út meet. **MAHART boats** run to: **Budapest** (2½-3hr., 2 per day, afternoon trip only, 650Ft); **Esztergom** (2hr., 2 per day, morning trip only, 600Ft); and **Szentendre** (1¼hr., 2 per day, 600Ft). **Visegrád Tours,** Rév u. 15 (tel. 39 81 60), can help with info. Turn right at the church in the town center; the office is at the very end of the street. (Open Apr.-Oct. daily 8:30am-5:30pm; Nov.-Mar. M-F 8:30am-5:30pm.) Although not particularly chipper, they have a few **private rooms** nearby. (Doubles 4200-4800Ft.) **Phone code:** 26.

ACCOMMODATIONS & FOOD. If you prefer to avoid the tourist agency, look for *Zimmer frei* signs along Fő út past the center. Also a few minutes past the center on Fő út, the brand new **Haus Honti,** Fő út 66 (tel. 39 81 20), offers spacious doubles and triples with TV and shower (5000, 6000Ft). **Elte Guest House,** Fő út 117 (tel. 39 81 65), is in a multi-level building 5min. down on the left. It offers carpeted rooms with bath, and—if you're lucky—a balcony. (2990Ft per person.) **Gulás Csárda,** Nagy Lajos u. 4 (tel. 39 83 29), takes as much care preparing their excellent Hungarian fare as they do folding their paper napkins origami-style. (Entrees 380-1250Ft. Open daily 11:30am-10pm.) For a sumptuous dessert and a terrace view of the Danube (or the parking lot, depending on where you sit), try **Ágasház** (tel. 39 76 16), across from the bus stop. Along with traditional Hungarian entrees (700-1400Ft), the restaurant serves breakfast and an indulgent assortment of pastries *à la mode.* (Open M-Sa 9am-11pm, Su 9am-10pm.) On a sunny day, the grassy banks of the Danube provide a perfect spot for a picnic. **ABC supermarket,** across from Visegrád Tours at the end of Rév u., sells all the necessities. (Open M-F 7am-7pm, Sa-Su 7am-3pm.)

SIGHTS & ENTERTAINMENT. King Béla's **Royal Palace** (Királyi Palota), built in 1259 in the foothills above Fő út, was thought to be a myth until it was discovered by archaeologists in 1934. (Tel. 39 80 26; fax 39 82 52. Open Apr.-Oct. Tu-Su 9am-5pm. 200Ft, students 160Ft.) During the second weekend of July, the grounds come alive once again for the **International Palace Games** (tel. (01) 166 17 80), complete with royal parades, knight tournaments, living chess, concerts, and medieval crafts. Named for a king imprisoned here in the 13th century, the hexagonal **Solomon's Tower** (Alsóvár Salamon Torony) at the end of Salamontorony u. once provided a fine view of Hungary's Camelot; the river is now a better vantage point. The **King Matthias Museum** inside displays a large Lion Fountain and other artifacts from the palace ruins. (Open May-Sept. daily 9am-4pm. 200Ft, students 100Ft.) Visegrád's main attraction, though, is the 13th-century **citadel,** visible for miles from its perch high above the Danube. (Open Apr.-Nov. daily 8:30am-6pm. 60Ft, students 35Ft.) Formerly a Roman outpost, the site commands a dramatic view of the river and surrounding hills. Catch a **minibus** (tel. 39 73 72; 900Ft) to the fortress, or make the arduous 30min. hike up **Kalvaria,** lined with icons depicting the Stations of the Cross. The citadel also offers a **wax museum** devoted to medieval torture. (Open daily 8am-6pm. 200Ft, students 160Ft.) To get into the 13th-century spirit, test your **archery** skills in front of the castle (60Ft per arrow).

ESZTERGOM

1000 years of religious history revolve around a solemn hilltop cathedral that makes Esztergom (ESS-ter-gom), nicknamed "the Hungarian Rome," worthy of its religious pilgrims. A basilica was originally built here in 1010, but the present Neoclassical colossus—Hungary's biggest church—was consecrated in 1856. One of the finest collections of religious ornamentation in Hungary rests inside; there is a view that exceeds it on top.

ORIENTATION & PRACTICAL INFORMATION. The **train station** is an easy 10min. walk from town. With the station at your back, turn left on the main street. Make a right onto Kiss János Altábornagy út, which becomes Kossuth Lajos u. as it proceeds toward the square. **Trains** connect Esztergom to **Budapest** (1½hr., 10 per day, 408Ft). Catch **buses** three blocks away from Rákóczi tér on Simor János u. (the street lined with fruit and clothing stands) to: **Budapest** (1¼hr., 3 per day, 350Ft, *InterCity* 440Ft); **Szentendre** (1½hr., hourly, 252Ft); and **Visegrád** (40min., hourly, 180Ft). **Buses** from **Budapest** leave from the M3 Árpád híd Metro station—follow the signs to the Volanbusz terminal. From the bus station in Esztergom, walk up Simor János u. toward the **street market,** which brings you directly to Rákóczi tér. Three **MAHART boats** (tel. 31 35 31) per day depart from the pier at the end of Gőzhajó u. on Primas Sziget island, stopping at **Visegrád** (1½hr., 600Ft) and **Szentendre** (3½hr., 650Ft) on the way to **Budapest** (5hr., 690Ft). **Grantours,** Széchenyi tér 25 (tel./fax 41 37 56), at the edge of Rákóczi tér, provides **maps** (150Ft) and will help locate central *panzió* rooms (doubles 4000-7500Ft) or cheaper, more distant **private accommodations.** (All private rooms 1550Ft. Open July-Aug. M-F 8am-6pm, Sa 9am-noon; Sept.-June M-F 8am-4pm, Sa 9am-noon.) **K&H Bank,** also on Rákóczi tér, has the best **exchange** rates in town, and cashes **traveler's checks** for no commission. (Open M-Th 8:15am-3pm, F 8:15am-1:30pm.) A 24hr. **currency exchange machine** and Cirrus/MC/Plus/Visa **ATM** stands outside. **Phone code:** 33.

ACCOMMODATIONS & FOOD. For a central location, several pensions are clustered around the square. **Platán Panzió,** Kis-Duna Sétány 11 (tel. 41 13 55), between Rákóczi tér and Primas Sziget, rents musty rooms with shared baths and a view of the courtyard rose garden. (Breakfast included. Hot water (be patient!). Check-out 10am. Singles 2000Ft; doubles 4000Ft.) **Gran Camping,** Nagy-Duna

Sétány (tel. 40 25 13), in the middle of Primas Sziget, rents tent space in a lush—but mosquito-infested—park on the banks of the Danube. (Tents 380Ft plus 250Ft per person.) **Csülök Csárda,** Battyány u. 9 (tel. 31 24 20), serves up fine Hungarian fare, adding over a dozen creative variations on ham-knuckle to the usual repertoire of roasts. (Entrees 780-1180Ft. Open daily noon-midnight.) **Szalma Csárda** (tel. 31 10 52), in the middle of Primas Sziget near the pier at the end of Gőzhajó u., serves fish straight from the Danube. (Entrees 420-700Ft. Open daily noon-midnight.) For picky eaters, a **Julius Meinl,** just off of Rákóczi tér, sells the usual **supermarket** fare. (Open M-F 6:30am-6:30pm, Sa 6:30am-1pm.)

SIGHTS. Climb to the top of the cathedral cupola (100Ft) for the **best view** of the bend, extending all the way to the Low Tatras in Slovakia, then descend into the solemn **crypt** to honor the remains of Hungary's archbishops. (Open daily 9am-4:45pm. 50Ft, free for pilgrims.) The **Cathedral Treasury** (Kincstáv), to the right of the main altar, is Hungary's most extensive ecclesiastical collection, including a treasure trove of ornate gold and silver relics spanning a millennium. The easy-to-miss jewel-studded cross labelled #78 in the case facing the entrance to the main collection is the **Coronation Cross** (Koronázási Eskűkereszt), on which Hungary's rulers pledged their oaths until 1916. (Open daily 9am-4:30pm. 200Ft, students 100Ft; English-language guide 80Ft.) On a smaller scale, the red marble **Bakócz Chapel,** to the left of the altar, is a masterwork of Renaissance Tuscan craftsmanship. It was dismantled during the Turkish occupation, then reassembled here from over 1000 separate pieces. Beside the cathedral stands the restored 12th-century **Esztergom Palace.** A **Castle Museum,** with pieces of St. István's original palace on display, is inside. (Tel. 31 59 86. Open Tu-Su summer 9am-4pm; off-season 10am-3:30pm. 160Ft, students 60Ft.) Don't pay the 50Ft to climb the roof; enjoy the view for free from the wall behind the cathedral. At the foot of the cathedral's hill, **Christian Museum** (Keresztény Múzeum), Berenyi Zsigmond u. 2 (tel. 31 38 80), houses a collection of Renaissance and Medieval religious art, including some of the world's finest tryptychs. (Open Tu-Su 10am-5:30pm. 200Ft, students 100Ft.)

THE ŐRSÉG

In the far west corner of Hungary, low-flying storks guard the pastoral region known as the Őrség. During the Cold War, authorities discouraged visitors and Hungarian citizens alike from entering the Őrség, as it was too close to the capitalist Austrian and Titoist Yugoslav borders. Thus, a region that had always been a little behind the times—electricity didn't arrive until 1950—became even more distanced from the pace of the modern world. From the religious monuments of Győr to the more offbeat museums of Sopron, from swimming in Tata to biking through Őriszentpeter, tourists are coming to catch this slice of timelessness.

GYŐR

The cobblestoned streets of Győr's (DYUR) inner city wind peacefully around a wealth of religious monuments, well-kept museums and prime examples of 17th- and 18th-century architecture. The horse-drawn carriages (when they appear) accompany rush-hour traffic, though, and Győr's industrial outskirts leave the city just real enough to placate the traveler weary of too much fairy-tale charm. Add a packed riverside waterpark, an array of terrace restaurants, and throngs of young people on weekend evenings, and you have a living, breathing combination of history and recreation that begs visitors to stay just one more day.

ORIENTATION & PRACTICAL INFORMATION

The **train station** lies only 5min. from the inner city; the underpass that links the rail platforms leads back to the **bus station.** To reach the center, head out the front of the train station and go right until you come to the bridge. Turn left just before the underpass, then cross the big street to pedestrian **Baross Gabor u.**

Trains: To **Budapest** (2½hr., 11 per day, 910Ft) and **Vienna** (2hr., 6 per day, 5116Ft).

Buses: To **Budapest** (2½hr., hourly, 910Ft).

Tourist Office: Tourinform kiosk, Árpád u. 32 (tel. 31 17 71). At the corner with Baross Gabor u. Free **maps.** Open June-Aug. M-F 8am-8pm, Sa 9am-3pm, Su 9am-1pm; Sept.-May M-Sa 9am-4pm.

Budget Travel: IBUSZ, Kazinczy u. 3 (tel. 31 17 00). A few blocks farther up Baross Gabor u. and a left on Kazinczy u. Less Győr-iented than Tourinform. Gives a 10% discount on international train and bus tickets for those under 26. Open June-Aug. M-F 8am-5pm, Sa 8am-noon; Sept.-May M-F 8am-4pm. MC/Visa.

Currency Exchange: OTP Bank, at the corner of Baross Gabor u. and Kisfaludy u. Good exchange rates. Open M 7:45am-4pm, Tu-F 7:45am-3pm. A Cirrus/Plus/MC/Visa **24hr. ATM** is outside. Cash AmEx traveler's checks in the post office (see below) at the *Postabank* desk for no commission.

Post office: Bajcsy-Zsilinszky út 46 (tel. 31 43 24). Open M-F 8am-8pm. **Postal code:** 9001. **Phone code:** 96.

ACCOMMODATIONS

In July and August, accommodations in downtown Győr overflow, making reservations essential. **Tourinform** (see above) can help you find a pension, dorm, or hotel room, and will make reservations if you call ahead. **IBUSZ** (see above) offers a few private doubles (from 2500Ft), but expect to pay a 30% surcharge if you stay fewer than four nights.

Hotel Szárnyaskerék, Révai Miklós u. 5 (tel. 31 46 29). Right across the street from the train station. If you forgive the icy reception, it's one of the best values in town. Doubles 3750Ft, with bath 5500Ft.

2sz. Fiú Kollégium (Boys' Dormitory No. 2), Damjanich u. 58 (tel. 31 10 08). Across the bridge from Baross Gabor u. and the city center. Freshly painted (though not particularly fresh otherwise) Open July-Aug. 3- and 4-bed dorms 1800Ft per person.

Széchenyi Istvan Főiskola Kollégiuma, Hédevári út 3, entrance K4 (tel. 42 97 22). Also across the Mosow-Dune River. Heading up Baross Gabor u. from the train station, turn right on Bajcsy-Zsilinszky u., then left onto Czuczor Gergely u. (which becomes Jedlik Ányos). Cross the bridge and take a sharp left onto Kúlóczy tér; from there, cross the parking lot and look for the Bufé. Entrance K4 is on the left. After 9pm enter at "K3" and walk across to your room. It's toilet paper-less, the showers are little more than a trickle, and there are no lockers, but you can't beat the price. Open July-Aug. Airy triples 1500Ft per person, students 900Ft.

Kiskút liget Camping (tel. 31 89 86), on Kiskút liget. Catch local bus #8 going toward the overpass in front of the train station; the stop is clearly marked. Year-round motel, as well as bungalows and a decent camping site. Open Apr.-Oct. 15. Tents 300Ft plus 300Ft per person. 2-person bungalows 2500Ft. Motel singles 2500F; doubles 3200Ft.

FOOD

The sprawling **Kaiser's supermarket** sits at the corner of Alany János u. and Aradi vértanúk. (Open M 7:30am-7pm, Tu-F 6:30am-7pm, Sa 6:30am-2pm.)

Sárkányluk (Dragon's Hole), Arany János u. 27 (tel. 31 71 16). Patrons love its meat dishes and family atmosphere. Open Tu-Sa 11am-9pm, Su 11am-3pm. MC/AmEx.

Matróz Restaurant, Dunakapu tér 3 (tel. 32 49 55). Off Jedlik Ányos facing the river. Fries up succulent fish dishes in a cozy atmosphere of old brick, fishnets, and dwarfish wooden chairs. Entrees 400-700Ft. Open daily 9am-10pm.

Paradiso, Kazinczy u. 20. The upstairs bistro offers standard Hungarian fare for a pittance. Don't venture downstairs unless you're in the market for something a little more racy. Entrees 250Ft. Open daily 9am-1am.

SIGHTS

Most sights in Győr lie within a small area near the center of town. With the McDonald's to your right, walk up Baross Gabor u. and make a left on Kazinczky u. to reach Bécsi Kapu tér, the site of the yellow, 18th-century **Carmelite church** (Karmelita-templom) and the remains of a **medieval castle** built to defend the town from the Turks. At Bécsi Kapu tér 5, a small branch of the **János Xanthus Museum** (Xantus János Múzeum) is built into the castle, housing an underground lapidarium filled with fragments of Roman ruins. (Open Apr.-Oct. Tu-Su 10am-6pm. 120Ft.) Just off the square at Kiraly u. 4 sits the house where Napoleon Bonaparte spent his only night in Hungary. Now called **Napoleon House** (Napólean Ház), it contains an upscale art gallery and music school. (Open Tu-Su 9am-5pm. 75Ft.)

Further up Baross Gabor u. on the left, the striking **Ark of the Covenant** (Frigylada szobov) statue, built by the king in 1731 with funds levied on his mercenaries to keep them impoverished and in line, marks the way to **Chapter Hill** (Káptalandomb). At the top, the **Episcopal Cathedral** (Székesegyház) has suffered constant additions since 1030. (Closed to the public M-Sa noon-2pm, Su 1-3pm.) Its exterior is now a hybrid of Romanesque, Gothic, and Neoclassical stylings. The Baroque splendor inside deserves more attention, with dozens of gilded cherubim swirling above magnificent frescoes. A priest fleeing Oliver Cromwell's regime in the 1650s brought the miraculous **Weeping Madonna of Győr** all the way from Ireland. On St. Patrick's Day 1697, legend has it that the image spontaneously wept blood and tears for three hours in compassion for persecuted Irish Catholics. On the opposite side of the cathedral, the Hédeváry chapel holds the **Herm of King St. Ladislas,** a medieval bust of one of Hungary's first saint-kings. For a larger dose of religious art, the **Ecclesiastical Treasury** (Egyházmegyei Kincstáv) hides in a small side alley leading off the square from the back right corner of the cathedral. It presents primarily 14th-century gold and silver religious accessories, but be sure to see the 15th- and 16th-century illuminated manuscripts as well. (Open Tu-Su 10am-4pm. 150Ft, students 75Ft. Labels in English.)

Coming from the river on Baross Gabor u., a left down Szabadsajtó u. brings you to Széchenyi tér, where you'll do well to visit the **Imre Patkó Collection** (Patkó Imre Gyűjtemény), Széchenyi tér 4. It is located in **Iron Log House** (Vastuskós ház), named for a stump into which traveling 17th-century craftsmen drove nails when they spent the night. The collection contains two fascinating floors of modern Hungarian art and an attic full of Asian and African works that Patkó amassed in his travels. (Open Tu-Su 10am-6pm. 120Ft, students 60Ft.) A short walk down Kenyér Köz from Széchenyi tér, the **Margit Kovács Museum** (Kovács Margit Gyűjtemény), Rózsa Ferenc u. 1, displays the artist's distinctive ceramic sculptures and tiles. (Open May-Oct. Tu-Su 10am-6pm; Nov.-Feb. 10am-5pm. 100Ft, students 80Ft.)

In summer, do as the locals do—splash in the water and enjoy the sun. Across the river from the center of town, thermal springs serve as the basis for a large **water park,** Cziráky tér and Tőltésszev u. 24, complete with swimming, saunas, massages, and water slides. The easiest way to there is to cross the main bridge from the city center at Jedlik Ányos, take a left get on the other side, and walk along the sidewalk until you come to another smaller footbridge on the left—cross this and the park is to the left. (Open M-F 6am-8pm, Sa-Su 7am-6pm. 400Ft, students 300Ft.) The **market** on the river changes into a **bazaar** on Wednesday, Friday, and Saturday mornings.

THE IRON ROOSTER CROWS AGAIN Against a random corridor wall in the János Xanthus Museum (see above) leans an unmarked iron rooster weathervane with a half-moon at its base. When Turks invaded and occupied Győr, they erected it on the town's highest tower and bragged that they would hold the town until the cock crowed and the half-moon changed phase. The Hungarians took the boast seriously and crowed like cocks under a full moon as they began the siege that eventually retook the city.

NIGHTLIFE

Győr has an active nightlife, with music spilling from every cellar bar onto streets full of teens in their Saturday-night best. Crowded at 5pm and still packed at midnight, the terrace of **Komédiás Biergarten,** in the courtyard at Czuczor Gergely u. 30 (tel. 31 70 80), inspires loud conversation and general merrymaking. (Amstel 200Ft. Open M-Sa. noon-midnight.) If you're wistful for a Guinness, head to **Dublin Gate Irish Pub,** Bécsikapu tér 8 (tel. 31 06 88), across from the yellow Carmelite Church. (Guinness 450Ft. Open daily noon-midnight.) A mean hangover is sure to follow a visit to **Trófea Borozó,** Bajcsy-Zsilinszky 16, with a selection of wines cheap enough to bring out the snob in anyone. (Open M-F 6am-10pm, Sa 7am-10pm. Cherry brandy 80Ft, *Unicuum* 130Ft.)

Győr frolics away June and July with **Győri Nyár,** a festival of daily concerts, drama, and the city's famous ballet. Buy tickets at the box office on Baross Gábor út or at the performance venue. Schedules are found at Tourinform and IBUSZ.

NEAR GYŐR: ARCHABBEY OF PANNONHALMA

Visible at a distance from Győr, the hilltop **Archabbey of Pannonhalma** (Pannonhalmi Főapátság) has seen ten centuries of destruction and rebuilding since it was established by the Benedictine order in 996. The working abbey now houses a 13th-century basilica, a staggering 360,000-volume library, a small art gallery, and one of the finest boys' schools in Hungary, all of which make it worth the short commute. Among the treasures to be found here are the oldest document bearing Hungarian words (see **Literature & Arts,** p. 265) and a charter from 1001 with St. Steven's peculiar John Hancock. Although the most recent renovation for the Pope's visit in 1996 left the abbey halls feeling more like a Hilton than a historical gem, Hungary's oldest graffiti is still visible in the wall: a soldier defending the hill against the Turks "was here" in 1578. For those with delusions of grandeur, Hungary's take on the sword-in-the-stone hides in the Gothic-Romanesque crypt beneath the Basilica; legend has it if you fit into St. Steven's wooden throne, you'll be the next king. You can hear **Gregorian chants** over the muzak every Sunday at the 10am mass. Classical music concerts also take place frequently in the acoustic halls of the abbey; inquire at **Pax Tourist** (tel. 96 57 01 91). To see the abbey, join an hourly tour group at the Pax Tourist office to the left of the entrance. English-speaking guides are available for the mandatory one-hour tour at 11am and 1pm in summer, but not the rest of the year. (Tel. (96) 37 01 91. Abbey open daily 8:30am-4pm. Hungarian tour with English text 400Ft, students 120Ft; English tour 650Ft, students 300Ft. AmEx/MC/Visa.)

GETTING THERE. Pannonhalma is an easy daytrip from **Győr** on the **bus** leaving from stand #11 (45min., 7 per day, 210Ft). Ask for Pannonhalma vár and look for the huge gates. Some of the buses only go as far as the town. The abbey is a 1km hike up from the town (about 15min.). Bring a snack—this is probably the only historical site you'll ever visit without a food stand nearby.

TATA

The quiet vacation town of Tata (TAW-TAW) stretches around lakes, canals, and a 14th-century castle, providing a restful training ground for the Hungarian Olympic team. If you'd rather go for the beach than the gold, the glassy lake is perfect for sunbathing, boating, and fishing. Visitors bask in the casual atmosphere and enjoy the views as the setting sun paints the local sky in shades of Esterházy yellow.

ORIENTATION & PRACTICAL INFORMATION. If you're traveling by train, make sure you don't get off at Tatabánya, one stop before Tata when coming from Budapest. From the station, exit on Gesztenye u., then take a left on Bacsó Béla u. About 10min. later, turn right on Somogyi Béla u., which ends at Országgyűlés tér. Bear left and you'll find yourself on Ady Endre u., Tata's main street. **Trains** from **Budapest's Keleti Station** (1½-2hr., 18 per day, 574Ft) pass through, but you can avoid the 1.5km hike into town by taking the **bus** from **Budapest's Árpád híd station** (1½hr., 2 per day, 594Ft). From the bus station, walk down the road toward the lake, and follow the shore as it curves to the left around the castle. Bear right onto Alkotmány u. when Bartok B. u. splits. A moment later, you'll be on Ady Endre u. **Tourinform** (tel. 38 48 06), Ady Endre 9, **exchanges cash,** offers a pocket-size **map** (170Ft), and helps with accommodations. (Open summer M-F 8am-4pm, Sa 8am-noon.) The **OTP Bank** on Ady Endre, to the left coming out of Tourinform, cashes **traveler's checks** for no commission. (Open M 7:45am-5pm, Tu-F 7:45am-4pm.) There is a Cirrus/Plus/MC/Visa **ATM** outside. The central **post office** lies off Országgyűlés tér opposite a church. (Open M-F 8am-6:30pm, Sa 8am-noon.) **Postal code:** 2890. **Phone code:** 34.

ACCOMMODATIONS & FOOD. Tata is a popular summer vacation destination for foreigners and Hungarians alike, so rooms fill quickly—call ahead. The **Hattyú Panzió,** Ady Endre u. 56 (tel. 38 36 53), supplies tidy, well-furnished doubles with shared bath (3500Ft). Several inexpensive options lie a bit farther out from the town center. **Patak Motel,** Fényes fasor 2890 Pf. 62 (tel. 38 28 53), offers clean, sunny doubles (3200Ft) and quads (5400Ft) with hall bathrooms. The lethargic reception may test your patience, but you can play hoops or ping-pong while you wait. Down the same road, **Fényes-Fürdö camping** (tel. 48 12 08; fax 38 14 91) rents four-person bungalows (4000Ft) and tents (1000Ft per person) in an extensive country-club with four swimming pools, tennis courts, and a laundromat. (Open May-Sept.) To reach both Patak and the campground, follow the *Bad-Camping* (an inadvertent combination of English and German)/*Fényes Fürdö* signs from the bus station. Coming from the town center, turn right down Ady Endre from the Spar, then turn left on the main road (út Május I) that leads off the far end of Országgyűlés tér. Then take a right onto Oroszlányi u. (across from the Profi Supermarket), which becomes Fényes fasor (20min.). If you're in a rush, take city bus #3 to "Fényes Fürdö" (departs every 30min. from the station). 10min. farther down Fényes fasor, *Zimmer frei* and *loras iskola* signs point left toward **Maestoso** (tel./fax 48 50 39). The fresh, bright pension in a peaceful field setting offers outstanding rooms with beautiful private bathrooms. (DM41. Breakfast included.) They also have a sauna (DM7), pool table, ping-pong, bike rentals, tanning salon and **horseback riding** (DM20 per hr.; 30min. lesson DM14).

At **Halaszcsárda,** Tópart u. 10 (tel. 38 01 36), one of many lakefront restaurants, fresh fish dishes can be enjoyed in the light of the setting sun over the lake. (Entrees 510-700Ft. Open Su-Th noon-10pm, F noon-midnight, Sa noon-1am.) A well-stocked **Supermarket Spar** sits across the street from Tourinform on Ady Endre. (Open M-F 6:30am-7pm, Sa 6:30am-2pm, Su 7am-noon.)

SIGHTS & ENTERTAINMENT. From the center, head down Alkotmány u. (the first left coming from Tourinform away from the SPAR) to the lake-shore and Tata's two main draws. Follow the lake to the right and you will quickly find yourself at the grassy, ruin-filled grounds of the **old castle** (Öregvár). Inside is Tata's main tourist attraction, **Kuny Domokos Múzeum,** covering two millennia of regional history. Breeze through the two lower floors and head for the third, which hides the wood, metal, and porcelain work of 18th-century master craftsmen. (Open Tu-Su 10am-6pm. 150Ft.) The real gem is the **Múzeum Presszó,** which has a glowing view of the lake from its rooftop terrace. The Baroque-style **Eszterházy mansion,** built in 1765 and now used as a hospital, sits a few meters farther down the shore. The family name came to be linked with the vibrant yellow color of the house's exterior. Today, "Eszterházy yellow" is a popular color for churches and monuments throughout the region. Nearby, a converted synagogue (the white building) across the street from the mansion houses a **Greek-Roman Statuary Museum** (Görög-Római Szobormásolatok Múzeum) and its collection of faux-ancient statues. They once lined the paths of **Angol Park,** Hungary's first English-style park, right off of Ady Endre u. Its wide paths, small waterfalls and public swimming pool maintain their elegance *sans* statuary. (Open Tu-Su 10am-6pm. 80Ft, students 50Ft.) On warm weekends, live bands play outside on the south shore of the lake. To the north, the DJ pumps dance mixes at **Lovas Disco,** just off Tanoda tér; follow the lights in the sky. (Cover 500Ft. Open F-Sa 10pm-2am.) Local youth party late at **Zsigmond borozó** (tel. 53 96 29), a hip bar located in underground caverns on the castle grounds. (Open daily 4pm-whenever the party ends.)

SOPRON

With soaring spires and winding cobblestone streets, the well-preserved historical monuments of Sopron's (SHO-pron) medieval quarter feel decidedly Austrian. Yet, as any local will remind you, Sopron is considered "Hungary's most loyal town." In 1920, the Swabians of Ödenburg (as Sopron was then called) voted to remain part of Hungary instead of joining their linguistic brethren in Austria, and boy did they feel stupid about it when the Soviets rolled into town. Fidelity notwithstanding, Sopron is deluged daily by Austrians drawn by low prices for medical care and sausage (especially sausage).

ORIENTATION

Belváros (Inner Town), the historic center, is a 1km-long horseshoe bounded by three main streets. **Ógabona tér** and **Várkerület** form an arc while **Széchenyi tér** connects the two longer roads near the train station. **Fő tér,** the site of many of the museums and notable buildings, sits within this region, at the end furthest from the train station. The **train station** is a 5min. walk from the city center on Mátyás Király út, which leads to Széchenyi tér, and becomes Várkerület, curving around the inner town. The **bus station** is also only 5min. from the center. Exit the station and make a right onto Lackner Kristóf út. A left at the Ciklámen Tourist office puts you on Várkerület near Fő tér.

PRACTICAL INFORMATION

Trains: To: **Budapest** (3-4hr., 7 per day, 1570Ft); **Győr** (1hr., 7 per day, 576Ft); and **Vienna** (1hr., 16 per day, 2410Ft).

Buses: To: **Budapest** (4hr., 5 per day, 1510Ft) and **Győr** (2hr., about 1 per hr., 654Ft).

Tourist Office: Tourinform, Előkapu u. 11 (tel. 33 88 92). Follow the trail of info signs to the shiny new office sitting right off of Várkerület u. Gives away free maps, advice, and accommodations info. Open M-F 9am-5pm, Sa 9am-noon.

Currency Exchange: To **exchange currency,** head to **Budapest Bank,** Színhaz u. 5, which also changes **traveler's checks** for no commission. Open M-Th 8am-5pm, F 8am-3pm. There is a Cirrus/Plus **ATM** outside Julius Meinl (see below), Várkerület 41.

Post Office: Széchenyi tér 7/10 (tel. 31 31 00). Just outside of Belváros. Open M-F 8am-8pm, Sa 8am-noon. **Postal code:** 9400. **Phone code:** 99.

ACCOMMODATIONS

Tourinform (see above) can get you settled into a comfy **private room** near the center. (Singles 1800Ft; doubles 2500Ft.) If you can speak German or Hungarian, **Ciklámen Tourist,** Ógabona tér 8 (tel. 31 20 40), on the way to city center from the bus station, can also set you up with a convenient private room. (Doubles 2500Ft, with bath 5000Ft. Open M-F 8am-4:30pm, Sa 8am-1pm.) If you're in the market, **Locomotiv Turist,** Várkerület 90 (tel. 31 11 11), locates the cheapest pension options. (Doubles from 4500Ft. TV, shower and fridge included. Open M-Sa 9am-5pm.)

Ringhofer Panzió, Balfi u. 52 (tel. 32 50 22; fax 32 60 81). From Széchenyi tér on Várkerület, take the second right onto Torna u. Go straight as the street becomes Bem u., then left onto Balfi u. Tourist tax 300Ft. Breakfast 350Ft. They also rent bicycles (1000Ft per day). Check-out 10am. Doubles with shower (3500Ft).

Talizmán Panzió, Táncsics u. 15 (tel. 31 16 20). Take a left on Ferenczi János u., past the bus station, then take a right onto Táncsics at the small green clock tower–it's on the left. Neat but somewhat scrunched doubles with beds so comfortable you'll forget the walls are closing in. Private TV and shower, but shared toilets. 3800Ft.

Lővér Campground (tel. 31 17 15), outside town on Köszegi u. Take bus #12 from the city center (one pick-up point is Erzsébet u. 2); the last stop is "Camping." Bus #12A also goes there–get off at its last stop on Köszegi u., follow the road curving left, and look for the fork with the "camping" sign, near the pastures. Open Apr. 15-Oct. 15. Threesome bungalows 2000-3800Ft; hut for two 2000Ft. Campsites 500Ft per tent; 750Ft per person.

FOOD

Of the many small grocery stores, the ubiquitous **Julius Meinl,** Várkerület 100-102, is among the best stocked. (Open M-F 6:30am-8pm, Sa 6:30am-3pm.)

Várkerület Restaurant, Várkerület 83 (tel. 31 92 86). Near Széchenyi tér, serves "house-proud dishes" in a great beer-garden surrounded by trees. Prompt service brings the meaty main courses (690-1250Ft) to warmly-lit tables in the dining room. Open daily 10am-midnight.

Pince Csárda, Széchenyi tér 4 (tel. 34 92 76). Upholds its good reputation with a tremendous array of chicken, venison, and veal dishes. Entrees 590-1850Ft. Open M-Th 10am-11pm, F-Sa 10am-midnight, Su 10am-4pm.

John Bull English Pub, Széchenyi tér 12 (tel. 31 68 39). A first-class emergency unit for all home-sick Brits, with one exception–the food is actually good here. Fantastic chicken, fish and veggie options with three types of genuine English beer on tap. Entrees 650-1450Ft. Guinness 700Ft. Open daily 10am-2am. MC/Visa.

SIGHTS

BENEDICTINE CHURCH. (Bencés Templom). Built in the 13th century by a happy herder whose goats stumbled upon a cache of gold, the Benedictine Church has been the site of the royal coronations for two queens and one king. Not bad for a place that has frolicking goats on the coat of arms above the main entrance. The small monastery *(kolostor)* next door also dates from the 13th century. Visitors can enter its Chapter Hall, a room full of textbook Gothic architecture enriched by taped Gregorian chants and ten sculptures of human sin. The nude, crouching, monkey-like figure represents avarice. *(On Fő tér. Open daily 10am-noon and 2-5pm.)*

OLD & NEW SYNAGOGUES. Two of the only medieval synagogues left standing after WWII, both are now museums dedicated to the daily life of the local Jewish community, expelled in 1526. **Old Synagogue** (Középkori Ó-Zsinagóga) was first built around 1300 and has been reconfigured to show the separate rooms for men and women, the stone Torah ark, the wooden *bima*, and the ritual bath well. *(Új u. 22. Open M and W-Su 9am-5pm. 100Ft, students 50Ft.)* **New Synagogue** (Új-Zsinagóga) is new only because it was built 50 years later. After centuries of neglect, its interior is now being restored—the exterior is visible through the courtyard at Szent György u. 12, on the opposite side of the block. *(Új u. 11. Open M 1-5pm, W-Th 9am-3:30pm, F 9am-noon.)*

FIRE TOWER. (Tűztorony). The main symbol of Sopron, the Fire Tower consists of a 17th-century spire atop a 16th-century tower on a 12th-century base straddling a Roman gate. Its clock is the source of the chimes heard throughout town. Squeeze up a spiral staircase to the balcony for a view of the surrounding hills. *(On Fő tér's north side. From the Tourinform office, walk away from Válkerület and through the nearby alley. The tower is past the parking lot. Open Tu-Su 10am-6pm. 120Ft, students 60Ft.)*

FABRICIUS HOUSE. The Gothic Fabricius House consists of three separate exhibits. The first and second floors hold a rather dry collection of antique furniture. The third-floor re-creations of life in 17th- and 18th-century Sopron are only slightly more riveting, with descriptions of how people made their beds when beds were made of straw. Tour guides thrust upon you a brief photocopied guide in your confessed *Sprache* as you enter each room. The best exhibit sits inside the vaulted cellar. Originally a Gothic chapel, and now the coolest place in town on a hot day, the high-vaulted ceiling of the **Roman Lapidarium** (Római Kőtár) houses stonework and monuments dating to Sopron's origins as the colony Scarbantia. *(Fő tér 6. Open Tu-Su 10am-6pm. 80Ft per exhibit, students 40Ft. Lapidarium 150Ft, students 80Ft.)*

STORNO HOUSE. (Storno-ház). Home to 19th-century Swiss-Italian restorers of monuments and cathedrals, Storno House's exterior restorations are unimpressive. However, its residents had impeccable taste in interior design, with furniture and artwork from the Renaissance to the 19th century. The guide says almost nothing—instead, she carries around a tape recorder with narration in Hungarian or German and points out each item as it's mentioned, like a flight attendant giving safety instructions. Unfortunately, most of the allure is lost on English speakers, who receive a flimsy fact sheet that can be read in two of the 40min. the tour takes. *(Fő tér 8. Open Tu-Su 10am-6pm. 80Ft, students 40Ft.)*

BAKERY MUSEUM. (Pékmúzeum). Illustrating the history of professional baking from the 15th to 20th centuries in the restored shop of a successful 19th-century baker, the Bakery Museum denies patrons the full sensory experience (there are no goodies for sale). *(Bésci út. 5. From Várkerület, enter onto Ikva-Dorfmeister u. near the small branch of the post office. Take the second left onto Jégverem Halász u. and follow it through Sas tér as it becomes Bésci út. Open Tu-Su 10am-2pm. 50, students 20Ft.)*

SOPRON MUSEUM. Housed in a dilapidated mansion, the Sopron Museum exhibits traditional Hungarian folk-crafts and costumes. The somewhat outdated English guide apologizes for not being the Liszt Museum, which resided here until 1989, and offers the current modest collection to disappointed tourists "by way of compensation." *(On the corner of Déak tér and Csatkai Endre u. From Várkerület, turn right onto Széchenyi tér, right again onto Erzsélet u., and take a final right onto Déak tér. Open Tu-Su 10am-6pm. 100Ft, students 50Ft.)*

ENTERTAINMENT

For information on cultural events in and around Sopron, visit Tourinform (see **Tourist Office,** above). Also, pick up a free copy of the monthly *Sopron Program,* which lists local events. Watch out for regular appearances by the Beatles, Hungary's popular take on the original mop-tops. During the **Sopron Festival Weeks** (June-July), the town hosts opera, ballet, and concerts. Some are set in the **Fertőrákos Quarry** caverns 10km away, reached by hourly buses from the bus terminal. (Quarry 30Ft for students. Concerts 500-600Ft.) Buy tickets for all events from the **Festival Bureau** on Széchenyi tér across from the post office. (Open M-F 9am-5pm, Sa 9am-noon; closed end of July and Aug.)

NIGHTLIFE

The Rockline and **The Dancing Bar,** in the parking lot at the intersection of Selmeci u. and Lacknev Kristóf u., one block up from the bus station moving away from the center. Sitting inside an amusement park, the lively scene borders on the carnival-esque. Sopron's youth get down to remixed Simon and Garfunkel favorites under flashing bulbs. M-Tu and F-Su cover 300Ft. Open daily 10pm-4am.

Cézár borozó, Hátsókapu 2 (tel. 31 13 37). Near Fö tér. The drink selection is so good, you'll never want to leave this 17th-century home. Open M-Sa 10am-9pm.

La Playa Cafe and Bar, Várkerlüct 22. So packed with Sopron youth that it's hard to appreciate the eclectic decor, complete with sombrero, sewing machine, and *Gone With the Wind* poster. Scarlett might have believed that "tomorrow is another day," but she wasn't dealing with a hangover brought on by Corona (350Ft) and Rolling Rock (125Ft). Open M, W-Th, and Su 6pm-1am, F-Sa 6pm-3am.

NEAR SOPRON: FERTŐD

27km east of Sopron, **Fertőd** (FER-tewd) is home to the magnificent Baroque **Eszterházy Palace,** Bartók Béla u. 2, nicknamed the "Hungarian Versailles." Miklós Eszterházy, known as **Miklós the Sumptuous** before he squandered his family's vast fortune, ordered the palace built in 1766 to host his extended bacchanal feasts, claiming boldly, "What the emperor can afford, I can afford as well." The mansion grounds, once home to an opera house, a Chinese pavilion, and a puppet theatre alone make a visit worthwhile. Although the interior is somewhat bare, the tour (1hr.) explains everything from the marble floors to the painted ceilings, including the cleverly concealed door in the prince's bedroom. Used as a stable and then a hospital during WWII, the mansion was restored with much-needed government funds directly after the 1957 revolution; the investment is now protected by the felt slippers visitors are required to don upon entrance. **Josef Haydn** spent 30 years composing here; **concerts** during the annual fall **Haydn Festival** recreate the premier performances of many of his most famous works. (Check at Tourinform in Sopron for a schedule.) The mansion hides behind an area of tall greenery, across from the parking lot with souvenir stands. (Tel. (99) 37 09 71. Open Apr. 16-Dec. 15 Tu-Su 9am-5pm; Dec. 16-Apr. 15 Tu-Su 9am-4pm. 600Ft, students 250Ft.)

GETTING THERE. Buses leave hourly for Fertőd from platform #11 in **Sopron's** station on Lackner Kristóf (45min., 265Ft). Buses continue on to **Győr** (2hr., 5 per day, 523Ft). There is a hotel inside the mansion; after a period of renovation, it should reopen in 2000. For reservations, particularly during the Haydn Festival in early fall, book with Ciklámen Tourist in Sopron.

SZOMBATHELY

Seat of Vas county and a major commercial crossroads between Transdanubia and Austria, Szombathely's (SOM-ba-tay; "Saturday's Place") sprawling streets wind haphazardly around 2000-year-old ruins and scattered baroque facades. The city has earned its name, filling each weekend with Austrian tourists looking for a taste of the Hungarian lifestyle—or at least good lager—out on the terrace of one of the city's many fine restaurants.

ORIENTATION

It takes only 20min. to walk the entire inner city of Szombathely. The town focuses around several squares, the largest of which is **Fő tér,** one of Hungary's largest squares and home of the main tourist offices. To get there from the **train station,** take **Széll Kálmán u.** to Mártírok tere. Turn left onto Király u., which ends in **Savaria tér,** a smaller square that opens onto the wide Fő tér. The **bus station** sits on the opposite side of the inner city; turn left on the street parallel to the station and follow it as it curves to the left. Cross Kiskar u. and then head straight to the narrow pedestrian Belsikátor, which ends in Fő tér.

PRACTICAL INFORMATION

Trains: Tel. 31 20 50. To: **Budapest** (3½hr., 7 per day, 1536Ft; *InterCity* 2¾hr., 4 per day, 1536Ft plus 310Ft reservation fee); **Győr** (2hr., 3 per day, 705Ft; *InterCity* 1¼hr., 4 per day, 705Ft plus 310Ft reservation fee); and **Keszthely** (2½hr., 3 per day, 820Ft). Tickets can be purchased at MÁV offices at the train station or at Király u. 8/A (tel. 31 23 79). Open M-F 8am-5pm, Sa 8am-noon.

Buses: Tel. 31 20 54. To: **Budapest** (3½hr., 3 per day, 2010Ft); **Győr** (2½hr., 5 per day, 862Ft); and **Keszthely** (2½hr., 4 per day, 702Ft).

Tourist Office: For English brochures and pamphlets go to **Városi Touristikai Iroda** (Town Tourist Office), Király u. 11 (tel. 34 18 10), off Fő tér. Open M-Th 8:30am-noon and 1-4:30pm, F 8:30am-1:30pm. For German info and maps (252Ft), Tourinform-licensed **Savaria Tourist** is a sure thing, with three central locations: Király u. 1 (tel. 32 58 31;

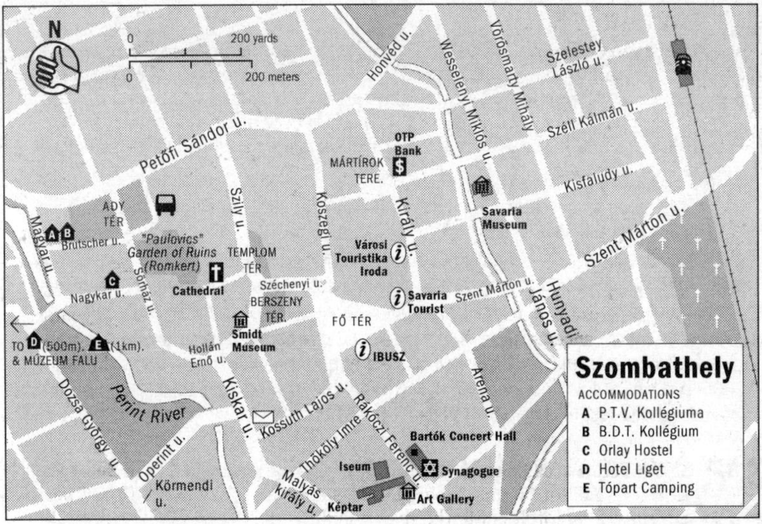

fax 32 58 30), Mártírok tere 1 (tel. 31 23 48), and Berzsenyi tér 2 (tel./fax 32 43 41). All three locations change currency and traveler's checks for no commission. Open M-F 8am-5pm, Sa 8am-noon.

Currency Exchange: OTP Bank, Király u. 10. Open M 7:45am-4pm, Tu-F 7:45am-3pm. Traveler's checks not accepted. A Cirrus/Plus/MC/Visa **ATM** stands just around the corner at Széll Kálmán u. 1.

Pharmacy: Fő tér 9 and 31 (tel. 31 25 83). Open M-F 7:30am-6:45pm, Sa 8am-1pm.

Medical Assistance: Doctor on call at Wesselényi Miklós u. 4 (tel. 31 11 00).

Post Office: Kossuth Lajos u. 18 (tel. 31 15 84). Open M-F 8am-8pm, Sa 8am-2pm. **Postal code:** 9700. **Phone code:** (0)94.

ACCOMMODATIONS

There aren't many private rooms available in Szombathely, and they're difficult to find on your own. **Savaria Tourist** offers centrally located doubles (3000-3800Ft) in the homes of elderly residents. **IBUSZ,** Fő tér 44 (tel. 31 41 41), also offers doubles (3640Ft) and a few singles (3120Ft), 15min. or less from the center. (Open June-Aug. M-F 8am-5pm, Sa 9am-noon; Sept.-May M-F 8am-4pm).

Orlay Hostel, Nagykar u. 1/3 (tel. 31 23 75), next to the bus station. Cross the street parallel to the station and walk left to the statue in the pedestrian area. Orlay is on the left across from the Xerox Center. Pristine rooms with linoleum floors and polyester comforters. More spacious than most, but the showers are curtain-less and shared. Open July-Aug. daily; Sept.-June Sa-Su only 3- to 8-person dorms 600Ft.

Puskás Tivadar Fém és Villamosipari Szakközépiskole Kollégiuma, Ady tér 2 (tel. 31 21 98), in the park opposite the bus lot. This hostel receives demerits for "excessive name length," "insufficient room size," and "not being open in the off season," but we love it anyway. Clean 1- to 4-bed rooms. Ask to speak to Dr. Öri Imréné (EW-ry EEM-ray-nay) to make a reservation. Open July-Aug. only. 850Ft per person.

Tópart Camping, Kenderesi u. 6 (tel. 31 47 66). Take bus #7 from the station to the lake terminal and walk 5min. to the other side of the lake. A picture-perfect campsite plagued by real-life mosquitoes. Open May-Sept. Tents 480Ft plus 360Ft per person. 2-person bungalows 2880Ft; 4-person bungalows with bath 4800Ft for 2 people, 7200Ft for 4. Tourist tax 120Ft.

FOOD

Szombathely offers a wide selection of restaurants, mostly along Fő tér's pedestrian walkway. **Julius Meinl** supermarkets sit at Fő tér 17 (open M-F 7am-10pm, Sa 7am-2pm) and also behind the bus station (open M 6am-6pm, Tu-F 6am-7pm, Su 6am-noon). They may not be the best stocked, but they accept MC and Visa.

Gődőr Étterem, Hollán Ernő 10/12 (tel. 31 06 87). Huge portions of Hungarian specialties from a menu so descriptive it makes your mouth water. Entrees 650-1890Ft. Open M-Th 11am-11pm, F-Sa 11am-midnight, Su 11am-3pm.

Saláta Bár, Belsikátir u. 3, off Fő tér. A dazzling array of cheap salads (90-260Ft). The make-your-own-meal-from-cabbage-cole-slaw-and-corn option leaves something to be desired, but the other food doesn't disappoint. Open M-F 8am-8pm, Sa 8am-6pm.

Belvárosi Vendéglo, Savaria tér 1 (tel. 31 49 67), near the end of Fő tér. This no-nonsense eatery has a quick staff, a well-stocked bar, and heaping plates of meat (650-2000Ft). Enjoy a smoke, a beer (0.5L Heineken 380Ft), and a steak (1890Ft) on the terrace with the rest of town. Open daily 8:30am-11pm.

SIGHTS & ENTERTAINMENT

Hungary's third-largest **cathedral,** was built in Baroque and Neoclassical styles in 1797. An Allied bombing raid in 1945 all but flattened the building; efforts at reconstruction have had little funding. To the right of the cathedral stands the entrance to **"Paulovics" Garden of Ruins** (Paulovics Romkert), Templom tér 1, the center of the city's original first-century AD Roman colony, with town walls, roads, a bathhouse, a partial palace, official buildings, and floor mosaics. From Fő tér, turn left onto Széchenyi u., then right onto Szily János u. and walk straight into Templom tér. (Tel. 31 33 69. Open Apr.-Nov. Tu-Sa 9am-5pm. 100Ft, students 60Ft.)

The spires of a late 19th-century Moorish-revival **synagogue** tower above the city. Its unchanged facade hides an interior that has been remodeled into a concert hall. A memorial outside remembers the 4228 Jews deported to Auschwitz from that spot during the Holocaust. Take Kossuth L. u. from the main square, keeping straight as it connects with Bejczy u. Make a right onto Thököly Imre u. and then a quick left onto Rákóczi Ferenc u. The synagogue sits one block away on the left. The **Art Gallery,** Rákóczi Ferenc u. 12, near the synagogue displays contemporary Hungarian art; the impressive collection is not done justice by the exhibition space, which feels somewhat like a hotel lobby. (Tel. 31 30 74. Open Tu-Su 10am-5pm. 100Ft, students 50Ft.) The **Smidt Museum,** Hollán Ernő u. 2, is a testament to Dr. Lajos Smidt's obsession with collecting just about anything he could get his hands on. Like a garage sale gone berserk, each case is packed with weapons, watches, coins, clothing, tableware, Roman artifacts, and ancient maps. Check out Franz Liszt's pocket watch and a beer mug inscribed with the largely unheeded warning *Bier ist Gift!* ("Beer is Poison!"). From Fő tér walk through the tiny Belsikátor u., to the main street, Hollán E. u. The museum is on the corner, right across the street. (Tel. 31 10 38. Open Tu-Su noon-5pm. 120Ft, students 80Ft.)

The **Savaria Museum,** Kisfaludy Sándor u. 9, unearths the roots of Vas county, including natural history dioramas and a Roman lapidarium in the basement. Watch your step in the first exhibit—the entire stretch of the floor has been modeled to reflect a topographical map of the region, complete with 2-inch graduations between altitude lines. Take Király u. left from Savaria tér, at the end of Fő tér, across from the McDonald's, then make the first right onto Kisfaludy Sándor. (Tel. 31 25 54. Open Tu-F 10am-5pm, Sa-Su 10am-4pm; Dec. to mid-Apr. closed Su. 120Ft, students 80Ft.) The **Village Museum** (Múzeum Falu), Árpád u. 30, on the outskirts of town consists of 150- to 200-year-old farmhouses transplanted from throughout the region. The rooms of each home are authentically furnished; the "owner's" clothes are even laid out. All maintenance is done using traditional techniques, although knowledge of them is rapidly dwindling; a century ago, a

LIVING IN THE PAST Before the Age of Enlightenment, when a sleepy Szombathely was only a glimmer in the eye of commercial traders, Kőszeg, a short distance to the north on the Austrian border, stood as the undisputed economic and political heart of the Őrség. Today, the small town still figures prominently in the Hungarian imagination (if no longer in its pocketbook), as the setting for a comic book tale of daring and do-right with a happy ending to match. Our fearless hero: Miklós Jurists, who made a stand in Kőszeg's castle against an onslaught of 100,000 Turks for nearly a month in 1532. In true save-the-world style, this story ends not in suicide or slaughter, but with a peaceful agreement—Miklós would raise the Ottoman flag and the Turks would retreat from the city. The cowed villains (in the Hungarian version, of course) kept their word, leaving the city at 11am on August 30th. Apocalypse had been averted, and the good people of nearby Vienna looked to Kőszeg as the home of their superhero savior.

The town today thrives on this tale of Hungarian chutzpah, with summer reenactments occurring daily at the castle (7 per day except M 10:30am-5pm), its main square littered with memorials to the epic event, and the town bells pealing at one hour before noon as a reminder of one man's stouthearted stand.

thatched roof could last 60 years, but nowadays no one can make them secure for more than 20. The English-speaking tour guide will explain everything, but is usually off on Saturdays. Take bus #7 from the train station to the lake terminus, then make a left onto Árpád út and walk along the lake shore until you reach the Museum parking lot a few minutes later. (Tel. 31 10 04. Open Apr.-Oct. 8 Tu-Su 10am-6pm. 120Ft, students 80Ft.)

On the west side of town, a series of **parks** is nestled around a romantic lake and island. Swimming is only allowed, however, in a huge **pool** across the street at Jazsai M. u. 2. (Open M-F 9am-8pm. 120Ft.) Around summer solstice, the parks host the **Szentivánéji Festivities,** with concerts by Hungarian bands, beer-drinking contests, and magic shows. A large abstract **monument,** dedicated to the **1945 liberation,** is set on Szombathely's highest hill.

NIGHTLIFE

On weekends and evenings, **Fő tér** is the hub of Szombathely's nightlife; impromptu concerts, planned summer performances, and ice cream stands all stay open late into the night. Enjoy a gooey pastry (100-240Ft) or ice cream concoction (300-470Ft) at **Claudia Cukrászda,** Savaria tér 1 (tel. 31 33 51; open daily 9am-10pm). **Ferences Söröző,** Aréna u. 1 (tel. 31 17 89), has a fine Hungarian menu (380-900Ft) and a wonderful location in the cellars of a former Franciscan monastery, but is best known for its great selection of lagers (0.5L Amstel draft 200Ft; open M-Sa 11am-11pm). Next to the synagogue, the **Szinfonia Café,** Rákóczi u. 3 (tel. 32 26 89), is a regular meeting place for musicians who perform in Bartok Hall. Red plush seats and a black-and-white bar give the impression that you're enjoying your coffee from the inside of a piano. (Open 2pm until guests leave.)

ŐRISZENTPETER

Rolling hills, cool forests, and beautiful countryscapes combine to make the Őrség a hiker's paradise, to which the centrally located Őriszentpeter (EW-ree-sent-PEH-ter) makes an excellent starting point. Foremost of the tiny Őrség villages, the town still regulates its busiest intersection with yield signs. For visitors here, the old bit about the journey being more important than the destination truly applies.

ORIENTATION & PRACTICAL INFORMATION. The quickest way to get to Őriszentpeter is to take the **train** to **Körmend** from **Szombathely** (45min., 14 per day, 146Ft), then follow the tracks to the left until you reach the bus station (6 buses per day to Őriszentpeter, 320Ft). **Buses** also arrive from **Szombathely** (2hr., 3 per day, 544Ft). No trains run to Őriszentpeter. The **bus station** in Őriszentpeter can be found at Kovács szer 1. There is no ticket office, just a **paper-products store** with a bus schedule in the window and indispensable **maps** (600Ft) of Őriszentpeter and the Őrség. (Open daily 7:15am-4:30pm.) Also consider buying a map in Szombathely before you arrive. The **pharmacy** is **Encián Gyógyszertá,** Városszer 26 (tel. 42 80 06; open M-F 7:30am-5pm, Sa 8am-noon). The **post office,** Városszer 106 (tel. 42 80 29), **exchanges money** for no commission. (Open M-F 8am-4pm.) The town's only **card telephone** awaits outside. **Postal code:** 9941. **Phone code:** 94.

ACCOMMODATIONS & FOOD. Once you arrive at the bus station, cross the bridge to the town center. Take a right and walk 10min. to reach a sign for **camping** up a short driveway to the left, just past the church. The reception is at **Savaria Tourist,** Városszer 57 (tel. 42 80 46 and 42 80 44); the same folks run the **Fogadó,** a local inn, and can also arrange **private rooms.** (Camping 500Ft per person; rooms from 2200Ft; 2-person bungalows with bath 2600Ft, extra bed 700Ft. Open mid-June-Sept. 24hr. reception.) They also rent sturdy **bikes** (500Ft per day). **Private rooms** are another alternative; keep an eye out for signs *(Szoba Kiádo* or *Zimmer frei).* They abound throughout the Őrség and usually come at a fairly modest price (1000-1500Ft).

The best food in town is at the **Bognár Étterem,** Kovács Szer 99 (tel. 94 42 80 27), 600m from the main intersection. Sit around a traditional clay stove and enjoy generous portions of Hungarian cooking in good company. (Entrees 450-900Ft. Open M-Sa 10am-11pm, Su 10am-4pm.) The **Centrum Étterem,** at the main intersection, dishes out huge main courses (600Ft) of local standbys. (Open M-F 6am-10pm, Sa-Su 7-10pm.) An **ABC Market** (open M-F 7am-noon and 1-5pm, Sa 7am-noon) and a few hard-nosed **bars** cluster around the main intersection to the right of the bus station. If you're ready for a slightly longer trek, purchase fresh homemade cheeses and yogurts at **Ferencz Porta,** Templom szer 11 (tel. 428 86 22). The young couple in charge would be happy to have you do some of their farm chores.

SIGHTS & ENTERTAINMENT. To begin, such a journey, enter the trail network just past Savaria Tourist, up an embankment to your left. Tiny **museums** freckle the Őrség, and more medieval **churches** stand here than anywhere in Hungary. Braver visitors might try knocking on nearby doors and asking for keys; this

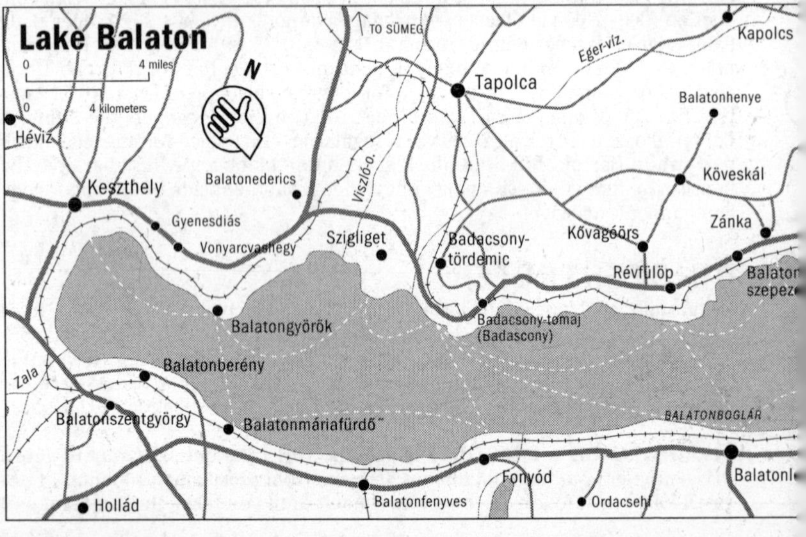

is also true for the many **artisans' studios** (marked *Fazekasház* for potters). **Bikers** have a number of appealing opportunities. The first is to start riding toward Savaria Tourist from the center; after 6km you will pass through the small village of **Szalafő.** Just before you reach the town, a sign to your left will point to a 13th-century **church.** Stop for a look, then continue past the town and over a bridge. Veer left, and at the top of the hill you'll find a now-empty **farm community,** preserved just as it was in the 19th century. Wander around the silent houses, built without chimneys to avoid the chimney taxes of the turn of the century, then peek in the windows to gain insight into what rural life was like in Hungary up to 1970. (Open Mar.-Nov. daily 10am-5pm. 100Ft, students 60Ft.) Farther past Szalafő lies **Fekete-tó,** with its huge peat bog, home to a number of rare, insectivorous plants. (Park open mid-May to mid-Oct. 7am-sunset; mid-Oct. to mid-May 7am-4pm.) Another route takes you down the road past the ABC as you leave town. About 12km south you'll encounter the villagers of **Magyarszombatfa,** who stoke backyard kilns to fire ceramic plates, bowls, and jugs built strong enough to slow-cook just about anything. On still another route, you can ride past the bus depot on your way out of town; this will lead you to **Batthyány Castle** in Körmend 26km to the north. (Open Tu-Su 10am-6pm.) Approximately 16km farther un Pankász (PUNK-ass), you'll find the 1256 **Romanesque Church.** Much closer to town, the famous 18th-century **wooden bell tower** stands at Dózsa György út 9/6.

LAKE BALATON

A Baywatch-inspired land of beaches, Lake Balaton has become one of the most coveted vacation spots in Central Europe. The waveless, freshwater lake is so warm and shallow that it feels more like a bath than the giant milky green body of water it is. Villas first sprouted along its shores under the Romans, and when a railroad linked the lake to its surrounding towns in the 1860s, the area became the summer playground of the Central European elite. More recently, it has grown into a favorite spot for German university students, who spend their infamous seven-day weekend with liquor flowing liberally on the waterfront. The commercialized south shore now sports such flashy resorts as Siófok and Balatonföldvár, while the north—with its elegant Festetics Palace, historic Tihany abbey, and welcoming vineyards—has cultural offerings that may surpass even its beaches.

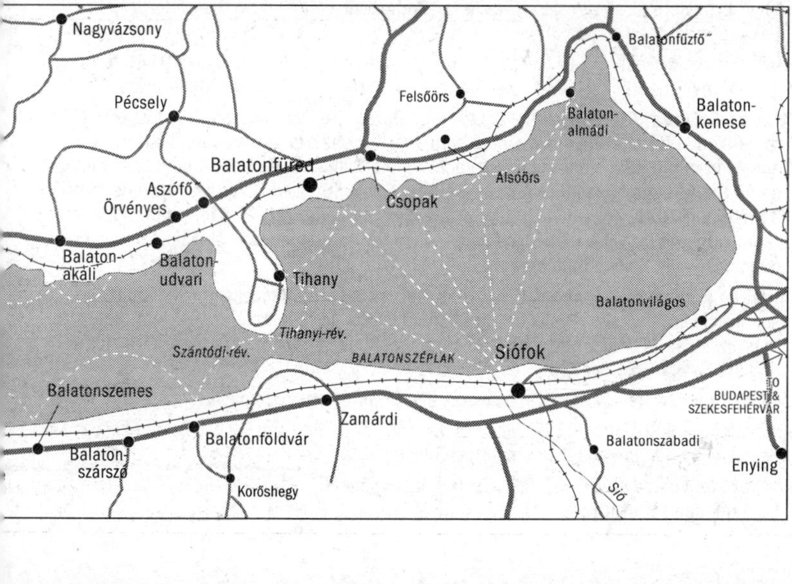

> Storms roll in over Lake Balaton in less than 15min., raising dangerous whitecaps on the otherwise placid lake. Amber lights on top of tall hotels and the Meteorological Research Center at Siófok's harbor give **weather warnings;** one revolution per two seconds means stay within 500m of shore; one revolution per second means swimmers must be within 100m and boats must be tied on shore.

SIÓFOK

The fact that more tourist offices per square kilometer congregate in Siófok than in any other Hungarian city says something about the number of surf-starved tourists who descend here annually. Siófok's street scene—filled with tacky t-shirt shops, pager-wielding teens, industrial strength discos, and low-riding convertibles with souped-up speakers—is the spitting image of a South Florida spring break, minus the palm trees. Siófok really has no sights to speak of (unless you count bronzed bodies) and the beach itself is not the Balaton's best bathing spot, but the lake provides ample excuse for bikinis, beer, and the high hedonism that rules Hungary's summer capital.

ORIENTATION

Siófok's proximity to Budapest and excellent transportation services make it an ideal base from which to explore the rest of the lake's offerings. The **train** and **bus stations** lie next to each other, roughly in the center of town. The main **Fő u.** runs parallel to the tracks, directly in front of the station, on the other side of an impeccably maintained lawn. A **canal** connecting the lake to the Danube divides the town. The **Arany-part** (Gold Coast) on the east side is home to the older, larger hotels, while the **Ezüst-part** (Silver Coast) on the west side hosts newer and slightly less expensive accommodations.

PRACTICAL INFORMATION

Trains: To **Budapest** (2½hr., hourly, 904Ft) and **Pécs** (3½hr., 3 per day, 1450Ft). Siófok also sits on the Budapest line to **Zagreb, Split, Ljubljana,** and **Venice,** as well as the Kaposvár line to **Prague.**

Buses: Express buses *(gyorsjárat)* leave for **Budapest** (2½hr., 6 per day, 1227Ft) and **Pécs** (3hr., 4 per day, 1303Ft).

Ferries: The quickest way to the north side of Balaton is by the hourly **MAHART ferry,** 10min. from the train station in the middle of the Strand. To **Tihany** (80min., 500Ft).

Tourist Offices: Tourinform, Fő u. 41 (tel. 31 53 55; fax 31 01 17; email tourinf@mail.datanet.hu; www.siofok.com), in the base of the wooden water tower across from the train station. English-speaking staff finds cheap accommodations and carries free **maps.** Open July-Aug. M-Sa 8am-8pm, Su 10am-12pm; Sept.-June M-F 9am-4pm. **IBUSZ,** Fő u. 61, 2nd floor (tel. 31 11 07; fax 31 14 81), a little farther down the street on the left. Exchanges money for no commission and books private rooms. Open M-F 8am-6pm, Sa 8am-3pm.

Currency Exchange: Postabank, Fő u. 176 (tel. 17 41 76). Exchanges currency for no commission and cashes AmEx traveler's checks for a 1% commission. A 24hr. Cirrus/Plus/MC/Visa **ATM** and **currency exchange machine** sit outside. Open M-F 8am-noon and 12:30-6pm, Sa 8am-1pm.

Police: Sió u. 14 (tel. 31 07 00). Well-acquainted with tourist complaints.

Pharmacy: Fő u. 202 (tel. 31 00 41). Stocks Western brands and such Balaton necessities as suntan lotion and condoms. Open M-F 9am-3:30pm.

Post Office: Fő u. 186 (tel. 31 02 10). **Telephones** stand outside. Open M-F 8am-7pm, Sa 8am-noon. **Postal code:** 8600. **Phone code:** 84.

ACCOMMODATIONS

Because of the preponderance of German tourists, prices in the Balaton are tied to the Deutschmark, making weekend trips relatively expensive for everyone else. Myriad agencies offer **private rooms,** although usually for a commission. **Tourinform** (see above) charges a 300Ft commission per night and will mediate in the negotiation of rates. Doubles in the center of town average 3000-5000Ft per person in July and August; prices drop slightly in the off season. **IBUSZ** (see above) offers doubles for 3000Ft in July and August, but without a reservation, you might end up paying more. There is a 30% surcharge for staying fewer than four nights. If you prefer to try your own luck, two residential streets close to the water—**Erkel Ferenc u.,** on the far side of the canal, and **Szent László u.,** to the left when leaving the train station—have rows of *Panzió* and *Zimmer frei* signs.

Tuja Panzió, Szent László u. 74 (tel. 31 49 96). Turn left as you leave the train station, and cross the tracks at your first opportunity. Hang an immediate right onto Ady Endie u., then turn left onto Tátra u. and right onto Szent László. The *panzió* will appear about 15min. later. Spacious doubles with a fridge for the pre-beach beer, a shower for the post-beach rinse, and satellite TV. 3000Ft per person; prices fall in the off-season.

Hunguest Hotel Azúr, Vitorlás u. 11 (tel. 31 20 33 or 31 22 59; fax 31 21 05), entrance on Erkel Ferenc u. With your back to the train station, go right onto Fő u. and right again onto Mártirok u. just before the Fő u. bridge. Take the first left onto Indóház u. and cross the bridge on the other side of the tracks. Follow the street as it curves right to become Vitorlás u., then go left on Erkel Ferenc u. After 5min. the huge hotel's guard booth will appear on the right. Immense and immensely popular. Extensive resort-style complex complete with barber shop, tennis courts, and weight room. Bright doubles with bathrooms 2400Ft. Reserve well in advance.

Aranypart Camping, Szent László u. 183/185 (tel. 35 25 19). 5km out of the town center. Take bus #2 15min. to the camping sign. The most affordable option, if you don't mind the commute to the beach. Open Apr.-Sept. No curfew, but bus service stops at 9:30pm; luckily, the lively crowd brings the party back to camp with them. Waterfront tent sites 700Ft per person; 2-bed bungalows with private patio 1200Ft. 120Ft tax.

FOOD

For beach provisions, a massive indoor fruit and vegetable **market** lies just across the canal off Fő u.; look for the **Vásárcsarnok** building. (Open M-F 7am-6pm, Sa 7am-1pm, Su 7am-noon.) Next to the market, buy your baked goods and beer at the **Julius Meinl grocery.** (Open M-F 6:30am-8pm, Sa-Su 6:30am-1pm.)

Csárdás, Fő u. 105 (tel. 31 06 42). Whips up traditional Hungarian dishes to the tune of live folk music. Ask for a table on the warmly-lit terrace to avoid immortalization in the "Family Trip to the Balaton" footage of the camcorder-wielding clientele. Entrees 850-1200Ft. Open daily 11am-11pm. Visa/MC/AmEx.

Restaurant-Café Kálmán, Kálmán Imre sétány 1. In the shopping shantytown next to the train station. The usual fried fare in an unusually classy setting. Entrees 800-1200Ft. Live music nightly 6pm. Open daily 10am-10pm.

Kristály Étterem, Petőfi sétány 1. Smack in the middle of the strand. Caters to the German hordes with their native favorites. Slightly less expensive than most. Entrees 400-1200Ft. Open daily noon-11pm.

SIGHTS & ENTERTAINMENT

Most attractions in Siófok pale in comparison with the **Strand,** which is a series of park-like lawns running to an extremely un-sandy concrete shoreline. There are public and private sections, with private spots charging around 150Ft per person, depending on the location and whim of the owner. The most popular section is the town park, but swimming isn't allowed. The largest private part lies just to the right as you face the water. (Open M-F 8am-7pm. 150Ft.) Most sections rent an assortment of wacky water vehicles (100-200Ft per hr.); pedal-powered contraptions—along with the usual bikes and mopeds—are available all along the Strand. (Bikes 500-600Ft per hr.; mopeds 800-900Ft per hr.)

For a taste of culture beyond the *Elvis Goes to Hawaii* variety, check out one of the German **operettas** performed nightly in the **Kultúrcentrum,** Fő tér 2, near the water tower (get tickets at Tourinform). In the first week of July, the town hosts an annual, four-day **International Folk Dance Festival.** Visit the **Kálmán Imre Múzeum,** Kálmán Imre sétany, next to the train station, for info on festival schedules and tickets as well as some delightful exhibits of the hometown boy's "picture-book" illustrations. (Open Tu-Su 9am-5pm. 100Ft.) Slightly more sober, the church at Fő u. 57 holds biweekly evening organ concerts. (500Ft, students 400Ft.)

NIGHTLIFE

Nightclubs of varying degrees of seediness line the lakefront. Many feature nude or semi-nude dancers; the ones with romance novel murals and sexy silhouettes may be more skin that you would like to see. Amphibious lounge lizards frolic to ABBA and the Bee Gees aboard MAHART **disco boats.** Music ranges from disc jockeys to live pop. (Cover 800Ft. Departs July 9-Aug. 21 nightly 7-9:30pm.)

Flört Disco, Sió u. 4. If you don't spot the yellow convertible throwing flyers, just follow the spotlights scoping the sky to this two-story Balaton institution. The top level is techno, the bottom is good old 80s standbys with plenty of bass and bikinis in between. Cover 600Ft. Open daily 9pm-5am.

Kajman Pub Disco, Fő u. 212. Swears it doesn't play techno, but still busts out the smoke machine and strobe lights for those special Cher disco mixes. Cover 500Ft. Open daily 10pm-4am.

Sörbár, Kálmán Imre étany. Just before the pedestrian overpass. A taste of home—if you're German. Boisterous beer garden with free-flowing *Zipfer* (300Ft) and *Weiselburger* (250Ft). Open daily 4pm-midnight.

NEAR SIÓFOK: SZÉKESFEHÉRVÁR

Known as the place where Árpád—the nation's Magyar forefather—first set up camp, Székesfehérvár is technically Hungary's oldest town. Today, Balaton-bound Budapesters treat themselves to a friendly, unpretentious city filled with historical significance, even if much of that history is still being excavated. The whimsical **Bory Castle** (Bory-vár), at Bory tér on the city's outskirts, could be the setting for the ultimate game of hide-and-seek. Over the course of 40 summers, architect and sculptor Jenő Bory built this iron, concrete, and brick mansion by hand as a memorial to his wife. The towers, gardens, crooked paths, winding staircases, and stone chambers are all crowded with works of art begging to be explored. Take bus #32 from the train station to the intersection of Kassai u. and Vágújhelyi u. (next to the white storefront with turquoise trim; tickets 100Ft on the bus, 70Ft at the terminal). From here, backtrack along Kassai u. and turn right on Mária Völgyi u. to Bory tér. (Open M-F 9am-5pm, Sa-Su 10am-noon and 3-5pm. 120Ft, students 60Ft.) In the center of town, the **King St. Stephen Museum** (Szent István Király Múzeum), Fő u. 6 (tel. 31 55 83), houses a permanent exhibition of archaeology, including a fantastic collection of Roman artifacts that are more than just bits and pieces. (Open Tu-F 10am-4pm, Sa-Su 1-5pm. 100Ft, students 50Ft.) The **Budenz House: Ybl Collection** (Budenz-ház: Ybl Gyűjtemény), Arany János u. 12, off Városház tér, (tel. 31 30 27), is home to the collection of the Ybl family, including exquisite 18th- to 20th-century Hungarian art and furniture. (Open Tu-Su 10am-4pm. 100Ft, students 50Ft.)

GETTING THERE. Trains chug along the lakeshore to **Siófok** (1hr., 18 per day, 353Ft), while **buses** pass through wide fields of corn (1hr., 6 per day, 304Ft). Trains run more frequently than buses, but the bus terminal is less than 5min. from the center. From the **bus station** (tel. 31 10 57), on Piac tér, walk away from the McDonald's onto Liszt Ferenc u., which leads directly to Városház tér. From the **train station** (tel. 31 22 93), on Béke tér, follow the "Centrum" sign in front of the station to Deák Ferenc u., the street that runs perpendicular to the tracks. After 15min., turn left onto the main Budai út, then right at the intersection with Varkörút. The inner city's gates will appear on your left after 5min.; follow Koronázo tér straight from the gates to central Városház tér. Or, pick up local bus #13, 34, or 35 from the train station and get off at the "Mozi" cinema stop on Varkörút (tickets from the train station paper shop 70Ft, from the driver 100Ft). Walk a few meters up Varkörút in the direction the bus was going, and enter through the city gates on your left.

NEAR SIÓFOK: BALATONFÖLDVÁR

A popular spot from the outset, Celts and then Romans settled the area of Balatonföldvár (BA-la-ton-FEWLD-var) long before the Magyars had even bought a copy of *Let's Invade: Eastern Europe.* At the turn of the century, the powerful Széchenyi family capitalized on its natural beauty and transformed the town into the lake-side resort of their dreams. With a large bank account and good taste to boot, the Széchenyis built an award-winning network of parks and promenades. The town has also been named "the most flowery city in Hungary;" a stroll through **Nagy Park,** across from the train station, quickly reveals why. The second weekend in June brings the **Földvárer Festival,** with folk music, amateur sport competitions, and an arts and crafts fair. The 1200m-long promenade along the lake borders a vintage Balaton-style **Strand.** Like any good Balaton town, Balatonföldvár sports its own floating disco, **Disco-ship M.S. Gulács,** departing from the main quay behind the train station for 2hr. of boat-rocking beats. (Cover 1000Ft, under 18 800Ft. Open Tu-W and F-Su 9pm.)

GETTING THERE. Széchenyi út, the main tourist artery, leads from the Strand up to Budapesti út, the town's residential center. **Trains** zig to neighboring **Siófok** (30min., hourly, 112Ft). With your back to the train station, walk right a few meters to Széchenyi út. **Buses** zag to **Siófok** (30min., hourly, 170Ft) from the bus stop on the main Budapesti út, next to the Julius Meinl supermarket. The **Siotour office,** in the pagoda at Széchenyi út 9/11 (tel. 34 00 99), offers free **maps** and helps with accommodations. (Doubles near the water 3000Ft per person. Open M-F 9am-6pm, Sa 9am-noon.) To get there from the bus stop, walk with the lake to your left a few meters, then take a left onto Széchenyi út toward the lake. **Phone code:** 84.

NEAR SIÓFOK: TIHANY

With its green hikes, luxurious homes, and extensive panoramas, the Tihany (TEE-hain) peninsula is known as the pearl of Balaton. Although every bit as touristy as the rest of the lake, Tihany retains a historical charm slightly more grown-up than its teeny-bopper beach-town brethren. The attraction that draws over a million visitors a year is the magnificent **Benedictine Abbey** (Bencés Apátság). Luminous frescoes and intricate Baroque altars make the interior distinctly photogenic; with so many blinding flashes going off at once, you might need to take a picture to see it properly. (Open daily 9am-5:30pm. 180Ft, students 90Ft.) Below the church, the 1060 **András I crypt** (I. András kriptája) contains the remains of King Andrew, one of Hungary's earliest kings and founder of the abbey. Next door, an 18th-century monastery has been reincarnated as the **Tihany Museum,** with contemporary psychedelic dreamscapes and large Roman artifacts displayed in a subterranean lapidarium. (Open Mar.-Oct. Tu-Su 10am-6pm. Included in church admission.) Follow the "Strand" signs along the Promenade behind the church to descend to the **beach** (open daily 7am-7pm; 200Ft), or continue a little longer along the panoramic walkway to **Echo Hill.** Named for its once "supercalifragilisticexpialidocious" echo, it is now just "super," due to landscape changes. Better yet, **hike** across the Peninsula on one of the many well-marked trails. It only takes an hour or two along the paths and dirt roads that pass through hills, forests, farms, and marshes. If you're lucky you'll never see another person, save for the occasional vineyard tender.

GETTING THERE. MAHART **ferries** are the fastest way to reach Tihany from **Siófok** (80min., hourly, 500Ft); overland transport can take up to 5hr. To reach the town from the ferry pier and neighboring Strand, walk toward the elevated road. Pass underneath and follow the "Apátság" signs up the steep hill to the abbey. Tihany's main drag, Kossuth Lajos u., sits just beyond the church at the top of the hill. Check out the **map** by the church before you leave, or pick one up at any of the tourist stands lining the Promenade (200Ft). **Postal code:** 8237. **Telephone code:** 87.

KESZTHELY

Sitting at the lake's west tip, Keszthely (KESS-tay) was once the toy-town of the powerful Festetics family, who left a legacy of 18th-century architecture, grand parks, and, most importantly, a magnificent Baroque mansion. In the midst of all this class, the main promenade hosts an eclectic mix of pricey restaurants, small street cafes, and rogue tattoo parlors typical of a Balaton resort. Unlike the rest of the lake, however, this town does not depend solely on the summer tide of tourism; a large student population is ready to pick up the slack after the tanned masses go home, and the nearby thermal spring attracts Austrians in any weather.

ORIENTATION & PRACTICAL INFORMATION. **Express trains** *(expressz)* run between Keszthely and **Budapest** (3hr., 5 per day, 1080Ft); **slow trains** *(személyvonat)* make the trip to **Szombathely** (2hr., 2 per day, 854Ft). **Buses** beat trains for local travel to **Balatonfüred** (2hr., 8 per day, 502Ft) and **Pécs** (3hr., 5 per day, 620Ft). Some buses leave from the terminal, while others use stops in the town center at either Fő tér or Georgikan u. Each departure is marked with an "F" or a "G" to indicate which stop it uses; check the schedules. The **train station** is adjacent to the **bus terminal** about 250m from the water and the MAHART **ferry pier.** In summer, **boats** run to and from **Badacsony** (2hr., 3 per day, 950Ft). The main **Kossuth Lajos u.** runs parallel to the shore, from **Festetics Palace** (Festetics Kastély) through the center at **Fő tér.** To reach the main square from the train station, walk straight up **Mártirok u.,** which ends in Kossuth Lajos u. Turn right; after 5min. you'll arrive in Fő tér. If you're coming from the ferry pier, walk toward the shore, and just after crossing the railroad tracks turn left on **Kazinczy u.** This leads directly to the train and bus stations. One of the best **Tourinform** offices on the Balaton, Kossuth Lajos u. 28 (tel./fax 31 41 44), sits on the palace side of Fő tér, with plenty of **maps** (240Ft) and info. (Open July-Aug. M-F 9am-6pm, Sa-Su 9am-1pm; Sept. and Apr.-June M-F 9am-5pm, Sa 9am-1pm; Oct.-Mar. M-F 8am-4pm, Sa 9am-1pm.) **IBUSZ,** Fő tér 6/8 (tel. 31 43 20), exchanges currency and books private rooms in town. (Open June-Aug. M-Sa 8am-6pm; Sept.-May M-F 8am-4pm.) **OTP Bank,** at the corner of Kossuth Lajos u. and Helikon u., **exchanges currency** and traveler's checks, both for no commission. (Open M-Tu and Th-F 7:45am-4pm, W 7:45am-5pm.) There is a **24hr. ATM** outside. You will pass the **post office,** Kossuth Lajos u. 48 (tel. 51 59 60), and the **card telephones** outside, on your way into town. (Open M-F 8am-6pm, Sa 8am-noon.) **Postal code:** 8361. **Phone code:** 83.

ACCOMMODATIONS. **IBUSZ** (see above) books central, private doubles with shower (3000Ft) and flats with kitchen (5000Ft) for longer stays (Visa/MC). **Zalatour,** Kossuth Lajos u. 1 (tel. 31 25 60; fax 31 43 01), also rents rooms, complete with bath and breakfast. (Singles 2700Ft; doubles 3000Ft. Open June-Aug. M-F 8am-6pm, Sa 8am-1pm; Sept.-May M-F 8am-4pm, Sa 8am-1pm.) If you'd like to avoid finder's fees, homes with *Zimmer frei* signs are plentiful, especially near the Strand, off Fő tér on Erzsébet Királyné u., and near Castrum Camping (see below) on Ady Endre u. Go up Kossuth Lajos and take a right on Szalasztó u. immediately before the palace entrance; Ady Endre will be on the right a few streets down. **Castrum Camping,** Móra Ferene u. 48 (tel. 31 21 20), has tent sites with all the amenities, including tennis, beach access, a restaurant, and nightly activities. (July-Aug. tents 620Ft, plus 990Ft per person. Sept.-June tents 480Ft, plus 690Ft per person. Tax 240Ft.)

FOOD. The fruit-and-flower **market** on Piac tér has been sitting on the same site since medieval times. At the center of the market's chaos, **Jééé supermarket** provides the essentials from the remaining three food groups. (Open M-F 6:30am-8pm, Sa 6:30am-6pm, Su 6:30am-1pm. Visa/MC.) Most of the restaurants around Fő tér are obscenely overpriced, but more reasonable options can be found farther from the center. The **Oázis-Reform Restaurant,** Rákóczi tér 3 (tel. 31 10 23), is not a mirage, although some vegetarians may think they're dreaming when they see the huge buffet of fresh, homemade dishes with no fried cheese or meat in sight. (150Ft per 100g. Open daily 11am-8pm.) **Corso Restaurant,** Erzsébet Királyné u. 23, nearer to the Strand in the Abbázia Club Hotel, draws on the rich fish stocks of Lake Balaton for its culinary delights. (Entrees 600-1500Ft. Open M-Sa 11am-10pm). **Donatello,** Balaton u. 1b (tel. 31 59 89), serves pizza and pasta in a lovely fish-pond courtyard. Somehow, it manages to retain its class despite the Teenage Mutant Ninja Turtle sign out front. (Entrees 330-870Ft. Open daily noon-11pm.)

SIGHTS. Keszthely's pride is the **Helikon Palace Museum** (Helikon Kastélymúzeum) in the **Festetics Palace** (Kastély). Built by one of the most powerful Austro-Hungarian families of the period, the storybook palace does Baroque architecture proud. Of the 360 rooms, tourists may visit only the central wing, but its mirrored halls, parquet floors, and extravagantly furnished chambers are enough to captivate. The somewhat-outrageous price is actually worthwhile, as it includes admission to the 90,000-volume, wood-paneled Helikon Library, an exotic arms collection that spans 1000 years, and an exhibit of the Festetics elaborate porcelain pieces. The well-kept **English park** around the museum provides a vast strolling ground with plenty of photo-worthy vistas. Popular chamber music **concerts** are frequently held in the mirrored ballroom; inquire at Tourinform (see above) for tickets. Follow Kossuth Lajos u. from Fő tér toward the Tourinform office until it becomes Keszthély u. You can't miss the palace—it's the only one on the block. (Open Tu-Su 9am-6pm; ticket office closes at 5:30pm. 1000Ft, students 600Ft. English or German tour 2000Ft.)

During the day, families throng to the **Strand,** on the coast to the right as you exit the train station. From the center, walk down Erzsébet u. as it curves right into Vörösmarty u. Go through the park on the left after the train tracks to reach the beach beyond. With rocks instead of sand and swamp instead of waves, it's a wonder that it's still so popular. (200Ft, children 100Ft.) Around the dock to the left of the main beach entrance glides a healthy population of **swans,** with benches on the shore for relaxing. If you have a moment, peek into the **Church of Our Lady** on Fő tér; its pastel green tower, built in 1896, conceals the main part of the structure, dating from 1386, which remains one of the most important standing works of Gothic architecture in Hungary. There are no Baroque frescoes here, but some beautiful stained glass and 14th-century wall paintings adorn the dark sanctuary.

NEAR KESZTHELY: HÉVÍZ

6km out of the city, Hévíz is home to the world's largest **thermal lake,** covered in gigantic lilies most of the year. The slightly-radioactive water is professed to have miraculous effects on locomotive disorders, supposedly once curing the beautiful, crippled daughter of the lord of Tátika Castle. At a calm-inducing 26-33°C (77-91°F), you too can live happily ever after, soaking in the hot springs all year-round. The 11-acre lake is surprisingly large, but the spring filling it pumps so fast that the water is entirely replaced every 28hr. To take advantage of this amazing spot, head out to the turn-of-the-century **bathhouse.** It sits on stilts above the center of the lake; the entrance is at Dr. Schüller Vilmos sétány 1 (tel. 34 04 55), across from the bus station. (Open daily 8:30am-5pm. 600Ft for 3hr.)

GETTING THERE. Buses leave hourly from **Keszthely's Fő ter** (30min., 120Ft) to transport you (and a busload of geriatric Germans) to Hungary's hottest hot tub.

NEAR KESZTHELY: SÜMEG

Only a short distance from the Balaton shore, Sümeg feels a world away. Its quiet streets are lined with Baroque architecture, and its ancient, besieged castle recalls a history beyond the memory of most Balaton resorts. Sümeg's **castle** (*vár;* tel. 35 27 37) is among Hungary's largest and best-preserved battlements, strategically perched atop a limestone outcrop 270m above the town. Built in the 13th century as a last defense against the invading Mongols, the castle stood up to the test of the Turks, standing until the Habsburg army, in the name of civilization, burned it in 1713. The stony walls were diligently restored in the 1960s, and the atmosphere inside is accordingly trippy, with magic shows, pony rides, archery ranges, and costumed characters performing to mandolin music. (Open daily 8am-8pm. 1000Ft, students and children 500Ft.) The **museum** inside exhibits medieval armor and the requisite torture chamber, full of pointy metal objects that could be rendered red-hot when necessary. (200Ft, students and children 100Ft.) Parents let the kids run free while they sample a glass of Badascony wine (0.2L 150Ft) from the small cellar. To get to the castle from the town center, walk up Vak Bottyán u. from the main Kossuth Lajos u., bear right at Szent Istvan tér and continue up the steep, cobblestone street. The castle's festivities may be the headliner in Sümeg, but it's the unprepossessing **Church of the Ascension** that quietly steals the spotlight. The mundane exterior conceals a frescoed marvel known to locals as the Hungarian Sistine Chapel; the comparison is slightly hyperbolic, but one can't help but be impressed by Franz Anton Maulbertsch's 1757 Rococo masterpiece. It seems that Maulbertsch knew how magnificent his work was: he's the one mugging for you in the first fresco to the right as you enter the church (the round cheese in his hand is supposedly a symbol of humility). The church sits about 200m from the center, at the corner of Deák Ferenc u. and Széchenyi György u.; follow Deák Ferenc downhill from the intersection across from the OTP bank on Kossuth Lajos u.

GETTING THERE. The best way to reach Sümeg is by **bus** from **Keszthely** (1hr., hourly, 159Ft). From the station at Flórián tér, cross Petőfi Sandor u. to Kossuth Lajos u., the town's central street. **Tourinform,** Kossuth Lajos u. 13 (tel. 35 24 81), on the main drag, will give you a map and help you find an affordable private room, but ask for a *Zimmer frei*—they only speak German. (Doubles 1500Ft, with bath 2000Ft. Open June-Aug. M-F 9am-5pm, Sa 9am-1pm; Sept.-May M-F 8am-4pm.) **Postal code:** 8330. **Phone code:** 87.

NEAR KESZTHELY: BADASCONY

Nestled at the base of a basalt outcrop jutting over the northern shore of the lake, the Badascony (BAD-uh-chone) region offers open wine cellars, relaxing hikes, and a welcoming beach-side marketplace. Technically, four resort towns lie at the foot of Balaton Hill (Badasconyhégy), but **Badascony-tomaj** is by far the most popular, and hence the one Hungarians refer to as Badascony. The town's main draw is the small community of **wine cellars** clustered on the southern face of the hill, where you can sample a vintage or purchase it by the 5L plastic jug (500Ft and up). The 3km walk up to the vineyards is not exactly pleasant on a blazing Balaton day; cheat a little instead and pick up one of the jeeps parked in front of the post office for a rough-and-tumble ride up the rocky slope. (500Ft per person, 800Ft round-trip; jeeps leave whenever four customers arrive.) Get off at the **Kisfaludy Ház** restaurant and sip on the region's finest wines (0.1L 100Ft; open daily 10am-11pm). Otherwise, wander back down the road and turn left onto the cobblestone Hegyalija u. for the less-pricey smaller cellars. One of the best is the **Bormúzeum Pince** (Wine Cellar Museum), Hegyaljau 6 (tel. 43 12 62); despite the name, its only dates you'll remember are from its fine vintages. (0.1L 60Ft. Open daily 10am-10pm.)

If you can still walk straight after a round of "samples," head farther uphill—about 100m past the spring next to Kisfaludy Ház—to try one of the Badascony's shady **hikes.** Fill up before you embark, as the soda stands (if not the crowds) end here. A short trek on the red trail leads to **Rose Rock** (Rózsakő), where legend has it that a couple who sit with their backs to the water will be married within a year. Local lore also has it that the Rock's daunting prophecy is the source of more break-ups than hook-ups, so proceed with caution. An hour's hike farther up rocky stairs will bring you to **Kisfaludy Tower** (Kisfaludy kiláto), where a predictably breathtaking vista rewards the journey. For those willing to make a day of it—or simply desperate to escape the tourist ranks—a **stone gate** *(kőkapu)* awaits still farther down the trail, a dramatic cliffside basalt formation resembling the gate to an airy underworld. Badascony's **beach** is rather small and swampy (open daily 8am-9pm; 200Ft, children 100Ft), but the carnival-esque **marketplace** around it captures the essence of a Balaton Strand, with blaring Ricky Martin, low-rent bikini stalls, and cheap *palascinta*.

GETTING THERE. Buses pass through town from **Keszthely** (1hr., 3 per day, 159Ft). If the wine makes a return to Keszthely impossible, **IBUSZ** (tel. 43 10 97) in the Il Capitano shopping center, just to the right of the pier heading away from the water, offers private rooms accessible by bus in the nearby Badascony town. (Doubles with shower 4000Ft. Open M-F 9am-6:30pm, Sa 9am-5pm, Su 9am-1pm.) **Postal code:** 8261. **Phone code:** 87.

SOUTHERN TRANSDANUBIA

Framed by the Danube to the west, the Dráva to the south, and Lake Balaton to the north, Southern Transdanubia is known for its rolling hills, sunflower fields, and mild climate. Once the southernmost portion of the Roman province of Pannonia, the region later suffered through the Turkish occupation, which ended in 1566 with the bloody battle of Szigetvár. This halted the Ottoman push toward Vienna; the Austro-Hungarian Empire rewarded its people with fine churches and elegant Baroque architecture, creating a charming cultural edge that remains today.

PÉCS

Nestled at the southern foot of the Mecsek mountains, Pécs's (PAY-ts) warm climate, incomparable views, and captivating architecture slow the pace of any walk through the city. With a 2000-year history, Pécs's monuments reveal a rich legacy of Roman, Ottoman, and Habsburg influence, and the city's many fine collections of modern art pick up where the sights leave off. This, along with a happening nightlife fueled by nearby colleges, make the city one of Hungary's most worthwhile weekend excursions.

ORIENTATION

Pécs rests on the knees of the Mecsek mountain range; conveniently, north and south correspond to up and down the hillside. Tourists bustle through the historic **belváros** (inner city), a rectangle bounded by the remnants of the city wall. The middle of the inner city is **Széchenyi tér,** where **Jokai u., Király u., Hunyadi Janos u., Ferencesek u.,** and **Janus Pannonius u.** converge, and where most tourist offices are located. Belváros is small enough for pack-toters to traverse on foot; it takes less than 20min. to cross it going downhill.

PRACTICAL INFORMATION

Trains: The station is just beyond the bottom of the city's historic district. 10min. by bus #30, 32, or 33 from the center of town. Or, with your back to the tracks, follow Jókai u. uphill as it becomes Széchenyi tér (20min.). Regular trains chug from **Budapest-Déli** station (3½hr., 3 per day, 1560Ft), as do *InterCity* trains (2½hr., 5 per day, 1920Ft, 300Ft reservation fee). Four trains per day leave for various towns around Lake Balaton. Purchase all tickets at the **MÁV travel office** in the station (tel. 31 24 43), or at Rákóczi út 39c (tel. 21 27 34; open M-F 9am-6pm).

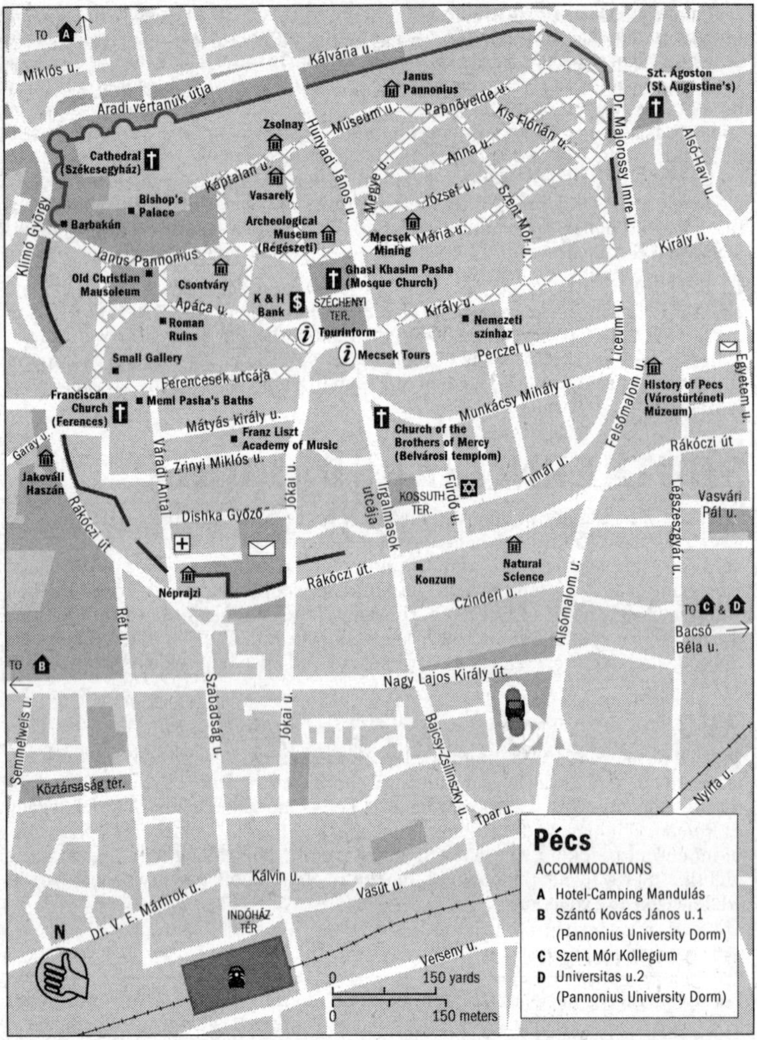

Buses: Tel. 21 52 15 and 21 56 65. At the intersection of Nagy Lajos Király út and Alsómalom u., a 15min. walk from the center. Hang a left onto Nagy Lajos Király út and look for Jókai u. on your right, which leads straight to Széchenyi tér. To **Budapest** (4½hr., 7 per day, 1750Ft).

Local Transportation: City bus tickets cost 80Ft at kiosks, and 100Ft on the bus.

Tourist Offices: Tourinform, Széchenyi tér 9 (tel. 21 11 34; fax 21 11 32). Offers free xeroxed **maps** and color maps (250Ft), sells phone cards and stamps, and exchanges currency. Also gives info on local entertainment and travel connections, but you'll have to do a bit of creative miming, as minimal English is spoken. Open June 16-Sept. 30 M-F 8am-5:30pm, Sa-Su 9am-2pm; Oct. M-F 8am-4pm, Sa 9am-2pm; Nov.-Apr. M-F 8am-4pm; closed May-June 15. **Mecsek Tours,** Széchenyi tér 1 (tel. 21 33 00; fax 21 20 44). Arranges travel, sells phone cards, exchanges money, and books rooms. English spoken. Open June-Aug. M-F 9am-5pm, Sa 9am-1pm; Sept.-May M-Sa 8am-3:30pm.

Currency Exchange: K & H Bank (tel. 23 31 00), on the corner of Széchenyi tér meets Jókai u. Cashes most traveler's checks and exchanges currency for no commission. Open M-Th 8am-4:30pm, F 8am-3:40pm, Sa 9am-noon. Cirrus/MC/Visa. **24hr. ATM** inside. Other ATMs are located at Mecsek Tours on Kiraly út, and at **OTP Bank,** Rákóczi út 44 (tel. 21 12 88), which also cashes traveler's checks and exchanges currency for no commission. Open M 7:45am-6pm, Tu-F 8am-5pm.

English Bookstore: International English Center, Mária u. 9 (tel. 31 20 10). New and used paperbacks and current English periodicals. Open M-F 10am-6pm. Also runs a cafe where you can read *National Geographic* over a hot cup of coffee (200Ft). Open July-Aug. M-F 10am-6pm; Sept.-June M-F 10am-8pm, Sa 9am-1pm.

Post Office: Jókai Mór u. 10 (tel. 21 44 22). Two-floor monster that offers so many services there's an info desk to guide you. **Poste Restante** available. Open M-F 8am-8pm, Sa 8am-2pm, Su 8am-noon. **Postal code:** 7621.

Internet Access: Matáv, Rákóczi u. 19 (tel. 22 53 35). Huge bank of computers equipped with English-language keyboards. 300Ft per 30min.; 500Ft per hr.

Phone code: 72.

ACCOMMODATIONS

For central accommodations, **private rooms** are the best budget option. **Mecsek Tours** (see above) has tons of listings with kitchens and common baths within walking distance from Széchenyi tér. (Singles 1500Ft; doubles 2100Ft; 30% surcharge for stays less than three nights.) Pécs's excellent bus system, however, makes cheap dorm rooms a little farther out almost as convenient.

Janus Pannonius University has several campuses around the city; dormitory rooms are nearly always available in July and August, but call ahead in September and June to see if there is space. **Universitas u. 2** (tel./fax 32 44 73). Take bus #21 from the main bus terminal to the wooded 48-as tér. Slightly rough around the edges, but the rooms are spotless. 3-bed dorms 900Ft. **Szántó Kovács János u. 1** (tel./fax 25 12 03). Slightly less central. Take bus #21 from the main bus terminal to Nendtvich Andor út. The university is across the main road and to the left. Neat triples with floor bathrooms and lacy curtains. The lower floors stay cooler, but offer less protection from mosquitoes. 900Ft. No curfew, but bus service ends at 11pm.

Szent Mór Kollégium, 48-as tér 4 (tel. 31 11 99). Take bus #21 to 48-as tér. Spiffy doubles in a gorgeous old building markedly lacking in linoleum. Hall bathrooms are cleaned daily, and toilet paper is never lacking. Sign up for laundry when you check in (100Ft per load). Common kitchen, but pots and pans are in short supply. 800Ft. Tourist tax 200Ft. Open June-Sept. 15.

Hotel-Camping Mandulás, Angyán János u. 2 (tel. 31 59 81). Take bus #34 from the train station to the hills above the city. The large camping complex—complete with its own post office and grocery store—offers accommodations in varying degrees of rusticity. Tents 600Ft, plus 600Ft per person. Breakfast 300Ft. Call Mecsek Tours (above) to reserve. Open Apr.-Oct.

FOOD

The countless restaurants, cafes, and bars that line Pécs's touristy streets are one of the city's biggest attractions. Reservations are necessary on Friday and Saturday nights at the more popular places, but a walk down Király u., Apáca u., or Ferencsek u., each packed with terraced cafes, should yield a table and an excellent dinner. When the money runs low, **Konzum,** on Kossuth tér, is the main supermarket. (Open M-F 6:30am-8pm, Sa 6:30am-2pm.)

DÓM Vendéglő Restaurant, Király u. 3 (tel. 21 00 88). Through the courtyard, it's the last door on the right. The interior is an impressive, if inexplicable, 2-level wooden reproduction of a church, complete with stained-glass windows. Serves various forms of roasted meat. Entrees 420-850Ft. Open daily 11am-11pm.

Caflisch Cukrászda Café, Király u. 32 (tel. 31 03 91). Possibly the best—and trendiest—cafe in town, despite Neil Diamond crooning in the background. Savor Hungarian sweets by the porcelain stove or enjoy the sun with a cold drink as Pécs strolls by. Pastries from 85Ft. Open daily 8am-10pm.

Liceum Söröző, Király u. 35 (tel. 32 72 84). Opposite the Liceum church and through a courtyard. Low prices make this a favorite of the student community. Everything is fried, but with 0.5L of *Gold Fassl* at 200Ft, no one seems to mind. Entrees 250-580Ft. Open M-F noon-10pm, Sa 6pm-11pm.

SIGHTS

CSONTVÁRY MUSEUM. The Csontváry Múzeum displays the works of Tivadar Csontváry Kosztka, a local artist who gained an international reputation despite less than 20 years of work. The well-assembled, well-lit exhibit brings the master's luminous skies to life, making it clear why the artist is known as a Hungarian Van Gogh. *(Janus Pannonius u. 11. Follow Janus Pannonius to the left from Széchenyi tér—the museum is on the left. Tel. 31 05 44. Open Tu-Su 10am-6pm. 250Ft, students 125Ft.)*

GHASI KHASIM PASHA INNER CITY PARISH CHURCH. (Ghasi Khasim Pase Belvarosi Templom). The ornate Baroque buildings on Széchenyi tér center around the striking Ghasi Khasim Pasha Inner City Parish Church. Aptly nicknamed the "Mosque Church," the elegant green-domed building is a former Turkish mosque, which itself was built on the site of an earlier Christian church. Verses from the Koran remain as decorative wall designs in the church's interior, and a former absolution basin—where the Turks washed their feet before entering the mosque—now serves as a baptismal font. The largest structure from the Ottoman occupation still standing in Hungary, the church is an exciting fusion of Christian and Muslim traditions; as such, it has become an emblem of the city. *(Open Apr. 16-Oct. 14 M-F 10am-4pm; Oct.15-Apr. 15 daily 10am-noon.)*

CATHEDRAL AND BISHOP'S PALACE. The neo-Romanesque cathedral *(bazilika)*, with its extraordinarily ornate altarpiece and frescoed chapels, stands proudly as Pécs's centerpiece. Masons have been piling on additions to its 4th-century foundation since the first bricks were laid. To the left of the cathedral, the Bishop's Palace is guarded by a 1983 statue of Franz Liszt that looks like it just came off the set of *The Wiz*. *(On Dóm tér. From Széchenyi tér, walk left on Janus Pannonius u., make the first right, and then go left on Káptalan to Dóm tér. Cathedral open M-Sa 9am-1pm and 2-5pm, Su 1-5pm; palace not open to the public. 220Ft, students 110Ft.)*

ZSOLNAY MUSEUM. There's nothing mass-produced at the Zsolnay Museum, which exhibits the finest pieces of the world-famous Zsolnay porcelain, handcrafted at the family workshop, which has been a Pécs establishment since the mid-19th century. *(Káptalan u. 2. Walk up Szepessy I. u. from the back of the Mosque Church, then turn left onto Káptalan u. Open Tu-Su 10am-6pm. 250Ft, students 125Ft.)*

ROMAN RUINS. Near the cathedral in the neighboring Szent István tér, 4th-century Roman ruins have been slowly decaying since Jupiter and Venus went out of business. Underneath lies the largest known burial site in Hungary. *(Cross Janus Pannonius from the cathedral or make the 5min. walk from Széchenyi tér—look for the sunken ruins on the left, in the park's corner. Open Tu-Su 10am-6pm.)*

BARBAKÁN. Surrounding Dom tér, the old city walls provide a popular walking spot. Follow along behind the cathedral to find the circular *barbakán*, a vestige of the great double-walled defense of the 15th century.

VASARELY MUSEUM. The neighboring Vasarely Museum houses the works of one of the most important 20th-century Hungarian artists, Pécs-born Viktor Vasarely, who was the founder of the Op-Art movement that defined the look of the 1960s. The graphic images will transport you to their era, and after 20min. of trippy 3D graphics, you'll probably have the headache to prove it. *(Káptalan u. 3. Open Apr.-Oct. Tu-Su 10am-6pm. 250Ft, students 125Ft.)*

SYNAGOGUE. The stunning 1869 Romantic synagogue is well worth a peek, with intricate paintings covering the ceiling and a fabulous Ark of the Covenant hiding in its sanctuary. The temple still holds services for the city's Jewish population, which today hovers at a mere 300; 88% of the prewar population was killed during the Holocaust. *(On Kossuth tér. Walk downhill from Széchenyi tér on Irgalmasok u.–the square on the left is Kossuth tér. Open M-F and Su 10am-11:30pm and noon-4pm. 60Ft, students 40Ft.)*

NIGHTLIFE

The flighty Pécs **nightlife** scene is one of the best in Hungary. It generally settles in the crowded, colorful bars near Széchenyi tér, especially on the first two blocks of Király u. For brain-busting beats and body piercings aplenty, the local alternative scene is unrivaled outside of Budapest.

Hard Rák Cafe, Ipar u. 7 (tel. 22 71 44), at the corner of Bajcsy-Zsilinszky u. The name refers to the music, not the American chain. Cave paintings will inspire your primal urges, if the liquor hasn't already. Live rock, alternative, and hard-core performances in summer on Friday and Saturday nights. Cover F-Sa 350Ft. Open M-Sa 7pm-6am.

Blues Pub, Apáca u. 2 (tel. 21 07 73). On weekends, this club attracts slightly more sophisticated Pécs youth looking for a place to converse, carouse, and consume one cigarette after another. This 5-level Surrealist structure of swirling mosaics will leave you dizzy after a few *Stella Artois* (200Ft). Open daily 11am-2am.

Rózsakert Söröző, Janus Pannonius u. 8/10 (tel. 31 08 62). Locals come here to enjoy a sobering breeze, live Hungarian gypsy music, and a lantern-adorned terrace. 0.5L *Gold Fassl* 180Ft. Open M-F and Su 11am-11pm, Sa 11am-midnight.

NEAR PÉCS: SZIGETVÁR CASTLE

In 1566, 50,000 Turks besieged the Croatian viceroy Miklós Zrínyi and his 2500 soldiers in **Szigetvár Castle.** After a month-long struggle, with their drinking water exhausted and the inner fortification in flames, Zrínyi's army decided to go out with a bang, opening the castle gates and launching a desperate suicidal attack against their aggressors. They were wiped out, but managed to take a quarter of the Turkish force with them, halting the Ottoman Empire's planned expansion into Vienna and ending Turkey's march on Europe. The castle ruins are remnants of a structure built well after the battle; the mostly red brick walls now house a pleasant park and the **Zrínyi Miklós Museum,** which chronicles the siege. (Open Tu-Su May-Sept. 9am-6pm; Oct.-Apr. 9am-4pm. 150Ft, students 75Ft.) The Szigetvár of the Turkish period is portrayed in the exhibits at the 16th-century **Turkish House,** Bástya u. 3. (Open May-Sept. Tu-Su 9:30am-2:30pm. 30Ft, students 15Ft.) The **Várostörténeti Museum and Turkish Cafe,** Vár u. 1 (tel. (0630) 74 29 34), lets visitors study the history of Szigetvár over a steaming cup of Turkish coffee and some sticky-sweet baklava. (30Ft, students 15Ft.)

GETTING THERE. Buses (tel. 31 26 58) from **Pécs** (40min., 14 per day, 426Ft) stop at the town's south end. Walk straight up Rákóczi u. 15min. to the castle. **Mecsek Tours,** on Zrínyi tér (tel. 31 01 16), sells **maps** (200Ft) of Szigetvár. (Open M-F 7:30am-4pm.) **Phone code:** 73.

THE GREAT PLAIN (NAGYALFÖLD)

Romanticized in tales of cowboys and bandits, Nagyalföld is an enormous grassland stretching southeast of Budapest over almost half of Hungary. Also called the *puszta*, meaning "empty plain," this tough region is certainly no longer empty, with arid Debrecen, fertile Szeged, and the vineyards of Kecskemét rising out of the flat soil like Nagyalföld's legendary mirages. Brimming with universities, fine art museums, and uniquely elegant architecture, these civilized spots offer an excellent opportunity to experience Hungarian high culture at its best. If you make it into the surrounding countryside, a visit to the Great Plain will acquaint you with the startling breadth of this small nation's heritage.

DEBRECEN

Protected by the mythical Phoenix, Debrecen (DE-bre-tsen; pop. 210,000) has risen from the ashes of over 30 devastating fires, the fate of a land-locked city on the dry Great Plain. Happily, the last rebuilding left the city with refreshing parks and wide boulevards where 19th-century architecture mixes comfortably with its modern counterparts—a relaxed urban setting that offers big-city action without the grit of big-city life. The unofficial capital of eastern Hungary and a university town, Debrecen draws youth from all over the world. This massive student population keeps the pace lively, whether lounging in Nagyerdei Park by day or pub-crawling through city streets until sunrise.

ORIENTATION

The town center is about a 15min. walk from the train station. With your back to the station, walk down **Piac u.**, the main street running perpendicular to the station. Piac u. ends in **Kálvin tér**, where the huge yellow **Nagytemplom** sits watching the city's center. Debrecen's other main hub lies about 3km farther along Piac u, which becomes Péterfia u. at Kálvin tér, running north to **Nagyerdei Park** and **Kossuth Lajos Tudományegyetem** (KLTE; Kossuth Lajos Technical University). The **bus station** is also about a 15min. walk from the center. Exit the station at Terminal 2 and make a left onto Arany János u.; continue until the street ends, then make a left onto Piac u., which leads directly to Kálvin tér.

PRACTICAL INFORMATION

Trains: Tel. 32 67 77. To: **Budapest** (3hr., 13 per day, 1530Ft; *InterCity* 2½hr., 5 per day, 1850Ft); **Miskolc** (2½-3hr., 5 per day, 920Ft); **Eger** (through Fúzesabony; 3hr., 3 per day, 786Ft); **Szeged** (through Cegléd; 3½hr., 7 per day, 1750Ft); and **Oradea, Romania** (destination Tîrgu Mureş; 3½hr. or more depending on border crossing, 1 per day, 1360Ft).

Buses: Tel. 41 39 99. At the intersection of Nyugari u. and Széchenyi u. To: **Tokaj** (2hr., 2 per day, 746Ft); **Szeged** (4-5½hr., 3 per day, 1990Ft); **Kecskemét** (5½hr., 2 per day, 1990Ft); **Miskolc** (2hr., every 30min.-1hr., 828Ft); **Eger** (2½hr., 4 per day, 1160Ft); and **Oradea** (3½hr., 1 per day, 704Ft).

Local Transportation: Don't be intimidated by Debrecen's public transportation system; you can't make a mistake, and it's by far the most convenient way to navigate the city. Tram #1 (the one and only) runs from the train station at Petőfi tér through Kálvin tér and then makes a loop around the park, past the university, and returns to Kálvin tér. Ticket checks are frequent and menacing (fine 2000-5000Ft, depending on how sympathetic the officer is to foreigners)—get tickets from the kiosk by the train station (80Ft) or pay the driver (100Ft). The price is always changing, so check on the back of the driver's seat to confirm. Once you board the tram, validate your ticket in the black contraptions. The tram is the best route to the town center from the train station; get off at the stop after the McDonald's for tourist offices and most other necessities.

Taxis: Tel. 44 44 44 or 44 45 55.

Tourist Office: Tourinform, Piac u. 20 (tel. 41 22 50; fax 31 41 39), in the cream-colored building on the right as you come from the train station just before Kálvin tér. Friendly agents fluent in English will provide **maps** and info on seasonal events and dormitory accommodations. Open June-Aug. daily 8am-8pm; Sept.-May M-F 9am-5pm.

Currency Exchange: OTP, Hatvan u. 2/4 (tel. 41 95 44), has fairly good rates, gives Cirrus/MC cash advances, accepts most traveler's checks, and has a 24-hour Cirrus/MC/Plus/Visa **ATM.** Bank open M-T, Th-F 7:45am-4pm, W 7:45am-5pm.

Luggage storage: At the train station. Open 24hr. 100-300Ft depending on size.

Pharmacy: In the center of town at Hatvan u. 1. Open M-F 8:30am-6pm, Sa 8:30-1pm.

Medical Assistance: Medical emergency room (tel. 41 43 33) is across the street from the bus station at the intersection of Erzsébet u. and Szoboszlój u.–look for the building with the blue and white *"Mentők, orro si ügyelet"* sign in front.

Post office: Hatvan u. 5/9 (tel. 41 23 74), faces the bank. Open M-F 7am-8pm, Sa 8am-2pm. **Postal code:** 4001.

Internet access: Internet Club, Timár u. 15 (tel. 34 96 62 or 45 87 99; email club@hermes.hu). From the train station, turn right onto Wesselényi u. and then take the first left (yes, the first) onto Teleki u. Another left brings you to Varga u. and the first right is Timár u. 300Ft for 30min., printing 20Ft per page. Open M-F 9am-8pm.

Phone code: 52.

ACCOMMODATIONS

Hajdútourist, Kálvin tér 2 (tel. 41 55 88; fax 31 96 16), arranges central private doubles (2500Ft, tax 120Ft; open M-F 8am-5pm; AmEx/MC/Visa); **IBUSZ** does the same on Széchenyi u. right near Piac u. (Doubles 2600Ft; triples 3200Ft. Open M-F 8am-5pm, Sa 8am-noon. AmEx/MC/Visa.) In July and August, many of the university dorms rent rooms (1500-2000Ft per person)—ask at Tourinform, but be warned: many of the dorms they list only rent rooms to groups, so let your fingers do the walking and call before trekking across the city.

Hotel Fönix, Barna u. 17 (tel. 41 33 55; fax 41 30 54). This sea-green hotel sits close to the train station, right off Piac u. Rooms are spotless, if occasionally stuffy–the windows are too high to see out. Singles 1920Ft; doubles 3440Ft, with shower 5640Ft; spare beds 920Ft extra. MC/Visa.

Hotel Stop, Batthyány u. 18 (tel. 42 03 01), occupying a pleasant courtyard near the center. From Kossuth tér head down Piac u. and walk left on Kossuth u.; Batthány u. will appear on the right. Don't be deceived by the lobby and exterior–the rooms are clean and bright. Doubles with shower 3900Ft; triples with shower and TV 4900Ft.

Termál Camping, Nagyerdei körút 102 (tel./fax 41 24 56), is hidden in Nagyerdei Park and is accessible from the train station by tram #1 or bus #10 or 14. Get off the tram once you're in the park–you should see Hotel Termál on the left–and follow the tram tracks for a few minutes until you hit Nagyerdei Körút at the intersection. Make a right, away from the tracks; the campground is about 5min. down the road. Reserve rooms one month in advance. Quads 2000Ft, with shower 4000Ft; July and Aug. 2200Ft, 5000Ft; tents 920Ft per person; caravans 1020Ft per person; 120Ft tax per person. Open May-Oct.

FOOD

The **University Dining Halls** offer lunch (100-250Ft per item) during the school year. (Cheap leftovers until approximately 4pm 50-100Ft. Open daily Sep.-June 11:30am-2:30pm.) Directly behind the main university building on Egytem tér, follow the center path straight through the park; bear right when you see the tennis courts—the "Menza" is on the 2nd floor of the white building. Otherwise, a tiny **supermarket** at Hatvan u. 8 is open 24hr.

Csokonai Söröző, Kossuth u. 21 (tel. 41 08 02). In the classy, candle-lit cellar, waiters accustomed to foreigners enthusiastically greet their customers and then allow them to try their luck with a roll of the dice for a free meal. The city's best menu includes English translations and photographs of its meaty dishes (475-1085Ft). Veggie soups and salads are also available (around 475Ft). Open M-Su noon-11pm.

Régi Posta Étterem, Széchenyi u. 6 (tel. 41 72 92). Attentive waiters serve almost only fried food at this restaurant named for an old stagecoach stop. Entrees 400-750Ft. Open M-Sa 10am-9pm, Su 10am-2pm.

Sütöde. As you walk down Kossuth u. from Piac u., make a right down the small alley directly before the Drogerie Markt. A small, store-front bread stand off Kossuth u., is where locals get breakfast and their daily supply of sweet-smelling baked goods. Breads sold by weight, 80Ft per kg. Open daily 7am-7pm.

SIGHTS & ENTERTAINMENT

Hungary's largest Protestant church and Debrecen's town symbol, the 1863 twin-spired **Nagytemplom** (Great Church; tel. 32 70 17), looms over Kossuth tér's northern end. The bell tower offers a great view of the town, but don't look down—the narrow, wooden stairs become progressively more rickety as you near the top. (Open M-F 9am-4pm, Sa 9am-noon, Su 11am-4pm. 40Ft, students 20Ft.) Hear the huge organ in action every Friday at noon (30min.; free). The **Református Kollégium,** Kálvin tér 16 (tel. 41 47 44), behind the church, was established in 1538 as a center for Protestant education. The present building housed the government of Hungary twice—in 1849, when Lajos Kossuth led the Parliament in the Oratory, and again in 1944. Today, it houses Calvinist schools, as well as a collection of religious art and an exhibit on the history of Protestantism in Debrecen. The highlight, though, is the 650,000-volume **library** which also displays 16th-century Bibles. (Open Tu-F 9am-5pm, Sa 9am-1pm. 60Ft, students 30Ft. Hungarian and German explanations.)

The **Déri Museum** (tel. 41 75 77), displays a collection ranging from local history to Japanese lacquerware. Upstairs see three awe-inspiring murals by Mihály Munkácsy of Christ's trial and crucifixion. Spot the artist's self-portrait in *Ecce Homo* as an old man in the crowd, next to the arch. Coming from Kossuth tér, walk to the left of the Great Church and take the first left onto Múzeum u.—it is on the right with the sculpture garden. (Open Nov.-Mar. Tu-Su 10am-4pm; Apr.-Oct. Tu-Su 10am-6pm. 200Ft, students 100Ft; special exhibits 100Ft. No cameras.)

Debrecen is famous for its young population—the largest in Hungary—and you'll find them all in **Nagyerdei Park,** which provides bike lanes, paddle boats, bars, tattoo salons, and an overabundance of leering single men sitting around in tank tops. The park's highlight, however, is the **municipal thermal bath,** where you can soak nude in steamy baths with other Debreceners or have a masseuse rub away the massive knots in your back from carrying that monster of a pack. (Open M-F 8am-noon and 1-6:30pm. Thermal bath 500Ft; 30min. massage 350Ft.) Debrecen hosts a series of summer events, ranging from equestrian competitions to musical performances and air shows. The fête season culminates in the hugely popular **Flower Carnival** parade on August 20 (reserve in the spring for accommodations during that weekend). Every spring, the **Jazz Days** festival features well-known musicians and bands (dates variable). The **International Military Band Festival** blows its horn every year in the last week of June. In July of even years, the **Béla Bartók Choir Festival** attracts great choirs from around the world. See Tourinform for schedules and tickets (usually 300-1000Ft).

Master the unmasterable—the Debrecen summer school at KLTE offers cheap and extremely popular **Hungarian language programs** for students from around the world. Contact Debreceni Nyári Egyetem, Egyetem tér 1, 4010 Debrecen Pf. 35 (tel./fax 48 91 17; email nyariegy@tigris.klte.hu; http://summer06.sum.klte.hu), in June. Then practice your new skills with the young, lively crowd in smoky **El Tornado,** Pallagi u. 2 (tel. 34 05 90), in Nagyerdei Park. (Open daily 5pm-4am.) This saloon-style pub even cranks out country music every once in a while (0.5L *Bor-*

sodi 130Ft). The more mellow **Yes Jazz Bár,** Kálvin tér 4 (tel. 41 85 22), is usually filled with low conversations set in time to the live jazz and blues. (*Guinness* 350Ft. Cover 100-300Ft. Open daily 2pm-2am.) A **cinema complex** (tel. 28 78 78) entertains and offers respite from the summer heat in three movie theatres. (Tickets 300-500Ft.) The month's schedule of Hollywood and foreign films—all subtitled in Hungarian—is posted on the door.

SZEGED

The easygoing charm of the Great Plain's cultural capital has prompted some to describe Szeged (SAY-ged) as a Mediterranean town on the Tisza. After an 1879 flood practically wiped out the city, streets were laid out in orderly curves punctuated by large, stately squares, giving Szeged a quiet cosmopolitan atmosphere closer to Europe's seaside cities than to anything in Hungary. Instead of the usual Baroque facades, rows of colorful Art Nouveau buildings line the busy walkways; the lively architectural mood is complemented by the boutiques, bars, and cafes that fill with university students come sundown.

ORIENTATION

Szeged is bisected by the **Tisza river,** with the city center on the west bank and the parks and residences of **Újszeged** (New Szeged) to the east. Szeged's downtown forms a semicircle against the river, with the curving **Tisza Lajos krt** as its circumference and **Széchenyi tér**—the grassy, main square—in the center. Across **Híd u.**

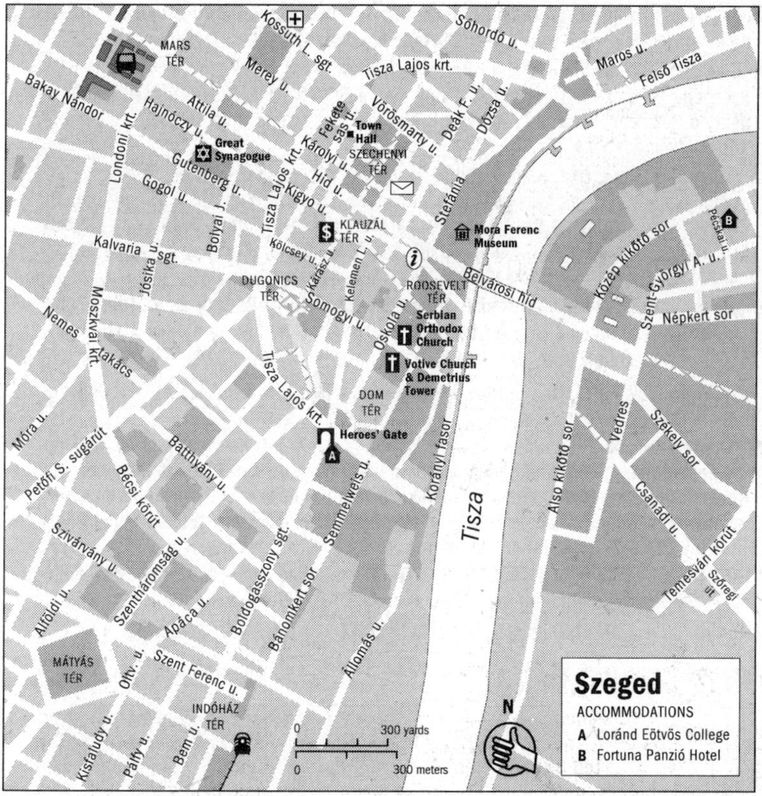

("Bridge St.") from Széchenyi, shops, travel bureaus, and cafes cluster on the pedestrian **Klauzál tér.** In spite of its status as the only planned city in Hungary, Szeged's streets can get confusing at times—happily, large, multilingual **maps** litter nearly every one of the city's squares. It's a 10-15min. walk from the bus station to the center; trains are about 20min. from the center in the opposite direction.

PRACTICAL INFORMATION

Trains: The main station, **Szeged pu** (tel. 42 18 21), sits on the west bank of the Tisza. Tram #1 transports you directly to the center, four stops from the station (see **Local Transportation,** below). Otherwise, it's a 15-20min. walk to Széchenyi tér. To: **Budapest** (2½hr., 15 per day, *InterCity* 1420Ft); **Debrecen** via **Cegléd** (3-4hr., 3 per day, 1709Ft); and **Kecskemét** (1hr., 15 per day, 650Ft, *InterCity* 910Ft). International cashier on 2nd floor. Open daily 6am-5:45pm.

Buses: Tel. 42 14 78. On Mars tér. From the station, cross the street at the traffic light and walk down Mikszáth Kálmán u., which intersects Széchenyi tér 10min. after becoming Károlyi u. To: **Budapest** (3½hr., 7 per day, 1590Ft); **Debrecen** (5¼hr., 2-4 per day, 1910Ft); **Eger** (5hr., 2 per day, 2140Ft); **Győr** (6hr., 2 per day, 2350Ft); **Kecskemét** (1¾hr., 10-14 per day, 820Ft); and **Pécs** (4½hr., 7 per day, 1705Ft).

Local Transportation: Tram #1 connects the train station with Széchenyi tér (4 stops) and continues 2 more stops to the corner of Pacsirta and Kossuth L. Sugár út, near the bus station. Facing the same direction as the tram, turn left on Pacsirta and walk two blocks to reach Mars tér. Tickets from kiosks 65Ft; from the driver 90Ft. The fine for riding ticketless is 1500Ft, and they *do* check.

Taxis: Tel. 470 470, 490 490, 480 480, and 488 488. Cheaper to call ahead. 100Ft base fare; 80Ft per km by phone, 120Ft per km on the street.

Tourist Office: Tourinform, Victor Hugo út 1 (tel./fax 31 17 11). From the tram stop at Széchenyi tér and Vár u., walk back along the tracks 1 block to Híd u. Turn left and then right on Oskola u., which runs along the river. The first right is Victor Hugo út. Free maps and accommodations info. Open M-F 10am-6pm.

Currency Exchange: OTP, Klauzál tér 5 (tel. 48 03 80). Cashes traveler's checks for no commission and gives MC/Visa cash advances. Open M-W and F 7:45am-4pm, Th 7:45am-5pm. **Budapest Bank Ltd.,** Klauzál tér 4 (tel. 48 55 85), doubles as a **Western Union.** Open M-Th 8am-5pm, F 8am-3pm. **K&H Bank,** Kárász u. 2, has a Cirrus/Plus/MC/Visa **24hr. ATM** and the best exchange rates.

Luggage Storage: At the train station. 60Ft 4am-4pm; 120Ft 4-11pm. Open 4am-11pm.

English Bookstores: Kőnyvesbolt, Kárász u. 16 (tel. 31 23 28). Open M-F 10am-6pm, Sa 9am-1pm. **Délhir Bolt,** Dugonics tér 1 (tel. 31 21 18). Open M-Sa 5am-8pm.

24hr. Pharmacy: Kígyó Richter Referenciapatika, Klauzál tér 3 (tel. 11 11 31). Ring the bell outside 8pm-7am.

Medical Assistance: Kossuth Lagos sgt. 15 (tel. 47 43 74). From the Town Hall, walk up the center of Széchenyi tér and turn left onto Vörösmarty u., then follow it as it becomes Kossuth Lagos sgt. 5min. later; the medical center will appear on the right at the intersection with Szilágyi u. Some English spoken. Open M-F 5:30pm-7:30am, Sa-Su 24hr. Ring the bell after hours. In an **emergency,** dial 1104.

Post Office: Széchenyi tér 1 (tel. 47 62 76). At the corner with Híd u. Open M-F 8am-8pm, Sa 8am-2pm, Su 8am-noon. **Postal code:** 6720. **Phone code:** 62.

Internet Service: PGM, Dugonics tér 11 (tel. 42 62 16). 150Ft per 30min.

ACCOMMODATIONS

Tourinform (see above) carries info on **private rooms** (central doubles with shower 1500-3000Ft) and other budget accommodations. University dorms are generally cheapest, especially for solo travelers, but are only open in July and August.

Fortuna Panzió, Pécskai u. 8 (tel./fax 43 19 07). Go across Belvárosi híd and take a left onto Szent-Györgyi Albert u.; turn left onto Pécskai u. after passing a huge hotel complex on the left. Worth the hot walk for that rare luxury in Hungary–air-conditioning. The spacious rooms are peaceful and bright, although the neighborhood dogs may interrupt your solace. Doubles with bath 5200Ft. MC/Visa.

Loránd Eötvös College, Tisza Lajos krt 103 (tel. 31 06 41). From Széchenyi tér, cross Híd u. and follow Kelemen as it becomes Zrinyi u. to Aradi Vértanúk tere, where two soldiers mark Hero's Gate. The hostel is to the left of the gate; its entrance is removed from the street, next to the restaurant. Cheap, central dorms with such necessities as mosquito-proof screens. Doubles 1800Ft first night, 1500Ft thereafter. Laundry service free.

Napfény, Dorozsmai u. 4 (tel. 42 18 00; fax 46 75 79). Take tram #1 to the last stop, go up the overpass, then turn left. After 10min., you'll see Napfény on the left. Next to international route E75, this hotel and campground feels like a typical highway motel. Tents 200Ft, plus 300Ft per person. Motel doubles 2100Ft.

FOOD

Szeged is home to Hungary's finest lunchmeat—Pick salami—and the best place for *halászle* (spicy soup made with fresh Tisza fish). The town's distinctive cuisine, combined with a hungry student population, makes dining out its favorite pasttime. The **non-stop ABC market** on Mars tér, near the corner of Londoni krt and Mikszáth Kálmán u., provides late-night munchies.

Roosevelt téri Halászcsárda (Sótartá Étterem), Roosevelt tér 14 (tel. 42 43 33). Next to the river. Sample the famously spicy *szegedi halászlé,* or try any of the *hallé* (fish soup) dishes with fiery green paprika on the side. Entrees 350-1500Ft. Open daily 11am-11pm.

At Aranykorona Étterem, Déak Ferenc u. 29 (tel. 32 17 50). Red velvet seats, a dungeon-style entrance, and waiters inexplicably decked out in leather are somewhat incongruous with the unpretentious menu. Entrees 490Ft-1390Ft. Open M-Th 11am-11pm, F-Sa 11am-2am, Su 11am-10pm.

Roxy Cafe and Pizzeria, Deák Ferenc u. 24. Chic restaurant serves pizzas (300-700Ft) and a daily vegetarian platter (490Ft) to Szeged's hippest university students. The perfect post-party, pre-hangover stop. Open Su-Th 10am-midnight, F-Sa 10am-2am.

Bounty Pub (tel. 32 65 00), on Roosevelt tér across from the Móra Ferenc Múzeum. This ship-like restaurant specializes in "Lava Rock grilling," a process in which gravy is steamed in with the meat. More than 70 types of whiskey (200-1900Ft) for sea-farers. Entrees 550-1000Ft. Restaurant open daily noon-midnight; bar open daily noon-3am.

SIGHTS

SYNAGOGUE. (Zsinagoga). Widely acknowledged as the most beautiful of its kind in Hungary, the 1903 synagogue is Szeged's absolute must-see. The temple's Moorish altar and gardens, Romanesque columns, Gothic domes, and Baroque facades are an awe-inspiring display of craftsmanship. The cupola, decorated with symbols of Infinity and Faith, seems to grow deeper the longer you look up into it; for a well-spent 100Ft, you can see it in its illuminated glory. Still a house of worship, the walls of the vestibule are lined with the names of the 3100 members of the congregation killed in concentration camps. *(Jósika u. 8. From Széchenyi tér, walk 4 Su-F 9am-noon and 1-6pm. If the building is locked, look for a woman cleaning the streets nearby; she also watches over the building. 150Ft, students 60Ft.)*

MORA FERENC MUSEUM. The riverside Móra Ferenc Museum houses an eclectic collection of 18th- to 20th-century folk art in a gorgeous Neoclassical palace. On your way upstairs, linger to inspect panoramic paintings of Szeged during the devastating flood of 1879. The first floor details the life of the long-vanished Avar tribe with an impressive series of papier-maché mannequins, complete with yarn hair. *(Roosevelt tér 1/3. From Széchenyi tér, turn right on Vár u., which brings you to Roosevelt tér. Tel. 47 03 70. Open Tu-Su Apr.-Oct. 10am-5pm; Nov.-Mar. 10am-3pm. 100Ft, students 50Ft.)*

VOTIVE CHURCH. (Fogadalmi Templom). The red-brick Votive Church pierces the skyline with its twin 91m towers. The 1880 cathedral was built after the great flood as a means of asking God's protection against future deluges. At least this monster is in no danger of washing away, with bulky towers sitting heavily on the square. Hungary's fourth-largest church, it houses a 10,000-pipe organ that often exerts itself for afternoon or evening concerts. Alongside the church stands the 12th-century **Demetrius Tower** (Dömötör Torony), Szeged's oldest monument, and all that remains of the church that originally stood on the site. On the walls surrounding the cathedral, the **National Pantheon** portrays the faces of 80 Hungarian history-makers. *(From Széchenyi tér, turn left onto Híd u. and then right on Oskola u., which leads to Dóm tér. Open M-Sa 9am-6pm, Su 12:30-6pm, but known to close haphazardly.)*

TOWN HALL. (Városháza). The yellow town hall, re-shingled with red-and-green ceramic tiles after the 1879 deluge destroyed most of the city, overlooks the grassy Széchenyi tér at the town's center. The bridge connecting the bright building to the drab one next door (which once held the tax office) was built to prevent Habsburg Emperor Franz József from having to walk up and down the stairs.

SERBIAN ORTHODOX CHURCH. (Palánki Szerb Templom). Smaller and brighter than the Votive Church, the 1778 Serbian Orthodox Church features impressive interior artwork. The iconostasis holds 60 gilt-framed paintings, while the ceiling fresco of God creating the Earth is covered with stars. *(Somogyi Béla u. 3. Open whenever there's someone around to collect the 100Ft admission.)*

HERO'S GATE. (Hősök Kapuja). Starting at Dóm tér and heading away from the center brings you to Hero's Gate, in the adjacent Aradi Vértanuk tér. It was erected in 1936 to honor Horthy's White Guards, who brutally cleansed the nation of "Reds." The propagandistic murals are now gone, but skeletal soldiers remain.

ENTERTAINMENT

The **Open-Air Theater Festival,** held from mid-July to mid-August, is Hungary's largest outdoor performance event. International troupes show off folk dances, operas, and musicals in an amphitheater, with the looming cathedral as a backdrop. Tickets (420-1500Ft) are sold at Deák u. 28/30 (tel. 47 14 66; fax 47 13 22; open M-F 10am-5pm) and at Tourinform (see **Practical Information,** above).

NIGHTLIFE

Szőke Tisza, 2 floors of disco fun docked just off of Roosevelt tér. Rock the boat alongside Szeged's disgruntled youth. *Kaiser* beer 150Ft. Open July-Aug. daily 9pm-4am.

Sing-Sing, on Mars tér. Disco ducks migrate here in colder weather. The DJ churns out popular beats for a ready-to-rave crowd. 0.5L *Amstel* 200Ft. Open daily 10pm-dawn.

Jate Klub, in the Toldi u. entrance to the central university building on Dugonies tér. During the school year, join *Szegedi* students on their own turf. With an area set aside for chatting–or chatting up–co-eds, undergraduate pretention never had such a great soundtrack. 0.5L *Rolling Rock* 150Ft. Cover 300Ft. Open Th-Sa 9pm-4am.

Grand Cafe, Deák Ferenc u. 18, 3rd Fl. (tel. 31 35 78). Skip the strobe lights and save your voice at Sophisticate Central. Mellow jazz glosses over the low conversation of young Hungarians. Red wine 170Ft. Generally open mid-afternoon to midnight.

HBH Bajor Serfőzde (Beer House), Deák Ferenc u. 4 (tel. 42 03 94). In the center of the city. Watch beer being made behind the bar and then disappearing down your throat. 150-254Ft per glass. Open M-Sa 11:30am-midnight, Su 11:30am-11pm.

KECSKEMÉT

Nestled amid vineyards, fruit groves, and the dusty *puszta* (plains), Kecskemét (CATCH-keh-MATE) lures tourists with its shady, park-like center and its famous *barack pálinka* (apricot brandy). First mentioned in 1368 as a market town, "the garden city" sprung up as the crossing point of traders' routes between Istanbul and Hamburg. The exceptional architecture culminates with the salmon-pink Art Nouveau town hall.

ORIENTATION

The town sprawls around a loosely connected string of squares. The largest, **Szabadság tér,** is orbited by three primary satellites, **Kossuth tér, Kalvin tér,** and **Széchenyi tér.** To get to Szabadság from the **train station,** turn left as you exit, take a quick right onto Rákóczi út, and walk straight for 10min. The **bus station** is around the corner on the right from the train station. If you don't want to walk, **local buses** head into town from a stop opposite the train station. Catch Volán bus #11 to get to the red-roofed bus depot in Széchenyi tér. From there, a right on Sík S. will quickly land you in the center.

PRACTICAL INFORMATION

Trains: Tel. 32 24 60. Kodály Zoltán tér, at the end of Rákóczi út. To: **Budapest** (1½hr., 13 per day, 786Ft); **Szeged** (1hr., 17 per day, 500Ft); and **Pécs** via **Kiskunfélegyháza** (5hr., 1153Ft).

Buses: Tel. 32 17 77. Kodály Zoltán tér. To: **Budapest** (1½hr., 26 per day, 710Ft); **Szeged** (1¾hr., 13 per day, 710Ft); **Eger** (2½hr., 3 per day, 1290Ft); **Debrecen** (5hr., 2 per day, 1507Ft); and **Pécs** (5hr., 3 per day, 1507Ft).

Local Transportation: Volán buses (75Ft from kiosks, 90Ft from the driver). Timetables are posted at most stops—service winds down around 10pm. The main local bus terminal is a block away from Kossuth tér; make a right from the terminal onto Sík S.

Tourist Offices: Tourinform, Kossuth tér 1 (tel./fax 48 10 65), in the town hall. From the train station, walk through the park to the left and down Rákóczi út. Continue straight past McDonald's, then head toward the huge pink building to your left; the office is on the building's corner. Get info on exploring the *puszta* here. Open summer M-F 8am-6pm, Sa-Su 9am-1pm; off-season M-F 8am-5pm, Sa 9am-1pm. **IBUSZ,** Kossuth tér 3 (tel. 48 69 55; tel./fax 48 05 57), to the right of McDonald's, behind the fountain as you come from the station. The staff will cheerfully assist with visas, pension rooms (see **Accommodations,** below) and international bus, train, and plane tickets. Discounts for those under 26. Open in summer M-F 8am-5:30pm, Sa 8am-noon. Visa/MC.

Currency Exchange: OTP, at the intersection of Szabadság tér and Arany János u., has the best exchange rates in town and also cashes traveler's checks, both for no commission. Open M-W and F 7:45am-4pm, Th 7:45am-5pm. An MC/Cirrus/Plus/Visa **ATM** sits outside. The branch next to the synagogue on Koháry I. krt. is open until 6pm.

Luggage storage: At the train station. 100Ft per day. Open daily 7am-7pm.

Pharmacy: Mátyás Király Gyógyszertár, Szabadság tér 1 (tel. 48 07 39). Open M-F 7:30am-8pm, Sa 8am-5pm.

Post Office: Kálvin tér 10/12 (tel. 48 65 86; fax 48 10 34). Open M-F 8am-8pm, Sa 8am-2pm. **Postal code:** 6000. **Phone code:** 76.

ACCOMMODATIONS

Summer brings all sorts of bargains, but winter travelers have fewer options. The best deals are in pensions, but some are overpriced. Most tourist agencies (see p. 329) will help in the quest for an affordable bed. **IBUSZ** rents private, fully loaded 4-bed flats near the center (3500-5000Ft), and can set you up with an equally convenient pension. (Doubles and triples 3500Ft, with shower 4000Ft.)

Hotel Pálma, Arany János u. 3 (tel./fax 32 10 45 and 32 20 94), in the heart of the city. From Tourinform, turn left past McDonald's; the hotel is in the sea-green building on the right. The beachy decor fails to hide the fact that this ex-college dorm is located in a strip mall. Recently renovated, with nice bathrooms. 4-person dorms with bunk beds, private showers, and phones. Beware of overheated top floor rooms. 2400Ft for 1 person; 4200Ft for 2 people; 4800Ft for 3 people.

Tanitóképzo Kollégiuma (Teacher's College), Piaristák tér 4 (tel. 48 69 77 and 48 73 48), 5min. from Kossuth tér. Coming from the train station, turn right just after the McDonald's and follow Sík S. to its intersection with Hornyik J. körút. From there, turn right; the Kollégiuma is on the left, facing the large church. Washing machine 150Ft. Doubles, triples, and quads 1200Ft per person.

Autós Camping, Csabay Gréza Krl. 5 (tel. 32 93 98). 15min. southwest of town on Volán bus #1 or 11. Get off at the swimming pool and follow the signs to this somewhat sandy site. Open mid-Apr. to mid-Oct. Tents space 500Ft plus 900Ft per person. 4-bed bungalows 4400Ft. Tax 100Ft; electricity and parking 400Ft each.

FOOD

Kecskemét is the home of apricots; not surprisingly, it is also the home of apricot brandy. Don't let the sweet name fool you: the stuff may taste great, but it will put hair on the chest of any greenhorn. An **Alföld supermarket,** Deák tér 2, just off Kossuth tér, serves the less adventurous. (Open M-F 6:30am-1pm.)

Liberté Coffee House, Syabadság tér 2 (tel. 48 03 50). Serves more than just coffee in leafy, terraced elegance. Hungarian specialties you've never seen before (like spare ribs). Entrees 590-1450Ft. Afterwards, grab dessert (100-450Ft) at the adjoining Fodor Cukrászada. Both open daily 10am-11pm.

Göröd Udvär Étterem, Hornyik J. 1 (tel. 49 25 13). Sit on doric stools at mosaic tables. This Greek oasis serves terrific *szuvlaky* (700Ft) and gyros (550Ft), plus a few traditional Hungarian dishes. Entrees 420-1000Ft. Open daily 11am-11pm.

Őregház Vendéglő, Hosszú u. 27 (tel. 49 69 73), next to Széchenyi krt., a 10-15min. walk from the center. Large portions of meat-n-potatoes Hungarian-style in a spacious neighborhood restaurant. Entrees 260-650Ft; 20% off Sa-Su. Open M-Th and Su 11am-10pm, F-Sa 11am-midnight.

SIGHTS

The salmon-colored **town hall,** Kossuth tér 1, was built in 1897 during the height of the Hungarian Art Nouveau movement. It is hard to miss, dominating Kecskemét's main square. If you hear a little Mozart chiming over the city, it's the hall's carillon working its magic. (Tel. 48 36 83; ask for Földi Margit. Tours by appointment daily 7:30am-6pm. 50Ft, in English 300Ft.) The 1806 Roman Catholic **Great Church** asserts itself with a gorgeous Neoclassical facade and an interior of elaborate frescoes. (Open Tu-F 9am-noon and 3-6pm.) You can brave its rickety wooden floors and wobbly stairs to find the best view in town atop the Church's **tower.** (Open June-Aug. daily 10am-8pm. 200Ft.) If you're not going to the *puszta,* at least hit the **Museum of Hungarian Folk Art** (Magyar Népi Iparművészet Múzeuma), Serfőző u. 19/a, a 10min. walk from the center. From the Tourinform office, turn left onto the main street and follow it as it becomes Petőfi and then Dózsa Gy. út. Take the first right after the Arpád Körút onto Lajita u., then the first left onto Serfőző; the museum is on the right. In addition to regional costumes, furniture, and ceramics, it displays a collection of painted Easter eggs and horse whips that will bring out the tenderfoot in anyone. (Tel. 32 72 03. Open W-Su 10am-6pm. 100Ft, students 60Ft.) The **Toy Museum** (Szórakaténusz Játékmúzuem és Műhely), Gáspár u. 11 (tel. 48 14 69), houses a fun collection of antique miniature trains, castles, and dolls, and also has hands-on workshops for children. (Open Mar. 15-Dec. 31 Tu-Su 10am-12:30pm, 1-5pm. 100Ft, students 50Ft. Toymaker's workshop open W and Sa 10am-noon and 1-5pm, Su 10am-noon.) The **Museum of Naive Artists** (Naív Művészek Múzeuma), Gáspár u. 11 (tel. 32 47 67), fills halls with the folksy, often intriguing work of local amateurs. Follow Deák Ferenc tér left from the Tourinform office. At the second major intersection, turn right onto Dobó István körút; the entrance is on the left behind the strip mall. (Open Tu-Su 10am-5pm. 150Ft, students 100Ft.) Across the square from the town hall, the **Kecskemét Gallery** (Kecskeméti Képtár), Rákóczi út 1, also displays the works of local artists, but its whimsical Art Nouveau building is the main attraction. (Tel. 48 07 76. Open Tu-Su 10am-5pm. 100Ft, students 60Ft.) The same could be said for the cupola-topped **synagogue** (now a conference center), Rákóczi út 2 (tel. 48 76 11), which houses 15 fake Michelangelo sculptures. (Open M-F 8am-9:30pm. 40Ft, students 20Ft.)

ENTERTAINMENT

Shakespeare may lose something in translation, but the elegant stage at the **Katona József Theater** *(Színhaz)*, Katona tér 5 (tel. 48 32 83), would make just about anything look good. (Summer drama and operettas 2000Ft, students 1600Ft; off-season 500-1000Ft. Box office open M-F 11am-6pm.) At **Club Robinson,** Akadémia krt. 2 (tel. 48 58 44), witness platform heels stomping to Abba. (0.5L beer 150Ft. Open daily 7pm-3am.) For a more laid-back evening, try **Kilele Music Cafe,** Jokai 34 (tel. 32 67 74). The sign outside may suggest a raging inferno, but the downstairs is more cool than hot, with live jazz on the weekends. (100-150Ft cover. 0.5L beer 200-300Ft. Open M-F noon-2am, Sa 6pm-4am, Su 6pm-1am.) Kecskemét has produced such greats as composer Zoltán Kodály (1882-1967) and author József Katona (1791-1830); its artistic tradition continues each March with the **Kecskemét Spring Festival,** featuring music, theater, and literary readings. In the last week of August and the first week of September, gain a few pounds at the **Hírös Food Festival,** when the Hungarian food industry dishes out its best creations.

NEAR KECSKEMÉT: BUGAC

Bugac (boo-GATS), a giant rural area 35km outside Kecskemét, abuts Kiskunság National Park. Sand lizards and vipers share the park with gray cattle, twisted-horned sheep, and the Mangalica pig. To make the most of your day, start with a visit to **Bugac Tours,** Szabadság tér 5/A, Kecskemét (tel. 48 25 00; fax 48 16 43; email bugac@mail.datanet.hu; www.datanet.hu/~bugac; open Apr.-Oct. 8am-8pm). The most popular destination for those with fast-shutter cameras is the 40min. **horse show.** Since the cowboys were constantly on the move due to raids, they taught their horses all kinds of tricks, such as lying down to hide. When the Nonius steeds perform now, it's all for show: tricks include sitting at the dinner table and shaking hands with their masters. The performance culminates with the breathtaking "Koch five-in-hand," in which a horseman drives a band of five horses at a staggering speed while he stands with one foot on the rumps of the two back horses. (Shows May-Sept. 15 at 1:15 and 3:15pm; Apr. and Oct. with enough people. Admission and a carriage ride 1600Ft, students 800Ft; without carriage ride 800Ft, students 400Ft. Carriage departs bus stop one hr. before show.)

The national park offers some lovely hikes and bike rides in the hilly juniper forest. **Táltos Panzió** (tel. 37 26 33; fax 37 25 80), next to Bugaci Karikás Csárda in Bugac-Felső, or **Bugac Tours** in Kecskemét, arrange **horseback riding** (1440-1800Ft per hr.), carriage rides (1000Ft per hr.), bike rentals, and wintertime sledding. At the bus stop where Beton út meets Főld út, a summer souvenir shop offers **tourist information** and directions. The national park **ticket office,** about 1km past the souvenir shop and right before Bugac-Puszta, offers info, but the staff's English ability depends on who is working that day. If you get hungry out on the range, try **Bugaci Karikás Csárda** (tel. 37 26 88), which has sated the appetites of the horse-mad British royal family (hence the pictures). The elegant Hungarian specialties (600-2500Ft) are more than a few steps above cowboy grub, but who says that budget travelers need to rough it *all* the time? (Open daily 8am-10pm. MC/Visa.)

PUTTING THE KOCH BEFORE THE HORSE

According to *puszta* folklore, German painter Koch, after his first visit to the region, painted a young *nagyaföld* cowboy leading a team of five horses speeding across the plain. Rather than riding normally, however, he painted the boy standing on the rumps of the last two horses—a romantic depiction of *puszta* daring that, whether merely the whim of the artist or a cover-up for some errant brush-stroke, had no basis whatsoever in reality. Nevertheless, the locals who saw the painting were inspired by the challenge and tried unsuccessfully to replicate the feat. Eventually, one skillful horsehand at Bugac succeeded in realizing Koch's boyishly macho vision of super-human skill. Today, the oft-performed trick forms the basis for an entire tourist industry on the *puszta* and is known as the Koch-five-in-hand.

GETTING THERE. **Bugac Karikás Csárda** and its *puszta*, where you'll find the horse shows, is about 6km north of Bugac and not directly accessible by public transportation, so be prepared to walk. The narrow-gauge **train** (tel. 32 24 60) leaves from **Kecskemét's little train station** (not the main station) on Halasi u. To get there, head down Batthyány u. from the center and cross the overpass (20min. walk). Or, take local bus #2 from the central bus terminal behind the Aranyhomok Hotel. (90Ft from the driver, 60Ft from a kiosk.) The train (1hr.) stops at four places in the Bugac area. The first, Bugac-Puszta, is *not* where the horse shows are. The next, Bugac town, is where to stop if you're looking for a private room. Bugac-Felső is the third stop and closest to the riding school. Bugaci Karikás Csárda (see below), the fourth stop, is about halfway between the town of Bugac and the horse shows; this is the most central stop. Continue from here along the tracks until a sand path crosses them, turn right, and follow the path to the Bugaci Karikás Csárda, where horse-show tickets are sold (10min.). For a good daytrip, take the 8:25am **train,** which meanders through the countryside to Bugac (350Ft, students 200Ft; buy tickets on the train). Other departures are at 2pm and 8pm. Return to Kecskemét either by the 6:35pm train or bus from Bugac. The Kecskemét Bugac Tours also arranges daytrips (see p. 329). **Buses** (45min., 6 per day, 300Ft) depart from the main **Kecskemét** station. There is no stop for Csárda; bring a brochure to show the driver, and remind him when you see the beige sign for Bugac Csárda. From the stop near a souvenir stand, follow the *green* sign to the ticket office to find out when the bus will be coming back.

NORTHERN HUNGARY

Hungary's northern upland is dominated by a series of six low mountain ranges running northeast from the Danube Bend along the Slovak border. Surrounding its leisurely towns, the same hills that yield unique vintage wines also provide endless opportunities for outdoor exploration. The Bükk and Aggtelek National Parks beckon hikers with their scenic trails and complex caves, while it seems that every town has its own distinctive export, from the Lipizzaner ponies of Szilvásvárad to the famous red and white wines of Eger and Tokaj, respectively. The result is a blessed pairing of alcohol and recreation, two joys of the traveler's life.

EGER

The siege of Eger Castle and István Dobó's subsequent defeat of the overwhelming Ottoman army figures prominently in Hungarian national lore. The key to victory: the strengthening powers of local *Egri Bikavér* (Bull's Blood) wine. The legacy remains alive today with the vibrant cellars of the Valley of the Beautiful Women and the dozens of historical monuments scattered throughout the city, an inviting combination that lends the city a feeling of perpetual sunshine. Eger seduces visitors with infectious tipsiness, gypsy musicians, and charming locals, found deep in its lively wine cellars or along its cobblestone streets.

ORIENTATION

Eger is centered around **Dobó tér,** the main square. Most of the main sights are within a 10min. walk of the square, except for the Valley of the Beautiful Women, which is 15min. southwest of the center. The **bus station** is just uphill from Dobó tér. To get to the center from the station, exit from terminal 10 and head right on **Barkoczy u.,** the main street in front of the station, then turn right on the first street, Brody u. Follow the stairs down to the end of the street and turn right onto Széchenyi u. A left down Érsek u. brings you to Dobó tér. The **train station** lies on the outskirts of town; take bus #11, 12, or 14 to get from the train station to the bus terminal (90Ft). Alternately, head straight from the station, take a right onto **Deák u.** and after about 10min., take a right onto **Kossuth Lajos u.** and an immediate left onto Széchenyi u. (between the cathedral and the Lyceum). A final right onto **Érsek u.** will bring you to Dobó tér (20min.).

PRACTICAL INFORMATION

Trains: Vasút u. (tel. 31 42 64). Sends trains to: **Budapest's Keleti station** (2hr., 5 direct per day, 1050Ft); **Füzesabony** (20min., 12 per day, 112Ft), which connects to **Budapest** and **Miskolc** (2nd leg 1½hr., total price 498Ft); **Szeged** (4½hr, 1 per day, 812Ft); **Szilvásvárad** (1¼hr., 6 per day, 180Ft). Budapest trains split in Hatvan—confirm with passengers or the conductor that your car is going to Budapest.

Buses: Barkóczy u. (tel. 41 05 52). To: **Budapest** (2hr., 15-22 per day, 1080Ft); **Szilvásvárad** (45min., every 30min.-1hr., 246Ft); **Aggtelek** (3hr., 1 per day, 8:45am departure, 5pm return, 910Ft); **Debrecen** (3hr., 3-6 per day, 1080Ft).

Tourist Office: Tourinform, Dobó tér 2 (tel./fax 32 18 07; email tourinfo@agria.hu). The English-speaking staff gladly provides accommodations info and good **maps**, and will research what they don't already know. Open M-F 9am-5:30pm, Sa-Su 10am-1pm.

Bank: OTP, Széchenyi u. 2 (tel. 31 08 06), gives AmEx/MC/Visa advances, and charges no commission on AmEx traveler's checks. A Cirrus/MC/Plus/Visa **24-hour ATM** stands outside. Open M, Tu, Th 7:45am-3:15pm, W 7:45am-5pm, F 7:45am-12:45pm; currency desk open M, Tu, Th until 1:45pm, W until 1:45 and 2:30-3:30pm, F until 11:45am.

Pharmacy: Dobó tér 2 (tel. 31 23 74), sells American and Western European brand names. Open M-F 7:30am-6pm, Sa 8am-12:30pm.

Post Office: Széchenyi u. 22 (tel. 31 32 32). **Telephones** are inside. Open M-F 8am-8pm, Sa 8am-1pm. **Postal code:** 3300.

Internet: PC Club, Mecset u. 2 (tel. 31 05 06), is accessible and open late. The staff is helpful at manipulating the Hungarian keyboards. The club is visible from the bridge leaving Dobó tér. Directly after crossing the bridge, make a left and the office faces the parking lot. 480Ft for 1hr. Open daily 10am-10pm.

Phone code: 36.

ACCOMMODATIONS

The best and friendliest accommodations are **private rooms;** look for *Zimmer frei* signs outside the city center, particularly on Almagyar u. and Mekcsey u. near the castle. (Around 2000Ft per person.) It's best to go knocking at lunchtime. **Eger Tourist,** Bajcsy-Zsilinszky u. 9 (tel. 41 17 24; fax 41 17 68), arranges private rooms in the center. (Around 3000Ft per person. Breakfast included. Open M-F 9am-5pm.)

Tourist Motel, Mekcsey u. 2 (tel. 42 90 14). A favorite of tour groups. The curfew-breaking 12-year olds can get loud, but the rooms are tidy and spacious. Doubles 2800Ft, with bath 3600Ft; triples 3450Ft, 4350Ft; quads 4800Ft, 5600Ft.

Eszterházi Károly Kollégiuma, Leányka u. 2/6 (tel. 41 23 99), is another cheap option, but the way is not well-marked. From Dobó tér with your back to the church, exit the square to the right, walking over the river and past the outdoor cafes. Turn right again on Dobó u., walk through Dózsa Gry. tér, and turn left as if to enter the castle. Take the stairs to the right just before the castle gate. After the underpass, you'll emerge on Leanyka u.; the Kollégiuma is the multi-leveled cement building on the left. 900Ft per person in triples and quads. Open July to early Sept. Call ahead.

Autós Caravan Camping, Rákóczi u. 79 (reserve through Eger Tourist), is 20min. north of the center on bus #5, 11, or 12. Get off at the Shell station and look for signs to the campground. 320Ft per person; 250Ft per tent. Open Apr. 15-Oct. 15.

FOOD

There are plenty of food options along Széchenyi u., but grocery stores are usually the cheapest and quickest way to eat. A giant **ABC supermarket** hides in its own little square, directly off Széchenyi u. between Sandor u. and Szt. Janos u. (Open M 6am-6pm, Tu-F 6am-6:30pm, Sa 6am-noon.) A daily **fruit and vegetable market** (spiced with paprika and the locals who grow it) sits just off Széchenyi u.—turn right on Arva Köz and the stands will be on the right. (Open in summer M-F 6am-6pm, Sa 6am-1pm, Su 6-10am; off-season M-F 6am-5pm, Sa 6am-1pm, Su 6-10am.)

HBH Bajor Söház, Bajcsy-Zsilinsky u. 19 (tel. 31 63 12), off Dobó tér directly across from the pharmacy, is a Bavarian beer house serving Hungarian standards such as cold brains, ham knuckles, and goose liver (entrees 599-1499Ft). Polyglot waiters and an English menu make the dining experience much less intimidating, if slightly less exotic. Open daily 10am-10pm.

Kulacs Csárda Borozó, (tel./fax 31 13 75), in the Valley of the Beautiful Women. The vine-draped courtyard keeps the crowds coming with a menu featuring Hungarian specialties and some rare, non-fried options. Meals 720-1100Ft. Open Tu-Su noon-10pm.

Stella Restaurant, Dobó tér 6/a (tel. 41 35 42). The billiards in the back attract the local 18-and-under set to this Hungarian-style pizzeria–potential toppings include roasted paprika, smoked ox tongue, and curded ewe cheese (380-880Ft).

Gyros Étterem, Széchenyi u. 10 (tel. 31 01 35), serves gyros (599Ft), souvlaki (595Ft), and small but tasty Greek salads (299Ft).

Dobos, Szécheny u. 6. Proves why Hungarians don't diet with its decadent pastries (75-120Ft). See for yourself with a Dobos Bomba (120Ft) and a cappuccino (260Ft). Open daily 9am-10pm.

SIGHTS

EGER CASTLE (EGRI VÁR). A symbol of Hungarian national pride, Egri Vár's innards include subterranean barracks, catacombs, a crypt, and, of course, a wine cellar. One ticket buys admission to the three museums in the castle: a **picture gallery** showing Hungarian paintings from as early as the 15th century; the **Dobó István Vármúzeum,** which displays excavated artifacts, armor, and an impressive array of weapons; and the **dungeon exhibition,** a collection of torture equipment that will inspire sadists and masochists alike. The 400-year-old **wine cellars** are also open to the public for tastings. Be careful, though, because the bar is in the same room as the hands-on archery exhibit where 10-year olds are taught to shoot long-bows.

ORIGINS OF A STRANGE NAME When Egri Vár was under siege by 100,000 Ottoman soldiers, Dobó István and his 2000 men downed mass quantities of the region's notorious wine. According to legend, the rich wine stained the beards of Hungarian soldiers red. When they failed to succumb to the overwhelming opposition, it was rumored among the Turks that the fierce Hungarians were quaffing the blood of bulls for strength. The rumor gave the vintage a name–Bull's Blood.

With real arrows. *(Tel. 31 27 44; ext. 111 to get information. Castle open daily 8am-8pm; museums open Tu-Su 9am-5pm; wine cellars open Tu-Su 10am-5pm; underground passages open M only. Castle 100Ft, students 50Ft; all three museums Tu-Su 300Ft, 150Ft; M 250Ft, 120Ft; wine cellars 60Ft. English tours 300Ft.)*

VALLEY OF THE BEAUTIFUL WOMEN (SZÉPASSZONYVÖLGY)

Start on Széchenyi u. with Eger Cathedral to your right. Make a right onto Kossuth Lajos u. and then a quick left onto Deák u., although the signpost on Kossuth Lajos u. directs you otherwise. Continue on Deák u. and make the first right onto Telekessy u., just before the Flintstone-esque "1956" monument. At the first big intersection, Telekassy u. becomes Király u. Continue straight; after about 10min., follow the fork to the left onto Szépasszony-völgy, after the cemetary. A few minutes later, the valley appears. Most cellars are open from around 10am and begin to close around 6 or 7pm. Some stay open as late as 4am, but the best time to visit is late afternoon. Little tasting glasses are free, 100mL shots run 30-50Ft, and 1L of wine is about 300Ft, less if you bring your own container.

After a morning of exploring Eger's historical sights, the early evening is well spent in the wine-cellars of the Valley of the Beautiful Women. Following World War II, cheap land made it possible for hundreds of cellars to sprout up on this volcanic hillside. Most of the 25 open cellars consist of little more than 20m of tunnels and a few tables and benches, but each has its own personality: some are subdued, while others are rowdy with Hungarian and Roma (gypsy) sing-alongs. Although locals pride themselves on white wines as well, Eger is Hungary's red wine capital; the most popular libations are the famous *Bikavér* and the sweeter *Medok*, or *Medina*. The valley is designed for people serious about buying, but many spend hours lingering in the friendly, smoky cellars, or outside chatting, wine-filled tupperware in hand. Visitors push coins into the spongy fungus on cellar walls—supposedly if your coin sticks, you'll return.

A good place to start is at **cellar #3,** where a South African woman will give you a thorough and entertaining introduction to the area's wines. *(Usually open 3pm-late.)* Other than her, you'll most likely be confronted with broken German. **Cellar #16** is usually still kicking when others have begun to close, probably because they serve the best *Medok* in the valley. Although the budget gospel dictates otherwise, the smart (and kind) thing to do here is to enjoy all the samples you want, and then buy a bottle of your favorite—this way the cellars can continue to give free tastings.

LYCEUM. The fresco in the library on the first floor of the Rococo Lyceum depicts an ant's-eye-view of the Council of Trent, out of which came the edicts of the Counter Reformation—hence the lightning bolt blasting a pile of heretical books. Upstairs, a small **astronomical museum** houses 18th-century telescopes and instruments from the building's old observatory. *(Open Tu-F 9:30am-1pm, Sa-Su 9:30am-noon. 200Ft, students 100Ft.)* A marble line in the floor represents the meridian; when the sun strikes the line through a pin-hole aperture in the south wall, it is astronomical noon. Two floors farther up, a **camera obscura** satisfies the peeping-tom in all of us. The mechanism projects a live picture of the surrounding town onto a table, providing a god-like view of the world below in a tower room so hot you won't forget your mortality. *(At the corner of Kossuth Lajos u. and Eszterházy tér.)*

EGER CATHEDRAL. Built in 1837 by Joseph Hild to be the largest in Hungary, this was quickly eclipsed by Hild's larger church in Esztergom. Half-hour **organ concerts** are held here from May to mid-October; the exquisite organist and soprano make the concerts well-worth the small admission price. *(The yellow Basilica on Eszterházy tér right off Széchenyi u. Concerts M-Sa 11:30am, Su 12:45pm. 300Ft, under 18 100Ft.)*

OTHER SIGHTS. The Baroque pink **Minorita Templom** (Minorite Church) in Dobó tér was built in 1773, and overlooks a statue of Captain Dobó and two Hungarian defenders, including a woman poised to hurl a rock upon an unfortunate Turk. Capture another Kodak moment at the 40m **Minaret,** the Ottomans' northernmost phallic symbol. From Dobó tér, walk down Mescet u. on the right—it leads right to the Turkish tower. The steep spiral staircase is not much wider than the average 20th-century person—only the intrepid make it to the top. *(Open daily 10am-6pm; closed in winter. 50Ft.)* The 18th-century **Szerb Ortodox Templom** (Serbian Orthodox Church) on Vitkovics u. at the town center's northern end drips with elaborate gilt ornamentation. Follow Széchenyi u. from the center and enter at #15. *(Open daily 10am-4pm.)*

ENTERTAINMENT

In summer, the city's **open-air baths** (a.k.a. swimming pools) offer a desperately needed respite from the sweltering city as well as curative power over ailments such as bone disease and "weariness." (Open May 1-Sep. 30 M-F 6am-7pm, Sa-Su 8am-7pm; Oct. 1-Apr. 30 daily 9am-7pm. Full-day swimming ticket 280Ft, 170Ft students and pensioners, 6-8am or 4:30-8:30pm only 100Ft.) Eger revels in its heritage during the **Baroque Festival,** held for two weeks in late July and early August. Nightly performances of operas, operettas, and medieval and Renaissance court music are held on Dobó tér, at the Basilica, and around the city. Buy tickets (300Ft, students 100Ft) at the place of performance. An international folk-dance festival, **Eger Vintage Days,** is held daily in the beginning of September. Ask at Tourinform (see **Practical Information,** p. 333) for schedules.

NEAR EGER: AGGTELEK

The spectacular **Baradla caves** wind for over 25km, straddling the Hungarian-Slovak border. In each chamber, a forest of dripping stalactites, stalagmites, and fantastically shaped stone formations tower over the visitor. The entrance (permitted only with a tour) in Hungary is at **Aggtelek** (AWG-tel-eck). A variety of tours are available, all in Hungarian (tel./fax (48) 35 00 06). Hour-long tours assemble daily at 10am, 1pm, 3pm, and in the high-season also at 5pm, and whenever more than 10 people assemble. (600Ft, students 300Ft.) More difficult, longer tours covering the entire main branch of the cave (5hr., 7km) can be arranged through Naturinform. (Tel. (48) 34 30 73; call ahead. 3200Ft, students 1600Ft.) A large chamber inside the cave with perfect acoustics has been converted into an auditorium, and the tour takes a dramatic pause here for a low-tech **light show** set to apocalyptic music. Another hall contains an Iron Age **cemetery** where 13 people, thought to be recent crime victims when the cave was first discovered, are buried. The tunnels along the tour are broad and well lit, but the guide turns the lights off as you pass to discourage stragglers. The caves' temperature is 10°C year-round, so bring a jacket.

GETTING THERE. The one daily **bus** leaves **Eger** at 8:45am, whizzes through **Szilvásvárad** at 9:25am, and arrives in Aggtelek at 11:25am (910Ft) in front of Cseppkő Hotel. The returning bus leaves from the same stop at 3pm; the one to **Miskolc** is at 5pm. To get to the cave from the bus stop, walk out behind the hotel and, with your back to it, cut across the field toward the street. Once on the road, the national park is to the right. Although slightly pricey, **Cseppkő Restaurant,** up the hill from the cave, has the only traditional food in town. (Entrees 685-1280Ft.)

SZILVÁSVÁRAD

Beloved for its carriages, Lipizzaner horses, and surrounding national parks, Szilvásvárad (SEAL-vash-vah-rod) trots along at its own dignified clip. One of only four places in the world to breed the prize-winning Lipizzaners, Szilvásvárad takes pride in its modest claim to international prominence—locals will attempt to bridge all language barriers whenever the "conversation" turns to horses.

ORIENTATION & PRACTICAL INFORMATION. **Trains** run to and from **Eger** (1¼hr., 8 per day, 202Ft). The town has two stations; get off at the first, Szilvásvárad-Szalajkavölgy. **Buses** are generally the most convenient way to get in and out of Szilvásvárad, running to **Eger** (45 min., every 30min.-1hr., 246Ft) and **Aggtelek** (1¾hr., 9:25am, 629Ft). The town's one big street, **Egri út,** extends straight from the Szilvásvárad-Szalajkavölgy train station and bends sharply at the race course's tollbooth-ticket office. The booth marks the entrance to **Szalajka u.**, which leads directly to the national park. Farther north, Egri út turns into **Miskolci út.** There is no bus station; after passing the looming concrete factories of Bükkszentmárton, Szilvásvárad is the next town. Don't get off at the first bus stop in town, unless you want to investigate the *Zimmer frei* signs. The second stop is on Egri út, within sight of Szalajka u. There is no tourist office in town, so get information and a basic map at the **Eger Tourinform** (see p. 333) before heading out. **Hiking maps** are available at the tollbooth-ticket office (150Ft) and are posted throughout the park along hiking trails. More detailed hiking maps of the surrounding mountains (200Ft) are available at the small **bank** behind the second bus stop on Egri út. (Tel. 35 41 05. Open M-F 8am-noon and 12:30-4pm.) **Phone code:** 36.

ACCOMMODATIONS & FOOD. Although Szilvásvárad seems perfectly scaled for a daytrip, accommodations abound. Although still the cheapest option, *Zimmer frei* prices (1500Ft with no amenities) rise during the Lipicai Festival. **Hegy Camping,** Egri út 36a (tel. 35 52 07) offers great views of the valley from the groomed campground. (500Ft per person, students 300Ft; tents 400Ft, more than 2 people 550Ft.) Bungalows come with bath. (Doubles 3000Ft; triples 4050Ft; quads 4600Ft; tax 300Ft per person. Open Apr. 15- Oct. 15.)

Csobogó, Szalajka u. 1 (tel. (30) 41 52 49), on the road to the national park, lies among all sorts of *büfé*, but stands out among the restaurants. In addition to traditional meals toned down for tourists, it offers a selection of "international" dishes, including vegetarian meals. (300Ft. Open daily 11am-8pm; summer Sa-Su until midnight.) For picnic supplies, the cheapest food in town is at the **Mini Coop Market,** Egri út 6. (Open M-F 6:30am-6pm, Sa 6:30am-1pm, Su 8am-noon.)

SIGHTS & ENTERTAINMENT. Although the town is only one street long, outdoor opportunities abound, from leisurely biking in the Szalajka Valley to hikes in the low Bükk mountains. **Horse shows** kick into action many weekends in the arena on Szalajka u., just to the right of the park entrance (400Ft per person). Or jump into the thick of things by learning how to drive a carriage, brandish a whip, or ride a steed. Many farms offer horse riding, especially in July and August. **Péter Kovács,** a round, friendly man, Egri út 62 (tel. 35 53 43), rents horses (1500Ft per hr.) and two-horse carriages (4500Ft). See where it all begins at **Lipicai Stables** (tel. 35 51 55), the stud farm for Szilvásvárad's Lipizzaner breed. Walking on Egri út away from the park entrance, make a left onto Enyves u. and follow signs to the farm. (Open for viewing daily 8:30am-noon, 2pm-4pm. 80Ft.) In late July, the extremely popular **Lipicai Festival** (call Lipicai Stables for information) ushers carriage drivers from all over the world for a grand three-day competition of horses and reins.

Shaded walks through the **Bükk mountains** and the **Szalajka valley** are beautiful, but not always relaxing—in June the trails swarm with school groups, packs of 14-year-olds, and families with more children than you can eat. At the **Fátyol waterfall,** the lazy trailside stream transforms into the most dramatic—and most popular—of the park's attractions. It only takes 45min. to walk here along the green trail, or 15min. by the little open-air train, which departs just to the right of the stop sign at the park's entrance. (100Ft, students 60Ft.) A 30min. hike along the green trail beyond the waterfalls leads to the **Istálósk cave,** home to a bear cult during the Stone Age (see **History,** p. 263). After clearing the brook, the trail becomes extremely steep—either bring a walking stick or wear shoes with good traction. One way of avoiding crowds is to **rent a bike** at Szalajka u. 28 (tel. (60) 35 26 95), just past the stop sign at the entrance to the park. The wide, flat paths are just rough enough to make it interesting. The shop also arranges trips to the local plateaus for groups of 10 or more for the cost of a day's rental. (500Ft for the first hour, 200Ft each additional hour, or 1200Ft per day. Open in summer daily 9am-dusk; off-season in good weather only.)

TOKAJ

Locals say that King Louis XIV called Tokaj (toke-EYE) vintage "the wine of kings and the king of wines." Although Tokaj is just one of many small towns at the foot of the Kopasz Mountains (er, hills) that produce unique whites, it lends its name to the entire class of wine. And rightly so—even the smell of wine hangs in the air above the wide, sunny streets of this town on the muddy Tisza river. If Tokaj gives the wine its name, the wine gives Tokaj its flavor, with days split between leisurely exploration of the famed local cellars and river fun on the opposite bank.

ORIENTATION & PRACTICAL INFORMATION. **Trains,** Baross G. u. 18 (tel. 35 20 20), chug to **Miskolc** (1hr., 12 per day, 348Ft) and **Nyíregyháza** (30min., 13 per day, 218Ft), which connects to **Debrecen** (from Tokaj 1½hr., 8 per day, 576Ft). **Buses** leave from the train station, but only service local towns. The trek from the train station to the town's center takes about 15min. on foot; with your back to the entrance of the station, walk left along the railroad tracks until you reach an underpass, then turn left on Bajcsy-Zsilinszky u. At the Hotel Tokaj fork, stay on the left road. It only takes 10min. to walk across Tokaj's center. The main **Bajcsy-Zsilinszky u.** becomes **Rákóczi u.** after the Tisza bridge, transforming again after **Kossuth tér.** to become **Bethlen Gábor u.** Some pensions' and wine cellars' brochures include primitive street **maps**—these may be the only ones you'll find. **Tokaj Tours/Tourinform,** Serház u. 1 (tel./fax 35 33 90), on the right side of Rákóczi u. as you walk into town, arranges private and hotel rooms (no fee), organizes tours of the region and wine tastings, and can set you up with a horse, canoe, or rafting tour. (Open M-F 9am-5pm, Sa 9am-1pm.) However, the office was closed in June 1999 and it is uncertain whether it will reopen. **Exchange currency** and traveler's checks or get MC/Visa cash advances at **OTP,** Rákóczi u. 35. (Tel. 35 25 21. Open M-Th 7:45am-3:15pm, F 7:45am-2:15pm.) There's a 24-hour Cirrus/MC/Plus/Visa **ATM** outside the bank. The **pharmacy** next to the Bacchus Etterem restaurant on Kossuth tér has regular hours; ring after hours for emergencies. (Open M-F 8am-5pm, Sa 8am-4pm, Su 8am-noon and 12:30-4pm.) The **post office** is at Rákóczi u. 24. (Tel. 35 24 17. Open M-F 8am-5pm, Sa 8am-noon.) **Postal code:** 3910. **Telephones** are sprinkled throughout the center and in the post office. **Phone code:** 47.

ACCOMMODATIONS & FOOD. See what Tokaj Tours has to offer, but *Zimmer frei* and *Szoba Kiadó* signs abound—your best bet is to walk along Rákóczi u. and venture down random streets to choose one you like. (Singles generally run 1500-2000Ft; doubles 3000-5000Ft.) Don't be afraid to bargain, but beware: your host may well talk you into sampling—and buying—her expensive homemade vintage. *Zimmer frei* etiquette dictates that you not go ringing on doors after 8:30 or 9pm. **Grof Széchenyi István Students Hostel,** Bajcsy-Zsilinszki u. 15-17 (tel. 35 23 55), the white building with the statue out front as you walk from the train station toward the center, is the best deal around, with fresh, recently renovated doubles (3800Ft with bath) and sparse but clean quads (3000Ft). Although they usually only cater to large groups, single travelers might still want to check it out on the way into town from the train station. (Open July-Aug. only; the reception is usually missing around lunch-time). **Lux Panzió,** Serház u. 14 (tel. 35 21 45), provides sunny rooms suffused with pink. Ask for the double with the shower in the room—it's the same price as those with a shower down the hall. (Doubles 3500Ft; triples 5200Ft; 125Ft tourist tax; all have bath, triples also have TV.) To get there, make a right onto Városháza-köz from Rákóczi u., just after OTP. The *panzió* is the last building on the left. If you think you're tougher than the mosquitoes that control the Tisza's banks (and you might want to think again), proceed across the river on the Tisza bridge (only 5min. from the center). The mega-center **Camping Tisza,** on the right as you cross the river, rents out waterfront campsites and tiny bungalows to the traveling hordes, keeping them busy until the

A MINI-GUIDE TO HUNGARIAN WINE Wine connoisseurs have been aware of the merits of Hungarian wines for years, and budget travelers have long appreciated the low prices. The exotic names on the labels, however, might intimidate those used to *Chardonnay*. The main local products are *Furmint*, a basic dry or sweet white wine, and *Hárslevelű*, a slightly more complex white. The famous *Aszú*, *Furmint* sweetened with "noble rot" (grapes which ripen and dry out more quickly than others in the same bunch), forms the basis for the various Hungarian whites. According to local lore, *Aszú* wine was invented when Máté Szepsi Laczkó neglected his harvest in 1630—fearing Turkish invasion, he left his grapes to rot on the vine. The fruit produces an extremely sweet dessert wine that soon became popular among farmers. *Szamorodni* is an aperitif that contains a mix of *Aszú* and regular grapes—when the bunches are harvested, the wine will be either sweet or dry depending on the proportion of dried up *Aszú* raisins to fresh grapes. Getting a little more technical, sweetness is measured in three, four, five, or six *puttony*—the number of baskets of *Aszú* grapes added (six is the sweetest; some say too sweet). Supposedly 1972, 1988, and 1993 were the best *Aszú* years. *Fordítás*, a dessert wine known for leaving its drinkers with a mean hangover in the morning, is made from the residue of grapes left over in the barrel after the *Aszú* is finished. To be an expert, or just look like one, sample wines in order from driest to sweetest, and do not *ever* swallow. But if the idea of wasting good wine offends your budget ethic, go ahead and drink up. We won't tell.

wee hours with a casino, souvenir shops, and a disco that churns out "the best" in 80s dance music. (Tents 800Ft per person; with vehicles 1000Ft; 2-person bungalows 2000Ft; 4-person 3600Ft. 2pm check-out.)

The informal **Bacchus Etterem,** centrally located at Kossuth tér 17 (tel. 35 20 54), serves up standard Hungarian foods (goulash 400Ft, pizza with ketchup 350Ft) on a lovely terrace; a 230-300Ft breakfast is also available. (Open M-Sa 8am-10pm, Su 9am-10pm.) The **ABC-Coop** supermarket, right in Kossuth tér, is by far the cheapest option. (Open M-F 6am-7pm, Sa 6am-1pm, Su 8-10:30am.)

SIGHTS & ENTERTAINMENT. Signs reading *Bor Pince* herald **private wine cellars** whose owners are generally pleased to let visitors sample their wares (50mL 90-500Ft, depending on the cellar.) Walk on in, or be bold and ring the bell if the cellar looks shut. The big flashy cellars on the main road are more touristy—explore the side streets for higher-quality wines. Serious commercialized **tasting** takes place at the best respected and largest of the lot: **Rákóczi Pince,** Kossuth tér 15 (tel. 35 20 09; fax 35 21 41). This 1.5km system of tunnels served as the imperial wine cellar for two centuries, until the end of WWI. In 1526, János Szapohjai was elected king of Hungary in the elegant and surprisingly large subterranean hall. Five-hundred years worth of dripping, spongy fungus keeps the cellar at 10°C regardless of the weather outside. **Wine tastings** and **group tours** of the cellar and hall usually occur on the hour, but can be pre-empted by tour groups. **Individual tours** can also be arranged at any time. (Open daily 10am-8pm. English-speaking guides available July-Aug. 1200Ft for the 30min. tour and a 6-glass wine-tasting. AmEx/MC/Visa.)

The young **Tokaji Hímesudvar cellars,** Bem u. 2 (tel. 35 24 16), not only produce phenomenal Aszú wines (their 1993 *5-puttonyos* received several international awards), but also offer immense tastings. The friendly, English-speaking Várhelyi family will be glad to guide you through the history of the region and the subtleties of the Tokaj wines. To get to the royal hunting lodge where the cellar is located, take the road to the left of the Catholic church in Kossuth tér and then follow the prominent signs to the cellar. (Open daily 9am-9pm. Tastings 280-1300Ft.) The **Tóth family cellar** at Óvár út 40, just off Rákóczi u. past the post office, produces five exceptional whites, including a 1988 *6-puttonyos Aszú.* (300Ft for 5 glasses.)

Tokaji Galléria, Bethlen Gábor u. 15, in an old red and cream Greek Orthodox Church, puts on free exhibitions by local artists that vary from funky paintings to landscape photography—check at Tokaj Tours to get a summer schedule of exhibitions. (Open June-Oct. Tu-Su 10am-4pm. 200Ft, students 100Ft.)

Outdoor recreation in Tokaj is becoming as popular as the wine that brings people here. **Vízisport Centrum,** at the campground to the left after crossing the bridge, rents bikes (500Ft per day) and canoes (1200Ft per day, 100Ft per half-hour), will drive you to the beginning of the Tisza for a long canoe trip (100Ft per km), and arranges horseback-riding (600Ft per hr., 1000Ft with trainer). **Camping Tisza** also rents canoes (4-seater 1000Ft per day).

With all the wine around, bars and discos aren't that common here. In summer, a **boat disco** floats on the river near Bajcsy-Zsilinszki u. across from Camping Tisza. The fun starts at 10pm with cheap beer and plenty of Hungarian hip-hop grooves, but don't forget the bug repellent. (Cover charge 250Ft. Open June-Aug. only.) **Veres Szekér Söröző,** Rákóczi u. 30-32, packs in students and young people for an after-dinner round. (0.5L beer 80-130Ft; 100mL wine 30-180Ft; pool 60Ft per game. Open daily 5pm-2am.)

LATVIA (LATVIJA)

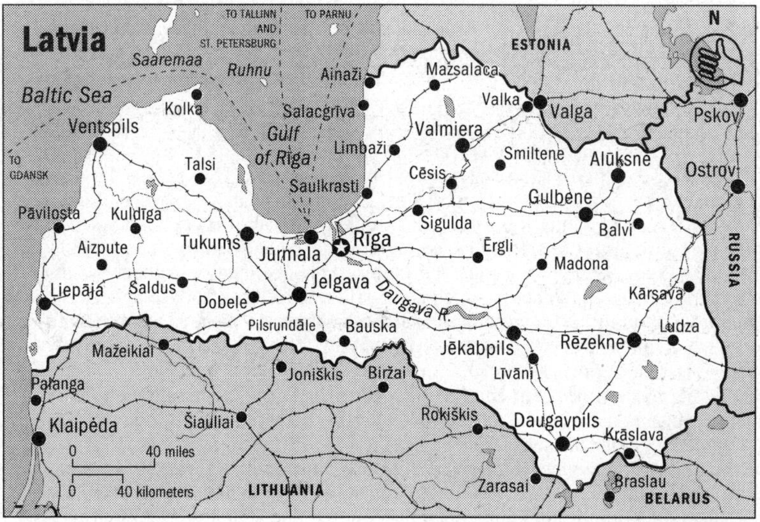

US$1 = 0.59LS (LATS)	**1LS = US$1.70**
CDN$1 = 0.40LS	**1LS = CDN$2.52**
UK£1 = 0.95LS	**1LS = UK£1.06**
IR£1 = 0.79LS	**1LS = IR£1.26**
AUS$1 = 0.38LS	**1LS = AUS$2.61**
NZ$1 = 0.31LS	**1LS = NZ$3.21**
SAR1 = 0.10LS	**1LS = SAR10.25**
DM1 = 0.32LS	**1LS = DM3.13**

PHONE CODES Country code: **371.** International dialing prefix: **00.**

Except for a brief period of independence ending with World War II, Latvia was ruled by Germans, Swedes, and Russians from the 13th century through 1991. A half-century of Soviet occupation left the legacy of a mass exodus of Latvians and a huge influx of Russians. With the smallest majority of natives of the three Baltic States, Latvia remains the least affluent and developed. Attitudes toward the many Russians who still live in the country are softening, but evidence of national pride abounds, from patriotically renamed streets bleeding with crimson-and-white flags, to a rediscovery of native holidays predating even the Christian invasions. Rīga, Latvia's only large city, is a westernizing capital luring more and more international companies. The rest of the country is mostly a provincial expanse of green hills dominated by tall birches and pines, dairy pastures, and quiet settlements.

HIGHLIGHT OF LATVIA

- The largest and most cosmopolitan of the Baltic capitals, **Rīga** draws visitors with its phenomenal museums and thumping discos. This birthplace of Baryshnikov also offers a wealth of fascinating daytrips to the countryside and seashore (p. 346).

LIFE & TIMES

HISTORY

Modern Latvia stands at the Baltic crossing of two historical and religious strains. Latgale, or southeastern Latvia, was historically tied to Catholic, Central European Lithuania and Poland. Northern Latvia, on the other hand, took the Estonian path, influenced mainly by Baltic and Lutheran powers.

Latvia has consistently struggled under the yoke of foreign rule. Problems began with the German **Confederation of Livonia,** which ruled over the territory for nearly 300 years. The confederation collapsed when Russian Tsar Ivan IV (the Terrible), invaded, beginning the 25-year **Livonian War** (1558-83) and a half-century of division. The 1629 Truce of Altmark brought an extended period of relative stability and freedom known as the **Swedish interlude,** achieved by ceding control of eastern Livonia to the Poles, while giving Rīga and the northern regions to Sweden. Sweden, however, was forced to cede the Livonian territories to Peter The Great under the Peace of Nystad in 1721, and with the **second partition of Poland** in 1795 the entire country fell under Russian control. Latvia continued to struggle for autonomy, but its independence efforts never achieved the vigor of its Baltic neighbors.

Reacting to the Bolshevik coup of November 1917, the **Latvian People's Council** finally proclaimed independence on November 18, 1918, establishing a government in Rīga led by **Kārlis Ulmanis.** Over the next few years, the country was overrun by battling armies. Latvians, Germans, White Russians, British, French, Estonians, Lithuanians, and the Red Army all fought for supremacy. By 1920, the Latvians were in control. Democratic coalitions ruled the country, and Ulmanis lasted four terms as prime minister, served a stint as benevolent dictator, and finally spent several years as president. As per the **German-Soviet Nonaggression Pact,** Latvia fell under the control of the USSR in 1938. However, Germany reneged on the Pact in 1941 and occupied Latvia itself. In 1945, the Red Army drove them back out.

Latvia was one of the wealthiest and most industrialized regions of the **Soviet Union.** But under Soviet rule, it was torn by radical economic restructuring, political repression, and a thorough **Russification** of its national culture. Immigrants from the rest of the USSR poured into the country, rarely bothering to learn the local language or to identify with the indigenous population, and subsequently dominated local politics. Within four decades, ethnic Latvians accounted for only half the population, a sharp drop from the three-quarters before the war.

Never reconciled to their incorporation into the Soviet Union, the Latvians were more than ready to take advantage of Soviet Premier Gorbachev's willingness to reform the Soviet system. Under **glasnost** and **perestroika,** Latvians protested *en masse* over the poor state of their environment and created the **Popular Front** of Latvia in 1988. The Communists were trounced in the 1990 elections. On May 4, 1990, the new legislature declared Latvia independent, but Soviet intervention sparked violent clashes in Rīga in 1991. Finally, after the failed Moscow coup in August, the Latvian legislature reasserted its **independence,** and the nation's sovereignty was recognized by most of the world in September 1991.

WHEN LIFE GIVES YOU LEMONS... Hey, having a disgruntled Russian population and a depressed economy isn't all bad, right? The former circumstance has given Latvia a fairly healthy vodka industry, while the latter has kept prices down and made distributors eager to get supply to a burgeoning international demand. Recently, smugglers took a page from the playbooks of collegiate binge drinkers, running their 300m pipeline down the throat of an Estonian border town en route from Rīga to Tallinn. The project was a smashing success (vodka costs 60% more in economically robust Estonia), until the international equivalent of an RA busted the party and confiscated the hardware. What's next...a toga party?

LATVIA TODAY

Latvia's transition to capitalism has been rocky. Initial glitches in the system led to problems with privatization and the failure of the Baltics' largest bank, but by 1995 most difficulties had been cleared up and the country was back on course. Since then, production has been rising, and the standard of living is beginning to approach pre-1991 levels again. Lax regulation has made Latvia the little Switzerland of ex-Communist countries; banking is booming.

Internal politics have been turbulent. The centrist-reform government is flanked by ultranationalist **Joachim Siegerist** and former KGB major **Juris Bojars,** all jockeying for position in the **Saeima** (Parliament). The country has also experienced a quick succession of Prime Ministers. However, President **Guntis Ulmanis,** interwar leader Kārlis Ulmanis's nephew, did manage to secure himself another term in June 1996 by sculpting a party comprising the LZS and the Latvian Christian-Democratic Union in alliance with the Latgalian Democratic Party. **Vilis Kristopans** became the new Prime Minister in the 1998 elections.

Latvia's most pressing problem may be its large Russian population, which constitutes 30.2% of the country. Due to Estonia's impending admission to the E.U., poor Latvia has become a punching bag for Russia, and its disenfranchisement of the remaining Russians led to an economic embargo in spring 1998. More lenient legislation was passed in response to the pressure, but many still view the Russians on their soil as a threat to Latvian culture and independence.

LITERATURE & ARTS

The legacy of the ancient Balts is powerful in Latvian literature. The **daina,** a folk song reflecting the pagan reverence of nature and a strong sense of ethics, has never left the Latvian memory. The first written literature, although late in coming, shows clear evidence of folk influence. The 17th-century poet **C. Fuereccerus** made use of the *daina's* stylistic elements, while **G. Mancelius,** founder of Latvian prose, simultaneously fought good-naturedly against the influence of the pagan songs.

The mid-19th century brought a national awakening as the country asserted its literary independence. The *daina*'s spirit was reflected in *Lāčplēsis (Bearslayer)*, **Andrējs Pumpurs's** 1888 national epic. Legend foretold that Pumpurs's hero would return to free Latvia, and believers say his 20th-century reappearance in the form of **Māra Zālite's** rock opera helped the cause.

Realism and social protest became important with the arrival of the New Movement in the last years of the 19th century. **Jānis Rainis** used folk imagery to depict contemporary problems, while his wife, **Aspazija,** fought for women's rights. The literary current shifted again with the 1905 Revolution as Latvians tried to break free from both imperialistic Russia and local German influence. Lyricism dominated, and the ethics of the *daina* were again invoked in the work of poet **Karlis Skalbe.**

New literary forms diversified Latvia's literature after the country achieved independence in 1918. **Jānis Akurāters's** romantic lyrics exhibit Nietzschean influence, while others, like **Kārlis Zariņš,** grappled with the aftermath of WWI. **Aleksandr Caks** used the ballad to caricature urban and suburban life, although his most outstanding work was *Marked by Eternity (Muzibas skartie)*, a haunting cycle about the Latvian riflemen of WWI. Many Latvian writers turned to psychological detail in the 20th century: **Mirdza Bendrupe's** Freudian prose explored the human psyche, **Eriks Adamsons** depicted modern neuroses, and **Anslavs Eglitis** reveled in intensifying human traits to the point of absurdity.

After WWII, Upītis became a leading writer, thanks in part to the political correctness of his texts. **Socialist Realism** failed to drown other trends, however. **Jānis Medenis,** exiled to a labor camp in Siberia, longed for a free Latvia in his poetry; **Imants Ziedonis** also managed to foster independent Latvian literature despite the authorities' tight censorship. **Martis Ziverts,** who wrote one-act plays, is generally regarded as the best 20th-century Latvian playwright.

READING LIST

The **Lithuanian Reading List** (p. 363) provides a good survey of Baltic history. *The Testimony of Lives: Narrative and Memory in Post-Soviet Latvia* by Vieda Skultans eloquently examines the recent difficulties experienced by Latvians.

FACTS AND FIGURES

- **Capital:** Rīga
- **Population:** 2,472,174
- **Land Area:** 64,610km^2
- **Geography:** Low plains
- **Languages:** Latvian, Russian
- **Religions:** 15% Lutheran, 15% Catholic, 8% Orthodox
- **GDP per capita:** US$2,162
- **Major Exports:** Forestry products

LATVIA ESSENTIALS

Irish, U.K., and U.S. citizens can visit Latvia for up to 90 days without a visa. Citizens of Australia, Canada, New Zealand, and South Africa require 90-day visas, obtainable at a Latvian consulate (see **Essentials: Embassies & Consulates,** p. 13) or the Rīga airport. Single-entry visas cost US$15; multiple-entry cost US$30; 24hr. rush processing costs US$60 (single-entry) or US$90 (multiple-entry). Allow ten days for standard processing. Send the application with your passport, one photograph, and payment by check or money order. For extensions, apply to the Department of Immigration and Citizenship (see **Rīga: Passport Office,** p. 348).

GETTING THERE & GETTING AROUND

Flights to Latvia use the Rīga Airport. **Air Baltic, SAS, Finnair, Lufthansa,** and others make the hop to Rīga from their hubs. **Trains** link Latvia to Berlin, Moscow, St. Petersburg, Tallinn, Lviv, Odessa, and Vilnius. Trains are cheap and efficient, but stations aren't well-marked, so get a map. The **suburban rail** system renders the entire country a suburb of Rīga.

Latvia's efficient long-distance **bus** network reaches Prague, Tallinn, Vilnius, and Warsaw. Buses, usually adorned with the driver's bizarre collection of Christian icons, stuffed animals, and stickers, are quicker than trains for travel within Latvia. Beware the standing-room-only long-distance jaunt. For daytrips from Rīga, you're best off taking the **electric train;** as a rule, a crowded train is more comfortable than a crowded bus. **Ferries** run to Rīga from Stockholm, Sweden and Kiel, Germany, but are slow and expensive. **Hitchhiking** is common, but hitchers may be expected to pay. *Let's Go* does not recommend hitchhiking.

PRIMARY BORDER CROSSINGS. Visas are not available at the border. While there is no official border crossing fee, you'll likely have to pay an unofficial US$20 fee to the border guards. Border crossings are quick. Traveling directly between Rīga and other capitals is the easiest way to enter Latvia.

Belarus: Daugavpils, LAT/Polatsk, BEL via Druya, BEL; connects Vidzeme and Latgale (p. 357) with Belarus.

Estonia: Valka, LAT/Valga, EST; connects Vidzeme and Latgale (p. 357) with Tartu (p. 258). Ainaži, LAT/Treimani, EST; connects Vidzeme and Latgale (p. 357) and Pärnu (p. 248).

Lithuania: Daugavpils, LAT/Zarasai, LIT; connects Eastern Latvia with Vilnius (p. 365). Jelgava, LAT/Joniškis, LIT; connects Rīga (p. 344) with Šiauliai (p. 380).

Russia: Rēzekne, LAT/Pskov, RUS (p. 625); connects Eastern Latvia with Northwest Russia (p. 596).

TOURIST SERVICES & MONEY

Look for the green "i" marking some tourist offices, but don't expect much help from them. At most, the Soviet "we'll get paid anyway" work ethic still reigns. Private tourist offices are much more helpful. The **Tourist Club of Latvia** is a stand-out, and **Latvijas Universitātes Tūristu Klubs** plans outdoor (and other) adventures, with prices geared toward students (see **Rīga: Tourist Offices,** p. 348).

The Latvian currency unit is the **Lat** (100 santīmi=1 Lat; abbreviated Ls). There are many **ATMs** in Rīga linked to Cirrus, MC, and Visa, and at least one or two in larger towns. Larger businesses, restaurants and hotels accustomed to Westerners accept **MC** and **Visa. Traveler's checks** are harder to use; both AmEx and Thomas Cook can be converted in Rīga, but Thomas Cook is a safer bet outside the capital.

COMMUNICATION

Latvia is by far the most difficult of the Baltic states from which to call the U.S.; there's no way to make a free call on a Latvian phone to an international operator. Most telephones take **cards** (available in 2, 3, 5, or 10Lt denominations) from post offices, telephone offices, and large state stores. Try to make **international** calls from a telephone office, although they may simply sell you a phone card for a booth. Access numbers include **AT&T Direct,** tel. 700 70 07 in Rīga, tel. 827 00 70 07 otherwise, and **MCI,** tel. 724 50 05. The gradual switch to digital phones has made making a connection comparable to cracking a safe—sometimes you must dial a 2 before a number, sometimes a 7, and sometimes an 8 from an analog phone. To call abroad from an analog phone, dial 1, then 00, then the country code. From a digital phone, simply dial 00, then the country code. Phone offices and *Rīga in Your Pocket* have the latest information on phone system changes. Ask for *gaisa pastu* if you want to send something by **airmail. Email** is only available in Rīga.

LANGUAGE

A blend of German, Russian, Estonian, and Swedish influences, **Latvian** (see **Glossary,** p. 815) is a member of the Baltic language group. Life, however, proceeds bilingually. **Russian** is hated but universally spoken; use it as a last resort. Many young Latvians study **English,** but don't rely on it. The older set know some **German.** *Alus* (beer) is a crucial word in any language. Key places are the *autoosta* (bus station), *stacija* (train station), *lidosta* (airport), *viesnīca* (hotel), and *pasts* (post office). To find an English speaker ask, *"Vai jūs runāyat angliski?"*

HEALTH & SAFETY

Bathrooms are marked with an upward-pointing triangle for women, downward for men. Latvians claim that Rīga **tap water** is drinkable, but boil it for 10 minutes to be safe. **Bottled water** is available at grocery stores and kiosks, although it is usually carbonated. Pharmacies are well-stocked with German brands of tampons, condoms, and band-aids. Most restrooms require you to bring your own toilet paper. If you feel threatened, *"Ej prom"* (EY prawm) means "go away"; *"Lasies prom"* (LAH-see-oos PRAWM) says it more offensively, and *"Lasies lapās"* (LAH-see-oos LAH-pahs; "go to the leaves"), poetic though it may be, is even ruder. You are more likely to find English-speaking help from your **consulate** than from the police.

> **! EMERGENCY NUMBERS.**
> **Police:** tel. 02. **Fire:** tel. 01. **Ambulance:** tel. 03.

ACCOMMODATIONS

College dormitories, which open to travelers in the summer, are often the cheapest places to sleep. The **Tourist Club of Latvia** lists budget lodgings, makes travel arrange-

A MIDSUMMER NIGHT'S EVE Everybody's favorite *jogānu rituālus* (pagan ritual), Līgo, inflames Latvia on June 23rd–Midsummer. Bonfires consume the hills as young lovers, sent to the woods to find the legendary fern flower that blossoms only on Midsummer's Eve, consume each other–passionately. Men don oak-leaf crowns to assert their fertility, and women wear flower wreaths; *dainas* (folk songs) fill the air, and the whole country stays up all night chasing down *Jānu* cheese with rivers of beer, merriment, and God knows what. The whole celebration–bigger than Christmas, New Year's, and Baryshnikov's birthday–results in a national hangover so severe that many establishments remain closed for the day after.

ments, and books accommodations (see **Rīga: Tourist Offices,** p. 348). In Rīga, **Patricia** provides English info and arranges homestays and apartment rentals for around US$15 per night (see **Rīga: Accommodations,** p. 350). Many towns have only one **hotel** (if any) in the budget range; expect to pay 3-15Ls per night.

FOOD & DRINK

Latvian food is heavy, starchy, and greasy. Big cities offer foreign cuisine, and Rīga is one of the easiest places to be a vegetarian in all the Baltics. Tasty national specialties include the holiday dish *zirņi* (gray peas with onions and smoked fat), *maizes zupa* (bread soup usually made from cornbread, and full of currants, cream, and other goodies), and the warming *Rīgas* (or *Melnais*) *balzams* (a black liquor great with ice cream, Coke, or coffee). Dark rye bread is a staple. Try *speķa rauši*, a warm pastry, or *biezpienmaize*, bread with sweet curds. Dark-colored *kaņepju sviests* (hemp butter) is good but too diluted for "medicinal" purposes. Latvian beer, primarily from the Aldaris brewery, is stellar, particularly *Porteris*.

CUSTOMS & ETIQUETTE

If a **tip** is expected where you're dining, it will most often be included in the bill. As elsewhere in the region, expect to be bought a drink if you talk with someone a while; repay the favor in kind. If you're invited to a meal in someone's home, bring a **gift** for the hostess (an odd number of flowers is customary). **Shops** sometimes close for an hour or two between noon and 3pm. Rīga is the melting pot of the Baltics. Clubs catering to **gays and lesbians** advertise themselves as such freely, although attitudes are far less tolerant outside the city.

NATIONAL HOLIDAYS

January 1, New Year's; April 21, Good Friday; April 23-24, Catholic Easter; May 1, Labor Day; 2nd Sunday of May, Mother's Day; June 23, Līgo (Midsummer Festival); June 24, Jāni (St. John's Day); November 18, National Day (1918); December 25-26, Ziemsvētki (Christmas); December 31, New Year's Eve.

RĪGA

Huge, restless, alluring, and slippery, Rīga remains a city without a handle, forever eluding the grasp of the terms and powers that have sought to contain it.

–David Beecher

The self-proclaimed capital of the Baltics, sprawling Rīga (pop. 826,508) feels strangely out of proportion as the capital of small, struggling Latvia. More Westernized and cosmopolitan than the rest of the country, Rīga envisions itself as the "Paris of the East," a city of fascinating museums, architectural splendor, and diplomatic importance. True, the city is more urbane and cultured than either Tallinn or

Vilnius and the *Jugendstil* buildings are stunning, but it nonetheless feels more like Las Vegas than Paris, with 24hr. casinos on every street, showgirls parading through posh hotels and cabarets, and the tell-tale tinted windows of German luxury automobiles. Rīga's seeming identity crisis makes sense in light of the city's history: founded in 1158 as an entirely Germanic metropolis, Rīga has suffered through Swedish, Polish, and, most recently, Russian control for hundreds of years. Independently Latvian for the first time in 1991, the city was left with a legacy of war and destruction. Not only was the city itself destroyed during WWII but the population was also decimated: the pre-war population was 500,000, but by 1945 it had dwindled to under 200,000. In the last nine years, Rīga and Latvia both have been coping with rebuilding, repopulation, new political and economic systems, and at long last testing out what it means to be Latvian (and not German or Russian). While the city has a long way to go to becoming a major European capital, it has admirably established a new identity as the cultural and social center of the Baltics. Like the freedom monument in the center of the city, Rīga stands above her surging and seedy streets with allusive and optimistic majesty.

GETTING THERE & GETTING AWAY

Airplanes: Lidosta Rīga (Rīga Airport; tel. 20 70 09), 8km southwest of Vecrīga. Take bus #22 from Gogol iela. **Air Baltic** (tel. 207 24 01) flies twice daily to **Tallinn** (US$207) and **London** (round-trip US$336). **Lufthansa** (tel. 728 59 01; fax 782 81 99) and **Finnair** (tel. 720 70 10; fax 720 77 55) fly to Western Europe.

Trains: Stacijas laukums (tel. 23 21 34), east of Vecrīga and north of the canal. It's really two stations, with long-distance trains in the larger building to the left as you face the station. Departures *(atiešanas)* listed on the board to the right as you enter. To reach **Berlin** and **Warsaw** on the Baltic Express, you must go via Vilnius. To: **Vilnius** (8hr., 1 per day, *coupé* 11Ls); **St. Petersburg** (13hr., 1 per day, *coupé* 23Ls); and **Moscow** (17hr., 2 per day, *coupé* 28Ls). **Suburban trains,** running as far as the Estonian border at Valka/Valga, leave from the smaller building. The Lugaži line includes Cēsis and Sigulda. Buy same-day tickets in the respective halls and advance ones in the **booking office** off the right side of the suburban hall. Open M-Sa 8am-7pm, Su 8am-6pm.

Buses: Tel. 721 36 11. 200m south of the train station along Prāgas iela, across the canal from the central market. Open daily 5am-midnight. To: **Kaunas** (7hr., 2 per day, 5-6Ls); **Tallinn** (5-6hr., 7 per day, 6-7Ls); **Vilnius** (6hr., 5 per day, 3.50-6Ls); and **Minsk** (10hr., 2 per day, 6.20-6.90Ls). Buses to **Prague** (30hr., 1 per week, 38Ls) and **Warsaw** (14hr., 1 per day, 15Ls) must be booked through **Eurolines** (tel. 721 40 80), at the bus station right of the ticket windows. Open M-F 9am-6pm, Sa 9am-7:30pm.

Ferries: Transline Balt Tour, Eksporta iela 1a (tel. 732 23 11), 1km north of Rīga Castle at the passenger port. Sails to **Stockholm** M, W, and F at 6pm, arriving at 11am the next day. Deck space 20Ls; 40Ls for a spot in a 4-place cabin with hall showers and toilets.

Local Transportation: Buses, trams, and **trolleybuses** run 5:30am-12:30am. Buy your tickets on board. 0.14Ls.

Taxis: Private taxis have a green light in the windshield. **Taxi Rīga** (tel. 800 10 10) charges 0.30Ls per km during the day, 0.40Ls per km at night.

Car Rental: Europcar Interrent Basteja bul. 10 (tel. 722 26 37; fax 782 03 60), rents Opels for US$96 a day. Open daily 9am-11pm.

ORIENTATION

Rīga's city center consists of a series of concentric half-circles along the banks of the **Daugava River,** engulfing **Vecrīga** (Old Rīga), which is bordered to the north by **Kr. Valdemāra iela** and to the south by **Marijas iela,** which becomes Čaka iela going northeast. **Pīlsētas kanāls** (the old city moat), surrounded by a park, marks the first circle; it's about a 15min. walk across. Beyond the canal, a ring of parks and boulevards designed in the 19th century make up the second circle; **Elizabetes iela,** 1km from the river, bounds this newer region. As the twisted streets of Vecrīga turn into the perpendicular avenues of the greater city, Rīga gradually seems less quaint and more like a dirty, sprawling metropolis. The city as a whole is neatly divided in half by **Brīvības bulvāris,** which leads from the outskirts to the **Freedom Monument** in the center, continuing through Vecrīga as **Kaļķu iela.** With the trains behind you, take a left onto the busy Marijas iela and right onto any one of the small streets beyond the canal to reach Vecrīga. You can buy it (0.60Ls) at kiosks, hotels, and travel agencies. Catch up on current and cultural events with the informative *The City Paper—The Baltic States,* generally available in the same places (US$1.50).

PRACTICAL INFORMATION

TOURIST & FINANCIAL SERVICES

Tourist Offices: Tourist services in Rīga lag far behind those in Tallinn and Vilnius. There is a good-humored and multilingual staff at **Patricia,** Elizabetes iela 22-26, 3rd Fl. (tel. 728 48 68; fax 728 66 50; email patricia@riga.mail.telia.com; www.rigalatvia.com), two blocks from the train station. Arranges homestays in Vecrīga (US$15 per person; breakfast US$5), and can help with Russian visas (6 days US$80). Open M-Sa summer 9am-9pm; off-season 9am-6pm. The most centrally located **Tourist Office** is at Skārņu iela 22 (tel. 722 17 31; fax 722 76 80; email tourinfo@latnet.lv), behind St. Peter's Church. **Balta Tourist Agency,** Basteja 10 (tel. 721 64 44; fax 724 31 00), gives out flight timetables. Open M-F 9am-6pm, Sa 10am-5pm.

Passport Office: For a visa extension, go to the **Department of Immigration and Citizenship,** Raiņa iela 5 (tel. 721 91 81), explain your situation, and pay the fee.

Embassies: Belarus, Jēzusbaznīcas 12 (tel. 732 25 50; fax 73 22 89). Open M-F 9am-1pm. **Canada,** Doma laukums 4, 4th Fl. (tel. 722 63 15). Open M-F 9am-5:30pm. **Russia,** Antonijas iela 2 (tel. 721 25 79), entrance on Kalpaka bulv. Open M-F 10am-1pm. **Ukraine,** Kalpaka bulv. 3 (tel. 33 29 56). Open M-F 10am-1pm. **U.K.,** Alunāna iela 5 (tel. 733 81 26). Open M-F 9am-5pm; visa section open 9:30am-noon. **U.S.,** Raiņa bulv. 7 (tel. 721 00 05). Open M-F 9am-noon and 2-4pm.

Currency Exchange: At any of the innumerable *Valutos Maiņa* kiosks or shops in the city. **Unibanka,** Kaļķu iela 13, has long hours, gives MC/Visa cash advances for a 4% commission, and cashes AmEx and Thomas Cook **traveler's checks** for a 3% commission. Open M-F 9am-9pm, Sa 9am-6pm. **24hr. exchange desks** are at branches at Basteja bulv. 14, Brīvības 30, and Merķeļa 10. Cirrus/MC/Visa **ATMs** are popping up all over.

American Express: Latvia Tours, Kaļķu iela 8 (tel. 721 36 52; fax 782 00 20). Cashes traveler's checks and holds mail. Open M-F 9am-6pm, Sa 10am-2pm.

LOCAL SERVICES

Luggage Storage: In the bus station, on guarded racks near the *Eurolines* office (0.20Ls per 10kg for 2hr.). Open daily 6:30am-10:30pm. At the train station, lockers (0.60Ls) are in the tunnel under the long-distance tracks. Open daily 5am-1am.

Bookstore: Aperto Libro, Kr. Baronas iela 31 (tel. 728 38 10). Free English newspapers. Open M 8am-7pm, Tu-F 10am-8pm, Sa 10am-7pm. MC/Visa. **Rastāmlietas Grāmatas Bērniem,** Elizabetes iela 85 (tel. 728 66 36), through a courtyard and on the right. English fiction on the 2nd floor. Open M-F 10am-7pm, Sa 10am-5pm.

Gay and Lesbian Hotline: Puškina 1a (tel. 951 95 51; email info@gay.lv). Open 9am-11pm; call before stopping by.

Laundromat: Miele, Elizabetes iela 85a (tel. 721 76 96), in the courtyard opposite the bookstore. Groaning machines take almost 2hr. to wash a load, so plan ahead. Wash 1.84Ls; dry 0.63Ls. 24hr. full-service 4.04Ls per load. Open 24hr. MC/Visa.

EMERGENCY & COMMUNICATIONS

Pharmacies: Grindex, Audēju 20 (tel. 721 33 40). Open M-F 8am-9pm, Sa 9am-5pm. MC/Visa. For late-night trips, try the 24hr. **Mēness aptieka,** Brīrības 121.

Post Offices: Stacijas laukums 1 (tel. 701 88 04), near the train station. Letter abroad 0.30Ls; postcard 0.20Ls. **Poste Restante** service at window #2. Open M-F 8am-8pm, Sa 8am-4pm, Su 8am-4pm. **Postal code:** LV-1050.

Internet Access: Latnet, Raiņa 29 (tel. 721 12 41). 0.22Ls per hr. Open M-Th 9am-6pm, F 9am-5pm. **Audalūzijas Suns,** Elizabetes iela 83/85 (tel. 724 28 26). 1.80Ls per hr. Open daily noon-10pm. **Elektroniskā Kafejnīca,** Elizabetes 83/85 (tel. 724 28 26). Six computers for 1.80Ls per hr. Open daily noon-10pm.

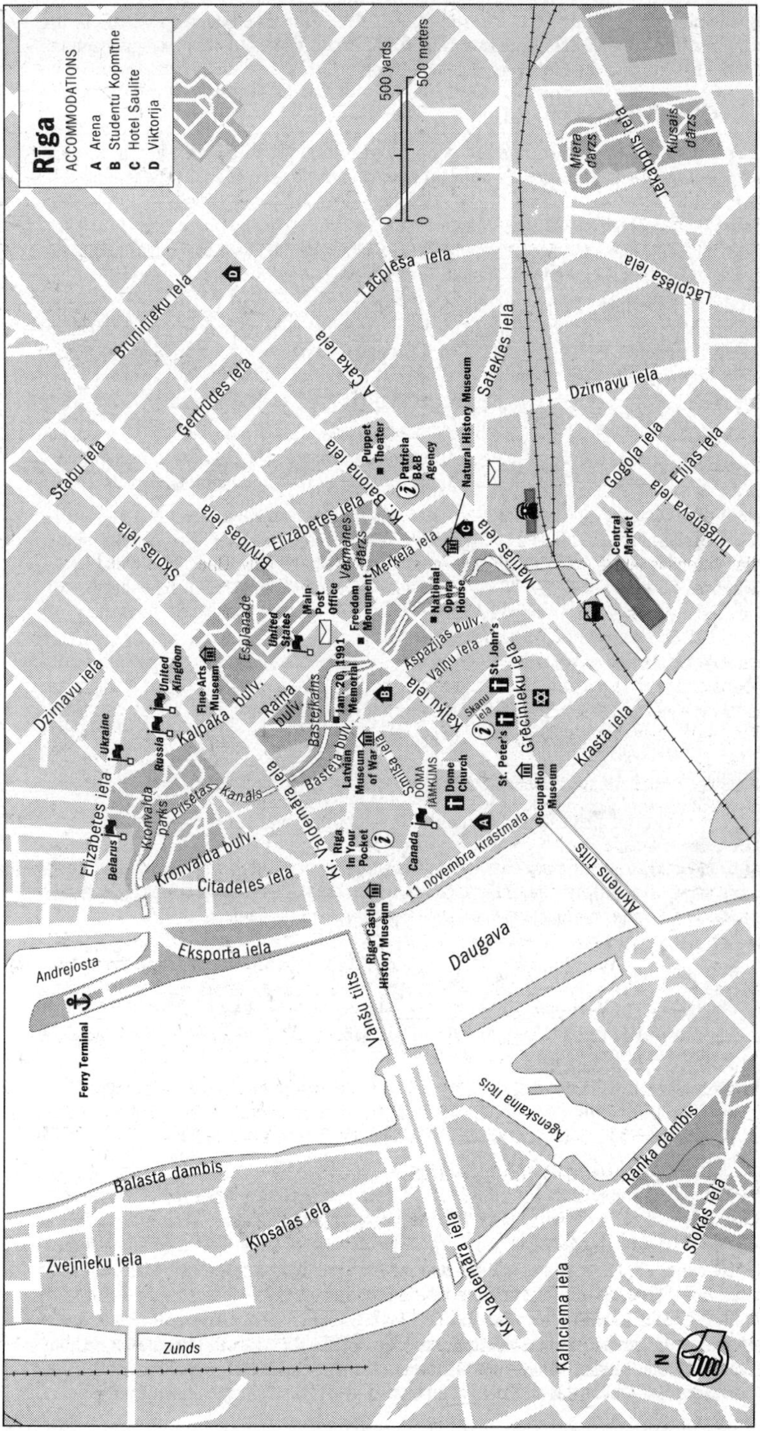
Rīga
ACCOMMODATIONS
A Arena
B Studentu Kopmītne
C Hotel Saulite
D Viktorija
500 yards
500 meters
0
0
Bruninieku iela
Stabu iela
Ģertrūdes iela
Skolas iela
Brīvības iela
A. Čaka iela
Lāčplēša iela
Elizabetes iela
Kr. Barona iela
Vērmanes dārzs
Merķeļa iela
Mārijas iela
Satekles iela
Dzirnavu iela
Gogoļa iela
Elijas iela
Turgeņeva iela
Jēkabpils iela
Miera dārzs
Klusais dārzs
Puppet Theater
Patricia B&B Agency
Natural History Museum
Central Market
Main Post Office
Freedom Monument
National Opera House
United States
United Kingdom
Fine Arts Museum
Esplanade
Kalpaka bulv.
Raiņa bulv.
Basteikalns
Jan. 20, 1991 Memorial
Aspazijas bulv.
Vaļņu iela
Kaļķu iela
St. John's
Skaņu iela
St. Peter's
Grēcinieku iela
Krasta iela
Dzirnavu iela
Ukraine
Russia
Elizabetes iela
Kronvalda parks
Pilsētas kanāls
Belarus
Kr. Valdemāra iela
Bastejа bulv.
Latvian Museum of War
Smilšu iela
DOMA LAUKUMS
Dome Church
Occupation Museum
Canada
Rīga In Your Pocket
Kronvalda bulv.
Citadeles iela
11 novembra krastmala
Rīga Castle History Museum
Akmens tilts
Eksporta iela
Andrejosta
Daugava
Ferry Terminal
Vanšu tilts
Āgenskalna līcis
Balasta dambis
Ķīpsalas iela
Zvejnieku iela
Ranka dambis
Slokas iela
Kr. Valdemāra iela
Kalnciema iela
Zunds
N

LATVIA

Telephone Office: Brīvības bulv. 19 (tel. 733 12 22). Smaller office at post office by the train station. Open 24hr. Cirrus/MC/Visa **ATM. Phone code:** 2 for all six-digit numbers; there is no phone code for seven-digit numbers.

ACCOMMODATIONS

Rīga's prices for decent rooms are generally the highest in the Baltics. If you are interested in a private room, try your luck with **Patricia** (see **Tourist Offices,** above).

Arena, Palasta iela 5 (tel. 722 85 83). In an unmarked building by Dome Cathedral, this is the cheapest place in town. 3Ls per person. Hall shower and kitchen; some rooms have sinks. Open Apr.-Oct. (the rest of the year circus performers live here).

Studentu Kopmītne (Student Dormitories), Basteja bulv. 10 (tel. 721 62 21). From the bus station, cross under the railroad tracks and take the pedestrian tunnel under the highway. Bear right onto Aspazijei bul., which becomes Basteja bul. Enter through the Europcar Interrent office on the edge of Vecrīga. Run by the University of Latvia for guest lecturers. 3-4Ls per person; with private bath 5-7Ls per person. Call ahead.

Saulite, Merķela iela 12 (tel. 22 45 46), directly across from the train station. Spiral staircase branches off to clean rooms and communal toilets. Singles 6Ls, with bath 16Ls; doubles 10Ls, 20Ls; triples 9Ls, 25Ls. Shared shower 0.40Ls. English spoken. MC/Visa.

Viktorija, Čaka iela 55 (tel. 701 41 11 and 701 41 61; fax 731 06 29 and 701 41 40). Eight blocks from the trains on Marijas iela (which becomes Čaka iela), or 2 stops on trolleybus #11 or 18. More expensive, newly renovated rooms with private bath, TV, and fridge, as well as cheaper rooms with peeling paint, plain rooms, and hallway toilets. Singles 8-9Ls, with bath 26Ls; doubles 10-12Ls, 38Ls. MC/Visa.

FOOD

Bleary-eyed women tend an insomniac's daydream: 24hr. food and liquor stores. Look for them along Elizabetes and Gertrūdes iela. The 24hr. **Interpegro,** Raiņa bulv. 33 (tel. 722 90 44), stocks liquor, water, fruits, vegetables, and more. Occupying five immense zeppelin hangars behind the bus station, **Centrālais Tirgus** (Central Market) is one of the largest in Europe. It has the best selection at the cheapest prices, but haggle, as vendors' prices vary. (Open M-Sa 8am-5pm, Su 8am-3pm.)

Alus Arsenāls (tel. 732 38 96), at Pils Laukums 4. Descend from the entrance on Arsenāla, or sit on the deck outside. Serves excellent, inexpensive Latvian cuisine. Entrees 3-4.50Ls. Service is faster inside. Open daily 11am-midnight.

LuLu Pizza, Gertrūdes iela 27. Best pizza in town. Slices 0.69-.95Ls; small and medium pizzas 2.50-5.50Ls. Open daily 8am-midnight. MC/Visa.

Kirbis (Pumpkin), Doma laukums 1 (tel. 949 54 09), directly across from the Dome Cathedral. A treat for vegetarians, with outstanding eggplant and mushroom dishes scooped out cafeteria-style. Entrees 2-4Ls. Open M-F 9am-11pm, Sa-Su 10am-11pm.

Tower, Smilšu 7 (tel. 721 61 55). An elegant international menu with offerings from fettuccine alfredo to T-bone steak. Outdoor seating in a medieval brick tower. Prices are moderate, but beware the hidden extras: 10% service charge and a whopping 0.60Ls for small glasses of water. Entrees 5-10Ls. Open M-F 11am-3am, Sa-Su noon-3am.

Rozamunde, Maza Smilsu 8 (tel. 722 77 98), one block off Filharmonija laukums. Wealthy foreigners dine at this small, elegant restaurant, which serves ample portions of Latvian cuisine. Live jazz 8-10pm. Entrees 8-16Ls. Open M-F 11am-11pm, Sa-Su noon-11pm.

Lido Bistro-Piceria, Elizabetes 65 (tel. 722 13 18). Cafeteria dining and a large, tiled interior somehow add up to one of the most popular fast-food places in Rīga. Greasy but decent meals 2-3.50Ls. Open daily 8am-11pm.

Hotel Latvija Express Bar, Elizabetes iela 55 (tel. 722 22 11), at the corner of Brīvības bul. past the Freedom Monument. Renowned breakfast joint serves small pancakes with jam (0.96Ls) and has 32 varieties of omelettes (0.81-4.21Ls). Open daily 7am-11pm.

SIGHTS

Most of Rīga's sights lie densely clustered in Vecrīga, but even the "modern" parts of town generally date from the mid-19th century and offer architectural pearls of their own. An exploration of Vecrīga should begin with the towering Freedom Monument, then branch out slowly to the side streets and hidden sights.

FREEDOM MONUMENT. In the center of the city stands the beloved Freedom Monument (Brivibas Piemineklis; "Milda," as she is affectionately known), raising her arms skyward, free at last from foreign occupiers. She was dedicated in 1935, during Latvia's brief tenure as an independent republic. To survive the subsequent 1940-41 occupation, she had to become a Soviet symbol. Intourist used to explain that the mighty figure represented Mother Russia supporting the three Baltic states (it actually shows Liberty raising up the three main regions of Latvia—Vidzeme, Latgale, and Kurzeme). *(At the corner of Raiņa bul. and Brīvības iela.)*

ST. PETER'S CHURCH. (Sv. Pētera baznīca). Towering above Rīga, St. Peter's dark spire is visible throughout the city. First built in 1209, the church as it is now dates from 1408. Its tower burned down during WWII and was rebuilt, complete with an elevator, in the 70s. From the top of the 103m spire, you can see the entire city and the Baltic. Inside exhibits cover the aforementioned fire. *(Proceed down Kaļķu iela from the Freedom Monument, then turn left on Skārņu iela. Open Tu-Su 10am-7pm. Church free; tower 1.50Ls, students 1Ls; exhibitions 0.50Ls, students 0.30Ls.)*

DOME SQUARE. Vecrīga's cobblestoned central square may feel timelessly serene, but in fact it only dates from 1936. The Latvian prime minister Kārlis Ulmanis (see **History,** p. 342) created the square by tearing down acoustically offensive buildings so his voice could be heard in a public address. On the far side of the square stands Rīga's centerpiece, **Dome Cathedral** (Doma baznīca), begun in 1226. The immense pipe organ inside is one of Europe's largest. *(Proceed down Kaļku iela from the Freedom Monument, then turn right on Šķūņu iela. Tel. 721 34 98. Cathedral open Tu-F 1-5pm, Sa 10am-2pm. 0.50Ls, students 0.20Ls. Concerts W and F at 7pm.)*

BASTEJKALNS. The central park of the ring near the old city moat **Pīlsētas kanāls,** Bustejkalns houses ruins of the old city walls. Across and around the canal, five red stone slabs stand as **memorials** to the dead of January 20, 1991, when Soviet special forces stormed the Interior Ministry on Raiņa bul. The dead included a schoolboy and two cameramen recording the events. At the north end of Bastejkalns, on Kr. Valdemāra iela, sits the **National Theater,** where Latvia first declared its independence on November 18, 1918. *(Tel. 732 29 23. Open M-F 10am-7pm, Sa-Su 11am-6pm.)*

THE THREE CEMETERIES. On the south end of **Mežaparks** lie the three main cemeteries of Rīga, powerful symbols of the struggle for Latvian nationhood. **Brothers' Cemetery** (Brāļu Kapi) is dedicated to soldiers who fell during the World Wars and the 1918-20 struggle for independence. The poet Jānis Rainis rests in the smaller **Rainis Cemetery** (Rainis Kapi), along with other nationalists, literary figures, and important Communists of the last 50 years. **Forest Cemetery** (Meža Kapi) is a peaceful area. *(Take tram #11 to Braļu Kapi, 11 stops from the starting point at the train station.)*

ST. JOHN'S CHURCH. (Sv. Jāņa baznīca). The small, 1927 St. John's Church was built by Dominicans but taken over by the Lutherans after the Reformation in 1582. It also served a stint as the city's armory. Through an alleyway on the left, **St. John's**

THE BOY WHO CRIED "NAPOLEON!" In 1812, Rīga was devastated by a single herd of cattle. Traveling happily through the countryside, the nefarious bovines raised a cloud of dust that was clearly visible to the city's residents. Believing the herd to be Napoleon's army, the people set fire to the city, razing 740 buildings and hundreds of acres of farmland. It was soon realized that the fearsome marauders were really only looking for grass and a good human to milk them. Meanwhile, Napoleon entered through a different route, wreaking his own havoc.

LATVIA

Courtyard (Jāņa sēta) is the oldest populated site in Rīga, where the first city castle stood; part of the old city wall is preserved here. *(Farther right on Skārņu iela on the corner with Jāņa iela. Tel. 722 40 28.Open Tu-Su 10am-1pm.)*

OTHER SIGHTS. To get a sense of the whole of Rīga, visit Zaķusalas island in the middle of the Daugava River, where the 98m high viewing platform of the **TV Tower** offers stunning panoramas. *(Take trolleybus #9 from behind the train station. Tel. 20 09 43.)* Continuing along Kaļķu iela from the Freedom Monument toward the river, you'll see three granite soldiers guarding the square **Latviešu strēlnieku laukums.** Dedicated during Soviet times to the crack team of Latvian riflemen who served as Lenin's bodyguards after the revolution, the statue was one of the few Soviet monuments not torn down. Explore the turn-of-the-century Art Nouveau creations of Mikhail Eisenstein (father of filmmaker Sergei Eisenstein) along Alberta iela. *(Heading along Elizabetes iela from the Daugava, take a left on Strelnieku, then a right on Alberta iela.)*

LATVIA

MUSEUMS

Some of the best museums of 20th-century Baltic history are in Rīga, ensuring that the horror of the 50-year Soviet occupation does not fade too quickly from memory.

Occupation Museum (Okupācijas muzejs), Strēlnieku laukums 1 (tel. 721 27 15). Behind the 3 granite soldiers on Latviešu strelnieku laukums. The finest museum in the Baltics. Top-notch exhibits with multi-lingual explanations. The initial Soviet occupation is depicted so vividly that you can almost hear the Red Army marching. Life in Soviet-Siberian concentration camps is vividly portrayed. Open daily 11am-5pm. Free.

Latvian Museum of War (Latvijas kara muzejs), Smilšu iela 20 (tel. 722 81 47). From the freedom monument, walk into the Vecrīga, turning right on Valnu iela. Located inside the cannonball-studded walls of Powder Tower. Rīga's most interesting military site, this huge museum jams the history of war, from the middle ages to the present, into eight floors. Open Tu-Su 10am-6pm. 0.50Ls, students 0.25Ls; foreign language tours 3Ls.

CROSSED SIGNALS Visitors to the Latvian Museum of War may be shocked to see frequent and prominent displays of red swastikas. Before running in terror from this apparent Baltic shrine to the Reich, know that the now-nefarious symbol (also called a fire cross, thunder cross, or sun wheel) was used by various peoples in Europe, South Asia, and the Americas long before it became synonymous with hate and prejudice. Latvia adopted a dark red version for its military standard when it gained statehood after WWI. Unfazed by the rise and fall of a certain German dictator in the following decades (after all, Latvia had first dibs), the nation's armed forces fought on under their misunderstood insignia, which they now proudly display, with a disclaimer for the historically short-sighted.

Motor Museum (Rīgas Motormuzejs), Eizenšteina 6. Take the rather infrequent bus #21 from Brīvības to the suburbs and get out at the Šmerļa iela stop in the Mežciems region. This highly-touted museum has a wacky collection of cars and related objects old and new, including Stalin's seven-ton armored Chaika limousine and Brezhnev's crashed Rolls Royce Silver Shadow, complete with wax test-dummies of the former dictators. Open Tu-Su 10am-6pm. 0.40Ls, students 0.20Ls.

Open-Air Ethnographic Museum (Etnogrāfiskais Brivdabas muzejs; tel. 99 41 06), on the shores of Juglas Lake (Juglas Ezers). Take tram #6 from Aspazijas iela in front of the freedom monument to the end of the line. Walk across the bridge and turn right onto Brīvības iela. The collection includes nearly 100 18th- and 19th-century buildings from all over Latvia. Open daily May-Oct. 10am-5pm.

History and Navigation Museum (Rīgas vēstures un kuģniecības muzejs), Palasta iela 4 (tel. 721 13 58 and 721 20 51), next to the Dome Cathedral. Describes Rīga's complex Germano-Russo-Swedish history. Open W-Su 11am-5pm. 1Ls, students 0.60Ls.

ENTERTAINMENT

Summer is the off season for ballet, opera, and most of the theaters around town; the rest of the year, purchase tickets at Teātra 10/12 (tel. 722 57 47; open daily 10am-7pm). The **Latvian National Opera** performs in the magnificent 19th-century Opera House on Aspazijas bul., where Richard Wagner once presided as director. After July, the **Latvian Symphony Orchestra** (tel. 722 48 50) has frequent concerts in the Large and Small Guilds off Filharmonija laukums, while smaller local and foreign ensembles perform throughout the summer in **Vāgnera zāle,** Vāgnera iela. (Open daily noon-7pm.) The ticket office, Amatu iela 6 (tel. 22 36 18), on the first floor of the Large Guild, sells tickets for nearly all concerts in Rīga. At the dome Cathedral, popular organ concerts (ėrģeļmūzikas koncerts) employ the third-largest organ in existence. Buy tickets at Doma laukums 1 (tel. 721 34 98), opposite the main entrace at *koncertzales kase.* (Open daily noon-3pm and 4-7pm.) The **Rīga Ballet** carries on the proud dancing tradition of native star Mikhail Baryshnikov.

Rīga has several **cinemas,** including the magnificent **Kino "Rīga,"** Elizabetes iela 61 (tel. 728 11 05), which shows American films with Latvian and Russian subtitles. (Tickets 1.50Ls; Tuesdays 0.70Ls). Check the paper for local listings.

LATVIA

NIGHTLIFE

Rīga doesn't sleep. Almost every day of the week in summer, into the early morning, young and old wander or stumble loudly through the streets of Vecrīga and the surrounding area. People drop into countless bars, but mostly gravitate toward the vast beer gardens of Doma laukums and the smaller ones at Filharmonija laukums. Rīga's *diskotekas* are multiplying, as are its casinos. Things get crowded on weekends, but keep in mind that Friday night is bigger and badder than Saturday, and that the most popular places change quickly. Some of the prime nightlife spots are in areas of town where it's undesirable to travel alone, so be prepared to find a friend or take a taxi. Rīga has two **gay** nightclubs, **Purvs** and **808,** below.

PUBS & BARS

Paddy Whelan's, Grēcineku iela 4 (tel. 721 02 49). Rīga's first Irish pub. Fast-flowing beer sates a noisy crowd of local students, backpackers, expats, and the occasional businessman. Guinness 1.20Ls. Open M-Th and Sa-Su 10am-1am, F 10am-2am. MC/Visa.

Pulkuedim Neviens Neraksta (Nobody Speaks to the Colonel), Peldu 26/28 (tel. 721 38 86). At night, trendy youth pack the backlit steel bridge, and a few even dance to the "alternative" (mainstream American rock) sounds. After 9pm, 1Ls cover on Saturday, 2Ls on Friday. Open Su-Th noon-3am, F-Sa noon-5am.

Ala (Cave), Audēju iela 11 (tel. 722 39 57). Go through a glass door, and walk through the building to the steep steps on the right. Subscribing to the "ant colony" school of bar design, tunnels and stairways connect little rooms of pool tables (2Ls per hr.), bars, slot machines, and young cave-dwellers. *Aldaris* 0.70Ls. Open daily 1pm-3am.

M (Maksims) Bars, Čaku iela 45 (tel. 27 45 41). Small, cozy black interior has wood paneling, low leather booths, and a high level of techno. The crowd grows progressively younger and more energetic as the night wears on. *Shashliks* 2.40-2.80Ls. Open 24hr.

CLUBS & DISCOS

Vernisāža, Terbātas 2 (tel. 709 24 00). Rīga's shiny new club is set to carry its nightlife into the 21st century. Descend the glass stairway into a smokey inferno complete with space-age lights and lasers, a moving stainless steel dance floor, and a rising central pedestal that takes dancers higher. Cover 5Ls. Open W-Su 11pm-6am.

Underground, Slokas 1 (tel. 761 54 56). One of the more popular clubs in Rīga, but trip there can be dangerous: the trek across the river from Vecrīga should not be made alone. Cover 3Ls. M, W-Th, and Sa 20+; F students only. Open M-F 9pm-6am, Sa 9pm-8am.

Hamlet Club, Jāņa Sēta 5 (tel. 722 99 38), in the heart of Vecrīga. Hosts the excellent Latvian Raubiško jazz ensemble Monday and Sunday nights at 9pm. Call ahead to reserve a table. Open daily 7pm-5am.

Groks Stacija (tel. 721 63 81), Kaļķu iela 22, near the Freedom Monument. The disco downstairs is meant to evoke a Metro stop, complete with fluorescent graffiti. *Aldaris* 0.60Ls. Open daily noon-5am, F-Sa until 6am.

Purvs, Matīsa 60/62. No signs, so just walk down the hall and inside. One of Rīga's 2 gay clubs. Neon-and-techno madness. Cover 0.50-1.50Ls. Open M and W-Sa 10pm-6am.

808, Kalniņa 8. Go into the drive and turn left. Rīga's other gay club. The fabulous lights and fun tunes make up for the somewhat cheesy decor. Cover 2Ls. Open daily 6pm-6am.

DAYTRIPS FROM RĪGA

DĀRZIŅI

The site of the **Salaspils Memorial,** this was where the Kurtenhof concentration camp was located during WWII. At the entrance to the memorial dedicated to 100,000 victims, the overhead inscription reads, "Behind this gate the earth moans." A huge concrete museum-memorial and six immense figures of suffering and defiance watch over barracks layered in flowers. A black box covered in wreaths emits a low ticking sound, like the pulse of a beating heart.

GETTING THERE. Electric trains travel frequently from **Rīga** to Dārziņi (*not* "Salaspils" on the Krustpils line; 20-30min., 14 per day, 0.25Ls).

PILSRUNDĀLE

In the late 18th century, **Ernst Johann von Bühren** employed 15,000 laborers and artisans to build his stately pleasure dome, a maze of 138 gilded ballrooms and cavernous halls. **Bartolomeo Rastrelli,** the Italian master who also planned St. Petersburg's Winter Palace (see p. 608), designed the palace in 1736; it wasn't until 1768 that the interior wall decorations were completed, by **Johann Michael Graff.**

Located in the heart of the Latvian countryside, the magnificent **Rundāles Palace** (Rundāles pils) served as a summer retreat for the Baltic German nobility. The motto under the eagle guarding the East Wing—"Faithfulness and Jealousy"—captures the story of its construction. Empress-to-be Anna married **Frederick, Duke of Courland,** who was bringing her to his estate in Jelgeva when he died en route. Abandoned among peasants, Anna was taken in by Von Bühren (Bīrons in Latvian), a local noble who became her adviser and lover. When she became Empress in 1727, Von Bühren suddenly found himself a rather wealthy count with the means to build an architectural symbol of his power. Used by the Soviets as a grain storehouse, hospital, and primary school, the palace was in a dismal state when restoration began in 1979; basketball hoops had been screwed into the walls of the parquet dining room. Up the grand staircase, now redone, is the **Gold Room** (Zelta Zāle), the marble and gold-leaf home to the throne, with dramatic murals and soldiers' graffiti from 1812. The **White Room** (Baltā Zāle) was the ballroom; plasterwork cherubs represent the four seasons and the four elements, and the Duchess's exotic boudoir is on display. It'll cost you more, but the exhibit of art recovered from churches brutalized by the Soviets is worthwhile; another exhibit showcases objects from the palace. (Ticket office tel. (239) 622 74. Open W-Su 10am-6pm. 1.20Ls, students 0.80Ls.) An English guidebook (0.15Ls) is available, as are info-packed tours (1½-2hr., 3Ls for an adult group; call (239) 621 97 to arrange in advance). The kitchen's immense fireplaces heated the ballroom year-round, cooking an estimated 1200 eggs and a full steer every day; refurbished, it now houses a **restaurant.**

GETTING THERE. To get there, you'll have to go through **Bauska,** connected to Rīga by **bus** (1¾hr., express 1¼hr.; 22 per day, last bus 8:20pm; 0.50-1.10Ls). Then take the bus to Jelgava; ask the driver to drop you off at "Pilsrundāle" (25min., 8-10 per day, 0.20Ls). From there, go left at the big Pilsrundāle sign, and walk 1.3km. The palace is around a hedge to the left. Half the daily buses go all the way to the hedge. Before leaving the Bauska station, ask for the times of returning buses.

SAULKRASTI

Saulkrasti, formed by the merging of the Neibāde, Pēterupe, and Katrinbāde villages, is a quiet seaside town of 5000. The sand on its beach is thick and dark, quite unlike the pale, cigarette-laden sable that awaits in crowded Jūrmala. Saulkrasti is attracting more and more beachgoers every year, but it's still ideal for relaxing by the waters of the Gulf of Rīga. The best way to lunch in Saulkrasti is to picnic on the beach. Stock up at the **"Giva" grocery store,** which is right where Raiņa iela meets Ainažu iela at Ainažu 8 (tel. 95 12 76; open 24hr.; MC). For prepared food, the **LN Saulkrasti Kafejnīca** (tel. 514 88) at the corner of Rīgas iela (what Ainažu becomes) and Murjāņu iela serves meals such as chicken filet (1.80Ls) and salad (0.60Ls) with *Aldaris* (0.50Ls; open noon-2am; MC).

GETTING THERE. The easiest way to get to Saulkrasti is by **commuter train** (1hr., 1-2 per hr., 0.54Ls). The Saulkrasti **train station** (tel. 95 13 37), a large, pale yellow building with cracks in the wall, also serves as the **bus station** (tel. 95 15 51). The station borders a paved road, Alfrēda Kalniņa iela, which you can take to the center of Pētrupe (it becomes Raiņa iela) by following it left out of the station, past the cemetery. For the beach, follow Raiņa past Unibanka into the woods.

JŪRMALA REGION

Since the late 19th century, Rīga has flocked in the summertime to this narrow spit of sand 20km from the capital between the Gulf of Rīga and the Lielupe River. In 1959, 14 towns were incorporated into the city-resort Jūrmala (YOUR-ma-la; pop. 60,000). It became a popular summer resort within the USSR, and as a result Latvian independence proved to be disastrous to the area. Nonetheless, Jūrmala is swiftly recovering as crowds of tourists once again inundate its beaches and shops.

Any of the towns between **Bulduri** and **Dubulti** are popular for sunning and swimming, but if you're looking for Jūrmala's social center, go to **Majori.** Trainloads of people file to the beach or wander along **Jomas iela,** Majori's pedestrian drag, lined with cafes, restaurants, and shops. From the train station, cross the road, walk through the cluster of trees in the small park, turn right, and you're there. Turn left off Jomas a few blocks after the tourist information center for the **Rainis and Aspazija Memorial Cottage,** Pliekšāna iela 5/7 (tel. 642 95), which displays both poets' works, books, and photos in the villa where Rainis died in 1929 (see **Literature & Arts,** p. 343). Hours can be irregular due to ongoing renovations. (Usually open M and W-Sa 10am-5pm. 0.50Ls, students 0.20Ls.)

The **tourist office,** Jomas iela 42 (tel. 642 76 and 644 93; fax 646 72), has **maps** (1Ls), brochures, and bustling, English-speaking employees willing to help with anything as they juggle phones. (Open M-F 9:30am-5:30pm, Sa-Su noon-5pm.) At **Orients,** Jomas iela 33 (tel. 620 82), cell-phone-toting tourists people-watch from the outdoor cafe tables at the start of the main pedestrian drag. (Dumplings with meat 1.8Ls; lobster salad 1.10Ls. Open daily 10am-midnight. MC/Visa).

The crowds that frolic in Majori taper off at either end of the beaches of Jūrmala. **Lielupe,** the town with beach access closest to Rīga, offers dramatic sand dunes. At the other end of Jūrmala, **Ķemeri** was once the prime health resort of the Russian Empire. Therapeutic mud baths, sulfur water, and other cures have operated here since the mid-18th century. The impressive white **Sanatorium,** built vaguely in the style of an Art Deco ocean liner in 1936, is an aging palace: it is in such major need of renovation as to make its future uncertain. It could always become a disco-bar.

GETTING THERE. A handful of towns dot the coast; from Rīga, beachless Priedaine is the first train stop in Jūrmala; the tracks then pass over the Lielupe river and quickly run through Lielupe, Bulduri, Dzintari, Majori, Dubulti, Jaundubulti, Pumpuri, Melluži, Asari, and Vaivari before heading back inland to Sloka, Kudra, and Ķemeri. The **commuter rail** runs one train every 30min. in both directions from 5am to 11:30pm. Trips to **Majori** take 35min. and cost 0.38Ls. **Public buses** (18 santīmi) and **microbuses** (0.20-0.30Ls) string together Jūrmala's towns. For the **Sanatorium,** the #6 bus to "Sanitorija Latvia" brings you close; take the paved road next to the bus stop and follow the street lights to the original, grand entrance.

KURZEME

Kurzeme, or Courland in English, originated as an autonomous region under Kuldīga apart from the Livonian Order. After the Great Northern War, both states were absorbed into Russia. Today, Kurzeme is the most rugged part of the country, where forests have not yet been cut to make way for civilization.

KULDĪGA

Legend has it that Kuldīga's (kool-DEE-ga) Rumba (the town's waterfall on the Venta River) formed after a rooster's call frightened the Devil, making him drop a sack of rocks into the river. Once the seat of the Duchy of Courland, Kuldīga was battered in the Great Northern War, never to regain its prominence. Relatively unscathed by Soviet rule, its Baltic red-tile-roofed architecture and views of the Venta make it one of the prettiest stops in the region.

ORIENTATION & PRACTICAL INFORMATION. Kuldīga lies about 150km west of Rīga. Its town center can be traversed in just 10min. The main street, **Liepājas iela,** intersects Baznīcas iela, which heads downhill to the castle park and the Venta river. The town center is a 15min. walk from the **bus station,** Stacijas iela 2. (Open daily 4:30am-9pm.) Buses arrive from **Rīga** (3-4hr., 7 per day, 2Ls). To get to the center, turn right out of the station and walk to the large brown and black barn. Take a left on Jelgavas iela and follow it until it turns into Mucenieku iela, then take a right on Putnu iela to reach Liepājas iela. The **tourist information office,** Pilsētas lankums 5 (tel. 222 59; mobile tel. 926 25 83), is located off Liepājas iela in the small kiosk and building in the town square. (Open M-F 9am-5pm.) **Exchange money** at **Zemes Banka,** Liepājas iela 15, which cashes AmEx traveler's checks and gives MC cash advances. (Open M-F 10am-4pm.) The **post office** is at Liepājas iela 34. (Open M-F 8am-6pm, Sa 8am-4pm.) **Postal code:** LV-3301. **Phone code:** (0)33.

ACCOMMODATIONS & FOOD. The Soviet **Viesnīca Kuršu,** Pilsētas laukums 6 (tel. 224 30; mobile tel. 829 35 73 98), stands tall, wide, and gray over the town square. Old but clean singles with curtainless, cold-water showers cost 6Ls (doubles 9Ls). If you like your water hot and need a TV, it's 12Ls (doubles 16Ls). A **cafe** on the first floor serves cheap Latvian fare. The new **Jāņa Nams Hotel,** Liepājas iela 36 (tel. 234 56), offers doubles with private bath. Go for the 22Ls room (bigger room and bigger TV). Use the **sauna** for 10Ls per hr.

Jāņa Nams Hotel has a **cafe** in front with a trendy half-brick interior that serves decent but modestly proportioned dishes (2-3.50Ls; open daily 7am-11pm). Crowded **Staburadze Kafejnica,** Liepājas iela 8 (tel. 222 75), a little closer to the river, provides some of the cheapest meals in town. Pork *carbonade* (fried in egg) with greasy fries is 1.66Ls. (Open M-Sa 11am-midnight, Su 11am-6pm.) **Rumba Cafe,** on Pils iela at the top of the castle park, has drinks and snacks but no full meals. (*Aldaris* 0.50Ls. Open daily 11am-1am.) For **groceries,** hit the **Tirdzniecības Centrs,** in the town square next to Viesnīca Kuršu. (Open daily 7am-10pm.)

SIGHTS. The most famous church in Kuldīga, **St. Katrina's** (Sv. Katrīnas baznīca), is a large white building on Baznīcas iela. Built in 1655, and rebuilt during the 19th and 20th centuries, the Soviets used it as a museum. (Services Su 10am-noon.) An 1807 **water mill** stands down the hill across the rickety wooden bridge (you could just walk along the street). Turn left onto the high bridge or bear right uphill for an impressive view of the river and its **waterfall.** Outside, the **Regional Museum** (Kuldīgas Novada Muzejs), Pils iela 5, a single-vaulted room of the castle—the top covered by earth and glass—forms part of a **sculpture garden.** (Open Tu-Su 11am-5pm.) The **Lutheran Church of St. Anne,** Dzirnavu iela 12, is a brick giant with green-coned tops. The stained glass near the pipe organ shows an absurd Soviet scene of bounty and family virtue. (Open daily 10am-5pm.)

VIDZEME

Along the rails running northeast from Rīga lie two slightly longer trips from the capital, both notable for the their outdoor activities and historic importance. Sigulda, the first stop, offers both caves and castles. Cēsis, farther out, is a major battle site from the quest for independence and the birthplace of the Latvian flag.

SIGULDA

The hills around Sigulda, 50km east of Rīga, boast legendary caves and the ruins of two castles, all connected by a string of nature trails in a picturesque stretch of the Gaujas Valley. Part of the Gaujas National Park, a bobsled run, bungee jumping, and hot-air ballooning make it a popular daytrip from the capital.

ORIENTATION & PRACTICAL INFORMATION. From the **bus** and **train stations,** walk up **Raiņa iela** to get to the town center. Continue as it turns into **Gaujas iela,** which in turn leads to **Turaidas iela. Trains** run from **Rīga** on the Rīga-Lugaži commuter rail line (1hr., 16 per day, 0.58Ls). **Buses** travel from **Rīga** (1½hr., 15-20 per day, 0.36-.70Ls) and drop passengers off at a station on the edge of Sigulda, at the corner of Gǎtes and Vizdemes. Turn right on Gǎtes and walk across the train tracks to reach the *autoosta* (bus station; open daily 6am-8pm). Bus #12 takes you to Hotel Senleja (0.15Ls) and the nearby **Turaida Castle;** buy **maps** here (0.50Ls). The **Sigulda Tourist Information Center,** Pils 4a (tel./fax 713 35), also sells maps (0.80Ls; open daily 10am-7pm). Just before Gaujas iela reaches the Gaujas Bridge, take a left on Peldu iela and follow it down 650m to get to **Makara Turisma Birojs,** Peldu iela 1 (tel. 737 24; fax 722 27 40). They **rent bikes** (5Ls per day) and **canoes** (1 day with return transportation 24Ls). The staff also organizes raft, ski, and bike adventures and even supplies ski instruction (Dec.-Mar.). **Exchange money** and get MC/Visa **cash advances** at **Latvijas Unibanka,** Rīgas iela 1 (tel. 711 99; open M-F 9am-5pm). The **post office** sits at Pils iela 2. (Open M-F 8am-noon and 1-5pm, Sa 8am-2pm.) **Postal code:** LV-2150. **Telephones** are at the post office. (Open daily 7am-9pm.) **Phone code:** 29.

ACCOMMODATIONS & FOOD. Hotel Senleja, Turaidas iela 4 (tel. 721 62; fax 790 16 11), offers small rooms in a Soviet-era lime-green edifice near the train station. Rooms come with TV and bath. (Singles 15Ls; doubles 22Ls. Tent space 2Ls.) To reach the **Hotel Véjupe,** Televizijas 19 (tel. 731 21), turn right onto Ausekla iela from the train station and follow it as it becomes Dárza iela and finally Televīzijas iela; the hotel is in a field. It rents spacious rooms and has a fallout shelter in the basement. Enjoy the sauna (5Ls per hr.) and bar. (Singles 8Ls; doubles 16-20Ls.)

Located inside the newer of the two local castles, **Pilsmuiža,** Pils 15 (tel. 713 95), is one of the best restaurants in the region. Ample portions of Latvian cuisine are carefully presented in the lodge interior or on a terrace overlooking the ruins of Sigulda Castle. (Entrees 2.50-5Ls. Open daily noon-2am.) The **Kafejnīca/Bistro,** Raiņa iela 1, across the street from the train station, is convenient. Salads, pork chops, chicken kebabs, and rice are all sold by weight. (Entrees 1.50Ls. Open daily 7am-10pm. MC/Visa.) There is a **grocery store** in the new complex next to the Kafejuīca. (Open M-Tu and Th-Su 8am-11pm, W 8am-10pm. MC/Visa.)

SIGHTS & HIKING. To reach **Turaida Castle** (Turaidas Pils), the largest and most impressive structure in the region, take bus #12 from the main bus station. Its restored brick fortifications are visible throughout the Gauja valley and surrounding hilltops. Work on the castle began in 1214, initiated by German crusaders seeking to convert the Liivs. Ascend the steep staircase of the main tower (restored in 1958) for views of the region. An adjacent building houses the **History Museum** (Siguldas novadpētniecības muzeja), Turaidas iela 10. It contains impressive displays on the history of the Liiv people, from their immigration to Latvia in the 3rd century to their near-elimination in the 12th-century crusades, complete with English descriptions and *faux* ancient music. (Open daily 10am-6pm. Admission to castle, tower, and museum 0.80Ls, students 0.40Ls.)

Walk 10-15min. back down the hill along Turaidas iela to reach the legendary **caves** of Sigulda. The chiseled mouth of **Gutman's Cave** (Gūtmaņa ala), inscribed with coats of arms and mottos from generations of Latvians and other visitors since the 16th century, continues to erode. Climb the wooden stairway behind the cave for a walk along the high ridge above the valley. After steep rises and falls, you'll arrive at the ruins of the 13th-century **Krimulda Castle** (Krimuldas pilsdrupas). There's barely anything left since the bulk of it fell in the 1601 Polish-Swedish war, but hints of magnificence make for a pleasant walk. Perched on a ridge to the right of Gauja iela, on the near side of the gorge, is the **Siguldas dome,** the new "castle" where the Russian Prince Kropotkin once lived. Behind, the immense ruins of **Siguldas Castle** (Siguldas pilsdrupas) are a mere glimmer of their former glory. Constructed by the German Order of Knights of the Sword from 1207 to 1226, the fortress was destroyed in the Great Northern War.

Hiking options abound. An excellent 2km walk follows the Gauja River to the steep **Piķenes Slopes,** where two caves, the deep **Devil's Cave** (Velna ala) and **Devil's Little Cave** (Mazā velnala), merit mention. The nearby spring is purportedly a **Fount of Wisdom** where ambitious mothers bathe their babes. Another good hike goes from Siguldas Castle down to the Gauja and heads upstream to cross **Vējupite creek.** Upstream another 100m, stairs rise to **Paradise Hil** (Paradīzes kalns), where 19th-century Latvian painter Jānis Rozentāls made the valley view famous. The **Gauja National Park Center,** Baznicas iela 3 (tel. 713 45), has 2hr. guided English tours. (Open daily 9am-5pm. Minimum 10Ls per guide, not including cable car and museum prices.) Call two days in advance to arrange tours.

ENTERTAINMENT. Sigulda's main attraction is its varied outdoor activities. Visible from the commuter rail, the Olympic-sized **bobsled and luge run** plummets from Sveices iela 13 (tel. 739 44; fax 790 16 67). From October to March, you can take the plunge—in summerdo it on wheels. (Open Sa-Su 10am-8pm. 3Ls.) From the bridge, a thin rope supports a tiny red **cable car.** This is the local **bungee jumping** base; call 762 51 for reservations. To go one-on-one with gravity, climb the wooden stairs, sign a release, and jump. (Open on weekends; 12Ls.)

Try **Dukšte Gunars** (tel. 761 16 14; mobile tel. 934 03 20) for **hot-air balloon** rides (60Ls per person per hr.); just don't float into Belarus. The **International Ballooning Festival** floats out of town in mid- to late May. Next to the Turaidas Museum, Turaidas 10, **horses** (tel. 745 84...for the owners, not the horses) are available for hire, with or without a trainer. (Open Tu-F noon-6pm, Sa-Su noon-7pm. 5Ls per hr.) Play **minigolf** (1Ls, children 0.50Ls) at Parka iela or **tennis** (open daily 11am-9pm; 1Ls per hour before 2 pm, 3Ls thereafter) across the street.

CĒSIS

The master of the Livonian Order (the German knights who controlled Latvia and Estonia from the 13th to the 16th century) once made his headquarters here in the center of present-day Gauja National Park. In 1919, Cēsis (TSEH-siss) was the site of a crucial battle in Latvian and Estonian rebellions againt Russia. During the brief period of independence that followed, the city became a popular resort, and today it is making a comeback among vacationers charmed by its medieval streets, majestic castle ruins, and the nearby hills and streams.

ORIENTATION & PRACTICAL INFORMATION. **Raunas iela** runs to the town center from the **bus and train station** (tel. 227 62; open daily 8am-2pm and 3-7pm) and empties into the main square, **Vienības laukums. Rīgas iela** and **Valnu iela,** heading downhill at the square's south end, meet at **Līvu laukums,** the original 13th-century heart of the city. **Lenču iela,** which runs away from Vienības laukums, travels to **Cēsu pils** (Cēsis Castle). From Rīga, Cēsis is easily reached via suburban **trains** (1½-2hr., 10 per day, 1.10Ls) and **buses** (2hr., 17 per day, 1.10Ls). Ask the cashier at the staiton to **store luggage.** Get your free **map** at Cēsis Hotel, Vienības laukums 1 (tel. 223 92). **Local transportation** consists of two buses (0.15Ls): bus #9 runs west to the Gauja River (catch it on Vienības laukums from the stop on the woodier side) while bus #11 runs east from the bus station along Poruka iela and down Lapsu iela

(M-Sa). The **tourist office,** Pils 9 (tel./fax 134 12 18 15), in the building on your right as you enter the castle grounds, functions best as a travel agency. (Open M-F 10am-4pm, Sa 11am-2pm.) **Exchange currency** upstairs at **Unibanka** (tel. 228 03), on Raunas iela, which cashes MC/Thomas Cook/Visa traveler's checks and gives MC/Visa cash advances. (Open M-F 9am-5pm, Sa-Su 9am-2pm.) The **post** and **telephone offices,** Raunas iela 13, sit at the corner of Vienības laukums. The post office (tel. 227 88) is housed in a new red brick building. (Open M-F 8am-6pm, Sa 8am-4pm.) The **telephone office** (tel. 078) is in the yellow building across the street. (Open daily 9am-7pm.) You can send a **fax** (tel. 234 81) for 1Ls. **Postal code:** LV-4100. **Phone code:** 241.

ACCOMMODATIONS & FOOD. **Putniņkrogs,** Saules iela 23 (tel. 202 90), isn't bad as far as Soviet-style accommodations go, and you can't beat the price. Follow the train tracks and the unmarked road to your right through the low bushes until it becomes paved. The hotel is the second brick building on the right after the dirt bike track; enter around the back. (Singles 3.50Ls; doubles 7Ls. Showers 0.50-1Ls) The **Cēsis Hotel,** Vienības Lakums 1 (tel. 412 01 22), is pure luxury, from the sumptuous lobby to the huge bed and sparkling private baths, but for a steep price. (Singles 28Ls; doubles 38Ls. Breakfast included. English spoken.) There is a **market** on Uzvaras Bulvaris between Vienības laukums and the tourist office. (Open 8am-4pm.) **Kafejnīca Raunis** (tel. 238 30), where Rauna iela meets the square, serves plentiful if somewhat bland main courses. (Entrees 1-2Ls. Open daily 8am-10pm.) The Hotel Cēsis has its own **Cafe Populare,** a bistro until 5pm and a full restaurant thereafter. (Entrees 1-2Ls.) For something more elaborate, try the **Restoran Alexu,** Vienības laukums 1 (tel. 223 92), also in the hotel. If you can decipher the calligraphied English menu, you'll find a wide array of Latvian, international, and vegetarian dishes. (Full meals 4-8Ls. Open daily noon-11pm.)

SIGHTS & ENTERTAINMENT. Built in 1206 by the Germans, the town's **castle** (tel. 226 15) was completed as a mighty fortress with 4m thick walls in the 1280s. By the late 16th century, the Livonian Order's power lapsed, but when Russia's **Ivan IV (the Terrible)** laid siege to the fortress in 1577, the men chose to fill the cellars with gunpowder and blow themselves up rather than surrender. It was later rebuilt, but when Russians invaded again in 1703 under **Peter the Great,** the castle was bombarded and left in its romantic, ruined state. Landscaped by a 19th-century baron, the surrounding park is mossy and peaceful. Ask an attendant to point out the **Lenin statue,** now resting under a giant wood crate resembling a coffin. **Cēsis History Museum** (Cēsis vēstures muzejs), Pils iela 9 (tel. 226 15), fills the two castles with coins and jewelry. More recent history awaits in the tower, with an exhibit on the 1919 1battle fought here against Russia. After viewing the displays, climb to the roof for a view of the other castle's ruins. (Open W-Su 10am-5pm. Castle 0.50Ls, students 0.30Ls; museum 0.50Ls, students 0.40Ls; tour 3Ls, in English 10Ls.)

Cēsis Brewery (Cēsu alus daritava), Lenču iela 9/11 (tel. 222 45), is the oldest brewery in Latvia, producing fine beverages since the 1870s. The shop parts with its wares for 0.23-0.26Ls a bottle. Tours are possible if you contact the director in advance (tel. 235 29; open M-F 8am-7pm, Sa 8am-5pm, Su 8am-1pm.) To access the older section of town, take Torņa iela from the parking lot by the castle. The Gaujas River flows on the east side of town, and a number of good **hiking** trails lead along the many cliffs lining the river. Bus #9 from the hotel on Vienības laukums leads 3km along Gaujas iela to the base of the trails. The best cliffs are to the south.

OUT, OUT DAMNED SPOT! In an effort to win back Cēsis from the Livonian Order that had taken the town in 1209, the Letgal tribe—ancestors of modern-day Latvians—went to battle against the knights in 1272. Legend has it that during the battle, the Letgal chief fell slain on a white sheet, staining it a deep crimson on two sides but leaving the middle section white. Some grief-stricken warrior flew the sheet and the tribe rallied around it. Today, that red-and-white pattern still adorns the Latvian flag, making it the second-oldest national banner in Europe.

LITHUANIA (LIETUVA)

US$1 = 4.00LT (LITAI) — **1LT = US$0.25**
CDN$1 = 2.69LT — **1LT = CDN$0.37**
UK£1 = 6.43LT — **1LT = UK£0.16**
IR£1 = 5.39LT — **1LT = IR£0.19**
AUS$1 = 2.60LT — **1LT = AUS$0.38**
NZ$1 = 2.12LT — **1LT = NZ$0.47**
SAR1 = 0.66LT — **1LT = SAR1.51**
DM1 = 2.17LT — **1LT = DM0.46**

PHONE CODES Country code: **370.** International dialing prefix: **810.**

Once the largest country in Europe, stretching into modern-day Ukraine, Belarus, and Poland, Lithuania has since faced oppression from tsarist Russia, Nazi Germany, and Soviet Russia. The first Baltic nation to declare its independence from the USSR in 1990, Lithuania has become more Western with every passing year. Its spectacular capital city of Vilnius welcomes hordes of tourists into the largest old town in Europe, recently covered in a bright new coat of paint from city-wide renovations. In the other corner of the country, the mighty Baltic Sea washes up against Palanga and Kuršių Nerija also called Curonian Spit.

HIGHLIGHTS OF LITHUANIA

■ Burgeoning **Vilnius** is often touted as the "New Prague" for its thriving art scene and sprawling Old Town (p. 365).
■ Quintessentially Lithuanian, **Kaunas** offers a taste of the country's eclectic folk culture and preoccupation with evil (p. 375).
■ Sun, fun, and sea lions welcome visitors to the beaches of **Klaipėda,** the Curonian Spit's premier beach town (p. 383).

LIFE & TIMES

HISTORY

Although the date of migrations of Baltic peoples to the region is a point of contention among scholars, it is clear that the people were well established by the beginning of the Christian era. From there on, a litany of would-be conquerors tested the resilience of the settlers, beginning with the Teutonic Order at the dawn of the Dark Ages. The Lithuanian tribes rose to the challenge, uniting under **Mindaugus,** who accepted **Christianity** in 1251 and was named the country's first king by Pope Innocent IV in 1253.

Lithuanian territory soon swelled to imperial proportions, swallowing modern Belarus and northern Ukraine, as **Gediminas** consolidated power in the 14th century. After his death, however, disputes weakened the state. **Jogaila,** grandson of Gediminas, married the 12-year-old Polish queen Jadwiga and became Wladisław II Jagiełło in 1385. With this union, Jogaila introduced **Roman Catholicism** to Lithuania, converting the nobility. Turning his attention to Poland, Jogaila delegated Lithuania to **Vytautus Didysis (the Great).** Together, they expanded their empire until the Vytautus's death in 1430, at which point Lithuania's grasp stretched from the Baltics to the Black Sea, from Vilnius to a mere 160km of Moscow.

Lithuania solidified its ties to Poland with the 1569 **Union of Lublin,** which heralded a period of prosperity and cultural development. In the mid-17th century, however, unrest among Ukrainian Cossacks, coupled with war against Sweden over Livonia, left the **Commonwealth of Two Peoples** (or Polish-Lithuanian Commonwealth) vulnerable. The three **Partitions of Poland** erased the Commonwealth from the European map, and Russia controlled all of Lithuania by 1815.

The country's subjugation followed the typical pattern: successive failed uprisings were followed by ever harsher reprisals. The tsars closed the 250-year-old University of Vilnius and banned the use of Lithuanian in public places. As Russia's empire began to crumble, Lithuania was subjected to the geopolitical whims of its mighty neighbors. German troops returned to Lithuania in 1915, 500 years after their last defeat, only to leave at the end of 1918, when the Soviets tried and failed to regain hold of the country. The Lithuanians expelled the Red Army in 1919, but during the confusion Poland took Vilnius and refused to give it up.

Deprived of its major city, Lithuania's independence was short-lived. A fragile parliamentary democracy collapsed in 1926 with a coup d'etat, as dictator **Antanas Smetona** quickly banned all opposition parties. Whatever autonomy remained disappeared with the 1939 **German-Soviet Nonaggression Pact** and subsequent treaties, which invited the Soviets to invade. In June 1941, the Soviets began pulling Lithuanians from their homes; **deportations** to Arctic or desert regions of the USSR displaced some 35,000. The Nazi victory over the Soviets only worsened, as Lithuania lost another 250,000 citizens, including most of its Jewish population.

The Soviets returned in 1944, although they were opposed by Lithuanian guerrilla fighters—at their height 40,000 strong—into the early 50s. It was not until the 60s that **Antanas Sniečkus** managed to solidify Soviet rule. Fortunately, Lithuania's industrial backwardness was ill-suited for Soviet designs and spared it from an influx of Russian immigrants. Resistance to the regime persisted through the stagnation of the 70s and 80s, as the republic, with the backing of the Catholic Church, generated more *samizdat* ("self-made" dissident publications) per capita than any other in the Soviet Union. **Mikhail Gorbachev's** reforms fell on dangerously fertile ground, and on March 1, 1990, Lithuania shocked the world when it declared **independence.** Moscow immediately retaliated, attempting futilely to disconnect the region's oil and gas resources. In a P.R. disaster for Gorbachev's *perestroika*, the Soviets launched an assault on Vilnius's radio and TV center, leaving 14 dead. Only in the wake of the failed Soviet *putsch* of August 1991 did Lithuania achieve any meaningful independence. Despite internal divisions, the country rejoiced on August 31, 1993, when the last Russian soldiers left Lithuania.

LITHUANIA TODAY

Lithuania got off to an early start on economic reforms, and has been labeled by investors—with the other Baltic states—as one of Europe's economic "tigers." Recently, however, many of its reforms have run aground. Approximately 80% of the population is officially poor, and disenchantment with government institutions has grown, due as much to corruption as the decline in GDP growth. An associate member of the **E.U.** since 1995, the country nonetheless remains heavily dependent on Russia for fuel and has therefore suffered from Russia's perpetual financial crisis. Meanwhile, Russia remains opposed to the **NATO** membership Lithuania seeks. Still, of the Baltic states Lithuania maintains the most cordial relations with its former ruler, due largely to the smaller Russian population on its soil.

Despite these setback, Lithuania has passed some very progressive legislation in its bid for full E.U. membership. In December 1998, its Constitutional Court ruled the death penalty illegal, and in January 2000 tobacco advertising was banned throughout the country. Newly elected Prime Minister Roland Paksas started his term off with just as much vigor, performing some daredevil stunts in his private plane at his inauguration.

LITERATURE & ARTS

Until the mid-18th century, books printed in Lithuanian were primarily of a religious nature. The **New Testament** was published in 1701 and the entire Scriptures in 1727. The first Lithuanian dictionary, the 1629 *Dictionarium trium linguarum* by **K. Sirvydas,** is also notable, as is the hexametric poem *The Four Seasons (Metai)*, written in 1818 by **Kristijonas Donelaitis.**

After 1864, many writers violated the ban on publishing Lithuanian works in Latin letters (as opposed to Cyrillic), seeking to overthrow Russian political and Polish cultural control. The first modern Lithuanian periodical was founded in 1883 by **Jonas Basanavicius;** the *Dawn (Ausra)* lent its name to the next literary generation. Known for both dramatic and lyric poetry, "the poet-prophet of the Lithuanian renaissance" was **Jonas Mačiulis,** whose 1895 *Voices of Spring (Pavasario balsai)* launched modern Lithuanian poetry. After independence, novelist and dramatist **Vincas Kreve-Mickevicius** was considered Lithuania's greatest writer, while **Jurgis Baltrusaitis** gained distinction as a lyrical poet. Ex-priest **Vincas Mykolaitis-Putinas** pioneered the modern Lithuanian novel with *In the Altar's Shadow (Altorių šešėly)*. The return to Soviet rule again gagged and shackled Lithuanian writers, but new expressive modes were attempted in the philosophical poetry of **Alfonsas Nyka-Niliunas,** and the novels of **Marius Katiliskis.** Socialist Realism was challenged by **Sigitas Geda** and **Judita Vaičiūnaitė** in poetry and drama, with a mix of Realism, mythological ambience, and urban Romanticism.

Both Lithuanian music and painting have been heavily influenced by the folk culture from which they emerged. Much of the visual arts' development has centered around the **Vilnius Drawing School,** founded in 1866, and much is also owed to the work of composer/painter **Mikolojus Ciurlionis,** who died in 1911. **Jonas Mekas,** born in Lithuania, was a prominent filmmaker of the last half-century.

READING LIST

The Baltic Revolution: Estonia, Latvia, Lithuania and the Path to Independence, by Anatol Lieven, reads smoothly, and contrasts the Baltic states' respective histories with a satisfying level of detail. Masha Greenbaum's *The Jews of Lithuania* is a must for anyone interested in Jewish history. On a different track, *There is no Ithaca: Idylls of Semeniskiai & Reminiscences* by Jonas Mekas is series of historical reflections from a Lithuanian who left the country to become an underground New York filmmaker.

FACTS AND FIGURES

- **Capital:** Vilnius
- **Population:** 3,705,992
- **Land Area:** 65,301km^2
- **Geography:** Plains, some marshland
- **Language:** Lithuanian, Russian, Polish
- **Religions:** 72% Catholic
- **GDP per capita:** US$2,585
- **Major Exports:** Textiles, chemicals

LITHUANIA ESSENTIALS

Citizens of Australia, Canada, Ireland, the U.K., and the U.S. do not need a visa for visits up to 90 days. Citizens of New Zealand and South Africa who have visas from Estonia or Latvia can use those to enter Lithuania; otherwise, regular 90-day visas are required. Send a completed application, one recent 33x44mm photo, your passport, application fee (by check or money order), and a stamped, self-addressed envelope to the nearest embassy or consulate (see **Embassies & Consulates,** p. 13). Single-entry visas cost US$20; multiple-entry visas US$40; transit visas (good for 48hr.) US$5; double-transit visas US$15. Regular service takes two weeks; rush service costs US$20 extra for 24hr. or US$15 extra for 72hr. service. Obtaining a visa extension may be a wild goose chase, but start at the Immigration Dept. in Vilnius, Virkių g. 3 #6 (tel. 75 64 53).

GETTING THERE & GETTING AROUND

Vilnius, Kaunas, and Klaipėda are easily reached by **train** or **bus** from Belarus, Estonia, Latvia, Poland, and Russia. **Planes** land in Vilnius from: **Berlin** (2hr., 540Lt); **Moscow** (2hr., 416Lt); **Stockholm** (2hr., 660Lt); and **Warsaw** (1¼hr., 270Lt), while **ferries** connect Klaipėda with German cities **Kiel** (34hr., 350Lt) and **Muhkran** (18hr., 140DM). Domestically, **buses** are faster, more common, and only a bit more expensive than the often-crowded **trains.** If you do ride the rails, two major lines cross Lithuania: one runs north-south from Latvia through Šiauliai and Kaunas to Poland, and the other runs east-west from Belarus through Vilnius and Kaunas to Kaliningrad, or on a branch line from Vilnius through Šiauliai to Klaipėda.

TOURIST SERVICES & MONEY

Tourist offices are generally knowledgeable and helpful. **Litinterp,** with locations in most towns, is generally the most helpful; they will reserve accommodations, usually without a surcharge. Vilnius, Kaunas, and Klaipėda each have an edition of the *In Your Pocket* series, available for 4Lt at newsstands and some hotels.

The unit of **currency** is the **Litas** (1Lt=100 centų), plural Litai. Since March 1994, it has been fixed to the U.S. dollar at US$1 = 4Lt. **Traveler's checks** can be cashed at most banks (usually for a 2-3% commission). Cash advances on **Visa** cards can usually be obtained with minimum hassle. **Vilniaus Bankas,** with outlets in major cities, accepts major credit cards and traveler's checks for a small commission. If you're planning on traveling off the touristed path, be aware that most places catering to locals don't take credit cards. **ATMs** are readily available in most cities.

PRIMARY BORDER CROSSINGS. There is no fee for crossing a Lithuanian border. Visas are not available at the border; however, Estonian and Latvian visas can double as a Lithuanian transit visa. Avoid crossing through Belarus to enter or exit Lithuania; not only do you need a transit visa for Belarus (US$20-30 at the border) but border guards will also demand an unofficial border crossing "surcharge." There are two rail routes that manage to avoid Belarus. The **Baltic Express** departs from Warsaw at 2:30pm on odd-numbered days, passes through Kaunas at 11:55pm, and arrives in Tallinn the next day at 1:10pm. There is also one overnight train between Warsaw and Šeštokai, LIT; it arrives at 6:30am, two hours before a Šeštokai-Kaunas-Vilnius train departs. Land travel in Lithuania often involves lengthy waits at customs, especially at the Polish border. It is easiest to visit Lithuania via Vilnius.

Belarus: Druskininkai, LIT (p. 380)/Hrodna, BEL (p. 76); connects inland Lithuania (p. 375) with Belarus (p. 64).

Latvia: Zarasai, LIT/Daugavpils, LAT; connects Vilnius (p. 363) to Eastern Latvia. Joniškis, LIT/Jelgava, LAT; connects Šiauliai (p. 380) with Rīga (p. 344).

Poland: Marijampolė, LIT/Suwałki, POL; connects with Kaunas (p. 375) with Białystok (p. 495).

Russia: Nida, LIT (p. 387)/Svetlogorsk, RUS (p. 637); connects Coastal Lithuania (p. 381) with the Kaliningrad region (p. 632). Tauragė, LIT/Sovetsk, RUS; connects inland Lithuania (p. 375) with the Kaliningrad region (p. 632).

COMMUNICATION

There are two kinds of public phones: the rectangular ones accept magnetic strip cards and the rounded ones accept chip cards. Both are sold at phone offices and many kiosks in denominations of 3.54Lt, 7.08Lt, and 28.32Lt. Calls to **Estonia** and **Latvia** cost 1.65Lt per minute; **Europe** 5.80Lt; and **U.S.** 7.32Lt. Most countries can be dialed directly. Dial 8, wait for the second tone, dial 10, then enter the country code and number. Access numbers include: **AT&T Direct,** tel. (8) 196; **BT Direct** tel. (8) 192; **Canada** tel. (8) 80 09 10 04; **Sprint Express,** tel. (8) 197. For countries to which direct dialing is unavailable, dial 8, wait for the second tone, and dial 194 or 195 for English-speaking operators.

Airmail *(oro pastu)* **letters** abroad cost 1.35Lt, postcards 1Lt. Airmail packages weighing up to 250g cost 4.80Lt plus a 1Lt registration fee. **EMS** international mail takes three to five days. The internet has yet to become a major force in Lithuania, so checking email outside major cities can be difficult.

LANGUAGE

Lithuanian is one of the only two languages left in the Baltic branch of Indo-european tongues (Latvian is the other). All "r"s are trilled. **Polish** is helpful in the south, **German** on the coast, and **Russian** most places, although it is not as prominent as in Latvia. You may need the words *atidarytas* (ah-tee-DAR-ee-tass; open), *uždarytas* (oozh-DAR-ee-tass; closed), *viešbutis* (vee-esh-BOO-tees; hotel), and *turgus* (tuhr-GUHSS; market). If someone seems to sneeze at you, they're just saying *ačiu* (aa-choo; thank you). For more, see the **Glossary,** p. 816.

HEALTH & SAFETY

A triangle pointing downward indicates men's **bathrooms;** an upward-facing triangle indicates women's bathrooms. Many restrooms are nothing but a hole in the ground. Well-stocked **pharmacies** are everywhere. Anything German with a picture of a man clutching his cranium is likely to be a reliable pain killer. Tylenol and ibuprofen dot the shelves. Drink bottled mineral water, and **boil tap water** for 10min. first if you must drink it.

! EMERGENCY NUMBERS.
Fire: tel. 01. **Police**: tel. 02. **Ambulance**: tel. 03.

ACCOMMODATIONS & CAMPING

Lithuania has several **Youth Hostels,** with plans for more to open. HI membership is nominally required, but an LJNN guest card (US$3 at any of the hostels) will suffice. The head office is in Vilnius (see **Vilnius: Practical Information,** p. 366). Their *Hostel Guide* is a handy booklet with info on bike and car rentals, reservations, and maps showing how to reach various hostels. Vilnius has a number of good budget accommodations, but elsewhere, you'll be lucky to find more than two cheap places. In that case, have **Litinterp** hunt something down for you.

FOOD & DRINK

Lithuanian **cuisine** is heavy and often very greasy. Keeping a vegetarian or kosher diet will prove difficult, if not impossible. Restaurants serve various types of *blynai* (pancakes) with *mėsa* (meat) or *varške* (cheese). *Cepelinai* are heavy, potato-dough missiles of meat, cheese, and mushrooms, launched from street stands throughout Western Lithuania. *Šaltibarščiai* is a beet and cucumber soup, not unlike cold borscht, prevalent in the east. *Karbonadas* is fried breaded pork fillet, and *koldunai* are meat dumplings. Lithuanian beer is plentiful and very good. *Kalnapis* is prevalent in Vilnius and most of Lithuania, *Baltijos* reigns supreme around Klaipėda, and the award-winning *Utenos* is widely available. Lithuanian vodka *(degtinė)* is also very popular.

CUSTOMS & ETIQUETTE

Reserve informal **greetings** for those you know personally. A *"laba diena"* (good day) whenever you enter a shop ensures good feelings, and you can never say *"prašau"* too many times (both "please" and "you're welcome"). Handshakes are the norm for men; women get handshakes and perhaps a peck on the cheek. **Tipping** is rare but becoming more common. In some places 10% is standard, although more often the waiter will just round the bill up. When eating in someone's home or, oddly enough, going to the doctor, bring a gift of flowers or chocolates. Feel free to **smoke** anywhere, except on the main pedestrian street in Kaunas, which is the country's only major smoke-free zone. **Homosexuality** is legal but not always tolerated, although Lithuania has the most nightclubs, hotlines, and services for gays and lesbians in the Baltics. Contact Vladimiras or Eduardas of the **Lithuanian Gay League** (tel./fax (2) 63 30 31; email lgl@gay.lt; www.gay.lt), P.O. Box 2862, Vilnius 2000. **SAPHO,** P.O. Box 2204, Vilnius 2049, is a prominent lesbian organization. Call 33 30 31 for info on events and accommodations for gay men.

NATIONAL HOLIDAYS

January 1, New Year's; February 16, Independence Day (1918); March 11, Restoration of Lithuanian Statehood; April 23-24, Catholic Easter; May 1, Labor Day; June 23, Rasos Šventi (Midsummer Night); July 6, Day of Statehood (Mindaugas Day); November 1, All Saints' Day; November 2, All Souls' Day; December 25, Christmas.

VILNIUS

Once a major Eastern European political and intellectual center, Vilnius (pop. 586,000) today is a small-feeling city of Baroque and Classical architecture, vast stretches of greenery, and a vibrant international community. Founded in 1321

LITHUANIA

after a prophetic dream by Grand Duke Gediminas, within 60 years Vilnius presided over the Polish-Lithuanian Commonwealth, the largest empire in Europe stretching from the Baltic to the Black Sea. By the 19th century, Vilnius's political perch had been supplanted by its significance as one of the world centers of Jewish scholarship (Warsaw and New York being the other two). The "Jerusalem of Europe"—its population was one-third Jewish—bore the Jewish Enlightenment and many influential Hasidic thinkers. Tragically, nearly all of Vilnius' Jews were killed during WWII at the Paneriai death camp. After the war, Vilnius fell into the grips of the USSR. While it definitely suffered at the hands of the Soviets, the city somehow managed to resist the mass Sovietization of other provincial capitals. As a result, millennial Vilnius feels much as it did at the turn of the 20th century: the most beautiful city in the Baltics, its landlocked geography gives it a decidedly Central European feel, prompting the cliched comparison with Prague, while the expanse of its Old Town is rivaled only by Kraków's. Undergoing reconstruction and enjoying the daily flood of new businesses, Vilnius is increasingly seen as the next Eastern European "it girl." With the Old Town's cafes frequented more and more by beer-guzzling ex-pats, and hostel beds quickly snatched up by the backpacking masses, time is running out to get in on the Vilnius secret.

GETTING THERE & GETTING AROUND

Airplanes: The airport *(oro uostas),* Rodūnės Kelias 2 (tel. 63 55 60), lies 5km south of town. Take bus #1 from the train station, or bus #2 from the Sparta stop of trolley bus #16 on Kauno g. (15-20min.). **LOT** (tel. 73 90 20; fax 63 27 72) flies to **Warsaw; SAS** (tel. 23 60 00; fax 23 31 39) to **Copenhagen; Estonian Air** (tel. 73 90 22; fax 26 03 95) to **Tallinn; Lithuanian Airlines** (tel. 75 25 88; fax 72 48 52) to **Berlin, Kiev, London,** and **Moscow.**

Trains: Geležinkelio g. 16 (tel. 63 00 86 and 63 00 88). Tickets for all trains are sold in the yellow addition left of the main station; windows #3 and 4 are specifically for trains to western Europe. Tickets for trains originating outside of Lithuania can be bought no earlier than 3hr. before departure. The **reservation bureau** (tel. 62 69 47) is in the main station hall on the right. Open M-F 9am-4pm. All international trains (except those heading north) pass through Belarus; you'll need a Belarussian visa to complete the trip (see **Belarus: Essentials,** p. 66). To: **Berlin** (22hr., 1 per day, 309Lt); **Kaliningrad** (7hr., 3 per day, *coupé* 65Lt); **Minsk** (5hr., 3 per day, *coupé* 52Lt); **Moscow** (17hr., 3 per day, *coupé* 128Lt); **Rīga** (7½hr., 1 per day, *coupé* 67Lt); **St. Petersburg** (18hr., 2 per day, *coupé* 108Lt); and **Warsaw** (11hr., 1 per day, *coupé* 115Lt).

Buses: Autobusų Stotis, Sodų g. 22 (tel. 26 24 82 and 26 24 83; reservations tel. 26 29 77 and 63 52 77), opposite the train station. Purchase tickets from the driver for short trips. **Tarpmiestinė Salė** covers long-distance buses; windows #13-15 serve destinations outside the former Soviet Union. Open daily 7am-8pm. To: **Kaliningrad** (8-10hr., 2 per day, 34-40Lt); **Minsk** (5hr., 8 per day, 19Lt); **Rīga** (6½hr., 5 per day, 25-40Lt); **Tallinn** (10hr., 2 per day, 81Lt); and **Warsaw** (9½hr., 4 per day, 60-65Lt).

Local Transportation: Buses and **trolleys** run only to Senamiestis's edges, but link the downtown with the train and bus stations and the suburbs. All lines run daily 6am-midnight. Buy tickets at any kiosk (0.60Lt) or from the driver (0.75Lt); punch them on board to avoid the hefty fine.

Taxis: State Taxis (tel. 22 88 88). 1.30Lt per km. **Private taxis** show a green light in the windshield; arrange the fare before getting in.

Car Rental: Hertz, Ukmergės g. 2 (tel. 72 69 40; fax 72 69 70), at the intersection of Ukmergės g. and Kalvarijų g. Best rates around.

ORIENTATION

From the **train** or **bus stations,** which are directly across from each other, walk east on **Geležinkelio g.** (right with your back to the train station), and turn left at its end.

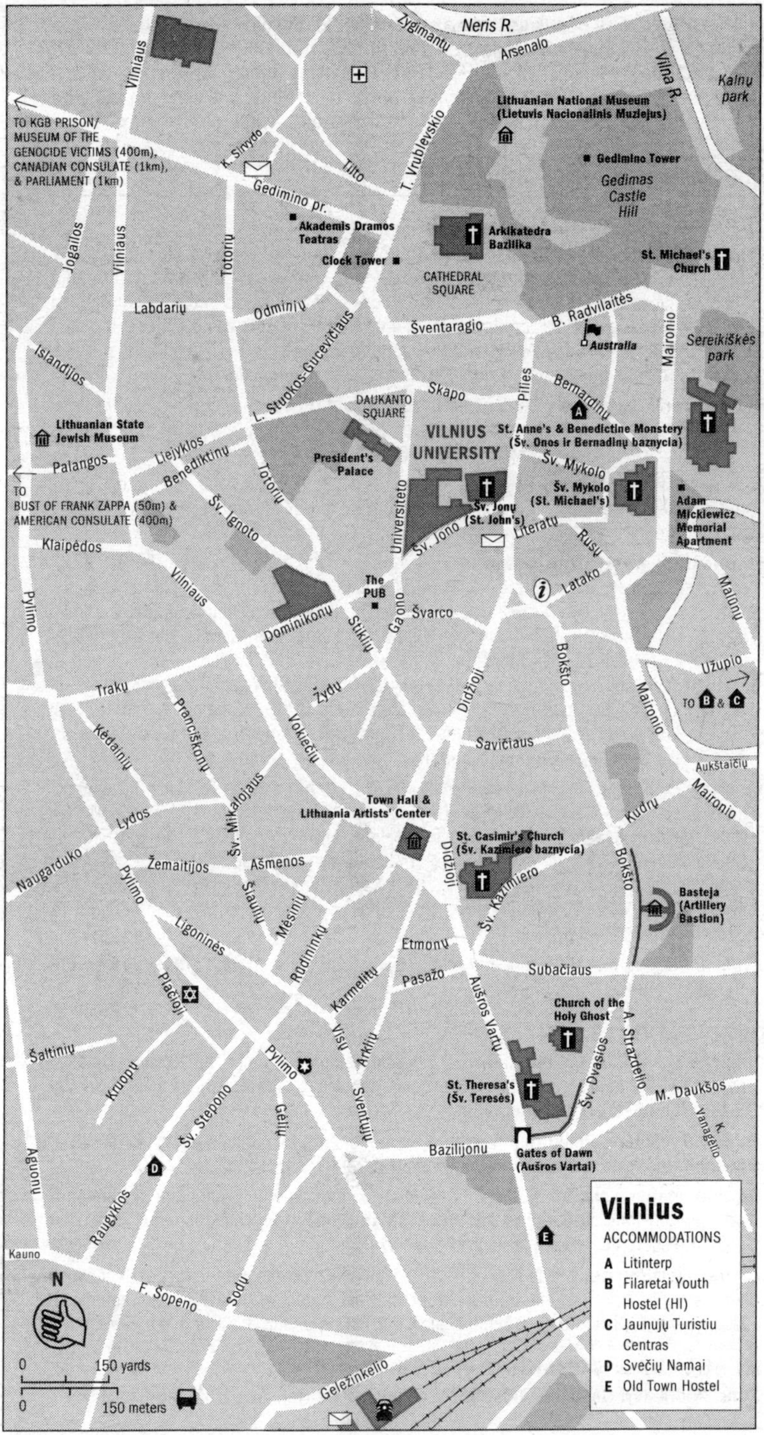
Neris R.
Zygimantų
Arsenalo
Vilnia R.
Kalnų park
Lithuanian National Museum (Lietuvis Nacionalinis Muziejus)
Gediminо Tower
Gedimas Castle Hill
TO KGB PRISON/ MUSEUM OF THE GENOCIDE VICTIMS (400m), CANADIAN CONSULATE (1km), & PARLIAMENT (1km)
Vilniaus
K. Sirvydo
Tilto
T. Vrublevskio
Gedimino pr.
Akademis Dramos Teatras
Arkikatedra Bazilika
Clock Tower
CATHEDRAL SQUARE
St. Michael's Church
Jogailos
Totorių
Labdarių
Odminių
Šventaragio
B. Radvilaitės
Australia
Maironio
Sereikiškės park
Islandijos
L. Stuokos-Gucevičiaus
Skapo
Bernardinų
Pilies
DAUKANTO SQUARE
Lithuanian State Jewish Museum
VILNIUS UNIVERSITY
St. Anne's & Benedictine Monstery (Šv. Onos ir Bernadinų baznycia)
Liejyklos
Benediktinų
President's Palace
Šv. Mykolo
Šv. Mykolo (St. Michael's)
Adam Mickiewicz Memorial Apartment
Palangos
TO BUST OF FRANK ZAPPA (50m) & AMERICAN CONSULATE (400m)
Šv. Ignoto
Universiteto
Šv. Jonų (St. John's)
Šv. Jono
Literatų
Rusų
Klaipėdos
The PUB
Latako
Malūnų
Vilniaus
Dominikonų
Stiklių
Gaono
Švarco
Pylimo
Bokšto
Didžioji
Užupio
TO B & C
Trakų
Žydų
Pranciškonų
Kėdainių
Vokiečių
Savičiaus
Maironio
Aukštaičių
Šv. Mikalojaus
Town Hall & Lithuania Artists' Center
Kudrų
Maironio
Lydos
St. Casimir's Church (Šv. Kazimiero baznycia)
Naugarduko
Žemaitijos
Ašmenos
Didžioji
Bokšto
Pylimo
Šiaulių
Mėsinių
Šv. Kazimiero
Basteja (Artillery Bastion)
Ligoninės
Rūdininkų
Etmonų
Subačiaus
Pasažo
Karmelitų
Aušros Vartų
Church of the Holy Ghost
Plačiosios
Visų
Arklių
A. Strazdelio
Šaltinių
Pylimo
St. Theresa's (Šv. Teresės)
Šv. Dvasios
M. Daukšos
Kruopų
Gėlių
Šventųjų
K. Vanagėlio
Šv. Stepono
Bazilijonu
Gates of Dawn (Aušros Vartai)
Aguonų
Raugyklos
Kauno
N
F. Šopeno
Sodų
0 150 yards
0 150 meters
Geležinkelio
Vilnius
ACCOMMODATIONS
A Litinterp
B Filaretai Youth Hostel (HI)
C Jaunujų Turistiu Centras
D Svečių Namai
E Old Town Hostel

LITHUANIA

This is the beginning of **Aušros Vartų g.**, which leads downhill through the gates of **Senamiestis** (Old Town) and changes its name first to **Didžioji g.** and then **Pilies g.**, before reaching the base of Castle Hill. Here, **Gediminas Tower** presides over **Arkikatedros aikštė** (Cathedral Sq.) and the banks of the river **Neris. Gedimino pr.**, the commercial artery, leads west from the square in front of the cathedral's doors.

PRACTICAL INFORMATION

TOURIST & FINANCIAL SERVICES

Tourist Offices: Tourist Information Centre, Pilies str. 42 (tel./fax 62 07 62; www.vilnius.lt), provides information about travel and events throughout Lithuania, organizes tours, and sells *Vilnius in Your Pocket* (4Lt). English and Russian spoken. Open M-F 9am-7pm, Sa noon-6pm. **Lithuanian Youth Hostels Head Office,** Filaretų g. 17 (tel./fax 25 46 27; email filaretai@post.omnitel.net), at the Filaretai Hostel (see below). Arranges travel and hostel reservations. Open daily 8am-5pm.

Budget Travel: Lithuanian Student and Youth Travel, V. Basanavičiaus g. 30, #13 (tel. 22 13 73). Great deals for travelers under 27. Sells student tickets for buses, trains, and planes. Open M-F 8:30am-6pm, Sa 10am-2pm.

Passport Office: Imigracijos Taryba, Verkių 3, #3 (tel. 75 64 53), 2km north of Senamiestis. Extends visas for those who demonstrate proof of need to stay in Lithuania (61Lt). Open M-F 9am-4:30pm.

Embassies: Australian Consulate, Radvilaitės 4 (tel./fax 22 33 69; email aust.con.vilnius@post.omnitel.net). **Belarus,** P. Klimo g. 8 (tel./fax 26 34 43). Visas at Muitinės g. 41 (tel. 63 06 26). Open M-Tu and Th-F 10am-4:30pm. **Canada,** Gedimino pr. 64 (tel. 22 08 98; fax 22 08 84). Open M-F 10am-1pm. **Russia,** Latvių g. 53/54 (tel. 72 17 63; fax 72 38 77; visa tel. 72 38 93; visa fax 72 33 75). Open M-Tu and Th-F 10am-1pm. **Ukraine,** Turniškių g. 22 (tel./fax 76 36 26). Visas at Kalvarijų 159, 2nd Fl. (tel. 77 84 13). Open M-Tu and Th-F 10am-1pm. **U.K.,** Antakalnio g. 2 (tel. 22 20 70; fax 72 75 79). Open M-F 9:30am-12:30pm. **U.S.,** Akmenų g. 6 (tel. 22 30 31; fax 31 28 19). Open M-Th 8:30am-5:30pm.

Currency Exchange: Geležinkelio 6 (tel. 33 07 63), to the right as you face the train station. Open 24hr. **Vilniaus Bankas,** Gedimino pr. 12 (tel. 68 28 12; fax 22 62 88). Gives MC/Visa cash advances for no commission. Also cashes AmEx and Thomas Cooke traveler's checks. Open M-Th 8am-3:30pm, F 8am-3pm. **Bankas Snoras,** A. Vivulskio g. 7 (tel. 26 27 71; fax 65 23 95). Cashes all traveler's checks and gives Visa cash advances for a 2% commission at circular blue and white kiosks throughout the city. Open daily 8am-8pm.

ATMs: Cirrus/MC machines lurk at **Vilniaus Bankas,** the airport, and **Lithuanian Savings Banks,** Vilniaus 16 and Piles 9.

LOCAL SERVICES

Luggage Storage: At the bus station. 1.50Lt per bag. Open daily 7am-10pm. In the tunnels under the train station. 1.50Lt per small bag, 2.50Lt for large bags and backpacks; 2Lt each additional day. Open 24hr.

English Bookstore: Penki Kontinentai (Five Continents), K. Stulginskio g. 5 (tel. 22 14 81), off Gedimino pr. Open M-F 9am-6pm, Sa 9am-1:30pm.

Gay Information Line: Tel. 63 30 31. Info about organizations, events, and accommodations for gay men. **Lithuanian Gay and Lesbian Homepage** (cs.ektaco.ee/~forter) lists gay and lesbian establishments in Lithuania.

Laundromat: Slayana, Latvių g. 31 (tel. 75 31 12), in Žvėrynas, 5min. west of Senamiestis across the Neris River. Take tram #7 from the train station or tram #3 from Senamiestis. Do-it-yourself wash and dry 12Lt; full service 20Lt. Detergent 3Lt. Open M-F 8am-3pm.

EMERGENCY & COMMUNICATIONS

24hr. Pharmacy: Gedimino Vaistinė, Gedimino pr. 27 (tel. 61 01 35 and 62 49 30).

LITHUANIA

Medical Assistance: Baltic-American Medical & Surgical Clinic, Antakalnio g. 124 (tel. 34 20 20), at Vilnius University Hospital. Open 24hr.

Post Office: Centrinis Paštas, Gedimino pr. 7 (tel. 61 67 59), west of Arkikatedros aikštė. Letter to the U.S. 1.35Lt. **Poste Restante** at the window that says *"iki pareikalavimo"*; 0.50Lt to pick up mail. Open M-F 7am-7pm, Sa 9am-4pm. **Postal code:** LT-2000.

Internet Access: Free email at the **Soros Foundation,** Šv. Jono g. 3/5 (tel. 22 38 06). Open M-F noon-8pm. Or, try the **Martynyas Mavydas National Library,** Gedimino pr. 51 (tel. 61 26 87). Library card (7Lt) required. Open M-F 8am-8pm, Sa-Su 10am-5pm.

Telephones: In the main post office (tel. 62 55 11). Phones take cards (from 8Lt) and allow direct dialing abroad (to Canada and the U.S. 7.32Lt per min.; Eastern Europe 3.57Lt per min.; Western Europe 5.80Lt per min.). **Phone code:** (8)22.

LITHUANIA

ACCOMMODATIONS

Old Town Hostel (HI), Aušros vartų g. 20-15a (tel. 62 53 57; fax 22 03 05; email livijus@pub.osf.lt), 100m from the "Gates of Dawn" in the Old Town. With your back to the train station, turn right on Geležinkelio and left on Aušros Vartų; the hostel is through the arch on the right. An outgoing proprietor and one huge dorm filled with raucous 20-somethings reminds you what budget travel is all about. Spotless shower and toilets. Large communal fridge and washing machine. Dorm beds 32Lt, non-members 34Lt. Singles and doubles next door 40-60Lt. Free email access, coffee or tea upon arrival, and a free beer at Rita's Slėtuvė. The owner runs trips to his friend's sauna in the country for 25Lt per person, plus gas money.

Litinterp, Bernardinų 7, #2 (tel. 22 38 50; fax 22 35 59; email litinterp@post.omnitel.net). With your back to the train station, turn right on Geležinkelio g. Take your third left onto Aušros Vartų g. Stay on this street until you reach a square; directly across you should see Didžiolji g. Follow this as it turns into Pilies g., then turn right on Bernardinų. More quiet and privacy than the Old Town, but slightly more expensive. Spotless and comfortable rooms. Shared bath. Singles 70-100Lt; doubles 120-140Lt. Apartment with kitchen and bath starting at 200Lt per night. Breakfast included. Reception M-F 9am-6pm, Sa 9am-4pm. Reservations recommended.

Filaretai Youth Hostel (HI), Filaretų g. 17 (tel. 25 46 27; fax 22 01 49; email filareta@post.omnitel.lt). Take bus #34, which leaves from the right of the station (across from McDonald's) to the seventh stop (10min.). Clean kitchen, satellite TV in the common room, hostel reservations in Russia and the Baltics, and local info, but without the Old Town's personal touch. Cozy, comfortable 2- to 8-bed dorms. First night 29Lt, non-members 31Lt; after first night 24Lt, non-members 26Lt. Washer/dryer 10Lt per load. Reception 7am-midnight. Curfew 1am.

Svečių Namai, Šv. Stepono 11 (tel. 26 02 54). With your back to the train station, head straight down Stoties and turn left on F. Šopeno, then right on Šv. Stepono. More privacy than other hostels. Large rooms with fold-out beds and kitchens. Shared bath. 40Lt per person. No English spoken.

Jaunujų Turistiu Centras, Polocko 7 (tel. 61 35 76). Take bus #34, which leaves from the right of the station (across from McDonald's) to the seventh stop (10min.). Aging, but still popular with Eastern European students. Kitchen and sparkling, renovated baths. Triples and quads 20Lt per person.

FOOD

The four French **Iki supermarkets** in Vilnius stock foreign foods, but are all rather far from Senamiestis. The most convenient one lies at Žirmūnų g. 2, just across the Žirmūnų bridge. (Open M-Sa 9am-10pm, Su 9am-8pm.)

RESTAURANTS

Trendy, inexpensive restaurants are popping up everywhere. A full meal can be as cheap as US$4-6, but quality and price are closely correlated. Check out translated menus and take notes before hitting a less touristed joint.

Ritos Slėptuvė (Rita's Hideaway), A. Goštauto g. 8 (tel. 62 61 17), west of Senamiestis along the Neris. *The* place to go. Funky American decor and "no sweat-suits allowed"–seemingly a subtle ban on the local mafia. 12" Chicago deep dish pizza (16-25Lt), chili (8Lt), and other American standards. Eat well for under 10Lt. Come before 4pm, after which the menus shrinks as the place becomes a **bar**. Live music Sunday nights; disco Fridays and Saturdays. Open M-Th 7am-2am, F 7am-6am, Sa 8am-6am, Su 8pm-2am.

Ritos Smuklė (Rita's Tavern), Žirmūnų g. 68 (tel. 77 07 86), next to an Iki supermarket. Too far to walk; take trolleybus #12, 13, or 17. Rita does Lithuanian, with traditional folk music and costumes. Great food! English menu, with highly amusing attempts at slang. Entrees 15-35Lt. Live folk music F-Sa 8-10pm. Open daily 11am-2am.

Stikliai Aludė (Beer Bar), Gaono g. 7 (tel. 22 21 09). This cozy, folksy, subterranean haunt is less pricey than Prie Parlamento, but just as good. Entrees 16-28Lt. Excellent local brew: *Biržai Grafas* 4.50Lt, *Kalnapilis* 3Lt. Open daily noon-midnight.

Prie Parlamento, Gedimino pr. 46 (tel. 62 16 06). A bit pricey, but extremely popular with yuppies-in-training. "The best lasagna in Lithuania" is cheap at 12.50Lt. Open M-F 8am-midnight, Sa-Su 10am-2pm.

LITHUANIA

CAFES & COFFEEHOUSES

Cafe Filharmonija, Aušros vartų g. 5 (tel. 22 13 83). Next to the National Philharmonic, and with the style to match. Of the sidewalk cafes near Aušros Vartų, this is the pick of the litter, marked by a golden "*Kavinė*" sign over the door and a relaxed crowd outside. Great for people-watching. Entrees 7-12Lt. Excellent ice cream 5-8Lt. Open daily 9am-11pm.

Užupio Kavinė, Užupio g. 2 (tel. 22 21 38), between Senamiestis and the Filaretų hostel. A meal with your intellectual pretensions? Potato pancakes with mushroom sauce 9.10Lt. 0.5L of *Dvaro* beer 6Lt. Open daily 11am-2am.

Cafe Afrika, Pilies g. 28 (tel. 61 71 90), smack in the center of it all. Look for the blue zebra sign and vibrant yellow decor. Soup, salad, and gourmet coffee for less than 12Lt. Open daily 10am-11pm.

SIGHTS

With the largest Old Town in Eastern Europe, Vilnius has no shortage of architectural wonders or historic spots, although its museums generally lag behind those in Rīga. The moment you reach the end of Geležinkelio g. and turn left, the 16th-century **Gates of Dawn** (Aušros Vartai), the only surviving portal of the old city walls, welcomes you in. Take a map, or just enjoy getting lost in the winding alleyways and crooked streets.

SENAMIESTIS (OLD TOWN)

Through the gates, enter the first door on the right to ascend the **Chapel of the Gates of Dawn** (Aušros Vartų Koplyčia), built in the 17th century around an icon said either to have been captured in Ukraine by Grand Duke Vytautas or to be a portrait of a 16th-century princess. The shrine is usually packed with locals either praying or selling holy paraphernalia. Head back to the street and through the doorway at the building's end to reach **St. Theresa's Church** (Šv. Teresės bažnyčia), known for its myriad Baroque sculptures, multicolored arches, frescoed ceiling, and stained glass. A few steps farther down, a gateway leads to the shockingly bright 17th-century **Church of the Holy Ghost** (Šv. Dvasios bažnyčia; tel. 62 95 95), seat of Lithuania's Russian Orthodox Archbishop. A functioning monastery, the church is the final resting place of Saints Antonius, Ivan, and Eustachius, martyred in 1371. Their bodies, usually clad in red in a glass case under the altar, wear white for Christmas and black for Lent. Beyond the gates, Aušros Vartų g. turns into Didžioji g., leading to the crown-topped **St. Casimir's Church** (Šv. Kazimiero bažnyčia), Didžioji g. 34 (tel. 22 17 15). Named after the country's patron saint, this is Vilnius's oldest Baroque church, built by the Jesuits in 1604 to ape the Roman Il Gesù church. In 1832, the church gained a Russian Orthodox dome; during WWI, the Germans made it Lutheran. With they returned in WWII and tore down the dome. After "liberating" Vilnius, the Soviets turned the temple into a shrine to atheism, but it's been back in the Catholic fold since 1989. (Open M-Sa 4-6:30pm, Su 8am-1:30pm.)

Didžioji g. broadens into **Town Hall Square** (Rotušės aikštė), an ancient marketplace dominated by the columns of the 18th-century **town hall,** now home to the **Lithuanian Artists' Center** (Lietuvos Menininkv Rumai). Didžioji g. continues north past **St. Nicholas's Church** (Šv. Mikalojaus bažnyčia), Šv. Mikalojaus g. 4 (tel. 62 30 69). Lithuania's oldest, St. Nicholas' was built in 1320 for the city's Hanseatic merchants. Shortly after the church, the street widens into a triangular square and merges with the pedestrian **Pilies g.,** lined with peddlers of amber, silver, and leather. The main entrance to **Vilnius University** (Vilniaus Universitetas) stands at the corner of Pilies g. and Šv. Jono g. Founded in 1579, the Jesuit university was a major player in the Counter-Reformation. On the east side of the main university courtyard, the 1387 **St. John's Church** (Šv. Jonų bažnyčia), Šv. Jono g. 12 (tel. 61 17 95), served as a science museum under the Soviets. Go through the arches opposite St. John's to the remarkable 17th-century **Astronomical Observatory,** once rivaled in importance only by Greenwich and the Sorbonne. The university **library,** Universiteto g., with more than five million volumes, remains one of Europe's largest. The **Church of the Holy Spirit** (Šventosios Dvasios bažnyčia), Dominikonų g. 8 (tel. 62 95 95), a gold and marble Baroque masterpiece last rebuilt in 1770, was the first Gothic church in Vilnius. (Open daily 7am-10am and 5-7pm.)

LITHUANIA

Continue north on Pilies g. (or Universiteto g.) to **Cathedral Square** (Arkikatedros aikštė), depicted on the 50Lt note. A church has stood here since 1387, when Grand Duke Jogaila converted his country to Catholicism in order to win the Polish throne (see **History,** p. 361). Today's 18th-century **cathedral** (Arkikatedra Bazilika; tel. 61 11 27) resembles a Greek temple, perhaps because this was once the site of the principal temple to Perkūnas, Lithuanian god of thunder. The contorted figures on the south wall depict grand dukes in ecstatic poses of religious fervor. Inside, peek into the early Baroque **Chapel of St. Casimir** (Šv. Kazimiero koplyčia), home to a royal mausoleum. (Open M-Sa 7am-1pm and 2:30-8pm, Su 7am-2pm.) Back out in the square, the octagonal 1522 **clock tower,** atop one of the lower fortress towers, is one of the city's best meeting points. Behind the cathedral, walk up the long path of the Castle Hill to **Gedimino tower** for a great view of Vilnius's spires.

From Cathedral Square at the base of the castle hill, follow B. Raduvilaites along the park and turn right on Maironio g. This leads south to Vilnius' Gothic treasure, **St. Anne's Church and Bernardine Monastery** (Šv. Onos ir Bernardinų bažnyčia), Maironio g. 8 (tel. 61 12 36). A red-brick structure built at the height of the Gothic style, St. Anne's is so beautiful that Napoleon supposedly wanted to carry it back to France. The Bernardine monastery in back, part of the city walls in 1520, partly houses the Art Academy and Design School of the University of Vilnius. Across the street, the Renaissance **St. Michael's** (Šv. Mykolo), Šv. Mykolo g. 9 (tel. 61 64 09), was built in 1625 to house a family mausoleum. (Open M 10am-5pm, W-Su 11am-6pm.) It is now home to the **Museum of Architecture.** The **Adam Mickiewicz Memorial Apartment** (A. Mickevičiaus Memorialinis Butas), Bernardinų g. 11 (tel. 61 88 36), sits on the road back toward Pilies g. The famous Lithuanian-Polish poet lived here in 1822 (see **Poland: Literature & Arts,** p. 401; open M-F 2-6pm, Sa 10am-2pm).

Cannons, armor, and rusty swords fill the **Artillery Bastion** (Bastėja), Bokšto g. 20/18 (tel. 61 21 49), a restored section of the city's 17th-century defenses against the Russians and Swedes. (Open W-Su 10am-5pm.) Cross Gedimino pr. to head south on Jogailos, which becomes Pylimo. The most random monument in Eastern Europe shoots skyward off Pylimo between Kalinausko 1 and 3. Its cap is a **bust of Frank Zappa** installed in 1995 after the Museum of Theater, Music, and Cinema turned it away.

THE OLD JEWISH QUARTER

Vilnius was once a center of Jewish life comparable to Warsaw and New York, with a Jewish population of 100,000 (in a city of 230,000) at the outbreak of World War II. Nazi persecution left only 6000 survivors by the time the Red Army retook the city in 1944. Only one of prewar Vilnius' 96 **synagogues** remains, at Pylimo g. 39 (tel. 61 25 33). The Nazis used it to store medical supplies; it's now undergoing its first exhaustive restoration. Fifty years of Soviet repression stalled any immediate post-war rebirth, but services are now held regularly on Saturday mornings, and commemorative plaques have started to appear on buildings. The **Lithuanian State Jewish Museum,** housed in two buildings at Pylimo g. 4 (tel. 61 79 17), offers a variety of exhibits testifying to the vitality of Yiddish culture in Lithuania and the tragedy of the Holocaust. An **exhibition on Jewish life** houses rotating exhibits and a permanent collection of items salvaged from the rubble of synagogues. The **Gallery of the Righteous** (Teisuoliu Gallerija; tel. 62 45 90 and 74 24 88) honors the Lithuanians who sheltered Jews during the war. The museum also arranges guided tours of Jewish Vilnius in English, Yiddish, Russian, and Lithuanian. (Open M-Th 9am-5pm, F 9am-4pm. Donations requested.) The **Green House,** Paménkalnio g. 12 (tel. 62 07 30; fax 22 70 83), set back from the street, chronicles the destruction of Vilnius's Jewish community through slides and photographs, including meticulous SS records of daily executions. It also documents where 90% of Lithuania's 240,000 Jews were exterminated during the war. Ben-Zvi (1884-1963) and Š.Z. Šazaras (1889-1974), Israel's second and third presidents, respectively, were both originally from Vilnius; their pictures now hang in the museum as testimony to the enduring vigor of the city's Jewish community. (Open M-Th 9am-5pm, F 9am-4pm. Donations requested.)

LITHUANIA

The **Genocide Memorial,** Agrastų g. 15, is only a 10-15min. train ride away in **Paneriai** (2Lt). Exit the train tracks on the left side and follow the road (Agrastų g.) straight to the memorial. Between 1941 and 1944, 100,000 people, including 70,000 Jews, were shot, burned, and buried here. Paved paths connect the pits that served as mass graves. (Open M and W-Sa 11am-6pm.) For more information on locating ancestors or on the Jewish Quarter in general, visit the **Jewish Cultural Centre,** Šaltinių g. 12 (tel. 41 88 09).

SOVIET VILNIUS

Don't miss the **Museum of Genocide Victims** (Genocido Aukų Muziejus), Gedimino pr. 40 (enter around the corner at Aukų g. 4; tel. 62 24 49), in the **old KGB prison.** One of the tour guides, G. Radžius, was once a prisoner in its cells; find someone to translate what he says. The stately building was originally constructed in 1899 by the Russian tsar to serve as a court, but it was captured by the Nazis during WWII and turned into a Gestapo headquarters. The officers of the *Abwehr*, a branch of the SS devoted to exterminating the Jews, held court downstairs. When the Soviets came to town, the building became Vilnius' KGB headquarters. The prison is still rife with torture and execution chambers; notice the dark, damp rooms in which prisoners were tortured and beaten, and then left to stand in solitude for as long as a week. There are also mounds of documents left by the KGB as they hastily left in 1991. (Open Tu-Su 10am-4pm. Tours in Lithuanian and Russian, captions in English.) Behind the Gedimino Tower, the **Lithuanian National Museum**

IT'S A SMALL GULAG AFTER ALL Apart from bringing freedom and opportunity for advancement to the millions formerly under its yoke, the fall of communism left former Soviet states with a slew of statues of the leaders of the glorious revolution and nowhere to put them. Enter Viliumas Malinaukas, a Lithuanian entrepeneur who wants to collect them all for a massive Soviet theme park. His plan: to place the statues in a strip of bogland he has filled and developed. He has already won the grace of the government, but not of all of the country. The older generation—who actually lived through communism—are particularly enraged at the plan to package their repression for tourists. And while Malinaukas claims that the park is meant to be educational, whether it's in good taste is another matter. Take, for example, the planned entrance to Leninland: a replica of the Vilnius train station from which thousands of Lithuanians were shipped to Siberia. One can only hope that an Aeroflot roller coaster isn't in the works.

(Lietuvis Nacionalinis Muziejus), Arsenalo g. 1 (tel. 62 94 26), recently underwent serious renovations; it now boasts a new red roof. Founded in 1855, the museum chronicles the history of the Lithuanian people through 1940. Don't miss the exhibit on the life and times of the 1918-40 independent Lithuanian republic. (Open W-Su 10am-5pm. 4Lt, students 2Lt, free with ISIC.)

The **parliament** sits at the west end of Gedimino pr., just before the Neris. In January 1991, the world watched as Lithuanians raised barricades to protect their parliament from the Soviet army. President Landsbergis later said that all of the deputies expected to become martyrs on the night of January 13, but the main attack came instead at the 326m **TV tower,** where 14 unarmed civilians were killed as the Red Army forced the station off the air. Crosses and memorials surround the spot today, and streets in the neighborhood have been renamed in honor of the 14 martyrs. The huge tower, visible from the city center, is reachable by trolleybus #11 going west from Skalvija on Žaliasis bridge's south end toward Pašilaičai (14 stops). Ascend the tower for a breathtaking view of the countryside. (Open daily 9am-9pm. 12Lt.)

EAST VILNIUS

Above Senamiestis's east side rises the **Hill of Three Crosses** (Trjių Kryžių kalnas), visible throughout all of Vilnius. White crosses were originally set here in the 18th century to commemorate seven 13th-century Franciscans crucified on the hill by pagan tribes. During Lithuania's first period of independence, a white stone memorial of three crosses appeared on the hilltop. Torn down by the Soviets in the 50s, the present monument is a 1989 copy; legend dictates that two of the crosses can be seen from anywhere in the city, while a third remains hidden. to reach the striking 1688 **St. Peter and Paul Church** (Šv. Apaštalv Petro ir Povilo bažnyčia), Antakalnio g. 1, take trolleybus #2, 3, or 4 from Senamiestis, or trolleybus #12 or 13 from Skalvija at the foot of the Žaliasis bridge three stops east to Meno mokykla. The church's humble founder is buried next to the door; his tombstone reads *Hic jacet peccator* ("Here lies a sinner").

ENTERTAINMENT

Vilnius's breakneck economic development has fostered a growing arts scene. In summer, music and dance festivals and pop concerts come to town; check *Vilnius in Your Pocket* or the Lithuanian morning paper *Lietuvos Rytas* for performances. Consult the tourist office at Gedimino pr. 14 (tel. 61 68 67; fax 22 61 18) for info on obtaining tickets. The **Academy Art Gallery** (Akademijos Galerija), Pilies g. 44 (tel. 61 20 94), one of the best of Vilnius' many new galleries, specializes in ceramics and graphic arts. (Open M-Sa noon-6pm.) See undubbed movies at **Lietuva Cinema,** Pylimo g. 17 (tel. 62 34 22), and **The Vilnius,** Gedimino pr. 5a (tel. 61 26 76). **Kino Centras Skalvija,** Goštauto g. 2 (tel. 61 05 05), shows the best foreign films in the city.

Lietuvos Naciolinė Filharmonija (National Philharmonic Orchestra), Aušros Vartų 5 (tel. 62 71 65 and 79 10 49), just north of the Senamiestis gates. Internationally renowned. Box office open M-F 10am-7pm, Sa-Su 10am-6pm; performances begin at 7pm. Tickets 10-150Lt. Also organizes the **Vilniaus Festivalis** (www.filharmonija.lt/vilnaiusfestivalis), a month of concerts starting in late May.

Operos ir Baleto Teatras (Opera and Ballet Theater), Vienuolio 1 (tel. 62 06 36; tickets tel. 62 07 27). Performances begin at 6 or 7pm.

Akademinis Dramos Teatras (Academic Drama Theater), Gedimino pr. 4 (tel. 62 97 71). From Neil Simon to Federico García Lorca. Box office open Tu-Su noon-6pm.

NIGHTLIFE

New discos, bars, and clubs are springing up daily to entertain the influx of foreigners and the city's younger crowd. Check out posters in Senamiestis or Prie Parlamento's bulletin board. Lithuanian hipsters Eduardas and Vladimiras organize a **gay disco** every Saturday night at a different venue. Call them (tel. 63 30 31) for more information (Cover 15Lt. Usually open F-Sa 10pm-6am.)

PUBS & BARS

The Pub (Prie Universiteto), Dominikonų g. 9 (tel. 61 83 93), in the heart of Senamiestis. Traditional English pub with heavy wooden interior and a cozy, 19th-century dungeon. The narrow brick courtyard is usually packed with foreigners and local students. Local bands play most nights. Wednesday night jazz. Cover 8Lt. Pint of *Pilsner Urquell* 10Lt. Open daily 11am-2am.

Amatininskv Užeiga, Didžiogi g. 19, #2 (tel. 61 79 68). Mingle with the locals at the bar or descend into the recently discovered medieval basement for a more intimate atmosphere. Open M-F 8am-5am, Sa-Su 11am-5am.

Savas Kampas (Your Corner), Vokiečių g. 4 (tel. 22 32 03). A laid-back option for a more mature set who like to hear 60s, 70s, and 80s tunes. Local Lithuanian bands play live on Friday and Saturday nights, when dancers hit the disco floor. Great mix of jazz, blues, and rock. Open daily midnight-3am.

CLUBS

Ministerija, Gedimino pr. 46 (tel. 62 16 06), in the basement of Prie Parlamento. Local studs practice American dance crazes—from six years ago. A "no techno" rule is mercifully enforced. 20+. Cover 5Lt. Open M-Th 6pm-2am, F-Sa 6pm-5am.

Ultra, Goštauto g. 12 (tel. 62 00 29). Frequented by a trendy younger crowd that gladly dances to anything with a beat. Cover 5Lt. Open Th-Sa 8pm-5am.

Naktinis Vilkas (Night Wolf), Lukiškių g. 3 (tel. 22 47 51). Popular student disco, full of Lenin memorabilia and Communist kitsch. Reputed to have the best singles scene in town. 21+. Cover M-Sa 5Lt. Open daily 8pm-6am.

NEAR VILNIUS: TRAKAI CASTLE

Trakai Castle sits in all its splendor on three islands in the middle of Lake Galvė near the small town of Trakai. Construction of the castle began in 1406 under Grand Duke Vytautas, who was replacing the ruins of a previous castle built on the main Trakai peninsula half a century earlier by his grandfather. It had been captured twice and later besieged by German knights, necessitating its recreation. Trakai Castle went through a lengthy process of restoration from 1952 to 1980; five stories of red bricks now tower over some of the most beautiful lakes and woods in Lithuania. A combined admission ticket is valid for both the castle's 30m brick **watchtower** and the **City and Castle History Museum.** Climb the watchtower's tight, circular staircases to the third floor to glimpse a magnificent view of the medieval courtyard below. The rooms in the tower chronicle the history of Lithuania after it came under the rule of tsarist Russia in 1795, as well as the history of the independent Lithuanian republic that existed between the wars. Across from the tower, the **City and Castle History Museum** (tel. 512 86) features Lithuanian period furniture from the 18th to 20th centuries, the clock collection of Bronius Kasperavicus, handmade marble postal stampers, and an immense and interesting collection of tobacco and opium pipes. (Open daily 10am-7pm. 7Lt, students and seniors 3.5Lt. 1hr. tours 40Lt, students 15Lt; foreign-language tours 50Lt; students 25Lt. Cameras and video cameras 2.50Lt.) Apart from the historic sights, give yourself at least 30min. to wander around the island, which affords amazing views of the surrounding countryside. The front courtyard inside the first line of defenses of the castle becomes the stage for the summer **Trakai Festival,** with performances of opera, ballet, and orchestral music. See *Vilnius in Your Pocket* or call tel. 62 71 12 for prices and schedules.

GETTING THERE. Trakai, 28km east of Vilnius, is an easy daytrip by **bus** (1hr., over 25 per day, 2.30-2.60Lt; buy your tickets on the bus). The last bus for Vilnius departs nightly at 9:07pm, but it occasionally leaves early. (Station open daily 5am-11:30pm.) The easiest way to navigate Trakai is by **boat;** boat owners are usually along the lake shore off Vytauto g. Don't forget to bargain—the going rate is 5-7Lt per hr. You can also rent boats from the tourist office to explore the islands (6Lt per hr., paddle boats 10Lt per hr.), or board a yacht in front of the castle for a guided tour (20-50Lt per hr.).

LIFE IN THE KARAITE LANE The Karaites, who constitute Lithuania's smallest ethnic minority, celebrated their 600th anniversary in Lithuania in 1997. Their sect was founded by Anon ben David in Babylon in the 8th century. Their beliefs (and their name; karaite is from the hebrew *gara*, "to read") emphasize the written laws of Judaism in the Torah. Grand Duke Vytautas brought back Karaite bodyguards and their families (300 total) from the Crimea after his 1397 campaign, and they have remained in Trakai ever since. Today, the 200 or so remaining Trakai Karaites make their homes in the wooden, cottage-lined, residential district along Karaimv g. Their square, green-roofed, 18th-century prayer-house, the Kinesė, stands quietly at Karaimv g. 30, where it is guarded by a black metal gate; come during services on Saturday mornings if you want a peek at the stained-glass windows inside.

INLAND LITHUANIA

The geographic heart of Lithuania also contains the figurative heart of its people. While the flashier capital and coastal resorts to the north attract foreigners' attention and investment, inland Lithuania has always been where the country turned when times went bad. Kaunas has rebuilt itself from countless razings to bear the standard of its nation's culture, and Šiauliai is home to the Hill of Crosses, a symbol of national resistance to communist rule.

KAUNAS

Burned to the ground 13 times, Lithuania's second-largest city has bounced back repeatedly, collecting new architectural monuments every time. Through it all, Kaunas (KOW-nas; pop. 410,800), has been called the most "Lithuanian" city in Lithuania and the "cradle of Lithuanian culture." It even served as the nation's provisional capital during the Lithuanian independence of 1918 to 1940, when Vilnius was in the hands of Poland. A contemplative, serene city, Kaunas keeps its unhurried pace despite the growing number of bars, restaurants, and shops.

ORIENTATION

At the confluence of the **Nemunas** and **Neris** rivers, Kaunas is on a peninsula pointing west, with **Senamiestis** (Old Town) at the western tip, the bus and train stations at the southeast point, and the hilly suburbs of **Žaliakalnis** in the north. **Naujamiestis** (New Town) fills the middle, bisected by the 2km pedestrian **Laisvės al.** At the fork with **Šv. Gertrūdos g.**, Laisvės al. merges with **Vilniaus g.** at the entrance to Senamiestis to lead directly to **Rotušės aikštė. Bus** #7 heads west from the stations on **Kęstučio g.**, turns left onto **I. Kanto g.**, then heads right on **Nemuno g.** From there, it cuts between Senamiestis and Naujamiestis by going north on **Gimnazijos g.**, and heads east along the avenue formed by three connected streets: **Šv. Gertrudos g.**, **F. Ožeškienės g.**, and **K. Donelaičio g.** Its route is never more than one block from Laisvės al. *Kaunas in Your Pocket*, an excellent yearly guidebook with detailed listings on the city (4Lt), is available at **Lintinterp** (see below).

PRACTICAL INFORMATION

Trains: Čiurlionio g. 16 (tel. 29 22 60), 1.5km southeast of Naujamiestis, at the end of Vytauto pr. To: **Rīga** (6hr., 1 per day, 35.60Lt, *coupé* 57.90Lt); **Kaliningrad** (15hr., 1 per day, 18.60Lt, *coupé* 52.60Lt); **Tallinn** (*Baltic Express* 12hr., odd-numbered calendar days, 87Lt); **Vilnius** (2hr., 15 per day, 7.30-8.70Lt); and **Warsaw** (9½hr., *Baltic Express* 1 per day, 67Lt). Go three stops on trolleybus #3, 5, or 7 from the train station to Gedimino, a block south of the end of Laisvės.

Buses: Vytauto pr. 24/26 (tel. 29 24 55; international reservations tel. 20 19 63; info tel. 22 19 42 and 22 19 55). To: **Klaipėda** (4hr., 9 per day, 26Lt); **Palanga** (4hr., 9 per day, 29Lt); and **Vilnius** (2hr., 1-2 per hr. 4am-9pm, 10.40Lt).

Hydrofoils: Raudondvario pl. 107 (tel. 26 13 48), in the trans-Neris town of Vilijampolė. Take trolleybus #7 from the train and bus stations, or #10 or 11 from the stop at the west end of Laisvės al.; get off at Kedainių, the third stop across the river. In summer, *Raketa* hydrofoils splash to **Nida** via **Nemunas** (4hr., 1 per day, 59Lt).

Local Transportation: Tickets for buses and trolleybuses are available from kiosks (0.60Lt) or the driver (0.70Lt). The best way to get around the city, however, is by the **maršrutinis taksis** vans that speed along bus routes in large numbers. To stop one, stick out an arm. Tell the driver where you want to get off (1Lt).

Taxis: State Taxi Co., tel. 23 66 66. 1Lt per km. **Private Taxi,** tel. 23 98 80.

Tourist Offices: Kaunas does not have a tourist office—don't be deceived by the "i" in front of **Delta/Tourist Information,** Laisvės al. 88 (tel. 20 49 11). Nevertheless, this travel agency sells **maps** (8Lt) and gives info on accommodations and sights. Open M-F 9am-6pm, Sa 10am-2pm. **Litinterp,** Kumelių 15, #4 (tel./fax 22 87 18), in Senamiestis, finds excellent private rooms in the old town. Buy any of the Lithuanian *In Your Pocket Guides* here. Open M-F 9am-6pm, Sa 9am-4pm.

Currency Exchange: Look for Valiutos Keitykla signs on Laisvės al. and Vilniaus g. **Lietuvos Taupomasis Bankas,** Laisvės al. 82 (tel. 20 66 36), gives MC **cash advances,** cashes AmEx/MC/Thomas Cook **traveler's checks,** and has a MC **24hr. ATM.** Open M-F 8am-4pm.

Luggage Storage: In a tunnel under the train station. 1Lt per bag. Open daily 8:30am-2:15pm, 3-8pm, and 8:30pm-8am. At the bus station, store luggage outside and to the left of the main building. 1Lt per bag. Open daily 7am-9pm.

Pharmacies: Aesculaturas, Gedimo 36 (tel. 20 48 02). English spoken. Open M-F 7:30am-6:30pm, Sa 9am-4pm. **Čemerys,** Savanoriu 66 (tel. 20 57 96), is open 24hr.

Gay & Lesbian Services: Lithuanian Movement for Sexual Equality, P.O. Box 973, 3026 Kaunas (tel. 79 12 93). For info on the scene call **Kęstas** at 79 12 93.

Post Office: Laisvės al. 102 (tel. 22 62 20). **Poste Restante** window #11; 0.50Lt per package. Open M-F 7:30am-6:30pm, Sa 7:30am-4:30pm. **Postal Code:** LT-3000.

Internet Access: Kavinė Internetas, Daukšos 12 (tel. 22 53 64). Open 10am-10pm.

Telephones: To the left as you enter the post office; card phones in the main lobby. Open daily 8am-10pm. **Phone code:** 827.

ACCOMMODATIONS & FOOD

Hard times have hit Kaunas' best budget accommodations; many have gone out of business. The only cheap option is **Litinterp** (see **Practical Information,** above), which arranges B&Bs. (Singles 60Lt; doubles 100Lt.) The eight carpeted floors of **Hotel Neris,** Donelaičio 27 (tel. 20 42 24), tower almost as high as the prices. This former Intourist giant is trying to go upscale; at least they got the overcharging part right. (Singles from 160Lt; doubles 200Lt; business suite 260Lt. Breakfast included. MC/Visa.)

The restaurant situation is much better. Dine well to live jazz among splatter-painted canvases in the cafe at **Astra,** Laisvės al. 76 (tel. 22 14 04). Good-sized international entrees run 20-35Lt. (Open M-Th 8am-midnight, F-Sa 8am-1am, Su 11am-midnight. Live music M-Th 8pm, F-Sa 10:30pm.) If you're looking to splurge, try **Tête-à-Tête,** Vytautos 56, considered by many the best restaurant in Lithuania. A few (but not many) entrees come in under 25Lt. (Open M-Tu noon-midnight, W-Su noon-2am.) **Venecija,** Muitinės 1-2 (tel. 22 89 17), satisfies the less generous budget with fantastic (if small) portions of Italian fare for 12-16Lt. (Open daily 11am-10pm.) **Pas Pranciška** (tel. 20 38 75), on Zamenhofo, offers simple, mid-range elegance. (Entrees 20-27Lt. Open M-F 9:30am-9pm, Sa-Su 10:30-9pm.)

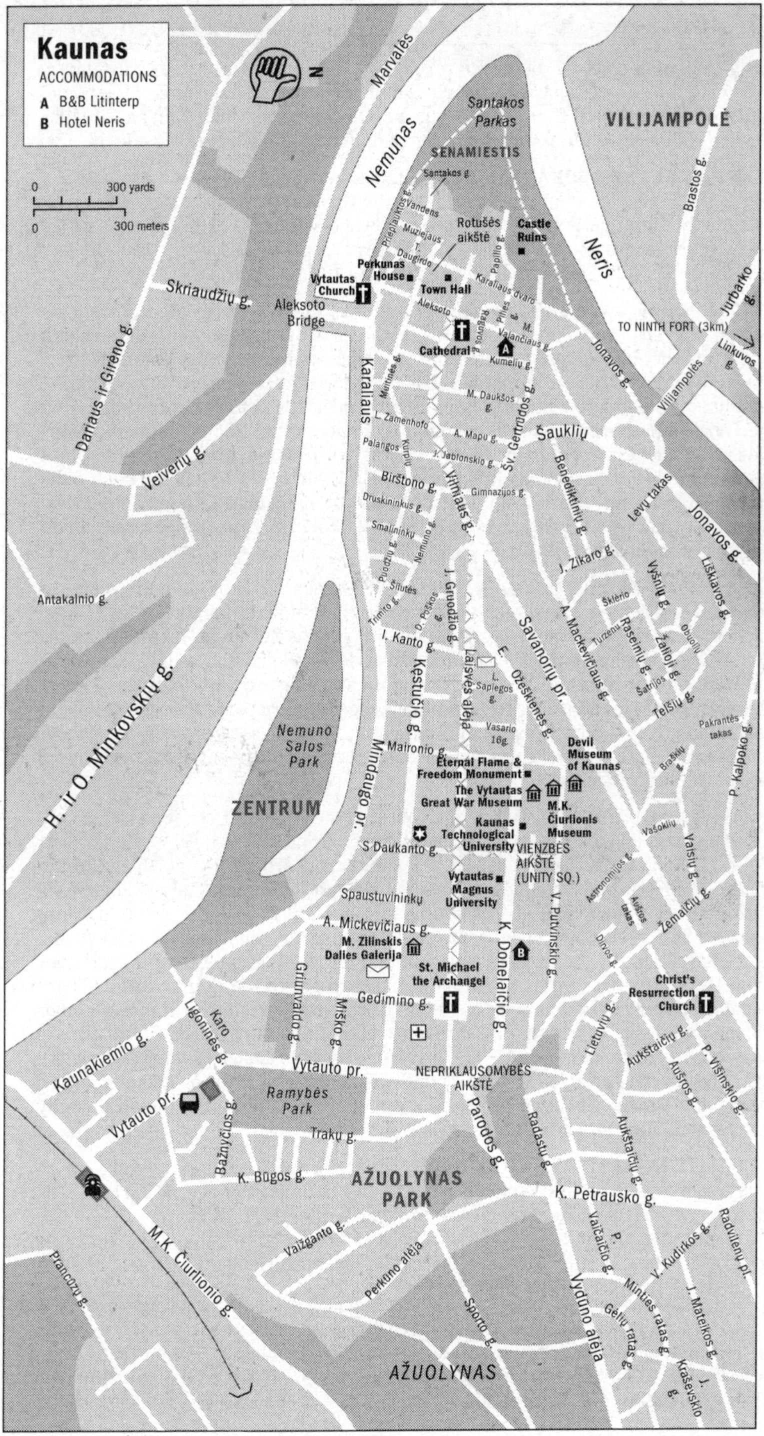
Kaunas
ACCOMMODATIONS
A B&B Litinterp
B Hotel Neris
0 300 yards
0 300 meters
N
Santakos Parkas
SENAMIESTIS
VILIJAMPOLĖ
Nemunas
Neris
Marvalės
Rotušės aikštė
Castle Ruins
Perkunas House
Vytautas Church
Town Hall
Cathedral
Aleksoto Bridge
Skriaudžių g.
Dariaus ir Girėno g.
Veiverių g.
Antakalnio g.
H. ir O. Minkovskių g.
TO NINTH FORT (3km)
Jonavos g.
Vilijampolės g.
Linkuvos g.
Jurbarko g.
Brastos g.
Šauklių
Karaliaus
Birštono g.
Vilniaus g.
Šv. Gertrūdos g.
Benediktinių g.
Levų takas
J. Zikaro g.
I. Kanto g.
J. Gruodžio g.
Kęstučio g.
Laisvės alėja
Savanorių pr.
A. Mackevičiaus g.
Maironio g.
Nemuno Salos Park
ZENTRUM
Mindaugo pr.
Eternal Flame & Freedom Monument
The Vytautas Great War Museum
Devil Museum of Kaunas
M.K. Čiurlionis Museum
Kaunas Technological University
VIENYBĖS AIKŠTĖ (UNITY SQ.)
S Daukanto g.
Vytautas Magnus University
Spaustuvininkų
A. Mickevičiaus g.
M. Zilinskis Dailes Galerija
St. Michael the Archangel
K. Donelaičio g.
V. Putvinskio g.
Christ's Resurrection Church
Gedimino g.
Vytauto pr.
NEPRIKLAUSOMYBĖS AIKŠTĖ
Ramybės Park
Kaunakiemio g.
Trakų g.
K. Būgos g.
AŽUOLYNAS PARK
K. Petrausko g.
Parodos g.
Radastų g.
Aukštaičių g.
Žemaičių g.
Vaižganto g.
Perkūno alėja
Sporto g.
Vydūno alėja
M.K. Čiurlionio g.
Prancūzų g.
AŽUOLYNAS
V. Kudirkos g.
Radvilėnų pl.
J. Mateikos g.

LITHUANIA

SIGHTS

Sights in Kaunas cluster around two regions. St. Michael's Church and Unity Square lie toward the end of Laisvės al, the city's main pedestrian boulevard; at the boulevard's other end you'll find Senamiestis and its cathedral, town hall, and smaller attractions. Pažaislis Monastery and Church and the Ninth Fort are outside the city.

ST. MICHAEL THE ARCHANGEL CHURCH. During an intense period of Russification in the 1890s, the church was built for the Russian garrison that came to man the nine forts around Kaunas. The sumptuous neo-Byzantine exterior is a feast for the eyes. *(In Nepriklausomybės, at the end of Laisvės al. opposite Senamiestis. Open M-F 8am-5pm, Sa-Su 9am-4pm. Services M-F noon, Sa 10am, Su 10am and noon.)*

UNITY SQUARE. (Vienybės aikštė). Two blocks down Laisvės al. and right on Daukanto g. lies Unity Square, depicted on the back of the 20Lt note. On the south side, **Vyatauto Didžiojo University** and the older **Kaunas Technological University** draw in a student population of more than 16,000. Across the street, in an outdoor shrine to Lithuanian statehood, busts of famous Lithuanians flank a corridor leading from the **Freedom Monument** (Laisves paminklas) to an eternal flame commemorating those who died for freedom in 1918-20. During Soviet occupation these symbols of nationhood disappeared, but emerged in St. Michael's in 1989. On a hill behind the Čiurlionis Museum (see below), **Christ's Resurrection Church,** a famous Modernist creation, waits to be finished. Started in 1932, construction stopped in 1940 on account of Stalin's meddling.

KAUNAS CATHEDRAL. (Kauno Arkikatedra Bažnyčia). One of Lithuania's largest churches, the cathedral is thought to have been first built during the 1408-13 Christianization of Low Lithuania on the orders of Vytautas the Great. Its breathtaking, vast interior, dating from 1800, is cut in sharp Gothic/Renaissance lines. A pillar at the back of the church on the side facing the old town square holds the **tomb of Maironis,** the beloved priest from Kaunas whose poetry played a central role in Lithuania's 19th-century National Awakening. *(Where Laisvės al. ends, Senamiestis begins; follow Vilniaus g. through an underpass and inside the medieval city walls, and then 3 blocks farther to the cathedral.)*

OLD TOWN SQUARE. (Rotušės aikštė). West of the cathedral, the **town hall,** a confused stylistic concoction constructed in stages from 1542 to 1771, presides over Town Hall Square in the city center. Up Karaliaus dvaro, off the north end of the square, the Neris and Nemunas rivers meet at **Santakos Parkas.** The remains of the 13th-century **Kauno castle** (pilis) stands here. Next to it is the decaying late-Baroque **St. Francis Church and Jesuit Monastery,** used by the Russians as an Orthodox Church and by the Soviets as a school. Follow Aleksoto g. toward the river from the southeast corner of Rotušės aikštė to get to the quirky 15th-century **Perkūnas House** (Perkūnas namas), a late-Gothic edifice built for Hanseatic merchants on the site of a temple to Perkūnas, god of thunder. *(Open Sa 11am-4pm, Su noon-4pm.)* At the end of the street is the Gothic **Vytautas Church** (Vytauto bažnyčia), also built in the early 1400s. In the southwest corner of Rotušės aikštė stands a **statue of Maironis.** His hand hides his clerical collar, a ploy that duped the silly Soviets into allowing the city to erect a statue of a priest.

PAŽAISLIS MONASTERY AND CHURCH. This vibrant Baroque ensemble with rich frescoes, sits on the Nemunas's right bank 10km east of central Kaunas. The church was designed by three Florentine masters in the 17th century. Used as a KGB-run "psychiatric hospital" and then as a tourist resort, the monastery was returned to the Catholic Church in 1990. Classical music concerts are held here, as is the much-touted **Pažaislis Music Festival** from May 30 to August 29. *(Take trolleybus #5 or 9 from the train station to the end of the line; the church is 1km down the road past a small beach. Tel. 75 64 85. Open Su 11am-6pm. Free tour after 11am mass.)*

NINTH FORT. (IX Fortas). Across the Neris from the castle lies the town of **Vilijampolė,** which gained infamy during WWII as the Jewish Ghetto of Kaunas, vividly immortalized in Avraham Tory's *Kovno Ghetto Diary*. The **Ninth Fort,** Žemaičių pl. 73 (tel. 23 75 74), a few kilometers north of the ghetto, was one of the nine forts constructed in the 1880s around Kaunas as the first line of defense against the German Empire. During WWII, it was used as a Soviet deportation center and killing ground until it became a Nazi concentration camp; still later, it served as the site of KGB atrocities. The museum focuses on the Nazis, but also includes newer exhibits on the mass deportations of Lithuanians in the 1940s and 50s, and the guerrilla resistance that continued until 1952. Part of the museum is housed in the prison cells of the fort, where 30,000 Jews were murdered. Inscriptions remain carved in the walls of the "dying cell." *(Local buses #23, 25, and 45 stop 1km away on Žemaičių pl. It's better to take any one of the intercity buses that stop at IX Fortas from the bus station (2-5 per hr. 2am-9pm). Open W-Su 10am-6pm. Each part of the museum 2Lt, students 1Lt. A tunnel connecting the prison with soldiers' barracks can be explored with a guide for 10Lt.)*

MUSEUMS

With a few notable exceptions, Kaunas' most interesting museums lie around Unity Square (Vienybės aikštė), off Laisvės al.

M. K. Čiurlionis Museum, Putvinskio 55 (tel. 22 14 17), in Unity Sq. Displays works by the revered artist and composer who sought to combine music and image to depict ideas in their pre-verbal state. High-quality 20th-century Lithuanian works fill the other halls. Open Tu-Su noon-6pm; closed last Tuesday of every month. 3Lt, students 1.50Lt.

Devil Museum (Velnių muziejus), Putvinskio g. 64 (tel. 20 84 72), across the street from the War Museum. More properly known by its less infernal moniker, the A. Žmuidzinavičiaus Art Collection. It displays over 2000 devils from Lithuania to Africa, Siberia, the Urals, and South America. Don't miss Devil Hitler and Devil Stalin chasing each other across bone-covered Lithuania. Open Tu-Su noon-6pm; closed last Tuesday of every month. 4Lt, students 2Lt.

Vytautas the Great War Museum (Vytauto Didžiojo Karo Muziejus), Donelaičio g. 64 (tel. 22 27 56), in Unity Sq. behind 2 soccer-playing lions. Houses all sorts of weapons and the aircraft in which 2 Lithuanian-Americans, Darius and Girėnas, tried to fly from New York to Kaunas non-stop in 1933; they crashed in Germany. Another exhibit follows Napoleon's journey through the Baltics en route to his ill-fated Russian campaign. Open W-Su 11am-5:15pm. 2Lt, students 1Lt.

Maironis Lithuanian Literature Museum (Maironio Lietuviu Literaturos Muziejus) Rotušes 13 (tel. 20 68 42), near the poet's statue in Senamiestis. In the 18th-century Baroque house where Maironis once lived, the museum preserves the poet's living quarters while exhibiting Lithuanian literature as a whole. Open W-Su 9am-5pm; closed last day of each month. 2Lt, students 1Lt.

Mykolo Žilinsko Dailės Galerija, Nepriklausomybės 12 (tel. 20 49 06), just south of St. Michael's. Hosts rotating exhibits of Modernist art and a collection of mummies, porcelain, and 19th-century paintings. Cézanne, Renoir, and Manet await on the upper levels. Open Tu-Su noon-6pm; closed last Tuesday of each month. 3Lt, students 1.50Lt.

ENTERTAINMENT

Locals are proud of the city's theaters, which unfortunately shut down in summer. Theater festivals occur at least two or three times a year; at other times, **Drama Academy Theater,** Muzikims 11 (tel. 22 31 85), picks up the slack, performing both classical and modern work. **Small Theater** (Mažasis Teatras), Daukšos 34 (tel. 22 60 90), stages alternative performances. **The Musical Theater** (Muzikinis Teatras), Laisvės al. 91 (tel. 20 09 33), performs operettas. The **Kaunas Philharmonic,** Sapiegos g. 5 (tel. 20 04 78), is well known for its classical concerts (9-15Lt). Some of Kaunas's outdoor bars offer live music in the evenings.

There are several folk and music festivals to keep the city busy in summer. Any excuse to revive traditional songs, dance, and dress is reason enough in Kaunas.

Mindaugas's Day (July 6th), celebrates the 1253 coronation of King Mindaugas by Pope Innocent IV, which unified the country.

Elfu šėlsmas, Laisves 85 (tel. 20 59 56). One of the hippest places in town, with barmaids in elfin skirts and boisterous patrons generating a lively atmosphere. Exposed-brick walls surround the packed bar and intimate tables. Live bands play to dancing revelers daily 10pm-midnight. 0.5L *Kalnapilis* 6Lt. Open daily 11am-4am. MC.

Amerika Pirtyje, Vytauto 71, at the Hotel Baltija. Rough wood, coiled rope, picnic tables, and an expansive dance floor make this stomping disco feel like a converted barn. Open M-W and Su noon-3am, Th noon-2am, F-Sa noon-4am.

Skliautai, Rotušės aikštė 26 (tel. 20 68 43). In the courtyard. Older sophisticates mellow out and enjoy the beer. 0.50L *Kalnapilis* 5Lt. Open daily 10am-midnight. MC.

NEAR KAUNAS: ŠIAULIAI

On a sunny morning in 1236, the German Knights of the Sword, returning from a campaign to Christianize Lithuania, were ambushed and massacred. The town founded on the site, Šiauliai (SEE-ow-oo-lee-eye; pop. 146,500), took its name from the shining sun *(saulė)* of that bloody day. To commemorate the bloodshed, people began the **Hill of Crosses** (Kryžių Kalnas), 14km northwest of the city. After the Lithuanian uprisings of 1831 and 1863, people from across the country brought crosses to remember the dead and the deported, and the collection grew. During Soviet occupation, the hill became a veritable mound of anti-Russian sentiment, and despite three bouts with a bulldozer, the memorial survived as Lithuanians replaced by night what the Soviets had destroyed by day. Independence has brought a new eruption of crosses, as emigrated Lithuanians and relatives of the exiled have returned to add their own monuments. In 1993, Pope John Paul II even added a crucifix of his own to the pile, which now rattles audibly in the breeze.

GETTING THERE. Šiauliai is best seen as a daytrip from Kaunas; **trains** make the connection (2hr., 5 per day, 6Lt). From the train station, walk left on Dubijos g., right on Višinskio, and left on Stoties to get to the bus station, Tilžės 109. **Buses** run north to **Joniškis, Meškuičiai, Rīga,** or **Tallinn** (15 per day); ask the driver to stop at Kryživ Kalnas—it's not a regular stop. Do *not* take a bus to Kryžkalnis; it's 30km south of Šiauliai. From the bus stop, a marked road leads down for about 2km. To get back, take any bus heading in that direction. The last train leaves at 5:45pm, and the last bus at 6pm.

DRUSKININKAI

Aside from being the much-ballyhooed home of Lithuanian artist Mikolojus Konstantinas Čiurlionis (see **Literature & Arts,** p. 362), Druskininkai (pop. 20,000), along the Nemunas river, is less than 10km from the Belarussian border. It houses over 40 sanatoria, and boasts several supposedly curative mineral springs. Poles used to flock to Druskininkai to put mud on their faces and bathe in its natural spring waters; after WWII, the town became a favorite vacation resort among Russians. These days, the Russians are gone, while the Poles are returning in droves. Spend a few hours among the town's still-whispering pines and you'll know why they—and Čiurlionis—held Druskininkai so close to their heart.

ORIENTATION & PRACTICAL INFORMATION. The **train station,** Gardino g. 3 (tel. 534 43), sends **trains** to **Vilnius** via **Parieče, Belarus** (you need a visa to get off; 4hr., 4 per day, 11.10Lt) and **Hrodna** (1½hr., 2 per day Sa-Su, 6Lt). Get to Hrodna on weekdays by boarding the 1:20 or 6:35pm train headed for Vilnius and switching to a Hrodna-bound train in Parieče (1½hr., 5.40Lt). **Buses** head from Gardino g. 1 (tel. 513 33), 400m north of the train station, to: **Vilnius** (2½hr., 4 per day, 13.20Lt); **Kaunas** (3hr., 7 per day, 13.20Lt); **Hrodna, Belarus** (1¾hr., 5 per day, 4-5Lt); and **Warsaw** (7-7½hr., 1 per day, 48Lt). To get to town, go left after exiting either station and walk down Gardiono g., which soon becomes V. Kudirkos g., and leads directly to the main artery, Čiurlionio g. (5min.). For maps and info, go to the **Tourist Information Center,** Gardino 1, (tel./fax 517 77; email druskininkutib@post.omnitel.net; www.druskonis.lt/info), upstairs from the bus station. (Open M-F 8:30am-5:30pm.) The bus station has **luggage storage** (0.50Lt). **Postal code:** LT-4690. **Phone code:** 233.

ACCOMMODATIONS & FOOD. **Druskininkai Hotel,** Kudirkos g. 43 (tel. 525 66; fax 522 66), on the corner of Taikos g., directly across the street from the Roman Catholic church. The spartan yet clean rooms are as cheap as they come in Druskininkai. (Singles with bath 50Lt; doubles 66Lt; triples 196Lt.) For pretty good Lithuanian eats, try **Ratnyčėlė,** Čiurlioni g. 56 (tel. 517 96), where a good-sized meal will cost less than 15Lt. (Open daily 9am-10pm.) The **French Bakery,** across the street and a few buildings to the right, sells pastries fresh out of the oven for a pittance. (Chocolate croissant 1Lt. Open 8am-7pm.)

SIGHTS. "You hear the murmur of the pines, so solemn, as if they were trying to tell you something," avant-garde artist, composer, and mystic Mikolojus Konstantinas Čiurlionis wrote in 1905. Čiurlionis was born and spent many of his days in Druskininkai, although, to the locals' regret, he died and was buried in Poland. The artist's unique works are kept alive at **M. K. Čiurlionis Memorialinis Muziejus,** Čiurlionio g. 35 (tel. 511 31), which tells the artist's story in four buildings, including the house in which he worked. The museum has mostly prints and focuses on the artist's life and times; for the originals, go to the M.K.C. Museum in Kaunas (see p. 379). Čiurlionis's evocative, mythical images are accompanied by recorded compositions—he intended the visual and audio components to be understood as one integrated form. (Open Tu-Su noon-6pm; closed last Tuesday of the month; 1Lt, students 0.50Lt.) **Piano concerts** on Sunday evenings in the summer feature Čiurlionis's own compositions, as well as those of Bach, Debussy, and Beethoven. (1hr. performances at 5pm. 8Lt.)

COASTAL LITHUANIA

In the opposite corner of the country from Vilnius lies Lithuania's Baltic beachfront property, a wonderful example of doing a lot with a little. The entire country seems to migrate to little Palanga in the summer. Further south, Klaipėda, among national powers by the winds of history, now guards Latvia's gateway to the thin Curonian Spit (or Neringa to the Lithuanians), in the middle of which, Nida is nestled among the dunes along the border with Kaliningrad.

PALANGA

If you hate magnificent beaches, charming streets filled with cafes and shops, and a rollicking nightlife, avoid Palanga at all costs. Amusement park rides and street vendors peddling all sorts of cavity-inducing goodies give this resort 25km north of Klaipėda a carnival air.

ORIENTATION & PRACTICAL INFORMATION

Palanga's main streets are **Vytauto gatrė,** running parallel to the beach past the bus station, and **J. Basanavičiaus,** which connects Vytauto g. to a boardwalk pier where tourists stroll out above the sea. The pedestrian **Meilės alėja** runs south of the pier alongside the beach, becoming **Birutės alėja** in Palanga Park and Botanical Garden. The **bus station,** Kretinjos 1 (tel. 533 33), sends buses to: **Kaunas** (3hr., 14-16 per day, 29Lt); **Vilnius** (4-5hr., 10-12 per day, 39Lt); and **Druskininkai** (5hr., 1 per day, 38.20Lt), among others. **Microbuses** leave for **Klaipėda** every 30min. from the bus station (20min., 2.50Lt; buy tickets from the driver). Get **tourist info** in English from the center right beside the bus info window at the station. (Open M-Sa 8am-8pm.)

Exchange money, cash AmEx/MC/Thomas Cook **traveler's checks,** and get MC **cash advances** at **Lietuvos Taupomasis Bankas,** Juratės g. 15/2 (tel. 512 09). **Western Union** services are available inside. (Open M-F 7:30am-6:30pm, Sa 8am-2pm.) The **post office,** Vytauto 53 (tel. 531 47), also exchanges currency. (Open M-F 8am-1pm and 2-6:30pm, Sa 9am-2pm.) The **telephone office** (tel./fax (8) 23 64 82 25), in the same building, has a MC **24hr. ATM. Postal code:** LT-5720. **Phone code:** 236.

ACCOMMODATIONS

Palanga is full of hotels to shelter the summer hordes, but finding inexpensive rooms can be tricky. All directions are given from the bus station.

"Palangos Žuvėdra" Viešbutis, Birutės alėja 52 (info tel. 538 52; registration tel. 532 53). Head left on Vytauto several blocks. Turn right onto Kestučio and left onto Birutės. A several-building complex close to the shore. Offers clean but bare doubles with shared bath (50Lt per person). Breakfast, lunch, and dinner 16.52Lt. Call ahead, as tour groups often rent the entire place out.

Vyturio Korpusas, Dariaus ir Girėno g. 20 (tel. 538 07). Go left on Vytauto g. to Danaus ir Gireno g. and right opposite the soccer fields. This circular complex includes a sauna and pool. Singles 78Lt; doubles 116Lt; triples 159Lt. Breakfast 8Lt; lunch 11Lt; dinner 8Lt. MC/Visa.

Pa Gryva, Plytų g. 71 (tel. 517 53 and 517 30). Take a left on Vytauto g., another left on Daiaus ir Girėno g., and a right on Plytų g. The prices, not the surly service, contribute to the popularity of this lifeless "rest home." Two doubles with soft beds share an old toilet and shower. Prices range from 20-45Lt per bed.

LITHUANIA

FOOD

The Palangan pedestrian will have no trouble finding food. Vytauto g. and J. Basanavičiaus g., among others, are lined with cafes blaring music onto the street. Every few meters a street vendor sells *čeburekai* (meat-filled dough pastries; 2Lt), *blyneliai su bananu* (pancake rolls with banana; 1Lt), or the more self-explanatory waffle-dipped-in-chocolate-on-a-stick (1.50-2.50Lt).

Monika, J. Basanavičiaus g. 12 (tel. 525 60). Don't be afraid to try the Mexican pizza (14Lt) at this somewhat classy "picerija." Veggie pizza 9Lt; other dishes 17-26Lt. Open daily 11am-midnight. Visa.

Senoji Dorė, Basanavičiaus 5, right at the head of the major pedestrian street. Healthy portions of Lithuanian cuisine. Dining flows from inside to outdoor under fishing nets and wood scaffolds. Entrees 16-28Lt. 5% service charge. Open 10am-midnight.

Elnio Ragas, J. Basanavičiaus g. 25 (tel. 535 05). This smoky neon lodge uses up lots of tongue in its dishes. If those and boiled pigs' ears (12Lt) aren't to your taste, there's always chicken fingers (7Lt). Open 11am until the last guest leaves. MC.

SIGHTS & ENTERTAINMENT

Palanga's pride and joy, the **Amber Museum** (Gintaro muziejus; tel. 535 01), is housed in the manor of the 19th-century magnates, the Tiškevičius family, in the heart of Palanga Botanical Gardens. The museum describes amber formations in great detail, provides examples of the many different types of amber, and displays a large portion of its 15,000 amber inclusions of primeval flora and fauna. (Open Tu-Su 10am-8pm; ticket office closes at 7pm. 5Lt, students and children 2.50Lt; admission good for the Clock Museum and Picture Gallery of Klaipėda 4.50Lt.) Just a little down Vytauto g. from the Botanical Garden toward Basanavičiaus g., is the **Dr. Jonas Šliūpas Memorial Gardens and House,** Vytauto g. 23a (tel. 545 59), where the famous "cultural worker and public man" lived from 1930-44. Dr. Šliūpas was a Lithuanian patriot who founded newspapers, participated in the brief Lithuanian government between the world wars, and worked as a doctor, high school teacher, and even brewmaster of Palanga. Much of his life was spent in the U.S., where he lived in exile and is buried today. (Open daily noon-7pm. Free. Captions in Lithuanian only.) Heading down J. Basanavičiaus g., the **Lithuanian Political Prisoners and Exiles Museum** (Lietuvos Politiniv Kaliniv ir Tremuntiniv Muziejus) is in a small yellow house on your left. It displays objects kept by prisoners in labor camps all over the Soviet Union, from a rosary made of bread to a small, embroidered bag containing Lithuanian soil. (Open W and Sa-Su 3-5pm. Donation requested.)

For recreation along Palanga's many paths, street vendors rent **bikes** (5-10Lt per hr.), **in-line skates** (7Lt per hr.), and a host of other wheeled vehicles. Or, go nuts with **minigolf** (15Lt, children 10Lt) next to Ritos Virtuvė on J. Basanavičiaus g. **Bumper boats** (5Lt for 3min.) are set up in front of the **Summer Concert Hall** (Vasaraos Koncertv Salė) at Vytauto g. 43 (tel. 522 10). The concert hall hosts **concerts** of the Lithuanian National Filharmonic and Klaipėdos Filharmonic, as well as visiting comedians, pop artists, and other performers. Many of the cafes lining Basanavičiaus g. and Vytauto g. feature live bands at night and a dance floor. **Kinoteatras Naglis,** Vytauto g. 82, shows Hollywood's latest attempts at cultural hegemony with Lithuanian subtitles and Dolby sound (8Lt).

KLAIPĖDA

Guarding the Curonian Lagoon with its fortress on the tip of the Neringa peninsula, Klaipėda (klai-PAY-da; pop. 201,500), Lithuania's third-largest city, may be a little too strategically located for its own good. For nearly 700 years, Klaipėda was anything but Lithuanian; briefly the Prussian capital in the 17th century, the town went to France in the 1919 Treaty of Versailles. It served as a German U-boat base during WWII, and was industrialized by the Soviets after the war. The legacy of conquest lives on in the city's architectural hodgepodge, while its location makes it an ideal base for tourist invasions of Lithuania's dramatic coast.

ORIENTATION

The **Danė River** divides the city into south **Senamiestis** (Old Town) and north **Naujamiestis** (New Town), while the Curonian Lagoon (Kuršių marios) cuts off **Smiltynė,** Klaipėda's Kuršių Nerija (Curonian Spit) quarter. All of mainland Klaipėda lies close to the **bus** and **train stations,** which are separated by Priestoties g. With your back to the bus station, turn left onto Priestoties and left again onto **S. Nėries g.** Follow S. Nėries g. away from the train station to its end, then take a right on **S. Daukanto g.** to reach the heart of the city. **H. Manto g.,** the main artery, becomes Tiltų g., then Taikos g., as it crosses the river into Senamiestis. Pick up *Klaipėda in Your Pocket,* with **maps** and info on Palanga and Nida (4Lt) at **Litinterp** (see below).

PRACTICAL INFORMATION

Trains: Priestočio g. 7 (tel. 21 46 14; reservations tel. 29 62 91). To **Vilnius** (5hr., 3 per day, 38Lt) and **Kaunas** (7½hr., 1 per day, 23Lt). Open daily 3:30am-10:30pm.

Buses: Butkų Juzės 9 (tel. 21 48 63; reservations tel. 21 14 34). To: **Nida** (2hr., 2 per day, 8Lt); **Kaunas** (2-4hr., 18 per day, 20-25Lt); **Kaliningrad** via **Sovetsk** (4hr., 2 per day, 25Lt); and **Vilnius** (4-7hr., 10 per day, 30-37Lt).

Ferries: The ferry landing, Žueju 8 (tel. 21 22 24), sends ferries to **Smiltynė** (10min., 1-2 per hr. 5:30am-2am, round-trip 1.40Lt, students and pensioners 0.70Lt. Ticket window open 5:15am-11:30pm. Call **Taurvita travel agency,** Taikos pr. 42 (tel. 21 78 00), for info and tickets. (Open M-F 9am-6pm.)

Local Transportation: City buses (0.60Lt per ride) and the wonderfully convenient **maršrutinis taksis** (route taxis) careen all over town. The latter pick up and deposit passengers anywhere along the way with flexible fares. Stick out an arm to hail one (1Lt 6am-11pm; 2Lt all other times). They serve the Curonian Split, going to Juodkrantė (5Lt), and Nida (7Lt) from Smiltynė.

Taxis: State company (tel. 000). 1.50Lt per km is the standard fare. The **private company** (tel. 31 12 11) is cheaper. 1.20Lt per km.

Tourist Office: Litinterp, S. Šimkaus g. 21/8 (tel. 31 14 90; fax 21 98 62; email litinterp@klaipeda.omnitel.net). Arranges private rooms in: Klaipėda (singles 60Lt; doubles 100Lt); Palanga (singles 100-120Lt; doubles 140Lt); and Nida (see p. 387). They also **rent bikes** (20Lt per day, US$100 deposit), sell **maps,** and answer questions. Open M-F 8:30am-5:30pm, Sa 10am-3pm.

Currency Exchange: At kiosks around the train station and the bus station, or at the many banks. **Vilnius Bankas,** Daržų g.13 (tel. 39 01 21), cashes AmEx/Thomas Cook traveler's checks for a 0.5% commission. Open M-F 9am-1:30pm and 2:30-4pm. There is a Visa **ATM** in the post office (see below).

Luggage Storage: Lockers at far end of the train station (0.50Lt for a small locker) or racks at the back of the bus station (1.50Lt per bag). Both open 5:30am-11:30pm.

Post Office: Liepų g. 16 (tel. 21 53 78), in an eccentric neo-Gothic brick building. Open M-F 8:30am-6pm, Sa 9am-4pm. **Postal code:** LT-5800.

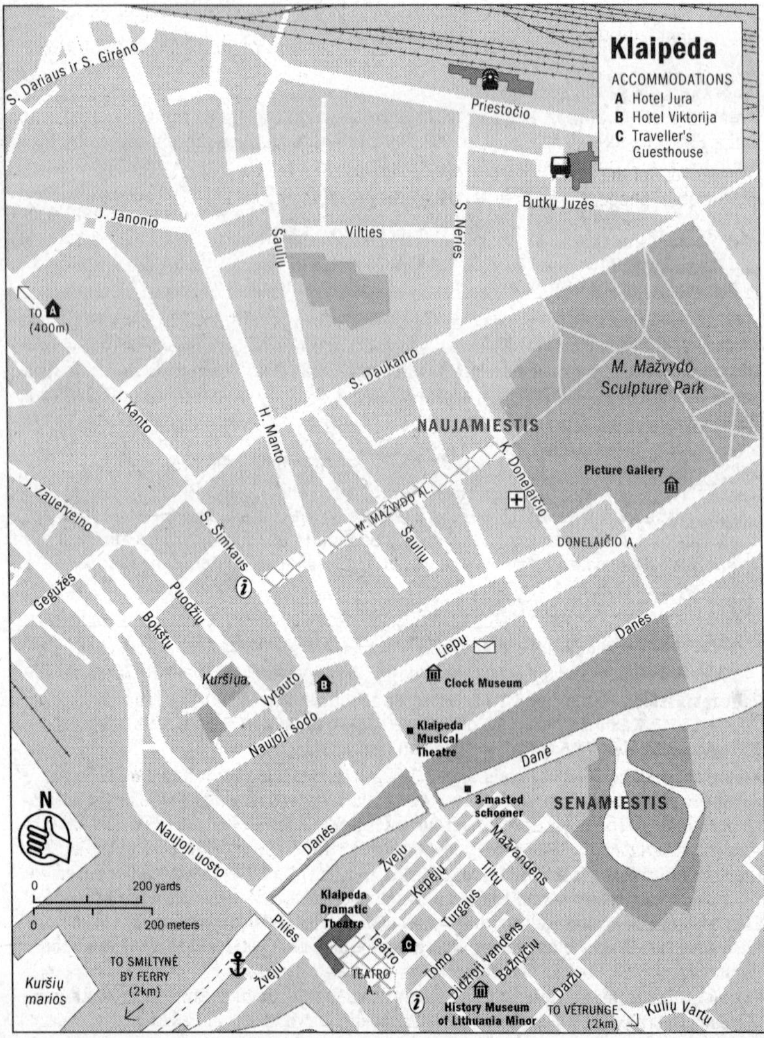

Internet Access: On the second floor of the **public library,** Tilžes 9 (tel. 25 89 02). Seven terminals open at 3Lt per hr. Open M-F 11am-7pm, Sa 10am-3pm.

Telephones: Central Telephone Office, Liepų g. 1 (tel. 25 54 46). Pay the attendant or use card phones. Open 24hr. **Phone code:** (0)26.

ACCOMMODATIONS

Litinterp (see **Practical Information,** above) arranges homestays with local families. (Singles 60Lt; doubles 100Lt. MC/Visa.)

Hotel Viktorija, S. Šimkaus g. 2 (tel. 21 36 70), on the corner with Vytauto g. The best location in town for the best price. Old rooms are clean but you'll have to hunt for functional toilets. Singles 45Lt; doubles 60-65Lt; private baths 120Lt. Hall shower 3.50Lt.

Klaipėda Traveller's Guesthouse (HI), Turgaus 3/4 (tel. 21 49 35; email oldtown@takas.lt), in the Old Town. Walk left from the train station (right from the bus station) down Trilapio, turn right on Liepu, then left H. Manto, which crosses the river. Turgaus is the second left after the bridge. Possibly the cheapest place to stay in town. Dorms 32Lt, 34Lt for non-members. Free beer and bike rental for reserving by email.

Hotel "Jura," Malūnininkų 3 (tel. 39 98 57; fax 21 16 93), in the northwest part of town. From the bus station, turn left onto Priestoties g. and follow it across the bridge as it changes names. Turn right onto Sportininkų and left onto Malūninkų. The lobby and second floor of this hotel have been beautifully renovated; new rooms come with Western furniture, phone, TV, and private baths. Singles 90Lt, renovated 150Lt; doubles 100Lt, 250Lt. Breakfast included. Sauna 70Lt per hr. MC/Visa.

LITHUANIA

FOOD

The **central market** is on Turgas aikštė (open daily about 8am-6pm), while the **IKI supermarket,** Mažvyado 7, has everything you could want in air-conditioned comfort within walking distance of the Old Town. (Open daily 9am-10pm.)

Skandalas, Kanto 44 (tel. 21 28 85). The only thing scandalous here is the Hollywood kitsch decor, which includes a pinstriped swing band nightly after 8pm. Excellent American cuisine—especially steaks—with rivers of beer to wash it all down. Lunch 25-35Lt. Open daily noon-3am. MC/Visa.

Lūja, H. Mauto 20 (tel. 25 94 45). An odd duck with fake straw umbrellas out front and an interior trying too hard for elegance. Big portions of German and Polish food. Entrees 10-30Lt. Open daily noon-midnight. MC/Visa.

Luiza Kavine, Puodžių 4 (tel. 21 98 82), opposite the gargantuan Hotel Klaipėda. Sit outside at the pleasant bar by the fountain. Squid stuffed with rice and vegetables 22Lt, stewed veal 15.40Lt, *Baltijos* 4.50Lt. Open daily 11am-midnight.

SIGHTS

MAINLAND KLAIPĖDA

The leafy park between Liepų g. and Daukanto g., **Mažvydo Sculpture Park** (Mažvydo Skulptūrų Parkas), once the town's central burial ground, was turned into a sculpture garden by the Soviets. From Egyptian sundials to Chinese candle clocks to a modern quartz watch-pen, every conceivable time-keeping device has a place at the **Clock Museum** (Laikrodžių Muziejus), Liepų g. 12 (tel. 21 35 31), in Naujamiestis, by the main post office. (Open Tu-Su 9am-5:30pm. 4Lt, students and pensioners 2Lt; "common ticket," also good for the Picture Gallery and Palanga's Amber Museum, 4Lt. Tours 20Lt, foreign-language 40Lt.) The **Picture Gallery** (Paveikslų), Liepų 33 (tel. 21 33 19), has some 19th-century portraits and plaster copies of Greek and Roman sculpture, but mostly excellent 20th-century work by Lithuanian artists. (Open Tu-Su noon-5pm. 3Lt, students 1.50Lt. Tours 20Lt.)

Klaipėda Theater (Klaipėdos Dramos Teatras; ticket tel. 21 25 89), Teatro aikštė, on the other side of Manto g., dominates the Old Town center. Built in 1857, the theater is famous as one of Wagner's favorite haunts, and infamous as the site where Hitler personally proclaimed the reincorporation of the town into the *Reich* in 1939. (Open Tu-Su 10am-2pm and 4-6pm.) In front, the **Simon Dach Fountain** spouts water over the symbol of Klaipėda, a statue of Ännchen von Tharau. The Klaipėda-born Dach wrote a song for the wedding of young Anna, expressing his love for her. The original statue disappeared in WWII; some say it was taken by the Nazis, who didn't want her back to Hitler during his speech. The copy standing today was erected by German expatriates in 1989. The fat lady sings at **Klaipėda Musical Theater,** Danės g. 19 (tel. 21 62 60), which houses operas and other musical events. (Ticket office open Tu-Su 11am-2pm and 4-7pm.) The **History Museum of Lithuania Minor** (Mažosios Lietuvos Istorijos Muziejus), Didžioji vandens g. (tel. 21 06 00), collects clothing, maps, rusty swords, coins, and buttons from the Iron Age to the present. (Open W-Su 10am-6pm. 2Lt, students 1Lt; Lithuanian tours W-F 15Lt.) The museum's backyard is home to a **Lenin statue** that, before 1991, graced the square next to Hotel Klaipėda. You need the museum director's (tel. 21 06 00) permission to see it. The square also includes several examples of exposed-timber *Fachwerk* buildings for which pre-war Klaipėda was well-known. Aukštoji g. is one of the best preserved areas of Senamiestis. Craftsmen's quarters from the 18th and 19th centuries today serve as shops, cafes, and boutiques.

SMILTYNĖ

The **Maritime Museum and Aquarium** (Jūrų muziejus ir Akvariumas), Tomo g. 10 (tel. 39 11 33), is housed in an 1860s fortress that protected the entrance to Klaipėda. The outer perimeter, buried deep in underground tunnels, displays the port's naval history. Sea lions now frolic in the inner moat. (Open June-Aug. Tu-Su 10:30am-6:30pm; May and Sept. W-Su 10:30am-6:30pm; Oct.-Apr. Sa-Su 10:30am-5:30pm. 5Lt, students 3Lt.) Sea lions kiss trainers and spectators in the **sea lion show** at 11am, 1pm, and 3pm (10Lt, students 5Lt), while the **Dolphinarium** stages shows at noon, 2pm, and 4pm next door (12Lt, students 6Lt). Both aquatic attractions are located in **Kopgalis,** at the head of the Spit, 1.5km from the ferry landing. To the east, several museums and displays line the road to a pier. The **Nature Museum** (Kuršių nerijos gamtos muziejus ekspozicija; tel. 39 11 79), near Landing 1, exhibits the region's natural and human history, including dioramas showing the villages buried by the shifting dunes. One building displays collected insects and plants, while another showcases stuffed mammals and birds; the bats are particularly interesting. (Open daily 11am-6pm. Free.) In the **Garden of Veteran Fishing Boats** (Žvejybos Laivai-veteranai), four forlorn ships sit on concrete pillars. The **Fishermen's Village** (Ethnografinė Pajūrio Žvejo Sodyba) is a reconstruction of a 17th-century settlement. (Open daily 24hr. 2Lt.) Forest paths lead west about 500m to the **beaches.** If you walk north before crossing over you can get a patch of sand to yourself. Signs mark gender-restricted areas for **nude bathing**—women to the right, men to the left, and the **public beach** in between.

NIGHTLIFE

The best bar hopping lies along H. Manto g., although most places close around midnight. A number of discos have opened recently to pick up the late-night slack. If you come in early June, a **Jazz Festival** will be in full swing.

Meridianas (tel. 21 68 51), Dauės Krautinė (river bank). The decks of this permanently moored schooner slope toward the bar. Old salts and sea pups alike imbibe while a skeleton (likely the only sober mate aboard) mans the keel. Disco down below from 10pm. Cover 20-30Lt. Open daily 3pm-5am.

Kalifornija, Laukininkų 17 (tel. 22 97 35), on the edge of town but still the most popular place around. Follow Taikos through Senamiestis away from the river. Take a left on

Smiltelės and a right on Vingio. A taxi will cost you 12Lt. Book a table well in advance, or just crowd the undersized dance floor. No cover. 20+. Open 10pm-6pm.

Baras Senamiestis, Bažnyčių 4 (tel. 25 18 44). Dark velvet attracts an older crowd. Art gallery upstairs. *Baltija* (dark) 4.50Lt. Open 11am-midnight.

NIDA

The magical rise of wind-swept, white-sand dunes has long drawn summer vacationers to Nida (pop. 2000), only 3km north of the Kaliningrad region on the Curonian Spit. From the immense sundial, you can look down on the summer home of Thomas Mann and beyond, to where the dunes shelter the lagoon from the Baltic.

ORIENTATION & PRACTICAL INFORMATION. From the hydrofoil port, **Taikos g.** runs west inland. Nida's other main street, **Naglių g.,** runs perpendicular, becoming Pamario g. The **bus station,** Naglių 18 (tel. 523 34), is more a schedule posted on the streetcorner than an actual building. **Microbuses** run to **Smiltynė** (1hr., 7Lt); buy tickets on board. The last one (11:45pm) should get you there to catch the 12:45am ferry back to **Klaipėda.** A **hydrofoil,** Naglių 16, runs to **Kaunas** (4hr., Tu-Su 1 per day, 49Lt; *kasa* open daily 12:30-3:30pm and 6-9pm). The **Tourist Information Center,** Taikos g. 4 (tel. 523 45; fax 523 44), opposite the bus and ferry stations, sells **maps** (3-5Lt), arranges homestays, and has good accommodation and transport info for the Curonian Spit. (Open M-Sa 9am-noon and 1-7pm, Su 9am-2pm.) **Exchange money** at **Lietuvos Taupomasis Bankas,** Taikos g. 5 (tel. 522 46), which also cashes AmEx and Thomas Cook **traveler's checks** and gives MC/Visa **cash advances.** (Open M-F 8:30am-12:30pm and 1:30-5:30pm, Sa 9am-1pm and 2-7pm, Su 10am-4pm.) The **post office,** Taikos g. 13, lies up the road. (Open daily 8am-5pm.) The adjacent **telephone office** (tel. 520 07) has cardphones. (Open daily 8am-11pm.) **Postal code:** LT-5870. **Phone code:** (8)259.

ACCOMMODATIONS & FOOD. The **tourist office** (see above) arranges bed-and-breakfasts (30-50Lt per person) for a 5Lt service charge. **Urbo Kalnas,** Taikos g. 32 (tel. 524 28), sprawled over a pine-covered hill above town, rents big, high-ceilinged rooms with clean hot showers, TV, and fridge. Just walk uphill along Taikos from the center. (Singles 150Lt; doubles 210Lt; triples 275Lt. Breakfast included.) **Litinterp** (tel. (26) 21 69 62), in Klaipėda (see p. 384), hikes its prices for **homestays** in Nida (singles 100-120Lt; doubles 140-150Lt).

The local specialty is *rūkyta žuvis* (smoked fish), which is best eaten with beer; selection varies from nondescript "fish" to eel and perch. **Seklyčia** (tel. 529 45), at the end of Lotmiško g. with wonderful views of the dunes, is considered the best restaurant in town. *Shashliks* and *blyni* are the cheapest meals. (Entrees 22-35Lt. Open daily 9am-3am.) **Ešerinė,** Naglių 2 (tel. 527 57), is a wacky collection of thatched-roofed, glass-walled huts. (Entrees 20-27Lt. Open daily 10am-midnight.) Nida's largest **grocery store** is **Gilija,** Naglių 29. (Open 8am-10pm.)

SIGHTS. The **Drifting Dunes of Parnidis** rise south of town, across the bay from the shore-side restaurants at the head of Naglių and Lotmiško. Walk along the beach or through forest paths to reach steps leading to surreal mountains and plains of white sand blowing gracefully into the sea from 100m above. The best views of the lagoon and the Baltic Sea are from a giant sundial at the top of the dunes. The nature preserve farther south is off-limits.

All of the **wooden houses** clustered along Lotmiškio g. are classified as historic monuments; another two whole villages of them are buried somewhere under the sand. From the center of town, walk along the promenade by the water and bear right onto Skruzdynės g. to reach the renovated **Thomas Mann House** (Thomo Manno Namelis; tel. 522 60) at #17. Mann built the cottage in 1930 and wrote *Joseph and His Brothers* here, but had to give it up when Hitler invaded. The house now contains photos of Mann and his family and newspaper articles on the writer. For the **Thomas Mann Festival** in July, the **Thomas Mann Cultural Center** puts on classical concerts in the house's living room.

MOLDOVA

US$1 = 10.97 LEI	10 LEU = US$0.91
CDN$1 = 7.36 LEI	10 LEU = CDN$1.35
UK£1 = 17.62 LEI	10 LEU = UK£0.57
IR£1 = 14.77 LEI	10 LEU = IR£0.68
AUS$1 = 7.14 LEI	10 LEU = AUS$1.40
NZ$1 = 5.81 LEI	10 LEU = NZ$1.72
SAR1 = 1.81 LEI	10 LEU = SAR5.50
DM1 = 5.94 LEI	10 LEU = DM1.68

PHONE CODES Country code: **373.** International dialing prefix is **00.**

Moldova, like the emblem on its flag, is a strange bird, with a long history of not knowing quite where to fit in. Occupying the area known as Bessarabia, but a long-time part of Moldavia (one of the three historical provinces of Romania), this region languished under Soviet rule for 45 years. While 70% of Moldova's land and people live on the west bank of the Nistru River (called the Dniestr by Russians), a high concentration of Russians and Ukrainians hold out on the other side, many clamoring for greater independence. Teetering on the brink of a post-Soviet abyss, Moldova clings to the edge of Europe, a silent battleground of the Slavic and Romanian cultures caught in the middle of an arduous economic transition.

HIGHLIGHT OF MOLDOVA

- The hospitable locals and stellar Indian food of **Chișinău** add to the intrigue of this quintessentially post-Soviet city (p. 393).

LIFE & TIMES

HISTORY

Moldovan history has been dominated by Russia and Romania, who have both long competed for the territories of **Bessarabia,** between the Prut and Dniester river, and **Transdniester**, literally "across the Dniester." Bessarabia has been the most contentious region, controlled by Scythia (1000 BC), Kievan Rus (10th and 12th centuries), Galician princes (early 13th century), and the Tatars (1241-1300s). The region enjoyed temporary new prosperity after its annexation by **Moldavia,** until the entire province was captured by the Turks. In the 15th century, **Ștefan cel Mare** expanded Moldavia's frontiers, pushing back Poles to the north and Turks to the south. But the Turks struck back, and by the time he came to power Ștefan's son, **Bogdan the One-Eyed** was paying tribute to them. For the next three centuries, its neighbors tore Moldavia apart—**Russia** occupied five times starting in 1711 and the 1812 **Treaty of Bucharest** legitimated their claim to the region.

Bessarabia's new rulers attempted to Russify the region's civil and religious institutions, but this had little effect on the largely illiterate peasants who remained culturally aligned with **Romania.** The birth of Romania as an autonomous kingdom in 1881 fueled the smoldering nationalism of the region but didn't erupt into a full-fledged unification movement until the **Russian Revolution of 1905.**

During **WWI,** the Central Powers tried to use Bessarabia to lure Romania to their side, but lost out to the Allies and their bait of Transylvania and Bukovina. In December 1917, Bessarabia renounced Russian rule and declared its autonomy. In response, the Bolsheviks invaded, only to be driven out by Romanian forces. Soon after, a grateful Moldavian state united with Romania, an agreement sanctified at

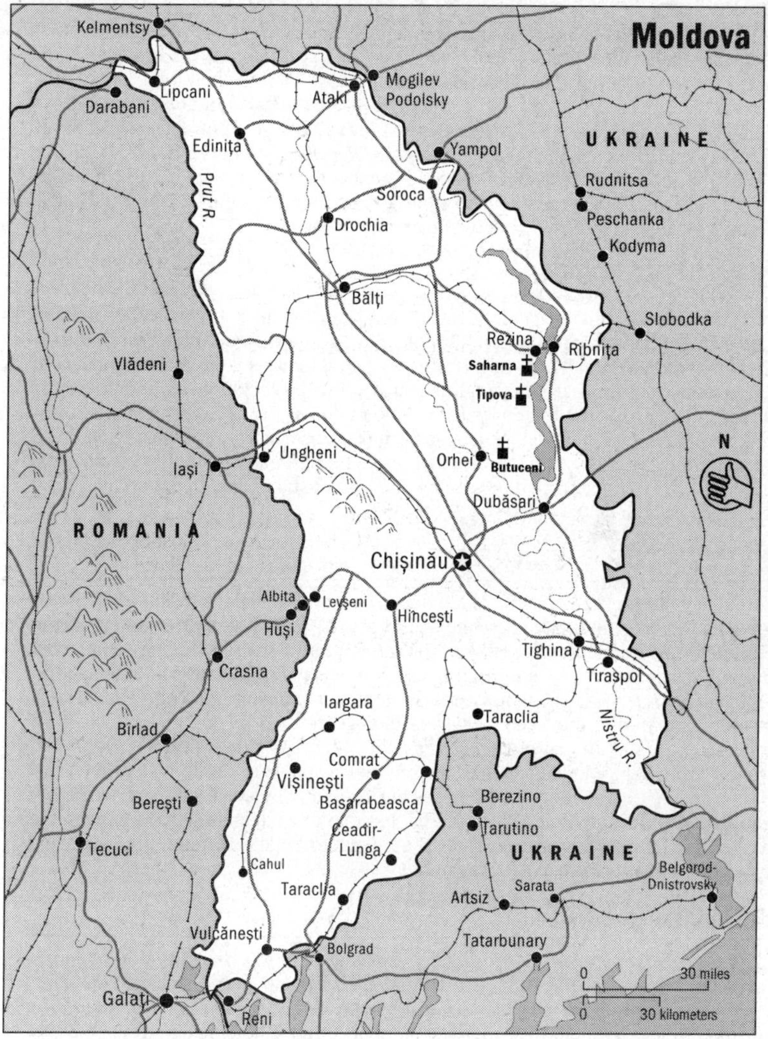

the **Paris Peace Conference** in 1920. The Soviets, refusing to accept Romania's claim to the land, established a tiny Moldavian state of their own in Transdniester. Meanwhile, because its exports had been geared toward Russia and not Romania, the regional economy stagnated.

In 1939, the Soviets invaded once again, attempting to unite central Bessarabia, northern Bukovina, and their miniscule Communist Moldavia. The Red Army appropriated Moldavian lands and expelled the German population to Western Poland. During **WWII,** Romania regained Bessarabia as Germany's ally, killing or deporting many Bessarabian Jews to make way for Romanian peasants. After the Axis defeat, however, the Russians reinvaded and integrated the region into the Soviet empire as the **Moldavian Soviet Socialist Republic.** Communist rule brought economic collectivization and industrialization as well as heavy **Russification.** Russia was made the official language and many Romanian-speakers were deported to the far reaches of the USSR as Russians and Ukrainians moved in.

Nationalism grew as the Soviet Union faltered in the 1980s, and on August 27, 1991, the **Republic of Moldova** declared independence. Finally free of Russia, a powerful nationalist movement in Moldova forced the government to reinstate the Latin alphabet and to adopt Romania's national flag and hymn as their own. These pro-Romanian tendencies alarmed the country's sizable Russian minority who feared reunification with Romania. Russian ultra-nationalists in **Transdniester** declared independence from Chişinău in September 1990. **Civil war** followed in 1992, with the Russian army aiding Transdniester and Romania backing Moldova. After a cease-fire in July of 1992, Transdniester emerged as an autonomous entity with **Igor Smirnov** as its leader.

MOLDOVA TODAY

Moldova approaches the millennium with internal strife, a breakaway province, and economic woes. On May 8, 1997, Moldovan President **Petru Lucinschi** (elected in December 1996) and Transdniester leader **Igor Smirnov** signed a **Memorandum of Understanding,** affirming a united Moldovan state with substantial autonomy for the Transdniester region. Nonetheless, the region remains firmly Soviet and refuses to acknowledge any Moldovan hand in its business. Russian troops in the region on an arms reduction mission have only heightened tensions. Meanwhile, **Ion Sturza**, elected Prime Minister in 1999, has his hands full stabilizing an economy whose currency devalued 50% in 1998.

LITERATURE & ARTS

Moldovan literature, like much of Moldovan history, is inextricably linked with that of Romania (see **Romania: Literature and Arts,** p. 476). During the Soviet era, art in Moldova suffered under the yoke of **Socialist Realism** (see p. 11). One of the most notable writers to surface during this period was **Andrei Lupan,** who managed to enliven the otherwise bland praise for the communist regime. **Ion Druta,** the greatest writer of the period, explored the psyche of the region's rural population in his 1963 novel *Ballads of the Steppes (Balade de câmpie)*. Although both Lupan and Druta wrote in Moldovan, much of their work was published only in Russian translation by the Soviet-controlled presses in Chişinău. Sovietization has had a more ambiguous effect on Moldova's **folk arts:** the state went to great lengths to preserve the native culture, but their efforts were negated by an economic program that eradicated much of the native way of life.

READING LIST

The *East European Monographs* series has several offerings on Moldovan history. Its broadest offering on modern Moldova is Donald Dyer's *Studies in Moldovan: The History, Culture, Language and Contemporary Politics of the People of Moldova*. Literary offerings in English translation are slim; your best bet is to look in anthologies of Romanian literature for Moldovan authors.

FACTS AND FIGURES

- **Capital:** Chişinău
- **Population:** 4,362,516
- **Land Area:** 33,700km^2
- **Geography:** Hilly plains
- **Language:** Moldovan, Russian
- **Religions:** 98% Orthodox
- **GDP per capita:** US$416
- **Major Exports:** Foodstuffs

MOLDOVA ESSENTIALS

Citizens of Australia, Canada, Ireland, New Zealand, South Africa, and the U.K. need visas and invitations to enter Moldova; citizens of the U.S. need visas, but not invitations. For U.S. citizens, single-entry visas (valid 30 days) cost US$30, multiple-entry visas run US$50-80 (depending upon length of stay), and transit visas are US$15 for single-entry, US$30 for double-entry. For other nationalities, single-entry visas are US$40 (valid 1 month), US$70 (2 months), or US$100 (3 months); single-transit visas cost US$20, and double-transit US$40. Regular service takes 5-7 days; 2-day rush service costs an additional US$20. Together with a visa application and invitation (if applicable), you must submit your passport, photograph, and fee by money order or company check to the nearest Moldova embassy or consulate (see **Essentials: Embassies and Consulates,** p. 13). U.S. citizens can also get visas at the airport in Chişinău, although getting one ahead before your trip will save your time and sanity. Invitations can be obtained from acquaintances in Moldova, or from Moldovatur after booking a hotel room in Chişinău. For a visa extension, visit the Ministry of Foreign Affairs, Consular Section, in Chişinău.

PRIMARY BORDER CROSSINGS. Visas and invitations are not available at the border. Expect to unofficially pay border officials at least US$20 to cross a Moldovan border. The easiest way into or out of Moldova is to take a direct bus or train from Chişinău to Bucharest, Kiev, or Odessa.

Ukraine: Edineţa, MOL/Mohyliv Podilsky, UKR via Ataki, MOL; connects Bălţi and Chişinău, MOL (p. 390) with Western Ukraine (p. 767). **Do not take any trains to Tiraşpol or Dubăsari, MOL,** both of which are in Moldova's politically unstable breakaway Trans-Dniestr Republic.

Romania: Leuşeni, MOL/Albita, ROM; connects Chişinău (p. 390) with Iaşi (p. 538), Romanian Moldova and Bukovina (p. 538), and the Black Sea Coast (p. 545).

GETTING THERE & GETTING AROUND

Trains connect Chişinău to Bucharest, Iaşi, Kiev, Moscow, Odessa, and Sofia. The Iaşi-Chişinău trip takes about 6hr., of which only 2hr. are spent in motion; border controls and wheel-changing (Moldovan rail tracks are of a larger gauge than Romanian ones) take up the rest. If you haven't seen bogies changed before, it's cool. Don't be surprised if border guards open your luggage. You will be given a sheet on which to **document the money you are changing.** Be sure not to lose it—it will be demanded by customs when you leave the country. Internally, trains from Chişinău go to Băltsi, Tiraşpol, and Ungleni, but the railroad network—built when Moldova and Ukraine were one country—crisscrosses their border in several places. **Buses** are generally the best way to get around Moldova, arriving in Chişinău from every direction inside Moldova and internationally from Bucharest, Odessa, and even Istanbul (via Romania, not Bulgaria). Beware the bus schedules posted at the station—they're often cryptic and just plain wrong. Ask the driver or the ticket salespeople instead. The efficiency of a bus driver's work is measured in number of heads per ride, so buses are always packed.

TOURIST SERVICES & MONEY

Moldovatur is the only show in town. For better or worse, its president is Moldova's Minister of Tourism. The Hotel Naţional office provides tours, hotel reservations, visa support, and some of the country's only English. It's not budget- or backpacker-oriented, but provides useful and friendly advice, a free map of Moldova and a 5 lei map of Chişinău (in French only, until *lei* grease the wheels of an English press).

The monetary unit, the **leu** (plural *lei*), is worth 100 *bani* (also called by the diminutive, bănuti). Unlike the currencies of many nearby countries, the Moldovan leu did not experience serious inflation in 1996-97, although Russia's economic woes have since done a number on its economy. Do not confuse the Moldovan leu with the Romanian currency of the same name. Black market sharks are common, but take care: it's better to have receipts for all currency exchanged to tame nasty customs officials (see above). **Bringing cash is necessary** since few places outside Chişinău take traveler's checks or give cash advances. U.S. dollars and Deutschmarks are easiest to exchange, but you can also change Russian rubles, Ukrainian hryvny, and Romanian lei. There are only one or two **ATMs** in the capital, and none anywhere else in the country.

COMMUNICATION

AT&T Direct and similar **phone** services are not yet available; collect calls also remain impossible. International service in the post office in Chişinău, although expensive (to the U.S. 9.80 lei per min.), is dependable to most countries. For local calls, either buy pay phone tokens or a Moldtelecom card for modern cardphones which are popping up all over Chişinău (from 12 lei). These cards can dial direct internationally (35 lei for 3min.), too—watch as your credits plunge like a post-Soviet economy. **Mail** is even slower than the average Eastern European mail (one week to Britain and 7-10 days to the US, they claim). Ask for *avion* if you want airmail, but tell your friends back home not to worry if they don't hear from you for some time. **Email** is cheap and usually available in Chişinău. For expensive efficiency, **DHL** has landed in both Chişinău and Tiraşpol.

LANGUAGE

As the official language of Moldova, **Romanian** was renamed **"Moldovan"** during the Soviet era for political reasons; despite some differences, the languages remain fundamentally the same. In 1989, the script was changed from Cyrillic back to the Latin alphabet, sparking a debate about whether the language should still be called Moldovan. Almost everybody speaks both **Russian** (see the **Russian Glossary,** p. 821, and **The Cyrillic Alphabet,** p. 807) and **Romanian** (see the **Romanian Glossary,** p. 819, and **Romania Essentials: Language,** p. 504). For the first year after the fall of the USSR, it was unusual to hear Russian spoken on the streets of Chişinău. Most ethnic Russians, aware of the changing times, tried either to leave or switch to Romanian, which they had avoided for decades. Now, however, Russian is back. In Chişinău and most urban centers (besides Bendu and Tiraşpol), it dominates in the tourist-oriented services and commercial life. Almost nobody speaks **English.** Most signs are bilingual (Moldovan-Russian). In the countryside, Russian drops like a rock; you may feel a bit like Koko the gorilla if you don't speak Romanian.

HEALTH & SAFETY

EMERGENCY NUMBERS.
Fire: tel. 901. **Police:** tel. 902. **Ambulance:** tel. 903.

Few travelers make it as far as Moldova; consequently, most Moldovans treat foreigners with a bit of suspicion. Women traveling alone are likely to feel uncomfortable. In Chişinău, streets are poorly lit at night, and it is unwise to stay out late. In the event of an emergency, try to get someone from the tourist office to accompany you or meet you at the hospital. Some British insurance plans are accepted by special arrangement, but American policies are not. Pharmacies in Moldova are generally well-equipped with western products, including condoms and feminine hygiene products.

ACCOMMODATIONS & FOOD

While not many hotels are geared toward the budget traveler, they remain inexpensive. Most rooms start at 200 lei. For the true budget traveler, private rooms are a clean and cheap option (14-40 lei). Moldovan cuisine is very much like Romanian fare. Highlights include *sarmale* (meat and rice in grape leaves), *plachinta* (cheese, cabbage, and melon pie), and ice cream topped with fruit. When ordering in a restaurant, remember that everything—including condiments—has a price.

CUSTOMS & ETIQUETTE

Moldova as a nation is under ten years old, and its customs and traditions still draw heavily on those of Romania and Russia. The countryside reflects the traditions of its Romanian peasantry, while more Russified urban dwellers carry on the customs of their Slavic forebears. One typical Moldovan attitude that seems to have grown out of living in such a delicate cultural balance is an uncommonly high level of **courtesy.** Moldovans are very helpful to travelers, especially those who impress with a few phrases in Russian or Romanian. Tipping in restaurants is common; give an extra 5-7% when you pay the bill.

On **homosexuality,** though, Moldova sticks to the old Soviet party line—it is unknown here, and therefore, discretion is highly advisable. The same is true for travelers of Jewish descent. Despite its location in the middle of the historic Pale of Settlement (to which the Jews were restricted), Moldova retains its Soviet-era anti-Semitism. While this may not present a problem, it will quickly become evident when travelers start discussing politics or Jewish history.

NATIONAL HOLIDAYS

January 1, New Year's; January 7-8, Orthodox Christmas; March 8, International Women's Day; April 30-May 1, Orthodox Easter; May 1, Labor Day; May 9, Victory Day; August 27, Independence Day.

CHIŞINĂU (КИЩИНЁВ)

The capital of Moldova, Chişinău (KEE-shee-nao; Russian kee-shee-NYOF; pop. 657,775) looks at first glance like a Soviet provincial city. Built on a rectangular grid, its sparseness is punctuated only by concrete monsters on a Stalinist scale. Subtly interspersed along broad, tree-lined side streets, however, are old churches and buildings that provide gracefully designed glimpses into the Romanian influence of pre-Soviet days. Indicators of the city's political, social, and economic future are as fascinatingly mixed as its architecture: marketplaces whirling with activity and booming entrepreneurial ventures coexist with highly bureaucratic bus rides and eerily quiet streets come night. In a country racked by political and economic instability, Chişinău sifts through the promises and prophesies, groping doggedly toward whatever the future may bring.

GETTING THERE & GETTING AROUND

Airplanes: The **airport** (tel. 52 54 12) is 12km from downtown; take bus #65 from the corner of Izmail and Stef. **Voiaj Travel,** bd. Negruzzi 10 (tel. 54 64 64), near Hotel Naţional, arranges flights on Air Moldova and other major airlines to: **Frankfurt** (2hr.; 1 per day M, T, and Th-Su; US$180); **Moscow** (2¾hr., 2 per day, US$155); **Athens** (3¼hr.; 1 per day T, W, and Sa; US$200); and **Istanbul** (3¼hr., 1 per day M-Th and Sa, US$190). Open M-Sa 8am-7pm, Su 9am-5pm. MC/Visa.

Trains: In the southwest corner of town (tel. 25 27 35). You can buy international tickets at the 2nd floor booth, but it's worth the 10 lei surcharge to go through **Moldovatur** if you don't speak the language. To: **Odessa** (2 per day, 50 lei); **Bucharest** (12½hr., daily, 150 lei); **Kiev** (14hr., 3 per day, 200 lei); **Minsk** (1 per day M and F, 110 lei); **Moscow** (31hr., daily, 340 lei); and **Varna** (21hr.; M, W, and F; 265 lei). Buy domestic tickets at the booth in the main station.

Buses: Str. Mitropolit Varlaam 58 (tel. 21 20 84). Coming up Ştefan cel Mare from the train station, take a right on Tighina and then a left on Mitropolit Varlaam where you see the buses. Do not trust the schedule posted in the lobby. Decrepit, crowded buses leave for: **Iaşi** (5 per day, 25 lei); **Odessa** (daily, 27.50 lei); and **Bucharest** (daily, 74 lei). Arrive at least 10min. early if you want a seat. Open daily 6:30am-6:30pm. **Kavasoglu lines** (tel. 54 98 22) and **Ozgüleu lines** (tel. 26 37 48) each run 2-7 buses to **Istanbul** from the train station (400 lei).

Local Transportation: Extensive but slow **trolley** system; buy tickets (0.50 lei, 0.75 lei on new buses; pay on board.) Scores of well-organized, efficient *marshrutki* (converted mini-vans) follow the same routes (numbers and destinations are on the windshield) and are a quick alternative (1 lei). Hold out your hand to hail one if you're not at a stop.

Taxis: tel. 907 and 908. State-run and ubiquitous. In theory, 1.50 lei per km in the city, but—at least with foreigners—drivers set the price before departing. If you're slick with Russian or Romanian, bargaining can work wonders.

ORIENTATION

Thanks to its grid lay-out, Chişinău is very easy to navigate. To get to the city center from the train station in the southeast corner of the city, walk through the park in front. On the left is the trolley station (near the vendors). Turn right, walk up to Hotel Cosmos, then veer left on **bd. Negruzzi;** after about 300m, it veers right and becomes **bd. Ştefan cel Mare.** This seemingly endless boulevard spans the city from southeast to northwest; most sights are clustered around it. About 10min. up from the train it is intersected by **str. Tighina;** turn right to find the marketplace and the **bus station.** Or, continue along bd. cel Mare 10min. to reach the central Piaţă Naţională. **Trolleys** #1, 4, and 8 run from the train station to the center.

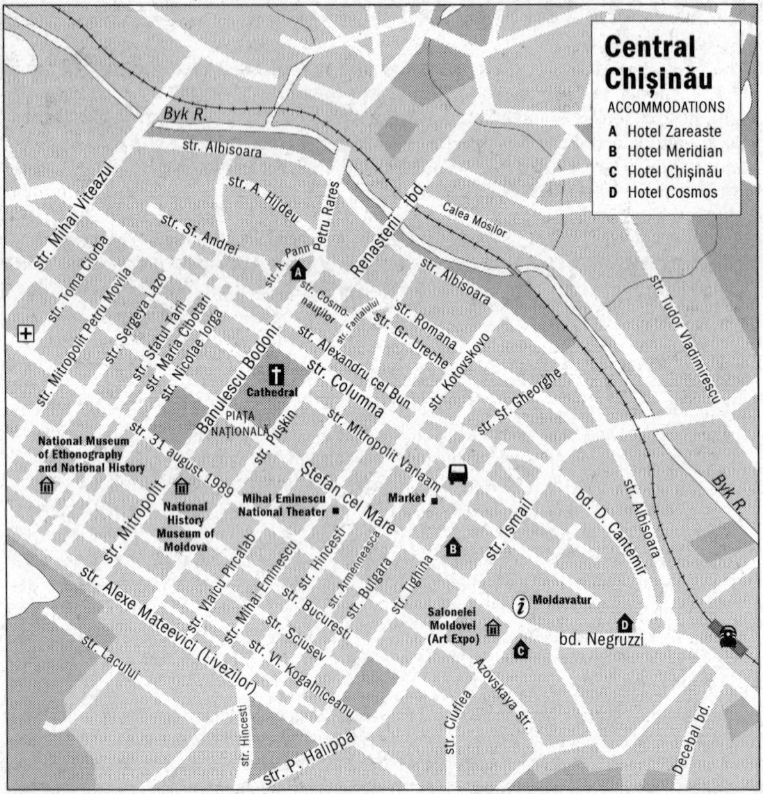

PRACTICAL INFORMATION

Tourist Office: Moldovatur, bd. Ştefan cel Mare 4 (tel. 26 04 88), on the 1st floor of Hotel Naţional. Arranges hotel reservations and tours, provides great city **maps** (5 lei), and speaks English. Open M-F 8:30am-5pm.

Embassies: U.S., str. Alexe Mateevici 103 (tel. 23 37 72; fax 23 30 44). Take trolley #7, 9, 10, or 24 to the university. Open M-F 9am-6pm; citizens' services W 2-4pm. Citizens of other countries should contact their embassies in Romania (see **Bucharest: Embassies,** p. 510).

Currency Exchange: One of the few businesses booming in Chişinău. All accept DM and US$. Romanian lei, Ukrainian hryvny, and Russian rubles are exchanged at bad rates. **Victoriabank,** 77 bd. Ştefan cel Mare (tel. 22 59 24), exchanges traveler's checks for a 1.5% commission and gives MC/Visa cash advances for a 2-3% commission. A Plus/Visa **ATM** stands outside.

Western Union: Windows #1 and 2 in **Banca de Economie al Moldovei,** bd. Ştefan cel Mare 6. Coming from the train station on bd. Ştefan cel Mare, the bank is in the row of shops on the right, just up the stairs past Hotel Naţional. Visa cash are advances also available. Open M-F 8:30am-3pm, Sa 9am-3pm.

English Bookstore: Libraria, bd. Ştefan cel Mare 6 (tel. 27 05 89), has a small selection of books in English. Open M-Sa 9am-7pm.

24hr. Pharmacy: Felicia Farmacia, bd. Ştefan cel Mare 128 (tel. 22 37 25). Well-stocked with feminine hygiene products and condoms.

Hospital: 1 Toma Ciorba.

Internet: Portal Internet, Renasterii 13, #102. Upstairs on the left. Surf the web for 8 lei per hr. Open daily 10am-midnight.

Post Office: Bd. Ştefan cel Mare 134, right across from city hall and the Mihai Eminescu Theater. Open M-Sa 8am-7pm, Su 8am-6pm. **Postal code:** 2012.

Telephones: Corner of str. Tighina and bd. Ştefan cel Mare, two blocks from Hotel Naţional. International service to the left as you enter. For international calls, dial 810 and the number; after the call is answered, dial 3. To: **Australia** and **U.S.** 17 lei per min.; **Ireland** and **U.K.** 8.50 lei per min. **Faxes** (fax 54 91 55) sent and received. To: **Australia** 44 lei per page; **U.S.** 34 lei per page; **Ireland** and **U.K.** 17 lei per page. Faxes open daily 8:30am-10pm. Telephones open 24hr., except for occasional coffee breaks. **Phone code:** (0)2.

MOLDOVA

ACCOMMODATIONS

Coopertiva Adresa, bd. Negruzzi 1 (tel. 54 43 92), across from Hotel Cosmos, rents **private rooms** (14-40 lei; all with TV). The staff speaks some English. (Open M-F 9am-9pm, Sa-Su 9am-6pm.) Approaching Hotel Cosmos from the train station, Coopertiva is on your left just after the traffic circle. Hotels in Chişinău are also affordable, but always ask to see your room before paying. All hotels levy a 9 lei tourist tax.

Hotel Meridian, str. Tighina 42 (tel. 27 06 20). Noisy and harried, but in a great spot; the entrance is up the steps and through the door next to the "Foto" and exchange booths in the market. Wonderful staff. 85 lei gets you a worn-out room with a fold-out couch for a bed. Rooms with real beds 200 lei. Hot water 6-8am and 9pm-midnight. Some English spoken.

Hotel Chişinău, bd. Negruzzi 7 (tel. 57 85 06). The lobby resembles a tiny, well-kept train station. Look closely; the dim hallways are actually pink. Old but clean rooms with fridge, TV, phone, and bath. Restaurant, exchange office, and room service available. Singles 150 lei; doubles 264 lei; triples 342 lei.

Hotel Zareaste, Anton Pann 4 (tel. 22 76 25). From the center go right down bd. Bodoni and left on Alexandru cel Bun. Pann is the first right; the hotel is on the right. Not the best location, but the bare rooms with TV, shared bath, and hot water are a bargain. Doubles 81.60 lei.

Hotel Cosmos, bd. Negruzzi 2 (tel. 54 27 57; fax 57 27 44). Parquet floors, checkered bedspreads, golden wallpaper, a massage parlor, and a restaurant and bar (live music; open daily 7:30am-11pm or later). Breakfast, hot water bath, and phone included. English spoken. Laundry service available. MC/Visa. Singles US$60; doubles US$48.

FOOD

As Moldova interacts with the outside world, it's learning a few important things about restaurants: they should be good, cheap, and everywhere. Unfortunately, everything on the table has a price; expect to be charged for ketchup. At the **market-place** off Ştefan cel Mare on str. Tighina you can find vendors selling fresh veggies, *buterbrod* (open-faced sandwiches with meat and veggies; 1-2 lei), fruit, and pastries. (Open in summer Tu-Su 6:30am-5pm; winter 7am-4pm.) Also look for **Alimentari** (food stores). **Gloria,** bd. Ştefan cel Mare 64, has staples, plus fresh meat and produce from the market. (Open daily 8am-3pm and 4pm-9pm.)

Barracuda, Puşkin 35 (tel. 20 21 02, 22 15 87, and 22 16 09). Quite possibly the best traditional food in Moldova. Sip fresh-squeezed juices as you peruse the English menu. Complete meals 25-100 lei. Open daily noon-11pm.

Restaurant Indian Tandoori, bul. Renasteri 6 (tel. 24 50 23; fax 24 21 34). Extensive menu of Indian classics. Entrees 20--80 lei. Open M-F noon-midnight, Sa-Su 3pm-midnight. MC/Visa.

Cactus Saloon and Restaurant, Armeneasca 24 (tel. 50 40 94), just off Bd. 31 Aug. 1989. Ever wonder what would have happened if Russia bordered Mexico? Soviet-Mex means sausage is in the salsa, but the result is delicious. Cowboy hats optional. Entrees 24-40 lei. Open daily 10am-10pm. MC/Visa.

La Bunel, Eminescu 50 (tel. 22 22 19). Hidden behind a large, green, uninviting metal gate, in a stone-walled courtyard teeming with ivy and singing birds. Moldovan entrees 12-24 lei. Open daily noon-midnight.

SIGHTS

NATIONAL HISTORY MUSEUM OF MOLDOVA. (Muzeul Naţional de Istorie a Moldovei). For such a young capital, Chişinău offers a remarkably strong collection of museums, starting with the National History Museum of Moldova. Outside, a she-wolf feeds Romulus and Remus, a symbol of south Bessarabia's Latin roots. Inside you'll find more of Moldova's cultural heritage, from ancient pottery to newspaper clippings from the nation's independence, with a fascinating coin collection along the way. *(Str. 31 August 1989 121a. From the center, take a right on Str. Puşkin followed by a right on Str. 31 August 1989; the museum is on the left. Tel. 24 43 25. Open Tu-Su in summer 10am-6pm; off-season 9am-5pm; closed last Friday of the month. Museum 0.50 lei, students 0.25 lei; treasury 2 lei, students 0.50 lei.)*

NATIONAL MUSEUM OF ETHNOGRAPHY AND NATURAL HISTORY. (Muzeul Naţiontal de Ethnografie şi Istorie Naturală). The National Museum of Ethnography and Natural History focuses on lions and tigers and bears. Don't miss the dinosaur skeleton unearthed in 1966. *(Str. Kogalniceanu 82. From the center, take a left on Bodoni and walk five blocks. Turn right on Kogalniceanu; the museum is three blocks down on the right. Tel. 24 00 56. Open Tu-Su 10am-6pm. 1 lei, students 0.75 lei.)*

A.S. PUSHKIN HOUSE AND MUSEUM. (Casa-Muzeu A.S. Pushkin). For the Moldovan take on Russian Pushkin-mania, visit the A. S. Pushkin House and Museum. Pushkin lived in Chişinău from 1820 to 1823 while he worked on *Eugene Onegin*. Some of the original manuscripts are on display here. *(Str. Anton Pann 19. Tel. 29 26 86 and 29 41 38. Open Tu-Su 10am-5pm. 2 lei.)*

ART EXPO. (Sala de Expozitii). Head down bd. Ştefan cel Mare toward the train station to the Art Expo, where 2m silver statues representing the classical arts—painting, writing, and sculpture—stand outside the wall. For souvenirs, head for the **Galerie Brancuşi,** in Sala de Expozitii, which also has cool temporary exhibitions. *(Open Tu-F 10am-5pm, Sa-Su 11am-4pm.)* Across the street, the stunning sky-blue towers of **Cioflii Church,** finished in 1876, are perhaps the most beautiful in Chişinău. *(Open daily 7am-8pm.)* A little further down, in front of Hotel Cosmos, stands the large statue of **Kotovski,** a bandit to Romanians, a Robin Hood to Soviets, who in the 1920s staged flash raids from across the Nistru River. Not as dramatic as Lenin's accomplishments, but then, Kotovski's statue is still standing.

PIAŢA NAŢIONALĂ. Up bd. Ştefan cel Mare, at the intersection with str. Puşkin, is **Piaţa Naţională,** the main square, with an 1846 triumphal arch along bd. Ştefan cel Mare. Behind it lie a **park** and the temple-like **cathedral** resembling a Stalin-sized, neo-Greek R2-D2. On the square's upper left corner stands the statue of the legendary **Stephen the Great** (Ştefan cel Mare). The statue, created in 1928, was moved around during WWII to avoid the Bolsheviks, but finally fell into the hands of the Soviets—who modified its inscription—in 1945. In 1972, it was set up in the park, but the 1990 National Revival brought it back to its original resting spot. The park also contains an alley with statues from the classics of Romanian literature.

CITY PARK. To reach the central **park,** complete with its very own lake, go about five blocks up str. Puşkin from the center until it ends. Turn right on Mateevici and look for the stairs on the left going down. Stroll through the cool wooded area and enjoy a picnic by the water, or even venture out in a rowboat from the small **beach.** *(Both located on the far side of the lake. Row boats 10 lei per hr.)* On the way you'll pass the **university;** many of the students who hang out at the cafes around here would welcome the chance to practice their English.

OTHER SIGHTS. A few blocks from the center toward the train station are the Corinthian columns and beige facade of the **Mihai Eminescu National Theater** (Teatrul Naţional Mihai Eminescu). *(Tel. 22 11 77. Ticket office open 10am-1pm and 2-6pm.)* Close by, two gentle lions guard the **Organ Hall;** check the board for concert schedules (usually at 6pm). A flag crowns the small tower above the charming facade of the nearby **City Hall.** A sizable crafts bazaar separates the two buildings.

MOLDOVA

NIGHTLIFE

Nightlife is lacking, probably because it isn't safe to go out alone after dark. The cafes near the opera house—on the right just past Piaţa Naţională—are popular with the younger crowd. **Chernaja Karakatiza,** across from the train station, is a major Russian disco. For a more Romanian crowd, head to **La Victor.** From the center, turn left on str. Vlaicu and then right on Varlaam. The club is tucked back on the right. The party begins nightly at 10pm.

NEAR CHIŞINĂU: VADUL LUI VODĂ

About 12km northeast of Chişinău, the relaxing riverside resort Vadul lui Vodă is a summertime haven for Russian-speaking Moldovans. On a hot summer day the beach is packed with Chişinău residents who come to burn calories swimming or skin roasting in the sun. The beach attracts a crowd eager to quench its thirst at the kiosks in this wooded retreat, but watch out for the hideous public toilets, contenders for the Eastern Europe Outhouse Hall of Shame.

GETTING THERE. Bus #31 runs here directly from the market in Chişinău, as do *marshrutki* (30 min., 3.50 lei). Ride the bus to the very end *(plaja),* where you'll see gobs of people in skimpy Speedos frolicking on the banks of the Nistru.

NEAR CHIŞINĂU: ORHEI

Old Orhei, or "a fortified place," became high-profile in the 15th century as a stop along trade routes running to the Far East. The town was destroyed in 1538 and never rebuilt, although its name was subsequently adopted by new Orhei. Archaeological excavations, a monastery, and a museum attract visitors today. New Orhei's small **history museum,** str. Renasterii Naţionale 23 (tel. 203 98), is free and worth seeing—it details the region's past all the way up to its 1991 independence, and has a small collection of stuffed birds, pinned butterflies and insects, and flora from the area. Subtitles are in Russian and Romanian. Turn left off bd. Ştefan cel Mare, the small street beside the town's newer-looking church. The museum is on the left. (Open Tu-Su 9am-5pm.)

GETTING THERE. The **bus** from Chişinău stops in **New Orhei** (1½hr., every 30min. from the stand past the main bus station, 6.30 lei). From here, buses leave for Old (Stari) Orhei each day at 6am and 12:45pm (the bus is headed for Trebujeni; 4 lei).

POLAND (POLSKA)

US$1 = 4.11ZŁ (ZŁOTY, OR PLN)	**1ZŁ = US$0.24**
CDN$1 = 2.76ZŁ	**1ZŁ = CDN$0.36**
UK£1 = 6.60ZŁ	**1ZŁ = UK£0.15**
IR£1 = 5.53ZŁ	**1ZŁ = IR£0.18**
AUS$1 = 2.67ZŁ	**1ZŁ = AUS$0.37**
NZ$1 = 2.18ZŁ	**1ZŁ = NZ$0.46**
SAR1 = 0.68ZŁ	**1ZŁ = SAR1.47**
DM1 = 2.22ZŁ	**1ZŁ = DM0.45**

PHONE CODES Country code: **48.** International dialing prefix: **00.**

Poland has always been caught at the threshold of East and West, and its moments of freedom have been brief. It is easy to forget that between 1795 to 1918, Poland simply did not exist on any map of Europe, and that its short spell of independence thereafter—like so many before it—was brutally dissolved. Ravaged by World War II and viciously suppressed by Stalin and the USSR, Poland has at long last been given room to breathe, and its residents are not letting the opportunity slip by. The most prosperous of the "Baltic tigers," Poland now has a rapidly expanding GDP, a new membership in NATO, and a likely future membership in the E.U. With their new wealth, the legendarily hospitable Poles have been returning to their cultural roots and repairing buildings destroyed in the wars, a trend popular with the growing legions of tourists that visit each year. Capitalism brought with it Western problems, like rising crime and unemployment, issues politicians have begun to recognize as serious. But there are few Poles complaining about the events of the past ten years. Political and economic freedoms have helped this rich culture to occupy its own skin once again, even if it's now wearing a pair of Levi's.

HIGHLIGHTS OF POLAND

- Flattened during WWII, reconstructed medieval fortifications and royal opulence make **Warsaw** a convincing fake (p. 406).
- If Vilnius is the "New Prague," much-adored **Kraków** is the old one (p. 422).
- Poland's liveliest music scene hides in the happening pubs of **Poznań** (p. 463).
- The sleepy fishing village of **Hel** is a slice of heaven as the home to the most beautiful (and deserted) beaches on the Baltic Sea (p. 490).
- The seven-day hike along the **Trail of Eagles' Nests** creeps through the heart of Poland, past limestone out-croppings and magnificent castle ruins (p. 454).

LIFE & TIMES

HISTORY

Between AD 800 and 960, a number of the West Slavic tribes occupying modern Poland joined to form small states. When **Prince Mieszko I** of the Piast dynasty converted to Catholicism in 966, he united many of the tribes, and his son, **Bolesław Chrobry** (the Brave), was crowned Poland's first king in 1025 (see **Gneizno,** p. 467).

Poland was devastated by the Mongols in 1241, but the 14th century—particularly under **King Kazimierz Wielki** (Casimir the Great)—developed into a time of prosperity and unprecedented religious and political tolerance. Poland became a refuge for Jews expelled from Western Europe, and Casimir III rebuilt the country's defenses, signed strategic peace treaties, and expanded Poland's territories. A university was founded at Kraków, the cultural and political and capital of Poland, in 1364.

The Piast dynasty ruled Poland until shortly after Jagiełło, grand duke of Lithuania, married Piast Princess Jadwiga in 1368, establishing the **Jagiełłon dynasty** and beginning the process of uniting Poland and Lithuania. After the death of Casimir III in 1370, Poland experienced increasing international difficulties, particularly with the **Teutonic Knights,** who took East Prussia and cut off access to the Baltic. In 1410, Poland and Lithuania defeated them at the **Battle of Grunwald,** thereby establishing the **Polish-Lithuanian Commonwealth** as one of the great powers in Europe.

The Renaissance reached Poland in the 16th century under **King Zygmunt I Stary** (Sigmund the Old). Shortly thereafter, Mikołaj Kopernik, an astronomer from Toruń better known by his Latin name, **Copernicus,** developed the heliocentric model of the solar system (see **Toruń,** p. 468). In 1569, the **Union of Lublin** created an elected kingship and legislature for Poland and Lithuania, and was quickly followed by the **Warsaw Confederation,** known for its religious tolerance.

In the early 17th century, the Swedish **Zygmunt III Waza** moved the capital to Warsaw. In 1648-67, the "Deluge" brought internal strife and a wave of Swedish invasions. **Jan III Sobieski** lifted the siege of Vienna in 1683, further exhausting Poland and leaving it vulnerable to attacks. Russia, Prussia, and Austria each took sizable chunks of the Polish-Lithuanian Commonwealth in 1772. Two decades later, Polish noblemen convened a special meeting of the Sejm to draft a state constitution. Signed on **May 3, 1791,** the new constitution was the second of its kind in the world; it established Catholicism as the national religion and set up a plan for the election of political leaders. In response to these attempts at independence, Russia and Prussia divided Poland again in 1793. The following year, **Tadeusz Kościuszko,** a hero of the American Revolution, led a peasant uprising against Russian rule. He ended up in prison, and Poland was divided one last time in 1795 (see **Racławice Panorama,** p. 456). The three **Partitions of Poland** removed Poland from the map of Europe for the next 123 years, during which time Russia crushed the nationalist spirit in the rebellions of 1831 and 1863.

Poland didn't win back its independence until 1918, after **Marshal Józef Piłsudski** had successfully pushed back a new invasion by the Red Army. A Polish delegation led by **Roman Dmowski** worked Polish statehood into the Treaty of Versailles. The Allies repatriated Poznań and West Prussia, as well as access to the port of Gdańsk, to the newly independent nation. From the 1920s until 1935, Piłsudksi ruled with only formal preservation of parliamentary authority. When the **German-Soviet Nonaggression Pact** was signed in August 1939, however, Poland's defense treaties became worthless. In September, Nazi and Soviet forces attacked Poland simultaneously from west and east. Germany occupied the western two-thirds of the country, while the Soviet Union got the rest. More than six million of Poland's inhabitants were killed, including three million Jews. As the Nazis lost control of the country to the Red Army, freedom fighters loyal to the government in exile in London initiated the **Warsaw Uprising** of 1944 to take back their city before the Soviets "liberated" it. The Germans retaliated mightily, however, while the Soviets bided time in the suburbs. When Red tanks finally rolled in, they took Warsaw with little opposition and inaugurated 45 years of Communist rule. The first few years brought mass migrations, political crackdown, and social unrest that contributed to the 1946 Jewish **pogrom.** Even after the country grudgingly submitted, **strikes** broke out in 1956, 1968, and 1970; all were swiftly and violently quashed.

In 1978, **Karol Wojtyła,** who authored religious plays and poems before entering the priesthood, became the first Polish pope, taking the name John Paul II. His visit to Poland during the following year helped to unite the Catholic Poles and was an impetus for the birth of **Solidarność** (Solidarity), the first independent workers' union in Eastern Europe, in 1980. Led by the charismatic **Lech Wałęsa,** an electrician at the Gdańsk shipyards, Solidarność activities resulted in the declaration of **martial law** in 1981 by head of Polish government **General Wojciech Jaruzelski,** allegedly as a means of protecting the Polish nation from a Soviet invasion. Wałęsa was jailed and released only after Solidarność was officially disbanded and outlawed by the government in 1982.

In 1989, Poland spearheaded the fall of Soviet authority in Eastern Europe. Solidarity members swept into all but one of the contested seats in the June elections, and **Tadeusz Mazowiecki** was sworn in as Eastern Europe's first non-Communist premier in 40 years. In December 1990, Wałęsa became the first elected president of post-Communist Poland. The government opted to swallow the bitter pill of capitalism all in one gulp by quickly eliminating subsidies, freezing wages, and devaluing the currency. This threw the already antiquated economy into recession and produced the first true unemployment in 45 years, a reality that led to the victory of the Left in the 1993 elections. Since this short period of rising crime and painful reform, though, Poland has bounded back toward economic and political stability.

POLAND TODAY

In Poland's tightly contested November 1995 presidential election, **Lech Wałęsa**—former leader of the Solidarity movement—lost to **Aleksander Kwaśniewski.** An 80s Communist and head of the ex-Communist Democratic Left Alliance, Kwaśniewski was elected on a platform of moderately paced privatization, increased emphasis on Christianity, and stronger ties with the West. Recently, however, the **Solidarity Electoral Action (AWS)** party has seen success in local elections, marked by the ascendance of **Jerzy Buzek** to the post of prime minister in October 1997.

Westward-looking Poland has developed Western-style problems, and public protests during 1996 against the rise in crime were the first demonstrations since the new government took control. **Anti-Semitism** also continues to be a problem in much of eastern Poland. Still, the country remains every bit a Western nation. In

March 1999, Poland became an official member of **NATO,** further enhancing its military and economic stability, and it is looking to join the **E.U.** by 2003. Despite problems caused by the Russian financial crisis, Poland's GDP is estimated to have grown by 4.5% in 1999, and foreign investment continues to pour in.

LITERATURE & ARTS

Like its social and political history, the course of Polish literature changed forever when the nation chose to follow Roman—not Byzantine—Christianity. Accordingly, Poland's medieval texts, mostly religious works and chronicles, were written in Latin. With the onset of the European Renaissance, Poland's Western alphabet and religion helped it become an immediate participant, and generated a literary culture that flourishes to this day. Sixteenth-century author **Mikolaj Rej,** the first to write consistently in Polish, is regarded as the father of Polish literature. His contemporary **Jan Kochanowski,** who remains one of the most important Slavic poets, challenged the poetic expectations of his time with *Treny (Laments)*, a cycle of poems about the death of his young daughter.

Diaries and pastoral poetry dominated Polish literature throughout the Baroque period, followed by the emphasis on drama and didactic poetry that defined the Polish Enlightenment. Loss of statehood in 1795 paved the way for **Romanticism,** which held nationalism as a primary ideal. The most prominent writers of this great period—**Adam Mickiewicz, Juliusz Slowacki,** and **Zygmunt Krasinski**—depict Poland as a noble, suffering martyr. Mickiewicz is widely regarded as Poland's "national poet," and his *Pan Tadeusz* is still considered the country's primary epic. **Cyprian Norwid,** a contemporary of Mickiewicz, was an innovative poet who furthered the developments of the already-productive period.

Another failed uprising in 1863 brought the Romantic period to an end. Characterized by naturalistic and historic novels, late 19th-century **Positivism** advocated simple work and participation in one's community. **Eliza Orzeszkowa** voiced such ideas in *Nad Niemnem (On the Banks of the Niemen)*, her novel about a pauperized noble's interaction with peasants. A rather different novel, Nobel Prize-winner **Henryk Sienkiewicz's** *Quo Vadis?*—a tale of early Christianity amid Roman decadence under Nero—argues that society rests on individual morality.

The daily grind provided inspiration only until the turn of the century; the early 20th-century **Młoda Polska** (Young Poland) movement was laden with pessimism and apathy. In his mystery-filled *Wesele* (The Wedding), one of the finest pieces of the period, playwright **Stanisław Wyspianski** addressed many of the problems that defined Poland in his era.

The post-WWII period gave birth to a number of internationally acclaimed voices in poetry and prose. **Witold Gombrowicz** explored the absurdities of nationality and selfhood in novels like *Trans-Atlantyk* and *Kosmos*. The "thaw" following Soviet attempts to enforce **Socialist Realism** brought about an explosion of new work addressing life under communism's thumb. **Zbigniew Herbert** developed the character *Pan Cogito*, while **Tadeusz Rózewicz** concentrated on very short, poignant lyric poems and plays. At the end of the next decade, the **Generation of '68** ushered in a new wave of authors whose poems and essays tackle the dilemmas of living at a historical crossroads. Recent Polish authors include Nobel Prize-winner **Czesław Milosz,** whose controversial *The Captive Mind (Zniewolony umysł)* remains an essential commentary on communist control of individual thought. In 1996, **Wisława Szymborska,** a prominent female poet, became the second Polish author in 16 years to receive the Nobel Prize.

Polish music is best defined by the work of **Frédéric Chopin**, a master composer and the first of many internationally acclaimed Polish instrumentalists (among them pianist **Artur Rubinstein**). Like Polish music, local painting is highly derivative of Western styles; among Poland's most respected artists were **Stanisław Wyspianski,** known for his portraiture, and **Jan Matejko,** famous for his giant historical canvases. Filmaker **Andrzej Wajda** is known for explorations of his country's internal conflicts; recently, Polish directors **Roman Polanski** and **Krzystztof Kieslowski** have achieved international fame.

READING LIST

Both *Heart of Europe: A Short History of Poland*, by Norman Davies, and *The Polish Way: A Thousand Year History*, by Adam Zamoyski, provide a good sense of Polish history, with all its quirks and intricacies. James Michener's best-seller *Poland* provides an outstanding fictional account of three Polish families over eight centuries. *Pan Tadeusz*, by Adam Mickiewicz, and *Teutonic Knights*, by Henryk Sienkiewicz, are both classics that include some interesting history, and *The History of Polish Literature* by the legendary Czesław Milosz covers the entire genre in a fascinating manner. Finally, *The River Midnight*, a highly acclaimed piece of historical fiction by new Canadian author Lilian Nattel, focuses on life in an 1894 Jewish village in Poland.

FACTS AND FIGURES

- **Capital:** Warsaw
- **Population:** 38,801,834
- **Land Area:** 312,685km^2
- **Geography:** Coastal plains, central lowlands, southern mountains
- **Language:** Polish
- **Religions:** 95% Catholic
- **GDP per capita:** US$3,271
- **Major Exports:** Maunfactured goods

POLAND ESSENTIALS

POLAND

Citizens of Ireland and the U.S. can travel to Poland without a visa for up to 90 days and U.K. citizens for up to 180 days. Australians, Canadians, New Zealanders, and South Africans all need visas. Single-entry visas (valid for 180 days) cost US$60 (children and students under 26 pay US$45); multiple-entry visas cost US$100 (students US$75); 48hr. transit visas cost US$20 (students US$15). A visa with a work permit is required of everyone seeking work in Poland. It is valid for 12 months and costs US$170 (students US$128). A visa application requires a valid passport, two photographs, and payment by money order, certified check, or cash; a visa with work permit also requires a work permit issued by the Labor Office or a certificate of employment. Regular service takes four days; 24hr. rush service costs an additional US$35. See **Essentials: Embassies & Consulates,** p. 13, for a list of Polish embassies. To extend your stay, apply at the local province office *(urząd wojewódzki)*.

GETTING THERE

LOT, British Airways, and Delta fly into Warsaw's **Okęcie Airport** from London, New York, Chicago, and Toronto (among other cities). **Trains** and **buses** connect to all neighboring countries, but **Eurail** passes are not valid in Poland. Almatur offers ISIC holders a discount of 192zł. **Wasteels** tickets and **Eurotrain** passes, sold at Almatur, Orbis, and major train stations, get those under 26 40% off international train fares. Thefts have been known to occur on international overnight trains; try not to fall asleep, or sleep in alternating shifts with a friend (for more on train safety, see **Safety & Security,** p. 26). **Ferries** run from Sweden and Denmark to Świnoujście, Gdańsk, and Gdynia.

GETTING AROUND

For all but daytrips, **PKP trains** are preferable to and, for long hauls, usually cheaper than buses. Train stations have boards that list towns alphabetically, and posters that list trains chronologically. *Odjazdy* (departures) are in yellow; *przyjazdy* (arrivals) are in white. **InterCity** and *Ekspresowy* (express) trains are listed in red with an "IC" or "Ex" in front of the train number. *Pośpieszny* (direct; also in red) are almost as fast. *Osobowy* (in black) are the slowest but are 35% cheaper than *pośpieszny*. All **InterCity,** *ekspresowy*, and some *pośpieszny* trains require seat reservations; if you see a boxed R on the schedule, ask the clerk for a *miejscówka*

PRIMARY BORDER CROSSINGS. Visas are not available at the Polish border. There is no fee for crossing. Fortunately, Polish customs are rather efficient and a border crossing takes minimal time. The cheapest way to cross a Polish/German border is to take a Polish train to the border and walk across, switching to a German train once in Germany. The easiest way to enter or exit Poland is to take a direct bus or train from Warsaw, Kraków, or Gdańsk to the capital of the neighboring country or region.

Belarus: Białystok, POL/Hrodna, BEL (p. 75) via Kuznica, BEL; connects Podlasie, POL (p. 494) with Belarus. Biała Podlaska, POL/Brest, BEL (p. 76) via Terespol, BEL; connects Małopolska (p. 421) with Belarus.

Czech Republic: Cieszyn, POL/Český Těšín, CZR (p. 449); connects Bielsko-Biała, POL (p. 447) with Ostrava, CZR and Moravia (p. 225). Szklarska Poręba, POL (p. 463)/Jablonec, CZR; connects Jelenia Góra, POL (p. 459) and Wrocław (p. 455) with Northern Bohemia.

Germany: Szczecin, POL (p. 474)/Prenzlau, GER; connects Pomorze (p. 474) with Berlin (p. 781). Słubice, POL/Frankfurt-Oder, GER or Gubin, POL/Guben, GER; connects Poznań, POL (p. 463) with Berlin (p. 781). Zgorzelec, POL/Görlitz, GER; connects Wrocław (p. 455) with southeastern Germany.

Lithuania: Suwałki, POL/Marijampole, LIT; connects Białystok (p. 495) with Kaunas (p. 375).

Russia: Braniewo, POL/Mamonov, RUS; connects Malbork (p. 486) and Gdańsk (p. 480) with Kaliningrad (p. 632). Bartoszyce, POL; connects Mazury (p. 493) with Kaliningrad (p. 632).

Slovakia: Nowy Sącz, POL/Stará Lubovňa, SLK via Piwniczna, POL; connects Kraków (p. 422) with Bardejov (p. 705). Zakopane, POL (p. 441)/Spišská Belá, SLK via Łysa Polana, POL; connects the Carpathians (p. 440) with the Slovak Tatras (p. 693). Spytkowice, POL/Dolný Kubin, SLK via Chyżne, POL; connects Kraków (p. 422) with Žilina (p. 684).

Ukraine: Przemyśl, POL (p. 439); connects Lviv, UKR (p. 767) to Kraków (p. 422) and Małopolska (p. 421).

(myay-SOOV-ka; reservation). Buy surcharged tickets on board from the *konduktor* before he or she finds (and fines) you. Most people purchase *normalny* tickets, while students and seniors buy *ulgowy* (half-price) tickets. **Beware:** foreign travelers are not eligible for discounts on domestic buses and trains—ISICs will get you nowhere. You risk a hefty fine by traveling with an *ulgowy* ticket without Polish ID. On Sundays, tickets cost 20% less. Train tickets are good only for the day they're issued. Allot plenty of time for long, slow lines. Better yet, buy your ticket in advance at the station or an Orbis office. Stations are not announced and are sometimes poorly marked.

PKS buses are cheapest and fastest for short trips. Like trains, there are *pośpieszny* (direct; marked in red) and *osobowy* (slow; in black). Purchase advance tickets at the bus station, and expect long lines. However, many tickets can only be bought from the driver. In the countryside, PKS markers (steering wheels that look like upside-down, yellow Mercedes-Benz symbols) indicate bus stops, but drivers will often stop if you flag them down. Traveling with a backpack can be a problem if the bus is full, since there are no storage compartments.

Though legal, **hitchhiking** is increasingly rare and more dangerous for foreigners. Hand-waving is the accepted sign. As always, *Let's Go* does not recommend hitchhiking as a safe form of transportation.

TOURIST SERVICES

The helpfulness of and services provided by travel agencies vary wildly, with city-specific offices generally more helpful than the bigger chains. In general, you can count on all offices to provide free info in English or German and to be of some help with accommodations for a nominal fee. **Orbis,** the state-sponsored travel bureau staffed by English speakers, operates luxury hotels in most cities and sells transportation tickets for longer journeys. **Almatur,** the Polish student travel organization, sells ISICs and helps find dorm rooms in summer. Both provide maps and brochures, as do **PTTK** and **IT** *(Informacji Turystycznej)* bureaus.

MONEY

The Polish **złoty**—plural *złote*—is fully convertible (1 *złoty* = 100 *grosze*). For cash, private **kantor** offices (except for those at the airport and train stations) offer better exchange rates than banks. **Bank PKO S.A.** cashes **traveler's checks** and gives MC/Visa **cash advances. ATMs** *(Bankomat)* are everywhere except the smallest of villages. **MC** and **Visa** are the most widely accepted ATM networks. Budget accommodations rarely, if ever, accept **credit cards,** although some restaurants and pricier shops will.

In January 1995, the National Bank cut four zeroes off all prices, and introduced new bills and coins. The old currency has been invalid since January 1, 1997. Learn the difference between old and new (posters at the airport and train stations depict the currencies), and never accept old currency. When changing money, it helps to ask for small bank notes (10zł or 20zł), since businesses and hostels may not be able to give change for the larger notes (50zł or higher).

COMMUNICATION

Mail is becoming increasingly efficient, although there are still incidents of theft. Airmail *(lotnicza)* usually takes a week to reach the U.S. For *Poste Restante*, put a "1" after the city name to ensure that it goes to the main post office. When picking up *Poste Restante*, you will usually have to pay a small fee (0.70-1zł). Most mid-sized towns and cities have at least one **internet club/cafe.**

Card telephones have become the public phone standard. Cards, which come in several denominations, are sold at post offices and some kiosks, and are necessary even for calling long-distance access numbers such as: **AT&T Direct,** tel. 00 80 01 11 11 11; **BT Direct,** tel. 0, 080 04 41 11 44; **Canada Direct,** tel. 00 80 01 11 41 18; **MCI WorldPhone,** tel. 00 80 01 11 21 22; **Sprint,** tel. 00 80 01 11 31 15. To make a **collect call,** write the name of the city or country and the number plus "*Rozmowa 'R'*" on a slip of paper, hand it to a post office clerk, and be patient.

POLAND

LANGUAGE

Polish varies little across the country. The two exceptions are the region of Kaszuby, whose distinctive, Germanized dialect is classified by some as a separate language, and Karpaty, where the highlanders' accent seems to have been thickened by the goat's milk they drink. In western Poland and Mazury, **German** is the most commonly known foreign language, although students will probably know **English.** Elsewhere, try English and German before **Russian,** which many Poles understand

POLSKI PHONE HOME? After making a call from one of Warsaw's spiffy new magnetic card telephones, you may find yourself accosted by any number of locals—from young girls to elderly gentlemen—staring at your card longingly and bargaining at you in Polish like a used-car salesman. Before you write these poor souls off as free-loaders who couldn't bother to buy their own phone card, know that the opposite is more likely true: they probably have plenty of cards and are looking to add yours to their collection. If you need confirmation of this bizarre factoid, most collectors will whip out their collection with great pride if asked. The cards with pictures on the back are the most coveted; if you find you're holding the Honus Wagner of phone cards—a 1999 Pope John Paul II—you'll have to fend off an ugly mob to escape.

but show an open aversion to speaking. Most Poles can understand **Czech** or **Slovak** if they're spoken slowly. Students may also know **French.**

The fully phonetic spelling is complicated by some letters not in the Latin alphabet: "*ł*" sounds like a "w"; "*ą*" is a nasal "on"; "*ę*" is a nasal "en." A dash above a consonant softens it: "*ó*" and "*u*" are both equivalent to an "oo." "*Ż*" and "*rz*" are both like the "s" in "pleasure"; "*w*" sounds like "v." A few consonantal clusters are easier to spit out than they seem: "*sz*" is "sh," "*cz*" is "ch," and "*ch*" and "*h*" are equivalent, and sound like the English "h." See the **Polish Glossary,** p. 817.

HEALTH & SAFETY

EMERGENCY NUMBERS.
Fire: tel. 998. **Police:** tel. 997. **Ambulance:** tel. 999.

Public restrooms are marked with an upward-pointing triangle for men and a circle for women. They range from pristine to nasty and can cost up to 0.70zł, even if they're gross. Soap, towels, and toilet paper all cost extra. **Pharmacies** are well-stocked, and at least one in each city will be open 24hr. There are usually clinics in major cities with private, Anglophone doctors. Expect to plunk down 30-70zł per visit. Avoid the state hospitals if you can help it. **Tap water** is theoretically drinkable, but **bottled mineral water,** available carbonated (*gazowana*) or flat (*nie gazowana*), will spare you from some unpleasant metals and chemicals. **Criminals** feed off naive Western tourists, and as unemployment grows, so do the ranks of con artists. Always be on your guard at big train stations. Be on the lookout for pickpockets, especially when aboard crowded public buses and trams.

POLAND

ACCOMMODATIONS & CAMPING

Grandmotherly **private room** owners drum up business at the train station or outside the tourist office. Private rooms are usually safe, clean, and convenient, but can be far from city centers. Expect to pay about US$10 per person. **Youth hostels** (*schronisko młodzieżowe*) abound and average 9-25zł per night. They are often booked solid, however, by school or tourist groups; call at least a week in advance. **PTSM** is the national hostel organization. **University dorms** transform into spartan budget housing in July and August; these are an especially good option in Kraków. The Warsaw office of **Almatur** can arrange stays in all major cities. **PTTK** runs a number of hotels called **Dom Turysty,** which have multi-bed rooms as well as budget singles and doubles. Hotels in generally cost 30-50zł per night. Many towns have a **Biuro Zakwaterowań,** which arranges stays in private homes. Rooms come in three categories based on location and availability of hot water (one is the best).

Campsites average US$2 per person; with a car, US$4. **Bungalows** are often available; a bed costs about US$5. *Polska Mapa Campingów* lists all campsites. Almatur runs a number of sites in summer; ask for a list at one of their offices.

FOOD & DRINK

Monks, merchants, invaders, and dynastic unions have all flavored Polish cuisine—a blend of dishes from the French, Italian, and Jewish traditions. Polish food favors meat, potatoes, and butter. It is less starchy than that of the Czech Republic, and less fiery than that of Hungary or Bulgaria.

A Polish meal always starts with **soup,** usually *barszcz* (beet broth), *chłodnik* (a cold beet soup with buttermilk and hard-boiled eggs), *kapuśniak* (cabbage soup), *krupnik* (barley soup), or *żurek* (barley-flour soup loaded with eggs and sausage). Filling **main courses** include *gołąbki* (cabbage rolls stuffed with meat and rice), *kotlet schabowy* (pork cutlet), *naleśniki* (cream-topped crepes filled with cottage cheese or jam), and *pierogi* (dumplings with various fillings—meat, potato, cheese, blueberry).

Poland bathes in **beer, vodka,** and **spiced liquor.** *Żywiec* is the most popular strong (12%) brew; *EB* is its excellent, gentler brother. *EB* also makes *EB Czerwone*, a darker, heavier, very-much-stronger variety. Other beers available throughout the country include *Okocim* and *Piast. Wódka* ranges from wheat to potato. *Wyborowa*, *Żytnia*, and *Polonez* usually decorate private bars. "Kosher" vodka is rumored to be top-notch, although what makes it kosher remains a mystery. The herbal *Żubrówka* vodka comes with a blade of grass from the region where the bison roam. It is sometimes mixed with apple juice *(z sokem jabłkowym). Miód* and *krupnik*—two kinds of meal—are beloved by the gentry, and many grandmas make *nalewka na porzeczce* (black currant vodka).

CUSTOMS & ETIQUETTE

Business hours tend to be Monday to Friday 8am to 6pm and Saturday 9am to 2pm. Saturday hours vary, as some shops in Poland distinguish "working" *(pracująca)* Saturdays, when they work longer hours, from "free" *(wolna)* ones, when hours are shorter. Unfortunately, each store decides for itself which Saturdays are which, so it may be difficult to prepare a shopping plan for any given weekend. Very few stores or businesses are open on Sunday. **Museums** are generally open Tuesday to Sunday, 10am to 4pm. They are ordinarily closed on holidays or the day after a holiday. In restaurants, tell the server how much change you want back, leaving the rest as a 10% **tip.** If you're paying with a credit card, give the tip in cash. When arriving as a **guest,** bring a female host an odd number of flowers. When addressing a man, use the formal *"Pan"*; with a woman, use *"Pani."* Most Poles eat meals at home; when they eat out, it's usually in the cafeteria-style *bary* and *bary mleczne*. It is not uncommon for **restaurants** to be mostly empty, especially in the evening. **Drinking** is common on the street, but **smoking** is often prohibited indoors. **Homosexuality** is legal and a frequent topic of media debate, although its practice remains fairly underground. When visiting religious sights, a donation is usually appreciated, and in the case of the Jewish cemeteries in Warsaw and Łódź, desperately needed for the upkeep and improvement of the grounds.

NATIONAL HOLIDAYS

January 1, New Year's Day; April 23-24, Catholic Easter; May 1, Labor Day; May 3, Constitution Day; June 22, Corpus Christi; August 15, Assumption Day; November 11, Independence Day (1918); December 25-26, Christmas.

WARSAW (WARSAWA)

Warsaw's motto, *contemnire procellas* (to defy the storms), has been put to the test often in the city's long history. According to legend, Warsaw (pop. 1,638,300) was created when the lucky fisherman Wars netted a mermaid (Polish *syrena*, now the city's emblem). She begged him to release her, and told him that if he and his wife established a city where the fantastic catch had been made, she would protect it forever. The mermaid has been very busy for the past 1000 years as invaders from the north, east, and west have all taken a shot at this bastion of Polish pride. Most recently, WWII saw two-thirds of the population killed and 83% of the city destroyed. Even that devastation was seen by the Varsovians as an opportunity to rebuild and revitalize.

Once again the world's largest Polish city (a title long held by Chicago), Warsaw is quickly throwing off its Soviet legacy to emerge as an important international business center. A crop of new skyscrapers has begun to emerge in the city center, while tourists now come to take in the museums, listen to the concerts, and feast in the many restaurants. The university infuses Warsaw with young blood, which keeps the energy high and the nightlife lively. All things considered, the *syrena* appears to have kept her promise.

GETTING THERE & GETTING AROUND

Airplanes: Port Lotniczy Warszawa-Okęcie, ul. Żwirki i Wigury (director's office tel. 650 30 00), referred to as "Terminal 1." Take bus #175 to the center (after 11pm, bus #611). Buy bus tickets at the Ruch kiosk in the departure hall or at the *kantor* outside. 2zł, students 1zł, extra ticket for a large suitcase or backpack. Open M-F 7:30am-6pm. **Airport-City Bus** (8zł, students 4zł; luggage free) is a faster way to the center. Open daily 5:30am-11pm, weekdays 3 per hr., weekends 2 per hr. Buy tickets from the driver.

Airline Offices: LOT, al. Jerozolimskie 65/79 (tel. 952 or 953), in Hotel Marriott. LOT flies directly to New York (9 per week) and Chicago (9 per week). Open M-F 9am-5pm. **British Airways,** ul. Krucza 49 (tel. 628 94 31; airport office 650 45 02 or 650 45 20), off al. Jerozolimskie. Open M-F 9am-5pm. **Delta,** ul. Królewska 11 (tel. 827 84 61). Open M-F 9am-5pm.

Trains: Warszawa Centralna, al. Jerozolimskie 54 (tel. 825 50 00; international info tel. 620 45 12; domestic info tel. 620 03 61.). Lines can be long, and most employees speak only Polish. Write down where and when you want to go, then ask them to write down which *peron* number to head for ("*Który peron?*" means "Which platform?"). Yellow signs list departures, white signs arrivals. To: **Berlin** (7-8hr., 6 per day, 136zł); **Budapest** (10hr., 2 per day, 201zł); **Kiev** (22-24hr., 3 per day, 136zł); **Minsk** (12hr., 4 per day, 110zł); **St. Petersburg** (26hr., 1 per day, 250zł); **Moscow** (27-30hr., 2 per day, 251zł); **Prague** (12-14hr., 2 per day, 153zł); **Vilinus** (12hr., 2 per day, 130zł); **Bratislava** (8hr., 2 per day, 164zł); and almost every corner of Poland, including **Poznań, Gdańsk,** and **Kraków** (3-4hr., several connections per day, 30-50zł).

Warning: Theft is rising on international overnight trains to and from Berlin and Prague, as well as in train stations. Travelers should be mindful of their safety and protect their property, and should avoid sleeping on night trains (see **train safety,** p. 26).

Buses: Warsaw sends buses from three separate stations:

PKS Warszawa Zachodnia, al. Jerozolimskie 144 (tel. 94 33, info tel. 524 41 45), shares a building, address, and bus stop with the Warszawa Zachodnia train station. It can be easily reached by taking the commuter train from the Warszawa Śródmiescie station (next to Warszawa Centralna; 2.40zł) or by taking bus #127 or 130 to Zachodnia station. Buses depart from here to the north and west. Check with the International Bus Information window for ever-changing schedules to places like Paris, Madrid, Vilnius, London, Copenhagen, and Prague. Window open M-F 8am-4pm.

PKS Warszawa Stadion lies on the other side of the Wisła; follow the directions to Zachodnia station and cross over the river. Buses head from here to the east and south.

Polski Express, al. Jana Pawła II (tel. 630 29 67), near Warszawa Centralna (see above), is a private company that offers faster and more comfortable bus service from Warsaw to **Gdańsk** (6hr., 2 per day, 37zł); **Kraków** (6hr., 2 per day, 32zł); **Łódź** (7 per day, 17zł); **Lublin** (4hr., 7 per day, 20zł); and **Szczecin** (9½hr., 1 per day, 32zł).

Local Transportation: Bus and **tram** lines are marked on some maps. Day trams and buses (including express lines) 2zł, with ISIC 1zł; night buses 4.20zł. Large baggage 1 ticket per piece. Daily pass 6zł, with ISIC 3zł; monthly pass 20zł, with ISIC 10zł. Buy tickets at most kiosks, or from the driver at night. Punch the ticket (on the end marked by the arrow and *tu kasować*) in the machines on board or face a 100zł fine, plus another 40zł for your pack. Bus #175 goes all the way from the airport to Stare Miasto by way of the central train station, the center of town, and ul. Nowy Świat; watch out for pickpockets. Bus #130 connects Zachodnia Station, Centralna Station, and Wilanów in the South. Warsaw's **Metro** has only a single line, which connects the southern border of town with the center. Ticket prices are the same as for the bus and tram.

Taxis: MPT Radio Taxi (tel. 919) or **Sawa Taxi** (tel. 644 44 44). Overcharging is still a problem; if possible, call these companies to arrange pickup. State-run cabs with a mermaid sign are generally safe. Fares start at 4zł plus 1.60zł per km; 2zł is the legal maximum per km.

Car Rental: Avis, at the Marriott Hotel (tel./fax 630 73 16). Open daily 8am-6pm. Airport office (tel. 650 48 72) open daily 7am-10pm.

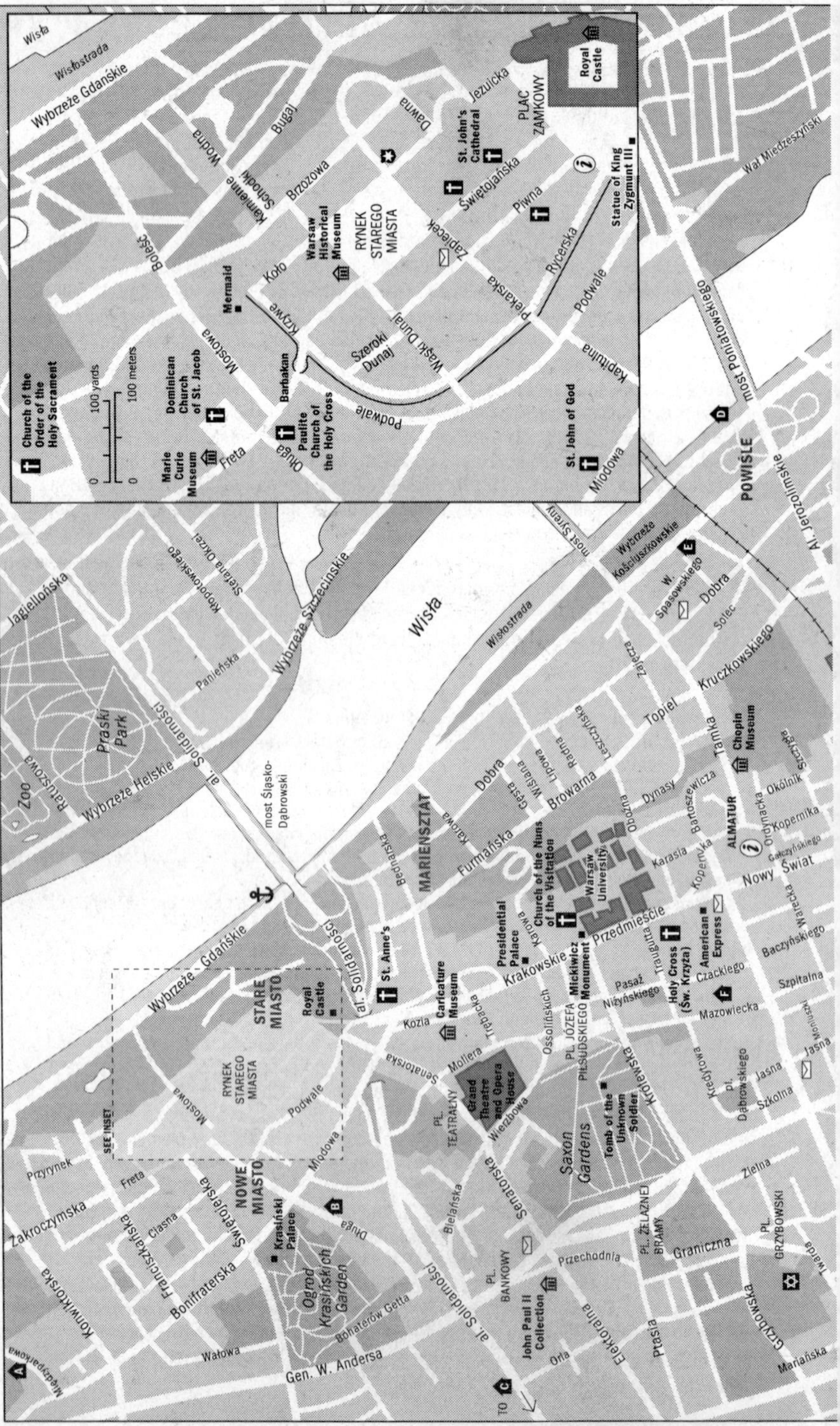

Wisła
Wisłostrada
Wybrzeże Gdańskie
Bugaj
Dawna
Jezuicka
Royal Castle
PLAC ZAMKOWY
St. John's Cathedral
Świętojańska
Statue of King Zygmunt III
Piwna
Brzozowa
Kamienne Schodki
Wodna
Bolesć
Warsaw Historical Museum
RYNEK STAREGO MIASTA
Zapiecek
Koło
Mermaid
Krzywe
Piekarska
Rycerska
Podwale
Wąski Dunaj
Szeroki Dunaj
Barbakan
Mostowa
Kapitulna
Church of the Order of the Holy Sacrament
Dominican Church of St. Jacob
0
100 yards
100 meters
Marie Curie Museum
Freta
Długa
Paulite Church of the Holy Cross
St. John of God
Miodowa
most Poniatowskiego
Wał Miedzeszyński
POWIŚLE
Al. Jerozolimskie
most Syreny
Wybrzeże Kościuszkowskie
W. Spasowskiego
Dobra
Solec
Kruczkowskiego
Topiel
Tamka
Chopin Museum
Szczyglia
Okólnik
Ordynacka
Kopernika
Gałczyńskiego
Nowy Świat
Warecka
Baczyńskiego
Szpitalna
Moniuszki
Jasna
Jagiellońska
Stefana Okrzei
Kłopotowskiego
Wybrzeże Szczecińskie
Panieńska
Praski Park
Ratuszowa
Zoo
Wybrzeże Helskie
al. Solidarności
most Śląsko-Dąbrowski
MARIENSZTAT
Bednarska
Karowa
Dobra
Browarna
Furmańska
Lipowa
Wiślana
Gęsta
Radna
Leszczyńska
Zajęcza
Dynasy
Oboźna
Bartoszewicza
Karasia
ALMATUR
Church of the Nuns of the Visitation
Warsaw University
Krakowskie Przedmieście
Presidential Palace
Mickiewicz Monument
American Express
Holy Cross (Św. Krzyża)
Traugutta
Pasaż Niżyńskiego
Czackiego
Mazowiecka
St. Anne's
Caricature Museum
Kozia
Trębacka
Ossolińskich
PL. JÓZEFA PIŁSUDSKIEGO
Królewska
Kredytowa
PL. Dąbrowskiego
Szkolna
Zielna
Wybrzeże Gdańskie
STARE MIASTO
Royal Castle
RYNEK STAREGO MIASTA
Mostowa
Podwale
SEE INSET
NOWE MIASTO
Miodowa
Senatorska
Moliera
PL. TEATRALNY
Grand Theatre and Opera House
Wierzbowa
Tomb of the Unknown Soldier
Saxon Gardens
Przyrynek
Freta
Zakroczymska
Świętojerska
Ciasna
Franciszkańska
Bonifraterska
Krasiński Palace
Długa
Ogród Krasińskich Garden
Bielańska
Senatorska
PL. BANKOWY
Przechodnia
PL. ŻELAZNEJ BRAMY
Graniczna
PL. GRZYBOWSKI
Twarda
Grzybowska
Ptasia
Elektoralna
John Paul II Collection
Orla
al. Solidarności
Bohaterów Getta
Gen. W. Andersa
Wałowa
Konwiktorska
Międzyparkowa
Mariańska
TO G
A
B
D
E
F

Warsaw
ACCOMMODATIONS
A Międzyparkowa Hostel
B Hotel Metalowcy
C Karolkowa Hostel
D Hotel Na Wodzie
E Hotel Belfer
F Hotel Mazowiecki
G Smolna Hostel
H Camping 1-2-3
I Camping Gromada
N
0 400 yards
0 400 meters
most Gen. Zygmunta Berlinga
Czerniakowska
Solec
Wioślarska
Gwardzistów
Rozbrat
Myśliwiecka
Łazienkowska
Szwoleżerów
29. Listopada
Kruczkowskiego
Śmigły-Rydz Park
Parliament (Sejm)
Canada
France
United States
United Kingdom
Ujazdowski Park
UJAZDÓW
al. Armii Ludowej
Agrykola
Botanical Garden
Old Orangery
Łazienki Park
Łazienski Palace
Chopin Monument
Al. Ujazdowskie
al. Szucha
Bagatela
Powiśle Railway Station
Military Museum
National Museum
Książęca
pl. Trzech Krzyży
Foksal
Smolna
Nowy Świat
Bracka
Krucza
Wilcza
Mokotowska
Koszykowa
Marszałkowska
L. Waryńskiego
pl. Konstytucji
Lwowska
Piękna
Hoża
Poznańska
Parkingowa
Zgoda
Orbis
Chmielna
Świętokrzyska
pl. Defilad
Palace of Culture and Science
CENTRUM
Śródmieście Railway Station
Warsaw Operetta
Marriott Hotel
Central Railway Station
Emilii Plater
Al. Jerozolimskie
TO INTERNATIONAL AIRPORT, H AND I
al. Jana Pawła II
Wojciecha Oczki
S. Noakowskiego
Warsaw Polytechnic University
al. Niepodległości
Nowowiejska
POLITECHNIKA
RONDO JAZDY POLSKIEJ
Park Marshal Józef Piłsudskiego
Lekarska
Filtrowa
Medical Academy
M. Langiewicza
Wawelska
Rektorska

ORIENTATION

Warsaw—Poland's main air and rail hub—sprawls over east-central Poland, 150km from the Belarussian border. The busy downtown area, **Śródmieście** is on the west riverbank of the **Wisła River,** which bisects the city. In the middle of it all, **Warszawa Centralna,** the main train station, lies on **al. Jerozolimskie**, between **al. Jana Pawła II** and **ul. Emilii Plater.** The nearby gargantuan Palace of Culture and Science hovers above **Parade Square** and its vast marketplace. A short walk along al. Jerozolimskie leads to the large intersection with **ul. Marszałkowska,** one of the city's main north-south avenues. This busy street leads north to **Ogród Saski** (Saxon Gardens) and the intersection serves as a major stop for most bus and tram lines. Al. Jerozolimskie continues east to the other main north-south avenue, **al. Ujazdowskie,** which intersects al. Jerozolimskie at **rondo Charles de Gaulle.** A left here runs north up **ul. Nowy Świat,** which becomes **ul. Krakówskie Przedmieście,** and leads directly to **Stare Miasto** (Old Town) and the Royal Palace. A right at rondo Charles de Gaulle leads to **al. Ujazdowskie,** which finds the Łazienski Palace by way of embassy row. Buy a **map** of the whole city, including the public transportation lines, from the tourist office in the back of the central train station's main hall.

PRACTICAL INFORMATION

TOURIST & FINANCIAL SERVICES

Tourist Offices: Informacji Turystycznej (IT), al. Jerozolimskie 54 (tel. 524 51 84; fax 654 24 47), inside the central train station. English-speaking staff provides **maps,** guidebooks, currency exchange, and hotel reservations. Open daily 9am-7pm. Also at pl. Zamkowy 1/13 (tel. 635 18 81; fax 831 04 64), by the entrance to Stare Miasto opposite the Royal Palace. Open M-F 9am-6pm, Sa 10am-6pm, Su 11am-6pm. Smaller offices at Zachodnia Station and the airport. English-language publications on sale include the indispensable *Warsaw Insider* (6zł) and the much less useful but occasionally interesting *Warsaw Voice* (6zł).

POLAND

Budget Travel: Almatur, ul. Kopernika 23 (tel. 826 35 12 or 826 26 39; fax 826 35 07), off ul. Nowy Świat. Sells international bus and ferry tickets as well as plane tickets at student discounts. Provides ISIC cards (32zł), and often has vouchers for hotels in major Polish cities. Open M-F 9am-6pm, Sa 10am-2pm. **Orbis,** ul. Bracka 16 (tel. 827 71 40 or 827 76 04; fax 827 76 05), entrance on al. Jerozolimskie near ul. Nowy Świat. Train, ferry, and bus tickets. Open M-F 8am-7pm, Sa 9am-3pm.

Embassies: Most near ul. Ujazdowskie. **Australia,** ul. Estońska 3/5 (tel. 617 60 81). Open M-Th 8:30am-1pm and 2-5pm. Visas: Piękna 2. Open M-F 8:45am-1pm. **Belarus,** ul. Ateńska 67 (tel. 617 39 54). **Canada,** ul. Matejki 1/5 (tel. 629 80 51). Open M-F 8am-4:30pm; visa department open 8:30-11am and 1-3pm. **Russia,** ul. Belwederska 49, bldg. C (tel. 621 34 53). Open W and F 8am-1pm. **South Africa,** ul. Koszykowa 54 (tel. 625 62 28). Open M-F 8am-12pm. **Ukraine,** al. Ujazdowskie 13 (tel. 629 32 01). Open M-F 10am-4pm. **U.K.,** al. Róż 1 (tel. 628 10 01). Open M-F 9am-noon and 2-4pm. **U.S.,** al. Ujazdowskie 29/31 (tel. 628 30 41). Open M-F 8:30am-5pm.

Currency Exchange: At hotels, banks, tourist offices, and private *kantori* (which have the best rates) throughout the city. **24hr. exchange** is available at Warszawa Centralna and the international airport departures area. For **traveler's checks** and **cash advances,** head to one of the branches of the **Bank PKO S.A.:** pl. Bankowy 2 (tel. 637 10 61), in the blue skyscraper; ul. Mazowiecka 14 (tel. 661 25 59); or ul. Grójecka 1/3 (tel. 658 82 17), in Hotel Sobieski. AmEx/Visa traveler's checks are cashed into dollars or *złoty* for a 1% commission. MC/Visa cash advances. All branches open M-F 8am-6pm, Sa 10am-2pm. Most branches also have Cirrus/MC ATMs**. 24hr. ATMs** are located at ul. Mazowiecka 14 and inside Hotel Sobieski, ul. Grójecka 1/3. 24hr. Euronet ATMs, which accept most major credit cards, are popping up everywhere.

American Express: ul. Krakówskie Przedmieście 11 (tel. 551 51 52; fax 828 75 56). Holds cardholders' mail and provides members with emergency cash advances. Exchange cash and AmEx traveler's checks for no commission. For **Poste Restante,** address mail to

"American Express Travel" (PL 00-069). Open M-F 9am-6pm. Services also available at the **Marriott Hotel.** Open M-F 8am-8pm, Sa-Su 10am-6pm. **24hr. AmEx ATMs** at American Express and at the airport.

Western Union: ul. Krakówskie Przedmieście 55 (tel. 826 20 21), in Prosper Bank S.A. Open M-F 8am-6pm, Sa 9am-1pm.

LOCAL SERVICES

Luggage Storage: At Warszawa Centralna train station, below the main hall. Lockers come in 3 sizes: "A" (6zł per day), "B" (9zł per day), and "C" (17zł per day). Open 24hr. Storage also available in Zachodnia Station; 4zł for a large pack.

English Bookstore: American Bookstore, ul. Koszykowa 55 (tel. 660 56 37; fax 660 56 38; www.abe.com.pl). Good but pricey selection of fiction, reference books, and periodicals. Open M-F 11am-7pm, Sa 11am-6pm. **Empik Megastore,** ul. Nowy Świat 15/17, on the corner of al. Jerozolimskie and ul. Nowy Świat (tel. 627 06 50), stocks a wide array of international newspapers. Open M-Sa 9am-10pm, Su 11am-7pm. AmEx/MC/Visa.

Gay and Lesbian Hotline: The Lambda Center Information Line (tel. 628 52 22) is available in English and Polish. They'll tell you what's up and where. Tu-W 6-9pm, F 4-10pm. Located at Tzernikowska 178 (#16), but call ahead before visiting.

Laundromat: ul. Karmelicka 17 (tel. 831 73 17). Take bus #180 north from ul. Marszałkowska toward Żoliborz, and get off at ul. Anielewicza; backtrack one block to ul. Karmelicka. Detergent 2.50zł. Wash and dry 19.50zł. Open M-F 9am-5pm, Sa 9am-1pm. Call ahead to make a reservation. Some English spoken.

EMERGENCY & COMMUNICATIONS

24hr. Pharmacy: Apteka Grabowski (tel. 825 13 72), at the central train station.

Medical Assistance: American Medical Center, ul. Wilcza 23 m. 29 (tel. 622 04 89; 24hr. emergency tel. 0 602 24 30 24; fax 622 04 97). Provides English-language medical and dental referrals, as well as guidance through the Byzantine Polish medical system. Call in an emergency and they will meet you at the hospital. General practice clinic open M-Sa 8am-6pm. **24hr. service and ambulance: Central Emergency Station**, ul. Hoża 56 (tel. 999 or 628 24 24).

Post Office: ul. Świętokrzyska 31/33 (tel. 826 75 11). The computer at the entrance doles out tickets; take a number and wait your turn. For stamps and letters, push "D." For packages, push "F." For **Poste Restante,** go in the room to the left and push "C" at the computer there Pick up at window #11 or 12. Letters abroad cost 5.90zł (20g), 6.30zł (20-50g), 6.90zł (50-100g), 9.20zł (100-250g). **Fax** bureau (fax 30 00 21). 14.10zł for the first 3min., 0.60zł for every min. afterwards. Open 24hr. **Postal code:** 00-001.

Internet Access: Lameriada Internet Cafe, ul. Piękna 68A (tel. 622 33 77). Only has five computers, but more may be added soon. 1hr. 8zł, 30min. 6zł, 15min. 3zł. Coffee 4.50zł. Tea 3.50zł. 0.5L *Żywiec* 5zł. Open M-Sa 11am-midnight, Su 1pm-midnight. **Casablanca,** ul. Krakówskie Przedmieście 4/6 (tel. 828 14 47; email cafe@cyberia.com.pl; www.cyberia.com.pl). To the right of Burger King. 8zł for 30min., 12zł per hr. Open daily 9am-midnight. **PDI,** ul. Nowogrodzka 12 (tel. 622 66 11; www.pdi.net). Through the gate and to the left; it's in the basement. Open M-F 9am-9pm.

Telephones: At the post office. Tokens and **phone cards** available at the post office and in many kiosks. **Directory assistance:** 913. **Phone code:** (0)22.

ACCOMMODATIONS

Rooms become scarce and prices rise in June, July, and August. Hostels are the first to go, so reserve at least a week in advance. Differences in hotel prices often do not reflect a difference in quality; some hotels just aim for the business traveler and charge more. For help finding **private rooms,** check with **Syrena,** ul. Krucza 17 (tel. 628 75 40 or 628 56 98), off al. Jerozolimskie. The staff speaks English. (Open M-Sa 9am-7pm, Su 9am-5pm. Singles start at 61zł; doubles at 84zł.) The city tourist offices (see **Tourist Offices,** p. 410) maintain a list of all accommodations in the city and can help with reservations. Hotels, and especially hostels, have many cancellations and no-shows; keep checking back even if they claim to be booked.

HOSTELS

Schronisko Młodzieżowe (HI), ul. Karolkowa 53a (tel. 632 88 29). Take tram #22 or 24 west from al. Jerozolimskie or the train station to "Okopowa." Cross at the corner near Pizza Hut and continue down al. Solidarności; the hostel will be to your right–follow the green IYH signs. Dorms are often overrun by school groups; the smaller rooms are more sedate. Kitchen and storage facilities, sterile bathrooms, and gorgeous showers. Doubles and triples include TV and fridge. 140 beds total. 7- to 14-bed dorms 21zł, non-members 28zł; bed in a triple or quad 38zł; singles 50zł; with bath 120zł; doubles 80zł, with shower 100zł. Sheets 3.50zł. Lockout 10am-5pm. Curfew 11pm.

Schronisko Młodzieżowe (HI), ul. Smolna 30, top floor (tel. 827 89 52), across from the National Museum. Close to the train station; take any tram headed east 3 stops to "Muzeum Narodawe." In a great location and accordingly busy all summer long: bathrooms are crowded and not sufficient for 120 people. Kitchen and storage available. Singles 40zł; bed in a double or triple 36zł; dorms 19.50zł, non-members 26zł. Sheets 2.50zł. 3-day max. stay. Call 2 weeks ahead. Lockout 10am-4pm. Curfew 11pm.

Schronisko Młodzieżowe (HI), ul. Międzyparkowa 4/6 (tel. 831 17 66), between 2 parks near the river. Take tram #2, 6, or 18 north from ul. Marszałkowska to "K.K.S. Polonia." It's on your left as you continue down the road. The least formal of the hostels in town, located in a tiny building in an old sports complex. The rooms–like the exterior–are a bit rugged, but they do the job; the same goes for the bathrooms. Caters to school groups and attracts few foreigners. 44 beds in 6-8 person dorms: under 26 10zł; otherwise 25zł. Sheets 5zł. Open Apr. 15-Oct. 15. Lockout 10am-5pm. Curfew 11pm.

HOTELS

Hotel Mazowiecki, ul. Mazowiecka 10 (tel. 682 20 65 or 682 20 69; tel/fax. 827 23 65). Hidden away a little more than a block from ul. Krakówskie Przedmieście off ul. Świętokrzyska. One of the poshest budget hotels in the downtown area, with hardwood floors and colorful carpeting. Mildew-free bathrooms. Bed in a double 65zł; bed in a triple or quad 50zł.

Hotel Metalowcy, ul. Długa 29 (tel. 831 40 20; fax 635 31 38). Take bus #175 from the train station to "pl. Krasińskich," backtrack to ul. Długa and turn right. Affordable and in a great location. Clean rooms (if you don't mind the occasional odd smell) and passable communal bathrooms. Small singles 47zł, with private bath 56zł; roomier doubles 88zł; quads with bath 144zł.

Hotel Belfer, ul. Wybrzeże Kościuszkowskie 31/33 (tel. 625 55 62; reservation tel. 625 26 00; fax 625 51 85). From the train station, take any tram east to "Most Poniatowskiego," then go north with the river on your right along the southbound lanes of Wybrzeże Kościuszkowskie. Cleaner, brighter, roomier, and correspondingly more expensive than Metalowiec. Some rooms have nice rooftop views. Singles 90zł, with bath 129zł; doubles 128zł, with bath 170zł. AmEx/MC/Visa.

Hotel Na Wodzie, ul. Wybrzeże Kościuszkowskie (tel. 628 58 83). From Most Poniatowskiego (see **Hotel Belfer,** above), walk down to the Wisła. Aldona and Anita, the twin ships that comprise Na Wodzie, will be moored to you left. Singles 65zł; bunk-bed doubles 85zł.

CAMPING

Camping "123," ul. Bitwy Warszawskiej 1920r. 15/17 (tel. 822 91 21; tel/fax. 823 37 48), by the main bus station. Take bus #127 to "Zachodnia" and cross the street at the traffic circle. Bitwy Warszawskiej is to the left. Close to downtown, well-shaded by trees, and near a popular swimming pool, this expansive complex includes a small hotel and bungalows. 10zł per person, children 4-10 5zł. Small tent space 8zł, large 10zł. Bungalows: double 64zł, with bath 95zł; triple 85zł, with bath 120zł. Hotel: double 95zł; triple 117zł; quad 137zł. English spoken.

Camping Gromada, ul. Żwirki i Wigury 32 (tel. 825 43 91). Take bus #175 (dir.: "Port Lotniczy") to "Akademia Medyczna." Cross the street, turn left, and follow the cheerful signs to the crowded campsite. 10zł per person; 6-9.30zł per tent space. Electricity 11zł. English spoken. Open Apr.-Sept.

FOOD

Countless food stands dot the square beneath the Palace of Culture, and many more can be found beneath the train station. For a decent meal, milk bars (*bar mleczny*) or proletarian-style **cafeterias** are an inexpensive and generally tasty option. There is a **24hr. grocery** at the central train station, as well as **Delikatesy,** ul. Nowy Świat 53 (tel. 826 03 22; open 7am-5am). Both are oases for late-night club crawlers and jet-lagged snackers. Some restaurants in Warsaw sell fish, poultry, and meat by weight. Ask in advance how much the average weight is to avoid a nasty surprise when the check arrives.

RESTAURANTS

Pod Samsonem, ul. Freta 3/5 (tel. 831 17 88). Between Stare Miasto and Nowe Miasto. Hearty Polish-Jewish cuisine is supposed to make you big and strong like Samson. Interior is decorated with photos of Jewish life in pre-war Warsaw. Meals 20-30zł. Open daily 10am-10pm. AmEx.

Bong Sen, ul. Poznańska 12 (tel. 621 27 13), just south of the train station (Poznańska runs parallel to al. Marszałkowska.) The decidedly Polish waitstaff won't create any illusion that you're in the Far East, but the authentic Vietnamese and Chinese cuisine will sure fool your mouth. Entrees 19-30zł. Open daily 11am-10pm. MC/Visa/AmEx.

Restauracja Ekologiczna "Nowe Miasto," Rynek Nowego Miasta 13/15 (tel. 831 43 79). Warsaw's first natural foods restaurant. Organically grown vegetarian entrees 20-50zł. Whole grain desserts, healthy soups, a variety of crepes, and an ensemble cast of salads, including *Juliet* and *Greek Theater* (19zł). Polish beer (0.5L *Żywiec* 9zł) and German wine. Outdoor seating available. Live music nightly 7-10pm. Open daily 10am-midnight.

Bar Mleczny Familijny, ul. Nowy Świat 39. A giant version of a Polish grandmother's kitchen. Full meals 2-6zł. Open M-F 7am-8pm, Sa-Su 9am-5pm.

Bar Uniwersytecki, ul. Krakówskie Przedmieście 16/18. As Polish and as fattening as it gets. Salad 1-2zł, soups 1zł, full meals 2-4zł. Open M-F 7am-8pm, Sa-Su 9am-5pm.

Zapiecek, ul. Piwna 34/36 (tel. 831 56 93), at the corner of ul. Piwna and ul. Zapiecek in Stare Miasto. German-tinged Polish cuisine; very tasty, but entrees are less than filling without side orders. Entrees 7-18zł, side orders 1-4zł. Outdoor dining. Open daily 11am-11pm. AmEx/MC/Visa.

Restauracja-Kawiarnia "Chmielna," (tel. 827 14 84), at the corner of ul. Chmielna and ul. Zgoda. Walk down al. Jerozolimskie from the city center toward the river, then turn left on ul. Krucza. Outdoor dining on a lively, pedestrianized street. Veggie lasagna 9.40zł; salads 4-7zł; entrees 6-19zł. Open M-Sa 11am-10pm.

Restauracja Boruta, ul. Freta 38 (tel. 831 61 97), on Rynek Nowego Miasta. Dine outside under the "Golden American" umbrellas. Entrees 15-35zł. Vegetarian menu. Open daily 11am until the last guest leaves. AmEx/MC/Visa.

Pizzeria Casa Mia, ul. Poznańska 37, just south of the Palace of Culture. A wide variety of pizzas prepared just for you. Pizzas 11-20zł. Open daily 10am-10pm.

Pod Herbami, ul. Piwna 21/23 (tel. 831 64 47). Looks like a medieval tavern, tastes like a Polish restaurant. Grilled salmon and other specialties run 20-30zł. Open M-Th and Su 11am-11pm, F-Sa 11am-1am. AmEx/MC/Visa.

Lody, Nowomiejska 9. The most popular ice cream shop in Stare Miasto. 1.20zł per scoop, with flavors like "smurf" and "tiramisu." Open daily 10am-7pm.

CAFES

Pożegnanie z Afryka, ul. Freta 4/6. The name means "Out of Africa," although most of the myriad coffees are actually South American; regardless, it's the best in town. Worth the wait for one of the 6 tables. Coffee 6-7zł. Open daily 11am-9pm.

Kawiarnia Bazyliszek, Rynek Starego Miasta 9/11/13 (tel. 831 32 35). A fancy cafe with relaxed outdoor seating. Great views of the restored splendor of Stare Miasto and the tourists here to see it. Tortes 3zł. Coffee 2zł. Open daily 11am-11pm.

Gwiazdeczka, ul. Piwna 40/42 (tel. 831 94 63), in Stare Miasto. The menu is full of innocent snacks and coffees (3-8zł). Beer and cocktails are ever-tempting alternatives (large *Żywiec* 5.50zł). Open daily 9am-10pm.

Casablanca, ul. Krakówskie Przedmieście 4/6 (tel. 828 14 47; www.cyberia.com.pl). To the right of Burger King. A little too Euro-chic for some, but the coffee (7zł) is a perfect companion for web-surfing. (see **Internet Access,** p. 411). Open daily 9am-midnight.

SIGHTS

Razed to something resembling the surface of the moon, Warsaw had to be almost entirely rebuilt after WWII. Thanks to the wonders of Soviet upkeep, though, most of the buildings look much older than their 50 years. Sights are very spread out, and exploring the city in full takes several days.

STARE & NOWE MIASTO

Warsaw's postwar reconstruction shows its finest face in the narrow, cobblestoned streets and colorful facades of **Stare Miasto** (Old Town), at the very end of ul. Krakówskie Przedmieście in pl. Zamkowy. To get here, take bus #175 or E3 from the city center to "Miodowa." At the right side of the entrance to Stare Miasto stands the impressive **Royal Castle** (Zamek Królewski). In the Middle Ages, it was home to the Dukes of Mazovia. In the late 16th century it replaced Kraków's Wawel as the official royal residence; still later it became the presidential palace. Burned down in September 1939 and plundered by the Nazis, the castle was elevated to martyrdom by Polish freedom fighters. Many Varsovians risked their lives hiding its priceless works in the hope that one day they could be returned. After Poland gained independence in 1945, the castle's plans and some of the treasures were retrieved, and for 30 years, thousands of Poles, Polish expats, and dignitaries worldwide sent contributions in hopes of restoring this symbol of national pride. Work began in 1971 and was completed in 1984. The kingly abode is an impressive example of restoration; visitors will marvel that anything so regal was built in the 1970s (see **Museums,** below). The **statue of Zygmunta III Wazy** stands proudly above the square in front of the castle. Constructed in 1644 to honor the king who transferred the capital from Kraków to Warsaw, it stood for 300 years before being destroyed in WWII. The king's crusading figure, now rebuilt, has watched over pl. Zamkowy for centuries; his vigil continues today, albeit over youngsters drinking beer on the steps below.

Jus up ul. Świętojańska from pl. Zamkowy sits Warsaw's oldest church, **St. John's Cathedral** (Katedra św. Jana). Decimated in the 1944 Uprising, the church was rebuilt after the war in Vistulan Gothic style. The 1339 case against the Order of Teutonic Knights, who had broken a pact made with Duke of Mazovia Konrad Mazowiecki, is hidden within its walls. Underneath are the **crypts,** wherein rest the dukes of Mazovia and such famous Poles as Nobel Laureate Henryk Sienkiewicz, author of *Quo Vadis*, and Gabriel Narutowicz, the first president of independent Poland. A side altar contains the tomb of Stefan Cardinal Wyszyński, primate of Poland from 1948-1981. (Open daily dawn-dusk, except during services.)

Ul. Świętojańska takes you past the beer gardens, flocks of pigeons, artists selling their wares, and tourists milling about in the restored Renaissance and Baroque **Old Town Square** (Rynek Starego Miasta). A stone plaque at the entrance commemorates its reconstruction, finished in 1953-54, and recalls the square's prewar history. On the *rynek*'s southeast side at #3/9, **Dom Pod Bazyliszkiem** immortalizes the Stare Miasto basilisk, a legendary reptile with a fatal breath whose stare brought instant death to all who crossed its path. Although the houses around the *rynek* were razed during the 1944 Uprising, large fragments of the ruins were used to reconstruct of many of the buildings.

Ul. Krzywe Koło (Crooked Wheel) starts in the northeast corner of the *rynek* and leads to the newly restored **Barbakan,** a rare example of 16th-century Polish fortification and a popular spot for locals and tourists to rest their feet to the tune of street performers. The **Little Insurgent Monument,** to the left near ul. Kilińskiego, honors the youngest soldiers of the 1944 Uprising. Around the barbakan are the remains of the walls that used to enclose Stare Miasto; they are marked by the **Mermaid** (Warszawska Syrenka), the symbol of the city.

The barbakan opens onto ul. Freta, the edge of Nowe Miasto. Despite its name, this is the city's second-oldest district. Also destroyed during WWII, its 18th- and 19th-century buildings have enjoyed an expensive facelift. The great physicist and chemist **Maria Skłodowska-Curie,** winner of two Nobel prizes, was born at ul. Freta 16 in 1867 (see **Museums,** p. 418). Ul. Freta leads to **New Town Square** (Rynek Nowego Miasta), the site of the **Church of the Holy Sacrament** (Kościół Sakramentek), founded in 1688 to commemorate King Jan III Sobieski's 1683 victory over the Turks (see **History** p. 399). Its stark interior is only a shade of its past glory, but the Baroque dome still inspires awe. (Open daily dawn-dusk.)

ROYAL WAY (TRAKT KRÓLEWSKI)

The 4km Royal Way, Warsaw's most attractive thoroughfare, begins on **pl. Zamkowy** at the entrance to Stare Miasto and continues along **ul. Krakówskie Przedmieście.** The Royal Way, so named because it leads south in the general direction of Kraków, Poland's former capital, is lined with palaces, churches, and convents built when the royal family moved to Warsaw. Traffic and crowds of tourists now detract from its once regal splendor. On the left as you leave pl. Zamkowy, **St. Anne's Church** (Kościół św. Anny), with a large figure of Christ above the entrance and beautiful gilded altar, dates from the 15th century but was rebuilt in the Baroque style. (Open daily dawn-dusk.) Farther down the street, a monument to Adam Mickiewicz, Poland's national poet (see **Literature & Arts,** p. 401), gazes toward pl. Piłsudskiego and Saxon Garden (Ogród Saski), which contains the **Tomb of the Unknown Soldier** (Grób Nieznanego Żołnierza). Urns hold earth from battlefields marked by Polish blood and the graves of Polish soldiers murdered by the Soviets in Katyń. The **changing of the guard** takes place on Sundays and national holidays at noon.

Warsaw is a requisite pilgrimage sight for **Fryderyk Chopin** fans (see **Literature & Arts,** p. 401). Chopin spent his childhood in the neighborhood near ul. Krakówskie Przedmieście, and gave his first public concert in **Pałac Radziwiłłów** (a.k.a. **Pałac Namiestnikowski**) #46/48, the building guarded by four stone lions. Today the Polish presidential mansion, an armed guard stands watch alongside his feline counterparts. A block down the road, the **Church of the Visitation Nuns** (Kościół Wizytek) once resounded with the romantic ivory pounding of the mop-topped composer. (Open daily dawn-dusk.) **Pałac Czapskich,** Chopin's last home before he left for France in 1830, provided the setting for many of his best-known compositions. Now the palace houses the **Academy of Fine Arts** and **Chopin's Drawing Room** (Salonik Chopinów; tel. 826 62 51). Enter through the gate at ul. Krakówskie Przedmieście 5; the entrance is on the left. (Open M-F 10am-2pm, closed holidays. 3zł, students 2zł.) Chopin died abroad at the age of 39 and was buried in Paris, but his heart belongs to Poland; it now rests in an urn in the left nave of **Holy Cross Church** (Kościół św. Krzyża). Other Chopin sights include the Chopin Museum (p. 418) and his birthplace, Żelazowa Wola (p. 421).

In front of Kościól św. Krzyża, a complex of rebuilt palaces on the left belongs to the **University of Warsaw** (Uniwersytet Warszawski), founded in 1816. **Pałac Kazimierzowski,** at the end of the alley leading from the main entrance to the university, now houses the rector's offices, but was once the seat of the School of Knighthood. Its alumni record includes General Tadeusz Kościuszko, who fought in the American Revolutionary War and later led an unsuccessful revolt against Russia. The **Copernicus Monument** (Pomnik Mikołaja Kopernika), an image of the famous astronomer, and **Pałac Staszica,** home of the Polish Academy of Sciences, mark the end of ul. Krakówskie Przedmieście. Trakt Królewski continues as **ul. Nowy Świat** (New World St.). The name of the street dates to the mid-17th century, when a new settlement was started here, composed mainly of working-class people. It was not until the 18th century that the aristocracy started moving in, embellishing it with ornate manors and residences. Today, there are wider and busier streets in the city, but none as enjoyable for a walk.

ŁAZIENSKI PARK

South of Stare Miasto along al. Ujazdowskie and Trakt Królewski, sprawls **Łazienski Park.** The park and the palaces within were built in the late 18th century for Stanisław August Poniatowski, the last king of Poland, but peacocks and swans rule the roost today. Take bus #116 or 195 from ul. Nowy Świat or #119 from the city center south to Bagatela. The park is just across the street. (Open daily dawn-dusk.) Near this entrance is the **Chopin Monument** (Pomnik Chopina), site of free concerts every Sunday at noon and 4pm from spring to autumn. Farther into the park is the striking Neoclassical **Pałac Łazienkowski,** also called **Palace on Water** (Pałac na Wodzie). This, like most palaces in the park, is the creation of benefactor King Stanisław August and his beloved architect Dominik Merlini. Galleries of 17th- and 18th-century art wait inside. (Open Tu-Su 9:30am-4pm, barring rain. *Kassa* closes at 3:15pm. 10zł, students 7zł. Guided tour in English 55zł.) Nearby, the **Old Orangery** (Stara Pomarańczarnia) served as not only a greenhouse for orange trees, but also as a theater and servants' quarters. **Stanisławowski Theater** celebrated its grand opening on September 6, 1788. In 1791, Stanisław August donated the theater to Wojciech Bogusławski, the "father of Polish theater." Bogusławski accepted the gift and opened the theater to the general public. In the west wing of Stara Pomarańczarnia, the 140 sculptures of **Gallery of Polish Sculpture** (Galeria Rzeźby Polskiej) trace the evolution of the genre from the end of the 16th century through 1939. (Open Tu-Su 9:30am-3:30pm. 5zł, students 3zł; guided tour in Polish 35zł, in English 55zł.) Just north of Łazienski along al. Ujazdowskie are the peaceful **Botanical Gardens.** (Open June-Aug. M-Th 9am-8pm, F-Su 10am-8pm; Sept. daily 10am-6pm; Oct. daily 10am-4pm. *Kassa* closes one hour before the gardens. 3.50zł, students 1.50zł.) Continuing north along al. Ujazdowskie, turn right on ul. Matejki and you will reach the **Sejm** (Parliament) and Senate building, built in 1925 and rebuilt after WWII. (Inside closed to the public.)

THE FORMER WARSAW GHETTO

Still referred to as the Ghetto, the modern **Muranów** neighborhood (literally, "walled"), north of the city center, holds few vestiges of the nearly 400,000 Jews—one-third of the city's population—who lived here prior to WWII. The **Umschlagplatz,** at the corner of ul. Dzika and ul. Stawki (take tram #35 from ul. Marszałkowska to "Dzika") was the railway platform where the Nazis gathered 300,000 of the Jews for transport to the death camps. A large monument, with writing in Polish, Hebrew, and Yiddish, now stands in its place. With the monument to your left, continue down Stawki and turn right on ul. DuBois, which becomes ul. Zamenhofa. You will pass a mound of earth with a stone monument on top marking the location of the underground command bunker of the **1943 ghetto uprising.** Further on, in a large park to your right stands the large **Monument of the Ghetto Heroes** (Pomnik Bohaterów). Nearby, a marker commemorates the **Relief Council for Jews,** the only organization working to rescue Jews from the Holocaust was sponsored and funded by its government in exile. Signs near the Monument indicate the future location of the **Museum of the History of Polish Jews.**

Continue along ul. Zamenhofa in the same direction, and turn right on ul. Anielewicza, continuing 5 blocks until you reach the **Jewish Cemetery** (Cmentarz Żydowski; tel. 838 26 22), in the western corner of Muranów (alternatively, take tram #22 from the city center to "Cm. Żydowski"). Thickly wooded and stretching for kilometers, the cemetery is the final resting place of 200,000 of Warsaw's Jews. Sadly, many of the tombstones are shrouded in undergrowth and thousands have long since disappeared. (Open M-Th 9am-3pm, F 9am-1pm. 3zł.)

The beautifully reconstructed **Nożyk Synagogue,** ul. Twarda 6 (tel. 620 43 24), north of the Pałac Kultury, on the other hand, is a living remnant of Warsaw's Jewish life. From the city center, take any tram north along ul. Jana Pawła II to "Rondo ONZ." Turn right on Twarda and left at the Jewish Theater (Teatr Żydowski). The only synagogue to survive the war, it was spared for use as a stable for the Wehrmacht. Today it serves as the spiritual home for the few hundred observant Jews who remain in Warsaw. (Open M-F 10am-3pm, Sa 9am-noon; staff will sometimes admit late arrivals. Morning and evening services daily; contact the synagogue for a schedules. 5zł.) The complex of buildings surrounding the old synagogue also houses **Our Roots,** ul. Twarda 6 (tel./fax 620 05 56), a Jewish travel agency that arranges English-language tours of Jewish Warsaw, Auschwitz, Treblinka, and Majdanek. (Open M-F 9:30am-1:30pm. Tours US$25-70.)

Early in the occupation of Warsaw, the Nazis confined Jews to the Ghetto, building a wall around the entire neighborhood. A small section of the **original ghetto wall** still stands between two apartment buildings on ul. Sienna and ul. Złota, just west of al. Jana Pawła II and near Warszawa Centralna station. Enter the courtyard at ul. Sienna 55; the wall is on the left. As the plaque indicates, two missing bricks now compose part of the Holocaust Memorial Museum in Washington, D.C. The ghetto was liquidated in 1943 after its residents, with minimal arms and resources, revolted against their captors.

COMMERCIAL DISTRICT

The center of Warsaw's commercial district, southwest of Stare Miasto and adjacent to the train station is dominated by the 70-story Stalinist Gothic **Palace of Culture and Science** (Pałac Kultury i Nauki; a.k.a "The Wedding Cake"), ul. Marszałkowska. Locals claim the view from the top is the best in Warsaw. Why? It's the only place from which you can't see the building. In reality, the Palace of Culture, while certainly not beautiful, is reviled more as a symbol of Soviet domination than for its aesthetics. The palatial eyesore houses over 3000 offices, exhibition and conference facilities, three theaters, several cinemas, a shopping center, a cafe, and two museums. (30th floor panorama open daily 9am-6pm. 7.50zł.) The **Museum of Evolution** (Museum Ewolucji; tel. 656 66 37; www.paleo.par.pl/museum/museum.htm.) has a collection of dinosaur fossils culled from a joint Polish-Mongolian expedition in the 1970s. There are also specimens of birds from the Amazons, some thought now to be extinct. (Open Tu-Sa 8am-4pm, Su 10am-2:30pm. 4zł, students 3zł.) The **Museum of Technology** (Muzeum Techniki; tel. 656 67 47) features an interesting exhibit on historic automobiles next to a less enthralling display on pneumatic valves. It also houses a **planetarium.** (Open Tu and Th 9am-5pm, W and F-Sa 9am-4pm, Su 10am-5pm. 4zł, students 2zł; planetarium 1zł.) Below, **pl. Defilad** (Parade Sq.), Europe's largest square (yes, even bigger than Moscow's Red Square) swarms with freelance bazaar capitalists.

POLAND

WILANÓW

After his coronation in 1677, King Jan III Sobieski bought the sleepy village of Milanowo, had its existing mansion rebuilt into a Baroque palace, and named the new residence Villa Nova (in Polish *Wilanów*). Over the years, a long line of Polish aristocrats have made the palace their home. One of the bluebloods, Duke Stanisław Kostka Potocki, thought it might be nice to share it with his subjects. In 1805, he opened it to visitors, thus founding one of the first public museums in Poland. Since then, **Pałac Wilanowski** (tel. 842 81 01) has functioned both as a museum and as a residence for the highest ranking guests of the Polish state. Inside are lovely frescoed rooms, countless 17th- to 19th-century portraits, and extravagant royal apartments. The 15zł/18zł ticket is technically for a spot in a slow-moving Polish-language tour, but it is better to break off and explore on your own (signs along the way in Polish, English, French, and Russian). To get here, take bus #180, 410, or 414 from ul. Marszałkowska, or bus #130 or 519 from the train station south to "Wilanów." Cross the street; the road to the palace will be to your right. (Open June 15-Sept. 15 M and W-Sa 9:30am-2:30pm, Su 9:30am-4:30pm; Sept. 16-June 14 9:30am-2:30pm. 15zł, students 8zł. Admission and guided tour for fewer than 5 people in English, French, German, Russian, Italian, or Spanish 100zł; for 6-35 people, 20zł per person.) The surrounding **gardens** form strict, formal patterns and feature an army of bottle-shaped topiary creations. (Open M and W-F 9:30am-dusk. 3zł, students 2zł.) Head down the steps to watch the lazy river among less sculpted greenery. The **Poster Museum** (Muzeum Plakatu; tel. 842 48 48; tel./fax 842 26 06), next to the palace, displays over 450 of its collection of 50,000 **posters** from the last century, from Soviet propaganda to old movie posters. (Open Tu-F 10am-4pm, Sa-Su 10am-5pm. 7zł, students 5zł; W free.)

PRAGA

The **Praga** neighborhood, connected to the Wisła from Stare Miasto by the Śląsko-Dąbrowski bridge *(most)*, offers a Victorian contrast to the contemporary architecture of the city center. Take tram #4 from ul. Marszałkowska to "Park Praski." To one side is the massive **Cathedral of St. Michael and St. Florian,** completed in 1902 and rebuilt after World War II. (Open daily dawn-dusk. Free.) On the other side of al. Solidarności is the lush **Park Praski,** which leads to the **Warsaw Zoo.** (Open daily 9am-7pm. *Kassa* closes at 6pm. 8zł, students 4zł.) A short walk farther along al. Solidarności ("Dw. Wileński" stop) leads to the **Russian Orthodox Church** (Katedra Kościóła Prawosławnego), a five-domed structure with a Byzantine layout and Renaissance facade. The traditional gold interior, including the elaborate iconostatis, is magnificent. (Open dawn-dusk. Sunday liturgy at 7:30, 8:30, and 10am.) A short walk due south with the river on your right will bring you to one of the universe's largest bazaars at ul. Targowa 54. (Open Apr.-Sept. M-F 6am-7pm, Oct.-Mar. M-F 7am-6pm.)

MUSEUMS

Royal Castle (Zamek Królewski), pl. Zamkowy 4 (tel. 657 21 78; www.zamek-krolewski.art.pl). Reconstructed just 20 years ago, the palace recreates the world of Poland's kings. Paintings, artifacts, and the stunning Royal Apartments are a sight to behold. Open M and Su 11am-6pm, Tu-Sa 10am-6pm. Tickets and guides at the *kassa*, inside the castle courtyard. *Kassa* open M and Su 10:50am-5pm, Tu-Sa 9:50am-5pm. 14zł, students 7zł. Tours 50zł extra.

John Paul II Collection, pl. Bankowy 3/5 (tel. 620 21 81, secretary tel. 620 27 25), in the old Stock Exchange and Bank of Poland building. Over 400 impressive paintings from a single private collection. Artists include Dalí, Titian, Rembrandt, Van Gogh, Goya, Renoir, and others. One of the most significant pieces is a massive mural of the Crucifixion by the Polish painter Gerson. Open Tu-Su 10am-5pm. *Kassa* open until 4pm. 5zł, children under 11 3zł. For a guide in Polish, add 1zł per person.

National Museum (Muzeum Narodowe), al. Jerozolimskie 3 (tel. 629 30 93). Founded in 1862 as a museum of fine arts and converted into a national museum in 1915, this is Poland's largest museum. Gives an impressive illustration of the evolution of Polish art while also housing a Gallery of Medieval Art and a Gallery of European Art, which include 14th- to 18th-century Italian works, 15th- to 16th-century German art, and 17th century Dutch and Flemish paintings. Open Tu-W and F 10am-4pm, Th noon-5pm, Sa-Su 10am-5pm. Closed Monday and the day after public holidays. 7zł, students 4zł, Sa free. Wheelchair accessible.

Museum of Pawiak Prison (Muzeum Więzienia Pawiak), ul. Dzielna 24/26 (tel. 831 13 17). Built in the 1830s as a model prison for common criminals, Pawiak later served as Gestapo headquarters under the Nazis. From 1939-1944, over 100,000 Poles were imprisoned and tortured here; 37,000 were executed and another 60,000 were transferred to concentration camps. The Nazis dynamited the prison during the 1944 Warsaw Uprising and it has never been fully rebuilt. Housed in a small, reconstructed section of the prison, the museum displays photographic exhibits and several intact cells. German, Polish, and English captions. Open W 9am-5pm, Th and Sa 9am-4pm, F 10am-5pm, Su 10am-4pm. Donation requested. Children under 14 not admitted.

Fryderyk Chopin Museum (Muzeum Fryderyka Chopina), ul. Okólnik 1 (tel. 882 74 71, ext. 34 or 35), enter from ul. Tamka. A small but fascinating collection of original letters, scores, paintings, and keepsakes, including the great composer's last piano (see **Literature & Art,** p. 401). Open May-Sept. M, W, F 10am-5pm, Th noon-6pm, Sa-Su 10am-2pm; closed holidays. 4zł, students 2zł. Audio guides 4zł.

POLAND

Polish Military Museum (Muzeum Wojska Polskiego), al. Jerozolimskie 3 (tel. 629 52 71 or 629 52 72). Could equip its own army with its collection of Polish weaponry and uniforms through the ages. Documents the nation's fight for independence during WWII. Open May 15-Sept. 30 W-Su 11am-5pm, Oct. 1-May 14 W-Su 11am-4pm. 3zł, students 1zł, F free. Guided tours in English 20zł. Library open W-F noon-3pm.

Maria Skłodowskiej-Curie Museum (Muzeum Marii Skłodowskiej-Curie), ul. Freta 16 (tel. 831 80 92; fax 831 13 04), in the Skłodowskis' former house. Founded in 1967, on the 100th anniversary of Maria's birth, the exhibit chronicles her life in Poland, emigration to France, and marriage to scientist Pierre Curie, with whom she discovered radium, polonium, and marital bliss. Open Tu-Sa 10am-4pm, Su 10am-2pm. 5zł, students 2zł.

Caricature Museum (Muzeum Karykatury), Kozia 11 (tel. 827 88 95). A collection of wonderful caricatures by Polish artists, focused primarily on Polish politics. Open Tu-F 11am-5pm, Sa-Su noon-5pm; closed the last Su of every month. 3zł, students 1.50zł.

Warsaw Historical Museum (Muzeum Historyczne Miasta Warszawy), Rynek Starego Miasta 42 (tel. 635 16 25). Chronicles the evolution of style in the city's architecture and clothing from the 13th century to the present. Open Tu and Th 11am-6pm, W and F 10am-3:30pm, Sa-Su 10:30am-4:30pm. 5zł, students 2.50zł, Su free.

Adam Mickiewicz Literary Museum (Muzeum Literatury im. Adama Mickiewicza), Rynek Starego Miasta 20 (tel. 831 40 61). Honoring Poland's national poet (see **Literature & Art,** p. 401), the permanent exhibition focuses on Mickiewicz's life and work. Open M-Tu and F 10am-3pm, W-Th 11am-6pm, Su 11am-5pm. 4zł, students 3zł.

ENTERTAINMENT

Classical concerts fill Pałac Na Wodzie in Łazienki on summer Saturdays. (Performances June-Sept. at 4pm. Tickets 15zł, students 10zł.) Inquire about concerts at the **Warsaw Music Society** (Warszawskie Towarzystwo Muzyczne), ul. Morskie Oko 2 (tel. 849 68 56). Take tram #4, 18, 19, 35, or 36 to "Morskie Oko" from ul. Marszałkowska. The society is to your left as you pass the Japanese Ambassador's residence on the right. From Oct.-May, concerts are held at the Society twice a week. (Th 6pm and Su 11am. Tickets available M-F 9am-3pm and just before concerts. 5zł.) The **Warsaw Chamber Opera** (Warszawska Opera Kameralme), al. Solidarności 76B (tel. 831 22 40), hosts a Mozart festival each year during early summer, with performances throughout the city. The **Chopin Monument** (Pomnik Chopina), nearby in Łazienski Park, hosts free Sunday performances by classical artists. (May-Oct. noon and 4pm.) **Teatr Wielki,** pl. Teatralny 1 (tel. 692 07 58; www.teatrwielki.pl), Warsaw's main opera and ballet hall, offers performances almost daily. (*Kassa* open M-F 9am-7pm, Su 10am-7pm, and one hour before shows. Tickets 6-90zł). The **National Philharmonic** (Filharmonia Narodowa), ul. Jasna 5 (tel. 826 72 81), gives regular concerts, but is closed in summer.

Jazz, rock, and blues fans have quite a few options, especially in the summertime, when Stare Miasto is enlivened with street music. **Sala Kongresowa** (tel. 620 49 80), in the Pałac Kultury on the train station side with the casino, hosts serious jazz and rock concerts with famous international bands. Enter from ul. Emilii Plater.

NIGHTLIFE

Warsaw has much in the way of post-pierogi revelry. A large variety of pubs attract big crowds and often have live music, and cafes (*kawiarnie*) around Stare Miasto and ul. Nowy Świat serve coffee and beer late into the night. In the summer, large outdoor beer gardens complement the pub scene. The late-night student scene can be incredible, especially on weekends. Don't miss the sunrise as you hike up al. Niepodległości from one of the student clubs back to the city center.

PUBS

Warsaw's pubs—despite their relatively high prices—are popular with both trendy locals and visitors looking for a comfortable nook. The extra cost is sometimes made up for by free concerts, creating a livelier atmosphere than at the cheaper, outdoor beer gardens.

Morgan's, ul. Okólnik 1 (tel. 826 81 38), enter on ul. Tamka under the Chopin Museum. Ollie Morgan runs this comfortable, friendly Irish haunt for expats and visitors. Ollie says he pours the best *Guinness* in Poland, and he's probably right (0.5L, 13zł). If you're hungry, try the Shepherd's Pie (19zł). Live music M and F-Sa at 9pm. Open daily 2pm-midnight.

Metal Bar, Rynek Starego Miasta 8 (tel. 635 32 72). Inside Stare Miasto, this bar features, well, a metal theme. Let those latent alloy fantasies fly with a cold glass of EB (0.5L, 5.50zł). Open M-Th and Su noon-midnight, F-Sa noon-2am.

Club Giovanni, ul. Krakówskie Przedmieście 24 (tel. 826 92 39), on the premises of Uniwersytet Warszawski. Enter from the street by way of the narrow stairway next to the main gate with music at the bottom. A hangout for a low-key student set at all hours, complete with faux-graffiti on the walls, foosball and comfy leather chairs. Live music Thursday nights. Plenty of beer on tap (8-10zł). Cheap food as well. Veggie pizza 12zł. Open M-Th 10am-1am, F 10am-3am, Sa 1pm-3am, Su 1pm-1am. AmEx/MC/Visa.

Harenda Pub, ul. Krakówskie Przedmieście 4/6 (tel. 826 29 00), at Hotel Harenda. Enter from ul. Karasia. Dimly lit, with pictures of the owners in bow ties doing chummy things like taking road trips and going on brewery tours. The outdoor seating has a nutty island theme. The friendly crowd usually stays until closing, but don't go for a Polish lesson. 0.5L *Żywiec* 8.50zł. F-Sa disco. Live jazz W 8pm. Open daily 8am-3am.

NIGHTCLUBS

Clubs are aimed at a young and energetic crowd. They tend to be hit-or-miss, depending on where people feel like meeting for the night. Posters around town have the latest info on special club and disco nights.

Underground Music Cafe, ul. Marzałkowska 126/134 (tel. 826 70 48; fax 826 70 47). Across form the Palace of Culture; walk down the steps in front of McDonald's. Top floor has a bar with ample seating, downstairs is an expansive dance floor. Beer 7-8zł. Frequently hosts live music; check the schedule posted outside. F disco, Sa house party. Cover: M-Th and Sa-Su free; Friday 25zł, students 15zł; Saturday 25zł, students 20zł; women get in free before 11pm. Open M-Tu 11am-1am, W-Th 11am-3am, F-Sa 11am-5am, Su 4pm-1am.

Park, al. Niepodległośći 196 (tel. 825 91 65). This international disco is one of the most popular student hangouts in Warsaw. Take bus #192 or night bus #604 from al. Jana Pawła II to "Bartorego" or take the Metro (which finally comes in handy) to "Pole Mokotowskie." Walk toward the downtown along al. Niepodlegtości. It will be on your right. Dance M 9pm-3am. Polish rock Tu 8pm-2am. Classic rock W 8pm-2am. Metal and punk Th 8pm-2am. Pop and rock F-Sa 9pm-3am. Reggae Su 10pm-2am. Cover: M 7zł; Tu-Th and Su 10zł, students 5zł; F-Sa 20zł, students 10zł.

Empik club, ul. Nowy Świat 15/17 (tel. 625 10 86). In the basement of the Empik Megastore; enter from al. Jerozolimskie. Hosts local bands of varied ilk, many of which are quite good. Live music M-Sa 9pm, Su 8pm. No cover. Open until the last guest leaves.

Jazz Club Akwarium, (tel. 620 50 72). Known for several years as the top spot in the city for live jazz, Akwarium was forced to relocate from ul. Emilii Plater 49 to make room for the new Warsaw Towers project. The move to a remodeled building on ul. Waryńskiego (take the Metro to "Politechnika") should be complete by mid-2000.

GAY & LESBIAN NIGHTLIFE

Unless visitors have come to Warsaw for a black eye, they do not advertise their homosexuality. Warsaw is largely a community of conservative businesspeople, and those gay clubs that do exist are rare and ephemeral. Establishments are often secluded and always discreet (on the outside, anyway). For the latest info, call the gay and lesbian **hotline** (tel. 628 52 22) for the best spot to hit and when. (Open Tu-W 6-9pm and F 4-10pm). Kiosks sell *Inaczej* and *Filo*—magazines listing gay entertainment throughout the country.

Między Nami, ("Our Place") ul. Bracka 20. A left off al. Jerozolimskie when coming from the Pałac Kultury; turn right on Bracka; it's the unmarked restaurant on your left. Mixed 20-30-something crowd during the day, mostly gay in the evening. Jazz every Monday night. Classy "industrial" interior. 0.5L *Żywiec* 5.50zł. Salads 8.50-9.50zł; entrees 5-15zł. Open M-Th 10am-10pm, F-Sa 10am-midnight, Su 4-10pm.

Koźla, ul. Koźla 10/12. One block left from Rynek Nowego Miasta, when facing away from Stare Miasto. No sign outside, but it's the only club on Koźla. A narrow staircase leads down to a small orange room with plenty of patrons crowding the bar and low couches. Decidedly gay. Open daily 5pm-2am.

Paradise, at the corner of ul. Wawelska and ul. Żwirki i Wigury, on the grounds of the "Skra" sports complex, next to the tennis courts. Take bus #175 (or night bus #611) to "Pomnik Lotnika." A bit farther out, with a large, bright dance floor, chill-out area, and a patio. During the day it's a gay pub with bright colors and mood lighting. Attracts men and women, younger than those at Między Nami (see above). Beer 5zł. Disco Th-Su nights. Cover 20zł, Th 10zł. Open M-Th and Su 10am-midnight, F-Sa 10am-6am.

NEAR WARSAW: ŻELAZOWA WOLA

The birthplace of Fryderyk Chopin, Żelazowa Wola is a must-see on any Chopin fan's itinerary (see **Literature and Arts,** p. 401). In the early 19th century, the town was the site of a large manor that belonged to Count Skarbek, for whom the composer's father, a Frenchman named Nicolas Chopin, worked as a French tutor. There he met and married Justyna Krzyżanowska, a distant cousin of the count. They had 4 children—3 daughters and Fryderyk, who was born February 22, 1810. The Chopin family did not remain at Żelazowa Wola for very long; they moved to Warsaw in October 1810. The **cottage** (tel. (46) 863 33 00) provides an interesting look at early 19th-century life. (Open May-Sept. Tu-Su 9:30am-5:30pm; Oct.-Apr. 9:30am-4pm. 8zł, children 4zł. Tours in English, Russia, Japanese, and German 40zł; in Polish, 20zł. Admission to park only 3zł; children, 1zł.) Although it lacks the family's original furniture, the interior is maintained in the style of the era. Among the momentos on display are the composer's birth certificate and his first *polonaise* (written at the tender age of 11). Every Sunday and on Saturdays in July and August, music fans gather here to listen to **concerts** of Polish musicians performing Chopin's work—probably the best reason to make the trip. (Concerts at 11am and 3pm on Saturdays, noon on Sundays). The schedule of music and performers, posted throughout Warsaw, is available at the Chopin museum (see **Warsaw: Museums,** p. 418); both change weekly. Concerts are free if you're content to listen from the park benches just outside the music parlor. The performers will come out to acknowledge the crowd afterwards. Seats in the parlor itself cost 20zł.

POLAND

GETTING THERE. Two **buses** daily pass through Żelazowa Wola (53km west of Warsaw) but none of the signs in Warsaw mention it. It is a regular stop on the route to **Kamion** (6.20zł) but tell the driver that you want to stop at Żelazowa Wola to be safe. Buses to and from Kamion are limited, and only the 9:45am bus actually puts you in Żelazowa Wola with more than enough time to take it all in (arrives at 11:10am; the other arrives after the museum closes, and there are no direct buses back after 4:30pm). Or, take a **commuter train** from **Warszawa Śródmieście** to the small town of Sochaczew (at least 20 per day, 6.20zł). A Sochaczew city **bus** runs to "Żelazowa Wola" every hour on weekdays, and every other hour on weekends. Each way, the trip costs 6-7zł and takes 1½-2½ hours, depending on transfers.

LESSER POLAND (MAŁOPOLSKA)

The Małopolska uplands lie in Poland's southeast corner, stretching from the Kraków-Częstochowa Uplands in the west, strewn thick with medieval castle ruins, to commercial Lublin in the east. Kraków, which suffered only minimal damage during WWII, remains Poland's cultural (and social) center, drawing flocks of local and global travelers. Daytrips from the city run the gamut of human accomplishment and suffering, from the salt caves at Wieliczka to the unspeakable horrors perpetrated at Auschwitz-Birkenau and Tarnów, a *Roma* town until the Nazi invasion. To the northeast, stand precariously preserved Sandomierz and Lublin, with another concentration camp, Majdanek on its outskirts. Along the Wisła, Kazimierz Dolny has long inspired Polish artists, while Zamość to the east was inspired by the artistry of Padua, Italy. Finally, near the Ukrainian border, Łańcut stands out for its castle and Przemśl for its decidedly Eastern feel.

KRAKÓW

Once tucked away behind the walls of Communism, Kraków (KRAH-koof; pop. 745,500) has quickly become a trendy, international city, recently earning a place on the E.U.'s list of Cities of Culture for 2000. But Kraków-adoration goes back much farther than the collapse of Communism. The ancient capital of Poland, Kraków protected centuries of Central European kings. As a result, the city garnered magnificent palaces, a multi-colored Old Town sprinkled with architectural gems, and the country's oldest—and best—university. Kraków suffered no major destruction over the centuries, and miraculously even survived WWII unscathed. Today, Kraków is Poland's only large city to make it to the 21st century with its original architecture intact. Unfortunately, the specter of destruction has never been far removed from blessed Kraków: the notorious Nowa Huta steelworks in the eastern suburbs are a grim reminder of the Stalinist era, and the Auschwitz-Birkenau death camp from the Nazi occupation lies only 70km to the west. It is this combination of vitality and darkness that lends the city its dynamism, as well as the protection and advocacy of all those that visit it. In the face of destructive pollution from the steelworks, UNESCO named Kraków on its original list of World Heritage Sites; today, UNESCO considers the city one of the 12 most important cultural monuments in the world. The flocks of tourists seem to agree, descending on the city to partake in its hip and splendid urban scene, peruse the galleries occupying the Old Town's ancient cellars, and chat until the wee hours in the city's underground network of pubs. By no means undiscovered, centuries-old Kraków is still *the* highlight of Poland.

GETTING THERE & GETTING AROUND

Airplanes: Balice airport (tel. 411 19 55 and 411 67 00), 15km west of the center. Connected to the main train station by northbound bus #208 (40min.) or express bus D (30min.). Major international carriers include Swissair, British Airways, Austrian Airlines, and LOT. Open 4am-midnight. **INT Express Travel Agency,** ul. św. Marka 25 (tel. 423 04 97; fax 421 79 06), is registered with most airlines. Open M-Sa 8am-8pm.

Trains: Kraków Główny, pl. Kolejowy 1 (tel. 624 54 39). To: **Berlin** (8hr., 2 per day, 110zł); **Bratislava** (7hr., 1 per day, 150zł); **Budapest** (11hr., 1 per day, 160zł); **Kiev** (22hr., 1 per day, 110zł); **Lviv** (10½hr., 1 per day, 60zł); **Prague** (8½hr., 1 per day, 150zł); **Vienna** (9hr., 2 per day, 145zł); **Warsaw** (4¾hr., 9 per day, 45zł). Tickets sold at the station and travel offices. Some trains to southeast Poland leave from **Kraków Płaszów,** pl. Dudzinskich 1 (tel. 933). Take the train from Kraków Główny or tram #3 or 13 from the center south to ul. Wielicka.

Buses: Tel. 936. On ul. Worcella, directly across from Kraków Główny. International tickets are sold by **Sindbad** in the main hall (tel. 266 19 21). Open M-F 9am-5pm. To: **Budapest** (11hr., 2 per week, 94zł); **Lviv** (10hr., 1 per day, 45zł); **Prague** (11hr., 3 per week, 140zł); and **Warsaw** (6hr., 3 per day, 35zł).

Local Transportation: Buy tickets at kiosks near **bus** and **tram** stops (1.50zł) or on board (1.80zł); punch them on board. Large backpacks need their own tickets (0.75zł). Night buses 3.50zł. Buy tickets in advance, as many kiosks are not open late. Day pass 6zł; weekly pass 15zł. 75zł fine if you're caught ticketless, 22zł if your bag is.

Taxis: Express Taxi (tel. 644 41 11). **Hellou** (tel. 644 42 22). **Major** (tel. 636 33 33).

ORIENTATION

The city fans outward in roughly concentric circles from the huge **Rynek Główny** (Main Market Square), located at the heart of the **Stare Miasto** (Old Town). The **Planty** gardens ring the Stare Miasto, and the **Wisła** river, snaking through the center, skims the southwest corner of **Wzgórze Wawelskie** (Wawel Hill). The **bus** and **train stations** sit opposite each other about 10min. northeast of the *rynek*. To reach the center, turn left out of the train station and right past the kiosks, then head through the underpass to the Planty gardens. Walk toward the crumbled city wall, turning left down ul. Szpitalna to the church. A right here leads to the *rynek*.

PRACTICAL INFORMATION

TOURIST & FINANCIAL SERVICES

Tourist Offices: Dexter, Rynek Główny 1/3 (tel. 421 77 06; fax 421 30 36). English-speaking staff organizes tours. Open M-F 9am-6pm, Sa 9am-1pm.

Budget Travel: Orbis, Rynek Główny 41 (tel. 422 40 35; fax 422 28 85). Sells international tickets, including *Wasteels.* Arranges trips to the Wieliczka salt mines and Auschwitz. English spoken. Open Apr.-Oct. M-F 8am-6pm, Sa 8:30am-3pm; Nov.-Mar. M-F 8am-6pm, Sa 8:30am-1pm.

Consulates: U.S., ul. Stolarska 9 (tel. 429 66 55; emergency tel. 422 14 00). Open M-F 8:30am-4:30pm. Observes American holidays.

Currency Exchange: At *kantory,* Orbis (see above), and hotels. *Kantory,* except those around the train station, have the best rates. **Bank PKO S.A.,** Rynek Główny 31 (tel. 422 60 22), cashes traveler's checks for a 1% commission (10zł minimum), gives MC/Visa cash advances, and has a **24hr. ATM**—nothing to boast about in Kraków. Open M-F 8am-7pm, Sa 10am-2pm. For a better rate, exchange your traveler's checks for US$ here and take the cash to a *kantor.* Most are open only during business hours, but the **Forum Hotel,** ul. M. Konopnickiej 28 (tel. 261 92 12), has a 24hr. currency exchange.

American Express: Rynek Główny 41 (tel. 422 91 80), in the Orbis office. Cashes traveler's checks for free, replaces lost checks, holds mail, receives wired money. Open Apr.-Oct. M-F 8am-6pm, Sa 8:30am-3pm; Nov.-Mar. M-F 8am-6pm, Sa 8:30am-1pm.

Luggage Storage: At Kraków Główny. 1% of value plus 3.60zł per day. Open 24hr.

English Bookstore: Odeon, Rynek Główny 5 (tel. 492 12 93). Open daily 9am-9pm. **Znak,** Sławkowska 1. Open M-F 10am-6pm, Sa 10am-2pm.

Laundromat: Ul. Piastowska 47, on the 1st floor of Hotel Piast. 3hr. drop-off. Wash 12zł; dry 12zł. Open daily July-Aug. 8am-8pm; Sept.-June 10am-7pm.

EMERGENCY & COMMUNICATIONS

Pharmacies: Look for "Apteka" signs. **Apteka "Pod Złotym Tygrysem"** ("Under the Golden Tiger"), Szczepańska 1 (tel. 422 92 93), just off Rynek Głowny. Posts a weekly list of 24hr. pharmacies in its window. Open M-F and Su 8am-8pm, Sa 8am-3pm.

Medical Assistance: Profimed, Rynek Główny 6 (tel. 421 79 97) and ul. Grodzka 26 (tel. 422 64 53). Some English spoken. Open M-F 8am-8pm, Sa 9am-1pm.

Post Office: Ul. Westerplatte 20 (tel. 422 51 63 and 422 86 48; fax 422 36 06). **Poste restante** at counters #1 and 3. Open M-F 7:30am-8:30pm, Sa 9am-2pm, working Sa 9am-4pm, Su 9-11am. **Postal code:** 31-045.

Internet Access: Available at **Club U Louisa** (see **Entertainment,** p. 429) for 5zł per hr. Open daily 11am-11pm. **Internet Cafe Looz,** Mikołajska 11 (tel. 422 37 97). Email 3zł per 15min., internet 8zł per hr. Open daily 10am-10pm.

Telephones: At the post office and opposite the train station, ul. Lubicz 4 (tel. 422 14 85 and 422 86 35). Both open 24hr. At the **Telekomunikacja Polska,** Rynek Głowny 18 (tel. 429 17 11; fax 423 00 19). Open daily 8am-10pm. **Phone code:** (0)12.

ACCOMMODATIONS

Reservations are prudent year-round, but necessary in summer. Call at least a couple days ahead. **Waweltur,** ul. Pawia 8 (tel. 422 16 40; fax 422 19 21), arranges private rooms. (Open M-F 8am-8pm, Sa 8am-2pm. Singles 64zł; doubles 96zł.) Locals also rent **private rooms;** watch for signs or solicitors in the train station.

Strawberry Youth Hostel, ul. Ractawicka 9 (tel. 636 15 00). Take tram #4, 8, or 13 from the train station to Urzędnicza. Backtrack to the intersection and go left up ul. Urzędnicza; after a short walk, go left on ul. Kazimierza Wielkiego, then right on Raclawicka. New hostel offering beds in doubles, triples and quads for 40zł. Check-out 10am.

Schronisko Młodzieżowe (HI), ul. Oleandry 4 (tel. 633 88 22). Take tram #15 from the train station and get off when the main drag turns into ul. 3-go Maja. Take the first right up 3-go Maja onto Oleandry. 350 cheap but dingy beds, 15min. by foot from the center. 2-bed dorms 24zł; 4- to 5-bed dorms 20zł; 6- to 8-bed dorms 18zł; 16-bed dorms 16zł. Flexible lockout 10am-5pm. Curfew midnight.

Dom Studentcki Zaczek, ul. 3-go Maja 5 (tel. 633 54 77). Opposite Hotel Cracovia, accessible by tram #15. Get off one stop after the museum at the start of ul. 3-ego Maja. Excellent location, but rooms might need dusting, the communal bathrooms could smell better, and the nearby disco may keep you up. Singles 55zł, with bath 65zł; doubles 65zł, 99zł; triples 75zł, 125zł. Check-out 10am.

Hotel Piast, ul. Piastowska 47 (tel. 637 49 33). Take tram #4 or 12 from the train station to "Wawel." Walk in the direction of the tram to the first intersection, then turn left. Go straight a few blocks and Piast will be on the left. The tidy rooms (some with balconies) teem with English speakers. Singles 50zł, with bath 85zł; doubles 110zł, 74zł; triples with bath 120zł.

Schronisko Młodzieżowe (HI), ul. Kościuszki 88 (tel. 422 19 51), inside the gates of a convent. Take tram #2 from the train station toward Salwator and get off at the last stop (15min.). Run by nuns, this heavenly spot is on the Wisła 20min. from the center, but school groups detract from the recently remodeled serenity. Clean toilets and baths but no shower. 8- to 36-bed dorms 9.75zł, nonmembers 15zł. Sheets 2.50zł. Reception daily 6am-3pm and 5-11pm. Lockout 10am-5pm. Strict curfew 11pm.

Hotel Saski, ul. Sławkowska 3 (tel. 421 42 22; fax 421 48 30). Gracefully faded regality and prime location make this hotel worth the price. Singles 110zł, with bath 200zł; doubles 145zł, 275zł; triples 185zł, 315zł. Check-out noon. MC/Visa.

Hotel Polonia, ul. Basztowa 25 (tel. 422 12 33; fax 422 16 21). Across from the train station. Convenient if you arrive too early or late to check into more affordable accommodations. Singles 140zł, with bath 220zł; doubles 164zł, 248zł; triples 170zł, 284zł. Breakfast 16zł.

Camping Krak, ul. Radzikowskiego 99 (tel. 637 21 22 and 637 29 57; fax 637 25 32). Take tram #4, 8, or 13 from the train station to Balicka Wiaduct. If it stops at Wesele, take bus #313 the last two stops. Walk down to ul. Armu Krajowej, the street under the tram line, and turn left. Tents 16zł per person; cars 18zł. Open May 15-Sept. 15.

FOOD

The many restaurants and cafes on and around the *rynek* satisfy Kraków's huge tourist population. Grocery stores surround the bus and train stations; more can be found near the *rynek*. Poland's infamous soft pretzels *(obwarzanki)* are sold by the street vendors for less than a złoty.

RESTAURANTS

Chimera, ul. św. Anny 3 (tel. 423 21 78), in the cellar and ivy garden. The oldest and most famous salad joint in town, Chimera remains popular, especially with students. Huge sampler of 6 of their 20 cruciferous creations costs 9zł; slightly smaller plate 6zł. Live music nightly 8pm. Open M-Tu 9am-11pm, W-Su 9am-midnight.

Vega Bar Restaurant, ul. św. Gertrudy 7. Elegant vegetarian eatery with dried chilis over the counter and lace-draped pianos. Tasty Polish fare 2-5zł. Open daily 10am-9pm.

Cafe Zakgtek, Grodzka 2 (tel. 429 57 25). Great fresh sandwiches (4-6zł) and salads. Breakfast 6zł. Open M-Sa in summer 8:30am-10pm; off-season 9am-7pm.

Jadłodajnia u Stasi, ul. Mikołajska 16. A one-person operation named after the owner's mom, Pani Stasia. Definitely low-budget. Famous for its traditional Polish food. Come early afternoon for the best selection, but be prepared to wait in line. Open M-F 12:30pm until the food runs out–usually 4-5pm.

Balaton, ul. Grodzka 37 (tel. 422 04 69). Divine Hungarian cuisine that always attracts crowds. Entrees 6-20zł. Open daily 9am-10pm.

Bar Mleczny Barcelona, ul. Piłsudskiego 1. A bastion of proletarian dining. The food's a little greasy–welcome to Poland. Entrees under 5zł. Open M-F 8am-6pm, Sa 8am-4pm.

Restauracja Ariel, ul. Szeroka 17 (tel./fax 421 38 70), in the old Jewish district of Kazimierz, a 15min. walk south of the *rynek*. Outdoor cafe tables and elegant, antique interior with a creative, non-kosher mix of Polish and Jewish cuisine (10-36zł). *Lots* of tour groups. Jewish music nightly 8pm; cover 20zł. Open daily 9am-11pm.

CAFES

Camelot, ul. św. Tomasza 17 (tel. 421 01 23). Popular with students, artists, and foreigners alike. Adorned with handcrafted wooden dolls and original paintings. Salad 14-18zł. Cabaret in the cellar at 8:15pm on Fridays in winter. Concerts every Wednesday and Saturday. Open daily 9am-midnight.

Cafe and Gallery Krzysztofory, ul. Szczepańska 2 (tel. 422 93 60), in the dim, smoke-filled cellar of the Dom Krzysztofory. A favorite of students and artists. The gallery has new exhibits every 2-3 weeks, and hosts performances in its avant-garde theater. Coffee 3zł. Cafe open daily 11am-9pm; gallery open daily 11am-5pm.

Kawiarnia Jama Michalika, ul. Floriańska 45 (tel. 422 15 61). More than a century old, this is one of Kraków's most famous, and best decorated, cafes. Former haunt of the Polish intelligentsia. Evening cabaret. Open daily 9am-10pm.

Pożegnania z Afryka (Out of Africa), ul. Św. Tomasza 21. A popular Polish chain with an antique feel, a thick aroma, and an extensive selection of rich coffees (around 5.50zł for a small pot). Imported beans sold in bulk. No smoking. Open daily 10am-10pm.

SIGHTS

Unlike Warsaw, Kraków was fortunate enough to be spared from destruction in World War II, but the fumes emitted by the Nowa Huta steelworks have since eroded Kraków's monuments. Designated a UNESCO World Heritage Site in 1978, the city has scraped off the grime to reveal the extensive beauty and character that makes Kraków one of Eastern Europe's most treasured cities.

WAWEL CASTLE

Tel. 422 51 55; fax 422 16 97. Castle open Tu and F 9:30am-4:30pm, W-Th 9:30am-3:30pm, Sa 9:30am-3pm, Su 10am-3pm; last admission 1hr. before closing. Cathedral open May-Sept. M-F 9am-5:15pm, Sa 9am-4:45pm, Su 12:15-5:15pm. Cave open May-Sept. daily 10am-5pm. Royal chambers 10zł, students 5zł; Oriental collection 5zł, students 3zł; treasury and armory 10zł, students 5zł; cathedral 6zł, student 3zł; cave 2zł. Apr.-Sept. Wednesday free; Oct.-Mar. Saturday free.

Wawel Castle (Zamek Wawelski) is one of the finest pieces of architecture in Poland. Begun in the 10th century but remodeled during the 1500s, the castle contains 71 chambers and a magnificent sequence of 16th-century tapestries commissioned by the royal family, among many other treasures. It is currently undergoing renovation, and not all of the rooms are open to the public. The **Crown Treasury** features the swords carried at many Polish coronations. The **Oriental Collection,** has an amazing display of 17th- and 18th-century porcelain from China and Japan, all intricately painted. Poland's monarchs were crowned and buried in the **Wawel Cathedral** (Katedra Wawelska), next to the castle. Karol Wojtyła, who grew up in Kraków, was archbishop here before he became Pope John Paul II. The cathedral houses ornate tombs of kings and others—poets Juliusz Słowacki and Adam Mickiewicz (see **Literature & Arts,** p. 401), and Polish and American military leader General Józef Piłsudski. The sarcophagus of King Kazimierz Jagiełłończyk was crafted by Wit Stwosz, who also designed the altar in Kościół Mariacki. St. Maurice's spear, presented by German Emperor Otto III in 1000 to the Polish prince Bolesław Chrobry (who became the country's first king in 1024), commemorates a spell of Polish-German friendship. Steep wooden stairs lead from the church to **Zygmunt's Bell** (Dzwon Zygmunta). It sounds only on major holidays, but when it does, its tones echo for miles. Outside, the **statue of Tadeusz Kościuszko** glorifies the Polish patriot who fought in the American Revolution and organized the 1794 revolt against Russia (see **History,** p. 399). The entrance to **Dragon's Cave** (Smocza Jama), the dwelling of Kraków's menace, is in the complex's southwest corner. If you've descended the hill, you've passed it.

KAZIMIERZ: THE OLD JEWISH QUARTER

Take tram #13 east from pl. Dominikańska, one block south of the rynek, and get off by the post office, at the intersection of ul. Miodowa and Starowiślna. Ul. Szeroka runs parallel to Starowiślna, on the right if you're looking in the same direction as the tram. By foot, the 15min. walk from the rynek leads down ul. Sienna past St. Mary's Church, and opposite the statue of Adam Mickiewicz. Eventually, ul. Sienna turns into Starowiślna. After 1km, turn right on Miodowa, then take the first left onto Szeroka.

South of the Stare Miasto lies Kazimierz, Kraków's 600-year-old Jewish quarter. Founded in 1335, Kazimierz was originally a seperate town. King Jan Olbrecht decided to move Kraków's Jews there in 1495 in order to get them out of the city proper. On the eve of WWII, 64,000 Jews lived in the Kraków area, many of them in Kazimierz, but Nazi policies forced most of them out. The 15,000 remaining were resettled in the overcrowded Podgórze ghetto in 1941. All were deported by March 1943, many to the nearby Płaszów and Auschwitz-Birkenau concentration camps. Kazmierz today is a focal point for the 5000 Jews still living in Poland, and serves as a starting point for those seeking their ancestral heritage.

The tiny **Remuh Synagogue** is surrounded by **Remuh's Cemetery,** one of Poland's oldest Jewish cemeteries. Beautiful but overrun, the cemetery holds graves dating back to the plague of 1551-52. On the eastern side, you'll find a 20m wall composed of tombstones recovered in 1959 from Nazi destruction. *(Szeroka 40. Open M-F 9am-4pm. 5zł, students 2zł. Services Friday at sundown and Saturday morning.)* **Temple Synagogue,** with a polychrome ceiling and 36 splendid stained-glass windows, was founded by the Association of Progressive Israelis in the early 1860s. It is under renovation through 2000, but for a small donation you can usually slip in the door and take a look. *(Miodowa 24.)* Poland's oldest synagogue, and the one most emblematic of Jewish architecture, **Old Synagogue** (Stara Synagoga) houses an interesting **museum** depicting the history, traditions, and art of Kraków's Jews. *(Szeroka 24. Tel. 622 09 62. Open W-Th and Sa-Su 9am-3pm, F 11am-6pm. 5zł, students 2.50zł.)* Built in 1644, **Isaac Synagogue** is Kraków's largest and newest synagogue. It offers continuous screenings of 5min. documentary films depicting the life of the district in 1936 and the Nazi evacuation of the Kraków Ghetto. *(Kapa 18. Open M-F and Su 9am-7pm; closed Jewish holidays. 6zł.)*

The **Jewish Bookstore Jarden** organizes tours, including a 2hr. tour of Kazimierz and the Płaszów concentration camp tracing the sites shown in the film *Schindler's List.* Płaszów is located in the south of Kraków and was completely destroyed by the Nazis on their retreat. Today, nothing remains apart from a long, overgrown field. *(Szeroka 2. Tel. 421 71 66. Open M-F 9am-6pm, Sa-Su 10am-6pm. Kazimierz tour 20zł, with Ghetto 25zł;* Schindler's List *sights 40zł; Auschwitz 80zł. Discounts for students and groups larger than 10.)* **The Center for Jewish Culture** is housed in the former Bene Emenu prayer house. It opened in November 1993 to provide a continuous series of cultural events and arrange heritage tours. *(Rabina Meiselsa 17. Tel. 423 55 87; fax 423 50 34.)*

STARE MIASTO (OLD TOWN)

At the center of the Stare Miasto spreads **Rynek Główny,** replete with seas of cafes and bars. It's a convenient central point for exploring the nearby sights.

ST. MARY'S CHURCH. (Kościół Mariacki). The two towers of St. Mary's were built by two brothers with different working styles: one hurried, the other deliberate. The hasty brother realized that the work of his careful sibling would put his own to shame, and killed him in a fit of jealousy. The murder weapon is on display in the Cloth Hall (see below). The deep blues and golds of the church's Baroque interior encase a 500-year-old wooden altarpiece carved by Wit Stwosz. Dismantled by the Nazis, the altar was rediscovered by Allied forces at the war's end. Now reassembled, its narration of the joy and suffering of St. Mary, complete with life-sized figures, is ceremoniously unveiled at noon each day. A trumpet call blares from the towers once in each direction every hour. Its abrupt ending recalls the destruction of Kraków in 1241, when the invading Tatars are said to have shot down the trumpeter in the middle of his song. *(At the corner of the* rynek *closest to the train station. Open daily noon-6pm. Altar 2.50zł, students 1.50zł.)*

CLOTH HALL. (Sukiennice). In the middle of the *rynek*, the yellow Italianate Cloth Hall remains as mercantile now as when cloth merchants actually used it: the ground floor is lined with wooden stalls hawking souvenirs. Upstairs, the **National Museum** (Muzeum Narodowe) houses a gallery of 18th- and 19th-century Polish classics. *(Tel. 422 11 66. Open Tu-W and F-Su 10am-3:30pm, Th 10am-6pm. Last admission 30min. before closing. 5zł, students 2.50zł.)* During the academic year, students cruise the area and wait for their friends under the **statue of Adam Mickiewicz,** Poland's most celebrated Romantic poet, between Cloth Hall and St. Mary's.

UL. FLORIAŃSKA. Ul. Floriańska runs from the corner of the *rynek* closest to the train station to the **barbakan,** the only remnant of the city's medieval fortifications. Ul. Floriańska was once part of the Royal Tract—the road leading to the castle—and many houses date from the 14th century. At the top of the street, **Floriańska Gate,** the old entrance to the city, is the centerpiece of the only surviving remnant of the city wall. In the 19th century, a local painter convinced city officials that the wall blocked the destructive north wind, thereby rescuing it from demolishment.

CZARTORYSKICH MUSEUM. Among other masterpieces, this museum displays Leonardo da Vinci's *Lady with an Ermine* and Rembrandt's *Landscape with a Merciful Samaritan*. It also exhibits objects of Polish historical significance, including full sets of armor bedecked with animal pelts and feathers. *(Ul. św. Jana 19. Ul. św. Jana runs parallel to ul. Floriańska. From the rynek, head to the end of the street; it will be on the right. Tel. 422 55 66. Open Tu-F 9am-5pm, Sa-Su 10am-3:30pm; last entrance 30min. before closing. 5zł, students 2.50zł; free Sundays. Cameras 15zł.)*

JAGIELLONIAN UNIVERSITY. (Uniwersytet Jagiełłoński). More than 600 years old, Kraków's Jagiellonian University ranks as the second oldest university in Eastern Europe (after Prague's Charles University). Astronomer Mikołaj Kopernik (Copernicus) and painter Jan Matejko are among its noted alumni. The university's oldest building, the 15th-century **Collegium Maius,** has an enchanting Gothic courtyard. *(Ul. Jagiełłonska 15. Walk down sw. Anny in the corner of the rynek near the Town Hall and turn left onto Jagiełłonska. Tel. 422 05 49. Open M-F 11am-2:30pm, Sa 11am-1:30pm.)*

UL. KANONICZA. Ul. Kanonicza runs parallel to ul. Grodzka, which extends from the corner of the *rynek* closest to the small **Wojciech's Church** (Kościół św. Wojciecha). This street, like Floriańska, was once part of the Royal Tract. Several galleries line the path to Wawel, including **Cricot 2,** a funky museum exhibiting the works of an avant-garde group once led by the late Tadeusz Kantor. *(Kanonicza 5. Tel. 422 83 32. Open M-F 10am-2pm. 5zł, students 2zł.)*

POLAND

CHURCHES AROUND UL. GRODZKA. Walking down Grodzka from the corner of the *rynek* closest to Wojciech's Church, turn right one block down ul. Franciszkańka. This will take you to the **Franciscan Church** (Kościół Franciszkański), which houses Stanisław Wyspiański's enormous *God the Father* stained-glass window, famous for its rippling colors. Pope John Paul II resided across the street in the **Bishop's Palace,** when he was still Cardinal Karol Wojtyła. A 1980 statue in the courtyard commemorates his 60th birthday. Walking straight down Grodzka, the **Church of St. Peter and St. Paul** (Kościół św. Piotra i Pawła) is notable as the first Polish church built in the Roman Baroque style. *(Open M-Sa 9am-5pm, Su 1-5pm. Crypt 1.50zł, students 1.10zł; tomb 16zł.)* Right next to it you'll find the 11th-century Romanesque **Church of St. Andrew** (Kościół św. Andrzeja), which sheltered many of Kraków's citizens as the city burned in the Tartar invasion of 1241.

ENTERTAINMENT

Dexter (see **Practical Information,** p. 423) offers brochures on each month's cultural activities. The **Cultural Information Center,** ul. św. Jana 2 (tel. 421 77 87; fax 421 77 31), sells the comprehensive monthly guide *Karnet* (2zł; www.karnet.krakow2000.pl) and tickets for upcoming events. (Open M-F 10am-7pm, Sa 11am-7pm.) Festivals abound in Kraków, particularly in summer. Some to note are the **International Short Film Festival** (late May), the **Festival of Jewish Culture** (end of June), the **International Festival of Outdoor Performances** (early July), and the **Jazz Festival** (Oct./Nov.). As a "European City of Culture," Kraków has chosen "Spirituality" as the main theme for its **Festival 2000.** The aforementioned tourist offices will have more details as the grand celebration approaches. Be sure to check the *Karnet* online before visiting in order to catch the events that will be going on.

As a rule, films in Poland are shown in their original language with Polish subtitles. **Kino Pod Baranani,** Rynek Głowny 27 (tel. 423 07 68), and **Kino Mikro,** ul. Lea 5 (tel. 634 28 97), are two of Kraków's more adventurous independent cinemas. Classical music buffs will appreciate **Filharmonia Krakówska** (tel. 422 09 58 and 422 94 77), performing regularly at ul. Zwierzyniecka 1, and at the **Opera Stage,** Plac Św. Ducha 1, whose box office is at the **J. Słowacki Theater** (tel. 423 17 00).

NIGHTLIFE

After a day of sightseeing in and around the *rynek*, stick around for the best clubbing opportunities in the city, frequented by both local students and tourists.

U Louisa, Rynek Główny 13 (tel. 421 80 92). Draws a diverse crowd with good, loud jazz and blues on weekends, a gallery of local photography, and a cybercafe (see **Internet Access,** p. 424). Beer 4-7.50zł. Cover 5-10zł. Open daily 11am until everbody leaves.

Free Pub, ul. Sławkowska 4 (tel. 423 13 11). Head under the archway, then down the stairs through the door on the right. Unmarked, so it's easy to miss. Mostly mellow 20- and 30-somethings. Beer 4.50zł. Open daily 4pm until the last guest leaves.

Jazz Club "U Muniaka," ul. Floriańska 3 (tel. 422 26 53). Cafe run by well-known Polish jazz musician, Janusz Muniak, who hosts jam sessions with his friends. Concerts Th-Sa 9:30pm. 15zł at the door. *Żywiec* 6zł. Open daily 5pm-midnight, 1am for concerts.

Pub Pod Papugami (Under the Parrots), ul. św. Jana 18 (tel. 422 82 99). Frequented by a quieter student crowd. 0.4L Guinness 9zł. Open M-F noon-2am, Sa-Su 4pm-2am.

Student Club, Rynek Główny 8 (tel. 429 38 37). A laid-back student hangout. Hosts a loud, smoky disco on F-Sa. *Żywiec* 5zł. Open daily from 9 or 10am until 3 or 4am.

Hali Gali, ul. Karmelicka 10 (tel. 438 08 68). Through the archway. A quiet bar where gay men can chat over a beer or coffee. Beer 4.10zł. Open Tu-Su 6pm-2am.

DAYTRIPS FROM KRAKÓW

AUSCHWITZ-BIRKENAU

An estimated 1.5 million people, mostly Jews, were murdered, and thousands more suffered unthinkable horrors, in the Nazi concentration camps at **Auschwitz** (Oświęcim) and **Birkenau** (Brzezinka). The largest and most efficient of the death camps, their names are synonymous with the Nazi death machine. Prisoners were actually held at the smaller **Konzentrationslager Auschwitz I,** which was—and still is—located within the limits of the town of Oświęcim. The grass and trees that have since grown among the eerily tidy red brick buildings seem almost collegiate, until the bitter irony of the inscription on the camp's gate—*Arbeit Macht Frei* (Work Makes You Free)—fully sinks in. Those prisoners who suffered the horrifying conditions at Auschwitz I escaped the immediate death waiting for those herded into **Konzentrationslager Auschwitz II-Birkenau**—the extermination camp created when the main Auschwitz crematorium was beyond its capacity.

Tours begin at the **museum** at Auschwitz. As you walk through the barracks, with nothing but a plate of glass between you and the remnants of thousands of lives—suitcases, shoes, glasses, and more than 100,000lbs. of women's hair—the sheer enormity of the evil committed here comes into focus. Other rooms, such as the second floor of Barrack 5, shock with minute detail, like the single pacifier atop a pile of children's clothing. There's an English showing every half hour of a **film** shot by the Soviet Army, which liberated the camp on January 27, 1945. Check the schedule at the movie ticket office (1.50zł). Children under 14 are strongly advised not to visit the museum. (Open daily June-Aug. 8am-7pm; May and Sept. 8am-6pm; Apr. and Oct. 8am-5pm; Mar. and Nov.-Dec. 15 8am-4pm; Dec. 16-Feb. 8am-3pm. Free. Guided tour in English daily at 11:30am, 3½ hr. 16zł. An English-language guidebook with maps of the camps is sold at the entrance for 3zł.)

Do not leave Oświęcim without visiting the starker and larger **Konzentrationslager Auschwitz II-Birkenau,** in the countryside 3km from the original camp, a 30min. walk along a well-marked route. Shuttles run here from the parking lot of the Auschwitz museum (Apr. 15-Oct. 31, hourly 10:30am-4:30pm, 1zł). Birkenau was constructed later in the war when massive quantities of Jews, Roma, Slavs, homosexuals, disabled people, and other "inferiors" were being brought to Auschwitz and a more "efficient" means of killing needed to be devised. Begin with the central watchtower, where you can view the immensity of the camp—endless rows of barracks, watchtowers, chimneys, gas chambers, and crematoria. Amazingly, this is only a small section of the original camp not destroyed by the Nazis as they tried to conceal their genocide. The crematoria and gas chambers are in ruins, but the train tracks leading to them have been reconstructed. The tracks end with a huge memorial to all those who died in the Auschwitz system. In the right corner of the camp lies a pond, still gray from the ashes deposited there half a century ago; fragments of bone can still be found in the area near the crematoria.

GETTING THERE. Buses run to Oświęcim from **Kraków's central bus station** (1½hr., 10 per day, 7.90zł; get off at "Muzeum Oświęcim"). **Trains** leave from **Kraków Główny** (1¾hr., 2 per day, 7.40zł), although times are not particularly convenient and trains may not be direct. More trains run from **Kraków Plaszów,** south of the center (see **Kraków: Trains,** p. 422). Tourist offices in Kraków also offer tours that include transportation and knowledgeable guides. From outside the Oświęcim train station, buses #2, 3, 4, and 5 drop visitors off at the "Muzeum Oświęcim" bus stop. By foot, turn right as you exit the station, go one block, and turn left onto ul. Więźniów Oświęcimia; the road stretches 1.6km to Auschwitz, which will be on the right.

WIELICZKA

The 1000-year-old **salt mine,** ul. Daniłowicza 10 (tel. 278 73 02 and 278 73 66; fax 278 73 33) in the tiny town of Wieliczka, is 13km southeast of Kraków. Pious Poles carved an immense 20-chapel complex 100m underground entirely out of salt; in 1978, UNESCO declared the mine one of the 12 most priceless monuments in the world. The most spectacular of the caverns is the 60m-by-11m **St. Kinga's Chapel,** complete with salty chandeliers, an altar, and relief works. A two-hour mandatory tour visits over 20 salt sculptures, ending at a cafe and souvenir shop. You can either stop here and take the lift 130m back to the surface, or go on to the **underground museum,** which gives a history of the salt mines and explains methods of extraction. (Open daily Apr. 16-Oct. 15 7:30am-6:30pm; Oct. 16-Apr. 15 8am-4pm. Tours 23zł, students 12zł. Cameras 6zł; video 11zł. English guide available in June at 12:30pm and five times daily July-Aug.; 28zł per person.)

POLAND

GETTING THERE. Orbis (see **Kraków: Orientation & Practical Information,** p. 423) organizes daily trips to the mine (3hr.; 100zł, students 75zł). Its **bus** leaves daily from Hotel Cracoiva at 3:05pm, and from PTTK Dom Turysty at Westerplatte 15 at 3:25pm. **Trains,** a cheaper option, also make the trip from Kraków (25min., hourly, 2zł), and private **minibuses** depart from the road between the train and bus stations (every 15min., 2zł). Look for the minibuses with "Wieliczka" on the door. Once in Wieliczka, follow the old path of the tracks and then the "*do kopalni*" signs.

TARNÓW

A Roma (gypsy) town before WWII, Tarnów still manages to preserve its legacy. Dedicated to "all travelers, past, present and, I hope, future," the **Ethnographic Museum,** ul. Krakówska 10 (tel. (014) 220 625; fax 261 585), traces the history of the Polish Roma since 1401, when they first arrived here. WWII saw 35,000 Polish Roma perish; today, only 20,000 remain. The museum exhibits a display on their history, art, and culture. In the summer, painted caravans await outside. The Roma flag—a red wheel against a green and blue background—symbolizes the people's nomadic tradition. (Open Tu and Th 10am-5pm, W and F 9am-3pm, Sa-Su 10am-2pm. 3zł, students 1.50zł. Cameras 5zł.)

GETTING THERE. Tarnów lies 82km east of Kraków. They are connected by **trains** (1½hr., 43 per day, 8-11zł) and **buses** (2hr., 24 per day, 13zł), both of which arrive at **pl. Dworcowy,** 15min. from the center. From the main bus station, turn right on **ul. Krakówska.** The museum is a 10min. walk, en route to the *rynek*.

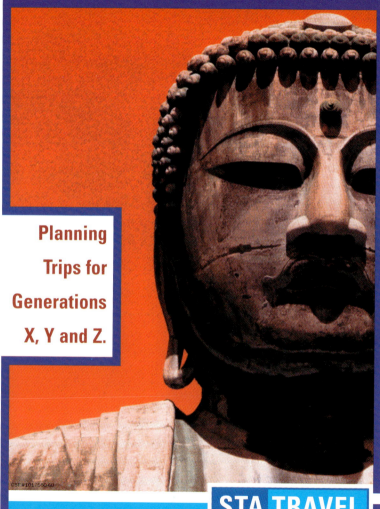

travel
The journey is the reward....
-Tao saying
Council Travel
Stop by one of our 65 offices listed
on www.counciltravel.com
Or call: 1-800-2COUNCIL

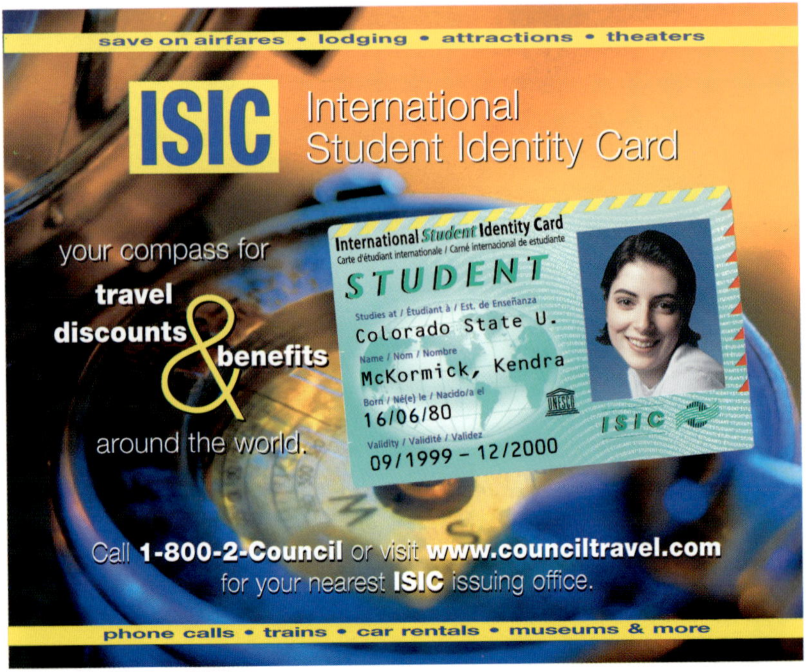
save on airfares • lodging • attractions • theaters
ISIC International Student Identity Card
International Student Identity Card
Carte d'étudiant internationale / Carné internacional de estudiante
STUDENT
Studies at / Étudiant à / Est. de Enseñanza
Colorado State U.
Name / Nom / Nombre
McKormick, Kendra
Born / Né(e) le / Nacido/a el
16/06/80
Validity / Validité / Validez
09/1999 - 12/2000
UNESCO
ISIC
your compass for
travel
discounts
&
benefits
around the world.
Call 1-800-2-Council or visit www.counciltravel.com
for your nearest ISIC issuing office.
phone calls • trains • car rentals • museums & more

SANDOMIERZ

The *małopolski* town of Sandomierz (SAN-do-myezh), chartered in 1241, is immaculate and charming. Named after Sudomir, its founder, the town suffered destruction by the Tatars in 1241-60 and a Swedish invasion in 1656. Only one fortification remains, but the *rynek*'s 15th-century apartments and dark underground system of wine cellars survived. Timely restorations to the crumbling hillside in 1967 kept this medieval operation from sliding into the Wisła. Now it's the perfect place to kick back, with captivating sights and outstanding cafes.

ORIENTATION & PRACTICAL INFORMATION. The **train station** (tel. 832 23 74), on ul. Lwowska, sits in the outskirts across the Wisła River. To reach the center, take bus #11; the bus stop is 100m ahead as you exit the train station. Get off at Brana Opatowska, which is opposite the old gate to the city. This street leads to the *rynek*. **Trains** chug to **Przemyśl** (3hr., 2 per day, 22-30zł) and **Warsaw** (4hr., 3 per day, 40-52zł). The **bus station,** ul. 11-go Listopada (tel. 322 302) is 20min. from the center. (Open daily 4:30am-9pm.) **Buses** roll to: **Kraków** (4hr., 2 per day, 20zł); **Lublin** (2½hr., 7 per day, 14zł); and **Warsaw** (3hr., 9 per day, 23zł). Taking a bus from one of these points is the easiest means of reaching Sandomierz; from smaller towns, the local tourist office can point out which ones pass through. Otherwise, you have to go through **Tarnobrzeg,** 15km south. Ul. 11-go Listopada links the bus station with the main drag, **ul. Mickiewicza.** A left on Mickiewicza leads past a park to **Opatowska Gate** (Brama Opatowska), the entrance to Stare Miasto. Inside the gate, a large **PTTK map** marks the way to the *rynek* straight ahead. The **PTTK tourist office,** Rynek 25/26 (tel. 832 23 05; fax 832 26 82), has free maps of the town. (Open M-F 8am-3pm.) Nearby bookstores also sell a map/city guide (2zł). Travel bookings are available at **Orbis,** Rynek 23 (tel./fax 832 30 40), next to PTTK. (Open M-F 8am-4pm, Sa 9am-1pm.) The **post office,** Rynek 10, doubles as a **currency exchange.** (Open M-F 8am-6pm, Sa-Su 8am-1pm.) **Postal code:** 27-600. **Phone code:** (0)15.

POLAND

ACCOMMODATIONS & FOOD. **Dom Noclegowy,** ul. Zamkowa 1 (tel. 832 22 19), down the hill from the *rynek*, offers simple singles (30zł) and doubles (60zł), some equipped with antique furnaces. Most importantly, communal bathrooms are odor-free. The larger **Hotel Dick,** Mały Rynek 2 (tel. 832 31 30), stands erect one block north of the *rynek*. From Opatowska Gate, just before the *rynek*, go left off ul. Opalowska. The hotel, a.k.a. Hotel Winnica, also has clean bathrooms. (Singles 49.50zł; doubles 67.50zł; triples 82.50zł; quads 96.50zł.)

Eateries in Sandomierz cluster around the *rynek*. **Restauracja 30,** Rynek 30 (tel. (0603) 55 12 14), offers animals cooked Polish-style for 10-12zł. (Open daily 10am-10pm.) **Winnica** (Vineyard), Mały Rynek 2 (tel. 832 35 91), in the same building as the hotel, also features traditional fare. (Entrees 8-18zł. Open daily 11am-10pm.) For something lighter, the **Kawiarnia "Retro,"** Rynek 5 (tel. 832 28 59), offers elegance and sweet snacks; the *kawa po sandomiersku* (4.50zł)—there's a whipped egg somewhere in there—is delicious. (Open daily 10am-9pm.)

SIGHTS. The Gothic **Opatowska Gate,** the only remnant of the town's fortifications, marks the entrance to Stare Miasto. The steep stairs to the top of the gate will reward you with a fantastic view of town. (Open daily 10am-6pm. 2zł, students 1.50zł.) Find it by heading down ul. Opatowska from the **Old Town Square** (Rynek Starego Miasta). Just a few steps from the *rynek*, take a left on ul. Oleśnicka off ul. Opatowska. This leads to the mysterious **Underground Tourist Route** (Podziemna Trasa Turystyczna)—yes, it's actually called that—through stone and brick chambers inhabited by Tatar ghosts. In these 14th-century cellars, wealthy merchants stored grain and wine made from the grapes of the vineyards that covered the sunny slopes surrounding Sandomierz. (Polish tours daily every 30min. 10am-5:30pm. 5zł, students 3.50zł.)

In the middle of the *rynek*, the Renaissance town hall houses a division of the **Regional Museum** (Muzeum Okręgowe), which features a model of 18th-century Sandomierz. (Open M and W-Su 9am-4pm. 3zł, students 2zł; children free Sa.) Ul.

Mariacka, off the *rynek*, takes you to the town's grandest monument, the 14th-century **cathedral.** (Open Tu-Sa 10am-2pm and 3-5pm, Su 3-5pm. Summer organ concerts W 6:30pm.) Continuing down ul. Mariacka, a right on ul. Zamkowa leads to **Kazimerz Castle.** Built in the 14th century by King Kazimierz Wielki and destroyed by the Swedes in 1656, the castle has recently undergone restoration—only the walls and skeleton reflect the original layout. Inside, the **archaeological exhibit,** ul. Zamkowa 14 (tel. 832 38 68 and 832 38 69), includes an 11th-century chess set. (Open Tu-Su 10am-5pm. 4zł, students 2zł.) Up at the top, the quiet **Kawiarnia Zamek** serves coffee, beer, desserts, amid darkness and children's artwork. (Open daily 11am-10pm.) The courtyard hosts a **music festival** in late June.

LUBLIN

Lublin (LOO-bleen) can fool visitors with the slow pace of its surroundings, but its residents know their city is anything but provincial. Long an incubator of social and religious movements, *Małopolska's* former capital served as the center of the Polish Reformation and Counter-Reformation in the 16th and 17th centuries, and later housed the only independent Polish Catholic university in the communist era. Today, despite unsightly apartment blocks on the outskirts of the city, a Bohemian presence has begun to thrive around the university and the Old Town.

ORIENTATION

The city's main drag, **ul. Krakówskie Przedmieście,** connects **Stare Miasto** (Old Town) in east Lublin to the **Catholic University of Lublin KUL** *(Katolicki Uniwersytet Lubelski)* in the west, becoming **al. Racławickie** along the way. Take bus #5, 10, or 13 to town from the bus station. On foot, head toward the castle and climb **ul. Zamkowa,** running from the castle gate to Stare Miasto. Changing names several times, Zamkowa emerges through **Brama Krakówska** (Kraków Gate) to become **Krakówskie Przedmiescie.** From the train station, take trolley #150 or bus #13 to the city center.

POLAND

PRACTICAL INFORMATION

Trains: pl. Dworcowy 1 (tel. 532 02 19; info tel. 933). To **Kraków** (4hr., 2 per day, 32.12zł) and **Warsaw** (2½hr., 10 per day, 22.50zł).

Buses: ul. Tysiąclecia 4 (tel. 776 649; info tel. 934). To **Warsaw** (3hr., 10 per day, 12zł). Polski Express service (20zł) runs odd hours and is worth the money for long rides.

Local Transportation: Buy tickets at kiosks. 10min. ride 1.40zł; 30min. ride 1.60zł.

Tourist Office: IT, ul. Narutowicza 54 (tel. 532 44 12). Walk or take bus #8, 9, or 11 south from the city center. Carries **maps** (5zł) and brochures, and can help find accommodations. Open M-F 9am-5pm, Sa 10am-2pm. Some English spoken.

Budget Travel: Orbis, ul. Narutowicza 31/33 (tel. 532 22 56; fax 532 15 30), handles international and domestic plane, train, and bus tickets, and is always excited to book rooms at their own hotels. Open M-F 9am-6pm, Sa 9am-2pm. English spoken.

Currency Exchange: *Kantor* have the best rates. **Bank PKO S.A.,** ul. Królewska 1 (tel. 532 10 16), accepts traveler's checks (5% commission) and offers MC/Visa cash advances. Open M-F 7:30am-6pm, Sa 10am-2pm. MC/Visa **ATMs** are all over town.

Pharmacy: ul. Krakówskie Przedmieście 49 (tel. 532 24 25). Open daily 8am-8pm; after hours, ring the bell.

Post Office: ul. Krakówskie Przedmieście 50 (tel. 743 67 61). **Fax** service (fax 532 50 61). Open M-F 7am-9pm, Sa 8am-9pm, Su 9am-4pm. **Poste Restante** at window #1. **Postal code:** 20-930.

Telephones: Outside the post office. **Phone code:** (0)81.

ACCOMMODATIONS

Room prices in Lublin are rising, but are still reasonable. Unfortunately, there are no good hostels or inexpensive hotels available in or directly around Stare Miasto. In the summer, **university dorms** serve as lodging, although they are a trek from the center. The tourist offices (see above) have information about these rooms.

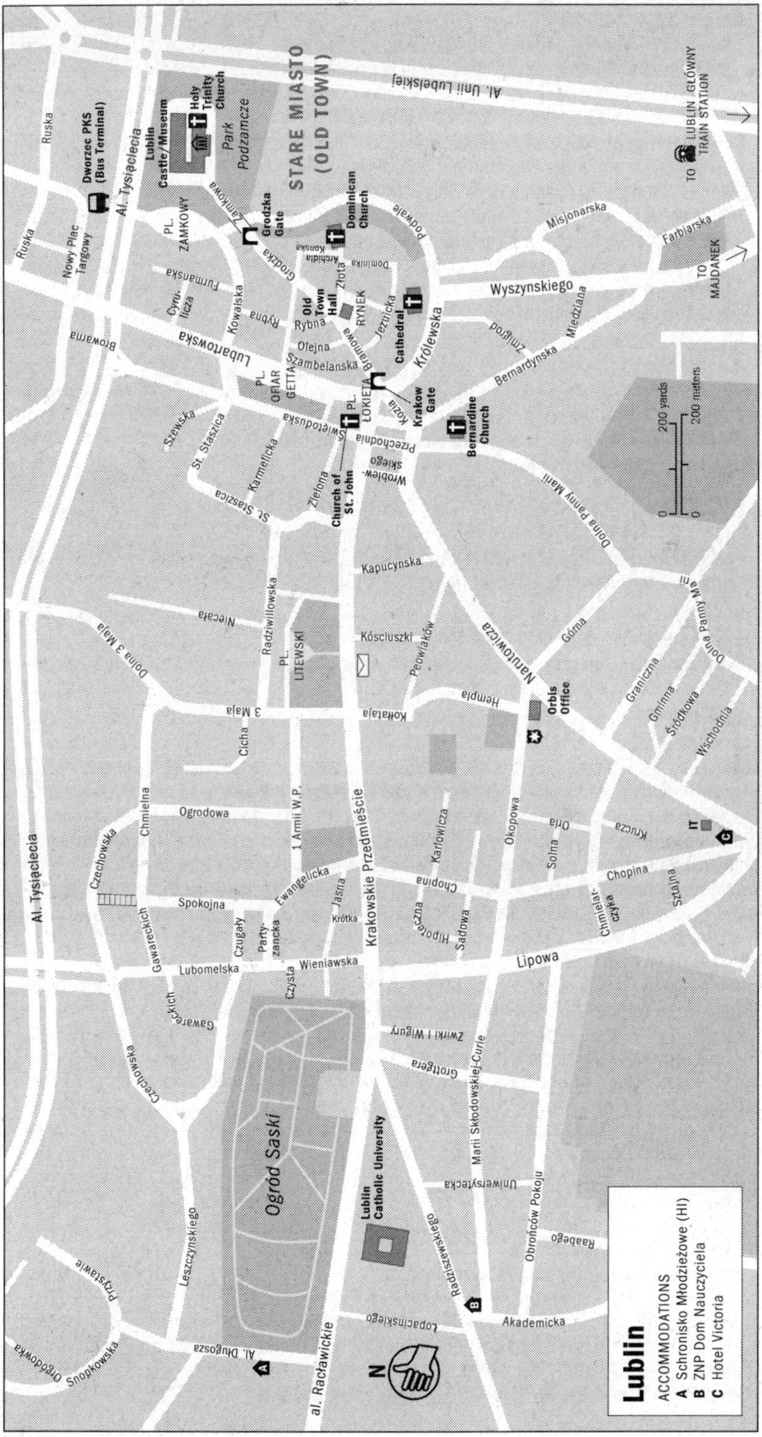
Lublin
ACCOMMODATIONS
A Schronisko Młodzieżowe (HI)
B ZNP Dom Nauczyciela
C Hotel Victoria
STARE MIASTO
(OLD TOWN)
Lublin Castle/Museum
Holy Trinity Church
Park Podzamcze
Dworzec PKS
(Bus Terminal)
Grodzka Gate
Dominican Church
Old Town Hall
RYNEK
Cathedral
Krakow Gate
Bernardine Church
Church of St. John
PL. ZAMKOWY
PL. OFIAR GETTA
PL. ŁOKIETA
PL. LITEWSKI
Orbis Office
IT
Lublin Catholic University
Ogród Saski
TO LUBLIN GŁÓWNY TRAIN STATION
TO MAJDANEK
200 yards
200 meters
Al. Unii Lubelskiej
Al. Tysiąclecia
Krakowskie Przedmieście
Lubartowska
Narutowicza
Lipowa
Królewska
Wyszynskiego
al. Racławickie
Al. Długosza
Akademicka
Marii Skłodowskiej-Curie
Radziszewskiego
Chopina
Okopowa
Ruska
Nowy Plac Targowy
Browarna
Kowalska
Grodzka
Zamkowa
Podwale
Misjonarska
Farbiarska
Bernardynska
Mledzlana
Świętoduska
Radziwiłłowska
Kapucynska
Kościuszki
Peowiaków
Hempla
Górna
Graniczna
Gminna
Środkowa
Wschodnia
Dolna Panny Marii
Dolna 3 Maja
3 Maja
Niecała
Chmielna
Ogrodowa
Spokojna
Czechowska
Gawareckich
Lubomelska
Wieniawska
1 Armii W.P.
Ewangelicka
Karłowicza
Hipoteczna
Sadowa
Solna
Orla
Krucza
Sztajna
Zwirki i Wigury
Grottgera
Uniwersytecka
Obrońców Pokoju
Raabego
Łopacinskiego
Leszczynskiego
Przystawie
Snopkowska
Ogrodowa
Szambelanska
Olejna
Rybna
Jezuicka
Bramowa
Złota
Dominikańska
Archidia Konska
Furmanska
Cyru- licza
Szewska
St. Staszica
Karmelicka
Zielona
Wróblewskiego
Przechodnia
Kozia
Zmigrod
Cicha
Kołłątaja
Czugały
Party- zancka
Czysta
Jasna
Krótka
Chmielar- czyka

POLAND

Schronisko Młodzieżowe (HI), ul. Długosza 6a (tel. 533 06 28), west of the center near the KUL. Walk to the end of the Ogród Saski and turn right on ul. Długosza. Turn left at the blue hostel sign after passing the colorful Warszałaty PSB Skolny. Isolated, but clean and quiet. Triples 19zł per person, non-members 20zł; 6-person dorm 16zł, non-members 18zł. Linen 4.50zł. Lockout 10am-5pm. Curfew 10pm.

Hotel Victoria, ul. Narutowicza 58/60 (tel. 532 70 11; fax 532 90 26). Take bus #8, 9, or 11 south from the city center. More upscale and closer to Stare Miasto than the other options. Well-lit, sparkling rooms. Singles 80zł; doubles with full bath 200zł. MC/Visa.

ZNP Dom Nauczyciela, ul. Akademicka 4 (tel. 533 82 85), near the KUL. From the Ogród Saski bus stop, cross the street and follow ul. Łopacińskiego until it turns into ul. Akademicka. Primarily for visiting teachers, but anyone can stay in one of its minimalist rooms. A good choice if you want to stay out late. Singles 64zł; doubles 72zł; single bed in a double 31zł; 6-person dorms 27zł.

FOOD

Lublin's eateries cluster around ul. Krakówskie Przedmieście. A dozen **beer gardens** are situated immediately outside the gate to Stare Miasto, and several more can be found inside. A well-stocked **delicatessen,** ul. Narutowicza 38/42 (tel. 534 37 72), is open daily 9:30am-10:30pm.

Pani Pizza, ul. Kósciuszki 3 (tel. 532 61 59), behind the post office. Ever-changing variety of big pizzas (4-10zł). Open M-Sa 10am-9pm, Su 11am-9pm.

Pod Basztab, ul. Królewska 6. A spotless milk-bar with a good selection. *Pierogi* 4zł, entrees 6zł. Open daily 10am-10pm.

Bar 21, ul. Krakówskie Przedmieście 21. The Polish take on fast food. Salads and platters like "Texas Chili" 6zł. Open M-Sa 10am-9pm, Su 11am-9pm.

Bar Turystyczny Mleczny, ul. Krakówskie Przedmieście 29. Spartan decor recreates communism for those who miss it. Soups 1.50zł, full meals 4-7zł. Open M-Sa 7am-6pm, Su 8am-5pm.

SIGHTS

The 19th-century ochre facades of **ul. Krakówskie Przedmieście** lead into the medieval Stare Miasto, home of Lublin's historical sights. Pl. Litewskim showcases an **obelisk** commemorating the 1569 union of Poland and Lithuania and a **Tomb of the Unknown Soldier.** Pl. Lokietka, east of pl. Litewskim, is home to the 1827 **New Town Hall** *(Nowy Ratusz)*, seat of Lublin's government. To the right begins ul. Królewska, with the grand **Cathedral of St. John the Baptist and St. John the Evangelist** (*Katedra Św. Jana Chrzciciela i Jana Ewangelisty*, 1586-1596). The cathedral's frescoes, gilded altar, and big barrel vault make it worth a visit.

Ul. Krakówskie Przedmieście travels through pl. Łokietka to the fortified **Kraków Gate,** which houses the **Historical Division of the Lublin Museum** *(Oddział Historyczny Muzeum Lubelskiego)*, pl. Łokietka 3. (Tel. 532 60 01. Open W-Sa 9am-4pm, Su 9am-5pm. 1zł.) Across the gate, ul. Bramowa leads to the *rynek*, lined with early Renaissance houses. In the *rynek's* center stands the 18th-century Neoclassical **Old Town Hall** *(Stare Ratusz)*. A walk along ul. Grodzka leads through the 15th-century **Grodzka Gate** *(Brama Grodzka)* to ul. Zamkowa, which runs to the massive **Lublin Castle** *(Zamek Lubelski)*. Most of the structure was built in the 14th-century by King Kazimierz Wielki (see **History,** p. 399), but was restored in the 19th-century with a neo-Gothic exterior. During the Nazi occupation, the castle functioned as a Gestapo jail; the prisoners were shot en masse when the Nazis had to make a hasty retreat.

Inside the castle, the **Lublin Museum** (tel. 532 50 01) features historical paintings, armaments, and ornamental art. While its collection is interesting, the Russo-Byzantine frescoes in the attached **Holy Trinity Church** are truly stunning. The panels were completed in 1418 and depict various biblical scenes. One of the few remaining examples of such art in Europe, the church is remarkably well maintained. (Open W-Sa 9am-4pm, Su 9am-5pm. 8zł for entry to both.)

NIGHTLIFE

Thanks to its large student crowd, Lublin has an impressive number of cafes and pubs and an active music scene. Stare Miasto is the center of the city's nightlife.

Colosseum Club, Radziszewskiego 8 (tel. 534 43 00), near the University. This booty-shakin' university favorite features a great bar and disco. Cover fluctuates with the size of the crowd. On the weekend, expect to pay 10zł if you're a man, half that for the ladies. The party starts at 8pm and rages until 1-4am.

Old Pub, ul. Grodzka 8 (tel. 743 71 27). Vibrant, pleasant, and popular with an older crowd. Sit at antique tables or enjoy the garden out back. 0.5L Kilkenny 9zł, 0.5L *Żywiec* 6zł. Open daily 11am-10pm. MC/Visa.

Cap Pub, across the street from Old Pub (above). A medieval-themed hangout popular with students. 0.3L *Żywiec* 3zł, 0.5L 4zł Open daily 4:30pm-2am.

Pub Non-Stop, Plac Łokietka 3 (tel. 534 65 69), next door to the Cap Pub. Lures young hipsters with the comfiest chairs in town. Open daily 8am-2am.

Jazz Pizza, ul. Krakówskie Przedmieście 55 (tel. 743 61 49). The full bar and frequent jazz concerts made all the more authentic by the wall-portraits of Dizzy Gillespie. Guinness 8zł, EB 4.10zł, pizza 6-8zł. Open M-Sa 2pm-midnight, Su 3-10pm.

Café NATO, ul. Kósciuszki 8. Celebrate Poland's acceptance into the Western military alliance at this dimly lit—and therefore trendy—basement bar. Tea 1.5zł, rum 8zł. Open M-F 10am-11pm, Sa-Su noon-11pm.

NEAR LUBLIN: MAJDANEK

The largest concentration camp after Auschwitz, **Majdanek** is all too near Lublin: it stands merely 4km from the city center, a 30min. walk down the road to Zamość (Road of the Martyrs of Majdanek; *Droga Męczenników Majdanka*). Approximately 235,000 people died here, including Jews, Poles, Danes, and others from all over Europe. **Majdanek State Museum** *(Panstwowe Muzeum na Majdanku)* was founded in 1944 after the liberation of Lublin. The Nazis didn't have time to destroy the camp, so the original structures stand in their entirety, including the gas chambers, the crematorium, the third field prisoners' barracks, the watchtowers, the guardhouses, and the electrified barbed-wire perimeter. (Museum open May-Sept. Tu-Su 8am-6pm; Mar.-Apr. and Oct.-Nov. Tu-Su 8am-3pm. Free; children under 14 not permitted. Tours in Polish 60zł, in English 100zł.)

A visit to Majdanek begins with the information building (tel. 744 26 48 or 744 19 55; fax 744 05 26), whose staff supplies free information in several languages and shows a 25min. documentary that includes the first footage taken after the camp's liberation. (Available in English, last showing 3pm. 2zł per person; min. 10zł per show.) Walking through the entire camp takes 1½-2hr. The route begins with the gas chambers; signs in Polish, English, French, Russian, and German explain Nazi methods of extermination and experimentation. Guardhouses #43-45 contain historical exhibitions, including statistical displays, prisoners' clothes, instruments of torture, and a sample of the 730kg of human hair exported from Majdanek to a fabric factory in Germany. Perhaps most shocking of all, guardhouse #52 is filled with the 800,000 pairs of shoes the Nazis took from victims of Majdanek and neighboring camps. At the end of the main path through the camp, the intact crematorium ovens sit next to the concrete dome of the mausoleum, which stands as a massive mound of ash and human bone. Black crows still patrol the area.

GETTING THERE. From Lublin, eastbound **bus** #28 from the train station, **trollies** #153 and 158 from al. Racławickie, and southbound trolly #156 from ul. Królewska all stop at the huge granite monument marking the entrance at Droga Męczenników Majdanka 67.

KAZIMIERZ DOLNY

Overlooking the mighty Wisła, this picturesque town has housed generations of Polish painters. Established by King Kazimierz Wielki in the 14th century (see **History,** p. 399), it's actually named in honor of Prince Kazimierz the Just, who in 1181 donated the settlement to a nunnery near Kraków. Kazimierz Dolny (KAH-zhee-myezh DOL-nih) burned down twice in the 16th century, Cossacks ransacked it during the 17th, and cholera and Swedes ravaged it in the 18th. Now, a mini-army of tourists and artists invade it daily, although most don't stay long enough to enjoy the town's most spectacular sight—sunset over the Wisła.

ORIENTATION & PRACTICAL INFORMATION. Some **buses** stop on the slow route between **Puławy** and **Lublin** (1½hr. to Lublin, 1 per hr., 6.30zł); others zoom to **Warsaw** (3½hr., 7 per day, 12zł). When coming from Lublin or Warsaw, Kazimierz will not be posted as the final destination—ask the driver if the bus is stopping there *(Czy ten autobus jedzie do Kazimierz?)*. When leaving Kazimierz by bus, don't assume that the driver will make the detour into the bus station—he or she will probably stop across the street just off the cobblestone **ul. Podzamcze.** If you've just arrived, follow ul. Podzamcze to the *rynek*. The **PTTK tourist office,** Rynek 27 (tel. 881 00 46), sells maps of town (3.50zł) and arranges private rooms. (Open May-Oct. M-F 8am-6pm, Sa-Su 10am-5:30pm; Nov.-Apr. M-F 8am-3pm, Sa-Su 10am-2pm. No English spoken.) A **pharmacy** sits at Rynek 17 (tel. 881 01 20; open M-F 8am-7pm, Sa 8am-3pm, Su 9am-2pm). The **post office,** ul. Tyszkiewicza 2 (tel. 881 05 15; fax 881 05 00), is a block west of the *rynek*. (Open May-Sept. M-F 8am-8pm, Sa-Su 10am-5pm; Oct.-Apr. M-F 8am-8pm, Sa 9am-1pm, Su 9-11am.) It also offers **currency exchange** (open M-F 10am-5pm), **telephones** (open daily 7am-9pm), and a MC/Visa **ATM.** There is **no bank. Postal code:** 24-120. **Phone code:** (0)81.

ACCOMMODATIONS & FOOD. Rooms in town are fairly limited, especially during summer weekends and during the **Festival of Folk Groups and Singer** *(Sogólnopolski Festiwal Kapel i Śpiewaków Ludowych)*, which takes place during the last week of June. It's especially important to call ahead for reservations during these times. **PTTK** (see above) arranges private singles (100zł) and doubles (140zł) in the area. Better rates can be found by looking at the advertised rooms around town. The clean, comfortable, and conveniently located **Youth Hostel Strażnica,** ul. Senatorska 23a (tel. 881 04 27), sits only one block southwest of the *rynek*. Walk down ul. Senatorska toward the river and follow it as it hooks to the left. Its 50 beds come in 2- to 10-person rooms. (Doubles and triples 28zł per person; dorms 24zł; sheets 4zł; breakfast included.) Next to Strażnica but more expensive is **Hotel Łaźnia,** ul. Senatorska 21 (tel. 881 02 98). Singles (100zł), doubles (140zł), and triples (170zł) are all lavishly decorated with hardwood floors and beautiful bedspreads. Keep going down ul. Senatorska to the Wisła, and walk along the bank to **Przystan Camping,** which offers a pretty space but limited facilities. (Tent and patch of grass 6zł.)

A **grocery** lies just south of the *rynek* at ul. Klasztorna 5. (Open M-F 6am-6pm, Sa 6am-3pm, Su 9am-2pm.) **Bistro U Zbyszka,** ul. Sadowa 4 (tel. 090 39 85 07), just west of the *rynek* off ul. Nadwiślańska, invites guests to cool off in its pool (4zł per hr.). (*Kiełbasa* 8zł. Open daily noon-2am.) An old-fashioned bakery with the freshest rolls in town, **Piekarnia Sarzyński,** ul. Nadrzeczna 6, is a few steps from the *rynek*. (Bread 5zł, tarts 8zł. Open daily 6am-9pm.) There is a popular fast food Polish eatery next door that servers *pierogi* and soups. **Restauracja Staropolska,** ul. Nadrzeczna 14 (tel./fax 81 02 50), is the town's culinary legend, serving Polish food at its best in the shade of spruce trees with correspondingly high prices. (*Barszcz* with meat dumplings 9zł. Open daily noon-10pm. MC/Visa/AmEx.)

SIGHTS & ENTERTAINMENT. Hike up to the **castle tower,** which used to alert the residents to passing boats on which they could levy tolls. From this lofty vantage point, you can see not only a long stretch of the Wisła, but also the castle at Janowiec. (Open Tu-Su 10am-5pm. Castle ruins and tower 2zł.) On your way up, stop by the 16th-century **Cathedral of St. John the Baptist and St. Bartholomew** *(Kosciól Farny sw. Jana Chrzciciela i sw. Bartlomieja)* and survey the lovely interior, as well as one of Poland's oldest (1620) and best-preserved organs. For an even better view, take a left by the *Zamek*, cross the road, and head up the trail to **Three Crosses Hill.** The crosses were erected in memory of those who died in an 18th-century plague. As you climb down the hill and return to ul. Zankowa, the **Galerie Dzwonnica,** ul. Zankowa 2, will be to your left. The gallery hosts an interesting collection of 20th-century Polish painting and photography. (2zł, students 1zł.) The **Museum of Goldsmithery** *(Muzeum Sztuki Złotniczej)*, ul. Senatorska 11/13, and the **Kamienica Celejowska** display a joint exhibit including ancient relics, modern ornamental art, paintings inspired by the town, and a display on the town's pre-war Jewish community. The **Museum of Natural History** *(Muzeum Przyrodnicze)*, ul. Pulawska 54 (tel. 881 03 26 and 881 03 41), a 10min. walk from the *rynek*, displays fossils and rocks from the Kazimierz region. (Museums open May-Sept. Tu-Su 10am-4pm; Oct.-Apr. 10am-3pm. Each museum 3zł, students 1.50zł.)

ZAMOŚĆ

Zamość, the dream of young aristocrat Jan Zamojski, sprang up in the 1580s. Having studied in Padua, Zamojski wanted to recreate its beauty in his homeland. He oversaw the building of a town hall, opulent houses, churches, an immense *rynek*, and one of only two fortresses in Poland to resist the Swedes in 1656. Touted by locals as the "Padua of the North," Zamość is now undergoing widespread restoration in an attempt to resuscitate its former beauty. The town square is a lovely place to relax with the locals among the town's storied arcades.

ORIENTATION & PRACTICAL INFORMATION. To get to the *rynek* from the **train station,** ul. Szczebrzeska 11 (tel. 638 69 44), turn right outside the front door and walk toward the spires of Stare Miasto on ul. Szczebrzeska. The road curves to the left after 5min. and turns into Akademicka, which deposits you right outside the cathedral. A right up Staszica here leads to the *rynek*. **Trains** run to **Lublin** (3hr., 2 per day, 11-16zł) and **Warsaw** (5hr., 1 per day, 30zł). For a **taxi,** call 96 22 or 919. To reach the *rynek* from the **bus station,** ul. Sadowa 6 (tel. 639 50 81), turn right up Sadowa, which turns into ul. Goninna. After 5min., turn right onto ul. Partyzantów. From here you can take any city bus (1zł) one stop to the beginning of the street and the edge of the old town. Or, walk left onto Lukasińskiego at the end of Partyzantów and take an immediate right onto Staszica. **Buses** go to **Lublin** (2hr., 37 per day, 12zł) and **Warsaw** (5hr., 5 per day, 31.50zł). The **ZOIT tourist office,** Rynek Wielki 13 (tel. 639 22 92; fax 627 08 13), in the town hall sells maps. **Bank Pekao S.A.,** ul. Grodzka 2 (tel. 639 20 40), cashes **traveler's checks,** gives MC/Visa cash advances, and has a Cirrus/MC/Visa **ATM** outside. (Open M-F 8am-6pm, Sa 10am-2pm.) The **pharmacy** is **Apteka Rektorska,** Rynek 2 (tel. 639 23 86; open M-Sa 8am-3pm). The **post office** and **telephones** are at ul. Kościuszki 9 (tel. 38 51 23; open M-F 7am-8pm, Sa 8am-3pm). **Postal code:** 22-400. **Phone code:** (0)84.

ACCOMMODATIONS & FOOD. Dom Turysty "Marta," ul. Zamenhofa 11 (tel. 639 26 39), is in the center of town. Follow the directions from the train station to the *rynek* (see above), then walk up ul. 1-Maja, passing the town hall on your left. Take the second right onto Zamenhofa with Dom Turysty on your right. This tourist hotel rents basic rooms with communal bathrooms, featuring clean showers and less clean toilets. (7-bed dorms 20zł; doubles 60zł.) To reach **Ośrodek Sportui Rekreacji,** Królowej Jadwigi 8 (tel. 638 60 11), follow the directions to the *rynek*, then take ul. Staszica to the cathedral and turning right down Akademicka. Turn left on Królowej Jadwigi; the building is next to a stadium. This lodging offers clean singles (72zł), doubles (90zł), triples (105zł), and quads (121zł), all with bath. Reserve 3-4 days in advance or sports teams will beat you to the beds. **Camping Duet,** Królowej Jadwigi 14 (tel. 39 24 99), is in a wooded area 5min. down the street. (Campsites 3zł per person; tents 6zł. 4-bed bungalows with bath and fridge 60zł for 1 person; 70zł for 2; 90zł for 3; 110zł for 4.)

Pleasant outdoor cafes encircle the *rynek*, but apart from them, culinary options in Zamość are limited. One tasty option is **Cafe-Restaurant Muzealna,** ul. Ormiańska 30 (tel. 638 64 94, ext. 40), next to the town hall. (Entrees 3.50-7zł. Open daily noon-midnight.) **Ratuszowa,** Rynek 13 (tel. 627 15 57), in the town hall, serves traditional Polish fare in a relaxed cafe setting. (Soups 2-4zł; entrees under 14zł. Open daily 9am-11pm.) A **grocery** is on the corner of Ormiańska and Bazyliańska. (Open M-Sa 6am-8pm, Su 8am-4pm.)

SIGHTS & ENTERTAINMENT. While the whole town is essentially one giant sight, the splendidly preserved **Armenian burgher houses,** ul. Ormiańska 22, 24, 26, 28, and 30, in the northeast corner of the *rynek*, are especially worthwhile. These houses, complete with intricate woodwork and bright interiors, are what remains from Zamość's economic heyday. House #26 is the headquarters of the **Muzeum Okręgowe** (tel. 638 64 94), which displays religious art. (Open Tu-Su 9am-4pm. 3zł, students 1zł.) A. Allori's *Annunciation* is inside the **cathedral,** ul. Kolegiacka; follow ul. Staszica from the *rynek* to get there. The region's religious riches—chalices, sculptures, and saints' relics—pack the adjoining **museum.** (Open May-Sept. M and Th-Sa 10am-4pm, Su 10am-1pm. 1zł.) If you're lucky, the cathedral's **bell tower** will be open (2zł). Follow the directions to the cathedral and cross Akademicka to reach war trophies and military weapons in **Arsenał Museum,** ul. Zamkowa 2 (tel. 638 40 76; open Tu-Su 9am-4pm; last admission at 3:30pm; 3zł, students 2zł).

Pool tables abound in the bars, and many residents and tourists head to the *rynek* for an evening *piwo;* unfortunately, the good times wind down before midnight. **Jazz Club Kosz,** ul. Zamenhofa 3 (tel. 638 60 41), hosts live jazz year-round; enter from the back of the building. (Open M-Sa noon-midnight, Su 4pm-midnight.) At the end of May, jazz musicians from Poland, Ukraine, and Belarus jam at the **Jazz in the Borderlands** (Jazz na Kresach) festival. In late September jazz singers gather for the **International Festival of Jazz Vocalists** (Międzynarodowe Spotkania Wokalistów Jazzowych.) Experimental theater groups take over Zamość's streets and theaters for the **Zamość Summer Theater Festival** (Zamojskie Lato Teatralne). Contact **Wojewódzki Dom Kultury (WDK),** ul. Partyzantów 13 (tel./fax 639 20 21), for info.

ŁAŃCUT

Apart from its castle, there isn't much to recommend the small town of Łańcut, but once you see it, you won't care about seeing anything else. Dominating the town economically and physically, the palace has a more intriguing history—and better art collection—than many small European cities.

ORIENTATION & PRACTICAL INFORMATION. **Buses** (tel. 21 21) roll to: **Przemyśl** (1½hr., 13 per day, 8zł) and **Rzeszów** (30min., 7 per day, 2.50zł). **Trains** (tel. 23 17) chug to: **Kraków** (2½hr., 9 per day, 12zł); **Przemyśl** (1hr., 23 per day, 8zł); and **Warsaw** (7hr., 2 per day, 40zł). From the **bus station,** ul. Sikorskiego, opposite the palace gardens, it's a 10min. walk along ul. Kościuszki to the *rynek*. Turn right as you leave the station. To get to the palace from the **train station,** ul. Kolejowa, call a **taxi** (tel. 20 00), or head along ul. Żeromskiego, across from the station, and take the first right onto ul. Grunwaldzka (30min.). To reach the *rynek*, turn right where ul. Grunwaldzka meets ul. Kościuszki, which leads to the palace gates. The **Trans-Euro-Tours tourist office,** ul. Kościuszki 2 (tel./fax 30 16), provides the scoop on hotels. (Open M-F 9am-5pm, Sa 9am-1pm.) **Postal code:** 37-100. **Phone code:** (0)17-225.

ACCOMMODATIONS & FOOD. The quiet **Hotel Zamkowy,** ul. Zamkowa 1 (tel. 26 71), in the palace park, attracts an international crowd and fills up fast. The rooms are clean and well priced. (Doubles 50-70zł, with bath 70-130zł; triples 70zł, 135zł. Check-out noon.) **Dom Wycieczkowy PTTK,** ul. Dominikańska 1 (tel. 45 12), off the *rynek*, occupies the old Dominican monastery. The spacious rooms have been renovated recently and the bathrooms are passable. (Doubles 20zł per person; 5-bed dorms 14zł.) The *rynek* contains a variety of cafes and fast-food joints. In the palace, **Restauracja Zamkowa,** ul. Zamkowa 1 (tel. 28 05), serves tasty soups (3-7zł) and entrees (10-27zł) in its stately dining hall. (Open daily 9am-9pm.) The four basic food groups are all available at the **grocery,** Super Sam Max, Rynek 29. (Open M-Sa 8am-9pm, Su 8:30am-8pm.)

SIGHTS. The **Łańcut Castle** (Zamek w Łańcucie) complex grants visitors a glimpse into the once lavish lifestyle of Polish nobility. Founded by King Kazimierz III Wielki in the middle of the 14th century (see **History,** p. 399), the town was fortified between 1610 and 1620 by the Lubomirski family, who acquired the castle after the death of Stanisław Stadnicki (a.k.a. the "Devil of Łańcut"). The Baroque fortress survived Swedish and Turkish sieges, but not Elżbieta Lubomirska z Czartoryskich, an 18th-century, lap-dog-loving duchess with French tastes and an eye for fine art. Under her direction, the castle was transformed to better suit her personal aesthetic. The Potocki family inherited the palace and continued to expand it. Although it was spared damage during WWII, the palace lost its soul when the last Lord of Łańcut fled Poland in 1944, taking 11 railway cars full of valuable artifacts with him. The new government turned the complex into a **museum** showcasing what was left of the furniture, architecture, and art. The **ticket office** (tel. 20 08; fax 20 12) is just inside the palace gate. The required tour includes the **Orangery** (Oranżeria), inside the palace grounds, and the **Powozownia,** the largest display of carriages in Europe. (Open Apr.-Sept. Tu-Sa 9am-4pm, Su and holidays 9am-3pm; Feb.-Mar. and Oct.-Nov. Tu-Su 9am-3pm. Tours 12zł, students 7zł.) Around the left side of the carriage building you'll find a small display of 16th- and 17th-century ruins, complete with hymnal accompaniment. (2zł, students 1zł.) The extensive park grounds surrounding the palace provide a serene and shady setting for walking or reading. The palace hosts an International **Music Festival** in mid-May and the **Interpretive Music Concert** (Kursy Interpretacji Muzycznej) every June. Outside the main palace gates and left onto ul. 3-ego Maja stands a **synagogue,** with impressive 18th-century polychromy. It may be closed, but be sure to take a peek through a window at the interior's bold colors.

PRZEMYŚL

Less than a *złoty*'s toss from the Ukrainian border, Przemyśl (PZHE-mysh-l) exhibits an Eastern flair matched by no other Polish city. Churches stand on every corner, and on Sundays the city resonates with the sound of Catholic masses broadcasting from the many outdoor loudspeakers.

ORIENTATION & PRACTICAL INFORMATION. The **bus station** is across the tracks from the **train station** at pl. Legionów; both are an 8min. walk from the city center. From the bus station, cross the train tracks through the tunnel marked "Peron 1, 2, 3, 4," at the far left of the bus station (facing the train tracks), and you will emerge at the train station. Take a diagonal left from Pl. Legionów onto Ul. Sowińskiego after Orbis, then turn right on **ul. Mickiewicza,** the main road that veers to the right again and becomes **ul. Jagiellońska.** To reach the *rynek,* head straight from ul. Mickiewicza along the much narrower **ul. Franciszkańska,** bearing left at the fork. **Trains** (tel. 678 40 31) go to: **Kraków** (4hr., 9 per day, 26-42zł); **Lublin** (4hr., 1 per day, 27zł); **Warsaw** (7hr., 4 per day, 69zł); **Lviv,** Ukraine (4hr., 3 per day, 39zł); and **Odessa,** Ukraine (18hr., 1 per day, 127zł). **Buses,** ul. Czarnieckiego (tel. 678 54 35), travel to: **Lublin** (4hr., 3 per day, 23zł); **Sanok** (2hr., 5 per day, 7.40zł); and **Lviv** (3hr., 1 per day, 15zł). Both the train and bus stations have **luggage storage** (2.80zł per day). **PTTK,** ul. Grodzka 1 (tel. 678 32 74 or 678 27 25), carries **maps** (3.50zł; open M-F 8am-3pm). **Orbis,** pl. Legionów 1 (tel. 678 33 66; fax 678 52 65), arranges international bus tickets. (Open M-F 8am-6pm, Sa 8am-2pm). **Bank PKO S.A.,** Ul. Jagiełłońska 7 (tel. 678 34 59), handles **traveler's checks** and MC/Visa cash advances (open M-F 8am-6pm, Sa 10am-2pm), but *kantory* give better rates on cash. A Cirrus/MC/Visa **ATM** sits outside the bank. The **pharmacy** (tel. 678 45 34) sits a little farther down ul. Jagiełłońska. (Open M-F 8am-6:30pm, Sa 8am-2pm.) The **post office** at ul. Mickiewicza 13 (tel. 678 32 70; open M-F 7:30am-8pm, Sa 8am-2pm,

Su 9-11am) has **telephones** (tel. 678 67 18; open daily 7am-9pm). **Postal code:** 37-700. **Phone code:** (0)10.

ACCOMMODATIONS & FOOD. Most hotels in town are occupied by traveling merchants from Russia and Ukraine, so reserving ahead is recommended. An exception is **Youth Hostel Matecznik (HI),** ul. Lelewela 6 (tel. 670 61 45), which has an inconvenient location but is popular with students. From the train station, head toward the center and turn right down ul. Jagiełłońska. The road curves to the left, then crosses the bridge on the right onto ul. 3-go Maja. Ul. Lelewela is on the left after 10min.; the hostel is the pink building set well off the road on the right (20min.). Alternatively, take local bus #2 or 14 from Mickiewicza (1.10zł; buy tickets at a kiosk) and get off at ul. 3-go Maja. (9zł per person. Check-out 9am. Curfew 10pm.) The central and immaculate **Dom Wycieczkowy PTTK "Podzamcze,"** ul. Waygarta 3 (tel. 678 53 74), sits down the hill off ul. Grodzka, which runs out from the *rynek*. (Doubles, triples, and quads 18zł per person. Check-out 10am.) A left onto Mickiewicza from the train station leads to **Lo Hotel Hala,** ul. Mickiewicza 30 (tel. 678 38 49). The clean but small rooms all have bath and shower. (Singles 57zł; doubles 73zł; triples 84zł; quads 105zł.)

You can buy milk or *wódka* at the **grocery,** pl. Na Bramie 5 (tel. 78 35 03), between the train station and the *rynek*. (Open M-Sa 7am-8pm, Su 8am-1pm.) The best eatery in town is **Pizzeria Margherita,** Rynek 4 (tel. 678 73 47), where you'll find 39 different kinds of pizza. (Small 3-7zł; large 6.50-13zł; spaghetti 6-13zł. Open daily 11am-11pm.) A busy pub next door has the same name. (Open M-Th and Su noon-midnight, F-Sa noon-2am.) **Polonia Restaurant,** ul. Franciszkańska 35 (tel. 678 57 78), serves tasty Polish cuisine. (Entrees 5-10zł. Open daily 9am-10pm.)

POLAND

SIGHTS. The twisting cobblestone streets of the city center and the paths along the river are ideal for strolling. From the *rynek*, a left onto Fredny as you're looking down ul. Grodzka leads to the austere **cathedral** at ul. Katedralna. Glance inside to see its richly decorated Renaissance interior and the ornate stained-glass windows. At the beginning of the *rynek* on ul. Franciszkańska sits another Renaissance building, **Kościół Ojców Franciszkanów,** featuring myriad golden sculptures and paintings. To get to the **Carmelite Monastery,** follow the directions to the cathedral, then continue on Kapitulna as it curves around to the left onto ul. Karmelicka. The monastery houses bells that ring on the hour and a silver-laced ceiling inside; its corresponding spike-steepled convent sits up the hill farther on ul. Tatarska. The white Renaissance castle *(zamek)* on ul. Zamkowa can be found by following the directions to the cathedral and turning right up ul. Zamkowa. (Open daily Apr.-Sept. 9am-6pm; Oct.-Mar. 10am-4pm.) Climb one of the towers for views of Przemyśl and the river San below. (1zł, students 0.50zł.) The castle theater stages three to four performances each year; check the gate for schedules.

Going toward ul. Franciszkanska from the *rynek*, turning right up Asnyka, and then left onto Katedralna brings you to BPA Śnigurskiego. Here, the **Museum Diecezalne,** ul. Śnigurskiego 2, has a room devoted to Polish Catholic, Ukrainian Greek Catholic, and Jewish artifacts, and a shrine to Pope John Paul II. Monks and nuns run the museum and encourage donations. To enter, push the button that says "museum" and go to the third floor. (Open May 3-Oct. 30 daily 10am-3pm.) Next door, **Museum Narodowe,** ul. Śnigurskiego 3, has an icon exhibit and a decent gallery of modern art. (Open Tu and F 10am-5pm, W-Th and Sa-Su 10am-2pm.)

THE CARPATHIANS (KARPATY)

The Polish Carpathians annually lure millions of Poles and foreigners to their superb hiking and skiing. In the skyscraping Tatry, Zakopane offers sky-high vistas at rock-bottom prices, while Szczyrk is a year-round mountain sport mecca of the Beskidy to the west and Sanok serves as a base for trips into the rounded hills of the Bieszczady to the east. In the midst of all this sport, Bielsko-Biała inspires with its history of religious tolerance as well as its spectacular scenery.

TATRAN MAPS. For a map of the Polish and Slovak Tatras, see p. 654-655 in the **Slovakia** chapter.

ZAKOPANE

Set in a valley surrounded by jagged Tatran peaks and soul-stirring alpine meadows, Zakopane (ZAH-ko-PAH-neh; pop. 100,000), Poland's premier year-round resort, buzzes with hikers and skiers. While prices in the Swiss and Austrian Alps are often untouchable, meals and lodging here are still reasonably priced. As an added bonus, the native highlander culture—which has inspired Polish writers, musicians, and artists—continues to thrive today in architecture, folk costumes, and the local dialect.

ORIENTATION

The **bus station** is on the corner of ul. Kościuszki and ul. Jagiełłońska. The **train station** lies across ul. Jagiełłońska. The center is a 10-15min. walk away along the tree-lined **ul. Kościuszki. Ul. Krupówki,** the dining and shopping hub, intersects ul. Kościuszki after 10-15min.

PRACTICAL INFORMATION

Trains: Ul. Chramcówki 35 (tel. 145 04). To: **Bielsko-Biała** (3½hr., 24 per day, 13zł); **Kraków Głowny** (3½hr., 12 per day, 13.82zł); and **Warsaw** (8hr., 5 per day, 21.38zł).

Buses: Ul. Kościuszki 25 (tel. 146 03). To: **Kraków** (2½hr., 22 per day, 10zł); **Warsaw** (8hr., 1 per day, 33zł); and **Poprad,** Slovakia (2½hr., 5 per day, 12zł). A **private express line** runs between Zakopane and Kraków in less than 2hr. (nonstop service, 7 per day, 10zł); buses leave from a well-marked stop on ul. Kościuszki, 50m toward the center from the bus station. Look for the "express" sign. Orbis (below) sells tickets.

Taxis: Radiotaxi, tel. 919, 120 87, and 142 32.

Bike Rental: Ital-Bike, Ul. Piłsudskiego 4a (tel. 206 26 87). Italian mountain bikes 5zł per hr., 20zł per 4hr., or 25zł per day. Open July-Aug. M-Su 10am-6pm. **Marek Malczewski Sport,** ul. Bronisława Czecha (tel. 120 05), near the "Pod Krokwią" campground. Turn right, take the first left and walk 100m from the campground; the shop is a mountain hut on your right–you'll see the bikes. Mountain bikes 5zł per hr. or 35zł per day. In-line skates 5zł per hr. Open daily 9am-7pm.

Tourist Offices: Tourist Agency Redykołka, ul. Kościeliska 1 (tel./fax 13 253; email king@zakopane.top.pl), arranges a variety of activities in Zakopane. They secure impeccable private rooms (20zł), private homes (50zł), and other accommodations, run a variety of English-language tours, and offer Dunajec rafting (90zł). Open July-Aug. and Dec.-Mar. M-Sa 9am-6pm, Su 10am-3pm; Sept.-Nov. and Apr.-June M-Sa 9am-5pm, Su 10am-1pm. Email in advance for priority service. **IT,** ul. Kościuszki 17 (tel. 122 11; fax 660 51), at the intersection with ul. Sienkiewicza. Walk right from the bus station up ul. Kościuszki, and look for a light alpine hut. English spoken. Sells **maps** (3-5zł) and arranges private accommodations (30zł per person). Open daily 8am-8pm.

Budget Travel: Orbis, ul. Krupówki 22 (tel. 146 09; fax 122 38). Sells plane, bus, and train tickets, and arranges daytrips (*Dunajec* rafting 58zł). Open July-Aug. and Dec.-Mar. M-Sa 9am-7pm; Sept.-Nov. and Apr.-June M-Sa 9am-5pm.

Currency Exchange: Bank PKO S.A., ul. Gimnazjalna 1 (tel. 685 05), north of and parallel to ul. Kościuszki, behind the bus station. Also at ul. Krupówki 71. Cashes traveler's checks for a 0.5% commission and gives MC/Visa cash advances. Open M-F 8am-6pm, Sa 10am-2pm.

ATMs: Cirrus/Plus/AmEx/MC/Visa in front of the bus station and on the right side of the "Granit" department store, ul. Kościuszki 3.

Luggage Storage: At the train station, 3.50zł per day. Open 1:30pm-1pm. At the bus station, 3zł per day. Open daily 8am-7pm.

Pharmacy: Ul. Krupówki 39 (tel. 633 31). Open M-F 8am-8pm, Sa 8am-3pm. List in the window posts names of 24hr. pharmacies.

Mountain Rescue Service: Ul. Piłsudskiego 63a (tel. 634 44).

Post Office: Ul. Krupówki 20 (tel. 638 58). Open M-F 7am-8pm, Sa 8am-3pm, Su 9am-noon. **Postal code:** 34-500.

Internet Access: Internet Cafe, Ul. Krupówki 30, in the Morskie Oko complex. Closed for renovation in 1999, but should reopen in 2000. 7zł for 30min. Open daily 10am-9pm.

Telephones: Ul. Zaruskiego 1 (tel./fax 144 21), in the post office building. Entrance on ul. Zaruskiego under the "Telekomunikacja Polska" sign. Phone cards and tokens sold, faxes sent, operator-assisted calls received. Open M-F 7am-9pm, Sa-Su 8am-9pm. **Phone code:** (0)18 20.

ACCOMMODATIONS

Since Zakopane sits at the summit of mountain tourism in Poland, it is crowded from July to September, around Christmas, during February, and around Easter. Prices skyrocket in high seasons by 50-100%. **Redykołka** (see **Tourist Offices,** above) is a popular source for private rooms and pensions. To find your own private room, look for *pokój*, *noclegi*, or *Zimmer* signs (25-30zł with some haggling). Hikers often stay in *schroniska* (mountain huts), but call at least three days in advance in summer to avoid being stranded.

The Cukiers, ul. Za Strugiem 10. From the bus station, go right up ul. Kościuszki toward the center, turn right onto ul. Krupówki, then left onto Kościeliska. Ul. Za Strugiem is 10min. up the road on the left. A friendly highlander family provides clean rooms decorated with original woodwork and intricately embroidered curtains. It's a 30min. trek, but their two houses are next to hiking trails. Doubles and triples with views of the Giewont peak 30zł per person. Reserve three days in advance with Mrs. Stanisława Cukier (tel. 666 29) or Mrs. Anna Puciło (tel. 629 20).

POLAND

Schronisko Morskie Oko (tel. 776 09), by the Morskie Oko lake, 7km from the bus out of Zakopane (carriages make the trip from the bus drop-off; see **Hiking,** below). Take the bus from the station to Łysa Polana, or a direct minibus from opposite the bus station (30min.). A gorgeous, popular hostel in an ideal hiking location. 3- to 6-bed dorms 32zł; 20zł in the old part of the hostel. Reception 8:30am-9:30pm. Call 4-7 days in advance.

PTTK Dom Turysty, ul. Zaruskiego 5 (tel. 632 07; fax 123 58). A large chalet in the center of town. Walk down ul. Kościuszki from the bus station; it turns into ul. Zaruskiego after the intersection with Krupówki. Spacious rooms and reasonable bathrooms with hot water. 4-bed dorms 28-34zł; 6- to 8-bed dorms 20zł; large dorms 17zł. 3zł surcharge for stays of only one night. The repertoir of their theater, **Teatr Witkacego,** includes plays by Arthur Miller, Shakespeare, Pinter, and Molière. Check-out 10am.

Schronisko Młodzieżowe (HI), ul. Nowotarska 45 (tel. 662 03). From the bus station, walk down ul. Kościuszki toward town, then take the second right onto ul. Sienkiewicza and walk two blocks. The hostel is across the street. Small rooms in a large, loud building. Showers open 5-10pm. 8- to 10-bed dorms 22zł. Doubles and triples in the renovated building next door 50zł. Breakfast included. Sheets 3.50zł. HI card required. Check-in 5pm. Check-out 10am.

Camping Pod Krokwią, ul. Żeromskiego (tel. 12 256), across the street from the base of the ski jump. From the train station, head south on ul. Jagiełłońska; at the church, make a right on ul. Witkiewicza and an immediate left on ul. Chałubińskiego. Follow ul. Czecha from the roundabout and turn right on ul. Żeromskiego. Tents 9zł per person, students 7ł; bungalows 30zł per person.

FOOD

Highlanders sell *oscypek* (goat cheese; 0.60zł), the local specialty, on the street. Vendors have a poor reputation regarding refrigeration; watch out for anything that might spoil. The many restaurants cater to tourists, overflowing with highland culture and charging accordingly. To escape, try the **grocery store,** Delikatesy, ul. Krupówki 41 (tel. 125 83; open M-Sa 7am-10pm, Su 8am-10pm).

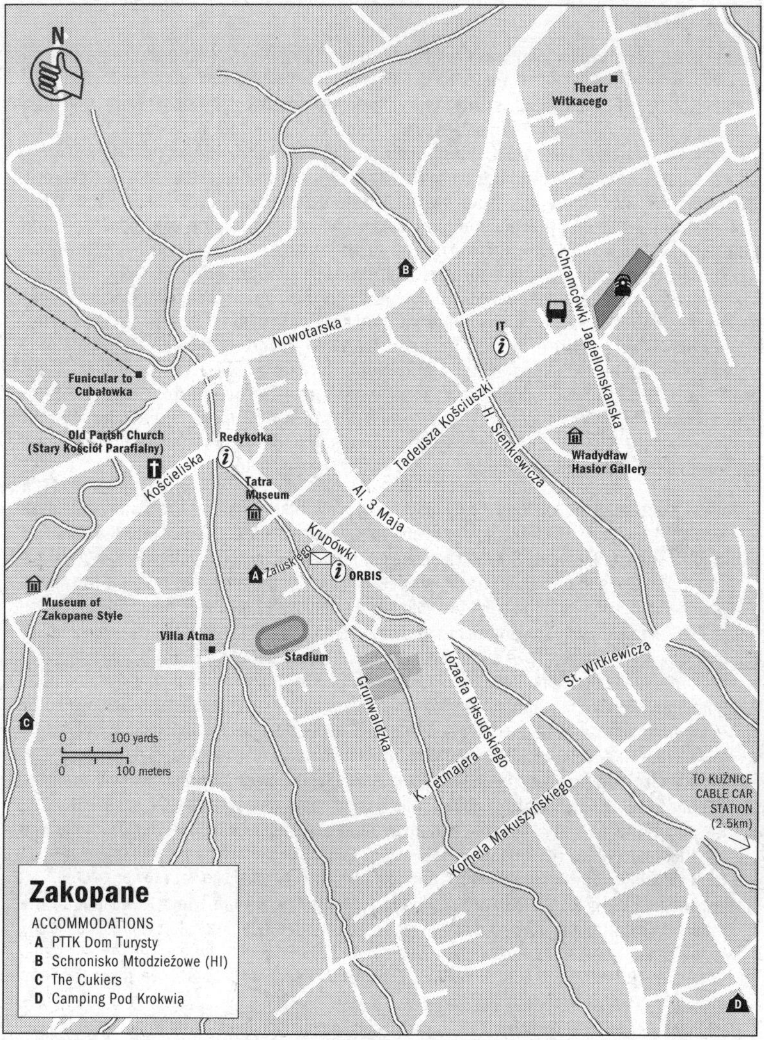

U Wandy, ul. Sienkiewicza 10. Heading toward the train station from town on ul. Kościuszki, turn right on ul. Sienkiewicza. The restaurant is on the right in a private home. Three large tables in a family dining room, complete with books and pictures. A home-cooked meal so immense that guests need help getting up. The small-of-stomach may want half-portions. Full meals 8-12zł. Open daily 2-6pm.

Karczma Sopa, ul. Kościeliska 52 (tel. 122 16). Walk 20min. west along historic ul. Kościeliska. Look for a barrel sign "Sopa" on the right. Fireplace, old musical instruments on the walls, and live Carpathian music daily at 7pm. Highland fare 8-23zł. Open daily 4pm-midnight.

Karczma Bąkowo-Zohylina, ul. Piłsudskiego 28a (tel. 120 45), has an open hearth inside and tables with an exceptional view of the Krokiew mountain and ski jump, scattered in a beautiful wild garden outside. Entrees 7.50-22zł. Open daily 11am-midnight.

Pizzeria Restauracja "Adamo," ul. Nowolarska 10 (tel. 152 90). Polish dishes are huge, as is the selection of 21 pizzas. Entrees 7-20zł. Open daily 11am-midnight.

HIKING

The magnificent **Tatran National Park** (Tatrzański Park Narodowy) shelters endless outdoor opportunities. Entrances to the park lie at the head of each trail. (3zł, students 1.50zł; off-season 2zł, students 1zł. Keep your ticket.) For dramatic vistas, catch a bus or minibus to **Kuźnice** (every 20min., 1.50zł), south of central Zakopane. Or walk along ul. Jagiełłońska, which becomes ul. Chałubińskiego, and then follow ul. Przewodników Tatrzańskich from the train station, to catch the 1955m **Kasprowy Wierch** cable car. (Open July-Aug. 7:30am-6:30pm; June and Sept. 7:30am-4pm; Oct. 7:30am-3pm. Round-trip 23zł, students 15zł.) The other popular cable car ascends **Gubałówka** (1122m) in the northern part of the city. To go up, walk north on ul. Krupówki to its end past the market. (Open daily 6:45am-8:50pm. 6zł one-way.) There are breathtaking views of Zakopane from the top, and highlander huts and sheep populate the slopes of Gubałówka. You can walk down (20min.) or take a leisurely stroll west (blue, black, and red trail) to **Butorowy Wierch** (20min.) and descend on a chairlift. (Open daily May-Sept. 9am-6pm; Mar.-Apr. and Oct. 9am-5pm; Jan.-Feb. and Nov. 9am-4pm; Dec. 9am-3pm.) Before hiking, buy the map *Tatrzański Park Narodowy: Mapa turystyczna* at a kiosk or bookstore. For an overview of the Tatras and safety information, see p. 693; for more hiking info, see **Camping & the Outdoors,** p. 38.

Dolina Kościeliska (full day): An easy and lovely hike crossing the valley of Potok Kościeliski. A bus shuttles from Zakopane to Kiry (every 30min., 2zł). From Kiry, a small road heads south toward Schronisko Ornak along a river; mountains hover on both sides and in front. It's about 1½hr. to the end of the road, and many trails lead off to various peaks and caves along the way. The valley is a popular day hike and bike route.

Sea Eye (Morskie Oko; 1406m; full day): The mountain lake Morskie Oko dazzles herds of tourists every summer. Take a bus from Zakopane's bus station (45min., 11 per day, 4zł) to Burnt Clearing (Polana Palenica), a.k.a. Bald Clearing (Łysa Polana), or take a minibus from opposite the bus station. The 9km hike leads up a road that can also be covered by horse and carriage (15zł each way). The trail is wildly popular and quite crowded, but all is forgiven when you reach the lake and the mountains surround you.

Mulch Valley (Dolina Chochołowska; full day): Take the westbound green trail from the entrance to Dolina Kościeliska at Kiry, which turns south onto a road after 3.5km. Head to the end of the road (1¼hr.) and go through a forested valley along the river. From there, a red trail takes off to Trzydniowiański Wierch (1765m), in the shadow of the higher Tatras, for a view back down the valley. It's a longer hike than Kościeliska with fewer people.

Giewont (1895m; 5hr.): Giewont's silhouette looks like a man lying down–hence the mountain's starring role in so many legends. The moderately hard blue trail (7km) leads to the peak. Begin at the lower cable car station in Kuźnice and follow signs to the peak. Chains anchored into the rock help with the final ascent up some steep rocks. The top affords a great view north over Zakopane.

Red Peaks (Czerwone Wierchy; 2122m; full day): The red trail leads west from the top of the cable car at Kasprowy Wierch (see above) along the ridge separating Poland and Slovakia. The ridge is part of the "West Tatras," a rounder, less rocky range running east of Kasprowy Wierch. It is characterized by the red blanket of grass that emerges in autumn. Four of the seven peaks along the way have paths that allow tired hikers to return to Zakopane. From the last peak, Ciemniak, the trail descends to Kiry, connected to Zakopane by bus.

Valley of the Five Polish Lakes (Dolina Pięciu Stawów Polskich; full day): One of the most beautiful hikes in the area. It departs from Kuźnice and leads along the blue trail to Hala Gąsienicowa. Refuel here at the mountain hut Schronisko Murowaniec, then continue to Czarny Staw (Black Tarn). On the incline to Zawrat Peak, you'll get to climb hand-over-hand up the chains. In the valley on the other side of Zawrat, another *schronisko* waits at Przedni Staw (Front Tarn) to shelter those exhausted by the hike or overwhelmed by the scenery. The blue trail ends 3km north (after several steep climbs and descents) at Morskie Oko, where you can eat, drink, or spend the night (see **Accommodations,** above). From the lake, a road travels down to Łysa Polana, which is connected to Zakopane by bus (9hr. hike; summer only). A shorter version of the hike (6hr.) begins at Łysa Polana.

Head in the direction of Morskie Oko (see above). A green path takes off to the right about 1hr. into the hike, after the waterfall Wodogrzmoty Mickiewicza. This heads to Dolina Pięciu Stawów Polskich. Once you reach Wielki Staw (Great Tarn), head east toward Przedni Staw and follow the trail to Morskie Oko.

Rysy (2499m; 8hr.): To claim you've climbed Poland's highest peak, follow the red trail from Schronisko Morskie Oko (see **Accommodations,** above) along the east lakeshore and up to Black Tarn (Czarny Staw). The arduous climb to Rysy begins in the tarn's southeast corner. Only for the fittest and only in good weather. You can also tackle Rysy from the Slovakia; see p. 696.

SIGHTS & ENTERTAINMENT

On a rainy day, check out **Old Parish Church** (Stary Kościół Parafialny), ul. Kościeliska, and its nearby cemetery. This small wooden church filled with awe-inspiring woodwork is the oldest in Zakopane. To find it, take a left at the bottom of ul. Krupówki onto ul. Kościeliska; the church will appear on the right a few minutes later. The **Tatra Museum** (Muzeum Tatrzańskie), ul. Krupówki 10 (tel. 152 05), across a little footbridge on the left, has exhibitions on the history of Zakopane and the customs of the *górale* (mountain people; open Tu-Su 9am-4pm; Tu-Sa 3zł, Su free). A branch of the museum, ul. Kościeliska 18 (tel. 136 02), displays different architectural styles common in Zakopane. (Open W-Su 9am-4pm.)

Bandit's Hut (Chata Zbójnicka; tel. 142 17; fax 639 87) on ul. Jagiełłońska is by far the best place for raucous and intoxicating mountain nights. From the center, walk up Kościuszki to the bus station. Turn right onto ul. Jagiełłońska and after 5min., head left up the gravel path with the big "Zbójnicka" sign. Mountain culture abounds here; enjoy an excellent shepherd's band and waitstaff who jitter to folk dances with willing partners. Some nights can get quite boisterous as evidenced by the collection of cut-off ties dangling from the ceiling. If the door is closed, beat on it—loudly. (Open daily 5pm-midnight.)

For a quieter evening, check out the cafes on ul. Krupówki. At **Piano-Cafe,** ul. Krupówki 63, you can try out the piano or just sit and talk around the flower-filled tables. (0.5L *Żywiec* 4zł. Open daily 3pm-midnight.) Nearby **Cafe Sanacja,** ul. Krupówki 45 (tel. 161 59), houses bizarre installations and *objets d'art;* look for bottles of beer kept in a birdcage when you enter. Make what you will of the huge-red-eye and corpse-of-an-eagle collage. Fortify your aesthetics with apple pie (4zł). (Open daily 1pm-midnight.)

Air-Sport, ul. Strążyska 13 (tel./fax 133 11), arranges paragliding over the Tatras. If you've never jumped before, try a tandem jump off Nosal Mountain (10-20min. flying time 100zł). Natural hot springs (1600m below ground) have been turned into the swimming pool complex **Basen Antalowka,** ul. Jagiełłońska 18 (tel. 639 34; open July-Sept. daily 6am-9pm; day pass 10zł). During the last week of August, Zakopane resounds with the **Festival of Highlander Folklore** (Misąrynardowy Festival ziem Gòrskich).

POLAND

NEAR ZAKOPANE: DUNAJEC GORGE (PRZELOM DUNAJCA)

A relaxing trip to the legend-packed Dunajec Gorge suits those no longer craving Tatran thrills. The two- to three-hour float on a wooden **raft** includes a Polish guide in traditional costume who navigates the cliff-bounded waterways, crossing the Polish-Slovak border for 1km of the ride. Look out for the seven large stone slabs on the hill; supposedly, they represent seven priests who were turned to stone as punishment for their trysts with a holy sister. Around the bend, the nun's silhouette is carved into the cliff. When the guide starts talking about a "kościól" (church), you know you're there.

GETTING THERE. The rafts travel from **Sromowce** to **Szczawnica**. (Daily May-Oct. Tickets 29zł; bags over 5kg require an additional ticket. Tel. (01826) 297 21. Office open daily May-Aug. 8:30am-5pm; Sept. 8:30am-4pm; Oct. 9am-3pm.) The easiest way to do the raft trip is by way of a tour from **Redykołka** (see **Zakopane: Tourist Offices,** p. 441), which costs only slightly more than bus and raft fare on your own. No English-speaking guides are offered, but you can ask for a leaflet explaining the history of the region. If you skip the tour, you can take direct **buses** that go to **Sromowce** from **Zakopane** at 9am and 1:45pm (1½hr., 9.20zł). Head in the direction of Szczawnica, but avoid the 12:50pm bus, which does not stop at Sromowce. **Minibuses** also make the trip, leaving from opposite the bus station around 9am (15zł). To catch a direct bus back to Zakopane (2hr., 5 per day, 9.80zł), walk 30min. down the riverside road to ul. Manifestu Lipcowego, which runs to the bus terminal. The last bus leaves at around 5:30pm, but you can catch another one to Nowy Tárg and connect from there if necessary.

SANOK

The cultural and economic hub of the Bieszczady, Sanok sits proudly atop a hill overlooking the San River. Under Communism, many rural churches were looted; as a result, the icon museum houses priceless pieces of local religious art. To make up for the looting, an open-air museum recreates the village life that has since been destroyed by war and time. With a wealth of outdoor activities only a short bus trip away and plenty of attractions in its own right, Sanok is an ideal base for trips to the Bieszczady mountains.

ORIENTATION & PRACTICAL INFORMATION. The **train** and **bus stations,** linked by an overpass, are a 15min. hike from the *rynek*. **Trains,** ul. Dworcowa (tel. 463 05 16), go to **Kraków** (4 per day, 27zł) and **Warsaw** (1 per day, 35zł). **Buses,** ul. Lipińskiego, head to: **Kraków** (5hr., 5 per day, 27zł); **Warsaw** (2 per day, 33zł); and **Przemyśl** (2hr., 7 per day, 7.60zł). A detailed map of town is posted across from the train station. To walk to the center, head right on ul. Lipińskiego from the bus station; eventually, it becomes **ul. Jagiełłońska.** After a steep hill, the latter curves to the right and turns into **ul. 3-go Maja,** which heads straight to the *rynek*. **Ul. Kościuszki** houses banks, grocery stores, and the post office; it juts out where ul. Jagiełłońska meets ul. 3-go Maja. **PTTK,** ul. 3-go Maja 2 (tel./fax 463 25 12), sells maps (3zł) and helps plan trips to the nearby national park and mountain area. (Open M-F 8am-4pm, Sa 8am-2pm.) They also have a *kantor* that **exchanges currency. Orbis,** ul. Grzegorza 4 (tel./fax 463 28 59), off ul. Kościuszki, books plane and train tickets. (Open M-F 9am-5pm, Sa 9am-1pm.) **Bank Pekao S.A.,** ul. Kościuszki 12, cashes **traveler's checks** and gives MC/Visa cash advances. (Open M-F 9am-5pm.) There's a MC/Visa **24hr. ATM** at Bank Depozytono Kredytowy across from Orbis. **Apteka Omega** doles drugs at ul. Kościuszki 22 (tel. 463 47 52; open M-F 7:30am-8pm, Sa-Su 9am-2pm). The **Mountain Rescue (GOPR)** headquarters are at ul. Mickiewicza 49 (tel. 463 22 04). The **post office** sits at ul. Kościuszki 26 (tel. 463 13 34; open M-F 7am-8pm, Sa 8am-2pm). **Postal code:** 38-500. **Phone code:** (0)13.

POLAND

ACCOMMODATIONS & FOOD. Sanok's rooms, while expensive, are of extremely high quality. The fastidious owners of **Hotel Jagiełłoński,** ul. Jagiełłońska 49 (tel. 463 12 08), near the station, offer some of the most dignified rooms in eastern Poland—spacious and outfitted with Oriental carpets, bathrooms, telephones, and TVs. (Singles 70zł; huge doubles with a couch 97zł; smaller doubles 86zł; triples 97zł. MC/Visa. Check-out 11am.) Just up the road on the right, **Hotel Turysta,** ul. Jagiełłońska 13 (tel. 463 09 22), has decent-sized rooms with tidy bathrooms. (Singles 60zł; doubles 80zł; triples 95zł.) To reach **Hotel PTTK,** ul. Mickiewicza 29 (tel. 463 10 13; fax 463 01 23), take bus #3 from the bus station and get off when the bus turns onto ul. Mickiewicza. Otherwise it's a 20min. walk: head straight through the *rynek* onto Cerkiewna. A left on Zamkowa leads to the intersecting Mickiewicza. Take a right and the hotel is immediately in front of you. It offers private baths, sized perfectly for dwarves. (Singles 42zł; doubles 36-94zł; triples 72zł.) **Hotel Błonie's campground,** al. Wojska Polskiego 1 (tel. 463 02 57; fax 463 14 93), set amid stadium lights, rents sites by the San. It's a 10min. walk from the train station; turn left onto Dworcowa and right onto Lwowska. This road bends to the right and meets Królowejbony, where you turn left. Al. W. Polskiego runs parallel on the left, but the campground is actually on the right; reception is inside the hotel.

(4.22zł per person; tent 3.50zł; car 3.20zł.) **Restaurant Max,** ul. Kościuszki 34 (tel. 463 22 54), cooks up an affordable selection of soups and other Polish cuisine (3-13zł; open daily 10am-10pm). **Restauracja Jagiełłońska,** at the hotel, is slightly more expensive, but delicious and not unreasonable (entrees 7-25zł; open daily noon-11pm). The **grocery store** with the longest hours is **Delta,** ul. Kościuszki 6 (tel. 463 68 08; open M-Sa 7am-10pm, Su 9am-9pm).

SIGHTS & ENTERTAINMENT. The **museum complex** in the castle (tel. 463 06 09), on ul. Zamkowa, is a must. The three-room **Muzeum Ikon** traces the stylistic progression of Ukrainian and regional icons from the 15th to 18th centuries. (Open M 11am-3pm, Tu-Su 9am-5pm. Tu-Su 3zł, students 2zł; Mondays free.) The adjoining **gallery** exhibits the creepy Surrealist works of local painter Beksiński. The walls of the 14th-century **parish church** in the *rynek* once witnessed the marriage vows of King Władysław Jagiełło—the founder of one of medieval Europe's most powerful dynasties (see **History,** p. 399).

The **skansen,** 2km north of town across the river San, recreates the village life of the region's main ethnic groups: the Łemks and Boyks. Follow Zamkowa out of the *rynek* and keep following the "Skansen" signs. It ranks among Europe's best open-air museums. The museum can also be reached by bus #3 from the *rynek.* Get off immediately after the bus crosses the river, take a sharp right onto ul. Rybickiego, and follow the signs to the *skansen.* Be sure to visit the 150-year-old schoolhouse displaying old textbooks and maps. At the far end of the park, trees and brush give way to open fields and sweeping vistas. (Open daily May-Oct. 8am-6pm; Nov.-Mar. 9am-2pm; Apr. 9am-4pm. 5zł, students 3zł. Guide for 20 people 20zł.) **Park Miejski** has outstanding views of the city and the valley. To get there, follow ul. 3-go Maja out of the *rynek* and turn right onto ul. Kościuski.

From Sanok, buses run regularly to **hiking** spots in the Bieszczady Mountains. The PTTK office (see above) has info on accommodations in Ustrycki Gorne, Wetlina, Kornacz, and Jezioro Sohna. Next door provides maps of hiking trails in those areas. In winter, cross-country and downhill **skiing** are popular. Not to be missed is the **Bieszczady National Park** (Bieszczadzki Park Narodowy), with its forests and diverse flora and fauna intact. Within the park is the highest peak in the Bieszczady, **Tarnica** (1346m). The park can be accessed from any of the villages listed and is connected to Sanok by frequent buses (30min.).

POLAND

BIELSKO-BIAŁA

A composite of two towns that once belonged to two duchies, Bielsko-Biała (BYEL-skoh BYAH-wah) is one of the only places in Poland where two religions—Catholicism and Lutheranism—thrive side-by-side. Thanks to its religious tolerance, but also to its textile and car manufacturing industries, Bielsko-Biała continues to do well for itself. It is a diverse and dynamic community, and, with the Carpathians as a backdrop, a beautiful one, too.

ORIENTATION

Bielsko-Biała has two centers: Bielsko's castle and *rynek* (town square) in the west, and the Biała's *rynek* in the east, separated by a 5min. walk along **ul. 11-go Listopada,** the main drag for shopping and service. Because of this, the town is trickier to navigate than most. To get to the Biała center from the train station, turn left out of the station down ul. 3-go Maja. After 15min., head down the stairs just past Hotel Prezydent to reach ul. 11-go Listopada.

PRACTICAL INFORMATION

Trains: Ul. Warszawska 2 (tel. 812 80 40; info tel. 933). To: **Bratislava** (5½hr., 2 per day, 80zł); **Katowice** (1½hr., 30 per day, 8zł); **Kraków** (2¾hr., 4 per day, 10zł); **Warsaw** (6hr., 5 per day, 25zł); and **Zakopane** (3hr., 2 per day, 19zł).

Buses: Ul. Warszawska 5 (tel. 812 31 25; info tel. 228 25). An overpass connects the bus station to the train station. To: **Oświęcim/Auschwitz** (1hr., 12 per day, 4.90zł) and **Kraków** (2¼hr., 20 per day, 13zł).

Tourist Office: Biuro Turystyczne Reisebüro Travel Agency, ul. Ks. Stojałowskiego 12 (tel. 812 27 77; fax 812 28 28). Follow directions to 11-go Listopada. Turn right onto Cechowa and left onto Ks. Stojałowskiego. Tourist office is over the river on the right. Sells maps, books rooms, and provides general info.

Budget Travel: Orbis, ul. 3-go Maja (tel. 812 40 00; fax 822 07 84). Arranges international rail and bus tickets. Open M, W, F 9am-5pm, Tu and Th 10am-5pm, Sa 9am-2pm.

Currency Exchange: Bank PKO S.A., ul. 11-go Listopada 15 (tel. 812 72 31). Exchanges currencies at stiff rates, cashes AmEx/Visa traveler's checks for a 1% commission (5zł minimum), and offers MC/Visa cash advances. Open M-F 8am-6pm, Sa 9am-1pm. *Kantory* congregate along ul. 11-go Listopada. **ATMs** can be found outside grocery stores.

Pharmacy: Apteka Podkorona, ul. Cechowa 4 (tel. 812 48 93), at the intersection with ul. 11-go Listopada. Open M-Sa 8am-8pm, Su 8am-2pm.

Medical Assistance: ul. Wyspiańskiego 21 (tel. 812 20 45). You will need a translator.

Post Office: ul. 1-go Maja 2 (tel. 15 10 01; fax 822 10 50). Open M-F 9am-6pm. **Poste Restante** at window #9. **Postal code:** 43-300.

Internet Access: Cyber Czad, ul. 11 Listopada 7 (tel. 822 94 14). Excruciatingly slow connection. 30min. 4zł, 1hr. 6zł, 2hr. 10zł, every subsequent hr. 5zł. Open M-Sa 10am-10pm, Su noon-6pm.

Telephones: Near the post office. **Phone code:** (0)33.

ACCOMMODATIONS

POLAND

Bielsko-Biała has plenty of places to spend a night. For the cheapest accommodations, look for signs advertising **private rooms** near the train and bus stations, or inquire at the tourist office.

PTTK Dom Wycieczkowy, ul. Krasińskiego 38 (tel. 812 30 19 and 812 62 62), 5min. from the bus and train stations. Turn left onto ul. 3-go Maja from the train station and right at the first street (ul. Piastowska). Krasińskiego is about 200m up on the left. Clean, spacious rooms with decent bathrooms. Doubles 46zł, with bath 66zł; triples 61zł, 96zł; quads and quints 18zł per person. Lockout 10am-2pm. Curfew 10pm-6am.

Pod Pocztą ("Under the Post Office"), ul. 1-go Maja 4a (tel. 815 16 92; fax 815 10 32). Turn left down ul. 3-go Maja from train station and walk 15min. to the post office; the hostel is just past it. Decent rooms, although hot water only rarely graces the communal bathrooms. Lame, loud disco downstairs will keep light sleepers awake on weekends. Singles 60zł, with bath 95zł; doubles 70zł, 120zł. Breakfast included.

Youth Hostel "Bolka i Lolka," ul. Komorowicka 25 (tel. 822 74 66). From the train station, go up to the overpass and left over all the rail lines. Walk straight down the street at the end to intersection with Michata Grażyńskiego. Turn here and head left onto Zmożka, which goes across the river to Komorowicka. Patronized by a younger crowd (i.e. schoolchildren). Some of the dorms (up to 8 beds) have TV. 16zł per person. Sheets 3zł. Checkout 10am. Lockout 10am-5pm. Curfew 10pm.

FOOD

Restaurants abound on and around the central ul. 11-go Listopada, as do grocery stores. **Savia,** ul. 11-go Listopada 38 (tel. 822 33 44), is one of the larger groceries. (Open M-F 6:30am-9pm, Sa 6:30am-8pm, Su 8am-4pm.)

Bar Mleczny, at the PTTK hostel (see above). Serves a reasonably good meal for the lowest price in town (8zł). Open M-F 8am-6pm, Sa 8am-4pm.

Restauracja Starówka, pl. Smołki 5 (tel. 812 24 24), off ul. Wzgórze. Offers Polish, French, and Chinese cuisine. The fountain at the entrance is an indication of upscale prices. Entrees 14-30zł. Open daily 10am-midnight.

Pizzeria Margerita (tel. 812 51 61), on ul. Cechowa. Serves pizzas (7-17zł) and a garden of salads (8-10zł). Open M-Sa 11am until the last customer leaves, Su from noon.

SIGHTS

Bielsko's modest 14th-century **castle** stands above pl. Chrobrego. From the main tourist office, turn left up Ks. S. Stojałowskiego. Cross ul. 3-go Maja into pl. Chrobrego and turn left onto Wzgórze. The entrance is located on the square's south end at ul. Wzgórze 16 (tel. 812 53 53). Its museum houses a collection of European paintings and sculptures. (Open Tu-W and F 10am-3pm, Th 10am-6pm, Sa 9am-3pm, Su 9am-2pm. 5zł.) The steeple of the early 20th-century **St. Nicholas's Cathedral** (Katedra św. Mikołaja), pl. Mikołaja 19 (tel. 812 45 06), can be seen from half the city. Follow directions to the castle and continue up Wzgórze to the *rynek*, then turn left down Kościelna. The church was bumped up from provincial status only a few years ago, when the Pope made the parish a bishopric. The grounds of the **Lutheran Church** (Kościół Ewangelicko-Augsburski), pl. Lutra 8 (tel. 812 74 71), feature Poland's only **statue of Martin Luther.** Follow directions to the castle but go straight through pl. Chrobrego up Nad Niprem.

The tall towers of **Providence Church** (Kościół Opatrzności Bożej), decorate ul. Ks. Stojałowskiego 64 (tel. 814 45 07); turn right from the tourist office and head down Ks. Stojałowskiego. Peek in at its Baroque interior, and don't miss the small gold pulpit depicting Jonah's escape from the whale. The **town hall** (*ratusz*), pl. Ratuszowy 1, stands near the tourist office. A striking piece of Neo-classicist architecture, the building houses the administrative offices of Bielsko-Biała.

Just a few kilometers south of Bielsko-Biała lies the sleepy town of **Żywiec** (ZHIH-vyets), home to Poland's best-known, hardest-hitting **brew** of the same name. Because the **Żywiec Brewery** is a long way down ul. Browarna, which often lacks a sidewalk, the fastest, safest way to the factory of bottled miracles is to take bus #1, 5, or 15 from the train station (1.40zł) to the "Browarna" stop; buy tickets at the kiosk next to the train station. **Trans-Trade Żywiec,** ul. Browarna 90 (tel. 61 27 01; tel./fax 61 57 73), is unmistakable—a modern complex of buildings with trucks and trains pouring in and out. Unfortunately, the brewery conducts tours only by special arrangement; call in advance. The *piwarnia* (beer garden) sells the freshest, cheapest beer in Poland; Żywiec products are sold at manufacturer's cost (0.5L 2.50zł) in a traditional setting. (Open daily 11am-10pm.) **Trains** connect Bielsko-Biała and Żywiec daily (40min., 23 per day, 3.90zł). The **bus station,** across the street from the train station, also connects the two (40min., 18 per day, 3.40zł).

POLAND

ENTERTAINMENT

The repertoire of the **Puppet Theater "Banialuka,"** ul. Mickiewicza 20 (tel. 822 10 46 and 822 10 47; fax 12 33 94), off the northwest corner of pl. Chrobrego, ranges from folk tales to classic dramas. (Closed during tours and from late June to Aug. Ticket counter open M-F 8am-4pm, Sa 4pm-5pm (subject to change), Su 9am-11am and 4pm-6pm. Tickets 4-12zł.). Across from the theater, relax at **Café Dziupla,** ul. Mickiewicza 15. This cellar pub offers a pool table as well as drinks (0.3L *Żywiec* 3zł) and music, and hosts a young crowd. (Live piano music Thursday 7pm. Open M-F 11am-11pm, Sa-Su 4-11pm.) **Bazyliszek Pub and Gallery,** ul. Wygórze 8, overlooks over the city from just past the castle. It has original art on the walls and a rattan bar serving *Okocim* (0.5L 4zł). Frequented by a more relaxed crowd, the bar is non-smoking and the radio is tuned to folk music. (Open Su-Th noon-midnight, F-Sa noon-2am.)

NEAR BIELSKO-BIAŁA: CIESZYN/ČESKÝ TĚŠÍN

The Olza River divides Polish Cieszyn (CHEH-shin) from Czech Český Těšín (CHESS-kee TYEH-shin). Walking across this natural boundary is **the cheapest way to cross the Czech/Polish border.** From the Cieszyn **bus station,** ul. Korfantego (tel. (033) 52 02 79), or the **train station,** ul. Hajduka 10 (tel. (033) 52 01 08), diagonally across from the buses, walk 15min. to the footbridge (Most Przyjaźni) into the Czech Republic. Walk up the short hill to ul. Korfantego and turn right. Take another right onto ul. Jana Michejdy and follow it until it hits ul. Zamkowa; a left here leads to the footbridge. Once across the border, continue straight on Hlavní to the railroad tracks, then turn left onto Nádražní. The **Český Těšín train station** (tel. (0659) 579 41), Nádražní, will be on the right (10min. walk from the bridge), while the **bus station** (tel. (0659) 578 41) on Jablunkovská is nearby—cross the train tracks and a main road and bear right. To cross back into Poland from the train station, you must head 400m farther down the river (there is a path through the park) toward the bus station.

The worn streets of 1000-year-old Cieszyn provide a few options for killing time between bus connections. As the story goes, King Leszko's three sons met at a well in what is now the town after a long trek. They were so overjoyed to meet that they founded a town around the well called Cieszyn ("happy"). To reach the *rynek* from the trains and buses, walk up the hill to ul. Korfantego and turn right. Instead of turning off for the footbridge, go uphill on Matejki. From the *rynek*, go down ul. Głęboka and turn left onto ul. Sejmowa. The first right on ul. Trzech Braci (Three Brothers) will take you down a steep cobblestone hill to the well where the brothers supposedly met. Near Most Przyjaźni stand the remains of Cieszyn's **medieval castle.** Ascend the hill, proceed through the brownish building's arch and into the park, and climb the **tower's** narrow wooden stairs for an amazing view of both Poland and the Czech Republic. (Tower open daily Apr.-Oct. 9:30am-5pm; Nov.-Mar. 9:30am-3pm. 2zł, students 1zł.)

GETTING THERE. **Trains** run from Cieszyn to: **Bielsko-Biała** (1¼hr., 9 per day, 4.80zł); **Kraków** (3hr., 1 per day, 10zł); and **Katowice** (1¾hr., 1 per day, 12.72zł). Trains leave Český Těšín to: **Brno** (3hr., 4 per day, 130Kč); **Olomouc** (1½hr., 4 per day, 96Kč); and **Prague** (5hr., 6 per day, 200Kč). The **bus station** (tel. (0659) 578 41) is on ul. Jablunkovská (see above). **Buses** head to: **Katowice** (1½hr., every hr., 10zł); **Bielsko-Biała** (1hr., 10 per day, 6zł); and **Kraków** (3hr., 6 per day, 18zł).

POLAND

SZCZYRK

Gymnastics for the English-speaking tongue ("shch" followed quickly by "irk"), Szczyrk's name comes from the sound that the Żylica stream makes as it passes through town—or so say the legends. Offering more hiking, mountain biking, ski jumping, and ski lifts than any other retreat in Poland, Szczyrk is a year-round tourist destination and the second-largest winter resort in the country.

ORIENTATION & PRACTICAL INFORMATION. Szczyrk is tucked away in a valley within the **Beskid Śląski** mountains, the western most part of the Carpathians. Frequent **buses** (30min., 2 per hr., 2.90zł) connect Szczyrk's Salmopolrun station to **Bielsko-Biała;** buses depart from platform #7. Buses to Szczyrk Salmopolrun from Bielsko-Biała platform 7. The town stretches for 8km along the **Żylica,** although most services are concentrated in the 2km centrum. Take a local bus from the station to "Szczyrk Centrum," and turn left on ul. Beskidzka to find the **tourist office,** ul. Beskidzka 41 (tel./fax 817 81 87). It offers detailed mountain biking and skiing info, as well as **maps** of the town and hiking trails. (Open M-F 8:30am-4pm, Sa 10am-2pm.) Bank PKO, ul. Beskidzka 12 (tel. 817 83 50), **exchanges currency.** (Open M-F 8am-6pm.) A **pharmacy** can be found at ul. Beskidzka 69. (Open M-F 9am-3pm, Sa 9am-7pm.) **Mountain rescue (GOPR)** is at ul. Dębowa 2 (tel. 817 89 86; emergency tel. 986). **Equipment rental,** including mountain bikes, is available next door at Dębowa 1 (tel. 817 87 89). The **post office,** ul. Beskidzka 101, also has **telephones.** (Open M-F 9am-6pm.) **Postal code:** 43-370. **Phone code:** (0)33.

ACCOMMODATIONS & FOOD. The pension **Beskidy,** ul. Myśliwska 4 (tel. 17 88 78), rents pleasant rooms with bath guarded by two rather protective dogs. (15zł per person; prices higher in winter. Open daily 10am-5pm.) Turn left from the "Centrum" bus stop on ul. Beskidzka and walk just pass its intersection with Górska, where it turns into Myśliwska. **Dom Turysty PTTK,** ul. Górska 7 (tel. 817 83 21; fax 817 89 79), is only a 10min. walk from the center of town, or a quick bus ride—get off at the "Szczyrk PTTK" bus stop. (Per person: doubles with bath 35zł; triples 22zł with bath 40zł; quads 40zł.) **Camping Skalite,** ul. Kampingowa 4 (tel. 817

87 60), can be found by turning right from the center and walking 15min. until you see the sign on the right. Or, take the bus to the "Szczyrk Skalite" stop. (Tents 7-11zł; 6.50zł per person; 3zł per child. Bungalow doubles 44zł; triples 54zł; both with bath. Reception 8am-6pm.)

Tourists have driven up the prices in many eateries; try the roadside kiosks or pizzerias for a cheap meal. Enjoy thick-crust pies (6-20zł) at **Pizzeria,** directly opposite ul. Beskidzka 30. (Open daily 11am-10pm.) Stop by the **Delicatesy** (tel. 817 85 85) on Beskidzka for hiking snacks. (Open M-Sa 7am-8pm, Su 10am-3pm.)

SIGHTS & HIKING. Most outdoor activity in the area focuses on **Skrzyczne,** the highest peak in the range (1257m). Two ski lifts ascend the slopes of Skrzyczne, an upper and a lower: a one-way trip costs 3.50zł, and a round-trip to the summit costs 14zł. (Lift runs daily July-Aug. 8:30am-6:30pm; Sept.-June 8:30am-5:30pm.) On a nice day the summit is packed with people catching rays, playing volleyball, or paragliding off the mountain, that is. Well-marked hiking and mountain-biking trails canvass both peaks; buy a map at a kiosk or info center, or check out the boards at the intersection of ul. Górska and ul. Beskidzka. The flatter bike trails are marked by circles; the steeper, hiking-only trails by lines. The longer green trails start by these map boards, while the more challenging red and blue trails begin by the "Szczyrk Kolejka" bus stop. The green trail from Szczyrk, opposite ul. Górska, leads to Skrzyczne's summit and on over to **Małe Skrzyczne** (1211m), **Kopu Skrzyczenska** (1189m), and **Malinowska Skała** (1152m), with some great panoramas along the way. A right at Malinowska Skała onto the red trail leads over Malinów peak (1115m) and past **Malinowa Cave** (Jaskinia Malinowa), which is on an offshoot just before the summit. The cave is home to 132m of passages and at least that many legends. Beware the 8m drop to the floor, traversed by a rickety metal ladder that shouldn't be trusted. Don't go in unless you have, at the bare minimum, climbing or caving experience, a rope and a light, and someone who knows your plans. After reaching the summit of Malinowa, the trail branches off again. Take the green trail to the right to reach Szczyrk Salmopol, where buses run back to the center. Or, you can walk the 4km back (5hr. round trip). For general info on hiking, see **Essentials: Camping & the Outdoors,** p. 38.

POLAND

SILESIA (ŚLĄSK)

West of Kraków, Silesia became Poland's industrial heartland when uncontrolled Five-Year Plans hemorrhaging away the land's coal, iron, and zinc and filled the gaps with heavy pollution. Farther west, Dolny (Lower) Śląsk managed to confine staunch bleeding, protecting its castles and Sudeten mountain spas. The regions' respective capitals, Katowice and Wrocław, reflect the varying impact of industrialization, and serve as bases for Catholic pilgrims to Częstochowa, and hikers to Jelenia Góra and Karpacz and Sklarska Poręba, two entrances to Karkonosze National Park.

KATOWICE

An industrial core and business magnet, Katowice (KA-toe-VEE-tseh) is not likely to be anyone's final destination, but most travelers in Poland find themselves in this major transport hub at some point. If you need money for a ticket, **Bank PKO,** ul. Chopina 1 (tel. 210 69 75 21 and 11 53 92 21), between the bus and train stations, gives MC/Visa cash advances and cashes traveler's checks. (Open M-F 8am-6pm and Sa 9am-1pm.) If you find yourself laid-over for the night, **Hotel Centralny,** ul. Dworcowa 9 (tel. 253 90 41), is directly behind the train station. The smoky, red-and-black decor might make you nervous, but the rooms are clean. (Singles 89zł, with bath 95zł; doubles 138zł, 142zł.) For dinner, **La Strada,** ul. Warszawska 3 (tel. 253 05 30 and 206 96 36), serves somewhat pricey pizza. (Vegetarian pie with artichokes and peppers 15zł; seafood spaghetti 16.50zł. Open daily noon-3am.) A **24hr. grocery** store is in the train station.

GETTING AWAY. The **train station,** in the heart of the city, has direct links to: **Berlin** (9hr., 2 per day, 125zł); **Bratislava** (5hr., 1 per day, 95zł); **Budapest** (8hr., 2 per day, 150zł); **Kiev** (24hr., 1 per day, 170zł); **Kraków** (2hr., 20 per day, 7zł); **Lviv** (12hr., 1 per day, 95zł); **Prague** (7hr., 2 per day, 125zł); **Vienna** (6hr., 2 per day, 130zł); and **Warsaw** (2½hr., 14 per day, 44zł). The **bus station,** only three blocks away on ul. Piotra Skargi (tel. 59 95 73), has connections to many western European countries, including Austria, France, Germany, U.K., Italy, Norway, and Spain.

CZĘSTOCHOWA

Częstochowa (CHEN-sto-HO-va) is Poland's Catholic Mecca. Every year, thousands make the pilgrimage to the monastery on Jasna Góra to see the most sacred of Polish icons, the *Black Madonna.* Even in this spiritual center, though, the legacy of communism remains: the monastery has a perfect view of towering smokestacks. Despite this reminder of dark days, the immaculate, tree-lined streets make Częstochowa warm and welcoming for international visitors.

ORIENTATION

Częstochowa lies about 100km northwest of Kraków. The main **train** and **bus stations,** connected at the south end of the train station's platform #4, are near the town center. **Al. Najświętszej Marii Panny (NMP;** Avenue of Our Lady) links the stations to **Jasna Góra.** From the train station, go right onto al. Wolności to get to al. NMP. Take a left to reach Jasna Góra.

POLAND

PRACTICAL INFORMATION

Trains: Częstochowa Główna, ul. Piłsudskiego 38 (tel. 324 13 37). To: **Katowice** (2hr., 37 per day, 15.30zł); **Kraków** (2hr., 7 per day, 20.24zł); **Warsaw** (3hr., 9 per day, express 42.76zł); and **Wrocław** (2½hr., 2 per day, 38.50zł).

Buses: Ul. Wolności 45/49 (tel. 24 66 16). Turn left onto ul. Wolności from the train station. To: **Kraków** (3hr., 5 per day, 16zł); **Warsaw** (4hr., 4 per day, 20zł); and **Wrocław** (4hr., 5 per day, 13.90zł).

Tourist Offices: WCIT, al. NMP 65 (tel. 324 13 60; fax 324 34 12). Fanatically organized; provides maps and detailed info on hotels. Open M-F 9am-6pm, Sa-Su 10am-6pm. **Jasnogórskie Centrum Informacji (IT),** ul. Kordeckiego 2 (tel. 365 38 88; fax 365 43 43), inside the monastery near the entrance to the cathedral. English-speaking staff sells maps and English guidebooks (3-25zł), arranges monastery tours in English (70-100zł, depending on group size), and makes reservations for Dom Pielgrzyma. Office also has a Cirrus/MC/Visa **ATM.** Office and ATM open June 1-Oct. 15 daily 7am-7:30pm; Oct. 16-Apr. 30 8am-5pm.

Currency Exchange: *Kantory* are throughout the city. **Bank PKO S.A.,** ul. Kopernika 17/19 (tel. 65 50 60), several blocks south of al. NMP off ul. Nowowiejskiego. Cashes traveler's checks for a 1% commission and gives MC/Visa cash advances. A PLUS/Visa **24hr. ATM** stands outside. Open M-F 8am-6pm, Sa 10am-2pm.

Luggage Storage: At the train station. 1.25zł per day, plus 0.32zł for every 50zł declared. Open daily 7:15am-1pm, 1:15-6:45pm, and 7:15pm-6:45am. Also at the monastery, for a donation. Open June-Oct. daily 6am-6pm; Nov.-May 7am-5pm.

Pharmacy: Ul. NMP 50 (tel. 24 62 74). Open M-F 8am-9pm, Sa 8am-2pm.

Post Office: Ul. Orzechowskiego 7 (tel. 24 44 43), between the bus and train stations. Open M-F 7am-9pm, Sa 7am-2pm. **Postal code:** 42-200.

Telephones: At the post office. **Phone code:** (0)34.

ACCOMMODATIONS

Reservations are strongly recommended all year, but are a must for early May and mid- to late August, when pilgrims descend en masse.

Dom Pielgrzyma im. Jana Pawla (The Pilgrim's House), ul. Wyszyńskiego 1/31 (tel. 24 70 11; fax 65 18 70), outside the west gate of the monastery. A large operation run by nuns and cigarette-smoking priests. Clean rooms with bath and a proliferation of religious paraphernalia. Singles 45zł; doubles 50zł; triples 75zł; quads 56zł. Curfew 10pm.

Dom Pielgrzyma—Hale Noclegowe, ul. Klasztorna 1 (tel. 65 66 88, ext. 224), just southeast of Jasna Góra's west gate. For the ascetic pilgrim. Single-sex bedrooms and communal bathrooms. No hot water. 3- to 10-bed dorms 11zł.

Youth Hostel, ul. Jasnogórska 84/90 (tel. 24 31 21), 15min. from the train station and 10min. from Jasna Góra. From al. NMP, go right onto ul. Dąbrowskiego, then left onto ul. Jasnogórska. At the hostel sign, go to the end of the alley. 12-18zł per person. Sheets 1.50zł. Open June-Aug. only.

Hotel Ha-Ga, ul. Katedralna 9 (tel. 24 61 73). A 5min. walk from the train station. Go left onto Piłsudskiego, then right onto Katedralna for 1 block. The hotel is on the right, through the gate after the Ha-Ga bar. Reasonably clean. Singles 45zł, with bath 50zł; doubles 50zł, 65zł; triples 60zł, 75zł; quads 70zł, 80zł.

Camping Oleńka, ul. Oleńki 10/30 (tel. 24 74 95), across the parking lot from the west gate of the monastery, near Dom Pielgrzyma. A sprawling complex with surprisingly clean and comfortable rooms; parties go late into the night. Kitchen facilities. Tent space 8zł per person. Triples 75zł; quads 100zł; quints 125zł, all with bath.

FOOD

If you are supplementing your pilgrimage with a fast, Częstochowa's culinary offerings won't move you to temptation. Kiosks serve cheap snacks, including *zapiekanki* (open-faced cheese and mushroom sandwiches). The enormous **Supermarket Billa,** a universal model for one-stop shopping, will bring tears of gratitude. It sits in the red building next to the bus station, across the street from the bus station. (Open M-F 9am-9pm, Sa 8am-8pm, Su 9am-4pm.)

Pod Gruszką (Under the Pear), al. NMP 37 (tel. 365 44 90), next to Almatur in a courtyard. Popular student hangout with a small selection of salads (15-20zł per kg) and *Żywiec* (4.50zł). More of a cafe/bar at night. Open daily 10am-10pm.

A. Blikle, al. NMP 49. A dainty, deep green cafe serving coffee (2.50zł) and tortes (1.50zł). Open M-Th 8am-8pm, F-Sa 8am-9pm, Su 10am-9pm.

Desperados, ul. Kościuszki 1A (tel. 66 41 85). Nachos, tacos, and enchiladas (9-14zł) served in a thematically arid setting. Happy hour 4-5pm with 2.50zł beer specials. Open M-Th and Su noon-10:30pm, F-Sa noon-midnight.

Bar Pierożek, ul. Kościuszki 7 (tel. 61 42 62). Cheap, basic spot serving typical Polish fare. Pierogi in five movements 4-5zł. Open M-F 11am-4pm, Sa noon-3pm.

Dom Pielgrzyma Cafe, next to the Pilgrim's House complex. Greasy, but hearty self-service cafeteria. Platters 4-9zł. Open daily 8am-8pm.

SIGHTS

Paulite Monastery (Klasztor Paulinów), on top of **Jasna Góra** (Bright Mountain), is *the* sight in town. The monastery, which resembles a Baroque fortress, was founded in 1382 by Duke Władysław Opolczyk, who also donated the *Blessed Mother and Child* painting in 1384. What the masses of pilgrims travel here to see, though, is the reportedly miraculous **Black Madonna** (Czarna Madonna). A Byzantine icon (ca. 500-700, although some believe it is a painting by St. Luke), it was desecrated in 1430 by Hussites but later restored. Two scars said to have appeared on the Madonna's cheek serve as a reminder of the sacrilege committed by the Hussites and as proof to the faithful icon's invincibility. The ornate 15th-century **Basilica** houses the icon inside the small **Chapel of Our Lady** (Kaplica Matki Bożej). Countless crutches, medallions, and rosaries strung up on the chapel walls attest to the faith of the pilgrims in the painting's otherworldly powers. (Chapel open daily 5am-9:30pm; icon revealed M-F 6am-noon and 1-9:30pm, Sa-Su 6am-1pm and 2-9:30pm. Free, but donations are encouraged.)

BLACK MADONNA Jasna Góra's pilgrimage tradition dates to the monastery's founding in 1382. That year, Prince Władysław II of Opole invited Paulite monks to Poland, giving them the Jasna Góra hill and the picture that has come to be known by its 20th-century appellation, the Black Madonna. According to tradition, the picture was painted by St. Luke on a plank of the table at which the Holy Family prayed and dined in Nazareth, although it is most likely a 6th- or 7th-century Byzantine icon. The annual 5 million pilgrims to Częstochowa come to get a glimpse at the two scars she is said to bear in testimony to her miraculous powers. They are attributed to the mishap of thieves (said to be followers of the Czech reformer Jan Hus, but more likely political opponents of the monastery's patron, King Władysław). According to legend, the picture increased in weight under the thieves' efforts until they were unable to carry it. In frustration, they slashed her face, immediately drawing a torrent of blood.

The monastery also houses a large **treasury** that contains priceless art works, many of them donated by pilgrims: monstrances, chalices, candelabra, liturgical vestments, and jewelry. (Open daily 9am-5pm.) The **Arsenal** exhibits weapons, military insignia, medals, and orders, including many from WWII. (Open daily 9am-5pm.) **Museum of the 600th Anniversary** (Muzeum Sześćsetlecia) commemorates the founding of the church and monastery; it also contains a collection of musical instruments. (Open daily 9am-5pm.) Climb up the **tower** and walk atop the fortifications for excellent views of the region. (Open Apr.-Nov. daily 8am-4pm.)

The largest pilgrimages and crowds converge on the monastery during the **Marian feasts and festivals.** These include: May 3 (Feast of Our Lady Queen of Poland), July 16 (Feast of Our Lady of Scapulars), August 15 (Feast of the Assumption), August 26 (Feast of Our Lady of Częstochowa), September 8 (Feast of the Birth of Our Lady), and September 12 (Feast of the Name Mary).

The neo-Gothic **Cathedral of the Holy Family** (Katedra św. Rodziny) is just on the other side of the train station off ul. Piłsudskiego. Follow ul. Katedra past Hotel Miły, and the cathedral looms on the right. One of the largest churches in Poland (100m end-to-end), it was erected in 1927. Facing the left wall as you enter the cavernous interior, note the large plaque honoring Roman Dmowski, the leader of Poland's right-wing nationalists in the interwar period; his image cringes at the street named for Józef Piłsudski, his arch-rival.

NEAR CZĘSTOCHOWA: TRAIL OF EAGLES' NESTS

Just when you've had it with crowded buses, churches, and regional history museums, a trip to the **Trail of Eagles' Nests** reminds you why you liked travel in the first place. Along the narrow 100km strip of land known as the **Kraków-Częstochowa Uplands,** numerous crags of Jurassic limestone erupt from rolling green hills. These outcroppings were often incorporated into the fortification of 12th-century **castles** built in the area, whose perches high on the rocky crags earned them the name "eagles' nests." As artillery grew more powerful, the effectiveness of the defensive walls diminished. By the 18th century, most of the fortresses had seriously deteriorated due to declining economic and political power; many were destroyed by Swedish invasions. Today, only a few remain whole, including **Wawel,** in Kraków, and **Pieskowa Skała** just northwest of Kraków. The ruins of the rest still lie along the uplands, waiting to be discovered by trail or bus.

A **hiking trail** that runs along the entire 100km takes about seven days to trek. **PTTK** in Kraków or Częstochowa can provide **maps.** The trail is marked by red blazes, and maps are regularly posted along the way. The route leads through many small towns where hikers can find tourist info, provisions, and accommodations. The two biggest attractions on the trail, the **ruins at Olsztyn** and the Pieskowa Skała Castle, are easy half-day trips from Częstochowa and Kraków, respectively.

To reach **Olsztyn Castle,** take **bus** #58 from ul. Piłsudskiego, across from the Częstochowa train station (30min., every 2hr., 1.20zł). Once there, it's hard to miss the ruins, which sit high above the town. The castle, originally constructed in the

12th and 13th centuries, consists of upper and lower parts later flanked by two outer castles. The Swedish army ransacked the complex in 1655. In the 18th century, locals appropriated bricks from the partially destroyed castle to rebuild the local church, further reducing the castle's glory. The sole preserved sections are in the **upper castle,** including two **towers.** Ghosts are rumored to haunt the castle; the two most prominent apparitions are Maciek Borkowic, imprisoned here for his rebellion against King Casimir the Great, and a young bride lost in the dungeon. If they don't appear, there's always the yellow and purple wildflowers, a spectacular view, and cows. Moo.

WROCŁAW

Wrocław (VROTS-wahv), the capital of Dolny Śląsk, straddles the Odra river. Since the city's elaborate post-war and post-communist reconstructions, only photographs recall Wrocław's destruction in WWII, when it became *Festung* (Fortress) Breslau under the Nazis, one of the last battlegrounds en route to Berlin. The city is rapidly developing, with streams of construction tape and uprooted rocks strewn everywhere. Beneath it all, Wrocław still charms visitors with the vast, antique grace of its many bridges, lush parks, and 19th-century buildings.

ORIENTATION

The political and social heart of Wrocław is its **rynek.** The **train** and **bus stations** lie 15min. southeast of the *rynek;* cheap accommodations cluster by the train station. With your back to the train station, turn left onto ul. Piłsudskiego, take your third right onto ul. Świdnicka, go past the **Kosciuszki pl.** (flanked by McDonald's and T.G.I. Friday's), over the **Podwale river,** and into the *rynek.* The bus station is behind the trains; cross ul. Sucha and go through the train station, then follow the directions from the train station. Or, you can catch any tram (in front of the Hotel Piast on ul. Piłsudskiego) going toward **pl. Dominikanski.** Once at the square, head down Oławska away from ul. Janickiego for 2min. to reach the *rynek.*

POLAND

PRACTICAL INFORMATION

Trains: Wrocław Głowny, ul. Piłsudskiego (tel. 68 83 33). A traveler's center with a 24hr. exchange booth, pharmacy, and eateries. Counters #17 and 18 handle international links. To: **Poznań** (1hr., 18 per day, 20zł); **Kraków** (4hr., 14 per day, 25zł); **Warsaw** (5hr., 9 per day, 29zł); **Dresden** (4½hr., 3 per day, 88zł); **Berlin** (5½hr., 3 per day, 87zł); **Budapest** (12hr., 1 per day, 151zł); and **Prague** (6½hr., 3 per day, 88zł).

Buses: Ul. Sucha 1 (tel. 61 22 99 and 61 81 22), behind the trains. Open daily 5am-11pm. Buses are generally slower and more expensive; avoid them. To: **Poznán** (3hr., 2 per day, 26zł); **Kraków** (destination "Krosno"; 7hr., 1 per day, 30zł); and **Warsaw** (8hr., 3 per day, 31zł).

Local Transportation: Tickets for **trams** and **buses** cost 1.60zł (students 0.80zł) per person and per backpack. 10-day pass 20zł. Express buses (designated by letters) 2.20zł. Night buses 2.60zł. Purchase tickets at kiosks; on the weekend, pay on board.

Taxis: HALLO Taxi, tel. 72 55 55. Avoid hailing a taxi on the street; if you must, agree on the price before the journey. From the train station to the *rynek* should cost 10zł.

Tourist Office: IT, ul. Rynek 14 (tel. 344 31 11 and 344 11 09; fax 44 29 62). Stocked with useful maps (4.50zł) and brochures. Open M-F 9am-5pm, Sa 10am-2pm.

Budget Travel: Almatur, ul. Kościuszki 34 (tel. 344 30 03 and 344 72 56; fax 344 39 51), in the student center "Pałacyk." Sells youth fare bus tickets and provides the skinny on student hostels. English spoken. Open M-F 10am-5pm, Sa 10am-2pm.

Currency Exchange: At *kantory* throughout the city and in the train station. **Bank PKO S.A.,** ul. Oławska 2 (tel. 344 44 54), cashes traveler's checks for a 1% commission (10zł minimum) and gives MC/Visa cash advances. Open M-F 8am-6pm, Sa 10am-2pm. **24hr. ATMs** throughout the city, including at pl. Solny 17 (Plus/Visa).

Luggage Storage: At the train station. 1.50zł per day, plus 0.27zł for every 100zł of declared value. Open 24hr. Also at the bus station. 4zł per day plus 1zł for every 50zł of declared value. Open 6am-10pm.

Pharmacy: Cefarm, ul. Kościuszki 53 (tel. 344 82 31). Open M-F 8am-9pm.

Medical Assistance: Tel. 343 63 69 and 999.

Post Office: ul. Małachowskiego 1 (tel. 344 17 17; fax 344 74 19), to the right when exiting the train station. **Poste Restante** at window 22. Open M-F 6am-8pm, Sa-Su 8am-3pm. **Postal code:** 50-415.

Internet Access: Cyberkawiarnia, ul. Kuźnicza 29a (tel. 72 35 71 and 44 75 28; fax 72 30 58). See **Entertainment**, p. 458.

Telephones: Outside the post office. **Phone code:** (0)71.

ACCOMMODATIONS

Check with the tourist office for info about **private rooms** or **student dorms.**

Youth Hostel (HI), ul. Kołłątaja 20 (tel. 343 88 56), directly opposite the train station on the road perpendicular to ul. Piłsudskiego. Clean, safe, and spacious. Dorms (and a few doubles) 13-18zł per person. Lockout 10am-5pm. Curfew 10pm. Call ahead.

Hotel Piast, ul. Piłsudskiego 98 (tel. 343 00 33), near the train station; look for the neon crown. For a quieter stay, request a room that does not face ul. Piłsudskiego. Clean 70s deco. Singles 40zł; doubles 70zł; triples 90zł; quads 110zł. Breakfast 10zł. Prices higher May-June and Sept.-Oct.

Hotel Podróżnik, ul. Sucha 1 (tel. 73 28 45), upstairs from the bus station. The ample rooms with bath are good for families. Doubles 90zł; quads 140zł.

Dom Nauczyciela, ul. Nauczycielska 2 (tel. 22 92 68; fax 21 95 02). Take tram #4 from the Hotel Piast stop toward Biskupin. Go left off pl. Grunwaldzki, then turn left again at the gas station. Singles 45zł; doubles 60zł; triples 70zł; quads 80zł; quints 90zł.

FOOD

There are several **24hr. grocery stores. Delikatesy,** pl. Solny 8/9 (tel. 343 56 85), is convenient to the *rynek*.

Bar Vega, ul. Rynek Ratusz 27a (tel. 344 39 34). Two modern, spiffy floors of fast veggie relief. The menus differ by floor—the upstairs has an international flair. Don't bother with a phrasebook for these imaginatively named dishes. Full meals under 5zł. Downstairs open M-F 8am-7pm, Sa-Su 9am-5pm; upstairs open M-F noon-6pm, Sa-Su 9am-5pm.

Bar Miś, ul. Kużniczna 48 (tel. 342 49 63). The polar bear on the sign (and the crowds) outside point the way to this popular bargain cafeteria. Full meals 4-5zł. Open M-F 8am-6pm, Sa 8am-5pm.

Spiż, ul. Rynek Ratusz 9 (tel. 344 68 56; fax 344 52 67). Restaurant and microbrewery. Beer lovers lounge in this cool shelter on summer evenings. Stick to the pub grub, which runs 5-10zł per entree. Open daily 10am-midnight.

Tutti-Frutti, pl. Kościuszki 1/4 (tel. 344 43 06). Endless ice cream desserts (5-12zł) and tortes (3-7zł). Bakery open M-Sa 9am-8pm, Su 9am-6pm; restaurant open daily 10am-10pm. Also at Rynek 22 (tel. 342 80 03; open 10am-midnight). AmEx/MC/Visa.

SIGHTS

RACŁAWICE PANORAMA & NATIONAL MUSEUM. The 120m-by-15m **Panorama** (see "Picturing an independent Poland," below) depicts the 18th-century peasant insurrection led by Tadeusz Kościuszko against the Russian occupation (see **History,** p. 399). 30min. headphone guides are available in Polish, English, French, German, and Spanish. Tickets are also valid for the **National Museum** (Muzeum Narodowe), in the brick building across the street. Check out the medieval Silesian paintings and sculptures, 16th- to 19th-century graphic art, and paintings by Canal-

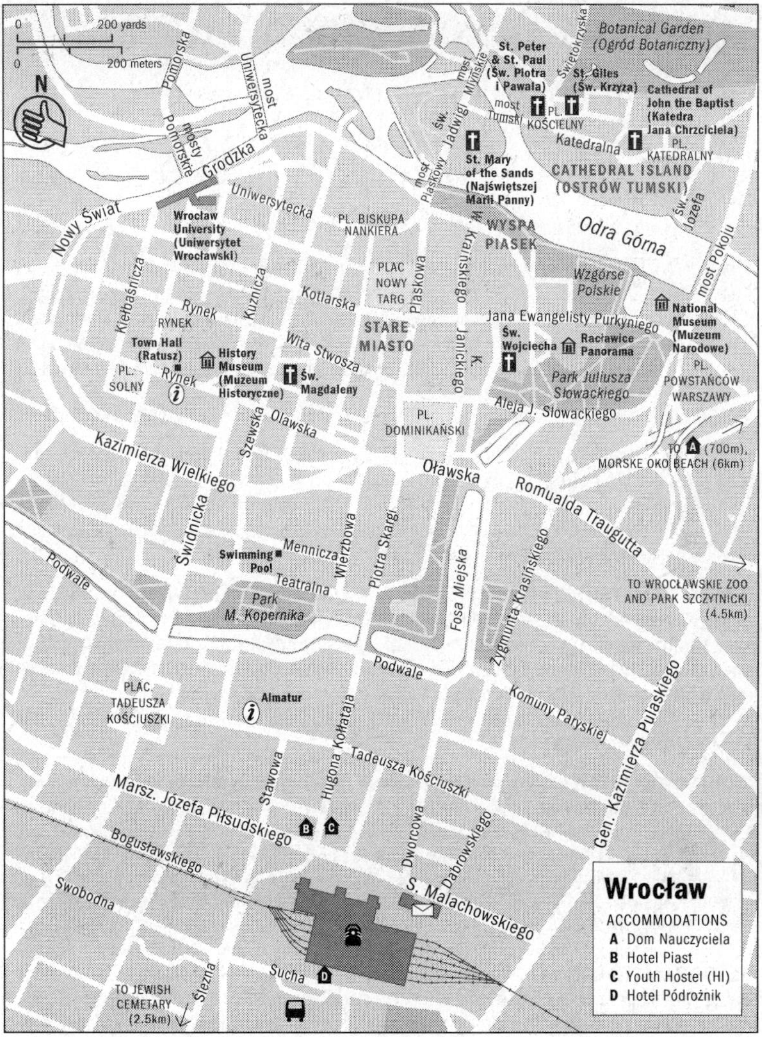

etto and Grottger. *(With your back to the town hall and the info office, bear left onto Kuźnicza for two blocks, and then right onto Kotlarska, which becomes ul. Purkyniego. The Panorama is several blocks down on the right, and the museum is at the end of the street on the left. Tel. 44 23 44; fax 336 39. Panorama open Tu-Su 9am-3pm; museum open M-W, F 10am-4pm, Th 9am-4pm, Sa-Su 10am-4pm. Joint admission 14zł, students 8zł.)*

CATHEDRAL ISLAND. (Ośtrów Tumski). The stately **Cathedral of St. John the Baptist** (Katedra św. Jana Chrzciciela) gives Cathedral Island its dignified character. Inside, a nun shows off the marble **Chapel of St. Elizabeth** (Kaplica św. Elżbiety; donation requested). Climb up the **tower** for an excellent view of the surrounding churches. *(From the National Museum, turn left over Most Pokuju, then left again onto Kard B. Kominka; soon you'll arrive at pl. Katedralny. Open daily 10am-5:30pm. 3zł, students 2zł.)* Bearing right down Kapitalna brings you to the **Botanical Gardens** (Ogród Botaniczny), ul. Sienkiewicza 23. *(Open M-F 8am-6pm, Sa-Su 10am-6pm. 3zł, students 2zł.)*

PICTURING AN INDEPENDENT POLAND The second most visited sight in Poland to the Black Madonna, the Racławicka Panorama depicts Jan Styka and Wojciech Kossak's version of the Racławice Battle, fought on April 7, 1794 between Russian troops and Polish peasants lead by Tadeusz Kościuszko (who had been a general in George Washington's Continental Army). The enormous painting (120m long and 15m high) was commissioned in 1894 to commemorate the Polish victory and one of the last gasps of an independent Poland. The third and final Partition of Poland occurred the following year, eliminating Poland from the map until 1918. The panorama was placed on public view in Lviv, at the time strongly Polish and part of Austria–the only Partitioning power tolerant enough to permit such nationalist expression. Damaged by a bomb in 1944, the painting was moved to Wrocław (along with much of Lwów) and put into storage. Officially, there were no specialists to restore it. In actuality, it was politically imprudent to permit Poles to glorify independence from Russia. With the rise of Solidarity in 1980, the painting was restored and made available for 30min. showings.

WROCŁAW UNIVERSITY. (Uniwersytet Wrocławski). The center of Wrocław's cultural life, the University houses many architectural gems. The most impressive is **Aula Leopoldina,** an 18th-century lecture hall with magnificent frescoes. *(Pl. Uniwersytecki 1. Go down Nankiera through its name change to Uniwersytecki. On the 2nd floor of the main University building. Open Th-Tu 10am-3:30pm. 2.50zł, students 1zł.)*

JEWISH CEMETERY. (Cmentarz Żydowski). Recently opened to the public, the **Jewish Cemetery** contains the remains of Ferdinand Lasalle and the family of Thomas Mann's wife, as well as fragments of Jewish tombstones dating from the 12th and 13th centuries found around Wrocław. *(Ul. Ślężna 37/39. Take tram #9 from the train station heading away from the center. Get off at the corner of Ślężna and Kamienna; go down Ślężna and the cemetery will be on your right. Tel. 67 82 36. Gates are open all week, but officially only on Sunday for a noon tour. 5zł, students 3zł.)*

AROUND THE RYNEK. The modern heart of the city, **Stare Miasto** (Old Town) centers around **Main Market Square** (Rynek Główny), the Renaissance and Gothic **town hall** *(ratusz)*, and the **History Museum** (Muzeum Historyczne). One exhibit focuses entirely on ul. Świdnicka, a central street so beautiful that the Germans tried to have its stones moved to their soil. Take time to look at the collections of armor and old silver, including an amazing scepter. *(Tel. 44 14 34. Open W-F 10am-4pm, Sa 11am-5pm, Su 10am-6pm. Cashier closes 30min. earlier. 4zł, students 3zł; free on Wednesday.)*

OUTDOOR ATTRACTIONS. Wrocławskie Zoo, the largest zoo in Poland, is famous for being much nicer to its feathered and fuzzy collection than its contemporaries. *(Ul. Wróblewskiego 1. Take tram #2 or 4 from the train station toward Biskupin and get off at ul. Wystawowa, next to a massive hall on the left. Open daily 9am-6pm; cashier closes at 5pm. 6zł, students 3zł.)* The **Morskie Oko beach,** in northeast Wrocław, has kayaks, tennis and volleyball courts, and a weight room. *(Ul. Chopina 27. Tel. 48 27 17. Open daily 9am-7pm.)* An indoor **swimming pool** exudes watery peace in the center of town. *(Ul. Teatralna 10. Tel. 44 16 56. Open M-F 10am-6pm, Sa 7:30am-2:30pm.)* The relaxing **Park Szczytnicki,** with a Japanese house on water, lies in the east part of the city in the fork of the Odra Miejska and Stara Odra rivers.

ENTERTAINMENT

For up-to-the-nanosecond cultural information, pick up a copy of **Co jest grane** *(What's Playing)*, free at tourist offices. Wrocław is famous for its student and experimental theater; check out the **Grotowski Center,** Rynek Ratusz 27 (tel. 44 53 20). May brings the international **Jazz nad Odrą** festival to Wrocław. Student clubs are the place to go for live music.

NIGHTLIFE

Szalony Koń (Crazy Horse), Rynek 36 (tel. 44 10 79), through the arched entry between two sports shops and down the hall, then down the stairs to the basement. In case the half-Chevrolet that graces the main room didn't clue you in, this place is badass. The stools are made from saddles, complete with stirrups. A big *EB Mocne* gives a tasty kick in the head (5.50zł). Occasional live concerts. Open Su-Th 3pm-2am, F-Sa 3pm until the last guest moseys on home.

Kawiarnia "Pod Kalamburem," ul. Kuźnicza 29a (tel. 44 75 28), in the university quarter theater. A decadent, Art Nouveau artists' corner. Large cups of viscous caffeine 3zł. Open M-Th 10am-11pm, F-Sa 11am-midnight, Su 4-11pm. Piano concerts F and Sa at 9pm. The adjacent **Cyberkawiarnia** peddles teas, coffees, and desserts with **internet access** on high-speed computers. 3zł per 30min. Open daily 10am-10pm.

Kalogródek, ul. Kuźnicza 29B, next to the Kawiarnia "Pod Kalamburem." In the center of the university district, students disperse themselves in amphitheater rank and file. Cheap beer (0.5L *Piast* 3zł; 0.5L *Grolsch* 4.30zł). Open daily 9am-10:30pm.

Millenium, (tel. 448 760). Twentysomethings gather in this chic underground joint to hear DJs "from around the world" spin acid, jazz, soul, funk, R&B, and house. Open M-Th and Su 5pm-3am, F-Sa 5pm-5am.

JELENIA GÓRA

In Poland's southwest corner, the land buckles along the Czech border to form the Sudety mountains. The crisp air and mineral springs in the Jelenia Góra valley have provided a welcome respite for centuries of city dwellers, including Goethe, Marysieńka Sobieska, and Henryk Sienkiewicz (see **Literature & Arts,** p. 401). At the foot of the Karkonosze range (part of the Sudety), Jelenia Góra makes a perfect starting point for treks to loftier hiking and skiing in Karpacz and Szklarska Poręba. Although not a destination in itself, the town's convenient bus and train connections and well-preserved facades in the *rynek* make it well worth a detour.

ORIENTATION & PRACTICAL INFORMATION. **Stare Miasto** is ringed by a street named **ul. Podwale** in the north and west and **ul. Bankowa** in the south. The **train station,** ul. 1-go Maja 77 (tel. 752 39 36), 15min. east of town, sees trains off to **Wrocław** (2½hr., 13 per day, 18.50zł) and **Warsaw** (8hr., 3 per day, 31zł). **Luggage storage** (5zł) is available here. Most **buses** stop at (and many leave from) the train station. To get to the center of town from the trains, turn right onto ul. 1-go Maja when leaving the train station. Bear slightly right at the first large intersection, and ul. 1-go Maja will lead you directly to Stare Miasto. The main **bus station,** ul. Obrońców Pokoju 1B (tel. 764 69 36), 10min. northwest of town, sends buses to **Wrocław** (3hr., 8 per day). From the bus station, make a left onto **Pokoju,** a right at the light, and a left onto **Jasna,** which brings you to the center. The **IT tourist office,** ul. 1-go Maja 42 (tel./fax 752 40 54), is two streets past the first large intersection with al. Wojska Polskiego. One of the most helpful, friendliest tourist offices in western Poland, it's well-equipped with brochures, maps (4-6zł), and advice. (Open M-F 8am-6pm, Sa 9am-1pm.) There is a **pharmacy, Apteka Karkonoska,** at ul. 1-go Maja 70 (tel. 752 77 18; open M-F 8am-7pm, Sa 8am-3pm). **Bank Zachodni,** ul. J. Kochanowskiego 8 (tel. 764 62 25), the second left after the train station, gives Visa cash advances and cashes traveler's checks for a 0.5% commission. **Western Union** services are also available. (Open M-Sa 8am-5pm, Su 8am-1pm.) There are Cirrus/Plus/Visa/AmEx **ATMs** outside Smok Restaurant (see below) and in the train station. The **post office,** ul. Pocztowa 9/10 (tel. 752 43 90), lies 2min. south of ul. 1-go Maja and one street past the IT office. (Open M-F 7am-9pm, Sa 8am-3pm, Su 9-11am.) **Internet Lab,** ul. 1-go Maja 60 (tel. 75 281 11) on the third floor, connects you for 6zł per hr. (Open M-F 9am-8pm, Sa 10am-2pm.) **Telephones** are outside the post office. **Postal code:** 58-500. **Phone code:** (0)75.

ACCOMMODATIONS. If you're visiting both Karpacz and Jelenia Góra, consider staying in Karpacz, where hotels are cheaper. Jelenia Góra's cramped **Youth Hostel Bartek,** ul. Bartka Zwycięzcy 10 (tel. 752 57 46), is off ul. Kochanowskiego two streets south of the train station. From ul. 1-go Maja, go left on ul. Kochanowskiego and turn left onto Bartka Zwyciezcy. (Bare-bones dorms 12-16zł. Lockout 10am-5pm. Curfew 9pm.) **Hotel Europa,** ul. 1-go Maja 16/18 (tel. 764 7231; fax 75 244 95), has modestly priced rooms 2min. from the *rynek.* (Singles 46zł, with bath 70zł; doubles 72zł, 150zł. Breakfast 10-15zł. MC/Visa/AmEx.) **Hotel and Camping Park,** ul. Sudecka 42 (tel. 752 69 42; fax 752 60 21), 15min. southeast of town on the road to Karpacz, hides in a petite park. (Tent space 6zł per person; tents 9zł. Doubles 60zł; triples 70zł.)

FOOD. For a cheap feast, **Karczma Staropolska,** ul. 1-go Maja 33 (tel. 752 23 50), serves tavern chow. (Entrees 4-8zł. Open daily 8am-10pm.) For a bit more, you can relax beneath the gleaming white arches of the pl. Ratuszowy arcade at one of the three restaurants on the west side of the square. **Pokusa** (Temptation), #12 (tel. 752 53 47), and **Retro,** #14 (tel. 752 48 94), offer traditional Polish food, while **Smok** (Dragon), # 15 (tel. 752 59 28), prepares pizza and Chinese dishes. All offer outside dining on the *rynek.* (Entrees at all three 8-20zł. Open daily 10am-10pm. MC/Visa/AmEx.) Many cafeterias on ul. 1-go Maja provide faster, cheaper options. **Bar Natura,** ul. 1-go Maja 60 (tel. 27 52 68 87), offers vegetarian pizza (3.50zł), soup (1.60 zł), and *pierogi* (1.50zł; open M-F 10:30am-6pm, Sa 9:30am-3pm).

SIGHTS & ENTERTAINMENT. Originally constructed at the turn of the 17th century after the Thirty Years' War, the market square **pl. Ratuszowy** had the good fortune to survive WWII without any major damage. Recent renovation has only enhanced the Baroque appearance of the buildings. In the middle of all this, the 1747 **town hall** *(ratusz)* displays its unadorned Classicist architecture.

POLAND

Walking back toward 1-go Maja from the town hall, the **Church of St. Erasmus and St. Pancras** (Kościół św. Erazma i Pankracego) stands tall at pl. Kościelny 4 (tel. 221 60). This basilica-style church boasts an elaborate 22m-by-11m altar. At the intersection of ul. Konopnicka and ul. 1-go Maja, **St. Anne's Chapel** (Kaplica św. Anny) is worth a glance—it originally formed part of the 16th-century town defenses. (Open M-Sa 9am-5pm. Free.) The 18th-century **Holy Cross Church** (Kościół św. Krzyża), down ul. 1-go Maja, sits in a walled park. Built in the shape of an Orthodox cross, the 1717 Baroque pulpit is composed of three pieces of limestone. The Michael Roeder **organ** here is one of Poland's largest. An hour's walk along the green-yellow path away from the bus station leads to the relaxing gorge **Pearl of the West** (Perła Zachodu), which has amazing views of the reservoir.

The 14th-century **Chojnik Castle,** atop a wooded hill in the suburb of **Sobieszów,** was left in ruins by a 17th-century lightning bolt. The castle tower offers extraordinary views of the mountain ranges. (Open daily in summer 10am-6pm; off-season 10am-4pm. 2zł, students 1zł.) **Hiking** opportunities abound; the black trail (50min.) is steeper and rockier than the red route (40min.). To reach the castle, 8km from town, take bus #7, 9, or 15 from the train station or from ul. Bankowa (30min., hourly, 1.20zł). Buy a ticket at a kiosk and get off after the bus turns right at Restaurant Pokusa. Backtrack a bit and follow the signs to Chojnik, across the river and south along dirt paths. If you call one month ahead, you can stay at **Schronisko PTTK "Chojnik"** (58-570 Jelenia Góra-Sobieszów; tel. 755 35 35), within the castle. (20-25zł per person. Open Apr. 15-Oct. 15.)

In September, the castle hosts the **Knights' Crossbow Tournament.** Other local festivals include the September 20-25 **Antiques and Oddities Market,** which crams pl. Ratuszowy with odds and ends sheltered from daylight for centuries. The week-long **International Street Theater Festival** fills the town's narrow streets with open-air performances of juggling and theatrics the first week in July; for information, contact the **Regional Cultural Center,** ul. Bankowa 28/30 (tel. 755 10 03).

NEAR JELENIA GÓRA: SZKLARSKA PORĘBA

Situated in the gentle valley of the Kamienna River, Szklarska Poręba is a year-round resort that hosts events of all stripes, ranging from cross-country skiing competitions to a motorcycle convention. The Czech border is only a few kilometers away, and **Karkonosze National Park** (see **Karpacz,** below), with its many appealing hiking options, is easy to reach. Follow the green trail 3km along the Kamienna River to Wodospad Szklarki, a 10m high waterfall. From here, the blue trail winds steeply up to **Mt. Szrenica** (2-3hr.). The red trail goes past the craggy cliffs of **Krucze Skały** (Ravens' Rocks) to **Huta Szkla Julia** (Julia Glassworks); the factory was established in the mid-19th century to continue the 600-year tradition of glass manufacturing. From the factory, the red trail climbs 25min. more to **Wodospad Kamieńczyka,** at 28m one of the highest waterfalls in the Sudety. The **Sudety Lift** to Mt. Szrenica is located 1km uphill from the town center at ul. Turystyczna 25a (tel. 717 30 35; fax 717 30 36). It takes you up 636m in two legs, but you can opt out of either one. (One-way, both legs 16zł, round-trip 18zł; children under 14 11zł, 14.50zł.) **MBIT,** ul. Jedności Narodowej 3 (tel. 717 24 94; tel./fax 717 24 49) exchanges money, sells **maps** (5-7zł) with all the hiking possibilities, and arranges private rooms (15-22zł), pensions (20-30zł), and mountain huts (8-30zł). They also help arrange **equipment rentals** (bikes, skis, rock-climbing, horses; open M-F 8am-6pm, Sa-Su 9am-7pm).

GETTING THERE. Trains (45min., 6 per day, 2zł) and **buses** run frequently to and from **Jelenia Góra** (40min., 25 per day, 3zł).

KARPACZ

Despite heavy tourism, a restful atmosphere persists in Karpacz. Together with Szklarska Poręba, it provides a main gateway to Karkonosze National Park (for ascents to Mt. Śnieżka and Mt. Szrenica, respectively). Surrounding mountains throw long shadows over thickly forested valleys, and the raw beauty of the landscape—even from within Karpacz itself—is stunning.

ORIENTATION & PRACTICAL INFORMATION. Karpacz's streets are poorly marked and follow the contours of the mountain, meandering uphill from the train station along **ul. 3-go Maja.** This main road is concealed from the station by trees and an incline—walk up the concrete stairs from the bus station and follow the short path to the left. Although there's no main station, **buses** stop regularly along the hill. Get off at the first stop after the **train station,** Karpacz Bachus, and either go uphill to the Karpacz tourist office or downhill to IT. **Trains** (tel. 61 96 84) and **buses** both head to **Jelenia Góra** (trains 35min., 3 per day, 2zł; buses 30min., 28 per day, 3zł). **Karpacz,** ul. 3-go Maja 52 (tel./fax 761 95 47), **exchanges currency,** arranges private rooms (30zł), and makes reservations at pensions and hotels. (Open M-F 9am-6pm, Sa 9am-4pm, Su 9am-1pm.) **IT,** ul. 3-go Maja 25a (tel./fax 761 97 16), is less helpful, but has brochures and indispensable **maps** (5zł), and arranges private rooms (20-30zł per person; open M-F 9am-6pm, Sa 9am-4pm, Su 9am-3pm). Ask at either tourist office about **equipment rental** (bikes, skis, rock-climbing, horses) and camping. **Bank Zachodni,** ul. 3-go Maja 43 (tel./fax 761 92 52), cashes **traveler's checks** for a US$1.50 commission. (Open M-F 9am-5pm.) It also has a Plus/Visa **ATM.** There's a **pharmacy, Pod Złotą Wagą,** at ul. 3-go Maja 82 (tel. 761 93 12; open M-F daily 9am-8pm, Sa 9am-3pm, Su 9am-1pm). The **post office** is at ul. 3-go Maja 21 (tel. 761 92 20; fax 761 95 85; open M-F 8am-6pm, Sa 9am-3pm, Su 9-11am). **Postal code:** 58-540. All **telephones** in Karpacz use magnetic cards, available at the post office and most kiosks. **Phone code:** (0)75.

ACCOMMODATIONS. Private rooms and **pensions** proliferate, especially on **Kościelna** street; the latter run 15-25zł. Unfortunately, some of them are open only part of the year—inquire at the Karpacz tourist office or at IT (see above) for cur-

POLAND

rent information. **Pension Celina** (tel. 761 94 55), right in the center of town at ul. Kościelna 9, has all the comforts of grandma's house. (30zł per person, plus 5zł if you're only staying one night. Private baths. Breakfast 5zł.) **D.W. Szczyt,** ul. Na Śnieżkę 6 (tel. 761 93 60), is at the uphill end of town next to Świątynia Wang—take the bus to Karpacz Wang. At 860m, the views from these comfortable rooms (25zł per person) are incomparable. Make reservations at the Karpacz tourist office. **FWP Piast,** ul. 3-go Mąja 22 (tel. 11 92 44), is downhill across the street from IT. Its spacious singles, doubles, and triples are drab, but the ping-pong is free. (25zł per person, with meals 40zł.)

FOOD. Tourists not pressured into taking meals at their hotel can opt to eat at another pension or at one of the few operations catering solely to the palate. **Astra,** ul. Obrońców Pokoju 1 (tel. 761 93 14), just uphill from IT, serves up large meals at slightly high prices. Potato dumplings with meat and salad (7zł), salmon filet with fries and salad (18zł), and spaghetti (7zł) are all reasonable options. (Open daily 10am-midnight.) The grocery store **Delikatesy,** ul. 3-go Mąja 29 (tel. 761 92 59), stocks everything necessary for a picnic in the mountains. (Open M-Sa 8:30am-9pm, Su 10am-6pm.)

SIGHTS & HIKING. The uphill hike to **Wang Chapel** (Świątynia Wang), ul. Śnieżki 8 (tel. 761 82 74), at the upper end of town, takes 90min., but is well worth it. This Viking church was built in southern Norway at the turn of the 12th century. In the early 1800s, it sorely needed a restoration no one could afford, so Kaiser Friedrich Wilhelm III of Prussia had it transported to Karpacz for the Lutheran community here. Gaping dragons' mouths, stylized lions, and intricate plant carvings adorn the temple. Organ concerts are held here on Saturday evenings in summer; check the schedule at the ticket office. (Open in summer M-Sa 9am-6pm, Su 11:30am-6pm; off-season M-Sa 9am-5:30pm, Su 11:30am-1pm. 3zł, students 2zł.)

Hikers of all ages aim for the crown of **Śnieżka** (Mt. Snow; 1602m), but there are multiple ways of reaching it. Śnieżka and most of the trails lie within **Karkonos National Park** (Karkonoski Park Narodowy; 1-day entrance fee 1zł, students 0.50zł; 3-day pass 2zł, students 1zł). To get to the summit as quickly (3-4hr.) and painlessly as possible, take the **Kopa chair lift** from ul. Strażacka, just south of ul. Karkonoska, or follow the black trail from Hotel Biały Jar until you see the lift on the left. (Runs daily 9am-6pm, weather permitting. One-way 9zł, students 7zł; round-trip 12zł, students 10zł.) From the top of the lift, the hike to the summit takes about an hour. A longer and less crowded trek starts at Świątynia Wang. Follow the blue route up to **Polana** (1080m; 1hr.), and then hike up to the scenic **Mały Staw** lake (another hr.). From here, it's 35min. to **Spalona Strażnica,** then an easy 30min. to the **Pod Śnieżką** pass (1394m); you can then ascend the peak (40min.).

Alternatively, you can take the red path up from behind Hotel Biały Jar's parking circle. Once you emerge above the tree line, it's difficult to ascend but still very manageable. The trek to Pod Śnieżką takes 2½hr., and the summit rises another 30min. away. Endurance hikers follow the blue trail from Świątynia Wang to Polana (1hr.), then the yellow path to the **Pilgrims** (Pielgrzymy) stone formations (1204m; 25min.). Continue along the yellow route to another petrified protrusion at **Sunflower** (Słonecznik; 35min.). Turning left here, the red trail travels to Spalona Strażnica and Pod Śnieżką (1hr.), one mound from Śnieżką.

There are two routes from Pod Śnieżką to the very top. The red **Zygzag** shoots straight up the north side—look for the cobblestoned path (20-30min.). The blue trail, **Jubilee Way,** winds around the peak (1hr.). Once there, there's a fee to climb to the **observatory,** which seems straight out of *The Jetsons.* (Open daily 10am-5pm. 2zł, students 1zł.) The lure of most of these hikes lies in the expansive views when above the tree-line.

GREATER POLAND (WIELKOPOLSKA)

A train ride through the *Wielkopolski* lowlands reveals stunning views of deep green fields and gently rolling hills, as well as a few dense woodlands. Except for a triad of urban centers—multi-faceted Poznań; Toruń home of Copernicus and gingerbread; and oft-neglected Łódź—Wielkopolska is as serene as it is culturally rich. Gniezno's coronation cathedral and Golub-Dobrzyń's castle testify that this region has long lain at the heart of Poland's religious and political history.

POZNAŃ

Poznań (POZE-nahn) has no defining tourist attraction. International trade fairs, a lively music scene, and delectable local food and architecture draw throngs for work and play. Just off the main streets, locals enjoy outdoor meals in the *rynek*, and students search for good beer in colorful watering holes.

ORIENTATION

Most everything in town can be found in the central **Stare Miasto** (Old Town). The train station, **Poznań Główny,** sits on ul. Dworcowa in Stare Miasto's southwest corner; the **bus station** is 500m down ul. Towarowa. On foot, exit the main hall of the train station onto **ul. Dworcowa** and follow it until it ends. Then go right onto **ul. Św. Marcin.** Continue to al. Marcinkowskiego. To get to **Stary Rynek,** the heart of Stare Miasto, go left and take the second right, ul. Paderewskiego (20min.). Or, catch any **tram** heading down Św. Marcin (to the right) from the end of ul. Dworcowa. Get off at the corner of Św. Marcin and Marcinkowskiego.

PRACTICAL INFORMATION

Trains: ul. Dworcowa 1 (tel. 866 12 12 and 869 38 11). To: **Berlin** (3hr., 7 per day, 116zł); **Gdańsk** (4-5hr., 7 per day, 30zł); **Kraków** (6-7hr., 8 per day, 36zł); **Warsaw** (3½hr., 19 per day, 34zł); and **Szczecin** (3hr., 14 per day, 26zł). Many of these are express trains, which cost 50% more.

Local Transportation: Tram and **bus** tickets are sold in blocks of time rather than per ride: 10min. 0.80zł; 30min. 1.60zł; 1hr. 2.40zł. Prices double 11pm-4am. Students are eligible for half-price *ulgowy* tickets. Tickets can be purchased at the Glob-Tour office in the train station or at the ubiquitous Ruch kiosks. 50zł fine for riding ticketless.

Taxis: Radio Taxi, tel. 919, 951, and 96 66.

Tourist Offices: Glob-Tour, ul. Dworcowa (tel./fax 866 06 67), in the main lobby of the train station. Tourist info in English, maps (6zł), and a **currency exchange.** Open 24hr. **Centrum Informacji Turystycznej (CIT),** Stary Rynek 59 (tel. 852 61 56), also sells maps (6zł) and provides info in English and German about sights and budget accommodations. Open M-F 9am-5pm, Sa 10am-2pm.

Budget Travel: EUROSTOP locations are sprouting up around town. The one at ul. Fredry 7 sells ISICs.

Currency Exchange: Bank Pekao S.A., ul. Św. Marcin 52/56 (tel. 855 85 58), has excellent rates and cashes traveler's checks for a 1% commission. Open M-F 8am-6pm, Sa 10am-2pm. Their **ATM** accepts Cirrus/MC/Plus/Visa. There are numerous *kantor*s and banks in the city, especially on ul. Św. Marcin.

Luggage Storage: At the train station, opposite Glob-Tour. 1.50zł plus 1% of luggage value. Open 24hr.

English Bookstore: Omnibus Bookstore, ul. Św. Marcin 39. Wide selection of paperbacks. Open M-F 10am-7pm, Sa 10am-4pm. MC/Visa/AmEx.

International Press: Empik Megastore, corner of pl. Wolności and ul. Ratajczaka. Open M-Sa 10am-10pm, Su 11am-5pm.

24hr. Pharmacy: ul. 23 Lutego 18 (tel. 852 26 25).

POLAND

Medical Assistance: ul. Szkolna 8/12 (tel. 999 and 852 72 11).

Post Office: ul. Kościuszki 77 (tel. 53 67 43). Open M-F 7am-9pm, Sa 8am-7pm, Su 9am-6pm. **Postal code:** 61-890.

Internet Access: Internet Club, ul. Garncarska 10 (tel. 853 78 18), to the right off Św. Marcin just past Hotel Royal. 6zł per hr. Open M-Sa 10am-10pm, Su 4-10pm.

Phone code: (0)61.

ACCOMMODATIONS

There are four year-round youth hostels, but only two are anywhere near the city center. During its fairs (Mar., June, Oct.), the city fills quickly with tourists and businesspeople, and most prices rise at least 10%. During these times, getting a decently priced room without calling ahead is virtually impossible. For **private rooms** (singles 37zł, during fairs 68zł; doubles 53zł, 96zł) contact **Przemysław,** ul. Głogowska 16 (tel. 865 83 06; fax 866 51 63; open M-F 9am-6pm, Sa 8am-2pm).

Schronisko Młodzieżowe (HI), ul. Berwińskiego 2/3 (tel. 866 40 40). Exit the train station through the tunnel toward McDonald's and turn left onto ul. Głogowska; ul. Berwiskińego is the 2nd street on the right. 52 beds in an old school. Clean rooms with thin mattresses. Self-serve kitchen. Doubles 20zł, non-members 23zł; dorms 15zł, 18zł. Sheets 4zł. Reception 5-10:30pm. Lockout 10am-5pm. Curfew 11pm.

Hotel Royal, ul. Św. Marcin 71 (tel. 853 78 84; fax 851 79 31), a short walk from the *rynek.* Large, comfortable rooms with well-kept baths. Singles 60zł, with bath 70zł; doubles 100zł; triples 150zł.

Hotel Dom Turysty, Stary Rynek 91 (tel./fax 852 88 93). Entrance on ul. Wroniecka. Exploit the cheap dorms of this upscale inn right on the *rynek.* Dorms 40zł. Other rooms, all with bath, 125-275zł. Breakfast included. Reception speaks good English. MC/Visa.

POLAND

FOOD

Two specialties capture the flavor of Poznań: *pyzy,* a cross between noodles and potato dumplings, and *rogale świętomarcińskie,* croissants with various fruit fillings sold by the kilo on November 11, St. Martin's Day. Middle eastern food is also big, reflecting Poznań's cosmopolitan flare. There are several **24hr. grocery stores** around town. Try **Prospero,** ul. Wielka 18 (tel. 52 33 07), for "just one more" bottle of the local fave *Lech Premium* (2.50zł). They have real food, too.

Restauracja Sphinx, ul. Św. Marcin 66/72 (tel. 852 07 02). Huge portions of Middle Eastern entrees and not-so-Middle Eastern pizza. Only the sphinx can explain the forest decor. Entrees 8-47zł, pizzas 8-12zł, salads 7-11zł.

Bar Mleczny Pod Kuchcikiem, ul. Św. Marcin 75. Traditional Polish food at unbeatable prices. Gorge yourself on *pyzy* and a bottle of Pepsi for 3.90zł. Entrees 1-3zł. Open M-F 8am-7pm, Sa 8am-4pm, Su 10am-4pm.

Cukiernia "U Marcina," ul. Św. Marcin 32 (tel. 852 67 88). Traditional Polish sweets, plus a small snack bar. Entrees 3-7zł. Open M-Sa 9am-8pm, Su 9am-7pm.

SIGHTS

Poznań seems to be more about doing than looking, but don't let all that action distract you from a number of noteworthy highlights. Opulent 15th-century merchant homes, notable for their rainbow paint-jobs and architectural flourishes, line **Stary Rynek.** The houses surround the **town hall** (*ratusz*), a multicolored gem deemed the finest secular Renaissance structure north of the Alps. The **Historical Museum of Poznań** (Muzeum Historii Poznania), Stary Rynek 1 (tel. 52 56 13), displays medieval artifacts, paintings, and the exquisite Chamber of Law. (Open M 9am-4pm; T, F, and Sa 9am-3pm; W noon-6pm; Su 10am-3pm. 3.20zl, students 2zl.) In front of town hall stands the menacing **1535 whipping post,** whose construction was funded with fines levied on maids for their risqué garb. Nearby is the city's most interesting museum, the **Museum of Musical Instruments** (Muzeum Instrumentów Muzycznych), Stary

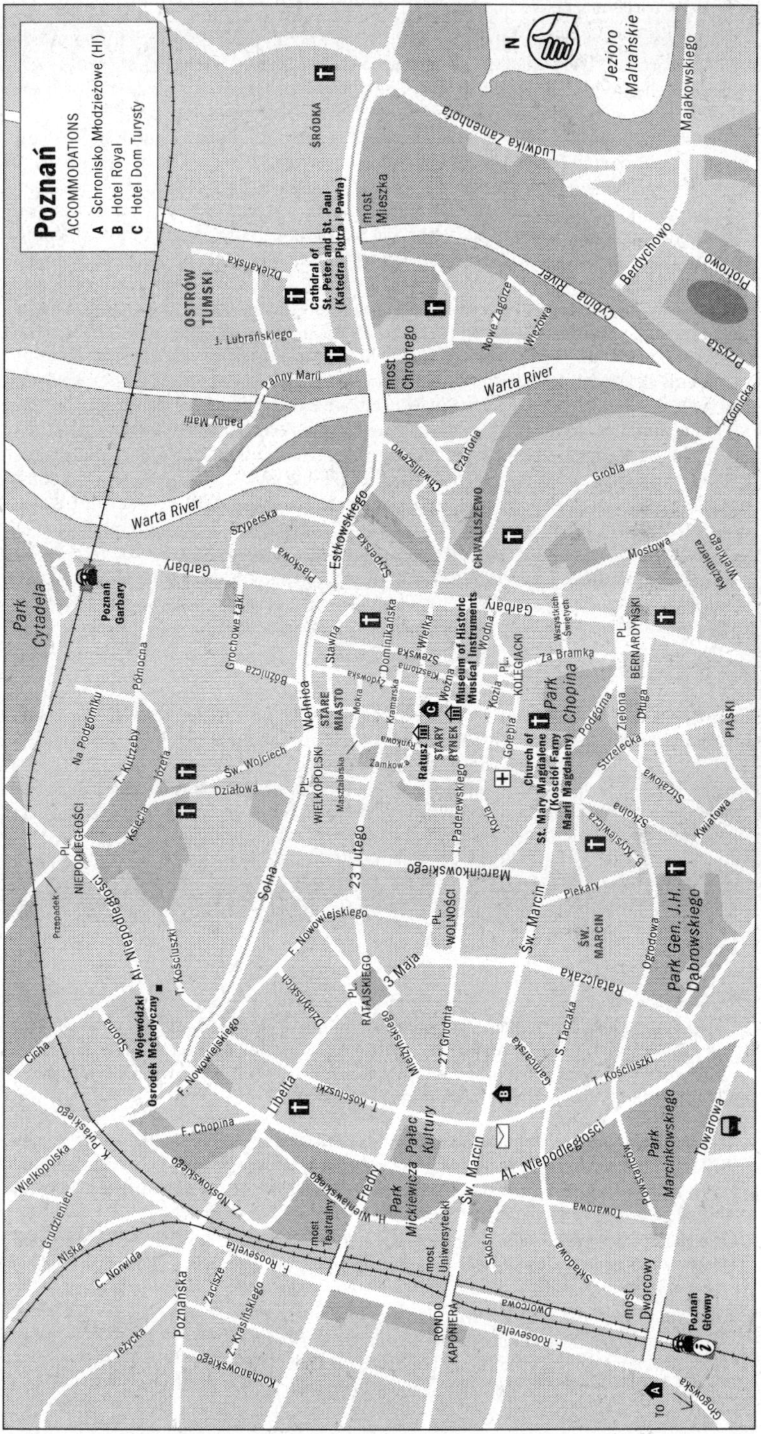
Poznań
ACCOMMODATIONS
A Schronisko Młodzieżowe (HI)
B Hotel Royal
C Hotel Dom Turysty
Jezioro Maltańskie
ŚRÓDKA
OSTRÓW TUMSKI
Cathdral of St. Peter and St. Paul (Katedra Piotra i Pawła)
most Mieszka
Ludwika Zamenhofa
Majakowskiego
Berdychowo
Cybina River
Piotrowo
Przysta
Warta River
most Chrobrego
Panny Marii
J. Lubrańskiego
Dziekańska
Nowe Zagórze
Wieżowa
Park Cytadela
Poznań Garbary
Garbary
Szyperska
Piaskowa
Estkowskiego
Chwaliszewo
CHWALISZEWO
Czartoria
Grobla
Mostowa
Kazimierza Wielkiego
Grochowe Łąki
Północna
Bóżnica
Na Podgórniku
T. Kutrzeby
Józefa
Św. Wojciech
Działowa
Księcia
PL. NIEPODLEGŁOŚCI
Al. Niepodległości
Przepadek
PL. WIELKOPOLSKI
Wolnica
STARE MIASTO
Stawna
Dominikańska
Wielka
Szewska
Klasztorna
Żydowska
Mokra
Kramarska
Wroniecka
Masztalarska
Zamkowa
Rynkowa
Ratusz
STARY RYNEK
Wożna
Museum of Historic Musical Instruments
Wodna
PL. KOLEGIACKI
Kozia
Gołębia
Za Bramką
Wszystkich Świętych
PL. BERNARDYŃSKI
Park Chopina
Church of St. Mary Magdalene (Kościół Farny Marii Magdaleny)
Podgórna
Zielona
Długa
PIASKI
Strzelecka
Szkolna
Szczałowa
Kwiatowa
B. Krysiewicza
I. Paderewskiego
23 Lutego
Marcinkowskiego
Solna
Św. Marcin
Piekary
ŚW. MARCIN
Ogrodowa
Park Gen. J.H. Dąbrowskiego
PL. WOLNOŚCI
F. Nowowiejskiego
Działyńskich
PL. RATAJSKIEGO
3 Maja
Ratajczaka
27 Grudnia
Garncarska
S. Taczaka
T. Kościuszki
T. Kościuszki
Wojewódzki Ośrodek Metodyczny
Sporna
Cicha
Libelta
Mielżyńskiego
Pałac Kultury
F. Chopina
K. Pułaskiego
Wielkopolska
Z. Noskowskiego
H. Wieniawskiego
Fredry
Park Mickiewicza
Al. Niepodległości
Park Marcinkowskiego
Towarowa
Towarowa
Powstańców
Grudzieniec
Niska
C. Norwida
most Teatralny
most Uniwersytecki
Skośna
Składowa
F. Roosevelta
Zacisze
Poznańska
Z. Krasińskiego
Jeżycka
RONDO KAPONIERA
Dworcowa
most Dworcowy
Poznań Główny
Kochanowskiego
TO A
Głogowska

POLAND

Rynek 45/47 (tel. 52 08 57). The collection's star, Chopin's piano, is backed by a chorus of instruments from Polynesia and Africa and an orchestra of antique music machines. (Open Tu 10am-5pm, W-Sa 9am-5pm, Su 11am-4pm. 3.20zł, students 2zł.)

Behind the town hall, on the *rynek*'s northeast corner, begins **ul. Żydowska** (Jewish St.), the center of the prewar Jewish district. Its **synagogue,** built in 1907, became a swimming pool in 1940. Opposite the synagogue, the **Parish Church of St. Mary Magdalene** (Kosciół Farny Marii Magdaleny) blesses the end of ul. Świętosławska with its frescoes and pink marble. (Open to the public except during masses. Organ concerts M-Sa at 12:15pm.) In **Ostrów Tumski,** the oldest part of town, stands the first Polish cathedral, **Cathedral of St. Peter and St. Paul** (Katedra Piotra i Pawła), encircled by 15 chapels. The original church was built in 968, soon after the first Polish bishopric was established in Poznań. Lost to fire in 1945, it was rebuilt after the war in a neo-Gothic style. The tombs of two famous Piasts are in the **Golden Chapel** (Kaplica Złota): Prince Mieszko I (d. 992) and his oldest son, Bolesław Chrobry (the Brave), the first king of Poland (d. 1025). In the underground crypt lie the remains of several 19th-century Polish nobles and of the original cathedral. (Open to tourists daily 9am-4pm, except during mass. Entrance to crypt 2zł, students 1zł.)

One of the most visible sights on ul. Św. Marcin hearkens from more recent history. The **park** on pl. Mickiewicz commemorates a 1956 clash over food prices between workers and government troops; 76 people died in the conflict. Two stark crosses knotted together with steel cable are emblazoned with the dates of workers' uprisings throughout Poland. An electronic recording tells the story from a console in front of the monument. (Free and in the language of your choice.)

In the hot summer months, take a dip in **Malta Lake** (Jezioro Maltańskie). Take tram #1, 4, 6, or 7 eastbound from the center and get off at ul. Zamenhofa. The year-round artificial **ski slope** lets you get a jump on ski season.

ENTERTAINMENT

Poznań's music and theater scene is lively but mercurial. The monthly **Poznański Informator Kulturalny, Sportowy i Turystyczny (IKS)** contains many useful phone numbers and info in English on all cultural events. (5zł; sold at bookstores and some kiosks.) Questions about music in town can be addressed to the **Music Society—Towarzystwo Muzyczne im. Henryka Wieniawskiego,** ul. Świętosławska 7 (tel. 852 26 42; fax 852 89 91), across from the Parish Church of St. Mary Magdalene. (Open M-F 9am-7pm.) The society hosts occasional classical performances, as well as the huge **International Theater Festival** at Malta Lake in late June and early July. Posters, pasted all over large stone columns near and along ul. Św. Marcin, alert passersby to local happenings.

NIGHTLIFE

Those seeking less formal entertainment (or simply a place to hang out) can choose from classy pubs, yards overflowing with kegs and music, and neon-and-smoke nightclubs. The *rynek*'s restaurants host outdoor cappuccino sipping and beer chugging amid 15th-century architectural wonders.

The Dubliner, ul. Św. Marcin 80/82 (tel. 853 60 81, ext. 147), located in the Zamek (Poznań Cultural Center). Enter on al. Niepodległości. A large, friendly pub with a devoted following. Irish food 8-20zł. 0.3L Guinness 9zł, pint 12zł. Live music in summer, Th-Sa 10pm. Open daily noon-midnight, or later.

Dziedziniec Zamkowy, in the courtyard of the Zamek, just past The Dubliner. A backyard party without the house to trash. Tap the keg for 4zł per glass. Cover 8-30zł. Hours vary and are posted outside.

Stajenka Pegaza (tel. 851 64 18), corner of ul. Fredry and ul. Wieniawskiego. The mix of fun-loving locals, tourists, and numerous draft beers more than make up for the remote location. Bring your favorite tape; they'll play it for you. *Żywiec* 4.50zł. Open M-F from 11am, Sa from noon, Su from 3pm until last customer leaves.

O'Morgan's, ul. Wielka 7 (tel. 852 83 83). A fledgling establishment run by the Irish owners of Morgan's in Warsaw. Best Guinness in town (pint 12zł). Open daily 1pm-1am.

NEAR POZNAŃ: GNIEZNO

Legend has it that Gniezno (g-NYEZ-no; "nest") was built as a perch by Lech, the mythical founder of Poland. The hamlet is a pocket of tree-lined neighborhoods and tiny shops around a diminutive town square. And with the refurbishments completed for the Pope's visit in June 1997, Gniezno is more charming than ever. What keeps the tourists (Papal and otherwise) coming is the massive **Gniezno Cathedral** (Katedra Gnieźnieńska), at the end of ul. Chrobrego, past the *rynek* and a short walk up ul. Tumska. The first Polish king, **Bolesław Chrobry** (the Brave), was crowned here in 1025, 25 years after Gniezno had become the seat of Polish archbishops (see **History,** p. 399). The town was Poland's capital until it was razed by Czechs in 1038, and the cathedral continued to host coronations into the 14th century. A foreboding statue of Bolesław (you'll recognize him from the 20zł note) guards the cathedral on the west side. The bronze door's 18 bas-reliefs depict the life and martyrdom of **Św. Wojciech,** whose remains rest here. Light coming in at odd angles illuminates the side altars but leaves the main altar, with its ornate spiraling columns, dark and somber. The gratings are nearly 700 years old. (Open M-Sa 10am-5pm, Su 1:30-5:30pm. 2zł. English displays toward the back.) The serene yard surrounding the parish buildings leads to the 12th-century **Church of St. George** (Kościół św. Jerzego) and the **Archdiocesan Museum,** ul. Kolegiaty 2 (tel. 426 37 78), which chronicles the history of Catholicism in Poland. Of particular note are the 14th-century robes, products of more than 20 years' labor. (Open May-Sept. Tu-Su 9am-4pm; Oct.-Apr. Tu-Su 9am-3pm. 2zł, students 1zł.) Gniezno's other main attraction is the **Museum of the Origins of the Polish State** (Muzeum Początków Państwa Polskiego), ul. Kostrzewskiego 1 (tel./fax 426 46 41), on the opposite end of Lake Jelonek from the cathedral. The main exhibit hall features an automated tour (available in English) through ancient artifacts, weapons, books, and scale models of buildings and cities. (Open May-June Tu-Su 9am-5pm, otherwise Tu-Su 10am-5pm. 3.50zł, students 2zł.)

GETTING THERE. Gniezno is linked by **train** to **Poznań** (50min., 21 per day, 6.60zł) and **Toruń** (1hr., 8 per day, 10zł) and by **bus** (20min.-2hr.; take the direct route; numerous buses daily, 6-8zł). To reach the *rynek* and cathedral, head out of the train station onto ul. Lecha. Turn onto ul. Chrobrego and walk 10min.

POLAND

NEAR POZNAŃ: BISKUPIN

The archaeological site on Lake Biskupin has unearthed artifacts of an Iron Age village (c. 1200 BC), and features a wooden reconstruction of the settlement. But the real attraction is the trip there on a **narrow-gauge railway.** The ride past farms, wildflowers, lakes, and streams is not to be missed.

The best introduction to the archaeological site is the **museum** (tel. 302 50 55) in the white building at the end of the entrance road. The exhibit hall waxes didactic about the region's culture, and displays original tools, personal items, pottery, Neolithic plant and animal remains, and evidence of trade with partners as far away as Egypt. The museum also displays human skeletons from the Neolithic Period (c. 10,000 BC), and much of the original settlement. To get to the actual **reconstruction,** head out the front door and back to the main road. Face the ticket booth and go right, following the arrows along a tree-shaded walkway. Along the right-hand row of houses, park employees wear the closest thing to period dress they could find and demonstrate Neolithic-era crafts. A little dingy named the *Diabel wenecki* ("Venice Devil") braves the lake every 30min., surveying the site from the water. (M-Sa 9am-5pm, Su 9am-4pm; 3zł at the main gate.) To check out the **experimental archaeology exhibit,** head back to the museum and go around to the right to find recreated bread ovens and animals related to those the inhabitants of Biskupin may have raised or hunted. (5zł, students 3zł.)

GETTING THERE. Follow the directions to **Gniezno** (see above) from Poznań. From Gniezno, **buses** travel to **Żnin** (1hr., hourly, 5.50zł; info tel. 302 04 92). From there, the train to Biskupin (the station is called **Żnin Wąsk**) is a right turn down ul. Dworcowa, which runs in front of the station (Apr.-Oct. 5 per day, last at 4:50pm, 4zł). Biskupin is the second stop. Once in Biskupin, head over the tracks and through the gate to the **ticket booth.** A **map** hangs near the gate.

TORUŃ

Toruń extols itself as the birthplace and childhood home of Mikołaj Kopernik—a.k.a. Copernicus—the man who "stopped the sun and moved the Earth" (see **History,** p. 399). After strolling the medieval cobblestoned streets, visiting the museum, and resting on the promenade along the river, you'll wonder why he ever left. In the city center, parishioners pray in 500-year-old churches and children play in the ruins of a Teutonic castle: Toruń has successfully matured into a modern city without losing its medieval charm.

ORIENTATION

Toruń lies 150km northeast of Poznań. The main **train station,** lies across the Wisła from most of the city. **City buses** #22 and 27 cross the river to the center; as you exit the main hall of the train station, take the tunnel just outside and to your left. Buy tickets at any of the Ruch kiosks in and around the station. Punch them when you board on both ends; students punch one end. (1.05zł; large luggage requires its own ticket.) To find the **tourist offices,** get off at pl. Rapackiego, the first stop across the river. Head away from the bus and through the little park; they're on your left. On foot, take ul. Kujawska left from the train station, turn right onto al. Jana Pawła II, and hike over the Wisła. Pl. Rapackiego is on the right, after **ul. Kopernika.** To reach the center from the **bus station,** walk away from the buses and through the small park that leads to **ul. Uniwersytecka.** Take a left onto Uniwersytecka and follow it until it intersects with Wały Gen. Sikorskiego. Head right onto Sikorskiego until pl. Teatralny. At pl. Teatralny, turn left onto ul. Chełmińska, which leads to **Rynek Staromiejski** (Old Town Square). Most of the town's sights are here or in **Rynek Nowomiejski** (New Town Square). From Rynek Staromiejski, take ul. Szeroka and veer left onto ul. Krolowej Jadwigi to reach Rynek Nowaniejski.

PRACTICAL INFORMATION

Trains: Toruń Głowny, ul. Kujawska 1 (tel. 94 36). To: **Warsaw** (3hr., 3 per day, 36zł); **Gdańsk** (2½hr., 6 per day, 26zł); **Poznań** (2hr., 5 per day, 21zł); and **Szczecin** (5hr., 2 per day, 27zł). International *kassa* sells Wasteels and Interrail. Open M-F 8am-5pm, Sa-Su 7am-7pm.

Buses: Dworzec PKS, ul. Dąbrowskiego 26, (tel. 655 53 32). To: **Warsaw** (4hr., 5 per day, 28zł); **Gdańsk** (3½hr., 3 per day, 28zł); and **Poznań** (3hr., 1 per day, 18zł). **Polski Express** buses leave pl. Teatralny for: **Warsaw** (3½hr., 14 per day, 23zł) and **Szczecin** (5½hr., 1 per day, 26zł). Tickets available at the Kolporter kiosk near the bus stop or at **Orbis** (see below). Students and seniors 30% off Tu-Th.

Taxis: Radio Taxi, tel. 91 91 through 91 99; 91 96 for wheelchair-accessible transport.

Tourist Offices: IT, ul. Piekary 37/39 (tel./fax 621 09 31; www.um.torun.pl). Very helpful English-speaking staff dispenses info and arranges accommodations. Open M and Sa 9am-4pm, Tu-F 9am-6pm, Su 9am-1pm; Sept.-Apr. closed Sunday. **PTTK,** pl. Rapackiego 2 (tel. 622 49 26; fax 622 82 28). Maps and brochures 3-6zł. 2hr. English tour of town 70zł. Open M-F 8am-5pm, Sa 9am-1pm. **Kompas,** ul. Kopernika 5 (tel. 621 05 87; fax 621 00 16). Buy your train tickets here to avoid long lines. Also sells international bus tickets and tours of Poland. Most of the friendly staff speaks English. Open M-F 9am-5pm, Sa 10am-1pm. **Orbis,** ul. Mostowa 7 (tel. 655 48 63; fax 654 91 44). Plane, rail, and bus tickets. Open M-F 9am-5pm, Sa 10am-2pm.

Currency Exchange: Bank PKO S.A., ul. Kopernika 38 (tel. 621 09 15), cashes AmEx/Visa traveler's checks for a 1% commission (5zł min.). AmEx/MC/Visa cash advances. Open M-F 8am-6pm. Private *kantors* exchange cash. **24hr. ATMs** abound along ul. Szeroka. AmEx/Cirrus/MC/Plus/Visa.

English Bookstore: Księgarnia Lingwista, ul. Szeroka 41 (tel. 621 01 08). Mostly reference books, but some fiction. Open M-F 10am-6pm, Sa 10am-2pm.

International Press: Empik Megastore, ul. Wielkie Garbary 18. Open M-F 10am-7pm, Sa 10am-4pm, Su 11am-5pm.

24hr. Pharmacy: Apteka Panaceum, ul. Odrodzenia 1 (tel. 622 41 59).

Medical Assistance: Szpital Bielany, ul. Św. Józefa 53/59 (tel. 610 01 10). Private doctors, ul. Szeroka 30 (tel. 652 12 32). 50zł per visit. Open M-F 9am-9pm, Sa 9am-3pm.

Post Office: Rynek Staromiejski 15 (tel. 621 91 00). Open M-F 8am-8pm, Sa 8am-1pm. Branch at train station open 24hr. **Postal code:** 87-100.

Internet Access: Internet Club Jeremi, Rynek Staromiejski 33 (tel. 663 51 00; fax 621 91 99; email jeremi@jeremi.pl). 13 computers, 4zł per hr. Open daily 9am til the last email.

Phone code: (0)56.

ACCOMMODATIONS

Toruń has no particular "crunch season"—most visitors are with school groups which are herded back onto buses at each day's end. Summer is the best season for budget lodgers, as student dorms open their doors and hostels expand their capacities. **IT** (see **Tourist Offices** above) can arrange stays at student dorms (20-25zł) and help with other accommodations. Vacancies fill fast, so call ahead.

Hotel Kopernik, ul. Wola Zamkowa 16 (tel./fax 652 25 73). Right by Rynek Nowomiejski, this is one of the best values and locations in town. Pleasant, newly renovated rooms and shabby but clean hall bathrooms. Singles 60zł, with bath 100zł; doubles 70zł, with toilet 90zł, with bath 110zł.

Hotel Trzy Koruna, Rynek Staromiejski 21 (tel./fax 622 60 31). You can't ask for a better location. Spacious rooms with TV. Singles 70zł; doubles 80zł, with bath 120zł; triples 90zł, 200zł. MC/Visa/AmEx.

Hotel Wodnik, Bulwar Filadelfijski 12 (tel. 622 60 49; fax 622 51 14), near the river. Bigger rooms than Trzy Koruna, all with satellite TV. Singles 80zł, with bath 115zł; doubles with bath 144zł; triples with bath 173zł. Swimming pool in summer. Wheelchair accessible. Some English spoken. MC/Visa/AmEx.

Schronisko Młodzieżowe (HI), ul. Św. Józefa 22/24 (tel. 654 41 07 and 654 45 80). From the train station, take bus #11 five stops to "Św Józefa." Basic rooms far from the city center. 100 beds in summer, 30 the rest of the year. Dorms 14zł, non-members 16zł; 2- to 4-person rooms 20zł, 24zł; singles (summer only) 32zł, 36zł.

FOOD

In the face of the slow spread of chains, Toruń still offers its centuries-old treat: **gingerbread** (*pierniki*). Originally sold by Copernicus' father to put his son through school, it is now hawked by the kilo in various forms, including chocolate-coated and Copernicus-shaped. There is a **24hr. grocery store** at ul. Chełmińska 22. The large market **Targowisko Miejskie** sits behind the "Supersam," one block north of Stare Miasto on ul. Chełminska. (Open daily 8am-4pm.)

Bar Mleczny, ul. Różana 1. This clean milk bar serves up primarily vegetarian Polish dishes, as well as a smattering of meat dishes. *Naleśniki,* the house-specialty pastries, come with a multitude of fillings. Try them with blueberries and cream (*z jagodami i śmietaną*) 3.90zł. Open M-F 9am-7pm, Sa 9am-4pm.

Pizzeria Browarna, ul. Mostowa 17 (tel. 622 66 74). Spacious booths and pinball. Very popular and crowded with students. Great pizza (6.50-18zł) and salads (8-14zł). Open daily 11am-midnight.

Stołówka Urząd Mraszałkowskiego, pl. Teatralny 2 (tel. 621 84 49). Enter at the "Bufet" sign and follow the enticing aroma through the underground passageways. A frugal diner's heaven: soup, entree, and side dish for 8zł. Open daily 8am-8pm.

Lotos, ul. Strumykowa 16 (tel. 621 04 97). Various Far Eastern specialties in a Far Eastern setting, with the requisite bamboo and a tropical fish tank. Try the "5 Flavored Chicken" (16.50zł). Vegetarian dishes 7-10zł. Open daily 11am-10pm. MC/Visa.

Kopernik Factory Store, ul. Żeglarska 25 (tel. 652 14 59), and Rynek Staromiejskie 6 (tel. 622 88 32). Stock up on Toruń's delicious *pierniki* in almost every imaginable form. Gets very crowded, so be patient while visions of gingerbread dance in your head. Prices range from 4zł for a small taste to 20zł per kg for "historical figures." Open M-F 10am-6pm, Sa-Su 10am-2pm.

SIGHTS

An astounding number of attractions are packed into Toruń's medieval ramparts, particularly in **Stare Miasto,** built by the Teutonic Knights in the 13th century.

DOM KOPERNIKA. The birthplace of renowned astronomer Mikołaj Kopernik (February 19, 1473) has been meticulously restored, and visitors can get a peek into the life of not only Copernicus, but also of 14th-century Toruń, with a miniature model of the city circa 1550. A "traditional" 16th-century sound and light show in five languages plays every 30min. *(Ul. Kopernika 15/17. Tel. 622 70 38. Open Tu-Su 10am-4pm. 3zł, students 2zł. Toruń model 4zł, students 3zł.)*

TOWN HALL. (Ratusz). This town hall, one of the finest examples of monumental burgher architecture in Europe, stands in the center of the tourist district. The original Gothic building's four wings were built in the late 14th century, and the turrets and other elements were added over the years. The town hall now contains the **Regional Museum** (Muzeum Okręgowe). Exhibits include the famous portrait of Mikołaj Kopernik from the late 16th century, likenesses of other prominent citizens, and some impressive modern Polish art. *(Rynek Staromiejski 1. Tel. 622 70 38. Open Tu-Su 10am-4pm. 3zł, students 2zł. Free Sundays. Medieval tower 2zł students 1zł.)*

TEUTONIC STRUCTURES. The Teutonic Knights' Castle continues to fascinate visitors. The 14th-century **toilet tower** served as its indoor plumbing and as a scatological defense—back in those days, one didn't just fart in the enemy's general direction. The 13th-century castle was destroyed by a city-wide burghers' revolt on February 8, 1454. *(Ul. Przedzamcze.)* The unique **Leaning Tower,** was built in 1271 by a knight of the Order as punishment for falling in love with a peasant girl. The 15m tower now deviates 1.5m from center at its top. It also houses a bar and souvenir shop, apparently so the broken-hearted can drown their tears in alcohol and capitalism. *(Ul. Krzywa Wieza 17.)*

CHURCHES. The **Cathedral of St. John the Baptist and St. John the Evangelist** (Bazylika Katedralna pw. św. św. Janów) is the most impressive of the many Gothic churches in the region. Built from the 13th-15th centuries, it mixes Gothic, Baroque, and Rococo elements. The tower contains Poland's second-largest bell, cast in 1500. The chapel witnessed Kopernik's baptism in 1473. *(At the corner of ul. Zeglarska. Open M-F 9am-2pm, Sa 9am-1pm, Su for masses only.)* The **Church of the Virgin Mary** (Kościół św. Marii), with its beautiful stained glass, has a less ornate feel than many Polish churches. A brief slide show and automated commentary tell its fascinating history. *(Across the rynek to ul. Panny Marii. 2zł.)*

OTHER SIGHTS. Opposite the town hall, **Artus Court** (Dwór Artusa) was designed in the 1880s by Rudolf Schmidt. The house was erected on the site of the original Renaissance building—also called Dwór Artusa—that had been the seat of patrician members of the Hanseatic League. *(Rynek Staromiejski 5.)* The building now houses the Toruń Orchestra. **House Under the Star** (Kamienica Pod Gwiazdą), originally a Gothic building, was later redone in Baroque style, with a modeled facade decorated with floral and fruit details. During reconstruction in the late 1960s, fragments of Gothic, late Renaissance, and Classical architecture were uncovered. Check out the exhibits on the arts of the Far East. *(Rynek Staromiejski 35. Tel. 622 11 33, ext. 16. Open W-Su 10am-4pm. 3zł, students 1zł.)* **Dom Eskenów** is opening an exhibit in January 2000 on Russian and German culture in Toruń from 1793 to 1920. *(Ul. Lazienna 16. Tel. 622 86 80. Open Tu-Su 10am-4pm. 2zł, students 1zł.)*

ENTERTAINMENT

Like its most famous son, Toruń's residents like to watch the stars come out, mostly from the pubs and cafes clustered around Rynek Staromiejski and along the Wisła. In Stare Miasto, music plays at the **Mix Club**, ul. Browarna 1 (tel. 621 93 20), off Rynek Nowomiejski. The entrance is around the corner from the pizza place next to ul. Wielkie Garbary 1. (Cover 5zł. Open Th-Sa from 8pm.) During the day, **Hotel Aeroklub Pomorski**, ul. Bielańska (tel. 622 24 74; fax 622 63 29), offers **skydiving** and **glider flying.** (450zł per hr. for 3 people, minimum 10min.)

Toruń also hosts a number of festivals, starting in May when **Probaltica**, the Baltic celebration of chamber music and arts comes to town, followed later that month by an **International Theater Festival.** In June and July, during the **Music and Architecture Festival**, classical concerts are held in different historic buildings each weekend. The fun moves outside with **Summer Street Theater** in July and August. The season ends late, in November, with the **National Blues Music Festival.**

Pub Czarna Oberża (Black Inn), ul. Rabiańska 9 (tel. 621 09 63). Local students favor this billiards and beer hangout. Impressive selection of imported beer, including Guinness and Kilkenny (0.4zł). *Żubrówka* vodka and apple juice 5.45zł. Also serves Vietnamese dishes (20-25zł). Open M-Th 1pm-midnight, F-Sa 1pm-1am, Su 2pm-midnight.

Kawiarnia Flisacza (tel. 622 57 51), on ul. Flisacza, overlooking the Wisła. Don't be scared away by the spikes and barbed wire; you're more than welcome to come in, nosh on cafe treats, and enjoy the...uh, ambiance. Open daily 10am-10pm.

NEAR TORUŃ: GOLUB-DOBRZYŃ

Just 42km from Toruń, Golub-Dobrzyń is worth a visit for its **Teutonic Castle** (Zamek Golubski) and a glimpse of small-town Polish life. Built between 1293 and 1306, the castle remains an imposing structure overlooking this tiny village. It hosts a **jousting tournament and medieval festival** on the third weekend in July, which draws quite a crowd. For info call the tourist bureau **PTTK**, located at the castle (tel. 683 24 55). The nearby town center has a small **rynek** and **St. Catharine's Church**, which should sate any lingering medieval fervor.

GETTING THERE. Frequent buses (about 1 per hr.) travel from **Toruń** to Golub-Dobrzyń (1hr., 5.40zł; buy ticket on bus). Look out for the large sign into town—the castle will appear just ahead. Stay on the bus as you pass the castle to your right and get off at the next stop. Backtrack and turn left onto **ul. Zamkova** to reach the castle. A right onto Zamkova leads to the center of town. (Castle open daily 9am-7pm; 5zł, students 3zł.)

ŁÓDŹ

Łódź (WOODGE; pop. 825,600), Poland's second-largest city, is often overlooked for international Warsaw to the northeast, picturesque Toruń to the north, or pious Częstochowa to the south. But strolling down the pedestrian al. Piotrkowska among historic buildings, busy shops, and student hangouts, it is difficult to imagine how Łódź could be ignored. Home to the largest ghetto in Europe and the famous Łódź film school, which has produced such luminaries as Andrzej Wajda and Krzysztof Kieślowski and, this 15th-century city has many surprises in store.

ORIENTATION

Restaurants and shops line **ul. Piotrkowska,** which runs north-south through the center of town and is closed to cars from **ul. Traugutta** in the north to **al. Marsz. Józefa Piłsudskiego** in the south. Accommodations and museums are nearby. The city center is within walking distance of both train stations. From **Łódź Fabryczna,** the main train station, cross **al. Jana Kilińskiego,** the wide street with multiple tram lines, and head toward Dom Kultury. Continue west two blocks to get to ul. Piotrkowska. From the **Łódź Kaliska** station, with your back to the entrance turn right on the highway (al. Włokniarzy), then left onto **al. Adama Mickiewicza,** which becomes al. Marsz. Józefa Piłsudskiego, and continue about 15min. to the intersection with ul. Piotrkowska.

PRACTICAL INFORMATION

Trains: Łódź Fabryczna PKP (tel. 935) sends trains to: **Warsaw** (2hr., 9 per day, 20zł). From **Łódź Kaliska** (tel. 934), trains chug to: **Toruń** (3hr., 5 per day, 23.68zł); **Kraków** (5hr., 2 per day, 28.76zł); and **Poznań** (4hr., 3 per day, 27.92zł). Posted train schedules provide info for both stations.

Buses: Łódź Fabryczna PKS (tel. 631 97 06) is attached to the Fabryczna train station. To: **Warsaw** (7 per day, 16zł); **Wrocław** (4-5hr., 3 per day, 25zł); **Kraków** (5hr., 6 per day, 27zł); and **Poznań** (3 per day, 32zł).

Local Transportation: Trams and buses cost 1.60zł (students 0.80zł) for a ride of up to 30min., 2.10zł up to 1hr., 2.82zł for 2hr., and 5.40zł for a full-day pass (students 2.70zł). Prices double at night. Buy tickets at kiosks around town.

Tourist Office: IT, ul. Traugutta 18 (tel./fax 633 71 69), in Dom Kultury, across al. Jana Kilińskiego from Łódź Fabryczna (see above). Enter in the back. An outgoing bunch with info on sights and accommodations. Open M-F 8:15am-4:15pm, Sa 10am-2pm.

Budget Travel: Orbis, ul. Piotrkowska 68 (flight info tel. 636 35 33; bus info tel. 633 21 14). Travel bookings and accommodations, especially helpful if you're Polish and planning a trip to Florida. Open M-F 9am-6pm, Sa 10am-3pm.

Currency Exchange: *Kantori* bumble around ul. Piotrkowska. **Pekao S.A.,** al. Piłsudskiego 12 (tel. 636 28 86), cashes traveler's checks for a 1% commission and gives MC/Visa cash advances. Open M-F 8am-6pm.

Luggage Storage: There is a locked storage room at Łódź Fabryczna. 1.50zł plus 0.40zł for every 50zł in declared value per day; go to *kassa* #9. Open daily 6:30am-1pm, 2:30-5:30pm, and 6:30-11pm. Storage is also available at the Kaliska station.

English Bookstore: Empik, ul. Piotrkowska 81 (tel. 632 83 55). Open M-F 10am-8pm, Sa 10am-6pm, Su 11am-5pm. MC/Visa.

24hr. Pharmacy: Apteka Hepatica, ul. Piotrkowska 35 (tel. 630 35 39).

Post Office: ul. Tuwima 38 (tel. 630 17 52). Open 24hr. **Poste Restante** at window #19. Open M-F 7am-9pm, Sa 9am-4pm. Fax service (fax 632 82 08). **Postal code:** 95-000.

Internet Access: Cybergrota Internet Cafe, ul. Więckowskiego 20 (tel. 632 81 00; kawiarnia.pactor.com.pl). Go through to the courtyard, then down to the basement. 2zł for 15min., 3zł for 30min., 5zł for 1hr.

Telephones: At the post office. Open 24hr. **Phone code:** (0)42.

ACCOMMODATIONS & FOOD

A number of budget options are centrally located around ul. Piotrkowska. To reach the **Youth Hostel (HI),** ul. Legionów 27 (tel. 630 66 80; fax 630 66 83), walk north (as the street numbers descend) along ul. Piotrkowska to the end and turn left on ul. Legionów. This super-classy establishment on the north end of town will make you feel like you're in a fancy hotel. Almost. It provides humongous, newly renovated singles with baths (35zł), doubles and triples (30zł per person), and 4- to 6-bed dorms (15zł, non-members 20zł; linen 4zł; lockout 10am-5pm; curfew 10pm). A little farther down the street, the **Hotel Garnizonowy,** ul. Legionów 81 (tel. 633 80 23), is being completely renovated and may yet emerge as a budget-travel paradise. In the meantime, there are simple, comfortable doubles (62zł) and quads (107zł). The hall bathrooms are reasonably clean but poorly maintained.

Inexplicably, pizza is the order of the day. Ul. Piotrkowska abounds with pizzerias where it's possible to get a nutritious, filling meal for under 10zł. The gleaming white **Pizzeria "Solo,"** ul. Piotrkowska 41 (tel. 630 01 32), serves a wide variety of good pizzas (small under 11zł, large 6.50-13.10zł), as well as Greek salads (2.40zł per 100g; open M-Th 11am-9pm, F-Sa 11am-10pm, Su noon-9pm). At **In-Centro Pizza,** ul. Piotrkowska 153 (tel. 636 99 92), prices are similar but tablesare scarce. (Open M-Sa noon-10pm, Su 1-10pm.) **Steakhouse Ramzes,** ul. Piotrkowska 40 (tel. 633 57 11), is a celebration of meat, with portions fit for a pharaoh. The steak is quite good, for Poland. (Steak 12-15zł, vegetarian pizza 10.50zł.) There is a **24hr. grocery** at al. Piłudskiego 12.

SIGHTS

JEWISH CEMETERY AND SYNAGOGUES. The most affecting and beautiful sight in Łódź, the sprawling Jewish cemetery (Cmentarz Żydowski), is the largest in Europe. There are more than 180,000 tombstones, some quite elaborately engraved; especially noteworthy is the colossal Poznański family crypt. Don't bother with the main gate at ul. Bracka; it's generally locked for security reasons. Near the entrance to the cemetery is a memorial to the Jews killed in the Łódź Ghetto. Signs lead the way to the **Ghetto Fields** (Pole Ghettowe), where Jews who died in the ghetto are buried in small but marked graves, something the local Nazi administration insisted upon. *(Take tram #1 from ul. Kilinskiego, #15 from ul. Legionów, or #19 from ul. Zachnodnia, north to the end of the line (30min.). Continue up the street to the first corner and make a sharp left turn onto the cobblestone ul. Zmienna before the car lot, and continue until the small gate in the wall. Open M-F and Su 9am-3pm, closed on Jewish holidays. 4zł admission goes toward maintenance; free for those visiting the graves of relatives.)* The **Jewish Community Center** (Gmina Wyznaniowa Żydowska) has more info and houses a new synagogue. Walk through the gates and it's the second building on the right. *(Ul. Pomorska 18. Tel. 633 51 56. Open M-F 10am-2pm. Services daily. English spoken.)* The **old synagogue**—the only one to survive the war—is generally kept closed, but visits can be arranged through the Jewish Community Center. *(Ul. Rewolucji-1905 28.)*

MUSEUM OF CINEMATOGRAPHY. (Muzeum Kinomatografii). International film giants Andrzej Wajda, Krzysztof Kieślowski, and Roman Polański (see **Literature & Arts,** p. 401) all got their start at Łódź's famous film school. They are now immortalized in the Museum of Cinematography, which is housed in a mid-19th-century mansion on al. Piłsudskiego. Rotating exhibits on Polish filmmaking are also featured, and local troupes occasionally put on productions here as well. *(Pl. Zwycięstwa 1. Take tram #25 from al. Kosciuszki and get off when you see a park on your right. Tel. 674 09 56. Open Tu-F 10am-3pm, Sa-Su 11am-3pm; closed last Su of the month. 3zł.)*

POZNAŃSKI PALACE. A block northwest of the monument at **pl. Wolności,** which crowns the northern end of ul. Piotrkowska, stands the grandiose Poznański Palace, named for a family of wealthy Jewish industrialists who lived there in the late 19th and early 20th centuries. The ornate gray building houses the **Łódź Historical Museum** (Muzeum Historii Miasta Łódźi), which begins in the vast and beautiful palace dining room and has exhibits on many of Łódź's famous sons and daughters, including pianist Artur Rubenstein and author Jerzy Kosinski. (see **Literature & Arts,** p. 401) *(Ul. Ogrodowa 15. Tel. 654 03 23; fax 654 02 02. Open Tu and Th-Su 10am-2pm, W 2-6pm. 4zł, students 2zł. Su free.)*

ŁÓDŹ FINE ARTS MUSEUM. (Muzeum Sztuki w Łódźi). The premier art collection in Łódź, the Fine Arts Museum is home to 20th-century works by artists like Max Ernst and Piet Mondrian, in addition to several Poles. *(Ul. Więckowskiego 36. Four blocks west of ul. Piotrkowska along ul. Więckowskiego. Tel. 674 96 98; fax 674 99 82. Open Tu 10am-5pm, W and F 11am-5pm, Th noon-7pm, Sa-Su 10am-4pm. 5zł, students 3zł; Tu-Th free.)*

THE LUCKY FEW Established in 1940 as the largest Jewish ghetto in Europe, Łódź's ghetto was remarkably lucky (as far as ghettoes go) during WWII. For the early part of the war, the ghetto doubled as a giant Nazi textile factory, supplying winter uniforms for German soldiers in Russia. As Nazi-controlled ghettoes throughout Europe were being liquidated in 1942, only the elderly, the infirm, and the young children of Łódź were deported to concentration camps; the ghetto had become too valuable as a source of labor for the Nazis to destroy. By 1944, it was the last remaining ghetto in Poland. Unfortunately, as the Red Army loomed only 150km away in August 1944, the Nazis decided it was at long last time to liquidate the Łódź ghetto; its 70,000 residents were deported to Auschwitz, Birkenau, and Majdanek. 800 "lucky" Jews remained as a cleaning crew, but as the Russians were about to capture Łódź, the Nazis decided to execute the remaining few and built a mass grave in anticipation. Fortunately, the swift advance of the Russians interrupted the execution, and the 800 ghetto residents were saved. Of those deported to concentration camps, some 20,000 survived–the highest number of survivors of any European ghetto. Their fortune was due to their late deportation; by the end of the war, the death camps were quickly declining in murderous "efficiency." Those interested in exploring the ghetto (many of whose buildings are still standing) or in seeking the graves of relatives buried in the Ghetto's Jewish Cemetery should contact the Jewish community center.

POMORZE

Pomorze, literally "along the sea," sweeps over the murky swamps and wind-swept dunes of the Baltic Coast. In the face of shifting sands and treacherous bogs, fishermen built villages here millennia ago. A few hamlets grew into large ports—Szczecin on the lower Odra River is the largest, while others like Świnoujście are building themselves up around their shoreline assets. Meanwhile, Woliński National Park shelters hiking trails and bison from the ills of tourism and industry.

SZCZECIN

Strategically situated on the Odra River, the port of Szczecin (SHCHEH-chin) has been the site of centuries of power plays. All that attention has luckily only benefitted the city, whose railways and waterways now sprawl kilometers from the center. The rows of historic buildings in the city center, along with the shipping port's friendly attitude, make Szczecin a popular starting point for tourists arriving from across the sea.

ORIENTATION

Szczecin sits near the German border at the mouth of the **Odra River,** about 65km from the Baltic Sea coast. You'll need a map, so visit a tourist office; get off the train at the **Szczecin Główny** train station (the bus stop is a block away) and walk out the front of the station, which faces the river. Go left (ul. Kolumba) and take the first left onto ul. Dworcowa. The main **tourist office** is at the end of this street. To the right, al. Niepodległości leads to **pl. Brama Portowa,** the center of Szczecin.

PRACTICAL INFORMATION

Trains: Szczecin Główny sits at the end of ul. 3-go Maja; take tram #3 north to the center. To: **Gdynia** (5hr., 6 per day, 32.12zł); **Poznań** (3hr., 13 per day, 26.24zł); **Warsaw** (6hr., 5 per day, 35.56zł, express 53.48zł); **Gdańsk** (5½hr., 5 per day, 33.80zł); and **Berlin** (2½hr., 5 per day, express 81.63zł).

Buses: Pl. Tobrucki, 2min. northeast of the train station. Tickets can be purchased either at the station or through Orbis (see below). Connections to: **Świnoujście** (3 per day, 10-19zł, depending on stops made) and **Toruń** (1 per day, 28zł).

Ferries: Ferries run run from Dworzec Marski (tram #6) to **Uznam** (1hr., July-Aug. 3 per day, Sept.-June 2 per day, 20zł).

Local Transportation: The city's numerous **tram** and **bus** lines run along most major roads. 1zł per 10min., 1.80zł per 40min., and 3.60zł per 2hr.; 5.10zł for all rides after 11pm. Schedules, route information, and tickets available at kiosks around town.

Taxis: City Taxi, tel. 433 53 35.

Tourist Office: Centrum Informacji Turystycznej (CIT), al. Niepodleglosci 1 (tel. 434 04 40; fax 433 84 20). Staff sells **maps** (6zł) and brochures (2-3zł) and makes hotel reservations. There is also a small tourist office in the train station (tel. 488 53 86) that has maps and gives information on buses and accommodations. Open 24hr.

Budget Travel: Orbis, pl. Zwycięstwa 1 (tel. 434 44 25), is particularly useful if you plan on crossing a border; it meets most travel needs and even has a **kantor.** Open M-F 10am-6pm, Sa 10am-2pm.

Currency Exchange: Pomorski Bank Kredytowy S.A., ul. Bogurodzicy 5 (tel. 488 00 33), and branches throughout the city. Cashes AmEx and Visa traveler's checks and gives AmEx/MC/Visa cash advances. Open M-F 8am-6pm. *Kantory* all over town exchange currency at similar rates. **24hr. ATMs** litter the town, including at the train station and along al. Niepodległości.

Luggage Storage: Downstairs by the exit to the platforms at the train station. 1.50zł, plus 0.32zł for every 50zł of declared value. Open 24hr.

24hr. Pharmacy: Ul. Więckowskiego 1/2 (tel. 434 26 27). From 7pm-8am, ring the bell. There is a 1.50zł surcharge for after-hours service.

International Press: Empik, al. Wojska Polskiego 2 (tel. 433 78 95), on the corner with bol. Krzywoustego. Sells *USA Today, London Times,* and other foreign newspapers. Open M-F 10am-7pm, Sa 10am-4pm.

Post Office: ul. Bogurodzicy 1 (tel. 440 13 02). Open M-F 8am-8pm, Sa 9am-2pm. **Postal code:** 70-405.

Telephones: At the post office, through a separate entrance on al. Niepodległości. Open 24hr. **Phone code:** (0)91.

ACCOMMODATIONS

For a list of Szczecin's spartan summer youth hostels contact **Almatur,** ul. Bohaterów Warszawy 83 (tel. 484 43 55; open M-F 10am-5pm). Budget accommodations in Szczecin become harder to find as the summer draws crowds to the city.

Youth Hostel (HI), ul. Monte Cassino 19a (tel. 22 47 61; fax 423 56 96). Take tram #1 or 9 from the train station or the center to ul. Felczarka. By foot, it's a short hike through downtown along ul. Wojska Polskiego, followed by a right on ul. Felczarka and a left onto ul. Monte Cassino. Large, often-crowded dorms. Singles with sink 33.30zł, non-members 40zł; 4- to 8-bed dorms 10.50zł, 17zł; 10- to 12-bed dorms 9.50zł, 15zł. Sheets 5zł. Bike rental (2zł per hr.) and luggage storage (2zł per day). Curfew 11pm.

Hotel Piast, pl. Zwycięstwa 3 (tel. 433 66 22). Take tram #1 or 9 to Brama Portowa. Ex-police barracks with a scenic downtown location. Spacious rooms, some with balconies. Singles 63zł, with bath 78zł; doubles 98zł, 118zł.

Hotel Gryf, ul. Wojska Polskiego 49 (tel. 433 45 66; fax 433 40 30). Slightly farther away (but still centrally located), Gryf, or 'Grf' as the decrepit sign would have it, offers well-kept rooms. Bring flipflops for the sticky-floored hall baths. Singles 65zł, with bath 80zł; doubles 95zł, 115zł; triples with bath 155zł. Breakfast included. AmEx/MC/Visa.

"Foundation in Support of Local Democracy" Hostel, ul. Marii Skłodowskiej-Curie 4 (tel. 487 04 72). In a white school building marked "Zachodniopomorska Szkoła Samorządu Terytorialnego." Take tram #1 or 9 to "Traugutta," continue two blocks, turn left, and walk to the street's end. The entrance is around the corner to the right. A crusader against post-communist hotel squalor with sunny rooms and wondrous bathrooms. Doubles 85zł, with bath 126.50zł; triples 103zł; quads 138zł. Call ahead.

FOOD

The Western fast-food invasion is in full force, but local cuisine is prepared to fight, allied with cheap Vietnamese cuisine (meals 10zł) and whole rotisserie chickens (12zł) at local kiosks. A large supermarket, **Extra,** is at ul. Niepodległości 27. (Open M-Sa 7am-10pm, Su 8am-10pm; MC/Visa.)

Bar Turysta, ul. Obrońców Stalingradu 6 (tel. 434 22 01), is just one of the many bars around town offering full meals for under 5zł. Open M-F 6:30am-7pm, Sa 8am-4pm, 1st and 3rd Su of month 8am-3pm.

Lucynka i Paulinka, ul. Wojska Polskiego 18 (tel. 434 69 22), treats browsers with luxury food items downstairs and sinful desserts, cups of coffee, and stiffer libations upstairs. Desserts and coffee start at 3zł. Open M-F 9am-10pm, Sa-Su 10am-9pm. MC/Visa.

Pod Muzami, pl. Żołnierza Polskiego 2 (tel. 434 72 09), is connected to the expensive Hotel Victoria. Brass mirrors and pink lighting dominate the decor; standard Polish fare runs 20-30zł. Dancing and live music nightly at 9pm. Cover M-F 6zł Sa-Su 10zł. Open M-Th and Su noon-4am, F-Sa noon-5am. MC/Visa/AmEx.

SIGHTS

A millennium of invasion, occupation, and re-occupation have left Szczecin's buildings with more than a few stories to tell. The Baroque **Port Gate** (Brama Portowa) lends a Prussian flavor to the downtown area, with female figures blowing trumpets, a Latin inscription commemorating Emperor Friedrich Wilhelm I, and a panorama of 18th-century Szczecin complete with Viadus, god of the Odra, leaning against a jug from which the river's waters flow. Originally called the Brandenburg and later the Berlin Gate, it was built in 1725 and spared during the removal of the city's fortifications in 1875 because of its architectural value. Friedrich Wilhelm would be proud.

Time has not been as kind, however, to some of the other structures downtown. A block away on ul. Wyszyńskiego, the 13th-century **Cathedral of St. John the Evangelist** (Katedra św. Jana Ewangelisty) looms over the city. Destroyed during WWII, it has been carefully restored to its original Gothic splendor, although its stained glass windows still need finishing. (Open daily 7am until the end of the last service, around 8pm.) Szczecin's past meets its present at the 870-year-old **Church of St. Peter and Paul** (Kościół św. Piotra i Pawla), where visitors can relive the parish's past few decades through the photo collages inside, including a visit from the Pope. On ul. Korsarzy, the giant, newly restored **Castle of Pomeranian Dukes** (Zamek Książąt Pomerańskich; tel. 434 73 91) overlooks the city from the site of Szczecin's oldest settlement. The seat of Pomeranian princes until 1630, it later belonged to Swedes, Prussians, and Germans. These days, it's occupied by an opera and theater group (not performing in the summer) and a **museum** (tel. 489 16 30; email cikit@zamek.szczecin.pl) housing the dukes' exquisitely decorated sarcophagi as well as temporary exhibits. (Open daily 10am-6pm; temporary exhibits closed Mondays. 3zł, students 2zł; temporary exhibits 5zł, 4zł.) The large courtyard is often the site of performances and concerts; check at the castle for upcoming events. Don't forget to climb the tall **tower** *(wieża;* 2zł) for a panoramic view of the entire region. Behind the castle stands the abandoned **Maiden's Tower of Seven Cloaks** (Baszta Panieńska Siedmiu Płaszczy), on ul. Panieńska, the only one of the medieval fortifications' 37 original towers to survive WWII.

Heading back to the market square from the castle leads to the old **town hall** *(ratusz)*, built in 1450. Rebuilt after WWII in original Gothic style, it houses one of the three branches of the **National Museum** (Muzeum Narodowe; tel. 488 02 49); this one illustrates Szczecin's history, from stones to cups and saucers. Another branch—a chronicle of Pomeranian art—is in the Baroque palace of the **Pomeranian Parliament,** ul. Stromłyńska 27/28 (tel. 433 60 70), north of Castle Hill two blocks west of Kościół św. Piotra i Pawla. (All branches open Tu and Th 10am-5pm, W and F 9am-3:30pm, and Sa-Su 10am-4pm. 4zł, students 2zł.) Finally, to take it all in from afar, take tram #6 north from the riverbank to its final stop at "Gocław" and climb the hill opposite to **Bismarck Tower** for a spectacular view.

ŚWINOUJŚCIE

A bustling resort with some of the best beaches on the Baltic Coast, Świnoujście is investing tourists' dollars to build a clean, inviting community that's almost as much fun to visit as saying its name (shuee-noh-OOSH-che).

ORIENTATION & PRACTICAL INFORMATION. Świnoujście occupies parts of two islands, **Wolin** and **Uznam,** linked by a ferry across the **Świna River.** The **train** and **bus stations** and the international **ferry terminal** are all on the Świna's east bank, near the port on Wolin Island. **Trains** travel to: **Szczecin** (2hr., 15 per day, 11.62zł, express 18.52zł) and **Warsaw** (8½hr., 1 per day, 36.10zł). **Ferries,** the fastest way to and from **Szczecin,** run from Dworzec Marski (tram #6) in Szczecin to **Uznam** (1hr., July-Aug. 3 per day, Sept.-June 2 per day, 20zł). On Wolin, **Polferries,** ul. Dworcowa 1 (tel. 321 30 06), next to the main dock, sends ferries to: **Copenhagen** (9hr., 5 per week, 166zł, students 150zł); **Malmö, Sweden** (10hr., 1 per day, 175zł, students 160zł); and **Ystad, Sweden** (9hr., 1 per day, 173zł, students 140zł). To get to the main part of town, on the west side of the river in Uznam, take the free **car ferry** (every 20min. 5am-11pm, every hr. midnight-5am) across the street from the train and bus stations, and 5min. up the road from the main ferry terminal; go left out of the ferry terminal on **ul. Dworcowa.** On the other side of the river, take a left, on ul. Władysław and then veer right on ul. Armii Krjowej at the small park. Ahead on your right will be **Centrum Informacji Turystycznej (CIT),** pl. Słowiański (tel./fax 322 49 99; email cit@fornet.com.pl), which issues free maps and brochures and helps find accommodations. (Open M-F 9am-5pm.) From here, ul. Piłudskiego runs right to the beach. To the left, ul. Grunwaldzka runs to the outlying part of town, including the youth hostel (see below). A 25min. walk down second right off Grunwaldzka, ul. Komstytucji 3 Maja, leads to the German border. **Bank PKO S.A.,** ul. Piłudskiego 4 (tel. 321 57 33), **exchanges money,** cashes **traveler's checks,** and produces credit-card cash advances. (Open M-F 8am-6pm, Sa 10am-2pm.) A **24hr. pharmacy,** ul. Piłudskiego 23 (tel. 321 25 15), provides a wide variety of drugs. (Open daily 8am-8pm; knock after hours.) The **post office** is at ul. Piłudskiego 1 (tel. 321 20 15; open M-F 8am-8pm, Sa 8am-6pm). **Postal code:** 72-600. **Phone code:** (0)97.

ACCOMMODATIONS & FOOD. Rooms are plentiful from September to June, but in July and August you'll need to call weeks ahead to avoid stratospheric prices. **Private rooms** (25-30zł), arranged through CIT (see above), are a good option. **Hotel Hutnik,** ul. Żeromskiego 15 (tel. 321 54 11), has cozy rooms near the beach. From the city center walk up ul. Piłudskiego, continue along ul. Energetyków and turn left on ul. Żeromskiego. (Per person: singles 48zł, off-season 42zł; doubles 44zł, 36zł; triples 41zł, 33zł; quads 37zł, 31zł.) For another 30zł you can eat three square meals a day. **Camping Relax,** ul. Słowackiego 1 (tel. 321 47 00; fax 321 39 12), also near the beach, offers tent space (7-13zł) and bungalows (triples 85-155zł; quads 115-196zł). A bit farther from both center and beach, the **Youth Hostel (HI),** ul. Gdyńska 26 (tel. 327 06 13), has free luggage storage and agreeable rooms. (Per person: doubles and triples students 11zł, non-students 15zł, non-members 20zł; quads 9zł, 13zł, 17zł. Reception 6-10am and 5-10pm.) Walk down ul. Grunwaldzka (10-15min.) then turn right on ul. Grodzka.

Food stands by the dozen line ul. Żeromskiego. Try the inexpensive and delicious *gofry* (hot Belgian waffles with whipped cream and strawberries), or corn-on-the-cob for just 3zł. More substantial appetites can find a grilled *kiełbasa* and *piwo* for only 4zł. Across from the post office at **Bar "Neptun,"** ul. Bema 1 (tel. 321 26 43), you can not only feast on inexpensive Polish dishes (12-25zł) and home-made carrot juice, but also get a chance to see the charismatic and multilingual Mr. Tomasz Strybel in action. (Open daily 8am-10pm.) **Restaurant Zhong-hua,** ul. Władysław 19 (tel. 322 20 16), serves up Chinese dishes. **Grocery Kama,** ul. Chopina 2 (tel. 327 04 73), has fresh bread, cheeses, and meats. (Open M-F 7am-9pm.)

SIGHTS & ENTERTAINMENT. Visitors flock to Świnoujście's main attractions: the shady parks and the Baltic shoreline, with its grassy dunes and relaxed beachcombing. The town's seafaring side becomes obvious from the ferry in. Colorful tugboats sit at the port, while sailors walk the streets; the **beach** and the **promenade** along ul. Żeromskiego are sights in and of themselves. There are, however, some notable buildings as well. In the old town hall in the city center, the **Fishing Museum** (Muzeum Rybołówstwa) chronicles Świnoujście's maritime past. (Open Tu-F 9am-3pm; Sa-Su 11am-3pm. 2zł, students 1.50zł.) The century-old **lighthouse,** to your right as you face the ocean, is one of the city's most enduring symbols.

As the sun goes down, the food stands along ul. Żeromskiego transform into places for good times and cheap beer; crowds of college-age fun-seekers also frequent the **nightclubs,** which are within easy walking distance. For a real culture shock, check out the **Manhattan,** ul. Żeromskiego 1 (tel. 321 26 11), with its New York City decor. (Cover in summer 6zł, off season free. Open daily 10pm-6am.)

WOLIŃSKI NATIONAL PARK

Amid quickly developing coastal resorts, Woliński National Park protects a pristine tract of Wolin Island containing glacial lakes, a bison preserve, and breathtaking views of the Baltic Sea. Pine-scented breezes stir its trails, while the dense woodland dampens the nearby road noise, leaving only silence and the cries of distant eagles. For those wary of the unabated Polish wilderness, fear not: the comforts of tiny Międzyzdroje, the best base for a trip into the park, are nearby.

ORIENTATION & PRACTICAL INFORMATION. Trains run to Międzyzdroje (MYEN-dzi-ZDROY-eh) from **Szczecin** (40min., 17 per day, 18.62zł) and **Świnoujście** (30min., 17 per day, 4zł). In the center of town at **PTTK,** ul. Kolejowa 2 (tel. 328 04 62; fax 328 00 86), you can obtain **maps** (3-6zł), **exchange cash,** and get info about the park and accommodations. Go right out of the train station/bus stop and follow ul. Kolejowa to the center. There is a large map of town posted outside the train station and maps of the park are posted at periodic intervals, so buying a map is not essential. However, the PTTK city/park map (5zł) is useful for hiking deeper into the woods. There is a MC/Plus/Visa **ATM** at ul. Zwycięstwa 1. A **pharmacy** (tel. 328 01 54) sits at ul. Zwycięstwa 9. (Open M-F 8am-8pm, Sa 8am-3pm.) The **post office** is at ul. Gryfa Pomorskiego 7, down the street from PTTK. (Open M-F 8am-8pm, Sa 8am-6pm.) **Postal code:** 72-510. **Phone code:** (0)91.

ACCOMMODATIONS & FOOD. In spite of Międzyzdroje's rapidly developing tourist industry, affordable accommodations still exist. **PTTK** (see above) arranges stays in private rooms (singles 32zł; doubles 40zł; triples 96zł) and runs the well-kept **PTTK Hotel** (tel. 328 03 82), in the same building as the office. (July-Aug. 40zł per person; Sept.-June 32zł.) They also run a second hotel during the summer at ul. Dąbrówski 11; enquire at the main hotel, on the way to the train station. **Camping Gromada,** ul. Bohaterów Warszawy 1 (tel./fax 328 07 79 and 328 05 84), has cabins (13-26zł per person) and tent sites (8-12zł) a few minutes from the beach. Continue down Kolejowa as it becomes Gryfa Pomorskiego and later Dąbrówski; Gromada is at the end of the street on the right. Inexpensive food can be found at the stands and restaurants along ul. Gryfa Pomorskiego and the beach.

HIKING. Although Międzyzdroje is rapidly drawing crowds as a prime beach resort, the true accolades still belong to **Woliński.** The park is immaculately kept, with three main **hiking trails** (red, green, and blue—marked on trees and stones every 30m); stick to them, or risk an encounter with park officials. All three can be accessed from Międzyzdroje—the red at the northeast end of **ul. Bohaterów**

Warszawy, the green at the end of **ul. Leśna** (follow the signs to the bison preserve), and the blue just off **ul. Ustronie Leśne.** Before hiking, a visit to the **Park Museum,** ul. Niepodległości 3, provides information about the area and a preview of nearby wildlife. (Open Tu-Su 9am-5pm. 2zł, students 1.50zł.)

The **red trail** alone makes the trip worthwhile. Part of a longer trek around Wolin Island, 15km along the Baltic coastline makes up the prime hiking leg of the trail. Only a short climb from the trailhead, **Kawcza Góra** is the first of many scenic outlooks on the Baltic Sea. Look closely and you just might see one of the park's famed eagles *(bieliki)*. Snaking along the cliffs, the trail never strays far from the shoreline, with sea breezes keeping hikers refreshed. The **green trail** (15km) heads into the heavily-forested heart of the park, rewarding the persistent hiker with serenity along glacial lakes. Just 1.2km from the trailhead is a **bison preserve** (rezerwat żubrów; open Tu-Su 10am-6pm; 2zł, students 1.50zł), home to deer, wild boar, eagles, and, of course, bison. After another 7km you'll come upon the lakes, and 7km after that lies the town of Kołczewo, from which you can ride a bus back to Międzydroje, or continue on to the end (another 3km), where the green and red trails meet. Or, take a bus from Kołczewo to Wisełka and join the red trail there. The **blue trail** wanders south, covering more than 20km as it winds to Wolin, the island's southernmost point. This jaunt heads into the park right off ul. Ustronie Lesne by the train station—go under the bridge and take a right. Less traveled than the other two trails, it is a perfect escape from the mobs of tourists in town.

TRI-CITY AREA (TRÓJMIASTO)

Trójmiasto, the tri-city area on Poland's Baltic coast, is rapidly developing into a major tourist destination. The three cities of Gdańsk, Sopot, and Gdynia encompass numerous historic buildings, great restaurants, a wide selection of shops, exciting cultural events and nightlife, and the best beaches in Poland. Efficient transportation allows visitors to find a room in one city and to see the sights of the other two, and to make any number of daytrips: to the fishing village Hel, the Malbork castle, Frombork, home of Copernicus in his last years, the former concentration camp at Sztutowo and beautiful Krynica Morska on the Curonian Spit.

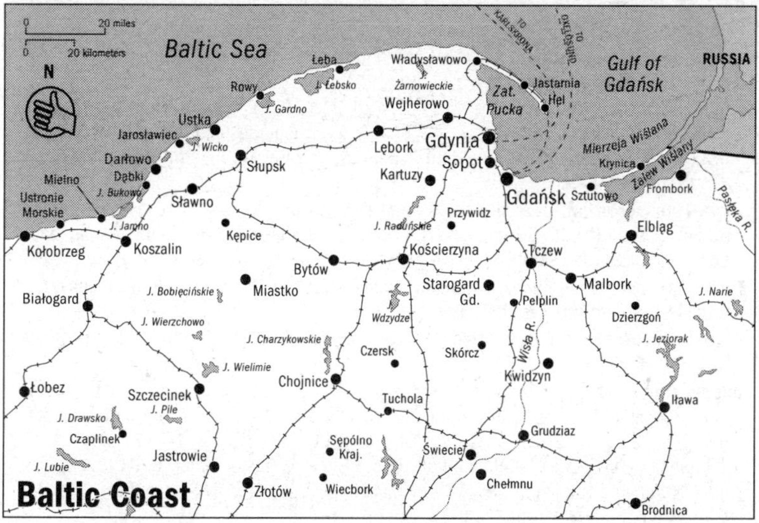

GDAŃSK

Gdańsk's (gh-DA-insk) strategic location on the Baltic Coast and at the mouth of the Wisła—helped it flourish architecturally and culturally, but has also put it at the forefront of Polish history for more than a millennium. Formerly the German city of Danzig, it saw the first deaths of WWII. At war's end, Gdańsk threw itself into creating a new identity while re-creating its previous appearance; but soon it was in the limelight again, serving as the birthplace of Lech Wałęsa's Solidarity movement. Today, Gdańsk is a multi-faceted gem, offering visitors a dizzying array of things to eat, drink, see, and do. From the beaches of Brzeźno to the parks of Oliwa, Gdańsk and its environs have matured without losing their charm.

ORIENTATION

While technically Gdańsk sits on the Baltic Coast, its downtown lies 5km inland. From the **Gdańsk Główny** train station, the city center lies a few blocks southeast, bordered on the west by **Wały Jagiellońskie** and on the east by the **Motława.** Take the underpass in front of the train station, go right, exit the shopping center, then turn left on ul. Heweliusza. Turn right on ul. Rajska and follow the signs to **Główne Miasto** (Main Town), turning left on **ul. Długa.** Długa becomes **Długi Targ** as it widens near **Motława,** one of the most beautiful parts of town and home to most of the sights and accommodations.

Gdańsk has a number of suburbs, all north of Główne Miasto. **Gdańsk-Brzeźno,** home to the city's beaches, is accessible by tram #13 from the train station. **Gdańsk-Oliwa,** famous for its cathedral, can be reached by commuter rail or by trams #6 and 12 from the train station. Also on trams #6 and 12 but closer to the center, the bustling **Gdańsk-Wrzeszcz** is home to a number of budget accommodations. Just north, on the tram line #2 and 8, **Gdańsk-Zaspa** has a major hospital.

PRACTICAL INFORMATION

Trains: Gdańsk Główny, ul. Podwale Grodzkie 1 (tel. 301 11 12). To: **Warsaw** (4hr., 18 per day, 32.12zł); **Kraków** (8hr., 10 per day, 36zł); **Berlin** (7hr., 2 per day, 123zł); **Prague** (17hr., 1 per day, 182zł); and **St. Petersburg** (36hr., 3 per week, 264zł). **Commuter trains (SKM)** run every 6-12min. to **Gdynia** (40min.) and **Sopot** (15min., 3zł, students 1.50zł). Punch your ticket at one of the *kasownik* machines before boarding.

Buses: Behind the train station via the underground passageway (tel. 32 15 32). To **Malbork** (1hr., 7 per day, 6.20zł) and **Frombork** (2hr., 5 per day, 12zł).

Ferries: Passenger ferries run May-Sept. to: **Sopot** (1½hr., 4 per day, round-trip 38zł, students 28zł); **Gdynia** (2hr., 3 per day, 49zł, 33zł); **Westerplatte** (50min., hourly 10am-6pm, 28zł, 16zł); and **Hel** (3hr. 2 per day, 49zł, 34zł). **Polferries,** ul. Przemysłowa 1 (tel. 343 18 87 and 343 69 78; fax 343 65 74; www.polferries.com.pl) sends ferries to **Oxelösund, Sweden** (19hr.; June-Sept. 1 per day, Oct.-May Tu, Th, and Su, departs 6pm; 210zł, students 180zł).

Local Transportation: Gdańsk has an extensive bus and tram system. 10min. 0.90zł; 30min. 1.80zł; 1hr. 2.70zł; daily pass 4.50zł. Prices higher at night. Students pay half-price, and baggage also needs a ticket. 63zł fine for riding ticketless.

Taxis: It's a bird, it's a plane, it's...**Super Hallo Taxi,** tel. 301 91 91. Not to be confused with the mild-mannered **Hallo Taxi,** tel. 91 97.

Tourist Offices: IT Gdańsk, ul. Długa 45 (tel./fax 301 91 51), in Główne Miasto. Open daily 9am-6pm.

Budget Travel: Orbis, ul. Podwale Staromiejskie 96/97 (tel. 301 21 32; fax 301 84 12). International and domestic ferry, train, and plane tickets. English tours of town. Open M-F 9am-5pm, Sa 10am-2pm. **Almatur,** ul. Długi Targ 11, 2nd Fl. (tel. 301 29 31; fax 301 78 18; email almatur@combidata.com.pl), in the Główne Miasto center. ISICs (32zł), info about youth and student hostels, international ferry tickets, and AVIS car rentals. Open M-F 9am-5pm, Sa 10am-2pm.

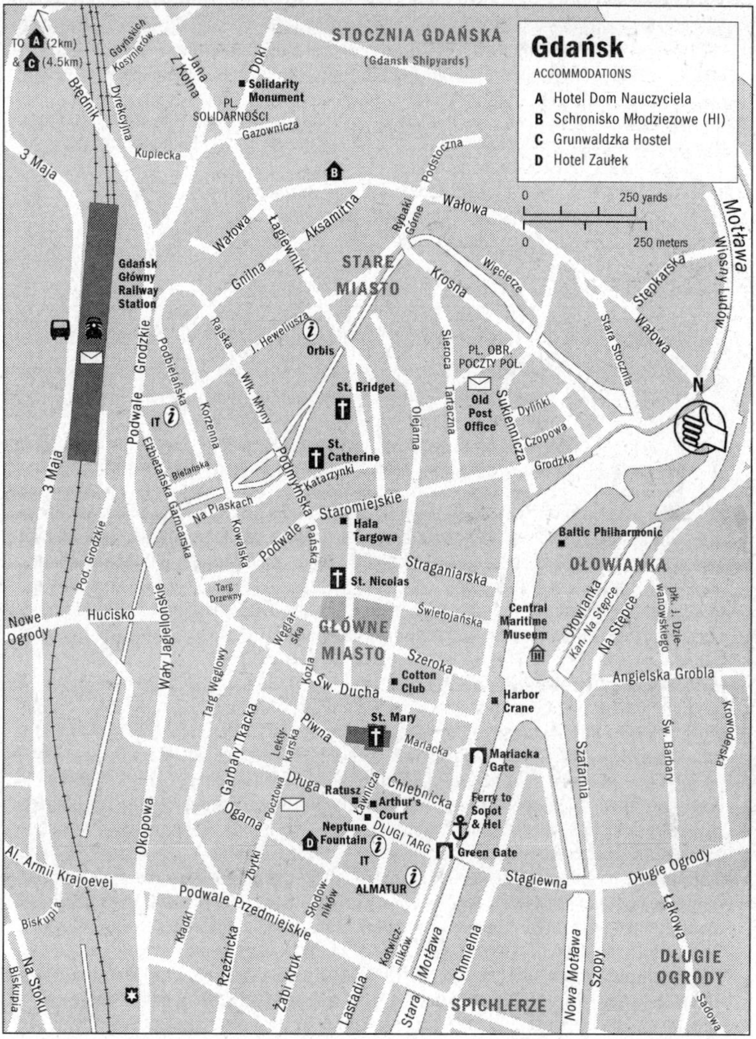

POLAND

Currency Exchange: At hotels, banks, *kantory,* and certain post offices. The train station has a 24hr. *kantor* and an AmEx/Cirrus/MC/PLUS/Visa **ATM.** Other 24hr. ATMs are located along ul. Długa and Długi Targ. **Bank Gdański,** Wały Jagiełłońskie 14/16 (tel. 307 92 12), cashes traveler's checks for a 1% commission, and provides AmEx/MC/Visa cash advances for no commission. Open M-F 8am-6pm. Orbis (see above) exchanges AmEx traveler's checks for no commission.

Luggage Storage: At the train station. 3.50zł. Open 24hr.

English Bookstore: English Books Unlimited, ul. Podmłyńska 10 (tel. 301 33 73). Open M-F 10am-6pm, Sa 10am-3pm. **Empik Megastore,** at the end of the underpass in front of the train station. Stocks English books and a wide selection of magazines and newspapers. Also sells music and **maps.** Open M-Sa 9am-9pm, Su 11am-7pm.

Late Night Pharmacy: At the train station (tel. 346 25 40). Closed 7:30-8am.

Medical Assistance: Private doctors, ul. Podbielańska 17 (tel. 301 51 68). A big blue sign on the building says "Lekarne Specjaliści." Visit 30-60zł. English spoken. Open M-F 7am-7pm. For **emergency assistance,** there is a hospital at al. Zwycięstwa 49 (emergency tel. 341 10 00), near the train station; with your back to the station, turn left and keep going. English spoken sporadically.

Post Office: ul. Długa 22/28 (tel. 301 88 53). Take a number and wait your turn. **Poste Restante** is around the back through a separate entrance. Open M-F 8am-8pm, Sa 9am-1pm. **Fax** bureau. **Postal code:** 80-801.

Internet Access: Rudy Kot Internet Music Cafe, ul. Garncarska 18/20 (tel. 301 86 49). Off Podwale Staromiejskie. 2.50zł per 30min. Open daily 10am-midnight.

Telephones: At the post office. **Phone code:** (0)58.

ACCOMMODATIONS

With Gdańsk's limited tourist infrastructure and increasing popularity, it is best to reserve well ahead, especially in the summer. If that proves impossible, private rooms are usually available, and can be arranged through **Gdańsk-Tourist** (Biuro Uslug Turystycznych), ul. Heweliusza 8 (tel. 301 26 34; fax 301 63 01), across from the train station. (Singles in the center 46zł, in the suburbs 37zł; doubles 76zł, 63zł. Open July-Aug. daily 8am-7pm; Sept.-June M-Sa 9am-5pm.) If you don't have luck inside, try the posse of elderly women milling abound out front.

Schronisko Młodzieżowe (HI), ul. Wałowa 21 (tel. 301 23 13). Cross the street in front of the train station, head up ul. Heweliusza, and turn left at ul. Łagiewniki and right on Wałowa; Gdańsk's most conveniently located hostel is on the left. **Kitchen** available; showers in basement. Attracts plenty of foreign guests. The building (and bathrooms) are quite old, but the rooms are decent. Luggage storage 1zł. Reception on the 2nd floor. Lockout 10am-5pm. Curfew 11pm. Single/doubles 26.75zł; triples/quads 16.05zł; dorms 12.84zł. "Seaside" tax 1zł, students 0.50zł. Sheets 3zł.

Schronisko Młodzieżowe (HI), ul. Grunwaldzka 244 (tel. 341 41 08). Take tram #6 or 12 north from the front of the train station and get off at "Abrahama" (unmarked), 14 stops later; you will see a complex of tram garages on the left (20-25min.). Turn right on ul. Abrahama, then right again on the highway-like Grunwaldzka; the hostel will be just ahead on the right. The rooms are immaculate and the bathrooms sparkle, but the location is less than ideal. Luggage storage 1zł. Reception 5-9pm. Lockout 10am-5pm. Curfew 10pm.Doubles 21.40zł, non-members 26.75zł; with bath 32.10zł, 37.45zł; quads 13.91zł, 16.05zł. Sheets 3zł.

Hotel Zaułek, ul. Ograna 107/108 (tel. 301 41 69). Ograna runs parallel to Długi Targ, one block south. The prices and location can't be beat, but you risk the occasional strange smell or tattered mattress. Fans of shower curtains will be sorely disappointed. Singles 50zł; doubles 65zł; triples 85zł; quads 100zł.

Hotel Dom Nauczyciela, ul. Uphagena 28 (tel. 341 55 87 and 341 91 16), in Gdańsk-Wrzeszcz. Take tram # 6 or 12 north from the train station to "Miszewskiego" (7 stops). Turn right on ul. Miszewskiego and take the next right onto Uphagena; the hotel will be ahead on the left, across from the tennis courts. Simple but clean rooms in an old building. Singles 43zł, with sink 63zł, with bath 118zł; doubles 60zł, 76zł, 166zł; triples 81zł, 90zł, 190zł; sinkless quads 92zł.

Camping #10, al. Gen. J. Hallera 234 (tel. 343 55 31), in Gdańsk-Brzeźno. Take tram #13 from the train station and get off on al. Hallera when you see an aqua-white building marked "spozywczy TOPAZ" on the right (20min.). The entrance is on the opposite side of the street, next to Nightclub Balladyna. Owned by Gdańsk-Tourist (see above), this large campground is a bit far from the center but right near the beach. Bungalows 24zł per person. Electricity and parking 82zł each. Reception 24hr. Tents 8-15.50zł plus 10zł per person.

FOOD

For fresh produce of all sorts, try **Hala Targowa** on ul. Pańska, in the shadows of Kościół św. Katarzyny, just off Podwale Staromiejskie. (Open M-F 9am-6pm, first and last Sa of the month 9am-3pm.)

Tan Viet, ul. Podmłyńska 1/5 (tel. 301 33 35). The Vietnamese cuisine is a little pricey, but worth every złoty. Exquisitely decorated interior, and each table features a small stone for warming food. Entrees 16-35zł. MC/Visa/AmEx.

La Pasta, ul. Szeroka 32 (tel. 301 51 91). No table service, but good food done cheap in a tasteful decor. Pizza and pasta 8-14zł. Open daily 11am-10pm.

Pizzeria Napoli, ul. Długa 62/63 (tel. 301 41 46). Lives up to its "Best in Town" sign, with 30 varieties of tasty pizza and spaghetti (12-30zł). Take-out and delivery available, but with a prime people-watching location like this, why go home? Open daily 11am-10pm. AmEx/MC/Visa.

U Szkota, ul. Chlebnicka 10 (tel. 301 49 11). This Scottish restaurant with a history serves up salmon, eel, trout, chicken, and beef (20-40zł). Kilted waiters add to the plaid experience. Open daily noon-midnight.

Bar Mleczny, ul. Długa 33/34 (tel. 301 49 88). Homestyle meat and veggie dishes in a traditional Polish cafeteria. Full meal 5-10zł. Open M-F 7am-6pm, Sa 9am-5pm.

Ha Long, ul. Szeroka 37/39 (tel. 305 90 64). Somewhat cheaper than Tan Viet, but still quite good, serving both Chinese and Vietnamese specialties. Entrees 14-30zł. Open daily 11am-10pm. AmEx/MC/Visa.

SIGHTS

GŁÓWNE MIASTO

Gdańsk was one of the first Polish cities to undergo an exhaustive postwar facelift; only a few buildings have yet to be fully restored. The handsome market square, **Długi Targ,** forms the physical and social center of Główne Miasto, where the original 16th-century facade of **Arthur's Court** (Dwór Artusa) faces out onto **Neptune's Fountain** (Fontanna Neptuna). The court, where medieval burgher held meetings, now houses one branch of the **Gdańsk History Museum** (Muzeum Historii Gdańska), noteworthy for its collection of model ships. (Open Tu and Th noon-7pm, F-Sa 10am-5pm, Su 11am-5pm; last entry 30min. before closing. 4zł, students 2zł.) The square hosts local artists and craftsmen, and visitors buy everything from original art to Gdańsk-themed t-shirts. Next to the fountain, where ul. Długa and Długi Targ meet, the 14th-century **ratusz** houses another branch of the **Gdańsk History Museum.** Don't miss the fantastic Red Chamber, with its ceiling covered with allegorical paintings by Baroque masters. Visit the museum's White and Winter Chambers to read a 1656 letter from Oliver Cromwell to Gdańsk authorities. Another, more sobering exhibit shows the state of Gdańsk right after WWII—including some of the actual rubble. For an extra 2zł you can climb the tower for an incredible view of the city. (Open same hours as museum, plus W 8-10pm.)

One block north of Długi Targ is Gdańsk's grandest house of worship, the 14th-century **Church of the Blessed Virgin Mary** (Kościół Najświętszej Marii Panny). Almost completely rebuilt after its destruction in WWII, the church reigns as Poland's largest brick cathedral. (Open M-Sa 9am-5:30pm. Donation requested.) For 3zł, visitors can climb the 405 steps to the top of the steeple. In the foreground of the view, from the top, you'll find the 15th-century **St. Nicholas's** (Kościół św. Mikołaja), ul. Wielkie Młyny, and behind it the 14th-century **St. Catherine's** (Kościół św. Katarzyny). Gdańsk's churches were often visited by Polish monarchs: King Władysław III Łokietek, who unified Polish principalities in the 14th century, supervised court trials in St. Catherine's. King Zygmunt III, who moved the capital from Kraków to Warsaw, received his electoral diploma in St. Nicholas's.

The cobblestone **ul. Mariacka,** behind the Church of the Blessed Virgin Mary, ambles to the river; street musicians playing medieval music complete the mood. After **Mariacka Gate,** the Motława River lies ahead, along with the numerous cafes and shops that line **ul. Długie Pobrzeże.** Going left along Długie Pobrzeże leads toward the huge Gothic **Harbor Crane,** which once set the masts of medieval ships. This and the ship *Sołdek* are part of **Central Maritime Museum** (Centralne Muzeum Morskie; tel. 301 69 38; fax 301 84 53; open daily 10am-6pm; 3zł, students 2zł).

From Podwale Staromiejskie, go north on Olejarna and turn right at the sign for **Gdańsk Post Office #1** (Urzad Poctowy Gdańsk 1), home of the stark **Memorial to the Defenders of the Post Office Square.** On Sept. 1, 1939, the employees of the post office put up a desperate defense against the German army, fighting until the building was engulfed in flames. Those who survived the blaze were summarily shot. There is also a museum commemorating the event. (Open W-Sa 10am-4pm, Su 10:30-2pm. 2zł, students 1zł.) Nearby is the simple brick **St. Bridget's Church** (Kościół św. Brygidy), ul. Profesorska 17, the parish of Lech Wałęsa. The flags of his trade union *Solidarność* fly high once again at **Gdańsk Shipyard** (Stocznia Gdańska) and at the **Solidarity monument,** pl. Solidarności, just north of the center at the end of ul. Wały Piastowskie. (See **History,** p. 400.)

GDAŃSK-OLIWA

The most beautiful of Gdańsk's many suburbs, **Oliwa** is the perfect spot for a brief respite from the big city. The fastest way there from the center of the city is on the commuter rail (15min., 2zł, students 1zł). Trams #6 and 12 will also get you there, but more slowly (30-35min.). From the Oliwa train station, go up ul. Poczty Gdańskiej, turn right on ul. Grundwaldzka, then turn left at the signs for the cathedral on ul. Rybińskiego. To the right you'll find the lush green shade and ponds of **Park Oliwski.** (Open daily May-Sept. 5am-11pm; Mar.-Apr. and Oct. 5am-8pm.) The oldest church in the Gdańsk area, the 13th-century **Oliwska Cathedral** (Katedra) is within the park's gates.. Gaze at the golden stars of the high Gothic cross vaults, or admire the surrounding ring of chapels. In back is the magnificent 18th-century Rococo organ, which the cathedral shows off several times daily to tourists. (Consult the free pamphlet "Informator Turystyczney," available at the Tourist Office, for a complete schedule.) During the summer, full-scale evening organ concerts can be heard twice a week during the **International Organ Music Festival.** (Tickets 5-10zł.) The **Oliwa Zoo,** nestled in a forest right outside Oliwa proper, houses such exotic animals as Andean condors and Bactrian camels from the Gobi Desert. Take bus #122 from Rybińskiego to get there. (Open daily May-Sept. 9am-7pm; Apr. 9am-6pm; Oct.-Mar. 9am-3pm. 6zł, students 3zł.)

POLAND

TRI-CITY LANDSCAPE PARK (TRÓJMIEJSKI PARK KRAJOBRAZOWY)

A massive, thickly wooded wilderness set in gently rolling hills to the west of the three cities, the Tri-City Landscape Park offers excellent hiking on its numerous well-maintained trails. Pick up a copy of the **map** "Nadleśnictwo Gdańsk" (6.90zł) at Empik Megastore to plan your route. The park is most easily reached from Oliwa. Follow the directions for the zoo (see above) and look out for a blue-and-white-marked path heading uphill to the right. From there, a short and pleasant hike along the blue trail leads to the **Sopot Kamienny Potoh train station,** where the commuter train can whisk you back to Gdańsk. The trail begins with a short but rigorous climb to the top of a small hill; immediate gratification awaits with a stunning view of the city and sea in the distance. From here on, it's all trees; follows the markings carefully, as unmarked trails often branch off confusingly from the main one. When you reach a small road just past high-tension power lines, turn left; the trail re-enters the woods about 5m further; the deceptive right arrow is for hikers coming in the opposite direction. The entire route is 10km and takes 2-3hr. When you reach Sopot, the markings disappear. As you descend past the small church, veer to the left onto ul. Małopolska and continue until you reach the train station; tickets are usually available at the nearby kiosks, but if you're coming through on a weekend after the buses have stopped running, bring tickets with you.

WESTERPLATTE

When Germany attacked on September 1, 1939, the little island fort guarding the entrance to Gdańsk's harbor gained the unfortunate distinction of being the target of the first shots of WWII. Its brave defenders held out for a week, until a lack of food and munitions forced them out. To get here, take bus #106 or 158 south from the train station to the last stop. **Guardhouse #1** has been converted into a museum housing a sparse exhibit on the fateful day. (Open May-Sept. 9am-4pm. 1.50zł, students 1zł.) The path beyond the museum passes the ruins of a command building and, farther up, the massive **Memorial to the Heroes of the Coast** (Pomnik Obrońców Wybrzeża). Climb the spiralling path lined by rose bushes to the top for a nice view of the shipyard and Baltic. On a clear day, you can see Hel Peninsula. Backtrack to the museum and head left to a **tank,** popular for military-themed snapshots, and a more serene **trail** along the rocky coastline.

BRZEŹNO

For some fun at the beach, Brzeźno—though it may not be as trendy as Sopot—is perfect. What it does have over Sopot is **Park Brzeźnieński,** a wondrous escape full of tall pine trees. Take tram #13 north from the train station to the last stop, "Brzeźno." Follow the footpath in the wooded area ahead to reach the beach. A few hundred meters to the left you'll find the **pier,** the center of beach activity, although the beach itself stretches beyond Sopot.

ENTERTAINMENT

Of the three cities that line this little stretch of the Baltic, Gdańsk draws the oldest and largest crowds to its incredible variety of activities. Street performances, often quite elaborate and captivating, liven up Długi Targ. The **Baltic Philharmonic** (Philharmonia Bałtycha), ul. Ołowianka 1 (tel. 305 20 40), performs free outdoor concerts during the summer; the audience listens from the other side of the Motłowa, near the end of Podwale Staromiejskie. Opera lovers can check out the **Baltic Opera** (Opera Bałtycha), al. Zwycięstwa 15 (tel. 341 01 34), in Gdańsk-Wrzeszcz. The summer brings various festivals, including street theater, a **Shakespeare Festival,** and the **International Organ Music Festival** at Oliwa (see **Sights,** above). In summer 2000, Gdańsk will host the famed **Cutty Sark Regatta.** Consult the tourist office for more info on these and other cultural events.

POLAND

NIGHTLIFE

Nightlife abounds. Długi Targ rages as crowds of all ages pack the pubs, clubs, and beer gardens late into the evening. 17th-century brewmaster/astronomer Jan Heweliusza, whose name and likeness grace Gdańsk's brew, would be proud.

U7, pl. Dominikański 7 (tel. 305 55 77), near the intersection of ul. Podwale Staromiejskie and ul. Podmłyńska. A massive entertainment complex in an old air-raid shelter. Named after its seven attractions: bowling (10-14zł), billiards (14zł per hr.), a sauna (10zł), solarium (0.60zł per min.), shooting range (10-20zł), fitness center (10zł), and of course, the bar (0.5L *Żywiec* 5zł, drinks 5-15zł). Open daily 9am-1am.

Jazz Club, ul. Długi Targ 39/40 (tel. 301 54 09). Well-located and extremely popular. A great spot for live music (F-Sa after 9pm) or a beer. Crowd is mostly over 30 but still kicking. 0.5L *Żywiec* 6zł. Occasional 5zł cover, depending on band. Open daily 10am until the last guest leaves.

Cotton Club, ul. Złotników 25/29 (tel. 301 88 13). Head here for jazz, or at least a jazzy atmosphere. Billiards downstairs (10zł per hr.). Beer 5-10zł. Open daily 4pm-until the last guest leaves.

Bar Kubicki, ul. Wartka 5 (tel. 305 54 60), on the Motława off the north end of Długie Pobrzeże. Good music, beer, friendly staff, and candles to boot. Beer 5zł, drinks 5-15zł. Open daily noon-until the last guest leaves.

Music Maker Pub, ul. Targ Rybny 9 (tel. 301 65 75), along the Motława near the end of ul. Podwale Staromiejskie. Empty during the day, this place fills up late for disco (nightly 10pm; cover 10zł), as the mostly student crowd shakes what their mamas gave them into the wee hours. 0.5L *Żywiec* 5zł. Open daily 3pm-late.

NEAR GDAŃSK: SZTUTOWO

Forty kilometers east of Gdańsk, the tiny village of Sztutowo (shtoo-TO-vo) would be unremarkable were it not for the **Stutthof Concentration Camp** (Obóz Koncentracyjny Stutthof). Although considerably smaller than many of the WWII-era centers around Poland, Stutthof was infamous as a forced labor, transit, and execution camp. Now, the **Stutthof Museum in Sztutowo** (Muzeum Stutthof w Sztutowie; tel. (055) 247 83 53) allows visitors to tour the original site and buildings, including the barracks, the gas chambers, and crematorium. (Open daily May-Sept. 8am-6pm; Oct.-Apr. 8am-3pm. Free. Visitors must be at least 14 years old and respectfully dressed.) The large brick building near the entrance once housed the Nazi administration, and now shows a short film about the camp (1zł. Minimum 15 people. Last showing at 4:30pm; no film Monday.) The remaining barracks house a Polish-language historical display, with explanations in German and English in one building. One structure to the left of the main gate is filled with the shoes of prisoners executed here. The map near the entrance will drive home the fact that the camp was in fact much larger than the area occupied by the museum.

GETTING THERE. Buses from **Gdańsk** run to Sztutowo hourly (6.20zł). Get off at the "Sztutowo Muzeum" stop, the second actual station outside the town of Stegna. Stand by the door to let the driver know you'd like to get off there. The museum is then just a short walk up **ul. Muzealna,** which is marked by a large stone monument. Head a little further down the road from Gdańsk to find the "Sztutowo Muzeum" stop for return buses (past the abandoned railway stop). Buses are more or less hourly, but be sure to stand somewhere visible or the driver might not stop.

POLAND

NEAR GDAŃSK: MALBORK

One of the many castles built by the **Teutonic Knights,** Malbork became the focal point of the Teutonic Order in the 1300s. The Teutons first came to the region in 1230 at the request of Polish Duke Konrad Mazowiecki to assist the nation in its struggle against the heathen Prussians. The Teutons double-crossed the Poles, however, establishing their own state on conquered Prussian soil in 1309, with Malbork as its capital. The great period of Teutonic castle-building lasted until the Order was defeated at the Battle of Grunwald in 1410. Malbork withstood several sieges, but the Poles finally defeated their arch-enemies in 1457 under the leadership of King Kazimierz Jagiełłończyk. For the next 300 years, Malbork served as a major arsenal and stronghold for the Kingdom of Poland. After the first partition of Poland in 1772, Malbork was incorporated into Prussia. Heavily damaged during WWII, the fortress was used by the Germans as a POW camp (Stalag XXB). After the fall of the Third Reich, Malbork returned to Poland.

Like most Teutonic castles, Malbork's layout is rectangular; it is unique, however, in that it is a complex of three huge castles. Construction began in the mid-1270s with the monastery that became the **Higher Castle.** It was to contain the main Church of the Virgin Mary, the Grand Masters' burial chapel, the chapter-room, the refectory, the dormitory, the treasury, kitchen facilities, a prison cell, and storerooms, all surrounded by a system of fortifications. Between 1335 and 1341, a **tower** and a **bridge** over the Nogat River were incorporated. The most splendid additions were those of the Grand Master Winrich von Kniprode, for whom Rhenish architect Nikolaus Fellenstein designed the impressive **Master's Residence** in the **Middle Castle.** Guest lodgings are also in this part of the castle, along with the **Grand Refectory,** where feasts were held. Finally, the 14th and 15th centuries saw the development of the **Lower Castle,** which included an armory, a chapel, an infirmary, servants' quarters, stables, and storerooms. (Open daily 9am-6pm; exhibitions and rooms open 9am-5pm; *kassa* 8:30am-5pm. 17zł, students 10zł. Mandatory 3hr. guided tour in Polish; English-speaking guide 90zł.)

GETTING THERE. Malbork makes a perfect daytrip from Gdańsk by **train** (40-60min., 25 per day, 8-11zł) or **bus** (1hr., 7 per day, 6.20zł). With your back to the station, walk right on ul. Dworcowa, then go left at the fork (sign points to

Elbląg). Go up and around the corner to a roundabout; the **Maltur tourist office,** ul. Sienkiewicza 15 (tel. 272 26 14), which sits near the traffic circle, provides brochures and maps of the area. (Open M-F 10am-4:30pm, Sa 10am-2pm.) To get to the castle, follow **ul. Kościuszki,** veer to the right on **ul. Piastska,** following the signs for the castle. **Phone code:** (0)55.

NEAR GDAŃSK: FROMBORK

Little Frombork is closely associated with the name and work of astronomer **Mikołaj Kopernik** (Copernicus), who lived here from 1510 until his death in 1543. It was in this town that Kopernik conducted most of his research and composed his revolutionary book, *De Revolutionibus Orbium Coelestium.* The tiny waterfront village surrounds a truly breathtaking and well-maintained cathedral complex perched majestically atop a hill. Follow the signs from the train and bus stops to get to the **cathedral.** Once you cross the wooden bridge, the *kasa* ahead on the right (tel. 243 73 96) sells tickets to **Muzeum Kopernika,** the cathedral, and the **tower** *(wieża).* The museum displays copies of *De Revolutionibus Orbium Coelestium* and a number of Kopernik's documents, including a scrap of paper that served as his Ph.D. diploma, circa 1503. (Open Tu-Su May-Sept. 10am-5:30pm; Oct.-Apr. 9am-3:30pm. 2zł, students 1zł.) Next door in the cathedral itself, the famous 17th-century **organ** has a seven-second reverberation and impeccable sound quality. (Open M-Sa 9:30am-5pm. Organ concerts twice daily, usually 11am and 3pm. 2zł, students 1zł.) A climb up the tower provides a phenomenal view of the cathedral, the town, and the Wisła lagoon. (Open M 9:30am-5pm, Tu-Sa 9:30am-7:30pm. 2.50zł, students 2zł.) Near the tower is the **planetarium** (tel. 243 73 92) with Copernicus-themed shows. (6 daily; 4zł, students 3zł.)

GETTING THERE. Frombork is best reached by **bus** from **Gdańsk** (2hr., 6 per day, 8-12zł). Taking the **train** entails changing in **Elbląg,** which may take up to four hours. The **train station** and the **bus stop** in Frombork are along **ul. Dworcowa,** with the docks right behind them. Return bus tickets must be purchased from the driver. In a parking lot opposite the train station stands a wooden hut with the familiar **IT** sign (tel. 243 75 00; open daily 8am-7pm). The main **tourist office,** Globus, ul. Elbląska 2 (tel./fax 243 73 54), sits across from the cathedral in the *rynek,* at the end of the path from the train station. (Open daily 9am-7pm.) **Phone code:** (0)55.

POLAND

SOPOT

As soon as you arrive in Sopot, you will realize that everything in this town exists to get you to and let you enjoy Sopot's incredible beaches. Simply put, Sopot is a beach resort. Let's re-emphasize this: beach beach beach. Beach. On the way there (to the beach, that is) you'll find wonderful shops, restaurants, bars, discos, street musicians, and more than a few rotisserie chicken stands, all of which make Sopot a fun place to be. But as soon you hit the famed 512m pier, look to either side, and remember why you're here.

ORIENTATION & PRACTICAL INFORMATION

Ul. Dworcowa begins at the train station and leads to the pedestrian **ul. Monte Cassino,** which runs along the sea to the **molo** (the 512m pier).

Trains: The **commuter rail (SKM)** connects Sopot to **Gdańsk** (15min., 4zł, students 2zł) and **Gdynia** (25min., 4zł, students 2zł). Trains depart from platform #1 every 6min. during the day and less frequently at night.

Ferries: Tel. 551 12 93. At the end of the pier. To: **Hel** (1½hr., 4 per day, round-trip 39zł, students 28zł); **Gdynia** (35min., 1 per day, 28zł, 19zł); **Gdańsk** (1hr., 1 per day, round-trip 38zł, 28zł); and **Westerplatte** (35min., 1 per day, 28zł, 9zł).

Tourist Office: IT, ul. Dworcowa 4 (tel. 550 37 83). In a little wooden house next to the train station. Helps with hotel reservations, arranges private rooms, and sells **maps** (3-6zł) of li'l old Sopot. Open M-F 8:30am-5pm, Sa-Su 8:30am-2pm. Accommodations bureau closed Sa and Su.

Budget Travel: Orbis, ul. Hafferna 7 (tel. 551 41 42; fax 551 74 86). Sells tickets for buses, ferries, and concerts around town, including at the Opera Leśna (see **Sights & Entertainment,** below). Open M-F 10am-6pm, Sa 10am-2pm.

Currency Exchange: Bank Gdański S.A., pl. Konstytucji 3 Maja 1 (tel. 551 02 99). Opposite the train station. Gives AmEx/MC/Visa cash advances, cashes traveler's checks, and has a MC/Visa **ATM.** Open M-F 8:30am-5pm, Sa 8:30am-2pm.

Post Office: Ul. Kościuszki 2 (tel. 551 59 51). The first street on the right heading down ul. Monte Cassino. Open M-F 8am-8pm, Sa 9am-3pm. **Postal code:** 81-701. **Phone code:** (0)58.

ACCOMMODATIONS

Sopot is one of Poland's most popular and expensive resorts, so reservations are a must in the summer. Consider renting a **private room;** stop by **IT** (see above) for help. (Singles 43zł; doubles 72zł; triples 85zł; quads 106zł.) If none of the following pan out, consider staying in Gdańsk, lest you want to see your złotys flutter away like a flock of seagulls.

Hotel Wojskowy Dom Wypoczynkowy (WDW), ul. Kilińskiego 12 (tel. 551 06 85; fax 626 11 33), is a 10min. walk from the pier. Facing the sea, turn right on ul. Granwaldzka; ul. Kilińskiego is the first left after ul. 3-go Maja. The TV-equipped rooms are a bit small, but are well-kept. Singles 61zł, with bath 76zł; doubles 122zł, 152zł; triples 183zł, 228zł; quads with bath 304zł. Breakfast included.

POLAND

Hotel Miramar, ul. Zamkowa Góra 25 (tel. 551 80 11; fax 551 51 64). On the opposite end of town near the Sopot Kamienny train station. From the pier and facing the sea, go left on ul. Powstańców Warszawy, which runs into ul. Hafferna, which in turn runs into al. Niepodległości. The hotel is just ahead on the right; *not* the aqua-green structure but the brown one behind it. The rooms are larger than those at WDW. Some have TVs and balconies, and all are 0.5km from the beach. AmEx/MC/Visa. Singles 80zł, with bath 125zł; doubles 90zł, 160zł; triples 150zł, 180zł; quads 220zł, 260zł.

Camping Nr. 19 (tel. 550 04 45), at the same address and phone number as Hotel Miramar (see above). Has a separate reception desk and entrance on ul. Niepodległości, 300m from the end of the path from the Sopot Kamienny Potok train station (go left). Outfitted with showers and a billiard hall; the 24hr. snack bar "Amigo" is next door. 11zł per person; tents 7-11zł; 4-person cabins 75zł, with bath 82zł.

FOOD

Even though ul. Monte Cassino now hosts Ronald McDonald and his big purple friend, a few spots continue to shine through the homogenized fog.

Bar Rybny Pod Strzechą, ul. Monte Cassino 42 (tel. 551 24 76). Serves simple but good fish dishes at unbeatable prices. Entrees 2-7zł. Open daily 10am-11pm.

La Mela, ul. Monte Cassino 16 (tel. 551 15 44). Cooks up a wide selection of Italian dishes, including pizza and lasagna. Entrees 8-22zł. Open daily 11am-9pm.

Saigon Restaurant, ul. Grunwaldzka 8 (tel. 551 33 74). One block south of the pier. Vietnamese meals hover around 12-20zł, but a few creep into the 30-40zł range. Open daily noon-10pm.

Cukiernia Wiedeńska, ul. Monte Cassino 11. Great for coffee, tea, and pastries. Everything under 4zł. Open M-F 7:30am-7pm, Sa 9am-5pm, Su 10am-4pm.

ENTERTAINMENT

As you may have gathered, Sopot's prominence is due largely to its **beach:** white, sandy, big, and adorned with all manner of recreation, from waterslides to outdoor theater. The most popular and extensive sands at the end of ul. Monte Cassino, where the famous **pier** (*molo*) begins. (M-F 1.90zł, students 0.90zł; Sa-Su 2.50zł, 1.40zł.) The town is just beginning to realize that the fun doesn't have to end when the tides come in, as evidenced by the growing number of street-side **cafes, pubs,** and **discos** along ul. Monte Cassino. **Pub FM,** ul. Monte Cassino 36 (tel. 551 33 59), offers traditional Polish fare (11-20zł) and Americanish steaks (39-42zł) to a youngish crowd, but most folks come here for the beer (0.5L Guinness 12zł) and cider. (Open daily 1pm-1am. MC/Visa/AmEx.) Pierside discos and nightclubs are the latest rage; **Fantom** (tel. 551 25 47; cover 10zł; open daily 10pm-late) and the misleadingly named **Non-Stop** (tel. 551 46 54; cover 10zł; open daily 10pm-late), both right next to the pier, are especially popular. **Opera Leśna,** an open-air theater, is a good place to get in on the local scene. Its open-air **rock and pop music festival** (tel. 551 18 12) dominates the area in mid-August; call ahead for tickets and info on other festivals and shows. Concerts on the pier are frequent in summer. On the beach, **Teatr Atelier** (info tel. 550 10 01) stages performances throughout the summer. **Sopocki Klub Tenisowy,** ul. Ceynowy 5/7 (tel. 551 35 69), rents out **tennis** courts. (14-30zł per hr.) And should your conscience bother you after a Saturday night of debauchery, the nearby **Parish Church of St. Andrew Bobala,** ul. Powstańców Warszawy 15, celebrates an English mass (Su 10am).

GDYNIA

Young Gdynia (gh-DIN-ya), mostly built only after WWI, is in no hurry to grow up. Although it lacks the history and tradition of Gdańsk and the glitz of Sopot, the town seems more than happy with its simple maritime life. Evening strolls along the waterfront reveal a little slice of nautical heaven; those looking for no-frills seaside living need look no farther.

POLAND

ORIENTATION & PRACTICAL INFORMATION. Despite its small size, the Gdynia Główna **train station** welcomes a large volume of **bus** and train traffic. The **commuter rail,** the cheapest and easiest way to get to Gdańsk (3zł) or Sopot (1.50zł), runs from *peron* (platform) one. Punch your ticket in a yellow *kasownik* box before getting on the train. **Trains** run to: **Warsaw** (4hr., 20 per day, 32zł); **Kraków** (7hr., 10 per day, 37zł); **Poznań** (4hr., 7 per day, 32.12zł); **Szczecin** (5hr., 6 per day, 32.12zł); and **Wrocław** (6hr., 6 per day, 35.12zł). **Buses** zoom to: **Hel** (2hr., 28 per day, 7.60zł); **Świnoujście** (8hr., 2 per day, 43zł); and **Warsaw** (7hr., 1 per day, 38zł). **Ferries** leave from al. Zjednoczenia 2 (tel. 620 26 42), on Skwer Kościuszki, to: **Gdańsk** (2hr., 11 per day, 24zł, students 17zł); **Hel** (1hr., 7 per day, round-trip 38zł, students 28zł); and **Sopot** (30min., 5 per day, 16zł, students 10zł). **Lion Ferry,** ul. Kwiatkowskiego 60 (tel. 621 36 23; fax 621 36 20), sends one ferry per day to **Karlskrona, Sweden** (13hr., 195zł). Gdynia is also blessed with an extensive public transit system. Rides cost 1.40zł, half that for students. If kiosks are closed, buy a book of five tickets (7zł, students 3.50zł) from the driver.

Any of the three roads running away from the train station will take you toward the beach and the pier. **Ul. 10-go Lutego** is the most direct. If you end up on ul. Jana Kolna, ul. Wójta Radtkiego, or ul. Starowiejska (which parallel ul. 10-go Lutego), take a right at the end of the street onto **pl. Kaszubski,** then turn left on ul. 10-go Lutego where it runs into the fountain-filled **Skwer Kościuszki.** For shopping, continue along pl. Kaszubski to **ul. Swiętojańska.** The **beach** is off Skwer Kościuszki. The **tourist office,** ul. 3 maja 27 (tel./fax 621 75 24), has free booklets on the tri-city area, sells maps (5zł), and helps with finding accommodations. (Open M-F 9am-5pm; Sa 9:30-1pm.) The *kantor* to the right of the ticket counters in the train station is always open and offers good rates. **Bank Gdański S.A.,** Skwer Kościuszki 14 (tel. 620 41 35), gives AmEx/MC/Visa cash advances and cashes AmEx/Visa **traveler's checks.** (Open M-F 8:30am-5pm, Sa 8:30am-2pm.) The **post office,** ul. 10-go Lutego 10 (tel. 621 87 11), is between the train station and Skwer Kościuszki. (Open M-F 7am-8pm, Sa 9am-3pm.) **Telephones** are at the post office. **Postal code:** 81-301. **Phone code:** (0)58.

ACCOMMODATIONS. Cheap sleeps are somewhat limited in the city center; look for private rooms. **Turus,** ul. Starowiejska 47 (tel. 621 82 65; fax 620 92 87), opposite the train station, will help you find one. (Singles 38zł; doubles 65zł. Open M-F 8am-6pm, Sa 10am-6pm.) To reach the **Youth Hostel (HI),** ul. Morska 108c (tel. 627 00 05), exit the train station through the tunnels under the platforms toward ul. Morska, then take bus #22, 25, 30, 105, 109, or 125 along ul. Morska for four stops. The entrance is in the back of building 108b. Rooms are basic but clean. Polish students and HI members get priority. (20zł, nonmembers 23zł. Sheets 2zł Reception daily 8-10am and 5-10pm.) **Hotel Lark,** ul. Starowiejska 1 (tel. 621 80 46), is at the end of the road to the right of the train station. Only a short walk from the sights and the beach. The rooms are decent, although the lighting is dim, and the hall bathrooms are well-kept. (Singles 77zł; doubles 111zł; triples 117zł. MC/Visa.)

FOOD. One of the most extensive markets in the tri-city area, **Hala Targowa** stretches between ul. Jana Kolna and ul. Wójta Radtkiego. You can get everything from fresh fruit, vegetables, and meat, to clothes, watches, and books, with numerous Russian vendors selling their wares at bargain prices. For a full sensory experience, check out the pungent "hall of fish." (Open M-F 9am-6pm, Sa 8am-3pm.) As in many seaside towns, there are food stands galore along the waterfront **Hala Rybna,** where a full meal can be had for less than 6zł. **Sphinx,** ul. 10 Lutego 11 (tel. 661 87 95), apparently catering to a crowd with diverse tastes, offers hearty Middle Eastern fare alongside pizza. A meal costs 10-30zł. (Open Su-Th 11am-midnight, F-Sa 11am-1am.) **Chang-Lin,** ul. Dworcowa 11a (tel. 20 81 07), a stone's throw from the train station, has a surprisingly extensive Chinese menu. (Entrees 11-30zł. Open daily noon-11pm.)

POLAND

SIGHTS & ENTERTAINMENT. The kiosks lining the **pier** on Skwer Kościuszki give it a carnivalesque atmosphere, and crowds hang around well after meals to relax by the sea. For more seaside views, walk along **bul. Nadmorski im. F. Nowowiejskiego.** The stroll also includes a few popular places to sit and watch others do the walking. Check out **Cafe Bulwar,** with the outdoor stage, one of Gdynia's more prominent meeting places. The cafe lies just south of Skwer Kościuszki and stays open until the last guest leaves. Those who feel inspired to get nautical will not be disappointed by the pier. The WWII destroyer **Błyskawica** is docked here, complete with crew. (Open Tu-Su 10am-1pm and 2-5pm. 3zł, students 1.50zł.) The 1909 sailboat **Dar Pomorza** (tel. 621 74 50) served as a school at sea for the Polish navy between 1930 and 1981, and has won several sailing competitions. (Open in summer Tu-Su 10am-6pm, off season 10am-4pm. 4zł, students 2.50zł.) The boat **Bożena** (tel. 651 06 85 ext. 206; after 3pm tel. 657 56 13) gives hour-long tours of Gdynia's port. (Open 8am-10pm. 11 tours per day. 10zł, students 8zł.) The **Oceanography Museum and Aquarium** (Muzeum Oceanograficzne i Akwarium), at the end of the pier, digresses on all things fishy. (Open daily 9am-7:30pm. 5zł, students 3zł.)

For theatrical entertainment, **Gdynia Musical Theater** (Teatr Muzyczny w Gdyni; tel. 621 60 24 and 621 60 25) puts on productions at pl. Grunwaldzki 1. Call for a schedule. Or, head over to disco **Tornado** (tel. 620 23 05), below the restaurant Róża Wiatrów on the pier. (Sa cover for men 15zł, women 10zł. Open F-Sa 9pm-4am.)

HEL

Go to Hel—really. For almost a millennium, the sleepy village of Hel has lived off the fish of the Baltic Sea and booty from boats stranded on the Hel Peninsula (Mierzeja Helska). Recently, the town has awakened to the sound of tourists walking its clean, wide, gorgeous beaches. Hel opens the gates to a day of relaxation, serving up outstanding fish and a heavenly change of pace from crowded resorts.

ORIENTATION & PRACTICAL INFORMATION. Frequent **trains** (2hr., 9 per day, 8.20zł) and **buses** (2hr., 1 per hr., 7.60zł) connect Hel to **Gdynia.** The road is lined with wind-swept dunes and awesome seaside views. The **train station,** as well as the first of the town's two bus stops, is a short walk from **ul. Wiejska,** the main street. Take **ul. Dworcowa** to the right (with your back to the station) as it follows a small park to intersect ul. Wiejska, and make a left to head into town. Hel can also be reached via **boat** from: **Gdańsk** (3hr., 2 per day, round-trip 49zł, students 34zł); **Sopot** (2hr., 4 per day, round-trip 39zł, 28zł); and **Gdynia** (1hr., 7 per day, round-trip 38zł, 28zł). It arrives at Hel's dock on **Bulwar Nadmorski,** a block from ul. Wiejska. When Hel freezes over (Nov.-Mar.), the ferry doesn't run. Tickets (tel. 675 04 37) are sold in the white kiosk by the ferry landing. (Open daily 9am-5pm.) The **post office,** ul. Wiejska 55 (tel. 675 05 50) also **exchanges currency.** (Open June-Aug. M-F 8am-6pm, Sa 9am-1pm, Su 9am-1pm; Sept.-May closed Su; *kantor* open 8-10am and 2:30-6pm). **Postal code:** 84-150. **Phone code:** (0)58.

ACCOMMODATIONS. The cheapest accommodations in Hel are **private rooms.** Look for the *wolne pokoje* signs along the road from the train station through town. There is also a **private accommodations bureau** (tel. 675 09 96), which can arrange a private room (30zł) or stays in a *pensjonat* (80zł). Their office is at ul. Obroncow Helu 7, Apt. #3, but they are most accustomed to dealing with customers by phone (they speak some English). If that plan gets shot to Hel, get in touch with the director of Fishing Museum (Muzeum Rybołówstwa), **Hanna Bulinska,** who may be able to put you up in her **pensjonat,** ul. Plażowa 5 (tel. 675 08 48), a large, white stucco house a few hundred meters west of the museum. (25zł per person.) **Tawerna "U Maćka,"** ul. Wiejska 82 (tel. 675 06 40), has several decent rooms, many with views of the sea. (Doubles 80zł, with bath 100zł; triple 100zł; quad 120zł. Breakfast included.) **Pensjonat Gwiazda Marza,** ul. Lesna 9b (tel. 675 08 59), has beautiful rooms on the way to the beach. (70zł per person.)

POLAND

FOOD. It'll be a cold day in Hel before anyone starves; the town feeds its guests well. Most eateries flank ul. Wiejska. The central **supermarket "Marina,"** ul. Wiejska 70, stocks groceries. (Open M-F 6am-7pm, Sa 6am-3pm, Su 10am-4pm.) Near the ferry landing, **Izdebka,** ul. Wiejska 39, a white-and-brown fisherman's hut built in 1844, sells a variety of fresh fish for 3-10zł. (Open daily 10am-8pm.) If you're in the mood for dessert, stop for coffee (1-2zł) and sweets (2-4zł) at **Maszoperia,** ul. Wiejska 110 (tel. 675 02 97), a 200-year-old hut with a traditional half-door. The name of this coffeehouse means "Fisherman's House" in the Kashubian dialect, but even vegans can enjoy the tiny eatery with its shady yard and homey interior. It's a popular meeting place, and if you ask nicely, they may take musical requests. (Open daily 10am-midnight.) If you feel like pork chops, **Bar Sami Swoi,** ul. Wiejska 117, provides combo meals of various meats and fishes for 9-14zł. (Opens daily at 10am.)

SIGHTS. If, like Odysseus, you arrive in Hel by boat, the first thing you'll see after the harbor is its oldest building. Hel's bells top the red-brick **Church of St. Peter and Paul** (Kościół św. Piotr i Pawla; 1417-32), on Bulwar Nadmorski, which now houses the **Fishing Museum** (Muzeum Rybołówstwa; tel. 675 05 52). The museum displays nets, canoes, boats, and fishing and boat-building techniques of the last thousand years. Check out the fishermen's ice skates, the net-mending needles, and the giant eel-catching combs. The second floor details the development of Hel and describes its role in WWII. For an extra 1zł, climb the **wooden tower,** which commands a magnificent view of the tri-city area, Hel's harbors, and Hel Town. (Open daily 9:30am-6pm. 3zł, students 2zł.)

One of the Baltic Coast's best-kept secrets is the **beach** at the end of ul. Leśna. Take a left off ul. Wiejska onto ul. Leśna, from which a wide footpath continues through a park to the other side of the *mierzeja* (15-20min.). **Ul. Wiejska,** the main artery, has retained much of its old character, thanks in part to **19th-century fishermen's houses** at #29, 33, 39 and 110. These low-set huts are made of pine and bricks, and are also notable for facing the street sideways. Following ul. Wiejska as it turns into ul. Kuracyjna eventually leads to a part of the Hel headland closed to visitors. The **Headland Battery,** site of the Polish defense of Hel at the beginning of WWII, is here. Concrete firing positions attest to the town's military history.

KRYNICA MORSKA

A small, popular seaside resort, Krynica Morska lies on the Curonian Spit (Mierzeja Wiślana), a narrow sandspit that stretches nearly 60km across the Baltic Sea. While the town itself features all the conveniences, comforts, and tackiness that you'd expect from a beach resort, Krynica Morska's setting sets it apart. On one side of town is the magnificent Baltic Sea and a gorgeous beach; just a short walk away is the serene Wiślany lagoon. Between the two, a pleasant pine forest provides shade and good hiking.

ORIENTATION & PRACTICAL INFORMATION. Krynica Morska is 70km east of Gdańsk and less than 20km from the Russian border, which intersects the **Curonian Spit. Buses** travel to and from **Gdańsk** (2hr., 15 per day, 7.60zł) and **Warsaw** (4hr., 2 per day, 40zł). There is also **ferry** service to **Frombork** (90min., 5 per day, round-trip 27zł, students 18zł). The main **bus stop** is on the eastern edge of town, along **ul. Gdańska,** the main thoroughfare. Looking back at where the bus came from, you can see the lagoon on the left; ferries leave from the pier here. There is a **map** of town along the path leading from the bus stop to the lagoon pier. Ul. Gdańska continues ahead through town. To the right, ul. Partowa leads up and over the hill. From its end, various roads and paths lead to the beach, about 10min. from the bus stop. There is a **pharmacy** at ul. Górników 15; take the first right off ul. Partowa when coming from ul. Gdańska and follow the signs. (Open M-F 8am-4pm, Sa 9am-1pm.) The **post office** is at ul. Gdańska 63. (Open M-F 8am-6pm, Sa-Su 9am-3pm.) **Postal code:** 82-120. Telephones are outside the post office and around town. **Phone code:** (0)55.

POLAND

ACCOMMODATIONS & FOOD. The best budget accommodations are **private rooms,** which are plentiful and easy to find; look for the *Wolne Pokoj* and *Zimmer frei* signs along ul. Gdańksa in the western part of town. Another good street to check is the unpaved ul. Rybacka, which runs parallel to ul. Gdańksa along the lagoon. From the bus stop, head west into town and turn left on ul. Bosmariska; Rybacka is the first right. *Pensjonats* offer pleasant and generally inexpensive quarters, but they tend fill up during the summer. **Pensjonat Riwera,** ul. Rybacka 37 (tel. 247 65 71), is family-run and offers 2- to 4-bed dorms with private bath, TV, and lagoon views. (30-40zł per person.) **Gospodarstwo Agroturystyczne Morszczyn,** ul. Krynica 4 (tel. 247 60 55), also has 2- to 4-bed dorms with bath. (25-30zł per person.) Ul. Krynica is a 10min. walk from the bus station, heading west (left) ul. Gdańska.

Krynica Morska is awash with eateries serving cheap and tasty fish, *pierogi*, and other favorites for less than 10zł. Those who lap up tackiness like a kitten does milk can check out **Bar Koga,** right off ul. Gdańska by the bus stop. The bar is impossible to miss: it's aboard a wooden ship "washed ashore." All the usuals (fish, chicken, *pierogi*, etc.) are served (fish 4.50zł per 100g), and patrons are invited to dance, every night and for free.

SIGHTS & ENTERTAINMENT. Krynica Morska is notable mostly for its natural beauty, although the Curonian Spit is historically significant as the route thousands of fleeing Germans took after Königsberg (Kaliningrad) fell to the Red Army in 1945. The **beaches** are the town's main draw. All lie on the Baltic and are quite nice: well-kept and wide with views of pine forests to either side. Right off the beach, numerous **trails** traverse the forest. Most are short and merely connect different parts of town, but they're still a pleasant diversion. Walking by the **lagoon,** with its calm waters and views of the mainland is also worthwhile. During the summer, **Lunapark** arrives to supplement the natural entertainment, offering rides and games. You can find the illustrious amusement park across from the lagoon near the bus stop. At night, many restaurants magically transform into **discos,** and put up tons of posters around town to announce this miraculous fact; just look for signs advertising "Dancing," followed by one to five exclamation points. there is usually no cover, but when there is (5-10zł), beer is included.

MAZURY

East of Pomorze, forested Mazury lives up to its nickname, "land of a thousand lakes." It would not be unfair to add, "and a thousand Germans," as the majority of tourists here are Germans who have come to find their roots in this former Prussian territory. The region is home to about 4000 lakes; the largest, Śniardwy and Mamry, each cover an area of more than 100 square km. The myriad canals, rivers, and streams are ideal for kayaking and sailing. Mrągowo is the last outpost of civilization for tourists venturing out into the wild and beautiful waters.

MRĄGOWO

Tiny, orange-roofed houses speckle the endless lakes and rivers (once part of a Scandinavian glacier) where Germans and other tourists come to boat, fish, kayak, swim, water-bike, water-ski, and ride horses. Known as Sensburg before 1947, Mrągowo (mrawn-GOH-voh) was named for Celesty Mrongowiusz, a patriot who fought the Germans so his countrymen could continue speaking Polish. His descendants have given up the struggle, and now most respond to *deutsch.* Shops and cafes crowd the narrow streets of the town center, but the surrounding hills and valleys swarm with more mosquitoes than tourists.

POLAND

ORIENTATION & PRACTICAL INFORMATION. The **train station** (tel. 741 61 70), on ul. Kolejowa, receives trains from other towns in the Mazury, such as **Olsztyn** (1½hr., 10 per day, 7.40zł), which has a large train station with many connections. To reach town from the Mrągowo train station, turn left on ul. Kolejawa, which runs in front of the station, then right on ul. Skłodowsklej. The **bus station** (tel. 741 32 11; fax 741 32 16) at the end of ul. Skłodowsklej, sends buses to **Warsaw** (4½hr., 7 per day, 27zł) and **Gdańsk** (5hr., 9:30am, 27zł). The station separates **ul. Warszawska,** a leg of Mrągowo's main thoroughfare, from **ul. Wojska Polskiego,** which leads out of town. With your back to the blue Mrągowo sign, bear right on ul. Warszawska to head into town (5min.). A right turn on **ul. Traugutta** drops down to **Jezioro Czos,** the biggest of the five *mrągowski* lakes. Ul. Warszawska becomes **ul. Ratuszowa,** and, then reluctantly becomes ul. Królewiecka. At ul. Ratuszowa 5, the large, wooden archway doors lead to **Mrągowoska Agencja Turystyczna** (tel. 741 81 51), which sells **maps** (5zł; open M-F 9am-1pm and 1:30-5pm, Sa 9am-2pm; some English spoken). For **currency exchange,** try one of the many *kantory* or **Bank Gdański S.A.,** ul. Ratuszowa 6 (tel. 741 29 72; fax 741 29 62), which also cashes traveler's checks for a 0.5% commission (5zł minimum) and gives MC/Visa cash advances. (Open M-F 8am-6pm, Sa 8am-2pm.) As an added bonus, the **24hr. ATM** outside is linked to all major networks and credit cards. The **post office,** ul. Królewiecka 39 (tel. 741 39 73; open M-F 7am-8pm, Sa 9am-2pm), has **phones** outside. **Postal code:** 11-700. **Phone code:** (0)89.

ACCOMMODATIONS & FOOD. The best deal in town is the central and comfortable **Hotel Garnizonowy,** ul. Kopernika 1 (tel. 741 22 11). From the bus station, turn left onto ul. Wojska Polskiego; Kopernika is the first left. (Singles 45zł; doubles 70zł, with bath 100zł.) The summer-only **Youth Hostel,** ul. Wojska Polskiego 2 (tel. 741 27 12; fax 741 24 61), right across from the bus station, is usually empty. Old but pleasant 1- to 4-bed dorms feature faded paintings and thriving plants. The showers in the basement are a little rustic. (14zł per person, students 9zł, non-students under 26 12zł. Sheets 7zł. Reception 6-10am and 5-10pm.) The simple yet clean **Hotel Meltur,** ul. Sienkiewicza 16 (tel. 741 59 00), has singles (48zł), small doubles (64zł), and large doubles with fridge (75zł). All rooms have private bath and TV, and all prices include breakfast. From the bus station, turn left on ul. Wojska Polskiego and then right on ul. Sienkiewicza (10min.).

Bars, snack shops, and ice cream joints pepper the town's main thoroughfare. **Biedronka** grocery store, ul. Skłodowskiej 1A, is adorned with giant lady bugs. (Open M-F 7am-8pm, Sa 8am-8pm, Su 9am-3pm.) Mrągowo's premier restaurant, **Restauracja Fregata** (tel. 741 22 44), just left off ul. Ratuszowa near ul. Dolny Zaułek, serves international and local cuisine. For a taste of the region, try the saucy *schab po mazursku* (Mazurian pork) for 13zł. (Entrees 6-19zł. Open daily 11am-10pm.) Follow the delicious smells wafting outside **Pizzeria "Margarita,"** ul. Królewiecka 5 (tel. 741 48 88), and dig into their pizza. (Small—plenty for one—7.50-9zł; large 9.50-13zł. Open M-F 10am-11pm.)

SIGHTS & ENTERTAINMENT. The last weekend in July (or first weekend in August), an amphitheater on the shore of Jezioro Czos holds a popular **Country Picnic Festival.** The main **beaches**—Plaża Orbisu, packed with canoeists, and Plaża Miejska—are both on Jezioro Czos. The coolest late-night draw in town **Bar Lasagna,** ul. Warszawska 7a (tel. 741 21 15), where locals gather until the wee hours to eat spaghetti (6zł) or *kiełbasa* (3.50zł), washing it all down with Polish beer (3.50zł; open daily 11am-1am). Local hipsters gather at **Milano,** ul. Królewiecka 53 (tel. 741 20 41), a disco that plays pop, rock, and—yes—*Polish* hip-hop.

NEAR MRĄGOWO: ŚWIĘTA LIPKA

During the Middle Ages, a Prussian tribal leader pardoned by the ruling Teutonic knights expressed his gratitude by placing the Virgin Mary's likeness in a local linden tree. Rumors of miraculous healing and epiphany soon attracted pilgrims to the so-called **Święta Lipka** (Holy Linden)—so many that the Teutons built a shrine to the arbor in 1320. Two hundred years later, the fickle knights switched religions, razed the Catholic shrine, and slowed the flow of believers by installing gallows (bodies included) around the tree. The gallows have since rotted away, and nothing deters the annual flocks of Germans from visiting the **Sanctuary of Our Lady** (Sanktuarium Maryjne). Amid lakes, craft shops, and a blossoming cemetery, the shrine guards an interior as breathtaking as its surroundings. Biblical paintings and a re-creation of the miraculous linden adorn the interior. Check out the elaborate, hand-forged gate and the frescoes inside the cloisters and church. The beautiful baroque organ is noteworthy for its mechanized ornaments: as the music picks up, glistening suns start swirling, baby-faced angels shake their golden bells, the archangel strums her *balalaika,* and golden trumpeters accompany the organ music. (Concerts June-Aug. F 8pm; M-Sa 7 performances per day, Su 5 per day.)

GETTING THERE. Five **buses** make the 30min. trip to Święta Lipka from **Mrągowo** on weekdays (3.60zł); two run on weekends. If you miss one of these, take the bus to **Kętrzyn** (40min., 16 per day, 4zł), and catch one of the many buses that run to Święta Lipka from there.

PODLASIE

Poland affords maximum environmental protection to this small, northeastern region, "the green lungs of Poland." Just a 2hr. train ride from Warsaw, Podlasie is decidedly rural. Wide-open fields are dotted with Poland's few Russian Orthodox villages and sluiced by the meandering Bug and Narew rivers. Białowieża Forest (Puszcza Białowieska), once the favorite hunting ground of Polish kings, is now a national park and the domain of the scarce European bison. Białystok, northwest of the preserve, is the region's hip capital.

BIAŁYSTOK

Only 60km from the Belarussian border, Białystok is a magnet for hawkers from Poland, Belarus, Lithuania, and Russia who come to stock up on Polish goods at one of the largest markets in Eastern Europe. A healthy influx of local students adds a cosmopolitan flair to this busy, multilingual, regional capital. Purported to be the birthplace of the famous *biały* roll, Białystok is the natural launching point for excursions to nearby Tykocin and to the scenic Białystok National Park (Białowieski Park Narodowy).

ORIENTATION

The downtown is organized along **ul. Lipowa,** which leads from the **bus** and **train stations** east to **Rynek Kościuszki,** the city center, and then on to **pl. Branickich.** If arriving by train, cross the tracks via the overpass leading to the bus station. Here, with your back to the bus terminal, go left on **ul. Bohaterów Monte Cassino** and turn right onto **ul. Świętego Rocha;** this leads directly to ul. Lipowa. Follow this street east to the *rynek* (15min.). Other major roads are **ul. Sienkiewicza,** which heads northeast and south from the *rynek*, and **ul. Piłsudskiego,** which parallels ul. Lipowa.

PRACTICAL INFORMATION

Trains: Ul. Kolejowa 1 (tel. 910). To: **Warsaw** (2½hr., 12 per day, 25zł); **Gdańsk** (8hr., 2 per day, 37zł); **Vilnius** (9hr., 1 per day, 54zł); **St. Petersburg** (26hr., 1 per day, 200zł); **Moscow** (27hr., 1 per day, 230zł); and **Kraków** (8hr., 1 per day, 35zł).

Buses: Ul. Bohaterów Monte Cassino 8 (tel. 936). To: **Białowieża** (2½hr., 2 per day, 11zł); **Warsaw** on Polski Express (3½hr., 4 per day, 19zł); **Mrągowo** (4hr., 2 per day, 22zł); **Minsk** (9hr., 2 per day, 40zł); and **Vilnius** (9hr., 1 per day, 40zł).

Local Transportation: Buy bus tickets at kiosks throughout the city. 1.40zł per ride, students 0.70zł. Baggage requires its own ticket. 70zł fine for riding ticketless.

Tourist Offices: Orbis, ul. Rynek Kościuszki 13 (tel. 742 16 27). Provides Western Union, MC/Visa cash advances, and currency exchange. Sells international train and bus tickets. Open M-F 9am-5pm, Sa 9am-2pm. **PTTK,** ul. Lipowa 18 (tel. 752 25 02 and 752 30 05), has a train schedule and can direct you to budget accommodations. Open M-F 8am-4pm.

Budget Travel: Almatur, ul. Zwierzyniecka 12 (tel. 742 82 09). Helps with student travel and accommodations. Open M-F 8am-4pm.

Financial Services: *Kantory* flank ul. Lipowa. **Bank PKO S.A.,** ul. Sienkiewicza 40 (tel. 743 61 00), cashes all major brands of **traveler's checks** for a 1% commission. Open M-F 8am-6pm, Sa 8am-2pm. There is a 24hr. Visa **ATM** at Rynek Kościuszki 16 and a MC ATM across the street.

Luggage Storage: At the train station, next to the toilets. 3zł. Open daily 8am-6pm.

English Bookstore: Empik, Rynek Kościuszki 6. Small but adequate collection of fiction, non-fiction, and magazines. Open M-F 9:30am-6:30pm, Sa 9:30am-3pm.

24hr. Pharmacy: Apteka Cito, ul. Skłodowskiej 4.

Post Office: Ul. Warszawska 10. Open M-F 8am-8pm, Sa 8am-2pm. A much smaller but more convenient branch is at Rynek Kościuszki 13 (tel. 742 42 30 and 742 28 12). Open M-F 8am-8pm, Sa 10am-4:30pm. **Postal code:** 15-900.

Internet Access: Internet Club Virus, ul. Biatówny 9/1 (tel. 732 75 76; email biuro@virus.com.pl), just off the Rynek. 3zł per 30min.; 5zł per hr.; 7.50zł per 90min. Call ahead weekend nights. Open daily 10am-10pm.

Telephones: At the post office.

Phone Code: (0)85.

ACCOMMODATIONS

For private rooms and pensions, **PTTK** (see **Practical Information,** above) directs tourists to the city's best steals.

Youth Hostel (HI), al. Piłsudskiego 7b (tel. 752 42 50). Bus #20 or 100 from the train station. Or, turn left on Św. Rocha, veer left when it meets Lipowa, and turn right onto al. Piłsudskiego. In a wooden house behind gray apartment buildings (10min.). Cramped-but-clean rooms with inch-thick mattresses. The director's understanding of the 10pm "curfew" allows for sharing drinks with guests into the wee hours. Sheets 4zł. 6- to 14-bed dorms 12.50zł, student members 7.50zł, non-members 17zł, student non-members 10zł.

Hotel Rubin, ul. Warszawska 7 (tel. 777 23 35), in a stately old building. Walk 15min. down ul. Lipowa, turn left on ul. Skłodowskiej, turn onto ul. Warszawska, and go 1 block past the park on your right. Or, take bus #2 or 21 from the train station and get off at the first stop on ul. Warszawska (15min.). Big rooms with tall ceilings. Doubles 60zł, with bath 120zł; triples 75zł, 150zł; 2-person apartment 140zł; 3-person 200zł.

Internat Nauczycielski, ul. Sienkiewicza 86 (tel. 732 36 64). 3 lengthy blocks up the street from Hotel Rubin. Enter through the courtyard in back. Rooms sparkle. Tends to fill up Fridays and Saturdays, when pedagogical students come to town to study for exams. Negotiable 10pm curfew. 2- or 3-bed dorms 20zł; 5- or 6-bed dorms 18zł.

FOOD

The city's best eateries are on **ul. Lipowa** and around **Rynek Kościuszki. Supersam,** ul. Skłodowskiej 16 (tel. 742 06 41), is a supermarket true to its name. (Open M-F 6am-9pm, Sa 7am-9pm, Su 7am-6pm. MC/Visa.)

Bar El'Jot, ul. Starobojarska 25 (tel. 732 63 16). A 10min. walk up ul. Sienkiewicza, on the right side. Small neighborhood haunt with a quiet terrace. More of a bar at night. Tasty entrees–including a powerful pepper-steak–4.50-8zł. Open M-Sa 11am-2am, Su 1pm-midnight.

Ananda Bar Wegetariański, ul. Warszawska 30 (tel. 741 33 36). 2 blocks past Hotel Rubin, Ananda is a much-needed respite for veggie lovers. If the Polish-only menu leaves you befuddled, rest assured that it's 100% vegetarian. Soups are particularly good. Full meals 10-20zł. Open M-F 11am-10pm, Sa-Su 1-10pm.

Savona Pizza, ul. Rynek Kościuszki 10 (tel. 743 51 35). Schizo romantic hole-in-the-wall pizza parlor features candlelit tables *and* music videos. Delectable pizza 5-14zł; spaghetti 6-9zł. Open M-Th and Su 9am-midnight, F-Sa 9am-2am.

SIGHTS

Though the interior of **Branickich Palace** (Pałac) is closed to tourists, this 18th-century mansion, which once belonged to a powerful aristocratic family, is worth a visit. Easily the most impressive building in Białystok, it is a Baroque reminder of the city's glorious past. Today, the Versailles-like structure is a bustling medical school. The **palace park and gardens,** which host occasional concerts, are open to the public. The entrance is just past Rynek Kościuszki across from pl. Jana Pawła II. (Open daily May-Sept. 6am-10pm; Oct.-Apr. 6am-6pm.)

The **Military Museum** (Muzeum Wojska), ul. Kilińskiego 7 (tel. 741 54 48), adjacent to the palace, collects Polish weapons, military dress, and historical records. The rooms bristle with cruel daggers, improbably huge swords, and the weapons of Poland's vanquished. The centerpiece is an exhibition of items relating to WWII, specifically the German march across Poland and the subsequent defeat of the Nazis. The collection includes posters, placards, and captured German materials. (Open Tu-Su 9am-5pm. 4zł, students 2zł.)

An architectural and historical curiosity stands a few paces down ul. Lipowa at the end of the *rynek*—a small **parish church** connected to a giant **cathedral.** In tsarist times, the Poles were forbidden to build any new Catholic churches. Their solution: attach a cathedral to the old church, even if the structures clashed. The inside warrants a look, too, but if you want to attend mass, arrive early or you'll be praying on asphalt and listening to the homily from the megaphones mounted outside.

A short walk to the west of the palace, the *rynek's* **town hall** *(ratusz)* originally served as a trade center. In 1940, it was demolished by the Russians, who planned to put a monument to Stalin in its place. The statue never materialized and the site remained vacant until the present building was constructed in 1958. Inside, the ground floor of the **Okręgowe Museum** (tel. 742 14 73) contains a gallery of Polish painting with a small but impressive collection of Neoclassical, Romantic, Impressionist, and Symbolist paintings. The lower level of the museum hosts a series of rotating exhibits. (Open Tu-Su 10am-5pm. 4zł, students 2zł.)

ENTERTAINMENT

For **nightlife**, either head to one of the watering holes around Rynek Kościuszki where locals meet for cheap beer and conversation, or ask local students where they like to hang. **Jazz Club Odeon,** ul. Akademicka 10/1 (tel. 742 49 88), is the hippest place in town. Enjoy the nightly jazz concert from the balcony over the stage, or take in the evening air out on the terrace. From the *rynek*, go right on ul. Sienkiewicza and left on ul. Akademicka. Odeon is hidden across from the palace garden. (Beer 3.50zł, whiskey and Coke 6.50zł. Jazz concerts daily 8-11pm. Open daily noon-2am.) If you feel like grinding to techno, visit **Klub Muzyczny Metro,** ul. Białówny 9A (tel. 732 41 54), off ul. Malmeda. (Beer 4zł. Open daily 6pm-4am.) For the latest films, head to **Kino Ton,** ul. Rynek Kościuszki 2 (tel./fax 743 53 82), which features English-language films with Polish subtitles. (Open daily noon-midnight. 11zł.) **Kino Pokaj,** ul. Lipowa 14, usually screens different films. (11zł.)

POLAND

NEAR BIAŁYSTOK: TYKOCIN

For a sobering reminder of Poland's Jewish past, visit tiny Tykocin, home to one of the most beautiful synagogues in Poland. Turn left from the central square onto ul. Złota (which becomes ul. Piłsudskiego) to find the renowned **synagogue.** Hebrew prayers and ornamental designs scroll around all four walls of the large 17th-century interior. Glass cases in front protect one of the synagogue's copies of the Torah. The synagogue once served the 2300 Jewish residents of Tykocin, almost 70% of the village's population. After the Nazis killed all but 150 of Tykocin's Jews, the synagogue was abandoned; restoration began in 1977. Today, not a single Jew is left in Tykocin; the last one left for Israel several years ago. The synagogue also exhibits Judaica—skillfully crafted silver menorahs and paintings chronicling Jewish struggles. Admission covers entrance both to the temple and to the **regional museum** next door. Housed in the Talmudic House, the museum features an interesting array of 17th- to 19th-century Polish household wares and visiting exhibitions. (Open Tu-Su 10am-5pm. 5zł, students 3zł.) On the other side of town, just past the *rynek*, stands the colossal **Holy Trinity Church** (Kościół św. Trójcy), an 18th-century structure whose two enormous towers loom over the market square.

GETTING THERE. Hop on a Tykocin bus from **Białystok** (1hr., 21 per day, 4.90zł).

NEAR BIAŁYSTOK: BIAŁOWIESKI PARK NARODOWY

Białowieża Primeval Forest (Puszcza Białowieska), a natural treasure of towering trees and Eastern European bison, sprawls out over oceans of flatland. Exploration begins in the sleepy town of **Białowieża.** Popular with Polish tourists, the preserve forms a small part of the park. A well-marked 4-5km path from the park entrance leads to the preserve (bike rental available; see below), but **only guided tours** (see below) may enter. About 250 of the lumbering bison remain; many were wiped out by hungry soldiers during WWI. If you don't want to pay the price for a tour of the preserve, stroll around the palace park into the **Natural History Museum** (Muzeum Przynodniczo-Leśne), next to Hotel Iwa. The museum houses exhibits on the history and topography of the region and displays a large number of stuffed local mammals and big, pointy teeth. (Open daily 9am-5pm.)

GETTING THERE. There is one **bus** that goes straight to **Białowieża** from **Białystok,** and it leaves at 6:30am (3hr., 11.10zł). An alternative is to take one of the frequent buses to **Hajnówka** (2hr., 24 per day, 7.10zł) and change there for **Białowieża** (45min., 8 per day, 3.90zł). Leave very early, as there may be a wait between buses. The main bus stop is not the final one. Once the bus reaches Białowieża, get off as you pass the post office and park gate on the left. Through the palace park entrance and uphill is **Hotel-Restauracja Iwa** (tel. (085) 681 23 85; fax 681 22 60), home of **Guliwer tourist office** (tel. 123 68 25), which arranges tours of the park. Both will re-open in late 1999 after the hotel completes renovations. Next door, **Dom Wycieczkowy PTTK** (tel. 681 25 05; email pttkbialowieza@sitech.pl) offers 3hr. group **tours.** (84zł for group of 25. English tour 105zł.)

ROMANIA (ROMÂNIA)

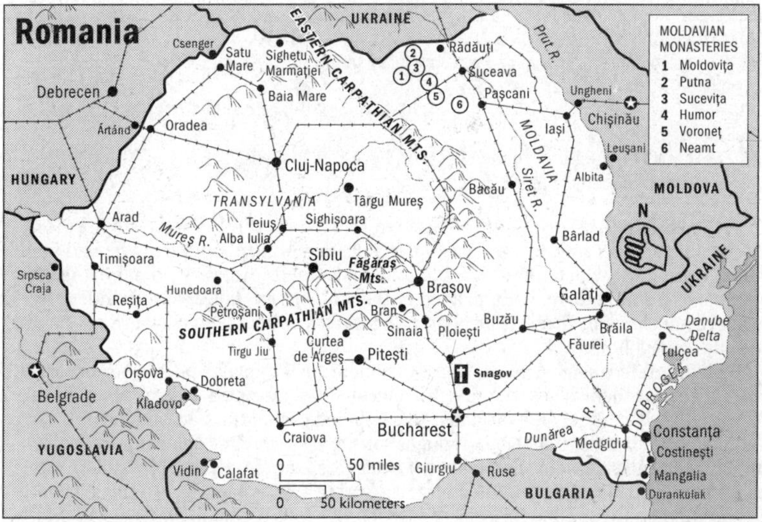

US$1 = 16,325 LEI (ROL)	**1000 LEI = US$0.06**
CDN$1 = 11,026 LEI	**1000 LEI = CDN$0.09**
UK£1 = 26,689 LEI	**1000 LEI = UK£0.04**
IR£1 = 21,960 LEI	**1000 LEI = IR£0.05**
AUS$1 = 10,674 LEI	**1000 LEI = AUS$0.09**
NZ$1 = 8697 LEI	**1000 LEI = NZ$0.12**
SAR1 = 2682 LEI	**1000 LEI = SAR0.37**
DM1 = 8839 LEI	**1000 LEI = DM0.11**

PHONE CODES Country code: **40.** International dialing prefix: **00.**

Romania, devastated by the lengthy reign of Communist dictator Nicolae Ceauşescu, now suffers under a government incapable of bridging its gaps with the West. The resulting state of flux has left the country disheartened, as the tourist industry flounders by with sights packaged far less smoothly than those of its more Westernized neighbors. Bucharest, the center of the country's political and cultural existence, has been swallowed by concrete apartment blocks and sterile Communist squares. Visitors who manage to avoid the beaten "Dracula" path and talk to common villagers, however, will discover that Romania runs far deeper than Ceauşescu's effects. The joy of travel here comes in peeling the layers off to the nation's recent history to find what lies underneath. Romanians go out of their way to make visitors feel at home, and travelers daring enough to explore will find a dynamic people eager to grow and hopeful in spite of their past.

LIFE & TIMES

HISTORY

The **Romanian** ethnographic tree has its roots in the **Thracian** tribes that settled in the region as early as 2000 BC. Contact with Greeks and then the Romans followed; the

HIGHLIGHTS OF ROMANIA

■ Explore the expanses of greenery, surprisingly good museums, and historical monuments of vast and hectic **Bucharest** (p. 506).
■ One of Romania's oldest cities, **Sibiu** is a portal to adventure in the Transylvanian Alps (p. 528).
■ Count Dracula's real castle and its gruesome history loom over the otherwise-peaceful **Curtea de Argeş** (p. 518).
■ After viewing the colorful frescoes of the secluded **Bukovina monasteries,** you *will* believe (p. 542).
■ The streets of tiny **Târgu Jiu** are blessedly lined with impressive works by internationally renowned modern sculptor Constantin Brancuşi (p. 530).

latter considered the flourishing Thracian (Dacian to the Romans) civilization threatening enough to warrant invasion. Hence, the 'Roman' in Romanian, and the vulgar Latin from which the Romanian tongue descends. Another primary component came from the **Slavs** who invaded in the 8th century. **Bulgarians** provided the final crucial element, Eastern Orthodox Christianity, which better integrated them with their neighbors.

With the ethnic melange more or less complete, the Romanian people began carving a space for themselves; the first Romanian state, **Wallachia**, was established in the early 1300s. The second, **Moldavia**, was founded east of the Carpathians in 1349. The fledgling states had it rough, though, constantly defending against invasion by the **Ottoman Turks**. Moldavia's **Ştefan cel Mare** (Stephen the Great; 1457-1504) was most successful in warding off their attacks. During his 47-year rule, he built 42 monasteries and churches, one for each of his victories (see p. 512, 517). Alas, with Stefan died successful resistance, as Moldavia and Wallachia became Turkish vassals.

For the next four centuries, Austria-Hungary, Russia, Turkey and the Polish-Lithuanian Commonwealth fought for control of the region. Internally, there were fleeting successes at creating a unified Romania. **Mihai Viteazul** (Michael the Brave) tried in 1599 when he invaded Moldavia and Transylvania, but Polish, Hungarian, and Ottoman attacks left Mihai dead and the country in tatters. Moldavia and Wallachia reunited in 1859 by electing **Alexandru Cuza** prince. This time, the union outlasted its ruler. **King Carol I** stamped out corruption, built the first railroads, and strengthened the army that, in 1877, finally won independence from Turkey (see **Constanţa: Sights,** p. 546). On the heels of Austria-Hungary's defeat in **WWI,** Romania managed to double its territory, gaining Transylvania, Bukovina and Bessarabia (modern-day **Moldova**). The population doubled, too, but expansion brought new minority groups and ethnic tensions.

The **German-Soviet Non-Aggression Pact** subjected Romania to a fate of its neighbors to the northwest, as it lost its new territory to the Axis powers. Forced to choose between the USSR and Germany, Romania's dictator, **General Antonescu,** hoping the Nazis would preserve an independent Romania, chose the latter. In 1944, **King Mihai** orchestrated a coup and attempted to surrender to the Allies. **The Big Three** had already decided Romania's fate, however, and the Soviets moved in and proclaimed the **Romanian People's Republic** on December 30, 1947.

Opposition was violently suppressed in the postwar era. More than 200,000 Romanians died in the purges of the 1950s alone, and farms were forcibly collectivized. In 1965, **Nicolae Ceauşescu** ascended to the top of the Communist Party. Although his attempts to distance Romania from Moscow's influence won praise from the West, his ruthless domestic policies were hardly laudable. His industrialization policies created useless, polluting factories. He exported domestic staples to cover the country's foreign debt. The average Romanian lacked food, heat, and even electricity at times. In the 80s, Ceauşescu began to "systematize" villages—demolishing them and transplanting the peasants to cinder-block ghettos.

By the late 80s, Ceauşescu had whipped Romania into a police state, but rebellion seethed under the surface. In 1989 a **revolution** as ruthless as the dictator it would overthrow erupted. What began as a minor event in Timişoara, when the dreaded **Securitate** (Secret Police) arrested a popular Hungarian priest, soon ripped through the country. Clashes with security forces in Bucharest on December 21-22 brought thousands of protesters to the streets. Ceauşescu and his wife were arrested, tried, and executed, all on Christmas Day.

The enthusiasm that followed these December days didn't last, though, as power was seized by **Ion Iliescu's National Salvation Front,** composed largely of former communists. Iliescu was himself a high-ranking communist official whom Ceauşescu pushed into minor positions because of his pro-Russian leanings. Despite his past, Iliescu won the 1990 presidential elections with 70% of the vote and began the moderate reforms on which he had run. In June 1990, Iliescu garnered international condemnation after calling on miners to repress student demonstrations in Bucharest; for three days, the miners terrorized the city, beating anyone resembling a protester. Revolution, it seemed, had changed little.

ROMANIA TODAY

In the first democratic transfer of power in Romania's history, **Emil Constantinescu** succeeded Ion Illiescu in November 1996. His **Romanian Democratic Coalition** (RDC) promised reforms, but has spent most of its time settling disputes among its member parties. Two years and two cabinets later, an E.U. report blasted the government for making no economic progress whatsoever. Nonetheless, the crisis in **Kosovo** has given President Constantinescu a chance to clamor anew for the **E.U. and NATO memberships** that were denied his country in 1997. Meanwhile, the **Hungarian Democratic Union in Romania**, feeling neglected by its coalition-mates, has taken the opportunity to accuse the government of "bloodless" ethnic cleansing of its constituents and other minorities. The intra-coalition bickering has led to apathy among voters, as the RDC loses public support to **right-wing nationalist parties**.

LITERATURE & ARTS

The earliest literary activity in the region actually stands apart from the national literature; the Roman poet **Ovid** wrote his last works while exiled near what is now Constanţa (see p. 546). The Romanian tradition has its roots in translations of Slavonia religious texts in the 15th century, a project that culminated with first Romanian translation of the **Bible** in 1688. Around this time the first Romanian poetry, written by a theologian named **Dosoftei** appeared in print, courtesy of a press in Poland. The 1700s brought Ottoman oppression, and it was not until the end of that century that literature could once again bloom. Much of the credit for this resurgence goes to the **Văcărescu family**: grandfather **Ienachita** wrote the first Romanian grammar, father **Alecu** wrote love poetry, and son **Iancu's** verse was so splendid that he, not his dad, is considered the father of Romanian poetry.

The first half of the 19th century saw the cultivation of new genres, and **Grigore Alexandrescu's** fables and satires, inspired by French literature, stand out among them. Building on these writers of the 1840s, the next generation—clustering around the literary magazine ***Junimea***—penned the great classics of Romanian literature. Emulating German culture, their works combined cosmopolitan awareness and a preoccupation with Romanian national identity. **Mihai Eminescu** (see p. 513 and p. 541), the Romanian national poet—often called the "Great Lost Romantic"—embodied **Romanticism** at its peak. His monumental poem "Luceafârul" drew on medieval history and folklore to create a fantasy world that the poet himself seemed to prefer to reality; he spent his last years in a mental asylum. The Junimea generation also fostered **Ion Luca Caragiale**, famed writer of satire and drama, and the storyteller **Ion Creangă** (see p. 513).

The interwar years saw the rise of the socially conscious novel. **Liviu Rebreanu** wrote of rural uprisings and the Great War, while **Mihail Sadoveanu** wrote on the place of the peasant in society. The lyric poem, Romania's strongest tradition, was also well-represented by the mathematically precise verse of **Ion Barbu,** and by **Tudor Arghezi,** heir to Eminescu's poetic legacy.

The end of WWII brought Nicole Ceaşescu's communist regime and the strictures of **Socialist Realism.** Arghezi was denied the right to publish but still managed to produce *1907*, one of his most mature works. **Geo Bogza** and **Mihail Beniuc** were among the prominent adherents to socialist realism, composing works that glorified the worker's state and its accomplishments. Some Romanian-born artists and scholars sought freedom in other lands and languages; absurdist dramatist **Eugène Ionesco** and religious scholar **Mircea Eliade** are the most prominent.

Folk arts also suffered under Ceauşescu. Nonetheless, some traditional crafts persist, to international renown. Most notable are the traditional crafts of **painting on glass** and the elaborate decoration of **easter eggs**. Folk music has found new life in the work of such contemporary composers as **Georges Enesco.** In the visual arts, **Constantin Brâncuşi** is the preeminent Romanian export and also one of the greatest modernist sculptors of the 20th century (see p. 530).

READING LIST

The most easily digestible primer to Romanian culture can be found in the verbosely titled *Taste of Romania: Its Cookery and Glimpses of its History, Folklore, Art and Poetry*. Acclimate yourself to the local proclivity for larded pork and sample the illustrations, folklore, and poetry interspersed throughout. For a more substantial and intriguing approach to said poetry, pick up *When the Tunnels Meet*, an anthology of recent Romanian verse translated by Irish poets, including Nobel laureate Seamus Heaney. For art lovers, *Constantin Brăncuşi: 1876-1957* is one of the best books on the sculptor and has lots of pretty pictures to boot. Finally, in keeping with *Let's Go's* mission to debunk cultural myths, we recommend *Dracula, Prince of Many Faces: His Life and Times* by Radu R. Florescu, for the real story of Vlad Ţepeş.

FACTS AND FIGURES

- **Capital:** Bucharest
- **Population:** 22,571,827
- **Land Area:** 237,500km^2
- **Geography:** Mountains
- **Language:** Romanian
- **Religions:** 86% Orthodox
- **GDP per capita:** US$1,379
- **Major Exports:** Textiles, minerals

ROMANIA ESSENTIALS

Americans do not need visas for stays of up to 30 days. Citizens of Australia, Canada, Ireland, New Zealand, South Africa, and the U.K. all need visas to enter Romania. Single-entry visas (US$35) are good for 60 days, multiple-entry visas (US$70) for 180 days, and transit visas (US$25) for four days. Obtain a visa at a Romanian embassy (see **Essentials: Embassies & Consulates,** p. 13) or at the border for no additional fee. To apply, submit a passport, payment by money order, and a letter stating the purpose of your visit and your approximate dates of departure and arrival. Get a visa extension at a local police station.

GETTING THERE

You can **fly** into Bucharest on Air France, Alitalia, British Airways, Delta, Lufthansa, or TAROM. **TAROM** (Romanian Airlines) is in the process of updating its aging fleet; it flies direct from Bucharest to New York, Chicago, and major European cities. The renovation of Bucharest's Otopeni International Airport has improved its notoriously bad ground services, but the airport is still far from ideal.

Trains head daily to Western Europe via Budapest. There are also direct trains to and from Chişinău, Moscow, Prague, Sofia, Vienna, Belgrade, and Warsaw. To buy **international tickets** in Romania, go to the **CFR** (Che-Fe-Re) office in larger towns. Budapest-bound trains leave Romania through either Arad or Oradea; when you buy your ticket, you'll need to specify where you want to exit, and they'll want to

PRIMARY BORDER CROSSINGS. Romanian visas can be obtained at any of the following border crossings for the standard visa price. There is no additional fee for crossing a Romanian border. The easiest means of crossing a Romanian border is to take a direct bus or train from Bucharest to the capital city of the neighboring country or region.

Bulgaria: Mangalia, ROM/Durankulak, BUL; connects the Romanian Black Sea Coast (p. 545) with the Bulgarian Black Sea Coast (p. 120). Giurgiu, ROM/Ruse, BUL; connects Southern Romania with Northern Bulgaria (p. 127). Calofat, ROM/Vidin, BUL; connects Southern Romania with Northwestern Bulgaria.

Hungary: Satu Mare, ROM/Csenger, HUN; connects Northern Romania (p. 537) with Nyíregyháza, HUN and Northern Hungary (p. 332). Oradea, ROM (p. 527)/Ártánd, HUN; connects the Western Carpathians (p. 524) with Debrecen, HUN (p. 322) and the Great Plain (p. 322). Arad, ROM/Szeged, HUN (p. 325) via Nădlac, ROM; connects Timişoara, ROM (p. 524) and Western Carpathians (p. 524) with Hungary's Great Plain (p. 322).

Moldova: Albita, ROM/Leuşeni, MOL; connects Iaşi (p. 538), Romanian Moldova and Bukovina (p. 538), and the Black Sea Coast (p. 545) with Chişinău (p. 393).

Ukraine: Suceava, ROM (p. 541)/Chernivtsi, UKR; connects Romanian Moldova (p. 538) with Western Ukraine (p. 767).

Yugoslavia: Timişoara, ROM (p. 524)/Srpsca Crnja, YUG; connects the Western Carpathians (p. 524) with Novi Sad and the Vojvodina region. Dobreta, ROM/Kladovo, YUG; connects the Transylvanian Alps (p. 527) with Niš and Serbia.

see your papers. An ISIC might get you a 50% discount, but don't count on it; technically, student discounts are for Romanians only.

Buses connect major cities in Romania to Athens, Istanbul, Prague, and various cities in Western Europe. Since plane and train tickets to Romania are often expensive, buses are a good—if slow—option. It is generally cheapest to take a domestic train to a city near the border and catch an international bus from there. Inquire at tourist agencies about timetables and tickets, but buying tickets straight from the carrier saves you from paying commission.

GETTING AROUND

CFR sells domestic **train** tickets up to 24hr. before the train's departure. After that, only train stations sell tickets. The timetable *Mersul Trenurilor* is useful in forming a plan of attack (L12,000; in English). Schedule info is available at tel. 221 in most cities. **Interrail** is accepted; **Eurail** is not.

There are four types of trains: *InterCity* (indicated by an "IC" on timetables and at train stations), *rapid* (in green), *accelerat* (red), and *personal* (black). International trains (often blue) are usually indicated by "i" on timetables. *InterCity* trains stop only at major cities such as Bucharest, Cluj-Napoca, Iaşi, and Timişoara, and have three-digit numbers. *Rapid* trains (also 3 digits) are the next fastest; *accelerat* trains have four digits starting with "1" and are slower and dirtier. The sluggish and decrepit *personal* have four digits and stop at every station. It's wise to take the fastest train you can, most often *accelerat*. Also opt for **first class** (*clasa-întîi;* wagons marked with a "1" on the side; 6 people per compartment) instead of **second class** (8 people per compartment); what you get for the extra money is well worth it. If you take second class in the summer, be prepared to spend your time hanging out in the hall with everyone else looking for some cool air. Only *personal* are well ventilated. If taking an **overnight train,** shell out for first class in a *vagon de dormit* (sleeping carriage). For holiday excursions or summer trips to the Black Sea, try to purchase tickets at least a day in advance.

Use the local **bus** system only when trains are not available. Buses are more expensive, but still as packed and poorly ventilated. Look for signs for the *autogară* (bus station) in each town.

Hitchhiking, although popular, remains risky; *Let's Go* does not recommend it. A wave of the hand, rather than a thumb, is the recognized sign. Some Romanians drive vans that become unofficial buses along popular routes. Big trucks, often traveling long distances, have also been reported to take passengers. The best places to hitch are at bus stops outside cities. A local Romanian, likely just as fed up with the transportation system as you, might help flag down a car and negotiate for you. Drivers generally expect a payment similar to the price of a train ticket for the distance traveled, although some kind souls will take you for free or accept whatever you can afford. Never hitchhike at night.

TOURIST SERVICES

ONT (National Tourist Office) used to be one of the most corrupt government agencies in Romania. Times have changed, but while you won't have to bribe anyone, the information you get will not necessarily be correct. ONT also moonlights as a **private tourist agency,** providing travel packages for a commission. Hotels and restaurants open and close all the time, and prices change with dizzying speed; double-check all important data. Get friendly locals to help you.

MONEY

The Romanian unit of currency is the *leu*, plural **lei** (abbreviated L). The banknotes are L500, L1000, L5000, L10,000, L50,000, and the new L100,000. While many establishments accept US$ or DM, you should pay for everything in *lei* to avoid being ripped off and to save your hard currency for bribes and emergencies.

Because many Romanians stave off the inflation demons by carrying dollars or Deutchmarks, **private exchange bureaus** litter the country; unfortunately, not many take **credit cards** or **traveler's checks.** Most banks will cash traveler's checks in dolalrs or Deutchmarks, then exchange them for *lei*, accumulating high fees in the process. Take the 20min. to walk around and see the going rates before plunking down your nice, reliable native bills. dollars and Deutchmarks are preferred, although other Western currencies can usually be exchanged somewhere. Always keep receipts for money exchanges. **ATMs,** which generally accept Cirrus, Plus, MC, and Visa and give *lei* at reasonable rates, are rare outside major cities.

ROMANIA

COMMUNICATION

Almost all public phones are orange and accept **phone cards,** although a few archaic blue phones take L500 coins. Buy L50,000 phone cards at telephone offices, major Bucharest Metro stops, and some post offices. Rates run L10,000 per min. to neighboring countries, L18,000 per min. to most of Europe, and L30,000 per min. to the U.S. International access numbers include: **AT&T Direct,** tel. 018 00 42 88; **BT Direct,** tel. 018 00 44 44; **Canada Direct,** tel. 018 00 50 00; **MCI WorldPhone,** tel. 018 00 18 00; and **Sprint,** tel. 018 00 08 77. They aren't kidding when they write "not available from all phones;" wait until major cities to call home. **Local calls** cost L500-1500 and can be made from any phone. Dial several times before giving up; a busy signal may just indicate a connection problem. It may be necessary to make a phone call *prin commandă;* that is, with the help of the operator at the telephone office, which, of course, takes longer and costs more. At the phone office, write down the destination, duration, and phone number for your call. Pay up front, and always ask for the rate per minute. At the post office, request *par avion* for **airmail,** which takes 10-19 days to reach the U.S.

LANGUAGE

Romanian is a Romance language; those familiar with French, Italian, Spanish, or Portuguese can usually decipher public signs. In Transylvania, **German** and **Hungarian** are widely spoken. Throughout the country, **French** is a common second language for the older generation, **English** for the younger. English-Romanian dictionaries are sold at book-vending kiosks everywhere. Spoken Romanian is a lot like Italian, but with three additional vowels: "*ă*" (pronounced like "e" in "pet") and the interchangeable "*â*" and "*î*" (like the "i" in "pill"). The other two characters peculiar to the Romanian alphabet are "*ş*" ("sh" in "shiver") and "*ţ*" ("ts" in "tsar"). At the end of a word, "*i*" is essentially dropped. "*Ci*" sounds like the "chea" in "cheat," and "*ce*" sounds like the "che" in "chess." "*Chi*" is pronounced like "kee" in "keen," and "*che*" like "ke" in "kept." "G" before "e" or "i" sounds like "j" as in judge and "gh" before those vowels is like "g" in girl.

HEALTH & SAFETY

EMERGENCY NUMBERS.
Fire: tel. 981. **Police:** tel. 955. **Ambulance:** tel. 961.

Most **public restrooms** lack soap, towels, and toilet paper, and those on trains and in stations smell awful. Worse yet, attendants charge L1000-1500 for a single square of toilet paper. Pick up a roll at a newsstand or drug store and carry it with you everywhere. You can find relief at most restaurants, even if you're not a patron.

Beware the manic **drivers** in congested Bucharest. Roads are currently undergoing a government-sponsored repair, but they still have potholes. In the country, watch out for unlit carriages and carts, as well as sheep and cows.

Drugstores *(farmacie)* are a crapshoot and may not have what you need. *Antinevralgic* is for headaches, *aspirină* or *piramidon* for colds and the flu, and *saprosan* for diarrhea. Condoms *(prezervative)* are available at all drugstores and at many kiosks. **Feminine hygiene** products are sold in cities.

ACCOMMODATIONS & CAMPING

While some **hotels** charge foreigners 50-100% more than locals, lodging is still relatively inexpensive. As a general rule, one-star hotels are on par with mediocre European youth hostels, so don't let the bed bugs bite—literally. Two-star places are decent, and those with three are good but expensive. In some places, going to ONT (in resorts, the *Dispecerat de Cazare*) and asking for a room may get you a price at least 50% lower than that quoted by the hotel.

Private accommodations are generally the way to go, but hosts rarely speak English; be aware that renting a room "together" means sharing a bed. Rooms run US$6-10 per person, sometimes with breakfast and other amenities. See the room and fix a price before accepting. Many towns allow foreign students to stay in **university dorms** at remarkably low prices. Ask at the local university rectorate; ONT *might* be able to help. **Campgrounds** are crowded and often have frightening bathrooms. Relatively cheap **bungalows** are often full in summer.

FOOD & DRINK

Romanian food is fairly typical of Central Europe, with a bit of Balkan and French thrown in. Romanians rarely eat out, which explains the paucity of decent restaurants; try to wrangle a dinner invite from a local. In the mountains or resorts, peasants sell fresh fruit and cheese. *Lapte* (milk) is fatty and often not homogenized; powdered milk is available in many shops. On the street, you can find cheap *mititei* (a.k.a. *mici;* barbecued ground meat) or Turkish-style kebabs, best in the morning when they'll still be warm. "Fast food" in Romania means pre-cooked and microwaved, and should be regarded with suspicion. *Ingheţată* (ice cream) is cheap and good. Harder to find, but worth the effort, are the delicious *mere în aluat* (doughnuts with apples) and the sugary *gogoşi* (fried doughnuts).

Bucharest is the only place where you'll find non-Romanian cuisine. Otherwise, lunch usually starts with a soup, called *supă* or *ciorbă* (the former has noodles or dumplings, the latter is saltier and usually has vegetables), followed by a main dish (usually grilled pork, beef, or chicken) and dessert. Soups can be very tasty; try *ciorbă de perişoare* (with vegetables and ground meatballs) or *supă cu găluşte* (with fluffy dumplings). Pork comes in several varieties, of which *muşchi* and *cotlet* are the best quality. Vegetarians should stick to salads, which are usually good and cheap, or pizza. For dessert, *clătite* (crepes), *papanaşi* (doughnuts with jam and sour cream), and *tort* (creamy cakes) can all be fantastic if they're fresh.

Some restaurants charge by weight (usually 100g) rather than by portion. If you order certain meats there is no way to predict how many grams you will actually receive and, therefore, how much you will have to pay. *Garnituri*, the extras that come standard with a meal, are usually charged separately, down to that dollop of mustard. As a rule, if the waiters put it in front of you, you're paying for it.

CUSTOMS & ETIQUETTE

It is customary to give (and receive) inexact change for purchases, generally rounding to the nearest L500. "Non-stop" cafes and kiosks can be found in all cities, but their names can be misleading; shops close arbitrarily when attendants run errands, wash the floor, or go home early. Romanians don't take **posted hours** very seriously, and many banks and businesses may be closed on Friday afternoons. Most weddings are on Saturday, meaning that nice restaurants will be booked that night but open on Sundays. **Churches** are open most of the day. Services are lengthy (2½hr. on Sunday), but people quietly come and go at all times.

Romanians take pride in their **hospitality.** Most will be eager to help, offering to show you around town or inviting you into their homes. When you're visiting, bring your hostess an odd number of flowers; even-numbered bouquets are only brought to graves. Especially in cities, Romanians dress well, and shorts are a rarity on even the hottest days. **Men** are usually fairly respectful of women. **Alcoholism** continues to plague the country. **Disabled travelers** will be hard pressed to find wheelchair-accessibility anywhere. Even if a hotel has an elevator, there are usually a few steps before the building's entrance.

Homosexuality has been legal in Romania since 1996, but public displays of affection remain illegal. Keep in mind that outside the major cities, many Romanians hold conservative attitudes toward sexuality, which may translate into harassment of gay, lesbian, and bisexual travelers. Homosexuals in Romania are well hidden, and gay hangouts are ephemeral when they exist at all. Nonetheless, Romanian women sometimes walk arm-in-arm without anyone batting an eye.

NATIONAL HOLIDAYS

January 1-3, New Year's; January 6, Epiphany; January 7, Orthodox Christmas; April 30-May 1, Orthodox Easter; May 1, Labor Day; December 1, National Day; December 25-26, Christmas.

BUCHAREST (BUCUREȘTI)

Once the fabled beauty at the end of the Orient Express, Bucharest (pop. 2,080,363) is fabled today only for its infamous communist makeover under Romanian dictator Nicolae Ceauşescu. During his 25 years in power, Ceauşescu managed to entirely undo the city's splendor; Neoclassical architecture, grand boulevards, and Ottoman traces were replaced with concrete blocks, wide highways, and Communist monuments. The city that was lucky enough to be spared war-time destruction was nonetheless ruined in a time of peace as the Ceauşescu regime demolished neighborhoods and razed churches; today, the metropolis is a somber ghost of its former self. Stray dogs, gypsy children, and rusted cranes fill the squares beneath the gargantuan Parliamentary Palace, a marble maze of rooms and chambers that stands as an opulent reminder of the city's sad fate. The parts of the city not standing in bitter memorial to the nefarious dictator are doubtless monuments to Romania's many post-Ceauşescu revolutions. Downtown streets and squares are marked by black crosses while the names of the square's themselves commemorate revolutionary victims and national dates of remembrance. Luckily, Romania's current government is slowly beginning to pull itself together, and as a result, is beginning to give Bucharest a desperately-needed face-lift. Newly restored parks and reconstructed historic buildings dot the cityscape while emerging museums provide indoor diversions from Communist monoliths. Romanians have been trying to forget the past 50 years, but it's proving impossible when the entire city stands as a crumbling historical testament.

GETTING THERE & GETTING AROUND

Airplanes: Otopeni Airport (tel. 230 00 22), 18km outside the city, is Bucharest's international airport. Buses from the airport to the Centru stop near Hotel Intercontinental Piaţa Universităţii (M2: Piaţa Universităţii). Bus #783 to Otopeni leaves from Piaţa Unirii every 20min. **Băneasa Airport** (tel. 232 00 20), connected with Piaţa Romană by bus #131 and Gara de Nord by bus #205, handles domestic flights. Buy **international tickets** at the **CFR/TAROM office,** Str. Brezoianu 10 (tel. 646 33 46). M2: Piaţa Universităţii. From Piaţa Universităţii, walk west on Bd. Carol I, left on Calea Victoriei, and right on Str. Eforie. CFR is down the street. The TAROM office at Piaţa Victoriei (tel. 659 41 85) sells domestic tickets. Both open M-F 7:30am-7:30pm, Sa 7:30am-1:30pm.

Trains: Gara de Nord (tel. 223 06 60) is the principal station. M3: Gara de Nord. L2000 fee to enter the station if you're not catching a train; this *almost* keeps things from being utterly chaotic. To: **Budapest** (12hr., 6 per day, L470,000); **Chişinău** (11hr., 1 per day, L179,000); **Istanbul** (20-24hr., 1 per day, L370,000); **Kiev** (30hr., 1 per day, L568,000); and **Sofia** (10hr., 3 per day, L350,000). **Gara Obor** (tel. 223 04 55), accessible by trolley #85 from Gara de Nord, #69 from Piaţa Universităţii, or M3: Obor, and **Gara Băneasa** (tel. 222 48 56), accessible by bus #301 from Piaţa Romană, are secondary stations that may be useful for travel to and from the Black Sea coast. **Tickets** can be purchased in advance at **CFR** (see **Airplanes,** above).

Buses: Filaret, Cuţitul de Argint 2 (tel. 335 11 40; M2: Tineretului), lies south of the Centru; the **Obor** and **Băneasa** train stations also connect with buses. Buses are the best way to reach Istanbul and Athens. To **Athens,** your best bet is **Fotopoulos Express** (tel. 335 82 49). To **Istanbul,** catch a **Toros** or **Murat** bus from outside Gara de Nord. **Double T** (tel. 613 36 42), affiliated with Eurail, can get you to Western Europe. All international bus companies hover near Piaţa Dorobanţilor.

Local Transportation: Buses, trolleys, or **trams** cost L2000 for one trip. Buy tickets from a kiosk; you can't always get them on board. Validate them to avoid a L50,000; police may try to get more from foreign tourists. **Express buses** take only magnetic cards (L10,000 round-trip), except #783. Unlimited day passes are available for all regular transportation lines (L6000) but not at all ticket kiosks. Pick-pocketing is a problem during peak hours. The **Metro** offers less crowded, very reliable service to all major points in Bucharest and runs 5am-11:30pm. Magnetic strip cards cost L4000 for 2 trips, L19,500 for 10 trips, or L6000 for a day pass. Hold onto your card; police only check cards once a month, but show no mercy.

Taxis: Getax, tel. 953. **Colbăcescu,** tel. 945, is rumored to be cheaper. Taxi drivers have long been overcharging foreigners; they can now do it legally by setting the meter on *"Tarif #2."* Expect to pay at least L1600 per km. Arrange the price *(preţul)* beforehand; L30,000-50,000 is probably the best you'll get. Never pay more than US$10. Be especially careful traveling from the train station. Learn the phrase *"prea mult"* (too much) and bargain harshly.

Car Rental: Avis (tel. 315 12 12), in Hotel Hilton, across the street from the National Art Museum on Calea Victoriei. M2: Piaţa Universităţii. Rents cars starting from US$33 per day for 1-3 days; US$28 for 4-6 days; US$24 for more than a week. Add US$0.33 per km. Insurance US$17. AmEx/MC.

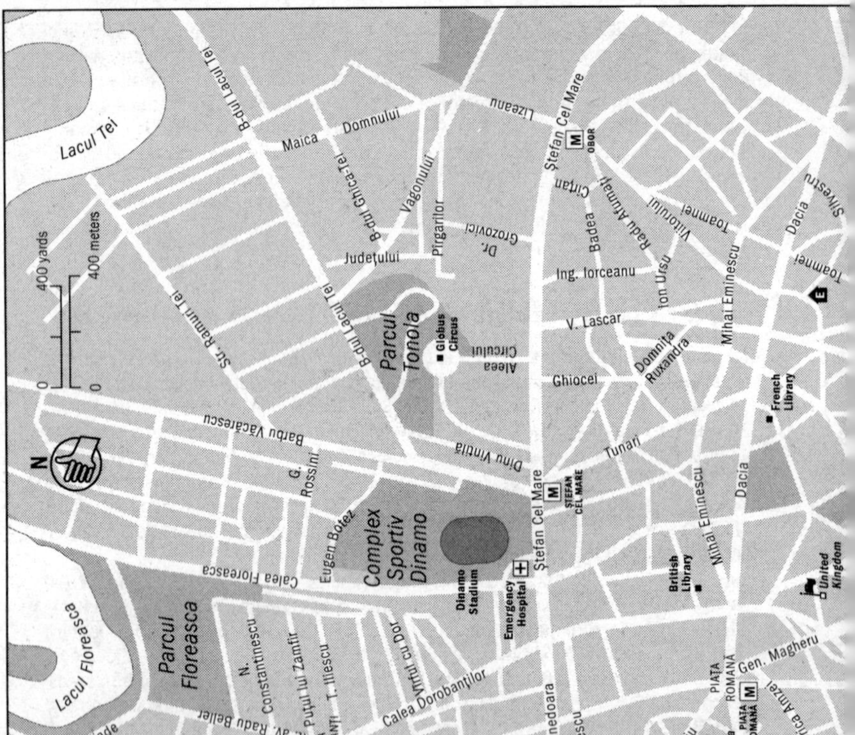
Lacul Tei
Lacul Floreasca
Parcul Floreasca
Parcul Herăstrău
Parcul Tonola
Complex Sportiv Dinamo
Dinamo Stadium
Emergency Hospital
Globus Circus
Village Museum
Geological Museum
Romanian Peasant Museum
Museum of Natural History
Art Collections Museum
Ministry of Foreign Affairs
British Library
French Library
Russia
Ireland
Canada
United Kingdom
Gara de Nord
GARA DE NORD
BASARAB
OBOR
ŞTEFAN CEL MARE
AVIATORILOR
PIAŢA VICTORIEI
PIAŢA ROMANĂ
PIAŢA CHARLES DE GAULLE
PIAŢA DOROBANŢI
PIAŢA VICTORIEI
PIAŢA ROMANĂ
400 yards
400 meters
0
0
N
B-dul Lacul Tei
Maica Domnului
Lizeanu
Ştefan Cel Mare
B-dul Ghica-Tei
Vagonului
Pirgarilor
Dr. Grozovici
Judeţului
B-dul Lacul Tei
Str. Ramuri Tei
Aleea Circului
Cirţan
Badea
Radu Alunaţi
Viitorului
Toamnei
Silvestru
Dacia
Toamnei
Ing. Iorceanu
Ion Ursu
Mihai Eminescu
V. Lascar
Domniţa Ruxandra
Ghiocei
Barbu Văcărescu
Dinu Vintilă
G. Rossini
Tunari
Eugen Botez
Ştefan Cel Mare
Mihai Eminescu
Dacia
Calea Floreasca
N. Constantinescu
Puţul lui Zamfir
T. Iliescu
Virtutul cu Dor
Calea Dorobanţilor
Gen. Magheru
Il. av. Radu Beller
Roma
Iancu de Hunedoara
Grigore Alexandrescu
Lascăr Catargiu
Biserica Amzei
Mircea Eliade
Jean Monnet
Teheran
Calea Dorobanţilor
Muzeul Zambaccian
Sofia
Ankara
Atena
Paris
Washington
Iorga
Dacia
Primăverii
Ing. Ermil Pangratti
Al. Alexandru
Tirana
Argentina
Orlando
Calea Victoriei
Bulevardul Aviatorilor
Popa Savu
Cimpia Turzii
Alexandrina
Maresal C. Prezan
Sevastopol
Frumoasă
Gl. Voievozilor
Popa Tatu
Dăniceni
Şoseaua Kiseleff
Arhitect Ion Mincu
Dr. Felix
Dr. Sergiu
Buzeşti
Barbu Delavrancea
Ady Endre
Petőfi Şandor
Scărlătescu
Veronica Micle
Dreaptă
G. Polizu
I. G. Duca
Mărăşti
Mareşal A. Averescu
Ion Mihalache
Grigore Manolescu
Banul Manta
Titulescu
Nicolae
Al. Cernat
Alexandru Ioan Cuza
Al Departeanu
Calea Griviţei
Ion Neculce
Gala Galaction
Turda
Dinicu Golescu
Bulevardul 1 Mai
C. Sandu
Plevnei
Orhideelor

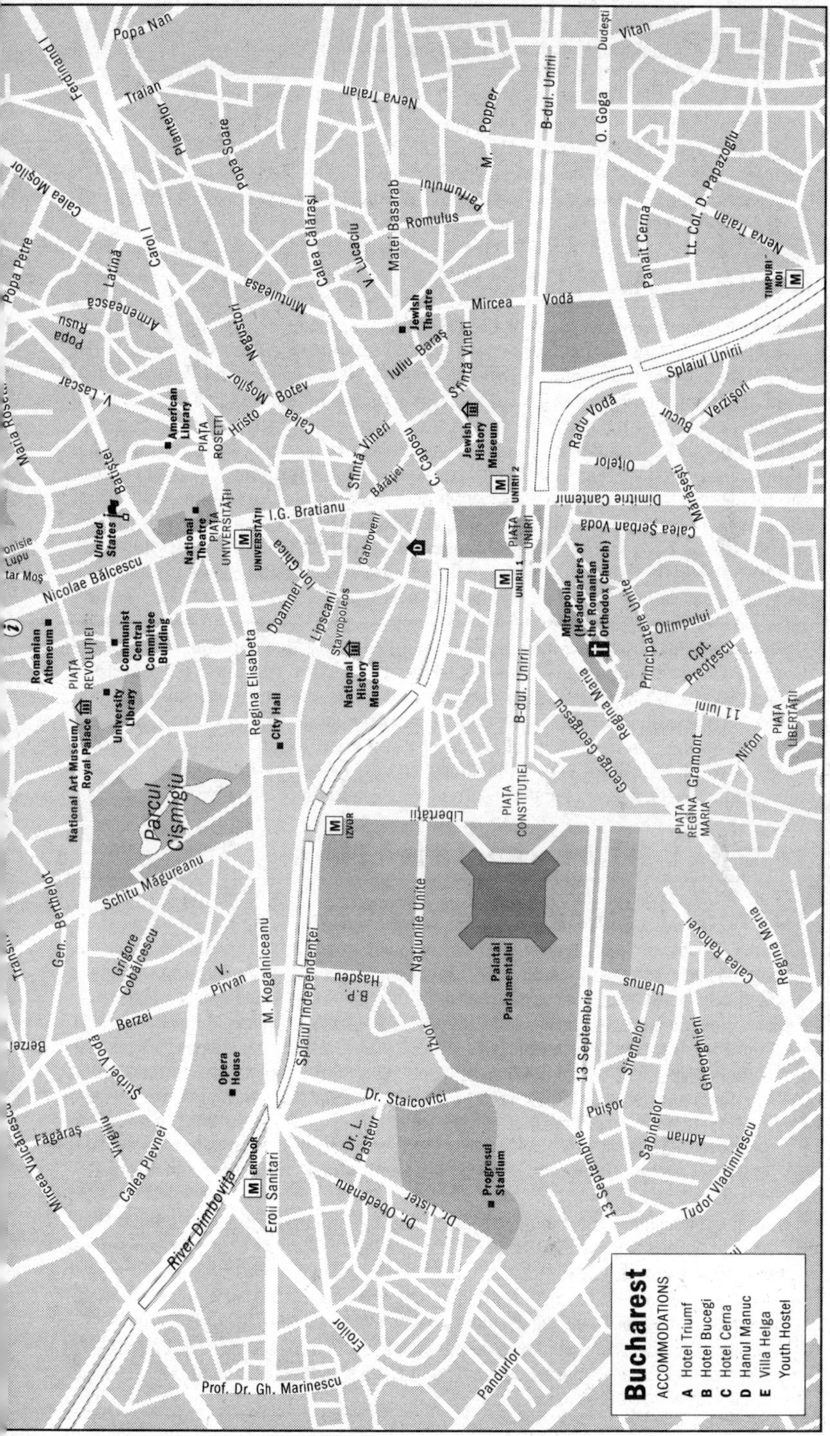
Bucharest
ACCOMMODATIONS
A Hotel Triumf
B Hotel Bucegi
C Hotel Cerna
D Hanul Manuc
E Villa Helga
Youth Hostel
National Art Museum/ Royal Palace
University Library
Romanian Atheneum
PIAȚA REVOLUȚIEI
Communist Central Committee Building
United States
American Library
National Theatre
PIAȚA ROSETTI
PIAȚA UNIVERSITĂȚII
UNIVERSITĂȚII
City Hall
National History Museum
Stavropoleos
Jewish Theatre
Jewish History Museum
UNIRII 2
PIAȚA UNIRII
UNIRII 1
Mitropolia (Headquarters of the Romanian Orthodox Church)
PIAȚA CONSTITUȚIEI
IZVOR
Palatul Parlamentului
PIAȚA REGINA MARIA
PIAȚA LIBERTĂȚII
TIMPURI NOI
Opera House
EROILOR
Progresul Stadium
Parcul Cişmigiu
River Dîmbovița
Popa Nan
Traian
Ferdinand I
Plantelor
Popa Soare
Nerva Traian
M. Popper
B-dul. Unirii
O. Goga
Dudeşti
Vitan
Calea Moşilor
Carol I
Latină
Popa Petre
Armenească
Popa Rusu
V. Lascar
Maria Rosetti
Batiştei
Nicolae Bălcescu
Negustori
Mântuleasa
Calea Călăraşi
V. Lucaciu
Matei Basarab
Romulus
Parfumului
Hristo Botev
Calea Moşilor
Iuliu Baraş
Sfîntă Vineri
Mircea Vodă
Panait Cerna
Lt. Col. D. Papazoglu
I.G. Bratianu
Ion Ghica
Doamnei
Lipscani
Gabroveni
Bărăţiei
C. Coposu
Dimitrie Cantemir
Calea Şerban Vodă
Radu Vodă
Oţetelor
Splaiul Unirii
Verzişori
Bucur
Mărăşeşti
Principatele Unite
Olimpului
Cpt. Preoţescu
11 Iunie
Nifon
Regina Maria
George Georgescu
Regina Elisabeta
Libertăţii
Naţiunile Unite
B.P. Haşdeu
Izvor
Splaiul Independenţei
M. Kogălniceanu
Schitu Măgureanu
Gen. Berthelot
Grigore Cobălcescu
V. Pîrvan
Berzei
Ştirbei Vodă
Gramont
Calea Rahovei
Uranus
13 Septembrie
Sirenelor
Gheorghieni
Puişor
Sabinelor
Adrian
Tudor Vladimirescu
Dr. Staicovici
Dr. L. Pasteur
Dr. Obedenaru
Dr. Lister
Eroii Sanitari
Eroilor
Făgăraş
Viitorului
Calea Plevnei
Mircea Vulcănescu
Pandurilor
Prof. Dr. Gh. Marinescu

Hitchhiking: Those hitching north take bus #783 to the airport. Those heading to the **Black Sea** and **Constanţa** take tram #14 from Piaţa Sf. Gheorghe, near Piaţa Universităţii on Bd. I.C. Brătianu. At the end of the line, they switch to bus #147 or 346 to get farther. To **Giurgiu** and **Bulgaria,** people take M2: Eroii Revoluţiei and then bus #275 to the end of the line. To **Piteşti** and **Western Romania,** travelers take the M1: Industriilor, then get on bus #150 (dir.: "Sat. Rudeni") and get off at what looks like a good hitching spot. Romanians hitchhike a good deal, but foreigners and women are better off not hitchhiking at all. It's no bargain, either; it is customary to pay what a comparable bus would cost. *Let's Go* does not recommend hitchhiking.

ORIENTATION

Bucharest lies some 60km from the Danube in southern Romania. The city is divided into six sectors that circle clockwise around the city. **Sector I** covers almost the entire northern portion of center, including **Piaţa Victoriei** and **Piaţa Romană,** some of downtown Bucharest's chicest squares, as well as the main train station, **Gara de Nord. Sector II** begins just east of the downtown area at the Ştefan cel Mare Metro stop and encompasses the entire northeastern quarter of the city; the **Obor** train station is in the center of this sector. **Sector III** is directly east of the center in the residential outskirts of the city. **Sector IV** is wedged into the southeast corner of the center, housing what remains of Bucharest's **Old Town** in addition to the eastern portion of the Civic Center. **Piaţa Unirii, Piaţa Universităţii,** and **Piaţa Revolutiei** are three of the city's most historically significant areas. **Sector V** stretches from the **Parliamentary Palace** into the city's southwest suburbs. **Sector VI** contains the westernmost residential neighborhoods.

The **main train station,** Gara de Nord, lies along the M3 Metro line just west of the Centru. Take a train headed toward Dristor II one stop to Piaţa Victoriei, then change to the M2 line headed toward Depoul. Take this train one stop to Piaţa Romana, two stops to Piaţa Universităţii, or three stops to Piaţa Unirii; all three stops are directly in the center of Bucharest and are a 15min. walk apart. It's also possible to take trolley #79 or #133. **Maps,** scarce elsewhere in Romania, are sold throughout Bucharest, especially by street vendors in Piaţa Universităţii.

PRACTICAL INFORMATION

TOURIST & FINANCIAL SERVICES

Tourist Offices: ONT, Bd. Magheru 7 (tel. 315 84 41, fax 312 09 15). M2: Piaţa Romană. ONT has an **exchange office.** Open M-F 8am-8pm, Sa 8am-3pm, Su 8am-1pm. A number of private tourist offices are at Gara de Nord. Info can also be found at major hotels.

Embassies: Canada, Str. Nicolae Iorga 36 (tel. 222 98 45). M2: Piaţa Romană. Open M-F 9am-5pm. **U.K.,** Str. Jules Michelet 24 (tel. 312 03 03). M2: Piaţa Romană. Open M-Th 8:30am-1pm and 2-5pm, F 8:30am-1:30pm. **U.S.,** Str. Tudor Arghezi 7/9 (tel. 210 40 42; after hours tel. 210 01 49; fax 211 33 60). M2: Piaţa Universităţii. A block behind Hotel Intercontinental. Consular services at Str. Nicolae Filipescu 26. Open M-Th 8-11:30am and 1-3pm, F 8-11:30am. Citizens of **Australia, Ireland,** and **New Zealand** should contact the U.K. embassy. Citizens of **South Africa** should contact their embassy in Budapest (see p. 241).

Currency Exchange: Exchange houses are everywhere, with rates posted out front. Many houses will refuse to give hard currencies for lei. Banks will usually extract a hefty commission (about 1.5% for traveler's checks). **ATMs** always give the best rate, and are located at most major banks, including **Banca Comerciala Romana** and **Bancorex,** near Piaţa Victoriei and Universităţii. Don't change money on the street—it's almost always a scam.

American Express: Marshall Tourism, Bd. Magheru 43, 1st floor, #1 (tel. 223 12 04). M2: Piaţa Romană. Replaces lost cards and checks, but by law cannot cash traveler's checks. Open M-F 9am-5pm, Sa 9am-1pm.

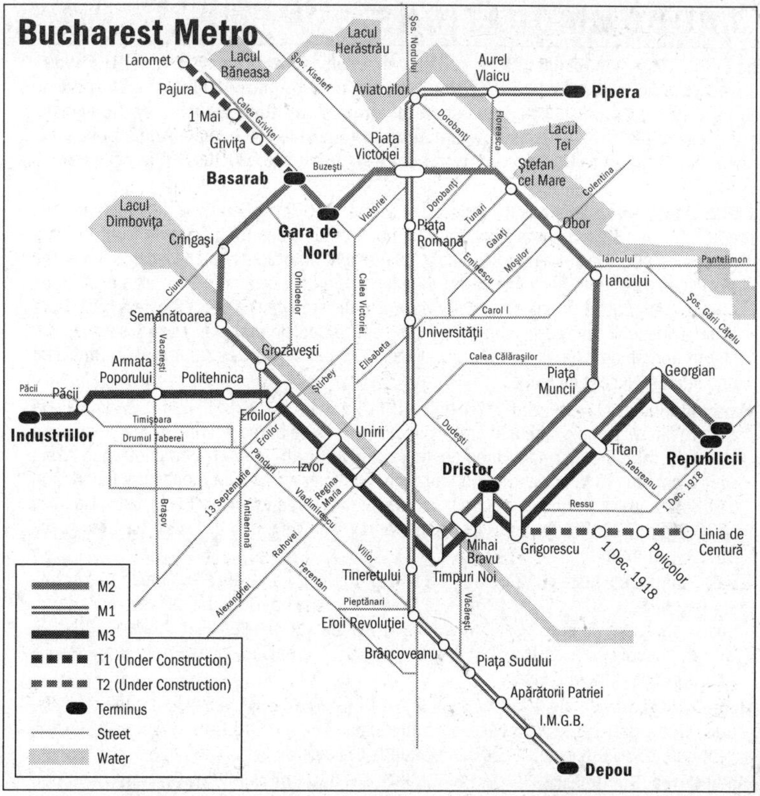

LOCAL SERVICES, EMERGENCY, & COMMUNICATIONS

Luggage Storage: Gara de Nord has one for foreigners and one for locals. Foreigners pay L4800-9600. Open 24hr.

International Press: Overpriced international magazines and newspapers are available at all major hotels. English-language Romanian publications are few: *Nine O'Clock* is a daily sometimes given out free at hotels; the weekly English edition of *Romania Libera* can be found at McDonald's.

24hr. Pharmacies: SF, Calea Victoriei 103-5 (tel. 650 78 38). **Farmadex,** Calea Moşilor 280 (tel. 211 95 60).

Medical Assistance: Spitalul de Urgenţă, Calea Floreasca 8 (tel. 212 19 43). M3: Ştefan cel Mare.

Post Office: Str. Matei Millo 10 (tel. 613 03 87). M2: Piaţa Universităţii. From the Metro, walk down Bd. Regina Elisabeta, turn right onto Calea Victoriei, and then left onto Str. Mille Constantin. Then take a right onto Str. Otetelesanu Ion; at the end of the street continue left onto Matei Millo. Open M-F 7:30am-8pm, Sa 7:30am-2pm. **Poste Restante** is three doors down, next to Hotel Carpati. **Postal code:** 70154.

Internet Access: Raffles, Calea Victoriei 25 (tel. 311 26 82). M2: Piaţa Universităţii, just south of Bd. Regina Elisabeta. L10,000 per 30min. Open M-Sa 10am-10pm. **Internet Cafe,** Bd. Carol I 25, (tel. 313 10 48). M2: Piaţa Universităţii. Head east on Bd. Carol I past Piaţa Rosetti. L15,000 for 30min. Open 24hr.

Telephones: Orange phone cards, L20,000 or L50,000, are good for domestic and international calls from throughout the city. Order collect calls at the **telephone office,** Calea Victoriei 37. Open M-F 7:30am-8pm, Sa 8am-2pm. **Phone code:** (0)1.

ACCOMMODATIONS

The ONT office (see **Tourist Offices,** p. 510) can arrange **private rooms** or **hotel** accommodations, but tourist offices in the train station may be more objective. During the school year (Oct.-June), Romanian students often share their rooms. Try the **dormitories** between M3: Grozăveşti and Semănătoarea. Otherwise, the accommodation scene is grim. It's difficult to find decent rooms for less than L300,000-400,000 per person.

Villa Helga Youth Hostel, Str. Salcâmilor 2 (tel. 610 22 14). M2: Piaţa Romană; bus #86, 79, or 133 two stops from Piaţa Romană or six stops from Gara de Nord to Piaţa (east along Bd. Dacia). From Bd. Dacia, take a right onto Str. Gemini Lascăr, a left at the triangular green, another left onto Str. Viitorlui, and a final right onto Str. Salcâmilor. Don't trust the supposed "staffers" at Gara de Nord; they're scam artists. The real staff, however, is friendly, funny, and provides 2-, 4-, and 8-bed dorms, free laundry service, and strong Romanian cigarettes. US$12 per day; $72 per week; $196 per month. Breakfast and kitchen access included.

Hanul Manuc, Str. Franceză 62/64 (tel. 313 14 15; fax 312 28 11). M1, 2, or 3: Piaţa Unirii. With McDonald's behind you, walk along the side of the square so the green is on your left. Take the first right, then continue straight to the end of a cobblestoned street with a church. To your right is the entrance. Formerly an ascetic monastery founded in 1808, it's now a luxurious, centrally located hotel. Huge rooms, all with bath. Doubles L630,000; L720,000 for an extra person. AmEx/MC/Visa. Call or fax at least one week ahead in summer.

Hotel Triumf, şos. Kiseleff 12 (tel. 222 31 72; fax 223 24 11). M2: Aviatorilor; bus or trolley #131, 205, 301, or 331 from Piaţa Lahovari to Arcul de Triumf. From the Arcul de Triumf, walk south on şos. Kiseleff; the hotel is on the left. Singles with shower L500,000, with bath L550,000; doubles L650,000, L700,000. Breakfast included. Laundry service L15,000 per item. MC/Visa.

Hotel Bucegi, Str. Witing 2 (tel. 637 52 25). M3: Gara de Nord. Across from the train station. Small, dark rooms with passable bathrooms. Singles L140,000; doubles L180,000, with bath L350,000; triples L240,000; quads L280,000.

Hotel Cerna, Str. Golescu 29 (tel. 637 40 87). M3: Gara de Nord. One-star hotel right next to the train station. Small but otherwise decent rooms. Singles L150,000, with bath L250,000; doubles L200,000, with bath L400,000; apartments L550,000.

ROMANIA

FOOD

Open-air markets offering all manner of veggies, fruits, meats, and cheeses abound in Bucharest—good ones are at Piaţa Amzei, Piaţa Matache, and Piaţa Latină. To reach Piaţa Amzei (M2: Piaţa Romană), cross the street in front of McDonald's at Piata Romană and head straight on Str. Take Ionescu. Piaţa Matache (M3: Gara de Nord) is a left down Calea Griviţei from the train station. The second street on the right leads to the market. To reach Piaţa Latină (M2: Piaţa Universităţii), start with your back to Hotel Intercontinental, turn left and walk east on Bd. Carol I for 10min. All three markets are open daily, but tend to be slower on Sundays. For excellent bread and pastries, try **Ana,** Str. Radu Beller 6 (tel. 230 67 00), and Calea Dorobanţilor 134 (tel. 230 57 32), both near Piaţa Dorobanţilor (M2: Aviatorilor or M3: Ştefan cel Mare; open M-Sa 8am-7:30pm, Su 9:30am-noon). **Grocery stores** are also plentiful—**Vox Maris Supermarket,** at Piaţa Victoriei, is open 24hr.

Taj Palace, Str. Radu Vodă 18 (tel. 330 67 15). M2: Piaţa Unirii. Walk away from McDonald's with the green to your right. Radu Vodă is the first right not along the water. Vegetarian-friendly. Feast on Indian dishes (entrees L40,000-60,000). Sitar music. Open noon-10pm.

Mes Amis, Str. Lipscani 82 (tel. 312 29 10). M2: Piaţa Unirii or Piaţa Universităţii. In a tiny alley between Lipscani and Gabroveni. Enjoy a light meal and drinks with artsy locals. Full meals L25,000-L35,000. Open daily noon-2am; food served until 11pm.

Carul cu Bere, Str. Stavropoleos 5 (tel. 313 75 60). M2: Piața Universității. Founded in 1879, the facade earned a place in ONT's photo album; the food isn't bad, either. Entrees up to L50,000. Live folk performances F-Su 8:30pm. Open daily 10am-1am.

Nicorești, Str. Maria Rosetti 40 (tel. 211 24 80). M2: Piața Romană; trolley #79, 86, or 226. Head east on Bd. Dacia to Piața Gemeni, then walk 2 more blocks and take a right onto Toamnei; it's after an intersection on the right. Often full on weekends, Nicorești has the best Romanian food in town. Open M-Sa 9am-10pm, Su 1-10pm.

Pescarul ("The Fisherman"), Bd. N. Bălcescu 9 (tel. 650 72 44). M2: Piața Universității, across from Hotel Intercontinental. Sailor decor goes overboard with the boat sticking out of the wall. Excellent seafood. Entrees around L40,000. Open M-Sa 10am-11pm.

Paradis 2, Str. Hristo Botev 10. M2: Piața Universității. Leave the square with Hotel Intercontinental on your left and take the second right. Middle Eastern entrees (including falafel) L20,000-40,000. Open daily noon-10pm.

Club Art Papillon, Str. Matei Voievod 66A (tel. 642 55 37). Trolleys #86 from Piața Romană and #90 from Piața Universității. A university hangout with live music during the school year. Entrees under L20,000. Open 24hr.

Casa Oamenilor de Stinta (COS), Piața Lahovari 9 (tel. 210 12 84). M2: Piața Romană. Head down Bd. Dacia with Bd. Maghera on your right until the first intersection with Str. Dorobanților. Turn right down Dorobanților; the restaurant is behind the house with the fantastic facade. Dine outside amid fountains or inside amid Baroque opulence. Be prepared to wait on the wait staff. Full meals L60,000-90,000. Open daily noon-midnight.

SIGHTS

Downtown Bucharest is a sprawl of concrete highrises, congested streets, and hundreds of rabid dogs. The memorials and sights worth seeing are not beautiful squares or opulent palaces; rather, Bucharest is worth exploring for the omnipresence of its history, for the sobering scars left on nearly every square and building by its recent revolutions and regimes.

CIVIC CENTER

In 1984, Ceaușescu set out to remodel Bucharest after Pyongyang, North Korea's quintessentially socialist capital. Using the 1977 earthquake as an excuse to "rebuild" the center, Ceaușescu's megalomaniacal vision was not about renewal; although he claimed to be creating "the first Socialist capital for the new Socialist man," he more likely wanted the new city to symbolize his own power. In order to create his perfect socialist capital, Ceaușescu destroyed 5 sq. km of Bucharest's historic center, demolishing over 9000 19th-century houses and displacing more than 40,000 Romanians. The result is today's Civic Center (Centru Civic), conveniently completed in 1989, just in time for his overthrow. The Civic Center is united by Bd. Unirii, intentionally built slightly larger than the Champs-Elysées, after which it was modeled. The western half, while ugly, has gone on to become an accepted part of Bucharest. The eastern half, however, was never completed and remains a wasteland of rusted cranes and skeletal structures; locals snidely call it "Hiroshima."

PARLIAMENTARY PALACE. (Palatul Parlamentului). With 12 stories, four underground levels, and 1100 rooms, the Parliamentary Palace is the world's third-largest building (after the Pentagon in Washington, D.C. and the Potala in Lhasa) and the incomprehensibly huge centerpiece of the Civic Center. Despite its original name—the People's House (Casa Poporului)—it is far from being a symbol of national pride. Ceaușescu demolished several historic neighborhoods and spent billions of dollars on his private palace, and the contrast between the palace's marble and wood opulence stands in stark contrast to the poverty of most Romanians. Although today this white monolith houses Romania's Senate and Parliament, Romanians still refer to it as the "Madman's Palace" (Casa Nebunului). *(M1 or 3: Izvor. For a more spectacular view, approach the palace from Piața Unirii. For tours, enter at entrance A1. Open daily 10am-6pm. Tours L30,000; camera privileges L30,000.)*

HEADQUARTERS OF THE ROMANIAN ORTHODOX CHURCH. Ceauşescu inexplicably spared Dealul Mitropoliei, the hill on its southwest side. Atop the hill sits the headquarters of the Romanian Orthodox Church, located in one of the largest cathedrals in Romania and one of the only churches not destroyed for the Civic Center. The cathedral also flanks the former **Communist Parliament building.** This impressive Baroque construction now belongs to the church and periodically hosts free religious concerts (especially around religious holidays). To avoid begging families, stray dogs, and crowds, try the ascent mid-day. *(M2: Piaţa Unirii. Head up Aleea Dealul Mitropoliei. Open M-Su 8am-7pm.)*

SIGHTS OF THE REVOLUTION

Bucharest is as marked by its 1989 revolution as it is by its 24 years under Ceauşescu. Streets and squares are marked with crosses and plagues commemorating the *eroilor revoluţiei Române*, or heroes of the 1989 revolution.

PIAŢA REVOLUŢIEI. The first shots of Romania's revolution were fired here on December 21, 1989. The square is surrounded by the newly refurbished **University Library** (Bibliotecă), which was gutted during the riots, and the **Central Committee Building.** Formerly the Communist Party headquarters, this Stalinist gem now houses government offices. Surprisingly near ground level is the balcony from which Ceauşescu delivered his final speech; the balcony is now marked by a white marble triangle with the inscription, *Glorie martirilor nostri* (Glory to our martyrs). Although the plaque points toward the balcony that held Ceauşescu, it actually commemorates the rioters themselves. Just down the street from Piaţa Revoluţiei on Bd. Nicolae Bălcescu is a black cross marking the spot where the first victim of the Revolution died. *(M2: Piaţa Universităţii. Walk up Bd. Brătianu from the Metro through its name-change to Bd. Bălcescu, and turn left onto Str. Rosetti.)*

PIAŢA UNIVERSITĂŢII. Another square central to Romania's recent revolutions, Piata Universităţii houses memorials to victims of both the 1989 and June 1990 revolutions. Demonstrators perished fighting Ceauşescu's forces here on December 21, 1989, the day before his fall. Crosses commemorating the martyrs line the center of the square, and defiant anti-Iliescu graffiti decorates university walls and the Architecture Institute, across from Hotel Intercontinental in the small Piaţa 22 Decembrie 1989. Piaţa 22 Decembrie 1989 was the sight of the June 1990 riots: students had been protesting the new ex-Communist government here in what they called the "Neo-Communist-free Zone" since April, and in June, Iliescu bussed in over 10,000 Romanian miners to violently squash the protestors. The rampage killed 21 students. *(M2: Piaţa Universităţii.)*

PARKS

One of Bucharest's few remaining beauties is her extensive park system. Scattered from the downtown to the suburban outskirts, the city's greenery was lucky to have been spared the crane and sledgehammer of Ceauşescu.

HERĂSTRĂU PARK. This sprawling park directly north of downtown is part nature preserve, part amusement park, part history lesson. At the southern end of the park on şos. Kiseleff stands the **Arcul de Triumf,** built to celebrate Romania's independence from Turkey in 1877. Within the park lies Bucharest's largest lake, which offers scenic strolls (periodically interrupted by meandering peacocks) to the small Island of Roses. The vast park is popular with families for its myriad diversions, from tennis courts and rowboat rentals to carousels and roller coasters. Also within the park is the **Ştrand,** a swimming pool/tennis court/beach complex. *(M2: Aviatorilor; bus #301, 331, or 131 from Piaţa Lahovari. The Metro station sits at the southern tip of the park, which sprawls along şos. Kiseleff. Open daily 9am-8pm; ştrand open May-Sept. 15 only. Lake tours L3000-L18,000. Boat rentals L20,000 per hr.; L20,000 deposit. Tennis L20,000-40,000 per hr. Pool L10,000, students L5000; Sa-Su L15,000.)*

CIŞMIGIU GARDENS. One of Bucharest's oldest parks, the Cişmigiu Gardens are filled with elegant paths and a small lake where you can rent paddle boats; the most famous walkways are "lovers' way," a tree-canopied trail, and the "writers' circle," a loop peppered with busts of literary heroes. The well-groomed park is, along with Herăstrău Park, the focal point of much of the city's social life during the summer. Elderly pensioners, young couples, football players, and chess whizzes abound. *(M2: Piaţa Universităţii. Just west of Piaţa Universităţii on Bd. Regina Elisabeta. Open daily 8am-8pm. Paddle boats L25,000 per hr. Photo ID required.)*

BOTANICAL GARDENS. One of downtown Bucharest's prime grassy knolls, the **Botanical Gardens** are a shocking contrast to the wasteland that is the neighboring Civic Center. Owned by the university, the gardens are also home to a greenhouse and a botany museum, making it one of the only viable parks to visit on a rainy day. The gardens were a main demonstration sight during the 1848 revolution. *(M1: Politehnica; M3: Grozăveşti or Semănătoarea. Şos. Cotroceni 32. Across from Cotroceni Palace. Open in summer daily 8am-7:30pm; off-season 9:30am-3:30pm; last entrance 30min. before closing. Museum and greenhouses open Tu, Th, and Su 9am-1pm. L3000.)*

OTHER SIGHTS

Several of modern Bucharest's most fashionable streets are sights in and of themselves; be sure to stroll along Calea Victoriei, şos. Kiseleff, Bd. Aviatorilor, and Bd. Magheru. The side streets just off Piaţa Victoriei and Calea Dorobanţilor, with names like Paris, Washington, and Londra, brim with villas and houses typical of the beautiful Bucharest that once was, and demonstrate that even an occasional communist monster can be successfully integrated into a neighborhood.

FREE PRESS HOUSE. (Casa Presei Libere). In the good old days, a statue of Lenin stood on the steps of the ironically named Free Press House, a Stalinist monstrosity that housed the state propaganda machine. The building was constructed in the 1950s, supposedly as a copy of either Moscow University, Moscow's Ukraina Hotel, or Warsaw's Palace of Science (exactly which is unclear, but hey, all Socialist architecture looks alike anyway). It still houses Romania's "free" national press. *(M2: Aviatorilor. Follow Bd. Prezan from the Metro to şos. Kiseleff. Turn right after the Arcul de Triumf and walk along Herăstrău Park for quite some time; the Soviet monster will rise unmistakably in front of you.)*

OBOR MARKET. If you're in the mood for something truly Romanian, visit the huge market at the Obor Metro stop. Among many other possibilities, you are likely to find eggs, raw wool, rusty nails, Bulgarian cigarettes, Turkish Levis, shower heads, fly paper, ceramic plates, and ducks. There are as many kinds of sellers as there are products; some are well established in air-conditioned stores at the adjacent mall, while others stand in the crowd calling out their price for smuggled goods, ready to look innocent when the police arrive. *(M3: Obor.)*

GHENCEA CEMETERY. This outlying cemetery is the final resting place for the Ceaşescu family. Nicolae and his wife Elena were buried here in 1989 under pseudonyms. Today, their graves are marked with their real names. Nicolae's grave is surprisingly visited by a steady stream of mourners, mostly die-hard communists and elderly Romanians, who keep it decorated with flowers and crosses. The *Condăctor's* grave is to the left of the central walkway, surrounded by a small black fence. Elena's grave is significantly more neglected on the other side of the walkway; she is marked only by a chipping, warped wooden cross. Their son, Nicu, is also buried here in a jarringly opulent tomb. *(From Piaţa Unirii, take bus #173, 203, 204, 214, or 303; or tram # 8, 47, 58.)*

MUSEUMS

Bucharest's museums vary widely in quality, but all are a welcome indoor break from the grim specter of Bucharest's streets. The new **Circului Park** is a delightfully bizarre outdoor museum of painted sculptures carved into tree trunks and makes for a pleasant afternoon stroll. (M3: Ştefan cel Mare. Just off Str. Ştefan cel Mare, after the circus at the end of Aleea Circului.)

Museum of the Romanian Peasant (Muzeul Tăranului Român), şos. Kiseleff 3 (tel. 650 53 60). M2 or 3: Piaţa Victoriei. Named the best museum in Europe 1996-1997 according to the foyer's plaques, and definitely Bucharest's museum star. The exhibits of religious iconography proves that the museum is finally shedding Ceauşescu's shackles, although his portrait hangs inside next to a painting of Stalin. Open Tu-Su 10am-6pm; last admission at 5pm. L10,000, students L3000.

Jewish History Museum of Romania (Muzeul de Istorie a Comunitaţilor Evreieşti din România), Str. Mămularai 3 (tel. 315 08 37). M2: Piaţa Unirii. Head up Bd. Corneliu Coposu from Piaţa Unirii, near Unirea. Take the first right across a parking lot between Unirea and the KMO store, and turn left at the very end of the street. The museum is on the right in the Great Synagogue. Many Romanian history museums disconcertingly skip the last 50-80 years, but not so with this one. The ground floor focuses on the history of Romania's Jewish community, while the first floor displays Jewish contributions to Romanian culture. The central sculpture mourns the 350,000 Romanian Jews deported and murdered by the Nazis. Ask the multilingual attendants to explain anything you don't understand. Open W and Su 9am-1pm. L5000.

Cotroceni Palace and National Museum (Muzeul Naţional Cotroceni), şos. Cotroceni 37 (tel. 410 05 81). M1: Politehnica. Head east on Bd. Iuliu Maniu and continue on şos. Cotroceni; the entrance is on the right. You must call ahead to visit. Originally built as a monastery, Cotroceni became home to Romania's crown prince Ferdinand. Despite a 1977 earthquake, the museum is in good shape thanks to renovations by Ceauşescu, who wanted to make the building into a hotel for diplomats. Check out the lovely Rococo flower room, the table where Mihai I signed his abdication in 1947, or see, from a distance, the current home of the president of Romania. Open M-F 9:30am-4pm. L25,000, students L15,000; temporary exhibits L10,000.

The Village Museum (Muzeul Satului), şos. Kiseleff 28/30 (tel. 222 91 10). M2: Aviatorilor; bus #205, 301, or 331. In Herăstrău Park. Although it's no substitute for the real Romanian countryside, this open-air museum excellently recreates peasant dwellings. Open W-Su in summer noon-6pm; off-season 8am-4pm. L25,000.

National Art Museum (Muzeul Naţional de Artă), Calea Victoriei 49/53 (tel. 313 30 30). M2: Piaţa Universităţii. In the Royal Palace in Piaţa Revolutiei. The permanent collection is still closed for renovations after the damages it sustained in the 1989 revolution, but there are some temporary exhibits. Open W-Su 10am-6pm. L10,000, students L5000; separate admission for each building.

ROMANIA

ENTERTAINMENT

Cinemas show a variety of foreign films, most from America and all with Romanian subtitles. Most cinemas look like renovated concert halls; the best view is typically from the first balcony. **Cinema Eforiei,** Str. Eforiei 2 (tel. 313 04 83), shows classic old American films for L8000. (M2: Piaţa Universităţii.) For complete film listings, check *Sapte Seri*, an entertainment guide available at most hotels and restaurants. Film prices run L8000-L20,000; students sometimes get half-price. Bucharest hosts some of the biggest **rock festivals** this side of Berlin; guests include rising indie groups as well as falling stars like Michael Jackson (who from the balcony of the Parliamentary Palace responded to screaming fans with "Hello, Budapest!") or, more recently, Metallica. Inquire at the tourist office.

Theater and **opera** are extremely inexpensive diversions in Bucharest. (Tickets L21,000-42,000.) Like every other European city, performances are on hiatus from June-September. Tickets are sold at each theater's box office and go on sale the Saturday before the performance. Seats tend to go quickly, but whatever is left is available for half-price 1hr. before showtime. If a performance is sold out, ask to speak to the manager; he or she may be able to provide you with house seats.

Teatrul Naţional, Bd. N. Bălcescu 2 (tel. 613 91 75). M2: Piaţa Universităţii. In Piaţa Universităţii. The center of theatrical activity in Bucharest. Huge banners outside announce the season's plays. Also home to the **Teatrul de Operetă** (tel. 313 63 48).

Teatrul Bulandra, Str. Schitu Măgureanu 1 (tel. 314 75 46). One of Bucharest's top theaters and the only one in town to (sporadically) perform in English.

Ateneul (tel. 315 68 75), Piaţa Revoluţiei. M2: Piaţa Universităţii. Holds excellent classical music concerts.

Opera Română, Bd. M.L. Kogălniceanu 70 (tel. 313 18 57). M1, 3: Eroilor. Stages top-notch opera for ridiculously inexpensive prices.

Teatrul Evreiesc, Str. Iuliu Barasch 15 (tel. 323 45 30). M2: Piaţa Unirii. Europe's only state-run Jewish theater. The shows are in Yiddish, and the Romanian headphone translations probably won't help. Performances run throughout the summer.

NIGHTLIFE

Pack a map and cab fare—streets are poorly lit and public transportation stops at 11:30pm. Bars and nightclubs around the center crawl with the *nouveau riche* and foreign businesspeople, while those in the M3: Semănătoarea and Grozăveşti are filled with students. Bucharest also suffers from the summer disease: clubs and popular hangouts slow down or close while everyone goes away for vacation.

R1, R2, R3 ("Regie"), and **Maxxx,** amid student dorms. M3: Semănătoarea and Grozăveşti. Take the last Metro (11:30pm) to Semănătoarea and let the noisy crowd lead you through the maze of dorms. First comes R2, on the right, followed after about 50m by R1—straight ahead—and R3—to the left. Maxxx is nearby. The most popular discos in town during the school year (Oct.-late June). Cheap beer (L10,000 or less per bottle; free beer Tu at R2), rave music (R1 and R2), mixed music (R3), and inevitable late-night jam sessions add to the great atmosphere. Cover for men L15,000; women free M-F, L10,000 Sa-Su. Open Oct.-late June daily 9:30pm-4am.

Backstage, Str. Gabroveni 14 (tel. 315 08 12). M2: Piaţa Unirii. A popular dance club in the Old Town that draws heavy drinkers and raucous dancers. L20,000 drink minimum. Open daily 8pm-5am.

Lăptărie, Bd. N. Bălcescu 2. M2: Piaţa Universităţii. At the National Theater. Enter where the theater and the operetta buildings meet and take the elevator to the top. At night, a terrace and bar entertain Bucharest's hippest. In winter, jazz concerts (L30,000-50,000) replace the summer attraction of movies shown out on the terrace (L10,000). Terrace open in summer daily 9:30pm-3am; bar open off-season daily 10am-2am.

Café Indigo, Str. Eforiei 2 (tel. 312 63 36). M2: Piaţa Universităţii. Jazz and blues sound off; Cinema Eforie, upstairs, plays American film classics. Open from 6am until late.

Club A, Str. Blanari 14 (tel. 315 68 53). M2: Piaţa Universitătii. Walk down Bd. Brătianu and take the 3rd right; Club A is on the right. Always crowded by 11pm, this club run by the University of Bucharest's School of Architecture draws an international crowd. Tu jazz, W blues, Th alternative, F-Sa disco, Su oldies. Cover Tu-Th men L15,000, women free; F-Sa L20,000. Open Tu-Su 9pm-5am. Closed in summer.

Swing House, Str. Gabroveni 30 (tel. 223 70 93). M2: Piaţa Unirii. Hyper dance club pulls an enthusiastic crowd. Live music nightly, with weekly swing performances. L30,000 drink minimum. Open daily 6pm-6am.

Dubliner Irish Pub, Bd. N. Titulescu 18 (tel. 222 94 73). M2, 3: Piaţa Victoriei. An expensive ex-pat haunt for those desperate to speak English. The best *Guinness* south of the Carpathians. Open daily noon-3am.

NEAR BUCHAREST: SNAGOV

Snagov is a tiny village 45km north of Bucharest, making it an ideal daytrip. On summer weekends, hordes descend upon **Snagov Park** where you can swim in the brownish lake, try waterskiing (L100,000), or call across the water for a boat to take you to **Snagov Monastery.** Here, allegedly, lies the grave of the infamous Vlad Ţepeş. It's difficult to identify a body without the head, though, which is supposedly in Turkey. Having learned his methods as a hostage in Turkey in his youth, this Wallachian prince—the model for the mythical **Count Dracula**—earned a reputation for impaling the heads of criminals and captured Turks, and then using them as decorative touches along the walls of his mansion. Vlad rebuilt the Snagov Monastery and added a jail for prisoners accused of high treason, a veritable *Who's Who* of Romanian heroes during the 1848 revolution. Today, only the church remains, and it's undergoing restoration. Ask the nun and priest who live on this lonely island to let you in. (English pamphlet L15,000.)

GETTING THERE. Trains head for Snagov daily; two leave **Bucharest** in the morning and two return in the evening (1hr., L12,000). The train does not leave you close to either the lake or the monastery. Some hitch from the train station or from Bucharest, but *Let's Go* does not recommend hitchhiking. You can avoid the hassle by going on a tour organized by Villa Helga. (US$40 per car; max. 4 persons. See **Bucharest: Accommodations,** p. 512.)

NEAR BUCHAREST: CURTEA DE ARGEȘ

Hiding in the foothills of the Făgăraș Mountains, Curtea de Argeș (CURT-ya DAR-jesh) preserves buildings that date back to the town's 14th-century heyday as Wallachia's capital. Noted for its monastery and the legend surrounding it, Curtea also serves as an excellent base for would-be-slayers seeking **Count Dracula's real castle, Cetatea Poienari,** 27km away. A bus from the station in Curtea de Argeș (take a right from the train station) takes you most of the way to the castle (40min., 4-7 per day, L7500). From here, continue on foot 500m along the main road until you see the Cetatea Poienari sign. The 1500 steps leading to the castle are appropriately tortuous, zig-zagging for 30min. up the mountain. Don't fear if you lose sight of both the start and the end of the trail: you're not lost, and the insects and goats will keep you company. The partially restored ruins eventually emerge from the clouds. (Open Tu-Su 9am-5pm. L2200. English brochure L5000.) **Taxis** (L100-125,000 round-trip) may seem an easier way to reach the castle, but they do not spare you the 1500-step climb.

GETTING THERE. Trains run from **Bucharest** to **Pitești** (*accelerat* 1½-2hr.), where a connection heads to Curtea (1hr., 6 per day, total trip L71,000). **Buses** run to **Sibiu** (4hr., 2 per day, L36,000), and are the only way to get north. A **tourist office** (open M-F 8am-4pm, Sa-Su 8-11am) awaits inside Hotel Posada, Str. Basarabilor 27. To reach the monastery from the train station, turn left and head right up the cobblestone Str. Castenilor. Go right at the small park, then left onto what becomes the main **Str. Basarabilor.** Yellow and blue signs point the way to "Mănăstirea Curtea de Argeș." At the fork past the hotel, take a right. The hotel is 1km past the train station; the monastery is another 500m. **Phone code:** (0)48

ROMANIA

SHE'S A BRICK...HOUSE The legend of the Curtea de Argeș monastery, learned by all Romanian school children, is no less gruesome than that of Vlad Tepeș. In 1512, Voievod Neagoe Basarab directed Master Manole to build the most beautiful church the world had ever seen. The best craftspeople were assembled to carry out his command, but work continually stalled–everything accomplished during the day was mysteriously destroyed at night. The builders redoubled their efforts, but the pattern continued. The solution finally came to Manole in a dream: unless human blood coursed through the church's stones, it could not possibly be erected. Since few unsuspecting travelers came through town, the workers naturally decided to entomb the first of their wives to arrive at the site the next morning. Only honest Manole did not warn his wife. She was buried within the walls of the monastery and work proceeded. As the men placed the last tiles on the roof, Basarab asked them whether they could ever build another church so beautiful. All answered that they could–and would–build another even more splendid. Furious that his church might be outdone, the prince removed all the ladders and scaffolding, leaving the craftsmen to die on the roof. Clever Manole attempted to fly from the roof with a pair of wings he fashioned, but he didn't get very far. A fountain across the street marks the site of his crash landing. (Monstery open daily 8am-7pm. L5000.)

TRANSYLVANIA

Though the name evokes images of a dark, evil land of black magic and vampires, Transylvania *(Ardeal)* is actually a region of green hills and mountains descending gently from the Carpathians to the Hungarian Plain, dotted with towns such as Cluj-Napoca with significant Hungarian populations. This is Romania's most Westernized region, due to geography and the influence of Austrian rule and ethnic minorities. Cities are cleaner, services better, and waiters friendlier. Even the speech is slower and more musical, with a few regional expressions such as *"fain"* (good, fine, or cool) and the Austrian *"Servus!"* (hello). The vampire legends, however, have their roots in the remarkable architecture: Transylvanian buildings are tilted, jagged, and more sternly Gothic than anywhere else in Eastern Europe, as a visit to ancient Alba Iulia will illustrate.

CLUJ-NAPOCA

The population of Cluj-Napoca (CLOOZH na-PO-ka), Transylvania's unofficial capital and student center, is not fully Romanian (a third of the population forms a vocal Hungarian minority). Nationalistic mayor Funar, however, wants to make sure that at least the town itself is as Romanian as possible. Consequently, the decorative street bulbs, bus and trolley tickets, and the benches in the center are all distinctively blue, yellow, and red, the colors of the Romanian flag. The city's name reflects its rich heritage—Napoca from the city's Roman name, Cluj (derived from Klausenburg) from medieval German domination and life under the Habsburgs. A better-run and more upbeat city than Bucharest most of the year, Cluj-Napoca loses much of its vitality with the student exodus in June.

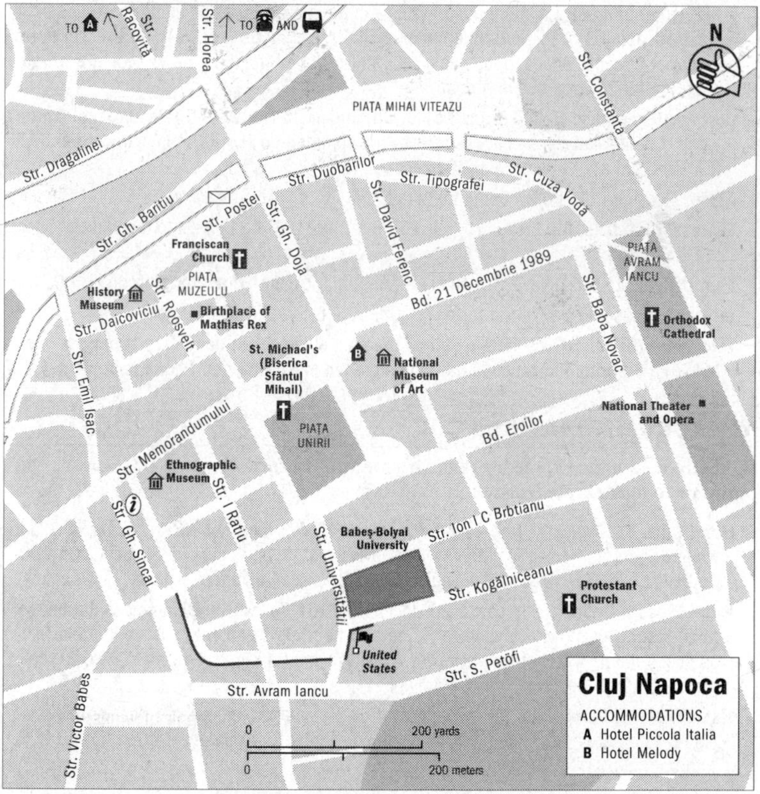

ORIENTATION

About 200km from Bucharest and 135km from the Hungarian border, Cluj is well connected to many Romanian cities by bus and train. From the **train station,** the **bus station** is a quick walk to the right and another right across a bridge. Buses #3 and 4, left and across the street from the train station, run to Piaţa Mihai Viteazul (round-trip L3300). Continue along the road away from the river and past McDonald's in the center of town, turning right on Bd. 21 Decembrie 1989 to reach the center. On foot, cross the street and head down Str. Horea, which changes to Str. Gh. Doja after crossing the river. The main square, **Piaţa Unirii** (1km), spreads at the end of Str. Gh. Doja.

PRACTICAL INFORMATION

Trains: CFR (tel. 19 24 75), Piaţa Mihai Viteazul. Open M-F 7am-7pm. To: **Alba Iulia** (2hr., 1 per day, *accelerat* L40,000); **Braşov** (5hr., 8 per day, *accelerat* L80,000); **Bucharest** (7hr., 7 per day, *accelerat* L45,600); **Budapest** (9-12hr., 4 per day, round-trip L400,000); **Sibiu** (4hr., 1 per day, *accelerat* L50,000); **Iaşi** via **Suceava** (9hr., 4 per day, *accelerat* L90,000); and **Timişoara** (5hr., 8 per day, *accelerat* L80,000).

Buses: Str. Giordano Bruno 3 (tel. 43 52 78), near the train station. To: **Budapest** (9hr., M-Tu and Th-F 7am, L180,000) and **Sibiu** (3-4hr., 1 per day, L80,000).

Taxis: Rows of cabs wait at the train and bus stations. Look for cabs with an official company sign listing a phone number and the price per km.

Tourist Office: OJT Feleacul, Str. Memorandumului (tel. 19 69 55), three blocks from Unirii, with an old city map in front. Open M-F 8am-8pm, Sa-Su 9am-12:30pm. Check with either to arrange a group tour of Cluj (with an English-speaking guide for groups of at least 10 people) or to **exchange currency.** OJT sells maps (L6000) and can get hotel rooms at cheaper prices, both within Cluj and beyond. May be able to secure a private room (US$9-20) or a bed in a dorm.

Currency Exchange: Bancă Transilvania, Bd. Eroilor 36 (tel. 19 45 67), off Piaţa Avram Iancu. Cashes traveler's checks for a 0.75% commission (L5000 minimum). Open M-F 8:30am-1pm and 3-7pm, Sa 9:30am-1pm.

ATMs: Along Str. Gh. Doja leading to Piaţa Unirii.

Express Mail: DHL, Bd. Eroilor 10 (tel. 19 06 92; fax 19 04 81), next to the church. Open M-F 9am-4pm.

Post Office: Str. Gh. Doja 33. Open M-F 7am-9pm, Sa 7am-1pm. **Postal Code:** 3400.

Internet Access: Kiro Internet Cafe, Str. Gh. Doja 6, 3rd fl. L10,000 per hr.

Telephone Office: Tel. 12 48 24. Behind the post office. Open daily 7am-10pm; fax open M-F 7am-8:30pm. Phones in Piaţa Unirii are open M-F 7am-9pm. **Phone code:** (0)64.

ACCOMMODATIONS

Lodging in Cluj is expensive, and private rooms hard to come by. Call well in advance to make arrangements.

Hotel Onix, Str. Albini 12 (tel. 41 40 76; fax 41 40 47) Take bus #3 to "Albini." Brilliant white exterior and gorgeous rooms with shower, phone, and color TV. Singles L285,000; doubles L320,000. Breakfast included. Call 1-2 days in advance, especially for singles.

Hotel Piccola Italia, Str. Racoviţă 20 (tel. 13 61 10). Follow Gh. Doja across the bridge, turn slightly left off what becomes Horea and head up the hill. Small hotel offers fairly spacious rooms with hot-water shower, TV, and use of a fridge. Singles L200,000; doubles L250,000. Reserve 2 days in advance.

Hotel Melody, Piaţa Unirii 29 (tel. 19 74 65). Restaurant, sidewalk cafe, and a risqué nightly cabaret show. Pricey, but the rooms are neat and modern. Doubles L240,000, with bath L350,000. Breakfast included. MC/Visa.

FOOD

Don't miss the chocolaty *Doboş Cluj,* a local specialty cake. A big indoor/outdoor **market** invades Piaţa Mihai Viteazul daily as long as it's light out, and sometimes even when it isn't. Part of the **Sora grocery store,** Bd. 21 Decembrie, across and farther down from Hotel Melody, is open 24hr.

Restaurant Panoramic, Str. Şerpuitoare 31 (tel. 43 20 80). Climb Cetăţuie Hill for the panoramic view, then follow the unpaved path behind Hotel Transilvania away from the cross monument (5min.) to reward yourself with a hearty dinner. Entrees (from L20,000) will wash away fatigue. Open M 3pm-midnight, Tu-Su noon-midnight.

Mary's, Str. Pavlov 27 (tel. 19 19 47), off Str. Gh. Bariţiu. Take the first metallic bridge after the one with the restaurant sign; the entrance is in the backyard. Candlelit interior or leafy terrace. Meat entrees under L25,000. Open daily noon-midnight. Call ahead.

Restaurant Privighetoarea (Nightingale), Str. Gh. Doja 16 (tel. 19 34 80). Savor delicious mushroom specialties and meat dishes (L20-45,000). Open daily 9am-11pm. MC/Visa

SIGHTS

PIAŢA UNIRII. Most strolls begin here, where the 80m Gothic steeple of the Catholic **Church of St. Michael** (Biserica Sf. Mihail) pierces the skyline. Ancient frescoes discovered during 1993 renovations shine anew. Near the entrance is an English summary of the church's history. *(Services daily 6:15 and 7:30am, Su 7, 8:45, 10, 11:30am, and 6pm.)* Around the corner you'll find the supposed **birthplace of Mathias Rex,** now home to the Art School. *(At the corner of the Piata and Str. Memorandumului, walk about 50m down Str. Matei Corvin.)*

BÁNFFY PALACE. The most notable of the palaces in the square, this is now home to the **National Museum of Art** (Muzeul Naţional de Artă), a collection focusing on Romanian work. *(Tel. 19 69 53. Piata Unirii 30. Open W-Su 10am-5pm. L6000.)*

PIAŢA AVRAM IANCU. In the square you'll find the Byzantine-Romanian **Orthodox Cathedral** (Catedrala Arhiepiscopală), built in 1933. *(Open Tu-F and Su 6:15am-8pm, M and Sa 6:30am-1pm and 5-8pm.)* The newly built **statue of Avram Iancu** in front is one of Mayor Funar's favorite projects; it replaced a Soviet tank. The **National Theater and Opera** (Teatrul Naţional şi Opera Română; tel. 19 53 63), also in the square, imitates Paris's Garnier Opera House. Performances run 2-3 times per week. Buy tickets at Piaţa Ştefan cel Mare 14. *(From Piata Unirii, head along either busy Str. 21 Dec. 1989—which commemorates the victims of the 1989 revolution—or Bd. Eroilor. Season Oct.-June. Open daily 11am-5pm. Best seats L20,000, students L4000. Tickets for Hungarian opera (Sept.-June) are sold at Emil Isaac 26-27 (tel. 19 34 68) at the end of Str. G. Baritiu. L20,500, students L6000.)*

ROMANIA

PIAŢA MUZEULUI. A 13th-century Franciscan **monastery** here is home to the Music High School. The **Franciscan Church** (Biserica Franciscanilor) has a Baroque interior that belies its foundation on a Roman temple site. The **Carolina Monument** used to grace Piaţa Unirii, but was moved next to the archaeological excavation to make room for the statue of Mathias Rex. Opposite is the **History Museum** (Muzeul de Istorie), with a 17th-century printing press and a flying machine built by a Cluj University professor in 1896. *(Str. Constantin Daicoviciu 2. Open Tu-Su 10am-4pm. L3000.)* The

MINCING WORDS Possibly the most disputed monument in Eastern Europe sits outside the Church of St. Michael. The equestrian likeness of the half-Romanian Cluj-born king Mathias Rex (Matei Corvin) was erected in 1902, when Transylvania was still part of the Austro-Hungarian Empire. Originally meant to symbolize harmony between Romania and Hungary, the statue has since come to symbolize ethnic tension. In 1933, historian Nicolae Iorga added an inscription denying that King Mathias had conquered Transylvania, which the Hungarians deleted in 1940. The communists diplomatically labeled the monument in Latin, but in 1992 nationalist Mayor Funar had Iorga's words reinscribed. Although UNESCO protects the statue, the quarrel continues.

Transylvania Ethnographic Museum (Muzeul Etnografiea al Transilvaniei) displays Romanian, Hungarian, and Saxon objects. *(Tel. 19 23 44. Str. Memorandumului 21. Open Tu-Su 9am-5pm. L3000, students L1500. To reach the square, head toward Casă lui Matei Corvin, turn left, then turn right again onto Str. Franklin Delano Rooswelt.)*

UNIVERSITY DISTRICT. The student area lies south of the main square on Str. Universitații. The 15th-century **Protestant Church** often hosts organ concerts. In front, a replica of the statue of St. George slays a dragon (the original is in Prague). Many of the townsfolk took refuge in this church when the town was attacked; halfway around the left wall of the church, above the secret escape door, is a partially buried cannonball. *(Kogblniceanu 21. Turn left on Str. Mihail Kogblniceanu.)* A block behind the church lies **Tailor's Bastion** (Bastionul Croitorilor), one of the remnants of the medieval defense wall. In front of the bastion, a statue of **Baba Novac,** wearing the national colors, whose Houdini-esque escape from a Turkish prison is legendary. The small **Orthodox Church** was the first Romanian Orthodox church in Cluj. The Ottomans did not permit Romanians to build an Orthodox church of stone until 1795, and then only outside the city walls. *(Off Universitatii, turn right on Str. Avram Iancu, and then left on Str. Bisericii Orthodoxe. Open daily 7:30am-7pm.)*

NEAR CETĂTUIE HILL. North of Piața Unirii, a short walk down Str. Gh. Doja leads to Piața Mihai Viteazul, named after the king of Muntenia who unified the Romanian principalities in 1600. Cross the bridge from Str. Gh. Doja and head left to the stairs to Cetățuie Hill; a dazzling view awaits. Down the hill and across the river lies the majestic but narrow **Parcul Central.** *(Rowboats rentals daily 8am-7:30pm. L5000 per person per 30min.)* The **Botanical Garden** (Grădină Botanica) might be the most relaxing and beautiful in Romania. *(Open daily 9am-7pm. L4000. A truly useful map L3000.)* From Piața Unirii, take Str. Napoca to Piața Blaja, then head left up to Str. Gh. Bilașcu. There's a Japanese garden with a pond and bridge, a Roman garden, greenhouses with waterlilies, orchids, and palm trees, and an ivy-clad tower.

NIGHTLIFE

Bars and clubs in this youthful city are plentiful, but empty out when the local students glut the sea-bound trains after the last bell in early July.

Diesel Club, Piața Unirii 17 (tel. 19 84 41), right across from Biserica Sfântul Mihail. Pass the ancient half-wall and descend to the centuries-old cellar. Thick vaults cordon off intimate rooms with couches and tiny black chairs where the 20-something crowd gathers to listen to jazz. 2-3 concerts per month; L10,000-15,000. Open 24hr.

Bianco & Nero, Universitătii 7-9 (tel. 19 65 01), next to the yellow Catholic church in the courtyard of the American Embassy Info Center at the University. Once the most popular disco in Cluj, now a bit more low-key. Cover F-Su L10,000, drink included. Cover W-Th L4000; students only (bring ID). Open W-Su 9pm-4am.

Hully Gully (tel. 42 68 93), on Str. Ciobanului. Take bus #4 to Mămăștur. A new dance club that draws all the business from its competitors. L10,000 cover; women L5000 Su. Open Th-Su 9am-4am.

ROMANIA

NEAR CLUJ-NAPOCA: THE APUSENI MOUNTAINS, BELIȘ, & SCĂRIȘOARA

The tiny, restful lake resort at **Beliș,** deep in the wilds of the **Apuseni Mountains** (Munții Apuseni), was all the doing of a dam downstream that created the artificial lake **Fântânele.** It's even possible to see a church steeple under the lake's surface when the water level falls. The resort entertains year-round with hiking, skiing, and water sports. More **hiking** awaits on the south side of the Apuseni; buy **maps** (L4000) at the reception of pricey hotel **Stațiunea Fântânele.** Some of the world's most spectacular frozen formations hang from **Scărișoara's Ice Cave** (Peștera Ghețarului). Visit in the spring before everyting melts. Guides may charge up to US$15-18. **Cetatea Ponorolui** lies a day's hike from Scărișoara on the Karstic-Padiș plateau. An underground river with lakes and 100m tall caverns runs under these three cliffs. The surrounding region of Podiş rewards the determined tourist with unspoiled beauty—serene streams, hidden caves, and dazzling views. **Maps** of the hiking trails are available in Beliş, or visit **Rural Eco-Tours Agro-Montan (RETAM),** Str. Libertătii 3 (tel./fax 43 03 30), for information on cycling, hiking, and accommodations in the mountains. RETAM also organizes tours (US$14-30 per day).

If you're staying in Beliş, **Pensiunea Geomolean** (tel. 25 15 30) is expensive, but a good value. Included in the price of a room are home-cooked meals and rides—on horses, in a motorboat, or in a romantic carriage with rather unromantic jolts. (US$30-35 per person.) The budget **Popasul Turistic "Brădet"** has doubles and triples (L25,000 per person) and tiny cabana beds (L18,000 per person). It's open only in summer, and there's only one shower, but guests can use the kitchen.

GETTING THERE. **Huedin** is the closest train station to Beliş (1hr. from Cluj-Napoca, 9 per day, L4700). A bus makes the 35km trek from Huedin to the resort (M-F 4 per day, Sa-Su 2 per day, L7000). From the station, turn right and head parallel to the tracks to reach the bus. To get to **Peştera Gheţarului,** take the **bus** from Cluj-Napoca to **Cîmpeni** (3½hr., 3 per day, L50,000). You'll need to get to the village of **Gîrda** (many hitch) to find a guide. Once there, follow the unpaved road along the Bistra River Valley (17km). Shortly after passing the river's source and hitting a fork in the road, the path merges with the red-stripe trail, which leads west to the cave. After 14km, it intersects an unpaved road that leads to Beliş (22km north) and Poiana Horea (7km north). To the south lies Albac (14km). Continue west another 12km to the cave.

ALBA IULIA

Alba Iulia (AL-bah YOO-lee-ah), the historic capital of Transylvania, reflects its regal legacy in almost every building of its old citadel. Churches, museums, and monuments testify to a history going back to the early Dacians 2000 years ago. More recently, King Ferdinand and Queen Maria were crowned here on October 15, 1922, appeasing Transylvanian nationalists and sealing Romanian unification.

ORIENTATION & PRACTICAL INFORMATION. The **train station** is a 15min. walk from the center. Walk straight from the station exit to the five-way intersection. Take a soft right, then walk five blocks. At the graveyard, take a left on **Str. Mihai Viteazul** to reach the hotels and tourist services in **Piaţa Iuliu Maniu.** Or, Maxi-Taxi **minivans** (Alba Iulia's answer to mass transit) run from the station to Piaţa Iuliu Maniu en route to the Cetate (L1500). **Trains** arrive from: **Bucharest** (6hr., 5 per day, L90,000); **Cluj-Napoca** (2hr., 4 per day, L36,000); **Sibiu** (2hr., 2 per day, L32,000); and **Timişoara** (5½hr., 3 per day, L32,000). The bus station (tel. 81 29 67), near the train station, sends **buses** to: **Cluj-Napoca** (3hr., 2 per day, L32,000). **ATMs** are available at most major banks, including the Bancomat near Piaţa Iuliu Maniu. Get as much internet as you can handle at the **Computer Club/Internet Cafe,** Avintlilui 3. (L10,000 per hr. Open 10am-10pm.) The **post office,** Piaţa Eroilor 2 (tel. 81 12 34), is in front of the statue of Romulus and Remus. (Open M-F 7am-8pm, Sa 8am-noon.) **Telephones** and **fax** are nearby in the big circular building. (Open daily 7am-9pm.) **Postal code:** 2500. **Phone code:** (0)58.

ACCOMMODATIONS & FOOD. **Mini-Hotel,** Str. Mihai Viteazul 6 (tel. 81 63 54), maintains doubles with modern (excluding the "consistent hot water" part of modern) communal bathrooms. Right at the first portal to the Citadel (L100,000). On the other side of the Citadel, **Hotel Cetate,** Str. Unirii 3 (tel. 81 17 80), spoils its clients with a multitude of freebies (local phone calls, mail service, wake up) and paid services (laundry L5000-25,000 per item). The hotel also boasts a bar, a restaurant, and bright rooms with bath. (Singles L464,000; doubles L510,000. Breakfast L40,000. MC/Visa.)

Restaurants and **groceries** line Piaţa Iuliu Maniu and Bd. Travsilvaniu across town. Piaţa Iuliu Maniu 14 is notable for cramming most food products known to man into its small space and the one next door. The **Mini-Hotel's restaurant** serves up myriad salads, entrees (L12,000-24,000) and *clătite* (crepes; L4000-7000) downstairs among bizarre green couches. (Open 24hr.) **Restaurant Transilvania** (tel. 81 11 95), in the hotel of the same name in Piața Iuliu Maniu, serves stellar Romanian food. (Meat dishes L30,000. Live folk music daily 7am-midnight. MC/Visa.)

SIGHTS. Str. Mihai Viteazul leads to the heart of the **Alba Carolina Citadel (Cetate).** After the citadel's first sculpted gate, a cobblestone ramp continues to the second portal, currently under renovation. The moat is a grassy field and the drawbridge a road, but it doesn't take much to imagine the stronghold as it was centuries ago. The **white obelisk** at the top of the ramp honors Horia, Cloşca, and Crişan, martyred leaders of the 1784 peasant uprising against the Hungarian overlords. The stairs to the left after the ornate arch lead to a great view, the very same one Horia enjoyed before his execution. Two more blocks up the fortress's central road, the **statue of King Mihai Viteazul,** who briefly united the Romanian principalities in 1600, comes into view (see **History,** p. 500). A right off Str. Mihai Viteazul at the monument leads to the **Museum of Unification** (Muzeul Unirii; tel. 81 33 00), which traces the development of Alba Iulia from the Dacians to contemporary times. The **Unification Hall** (Sala Unirii), garnished on the outside with a row of busts, centers around the table on which the charter unifying Transylvania and Romania was signed. (Both open Tu-Su 10am-5pm; ticket office closes at 4:30pm. L4000, students L2000; Sala Unirii L3000, students L1500.)

The 1246 **Roman Catholic Cathedral** rises on Str. Mihai Viteazul. Although the exterior is under construction, the inside is open to visitors; enter through the main gate. The church holds the tombs of the Huniade family, including Iancu de Hunedoara, "the White Knight of the Christians," who checked the 15th-century Ottoman invasion. While organ concerts occassionally pipe up, the rosewood sculptures in the alcoves are a more consistent attraction. For a guide in English, French, or German (L1000), enter the wooden door left of the Cathedral's exit and knock on the first door on the right. (Open M-F and Su 8am-5pm.) The **Orthodox Cathedral** (Catedrala din Alba Iulia), ahead to the right behind some orangey-brown columns, is usually referred to as the **Coronation Cathedral** (Catedrala Încoronării), since it was built for the coronation of King Ferdinand and Queen Maria in 1922. (Open M-Sa 6:30am-9pm, Su 7-9pm.) The cathedral was constructed on the site of the Roman Apoulon fortress. On the far side of the citadel from the Mihai Viteazul statue, the **Batthyaneum Library** (Biblioteca), Str. Bibliotecii 1 (tel. 81 19 39; officially open only to scholars), contains the 810 **Codex Aureus,** a work of gold-ink calligraphy done for Charlemagne.

WESTERN CARPATHIANS

The Carpathians roll westward into the marshland traditionally known as the Banat and toward the Great Plain of Hungary. Indeed, the entire region is a means to a westward end: Timişoara is Romania's most Western-spirited city while Oradea is the main transportation link to Hungary.

TIMIŞOARA

In 1989, 105 years after becoming the first European city illuminated by electric street lamps, Timişoara (Tee-mee-SHWAH-rah; pop. 325,000) ignited a revolution that left communism in cinders. Romania's westernmost city, Timişoara has always been on the forefront of its nation's cultural and economic change. Calmer and cleaner than Bucharest, but as student-filled, Timişoara remains a dynamic city.

ORIENTATION

Timişoara lies only 75km from the Hungarian border. By train, get off at **Timişoara Nord** rather than Timişoara Est. Trolley #11 and 14 run from the station to the center (round-trip L3000); get off when you see **Piața Victoriei** with its white Opera and the multicolored Metropolitan Cathedral. Trolley #1 runs by the Opera; get off when the tram turns left and backtrack a little. Or, turn left outside the station and follow **Bd. Republicii** to the opera. To the left and up a bit, **Str. Alba Iulia** leads to **Piața Libertății;** to the right, **Piața Victoriei** gathers crowds.

PRACTICAL INFROMATION

Trains: CFR Agentie de Voiaj, Piața Victoriei 2, 2nd floor (tel. 19 18 89). Sells tickets a week in advance. Open M-F 8am-8pm. To **Bucharest** (8hr., 8per day, *rapid* L170,000) and **Budapest** (5hr., 2 per day, round-trip L450,000).

Tourist Office: Colibri Travel and Tourism, Bd. C. D. Loga 2 (tel./fax 19 40 74), near Cinema Capitol. Friendly staff offers old but helpful **maps** for free, but specializes in tours. Open M-F 9am-5pm.

Currency Exchange: Exchange offices abound, especially on Str. Alba Iulia. On the ground floor of the Bega supermarket next to Hotel Continental. From Piața Libertății, take a right and follow the tram tracks 4 blocks. Change US$ or DM at bad rates. Open daily 10am-10pm. There is a Visa/MC/Cirrus/Plus **ATM** ahead and to your right as you stand with your back to the Opera.

English Bookstore: Mihai Eminescu, Măceşilor 2 (tel. 19 41 23), in the main square near Restaurant Bulevard. The English section is to the left of the entrance. Open M-F 9am-6pm, Sa 9am-2pm.

Post Office: Str. Piatra Craiului, off Bd. Republicii and Piața Victoriei. Open M-F 7am-8pm. **Postal code:** 1900.

Internet Access: Internet Cafe, Bd. Pîrvan Vasile 14 (tel. 29 30 32). On the left after you cross Michelangelo bridge; enter around back. Speedy connection. L10,000 per hr. Open 24hr.

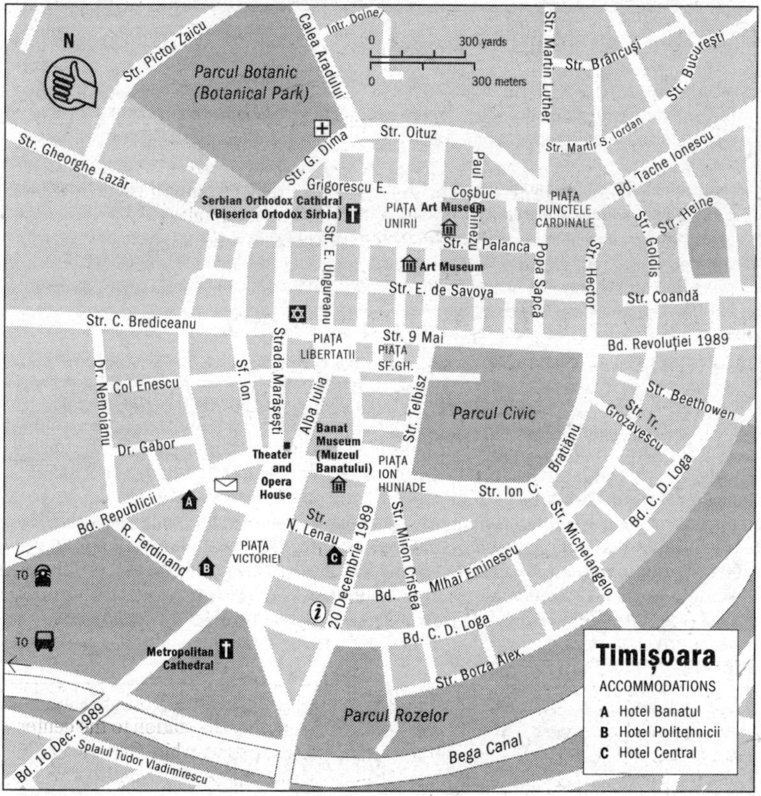

Telephones: Walking toward the Metropolitan Cathedral from the Opera, take the 1st left after the Romulus and Remus statue. Office is 50m ahead on the right. A machine out front sells L50,000 phone cards. Open daily 7am-1pm and 2-9pm. **Phone code:** (0)56.

ACCOMMODATIONS

Old **hotels** in Timişoara are cheap and decent. **Private rooms** are hard to find, but students might get lucky in the dorms on Bd. Dr. Victor Babeş in Complexul Studenţesc. Cross the bridge following Str. R. Ferdinand, continue down Str. Mihai Viteazul, and take a left onto Bd. Dr. Victor Babeş. (US$1-2. Open July-Aug.)

Hotel Banatul, Bd. Republicii 3-5 (tel. 19 19 03; fax 19 01 30). Rooms are decent, but the psychedelic decor may throw you off at first. Singles L70,000, with bath L120,000; doubles L120,000, L180,000; triples L180,000, L290,000. Breakfast included.

Hotel Central, Str. Lenau 6 (tel. 19 00 91). From the Opera, take the first left off Piaţa Victoriei. Very modern facilities and friendly staff. Clean rooms with TV and phone. Doubles with bath L240,000. Breakfast included.

Politehnicii, Str. Ferdinand 2 (tel. 22 00 00). Decent rooms in a good location. Singles L130,000; doubles L240,000. Breakfast included.

FOOD

Food is plentiful and fairly inexpensive. An **outdoor market,** Piaţa 700, sells fruits and veggies at the corner of Str. C. Brediceanu and Str. Paris. (Open daily 7am-9pm; slower on Sundays.) Don't miss the exquisite **kandia chocolates,** a local specialty, available at almost any kiosk in the center. Grocery stores and 24hr. snack shops abound in the Piaţa Victoriei area.

Braseria Opera (tel. 19 07 90), near the Opera. Grill/pizzeria with reproductions of turn-of-the-century paintings on the walls. Waitresses in short red skirts balance opera-themed dishes to the latest Eurobeat hits. Thick-crust pizza L20,000-40,000. Open daily 9am-midnight.

Restaurant N&Z, Str. Alba Iulia 1 (tel. 19 39 77), just before Piaţa Libertăţii on the left. This young, modern restaurant welcomes customers with sleek metal chairs and cable TV. Meaty entrees less than L30,000. Open daily 9am-midnight.

Fram (tel. 19 68 63), off Piaţa Victoriei, almost directly across from the telephones. Every sweet tooth's dream: real hot chocolates, *clătite,* and ice cream. Sweet prices as well. L2000-20,000. Open daily 9am-9pm.

SIGHTS

The tourist hub revolves around Piaţa Victoriei, with the **National Theater** and **Opera House** (Teatrul Naţional and Opera Timişoara) on one side, and Metropolitan Cathedral on the other. Off the square but near bleached **opera** (built on pillars because the place was originally a swamp), the old **Huniazilor Castle** houses the **Banat Museum** (Muzeul Banatului) which traces Timişoara's history. A comprehensive display of artifacts extends from pre-history to 1989, but mysteriously skips the 40 years following WWII. (Open Tu-Su 10am-4:30pm. L4000, students L2000, plus L2000 per photo taken.) **Metropolitan Cathedral,** across the square from the Opera, was built between 1936 and 1946 in Moldavian folk style, with a rainbow-tiled roof and 8000kg bells. (Open 24hr. Services M-F 6pm, Su 10am and 6pm.) An impressive **museum** downstairs displays religious artifacts; enter down the stairs in the front right corner of the church. (Open W-Su 10am-1pm. Free.) Piaţa Victoriei was a gathering place for protesters during the uprising against Ceauşescu. The wooden *troika* across the street and plaques at the entrance record the sacrifices made by the young revolutionaries of December 1989.

The **Park of Roses** (Parcul Rozelor) is worth the walk. With the Cathedral behind you, turn right and head straight down Bd. Loga past Str. 20 Decembrie 1989. Any right in the next few blocks will bring you to a park entrance. True to its name, the park has intimate white benches surrounded by hundreds upon hundreds of roses. Ideal for lovers during the day, it often hosts free concerts at night.

Str. Alba Iulia travels from Piața Victoriei past numerous shops to **Piața Libertății,** the old city center. The old **town hall,** Str. Ungureanu 1, houses an **Art School.** A Baroque-Renaissance structure from the 1700s, it is now the oldest edifice in Timișoara. On the left, Str. Ungureanu runs under the clock towers of the mustard-colored 1743 **Serbian Church** (Biserica Ortodoxă Sârbă), Str. Ungureanu 12. (Open M-F 7:45-9am, Sa 4-6pm, Su 10am-12:30pm.) Behind the church lies **Piața Unirii,** where the lamp posts and pavement were designed to appear turn-of-the-century. One of the paving stones has a map of the old citadel of Timișoara engraved on it. The quiet square's **Catholic Cathedral** (Domul Romano-Catolic) has survived many a battle since its construction in 1754. The **Old Prefecture** has a superb Baroque facade (under renovation). Water from the central fountain is said to be a remedy for stomach ailments. It certainly tastes like medicine.

ENTERTAINMENT

The **opera** ticket office is just up from the building, on Str. Mărășești. (Open Tu-Su 10am-12:30pm and 5-7pm. Tickets L15,000, students half-price.) To get to the **Crossroads Blues Club,** Str. Gh. Doja 34 (tel. 20 14 40), take a cab or walk down Bd. 16 Decembrie 1989 (the big street leading away from Piața Victoriei to the right as you face the Metropolitan Cathedral) and take the second left after the bridge. The bar is below street level. Enjoy good wine (L35,000-45,000 per bottle) and blues with a cool young crowd. (Live music monthly. Open M-Th and Su 6pm-2am, F-Sa 6pm-4am.) **Discoland** (tel. 19 80 08), near the Opera, is the reigning disco in town. (Cover Sa-Su L20,000, M-F L10,000; students free Th and Su all night, F-Sa 10-11pm. Open daily 10pm-4am.) **Discoteca Ștrand Termal** has a popular pool (L10,000). Turn left after crossing the Michelangelo Bridge from the center.

ORADEA

Only 20km from Romania's northwest border, Oradea (oh-RA-day-ah) will most likely be visited en route to or from Hungary. The downtown might have enough shops and restaurants to keep you occupied for a few hours between trains, but the town dies after the last train of the day leaves. **Banca Natională a României,** Parcul Traian 8, can do some last-minute forint/lei converting. If you do get stuck in Oradea overnight, skip the train station and crash at **Hotel Parc,** Str. Republicii 5 (tel. 41 16 99), whose luxurious rooms just might make you forget how utterly bored you are. (Singles L90,000; doubles L210,000, with bath L310,000). **Restaurant Oradea** (tel. 13 43 39), on Str. Republicii near the CFR travel agency, is convenient and calming, with muzak droning on as sonic wallpaper. (Entrees L30,000-40,000. Open daily 10am-1am.) **Postal code:** 3700. **Phone code:** (0)59.

GETTING AWAY. Trains whisk you away to: **Timișoara** (3-4hr., 2 per day, *accelerat* L50,000); **Budapest** (3hr., 4 per day, round-trip L400,000); and **Bucharest** (11hr., 1 per day, *accelerat* L100,000). To reach the center, take the tram that departs across the street from the station three stops to Str. Republicii (L3000). **Luggage storage** is available at Bagaje de Mână in the train station. (L7000-14,000. Open 24hr.)

TRANSYLVANIAN ALPS

The Southern Carpathians have protected the inhabitants of Munteria from almost every invader. The citadels and castles guarding Brașov and the fortress at Bran recall those who tried to tame this difficult region. But that intractable wilderness has remained largely untamed to this day, creating wonderful opportunities for hiking from Păltiniș, Sinaia, Poiana, Poiana Brașov, and into the Făgăraș Mountains. Both folk and high art can be found, as well, from marvelously preserved Sighișoara to the jazz festival at Sibiu and the sculpture gardens of Târgu Jiu.

SIBIU

One of Romania's oldest cities, Sibiu (SEE-bee-oo) was founded by German colonists in the 12th century and remains a town of medieval monuments and colorfully ornate houses. Culturally, Sibiu is marked by German and Hungarian influences, and socially, by a lethargic pace of life. This dormant volcano, however, erupts suddenly during the jazz festival in May.

ORIENTATION

To reach the center from the train station, walk 10min. up **Str. Generalu Magheru** (continue left at the fork) to **Piața Mare,** marked by a statue of Gheorghe Lazăr, founder of Romania's school system. The 18th-century **Roman-Catholic Church** separates Piața Mare from **Piața Mică.** From Piața Mare, continue straight up **Str. Nicolae Bălcescu** to **Piața Unirii.** This *piața* is only a few minutes away from the train station by **trolley** T1 or T2 (L3000 for 2 trips); get off at the third stop, when you see the Dumbrava department store or Hotel Bulevard. Go through the underpass to Hotel Bulevard, then turn right onto the pedestrian Str. Nicolae Bălcescu.

PRACTICAL INFORMATION

Trains: on Str. Generalu Maghero. To **Bucharest** via **Brașov** (5-8hr., 5 per day, *accelerat* L35,600). **CFR,** Str. N. Bălcescu 6. Near Hotel Împaratul Romanilor. Sells train tickets. Open M-F 7:30am-7:30pm.

Tourist Office: Prima Ardeleanu, Piața Unirii 1 (tel. 21 17 88). Free, new tourist maps. Open M-F 10am-7pm, Sa 10am-2pm.

Currency Exchange: EDF Asro, Str. N. Bălcescu 41 (tel. 21 50 57). Enter the alleyway, go up the first stairway on the left, and take a left at the landing. Exchanges currency and cashes traveler's checks for a reasonable commission (L1000 per L20,000). Open M-F 9am-6pm. Cirrus/MC/Visa **ATMs** are at **Banca Comerciala Română,** across from CFR on Str. N. Bălcescu, and on Calea Dumbrăvii.

English Bookstore: Thausib, Piața Mică 3 (tel. 21 57 74). Open M-F 9:30am-5:30pm, Sa 10am-2pm.

Post Office: In the light gray building at the corner of Str. Metropoliei and Str. Poștei. Open M-F 7am-8pm, Sa 8am-1pm. **Postal code:** 2400.

Internet Access: PVD-Net Group, Str. N. Bălcescu 5 (tel./fax 21 67 71; pvdnet.logicnet.ro). L6500 per 30min., L10,000 per hr. Open M-F 9am-6pm.

Telephones: At beginning of Str. N. Bălcescu. Open M-Sa 7am-7pm. **Phone code:** (0)69.

ACCOMMODATIONS

At the train station, look for locals offering **private rooms** (L70,000-90,000).

Hotel Bulevard, Piața Unirii 2/4 (tel. 21 60 60; fax 21 01 58). Ideal location. Majestic exterior, friendly staff, and modern rooms with small beds, private baths and nonstop hot water. Singles L230,000, with TV, fridge, and that special touch of class L260,000; doubles L490,000, L630,000. Breakfast included.

Hotel Parc, Str. Școala de Înot 3 (tel. 42 44 55). From the train station, take tram T1 or T2 four stops, backtrack, take two consecutive lefts, and walk down the street. Far from the center, but worth the trip. Singles with shower L200,000; doubles L300,000.

Hotel La Podul Minciunilor, Str. Azilului 1 (tel. 21 72 59). Walk down the stairs from the Bridge of Lies in Piața Mare and take the first left onto Str. Azilului; the hotel is on the right. Knock on the shutters if the gate is closed. Laundry available. TV and bath (reliable hot water) are standard for all 3 rooms. Singles L200,000; doubles L300,000.

FOOD

To reach an **outdoor market,** take a right onto Bd. Corneliu Coposcu from Dumbrava, then another right at the bus stop lined with street vendors. Fruit, vegetable, and flower sellers start business as early as 7am; the market winds down around 8pm. Munch around the clock at **Juventus Non-Stop,** Str. N. Bălcescu 40.

Crama Sibiul Vechi (Wine Cellar of Old Sibiu), Str. Papiu Ilarian 3 (tel. 21 04 61). Below street level. Features carved-wood chairs with animal-fur cushions and waiters in folk costumes serving filling meals (L40,000) with enough booze to intoxicate an elephant. Open daily noon-midnight.

Împaratul Romanilor, Str. N. Bălcescu 4 (tel. 21 65 00). Formal attire is a must in this starched, white-tablecloth decor. A large variety of meat entrees L20-35,000. A live band will sometimes play an evening tango, but the dance floor is under-used. Open daily 7am-midnight. MC/Visa.

Restaurant Bufnița, Str. N. Bălcescu 45 (tel. 21 03 44). Intimate atmosphere with painted porcelain lamps. Entrees L15-20,000. Open daily 8am-midnight.

SIGHTS

Piața Mare, the center of Sibiu's Old Town, once hosted myriad festivals and the occasional public execution. The plaza lies in the shadow of the massive **Roman Catholic Church** (Biserică Romano-Catolică), a beautifully restored 18th-century monument built by the Austrians after they conquered Transylvania in a failed attempt to re-convert the Saxons to Catholicism. Under the arch at Piața Mică 11 stands the **Ethnographic Museum,** which displays a collection of objects from central Africa in addition to two temporary exhibits. The museum even has a 2500-year-old mummy. (Open in summer Tu-Su 10am-6pm; off-season Tu-Su 9am-5pm. L10,000, students L5000.) After reaching Piața Mică from Piața Mare, head right until you see the small **Bridge of Lies** (Podul Minciunilor). Legend has it that young lovers would meet in the square, declare their undying love, and agree on another rendezvous.Few couples ever saw each other again, hence the bridge's name.

The ornate **Brukenthal Museum** (Muzeul Brukenthal) in Piața Mare is definitely still worth a visit, although some of its finest paintings were stolen in the 1960s. The gallery on the second floor has strong Dutch and Italian art collections, and Transylvanian painting decorates the first floor. (Open Tu-Su 9am-5pm; last entrance at 4:30pm. L22,000, students L11,000. English tour for groups of 5 L50,000.) Take a left upon leaving to find the second museum named for former Transylvanian governor Samuel von Brukenthal, the Gothic **Brukenthal History Museum,** Str. Mitropoliei 2. It has a well-preserved collection of Roman coins, a good stock of medieval and modern weapons, and the requisite rooms of "anthropological finds" (clay pots). (Open Tu-Su 9am-5pm; last entrance at 4pm. L16,000, students L8000.) Romania's second-largest **Orthodox Cathedral** (Catedrala Ortodoxă), on Str. Mitropoliei, is a quarter-scale copy of Istanbul's St. Sophia. Unlike its Turkish counterpart, Sibiu's gorgeous cathedral is in excellent condition and is still in use. (Open daily 6am-8pm.)

ROMANIA

ENTERTAINMENT

Every May and June, Sibiu heats up for Romania's biggest **jazz festival. Teatru Radu Stanca,** next to the Dumbrava department store, sometimes shows plays and American movies and hosts an international **theater festival** in June. **Cinema Tineretului,** Aleea Odobescu 4 (tel. 21 14 20), in the big white building under the Teatrul Gong sign, shows American movies during the day. To get there, take a right on Str. Poștei after the post office and go down the stairs. (Shows 11am-5pm. L8000, first show L5000.) The cinema becomes the attractive **Discoteca Piramid** at night, where you can dance like an Egyptian. (Open 9pm-5am. Sa-Su cover L10,000 after 10pm.)

NEAR SIBIU: PĂLTINIȘ

In the Cibin Mountains (Munții Cibinului), 35km from Sibiu, Păltiniș (pall-tee-NEESH) is Romania's oldest (1894), highest (1440m), and possibly smallest mountain resort. Its beautiful location, fresh air, and numerous hiking opportunities have made Păltiniș a favorite of everyone from modern Romanian philosophers to crowds of German tourists. In winter, Păltiniș becomes a major **ski** center. In summer, many businesses shut down, since most visitors are either daytrippers or destined for loftier locales along the hiking trails *(trasee turistice)*. Open year-round, the **red dot trail** leads northwest toward **Cibinului Gorge** (Cheie Cibinului; 5km). The **red cross/red stripe trail** (4½hr. round-trip) follows an unpaved road for part of the way to **Old Woman's Peak** (Vf. Bătrâna; 1911m). Staying on the red-stripe trail for 25km (7hr.) to **Cîndrel Peak** (2244m) is more difficult, but more visually rewarding. (Trails open summer only.)

On the main street, the kiosk to the left of **Gasthaus zum Hans** sells **hiking maps** (L18,000; open Tu-Su 10am-6pm). Stock up on food in Sibiu before coming to Păltiniş; there's no grocery store, and only the restaurant at the Cabana opens for dinner. (Entrees L5000-15,000. Open daily 8am-10pm.) **Phone code:** (0)69.

GETTING THERE. A comfortable **bus** connects Sibiu's train station to Păltiniş (1hr., 3-4 per day, L13,000; pay the driver). The buses are actually about 50m in front of the bus station (autogară), which is next to the train station. Sibiu's **Agenţia de Turism—Păltiniş,** Str. Tribumei 5 (tel. 21 83 19), off Piaţa Unirii, has bus schedules. Ride the bus to the **ski lift** (open in winter 9am-4:30pm). Follow the signs to start hiking the red triangle or red cross **trails.** To get to the red dot trail, follow the ski lift to the main street and turn right.

NEAR SIBIU: FĂGĂRAŞ MOUNTAINS

The Făgăraş mountain range extends more than 60km from the Olt Valley to the Piatra Craiului mountains; the tallest peaks, Moldoveanu and Negoiu, are both higher than 2500m. Wildflowered meadows, shrouded summits, and superb views of Wallachian plains and Transylvanian hills cure all fatigue. With a bit of luck, you might even spot a jumpy black goat or a delicate edgy flower, both of which are found exclusively in this range. Be sure to bring adequate supplies and a map; look for a rudimentary one in Păltiniş or Sibiu, or pick up *Drumeţi În Carpaţi* in Bucharest or Bran (about L50,000). The hiking season lasts from July to mid-September, but the mountains are never crowded. Always be prepared for cold, snowy summits. The range can be traversed in about seven days; the usual route is from west to east, starting in Transylvania. It is possible to sleep in a cabana, but be prepared to camp if necessary. Cabana facilities vary; some may offer just sleeping sacks (L50,000 per person), while others offer doubles with bath (L125-300,000). Call **Cabana Salişte** in Sibiu (tel. 21 17 03) to make reservations for the more upscale cabanas. Cabana Sur, formerly on the red path, has burned down.

Custura Sărăţii (1hr. east of the Puha Saddle) is the ridge trail's most spectacular and difficult portion; for 2hr. you'll cling to rocks on a path sometimes less than a foot wide, with drop-offs on either side (an alternate path avoids this route). Many end their hike with a descent into the **Sîmbăta Valley** (red triangle trail); the ridge ends at Cabana Plaiul Foii near the Piatra Craiului mountains, about 30km from Braşov. To get down to the valley, however, you may have to backtrack to find a suitable descent trail. *Nobody* should hike alone in the Făgăraş. See **Essentials: Camping & the Outdoors,** p. 36, for more hiking tips.

GETTING THERE. Countless itineraries are possible; most start in the **Olt Valley** on the railroad from Sibiu to the south. A majority of hikers enter the ridge at **Lac Avrig,** a glacial lake reachable by the red cross and blue dot trails, or the **Puha Saddle** (Şaua Puha). You can reach both from the sleepy town of **Avrig** (1hr., 9 per day from Sibiu, *personal* L7100). Plan a day's hike from Avrig to reach the trails.

TÂRGU JIU

Despite a history that begins in the 13th century, it is the Constantin Brâncuşi National Cultural Assembly (Complexul Cultural National Constantin Brâncuşi) alone that keeps the town of Târgu Jiu (TIR-goo dj-IOO) from passing almost entirely unnoticed. These world-renowned, open-air works by Brâncuşi (bran-CHOOSH), one of the world's most noted modern sculptors, make Târgu Jiu one of the most artistically rich towns in Romania.

ORIENTATION & PRACTICAL INFORMATION. **Trains** run to: **Bucharest** (5hr., 4 per day, *accelerat* L60,000) and **Cluj-Napoca** (6hr., 1 per day, L30,000). **Store luggage** at the train station (L7000-14,000; open 24hr.). The main **bus station** is next to the train station. To reach the center, exit the train station and take a right onto Bd. Republicii; continue straight until the intersection with Str. Unirii. To reach Str. Eroilor, parallel to Str. Unirii, turn left onto Str. Unirii and then right onto either Str. Griviţa or Str. Victoriei. Or, take a bus from the train station to Parcul Central (L2500). The **tourist office,** OJT, Str. Eroilor 6 (tel./fax 21 40 10), connected to Hotel Gorj, has old but helpful **maps** (L5000) and helps find rooms in hotels. (Open M-F 10am-3pm.) Exchange money at **Banca Comercială Română (BCR)** at the intersection of Unirii and Republicii (tel. 21 40 18; fax 21 26 30), or at **Banc Post,** Str. T. Vladimirescu 17 (tel. 21 34 91; fax 21 80 72). There is a **pharmacy** at Str. Unirii 2 (tel. 21 31 03; open M-F 7am-8pm, Sa 7am-7pm, Su 7am-1pm). The **post office** and **telephones,** Str. Traian 1, off Str. Eroilor. (Open M-F 8am-8pm, Sa 9am-noon.) **Postal code:** 1400. **Phone code:** (0)53.

ACCOMMODATIONS & FOOD. The excellent **Hotel Gorjul,** Str. Eroilor 6 (tel. 21 48 15), conveniently located close to Parcul Central, offers decent rooms with bath and TV. (Singles L300,000; doubles L380,000; triples L420,000. Breakfast included.) **Hotel Tineretului,** Bd. N. Titulescu 26 (tel. 24 46 82), is cheaper, but more remote. Take a taxi. (Doubles with bath L130,000; triples L195,000.) Try the terrace bar-restaurant **Lider,** Str. Eroilor 11 (tel. 21 90 02), which boasts no less than 16 types of pizza and 45 entrees. (Pizza and entrees L20,000-40,000. Open 24hr.) For an almost home-cooked meal, try the more expensive **Restaurant Sohodol,** Str. 30 Decembrie 1989 2 (tel./fax 21 03 63). Full meals for L45,000. (Open daily 8am-1am.)

SIGHTS & ENTERTAINMENT. There are two clusters of sculptures at opposite ends of Str. Eroilor: one in Parcul Central and one in Parcul Tineretului. The sculptures, created between 1937-38 and dedicated to the Romanian soldiers who died in WWI, were originally designed by Brâncuşi to lie in a straight line at either end of the town along Str. Eroilor (Heroes' Street). The town, however, has since expanded to envelop the artwork. **Parcul Tineretului,** at the east end of Calea Eroilor (in the triangle formed by Str. Craiovei, Calea Bucureşti, and Str. Tudor Vladimirescu) is dominated by the impressive **Column of Infinity** (Coloana Infinitului) that lies at the center. At the other end of Calea Eroilor, close to the banks of Jiu River, lie the other three sculptures. From Eroilor, the series begins with the arched **Kissing Gate** (Poarta Sărutului), made of special *Bampodoc* stone. Next you'll find **Aleea Scaunelor**, a long alley lined with 30 squat, round seats. Finally, at the end of Aleea Scaunelor, the **Table of Silence** (Masa Tăcerii) sits, also made of *Bampodoc* stone and made in the ancient Dacian style. The 12 hourglass-shaped chairs are said to symbolize the 12 months of the year. If you still want more of Brâncuşi, catch an early bus to **Hobita** (29km, L14,000) where you can visit his birthplace, **Casa Memorială Brâncuşi,** in the center. On the outskirts, you can watch aspiring sculptors at the **Brâncuşiana International Sculpture Camp** (Tabbra de creatie "Brâncuşiana").

BRAŞOV

Established as the center of Carpathian defense, Braşov (BRA-shohv) later became an international crossroads and is now an ideal starting point for excursions into the mountains. The fortresses surrounding the city testify to its former role in defending the mountain pass, and the cosmopolitan population further reflects its rich history. The exquisite city center, with museums, restaurants, churches, and cable cars to nearby mountain tops demonstrate that Braşov is now as suited to tourism as it has been to its other, more sinister roles.

ORIENTATION & PRACTICAL INFORMATION. **Trains** go to **Bucharest** (3-4hr., up to 25 per day, *accelerat* L40,000) and **Cluj-Napoca** (5-6hr., 6 per day, L70,000). Train info can be found at **CFR** on Str. Republicii. (Open M-F 8am-7pm, Sa 9am-

1pm.) To get to town from the station, take bus #4 toward Piața Unirii (L3000 for 2 rides) to the main **Piața Sfatului** (10min.); descend in front of **Biserica Neagră,** a big, dark Gothic church. Or, on foot, cross the street in front of the train station and head straight down Bd. Victoriei; then follow Str. Mihail Kogălniceanu around the civic center until it ends. At the fork, take the soft right onto Bd. 15 Noiembrie (it becomes Bd. Eroilor) and turn left on Str. Republicii or Str. Mureşenilor (2km). To get to from Piața Sfatului to the bus station, walk up Bd. Eroilor, turn right onto Str. Mureşenilor, and then left at the plaza. Buy bus tickets at the booths on the elevated sidewalk. (Open M-Sa 5:30am-8pm, Su 7am-7pm.) Another main bus station is **Autogară 2,** sometimes called **Gara Bartolomeu,** on the western edge of the city. Take a taxi or one of the trolleybuses that go down Str. Stadionului. **Odeon "D" Travel,** Str. Mureşenilor 28 (tel. 14 28 40), offers info about transportation and hotels. (Open M-F 9am-1:30pm and 2-6pm, Sa 9am-1pm.) Hotel Aro-Palace, Bd. Eroilor 9, offers free **maps** of the city. From Piața Sfatului, walk right on Str. Mureşenilor until it intersects Bd. Eroilor at the bus station and turn right. A Cirrus/MC/Visa **ATM** sits next to the entrance of Hotel Aro's restaurant. **Exchange currency** at any bureau on Piața Sfatului or on nearby streets. **IDM** (tel. 41 02 19), in the circular building at the intersection of Bd. Eroilor and Str. Republicii, cashes AmEx **traveler's checks** and gives MC/Visa **cash advances** for no commission. (Open M-F 7:30am-9pm, Sa 9am-6pm, Su 9am-5pm.) A **pharmacy,** Aurofarm, is at Str. Republicii 27 (tel. 41 12 48), near the Bayer sign. (Open daily 8am-8pm.) The **post office,** Str. Nicolae Iorga 1 (tel. 41 51 64), is on the street that parallels Bd. Eroiler across the long Parul Central. **Phones** are inside the post office building. (Open daily 6:30am-10pm.) **Postal code:** 2200. **Phone code:** (0)68.

ACCOMMODATIONS & FOOD. **Private-room** hawkers descend on tourists when they arrive at the train station. In general, they offer good rooms (US$10-15). To go through an agency, try **EXO,** Str. Postăvarului 6 (tel. 14 45 91), near the city center. From Piața Sfatului, walk down Str. Republicii and turn right onto Diaconu Coresi. The next left is Str. Postăvarului. EXO finds rooms starting at L120,000 per person. (Open M-Sa 11am-8pm, Su 11am-2pm.) **Hotel Postăvarul,** Politehnicii 2 (tel. 14 43 30), shares an entrance with Hotel Corona; enter under the Hotel Corona sign. To get there, follow the pedestrian Str. Republicii away from Piața Sfatului, and take the last right before the end of the street. It offers spacious singles with toilets and sinks. (Singles L235,000; doubles L320,000, with bath L360,000; triples L480,000. Breakfast included.)

ROMANIA

A daily **market** on Str. Nicolae Bălescu, two blocks from the intersection with Bd. Eroilor, provides a cheap array of fruits, vegetables, and other fresh and packaged foods. (Open M-F 7am-7pm, Sa 7am-2pm.) The most notable restaurant is **Crama,** Piața Sfatului 12 (tel. 14 39 81), in the 16th-century Hirschner house. Eat meat (from L30,000) and drink wine (700ml L30,000-70,000) while watching traditional dances. (Open Tu-Su 7pm-2am.) **Restaurant Intim,** Str. Mureşenilor 4 (tel. 14 17 46), goes for an intimate feel with drawn curtains and red upholstered walls. It serves breakfast (under L12,000) as well as lunch and dinner to a diverse clientele. (Entrees L15,000. Open daily 7am-8pm.)

SIGHTS. **Piața Sfatului** and Str. Republicii are perfect for a stroll, and many historical sights have signs in English. The **History Museum** on the square used to be the city hall and courthouse; legend holds that the condemned had to jump from the tower to their deaths. Its renovation should be completed by the summer of 2000. (Open Tu-Su 10am-6pm. L4000, students L1000.) The small museum holds archives and artifacts of Braşov and nearby regions. Beyond the square along Str. Gh. Barițiu looms the Lutheran **Black Church** (Biserica Neagră), Romania's most celebrated Gothic church. It received its name after being charred by fire in 1689. Keep your grubby hands away from the church's 17th- and 18th-century Anatolian carpets, or pay a hefty fine. (Open M-Sa 10am-5pm. L5000. No photos.)

The city gate, **Poarta Schei,** was built in 1828 to separate the old German citadel from the Romanian *schei*—a quiet area of old-style houses. From the main square, follow Str. Apollonia Hirschner and turn right onto Str. Poarta Schei. Behind the *poarta*, Str. Prundului leads to Piaţa Unirii and its two attractions: the black-towered, icon-filled **St. Nicholas Church** (Biserică Sfântu Nicolae), built in 1495, and **Romania's First School** (Prima Şcoala Românească; open 9am-5pm; L10,000, students L5000). The small **Ethnographic Museum,** Bd. Eroilor, exhibits Transylvanian folk costumes and ceramics and sells folk crafts. (Open Tu-Su 10am-6pm. L4000. Guides in English, French, and German, L20,000.) To see the mountains without too much exertion, **cable cars** *(telecabina)* climb up Muntele Tâmpa from Aleea T. Brediceanu. Look for steep, stone steps off the main path. (One-way L10,000, round-trip L15,000. Open M noon-6pm, Tu-F 10am-7pm, Sa-Su 10am-8pm.) To climb a road less traveled, trails on Aleea T. Brediceanu lead to the majestic **Weaver's Bastion** and other **medieval ruins.**

ENTERTAINMENT. Cultural activities abound in Braşov. **Operas** tend to be low on production but big on vocal talent. (Box office open daily noon-4pm. L15,250, students L10,500.) Tickets (tel. 14 41 38) are sold on Str. Republicii at Agenţia Teatrală de Bilete. Local students shake their booty at ephemeral **discos;** ask around for the current hot spot. Unfortunately, most of the permanent entertainment options are strip clubs. In late summer, Piaţa Sfatului holds the international **Golden Stag** (Cerbul de Aur) festival, which in the past has starred Ray Charles and MC Hammer.

NEAR BRAŞOV: BRAN

It's a dark and stormy night in the 19th century. As rain crashes down on the roofs of Bran and lightning illuminates its looming castle, an unfamiliar chariot navigates the Bran Pass—the tight road between the old principalities of Transylvania and Wallachia. This chariot was long thought to have belonged to Bram Stoker, who was said to have been so impressed by the scene that he wrote a book about it: *Dracula*, which was soon to become the seed of the vampire myth and its zillions of re-interpretations. Unfortunately, this myth is no more true than the vampire story itself; Stoker, in fact, never visited Romania. Sadly, the book also established Romania as a backwards and superstitious country in the Western imagination. In reality, **Vlad Ţepeş Dracula** (literally Vlad the Impaler, son of Dracul), had little to do with either this overly restored edifice or vampires. As Prince of Wallachia (1448, 1456-62, and 1476-77), he was charged with protecting the Bran pass, which played a crucial role during the Middle Ages in the development of Romanian trade. Today, Bran is a small town with a big castle of mythic importance, although it's not as beautiful or impressive as many other fortresses scattered across Romania.

ROMANIA

DRACULA, UNCENSORED While Bran castle may be underwhelming, the gruesome exploits of its temporary tenant make the hack horror novel pale in comparison. Born in Sighişoara in 1431, Vlad Ţepeş' father (also Vlad) was a member of the Order of the Dragon, a society charged with defending Catholicism from the infidel. Hence the name by which he ruled: Vlad Dracul ("Dragon"), and his son's moniker Dracula, "son of the dragon," which was corrupted to "son of the devil" as word of his atrocities spread. In 1444, Vlad's father shipped his two sons off to a Turkish prison to placate an Ottoman ruler. In his five years there, Vlad learned the tortures for which he would become infamous. His personal favorite of these was impalement: a victim was pulled down a stake driven up his anus by two horses tied to his spread legs. When the Turks invaded Walachia in 1462, they were met by some 20,000 of their kinsmen impaled in this manner outside Dracula's territory. The Turks, horrified, retreated. Dracula also practiced such terror tactics on his own people. In order to combat poverty in his realm, for example, the benevolent ruler invited the destitute and disabled to his palace for a banquet... and then had them burned to death. By the height of his rule, his subjects were so scared into obedience that Dracula placed a gold cup in Tirgovişte square; it remained there undisturbed for the length of his reign.

The castle at Bran, which overlooks the pass, may have been the physical model for Stoker's, but Țepeș actually resided in a castle near Curtea de Argeș (see p. 518). Despite its lack of blood-sucking significance, the castle contains a number of interesting exhibits, including an **ethnographic village** (with rather poor English and French translations) and a **museum** featuring Bran's economic, rather than mythic, importance. (Open Tu-Su 9am-6pm. L30,000, students L20,000.) If you're in a group, you can get an excellent tour of the castle, including all the details (real and fictional) of Țepeș' life. **Hiking maps** are available near the entrance to the castle complex (L20,000-25,000). Follow the yellow triangle, red cross, or red stripe trails on Str. Valeriu Lucian Bologa to Omu peak (6-7hr.; see **Sinaia,** p. 534).

GETTING THERE. To get to Bran from Brașov, take a taxi or one of the many trolleybuses to "Autogară 2" (officially called "Gară Bartolomeu"), where the **bus** to Bran departs; pay the driver (45min., 1 per hr., L8000). To reach the castle, get off at the main bus stop by the sign that says "Cabana Bran Castle—500m." Then take the main road back toward Brașov and take the first right. The **tourist office, Compania Bran** (tel. 23 66 42 and 23 68 84), has recently moved; it is now 2-3km back toward Brașov on the main road. For tourist information, call 23 68 84. (Open daily 8am-6pm.) **Phone code:** (0)68.

NEAR BRAȘOV: POIANA BRAȘOV

About 13km from Brașov, this mountain niche has long been vying with Sinaia for the title of Romania's best alpine resort. The beautiful green valley is perfect for **hiking** or **skiing.** Trails here are accessible to the average hiker, and the view atop **Mt. Postăvarul** (1802m) is glorious. **Centrul de Echitatie** (tel. 26 21 61), off the parking lot to the right when coming from Brașov, offers ponies, carriage rides, and horses. (Open daily 8am-8pm.) In summer, swimming, tennis, and track facilities draw visitors to the town. In winter, in addition to ten **downhill ski runs,** Poiana Brașov offers **cross-country skiing** and **ice skating.** Ski schools and rentals abound behind Hotel Teleferic at *telecabina* (cable-car) Poiana-Kanzel, and behind Hotel Sportul at *telecabina* Capra Neagra. (Open daily summer 9am-9pm; off-season 8:30am-4pm. L20,000 round-trip.) Hikers have a choice of four main trails from Poiana Brașov. The **blue stripe** trail leads to Rîsnou, while the **yellow stripe** winds its way back to Brașov. You can take either the **red cross** or the **blue cross** to Cabina Potavarala; the former is the less steep of the two.

GETTING THERE. Buses for Poiana Brașov leave from the station in **Brașov** on Bd. Eroilor (2-3 per hr., L3500). Bus #20 leaves from the far end of the bus platform. Once in Poiana Brașov, examine the map signs where the bus drops you off. Poiana Brașov's **tourist office** (tel. 26 23 89) offers great one-day excursions (L80,000-400,000; discounts for large groups), including a trip (US$7) to Bran castle. (Open M-F 8am-3pm.) To get there from the bus station, turn away from the mountain and take the street veering to the right from the bus parking lot. **Postal code:** 2209. **Phone code:** (0)68.

ROMANIA

SINAIA

Wedged into the Prahova valley and flanked by the Bucegi mountains on both sides, Romania's most celebrated year-round alpine resort made its mark as a favorite getaway of Romania's first royal family in the late 1800s. With its elegant villas and park, Sinaia retains an aristocratic aura. The palace and monastery combine with slopes and magnificent hiking trails to draw throngs of sightseers, skiers, and hikers, who mingle with locals and the occasional black-clad monk. Meanwhile, the town itself offers the metropolitan best of alpine Romania.

ORIENTATION & PRACTICAL INFORMATION. Trains run hourly to **Bucharest** (2hr., *accelerat* L40,000) and **Brașov** (1hr., L20,000). From the station, cross the street, climb two flights of stairs, and take a left onto a cobblestone ramp at the first landing. Climb the first steps and take two left turns onto **Bd. Carol I,** the main street. Large hotels, including the Hotel Palace (see **Accommodations,** below), provide **info** and bad **maps** of Sinaia and the trails (L4000). Good maps are available at the base of the cable cars for a hefty price (L20,000). **Commercial Bank,** Bd. Carol I 49, has it all: traveler's check exchange (M-F 8am-noon), credit card advances, an Cirrus/MC/Plus **ATM,** and steep commissions. **Telecabinas** (cable cars) whisk you to Cota 1400 (elevation not surprisingly 1400m) from behind Hotel Montana. (Runs M-F 8am-4pm, Sa-Su 8am-5pm. L15,000.) From Cota 1400, take another *telecabina* to Cota 2000. (Runs M-F 8:45am-3:45, Sa-Su 8:30-4pm. L10,000.) In an emergency, contact the **mountain rescue** squad, Bd. Carol I 47 (tel. 31 31 31). The **post office** is across the street and to the left. A **telephone office** and train ticket information booth are inside. (Open M-F 7am-8pm.) **Postal code:** 2180. **Phone code:** (0)44.

ACCOMMODATIONS & FOOD. Locals await tourists at the train station with offers of *o cameră* (private rooms; US$5-15). On the trail, stay in a mountain *cabana* (L300,000). Sinaia's priciest hotels, which are geared toward foreigners, offer many amenities, but prices are as steep as the peaks in mid-summer and during winter holidays. **Complex Economat** (tel. 31 11 51), in the park of Castelul Peleş, offers surprisingly decent prices for a good hotel (one-star singles L125,000, two-star L175,000; doubles L200,000, L300,000. MC/Visa.) Redeem your L25,000 breakfast credit at the welcoming but pricey **restaurant** downstairs. (Entrees L40,000. Open M noon-10pm, Tu-Su 7am-11pm.) Luxurious **Hotel Palace** lies at Str. Octavian Goga 11 (tel. 31 20 51). Instead of making a left onto Bd. Carol I, keep to the right and wind around the park; the hotel is the imposing white building on the right. Reservations are essential. (Singles from L185,000; doubles L270,000. Up to 30% discount for stays of more than 1 night. L30,000 breakfast credit.) **Hotel-Restaurant Furnica,** Str. Furnica 50 (tel. 31 18 51), has simple rooms (singles L150,000; doubles L250,000) and tasty meats (up to L30,000; open daily 7:30am-11pm).

SIGHTS & HIKING. The Romanian royal family chose to live in Sinaia when they weren't at Cotroceni in Bucharest. They began the construction of **Peleş Castle** (Castelul Peleş) in 1873 under the watchful eyes of Carol Hollenzollern-Sigmaringen, who finished it ten years later as King Carol I of a newly independent Romania (see **History,** p. 499). The enormous fortress features ornate rooms with woodwork from all over Europe, Venetian mirrors, 15th-century Spanish armor, and a number of Rembrandt duplicates. It also has central heating, electric lights, and an elevator, all built nearly 125 years ago. (Open W-Su 9am-5pm; last entry 4:15pm. L50,000, students L25,000.) Electricity and German design are the only similarities between Carol I's Peleş and the equally striking **Pelişor,** built nearby in the early 20th century as a summer residence for King Ferdinand, but designed and decorated by his wife, Queen Maria. An aspiring painter and writer, Maria wanted Pelişor to house artists and intellectuals. She designed it to fit modern tastes; hence the French and Art Nouveau interior featuring bright, open spaces with simple wooden furniture, often painted white. Vases and colored stones cover the bookcases and tabletops, while Maria's own paintings and stained glass decorate the walls. (Open Tu 12:15-4:15pm, W-Su 9:15am-4:15pm. L40,000, students L20,000.) If you visit one of the houses, be sure to see the other as well; the stylistic changes wrought by 30 years are truly astounding. Both feature well-informed, multilingual tour guides.

The *telecabina* (cable car) to Cota 1400 (L15,000, round-trip L25,000) leads to alpine **hikes** and summer **hang-gliding. Ski slopes** descend from Cota 2000, which can be accessed by *telecabina* (L10,000, round-trip L18,000) or, in winter, *teleschi* (ski lifts). Along the Bucegi range, the **yellow stripe trail** leads obsessive hikers on a strenuous four-hour climb from Cota 2000, past **Babele** (2200m; accessible by cable car—see Buşteni below), to **Omu** (2505m), the highest peak of the Bucegi. The Babele rocks are said to represent two *babe* (women) and a Sphinx. From Cabana Babele, the mountain cabin, follow the **blue cross trail** to the 42m **Heroes' Cross** (Crucea Eroilor, a.k.a. Crucea Caraiman; 1hr.), a monument to Romanians killed in WWI. Flashlight-equipped spelunkers go farther on to **Cheile Peşterii,** a pitch-black but easily reached cave. Cable cars stop running weekdays at 4pm, although the system isn't quite as orderly as the signs make it seem. Helpful **maps** are available for L10,000 on the steps in front of the *telecabinas*. Most trails are extremely dangerous and thus inadvisable in the winter. They are recommended only for experienced hikers in summer. Dance your acrophobia away at the **Blue Angel** (tel. 31 26 17), across from Hotel Montana. (Open M-F and Su 9pm-3am, Sa 9pm-4am. Cover L15,000.)

NEAR SINAIA: BUŞTENI

Hikers seeking a quick trip to the natural sights of the Bucegi range should head to the *telecabina* in Buşteni. Opposite the train station in Buşteni stands a small stone **church** built by King Carol I and Queen Elisabeta in 1889. Buşteni is also a good jumping-off point for a number of short, easy hikes, including the **blue triangle** path (3-4hr.) that starts from the Buşteni train station. Pick up supplies and an indispensable **hiking map** in Sinaia before heading on to Buşteni; if necessary, you may be able to find a good map at the bottom of the *telecabina* lines.

GETTING THERE. You can take either a **train** from **Sinaia** (10min., 23 trains per day, L3000), or one of the less frequent but more comfortable **minibuses** (L3000). To hit the Bucegi trails, take a left onto the main road and walk past the sloping-roofed **Hotel Caraiman.** A ways down the road, take a right at the Hotel Silva sign on the bridge and walk up the aptly named Str. Telecabinii. Behind the hotel hides the *telecabina* to Babele (15min., M-F 9am-4pm, Sa-Su 9am-4:45pm, L30,000). After Babele, the *cabina* continues to Cheile Peşterii (see **Sinaia: Sights,** p. 535).

SIGHIŞOARA

Sighişoara (see-ghee-SHWAH-rah) is perhaps the most pristine and enchanting medieval town in Transylvania. Surrounded by mountains and crowning a green hill, its gilded steeples, old clocktower, and irregularly tiled roofs have survived centuries of attacks, fires, and dozens of floods.

ORIENTATION & PRACTICAL INFORMATION. Trains run to **Bucharest** (5hr., 10 per day, *accelerat* L70,000) and **Cluj-Napoca** (3½hr., 4 per day, L40,000). To reach the center from the train station, take a right onto **Str. Libertăţii,** then take your first left onto **Str. Gării.** Veer left at the Russian cemetery commemorating the victory over fascism. From there, turn right and cross the footbridge over river **Târnava Mare,** then walk down Str. Morii, the street behind Sigma. A right at the fork leads to Str. O. Goga and the Citadel; a left leads to the main **Str. 1 Decembrie 1918** after a block. **Store luggage** at the train station. (L7100 or 14,200 per item, per day. Open 24hr.) **OJT Agenţie de Turism,** Str. 1 Decembrie 1918 10 (tel. 77 10 72), helps find rooms in hotels, organizes tours with an English speaking guide (US$10-15 per hr. for groups of at least 10), and sells maps for L10,000. (Open M-F 9am-5pm, Sa 9am-1pm. **Exchange bureau** open M-F 8am-8pm, Sa 9am-1pm.) **IDM exchange office,** Str. Hermann Oberth 15 (tel. 77 49 49), accepts AmEx, MC, and Visa, and most traveler's checks. (Open M-F 8am-8:30pm, Sa 9am-1pm.) There is a **Western Union** (open M-F 8:30am-3pm) and an **ATM** at the Bancorex on 1 Decembrie 1918. Log onto cyberspace **Internet Cafe,** 1 Decembrie 1918 15, for L10,000 per hr. (Open daily 8am-8pm.) Farther down, as Str. 1 Decembrie 1918 becomes Piaţa H. Oberth, lies the almighty **post and telephone office.** (Post open M-F 7am-8pm. Phones daily 7am-8pm.) **Postal code:** 3050. **Phone code:** (0)65.

ACCOMMODATIONS & FOOD. At **Bobby's Hostel,** Str. Tache Ionescu 18 (tel. 77 22 32), the company will likely be great, although the rooms can be sterile. Young people from all over stop here. Enjoy communal showers with hot water for an hour twice a day. Washing machines (L5000 per load) and cable TV are also available. (Doubles L90,000; quads L75,000; 10-bed dorms L60,000 per person. Open June 15-Aug. 30, but Bobby may have room in the off season.) In the Citadel, try **Restaurant Cetate,** Piaţa Cositorarilor 5 (tel. 77 15 96), under the big metal dragon sign. Dracula's dad, they claim, might once have lived here. The traditional meals and medieval decor are truly worth the extra *lei*. (*Ciorba* L8,000-20,000; beef entrees L25,000-40,000. Open daily 10am-10pm.) Downtown, **4 Amici,** Str. Morii 7 (tel. 77 25

69), serves pizza and other Italian fare (L25,000-40,000). Listen to music while watching your pie being made, or peruse the Italian magazines on the tables. (Open daily 11am-2am.) The small **grocery stores** along Str. 1 Decembrie 1918 will satisfy any remaining pangs of hunger.

SIGHTS & ENTERTAINMENT. The **Citadel** (Cetate), built by Saxons in 1191, is now a tiny medieval city-within-a-city. Its winding streets, filled with explanatory signs in Romanian, German, and English, can keep tourists busy for up to a day. Enter the Citadel through the **Clock Tower** (Turnul cu Ceas), off Str. O. Goga. The **history museum** (tel. 77 11 08) inside this old tower displays everything from Roman furniture to Apollo-program rocket science. (Open M 10am-3:30pm, Tu-F 9am-6pm, Sa-Su 9am-4pm. L10,000, students L5000. Signs in English.) Climb to the top to see the clock's mechanism and an expansive view of the area. Slightly to the left as you leave the Clock Tower, the four-room **Museum of Medieval Armory** offers a small exhibit on Vlad Ţepeş (Dracula), as well as arms from all over the world. (Open Tu-Su 10am-3:30pm. L6000, students L3000.) From the clock tower, walk straight past the house of Vlad Dracul (Vlad Ţepeş's father) and take a left onto Str. Şcolii to reach the 170-step **covered wooden staircase.** These lead to the **School on a Hill,** whose steps were built to make the climb easier for lazy 17th-century students. The newly-restored 1937 **St. Treime Cathedral** (Catedrala Sfânta Treime) lies along Str. A. Şaguna. Look for the large black and white church on the right after the Russian cemetery. Set on the banks of the River Târnava Mare, the Cathedral is breathtaking at sunset. **Church of the Monastery** (Biserica Mânăsterii), near the clock tower, offers a brochure in English (L2000) about Sighişoara's Lutheran churches, including the prominent **Hill Church,** next to the School on a Hill. (Open M-Sa 10am-6pm.) Once a year, in July or August, the town hosts a huge **medieval festival.**

NORTHERN ROMANIA

Nestled up against Ukraine and Hungary, the Maramureş region of northern Romania is known for its stunning woodcarving and reverence for secular traditions. Many residents make and wear folk costumes, especially to church and during feasts and holidays. Otherwise, the bucolic region comes to life only in July, during the International Festival of Traditional Village Music held at Vadu Izei, 6km away from Sighetu-Marmaţiei (on the Baia Mare route). These days, few visitors find reason to venture into the area's rolling hills, but those who do are rewarded with the peaceful, seldom-seen traditions of village life.

SIGHETU-MARMAŢIEI

The northern village of Sighetu-Marmaţiei (see-GHEH-too mar-MAH-tsee-ay; or just Sighet) blends together tiny shops and towering church steeples on its main street. Meanwhile, locals wear a modernized version of the traditional costume, making streets on the periphery seem like they belong in a rural hamlet.

ORIENTATION & PRACTICAL INFORMATION. The scenic **train** ride from **Cluj-Napoca** (7hr., 1 per day, L45,000) is worth every *leu.* Trains run to **Bucharest** (13½hr., 1 per day, L100,000) and **Timişoara** (12hr., 1 per day, L65,000). To reach the town center, walk four long blocks down Str. Iuliu Maniu away from the train tracks to the yellow church. The best **map** of town is posted on a large board several blocks down from here, at the other end of the center. **Banca Comercială,** Str. Iuliu Maniu 32, accepts Visa and cashes all kinds of traveler's checks for a 2.5% commission. (Open M-F 8am-2:30pm.) The **post office** is at Str. Bogdan Vodă—cross the square from OJT and take a left. (Open M-F 7am-8pm, Sa 8am-noon.) Continue down the street and turn left at the small garden with a statue to find the **telephone office,** Str. Dragoş Vodă 2. (Open daily 7am-9pm.) **Postal code:** 4925. **Phone code:** (0)62.

ACCOMMODATIONS & FOOD. Ask at the reception of Hotel Tisa (see below) about superb **private rooms** with hot-water baths and English-speaking hosts (L120-300,000). The rooms are in private houses in Vadu Izei, 6km away from Sighet on the Baia mare route. Don't let the distance scare you—hosts will often pick you up with a car, or you can take a bus to the village (10 per day, L2500). **Mini-Hotel Măgură,** Str. Iuliu Maniu 44, 300m down the road from the train station, is your best bet for budget sleeps. The communal bathroom is decent at best. (Singles L60,000; doubles L75,000.) **Hotel Tisa,** Piața Libertății 8 (tel. 31 26 45), offers clean rooms with color TV and hot water bath. (Singles L225,000; doubles L300,000. Breakfast included.) In the center, tons of little eateries and patisseries offer variety at low prices. For a real restaurant experience, **Restaurantul Curtea Veche** (tel. 31 32 75), on the second floor of the building that faces the yellow church, serves traditional Romanian meals (L30-40,000).

SIGHTS. The **Memorial to the Victims of Communism and the Resistance** (Memorialul Victimelor Comunismului și al Rezistenței), on Corneliu Coposu Bvd., has earned worldwide acclaim and UNESCO patronage. The silent walls of this jailhouse-turned-museum witnessed the death of the Romanian elite, as the Communist Party imprisoned countless professors, doctors, ministers, generals, and other intellectuals opposed to the Red wave. A partial list of those exterminated between 1952 and 1955 hangs on the facade of the sobering sight. To reach the museum take the first right (off the main street) after the town hall. (Open W-Su 10am-6pm. L2,000.) The decaying Soviet-era **Holocaust Memorial** (down Str. A. Muresan off Pța. Libertății) commemorates the 38,000 Maramureș Jews killed by the Nazis. The **Outdoor Folk Architecture Museum** (Muzeul de Arhitectura și Artă Populară), Str. Bicazului, on the Dobăieș Hill, is reachable from the center by bus (hourly, L1600). Get off when you see a sign for "Muzeul Statulai." Near the old tracks, turn left up Str. Muzeului, as the sign indicates. The museum is an idealized village, and the most beautiful peasant houses in Maramureș are transplanted here; make sure the English-speaking guide doesn't forget to open them. The interiors reveal intricately furnished rooms embellished with handmade carpets, covers, and more. (Open Tu-Su 10am-6pm. L5000, students L2000, disabled free.)

ROMANIAN MOLDOVA AND BUKOVINA

Eastern Romania, which once included the neighboring Republic of Moldova, extends from the Carpathians to the Prut River. Moldavia, as this region was once called, saw its greatest glory in the late-15th century under the rule of Ștefan cel Mare (1457-1504; see **History,** p. 499). Somewhat underdeveloped today, its northern landscape rolls into green, gentle hills that contain some of Romania's most beautiful churches and villages. Active social life can only be found only in the culturally rich 19th-century capital, Iași. Farther north, the Bukovina monasteries near Suceava preserve a distinctive religious ornament that defies imitation.

IAȘI

The intoxicating perfume of lindens in summer is as omnipresent in Iași (yee-ASH; pop. 339,889) as church steeples and, from October to June, university students. During the second half of the 19th century, this city was one of Romania's administrative and cultural centers. Its spiritual life revolved around the Junimea society, founded by the country's top writers, nobles, and intellectuals. They looked westward, filling Iași with Neoclassical homes and palaces. These buildings, remarkably well preserved after 45 grinding years of Soviet communism, draw throngs of tourists to the city's lovely modern streets, some of the cleanest in Romania.

ORIENTATION

To reach Iași's center, walk up the slope leading away from the train and bus stations, take a right on **Str. Arcu** (which becomes **Str. Cuza Vodă** at Piața Unirii), and follow the tram tracks. After a block you'll hit **Piața Unirii.** The center is equally accessible via tram #1 or 3 from directly in front of the train station and across the street from **Vama Veche** (Old Customs Tower). Ticket checkers are exceptionally diligent, so stamp your ticket (L3100 round-trip) immediately.

PRACTICAL INFORMATION

Trains: Str. Silvestru. To: **Bucharest** (6hr., 10 per day, *accelerat* L100,000); **Chișinău** (7hr., 1 per day, L90,000); and **Timișoara** via **Cluj-Napoca** (16hr., 2 per day, *accelerat* L120,000). **CFR,** Piața Unirii 9/11 (tel. 14 76 73), sells tickets. Open M-F 8am-8pm.

Buses: Str. Arcu (tel. 14 65 87). To: **Brașov** (7hr., 1 per day, L100,000); **Chișinău** (4hr., 4 per day, L90,000); and **Ungheni** (2hr., 2 per day, L25,000).

Tourist Offices: Several agencies along Str. A. Panu and behind the Hotel Moldova offer guided tours and private rooms. **Libraria Junimea,** Piața Unirii 4 (tel. 11 46 64), sells very useful **city maps** (L8000). Open M-F 9am-8pm.

Currency Exchange: IDMs litter the city—the most central is at Piața Unirii 12, in Cinematograf Victoria. Changes AmEx, DC, MC, Visa, and Australian traveler's checks, and gives cash advances on MC/Visa for no commission, but at unfavorable rates. Open M-F 9am-5pm, Sa 9am-1pm.

Luggage Storage: At the train station. L7100 per day for small, L14,200 for large. Also at the bus station (L8000).

Post Office: Str. Cuza Vodă 3 (tel. 11 59 85). Open M-F 7am-8pm, Sa 8am-noon. **Postal code:** 6600.

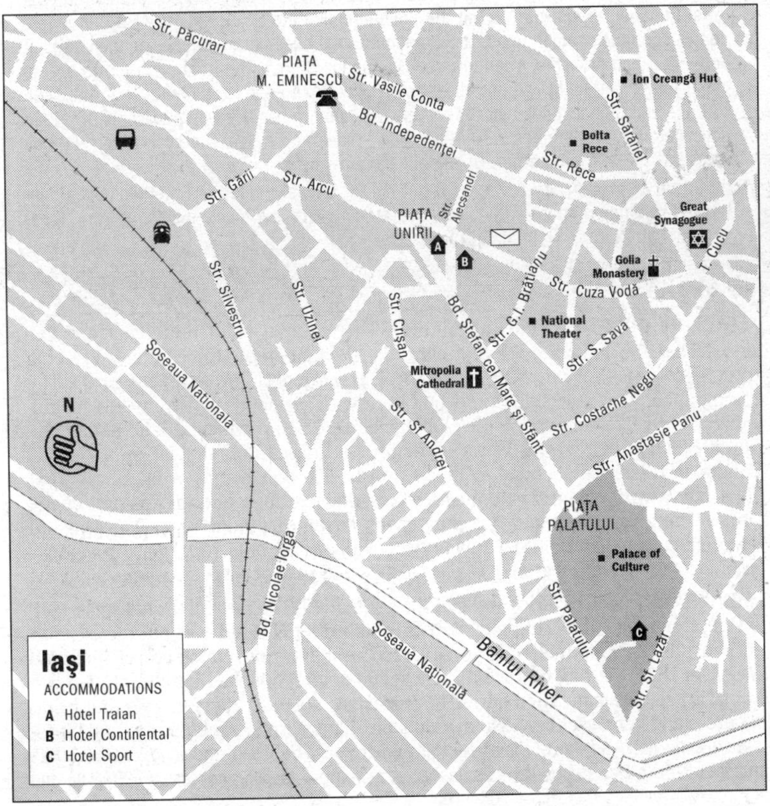

Telephones: Str. Lăpuşneanu 17. From Piaţa Unirii, walk to Hotel Traian, and go down Str. Lăpuşneanu past the hotel on the right; the office is past a small church, on the left. Open daily 7am-9pm. **Phone code:** (0)32.

ACCOMMODATIONS

Private rooms are hard to come by. Mrs. Dincă, Str. Cuza Vodă 6, Bl. Plomba, et. 1, apt. 5 (tel. 11 57 67), has some rooms downtown (US$10 per person). Iaşi also has some excellent hotel options.

Hotel Traian, Piaţa Unirii 1 (tel. 14 33 30). Central location. Pastel, silk-covered furniture echo the Rococo architecture. All rooms have bath and TV. Doubles L480-580,000; Triples L600-750,000. L45,000 breakfast credit included. MC/Visa.

Hotel Continental, Str. Cuza Vodă 1-4 (tel. 11 43 20). Good location. Decent rooms with TV and phone. Singles with bath are a steal at L180,000. Doubles L240,000, with bath L320,000; triples L324,000.

Hotel Sport, Str. Sf. Lazăr 76 (tel. 23 28 00), two blocks behind Palatul Culturii. Tidy doubles with shower L150,000; triples L180,000.

FOOD

For a limited selection of groceries, try the modern **Rodex,** Str. Arcu 3/5, in the basement under the TAROM office. (Open 24hr.) The **market** is at Piaţa Mihai Eminescu near the intersection of Str. Copou and Bd. Independenţei.

Bolta Rece (Cold Ceiling), Str. Rece 10 (tel. 11 25 67). Walk down Str. Cuza Vodă past Hotel Continental and turn left at the Philharmonic onto Str. Brătianu. At Bd. Independenţei, continue straight across the street onto what becomes M. Eminescu, then turn left onto Str. Rece after the green-towered Sf. Teodor church. The Romanian motto on the menu reads, "All things go and disappear/ Only Bolta Rece is still here," and the Latin over the entrance testifies that the *Universitas Vinorum* has been here since 1786. Head downstairs for tasty entrees (L30-40,000) in a place where great writers used to get drunk (wine L40-80,000 per bottle). Open daily 8am-midnight.

Restaurant Dumărea, Str. A. Panu 50 (tel. 14 02 51), to the left of Hotel Moldova under the red awning. Intimate eatery, with live modern and folk music nightly at 7pm. Meat entrees L15-25,000. Open daily 7am-11pm.

SIGHTS

PALACE OF CULTURE. (Palatul Culturii). The massive, neo-Gothic **Palace of Culture,** marked by a clocktower that plays the 1859 union of Moldova and Walachia anthem, contains four museums: **Historical, Ethnographic, Art,** and **Polytechnic.** The ethnographic wing starts on the second floor with agricultural instruments, including waterwheels and wooden olive-oil machines. The art wing exhibits Italian and Dutch Renaissance works. **Voivodes' Hall** (Sala Voievozilor) displays portraits of Romanian rulers from Traian to King Carol II. The polytechnic wing, on the first floor, teems with centuries-old music boxes, phonographs, and the first automatic piano. The ethnographic wing showcases a rich display of the 5000-year-old Cucuteni culture, characterized by pottery with swirl motifs. *(Open Tu-Su 10am-5pm. History, art, and ethnographic museums each L3000; polytechnic L4000, students L2000.)*

TREI IERARHI. The exterior walls of the gorgeous Trei Ierarhi church display Moldavian, Romanian, and Turkish patterns in raised relief. Gold covered the exterior until invading Tatars melted it down in 1653; the interior retains its original gold sheen. In 1821, the flag of the Eteria, a secret society for the liberation of Greece from Turkey, was sanctified here. The **monastery,** home to the country's first printing press and later a school, displays valuable manuscripts, books, icons, and tapestries. *(On the left-hand side of Ştefan cel Mare. Church open daily 9am-noon and 3-7pm. L3000, students L1500. Free during services; just don't look like a tourist. Services: M-F 9-10am and*

5:30-7pm, Su 9am-12:30pm and 6-7pm. Monastery open 9am-noon and 3-7pm. Monastery L3000, students L1500. Decent attire required. Photographs prohibited.)

NATIONAL THEATER. Past the **city hall** and the 1894 National Theater, a statue commemorates the theater's founder, Vasile Alecsandri, a leader of the 1848 revolution and an important literary and political figure. *(Box office: Str. Ştefan cel Mare 8. Near Bancorex and beyond the 1833 Mitropolia Cathedral. Tel. 11 48 49. Box office open M-F 10am-1pm and 5-6:30pm, Su 10am-noon. No opera tickets sold Friday, no theater tickets sold Wednesday. Tickets up to L15,000, students half-price. Season runs Sept.-June.)*

ION CREANGĂ HUT. Writer Ion Creangă, "Romania's Mark Twain" (see **Literature & Arts,** p. 501) spent his last years in Iaşi. Creangă was born a peasant and pursued a career as a priest until he was expelled for shooting crows in the churchyard. He turned to writing and became famous in the Junimea circle for his storytelling. His most important work, *Amintiri din copilarie (Memories of My Boyhood)*, depicts life in his native village. On March 1, huge parties honor Creangă's birthday. *(Str. Simion Bărutiu 4. Where Golia meets Bd. Independentei, crawl up Str. Sărăriei 20min., past #120 and follow the signs to "Bojdeuca." Open Tu-Su 10am-5pm. L2500.)*

MIHAI EMINESCU TREE AND MUSEUM. Inside **Copou park,** created by Prince Mihail Sturza in 1836, is the famous **Mihai Eminescu linden,** the tree that shaded Romania's great poet as he composed (see **Literature & Arts,** p. 501). Eminescu, who was born in Bukovina (which at the time belonged to Austria), studied in Vienna and Berlin, and returned to Iaşi briefly before moving to Bucharest. Statues of several writers and satirists, including Creangă (see above), Eminescu, and Veronica Micle, line a nearby promenade. *(On Bd. Copou, reachable by bus #35 from Piaţa Unirii.)* The adjacent **Eminescu Museum** exhibits pictures of the poet and some of his documents. *(Open Tu-Su 10am-5pm. L2000 per person.)*

OTHER SIGHTS. The Romanian government moved to Iaşi while Bucharest was occupied by the Germans during WWI. The last house on the right before Bd. Copou is that of **General Berthelot,** who was sent by the French government to help the Romanians during this period. *(From Bojdeuca, walk a few yards past the Bojdeuca sign on Str. Sărăriei, turn left on Str. Ralet, and continue on Str. Berthelot just to the left.)* After turning right on Bd. Copou you'll see the Neoclassical **Alexandre Ioan Cuza University** on the left; it was designed by the French architect Le Bland and built between 1893 and 1897. The late 17th-century **Cetăţuia Monastery** perches on a hill 4km south of the center. Intended as an imitation of Prince Duca's Biserica Trei Ierarhi, it boasts panoramas to match. *(Head for Hotel Conest, then follow the Nicolina bridge toward the train tracks. Follow the tracks to the left to the bell-tower of Beautiful Monastery (Frumoasa). Cross the tracks via the underpass to get to the front gate, then head up the hill.)*

SUCEAVA

Moldova's capital under Ştefan cel Mare, Suceava (soo-chay-AH-vah) opened its gates to Mihai Viteazul in 1600, completing his conquest of the Romanian provinces. Although the modern town may not impress visitors with its beauty or social activity, it serves as a useful base for exploring Bucovina's monasteries.

ORIENTATION & PRACTICAL INFORMATION. Suceava lies 100km northwest of Iaşi near the foothills of the Carpathians. There are two **train stations:** the main **Suceava,** Str. Lorga 7 Cart. Burdujeni (tel. 21 38 97), and **Suceava Nord,** Str. Gării 4 Cart. Iţcani (same tel.). **Trains** run to: **Bucharest** (6½hr., 11 per day, *accelerat* L90,000); **Iaşi** (2hr., 6 per day, *accelerat* L40,000); **Timişoara** (13½hr., 3 per day, *accelerat* L120,000); and **Moscow** (14½hr., 1 per day, L1,000,000). Buy tickets at **CFR,** Str. Bălcescu 8 (tel. 21 43 35; open M-F 8am-8pm; international tickets 8am-2pm). To get downtown from the train station, take trolley #2 (15min., L2600 round-trip) six stops to the *centru* (or bus #1 from Suceava Nord). Get off where unimpressive ruins surround a beige stone tower. The **bus station** is at Str. Alecsandri 2 (tel. 21 60 89). **Buses** run to: **Chernivtsi, Ukraine** (Cernăuţi; 3hr., 9 per day, L50,000); **Iaşi** (3hr., 1 per day, L40,000); and **Chişinău** (1 per day). To reach the center, with your back to the station, head right onto the pedestrian walkway, which leads to the perpendicular Str. N. Bălcescu. **ONT,** Str. Bălcescu 2 (tel. 22 12 97; fax 21 47 00), in the main square, offers **maps** (L10,000), arranges car tours of the monasteries (US$50-60 per day, driver included), and books rooms. (Open M-F 8am-4pm.) **Exchange currency** at one of the banks around Str. N. Bălcescu and Str. Ştefan cel Mare, but expect bad rates and fees. **ATMs** are a better bet; there's one at Banca Comercială a Romană (BCR), next to the history museum, and another around the corner from the post office (Cirrus/Plus/MC/Visa). There's a **24hr. pharmacy** next door to ONT (MC/Visa). Log onto the **internet** at Warp Net Technologies for L20,000 per hr. The **post office** is on Str. Dimitrie Onciul in a low brick building. (Open M-F 7am-8pm, Sa 8am-noon.) **Telephones** (Str. Meseriaşilor) are on the first side street to the right after CFR, walking up Str. Bălcescu from ONT. (Open daily 7am-10pm.) **Postal code:** 5800. **Phone code:** (0)30.

ACCOMMODATIONS & FOOD. Ask at **Bucovina Estur,** Str. Ştefan cel Mare 24 (tel. 22 32 59), across the *piaţa* from ONT, about rooms in Suceava and the area. (Hot water and color TV. US$12-25 per person.) **ONT** (see above) can arrange hotel rooms for US$13 a night. **Hotel Gloria** (formerly al Partidului), Str. V. Bumbac 48 (tel. 52 12 09), off Str. Nicolae Bălcescu and to the right of Hotel Suceava, offers bright rooms with color TV. (Singles L100,000; doubles L160,000, with bath L250,000. Breakfast included. Call 1-3 days in advance.) **Hotel Autogară** (tel. 21 60 89), above the bus station, might not be in the nicest neighborhood, but it features sunny new doubles with great private bathrooms for L150,000 per person. On Str. Petru Rareş between Str. Alecsandri and Str. Ştefan cel Mare, the huge **Piaţa Agroalimentară Market** sells the requisite fruits and veggies. (Open daily dusk-dawn.)

SIGHTS. The ruins of the **Royal Fortress** (Cetatea de Scaun) sprawl in **Parcul Cetăţii,** east of Piaţa 22 Decembrie. Take a left on Bd. Ipătescu, a right on Str. Cetăţii (a gravel path), walk down the hill, and go up the path and stairs. The ruins are in excellent shape, considering they were built around 1388, when Prince Petru Muşat I of Moldavia moved his capital here; Ştefan cel Mare added 3m-thick walls. The defenses resisted the 1476 siege of Sultan Mahomed II, conqueror of Constantinople, but not the 1675 Ottoman attacks. (Open daily 8am-9pm. L5000.) From the cafe in front of the fortress, follow the fence into the woods and take a right to reach a rather dark park with pleasant gardens (during the day, that is—at night it's probably wise to stay away) and a 22m **statue of Ştefan cel Mare.** More medieval ruins are scattered around neighboring hills.

Back in town, check out the dark, impressive **St. John the New Monastery** (Mănăstirea Sf. Ioan cel Nou). From the main square, turn right on Bd. Ipătescu, then left on Str. Ioan Vodă cel Viteaz. Thousands come from Bucovina for the June 24 **Sânzâiene festival**—a celebration of the local St. John—in which his mummified remains are removed from the monastery's church and paraded in a religious procession. According to legend, John was decapitated at Cetatea Alba and brought back to Suceava by Prince Alexandru cel Bun. (Open daily 5:45am-8pm.) The **History Museum** (Muzeul Bucovinei Secţia de Istorie), Str. Ştefan cel Mare 33 (tel. 21 64 39), is one of the better collections of its kind in Romania. Among the in-depth presentations is a French wax reconstruction of Ştefan cel Mare's throne room. (Open Tu-Su 8am-7pm. L6000, students L3000.)

NEAR SUCEAVA: BUKOVINA MONASTERIES

Bukovina's painted monasteries, hidden among green hills and rustic farming villages, have witnessed many attacks over the centuries; recently, they have endured early Soviet-era policies forcibly ending the monastic life in favor of "reintegration." Built 500 years ago by Ştefan cel Mare and his successors, the exquisite structures serenely mix Moldavian and Byzantine architectures, Romanian soul, and Christian dogma. Most of the monasteries are small, with stone walls and wooden roofs, surrounded by living quarters for monks or nuns and heavy stone walls that never quite deterred looters. Unfortunately, getting to them on public transport can be a trial of faith; instead, try one of the tours organized by ONT (see above). Young people often hitch, especially during summer. Wear long sleeves and a long skirt or pants, or else borrow a skirt to wear over your shorts. Chew gum at your own risk. Smoking is prohibited, as is photography of the cloistered.

VORONEȚ & HUMOR

To reach Voroneț from Suceava, take a ***train*** *to* ***Gura Humorului*** *(1¼hr., 9 per day, L13,000), or a* ***bus*** *(1hr., 2 per day, L18,000). Or, take a bus from Varna through Suceava toward* ***Vatra Dornei*** *stopping at Gura Humorului (1¾hr., M-F 3 per day, Sa-Su 2 per day, L25,000). From there, catch the bus for Voroneț (10min., M-F 4 per day, L6000). To find the bus, turn right on Ștefan cel Mare with your back to the train station. To walk to the monastery, keep going, and after less than 1km take a left onto Cartierul Voroneț, which heads toward Voroneț (5km). To get to Humor, walk right on Ștefan cel Mare from the train or bus station and walk to the heart of Gura Humorului. At the fork near a park on the right, follow Str. M. Humorulu to the left and continue 6km to the monastery. Open daily 8am-8pm. L5000, students L2500.)*

Voroneț Blue (Albastru de Voroneț) is a phrase that haunts Romanian imaginations, from schoolchildren to art conservationists searching for a modern equivalent of its 15th-century paint. The blue that brought the monastery its legendary fame is also the source of its postponed restoration, since most work has to be put off until the paint is reproduced. Voroneț's **frescoes** are incredible; the *Last Judgment* mural on the east wall is a masterpiece. The damned wear the faces of Moldavia's enemies, the Turks and Tatars; the blessed look ethnically Moldavian, and angels sport regional musical instruments. God sits above Jesus at the very top of the wall, and angels roll up the Zodiac around him, a demonstration of the passing of earthly time. *Jesse's Tree*, on the south wall, displays the genealogy of Jesus, while the north wall depicts scenes from Genesis and Adam's pact with the Devil. The church was built in 1488 by Ștefan cel Mare, supposedly on the advice of St. Daniel. The gold-covered iconostasis is made from *tisa* wood, which can last up to 1000 years. **Humor,** which dates from 1530, is 6km north of Gura Humorului. The south wall depicts the Virgin Mary's life; based on a poem by the patriarch of Constantinople, it represents her saving Constantinople from a Persian attack in 626. With an eye toward staying current, the artist substituted Turks for Persians and added weapons typical of the 16th century. He painted himself in as a cavalier running a Turk through with his spear.

ROMANIA

MOLDOVIȚA

From Suceava, take a ***train*** *to* ***Vama*** *(1½hr., 8 per day) and switch for the train to* ***Vatra Moldoviței,*** *2km east of Moldovița (35min., 3 per day, 5th stop, L20,000 for whole trip).* ***Buses*** *also run from Suceava through Vama to* ***Vatra Dornei*** *(1¾hr., M-F 3 per day, Sa-Su 2 per day, L25,000). L5000, students L1500. Photos L10,000. Video L25,000.*

Moldovița is the largest of the painted monasteries, and its frescoes are among the best-preserved. Built in 1532 and painted in 1537, it has a *Last Judgment*, a *Jesse's Tree*, and a monumental *Siege of Constantinople*. The siege of 626, painted on the exterior wall to the right of the entrance, depicts the ancient fortress in an uncanny 16th-century light. The monastery was closed from 1785 until 1945, and the north wall is badly weathered. Elaborately carved grapevine columns painted with gold jut out from the iconostasis. As in most of the monasteries, the founder is painted *"al fresco"* inside the nave, presenting the church to Jesus. The museum houses the wooden (now seatless) throne of Prince Petru Rareș, founder of many monasteries. Opposite the throne in the main room is the *Pomme d'Or* prize awarded to Bukovina in 1975 in recognition of its artistic importance. Be sure to see the giant **religious tome** donated by Catherine the Great.

SUCEVIȚA

Sucevița lies 29km north of Moldovița (see above). From Suceava, catch the ***train*** *to* ***Rădăuti*** *(2hr., 7 per day, L1300). Turn left from the train station and follow the road right to reach the bus station, from which* ***buses*** *run to* ***Sucevița*** *(30min., M-F 4 per day until 6pm, Sa-Su 3 per day until 3pm, L15,000). The* ***Moldovița-Rădăuți*** *bus between the Sucevița and Moldovița monasteries features incredible scenery (1hr., 1 per day, L10,000). Open daily 6am-9pm. L5000, students L3000. Photos in courtyard only.*

Sucevița is beautifully set in fortified hills. On sunny days its white walls shine, making it look more like a citadel than a monastery. The frescoed south wall presents a *Genealogy of Jesus* and a *Procession of Philosophers,* which portrays Pythagoras, Socrates, Plato, Aristotle, and Solon in Byzantine cloaks. Plato is carrying a small coffin of bones on his head. The shade of green you see is unique to Sucevița. Unlike the north faces of the other monasteries, Sucevița's is well-preserved; souls climb a heavenly ladder of 30 rungs, each representing a virtue and a sin. The west wall remains unpainted—the artist fell from the scaffolding, and his ghost supposedly prevents completion. The black stone head under the arch represents a woman who hauled stone for the construction with her oxen for 30 years. Inside, a *Last Judgment* decorates the wall under the balcony's Zodiac ceiling, next to an illustration of the martyred **St. John the New** returning from Cetatea Alba. The pro-nave depicts the deaths of 420 Orthodox saints, while the chamber contains an iconostasis carved from *tisa* wood. The **tomb room,** painted with scenes from Jewish history, houses the tombs of the **Movila** dynasty. A tiny door on the left leads to an emergency hiding place for relics and precious icons. The nave depicts scenes from the life of Jesus, and the altar boasts two iconostases. The tomb room is currently under renovation. The museum in one of the old towers displays intricate tapestries, religious icons, and books.

PUTNA

For the scenic ride to ***Putna,*** *catch direct* ***trains*** *from Suceava, 75km southeast (2½hr., 5 per day, L15,000). The last train leaves Putna around 9pm. The monastery lies 1km from the train station. Exiting the platform, take a right and then a left at the first intersection, and keep walking. Monastery open daily 8am-8pm. Free. Photos L10,000. Museum open daily 9am-5pm. L5000, students L1500. Church open daily 9am-5pm. Free. No photos. Music at the entrance gate, in the shop on the right; L10,000 per cassette.*

Immaculately white and beautifully simple, Putna Monastery deceptively appears to be newer than its counterparts. Only one tower has survived the ravages of history, which have included fires, earthquakes, and attacks; not even the frescoes remain. The complex encompasses the marble-canopied **tomb of Ștefan cel Mare** (see **History,** p. 499), among others, and a wide-ranging **museum.** Putna also boasts the only collection of recorded music of the monasteries. In the church, Ștefan decays down on the right; his sons occupy the nearer tombs. Built in 1469, Putna was the first of 38 monasteries founded by Ștefan, who built one church after each battle he won. He left Putna's location up to God: climbing a nearby hill to the left of the monastery (marked by a cross), he shot an arrow into the air. A piece of the oak it struck is on display at the museum, along with a number of manuscripts and religious garb. Midway to the railway station along the main road, stop by the 14th-century **Wooden Church Dragoș Vodă** (Biserica de lemn Dragoș Vodă). There are good **hiking trails,** but no map. Tourists flood Putna on July 2, Ștefan's Day.

NEAMȚ

Passage to the monastery runs through ***Târgu Neamț*** *on the Suceava-Buzău-Bucharest* ***train*** *line: switch at* ***Pașcani*** *(1hr. from Suceava) onto a personal train to* ***Târgu Neamț*** *(45min., 4 per day, L20,000 total). Buses from Suceava also head straight for the center of Târgu Neamț (2hr., 2 per day, L22,500). Getting between the bus and train stations is tricky; ask a taxi to take you to the autogară (up to L25,000), or head for Str. Cuza Vodă. Catch the bus at the autogară to Mânăstirea Neamț (35min., M-F 4 per day, Sa-Su 3 per day, L8700). Open daily 8am-7:30pm. No photos.*

Fields of clovers and buttercups cradle **Neamț Monastery,** 12km northwest of Târgu Neamț. A giant throne looks upon a 6th-century *Madonna and Child* known as "the miracle-worker." Presented to Alexandru cel Bun in 1424 by the Byzantine Empire, the icon was nearly lost in a Turkish attack. Legend has it that the Madonna's piercing eyes paralyzed the Turk who stole it; stricken, he swore to renounce Allah if the icon saved him. He died a monk at the monastery. The chandelier holding eight ostrich eggs, symbols of eternal life. On the path to the church a placard indicates where the bones of a saint were discovered in 1986. The monks first decided to excavate this spot because small stones supposedly stood up whenever a non-Christian walked by.

The covered remains of the saint are on display inside the church. The **museum,** once home to the calligraphy school that nurtured Moldova's first historians, contains icons, priestly garb, and prince-writer Dimitrie Cantemir's 1821 *Descriptio Moldoviae;* at 45cm by 32cm, it is the largest printed Old Romanian book.

BLACK SEA COAST

The land between the Danube and the Black Sea has weathered a troubled history. Conquered by the Turks in the 14th century, it remained part of the Ottoman Empire until 1877, when it was ceded to Romania as compensation for losing part of Moldavia to its treacherous ally Russia (see **History,** p. 500). Beautiful beaches stretch to the south, while the interior valleys and rocky hills, holds Roman, Greek, and early Christian ruins and produces some of Romania's best wines. Crowds packed the area in the past, but now prices are too steep for many Romanians, particularly during high season (mid July-Aug.). If you tire of the plastic resorts, take refuge to the north in where the mighty Danube meets the Black Sea.

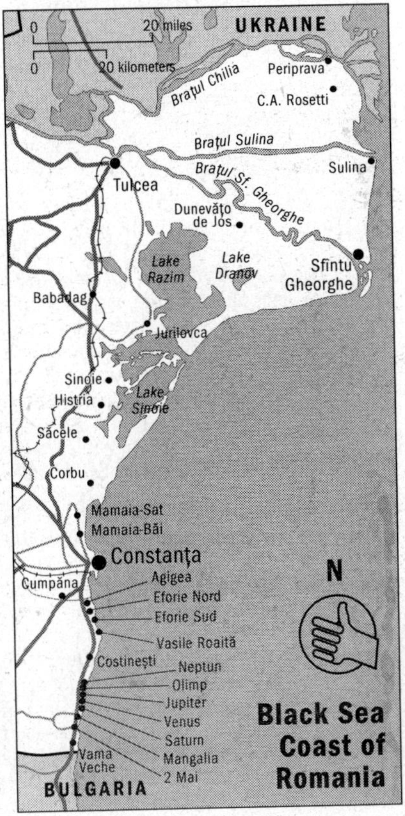

CONSTANȚA

Over the last 2500 years Constanța (con-STAN-tsa; pop. 348,575) has been the prize of many rulers, but today it serves as a mere jumping-off point to other nearby beach resorts. Dozens of dormant mechanical cranes, reminders of the city's stint as a communist-planned commercial port, still loom over the town. Beyond the tourist traps of Str. Ștefan cel Mare, though, one can still find haunting Orthodox churches and a tree-lined boulevard with old men playing backgammon.

ORIENTATION & PRACTICAL INFORMATION. Constanța, 225km east of Bucharest, is north of most Black Sea resorts. **Trains** head for every corner of the country, largely via **Bucharest** (2¾-3hr., up to 16 per day in high season, *accelerat* L100,000). Buy tickets in advance from June to August; a seat reservation is required for a *rapid* or *express* train—only on the *accelerat* and *personal* can you squeeze in the hallway. Most trains and buses depart from Constanța's main **train** and **bus stations,** which are next to each other, but northbound buses leave from **Autogară Tomis Nord** (5 stops on trolley #100 from the train station, then head left). To get downtown from the train station, take trolley #40 or 43 and get off where Bd. Tomis intersects Bd. Ferdinand (4 stops). Buy tickets (round-trip L3200) from kiosks in front of the station. Validate your ticket or suffer a L40,000 fine. Cash **traveler's checks** for no commission or get a **cash advance** on Visa or AmEx at the **Trans Danubius Tourist Office,** Bd. Ferdinand 36 (tel. 61 58 36 and 61 94 81). The agency can arrange you a car (with driver) for US$0.35 per km, insurance and gas included.

(Open M-Sa 9am-8pm, Su 9am-2pm.) **Internet access** is available at **Space Games,** Bd. Tomis 129 (tel. 61 47 65; L15,000 per hr.; open daily 24 hr.). Near Bd. Tomis and Str. Ștefan cel Mare are the **post office** (open M-F 7am-9pm, Sa 8am-noon) and a bay of **telephones. Postal code:** 8700. **Phone code:** (0)41.

ACCOMMODATIONS & FOOD. While it's difficult to find a cheap bed in Constanța, the quality far surpasses that of other coastal towns. **Private rooms**—many within five minutes of the Mamaia beach, although a bit far from Constanța's center—provide an affordable alternative (US$5 and up). **Cazare la Particulari,** Str. Lăpușneanu (tel. 65 55 56), can arrange singles (L180,000) or doubles (L230,000). From the train station, take tram #100 to the end of the line and look for the hotel/restaurant complex on the right. (Open mid-June to mid-Sept. M-Sa 9am-5pm, Su 9am-1pm.) To reach **Hotel Astoria,** Str. Mircea cel Batrîn 102 (tel. 61 60 64), take trolley #40 or 43 downtown, then continue on Bd. Ferdinand away from the train station. Turn left when you hit the water; it's a bit past Hotel Sport. Offers clean rooms with cushy beds, dilapidated TVs, and baths near the water. (Singles L160,000; doubles L240,000; quads L260,000. Breakfast included.)

Turning right on Bd. Ferdinand from the train station will bring you to Bd. Tomis and its abundant pizzerias. **Restaurant Les Barons,** Bd. Tomis 78 (tel. 61 54 15), offers delicious food and high-class service in a sober black-and-white decor. (3-course meal US$6.50. Open daily 9:30am-midnight. MC/Visa.) At the corner of Bd. Tomis and Bd. Ferdinand, the **Grand supermarket** has it all, all the time. (Open 24hr.) A covered outdoor **market** is near the intersection of Str. Ștefan cel Mare and Str. Mihăileanu. To get there, head back toward the train on Bd. Ferdinand past the Trans Danubius office and go right on Str. Mihăileanu. (Open daily dawn to dusk.)

SIGHTS & ENTERTAINMENT. With your back to the train station, turn right down Bd. Tomis to reach the center of the **Old Town.** Continue along Bd. Tomis, following it until it curves left and ends in Piața Ovidiu to reach the **statue of Ovid** (see **Literature & Arts,** p. 501), who penned some of his most famous poems while in exile here. He was ostensibly exiled for writing *The Art of Love*, although the real reason was more likely his practice of that art with Emperor Augustus's daughter. The epitaph on the statue is a Romanian translation of Ovid's verse: "Here lies Ovid. The singer of delicate loves, killed by his own talent. Oh, passer-by, if you have ever loved, pray for him to rest in peace." Ovid's actual resting place is not under the statue, but somewhere in the Black Sea. The nearby **Museum of National and Archaeological History** (Muzeul de Istorie Națională și Arheologie), Piața Ovidiu 2 (tel. 61 45 83), displays several items from the Roman past, and recounts the 19th-century War of Independence from Turkey with particular flair (see **History,** p. 500). (Open in summer daily 9am-8pm; off-season W-Su 9am-5pm. L10,000. Pictorial guide in English L10,000.) **Excavations** of a Roman port with the **world's largest floor mosaic** are hidden behind the Roman columns to the right of the museum. The mosaic is preserved from the 4th century BC and was discovered only in 1959. Walk behind the museum to better admire the mosaic and the surrounding brickwork. (Open in summer daily 9am-8pm; off-season Tu-Su 9am-5pm. L20,000. Explanations written in English.)

The **mosque** off Piața Ovidiu on Str. Arhiepiscopiei is one of the few remaining vestiges of the Turkish domination. It is decorated with one of the largest **Oriental carpets** in Europe, woven in the 18th century in Turkey and presented as a gift to the mosque by the Sultan himself. Built in 1730, the mosque was reconstructed by King Carol I in 1910 and sports a 50m **tower.** If you come for services, wash your hands, feet, and face in the courtyard. (Open June-Sept. daily 10am-5:30pm; Oct.-May during services only. Services F 1pm. L4000.) The **Naval History Museum** (Muzeul Marinei Romane), Str. Traian 53 (tel. 61 90 35) dazzles with its stockpile of instruments, uniforms, documents, and models. Str. Traian runs roughly parallel to Bd. Tomis but hooks off to hug the coast. (Open in summer Tu-Su 10am-6pm; in off-season 10am-5pm. L15,000.) The **archaeological park** opposite Trans Danubius offers urban respite among 2000-year-old Greek amphorae and Roman sarcophagi.

Closer to the sea sits the **Orthodox Cathedral of St. Peter and St. Paul** (Catedrala Ortodoxă Sf. Petru și Pavel), Str. Arhiepiscopiei 25, built in 1877 following Romania's independence from Turkey. (Open daily 7am-7pm.) The statue-lined waterfront promenade is about as close to the water as you want to get (clean beaches are scarce in Constanța) but if you're eager to explore the sea from here anyway, **boat tours** can be chartered from the main boardwalk. (L15,000 per person, if at least 6 people show up.)

RESORTS NEAR CONSTANȚA

The coast to the south of Constanța is lined with sandy beaches and 70s revival tourist resorts. Most towns are similar; nearly all have the requisite amusement parks and campsites. **Costinești** is especially popular with young Romanians while **Neptun** has the most luxurious amenities. Resorts are open during the high season (late June-mid-Sept.) and on May 1, a school holiday. July and August, the peak of high season, bring heavy crowds and high prices.

Buses run south from Constanța toward **Mangalia** (40km, 3 per hr. until 7:30pm, L4600). More comfortable private **minibuses** to Mangalia usually cost L7000, but hit L15,000 in the evening after the trains and buses stop running. **Minivans** connect the constellation of resorts near Mangalia late into the night (L2000-11,000, depending on how far you're going). **Trains** run hourly and are a bit less expensive, but not enough to make them preferable to the minibuses. All the resorts on the coast have the same **postal** (8700) and **phone** (041) **codes** as Constanța.

EFORIE NORD, EFORIE SUD, & COSTINEȘTI. Closest to Constanța are **Eforie Nord** and **Sud,** the oldest resort towns. Although they're beginning to show their age, they're still large and popular, and are especially renowned for their mud baths near **Lake Techirghiol.** The lake water is rumored to be so salty that you can't sink, although *Let's Go* doesn't recommend testing this. Reach the Efories from **Constanța** (Eforie Nord precedes Eforie Sud by 2min.) by **train** (20min., up to 19 per day, *accelerat* L2500), or take the infrequent **bus** #12 (L2600). In Eforie Nord, **Hotel Bega** (tel. 74 19 53) *almost* overlooks the sea. (Doubles July 11-Aug. L220,000; off season L140,000). **Hotel Apollo,** near the center of Eforie Nord, offers drabber doubles. (July-Aug. L300,000; off-season L100,000.) Continue away from the center on the seaside Bd. T. Vladimirescu and turn left after Maxim Disco to find **Camping Meduza,** Str. Sportului (tel./fax 74 23 85; July-Aug. L11,000 per day, off season L9500 per day; tourist tax L15,000; electric lights L3500).

Costinești, south of the Efories, is the coastal hot spot. Wonderfully crowded with young Romanians, it offers loud fun and cheap prices. Unfortunately, hot running water is rare; even posh hotels have at most two hours of hot water per day (7-8am and 6-7pm), and at the cheapest places you might be hard pressed to find running water at all. Those arriving by bus sometimes hitch the 4km from the bus stop; otherwise, they take **bus** #12 (L4500). The **train** drops you closer to town; get off at **Costinești Tabără** and circle right around the lake. After trains stop running around 9pm, try to catch a minibus going back to Constanța. **Hans Exchange,** at the entrance to town, takes MC/Visa and cashes **traveler's checks** for a high 6% commission. (Open daily 9:30am-10pm.) Try to stay in Constanța, but if you miss the last bus back, **Albatros/Belvedere** (tel. 73 40 15), on the main street under the "Recepție Perla" sign, provides tidy two-room villas with only cold water close to the sea. Albatros has nicer rooms, but Belvedere is cheaper. (July-Aug. L90,000-150,000; off season L60,000-100,000.)

Cheap meals abound near the train station and on the main street. (L7000 per person.) Beware: if places label their food "fresh," it probably means it's not. At night, follow the hordes to **Disco Ring,** where disgruntled youth boogie all night to eclectic music, including occasional live bands. (Open nightly 9:30pm-4am. Cover L10,000.) Renting a **boat** for a spin around the lake is also popular in the evening. (L15,000 per hr.)

VENUS, SATURN, NEPTUN, OLIMP, & JUPITER. **Venus** rose from the foam of Saturn's seas to create one of the best **beaches** on the coast. To reach **Saturn,** take the train to **Mangalia** (1hr., 16 per day in high season, *personal* L8100), exit the train station and head down the street with the covered market. Continue until you reach the beach. From Saturn, it's a 20min. walk through the resort to nearby Venus, or you can catch one of the **minibuses** patrolling the coasts for confused tourists (L5000). Staying in Saturn is fairly inexpensive: at the height of the season, stay at a one-star hotel. (Doubles L108,000; triples L159,000.) Camping is even cheaper. (L9600 per day; L15,000 tourist tax.) The cheapest accommodation in the area, however, is the popular **free camping** zone across the highway from the beach and sandwiched between Venus and Saturn. Alternatively, some vacationers accept offers of **private rooms.** (Off-season around US$10, summer $20.) Prior to 1999, the best place to get a bite to eat in the center of town was the **Gradina de Vara,** which has recently been shut down; supposedly, it will soon be replaced by a renovated restaurant named **Grădina Dunăreă** by summer 2000. Dancers get funky under a disco ball at **Bowling Saturn** (tel. 75 17 40), the cheapest and most popular—but certainly not the only—**disco** in town. (Open nightly 8:30pm-5am. No cover but L5000 drink min.)

Neptun, site of Ceauşescu's summer villa, is the shining star of this solar system—a highbrow resort with carriage rides, hot water, and probably the best food on the coast. **Trains** run to Neptun from **Constanța** (50min., 16 per day, *accelerat* L5800). Exchange **traveler's checks** at **Banca de Comerț Exterior** (tel. 73 19 34; commission 1.5% on total sale plus 0.2% per check, min. US$5; open M-F 8:30am-2pm). The Neptun **post office** has **telephones.** (Open M-F 7am-9pm, Sa 8am-4pm.) The **Dispecerat de Cazare,** in the Topkapî shopping center (tel. 73 13 10; fax 63 90 02), helps find rooms for prices lower than the hotels. (Singles in a 2-star hotel US$13-15; 3-star hotel US$20. 10% commission. Open May-Sept. daily 24hr.) Two-star hotels, such as **Apollo** (tel. 73 16 16) and **Romanța** (tel. 73 10 23), offer clean, spacious rooms with hot running water. (Singles L270,000; doubles L400,000. Breakfast included.) Feast on grilled sturgeon and quality wines while enjoying live dance shows at the **Rustic** (tel. 73 10 26). Reserve with your hotel's tourist office or directly with the restaurant. (Entrees under L50,000. Show L25,000: modern music 8-9pm, folk dance show 9-11pm. Open daily 10am-4pm and 8pm-1am.) **Disco Rainbow** (tel. 73 18 12) is a magnet for the coastal youth. (Open daily 9pm-5am. Cover 9-10pm L5000, after 10pm L10,000.)

Wedged between Neptun and Venus, **Olimp** and **Jupiter** enjoy neither the popularity of the first nor the beaches of the second. But accommodations are cheaper (1-star hotels: singles L70,000, doubles L90,000; 2-star hotels: singles L85,000, doubles L135,000; private rooms L50,000-70,000), and Neptun and Venus are both a 10-20min. walk away. And if you're tired of swimming, practice your swing at **Mini-Golf Marea Neagră,** close to the beach, off the main street. (Open daily 10am-2am. L10,000.)

MANGALIA, 2 MAI, & VAMA VECHE. The **railway** terminus of Mangalia sees scores of trains dump beachgoers onto the sunburnt streets of this city. (1hr., June-Aug. up to 19 per day from Constanța, L8000-12,000; **luggage storage** L4800-9600.) To get back a little faster, take one of the **buses** or **minibuses** across the street from the train station. **Centru de Cazare** (tel. 75 37 61), also across from the train station, finds **private rooms** in Mangalia (high season L50,000 per person) and discounted **hotel** rooms in Venus. (L80,000, for longer stays L100,000; commission L50,000 for 1-10 days; open daily 9am-6pm.) You can buy groceries at a **covered market** on the side street, Str. Ion Creangă, leading away from the station.

Mangalia is a great site from which to explore more pristine beach towns, such as nearby **2 Mai** (6km) and **Vama Veche** (11km). A few Coca-Cola signs indicate that 2 Mai's natural beauty might not outlive the first stage of Romanian privatization, but Vama Veche remains untouched. You can hike to them, take one of the minibuses that leaves every 20min. in high season (L8000; hourly in the off season), or catch bus #14 from Mangalia (4 per day 6am-6pm; L3000). For Vama Veche, get off at the second-to-last stop, lest you want to cross the border into Bulgaria. These less-touristed villages offer tent space and **private accommodations.** (L45,000-60,000; set the price before you move in.) Young people often **camp** at the south end of the nude beach in 2 Mai. (Tent space L9500 per person. Parking L3000.) Another campground at a beach chaperoned by industrial cranes lies in the north part of 2 Mai, a block away from the bus #14 stop. (Tents L11,000 per person. Parking L4000.) At Vama Veche, camp on the quiet beach. (L10,000 per person. Parking L4000.) In 2 Mai, dine at the hip restaurant **Şuberek's.** (Open daily 8pm-5am. Pizza L9000; Turkish honey cake with nuts L3000.)

HISTRIA. A Hellenic colony first mentioned by the Greek historian Strabo in the 5th century BC, the town of Histria was rediscovered in the early 20th century by Romanian archaeologist Vasile Pârvan. The excavations are about 30km north of Constanţa, on the shore of Lake Sinoe (a lagoon separated from the sea by a thread of sand). **Buses** leave from Constanţa's Tomis Nord station (1-1½hr., 4 per day, L10,200); unfortunately, they drop you off an invigorating 7km hike from the site. A taxi from Constanţa will set you back at least L350,000. The **museum** and **excavations** follow the city's 14 centuries of recorded history, from the 7th century BC to the 7th century AD. The museum's explanations are in Romanian, while the ruins' are in French and German as well. An English brochure to the museum is available for L10,000. The city is named for the Danube (*Istros* in Greek), which returned the favor by ultimately causing Histria's decay, blocking the city harbor with mud. It's no gleaming white marble utopia (or democratic slave-society, as the 20-year-old descriptions call it), but the fairly extensive ruins give you a feel for the town—note the tavern conveniently located by the basilica. Filled with greenery, the crumbling houses overlooking the lake would make any Romantic painter drool. (Open daily 8am-6pm. L20,000.)

RUSSIA (РОССИЯ)

US$1 = 26R (RUBLES)	**10R = US$0.39**
CDN$1 = 17R	**10R = CDN$0.57**
UK£1 = 41R	**10R = UK£0.24**
IR£1 = 35R	**10R = IR£0.29**
AUS$1 = 17R	**10R = AUS$0.59**
NZ$1 = 14R	**10R = NZ$0.73**
SAR1 = 4.25R	**10R = SAR2.33**
DM1 = 14R	**10R = DM0.71**

PHONE CODES Country code: **7.** International dialing prefix: **810.**

Seven years after the fall of the Evil Empire, we still don't understand Russia, and it still doesn't understand us. The current paradoxes in which it exists go well beyond any of the clichés visited upon it by Western journalists. Vaguely repentant former communists man the ship of state under the standard of the market, while impoverished, outspoken pensioners long for a rosy-tinted Soviet past. Heedless of the failing provinces, cosmopolitan Moscow indiscriminately gobbles down hypercapitalism, while St. Petersburg struggles not to resemble a ghost capital. Conservative monarchists, believers in the fundamental Orthodoxy of the Russian soul, rub elbows, and none too gently, with conservative Communist-nationalists, believers in Russian greatness through nuclear weapons. Neither have much affection left for the West, by whom most Russians feel profoundly betrayed.

Russia is in many ways the ideal destination for a budget traveler—inexpensive and well-served by public transportation, with hundreds of neglected monasteries, kremlins, and churches. At the same time, it is a bureaucratic nightmare that would have made Trotsky blush, and you can't exactly skip through in a day. Still, if Russia does not collapse into a group of feudal strongholds, it can offer you the world (or half the world, at least), from the capital's rousing nightlife to Lake Baikal, the world's deepest lake, and from lavishly decorated medieval cathedrals to rusted glimpses of life as it was before the Iron Curtain fell.

HIGHLIGHTS OF RUSSIA

- Just a few years after the fall of the Iron Curtain, **Moscow** is one of the brashest and most overwhelming cities in Europe (p. 561).
- Peter the Great built **St. Petersburg** on top of a Finnish swamp; today, its 40 islands house splendid palaces and the Hermitage, Europe's largest art collection (p. 596).
- When the French Alps want the cookies on the top shelp, they ask **Mt. Elbrus,** the highest peak in the Caucasus and in Europe (p. 650).
- The **Altai Republic** is the most devastatingly beautiful place in the world; we hope you like long train rides (p. 659).
- **Lake Baikal** is Russia's natural marvel: the deepest and oldest lake in the world, it contains one-fifth of the world's freshwater (p. 664).

LIFE & TIMES

HISTORY

Throughout its millennium-long history, Russia's ideology and theology have isolated it from Western Europe. In AD 988, the first great Slavic empire, **Kievan Rus,** chose Constantinople and **Eastern Orthodoxy** over Rome. But this isolation was minimal compared to that which the **Mongols** (or **Tatars**) visited on the region during their 300-year rule. As the rest of Europe underwent Renaissance and Reformation, Russian cities lay prostrate to their overlords. By the time **Ivan III** finally threw off the Mongol yoke and set Moscow on a path to dominance, Russia lagged far behind its neighbors to the West.

Ivan IV (the Terrible) was the first ruler to take the title "tsar." He conquered neighboring Kazan and expanded into the European sphere, but alienated his generals and killed his oldest son and heir with his own hands. Ivan's second son, **Fyodor I,** proved too weak to rule alone; his brother-in-law **Boris Godunov** secretly ruled in his stead. When Fyodor died childless in 1598, Boris became tsar, marking the end of the Rurik dynasty. Conspiring against Godunov, the Russian **boyars** (nobles) brought forward a pretender named Dmitry who claimed Fyodor I had been his father. After Godunov's mysterious death, the *boyars* crowned this **"False Dmitry"** tsar. A decade of unprecedented instability and chaos followed, with the *boyars* striving for ever greater control over a succession of weak tsars. Finally, in 1613, **Mikhail Romanov** ascended to the throne, ushering in the dynasty that ruled until the Bolshevik Revolution of 1917.

Peter the Great, whose reign began in 1682, dragged Russia kicking and screaming Westward. Peter created his own elite and built St. Petersburg, his "window to the West," in the middle of a Finnish swamp. He killed innumerable workers in the process, hung the opposition, traipsed around Europe causing even more damage than the average *Let's Go* traveler, and left Russia with a permanent crisis of cultural identity when he died in 1725. With no male heir to the throne, the nobles took the opportunity to install a string of rulers firmly under their collective thumb, until the reign of **Catherine the Great.** The meek, homely daughter of an impoverished Prussian aristocrat, Catherine came to Russia to marry heir to the throne Peter III, whom she promptly overthrew after he came to power. Catherine extended the empire and partook of certain modish Enlightenment trends, but also increased landowners' power over their dominions.

Napoleon's invasion in 1812 foundered as the Russians burnt their crops and villages as they retreated, leaving the French to face the harsh winter *sans* supplies. Victory over the little Corsican brought prestige and new contact with the rest of Europe, but led to internal strife. Russian officers, returning from the West attempted a coup on December 14, 1825. Some **Decembrists** were hanged, most were exiled to Siberia, and for the next 30 years, Tsar Nicholas I made sure to stifle all dissent.

The 1840s saw a marked split in the intelligentsia between **Westernizers** like **Vissarion Belinsky,** who considered Russia a backwards, despotic country in need of reform, and the **Slavophiles,** who insisted that serfdom and autocracy were just bends along Russia's "special path" to saving Christianity and the world. The Westernizers bred a radical wing that would later take to Marxism and, more recently, consumer capitalism; Slavophilism, more amenable to the tsars, remains to this day the banner of extreme nationalism.

Polemics and politics became increasingly extreme as the century progressed. Russia's loss to the West in the **Crimean War** (1853-1856) spurred reforms that included the **emancipation of the serfs** in 1861. Alexander II soon slowed the pace of reform, however, which prompted the radicals to move against him; he was assassinated shortly thereafter.

The famine, peasant unrest, terrorism, and strikes of the late 1800s culminated in the failed **1905 Revolution.** Tsar **Nicholas II** established a progressive congressional body, the **Duma,** and made vague attempts to address the demands of his people. However, **WWI,** stalemate with the Duma, and fermenting revolution led him to abdicate in March 1917. The organizational genius **V.I. Lenin,** leader of the Bolsheviks, steered the bloodless coup of October 1917: a few well-placed words to **Aleksandr Kerensky,** leader of the provisional government, and a menacing ring around the Winter Palace turned the nation Red. A **Civil War** followed the October Revolution, but Lenin died soon after the Red Army triumphed, and infighting began as **Joseph Stalin** eliminated his rivals.

Stalin implemented **five-year plans,** forced collectivization of Soviet farms, and filled Siberian labor camps with regional quotas. Priority was given to national defense and heavy industry, which led to shortages of consumer goods. His numerous purges killed millions. Among world leaders, Stalin was able to find only one chum—**Hitler.** After purging most of his top generals, Stalin brought the USSR into **WWII** unprepared. Fortunately, a long winter combined with the skillful tactics of military commander **Georgy Zhukov** helped the USSR fend off Hitler's treachery, much as it had foiled Napoleon's ambition. The **Battle of Stalingrad** (today **Volgograd,** p. 643), in which 1.1 million Russian troops are thought to have been killed, broke the German advance and turned the tide of the war on the Russian front. In 1945, the Soviets pushed through to Berlin and gained status as a postwar superpower.

In 1949, the Soviet Union formed the Council for Mutual Economic Assistance, or **COMECON,** which incorporated all the Eastern European countries, reducing them to satellites of the Party's headquarters in Moscow. After Stalin's death in 1953, **Nikita Khrushchev** emerged as the new leader of the Union. In his 1956 "secret speech," he denounced the terrors of the Stalinist period. A brief political and cultural **"thaw"** followed in the early 60s, until 1964, when Khrushchev was ousted by

Leonid Brezhnev, who stayed in power until 1983, overseeing a period of political repression that witnessed the exile of writers such as **Alexsandr Solzhenitsyn** and **Joseph Brodsky.** Internal dissent was quashed as well, as in the case of exiled physicist **Andrei Sakharov,** the reluctant father of the Soviet H-Bomb who had become a staunch advocate of disarmament. **Yuri Andropov** and **Konstantin Chernenko** followed Brezhnev in laughably quick succession. The geriatric government finally gave way to 56-year-old firebrand **Mikhail Gorbachev** in 1985. As the decline of the aging elite consumed political circles, the army became frustrated with its losses in the war with Afghanistan. Gorbachev's political and economic reforms were aimed at helping the country regain the status of a superpower. Reform began slowly, with **glasnost** (openness) and **perestroika** (rebuilding). The state gradually turned into a bewildering hodge-podge of near-anarchy, economic crisis, and cynicism. Gorbachev became the architect of his own demise; despite popularity abroad (and the 1990 Nobel Peace Prize), discontent with his reforms and a failed right-wing coup in August 1991 led to his resignation, the dissolution of the Union, and **Boris Yeltsin's** election as President of Russia. Homesick fragments of the Union have banded together as the **Commonwealth of Independent States,** but many others have gone their own way, most of them Westward with varying degrees of success.

RUSSIA TODAY

The constitution ratified in December 1993 gave the presidency sweeping powers, a provision whose shortcomings **President Boris Yeltsin's** tenure has exposed. Apparently lacking any political imagination whatsoever, Yeltsin has been least lethargic when dealing with his cabinet and advisors—he's gone through them as if they were vodka. What economic policies he did attempt came crashing down in August 1998, when the pyramid schemes Russia had played with its natural resources and bond sales were halted abruptly. The ruble was devalued in an attempt to lessen the country's foreign debt. As a result, **inflation** skyrocketed, hitting 84% by the end of 1998. Those with money in the bank languished in financial limbo, unable to withdraw their savings. Those with rubles in hand have frantically bought up available resources through the nation's feeble distribution network. Citizens have resorted to bartering for basic goods.

The crisis in **Kosovo** has staved off popular revolt by giving Russians someone to hate other than their own government. Historical ties to Serbia and ignorance of **Slobodan Milosovic's** ethnic cleansing have created among the populace the impression that Uncle Sam is picking on their little Slavic brother for no good reason. At the height of the conflict, **anti-American sentiment** ran rampant, especially in cities.

With the end of Yeltsin's term mercifully approaching in 2000, the country is already looking for his successor. Media darling **Vladimir Zhirinovsky** has gone from force to farce, and former **General Alexander Lebed,** who won the Krasnoyarsk governorship in early 1998, appears to have expended his fifteen minutes of political fame. Yeltsin's most recently sacked Prime Minister **Yevgeny Primakov** has hinted at running, but his support will likely diminish now that he is out of a job. That leaves Moscow mayor **Yuri Luzhkov**, who enjoys strong support among industry, finance and media bigwigs, as the frontrunner.

LITERATURE & ARTS

Ever since Catherine the Great committed **Alexander Radishchev,** who had written an awkward protest against serfdom, to a mental asylum, arts and politics in Russia have been inextricably bound together. The country's first and most beloved literary figure, **Aleksandr Sergeevich Pushkin,** was sympathetic to the Decembrist revolution, but ultimately chose aesthetics over politics. His novel in verse, *Eugene Onegin* (1822-1829), was a biting take on the poet's own earlier Romanticism. Pushkin could not escape the intrigues of the royal court, however, and his death in a duel with a French officer is thought by some to have been a set-up. With his eulogy to Pushkin, **Mikhail Lermontov** accepted the poet's legacy, which included his own stint in exile and death in a duel. Meanwhile, **Mikhail Glinka** took inspiration from Pushkin to pen one of the first great Russian operas, *Ruslan and Lyudmila*.

The 1840s saw a turn, under the goading of Westernizing critic **Vissaron Belinsky,** to the realism and social awareness that would produce the masterpieces of Russian literature. While **Nikolai Gogol's** short stories, with their absurdist wordplay, were hardly realist, they were read at the time as masterful satire. **Ivan Turgenev's** *Fathers and Sons* was less ambiguously social, sadly recording the severance of the intellectual generations of the 40s and 60s. **Fyodor Dostoevsky's** works, including *Crime and Punishment* and *The Brothers Karamazov*, have long outlasted various revolutionary and religious quests to save Russia. The same can be said for **Lev Tolstoy,** whose psychological epics like *Anna Karenina* and *War and Peace* preceded the religious polemics of his old age. The 1890s saw the rise of **Maxim Gorky,** whose "tramp period" fictions explored the dregs of Russian society and foreshadowed his part in the Bolshevik Revolution. Realism's last great voice belonged to **Anton Chekhov,** whose short stories distilled the power of his verbose predecessors and whose plays are still part of repertoires worldwide.

Music of the late 1800s was less dominated by one ideology than was literature. **Peter Illych Tchaikovsky** was closest to Belinsky's West-minded school, tempering native melodies with European restraint, while the work of **Modest Mussorgsky** and **Nikolai Rimsky-Korsakov** was bombastically Slavophilic.

The early 20th century brought revolutionary ferment and artistic experimentation. Visual arts gained the prominence music and literature had long enjoyed, with forays into **Symbolism** and **Abstraction,** the latter as pioneered by **Vasily Kandinsky. Natalya Goncharova** dabbled in **Futurism** early before working as a designer for the avant-garde **Ballets Russes.** Music was dominated by the lyrical piano concertos of **Sergey Rachmaninov** and the stylistic breakthroughs of **Igor Stravinsky.** Literature experienced its **Silver Age,** with poets pursuing art for art's sake and emulating French symbolism. **Aleksandr Blok,** whose talents may have exceeded those of the beloved Pushkin, tinted his verse with mystic and apocalyptic hues. For Blok and others, the Bolshevik revolution of 1917 seemed only to heighten the excitement in the air. It was during the 20s that **Formalism** as proposed by such luminaries as **Mikhail Bahktin** garnered attention for its structuralist readings of literary texts. Meanwhile, painters of the **Constructivist** school experimented with clean, geometric forms, and **Sergei Eisenstein,** considered by some the greatest filmmaker to ever live, revolutionized film theory with his visual montages. But communism soon mandated **Socialist Realism,** a coerced glorification of international socialism. Visual artists were limited to painting canvases with such bland titles as "The Tractor Drivers' Supper." The regime turned its purges on the *literarati:* lyric poet **Anna Akhmatova** lost her husband to a firing squad and was subject to internal exile, as was **Boris Pasternak**, for his Civil War epic *Doctor Zhivago*. Some artists such as **Vladimir Nabokov** left their homeland to escape censorship; others, including the bitingly sarcastic composer **Dmitri Schostokovich,** persevered under the censor's watchful eye. Literature pushed on also, as **Mikhail Bulgakov** (for Bulgakov's house, see **Ukraine: Sights,** p. 747) slipped the leash of Socialist Realism with *The Master and Margarita* (whose publication was suppressed for some thirty years, until 1966, and then only in the West). The early sixties brought a "thaw" that allowed **Joseph Brodsky's** verse and **Alexander Solzhenitsyn's** shocking *One Day in the Life of Ivan Denisovich*, detailing life in a labor camp, to emerge. Leonid Brezhnev plunged the arts into an ice age from which it has yet to fully recover. Postmodernists like **Dmitry Prigov** and **Lev Rubenstein** can publish freely, but the fabric of their world has hardly changed. **Lyudmilla Petrushevskaya,** for one, writes of people as unhappy as they were before.

READING LIST

The literature on Russia, like its armed forces, is immense and unmanageable, but certain books are particularly worthwhile. James Billington's *The Icon and the Axe* is the classic study of Russian culture. Orlando Figes's *A People's Tragedy* is an amazing panorama of the Russian revolution. The most profound Western book on 19th-century Russian thought is probably Isaiah Berlin's *Russian Thinkers*, while Vladimir Nabokov's *Lectures on Russian Literature* are the best introduction 19th-century Russian literature could hope to have. Joseph Brodsky's essays in *Less Than One* pay eloquent homage to 20th-century poets. Richard Pipes's *The Russian Revolution* remains the seminal history of the revolutionary period, while among accounts of Stalinism, nothing can match the moral force and courage of Solzhenitsyn's *The Gulag Archipelago*. In the past several years, a number of "I-went-to-Russia-and-boy-was-it-crazy" books have popped up; these should be avoided, and don't even think of writing one yourself. An exception is David Remnick's fine study of the fall of the Soviet Union in *Lenin's Tomb*.

FACTS AND FIGURES

- **Capital:** Moscow
- **Population:** 146,230,610
- **Land Area:** 17,075,400km^2
- **Geography:** Western lowlands, eastern mountains
- **Language:** Russian
- **Religions:** 74% nonreligious, 16% Russian Orthodox, 10% Muslim
- **Average Income per capita:** US$794
- **Major Exports:** Fossil fuels

RUSSIA ESSENTIALS

Citizens of Australia, Canada, Ireland, New Zealand, South Africa, the U.K., and the U.S. all require a visa to enter Russia. All Russian visas require an invitation stating the traveler's itinerary and dates of travel. They are inherently difficult to get without a Russian connection. Travel agencies that advertise discounted tickets to Russia often are also able to provide visas. **Info Travel,** 387 Harvard St., Brookline, MA 02146 (tel. (617) 566-2197; fax 734-8802; email infostudy@aol.com), and **Academic Travel,** 1302 Commonwealth Ave., Boston, MA 02134 (tel. (617) 566-5272; fax 566-3534; email academictr@aol.com), both provide invitations and visas to Russia starting at US$145. The price goes up if they have less than two weeks' notice. A larger but significantly more expensive operation is **Russia House.** In the **U.S.,** they are at 1800 Connecticut Ave. NW, Washington, D.C. 20009 (tel. (202) 986-6010; fax 667-4244; email lozansky@aol.com). In **Russia,** contact them at 17 Leningradsky Prospekt, Moscow 125040 (tel. (095) 250 01 43; fax 250 25 03; email aum@glasnet.ru). Invitations and visas are available at fairly exorbitant prices (to Russia starting at US$275; Ukraine US$175; Belarus US$175).

The following organizations can also supply invitations and/or visas for individual tourists, but generally require that you book accommodations for your stay in Russia with them. Prices vary dramatically, so shop around.

Host Families Association (HOFA), 5-25 Tavricheskaya, 193015 St. Petersburg, Russia (tel./fax (81) 22 75 19 92; e-mail hofa@usa.net). Arranges homestays in more than 20 cities of the former Soviet Union. Visa invitations available for HOFA guests to Russia, Ukraine, and Belarus. Singles US$30, doubles US$50. Occasional 20% discounts for non-central locations and Russian-speaking students.

Red Bear Tours/Russian Passport, Suite 11, 401 St. Kilda Rd., Melbourne 3004, Australia (tel. (613) 98 67 38 88; fax 98 67 10 55; email passport@werple.net.au; www.travelcentre.com.au). Provides invitations to Russia and the Central Asian Republics, provided that you book accommodations with them. Also sells rail tickets for the Trans-Siberian, Trans-Manchurian, Trans-Mongolian and Silk routes and arranges tours.

Traveller's Guest House, Bolshaya Pereyaslavskaya 50, 10th Fl., Moscow, Russia 129401 (tel. (095) 971 40 59; fax 280 76 86; email tgh@glas.apc.org). Arranges visa invitations, makes reservations, gets train tickets, and registers you upon arrival. For more, see **Moscow: Accommodations,** p. 569.

If you have an invitation from an authorized travel agency, apply for the **visa** in person or by mail at a Russian embassy or consulate (see **Essentials: Embassies & Consulates,** p. 13). Bring an original of your invitation; your passport; a completed application (available from an embassy or consulate); three passport-sized photographs; a cover letter stating your name, dates of arrival and departure, cities you plan to visit in Russia, date of birth, and passport number; and a money order or certified check for the amount of the visa fee made out to the embassy or the nearest consulate. (Single-entry, 60-day visas US$70 for 2-week processing, US$80 for 1-week service, US$110 for 3 business days; double-entry visas US$105, US$125, and US$145; prices change constantly, so check with the embassy.) If you have even tentative plans to visit a city, have it put on your visa. Many hotels will **register your visa** for you on arrival, as should the organizations listed above. However, they can only do that if you fly into a city where they are represented. If you enter the country elsewhere, you'll have to climb into the seventh circle of bureaucratic hell known is the central OVIR (ОВИР) office (in Moscow called UVIR—УВИР) to register. Many travelers skip this purgatory, but it is the law and taking care of it will leave one less thing over which bribe-seeking authorities can hassle you. OVIR is also where you should attempt to extend your visa, but it's far better to get a visa for longer than you plan on staying than to hang yourself with red tape.

GETTING THERE

In a perfect world, everyone would fly into St. Petersburg or Moscow, skipping customs officials who tear packs apart and demand bribes, and avoiding Belarus entirely. But it's not a perfect world, and you'll most likely find yourself on a westbound **train.** If that train is passing through Belarus, you may need a US$20-30 transit visa, although you can sometimes get by with a Russian one. If you wait until you reach the border, you'll likely pay more and risk missing your train. Finnord **buses** leave for St. Petersburg four times per day from Lahti, Finland, and are cheaper than trains.

Upon your entrance to the country, you'll be given a **Customs Declaration Form** to declare all your valuables and foreign currency; don't lose it. Everything listed on the customs form must be on you when you leave the country. You may not export works of art, icons, old samovars (pre-electric models), or anything published before 1945. Keep receipts for any expensive or antique-looking souvenirs. You cannot bring rubles into or out of the country.

GETTING AROUND

Foreigners are officially required to pay inflated Intourist prices for **domestic plane and train tickets;** passports are required. If you get a Russian friend to buy your ticket, be warned that the name of the buyer is printed on the ticket and will be checked against your passport on board. You can buy tickets in different cities, but it's best to buy round-trips from the Moscow or St. Petersburg central offices.

If you plan far enough ahead, you'll have your choice of four **classes.** The best is *lyuks* (люкс), or *2-myagky* (2-person soft; мягкий)—a place in a two-bunk cabin in the same car as second-class *kupeyny* (купейний), which has four bunks. Both classes have the same type of beds: almost comfortable, with a roll-up mattress and pillow. On hot summer nights, air conditioned *lyuks*, which are only available on major lines, may be worth the added cost. The next class down is *platskartny* (плацкартный), an open car with 52 shorter, harder bunks. Aim for places 1-33. Places 34-37 are next to the unnaturally foul bathroom, while places 38-52 are on

BEFORE YOU GO. See **Essentials: Before You Go,** p. 23, for info on how to find the latest travel advisories. In August 1999, the U.S. State Department issued a travel advisory regarding bringing Global Positioning Systems (G.P.S.), cellular phones, and other radio transmission devices into Russia. Failure to register such devices can (and does) result in search, seizure, and arrest.

RUSSIA

PRIMARY BORDER CROSSINGS. Russian borders are notoriously difficult to cross. Be prepared for long delays, difficult border guards, lots of miscommunication, confiscated passports, ripped-open backpacks, and bribes (usually US$20). Save yourself unnecessary hassle by taking only direct buses and trains from Moscow or St. Petersburg to neighboring capitals. Under no circumstances are visas available at the border.

Belarus: Smolensk, RUS/Orsha, BEL via Krasnol, BEL; connects Northwest Russia (p. 596) with Belarus. Novozybkov, RUS/Homel, BEL; connects the Volga Region (p. 638) with Belarus.

Estonia: Ivangorod, RUS/Narva, EST; connects St. Petersburg (p. 596) and the Northwest (p. 596) with northeastern Estonia.

Finland: Vyborg, RUS (p. 631)/Kouvola, FIN; connects Northwest Russia (p. 596) with Helsinki (p. 788).

Latvia: Pskov, RUS (p. 625)/Rēzekne, LAT; connects Northwest Russia (p. 596) with Eastern Latvia.

Lithuania: Svetlogorsk, RUS (p. 637)/Nida, LIT (p. 387); connects the Kaliningrad region (p. 632) with Coastal Lithuania (p. 381). Sovetsk, RUS/Tauragė, LIT; connects the Kaliningrad region (p. 632) Inland Lithuania (p. 375).

Poland: Mamonov, RUS/Braniewo, POL; connects Kaliningrad (p. 632) with Malbork (p. 486) and Gdańsk (p. 480). Sepopol, POL; connects Kaliningrad (p. 632) with Mazury (p. 493).

Ukraine: Rostov-na-Donu, RUS (see p. 646)/Donetsk or Maryupol, UKR; connects Southern Russia, including the Caucasus (p. 646) and the Volga Region (p. 638), with Crimea (p. 750). Belgorod, RUS/Charkiv, UKR via Kozacha Lopan, UKR; connects Northern Russia to Ukraine.

the side of the car and get horribly hot during the summer. Women traveling alone can try to buy out a *lyuks* compartment for security, or can travel *platskartny* with the regular folk and depend on the crowds to shame would-be harassers into silence. *Platskartny* is also a good idea on the theft-ridden St. Petersburg-Moscow line, as you are less likely to be targeted there. This logic can only be taken so far; the *obshchy* class may be devoid of crooks, but you'll be traveling alongside livestock. All first and second class cars are equipped with samovars that dispense scalding water for soups, hot cocoa, and coffee. In the upper classes, the car monitor will provide **sheets** for free or for around US$1; in *platskartny*, the grumpier monitors won't even let you use the mattress unless you've paid for sheets. *Elektrichka* (commuter rail; marked on signs as пригородные поезда; *prigorodnye poezda*) has its own platforms at each station; buy tickets at the *kassa*. These trains are often packed, especially on weekends, so expect to stand.

Russia boasts a vast, not-so-reliable **air** system monopolized by **Aeroflot,** infamous for its aging fleet and disastrous safety record. Nascent alternative **Transair** services only select cities. **Buses,** slightly less expensive and less crowded than trains, are your best bet for for shorter distances. On the Hungarian **Ikarus** buses, you'll get seated in a fairly comfy reclining chair, and should be able to store luggage for free.

Hailing a **taxi** is indistinguishable from hitchhiking, and should be treated with equal caution. Most drivers who stop will be private citizens trying to make a little extra cash (despite the recent restriction on this technically illegal activity). Those seeking a ride should stand off the curb and hold out a hand into the street, palm down; when a car stops, riders tell the driver the destination before getting in; he will either refuse the destination altogether or ask *Skolko?* (How much?), leading to protracted negotiations. Non-Russian speakers will get ripped off unless they manage a firm agreement on the price—if the driver agrees without asking for a price, you must ask *skolko?* yourself (sign language works too). Never get into a car that has more than one person in it. While this informal system might seem dicey, officially labeled taxis can also be expensive and dangerous, with reports of kidnappings and muggings.

TOURIST SERVICES & MONEY

Russian tourist centers exist to make money on tours and tickets, not to help confused tourists, so don't expect brochures, maps, or even common courtesy. Yet trying won't hurt, and polite, even apologetic, inquiries can yield unexpectedly fruitful results.

The **ruble** was redenominated in 1998, losing three zeros. The old currency is gradually being fazed out, although some prices are still quoted in thousands. Government regulations require that you show your passport when you exchange money. Find an *Obmen Valyuty* (currency exchange; Обмен Валюты) sign, hand over your currency—most places will exchange U.S. dollars and Deutschmarks, and some also accept French francs and British pounds—and receive your rubles. **Do not exchange money on the street.** Banks offer the best combination of good rates and security. You'll have no problem changing rubles back at the end of your trip (just keep exchange receipts), but it's best not to exchange large sums at once, as the rate is unstable.

ATMs (*bankomat;* банкомат) linked to all major networks and credit cards can be found all over most cities, but are highly unreliable. Big establishments now accept major **credit cards.** Main branches of banks will usually accept **traveler's checks** and give cash advances on credit cards, most often Visa. Although you'll have to pay in rubles, keeping dollars on you is a wise precaution. Be aware that most establishments do not accept crumpled, torn, or written-on bills of any denomination. Russians are also wary of the old US$100 bills; bring the new Benjamins if you bring any at all.

COMMUNICATION

Old local **telephones** in Moscow take special tokens, sold at Metro *kassy;* in St. Petersburg, they take Metro tokens. However, these old public phones are gradually becoming obsolete; the new ones take phone cards, are good for both local and intercity calls, and often have instructions in English. Phone cards are sold at central telephone offices and newspaper kiosks. You can make **intercity** calls from private homes, telephone offices, your hotel room, or *mezhdugorodnye* (междугородные) phone booths. It will take awhile, but you can usually get through. Dial 8, wait for the tone, then dial the city code.

Direct **international** calls can be made from telephone offices and hotel rooms: dial 8, wait for the tone, then dial 10 and the country code. You cannot call collect, unless using AT&T service (same access number as listed below), which will cost your party dearly (US$8 first min.; US$2.78 each additional min. to the U.S.). Prices for calls to the U.S. range from 9R per minute to 25R, depending on where you're calling from. To make calls from a telephone office, you can buy tokens or phone cards, or simply prepay your calls (depending on the city) and use the *mezhdugorodnye* telephones; be sure to press the *otvet* (reply; ответ) button when your party answers or you won't be heard. If there are no automatic phones, you must pay for your call at the counter and have it dialed for you by the operator. Several hotels in Moscow now have direct-dial booths operated by a special card or credit card. The cost is astronomical (at least US$6 per min. to the U.S.). Access numbers include: **AT&T Direct,** tel. 755 50 42 in Moscow, tel. 325 50 42 in St. Petersburg; **Australia Direct,** tel. 810; **BT Direct,** tel. 810 80 01 10 10 44; **Canada,** tel. 755 50 45 in Moscow, tel. 747 33 25 in St. Petersburg; **MCI WorldPhone,** tel. 747 33 22 in Moscow, tel. 960 22 22 in St. Petersburg. When calling from another city, dial 8-095 or 8-812 before these codes; you pay for the phone call to Moscow or St. Petersburg in addition to the international connection. Calling into the country is much less frustrating. Most countries have direct dial to Moscow and St. Petersburg; for other cities, go through the international operator.

Mail service will take 2-3 weeks to get anwhere, if it gets there at all. Domestic mail will usually reach its destination; from abroad, send letters to Russian recipients via friends who are traveling there, and do the same to get mail out. Airmail, if you want to risk it, is *avia* (авиа). A letter to the U.S. will cost 7R. If you're sending anything other than paper goods into the abyss that is the Russian mail system, you'll need to fill out a customs form at the post office. **AmEx** card- and traveler's check-holders can receive letters (but not packages) at the AmEx bureaus in Moscow and St. Petersburg; this strategy is usually more reliable than Russian mail. They will hold your mail for 30 days. **DHL** operates in most large cities. Central post offices can often send and receive **faxes.** With a mail system mired in communist inefficiency and a phone system with very capitalist rates, **email** is your best bet for keeping in touch—if you can find it. Seek out university campuses and post offices when internet cafes are not available.

LANGUAGE

Take some time to familiarize yourself with the **Cyrillic** alphabet. It's not as difficult as it looks and will make getting around and getting by immeasurably easier. Once you get the hang of the alphabet, you can pronounce just about any Russian word, although you will probably sound like an idiot. For more info on Cyrillic, see p. 807. Although more and more people are speaking **English** in Russia, come equipped with at least a few helpful Russian phrases. See the **Glossary,** p. 821.

Note that улица (*ulitsa;* abbreviated ул.) means "street," проспект (*prospekt;* пр.) means "avenue," площадь (*ploshchad;* пл.) means "square," and бульвар (*bulvar*; бул.) is "boulevard." Кремль (*kreml';* fortress); рынок (*rynok,* market square); гостиница (*gostinitsa;* hotel); собор (*sobor;* cathedral); and церков (*tserkov;* church) are also good words to know.

HEALTH & SAFETY

EMERGENCY NUMBERS.
Fire: tel. 01. **Police:** tel. 02. **Ambulance:** tel. 03.

Russian bottled water will be mineral water; you may prefer to boil or filter your own, or buy foreign **bottled water** (the Finnish kind is cheap) at a supermarket. Water in much of Russia is drinkable in small doses, but not in Moscow and St. Petersburg; boil it to be safe. A gamma globulin shot will lower your risk of hepatitis A (see **Health,** p. 28). Check the expiration date before buying any packaged snack. Men's **toilets** are marked with an "M", women's with a "Ж." The 0.5-5R charge for public toilets generally gets you a hole in the ground and a measured piece of toilet paper; get into the habit of carrying your own. **Pharmacies** are among the few places where the positive effects of capitalism are apparent, with all sorts of Western medicine and hygiene products. For **medical emergencies,** either leave the country or go to the American Medical Centers at St. Petersburg or Moscow; these clinics have American-born and trained doctors and speak English. Traveler's health insurance is a must (ISIC provides some coverage; see **Essentials,** p. 34); it will cover the aforementioned foreign clinics, or even evacuation.

Reports of **crime** against foreigners are on the rise, particularly in Moscow and St. Petersburg. Although it is hard to look Russian (especially with a huge pack on your back), try not to flaunt your true nationality. Your trip will be that much more pleasant if you never have to file a crime report with the local *militsia,* who will not speak English and will probably not help you. Reports of mafia warfare are scaring off tourists, but unless you bring a shop for them to blow up, you are unlikely to be a target. After the recent eruption of violence in the Northern Caucasus, the Dagestan and Chechnyan regions of Russia are best avoided.

ACCOMMODATIONS

The only **hostels** in Russia are in St. Petersburg and Moscow, and even those average US$18 per night. Reserve well in advance, especially in summer. Hotels offer several classes of rooms. "Lux," usually two-room doubles with TV, phone, fridge, and bath, are the most expensive. "Polu-lux" rooms are singles or doubles with TV, phone, and bath. Rooms with bath and no TV, when they exist, are cheaper. The lowest priced rooms are *bez udobstv* (без удобств), which means one room with a sink. Expect to pay 150-250R for a single in a budget hotel. As a rule, and in small cities in particular, only cash is accepted as payment. In many hotels, hot water—sometimes all water—is often turned on only a few hours per day. Reservations are not necessary in smaller towns, but they may help you get on the good side of management, which is often inexplicably suspicious of backpackers.

University dorms offer cheap rooms; some accept foreign students for about US$5-10 per night. The rooms are liveable, but don't expect sparkling bathrooms or reliable hot water. Make arrangements with an institute from home. **Homestays,** often arranged through a tourist office, are often the cheapest (50-100R per night) and best option in the countryside.

FOOD & DRINK

Russian cuisine is a medley of dishes both delectable and disgusting; tasty borscht can come in the same meal as a bit of *salo* (pig fat). As a rule, the quality of both the ingredients and the preparation improves vastly the farther south you travel. If you are stuck in the culinary wasteland of the upper latitudes, look for a Georgian or Azerbaijani restaurant for some respite. The largest meal of the day, *obed* (lunch; обед), is eaten at midday and includes: *salat* (салат), usually cucumbers and tomatoes or beets and potatoes with mayonnaise or sour cream; *sup* (soup; суп), either meat or cabbage; and *kuritsa* (chicken; курица) or *myaso* (meat; мясо), often called *kotlyety* (cutlets; котлеты) or *beefshteaks* (бифштекс). Ordering a number of *zakuski* (Russified *tapas;* закуски) instead of a main dish can save money and add variety. Dessert includes *morozhenoye* (ice cream; мороженое) or *tort* (cake; торт) with *cofe* (coffee; кофе) or *chai* (tea; чай), which Russians will drink at the slightest provocation. A **cafe** (кафе) or *stolovaya* (cafeteria; столовая) is cheaper, but the latter may be unsanitary.

One can find basic Russian food on the street, at stores, or at the market. **Dietas** (диета) sell goods for people on special diets (such as diabetics); **produkty** (продукты) and **gastronoms** (гастроном) offer a variety of meats, cheeses, breads, and packaged goods. The larger **universam** (универсам) simulates a supermarket with its wide variety. The **market** (*rynok;* рынок) sells abundant fruits and vegetables, meat, fresh milk, butter, honey, and cheese. Wash and dry everything before you eat it—Russian farmers use pesticides as if they were going out of style. Milk may not be pasteurized. **Bulochnaya** (bakeries; булочная) sell fresh bread daily and, sometimes, sweet rolls, cakes, and cookies.

The **kiosks** found in every town act as mini-convenience stores, selling soda, juice, candy bars, and cookies; point to what you want. On the streets, you'll see a lot of *shashlyki* (barbequed meat on a stick; шашлыки) and *kvas* (квас), an alcoholic dark-brown drink (see **"Just for the Taste,"** p. 736). Kiosks often carry alcohol; imported cans of beer are safe (though warm), but be wary of Russian labels—you have no way of knowing what's really in the bottle. *Zolotoye koltso*, *Russkaya*, and *Zubrovka* are the best vodkas; the much-touted *Stolichnaya* is mostly made for export. *Moskovskaya* is another known name. Among local beers, *Baltika* (Балтика; numbered 1 through 7) is the most popular and arguably the best. *Baltika* 1 is the lightest (10.5%), *Baltika* 7 the strongest (14%). *Baltikas* 4 and 6 are dark; the rest are lagers. Numbers 3 and 4 are the most popular; 7 is extreme.

Vendors do not provide **bags** for merchandise. You can usually buy plastic bags in stores, at markets, and on the streets, but bring your own to be safe. In stores, especially the older Soviet throwbacks, decide what you want, then go to a *kassa* and tell the person working there the item, the price, and the *otdyel* (department; отдел) from which you are buying. The person will take your money and give you a receipt. You then take the receipt back to the *otdyel*, give it to the person working there, and they will give you what you want.

CUSTOMS & ETIQUETTE

Decades of collective lifestyle forced people very close together; as a result, the notion of personal space is almost nonexistent in Russia. People pack tightly in lines and on buses, tolerating the discomfort with stoic patience. When boarding a bus, tram, or Metro car, forceful shoving is required. On public transportation, it's polite for women to give their seats to elderly or pregnant women and women with children. For men, it's gallant to yield a seat to all women. It's okay for everybody (especially *babushki*) to push and shove if polite requests don't get you anywhere. On trains, even the hottest day of the summer, you will find the windows closed "for the winter" (no, there is no air-conditioning). If you luck out with a single window that does open, Russians will close it anyway—there's a national fear of drafts.

In St. Petersburg and Moscow (but nowhere else) a 5-10% **tip** is becoming customary. Most establishments, even train ticket offices, close for a **lunch break** sometime between noon and 3pm. Places tend to close at least 30 minutes earlier than they should, if they choose to open at all. "24hr." stores often take a lunch or "technical" break and one day off each week.

The concept of **sexual harassment** hasn't reached Russia yet. Local men will try to pick up women and will get away with offensive language and actions. The routine starts with an innocent-sounding *"Devushka..."* (young lady); just say *"Nyet"* (No) or simply walk away. Locations and intensity of pursuit vary, with intentions ranging from playfulness to physical abuse. And no, they don't wear deodorant—it's considered fine for Russian men to smell. Solo female travelers can only expect more of this treatment. Women should not travel alone in the Dagestan region, where a number of disappearances and rapes have been reported of late.

The laws outlawing **homosexuality** were taken off the books about seven years ago, but gay, lesbian and bisexual travelers should not expect tolerance of public displays of affection outside of the gay clubs that have sprung up in Moscow and St. Petersburg. Travelers of African or Indian decent will often receive rude treatment in stores or restaurants, as Russians **discriminate** against even their own non-Slavic citizens in the south.

When visiting friends, bring flowers, cookies, or candy. Russians tend to dress up to go visiting, even if it's just across the street. Visiting a museum in shorts and sandals is disrespectful (they will give you a very hard time at the Hermitage). Many locals say that criminals spot foreigners by their sloppy appearances, so dress up and don't smile when stared at. For polite requests, use first names and patronymics, which are middle names derived from one's father's first name (i.e. "Mikhailovich" from Mikhail for men, or "Mikhailovna" for women).

NATIONAL HOLIDAYS

January 1-2, New Year's; January 7, Orthodox Christmas; February 23, Defenders of the Motherland Day; March 8, International Women's Day; April 30, Orthodox Easter; May 1-2, Labor Day; May 9, Victory Day; June 12, Independence Day; November 7, Day of Accord and Reconciliation; December 12, Constitution Day.

MOSCOW (MOCKBA)

Like very few cities on earth, Moscow (pop. 8,400,000) has an audacity of place, a sense of itself as a focal point in world history. Its rings of streets, emanating from the Kremlin like the early Muscovite conquests and spiraling into a crumbling wasteland on the peripheries, mirror the permanent condition of its residents: destined to live on the margins of a system they don't understand and didn't authorize, flinging themselves into the center only to return at the end of the day, drab and wasted, to their concrete blocks. Destroyed by murderers and rebuilt by prisoners, the city's every building could plaque its tale of horror next to some memento from a Lenin guest appearance (c. 1918). This, one could say, has always been one of the dark places of the earth.

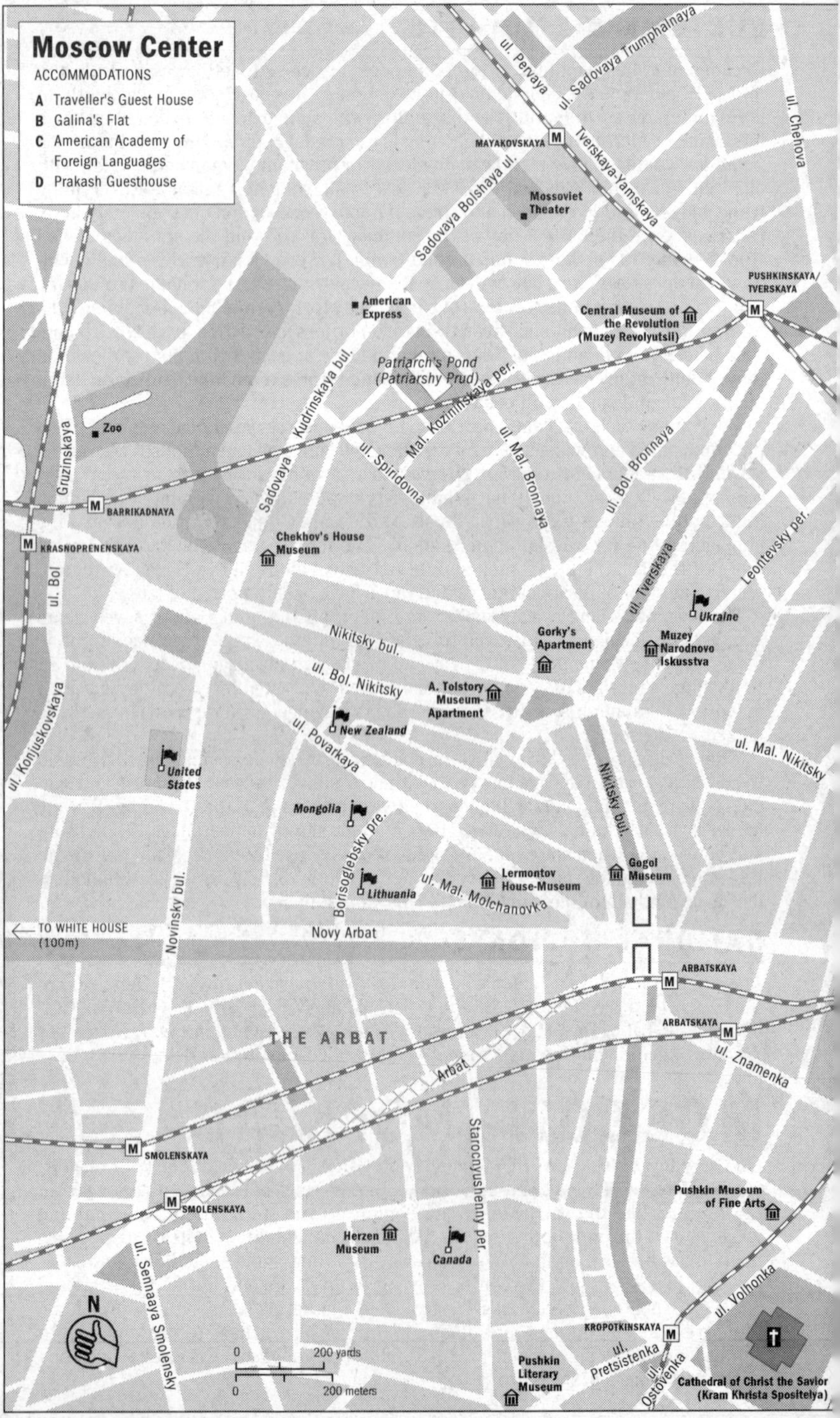
Moscow Center
ACCOMMODATIONS
A Traveller's Guest House
B Galina's Flat
C American Academy of Foreign Languages
D Prakash Guesthouse
ul. Pervaya
ul. Sadovaya Trumphalnaya
ul. Chehova
MAYAKOVSKAYA
Tverskaya-Yamskaya
Sadovaya Bolshaya ul.
Mossoviet Theater
PUSHKINSKAYA/TVERSKAYA
American Express
Central Museum of the Revolution (Muzey Revolyutsii)
Patriarch's Pond (Patriarshy Prud)
Mal. Kozinhskaya per.
Sadovaya Kudrinskaya bul.
Zoo
Gruzinskaya
ul. Spiridovna
ul. Mal. Bronnaya
ul. Bol. Bronnaya
BARRIKADNAYA
KRASNOPRENENSKAYA
Chekhov's House Museum
Leontevsky per.
ul. Tverskaya
ul. Bol
Ukraine
Gorky's Apartment
Muzey Narodnovo Iskusstva
Nikitsky bul.
ul. Bol. Nikitsky
A. Tolstory Museum-Apartment
New Zealand
ul. Konjuskovskaya
ul. Povarkaya
ul. Mal. Nikitsky
United States
Nikitsky bul.
Mongolia
Borisoglebsky pre.
Gogol Museum
Lermontov House-Museum
Lithuania
ul. Mal. Molchanovka
TO WHITE HOUSE (100m)
Novy Arbat
Novinsky bul.
ARBATSKAYA
ARBATSKAYA
THE ARBAT
ul. Znamenka
Arbat
Starocnyushenny per.
SMOLENSKAYA
SMOLENSKAYA
Pushkin Museum of Fine Arts
Herzen Museum
Canada
ul. Sennaaya Smolensky
N
ul. Volhonka
KROPOTKINSKAYA
0
200 yards
0
200 meters
Pushkin Literary Museum
ul. Pretsistenka
ul. Ostovenka
Cathedral of Christ the Savior (Kram Khrista Spositelya)

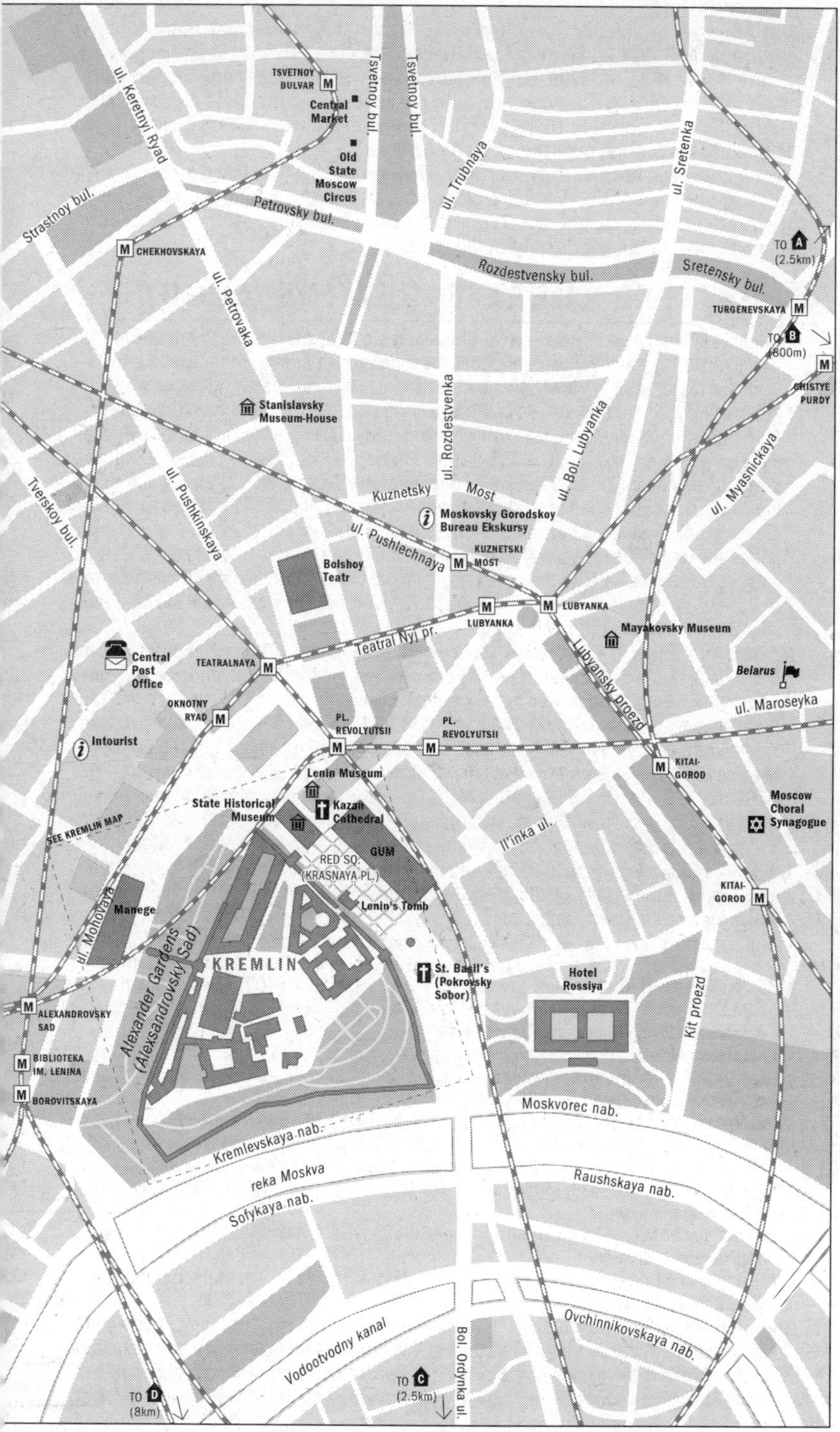
TSVETNOY BULVAR
Central Market
Old State Moscow Circus
Tsvetnoy bul.
Tsvetnoy bul.
ul. Keretnyi Ryad
Strastnoy bul.
Petrovsky bul.
ul. Trubnaya
ul. Sretenka
CHEKHOVSKAYA
ul. Petrovaka
Rozdestvensky bul.
Sretensky bul.
TO A (2.5km)
TURGENEVSKAYA
TO B (800m)
CHISTYE PURDY
Stanislavsky Museum-House
ul. Rozdestvenka
ul. Bol. Lubyanka
ul. Myasnickaya
Tverskoy bul.
ul. Pushkinskaya
Kuznetsky Most
Moskovsky Gorodskoy Bureau Ekskursy
ul. Pushlechnaya
KUZNETSKI MOST
Bolshoy Teatr
LUBYANKA
LUBYANKA
Mayakovsky Museum
Teatral Nyj pr.
Central Post Office
TEATRALNAYA
Lubyansky proezd
Belarus
ul. Maroseyka
OKNOTNY RYAD
PL. REVOLYUTSII
PL. REVOLYUTSII
Intourist
KITAI-GOROD
Lenin Museum
State Historical Museum
Kazan Cathedral
Moscow Choral Synagogue
SEE KREMLIN MAP
Il'inka ul.
RED SQ. (KRASNAYA PL.)
GUM
Manege
Lenin's Tomb
KITAI-GOROD
ul. Mohovaya
Alexander Gardens (Alexsandrovsky Sad)
KREMLIN
St. Basil's (Pokrovsky Sobor)
Hotel Rossiya
ALEXANDROVSKY SAD
Kit proezd
BIBLIOTEKA IM. LENINA
BOROVITSKAYA
Moskvorec nab.
Kremlevskaya nab.
reka Moskva
Raushskaya nab.
Sofykaya nab.
Ovchinnikovskaya nab.
Vodootvodny kanal
Bol. Ordynka ul.
TO C (2.5km)
TO D (8km)

But Moscow is prettier now, its center restored by a corrupt but adorably chubby mayor to its 19th-century magnificence. Stalin's gargantuan edifices stand like little more than monster-land anachronisms, and if one keeps to the 16th-century sidestreets and does not stray into the suburbs—one should not stray into the suburbs—it's possible to see what Napoleon saw with the city at his feet, golden domes sparkling over the expanses of Asia.

Post-ideological, post-apocalyptic, post-whatever the hell you want, Moscow is in your face, like the endless leather-jacketed hoods hanging about countless alleyways. A brutal, tiring capital, not so unsafe as it is maddening, Moscow at the millennium is most definitely the end of the world.

GETTING THERE & GETTING AROUND

Airplanes: International flights arrive at **Sheremetyevo-2** (Щереметьево-2; tel. 956 4666 and 578 9101). Take the van under the "автолайн" sign in front of the station to M2: Rechnoy Vokzal (20min., every 10min. 7am-10pm, 10R). Alternately, take bus #551 to M2: Rechnoy Vokzal (Речной Вокзал) or bus #517 to M7: Planyornaya (Планёрная), 10R. Buses run 24hr. Most domestic flights and many flights within the former-USSR originate at **Vnukovo** (Внуково; tel. 436 2109), **Bikovo** (Биково; tel. 558 4738), **Domodedovo** (Домодедово; tel. 323 8565), or **Sheremetyevo-1** (tel. 578 2372). Buy tickets at the *kassa* (касса) at the **Tsentralny Aerovokzal** (Central Airport Station; Центральный Аэровокзал), 2 stops on tram #23 or trolley #12 or 70 from M2: Aeroport (sign on front of bus should say Центральный Аэровокзал). Check the express-bus schedules posted outside the station. Taxis to the center charge more than you ever dreamed possible, up to US$60—make sure to bargain (in June 1999 you could get it down to US$25). Agree on a price before you get into the cab.

Airlines: Air France, ul. Korovy Val 7 (Коровый Вал; tel. 234 3377; fax 234 3393). Open M-F 9am-6pm. Also at Sheremetyevo-2, 6th floor (tel. 578 3156). Open M-Sa 5:30am-11pm, Su 1-6pm. **British Airways,** Krasnopresnenskaya nab. 12, 19th floor, #1905 (Краснопресненская; tel. 258 2492; fax 258 2272). Open M-F 9am-5:30pm. **Delta,** Krasnopresnenskaya nab. 12, 11th floor, #1102a (tel. 258 1288; fax 258 1168). Open M-F 9am-5:30pm, Sa 9am-1pm. **Finnair,** ul. Kuznetsky most 3 (Кузнецкий мост; tel. 292 1762; fax 292 4948). M6: Kuznetsky Most. Open M-F 9am-5pm. Also at Sheremetyevo-2 (tel./fax 578 2718). **Lufthansa,** Olimpysky pr. 18/1 (Олимпийский; tel. 975 2501; fax 971 6784), in Hotel Olympic Penta. M4, 5: Prospekt Mira. Open M-F 9am-5:30pm.

Trains: Moscow has 9 train stations, arranged around the *koltsivaya linia* (**circle line;** кольцывая линия; M4) of the Metro. At all train stations, platform numbers are announced as the trains are arriving.

Leningradsky Vokzal (Ленинградский), Komsomolskaya pl. 3 (tel. 262 4281, 262 9143, and 262 6038). M1, 4: Komsomolskaya. To: **St. Petersburg, Finland,** and **the Baltics.**

Kazansky Vokzal (Казанский), Komsomolskaya pl. 2 (tel. 264 6409, 266 2736, and 266 2542), opposite Leningradsky Vokzal. To the east and southeast, including **Volgograd, Kazan, Rostov-na-Donu,** and **Central Asia.**

Yaroslavsky Vokzal (Ярославский), Komsomolskaya pl. 5 (tel. 921 0817, 266 0301, and 266 0595). To: **Siberia** and the **Far East.** The starting point for the legendary Trans-Siberian Railroad (see **Trans-Siberian Railroad,** p. 655).

Paveletsky Vokzal (Павелецкий), Paveletskaya pl. 1 (tel. 235 6807, 235 3960, and 235 4673), and **Kursky Vokzal** (Курский), ul. Zemlyani Val 29/1 (tel. 924 9243, 262 8532, and 266 5652). To: **Crimea, Eastern Ukraine, Georgia, Azerbaijan,** and **Armenia.**

Rizhsky Vokzal (Рижский), Rizhkaya pl. 79/3 (tel. 971 1588, 281 0118, and 266 1176). To: **Latvia** and **Estonia.**

Belorussky Vokzal (Белорусский), pl. Tverskaya Zastava 7 (tel. 251 6093). To: **Warsaw, Minsk,** and **Kaliningrad.**

Kievsky Vokzal (Киевский), pl. Kievskovo Vokzala (tel. 240 1115). To: **Bulgaria, Romania, Slovakia,** and **Ukraine.**

Train Tickets: Buying a train ticket in Russia can be enormously frustrating. If you don't speak Russian you may want to buy through **Intourist** or your hotel: you'll pay more, but you'll be spared the hassle of the *vokzal* (station; вокзал) experience, where you can expect long lines and longer red tape as you're shuffled, often for no good reason, from one ticket window to another. Russian speakers should buy tickets for the *elektrichka* (local trains) at the *prigorodnaya kassa* (local ticket booths; пригородная касса) in each station. Tickets for longer distances can be bought at the *Tsentralnoe Zheleznodorozhnoe Agenstvo* (**Central Train Agency;** Центральное Железнодорожное Агенство), to the right of Yaroslavsky Vokzal (see below). Purchase tickets at window #10 or 11. A complete schedule of train stations, trains, destinations, and departure times is posted on the left side of the hall. *Kassa* open daily 8am-1pm and 2-7pm. If you have to catch a train and the Central Train Agency is closed, go to the **24hr. Intourist *kassa*** on the 2nd floor of Leningradsky Vokzal (entrance #3, windows #19 and 20; see below). They are supposed to sell tickets to St. Petersburg only, but they have been known to bend the rules when everything else is closed. If you plan to take the **Trans-Siberian Railroad,** you're probably better off with Traveller's Guest House (see **Russia Essentials,** p. 555). They will explain how the TSR works and can arrange a special ticket that allows you to get on and off the train at all major cities along the trek across Asia. Your ticket will have your name and seat on it and tells you at which *vokzal* to catch your train. The main ticket office in Moscow for foreigners buying international and domestic tickets is **Intourtrans Glavnoe Zheleznodorozhnoe Agenstvo** (Main Ticket Office; Главное Железнодорожное Агенство), Maly Kharitonevsky per. 6 (Малый Харитоневский; tel. 262 0604). M5: Turgenevskaya. Take a right off ul. Myasnitskaya (Мясницкая) and walk into the connected building on the right. Open daily 8am-1pm and 2-7pm. There is another office in **Gostinitsa Intourist** (see **Tours,** p. 566). Same hours as main office, but limited ticket availability.

Local Transportation: The **Metro** is large, fast, and efficient–a masterpiece of Stalinist urban planning. It stops within a 15min. walk of any place in town and is a continual reminder that 13 million people do live in Moscow–and all of them ride the Metro. Passages to different lines or stations are indicated with a blue-and-white sign of a man walking up stairs; individual exit signs indicate nearby street names. A station serving more than one line may have more than one name. Trains run daily 6am-1am, but plan to catch one by 12:30 to be safe. Rush hours are 9-10am and 5-6pm. Buy token-cards (4R) from the *kassa* inside stations. **Bus** and **trolley** tickets are available in gray kiosks labeled "проездные билеты" and from the driver (4R). Punch your ticket when you get on, especially in the last week of the month when ticket cops are out to fill their quotas–the fine for not doing so is 10R. *Edinye bilety* (monthly passes; единые билеты) let you ride on any form of transportation (240R). Buy them after the 20th of the preceding month. Monthly Metro passes are more cost-effective (120R). Purchase either from the *kassa.* Metro maps are on the wall inside the entrance to every station; consult the maps (in both Cyrillic and English) in the front and back of this book.

Taxis: If you don't speak Russian, it's tough to get a fair rate. Most drivers charge by destination—agree on a price by haggling before you set off. Taxi stands are indicated by a round sign with a green T. Consult *Moscow Business Telephone Guide* to order one over the phone. Meters tend to be purely ornamental, although a new law decrees that they must be used. Make sure the driver turns it on. Try to avoid taxis unless you know Moscow, as it is easy to get ripped off. Many travelers choose the cheaper option of getting a ride with natives (see p. 557).

WE BRAKE FOR NO ONE. Moscow drivers are notorious–unbelievably fast and blissfully ignorant of the gentle art of yielding to pedestrians. Should you dare venture from your curbside security onto the blacktop, they will honk, they will yell, they will gesticulate obscenely, but they will not touch their brakes. One day of such confrontations will suffice to convince you that the underpasses beneath intersections are there out of dire necessity. While crosswalks are islands of safety in many countries, here they're not much more than zebra lines on the road. Crossing at stop-light intersections is the only relatively safe bet, as the "walk" sign is illuminated just long enough to allow a mad dash across the road. The only time that cars *might* stop for you would be if you're female, alone, and out at night–and that's only because they think you're a prostitute. On the roads of Moscow, there are pedestrians and there are drivers. And pedestrians are most decidedly not wanted.

Car Rental: Alamo, pr. Mira 44 (tel. 284 3741; fax 284 3741; email alm@centro.ru). M4, 5: Prospekt Mira. US$95 per day. Unlimited mileage and insurance included. Min. 3-day rental. **Hertz,** ul. Chernyakhovskovo 4 (Черняховского; tel. 937 3274; fax 956 1621; email hertz.mos@co.ru). US$146 per day. Unlimited mileage and insurance included. **Budget,** ul. Verkhniya Radishchevskaya 16, kor. 1, room #8 (Верхняя Радищевская; tel. 915 5237; fax 915 5940). US$115 per day. Unlimited mileage, insurance included. Min. 3-day rental. Open M-F 9am-7pm.

ORIENTATION

A series of concentric rings radiates from the **Kremlin** (Kreml; Кремль) and **Red Square** (Krasnaya ploshchadz; Красная Площадь). The outermost street, **Moscow Ring Road,** marks the city limits, but most sights lie within **Sadovoe Koltso** (**Garden Ring;** Садовое Кольцо). To the east of Red Square and the Kremlin is the 9th-century neighborhood, **Kitai-Gorod,** packed with towering churches and bustling commercial thoroughfares. Semi-circling around the Kremlin and Kitai-Gorod to the north is **Beliy Gorod** (White Town), Moscow's nicest residential district and home to most of the city's cultural life, including the Pushkin Museum of Fine Arts and the Bolshoy Theater. **Ul. Tverskaya** (Тверская), one of Moscow's main shopping streets, begins in Beliy Gorod and continues north along the green line. **Zemlyanoy Gorod,** the next concentric circle out from Beliy Gorod, is the dividing line between the bourgeois center and the outskirts of the city. Zemlyanoy Gorod has the highest concentration of literary homes (see **Houses of the Literary & Famous,** p. 583) as well as the **Arbat** (Арбат) and **Novy Arbat** (Новый Арбат), Moscow's poshest and most commercialized streets, respectively. The old working-class neighborhood, **Krasnaya Presnya,** lies just to the southwest of Zemlyanoy Gorod and is notable primarily as the home to Russia's White House and the highest proportion of New Russians. **Zamoskvareche** and **Krimskiy Val,** the neighborhoods directly south of the Kremlin, Red Square, and the Moskva River, are home to myriad pubs, mansions, and monasteries, as well as **Gorky Park.** The suburbs to the north and south are a concrete wasteland of apartment blocks and Soviet exposition centers.

If you familiarize yourself with the Cyrillic alphabet and orient yourself by the Metro, it's difficult to get lost. An extensive city map in English can be bought (20R) at the book store **Slavyanka** (Славянка), ul. Kuznetsky most 9. Many other maps are outdated, so be sure to check the year of publication. See this book's color insert for English and Cyrillic maps of the Metro and the city.

PRACTICAL INFORMATION

TOURIST & FINANCIAL SERVICES

Tourist Offices: Intourservice Central Excursion Bureau, Nikitsky per. 4a (Никитский; tel. 203 7585; fax 200 1243). M1: Okhotny Ryad.

Tours: Main office of **Intourist,** ul. Mokhovaya 13 (Моховая; tel. 292 1278). Arranges English-language tours of the Armory Chamber and Kremlin (M-W and F-Su 11am) and sightseeing tours by bus (daily at 2:30pm). Haggle with the English-speaking tour guides at the Kremlin *kassa.* **Moskovsky Gorodskoy Bureau Exkursy** (City of Moscow Bureau of Excursions; Московский Городской Бюро Екскурсий), ul. Rozhdestvenka 5 (Рождественка; tel. 923 8953). Excellent 1½hr. bus tours of the main sights. Tours leave from Krasnaya pl., between the Lenin Museum and GUM; look for the person with the microphone. Daily 9am-8pm. 100R. Russian only.

Budget Travel: Student Travel Agency Russia (STAR), ul. Baltiyskaya 9, 3rd floor (чл. Балтийская; tel. 797 9555). M2: Sokol. Discount plane tickets, Interrail and Eurobus passes, ISICs, worldwide hostel booking, and Trans-Siberian tickets. Open M-F 10am-6pm, Sa 11am-4pm. **Moskovsky Sputnik** (Московский Спутник), Maly Ivanovsky per. 6, kor. 2 (Малый Ивановский; tel. 924 03 17). M5, 6: Kitai Gorod. Student travel, visas, and tickets. Open M-Th 9am-1pm and 2-6pm, F 9am-1pm and 2-7pm.

Passport Office: UVIR (ЧВЦР), ul. Pokrova 42 (Покрова). M1: Krasnye Vorota. From the Metro, turn right onto Sadovaya Chernogryazskaya, and continue down until ul. Pokrova (10min.) and turn right. UVIR is possibly the seventh ring of Russian bureaucratic hell—to avoid an unpleasant encounter, secure a visa invitation and stamp from your first night's accommodation whenever possible. Most hotels register you automatically and give you a card to prove you're staying there.

Embassies: Australia, Kropotkinsky per. 13 (Кропоткинский; tel. 956 6070; fax 956 6170). Consular services (tel. 924 7095; fax 239 9948). M3: Smolenskaya. Open M-F 9am-12:30pm and 1:30-5pm. **Belarus,** ul. Maroseyka 17/6 (Маросейка; tel. 923 3838; fax 928 6403). Consular services (tel. 924 7095; fax 928 6403). **Canada,** Starokonyushenny per. 23 (Староконюшенный; tel. 956 6666 and 956 6158; fax 232 9948). Consular services (tel. 956 6666; fax 232 9950). M1: Kropotkinskaya. Open M-Tu and Th-F 8:30am-1pm and 2-5pm. **China,** ul. Druzhby 6 (Дружбы; tel. 238 2006 and 143 1540; fax 938 2132). Consular services (tel. 143 1540; fax 956 1169). **Estonia,** Maly Kislovsky per. 5 (Кисловский; tel. 290 5013 and 291 5807; fax 202 3830). Consular services at Kalzhny per. 8 (Калжний; tel. 290 3178; fax 291 1073). M3: Arbatskaya. Open M-Th 10am-noon. **Ireland,** Grokholsky per. 5 (Грохольский; tel. 742 0907; fax 975 2066). Consular services (tel. 742 0901; fax 742 0920). M4, 5: Prospekt Mira. Open M-F 9:30am-1pm and 2:30-5:30pm. **Lithuania,** Borisoglebsky per. 10 (Борисоглебский; tel. 291 1501; fax 202 3516). Consular services at Borisoglesky per. 11 (tel. 291 1501; fax 291 7586). M3: Arbatskaya. Open M-F 9-11:30am. **Mongolia** consular section, Spasopeskovsky per. 711 (Спасопесковский; tel. 241 1548, 244 7867; fax 291 6171). **New Zealand,** ul. Povarskaya 44 (Поварская; tel. 956 3579; fax 956 3583). Consular services (tel./fax 956 2642). M4, 6: Krasnopresnenskaya. Open M-F 9am-5:30pm. **South Africa,** Bolshoy Strochinovsky per. 22/25 (Большой Строчиновский; tel. 230 6869; fax 230 6865). Open M-F 9am-5pm. **U.K.,** Sofiyskaya nab. 14 (Софийская; tel. 956 7200; fax 956 7420). Consular services (tel. 956 7250; fax 956 7440). M1, 3, 8: Borovitskaya. Open M-F 9am-5pm. **Ukraine,** Leontyevsky per. 18 (Леонтьевский; tel. 229 1079; visa tel. 229 6922), off ul. Tverskaya. M3: Tverskaya. Open M-F 9:15am-12:30pm. **U.S.,** Novinsky 19/23 (Новинский; tel. 252 2450 through 56; emergency tel. 230 2001; fax 956 4261). Consular section (tel. 956 4242 and 255 9555) can only help you with major passport/visa problems. M6: Krasnopresnenskaya. Flashing your U.S. passport will let you cut the outrageously long lines. Open M-F 9am-6pm.

Currency Exchange: Banks at almost every corner; check ads in English-language newspapers. The pamphlet *Moscow Express Directory,* updated biweekly and free in most luxury hotels, lists the addresses and phone numbers of many banks, as well as places to buy and cash traveler's checks. Few besides main branches of large banks will change traveler's checks or issue cash advances; a posted sign is no guarantee. Nearly every bank and hotel has an **ATM.** A particularly reliable one stands in the lobby of the Gostinitsa Intourist Hotel (Cirrus/MC/Plus/Visa). There is an **AmEx ATM** in the lobby of the AmEx office (see below). Money can be withdrawn in US$ or rubles. US$5 service charge per transaction. Beware of ATMs protruding from the sides of buildings on the Arbat; not only do they work irregularly, but standing out in the middle of a busy street getting money invites muggers.

American Express: ul. Sadovaya-Kudrinskaya 21a, Moscow 103001 (Садовая-Кудринская; tel. 755 9024; fax 755 9004). M2: Mayakovskaya. Exit the Metro and cross through the street/parking lot directly ahead and take a left onto ul. Bolshaya Sadovaya (Большая Садовая), which becomes ul. Sadovaya-Kudrinskaya. Travel assistance for all; banking services for members. One of the only places that will cash traveler's checks in Moscow. Mail held for members and traveler's check holders. Open M-F 9am-5pm, Sa 10am-2pm. 24hr. **AmEx ATM** in lobby.

Western Union: Rossiyski Credit (Российски Кредит), Usacheva 35 (Усачева; tel. 119 8250), left entrance. M1: Sportivnaya. Exit to the right; it's on the right, next to the Global USA Shop. Open M-F 9am-7pm, Sa 9am-3pm.

LOCAL SERVICES

English-Language Bookstores: Angliyskaya Kniga (Английская Книга), ul. Kuznetsky most 18 (tel. 928 2021). M6: Kuznetsky most. Moscow's largest selection, imported straight from Britain. Open M-F 10am-7pm, Sa 10am-6pm. AmEx/MC/Visa. **Shakespeare and Co.,** Pervy Novokuznetsky per. 5/7 (tel. 951 9360). M2: Novokuznetskaya. Carries books from *The New York Times* best-seller list. Open M-Sa 9am-7pm.

English-Language Press: Two free English-language newspapers are easy to find in hotels and restaurants across the city. *The Moscow Times* (more widely read and distributed) and *The Moscow Tribune* have foreign and national articles, sports, etc. for news-starved travelers. Both also have weekend sections (on Fridays) that list exhibitions, theatrical events, English-language movies, and housing and job opportunities. An "alternative" paper, *The eXile,* is one of the most irreverent and offensive papers on Earth, and is therefore a must-read, if only for comic relief. Its nightlife section is brutally and indispensably candid. It enlightens the expat world every other Friday, and is available at the most expatriate of establishments, such as the Starlite Diner (see **Restaurants,** p. 571). The *Moscow Business Telephone Guide* and *What and Where in Moscow,* both free, are excellent info resources. Foreign publications such as *Time, Newsweek,* and *The International Herald-Tribune* (100-150R) are available at major hotels.

Cultural Centers: The Western powers have all ganged up, putting their cultural centers in the same building: **Foreign Library,** ul. Nikoloyamskaya 1, 3rd floor (Николоямская). M4, 7: Taganskaya. The **American Cultural Center** (tel. 956 3022 and 215 7985) has a library full of reference materials. The **French Cultural Center** (tel. 915 3669) and the **British Council Resource Centre** (tel. 915 3511) are next door. Bring your passport, you expat, you! All open M-F 10am-8pm.

Gay and Lesbian Organizations: Treugolnik (Треугольник; tel. 932 0100), and **AIDS Infoshare Russia** (tel. 110 2460). Both carry info on gay and lesbian life in Russia.

Laundromat: Traveller's Guest House (see **Accommodations,** p. 569) does your laundry for 25R per load. **California Cleaners,** Leninsky pr. 111/3 (tel. 956 5284), and 12 other locations around Moscow. For free pickup and delivery call 497 0005 or 497 0011. Wash and dry US$2 per kg, slightly more for ironing.

EMERGENCY & COMMUNICATIONS

Emergencies: Call your embassy for passport and visa problems. Call 299 1180 to report offenses *by* the police. **Lost children:** tel. 401 9982. **Lost credit cards:** tel. 956 9006 for AmEx, tel. 956 3456 for MC and Visa. **Lost property:** Metro tel. 222 2085; other transport tel. 923 8753. **Lost documents:** tel. 200 9957.

24hr. Pharmacies: Leningradsky pr. 74 (Ленинградский; tel. 151 4570). M2: Sokol. Kutuzovsky pr. 14 (Кутузовский; tel. 243 1601). M3: Kutuzovskaya. 40-Letia Oktyabrya pr. 4, bldg. 2 (40-летия Октабря; tel. 350 0594). M9: Lyublino.

Medical Assistance: American Medical Center, 2 Tverskoy-Yamskoy per. 10 (2-ой Тверской-Ямской; tel. 956 3366; fax 956 2306). M2: Mayakovskaya. American joint venture offering walk-in medical care for hard currency. Most experienced Western medical clinic in Moscow. Pharmacy and X-ray on premises. US$215 per visit. Monthly membership US$55, students US$40. Open M-F 8am-8pm, Sa 9am-5pm; 24hr. for emergencies, although you will pay more. **Mediclub Moscow,** Michurinsky pr. 56 (Мичуринский; tel. 931 5018 and 931 5318). M1: Prospekt Vernadskovo. Private Canadian clinic offering full-scale emergency service. Medical consultations US$90-120. Payment in rubles or by credit card only (MC/Visa). Open M-Th 9am-8pm, F 9am-6pm, Sa 10am-2pm.

Internet Access: Internet Chevignon Cafe, Stoleshnikov per. 14, 2nd floor (Столешников пер.; tel. 733 9206). M2: Tverskaya. Exiting the Metro, walk downhill on Tverskaya and turn left onto Stoleshnikov. Enter through the Levi's shop on the 1st floor. Buy a drink and you'll have 30min. of access; purchase additional drinks for additional time. *Baltica,* espresso, and Coca-Cola 29R. Open daily noon-midnight. **Partiya Internet Cafe** (Партия), Volgogradsky pr. 1 (Волгоградский). M6: Proletarskaya. US$3 per hr. Open daily 10am-8pm. **VDNKh** (ВДНХ) **Metro Exhibition Hall.** From the Metro, take the ВВЦ exit and head left past the statue through the main gates to the exhibition hall. At the back of the hall on the 2nd floor there is an internet kiosk. 85R per hr. Daily 10am-6pm.

Post Offices: Moscow Central Telegraph, ul. Tverskaya 7, a few blocks uphill from the Kremlin. M1: Okhotny Ryad. Look for the globe and the digital clock in front. **International mail** service open M-F 8am-2pm and 3-9pm, Sa 8am-2pm and 3-7pm, Su 9am-2pm and 3-7pm. Address mail: "Москва 103009, До востребования (POSTE RESTANTE), FU, Jenny." **Faxes** and **telegrams** at window #1. Telegrams to the U.S. about 4.50R per word. Faxes 7.8R per page domestic, 20R to Europe, 36R to the U.S., Australia, and Africa. Window #32 sends letters, but not packages, abroad. Open daily 8am-10pm. **Poste Restante** also at the **Gostinitsa Intourist Hotel post office,** ul. Tverskaya 3/5, just past reception and to the right. Address mail "MCCARTHY, Kate, До востребования, K-600, Гостиница Интурист, ул7 Тверская 3/5, Москва." To mail **packages** (paper-made contents only, books, manuscripts, etc.), bring them unwrapped to the Intourist post office or to Myasnitskaya 26 (Мясницкая); they will be wrapped and mailed while you wait. Intourist post office open M-F 9am-noon and 1-6pm. Regular letters (7R, postcards 5R) theoretically take up to 2 weeks; *zakaznoe* (special delivery; заказное; 8R) 10 days. **Postal code:** 103009.

Telephones: Moscow Central Telegraph (see **Post Offices,** above). To **call abroad,** go to the 2nd hall with telephones. Collect and calling card calls not available. Prepay at the counter for the amount of time you expect to talk. You will then be given the number of a stall from which to dial directly. Use the *mezhdunarodnye telefony* (**international telephone cabinets;** международные телефоны). To get a refund if you do not reach your party, you must stand in line again at the same counter. Calls to Europe run US$1-1.50 per min.; to the U.S. and Australia about US$2-3. Open 24hr. International calls can also be placed from private homes (dial 8-10-country code-phone number); private homes are also often the *only* way to use a calling card. For calling card access numbers, see **Russia Essentials: Communication,** p. 558. **Local calls** require new phonecards, available at some Metro stops and kiosks. **Phone code:** (0)95.

ACCOMMODATIONS

Just about everything can be found in Moscow these days—except budget accommodations. The lack of a hard-core backpacking culture results in slim pickings and over-priced rooms. In summer, make sure to call at least a week ahead. Women standing outside major rail stations rent **private rooms** or **apartments** (as low as 200-250R per night; don't forget to haggle); just look for the signs advertising rooms (*sdayu komnatu;* сдаю комнату) or apartments (*sdayu kvartiru;* сдаю квартиру). If you're interested in a **homestay,** book it in advance (see **Russia Essentials,** p. 551). The **Moscow Bed & Breakfast** (U.S. tel. (1)603-585-3347; fax (1)603-585-6534; email jkates@top.monad.net) is an American-based organization that rents out apartments in the city center; contact them before you arrive in Moscow. (Singles US$35; doubles US$52) The places below are as cheap as it gets.

RUSSIA

Traveller's Guest House, ul. Bolshaya Pereyaslavskaya 50, 10th floor (Большая Переяславская; tel. 971 4059; fax 280 7686; email tgh@glas.apc.org). M4, 5: Prospekt Mira (Проспект Мира). From the Metro, walk north along pr. Mira (approx. 10min.) and take the 3rd right on Banny per. (Банный). Hang a left at the end of the street. TGH is the white, 12-story building across the street. The only hostel-like accommodation in Moscow, TGH is *the* place to meet other budget travelers and get travel advice. All information is printed in English, which the management speaks fluently. Spotless rooms and kitchen facilities. Dorms US$18; singles US$36; doubles US$48, with private bath US$54. Laundry service US$2 for 3-5kg. Airport pickup and drop-off (US$40). Visa invitations for Russia (US$40; allow several days to 1 week). Phone cards for calls abroad sold (from 140R). Reserve a week ahead; retain copies of all reservation forms and receipts. Checkout 11am. MC/Visa.

Galina's Flat, ul. Chaplygina 8, #35 (Чаплыгина; tel. 921 6038), in a beautiful old neighborhood. M1: Chistye Prudy. From the Metro, head down bul. Chistoprudny (Чистопрудный) past the statue of the poet Griboedov. Take the first left onto

Kharitonyevsky per. (Харитоньевский) just after the blue Kazakh Embassy and then the second right on Chaplygina. Go through the courtyard (under the blue sign), hang a right, and enter the building with the "Уникум" sign next to the doorway; the flat is on the 5th floor, on the right-hand side. Galina and her sidekick Sergei welcome you to their homey Russian apartment. Easygoing atmosphere. 5-bed dorm US$9; comfortable double US$11 per person. If an 8th person arrives, an extra cot will appear. Hot showers. Kitchen facilities. Only 8 beds, so call ahead.

American Academy of Foreign Languages, ul. Bolshaya Cheryomushinskaya 17a (Большая Черёмушинская; tel. 129 4300; fax 123 1500). M5: Akademicheskaya (Академическая). From the Metro, turn left at the Ho Chi Minh statue and walk 15min. on ul. Dmitriya Ulyanova (Дмитрия Ульянова), then left at the trolley tracks on Bolshaya Cheryomushinskaya. Clean, if uninspiring, rooms. Bed in a triple 100R; in a quad 80R; 2-room "lux" suites 500R for a single, 550R for a double; half-lux suites 450R. Baths shared by 2 rooms. 25% discount if you call ahead, but even at the American Academy of Foreign Languages, the voice on the other end may not speak English.

Prakash Guesthouse, ul. Profsoyuznaya 83, kor. 1 (2nd entrance), 3rd floor, (Профсоюзная; tel. 334 8201 and 335 0876; fax 334 2598; email prakash@matrix.ru). M5: Belyaevo (Беляево). From the Metro, take the exit nearest the last car of the train and go all the way to the right of the tunnel; exit from the last stairway on the left side. The guest house is in the fourth building on your right. Enter from the third entrance, right of the main entrance and to the rear of the building. Office is on the second floor, first door. Call ahead, and they'll meet you at the Metro. Friendly but remote lodge caters (but not exclusively) to Indian guests. Will arrange accommodations and train tickets to St. Petersburg. Shower, toilet, and telephone for local calls in each room. Singles US$30; doubles US$40; bed in a 5-bed dorm US$15. Breakfast US$6. Dinner US$12. Free email. Reception 7am-11pm; call ahead if you're arriving earlier or later. MC/Visa.

FOOD

Eating out in Moscow can be incredibly expensive, but it doesn't have to be. Avoid the tourist-targeted venues and follow the natives to local eateries—you'll be well rewarded with home-cooked meals at wallet-friendly prices. Many restaurants list prices in U.S. dollars to avoid having to change their menus to keep up with inflation, but payment is almost always in rubles. Russians tend to eat late in the evening, so you can avoid the crowds by eating earlier. Scattered bread stands, increasingly rare in central Moscow but quite common at outdoor market areas, are still an excellent choice for sweet and savory pies (3-5R).

RESTAURANTS & CAFES

THE ARBAT

Praga (Прада), Arbat 2 (tel. 290 3137), near the corner of Novy Arbat. M3: Arbatskaya. Home of the famous "Praga" torte sold all over Moscow. The bakery next door sells delectable pastries and mini-cakes for 5R apiece. Open daily 9am-8pm.

Evropeyskoe Bistro (Европейское Бистро), Arbat 16 (tel. 291 7161), with an orange-and-blue awning. Serves cafeteria style "Eurofood"–Russian cuisine with a snazzy name. Patio seating facilitates people-watching. Complete meals 150-200R. Open daily 8am-midnight.

Cafe-Bar "Reconee," Arbat 43 (tel. 241 7846). M3: Smolenskaya. Beats your average cafe fare. The owner is friendly, the menu extensive, and the food cheap (for the Arbat). Fabulous people-watching and even more fabulous borscht (35R). Full meals 150R. Live country music Th-Su 6-11pm. Open daily 11am-11pm.

NEAR THE PUSHKIN MUSEUM OF FINE ARTS

Mama Zoya's, Sechenovsky per. 8 (Сеченовский; tel. 202 0445). M1: Kropotkinskaya. Exiting the Metro walk 4 blocks down ul. Ostozhenka (Остоженка) and take a right on Sechenovsky. Turn right at the Mama Zoya's sign and head to the basement in the back of the building. Mama cooks up inexpensive, home-style Georgian feasts. Entrees 35-55R. Live Georgian music. Open daily 11am-midnight.

Patio Pizza, ul. Volkhonka 13a (Волхонка; tel. 298 2520), opposite the museum. M1: Kropotkinskaya. Also at Tverskaya 3 (M1: Okhotny Ryad). This place rocks, and everyone in Moscow knows it–the food and prices have the crowds lining up after 7pm. Fast service and delicious thin-crust pizzas. One of the only restaurants in Moscow whose concept of salad actually includes vegetables. Pizzas around US$8, all-you-can-eat salad bar US$6. Open daily noon-midnight. AmEx/MC/Visa.

Krizis Zhanra, per. Prechistensky 22/4 (Пречистенский; tel. 241 2940). M1: Kropotkinskaya. From the Metro, walk down ul. Prechistenka (Пречистенка) away from the Church of Christ the Savior. Take the third right onto Prechistensky. Walk through in the gate across from the Danish embassy into a courtyard and turn left; the entrance is the first large door on the left. Caters to pensive, artsy types–bring your *Crime and Punishment.* Snacks and beers 200-250R. Open Tu-Su noon-1am.

OFF UL. TVERSKAYA

Moscow Bombay, Glinishchevsky per. 3 (Глинищевский; tel. 292 9731; fax 292 9375). M6: Pushkinskaya. Exiting the Metro, walk 5min. downhill on Tverskaya and turn left onto Glinishchevsky. English menu surprises with pages of Indian and European specialties, including a full page of vegetarian options. Appetizers US$4-6, *naan* US$2, entrees around US$9. 10% student discount. Reservations recommended, especially on weekends. Open daily noon-midnight. Visa/MC.

Cafe Margarita (Кафе Маргарита), ul. Malaya Bronnaya 28 (tel. 299 6534), at the corner of Maly Kozikhinsky per. (Малый Козихинский). M2: Mayakovskaya. Exiting the Metro, take a left onto Bolshaya Sadovaya, then left again onto Malaya Bronnaya. A super-trendy cafe opposite the Patriarch's Ponds, where Bulgakov's *The Master and Margarita* begins. Enjoy the house specialty–tomatoes stuffed with garlic and cheese–or just sip a cup of tea and watch unemployed artists gossip and smoke the afternoon away. Hearty Russian meals 400R. Live piano music after 7pm (cover 15R). Open daily 1pm-midnight.

Starlight Diner, ul. Bolshaya Sadovaya 16 (Большая Садовая; tel. 290 9638). M2: Mayakovskaya. Look for the neon and chrome. Another location at ul. Korovy Val 9 (tel. 230 3268). M4: Oktyabrskaya. This place is authentic–they flew it in from Florida. Large selection of American favorites, for those times when wings and nachos are a must. Burgers US$7-9, entrees US$18. Drink menu extensive but expensive (US$6-7). Open 24hr. Visa/MC.

Tram, ul. Malaya Dimitrovka 6 (tel. 299 0770). M6: Pushkinskaya. Exiting the Metro, walk alongside the park past the statue of Pushkin and take the first left at Malaya Dimitrovka. Below the LENKOM theater, this drama-themed establishment serves above-average Russian food at equally above-average prices. A four course meal averages US$25-30. Open 24hr.

NEAR THE TRAVELLER'S GUEST HOUSE

Zaydi i poprobuy ("Drop In and Try"; Зайди и попробуй), pr. Mira 124 (Мира; tel./fax 286 8165). M5: Rizhskaya, then take the trolley a couple of stops north. Entrance on Malaya Moskovskaya ul. (Малая Московская). Drop in, indeed, since the restaurant lies below street level. The best of Russian cuisine at the lowest of Russian prices. Full meals 150R. Open daily 11am-11:30pm.

Flamingo, pr. Mira 48. M4: Prospekt Mira. Look for the large, pink flamingo on the door. Chintzy decor and mafioso-wannabes aside, this is the place for larger-than-average portions of better-than-average Russian food. The *blini* filled with meat or cabbage (80R) are divine. Eat, drink, and be merry for 250-300R. Musicians play everything from Russian classics to Mack the Knife. Open daily noon-1:30am.

FILI

Cafe Kitayskoy Kukhni ("Cafe of Chinese Cooking;" Кафе Китайской Кухни), ul. Krasnaya Presnya 30 (Красная Пресная; tel. 252 3384). M6: Ulitsa 1905 goda. Turn left from the Metro stop; it's on the left marked by a yellow neon sign. The interior is small and dimly lit, but the Chinese food is cheap. There is no English menu; look at what the Russian customers get and point. Portions are small so get several dishes and share. Dinners 150R. Open daily 11am-11pm.

WEST OF GORKY PARK

Guria's, Komsomolsky pr. 7/3 (Комсомольский; tel. 246 0378), on the corner of ul. Frunze, opposite St. Nicholas of the Weavers. M1, 4: Park Kultury. Superb Georgian fare for some of the city's lowest prices. Cabbage leaves stuffed with rice and meat (40R) are a must. Entrees 30-50R. Open daily noon-11pm.

THE CHAINS (OR, HOW UNCLE SAM WON THE COLD WAR)

McDonald's (Макдоналдс—not that you need the Cyrillic, ye seeker of the Golden Arches). Ronald now has 21 corporate outlets in Moscow, included here because *Let's Go* endorses the steady homogenization of world culture. Bolshaya Bronnaya 29 (Большая Бронная), M6: Pushkinskaya, and ul. Arbat 50/52 (Арбат), M3: Smolenskaya, are the biggest. Big Mac 33.50R. Large fries (*bolshaya portsiya kartofel-fri;* большая порция картофель-фри) 22.50R. Open daily 8am-midnight.

Russkoe Bistro (Русское Бистро). Moscow's stellar, cheaper answer to McDonald's, with locations all over town (particularly near the Pushkinskaya Metro, where you can see *three* of them at once). Traditional food, fast. Pre-made salads 13-15R, pies with sweet and savory fillings 25-30R. Open daily 9am-midnight.

Rostik's (Ростик'с). Moscow's Kentucky Fried Chicken, the largest of these popular eateries is located diagonally across from M2: Mayakovskaya; another inside GUM. Look for the deranged, grinning rooster holding a fork and knife. 3 pieces of "Rostik's original" chicken 55R, salads and soups 10-20R. Open daily 10am-11pm.

Baskin Robbins, on the Arbat, near Arbat 20. M3: Arbatskaya (Арбатская). The not-always-31 flavors might be overpriced, but they nonetheless provide a refreshing change from typical Russian ice cream bars. Small scoop 16R. Open daily 10am-10pm.

SUPERMARKETS

The number of supermarkets is increasing just as the need for them is decreasing—many goods can be found more cheaply in kiosks and in smaller, neighborhood markets selling Russian and foreign food. If nothing else, the convenience of knowing you can find everything you need without being trampled is tempting. Listed below are a few of the largest.

Eliseevsky Gastronom (Елисеевский), ul. Tverskaya 14 (tel. 209 0760). M2: Tverskaya. With stained glass, high Baroque ceilings, and high-flying chandeliers, Moscow's most famous grocery is as much a visual spectacle as it is a place to buy food. Stocked with foreign goods. Higher prices than most other groceries (if you dare demean it by calling it a grocery). Open M-F 8am-9pm, Sa 10am-7pm.

Gastronom Tsentralny, ul. Bolshaya Lubyanka 1½ (Большая Любянка), behind Lubyanka Prison. M1, 7: Lubyanka. This 24hr. supermarket stocks everything, but with a 20% price-hike 10pm-7am—you pay for that midnight snack. AmEx/MC/Visa.

Dorogomilovo (Дорогомилого), ul. Bolshaya Dorogomilovskaya 8 (Большая Дорогомиловская). M4: Kievskaya. Left of McDonald's, across the park from Kievsky Vokzal. The least expensive of the new supermarkets that stock Western foods. Open M-Sa 9am-9pm, Su 9am-7pm.

Stockmann, M2, 4: Paveletskaya. Facing the station, walk left 2 blocks; the glassed-in store is behind the white curtains. Cheaper than most, this Finnish grocery emporium accepts credit cards only. Open daily 9am-9pm.

MARKETS

Georgians, Armenians, Uzbeks, and other rural folk cart their finest produce to Moscow's many markets. A visit is worthwhile just for the sights: sides of beef, piles of tomatoes, peaches, grapes, jars of glowing honey, and huge pots of flowers crowded together in a visual bouquet. Wash fruit and vegetables with bottled water before eating. The **central market** (M8: Tsvetnoi Bulvar), next to the Old Circus, has reopened after a recent reconstruction. The alternative is the **Rizhsky Market** (M5: Rizhskaya). Otherwise, impromptu markets spring up around Metro stations; some of the best are at Turgenevskaya, Kuznetsky Most, Aeroport, Baumanskaya, and between Novoslobodskaya and Mendeleevskaya. In general, people appear with their goods around 10am and leave by 8pm, although stragglers stick around until 10pm. Produce, sold by the kilogram, is far cheaper than in the grocery stores; bags are never provided, so bring your own.

SIGHTS

Moscow's sights reflect the city's strange history: one can choose from 16th-century churches or Soviet-era museums, but there's little in between. The city also suffers from the 200 years when St. Petersburg was the tsar's seat—there are no grand palaces, and the city's art museums, although impressive, pale in comparison with the Hermitage. Tourists will notice that the political upheaval of the last decade has taken its toll on the museums dedicated to Lenin, Marx, and Engels, which are closed indefinitely while their political significance is reassessed. Yet the "political reconstruction" of the capital has also led to physical renovation, and the city seems to be constantly under construction, with new buildings going up practically overnight. A massive restoration and reconstruction effort for Moscow's 850th anniversary celebration has left some sights temporarily out of commission. Despite the fact that 80% of Moscow's pre-revolutionary splendor was torn down by the Soviet regime, the capital still packs enough sights to occupy you for over a week.

RED SQUARE

There is nothing red about it; *krasnaya* meant "beautiful" long before the Communists co-opted it. Red Square (Krasnaya ploshchadz; Красная площадь), a 700m-long lesson in history and culture, has been the site of everything from a giant farmer's market to public hangings, from political demonstrations to a renegade Cessna's landing. On one side, the **Kremlin** stands as both the historical and religious heart of Russia and the seat of the Communist Party for 70-odd years; on the other, **GUM,** once a market, then the world's largest purveyor of Soviet "consumer goods," is now an upscale shopping mall. At one end, **St. Basil's Cathedral** (Pokrovsky Sobor; Покровский Собор), the square's second oldest building, rises high with its crazy-quilt onion domes; at the other end sit the **History** and **Lenin Museums.** Lenin's historical legacy has come into question, and his name and face are coming down all over Moscow; the Party is finally over, but Lenin's mausoleum still stands in front of the Kremlin, patrolled by several scowling guards. Moscow's mayor has built a church to block the largest entrance to the square, ensuring that Communist parades will never again march through. Begin your sightseeing here, and make sure to enter with your eyes closed, then open them to get the full effect.

KREMLIN (KREML; КРЕМЛЬ)

__Open__ M-W and F-Su 10am-5:30pm. Armory and Diamond Fund open M-W and F-Su 10-11:30am, noon-1:30pm, 2:30-4pm, 4:30-6pm. __Entrance__ to all cathedrals 200R, students 110R; 90R, students 45R after 4pm. Camera privileges 30R. Armory 280R, students 140R. Diamond Fund 100R. Buy tickets at the kassa in Alexander Gardens, on the west side of the Kremlin, and enter through Borovitskaya gate tower in the southwest corner. English-speaking guides offer __tours__ at outrageous prices; haggle away. Local hotels also offer tours. Large bags and cameras must be checked (5R) before entering the Diamond Fund.

Like a spider in her web, the Kremlin sits geographically and historically in the center of Moscow. Here, Ivan the Terrible reigned with his iron fist and Stalin ruled the lands behind the Iron Curtain. Napoleon simmered here while Moscow burned, and the Congress of People's Deputies dissolved itself here in 1991, ending the USSR. But despite the tremendous political history of this one-time fortress, its magnificent churches are the real attraction. Much of the Kremlin is still government offices; the watchful police will blow whistles if you stray into a forbidden zone.

Follow the eager masses to **Cathedral Square,** home of the most famous gold domes in Russia. The first church to the left, **Annunciation Cathedral** (Blagoveshchensky Sobor; Благовещеиский Собор), guards the loveliest iconostasis in Russia, with luminous icons by Andrei Rublyov and Theophanes the Greek. Originally only three-domed, the cathedral was elaborated and gilded by Ivan the Terrible. The second, southeast entrance is also his work; Ivan's four marriages made him ineligible to enter the church so he was forced to stand in the porch during services as penance. Across the way, the square **Archangel Cathedral** (Arkhangelsky Sobor; Архангельский Собор), gleaming with vivid icons and frescoes, is the final resting place for many tsars prior to Peter the Great. Ivans III (the Great) and IV (the Terrible) are behind the south end of the iconostasis; Mikhail Romanov is in front. Directly behind the Cathedral is **Tsar Bell** (Tsar-kolokol; Царь-колокол). The world's largest, this bell has never rung and never will: an 11.5-ton piece cracked off after a fire in 1737.

The center of Cathedral Square is **Assumption Cathedral** (Uspensky Sobor; Успенский Собор), the oldest cathedral in the Russian state. The icons on the west wall are from the 15th century; the others are from the 1640s. Ivan the Terrible's throne still stands in the armory, and Napoleon, securing his excellent reputation with the Russians, used this place as a stable in 1812. To the right of Uspensky Sobor is **Ivan the Great Belltower** (Kolokolnya Ivana Velikovo; Колокольня Ивана

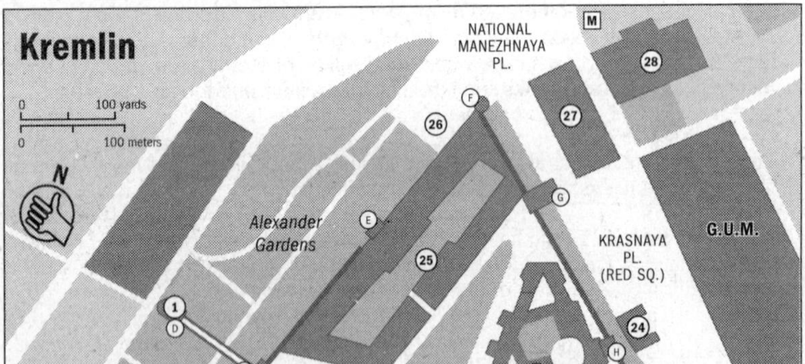

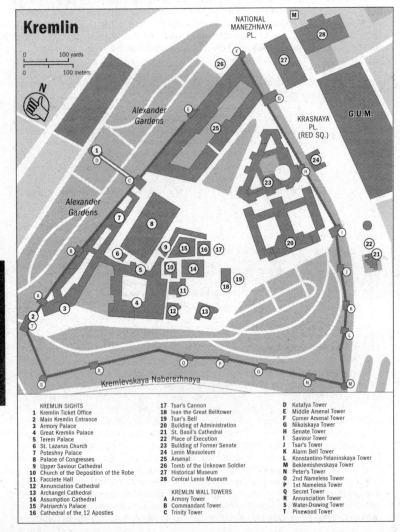

KREMLIN SIGHTS
1 Kremlin Ticket Office
2 Main Kremlin Entrance
3 Armory Palace
4 Great Kremlin Palace
5 Terem Palace
6 St. Lazarus Church
7 Poteshny Palace
8 Palace of Congresses
9 Upper Saviour Cathedral
10 Church of the Deposition of the Robe
11 Facciete Hall
12 Annunciation Cathedral
13 Archangel Cathedral
14 Assumption Cathedral
15 Patriarch's Palace
16 Cathedral of the 12 Apostles
17 Tsar's Cannon
18 Ivan the Great Belltower
19 Tsar's Bell
20 Building of Administration
21 St. Basil's Cathedral
22 Place of Execution
23 Building of Former Senate
24 Lenin Mausoleum
25 Arsenal
26 Tomb of the Unknown Soldier
27 Historical Museum
28 Central Lenin Museum

KREMLIN WALL TOWERS
A Armory Tower
B Commandant Tower
C Trinity Tower
D Kutafya Tower
E Middle Arsenal Tower
F Corner Arsenal Tower
G Nikolskaya Tower
H Senate Tower
I Saviour Tower
J Tsar's Tower
K Alarm Bell Tower
L Konstantino-Yelaninskaya Tower
M Beklemishevskaya Tower
N Peter's Tower
O 2nd Nameless Tower
P 1st Nameless Tower
Q Secret Tower
R Annunciation Tower
S Water-Drawing Tower
T Pinewood Tower

Велнкого). It is visible from 30km away thanks to Boris Godunov (the one pre-Peter tsar not buried in the Kremlin—he's in Sergiev Posad), who raised the tower to 81m. Behind the Assumption Cathedral stands the **Patriarch's Palace** (Patriarshy Dvorets; Патриарший Дворец), site of the Museum of 17th-Century Russian Applied Art and Life, and **Church of the Twelve Apostles** (Sobor Dvenadtsati Apostolov; Собор Двенадцати Апостолов), built by Patriarch Nikon in the 17th century as revenge against Ivan the Terrible's extravagant St. Basil's Cathedral.

The **Armory Museum and Diamond Fund** (Oruzheynaya i Vystavka Almaznovo Fonda; Оружейная и Выставка Алмазного) lies just to the left as you enter. All the riches of the Russian Church and those of the state not in the Hermitage can be found in these nine rooms. Room 3, on the second floor, holds the legendary **Fabergé eggs**—each opens to reveal an impossibly intricate jewelled miniature. Room 6 holds thrones and other royal necessities, such as crowns and dresses (Empress Elizabeth is said to have had 15,000 gowns, only one of which is on display). Room 9 contains royal coaches and sleds—Elizabeth (not one for understatement) had her sled pulled by 23 horses. The display is a must-see to comprehend the opulence of the Russian court. The Diamond Fund, in an annex of the Armory, has still more glitter, including a 190-carat diamond given to Catherine the Great by Gregory Orlov, a "special friend." The only other place inside the Kremlin you can actually enter is the **Kremlin Palace of Congresses,** the square white monster built by Khrushchev in 1961 for Communist Party Congresses. It's also a theater, open in summer for concerts and ballets.

STATE DEPARTMENT STORE GUM. (Gosudarstvenny Universalny Magazin; Государственный Универсальный Магазин; ГУМ). Built in the 19th century, GUM was designed to hold 1000 stores, and its arched, wrought-iron-and-glass roofs resemble a 19th-century train station. During Soviet rule, going to GUM was a depressing experience; the sight of 1000 empty stores is pretty grim. These days, however, it is depressing only to those who can't afford it (which is almost everyone). The complex has been completely renovated and is a shopping mall of which any American metropolis would be proud. Some stores quote prices in U.S. dollars or Deutchmarks, pay in rubles. Gucci, Pierre Cardin, Calvin Klein, and Benetton all call GUM home. *(M3: Ploshchadz Revolutsii (Площадь Революции). From the Metro, turn left, then left again at the gate to Red Square. Tel. 929 3381. Open daily 9am-9pm.)*

ST. BASIL'S CATHEDRAL. (Pokrovsky Sobor or Sobor Vasiliya Blazhennovo; Собор Василия Блаженного). There is perhaps no more familiar symbol of Moscow than St. Basil's Cathedral . Completed in 1561, it was commissioned by Ivan the Terrible to celebrate his 1552 victory over the Tatars in Kazan. The nine main chapels are named after the saints' days on which Ivan won his battles, but the cathedral itself used to bear the moniker of a holy fool, Vasily—Basil in English—who correctly predicted that Ivan would murder his own son. Before the Kazan victory, Vasily died and was buried in the church that once stood on this ground. The grand cathedral that replaced it has seen the addition of a few minor domes since Ivan's time, as well as the colorful patterns for which the domes are known. The maze-like interior—unusual for Orthodox churches—is filled with intricate but reconstructed frescoes. Downstairs, an exhibit traces the history of the church and Ivan's campaign against the Tatars, all in Russian. *(M3: Ploshchadz Revolutsii (Площадь Революции). Open W-M 10am-5pm; kassa closes at 4:30pm. 75R, students 38R. Buy tickets from the kassa to the left of the entrance, then proceed upstairs.)*

LENIN'S TOMB. (Mavzoley V.I. Lenina; Мавзолей В.И. Ленина). In the glory days, this squat red structure in front of the Kremlin was guarded by fierce goose-stepping guards, and the line to get in was three hours long. The guards have now been replaced by teenage cadets, and the line has completely vanished, which makes getting in Lenin's tomb—at least when it's open—a cinch. No photos are allowed of Vlad's embalmed remains, and bags must be checked at the cloakroom in Aleksandrovsky Sad. Pulling out a camera in the tomb might get you escorted out to the gates of Red Square. Entrance to the mausoleum also gives access to the **Kremlin wall,** where Stalin, Brezhnev, Andropov, Gagarin, and John Reed (author of *Ten*

Days that Shook the World) are buried. As you admire the mausoleum on your stroll around Red Square, note the balcony on top, where Russia's leaders stood during May Day and November 7 parades. Rumor has it that the plushest bathroom in Moscow is hidden somewhere in the back. Unfortunately it is not open to the public. *(Open Tu-Th and Sa-Su 10am-1pm.)*

KAZAN CATHEDRAL. (Kazansky Sobor; Казанский Собор). The orange and gold birthday-cake Kazan Cathedral has been reopened for services after being demolished in 1936 to make way for May Day parades. The interior of the faithful 1990s reconstruction is plainer than that of most Russian churches, and the iconostasis is free of gold Baroque madness. With a healthy mix of tourists and worshippers, you needn't worry too much about the rules on the door. *(M3: Ploshchadz Revolutsii (Площадь Революции). Stands opposite St. Basil's on Pl. Revolutsii, and just to the left as you exit the Metro. Open daily 8am-7pm. Services 8am and 5pm.)*

ALEXANDER GARDENS. (Aleksandrovsky Sad; Александровский Сад). More than just the place to buy kremlin tickets, the Alexander Gardens are a green respite from the carbon monoxide fumes of central Moscow. At the north end of the gardens at the **Tomb of the Unknown Soldier** (Mogila Neizvestnovo Soldata; Могила Неизвестного Солдата), an eternal flame burns in memory of the catastrophic losses suffered in WWII, known in Russia as the Great Patriotic War. Twelve urns containing soil from the Soviet Union's "Hero Cities," which withstood especially heavy casualties, stand there as well. It used to be the trendy (and macabre) spot to get your picture taken on your wedding day—that and Lenin's mausoleum. *(M3: Ploshchadz Revolutsii (Площадь Революции), to the left of the exit.)*

MONASTERIES, CHURCHES, & SYNAGOGUES

If the grime and bedlam get to you, escape to one of Moscow's hidden synagogues, churches, or monasteries. Before the Revolution, the city had more than 1000 operational churches; today, there are fewer than 100. At all Orthodox monasteries, shorts are not permitted and women must cover their heads.

CATHEDRAL OF CHRIST THE SAVIOR. (Khram Khrista Spasitelya; Храм Христа Спасителя). No one should leave Moscow without visiting the city's most controversial landmark, the enormous, gold-domed Cathedral of Christ the Savior, visible from just about anywhere in west Moscow. Believe it or not, the city government of Moscow, led by Mayor Yury Luzhkov, constructed the cathedral that stands here today in a mere two years, on the site of the former Moscow swimming pool. Nicholas I had originally placed a cathedral on this spot to commemorate Russia's victory over Napoleon, but in 1934 Stalin had it dynamited, claiming it interfered with the city's bi-annual military parades. The minute the church was leveled, however, the truth came out: Stalin intended to erect a "Palace of the Soviets," which he wanted to be the tallest building in the world, on the spot. The so-called "Palace" was to be topped with a 100m statue of Lenin (the world's tallest statue). The ground on which the great building was to stand ultimately proved to be too soft to hold a building of such weight, and after Stalin's death Khrushchev abandoned the project and instead turned the site into the Moscow outdoor swimming pool. Although 20,000 people per day used the pool, in the early 90s it was discovered that vapor from the heated water damaged paintings at the nearby Pushkin Museum, so the pool was closed. In 1994-95 a controversy erupted over what was to become of the site; the Orthodox Church and Moscow's mayor finally won out to raise funds to build the US$250 million cathedral that stands here today. As for where they got the money—well, let's just say it was a miracle. The beautiful gold-domed monolith is worth a visit, although in summer 1999, the interior was closed to the public due to ongoing construction. *(M1: Kropotkinskaya. Between ul. Volkhonka (Волхонка) and the Moscow River.)*

NOVODEVICHY MONASTERY & CEMETERY. (Новодевичий Монастырь). Among the most famous of Moscow's monasteries is the Novodevichy Monastery. You can't miss the high brick walls and golden domes, although both are in need of some repair. Tsars and nobles kept the coffers filled by exiling their well-dowried wives and daughters here when they grew tired of them. Buried within the monastery's walls are some well-known 16th-century Russians, but all the truly famous folks are entombed at the cemetery next door. Just wandering the grounds is rewarding, but a few of the buildings are also open. The **Smolensk Cathedral** (Smolensky Sobor; Смоленский Собор), in the center of the convent, shows off Russian icons and frescoes. English/Cyrillic keys decode the maze of scenes elaborately depicted on the walls. Other buildings of interest include **Assumption Church** (Uspenskaya Tserkov; Успенская Церковь), to the right of Smolensky, and a small three-room **exhibit hall** at the far end of the grounds. *(M1: Sportivnaya. Take the exit out of the Metro that does not go to the stadium. Take a right and the monastery is several blocks down on the left. Tel. 246 8526. Open M and W-Su 10am-5:30pm; cathedrals close at 4:45pm. Closed 1st Monday of each month. Avoid Sunday, when tour buses hog the place. Entrance to the grounds 25R, students 14R; Smolensk Cathedral 56R, students 30R; special exhibits 56R, students 30R.)*

Exiting the monastery gates, turn right and follow the exterior wall back around to the **cemetery** (*kladbishche;* кладбище)—a massive pilgrimage site which cradles the graves of Gogol, Chekhov, Stanislavsky, Khrushchev, Shostakovich, Mayakovsky, Bulgakov, and other luminaries. The tombstones are often highly artistic representations—visual or symbolic—of the deceased. Once closed to prevent crowds from flocking to Khrushchev's tomb (straight through the entrance at the back of the cemetery), it is now open to the public. The writers are conveniently clustered near each other. *(Open in summer daily 9am-7pm; in off-season daily 9am-6pm. 20R; buy tickets at the small kiosk across the street from the entrance. Cyrillic maps of cemetery 5R.)*

MOSCOW CHORAL SYNAGOGUE. First constructed in the 1870s, the Moscow Choral Synagogue is a much-needed break from the city's ubiquitous onion domes. Although it functioned during Soviet rule, KGB agents stationed across the street were instructed to take pictures of anyone entering (later to be used as negative evidence), thus preventing all but the boldest of Moscow's Jews from participating in services. Today more than 200,000 Jews officially live in Moscow, and services are increasingly well attended, especially on holidays. The synagogue has two prayer rooms; the main room is marked by 10 chandeliers and a patterned square ceiling that protects the upper level, where women must sit. The graffiti occasionally sprayed on the building serves as a sad reminder that anti-Semitism in Russia is not dead. Regular services are held every morning and evening, presided over by Swiss rabbi Pinchas Goldsmith. A **restaurant** on the premises serves kosher food. *(Bolshoy Spasoglinishchevsky per. 10 (Большой Спасоглинищевский). M5, 6: Kitai-Gorod. Go north on Solyansky Proezd (Солянский Проезд) and take the first left. Tel. 923 9697. Open daily 9:30am-6pm; Sabbath services Sa 9am. Restaurant open Su-M 9am-6pm.)*

CHURCH OF ST. NICHOLAS OF THE WEAVERS. (Tserkov Nikoly v Khamovnikakh; Церковь Николы в Хамовниках). One of Moscow's better-known churches, St. Nicholas of the Weavers attracts (or, perhaps, assaults) passersby with a colorful facade. It looks like Hansel and Gretel's witch designed it, with deliciously artificial green-and-orange trimming. Entering off ul. Frunze gives you the best view of the low ceilings and equally vivid interior. *(M1, 4: Park Kultury. Located at the corner of Komsomolsky pr. and ul. Frunze (Фрунзе) across from the popular restaurant Guria's. Open M-Sa 8am-7pm, Su and holidays 7am-7pm. Service begins at opening.)*

DANILOVSKY MONASTERY. (Даниловский). This monastery is home to the Patriarch, head of the Russian Orthodox Church. A map on the left side of the entrance to Danilovsky explains the different buildings. The well-preserved and recently restored pastel exterior is complemented by stunning grounds and long-robed monks; unfortunately, visitors can see no more than these exterior views. Charming and peaceful, it's worth a visit. The Patriarch's office is hard to miss, marked by an enormous mosaic of a stern-looking man watching over the visitors to his domain. *(M8: Tulskaya. Turn right from the Metro and then take another right onto Danilovsky vul. The monastery is 3-4 blocks down on your right. Open daily 6am-8pm. Services M-F 7am and 5pm, Sa-Su 9am and 5pm.)*

DONSKOV MONASTERY. (Донсков). The least famous of Moscow's monasteries, Donskov is, as a result, the most authentic and serene. Since the fall of communism, the red-brick Donskov has once again gained a congregation, but not quite equal to its 1591 prestige. Still, on Russian Orthodox holidays the monastery teems with life, and on other days it sits peacefully in the golden sunlight. The main church lies directly opposite the entrance. Its beautiful interior is covered with traditional frescoes. The smaller church to the right presents a less-ornate display characteristic of the older Orthodox style. *(M5: Shabolovskaya. From the Metro, head right on Shabolovka until the first main street and turn right again. Tel. 952 1646. Open daily 7am-7pm. Services daily at 8am and 5pm.)*

SPASO-ANDRONIKOV MONASTERY. (Спасо-Андроников). Dating from the 1360s, Spaso-Andronikov is famed for its preservation of life-sized 16th-century icons and a biblical text from the 14th century. Master of iconography Andrei Rublyov was once a monk here and is buried inside. The tiny **Museum of Andrei Rublyov** (Muzey Andreya Rublyova; Музей им. Андрёя Рублева), on the grounds of the monastery, showcases several beautiful icons but, unfortunately, nothing by Rublyov. *(Andronikovskaya pl. (Андрониковская). M7: Ploshchadz Ilicha. On the banks of the Yauza river, which branches off from the Moscow River. Tel. 278 1467. Open M-Tu and Th-Su 11am-6pm; closed last Friday of the month. Kassa closes 5:30pm. 35R, students 10R.)*

OTHER CHURCHES. An 18th-century ecclesiastical gem, **Church of St. John the Warrior** (Tserkov Ioanna Voina; Церковь Иоанна Воина), takes its name from the patron saint of the tsar's musketeers. *(Ul. Bolshaya Yakimanka 54 (Большая Якиманка). M4, 5: Oktyabrskaya. Open 24hr. Services Tu-Su at 5pm.)* **Yelokhovsky Cathedral** is perhaps Moscow's most beautiful operational church. Built in 1845, only the gilded interior outshines the brilliant turquoise exterior. The cathedral has the grand honor of being one of the main administrative locations of the burgeoning Russian Orthodox Church. *(Ul. Spartakovskaya 15 (Спартаковская). M3: Baumanskaya. Services M-Sa 8am and 6pm; Su 6:30, 9:30am, and 6pm.)*

REGIONS FOR WALKING

ARBAT. A pedestrian shopping arcade, the Arbat was once a showpiece of *glasnost* and a haven for political radicals, Hare Krishnas, street poets, and *metallisty* (heavy metal rockers). Today, the flavor of political rebellion has been replaced by the more universal taste of capitalism, including McDonald's, Baskin Robbins, and Benetton. Popular with native Muscovites, the Arbat nevertheless is peppered with kiosks tempting tourists with everything from *madryoshka* dolls to Soviet military caps. Midway up, on a side street, is a sadly dilapidated graffiti wall dedicated to rocker Victor Tsoi of the Soviet group Kino, who was idolized by many young Russians before his death in a car crash early in the decade. A quick bite or a leisurely meal in one of many outdoor cafes provides the ideal venue for extensive people-watching. Intersecting but almost parallel with the Arbat runs **Novy Arbat,** a thoroughfare lined with foreign businesses (such as the Arbat Irish House), and massive Russian stores like the famous **Dom Knigi,** a giant bookstore, and **Melodiya,** a top record store. *(M3: Arbatskaya.)*

PUSHKINSKAYA PL. This square in central Moscow has inherited the Arbat's mantle of political fervor. Missionary groups evangelize while amateur politicians gather here to argue and hand out petitions. All the major Russian news organizations are located in this region, perhaps explaining why the square is the center of free speech. Everything on the square is large—from the golden arches to the **Kinoteatr Rossiya,** Moscow's largest movie theater, which brought *Terminator* to the masses. Follow ul. Bolshaya Bronnaya, next to McD's, down to the bottom of the hill, turn right, and follow ul. Malaya Bronnaya to **Patriarch's Pond** (Patriarshy Prud; Патриарший Пруд), where Mikhail Bulgakov's *The Master and Margarita* begins. This area, known as the Margarita, is popular with artsy students and old men playing dominoes by the shaded pond. *(M6: Pushkinskaya. Halfway up ul. Tverskaya from Krasnaya pl.)*

NATASHA AND THE AMAZING TECHNICOLOR DREAMCOAT Bold blue spirals swirling feverishly against a shockingly orange background. Strands of purples and greens speckled with brilliant flecks of gold. The spires of St. Basil's Cathedral, perhaps? Not quite. And did we mention the zebra stripes? Still perplexed? Usually colorful, often creative, and always downright crazy, Moscow fashion is storming the streets like a school of mildly deranged tropical fish. Garish colors and peek-a-boo à la Russe are enough to make a Mardi Gras parade look like a funeral procession. "But wait," you say. "How will I blend in—aren't I supposed to dress like a native?" Just remember one word: cloth. So long as an ensemble is composed entirely of cloth, you can't go wrong. So go ahead, pair that purple-and-orange faux snakeskin leopard-print skirt with the pink-and-blue flowered mesh halter top. Both cloth. Get it? A match made in heaven. At least for Natasha.

OTHER AREAS FOR WALKING. Soviet and Old Russian architecture face-off on **ul. Razina** (Разина), where the on- and off-ramp of the **Rossiya,** the world's largest hotel, slither around a series of lovely churches. Turn right out of GUM down **Nikolskaya ul.** to reach **pl. Lubyanka,** the current home of FSB (a shinier, happier KGB) headquarters and formerly the site of a huge stone Felix Dzerzhinsky, the organization's founder. *(One left turn past St. Basil's Cathedral.)* One need not wander far to find **Stalinist architecture** in Moscow, but **Kutuzovsky pr.** is particularly blessed with the neo-Classical grandiloquence of the Soviet 30s. *(M3: Kievskaya.)* Several kilometers past the former residences of the Soviet elite, the recently opened **Victory Park** (Park Pobedy; Парк Победы), is a popular gathering point. The entire park and its museum (see **Historical Museums,** p. 582) were built as a lasting monument to WWII, in which 27 million Russians perished. The main square showcases stones, each inscribed with a year that the Soviet troops fought in the war (1941-45). The gold-domed **Church of St. George the Victorious** (Khram Georgiya Pobedanosnova; Храм Георгия Победоноспого) commemorates those who died in battle. *(M3: Kutuzovskaya.)*

PARKS

GORKY PARK. In summer, droves of out-of-towners and young Muscovites promenade, relax, and ride the roller coaster at Moscow's **amusement park.** In winter, the paths are flooded to create a park-wide **ice rink.** Those seeking an American-style amusement park will be disappointed—attractions are far outnumbered by ice cream kiosks, and the rides are on their last legs. However, the park is a must-see for its symbolic and historical significance. Night may be the best time to go; the rides are illuminated and the hordes of young children are home sleeping. *(M1, 4: Park Kultury or M4, 5: Oktyabrskaya. From the Park Kultury stop, cross Krimskiy most. From Oktyabrskaya, walk downhill on Krimskiy val. and enter through the main flag-flanked gate. Park open daily 10am-midnight. General admission 15R. Most rides 40-70R.)*

VDNKh. The **Exhibition of Soviet Economic Achievements** (Vystavka Dostizhenii Narodnovo Khozyaystva—VDNKh; Выставка Достижений Народного Хозяйства—ВДНХ) has changed much since its original conception. Now that it has been conclusively demonstrated that there were no Soviet economic achievements, this World's Fair-esque park filled with pavilions (each more garish than the next) has become, ironically, a large department store. Pavilions proclaim "Atomic Energy" and "Education" right above signs reading "Stereos" and "Shoes." It's a fun place for a midday walk—weekends provide comical people-watching opportunities. At the far end is the **Space Pavilion,** where you can see the rocket that launched Sputnik, topped by a giant Lenin statue. Beneath the statue is the **Space Museum,** equally garish in its Star Trek-esque displays of life in space and aboard Sputnik, complete with cosmonaut food: freeze-dried borscht. You can even have your photo taken in Yuri Gagarin's original space suit. *(M5: VDNKh (surprise, surprise). Exiting the Metro, go left* *down the kiosk-flanked sidewalk. Enter through the large main gate. Shops open 10am until dark. Space Museum, pr. Mira 111. Tel. 283 7914. Open Tu-Su 10am-7pm; closed last Friday of the month. 40R, children 8R; space suit photo 50R.)*

KOLOMENSKOE SUMMER RESIDENCE. The tsars' summer residence sits on a wooded rise above the Moskva River. Peter the Great's 1702 log cabin and Bratsk Prison, where the persecuted Archpriest Avakum wrote his celebrated autobiography, have been moved here from Arkhangelsk and Siberia, respectively. At the complex's edge, overlooking the river, stands the 16th-century **Assumption Cathedral** (Uspenskaya Sobor), the first example of a brick church built like a traditional wooden building (St. Basil's is the more famous example). Note the gold double-headed eagle at the top of the entrance gate: this emblem of the Romanovs, made of plastic, was installed in 1994. Red-coated guards with handy axes and swords patrol the grounds, an authentic if kitschy blast from the past. *(M2: Kolomenskaya. Follow the exit signs to "к музею Коломенское." Exiting the Metro, turn right and walk about 400m down the shaded, merchant-lined path to the main entrance gate. Grounds open daily 7am-10pm. Free. Museums open Tu-Su 11am-6pm. 15-20R; buy tickets at the kassa.)*

TSARITSYNO. This Tsar's park is most famous for its unhappy history. Conceived for Catherine the Great, the project was headed by Vasily Bazhenov, a Paris-educated serf, and included several pavilions, a system of palaces, arches, bridges, and trails. Bazhenov had barely set up some pavilions and started the palaces when capricious Catherine changed her mind and canceled the project. Bazhenov was devastated, but the blueprints survived. The Soviet authorities began restorations of the palaces many a time, but always ran out of funds. Two years ago some of the palaces were completed, along with the arches and bridges. Now, the red and white buildings, fragile and exotic, stand out against the gray Moscow sky. Many believe the place was cursed some 250 years ago, and its bad luck still looms over the ancient oak and linden trees. It is not, of course, a fairy tale, and this park, like all the others, has drinking, swearing, and littering Muscovites. At least here you can chalk it up to the curse. *(M2: Orekhovo. Exit "к парку" from the front of the train platform and then follow the main alley (directly ahead when you exit) all the way to the palaces.)*

IZMAYLOVSKY PARK. (Измайловский Парк). Izmaylovsky Park is known better for its colossal weekend market, **Vernisazh** (Вернисаж), than for its lush greenery. Arrive late Sunday afternoon, when people want to go home and are willing to make a deal. Comparison shop—the first painted box you see will not be the last, guaranteed. *Everything* is sold here, from carpets and samovars to military uniforms and old Soviet money. You'll also find jewelry, shawls, old books, t-shirts, and Russia's favorite folk art: painted wood—boxes, eggs, spoons, and cutting boards, all decorated with designs and flowers. And, of course, the ubiquitous *matryoshki*. *(M3: Izmaylovsky Park. Go left and follow the hordes. Open daily 9am-5:30pm.)*

OTHER PARKS. Although Moscow is filled with serene green areas, one of the largest and most popular with small children is **Krasnaya Presnya** (Красная Пресня), a leafy oasis with scattered playgrounds and wooden houses. With fewer hot dog and ice-cream kiosks than most other parks, Krasnaya Presnya caters mostly to the simple pleasures of the under-10 crowd. *(M6: Ulitsa 1905 goda. Walk down ul. 1905 goda until Mezhdunarodny and turn right.)* At the **Zoopark** (Зоопарк), you can see animals that are generally too big for their cages, and watch Russian children feed cotton candy to everything in reach. Animal lovers should stay away; it's a bit like watching calves caged for veal. *(On both sides of ul. Bolshaya Gruzinskaya (Большая Грузинская). Tel. 255 5375. Open Tu-Su 10am-8pm; kassa closes at 7pm. 15R.)*

MUSEUMS

Moscow boasts an impressive collection of museums of national and international stature; the most renowned are listed below. The **Moscow Metro,** one of the most beautiful in the world, is worth a tour of its own. All stations are unique, and those inside the Circle Line are elaborate, with mosaics, sculptures, stained glass, and crazy chandeliers. It's only 4R, and you can stay as long you as like, with no *babushka* in the corner to yell at you. Stations **Kievskaya, Mayakovskaya** (with lovely, not-entirely-socialist-realist ceiling murals), and **Ploshchadz Revolutsii** (with a statue on each step) are particularly good, as are **Komsomolskaya, Rimskaya,** and **Mendeleevskaya.** Note the atomic-model light fixtures in the Mendeleevskaya station. *(Open daily 6am-1am.)*

ART MUSEUMS

Tretyakov Gallery (Третьяковская Галерея), Lavrushensky per. 10 (Лаврушенский; tel. 230 7788), in Zamoskvareche. M7: Tretyakovskaya. Exiting the Metro, turn left and then left again, followed by an immediate right onto Tolmachevsky per. (Толмачевский пер). Walk two blocks and take a right onto Lavrushensky per. Founded through Tretyakov's 1892 donation of his private collection, this gallery is a veritable treasure chest of Russian national art. 18th- and 19th-century portraits and 19th-century landscapes comprise most of the collection. The heart of the gallery is its magnificent collection of icons, the subject of heated debate of late; many of the churches from which they were taken wish to reclaim them. Although the collection contains several modern works (including Malevich's immortal *Black Square*), the museum's shining star is the 12th-century Vladimir *Virgin Mary* icon, taken from Constantinople. The icon hung for centuries in the Kremlin's Assumption Cathedral, allegedly protecting Moscow from the Poles. Plan to spend several hours wandering through the more than 60 rooms. Open Tu-Su 10am-8pm. 175R, students 100R.

Pushkin Museum of Fine Arts (Muzey Izobrazitelnykh Iskusstv im. A.S. Pushkina; Музей Изобразительных Искусств им. А.С. Пушкина), ul. Volkhonka 12 (tel. 203 9578). M1: Kropotkinskaya. Across from the Cathedral of Christ the Redeemer. The museum houses a large collection of European Renaissance, Egyptian, and Classical art. Russia's second most famous art museum (after St. Petersburg's Hermitage), the Pushkin was founded in 1912 by poet Marina Tsvetaeva's father, who wanted his art students to have the opportunity to see original specimens of Classical art. Today—likely much to his chagrin—those originals hang alongside several mere reproductions. It gained the majority of its impressive exhibits after the October Revolution decreed that no museum would contain private possessions. The Egyptian art on the first floor and the French Impressionists (including some great Monets) on the second are the largest draws and most noteworthy collections. The aquamarine building to the left of the main entrance houses the three-floor **Museum of Private Collections,** which exhibits famous foreign and Russian art from the 19th and 20th centuries. The museum began when Ilya Siberstein donated his collection to the state and asked that it be placed in the old Prince Yard Hotel, frequented by Ilya Repin and Maxim Gorky. Open Tu-Su 10am-7pm; *kassa* closes at 6pm. Private Collection closes at 5pm. 150R, students 80R.

State Tretyakov Gallery (Gosudarstvennaya Tretyakovskaya Galereya; Государственная Третьяковская Галерея), ul. Krymskiy Val 10 (Крымский Вал; tel. 238 1378). M1, 4: Park Kultury. Directly opposite the Gorky Park entrance on the right side. Built to house newer works and exhibitions of Russian art, it shares a building with the Central House of Artists; the Tretyakov is the building in back, with an entrance to the right side. Comprehensive Russian art exhibits: the ground floor usually hosts contemporary art, while the 2nd floor showcases various 19th-century artists. The top floor contains the permanent exhibit, a huge retrospective of Russian art from 1910-1930, which intelligently describes the development of Socialist Realism (see **The Iron Curtain and the Cold War,** p. 10), a cubist fan's heaven. Behind the gallery to the right lies a makeshift **graveyard for fallen statues.** Once the main dumping ground for decapitated Lenins and Stalins, it now contains plaques and neat pathways to ease your journey among sculptures of Gandhi, Einstein, and Niels Bohr. Stalin himself, nose broken, lies uncomfortably on his elbow, and the unfortunate Khrushchev's head rolls in the grass. In the background, note the enormous statue of Peter the Great; a bronze atrocity, it is one of Moscow's most controversial monuments. Open Tu-Su 10am-8pm; *kassa* open until 7pm. 175R, students 100R.

Central House of Artists (Tsentralny Dom Khudozhnika; Центральный Дом Художника), ul. Krymsky Val 10 (tel. 238 9634). M1, 4: Park Kultury. In the same building as the State

Tretyakov Gallery (see above). Houses numerous small exhibits. Cutting-edge Russian art as well as fast-changing progressive historical exhibits. Consult *The Moscow Times* for info, or go to the auction hall and start a private collection of your own. Open Tu-Su 11am-8pm. *Kassa* closes at 7pm. 15R.

All-Russia Museum of Decorative and Applied Folk Art (Vsye-rossiysky Muzey Dekorativno-Prikladnovo; Все-российский Музей Декоративно-прикладного), Delegatskaya ul. 3 (Делегатская; tel. 923 1741 and 921 0139), just north of the Garden Ring. M8: Tsvetnoi Bulvar. This is what the junk they sell on the Arbat is supposed to look like. The first building, where you buy your tickets, contains rooms of fine-quality painted and lacquered wood, 17th- and 18th-century textiles, and samovars. The second building at ul. Delegatskaya 5 is more interesting—the first room juxtaposes traditional Russian peasant costumes of the last century with what the St. Petersburg glitterati were wearing in the same period. Open M-Th and Sa-Su 10am-6pm; last entrance at 5pm. Closed last Thursday of each month. 60R, students 25R.

Universal Art Gallery, Petrovsky bul. 14 (tel. 200 3827), on the premises of the Modern Drama Academy. M8: Tsvetnoi Bulvar. Impressive collection of Russian Impressionism and Realism from the 1930s-60s, including works by Radimov and Ioganson. Socialist Realist paintings and graphics. Open M-F 2-7:30pm, Sa 2-5pm.

ART GALLERIES

Manezh (Манеж), Manezhnaya pl. (Манежная; tel. 202 8250). M1: Okhotny Ryad. A big yellow building with white columns across from the main entrance to the Alexander Gardens. Enter from the north end, on the square. A one-time riding school for the military is now the Central Exhibition Hall and often features interesting modern Russian exhibits.Open M-Sa noon-7pm. Special exhibits are usually open 10am-6pm.

Exhibition Hall of the Russian Academy of Art, ul. Prechistenka 21/12 (tel. 201 7425). M1: Kropotkinskaya, near the Pushkin Literary Museum, two to three blocks down on the left side. A well-visited exhibit hall displays the work of trendy artists, including some from the Soviet period. Exhibits change periodically. Open W-F noon-8pm, Sa-Su 10am-6pm. *Kassa* closes 1hr. earlier. 60R, students 25R.

MARS Gallery, ul. Malaya Filevskaya 32 (Малая Филевская; tel. 146 8426; fax 146 6331). M3: Pionerskaya. Widely known for contemporary and avant-garde art. Check *The Moscow Times* for exhibits. Open Tu-Su noon-8pm.

SpiderMouse, Leningradsky pr. 58 (tel. 287 1360; email spider@ica.msk.ru). M2: Aeroport. The most cutting-edge gallery in Moscow. If the name doesn't clue you in to the über-hipness of this basement space, the sophisticated (or incomprehensible) installations will. Open Th-Sa 5-8pm.

HISTORICAL MUSEUMS

Central Museum of the Revolution (Muzey Revolyutsii; Музей Революции), ul. Tverskaya 21 (tel. 299 6724). M6: Pushkinskaya. Exiting the Metro, walk one block uphill on Tverskaya and walk through the gates on the left. Housed in the former mansion of the Moscow English club, covers Russian history from the revolution to today in exhausting detail. Perhaps a sign of the ever-changing times, this Soviet archive complements its Cold War propaganda posters with newly displayed statistics on the ill effects of socialism. Even their beat-up trolley has a recent story to tell: it was the one damaged in the August 1991 coup that clinched Yeltsin's support. The museum shop on the 1st floor best reflects a revolutionizing Russia. One of the best places to buy Soviet medals, this store also stocks old posters and t-shirts with slogans like "The Party is Over." Museum open Tu, Th, and Sa 10am-6pm, W 11am-7pm, Su 10am-5pm. 10R.

State Historical Museum, Krasnaya pl. 1 (924 4529). M2, 3: Ploshchadz Revolutsii. Across from Lenin's Tomb in Red Square. Although only a fraction of the museum's galleries have re-opened after an 11-year renovation, the exhibits that are open are impressive, tracing Russian history from the Neanderthals to the Kievan Rus dynasty to modern Russia. Unclear whether the huge rhinoceros is also supposed to be Russian. Two highlights are new additions: an exhibition hall devoted to the Tsars (including both portraits and thrones) and a cinema showing Western and Russian films. Open M and W-Su 11am-7pm; last entrance at 6pm. Closed the first Monday of the month. 120R, students 60R.

Central Museum of the Armed Forces of the USSR (Tsentralny Muzey Vooruzhennykh Sil SSSR; Центральный Музей Вооруженных Сил СССР), ul. Sovetskoy Armii 2 (Советской Армии; tel. 281 4877). M4: Novoslobodskaya, then walk 10min. down ul. Seleznevskaya (Селезневская) to the square/rotary. Pass a huge theater on your left, and bear right at the fork. The museum is 1 block down on the right. Tanks, guns, and propaganda posters from WWII, including the milepost 41 marker from the Moscow-Leningrad highway, the closest the Nazis ever got to Moscow. Open W-Su 10am-5pm. Closed second Tuesday and the last week of each month. 90R, students 40R.

Borodino, Kutuzovsky pr. 38 (tel. 148 1967). M3: Kutuzovskaya, then 10min. to the right down Kutuzovsky pr. A giant statue of Commander Kutuzov stands in front of the large circular building that houses the Borodino panorama and museum. Commemorating the bloody battle against Napoleon in August 1812 (see **History,** p. 552), the 360° painting and accompanying exhibitions usually draw long lines. Open M-Th and Sa-Su 10am-4:45pm. Closed last Thursday of each month. 60R.

Museum of the Great Patriotic War (Muzey Otechestvennoy Voyny; Музей Отечественной Войны), pl. Pobedy (tel. 449 8044). M3: Kutuzovsky. Devoted to the soldiers and heroes of the "Great Patriotic War" (WWII). This was one of Mayor Luzhkov's most ambitious building projects, and he succeeded more at making it look like a shopping mall than a museum. In the park behind the museum is the **Museum of War Technology** (Muzey Voyennoy Tekhniki; Музей Военной Техники), an outdoor display of several WWII fighter planes and helicopters, including an American Douglas DC-3 that was given to the Russians. Open Tu-Su 10am-6pm. Free.

Bakhrushin Theater Museum, ul. Bakhrushina 31 (Бахрушина; tel. 953 44 70). M2 or 4: Paveletskaya, and turn left (across the street from the station). One of the numerous theater museums in Moscow, it celebrates one of Russia's great art forms with a chronologically arranged permanent exhibit of costumes, dressers, programs, photos, and intricately crafted theatrical creations. The pamphlet at the desk tells you everything, in English. Open M noon-6pm, Tu-Su noon-7pm. 5R.

HOUSES OF THE LITERARY AND FAMOUS

Russians take immense pride in their formidable literary history, preserving authors' houses in their original state, down to half-empty teacups on the mantelpiece. Each is guarded by a team of fiercely loyal *babushki*. Plaques on buildings throughout the city mark where writers, poets, artists, and philosophers lived and worked; the highest concentration of homes is in Zamlyonoy Gorod.

Lev Tolstoy Estate, ul. Lva Tolstovo 21 (Льва Толстого; tel. 246 9444). M1, 4: Park Kultury. Exiting the Metro, walk down Komsomolsky pr. toward the colorful Church of St. Nicholas of the Weavers; turn right at the corner on ul. Lva Tolstovo. The estate is three blocks up on the left. The author lived here in the winters of 1882-1901. One of the most perfectly preserved house-museums in Moscow–it seems as if the author and his family have just stepped out for a walk and will be back at any moment. Tolstoy was apparently a man of habit; he always drank barley or acorn coffee, dined at 6pm every evening, and when writing *The Resurrection* sat in the study here between exactly 9am and 3pm every day, without once raising his head from the page. Tolstoy's 13 children are well-represented, too, providing a more comprehensive sense of the author as a father. Helpful explanations of each of the rooms are provided in English. The *kassa* is to the right of the entrance gate or, if that is closed, in a small building down a path to the left, inside the entrance. Open in summer Tu-Su 10am-6pm; *kassa* open until 5pm. Off-season 10am-3:30pm. Closed last Friday of the month. 50R, students 5R.

The White House. M4: Krasnopresnenskaya. From the Metro, take a left and follow the trail of red ribbons and makeshift monuments. You can't visit this symbol of the 1993 political upheaval but since you've probably already seen it on TV, stroll by and see what it's like in times of relative peace. Yeltsin climbed atop a tank here, brandishing the flag of the Russian Federation, and declared himself the only legitimate ruler of the country. Not long after, Yeltsin switched positions when he bombarded an anti-reformist Parliament with cannonfire during the October 1993 coup. The building has since been renovated, but if you look closely you can still see bullet holes in the fence.

Tolstoy Museum, ul. Prechistenka 11 (Пречистенка). M1: Kropotkinskaya. From the Metro, walk three blocks down Prechistenka in the opposite direction from the Cathedral of Christ the Savior; the museum is on the left. This airy yellow and white building in the neighborhood of Tolstoy's first Moscow residence has been carefully constructed to showcase purely his literary genius. Individual rooms are dedicated to his major works, including *War and Peace, Anna Karenina,* and *The Resurrection,* and display original text, paintings, letters, and historical documents providing clues as to the motivation behind Tolstoy's legendary masterpieces. Literature buffs should take note of the numerous portraits of Pushkin's daughter, the physical model for Anna Karenina. Each room contains explanations in English, and the *babushki* will earnestly point out anything you may have missed. Open Tu-W 10am-6pm; *kassa* closes at 5pm. 40R, students 20R.

Gorky's Apartment, ul. Malaya Nikitskaya 6/2 (Малая Никитская; tel. 290 5130). M3: Arbatskaya. From the Metro, cross Novy Arbat and turn right onto Merzlyakovsky per. (Мерзляковский пер). When you get to the small park, cross through it and the apartment will be directly across from you. Entrance is on the street just to the left on ul. Apiridonova through the small courtyard. A pilgrimage site more for its architectural interest than for its collection of Maxim Gorky's possessions. Designed by Shekhtel in 1906, this is one of the best examples of Art Nouveau. The main staircase is modeled to project the feeling and movement of waves on the sea. Each room contains explanatory information in English. Open W and F noon-7pm, Th and Sa-Su 10am-5pm. Closed last Thursday of the month. Free; 5-10R donations are requested.

Mayakovsky Museum (Muzey im B.B. Mayakovskovo; Музей им. В. В. Маяковского), Lubyansky pr. 3/6 (Лубянский; tel. 921 9560). M1, 7: Lubyanka. Look for the bust of Mayakovsky surrounded by huge crimson metal shards; the museum hides in the building behind it. The avant-garde poet and artist lived here in a communal apartment from 1919. His room is preserved at the top of the building, the eye of a storm of steel girders and shards of glass, chronicling his initial love affair with the Revolution (communist propaganda wallpapers the museum) and his travels abroad. His apartment is a fascinating achievement in Futurist museum design: chairs sit at bizarre angles and hang from the walls, convoluted red metal in the shape of fire climbs the spiral staircase, and green paint spills everywhere. Mayakovsky shot himself in this flat in 1930. Open M-Tu and F-Su 10am-6pm, Th 1-9pm. 30R, tour 850R.

Stanislavsky Museum-House (Muzey-dom Stanislavskovo; Музей-дом Станиславского), Leontyevsky per. 6 (Леонтьевский; tel. 229 2442 and 229 2885). M6: Pushkinskaya. Walk down ul. Tverskaya and take a right onto ul. Leontevsky. The respected theater director held lessons in his home, the rooms of which have different themes. More interesting than his upstairs apartment, however, are the collections of costumes in the basement used for famous productions of Gogol's *Government Inspector* and Shakespeare's *Othello.* Open Th and Sa-Su 11am-6pm, W and F 11am-8pm. Closed last Thursday of each month. 60R.

Pushkin Literary Museum (Literaturny Muzey Pushkina; Литературный Музей Пушкина), ul. Prechisterka 12 (Пречистерка), at the corner of Khrushchevsky per. (Хрущевский). M1: Kropotkinskaya. If you haven't seen Pushkin-worship first-hand, this carefully tended museum will either convert or frighten you. See Pushkin's thrilling first editions, as well as his famous drawings and marginalia. The museum was closed in summer 1999 for renovations but is expected to reopen by summer 2000.

Chekhov's House Museum, ul. Sadovaya-Kudrinskaya 6. M6: Barrikadnaya. Chekhov lived here from 1886 until 1890, both writing and receiving patients—but you won't get as good a feel for the author/doctor as he did for the Russian psyche. Open Tu, Th, and Sa-Su 11am-6pm, W and F 2-7pm; last entrance 1hr. earlier. Closed last day of each month and if the temperature drops much below zero.

Lermontov House-Museum (Dom-muzey Lermontova; Дом-музей Лермонтова), ul. Malaya Molchanovka 2 (Малая Молчановка; tel. 291 5298), off Novy Arbat. M3: Arbatskaya. Pushkin's fiery poetic heir lived in this small house—appropriately preserved and guarded. Enter through the white gate to see another example of fairly well-to-do 19th-century life. Open Th and Sa-Su 11am-6pm, W and F 2-8pm. Closed last Friday of each month. 30R.

Gogol Museum (Музей Гоголя), Nikitsky bul. 7 (tel. 291 1240). M3: Arbatskaya. Cross Novy Arbat and take the first right onto Nikitsky bul. through the large courtyard on the left; the entrance is on the right. Only 2 small rooms inside a library, but it provides a glimpse of the brilliant 19th-century writer's life and his meager possessions–without costing a ruble. Open M and W-F noon-6:45pm, Sa-Su noon-3:45pm.

ENTERTAINMENT

Moscow is a large, fast-paced metropolis, with the recreation options to prove it. Renowned theater, opera, and ballet provide a healthy injection of culture to go with *Tverskaya Tyomnaya* on the street. Fortunately for movie-goers, many new movie theaters offer imports in their original English. Of these, **American House of Theater,** Radisson-Slavjanskaya Hotel (tel. 941 8747; M4: Kievskaya) is the largest. The *eXile* provides detailed theater listings and show times. **Moskva Movie Theater,** Triumphalnaya pl. 1 (tel. 251 5860), to Mayakovsky's left, is the only cinema in Moscow that consistently shows new Russian films, even when they're pretty awful. (US$4.) **Muzey Kino,** Drushinikovskaya ul. 15, tucked around on the left side of the Cinema Center building (M6: Krasnopresnenskaya), shows film classics, some of which are subtitled. Check the Friday *Moscow Times* for listings.

THEATER, BALLET, & OPERA

Summer is the wrong season for theater in Moscow. Russian companies not on vacation are usually on tour and the only folks playing in Moscow are touring productions from other cities, which, with the exception of those from St. Petersburg, tend to be of lesser quality. Starting in September and running well through June, however, Moscow boasts some of the world's undisputed best theater, ballet, and opera, as well as excellent orchestras. If you buy tickets far enough in advance and don't demand front row center, you can attend very cheaply (US$2-5). Tickets can usually be purchased from the *kassa* located inside the theater. (Usually open noon until right before the performance.) Tickets to most events are also sold at the "Театры" kiosks around the city.

Scalpers and Intourist (see **Tours,** p. 566) often snatch up tickets to performances at the Bolshoy and the Tchaikovsky Concert Hall, so if you have no luck at the box office, hang outside the theater. Scalpers look around a lot and ask if tickets are needed with the not-so-subtle *"Bilety nada?"* or *"Bilety nyzhny?"* ("Need tickets?"). Haggle over what you think is a fair price. Always check back at the *kassa* to be sure you're not getting hosed. At the *kassa*, ask for the cheapest tickets *("samiy deshoviy")*, which usually go for 30-250R at the Bolshoy Theater and 30-100R at the Tchaikovsky Concert Hall.

Bolshoy Teatr, Teatralnaya pl. 1 (Большой Театр; tel. 292 0050; fax 292 9032). M2: Teatralnaya. Literally, "The Big Theater." Home to both the opera and the world-renowned ballet companies, Bolshoy performances are consistently excellent. Champagne and caviar served at intermission under crystal chandeliers. *Kassa* open noon-7pm. Daily performances Sept.-June at 7pm. Tickets 30-1000R.

Maly Teatr, Teatralnaya pl. 1/6 (Малый Театр; tel. 923 2621). M2: Teatralnaya. Just north of the Bolshoy. Affiliate at Bolshaya Ordynka 69. The "Small Theater" shows a different production every night, mostly Russian classics of the 19th and 20th centuries, including Tolstoy and Chekhov. All performances in Russian. *Kassa* open Tu-Su 12:30-3pm and 4-6:30pm. Daily performances at 7pm. Tickets start at 20-35R.

Musical Operetta Theater, ul. Bolshaya Dmitrovka 6 (tel. 292 6377), just east of the Bolshoy. Completes the M2: Teatralnaya theater triumverate. Famous operettas staged year-round. Performances begin at 7pm. Tickets 25-250R.

Tchaikovsky Conservatory's Big and Small Halls, Triumfalnaya pl. 4/31 (tel. 229 0378). M2: Mayakovskaya. During intermission, locals sneak into the Bolshoy Zal (Grand Hall;

Большой Зал) to admire its pipe organ and chandeliers. Scalpers may lie and say no tickets are available when the *kassa* will sell them more cheaply. Concerts almost daily at 7pm plus Sunday at 2pm. *Kassa* in big hall open daily noon-7pm. Tickets can range from 100 to several thousand rubles, depending on the program. Back-row tickets for the Maly Zal (Small Hall; Малый Зал) just 5R.

Leninsky Komsomol (LENKOM), ul. Malaya Dmitrovka 6 (tel. 299 9668). M6: Pushkinskaya. Director Mark Zakharov is well known in Russia and attracts crowds to see dramas such as *Figaro* and *Chaika* and bright, Broadway-style musicals. Performances noon and 7pm. *Kassa* open daily 1-3pm and 5-7pm. Tickets around 50-150R.

Taganka Theater (tel. 915 1217). M4, 6: Taganskaya. Directly across the street from the ring line exit. This avant-garde theater is the only reason to come to this oppressive square on the loud and dusty Garden Ring. *Kassa* open daily 1-3 and 5-7pm.

Stanislavsky Theater, ul. Tverskaya 23 (tel. 299 7224). M2: Tverskaya. Mostly avant-garde productions. *Kassa* open in winter daily noon-7pm.

CIRCUS

Great Moscow Circus, pr. Vernadskovo 7. M1: Universitet. It was the greatest show on earth, but all the big stars defected or died; now it's the greatest show in Moscow. Performances Tu-F 7pm, Sa-Su 11:30am, 3, and 7pm. *Kassa* open daily 11am-3pm and 4-7pm. Tickets start at 50R, children under 6 free.

Old State Moscow Circus, Tsvetnoi Bulvar 13 (tel. 200 0668). M8: Tsvetnoi Bulvar. Turn right and walk half a block; it's on the right, newly renovated. Traditional street circus. Animal acts in the first half and a glittery acrobatic performance in the second. Great for non-Russophones. Don't miss the motorcycle acrobat act of Oleshchenko and Shavro or Piotr Prostetsov's trained dogs. Erotic dancers complete the spectacle. Shop around among the eager scalpers outside. Performances M and W-F 7pm, Sa 7 and 8pm, Su 1, 3, and 7pm. *Kassa* open daily 11am-7pm. Tickets 100-150R.

BANYAS

If weeks of traveling on sweltering, crowded trains and living out of a backpack crammed with smelly t-shirts have you feeling not-so-fresh, a trip to a Russian *banya* is in order. Similar in theory to a Turkish bath, the *banya* experience is a cyclical whirlwind of hot and cold extremes that rejuvenate via shock therapy. Segregated by sex, the men's and women's sections of each *banya* are divided into four rooms. First stop is the dressing room, staffed by attendants who rent linen, assign places, and sell drinks and snacks. Next comes the shower room, the self-explanatory step. The *paulka* (steam room) is the third and most lavishly praised room of the *banya.* With temperatures upwards of 110°F and the steamy air thick with the fragrance of scented oils, the steam's magic will draw out your tensions, along with a lot of sweat. Before you pass out, escape to the cooling relief of the dipping pool, designed to quickly lower the body temperature. The final stage is a return to the *paulka,* this time engaging in the quasi-masochistic tradition of the birch branches. While showering, soften a bundle of birch branches with hot water, then beat yourself vigorously to exfoliate dead skin, improve circulation, or simply blend in with the locals. *Banya* sessions typically last two hours; prices are listed for the standard experience, but myriad other services, including massages and manicures, can be enjoyed at an additional cost. Save a few rubles by bringing a towel, sheet, and soap and shampoo.

Sandunovsky Bani (Сандуновские Бани), ul. Neglinnaya 14 (Неглиння; tel. 925 4631), one block behind the main building. M1: Kuznetsky Most. Moscow's oldest and most luxurious *banya* features high ceilings, clean and cavernous rooms, and classical statues. 2hr. sessions 150-250R, depending on level of luxury. A full range of extra services available, with massages starting at 150R. Open daily 8am-10pm.

Bani Na Presnye (Бани На Пресне), Stolyarnii per. 7 (Столярни; tel. 255 0115). Large but sparsely decorated, this modern *banya* is crowded on weekends. Ice-cold dipping pool and refreshing lemon-infused chai tea (25R a pot). 2hr. sessions 200R, more on weekends. Open M and W-Su 8am-10pm, Tu 2-10pm.

Astrakhanskye (Астраханские), Astrakhansky per. 5/9 (Астраханский; tel. 280 4329). M4: Prospekt Mira. A 20min. walk from the Traveller's Guest House. Less extravagant but no less effective than the other *banyi;* no dipping pool means you cool off in the shower. 2hr. session 175R. Massages start at 100R. Open Tu-Su 8am-11pm.

NIGHTLIFE

Moscow's nightlife boasts the most kickin' action this side of the Volga, and certainly the most varied, expensive, and dangerous in Eastern Europe. While Moscow may not be New York or London, it certainly thinks it is—with the cover charges to prove it (usually 100R). Restaurants often transform into dance clubs after dark, while myriad casinos stay open all hours of the night. Check the weekend editions of *The Moscow Times* or *The Moscow Tribune* for club reviews and music festival listings, including the annual jazz festival. *The Moscow Times's* Friday pull-out section, *MT Out*, provides an excellent synopsis of each week's events, as well as up-to-date restaurant, bar, and club reviews. Cheaper and more popular bars on isolated streets may be a better time than the dark, *faux*-elegant, and fully expensive "bars" close to the center, which cater to New Russians or to no one at all.

HUNGRY FOR MORE Almost as much of a Moscow landmark as the Kremlin, the Hungry Duck was known internationally for its debaucherous parties and Sodom-and-Gomorresque Ladies' Nights. Women were cattle-called into the bar hours before men to consume mass quantities of alcohol and participate in strip shows and bar-dancing. By the time the women were too drunk to protest, hordes of desperate men—American backpackers, mafiosos, and Russian businessmen alike—were let loose, and the floodgates of testosterone were opened. If the live sex shows weren't enough, bathrooms, bars, and not-so-dark corners all became impromptu bordellos as the masses got busy to the sonic sex pulsing over the sound system. Floors were sticky with sweat, vomit, and God knows what other bodily fluids while bathrooms were crowded with heaps of limp drunks. By the end of a Ladies' Night, over 200 people would get laid, at least three plastered women would have to be carried out of the bar, and more than a few fights broke out. Sadly (or maybe not so), the Hungry Duck closed without explanation in 1999, leaving Moscow nightlife with quite a void to fill. The capitalist mastermind behind this pumping, thumping den of sin (Ladies' Night racked in millions of rubles), has opened a new venue, the Chesterfield Cafe, but it's unclear whether this subdued expat haunt can become Moscow's next Babylon.

KITAI-GOROD

Propaganda, Bolshoy Zlatoustinsky per. 7 (Большой Златоустинский; tel. 924 5732). M5, 6: Kitai-Gorod. Exiting the Metro, walk down ul. Maroseika and take a left on Bolshoy Zlatoustinksy per.; the club is on the right. Once voted one of the best clubs in Europe, Propaganda is the best place in Moscow to dance without feeling like you're in a meat market. Hip, unpretentious student crowd boogies to top American and European DJs. Hopping, even on Sunday, but gets extraordinarily hot. Beers 50-65R. Cover F-Sa 70R. Open M-Th and Su noon-2am, F-Sa noon-6am.

Fiesta, Pushechnaya ul. 9 (923 6158). M1: Kuznetsky Most. Just left of the Metro station. A worthy successor to the internationally infamous Hungry Duck (see **"Hungry for More,"** attached). Tuesday and Friday are Ladies' Night: women drink free while watching male strippers. Wednesday is Octoberfest: all-you-can-drink beer for 200R. Thursday is Latin Night: 2-for-1 Corona and an erotic dance by a 250-pound woman thrown in for good measure. Beers 60-90R. Cover for men 100R, women 30R. Open daily 6pm-6am.

Respublika-Respublika, ul. Nikolskaya 17 (tel. 928 4692). M2, 3: Pl. Revolutsii. Follow the signs to ul. Nikolskaya and walk away from Red Square. The bar is well-marked, on the left side of the street. A new addition to Moscow nightlife. Great dance music, spacious layout, and a student crowd. Beers 60R. No cover. Open daily 6pm-6am.

Chesterfield Cafe, Zemlyanoi val 26 (tel. 917 0150). M3: Kurskaya, opposite the train station. About as American as you can get in Moscow, prices included. Packed on weekends. Beer 70-110R. Cover Su-Th for men 50R, women free; F-Sa 60R, 50R. Open daily noon-6am.

ARBAT

Sports Bar, Novy Arbat 10 (tel. 290 4311). M3: Arbatskaya. A true paradise for Eurosport fans: 8 TVs at the bar and a large screen so you can catch it from every angle. The two floors fill up fast for big games; at other times, the second floor is the place to shoot pool, throw darts, and watch New Russians compare their New Cellular Phones. The disco is a late-night hotspot. Higher drink prices than your neighborhood sports bar—think 100R per beer. Live music nightly 8-11pm. Happy Hour 5-8pm featuring 2-for-1 beer. Bar open daily noon-6am; disco 11pm-6am. AmEx/MC/Visa.

Master, ul. Pavlovskaya 6 (Парлобская; tel. 237 1742). M3: Arbatskaya. Mostly filled with student types, but New Russians are learning the ins and outs of techno, too. Come on Friday, when it's packed. Upstairs is hard-core techno, downstairs commercial techno, everywhere is techno, techno. Cover M-Th and Su men 60R, women 30R; F-Sa US$20, US$10. Open daily 11pm-7am.

NEAR THE PUSHKIN MUSEUM OF FINE ARTS

Krizis Zhanra, Bolshoy Vladsyevsky per. 4 (Пречистенский; tel. 241 1928). M1: Kropotkenskaya. From the Metro, walk down ul. Prechistenka (Пречистенка) away from Church of Christ the Savior down Gogolevskii bul. Take a left onto Gagarinskii per. and after 5min. turn left onto Vladsyevsky. The bar is hidden in the first courtyard on the left. One of the best places in Moscow to grab a beer. Extremely popular with local and foreign students. Live concerts pack 'em in daily 7-10pm—arrive early. Czech beers 50R. Open daily noon-midnight.

Rosie O'Grady's, ul. Znamenko 9/12 (Знаменко; tel. 203 9087). M8: Borovitskaya. Go right out of the Metro, then right on ul. Znamenko. Rosie's is on the left, at ul. Marxa i Engelsa. Typical Irish pub frequented by American and British expats, with the occasional Russian yuppie. *Baltika* 50R, Guinness 100R. Open daily noon-late.

ZAMOSKVARECHE AND GORKY PARK

TaxMan, Krymsky Val. 6 (Крымский Вал; tel. 238 0864). M5: Oktyabrskaya. Exiting the Metro, walk downhill on Krymsky val. TaxMan is on the right side of the Central House of Artists, opposite the entrance to Gorky Park. Inexpensive drinks and musical variety attract students. Pool tables and an arm-wrestling table for a little healthy competition. Draft beer 40R. Cover varies. Open daily noon-6am.

Moosehead Canadian Bar, ul. Bolshaya Polyanka 54 (Большая Полянка; tel./fax 230 7333). M4: Dobryninskaya. Take a left exiting the Metro onto Bolshaya Polyanka; Moosehead is in a little enclave on your left. Loud, nondescript Western bar could be in any North American city, from Winnipeg to Williamstown. Best Buffalo wings in Moscow (3 for US$1 every W). Beers US$2-3. Happy Hour M-F 6-8pm. Open Su-Th noon-1am, F-Sa 3pm-5am.

M7: TRETYAKOVSKAYA

Bednye Lyudi (Бедные Люди; Poor Folks), ul. Bolshaya Ordynka 11/6 (Большая Ордынка; tel. 951 3342). M7: Tretyakovskaya. Follow the signs to ul. Bolshaya Ordynka out of the Metro, and walk toward Red Square. The club is on a side street to the right. Converted basement has live rock/alternative nightly. Separate rooms for dancing, chatting, and billiards make it a favorite haunt for young Russians. Beer 20-55R. Cover Su-Th 60R; F-Sa 100R. Open daily 5pm-5am.

Trety Put' (Третий Путь), ul. Pyatnitskaya 4 (Пятницкая; tel 231 8734). M7: Tretyakovskaya. Welcome to your Greenwich-Village-loft-turned-nightclub-and-bar, featuring a number of little rooms where you can watch videos, play chess, or dance to psychedelic music. Live house, techno, and experimental music. Young grunge and alternative crowd. Cover hovers around 20R. Open Th-Sa 9pm-2am.

OUTSIDE THE CENTER

Chance (Шанс), ul. Volocharskovo 11/5 (Волочарского; tel. 956 7102), in Dom Kultury Serp i Molot (Дом Культуры Серп и Молот). M7: Ploshchad Ilicha. Walk down ul. Sergia Radonezhskovo all the way through the third open driveway on your right. When you see tram tracks on the road, turn and walk up the stairs. It's on top of the hill, straight ahead. The oldest and most popular gay club in Moscow, with 3 bars, a restaurant, nightly strip shows, and aquariums–some with naked men in them. Although the club is popular with everyone and the crowd is a mixture of ravers, punks, students, and New Russians, it's 90% gay. Downstairs is dance music, upstairs Russian pop. Plush sofas ensure you get to know even those too timid to dance. Very Euro–black attire is *de rigeur.* Beers 40-60R. Cover after midnight US$5. Open daily 11pm-5am.

John Bull Pub, Kutuzovsky pr. 4 (tel. 243 56 88). M4: Kievskaya. Take a left; it's behind the Ukraine hotel. Another expat favorite. An English pub with US$5 draft beers. Live pop bands, karaoke, blues, and jazz nights. Open Su-Th noon-midnight, F-Sa noon-3am. AmEx/MC/Visa.

NEAR MOSCOW: SERGIEV POSAD (СЕРГИЕВ ПОСАД)

Possibly Russia's most famous pilgrimage point, Sergiev Posad attracts wandering Orthodox believers with a mass of churches huddled at its main sight—**St. Sergius's Trinity Monastery** (Troitsko-Sergieva Lavra; Троицко-Сергиева Лавра). During Soviet times, Sergiev Posad was called Zagorsk, and the town is still called this by many locals. Approximately 60km from Moscow, it's the closest town on the Golden Ring to the capital. After decades of state-propagated atheism, the stunning monastery, founded in the 1340s, has again become a religious center, and monks pace the paths between the colorful collection of churches and gardens. The patriarch of the Russian Orthodox Church, also known as the Metropolitan, resided here until 1988, when he moved to the Danilovsky Monastery in Moscow (see **Monasteries, Churches, & Synagogues,** p. 578). Although entrance into the *lavra* (the highest monastic order) is free, there are separate fees for the wall's ramparts, the folk art exhibit, the art museum, and the historical museum. Those wishing to photograph the site must pay 100R for the privilege—if you don't plan on taking pictures, be sure to keep your camera out of sight or you'll be charged anyway. Each church is exquisite, but Russian Orthodoxy's opulent colors come out in the **Trinity Cathedral,** where the numerous covered heads and quickly crossing hands captivate the visitor as much as the gilded Andrei Rublyov icons. The **Refectory** delights with its breath-taking display of ecclesiastical opulence, including a magnificently frescoed ceiling. The **Chapel-at-the-Well** has an appropriately superstitious history—one day, a spring with magical healing powers allegedly appeared inside a tiny chapel in the monastery. *Babushki* still come here with empty bottles to carry the holy water home. Next door, **Assumption Cathedral** (Uspensky Sobor; Успенский Собор), was modeled after the eponymous cathedral in Moscow's Kremlin and proves it's equal in splendor. Outside the door on the left is the grave of Boris Godunov, who, among other things, has the distinction of being the only Russian tsar not buried in Moscow's Kremlin or St. Petersburg's St. Peter and Paul Cathedral. As with any active Orthodox monastery, women should respectfully cover their heads.-

RUSSIA

GETTING THERE. *Elektrichki* (commuter trains) run to Sergiev Posad from **Moscow's Yaroslavsky Vokzal** (1½hr., every 30-40min., 25R round-trip). Departure times are listed on a white board immediately outside the *prigorodnaya kassa* (suburban cashier; пригородная касса), where the tickets are sold. Any train with the destination "Sergiev Posad" or "Aleksandrov" (Александров) will get you there. The announcement boards in front of the trains often do not work, but tiny strips on the sides of the trains show their destinations. Alternatively, purchase a 12R one-way train ticket there and catch the "Москва-ВВЦ" bus outside the main Sergiev Posad *kassa* (10R, every 15min.).

GOLDEN RING (ЗОЛОТОЕ КОЛЬЦО)

To the north and west of Moscow lie a series of towns known as the Golden Ring (Zolotoye Koltso), home to ancient churches and kremlins widely considered to be the most beautiful in Russia. Many of them reached their zenith in the 12th century, as power shifted north with the weakening of Kiev, and have spent the subsequent years trying to maintain their importance in a constantly changing nation. Vladimir and Suzdal were once Russian capitals, and still maintain kremlins of extraordinary elegance; Yaroslavl was the capital of its own principality in the 13th century and is today one of the most pleasant and attractive cities in Russia. An array of architectural monuments and slow pace of life make the Golden Ring a truly unique part of Russia.

YAROSLAVL (ЯРОСЛАВЛЬ)

Yaroslavl (yi-ra-SLAH-vl) acquired its wealth and prosperity from 16th-century trade with the Middle East and the West, and has fought hard to have things its own way. Case in point: when Prince Yaroslav the Wise considered settling here, the townspeople chased him out of town with a wild bear. This century, the citizens of Yaroslavl have fought just as fiercely to ward off Soviet architectural monstrosities. With its wide, green boulevards, romantic river walks, numerous parks, and proximity to Moscow, Yaroslavl offers the best of two worlds—provincial charm with capital-city comforts.

ORIENTATION

Yaroslavl lies on the west bank of the **Volga** river, 280km northeast of Moscow. It straddles the **Kotorosl** river, with most of the sights and churches along the north bank. Locals call the corner where the Kotorosl meets the Volga *strelka* (the promontory; стрелка). From Glavny Vokzal, the **main train station** (Главный Вокзал), ul. Svobody (Свободьи) leads to the center at **pl. Volkova,** the origin of most bus lines. Ul. Kirova (Кирова) runs east out of this square toward the Volga. **Ul. Komsomolskaya** (Комсомольская) and **ul. Pervomayskaya** (Первомайская) are the center's main north-south thoroughfares; at the southern end the streets converge on **pl. Bogoyavlenskaya** (Богоявленская). Here, the six-lane Moskovsky pr. (Московский лр) runs south across the Kotorsol to **Moskovsky Vokzal,** the secondary train and primary bus station. From Moskovsky Vokzal, cross Moskovsky pr. and take trolley #9 three stops to pl. Volkova. From Glavny Vokzal, trolley #1 will bring you to pl. Volkova in six stops. In an attempt to avoid name-change confusion, street signs often list a whole genealogy of names, resulting in posts bearing up to four different plates. Cyrillic **maps** of the center are sold at Gostinitsa Volga (10R; see **Accommodations,** p. 592). It's best to avoid Yaroslavl around June 20th, commencement day for the town's two military academies.

PRACTICAL INFORMATION

Trains: Glavny Vokzal (tel. 79 21 12 and 79 21 11), connected to pl. Volkova by trolley #1. Trains run to: **Vologda** (4hr., 2-3 per day, 40-43R); **Moscow** (4½hr., 13 per day, 44-48R); and **St. Petersburg** (12hr., 2 per day, 80-113R). From **Moskovsky Vokzal,** on trolley lines #5 and 9 from Bogoyavlenskaya pl., trains leave for: **Nizhny Novgorod** (9½hr., 1 per day, 65R). *Kassa* #4 open 24hr. You're best off, however, buying a round-trip ticket in Moscow.

Buses: Avtovokzal, to your left as you exit Moskovsky Vokzal. Buses to: **Vologda** (5hr., 1 per day, 52R) and **Vladimir** (6hr., 1 per day, 45R).

Local Transportation: Yaroslavl's local transportation system is excellent, by Russian standards; trolleys and buses stop every 2min. Trolley #9 runs up and down Moskovsky pr. through pl. Volkova to Leninsky pr. (Ленинский). Trolley #1 travels from Glavny Vokzal to the center. Buy tickets (1R) at the light-blue kiosks next to main stops labeled "яргортранс продажа проездных документов"; once aboard hand your ticket to the person with the black waist pouch. 8R fine for being caught ticketless.

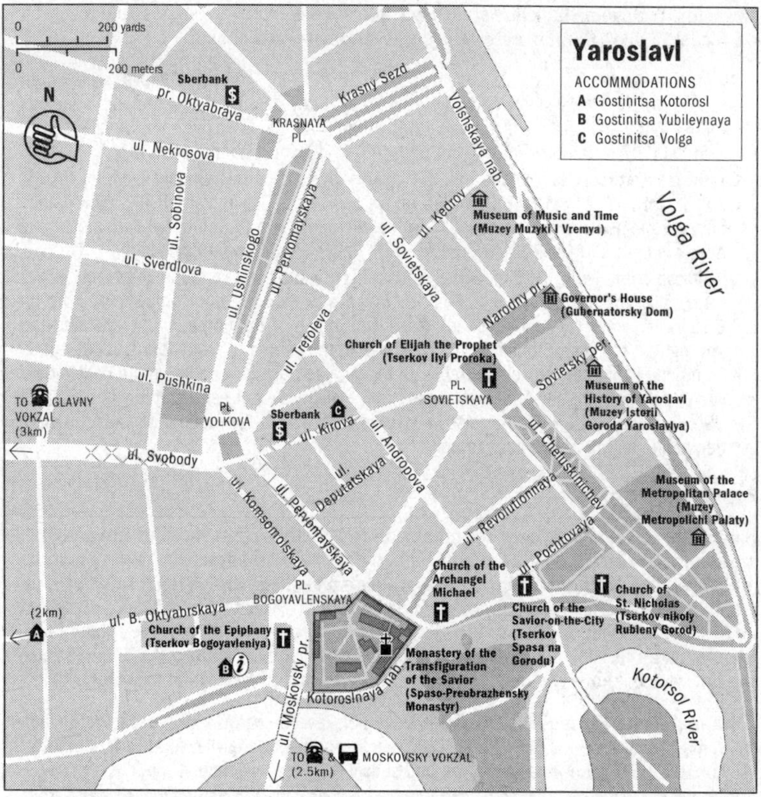

Tourist Office: Intourist, Kotoroslnaya nab. 11a (Которосльная; tel. 22 93 06 and 30 50 58; fax 30 54 13), on the 1st floor of Gostinitsa Yubileynaya. English-speaking staff will lead tours, sell pamphlets, or book hotel rooms for less than most places, but for a commission.

Currency Exchange: One of the best options is **Sberbank,** ul. Kirova 16, which also cashes AmEx and Thomas Cook **traveler's checks** for a 3% commission. Open M-Th 8:30am-1pm and 2-6:30pm, F 8:30am-1pm and 2-4pm. **SBS Argo,** ul. Pyatnitskaya 6, near the intersection of ul. Pobedy and ul. Republikanskaya, has a 24hr. Cirrus/Plus/MC/Visa **ATM** and offers cash advances on these, both for a 2% commission.

Luggage Storage: Available at Glavny Vokzal for 8.50R per day. Open 24hr.

Post Office: 22/28 Bogoyavlenskaya pl. (Богоявленская; tel. 22 37 28), opposite the monastery and down ul. Komsomolskaya from pl. Volkova. Open M-Sa 8am-8pm, Su 8am-6pm. **Postal code:** 150000.

Telephone Office: In the same building as the post office. Prepay at the counter to get a booth. 3 tones mean the call has yet to go through. Press the "ответ" button when someone answers. Buy tokens for local and intercity calls (0.45R and 2.85R) at the same booth; for the latter, use phones labeled "междугородный автомат" *(mezhdugorodny avtomat),* which malfunction frequently. Open 24hr. **Phone code:** (0)852.

RUSSIA

ACCOMMODATIONS

Yaroslavl has always been popular among both Russians and foreigners, and for that reason its hotel prices are high. Foreigners are consistently charged more than

Russians. With some luck and some sacrifice of convenience, it is possible to get by on a tight budget. Rooms are scarce come summer—call ahead.

Gostinitsa Volga (Волга), ul. Kirova 10 (tel. 22 91 31). From pl. Volkova, walk south toward pl. Bogoyavlenskaya and take a left on ul. Kirova. Excellent location and spacious rooms, but watch out for the mosquitoes. Some hall toilets have seats. Singles 260R, with bath 360R; doubles 440R, with bath 540R. Check-out noon.

Gostinitsa Kotorosl (Которосль), ul. B. Oktyabrskaya 87 (Б7 Октябрьская; tel. 21 24 15; English info tel. 21 15 81). One stop on tram #3 from Glavny Vokzal. This pink palace offers brand-new rooms at reasonable rates. All rooms with TV and telephone; most have a private bath. Singles 260R; doubles 506R. English and German spoken.

Gostinitsa Yubileynaya (Юбилейная), Kotoroslnaya nab. 11a (Которосльная; tel. 22 41 59; English info tel. 22 45 94). From pl. Volkova, walk down Komsomolskaya ul. to pl. Bogoyavlenskaya (Богоявленская). Pass the Church of the Epiphany on your left and turn right at the river. Intourist's first choice–and thus home to many tour groups–this 7-floor hotel is nonetheless comfortable. In the summer, ask for a room on the back side if you're not springing for A/C; front ones have a nice view but get incredibly hot. Singles US$30; doubles US$50. Intourist may be able to chip a few dollars off these figures, depending on the size of your group.

FOOD

Sidewalk cafes hawking beer, ice cream, and sweet rolls reign supreme in Yaroslavl, where actual restaurants seem outnumbered by old cathedrals. Stock up on fruits and vegetables at the *tsentralny rynok* (**central market;** центральный рынок), ul. Deputatskaya 1 (Депутатская; open M-Sa 8am-6pm, Su 8am-4pm). The central and crowded **gastronom** on Kirova 13 sells just about everything else. (Open daily 8am-noon and 1-9pm.) Two Western-style grocery stores at ul. Ushinskovo 10 and 12 are the only places that sell non-carbonated bottled water. (Open daily 8am-9pm.)

Staroye Mesto (Старое Место), ul. Komsomolskaya 3, off pl. Volkova, facing ul. Pervomayskaya. A dark, brick-vaulted cellar serving authentic Russian fare. Only six tables. For 100-150R you will leave stuffed and satisfied. Open daily noon-10pm.

Cafe Aktor (Актор), ul. Kirova 5 (tel. 72 75 43). Follow the Russian cartoons up the stairs to this chic little cafe. Mannequins on the mock stage watch you gorge yourself on tasty Russian specialties, including stuffed cabbage (30R). Full meals with beer 125R. Open daily 8am-11pm.

Cafe Lira (Лира), Volzhskaya nab. 43 (tel. 22 21 38), one block south of the river station. The food is unexciting, but for romance this Volga spot, complete with heart-shaped napkin holders, can't be beat. Full meals 140R.

SIGHTS

MONASTERY OF THE TRANSFIGURATION OF THE SAVIOR. (Spaso-Preobrazhensky Monastyr; Спасо-Преображенский Монастырь). The fortified Monastery of the Transfiguration of the Savior, pl. Bogoyavlenskaya, has been guarding the banks of the Kotorosl since the 12th century. The high white walls surround a number of buildings and exhibitions, which, frustratingly, all have separate entrance fees. Enter the grounds through the **Holy Gate** (Svyatye Vorota; Святые Ворота), on the side facing the Kotorosl. If you climb to the top of the popular **bell tower** (*zvonnitsa;* звоница) just inside, you'll be rewarded with a spectacular view of the city. *(Open daily 10am-5:30pm. 10R, students 4R.)* The 15th-century **cathedral** in the center displays an odd assortment of stuffed animals, but is usually passed over by visitors for the real thing: **Medveditsa Masha,** a ten-year old bear, was found as a cub and installed in the monastery. Masha more than pays for her supper, delighting tourists by posing for cameras. She looks cuddly, despite being far too big for her tiny cage. The most appealing exhibits within the monastery complex include the **Old Russian and National Applied Art exhibit** (Drevnerusskoye i Narodno-Prikladnoye Iskusstvo; Древнерусское и Народно-Прикладное

Искусство), devoted to national crafts and icons of the Yaroslavl school (7R, students 3R); **Monuments of the Transfiguration Monastery** (Pamyatniki Spasskovo Monastyrya; Памятники Спасского Монастыря), which describes the history of medieval structures on the grounds (6R, students 2R); and the **exhibit on *Lay of Igor's Expedition*** (Ekspozitsiya Slovo o Polkye Igoreve; Экспозиция Слово о Полке Игореве), dedicated to the discovery and publication of one of the first literary creations of Old Russia, dating from the 12th century and found on the monastery grounds in the late 18th century. (6R, students 2R.) At times the exhibits are difficult to understand, as foreign-language guides are not available. *(Monastery open daily 8:30am-7pm. Exhibitions open Tu-Su 10am-5:30pm; kassa closes at 4:30. 6R, students 2R. Entrance free with purchase of tickets to museum.)*

CHURCH OF THE ELIJAH THE PROPHET. (Tserkov Ilyi Proroka; Церковь Ильи Пророка). Perhaps Yaroslavl's most beautiful church, the Church of Elijah the Prophet lies on Sovetskaya pl. (Советская) at the end of ul. Kirova. Built in the 17th century in traditional Yaroslavl style, its original frescoes complement the elaborate and lovingly-restored iconostasis. The low ceilings in the two ante-chambers allow for detailed study of the magnificent wall paintings. *(Open M-Tu and Th-Su 10am-1pm and 2-6pm. 10R, students 3R. Photos 20R.)*

ART MUSEUM. (Khudozhestvenny Muzey; Художественный Музей). The Art Museum has two branches. The first, **Museum of the Metropolitan Palace** (Muzey Metropolichi Palaty; Метрополичьи Палаты), displays the best of Yaroslavl's icons but, with its higher prices, is sadly under-visited. *(Volzhskaya nab. 1. Tel. 22 34 87 and 22 96 65. Open Sa-Th 10am-5:30pm; kassa closes 4:30pm. 30R.)* The modern branch, in the former **Governor's house,** displays 18th- to 20th-century Russian paintings and sculpture, most the work of local artists. *(Volzhskaya nab. 23. Tel. 30 35 04. Open Tu-Su 10am-6pm; kassa closes 5pm. 10R, students 4R.)*

CHURCH OF THE EPIPHANY. (Tserkov Bogoyavleniya; Церковь Богоявления). Across from the monastery and farther from the Volga, the red-brick Church of the Epiphany shows off one frescoed room fragments of frescoes recovered from destroyed Yaroslavl churches. The main room has an ornately carved Baroque iconostasis and a mixture of beautiful frescoes in dire need of restoration. Concerts are often held here at 6pm—ask at the monastery. *(Pl. Bogoyavlenskaya. Open W-M 10am-5pm. Knock on the door if the church seems closed. 10R, students 4R. Photos 10R.)*

CHURCH OF THE ARCHANGEL MICHAEL. (Tserkov Arkhangela Mikhaila; Церковь Архангела Михаила). Across from the corner of the monastery nearest the *strelka*, the Church of the Archangel Michael thrusts a similar set of red brick and green domes skyward, and also shelters frescoes by local artists. *(Open daily 9am-8pm. Services F-Sa 5pm, Su 9am.)*

OTHER MUSEUMS. The **Museum of the History of Yaroslavl** (Muzey Istorii Goroda Yaroslavl; Истории Города Ярославль) is a small museum filled with engravings, furniture, photos, and clothes from throughout Yaroslavl's history. *(Volzhskaya nab. 17/2. Tel. 22 25 40. Open W-M 10am-6pm; kassa closes 5pm. 6R, students 2R.)* The tiny but enchanting **Museum of Music and Time** (Muzey Muzyki i Vremya; Музыки и Время) is housed in a restored 19th-century brick house. This hands-on museum brings out the child in everyone, encouraging visitors to play with artifacts including a player piano and a variety of music makers. *(Volzhskaya nab. 33. Open daily 10am-7pm. 10R, students 5R.)*

NIGHTLIFE

For better or worse, nightlife here seems wed to Russian pop. One of the cooler and friendlier places in town is the well-attended **Arsenal Bar,** right on the Volga below Volzhsky Spusk, in the old Arsenal Tower. (Open daily 10am-4pm and 5pm-1am.) **Club Yuta** (Клуб Юта), ul. Respublikanskaya 79 (Республиканская; tel. 21 34 24), kicks it from 9pm to 2am, but the crowd is often local and exclusive. (Open Th-Su. Cover for men 20R, for ladies 10R.) In summer, many locals drive to Volzhskaya nab., open their car doors, blast the radio, and simply stroll on the street.

VLADIMIR (ВЛАДИМИР)

Once the capital of Russia and headquarters of the Russian Orthodox Church, Vladimir (vlad-IH-mir) suffered at the hands of the Tatars, and eventually fell to Moscow in the early 14th century. Until that time, it had rivaled Kiev in size and splendor. Now marked by 12th-century white stone monuments and splendid cathedrals, this city of 360,000 has old-world charm to spare. Some of the oldest and most striking churches in the Golden Ring are offset here by proud, rejuvenated commercial industries; together they are a fitting union of the city's imperial past and the more sedate present.

ORIENTATION & PRACTICAL INFORMATION. The old city stretches the length of a small ridge, along whose crest runs **ul. III Internatsionala** (III-его интернационала), increasingly known by its new name **ul. Bolshaya Moskovskaya** (Большая Московская), a 5min. walk uphill from the train station. Nearly everything of interest to tourists is on or near this street. **Trains** run from the station on Vokzalnaya ul. (Вокзальная) to: Moscow's **Kursky Vokzal** (3hr., 8 per day, 55R) and **Nizhny Novgorod** (4hr., 6 per day, 30-90R). **Buses** depart from across the street from the train station to: **Moscow** (3½hr., many per day, 35-40R); **Nizhny Novgorod** (5½hr., 2 per day, 50R); and **Yaroslav** (5hr., 1 per day, 47R). Vladimir's tourist office, **Excursionnoye Byuro** (Экскурсионное Бюро), ul. III Internatsionala 43 (tel. 34 42 63), arranges English-language tours of Vladimir (40R per person, plus additional surcharges depending on group size) and Suzdal (60R, additional charges; open M-Th and Sa-Su 8:30am-5:30pm, F 8:30am-3pm). The bank offering the most service is **Inkombank,** 4 ul. Spasskaya (Спасская), not far from the Golden Gates, which gives MC/Visa cash advances and cashes traveler's checks (US$5 min.) for a 2% commission. It also has an **ATM,** albeit inside the bank. (Open M-F 9am-1pm and 1:30-5pm, Sa 9am-1pm and 1:30-3pm.) The main **post office** is at ul. Podbelskovo 2; head down ul. Muzeynaya near the Excursionnoe Byuro, then turn left on Podbelskova. (Open M-F 8am-8pm, Sa-Su 8am-6pm.) **Postal code:** 600000. Enjoy astoundingly fast **internet** connections on the 3rd floor of ul. Gagarina 2. Walk south on ul. III Internatsionala, then take a right on ul. Gagarina (Гагарина) at the first traffic signal after Cathedral Square. (Open M-F 8am-6pm, Sa 8am-1:30pm. 0.75R per min.) The train station houses a 24hr. **telephone office** that serves only Russian cities. A 25R **telephone card** is required to use these phones (good for about 4min. to Moscow). For 5-digit numbers, insert a "2" between the dialing code and the phone number. For **international calls,** head to Peregovorny Punkt (Переговорный Пункт), Gorkovo 60 (Горького). Take trolley #2 or 8 down ul. Gagarina between the Cathedrals and the Golden Gate off ul. III Internationala to pl. Lenina. (Open 24hr.) Or, they can be placed from the Gostinitsa Vladimir (see **Accommodations,** below). Calls to Europe are US$2 per minute, while calls to the U.S. are a whopping US$4 per minute. **Phone code:** (0)922.

ACCOMMODATIONS & FOOD. Heading uphill on the far left path from the train station leads to **Gostinitsa Vladimir** (Гостиница Владимир), ul. III Internatsionala 74 (tel. 32 30 42; fax 32 73 33). Blissfully untroubled by competition, it rents clean and pleasant rooms with sinks. (Singles 100R, with bath 310R; doubles with bath 400R.) Write ahead to reserve, and expect a 25% first-night surcharge if they can save you a spot. The **grocery** next door is well-stocked and has great bread (3-4R per loaf) when it's hot from the oven. (Open M-F 9am-8pm, Sa 9am-7pm, Su 9am-5pm.) For cheap and greasy fare, the **Pirozhki Bar** at ul. III Internatsionala 22 (*pirozhki* 8R, entrees 5-15R; open M-F 8am-8pm and Sa 8am-5pm) and the **Pizzeria,** ul. III Internatsionala 14 (pizza 25R; open daily 11am-3pm and 4-10pm) are tops. For a bit more money and a lot less grease, **U Zolotykh Vorot** ("By the Golden Gates;" У Золотых Ворот), ul. III Internatsionala 15 (tel. 23 116), will turn out a tasty Russian meal; those with a lucky streak may choose to play a hand at the adjoining casino as well. (Full meals 150R. Open daily noon-1am.)

SIGHTS. From the Soviet monuments in Sobornaya Ploshchadz on ul. III Internatsionala, head diagonally down through the trees to the 12th-century **St. Dmitry's Cathedral** (Dmitrievsky Sobor; Дмитриевский Собор), the only surviving building of Prince Vsevelod III's palace. Lavishly carved in stone, the cathedral's outer walls display the stories of Hercules, King David, and Alexander the Great, but locked doors prevent visitors from viewing the Byzantine frescoes inside, as a major restoration project is underway. Vladimir's **Assumption Cathedral** (Uspensky Sobor; Успенский Собор) lies a bit farther up the ridge; it once guarded the famous Virgin Mary icon now housed by Moscow's Tretyakov Gallery (see **Moscow: Sights,** p. 573). Fortunately, Tretyakov couldn't take the frescoes by renowned artists Andrei Rublyov and Daniil Chiorny. The cathedral was begun in 1158, and in 1189 received four more domes and two more aisles—try to ignore the 19th-century bell tower. (Open Tu-Su 1:30-5pm. Free. Respectful attire required.) Between the two cathedrals is yet another regional **Picture Gallery,** ul. III Internatsionala 58 (tel. 22 24 29), displaying paintings from the 18th-20th centuries. (Open Tu and F 10am-4pm, W-Th and Sa-Su 10am-5pm. 25R, students 10R.) The park in front, with its wooden statues of Snow White and the Seven Dwarves, is probably more fun. Farther down the hill, the brick **Museum of the History of Vladimir** (Muzey Istorii Vladimirskovo Kraya; Музей Истории Владимирского Края), ul. III Internatsionala 64 (tel. 34 22 84), has a satisfying—if predictable—collection of artifacts from the stone age through 1917, including mammoth tusks, suits of armor, and a model of the city as it looked in the 12th century. (Open Tu and F-Su 10am-4:30pm, W-Th 10am-3:30pm; closed last Thursday of each month. 25R, students 10R.) Down the street are the remains of the **Nativity Monastery** (Rozhdestvensky Monastyr; Рождественский Монастырь), Aleksandr Nevsky's former burial site. Peter I schlepped the poor guy's remains to Petersburg in the 1600s, robbing the monastery of its only worthwhile attraction. (Open daily for worship only 4-5pm, although the grounds are open during the day.)

The 12th-century **Golden Gate** (Zolotye Vorota; Золотые Ворота; tel. 22 25 59) stands triumphant—and somewhat foolish—in the middle of ul. III Internatsionala, marking the end of the old city. (Open W-M 10am-5pm; closed last Friday of each month. 25R, students 10R.) You can climb to the top for an outstanding view. The early-20th-century **Trinity Church** beyond Zolotye Vorota houses an exhibit of **crystal** and **lacquer crafts** (tel. 22 48 72), as well as a large room filled with gadgets from the surrounding region. (Open M and W 10am-4pm, Th-Su 10am-5pm; closed last Friday of the month. 25R, students 10R.) The **Exhibit of Old Vladimir** (Vystavka Starovo Vladimira; Выставка Старого Владимира; tel. 254 51), in a water tower near the gates, displays assorted items from life in 19th-century Vladimir and offers a panoramic view of the old city. (Open Tu and F-Su 10am-5pm, W-Th 10am-4pm; closed last Thursday of each month. 20R, students 10R.)

Vladimir is also famous for its **choirs.** Eduard Markin's Boys' Choir holds Saturday concerts of old Russian hymns and folk songs in an old church on ul. Georgievskaya (Георгиевская), a rock road rolling off ul. III Internatsionala around building 26. The **Zavazalsky Choir** (Khor Zavazalskovo; Хор Завазальского) often performs in the Planetarium building, ul. III Internatsionala 66a (tel. 34 22 90), which was formerly the Nikolo-Kremlevskaya church. (Open M-Sa 10am-4pm.)

NEAR VLADIMIR: SUZDAL (СУЗДАЛ)

Set in a fertile countryside of lazy streams, dirt roads, free-roaming chickens, and goats, Suzdal (SOOZ-dull; pop. 10,000) looks, miraculously, much as it always has. Until the 12th century, Suzdal's **kremlin** ruled the Rostov-Suzdal principality; now it offers an array of attractions drawing tourists from around the world. Although vegetation and time have softened the profile of the mighty fortress, the star-studded blue domes of the **Nativity Cathedral** (Rozhdestvensky Sobor; Рождественский Собор) still dazzle. Brightly-colored frescoes and ornately-carved arches decorate the early 13th-century church. Unfortunately, the cathedral is sometimes closed to visitors, as even the slightest change in humidity can damage the frescoes. The nearby **History of Suzdal** exhibit displays irregularly-shaped coins of Ivan the Terrible, a huge and ornate ceramic oven, and a mock-up of Suzdal in olden-times. Also within the kremlin, the **Museum of Old Russian Painting** (Muzey Drevnerusskoy Zhivopisi; Музей Древнерусской Живописи) displays icons of the Suzdal school from the 13th through 17th centuries. (Museums and cathedral open M, W-Su 10am-6pm, closed last Friday of the month. 15R, students 5R; photos 8R.) Gift shops in both towns sell a handy guide to Suzdal for 29R. For directions to accommodations or restaurants, visit the friendly **Excursionnoe Byuro,** ul. Lenina 22 (tel. 209 37), which also leads tours (with prior notice) in English and German. **Postal code:** 601260. **Phone code:** (0)9321.

GETTING THERE. Buses run to Suzdal from **Vladimir** (50min., every 40-50min., 8R). Departure times are listed on a white board outside the bus station. From the station, turn left onto ul. Vasilevskaya for the 25min. walk to ul. Lenina, or take the trolley (every 10-15min., 1R).

THE NORTHWEST (СЕВЕРО-ЗАПАД)

Lakes and monasteries shine like cool diamonds in the frigid forests of Russia's northwest territory, in whose landmarks one can read the history of Imperial Russia. The story begins with Novogorod, which stood as Moscow's northern rival at its peak. The hard-won fortress at Schlisselburg symbolizes the will of one man to give his nation a window to the west, and the grad that Peter built endures as the Northwest's crown jewel. St. Petersburg is set among smaller, well polished gems, the palaces at Pushkin, Peterhof, and Pavlovsk, which testify to the decadence into which the royalty soon fell. The island of Valaam, on the other hand, is a quiet reminder of natural, unadorned beauty. Finally, Pskov stands alone as the crushing final chapter, the city where the last of the Romanovs lost his throne.

ST. PETERSBURG (САНКТ-ПЕТЕРБУРГ)

Remember, St. Petersburg is Russian...but it is not Russia.

—Tsar Nicholas II

St. Petersburg (pop. 4,200,000) is a symbol—an ideal of progress and Westernization, where Russia suddenly becomes wide boulevards, glorious palaces, and artistic revelry. Almost Scandinavian in its mood, St. Petersburg is marked by a distinctly un-Russian opulence. This splendor is exactly what Peter intended when he founded St. Petersburg in an attempt to create a "Window to the West" in 1703. The city was built atop a drained swamp on the Gulf of Finland, a strategic location for the new capital intended to drag Russia from its backward roots in "Asiatic" Moscow and Byzantium toward the more advanced countries of the West. The city was constructed to impress—and it does just that—but as a result, it often leaves an impression of self-consciousness and artificiality, as if it were merely an elaborate period costume-drama rather than a real (albeit anachronistic) Russian metropolis. While Peterites revel in the excess of Russia's "cultural capital," they can never quite escape the horrors of the city's past: St. Petersburg was the violent setting of both the 1905 and 1917 revolutions, as well as the brutal 900-day siege of Leningrad by the Nazis. Indeed, the city's artistic and historic legacies are etched on every street and square; the splendid palaces of Peter and Catherine have inspired the masterpieces of Dostoevsky, Gogol, Tchaikovsky, and Stravinsky, while the seedy cafes and dark courtyards of the city's underbelly fostered the revolutionary dreams of Lenin, Trotsky, and Rasputin.

The Soviets chose to neglect the graceful northern capital for the more brazen Moscow, and within a few years of post-Communist life, St. Petersburg was plagued by so many mafiosos that she was likened to Chicago in the 1920s. The city has returned to its original name; St. Petersburg was shunned as too Germanic-sounding in WWI and became Petrograd, which the Bolsheviks later traded in for the more proletarian Leningrad. Luckily, the worst is past. The Hermitage is slowly cleaning up and expanding, primed to resume its place as Europe's premier museum. Likewise, Peterites are managing once again to frolic in the city's intense nightlife, which climaxes during the famed Midsummer White Nights, when the sun never sets and the city never sleeps. Moscow may be the embodiment of Mother Russia's bold, post-apocalyptic youth, but St. Petersburg remains the majestic and mysterious symbol of Peter's great Russian dream.

GETTING THERE & GETTING AROUND

Airplanes: The main airport, **Pulkovo** (Пулково), has two terminals: Pulkovo-1 for domestic and Pulkovo-2 for international flights. M2: Moskovskaya. From the Metro, take bus #39 for Pulkovo-1 (30-40min.), or bus #13 for Pulkovo-2 (25-30min.). Hostels can usually arrange for a taxi (usually US$30-40). **Air France,** Bolshaya Morskaya 35 (Большая морская; tel. 325 8252). Open M-F 9am-5pm. **British Airways,** ul. Malaya Konyushennaya 1/3 (Малая конюшенная; tel. 329 2565). Open M-F 9am-5:30pm. **Delta Airlines,** Bolshaya Morskaya 36 (tel. 311 5819 and 311 5820). Open M-F 9am-5:30pm. **Finnair,** Malaya Morskaya 19 (Малая Морская; tel. 315 9736 and 325 9500). Open M-F 9am-5pm. **Lufthansa,** Voznesensky pr. 7 (Вознесенский; tel. 314 4979). Open M-F 9am-5:30pm. **SAS/SwissAir,** Nevsky pr. 57 (tel. 325 3250). Open M-F 9am-5pm.

Trains: Tsentralnye Zheleznodorozhnye Kassy (Central Ticket Offices; Центральные Железнодорожные Кассы), Canal Griboedova 24. Open M-Sa 8am-8pm, Su 8am-4pm. Foreigners must purchase domestic tickets at **Intourist** windows #100-104 and international tickets at windows #90-99 on the 2nd floor. Expect long lines and few English-speaking tellers. For information on prices, go to ticket window #90; 4R per question. Prices vary slightly depending on the train running (see **Getting Around,** p. 556). There are also Intourist offices at each of St. Petersburg's four train stations. For schedule and fare info in Russian, call 168 0111 or 162 3344. Check your ticket to see which station your train leaves from.

Varshavsky Vokzal (Варшавский Вокзал). M1: Baltiskaya (Балтийская). To: **Rīga** (12hr., 1 per day, 1049R); **Tallinn** (8hr., 1 per day, 477R); **Vilnius** (11hr., 1 per day, 822R); and **Warsaw** (27hr., 1 per day, 1123R).

Vitebsky Vokzal (Витебский Вокзал). M1: Pushkinskaya (Пушкинская). To: **Kiev** (26-32hr., 2 per day, 725R) and **Odessa** (36hr., 1 per day, 870R).

Moskovsky Vokzal (Московский Вокзал). M1: Pl. Vosstaniya. To: **Novgorod** (5hr., 1 per day, 400R); **Moscow** (6-9hr., 15 per day, 305R); and **Sevastopol** (36hr., 1 per day, 997R). Anna Karenina threw herself under a train here.

Finlyandsky Vokzal (Финляндский Вокзал). M1: Pl. Lenina (Ленина). To **Helsinki** (5hr., 2 per day, 1134R).

Buses: nab. Obvodnovo Kanala 36 (Обводного Канала; tel. 166 5757; international info tel. 166 8101). M4: Ligovsky pr. Take tram #19, 25, 44, or 49, or trolley #42, from the M1 stop across the canal. Facing the canal, turn right and walk two long blocks. The station is on your right; enter through the back. Cheaper and more comfortable than trains during the day, but queue up early for the over-booked short-distance jaunts. Buy tickets several hours before departure to avoid a 3R surcharge for advance booking. One-way tickets only. Open daily 5:30am-midnight. Advance ticket booth open daily 8am-2pm and 3-8pm. Destinations in **Finland, Estonia,** and **Belarus.** (1-2 trains per day to capitals and major cities). Baggage 2-5R extra, depending on destination.

Local Transportation: The **Metro** (Метро) is a comprehensible, efficient, and safe method of exploring the city. Runs daily 5:30am-12:30am. Four lines run from the outskirts of the city through the center. A Metro **token** (*zheton;* жетон) costs 3R. Stock up, as lines are ridiculous at peak hours. **Buses, trams,** and **trolleys** run fairly frequently, depending on the time of day. Read the list of stops posted on the outside of the bus. Trolleys #1, 5,

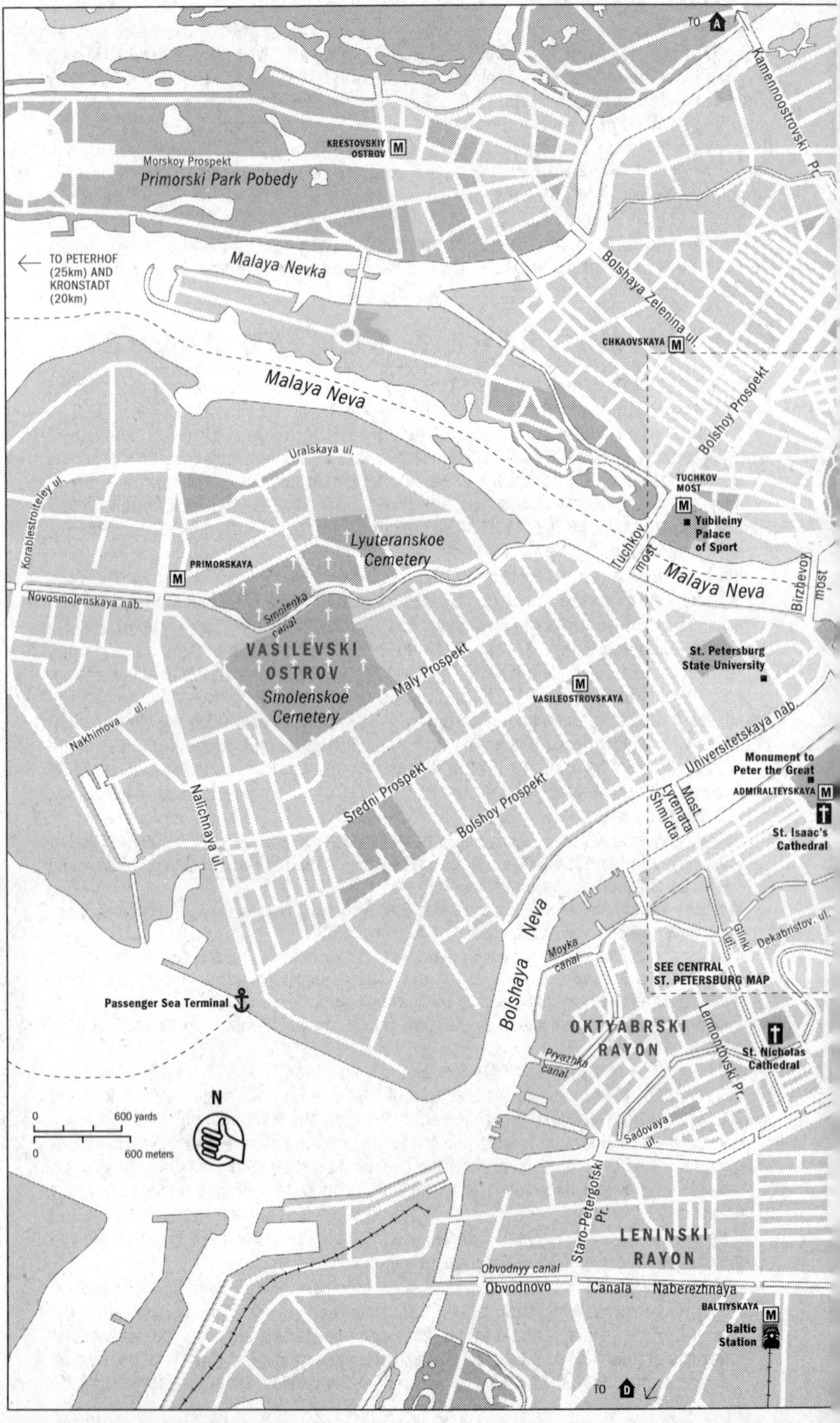
TO A
Kamennoostrovski Pr.
KRESTOVSKIY OSTROV
Morskoy Prospekt
Primorski Park Pobedy
TO PETERHOF (25km) AND KRONSTADT (20km)
Malaya Nevka
Bolshaya Zelenina ul.
CHKAOVSKAYA
Malaya Neva
Bolshoy Prospekt
Uralskaya ul.
Korablestroiteley ul.
TUCHKOV MOST
Yubileiny Palace of Sport
Lyuteranskoe Cemetery
PRIMORSKAYA
Tuchkov most
Malaya Neva
Birzhevoy most
Novosmolenskaya nab.
Smolenka canal
VASILEVSKI OSTROV
Smolenskoe Cemetery
Maly Prospekt
VASILEOSTROVSKAYA
St. Petersburg State University
Universitetskaya nab.
Nakhimova ul.
Monument to Peter the Great
ADMIRALTEYSKAYA
Nalichnaya ul.
Sredni Prospekt
Bolshoy Prospekt
Lytenata Shmidta Most
St. Isaac's Cathedral
Neva
Moyka canal
Glinki ul.
Dekabristov. ul.
SEE CENTRAL ST. PETERSBURG MAP
Passenger Sea Terminal
Bolshaya
OKTYABRSKI RAYON
Lermontovski Pr.
St. Nicholas Cathedral
Pryazhka canal
N
0 600 yards
0 600 meters
Sadovaya ul.
Staro-Petergofski Pr.
LENINSKI RAYON
Obvodnyy canal
Obvodnovo Canala Naberezhnaya
BALTIYSKAYA
Baltic Station
TO D

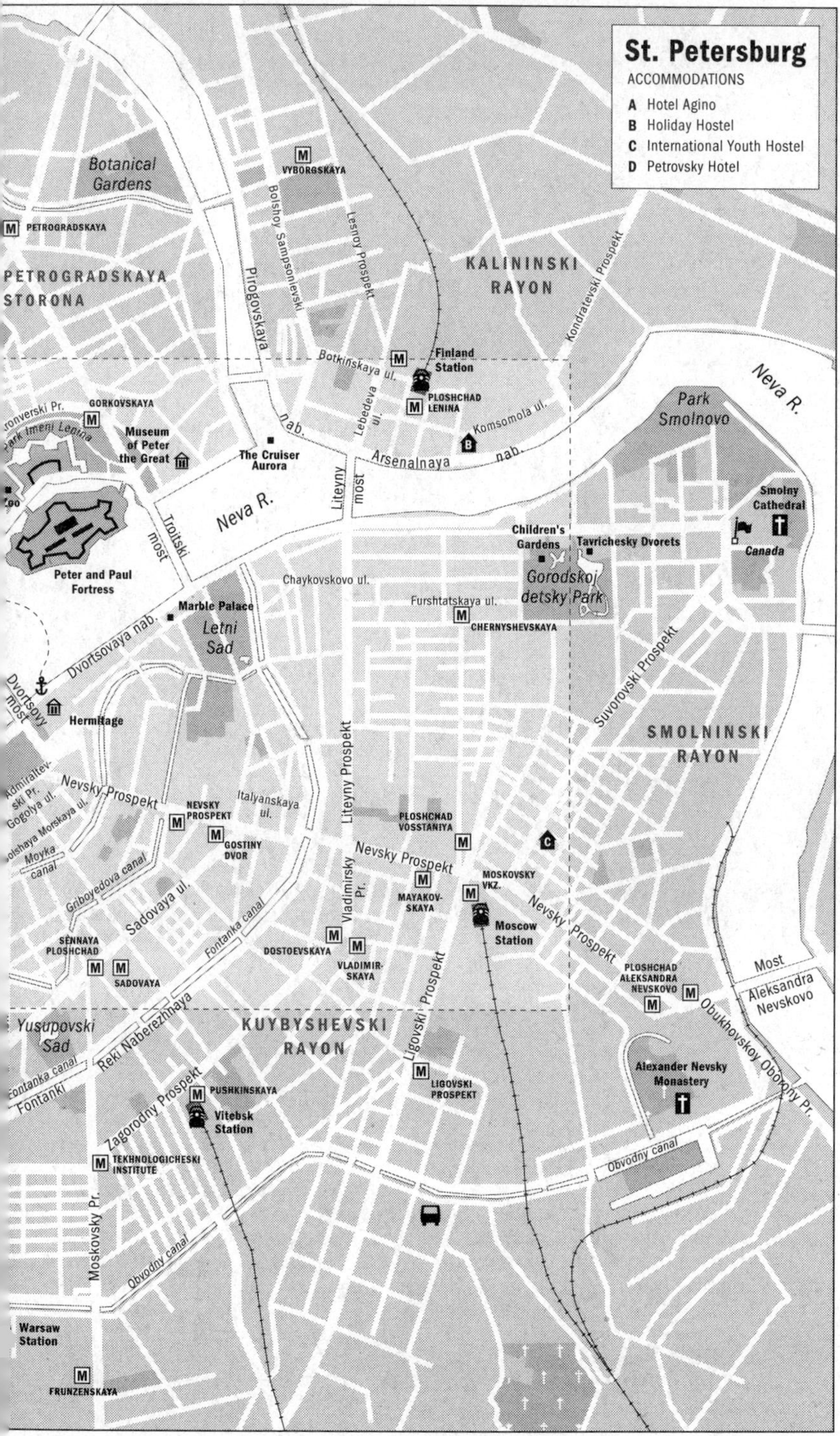
St. Petersburg
ACCOMMODATIONS
A Hotel Agino
B Holiday Hostel
C International Youth Hostel
D Petrovsky Hotel
Botanical Gardens
PETROGRADSKAYA
VYBORGSKAYA
Bolshoy Sampsonievski
Lesnoy Prospekt
KALININSKI RAYON
Kondratevski Prospekt
PETROGRADSKAYA STORONA
Pirogovskaya
Botkinskaya ul.
Finland Station
PLOSHCHAD LENINA
Lebedeva ul.
Neva R.
Park Smolnovo
GORKOVSKAYA
Museum of Peter the Great
The Cruiser Aurora
nab.
Arsenalnaya
nab.
Komsomola ul.
Liteyny most
Neva R.
Troitski most
Peter and Paul Fortress
Children's Gardens
Tavrichesky Dvorets
Smolny Cathedral
Canada
Gorodskoj detsky Park
Chaykovskovo ul.
Furshtatskaya ul.
CHERNYSHEVSKAYA
Marble Palace
Letni Sad
Dvortsovaya nab.
Dvortsovy most
Hermitage
Suvorovski Prospekt
SMOLNINSKI RAYON
Liteyny Prospekt
Admiraltevski Pr.
Gogolya ul.
Bolshaya Morskaya ul.
Nevsky Prospekt
NEVSKY PROSPEKT
Italyanskaya ul.
PLOSHCHAD VOSSTANIYA
GOSTINY DVOR
Moyka canal
Griboyedova canal
Nevsky Prospekt
Vladimirsky Pr.
MAYAKOVSKAYA
MOSKOVSKY VKZ.
Moscow Station
Nevsky Prospekt
Sadovaya ul.
Fontanka canal
SENNAYA PLOSHCHAD
SADOVAYA
DOSTOEVSKAYA
VLADIMIRSKAYA
Ligovski Prospekt
PLOSHCHAD ALEKSANDRA NEVSKOVO
Most Aleksandra Nevskovo
Obukhovskoy Oborony Pr.
Yusupovski Sad
Reki Naberezhnaya
KUYBYSHEVSKI RAYON
Fontanka canal
Fontanki
Zagorodny Prospekt
PUSHKINSKAYA
Vitebsk Station
LIGOVSKI PROSPEKT
Alexander Nevsky Monastery
TEKHNOLOGICHESKI INSTITUTE
Obvodny canal
Moskovsky Pr.
Obvodny canal
Warsaw Station
FRUNZENSKAYA

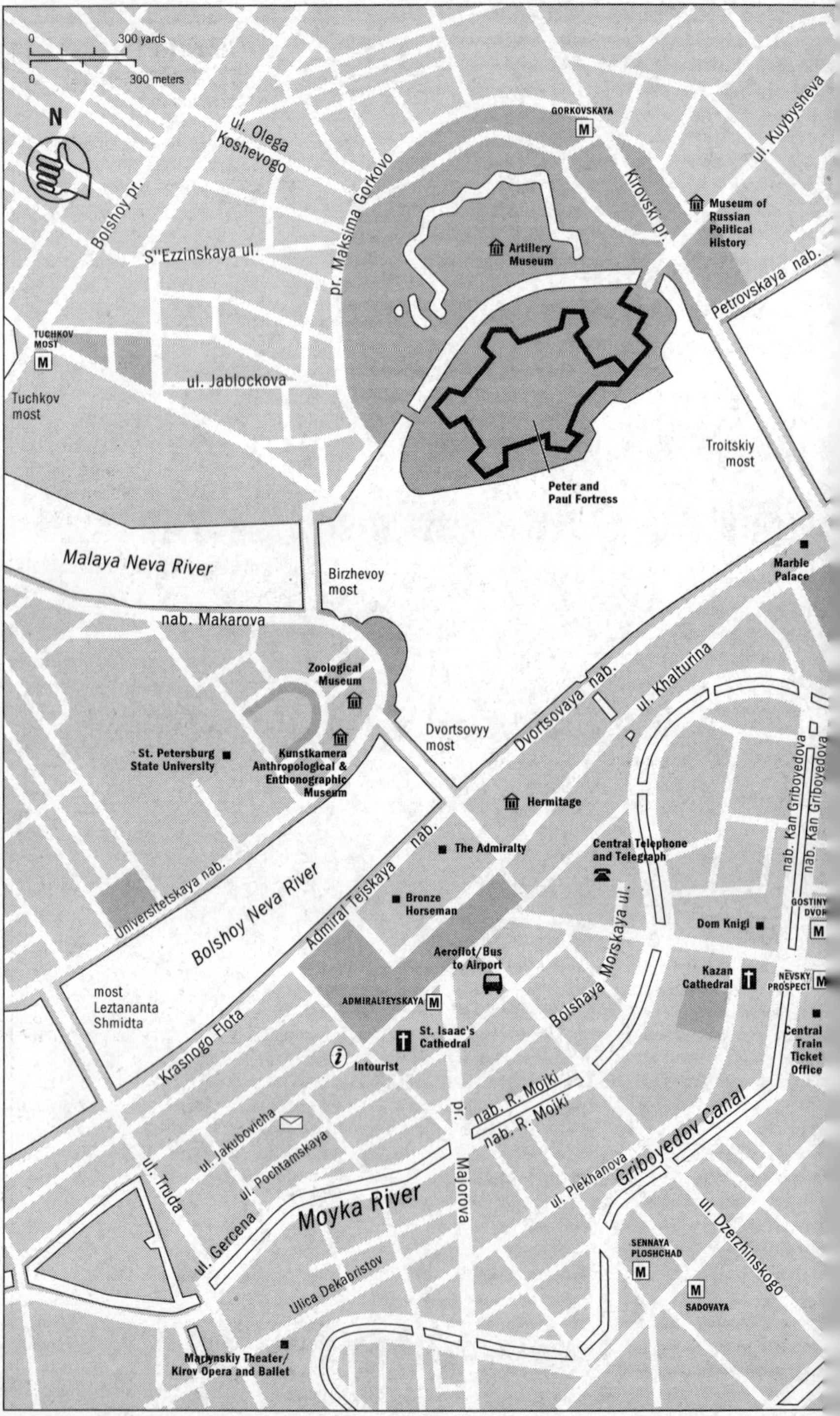
0
300 yards
0
300 meters
N
GORKOVSKAYA
M
ul. Kuybysheva
ul. Olega Koshevogo
pr. Maksima Gorkovo
Kirovski pr.
Museum of Russian Political History
Bolshoy pr.
S"Ezzinskaya ul.
Artillery Museum
Petrovskaya nab.
TUCHKOV MOST
M
ul. Jablockova
Tuchkov most
Troitskiy most
Peter and Paul Fortress
Malaya Neva River
Birzhevoy most
Marble Palace
nab. Makarova
Zoological Museum
ul. Khalturina
Dvortsovaya nab.
Dvortsovyy most
St. Petersburg State University
Kunstkamera Anthropological & Enthonographic Museum
nab. Kan Griboyedova
nab. Kan Griboyedova
Hermitage
nab.
The Admiralty
Central Telephone and Telegraph
Universitetskaya nab.
Bolshoy Neva River
Admiral Tejskaya
Bronze Horseman
Bolshaya Morskaya ul.
GOSTINY DVOR
Dom Knigi
M
Aeroflot/Bus to Airport
Kazan Cathedral
NEVSKY PROSPECT
M
most Leztananta Shmidta
ADMIRALTEYSKAYA
M
St. Isaac's Cathedral
Central Train Ticket Office
Krasnogo Flota
Intourist
pr. Majorova
nab. R. Mojki
nab. R. Mojki
Griboyedov Canal
ul. Jakubovicha
ul. Pochtamskaya
ul. Plekhanova
ul. Truda
Moyka River
ul. Dzerzhinskogo
ul. Gercena
SENNAYA PLOSHCHAD
M
M
SADOVAYA
Ulica Dekabristov
Mariinskiy Theater/ Kirov Opera and Ballet

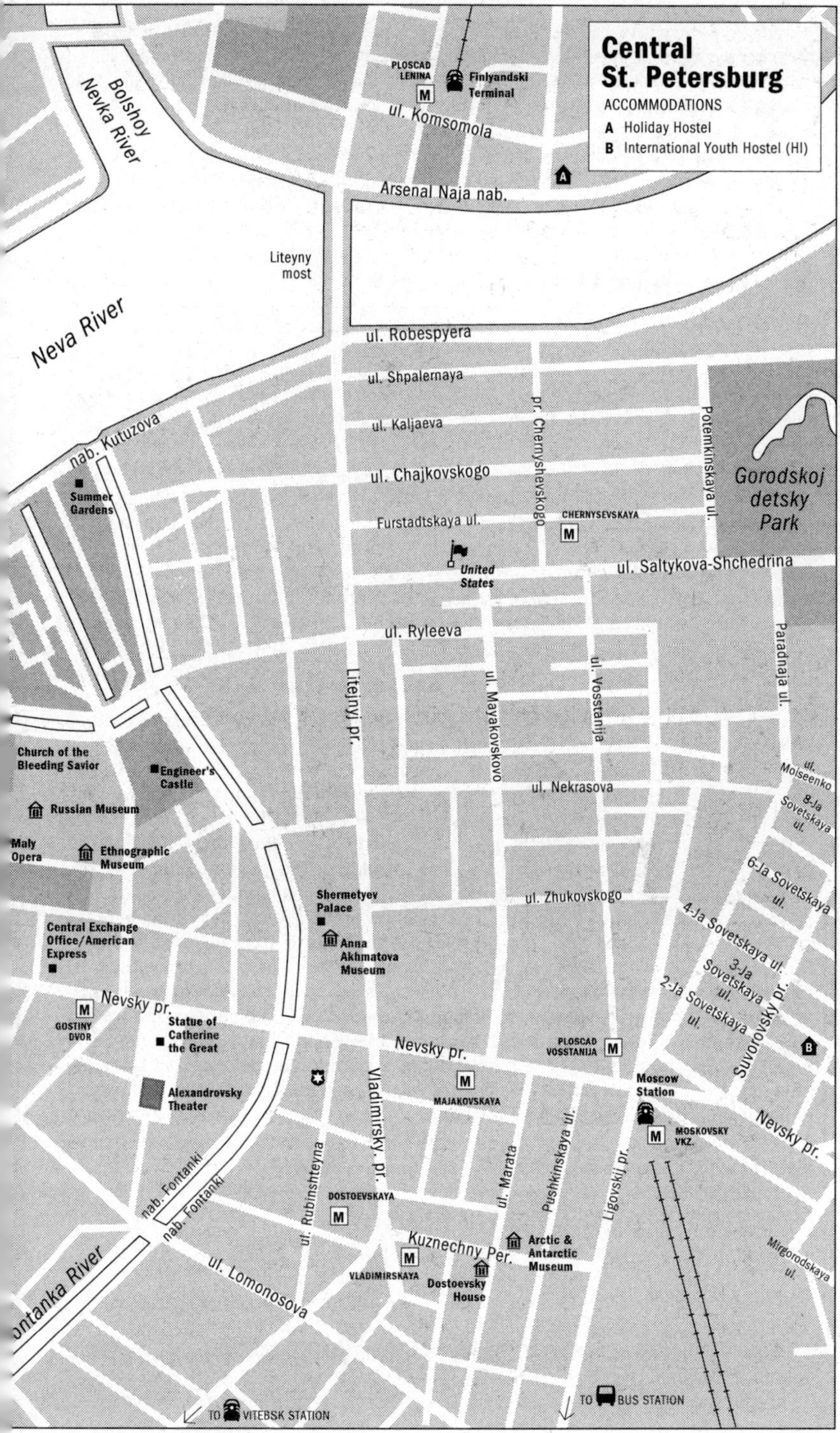
Central St. Petersburg
ACCOMMODATIONS
A Holiday Hostel
B International Youth Hostel (HI)
Bolshoy Nevka River
Neva River
Liteyny most
Ploscad Lenina
Finlyandski Terminal
ul. Komsomola
Arsenal Naja nab.
ul. Robespyera
ul. Shpalernaya
ul. Kaljaeva
ul. Chajkovskogo
Furstadtskaya ul.
pr. Chernyshevskogo
Chernysevskaya
Potemkinskaya ul.
Gorodskoj detsky Park
ul. Saltykova-Shchedrina
United States
ul. Ryleeva
nab. Kutuzova
Summer Gardens
Litejnyj pr.
ul. Mayakovskovo
ul. Vosstanija
Paradnaja ul.
ul. Moiseenko
8-Ja Sovetskaya ul.
ul. Nekrasova
Church of the Bleeding Savior
Engineer's Castle
Russian Museum
Maly Opera
Ethnographic Museum
6-Ja Sovetskaya ul.
Shermetyev Palace
Anna Akhmatova Museum
ul. Zhukovskogo
4-Ja Sovetskaya ul.
3-Ja Sovetskaya ul.
2-Ja Sovetskaya ul.
Suvorovsky pr.
Central Exchange Office/American Express
Nevsky pr.
Gostiny Dvor
Statue of Catherine the Great
Ploscad Vosstanija
Moscow Station
Alexandrovsky Theater
Majakovskaya
Moskovsky Vkz.
Vladimirsky. pr.
ul. Rubinshteyna
ul. Marata
Pushkinskaya ul.
Ligovskij pr.
nab. Fontanki
Dostoevskaya
Fontanka River
Kuznechny Per.
Arctic & Antarctic Museum
Vladimirskaya
Dostoevsky House
ul. Lomonosova
Mirgorodskaya ul.
TO VITEBSK STATION
TO BUS STATION

and 22 go from pl. Vosstaniya to the bottom of Nevsky pr., near the Hermitage. Buses are often packed and brutally hot in the summer. Bus, tram, and trolleys run 6am-midnight; tickets (2R) should be purchased from the driver. Be sure to punch them on board (the fine for not doing so is 9R). And, yes, they do check. A **monthly transportation card** is good for unlimited public transportation; purchase one at any Metro station at the start of the month.

Taxis: Both marked and private cabs run throughout St. Petersburg. Fares are flat and based on your destination. They are safe for the most part, but never get into a car with more than one person already in it.

ORIENTATION

St. Petersburg is 6hr. east of Helsinki and 9hr. northwest of Moscow. It sits at the mouth of the **Neva river** (Нева) on the **Gulf of Finland** (Finsky Zaliv; Финский Залив), occupying 44 islands interspersed among 50 canals. The city center lies on mainland St. Petersburg between the south bank of the Neva and the north bank of the **Fontanka River. Nevsky Prospekt** (Невский Проспект), running through this downtown area, is the cultural heart of the city. Most of St. Petersburg's major sights—including the Winter and Summer Palaces, the Hermitage, and the city's three main cathedrals—are on Nevsky pr. South and east of the Fontanka on the mainland are the **Liteyny, Smolny,** and **Vladimirskaya** districts. These are central St. Petersburg's newest neighborhoods, developed primarily in the late 19th century, and house the Smolny Institute and the Aleksandr Nevsky Monastery. **Moskovsky Vokzal** (Moscow Train Station; Московский Вокзал), the city's main train station, is in the middle of this district, located near the midway point of Nevsky pr.; **Vitebsky Vokzal** (Витебский Вокзал) is at the southern edge of this district on Litiyny pr. (Литеиний пр.). East of the downtown and across the Neva sprawls **Vasilevsky Island,** the city's largest island and originally intended site of Peter's dream-city. Most sights on the island are St. Petersburg's oldest and are congregated on the island's eastern edge in the **Strelka** neighborhood. The western portion of the island is a sprawl of grid-patterned streets and apartment complexes; the city's **Sea Terminal,** the port for all ferries arriving in St. Petersburg, is at the island's far western tip on the Gulf coast. On the north side of the Neva and across from the Winter Palace is a small archipelago housing the Peter and Paul Fortress, the **Petrograd Side** residential neighborhood, and the wealthy **Kirov Island** trio; this is the historic heart of St. Petersburg. North and south of the downtown on the mainland are the southern suburbs and the **Vyborg Side** neighborhoods; both are vast expanses of tenements and factories and are of little interest to most tourists aside from the train stations they house, including **Finlyandsky Vokzal** (Finland Train Station; Финляндский) in the north and **Varshavsky Vokzal** (Warsaw Train Station; Варшавский) in the south. In an appropriate expression of Peter's grand dream, St. Petersburg *sprawls;* the easiest means of navigation is the **Metro,** efficient and convenient but always packed at rush hour. In the center, **trolleybuses** have more frequent stops; #1, 5, and 22 go up and down Nevsky pr. The city makes promenading a pleasure, and fortunately most major sights are close together.

PRACTICAL INFORMATION

TOURIST & FINANCIAL SERVICES

Tourist Office: Ost-West Contact Service, ul. Mayakovskovo 7 (Маяковского; tel. 327 3416; fax 327 3417). Free info, from clubs to pharmacies to international airline tickets (international only). Arranges homestays (US$20 in center, US$15 elsewhere), boat and bus tours, and theater tickets. Open M-F 10am-6pm, Sa noon-6pm.

Budget Travel: Sinbad Travel (FIYTO), 3-ya Sovetskaya ul. 28 (3-я Советская; tel. 327 8384; fax 329 8019; email sindbad@ryh.spb.su; www.spb.ru/ryh). In the International Hostel. Geared toward students and budget travelers. Arranges plane, bus, ferry, and train

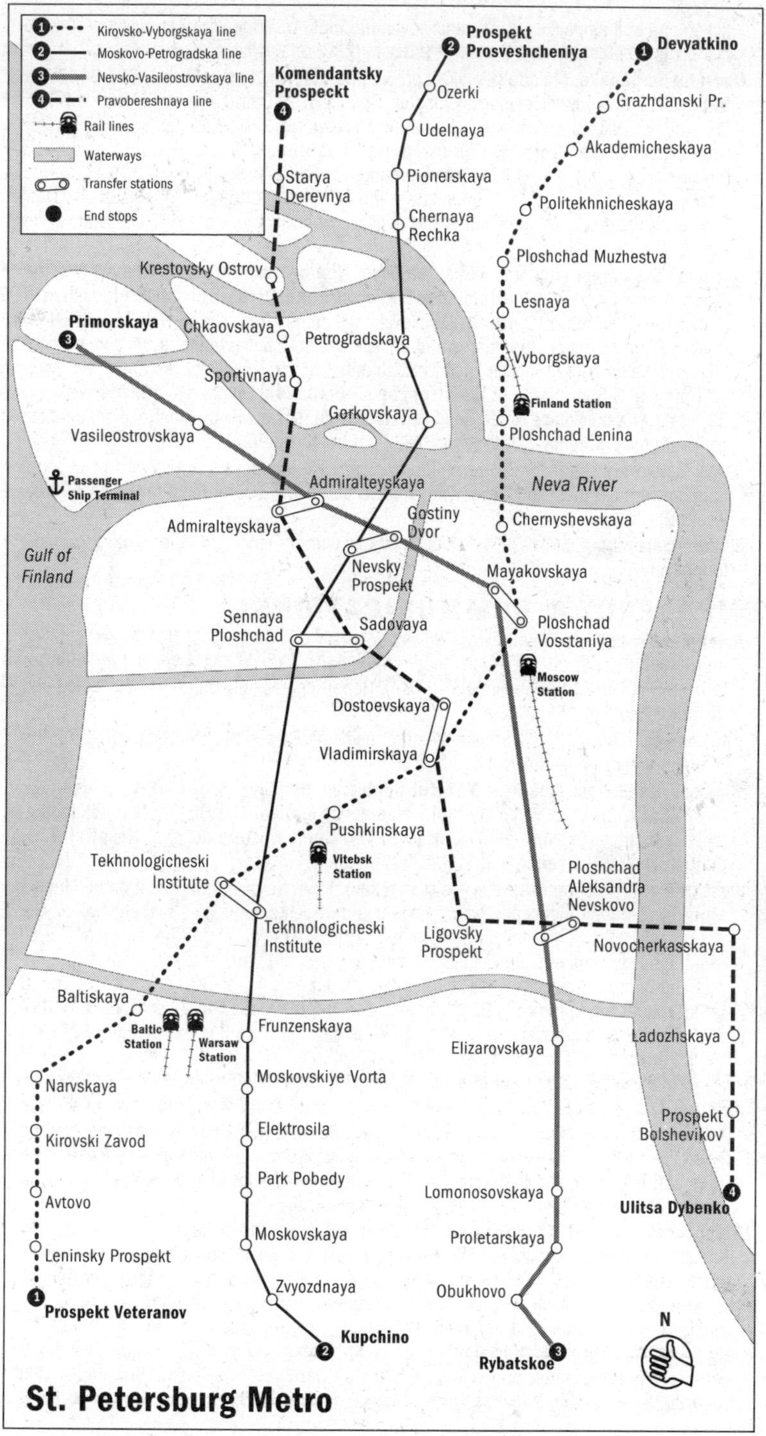

Kirovsko-Vyborgskaya line
Moskovo-Petrogradska line
Nevsko-Vasileostrovskaya line
Pravobereshnaya line
Rail lines
Waterways
Transfer stations
End stops
Prospekt Prosveshcheniya
Devyatkino
Komendantsky Prospeckt
Ozerki
Grazhdanski Pr.
Udelnaya
Akademicheskaya
Starya Derevnya
Pionerskaya
Politekhnicheskaya
Chernaya Rechka
Ploshchad Muzhestva
Krestovsky Ostrov
Lesnaya
Primorskaya
Chkaovskaya
Petrogradskaya
Vyborgskaya
Sportivnaya
Finland Station
Gorkovskaya
Ploshchad Lenina
Vasileostrovskaya
Passenger Ship Terminal
Admiralteyskaya
Neva River
Gostiny Dvor
Chernyshevskaya
Admiralteyskaya
Gulf of Finland
Nevsky Prospekt
Mayakovskaya
Sennaya Ploshchad
Sadovaya
Ploshchad Vosstaniya
Moscow Station
Dostoevskaya
Vladimirskaya
Pushkinskaya
Vitebsk Station
Tekhnologicheski Institute
Ploshchad Aleksandra Nevskovo
Tekhnologicheski Institute
Ligovsky Prospekt
Novocherkasskaya
Baltiskaya
Baltic Station
Warsaw Station
Frunzenskaya
Elizarovskaya
Ladozhskaya
Narvskaya
Moskovskiye Vorta
Kirovski Zavod
Elektrosila
Prospekt Bolshevikov
Park Pobedy
Avtovo
Lomonosovskaya
Ulitsa Dybenko
Moskovskaya
Proletarskaya
Leninsky Prospekt
Zvyozdnaya
Obukhovo
Prospekt Veteranov
Kupchino
N
Rybatskoe

St. Petersburg Metro

RUSSIA

tickets, as well as package tours and adventure trips. US$5 fee for train tickets. 10-80% discounts on plane tickets. Open M-F 9:30am-5:30pm. English spoken.

Consulates: Canada, Malodetskoselsky pr. 32 (Малодетскосельский; tel. 325 8448; fax 325 8393). M1: Tekhnologichesky Institut. Open M-F 9:30am-1pm and 2-5pm. **U.K.,** pl. Proletarskoy Diktatury 5 (Пролетарской Диктатуры; tel. 325 6036; fax 325 6037). M1: Chernyshevskaya. Open M-F 9am-1pm and 2-5pm. **U.S.,** ul. Furshtatskaya 15 (Фурштатская; tel. 275 1701; 24hr. emergency tel. 274 8692; fax 213 6962). M1: Chernyshevskaya. Open M-F 9:15am-1pm and 2-5:30pm. Citizens of **Australia** and **New Zealand** should contact their embassies in Moscow but can use the U.K. consulate in an emergency.

Currency Exchange: Look for "Обмен валюты" (*obmen valyuty*) signs everywhere. The black market no longer exists. **Central Exchange Office,** ul. Mikhailovskaya 4 (Михайловская; tel. 110 4909). Off Nevsky pr. across from Grand Hotel Europe. M3: Gostiny Dvor. All major credit cards and traveler's checks accepted for a 3% commission, but expect a long wait. Shorter lines for cash and AmEx traveler's checks. Open M-F 9am-1:30pm and 3-6pm, Sa-Su 9:30am-2pm and 3-6pm. **24hr. exchange office,** Nevsky pr. 57, at the Nevsky Palace Hotel. Keep your exchange receipts if you plan to change rubles back into hard currency, but they still might not be accepted.

ATMs: Банкомат *(bankomat)* are multiplying rapidly. All upscale hotels and most large banks now have them; on Nevsky pr., there's one every 100m. Most take Cirrus/Plus/Visa/MC.

Laundry Service: Tel. 560 2992. Pick-up, next-day laundry service. 45R for 4.5kg, plus 45R for delivery.

EMERGENCY & COMMUNICATIONS

Emergencies: Police and ambulance drivers generally do not speak English. There is now a multilingual police office which deals specifically with crimes against foreigners at Ligovsky Pr. 145 (24hr. hotline 164 9787). Report crimes immediately to this office and to your consulate.

Pharmacies: Nevsky pr. 22. Stocks Western medicines. Open M-F 8am-9pm, Sa-Su 24hr. At night, enter through the back.

Medical Assistance: American Medical Center, ul. Serpukhovskaya 10 (Серпуховская; tel. 326 1730; fax 326 1731; 24hr. emergency hotline 310 9611). M1: Tekhnologichesky Institut (Технологический Институт). Staffs western doctors. **Hospital #20,** Gastello ul. 21 (Гастелло; tel. 108 4090), treats foreigners.

Post Office: ul. Pochtamtskaya 9 (Почтамтская). From Nevsky pr., go west on ul. Malaya Morskaya (Малая Морская), which becomes ul. Pochtamtskaya. It's about two blocks past Isaakievsky Sobor on the right, before an overhanging arch. Change money or to make intercity or international calls. Mailing services are unreliable for international letters and parcels—the extra 8-10R for certified mail may help the post office to not lose it. International airmail letters 7R; postcards 5R. International mail is sent from window #24. For **Poste Restante,** address mail: "WAGNER, Kate, До Востребования, 190 000 Санкт-Петербург, Главпочтамт, Russia." Held up to one month at windows #1 and 2. Open M-Sa 9am-7:30pm, Su 10am-5:30pm.

Internet Access: Tetris Internet Cafe (Тетрис), Chernyakhovskovo 33 (Черняховского; tel. 164 4877; email postmaster@dux.ru; www.dux.ru). M4: Ligovsky Prospekt. Exit the Metro, turn left onto Ligovsky pr. and walk straight for 5min. 80R per hr. Both **Hostel Holiday** and **International Youth Hostel (HI)** (see **Accommodations,** p. 605) let you send and receive email free at the hostel's web address only.

Telephones: Central Telephone and Telegraph, Bolshaya Morskaya ul. 3/5 (Большая Морская). Facing the Admiralty, it's right off Nevsky pr. near Dvortsovaya pl. For intercity calls, use one of the *mezhdugorodny* (междугородный) phone booths; they take special grooved *zhetony* (tokens; жетоны) sold across from the booths (3R). Prepay your phone call in the *kassa* in the 2nd (for intercity) or 3rd (for international) hall, and get change for unspent time. English instructions available. When making long-distance calls, dial 8 and wait for the tone before proceeding. When your party answers, push the round button bearing an arrow for a few seconds. Open M-F 9am-12:30pm and 1-8pm, Su 9am-

12:30pm and 1-5pm. **Intercity calls** can also be made from any public phone on the street that takes phone cards (25 units 55R, 400 units 331R; 1 unit per min. for local calls; 54 units per min. to U.S.). Cards are good for both local and intercity calls; they can be purchased at the Central Telephone Office or news kiosks and are good for both local and intercity calls. Certain phones also take Metro tokens for local calls. For **AT&T Direct,** call 325 5042; you can also use this service to call collect from most international phones, except credit card phones. **Phone code:** 812.

> The pipes and drainage system in St. Petersburg have not changed since the city was founded. There is no effective water purification system, making exposure to giardia very likely. Always boil tap water at least 10min., dry your washed veggies, and drink bottled water. For more info, see **Essentials: Health,** p. 28.

ACCOMMODATIONS

Nowhere is Russia's politico-economic flux more apparent than in the accommodations industry. Where once travelers were assigned a hotel by Intourist, now they can choose among deluxe new joint ventures, old Intourist dinosaurs, **hostels,** and **private apartments.** *The St. Petersburg Times* lists apartments for rent, both long- and short-term; pick up a free copy in the Grand Hotel Europe or at one of the hostels. The International Youth Hostel's *Traveler's Yellow Pages* has current listings of accommodations options.

That said, budget accommodations are rare and not very "budget." Russian speakers may want to consider a **homestay,** which can be arranged by the **Host Families Association (HOFA;** tel./fax 275 1992; email alexei@hofak.hop.stu. neva.ru), based at the St. Petersburg Technical University. They provide bed and breakfast in apartments within 5km of the city center. The most economical B&B package includes only room and breakfast: if your host meets you at the station or treats you to a homemade dinner, expect to be charged extra. Also available are deluxe B&B (includes dinner) and full service (all meals and a car) packages. Rates are cheaper if you go hunting on your own.

The national **Russian Youth Hostels Association (HI)** in St. Petersburg accepts reservations by phone, provides assistance with visas, books train tickets, and provides rides to the airport. They also sell maps and bottled water.

Hostel "Holiday" (HI), ul. Mikhailova 1 (Михайлова; tel. 542 7364; fax 325 8559; email postmaster@hostelling.spb.su; www.spb.su/holiday). M1: Pl. Lenina. Exit at Finlyandsky Vokzal, turn left on ul. Komsomola (Комсомола), then right on ul. Mikhailova. Just before the river, turn left into a courtyard, then right. Look for their sign on the wall ahead. Large, rooms overlooking the Neva. Internet access and visa support (single-entry US$30). Beds range from rock-hard to low-slung. Hall baths and toilets, minus the toilet paper. Doubles US$38 per person; 3- to 5-bed dorms US$14. Breakfast included. US$1 discount for HI members; US$2 after 5 days. Check-out 11am. Call ahead.

International Youth Hostel (HI), 3-ya Sovetskaya ul. 28 (3-я Советская; tel. 329 8018; fax 329 8019; email ryh@ryh.spb.ru; www.spb.ru/ryh). M1: Pl. Vosstaniya. Walk along Suvorovsky pr. (Суворовский) for 3 blocks, then turn right on 3-ya Sovetskaya ul. A tidy hostel in a pleasant neighborhood with all the Soviet basics. Communal showers available 8-11am and 7-11pm. Minimal kitchen; laundry service (US$4 for 4kg); TV. Send email after 6pm. Tickets for ballet, theater, trains, etc.; city tours also offered. English films Sa-Su 8pm. 2- to 5-bed dorms US$17, ISIC holder US$18, nonmembers $19. Breakfast included. Check-out 11am. Curfew 1am. The hostel is a member of the International Booking Network (IBN), so you can book all other IBN hostels from here or vice versa. MC/Visa.

Petrovsky Hostel, ul. Baltiyskaya 26 (Балтийская; tel. 252 7563; fax 252 4019). M1: Narvskaya. From the Metro, turn left on pr. Stachek (Стачек) to ul. Baltiskaya. The hostel is a few blocks ahead on your left. Although a little ways from the center, this is a solid, cheap option; just beware the grungy hall baths and toilets. Kitchen, common room with TV. Sheets not included. Clean 2- to 3-bed dorms 130R. Check-in by midnight. Check-out 11am.

Hotel Olgino (Отель Ольгино), Primorskoe Shosse 18 (Приморское Шоссе; tel. 238 3671; fax 238 3463). M2: Chernaya Rechka. Then take bus #110 (20-25min.). The campsite and recently renovated hotel just outside the city is not worth the inconvenience unless you are traveling by car. Showers and kitchen on-site. Sauna (250R for 2hr.) and horse rentals. Camping US$7 per person; parking US$2. Singles and doubles US$22. Some English spoken.

FOOD

St. Petersburg's menus vary little, but many restaurants harbor top-secret methods of preparing old Russian favorites worth tasting. The few great restaurants fill up fast, and getting there often requires a hefty walk. Unfortunately, even in highly touristed regions, menus are often exclusively in Cyrillic.

RESTAURANTS

Kafe Hutorok (Хуторок), 3-ya Sovetskaya ul. 24. M1: Pl. Vosstaniya. This randomly Polynesian basement cafe whips up amazing Russian food. Entrees 75-125R. Don't leave without trying the cherry dumplings. Open 10am-11pm.

Tblisi (Тблиси), ul. Sytninskaya 10 (Сытнинская; tel. 232 93 91). M2: Gorkovskaya. Follow the wrought-iron fence that wraps around Park Lenina away from the fortress until you see the Sytny (Сытный) market. Tblisi is just behind it. The owners are eager to suggest their Georgian favorites. Entrees 40-50R; *tolmas* (meat wrapped in grape leaves) 41R. Lunch specials daily noon-5pm; 25R. Open daily noon-11pm.

Green Crest (Грин Крест), Vladimirsky pr. 7 (Владимирский). M1: Vladimirskaya; M4: Dostoevskaya. "Ecological oasis in this gastronomical desert," reads the welcoming sign at the door. 12 varieties of picturesquely displayed fresh salads; a full plate lets you sample several of your choice. Quite possibly the only non-smoking eatery in St. Petersburg, so breathe deep. Open daily 9am-11:30pm.

Koreysky Domik, (Корейский Домик), Izmailovsky pr. 2 (Измайловский; tel. 259 9333). M1, 2: Tekhnologicheski Institut. Authentic South Korean cuisine. Delicious soups, including Korean vegetable (meat based) 24R; "big bowl" specials 50-60R. Full meals up to 200R, but well worth it. Open daily 1-11pm.

Tandoor (Тандур), Voznesensky pr. 2 (tel. 312 3886). M2: Nevsky Prospekt. On the corner of Admiralteysky pr., two blocks to the left after the end of Nevsky pr. Enjoy Indian cuisine served by Russian boys in Aladdin costumes, complete with gold shoes. Dinner runs US$15-25. Lunch special daily noon-4pm; US$10. Open daily noon-11pm.

La Cucaracha, nab. Fontanki Reki 39 (Фонтанки Реки; tel. 110 4058.) M3: Gostiny Dvor. Hold back your cockroach jokes, cynical wanderer; any bugs around here were scared off by the over-the-top Tex-Mex decor and live music on Tuesday, Thursday, and Friday evenings. The chicken fajitas (129R) are a shot of adrenaline to the over-borschted palate. Full meals 150-200R. Happy hour 6-8pm. Open daily noon-1am.

FAST FOOD

Fast food venues are springing up all over St. Petersburg, many open 24hr. Plenty serve hamburgers and french fries, and several chains have fairly good Russian food. For those craving good old American fare, **Pizza Hut, KFC,** and **Baskin-Robbins** are all over town. Or, bask in the glow of the Golden Arches at **McDonald's,** 11 Bolshaya Morskaya, two blocks from St. Isaac's Cathedral. (Open 24hr.)

Koshkin Dom (Cat's House; Кошкин Дом), Liteyny pr. 23 (Литейний) and ul. Vosstaniya 2. M1: Pl. Vosstaniya. Carnivores can tear into Russian entrees and soups for 15-50R. Both locations open 24hr.

Bistro Maslenitsa, (Бистро Масленица), Nevsky pr. 27 (tel. 558 8748). M2: Nevsky Prospekt. This small, bustling cafe proves there's more than one way to stuff a blini—in fact, there's 15 by their count. Blini 5-25R. Open 24hr.

Minutka (Минутка), Nevsky pr. 20. M2: Nevsky Prospekt. Large sandwiches, small prices. Vegetarian 12-inch subs 55-75R. Prepared salads (mostly meat) 35-40R. Open daily 10am-10pm.

CAFES

Cafes have long been pivotal to St. Petersburg culture, inspiring Dostoevsky's frightening tales of Russian urban life and Lenin's dreams of revolution. Unfortunately, many of the city's most famous and elegant cafes were replaces with sterile and faceless Soviet-era cafes, which inspired the communist era's counter culture. Today's mainstream cafes hold only vague echoes of past debates as the younger generation seeks refuge in bars instead. Fortunately, cafes remain cheap, offering the few truly inexpensive meals in St. Petersburg.

Idiot (Идиот), nab. Moyki 82 (Мойки; tel. 315 1675). M4: Sadovaya. 5min. down the Moyka from Isaakievskaya pl. This spacious but homey cafe captures the feel of a Silver Age salon. Couches invite leisurely reading; books are available in the entrance hall (English titles 17R each). Homemade Russian meals 100R. Happy hour 6:30-7:30pm; 2-for-1 beer or wine. Open daily noon-11pm.

Kolobok (Колобок), ul. Tchaikovskovo 40 (Чайковского). M1: Chernyshevskaya. Turn right on pr. Chernyshevskovo for one block until ul. Chaykovskovo. Cheap, greasy, and fast. Sweet and savory rolls 4-10R; entrees 25-50R. Open daily 7:30am-8pm.

Kafe Kolokolchik (Little Bells; Кафе Колокольчик), per. Krylova 1 (Крылова). M3: Gostiny Dvor. At the corner of ul. Sadovaya; enter through the iron gates. Light, uninspired meals 20-40R; coffee 10-20R; beer 25-35R. Open daily noon-4pm and 5-9pm.

SUPERMARKETS

Magazin #11 (Магазин), Nevsky pr. 105. M1, 3: Pl. Vosstaniya. The usual elevated supermarket prices but a bigger selection than most. Probably the only place in town that stocks herbs and spices. Open daily 10am-10pm.

Eliseevsky (Елисеевский), Nevsky pr. 56. M2: Nevsky Prospekt. Across from pl. Ostrovskovo. A gastronomical and decorative delight. Fancy stained glass and elaborate chandeliers elegantly frame Russian delicacies. Open daily 9am-1pm and 2-9pm.

Produkty (Продукты), ul. Komsomola (Комсомола). M1: Pl. Lenina. 5min. from Hostel Holiday. The only reasonably priced supermarket in St. Petersburg. Open 24hr.

MARKETS

Markets stock fresh produce, meat, cheese, bread, pastries, honey, and the occasional greasy prepared dish, but are more expensive than state-owned stores. They are a truly Russian experience and require energy on the part of all involved. Sellers easily spot foreigners and try to cheat them; watch out for fingers on the scales and count your change. If you are not satisfied, simply walk away; a simple *nyet* will do wonders to bring the price down. Bargaining is what these places are all about. Don't forget to bring bags and jars, although some vendors provide them for a couple of rubles. The **covered market,** Kuznechny per. 3 (Кузнечьный), just around the corner from M1: Vladimirskaya, and the **Maltsevski Rynok,** ul. Nekrasova 52 (Некрасова), at the top of Ligovsky pr. (Лиговский; M1: Pl. Vosstaniya), are the biggest and most exciting.

RUSSIA

SIGHTS

St. Petersburg is a city obsessed with its glory days. Citizens speak of the time "before the Revolution" as though it had occurred only a few years ago, and of dear old Peter and Catherine as if they were first cousins. Even if you don't go inside any of St. Petersburg's major sights, take the time to stroll through the city to experience the grace of its architecture.

THE HERMITAGE

Dvortsovaya nab. 34 (Дворцовая). M2: Nevsky Prospekt. Exiting the Metro, turn left and walk down Nevsky pr. to its end at the Admiralty. Head right, onto and across Palace Square. Tel. 110 9657. Open M-Sa 10:30am-6pm, Su 10:30am-5pm; cashier and upper floors close 1hr. earlier. Kassa located on the river side of the building. 250R, students free. Cameras 75R; video 200R. Lines can be long, so come early or on a weekday. Students should buy tickets at kassa #5. Allow at least 3-4hr. to see the museum, although an entire day is better. It's easy to latch onto a tour group, especially if you understand Russian.

Originally a collection of 225 paintings bought by Catherine the Great in 1764, the **State Hermitage Museum** (Эрмитаж), the world's largest art collection, rivals both the Louvre and the Prado in architectural, historical, and artistic significance. After commissioning its construction in 1769 and filling it with works of art, **Catherine II** (the Great) wrote of the treasures: "The only ones to admire all this are the mice and me." This, to the public's great fortune, is no longer true; the collection was made public in 1852. The **Winter Palace** (Zimny Dvorets; Зимний Дворец), commissioned in 1762, reflects the extravagant tastes of the Empress Elizabeth, Peter the Great's daughter, and the architect Rastrelli. By the end of the 1760s, the collection amassed by the empress had become too large for the Summer Palace, and Catherine appointed Vallin de la Mothe to build the **Small Hermitage** (Maly Hermitage; Малый Эрмитаж), where she could retreat by herself or with one of her lovers. The **Big Hermitage** (Veliky Hermitage; Великий Эрмитаж) and the **Hermitage Theater** (Hermitazhny Teatr; Эрмитажный Театр) were completed in the 1780s. Stasov, a famous imperial Russian architect, built the fifth building, the **New Hermitage** (Novy Hermitage; Новый Эрмитаж), in 1851. The tsars lived with their collection in the Zimny Dvorets and Hermitage complex until 1917, after which the museum complex was nationalized.

Today, the museum takes up all five buildings, although the Hermitage Theater is often closed. Buy an indispensable English floor guide (5R) at the souvenir tables near the *kassa;* otherwise, consult those found on each level. The rooms are numbered, and the museum is organized chronologically by floor, starting with **Egyptian, Greek,** and **Roman** art on the ground floor of the Small and Big Hermitages, and **prehistoric artifacts** in the Winter Palace. On the second floors of the Hermitages are collections of 17th- and 18th-century **French, Italian,** and **Dutch** art. In rooms 226-27, an exact copy of **Raphael's Loggia,** commissioned by Catherine the Great, stands just as in the Vatican.

Room 189 on the Summer Palace's second floor, the famous **Malachite Hall,** contains six tons of malachite columns, boxes, and urns, each painstakingly constructed of thousands of matched stones to give the illusion of having been carved from one massive stone. If you wondered why the revolution occurred, decadence like this might explain. The Provisional Government of Russia was arrested in the adjacent dining room in October 1917. On the third floor of the Winter Palace (the only building with three floors) you'll find **Impressionist, Post-Impressionist,** and **20th-century** European and American art. If you're running late, visit them first—the museum closes from the top down.

In June 1997, the museum received a US$1.6 million grant from IBM to provide wider electronic access to the Hermitage treasures for internet visitors (www.hermitage.ru/indexeng.htm); computers opposite the ground-level cafe allow you to explore the collection's many rooms before setting off. It is impossible to absorb the whole museum in a day or even a week—indeed, only 5% of the three-million-piece collection is on display at any one time. Rather than attempting a survey of the world's artistic achievements, pick a building or time period to focus on.

The **Palace Square** (Dvortsovaya Ploshchadz; Дворцовая Площадь), the huge windswept expanse in front of the Winter Palace, has witnessed many turning points in Russia's history. Here, Catherine took the crown after overthrowing her husband, Tsar Peter III. Later, Nicholas II's guards fired into a crowd of peaceful demonstrators on "Bloody Sunday" in 1905, leading to the 1905 revolution. And here, Lenin's Bolsheviks seized power from Kerensky's provisional government during the storming of the Winter Palace in October 1917. Today, vendors peddle ice cream and quickly-drawn portraits while the angel at the top of the **Alexsander Column** (Aleksandriyskaya Colonna; Александрийская Колонна) waits for another riot. The column commemorates Russia's defeat of Napoleon in 1812. The inscription on the Hermitage side reads, "To Aleksandr I from grateful Russia"; the angel's face is said to resemble the Tsar's. The column itself weighs 700 tons, took two years to cut from a cliff in Karelia, and required another year to bring to St. Petersburg. With the help of 2000 war veterans and a complex pulley system, it was raised in just 40min. and is held in place by its massive weight alone.

ST. ISAAC'S CATHEDRAL

M2: Nevsky Prospekt. Exiting the Metro, turn left and walk to the end of Nevsky pr. Turn left onto Admiraltevsky pr.; the cathedral sits at the corner of Admiraltevsky and Voznesensky pr. Tel. 315 9732. Open Tu-Su 11am-7pm; colonnade open 11am-6pm. The kassa is to the right of the cathedral. 200R, students 80R; colonnade 100R, students 40R. Foreigners buy tickets inside the church. Museum open M and Th-Su 11am-5pm, Tu 11am-4pm. 15R.

Glittering, intricately-carved masterpieces of iconography await beneath the dome of **St. Isaac's Cathedral** (Isaakievsky Sobor; Исаакиевский Собор), a massive example of 19th-century civic-religious architecture. On a sunny day, the 100kg of pure gold that coats the dome shines for miles; 60 laborers died from inhaling mercury fumes during the gilding process. The cost of building this opulent cathedral was well over five times that of building the Winter Palace. The job took 40 years, due in part to architect Auguste de Montferrand's lack of experience and also to a superstition that the Romanov dynasty would fall with the cathedral's completion. The cathedral stood finished in 1858, the Romanovs fell in 1917, and while we're at it, Rasputin was probably a charlatan, but that's all water under the mystic bridge. The interior overwhelms for the first few minutes, but after getting used to the grandeur of the place, its details merit a look. Some of Russia's greatest artists have worked on the murals and mosaics inside and because a 1931 Soviet decree named the cathedral a museum, the paintings have their titles explained in English. The cathedral still holds religious services. The chips in the marble columns outside were caused by German artillery fire during the siege of Leningrad.

Despite the fact that the cathedral's glowing dome would make a convenient "reference point #1" for the Luftwaffe siege during WWII, the starving citizens of Leningrad planted cabbages in the square directly in front. In an admirable display of restraint, however, they never touched the unique collection of seeds from all over the world stored in the Vavilov Institute of Plant Breeding on the other side of the square. Photographs of the cabbage field are displayed at the somewhat depressing "Leningrad During the War Years and the Siege" exhibition in **Rumyantsev House,** Angliyskaya nab. 44 (Английская), along the embankment, 5min. from the Admiralty heading in the opposite direction of the Hermitage. A blue-and-white sign at Nevsky pr. 14, close to the Admiralty, is yet another reminder of the 900-day siege. It reads, "Citizens! During artillery bombardments this side of the street is more dangerous."

FORTRESS OF PETER & PAUL

M2: Gorkovskaya. Exiting the Metro, turn right on Kamennoostrovsky pr. (Каменноостровский), the street in front of you (there is no sign). Follow the street to the river, and cross the wooden bridge to the island fortress. Tel. 232 9454. Open M and Th-Su 11am-6pm, Tu 11am-5pm; closed last Tuesday of each month. Peter's Cabin open M W-Su 10am-5:30pm; closed last Monday of the month. Aurora open Tu-Th and Sa-Su 10:30am-4pm. US$3, students US$1.50; additional charges for special exhibitions. Cabin 25R, students 15R. Purchase a single ticket for all museums at the kassa located in the "boathouse" in the middle of the island or in the smaller kassa to the right just inside the main entrance.

Across the river from the Hermitage, the walls and golden spire of the **Fortress of Peter and Paul** (Petropavlovskaya Krepost; Петропавловская Крепость) beckon. In summer, locals try to sunbathe on the rocky embankment; in winter, walruses and masochists in Speedos swim in holes cut through the ice. Construction of the fortress began on May 27, 1703, a date now considered the birthday of St. Petersburg.

Originally intended as a defense against the Swedes, it never saw battle; Peter I defeated the northern invaders before the bulwarks were finished. With the Swedish threat gone, Peter turned the fortress into a prison for political dissidents; sardonic etchings by inmates now cover the citadel's stone walls. The fortress currently houses a gold-spired cathedral that gives the complex its name.

Inside, the **Peter and Paul Cathedral** (Petropavlovsky Sobor; Петропавловский Собор) glows with rosy marble walls and a breath-taking Baroque iconostasis. From the ceiling, cherubs keep watch over the graves of Peter the Great and most of his successors. Before entering the main vault you will pass through the recently restored **Chapel of St. Catherine the Martyr**. The bodies of the Romanovs—Tsar Nicholas II, his family, and their faithful servants—were entombed here on July 17, 1998, the eightieth anniversary of their murder at the hands of the Bolsheviks. Just outside the church, Mikhail Shemyakin's controversial bronze statue of Peter the Great at once fascinates and offends Russian visitors with its scrawny head and elongated body. **Nevsky Gate** (Nevskoe Vorota; Невское Ворота), site of many an execution, stands beyond the statue, to the left. Plaques on the wall mark the water level of the city's worst floods. **Trubetskoy Bastion** (Трубецкой Бастион), in the fortress's southwest corner, is a reconstruction of the prison where Peter the Great held and tortured his first son, Aleksei. Dostoevsky, Gorky, Trotsky, and Lenin's older brother also spent time here. Plaques in Russian next to each cell identify other notable inmates.

Like a set of *matryoshki* dolls, the small brick house, set back in a park on the Petrograd Side of the fortress, shelters another house, **Peter's Cabin** (Domik Petra Pervovo; Домик Петра Первого). This was the first building constructed in St. Petersburg, and served as home to Peter I while he supervised the construction of the city. Now it's a shrine, with exhibits on the founding of the city and the Tsar's victory over Sweden; don't be surprised if the furniture is more exciting. Continue along the river past Peter's Cabin to the cruiser **Aurora** (Avrora; Аврора). Initially deployed in the Russo-Japanese war, the ship later played a critical role in the 1917 Revolution when it fired a blank by the Winter Palace, scaring the pants off Kerensky and his Provisional Government. Inside there are exhibits on revolutionary and military history.

ALEXSANDER NEVSKY MONASTERY

M3, 4: Pl. Aleksandra Nevska. Lazarus Cemetery lies to the left of the entrance, Tihkin to the right. Cemeteries open M-W and F-Su 10am-7pm. Cathedral services M-Sa 6am, 10am, and 5pm; Su 7am, 10am, and 5pm. Admission to both cemeteries 20R, students 10R. Cameras 10R; video 20R. Free admission to cathedral, but donations requested. No shorts allowed in the monastery, and women must cover their heads.

RUSSIA

A major pilgrimage spot and a peaceful place to stroll, **Alexsander Nevsky Monastery** (Aleksandro-Nevskaya Lavra; Александро-невская Лавра) derives its name and fame from Prince Aleksandr of Novgorod, whose body was moved here by Peter the Great in 1724. In 1797, it received the highest monastic title of *"lavra,"* bestowed on only four Orthodox monasteries. Placement of the dead has always been a concern of Russian Orthodoxy; cemeteries are of major importance, and gravestones are carefully sculpted. Many of the tombs in Aleksandro-Nevskaya Lavra's two cemeteries are extremely elaborate. A cobblestone path lined with souvenir-sellers and beggars connects the cathedral and the two cemeteries.

The 1716 **Lazarus Cemetery** (Lazarevskoye Kladbishche; Лазаревское Кладбище) is the city's oldest burial ground. Going around the edge of the cemetery to the left leads to the plain black tomb of **Natalya,** the wife of Aleksandr Pushkin. Smack in the tiny cemetery's middle lie the graves of two famous St. Petersburg architects: **Andrei Voronikhin,** who designed the Kazan Cathedral (see p. 612), and **Adrian Zakharov,** architect of the Admiralty (see p. 612). The **Tikhvin Cemetery** (Tikhvinskoye Kladbishche; Тихвинское Кладбище), next to Lazarus Cemetery, is newer and larger, and is the permanent home of a still more distinguished group. **Fyodor Dostoevsky** could only afford to be buried here thanks to the Russian Orthodox Church; his grave is around to the right, fairly near the entrance and always strewn with flowers. Continuing along the cemetery's right edge, you arrive at the cluster of famous musicians: **Mikhail Glinka,** composer of the first Russian opera and a contemporary of Pushkin's, and **Mikhail Balakirev,** to the left of Glinka, who taught **Nikolai Rimsky-Korsakov.** Balakirev's famous pupil's grave is recognizable by its unfriendly angels and white marble Orthodox cross. Many are drawn to **Aleksandr Borodin's** grave by the gold mosaic of a composition sheet from his famous String Quartet #1. **Modest Mussorgsky, Arthur Rubinstein,** and **Pyotr Tchaikovsky** are in magnificent tombs next to Borodin. Once Tchaikovsky's homosexuality was discovered and publicized, the Conservatory deemed it more appropriate that the musician commit suicide than disgrace its hallowed halls. Whether the composer truly complied or was murdered is, like most of Russian history, still unclear, but black angels watch over his tomb. The tomb left of the entrance is that of **Igor Stravinsky.**

The **Church of the Annunciation** (Blagoveshchenskaya Tserkov; Благовещенская Церковь), farther along the central stone path on the left, was the original burial place of the Romanovs, who were moved to Peter and Paul Cathedral in 1998 (see p. 609). The church is currently under renovation. The **Trinity Cathedral** (Troitsky Sobor; Троицкий Собор), at the end of the path, is a functioning church, teeming with priests in black robes and *babushki* devoutly crossing themselves and kissing icons. The large interior contains many altars and icons. It is often possible to join English tours at the monastery; ignore the herd mentality and focus on the knowledgeable guide.

SMOLNY INSTITUTE & CATHEDRAL

Take bus #136, 134, or 46 from the stop across the street from M1: Chernyshevskaya to the Smolny (Смольный) complex. Or, just head north 20min. on Suvorovsky pr. (Суворовский) from Nevsky pr. Tel. 271 7632. Open Su-Tu and Th-Sa 11am-6pm, W 11am-5pm; kassa closes 45min. earlier. Performances Sept.-May. Exhibition 100R; tower 100R.

Once a prestigious school for aristocratic girls, the **Smolny Institute** earned its place in history when Trotsky and Lenin set up the headquarters of the **Bolshevik Central Committee** here in 1917 and planned the Revolution from behind its yellow walls. Now it is the municipal office of St. Petersburg. The gate to the buildings at the end of the drive read, from left to right, "First Soviet of the dictatorship of the proletariat" and "Proletariats of all nations, unite!" Farther down, again from left to right, are busts of Engels and Marx. Next door the blue-and-white **Smolny Cathedral** (Smolny Sobor; Смольный Собор) rises, notable for combining Baroque and Orthodox Russian architectural styles. The church now functions as an exhibition and concert hall. Climb to the top of a 68m high bell tower and survey Lenin's—er, Peter's—city.

SUMMER GARDENS & PALACE

M2: Nevsky Prospekt. Turn right on nab. Kanala Griboedova, cross the Moyka, and turn right onto ul. Pestelya. The palace and gardens are on your left, behind the Russian Museum and directly across the river from Petropavlovskaya Krepost. Tel. 314 0456. Garden open daily in summer 8am-11pm; off-season 8am-7pm. Palace open M and W-Su 10am-6pm; closed the last Monday of the month. 50R, students 25R; Tea and Coffee Houses 5R each.

The **Summer Gardens and Palace** (Letny Sad i Dvorets; Летний Сад и Дворец) are lovely places to rest and cool off. Two entrances at the north and south lead to long, shady paths lined with replicas of Classical Roman sculptures and busts. In the northeast corner of the Garden, you'll find Peter's **Summer Palace.** The Tsar lived downstairs, surrounded by heavy German furniture and lots of clocks, while upstairs resided his kids and wife Cathy, who upon his death became Russia's first tsarina. Lots of 18th-century paintings and Petrobilia await inside, but you must join a Russian tour to see it. Buy your ticket, and wait outside until they invite you in. The **Tea House** (Chayny Domik; Чайный Домик) and **Coffee House** (Kofeyny Domik; Кофейный Домик), also in the Garden, hold temporary exhibitions.

Mars Field (Marosovo Pole; Маросово Поле), so named because of military parades held here in the 19th century, extends next to the Summer Gardens. The broad, open park is now a memorial to the victims of the Revolution and the Civil War (1917-19). There is a monument in the center with an eternal flame. Don't walk on the grass; you'd be treading on a massive common grave.

ALONG NEVSKY PROSPEKT

The easternmost boulevard of central St. Petersburg, Nevsky pr. is the city's equivalent of the Champs-Elysées or Unter der Linden. Like nearly everything else in the city, Nevsky pr. was constructed under Peter the Great. In accordance with his vision for St. Petersburg, the avenue is of epic scale, running 4.5km from the Neva in the west to the Alexander Nevsky Monastery in the east; the golden dome of the Admiralty is visible all the way from pl. Vosstaniya, two-thirds of the way down the avenue to the monastery. In addition to housing many of St. Petersburg's most monumental sights, Nevsky pr. is also notable for its chronology of architectural styles and vibrant street life.

ADMIRALTY. (Admiralteystvo; Адмиралтество). The Prospekt begins at the Admiralty, whose golden spire—painted black during WWII to disguise it from German artillery bombers—towers over the Admiralty gardens and Dvortsovaya pl. The height of the **tower**—one of the first buildings in early St. Petersburg—supposedly allowed Peter to supervise the continued construction of his city. He also directed Russia's new shipyard and navy from its offices. The **gardens,** initially designed to allow for a wider firing range when defending the shipyard, now hold the statues of important Russian literary figures. *(M2: Nevsky Prospekt. Exit the Metro, turn left and walk to the end of Nevsky pr.)*

BRONZE HORSEMAN. Etienne Falconet's Bronze Horseman stands as a symbol of the city and its founder's massive will. Catherine the Great commissioned the statue as a "gift" to her father-in-law in 1782. It shows Peter, mounted on a rearing horse and crushing a snake. The snake symbolizes both Sweden, which Peter I defeated in the Northern War, and the "evils" of Russia over which he triumphed. The horse stands on a rock from the site outside St. Petersburg where Peter first surveyed the city; the wave behind him represents the sea (St. Petersburg was Russia's first seaport to the west). *(M2 Nevsky Prospekt. Exiting the Metro, turn left and walk to the end of Nevsky pr.; the statue is to the left of the Admiralty as you face it.)*

KAZAN CATHEDRAL. (Kazansky Sobor; Казанский Собор). The colossal edifice across the street from Dom Knigi, the Kazan Cathedral was modeled after St. Peter's in Rome but designed and built by Russian architects (and left to decay by the Soviets). Formerly the **Museum of the History of Religion and Atheism,** now the **State Museum of the History of Religion,** its gold cross was restored in 1994. The cathedral, completed in 1811, was originally created to house **Our Lady of Kazan,** a now-lost sacred icon of the Romanovs. The few remaining icons, robes, and Bibles are displayed in glass cases, but pale in comparison to their home and are not worth the admission fee. *(M2: Nevsky Prospekt. Tel. 311 0495. Open M-Tu and Th-F 11am-6pm, Sa noon-6pm, Su 12:30-6pm; kassa closes at 5pm. Morning services M-Sa 9am, Su 10am. Cathedral is free; museum 45R, students 22R.)*

CHURCH OF THE BLEEDING SAVIOR. (Spas Na Krovi; Спас На Крови). The colorful Church of the Bleeding Savior, a.k.a. the Savior on the Blood, sits on the site of Tsar Aleksandr II's 1881 assassination. Reopened after 20 years of Soviet condemnation, the church has been beautifully renovated. The walls are covered with 7000 square feet of mosaics, restored to correspond with the designs of the original Russian artists. In the center of it all sits a bust of Tsar Aleksandr II. The adjacent chapel houses various temporary exhibitions. *(M2: Nevsky Prospekt. Three blocks off Nevsky pr. up on the Griboyedov canal from the House of Books. Tel. 315 9732.)*

OSTROVOSKOVO SQUARE. (Pl. Ostrovskovo; пл. Островского). One of the most tranquil squares in the city, Ostrovoskovo Square is home to a monument to Catherine the Great surrounded by the principal political and cultural figures of her reign: Potemkin, her favorite; Marshall Suvorov; Princess Dashkova; and poet Derzhavin, among others. To the right is St. Petersburg's main public library, decorated with sculptures and reliefs of ancient philosophers. The oldest Russian theater, **Alexsandrovsky** (Александровский), built by the architect Rossi in 1828, is behind Catherine's monument. The first production of Gogol's *The Inspector General* was staged here in 1836. On ul. Zodchego Rossi, behind the theater, you'll find the **Vaga-**

nova School of Choreography, which graduated such greats as Vaslav Nizhinsky, Anna Pavlova, Rudolf Nureyev, and Mikhail Baryshnikov. *(M3: Gostiny Dvor. Exit the Metro and head right on Nevsky pr. The square is on the right.)*

SHEREMETYEV PALACE. (Dvorets Sheremetevykh; Дворец Шереметьевых). Constructed in the early 1700s as a residence for Peter the Great's marshal, Boris Sheremetyev, Sheremetyev Palace underwent numerous alterations throughout the 18th century. After the Revolution, it briefly housed the Museum of Russian Everyday Life, but eventually neglect left it in decay. Major restoration has been underway since 1990; the two rooms currently open contain a permanent exhibition on music in St. Petersburg. The palace's music room hosts occasional concerts. *(M3: Gostiny Dvor. Nab. Fontanki 34. Tel. 272 38 98. Open W-F 2-6pm, Sa-Su noon-6pm; closed last Wednesday of the month. 20R, Russians 3R. Concerts Oct.-May. 5R.)*

UPRISING SQUARE. (Ploshchadz Vosstaniya; пл. Восстания). Some of the bloodiest confrontations of the February Revolution took place in Uprising Square, highlighted by the moment the Cossacks turned on police during a demonstration. The obelisk in the center, erected in 1985, replaced a statue of Tsar Aleksandr III that was removed in 1937. Across from the train station, the green Oktyabrskaya Hotel bears the words "Город-герой Ленинград" (Leningrad, the Hero-City), in remembrance of the crippling losses suffered during the German siege. *(M1: Ploshchadz Vosstaniya. The halfway point of Nevsky pr., near Moskovsky Vokzal.)*

OCTOBER REGION

St. Petersburg's most romantic quarter, the October Region (Oktyabrsky Rayon; Октябрьский Район) sees canal Griboedova meander through quiet neighborhoods with leafy parks.

YUSUPOVSKY GARDENS. (Yuspuovsky Sad; Юсуповский Сад). On the outer borders of the October Region, the large park Yusupovsky Gardens, named after the prince who succeeded in killing Rasputin only after poisoning, shooting, and ultimately drowning him, provides an island for peaceful picnics.

ST. NICHOLAS' CATHEDRAL. (Nikolsky Sobor; Никольский Собор). A magnificent blue-and-gold structure, St. Nicholas's Cathedral was constructed in striking 18th-century Baroque style. The bells atop the spectacular tower are supposed to have special mystic powers. Inside, low ceilings make the smell of burning wax overpowering. *(M4: Sadovaya. Turn right off ul. Sadovaya and cross the canal onto ul. Rimskovo-Korsakovo (Римского-Корсакого), near the Marinsky Theater and Conservatory. Enter across from the bell tower. Services daily at 10am and 6pm.)*

LARGE CHORAL SYNAGOGUE OF ST. PETERSBURG. St. Petersburg's only functioning synagogue, the Large Choral Synagogue of St. Petersburg, is also Europe's second-largest. The synagogue celebrated its 100th anniversary in 1993 and has only around 70 regular members, down from 5000 in 1893. Make sure that the knowledgeable guides show you the wedding hall. *(Lermontovsky pr. 2. M4: Sadovaya. Turn right off ul. Sadovaya and cross the canal onto ul. Rimskovo-Korsakovo, continuing to Lermontovsky pr. and turning right. Tel. 114 1153. Open daily 9am-9pm. Morning and evening services daily—call for times.)*

OTHER SIGHTS

MENSHIKOV PALACE. In the middle of the Strelka district on Vasilevsky Island (Vasilevsky Ostrov; Васильевский Остров), Menshikov Palace is an unassuming yellow building with a small courtyard. Aleksandr Menshikov was a good friend of Peter I and governor of St. Petersburg. Peter entertained guests here before he built the Summer Palace, and then gave it to the Menshikovs, who employed Catherine I as a serving-girl before she became Peter's second wife. The museum displays a "Russian Culture of Peter's Time" exhibition, with fragments of original 18th-century interiors and Dutch tiles. *(Universitetskaya nab. 15 (Университетская). M3: Vasileostrovskaya. It's better, however, to cross the bridge north of the Admiralteystvo and walk left. Tel. 213 11 12. Open Tu-Su 10:30am-4:30pm. 30R, students 6R.)*

PISKAROV MEMORIAL CEMETERY. (Piskarovskoye Memorialnoye Kladbishche; Пискаровское Мемориальное Кладбище). To understand St. Petersburg's obsession with WWII, come to the remote and chilling Piskarov Memorial Cemetery. Close to a million people died during the 900 days that the German army laid siege to the city; this cemetery is their grave. An eternal flame and grassy mounds bearing the year are all that mark the dead. The place is nearly empty, yet the emotion is palpable—this is the grave of a Hero City. The monument reads: "No one is forgotten; nothing is forgotten." *(Stop at M1: Ploshchadz Muzhestva (Площадь Мужества) and go left to the street. At the corner, cross Nepokorennykh pr. (Непокоренных) in front and catch bus #123 from the shelter. Ride about six stops (7-10min.). On the right will be a large flower shop and on the left the cemetery, recognizable by a low granite wall and two square stone gate buildings, each with four columns.)*

MUSEUMS

There are three kinds of museums in St. Petersburg: the giant, famous ones, fast-disappearing Soviet shrines, and recreated homes of cultural figures. The first are a must, despite high foreigner prices and yammering tour groups. The second appeal largely to lovers of the absurd and/or military history. The third are pilgrimage sites for those seeking such relics as a famous author's pen and toothbrush, but are less revealing for those who don't read Russian.

A MUSEUM-GOER IN A STRANGE LAND Like many in Eastern Europe, museums in Russia charge foreigners much higher rates. In desperation, some travelers don a fluffy fur hat, snarl a little, push the exact number of rubles for a Russian ticket toward the *babushka* at the *kassa,* and remain stoically mute. Go ahead and try; it might work. Once inside, don't worry about forgetting to see anything–the *babushki* in each room will make sure of that. Many museums, with floors made of precious inlaid wood, will ask visitors to don *tapochki,* giant slippers that go over your shoes and transform the polished gallery floor into a veritable ice rink. There are no guardrails–only irreplaceable imperial china–to slow your stride. Make sure your slippers fit well, or after navigating dozens of slippery wooden exhibition rooms you will meet an unfortunate end on the marble stairs.

Russian Museum (Russky Muzey; Русский Музей; tel. 219 1615; fax 314 4153). M3: Gostiny Dvor. In the yellow 1825 Michael Palace (Mikhailovsky Dvorets), behind Pushkin's monument. Go down ul. Mikhailovsky past the Grand Hotel Europe. Enter through the basement in the right corner of the courtyard; go downstairs and turn left. Or, enter through the Benois Wing on Gribodova Canal. Boasts the 2nd-largest collection of Russian art after Moscow's Tretyakov Gallery, and the title of first public museum of Russian art (1898). 12th- to 17th-century icons, 18th- and 19th-century paintings and sculpture, and Russian folk art arranged chronologically. Benois Wing with modern art and such controversial exhibitions as "The Color Red in Russian Art." The 20th-century collection may disappoint, with nary a Kandinsky or Chagall in sight. Open M 10am-5pm, W-Su 10am-6pm; *kassa* closes at 5pm. 140R, students 70R.

Ethnographic Museum (Muzey Etnografii; Музей Этнографии), Inzhenernaya ul. 4, bldg. 1 (tel. 210 4320). Next to the Russian Museum. Hands-on exhibitions of the folk traditions, arts, crafts, and cultures of the 15 former Soviet republics. Open Tu-Su 11am-6pm; *kassa* closes at 5pm. 20R, students 10R.

Kunstkamera Anthropological and Ethnographic Museum (Muzey Antropologii i Etnografii–Kunstkamera; Музей Антропологии и Этнографии–Кунсткамера; tel. 218 1412). Facing the Admiralty from across the river. A natural history museum with a morbid twist. "Lives and habits" of the world's indigenous peoples join Peter's anatomical collection, featuring severed heads and deformed fetuses bathed in formaldehyde. Open M-W and F-Su 11am-5pm. 50R, students 20R.

Zoological Museum (Zoologicheskiy Muzey; Зоологический Музей), Universitetskaya nab. 1 (tel. 218 0112). Right next door to the Anthropological and Ethnographic Museum. Contains 40,000 animals, fish, insects, and specimens, including a stuffed mammoth. Open M-Th and Sa-Su 10:50am-4:50pm. 15R.

Theater and Music Museum (Muzey Teatralnovo i Muzykalnovo Iskusstva; Музей Театрального и Музыкального Искуства), pl. Ostrovskovo 6, 3rd fl. (tel. 311 2195). M3: Gostiny Dvor. Posters, programs, set designs, and elaborate costumes. Tickets to concerts and lectures (5-25R) in the small concert room sold at entrance. Open W 1-7pm, Th-Su 11am-6pm; closed last Friday of the month. 30R, students 10R.

Museum of Russian Political History (Muzey Politicheskoy Istorii Rossii; Музей Политической Истории России), ul. Kuybysheva 2/4 (tel. 233 7052). M2: Gorkovskaya. Go down Kronverksky pr. toward the mosque and turn left on Kuybysheva. The museum is located in the mansion of Matilda Kshesinskaya, prima ballerina of the Mariinsky Theater and a lover of Nicholas II. It displays a range of Soviet propaganda, focusing on the 1905 and 1917 revolutions, including a printing press, revolutionary items, and other artifacts. Upstairs exhibits focus on modern Russia, with several photos of a tipsy-looking Boris Yeltsin. Open M-W and F-Su 10am-6pm. 60R, students 30R.

Pushkin Museum (Muzey Pushkina; Музей Пушкина), nab. Reki Moyki 12 (Реки Мойки; tel. 311 3801). M2: Nevsky Prospekt. Walk right on Nevsky from the Metro, then turn right onto nab. Reki Moyki and follow the canal; it's the yellow building on the right. Enter through the courtyard; the *kassa* and museum entrance are on the left. Former residence of Russia's adored poet. Personal effects of the poet, and many drafts and sketches (Pushkin apparently loved to draw funny-looking people in his margins). In the library where Pushkin died, the furniture is original, and the clock is stopped at the time of his death. Interesting to literary buffs, but not many others. Open M and W-Su 10:30am-5pm; closed last Friday of the month. 20R, students 10R, plus another 40R for the mandatory taped tour.

Dostoevsky House (Dom Dostoevskovo; Дом Достоевского), Kuznechny per. 5/2 (Кузнечный; tel. 164 6950). M1: Vladimirskaya, around the corner to the right. Dostoevsky wrote *The Brothers Karamazov* here; his notes and bills, on display, are in perfect order, thanks to his wife and secretary, Anna. The area resembles Dostoevsky's St. Petersburg, although *Crime and Punishment* junkies should check out Sennaya pl. (Сенная), the setting of the book's grisly murder. Expensive neighborhood tours available. Open Tu-Su 11am-6pm; *kassa* closes 5:30pm; closed last Wednesday of each month. 70R, students 10R. Film versions of Dostoevsky's novels Sa-Su at noon. 20R, students 10R.

Anna Akhmatova Museum (Muzey Anny Akhmatovoy; Музей Анны Ахматовой), Fontanki 34 (tel. 272 18 11). Enter at Liteyny pr. 51, through an archway; keep left and follow the signs. In a wing of the Sheremetev Palace. Personal possessions of the poet whose courageous Soviet-era writings made her a national hero. Akhmatova lived here from 1933-41 and again in 1944-54. Open Tu-Su 10:30am-5pm; closed last Wednesday of each month. 70R, students 35R. Tours in Russian only.

Artillery Museum (Artillerysky Muzey; Артиллерийский Музей; tel. 238 4704). M2: Gorkovskaya. One of the oldest museums in the city. Opened in 1756, it moved to its present site—in an old arsenal—in 1868. There are lots of cannons, including the toy one little Peter the Great played with, as well as tanks in the courtyard. Open W-Su 11am-5pm; closed last Thursday of each month. 100R, students 50R.

Arctic and Antartic Musuem (Muzey Arktiki i Antarktiki; Музей Арктики и Антарктики; tel. 113 1998 and 311 2549). M3: Mayakovskaya. On the corner of Kuznechny per. and ul. Marata (Марата). Model ships, nautical instruments, and most everything else Arctic expeditions would have used. Fox-furs and stuffed wolves glorify humankind's invasion of the wild. Open W-Su 10am-5pm; *kassa* closes at 4:30 pm; closed last Saturday of each month. 75R, students 25R.

ENTERTAINMENT

St. Petersburg's famed White Nights lend the night sky a pale glow from mid-June to early July. In summer, couples stroll under the illuminated night sky and watch the bridges over the Neva go up at 1:30am. Remember to walk on the same side of the river as your hotel—the bridges don't go back down until 4-5am, although some close briefly between 3 and 3:20am.

The city of Tchaikovsky, Prokofiev, and Stravinsky continues to live up to its reputation for classical performing arts. It is fairly easy to get tickets to world-class performances for as little as 20-30R, although many of the renowned theaters are known to grossly overcharge foreigners. Buying Russian tickets from scalpers will save you money; be *very* sure that they aren't for last night's show. If you do get Russian tickets, dress up and speak no English, or the ushers may ask to see your passport. The **Mariinsky Ballet,** one of the world's best companies and the place where Russian ballet won its fame, often has cheap tickets. Sprinkled across the city are a few large concert halls. In the third week of June, when the sun barely touches the horizon, the city holds a series of outdoor evening concerts as part of the **White Nights Festival.** Check kiosks, posters, and the monthly *Pulse*, published in English and free at most upscale hotels, for more info. The theater season ends around the time of the festival and begins again in early September, but check for summer performances at ticket offices at Nevsky pr. 42, across from Gostiny Dvor, or at kiosks and tables near Isaakievsky Sobor and along Nevsky pr. It may be more productive to try the *kassa* of the theater where the performances are held. A monthly program in Russian is usually posted throughout the city.

In general, theaters start selling tickets 20 days in advance, and only cheap ones are still available by the day of the performance. *Yarus* (ярус) are the cheapest seats, and, close to the start of a performance, some viewers manage to sneak into this section for free. Performances often start a few minutes late. Russians dress up for the theater and consider foreigners who arrive for a performance in everyday clothes an insult to their culture.

For the most part, Russian performers are at their best when doing Russian pieces. While the Maly Opera's rendition of *La Traviata* may be the worst Italian opera you've seen, Tchaikovsky's *Queen of Spades (Picovaya Dama; Пиковая Дама)* will easily make up for it; likewise, choose Prokofiev over Strauss at any orchestral performance. As with opera and orchestral music, Russian plays in Russian are generally better than Shakespeare in Russian. The Russian circus, while justly famous, is not for animal lovers. In fact, even those who come garbed in fur coats and hats may want to run home and throw red paint on themselves after seeing a bear whipped into walking a tightrope. Nonetheless, the circus can be amusing and, of course, you don't need to speak Russian to enjoy it.

BALLET & OPERA

Mariinsky Teatr (Марийнский), a.k.a. the "Kirov," Teatralnaya pl. 1 (Театральная; tel. 114 4344). M4: Sadovaya. Walk 10min. along canal Griboyedova, then turn right onto the square. This imposing aqua building where Tchaikovsky's *Nutcracker* and *Sleeping Beauty* both premiered is one of the most famous ballet halls in the world. Pavlova, Nureyev, Nizhinsky, and Baryshnikov all started here. For two weeks in June, the theater hosts the **White Nights Festival,** for which tickets are relatively easy to get. Tickets (15R and up) go on sale ten days in advance. Matinees Sept.-June 11:30pm; evening performances 7pm. *Kassa* open W-Su 11am-3pm and 4-7pm.

Maly Teatr (Малый Театр), a.k.a. "Mussorgsky," pl. Iskusstv 1 (Искусств; tel. 219 1978), near the Russky Muzey. Open July-Aug., when the Mariinsky is closed. Similarly impressive concert hall hosting excellent performances of Russian ballet and opera. Tickets for foreigners up to 200R, Russians 5-30R. *Kassa* open daily 11am-3pm and 4-8pm. Performances 7pm. Bring your passport; documents are checked at the door.

Conservatoriya (Консерватория), Teatralnaya pl. 3 (tel. 312 25 19), across from Mariinsky Teatr. M4: Sadovaya. Excellent student ballets and operas often performed here. Evening performances M-F 6:30pm, Sa-Su 6pm. Matinees at noon. Tickets from 10R. *Kassa* open daily noon-6pm.

CLASSICAL MUSIC

Shostakovich Philharmonic Hall, Mikhailovskaya ul. 2 (tel. 118 4257), opposite the Grand Hotel Europe. M3: Gostiny Dvor. Large concert hall with both classical and modern concerts. Acoustics are flawed due to its original use for Boyar Council meetings, which had no need for such subtleties. One of the few arenas offering cheap tickets to foreigners. Tickets from 10R, depending on the concert and day. The Philharmonic is on tour for most of the summer.

Akademicheskaya Kapella (Академическая Капелла), nab. Reki Moyki 20 (tel. 314 1048). M2: Nevsky Prospekt. Small hall for choirs, solos, and small orchestras. Concerts at 7pm. Prices from 10R. *Kassa* open daily noon-3pm and 4-7pm.

Glinka Maly Zal, Nevsky pr. 30 (tel. 312 4585). Part of the Shostakovich Philharmonic Hall, but has better acoustics than in the main hall. Tickets from 20R, depending on the concert and day. Concerts 7pm. *Kassa* open daily 11am-3pm and 4-8pm.

THEATER

Aleksandrinsky Teatr (Александринский Театр), pl. Ostrovskovo 2 (tel. 110 4103). M3: Gostiny Dvor. Turn right on Nevsky pr., then right at the park with Catherine's statue. Ballet and theater—mostly Western classics like *Hamlet* and *Cyrano de Bergerac*. Attracts some of Russia's most famous actors and companies; St. Petersburg citizens wait in line for hours to see some Moscow troupes. Summer ballet season starts July 25. Performances throughout the summer at 11am and 7:30pm. Tickets available 20 days in advance (10-50R). *Kassa* open daily 11am-3pm and 4-8pm.

Bolshoy Dramatichesky Teatr (Большой Драматический Театр), nab. Reki Fontanki 65 (Реки Фонтанки; tel. 310 0401). M3: Gostiny Dvor. Conservative productions of Russian classics. Tickets 8-70R. *Kassa* open daily 11am-3pm and 4-6pm.

CIRCUS

Tsirk (Цирк; Circus), nab. Fontanki 3 (tel. 314 8478), near the Russky Muzey. M3: Gostiny Dvor. Russia's oldest traditional circus, made more interesting by a non-traditional live orchestra. Tickets from 10R. Matinees 11:30am, afternoon shows 3pm, evening shows 7pm. Closed mid-July to mid-Sept. *Kassa* open daily 11am-4pm.

NIGHTLIFE

During the pre-Gorbachev era, St. Petersburg was the heart of the Russian underground music scene; today, the city still hosts a large number of interesting clubs. There are plenty of expensive dance clubs for Russian *biznessmeni* too, but better evening fare is tucked away in former bomb shelters off the main drag. Be careful going home late at night, especially if you've been drinking—loud, drunk foreigners might as well be carrying neon signs saying "rob me!" Taking taxis home is common and fairly safe, but check to see when your bridge rises or you may be stuck on the wrong side of the river. Clubs last no longer than most high school relationships; the hip scene tends to get infatuated and then grow quickly bored. HI hostels can often recommend the newest places. Check the Friday issue of *St. Petersburg Times* and *Pulse* for current events and special promotions. For info on jazz clubs around St. Petersburg, call Jazz-inform (tel. 327 3865).

Metro, Ligovsky Prospekt 174 (tel. 166 0204). M4: Ligovsky Prospekt. From the Metro, turn left on Ligovsky and follow it for 10min. to the neon sign. Three bars, two dance floors (pop downstairs, techno up), a young crowd, and scantily clad bartenders. One of the hottest spots in town at press time. Draft beer 35-75R per pint; mixed drinks 45-80R. Cover M-Th and Su 36-45R; F-Sa 54-90R. Open daily 9pm-4am.

Mama, ul. Malaya Monetnaya 3b (Малая Монетная; tel. 232 3137). M2: Gorkovskaya. Very hip, very young, very techno and raging very late. Hardcore Fridays, jungle Saturdays. Beer on tap 30-55R. Cover 60R. Open F-Sa 11:50pm-6am.

JFC Jazz Club, Shpalernaya ul. 33 (Шпалерная; tel. 272 9850). M1: Chernyshevskaya. Go right for four blocks on pr. Chernyshevskovo (Чернышевского), then turn left on Shpalernaya and look for the small sign on the left. The best local jazz in a relaxed, expat setting. Arrive early or call ahead for a table. Cover 35R. Open daily 7pm-10pm.

Moloko (Milk; Молоко), Perekupnoy per. 12 (Перекупной; tel. 274 9467). M3, 4: Pl. Aleksandra Nevskovo. Walk up Nevsky pr. three blocks, then turn right. Small rock club featuring various local bands and friendly local students. Cover 20-30R. Open Th-Su 7-11pm.

The Shamrock, ul. Dekabristov 27 (Декабристов; tel. 219 4625). M4: Sadovaya. Across from the Mariinsky in Teatralnaya pl. A shining example of Ireland's second-largest export, this authentic Irish bar is a fun place to down a beer or two (or three). Western music and a young but clean-cut crowd. Pint of Guinness or Kilkenny 35R. Live Irish music on weekends. Open daily noon-2am.

GAY & LESBIAN NIGHTLIFE

69 Club, 2-aya Krasnoarmeiskaya 6 (2-ая Красноармеиская; tel. 259 5163). M1: Technologichesky Institut. Popular with both gay and straight clubbers. Pop and Eurodance with splashes of techno. Drinks are steep (50-100R) but not stiff. Male strippers perform at 2am. Cover 30-120R. Open daily 11pm-4am.

Jungle, ul. Blokhina 8 (tel. 238 8033). Gay club on the Petrogradskaya Storona. No sign—spot the aquamarine door and go upstairs. Admittance based on membership, but foreigners are welcome. Call in advance. Eurodance with some Russian pop. Erotic and drag shows 1:45am. Cover 30-50R, men free 11-11:30pm. Bring ID—no one under 17 is allowed, although exceptions are common. Open F-Sa 11-6am.

DAYTRIPS FROM ST. PETERSBURG

Ride the suburban *elektrichka* trains out of St. Petersburg to witness the Russians' love of the countryside. Most residents of St. Petersburg own or share a *dacha* outside the city and go there every weekend; families crowd outgoing trains loaded with groceries, pets, and sometimes lumber for a new construction project. The tsars were no different; they, too, built country houses, and several such palaces have been restored to their original opulence. The three palaces stand on what was German territory during the siege of Leningrad from 1942 to 1944. All were burned to the ground during the Nazi retreat, but Soviet authorities provided the staggering sums of money necessary to rebuild these symbols of rich cultural heritage during the postwar reconstruction. Today, they provide wholly worthwhile daytrips from St. Petersburg. Although Peterhof and the Catherine Palace in Pushkin have small cafes nearby, they are grossly overpriced, so bring a picnic lunch to eat in the idyllic parks. Wear a jacket if your destination is Peterhof—the grounds run up against the Gulf of Finland and the garden can get quite windy.

PETERHOF (ПЕТЕРГОФ)

Formerly known as Petrodvorets (Петродворец), this is the largest and most thoroughly restored of the palaces. The entire complex at Peterhof is 300 years old, although many of the more recent tsars added their own personal touches. The **Grand Palace** (Bolshoy Dvorets; Большой Дворец; tel. 427 9527) was Peter's first residence here, but his daughter, Empress Elizabeth, and later, Catherine the Great greatly expanded and remodeled it. The rooms have been returned to their previous glory, reflecting the conflicting tastes of various tsars and the interior fashions from early Baroque to Neoclassicism. A palace tour (in English) is worthwhile.

Golden cherubs guard the ceremonial stairs to the palace. Just before the throne room, the **Chesma Gallery,** a room larger than most one-family homes, depicts the 1770 Russian victory over the Turks at Chesma Bay. Aleksandr Orlov supposedly arranged for a frigate to explode in front of the painter to ensure the images' authenticity. Farther along, two Chinese studies flank a picture gallery that contains 360 portraits by the Italian Pietro Rotari; all are of the same eight women dressed in different outfits of authentic 18th-century silk. Apparently his widow, strapped for cash, sold the whole lot to Catherine the Great. The last room on the tour—**Peter's study,** lined with elegantly carved oak wood panels—is a rest for the eyes after all the opulence. Much of the room inexplicably survived the Nazi invasion (unlike the rest of the grounds); the lighter panels are reconstructions, some of which took 1½ years to complete. (Open Tu-Su 10:30am-6pm; *kassa* closes at 5pm; closed last Tuesday of the month. Tours 10:30am-noon and 2:45-4:15pm. 200R, students 100R. Cameras 80R; video 200R. Handbags must be checked, 1R.)

Below the Grand Palace, the **Lower Gardens** are perfect for a post-palace picnic along on the shores of the Gulf of Finland. Most of the fountains are reconstructions, as post-war Germany couldn't remember what they did with the stolen originals. (Open daily 9am-9pm. 100R, students 50R. Fountains flow May-Sept. M-F 11am-8pm, Su 11am-9pm.) To the right of the gardens, a **Wax Museum** contains figures of the residents of Peterhof. (Open daily 9am-5pm. 100R, students 50R.) From the Wax Museum and the nearby quay, the view up the cascade with the Grand Palace as a backdrop is stunning. Look the other way to see the shores of Finland across the gulf. Follow the sound of children's shrieks and giggles to the **"joke fountains,"** which, activated by one misstep, splash their unwitting victims.

On the other side of the garden stands **Monplaisir,** where Peter actually lived (the big palace was only for special occasions). Smaller and less ostentatious than its neighbors (he was the tsar with good taste), it is graceful and elegant. The place is peaceful even on the busiest Saturdays. (Open M-Tu and Th-Su 10:30am-6pm; closed last Thursday of the month. 70R, students 35R.) Next door is the **Catherine Building** (Ekaterininsky Korpus; Екатерининский Корпус), where Catherine the Great laid low while her husband was (on her orders) being overthrown. (Open M-W and F-Su 10:30am-6pm; closed last Friday of each month. 70R, students 35R.)

The **Hermitage Pavilion,** in the woods of the eastern part of the lower park, is symmetrically opposite Monplaisir. The 124 pieces of 17th- and 18th-century European art in the first floor hall are well worth seeing. The kitchen affords a behind-the-scenes look at gala receptions, including 18th-century kitchenware. (Open Tu-Su 10:30am-5pm; closed last Thursday of the month. 18R, students 9R.)

GETTING THERE. The fastest and most exciting way to get to Peterhof during the summer is to take the **meteor** (hydrofoil; метеор) from the quay on Dvortsovaya nab. (Дворцовая) in front of the Hermitage (30min., every 30min. from 9:30am, 150R). Peterhof is also an easy trip by *elektrichka* from the Baltiysky vokzal (Балтийская; M1: Baltiyskaya; 40min., every 15min., 8R). Buy round-trip tickets from the ticket office (*prigorodnaya kassa;* Пригородная касса) in the courtyard—ask for "NO-viy Peter-GOFF, too-DAH ee oh-BRAHT-nah." Get off at Novy Peterhof (the destination of the train is posted on signs in front of the track). Be sure to sit in the first few cars on the train, or you might not see the sign for the station until you're chugging away from it.

TSARSKOYE SELO/PUSHKIN

About 25km south of the city, Tsarskoye Selo ("Tsar's Village") surrounds Catherine the Great's summer residence, a gorgeous azure, white, and gold Baroque palace overlooking sprawling, English-style parks. The area was renamed "Pushkin" during the Soviet era—most Russians and train conductors still use that name. Built in 1756 by the architect Rastrelli before he began work on the Winter Palace, this opulent residence was remodeled by Charles Cameron under the orders of Catherine the Great; she had the good taste to remove the gilding from the facade, desiring a modest "cottage" where she could relax. The Baroque Palace, named **Catherine's Palace** (Ekaterininsky Dvorets; tel. 466 6669) after Elizabeth's mom Catherine I, was largely destroyed by the Nazis; each room exhibits a photograph of it in a war-torn condition. The **Amber Room** suffered the most; its walls were stripped and probably lost forever (one rumor places the hidden furnishings somewhere in Paraguay). Even the exorbitant entrance fees don't suffice to repair these mansions completely. Still, many of the salons, especially the huge, glittering **Grand Hall** ballroom, have been magnificently restored. Elizabeth used to hold costume parties here. Today there is ample space for you to waltz around. The "golden" suites—so named for their lavish Baroque ornamentation—now hold those of the original furnishings that survived WWII. North of the main staircase more rooms wait, one displaying a number of exquisite artifacts from East Asia. Latch onto one of the many English-speaking tours. (Open W-M 10am-5pm; closed last Monday of the month. 186R, students 92R. Photos 86R.)

Many visitors choose to bring a picnic and wander through the surrounding parks. (Open daily 10am-8pm. 50R, students 25R; free after 6pm.) Aleksandr I's palace, although closed to the public, stands guard over a wild forest. The rest of the 1400-acre **Catherine Park** is a melange of English, French, and Italian gardening styles. The **Great Pond** is the centerpiece of the English section; it is possible to rent rowboats here in summer. To the east lies the Italian-landscaped park where Catherine would ramble with her dogs. Some believe Catherine loved Muffy and Fido (or the Russian equivalent) more than her children; they now rest in peace under the Pyramid. Numerous other structures are scattered around the pond. Next to Catherine's Palace, the **lycée** (tel. 476 6411) schooled a 12-year-old Pushkin, one of the school's first students. His cubbyhole can still be seen through hordes of awestruck Russians, along with the classrooms, laboratory, and music rooms. (Open M and W-Su 10:30am-4:30pm. 20R, students 10R.)

GETTING THERE. Take any *elektrichka* from Vitebsky vokzal (M1: Pushkinskaya). To buy your ticket, go to a gray, bunker-like building behind the station to the right. Ask for "Pushkin" (tickets 6R). Ask for "too-DAH ee oh-BRAHT-nah" if you want a return ticket. Don't be worried that none of the signs say Pushkin; all trains leaving from platforms 1-3 stop there. It's the first stop that actually looks like a station, recognizable by the large number of people (30min.). The conductor should mumble "Pushkin" at some point before you arrive. Once at the station, it's a 15min. walk or 10min. ride on bus #371 or 382 (2R) to the end (you're less likely to get lost on the bus). There will be a yellow building on the left; the palace is visible through the trees on the right. Or, take a **charter van** right to the entrance (2R).

PAVLOVSK (ПАВЛОВСК)

Catherine the Great gave the park and gardens at Pavlovsk to her son Paul in 1777, perhaps because she wanted to keep her eye on him. The largest **park** of all the outlying palaces, Pavlovsk's lush, shady paths wind among wild foliage, classical statuary, bridges, and pavilions. The **Three Graces Pavilion,** just south of the main palace, is renowned for the beauty of the central sculpture, carved by Paolo Triscorni in 1802 from a single piece of white marble. To the east lies the **Monument to Marie Fyodorovna,** widow of Paul I. Marie retreated to Pavlovsk after her husband's assassination, and her hand can be seen in much of the park today. (Open daily 9am-8pm. 12R, students 6R.)

Paul's **Great Palace** is not as spectacular as his mother's at Tsarskoye Selo, but is nonetheless a worthwhile visit. The marble columns and sculpted ceilings of the **Greek Hall** are particularly noteworthy, as is the **Gala Bedroom.** Marie Fyodorovna's apartments are among the few examples of modest royal taste. Plundered, burnt and mined by the Nazis, the palace was the hardest hit of those near St. Petersburg, making its current restored state all the more remarkable. (Open M-Th and Sa-Su 10am-5pm. 30R, students 15R.)

GETTING THERE. Although visits to Pushkin and Pavlovsk can be combined in one day, a leisurely visit is more enjoyable. To reach Pavlovsk, get off at the *elektrichka* stop after Tsarskoye Selo/Pushkin on trains leaving from platforms #1-3 at Vitebsky vokzal. To get to the palace from the train station, take bus #370, 383, or 383A. To get to Pushkin from Pavlovsk, take bus #370 or 383 from the Great Palace, or bus #473 from Pavlovsk Station (3R).

SHLISSELBURG (ШЛИССЕЛЬБУРГ)

About 35km east of St. Petersburg, on a small island at the estuary of the Neva river, is the medieval fortress Shlisselburg, also known as Oreshek ("a tough nut";

Орешек). The fortress played a key role during the Swedish campaign of Peter the Great, who appropriately named it Shlisselburg, the key-city, but it has fallen into decay since state subsidies were cut off. The ruins of Shlisselburg still hide both centuries of history and remarkable architecture; absorb it all in a leisurely, tourist-free setting.

The merchants of Novgorod built the original **fortress** in 1323, calling it "Oreshek" after the island Orekhovy ("nut island"; Ореховый), and used it as a trading outpost. When the pier burned down in 1352, the clever Novgorodians replaced it with a stone structure. Oreshek became a strategic military point in the 15th century, and was therefore rebuilt from scratch as a fortress with six towers and drawbridges. Ultimately, it spent most of the 17th century under Swedish control. October 1702 saw the forces of Peter the Great retake the fortress and rename it Shlisselburg. In a legendary letter, Peter wrote: "Tough was this nut indeed, but luckily we cracked it; our artillery worked true wonders." From that point on, it was the central base for Peter I's expeditions against Sweden.

As with many fortresses, later in the century the fortified island became a prison for intellectuals, writers, revolutionaries, and other political undesirables. Continuing around to the left through an archway leads to a small courtyard and the **Old Prison,** built in 1789. Between 1826 and 1834, the Old Prison held members of the Decembrist group that, in 1825, attempted to overthrow the tsarist regime. From 1884 to 1906, it held death-row revolutionaries, including **Aleksandr Ilyich Ulyanov,** elder brother of Vladimir Ilyich Ulyanov, a.k.a. **Lenin.** Aleksandr was arrested for plotting the assassination of Tsar Alexander III; he was executed at Shlisselburg on May 8, 1887. His death marked the beginning of his younger brother's deep resentment of the tsarist government. Inside the Old Prison, a **museum** details the building's history. The **3rd Cell** shows the fine amenities each Decembrist received, while the even grimmer **4th Cell** depicts what later revolutionaries endured. The first prisoners of Shlisselburg were members of the royal family; in the early 18th century, the displeased Peter sent his first wife Evdokiya Lopukhina and his sister Maria Alekseevna here.

Ahead of the main yard and to the left stands the **New Prison** (1884), darker and danker than even the Old Prison. It too has a **museum** displaying photos and living conditions of inmates. The far right door in the courtyard leads outside the fortress walls. (If the door is closed, ask the attendant to unlock it.) From here, magnificent view of Ladoga Lake opens up. During the Nazi's 900-day siege of Leningrad, the only road connecting the city with the mainland, known as "The Road to Life," ran across Ladoga. Ships in the summer and trucks in the winter (when Ladoga froze) carried ammunition and food supplies to the besieged city. Outside, an Orthodox Cross marks the **communal grave** of soldiers of the Northern War and WWII. Toward the left around the perimeter stands the **overseer's building,** built in 1911 and bombed completely by the Nazis. Beyond that, the **Fourth Prison** building, also constructed in 1911, held revolutionaries until the revolution of 1917 when all the prisoners of Shlisselburg were freed. An **exhibition and monument** to the battle at Shlisselburg during WWII, when the Nazis attempted to obliterate the fortress, marks the middle of the yard. To the right of the monument you can see a fragment of the 14th-century **Novgorodian fortress**—a precious archaeological find excavated in 1969. (Fortress open summer daily 10am-5pm. Prison museums open approximately same hours, with random lunch breaks. Admission to all sights 140R, students 70R.)

GETTING THERE. To reach the fortress, catch **express bus** #575 from M4: Ulitsa Dybenko; buy the ticket from the conductor (1hr., every 30min., M-F 12R, Sa-Su 16R). Ride past the "Шлиссельбург" stop to the last stop, "Петрокрепость" (Petrokrepost). From the bus station, walk across the bridge and turn left, heading toward the river. Turn right at the statue of Peter the Great that stands in a shady little cove. On your left awaits the **ferry** (3min., 6 per day, last ferry back leaves at 4:30pm, round-trip 10R).

VALAAM (ВАЛААМ)

If you're interested in visiting a Karelian island but not its uneventful capital, Petrozavodsk, you can take a boat trip directly from St. Petersburg to Valaam in Lake Ladoga. Once a refuge for Russian monks and now a famous **nature preserve,** accessible only by tourist boats, **Valaam Island** offers a romantic escape amid granite cliffs, pine trees, and clear waters. Currently Karelian, the island has changed its "nationality" several times since the 13th century, when a Russian Orthodox **monastery** was founded here. Destroyed by the Swedes four centuries later, the monastery was "resurrected" (and used as a prison) by Peter the Great in 1715 after his victory over Sweden. By the end of the 19th century, Valaam possessed an awe-inspiring, five-domed **cathedral** of the transfiguration, as well as a whole range of agricultural and church buildings. In 1917 the island became a Finnish territory, but was regained by the Soviets in 1940 at the end of the war with Finland. At that point, the monks packed up their sacred possessions and left the island for Finland, leaving the remnants of the monastery for tourists. Today, the monastery is again being restored by monks. Valaam is primarily a place to enjoy nature. You can swim in the waters off the island, or hire a local fisherman to take you to one of the smaller islands, where there are a number of chapels.

GETTING THERE. There is a two-night, one-day cruise to Valaam only (860R) or a three-day, four-night trip to both islands (1500R). The trip embarks from St. Petersburg's Rechnoy Vokzal (River Station; Речной Вокзал), pr. Obukhovskoy 95 (Обуховской; M3: Proletarskaya), every three days. **ETUS Tour,** Ligovsky pr. 64 (Лиговский; tel. 164 5958), in St. Petersburg, books these popular tours. (Open M-F 11am-5pm.)

NOVGOROD (НОВГОРОД)

Founded in the 9th century by Prince Rurik, Novgorod blossomed during the Middle Ages. In its heyday, it was home to almost twice its current population, victor over the Mongols, and challenger to Moscow for Slavic supremacy. Moscow ultimately won out, and Ivan III and Ivan the Terrible subjugated the upstart city (see **History,** p. 551). Novgorod lives on as Russia's best-preserved metropolis; many of the 140 churches and 50 monasteries built between 1100 and 1500 are still standing. Bigger and better restored than Pskov, Novgorod makes a good introduction to early Russia.

ORIENTATION

Novgorod's heart remains its **kremlin,** from which a web of streets spin outward from the west side of the river. The train station, bus station, and telephone office all lie on the outermost street, **ul. Oktyabrskaya** (Октябрьская). **Pr. Karla Marxa** (Карла Маркса) runs from the train station to the earthen walls that surround old Novgorod. Follow ul. Ludogoskaya (Лудогоская) from the walls, through **pl. Sophiskaya** (Софиская) to the kremlin. The river's east side is home to major hotels and churches; Yaroslav's court is also on this side. Purchase **maps** (25R) at **Gostinitsa Intourist,** or from the kiosk at the kremlin's east side. The latest 1994 edition only partially reflects the many changes in street names. Novgorodians use the old and new names interchangeably, and two signs often adorn one corner.

PRACTICAL INFORMATION

Trains: To: **St. Petersburg** (5hr., 3 per day, 42R) and **Moscow** (8hr., 2 per day, 100R). More expensive than buses, but more comfortable. Tickets are at Intourist *kassa* #1, open 24hr.

Global connection with the AT&T Network

AT&T direct service

Exploring the corners of the earth? We're with you. With the world's most powerful network, **AT&T Direct® Service** gives you fast, clear connections from more countries than anyone,* and the option of an English-speaking operator. All it takes is your AT&T Calling Card. And the planet is yours.

For a list of AT&T Access Numbers, take the attached wallet guide.

AT&T

*Comparison to major U.S.-based carriers.

AT&T

AT&T Direct® Service

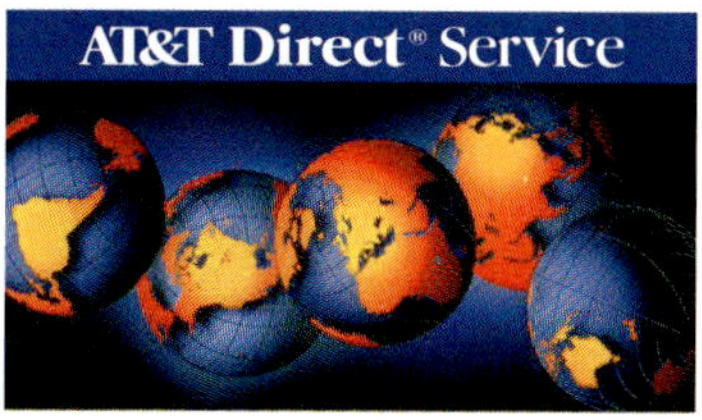

AT&T Access Numbers

Austria●	**0800-200-288**
Albania●	**00-800-0010**
Armenia●▲	8◆10111
Bahrain	800-000
Belgium●	**0-800-100-10**
Bulgaria▲	00-800-0010
Croatia	**0800-220111**
Czech Rep.▲	**00-42-000-101**
Cyprus●	080-90010
Denmark	**8001-0010**
Egypt●(Cairo)	**510-0200**
(Outside Cairo)	**02-510-0200**
Estonia	**800-800-1001**
Finland●	**9800-100-10**
France	**0-800-99-0011**
Germany	**0800-2255-288**
Greece●	**00-800-1311**
Hungary●	**00-800-01111**
Ireland✓	**1-800-550-000**
Israel	**1-800-94-94-949**
Italy●	**172-1011**
Luxembourg†	**0-800-0111**
Macedonia, F.Y.R. of ○	**99-800-4288**
Malta	0800-890-110
Monaco●	**800-90-288**
Morocco	002-11-0011
Netherlands●	**0800-022-9111**
Norway	**800-190-11**
Poland●▲	**00-800-111-1111**
Portugal▲	**0800-800-128**
Romania●	**01-800-4288**
Russia●▲	
(Moscow)◗	**755-5042**
(St. Petersburg)◗	**325-5042**
Saudi Arabia◇	**1-800-10**
South Africa	**0-800-99-0123**
Spain	**900-99-00-11**
Sweden	**020-799-111**
Switzerland●	**0-800-89-0011**
Turkey●	**00-800-12277**
U.K.▲✜	**0800-89-0011**
U.K.▲✜	**0500-89-0011**
U.A. Emirates●	800-121

FOR EASY CALLING WORLDWIDE

1. Just dial the AT&T Access Number for the country you are calling from.
2. Dial the phone number you're calling. *3.* Dial your card number.

For access numbers not listed ask any operator for **AT&T Direct®** Service. In the U.S. call 1-800-331-1140 for a wallet guide listing all worldwide AT&T Access Numbers.

Visit our Web site at: www.att.com/traveler

Bold-faced countries permit country-to-country calling outside the U.S.

- ● Public phones require coin or card deposit.
- ▲ May not be available from every phone/payphone.
- ◗ Additional charges apply outside the city.
- ◇ Calling available to most countries.
- ◆ Await second dial tone.
- ✓ Use U.K. access number in N. Ireland.
- ✜ If call does not complete, use 0800-013-0011.
- † Collect calling from public phones.
- ○ Public phones require local coin payment through the call duration.

When placing an international call ***from*** the U.S., dial 1 800 CALL ATT.

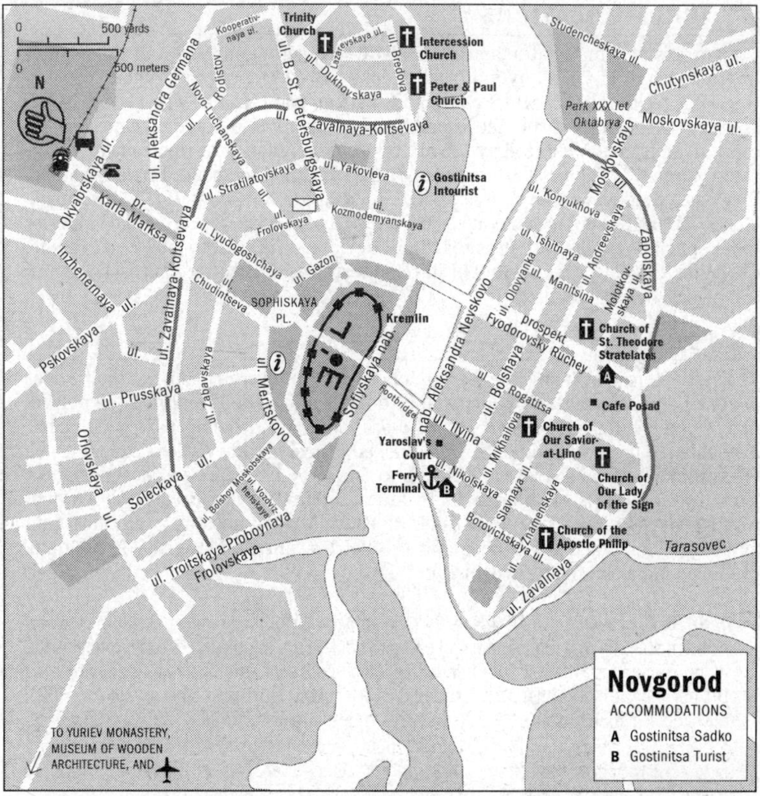

Buses: To the right as you face the train station, in a small white building labeled "Автостанция." Station open 5am-10pm. Buses run to: **Moscow** (10hr., 1 per day, 90R); **St. Petersburg** (3½hr., 1 per day, 46R); and **Pskov** (4½hr., 2 per day, 41.40R).

Tourist Office: Ul. Meretskovo 2 (Мерецкого), on the 2nd floor of a small brick building on the left side of the square in front of the kremlin. English tours of Novgorod (2R) and the kremlin (4R), but no maps or brochures. Open M-F 9am-6pm.

Currency Exchange: Ul. Velikaya 16 (Великая), inside Gostinitsa Intourist. Exit the kremlin to the right, cross the park, and continue on to the river. Follow Velikya along the water past the odd-looking theater. Exchanges any hard currency, but only has good rates for dollars. Also at any "Обмен Валюты" sign.

ATM: AmEx/MC/Visa accepted in the telephone office (see below).

Luggage Storage: In the train station (11R per day). Open 24hr. Also in the bus station (4R). Open daily 5am-9:30pm.

Post Office: Ul. B. Sankt Peterburgskaya 9. Open M-F 9am-2pm and 3-7pm, Sa 9am-4pm. **Postal code:** 173001.

Telephone Office: Opposite the train station on ul. Oktyabrskaya. Phones on the right are for direct calls. Prepay at the *kassa* for a booth number, then get change if you have time left. For international calls either dial direct or pay in advance (the wait for international calls can be 1hr.). 1min. to the **U.S.** 25.20R. Or, call **AT&T Direct** or a similar service in Moscow (see p. 558). Tokens for local calls 6R, intercity calls 3.15R. Phones open 24hr. You can also send **faxes** to **Australia, Canada, New Zealand,** and the **U.S.** for 47.60R per page. To **Europe** 20.40R. Fax desk open M-F 8am-10pm, Sa 9am-8pm. **Phone code:** 81622.

RUSSIA

ACCOMMODATIONS

Novgorod's accommodations provide a wide range of comforts and prices. **Gostinitsa Sadko** (Садко), ul. Fyodorovsky Ruchey 16 (Фёдоровский Ручей; formerly Gagarina; tel. 66 30 04), features a friendly staff, spacious rooms with private baths, and a remote location. From the kremlin, cross the foot bridge and take the first left onto ul. Bolshaya Moskovskaya. Walk two blocks, then turn right onto Fyodorovsky Ruchey. (Singles 200R; doubles 314R. Breakfast included. English spoken. MC/Visa.) **Gostinitsa Turist** (Турист), nab. Aleksandra Nevskovo 19/1 (Александра Невского; tel. 341 85) is sometimes called the Hotel Russia. The crumbling exterior hides spacious rooms with private baths; some have views of the beloved kremlin. From the kremlin, cross the foot bridge and walk past the walls of Yaroslav's court. (Singles 250R; doubles 350R.)

FOOD

The few eateries with any kind of ambience cater to tourists and raise their prices accordingly. Frequented by locals and tourists alike, the kremlin is the perfect place for a picnic; try *shashlyky* and *sloyki* (слойки; a delicious pastry with jam), available at an outdoor stand. A well-stocked grocery store, **Vavilon** (Вавилон), ul. Oktyabrskaya 10, is another alternative to fancy dining in Novgorod. (Open daily 9am-11pm.) There is a market on ul. Fyodorovsky Ruchey (formerly Gagarina) that runs from Aleksandra Nevskovo to ul. Bolshaya Moskivskaya. In addition to fruit and vegetables, you'll find clothes, shoes, toiletries, and anything else you can think of. (Open M-Sa 8am-7pm, Su 8am-4pm.)

Detinets (Детинец; tel. 746 24), within the stone walls of the kremlin. Rough brick walls, wooden spoons, and real candles take diners back to the middle ages. Tour groups fill the place; call ahead. The 1st floor bar serves jolly *medovukha,* an alcoholic honey drink, for 9R per mug. *Golubtsy* (stuffed cabbage; 36R), mushrooms with sour cream (30-40R), and *shchi* (cabbage soup; 37.50R). Open M noon-midnight, Tu-Su 11am-11:30pm.

Pri Dvore (При Дворе; tel. 743 43). In the park outside the kremlin. *Shashlyky* grilled outside (15R). Sandwiches (from 10R) and hot dishes (18-30R) are served from the bar inside. Live music at night M and W-Su. Open daily 11am-4pm and 6-11pm.

Skazka (Fairy Tale; Сказка), ul. Meretskovo 13 (tel. 771 60). To the left of the square in front of the kremlin. Go left through the park about 150m; the restaurant occupies the corner of ul. Meretskovo and ul. Chernyshevskovo (Чернышевского). Veggie salads 18-35R. Open daily noon-midnight. Call ahead. In the **dessert hall,** snack on sandwiches, hot dogs (5-8R), or ice cream (7.50R). Open 11am-11pm.

SIGHTS

THE KREMLIN. Sometimes known as *detinets*, a small kremlin, Novgorod's pride and joy is impressive nonetheless. Its walls, 3m thick and 11m high, and nine spiraling towers protect most of the city's sights, which are clustered around a grassy park. To the immediate right of the lakeside entrance, bells are arranged at the base of the **belfry;** at the west gate stands **clock tower** (*chasovnya;* часовня). The tower's bell used to call citizens to meetings of the city council, until the Ivans did away with both the bell and the council. *(Both open daily 6am-midnight. Free.)* Entering the kremlin from the west side of the river, the golden-spired building to the left is **St. Sophia's Cathedral** (Sofiysky Sobor; Софийский Собор), the oldest stone building in Russia. This 11th-century Byzantine cathedral, with intricately carved western doors depicting scenes from the Bible, is most imposing from the outside. A shadowy interior obscures the few remaining icons; most are in the museum. With the exception of the inside of the dome, the frescoes were painted fresh in the 19th century. The golden dove atop one of the cupolas safeguards the city. According to legend, as long as the dove remains, there will be peace in the city, and as long as Sofiysky Sobor stands, Novgorod will weather all troubles. *(Open daily 8am-8pm; services 10am and 6pm.)* Next to the clock tower sits the **Faceted Chamber** (Granovitaya

Palata; Грановитая Палата), a monument to religious devotion with an elaborate collection of golden artifacts. The collection can only be toured with a guide (in Russian). Buy your ticket at the museum and wait for a group to gather. *(Open Th-Tu 10am-6pm; closed last Friday of the month. 28R, students 14R.)* The exhibits in the **Novgorod United Museum,** inside the classical structure within the kremlin, lead visitors through the city's history. Architectural finds and birch bark inscriptions dominate the first few rooms but give way to typical displays of the tsarist era (medals, uniforms, and portraits). The proud red Soviet rooms are more interesting. The second floor holds famous icons; the city hung one, of the Virgin Mary, on its gates to save itself from the Suzdal. When the icon began to cry, the besieging army fled in terror. Lamentably, the 20th-century art has no such story to accompany it, although it could certainly use one. *(Open M and W-Su 10am-6pm; closed last Th of each month. 28R, students 14R. Photos 15R, video 35R.)* In the center of the kremlin park, directly in front of the museum, stands the **Russian Millennium** (Tysyacheletie Rossii; Тысячелетие России). It was built in 1852 as one of three identical bell-shaped monuments; the second stands in St. Petersburg, the third in Kiev. Engraved in the bronze are a thousand years of Russian history, with an emphasis on pain—note the number of fallen men holding daggers. The old favorites—Rurik, Prince Vladimir of Kiev, and Peter the Great—are all here. The sculpture atop the bell represents Russia's 988 adoption of Christianity.

YAROSLAV'S COURT. (Yaroslavovo Dvorishche; Ярославово Дворище). Across the footbridge from the kremlin lies **Yaroslav's Court,** the old market center and the original site of the palace of Novgorod princes. It contains what's left of the 17th-century waterfront arcade, several 13th-and-16th-century churches, and the market gatehouse (now a museum). The nearby **Novgorod horseman** guarding the kremlin walls commemorates the city's longevity, but only by default. Designed for Moscow after WWII, the statue was sent to Novgorod after the capital rejected it.

YURIEV MONASTERY. (Yuriev Monastyr; Юриев Монастырь). Dating from 1030, Yuriev Monastery is one of the three working monasteries around the city. Take bus #7 (1.50R) from pl. Pobedy to the airport. Go left at the fork around a small church; the monastery is just ahead. Its whitewashed buildings standing amid broad, windy marshes have an almost mystical quality to them. From here you can see Lake Ilmen, the site of the 9th-century Rurik's court, from which the state of Russia originated. The twin-domed **St. George's Church** (Georgievskaya Tserkov; Георгиевская Церковь), dating to 1119, houses icons dating from the 12th century, as well as a unique, round pulpit (*kafedra;* кафедра). The church is undergoing extensive reconstruction. On the way out note the bright blue cupolas of **Khristovozdvizhenskaya;** golden stars symbolize the monastery's high status. *(Open W-M 7am-9pm. 16R, students 10R. Photography 15R. Women must wear skirts, rentable for 5R.)*

PSKOV (ПСКОВ)

Since its first mention in an historical account in 903, Pskov has been an important border trading post. Its recently renovated fortress walls, 6m thick to withstand sieges from neighboring countries are reminders of its vulnerability to trading partners and neighbors. This century, Pskov saw the end of yet another siege, when Nicholas II abdicated the throne here in March 1917. While it is not as pretty as Novgorod, Pskov offers visitors a more intimate look into its history.

ORIENTATION

The **bus** and **train stations** are next to each other on Vokzalnaya ul. (Вокзальная). It intersects with the end of the **Oktyabrsky pr.** (Октябрьский пр.) a couple of blocks to the right as you exit either station. Oktyabrsky pr., Pskov's main axis, is home to Gostinitsa Oktyabrskaya, as well as the telephone and post offices. In the main square, **Oktyabrskaya pl.** (Октябрьская), it intersects with **ul. Sovetskaya** (Советская), which runs up to the kremlin in the town's north end. The **Velikaya** (Великая) and **Pskova** (Пскова) **Rivers** meet at the northernmost corner of the kremlin. Across the Velikaya is Gostinitsa Sputnik, and farther along **Rizhsky pr.** (Рижский) sits Gostinitsa Rizhskaya. The old outer town walls run for 9km along the river and **ul. Sverdlova** (Свердлова), past Pskov's two large parks. City **maps** are usually available at Gostinitsa Oktyabrskaya.

PRACTICAL INFORMATION

Trains: To: **Moscow** (12hr., 2 per day, 230R); **St. Petersburg** (7hr., 2 per day, 88.60R); and **Tallinn** (6½hr., departs daily 2:50am, 520R). Ticket office open 24hr.

Buses: The best way to and from Pskov, unless you're going to Moscow. To: **Novgorod** (4½hr., 2 per day, 44R); **Pechory** (1½hr., 8 per day, 14.40R); and **St. Petersburg** (7hr., 2 per day, 41R). Each *kassa* sells tickets for different destinations, indicated above the windows. *Kassa* open daily 8am-1pm and 2-7pm; station open 5am-10pm.

Local Transportation: Buses #1 and 17 depart in front of the train station. Bus #17 stops in front of Gostinitsa Rizhskaya. Bus #1 stops just after Gostinitsa Oktyabrskaya. Buy tickets from the conductor (2R).

Tourist Offices: Intourist, Rizhsky pr. 25, 3rd Fl., #330 (tel. 46 75 13 and 46 17 63; fax 44 74 33). In Gostinitsa Rizhskaya, over the bridge from Oktyabrskaya pl. (10min.). Or, take bus #2, 14, or 17. Arranges city tours in English (190R without transportation), but does little else. Open M-F 9am-7pm. A **tourist bureau** (tel. 219 06 and 239 88; fax 72 32 57), on the right just after the entrance to the kremlin, provides historical pamphlets and brochures. Open M-F 9am-1pm and 2-5:30pm, Sa 9am-2pm.

Currency Exchange: Oktyabrsky pr. 23/25 (tel.16 03 37). Next to Sberbank (Сбербанк) across the street from Gostinitsa Oktyabrskaya. **Traveler's checks** cashed for a 2% commission. Open M-F 9am-2pm and 3-8pm, Sa 9am-3pm. Better exchange rates at most "Обмен Валюты" signs.

Luggage Storage: In the train (11R per day) and bus (6R per day) stations. Open 24hr.

Post Office: Obscured by trees on the north side of pl. Oktyabrskaya. Open M-F 9am-2pm and 3-7pm, Sa 9am-2pm. **Postal code:** 180000.

Telephones: Oktyabrsky pr., in a large gray building opposite the statue of Kirov between ul. Nekrasova (Некрасова) and ul. Gogolya (Гоголя). Prepay for intercity and international calls; you will receive change if there is time left. To St. Petersburg 3.15R per min.; to the U.S. and Australia 25.20R per min.; to Europe 20.48R per min. Open 24hr. **Faxes** at *kassy* 5 and 6. Open daily 7:30am-10:30pm. **Phone code:** 81122.

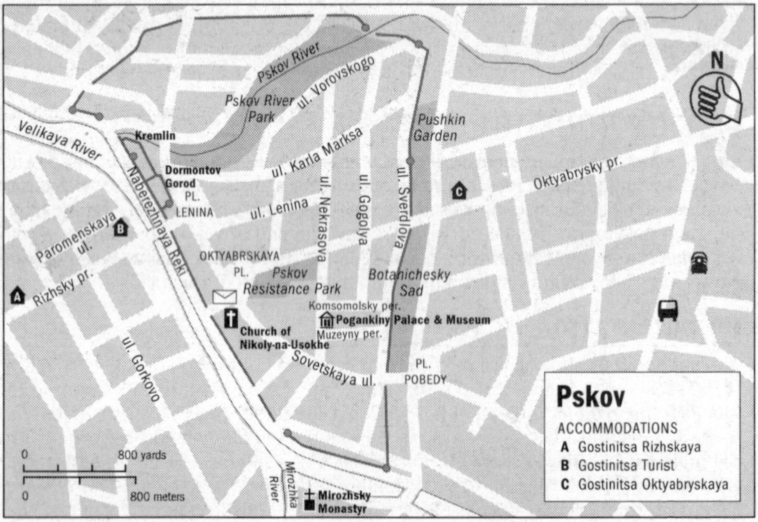

ACCOMMODATIONS

Most hotels offer reasonably priced rooms, but there aren't any incredible values; you pay for what you get. For slightly higher prices, **HOFA** (see **St. Petersburg: Accommodations,** p. 605) provides homestays (170R per night).

Gostinitsa Rizhskaya (Рижская), Rizhsky pr. 25 (tel. 243 01). Hop on bus #17 from the train station (2R). Tries for Western chic with its posh lobby and wide, carpeted hallways, and almost pulls it off. Small bathtub, shower, and toilet in each room. Singles 300R; doubles 400R. TV, phone, and fridge extra. English spoken.

Gostinitsa Turist (Турист), ul. Paromenskaya 4 (Пароменская; tel. 44 51 50). Bus #17 stops just past the bridge. Tucked between Upeniya Paromenya and Velikaya, this establishment, with its dingy halls and dingier rooms, begs the question: "Am I *really* this cheap?" Doubles and triples with private bath 63R per person.

Gostinitsa Oktyabrskaya (Октябрьская), Oktyabrskaya pr. 36 (tel. 399 12). Take bus #1 or 17 from the train station. The hotel is on your right, just before a park with a monument to Pushkin and his nurse. Cold stone building with cold stone floors and cold stone staff. Small, musty rooms with firm beds and clean sheets. Sinks have cold water only, and bathrooms have no toilet paper. 3rd fl. showers 5R. Singles 180R; doubles 360R; triples 90R per person.

FOOD

Restaurants here sell a variety of salty, fatty, potato-oriented foods. Kiosks aren't much better, peddling mostly cookies, crackers, chips, and beer. Greener fare can be found at the **Central Market** (Tsentralny Rynok; Центральный Рынок), or from the *babushki* on the street. The market is off pr. Karla Marxa (Карла Маркса) down a dirty, narrow street about 50m past a church that's being renovated. Behind a fence, it's the large building labeled "РЫНОК" in huge letters. (Opens at 8am.) The "24hr." supermarket, **Rostek-Market** (Ростек-Маркет), Oktyabrsky pr. 16, near Gostinitsa Oktya, is well-stocked with local and imported goodies, but it interrupts its regularly-scheduled programming for a "technical break" from 2:30 to 3pm daily. Many markets take most of Monday off altogether.

Cafe Cheburechnaya (Кафе Чебуречная), Oktyabrsky pr. 10A. In an orange clapboard building; enter from behind. This Georgian greasy spoon is very popular with locals. Old-school Soviet decor surrounds you, from the abacus to the reel-tape player. Specializes in *chebureki* (greasy but tasty meat pies; 5R). Open daily 11am-6pm.

Uyut (Уют; Comfort), lurking behind Cafe Cheburechnaya. A Russian cafe with a shady interior. Basic menu. Pastries 3-7R; sandwiches 9-18R; lunch plates 15-25R; extensive drink list. Nightly variety show midnight-1:30am; 20R. Open daily 11am-5am.

Aurora (Аврора), Oktyabrsky pr. 36, connected to Gostinitsa Oktyabrskaya. Russian pop tries—but fails—to rejuvenate this aging haven of vodka-shooting middle-aged women. The food is good, and the experience is not to be missed. Cheesy chicken and greasy fries 35R; borscht 10.90R; entrees 18-35R; various St. Petersburg beers 9-15R. Open M-Th and Su 1pm-midnight, F-Sa 1pm-2am.

SIGHTS

KREMLIN. With its thick stone walls topped by authentic wooden roofs and spires, the kremlin seems to hold time at bay outside its arched portals. In contrast to the numerous attractions within Novgorod's kremlin, the interior courtyard here has only one building: the golden-domed **Trinity Cathedral** (Troitsky Sobor; Троицкий Собор). Founded in the 10th century by Saint Olga (Russia's first Christian monarch who married Prince Igor of Kiev and was later beatified) on her way to nearby Novgorod, this is actually the fourth cathedral to stand on this spot. The current structure, covered with 17th-century frescoes, which exemplify the Pskovian school of icon painting, was built in 1869. Those closest to the ceiling are the oldest and most valuable. Kerchiefed *babushki* are the curators of this holy place, diligently polishing brass and sweeping the floors. *(From the train station, take bus #1 or 17; get off when you spot the kremlin walls. Kremlin open 24hr. Church open 8am until the end of the evening service. Services daily 8-11am and 6pm-late. Free, but donations appreciated.)*

DOVMONTOV'S CITY. (Dovmontov Gorod; Довмонтов Город). A small courtyard adjacent to the kremlin Dovmontov's City, named for Prince Dovmont, contains the foundations of nine churches built between the 12th and 15th centuries. The overgrown ruins aren't much to look at, but the idea of the once-thriving religious center is impressive. *(Follow the directions to the kremlin, and look for the courtyard.)*

POGANKIN PALACE & MUSEUM. (Pogankiny Palaty i Muzey; Поганкины Палаты и Музей). The wealth and heritage of Pskov rest in Pogankin Palace and Museum, originally the home of a wealthy 17th-century merchant. Vaulted ceilings and well-lit cases of coins and handicrafts greet visitors on the first floor. The second floor is populated by students copying the icons on display with meticulous detail. Next to the main hall is the picture gallery, where the local take on post-modernism is on display. *(On Komsomolsky per. (Комсомольский), at the intersection with Sovetskaya ul. Enter through the new wing— walk past Soviet art and history and the glaring guards, through the courtyard to the main house. Open Tu-Su 11am-6pm; closed last Tu of the month. 30R, students 15R.)*

OTHER SIGHTS. With more **churches** than restaurants and hotels combined, Pskov is clearly still a spiritual center. Unfortunately, most desperately need repair and are closed to the public. **Transfiguration Cathedral** (Spaso-Preobrazhensky Sobor; Спасо-Преображенский Собор) dates from 1156 and features spectacular art-book-like frescoes typical of the Pskov region. The place is certainly worth a visit; Russians hold it in understandably high esteem. *(Open Tu-Su 11am-5pm. 15R, students 10R. English tour 85R.)* Several old churches, including the 16th-century **Nikol-na-Usokhe** (Николь-на-Усохе), are scattered around the main Oktyabrskaya pl. To see the interior of a typical Pskov church in all its splendor, head to Pechory.

NEAR PSKOV: PECHORY MONASTERY

If you happen to be in Pskov overnight, **Pechory Monastery** (Pechory Monastyr; Печоры Монастырь) is a good excursion for the next day; it is possible to go in the morning and be back in time for an afternoon bus. Founded in 1473, the monastery had over 200 brothers in the 16th century, when it doubled as a fortress. Today the complex is home to around 60 monks. The yellow and white **Assumption Cathedral** (Uspensky Sobor; Успенский Собор) stands just through the main entrance. (Cathedral services daily 6am and 6pm.) The door on the left leads to the sacred caves, where monks and hermits are sealed in the walls. (Caves closed to visitors except at 9:30am, after the morning service. Free, but donations appreciated.) Next to the cathedral stands a whitewashed belfry whose facade is graced by a remarkable golden-winged angel. A few steps down, the beautiful flower garden surrounds a sacred water fountain, which serves as the site of regular pilgrimages; besides being sacred, the water is reputedly potable; tours 100R. The golden-domed 1827 **St. Michael Church** (Mikhaylovskaya Tserkov; Михайловская Церковь) stands beyond the "no entrance" (Нет Входа) sign. (Complex open daily 8am-5pm. Call 215 93 to arrange a tour. Tours in English or German 250R. Photos 40R, payable to gatekeeper. Women must cover their head and wear skirts, which can be borrowed at the monastery entrance.)

GETTING THERE. Buy a ticket to Pechory at the **Pskov** bus station (14.40R); get one back to Pskov as soon as you arrive, unless you want to camp out with the monks. Schedules vary, but the last bus leaves at 8:45pm. The monastery is to the right at the end of Yurevskaya ul. (Юревская). Go left out of the station and take the first right.

KARELIA (КАРЕЛИЯ)

Rolling hills and vast forests dominate Karelia, once the fingertips of Russia outstretched northwest hand and now an autonomous region. That political independence, the Scandanavian flavor of Petrozavodsk and Vyborg, and the rustic splendor of the wooden structures at Kizhi all seem to sugest that perhaps the empire never did have a very good grip on this region between Petersburg and the Arctic Circle. It is also a region of profound natural beauty: among Karelia's 60,000 lakes are Ladoga and Onega, the largest in Europe and second-largest in Russia, bettered only by Siberia's mighty Lake Baikal.

PETROZAVODSK (ПЕТРОЗАВОДСК)

With clean air, small, quiet streets, a Ben & Jerry's in the center, and a lake to call its own, Petrozavodsk is seems a complete departure from the rest of Russia. Founded in 1703, the same year as St. Petersburg, Petrozavodsk (Peter's Factory) was originally a foundry and armaments plant; tsars later exiled misbehaving intellectuals and disfavored politicians here. Today, brimming with modern fountains and sculptures, the waterfront city is ideal for a stroll with ice cream cone in hand.

ORIENTATION

The main arteries, **pr. Lenina** (Ленина) and **pr. Karla Marksa** (Карла Маркса), intersect at the center of the city. Pr. Lenina begins at the **train station** and runs to **Lake Onega.** It's a worthwhile walk, but you can also take trolley #1 (2R) to the embankment. Everything necessary is within two blocks of this main road. Pr. Marksa leads to a **dock** where speedy ferries sail to the Kizhi Islands.

PRACTICAL INFORMATION

Trains: To: **Moscow** (8-11hr., 5 per day, 709R) and **St. Petersburg** (9hr., 2-3 per day, 139R). Buy tickets at the Intourist *kassa* marked "International Booking." Trains from St. Petersburg leave from Moskovsky Vokzal (Московский Вокзал; see **St. Petersburg: Transportation,** p. 597).

Tourist Office: Intourist, pr. Lenina 21 (tel. 77 63 06), in Gostinitsa Severnaya, is a good source for train tickets if the *kassa* by the station is out. Also offers **bus tours** (min. 15 people) to **Martsialnye Vody,** Russia's first mineral spa, and a nature reserve at **Kivach.** Open M-F 9am-1pm and 2-5pm.

Currency Exchange: All along pr. Lenina. Traveler's checks cashed for a 5% commission. Usually open M-Sa 10am-6pm. **Industry Construction Bank,** inside the Lotis (Лотис) store on pl. Gagarina (пл. Гагарина) in front of the train station, gives Visa/MC cash advances. Open Tu-F 11am-3:30pm and 4-6:30pm, Sa 11am-4:30pm. There is an **ATM** in the telephone office (see below).

Luggage storage: At the train station, in the same building as the ticket office. 11R per day. Open 24hr.

Post Office: Ul. Sverdlova 29 (Свердлова). On pr. Lenina, pass Gostinitsa Severnaya, take a right onto ul. Andropova, and a left onto Sverdlova. The post office is the building with the clock tower. **Poste Restante** at *kassa* #2. English spoken. Open M-F 8am-8pm, Sa 9am-6pm. **Postal code:** 185035.

Internet Access: Computer Center Splayn (Сплайн), pr. Lenina 9 (tel. 77 13 89). 15R per hr. Open M-F 10am-7pm, Sa 11am-4pm.

Telephones: Ul. Sverdlova 31, next door to the post office. Prepay for intercity calls at the *kassa*, get a booth, and get change for time not used. International calls can be ordered in advance, or purchase a phone card for 130R (this buys a 14min. call to the U.S.). Open 24hr; *kassa* open daily 8am-10pm. **Phone code:** 814.

ACCOMMODATIONS

Anyone not holding a Karelian passport will pay higher prices; the prices quoted below are for non-Karelians and non-Russians.

Gostinitsa Severnaya (Гостиница Северная), pr. Lenina 21 (tel. 76 20 80; fax 76 22 55). A 10min. walk from the train station down pr. Lenina reveals this hotel, located in one of the most beautiful old buildings in town. The grand foyers give way to bare corridors and simply appointed rooms, but friendly service, a decent restaurant, and the central location make it the best stay in town. Staff speaks some English. Singles 220R, with bath 420R; doubles 440R. 25% reservation fee. Visa/MC.

Gostinitsa Karelia (Карелия), nab. Gyullinga 2 (Гюллинга; tel. 55 73 58 and 55 88 97). Walk 5min. from the ferry dock, head down pr. Marksa from pr. Lenina, and turn right onto ul. Lunacharskovo (Луначарского). Pass the fountain and take the first left directly overlooking the water. 10-story brick tower offers closet-sized singles (300R) with TV, phone, and primitive but functional bathrooms. Doubles 400R.

FOOD

English menus are unheard of in Petrozavodsk, and waitstaff are less than eager to interpret. When in doubt, stick to basics like *shchi* (cabbage soup; щи) and *shashlik* (shish kabob; шашльик). Stock up for long train rides at any of the "24hr." shops (closed 8-9am).

Ben & Jerry's, Krasnaya ul. 8 (Красная; tel. 77 41 08), on the corner of ul. Andropova. From the train station, walk down pr. Lenina, then go left onto ul. Andropova and take the first left onto ul. Krasnaya. Tie-dye and cow spots abound, but glassy-eyed Playstation gladiators don't seem to notice (20R per hour). The ice cream and cones are made on the premises. (2 scoops 9R, with cone 11R.) Open daily 10am-8pm.

Shashlychnaya Kavkaz (Щашлычная Кавказ), ul. Andropova 13/16 (Андропова; tel. 77 09 45), at the corner of pr. Lenina. Dim lighting, wood paneling, and the buzz of conversation fill this shish kebab heaven. Try *kharcho* (spicy meat and rice soup; харчо; 9.72R) or *shashlik* (39.60R). Open daily 11am-4pm and 5-10pm.

Restoran Petrovsky (Ресторан Петровский), ul. Andropova 1 (Андропова; tel. 77 09 92), on the corner of pr. Marksa and ul. Andropova, behind the statue on pr. Lenina. Low vaulted ceilings, whitewashed walls, high-backed chairs, earthenware, and wrought-iron gates between rooms recreate the days of Peter the Great. Salads 10-20R; baked fish 19R; *myaso po-petrovsky* (juicy meat in a clay pot with mushrooms; мясо по-петровский; 37.23R). Open daily noon-5pm and 6pm-midnight.

SIGHTS

Lined with eye-catching sculptures and open-air techno cafes, the breezy **waterfront** on Onega Lake between pr. Lenina and the ferry dock is the center for summer activity. The views and sculptures are spectacular; note the delightfully freakish "Fisherman," designed by American Rafael Consuegra. The **Museum of Local Karelian Culture** (Karelsky Kraevedchesky Muzey; Карельский Краеведческий Музей), pr. Lenina 1 (tel. 77 27 02 and 77 94 79), displays exhibits ranging from old cannons made by the city's armaments factory to modern Karelian folk paintings. (Open M-Th and Sa 10am-5:30pm. 25R, students 15R; Sundays free. Cameras 10R. English tour 90R.)

One of the few working churches in Petrozavodsk, **Krestovozdvizhenskaya Church** (Крестовоздвиженская Церковь), ul. Volkhovskaya 1 (Волховская), is in a slightly rough neighborhood at the corner of ul. Pravdy. From pr. Marksa, pass a Finnish-language theater on the right, then turn right over the bridge and through the park onto ul. Pravdy (Правды). The yellow-and-white church with its bright blue cupolas, elaborate iconostasis, and pleasantly overgrown cemetery are on the left, and are only worth the walk if you *really* love churches. On the way to the church, on pl. Kirova, you'll pass the columned wonder that is the **Musical and Russian Drama Theater** (Muzykalny i Russky Dramatichesky Teatr; Музыкальный и Русский Драматический Театр). Meanwhile, restorations of the famous **Alexander Nevsky Cathedral** (Sobor Aleksandra Nevskovo; Собор Александра Невского) are going well; the golden cupolas are shining, and the left side is now a bright yellow.

NEAR PETROZAVODSK: KIZHI (КИЖИ)

A 90min. boat ride from Petrozavodsk, Kizhi is a serene island with a wonderful outdoor museum of 18th-century wooden architecture. An ancient pagan ritual site that drew Russian Orthodox colonizers in the 12th century, the 5km long island now draws tourists from all over the world. Wooden buildings, most of them moved from the nearby villages around Lake Onega, dot the southern part of the island to form an **open-air "museum."** You must pay to enter, but once inside, you are free to explore both the architecture and natural beauty of what the Karelians call "our Greece." The natural wood domes of the **Church of the Transfiguration** (Preobrazhenskaya Tserkov; Преображенская Церковь) are visible above the trees. Unfortunately, the iconostasis inside cannot be viewed: entry is prohibited due to its state of eternal (and futile) renovation. Despite UNESCO protection, no one has figured out how to restore the church, built in 1714 without a single nail. The 14th-century **Church of the Resurrection of Lazarus,** the oldest wooden church in Russia, was moved here from the former Murom monastery. This church is open to visitors, as are the nearby *banya*, barn, and a Goldilocks trio of peasant houses, preserved in all their fairy-tale splendor. The house of **"Wealthy Peasant Oshevnev"** (1876) was built to accommodate 22 people, and is stuffed with a variety of peasant possessions. A covered courtyard—a conventional way to expand living quarters—is attached in back. The houses of **"Poor Peasant Shchepin"** and **"Average Peasant Yelizarov,"** are strikingly similar to Oshevnev's, although they were brought from different regions and have fewer possessions inside. A stroll through the complex should take three hours—which is all the time you'll have between the ferry's arrival and departure. (Open May 25-Oct. 15 daily 8am-8pm; Oct. 16-May 24 11am-3pm. 45R, with tour 50R; students 22R, 25R.)

GETTING THERE. To catch the **ferry** from **Petrozavodsk,** take ul. Lenina from the train station to the waterfront and follow the sculpture-lined path to the right. Buy tickets in the gray building (labeled "Водохный Вокзал") on the right. Walk through the first door of the building to get to the ferry *kassa*. (Open 7:30am-8pm.) Boats to **Velikaya Guba** (Великая Губа), beyond Kizhi, leave frequently, starting at 9am; boats also leave for Kizhi directly (2 per day at noon and 1pm; buy your ticket the day before if possible), but these are mostly on weekends and often full. Double-check the departure times in Kizhi or risk seeing more of the museum than you might like to. The last boat leaves Kizhi at 8:30pm (mid-May to mid-Nov. or until the lake freezes over, 1¼hr., round-trip 73.50R).

VYBORG (ВЫБОРГ)

Since its founding some 700 years ago, Vyborg has been shuffled between Russia, Sweden, and Finland many times. The whole tiff began when Peter the Great took the city from the Swedes in 1709. Vyborg's trademark castle, built by the Swedes but expanded by the Russians, attests to the strife of that period. A century of stability began when the Grand Duchy of Finland took control in 1818, but Russia regained the city when the Bolsheviks came to power, and it hasn't let it go since.

ORIENTATION & PRACTICAL INFORMATION. From the **train station,** walk 5min. down **Leningradsky pr.** (Ленинградский) to the market; the castle's tower can be seen from anywhere in town. Vyborg's other major avenue is **ul. Krepostnaya** (Крепостная), which intersects Leningradsky two blocks after the turn-off for the marketplace. **Trains** run to: **St. Petersburg's Finlandsky Vokzal** (hourly 6am-9:30pm, 28R) and **Helsinki** (daily at 2:10am). Bring a pillow—the seats are flat pieces of wood. Bus trips to Helsinki are organized by the travel agency inside Hotel Druzhba, ul. Zheleznodorozhnaya 5 (Железнодорожная). Also in Hotel Druzhba is a **currency exchange,** which cashes traveler's checks for a 5% commission, and a MC/Visa **ATM. Store luggage** in the train station, downstairs and to the right (11R for 24hr.). To reach the **post office** from the market, turn left onto ul. Krepostnaya and take the second left onto ul. Sovetskaya (Советская); the post office is the first door on the left. (Open M-F 8am-8pm, Sa 10am-4pm.) To reach the **telephone office** (open 24hr.) from the train station, take the second left off ul. Leningradsky as you walk into town, then take the third left and another quick left onto ul. Mira (Мира). **Postal code:** 188900.

ACCOMMODATIONS & FOOD. Hotels cater to and are packed with vacationing Finns seeking their cultural heritage (or, more likely, cheap shopping). **Korolenko Boat Hotel** (tel. 344 78), docked on ul. Zheleznodorozhnaya is well-kept, although its bathrooms could use a good swabbing. (Tiny cabins with portholes 400R per person; groups 300R per person. Some English spoken.) The **Vyborg Hotel,** pr. Leningradsky 19 (tel. 223 83) charms guests with its diminutive size. (Doubles 1200R; triples 1400R. All rooms have TV and private bath. MC/Visa.) There are a wide variety of food options in Vyborg, with affordable eateries at almost every corner. For groceries, try **Zhkolog** (Жколог), ul. Krepostnaya 13 (Крепостная). (Open daily 9am-2pm and 3-9pm.) **Restaurant Druzhba** (tel. 257 44), inside Hotel Druzhba, welcomes guests with their English menu and friendly staff. Get there early, before the bar gets loud. (Entrees from 35R. Open daily 7am-midnight.) **Nord-Vest** (Норд-Вест) at the head of the marketplace, is a haven for the hungry any time of day. (Entrees 45-99R. Open 24hr.)

SIGHTS. Vyborg's primary (single) attraction is its **castle,** standing watch from an island in the bay. Construction began in 1293, although the tower and most other characteristic embellishments were added in the 16th century. The **museum** inside the castle is not to be missed. The most interesting exhibit, found in the Customs Room, traces the history of Russo-Finnish smuggling from gold bullion to cocaine. The **castle tower,** over 48m high, offers a spectacular view of the entire city. (Museum open M-W and F-Su 11am-7pm. Tower open daily 10am-7pm. Combined admission 30R, students 10R.)

THE KALININGRAD REGION (КАЛИНИНГРАДСКАЯ ОБЛАСТЬ)

History and fate have conspired to leave the Kaliningrad region *(Kaliningradskaya Oblast)* part of Russia. The region, initially the German province of East Prussia, was thrust into isolation by Poland's acquired "corridor to the sea." At the end of World War II, Kaliningrad was captured by the Soviets, but was then left behind when the Soviet Union unraveled. Suddenly, it had become an island of armed, confused Russians severed from the Motherland by the newly sovereign Latvia, Lithuania, and Belarus. Over time, it became a home for 40,000 ethnic Germans, deported to Siberia by Stalin in the 40s and 50s, now seeking refuge from the harshness of the Russian Far East while waiting to return to Germany. As they have tried to make sense of their new position, the rest of the world has generally left them alone. Visitors can still enjoy the unspoiled beaches of Svetlogorsk and the Curonian Spit, which no one, in their rush to leave, has bothered to explore.

KALININGRAD (КАЛИНИНГРАД)

Sovietization was accomplished so completely after the Red Army's 1945 occupation that a contemporary observer would hardly suspect that Kaliningrad existed as a German city for 700 years. Home to philosopher Immanuel Kant, the former Königsberg (King's City)—appropriately named for its importance in Prussia—was virtually razed during WWII. The erstwhile German inhabitants have all but disappeared—killed in conflict, deported to Germany, or exiled by Stalin to Siberia. For security reasons, the city, renamed after Stalin's henchman Mikhail Ivanovich Kalinin (who himself never set foot here), was only opened to tourists in 1991; a flood of German tourists looking for their roots soon followed, but it still remains most associated with the 200,000 Russian soldiers and sailors of the Soviet Baltic Fleet stationed here. Kaliningrad remains an island of confusion, edging economically ahead of the rest of Russia, but lagging far behind its Baltic neighbors. While far from picturesque, Kaliningrad offers a glimpse Russian without leaving Europe too far behind.

ORIENTATION

From the bus and southern train stations, both on **pl. Kalinina** (Калинина), **Leninsky pr.** (Ленинский), the main artery, runs north across the **Pregolya River** (Преголя) and **Kneiphof Island,** home of the **cathedral.** Past the hideous House of Soviets to **Tsentralnaya pl.** (Центральная), it veers left to extend to its terminus, **pl. Pobedy** (Победы). Just before there, **pr. Mira** (Мира) veers left toward the zoo, while **ul. Chernyakhovskovo** (Черняховского) travels east toward the central market and the amber museum. Obtainable at many bookstores and kiosks, the **map,** "План города для туристов" (*Plan goroda dlya touristov*; city map for tourists; 21R), shows the locations of museums, sights, and accommodations.

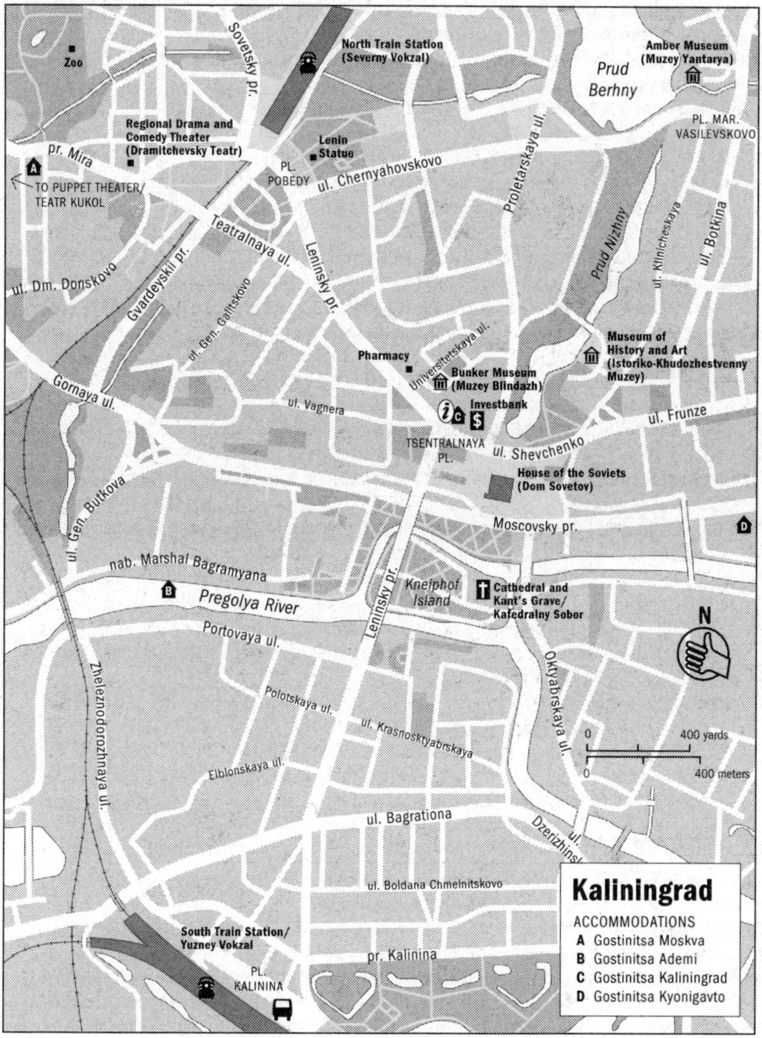

PRACTICAL INFORMATION

Trains: Yuzhny Vokzal (Южный Вокзал; South Station; tel. 49 99 91 and 49 26 75), on the south side of pl. Kalinina, handles international connections. Open 4am-midnight. To: **Moscow** (22hr., 1 per day, *platskartny* 324R); **St. Petersburg** (22hr., 1 per day, *platskartny* 391R); **Vilnius** (8hr., 1 per day, 268R); and **Gdynia,** via **Gdańsk** and **Malborg** (5hr., 1 per day, 180R). International *kassa* upstairs to the right of exit; open 8am-1pm and 2-8pm. Local *kassa* left of the exit. **Severny Vokzal** (Северный Вокзал; North Station; tel. 49 26 75), north of pl. Pobedy, in front of the big pink building that once held the local KGB headquarters, sends trains to Baltic Coast cities. To **Svetlogorsk** (1hr., 10 per day, 8R) and **Zelenogradsk** (35min., 6 per day, 6.40R). Most trains leave Yuzhny Vokzal about 10min. before arriving at Severny Vokzal.

Buses: pl. Kalinina, just east of Yuzhny Vokzal (tel. 44 36 35). To **Gdańsk** (5hr., 2 per day, 125R) and **Warsaw** (8-9hr., 2 per day, 200R). *Kassa* open daily 5:30am-2pm and 3-11:30pm.

Local Transportation: The transportation system in Kaliningrad is undergoing a massive overhaul. **Buses,** which are now privatized, will speed your journey. Prices (2-3R) are posted in bus window; pay the conductor if there is one, or the driver when you get off if not. Some lack numbers, so you may have to look for your destination written on the front. Slower public **trams** traverse the city (1R); trams #2 and 3 run from pl. Kalinina to pl. Pobedy via pl. Tsentralnaya, connecting the southern and northern train stations, while tram #1 runs east to west from beyond the zoo toward the market.

Taxis: In every major square, especially at the train stations, Gostinitsa Kaliningrad, the zoo, and pl. Pobedy. Agree on a price before setting off.

Tourist Office: Gostinitsa Kaliningrad (Гостиница Калининград), Leninsky pr. 81, on the north end of Tsentralnaya pl. Bare-bones services. **Noktyurn** (Ноктюрн; tel./fax 46 95 78), to the left of the lobby. No train tickets. Open M-Sa 8am-6pm.

Currency Exchange: Kiosks with "Обмен Валюты" signs dot major downtown intersections, including one inside the train station, on the right near the exit. **Investbank** (Инвестбанк), Leninsky pr. 28 (tel. 43 11 62), immediately to the right of Hotel Kaliningrad (see above). Accepts AmEx **traveler's checks** and gives MC/Visa cash advances, both for a 2% commission. There is also a 24hr. MC ATM outisde, and a MC/Visa one outside Hotel Kaliningrad, but don't be surprising if neither is working. Branch offices are popping up throughout Kaliningrad. Open M-Sa 9:30am-1pm and 2-4pm.

Luggage storage: Buy a *zheton* at one of the bus station *kassa* for 2.60R. Open M-Sa 6am-10pm, Su 6am-6pm.

Pharmacy: Apteka (Аптека), Leninsky pr. 63/67 (tel. 43 27 83). Fairly current compared to other stores in the city, which isn't saying much. Open daily 8am-8pm.

Post Office: Out of the way at ul. Leonova 22 (Леонова; tel. 21 52 33). A right off pr. Mira, past Gostinitsa Moskva. Open M-F 9am-6pm, Sa 10am-6pm. *Poste Restante* at window #21. **EMS** at window #8 (tel. 27 34 95). **Branch office** at ul. Krasnooktyabrskaya 6/12 (Краснооктябрьская; tel. 44 33 15), to the right of Leninsky pr. before the river. Shorter lines, but no **EMS. Postal code:** 236 000.

Telephones: Ul. Leonova 20, through the back entrance to the post office. **Faxes** inside. Open daily 8am-9pm. **International Telephone Center** (tel. 45 15 15; fax 46 95 90), inside Hotel Kaliningrad, on the left as you enter. Connecting to Moscow to reach AT&T or MCI operator costs 4R per min.; faxes 28R per min. to Australia and the U.S. Open daily 7:30am-11pm. **Phone code:** 0112.

ACCOMMODATIONS

The creation myth of accommodations in Kaliningrad: First there was nothing. Then, the Germans came, and they were not pleased. So, Kaliningrad built for the Germans many fine hotels, but the Germans were still not pleased, and the Germans decided to go to Florida (or at least elsewhere in Poland). Then the ruble was devalued, and the many fine hotels were not pleased, because they couldn't get much money out of the Russians, there only clientele after the Germans left. But then came you, the budget traveler, and you will be quite pleased indeed.

Gostinitsa Ademi (Адеми), nab. Marshala Bagramyana (наб. Маршала Баграмяна; tel. 46 16 62; fax 46 16 41). From Leninsky pr., cross the bridge heading toward Tsentralnaya pl.; the hotel is the third ship on the left. Good location, upscale facilities, and rock-bottom prices. Singles with shared bath 160R; doubles with shared bath 180R, with private bath 350R; triples with private bath 400R. Sauna, restaurant, bar, business center, and casino on premises. English-speaking reception.

Gostinitsa Kaliningrad (Гостиница Калининград), Leninsky pr. 81 (tel. 46 94 40), on the north side of Tsentralnaya pl. The fanciest digs in town, and the interior even looks stylish...if you compare it to the nearby House of Soviets. Also houses a tourist bureau, exchange office, phone center, and a business center. Singles US$48; doubles US$67. Reception speaks German, but no English. Open 24hr. MC/Visa/AmEx.

Gostinitsa Kyonigavto (Кёнигавто), Moskovsky pr. 184 (tel. 46 76 52; fax 46 07 22), on the right side of the street walking from the city center. Take tram #8 or 10 from Yuzhny Vokzal to Moskovsky Universam (Московский Универсам—a grocery store on Moskovskaya pr.), cross the street, and take bus #2 or 5 for 5 long blocks. The hotel is set back from the road by the parking lot in front. Newly remodeled rooms, each with bathroom, TV, and shower. Singles 300R; doubles 350R. Breakfast included. One-time visa registration fee 17R. Parking 25R. Reception and bar open 24hr.

Gostinitsa Moskva (Москва), pr. Mira 19 (tel. 27 20 89), a few blocks past pl. Pobedy and just past Baltika stadium on the left, across from the zoo. Take any tram in the direction of "Парк Калинина" (Park Kalinina). Where Russians from other cities stay when they're in town. Communication center on the 1st floor is more convenient than the nearby post office. Somewhat musty rooms and iffy hot water. Singles 160R, with shower 180R; doubles with shower 250R; triples without shower 150R.

FOOD

While eating out in Kaliningrad remains a largely disappointing experience, some nice places can be found and new eateries are slowly appearing. For groceries, head to the **central market** (tsentralny rynok; центральный рынок), where ul. Chernyakhovskovo intersects ul. Gorkovo, originally built for a 1930s trade exhibition. (Open daily 9am-6pm.) Several reasonably well-stocked supermarkets lie along Leninsky pr, between Tsentralnaya pl. and pl. Pobedy.

Pri Svechakh (При Свечах; By Candlelight), on the terrace of the Dramatichesky Teatr (tel. 21 77 71). The best outdoor cafe in the city. Relax and watch the city rush by over a cold *EKU Pils* (10R) and real sandwiches.

Oleg's Uzbek Kitchen, Staraya Bashnya (Старая Башня), Kiosk #52/54, in front of the House of Soviets. Ignore the less-than-exclusive address; this is a real sit-down palce with real and bountiful ethnic specialties for 30-50R. Open daily noon-11pm.

Cafe City Papa (Сытый Папа), Moskovskay pr. 123. Small well-appointed bar/cafe with comfy booths and outdoor seating. Smallish portions of simple, tasty staples for 10-50R. Open M-Sa 10:30am-7pm.

SIGHTS

CATHEDRAL. Kaliningrad's former pride and joy is the old **Cathedral,** which ages away on large Kneiphof Island in the middle of the Pregolya river. Damaged by fire way back in 1544, funds are only now being raised to build a new roof and restore the towers. Meanwhile, the burnt-out shell stands as both a reminder of Kaliningrad's German heritage and a monument to the Russian conquest of the city, while the plastic surgery progresses with the ebb and surge of German tourism. Inside, you can see the vandalized and eroding tombs lining the cathedral's walls, or climb the mythical steps made famous by German Romantic writer E.T.A. Hoffmann. The **Kaliningrad Symphony** occasionally holds concerts here; inquire within. Walk around (outside) to the back of the cathedral to find the immaculately kept **grave of Immanuel Kant** (1724-1804), the German philosopher who spent his entire life in Königsberg and taught at the local university. Kant's grave is enclosed by pink marble colonnades, probably to protect him from the busloads of German tourists who visit him daily. Other Kant paraphenalia, including a maccabre copy of his death mask, are in the **museum** upstairs in the cathedral. Behind the cathedral, not far from Kant's remains, is a monument erected in 1991 by Prussian-born Germans to **Julius Rupp** (1809-1884), one of Königsberg's famous pastors, whose house once stood on this spot. Rupp founded a new, unofficial religious order that he called *Druzya Sveta* (Друзья Света; Friends of the World), which stood for harmony among all peoples and religions. Although Rupp was chastised for his views in the 19th century, he has remained one of Königsberg's most influential thinkers, eventually passing on many of his beliefs to German artist Käthe Kollwitz, his niece. *(Tel. 21 25 83. Open daily 9am-5pm. 3DM (pay in rubles), foreign students 10R.)*

AMBER MUSEUM. (Muzey Yantarya; Музей Янтаря). Located in one of Königsberg's seven remaining **City Gates,** this is perhaps the city's finest and most interesting museum. Nearly 90% of the world's amber comes from nearby Yantar, much of it smuggled out illegally every year, and these are the best specimens of the lot. The museum's three floors display amber crowns, jewelry boxes made for Catherine the Great, one of the world's largest single pieces of amber (weighing in at 4.28kg), and even the poor insects who met their fate inside various gems as they hardened. Amber souvenirs are sold downstairs, but better prices can be found elsewhere. *(Tel. 46 12 40. Open Tu-Su 10am-6pm, kassa closes at 5:30pm. 10R, students 3R.)*

BUNKER MUSEUM. (Muzey Blindazh; Музей Блиндаж). This underground complex has taken over the network of rooms from which the Nazis directed their defense of Königsberg before the city was finally conquered by Soviet forces on April 9, 1945. The museum presents the capture of the city in great detail; unlucky Room 13 has been left exactly as it was when the commander signed the city over to the Red Army. Some of the displays have been translated smugly into German, while signs in English outside each room explain the contents' significance. *(Off Leninsky pr., on ul. Universitetskaya (Университетская), opposite the garden of the University of Kaliningrad. Tel. 43 05 93. Open daily 10am-5:30pm. 10R, students 5R.)*

HOUSE OF SOVIETS AND ENVIRONS. Since 1255, when Teutonic knights first arrived in this area, a castle guarded the hill east of what is now Tsentralnaya pl. As part of the concerted effort to turn Königsberg into a truly Soviet city, that castle was blown up in 1962 and replaced by Kaliningrad's, the **House of Soviets** (Dom Sovetov; Дом Советов) an H-shaped monstrosity that, after 35 years, stands incomplete even as it begins to crumble. Meanwhile, the nearby **Gallery of Artists** (Khudozhestvennaya Galereya; Художественная Галерея), displays local artwork and exhibits on the history of the *oblast*. *(Moskovsky pr. 60/62. Tel. 46 72 49. Open Tu-Su 11am-6:30pm. 10R.)*

MUSEUM OF HISTORY AND ART. (Istoriko-Khudozhestvenny Muzey; Историко-Художественный Музей). The second floor of this gallery is devoted to the heroic Soviet army and its 1945 conquest of the depraved German city of Königsberg. There is also a newer, less bombastic display on the war in Afghanistan. Rotating exhibits of modern artists from the former Soviet Union comprise the third floor. *Klinicheskaya (Клиническая) 21. From Tsentralnaya pl., walk up the north side of the House of Soviets along ul. Shevchenko, which becomes ul. Klinicheskaya and snakes aroung Nizhny Lake. the museum is halfway up the lake. Tel. 45 39 02. Open Tu-Su 10am-6pm. 10R, students 5R.)*

OTHER MONUMENTS TO SOVIET GLORY. In the middle of **pl. Pobedy** (Victory Square) stands a 7m **statue of Lenin,** one of the last monuments from the Soviet era still standing (unless you count Kaliningrad itself). If you liked that, don't miss the genial-looking statue of **Mikhail Ivanovich Kalinin,** waving to the city named after him that he never saw, from outside Yuzhny Vokzal. Two blocks to the left of Lenin, at Sovetsky pr. 3-5, a glorious pink-and-white Prussian building, former home of the Kaliningrad **KGB.**

ZOO AND STADIUM. Wrestling baby bears welcome you to the **zoo**, on pr. Mira, across from Gostinitsa Moskva; their older relatives have learned to do tricks for tourists offering food (against the rules, of course). Once among the top five zoos in Europe, it turned 100 in 1996 and is showing its age. Don't be surprised if you see a common housecat playing the part of his bigger cousins in the feline cages. *(Tel. 21 89 24. Open 9am-8pm. 10R.)* The **stadium** across from the zoo is home to Kaliningrad's beloved soccer team, Baltika. It is worth seeing the team play if you are a soccer fan, but beware the rowdy crowd of drinking men.

ENTERTAINMENT

The **Puppet Theater** (Teatr Kukol; Театр Кукол; tel. 21 29 69) in **Luise Church** in the **Kalinin Park of Culture and Rest** (ПКиО; *PKiO*) is two stops past the zoo on tram #1 or 4; trolleybus #3, 4, or 6; or bus #3, 5, 14, or 105. (Box office open M-F 10am-5pm.) Frequent **organ concerts** resound in the large brick church at ul. B. Khmelnitskovo 63a (Б. Хмельницкого), several blocks northeast of Yuzhny Vokzal. Prices and times fluctuate; check posters for details. There's also the **Dramatichesky Teatr,** pr. Mira 4 (Драматический Театр; tel. 21 24 22), in a Weimar-era residence east of the zoo. Ask the friendly director Anatoly Kravtsov for a tour of the remarkable building. (Open daily 9am-9pm; tickets to performances run 10-15R.) The German government has recently built a cultural center for the large number of ethnic Germans who have arrived in Kaliningrad from central Asia. The **Deutch-Russiches Haus** (Немецко-Русский Дом), ul. Yaltinskaya 2a (Ялтинская; tel./fax 46 96 82 and 45 06 31), off Moskovsky pr., offers German-language drama, German courses, and other events for anyone interested in the history of German-Russian relations. (Open Tu-Sa 9am-6pm.)

NIGHTLIFE

Nightlife in Kaliningrad is slowly reviving, although much of it revolves around casinos. At **Diskoteka Vagonstra** (Дискотека Вагонстра), on ul. Radishcheva (Радищева) in a cavernous, unmarked gray building, *mafiosi* shimmy with students and soldiers till dawn. Take tram #1 or 4 five stops past the zoo, and follow ul. Vagonstroitelnaya (Вагонстроительная), the street immediately behind the tram as you get off. The first street on the right is ul. Radishcheva.

NEAR KALININGRAD: SVETLOGORSK (СВЕТЛОГОРСК)

Formerly the German town of Rauschen, this pleasant seaside resort was used by Soviet officials as a spot for rest and relaxation. Today, German tourists have returned to Svetlogorsk. Those old enough to remember can tell you that much of the old charm is still here—tall pines line quiet streets with lovely old villas perched above the Baltic. The main attraction here is the beach, which is quite pleasant (if a bit narrow) and where vendors hawk a good selection of **amber** for reasonable prices. At the east end of the promenade sits a **sundial,** purportedly the largest in Europe. At ul. Lenina 5, on the outskirts of town, stands a small **chapel,** opened in 1994 in memory of the 34 people who died when a Soviet military aircraft crashed into a kindergarten on the site. Among the dead were 23 children. The incident was covered up until 1991, when the Russian Orthodox Church decided to build the chapel.

GETTING THERE. A convenient daytrip from Kaliningrad, Svetlogorsk is beat reached by train; buses also run but tend to be overcrowded. Trains from **Kaliningrad** (1hr., 13 per day, 8R) stop at both Svetlogorsk 1 and Svetlogorsk 2; 2, the last stop, is much closer to the center of things. In front of Svetlogorsk 2, **ul. Lenina** (Ленинна) runs east-west, parallel to the sea. The downright impatient can take chairlift from behind the station directly to the beach. (Runs daily 10am-8pm. 3R). Otherwise, a left down ul. Lenina leads to the center of town (5min.).

KURSHSKAYA KOSA (КУРЩСКАЯ КОСА)

Nearly 80km long and never more than 4km wide, the Kurshskaya Kosa (Curonian Spit) is essentially a giant sandbar. On it, however, rests the most stunningly beautiful landscape in the region. Lush pine forests cover all but the western side, molded by Baltic winds into a series of famed sand dunes. The eastern side faces the calmer waters of the Kurshisky Zaliv (Curonian Lagoon), and is home to a few villages, including tiny Rybachii (Рыбачий), the best base for exploring the Spit.

ORIENTATION & PRACTICAL INFORMATION. There are three main settlements along the Spit; Lesnoe (Лесное) to the south, Morskoe (Морское) to the north near the Lithuanian border, and Rybachii in between. The area is only accessible by mass transit, as those traveling by car who are not Kaliningrad residents must obtain special permission. Some buses between Klaipeda and Kaliningrad travel up the Spit, but non-Russian speakers will have trouble determining which. A better option is a **train** (40min., 6 per day, 8R) or **bus** (50min., at least hourly, 8R) to **Zelenogradsk** (Зеленоградск), just south of the Spit. From there you can catch a bus to Morskoe or Klaipeda that will stop in Rybachii (40-45min., 8 per day, 9R). Buy tickets in the train station building facing the buses; just ask for a ticket to Rybachii and the time of departure will be printed on it. Rybachii's "bus station" (a blue hut) is on the main drag ul. Pobedy (Победы). Turn right to reach most everything in town. In this direction, Pobedy ends at the main highway; the road to Morskoe and Klaipeda is straight ahead, while Zelenogradsk is to the left. A second bus stop, where some buses may stop, also lies here. There is a small **post office,** with telephones, at ul. Pobedy 29. (Open M-Sa 9am-5pm.) A large **map,** with English notation, is just a short walk down the road toward Zelenogradsk.

ACCOMMODATIONS & FOOD. Rybachy boasts one place to stay, the **ZRP Rest Home,** which offers sparse but clean rooms with shared baths for 5-10R person. Some overlook the lagoon, but none have telephones.

Many visitors come just to eat Rybachy's fantastic restaurant, **Tracter** (Трактирь), at the end of ul. Pobedy along the higway. Their specialty is locally-caught seafood, including delicious fried eel and fish soup, but it also does meats and salads pretty well. Everything is served with generous side dishes (a rarity in Eastern Europe) of veggies, bread, and red caviar. (Entrees 90-150R, soup 30R. Open daily noon-4am). Tracter is also building a log-cabin hotel adjoining the restaurant that should be completed by early 2000.

SIGHTS & HIKING. Tourist infrastructure on the Spit ranges from minimal to non-existant, so don't expect visitor centers or even many hiking trails. There are a few access points to the sea and the lagoon between towns; these usually have a bus stop. Otherwise, scores of unpaved roads and unmarked footpaths crisscross the forest. Most of these lead to private homes or nowhere at all, the product of grazing cattle. The one **hiking trail** in the area is about 15min. from Rybachy down the road toward Zelenogradsk, but it is not to be missed. Look for signs along the road in Russian, German and English for Excursion Route "Island" (Остов); the trailhead is on the right just after the lake on your left. An gentle 3.5km loop, it was built in 1998 by a group of international environmentalists. Follow the wooden arrows (some of which are missing, in which case follow the bigger path) to the top of Müller's Hill, the highest point on the Spit. Climb the taller of the two observation towers for a view that will make even the most jaded hiker gape in awe. The entire Spit is visible, from Lesnoe to Lithuania and from idyllic Rybachy on the lagoon to the shimmering Baltic. From here, the trail descends into a pleasant pine forest whose trees slant to one side from the force of the wind. This part of the trail is especially poorly maintained, and you may even find yourself forced back the other way to return to town. Once there, take a walk down by the **beach;** head down the road toward Klaipeda and Morskoe. Just after a bend (10min.), a power line crosses the road; turn left here onto the path under it. Continues straight until you reach the vast and empty sands.

THE VOLGA REGION (ПОВОЛЖЬЕ)

The longest river in Europe, the 3700km Volga is Russia's main trade artery, linking Moscow with five seas and oceans. The fertile triad of the Volga, the Don, and the Oka gave birth to Russian civilization around the 7th century. The Slavs prospered

Southern Volga Region and Caucasus

here until the first wave of Mongol invasions forced them north. But even northern forests and powerful fortresses provided insufficient protection, and they were soon overrun—within half a century, the Russians were able to push back south to Azov and reclaim their ancestral lands. Previously closed to foreign visitors, war-scarred Volgograd and bustling Nizhny Novgorod display Russia's grisly past and its scrounging, capitalist present, while Rostov-na-Donu serves as a gateway to future journeys southward.

NIZHNY NOVGOROD (НИЖНИЙ НОВГОРОД)

According to a Russian proverb, St. Petersburg is Russia's head, Moscow its heart, and Nizhny Novgorod (NEEZH-nee NOHV-guh-rud, formerly Gorky; pop. 1,400,000) its pocket. The city has always been more accepting of Western culture than most of Russia, and a strategic position on the Volga and Oka rivers, combined with a population of 1,500,000 (the third-largest in Russia) have made it a crossroads for Russia's urban and provincial economies. From the city's kremlin, rulers have long regulated trade and repelled Mongol invaders; today, they oversee its transition from a peripheral outpost to a center of privatization, with Pepsi, Marlboro, and Jeep Cherokee ads popping up on even the dustiest of side streets.

ORIENTATION

The **Oka** and **Volga** rivers twist through Nizhny Novgorod, with the main attraction, two-tiered **Central Nizhny,** on the bank opposite the train and bus stations. The first level of Central Nizhny includes the river station and ul. Rozhdestvenskaya (ул.

Рождественская); the second sits uphill and houses the kremlin, the Gorky mususm, and the art museum. The main pedestrian street, lined with stores, restaurants, and, cafes, **ul. Bolshaya Pokrovskaya** (ул. Большая Покровская) runs from the kremlin to **pl. Gorkovo** (пл. Горького). From the train station, take any bus labeled "МИНИНА" to pl. Minina, the city center. **Verzhne-Volzhskaya nab.** (Вержие-Волжская наб.) originates in pl. Minina, and rises up to the top of a cliff overlooking the river. The **Nizhny Novgorod Fairground,** on the bank of the Oka and near pl. Lenina (Ленина), is also a useful reference marker.

PRACTICAL INFORMATION

Trains: Moskovsky Vokzal (Московкий Вокзал), across the river from the kremlin. Trains to: **Kazan** (9hr., 1 per day, 125R) and **Moscow** (8hr., 6 per day, 3 of which are night trains, 80-100R), via **Vladimir** (4hr., 6 per day, 55R).

Buses: Coming out of the train station, the *avtovokzal* (автовокзал) is a 5min. walk to the left. Buses are generally more crowded than trains. To: **Moscow** (9hr., 7 per day, 150R) and **Vladimir** (5hr., 2 per day, 100R). Open daily 6am-10:30pm.

Local Transportation: Nizhny is clearly organized, but bigger than most Russian cities. A 1-day pass for buses and express buses (denoted by "з" after the number) costs 2R; a 5-day pass is 9.50R. On trams and trolleys, pay the conductor or driver 1R. Taxi-buses (marked with a "T" prefix) are 2R. Most destinations are marked on the front of the bus. Any bus or trolley labeled "Московский Вокзал" goes across the river to the train station and stops at the ferry station and Tsentralnaya Gostinitsa (Центральная Гостиница). Any bus or tram with "#1 Минина" on the side goes to pl. Minina and pl. Gorkovo. Public transportation runs until 11:30pm, which may explain why the restaurants and bars on ul. Bolshaya Pokrovskaya close at 10 or 11pm.

Taxis: Taxis are safe, but most drivers never turn on their meters. The "official" prices are posted on the sides of the cabs: 3R initial charge plus 3R per km. Be prepared to be asked how much you expect to spend, then approximate the distance and haggle. A ride from the train station to pl. Minina will run 15-20R.

Tourist Office: Intourist, pl. Lenina, in Tsentralnaya Gostinitsa, Rm. 814. Plane and rail bookings from an English-speaking staff. Open M-F 9am-6pm.

Currency Exchange: Gostinitsa Oktyabrskaya (Октябрьская), Verzhne-Volzhskaya nab. 5. Cashes traveler's checks for a 3% commission, and gives cash advances on MC/Visa. Open daily 8:30am-1:30pm and 2:30-6:30pm. **Inkom Bank** (Инком Банк), ul. Varvarskaya 32 (Варварская; tel. 37 94 42), also gives Visa cash advances. Open M-Sa 8:30am-1pm and 2-8pm. An **ATM** (банкомат), ul. Bolshaya Pokrovskaya 24, takes Cirrus/MC/Plus/Visa.

Luggage Storage: Downstairs from the entrance to the train station, to the left. Look for the "Камерю Овранениуа" sign. No lockers–baggage room only. 14R for 24hr.

Emergency number: 03. Ask for *"skoral pomuch."*

Post Office: ul. Bolshaya Pokrovskaya 56, at pl. Gorkovo, on the left and up the stairs as you walk toward pl. Gorkovo. Open daily 8am-8pm. **Postal code:** 603000.

Telephones: Around the corner and to the left of the Post Office when walking toward pl. Gorkovo. Pay at window #4. Dial 8, wait for the tone, then dial 10 plus the country code and phone number, and then a 3 when you hear an answer. They'll also dial for you inside

LET GRANDMA ON THE TRAIN They push harder than anyone on the buses and Metro. They bundle up to the ears on even the hottest days in scarves and winter coats, then strip down to teeny-weeny bikinis and sunbathe on the banks of the Neva. They are *babushki,* and they mean business. Technically, *babushka* means grandma, but under the Soviet system—when it became alright to be rude—Russians began using it as a generic term for elderly women. In any case, be warned: if a *babushka* gets on the Metro, no matter how hardy she looks or how weak you feel surrender your seat, or prepare for the verbal pummeling of a lifetime.

the post office. Local calls 1R; to the U.S. 8am-8pm 22-37R per min., 8pm-8am 15-28R per min. Dial 30 45 01 for the operator. Phone bank open M-Sa 8am-10pm, Su 8am-6pm. **Phone code:** 8312.

ACCOMMODATIONS

Most hotels in Nizhny Novgorod gladly accept foreigners, although each has its own approach to pricing. Foreigners are usually charged 150-200% more than Russians, but some enlightened establishments have become more egalitarian.

Gostinitsa Tsentralnaya (Гостиница Центральная), ul. Sovetskaya 12 (Советская; tel. 77 55 82). With your back to the train station, turn left and walk 10min.; it's the big gray building next to the Trade Fair. Spectacular view of the Oka. Sauna, massage parlor, and 24hr. room service. Singles with bath, TV, telephone, and refrigerator 300R; doubles 400-500R.

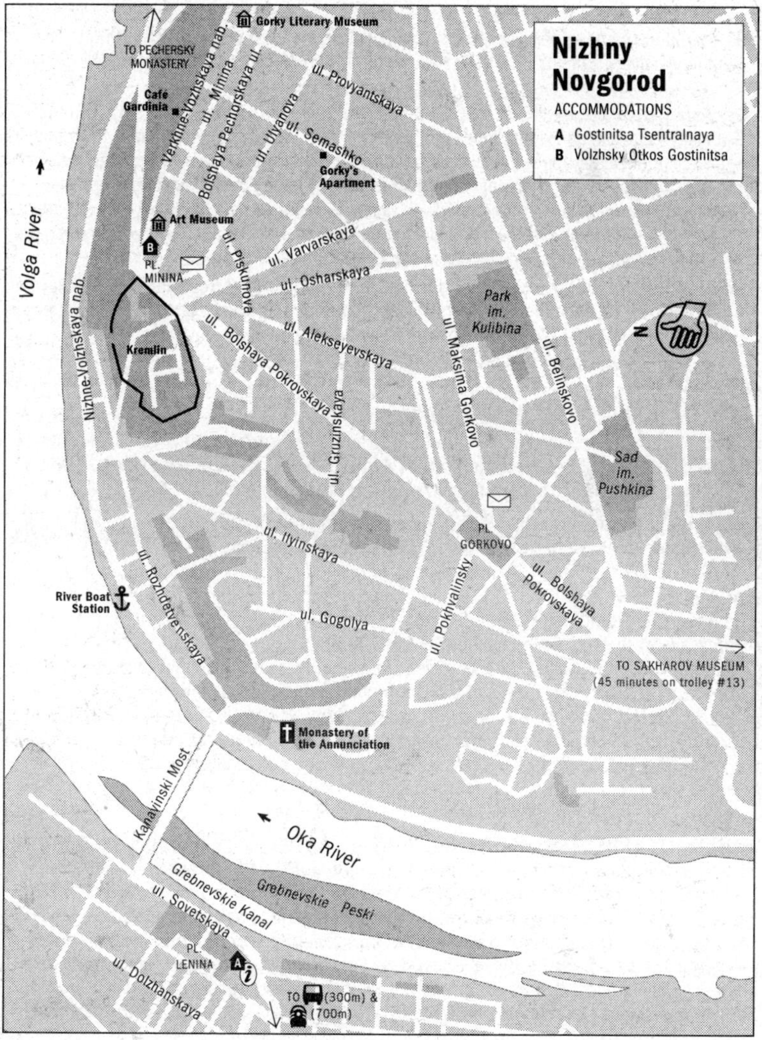

Gostinitsa Volzhsky Otkos (Гостиница Волжский Откос), Verzhne-Volzhskaya nab. 2a (tel. 39 19 71, reservation tel. 39 19 51; fax 36 38 94). Take any of the numerous buses from the train station to pl. Minina. Facing the kremlin, walk to the right, then turn left at the river. Big and gray in a quiet neighborhood facing the Volga, and an easy walking distance from the center (although far from the train station). English-speaking staff does not overcharge foreigners. Most rooms have TV and all have phones.Singles 150R; doubles 400-500R.

FOOD

The recent explosion of private enterprise has brought a slew of new cafes. Many flank ul. Bolshaya Pokrovskaya. Do-it-yourselfers go to the **Torzhok grocery store** (Торжок) on ul. Bolshaya Pokrovksaya near ul. Piskunova (Пискунова; open 24hr.), or the **Dmitrievsky grocery store** (Дмитриевский) on ul. Piskunova (open daily 8am-8pm). The **Mytny Rynok** (Мытный Рынок), between #2 and 4 on ul. Bolshaya Pokrovskaya, vends fruits, vegetables, and meat in the summer. (Open daily 6am-7pm.)

Cafe Arlekin (Кафе Арлекин), ul. Bolshaya Pokrovskaya 8A (tel. 33 99 07). Outdoor seating flanks the bustling ul. Bolshaya Pokrovskaya. A limited selection of moderately priced salads (10-20R) and meat dishes (25-50R). Open daily 10am-10pm.

Gardinia (Гардиния; tel. 36 41 01), Verzhne-Volzhskaya nab., across from Gostinitsa Oktyabrskaya. Started by the first American "beeznesman" in town, this smart little cafe above the Volga serves American drinks to wealthy Russians. Cafeteria-style options include fried potatoes, soups, and spaghetti. Entrees 50-65R. Open daily 9am-10pm.

Russkye Pelmeni (Русские Пельмени), ul. Bolshaya Pokrovskaya 24 (tel. 33 21 07). *Pelmeni,* a sort of Russian ravioli, are served in bouillon or with cheese, sour cream, and butter. With salad, soup, and drinks for under 35R. Open daily 10am-9pm.

Houston Bar & Café (tel. 36 02 00), across from Gardinia and Gostinitsa Oktyabrskaya. Eat mediocre American food under pictures of Elvis and 1970s basketball stars. Entrees 50R-100R, drinks 5-50R. Open M-F 1pm-2am, Sa-Su noon-2am. MC/Visa.

SIGHTS

For a city known as Russia's pocket, Nizhny Novgorod offers a relative dearth of sights. When you get tired of strolling the kremlin, be sure to enjoy one of **Tourboat Moskva's** (Москва) great two-hour rides around the Volga and Oka rivers. (Boats across from the Hotel Tsentralnaya depart nightly at 6pm. 25R.)

KREMLIN. Resting atop one of the Volga region's few hills, the fortress surveys a vast expanse, making the town a formidable bastion against the armies of Genghis Khan in the 12th century (see **History,** p. 551). Today, it serves as a reminder of the city's legacy as an important border outpost. The kremlin's 8m thick walls still act as a defense: the premises house a bank, an art museum, the local governor and mayor's offices, and the 1631 **Archangel Cathedral** (Arkhangelsky Sobor; Архангельский Собор), now a museum of the city's history. The courtyard boasts an impressive collection of WWII-era tanks, jeeps and aircraft, all of which can be climbed on like a jungle gym. The **Art Museum** (Khudozhestvenny Muzey; Художественный Музей), also within the kremlin walls, exhibits Russian art from the 15th- to 20th- centuries, including 18th- and 19th-century portraits of tsars and other Russian notables. *(To find the museum, bear right after entering the kremlin and head back to the large white building. Open M and W-Su 10am-5pm. 20R, students 10R. Photos 100R. English labels.)*

GORKY LITERARY MUSEUM. (Literaturny muzey im. Gorkovo; Литературный Музей им. Горького). The best part of this museum is the building housing it—a 19th-century mansion complete with mirrors, cherubs, velvet wallpaper, and carved wood. The inside shows the literary and cultural achievements of Gorky's contemporaries (see **Literature and Arts,** p. 553), including a few handwriting specimens. *(Ul. Minina 26. Tel. 36 65 83. Open W-Su 9am-5pm. 3R. Friendly, energetic staff offers worthwhile guided tours in Russian, 5R per person.)* True Gorkyphiles may wish to visit **Gorky's Apartment** (Kvartira A. M. Gorkovo; Квартира А. М. Горького), featuring some great pictures from his mustached youth. Gorky lived here from 1902 until 1904. *(Ul. Semashko 19 (Семашко). With your back to Gostinitsa Oktyabrskaya turn left and head to pl. Minina. Take another left and walk a few blocks, then turn right onto Semashko. Tel. 36 16 51. Open Tu-W and F-Su 9am-5pm.)*

SAKHAROV MUSEUM. (Muzey Sakharova; Музей Сахарова). The father of the Soviet H-bomb who became an adamant opponent of the arms race and eventually won the Nobel Peace Prize, Andrei Dmitryevich Sakharov (see **History,** p. 553) lived on the first floor of this typically Soviet apartment block while under house arrest from 1980-86. Under guard and deprived of visitors or even a telephone, he nonetheless chose to have his huge, 4 bedroom flat draped in green, late '70s wallpaper, now yours to enjoy. *(Pr. Gagarina 214 (Гагарина). Reachable by trolley #13 from pl. Minina or bus #43 from the Trade Fair down pr. Gagarina to* "Музей Сахарова" *(about 45min. from pl. Minina). Cross the street, and it's just to the right. Tel. 66 86 23. Open M-Th, Sa-Su 9am-5pm. 8R. Reservations necessary for English tours, 12R per group.)*

MONASTERIES. The operational **Monastery of the Annunciation** (Blagoveshchensky Muzhskoy Monastyr; Благовещенский Мужской Монастырь) was founded in 1221, and after a period of sad Soviet dilapidation, reopened in 1993. Most of the surviving structures date from the 17th-century. The **cathedral** and **church** are open to the public, while the **planetarium** stands as a reminder of Soviet-era secularization. *(Up the hill a short distance from where ul. Rozhdestrenskaya ends and the bridge over the river begins. Buses stop right at the bottom of the hill before the monastery.)* The interior of the **Pechersky Monastery** (Печерский Монастырь), on the lower banks of the Volga, is closed; the crumbling building and overgrown foliage tell the story on their own. *(Take bus #24 or 74 to "Автовокзал" then walk down the street across from the stop. Free.)*

VOLGOGRAD (ВОЛГОГРАД)

Memories of World War II still haunt Volgograd (VUHL-guh-GRAHD, formerly Stalingrad). Here, the remnants of the Nazi Sixth Army surrendered to Soviet troops on January 31, 1943. The 200-day battle, perhaps the war's worst, left 91% of the city in ruins and an estimated two million dead. The city was rebuilt as a monument to the fallen—statues and plaques commemorating the battle fill Volgograd's wide streets, which are in most cases named for the heroes and regiments of the battle. As in Minsk, the rebuilding seems to have given Soviet urban planners free reign to produce an ideal, rationally organized city: Volgograd is rectilinear, scaled as if the statues would be walking around, and sprinkled with gracious Neoclassical buildings. Not even the balmy breeze off the Volga can dissipate the pall of history over the city, but the *babushki*, teeny boppers, families and mafiosos living here all seem to push forward nonetheless.

ORIENTATION

Crescent-shaped Volgograd stretches around a bend in the Volga, 800km south of Ulyanovsk and 1000km southeast of Moscow. The **Volga-Don Canal,** which begins in Volgograd's southernmost region, links the city with Rostov-na-Donu, 500km to the west, and with the Azov and Black Seas beyond. The main hotels and most of the restaurants and shops lie between the train and ferry stations. From the train station, head for the neon **Gostinitsa Intourist** (Гостиница Интурист) sign to your left atop a large building. This hotel stands in central **pl. Pavshikh Bortsov** (пл. Павших Борцов), and the wide, tree-lined **alleya Geroev** (Avenue of Heroes; аллея Героев) leads from here across **pr. Lenina** to the river. **Mamaev Kurgan** (Мамаев Курган), home to Volgograd's most moving sights, is a 100m high hill at the end of pr. Lenina. A kiosk in the ticketing hall of the train station sells city **maps** (8R).

PRACTICAL INFORMATION

Trains: Volgograd-1 vokzal (tel. 005, 30 21 64, or 30 21 75), on ul. Kommunisticheskaya. To: **Rostov-na-Donu** (16hr., 1 per day, 350-400R); **Pyatigorsk** (20hr., 1 per day, 300R); and **Moscow** (27hr., 2 per day, 750R). Foreigners may buy tickets at an ordinary *kassa.*

Buses: Avtovokzal Tsentralny (Автовокзал Центральный), ul. Bolonina 11 (Болонина; tel. 37 72 28). Cross the tracks behind the train station, take a right at the bottom of the steps heading down from the bridge and paralleling the tracks—don't go all the way across the bridge. To: **Rostov-na-Donu** (10-11hr., 4 per day, 101-110R) and **Pyatigorsk** (13hr., 2 per day, 131R).

Local Transportation: The **metrotram** (метротрам) runs from the train station and along pr. Lenina (Ленина). It travels underground in the center, but otherwise resembles its tram half more than its metro half. Tickets (2R) are sold at kiosks by above-ground stops and at ticket counters underground. The stop closest to alleya Geroev is "Комсомольская" (Komsomolskaya). **Buses** link the train station with the city's outer parts. They are heavily patrolled by officers eager to collect 8R from the ticketless, so be sure to buy your ticket (2R) before you board. The *kassa* may look closed—just shove your money in and a hand will take it (hopefully). In principle, buses run till midnight, but many drivers call it a day around 10pm.

Tourist Office: The bureau in **Gostinitsa Intourist,** ul. Mira 12 (Мира; tel. 33 75 78; fax 36 16 48), will answer questions in English. They also sell cheap Soviet-era pamphlets celebrating glorious Volgograd's virtues.

Currency Exchange: There are neither **ATMs** nor establishments that cash traveler's checks in town.

Luggage Storage: Kamera khraneniya (Камера Хранения), in the basement of the train station. 19-79R per day. Open daily 8am-6pm and 7pm-7:30am.

Pharmacy: Apteka (Аптека), alleya Geroev 5 (tel. 36 19 75). Open daily 8am-8pm.

Post Office: pl. Pavshikh Bortsov (tel. 36 10 78), right across ul. Mira from Gostinitsa Intourist (see **Tourist Office,** above). Pleasant central rotunda where you can write letters under Lenin's watchful eye. **Poste Restante** (*do vostrebovanya;* до востребования) at window #11. **Photocopying** (1.50R per page), **internet,** and fax in **telegraph office** to the left after entering the post office. Open M-F 8am-7pm, Sa-Su 8am-6pm. **Postal code:** 400066.

Telephones: Phones take *zhetony* (жетоны; tokens), sold at the telegraph office (see above); phone cards (75.60R) are for sale in the **telephone office,** on the left, which is also the place for international calls. To the U.S. 25.80R per min. Both offices open 24hr. **Phone code:** 8422.

ACCOMMODATIONS

Despite its large student community, Volgograd does not offer much in the way of budget accommodations. The larger, centrally located hotels are inordinately expensive, while budget rooms on the fringe of town are hard to find. **Private rooms** are the cheapest option; *babushki* advertise space in their apartments outside the more expensive hotels. (50-70R per night.) If sleeping next to an old woman's cat

RUSSIA

doesn't appeal to you, try **Gostinitsa Turist** (Турист), nab. 62-y Armii 3 (62-й Армии; tel. 34 12 43). Take the metrotram or walk 30 min. down pr. Lenina to Mamaev Kurgan and go almost to the river. The Turist is a tall building on your left offering ordinary rooms with bath and patented Russian service-without-a-smile. (Singles 185R; doubles 250R.) **Gostinitsa Intourist,** ul. Mira 14 (tel. 36 45 53; fax 36 16 48) offers a central location, comfortable rooms, and a couple of out-of-tune pianos for aspiring Rachmaninoffs. (Singles with sink and toilet 352.67R, with bath 650R; doubles 832R. Breakfast included. Low-end prices may rise if renovations occur. Partial compensation if amenities fail. AmEx/MC/Visa. Fax to reserve.)

FOOD

The **tsentralny rynok** (central market; центральный рынок), ul. Sovetskaya 17 (Советская), has entrances on ul. Komsomolskaya (Комсомольская) and pr. Lenina, behind the Central Bank. (Open M 7am-4pm, Tu-Sa 7am-7pm, Su 7am-5pm.) **Cafes** serving alcohol, ice cream, and shashliks (10-15R) abound along the river and near alleya Geroev, but monuments far outnumber sit-down restaurants. **Drakon** (Дракон), pr. Lenina 10 (tel. 36 77 46 or 36 78 94), is near the intersection of pr. Lenina and alleya Geroev. The faux-Chinois decor fools no one—this place is Russian dining through and through. The only "dragon" is the pet alligator in the fishtank. (Entrees 35-100R. Open daily noon-2am. Visa.)

SIGHTS

When it was completed in 1967, Russians flocked to Volgograd's **Mamaev Kurgan monument complex.** New revolutions and new problems have directed their attention elsewhere, but first-time visitors will be impressed by the measurements—and perhaps even moved by the presence—of the Motherland statue. Mamaev Kurgan's strategic **peak** changed hands 13 times in the course of the Battle of Stalingrad, and the earth became so clogged with shrapnel that for two years nothing would grow on the mound. Today, trees dedicated to individual soldiers cover the slopes. The stairs to the peak teem with graffiti shouting Party slogans like Stalin's murderous dictum "Ни шаг назад" (Not one step back). Farther up, statues of stoic Soviets carrying their wounded commemorate the sufferings of the brutalized country. Towering above it all is the 52m tall **Motherland** statue (Mat' Rodina; Мать Родина), recalling the French revolutionary painting, "Liberty Leading the People," on a monumental scale. The Russian soldiers guarding the eternal flame on the way up put on an impressive gun-twirling routine. Metrotram runs here, as do buses #8, 9, 12, and 13.

For a glorification of the Russian defense of Stalingrad that verges on heady Soviet kitsch, try the **Panorama Museum** (Muzey-Panorama; Музей-Панорама), ul. Chuykova 2 (tel. 34 67 23). With alleya Geroev on your right walk along pr. Lenina for a few blocks, turn right onto ul. Gagarina, and then left onto ul. Chuykova. The museum, which resembles a nuclear cooling tower, is on your right. It presents a blow-by-blow account of the Soviet counterattack, with such aids to the imagination as uniforms, walk-in pillboxes with menacing tanks visible at the loopholes, and hard-hitting photos of the countless dead. The painted panorama on the second floor, however, is more compelling than the artifacts surrounding it. (Open in summer Tu-Su 10am-6pm; in off-season Tu-Su 10am-5pm, closed last Friday of the month. *Kassa* closes ½hr. before museum. 25R for foreigners, 15R for Russians, 10R for children.) A gutted **mill,** preserved to demonstrate the wartime destruction, crumbles by the Muzey-Panorama. Across the street stand the remains of **Dom Pavlova** (Дом Павлова), where Sgt. Yakov Pavlov and 23 soldiers held out for 58 days against German attacks.

The centrally located **Fine Arts Museum** (Muzey Izobrazitelnikh Iskusstv; Музей Изобразительных Искусств), pr. Lenina 21 (tel. 36 39 06), has refreshingly little to do with the war, except in that its predecessor's destruction led to the donation of works from the Hermitage and Tretyakov Gallery, among others. It's an above-average collection of less-then famous artists. (Open Th-Tu 10am-5:30pm. 10R, students

8R.) To beat the heat, hang out on the south edge of the city by the mouth of the **Volga-Don Canal,** guarded by a dapper Lenin on one side and a bare pedestal where Stalin once stood on the other. Near the triumphal arch of the canal's first lock, local teenagers jeer and spit at passing cruise ships.

ENTERTAINMENT

With streets thronged with students by day, Volgograd should be jumpin' at night. Unfortunately, it's likely to be just you, the monuments, and a few bottles of Baltika #6. What action there is can be found down by the river as discotheques putter along and makeshift stages occasionally host local bands and their renditions of current hits. The **stadium,** one stop before Mamaev Kurgan on the metrotram, hosts Russia's top **soccer** league; game announcements are posted outside. The handsome, domed **Planetarium,** ul. Gagarina 14 (Гагарина; tel. 36 34 83), has astronomy for children and adults, as well as films of the city's reconstruction. (Daily shows scheduled for 10am, noon, 2, and 4pm; a given show will materialize if at least 15-20 people show up; at least 1 occurs per day. 10R.) The **Puppet Theater** (Teatr Kukol; Театр Кукол), pr. Lenina 15 (tel. 33 06 49), stages performances mainly for children. (Shows Sa-Su 11am. *Kassa* open Tu-F 11am-1:30pm and 2:30-6pm, Sa-Su 10am-1:30pm and 2:30-5pm. Admission varies, typically 4.50R.) Stop at the **Big Top Circus** (Volgograd Tsirk; Волгоград Цирк), ul. Krasnoznamensk (Краснознаменск; tel. 36 31 06; daily shows in the summer). To reach the **beach** on the vast Volga's other side, take a quick ferry to **Krasnoslobodsk** (Краснослободск) from terminal #12 at the river station (15min., 1 per hr. 6am-10pm, 10R).

ROSTOV-NA-DONU (РОСТОВ-НА-ДОНУ)

Rostov-na-Donu (pop. 1,000,000) has little to recommend it other than its status as the hub of southbound transportation. If you find yourself laid-over here (a fate equalled only by a delay in Kazan), the cheapest accommodations in town are at the **Gostinitsa** in the train station, which will put you in a scruffy but clean double with TV, balcony, and hall bath for 162R. If you want to explore a little, take any of the buses from the train station; all of them make stops on the main drag, **ul. Bolshaya Sadovaya** (Большая Садовая). On Sadovaya you'll find Russian specialties served in an elegantly mellow atmosphere at **Druzhba** (Дружба), ul. Bolshaya Sadovaya 88. (Entrees 40-80R, soups and appetizers 10-30R. Open daily from 11am until the last guest leaves.) **Mostbank,** on the left side of Voroshilovsky pr. coming from ul. Bolshaya Sadovaya **exchanges currency,** cashes **traveler's checks,** has an indoor **ATM** (Cirrus/MC/Plus/Visa) and offers MC/Visa **cash advances** for a 3% commission.

GETTING AWAY. Trains depart to: **Kiev** (22hr. 2 per day, 390R); **Sochi** (10hr. 4 per day, 88R); **Pyatigorsk** (10hr., 2 per day, 230R); **Moscow** (24hr., 2 per day, 170R); and **Volgograd** (14hr. 1 per day, 90R). Meanwhile, **buses** leave as quickly as possible for: **Azoz** (1hr., every 20min., 5R) **Simferopol** (10hr., 1 per day, 225R); **Volgograd** (9½hr., 3 per day, 100R); **Pyatigorsk** (10hr., 1 per day, 115R); and **Sochi** (in summer 14hr., 1 per day, 95R).

THE CAUCASUS (КАВКАЗ)

> "The air is pure and fresh as a child's kiss, the sun is bright, the sky is blue. What more can one wish? What need have we here of passions, desires, regrets?"
>
> —Mikhail Lermontov, *A Hero of Our Time*

As the above quote suggests, Russia's literary giants found something mightier in this land than its warring inhabitants and bloodshed. "It was here," wrote Gogol, "that Pushkin summoned all his soul's powers and tore from the last chains which still clutched at free thought" while serving out his exile. Lermontov was also exiled here, during which time he produced the first great Russian novel *A Hero of Our Time*, a fact which the town of Pyatigorsk will remind you of, none too subtly. Beach resort Sochi and hiking and skiing destinations Prielbruyse, Dombay, and

Krasnaya Polyana remain stable and inviting, despite the exploits of Chechyan guerrillas that tear through the headline. Equally unchanged are the pale, eternal cones of Mt. Elbrus—a dormant volcano and the highest mountain in Europe—which loom over the Caucasian range, a symbol of the freedom of the mountains and the volatility that threatens them.

> Because of nearby instability in the Southern Caucasus, always hire a guide before setting out for a hike in the mountains. While the Northern Caucasus are safe to explore, unfamiliarity with the region could lead you to a dangerous border with such breakaway republics as Chechnya or Abkhazia. See **Essentials: Safety & Security,** p. 22, for more information.

PYATIGORSK (ПЯТИГОРСК)

Long the most stable region in the Caucasus, and a centuries-old vacation mecca for Russians, foreigners have only recently discovered the North Caucasus. Pyatigorsk is the biggest of the five cities at the base of the northern mountains, and is probably the most convenient place to start a trek. Despite a decrease in tourism, it is still a resort town, speckled with spas and sanitoria. Invalids, hypochondriacs, and poets have all bathed in the supposedly magical (and certainly mineral-laden) springs of these mountains. For the more adventurous traveler, Pyatigorsk's students and mafiosos guarantee a few non-therapeutic activities come night.

ORIENTATION

Pyatigorsk nestles against the southeast side of **Mt. Mashuk** (933m), 10km south of the Beshtau peaks. **Pr. Kirova** (пр. Кирова) probably qualifies as Pyatigorsk's main street; it runs from the main **Pyatigorsky train station** to **Park Tsvetnik** (Парк Цветник) on the mountain's flanks. From the train station, take tram #2 until it veers left. At that point you can either keep riding to the Lermontovskaya (Лермонтовская) train station and most of the cheaper accommodations, or get off and take tram #4, which continues up pr. Kirova to the city center around ul. Kraynevo (Крайнего).

PRACTICAL INFORMATION

Trains: Long-distance tickets are available at **Pyatigorsky vokzal** (info tel. 502 91) a stop on tram lines #1, 2, 3, 6, and 7. Trains run to: **Sochi** (14hr., every other day, 460-720R); **Kiev** (31hr., every 2 days, 506-750R); **Moscow** (34hr., 2 per day, 350-520R); and **St. Petersburg** (46hr., 1 per day, 290-480R). The *elektrichka* (electric commuter rail) runs from 5am-11pm.

Buses: Glavny autovokzal can be reached by taking tram #4 to the intersection of ul. Kraynevo and pr. Kirova. Buses roll to: **Rostov na Donu** (10hr., 1 per day, 91R). A few buses and *marshrutnye* (fixed-route taxis—a bit pricier than buses but a lot cheaper than taxis) leave from **Gorachevsky autovokzal,** at tram #4's last stop, "Ludmila" (Лудмила). Others still leave from the **Verkhny Rynok,** a few blocks up ul. Mira from the "Mira" stop on trams #2 and 4. The convenience of a direct *marshrutnye* might not outweigh the frustration of trying to find it.

Local Transportation: Buses are rare, inefficient, and crowded in Pyatigorsk, but **tram #4,** affectionately called the *chetvyorka,* makes up for it. It runs from the Lermontovskaya train station to the Gorachevsky bus station, stopping at Park Tsvetnik, the University (stop "Universam" for the department store), and the lower market. **Tram #2** is also helpful, running between the two train stations. All trams are 2R; pay when the conductor tracks you down.

Tourist Office: Bureau Puteshestviye (Бюро Путешествие), ul. Kraynevo 74 (ул. Крайнего; tel. 500 54). With the post office behind you, walk about 2 blocks down ul. Kraynevo and enter through the lime-green gate on the right. When you get there, however, you might find yourself rerouted to the Bureau's kiosk at tram #4's "Tsvetnik" stop (tel. 559

RUSSIA

42). Arranges trips to local mountains, including Prielbrusye (55R) and Dombay (65R). Also arranges guides for hard-core hikers. Open M-Sa 9-noon and 1-5pm. **Maps** of Pyatigorsk (8R) and the nearby mountains (14R) are sold at kiosks all over, and at **Magazin Kartograf,** ul. Gorkovo 4 (tel. 528 09), off ul. Kirova and a block up from Pyatigorsky vokzal.

Budget Travel: Pyatigorsk State Pedagogical University has a mountain campsite called Damkhurts (Дамхурц), to which it occasionally sends groups of students for a few weeks. If your timing is right, you could go on an outing for about 1200R. Contact Aleksandr Grankin, head of the Student Union on the 6th floor of the university, up ul. Kalinina from tram #4's "Universam" (Универсам) stop.

Passport Office (OVIR): From the intersection of pr. Kirova and pr. 40-let Oktyabrya, go toward the pillared gates to the amusement park (the only direction with no tram tracks); turn left before the gates and then right into the courtyard of the OVIR building. Registering costs 40R, but is not necessary if you've already registered in Russia.

Currency Exchange: Intourist (tel. 490 18), up ul. Kraynevo from the post office, offers **currency exchange,** not much else.

Luggage Storage: In Pyatigorsky vokzal. Walk between the dysfunctional automated lockers to the window with the living, breathing person. 10R per piece for 24hr. Open 24hr.

Post Office: ul. Kraynevo 52. Tram #4: Kraynevo. Open M-Sa 8am-7pm, Su 8am-6pm. **Postal code:** 357500.

Telephones: International and intercity calls can be made from **Mezhdugorodny Telefon** (Междугородный Телефон), ul. Kraynevo 54. Buy your **tokens** (1.60R) at the post office kiosk, then head across and up the street. Open 24hr. **Phone code:** 86533.

ACCOMMODATIONS

Pyatigorsk State University Dorm #4, up ul. Dvesti-Devyanosta-Pyaty Strelovoy Divizii (295 Стреловой Дивизии) from the Lermontovskaya rail stop (terminus of trams #2 and 4) toward the Lermontov Duel Site. Ask for the *kommandant,* Galina Maksimovna. Students often go away in early summer, leaving locked rooms and few vacancies, but Galina may be able to find you something, either in the dorm proper or in affiliated rooms. You can help students with their English homework. 30R per night.

Gostinitsa Pyatigorsk, ul. Kraynevo 62 (tel. 567 03), up the hill and on the same side of the street as the post office. Ordinary rooms for ordinary Russians. Small double with sink 130R; larger double 250R. Hall bathroom, *sans* toilet paper. Shower 10R.

Gostinitsa Intourist, ul. Kosta Hetagurova (Коста Хетагурова; tel. 490 18). From the train station take tram #4 to "Kraynevo" (Крайнего). Walk uphill past the telephone and post offices, and the Gostinitsa will loom on the right. Enormous, expensive rooms with bath, TV, and phone for 400R. Casino, bars, and restaurant inside.

RUSSIA

FOOD

Quality fruits and vegetables abound in the market, just up ul. Kraynevo from the post office. While myriad cafes line pr. Kirova, finding a good restaurant in Pyatigorsk is still as tough as finding a good restaurant in, well, Russia.

Cafe Tals (Кафе Талс), ul. Kirova 68 (Кирова; tel. 574 50). Little more than Russian street food after a shave and a shower, but it's cheap, tasty, and quasi-instantaneous. Pastries (1-3R), meat rolls (5R), and juices (15R per liter). Open daily 8am-8pm.

Pizza Roma, with 2 locations: pr. Kalinina 2 (tel. 519 28), down the hill from the gate to the Duel Site, and ul. Kirova 29a, in front of the "Tsvetnik" stop on tram #4. Let not the height of the prices nor the shame of patronizing this American-chain affiliate prevent you from sampling the offerings. Their creative slogan says it all—"We are the Best." Pizzas 50-135R. Hamburger 35R. Open 10am-11pm.

Cafe Na Stipendiyu (Кафе На Стипендию), ul. Kozlova 39 (Козлова; tel. 734 43), on the corner of ul. Bulvarnaya opposite the "Universam" stop on trams #2 and 4. Remarkable salads (10-25R) and ice cream (10-20R) complement inexpensive but ordinary entrees (9-15R). Caters to students. Fast and friendly. Open 10am-10pm.

SIGHTS & ENTERTAINMENT

You don't know much about Pyatigorsk unless you've read **Lermontov's** *A Hero of Our Time*, a novella about an officer's adventures in the Caucasus (see **Literature & Arts,** p. 553). In real life, Pyatigorsk is perhaps most famous for being the site of the Russian writer Lermontov's death; "Pushkin began his exile here," Belinsky wrote of the region, "and Lermontov ended it here." The poet was challenged to a duel by a Major Martinov, whose sister Lermontov had insulted years earlier in St. Petersburg. Upon meeting the Major again, Lermontov composed a witty epigram that went something like, "The Major's saber hangs down to his knees." It is a matter of some historical debate whether there was some conspiracy, or whether the Major was just very touchy about his saber, but a duel followed shortly thereafter. Without walking to the barrier, Lermontov fired into the air. His opponent, cowardly scoundrel that he was, then walked up to the barrier (without tripping over his saber) and fired, killing Russia's greatest living poet. The series of events eerily resembled both Pushkin's duel and that of Lermontov's fictional character Pechorin. To get to the **Duel Site** and its sculpted vultures, walk up the hill from Lermontovskaya station, past the university dorms, and through the stone gates across the street. There is a well-labeled map at the park entrance that shows the duel site, as well as other attractions around Mt. Mashuk. Turn left when the road forks for a pleasant 3-4hr. hike around the mountain; go straight up to reach most of the sights, except the duel site.

Two kilometers into the longer hike are the **Gates of Love,** a graffiti-ridden stone arch rumored to secure a lifetime of love to those who pass under it. Twenty minutes beyond that is **Proval,** a light blue, bubbly, and sulfurous spring and underground lake; Lermontov himself once bathed here. Pyatigorsk's springs are said to have magical healing powers. They may, for example, cure a digestive tract that has been grumpy since one's arrival in a land where little is safe to eat or drink. There is no longer a bridge over the spring (a man and his cow, it seems, fell through and broke it), but a tunnel in the hillside lets you admire the water up close. (Open daily 8am-7pm.) If you want to get even closer, you can join the crowds bathing in the outflow across the street. A little farther up the road and down a few flights of stairs, **Spring #24** is across the street and down the stairs from the cave, and offers cold—albeit sulfurous—**water.** (Open daily 7-8am, 12:30-1:30pm, and 5-6pm. Free, but bring a cup.) If you want to enjoy the springs without the accompanying hike, take bus #1 or 15 to "Proval."

Walking up the hill from Proval and then left down a divided pedestrian street leads to the **Academic Gallery** (Akademichskaya Galereya; Академичская Галерея), which houses a butterfly collection that would wow Nabokov. (Open daily 9am-5pm. 5R.) The Aeolian harp, from Lermontov's *A Hero of Our Time*, used to stand under the small rotunda behind the Gallery, but now the fine view is the promontory's only attraction. Between the look-out point and the gallery, the **Grotto of Lermontov** reminds the traveler once again of the poet.

Park Tsvetnik can be found down the stairs from the Gallery or by taking tram #4 to "Tsvetnik." In the park lies the **Theater of Musical Comedy** (Teatr Muzikalnoy Komedii; Театр Музыкальной Комедии), ul. Kirova 17 (tel. 522 21), which puts on nightly shows for 45-60R. (Ticket window open daily 9am-noon and 1-7pm.) Continue down the hill to the gardens in front of the light blue **Lermontov Gallery** (Lermontovnaya Galereya; Лермонтовная Галерея), and see if you can beat one of the many old men playing chess onto the benches. At the base of the park stands the Lermontov Statue, and a right on ul. Karla Marxa (Карла Маркса) will take you to his house, **Domik Lermontova** (Домик Лермонтова), ul. Lermontova 4 (tel. 527 10), where the duel challenge was issued. (Open W-Su 10am-5pm. 10R, with tour 15R.)

For activities that involve **no Lermontov whatsoever:** a **cable car** travels to the top of Mt. Mashuk, offering a view of snow-capped peaks on a very clear day. (*Kassa* open daily 10am-5:15pm. 10R each way.) Bus #15 stops right under the cable. The **amusement park** in Park Kirova is ideal for those traveling with children—and, of course, for the young at heart. (Park open daily 10am-9pm.) A wild spinning ride called "The Waltz" costs 5R—you must be as tall as Lermontov to ride.

Unless you crash a dorm party, the best **nightlife** in town is at **Syedmoye Nyebo** (Seventh Heaven) on top of the Gostinitsa Beshtau (see **Accommodations,** p. 648). (Open daily 5pm-midnight, or until 1 or 2am if there are enough people; best on Th-Sa nights. Men 10R, women free.)

NEAR PYATIGORSK: DOMBAY (ДОМБАЙ)

A bustling winter ski resort, Dombay in the summertime is small, quiet, devastatingly beautiful, and inexpensive. More importantly, it is a superb base for hikes into the surrounding mountains, most of which are protected as part of the Teberdinsky Preserve (Teberdinsky Zapovednik).

If you're content with mountain views from a gondola lift, you would be best served by an **organized tour** from Pyatigorsk. (62R at the tourist bureau kiosk; see **Pyatigorsk: Orientation & Practical Information,** p. 647). If you're engaging in serious hiking, forgo the tour for an **instructor** who can steer you away from dangerous areas on the Georgian border. (Day-long outing 50-300R.) There are, fortunately, plenty of **day-hikes** within striking distance. One of the most stunning begins as a continuation of the main road through the village. After losing itself briefly in boulders, the trail climbs over a small waterfall, through deciduous forests and up to a fantastically fragrant alpine meadow called **Bear Glade** (Medvezhaya Polyana; about 1hr. of moderately strenuous climbing). From here, it continues up to a saddle on the ridge. A longer, less steep, and more heavily hiked trail starts as a continuation of the road above Gostinitsa Gorniye Vershiny. The first 90min. of the hike pass through **Camp Alibek** (accessible by car) and a mountainous **grave site,** a solemn tribute to climbers who have died in these mountains. The trail later splits; the left fork, rarely traveled, leads to a magnificent **waterfall** and, across the stream, a giant glacier. The less strenuous right fork leads to a serene, cold lake (2hr.). On both, thousands of beautiful **butterflies** flutter by the alpine flora. **Hiking maps** are available at a kiosk below Gostinitsa Gorniye Vershini for 15R. For more accessible views, a **ski-lift** will take you above the tree-line. (Runs daily 8am-5pm. Round-trip 30R.)

Backtracking from the bus stop over the bridge and past the natural mineral-water spring (*narzan;* нарзан) will take you to the slightly upscale **Gostinitsa Dombay** (tel. 581 69 or 581 60), which has bright, clean singles, doubles, and triples for US$20 per person (add 30R for three meals). Numerous little cafes, such as the **Kafe Alibek,** line the strip near the bus stop, but cheaper and (surprisingly) better meals are available at any of the *shashlik* stands. (*Shashlik*, sauces, veggies, and bread 50-70R.) Beware: nothing in town is open after 6pm. **Postal code:** 357191.

GETTING THERE. If you're not on an organized tour, getting to Dombay requires patience, flexibility, and good bargaining skills. A bus runs daily between Pyatigorsk and **Teberda,** about 16km north of Dombay (5hr., 3:30pm, 37R); but unless you want to hitch you're better off taking a morning bus from Pyatigorsk to **Cheresk** (2½hr., 8 per day, 22R) and from there a bus to Teberda (2hr., 6 per day, 25R). There are no buses to Dombay, but locals masquerading as taxis often wait at the Teberda bus station (25R with haggling). Hitching is also very common, although not recommended by *Let's Go*.

NEAR PYATIGORSK: PRIELBRUSYE (ПРИЭЛЬБРУСЬЕ)

At 5642m, volcanic Mt. Elbrus is the tallest mountain in Europe. The sizeable valley in its shadow contains numerous villages, camps, and settlements known collectively as Prielbrusye (literally "around Elbrus"). The highest and most convenient of the villages are Terskol and Cheget. Although landslides caused by deforestation have made much of the valley less pristinely beautiful than Dombay, the peaks here are even more stunning. Figure out whether you prefer rocks and ice or flowers and butterflies, and plan your trip accordingly.

Although it is often climbed by Russians and foreigners alike, if you're planning to tackle Elbrus, you should know what you're doing or take a guide who does. The surrounding area affords plentiful hiking opportunities for the less ambitious. A particularly satisfying hike leaves from the lower corner of the market below Gostinitsa Cheget. After following the rushing mountain streams briefly, the track starts winding up the hillside through a series of extraordinarily colorful meadows. About 90min. into the hike, at roughly the height of the slag-heap opposite, a goat-trail heads away from a hairpin turn toward the blue-green tinted **Donuz-Orunkel Lake.** Watch for **avalanches** across the valley, especially in the spring or during abnormally warm weather. Above the lake, another trail doubles back, leading to the top of the chair-lift from Cheget and impressive views of Elbrus. At this point, you can give your knees a break and ride down. (Supposedly runs daily 9am-2:45pm, but check in town. 20R.) A helpful **trail map** (25R) is sold in town or, on the weekends, at the newsstand below Gostinitsa Cheget.

The **Gostinitsa Cheget** (tel. 713 39) is a short walk down the road from Terskol, with run-down but clean rooms (US$20 per person). Hot water is available. For food, you can shop at one of the moderately overpriced stores in Terskol, or try any of the vendors or cafes. One option is **Cafe Goryanka,** at the turn-off for Cheget. (Entrees 15-40R.) **Postal code:** 361605. **Phone code:** 86639.

GETTING THERE. Getting to Prielbrusye takes a little work if you're not purchasing a packaged tour (Sa-Su, 55R at the tourist bureau's kiosk). **Buses** run from Pyatigorsk to **Nalchik** (2hr., 12 per day, 22R) and **Baksan** (2hr., 6 per day, 22R), from both of which **mini-buses** (*marshrutniye*) run to Terskol at least once a day on the weekends. Mini-buses run rarely if ever during the week, leaving you to hitch or pay for a **private ride** to Terskol (25-40R is reasonable).

SOCHI (СОЧИ)

In an earlier era, admirers dubbed Russia's Black Sea coast the "Caucasian Riviera," but Sochi now aspires to be the next Miami. Its beachfront—gaudy, raucous, and packed with thonged Russians (women and, alas, men alike) ranging from rare to well-done, represents the concerted effort of the city's population to extract a year's income from three months of tourism. Nevertheless, Sochi's subtropical climate, hilly streets, warm waters, and pebble beaches are intoxicating enough to forgive the crowds, if not forget them. Once a bastion of the aged and decrepit, Sochi is increasingly attracting hip-hoppy youngsters and foreigners. Open late, incredibly modern, and favoring Roman over Cyrillic, Sochi is not the place to experience traditional Russian culture—which may be precisely why so many Russians want to be here.

ORIENTATION

Greater Sochi extends 145km along the Caucasian coast of the Black Sea, from Tuapse to the border of Abkhazia. The city center is roughly 1400km south of Moscow, at the same latitude as Marseilles. To the north are the resort towns of Lazarevskoye and Dagomys; south are Khosta and Adler. Central Sochi has two focal points: the **train station** and the **seashore.** Exiting the train station, turn left on **ul. Gorkovo** (Горького) and follow it on foot, or take any bus to Gostinitsa Moskva on **Kurortny pr.** (Курортный), which runs along the shore. Going straight across Kurortny pr. leads to the **port** and the beaches; turning right onto Kurortny takes you to the **Park Riviera. Ul. Roz** (Роз) and **ul. Moskovskaya** (Московская) both run perpendicular to ul. Gorkovo, continuing out from the train station exit (ul. Roz is farther to your right), while **ul. Vorovskovo** (Воровского) parallels Gorkovo, a block or so farther from the train station. **Maps** (8.50R) are available at newsstands.

PRACTICAL INFORMATION

Trains: Zheleznodorozhny vokzal, ul. Gorkovo 56 (tel. 92 30 44). Sochi still clings to a 2-tier pricing system—foreigners must buy tickets at the international *kassa* (#8), typically for 3-4 times the Russian rate. To: **Moscow** (34-41hr., 1 per day, 450R)—choose a train via Aiksi (Аикси), Russia, *not* Kharkiv, Ukraine, or risk meeting dollar-hungry border officials; **Rostov-na-Donu** (16hr., 6 per day, 250R); and **Kiev** (34hr., 3 per week, 350R).

RUSSIA

> **!** The nearby mountains give the resort potential for a scenic adventure, but they also mark the border with Georgia's breakaway republic, Abkhazia. The crowds have returned to Sochi, but border guards with machine guns still keep many of the most beautiful mountain hikes and coastal cruises off-limits. If you do decide to savor the natural surroundings, take a guide. See **Essentials: Safety and Security,** p. 22, for more information.

Open daily 8am-1pm and 2-7pm.The *elektrichka* runs north along the coast via Dagomys to **Tuapse** (2½hr., 5 per day, 10R). Railway officials at these smaller stations might be more likely to overlook official policy and charge only the Russian rate.

Buses: Avtovokzal, ul. Gorkovo (tel. 99 65 69). Shuttles head to **Adler** (1hr., every 15min., 4-6R) and **Dagomys** (30min., every 30min., 4R). Long-distance buses run to **Rostov-na-Donu** (15hr., 2 per day, 104R) and **Pyatigorsk** (17hr., 2 per day, 125R). *Kassa* open daily 6-10am, 11am-4pm, and 5-10pm.

Ferries: Tel. 99 72 55. Still under renovation; port service has been cut back. To **Istanbul** (20hr., 2 per week, 1200R) and **Trabzon,** Turkey (11hr., 1 per day, 600R). Temporary *kassa* to the right facing the Morskoy Vokzal. Local boats leave for **Dagomys** (1hr., 6 per day, 40R), but the bus or *elektrichka* is more efficient.

Local Transportation: Buses (1-3R, pay on board) make life easier. Stops are marked on the side of bus. Bus #4 goes to the base of Gora Akhun and continues on to Adler. Mini-buses *(marshrutniye)* stop less and are faster, but cost 3R. Both are scarce after dark.

Taxis: Easy to find. Haggling may bring the price down to 10 times the cost of a bus.

Tourist Offices: The bureau outside Gostinitsa Moskva, at the intersection of Gorkovo and Kurortny Pr., offers daytrips to tourist attractions around Sochi, as do the many booths along the beach. A typical price is 60-90R.

Financial Services: Vneshtorg Bank, ul. Karla Libknekhta 10, across from the train station, exchanges currency and gives MC/Visa cash advances and cashes traveler's checks for a 2% commission. A Visa **ATM** is at **Mosbiznesbank,** ul. Gorkovo 15.

Passport Office: UVIR (ОВИР), ul. Gorkovo 60 (tel. 62 27 68). Registration is desirable but not compulsory if you've registered elsewhere in Russia. Most hotels will register you automatically. Open Tu-W and F 10am-noon and 3-5pm, Sa 10am-noon.

Luggage Storage: Temporarily in the old round building to your left as you exit the train station. May soon return to the station. 14R per day. Open 24hr.

Post Office: ul. Vorovskovo 1 (tel. 92 20 15), corner of Kurortny pr. **Poste Restante** *(do vostrebovanya)* service available. For **express mail** (tel. 92 28 10), enter to the right facing the main entrance. Open M-Sa 8am-7pm, Su 8am-6pm. **Postal Code:** 354000.

Internet Access: Ultima Internet Club (tel. 99 84 97) offers full internet access and email for 30R per hr., although you might have to wait for Tomb-Raiding Russian teens.

Telephones: The last of the old, free public phones are being replaced by the card-operated, money-gobbling variety. Cards (25R for local calls, 75R for intercity/international) are for sale at the central **telephone office,** ul. Vorovskovo 6, opposite the post office. Open 24hr. **Phone code:** 8622.

RUSSIA

ACCOMMODATIONS

The moment you step off the bus or train in Sochi, you're bound to be accosted by a mob of *babushki* requesting the honor of your presence in their homes. Be aware, however, that the nice old lady you meet at the train station may not be the one who owns the room she's advertising, but rather just a field agent for higher-ups in the *babushka* chain of command. It's best simply to get a phone number and an address and check the place out for yourself, although it's more convenient to be shown the way. Expect to pay 70-150R a night in the summer; most expect at least a two-night stay. Elderly landladies are often happy to prepare meals and do laundry at mutually agreeable rates. If you want a slightly more official version of this process, the **Resort Bureau,** to the right of the *Prigorodniye kassy* (Пригородные Кассы) in the train station, can help find an apartment.

Gostinitsa Primorskaya (Приморская), Sokolova 1 (Соколова; tel. 92 57 43; fax 92 40 06), between Kurortny pr. and Leningrad Beach. A palatial, old, yellow-and-white building with basic but cheerful salmon rooms. Hall toilets of the hole-in-the-ground variety. Singles with sink and TV 200R; doubles 300R. 1st-floor shower 10R. Call ahead.

Gostinitsa Chaika (Чайка), ul. Moskovskaya 3 (tel. 92 03 88), facing the train station across ul. Gorkovo. Large but aging rooms with balconies overlooking the station. Singles with bath and TV 150-170R; doubles 220-290R.

Gostinitsa Magnolia (Магнолия), Kurortny pr. 50 (tel. 92 14 36). Co-managed with the cheaper Gostinitsa Sochi next door. Bright, expensive rooms with garish bedspreads, or basic cheap ones. Gigantic hall showers; no seats or paper in hall toilets. Singles with sink 130-185R; with shower, fridge, TV, and phone 220R; doubles 250R, 260R.

FOOD

A **market** in front of Gostinitsa Chaika sells a variety of goods. Overpriced cafes with a dismally predictable bill of fare (hot dogs and *shashliks*) line the beach.

Cafe Kashtan (Каштан), ul. Roz 115, a block away from the train station, is largely bypassed by the tourist hordes. Daily Caucasian specialties run 10-25R. Open daily 11am-11pm.

Cafe Natasha (Кафе Наташа), ul. Vorovskovo 3, behind the post office, serves spicy Georgian meats and beans. Entrees are 25-40R, and *zakuski* cost 10-15R. Open daily 8am-midnight.

Shashlychnaya Akhun Cafe, at the base of the tower at Mt. Akhun. Delicious mountain concoctions. Kebabs 25-40R; vegetarian options available. Open daily 8am-10pm.

SIGHTS

Sochi is home to a remarkable **arboretum** (*dendrary;* дендрарий), Kurortny pr. 74 (tel. 92 36 02), whose international trees and plants provide blessed shade on a hot afternoon. (Open daily 8am-8pm. 10R, with tour 18R; children under 10 half-price.) Take bus #11 to "Svetlana" (Светлана) and keep walking, or take the cable car from Kurortny pr. to an observation post at the top of the park, from which you can walk back down through the park. (Open Tu-Su 8am-8pm. 30R, with tour 40R.) For cheaper but less exquisite shade, try **Park Riviera,** ul. Yegorova 1 (Егорова), on the north side of the ferry terminal across the Sochi river. It's a pretty park full of evergreens, outdoor cafes, marble statues of deer, and the occasional war monument. Enterprising folks sell ice cream, toys, and semi-pornographic paintings to strolling vacationers. The **Garden of Russo-Japanese Friendship,** on Kurortny pr. near the Magnolia Hotel, is a pleasant oddity as well. On a rainy day, visit the **History of the Resort-City Museum** (Muzey istorii goroda-kurorta; Музей истории города-курорта), ul. Ordzhonikidze 29 (Орджоникидзе; tel. 92 23 49 and 99 88 48), with its motley collection of local archaeological finds, butterflies, and astronaut gear. (Open Tu-Sa 9am-6pm, Su 10am-6pm; closed 1st day of the month; *kassa* closes 30min. before museum. 15R.) There's also the refreshingly deserted but otherwise unimpressive **art museum** (*khudozhestvenny muzey;* художественный музей), Kurortny pr. 51 (tel. 99 99 48; open Tu-Su 10am-5:30pm; 8R, students 3R).

A rewarding trip from Sochi, **Mt. Akhun** (Gora Akhun) has an **observation tower** commissioned by Stalin at its summit, which commands magnificent views of the sea and surrounding mountains. (Open daily 9am-6pm. 5R.) Take bus #4 to the Sputnik stop and either hike the 11km up the paved road or backtrack across the bridge, where taxis hover, eager to take you one-way (100-150R) or round-trip (200R if you haggle). If you're hiking, start early and don't expect a ride down. The excursion bureau in Sochi is a better bet—they'll bus you there and back for 60R.

BEACHES

Follow behind (but not too close behind) the thonged throngs to the **beach,** Sochi's main draw. The city beaches tend to be crowded—if you're not in the mood to mingle, there are long stretches of quieter beach to the north, many accessible by *elektrichka*. Hotel beaches (50-70R) are less crowded. If sun and water lose their appeal, rent a **banana-boat** (60R per person for 10min.) or a **jet-ski** (350R for 10min.). Near the ferry terminal is a **Waterslide Park** (Akva Park Mayak; Аква Парк Маяк), good for a break from the beach-going, if not the crowds. (Open daily 8am-8pm. 150R, children 100R.)

If your vision of relaxation does not include dozens of screaming Russian families, take a daytrip from Sochi to **Dagomys.** Situated 12km north of greater Sochi, it offers emptier, cooler, and pricier beaches for those willing to make the trip. From the Sochi bus station, take one of the many buses to Dagomys (30min., every 30min., 5R), or one of the *marshrutniye* labeled "Dagomyskoe Passazhirskoe" (Дагомыское пассажирское; 20min., every 40min., 6R). The **Dagomys Complex** is on a hill above the beach, but the buses and *marshrutniye* will drop you at the bottom. To get to the complex, exit the bus at the "Dagomyskoe Passazherskoe" stop, cross the street, and walk 15min. up ul. Leningradskaya. Alternatively, take an overpriced taxi (40R if you haggle). With the Gostinitsa Olympiysky on your left, continue along ul. Leningradskaya, walk past the mountainous, two-humped Gosinitsa Dagomys, and continue along the path until you reach the vertical lift; this will drop you at the beach (20R).

ENTERTAINMENT

The city has a flourishing cultural life, with a major annual **independent film festival** the first ten days of June and an **art festival** in September. During the peak tourist season in July and August, theater troupes, orchestras, and rock bands come to play for the vacationing elite. Despite its name, the **Winter Theater** (Zimny Teatr; Зимний Театр), ul. Teatralnaya 2 (Театральная; tel. 99 77 06), down ul. Teatralnaya from Kurortny pr., puts on more shows in the summer. (Tickets 30-50R).

Many of the small **bars** lining the beach have live music after dark, but those who need an entire building to contain their dance moves will be comforted by the presence of the two-story techno **Discoclub Cascad** (Дискоклуб Каскад), on pr. Kurortny between the sea port and the Magnolia. (Open nightly 9pm-3am. Cover for men 30R, ladies 10R.) If you missed sunbathing with Sochi's elite, you can party with them at **Eighth Heaven** (Vosmoye Nebo; Восьмое Небо), ul. Alleya Cheltechema off Korortny pr. (Open nightly 9pm-5am. 120R cover.)

NEAR SOCHI: KRASNAYA POLYANA (КРАСНАЯ ПОЛЯНА)

Telephone numbers are being standardized in Krasnaya Polyana. Current numbers will have a 430 added to the beginning; the last 3 digits remain the same.

This high-altitude village on the Western edge of the Caucasus range acts as a wintertime ski resort. In summer, the area offers fine **hiking.** If you intend a serious hike into the nearby **Caucasus Preserve,** you must obtain permission from the relevant bureaucrats in Adler. At the very least, make sure you're not wandering toward the Georgian border or trampling indigenous flora. More modest hikes are, of course, possible, including the six-hour climb to the alpine lake from the **rescue station** (*spasitelnaya stantsiya*; спасительная станция; tel. 49 44 22), whose friendly staff are glad to share their detailed knowledge of the area with visitors.

The Olympic Committee's decision that the situation in nearby Georgia made Sochi an unwelcome site for the 2002 Winter Olympics means that intrepid hikers and skiers have several more years to enjoy an unspoiled Krasnaya Polyana. *If* you make it here: the ride to town is an adventure in itself, part of whose allure is the uncertainty of survival. The bus zips blithely along a tortuous cliffside road clearly intended for a tiny horse-drawn cart. In one tunnel, after the most frightening part of the road, you will be relieved to see the candlelit **icon of the Virgin Mary.** In town, across from the museum, the **Restaurant Shater** (Шатер; tel. 43 03 38) has great timber beams, outdoor dining, and a fine view. Entrees run 30-40R. Locally produced honey is sold outside. **Postal code:** 354 392. **Phone code:** (8)8622.

GETTING THERE. From Sochi, take express bus #4э to the end of the line at **Adler Market,** where you can buy tickets for bus #135 (2hr., hourly, 15R). Seats sell out fast, so arrive early or ask the driver to let you stand (for the full fare).

THE TRANS-SIBERIAN RAILROAD

The lifeline that connects the gilded domes and tinted windshields of Moscow with the rest of her proud but crumbling empire, the Trans-Siberian railroad is a trip through Russia in the fullest sense. Over the course of 6½ days, the train rolls through 9289km, two continents, and seven time zones, over endless *taiga* and titanic rivers. While the exterior journey is certainly spectacular, travelers will likely remember most what goes on inside the train. Whether you find yourself riding with a nightgowned *babushka* and her bucket of berries or middle-aged men who drink vodka before bed and beer for breakfast, the ride is a crash-course in Russian culture. For years, the Trans-Siberian was a mysterious voyage past closed cities and missile silos attempted by only the most intrepid of travelers. Today, agencies in both Asia and Russia have cracked this tough nut, providing help with tickets and visas. While backpackers and tours have discovered the Trans-Siberian, it remains an exotic, unpolished journey that can't be matched.

LOGISTICS. The term "Trans-Siberian" actually does not refer to a single train, but to three sets of rail tracks and the numerous trains that run along them. The **Trans-Siberian** line links Moscow and Vladivostok, the **Trans-Mongolian** connects Moscow with Beijing via Ulaanbaatar, Mongolia, and the **Trans-Manchurian** loops through Manchuria en route to Beijing. Most westerners buy a ticket at one end for the entire trip, but it is possible to travel point-to-point. In addition to the well-known trans-continental trains, there are many shorter (and dirtier) intercity lines. You'll need **visas** to enter China and Mongolia; the Chinese visa is best obtained in Moscow (see **Moscow: Practical Information,** p. 566), while a Mongolian visa can be picked up either in Moscow (see **Moscow: Orientation & Practical Information,** p. 566), Irkutsk (see **Irkutsk: Orientation & Practical Information**, p. 644), or Ulan Ude.

COSTS. The cost of a Trans-Siberian ticket depends on myriad variables, including where and when you buy it, who you buy it from, how far you're going, what class you want, whether you're Russian or foreign, and whether the salesperson likes you. Tickets are most expensive in and around Moscow, but are still cheaper than buying a string of tickets from town to town. Summer prices are always higher than winter prices. If you're only making a few stops, you're best going through the **Traveller's Guest House** in Moscow (see p. 569) which offers several different types of Trans-Siberian tickets for a $20 commission. More importantly, they'll explain in excellent English how the railroad works and can help you choose the ticket best suited to your itinerary. To: **Beijing via Mongolia** US$190; **Beijing via Manchuria** US$210; **Vladivostok** US$85; and **Ulaanbaatar** US$180. All prices are for second class. A less expensive way to get tickets if you speak Russian is to buy them yourself from **Tsentralnoe Zheleznodorozhnoe Agenstvo** (Central Train Agency; Центральное Железнодорожное Агенство) in Moscow (see p. 565).

DEPARTING. All Trans-Siberian **trains** depart from Moscow's **Yaroslavsky Vokzal** (see **Moscow: Practical Information,** p. 564). The better, long-distance trains, called *firmeny* (private), offer cleaner facilities but can also cost twice the regular *skory* (fast) trains. Local color aboard *skory* makes for an entertaining short trip, but offensive drunks and more offensive odors make the *firmeny* worth the money for trips longer than 24hr. From Moscow, the *firmeny* trains are: **train #2 (Rossia)** departing for **Vladivostok** at 3:25pm on odd days; **train #10 (Baikal)** to **Irkutsk** and **Lake Baikal,** departing at 9:25pm on odd days; **train #4 (The Chinese Train)** to **Beijing** via **Ulaanbaatar,** the cleanest and best train, departing Tuesdays at 9:03pm; **train #20**

(The Russian Train) to **Beijing** on the Trans-Manchurian, departing Fridays at 8:25pm; and **train #6** to **Ulaanbaatar,** departing Wednesdays and Thursdays at 9pm. *Firmeny* trains usually have a plaque on the side of each car stating the train's name. In all cases, "odd" (нечетный) and "even" (четный) refers to calendar days.

LIFE ABOARD THE TRAIN. Two attendants—*provodnik* (male) or *provodnitsa* (female)—sit in each train wagon to make sure all goes smoothly; they offer tea (1R) more cheaply than the restaurant car. Try to avoid the first or last *coupé* in the wagon; these neighbor the toilets and, especially on non-*fermeny* trains, the stench can become unbearable after several days (on *fermeny* trains they're cleaned several times per day). Always carry your own toilet paper. A posted schedule in each wagon lists arrival times for each *stoyanka* (stop; стоянка). When the train stops for longer than 15min., locals come out to hawk food to passengers, but there are other feeding options (see **"I'll Get That To Go,"** below). Depending on the train, Moscow and Perm are separated by about 22hr., another 6½hr. gets you to Yekaterinburg, and 23hr. more stand between you and Novosibirsk. From Novosibirsk, it's 32hr. more to Irkutsk. Another 8hr. gets you to Ulan Ude, and it's a mere day from there to Ulaanbaatar, which is 36hr. from Beijing.

TRAIN TIME. The Trans-Siberian traverses 7 time zones, but all train arrivals and departures are listed in Moscow time at stations as well as in *Let's Go.*

POSSIBLE STOP: YEKATERINBURG (SVERDLOVSK)

The site of the Romanov family's brutal assassination in 1918 and hometown of Boris Yeltsin, Yekaterinburg (Sverdlovsk as far as the railroad is concerned; pop. 1,300,000) has lost some appeal after the royal remains took the Trans-Siberian back to St. Petersburg in 1998 for their interment. If you end up here, take trolley #1, 8, or 9, or a bus with "пр. Ленина" on it to get to the main street, **ul. Lenina.** The **U.S. Consulate** is at ul. Gogolya 15, 4th Fl. (Гоголя; tel. 56 47 44). The **British Consulate** is next door. Cash **traveler's checks,** receive **cash advances,** or use the **24hr. ATM** at **Most Bank,** ul. Mamina-Sibiryaka 145. (Open M-Th 9am-12:30pm and 2-4pm, F 9am-12:30pm and 2-3pm.) Another ATM sits at Yakova Svedlova 22 (Якова Свердлова), 10min. from the station. Yekaterinburg has a busy cafe scene, but for a meal go to **Bistro Express** (Бистро Экспресс), ul. Lenina 46, which serves standard Russian grub at better-than-standard prices. (Entrees 15-25R.) Given enough time, you can have a **shower** at track #1—look for the "Душ" *(dush)* sign. If you fall in love with this industrial hot-bed, **Gostinitsa Bolshoy Ural,** Krasnoarmeyskaya 1 (Красноармейская), has a spot for you in four-person room for 60R.

I'LL GET THAT TO GO If you ride the Trans-Siberian the way most Russians do, you'll spend most of your time eating. The thought of munching for six days straight might not appeal to the Stairmaster set, but if you plan properly, it can be six days of bliss. Above all, keep an open mind about trying new things–and about sticking to the tried-and-true when necessary. At every stop longer than 15min., a flock of *babushki* and little boys will storm the platform hawking water, ice cream, meat pies, and vegetables. Near Lake Baikal you'll also see smoked fish. None of this is enough for a hearty meal, but it does fill in the caloric cracks. Back on board, *firmeny* trains all pull restaurant cars, featuring the ethnic food of whichever country the train is rolling through that day. While it affords a great opportunity for Westerners to bemoan the state (or lack) of Russian civilization, it's also the best value on the rails. But the best culinary experiences are more spontaneous. If you're lucky, a Russian family will bring the better half of their vegetable garden aboard and treat the car to a feast. The first course is usually *Baltika #3* and dried fish. Then comes vodka, chased down by a little juice. Finally, the meal: cucumbers, tomatoes, dill, bread (dark, of course), sausage, and roast chicken, all seasoned with a film canister of salt. Eat until the sun goes down, finish the vodka, and hit the sack.

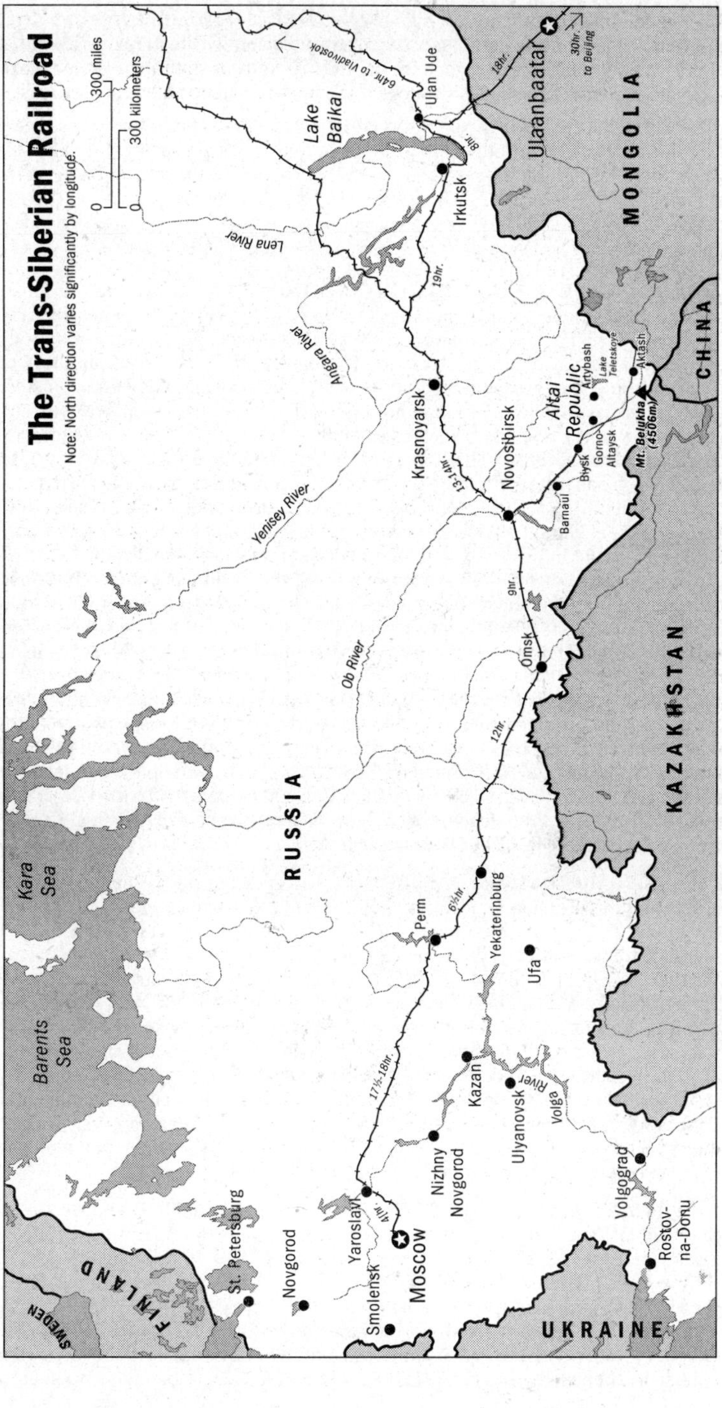
The Trans-Siberian Railroad
Note: North direction varies significantly by longitude.
0
300 miles
0
300 kilometers
Kara Sea
Barents Sea
RUSSIA
FINLAND
SWEDEN
UKRAINE
KAZAKHSTAN
CHINA
MONGOLIA
St. Petersburg
Novgorod
Smolensk
Moscow
Yaroslavl
4hr.
Nizhny Novgorod
17½-18hr.
Kazan
Ulyanovsk
Volga River
Volgograd
Rostov-na-Donu
Perm
Ufa
6½hr.
Yekaterinburg
12hr.
Omsk
Ob River
9hr.
Novosibirsk
Barnaul
Biysk
Gorno-Altaysk
Altai Republic
Artybash
Lake Teletskoye
Aktash
Mt. Belukha (4506m)
Yenisey River
13-14hr.
Krasnoyarsk
Angara River
19hr.
Lena River
Irkutsk
Lake Baikal
8hr.
Ulan Ude
64hr. to Vladivostok
18hr.
Ulaanbaatar
30hr. to Beijing

RUSSIA

NOVOSIBIRSK (НОВОСИБИРСК)

For a city of 1.4 million built almost entirely by Soviets, Novosibirsk isn't half-bad. Unlike many of its Siberian comrades, this mid-continental transport hub shows signs of post-capitalist life. The parks don't look like abandoned lots, unfinished buildings make up much less than half the city, and citizens are getting on with life rather than lamenting Soviet glory days. There's nothing particularly charming or exciting about Novosibirsk's riverside sprawl, but with a handful of western-style restaurants and decent hotels, it's a good stop on the way to Asia or the Altai.

TIME CHANGE. Novosibirsk is 3hr. ahead of Moscow time (GMT+6).

ORIENTATION & PRACTICAL INFORMATION. The **train station,** ul. Shamshurina, sends trains to: **Moscow** (48-52hr., 5-6 per day, 900R); **Yekaterinburg** (22hr., 7-8 per day, 500R); and **Krasnoyarsk** (13hr., 5-6 per day, 300R). Novosibirsk also serves as a gateway to Central Asia. Connections can be made to various cities, but the main route, the Turkistan-Siberian railway, goes to **Almaty, Kazakhstan** (35-40hr., every other day, 1030R). The following Trans-Siberian services stop in Novosibirsk (in Moscow time): **train #2** to **Vladivostok** (4 days, odd days 4:50pm, 1000R); **train #4** to **Beijing** via **Ulaanbaatar** (Th 9:15pm, 3000R); **train #20** to **Beijing** (Su 8:55pm); and **train #6** to **Ulaanbaatar** (F and Sa 9:15pm, 1700R). **Store luggage** at the train station (14-20R; open 24hr.). The **Metro** (2.50R) connects the city center, **pl. Lenina,** to the train station at Garina-Mikhailovskovo (Гарина-Михайловского). From the train station, walk out into the city and then underground where you see the "M." Take the Metro one stop to Sibirskaya (Сибирская), then walk upstairs to change stations; one more stop takes you to pl. Lenina. The Sibirskaya Metro is close to the circus, the Ascension Church, the market, and the stadium. Buy a **map** (35R) at **Tsentralny Dom Knigi** (Центральный Дом Книги), Krasny pr. 29. (Open M-Sa 10am-2pm and 3-7pm.) **Alfa Bank** (Альа Банк), Dimitrova 1 (Димитрова), across from New York Pizza, has the city's most versatile **ATM** (MC/Visa; open M-Sa 9-6pm). There is a **pharmacy,** ul. Chaplygina 58 (tel. 23 32 07), at the corner of Krasny pr. and across the street from St. Nicholas's Church. (Open daily 8am-8pm.) The **post office** is at ul. Sovetskaya 33 (tel. 22 05 83; open M-F 8am-7pm, Sa-Su 8am-6pm). The **telephone office,** ul. Lenina 5 (tel. 22 02 28), is up the block and to the left. (To the U.S. 27R per min.; to Moscow 4.10R per min. Open 24hr. **Internet access** 15R per hr. Open M-Sa 9am-9pm.) **Postal code:** 63 00 99. **Phone code:** 38 32.

RUSSIA

ACCOMMODATIONS & FOOD. Novosibirsk has two clean, mid-range hotels that differ mainly in location. **Hotel Novosibirsk** (Новосибирск; tel. 20 11 20; fax 21 65 17), is across from the train station. (Singles 190R, with bath 350R; doubles with bath 450R. Edible Russian breakfast included.) **Hotel Tsentralnaya** (Центральная), ul. Lenina 3 (tel. 22 72 94; fax 22 76 60), is as central as you can get. Take the Metro to Pl. Lenina, then head down ul. Lenina (to the right of the supermarket) one block. (Singles with bath 367R; dorms 126R.)

A large **market** on ul. Krylova (Крылова) covers nearly as much area as the stadium it borders. (Open daily 8am-7pm.) **Gastronom,** Krasny pr. 30, offers indoor shopping. (Open daily 8am-9pm.) For pizza as good as any you'll find in Manhattan (at a third of the price), head to **New York Pizza,** Dimitrova 4. (Open 24hr.) For finer dining, Siberian yuppies flock to **Nikolai's** (Униколая), ul. Lenina 11, behind the wooden cottage. (Entrees 80-140R. Open daily 9am-9pm.)

SIGHTS & ENTERTAINMENT. The popular **Novosibirsk Picture Gallery** (Novosibirskaya Kartinnaya Galereya; Новосибирская Картинная Галерея), Krasny pr. 5 (tel. 22 20 42), features a permanent exhibit of Russian artists of the 18th to 20th centuries. Most of the collection looks like it came from a sidewalk sale, but there are a few powerful landscapes. (Open M and W-Su 11am-7pm. 25R, students 15R.) Up Krasny pr. from the gallery, the tiny, gold-domed **St. Nicholas's Church** (Chasovnya vo imya Svyatitilya Nikolaya; Часовня во имя Святитиля Николая) supposedly sits in the exact middle of Russia. (Open daily noon-5pm.)

The larger **Ascension Church** (Khram Vozneseniya Gospodnya; Храм Вознесения Господня), at the intersection of ul. Gogolya (Гоголя) and ul. Sovetskaya, flaunts a heavenly blue ceiling with classical paintings and a dazzling white-and-gold iconostasis. (Services M-F 9am and 5pm; Su 7am, 10am, and 5pm.) The **Regional Museum** (Kraevedchesky Muzey; Краеведческий Музей), Krasny pr. 23 (tel. 18 17 73), displays Russian pottery and other items from the Novosibirsk *oblast*. (Open M-F 10am-6pm. 3R, students 2R.) If you've got some time, **Obskoe More** (Обское Море), a huge lake created by a dam in the Ob River, offers fresh air and swimming. Go to the main train station and catch a suburban train to "Обское Море."

ALTAI REPUBLIC (РЕСПУБЛИКА АЛТАЙ)

The Altai Republic, a vast, mountainous region and semi-independent republic jutting south from central Siberia and bordering Kazakhstan, Mongolia, and China, is considered by many of those who have made it here to be the most devastatingly beautiful place on earth. With wild rivers and thick forests, an endless semi-desert steppe, and snow-capped peaks (to say nothing of the mighty Siberian yak), the Altai is a blizzard of natural wonders. Of the world's great mountain ranges, it is also among the hardest to reach and the worst-equipped to handle independent travelers. Without a guide it's difficult to see the most spectacular areas, and any worthwhile trip from Novosibirsk will take at least a week. Still, travelers who have the time, money, or chutzpah to do it alone are unlikely to find a more rewarding destination on the face of the earth.

REGIONAL ORIENTATION

The largest city near the Altai is **Novosibirsk.** From there, you can purchase a spot in an adventure tour or hire a guide (see below), or you can take the train to **Barnaul** or the overnight to **Biysk** (see below), southern Siberian towns that may afford the last opportunity to pick up supplies. **Gorno-Altaysk** (see below), the republic's administrative center and, as it happens, the only real town in the Altai, is located in the Altai's northwest corner. The **Chuysky Trakt** (Чуйский Тракт), a.k.a. **M-52,** heads through the Altai; buses ply this route daily from Gorno-Altaysk heading to tiny **Kosh-Agach** (Кош-Агач) in the southeast. Most other roads are unpaved.

There are three major trekking and camping regions. **Mt. Aktru** (Актру) is the second-highest mountain in the Altai at 4174m. It is southwest of **Aktash,** which is 12hr. down the Chuysky highway from Gorno-Altaysk. The **Lake Teletskoye** (Телетское) region is the most accessible, lying on a road leading east from Gorno-Altaysk to the fishing village of Arlybash. **Mt. Belukha** (Белуха), the tallest mountain in the Altai at 4506m, can be reached from Tyungur, where there are several tourist bases. Tyungur is approachable via Ust-Koksa along a road that branches off the Chuysky Trakt after the Seminsky Pass.

TREKKING THROUGH THE ALTAI

For travelers accustomed to even the cheapest hotels and public transportation, the Altai can be a difficult place to travel. Bus service into the wilderness is limited and there is virtually nothing in the way of accommodations. The most spectacular wilds are only accessible on foot or raft and require the guidance of a local to reach them safely. All but the most experienced hikers are advised to hire a guide. As always, do not set off on a solo excursion. For more information on safe hiking and wilderness travel, see **Camping & the Outdoors,** p. 38. With or without a guide, travel in the Altai falls into several categories:

TREKKING. Most treks begin a day's drive from Gorno-Altaysk and take you even deeper into the wilderness. It's the most spectacular way to see the Altai, but it almost certainly requires a guide and no less than 10 days.

RAFTING. The Altai is renowned for some of the best rafting in the world. Low-difficulty rivers include Sema (Сема; accessible from Shebalino village), Ursul (Урсул; from Seminsky Pass), Chemal and Kuba (Чемал, Куба; from Chemal camp), and Chuya (Чуя; from Chibit). More problematic rivers requiring guides include Chulyshman (Чулышман; from "Ust-Ulagan" camp), Katun (Катунь; from Yaloman), and Bashkaus (Башкаус; from Kosh-Agach).

TOURBAZY. The Altai is filled with *tourbazy*, small companies/hotels aimed at tourists hoping to enjoy the wilderness in comfort. Unfortunately, the quality of Altai *tourbazy* varies wildly. While you could find yourself in a beautiful lakeside room, you could also find yourself stuck next to an outhouse under a leaky roof.

CAR-CAMPING WITHOUT A GUIDE. Most Russians see the Altai through the windows of an automobile. In the summer, families pack the car with *kasha* and kids and head down the M-52 to a nice place by the river to pitch a tent. Although this strategy won't get you to the most isolated parts of the Altai, the M-52, especially between Ongudai (Онгудай) and Kosh-Agach (Кош Агач), has no shortages of spectacular scenery. If you don't have a car, there are buses that follow the route. The only problem with going by bus is having to camp. Buses take all day to reach places like Kosh-Agach and Aktash from Gorno-Altaysk, and the only hotel en route that was definitely open in the summer of 1999 was on Seminsky Pass, at the Western end of the M-52. Although camping is basically unrestricted in the Altai, there is no telling what type of hassles you might encounter from locals, border guards, or hungry dogs. *Let's Go* does not recommend camping without a guide.

TOURING THE ALTAI

Hiring Altai guides, as imperative as it is, can also be extremely frustrating. Not only are most firms difficult to contact, but it's often hard to know exactly what you'll be getting. It is best to know exactly what kind of trip you want before making calls. When you talk to a firm, be very specific about your plans and have them send an itinerary before you agree to anything. Prices are not cheap, but they are negotiable. All guides are based out of Novosibirsk. Start calling **two months ahead.**

Brothers Govor (Братья Говор), ul. Spartaka 4, Novosibirsk (tel. (3832) 23 49 79; email Oksana Shavorskaya at oash@hotmail.com). Pass the Novosibirsk Picture Gallery and turn right onto ul. Spartaka. Go over the bridge and take your first left; before the first building, go right and down the hill. Contact director Valerya Govor or Oksana Shavorskaya, the company interpreter with a fluent command of English. Not the cheapest option but definitely the best way to get to high altitudes. 13-day tour of the Belukha region US$650 per person; 10- to 12-day rafting trip along the Bra and Katun rivers from Teletskoe Lake US$400 per person. Open M-F 9am-6pm.

Central Travel Bureau (Центральное Бюро Путешествий) Krasny pr. 25, rm. 203, Novosibirsk (Красный; tel. 22 77 70). Contact: Irina Liftshits (tel. 22 09 77; fax 22 01 86; email center@mail.cis.ru). Places travelers on hiking trips or at *tourbazy* throughout the Altai. Open M-F 10am-6pm.

Siberia (Сибирь; tel. (3832) 21 53 53 or 21 95 11; fax 21 12 27), in the Hotel Novosibirsk, in Novosibirsk. Cheaper than most, but in the Altai—as in life—you get what you pay for. Rafting tours along the Katun River 60-150R per person per day. Trips to Teletskoye Lake 170-250R per day. Open M-F 9am-6pm.

GETTING TO THE ALTAI: BIYSK

The best thing about Biysk is that you don't have to spend too much time here. The daily overnight train from **Novosibirsk** arrives at 8:00am, leaving you plenty of time to head across the parking lot for the 8:30am bus to **Gorno-Altaysk** (2hr., 30R). If you miss that, buses to Gorno run all day every other hour. On your way back, make sure to get on the 4:00pm bus in Gorno to avoid spending the night in Biysk; the train back to Novosibirsk leaves around 8:00pm. If you do get stuck, **Hotel Tsentralny** is cheap and better-maintained than most. Walk straight from the train station to the tram tracks, then head toward the center of town three stops. The hotel is the tall building on your right. (Singles with bath 150R.)

GETTING TO THE ALTAI: GORNO-ALTAYSK

Surrounded by hills that are a little taller than grimy apartment buildings, Gorno-Altaysk is slightly nicer than the average Russian town, but it's definitely not the reason to come to the Altai. Gorno is a good base, but most of the spectacular wilds are still a day's drive away. **Buses** run to: **Biysk** (2hr., 7 per day, 30R); **Seminsky Pass** (5 per day, 47R); **Ongudai** (6hr., 3 per day, 28R); **Aktash** (2 per day, 100R); and **Kosh-Agach** (12hr., 3 per week, 127R). From the station, take bus #1, 3, or 105 to reach **Hotel Gorny Altai,** ul. Erkimena Palkina 5 (Эркимена Палкина), which offers clean rooms with sinks, telephones, and not-so-clean hall toilets. (Singles 150R; doubles 200R.) Dining options are Slim to None, and Slim's visa is running out. Try the cozy kitchen of Hotel Gorny Altai which serves hearty goulash with cucumber salad for 25R. Also try the **grocery store/greasy spoon** at Kommunisticheskaya 6. Gorno-Altaysk may not overwhelm you with fun, but there is a cool **Regional Museum** (Krayevedchesky muzey; Краеведческий Музей) on ul. Choroz Gurkina. The third floor features landscapes by local artists that make an excellent prelude to trekking into the Altai. (Open W-Su 10am-4:30pm. 6R, students 2R.)

KRASNOYARSK (КРАСНОЯРСК)

Founded as a Cossack fort in the 17th century, Krasnoyarsk straddles the 2km-wide Yenisey River and is the capital of Krasnoyarsk Kray. During the Cold War, Krasnoyarsk was closed to foreigners because of its defense industry, but today it's trying to use its history and natural resources to escape Siberian anonymity. The efforts haven't paid huge dividends, but the city does have enough commercial activity and pre-revolutionary architecture to distance it from most other truck-side civilization muscled out of the taiga.

TIME CHANGE. Krasnoyarsk is 4hr. ahead of Moscow time (GMT+7).

ORIENTATION & PRACTICAL INFORMATION. The city straddles the Yenisey River, but almost everything of interest, with the exception of the Stolby Nature Reserve, lies on the north bank. The **train station,** ul. Tridsatovo Iyulia (30-го Июля; tel. 29 34 34), on the north bank slightly west of the city center, sends trains to: **Irkutsk** (19hr., 1-5 per day, 330R); **Novosibirsk** (14hr., 2-6 per day, 300R); and **Vladivostok** (3 days, 1-3 per day, 820R). Along the **Trans-Siberian** (in Moscow time): **Moscow** (train #1 even days 2:56pm, #3 Sa 3:38am, #5 M and W 3:38am; 1000R); **Vladivostok** (train #2 daily 5:13am, from 800R); **Beijing** (train #4 F 9:13am, train #20 M 9:16am; 1500R); and **Ulaanbaatar** (46hr., train #6 Sa-Su 9:37am, from 1000R). International tickets must be purchased at the downtown ticket office, ul. Robespiera 20. (Open M-F 8am-7pm, Sa-Su 9am-6pm.) Coming straight out of the train station, take bus #55 from the parking lot on your right to the Hotel Krasnoyarsk (3-4 stops)—this is as close to a center as you get. Bus #135 leaves the suburban bus station, ul. Karla Marxa, behind Hotel Krasnoyarsk, for the **airport,** 50km north of town (1hr., every 30min. 6am-11pm, 15R). **Store luggage** in the basement of the train station (12R; open 24hr.). Krasnoyarsk's three main streets, **ul. Lenina** (Ленина), **pr. Mira** (Мира), and **ul. Karla Marxa,** all run west-east from the train station, parallel to the river. There is no tourist office, but the friendly folks at **Service-Center Trans-Sib** (Сервис-Центр Транс-Сиб), on the 3rd floor of the train station (tel. 29 26 92; fax 21 65 71), will provide all the help you'll need. They reserve domestic train tickets and provide international telephone and fax services. (Open M-F 9am-8pm.) You can snag a **map** in the lobby of Hotel Krasnoyarsk. **Exchange currency** at **Most Bank** (Мост Банк; tel. 23 69 82), in the tower across the street from Hotel Krasnoyarsk. They also give MC and Visa cash advances for a 1.5% commission, cash traveler's checks for no commission, and house a **24hr. ATM.** (Open M-F 9:30am-6pm, Sa 9:30am-3pm.) **Internet Cafe MaxSoft,** ul. Uritskovo 61, 4th fl. (tel. 65 13 85), is all internet and no cafe. (40R per hr.) The **post office** is at ul. Leninia 62 (tel. 27 06 41; open M-Sa 8am-1pm and 2-7pm). An international **telephone office** is just across the street. (To: U.S. 24R per min; U.K. 19R per min.; Moscow 7R per min. Open daily 7am-10pm.) **Postal code:** 660 049. **Phone code:** 3912.

ACCOMMODATIONS & FOOD. **Hotel Krasnoyarsk** (tel. 27 37 69; fax 27 02 36), on the corner of ul. Venbauma and ul. Karla Marxa, is the most convenient option. Take bus #55 from the train station. (Singles 460R; bed in a double 230R. Breakfast included.) If you feel like saving a few rubles and roughing it, head to the river in front of Hotel Krasnoyarsk and walk along it 5-10min. away from the train station. **Mikhail Godenko** (tel. 29 04 81) is the hotel-ship permanently anchored along ul. Dubrovinskovo. (Singles 135R; doubles 205R.) Next door, **Restauran Volna** (tel. 29 04 81) has the typical Russian menu, complete with *shashlik* (42R). Cheaper options include the **24hr. cafe,** on the 3rd floor of the Hotel Krasnoyarsk, and **Russo Pizza,** pr. Mira 111. (Slices 15R. Open daily 11am-midnight.)

SIGHTS & ENTERTAINMENT. Although he studied in St. Petersburg and is buried in Moscow, the Russian 19th-century painter Vasily Ivanovich Surikov was born and raised in Krasnoyarsk, and his estate has now been turned into the **Surikov Museum** (Muzey Surikov; Музей Сурикова), ul. Lenina 98 (tel. 23 15 87). Inside the elegant wooden house, ten rooms on two floors showcase Surikov's life and work. (Open Tu-Su 11am-7pm. 3R, students 2R.) A block to the south, the **Central Geological Museum of Siberia** (Muzey Geologoy Tsentralnoy Sibiry; Музей Геологой Центральной Сибирий), pr. Mira 37 (tel. 27 74 40), in a blue-and-white building, is a rock collector's dream, showcasing minerals and stones found nowhere else on earth. The museum shows the mineralogical riches of the Krasnoyarsky Kray, where 98% of Russia's platinum and the second-largest chunk of pure gold have been unearthed. If you want to see the rocks in their natural state, the museum's director Victor Covlook (tel. 27 62 62; email geomuseum@krsk.ru) can arrange a **backpacking expedition.** (Open M-F 9am-4pm. 1R, students 0.50R; if you're alone they may charge you the 10R tour group fee.) Around the corner, the gold-domed pink-and-white **Russian Orthodox Church** (Pokrovsky Kafedralny Sobor; Покровский Кафедральный Собор), ul. Surikova 26, was built in the late-18th century. (Open daily 8am-7pm. Services at 9am and 5pm.) Farther east, the **Surikov Art Museum,** ul. Parizhskoy Kommuny 20 (Парижской Коммуны), at the corner of ul. Karla Marxa, displays more of Surikov's works alongside paintings by other Siberian artists. (Open Tu-Su 10am-6pm. 10R, students 3R.)

Another attraction is the **Museum-Ship St. Nicholas** (Muzey-Parakhod Sv. Nikolay; Музей-Пароход Св. Николай; tel. 23 94 03), at the east end of ul. Dubrovinskovo, near the Philharmonic Hall. In 1897, this ship carried Lenin up the Yenisey to his exile in Shushensk. Another time, it transported Tsar Nicholas II, and now the museum features wax figures of Lenin and Tsar Nicholas II as well as a Samovar exhibit. (Open Tu-Su 11am-6pm. 3R, students 2R.) Although Lenin's route to exile took him well past Krasnoyarsk, Vlad left an enormous statue of himself to guard the entrance to the slightly depressing **Central Park** (Tsentralny Park; Центральный Парк), located off ul. Dubrovinskovo toward the train station.

RUSSIA

IRKUTSK (ИРКУТСК)

A Siberian trading post for three centuries, Irkutsk is one of the few eastern metropoles that sprang up *before* the Trans-Siberian's tracks were laid. A bazaar for fur-traders and a den for desperate gold-diggers, Irkutsk developed as a feisty mix of high culture and window-smashing brawls. This pit of unchecked capitalism said "*nyet*" to the Revolution in 1917, welcomed the retreating White troops, and didn't turn Red until 1920. Today, Irkutsk is much less of an anomaly, as it stumbles through the same economic malaise as the rest of Russia. Nonetheless, the city's grand (if crumbling) brick facades and the colossal beauty of nearby Lake Baikal have made it the most popular stop for Trans-Siberian travelers.

TIME CHANGE. Irkutsk is 5hr. ahead of Moscow time (GMT+8).

ORIENTATION & PRACTICAL INFORMATION. The Angara River bisects the town; the old city center and all the sights lie on the right bank, while the train station and some budget accommodations sprawl along the residential left bank. The **train station,** on ul. Vokzalnaya (tel. 43 17 17 and 29 65 01), chugs to: **Moscow** (3½ days, 1-3 per day, 1300R); **Krasnoyarsk** (19hr., 3-4 per day, 360R); and **Ulan Ude** (8hr., 3 per day, 190R). The following Trans-Siberian trains pass through (in Moscow time): **train #2** to **Vladivostok** (odd days 1:19am, 1100R); **#4** to **Beijing** (Sa 3:43am, 2400R); **#6** to **Ulaanbaatar** (Su-M 3:43am, 1100R); and **#20** to **Beijing** (Tu 3:33am, 2400R). Foreigners must purchase tickets from *kassa* #6 or 7 (tel. 28 28 20) in the suburban ticketing hall (the one with the glass doors). To **store luggage,** exit the station, go left, and keep going until the other side of the post office (12R).

There is no official tourist office, but the **Irkutsk-Baikal Service Department** in the lobby of Hotel Intourist, ul. Gagarina 44, 3rd Fl., #308 (tel. 25 01 61 67), is the next best thing. The agency sells **tickets** for planes and the theater, and hands out free info on Irkutsk. (English spoken. Open M-F 8:30am-6pm.) Buy **maps** (15R) at the kiosk in the lobby. The **Mongolian consulate,** ul. Lapina 11 (tel./fax 34 21 43 and 34 24 47), can arrange **visas** if you have a passport-sized photo ready for them. (No invitation needed for 7-day tourist visa. 72hr. service US$25; 24hr. service US$50. Transit visa available with ongoing train ticket and valid Chinese visa for US$15. Open M-F 9am-1pm and 2-6pm.) Only **Vneshtorg-bank** (Внешторг-Банк), ul. Sverdlova 40, #201 (tel. 24 39 16), cashes **traveler's checks** (2% commission plus US$0.50 per check). You can also get MC/Visa cash advances for a 2% commission. (Open M-F 9:30am-4pm.) There is a MC/Visa **ATM** at Alfabank, B. Tagarina 58 (Б. Тагарина), two blocks from the Intourist heading away from the main bridge. The best place to check **email** is at the unnamed store across from the Stratosphere nightclub at Greznova 14 (Грезнова; ul. Karla Marxa on older maps; 14R per hr.; open 10am-10pm). The main **post office,** ul. Stepana Razina 23 (Степана Разина; tel. 33 26 92), holds **Poste Restante.** (Open M-F 8am-8pm, Sa-Su 9am-6pm.) The **telephone office,** ul. Proletarskaya 12 (Пролетарская), is across from the circus. (Open 24hr.) **Postal code:** 664000. **Phone code:** 3952.

ACCOMMODATIONS. Amerikansky Dom (Американский Дом), ul. Ostrovskovo 19 (Островского; tel. 43 26 89; fax 27 92 77), is owned by Lida Sclocchini, the Russian widow of the man from Philadelphia whose early-80s love affair was the basis for the film *From America With Love.* With the train station behind you, follow the tram tracks up the hill to your left and veer to the right when the tracks fork to the left. From there, walk up two blocks, take a right after a cluster of kiosks, and then take the second real left onto ul. Kaiskaya (Каиская). Ul. Ostrovskovo (unmarked) is about 400m ahead on the right, on the street below the main drag at the top of the hill; Amerikansky Dom is 30m down on your right (15-20min.). Or, take a taxi from the station (20-30R). The clean, Western-style house has hot water but only seven beds that fill quickly with Trans-Siberian backpackers; call ahead. (US$20. Laundry US$5.) **Hotel Angora,** ul. Sukhe-Batora 7 (tel. 25 51 06; fax 25 51 03; Сухе-Батора) has cheaper rooms right in the center of town, if you don't mind telephone calls to your room advertising prostitutes for the evening. Not surprisingly, the mattresses are a little worn-out. (Singles 325R; doubles 440R. Hot water and breakfast included.)

FOOD. A **supermarket,** Magazin Okean (Магазин Океан), at the corner of ul. Sverdlova and Stepana Razina, sells everything from fruit to film. (Open M-F 9am-9pm, Sa 9am-8pm.) The central market hawks fresh fruit, veggies, and meat. (Open daily 8am-8pm.) Any form of transport that reads "рынок" *(rynok)* will do. **Cafe Sport Express** (tel. 33 48 30), in the stadium, serves killer *pelmeny* (16R) and other cheap, delicious dishes. (Open daily 10am-9pm.) **Cafe Karlson** (Карлсон), ul. Lenina 15 (tel. 33 30 97), is central and the food doesn't taste bad, which is more than most places can say. (Entrees 16-20R. Open daily 10am-midnight.)

SIGHTS. Irkutsk's most illustrious residents were the Decembrists, who arrived as exiles in the 19th century. Unfortunately, only one of their houses was

RUSSIA

open to the public in the summer of 1999: **Muzey-Dekabrista Volkonskovo** (Музей-Декабриста Волконского), ul. Volkonskovo 10 (tel. 27 57 73), waits on a dusty side street just off of ul. Timiryazeva (Тимирязева). To get there, take trams #1-4 to Dekabersky Sabitiye and walk around the big domed church. (Open Tu-Su 10am-6pm; *kassa* closes at 5:30pm. 15R, students 10R.) A block away, **Prince Sergey Trubetskoy's house-museum** (Музей Трубецкого), ul. Dzerzhinskovo 64 (Дзержинского; tel. 27 57 73), exhibits his books, furniture, tapestried icons, silverware, and photos of his jail cell. (Theoretically open M and Th-Su 10am-6pm; *kassa* closes at 5:30pm. 15R, students 4R.) Near the river, the **Regional Museum** (Kraevedchesky Muzey; Краеведческий Музей), in a pink Victorian building at ul. Karla Marxa 2 (tel. 33 34 49), exhibits furs, skis, Buddhist masks, drums, woven icons, music shells, and pipes of local Siberian tribes. (Open Tu-Su 10am-6pm. 3R.) Antique clothes and old-style Russian furniture wait next door. The **Sukachev Art Museum** (Khudozhestvenny Muzey Imeni Sukacheva; Художественный Музей Имени Сукачева), ul. Lenina 5 (tel. 34 42 30), houses Chinese vases, Siberian paintings of the 16th to 20th centuries, and a display of the works of the *peredvizhniky* (traveling artists). (Open W-Su 10am-6pm. 30R, students 20R.) The elegant, gold-columned iconostasis in **Znamensky Monastery** (Знаменский Монастырь), north of the town center on ul. Angarskaya (Ангарская), is brightened by a golden chandelier-lit interior. Take trolley #3 or buses #8, 13, or 31 to the first stop past the northern bridge, or walk along ul. Frank Kamenetskovo (Франк Каменецкого), bear right at the fork, and carefully cross the street to the blue-green domes. (Open daily 8:30am-8pm. Services daily 8:30 and 11am.) **Epiphany Church** (Bogoyavlensky Sobor; Богоявленский Собор) and **Savior's Church** (Spasskaya Tserkov; Спасская Церковь), dominate the area north of the center. The latter also houses a museum. (Open M and W-Su 10am-5:30pm. 30R.) Irkutsk's light blue **synagogue,** ul. Karla Libknekhta 23 (Карла Либкнехта; tel. 27 53 67), off ul. Karla Marxa, holds services Saturdays at 10:30am. (Open M-F 10am-5pm.) A **mosque** stands at Karla Libknekhta 86.

ENTERTAINMENT. At dusk, locals head to the obelisk on the river at the end of Greznova to drink beer and watch the sunset. When it gets dark, those who don't have kids to put to bed head across the cove to **Youth Island** (Ostrov Yunosty; Остров Юности) to drink more and dance until morning. (Cover 20R. Open F-Sa 11pm-3am.)

RUSSIA

LAKE BAIKAL (ОЗЕРО БАЙКАЛ)

At 1637m, Lake Baikal is the **deepest freshwater body of water** in the world, containing one-fifth of the earth's fresh water supply. At twenty-five million years old, it is also the world's oldest lake (most aren't older than 100,000 years). Surrounded by snow-capped peaks, its waters teem with species found nowhere else in the world—translucent shrimp, oversized sturgeon, and deepwater fish that explode when brought to the surface. The *nerpa* freshwater seal lives 3000km from its closest relative, the Arctic seal, and no one knows quite how it got here. One deepwater fish has evolved into a gelatinous blob of fat—so fatty, in fact, that locals stick wicks in its lipidinous lumps and use them as candles.

Baikal's **shores** are no less fascinating than its waters. Reindeer, polar foxes, wild horses, brown bears, wild boars, and nefarious Siberian weasels hide in the surrounding mountains while glacial lakes melt into ice-cold waterfalls. Buryat *ger* (tent) communities border the edges. Painted rocks and "wishing" trees strung with colored rags recall the area's shamanistic heritage; the Buryat region to the northeast counts 45 Buddhist monasteries. Deserted gulags (where many lamas and shamans spent their last days under an atheist regime) pepper the outskirts.

In recent years, authorities and international organizations have begun initiatives to preserve the region. **Barguzinsky National Reserve** (Barguzinsky Zapovednik; Баргузинский Заповедник), on Baikal's east shore, was Russia's first national reserve. **Pribaykalsky National Park** (Прибайкалский Национальный Парк) encom-

THE UNDERWATER RAILROAD In winter, Lake Baikal freezes, and the extraordinarily deep ice enables ferry routes to become roads for trucks. The sturdiness of the ice was first tested during the Russo-Japanese War (1904-05) when the Russian Army—foreshadowing such future Russian engineering brilliance as the draining of the Aral Sea and Chernobyl—built train tracks over the ice in order to get troops to the front lines faster. Those tracks now have the distinction of being the farthest-underwater railway in the world.

passes much of the lake's west coast, and is the closest reserve to Irkutsk. When fog doesn't obscure the forest tops, views reach over pine-trees and crystal-clear water. Some days, visibility is better in the water (30m) than on land. **Olkhon Island,** also part of the park, is a prime spot for seal watching.

LISTVYANKA. The most popular destination for daytrippers is a tourist-friendly town of 2500 where meandering cows battle tourists and their cars for control over the one and only real street, ul. Gorkovo (Горького), which runs from the boat dock to the typically concrete Intourist Hotel. Yeltsin and German Chancellor Helmut Kohl stayed in this hotel (not in the same room) during their 1993 trip to Lake Baikal. **St. Nicholas's Church,** ul. Kylekova 88 (tel. 571), built in gratitude for a miraculous ship rescue, sits in a small valley away from the lake, making for a great stroll. Backtrack from the boat terminal, go left with your back to the docks, and turn right when you see a green spire to your right. Plain white walls and detailed, golden-framed icons wait inside the church. (Open M-F 10am-6pm. Services Sa-Su 8:30am-noon and 1-7pm.)

Housing is not hard to find. The cheapest option is upstairs from the national park office at ul. Gorkovo 39, 20m from the lake. Downstairs, you can get info and **maps** (15R) of Lake Baikal and the surrounding area. (2-person dorms 105R.) The owners of **Traktir** (Трактир), ul. Chipaeva 24, will put you up in their gorgeous wooden house and let you use their *banya.* (US$25 per person. Breakfast included.) They also arrange **picnic tours** of Baikal for about US$35 per person. For longer stays, try the cheap accommodations on **Okhon Island.** Transport by bus or hydrofoil runs several times a week. **Bistro** (Бистро), by the boat docks, sells decent food. (*Pelmeny* 18R. Open daily 10am-10pm.) Take a left out of the boat dock to get to the **post office,** ul. Gorkovo 49. (Open M-F 8:30am-1pm and 3-5:30pm, Sa 8:30am-noon; closed last Thursday of each month.) There is nowhere reputable or competent to **change money** in town, so plan accordingly.

GETTING THERE. Buses run to **Listvyanka** (1¼hr., 4 per day 9am-7pm, 4 return trips 7am-6pm, 18R) from **Irkutsk's bus station,** ul. Oktyabrskoy Revolutsiye 11 (tel. 27 24 11). A quicker, more interesting way to get to Listvyanka is to take a **hydrofoil** from **Irkutsk's "Ракета" terminal** (tel. 23 80 53), on ul. Solnichnaya south of town (1hr., M-F 8:30am departure, 10:50am return, more on weekends, 23R). Buy tickets at least a day ahead for the hydrofoil, and expect a long schlep to the dock. From ul. Lenina in Irkutsk, take bus #16 or trolleybus #5 to the terminal (20min., 2R).

RUSSIA

ULAN UDE (УЛАН УДЕ)

For all intents and purposes, Ulan Ude is where Slavic Russia meets its Asian counterpart, where the world's largest bust of Lenin sits ignored by local Buddhists. The Buryat people roamed the region semi-nomadically long before the Russians arrived. While most Buryats have today adopted the Russian language, native culture still permeates, from the ubiquitous *pozy* (traditional meat dumplings) to the local *datsan* (Buddhist monastery).

TIME CHANGE. Ulan Ude is 5hr. ahead of Moscow time and is in the same time zone as Mongolia and China (GMT+8).

ORIENTATION & PRACTICAL INFORMATION. Ulan Ude's main square, **pl. Sovetov** (Советов), lies 0.5km south of the station; take bus #10 or 36 to reach it (3R). The main artery, **ul. Lenina,** runs south from pl. Sovetov. The **train station** (tel. 34 25 31), just off ul. Revolutsiye 1905-a goda, lies north of the city center, and sends trains to: **Irkutsk** (8hr., 4-5 per day, 188R); **Ulaanbaatar** (24hr., 1 per day, 231R); and **Beijing** (2 per week, 560R). Ulan Ude is the last (or first, depending on the direction you're traveling) major Russian city on the Trans-Mongolian line. The following Trans-Siberian **trains** pass through the city (in Moscow time): **train #2** to **Vladivostok** (odd days at 8:05am, 650R); **#4** to **Beijing** (Sa 11:35am, 1743R); **#20** to **Beijing** (Tu 11:25pm, 2183R); and **#6** to **Ulaanbaatar** (Su-M 11:35am). Foreigners must purchase tickets from the Intourist *kassa* on the second floor of the station; look for the door with the "Международные Кассы" sign. In the lobby of Hotel Buryatiya (Бурятия), just off ul. Lenina, you can cash **traveler's checks** (M-F 9am-1pm and 2-4pm) and receive MC/Visa **cash advances** (M-F 9am-6pm). The lobby also houses the city's most convenient **ATM. Store luggage** in the center hall of the train station (backpacks 6R). Purchase newer **maps** (10R) at **Dom Knigi** (Дом Книги), ul. Lenina 36. (Open M-Sa 10am-7pm.) A **24hr. pharmacy** can be found at ul. Lenina 29 (tel. 21 24 37; ring bell midnight-6am). Take the tram from Hotel Buryatiya to the first stop across the river and the **main post office,** ul. Lenina 61 (tel. 21 51 31). **Internet access** (1R per min.; open daily 9am-6pm), **fax,** and **24hr. international phone service** are available in the **business center** (бизнес центр), ul. Babushkina 20 (Бабушкина). **Postal code:** 670000. **Phone code:** 3012.

ACCOMMODATIONS & FOOD. The best bargain is **Hotel Barguzin** (Баргузина), ul. Sovietskaya 28 (tel. 21 57 46). Take bus #36 from the train station and ask the driver for the hotel by name, or take bus #10 to pl. Sovietov, walk two blocks down ul. Lenina, and go right on ul. Sovietskaya. Rooms don't have hot water, but a shower on the 2nd floor does (singles with bath 130R; doubles 266R). The more upscale **Hotel Geser,** ul. Ranzhurova 11 (Ранжурова; tel. 21 61 51), has a friendly, English-speaking staff. Head up Lenina to the post office, then turn left and walk 2min.; look for the hotel restaurant's sign. (Singles with bath 220R; doubles 440R. Breakfast included.) Both hotels have **24hr. cafes.** Numerous small cafes line ul. Lenina. **Kinsburger** (Кинсбургер), ul. Lenina 21 (tel. 21 52 53), serves a decent hamburger (7000R) and *Buryat kroket* (крокет), a dumpling filled with potatoes, lettuce, and some meaty stuff called *farsh.* (Open daily 8am-1am.) **Poznaya** (Позная), on the corner of ul. Lenina and ul. Sovetskaya, serves great *pozy* (7R), although they may sell out by 7:30pm. (Open daily 10am-9pm.)

SIGHTS & ENTERTAINMENT. Begin your tour of Ulan Ude at the city's main square, **pl. Sovetov,** which is crowned by an enormous figurehead of Vladimir Ilyich Lenin. The *Guinness Book of World Records* lists it as the largest bust in the world, and this sounds about right—it's big. The Soviet-era structures around pl. Sovetov house Buryat Republic government offices. At the southwest corner of the square, on the corner of ul. Lenina, stands the yellow **Buryat State Academic Theater of Opera and Ballet** (Бурятский Государственный Академический Театр Оперы и Балета), a classical-style building with two horsemen perched to guard the front entrance; the steps on the theater's rear side afford stunning views of the downtown area and the surrounding mountains. (Season runs Oct.-May.)

RUSSIA

The recently opened **Museum of Buryat History** (Muzey Istorii Buryatii; Музей истории Бурятии), ul. Profsoyuznaya 29 (Профсоюзная; tel. 21 65 87), off ul. Kommunisticheskaya by Hotel Buryatia, was first founded in 1923 but closed down, supposedly for renovation, in 1980. True renovations began only after Ulan Ude celebrated the 250th anniversary of Buddhism in Russia in 1992, and it finally reopened to the public in May 1997. Today the museum includes exhibits on the history of the city and the БАМ (BAM), the costly second Trans-Siberian railway. There is also a huge collection of Buddhist paraphernalia. (Open Tu-Su 10am-6pm. 50R.) Walking four blocks south on ul. Kommunisticheskaya away from pl. Sovetov brings you to ul. Kirova (Кирова) and the local **Buddhist shrine** (*lamrim;*

лампим), right next to the hardware store. Walk past the black gate and ask to take a peek inside. The surrounding 18th- and 19th-century **wooden houses** comprise the oldest part of town.

The two most interesting sights lie outside the city limits. The **Ethnographic Museum** (Etnograficheskу Muzey; Етнографический Музей; tel. 33 57 54), 10km north of the city center, can be reached by bus #8 (every 30min., 2R) from in front of the Lenin bust at pl. Sovetov. Ask the driver to drop you off at "Etnograficheskу Muzey," then walk about 1km down the road that veers left from the bus stop (15min.); the museum will appear after the green fence on the right ends. The museum is an open-air complex of reconstructed buildings meant to depict the traditional way of life in the region. The "Buryat complex" consists of several *ger* (traditional Buryat tent-homes, also known as *yurts*), and the "Russian old-life complex" features a nearly perfect copy of a wooden Russian country church. (Open Tu-Su 9am-6pm; *kassa* closes at 5pm. 20R.) An adjoining **zoo** squeezes camels, deer, horses, bears, and a very unhappy wolf into veal-ranch-sized cages.

The most fascinating building in the Buryat region is in the hamlet of **Ivolga** (Иволга), 28km west of Ulan Ude. In the middle of the hills stands **Datsan-Ivolga,** a large Buddhist monastery complete with a yellow, curved roof, a white picket fence with Buddhist prayer drums, and a village full of Mongolian-trained Buddhist lamas. (Visit in the morning or early afternoon. Free.) Built in 1972, the shrine served as the center of Buddhism in the former Soviet Union. In the main temple are several Buddhist scriptures handwritten in Tibetan and Sanskrit and a display of gifts. Around the edge of the complex are 120 prayer drums, each inscribed with sacred scripture. The lamas' houses are behind the complex. From the bus station in Ulan Ude (two blocks to the left from Hotel Barguzin) buses leave at 7am, noon, and 4pm.

ULAANBAATAR, MONGOLIA

With half a million people, booming tourism, and enough land to fit a population several times its size, the capital of Mongolia is a sprawling desert oasis. Ulaanbaatar is the main stop on the Trans-Mongolian Railroad, which connects the Trans-Siberian Railroad in the north with Beijing in the southeast. While the best parts of Mongolia lie out in the countryside, "UB" is still one of the best stops between Moscow and Beijing.

ORIENTATION & PRACTICAL INFORMATION. Mongolia requires that tourists possess a valid **passport** and a **visa,** which can be arranged with little hassle at the Mongolian embassies in Moscow (tel. (7-095) 229 67 65; fax 291 61 71), London (tel. (44-0171) 937 01 50; fax 937 11 17), and Washington, D.C. (tel. (1-202) 298-7117; fax 298-9227). The unit of **currency** is the **tugrik** (T), 1006 of which equalled US$1 in the summer of 1999. Map labels and street names are in Mongolian and sometimes in Russian. The center of town is **Sukhbaatar Square,** marked by a small statue of the patriot for whom it is named. To get there from the train station, take bus #4 (T100). The **train station** is on Teeverchid St. International tickets must be bought at the **International Railway Ticketing Office;** exit the train station, turn left, and walk about 2min. to the yellow building set back from the road on the right. The office on the second floor has a **currency exchange** that cashes traveler's checks and gives AmEx/MC/Visa cash advances for a 4% commission. (Open M-F 9am-1pm and 2:30-5pm.) For general info and maps of the city, head to **Hotel Ulaanbaatar,** a block past Sukhbaatar Square as you come from the train station. **Juulchin Tourist,** Chinghis Khaan 5B (tel. 32 84 28; fax 32 02 46; email jlncorp@magicnet.com; www.mol.mn/juulchin), behind the Bayangal Hotel, arranges trips to the Gobi Desert, the ancient capital of Karakorum, and the lake regions. The **post office** is on the corner of Enkh Tayvan Ave. and Sukhbaatar St. (Open M-F 7:30am-9pm, Sa 8am-8pm, Su 9am-8pm.) The **telephone office** is in the same building. (To: North America T2374; Australia T3000 per min; Europe T2000 per min. Open 24hr.) **Postal code:** 210613. **Mongolia country phone code:** 976. **Ulaanbaatar city phone code:** 1.

ACCOMMODATIONS & FOOD. Ulaanbaatar has some of the best accommodations on the Trans-Siberian route. Most mid-range hotels in the capital accept major credit cards, and the staffs generally speak good English. For a truly Mongolian experience, head to **Gana's Guest House** (tel./fax 36 73 43; call in advance, and Gana will send someone to pick you up at the train station) near the Gandan Hiid monastery. With your back to the train station, turn right, walk 5min. and take the first hard left. You will pass two intersections and ascend a hill; signs on the right side of the road lead the way. The guest house consists of five to six Mongolian *ger*, with four to five beds each, occupied by rustic Europeans. The hot shower and outhouses are in back, but the incredibly comfy beds and great views more than make up for the inconvenience. (*Ger* US$5; dorms US$3.) For something a little more socialist, head to **Serge's Guest House,** 50 Enchtaivan St. Follow the directions to Gana's, but turn right at the second major intersection. Serge's is the pink door in the first building on the right. (4-person dorms US$5.)

For decent pizza (T1000-2000) and Anglophone company, head to the **Khan Brau Restaurant and Pub,** a block up from Sukhbaatar on the left side of Chengis Ave. For quality Mongolian fare, follow the locals to the **cafeteria** in the little blue building on Ikh Tyruu St., 100m after it bears right and away from the monastery.

SIGHTS. Ulaanbaatar is particularly impressive for its Buddhist monasteries. Closest to the train station, on Ikhtoyruu St. (follow directions to Gana's Guest House, above), is the **Gandan Hiid.** Built in 1840, the monastery is named for a monk employed as a KGB agent to spy on the Mongolian Buddhists for the Soviets. (Open 24hr. Free.) Opposite Sukhbaatar Sq., between Chinghis Khaan Ave. and Marx St., stands the fantastic **Monastery-Museum of Choijin Lama,** a complex of four temples. If no one else is around, one of the ladies working at the door might give you a personal tour. (Open daily 10am-5pm. T2000; photos T5000.) The **Museum of Natural History,** at the corner of Khuvsgalchid Ave. and Sukhbaatar St., is a three-floor chronicle of the history of humans in Mongolia. The clothing and jewelry displays on the second and third floors are worth seeing. (Open daily 10am-4pm. T1500.) Finally, if you're not convinced that UB is an ex-pat haven, just stop by **Scrolls English Bookstore** (tel. 31 44 74) on Khuvagalchid Ave. between the Wrangler Jeans store and Millie's Cafe.

SLOVAKIA (SLOVENSKO)

US$1 = 41SK (SLOVAK KORUNY)	**10SK = US$0.24**
CDN$1 = 28SK	**10SK = CDN$0.36**
UK£1 = 66SK	**10SK = UK£0.15**
IR£1 = 56SK	**10SK = IR£0.18**
AUS$1 = 27SK	**10SK = AUS$0.37**
NZ$1 = 22SK	**10SK = NZ$0.46**
SAR1 = 6.83SK	**10SK = SAR1.46**
DM1 = 22.43SK	**10SK = DM0.44**

PHONE CODES Country code: **421.** International dialing prefix: **00.**

After centuries of nomadic invasions, Hungarian domination, and Soviet industrialization, Slovakia has finally emerged as an independent country. Freedom has introduced new challenges, though, as the older generation reluctantly gives way to their chic, English-speaking offspring. The nation remains in a state of generational flux between industry and agriculture, unable to muster the resources necessary for an easy Westernization and unwilling to return to its past. This leaves a strange mixture of fairy-tale traditionalism and easy-going youth, which combine with low prices to create a haven for budget travelers. From tiny villages to the busy streets of its capital, Slovakia is coming to grips with progress, as the good old days retreat to castle ruins, pastures, and the stunning Tatras above.

HIGHLIGHTS OF SLOVAKIA

- A combination of glitzy resorts and tiny mountain villages, the **High Tatras** (p. 693) offer many of the best hiking opportunities in Europe.
- The *château* at **Bojnice** (p. 684) looks straight out of Disneyland...or maybe the palace at Disneyland looks straight out of Bojnice. But only one's real, and it's not in L.A.
- In the heartland of Slovakia, an oasis of...Andy Warhol? A museum in **Medzilaborce** (p. 704) founded by his brother hosts a collection of his work and memorabilia.

SLOVAKIA

LIFE & TIMES

HISTORY

Slovakia's history is that of an embattled border region, susceptible to the whims and invasions of its more powerful neighbors. Its first settlers were the **Western Slavs** in the 6th and 7th centuries. In 870, Slovakia was incorporated into the **Great Moravian Empire** along with Bohemia, southern Poland, and western Hungary. When **Magyars** invaded in 896, Slovakia was shuffled off to another power, the **Kingdom of Hungary.** In the wake of economic devastation caused by Tartar attacks in the 13th century, the Hungarians pushed the Slovak-inhabited region off onto **Saxon** landlords. For a few decades at the start of the 14th century, a local ruler, **Matús Čák,** managed to handle his tenants fairly well; alas, that soon gave way to another 200 years of Hungarian rule.

After the Hungarian defeat by the Ottomans at the 1526 **Battle of Mohács,** the **Habsburgs** inherited Slovakia. They moved their capital north to Bratislava in 1536, and from that base, managed to wrench all of Hungary free from Turkish hands and eventually rebuild the region. They also had some religious spring cleaning to do, replacing Slovakia's **Lutheranism** and **Calvinism** with **Roman Catholicism** (see p. 663, 670); not surprisingly, religious wars followed throughout the 17th century.

In the 19th century, a Slovakian nationalist movement led by **L'udovít Štúr** emerged in the Kingdom of Hungary. The tumultuous **Revolution of 1848** brought little change to Slovakia but disaster to its Hungarian overlords. After the establishment of the **Austro-Hungarian Dual Monarchy** in 1876, Hungary regained control of Slovakia which remained one of the most subjugated nations in the Austro-Hungarian Empire. Without its own province, Slovakia lived directly under Hungarian rule. Ignoring the wise advice of Hungarian intellectuals, the Hungarian government, particularly under **Tisza,** intensified the policy of Magyarization, forcing many Slovaks to leave their homeland and alienating those who stayed behind.

The Slovak national movement continued to blossom through the turn of the century and on October 28, 1918, six days before Austria-Hungary sued for peace, Slovakia was attached to Bohemia, Moravia, and Sub-Carpathian Ruthenia to form **Czechoslovakia**, a new state in the heart of Europe with its capital at Prague. Fortunately, the new state was able to repel an invasion of Slovakia by the Hungarian Communist **Bela Kun** in 1919 and secured the withdrawal of Romanian troops from Ruthenia. It became a **liberal democracy** based on the American model, one of the world's wealthiest nations, and the only state in Central or Eastern Europe not to fall to fascist, authoritarian, or communist rule.

As Adolf Hitler plotted his territorial ambitions, Czechoslovakia was one of his first targets. Abandoned by Britain and France in the **Munich Agreement** of September 1938, Slovaks clamored for autonomy. A month later, they got their wish, as Slovakia was proclaimed an autonomous unit within a federal Czecho-Slovak state. But as spring came, the fledgling **Second Republic** buckled as German troops invaded Bohemia and Moravia. As Hitler occupied Prague, Slovakia emerged as a collaborative Nazi puppet under the rule of **Monseignor Tiso.** Hungary took the opportunity to kick its neighbor while it was down, helping itself to the province of Ruthenia. Nonetheless, the Slovaks persisted, staging the two-month **Slovak National Uprising (Slovenské Národné Povstanie; SNP),** against Tiso and the Nazis in August 1944 (see **Banská Bystrica: Sights and Entertainment,** p. 683).

After **WWII,** Slovakia returned to the democratic Czechoslovakia. Unfortunately, things did not go smoothly. The new state lost Ruthenia again, this time to the Soviets, and took out its frustrations internally by expelling Slovakia's ethnic Hungarians and Saxons. **Communists,** led by **Klement Gottwald,** won 36% of the vote in 1946 and soon dominated through a leftist coalition. In February 1948, as the Popular Front government fell apart, they mounted a Soviet-backed coup. Although the 1948 constitution guaranteed equal status for their state, Slovaks were still wary of a Czech-dominated government. Indeed, it took a Slovak, **Alexander**

Dubček, to shake the regime out of its subservience to Moscow. Dubček introduced his **"Prague Spring"** reforms in 1968, but Soviet tanks immediately rolled into Prague, crushed his allegedly disloyal government, and plunged the country back into totalitarianism. Bratislava was dubbed a "capital city," and rural Slovakia underwent heavy industrial development. The communists remained in power until the **Velvet Revolution** of 1989. **Václav Havel** was appointed President and the government introduced a pluralistic political system and a market economy. In this fertile political environment, Slovak nationalism blossomed into a **Declaration of Independence** in 1993. After centuries of conquest, alliance, and betrayal, Slovaks had an independent state to call their own.

SLOVAKIA TODAY

Coming out of the 1993 Velvet Revolution with only 25% of former Czechoslovakia's industrial capacity and even less of its international reputation, Slovakia has had more trouble adjusting to the post-Eastern Bloc world than its former partner. Relations with Hungary and the Czech Republic are strained. Political instability has isolated Slovakia from the West and potential membership in both the **E.U.** and **NATO**. The primary instigator of this instability has been **Vladimir Mečiar**. Inexplicably popular, he has thrice been elected prime minister and thrice been removed. During his terms, he has violated the country's constitution, cancelled presidential elections and referendums on NATO membership, and even granted amnesty to terrorists suspected of kidnapping the son of former president **Michal Kovac**. Although Mečiar has dropped off the political radar after losing power in the September 1998 elections, the damage he wrought is just now being repaired, Only in May 1999 did the country achieve the two-fifths majority needed to elect **Rudolf Schuster,** former mayor of Košice, president. With his election come promises of further Westernization and, of course, a brighter future.

LITERATURE & ARTS

Mirroring the nation's political history, art in Slovakia had to struggle long and hard to escape the orbit of neighboring traditions. The Slovak tongue, for example, only emerged as a literary language distinct from Czech in the 18th century, and even then only because a decline in literary Czech left room for it to flourish. Early examples of the Slovak novel, such as **Ignác Bajza's** *René* (1785), were written in a Slovak dialect of Czech, rather than a distinct language. **Ján Holly's** lyrics and idylls of this period owe a tremendous debt to folk poetry. The Slovak literary tradition really got started with the 19th century linguist and nationalist **L'udovít Štur,** whose "new" language based on the Central Slovak dialects inspired a string of national poets. Foremost among these was **Andrej Sládkovič,** author of the national epic *Marína* (1846). Sládkovič's contemporary, the poet and revolutionary **Janko Král,** launched an enduring tradition of Slovak Romanticism with his ballads, epics, and lyrics, a tradition followed by the rustic poets **Svetozar Vajansky** and **Hviezdoslav.**

The 19th century also saw the dawn of classical music in the region, with works by such composers as **Frico Kafenda.** Visual artists of the early 1800s looked abroad for inspiration, but toward the end of the century, painters such as **Mikolaš Ales** and **Joza Uprka** turned their attention back to Slovakia. Slovak painters in Prague before the WWI developed a style known as **descriptive realism** which dominated in Slovakia until the 1960s.

In the wake of WWI, Slovak nationalism and literature matured concurrently. More cosmopolitan influences began to appear alongside Romanticism: **E. B. Lukáč** introduced **Symbolism** to the Slovak tradition while **Surrealism** found a champion in **Rudolf Fabry.** The long-established primacy of the lyric began to give way to novels and short stories. As in poetry, rural themes and village life took center stage, often as an object of celebration, but increasingly as the butt of scorn and ridicule. **Janko Jesenký** savaged the regional poo-bahs of the post-war government in his novel *The Democrats (Demokrati)*. Meanwhile, **Andrej Ocenasa** led a prominent generation of composers who blended classical and folk strands in their works.

Just as totalitarianism inspired the likes of Kafka in Prague, communist rule after WWII inspired reaction among the Slovak literati. **Ladislav Mnačko** was one of the first writers in Eastern Europe to speak out against Stalinism, in his 1967 novel *The Taste of Power*. Around the same time, **Jan Kadar** directed *The Shop on Main Street*, the best known Slovak contribution to world cinema.

READING LIST

Literature on and from Slovakia in English is particularly difficult to find, owing perhaps to the dominance of other states and traditions in the region's history. For one-stop Slovak history, Stanislav Kirschbaum's *A History of Slovakia: The Struggle for Survival* is a well-researched (if somewhat biased) study of the Slovak people through centuries of conquest. Equally comprehensive is Peter Petro's *A History of Slovak Literature*, which explores the literary tradition with a keen eye to its political and cultural interactions.

FACTS AND FIGURES

- **Capital:** Bratislava
- **Population:** 5,404,268
- **Land Area:** 49,036km^2
- **Geography:** Mountains; plains near the Hungarian border
- **Language:** Slovak, Hungarian
- **Religions:** 60% Catholic
- **GDP per capita:** US$3,494
- **Major Exports:** Semimanufactured materials

SLOVAKIA ESSENTIALS

Citizens of South Africa and the U.S. can visit Slovakia without a visa for up to 30 days; Canada and Ireland 90 days; and the U.K. 180 days. Citizens of Australia and New Zealand need a 30-day visa (single-entry US$21; double-entry US$32; 90-day multiple-entry US$52; 180-day multiple-entry US$93; transit US$21). Apply to an embassy or consulate in person or by mail; processing takes two days. Submit your passport (which must be valid for eight months from the date of application), company check or money order for the fee, one visa application per planned entry, and two passport photos for every application. Travelers must also register their visa within three days of entering the Slovakia, although hotels will do this automatically. If you intend to stay longer or obtain a visa extension, you must notify the Office of Border and Alien Police in the town where they are staying in the first three business days of their arrival. For a list of Slovak embassies and consulates, see **Essentials: Embassies & Consulates,** p. 13.

GETTING THERE & GETTING AROUND

International bus and rail links connect Slovakia to its neighbors. Large train stations operate **BIJ-Wasteels** offices, which offer 30% discounts on tickets to European cities, except Prague, for those under 26. **EastRail** is valid in Slovakia; **Eurail** is not. As everywhere, you'll pay extra for an InterCity or EuroCity fast train, and if there's a boxed R on the timetable, a *miestenka* (reservation; 7Sk) is required. If you board the train without a reservation, expect to pay an additional 150Sk fine. International ticket counters have multilingual signs.

Larger towns on the **railway** have many *stanice* (train stations); the *hlavná stanica* is the main one. Smaller towns have only one, and tiny villages usually have just a decaying hut with an illegible schedule. Tickets must be bought before boarding the train, except in the tiniest towns. **ŽSR** is the national train company; every information desk has a copy of **Cestovný poriadok** (58Sk), the master schedule, which is also printed on a large, round board in most stations. *Odchody*

PRIMARY BORDER CROSSINGS. Visas are not available at the Slovak border and there is no fee for entering or exiting Slovakia. In general, Slovak customs are quick and painless; a border crossing should add no extra time to your journey. As always, it's easiest to take a direct train or bus from Bratislava to the nearest major city in the neighboring country.

Austria: Bratislava, SLK (p. 676)/Vienna, AUS (p. 792) via Jarovce/Kittsee. Morava sv. Ján, SLK/Hohenau, AUS; connects northwestern Slovakia with northeastern Austria.

Czech Republic: Kúty, SLK/Břeclav, CZR; connects Bratislava (p. 676) with Moravia (p. 225). Trenčín, SLK/Brumov-Bylnice, CZR; connects Central Slovakia (p. 682) with Moravia (p. 225).

Hungary: Bratislava, SLK (p. 676)/Rajka, HUN; connects southwestern Slovakia with Győr (p. 296). Komárno, SLK/Komárom, HUN; connects southwestern Slovakia with the Őrseg (p. 296). Štúrovo, SLK/Esztergom, HUN (p. 295); connects southwestern Slovakia with the Danube Bend (p. 292). Lučenec, SLK/Salgótarján, HUN; connects Central Slovakia (p. 682) with Miskolc and Northern Hungary (p. 332). Košice, SLK (p. 699)/Tornyosnémeti, HUN; connects Šariš (p. 698) with Northern Hungary (p. 332).

Poland: Stará Lubovňa, SLK/Nowy Sącz, POL via Piwniczna, POL; connects Bardejov (p. 705) with Kraków (p. 422). Spišská Belá, SLK/Zakopane, POL (p. 441) via Ľysa Polana, POL; connects the Slovak Tatras (p. 693) with the Carpathians (p. 440). Dolný Kubin, SLK/Spytkowice, POL via Chyżne, POL; connects Žilina (p. 684) with Kraków (p. 422).

Ukraine: Sobrance, SLK/Užhorod, UKR (p. 778); connects Šariš (p. 698) with Western Ukraine (p. 767).

(departures) and *príchody* (arrivals) are posted on yellow and white signs, respectively, but don't always believe information about platforms—check the station's display board for the right *nástupište* (gate). Reservations are sometimes required and generally recommended for *expresný* trains and first-class seats, but are not necessary for *rychlík* (fast), *spešný* (semi-fast), or *osobný* (local) trains. Trains usually run on time. Station **locker** instructions probably won't be in English. Insert a 5Sk coin, choose a personal code on the *inside*, insert your bag, and try to shut the door. If it does not lock, throw a loud tantrum, and try another locker. Repeat 10 times. If this fails, go to the luggage window. To reclaim your bag, arrange the outer knobs to fit your personal code. Sometimes the aging circuit takes a few seconds to register and open. Left luggage offices (10-20Sk) are easier.

In many hilly regions, **ČSAD** or **SAD buses** are the best and sometimes the only option. Except for very long trips, buy the ticket on the bus. Schedules seem designed to drive foreigners batty with their many footnotes; the most important are as follows: **X** (it actually looks like two crossed hammers), weekdays only; **a,** Saturdays and Sundays only; **r** and **k,** excluding holidays. **Numbers** refer to the days of the week on which the bus runs—1 is Monday, 2 is Tuesday, and so forth. *"Premava"* means including; *"nepremava"* is except; following those words are often lists of dates (day, then month). In the summer, watch out for July 5, when the entire country shuts down for Sts. Cyril and Methodius Day.

The rambling wilds and ruined castles of Slovakia inspire great **bike** tours. The Slovaks love to ride bicycles, especially in the Tatras, the foothills of West Slovakia, and Šariš. **VKÚ** publishes color-coded maps of most regions (70-80Sk).

TOURIST SERVICES & MONEY

The main tourist information offices form a loose conglomeration called **Asociácia Informačných Centier Slovenska (AICS);** look for the green logo. The offices are invariably on or near the town's main square; the nearest one can often be found by dialing 186. English is often—but not always—spoken here; accommodation bookings can usually—but not always—be made; and the staff is usually—but not always—delightful. **SATUR,** the Slovak branch of the old Czechoslovakian Čedok, seems more interested in flying Slovaks abroad on package tours, but may be of some help. **Slovakotourist** can be of assistance when available.

After the 1993 Czech-Slovak split, Slovakia hastily designed its own currency, which is now the country's only legal tender. One hundred **halér** make up one Slovak **koruna (Sk). Všeobecná Úverová Banka (VÚB)** has offices in even the smallest towns and cashes **traveler's checks** for a 1% commission. Most offices give **MC** cash advances and have Cirrus/Plus/MC/Visa **ATMs,** called **Bankomats**—look for the red and black signs. Many **Slovenská Sporiteľňa** bureaus handle **Visa** cash advances and have Visa **ATMs.** Leave your **AmEx** at home—it's useless in Slovakia.

COMMUNICATION

Slovakia has an efficient **mail** service. Almost every *pošta* (post office) provides **Express Mail Services,** but to send a package abroad, a trip to a *colnice* (customs office) is in order. **Poste Restante** mail with a "1" after the city name will arrive at the main post office. Even in small towns, **cardphones** are common, and although they sometimes refuse your card (150Sk), they're much better than the coin-operated variety. Long-distance access numbers include: **AT&T Direct,** tel. 00 42 10 01 01; **BT Direct,** tel. 080 00 44 01; **Canada Direct,** tel. 00 42 10 01 51; **MCI WorldPhone,** tel. 00 42 100 112; **Sprint,** tel. 00 42 18 71 87. Slovakia's only **English-language newspaper** is the weekly *Slovak Spectator* (24Sk), available at the Bratislava and Banská Bystrica Interpress stores. It is geared toward a business audience, but it has some useful listings and publishes an annual glossy *Spectacular Slovakia* brochure (75Sk) for tourists. Other English-language finds are likely to be dreary government propaganda.

LANGUAGE

Slovak, closely related to **Czech,** is a tricky Slavic language, but any attempt will be appreciated. **English** is not uncommon among Bratislava youth, but people outside the capital are more likely to speak **German.** You may not find any English-speakers, even in the tourist office. **Russian** is understood, but not always welcome. When speaking Slovak, the two golden rules are to pronounce every letter—nothing is silent and it's all phonetic—and to emphasize the first syllable. Accents on vowels affect length, not stress. Flick the "r" off the top of your mouth.

HEALTH & SAFETY

! **EMERGENCY NUMBERS.**
Fire: tel. 150. **Police:** tel. 158. **Ambulance:** tel. 155.

Tap water varies in quality and appearance—sometimes crystal clear, sometimes chlorine-cloudy—but is generally safe. If it comes out of the faucet cloudy, let it sit for 5min. while the nastiness settles to the bottom; it'll be clear and drinkable. A reciprocal agreement between Slovakia and the U.K. entitles Brits to free medical care here. *Drogerie* (drugstore) shelves heave with Western brand names; obtaining supplies shouldn't be hard. Tampons are *tampony*, a band-aid *plaster*, and aspirin *aspirena*.

ACCOMMODATIONS & CAMPING

Foreigners will often pay up to twice as much as Slovaks for the same room. Finding cheap accommodations in Bratislava before the student dorms open in July is impossible, and without reservations, the outlook in Slovenský Raj and the Tatras can be bleak. Otherwise, it's not difficult to find a bed as long as you call ahead; just don't expect an English-speaker on the other end. The tourist office, **SATUR,** or **Slovakotourist** can usually help. **Juniorhotels (HI),** although uncommon, are a step above the usual hostel. In the mountains, **chaty** (mountain huts/chalets) range from plush quarters for 400Sk per night to a friendly bunk and outhouse for 150Sk. **Hotel** prices fall dramatically outside Bratislava and the High Tatras, and they are rarely full. **Pensions** *(penzióny)* are less expensive than hotels, and often more fun. Two forms of *ubytovanie* (lodging) cater mainly to Slovaks and offer super prices for bare-bones rooms: **stadiums** and sport centers often run hotels on the lot for teams and fans (the requisite ground-floor pubs are always hoppin'), and **workers' hostels** generally offer hospital-like rooms with no pub. **Campgrounds** lurk on the outskirts of most towns, and many offer bungalows for travelers without tents. Camping in national parks is illegal.

FOOD & DRINK

Slovakia emerged from its 1000-year Hungarian captivity with a taste for paprika, spicy *gulaš*, and fine wines. The good news for vegetarians is that the national dish, *bryndžové halušky*, is a plate of dumpling-esque pasta smothered in a thick sauce of sheep or goat cheese; the bad news is that it sometimes comes flecked with bacon. The Slovaks like their dumplings *(knedliky)*, but—unlike in the Czech Republic—it's often possible to escape them and have potatoes *(zemiaky)* or fries *(hranolky)* instead. Slovakia's second-favorite dish is *pirohy*, a pasta-pocket filled with potato or *bryndžou* cheese, topped with bacon bits. *Pstruh* (trout), often served whole, is also popular. *Kolačky* (pastry) is baked with cheese, jam or poppy seeds, and honey.

White wines are produced northeast of Bratislava in the Small Carpathians, especially around the town of Pezinok. *Riesling* and *Müller-Thurgau* grapes are typically used, and quality varies greatly. *Tokaj* wines are produced around Košice. You can enjoy any of these at a *vináreň* (wine hall). *Pivo* (beer) is served at a *pivnica* or *piváreň* (beerhall). The most-favored Slovak beer is *Zlatý Bažant*, a light, slightly bitter Tatran brew. Slovakia produces several brandies: *slivovica* (plum), *marhulovica* (apricot), and *borovička* (juniper-berry).

CUSTOMS & ETIQUETTE

Tipping is common in restaurants; most people round up to a convenient number by refusing change when they pay, with 8-10% being generous. Most **museums** close Mondays, and **theaters** take a break during July and August. Like Poland and unlike the Czech Republic, Slovakia is intensely Roman Catholic, resulting in social mores that are often quite conservative. Although **homosexuality** is legal, a gay couple walking down the street might encounter stares or insults, although often everyone is so shocked, though, that no one interferes. **Ganymedes,** the national gay organization, runs hotlines around the country, but few employees speak English. **Grocery store attendants** will accost you if you don't grab a basket by the entrance. And, more often than not, restaurant **toilets** will be locked with the key *(kluč)* hanging up by the bar.

NATIONAL HOLIDAYS

January 1, Independence Day; January 6, Epiphany; April 21, Good Friday; April 23, Easter; May 1, Labor Day; July 5, Sts. Cyril and Methodius Day; August 29, Anniversary of Slovak National Uprising; September 1, Constitution Day; September 15, Our Lady of the Seven Sorrows; November 1, All Saint's Day. December 24-26, Christmas.

BRATISLAVA

Perched directly between Vienna and Budapest, Bratislava (pop. 452,053) is experienced most often as a passing blip, a blur of highrises and hills on the way to bigger, more cosmopolitan cities. Indeed, the city has little to offer most travelers: Soviet-style apartment blocks, polluted roadways, and crumbling buildings are the main attractions, reminders of the city's history of oppressive rulers: Habsburgs, Magyars, Soviets and, some would say, Czechs, whose hipper capital to the north looms over Bratislava's tourist industry as a reminder of the disappointments of post-Czechoslovak independence. While it's tempting to follow suit and pass Bratislava by, the city might actually surprise those who take the time to discover it. Its cobblestoned Old Town is full of relaxing cafes, talented street musicians, surprisingly stylish natives, and several stunning Baroque buildings, while the outskirts of town are laced with vineyards and castle ruins. Above it all towers Bratislava Castle, symbol of Slovak national pride. If nothing else, Bratislava offers a glimpse into the psyche of a nation struggling to redefine itself.

GETTING THERE & GETTING AROUND

Airplanes: M.R. Štefánik International Airport (info tel. 48 57 33 65), 8km northeast of the city center. To reach the city center, take bus #24 from the airport to the train station and switch to tram #1, getting off at "Poštova" on Nám. SNP. Flights are very infrequent. It is better to use the much larger airport in nearby Vienna. The following carriers have local offices: **Austrian Airlines** (tel. 54 41 16 10), **British Airways** (tel. 39 98 01), **ČSA** (tel. 36 10 38), **Delta** (tel. 54 43 47 18), **LOT** (tel. 36 40 07), **Lufthansa** (tel. 36 78 14), and **Tatra Air** (tel. 43 29 23 06).

Trains: Bratislava Hlavná stanica (info tel. 39 59 04 and 50 58 44 84), north of the center. From the center, head up Štefánikova, turn right onto Šancová, and then left up the road that goes past the waiting buses. International tickets at counters #5-13. **Wasteels** office at the front of the station sells discounted international tickets to those under 26. Open M-F 8:30am-4:30pm. To: **Vienna** (1½hr., 3 per day, 248Sk); **Budapest** (2½-3hr., 7 per day, 660 Sk, Wasteels 245Sk); **Prague** (5hr., 7 per day, 350Sk); **Warsaw** (8hr., 1 per day, 1400Sk, Wasteels 342Sk); **Kraków** (8hr., 1 per day, 1080Sk, Wasteels 205Sk); and **Berlin** (10hr., 2 per day, 3600Sk, Wasteels 2497Sk).

Buses: Mlynské nivy 31 (info tel. 09 84 22 22 22), east of the center. To: **Vienna** (1½hr., 10 per day, 400Sk); **Prague** (5hr., 8 per day, 247Sk); and **Budapest** (4hr., 2 per day, 400Sk). Services the rest of Slovakia more frequently and consistently than trains. Check ticket for bus number *(č. aut.)* as several different buses may depart from the same stand simultaneously.

Hydrofoils: Lodná osobná doprava, Fajnorovo nábr. 2 (tel. 36 35 18; fax 536 22 31), along the river. A scenic alternative to trains for Danube destinations. To: **Vienna** (1½hr., 1-2 per day, round-trip 360AS, one-way 210AS); **Budapest** (4hr., 1-2 per day, round-trip 1000AS, one-way 680AS); **Devín Castle** (2 per day, round trip 90Sk, one-way 70Sk). Book tickets at least 48hr. in advance and show up at least 30min. early. Discounts for children. Major credit cards accepted. Summer only.

Local Transportation: All daytime trips on **trams** or **buses** require a 10Sk ticket good for one trip and sold at kiosks or the orange *automats* found at most bus stations. **Night buses** marked with black and orange numbers in the 500s require 2 10Sk tickets. They run at midnight and at 3am. Trams and buses run 4am-11pm. Most trams pass by Nám. SNP while most buses stop at the north base of Nový Most. Joyriding will cost you 1000Sk; authorities *do* check during the day. Tourist passes sold at some kiosks: 24hr. 45Sk, 48hr. 80Sk, 3 days 100Sk, 7 days 150Sk.

Taxis: Otto Taxi (tel. 54 77 75 77), BP (tel. 65 42 22 22), or FunTaxi (54 77 74 77).

Hitchhiking: Those hitching to **Vienna** cross most SNP and walk down Viedenská cesta. This road also heads to **Hungary** via Győr, although fewer cars head in that direction. A destination sign might help. Hitchers to **Prague** take bus #121 or 122 from the center to the Patronka stop. Hitching is legal (except on major highways) and common, but not recommended by *Let's Go*.

ORIENTATION

The **Dunaj** (Danube) runs east-west across Bratislava. The city's southern half consists of little more than a convention center, an amusement park, and miles of post-war high-rises. **Nový Most** (New Bridge), the spaceship-like bridge connecting the two sections, becomes the highway **Staromestská** to the north. The **castle** towers on a hill to the west, while the city center sits between **Nám. SNP**, the administrative center of town, and the river. Don't get off at the **Nové Mesto train station;** it's much farther from the center than **Hlavná stanica** (main station). From the station, take tram #1 to "Poštová" at Nám. SNP. From the bus station, take trolley bus #215 to the center, or turn right onto Mlynské nivy and walk 10min. to Dunajska which leads to Kamenné nám., the center of town.

Bratislava is in the midst of reforming its telephone system. Businesses often receive no more than three weeks' notice before their numbers change. The eight-digit numbers provided in these listings are the updated numbers and thus the least likely to change—but nothing is guaranteed.

PRACTICAL INFORMATION

TOURIST & FINANCIAL SERVICES

Tourist Offices: Bratislavská Informačná Služba (BIS), Klobučnicka 2 (tel. 54 43 37 15 and 54 43 43 70; fax 54 43 27 08; email bis@isnet.sk; www.isnet.sk/bis). Sells **maps** (28Sk), gives city tours, and books rooms for a 50Sk fee. Budget prices available July-Aug. only. (Singles 300Sk, at other times 900Sk). Open M-F 8am-7pm, Sa-Su 8:30am-1:30pm. Branch in the **train station annex** open June-Sept. M-F 9am-6:30pm, Sa-Su 10am-6:30pm; Oct.-May M-F 8:30am-6pm, Sa-Su 9am-2pm.

Embassies: Canada (honorary consulate), Kolárska 4 (tel. 36 12 77; fax 36 12 20). Open M and W 3-5pm. **South Africa,** Jančova 8 (tel. 54 41 15 82; fax 54 41 25 81). Open M-F 9am-noon. **U.K.,** Panská 16 (tel. 54 41 96 32; fax 54 41 00 02). Visa section open M-F 9-11am. Other sections by appointment only. **U.S.,** Hviezdoslavovo nám. 4 (tel. 54 43 08 61 or 54 43 33 38; after hours emergency tel. (0903) 70 36 66; fax 54 41 51 48). Open M-F 8am-4:30pm; visa section open M-F 8-11:30am. The nearest embassy for **Australians** and **New Zealanders** is in Vienna. In an emergency, they should contact the British Embassy, as should **Irish** citizens.

Currency Exchange: VÚB, Gorkého 9 (tel. 59 55 79 76; fax 59 55 80 90). Cashes traveler's checks for a 1% commission and handles MC/Visa **cash advances.** Open M-W and F 8am-5pm, Th 8am-noon. A **24hr. currency exchange machine** outside Bank Austria at Mostová 6 changes US$, DM, UK£, and several other western European currencies into Sk for no commission. **ATMs** are all over the center and at the train station. Virtually all of them accept Cirrus/MC/Maestro/Plus/Visa.

American Express: Tatratour, Mickiewiczova 2 (tel. 52 93 28 11; fax 31 78 88; e-mail: tttour01@isternet.sk). Changes cash for a 1% commission and traveler's checks for a 2% commission. Holds mail for AmEx members. Open M-F 9am-6pm, Sa 9am-noon.

LOCAL SERVICES & COMMUNICATION

Luggage Storage: Finicky lockers at the train and bus stations (5Sk). Better to use the luggage storage rooms. 10Sk at the bus station; 20Sk in train station. Open 6am-6pm.

English Bookstore: Big Ben Bookshop, through the arch at Michalská 1 (tel. 54 43 36 32; fax 54 43 36 92; email bigbenşinternet.sk; www.bigbenbookshop.com). Extensive selection. Open M-F 9am-6pm, Sa 10am-1pm. **Interpress Slovakia** (tel. 54 41 07 41), on the corner of Sedláska and Michalská, carries a large range of foreign press. Open M-Sa 7am-10pm, Su 10am-10pm.

Laundromat: INPROKOM, Laurinská 18 (tel. 36 32 10). Same-day service 7-48Sk per garment; slower service 4-30Sk. No self-service. Open M-F 11am-6pm.

Gay Help Line: tel. (090) 53 61 13 23. Open Tu and Th 6-8pm.

24hr. Pharmacy: The most central one is at Nám. SNP 20 (tel. 54 43 29 52), on the corner of Gorkého and Laurinská.

Internet Access: Klub Internet, Vajanského nábr. 2 (tel. 59 34 91 96; email tatrashop@tatrahome.sk). At the back of the National Museum on Múzejná. 7 speedy PCs (2Sk per min.). Open M-F 9am-9pm, Sa-Su noon-9am.

Post Office: Nám. SNP 35 (tel. 54 43 12 41). **Poste Restante** at counter #5. Open M-F 7am-8pm, Sa 7am-6pm, Su 9am-2pm. **Postal code:** 81000 Bratislava 1.

Telephones: On Nám. SNP, Františkánské nám., and behind the National Theater. **Phone code:** 7.

ACCOMMODATIONS

Bratislava's tourist agencies seem to rent out everything but retirement homes and orphanages to the summer's Vienna-bound crowds. During July and August, several dorms open up as hostels. Until then, good deals are hard to come by. Most cheap beds are near the station on the north side of town, a 20min. walk or 5min.

tram ride from the center. Pensions or **private rooms** (see **BIS,** above) provide a cheap and comfortable alternative.

Pension Gremium, Gorkého 11 (tel. 54 13 10 26; fax 54 43 06 53). Central location just off Hviezdoslavovo nám. Fluffy beds, sparkling private showers, and huge fans for those muggy Slovakian nights. Popular cafe downstairs. English-speaking reception. Singles 890Sk; doubles 1290Sk. Light breakfast included. Only one single and 4 doubles, so call several days ahead. Check-out 9am. MC/Visa.

Youth Hostel Bernolak, Bernolákova 1 (tel. 39 77 21; fax 39 77 24). From the train station, take bus #23, 74, or 218, or tram #3 to "Račianské Mýto." From the bus station, take bus #121 or 122. All rooms have baths. 300Sk per person; 10% discount with Euro26, HI, and ISIC. Check-out 9am. Open July 1-Sept. 15.

Výskumný Ústav Zváračský, Ponierska 17 (tel. 504 67 61). Take tram #3 from the train station to "Ponierska." A worker's hostel whose concrete-box exterior conceals sparse singles (350Sk) and doubles (700Sk). Shared bath. Check-out 9am. Curfew midnight.

Youth Hostel, Wilsonova 6 (tel. 397 735). See directions for YH Bernolak–Wilsonova runs parallel to Bernolákova. Remarkable only for the price: 2- to 4-bed dorms 180Sk per person; 30% discount with Euro26, HI, or ISIC. Check-out 9am. Open July-Aug.

Autocamping Zlaté Piesky, Senecká cesta 2 (tel. 25 73 73), in suburban Trnávka. Take tram #2 or 4 or bus #215 from the train station to the last stop and cross the footbridge. Campground and bungalows down by the lake, far from town. 100Sk per person, 90Sk per tent. Bungalow doubles 650Sk; triples 900Sk.

FOOD

While the city center is bursting with red-canopied cafes, virtually none serve food. A few of Bratislava's restaurants serve the region's spicy meat mixtures with west Slovakia's celebrated **Modra** wine. If that fails, you can always chow at one of the ubiquitous burger or chicken stands. Offering respite from both cost and confusion is **Tesco Potraviny,** Kamenné nám. 1, a grocery and department store. (Open M-W 8am-7pm, Th 8am-8pm, F 8am-9pm, Sa 8am-5pm, Su 9am-5pm).

Prašná Bašta, Zámočnícka 11 (tel. 54 43 49 57). Dark alcoves with funky sculptures inside and a leafy terrace outside. Ocassional live music. Excellent traditional Slovak dishes 88-175Sk. Open daily 11am-11pm.

Cafe London, Panská 17 (tel. 54 43 12 61), in the British Council's courtyard. For those saturated with sheep's cheese, Cafe London offers the respite of good, old-fashioned sandwiches and other light meals (52-118Sk). Open M-F 9am-9pm.

Vegetarian Jedáleň, Laurinská 8. A cafeteria-style lunch spot popular with both local businessfolk and young Slovak herbivores. Menu changes daily and features such dishes as vegetable risotto and sheep's cheese *halušky* (minus the bacon). Prices hover around 50-100Sk. Open M-F 11am-3pm.

Antica Gelateria del Corso, Michalská 14-16 (tel. 54 4193 38). Great service, with a large selection of Italian entrees (60-250Sk). Open daily 10am-midnight.

YOU WANT FRIES WITH THAT? The only thing less comprehensible to Westerners than a Slovakian menu is a menu at one of Bratislava's many burger stands. A *syrový burger* (cheeseburger) costs less than a *hamburger so syrom* (hamburger with cheese) because, as the stand owner will explain with humiliatingly clear logic, a cheeseburger is made of cheese—*only* cheese. A *pressburger*, named after Bratislava's former moniker Pressburg, consists of bologna on a bun, and hamburgers are actually ham. Everything comes boiled, except, of course, the cheese.

SIGHTS

AROUND NÁMESTÍ SNP

Nám. SNP, commemorating the bloody but ultimately unsuccessful Slovak National Uprising against the fascist regime (see **History,** p. 670), together with the adjoining Kamenné nám., comprise the heart of the modern city. A walk left down Klobučnícka leads to **Primaciálné nám.** To the left, on Klobučnícka, is the main tourist office, and a CD shop that doubles as the entrance to a museum devoted to the 19th-century Austrian composer and pianist **Johann Nepomuk Hummel.** *(Open Tu-Su 1-5pm. 15Sk.)* On the square itself stands the Neoclassical **Primate's Palace** (Primaciálny Palác), dating from 1781. In 1805, Napoleon and Austrian Emperor Franz I signed the Peace of Pressburg (the German name for Bratislava) there, two weeks after the decisive French victory at Austerlitz. Buy tickets on the second floor and head upstairs to see the **Hall of Mirrors** (Zrkadlová Sieň), where it all happened, as well as some 17th-century English tapestries and a small Baroque church. *(Primaciálne nám. 1. Open Tu-Su 10am-5pm. 20Sk, children under 15 free.)*

A walk down Klobučnícka from the center and straight through Primaciálné nám. ends at **Hlavné nám.,** a popular spot for tourists perusing souvenir stands. In the early evening, the square is overrun with loud 14-year-olds and crusty bongo players. Hlavné nám. is also home to the **Town History Museum** (Muzeum História Mesta). You don't need a ticket to see the wonderful 1:500 scale model of 1945-55 Bratislava just inside. The rest of the collection includes a battery of untranslated Slovak notices describing the medieval town and a series of galleries illustrating Bratislava's development. *(Hlavné nám. 1, in the Old Town Hall (Stará Radnica). Tel. 33 34 01. Open Tu-F 10am-5pm, Sa-Su 11am-6pm. 25Sk, students 10Sk.)*

St. Martin's Cathedral (Dóm sv. Martina) is a fairly unspectacular Gothic church where the kings of Hungary were crowned for three centuries. It is now undergoing renovations to restore some of its former glory. *(From Nám. SNP take a left down Michalská, a right down Prepoštská, and a left down Kapitulská.)* Nearby, the 13th-century **St. Michael's Tower** (Michalská Brána) is the only preserved gateway from the town's medieval fortifications. Trot up to the top for a view of the city. *(Open M and W-F 10am-5pm, Sa-Su 11am-6pm. Last entry ½hr. before closing. 20Sk.)* The **Museum of Jewish Culture** (Muzeum Židovskej Kultúry) preserves valuable fragments of a nearly vanished population: **Schlossberg,** the old Jewish quarter, was bulldozed in the name of "progress." *(Židovská 17. Cross the freeway on the far side of St. Martin's via the overpass. Tel. 54 41 85 07. Open M-F and Su 11am-5pm. Last entry 4:30pm. 50Sk.)* **Grassalkovich Palác** is the grandest of the city's many Hungarian aristocratic residences. So grand, in fact, that former Premier Mečiar turned it into the **Presidential Palace.** Behind the castle, the **Grassalkovich Gardens** once offered escape from the noisy chaos of the square, but now that the Premier lives there, the entire complex is closed to the public. *(Hodžovo nám. 1. Head up Poštová from Nám. SNP.)*

AROUND HVIEZDOSLAVOVO NÁMESTÍ

More than a square, Hviezdoslavovo nám. is actually a park surrounded by 19th-century architecture. The 1886 **Slovak National Theater** (Slovenské Národné Divadlo) stands at the square's end nearest the center. The nearby **Nám. L'udovita Štura** celebrates L'udovit' Štur, who codified the Slovak language in the 19th century as distinct from Czech (see **Literature & Arts,** p. 671). *(Walk down Štúrova from Kamenné nám., take a right onto Jesenského, and then a left onto Mostová.)* The **Slovak National Museum** (Slovenské Národná Muzeum) houses the region's archaeological finds, including casts of local Neanderthal skeletons. *(Vajanského nábr. 2. Take a right off Štúrova onto Jesenského, a left onto Palackého, another left onto Kúpemna, and still another left onto Vajanského. Tel. 59 34 91 11. Open Tu-Su 9am-5pm. 20Sk, students 10Sk. Special exposition tickets 20Sk for 30min.)* The nearby **Slovak National Gallery** displays well-preserved sculpture, frescoes, and paintings from the Gothic and Baroque periods. The garden outside is free and showcases a combination of bizarre and beautiful modern sculptures. *(Rázusovo nábr. 2. Follow* *the directions to the National Museum but take a right on Vajanského, continuing down to Rázusovo nábr. Tel. 533 42 76. Open Tu-Su 10am-6pm. 25Sk, students 5Sk, children under 6 free.)* **New Bridge** (Nový Most), whose reins are held by a giant flying saucer, can be reached most directly by continuing down Rázusovo nábr. from the National Gallery. *(10Sk to climb to the top.)*

BRATISLAVA CASTLE (BRATISLAVSKÝ HRAD)

Visible from the Danube's banks to the center's historic squares, the four-towered Bratislava Castle is Bratislava's defining landmark. Of strategic importance for more than a millennium, the castle's heyday came in the 18th century, when Austrian Empress Maria Theresa held court there. The castle was destroyed by fire in 1811 and by bombs during WWII; what is left today is largely communist-era restoration, which *almost* succeeded in capturing the castle's former glory. The view of the Danube passing from Austria through Slovakia and into Hungary is more impressive than the castle itself. The **Historical Museum** (Historické Muzeum), inside, displays temporary exhibits from the Slovak National Museum. *(Open Tu-Su 9am-5pm. 30Sk, students 15Sk.)*

DEVÍN CASTLE

Slovakia's best-loved castle ruins perch on a promontory 9km west of downtown Bratislava. The fortress itself overlooks the confluence of the mighty Morava and Dunaj rivers. Fortified by Slavs in the 9th century, this large outcrop has since fallen under the control of Magyars, Napoleon, and finally, after years of neglect, Slovaks. Under Communist control, the castle grew to symbolize totalitarianism, sheltering sharpshooters who were ordered to fire at anyone walking the beach alongside the Morava, which marks the Austrian border. Paths wind through the rocks and ruins, while a **museum** shows off local archaeological finds. *(Take bus #29 to Devín from below Nový Most and get off at the Strbska stop. Continue on the main road 200m in the same direction, and turn left just before the bridge onto the second, unmarked street by the white stone fence. The parking lot at the end of this street leads to the castle. Museum tel. 65 73 01 05. Open Apr. 24-Oct. 31 Tu-Su 10am-5pm, last entrance 4:30pm. 40Sk, students, seniors, and children 10Sk; museum 50Sk, students, seniors, and children 10Sk.)*

ENTERTAINMENT

For film, concert, and theater schedules, get a copy of *Kám v Bratislave* at BIS (see **Tourist Offices,** p. 678). Although it's entirely in Slovak, the info is easy to decipher. **Slovenská Filharmonia** plays regularly at Palackého ul. 2; the box office is around the corner on Medená (tel. 54 43 33 51; open M-Tu and Th-F 1-7pm, W 8am-2pm). The Filharmonia as well as most theaters vacation in July and August. Tickets to the **Národné Divadlo** (National Theater) are sold at the box office at Laurinská 20. (Open M-F noon-6pm. Tickets from 50Sk.) A dozen **cinemas** are scattered across the city; unfortunately, most films are dubbed into Slovak. In late September and early October, the **Bratislava Music Festival** brings dozens of acts to the city.

NIGHTLIFE

Alligator Club, Laurinská 7. Bratislava's sleekest 20-somethings gather at this basement pseudo-diner to hear live rock and blues nightly at 7pm. Excellent selection of mixed drinks (80-120Sk). Open M-F 10am-midnight, Sa 11am-midnight, Su 11am-10pm.

Dubliner, Sedlarská 6 (tel. 54 41 07 06). Bratislava's *ersatz* Irish pub grows lively after dinner. And instead of the usual 1916 proclamation, an *Irish Post* from 1939 charts Hitler's grab for Czechoslovakia. Expensive Guinness and Kilkenny (75Sk); local brands are also pricey (45Sk). Open M-Sa 10am-1am, Su 11am-midnight.

Krater, Vysoka 14 (tel. 31 74 08). When this eatery turns into a disco over the weekend, Bratislava gets up and dances. Cover 20Sk. Disco open F-Su 8pm-3am.

CENTRAL SLOVAKIA

Rail connections are poor but journeys spectacular in the hills of central Slovakia, where medieval miners once dug into the richest gold and silver deposits in Europe. Nestled between Bratislava and the snow-capped Tatra mountains, the region is now a barely-touristed blend of Slovak folk tradition and the endless possibilities for hiking, biking, fishing, hang-gliding, and virtually any other activity you can think of. It's tempting to pass Central Slovakia by for her more glamorous neighbors to the northeast, but those who stop to explore the wealth of history and outdoor opportunities will be extravagantly rewarded.

BANSKÁ BYSTRICA

Like the hills surrounding this Renaissance town, Banská Bystrica (BAN-ska bis-TREE-tsah) is lush and relaxing. The old town center is a lively, car-free square, filled with dozens of outdoor cafes (serving surprisingly good coffee), some of the best folk-art boutiques in Slovakia, and mellow locals strolling with ice cream in hand. While the town center is a fine place to relax, the surrounding hills make a magnificent playground for biking, hang-gliding, and light hiking. Adventure seekers will likely find Banská Bystrica boring, but its burbling fountains and beautiful vistas make it an ideal place to rest up en route to or from the Tatras.

ORIENTATION & PRACTICAL INFORMATION. The railway lines around Banská Bystrica provide gorgeous rides through the hills and valleys—it's just a shame the connections are so poor. **Trains** (tel. 414 21 32) run to **Bratislava** (4hr., 2 per day, 169Sk) and **Košice** (4hr., 1 per day, 178Sk). **Buses** (tel. 09 84 22 23 33) go to **Bratislava** (4hr., 21 per day, 160Sk) and **Liptovský Mikuláš** (1½hr., 6 per day, 64Sk) and **Košice** (4hr., 5 per day, 160Sk). The bus terminal is next door to the train station, where **24hr. luggage lockers** cost 5Sk. To get to the town center, walk past the gas station behind the bus station and cross cesta K. Smrečine into the gardens. Take the pedestrian underpass under the highway and continue along cesta K. Smrečine; a left onto Horná at the glass pyramid bookstore brings you to Nám. SNP, the town center (15min.). Alternatively, the city bus (there's only one and it's a minibus) takes people right to the city center. Get off at the Nám. S. Moyzesa stop (5Sk). **Kultúrne a Informačné Stredisko (KIS),** Nám. S. Moyzesa 26 (tel./fax 543 69; email pkobb@isternet.sk), between Horná and Nám. SNP, has leaflets about cultural events, free maps, and info on Banská Bystrica's accommodations, and if asked they will book private rooms at no fee. (Open June 15-Aug. 31 and Dec. 15-Mar. 15 M-F 9am-7pm, Sa 8am-noon; the rest of the year M-F 9am-5pm). **VÚB,** Nám. Slobody 1 (tel. 450 55 11) and Dolná 17 (tel. 450 34 88) off Nám. SNP, **exchanges currency** and cashes traveler's checks for a 1% commission. (Open M-W and F 7:30am-4:30pm, Th 7:30am-noon.) There's a Cirrus/MC/Visa **ATM** outside the tourist office. **Interpress Slovakia,** Dolná 19, sells English-language journals and newspapers. (Open M-F 7am-8pm, Sa 8am-2pm, Su 11am-6pm.) Several **pharmacies** operate around Nám. SNP, sometimes posting addresses of late-closing places in the window; try **Lekáreň pod Branon** through the passageway at Nám. SNP 14. (Open M-F 8am-6pm.) **Klub Internet,** Horná Strieborná 8, has 3 fast computers for internet access. (Open M-F 9am-7pm, Sa 9am-noon, 2pm-7pm, Su 2pm-7pm. 1hr. 50Sk.) The **post office** is at Horná 1 (tel. 415 26 37), just off Nám. SNP next to the tourist office. (Open M-F 8am-8pm, Sa 8am-noon, Su 8-10am.) A **card phone** stands outside; coin-operated phones are inside the building. More phones can be found under the arch at the intersection of Narodná ul. and Nám. SNP. **Postal code:** 97400. **Phone code:** (0)88.

ACCOMMODATIONS & FOOD. Summer visitors should ask **KIS** (see above) about temporary **hostel** arrangements. The best option is to get them to book **private rooms**, which are often comfortable *and* affordable. Failing this, **Hotel Turist ATC,** Tajovského 68 (tel. 423 07 45), is a year-round hostel providing beds in minimalist dorms 15min. from the center. Turn right on Horná Strieborna from the far end of Nám. SNP opposite the clock tower, then head left down J.G. Tajovského. (200Sk per person.) **Hotel Národný dom,** Národná 11 (tel. 412 37 37; fax 412 57 86), off Nám. SNP, is admirably central, and thoughtfully provides its guests with small metal shoehorns. Comforters are super-fluffy but showers are rather rusty. There's a cafe in the building and the opera house is next door; things get noisy at night. (Singles 700Sk; doubles 1080Sk; triples 1380Sk; all with shower except for two triples at 740Sk. Visa/MC/AmEx.)

Tops for food is **Copaline Baguette,** Dolná 1 (tel. 412 58 68), which stuffs fresh French bread with ham, cheese, eggs, shrimp, salmon, and anything else they can think up—just point at the *sendvič* you want (40-90Sk), and for dessert try the tasty chocolate *pudink* (16Sk) while you're at it. (Open M-F 6:30am-midnight, Sa-Su 8am-midnight.) **Slovenská pivnica,** Lazovná 18 (tel. 415 50 36), off Nám. SNP, serves traditional Slovak dishes (36-78Sk) in an underground bunker. (Open M-Sa 11am-10pm.) Find groceries at **Prior** on the corner of Horná and cesta K. Smrečine, by the pyramidal bookstore. (Open M-F 8am-7pm, Sa 8am-1pm. MC/Visa.)

SIGHTS. A cluster of the town's oldest buildings stand on Nám. Š. Moyzesa. The tourist office is on the ground floor of the **barbakan** fortification in the middle of the square; next door, the restored **Pretórium** (tel. 412 48 64)—once the town hall, now the **Galleria**—displays three floors of local avant-garde art. (Open Tu-F 9am-5pm, Sa-Su 10am-4pm. 20Sk, students 5Sk.) The large church behind the Galleria and barbakan fortification is the Romanesque **Church of the Virgin Mary** (Kostol Panny Márie), which sports a fine Baroque ceiling and an even finer Gothic altarpiece by Majstr Pavel of Levoča (see **Levoča,** p. 689). Wandering onto **Nám. SNP** from the tourist office, the **Museum of Central Slovakia** (Stredoslovenské Múzeum), Nám. SNP 4, has a historical collection well-presented in a restored Renaissance house. (Open M-F 9am-noon and 1-5pm, Su 1-5pm. 15Sk, 8Sk students. English language pamphlet 3Sk.)

Two exhibitions outside the square deserve visits. Go left from the tourist office down Horná to get to **Skuteckého dom,** a restored 19th-century neo-Renaissance villa at Horná 55 (tel. 412 54 50) that displays the state's collection of paintings by local artist Dominik Skutecký (1849-1921), a dogged realist in the age of Impressionism. (Open Tu-Su 10am-5pm. 10Sk, students 4Sk, children 2Sk. Ask the staff to lend you the glossy English catalog.) The **Museum of the Slovak National Uprising** (Múzeum Slovenského Národného Povstania) is in an oddly shaped building in the gardens of Kapitulská. Banská Bystrica was the rebels' headquarters during the eight weeks of fighting that began when Nazi forces entered puppet ally Slovakia's territory on August 29, 1944 (see **History,** p. 670). The museum charts the course of the failed insurrection and the grim Nazi reprisals that followed, and sets the SNP in the wider context of WWII, the "independent" Slovak state of Josef Tiso, and the deportation of the Slovak Jews organized by his regime. No written English help is given, but any knowledge of WWII helps make sense of the exhibits. Turn right from the tourist office into Nám. SNP, then an immediate left onto Kapitulská. (Open Tu-Su 9am-6pm. 20Sk, students 10Sk.)

ENTERTAINMENT. For more active entertainment, Banská Bystrica offers myriad outdoor adventures, including bike rental, hiking, horseback riding, and rock climbing. To reach **Spedik-Jahn** (tel. 419 73 80), a travel agent in the village Tajov that rents bikes (2hr. 60Sk, 4hr. 40Sk, 8hr. 30Sk, 1wk. 900Sk), take the city bus from the bus station to **Tajov.** The bus runs hourly during the week and every two hours on weekends (7 km, 10Sk). Popular hiking trails run from the ski area Donovaly. Take the bus from the bus station to **Donovaly** (25 km, 20Sk). **Škola Paragliding Donovaly,** Mistriky 230 (tel. 419 97 32), runs a paragliding school for around 2400Sk, as does **Pegas Paragliding,** na Uhlisten 26 (tel. 411 36 84; 3300Sk; 10% student discount). Call ahead for both. **Pony Farma-Suchý Urch,** Jazdiareň Uhlisko (tel. 415 45 90), offers horseback riding for all levels.

Cinemas are the primary evening entertainment in Banská Bystrica. Almost all show Hollywood flicks and almost all are subtitled in Slovak—look for *titulky* on the cinema's posters around town to verify subtitling. The two main cinemas are **Kino Hviezda,** Skuteckého 3 (tel. 412 35 15 or 414 20 74; cinema.web.sk/kino), and **Art Kino,** Nám. Slobody 3 (tel. 415 24 66). Tickets are 35-60Sk depending on popularity and date of release. Otherwise, **Piváreň Perla,** Horná 52, is a lively local favorite where copper vats of *Perla* bubble right behind the bar while locals chain-smoke in front of it. Both barflies and businessfolk enjoy the quality microbrew (12Sk) on communal tables and benches. Ignore the stares; don't be shy about scooting right in. (Open M-Sa 8am-11:30pm.) The town's well-known **Rázcesti puppet theater,** Kollárova 18 (tel. 412 41 93), offers popular Slovak shows. (Box office open Sept.-June M-F 2-4pm. Tickets 30-50Sk.)

NEAR BANSKÁ BYSTRICA: BOJNICE

Unlike other castles in Slovakia, which tend to be disappointing ruins or reconstructions, the **chateau** at Bojnice remains an impressive fairy-tale of turrets, caves, princesses, and spiraling staircases. Originally a 12th-century wooden fortress for a Benedictine Monastery, the castle was traded between noble families for 700 years until Count Jan Pálffy inherited it in 1852. Bojnice today is a result of Pálffy's lifelong effort to "remodel" the palace in the style of a Loire-valley chateau; the castle easily outdoes any other in Slovakia in both opulence and splendor. The guided tour visits galleries, gardens, hunting rooms, bedrooms, a citadel, a chapel, a crypt, a cave, medieval washrooms, and the magnificent Oriental and Golden Halls. You'll be mesmerized, if not by the stunning rooms and vistas of the basin region, then by the costumed noblewomen who haunt the hallways and turrets. (Open May-Sept. Tu-Su 9am-5pm; Oct.-Apr. Tu-Su 10am-3pm. Slovak tour every 15min. except noon-12:30pm; English tour whenever there are 10 people. Slovak tour 50Sk, English 100Sk, students 60Sk. Cameras 30Sk. Excellent English guidebook 7Sk.) If you prefer real ghosts, come in early May for the **International Festival of Ghosts and Spirits.**

After romping about, satisfy your inner child (or your real children) by heading next door to the **Bojnice Zoo,** the oldest in Slovakia. Admire the bears, zebras, and...donkeys. (Open daily June-Aug. 7am-7pm; Sept.-Oct. 7am-4:30pm; Nov.-Feb. 7am-3:30pm; Mar.-May 7am-6pm. 35Sk, students 20Sk. Video camera 10Sk; camera 5Sk.) A water-park, **Kupalisko Čajka,** sits just up the road from the castle on ul. Zámok headnig away from the zoo. Huge indoor and outdoor pools are usually packed with swarms of children and bikinied pre-teens, but offer cheap and refreshing relief from the sweltering heat. (Open daily 9am-7pm. 30Sk, students and children 15Sk; 2-4pm 25Sk, 10Sk; after 4pm 10Sk, 5Sk.) There are only a few restaurants in Bojnice; the best is **Pizzeria Charlie,** Hurbanovo nám. (tel. 543 17 28), with good pizza (69-112Sk), big salads (50-100Sk), and a huge selection of excellent ice cream sundaes (50Sk); beer is 35Sk. (Open daily 10am-midnight.) **Phone code:** (0)862.

GETTING THERE. The only way to reach Bojnice is by **bus** via **Prievidza.** Buses to Prievidza run from: **Banská Bystrica** (1-2hr., hourly, 85Sk); **Bratislava** (2½hr., 12 per day, 120Sk); **Liptovský Mikuláš** (3½hr., 2 per day, 110Sk); and **Prešov** (6hr., 2 per day, 150Sk). From the Prievidza bus station, catch local bus #3 (stop: "Bojnice-Kúpelé") or #9 (stop: "Bojnice-Čajka"). Both cost 6Sk and stop first at Hurbanovo nám., Bojnice's center, and then at the castle (10min.). From the Prievidza bus station, turn left onto ul. A. Hlinku, which goes into ul. Hviezdoslavova. Turn right onto Pribinovo nám. to reach Nám. Slobody, the center of Prievidza.

ŽILINA

Although there isn't much to do in Žilina (ZHI-li-na), its arcaded squares and position on a major railway make it the ideal base for an adventure in the nearby Malá Fatra mountains. **Selinan,** a travel agency-*cum*-tourist office at Burianova Medzierka 4 (tel. 62 14 78, fax 62 31 71), is on a small street parallel to Farská ul., off Mariánske nám. They sell VKÚ hiking **maps** of the nearby mountains. (Open May 15-July M-F 8am-

6pm; Aug. M-F 8am-5pm; Sept.-May 14 M-F 8am-4:30pm.) **VÚB,** on the corner of Nám. A. Hlinku and ul. Narodná, **exchanges currency** and cashes **traveler's checks** for a 1% commission. (Open M-W and F 8am-noon and 1-4pm, Th 8am-noon.) A Cirrus/Visa/MC **ATM** operates outside the main entrance of the huge Tesco on Nám. A. Hlinku.The best place to stay is at the **Hospital Hostel,** ul. Vojtecha Spanyola 43 (tel. 453 27). Spacious singles with balcony and bath are a meagre 200Sk and only 10min. from the center and 15min. from the train station. From the train station, turn left onto ul. Hviezdoslava. Turn right onto ul. L. Maja at the bus station. Just after this turns onto Veľká Okružná ul., turn left onto ul. Vojtecha Spanyola. Don't go through the main hospital gates; instead, walk on about 50m. Past the bus stop, there is a small path on the left that goes straight to the hostel. (Check-out 9am. No curfew.) **Bagetéria,** Nám. A. Hlinku 5, has a range of meat and vegetarian baguettes (27-39Sk); just point to the sandwich you want. (Open M-Sa 7am-9pm, Su 9am-9pm). To stock up on carbos for hiking, **Tesco** (tel. 63 07 34) on Nám. A. Hlinku has groceries on the ground floor. (Open M-F 8am-8pm, Sa 8am-6pm, Su 8am-2pm.)

GETTING AWAY. The **train station** sits on ul. Hviezdoslava. Trains run to: **Bratislava** (2½hr., 14 per day, 155Sk) and **Košice** (3-4hr., 7 per day, 180Sk). The **bus station** is almost opposite the train station on the corner of ul. Hviezdoslava and ul. L. Maja. **Buses** head to: **Bratislava** (3hr., 5 per day, 155Sk) and **Banská Bystrica** (2hr., 17 per day, 70Sk). To get to the town center, walk straight out of the train station and through the underpass; ul. Narodná stretches up from the underpass to the new town square, Nám. A. Hlinku. Go straight through the square, head up the stairs to Farská ul., and you'll arrive in Mariánske nám., the old town square.

NEAR ŽILINA: MALÁ FATRA

The Malá Fatra mountains offer panoramic views, deep valleys, and amazing waterfalls at every height. The range is a wonderland of natural splendor for everyone, whether you're out for a day hike or planning on staying at *chaty* along the way (beds less than 150Sk).

While there are higher mountains in the range, the most excitement can be found on the slopes of **Veľký Rozsutec** (1610m). The **best hike** in the region begins not in Žilina but in **Štefanová.** Take the Terchova-Vrátna bus from platform #10 in Žilina to Štefanová (26Sk) and follow the yellow trail to **Sedlo Vrchpodžiar.** A right onto the blue trail just after the saddle goes straight up a tumbling mass of waterfalls and rapids known as **Horne diery.** The trail is laddered and stained most of the way, but it is not an ascent for the fainthearted. Continue along the blue trail to **Sedlo Medzirozsutce;** a left onto the red trail leads to the summit, with a few helpful chains along the way. Descend by continuing on the red trail until it intersects with the green trail near **Sedlo Medziholie.** A right onto the green leads back down to Štefanova (round trip 5hr.).

At 1708 meters, **Veľký Kriván** is the highest peak in the range. Take the bus from platform #10 in Žilina to **Terchova, Vrátna** (26Sk), which takes you through the village of Terchová and Vrátna Valley, considered the most beautiful valley in Slovakia. Get off at **Chata Vrátna** at the end of the road; the green trail will take you straight up to **Snilovské Sedlo.** Following the green trail to the red brings you to the summit (3hr.). The red trail travels the entire ridge, so any combination of mountains can be planned. One takes you along 4km of beautiful vistas (and sharp winds) on the ridge line to **Poludňový grúň** (1460m); from the green trail at Snilovské Sedlo, turn left onto the red trail. Once at Poludňový grúň, take a left onto the yellow trail to descend back to Chata Vrátna (round-trip 8hr.). A chairlift also operates daily 8:30am-4:30pm, weather permitting. (90Sk, students 50Sk.) Take the lift from Chata Vrátna to its end just before Snilovské Sedlo to reach the green trail. Continue a bit farther on the green and then take a right onto the red to reach the Veľký Kriván summit. To descend, just hop back on the lift, or backtrack to the green trail and follow it down to Chata Vrátna. Dress warmly for all these hikes, as the wind above tree level is cold and gusty. And don't leave Žilina without VKÚ map 110 from Selinan (70Sk; see p. 684).

LIPTOVSKÝ MIKULÁŠ

Despite its fame as the place where Slovak folk hero Juraj Jánošik was stuck on a spike in 1713, Liptovský Mikuláš (LIP-tov-skee MEE-koo-lash) is an unexciting town with a drab modern center. It is, however, a good base for trips to the nearby Nízké Tatry (Low Tatras), which are much less crowded than their taller Carpathian cousins farther north, and only a short bus ride from Liptovský Mikuláš. If you're determined to see something in town stop by the **Jewish synagogue** (Židovská synagogá) on Hollého. Outside by the door is a wrenching bronze memorial to the 885 local Jews murdered by the Nazis: their names are recorded in the Múzeum Janka Kráľa. (Drop by the Múzeum to be let in the synagogue.) Finding a bed shouldn't be hard. Ask the tourist office about private rooms in town, or if workers' hostels are taking tourists. (Hostels average 150-200Sk per person; pensions 200-400Sk per person.) Otherwise, try the central **Hotel Kriváň,** Štúrova 5 (tel. 552 24 14; fax 552 42 43), directly across the square from the tourist office. Tidy, if miniscule, rooms. (Singles 250Sk, with bath or shower 350Sk; doubles 350Sk, 500Sk; triples 400Sk, 750Sk.) Enjoy Slovak TV in some triples, for a little extra. Get chocolate bars and other hiking snacks at the grocery in the **Prior** building on Nám. Mieru. (Open M-F 8am-7pm, Sa 7am-1pm.) The tourist office, **Informačné Centrum,** Nám. Mieru 1 (tel. 552 24 18; fax 55 14 48; email infolm@trynet.sk), on the northern side of the square in the Dom Služieb complex, sells local hiking maps (ask for VKÚ sheet 122 or 123; 78Sk; open June 15-Sept. 15 and Dec. 15-Mar. 31 M-F 8am-7pm, Sa 8am-2pm, Su noon-6pm; Sept. 16-Dec. 14 and Apr.-June 14 M-F 9am-6pm, Sa 8am-noon). **VÚB,** Štúrova 19 (tel. 552 23 57), exchanges currency, cashes traveler's checks for a 1% commission, and has a Cirrus/EC/MC **24hr. ATM.** (Open M-W and F 7:30am-4:30pm, Th 7:30am-noon.) **Postal code:** 03101. **Phone code:** (0)849

GETTING AWAY. The **train station** (tel. 552 28 42) lies on Štefánikova, and the **bus station** (tel. 552 36 38) is the asphalt lot directly outside. **Trains** run to: **Poprad** (1hr., frequent, 30-50Sk); **Košice** (2hr., frequent, 120Sk); and **Bratislava** (4hr., 7 per day, 192Sk). **Buses** run to: **Poprad** (1-2hr., 5 per day, 46Sk), **Košice** (3-4hr., 2 per day, 140Sk); and **Bratislava** (4hr., 4 per day, 210-230Sk). The **town center** is an easy 10min. walk from the bus and train terminals. Follow Štefánikova toward the gas station at the bus station's far end, then turn right onto Hodžu.

NEAR LIPTOVSKÝ MIKULÁŠ: NÍZKE TATRY

Liptovský Mikuláš is a popular base for hiking in the **Nízke Tatry,** or Low Tatras. Despite their name, these mountains are not to be underestimated: their highest peaks still reach well above the tree-line. If your first instinct is to get to the top of the tallest peak in the range—**Mt. Ďumbier,** at 2043m—here's one way to do it. Catch an early bus from platform #11 at Liptovský Mikuláš's bus station to **Liptovský Ján Kúpele** (20min., hourly, 10Sk) and hike the blue trail up the Štiavnica river and onto the **Ďumbierske Sedlo** by **Gen. M.R. Štefanika Hut** (Chata generála M.R. Štefanika; about 5hr.). Then follow the red trail to the ridge, which leads to the summit (1½hr.). Going back down the ridge and following the red sign leads to the neighboring peak, **Chopok** (2024m, the second-highest in the range). At the hut there, **Kammená chata,** you might be able to snag a bed (120Sk) as well as a *Martiner* draft beer (30Sk) or a mug of tea (10Sk). From Chopok, it's a mellow walk down the blue trail to the bus stop at **Jasná** (1½hr.), but you may prefer the view from the chairlift. (Runs weather permitting June-Sept. 8:30am-4pm; Dec.-Mar. 8:30am-3:30pm. 85Sk.) For more on hiking, see **Camping & the Outdoors,** p. 38.

For a shorter hike, catch a bus from platform #3 at Liptovský Mikuláš to the "Jasná" stop at Hotel Ski, 1km downhill from Jasná (30min., 15 per day, 12Sk), where signs point up the mountain toward the chairlift (times and prices same as above). Once at the top, follow the blue trail to the summit (1hr.)—watch out for wind gusts. To get down, take the chairlift or follow the blue trail to Jasná Hotel Grand, where a bus will whiz you back to Liptovský Mikuláš. With the VKÚ maps (see **Informačné Centrum,** p. 686), it's possible to compose endless variations on the Chopok-Ďumbier theme; all the trails are well-marked and easy to follow.

WHERE'S JURAJ'S EPIC FILM? A cross between Robin Hood and William Wallace, Juraj Jánošík (1688-1713) is legendary throughout central Slovakia. Juraj's saga begins when his father was beaten to death by their landowner for taking time off to properly bury his wife. This horror prompted Jánošík to take to the hills as a champion of the people. For two years, Jánošík and his loyal followers stole from the rich and gave to the poor, until he was caught by a lord in 1713. He was sentenced to death by hanging—from a hook through his rib cage—in the central square of Liptovský Mikuláš. Terchová, Jánošík's birthplace, is on the way from Žilina to Vrátna Dolina. As the bus turns toward the mountains you'll see a huge aluminum statue of the hero overlooking the town.

Demänovská ľadová jaskyňa, an **ice cave** midway between Liptovský Mikuláš and Jasná, is yet another treasure. Take the bus from Liptovský Mikuláš to Jasná at stop: "Kamenná chata" (15min.), and follow signs up the hill to a valley view and the cave entrance (15min.). The cave features the bones of prehistoric bears and signatures of 18th- and 19th-century visitors. The last part of the tour brings visitors to a frozen waterfall draped beneath bleached stone. Be sure to bring a sweater—it is an *ice* cave, after all. (Open May 15-May 30 and Sept. 9am-2pm; June-Aug. 9am-4pm. 40min. tours leave every 1-2hr. 80Sk, students 60Sk.)

Also ask at the Liptovský Mikuláš tourist office (see p. 686) for info on watersports, paragliding, horseback riding, and rock climbing in Demänovská valley. **Rent bikes** from Cycloturistika. (1hr. 60Sk, 4hr. 220Sk, 1 day 300Sk; 4hr. personal guide 500Sk.) Ask at the tourist office for Orava Litpov Horehronie, a hiking and cycling **map** and guide book (125Sk). Windsurfing, boating, canoeing, and swimming—often with instruction—are available at **Autocamping Liptovský Trnovec,** (tel./fax 973 00), 6km from Liptovský Mikuláš on Liptovský Mara lake. The tourist office can offer more details.

SPIŠ

Most tourists know Spiš (SPISH) only as neighbor of the Tatras and home of Kežmarok. But to the east, flatter land leads to tiny towns where villagers walk their cows and the lawnmower has not yet replaced the scythe. In the minds of romantics, the white sprawling ruins of Spišský hrad rule the region, and Levoča, home of the world's tallest Gothic altar, bustles with the wealthy merchants who placed it there. For centuries an autonomous province of Hungary with a large Saxon population, Spiš made its last bid for independence in 1918, before being folded up into Czechoslovakia until the Velvet Revolution in 1993. Today, the region boasts one of Slovakia's most exhilarating national parks (Slovenský Raj) and a collection of churches and ruins that merit exploration.

KEŽMAROK

Prosperous Kežmarok (KEZH-ma-rok) has always been marked by conflict: the townsfolk against the rulers in the castle, the Catholics against the Protestants, and everybody against neighboring Levoča. As late as 1918, the townsfolk proclaimed their own republic, but were quickly incorporated into the new Czechoslovak state. These struggles manifest themselves in Kežmarok's finest buildings—three remarkable churches and the old castle—making a day here a pleasant visit. Cheap accommodations and a train line to Poprad also make it a feasible base for exploring the nearby peaks of the Vysoké Tatry.

ORIENTATION & PRACTICAL INFORMATION. **Trains** run to and from **Poprad** (20-30min., 12 per day, 9Sk) from the stately, bright yellow station (tel. 32 89) northwest of town. **Buses** leave from under blue-and-yellow canopies opposite the trains for: **Levoča** (1hr., 11 per day, 29Sk); **Starý Smokovec** (40min., 17 per day, 22Sk); **Tatranská Lomnica** (30min., 28 per day, 14Sk); and **Poprad** (20-30min., several per hr., 12Sk). To get to the center, cross the footbridge (*not* the main transport bridge) at the base of the train station and follow MUDr. Alexandra to the main **Hlavné nám.,** where the Baroque tower of the town hall *(radnica)* rises above two-story dwellings. Hiding in an alcove at Hlavné nám. 46, the tourist office **Kežmarská Informačna Agentura** (tel./fax 52 40 47; email: infokk@kk.sinet.sk) sells a handy **map** of town (12Sk) and books private rooms and pensions for 200-250Sk. (Open in summer M-F 8:30am-5pm, Sa-Su 9am-2pm; off-season M-F 8:30am-5pm, Sa 9am-2pm.) **Slovenská Sporiteľňa,** MUDr. Alexandra 41 (tel. 52 30 41), **exchanges currency** for no commission and cashes AmEx/MC/Visa **traveler's checks** for a tiny commission. (Open M and Th-F 8am-4pm, Tu 8am-1pm, W 8am-5pm.) An MC/Visa **ATM** stands outside. The pharmacy, **Lekáreň Luna,** sits at Hviezdoslavova 9. (Open M-F 7:30am-5pm, Sa 8am-noon.) The **post office,** Mučeníkov 2 (tel. 52 28 22), lies where Hviezdoslavova becomes Mučeníkov. (Open M-F 8am-noon and 1-4:30pm, Sa 8am-noon.) **Postal code:** 06001. **Phone code:** (0)968.

ACCOMMODATIONS & FOOD. Except for the second weekend in July, when Kežmarok hosts a European folk arts festival, there shouldn't be a problem finding cheap accommodations, and the tourist office (see above) is always there to help. **Penzión No. 1,** Michalská 1 (tel. 52 46 00), with cottage-style rooms, a sports-friendly garden, and a quiet cellar den, couldn't be more welcoming. Turn left out of the station; it's the first building you come to. Ring the bell upon arriving. (Doubles and triples 200Sk per person; with the divine breakfast 250Sk.) Security heavies have replaced receptionists at the ski-lodge **Hotel Štart** (tel. 52 29 15; fax 52 29 16), off Pod lesom behind the castle, but rooms are more welcoming. From the train station, turn left and walk 10min. down Michalská. Turn right at the bridge onto Nižná brána, and take the first left onto Pod lesom. The hotel is to the left, up a hill after the intersection with Sverná. (Up-to-4-person rooms 200Sk, with bath 270Sk. Check-out 9am.)

For a cheap Slovak meal, try **Restaurant Tiffany,** Hlavné nám. 40, which features a beer garden and a rare non-smoking area out back. (Entrees 40-80Sk; beer 15Sk. Open M-Sa 8am-10pm, Su 9am-9pm.) **Barónka Restaurant,** Hlavné nám. 46 (tel. 52 45 01), behind the tourist office, serves its take on Slovak standards (45-125Sk) amid Van Gogh prints. (Open M-F 10am-11pm, Sa-Su noon-10pm.) A **grocery,** MUDr. Alexandra 35, stocks staples. (Open M-Sa 7am-10pm, Su 8am-9pm.)

SIGHTS. From the main Hlavné nám., a walk down Hviezdoslavova leads to Kežmarok's highlight, the **Wooden Articulated Church** (Drevený Atikulárny Kostol). Three anti-Protestant regulations governed its construction in 1717: the church had to be built outside the town walls, hence the location; it could not have a foundation, hence the sinking sensation; and it had to be financed with parish funds alone, hence the decision to build it entirely out of wood. The astonishing Baroque interior of yew and lime bursts with imagination and resourcefulness; the porthole-shaped windows are the mark of the Swedish sailors who helped build it. You may have to wait outside while a tour is finishing, but it's well worth it, as is the English pamphlet describing the church's construction. When it sank too low for comfort, local Protestants erected the colossal **New Evangelical Church** (Nový Evanjelický Kostol) a mesmerizing blend of Romanesque, Byzantine, Renaissance, and Middle Eastern styles. The facade is more impressive than the sparse interior. The Kežmarok-born Imre Thököly, exiled to Turkey for fighting the Habsburgs, now rests peacefully in his own private vault. (Both churches open June-Sept. daily 9am-noon and 2-5pm; Oct.-May Tu and Th 10am-noon; no tours during services Su 9-10:15am. Slovakian tour 20Sk, students 10Sk.) The last of the town's three churches, the **Church of the Holy Cross** (Kostol sv. Križa) stands in the middle of Staré Mesto, dominating Nám. Požiarnikov. From Hlavné nám. walk down MUDr. Alexandra and turn right onto Nám. Požiarnikov. Knock at the priest's office behind the church to be let in. The interior boasts several 15th-century Gothic altars, two organs, and some fine frescoes.

I PROCLAIM IT HIGHLY UNSAFE! Dr. Vojtech Alexander, a pioneer in the field of radiology, was born in Kežmarok in 1857. He is famous for owning and using the first X-ray machine in Hungary, now on display at the Kežmarok Museum. One of his most important tasks was testing the safety of his ground-breaking machine; Dr. Alexander, one of the bright lights of his day, decided to make his determination by photographing his own unborn son. After undergoing constant exposure to a primitive X-ray machine during crucial stages of development, the child was born with severe mental deficiencies. Some speculate it was the effects of the machine; others simply say that he took after his old man.

Hlavné nám. and Nová culminate at the impressive **Kežmarský castle,** Hradné nám. 42 (tel. 52 41 53). Owned by the powerful Habsburgs, Thurzos, and Thökölys, and often at war with the town, the 15th-century fortification fashionably confounds styles with a Renaissance decor hanging from its stocky Gothic frame. The courtyard contains the foundations of a 13th-century Saxon church. The compulsory Slovak tour of the **Kežmarok Museum** (tel. 52 26 18) is boring unless you buy the English guidebook (6Sk) from the ticket office. Among the stops is an exhibit on Dr. Vojtech Alexander (see **I Proclaim it Highly Unsafe!,** below), a radiology pioneer. (Open May-Sept. Tu-F 9-11:30am and 1-4:30pm, Sa-Su 9am-4pm; Oct.-Apr. Tu-Su 9am-4pm; tours every 30-60min. 20Sk, students 10Sk.)

ENTERTAINMENT. The **Castellan Club** (tel. 52 27 80), hosts the party nightly at the head of Starý trh, underneath the castle. Shake down under disco lights, shoot some pool, or just watch the fish behind the bar (*Zlatý Bažant* 25Sk; open M-Th and Su 8:30pm-3am, F-Sa 8:30pm-5am; women free, men 30Sk). **Kino Iskra,** Hlavné nám. 3 (tel. 52 25 41), in the Poľnobank building, shows Hollywood flicks (40-60Sk).

LEVOČA

The wealth of medieval Levoča (LEH-vo-cha) was due to both its position on Hungarian trading routes and the "Law of Storage," the imperial concession that forced merchants passing through to offer all they had at wholesale prices. Artistic distinction was added to this commercial prosperity in the early 16th century, when Majster Pavol's workshop pioneered an expressive style of wood-carving and erected the world's tallest Gothic altar. Today's town feeds off this illustrious past just as it preyed on merchants, catering to two kinds of visitors: tourists inspecting the walled medieval center, and Catholics assembling for the annual Festival of Marian Devotion in early July.

ORIENTATION & PRACTICAL INFORMATION. Relegated to a sidetrack on Slovakia's railway system, Levoča can only be reached by bus. The **bus station** (tel. 451 22 30) rarely opens its info booth, but departure times are listed on a large billboard. **Buses** run to: **Košice** (2hr., 12 per day, 140Sk); **Poprad** (30min., 36 per day, 22Sk); and **Prešov** (2hr., 29 per day, 138Sk). To get to the center, turn right out of the station and walk 100m up to the intersection with the main road, **Probstnerová cesta.** Walk straight through, then continue following the footpath to the right uphill, past the statue of Jesus, and to the right onto **Nová.** Nová leads straight to the main square, **Nám. Majstra Pavla** (15min.). There's an infrequent **local bus** (5Sk) that covers the same distance more circuitously; catch it on the small road to the left of the station. The helpful **tourist office,** Nám. Majstra Pavla 58 (tel./fax 451 37 63), books *penzióny* and private rooms. (300Sk per person. Open May-Sept. M-F 9am-5pm, Sa-Su 9:30am-2pm; Oct.-Apr. M-F 9:30am-4:30pm.) The small **VÚB,** Nám. Majstra Pavla 28 (tel. 451 43 16), cashes **traveler's checks** for a 1% commission. (Open M-W and F 7:45am-noon and 1-3:45pm, Th 7:45-11:45am.) Its Cirrus/MC **ATM** is across the square in the corner by Uholná. **Slovenská Sporiteľňa,** Nám. Majstra

Pavla 56, has a Cirrus/Plus/MC/Visa **ATM.** The **pharmacy** at Nám. Majstra Pavla 13 (tel. 451 24 56), posts a list of pharmacies open weekends in its window. (Open M-F 7:30am-5pm.) The **post office** is at Nám. Majstra Pavla 42 (tel. 451 24 89; open M-F 8am-noon and 1-4:30pm, Sa 8-10:30am). **Postal code:** 05401. **Phone code:** (0)966.

ACCOMMODATIONS & FOOD. Except for the first weekend in July, when some 250,000 pilgrims invade the town, finding accommodations shouldn't be a problem. The tourist office can point you toward private rooms (see above) and nearby campsites. Most cheaper accommodations lie outside the medieval center, but not too far. An exception is the splendid, family-run **Penzión Šuňausky,** Nová 59 (tel. 451 45 26; mobile tel. 09 05 31 89 90). Follow the directions above to the center; the pension is on Nová on the left. The accommodating German- and English-speaking proprietors rent out sparkling, cozy dorms. A shared kitchen, garden, and delicious breakfast are all included. (Call at least two days ahead. 300Sk.) For **Hotel Texon,** Franciscího 45 (tel. 451 44 93), catch the local bus from the bus station or in front of the post office and hop off at the white Obchodné centrum Texon building. Reception is usually empty and the hotel locked; check the bar, or just go through the tourist office, which has keys to the place. Every two dorms share a bathroom. (180Sk per night for 2 nights; 150Sk for longer stays. Check-out noon.)

There's a **grocery** at Nám. Majstra Pavla 45. (Open M-F 6:45am-7pm, Sa 6:45am-1pm, Su 7:30am-noon.) The popular **U 3 Apoštolov,** Nám. Majstra Pavla 11 (tel. 451 23 52), is Slovakian food done right (52-149SK), including some veggie dishes with no fried cheese (25-66Sk). The modern art on the wall is yours—for 9000Sk. (Open M-Sa 9am-10pm. Su 10am-10pm.) The cafeteria-style **Vegetarián,** Uhoľná 3 (tel. 451 45 76), is a cheaper lunchtime alternative, with four dishes each day (40-47Sk), soups (6-8Sk), and salads (7-8Sk). It also doubles as a health-food store, selling tofu, muesli bars, and soy milk. (Open M-F 10am-3pm.)

SIGHTS. Levoča's star attraction is the 14th-century **St. Jacob's Church** (Chrám sv. Jakuba), home to the world's tallest Gothic altar (a staggering 18.62m) carved by Majster Pavol from 1507-1517. Highlights are an incredibly detailed (and quite comical) depiction of the Last Supper; the 2.5m statues of James, Mary, and John the Evangelist; and the smaller Church Fathers above. To the left of the altar, a medieval mural depicts the seven deeds of bodily mercy and the seven deadly sins. Another mural presents the sad tale of St. Dorothy. Thrust into a pagan land, she was given the choice of heathenry with a rich husband or chaste Christianity with a torturous death. What could she do? She was a saint, after all. Putting 5Sk into the automatic info box yields commentary on the sculptures in English or Hungarian. (Open summer M 11am-5:15pm, Tu-Sa 9am-5:15pm, Su 1-5:15pm; off-season M 11am-4pm, Tu-Sa 9am-4pm, Su 1-4pm. 40Sk, students 20Sk. No sleeveless shirts.)

Three branches of the **Spišske Museum** dot Nám. Majstra Pavla. By far the best is **Dom Majstra Pavla** at #20, with an exhibition on the master's work that contains high-quality facsimiles of much of his best stuff and allows you to get much closer to the Last Supper than you can in the church itself. The museum staff shows a 20min. video about Levoča's history—it's in English and just might persuade you that the town is more than a one-majster show. The **town hall** *(radnica)*, in the middle of the square, is more interesting for its architecture than for the exhibit of armor and local crafts it houses. According to legend, the white lady now painted on one of the doors betrayed the town by giving the city's keys to her lover—an officer in the invading Hungarian army. The **Cage of Shame** (Klietka Hanby), the oversized birdcage in the square, is where women of supposedly loose morals were pilloried in the 16th century. The **third branch** at #40, is an only moderately interesting collection of local painting and woodwork. (All open May-Oct. Tu-Su 9-11:30am and noon-5pm; Nov.-Apr. Tu-Su 9-11:30am and noon-4pm. Each 15Sk, students 5Sk.) The neo-Gothic **Basilica of the Virgin Mary** (Bazilika Panny Marie), 3km from Levoča and clearly visible from the town, stands on top of Mariánská hora. It attracts 250,000 pilgrims in the first weekend in July for the Festival of Marian Devotion, culminating in a 10am mass on Sunday, led by the Pope himself in 1995.

NEAR LEVOČA: SPIŠSKÉ PODHRADIE & ŽEHRA

There's nothing to see in Spišské Podhradie (SPISH-skay POD-hra-dyeh) itself, but on the hills above the valley are two of Slovakia's finest monuments. West of town, walled **Spišska Kapitula,** the region's religious capital, contains **St. Martin's Cathedral** (Katedrála sv. Martina), and its medieval frescoes. The clergy were driven out by scientific socialists in 1948, but have since recolonized. From the bus stop, walk left through the gardens and over the river; the main road here winds up and around to the cathedral (15min.). Get your tickets from the info building 10m from the church. (Open May-Oct. daily 9am-6pm. 20Sk, students with ISIC 10Sk. No sleeveless shirts.) The gleaming white magnificence of **Spišský castle,** central Europe's largest, sprawls over the opposite mountain. There's been a fortified settlement here for two millennia, but the present ruins are the remains of the 12th- to 15th-century Hungarian castle that dominated the Spiš region until it burned down in 1780. Many paths lead to the castle (check the info map at the castle end of the main square), but the most satisfying is the grassy 2km trek from the left side of the town's cemetery. With your back to the departing-times board at the bus stop, head right to the main square. Follow it left out of town; the cemetery will be on your left over a bridge. Watch out for cow patties. The ruins, while clearly a castle, are ruined enough to leave little in the way of interesting exploration, and the living quarters are off limits. The view from the top turret, however, is spectacular.

The real highlight of the day is the church at **Žehra,** about 3km away. From the castle entrance, descend to the parking lot and hike the yellow trail from the other side, past the limestone crags and down into the wide valley. The **Church of the Holy Spirit** (Kostol Svätého Duchá) is easy to spot with its onion-domed tower. Its interior is plastered with remarkable 14th-century frescoes uncovered in the 1950s. The church is usually locked, but the priest, at house #87 nearby, will open it up for visitors. It's about 6km along the road back to Spišské Podhradie.

GETTING THERE. Buses head to the center of town from **Poprad** (1hr., hourly until 9pm, 50Sk); **Levoča** (20min., hourly until 9:30pm, 12Sk); and **Prešov** (1½hr., 12 per day until 7pm, 85Sk). For fuel, try the **grocery** at Marianské nám 4. (Open M-F 5:30am-noon and 12:15-6:45pm, Sa 5:30am-1:45pm, and Su 7:30am-3:45pm.) **VÚB,** Marianské nám. 34 (tel. 81 11 49), cashes **traveler's checks.** (Open M-W and F 8am-noon and 1-4:30pm, Th 8:30am-2pm.)

SLOVENSKÝ RAJ

South of Poprad and on the other side of the Nízke Tatry lies the Slovenský Raj (Slovak Paradise) National Park. Fast-flowing streams have carved deep ravines into the limestone hills, while hikers and skiers have carved their own trails between tiny villages cut off from the rest of Slovakia.

ORIENTATION & PRACTICAL INFORMATION. Nestled in a gorge on the shores of manmade lake Palčmanská Maša, **Dedinky** (pop. 400) is the largest town on Slovenský Raj's southern border. The easiest way to get there is to catch the **bus** from **Poprad** (dir. Rožňava; 1hr., 6 per day, 33Sk). The bus stops first at the **Dobšinská ľadová jaskyňa,** then at the village **Stratená,** and finally at a junction 2km south of Dedinky. Watch for the huge blue road sign at the intersection, and then the smaller blue signs to Dedinky, just before the bus stop. From here, you're in for a hike. From the intersection, walk down the road that the bus didn't take. The road curves down into the basin and comes to an intersection. Turn right and find the disused railway station and a big dam. Cross the dam, turn right and walk 10min. to Dedinky. Or, take the slightly steeper yellow trail that branches off to the right 200m from the intersection. When you reach the road at the bottom, turn left and the dam is right there. This way is about 5-10min. quicker, or 15min. if you end up rolling down the steep pitch.

Pick up a copy of **VKÚ sheet 124**—one of the excellent green hiking maps (70-80Sk)—before entering the region, or at Hotel Priehrada (see below). A **chairlift** runs from Hotel Priehrada up to Chata Geravy. (Runs every hr. July-Aug. M 9am-3pm, Tu-Su 9am-4:30pm; June M 9am-3pm, Tu-Su 9am-4pm; Sept.-May daily 9am-2:45pm. 30Sk, round-trip 60Sk.) **Tókóly Tours** (tel. (0965) 449 33 10; open in summer daily 9am-6pm), along the town's only road 200m from Hotel Priehrada, rents four-person **rowboats** (40Sk per hr.) and two-person **paddle boats** (50Sk per hr.). Street **bikes** are 20Sk per hr. Dedinky's **post office** hides behind the wooden tower near the bus stop in the center of town. (Open M-F 8am-10pm and 12:30-3pm.) **Postal code:** 04973. **Phone code:** (0)942.

ACCOMMODATIONS & FOOD. It is wise to book ahead in July, August, and January. In Dedinky, **Hotel Priehrada** (tel. 982 12; fax 982 21) rents dated but comfortable rooms with shared baths and views of the lake and *chaty* behind the hotel for 200Sk. (Lower prices Sept. to mid-Dec. and Apr.-June.) It also has a preposterously cheap **campsite** in front of the lake. (Tents 20Sk, plus 20Sk per person. Check-out 10am in hotel, 9am in huts.) **Penzión Pastierňa,** Dedinky 42 (tel. 981 75), has good rooms (200Sk per person) and a restaurant downstairs serving the usual Slovak fare (66-141Sk) with three vegetarian dishes (37-49Sk) and wine (25Sk). Turn right from the bus stop in the town center and right again at the second turn. (Open daily 8am-10pm.) The chairlift behind Hotel Priehrada will take you to **Chata Geravy,** a great starting point for hikes that also has small rooms with huge pillows. (180Sk; check for vacancies at Hotel Priehrada before going up; guests at Chata Geravy get a special 30Sk round-trip rate on the chairlift.) Carbo-load at the **grocery** in Dedinky (open M-F 7am-6pm, Sa 7am-5pm, Su 9am-5pm), or at the one at the base of the ice-cave trail (see below; open M, W, F 7am-10am and 1-4pm, Tu noon-3pm, Th 10am-3pm, Sa 8-11am). Other than the restaurant in Penzión Pastierňa, there is really only the uninspiring restaurant in Hotel Priehrada. (Full meals 30-110Sk.) Another much pricier restaurant sits at the bottom of the ice caves. (Entrees 100-130Sk. Open daily 9am-5:30pm.)

SIGHTS. Some 110,000 cubic meters of water are still frozen from the last Ice Age in the form of a giant underground glacier in the 19km stretch of the **Dobšinská Ice Caves** (Dobšinská ľadová jaskyňa). The 30min. tour covers only 475m of the cave, but that's awe-inspiring enough, with hall after hall of frozen columns, gigantic ice wells, and hardened waterfalls. To get here from Dedinky, take the 7:29, 11:19am, or 2:41pm train two stops (8Sk, 10min.). The one road from the cave train station leads 100m out to the main road. Turn left and the cave parking lot is 250m ahead. From the parking lot, the blue trail leads up a steep incline to the cave (20min.). Bring a sweater—the cave temperature hovers between -3.8° and 0.5°C year-round. Buses (8Sk) also leave for the cave from outside Hotel Priehrada weekdays at 9:04, 9:22, and 9:52am and drop you right in the cave parking lot. (Open May 15-June and Sept. 9:30am-2pm; July to Aug. 9am-4pm. Hourly Slovak tours 80Sk, students 60Sk, children 40Sk; in English 130Sk, 100Sk, 60Sk. 20-person min. for English tours. Cameras 100Sk.)

HIKING. This is a national park, so camping and fire-lighting are prohibited. Cascade trails are one-way—you can go up, but not down. Most trails are closed November to June to those without certified guides.

Biele vody (White Waters; 1½hr.): The trail in all the pictures. The hike up one of the park's many rapids involves ladder and is one-way, so there's no turning back, even for vertigo. From Hotel Priehrada in Dedinky, take the red trail to Biele Vody. The blue cascade trail will be on the left. Chata Geravy (see above) waits at the top, and the green trail leads back down, or ride the roller-coaster chair lift. The river tumbles through the greenery the whole way up the trail, making for lovely sights and sounds.

Havrania skala (Crow's Cliff; 3hr.): This hike is remarkable mainly for the views from the top. From Stratená bus stop, the green trail leads up the hill to the underwhelming spring Občasný prameň (1hr.); from Chata Geravy, it's 1½hr. through hillside meadows

SLOVAKIA

along the yellow trail. From the spring, it's a 30min. climb up the steep, earthy yellow trail to the top of Havrania skala and a gorgeous view. The yellow trail continues downhill steeply for 1hr. to meet the road just west of Stratená—turn left at the tarmac.

Vemký sokol (6-8hr.): A more demanding hike into the heart of Slovenský Raj and up its deepest gorge. Follow the road west from Stratená or east out of the ice caves. At the head of the big U-bend, take the green trail north, over the Sedlo Kopanec (987m), and along the stream. Turn right onto the road and take the red path to the bottom of the gorge. The one-way yellow trail leads up the ravine, criss-crossing the mountain stream. Your feet will get wet and muddy, the logs are slippery, and some of the walkways inspire belief in a Supreme Being. From the top, the red path returns to Chata Geravy and the descent to Dedinky. Those who don't like wet feet can follow the red trail from the bottom of the gorge to the top around the northern edge (30min. longer).

THE HIGH TATRAS (VYSOKÉ TATRY)

The High Tatras are mesmerizing. Spanning the border between Slovakia and Poland, the jagged mountains are home to hundreds of addictive hiking and skiing trails along the highest peaks in the Carpathian range (2650m). Millions of visitors pack the slopes and trails each year—the trains are always crowded and the trails overrun with scampering tots (who knew 4-year-olds made good mountaineers?). Unlike in the Tatra's western counterparts, however, budget accommodations are still easy to find—including cheap beds in the mountain *chaty* (huts)—and a ridiculously cheap mountain railway means it often doesn't matter where you stay. If you climb high enough, you just might leave the screaming children behind long enough to have a moment alone with the mighty Tatras.

> **!** The Tatras are a wonderful place for a summer hike, but in the winter a guide is almost always necessary. The snowfall in the Tatras is very high and avalanches frequent. Each year, dozens of winter hikers in the area die, often on "easy" trails. Check with a mountain rescue team, a local outdoors store, or a tourist office before going anywhere without an escort.

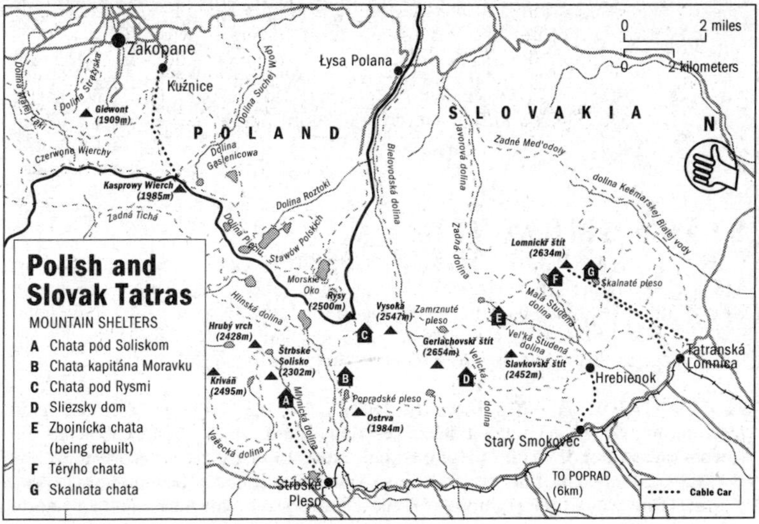

POPRAD

Poprad was born when Czechoslovakia linked four sleepy mountain villages with drab apartment blocks. It's not a pretty place, but it does boast super transport lines to the Vysoké Tatry and the towns of the Špiš region, as well as a looser accommodation scene than in the mountain resorts. Aside from these conveniences, Poprad has little to offer the traveler, and most travelers stop here only long enough to change trains on the way to the Tatras, which, when they aren't enshrouded in clouds, cast their jagged shadow over the town and nearby villages.

Even if you're not spending the night in Poprad, the tourist office, **Popradská Informačná Agentúra,** Nám. sv. Egídia 114 (tel. 161 86 and 72 17 00; email infopp@pp.psg.sk), is worth a stop; the English-speaking staff sells **VKÚ sheet 113** of the High Tatras (70Sk), has info on all sorts of recreation, and can help with accommodation anywhere in the region. (Open M-F 8am-6pm, Sa 9am-1pm.) **VÚB,** Mnohel'ova 9 (tel. 605 11 11), cashes AmEx and Visa traveler's checks for a 1% commission. (Open M-W and F 8am-5pm, Th 8am-noon.) Cirrus/MC/Maestro/EC/ Visa **ATMs** are around the corner and all over town. **Store luggage** at the train station. (Lockers 5Sk; 10-20Sk per day at the office. Open 24hr.) If you're staying in Poprad, the cheapest accommodations are at **Domov Mládeže,** Karpatská 9 (tel. 634 14), a large workers' hostel that doubles as a tourist hostel in summer. Walk down Alžbetina away from the train station toward the bus station, then go right onto Karpatská. (Singles and 2- to 4-bed dorms with bath 150Sk; 200Sk for 1 night. Check-out 9am.) Or, stay in one of the paisley rooms at **Hotel Gerlach,** Hviezdoslavova 2 (tel. 72 19 45; fax 636 63). Take Alžbetina between the bus and train stations and turn left on Hviezdoslavova; Gerlach is on your right. (Singles 350Sk; doubles 450Sk, with shower 600Sk; triples with bath 700Sk. Check-out noon.) There's a **supermarket** on the top floor of **Prior** at Mnohel'ova and Nám. sv. Egídia. (Open M-F 8am-7pm, Sa 8am-2pm, Su 10am-4pm.) If you have time to linger, **Egídius** (tel. 72 28 98), Mnohel'ova 18, has an outdoor beer garden, a classy cellar restaurant, and an candle-lit cafe upstairs. (Full meals 45-160Sk. Open daily 11am-11:30pm.) Should you find yourself here in the evening—and you're not too tired from hiking—you can drink in the shadow of an old church and enjoy live music at **Vináreň sv. Juraj,** Sobotské nám. 29. (*Zlatý Bažant* 28Sk; open Tu-Th 3pm-2am, F-Sa 5pm-5am, Su 4pm-midnight.) **Postal code:** 05800. **Phone code:** (0)92.

GETTING AWAY. Trains (tel. 72 18 30) leave from the north edge of town to **Košice** (2hr., 25 per day, 79Sk) and **Bratislava** (4hr., 12 per day, 234Sk). Tatranská Električká Železnica (TEŽ; electric train) connects Poprad with the **Tatran resorts** (every hr., up to 22Sk), but buses are generally quicker and more frequent, if less fun. **Buses** (tel. 625 55; info window open M-F 7am-3pm), near the train station at the corner of Wolkerova and Alžbetina, head to: **Zakopane, Poland** (2hr., 2 per day July-Aug. and Dec.-Mar.; 80Sk); **Banská Bystrica** (2½hr., 18 per day, 120Sk); **Košice** (2hr., 9 per day, 100Sk); and **Tatran resorts** (20-30Sk). To get to the center, walk up Alžbetina, which runs between the bus and train stations. Take the first left onto Hviezdoslavova, then the first right onto Mnohel'ova. This leads to Nám sv. Egída.

STARÝ SMOKOVEC

Starý Smokovec (STAH-ree SMO-ko-vets) is the High Tatra's most central resort and, founded in the 17th century, one of the oldest. Cheap sleeps down the road in Horný Smokovec make it easily accessible to the budget traveler. The town itself is a little bland (one street of hotels and grocers) and tackily geared toward tourists, but the trails leading up into the mountains are nothing short of spectacular.

ORIENTATION & PRACTICAL INFORMATION. TEŽ **trains** arrive from **Poprad** (30min., hourly, 12Sk) and **Tatranská Lomnica** (15min., every 30min., 8Sk) at the town's lowest point, south of Hotel Grand. **Buses** to many Tatra resorts stop in a parking lot just east of the train station. A **funicular** runs to Hrebienok every 30-40min. (One-way 70Sk; round-trip 80Sk.) There are no street names, but good signs point to hotels, restaurants, and services. Facing uphill, head up the road that runs just left of the train station, then cross the main road veering left. The friendly staff of **Tatranská Informačná Kancelária** (tel. 44 23 34 40; fax 442 31 27), in Dom Služieb, provides weather info and sells hiking maps, including the crucial **VKÚ sheet 113** of the High Tatras (70Sk; open M-F 8am-5pm, Sa 9am-1pm). **Slovenská Sporiteľňa** (tel. 442 24 70; fax 442 32 53), also in Dom Služieb, cashes traveler's checks and has two machines outside: one changes currency for a 1% or 20Sk commission, the other is a Cirrus/MC/Plus/Visa **ATM.** (Bank open M 7:30am-noon and 12:30-3pm, Tu 7:30am-12:30pm, W 7:30am-noon and 12:30-4:30pm, Th-F 7:30am-noon and 12:30-2:30pm.) **T-ski** (tel. 442 32 00), in the ski lift station, offers everything from ski classes to river-rafting trips, and rents **sleds** (50Sk per day), **skis** (190-390Sk), and mountain **guides** (from 4000Sk per day; open daily 9am-5pm). There's a **pharmacy, Lekáreň U Zlatej Sovy** (tel. 442 21 64), on the second floor of Dom Služieb. (Open M-F 8am-noon and 12:30-4:30pm, Sa 8am-noon.) The **post office** (tel. 442 24 71) lies near the train station. (Open M-F 7:30am-4pm, Sa 8-10am.) **Postal code:** 06201. **Phone code:** (0)969.

ACCOMMODATIONS & FOOD. Up the road from the train station on the way to Dom Služieb, an **InfoPanel** displays info on hotels, pensions, and hostels in the greater Smokovec area and has a free phone for reservations. Most budget options are along the road running east out of Starý Smokovec in the hamlet of **Horný Smokovec.** Turn right on the main road from the train or bus stations and walk 10min. to **Hotel Šport** (tel. 442 23 61; fax 442 27 19), a mega-complex that includes a restaurant, cafe, sauna, swimming pool, and massage parlor. (Singles 415Sk; doubles 720Sk; triples 1015Sk. Breakfast included. Book at least one week ahead.) Another 15min. along the road (or two stops on the TEŽ toward Tatranská Lomnica), and down a short path through the trees, is **Hotel Junior Vysoké Tatry** (tel. 442 26 61; fax 442 24 93), a young hostel with compact rooms, shared baths, a disco, and foosball. (Singles 230Sk; doubles 360Sk; triples 490Sk; quads 560Sk; with ISIC, singles 200Sk. 10Sk cheaper off-season; 30% MC discount. Breakfast included. Book one week ahead.) If you're intent on staying in Starý Smokovec, **Hotel Smokovec** (tel. 442 51 91; fax 442 51 94), above the train station, offers pricey but beautiful rooms. (2-, 3-, and 4-person dorms 730, 680, and 620Sk in summer; 620, 570, and 520Sk off-season. Pets 150Sk. Check-out 10am.)

Grocers clutter Starý Smokovec, with five on the main road just above the bus and train stations. The largest is the *potraviny* in the shopping block above the bus station. (Open M-F 7:45am-7pm, Sa-Su 8am-3pm.) Decent restaurants, however, are sparse. The mountain-hut **Restaurant Koliba** (tel./fax 22 04) is one notable exception. Facing downhill, head into the parking lot to the right of the train station and across the tracks. Don't leave without trying their infamously flaming *Tatranský Čaj* (Tatran tea; 33Sk; Slovak meals 45-185Sk; open daily 11am-9pm). **Bistro Tatra,** just above the bus station, is for those who like their Slovak fare served extra-fast. (Entrees 20-100Sk. Open daily 10am-9pm.)

HIKING. The funicular to **Hrebienok** (1285m) leads right to the heart of hiking country; if you want to hike it, start at the funicular station behind Hotel Grand (behind the train station) and head 30min. up the green trail. Deluxe hut **Volopády Bilikova Chata** (tel. 442 24 39) sits at the funicular station offering hot toddies, food, and beds (300Sk per person). Another 20min. from Hrebienok, the green trail leads north to the foaming **Studeného Potoka** (Cold Waterfall). The incline is small, the hike is through the trees, and the waterfall is well worth it. The eastward blue trail descends gradually from the waterfall through the towering pines to **Tatranská Lomnica** (1½hr.), while the yellow trail plunges sharply down along the river to **Tatranská Lesná** (1½hr.). A TEŽ train can whisk you from Tatranská Lomnica and Tatranská Lesná back to Starý Smokovec. The long, red **Tatranská magistrála** trail travels west from Hrebienok breaking the tree-line at **Sliezsky Dom** (2hr.; 1670m; tel. 442 52 61; 240Sk per person), then zig-zagging down to **Chata Nu Popradskom**

WHAT'S NEXT, EQUALITY? A display in Kežmarok castle (see p. 688) tells the tales of the first climbers to conquer the high Tatras, a group that included many men and one extraordinary woman. Beata Laška demanded to be a part of the expedition, then successfully kept up with the men around her as they reached the summit. Rather than praising Beata for the difficulties she overcame, though, her husband Albert (17 years her junior) declared her "insubordinate" and "brash," imprisoned her, and enjoyed the fruits of her fortune for the rest of his days. Beata spent the final six years of her life going mad in the castle dungeon.

Plese, a.k.a. **Chata Kapitána Moravku** (1500m; 5½hr.; tel. 449 21 77; 230Sk per person in summer, 170Sk off-season) on the shore of the lake **Popradské Pleso.** From here, the red trail continues to **Štrbské Pleso** (7hr. from Hrebienok). Before Popradské Pleso there are three trails back to civilization, two to Tatranská Polianka, and one to Vyšné Hágy (1-2hr. each). A more daunting blue trail branches north from the *magistrála* 20min. west of Hrebienok to climb one of the highest Tatran peaks, the stony **Slavkovský Štít** (2452m; about 8hr. round-trip from Hrebienok; for advanced hikers only).

The *magistrála* also heads north from Hrebienok to the lake **Skalnaté Pleso,** and its nearby *chata* (2hr.). The hike to **Malá Studená Dolina** (Little Cold Valley) is also fairly relaxed; take the red trail from Hrebienok to **Zamkovského chata** (1475m; tel. 442 26 33; 220Sk per person) and onto the green trail to **Térého Chata** (2015m; 4hr.; tel. 442 52 45; 200Sk per person), which climbs above the tree-line to a high lake.

An intense 6hr. hike traverses the immense **Veľká Studená Dolina** (Big Cold Valley) to **Zbojnícka Chata.** (*Chata* closed in 1999 due to fire; slated to re-open summer 2000.) From Sliezsky Dom (see above), take the green trail to **Zamrznuté Pleso** (Cold Lake; 2047m), turn right onto the blue trail at the lake, and follow the crashing **Veľký Studený Potok** (Big Cold Stream), to Studeného vodopády (waterfall), via Zbojnicka Chata. From here, the green trail returns to Hrebienok, spending much time above the tree-line. (All trails open July-Sept. All of the *chaty* double as restaurants, but they're the only restaurants, so pack plenty of carbs.)

NEAR STARÝ SMOKOVEC: ŠTRBSKÉ PLESO

The hotels and ski-jump towers that clutter placid **Štrbské Pleso** (Lake Štrbské; SHTERB-skay PLAY-so) seem to be trying to recapture the spirit of the 1975 "Interski" Championship, while gaggles of school kids add screams and whistles to the mess. After all, one can't expect to enjoy the Tatras' most-beloved ski resort alone.

The town is the range's highest settlement and a great starting point for hikes. Just one lift runs in summer, hoisting visitors to **Chata pod Soliskom** (1840m) overlooking the lake and the expansive plains behind Štrbské Pleso. A small restaurant under the top lift station, **Bivak Club,** offers tea (15Sk), Tatran fast food (30-50Sk), and, of course, beer (25Sk). The lift is 10min. up the road from the trains—follow the signs or the yellow trail. (Runs June-Sept. 8am-3:30pm. July-Aug. one-way 85Sk, round-trip 120Sk; June and Sept. 60Sk, 85Sk.) Once at the top, hike the red trail to the peak of **Predné Solisko** (2093m); the only route is the steep blue trail back down to Štrbské Pleso.

Two magnificent day hikes start from Štrbské Pleso, both involving stretches with chains. For both, dress warmly and bring plenty of food and water. The yellow route heads from the east side of the lake (follow the signs to Hotel Patria) out along **Mlynická Dolina** to mountain lakes and **Vodopády Skok** (waterfall). It then crosses **Bystré Sedlo** (saddle; 2314m) and circles **Štrbské Solisko** (2302m) before returning to Štrbské Pleso (about 7hr.). Along the way are some steep ascents and descents that take you well above the tree-line. Turn left where the yellow trail ends at the red trail 30min. from Štrbské Pleso to get back to town. The second hike takes you to the top of **Rysy** (2499m) on the Polish-Slovak border, Poland's highest peak and the highest Tatra scalable without a guide. From Štrbské Pleso, follow the *magistrála* to **Chata Kapitána Moravku** (1500m; tel. 449 21 77; 230Sk per person), also known as Chata Popradské Pleso. From here, take the blue trail up the side of the valley and turn right onto the red trail after 30min. to tackle Rysy. Go past the lakes **Zabie Plesá** to **Chata pod Rysmi** (2250m; 120Sk per person), where there is free hot tea for anyone who brings up 5kg of supplies from Chata Kapitána Moravku. (Pick up a bag from the tiny shelter where the blue trail meets the red near Chata Kapitána Moravku.) Rysy is 40min. from the *chata;* allow 8-9hr. for the round-trip. This hike is for advanced hikers and should be tried only in good weather. The stretch from Štrbské Pleso to Chata Kapitána Moravku (1¼hr.) is part of the *magistrála* and attracts many hikers. with its views of the valley. A green trail branches off after 30min. and rolls by the **Hincov Potok** (stream) to the *chata* and its lake.

From the *chata*, the 15min. yellow trail (open July-Oct.) leads south to the **Symbolic Cemetery** (Symbolický cintorín; 1525m). Built between 1936 and 1940 by painter Otakar Štafl, the field of painted crosses, metal plaques, and broken propeller blades serves as "a memorial to the dead, and a warning for the living," for those who have died and those who are still climbing in the Tatras. The trail ends at a paved blue path. The weary can descend the blue trail to the Popradské Pleso TEŽ stop (45min.), but backtracking to Štrbské Pleso is far more interesting. The *magistrála* continues from the *chata* for hours along scenic ridges to **Hrebienok** (see **Starý Smokovec: Hiking,** p. 694). There's a steep climb up the face of **Ostrva** (1984m) to the **Sedlo pod Ostrvou** (Ostrva saddle; 1966m), but it levels off after that.

GETTING THERE. TEŽ **trains** leave hourly from Štrbské Pleso for: **Starý Smokovec** (30min., 16Sk); **Tatranská Lomnica** (45min., 22Sk); and **Poprad** (1¼hr., 22Sk). The infrequent **buses** to **Poprad** are faster (50min., 20Sk). Budget travelers should leave the town before dusk, since hotel prices are higher than the elevation. Cheap beds are just a short train ride away in Starý Smokovec and Tatranská Lomnica.

TATRANSKÁ LOMNICA

Among Tatran resorts, charming Tatranská Lomnica (TA-tran-ska LOM-nee-tsa) is clearly *the* place to stay. The snow is deep, the sleeps are cheap, and the tourists are not nearly as offensive as those in Starý Smokovec. In summer, few trails lead directly from town; the ear-popping lift to Lomnica Štít is the town's main attraction. Thanks to frequent TEŽ trains, however, all of hiking country is close by.

ORIENTATION & PRACTICAL INFORMATION. **Buses** are the best way to get here from **Poprad** (30min., hourly, 16Sk). **TEŽ trains** (tel. 967 884) run from **Starý Smokovec** and **Štrbské Pleso.** With nameless streets and scattered buildings, the village can be confusing, but excellent signs to restaurants, hotels, and services are everywhere and most everything is within spitting distance of the train station. The **information board** halfway between the train stop and Hotel Lomnica, away from the tracks, displays the location of hotels, pensions, and restaurants, and has a free phone to call for reservations and neat buttons to push to find out whether rooms are available. **Currency exchanges** pop up around town, including at **Slovenská Sporiteľňa** (tel. 96 72 59; fax 96 76 67), in the woods behind the train station, which cashes traveler's checks and has a 24hr. Cirrus/MC/Plus/Visa **ATM.** (Open M 7:30am-3pm, Tu 7:30am-1pm, W 7:30-11:30am and noon-5pm, Th-F 7:30-11:30am and noon-3pm.) **Poľnobank,** along the track across from the railroad station, has another ATM (Cirrus/EC/Maestro/MC). **WR Šport** (tel. 446 72 16; open daily 8am-6pm), in the back of Slalom Restaurant, on the main road near the train stop, rents bikes and in-line skates (both 300Sk per day; 80Sk per hr.), and skis (250Sk per day; boots and poles included). The **post office** (tel. 96 72 00) lies behind the train station. (Open M-F 7:30-11:30am and noon-4pm, Sa 8-10am.) **Postal code:** 05960. **Phone code:** (0)969.

ACCOMMODATIONS & FOOD. To camp or not to camp, that is the question. If you don't have a tent, don't fret—virtually all of the hotels and pensions in town are remarkably cheap. **Penzión Bělín,** in the center of town (tel. 446 77 78), is by far one of the best. The friendly, English-speaking staff rents out warm rooms in their giant orange house for bargain prices. There are kitchens and satellite TVs in each floor's common room. Follow the sign from the info board into the gardens. At the second path junction (50m), take the left path that heads up to the road. Turn right and Bělín is right in front of you. (2- to 4-person dorms 200Sk.) If you feel like gittin' jiggy with nature, follow the road out of town to the campsites on the edge of the national park. The large **Eurocamp FICC** (tel. 446 77 41; fax 446 73 46), 4km from town, has its own train stop (hourly from town, 6Sk). It rents 100 spacious bungalows with spotless showers. (Tents 90Sk, plus 100Sk per person. Doubles with bath 1000Sk; quads 1800Sk.) A sports store **rents bikes** (250Sk per day), in-line skates (50Sk per day), and skis (180Sk per day; open daily 8am-8pm). There is also a grocery store, disco, restaurant, bar, and movie theater on the premises. From Eurocamp, 10min. heading away from the mountains leads to **Šport-camp** (tel./fax 446 72 88) and its tiny, shiny 14- to 20-bed dorms with shared showers and tent sites. (Tents 70Sk, plus 100Sk per person. Dorms 200Sk. Showers 12Sk after first night. Reception 7am-10pm.)

There's a **supermarket** just behind the main train station building. (Open M-F 7:45am-7pm, Sa 7:45am-3pm, Su 8am-3pm.) Restaurants line the train tracks and the main road, but most are insufferably touristy. The wonderful **Reštaurácia Júlia** (tel. 46 79 47), 200m below the station (follow the sign), somehow manages to transcend the pervasive kitsch with its Slovak specialties. (Entrees 55-200Sk. Open M-F and Su 11:30am-9pm, Sa 11:30am-9:30pm.) The **Country Bar** in Hotel Slovakia (tel. 446 79 61), left on the main road from the stations, is your only option if you're eating late. (Entrees 55-102Sk. Open daily 6pm-midnight.)

SIGHTS & HIKING. Get tickets early for the remarkable lift up to **Lomnický Štít** (2634m), the Tatras' second-highest peak. Follow the signs around town to either of the two *lanova drahy* mini-cabins that ride up to the glacial lake of **Skalnaté Pleso** (1751m). The older, 32-person car goes hourly from behind Grandhotel Praha, while the newer, 4-person lift runs continuously if there's demand (hourly otherwise) from behind Hotel Horee. (Open 7am-7pm; last ascent 4pm. Round-trip 300Sk in-season; 260Sk off-season.) From the lake, the Grandhotel Praha mini-cabins ascend to the summit while a chairlift plows to **Lomnické Sedlo.** (Both 400Sk round-trip.) A 540Sk day ticket can be obtained for skiing the excellent trails from Skalnatá Chata to Tatranská Lomnica. On a clear day, the peak offers a staggering view of just about everywhere. The craggy mountain peak has good picnic spots; at the lake, **Skalnatá Chata** is an admirable refreshment stop. Dress warmly—it snows up here even in July.

Hiking is generally better from Starý Smokovec or Štrbské Pleso, but a few full-day hikes are accessible from Tatranská Lomnica's lift. The red *Magistrála* trail heading southwest from **Skalnaté Pleso** toward **Lomnická vyhliadka** (1529m) and then to **Zamkovského Chata** (2hr.) is challenging but well worth the view (see **Hiking: Starý Smokovec,** p. 695). The blue trail from the info board in town to **Vodopády Studeného Potoka** (Cold Waterfalls) and back to Tatranská Lesná is gentler (4½hr.).

ENTERTAINMENT. While most people in Tatranská Lomnica are too exhausted from skiing and hiking to function beyond 8pm, there are a few options for night action. **Kino Tatry** (tel. 446 72 19), in the Tatranské Kulturne Centrum, probably requires the least energy with the usual mindless Hollywood films in all their English splendor. From the bus or train station, turn right onto the main road and then right again at the Muzeum Tanaf signs; the center is next door to the museum. (Shows at 5:15 and 7:30pm. 40-50Sk.) **Oaza Disco Bar** is in the same building and plays 60s rock under laser lights and gaudy wallpaper for seasoned locals and a few brave tourists. (Open M-Th and Su 3pm-midnight, F 3pm-2am, Sa 3pm-3:30am).

ŠARIŠ

Tucked away in the green hills of east Slovakia, Šariš is still struggling to deal with many of the political events of the last 80 years. For many years a borderland against Turkish invasions, the region and its sleepy towns still stand behind bastions built to repel the Saracens. German-speaking tourists are less common here, with English in the running for second language. But lest you think that Šariš is nothing but folk tales and chiming bells, two giant Campbell's soup cans beckon you to a shrine to native-son Andy Warhol in the miniscule town of Medzilaborce.

KOŠICE

Now Slovakia's second-largest city, Košice (KO-shih-tseh; pop. 240,915) struggles mightily to avoid the pitfalls of most big towns. Its Old Town and central square were painstakingly renovated to be sheltered from the political and economic change around them; but inevitably, the size, noise, and dirt make their presence known. Still, while the medieval gold craftsmen who founded the town would wince at Košice's blast furnaces and steel foundries, they would also tap their feet to the music of the *Glockenspiel* bells and laugh at the children who play in the wrought-iron Art Nouveau fountains on its streets.

ORIENTATION

Košice's **Staré Mesto** (Old Town) lies close to the **train station.** To get to the central **Hlavná** and the tourist office, exit the station and follow the "Centrum" signs across the park that lies just to the right of the train station. You'll arrive at Mlynská, which intersects Hlavná opposite the church.

PRACTICAL INFORMATION

Trains: Tel. 613 20 68. On Predstaničné nám. To: **Bratislava** (5hr., 14 per day, 280Sk); **Prague** (9hr., 4 per day, 540Sk); **Budapest** (4hr., 4 per day, 753Sk); **Kraków** (6hr., 1 per day, 733Sk); **Lviv** (6hr., 1 per day, 733Sk); and **Kiev** (12hr., 1 per day, 1218Sk).

Buses: Tel. 625 16 19. Next to the train station. Buses are bumpier and more expensive than trains, but sometimes faster for local trips, and always more scenic. To **Bratislava** (5hr., 12 per day, 305Sk) and **Brno** (10½hr., 5 per day, 430Sk).

Local Transportation: Trams and **buses** traverse the city and its suburbs. Tickets 8Sk from kiosks and little orange boxes at bus stops.

Taxis: Rádio Taxi (tel. 163 33). **Classic Taxi** (tel. 622 22 44). **CTC** (tel. 43 34 33).

Tourist Offices: Mestské Informačna Centrum, Hlavná 8 (tel. 625 88 88). Dispenses info on hotels and cultural happenings. Open M-F 9am-6pm, Sa 9am-1pm. **Tatratour,** Alžbetina 6 (tel. 622 48 72), near the cathedral. Cashes traveler's checks for a 1% commission and reluctantly arranges pensions for 600Sk per person.

Currency Exchange: VÚB branches are liberally sprinkled throughout the city; the one at Hlavná 8 (tel. 622 62 50) cashes traveler's checks and exchanges currency for a 1% commission, and gives MC cash advances. Open M-W and F 7:30am-4:30pm, Th 7:30am-noon. Cirrus/MC **ATMs** spit magic cash in front of many VÚB branches.

Luggage Storage: At the train station. 10Sk per bag under 15kg.; heavier bags 20Sk. Small lockers 5Sk. Open daily 2:35am-12:15pm, 1-7pm, and 7:45pm-1:50am.

English Bookstore: ArtForum, Mlynská 6 (tel./fax 623 26 77). A small selection. Open M-F 9am-7pm, Sa 9am-1pm.

24hr. Pharmacy: Ratislavova 43 (tel. 622 65 90).

Post Office: Poštová 20 (tel. 622 26 37). Open M-F 7am-7pm, Sa 7am-2pm. **Postal code:** 04001.

Telephones: Around Hlavná and outside the post office. **Phone code:** 95.

ACCOMMODATIONS

Although accommodations generally cost more in Košice than in smaller towns, a few hotels and *penzións* are reasonable; the tourist office keeps a list of possibilities. In July and August, student dorms are the cheapest option (about 100Sk per night), but are very far from the center.

Tourist Hotel Metropol, Šturová 32 (tel. 625 59 48), is a godsend. Three stops away on tram #6 or bus #11, 16, or 30 from the train/bus station, or a 15min. walk along Šturová. Walk left out of the bus station and turn the corner onto the main road. Šturová is the road running opposite McDonald's. You'll see a sign for Metropol on your left; walk through the gate into a flower-filled yard with a fountain. Turn left and go upstairs for the reception. Sauna 80Sk per 2hr. Great restaurant on premises. Info posted on trips and hikes in the region. Check-out 10am. 50 beds in triples and quads 300Sk.

Hotel Európa, Protifašistických Bojovníkov 1 (tel. 622 38 97), across the park in front of the train station and bridge. A run-down, 19th-century hotel with bathroom tiles that seem to date from the Hungarian occupation. Communal toilets and a unisex shower room with a locking door. Check-out 10am. Singles 480Sk, with shower 570Sk; doubles 740Sk; triples 950Sk; suites with private bath and fridge 1060Sk.

Hotel Kohal, Trieda SNP 61 (tel. 42 55 72). Take tram #6 in front of the train/bus station to a roundabout at Toryská and Trieda SNP. Get off at the Ferrocentrum stop, after the tram turns right onto Trieda SNP. Kohal is on your right, offering basic comforts. Check-out 11am. Visa/MC/AmEx. Hostel singles 210Sk; doubles 400Sk. Breakfast 90Sk.

Penzión Rozália, Oravská 14 (tel. 633 97 14). From the train station, take tram #6 to Amfitéater (20min.) and walk up Stará spišská cesta, behind you near the amphitheater. After 10min., Oravská appears on the right; ring the bell at #14. Small rooms overlooking a garden. Singles 250Sk, with bath 600Sk; doubles 500Sk, 800Sk. Call ahead.

FOOD

From the roof-top terrace of Ajvega/Veža to the sweet temptations of Aida, Košice is a food emporium. Vegetarians need look no further, and connoisseurs of Slovak cuisine will find enough *knedle* (dumpling) to keep them happy for months. For **groceries,** try the **Tesco** at Hlavná 109 (tel. 62 29 80; open M-F 8am-8pm, Sa 8am-5pm, Su 8am-4pm).

Ajvega, Orlia 10 (tel. 622 04 52), off Mlynská. Veggie pasta, pizza, soups, and salads. The "Vitaminové bomby" salads live up to their name, exploding with fresh color (55Sk). Huge menu includes half-portions (41.30-49.30Sk). On the 2nd floor, up a winding staircase, is **Restaurant Veža** (the tower), with a more elegant decor, the same menu, and a roof-top terrace. Open daily 11am-10pm.

Reštaurácia Veverička, Hlavná 97 (tel. 622 33 60). Look for the pair of squirrels over the shiny-dark wood. Outdoor seating. Good and cheap Slovak fare 35-86Sk. Open daily 9am-10pm.

Pizzeria Venezia, Mlynská 20 (tel. 622 44 44). People-watch while eating pizza (118-138Sk) or spaghetti (70-158Sk) on the terrace. Open daily in summer 9am-midnight; off-season 10am-midnight.

Cukráren Aida, Poštová 4. Draws crowds for its sweets (7-40Sk) and fabulous ice cream (4Sk per scoop). Open daily 8am-10pm.

SIGHTS

The streets of Košice's Staré Mesto provide a few full days of good walking. Bulbous **Hlavná** marks the heart of historic Košice, with the centerpiece **Cathedral of St. Elizabeth** (Dom sv. Alžbety) at its widest point. Begun in 1378 as a high-Gothic monument, the cathedral has undergone repeated confused renovations; it now stands as a conglomeration of almost every style known to Western architecture. In 1900, restorers built a crypt under the cathedral's north nave. Transported from Turkey in 1906, Košice's revolutionary hero, **Ferenc Rakóczi II,** has proven to be less trouble in a sarcophagus. The cathedral's little brother next door, the **Chapel of St. Michael** (Kaplnka sv. Michala), serves as a mortuary. (Under renovation until Oct. 2000.) Outside, a relief of St. Michael weighs the souls of the dead. On the other side of the cathedral, the barren facade of **Urban's Tower** (Urbanova veža) seems almost two-dimensional next to the ornaments of St. Elizabeth's. A closer look, however, reveals 36 tombstones lining the exterior, one of which dates from the 4th century. Outside St. Michael's, stairs lead down to a free **underground museum,** home to the ruins of the town's fortifications. (Open July-Sept. 15 Tu-Su 11am-7pm; tours every 30min.)

Walking down Mlynská from the cathedral toward the train station leads to the 19th-century **Jacob's Palace** (Jakabov palác), built of stones discarded from the cathedral. Currently occupied by the British Council, the palace served as the temporary home of Czechoslovakia's president in the spring of 1945. Backtrack to the center and head left down Puškinova to the closed **synagogue.** A strikingly graphic memorial to local Jews deported to concentration camps hangs outside. Behind the cathedral on Hlavná, at the other side of the fountain (which dances to music in the afternoons and evenings), stands the neo-Baroque **State Theater** (Štátne divadlo), built the end of the 19th century.

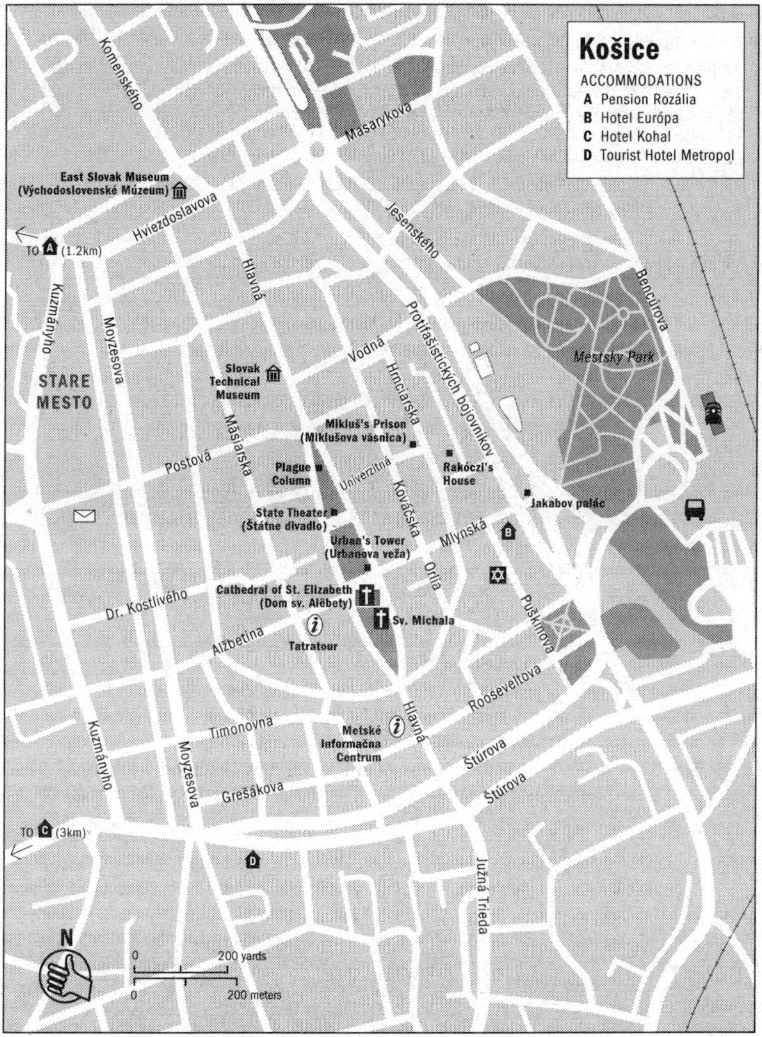

Past the theater on Hlavná, the 14m **Plague Column** (Morový sloup) commemorates the devastating outbreak of 1710. Running right from Hlavná between the Column and the theater, Univerzitná leads to two museums, **Mikluš's Prison** (Miklušova väznica) and **Rakóczi's House,** both at Hrnčiarska 7. The ticket office for both lies behind the gate at Hrnčiarska. Housed in the former city jail, Mikluš's prison reveals life behind bars from the 17th to 19th century, including prisoner graffiti, death verdicts, and torture instruments. The tour leads through reconstructed prison chambers, many with unflattering sketches of the executioners, and photo collections of actors demonstrating the various methods of torture and annihilation. Rakóczi's House is a shrine to Ferenc Rakóczi II, Hungary's anti-Habsburg national hero. The museum contains furniture and an entire room from Rakóczi's home in Turkey, where he died in exile. (Museums open Tu-Sa 9am-5pm, Su 9am-1pm. 20Sk, students 10Sk.)

At the northern end of Hlavná, past the Plague Column, stands the **East Slovak Museum** (Východnoslovenské Múzeum), Hviezdoslavova 3. Inside the building to the right, recent history shines with examples of the region's folk and religious art such as dancing saints, gigantic Jewish wedding bands, and a life-sized sculpture of a knight on horseback descending upon a peg-legged beggar. To the left, prehistoric remnants illuminate the saga of the Celts, Germans, and Slavs who settled the region. The museum's pride, however, awaits downstairs behind a two-ton door. In 1935, while laying foundations for a new finance headquarters at Hlavná 68, workers discovered a copper bowl filled with 2920 gold *tholars* and a Renaissance gold chain over 2m long. The vault has them on display. (Tel. 622 30 61. Open Tu-Sa 9am-5pm, Su 9am-1pm. 20Sk, students 10Sk)

ENTERTAINMENT

Fans of high and low culture alike will not be disappointed by Košice. Information and tickets for Košice's **philharmonic** and four **theaters** are available at the tourist office, Hlavná 8; beer and wine halls are plentiful in the town center.

Jazz Club, Kovasča 39 (tel. 622 42 37). Not much jazz, but its damp and crowded cellars echo with disco, oldies, and salsa. Cover 55Sk, plus 50Sk for live music. Open daily 5pm-2am.

Country Club Diera, 14 Poštová (tel. 622 05 51). Quenches the Slovak thirst for Bluegrass. Bartenders serve tequila shots and seven types of whiskey behind pictures of Annie Oakley and Davy Crockett. Thankfully, the beer isn't American. Open M-Th 11am-2am, F 11am-3am, Sa 6pm-3am.

Kaviaren Urbana (tel. 623 25 34), located in the 1628 Urbanova Veža, next to the cathedral. Watch the cascading singing fountain in front of the Divadlo Janka Boradáča while sipping your *Pilsner* (35Sk). Open M-Sa 10am-10pm.

Bar u Slona (Under the Elephant), Hlavná 37 (tel. 622 62 31), hidden in a romantic courtyard. Enter at the brass elephant standing on one leg and its trunk. Pizza 48-58Sk. *Heineken* 68Sk, *Plzen* 33Sk. Open M-Sa 10am-11pm, Su 2-11pm.

PREŠOV

More than a millennium ago, the first Slavic agricultural estates were already in place where Prešov (preh-SHUV; pop. 92,687), Slovakia's third-largest city, now stands. Those rural roots have grown into the rugged feel lingering among the historic buildings and monuments that form modern-day Prešov. While not an overly exciting city, it stands at the crossroads of cultures, where Gypsies, Magyars, Ukrainians, and Slovaks co-exist in a calm that can't help but mesmerize.

ORIENTATION & PRACTICAL INFORMATION. Prešov's stem, **Košická,** sprouts straight from the train station, blooming into **Masaryková,** then **Hlavná,** home of the Church of St. Nicholas. Northbound **buses** and **trolley-buses** (all except

#19 and 31) travel between the station and the center; take the walkway under Masaryková and purchase an 8Sk ticket from the orange automats at major stops, or from a kiosk. Otherwise, the center is a 20min. walk left from the train station along Košická, or a 50Sk taxi ride away. **Trains** (tel. 73 10 43) travel to: **Košice** (50min., 18 per day, 24Sk); **Bratislava** via **Kysak** (4½hr., 11 per day, 282Sk); and **Kraków** (5½hr., 3 per day, 639Sk). **Buses** (tel. 73 13 47 and 72 45 91), opposite the train station, travel to **Košice** (30-45min., 3 per hr., 26Sk) and **Poprad** (1½hr., hourly, 68Sk). **Metské Informačna Centrum,** Hlavná 67 (tel. 186 and tel./fax 73 11 13), provides info on the town and hotels. (Open May-Oct. M-F 8:30am-5:30pm, Sa 9am-noon; Nov.-Apr. M-F 8am-4:30pm.) **Exchange currency** at **Istrobanka,** Hlavná 75, which has good rates and an MC **ATM.** (Open M and W 8am-5pm, Tu and Th 8am-4pm, F 8am-2pm.) **Poštová Banka,** Hlavná 114 (tel. 72 15 99), cashes all **traveler's checks** for a 1% commission, exchanges currency, and houses an ATM. (Open M 8am-noon and 1-4:30pm, Tu and Th-F 8am-noon and 1-4pm, W 8am-noon and 1-6pm.) There is also a Cirrus/MC/Visa **ATM** at the bus station opposite stand #11. There is a **24hr. pharmacy** at Sabinovská 15 (tel. 71 94 05). Walk down Hlavná away from the train station, and Sabinovská is over the main road. Surf the **internet** at Meladova 8 for 40Sk per hr. (Open M-Su 9am-midnight.) The **post office,** Masarykova 2 (tel. 326 43), sits just south of the city center. (Open M-F 8am-7pm, Sa 8am-1pm.) **Telephones** stand outside. **Postal code:** 08001. **Phone code:** (0)91.

ACCOMMODATIONS & FOOD. Many inexpensive rooms hide in Prešov's suburbs, and since tourists aren't common, vacancies are. To get to **Turistická Ubytovaňa Sen,** Vajanského 65 (tel. 73 31 70), take a bus toward the center. Get off at the third stop, "Na Hlanéj," at the entrance to the main square. Follow the departing trolley and take the first right onto Metodova. Vajanského is 5min. up; turn left and the hostel is on the right. It rents 27 beds and one shower and is close to the center. (Check-out 10am. 200Sk.) 200 beds fill up the 10 floors of **Penzión Lineas,** Budovatelská 14 (tel. 72 33 25, ext. 28; fax 72 32 06). From the station, walk toward the town center, take the first left on Škultétýho, and left again at Budovatelská. (Check-out 11am. Doubles with bath 450Sk.) **Penzión Andreas,** Jarková (tel. 72 32 25), offers six lovely rooms in the center of town. Follow the bus directions for Turistická Ubytovaňa Sen, then follow the tram to Florianova. Turn left here and left again onto Jarková. The pension is on the left. (Call one week ahead. 400Sk; apartment double 1800Sk.)

Prešov boasts a well-spring of stellar restaurants. For do-it-yourselfers, there's a **Tesco** at Legionarova 1, where Hlavná becomes Masarykova. (Open M-Th 8am-7pm, F 8am-8pm, Sa 8am-4pm, Su 8am-1pm.) **Florianka,** Baštová 32 (tel. 73 40 83), sits through the archway next to Slovakia's best hotel and restaurant management school, which has made this former firehouse its training ground. Sip *Zlatý Bažant* beer (25Sk) by the old pushcart fire truck outside or enjoy hot meals in the restaurant's blazing red interior. The student chefs get high marks for food and service. (Chicken breast 62Sk; bean soup and stuffed peppers 52Sk. Open M-F 11am-7pm.) **Senator,** Hlavná 67 (tel. 773 11 86), overlooking Staré Mesto, serves vegetarian dishes (41-60Sk) and meatier Slovak fare. (Entrees 40-150Sk. Open M-F 10am-10pm, Sa-Su 11am-10pm.) There is also a wine and beer hall attached. (Open daily 3pm-midnight.) **Bagetéria,** Hlavná 36 (tel. 773 26 02), serves baguette sandwiches (30-50Sk) with and without meat. (Open M-F 6am-10pm, Sa 7:30am-10pm, Su 8am-10pm.) Down the street from Bagetéria, **Veliovič Cukráreň,** Hlavná 28, supplies sweets (6-10Sk), hefty desserts (banana splits 45Sk), and cappuccino (20Sk; open M-F 8am-9pm, Sa-Su 9am-9pm).

SIGHTS. Hlavná's Renaissance houses stand back in deference to the town's older **Church of St. Nicholas** (Kostol sv. Mikuláša). The Gothic cathedral's distinctive turrets attest to Saxon influence in Prešov during the late Middle Ages. The church opens its doors only irregularly other than for services; sleeved shirts will spare you glares. Near the church at Hlavná 86, the 16th-century **Rákoczi Palace,**

NEW YORK, PARIS, PREŠOV At first glance, it may seem that one of these places is "not like the others." Prešov's residents proudly broadcast, however, that the 49th parallel runs right through the city's Hlavná ul., placing it on a direct line with the City of Light and the City That Never Sleeps. Souvenirs and advertising pair New York with the Statue of Liberty, Paris with the Eiffel Tower, and Prešov with a bottle of beer. It seems, however, that the person who dreamed up this bit of geographical trivia might have had a few too many of those bottles of beer: while Prešov and Paris are indeed in cosmic alignment, New York hovers around the *41st* parallel.

with its attic gable of plants and saints, houses the **City Museum** (Krajské múzeum; tel. 73 47 08). The exhibition on fire moves from making it in the Stone Age to fighting it in more recent eras, concluding with old fire trucks parked out back. A new exhibit upstairs is dedicated to another element: moving photographs from a 1998 flood that ravaged a nearby village. (Open Tu-F 9am-noon and 12:30-5pm, Sa 9am-1pm, Su 1-5pm. 20Sk, students 10Sk.) Farther down the street, at #62, stands the 19th-century **Russians' Clubhouse** (Ruský Dom), the community center for this tiny minority group. A second-floor office sells books on Rusin history and culture, as well as the local Rusin newspaper. The hammer-and-sickle-adorned column outside seems even more anachronistic than the nearby statue of Neptune. The latter was given to the town by a 19th century Jewish merchant as thanks for allowing him to settle in Prešov. Amble down to the Greek Orthodox **St. John's Cathedral** (Katedrálny chrám sv. Jána Krstiteľa), at the base of Hlavná, to peek at the breathtaking altar. On the west side of Hlavná, the restored Gothic **Šarišská Gallery,** Hlavná 51, features Slovak art. (Tel. 72 54 23. Open Tu-F 9am-5pm, Sa 9am-1pm, Su 2-6pm. 10Sk, students 5Sk; Su free.)

Heading west from the town hall on Hlavná, the narrow, medieval Floriánova leads to **St. Florian's Gate** (Brána sv. Floriána), a remnant of Prešov's early Renaissance fortifications. In northwest Staré Mesto, just left off Hlavná at Švermova 56, sits the **synagogue,** with its ornate interior and 1991 monument to Prešov's 6000 victims of the Holocaust and the Tiso regime. If the doors are closed, you can still see the interior via the **Judaica Museum,** on the upper balcony. (Tel. 73 16 38. Open Tu-W 11am-4pm, Th 3pm-6pm, F 10am-1pm, Su 1-5pm. 40Sk, students 5Sk.)

NIGHTLIFE. There's a surprising amount of nightlife in this placid town—see for yourself at any of Prešov's numerous pubs, *vinareňí*, and nightclubs. For relaxation before the revelry, the town has two theaters and a fine **Wine Museum,** Floriánova ul. (tel. 73 31 08). This drinking establishment in the basement of the town hall serves more than 1000 varieties of wines for 60-20,000Sk per bottle. A 1763L wine barrel and 1.2m double-barreled-shotgun wine bottle wait at the end. (Open M-F 8am-7pm, Sa 8am-noon. 40Sk; 20Sk per person for groups of 5 or more.) **Piváreň Smädný Mních,** Svätoplukova 1 (tel. 72 18 04), on a side passage, features the "Thirsty Monk" (16Sk) and many happy locals. Just don't try swinging on the wagon-wheel chandeliers. (Open M-F and Su 9am-10pm.) The foot-tapping live folk music at **Vinaren Neptun,** Hlavná 62 (tel. 73 25 38), provides a refreshing break from Abba and friends. (Open M-Th and Su 8am-10pm, F-Sa 8pm-3am.) But if it's Abba you want, the red-lighted **Alpa,** Kováčska 3 (tel. 72 52 52), is the place to be. Dress up and dress tight. (Open daily from 8pm-3am.)

NEAR PREŠOV: MEDZILABORCE

While Medzilaborce (pop. 6000) isn't anything spectacular, it can claim one peculiar attraction: its **Museum of Modern Art** (Múzeum Moderného Umenia), on A. Warhola. From the train station, turn left onto Dobranského, which becomes A. Warhola; look for the two Campbell's soup cans guarding the entrance. The museum was established by John Warhol, brother of Andy, in memory of his sibling and parents. The location is not as random as it might initially seem—the Warhol family migrated to the U.S. after WWII from the tiny village of Miková near

Medzilaborce. Andy (or Andrej, as his birth certificate would have it) was born two years later. The museum houses a couple of Warhol originals, as well as possessions important to Warhol family history, such as the dress worn by the Warhol boys for their Baptism. The biographical information on Warhol—emphasizing his humble beginnings and shy demeanor—is particularly interesting in light of the very high profile he kept after achieving stardom. Also on display are works by Andy's brother Paul, which range from experiments with the screenprinting made famous by his brother to decorative pieces made from colored eggs; works by Paul's son James; and other, less nepotistic temporary exhibits. (Tel. 210 59. fax 210 69 Open Tu-Su 9am-5pm. 20Sk, students 10Sk. Cameras 50Sk; video 100Sk.)

GETTING THERE. The best way to reach Medzilaborce from **Prešov** is to catch a train to **Humenné** (1½hr., 10 per day) and then switch trains to Medzilaborce (1¼hr., 14 per day.) The whole trip will cost 74Sk. Catching the 8:50am train to Hummené will let you make the trip without staying over. But if you're not an early riser (and what aspiring pop artists are?), you can crash at **Športklub,** Mierova 20 (tel. 218 55). From the museum, A. Warhola continues over the river and becomes Mierova. The hotel is on the left just after the rail crossing. (4-bed dorms with hot water and shared bath 250Sk. Check-out noon.)

BARDEJOV

For the last 500 years, the monuments of Bardejov (bar-day-YOV) have been dancing with disaster. The troubles began in 1494, when the vault of the Church of St. Aegidius collapsed only months after its construction. Turkish armies, an earthquake, and three fires left the town in ruin, but the citizens have kept coming back with a vengeance. Bardejov's most recent restoration won a UNESCO heritage gold medal in 1986. Today, the few tourists that come to town do so for the healing springs in nearby Bardejovské Kúpele, although the town's peaceful beauty is an attraction in its own right.

ORIENTATION & PRACTICAL INFORMATION. The quickest way to and from Bardejov is by **train** to **Prešov** (1½hr. 9 per day, 30Sk) or **Kraków** (6½hr., 3 per day, 758Sk). The **bus station,** next to the train station, sends buses to **Poprad** (2½hr., 10 per day, 80Sk) and **Košice** (1¾hr., 14 per day, 50Sk). From the train station, turn left and take the stone path to the right through the ruined, lower gate of Staré Mesto onto Stöcklova. Follow Stöcklova around to the left and turn right onto Paštová to reach **Radničné nám.,** the main square. The **tourist office,** Radničné nám. 21 (tel./fax 472 60 72), displays a green and white "I." (Open May-Oct. 15 daily 10am-6pm; Oct. 16-Apr. daily 8am-4pm.) **Exchange currency** at **VÚB,** Kellerova 1 (tel. 472 26 71), or cash AmEx/Visa **traveler's checks** for a 1% commission. The bank also has a Cirrus/MC **ATM.** (Bank open M-W and F 8am-5pm. ATM open daily 6am-10pm.) **Poľnobanka,** Dlhý rad 17 (tel. 474 67 45), does the Visa cash advance thang. (Open M-F 8am-2:30pm). A **pharmacy** sits at Radničné nám. 43. (Open M-F 8:30am-noon and 1-4:30pm.) The **post office** is at Dlhý rad 14 (tel. 472 20 96; open M-F 7:30am-1:30pm, Sa 8-11:30am). The outer foyer office sells phone cards (open M-F 7am-5:30pm). **Telephones** stand outside. **Postal code:** 08501. **Phone code:** (0)935.

ACCOMMODATIONS & FOOD. Popular with teenage Slovaks and the only consistent option in town, **Športhotel,** Katuzovovo 31 (tel. 472 49 49; fax 472 82 08), is 15min. from the train station. Turn right from the station and follow Slovenská; take the first left onto Kúpelná, and, after 200m, a right on Kellerova (the street isn't well marked, but you'll see a bridge when you turn). Take the first left after the bridge and the hotel will appear on the right. (Hot water 4-10pm. Check-out 10am. Call ahead. Doubles with bath 500Sk; triples 700Sk; quads 800Sk.)

Restaurants in Bardejov are affordable, but few rise above the rabble of snack bars and drab beer halls. **U Zlatá Koruny,** Radničné nám. 41 (tel. 472 53 10), is one exception, serving a variety of wines and elegant entrees for 30-120Sk. They also have a self-service deli (enter on the side of the restaurant), and salads sold by weight. (Open M-Th and Su 9am-10pm, F-Sa 9am-11pm.) **Reštaurácia Na Bráne,** Jiráskova 3 (tel. 472 23 48), at the end of Hviezdoslavova, looks like a dark beer hall, but the food (entrees 32-85Sk) is simple and good. (Open M-F 8am-9pm, Sa-Su 8am-7:30pm.) Next to the natural science chapter of the Bardejov museum sits the **Bagetéria,** Rhodýho 4. Design your own sandwich or salad from well-displayed greens, cheeses, and breads (7-38Sk), and enjoy the CD collection and original graphics on the walls. (Open M-Th and Su 10am-11pm, F-Sa 10am-midnight.)

SIGHTS. Bardejov may be the only town in Šariš where the square's centerpiece isn't a church. The maple tree at the south end is a gift from the U.S., brought in 1991 by former vice-president Dan Quayle. The **town hall** *(radnica)*, Radničné nám. 48 (tel. 74 60 38), now serves as one of the town's museums, displaying historic trinkets. Among them is the key to the city, which the mayor's wife passed to her treacherous Turkish lover in 1697; she was later executed for her deceit. The **ikony** exhibition, Radničné nám. 27 (tel. 472 20 09), houses a huge collection of Orthodox icons. The "Nature of Northeastern Slovakia" display in the **Prírodopisné Museum** (tel. 72 26 30), on Rhodýho 4, will tickle the animal-stuffer in you. (Museums open May-Oct. 15 Tu-Su 8:30am-noon and 12:30-5pm; Oct. 16-Apr. Tu-Su 8am-noon and 12:30-4pm. 25Sk, students 10Sk). All museums (including Bardejovské Kúpele; see below) join under the auspices of Šarišské Museum, Radničné nám. 13 (tel. 474 60 38), the office headquarters, which should not be mistaken with the actual exhibitions.

The **Church of St. Aegidius** (Kostol sv. Egídia), at the downhill end of Radničné nám., contains 11 Gothic wing altars crafted between 1450 and 1510. In the 17th century, iconoclastic Calvinists took over the town and the church. Fortunately, they compromised with the town's merchants and let the altars stay as long as they remained shut. The biggest and most valuable is the 15th-century **Nativity Altar.** (Open M-F 9am-5pm, Sa 10am-5pm, Su 11:30am-3:30pm. 20Sk.) A walk down Veterna, over the main road and left up Pod lipken leads to the **Church of the Holy Cross** (Kostol sv. Kríža), which stands watch over Bardejov's cemetery. A forest path leads past 14 stark Stations of the Cross before reaching the weed-filled graveyard. A full panorama of Bardejov's valley stretches below, but watch out for the stinging nettles. Veterna ends at one of Bardejov's **bastions,** which first served as a crossroads beacon and later as the local beheading stock. The tourist office has pamphlets on all the **walking tours** possible around Bardejov and its 14th-century towers. One focuses on the history of Bardejov's Jewish quarter at ul. Mlynská, west of the city center, where there is a closed **synagogue** and a memorial plaque to the more than 7,000 Bardejov Jews who perished during the Holocaust.

NEAR BARDEJOV: BARDEJOVSKÉ KÚPELE

About 5km from Bardejov, Bardejovské Kúpele works wonders with its springs and country air. Actual curing stations are off-limits, but several free fountains spurt with the spa's acidic water. The complex is an awkward collection of 18th- and 19th-century buildings in need of a paint job and more recent (less ornate) hotels, all laced together by sidewalks and fountains. The spa reached its zenith in the late 18th and early 19th centuries with such clientele as Alexander I of Russia, Emperor Joseph II of Austria-Hungary, and the wives of Austrian Emperor Franz Joseph and Napoleon, but WWI and the fall of the Empire cut the spa off from Hungarian aristocrats. On the resort's outskirts, Slovakia's oldest folklore exhibition sits in a hectare replica of Šariš village life. In summer, the **skansen** (or Múzeum Ľudovej; tel. 472 20 72) hosts regular folk festivals and craft days. (Open May-Sept. Tu-Su 9:30am-noon and 12:30-5pm; Oct.-Apr. Tu-Su 8am-noon and 12:30-3:30pm. 20Sk, students 10Sk.)

GETTING THERE. To get to Bardejovské Kúpele, take **bus** #2, 7, 10, or 12 to the end of the line (20min.) from the front of the train station

SLOVENIA
(SLOVENIJA)

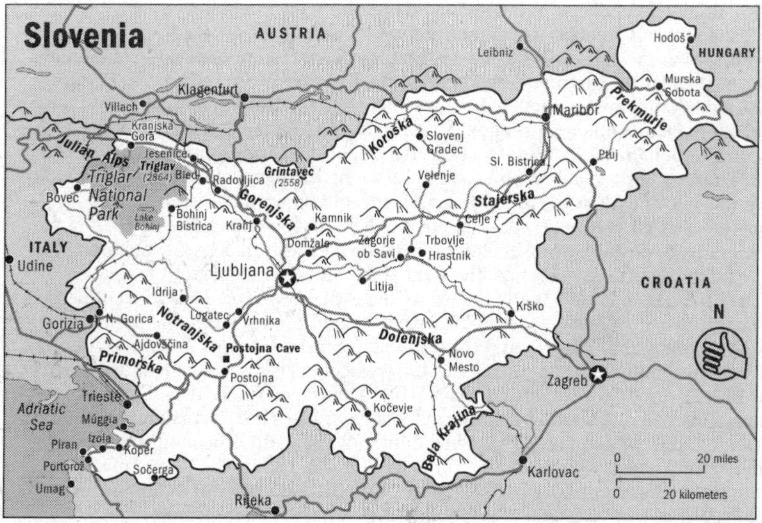

US$1 = 183SIT (SLOVENIAN TOLARS)	**100SIT = US$0.54**
CDN$1 = 123SIT	**100SIT = CDN$0.80**
UK£1 = 294SIT	**100SIT = UK£0.33**
IR£1 = 247SIT	**100SIT = IR£0.40**
AUS$1 = 119SIT	**100SIT = AUS$0.83**
NZ$1 = 97SIT	**100SIT = NZ$1.01**
SAR1 = 30SIT	**100SIT = SAR3.25**
DM1 = 99SIT	**100SIT = DM1.01**

PHONE CODES Country code: **386.** International dialing prefix: **00.**

Slovenia, the most prosperous of Yugoslavia's breakaway republics, has reveled in its independence, modernizing rapidly while turning a hungry eye toward the West. It has quickly separated itself from its neighbors, using liberal politics and a high GDP to gain entrance into highly sought-after trade and security alliances. For a country half Switzerland's size, Slovenia, on the "sunny side of the Alps," is also extraordinarily diverse: in a day, you can breakfast on an Alpine peak, lunch under the Mediterranean sun, and dine in a vineyard on the Pannonian plains.

HIGHLIGHTS OF SLOVENIA

- Youthful **Ljubljana** feels like a slice of Western Europe in the Balkans (p. 713).
- Hike through the Triglavski National Park for adrenalized adventures in **Blejski Vintgar,** complete with waterfalls, icy pools, and white-water rapids (p. 721).

LIFE & TIMES

HISTORY

Slovenes are descendants of the **West Slavs** who migrated to the Eastern Alps in the 6th century, absorbing the existing Roman, Celtic, and Illyrian cultures. In 623, a Slavic kingdom emerged under **Samo** (623-658) but soon fell to the Franks after 748. Although the Slavs were assimilated into the Magyar and Bulgarian tribes, the tribal duchy of **Carinthia**—precursor of modern Slovenia—survived.

Following the fall of the Frankish Empire in the 10th century, Slovene lands were given to the German kingdom, and the Slovenes were reduced to serfdom. The kingdom was not secure, however, and the territory occupied by Slovene speakers changed hands frequently, falling briefly under Slavic rule in the 13th century when **Otakar II** of Bohemia tried to establish a Slavic empire. From 1278 to 1335, all but Istria (nabbed by Venice), fell to the **Habsburgs.** Habsburg rule, while stifling, allowed Slovenes to reach high levels of literacy and technological development, as well as the early development of a market economy. The last half of the 19th century saw a growing hunger for a national identity, marked by the first Slovene political parties and the codification of the Slovene language.

In 1918, Slovenia reluctantly agreed to join the newly formed Kingdom of Serbs, Croats, and Slovenes (renamed **Yugoslavia**—Land of the South Slavs—in 1929), with the capital in Zagreb, and thus Slovenia ceased to be a part of the Austro-Hungarian empire. The new state was too weak, however, to withstand the attacks of Hitler's armed forces during **WWII.** When Yugoslavia fell in 1941, Slovenia was partitioned among Germany, Italy, and Hungary. After the German attack on the Soviet Union in summer 1941, Christian Socialists and other left-wing groups joined the Yugoslav partisan army of **Josip Broz Tito.** Led by the Communist party, the army was eventually recognized by the British and Americans as an ally against Hitler, and as such, was supplied with arms to continue their fight.

By 1945, partisans occupied all of Yugoslavia, and once again a unified state emerged, this time with Tito in command and the capital in Belgrade. Tito liquidated Slovene politicians and leaders who failed to cooperate with the Communists; tens of thousands of Slovene patriots were murdered at **Kočevje.** The 50th anniversary of this mass murder was commemorated in 1995, ending five decades of silence. Starting in 1948, as a rift formed between Tito and Stalin, Yugoslavia began to introduce a market economy. Slovenia was soon acknowledged as the economically strongest and most Westernized of the Yugoslav republics. Upon Tito's death in 1980, confusion undermined the seeming peace and stability of the country. Long-suppressed **ethnic conflicts** threatened to tear Yugoslavia apart. The Communist Party's attempts to find a replacement for Tito failed. Without the fear of a strong hand in Belgrade, opposition speedily emerged in Slovenia.

In April 1990, Slovenia held the first contested elections in Yugoslavia since before WWII, bringing to power a center-right coalition that called for independence. On June 25, 1991, Slovenia seceded from the federation. The Yugoslav army responded with force, but after 10 days of violent clashes, it gave up the fight; Serbia, the driving force behind Yugoslavia and the conflict, had no border claims against the Slovenes, and no large Serbian minority lives in Slovenia. The final steps to independence were the new Slovene constitution of December 1991 and its recognition by the European Community in 1992.

SLOVENIA TODAY

On July 12, 1995, the European Commission approved Slovenian associate membership in the **E.U.** The terms were favorable, but problems may arise because of the stipulation that Slovenia revise the 1975 **Osimo Agreements** with Italy, which might allow the re-acquisition of Slovene lands by Italians forced out after WWII. Whether or not this is unacceptable to Slovenia, accession is not likely to happen until 2003. Currently, the Liberal Democratic Party (LDS; made up of former Communists), in coalition with two smaller conservative parties, holds power in the **Skupšcina Slovenije** (Assembly of Slovenia), with **Janež Drnovsek** of the LDS as Prime Minister. **Milan Kučan** won re-election as president in February 1997. Slovenia has gained membership in international organizations such as the Council of Europe, the IMF, the World Bank, the World Trade Organization, and the Central Europe Free Trade Area. While **NATO** disappointed Slovenia by denying it membership in its first round of expansion, the nation is preening itself for inclusion in the anticipated second round. Slovenia recently replaced Poland as a non-permanent member of the UN Security Council through 1999. Although the process of economic reform is far from over, the pains of transition have so far been easier to bear here than in many parts of Eastern Europe; Slovenia's per capita GNP is far above that of most Eastern European countries.

LITERATURE & ARTS

Although Slovenian literature and art dates back to the 11th century, most early works were purely devotional and religious. In fact, from the 11th to the 19th century, Slovenia's main contribution to international art was the Renaissance composer Jakob Petelin Gallus-Carniolus, known in the rest of the world as **Jacob Handl.** In the 19th century, however, Slovene literature emerged as an important national art form with the codification of the language by **Jernej Kopitar** in 1843 and the writings of the Romantic poet **France Prešeren** (see **Ljubljana: Sights,** p. 716). The early 19th century's greatest Slovene poet, Prešeren was instrumental in revitalizing Slovene literature through his use of Western European literary models in his patriotic poems. Throughout the later **Realist** period (1848-1899), writers such as **Fran Erjaveć** focused on folkloric themes with a patriotic flavor; the first Slovene novel, *The Tenth Brother* (*Deseti brat)*, by **Josip Jurčič,** was published in 1866.

The prevalence of the Romantic themes of nationalism and freedom from foreign influence didin't stop Western European ideas from molding the Slovene **Modernist** and **Expressionist** movements in the first half of the 20th century. Modernist prose flowered in **Ivan Čankar's** 1904 *The Ward of Our Lady of Mercy (Hisa Marije pomocnice)* and his 1907 *The Bailiff Yerney and His Rights (Hlapec Jernej in njegova pravica)*, while Expressionism showed the social and spiritual tensions brought on by WWI in the poetry of **Tone Seliskar, Miran Jarc,** and **Anton Vodnik,** and in the plays of **Slavko Grum.** Coinciding with the Modernist and Expressionist movements in Slovene literature, architect **Jože Plečnik** was a major figure in the development of **Art Nouveau.** While he designed buildings in both Vienna and Prague, his masterpiece is his transformation of his hometown, Ljubljana, from a provincial city to a cosmopolitan capital (see **Ljubljana: Sights,** p. 716).

The advent of Soviet **Socialist Realism** crushed many of the modern and avant-garde trends that had diversified the Slovene literary movement. Disillusionment was the theme of **Bozo Vodusek's** caustic sonnets. The aftermath of WWII shaped poet/dramatist **Matej Bor's** 1958 *A Wanderer in the Atomic Age (Sel je popotnik skozi atomski vek)*. **Cene Vipotnik, France Balantič,** and especially **Jože Udovič** contributed to Slovene literature's continued growth. At the end of the 70s, a number of Slovenian writers, including **Vitomis Zupan, Igor Torkar,** and **Jože Snoj,** came out with books that dealt with Stalinism in Slovenia. The postmodern trend of the 80s showed up in the so-called **"Young Slovenian Prose"** movement, which had its strongest representation in short prose pieces. Today, Slovenian literature is widely translated, especially into German, and enjoys a level of activity rivaling its glorious past. Two current stars in international literature include poet **Tomaž Šalamun** and Ljubljana-based cultural critic and essayist **Slavoj Žižek.**

READING LIST

Interesting accounts of Slovenia's history are rare. An exception is Jill Benderly's *Independent Slovenia: Origins, Movements, Prospects*, a volume of essays exploring the peaceful transition to Slovenian independence with writings from economic theorists, Slovenia's foreign minister, punk sociologists, and radical feminists. A more sensual approach to Slovenia is delivered in native Slovene Roman Latković's travelogue *Bewitching Istria: A Never-Ending Story.* Of course, no reading about Slovenia is complete without a foray into the wacky yet brilliant world of cultural critic Slavoj Žižek. *The Žižek Reader* offers an entertaining introduction to the work of this flamboyant essayist who has been described as an "arresting, insightful and scandalous thinker."

FACTS AND FIGURES

- **Capital:** Ljubljana
- **Population:** 1,955,000
- **Land Area:** 20,256km^2
- **Geography:** Mostly mountains and plateaus
- **Language:** Slovenian
- **Religions:** 96% Catholic
- **GDP per capita:** US$8,634
- **Major Exports:** Machinery, transport equipment

SLOVENIA ESSENTIALS

Australian, Canadian, Irish, New Zealand, U.K., and U.S. citizens can visit visa-free for up to 90 days. South Africans need visas (180-day single-entry or transit US$35; 180-day multiple entry US$70). Apply by mail or in person in your home country (see **Essentials: Embassies and Consulates,** p. 13). Processing takes a few days, and requires your passport and the fee in the form of a money order.

PRIMARY BORDER CROSSINGS. Visas for Slovenia cannot be purchased at any border crossing. There is no entry fee required at the border. The easiest way into or out of Slovenia is to take a direct bus or train from Ljubljana to the capital city of the neighboring country.

Austria: Jesenice, SLN/Villach, AUS via Karavanški predor, SLN; connects the Julian Alps (p. 719) with Klagenfurt, AUS.

Croatia: Sočerga, SLN/Sočerga, CRO; connects Slovenian Istria (p. 725) with the Gulf of Kvarner, CRO (p. 153). Potorož, SLN/Umag, CRO; connects Slovenian Istria (p. 725) with Croatian Istria (p. 149).

Hungary: Murska Sobota, SLN/Őriszentpéter, HUN (p. 307); connects eastern Slovenia with the Őrseg (p. 296) and Lake Balaton (p. 309).

Italy: Koper, SLN/Múggia, ITA via Fernetiči, SLN; connects Slovenian Istria (p. 725) with Trieste, ITA. Novy Gorica, SLN/Gorizia, ITA; connects the Julian Alps (p. 719) with Udine, ITA.

GETTING THERE & GETTING AROUND

Slovenia is easily accessible by train, or plane. There are three international **airports,** but commercial flights all arrive at the **Ljubljana Airport,** which has regular bus service to the city 25km away. The national carrier **Adria Airways** flies to European capitals. A regular **hydrofoil** service also runs between Venice and Portorož.

Trains are cheap, clean, and reliable. You can usually find a seat on local trains, although it's best to avoid peak commuting hours near Ljubljana. Round-trip tickets are 20% cheaper than two one-way tickets. For most international destinations, travelers under 26 can get a 20% discount; check at the Ljubljana station (look for the **BIJ-Wasteels** logo). Domestic tickets are available for ISIC holders at a 30% discount. In both cases ask for a *"popust"* (discount). *"Vlak"* means train, *"prihodi vlakov"* means arrivals, and *"odhodi vlakov"* means departures. Schedules usually list trains by direction; look for trains that run *dnevno* (daily).

Buses are roughly 25% more expensive, but run to some otherwise inaccessible places in the mountains. Tickets are sold at the station or on board; put your luggage in the passenger compartment if it's not too crowded. All large backpacks cost 200Sit extra. For those traveling by **car,** the **Automobile Association of Slovenia's** emergency telephone number is 987. *Let's Go* does not recommend **hitchhiking,** which is extremely uncommon in Slovenia. If not traveling by bus or train, most Slovenes transport themselves by **bike.** Nearly every town has a bike rental office.

TOURIST SERVICES & MONEY

Tourist offices are located in most major cities and tourist spots. The staff are generally helpful, speak English and German, provide basic information, and assist in finding accommodations. The main tourist organization in Slovenia is **Kompas.**

The national **currency** is the Slovenian **tolar** (Sit). Currency prices tend to be stable and are set in Deutschmarks (DM) rather than dollars (US$). **Banks** are usually open Monday-Friday 8am-5pm and Saturday 8-11am. Rates vary, but tend to be better in major cities. Some establishments charge no commission, a fact reflected by worse rates; post offices have the worst of all. Almost everyone—from restaurants and shops to train stations—accepts major **credit cards,** including AmEx, but the most widely endorsed is MC, followed by Visa. There's a 20% **value-added tax,** but for purchases over 9000Sit, it is refundable at the border (ask the store salesperson for a tax-free check). There is one **ATM** in Ljubljana, but they are nonexistent outside the city. You can, fortunately, withdraw money from bank tellers. Two major Slovenian banks are Ljubljanska Banka and Gorenjska Banka.

COMMUNICATION

Mail is the cheapest and most reliable means of communication. **Post offices** are usually open Monday-Friday 8am-7pm and Saturday 8am-noon, with night and Sunday service in larger cities. To send letters via airmail, ask for *letalsko.* Air mail takes 1-2 weeks to reach North America, Australia, New Zealand, and South Africa. Postage rates are very reasonable. To the U.S., letters cost 105Sit and postcards cost 95Sit; to the U.K. 100Sit for letters, 90Sit for postcards; to Australia and New Zealand 110Sit and 100Sit. While at the post office, purchase a **magnetic phone card** (750Sit per 50 impulses, which yields 50 local calls or 90 seconds to the U.S.). For **MCI WorldPhone** call 080 88 08. Similar services for other phone companies are not yet available, but should be by 2000. Call 901 for English-speaking operator-assisted collect calls. If you want to call collect from a post office, say *"P.O. pogovor."* Calling the U.S. is expensive (over US$6 per min.). If you must, try the phones at the post office and pay when you're finished.

> **PHONE CHANGES.** Slovenia is in the process of changing all of its phone numbers. Although we've accounted for as many as possible, most aren't changing until January 2000, and therefore some of the numbers we list will be wrong. When you call a changed number, a voice will tell you in both English and Slovenian what the new number is.

LANGUAGE

Slovene, a Slavic language, employs the Latin alphabet. Most young people speak at least some **English,** but the older generation (especially in the Alps) is more likely to understand **German** (in the north) or **Italian** (along the Adriatic). Many cities along the Italian border are officially bilingual. The tourist industry is generally geared toward Germans, although most tourist office employees speak English.

When speaking Slovene, "*č*" is pronounced "ch," "*š*" is "sh," and "*ž*" is pronounced is "zh." "*R*" is at times a vowel (pronounced "er"), while "*v*" and "*l*" turn silent at the strangest times. Phrases essential to winning the natives over include *"dober dan"* ("hello"), *"prosim"* ("please"), and *"hvala lepa"* ("thank you very much.") The words most frequently used in this chapter are *"Stari Grad"* ("Old Town"), *"Trg"* ("square"), *"cesta"* ("road"), *"cerkev"* ("church"), *"most"* ("bridge"), and *"lekarna"* ("pharmacy"). For more words, see the **Slovenian glossary,** p. 824.

HEALTH & SAFETY

EMERGENCY NUMBERS.
Fire: tel. 112. **Police:** tel. 113. **Ambulance:** tel. 112.

Slovenia's **climate** varies by region: Mediterranean near the Adriatic, Alpine in the mountains, moderately continental on the eastern plains, and pleasant everywhere in summer, although snow may strew the Alps as late as June. A Slovene proverb says that if it *doesn't* rain on May 15, it *will* rain for 40 days afterwards, but don't use this as a reason to avoid spring visits—even the groundhog isn't always right.

Crime rates, especially for violent crime, are very low in Slovenia. Even in the largest cities, friendly drunks and bad drivers are the greatest public menace. The occasional unwanted ogles and pick-up lines do occur.

Medical facilities are nearly up to Western standards, although there are very few English-speaking doctors. Fortunately, there is a hospital for foreigners in Ljubljana (see **Ljubljana: Practical Information,** p. 714). U.K. citizens receive free medical care with a valid passport; everyone else must pay cash. **Pharmacies** are also stocked to Western standards, although brand names will be different; ask for *obliž* (band-aids), *tamponi* (tampons), and *vložki* (sanitary-pads) in Slovenian.

ACCOMMODATIONS & CAMPING

At the height of tourist season prices are steep, services slow, and rooms scarce. The seaside, packed as early as June, is claustrophobic in July and August. Tourists also tend to swarm to the mountains during these months, and student rooms are generally available late June to early September. **Hotels** fall into five categories (L (deluxe), A, B, C, and D) and tend to be expensive. **Youth hostels** and **student dormitories** are cheap, but are generally open only in summer (June 25-Aug. 30). **Pensions** are pricey and **hotels** impossible. The best option is to rent **private rooms**—prices vary according to location, but rarely exceed US$30, and most rooms are good. Inquire at the tourist office or look for *Zimmer frei* or *sobe* signs on the street. **Campgrounds** can be crowded, but are generally in excellent condition. Bungalows are rare. Reserve all accommodations at least three days in advance.

FOOD & DRINK

For mouth-watering homestyle cooking, try a *gostilna* or *gostišče* (interchangeable words for a restaurant with a country flavor, although a *gostišče* usually also rents rooms). A good national dish to start with is *jota*, a soup with potatos, beans and sauerkraut. *Svinjska pečenka* (roast pork) is tasty, but **vegetarians** should look for *štruklji*—large, slightly sweet dumplings eaten as a main dish. In a pinch, vegetarians can always rely on the abundance of Italian pizzerias for meatless dishes. Fast food is not nearly as appetizing: the most popular street food in Ljubljana is horse burger. Slovenes savor their desserts; one of their favorites is *potica*, which consists of a sheet of pastry that is spread with a rich filling and rolled up. The most popular filling is made from walnuts.

The country's **wine** tradition, dating from antiquity, was fostered during the Middle Ages. Look for familiar grape varieties on the label. *Renski Rizling* and *Šipon* are popular whites. Slovenia produces many unique red wines, including the light *Cviček*, from the central region, and the potent *Teran*, from the coast. The art of brewing is centuries old here as well; good beers include *Laško* and *Union*. For something stronger, try *ganje*, a strong fruit brandy. The most enchanting alcoholic concoction is *Viljamovka*, distilled by monks who know the secret of getting a full pear inside the bottle. **Tap water** is drinkable everywhere.

CUSTOMS & ETIQUETTE

Slovenians welcome foreigners to their country with open kitchens. If you are fortunate enough to be invited into someone's home, remember to bring an odd number of **flowers.** At restaurants and cafes, the bill is never split; one person pays for everything, and any evening up can be attended to later. **Tipping** is not expected, although rounding up will be appreciated. In general, **business hours** are Monday to Friday 8am-5pm, Saturday 8am-noon. Although anti-gay acts are rare, attitudes toward **homosexuals** range from unsure to unfriendly. Slovenes dress stylishly, so be prepared for quizzical stares if you romp around in jeans and a t-shirt.

NATIONAL HOLIDAYS

January 1-2, New Year's; February 8, Culture Day (Prešeren Day); April 23-24, Easter; April 27, National Resistance Day (WWII); May 1-2, Labor Day; June 25, National Day; August 15, Assumption; October 31, Reformation Day; November 1, Remembrance Day; December 25, Christmas; December 26, Independence Day.

LJUBLJANA

If you are arriving in Ljubljana (pop. 270,000) after some time in Central Europe, the prices will stop you in your carefree currency tracks. The city also suffers from two significant architectural scars: an 1895 earthquake which leveled everything but a few Roman walls, and intensive Socialist urban planning. Despite the high prices and the lack of a true cosmopolitan feel, however, Ljubljana manages to find its niche among European capitals. With students comprising 10% of its 350,000 inhabitants, student bars and clubs can be found on literally every corner. Furthermore, the beautifully organized city center—designed by Jože Plečnik (see **Literature & Arts,** p. 709)—is worthy of the social life it houses. His columns and pyramidal structures testify to the decidedly social core of a city swept with weeping willows. Grin and bear the prices, enjoy the fast pace of student life, and watch people stroll with romantic ease as the green Ljubljanica River ambles along.

GETTING THERE & GETTING AROUND

Airplanes: A shuttle (tel. 64 08 39) goes from major hotels to the **airport** (tel. (064) 22 27 00), 23km away in Brnik. 3500Sit, 4000Sit round-trip. Reservations, made through hotels, are required. You can also take the public bus from the #28 stop (1hr., 480Sit). Buses depart M-F hourly 7am-8pm, Sa-Su 6am, 9am, and every odd hour until 7pm. **Adria Airways,** Gosposvetska 6 (tel. 31 33 12 and 32 16 67); **Austrian Airlines,** Dunajska 107 (tel. 168 40 99); **Lufthansa,** Gosposvetska 6 (tel. 32 66 69); **Swissair,** Dunajska 156 (tel. 169 10 10); **British Airways,** Slovenska 56 (tel. 300 10 00).

Trains: Trg O.F. 6 (tel. 291 33 32). To: **Budapest** (9hr., 2 per day, 6300Sit); **Munich** (6hr., 3per day, 9000Sit); **Trieste** (3hr., 4 per day, 2900Sit); **Venice** (6hr., 3 per day, 4300Sit); **Vienna** (6hr., 2 per day, 7700Sit); and **Zagreb** (2½hr., 7 per day, 2200Sit).

Buses: Trg O.F. 4 (tel. 134 38 38), in front of the trains. To: **Zagreb** (3hr., 4 per day, 2270Sit); and **Rijeka** (3hr., 1 per day, 1770Sit).

Local Transportation: Buses run until midnight. Drop 130Sit in change in the box beside the driver, or buy 80Sit tokens *(žetoni)* at post offices and newsstands. One-day (280Sit) and weekly (1400Sit) passes are sold at **Ljubljanski Potniški Promet,** in the red kiosk in front of Slovenska cesta 55.

Taxis: Tel. 97 00 through 97 09, or catch one on the street. About 150Sit per km.

Car Rental: Kompas Hertz, Miklošičeva 11.

Bike Rental: At the bus station. 500Sit per hour, 2500Sit per day. Open daily 5am-6pm.

ORIENTATION

Central Ljubljana envelopes the curvy Ljubljanica River, which roughly separates day from night—the concrete business district from the picturesque **Stare Miasto** (Old Town). The **train** and **bus stations** are on **Trg Osvobodilne Fronte (Trg O.F. or O.F. Square).** To get to the city center, stand with your back to the train station, turn left, walk past the small park, then take a right onto the first street, **Resljeva.** Follow Resljeva, then bear right on **Trubarjeva cesta,** which leads to **Prešernov Trg,** the main square. After crossing the **Tromostovje** (Triple Bridge), you'll see Stari Miasto at the castle hill's base; the tourist office is on the left at the corner of Stritarjeva and Miklošičeva. To reach **Slovenska,** walk up **Čopova** from Prešernov Trg.

PRACTICAL INFORMATION

TOURIST & FINANCIAL SERVICES

Tourist Office: Tourist Information Center (TIC), Stritarjeva 1 (tel. 306 12 35 and 306 12 15; fax 306 12 04; email pcl.tic-lj@ljubljana.si). Offers free maps and excellent brochures—including the useful *Where?* and *Events* (in English, free)—and arranges accommodations. Open M-F 8am-7pm, Sa 9am-5pm, Su 10am-6pm. The branch at the train station (tel. 133 94 75) is open June-Sept. daily 8am-9pm; Oct.-May daily 10am-6pm.

Budget Travel: Erazem, Trubarjeva cesta 7 (tel. 133 10 76; fax 133 20 84), in Stari Miasto. Geared toward students. Open M-F 10am-5pm.

Embassies and Consulates: Australia, Trg Republike 3 (tel. 125 42 52; fax 126 47 21). Open M-F 9am-1pm. **U.K.,** Trg Republike 3 (tel. 125 71 91; fax 125 01 74). Open M-F 9am-noon. **U.S.,** Pražkova 4 (tel. 30 14 27; fax 30 14 01). Open M, W, and F 2-4pm, Tu and Th 9am-noon and 2-4pm.

Currency Exchange: Currency exchanges *(menjalnice)* abound. **Ljubljanska banka** has branches all over the city that change money and cash traveler's checks for decent rates and no commission. The worst rates are at the post office; the best are in **Upimo,** Šubičeva 1 (open M-F 8am-6:30pm, Sa 8:30-1pm).

ATMs: The only **ATM** is on Trg Republike in the Maximarket archway next to the travel office (Cirrus/MC; 24hr.). Money can be drawn using AmEx/MC/Visa cards in banks at *"tolarsko i devinzno poslovanje"* counters. **Ljubljanska banka** at Čopova 3 does this on the 1st floor, counter #10. Open M, W, and Sa 9am-noon, Tu 2-5pm, Th 3-5pm.

American Express: Trubavjeva 50 (tel. 133 20 28).

LOCAL SERVICES & COMMUNICATIONS

Luggage storage: At the train station. Look for *"garderoba"* signs. 180Sit per day. 24hr.

English Bookstore: MK-Knjigarna Konzorcij, Slovenska 29 (tel. 21 98 33 and 21 98 36). Good selection of English-language books, as well as international magazines and newspapers. Open M-F 8am-7:30pm, Sa 8am-1pm. **Kocbekova knjigarna,** Slovenska 55 (tel. 31 07 36), is smaller but homier. Open M-F 8am-7pm, Sa 8am-1pm.

Laundromat: Tic, Student Campus, Cesta 27 Aprila 31, Building 9 (tel. 27 43 97). Self-service. 3000Sit per 5kg load. Open M-F 8am-2pm and 4-7pm, Sa 8am-2pm.

24hr. Pharmacy: Miklošičeva 24 (tel. 31 45 58).

Medical Assistance: In an emergency, call **Bohoričeva Medical Centre,** Bohoričeva 4 (tel. 32 30 60), or **Klinični center,** Zaloška 7 (tel. 133 62 36 and 131 31 13).

Crisis Hotline: Hotline for Women, Metelkova 24 (tel. 133 05 89).

Post Office: Slovenska 32. **Poste Restante** received at Pražakova 3 (tel. 174 15 01), parallel to Trg O.F. Held for 1 month at the counter labeled *"poštno ležeče pošiljke."* Open M-F 7am-8pm, Sa 7am-1pm. **Postal code:** 1106.

Internet Access: Podhod, Plečnikov Trg, between Maximarket and Kongresni Trg. 2 free computers at the back of club. Ask for internet card at the bar. **K-4,** Kersnikova 4. Open daily 9am-7pm. Closed July-Sept. Free.

Telephones: Around the post office, and all over town. Magnetic phone cards available in post office and newsstands (100 impulses for 1700Sit). There are 24hr. phones in the post office on Trg O.F., to the right of train station. **Phone code:** (0)61.

ACCOMMODATIONS

Ljubljana is not heavily touristed by backpackers, and therefore lacks true budget accommodations. On top of that, there is a nightly **tourist tax** (185Sit). Finding cheap accommodations is easier in July and August, when high school dormitories open their doors to tourists. **TIC** (see **Tourist Office,** above) will attempt to find a private single (2200-3500Sit) or double (4000-5500Sit).

Dijaški Dom Tabor (HI), Vidovdanska 7 (tel. 31 60 69 and 32 10 67; fax 32 10 60). From the train station, turn left and walk alongside the park. Turn right on Resljeva, left on Komenskega, and left again on Vidovdanska. Clean, with a friendly staff. Reception has 2 computers with **internet access.** 180 beds in doubles and triples with shared bath. 2200Sit with student ID. Generous breakfast 400Sit. **Laundry** 1000Sit. Check-out 11am. Unenforced 10pm curfew. Open June 25-Aug. 28.

Dijaški Dom Bežigrad, Kardeljeva pl. 28 (tel. 34 28 67; fax 34 28 64). Turn right at the train station and walk to the large crossroad with Slovenska. Take bus #6 (to Črnuče) or #8 (Ježica) and get off at "Stadion" (5min.). Walk past the red London phone booth to the crossroads. The path through the park on your right will take you to the reception. The rooms are ugly and a bit worn out, but the staff is friendly, it's clean, and it has the best water pressure in town. Singles 2600Sit, with shower 3000Sit; doubles 1800Sit, 2600Sit; triples 1800Sit, 2200Sit. Open mid-June to Aug., weekends only Sept.-May.

Dijaški Dom Ivana Cankarja, Poljanska 26-28 (tel. 174 86 00). From the stations, go straight on Resljeva, then left on Poljanska; look for the Pinki restaurant sign at #22. Turn right and go into the courtyard. Reception is on the other side of the complex. Singles 2300Sit; doubles and triples 1800Sit. Breakfast 470Sit, lunch 750Sit, dinner 660Sit. 10% discount for students and large groups. Open June 25-Aug. 30.

Bellevue, Pod gozdom 12 (tel. 133 40 49; fax 133 40 57). From the train station, turn right and follow Trg O.F. to the crossroads. Cross the street, continue on Tivolska, then take a right onto Celovska. Cross the street and walk along the park to the parking lot, and from there follow the curving street uphill. Majestically situated in the greenery of Tivoli Park. Singles 3300Sit; doubles 6600Sit; triples 9900Sit. Breakfast included. Reservations recommended. 24hr. reception. May be closed for part of 2000.

Autocamp Ježica, Dunajska 270 (tel. 168 39 13; fax 168 39 12). Follow directions to Dijaški dom Bežigrad (see above), but take bus #8 and get off at "Ježica." Bungalows: singles 5000Sit; doubles 7600Sit; triples 11,400Sit.

FOOD

The cheapest places to eat are **cafeterias,** where university students cash in their government-subsidized *studentske bone* (student tickets). At the one in the basement of Maximarket on Trg Republike you can get an appetizer, soup, main dish, and dessert for 800Sit. (Open M-F 9am-4pm, Sa 9am-3pm.) The same basement also houses the largest **grocery store** in town. (Open M-F 9am-8pm, Sa 9am-7pm.) Look for the huge outdoor market at Vodnikov Trg next to the cathedral. (Open M-Sa 9am-6pm, Su 9am-2pm.) Fast food stands abound, featuring such favorites as the *burek*—fried dough filled with meat (*mesni*), cheese (*sirov*), or a pizza mixture—and the horseburger (*konji burger*), made out of, yes, horse meat.

Italijanska kuhinja pri Albertu in Adrianu, Trubarjeva 36 (tel. 134 37 19). Albert and Adrian succeed in making this look like a mom's kitchen: warm and cozy with dry flowers and a plush carpet. Risotto 800-1200Sit, spaghetti 800-1400Sit, with many veggie options. 0.5L *Laško* or Union 290Sit. Open M-W 10am-10pm, Th-Sa 10am-midnight.

Pizzeria Foculus, Gregorčičeva 3 (tel. 21 56 43), between Slovenska and Prešernova. Delicious pizzas with several vegetarian combinations 700-900Sit. Open M-F 10am-midnight, Sa-Su noon-midnight.

Gostilna Pri Pavli, Stari Trg 21. Serves huge portions of *Ljubljanski zrzek* (steak Ljubljana style, 1000Sit), ham and vegetable omelettes (600Sit), and spaghetti with mushrooms (550Sit) in a boxy, Eastern European setting. Open M-F 7am-10pm, Sa 7am-3pm.

Kitajska Restauracija Shanghay, Poljanska 14 (tel. 133 80 54). Chinese food that proves a welcome alternative to Ljubljana's cuisine, but at a price. Soups 300-350Sit, entrees 750-1100Sit. Open daily 11am-11pm.

Dajdam, Cankarjeva 4. Cheap buffet with the charm of a trough. Set menu 750-950Sit, set vegetarian menu 850Sit. Open M-F 6am-9pm, Sa 7am-4pm, Su 10am-6pm.

SIGHTS

The best way to see the city is to meet in front of the **city hall** *(rotovž)*, Mestni Trg 1, for the two-hour **walking tour** in English and Slovene. (June-Sept. daily 5pm; Oct.-May Su 11am. 700Sit, students and seniors 500Sit. Tickets may be purchased from TIC, hotel receptions, or from the guide prior to the tour.)

In front of the city hall spurts a fantastic fountain, wrought by the local master Francesco Robba in 1751, embellished with allegorical sculptures of three rivers—the Ljubljanica, Sava, and Krka. A short walk from the city hall down Stritarjeva and across the Triple Bridge brings you to the main square, **Prešernov Trg.** The square was christened in honor of France Prešeren, the most famous Slovene poet, whose statue stands here (see **Literature & Arts,** p. 709). The square is dominated by the Neoclassical **Franciscan Church** (Frančiškanska cerkev) built in the 17th century. Robba also crafted the impressive altar inside. Don't miss the fabulous glass waterfall on the church's outside back wall.

The **Triple Bridge** (Trojmostovje) is an attraction in itself. It dates from the 1930s, when revered architect Jože Plečnik (see **Literature & Arts,** p. 709) modernized the old Špitalski most by supplementing the stone construction with two footbridges. They now provide a majestic entrance to Old Ljubljana. Cross the bridge back to the Old Town and take a left along the water and its gorgeous arcades, also designed by Plečnik. On your right, the **cathedral** *(stolnica)* occupies the site of an old Romanesque church dedicated by the boatmen and fishermen of Ljubljana to their patron, St. Nicholas. Today's cathedral dates from the early 18th century; little original artwork remains, but visitors can still admire the 15th-century Gothic *Pietà,* the impressive triple organ, and the gold leaf trim. (Closed noon-3pm.)

At the end of Vodnikov Trg sprawls the **Dragon Bridge** (Zmajski most), built in 1901 to replace the old wooden "Butcher's Bridge." Originally named after the Emperor Franz Joseph, the locals never accepted it as such; the dragons of Ljubljana's coat of arms, which adorn the bridge, gave it the current name. On the opposite side of Vodnikov Trg, the narrow path Studentovska leads uphill to **Ljubljana Castle** (Ljubljanski Grad). The castle dates from at least 1144, but was almost entirely destroyed by an earthquake in 1511; the present buildings date from the 16th and 17th centuries. Currently under renovation, the castle has little to offer aside from occassional exhibits, a tower with a view of the city, and a mesmerizing double-helix staircase. (Open daily 10am-9pm. 200Sit, students 100Sit.)

The bridge at the beginning of Mestni Trg leads to the site of the **former Jewish ghetto,** Židovska ul. A left on Gosposka brings you to the gray and orange **National University Library** (Narodna in Univerzitetna Knjižnica), built by the omnipresent Plečnik, and connected to the ruins of a Roman wall on **French Revolution Square** (Trg Francoske Revolucije). The square and its environs were once occupied by the Teutonic Knights; the neighborhood **Križanke,** the Slovene translation of their name, still commemorates them. In the square, the Knights set up a monastery, which was abandoned in the 18th century. It was restored under Plečnik's guidance, and now hosts music, theater, and dance performances for the **Ljubljana International Summer Festival** (mid-July to Sept.; see **Entertainment,** below).

Behind the Ursuline Church on Slovenska cesta is **Trg Republike,** home to the Parliament, the colossal Maximarket, and the even-bigger **Cankarjev dom,** the city's cultural center. Nearby, on Cankarjeva, stands one of Ljubljana's most notable structures: **Cyril and Methodius' Church** (Crkva Ciril in Metodja), the only Serbian Orthodox church in the country. (See **"What's in a name?,"** p. 8.)

MUSEUMS

Ljubljana's museums cluster around the Slovenian Parliament near Trg Republic. All are closed Mondays.

The Plečnik Collection (Plečnikova zbrika), Karunova 4 (tel. 33 50 66 and 33 50 67). Part of the Architectural Museum (Architekturni mezej). Walk up Slovenska, turn left on Zoisova, then right onto Emonska. Cross the bridge, and the museum lies behind the church. In a house that Plečnik built for himself, this museum chronicles the work and ascetic life of this genius bachelor. Open Tu and Th 10am-2pm or by appointment one week in advance. Guided tours only; available in English. 600Sit, students 300Sit.

Modern Gallery (Moderna Galerija), Cankarjeva 15 (tel. 21 41 01). A good-sized collection of 20th-century Slovenian paintings and sculptures. Open June-Aug. Tu-Sa 10am-7pm, Su 10am-1pm; Sept.-May Tu-Sa 10am-6pm. 500Sit, students 300Sit.

National Museum (Narodni Muzej), Muzejska 1 (tel. 21 88 86). Detailed exhibits on archaeology, culture, and Slovenian history. The left wing of the 1st floor contains the Museum of Natural History. Although a bit dry as a whole, the giant mammoth and the ground-floor lapidarium from Ljubljana's Roman days are themselves worth the price of admission. Open Tu-W and F-Su 10am-6pm, Th 10am-8pm. 500Sit, students 300Sit, groups of 7 or more 250Sit; Su free. Ask for English guidebook.

Tivoli Castle (Tivolski Grad), Pod turnom 3 (tel. 126 52 40). From Cankerjeva, follow Jakopičevo sprehajališče in Tivoli Park. Home to the International Center of Graphic Art, the castle features temporary exhibits, and hosts the International Biennial of Graphic Art. Open Tu-Sa 10am-6pm, Su 10am-1pm. 200Sit, students 100Sit.

National Gallery (Narodna Galerija), Cankarjeva 20 (tel. 21 97 16). Houses the creations of Slovenian artists from the 13th to 20th centuries. Open Tu-Su 10am-6pm. 500Sit, students 300Sit, Sa afternoons free.

ENTERTAINMENT

Just as the neighboring Zagreb seems to host all the fairs of the world, Ljubljana boasts a wide variety of festivals, including the **International Jazz Festival** in late June and early July, the **Ljubljana International Film Festival (LIFF)** in November, and the vaguely titled **International Summer Festival** in July and August, a conglomeration of opera, theater, and musical performances. **Slovene Music Days** gets it all started in mid-April. Most festivals take place in **Cankarjev dom,** Prešernova 10 (tel. 22 28 15), the major concert and congress hall, or the outdoor **Križanke Summer Theatre,** part of **Festival Ljubljana,** Trg Francoske revolucije 1 (tel. 126 43 40). Cankerjev dom also hosts the **Slovene Symphony Orchestra** (Oct.-June; tickets 800-3000Sit; box office in basement of Maximarket) and **Galerija CD,** which has 6-7 exhibitions each year featuring mostly Slovenian artists. (Open Tu-Sa 10am-7pm, Su 10am-2pm. 500Sit, students 300Sit.) The **opera house** at Župančičeva 1 (tel. 25 46 80) hosts performances from September to June (tickets 800-3000Sit). **Tivoli Hall,** a sports arena in the center of Tivoli Park, hosts basketball, hockey, and rock concerts. Inquire about these and all other events at **TIC** (see **Tourist Office,** p. 714) or Festival Ljubljana (see above).

NIGHTLIFE

If Ljubljana's cultural options don't suit your fancy, join Ljubljana's large student population at the cafes or bars on Trubarjeva, Stari Trg, and Metni Trg.

Casa del Papa, Celovška 54a (tel. 134 31 58). A clean, well-lighted place that pays homage to Hemingway with its decor as well as the latin beats from the club downstairs. Too high-brow for the student crowd. Serves beer (0.5L 400Sit), coffee (150Sit), and sandwiches (350-450Sit). Open daily 11am-2am.

Le Petit Cafe, Trg Francoske revolucije 4 (tel. 12 64 88). Placed strategically next to the university library, this francophile cafe is *the* student hangout in Ljubljana. Parisian music, of course. Try the iced coffee (400Sit). Cakes 400-600Sit. Open M-F 7:30am-11pm, Sa 9am-11pm, Su noon-9pm.

Jazz Club Gajo, Beethovnova 8 (tel. 125 32 06). Run by a wonderful couple who host free jazz whenever business is brisk (usually 2-4 days per week). Tourists, students, and embassy staff squeeze in even on silent nights for the jazz juice–a blend of banana, kiwi, and orange (300Sit). Open M-F 10am-2am, Sa-Su 7pm-midnight.

K-4, Kersnikova 4 (tel. 131 70 10). Student-run cafe/bar/club/cyber hangout. DJ or live music nightly. Remodeled annually and always hip. Sunday is gay night. Cover 200-1000Sit, students 40% off. Open Oct.-June daily 9am-4am (clubbing starts at 9pm).

NEAR LJUBLJANA: POSTOJNA

A single cavern of the two-million-year-old **Postojna cave** (Postojnska Jama) would justify the trip. More amusement park than cave, it contains an astonishing array of plant-like stalagmite columns, alabaster curtains of stone, gorges, rivers, and multi-colored stalactites (the cave's youngest stalactite is 74 years old and hangs like a small drop of water). A 15min. walk northwest of the town brings you to the **jama** (cave), Jamska cesta 30 (tel. 25 041). Follow the signs from the center of town. The obligatory tour covers only 20% of the cave's 27km and lasts an hour and a half; part is on foot and part on a train. Bring a jacket or rent a cloak for 100Sit; the temperature in the cave is a constant 8°C. The final "hall" of the tour has amazing acoustics and hosts occasional musical performances by Slovene groups. (Open May-Sept. daily 9am-6pm, Oct.-Apr. daily 10am-4pm. Tours leave May-Sept. on the hour, Oct.-Apr. on even hours. 1900Sit, students 950Sit. Tours in Slovene, English, French, Italian, and German.)

Nearly impossible to reach but worth the effort is **Predjama Castle** (Predjamski grad; tel. (067) 56 82 60), 9km from Postojna. Carved into the face of a huge cliff, the former home of the robber baron Erazem is, as the brochure calls it, "almost arrogant in its simplicity." (Open M-F 10am-4pm, Sa-Su 10am-5pm; 600Sit, students 300Sit.) On the last Sunday in August, a colorful knights' tournament takes place outside the castle. During the school year, two local school buses go to **Bukovje,** 2 km from the castle (15 min., M-F only, 270Sit). You can also walk from Postojna, and although hitchhikers may be accommodated, passing cars are rare.

GETTING THERE. The town is reachable from **Ljubljana** by **bus** (1hr., every 30min., 900Sit) or **train** (1hr., 22 per day, 780Sit). Both buses and trains head for Istria so you may want to stop in Postojna on your way to the coast.

THE JULIAN ALPS (JULIJSKE ALPE)

Arnold Rikli, founder of the Climatic Health Resort in Bled, declared that "water of course is good, air is even better, and light is the best." Covering northwest Slovenia, the Julian Alps fuse all three elements perfectly. Although they are not as high as their Austrian or Swiss cousins (Mt. Triglav peaks at 2864m), they are no less stunning. Whether you're looking for wilderness near Lake Bohinj, authentic cultural festivities in Kranjska Gora, or the well-groomed spas of Bled, the Julian Alps offers something for every taste.

BLED

Bled has all of the beauty and exquisite stillness of a postcard: green Alpine hills, snow-covered backdrop peaks, a translucent blue-green lake, and a stately castle poised above the panorama. The tranquility of Blejsko Jezero (Lake Bled) is conducive to rejuvenation—people have been coming here for centuries to recuperate in spas or to lose themselves in the splendor of a warm summer evening. This internationally known resort is a paradise, but one that is perhaps a bit too pristine: nothing stays open past 11pm and even the swans seem to have been groomed recently.

ORIENTATION & PRACTICAL INFORMATION. Trains stop at the **Lesce train station** (tel. 74 11 13), 5km from Bled on the Ljubljana-Salzburg-Munich line (1hr., 450Sit). From there, take one of the frequent **commuter buses** (10min., 200Sit) to Bled. These stop on **Ljubljanska,** the main street, and at the main **bus station** at cesta Svobode 4 (tel. 74 11 14), closer to the youth hostel and the castle. Alternatively, arrive directly by bus from Ljubljana (1½hr., every hr., 880Sit). It is also possible to rent a car at **Kompas Hertz**, Ljubljanska 7. (Open M-F 7am-noon, 5-9pm, Sa 7am-1pm.) Bled is spread around the lake, with most buildings clustered along the eastern shore. Ljubljanska leads straight to the water. For tourist info, visit **Turističko društvo,** cesta Svobode 15 (tel. 74 11 22; fax 74 15 55), where you can pick up a copy of the illustrated *Bled Tourist News* and a handy **map** of Bled. (Open July and Aug. 8am-10pm, Su noon-6pm; June and Sept. 8am-8pm, Su noon-6pm; Nov.-Feb. M-Sa 9am-5pm, Su noon-6pm; Mar.-May and Oct. 8am-7pm, Su noon-6pm.) An all-purpose **shopping center** is at Ljubljanska 4. **Currency exchanges** have bad rates and extract large commissions. The first place to go is **Gorenjska Banka,** cesta Svobode 15 (tel. 74 13 00), which exchanges cash and traveler's checks and withdraws C. (Open M-F 9-11:30am, 2-5pm, S 8-11am). **Kompas Bled,** Ljubljanska 4 (tel. 74 15 15; fax 74 15 18), is another option, exchanging cash and traveler's checks for a 3% commission. (Open M-Sa 8am-7pm, Su noon-4pm.) There are **no ATMs** and there is **no internet access** available in Bled. There is a **pharmacy** at Prešernova 36 (tel. 74 15 22; pen M-F 7am-7:30pm, Sa 7am-1pm). In an **emergency,** call 74 14 00. The **post office** is at Ljubljanska 4 (tel. 74 80 20; open July-Aug. M-Sa 7am-8pm; Sept.-June M-F 7am-7pm, Sa 7am-noon). **Postal code:** 4260. **Phone code:** (0)64.

ACCOMMODATIONS. **Private room** prices vary according to season. **Kompas Bled** (see above) can arrange singles for 2000Sit and doubles for 1600Sit per person. (200Sit additional tax per night; stays of less than 3 nights cost 30% more.) Finding a private room yourself may save money; look for *sobe* signs, particularly on Prešernova cesta and Ljubljanska. The newly renovated **Bledec Youth Hostel,** Grajska cesta 17 (tel. 74 52 50), is a bright supernova in the backpacker's dark sky. Everything from the stylish wooden furniture to the private bathrooms and showers is brand-new and *clean!* With your back to the bus station, turn left and walk on the street all the way to the top. (2600 Sit with breakfast; 2000Sit with ISIC, FIYTO, GO25 or PZS-IYHF; prices 20% higher with no student ID. Tourist tax included. Book one day in advance. Reception daily summer 7am-8pm; off-season 7am-7pm. Checkout 10am.) **Camping Zaka-Bled,** cesta Svobode 13 (tel. 74 82 00; fax 74 82 02), sits in a beautiful valley on the opposite side of the lake. Walk around the bus station and go downhill on cesta Svobode. When you get to the lake, walk along the water to your right for about 25 minutes, until you get to the camp on the opposite side. Refrigerators, electrical connections, sand volleyball, tennis and basketball courts, a store, a restaurant, and a beach are all available—alas, no bungalows. (1240Sit per person; tourist tax 177Sit. Check-out 3pm. Open Apr.-Oct.)

FOOD. As long as you don't require a lakeside restaurant, prices aren't much higher than in the rest of Slovenia. **P-hram,** cesta Svobode 19a (tel. 79 12 80) serves Slovenian main courses for 550-900Sit—including delicious *kranjska klobasa* (Carniolan sausage, 700Sit. Open daily 9am-11pm). Locals recommend **Gostilna pri Planincu,** Grajska cesta 8 (tel. 74 16 13), near the bus station. This bar/restaurant serves entrees (600-1250Sit) including pizzas (600-850Sit; open daily 9am-11pm). **Kitajska Restavracija Peking,** Ulica narodnjich Herdinov 3, is a little Asian island in the Julian Alps, offering springrolls (600Sit) and Chinese entrees (850-1400Sit) to the locals. (Open daily noon-11pm.) If all else fails, try **Market Špecerija,** Ljubljanska 4. (Open M-Sa 7am-7pm, Su 9am-noon.) The interior of **Franci Šimon,** Grajska cesta 3 (tel. 74 16 16), is conducive to brooding, but the terrace has marble tabletops and shares a low fence with the neighbor's garden. (Tortes 80-350Sit; coffee 110Sit. Open daily 7:30am-10pm.)

SIGHTS & ENTERTAINMENT. A stroll around the lake's 6km perimeter should take about two hours. On the **island** in the center stands the **Church of the Assumption** *(Cerkev Marijinega Vnebovzetja)*, which has stood there since the 9th century. Although today's structure actually dates from the 17th century, a unique pre-Romanesque apse remains. There are many ways to approach the island. At the managed swimming area below the castle, **boat rentals** cost 1000Sit per hour for a three-person boat or 1200Sit for a five-person boat and require a 1000Sit deposit. You can also travel via **gondola** from various points along the shore. (Roundtrip 1½hr., 1500Sit.) Gondolas depart when they are full and the church opens when they arrive. Swimming to the island is permissible, but padding into the church dripping wet is not. Dive in from any beach without a No Swimming sign; swimmers tend to hang out on the western shores. The managed swimming area charges 600Sit for full-day entrance to its concrete beach. Use of the **waterslide** is included in the entrance fee. (Open daily 7am-7pm. 500Sit after noon; children 400Sit; locker rental 300Sit; chair rental 100Sit.) The water is warm in summer but becomes a huge ice-skating rink in winter.

The 16th-century **Bled castle** *(Blejski grad)* rises 100m above the water. The official path to the castle is on Grajska cesta, although there are several more pleasant hikes through the forest. From the lake, go to St. Martin's Church (Cerkev sv. Martin) on Kidričeva cesta then follow the path up the hill. The castle houses a splendid museum of history of the Bled region with furniture, weapons, and a skeleton of an Alpine Slav woman from a nearby evacuation site. (Open daily 8am-7pm. Adults 500Sit; students 400Sit; children 250Sit.) Numerous **hiking paths** snake from the lake into the neighboring hills, and **mountain bikes** of varying quality can be rented at the **Kompas Bled** tourist agency. (500Sit per hr., 1000Sit per ½-day, 1500Sit per day. See **Orientation and Practical Information,** above.)

From mid-June to September, **concerts** and traditional cultural activities take place on the island, on the promenade, and in the hotels. The Tourism Association and tourist agencies (see **Orientation & Practical Information,** above) carry a free monthly brochure filled with events which run the gamut from folklore shows to entertainment programs for children. For such an enchanting place, the nightlife, surprisingly, is not. The adolescent crowd gathers at the **Club Libra Royal,** on the ground floor of the shopping complex on Ljubljanska cesta. The dance floor's attempt at sophistication sadly fails, but it does have an all-night disco. (One free drink included in 500sit cover charge. Closes around 5am.) Those more uniformly on the 20s side of youngish hang out at **Pub,** cesta Svobode 8a (tel. 74 22 17), under Hotel Jelovica. The Irish name is backed up by all the necessary accessories. (Open daily 7am-midnight. 0.3L Union 200Sit, 0.3L Guinness 300Sit.)

NEAR BLED: BLEJSKI VINTGAR

The 1.6km long Vintgar gorge carves through the rocks of the Hom and Burt hills of the **Triglav National Park** *(Triglavski Narodni Park)*, traced along the way by the waterfalls, pools, and rapids of the Radovna River. The part of the park that passes through the gorge winds over a series of bridges leading to the 16m high **Šum waterfall.** The walk through the gorge nears paradise, and of course, paradise isn't free. (Park admission 400Sit, children 100Sit.)

GETTING THERE. You can walk the approximately 3km distance from Bled—just follow the signs out of town, or take one of the frequent buses to Podhom (180Sit) and follow a well-marked 1.5km route. During summer, **Alpetour** (tel. 74 11 14) runs a special bus once per day. (July 1-Sept. 30, 9:30am, one-way 250Sit.) Once at the waterfall, you may return the same way, or follow the signs to Sv. Katarina-Bled (1hr.).

LAKE BOHINJ (BOHINJSKO JEZERO)

Although it's only 30km southwest of Bled, Bohinjsko (BOH-heen-sko) Jezero's unmitigated natural character is worlds away. Protected by its position within the borders of Triglav National Park, this glacial lake—together with its surrounding wildflowers, waterfalls, and windy peaks—stands at the center of Slovenia's alpine tourism universe. Some travel here for the water sports, but most come to ascend the heights and experience mountain hospitality on their return.

ORIENTATION & PRACTICAL INFORMATION. The nearest town is Bohinjska Bistrica 6km to the east. The lake itself is defined by three villages: Ribčev Laz, Stara Fužina and Ukanc. One **train** per day arrives in Bohinjska Bistrica directly from **Ljubljana** (2hr.), and four more come via **Jesenice** (you may need to change trains). All buses go from **Ljubljana** (2¼hr., every hr., 1300Sit) and pass through **Bled** (35min., 460Sit) and **Bohinjska Bistrica** (10min., 200Sit). These take you either to Hotel Jezero in Ribčev Laz, or all the way to Hotel Zlatorog in Ukanc on the other side of the lake. You should find everything you need in **Ribčev Laz,** on the water's edge—just ask at the **tourist office,** Ribčev Laz 48 (tel. 72 33 70; fax 72 33

30; email tdbohinj@bohinj.si). They also exchange cash for a 3% commission. (Open July-Aug. M-Sa 7:30am-9pm, Su 9am-3pm; Apr.-June and Sept.-Oct. M-Sa 8am-7pm; Nov.-Mar. 8am-5pm.) Drop by **Alpinsport,** Ribčev Laz 53 (tel./fax 72 34 86 and 65 00 36), near the bridge, to rent a mountain **bike** (700Sit per hr., 1900Sit for 3hr., 2900Sit per day), or to get gear for **kayaking** (700Sit per hr., 2500Sit for 3hr., 3200Sit for 5hr., 3900Sit per day) and **canoeing** (700Sit per hr., 3000Sit for 3hr., 4000Sit for 5 hr., 4900Sit per day). **Paragliding** trips are also available. (7000-9000Sit per jump.) Open daily Sept.-June 10am-5pm, July-Aug. 9am-6/7pm.) The lake has no **pharmacy;** the closest to be found is in Bohinjska Bistrica, Triglavska 15 (tel. 72 16 30; open M-F 8am-7:30pm). The nearest **bank** is **Gorenjska Banka,** Trg Svobode 26 (tel. 72 16 10; open daily 9-11:30am and 2-5pm). The **post office** on Ribčev Laz 47 exchanges cash for no commission and traveler's checks for a 3% commission, but at a slightly worse rate than the tourist office. (Open M-F 8-9:30am, 10-11:30am, and 4-6pm, Sa 8am-noon.) **Postal code:** 4265. **Phone code:** (0)64.

ACCOMMODATIONS. The tourist office (see above) arranges rooms. (July-Aug. 1600-2500Sit per person, off season 1300-2200Sit per person; 154Sit additional tourist tax, 20% more for a single, 30% more for stays less than three nights.) To reach **AvtoCamp Zlatorog,** Ukanc 2 (tel. 72 34 82; fax 72 34 46), take a bus to the Hotel Zlatorog (see **Orientation & Practical Information,** p. 721) and backtrack for a few minutes. Located on the west side of the lake, it usually has spaces available. (July-Aug. 1600Sit, May-June and Aug.-Sept. 1000Sit; children under 14 pay half-price.) The tourist office operates **Camping Danica,** 4264 Bohinjska Bistrica (tel. 72 10 55 and 74 60 10; fax 72 33 30), just outside of Bohinjska Bistrica but not on the lake. Get off the bus/train in Bohinjska Bistrica and continue in the direction of the bus toward the lake at the end of town; the campground will be on your right. (July-Aug. 1100Sit per person, off season 800Sit per person; 100Sit additional tourist tax, 10% discount for stays over 7 days.) There are occasional private rooms—look for *sobe* (room) signs, especially in Ukanc. Hotels think in Deutchmarks, so be prepared (40-90DM per night).

FOOD. The smell of sizzling fresh fish entices visitors into excellent, if pricey, local restaurants. **Restaurant Rožič,** Ribčev Laz 42 (tel./fax 72 33 93), offers a combination of the traditional Slovenian peasant cuisine and Balkan grill. Rožič's daily tourist menu (1300Sit), pizza (900Sit), and pasta (700Sit) attract many visitors. (Open daily 7am-10pm.) **Gostišče Kramar,** Stara Fužina 3 (tel. 72 36 97), is slung low over the lake; its wood-burning stove and wicker chairs hover scarcely a meter above the water. The large windows provide an astounding and unobstructed view of the peaks through thin bands of reflective watery light. Follow the dirt path on your left after the stone bridge. The restaurant will appear after 10min. (Pizza 600-850Sit; grilled octopus 1100Sit; milkshakes 350Sit. 0.5L *Laško* 280Sit; coffee 120Sit. Open daily 11am-midnight.) **Restaurant Triglav,** Stara Fužina 23 (tel. 74 82 38), brings in enough tourists to offer an affordable daily menu including soup, entree, salad, and dessert (1300Sit). To find it, cross the bridge next to the church on Lake Bohinj, and walk 10min. to the next village—the view of the lake justifies the higher prices. (Open daily 11am-11pm.) The **Mercator supermarket,** Ribčev Laz 49, is by the tourist office. (Open M-F 7am-7pm, Sa 7am-5pm.)

SIGHTS & HIKING. Hiking is plentiful around Lake Bohinj, but there are a few strictly Slovenian rules of the road. Trails throughout Slovenia are marked with a white circle inside a red circle; look for the blazing sign on trees and rocks. A bend in the trail may be marked by a bent red line. When trails separate, a sign usually indicates which one is headed where. In Slovenia, hikers always greet each other on the path. As old-timers will remind you, the person ascending the path should speak up first; respect belongs to those who have already conquered the hill. **Mountain bikes** are not allowed on the trails, but they can be fun on the forest roads *(gozdna pot)* and specially marked rough dirt roads *(poljska pot)*. See **Essentials: Camping and the Outdoors,** p. 38, for general info about hiking and safety.

COMING TO A HEAD...OR THREE Slovenia's highest peak, Mt. Triglav (2864m), may not seem like much of an ascent until you realize that, on a clear day, the sea is visible from the summit. Originally worshipped by pre-Christian Slovenes, "Three Heads" was first conquered by one in 1778, and since then the mountain has become a symbol of the country's identity. The three-peaked contour was the symbol of the Liberation Front when Slovenia was occupied during WWII, and today has a place on the national flag and coat of arms. Politicians make the hike to show off their national spirit. If you reach the summit, you will be treated like a hero on your return: it's the one way of truly becoming a Slovene. Don't forget to leave your name in the book at the top. A good route up Mt. Triglav begins at Bohinjsko Jezero. Some have done it in one day, but two days provide for a safer and more enjoyable journey. There is an abundance of mountain huts along the way. For 760Sit, *How to Climb Triglav* details all the options.

Any number of trips can be made from the shores of Bohinj, from the casual to the nearly impossible. Several good **maps** are available; the ones that cover the most area without losing too much detail are *Triglavski Narodni Park* (1200Sit) and *Triglav* (1600Sit), for purchase at the tourist office. Biking around Lake Bohinj is only allowed on the northern and eastern sides, near Ribčev Laz and Stara Fužina. The most popular and accessible destination is **Savica Waterfall** (Slap Savica), where the Bohinj river starts. Take a bus from Ribčev Laz to "Bohinj-Zlatorog," get off at Hotel Zlatorog, and follow the signs uphill to Savica Waterfall (1hr. to the beginning of the trailhead at Koča pri Savici, then 20min. to the waterfall). If you're brave enough to forego the bus, turn left at the lake in Ribčev Laz and follow the scenic road along the lake and past Ukanc to Savica Waterfall (3hr.). Along the way you'll pass the **Church of the Holy Ghost,** built in 1743, and a sobering **Austro-Hungarian WWI Cemetary.** Once at the entrance to the powerful 60m waterfall, it's a 300Sit fee (200Sit students, 150Sit children) to continue on. Adventurers can return along a different trail that skirts the north side of Lake Bohinj. Look for its entrance at Koča pri Savici, and keep to the westbound trail on your left (3hr.).

If, instead of turning back, you follow the signs toward **Black Lake** (Črno Jezero), you'll come to yet another liquid Alpine gem (1½hr.). The hiking is very steep here; be extremely cautious. Shortly after reaching the ridge line, a trail to the right *(Dol Pod Stadorjem)* leads to Mt. Viševnik. Turn south from this peak to **Pršivec** (1761m; 2½hr.), where the view of the lake is breathtaking. Return the way you came, or follow the trail east to return along the ridge to **Stara Fužina** and **Ribčev Laz** (2½hr.). If you opt for the latter, be advised that for the first hour and a half your hat will be providing the only shade around.

The more traditional (but equally difficult) way to reach Pršivec is from Stara Fužina. Cross the bridge in Ribčev Laz and follow the road to the next village, Stara Fužina. Walk straight through town to Pension Rabič (20min.). Once there, you'll have to pass through a closed gate, which is perfectly legal as long as you're not behind a steering wheel. After **Devil's Bridge** (Hudičev most), built by Mr. Devil himself, Italian builder Diavollo, follow the leftmost road at the fork (*not* the trails along the river pointing toward Korita Mostnice). Continue along the marked carriage path that leads into the woods on the left. This will take you to the road; follow it for 50m and then turn left at the crucifix. From here, signs lead to **Vogar** (1hr.) and **Pršivec** (4hr.). The path to Vogar winds steeply through a forest and is paved with rocks.

While resting between hikes, you can take in a bit of Alpine culture. The key to the 15th-century **Church of John the Baptist** on Lake Bohinj, which is closed until summer 2000, can be found at the tourist office. The **Alpine Highlander Museum,** 1.5km north in Stara Fužina, exhibits materials from the life of a 19th-century highlander. (Open July-Aug. Tu-Su 11am-7pm; Jan.-June and Sept. Tu-Su 10am-noon and 4-6pm. 150Sit. The curator, Mrs. Lidija Mlakar, lives at Stara Fužina 179, tel. 72 30 95.) A few kilometers to the east in **Studor** sits a 100-year-old peasant house-turned-museum at #16; contact Gregor Resman, Studor 14a (tel. 72 35 22; open July-Aug. Tu-Su 11am-7pm, Jan.-June and Sept.-Oct. Tu-Su 10am-noon and 4-6pm).

Amor Club in Ribčev Laz, right next to the tourist office, morphs into a disco from 9pm-midnight. Lake Bohinj hosts several festivals during the summer months. **Midsummer Night** (Kresna Noč) in mid-August is the most spectacular, with candles and fireworks decorating the night sky. The **Peasant's Wedding Day** at the end of July and the mid-September **Cow Ball** (Kravji bal) in Ukanc offer more traditional—if stranger—forms of entertainment. For further information, visit the tourist office (see above).

KRANJSKA GORA

Home to jagged peaks, fields of yellow grass, and a curious museum of traditional folk fashion, Kranjska Gora offers a happy combination of nature and culture. Lucky visitors get to explore the unique Zgornjesarska Valley, without missing out on any traditional elements of the Alpine resort lifestyle. In addition, the town hosts a variety of festivals and events, and is only a short distance away from the Austrian and Italian borders.

ORIENTATION & PRACTICAL INFORMATION. The entire village is spread along **Borovška cesta.** To get there from the **bus stop** on Koroška cesta, backtrack on Koroška and take the first left onto **Kolodvorska cesta,** continuing to the end of the street. A right turn on Borovška will take you past a church and into the center of town. **Buses** go to and from **Bled's** Lesce train station (45min., every hr., 630Sit) and **Ljubljana** (2¼hr., every hr., 1440Sit). The tourist information center, **Turistično društvo Kranjska Gora,** Tičarjeva 2 (tel. 88 17 68; fax 88 11 25; email infoşkranjska-gora.si), is located in the center of town on the corner of Tičarjeva and Borovška. They arrange private rooms, exchange traveler's checks for a 3% commission, and sell postcards and souvenirs. (Open daily 8am-7pm.) There is a **pharmacy,** Lekarna Kranjska Gora, at Naselje Slavka Černeta 34 (tel. 88 17 85; open M-W and F 7:30am-3pm, Th noon-7pm, Sa 8am-1pm). The **post office** is at Borovška 92 (tel. 88 17 70; fax 88 14 67). They exchange cash for no commission. (Open M-F 8am-7pm, Sa 8am-noon.) **Telephones** are in the post office. **Postal code:** 4280. **Phone code:** (0)64.

ACCOMMODATIONS & FOOD. There are no *sobe* (room) signs around the village because all **private rooms** are arranged through the Turistično društvo (See above. July-Aug. 2,200Sit; June and Sept. 1700Sit; Apr.-May and Oct.-Dec. 1,500Sit; 154Sit additional tourist tax, 20% more for less than three nights, and 1000Sit extra for a single.) There are neither budget hotels nor camping in town.

The **Emona Merkur Market,** Borovška 92, has a counter service restaurant called **Bife,** providing inexpensive food under the penetrating stare of a huge yellow bird in a baseball cap. (Goulash 550Sit, risotto 450Sit. Open M-Sa 7am-7pm, Su 7am-noon.) Further down the street from the tourist information center is **Gostilna Bor,** Tičarjeva 10 (tel. 88 12 69). Its warm red candles and wooden ceiling give it a cozy mountain hut feel, appreciated by many a motorbiker. (Omelettes made-to-order 720Sit, chef's choice vegetarian plate 830Sit. Open M-Th and Su 10am-10pm, F-Sa 10am-11pm.) **Gostilna pri Martinu,** Borovška 61 (tel. 87 90 30), has set menus for 1100Sit, as well as a space for folk dances with live music called **Martinov Kevdr.** (Restaurant open daily 10am-11pm, dance area open F-Sa 5pm-midnight.)

SIGHTS & ENTERTAINMENT. You can rent **mountain bikes** at **Šport Bernik,** Borovška 88a (tel. 88 14 70; fax 88 16 82), to explore the hills of Kranjska Gora. (1hr. 400Sit, half-day 1000Sit, day 1600Sit. Open daily 8am-6pm.) **Walking maps** of the area with 17 marked routes are available from the tourist information center (1300Sit). Look for the village **Podkoren** (3km from Kranjska Gora toward the Austrian border), known for its well-preserved folk architecture. It also harbors the natural reserve **Zelenci,** which is the outspring of the Sava Dolinka River. **Rateče,** a small village with alpine houses 7km from Kranjska Gora, sits below **Pec** (1510m) and near the three-way border of Slovenia, Austria, and Italy. One of the most interesting hikes in the area runs through the **Planica valley** to the mountain of **Tamar.** From the town, follow the abandoned railroad westward. After passing the ski lifts that dominate the view to the left, you'll reach the old railroad station in Rateče. Turn left into the Planica valley to enjoy an amazing view of Mojstrovka, Travnik, and Šit mountains. Continuing past the ski ramps for 30min. will lead to the mountain home **Tamar,** from which **Jalovec**—the symbol of Slovenian mountaineers and among the most beautiful Slovenian mountains—can be seen.

The Liznjek House (Muzej Jesenice-Liznjekova hiša), on Borovška 63 (tel. 88 19 99) is the former home of an 18th-century wealthy estate owner, preserved with all its belongings, including the equipment of an 18th-century kitchen. (Open Jan.-Mar., May-Oct., and Dec. Tu-F 10am-5pm, Sa-Su 10am-4pm. 350Sit, students 300Sit.) The village's nightlife consists largely of sleeping. However, during summer it wakes up for 3 months of festivities including concerts, fashion shows, farm markets, and sports events. Consult the tourist information center for a free seasonal booklet. The **Hotel Larix,** Borovška 99 (tel. 88 15 75), has **billiards** from 5pm for 150Sit per game. Check your bad self out at the **Caffe Bar Pinki,** Borovška 91 (tel. 88 16 47), in the oversized mirrors. (0.5L Union 270Sit. Open daily 9am-11pm.)

ISTRIA

Though Slovenia claims only 40km of the Adriatic coast, this stretch of green bays and old coastal towns has developed its own Italian flavor, with palm trees and fishing boats dotting the shore. Koper, with its extensive transport, facilitates jaunts between Venetian-tinged Piran (home of the best accommodations) and the beachside fun of Portorož.

KOPER

With no beaches, too much industry, and plenty of trains, Koper serves primarily as the accommodation and transportation hub for Slovenian Istria. **Dijaški Dom Koper**, Cankarjeva 5 (tel. 27 32 50; fax 27 31 82), is the only youth hostel in Slovenian Istria. The hostel is 1km from the train and bus station: turn right leaving the station and follow Kolodvorska cesta toward the city center. After passing through Kosovelov Trg, walk up Manesiceva to Trg Brolo and take a right onto Cankarjeva. Tidy and close to the center of town, with hallway bathrooms that appear brand new. (380 beds, most in triples; 1966Sit per person if you stay less that 3 nights, otherwise 1512Sit; 83Sit tourist tax; students 10% off. Open June 15-Aug. 23.) For traditional Slovenian fare in a rustic setting, the charming **Gostišče Istrska Klet,** Župančičeva 28, offers *kranjska klobasa* (Carolinian Sausage; 700Sit) and seafood *risotto* (700Sit; open M-F 6:30am-9pm). **Phone code:** (0)66.

GETTING AWAY. The **train** and **bus station** is at Kolodvorska 11 (bus tel. 346 20; train tel. 312 21). Direct **buses** arrive from **Ljubljana** (2¼hr., 13 per day, 1730Sit); **Portorož** (35min., 9 per day, 340Sit); **Piran** (40min., 9 per day, 380Sit); **Trieste, Italy** (45min., 17 per day, 420Sit); **Pula,** Croatia (3¼hr., 2 per day, 1800Sit); and **Poreč,** Croatia (2hr., 3 per day, 1160Sit). **Trains** from **Ljubljana** are less frequent but cheaper (2¼hr., 4 per day, 1500Sit).

PORTOROŽ

If Slovenian Istria were condensed into one town, with Koper as the bus station and Piran the museum, Portorož (port-oh-ROZH) would provide the entertainment. While it is the most heavily touristed of the three, the grassy beach, seaside restaurants, holiday feel, and deep blue tide make it well worth battling the crowds: if you come to join masses of Europeans at play, the exuberance of Portorož almost eclipses its plastic feel.

ORIENTATION & PRACTICAL INFORMATION. **Buses** arrive from **Ljubljana** and **Postojna** (2½hr., 9 per day, 1500Sit from Ljubljana). **Trains** arrive in nearby Koper from **Ljubljana** (2¼hr., 4 per day, 1500Sit); a bus connects to **Portorož** (35min., 9 per day, 340Sit). Thomas Mann wrote that Venice should be entered only by sea; accordingly, a **catamaran** makes the **Portorož-Venice** trip (Apr.-Oct. F-Su, July-Aug. also on Tu; departs 8am; 2½hr.). For a **taxi** call 735 55. Most streets start from **Obala,** the waterfront boulevard, and head uphill. The bus station is just meters from the sea; across the street by the sea stands the main **tourist office, Rosetour,** Obala 16 (tel. 667 52 91; fax 667 63 64), which rents **mountain bikes** (2hr. 950Sit, 6hr. 1360Sit, 1 day 2450Sit), and arranges **accommodations.** (Singles 2900Sit; doubles 4690Sit; triples 6290Sit; 50% surcharge for a stay of less than 3 nights, 240Sit tourist tax.) During peak seasons they may refuse to help you unless you stay for a week. Mention that you read about them in *Let's Go* for a 20% discount on rentals and excursions. (Open July-Aug. daily 8am-10pm, Sept.-June M-Sa 8am-noon and 4-7pm.) **Atlas Express,** Obala 55 (tel. 732 64 and 74 67 72; fax 74 88 20), also rents mountain bikes (2hr. 950Sit, 6hr. 1400Sit, 1 day 2500Sit) and **scooters** (2hr. 2800Sit, 6hr. 5500Sit, 1 day 6600Sit), offers excursions made to order, sells tickets for organized trips, and exchanges currency. (Open daily 8am-8pm.) There is a **pharmacy,** Lekarna Portorož, at Obala 41 (tel. 747 22 20). To get there, walk down Obala, turn right into the Hotel Palace Courtyard, and follow the sign. (Open M-F 8:30am-8pm, Sa 8:30am-1pm.) The **post office** is at K Stari cesta 1 (tel. 74 67 57). They **exchange cash** and **traveler's checks** for no commission. (Open M-Sa 8am-9pm.) There is **24hr. ATM** (Cirrus/MC) at Obala 53. **Postal code:** 6320. **Phone code:** (0)66.

ACCOMMODATIONS & FOOD. As a rule, hotels and **pensions** are expensive and crowded, although prices drop drastically off-season. **Private rooms,** offered by the tourist offices, remain the least expensive option (see above). To find a room on your own, look for *Sobe* or *Zimmer frei* signs along Obala. **Lucija** (tel./fax 77 10 27), a nearby campground, is accessible by bus from the station (every 20min., 120Sit). It offers minigolf, rowing, sailing, surfing, swimming, tennis, and waterskiing facilities. (1770Sit per person; no bungalows). Faceless restaurants line the coastal side of Obala. Locals deny the existence of budget restaurants in Portorož, but there is a large supermarket, **Mercator Degro,** Obala 144, next to the bus station. (Open M-Sa 7am-8pm, Su 8-11am.)

PIRAN

In the center of Piran (5km from Portorož), a statue of the native-born violinist and composer Giuseppe Tartini, his bow poised as if the town were itself an orchestral cadenza, sweeps over the square bearing his name. Medieval Venice, under whose rule Piran flourished, seems to sigh through the richly colored shutters. With only 5,000 inhabitants, the town occupies no more than a tiny peninsula, but its beauty surpasses that of its larger neighbors.

ORIENTATION & PRACTICAL INFORMATION. Facing the sea, take a right from the bus stop along the quay to the marina, then to the central **Tartinijev Trg.** Buses arrive in Piran from **Ljubljana** through **Koper** (40min., 9 per day, 380Sit), and **Trieste** (1½hr., 6 per day, 780Sit). The **tourist service office,** Tartinijev Trg. 2 (tel./fax 74 02 20), sells great maps (690Sit) of Piran. (Open Tu-Sa 10am-5pm, Su 10am-2pm.) They also organize tours of Slovenian Istria in English (3000-8000Sit, by appointment) and plan to connect Piran to the internet in the near future. To book a private room, visit **Turistbiro,** Kidričevo nabr. 4 (tel. 74 61 99, 74 63 82, and 74 60 95; fax 74 61 99; email zasebne.sobeşsiol.net), at the corner of Tomažičev Trg. To get there from the bus, walk toward the tip of the peninsula until it pops out. (July-Aug. singles 3100-3400Sit; 30% cheaper off-season; doubles 4700-5200Sit; 50% surcharge for less than 3 nights; daily tourist tax 190Sit. Open daily 9am-1pm and 4-7pm.) There is a **pharmacy** at Tartinijev Trg 4 (tel. 74 01 50); ring the bell outside.

(Open M-F 8am-7pm, Sa 8am-1pm, Su 9am-noon.) **Banka Koper,** Tartinijev Trg. 12, **exchanges cash** and **traveler's checks**. (Open M-F 8:30am-noon and 3-5pm, Sa 8:30-noon.) The **post office,** Leninova 1 (tel. 74 62 32), also exchanges cash and traveler's checks for no commission. (Open M-F 7:30am-9pm, Sa 7:30am-8pm, Su 8-11am.) **Telephones** are at the post office and card phones are at the corner of Zelenjavni Trg. **Postal code:** 6330. **Phone code:** (0)66.

ACCOMMODATIONS & FOOD. The proprietor of **Penzion-Val,** Gregorčičeva 38a (tel. 745 99; fax 74 69 11), near the lighthouse, contends that he runs the best pension in all of Slovenia. He may very well be right, and a bed with breakfast is only 2700Sit per person (no minimum stay). To get there from the bus, just keep walking toward the tip of the peninsula; you can't miss it. He also runs a **restaurant** outside the pension with a tourist menu (1000Sit) and pasta from 700Sit. (Open daily 8am-3pm and 6-10pm.) For budget food, **Pizzeria Surf,** Župančičeva ul. 21 (tel. 74 11 75), offers pizza (600-1000Sit) and a self-serve salad bar (600Sit; open daily 10am-11pm.) Interchangeable restaurants line the shore. **Supermarket Kras** is at Zelenjavni Trg. 1, with an **outdoor market** out front. (Open M-Sa 7am- 8pm, Su 8am-noon.)

SIGHTS. Although you'll be tempted to jump in the sea anywhere along the peninsula, waiting until after you stroll along Piran's streets is well worth it. A short walk uphill from Tartinijev Trg is Piran's most prominent church, the Gothic **Church of St. George** (Crkva sv. Jurja) first built c. 600 and rebuilt in the 14th century. The church itself is closed for renovation, but its terraces offer amazing views of the sea. A walk along the quay brings you to the **lighthouse** at the end of the peninsula. The **aquarium,** Tomažičeva 4, on the water opposite the marina, has an enormous variety of Marine life in 25 tanks. (Open daily 9am-10pm. 350Sit, children 250Sit.)

UKRAINE (УКРАЇНА)

US$1 = 4.50HV (HRYVNY)	**1HV = US$0.22**
CDN$1 = 3.02HV	**1HV = CDN$0.33**
UK£1 = 7.23HV	**1HV = UK£0.14**
IR£1 = 6HV	**1HV = IR£0.16**
AUS$1 = 2.93HV	**1HV = AUS$0.33**
NZ$1 = 2.39HV	**1HV = NZ$0.41**
SARI = 0.74HV	**1HV = SAR1.31**
DM1 = 2.44HV	**1HV = DM0.40**

PHONE CODES Country code: **380**. International dialing prefix: **810**.

Stuck between the stubbornly nostalgic heart of Russia and a bloc of nouveau-riche E.U.-aspirants, vast and fertile Ukraine stumbles along on its own path. Kiev, for centuries the cradle of Russian culture, now finds itself besieged by Western Ukraine with its Uniate congregations in lavish Polish cathedrals, its bold rhetoric of Ukrainian nationalism, and its traditional affinity for Europe; on the other side is the lovely Crimea, whose predominantly Russian population longs for the Motherland. East-central Ukraine, meanwhile, is an industrial wasteland and home to the infamous, still-functioning Chernobyl nuclear power plant.

There is nothing quaint or pretty about an industrial nation that has turned into a giant cluster of subsistence farmers, but it is an absolutely unique travel experience. Decades off the beaten path, "tourism" in Ukraine is like nothing in the rest of modern Europe. Quality museums in the cities cost nothing and are empty, medieval castles in the west still loom dark and unsupervised, and the Black Sea Coast, even after years of Soviet tourism, retains an untouchable natural magnificence. There are treasures here, but you'll have to find them yourself. Ukraine, with enough troubles of its own, isn't inclined to play host.

HIGHLIGHTS OF UKRAINE

- Once the seat of the Kievan Rus dynasty, modern **Kiev** exists in a time warp, as if its tree-lined streets and riverside vistas were still sheltered by the Iron Curtain (p. 737).
- **Lviv** really is an undiscovered jewel; you have only the Ukrainian visa authorities to thank (p. 767).
- Khrushchev gave **Crimea** to Ukraine, and the Russians didn't object (p. 750). Idiots!
- Former USSR party town, **Odessa** still hums, just at a lower frequency (p. 761).

LIFE & TIMES

HISTORY

Recorded Ukrainian history dates from the **Kievan Rus** dynasty that sprang from the infiltrations of Viking (Varangian) warrior-traders into the Dnipro River region in 882. They grew wealthy from the new north-south fur trade among Constantinople, Novgorod, and Baltic trade organizations. Kievan aristocracy, although of Varangian stock, quickly became Slavicized, adopting the Cyrillic alphabet and **Christianity.** Prince **Volodymyr the Great** welcomed missionaries from **Constantinople** and was baptized in 988. With Christianity came a flow of Byzantine thought and culture of which Kievan Rus grew so enamored that it tried to conquer its southern neighbors three times. Volodymyr's son **Yaroslav** promoted architecture, art, music, and the development of written Old Church Slavonic (see p. 746). Unfortunately, Yaroslav's rule marked the high before the crash, as changes in trade routes and squabbling over succession left the empire a prime target for invasion.

Invasion is exactly what **Genghis Khan** had in mind when he moved into Ukraine in the 1230s; grandson Batu eventually sacked Kiev in 1240. Batu's death halted the **Golden Horde's** march into Europe but not Mongol rule in Ukraine, which persisted as late as 1783 in the Crimea. By the mid-14th century, Ukraine proper was ruled by the Horde, Lithuania, and Poland, while serfdom and Roman Catholicism slowly were working their way in from the West. Meanwhile, **Cossack** warriors living in eastern Ukraine came under the employ of the Polish government as soldiers against Constantinople and Muscovy. But the Cossacks, who were as adept at fighting for themselves as for Poland, got uppity. In 1648, a legendary rebellion led by *hetman* (commander-in-chief) **Bohdan Khmelnitsky** defeated the Poles and won Kiev and Lviv. A crucial 1654 agreement with Moscow brought an ally into the war with Poland, but Khmelnitsky's death left confusion that led to a period of decline known as **"the Ruin."** By 1667, the nation was forced to accept a treaty cutting Ukraine along the Dnieper River. Russia won the east (Left Bank), including Kiev and Odessa, and the west went to Poland. Under the **Russian empire,** most of Ukraine was reorganized into Russian provinces. Jews were restricted to the Right Bank, which became known as the **Pale Settlement,** with Odessa growing into a large metropolis and Jewish center. Native culture was given a freer reign in Western Ukraine and its capital city, Lviv, which fell into Austro-Hungarian hands after the **First Partition of Poland** in 1772.

The 19th century saw Ukraine become a more vital part of the Empire, as Odessa society under Governor **Mikhail Vorontsov** hosted Pushkin for part of his exile (see **Alupka,** p. 760). Ukrainian nationalism also resurfaced, led by the poet and painter

Taras Shevchenko, who sought to revitalize the Ukrainian language and establish a free and democratic state. Shevchenko was arrested and exiled to Central Asia and **Aleksandr II** soon issued a decree banning publication, stage performances, and public readings in Ukrainian. Ukraine declared its independence in 1918, but the **Bolsheviks** set up a rival government in Kharkiv and seized complete power during the Civil War (1918-20); the Poles took Lviv and Western Ukraine only to lose them again in 1940. The next 70 years saw one tragedy after another, as this "bread basket of Russia" bore the brunt of Stalin's murderous collectivization of agriculture, Nazi invasion, a long-standing ban against Ukrainian in Soviet schools, and the 1986 meltdown at the **Chernobyl** nuclear power plant.

Ukraine pulled out of the Soviet Union on December 1, 1991, following an overwhelming vote by 93% of its population for complete **independence.** But the Soviet legacy was not so easily shed: ownership of the Black Sea Fleet at Sevastopol was in dispute, as was the status of the Crimea. Voting in the 1994 presidential election split along regional lines, but President **Leonid Kuchma's** initial policies aimed for Westernization (see below), despite his Russophilic campaign.

UKRAINE TODAY

Ukraine is in pretty bad shape. GDP has shrunk 72% since the nation declared independence. Political squabbling has stalled the magic market-reform bill, exacting its payment in jobs and production. The new **hryvnia,** once remarkably stable, has gone sour as the nation's creditors, most notably the **IMF,** have grown sick of the lack of financial reform. Ukraine remains rudderless, its state publications still looking like poorly done Communist propaganda sheets.

Democracy has not arrived in any real sense whatsoever, although its stepsister capitalism can be spotted in parts of Kiev and Odessa. With a piddling 6% approval rating and the humiliating defeat of his candidate in the 1999 Kiev mayoral election, there is little chance that President Leonid Kuchma will be around for another term. The leading candidates for his job are: ex-KGB chief Yevhen Marchuk on the right; and on the left Alexander Moroz, leader of the Socialist Party; parliament Speaker Alexander Tkachenko; and Communist Party head Pyotr Simonenko, all of whom favor reunification with Russia in lieu of real change. Reformers and crusaders are few and far between, as factories stand still, agriculture tries to rid itself of Communist collectivization, and technological industries try to cope with "brain drain" to Moscow and Israel. Perhaps most devastating, however, is the communist work ethic—the old joke, "they pretend to pay us, and we pretend to work" still rings true as wage arrears continue and workers at hotels, train stations, and stores slack off accordingly.

LITERATURE & ARTS

Ukraine's written tradition shares its roots with Russia's and Belarus's in the histories and sermons of the Kievan Rus. Translations from the original **Old Church Slavonic** gave way to original works, characterized by their stylized writing and exuberant praise of the empire. Perhaps the most important literary endeavor of this era was *The Song of Igor's Campaign (Slavo o polku Ihorevi)*, a largely symbolic epic unsurpassed in the courtly tradition. (**Vladimir Nabokov** rendered the epic in English in 1960.) The visual arts developed also, with Byzantine influences on architecture, manuscripture, and iconography. Further artistic progress was quashed, however, when the Lithuanian-Polish alliance swallowed Ukraine.

After a long dormancy, Ukrainian literature re-emerged in the 17th and 18th centuries. The most accomplished author of the period, **Ivan Kotliarevsky,** virtually created the Ukrainian vernacular with his comic travesty of Virgil's *Aeneid*, called the *Eneïda.* The **Romantic** movement of the 1830s rediscovered folk tales and added a nationalist tinge to the nascent Ukrainian style. In Kiev, **Mykola Kostomarov, Panteleymon Kulish,** and **Taras Shevchenko** (see **Kiev: Sights,** p. 746) joined the **Brotherhood of Sts. Cyril and Methodius** devoted to increasing Ukrainian national consciousness.

Shevchenko's brilliantly crafted poems, which sometimes resemble folk songs, speak of Ukrainian autonomy and idealize the Cossack period. He was also a painter, and his work straddles Classicism and an emerging Realism.

Realism worked its way into literature in the form of social commentary. **Marko Vovchok** wrote of the serfs' plight and the oppression foisted on her country by the Russians. Meanwhile, composer Mykola Lysenko dominated secular music with output ranging from piano concertos to an opera of Nikolai Gogol's *Taras Bulba*.

The early 20th century saw a dramatic outburst of artistic activity. Literary movements overtook one another rapidly: the Modernism of **Lesya Ukrainka** (the country's foremost poetess) gave way to decadent Realism in prose and Symbolism in verse. Another, newly developed movement, Futurism, gave Ukraine one of its greatest poets of the century, **Mykola Bazhan.** In the visual arts, **Monumentalism** dominated painting while **Neo-Baroque** dominated in the graphic arts. Communist-imposed **Social Realism** rained on the artistic parade, with mass censorship and Stalinist purges of dissenting writers. Creativity lay dormant until Nikita Kruschev's **thaw** of the early 60s, when it burst forth in expressionistic paintings of communist horrors, and in the works of aptly-named **Writers of the Sixties,** Vasyl Stus, Lina Kostenko, others, who wrote just enough to warrant even tougher repression in the coming decades. The result was a coma that the arts—at least among non-exiles—are just beginning to awaken from.

READING LIST

For an overview of Ukrainian history that goes to great lengths to debunk the myths that such surveys too often perpetuate, pick up *Borderland: A Journey through the History of Ukraine* by *Economist* journalist Anna Reid. For more depth, Miron Dolot offers a riveting memoir of Stalin's forced collectivization of agriculture, bleakly titled *Execution by Hunger: The Hidden Holocaust.* Author Glenn Cheney captured a more recent national tragedy in his travelogue *Journey to Chernobyl: Encounters in a Radioactive Zone.* Finally, if chasing radiation isn't your game, cozy up with the country's best young poets and prose writers in *From Three Worlds: New Ukrainian Writing*, edited by Ed Hogan.

FACTS AND FIGURES

- **Capital:** Kiev
- **Population:** 51,150,408
- **Land Area:** 603,700km^2
- **Geography:** Plains
- **Language:** Ukrainian, Russian
- **Religions:** 29% Ukrainian Orthodox 7% Uniate, 4% Protestant
- **Average Income per capita:** US$955
- **Major Exports:** Ores and metals

UKRAINE ESSENTIALS

All foreign travelers arriving in Ukraine must have a **visa,** which requires an **invitation** from a citizen or official organization, or a tourist voucher from a travel agency. Regular single-entry visa processing for Americans at a Ukrainian embassy or consulate (see **Essentials: Embassies and Consulates,** p. 13)—with invitation in hand—takes up to nine days (mailing time not included; enclose pre-paid FedEx envelope to speed the return). Singles entry visas cost US$30; double-entry US$80 and multiple-entry US$120, not including the $US45 processing fee. Three-day rush service costs US$60 (double-entry US$120). Submit a completed visa application, an invitation or confirmation from a hotel in Ukraine, your passport, one passport-size photo, and payment by money order or cashier's check. Anyone planning to work in Ukraine must have an additional letter stating the purpose of the work; the letter has to come from an official Ukrainian agency, even if you will be working for a foreign company. See **Russia: Essentials,** p. 551, for a list of organizations that arrange invitations and visas.

If you arrive in the **Kiev airport** without a visa, you can get a tourist voucher-*cum*-invitation, which will allow you to buy a visa and proceed through **customs.** Declare all valuables and foreign currency above US$1000 (including traveler's checks) in order to settle your tab when leaving the country. The process takes several hours. Most foreigners arriving at Kiev's Borispol airport must purchase a $3 per week health insurance policy for their stay in the Ukraine, in addition to any other policies they may already own.

Upon arrival, check into a hotel or register with the hall of nightmares that is the **Office of Visas and Registration** (UVIR; ОВИР), in Kiev at bul. Tarasa Shevchenka 34 (Тараса Шевченка), or at police stations in smaller cities, within your first three days in the country. Visas may also be extended here. If you do not get your visa registered, you may get hassled when trying to leave. **Do not lose the paper given to you when entering the country to supplement your visa;** it is required to leave and begging the immigration officials to kick you out of the country will do no good. Once you depart Ukraine, your visa becomes invalid. If you have a double-entry visa, you'll be given a re-entry slip (*vyezd;* въезд) when you arrive.

If you need help getting an **invitation,** try Diane Sadovnikov, a former missionary living and working in Ukraine. Together with her husband Yuri, she arranges accommodations, airport drop-off/pick-up (US$20-30), invitations (US$35), phone calls, and faxes. It's best to fax Diane a month in advance (U.S. tel./fax (757) 463-6906, Ukraine tel./fax 044 516 2433; email ims-travel@imb.net).

PRIMARY BORDER CROSSINGS. Visas and invitations for Ukraine cannot be purchased at the border; however, paying a border official US$20-50 may buy you an entry. Visas can be purchased at the Kiev airport. Expect to be asked to "unofficially" pay at least US$20 whenever you cross a Ukrainian border. Allow several hours to cross a Ukrainian border. As always, the easiest way to cross a Ukrainian border is to take a direct bus or train from Kiev, Lviv, Odessa, or Simferopol to the capital city of the neighboring country or region.

Belarus: Kovel, UKR/Brest, BEL (p. 76) via Makrany, BEL/UKR; connects Western Ukraine (p. 767) and Belarus.

Hungary: Uzhhorod, UKR (p. 778)/Nyíregyháza, HUN via Chop, UKR; connects Western Ukraine (p. 767) with Hungary.

Moldova: Mohyliv Podilsky, UKR/Edineţa, MOL via Ataki, MOL; connects Western Ukraine (p. 767) with Bălţi and Chişinău, MOL (p. 390). Do not take any trains to Tiraspol or Dubăsari, MOL, both of which are in Moldova's politically unstable breakaway Trans-Dniester Republic.

Poland: Przemyśl, POL (p. 439); connects Lviv, UKR (p. 778) to Kraków, POL (p. 422) and Małopolska (p. 421).

Romania: Chernivtsi, UKR/Suceava, ROM (p. 541) via Porubne, UKR; connects Western Ukraine (p. 767) to Romanian Moldova (p. 538).

Russia: Donetsk or Maryupol, UKR/Rostov-na-Donu, RUS (see p. 646); connects Crimea (p. 750) to Southern Russia, including the Caucasus (p. 646) and the Volga Region (p. 638). Charkiv, UKR/Belgorod, RUS via Kozacha Lopan, UKR; connects Ukraine to Northern Russia.

Slovakia: Uzhhorod, UKR (p. 778)/Sobrance, SLK; connects Western Ukraine (p. 767) with Šariš (p. 698).

GETTING THERE

Air Ukraine International (U.S. tel. (800) 876-0114; Kiev tel. 216 70 40 and 276 70 59; fax 216 76 09) flies to Kiev, Lviv, and Odessa from a number of European capitals, as well as from Chicago, New York, and Washington, D.C. Air France, ČSA, Lufthansa, LOT, Malév, SAS, and Swissair also fly to Kiev, generally once or twice a week. **Trains** are much cheaper, run frequently from all of Ukraine's neighbors, and are the most popular way of entering the country. When coming from a non-ex-Soviet country, expect a two-hour stop at the border while the wagons get their wheels changed. **Buses** are a pain unless you're traveling short distances. However, taking a bus from Przemyśl, Poland to Lviv saves money and time. **Ferries** across the Black Sea are limited to a few routes from Odessa and Yalta to Istanbul.

GETTING AROUND

Trains go everywhere and offer dirt-cheap comfort; unfortunately, getting the **tickets** could drive you batty. For long-distance travel, try to buy tickets a few days in advance. If you're leaving from a town that's not the start of the train route, however, you'll only be able to obtain same-day tickets. You can also try to plead with the conductor, who will charge the cost of the ticket, pocket the money himself, and find you a seat. In larger towns, foreigners need to buy their tickets from a separate Intourist window, but in most towns you get to line up with the locals.

On most trains within Ukraine there are two classes: *platzkart*, where you'll be crammed in with *babushki* and their baskets of strawberries, and *coupé*, less crowded but still with disgusting bathrooms. Unless you are determined to live local, pay the extra two dollars for *coupé;* it can make the difference between dreading and tolerating a long trip. When traveling between Lviv and Kiev, choose trains #92 (to Kiev) and 91 (to Lviv)—both have special "Grand-Tour" cars (Гранд-Тур) that are even cozier (60hv). Except in Kiev, where **platform** numbers are posted on the electronic board, the only way to figure out which platform your train leaves from is by listening to the distorted announcement. In large cities, trains arrive well before they are scheduled to depart, so you'll have a few minutes to show your ticket to cashiers or fellow passengers, look helpless, and say "платформа?" (plaht-FORM-ah?) For some stellar advice on post-Soviet train travel, see **Russia: Getting Around,** p. 556.

Buses are a bit more expensive, a lot less comfortable, but the best way to go short distances. In large cities, buy tickets at least the night before leaving at the regular ticket-windows. In smaller cities, the *kasa* will start selling tickets only an hour before the bus departs. Sometimes, they'll direct you to buy the ticket from the driver, but always try the *kasa* first. Each platform has its buses posted. **River transport** is infrequent, but some routes do exist. Kiev hydrofoils go only as far as Chernihiv. The port agents know more than the Intourist offices, which feign ignorance. Within cities, private **taxis** are indispensable (see p. 556).

TOURIST SERVICES

In theory, the breakup of the Soviet Union brought about the demise of the official state travel agency, **Intourist,** which was responsible for foreigners traveling in Ukraine. In reality, they still have an office in almost every city, sometimes under another name, and offer hard-to-find train tickets. However, they're used to dealing with groups, to whom they sell "excursion" packages to nearby sights, rather than individuals. Smaller tourist offices—if they exist—may be more helpful and have cheaper services. Don't be surprised if they don't have maps or speak English.

MONEY

In September 1996, Ukraine decided to wipe the extraneous zeros off most prices by replacing the **karbovanets** (Krb; a.k.a. kupon) with a new currency, the **hryvnia** (hv; plural hryvny; гривна); each hryvnia is worth 100,000 karbovantsi. **Exchanging** U.S. dollars and Deutschmarks is fairly simple, since Ukrainians frequently use the two currencies themselves; *Obmin Valyut* (Обмін Валют) kiosks in the center of most cities offer the best rates. Other currencies pose difficulties; **traveler's checks** can be changed into dollars for small commissions in many cities, although it can be time-consuming. **X-Change Point** (available in Kiev, Odessa, Yalta, Uzhhorod, Dnipropetrovsk, and Lviv) is a rare Renaissance thinker in the Dark Ages of Ukrainian finance—they have **Western Union** and can give Visa cash advances. Most banks will give MC/Visa cash advances for a high commission; this, too, will probably take a long time. The lobbies of fancier hotels usually exchange U.S. dollars at lousy rates. **Private money changers** lurk near legitimate kiosks, ready with brilliant schemes for ripping you off. **Do not** exchange money with them; it's illegal and they might slip you a wad of useless *karbovantsi.* There are **ATMs** in the larger cities.

COMMUNICATION

Mail is cheap but slow (min. 2-4 weeks from Kiev to any foreign destination). From other cities, it may never arrive, or even be picked up. Trust not street corner mail boxes; going straight to the post office is safest. The easiest way to mail letters is to buy pre-stamped envelopes at the post office.

Telephones are stumbling toward modernity, as a few central telephone centers spiff themselves up. The easiest way to make international calls with a calling card or collect is with **Utel** (Ukraine telephone). Buy a Utel phonecard (sold at most Utel phone locations) and dial the number of your international operator (counted as a local call): **AT&T,** (8) 100 11—wait for another tone after the 8; **BT Direct,** (8) 10 04 41; **Canada Direct,** (8)100 17; **MCI,** (8) 100 13; **Sprint** (8) 100 15. Utel phones can be found in expensive hotels, city telephone centers, and some expensive restaurants. If you don't have a calling card, order your international call at the central telephone office. Estimate how long your call will take, pay at the counter, and they'll direct you to a booth. Order intercity calls at the post office and pay up front; in some cities, pay phones marked "Міжміський" *(mizhmisky)* work with tokens, as do Utel phones. **Local calls** from gray pay phones generally cost 10-30hv.

With the mail and phone systems in the states they're in, **email** may be your quickest and easiest options. Internet access is widespread and fairly reliable, save a few bad connections in the Crimea.

LANGUAGE

Your trip will go more smoothly if you can throw around a few words of **Ukrainian** or **Russian** (see **Glossaries: Ukrainian,** p. 824, and **Russian,** p. 821). In Crimea and most of east Ukraine, Russian is more common than Ukrainian; even in Kiev, most people speak Russian (although all official signs—such as those on the Metro—are in Ukrainian). In west Ukraine, Ukrainian is preferred, and **Polish** is often understood. *Let's Go* uses Ukrainian names in Kiev and Western Ukraine, and Russian in the Crimea and Odeshchina.

The Ukrainian alphabet resembles Russian (see **The Cyrillic Alphabet,** p. 807), but with a few character and pronunciation differences. The most notable additions are the "i" (*ee* sound) and the "ï" (*yee* sound)—the "и" is closest to "s*i*t." The rarely used "є" sounds like "ye" in "yep!" The "ґ" (hard "g") has been reintroduced since independence but is not yet widely used, and the "г," pronounced "g" in Russian, comes out like an "h." Roll your "r"s, but not too flamboyantly.

Words that appear frequently in this chapter include: *apteka* (аптека; pharmacy); *avtovokzal* (автовокзал bus station); *hastronom* (гастроном; supermarket); *hostinitsa* (гостініца; hotel or guest house); *kostyol* (костьол; church); *rynok* (ринок; market); *sobor* (собор; cathedral); *tserkva* (церква; church).

HEALTH & SAFETY

! EMERGENCY NUMBERS.
Fire: tel. 01. **Police**: tel. 02. **Ambulance**: tel. 03.

While Ukraine is neither violent nor politically volatile, it is poor and its people desperate. Keep your foreign profile low, watch your belongings, and don't make easy acquaintances, especially on the street. Don't be afraid to initiate contact; people who don't go out of their way to approach you can generally be trusted. The risk of **crime,** although made much of, isn't much greater than in the rest of Eastern

Europe. Travelers who have been harassed by the police say it's possible to get back on the law's good side with a US$20 bill. It's a wise idea to **register** with your embassy once you get to Ukraine. This makes the process of recovering a lost passport much quicker. For more information, see **Safety & Security,** p. 22.

Authorities recommend boiling water for 10min. before drinking it, and bottled water is even safer. It is extremely difficult, however, to find non-carbonated bottled water outside Kiev. Fruits and vegetables from open **markets** are generally safe, although storage conditions and pesticides make thorough washing imperative. Meat purchased at public markets should be checked very carefully and cooked thoroughly; refrigeration is a foreign concept and insects run rampant. Don't trust the tasty-looking hunks of meat for sale out of buckets on the Kiev subway—they are not safe. Embassy officials declare that Chernobyl-related **radiation** poses minimal risk to short-term travelers, but the region should be given a wide berth. For more on Chernobyl, see p. 729. Public restrooms range from yucky to scary. Pay **toilets** (*platny;* платній) are cleaner and (gasp!) might provide toilet paper, but bring your own anyway.

Pharmacies are quite common, and medications prescribed by local doctors are usually available. Aspirin is the only painkiller on hand, but plenty of cold remedies and bandages are available. In large hotels, imported medications may be available for hard currency. **Sanitary napkins** (гігієнічні пакети; hee-hee-eh-NEE-chnee pak-YET-ih), **condoms** (презервативи; prey-zer-vah-TIV-ih), and **tampons** (прокладки; proh-KLAHD-ki) are intermittently available at kiosks.

Women traveling alone are likely to be harassed in one way or another. Ukrainian women never go to restaurants alone, so expect to feel conspicuous if you do, even in the middle of the day. Even hotel restaurants may be uncomfortable; small cafes and cafeterias are safer options. There is not much **racial diversity** in Ukraine today. Although non-Caucasians may experience discrimination at stores, restaurants, and hotels, the biggest problems come from the militia, which frequently stops people who they suspect to be non-Slavic.

ACCOMMODATIONS

Not all hotels accept foreigners, and those that do often charge them many times more than what a Ukrainian would pay. Hotels fall into two categories, **"hotels"** and **"tourist bases"**—called "Турбаза" (TOOR-bah-zah), usually part of a complex targeted at motoring tourists, but otherwise indistinguishable from hotels. Although room prices in Kiev are astronomical, singles run anywhere from 5hv to 90hv in the rest of the country. The phrase "самое дешёвое место" (SAHM-ah-yih dih-SHOHV-o-ye ME-stoh) means "the cheapest place." More expensive hotels aren't necessarily nicer, and in some hotels, women lodging alone may be mistaken for prostitutes. Most cities have cheap hotels above the train stations—these are usually seedy and unsafe.

Tourism is slow, so hotels usually have vacancies. They may hold on to your passport during your stay, although you can get it back if you politely suggest you'd rather keep it with you. You will be given a *vizitka* (hotel card; визитка) to show to the hall monitor (*dezhurnaya*; дежурная; or *cherhova*; чергова) to get a key; surrender it on leaving the building. **Bathroom conditions** are usually adequate, although Ukraine is generally a bring-your-own-toilet-paper country. Hot water is a godsend when you find it; some places have no water at all for a few hours every day. Valuables should never be left unattended; ask at the desk if there's a **safe.**

Private rooms can be arranged through overseas agencies or bargained for at the train station. Prices run 2-10hv per person, but conditions vary. During the summer, **university dorms** might put you up for a couple of nights, depending on whether the *kommandant* likes you; come during business hours to see this powerful bureaucrat. A bed usually costs 2-10hv. Most cities have a **campground,** which is a remote hotel with trailers for buildings. The old Soviet complexes can be quite posh (and quite expensive), with saunas and restaurants. Free camping is illegal, and enforcement is merciless.

FOOD & DRINK

Ukraine is simply not going to make your tummy happy. New, fancy restaurants are popping up to accommodate tourists and the few Ukrainians who can afford them. There are few choices between these and the *stolovaya*, dying bastions of cheap, hot food. There is usually a choice of two soups, two entrees, and some *kompot* (a homemade fruit drink). The busier it is, the fresher the food. Non-fresh *stolovaya* food can knock you out of commission for hours, while a good *stolovaya* meal is a triumph of the human spirit. If not, they know something you don't. Most restauranteurs' reactions to **vegetarians** are hostile, and the meat-free menu rarely has more than mushrooms (*hribi*; гриби). When you ask for an entree without meat *(bez myaso)*, make sure they don't just bring you another kind of meat. Be aware that most Ukrainian restaurants do not include side dishes with their entrees. If you want a pickle with your *pierogi*, you'll have to order it.

Produce is sold by the kilogram at jam-packed warehouse **markets.** Bring a bag or buy one at nearby kiosks. Markets are open daily, usually by 7am, and close no earlier than 5pm. **State food stores** are classified by content: *hastronom* (гастроном) packaged goods; *moloko* (молоко) milk products; *ovochi-frukty* (овочі-фрукты) fruits and vegetables; *myaso* (мясо) meat; *hlib* (хліб) bread; *kolbasy* (колбаси) sausage; and *ryba* (риба) fish. Pay the cashier first for the item you want (just tell her the price), then trade your receipt for the products at the counter. In the suburbs, there is one store per designated region, simply labeled *mahazyn* (store; магазин). Kiosks often have the same products as expensive Western stores for much cheaper (this applies only to non-perishables, however; kiosk dairy and meat are not safe).

Liquor is cheap and available everywhere. A half-liter bottle of *Stolichnaya* costs about 3hv and is generally tastier than the moonshine *(samohonka)* Ukrainians might offer you in their homes. The quality of **beer** varies. *Obolon* (оболонь) is the most popular, but Lviv's *Zoloty kolos* (Золотий Колос) and *Lvivske* (Львiвськe) are of higher quality. Don't miss out on *kvas* (квас), an unholy but delicious mix of fermented bread and water poured for kopeks from huge kegs in the street. At mealtime, don't count on free water. Few eateries carry water and those that do charge more for it than juice.

CUSTOMS & ETIQUETTE

Arrive at parties bearing flowers, vodka, or pastries for the hosts, and expect chit-chat to soon evolve into political discussion. Unless you know the situation in Ukraine well, confine your comments to the beauty of the countryside and the hospitality of its people. Topics such as abortion and **homosexuality,** although not taboo, provoke a negative reaction; being homosexual will provoke an even worse reaction. Dinners can last long into the evening; if you try to leave early, you may offend your hosts. Not eating your food is equally insulting. Although locals don't usually leave **tips,** most expats give 10% of the meal's price. Large backpacks give away your foreignness, as does sloppy dress. Women and girls are often dressed up, or rather, hardly dressed; shorts, if worn at all, are fancy and normally accompanied by dress shoes.

JUST FOR THE TASTE When the sun is high and the steppe is hotter than a Saharan parking lot, Aussies thirst for a *Fosters*, Czechs a *Pilsner*, and Yankees a *Bud*, but a true Ukrainian won't have anything other than a ladle of **kvas** (квас). In Kiev you'll see it served from siphons, in the provinces from rusty cisterns. The taste—kind of like beer without the hops—varies depending on the container, but it all comes down to acidic bread bubbles; the drink is based on a sourdough solution that rushes tingling into your bloodstream. It's so addictive that Kiev drinks *kvas* all summer, even in the rain, when groups of young tots, middle-aged shoppers, and love-struck teenagers huddle around toothless tap-masters, all under one leaky umbrella.

NATIONAL HOLIDAYS

January 1, New Year's; January 7, Orthodox Christmas; March 8, International Women's Day; April 28, Good Friday; April 30, Orthodox Easter; May 1-2, Labor Day; May 9, Victory Day (1945); June 18-19, Holy Trinity; June 28, Constitution Day; August 24, Independence Day (1991).

KIEV (КИЇВ)

...Most often of all I soothe my aged imagination with pictures of gold-domed, garden-cloaked and poplar-crowned Kiev.

–Taras Shevchenko (from exile)

Straddling the wide Dnipro River and layered with hills and greenery, Kiev (pop. 2,630,200) is a becoming place, although it still hasn't quite figured out how to become a thriving capital(ist) metropolis. Once the USSR's third largest city—and now Ukraine's center for everything—Kiev should share the vibrancy and vivacity that other newly liberated Eastern European cities possess. In many ways the city does, with rich (albeit crumbling) sights and a relative lack of tourists. Nonetheless, locals still prefer to store their money in dollars under their pillows, its roundabout route to the 20th century continues to baffle travelers accustomed to regular train schedules, and visiting Americans are more likely to be shopping for wives than for tourist kitsch.

GETTING THERE & GETTING AROUND

Airplanes: Kiev-Boryspil Airport (Київ-Бориспіль; tel. 296 75 29), 30min. (by car) southeast of the capital. Cash-only exchange office. **Buses** (25hv per person) leave from the front of the terminal at 2:20pm and 3pm and drop passengers off at Hotels Dnipro and Rus. The city bus or a *marshrutne taksi* (маршрутне таксі) is cheaper–both dump the newly arrived at MR: Livoberezhna (Лівобережна; every 2hr., 2.50hv). Buy your ticket on the bus. It's worth taking a **taxi** to the Hostinitsa Druzhba, or elsewhere on the south side of town; US$40 should be haggled down to $20. The private company **Taksys** (Таксис; tel. 295 95 08) charges 60hv. Purchase tickets at airline offices throughout the city:

- **Air Ukraine,** pr. Peremohy 14 (tel. 216 70 40 or 276 70 59; fax 216 76 09). Open M-F 10am-5pm.
- **Austrian Airlines/Swissair,** Chervonoarmiska vul. 9/2 (tel. 244 35 40 or 244 35 41). Open M-F 10am-5pm.
- **British Airways,** Yaroslaviv Val. vul 5 (tel. 247 66 44). Open M-F 9am-6pm, Sa 10am-2pm.
- **Malév,** Volodymyrska vul. 20 (tel. 229 36 61). Open M-F 10am-5pm.
- **Air France,** Velyka Zhytomyrska 6/11 (tel. 464 10 10). Open M-F 9am-5pm.
- **ČSA,** vul. Ivana Franka 36 (tel. 246 56 28). Open M-F 9am-5pm.
- **LOT,** next to ČSA (tel. 246 56 20). Open M-F 9am-5pm, Sa 10am-2pm.
- **KLM,** vul. Ivana Franka 29 #2 (tel. 246 55 85). Open M-F 10am-5pm.
- **Lufthansa,** vul. Khreshchatyk 14-16 (tel. 229 62 97; fax 229 29 72). Open M-F 9am-5:30pm.

Trains: Kiev-Passazhyrsky (Київ-Пассажирський; schedule info tel. 005), Vokzalna pl. MR: Vokzalna. When you enter the main ticketing room on the 1st floor, arrivals are listed on the right and departures on the left. **Tickets** can be purchased at the Intourist window on the 2nd floor. Beware clerks who demand you pay an unreasonable price in U.S. dollars. Open daily 8am-1pm, 2-7pm, and 8pm-7am. There are also potential ticket-buying intermediaries on the main floor, including **Advance-Ticket Kasas,** bul. Shevchenka 38. MR: Universytet (Університет). Cross and go left down Shevchenka. No passport required. Open M-F 8am-8pm, Sa-Su 9am-6pm. If you don't feel like a wait, try **Intourist,** vul. Hospitalna 12 (tel. 224 25 59). Scalpers add 4-6hv to the price, but may have some tickets that are otherwise unavailable. Ask a clerk to check if the ticket is valid before paying by saying *"Pro-VER-teh, po-ZHA-lus-tah, EH-tot bee-LYET"* ("Please, check if this ticket is

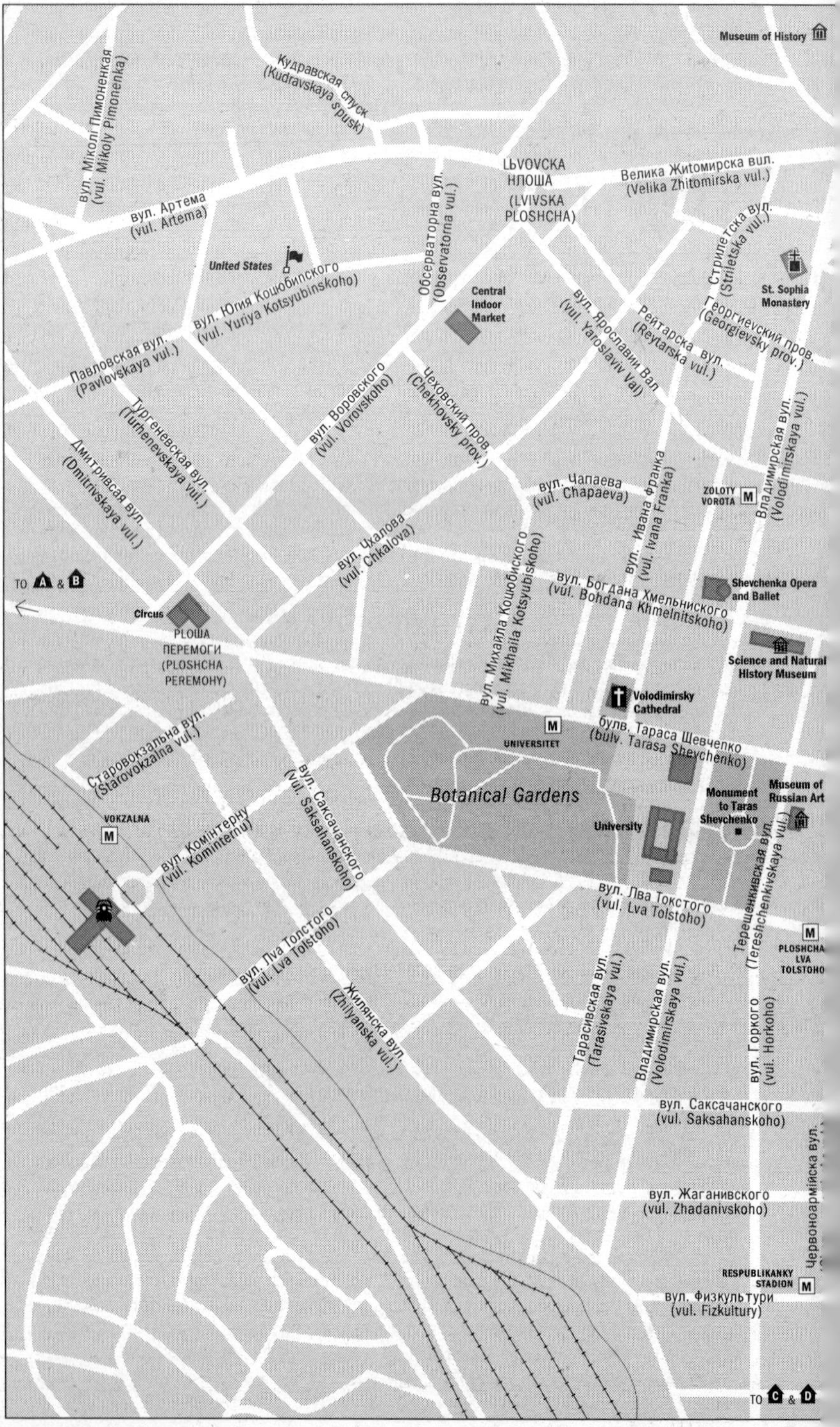
Museum of History
Кудравская спуск
(Kudravskaya spusk)
вул. Миколі Пимоненкая
(vul. Mikoly Pimonenka)
ЬВОVСКА
НЛОША
(LVIVSKA
PLOSHCHA)
Велика Житомирска вул.
(Velika Zhitomirska vul.)
вул. Артема
(vul. Artema)
Обсерваторна вул.
(Observatorna vul.)
United States
вул. Югия Кошобинского
(vul. Yuriya Kotsyubinskoho)
Стрилетска вул.
(Striletska vul.)
St. Sophia Monastery
Central Indoor Market
вул. Ярослави Вал
(vul. Yaroslaviv Val)
Рейтарска вул.
(Reytarska vul.)
Георгиевский пров.
(Georgievsky prov.)
Павловская вул.
(Pavlovskaya vul.)
вул. Воровского
(vul. Vorovskoho)
Чеховский пров.
(Chekhovsky prov.)
Тургеневская вул.
(Turhenevskaya vul.)
Дмитривсая вул.
(Dmitrivskaya vul.)
Владимирская вул.
(Volodimirskaya vul.)
вул. Чапаева
(vul. Chapaeva)
Ивана Франка
(vul. Ivana Franka)
ZOLOTY VOROTA
вул. Чхалова
(vul. Chkalova)
вул. Михайла Кошобиского
(vul. Mikhaila Kotsyubiskoho)
TO A & B
Shevchenka Opera and Ballet
вул. Богдана Хмельниского
(vul. Bohdana Khmelnitskoho)
Circus
PLOША
ПЕРЕМОГИ
(PLOSHCHA
PEREMOHY)
Science and Natural History Museum
Volodimirsky Cathedral
UNIVERSITET
булв. Тараса Шевченко
(bulv. Tarasa Shevchenko)
Старовокзальна вул.
(Starovokzalna vul.)
вул. Саксачанского
(vul. Saksahanskoho)
Botanical Gardens
Monument to Taras Shevchenko
Museum of Russian Art
University
VOKZALNA
вул. Комінтерну
(vul. Kominternu)
Терещенкивская вул.
(Tereshchenkivskaya vul.)
вул. Лва Токстого
(vul. Lva Tolstoho)
вул. Лва Толстого
(vul. Lva Tolstoho)
PLOSHCHA LVA TOLSTOHO
Жилянска вул.
(Zhilyanska vul.)
Тарасивская вул.
(Tarasivskaya vul.)
Владимирская вул.
(Volodimirskaya vul.)
вул. Горкого
(vul. Horkoho)
вул. Саксачанского
(vul. Saksahanskoho)
Червоноармійска вул.
вул. Жаганивского
(vul. Zhadanivskoho)
RESPUBLIKANKY STADION
вул. Физкультури
(vul. Fizkultury)
TO C & D

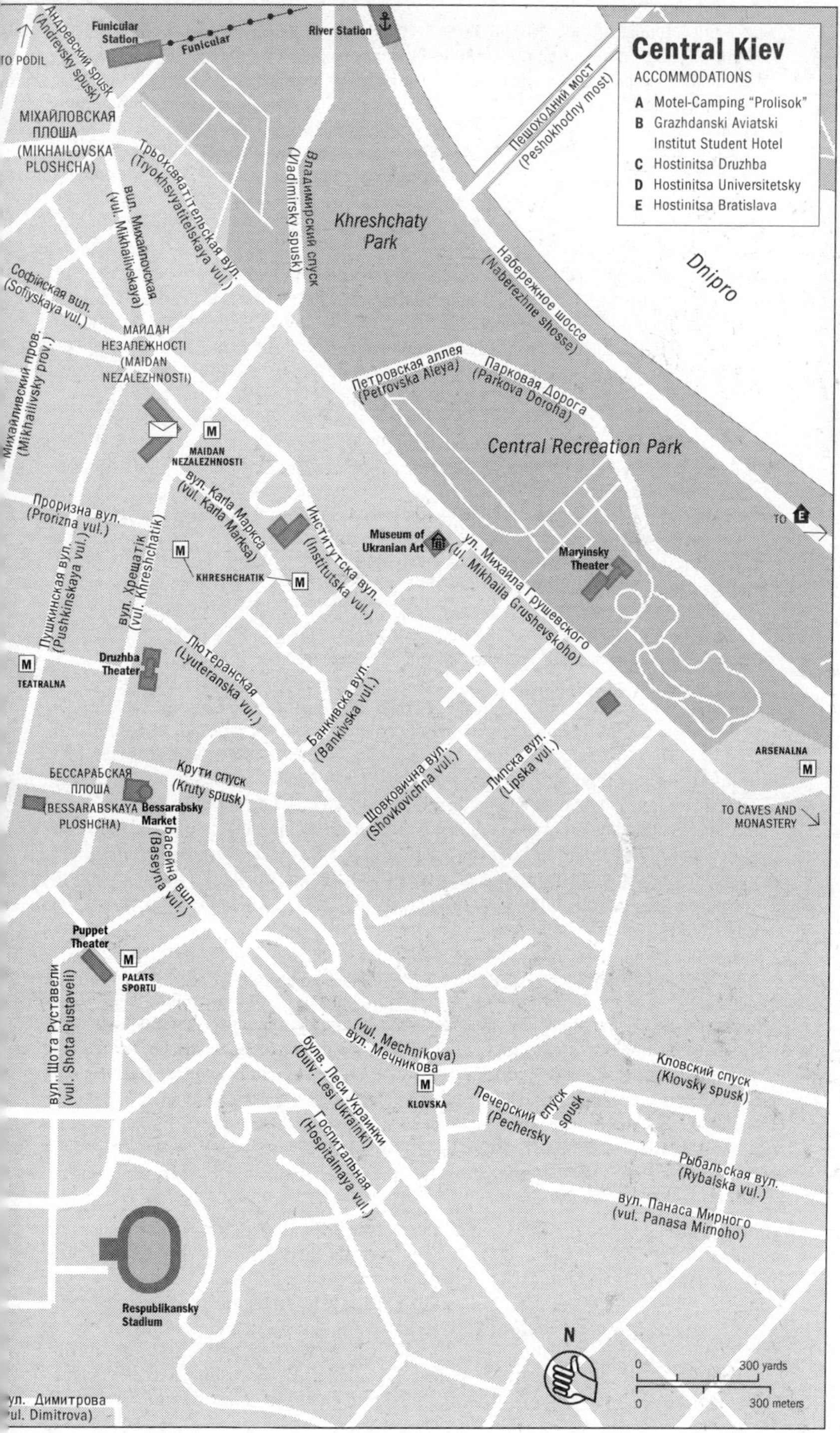
Central Kiev
ACCOMMODATIONS
A Motel-Camping "Prolisok"
B Grazhdanski Aviatski Institut Student Hotel
C Hostinitsa Druzhba
D Hostinitsa Universitetsky
E Hostinitsa Bratislava
TO PODIL
Funicular Station
Funicular
River Station
Андревский spusk (Andrevsky spusk)
МІХАЙЛОВСКАЯ ПЛОША (MIKHAILOVSKA PLOSHCHA)
Трьохсвятительская вул. (Tryokhsvyatitelskaya vul.)
вул. Михайловская (vul. Mikhailivskaya)
Владимирский спуск (Vladimirsky spusk)
Пешоходний мост (Peshokhodny most)
Khreshchaty Park
Dnipro
Набережное шоссе (Naberezhne shosse)
Софійская вул. (Sofiyskaya vul.)
Михайливский пров. (Mikhailivsky prov.)
МАЙДАН НЕЗАЛЕЖНОСТІ (MAIDAN NEZALEZHNOSTI)
Петровская аллея (Petrovska Aleya)
Парковая Дорога (Parkova Doroha)
Central Recreation Park
MAIDAN NEZALEZHNOSTI
вул. Карла Маркса (vul. Karla Marksa)
Прорizна вул. (Prorizna vul.)
Институтска вул. (Institutska vul.)
Museum of Ukranian Art
ул. Михайла Грушевского (vul. Mikhaila Grushevskoho)
TO E
Maryinsky Theater
Пушкинская вул. (Pushkinskaya vul.)
вул. Хрещатік (vul. Khreshchatik)
KHRESHCHATIK
TEATRALNA
Druzhba Theater
Лютеранская (Lyuteranska vul.)
Банкивска вул. (Bankivska vul.)
Липска вул. (Lipska vul.)
ARSENALNA
БЕССАРАБСКАЯ ПЛОША (BESSARABSKAYA PLOSHCHA)
Крути спуск (Kruty spusk)
Bessarabsky Market
Шовковична вул. (Shovkovichna vul.)
TO CAVES AND MONASTERY
Басейна вул. (Baseyna vul.)
Puppet Theater
PALATS SPORTU
вул. Шота Руставели (vul. Shota Rustaveli)
(vul. Mechnikova) вул. Мечникова
KLOVSKA
Кловский спуск (Klovsky spusk)
булв. Леси Украинки (bulv. Lesi Ukrainki)
Печерский спуск (Pechersky spusk)
Госпитальная (Hospitalnaya vul.)
Рыбальская вул. (Rybalska vul.)
вул. Панаса Мирного (vul. Panasa Mirnoho)
Respublikansky Stadium
N
0 300 yards
0 300 meters
вул. Димитрова (vul. Dimitrova)

valid"). If Intourist or the *kasa* claim not to have tickets, try again both 6 and 2 hours before the train leaves. To: **Ivano-Frankivsk** (16hr., 2 per day, 15hv, *couchette* 24hv); **Kamyanets-Podilsky** (11hr., 3 per day, 11hv, *couchette* 20hv); **Lviv** (12hr., 5 per day, 14hv, *couchette* 21hv); **Odessa** (11hr., 5 per day, 22hv, *couchette* 34hv); **Simferopol** (18hr., 4 per day, 21hv, *couchette* 47hv); and **Uzhhorod** (19½hr., 3 per day, 16hv, *couchette* 25hv). For **international tickets,** you will need to present your passport so they can charge you a higher price. To: **Bratislava** (18hr., 1 per day, 194hv); **Budapest** (25hr., 1 per day, 192hv); **Minsk** (12-13hr., 1 per day, 30hv, *couchette* 47hv); **Moscow** (15-17hr., 15 per day, 43-63hv); **Prague** (34hr., 1 per day, 197hv); and **Warsaw** (15hr., 1 per day, 82hv).

Buses: Tsentralny Avtovokzal (Центральний Автовокзал), Moskovska pl. 3 (Московьска; tel. 265 04 30). A 10min. walk past Libidska, the last stop on the MG line. Take a right and then a left out of the Metro, and look for bus #4. If it isn't available, walk 100m to the big highway, then take a right and follow it for 300m. Long-distance destinations: **Kharkiv** (2 per day, 17hv); **Minsk** (2 per day, 21hv); and **Moscow** (2 per day, 42hv). Stations serving other destinations include:

Darnytsa (Дарница), pr. Gagarina (Гагаріна; tel. 559 46 18), sends buses to **Dnipropetrovsk** (9hr., 18hv) and **Pereyaslav-Khmelnitsky** (1½hr., 3hv).

Pivdenna (Південна), pr. Akademyka Hlushkova 3 (Академика Глушкова; tel. 263 40 04), connects to **Odessa.**

Podil (Поділ), vul. Nyzhni Val 15a (Нижній Вал), sends buses to the **Crimea.** From MB: Kontraktova pl. (Контрактова), walk northwest along vul. Konstyantynivska (Констянтинівська) and hang a left onto vul. Nyzhny Val.

Local Transportation: Kiev's **Metropoliten** is efficient for the few places it serves, but leaves large areas between its 3 lines and does not reach the university dorms. Buy clear blue tokens at the "Каса" *(Kasa)* for 0.30hv or a monthly pass from a numbered kiosk for 10hv. Monthly passes are good on all public transportation. If you buy one, slide it through the slot on top of the turnstile. The stations' signs are all in Cyrillic—consult your handy *Let's Go* subway map. "Перехід" *(perekhid)* indicates a walkway to another station, "вихід у місто" *(vykhid u misto)* an exit onto the street, "вхід" *(vkhid)* an entrance to the Metro, "нема вхіду" *(nema vkhidu)* no entrance. Make use of Kiev's extensive system of **trams, trolleys,** and **buses**. Trolleys and buses with identical numbers may have very different routes; a route map is a worthwhile investment (see **English Bookstore,** p. 742). Buy tickets at numbered kiosks (0.30hv) or from a conductor with a badge and tickets in hand, and punch them on board to avoid a 6hv fine (or jail!). Transport runs 6am-midnight, but some buses travel later. Occasionally, techno-blaring private **"marshrutne taksi"** will run the same route twice as fast and for 0.10hv more, but you have to tell the driver where to stop.

Taxis: Avoid taxis when you can, as they overcharge foreigners. If you can't, give the driver an address *near* your hotel; he won't assume so quickly that you're a businessperson on an expense account. Some are almost always available at **Maydan Nezalezhnosti. State taxis** (tel. 058), identifiable by the checkered sign on top, are more consistently priced. The private company **Taksys** (Таксис; tel. 295 95 08) is a little bit cheaper at 0.36hv per min. from 6am-11pm and 0.40hv per min. from 11pm-6am. 50hv to the airport. Taxi-like **private cars** are cheaper; agree on a price before getting in. Hold your arm down at a 45° angle to hail a ride. *Let's Go* does not recommend private rides.

Car Rental: Avis, Hospitalna 4, #404 (tel. 294 21 04).

ORIENTATION

Although the city straddles the **Dnipro River** (Дніпро), almost all its attractions and services lie on the right (west) bank. The **Metro's** three intersecting lines—blue (MB), green (MG), and red (MR)—cover the city center but leave most of the outskirts to trolleys and trams. The **train station** lies at MR: Vokzalna (Вокзальна). Two stops away is the **Khreshchatyk** (Хрещатик) stop and its corresponding street, a broad and busy post-war boulevard. Parallel to vul. Khreshchatyk and just up the hill runs the stately, tree-lined Volodymyrska vul. (Володимирьска). Bul. Shevchenka (Шевченка) and vul. Khmelnitskoho (Хмельніцького) run perpendicular to these. Along the west bank of the Dnipro, **Khreshchaty Park** covers the slope that runs from the city center to the water's edge. The heart of Kiev is vul. Khreshchatyk's **Maydan Nezalezhnosti** (Майдан Незалежності), a fountain-filled fun spot next to the post office. You can buy **maps** (3-5hv) here or in any kiosk.

PRACTICAL INFORMATION

TOURIST & FINANCIAL SERVICES

Tourist Offices: Kiev still lacks decent tourist offices. The **Ukraine Hotel**, Tarasa Shevchaka blvd. 5 offers guidance. MB: Ploshcha Iva Tolstovo.

Embassies: Belarus, vul. Yanvarskoho Vossttanaya 6 (Январского Восстанія; tel. 290 02 01). Open M-F 10am-5pm. **Canada,** vul. Yaroslaviv Val 31 (Ярославів Вал; tel. 464 11 44). Open M-Tu and Th-F 8:30am-noon. **Latvia,** vul. Desyatynia, 4/6 (Десятиниа; tel. 229 23 60). Open M-F 10am-5pm. **Russia,** pr. Kutuzova 8 (Кутузова; tel. 294 79 36 or 294 63 89). Open M-Th 9am-6pm, F 9am-5pm. **U.K.,** vul. Desyatynya 6 (tel. 462 00 11; fax 462 00 13). Open M-F 9am-5:30pm. **U.S.,** vul. Yu. Kotsyubinskoho 10 (Ю. Коцюбинського; tel. 246 97 50; emergency tel. 216 38 05; fax 244 73 50; consular services fax 216 33 93; email consular@usemb.kiev.ua; www.usemb.kiev.ua). From Maydan Nezalezhnosti, take trolley #16 or 18 from the top of the square to the 4th stop, and walk down between the Nike and the fruit stores. American embassy services M-F 8:45-11:45am.

Currency Exchange: *Obmin-Valyut* (Обмін-Валют) windows are on every street and alley. They usually take only US$ and DM. Rates tend to be good, as they are primarily for locals who keep their money in dollars. New booths that cash traveler's checks and give MC/Visa advances usually have bad rates or high commissions. **Legbank** (Легбанк), vul.

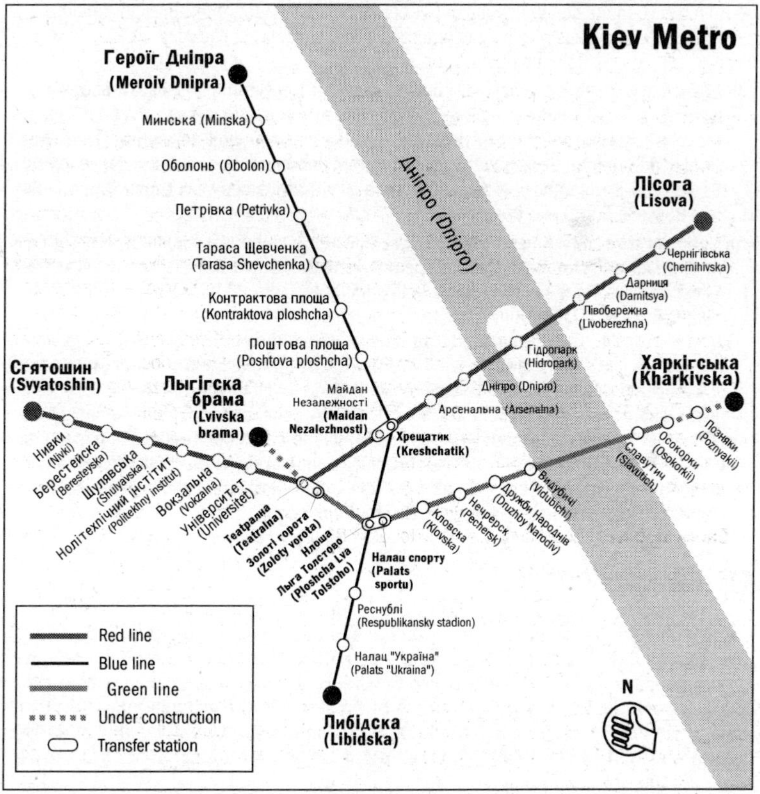

Shota Rustaveli 12 (Щота Руставелі). From MB/G: Palats sportu (Палац спорту), go northwest on vul. Rohnydinska (Рогнидінська) and turn right on Rustaveli. Good rates and low commissions: 3% for MC/Visa; 2% for traveler's checks if over US$250, otherwise flat US$5 commission. Open M-F 9am-7pm, Sa 9am-6pm. **National Bank of Ukraine,** on the corner of Institutska and Khreshchatyk, does everything for a 3.5% commission. They also offer **Western Union** services. Open daily 9am-1pm and 2-8pm. There are **ATMs** in TSUM on vul. Khreshchatyk, and in Hotel Kyivska.

LOCAL SERVICES, EMERGENCY, & COMMUNICATIONS

Luggage Storage: At the train station (look for Камери Схову), down the stairs outside the main entrance (2hv). Open daily 8am-noon, 1-7:30pm, 8pm-midnight, and 1-7:30am. The **Hotel Rus,** Hospitalna 4, is safer and open to non-guests (3lv). 24hr.

English Bookstore: Znaniya (Знанія), bul. Khreshchatyk 44 (tel. 224 82 19), has the widest selection, which isn't saying much. Open M-F 10am-2pm and 3-7pm. The lobby of **Hotel Kyivska** (Київська, formerly Hotel Intourist), behind Hotel Rus at vul. Hospitalna 12, stocks *The Kiev Post*—a weekly **free English newspaper.**

24hr. Pharmacy: Apteka, the purple building on the corner of vul. Khmelnytskoho and vul. Ivana Franka 25/40 (Івана Франка; tel. 224 29 88), sparkles with sanitized cleanliness and carries high-quality products. Open 24hr.; ring the bell 8pm-8am.

Medical Assistance: Check with the **U.S. Embassy** (see above) for a list of safe hospitals. **Emergency Care Center,** vul. Mechnikova 1 (tel. 227 92 30), also has a **dental clinic** (tel. 227 42 40). The **American Medical Center,** vul. Berdicherska 1 (tel. 211 65 55; fax 211 65 57), will cost you dearly.

Internet Access: Kiber Cafe (Кібер Кафе), Proresnaya 21 (tel. 228 05 48; email admin@cybercafe.com.ua). Smoky but centrally located and often packed during evenings with Ukrainians playing computerized cards and expats checking email (12hv per hr.). Open daily 10am until the last user leaves.

Post Office: vul. Khreshchatyk 22, next to Maydan Nezalezhnosti. **Poste Restante** at counters #29-30. Address mail to: "PARR, Richard, Poste Restante, 252001 Київ-1, Почтамт до Востребоваиия, UKRAINE." Pre-stamped airmail envelopes (1.42hv at counter #1) are the easiest way to send international mail. To mail packages, enter on the Maydan Nezalezhnosti side. Also houses a full-service copy/fax center. Open M-Sa 8am-8pm, Su 9am-7pm. **Postal code:** 252 001.

Telephones: Myzhmisky Perehovorny Punkt (Мижміський Переговорний Пункт), at the post office, or **Telefon-Telefaks** (Телефон-Телефакс), around the corner (entry on Khreshchatyk). Some phones require that you dial an initial "8." To: Moscow 0.60hv per min.; Ireland and U.K. 3.90hv; U.S. 4.64hv; Australia, New Zealand, South Africa 5.76hv. Window #3 puts calls through to North America. State the number of minutes you want and pay up front. Both offices open 24hr. They insist they can't dial AT&T or MCI operators, but Utel phones will do the trick. When making an international call from a private phone, dial 8, wait for a tone, then dial 10, country code, city code, and number. Calls within Kiev require phone cards (0.50hv). **Utel phone cards** are available in denominations of 10hv, 20hv, and 40hv at the post office and upscale hotels. Utel phones can be found in the post office, the train station, hotels, fancy restaurants, and Dom Ukrainsky (Дом Український), across from Hotel Dnipro. **Phone code:** (0)44.

ACCOMMODATIONS

Accomodations in Kiev suffer from an unfortunate combination of capitalist prices and socialist quality. Unless you have money to spare, be prepared to stay in a Soviet subdivision like the rest of the city. **Diane Sadovnikov,** a former missionary, and her husband Yuri (see **Ukraine Essentials,** p. 729) arrange lodgings in a private apartment (45-75hv per person) not far from MR: Darnytsa, and can also place you with a family or help make hotel/dorm reservations (possibly at a discounted rate). It's best to fax them a month in advance. (Home tel./fax 044 516 24 33; email ims-travel@imb.net.)

Hostinitsa Druzhba (Дружба), bul. Druzhby Narodiv 5 (Дружби Народів; tel./fax 268 33 87). MB: Libidska. Go left then right to exit the Metro. Then, go straight for 100m and turn left before the overpass onto the major road. The hotel is 100m up on the left. If the staff were friendlier and the price a little lower, one might call this a good hostel. But hey, the bathrooms work and it's on a Metro line. Singles 55hv; doubles 112hv, with shower 168hv; 3-bed room 58hv per person. Call ahead and confirm by fax. Be persistent if you want them to give you the cheapest room.

Grazhdanski Aviatski Institut Student Hotel, vul. Nizhinska 29E (Ніжінська; tel. 484 90 59). From behind MR: Vokzalna, ride 6 or 7 stops on tram #1K or 7 to "Граматна" *(Hramatna)*, until it stops in front of a huge, broken-down gray building. Backtrack 1½ blocks, swing a right onto vul. Nizhinska, cross at the first intersection with a trolleybus, then follow the path into the complex. Keep the first building on your right as you walk diagonally to block "Д." After passing Д on the right, the door lies 100m further, also to your right. 50min. from the city center. Their clean rooms are the best deal around if you don't mind the trek. Singles 36hv; spacious doubles 44hv. 2 rooms share a bath.

Hostinitsa Bratislava (Братіслава), vul. Malishka 1 (Малішка; tel. 551 76 44). MR: Darnitsya (Дарніця). Take 2 lefts to get out of the Metro. Head right across the park; Bratislava is the concrete beast to the left. Spotless bedrooms and bathrooms with a bar, exchange kiosk, drugstore, Western Union, and newspaper stand downstairs. Singles with bath US$53; doubles with bath US$142. Breakfast included. English spoken. MC/Visa/AmEx.

Hostinitsa Universitetsky (Университетский), vul. Lomonosova 81 (Ломоносова; director's tel. 266 74 44). MB: Libidska. Go right then left through the Metro tunnels to bus #38. Take it to the end at "Ковалевської" *(Kovalevskoy)*, then go a little farther to the two 9-story buildings (45min. from center). *Avtosvit* (автосвіт) minibuses won't stop unless you flag them down (0.50hv). Primarily for Ukrainian students, but if you call the director beforehand and ask for him when you show up, you can usually get a room. Spacious doubles with shower, kitchen, and balcony 40hv; with TV and fridge 66hv. Barer rooms for 10hv.

Motel-Camping "Prolisok," pr. Peremohy 179 (tel. 444 12 93). From MR: Svyatoshin (Святошін), take trolley #7 west to "Автостанція Дачна" *(Avtostantsiya Dachna)* and walk 2km down the highway on the left. Bus #30 stops at the front gate, but only comes every 20min. Enter just before the pedestrian overpass. Pitch your *platka* (tent) in pleasant surroundings for 12hv per person. Doubles 200hv. Trailer parking, restaurant, and sauna attract foreign truck drivers. Utel phone on premises. MC/Visa.

FOOD

Despite Kiev's rosy outward appearances, recent economic problems have forced a number of young restaurants to close up shop. What remains are high-priced even by Western standards and cater almost exclusively to foreigners and the few Ukrainians who can afford them. Check out the *Kiev Post* for their ads. If you don't mind the tab, **Arizona, Bombay Palace,** and the outrageously priced **San Tori** are among the most popular. Locals choose Kiev's specialty drinks over munchies—vendors sell *Stolichnaya* vodka, *kava po-skhidnomu* (eastern-style coffee; кава по-східному), and good-old *kvas* (квас; 0.5L 0.30hv in the most touristed areas). For those on a tight budget, the best option is a trip to one of Kiev's *rynki* (markets). The ubiquitous *hastronomy* (supermarkets; гастрономи) usually close around 7pm. Their Western equivalents have sprung up in the center; although they can be good for refrigerated meat and other rarities, many of the same items can be found at *hastronomy* for much lower prices. As the name backwardly suggests, **7/24** on vul. Baseyna 1/2 (Басеїна; tel. 221 58 57), behind Bessarabsky Rynok, is always open. MC/Visa.

RESTAURANTS

Pantagruel (Пантагруель), vul. Lysenko 1 (Лисенко; tel. 228 81 42), right next to MG: Zoloty Vorota. Authentic Italian food prepared by an authentic Italian chef in an authentic Italian cellar. Rigatoni with spicy sauce 12hv, other entrees 16-22hv. Outdoor seating in the summer. Live music F-Sa 8-10pm. English-language newspapers sold. Open M-Th, Su 11am-11pm, F-Sa 11am-2am.

Pizza Lola (Піцца Лола), vul. Lva Tolstoho 8 (Льва Толстого; tel. 224 74 23). MB: Ploshcha Lva Tolstovo. Follow the street for 2min.; Lola's is in the basement on the left. Full of molten cheese, these Ukrainian pizzas put Italy to shame. To avoid fighting for a table, have them put your personal circle of joy in a box and walk a block up the street to eat in the park. One-person cheese pizza 10hv, with 2 toppings 15hv. 0.5L beer 3.50hv. Soda water 0.50hv. Open daily 11am-9pm, in summer until 10pm.

Caribbean Club (Карібіан Клуб), vul. Kominterna 6 (tel. 244 42 90). A low-key restaurant/bar with a surprisingly accurate—for the former Soviet Union—Caribbean atmosphere. Barbeques outside on the patio every evening in the summer. Entrees 20-30hv.

Shelter, vul. Khreshchatyk 15. A cheap option on Kiev's priciest street and a favorite among teens. International fast food from Mexico, China, and the U.S. will run you 10hv. Downstairs a blues bar offers live music nightly in the winter. MC/Visa.

Mr. Snack (Мистер Снак), vul. Horodetskoho 4 (Городецького; tel. 228 29 87). M: Maydan Nezalezhnosti. Strategically located near nightlife and conveniently open until 1:30am. Pizza, ice cream, pastries, and hot sandwiches (3 fillings 6.5hv).

Cafe Starokyivske (Кафе Старокиївське), 41 Chervonoarmiska vul. MB: Ploshcha Lva Tolstovo. Nonexistent atmosphere, but hearty, cafeteria-style Ukrainian food for 5hv. Open daily 10am-10pm.

CAFES

Cafe Panorama (Кафе Панорама; tel. 417 74 89). Walk down Andraivesky uzviz, 25m past St. Andrew's Church, past the main pointing statue and up the steep wooden steps that eventually appear on the right. Quiet outdoor seating and glorious views from its perch above Kiev. Simple beef or chicken *shashlik*15hv. 0.5L *Obolon* 5hv. Open daily in summer 11am-11 pm.

Kavyarnya Svitoch (Кавярня Світоч), vul. Velyka Zhytomyrksa 8a (tel. 264 08 09). On the right as you follow the street from Mikhailivska pl. This famous Lviv confectioner opened its Kiev outlet in 1995; the cafe is next door. *The* place for black coffee (2hv) and dark chocolate (0.20-2hv). Popular with students. Open daily 9am-9pm.

Cafe U Georga (Кафе У Георга), vul. Khreshchatyk 10. MB/R: Maydan Nezalezhnosti. The main street's best grotto for a lunchtime shot of vodka (1hv). A semicircular counter, no tables, loud music about love and San Francisco, and vodka-loving regulars. Espresso 0.70hv. Open daily 10am-9pm.

MARKETS

Ukraine has a European passion for fresh food, but so do the occassional swarms of flies. The French have their *marchés*, the Kievans their *rynki*.

Bessarabsky Rynok (Бессарабский Ринок; tel. 224 89 34), at the intersection of vul. Khreshchatyk and bul. Shevchenka. No mere gaggle of *babushki* selling berries. On the edge of Kiev's chi-chi-est neighborhood, Bessarabsky offers the best meat and produce the Ukrainian countryside has to offer.

Volodymyrsky-Kolhospny Rynok (Володимирский-Колгоспний Ринок), vul. Telmana (Тельмана), between vul. Chervonoarmiska and bul. Horkovo (Бул Горького). MB/G: Palats Ukraina (Палац Україна). Even larger than the Bessarabsky. Plenty of food, flowers, clothes, tapes, and unhappily-caged animals. Open daily 10am-7pm.

SIGHTS

A millennium as Ukraine's capital has left Kiev with a store of historical sights. The Soviets donated their fair share of mutant monuments, but with creeping capitalism modern architecture has begun to infiltrate. While older mementos remain, the ruins may soon be lost in the city's remodeling.

VUL. KHRESHCHATYK & ENVIRONS

Downtown Kiev centers around **vul. Khreshchatyk,** a broad commercial avenue built after WWII into a monument to Soviet-style bigness, although the surrounding buildings have retained a surprising amount of character. On weekends, the street is closed to traffic as Kievans come out to shop, stroll, and even ride horses.

KIEV 3, NAZIS 0 Following the devastating Nazi invasion of Kiev in September 1941, a German soldier discovered that one of his prisoners was a member of the city's *Dynamo Kiev* soccer team. Officers quickly rounded up the other players, and arranged a "death match" between them and the German army team. Despite the Dynamos' weakened condition and a referee dressed in a Gestapo uniform, they won the game 3-0. Shortly thereafter the entire team was thrown into a concentration camp, where most of them perished in front of a firing squad. Their memory—and Kiev's pride—lives on in a monument overlooking Khreshchaty Park.

Khreshchatyk begins at the intersection with bul. Shevchenka, where **Lenin**, surrounded by inspirational sayings, gazes off into the future. Across the street, **Bessarabsky Rynok** (see **Markets**, above) is one of the most ornate markets of its kind. Walking along vul. Khreshchatyk, check out the **central department store TSUM** (ЦУМ), Khmelnytskoho 2, on the corner, which sells everything from guitars to lawn chairs to coffee cake. But don't let the fancy new facade fool you; it's still run like a state store. (Open M-Sa 9am-8pm. MC/Visa.)

Continuing up vul. Khmelnytskoho, you'll reach the recently built and highly nationalistic **Museum of Ukrainian Literature** (Muzey Literatury Ukrainy; Музей Літератури України), on the left at #11. The museum traces Ukrainian literature from its inception to the present, quoting Ivan Franko and Taras Shevchenko the entire way. English-speaking guides are available only through Intourist for an exorbitant rate, but the museum staff will happily explain everything in Ukrainian. (Open M-Sa 9am-5pm. Admission 2.40hv.) Farther up at Khmelnyskoho 15 is the **National Science Museum**, which has sections devoted to archaeology, geology, botany and zoology. (Open M-Tu, F-Su 10am-3pm. 1.50hv.)

Back on vul. Khreshchatyk, the **archway** to vul. Lyuteranska (Лютеранська) leads to a quiet, residential neighborhood along a street lined with pretty stone facades. The next archway leads to Kiev's most cosmopolitan area, a passage with fancy, high-priced cafes and bars. **Independence Plaza** (Maydan Nezalezhnosti; formerly October Revolution Square) is the very center of town. Book vendors, musicians, hipsters, and those gathering to talk away the evening over tankards of beer or *kvas* fill the terrace around the large fountains. Right-wing, left-wing, and tourist propaganda is sold along the fountain walls while the occasional street performer pleases crowds. At night, the Metro stop underneath shelters Kiev's best street musicians. The square saw revolution in 1905 and, later, the execution of Nazi war criminals. The **statue of Archangel Michael** was unveiled in 1996 and displays on its base the distances from Kiev to all the capitals of the world.

Just past the square to the right is vul. Institutska (Институтська), another facade-filled promenade. Uphill to the left glows the bright-yellow **Palace of Culture** (Palats Kulturny; Палац Культурни), today one of Kiev's largest concert halls and a Neoclassical rival to the Rococo **National Bank of Ukraine** (Natsionalny Bank Ukrainy; Національний Банк України), also on the left.

KHRESHCHATY PARK

Referred to by locals as the "Yoke," the silver croquet wicket that towers over the park is the **Arch of Brotherhood**, a monument to the 1654 Russian-Ukrainian union (see **History**, p. 729) that now serves as a popular meeting spot for romantic unions, with couples enjoying the view of the Dnipro below. To the left across Volodymyrsky uzviz is **Prince Volodymyr** brandishing a cross and overlooking the river in which he had the whole city baptized in 988—despite freezing temperatures—making Orthodox Christianity the official religion of Kievan Rus. Go right at the arch and into the park for the monument to **brave soccer players** (see above).

Farther to the right and atop the hill stands the **Maryinsky Palace**, built by Bartolomeo Rastrelli, who also designed Kiev's St. Andrew's Church and much of St. Petersburg. The palace was built for Tsaritsa Elizabeth's visit in the 1750s, but, alas, not for your visit—it is closed to the public. Across from the lovely garden (also closed) stands a statue of the Ukrainian poet and revolutionary **Lesya Ukrainka** (see **Literature & Arts,** p. 731), gazing sensitively at the splendor of aristocrats and pondering the plight of Ukrainian workers. The park leads toward the Arsenalna Metro stop, but if you resist its rigid paths, you might find the **grave of Prince Askoldel,** who was murdered by the usurping Prince Oleg in 882. The park is enormous, with each monument tucked away in its own corners; you'll do best to just wander to the birds' songs.

BUL. TARASA SHEVCHENKA

A walk past Lenin's metal figure takes you up a street that, although broad and busy, is among Kiev's prettiest. The boulevard is dedicated to the poet **Taras Shevchenko,** whose paintings and poetry re-invented the Ukrainian language in the mid-19th century (see **Literature & Arts,** p. 730). Banished in 1847, he never returned to Kiev. At #12 stands the **Taras Shevchenko Museum** (tel. 224 25 56), one of the largest and most beautiful literary museums in the former USSR. (Open Tu-Su 10am-5pm; closed last Friday of the month. 1hv, students 0.30hv. English tours 20hv, students 10hv.) The museum contains a huge collection of Shevchenko's sketches, paintings, and prints, as well as some of his correspondence and poetry. Exhibits are labeled in both Ukrainian and Russian. On the left side of the street, inside one of Kiev's many parks, a famous monument to the hero stands at least 1½ times taller than Lenin's paltry form. He faces his namesake **university,** which still leads independent thought in Ukraine. The university's students gather around the park benches nearby to contemplate some Taras. Farther up stands the many-domed ochre **Volodymyrsky Cathedral,** bul. Tarasa Shevchenka 20, built to mark 900 years of Christianity in Kiev. Its interior holds examples of Byzantine and Art Nouveau styles. A **botanical garden** offers some shade across from the cathedral. (Open 9am-9pm. 0.30hv, students 0.10hv.)

ST. SOPHIA & ENVIRONS

The enormous and elaborate **St. Sophia Monastery Complex,** Volodymyrska vul. 24, is what many tourists come to Kiev to see: golden onion domes, decorated facades, and exquisite Byzantine icons from the 11th century. The interior mosaics are not to be missed, although not all of them have been restored. The monastery was the cultural center of Kievan Rus and is still the focal point of the increasingly complex question of Ukrainian nationalism. In July 1995, the government denied the Uniate Church's desire to bury its patriarch here. When the funeral procession led by the Ukrainian nationalist militia attempted entry into the complex, they were violently rerouted by the police. (Open M-Tu, F-Su 10am-5:30pm, W 10am-4:30pm. 6hv. Architectural museum and exhibitions an additional 2hv. 1hr. tours: 10hv. Cameras 10hv.)

300m down Volodymyrska vul. stands **Golden Gate** (Zoloty Vorota; Золоти Ворота). Actually made of wood and stone, it has marked the entrance to the city since 1037. As legend has it, the gate's strength saved Kiev from the Tatars during the reign of **Yaroslav the Wise,** whose statue stands nearby (see **History,** p. 729). A **museum** devoted to the gate is inside. (Open May-Oct. M-W and F-Su 10am-5pm. Admission 2hv, students 1hv.)

Back by the entrance to St. Sophia lies pl. Khmelnytskoho, a square of gorgeous 18th- and 19th-century buildings supervised by the statue of national hero **Bohdan Khmelnitsky.** Khmelnitsky (1595-1657) led Ukrainian Cossacks and peasants in a revolt against Polish rule in the mid-17th century, only to end up signing a 1654 union treaty with Russia that eventually ceded control of Ukraine to the tsars.

Continuing down vul. Volodomyrska brings you to the recently upgraded **Mikhaylivska pl.** (Михайлівська). The sprucing-up accompanied a new statue of **Princess Olga,** grandmother of Volodymyr I and perhaps the first Christian in Kievan Rus. She is surrounded by **St. Cyril, St. Methodius** (see **What's in a name?,** p. 8) and **St. Andrew the Apostle,** who is believed to have blessed these lands centuries before the founding of Kiev. Behind the princess and to her left stands the monumental **Ministry of Foreign Affairs,** which we've measured to be 90% pillar, 10% building.

Guarding the top of Mikhaylivska pl. is the soon-to-be very snazzy **Mykhailivskhyi Zolotoverkhy Monastery** (Monastyr; Михайлівский Золотоверхий Монастир). The monastery was undergoing renovations in the summer of 1999, but those you can't wait can tour the **museum.** (Open Tu-Su 11am-5pm.) To the right of the monastery, vul. Tryokhsvyatytelska passes a series of smaller churches as it winds its way down to **Volodymyrska Hirka** (Володимирска Гірка) park, full of tiny pavilions and sculptures by folk artists. The park is also rumored to be a **gay cruising spot.**

A right on vul. Tryokhsvyatytelska (Трьохсвятительска) as you face Olga leads to several interesting churches. First on the left sits the petite, white-washed, and onion-domed **Church of the Holy Apostle John** (Khram Svyatoho Apostola Ioana Bohoslava; Храм святово апостола Іоана Богослава). Entrance is free, but many visitors buy a small candle (0.20hv) from the priests at the door. The dark, plain interior shelters richly colored, gilded icons. (Open daily 8am-8pm.) Continuing down the street on the right, the stolid **Church of St. Oleksandr** (Kostyol sv. Oleksandra; Костьол св. Олександра) mixes serenity with holy chatter in many tongues; it offers masses in 7 languages. (Open daily 7am-8pm; English mass Su 6pm.)

ANDRIVSKY UZVIZ & THE PODIL DISTRICT

The easiest way to see the cobblestone **Andrivsky uzviz**—a winding road lined with cafes, souvenir vendors, and galleries—is to ride up and walk down. A **funicular** can transport you up Andrivsky uzviz from MB: Poshtova. (Every 5min. daily 6:30am-11pm, 0.30hv.) As you walk down, look for signs offering "Виставка" (exhibition) of local artists' work. Be prepared to bargain if you want to buy anything. Next to the entrepreneurs selling real Ukrainian pipes and Soviet Army hats, some independent galleries show the newest and boldest work Ukrainian visual artists have to offer, but most just sell touristy paintings of the **St. Andrew's Cathedral** (closed for renovations). The edifice in question dominates the street; if you read Russian, you can learn about it and the avenue below at the **Andrivsky Uzviz Museum** at #22 (tel. 416 03 98; open W-Su 11am-7pm; 1hv).

Before starting the climb down, ascend the gray steps to the left at the crossroads of Desatynia, Andrivsky, and Volodymyrska, and walk through the ruins of **Tithe Church** (Desatinia Tserkva; Десатиниа Церква), which converted pagan Kievans to Christianity in the 10th century. The oldest stone church of Kievan Rus (c. 989-96), it endured for centuries only to be deliberately destroyed in 1937. Next to the great view on the other side of the ruins, you'll find the **National Museum of Ukrainian History** (Natsionalny Muzey Istorii Ukrainy; Національний Музей Історії України), vul. Volodymyrska 2 (tel. 228 65 45), which houses exhibits from the Stone Age to the present. (Open M-Tu and Th-Su 10am-6pm, closed last Thursday of each month. 4.80hv. Tours available in Ukrainian and German.) Out front lie the foundations of the Old City, preserved under glass. Back on Andrivsky uzviz, past the museum, **Bulgakov's House** at #13 (tel. 416 31 88) tells you all you need to know about Mikhail Bulgakov's *White Guard*, (see **Russia: Literature and Arts**, p. 730) a sympathetic look at a White Army family in Kiev during the Civil War, but the museum is confusing if you haven't read the book. (Open M-Tu and Th-Su 10am-6pm. 2hv, students 1hv. 45min. tour in English or French 10hv.)

Andrivsky uzviz spills out onto **Kontraktova pl.**—the center of **Podil,** Kiev's oldest district and the city center in the 10th and 11th centuries. This pleasant neighborhood is home to a wealth of small **churches.** In the *ploshcha*'s north corner lies the yellow **Kiev-Mohyla Academy,** the oldest university in this part of the world. Closed by the Communists, it graduated its first new class in 1996. Just east of the *ploshcha* lies the **Chernobyl Museum,** Provulok Zhorevii 1 (tel. 417 54 22). Powerful imagery conveys the magnitude of the disaster, and helps explain why the Soviet Union fell apart. Ask about the video, usually shown during tours, that shows the explosion. (Open M-Sa 10am-6pm; closed last Monday of the month. Free.)

BABYN YAR & ST. CYRIL'S

The moving WWII monument at **Babyn Yar** (Бабин Яр) marks the graves of the first victims of the Nazis, buried in September 1941. Although the plaques state that

100,000 Kievans died here, current estimates double that figure. Many of the victims—most of them Jews—were buried alive. Take trolley #27 eight stops from MB: Petrivka or trolley #16 from Maydan Nezalezhnosti about 10 stops. The monument—a large group of interlocking figures—stands in the park near the TV tower, at the intersection of vul. Oleny Telihy and vul. Melnykova.

From Babyn Yar, four stops on trolley #27 northeast (catch it on the same side of vul. Telihy as Babyn Yar) toward MB: Petrivka take you to **St. Cyril's Church** (Kyrylivska Tserkva; Кирилівська Церква), the multi-domed shelter of Kiev's best frescoes. The church's opulence rivals St. Sophia's. From the trolley stop, ascend the stairs to your right. An English version of the church's history is available inside. (Open M-W and Sa-Su 10am-6pm, Th 10am-5pm. Admission 6hv, students 5hv, Ukrainians 2hv.)

LAVRA AND ENVIRONS

MR: Arsenalna. Turn left as you exit and walk 20min. down vul. Sichnevoho Povstaniya. Trolleybus #20 can also take you here (2 stops going left from the Metro toward the river). Open daily 9:30am-7pm; in off-season until 6pm. General admission 8hv, students and Ukrainians 4hv. Jewelry Museum 3hv, students 1hv. Miniatures Museum 2hv, students 1hv. Tours in Russian free; private tours in English 80hv.

Kiev's oldest and holiest religious site, the mysterious **Kiev-Pechery Monastery** (Kievo-Pecherska Lavra; Київо-Печерська Лавра) deserves a full day of exploration. Most of the sights are in various states of much-needed renovation that should soon have the monastery sparkling. Although this was once the center of Orthodox Christianity, its monks were subsequently mummified and entombed in the **caves**—the most interesting part of the complex. (Open M, W-Su 9-11:30am and 1-4pm.) Buy a candle (0.50-1hv) as you enter if you want to see anything. Women should cover their heads and shoulders; men should wear pants. When in the caves, you're only allowed to look at the monks whose palms are facing up. People offer unofficial tours of the underground as you enter the complex for around US$10, but the caves are pretty self-explanatory. There are numerous churches, gardens, and museums on the grounds, as well as the Italian Embassy. Most noteworthy are the 18th-century **Great Cave Bell Tower** (Velyka lavrska dzvinytsya; Велика лаврська дзвіниця), which offers fantastic views of the river and apartment blocks on the horizon mingling with golden domes (open daily 9:30am-8pm; admission 2.50hv, students 1hv), and the 12th-century **Holy Trinity Church** (Troitska Nadzramna Tserkva; Троїцка надзрамна церква), which serves as the entrance to the monastery. The church's interior (take a left upon entering) contains some beautiful frescoes, a 600kg censer, and the ruins of an ancient church. Be sure to step into the functioning **Refractory Church,** home to one of the longest and most decorative domes in the complex.

The monastery, a former fortress with 2m thick walls to prove it, is also a nice place just to perambulate. Some museums require a separate ticket, but the general admission ticket lets you into the **Museum of Books and Bookmaking** (Muzey Knigi i Knigopechataniya; Музей книгі і кигопечатанія), which details the history of book and printing development in Ukraine, and the **Museum of Historical Treasures** (Muzey Istoricheskikh Dragotsennostey; Музей Історіческих драгоценностей), which displays all sorts of precious stones and metals, both ancient and modern. The ticket shows a map of the complex, but the labels are in Cyrillic only. (Open M, W-Su 9:30am-4pm.)

A left as you exit the monastery will lead to a WWII victory spike and eternal flame, as well as a marvelous view of the river. Farther along the same road is the gigantic titanium **Motherland statue,** a.k.a. huge lady with little sword. The sword used to be bigger but was shortened when the monks raised a stink about it being higher than the bell tower. The statue, which also celebrates the WWII victory, was designed by the wife of the sculptor of the Volgograd Motherland statue (see p. 643). Plans to tear down the tin lady and replace her with a monument to the victims of Chernobyl have not yet come to fruition, but the statue might fall of its own accord due to poor construction. Beneath the metal mama lies the **Museum of the**

Great Patriotic War (Muzey Velykoi Otchyznenoi Viyny; Музей Великої Отчизненої Війни), Sichnevoho Povstaniya 33 (tel. 295 94 52), which illustrates the stages of WWII with panoramas, videos, pictures, and weapons. (Open 9am-7pm. 3hv, students 2hv. Russian or Ukrainian tours 10hv, students 5hv.)

ENTERTAINMENT

SPORTS & THE OUTDOORS

During the soccer season (late spring to autumn), don't miss **Dynamo Kiev,** one of the top teams in Europe. Check with the *kasa* at the Respublikansky Stadium, vul. Chervonoarmiska. MB: Respublikansky stadion.

On hot summer days, locals head out to **Hidropark** (Гідропарк), an **amusement park** and **beach** on an island in the Dnipro. (MR: Hidropark.) Tucked in a corner near the bridge, **Venice Beach of Ukraine** hosts young buffs lifting spare automobile parts to keep in shape. The beach has showers, toilets, and changing booths, and no one seems to charge admission. **Rent boats** at *Otdykh na vode—Fregat* (Отдых на воде—Фрегат), on the east shore of Hidropark, near the Metro bridge. (Boat or waterbike 3hv per hr. Open daily 9am-8pm, last rental 6pm.) The free beach is also a hot pickup spot for the college-age crowd. In the evenings, make-shift hoops games can be found on the bumpy but playable courts on the Western bank close to the Metro. **Spike Bowling Club,** Peremohy 84 (tel. 442 64 64), hosts Kiev's pin-topplers.

The daily and weekend **bazaars** in the summer at Respublikansky Stadion and Vokzalny are experiences in themselves, even if you don't buy any of the myriad sodas and cigarettes hauled in from all over the former Soviet Union. Everything is wholesale—buy in bulk and start your own kiosk. The festival **Kiev Days** takes place the last weekend in May, and Andrivsky uzviz is jam-packed with *shashlik* stands, orchestras, and craftspeople from all over.

PERFORMANCES

Most of Kiev's theaters close in summer. For **tickets,** check with any *teatralna kasa* (театральна каса; open Tu-Su 9am-5pm; tickets 8-10hv; check the *Kiev Post* for listings). Most shows are in Ukrainian or Russian. Every March, however, international troupes come for a two-week multilingual **theater festival. Kinopanorama,** S. Rustaveli 19 (tel. 227 11 35), and the new **Kino Palats,** vul. Institutska 1, right across from Maydan Nezalezhnosti, show the last movie of the night in English, after all the Ukrainians are in bed.

Philharmonic, Volodymyrsky uzviz 2 (tel. 229 62 51). Classic and classical. *Kasa* open M 3-7pm, Tu-F noon-7pm.

Shevchenka Opera and Ballet Theater, Volodymyrska vul. 50 (tel. 224 71 65 or 229 11 69). MRG: Teatralna. Huge and imposing. Several shows each week at noon and 7pm. Ticket office open M 3-7pm, Tu-Su 11am-2pm and 3-7:30pm.

Operetta (Оперетта), vul. Vesyl Kyivska 5313, on the corner of vul. Zhylyanska (Жилянська). MB: Respublikansky stadion. Favorites by Kalman, Lehar, and Strauss.

Kiev Youth Theater (Kyivsky Molody Teatr; Київский Молодий Театр), vul. Prorizna 17 (tel. 224 62 51 or 228 73 92). Possibly Kiev's best theater, but it can get expensive.

NIGHTLIFE

Perhaps it is the many cathedrals looming overhead, or that by midnight many people are too drunk to walk, but when it comes to nightlife Kiev simply doesn't live up to its big-city billing. Most citizens are content to spend their twilight hours sucking on an *Obolon* outdoors, and to call it a night shortly after the sun sets. But while there will be no dancing on barstools, there are plenty of mellow watering holes where the taps are kept open and the occasional jazz chord can be heard.

BARS

Club Sofia, vul. Sofiivska 7 (Софіївська; tel. 229 88 16), off Maydan Nezalezhnosti. Formerly known as "Eric's Bar," it's now informally known as "Eric's Bar #1," since Eric now owns several bars and clubs throughout Kiev. This smoky cellar will be jam-packed with young artists, intellectuals, foreigners, and Ukrainians in the evening. *Obolon* 5hv. Open daily noon-1am.

Rock Cafe (Рок Кафе), vul. Horodetskoho 10 (tel. 228 36 38). MG: Maydan Nezalezhnosti. Walk 300m along the street to the right of the giant steps; the cafe is on your right. Easygoing coffeeshop where unpretentious expats hang with their local acquaintances, but evolves into a busy bar at night. Coffee or half-glass of sparkling water 3hv. Outdoor seating. Pool 4hv per game. 0.5L *Obolon* 5hv. Open daily 11am-3am.

The Cowboy Bar, vul. Khreshchatyk 15 (tel. 228 17 17), at the far end of the *pasazh.* A piece of Ukraine-generated America on Kiev's Euro-trash street. Raw, unpainted wood, cigarette smoke and live blues, jazz, and country music nightly after 9pm. Behind the bar, a "Wanted" poster promises a reward for the capture of "Robber Boss Wild Bill." *Obolon* 6hv. Cover 10hv. Open daily 6pm-6am.

O'Brien's Pub, vul. Mikhailyska 17a (Михайлівська; tel. 229 15 84), off Maidan Nezalezhnosti. The new Irish cellar in town, full of British expats, and perhaps the most relaxed drinking atmosphere outside Khreshchaty Park. Open daily 8am-2am.

Miami Blues, vul. Chervonoarmiska 114 (Червоноармійська; tel. 264 19 31). Expensive and remote, but a fascinating look at Ukrainian yuppie culture. Live jazz M and Th-F and an adventurous drink menu: try the fruity *lemon fleep* or the local mafia favorite *BMW.* Outdoor seating. Open 24hr., but dies out around 1am.

Portofino (Портофино), vul. Sofiivska 5 (Софіївська; tel. 229 87 71). Offers pool tables and bars inside and out where you can listen to the best of Russian disco in plastic deck chairs. Next to Club Sofia (see above). *Obolon* 5hv. Open daily 11am-midnight.

DANCING

Kiev's most popular discos pale next to the shining stars of Moscow, but keep your ears open for occasional raves. **Al Capone,** Kostyantynivska 26, is the boss of late night boogying. A converted cinema, it is the latest venture of "Eric," don of Kiev nightlife. Check Club Sofia for a listing of his new discos. Disco **New York,** Perova 2 (tel. 552 51 44), near Park Peremchy, also has a loyal following. **Club Hollywood,** vul. Frunze 134 (Фрунзе; tel. 435 40 68), is a haven for those in the fast lane who can afford the 20-30hv covers. Dress up or you *will* be kicked out.

GAY AND LESBIAN ENTERTAINMENT

In the eyes of many Ukrainians, homosexuality is simply not acceptable. Discrimination and homophobia are widespread, and thus the gay scene in Ukraine has failed to take off the same way it has in Moscow. Yet gay nightlife, previously limited to private parties and irregular club venues, is slowly developing. The safest and most popular **cruising area** is the so-called "Walk of Shame," which runs along the Khreshchatyk-Bessarabska pl. promenade from Bessarabsky Rynok to the recently opened McDonald's near the Metro. The bread store across Khreshchatyk from the Bessarabsky Rynok is also known as a place to meet gay men. In the summer, the scene is revived substantially, thanks to Hidropark; follow the mob to **Youth Beach** (Molodizhny Plyazh). There, buy a 1hv boat ride to the beach opposite, where the crowd is mixed and clothes are optional. There's also an all-gay beach nearby, but it's muddy. The **lesbian** scene is still very much underground.

CRIMEA (КРЫМ)

TIME ZONES. Turn your watch forward one hour from Kiev time for the Crimea (GMT+3).

Thanks to its position on the Black Sea Coast, the Crimea (in Ukrainian, "Крим") has been a traveling and trading thoroughfare since antiquity. Tsars and Mongol princes built palaces here, the workers of the former Soviet Union flocked here for state-sponsored holidays, and now capitalists are trying to find their place (and a few rubles) along the rocky shores. From Simferopol, redeemed only by its rail connections and the splendor of nearby Bakchisarai, travelers can reach the sandy

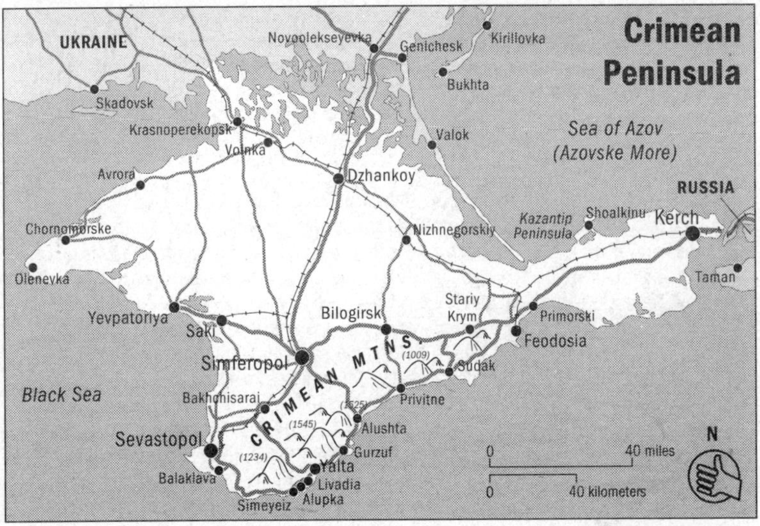

shores of Feodosia or the maritime history of Sevastopol. Others rave the month of August away atop the nuclear reactor at Kazantip. Finally, there's Yalta, where tourists have spooked the ghost of Chekhov away to his summer home at Gurzuf. Livadia, where Roosevelt, Churchill, and Stalin divided up the post-WWII world, and Alupka, a testament to the decadence of empire, also lie beyond the city.

SIMFEROPOL (СІМФЕРОПОЛЬ)

God made the Crimea, and all Simferopol (sim-fer-ROH-pul) got was a lousy train station. As a result, poor Simferopol should only be visited as a means to a southward end. **Bank Aval,** ul. Naberezhnaya 32 (tel. 27 37 37), exchanges currency, offers Western Union services, gives MC/Visa cash advances for a 3% commission, and cashes traveler's checks for a 2% commission. (Exchange services Sa-Su 9am-noon.) The best place to sleep is on the train out of town, but if you have a lay-over, stay at the central **Gostinitsa Ukraina** (Украина), ul. Rozy Lyuksemburg 7-9 (tel. 51 01 65), which offers aging but decent rooms. (Singles 41hv, with bath 92hv; doubles 60hv, 110hv; triples72hv.) You'll have to eat, too: try the **Restoran Latysh** (Латыш; tel. 27 88 63), ul. Rozy Lyuksemburg 4, which specializes in kosher food. (Entrees 6-15hv. Open daily 11am-midnight.)

GETTING AWAY. Trains run everywhere: **Kiev** (15hr., 4 per day, 45hv); **Lviv** (32hr., 1 per day, 35hv); **Minsk** (35hr., 3 per week, 70hv); **Moscow** (28hr., 4 per day, 70hv); and **Odessa** (14hr., 1 per day, 20hv). Tickets for the *elektrichka* (electric train) are sold behind the main station building. These head to **Sevastopol** (2½hr., 7 per day, 2.25hv) via **Bakhchisarai** (45min., 1.50hv). **Buses** are in high demand; be sure to buy tickets in advance. They drive to: **Feodosia** (2hr., hourly 7am-7pm, 5.87hv); **Bakhchisarai** (1hr., 5 per day, 2.20hv); **Sevastopol** (2hr., 9 per day, 5.07hv); **Kazantip** (4hr., 3 per day, 20hv); and **Rostov-na-Donu** (14hr., 1 per day, 47hv). Buses for **Yalta** leave from the train station (2hr., every 30min., 4.65hv). From the **train station,** ul. Gagarina (Гагарина; tel. 005), trolleys #2 and (by a roundabout route) 6 travel to the **bus station** via the city center.

NEAR SIMFEROPOL: BAKHCHISARAI (БАХЧИСАРАЙ)

Amid the dry, solemn cliffs of the Central Crimean steppe, the ancient town of Bakhchisarai makes up for Simferopol's lack of historical and architectural excitement. An outpost of the Byzantine Empire at the end of the 6th century and subse-

WHO OWNS CRIMEA? In the 5th century BC, Herodotus first recorded that Scythians and Greeks dwelled in Crimea, but invaders have been joining the beach party ever since. The Sarmatians followed the Scythians a century later, and were then supplanted by Romans, Ostrogoths, Huns, Slavs, Khazars, and Varangians. Byzantium ruled the peninsula until the great Batu Khan (grandson of Genghis) took the region and opened Crimea to trade. Pleased with the land, many Mongols settled and became the indigenous Crimean Tatars.

Crimea remained autonomous until Russia annexed it in 1783 and refurbished it as a beach resort extraordinaire. The 1854 Crimean War saw France and Britain clash with Russia over the city of Sevastopol. The Russians evacuated, leaving the Tatars to revive their national heritage, language, and culture. In 1917, the Tatars put together a *Kurultay*—Tatar National Constituent Assembly—which declared their autonomy against the will of the Bolsheviks. Russia soon regained control and paid its citizens to settle the city, and on the night of May 18, 1944, Stalin had the entire Crimean Tatar population, largely collaborating with the Germans, shipped to Uzbekistan.

Crimea was officially incorporated into Ukraine in 1954 as a "gift" from Khrushchev; it proved a costly gesture. Russians, still in denial, continue to flood the resorts while Ukraine reaps the financial rewards. The Tatars have also returned *en masse* over the past five years to demand their land back. Amid the turmoil, Crimea's future remains unclear; the only certainty is that the peninsula's growing popularity and lucrative tourist industry are bound to attract even more heated claims to the region.

quently the seat of Tatar power, the town now holds three of the Crimea's most evocative monuments. The **Khan's Palace** (Khansky Palats; Ханський Палац) was first built in the early 16th century by the second Crimean Khan, although much of what remains was added piecemeal over the centuries. The palace houses many finely decorated rooms stocked with delicate fabrics and dishware, but most delightful are the **courtyards** and **fountains.** In one courtyard the Khan confined his black-market harem. In another, the Fountain Courtyard, trickle the **Golden Fountain** and the famous 1764 **Fountain of Tears,** supposedly built by a disconsolate khan who had fallen in love with a dying slave; two roses are retained in perpetuity to catch the fountains tears. Pushkin re-immortalized the fountain in his poem "Bakhchisarai Fountain" ("Bakhchisaraisky Fontan"; Бахчисарайский Фонтан). To reach the palace from the train station, head up the hill away from the tracks and straight across the first intersection (*not* left uphill or right downhill). Keep going straight up the valley for 30min. On a hot day, a taxi from the train station can make the hike a lot easier (8-10hv). The palace, on your right, is unmistakable. (Open daily 9am-5:30pm. Closed last day of the month. 8hv, students 5hv.) The adjoining late-16th-century **mosque** with graceful minarets can be visited for free. Farther up the valley is the **Assumption Monastery** (Uspensky Pecherny Monastir; Успенский Печерний Монастир). Carved out of a cliff in the 15th century, this monastery was central to Orthodox Christian life in Crimea. Although restorations keep much of the monastery off limits, its location commands one of the best views in all of the Central Steppes. To get there from the Khan's palace, continue up the road for 20-30min. and bear right at the small parking lot.

As the former location of what is now Bakhchisarai and site of Byzantine and early Tatar remains, the higher-up **Jews' Fortress** (Chufut-Kale; Чуфут-Кале) is indeed an impressive stronghold: it is a fortification created entirely by nature. The settlement received its current name when the capital of the Crimean Khanka moved to Bakhchisarai in the early 16th century leaving only Jews and Armenians behind. The dry white cliffs it surveys may have repelled invaders for centuries, but more recently they have invited a new invasion: the film industry. These powerful, brooding cliffs have popped up in Indian and British films, and most recently in an American blockbuster starring Chuck Norris. Among the most interesting sights in the old city are the **Kansas,** or prayer houses, not far from the entrance, the domed 1437 **mausoleum,** near the arched gate in the 6th-century Byzantine wall, and a fascinating 15th-century **cave complex,** with two stories, a central pillar, and hollows for wine production and storage, just beyond the Byzantine wall near the far side of the headland. The Jews' Fortress is about 1km up the road from the monastery; bear left into what locals call the *Balky* (Велика; Hollow) and left again up the hillside. (6hv, students 4hv.)

With very scarce accommodations in Bakhchisarai and excellent connections to the otherwise-drab Simferopol, Bakhchisarai is best explored en route to other Crimean cities or as a daytrip from Simferopol. Bring a water bottle if you're planning to hike—it can get pretty hot, and the touristy refreshment stands up the valley are sorely overpriced. The local specialty, *Moloko*, consisting of cannabis boiled in goat's milk, is regrettably illegal and not found in restaurants. Discretion is your friend if you try to procure this magic potion; *Let's Go* does not recommend *moloko*.

GETTING THERE. The *elektrichka* is the cheapest and fastest transport (45min., 7 per day, 1.07hv); several daily buses also make the trip (1hr., 5 per day, 1.71hv) from the Simferopol *Avtovokzal.*

FEODOSIYA (ФЕОДОСИЯ)

If you don't think the smooth rocks of Yalta feel much like a beach, head east. Outside Feodosiya, founded as the ancient slave-trading town of Theodosia, the 16km stretch of bronzed sand speckled with sea-worn shells has attracted vacationers for centuries. From the **bus station** head past the little church, turn right on ul. Fedko (Федко), and cross the bridge over the tracks to reach the **beach.** Beaches with toilets and shower cost 2hv; free beaches without amenities are farther out to your left. Continuing down ul. Fedko (to your right facing the sea), turn left across the park, then right on pr. Lenina to reach the city center. Or, city **buses** #2 and 4 run along ul. Fedko. In the center, on the corner of ul. Gallereynaya and pr. Lenina, stands the **I. K. Aivazovsky Museum,** in the building where the well-known painter lived and worked on his stunning maritime scenes from 1848 to 1900. The most famous work in this collection is *Poseidon's Journey on the Sea*, portraying a sombre and terrifying sea god surrounded by thunderclouds. Other exhibits portray Aivazovsky himself, who was by all accounts a strange man, particularly toward the end of his life, when he grew sideburns that would have put Pushkin (posthumously) to shame. (Open Th-M 10am-5pm, Tu 10am-2pm. 5hv, students 2.50hv.) Feodosiya also boasts a 14th-century **Genoese fortress,** farther south along the waterfront from the city center along ul. Gorkovo and up a hill. In the valley below the fortress, a pair of diminutive but appealing **Armenian churches,** also from the 14th century, are beginning to recover from Soviet-era neglect.

If spending the night in Feodosiya, the **Astoriya** (Астория), pr. Lenina 9 (tel. 323 16 and 323 27), has clean and relatively affordable rooms. (Singles with sink and TV 18.76hv, with toilet 30.23hv, with bath 48.05hv; doubles 31.66hv, 39.84hv, 57.37hv. Hall shower 2hv. Call ahead in summer.) A *Kvartirnoy Byuro* at the bus station will arrange a **private room** or apartment for upwards of 3hv per night. If the beachfront hot-dog kiosks don't tickle your fancy, there's the **Cafe Assol** (Ассоль) at the intersection of ul. Libnekhta (Либнехта) and ul. Galereina (Галереина), which serves kebabs (5hv) and other entrees (4-8hv; open daily 9am-11pm).

GETTING THERE. Buses connect Feodosia with **Simferopol** (3hr., 11 per day, 9hv) and **Yalta** (3hr., 12 per day, 13hv). Many buses on the **Simferopol-Kerch** route (11 per day, 9hv) pass through Feodosia. **Phone code:** (0) 6562.

KAZANTIP (КАЗАНТИП)

If you thought Moscow's clubs were overpriced and Kiev's discos weren't disco enough, head to the Kazantip Peninsula on the Azov Sea when August rolls around. From July 20 to August 27, the hippest German and Eastern European DJs congregate here and mix up a unique barrage of techno beats. The rave has been gaining momentum, and last year nearly 10,000 ravers came here to celebrate the end of the summer. Different DJs mix nightly on or near the beach, and endless nights of dancing and swimming ensue, all in the shadow of a looming, never-used **nuclear reactor.**

Everything goes down in **Sholkinu** (Шёлкину), the largest of the small towns on the peninsula, where the buses to Kazantip from **Simferopol** (4hr., 3 per day, 20hv) stop. The **post office** (open M-F 8am-1pm and 3-6pm, Sa 8am-1pm and 3-4pm) and the **telephone office** (open 24hr.) are next to Gostinitsa Bris. It's free to pitch a tent anywhere, and if you walk toward the beach almost everyone in town will offer you a room in their home (20-30hv). The **Gostinitsa Bris** (Гостиница Брыс; tel. 687 08), two blocks behind the bus station and to the left, also offers rooms. (Doubles and triples 32hv. Shared bathrooms.) A number of predictable but inexpensive cafes lie around the bus stop and the beach, including the **Tantsuyushchi Delfin** (Dancing Dolphin; Танцюущий Делфин), across from the bus stop. (Entrees 4-8hv.) **Postal code:** 334640. **Phone code:** 06557.

SEVASTOPOL (СЕВАСТОПОЛЬ)

The Black Sea cuts an inlet into the southwestern tip of Crimea, forming a perfect natural harbor. Positioned so ideally, Sevastopol had no choice but to become a focal point in world history. It achieved international significance first in the Crimean War and later in WWII, when its tragic losses placed it among the ranks of the Soviet "Hero Cities." Rebuilt before ornament had become taboo in Soviet circles, central Sevastopol is elegant and formal. Russia and Ukraine still quarrel over the ownership of the city's Black Sea Fleet, and young sailors from both countries fill the streets. Fortunately, the end of the Cold War has lifted the city's shroud of secrecy and its ban on foreigners, so you need not fear Sevastopol's uniformed masses—but don't pick fights.

ORIENTATION

Greater Sevastopol is impossibly complicated, with poorly marked streets on several peninsulas jutting into the harbor in every possible direction. Happily, the center of town is confined to a single peninsula, on the south side of the harbor. The hilly interior of the west-pointing peninsula is circumscribed by the main streets **ul. Lenina** (Ленина) to the north, **ul. Bolshaya Morskaya** (Болшая Морская) in the southeast, and **pr. Nakhimova** (Нахимова) to the southwest. Ul. Bolshaya Morskaya and pr. Nakhimova meet at **pl. Lazaryova** (Лазарёва). **Primorsky bul.** is the pedestrian street beside pr. Nakhimova. From the **train station,** cross the footbridge over the tracks and take trolleybus #7 or 9 going right. The city center is ill-defined, but both buses stop within sight of **Gostinitsa Sevastopol,** a reasonable starting place. **Maps** (4-6hv) remain scarce; try **Soyuzpechat** (Союзпечать) kiosks.

PRACTICAL INFORMATION

Trains: Tel. 52 30 77 and 36 60 74. Daily to: **Moscow** (28hr., 75hv); **Kiev** (19hr., 30hv); and **St. Petersburg** (37hr., 84hv). *Elektrichka* (commuter rail) runs to **Simferopol** (3hr., 6 per day, 2.20hv). Most other trains pass through Sevastopol. Being in the train station between 10pm and 4am costs 2hv.

Buses: Pl. Revyakina 3. Across a few tracks behind the train station or one stop farther on trolleybus #7. To: **Simferopol** (2½hr., 4 per day, 1.50hv); **Yalta** (2hr., 10 per day, 5.25hv); and **Rostov-na-Donu** (14hr., 1 per day, 50hv). Open daily 6am-6pm.

Ferries: A car and passenger ferry leaves from Artilleriyskaya Bay behind Gostinitsa Sevastopol for the north shore (Severnaya Storona), landing near pl. Zakharova (20min., hourly, 1.50hv). A passenger boat leaves from a nearby dock for **Uchkuyuvka Beach,** on the open sea north of town (20min., every 40min., 2.50hv).

Local Transportation: Trolleybuses (0.30hv) are efficient and convenient. #12 runs up ul. Bolshaya Morskaya. #7 and 9 circle the center, stopping at the train station.

Tourist Offices: Excursion offices are common on Primorsky bul., offering guided tours of Crimean sites and of the city and boat tours of the harbor and its ships. Pricey, but convenient. 20-30hv.

Visa Registration: OVIR, ul. Pushkina 12. Between the upper part of ul. Lenina and the sea. Open M and F 10am-noon and 2-4pm, Tu 2-4pm.

Currency Exchange: Everywhere, with the best rates in Crimea. Only banks having Western currency or rubles. **Bank Aval,** ul. Suvorova 39 (tel. 46 05 75 and 46 01 75), near the intersection of ul. Bolshaya Morskaya and ul. Admirala Oktyabrskova; head upstairs and through the arched door. Gives MC/Visa **cash advances** for a 3% commission, and cashes AmEx and Thomas Cook traveler's checks for a 2.5% commission. **Western Union** available here. Open M-F 9am-noon and 1-3pm. There are **no ATMs.**

Luggage Storage: In the train station's back entrance. 1.50hv per 24hr. Open daily 8-11am and noon-8pm.

Pharmacy: Gedeon Richter, ul. Lenina 34. Open M-F 8am-7pm, Sa 10am-6pm, Su 9am-4pm.

Post Office: ul. Bolshaya Morskaya 21. Open M-F 8am-7pm, Sa-Su 8am-6pm. **Postal code:** 335011.

Telephones: In the post office, on the ground floor and to the left. Local phones use old 10-kopek coins. To: North America 9.80hv per min.; Western Europe 6.75hv per min.; Australia 9.20hv per min. Open daily 8am-7pm. **Phone code:** (0)692.

UKRAINE

ACCOMMODATIONS

For an extended summertime stay, it's hard to beat the **private rooms** aggressively advertised by *babushki* in the train station for 10-20hv.

Komnata Otdykha (Room of Rest; Комната Отдыха), at the train station, straight behind the *prigorodnye kassy* (local ticket counters) beyond the bridge. Knock at the top of the staircase. The cheapest alternative to a private room. Bed in a 6- or 4-person dorm 12hv; doubles 18hv. "Lux" double or triple with bath 22hv.

Gostinitsa Sevastopol, pl. Nakhimova 8 (tel. 52 36 82), accessible by trolleybuses #1, 3, 7, and 9. Ordinary Russian rooms. Hot water hall showers 2.50hv for 30min. Singles 30hv, with sink 33hv, with bath, telephone, and fridge 72hv; doubles 42hv, 56hv, 84hv; triples 66hv, 84hv, 92hv.

Gostinitsa Krym (Крым), ul. 6 Bastionnaya 46 (6 Бастионная; tel. 52 22 53), up ul. Admirala Oktyabrskova from ul. Bolshaya Morskaya. Also on trolleybus line #5. A Soviet behemoth. Hot water 7-10pm. Singles with bath 60hv; doubles 60hv; triples 72hv.

FOOD

The **central market** lies downhill from pl. Lazaryova at the intersection of ul. Partizanskaya (Партизанская) and ul. Odesskaya (Одесская). (Open Tu-Su 8am-5pm.) An elegant and well-stocked **Gastronom** sits at pr. Nakhimova 5. (Open M-Sa 8am-2pm and 3-8pm, Su 8am-3pm.)

Restoran Dialog (Диалог), next to the post office. An old-school *stolovaya* (cafeteria) repackaged as a slick new cafe. Entrees 3-8hv; salads 1-7hv. Open daily 9am-10pm.

Restaurant Nikita, Shestakova 1a, diagonally uphill from pl. Lazaryova. A respectable effort at world cuisine, with a pardonable emphasis on the ex-Soviet world. Entrees 8-12hv. Open daily 11am-midnight.

Medzhik Burger, on ul. Bolshaya Morskaya and uphill from the ferries. Look for the revolving chef sign. Russo-Ukrainian-American fast food. Pizza 10hv; *pelmeni* 3hv; burger 4hv. Open daily 9am-9pm.

SIGHTS & ENTERTAINMENT

Nearly everything in Sevastopol is maritime. The **Museum of the Black Sea Fleet** (Muzey Chornomorskovo Flota; Музей Чёрноморского Флота), ul. Lenina 11 (tel. 52 22 89 and 52 03 92), founded in 1869, displays model ships, naval paintings, and personal effects of notable sea-dogs. (Open in summer 10am-5pm; off-season W-Su 10am-5pm. Closed last Friday of every month. 8hv, students 5hv.) The small but well-kept **aquarium,** pr. Nakhimova 2, attracts crowds with its sky-lit central tank of sharks and stingrays. (Open in summer daily 9am-7pm; off-season Tu-Su 9am-7pm; *kassa* closes at 6pm. 6hv, students 2hv.) The pseudo-Byzantine **St. Vladimir's Cathedral,** on the crest of the peninsula near ul. Marata (Марата), is the not-so-watery resting place of Orthodox admirals. (30min. visits 2hv.) The massive, circular **Panorama Museum** (tel. 52 21 46), in the park at the high-numbered end of ul. Lenina, presents a somewhat pro-Soviet (and who can blame them) look at the 1941-42 battle of Sevastopol. (Open in summer daily 9am-6pm; off-season Tu-Su 9am-5pm. Mandatory 40min. tour 6hv, students 4hv.) A nearby **amusement park** has bumper cars (2hv), a "chamber of fear" (2hv), and a one-car roller coaster called the "American Mountains" (3hv; open daily 9am-8pm).

To get to the **beach,** head out of town, away from the dirty harbor. Take the boat (see **Ferries,** above) or trolleybus #10 to its terminus, **Plyazh Omega,** a vaguely horseshoe-shaped bay ringed by mixed rocks and sand. Rent a boat (8hv per hr.), a pedal boat (6hv per hr.), a catamaran (12hv per hr.), or windsurfing gear (6hv per hr.) at the boat station. (Open daily 9am-9pm; windsurfing 10am-6pm.) Beachfront bars are largely interchangeable; most charge 4-6hv for domestic beer.

For the best nightlife, head to **Bunker** (Бункер), ul. Marata 5 (Марата). Look for the orange sign down the alley near ul. Lenina 32, and head down tunnel after strangely painted tunnel. The club itself, safe from nuclear holocaust 37m underground, hosts rock groups from all over Russia and Ukraine. (Bottle of wine 2.20hv; beer 3-7hv. Cover 5hv. Best from 7 or 8pm to midnight.)

YALTA (ЯЛТА)

The gaudy Yalta waterfront, with its hot dog vendors and computerized astrology stands, dashes any illusion that this is still the city of Chekhov, Rachmaninov, and Tolstoy. Prices here are still cheap by European standards, but have risen beyond the reach of many former Soviets. The trash littering Yalta's hillsides and the *babushki* pawing through rubbish heaps serve as a reminder that this is not paradise on Earth. Nonetheless, there are still spots in Yalta where the houses, with their characteristic balconies (minus Humphrey Bogart), line streets covered by trees. With a little social irresponsibility you can enjoy Yalta for what it is: a lovely, historical city weathering the storm of capitalism the best it can.

ORIENTATION

Pedestrian **nab. Lenina** (Ленина) runs most of the length of the waterfront *(naberezhnaya).* From the bus and trolley stations, take trolleybus #1 uphill. It quickly turns around and runs down **ul. Moskovskaya** (Московская) past the **circus** and **market** to **Sovetskaya pl.** (Советская), where you can get off and walk two blocks toward the sea. At this point, turning left will get you to the old quarter and the cheaper hotels, and a right will start you on the slippery slope to hedonism that is nab. Lenina. Farther down the waterfront, the pedestrian **ul. Pushkinskaya** (Пушкинская) veers inland to Kinoteatr Spartak, also a major stop on trolleybus #1. **Maps** are 3-5hv at newsstands; newer ones are available at Hotel Yalta.

PRACTICAL INFORMATION

Buses: Moskovskaya ul. 57 (tel. 34 20 92). To: **Simferopol** (2hr., every 30min., 4.50hv); **Sevastopol** (2½hr., 4 per day, 5.15hv); and **Feodosia** (5hr., 3 per day, 12hv). Across the street is the **trolleybus station,** which has slightly slower (2½hr.) but more comfortable trolleys going to the **Simferopol train station** (4.25hv), the Simferopol **airport** (5.05hv), and **Gurzuf** (0.85hv) every 20min. Advance tickets are available above and behind the ordinary ticket *kassa.*

Water Shuttles: Every 40min. to: **Alupka** (1¼hr., 6hv) via **Livadia** (20min., 4hv) and **Gurzuf** (45min., every 2hr., 3hv). Buy tickets in front of the Casino Diana; otherwise you may end up buying a more expensive "excursion" for 10-15hv more.

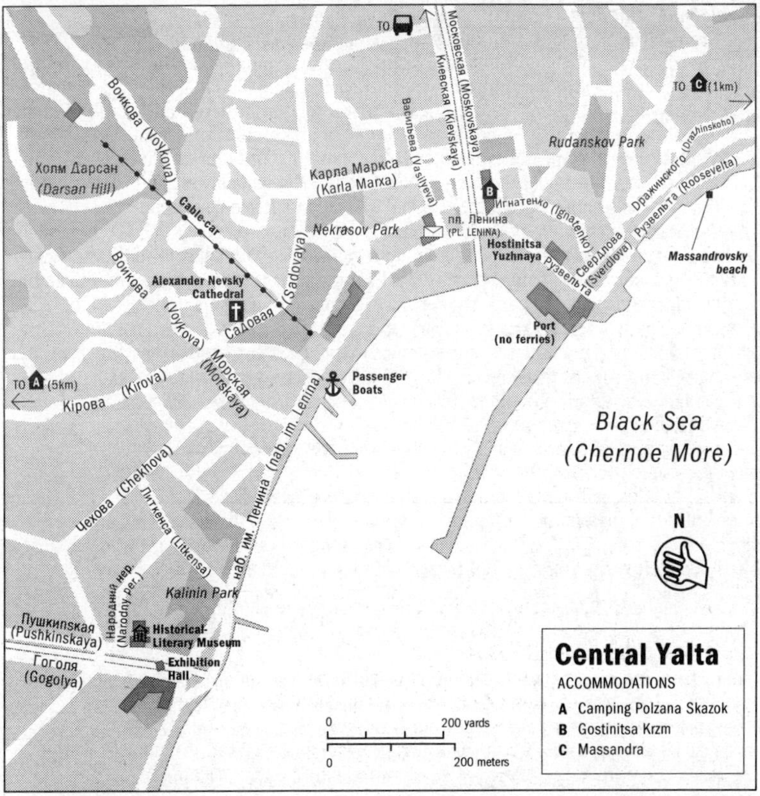

Local Transportation: Trolleys run throughout the city; trolleybus #1 covers most of the central area (0.30hv). The trolleybus that stops on ul. Moskovskaya heads to the train station, while the one with a stop across from Discoclub Saturn runs toward Kinoteatr Spartak and the Pushkin Museum.

Financial Services: Currency exchanges are everywhere and are all part of a cartel offering uniform rates. A few near the post office charge half a percent less. A window in the central telephone office offers **Western Union** and gives MC/Visa **cash advances** for a 3% commission. **Ukreksimbank,** Moskovskaya ul. 31a, next to the circus at the Tsirk stop, cashes all major **traveler's checks** for a 2.5% commission.

Tourist Office: Intourist, ul. Drazhinskovo 50, in the Hotel Yalta, gears its pricey English tours to large groups, but does have good city **maps** (5hv). Open daily 9am-5pm.

Luggage Storage: At the bus station. 0.90hv for 24hr. Open 8am-noon and 1-8pm.

24hr. Pharmacy: Botkinskaya ul. 1 (Боткинская). Between 8pm and 8am (Sa 6pm-11am), knock at the *dezhurnaya*'s door, Botkinskaya 3.

Post Office: pl. Lenina. **Poste Restante** *("do vostrebovanya")* at the window farthest from the entrance. Open daily 8am-8pm. **Postal code:** 334200.

Internet Access: Internet Cafe, ul. Marshaka 9, hidden behind Kinoteatr Spartak and up the stairs. Not a cafe at all. 4hv per hr., although you'll have to compete with teenage boys playing Quake. Open 24hr.

Telephones: Moskovskaya ul. 9, down an alleyway. Buy tokens for local (0.15hv) or intercity calls (0.70hv). To the U.S. 9.80hv per min. Fax 0.20hv per page. Telephones open 24hr.; fax open daily 8am-noon and 1-7:30pm. **Phone code:** (0)654.

ACCOMMODATIONS

The prices at Yalta's beachside hotels have increased dramatically and may continue to do so. Lone travelers will have difficulty getting a place in a double. Book ahead. Bus station *babushki* often offer unbeatable deals on **private rooms.** 20-30hv is a good rate, but expect to pay more as you get closer to the waterfront.

Hostinitsa Krym (Крым), Moskovskaya ul. 1/6 (tel. 32 60 01; reservations tel. 32 78 73). Colorless but livable rooms in a very central location. Singles 33hv; doubles 45hv; triples 55hv. Shower 2.25hv. Hot water 7-10pm. Registration 2.55hv. Call ahead.

Massandra (Массандра), ul. Drazhinskovo 48 (Дражинского; tel. 35 25 91), a 15min. trudge from the town center but not far from the beach. All doubles; if you come alone they'll give you a roommate. Airy and attractive rooms. Place in a double 30hv; with bath, TV, fridge, and toilet 45hv. Hall shower has hot water 7-9pm (2hv).

Motel-Camping Polyana Skazok (Поляна Сказак), ul. Kirova 167 (Кірова; tel. 39 52 19). Take bus #11, 26, or 27 from the bus station to "Поляна Сказок," then head uphill along a busy but otherwise pretty country road (20min.). They don't allow tents, but it's cheap (cheaper with a caravan) and in a nice spot. 2-person bungalow 30hv (shared showers and toilets); motel doubles 50-63hv.

FOOD

Many sit-down **restaurants** along nab. Lenina serve food with their liquor for excessively high prices. Seek refuge in the city's **cafeterias** and **stolovayas;** they are the last bastions against the hot dog and pizza epidemic plaguing the former Soviet Union. A well-stocked and better-adorned **Gastronom** (Гастроном), nab. Lenina 4, sells bread for pennies. (Open daily 8am-3pm and 4-8pm.) The **market** across from the circus, accessible by trolleybus #1, has bountiful produce. (Open 8am-8pm.)

Cafe Siren (Сирень), ul. Roosevelta 4 (Рузвелта). The song of this cafeteria's mascot will lure you to freshly prepared Russian food. Full meals 5-6hv. Open daily 8am-9pm.

Russkye Bliny, ul. Morskaya 4/2, a block above the waterfront. A popular option for a quick meal. *Bliny* with jam 1.60hv; entrees 4-8hv. Open daily 8am-11pm.

Cafe Krym (Крым), Moskovskaya ul. 1/2, in the same building as Gostinitsa Krym. Simple Russian food similar to what you'll find at the Siren, but cheaper and not as heavily frequented. Full meals 5hv. Open daily 7am-8pm.

SIGHTS & ENTERTAINMENT

If **Anton Chekhov** is your deity of choice (see **Russia: Literature & Arts,** p. 554), Yalta is your Mecca, or at least Medina. The author lived here for the last five years of his tuberculosis, and you can practically retrace his every step from monuments and plaques. On nab. Lenina at the entrance of Gurman, you can see where he once slept, and on ul. Litkensa (Литкенса) you'll find the **school** where he taught. At ul. Kirova 112, you can explore the **house** he built, the garden he planted, and the **museum** (tel. 39 49 47) his sister dedicated to him, all remarkably well-preserved. The museum displays manuscripts, old editions, and the room where the author entertained luminaries, including Rachmaninov and Tolstoy. Bus #8 rolls here every 40min. from Kinoteatr Spartak on ul. Pushkinskaya. Or, take the much more frequent trolleybus #1 to Pionerskaya (Пионерская), cross the street and walk up the hill. (Open Tu-Su 10am-5:15pm. 10hv, students 5hv.) To check out more recent trends in Russo-Ukrainian art, drop by the **Art Exhibition Hall,** ul. Gogolya 1, which straddles the waterway with monthly exhibits. (Open Tu-Su 10am-8pm. 6hv.)

Up the street, the **Yalta Historical Museum,** ul. Pushkinskaya 5a, displays fragments of the city's past, including amphorae, a Roman bust, and numerous 19th-century postcards. (Open Tu-Su 11am-6pm. 6hv, tour 15hv.) If this collection stretches the limits of your eclecticism, you'll be relieved to find the **Museum of Turn-of-the-Century Noble Life,** ul. Ekaterininskaya 8 (Екатеринская), and the **Museum of Lesya Ukraina** (tel. 32 16 34; see **Literature & Arts,** p. 731), upstairs in the same beautiful Moorish-style building. The former displays furniture and other possessions of well-known (or at least well-to-do) Russians, while the latter pays tribute to the famous Ukrainian writer who lived here briefly in 1897. (Both open Tu-Su 10am-6pm; closed last day of month. 5hv each.) For tamer specimens of Yalta's domestic architecture, consider a stroll among the back streets; ul. Chekhova and ul. Kirova are both well endowed.

Yalta's shady parks provide an intermediate level of cool between the bracing sea and scorching sun. In **Seaside (Primorsky) Park Gagarina,** at the southwest end of nab. Lenina, you can find an **Exotic Fish Aquarium.** The rather sad-looking inhabitants include some piranhas and a pair of very confused baboons. (Open daily 9am-8pm. 3hv.) The **city circus** (info tel. 32 75 45) is at the Tsirk stop on ul. Moskovskaya, trolleybus #1. (Shows May-Sept. Th and Sa 7pm, and F and Su 4pm. *Kassa* open 10am-8pm if there's a show, 10am-6pm if not. Tickets 5-10hv.) For a view of Yalta's ramshackle rooftops and the sea, take the chairlift from behind Casino Diana on nab. Lenina to a **mock Greek temple.** There, you'll find an irreverent statue of Zeus, unperturbed that the only idol worshipped here is Coca-Cola. (Open June-Oct. daily 10am-3am. Round-trip 8hv.)

Near the Polyana Skazok Campground lies the **Fairy-Tale Meadow** (Polyana Skazok; Поляна Сказок), with oversized sculptures of characters from Russian and Ukrainian fairy tales, including Snow White. (Open summer 9am-6pm; off-season 9am-5pm. 5hv.) To get to the **Uchan Su Waterfall,** keep going up the road to Polyana Skazok past the campground. Turn right up the hill after the bridge, follow the sign to Detsky Lager Isary (Детский Лагерь Исары), and promptly turn right onto one of the footpaths uphill. Stay on the bluffs with the stream below to your right and climb. At some point, the trail should cross the stream. There are lots of unmarked trails, but it's hard to get badly lost: down leads to civilization, up to cliffs. The waterfall itself—more of a water-trickle—is not nearly as interesting as the hike there. Many a newlywed has left a tatter of clothing on the wishing trees under the falls. Wooden steps take you partway up the cliff for a fair view.

Yalta has many **beaches;** follow the seashore either way from the harbor. City beaches cost 1.50hv, commercial ones 3hv, although some are free after 6pm; most are crowded and all lack sand. If boredom strikes, there are always **jet-skis** or **hydroplanes** (6hv per min.), or the more reasonable **carousel** (1hv per 5min.). Inflatable **mattresses** cost 2hv per hr.

NIGHTLIFE

Nightlife in Yalta tends to be sedate. People chat, stroll, and enjoy the night air around Pl. Lenina and the *naberezhnaya.* One strategy is to start out with a wine-tasting at **Crimea Wines,** on nab. Lenina in the Casino Diana building. (Tastings every 1½hr. from 2:30-8:30pm. 15hv.) Then head to **Guinness,** ul. Sverdlova 7, for a pint (8hv). Finally, polish your night off by getting ill on the **spinning rides** (5-10hv) along the waterfront. A more conventional approach would be to do your gyrating at **Discoclub Saturn,** which advertises pop from 9pm-1am and "Ravoanimation" from 1-6am; it doesn't really get going until midnight.

NEAR YALTA: GURZUF (ГУРЗУФ)

Eighteen kilometers up the coast from Yalta, Gurzuf looks like it was built by a committee of artists tired of searching for the picturesque. Its steeply twisting stair-step streets, colorful overhanging houses, and a-little-too-perfectly-placed vegetation all add to this sense. In addition, the town harbors the **Dacha Chekhova,** ul. Chekhova 22, where the ailing Chekhov sought peace and quiet, and later began *The Three Sisters*. The house, now a museum, contains a furnished room, a literary museum room, and exhibits by local artists. Follow ul. Leningradskaya to the police station and turn right down the stairs; take a left onto ul. Chekhova when you can descend no farther. (Open in summer daily 10am-6pm; off-season W-Su 10am-6pm. 8hv, students 3hv. The rocky beach below the *dacha* is free with museum entry, 1hv otherwise.) Gurzuf is also home to a dull little **Pushkin Museum,** centered around the two months he spent here as a young man. It's in the Sanatorium Pushkina, down the waterfront toward Yalta— tell the gatekeeper you're visiting the museum and head through the park to your left. (Open W-Su 10am-5pm. 4hv, students 2hv.) The rocky mass at the upper end of ul. Leningradskaya contains a **tunnel** leading to an impressive view of cliffs and sea. Ask to see the *"tunel v skalye"* at the gate to Camp Artek in the middle of the black iron fence on the right, then go right and follow the green fence to the tunnel entrance. Higher up are the scant remains of a Genoan fortress, partly obscured by signs forbidding climbing. Gurzuf's **beaches** (1-2hv) are pretty ordinary, but renting a **paddleboat** (7hv per hr.) might make things more interesting.

For economical fare try **Pelmennaya,** up the beachfront toward Chekhov's *dacha* at the second bend in the road. Geared toward hibernating Russians, the food is cheap and filling. (Entrees 1.50-5hv. Open daily 8am-8pm.) **Postal Code:** 334284. **Phone code:** (0)654.

GETTING THERE. Gurzuf is most pleasantly reachable from **Yalta** by **boat** (50min., every 2hr., 5hv) and most cheaply by **bus** #31, from the 7th platform of the **Avtovokzal** (45min., hourly, 0.65hv).

NEAR YALTA: LIVADIA (ЛИВАДИЯ)

Only an hour's hike or a 15min. boat ride away, Livadia hosted the imprecisely named **Yalta Conference.** Churchill, Roosevelt, and Stalin met for a week in February, 1945 at Tsar Nicholas II's summer palace to hash out postwar territorial claims. Secretly, the Russians committed to enter the war against Japan after the German defeat (which Stalin did two months after the German surrender, when the atom bomb on Hiroshima had decided things), and Roosevelt and Churchill agreed to return all Soviet POWs. Some considered the conference a great cave-in on the Anglo-American side, particularly regarding the Soviet presence in Eastern Europe. A second school of thought, led by ideologically confused tour guides, thinks the conference guaranteed "50 years of peace."

The **Great Palace** (Veliky Dvorets; Великий Дворец), built in 1911, is worth the visit regardless of its historical significance. The lower level commemorates the conference, while the upper level houses the royalist **Nicholas II museum.** The palace's exquisite marble and wood interior, the tiled Arab Courtyard, and the view from Nicholas' windows all amply demonstrate that it was good to be tsar. That is, until the masses revolted. The guides will make you don felt slippers inside, which will stay on your feet about as well as Roosevelt, Churchill, and Stalin stuck to the agreement reached within. (Open in summer daily 10am-6pm; off-season Th-Tu 10am-4pm. 8hv, students 6hv).

GETTING THERE. Buses #26 and 27 run to Livadia from **Yalta** (10min., every 30-40min., 0.65hv). **Minibuses** (*marshrutky*) labelled "Лівадія" head to Livadia from throughout **Yalta** for slightly higher prices. There is also a **water shuttle** (15min., hourly, 3hv). From the dock, head left a few hundred meters; tell them you're going to the "leeft" (Лифт) if they try to charge you entry to the beach. Turn right into the cool passage. (Elevators run daily 7am-1pm and 4-6pm. 0.25hv.) Head through the elegant **park** from the top of the second elevator to get to the palace.

NEAR YALTA: ALUPKA (АЛУПКА)

Alupka is home to the most extravagant *dacha* in Greater Yalta. **Dvorets Vorontsova** (Дворец Воронцова) is a still-active compound built by the wealthier-than-thou regional governor, Count Mikhail Vorontsov (see **History,** p. 729). Construction of the palace took over 30 years, finishing in 1841. Most of the grounds and exterior can be visited for free, but a look inside will cost you 6hv. Of particular interest are the **Blue Drawing Room** (Golubaya Gostinnaya) and the **Great Hall.** The exterior is an unlikely blend of Gothic Revival and Moghul stylings. The south side, facing the sea, has a particulary bizarre and magnificent facade. (Open May-Sept. daily 9am-5pm; Oct.-Apr. Tu-Th and Sa-Su 9am-5pm.) 1km back up the coast toward Yalta (take the road through the park from the palace exit), past a summer house com-

PRAISE ALLAH, AND MOTHER RUSSIA, TOO Six lions—a truly impressive marble one by the Italian master Leone Bonani, and five goofy-looking knock-offs by his students—guard a portico of the castle with an Arabic invocation to Allah. What this is doing in Ukraine is unclear. Apparently, the English architect who designed the palace thought the Black Sea here looked a lot like the Indian Ocean, and copied the design of an Indian mansion and its inscription, "All Praise to Allah." The story has it that when Tsar Nicholas I came to the palace, he was offended by its extravagance. Vorontsov merely pointed to the lettering, explaining to the tsar that, after all, all praise is due to Russia.

manding a fine view, a **cable car** leads up to the top of some substantial cliffs. (Runs M-W and F-Su 9am-5pm; last car descends at 6pm. Round-trip 15hv.) The trip is best on a clear day. To avoid retracing your steps, continue along the same road to a large, inverted cement triangle, then head downward toward the shore. From here you can take a **boat** back to **Yalta** (2hv). Note the statue crawling from the sea near the dock. By the lower cable-car station, the **Cafe Khashta Bash** (Хашта Баш; tel. 72 12 85), whose most exotic feature is its Tatar name, serves a reasonable selection of non-hot-dog, non-*shashlyk* dishes, with an emphasis on seafood. (Entrees 8-15hv).

GETTING THERE. To get to Alupka, take the **ferry** (1¼hr., hourly, 6hv), or, if you must, **bus #27** (1½hr., every 40min., 1.80hv) from the **Yalta** bus station.

ODESHCHINA (ОДЕШИНА)

South of Kiev and west of Crimea spreads the Ukrainian steppe and wooded half-steppe. While other regions of the East Slavic diaspora shook themselves free of the Mongol yoke in the 15th century, this area languished under various overlords (most notably the Ottoman Turks) until the end of the 18th century, when fellow Slavs from Moscow and St. Petersburg brought liberation. With Russian rule came a curious mix of Russian and French culture, blended with the influence of Jews who under the Pale of Settlement were herded from all over Russia into this small corner of the empire. The Odeshchina region, with Odessa at its heart, has fed off the diversity and has maintained an unusually independent and spirited identity.

ODESSA (ОДЕССА)

With the help of luck, Catherine the Great's patronage, and its location on the sea, Odessa (pop. 1,046,400.) long ago became an important port with all the attendant prosperity and corruption. Today, that splendor endures, having weathered Romanian occupation during WWII with relatively little damage. Although Odessa lays some claim to Pushkin, exiled here, the city's true literary son is Isaac Babel, who told stories of the colorful Jewish mafia in Odessa's Moldovan neighborhood. Not surprisingly, Odessa has taken to post-Soviet crime like a swan to water, becoming one of the parent cities of the Russian mafia. But with the shell of past greatness cracking under its own unused weight, the party town of the former USSR still hums, just at a lower frequency.

GETTING THERE & GETTING AROUND

Trains: pl. Privokzalnaya (Привокзальная), at the south end of ul. Pushkinskaya. Trams #2, 3, and 12 run along ul. Preobrazhenskaya to the west end of ul. Deribasovskaya. Buy international (non-former-USSR) or advance tickets in the *Mizhnarodny Zal* (International Room; Мижнародний Зал), to your left as you enter the building (window #19). Open daily 8am-noon and 1-7pm. Tickets are also available at the **Central Ticket Bureau,** ul. Srednefontanskaya (Среднефонтанськая), reachable by bus #136 or 146 or the more frequent tram #17 or 18 (from across the park). Head to stop: Sredni Fontan (Central Fountain) and look for the "Центральные Железнодорожные Кассы" sign. The **luna**

Interservice office (see **Tourist Office,** below) helps with buying tickets. To: **Kiev** (12hr., 2 per day, 46hv); **Lviv** (16hr., 1 per day, 45hv); **Simferopol** (13hr., 1 per day, 26hv); **Chișinău** (6hr., 3 per day, 16hv); **Moscow** (26hr., 3 per day, 121hv); **St. Petersburg** (35hr., 1 per day, 112hv); and **Rīga** (49hr., 95hv).

Buses: Ul. Dzerzhinskovo 58 (Дзержинского). Take tram #5 from the train station or 15 from downtown. Both stop four blocks north of the station. Buy tickets at the station at least the night before, or you'll be standing the entire ride. To: **Kiev** (12hr., 4 per day, 35hv); **Simferopol** (8hr., 2 per day, 26hv); and **Chișinău** (6hr., every 3hr., 13hv).

Ferries: Schedules are unpredictable. **Morskoy Vokzal** (Морской Вокзал), ul. Suvorov 12 (Суворов). Eugenik Travel (see **Tourist Office,** below) sells tickets to: **Yalta** (1 every 5-6 months, 130hv); **Istanbul** (1-2 days, 3 per week, US$75-90; pay in US$); and **Haifa** (2-3 days, 1-2 per month, if that). Open M-F 9am-5pm, Sa-Su 10am-2pm.

Local Transportation: The train station and pl. Grecheskaya are main end points. Info in Russian available inside the train station (2hv per question). **Trams** and **trolleybuses** cost 0.30hv and run almost everywhere 7am-midnight. Watch out for pickpockets. **Buses** (0.50-0.60hv) are confusing, but locals can point you to the one you need.

Taxis: Speedy **marshrutne** (2-3hv) have numbers indicating which trolleybus route they are taking. Nice new yellow taxis are on the expensive side, so haggle away. Don't pay more than 4hv from pl. Grecheskaya to the train station. Gypsy cabs, hailed by holding out your palm while facing traffic, are cheaper.

ORIENTATION

Odessa occupies a 50km strip along the Black Sea. Its center is bounded by a **train station** to the south and a **port** to the north. All streets, have been recently renamed and labeled in both Ukrainian and Russian, but since almost no one in Odessa speaks Ukrainian, most maps are only in Russian; *Let's Go* lists Russian names. Coming out of the train station, walk right across the park to the stop opposite **Spartak stadium** (Спартак), and take trolley #5 or 9 to central **pl. Grecheskaya** (Греческая), right off Odessa's most famous street, **ul. Deribasovskaya** (Дерибасовская), reachable by tram #2, 3, or 12 from the station. Heading toward Shevchenko Park, it crosses **ul. Pushkinskaya** (Пушкинская). A right onto ul. Pushkinskaya from ul. Deribasovskaya leads to the train station. A left on the tree-lined **Primorsky bul.** (Приморский) leads to a great view of the sea. Odessa's beaches stretch for kilometers east of the center and are reachable by trolleybus #5 or 9 from pl. Grecheskaya. Detailed **maps** are available throughout the city (3-5hv) or at Hotel Krasnaya (Красная; 6hv). Pick up a copy of the free weekly *Odessa Post* at a hotel or Mick O'Neil's Irish pub.

PRACTICAL INFORMATION

TOURIST & FINANCIAL SERVICES

Tourist Office: Eugenik Travel in Morskoy Vokzal arranges tours of the catacombs, the city, and the rest of Ukraine. Open daily 9am-6pm. **Yuna Interservice** (Юна Интерсервис; tel. 25 22 46), next to Hotel Krasnaya, arranges plane and train tickets for a 6hv charge. Open daily 9am-2pm.

Visa Registration: **OVIR (**ОВИР**),** Krasny Pereulok 5 (Красный Переулок; tel. 25 89 74). If you have already registered in Ukraine, you needn't register here, but check to be safe. They may send you to another registration office on the 2nd Fl. of vul. Bunina 37 (Бунина). Keep the registration card to avoid a heavy "fine" at the border.

Tourist Police: Sped-Sluzhba (special service), ul. Zhukovskovo 42 (Жуковского; tel. 28 22 66), at the intersection with ul. Preobrazhenskaya (Приображенская; formerly Советской Армий). On the 2nd floor, to the left. Deals with crimes by and against foreigners, but don't expect any knights in shining armor.

Currency Exchange: Ridvenny Bank (Ридвенний; tel. 23 08 28), downtown on the corner of ul. Shchepkina (Шепкина) and Preobrazhenskaya, cashes traveler's checks and gives cash advances for a 3% commission. Open M-F 9am-1pm and 2-6pm, Sa 10am-7pm. **Bank Pivdenny,** in Morskoy Vokzal, cashes major traveler's checks for a US$10 commis-

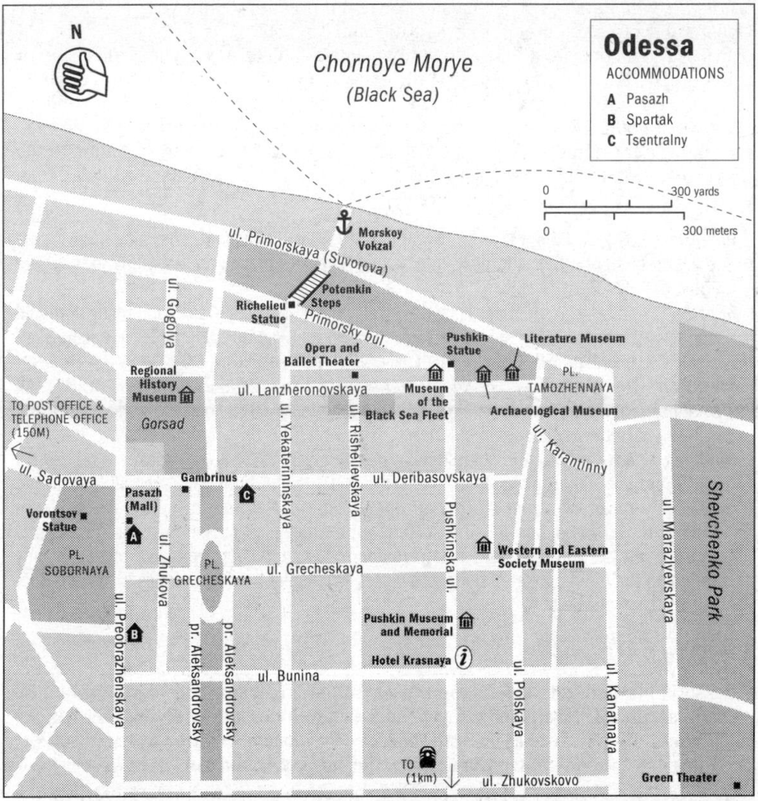

sion. Open daily 9am-6pm. Cirrus/MC/Visa **ATMs** can be found in Mick O'Neil's (see **Nightlife,** p. 767) and in the lobby of Hotel Londonskaya at Primorsky bul. 11. Exchange US$ and DM at any *Obmin Valyut* (Обмін Валют) for similar rates.

EMERGENCY & COMMUNICATION

24hr. Pharmacy: Tel. 28 70 71. In the train station.

Medical Assistance: Polyklinik, Primorsky bul. 12 (tel. 22 43 87 and 25 91 90). Inside the courtyard, 1st door on the left. Reception on 3rd floor. Treats foreign patients.

Post Office: Ul. Sadovaya 10. Open M-Sa 8am-8pm, Su 8am-6pm. **Poste Restante** at counter #16; pre-stamped airmail envelopes (*konvert s markami;* конверт с марками) and packages at counter #19. **Postal code:** 270 015.

Internet Access: Ul. Sadovaya 16. Offers a fast connection for 5hv per hr. Open daily 10am-11pm.

Telephones: At the post office. Prepay international and intercity calls to the left as you enter. To **U.S.** US$2.50 per min. Open 24hr. Local calls require phone cards, sold at the post office and used in blue or yellow booths around town. **Utel** cards and phones can be found at Mick O'Neil's and Morskoy Vokzal. **Phone code:** (0)482.

ACCOMMODATIONS

Private rooms are the cheapest option (from US$5 per person), but you'll be lucky to get anything near the center. Train-station hawkers are recognizable by their signs—some variation on "Сдаю Комнату." Ask *"Skolko?"* (How much?). The *babushki* will start at US$10; haggle down and don't pay until you see the room. Collateral is often required for keys in July and August.

Prices are inconsistent in the downtown **hotels**—make sure a ghost television or refrigerator isn't added to your bill. Truly budget-minded travelers request "*samoye deshovloye mesto*" (the cheapest place), which lands you in a triple or quad. Most hotels overcharge foreigners and have infrequent hot water; some even turn the water off midnight to 6am. Take tram #3 or 12 from the train station to the downtown hotels, all near noisy pl. Grecheskaya and ul. Deribasovskaya. Make sure to get a room away from the street.

Pasazh (Пасаж), ul. Preobrazhenskaya 34 (tel. 20 48 49). This fairly charming hotel is next to the real Pasazh. Pleasant, boxy little rooms. Singles with sink and TV 40hv, with shower 75hv; doubles 64hv, 138hv.

Spartak (Спартак), ul. Deribasovskaya 25 (tel. 26 89 23). Old, grand, and trying to regain respectability, but a bit more worse for wear than its neighbors. No water midnight-6am. Singles with sink and TV 60hv, with shower 86hv; doubles 60hv, 90hv.

Tsentralny (Центральный), ul. Preobrazhenskaya 40 (tel. 26 84 06 and 26 86 07). An elegant marble staircase complements the fine location. Spacious rooms are bright but aging, and hot water is sporadic. Singles 40hv, with bath 65hv; doubles 52hv, 84hv.

Camping "Delfin" (Кемпинг "Дельфин"), dor. Kotovskovo 307 (Котовского; tel. 55 50 52). From the train station, take trolley #4 or 10 to the terminus (a small loop in the road) and transfer to tram #7; get off 20min. later at Лузанивка *(Luzanivka)* and continue 500m. Or, take bus #130 or 170 from pl. Grecheskaya. Remote even for a campground, but the friendly staff, cheap restaurant, sauna, bar, and private beach may appeal to the most budget of budget travelers. Infrequent hot water. English spoken. Bungalows 22hv per person.

FOOD

Odessa is blessed with a few good restaurants, a market, and plenty of quality Ukrainian cafes. Ul. Deribasovskaya teems with outdoor cafes serving beer, vodka, and cutlets. The **Privoz mega-market** (Привоз), Privoznaya ul., near the train station, provides more food than the port can handle, and other curiosities.

Steakhouse (Стейкхаус), ul. Deribasovksaya 20 (tel. 28 77 75). Enjoy a prime slice of meat at the city's best people-watching locale. Veal, chicken, cow, or fish 16-50hv.

Kartoplyanki (Картоплянки), ul. Ekaterinskaya 3. A busy Ukrainian eatery in the center serving excellent food. Entrees 6-10hv. Open daily 8am-10pm.

Na Deribasovskaya (На Дерибасовская), on the corner of Deribasovskaya and ul. Maydan. A popular place. Entrees starting at 8hv.

Pan Pizza (Пан Пицца), in a booth in the big *gastronom* on ul. Deribasovskaya, and also nearby at Ekaterinskaya 45. Decent pizza (for Russia) 8hv.

Student Stolovaya (Студентичная Столовая), ul. Grecheskaya 19. Food for the brain, as cheap as it gets.

SIGHTS

CATACOMBS. When Odessa was a young city, the nearest rock source was directly underground. Over time, this circumstance produced the world's longest series of catacombs. During the 2½-year Nazi occupation, the city's resistance was based here, and the city has set up an excellent museum in its honor. Due to people getting lost in the extensive network of caves, all of the entrances but one have been closed, and you must be with a tour group to enter. The subterranean museum re-creates the resistance camp—the well, bathrooms, and sitting room (with a picture of Stalin torn down repeatedly during *perestroika*)—where 30 men and women held out for six months against German attacks. At Guard Point #1, soldiers had to sit in two-hour shifts in complete darkness to wait for German attackers. Graffitied rocks have been transported from the original site; one declares "Blood for blood; death for death." This understated and haunting complex is now one of the most moving WWII memorials in the former USSR. *(Tours in Russian, Ukrainian, or English through Eugenik Travel (see Tourist Offices, p. 762) in the Morskoy Vokzal. 3hr. English tour 50hv. Russian tours usually leave at 11am and 1pm from train station; look for signs out front for "экскурсии." 5-10hv. Or, spend a lot more and get an English-speaking guide and car from the service bureaus at Hotel Krasnaya or Londonskaya.)*

411TH BATTALION MONUMENT. Far from the busy commercial center lies the Memorial Complex of the 411th Battalion, one of Odessa's more entertaining monuments. The typical armaments of the Soviet forces are here in all their glory, spread over a large park. You'll think the guns and torpedoes are impressive until you get to the other end of the park and see the tanks (even the turrets move), the bomber, and—yes—the battleship, carried here in pieces via tractor-trailer. They're all free for you to climb on, in, and around, but you'll have to share the fun with dozens of little boys and girls making "ratt-ta-tatt-tatt" noises as they aim the big, bad guns. There is a small **museum** by the battleship. *(The complex is on ul. Amundsena (Амундсена), reachable from the train station by bus #108 or 127 or tram #26. 30-40min. Museum open Sa-Th 10am-6pm. 2hv.)* The cliffs along the rocky **coast** are a short walk from behind the bus stop. At high tide, the sea provides its own violent spectacle.

AROUND UL. DERIBASOVSKAYA. Street culture centers on ul. Deribasovskaya where jazz musicians play, mimes tailor their performances to the wishes of the most generous donors, open-air cafes attract young hipsters, and *biznesmeni* swagger with their cell phones. At **Gorsad** on the west end of ul. Deribasovskaya, artists sell elegant handiwork. Across the street is the famous **Gambrinus** (see p. 767). From ul. Deribasovskaya's west end, cross ul. Preobrazhenskaya to see the **statue of Mikhail Vorontsov,** Odessa's powerful governor during the 1820s. The statue is swell, but it's a poor substitute for the cathedral that used to stand here. The church was destroyed in 1936 in an effort to quell the ecclesiastical forces threatening Soviet rule. The square is still called **Cathedral Square** (Soborna pl.). A block to the left on ul. Preobrazhenskaya you'll find the superbly aromatic **flower market,** where old women advise suitors which flowers to buy their sweethearts.

POTEMKIN STAIRS. (Potomkinskaya Lestnitsa; Потёмкинская Лестница). The concrete statue of the **Duc de Richelieu,** the city's founder, stares down the Potemkin Stairs toward the port. Director Sergei Eisenstein used the stairs in his 1925 silent epic *Battleship Potemkin*, and the name stuck. In the film, the stairs were the original site of the visual cliché of a baby carriage careening wildly downhill. *(Above Morskoy Vokzal and the waterfront; a left off ul. Deribasovskaya.)*

PRIMORSKY BUL. This shady street is a prime people-watching spot and home to some of the finest facades in Odessa. The statue of **Aleksandr Pushkin** turns its back unceremoniously to the city hall, which refused to help fund its construction. On either side of the city hall are Odessa's two symbols: **Fortuna,** goddess of fate, and **Mercury,** god of trade. To the left is the long, white **Mother-in-Law Bridge,** built, they say, so an elderly lady could more easily visit her son-in-law, a high-ranking Communist official. More beautiful buildings lie farther down ul. Gogolskaya, including the **House of Scientists,** a club for the intelligentsia. *(Running parallel to the waterfront and ul. Primorskaya; above Morskoy Vokzal and the Potemkin Stairs.)*

UL. PUSHKINSKAYA. Quite possibly Odessa's most beautiful street, ul. Pushkinskaya's namesake poet lived here during his exile; his house is now a museum (see **Museums,** p. 766). The **Filarmoniya** (Филармония), built from 1894 to 1899, looks out sternly from the corner of ul. Pushkinskaya and ul. Rozy Lyuksemburg (Розы Люксембург). It's one of only two surviving opera houses constructed with special 19th-century acoustics (the other is Milan's La Scala). A bit farther down, the large, gray **Brodsky Synagogue** used to be the center of Odessa's large Jewish community; today it contains an archive. A left at the Filarmoniya leads toward **Park Shevchenko,** a vast stretch of greenery that separates the city from the sea; at the entrance stands a **monument** to the poet Taras Shevchenko (see **Literature & Arts,** p. 730); within you will find the familiar Soviet spike and eternal flame. *(From Primorsky bul., turn right onto ul. Pushkinskaya.)*

CAPITALISM. Commerce is what port towns are all about, and Odessa is no exception. First and foremost is the fabulous **Privoz market.** Several acres large, the market supplies just about everything you can imagine. Roughly speaking, fruit and vegetables are in the middle, milk products are in the northeast corner, with hardware and clothes around the edges. Keep a hand on your wallet—pickpocketing is rampant. *(Left of the train station on Privoznaya ul. Open daily 8am-6pm.)* Odessa's **Tsentralny Universalny Magazin** (ЦУМ), ul. Pushkinskaya 72, is another shopping heaven. *(Open daily 9am-7pm.)* Along ul. Rishelevskaya, **state department stores** sell everything from cloth to low-priced cassettes. The **Pasazh** (Пасаж), next to Hotel Pasazh, is a passageway leading from ul. Preobrazhenskaya to ul. Deribasovskaya. It is filled with expensive shops and fashion-conscious shoppers.

BEACHES. The farther from the center you go, the cleaner the beaches are, but none of them hold a candle to the ones in Crimea. Most are reachable either by public transportation or on foot. The shoreline from Park Shevchenko up to Arkadiya Beach makes a good path for an early-morning jog. **Arkadiya** (Аркадия), the city's the most popular on summer nights, is the last stop on trolley #5. Or, take bus #129. **Golden Shore** (Zolotoy Berig; Золотой Берег) is farther away, but boasts the most impressive sea and surf. Trams #17 and 18 stop here and at the **Chayka** (Чайка) and **Kurortny** (Курортный) beaches. **Chornomorka** (Чёрноморка), the beach of the proletariat, lies just outside a high-rise monstrosity of a neighborhood. Take tram #29 to the terminus and keep going. Tram #5 stops at **Lanzheron** (Ланжерон), the beach closest to central Odessa, and at **Vidrada** (Видрада), but you may want to walk the pleasant **forest road** leading into town through Park Shevchenko instead.

MUSEUMS

Museum of the Black Sea Fleet (Muzey morskovo flotu; Музей морского флота), ul. Lanzheronovskaya 6 (Ланжероновская; tel. 24 05 09), near the Opera and Ballet Theater. Boasts a unique collection of dozens of models of old ships in what was once a luxury club for 19th-century dandies. A few WWII cannons are included for good measure. Open M-W and F-Su 10am-3pm. 5hv, children 2hv. Russian tour 10hv.

Archaeological Museum (Arkheologichesky muzey; Археологический музей), Lanzheronovskaya 4. Houses artifacts found in the Black Sea region from ancient Greek and Roman times, including a noteable collection of gold coins stored in a basement vault. You'll have to convince the *babushka* to let you have a peek, since only large tour groups are "officially" admitted. Open Tu-Su 11am-5pm. 5hv.

Literature Museum (Literaturny muzey; Литературный Музей), Lanzheronovskaya 2 (tel. 22 32 13). A fascinating look at the city's rich intellectual and cultural heritage through its books, prints, and photos, with an emphasis on Pushkin and Gogol. The collection includes the famous letter from Vorontsov to the Tsar asking that Pushkin be sent out of Odessa "for his own development," because he "is getting the notion into his head that he's a great writer." Exhibits are labeled only in Russian. Open Tu-Su 10am-5pm. 6hv, students 2hv. Russian guide 8hv, English guide (when available) 25hv.

Pushkin Museum and Memorial (Literaturno-memorialny muzey Pushkina; Литературно-мемориальный музей Пушкина), ul. Pushkinskaya 13 (tel. 24 92 55). The 1821 building's noteworthy facade faces away from the sea to avoid salt-air damage; it was Pushkin's residence during his brief exile here from the St. Petersburg nightlife (see **Literature & Arts,** p. 730). Open daily 9am-4pm. 3hv, students 1hv.

ENTERTAINMENT

Ul. Deribasovskaya is pure entertainment, especially in Gorsad—the art hangout and bazaar. The **Teatr Opery i Baleta** (Opera and Ballet Theater; Театр Оперы и Балета), at the end of ul. Rishelevskaya, has shows nightly. Odessa's elite arrive in their most dashing attire. Sunday matinees begin at noon, and evening performances (W-Su) start at 6pm. Buy tickets a day in advance, or at least that morning, from the ticket office to the right of the theater. (Open M-F 10:30am-5pm, Sa-Su 10:30am-4pm. 15-25hv, US$3-35 when a major act comes to town.) **Zeleny Teatr**

(Green Theater; Зеленый Театр) performs in Park Shevchenko on summer weekends at 6pm. For tickets, go to the **Central Theater Office** (Центральная театральная касса), ul. Deribasovskaya 10. (Open daily 11am-5pm.) The **Filarmoniya ticket office** is in the Filarmoniya, Pushkinskaya 17. Schedules are as unpredicatable as the economy. (Open 11am-7pm. Season: Sept.-June. 5-15hv.)

NIGHTLIFE

Odessa, the party town of the former USSR, truly never sleeps. The restaurants, cafes, and bars on ul. Deribasovskaya hop all night with beer, vodka, and music ranging from Euro-techno to Slavic folk. The street is pure entertainment, especially near Gorsad, the local hangout for artists and newlyweds. For younger and more light-footed entertainment, discos around Arkadia (trolley #7 from the train station, #5 from pl. Grechskaya), such as bul. Frantszusky's **Cosmo, Rio,** and **Contiki,** fit the bill. (Drinks 5-7hv. Cover 15hv.)

Gambrinus (Гамбринус), Deribasovskaya 31 (tel. 22 51 51), at the intersection with ul. Zhukova (Жукова). The dark, spacious interior resembles a beer hall, with tables made of beer vats. Two old men play Slavic folk tunes on violins while you drink decent draft beer (0.5L 5-8hv) and munch on excellent snacks. A historical landmark that was the center of Odessa's cultural scene before the Revolution, it can still sustain hours of drunken literary talk. Open daily 10am-11pm.

Mick O'Neil's, Deribasovskaya 52. Odessa's elite gather here to get noticed as they talk on cell phones and drink imported beer (0.33L 8-10hv) or fancy fruit shakes (12hv). Mick's has gobbled up Odessa's night scene with its sparkling interior, satellite TV, decent food, and groovin' live music (8-11pm). But don't expect to run into any local students–this place is for foreigners and local *biznesmeni* only.

Kafe Bar (Кафе Бар), at Dvorets Sporta (Sports Palace; Дворец спорта) on pr. Shevchenko (Щевченко). A hip spot, packed even on weeknights. Its style may be getting a bit cramped by the two high-rises under construction on either side. Dance the night away in the parking lot with students and *mafiosi* alike. Open nightly 10pm-4am.

WESTERN UKRAINE (ЗАХОД УКРАЇНИ)

Clinging tenaciously to its Habsburg and Polish roots, Western Ukraine is trying to break free of Moscow's grip and strengthen its own identity. Led by its lovely and forgotten capital, Lviv, this part of the country has a language and culture distinct and independent from Russified Kiev—and the people are proud of it. Bouncing along country roads between welcoming Kamyanets-Podilsky, bustling Ivano-Frankivisk or restful Uzhhorod, you may just find yourself next to a *babushka* who has never met a Westerner, who depends on her cabbage crop for basic survival, and is happy to tell you all about it.

LVIV (ЛЬВІВ)

Dear Abby,

Divorced from Poland in 1945 after 600 years of ups and down, I just went through a breakup with the USSR, for whom I had cooked and slaved for over 45 years. I'm living with my mother now, old Kiev, but we don't even speak the same language! In spite of my age, I feel ready to be conquered by the world. My Polish half-sister, Kraków, tells me that living with tourists creates all sorts of ills, but I just want to be loved, admired, and remembered. My steeple-filled city center teems with energy that can't be found anywhere else in Ukraine, and, if I do say so myself, I'm fun! Why won't anyone enter my gates?

Worthy and waiting, Lviv.

UKRAINE

ORIENTATION

The center of town is **pl. Rynok** (Ринок), the old market square. Around it, a grid of streets forms the **Old Town,** where most of the sights are found. A few blocks back toward the train station, **pr. Svobody** (Свободи) runs from the Opera House to **pl. Mitskevycha** (Міцкевича). Tram #1 runs from the main train station to the Old Town's center, tram #6 to the north end of pr. Svobody. Tram #9 goes from the Old Town to the station. It's a 40min. walk. Unless otherwise stated, assume that English is not spoken anywhere.

PRACTICAL INFORMATION

Trains: pl. Vokzalna (Вокзальна; tel. 748 20 68). **Tickets** available at Intourist windows #23-25 on the 2nd floor. To: **Kiev** (11-16hr., 8 per day, *coupé* 40hv); **Odessa** (14hr., 3 per day, *coupé* 40hv); **Bratislava** (18hr., 1 per day, 265hv); **Budapest** (14hr., 1 per day, 211hv); **Przemyśl** (3½hr., 3 per day, *coupé* 42hv); **Kraków** (8hr., 2 per day, 8hv); **Warsaw** (13hr., 1 per day, 82hv); **Moscow** (29hr., 4 per day, *coupé* 130hv); and **Prague** (21hr., 1 per day, 383hv).

Buses: The **main station,** vul. Stryska (Стрийська; tel. 63 24 73), on the outskirts of town, has extensive regional service as well as service to Poland. From town, take trolley #5 or bus #71. From the station, bus #18 goes to the train station, where trams into town are frequent. To: **Przemyśl** (4hr., 14 per day, 23hv); **Kraków** (7-9hr., 1 per day, 57hv); and **Warsaw** (10hr., 4 per day, 57hv). Lviv also has a series of smaller, more regional stations. The one at vul. Khmelnytskoho 225 (tel. 52 04 89), can be reached by bus #4 from vul. Shevchenka. Buses to **Brest** (8hr., 2 per day, 20hv). There is a station with buses to **Zhovkva** at vul. Bazarna (Базарна; tel. 33 80 55). In general, buses run more frequently to regional destinations, but they are usually stopped at borders, the stations are harder to reach, and the trip is longer. For long-distance destinations, buy tickets a day in advance from **Avtokasa,** Teatralna 26 (Театральна; tel. 72 76 43). Open daily 9am-2pm and 3-7pm. Buy advance tickets to Poland at window #1; same-day at window #2.

Local Transportation: Buy tickets (0.30hv for **trams** and **trolleys,** 0.40-0.50hv for **buses**) on board from the conductor (not the driver). Controllers are vigilant and eager to slap freeloaders with a 5hv fine. Some kiosks sell a recent public transit **map.** Tram lines are marked in brown, trolley in red, and bus in blue. In the Old Town, pl. Halitska (Галицька) is a hub for buses.

Tourist Offices: Lviv Intourist (tel. 72 67 40; fax 97 12 87), in the Hotel George (see **Accommodations,** p. 769), plans guided **tours** (US$30 for 1-3 people; US$75 for a group of 6; US$30 for a car) in various languages, including English, and has a lot of info about the city. They are none too friendly to people who are not paying for a tour. Open M-F 9am-5pm. For other questions, the friendly staff at the service desk of the **Grand Hotel** speak English and assume you're staying there if you let them.

Currency Exchange: The exchange in **Hotel George** cashes **traveler's checks** and gives MC and Visa cash advances for a 3% commission. It's best to get US$ or DM and then exchange them at better rates elsewhere. Open daily 9am-5pm. **Avalbank** (Авальбанк), vul. Slovatskoho 1 (Словацького; tel. 97 18 17), in the post office, cashes AmEx/Thomas Cook traveler's checks and provides MC/Visa cash advances for a 4% commission. The Cirrus/MC/Visa **ATM** on the 1st floor of the post office charges a US$3 flat fee. Open M-F 9am-12:30pm and 2-5:30pm.

Western Union: X-Change Points, on the 2nd floor of the post office. Open M-F 9:30am-5pm, Sa 9:30am-2pm.

Luggage Storage: At the **Hotel George,** 1hv per bag per day. At the train station, 1.5hv.

English Bookstore: pl. Mitskevycha 8. Everything from Emily Brontë to Michael Crichton. Also sells a great city **map** for 2hv. Open M-F 10am-6pm, Sa 10am-4pm.

24hr. Pharmacy: Apteka #28 (Аптека), vul. Zelena 33 (Зелена; tel. 75 37 63).

Post Office: vul. Slovatskoho 1 (tel. 72 39 43), a block from Park Ivana Franka, to the right as you face the university. **Poste Restante** on the 2nd floor. Open M-F 8am-8pm, Sa 8am-6pm, Su 8am-2pm. **Postal code:** 290 000.

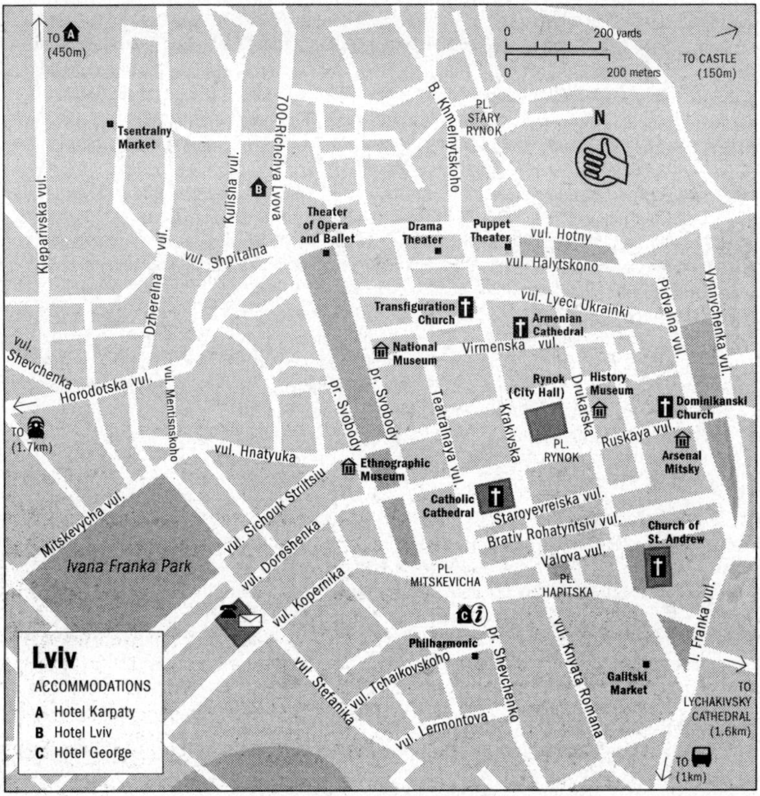

Internet Access: Internet Cafe, pr. Shevchenka 3 (tel. 72 36 30), across from Hotel George. Runs a Windows knock-off that crashes often. Open daily 10am-8pm. If this fails, take tram #9 to "Intehrator" (Інтегратор), and head to **Kseprokopii** (Ксепрокопії; tel. 97 02 51), vul. S. Banderi 35 (С. Бандери). Here you can find the real thing, but with a slow connection. Also try **Vavylon** (Вавилон), pr. Shevchenka 3 (tel. 72 36 30), which offers access for 7hv per hr.

Telephones: vul. Doroshenka 39 (Дорошенка), behind an unmarked door around the corner from the post office. For local and inter-city calls, buy *zhetony* (tokens; жетони; 0.20hv) at the telephone office or at kiosks. Pick up the phone, wait for the dial tone, and deposit your *zheton* only when the person answers. Intercity calls can be made only from the telephone office or from telephones that say "Міжмиськи" (*mizhmysky*; intercity). Open daily 7am-midnight. Sending **faxes** (fax 75 37 29) costs 14.22hv per page to the U.S. **Utel** cards available at Hotels George, Sputnyk, Lviv, and Karpaty, the telephone center, and the post office. **Phone code:** (0)322.

ACCOMMODATIONS

Responding to increasing tourist demand, Lviv has renovated some old Intourist haunts. A few years ago, the Grand Hotel opened its gleaming salons to the public, but not to the budget traveler (US$215 per room)—although you might want to exploit its downstairs bathroom. Prices are rising, but the city is still much more affordable than Kiev. Many student dorms open up in July and August—the best way to get in is to go through Hotel George's service bureau (call in advance).

Hotel George (Готель Жорж), pl. Mitskevycha 1 (tel. 72 59 52). Take tram #1 from the train station to "Дорошенка" *(Doroshenka).* Walk another block, and head right at the park. The hotel is the big pink building at the end. In the city's center, this beautiful turn-of-the-century hotel is both part of the scenery and the perfect place from which to see it. Friendly, English-speaking staff. Rooms in the recently restored building cost a measly 90% extra for foreigners (compared to the usual 300-600%). Large singles 73hv, with bath 302hv; doubles 83hv. Breakfast included.

Hotel Lviv, ul. 700-richna Lvova 7 (tel. 79 22 70), a few blocks north of pr. Svobody. Take tram #6 from the train station to the first stop after you see the Opera House on your right. Walk back to the Opera House and take a right onto Tsvova (Цвова). The hotel is in the second block on your left. A bit noisy, but it's in the middle of town. Spartan singles with TV 30hv, with bath 54hv; doubles 30hv, 84hv. Hot water available 6-11am and 6-11pm.

Hotel Karpaty (Карпати), vul. Kleparivska 30 (Клепарівська; tel. 33 34 27). From the Opera House, walk straight, bear right onto Shevchenka when the road splits, then take a right onto vul. Kleparivska. Continue straight past Tsentralny Rynok until you see the hotel on your right (20min.). Tram #4 from vul. 700-richna Lvova also stops near the hotel. Clean, agreeable rooms. Singles with bath 30hv; doubles 60hv. Hot water for 90min. in morning and afternoon and 1hr. at night. Bring your own toilet paper.

FOOD

Pl. Rynok is the restaurant and cafe center of Lviv; the most convenient (and expensive) **market** is **Galytsky Rynok** (Галицький Ринок), behind the flower stands across from St. Andrew's Church, a block from Hotel George. Fresh berries, honey, and vegetables line the path to the market. (Open in summer daily 7am-6pm.) A little farther out is the cheaper and bigger **Tsentralny Rynok** (Центральний), known as **Krakivsky Rynok** (Краківський) by locals. (Open M-Sa 6am-9pm.) There are several 24hr. grocery stores; **Mini Market,** vul. Doroshenka 6 (Дорошенка; tel. 72 35 44), is a block from the Grand Hotel.

RESTAURANTS

Lviv is full of quick eateries serving decent Ukrainian fast food (beef and potatoes, borscht, etc.). There are also several elegant-looking restaurants that serve cuisine of a jarringly lower caliber than their atmosphere suggests.

Mediviya (Медівія), vul. Krakivska 17 (tel. 72 91 41), not far from pl. Rynok. The wooden picnic tables in this small room are often packed. Fresh and cheap traditional food cooked by Ukrainians, for Ukrainians. Delicious *chanakhy* (bean soup with potatoes and meat; Чанахи) 1.94hv. Open daily 10am-10pm.

Pizza Pronto (Пицца Пронто), Horodetska 61 (Городецька), not far from pr. Svobody. Great pizza, but not pronto. Small, bubbling, cheesy pies 5-8hv, large 10-15hv; spaghetti 3hv. Open daily 10am-10pm.

Videnska Kavyariya (Віденська Кавярия), pl. Svobody 12 (tel. 72 20 21). Lviv's hottest place to have dessert, but they serve a great dinner as well. Sit outside in the wicker chairs and chat with expats. Entrees 6-12hv.

Akropolis (Акрополіс), vul. Shota Rystaveli 2 (tel. 76 20 82). Follow vul. I. Franka until it intersects with vul. Zelena (Зелена); Shota Rystaveli shoots off Zelena. This sparkling new establishment is a favorite among locals. Entrees 5-9hv. Point to what you want—it comes with loads of rice and salad. Open daily 11am-11pm.

CAFES

Lviv is a city of coffee and cafes; there are even songs about it. Most are meant for people having a cup o' joe with friends, and a few have their own particularly trendy atmosphere. If a cappuccino costs more than 0.80hv, you're paying Intourist prices.

Italiisky Dvoryk (Італійський Дворик), pl. Rynok 6. Here, Lviv's hippest sip coffee or juice among Renaissance statues and arches in the courtyard of a 16th-century Italian merchant's house. A museum upstairs contains his chicest belongings. Not Lviv's best coffee, but undoubtedly its best setting. Coffee 1.20hv. Open daily 10am-8pm.

Bernardinsky Dvorik (Бернардінський Дворік), behind and to the left of St. Andrew's Church. Lit by a fireplace in winter, the near darkness absorbs the low rumble of conversation. Coffee 1hv. Open daily noon-midnight.

Mandriki (Мандрікі), vul. Hnatyuka 4 (Гнатюка). Good coffee (0.80-0.90hv), folk carvings, and oak tables. Open daily 10am-4pm and 5-9pm.

SIGHTS

Lviv's historical sights are a classic example of the whole being greater than the sum of its parts. Together the city's museums, churches, and ancient tenement houses create a city as splendid as St. Petersburg or Prague; taken alone, the same buildings smack of provinciality. The best way to enjoy the city is to wander around the streets and poke your head into whatever looks worthwhile. If you are specifically interested in seeing churches, the best time is between 5 and 7pm, when doors open for the faithful.

OUTSIDE THE OLD TOWN

Before you venture into the heart of the city, a great way to introduce yourself to Lviv is to climb up to **High Castle Hill** (Vysoky Zamok; Высокий Замок), where the television tower now stands. Follow vul. Krivonoca (Кривоноса) from its intersection with Hotny and Halytskono. Go until you pass #39, then take a left down the long dirt road and begin to wind your way up around the hill counter-clockwise.

Back on vul. Lychakivska, head down vul. Mechnykova (Мечникова) to the white-washed chapel and **Lychakivsky Cemetery** (Lychakivsky Tsvyntar; Личаківський Цвинтар); tram #7 also stops right out front. Inside Lviv's most famous necropolis, the tombs of Polish nobles lie beside the simple graves of local residents. Hidden from the sun by a heaven of trees, Lychakivsky's paths provide a pleasant strolling ground. For the most instructive visit, follow Mechnykova down past the large empty space to the main gate. Upon entering, follow the path to the right to visit the graves of famous Ukrainian artists. On its left side, a hammer-armed Stakhanovite decorates the eternal bed of **Ivan Franko** (Іван Франко), a nationalist poet. Across the path from Franko sleeps **Lyudkevich** (Людквевич), Ukraine's favorite composer. A gorgeous man playing a stone lyre attempts to revive the golden voice of **Solomiya Kruzhelnytska** (Соломія Кружельницька), in whose honor Lviv holds its November opera festivals. Continuing on the main path, bearing left past the gymnast **Chukarin,** lies the sepulcher of artist **Volodymyr Ivasyuk** (Ивасюк), marked by the standing figure of a young hunk looking for inspiration. At his tomb, turn right off the alley and walk 100m to reach the rows of graves of Ukrainian, Polish, and foreign soldiers who died defending Lviv during 1918-19. The central arch hails them with a typical Latin motto: *Morti svnt vt liberi vivamvs*—"They died so we may live free." (Open daily 9am-9pm. 1hv.)

About 1km south of the city center is the splendidly manicured **Strysky Park** (Стрийський Парк), with swans, a greenhouse, and fountains. Vul. Ivana Franka courses south to vul. Stryska, which borders the garden.

OLD TOWN

The heart of the city is **pl. Rynok,** the historic market square surrounded by a collage of richly decorated merchant homes dating from the 16th to 18th centuries. The square gazes lovingly at the **town hall** (ratusha), a 19th-century addition. Its corners are guarded by statues of Diana, Venus, Neptune, and Cupid. Just beyond the gaze of trident-armed Neptune is pl. Katedralna (Катедральна), where the main attraction is the Polish **Catholic Cathedral** (Katolitsky Sobor; Католицкий собор). The huge, decorated columns and dark, apocalyptic frescoes make this one of Ukraine's grandest cathedrals. The church contains four altars along each nave and a ninth one to the right of the main altar, each worth a lengthy *tête-à-tête.* (Open M-Sa 6am-noon and 6-8pm, Su and holidays 6am-3pm and 5:30-8pm.) Next door stands the small, Renaissance **Boym's Chapel** (Kaplytsya Boimiv; Каплиця Боїмів), which is the only example of Lviv's religious architecture that's more a tourist attraction than a house of worship. The tiny one-room chapel was commissioned by a rich

Hungarian merchant, Boim, and contains the rotted skeletons of 14 members of his family. Gaze up at the ceiling for a head-spinning view of the dome's spiral decorations. Lacking noble origins, Boim bought himself the title of consul, which gave him the right to an "emblem;" it hangs in the upper left corner. (Open Tu-Sa 10am-5pm. 0.50hv, students 0.20hv.)

Head down Halitska (Галицька) and take a left by pl. Mitskevicha to find the stone-gray, 17th-century Bernardine Monastery, now the Greek Orthodox **Church of St. Andrew.** The massive **Assumption Church** (Uspenska Tserkva; Успенська Церква) is just up vul. Pidvalna (Підвальна); enter through the archway. Every icon was painted by a scholarly monk. The out-of-place main altar is a reminder of the Russian Orthodox church's brief spell under Greek Orthodox supervision. Next to the church, **Kornyakt's Tower** (Bashta Kornyakta; Башта Корнякта) hoists a bell 60m above ground.

Heading up vul. Federova, then left on vul. Virmenska, lands you at the barricaded **Armenian Cathedral** (Virmensky Sobor; Вірменський собор). It seems so out of place that one would never guess it has stood here since the 14th century. Down the hill, a passage runs from vul. Virmenska to vul. Lesy Ukrainky (Леси Українки) in the ecclesiatic back alleys between the church and the bishop's hearth. On vul. Lesy Ukrainky, a left steers you to **Transfiguration Church** (Preobrazhenska Tserkva; Преображенська церква). The polished interior is definitely worth a peek.

PROSPEKT SVOBODY

The dazzlingly complex exterior of the **Theater of Opera and Ballet** (Teatr Opery a Baletu; Театр Опери а Балету; see **Entertainment,** p. 773) dominating the main square is surpassed only by its interior's gilded sculptures. It opens onto a pedestrian mall that runs down the middle of pr. Svobody. Exiting the theater, a walk down the boulevard's right side leads past shops and hotels, lodged in the facades of old Polish apartments. On the left, behind pr. Svobody 24, is a **market** where local artists and craftsmen display their work and old *dedushki* try to sell their Soviet souvenirs; most of the "art" looks ready for export to seedy American motels. The promenade that runs through the center of the boulevard is popular for early-evening ice cream strolling and intense chess matches (try your luck, if you dare: the bet is usually 1hv per game). At the end of pr. Svobody, the **Mickiewicz statue** honors the Polish poet and patriot and serves as the site of concerts, heated political discussions, and the occasional Hare Krishna sing-along.

IVANA FRANKA PARK

From pr. Svobody head down Hnatyuka, then take a left on Sichovka Stritsiv to **Ivana Franka Park** (Park im. Ivana Franka; Парк ім. Ивана Франка), which faces the grand columned facade of **Lviv University.** Franka looks kindly down to the right on the students. Walk all the way uphill through the park to be rewarded by the ochre-walled, gold-studded **St. Yura's Cathedral** (Sobor sv. Yura; Собор св. Юра). The interior of this 18th-century wonder houses an elaborate, glistening altar. Outside, note the equestrian dragon-slayer Yura perched over the entrance. (Open daily 7am-1pm and 3-8pm.) Toward the train off vul. Horodetska is **St. Elizabeth's Cathedral.** Constructed by Poles when they first settled in Lviv, its spires purposefully reach higher than St. Yura's domes to assert the dominance of Polish Catholicism over Ukrainian Orthodoxy.

MUSEUMS

There are enough museums around Lviv to provide you with cocktail party fodder for a year; whether it's *good* fodder you'll need to decide for yourself.

National Museum (Natsionalny Muzey; Національний Музей), on pr. Svobody. Even the impressive front of this museum commands attention: part of the town's original city walls and gates still stand next to it. The main gallery offers two permanent exhibits and a rotating modern foreign art display. Several rooms of 14th- to 19th-century icons and two wings of excellent 19th- and 20th-century Ukrainian paintings. Open M-W 11am-5pm, Sa-Su noon-6pm. 1hv, students 0.50hv; students free Mondays.

Art-Cultural Center "Dzyha" (Kulturno-Mystetsky Tsentr "Dzyha"; Культурно-Мистетський Центр "Дзига"), vul. Virmenska 35, (tel. 72 74 20). Lviv's newest museum. Funky exhibitions of contemporary sculptures, paintings, photos, and prints. Concerts are held weekly, usually Saturday or Sunday; look for notices in the building. Friday is jazz night. Open daily 10am-7:30pm. Free.

History Museum (Istorychny Muzey; Історичний Музей), pl. Rynok #4, 6, and 24. The museum at pl. Rynok 4 recounts the history of Lviv during the World Wars. The adjoining **Italian Courtyard,** pl. Rynok, 6, presents military clothing, paintings, and other household treasures of the Italian *mascalzone* (rascals) who lived here in the 16th century. #24 has three floors of various medieval artifacts. Open Th-Tu 10am-5pm. Separate tickets for each exhibition, from 0.30-1hv.

Museum of Architecture (Shevchenkivsky Hay; Шевченківський Гай). Take tram #2 or 7 to Mechikova (Мечнікова), or walk along vul. Lychakivska to vul. Krupyarska and head all the way up the hill, bearing right at the top to reach the outdoor museum. Lying on a vast park, it hosts a collection of wooden houses from all around western Ukraine, one of which is now an active church. Open Tu-Su 11am-7pm. 0.60hv.

Mitsky Arsenal (Міцький арсенал), vul. Pidvalna 5 (Підвальна), wields iron examples of the many implements humans have employed to kill each other. Open Th-Tu 10am-5pm. 1hv, students 0.50hv; Russian tours 4hv, students 1.50hv.

Ethnographic Museum (Muzey Etnohrafii; Музей Этнографії), pr. Svobody #15. At the corner of vul. Hnatyuka. Harbors an exhibit of Ukrainian dress, archaeological artifacts, painted eggs, and embroidery. It's worth a look inside, if only for the fabulous marble staircase and lofty decorated ceilings. Open W-Su 10am-6pm. 0.50hv, students 0.20hv; tours 3hv, students 1.50hv; exhibitions 1hv.

ENTERTAINMENT

Pr. Svobody fills up after lunch with sexagenarians singing wartime and harvest tunes to accordion accompaniment. By 8pm, sounds of light jazz from sidewalk cafes fill the avenue, coffeehouses cloud up with smoke and reverberate with political discussion, and auditoriums echo with arias or tragic monologues. Only here, in Ukraine's cultural capital, can you feast on such fun for pennies, so don't get stuck in your sweet Hotel George digs.

Opera, experimental drama, cheap tickets, and an artistic population make Lviv's performance halls the second most frequented institution after cafes. Theaters post their schedules by the front entrance, although many host only irregular performances in the summer. Tickets range from 2 to 5hv, so it's the perfect time to snag that front-row seat. Purchase tickets at each theater's *kasa* or at the *teatralny kasy* (ticket windows; театральни каси), pr. Svobody 37. (open M-Sa 10am-1pm and 2:30-6pm).

Teatr Opery a Baletu (Театр Опери а Балету), pr. Svobody 1 (tel. 72 88 60). You don't have to love opera, and you don't even need a tux; you just have to go. Great space, great voices, great sets—a paradise in gilded Eden. Catch a Verdi or a Rossini from the front row for 5hv.

Philarmonia (Філармонія), vul. Tchaikovskoho 7 (tel. 75 21 01), around the corner from the George. Less frequent performances than the Opera, but with many renowned guest performers, usually from Kiev or Russia. Tickets 2-5hv.

Maria Zankovetskoi Ukrainian Theater (Ukrainsky Teatr Marii Zankovetskoi; Украïнский Театр iм. М. Заньковецькоï), Lyeci Ukrainki 1 (tel. 72 07 51). Famous throughout the land, this crumbling house of drama produces both classical and experimental Ukrainian plays.

Lvivsky Dukhovny Teatr "Voskresinnya" (Львівський Духовний Театр "Воскресінія"), pl. Hrihorenka 5 (Григоренка; tel. 74 13 00), at the end of vul. Hnatyuka, heading from the Ethnographic Museum on pr. Svobody. Voskresinnya presents 20th-century works—from Chekhov to Beckett—in Ukrainian. The theater's fame rests on the innovation of its shows.

NIGHTLIFE

After singing all day in the streets and buzzing up in the java houses, at night Lviv sits down in its squares and patios for yet another sing-along or final cup. For an evening free of partisan arias, stop for a shot of whatever at a club-cafe, swig some steins at Zoloty Kolos, or move to the groove at Vavylon. The closest **gay** life comes to being organized is the cruising area on pr. Svobody—from the Opera to the Shevchenko statue. Check for notices in the basement of the Puppet Theater.

Club-Cafe Lyalka (Клуб-Кафе Лялька), vul. Halytskoho 1 (Галицького), below the Teatr Lyalok (Puppet Theater). Downstairs, artsiness fights artfulness for supremacy. Shabbily dressed artfuls do shots while arguing with the sophisticated black-clad wine-sippers. A wall of posters advertises past and future concerts; speakers exude soft Italian rock or Australian pop; graffitied bedsheets hang from the ceiling. A little slow on weeknights, but the place to be when they turn the disco ball. Jazz on Wednesdays. Cover 5hv disco nights. 100mL wine 2hv, coffee 0.60hv. Open M-F 1-11pm, Sa-Su 11am until 1 or 2am.

Vavylon (Вавилон), pr. Shevchenka 3 (tel. 72 36 30), across from the George. Communicate with far-off lands in the **cyber cafe** while sipping cappuccino into the wee hours; debate with local hipsters in the bar while shooting *Stoli;* or practice your body language in the adjacent dance club—all under one roof for a 10hv cover. No cover for cyber cafe. Open daily 10am-2am.

Zoloty Kolos (Золотий Колос), vul. Kleparivska 18 (Клепарівська; tel. 33 04 89). The USSR's best brewery continues to bubble-up the ex-USSR's best beer. (Bottles 1.05hv.) Descend into the spacious, cobblestone-walled cellar to enjoy hops-n-malt (0.5L for 1.30hv). When *Zoloty Kolos* is unavailable, the weaker but equally tasty *Lvivske Pivo* foams. Open daily 10am-11pm.

Club-Cafe za Kulisamy (Клуб-Кафе за Кулісами), vul. Tchaikovshoho 7, on the 2nd floor of the Philharmonic. Entrance to the left, but not well marked. Everybody here knows each others' names, but not yours. Sounds of practicing Philharmonic artists leak in. Hard liquors and suds available, but they somehow seem out of place—it's java and Marlboro all the way. Beyond mellow. Coffee 0.70hv. Open daily noon-midnight.

NEAR LVIV: OLESKO (ОЛЕСЬКО)

The 14th-century **castle** (zamok) at Olesko, 70km from Lviv, has been destroyed repeatedly, yet still sits majestically atop a hill overlooking fields and more fields. There is nothing spectacular about the castle, but if you're in the mood for a day-trip, you'll have a great time (as long as you remember to bring lunch). A **museum** inside the castle holds 15th- to 18th-century wooden sculptures, icons, paintings, and battle tapestries. (Open Tu-Su 11am-5pm. 2hv; Ukrainian tours 10hv, students 5hv.) Even more interesting is the castle itself. In the cellar, you can see a split in the walls, one of the only signs left of the destruction caused by a 19th-century earthquake (some cracks were as large as 3m). The dim and damp walls of the cellar also hide an empty **treasury** and an old **well** that was 42m deep before the earthquake. Across from the museum, the 18th-century **Capuchin Church and Monastery** (Monastyr Ordena Kaputsyn; Монастирь Ордена Капуцинь) belongs to the castle museum, but is closed.

GETTING THERE. Buses arrive from both **Lviv's main station** and the station on vul. Khmelnytskoho (see **Lviv: Orientation & Practical Information,** p. 768). Once in Olesko, turn left from the bus station and head straight to the church; turn left, and go straight again. The 15min. walk leads right through the rooster-filled town. Six buses per day go back to Lviv (3hv); the last one is at 4:45pm. Hotel George (see **Lviv: Accommodations,** p. 770) offers excursions for a whopping US$50.

KAMYANETS-PODILSKY (КАМЯНЕЦЬ-ПОДІЛСКИЙ)

Cleaved by the Smotrych River Canyon and packed with once-grand churches, Kamyanets-Podilsky (ka-mya-NYETS po-DIL-skee) has all the geography of an attractive destination. What's more, this Soviet Salzburg is also the kind of undiscovered place where foreigners are still a novelty and the whole town turns out for a wedding. After the anonymous shuffle of Eastern European metropolises, personable Kamyanets-Podilsky is a welcome respite.

ORIENTATION & PRACTICAL INFORMATION

Kamyanets is separated into the **Old Town,** an island of cobblestoned streets and historic buildings in a gorge carved by the Smotrych River, and the **New Town,** a grid of boulevards where the majority of the town's business (i.e., lounging in cafes and drinking beer) takes place. **Bul. Knyaziv Koriatovychiv** (Князів Коріатовичів) runs right through the middle of the New Town, from the Old Town bridge to the market (ринок; *rynok*) and the bus station. For a city in the middle of Ukraine, Kamyanets-Podilsky is horrendously difficult to reach. When they're working, **buses** run to: **Chernivtsi** (hourly, 7am-8pm, 4.30hv) via **Khotyn** (1hv); **Lviv** (daily, 12hv); and **Kiev** (2 per day, 18.20hv). With your back to the bus station, a right leads down bul. Knyaziv Koriatovychiv into the center of town, while a left and then another left at the first intersection leads to the train station. **Trains** puff to **Kiev** (12hr., 2 per day, 14hv, *coupé* 22hv); and **Chernivtsi** (5½hr., departs 2:10am, 15hv, *coupé* 19hv), passing through Moldova; expect guards to demand a $20-30 "additional charge" at the border. To reach the center from the train station, take **bus #5** from vul. Hrushevska at the end of Chervonoarmiska vul. At its far end of **Pl. Saborna** (Саборна) is Hotel Ukraina (Україна); on the second floor, **Avitsenna-Transit Tourist Office** (Авіценна-Транзит; tel. 323 00) sells maps and brochures (3-4hv), and organizes excursions to Khotyn (English tour 10hv per person; open M-Sa 8am-10pm). From Hotel Ukraina, a left on vul. Lesy Ukrainky (Леси Українки) and then a right onto vul. Knyaziv Koriatovychiv crosses the **Smotrych River** (Смотрич) into the Old Town. On the edge of the market square **Bank Aval** (Аваль; tel./fax 318 40) exchanges cash and gives MC/Visa cash advances. (Open M-F 8:30-5:30.) The **post office** (open M-F 9am-6pm, Sa 9am-3pm) and **24-hour telephone bureau** sit near the Hotel Ukraina on pl. Saborna, but Utel is not available there. **Postal code:** 281 900. **Phone code:** (0)3849.

ACCOMMODATIONS & FOOD

Hotel Ukraina, vul. Lesi Ukrainky 32 (tel. 391 48), has a monopoly on the Kamyanets hotel business, but the prices are excellent, the service is friendly, and the rooms are clean. The restaurant next door can be noisy late at night. A cafe on the second floor serves breakfast (omelette, coffee, and bread 2hv) and dinner. (Singles 15hv; doubles 28hv, with bath 68hv.)

Locals frequent the **Restaurant Ukraina** for lively music and the legendary *myasa ukraina* (3.62hv): steak smothered in whipped egg, stir-fried mushrooms, onions and melted cheese. (Full meals 5-7hv.) In the Armenian marketplace in the Old Town, **Mriya's** (Мрія) serves the hungry traveler cabbage, pickles, and cutlets for less than 1hv apiece. (Open M-F 8am-7:30pm, Sa-Su 8am-4pm.) **Stara Fortetsya** (Стара Фортеця), bul. Skhidny 1 (Східний), occupies the building of a former synagogue. From the Old Town, turn left just after crossing the bridge onto a shady cobblestoned street and walk three minutes until the sign for the restaurant next to the defense tower. The smiling waiter will help you put together a more-than-filling meal (3.50-5hv) while you gaze out over the Smotrych canyon. Come night, this serene eatery transforms into a **disco.** (Restaurant open daily 11am-9pm; disco open daily 7pm-6am. Cover 1hv.) The real party, however, is back in New Town at **New York Club and Bar,** two blocks down vul. Ukraina from the hotel. Warm up with cognac shots (2.80hv) and a chaser of Slovakian beer (2.50hv) downstairs, then dance 'til dawn under the disco ball. (Opens at noon, disco closed M.)

SIGHTS

Kamyanets-Podilsky's Old Town is eerily quiet; at times it seems the German army pulled out a few hours ago, leaving only the goats to welcome the Russian advance.

This timeless quality enhances the beauty of the neighborhood's churches, squares, and stately old homes.

FORTRESS. The most famous of the town's aged structures, this fortification was originally built of wood in the 11th century and rebuilt in the 1400s, when its residents realized the difficulty of defending a wooden fortress against fire. Some stroll through what's left of the walls; others pick apples from the trees in the courtyard. The tower in the far right corner is scalable, but use caution on the steep and shoddy ladders. Behind the fortress walls is the "new castle," built in the 17th century. Its grass-covered walls provide the best views of the surrounding city and fields. *(Just over the Turkish bridge on the far end of the Old Town. Open M-F 9:30am-6pm, Sa-Su 9:30am-7pm; ethnographic museum in the castle walls closes 1hr. earlier. 1hv.)*

CATHEDRAL OF ST. PETER AND ST. PAUL. (Kafedralny Petropavlivsky Kostyol; Кафедральный Петропавліска костьол). Flanked by an 18th-century tower and surrounded by gardens, the cathedral dates from the 1400s. Although smaller than other churches, its elegantly understated interior has been recently restored, and now contains several delicate marble figures, including a shrine to the Virgin Mary on the right as you enter. Outside, a Muslim minaret, a remnant from the cathedral's stint as a Turkish mosque, is now topped with another Blessed Virgin—placed there by the Poles in 1756, perhaps to mock the Turks. The partition of Poland began shortly thereafter. *(Vul. Tatarska 20. Cross the bridge and take the second left onto vul. Tatarska.)*

OTHER CHURCHES. Behind Peter and Paul's minaret is a look-out point from which the castle (*zamok*) and blue-domed **Church of St. George** can be seen on the opposite bank. Just beyond the central park in the Old Town stands the 16th-century **Dominican monastery** (Dominikansky Kostyol; Домініканський костьол), still fortified against the infidels. An ill-timed fire gutted the complex toward the end of renovations, but its charred shell merits a look. Between the Armenian market and the Turkish bridge is the Roman Catholic **Trinitarian Church** (Trynitarsky Kostyol; Тринітарський костьол), with an inscription boldly proclaiming, "Everything will not be like this" ("Всё так не будет"). Prophetic, considering the current sorry condition of the church's red facade.

ON THE OLD POSTAL ROAD. A number of curious defense bastions stand watch over the Smotrych. At the north end of vul. Tatarska, past the Cathedral of St. Peter and St. Paul, **Old Postal Road** (Staropochtovy Uzviv; Старопочтовий узвив) drops down on the left past the **Stefan Batory Tower** (Bashta Stefana Batoriya; Башта Стефана Баторія)—named after a victorious Polish king. Its stone **Windy Gate** (Vitryana Brama; Вітряна брама) is famed for having knocked Peter the Great's hat from his head. The **Polish Gate** (Polska Brama; Польска брама) a bit farther on was used in tandem with the **Ruthenian Gate** (Ruska Brama; Руська Брама) to flood the canyon in the event of an attack.

IVANO-FRANKIVSK (ІВАНО-ФРАНКІВСЬК)

With its streets torn apart by sewer construction, students eager to practice their "beezness" English, and fledgling capitalists out to make a quick hryvnia, Ivano-Frankivsk is working hard to catch up with the West. The city has its work cut out for it, though, given its position in the middle of poor Ukraine, but that doesn't mean that budget travelers can't enjoy what progress has been made. The 19th-century architecture packed along the shady streets is worth a look.

ORIENTATION & PRACTICAL INFORMATION. Trains, pl. Pryvokzalna (Привокзальна; tel. 21 22 23 or 21 20 05), chug to: **Kiev** (14hr., 1 per day, 12hv, *coupé* 30hv); **Chernivtsi** (3½hr., 1 per day, 1hv); **Lviv** (3½hr., 5-6 per day, 8hv, *coupé* 13hv); **Odessa** (22hr., odd days, 27hv, *coupé* 41hv); **Brest, BEL** (17hr., even days, 33hv, *coupé* 53hv); **Minsk, BEL** (41hv, *coupé* 64hv); and **Przemyśl, POL** (6hr., 1 per day, 29hv). **Buses** (tel. 238 30), next door, go to: **Chernivtsi** (3½hr., 8 per day, 6.30hv);

Lviv (3½hr., 8 per day, 6hv); **Przemyśl, POL** (1 per day, 25hv); **Yaremcha** (2hr., 10 per day, 3hv); and **Prague** (1 per day, 132hv). **Local transportation** consists of buses and trolleybuses (0.20hv) and minivans (*mashruty*; 0.35hv) that travel bus routes. When you leave the front door of the train station, head for the far right corner of the square and take a left on **vul. Hrunvaldska** (Грунвалдська), which turns into **vul. Hrunshevskoho** (Грушевського). Walk down to **vul. Melnychuka** (Мельничука) and turn right onto it to reach **pl. Rynok** (пл. Ринок), the old city center; the new one at **pl. Vychevy** (Вичеви), is a few streets farther down. The main pedestrian street, **vul. Nezalezhnosti** (Незалежності), shoots off from here. The **tourist agency Auscoprut** (tel. 234 01; fax 314 02), in the posh **Hotel Roxolana,** vul. Hrunvaldska 7-9, is staffed with friendly English-speakers who sell old but useful **maps** (1hv) and offer guided tours of five destinations outside of town, including Yaremcha. They also have a train schedule and arrange tickets for a 20hv fee. (Open daily 9am-6pm.) For **currency exchange,** kiosks—which change dollars, marks, and hryvny—are your best bet. **Ukrainsky Bank** (tel. 55 97 01), on vul. Komarova (Комарова), will change Thomas Cook **traveler's checks** for a 4% commission and give MC/Visa **cash advances** for a 3% commission. (Open M-F 10am-2pm and 3-6pm.) **Luggage storage** is 7hv at the train station, or free for guests of most hotels. There is a **24hr. pharmacy,** Avitsena Pharm (Авіцена Фарм; tel. 311 91) at Hetmana Mazly 27a (Гетьмана Мазли). The **post office** is at vul. S. Striltsiv 13 (С.Стрільців). Go around the corner to the pl. Vichevy entrance for **Poste Restante** and to send packages. Address mail to: "Peter PIHOS, Ivano Frankivsk 284000, Поштамт до Запитанне."(Open M-F 8am-7pm, Sat 8am-6pm, Su 9am-5pm.) Across the square, **Tsentralny Mizhmisky Perehovorny Punkt** (Центральний Мижміський Переговорний Пункт), vul. Vitovskovo 2 (Витовьского; tel. 241 25 or 220 99), charges 16.57hv per minute for calls to Australia and New Zealand, 14.23hv to the U.S. and Canada, and 8.89hv to the U.K. (Open daily 7am-11pm.) **Utel phones** sit in Hotels Roxolana, Ukraina, Dnister, and Tourbaza Prykarpattya. **Postal code:** 284000. **Phone code:** 803422.

ACCOMMODATIONS & FOOD. Centrally located, the **Hotel Dnister** has no frills and, fortunately, no major problems, although you'll have to share the hot showers and clean bathrooms. (Singles 45hv; doubles 74hv. 120hv for your own shower and bath.) The nicest place in town, **Hotel Ukraina,** vul. Nezalezhnosti 40 (tel. 226 09), is centrally located and has rooms with bath and hot water, TV, phone, and fridge (Singles 54hv; doubles 88hv.) Fresher air and friendlier environs can be found at **Tourbaza Prykarpattya** (Турбаза Прикарпаття), vul. Hetmana Mazepy 140A (Гетмана Мазепи; tel. 302 98). It's on the outskirts of town, but reachable by bus #8 or 14 from the train station (15-20min.). In the summer of 1999, construction forced these buses to stop elsewhere: #14 at the corner of Hrunvaldska and #8 a block away at the corner of Lepkoho and Byor Donstova (Донцова). Get off after the lake comes into view. The rooms are fresh and clean with hot water and toilet. (Singles 50hv; doubles 80hv; bed in a quad 24hv.)

Though many restaurants lie near the center, few offer much more than Soviet standards. Grocery stores or the market may be your best bet. **Orelya** (Опеля), at vul. Hrushevska 20, is small but has some Western products. (Open 8am-9pm.) A slightly pricier 24hr. grocery is near Hotel Ukraina. The enormous, cheap **market** on vul. Dnistrovska (Дністровська) operates daily 8am-6pm, but Sundays are the main days. The only restaurant of note is the classy new **Restauran Slovan** (Слован), vul. Komarova 4 (Комарова; tel. 225 94), off vul. Nezalezhnosti and on the way from the train station to Dnister. (Turkey and steak fillets 6.50-8hv. Open daily 10am-midnight.) For breakfast or lunch, locals duck into **Pirizhkova** (Пріжікова) for *pierogi* (0.38-0.60hv; open M-F 8am-8pm, Sa-Su 9am-8pm).

SIGHTS & ENTERTAINMENT. Some of the oldest, richest, and most beautiful homes in Ivano-Frankivsk line **vul. Shevchenka.** Every aging house and street in the center has a story; if you know Ukrainian, you can read about them at the Auscoprut tourist office. Looking a bit like a lighthouse, the 1666 **town hall** (*ratusha*) beckons from the heart of pl. Rynok. It now houses the **Regional Museum**

(Kraeznavchy Muzey; Краезнавчий Музей) which exhibits the 800-year-old sarcophagus of King Yaroslav Osmomsyl. Local paintings and old furniture figure prominently in the temporary exhibitions. (Open Tu-Su 10am-5:30pm. 3hv, students 1hv.) A plaque on the corner of the *ratusha* commemorates the life of Alexei Dovbusha's friend and fellow conspirator, Vasyl Bayurok (Васил Баюрок; see **Near Ivano-Frankivsk: Yaremcha,** p. 778), who was killed here by Polish landlords. Around the corner, the **State Art Museum** (Derzhavny Khudozhny Muzey; Державний Художний Музей) resides in a Ukrainian Greek Catholic Church. The museum displays the chronological development of Galician art, focusing on icons from the 16th through 19th centuries. Ancient books, paintings, and sculptures also line the walls. (Open Su-Th 10am-6pm. 0.50hv, students 0.20hv.) At the other end of the same square stands an impressive **Greek Catholic church** rich with icons. One of the few holy places to remain open during the Soviet era, it was converted to Russian Orthodoxy in 1955 and didn't return to its Greek Catholic roots until 1990. Back on vul. Melnychka you'll find the modern and imposing government building. The two statues holding traditional Ukrainian instruments symbolizes the relationship between local and state government, with the smaller part of the central shaft representing the local government, and the larger part standing for Mother Ukraine. Although they stand in harmony, it's clear who apportions the regional funding. Farther out of the center, behind the theater, lies the **Shevchenka park,** formerly a cemetery. Some graves were transplanted during its construction, but many, particularly those belonging to Jews, were destroyed.

When you're lucky, intricate rugs, embroidered clothing, carved wooden boxes, and other handicrafts can be found at the **flea market** (bazar; базар), but mostly it's just a good place to stock up on soap. Don't be afraid to bargain. Surrounding towns sell similar goods at similar (or better) prices. (Open daily about 8am-6pm.)

Ivano-Frankivsk gets its evening entertainment May through July at the **Oblasny Muzichno-Dramatychny Teatr** (Обласний Музічно-Драматічний Театр), vul. Nezalezhnosti 42 (tickets 1-3hv), and **Filharmonia** (Філармонія), vul. Lesya Kurbasa 3 (Леся Курбаса; tickets 5-20hv). Most other entertainment ends early. University students staff **Cafe Maestro** (Маэстро), vul. Vahilevycha 8 (Вагилевича), off vul. Nezalezhnosti, and their friends all join them for beers there. A rattling TV, crowded tables, and hot-burning lights enliven this mellow basement bar. (Bottled beer 3-4hv. Open 11am-midnight.) An outdoor dance floor and cheap beer make **Kafe Pid Lylykom** (Під Лиликом), vul. Shevchenka 12, a rowdy summertime favorite with students and artists (Cappucino 1hv, 0.5L *Obolon* 1hv. Open daily 10am-11pm.)

UZHHOROD (УЖГОРОД)

Uzhhorod may not be the busiest of Trans-Carpathian border towns, but that makes it an ideal rest stop for travelers heading north or south. 800 years of Austro-Hungarian rule has left a pleasant (if unspectacular) downtown where the most popular pastime is watching the river roll by. Although the town did not escape Socialist urban planning untouched, winding cobblestone streets lend it an aura more Central European than Soviet. Don't go out of your way to find Uzhhorod, but if you are passing through, the banks of the Uzh are a perfect place to unwind.

ORIENTATION & PRACTICAL INFORMATION. Uzhhorod straddles the **Uzh** (Уж) River. The **train** and **bus stations** are both on the south side. To reach the center of town, take a right out of the train station and head down vul. Pidhradska two blocks to vul. Mukachivska. Take a left here, and head through the square at the end of the street. Take a final right and cross the pedestrian bridge. **Trains** run to: **Budapest** (5hr., 1 per day, 150hv) and **Prague** (14hr., 1 per day, 300hv). Domestic trains run to: **Kiev** (18hr., 2 per day, 16hv, *coupé* 37hv); **Lviv** (7hr. or overnight, 3 per day, 8.10hv, *coupé* 16hv); and **Chernivtsi** (12hr., 1 per day, 10.15hv, *coupé* 15.50hv). **Buses** rumble to: **Lviv** (7hr., 2 per day, 19hv); **Ivano-Frankivsk** (9hr., 2 per day, 13hv); **Bratislava** (2 per day, 67hv); and **Prague** (1 per day, 101hv). Many **buses** (1hr., 2.23hv)

THE ARTIFICIAL FAMINE In 1930, the first of the USSR's five-year plans collectivized agriculture and set state quotas for agricultural production. For most Russian farmers, who had long practiced communal farming, this mandate changed their work habits little. In Ukraine, however the policies were met with fierce opposition, as farmers destroyed their livestock in protest. Stalin, in order to break the resistence, raised grain quotas for the Crimea, the Caucasus, the lower Volga, and part of Belarus to impossible levels, leaving the peasants nothing of their labors. Exit visas for the region prohibited, and taking from the harvest before the state had had its "share" was punishable by death. The effects were devastating: the most conservative estimates put the deathtoll from starvation winter 1932-summer 1933 and 4.8million, not including the atrocities committed by the thousands of troops sent to enforce collectivization. Stalin himself confessed to "ten of millions" of deaths in a conversation with Sir Winston Churchill in August 1942. Historians, pouring over what Soviet records they could find, put the official number at 6-8 million, comprable to the horrors of the Holocaust that followed a decade later and whose shadow has tragically obscured the suffering of Ukrainian people from the Western consciousness for decades.

and trains (2hr., 3.50hv) run daily to **Mukachiv,** where there are additional international connections. International train tickets can be bought at the **Zaliznichni Kvytkovi Kasa** (Залізнічні Квиткові Каса), vul. Lva Tolstoha 33 (open daily 8am-5pm), but for non-Uzhhorod routes, call **Intourist** (tel. 938 29 58). **Luggage storage** (2hv) can be found in the building just to the right of the train station as you exit. Near the pedestrian bridge, the **Ukraine Export-Import Bank,** pl. Petefi, 19 (Петефі; tel. 122 62), will cash **traveler's checks** for a 2% commission. (Open M-Th 9am-12:45pm and 2-4pm, F 9am-12:45pm and 2-3pm.) Take an immediate left after the bridge and head down to Hotel Zakarpattya, nab. Nezalezhnosti 6 (Незалежності) for **Utel phones.** (Calls to the U.K. 5.95hv per min.; U.S. 9.48hv per min.) Around the corner from the hotel is the **post office**. (Open M-F 7am-6pm, Sa 7am-5pm.) Uzhhorod's pride and joy, the **X-Change Point,** is on the 2nd floor, and offers **Western Union** services, cashes **traveler's checks,** and gives MC/Visa cash advances for a 5% commission. (Open M-F 9am-5pm, Sa 10am-1pm). **Postal code:** 294 000. **Phone code:** (0)3122.

ACCOMMODATIONS & FOOD. It's a 10min. hike from the train station, but **Turbaza Svitanok** (Турбаза Світанок), vul. Koshytska 30 (Кошицька; tel. 343 09), is ideal for the budget traveler. From the pedestrian bridge, take a left at the Hotel Koruna, followed by a right and another left. Follow this street as it bears right and uphill into Zhulanatska (Жуланацька). Take a left at the next major intersection and go straight until you come to vul. Sobranetska (Собранецька). Take a right and walk 5min. uphill. Not only will they lodge and feed you, but this is the main **tourist office** for treks into the Carpathians. Ask for a brochure with the names and locations of all the other *turbazi* in the Ukrainian Carpathians. (Singles 16.80hv; doubles 33.60hv; bed in a double with shower 24hv. Sporadic hot water.) The **cafeteria** across the street could put a Ukrainian grandmother to shame. (Meals 1-2hv. Open 8:30-9:30am, 1:30-3pm, and 6:30-8pm.) **Cafe Mala Rafanda** (Мала Рафанда), vul. Rakotsi 24 (Ракоці), offers a departure from the standard Ukrainian fare. Popular with the younger crowd, Mala serves *pelmeni* (2hv) and a luscious chocolate dessert (0.75hv). It's also a small **grocery** store selling cereal and other snacks. (Open daily 6:30am-10pm.)

SIGHTS & ENTERTAINMENT. Uzhhorod's three main tourist attractions are found next to one another, making for painless sightseeing for the weary traveler. To reach the majestic **Kafedralny Cathedral** (Kafedralny Sobor; Кафедральний собор), take a right from the base of the pedestrian bridge facing the Hotel Koruna. At the Philharmonia building take a left up the stairs. Come out of the alley and head diagnonally to your left; the cathedral will appear in front of you. Follow the road in front of the cathedral to its end to reach a small **castle** (*zamok;* замок) featuring some statues, a museum, and stunning views of the nearby foothills. The castle joined the predictably unsuccessful 1704 Trans-Carpathian revolt against the Habsburgs. The extensive museum has exhibits on traditional Carpathian clothing and natural history with a diorama of big, ugly bears. (Open Tu-Su 9am-5pm. 0.80hv.) Across the way, the **Folk Architecture and Life Museum** (Muzey Narodnoi Arkhitektury i Pobutu; Музей Народної Архітектури і Побуту), an open-air display at vul. Kapitulna 33 and 33a (Капітульна), consists of a dozen original wood and stone huts typical of the region, and a wooden church built without nails. (Open W-M 9am-5pm. 1hv, students 0.50hv.)

For nightlife, try the graffiti-plastered **Cafe Teraca** at 22 Koshytska, down the street from Svitanock. In the summer, the party is on the roof deck. (Open daily 10am-1am; disco F 8pm-2am, Sa 8pm-5am.) Also check out **Bar on the Uzh** (Бар Над Ужем) for an *Obolon* (1.60hv), or to contemplate the river. Or, dance downstairs in the evening. (Open daily 8am-1am.)

GATEWAY CITIES

BERLIN, GERMANY

US\$1 = DM1.85 (DEUTSCHMARKS)	**DM1 = US\$0.54**
CDN\$1 = DM1.25	**DM1 = CDN\$0.80**
UK£1 = DM3.02	**DM1 = UK£0.33**
IR£1 = DM2.48	**DM1 = IR£0.40**
AUS\$1 = DM1.21	**DM1 = AUS\$0.83**
NZ\$1 = DM0.90	**DM1 = NZ\$1.02**
SAR1 = DM0.30	**DM1 = SAR3.49**

PHONE CODES Country code: **49.** International dialing prefix: **00.**

What has always made Berlin remarkable is its ability to flourish in times of adversity. Raised in the shadow of global conflict, post-WWII Berliners responded with a storm of cultural activity and the type of free-for-all nightlife you might expect from a population with its back against a Wall. The fall of the physical and psychological division between East and West in 1989 symbolized the end of the Cold War, and Berlin was officially reunited to widespread celebration on October 3, 1990. But the task of uniting Berlin's twin cities has proven no easier than that of stitching together both halves of the country; it seems that Eastern and Western Berliners don't really like each other as much as they once imagined they would. But as Karl Zuckmayer once wrote, "Berlin tasted of the future, and for that one happily accepted the dirt and the coldness as part of the bargain."

! Although Berlin is by far the most tolerant city in Germany, economic chaos has unleashed a new wave of right-wing extremism, particularly in the outer boroughs of Eastern Berlin. While it's unlikely that you'll encounter neo-Nazi skinheads, it is important for people of color as well as gays and lesbians to take precautions when traveling in suburban East Berlin or on the S-Bahn late at night.

GETTING THERE & GETTING AROUND

Airplanes: Tel. (0180) 500 01 86 for all airports. **Flughafen Tegel** is Western Berlin's main airport. Take express bus X9 from Bahnhof Zoo, bus 109 from U7: Jakob-Kaiser-Platz, or bus 128 from U6: Kurt-Schumacher-Platz. **Flughafen Tempelhof** handles domestic and European flights. U6: Platz der Luftbrücke. **Flughafen Schönefeld,** southeast of Berlin, handles intercontinental flights and those to the former USSR. Take S9 or 45 to Flughafen Berlin Schönefeld, or bus 171 from U7: Rudow.

Trains: Tel. (0180) 599 66 33. Most trains arrive at both **Zoologischer Garten (Bahnhof Zoo)** in the West and **Ostbahnhof** in the East, although some from the former GDR only stop at the latter. Many connect to **Schönefeld** airport. To: **Prague** (5hr., 4 per day, DM127); **Warsaw** (6hr., 4 per day, DM49); and **Kraków** (10½hr., 4 per day, DM51).

Buses: ZOB (Central Bus Station; tel. 301 80 28), by the *Funkturm* near Kaiserdamm. U2: Kaiserdamm or S4, 45, or 46: Witzleben. Buses are often cheaper than trains.

Hitchhiking: *Let's Go* does not recommend hitchhiking. It's illegal to hitch at rest stops or on the highway. Those heading west and south take bus 211 to the Autobahn entrance ramp from S1, 7: Wannsee. Those heading north walk 50m to the bridge on the right from S25: Hennigsdorf. **Mitfahrzentralen: City Netz,** Joachimstaler Str. 17 (tel. 194 44), arranges **ride-sharing.** U9, 15: Kurfürstendamm. Open M-F 9am-8pm, Sa-Su 9am-7pm.

Local Transportation: BVG (Berliner Verkehrsbetriebe; tel. 194 49), in the bus parking lot outside Bahnhof Zoo (tel. 25 62 25 62). While it is impossible to tour Berlin on foot, the extensive **bus, Straßenbahn** (streetcar), **U-Bahn** (subway), and **S-Bahn** (surface rail) systems are extensive and efficient. Berlin is divided into 3 transit zones: **Zone A** (downtown Berlin); **Zone B** (almost everywhere else); and **Zone C** (outlying areas including Potsdam and Oranienburg). The *Liniennetz* map is free at any tourist office or subway station. U- and S-Bahn lines generally do not run 1-4am, although most S-Bahn lines run every hr. on weekend nights and the U9 and 12 run all night F-Sa. **Night buses** (designated "N") run every 20-30min.; pick up the free *Nachtliniennetz* map at the BVG. A single **ticket** (*Langstrecke* AB or BC DM3.90; or *Ganzstrecke* ABC DM4.20) is good for 2hr., but passes are usually better values. A **Tageskarte** (AB DM7.80, ABC DM8.50) is valid until 3am the next day. A **Gruppentageskarte** (AB DM20, ABC DM22.50) allows up to 5 people to travel together on the same ticket. The **WelcomeCard** (DM29) is valid on all lines for 72hr. The **7-Tage-Karte** (AB DM40, ABC DM48) is good for 7 days of travel. Buy tickets from *Automaten* (machines), bus drivers, or ticket windows in the U- and S-Bahn stations. Cancel your ticket in the **validation box** marked *"hier entwerten"* before boarding, or face a steep fine (DM60).

Taxis: Tel. 26 10 26, 21 02 02, or 690 22. Call at least 15min. in advance. Women may request a female driver. Trips within the city usually cost less than DM20.

Bike Rental: Hackescher Markt Fahrradstation, downstairs at S3, 5, 7, 9, 75: Hackescher Markt. Also try the red trailer off the **Lustgarten.** DM5 per day. Same S-Bahn stop.

GATEWAY CITIES

ORIENTATION

Berlin is an immense conglomeration (eight times the size of Paris) of two once-separate cities: the former East, which contains most of Berlin's landmarks, historic sites, and cookie-cutter concrete socialist architectural monsters, and the former West, which functioned for decades as an isolated Allied protectorate.

The commercial heart of the united city lies in Western Berlin southwest of the **Tiergarten,** centered around **Bahnhof Zoo** and **Kurfürstendamm (Ku'damm).** Southeast of Ku'damm, **Schöneberg** is the nexus of the city's gay and lesbian community. North of Ku'damm, **Charlottenburg** is home to cafes, restaurants, and *pensionen.* **Straße des 17. Juni** runs east from Charlottenburg through the Tiergarten to the triumphant **Brandenburg Gate** on the other side, opening onto **Unter den Linden,** Berlin's most famous boulevard. The broad, tree-lined throughway cuts through **Mitte** and empties into **Alexanderplatz,** the commercial center of Eastern Berlin. The west-east Spree River splits between Mitte and Alexanderpl., forming the **Museumsinsel** (Museum Island), Eastern Berlin's cultural epicenter. Heading south from the Brandenburg Gate and the **Reichstag,** Ebertstraße runs haphazardly through construction sites to **Potsdamer Platz.** Southeast of Potsdamer Pl. lies **Kreuzberg,** home to radical leftists, Turks, punks, and homosexuals. Northeast of the city center, **Prenzlauer Berg,** a former working-class-suburb-turned-squatter's-paradise, rumbles with as-yet-unrestored pre-war structures and sublime cafes. Southeast of Mitte, **Friedrichshain** is emerging as the center of Berlin's counterculture.

For visits of more than a few days, the blue-and-yellow **Falk Plan** (DM11) can be useful. Dozens of streets and subway stations in Eastern Berlin have been renamed in a purge only recently completed; be sure your map is up-to-date.

PRACTICAL INFORMATION

TOURIST & FINANCIAL SERVICES

Tourist Offices: www.berlin.de. Most tourist offices sell city maps (DM1) and book same-day hotel rooms (from DM50, plus DM5 fee). **Euraide** is in Bahnhof Zoo, to the left and down the passage on your right as you face the *Reisezentrum.* Open daily 8am-noon and 1-6pm.

Tours: Berlin Walks (tel. 301 91 94) offers a range of English-language walking tours, including **Infamous Third Reich Sites, Jewish Life in Berlin,** and the **Discover Berlin Walk** (2-3hr.). Tours depart at 10am from the taxi stand in front of Bahnhof Zoo; Discover Berlin Walk in summer also 2:30pm. All tours DM15. **Insider Tour** provides a thorough

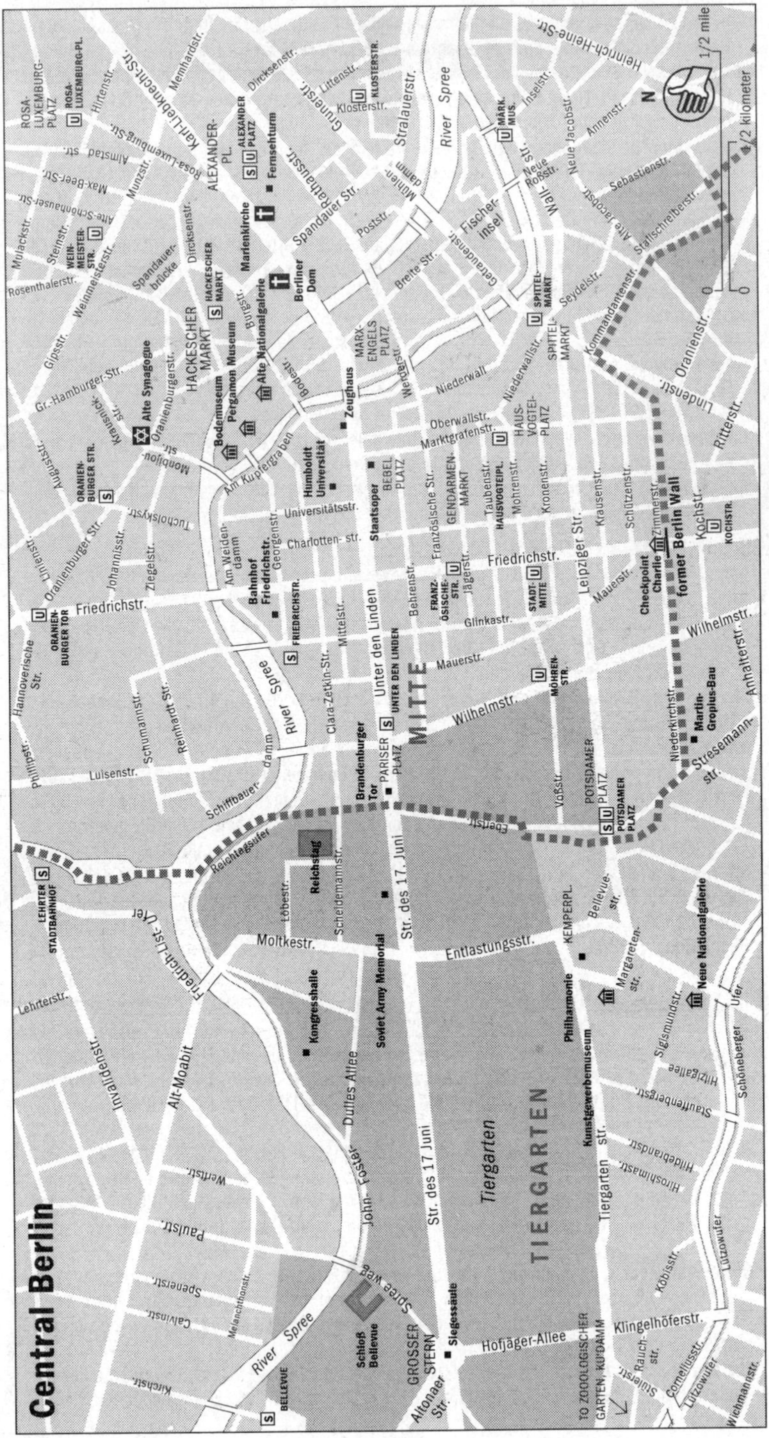
Central Berlin
TIERGARTEN
Tiergarten
MITTE
River Spree
Reichstag
Brandenburger Tor
PARISER PLATZ
Unter den Linden
Str. des 17. Juni
Siegessäule
GROSSER STERN
Schloß Bellevue
Kongresshalle
Soviet Army Memorial
Philharmonie
Kunstgewerbemuseum
Neue Nationalgalerie
Martin-Gropius-Bau
Checkpoint Charlie
former Berlin Wall
POTSDAMER PLATZ
LEIPZIGER STR.
Friedrichstr.
Bahnhof Friedrichstr.
Staatsoper
Humboldt Universität
Zeughaus
Alte Nationalgalerie
Pergamon Museum
Bodemuseum
Berliner Dom
Marienkirche
Fernsehturm
Alte Synagogue
ALEXANDER-PL.
HACKESCHER MARKT
GENDARMEN-MARKT
BEBEL PLATZ
MARX-ENGELS PLATZ
SPITTEL-MARKT
HAUS-VOGTEI-PLATZ
KEMPERPL.
Fischer-insel
LEHRTER STADTBAHNHOF
TO ZOOLOGISCHER GARTEN, KU'DAMM
Moltkestr.
Entlastungsstr.
Hofjäger-Allee
Alt-Moabit
Invalidenstr.
John-Foster-Dulles Allee
Wilhelmstr.
Stresemann-str.
Kochstr.
Oranienstr.
Lindenstr.
1/2 mile
1/2 kilometer
N

historical narrative and hits all the major sights (3½hr.). Departs from the McDonald's by Bahnhof Zoo Mar.-Nov. daily at 10am and 2:30pm. DM15.

Budget Travel: STA, Goethestr. 73 (tel. 311 09 50). U2: Ernst-Reuter-Platz. Open M-W and F 10am-6pm, Th 10am-8pm. **Kilroy Travels,** Hardenbergstr. 9 (tel. 313 04 66), 2 blocks northwest of Bahnhof Zoo. Open M-F 10am-6pm, Sa 11am-1pm.

Embassies: The locations of embassies remain in flux; for the most up-to-date info, call 20 18 60. **Australia,** Friedrichstr. 200 (tel. 880 08 80). U2, 6: Stadtmitte. Open M-F 9am-noon. **Canada,** Friedrichstr. 95 (tel. 20 31 20; fax 20 31 25 90), on the 12th fl. of the International Trade Center. S1, 2, 3, 5, 7, 9, 75, or U6: Friedrichstr. Open M-F 8:30am-12:30pm and 1:30-5pm. **Ireland,** Ernst-Reuter-Platz 10 (tel. 34 80 08 22; fax 34 80 08 63). U2: Ernst-Reuter-Platz. Open M-F 10am-1pm. **New Zealand,** Friedrichstr. 60. U6: Oranienburger Tor. **South Africa,** Douglasstr. 9 (tel. 82 50 11; fax 826 65 43). S7: Grunewald. Open M-F 9am-noon. **U.K.,** Unter den Linden 32-34 (tel. 20 18 40; fax 20 18 41 58). S1, 2, 3, 5, 7, 9, 25, 75, or U6: Friedrichstr. Open M-F 8:30am-5pm. **U.S. Citizens Service,** Clayallee 170 (tel. 832 92 33; fax 831 49 26). U1: Oskar-Helene-Heim. Open M-F 8:30am-noon. **U.S.** (consulate), Neustädtische Kirchstr. 4-5 (tel. 238 51 74; fax 238 62 90). S1, 2, 3, 5, 7, 9, 25, 75, or U6: Friedrichstr.

Currency Exchange: Wechselstube, Joachimstaler Str. 1-3, near Bahnhof Zoo. Good rates and no commission. Open M-F 8am-8pm, Sa 9am-3pm.

American Express: Uhlandstr. 173 (tel. 88 45 88 21). U15: Uhlandstr. Mail held. No commission on AmEx traveler's checks. Open M-F 9am-5:30pm, Sa 9am-noon.

GATEWAY CITIES

EMERGENCY & COMMUNICATIONS

Emergency: Police, tel. 110. Station at Platz der Luftbrücke 6. **Ambulance** and **fire,** tel. 112.

Crisis Lines: English spoken at most crisis lines. **American Hotline,** tel. (0177) 814 15 10. Crisis and referral service. **Sexual Assault Hotline,** tel. 251 28 28. Open Tu, Th 6-9pm, Su noon-2pm. **Schwules Überfall** (gay bashing), tel. 216 33 36. Hotline and legal help. Open daily 6-9pm.

Pharmacies: Europa-Apotheke, Tauentzienstr. 9-12 (tel. 261 41 42), near Bahnhof Zoo. Open M-F 9am-8pm, Sa 9am-4pm. For info about **late-night pharmacies,** call 011 89.

Medical Assistance: The American and British Embassies have a list of English-speaking doctors. **Emergency Doctor** (tel. 31 00 31) and **Emergency Dentist** (tel. 89 00 43 33).

Post Office: Budapester Str. 42, opposite the Europa-Center near Bahnhof Zoo. Address mail to be held: *Postlagernde Briefe* für Jordan KNIGHT, Postamt in der Budapester Str. 42, **10787** Berlin, Germany. Open M-Sa 8am-midnight, Su 10am-midnight.

Internet Access: Alpha, Dunckerstr. 72 (tel. 447 90 67), in Prenzlauer Berg. U2: Eberswalder Str. DM12 per hr. Open daily 3pm-midnight. **Cyberb@r,** Joachimstaler Str. 5-6, near Bahnhof Zoo on the 2nd floor of Karstadt Sport department store. DM5 per 30min.

Phone code: (0)30.

ACCOMMODATIONS

Same-day accommodations aren't impossible to find even in summer, although, as always, it's best to call ahead. If arriving on a weekend or during the **Love Parade** (in mid-July), book ahead. For DM5, **tourist offices** find rooms in hostels, *Pensionen*, and hotels, but be prepared to pay DM70 for singles, DM100 for doubles.

Circus, Rosa-Luxemburg-Str. 39-41 (tel. 28 39 14 33; fax 28 39 14 84; email circus@mind.de), near Alexanderpl. U2: Rosa-Luxemburg-Platz. A heroic effort at hostel hipness, with cheap internet and a disco ball in the lobby. Sheets DM3. Bikes DM12 per day. Reserve ahead and reconfirm a day before. 5- to 6-bed dorms DM25-35; 4-bed DM27; 3-bed DM30; 2-bed DM35; singles DM45.

Clubhouse Hostel, Johannisstr. 2 (tel. 28 09 79 79). S1, 2, or 25: Oranienburger Str., or U6: Oranienburger Tor. Great location in the center of the Oranienburger Str. club and bar scene. Breakfast DM5. Internet DM1 per 5min. Call 2-3 days ahead. 8- to 10-bed dorms DM25; 5- to 7-bed DM30; 2-bed DM40.

The Backpacker/Mitte, Chausseestr. 102 (tel. 262 51 40; fax 28 39 09 35; email backpacker@snafu.de; www.backpacker.de). U6: Zinnowitzer Str. An English-speaking haven filled with whirlwind-tourers. Eager staff with tips on sightseeing and nightlife. Sheets DM5. Laundry DM5. Bikes DM10-12 per day. Reception 7am-10pm. 5- to 6-bed dorms DM25-29; 4-bed DM31; 3-bed DM33; 2-bed DM38.

Pension Berolina, Stuttgarter Pl. 17 (tel. 32 70 90 72; fax 32 70 90 73). S3, 5, 7, 9, 75: Charlottenburg or U7: Wilmersdorfer Str. Simple, spartan rooms, but the prices get 2 thumbs up. Shared bathrooms. Breakfast DM8. Reservations recommended. Singles DM50; doubles DM60; triples DM70; quads DM80; quints DM90.

Hotel-Pension Cortina, Kantstr. 140 (tel. 313 90 59; fax 31 73 96). S3, 5, 7, 9, or 75: Savignyplatz. Bright, convenient, and hospitable. Breakfast included. Dorms DM35-60; singles DM60-90; doubles DM90-150.

FOOD

The most typical Berlin food is Turkish, and every street has its own Turkish *Imbiß* or restaurant. The *Döner Kebab*, a lamb/salad sandwich, has cornered the fast-food market, with falafel running a close second (each DM3-5). The leisurely breakfast is a gloriously civilized institution in Berlin cafes, often served well into the afternoon. **Aldi, Plus, Edeka,** and **Penny Markt** are the cheapest supermarket chains; most are open Monday to Friday 9am to 6pm and Saturday 9am to 4pm, although some are open as late as 8pm on weekdays. At Bahnhof Zoo, **Ullrich am Zoo,** below the S-Bahn tracks, and **Nimm's Mit,** near the *Reisezentrum*, have longer hours. (Both open daily 6am-10pm.) The best **open-air market** fires up Saturday mornings on Winterfeldtplatz, although almost every neighborhood has one. For cheap vegetables and enormous wheels of *Fladenbrot*, check out the **Turkish market** in Kreuzberg, along Maybachufer on Fridays (U8: Schönleinstr.).

Käse-König, under the *Fernsehturm*. S3, 5, 7, 9, 75 or U2, 5, 8: Alexanderplatz. Serves cheap German food in a GDR-style canteen to a mix of students and hard-hats. Bockwurst DM1; schnitzel DM2.70. Open M-F 9am-6:30pm, Sa 9am-6pm.

Mensa TU, Hardenbergstr. 34 (tel. 311 22 53), 10min. northeast of Bahnhof Zoo. Cheap, decent food. Meals DM4-5 for students, others DM6-7. Open M-F 11:15am-2:30pm.

Baharat Falafel, Winterfeldtstr. 37. U1, 2, 4, or 15: Nollendorfplatz. The best falafel in Berlin (DM5-6). Juice DM3-6. Open daily 11am-2am. Closed last week in July.

Amrit, Oranienstraße 202-203 (tel. 612 55 50). U1, 15: Görlitzer Bahnhof. Possibly Berlin's best Indian restaurant. Fabulous vegetarian dishes like *palak paneer* (DM11) as well as delectably spicy meat entrees. Open M-Th and Su noon-1am, F-Sa noon-2am.

Die Krähe, Kollwitzstr. 84 (tel. 442 82 91), off Kollwitzpl. U2: Senefelderplatz. Changing weekly menu. Breakfasts under DM10; crunchy salads DM12; Sunday buffet DM13.50. Open M-Th 5:30pm-2am, F-Sa 5:30pm-3am, Su 10:30am-2am.

Trattoria Ossena, Oranienburger Str. 65 (tel. 283 53 48). More substantial fare than most cafes in the area. Delicious Italian pastas and enormous pizzas. Most meals under DM20, many large enough for 2. Open daily from 5pm.

Café Hardenberg, Hardenbergstr. 10 (tel. 312 33 30), opposite the TU *Mensa*, but with more atmosphere. Funky music and artsy interior. Order sizzling breakfasts (DM5-12) day or night. Salads and pasta DM5-13. Open M-F 9am-1am, Sa-Su 9am-2am.

SIGHTS

It's impossible to see all of sprawling Berlin on foot, but many major sights lie along the route of **bus 100,** which travels from Bahnhof Zoo to Prenzlauer Berg via the Siegessäule, Brandenburg Gate, Unter den Linden, Berliner Dom, and Alexanderplatz. To add an element of thrill, climb up to the second floor of the double-decker bus and sit in the very first row: the view is unbeatable, and you'll feel like you're on an amusement park ride (day pass DM7.80, 7-day pass DM40).

MITTE

For decades a barricaded gateway to nowhere, the opened **Brandenburg Gate** (Brandenburger Tor) symbolizes reunited Berlin, connecting Unter den Linden on the east with the Tiergarten park and Straße des 17. Juni on the west. Built during the reign of Friedrich Wilhelm II as an emblem of peace, the locked gate embedded in the Berlin Wall was a symbol of Cold War division. The **Berlin Wall** itself is a dinosaur, with only fossil remains. Fenced overnight on August 13, 1961, the 165km wall separated families and friends, sometimes even running through homes. Portions are preserved near the *Ostbahnhof* and by Potsdamer Platz; the longest remaining bit is the brightly painted **East Side Gallery** (S3, 7, 9: Ostbahnhof). **Potsdamer Platz,** cut off by the wall, was once a major Berlin transportation hub, designed under Friedrich Wilhelm I to approximate Parisian boulevards; the surrounding area is now the world's largest construction site. Just south of Potsdamer Platz stands the **Martin-Gropius-Bau,** Stresemanstr. 110. The decorous edifice was designed by Martin Gropius, a pupil of Schinkel and uncle of *Bauhausmeister* Walter Gropius. The popular **Haus am Checkpoint Charlie,** Friedrichstr. 44 (U6: Kochstr. or bus #129), a museum on the site of the famous border crossing point, is a fascinating mixture of Western tourist kitsch and Eastern earnestness. (Tel. 251 10 31. Open daily 9am-10pm. DM8, students DM5.)

WESTERN BERLIN

Just north of the Brandenburg Gate sits the imposing, stone-gray **Reichstag,** former seat of the parliaments of the German Empire and the Weimar Republic, and as of 1999, home to the German parliament, the *Bundestag*. Shortly after Hitler became Chancellor in 1933, a mysterious fire in the Reichstag provided a pretext to declare a state of emergency, giving the Nazis broad powers to arrest and intimidate opponents. In the heart of **Tiergarten** (bus #100, 187, or 341 to Großer Stern), in the center of old Berlin, the slender 70m **victory column** (Siegessäule), topped by a gilded statue of winged victory, commemorates Prussia's triumph over France in 1870. Climb 285 steps for a panorama of the city. (Open Apr.-Nov. M 1-6pm, Tu-Su 9am-6pm. DM2, students DM1.)

Charlottenburg Castle (Schloß Charlottenburg; U7: Richard-Wagner-Platz or bus #145 from Bahnhof Zoo to Luisenpl./Schloß Charlottenburg), the vast, bright Baroque palace built by Friedrich I for his second wife, Sophie-Charlotte, presides over a carefully landscaped park. Seek out the **Palace Gardens,** with their small lakes, footbridges, fountains, and carefully planted rows of trees surrounding the **Royal Mausoleum.** (Tel. 32 09 11. Castle open Tu-F 9am-5pm, Sa-Su 10am-5pm; mausoleum open Apr.-Oct. Tu-Su 10am-noon and 1-5pm; garden open Tu-Su 6am-9pm. Entire palace complex Tageskarte DM15, students DM10.)

EASTERN BERLIN

The Brandenburg Gate opens east onto **Unter den Linden,** once one of Europe's best-known boulevards and the spine of pre-war Berlin. Beyond Friedrichstr., many neighboring 18th-century structures have been restored to their original splendor, although GDR excesses still mar the landscape. Amid the architectural terror at the intersection of Friedrichstr. and Unter den Linden rises the stately **German State Library** (Deutsche Staatsbibliothek); the shady, ivy-covered courtyard houses a pleasant cafe. Beyond the library is **Humboldt University,** whose hallowed halls have been trodden by the likes of Einstein, Hegel, Marx, and the Brothers Grimm. Next door, the **New Guard House** (Neue Wache) was designed by Schinkel in unrepentant Neoclassical style. Buried inside are urns full of earth from the Buchenwald and Mauthausen concentration camps, as well as the battlefields of Stalingrad, El Alamein, and Normandy. Across the way is **Bebelplatz,** where on May 10, 1933, Nazi students burned nearly 20,000 books by "subversive" authors. The building with the curved facade is the **Old Library** (Alte Bibliothek).

Berlin's most impressive ensemble of 19th-century buildings is a few blocks south of Unter den Linden at **Gendarmenmarkt.** The twin cathedrals **Deutscher Dom** and **Französischer Dom** grace opposite ends of the square; in between lies the Neoclassical **Schauspielhaus,** Berlin's most elegant concert space. After crossing the Schloßbrücke over the Spree, Unter den Linden passes by **Museum Island** (Museumsinsel), home of four major museums (see **Museums,** below) and the **Berliner Dom** (S3, 5, 7, 9, 75: Hackescher Markt). The beautifully bulky cathedral was severely damaged by bombs in 1944; it emerged from its 20-year restoration with a stunning interior. (Open daily 9am-7:30pm. DM5, students DM3.) To the left stands the pillared **Altes Museum.** The **Lustgarten** in front, normally a pleasant collection of trees and benches, will be completely overhauled in the next few years to look as it did in the 19th century. Across the street, the Lustgarten turns into Marx-Engels-Pl. under the amber-colored **Palace of the Republic** (Palast der Republik), where the GDR parliament met. Crossing the Liebknecht-Brücke leads you to a small park on the right-hand side of the street, which used to be collectively known as the **Marx-Engels Forum;** the park has not been renamed, but the street is now called Rathausstr. On the other side of Museum Island, Unter den Linden becomes Karl-Liebknecht Str., and leads into the monolithic **Alexanderplatz.** The undisputed landmark of the district is the **television tower** (Fernsehturm), the city's tallest structure. (Open daily Mar.-Oct. 9am-1am; Nov.-Feb. 10am-midnight. DM9.)

MUSEUMS

Berlin is one of the world's great museum cities. The **Staatliche Museen Preußischer Kulturbesitz (SMPK)** runs the four major museum complexes: **Museum Island** (S3, 5, 7, 9: Hackescher Markt; bus #100: Lustgarden); **Tiergarten-Kulturforum,** on Matthäikirchplatz (walk up Potsdamer Str. from S1, 2, 25, or U2: Potsdamer Platz); **Charlottenburg** (U7: Richard-Wagner-Platz, or bus #145 from Bahnhof Zoo to Luisenpl./Schloß Charlottenburg); and **Dahlem** (U2: Dahlemdorf). The **Alte Nationalgalerie,** Bodestr. 1-3, and **Bodemuseum,** Monbijoubrücke, are closed for renovations until 2001 and 2004, respectively. SMPK admission prices are standardized (DM4, students DM2). A one-day *Tageskarte* (DM8, students DM4) is valid for all SMPK museums; a *Wochenkarte* (DM25, students DM12.50) is valid for an entire week. The first Sunday of the month is free.

Painting Gallery (Gemäldegalerie; tel. 20 90 55 55), Tiergarten-Kulturinform. Rightly one of Germany's most famous museums. Stunning and enormous collection by Dutch, Flemish, German, and Italian masters, including works by Rembrandt, Breughel, Vermeer, Raphael, Titian, Botticelli, and Dürer. Open Tu-Su 10am-6pm. SMPK prices.

Pergamonmuseum (tel. 203 55 00), on Museum Island. One of the world's great ancient history museums, thanks to Heinrich Schliemann, who traversed the world, pillaged the debris of ancient civilizations, and reassembled it at home. Mind-boggling exhibits: the entire Babylonian Ishtar Gate, the Roman Market Gate of Miletus, and the Pergamon Altar of Zeus. Open Tu-Su 9am-6pm. *Tageskarte* required. Free audio tours.

Sammlung Berggruen, Schloßstr. 1 (tel. 326 95 80), across the street from the Ägyptisches Museum. Five floors of a spiral staircase provide a comprehensive overview of Picasso's work and influences. Open Tu-F 10am-6pm, Sa-Su 11am-6pm. SMPK prices.

Neue Nationalgalerie, Potsdamer Str. 50 (tel. 266 26 62), in the Tiergarten. Sleek van der Rohe building contains a collection of large works–the first 2 floors are enough to make Atlas cry. SMPK ticket will get you into the permanent collection of Kokoschka, Kirchner, and Beckmann, but special exhibits occupy two-thirds of the building (DM12, students DM6). Open Tu-F 10am-6pm, Sa-Su 11am-6pm.

NIGHTLIFE

Berlin's nightlife is absolute madness, a teeming cauldron of debauchery. Bars, clubs, and cafes jam until at least 3am and often stay open until daylight; on weekends, you can dance non-stop from Friday night until Monday morning. If at all possible, try to hit Berlin during the **Love Parade,** usually held in the second weekend of July, when all of Berlin just says "yes" to everything. The best nightlife areas in Berlin include: **Kreuzberg, Potsdamer Platz,** Mitte's **Oranienburger Str.,** and its intersection with **Friedrichstr.** The social nexus of **gay and lesbian** nightlife centers around **Nollendorfplatz** and the gay neighborhood (Schwuler Kiez) of **Schöneberg.** For up-to-date events listings, pick up a copy of the amazingly comprehensive *Siegessäule* (free), named after the phallic monument.

Sage Club, Brückenstr. 1, in Kreuzberg. U8: Heinrich-Heine-Str.; bus N8. Fast-paced dance club corners the techno and house market. Bring your lycra and leather. Cover DM10-25. Get into the groove Th-Su from 11pm.

Tresor/Globus, Leipziger Str. 126A (tel. 229 06 11), in Mitte. U2, or S1, 2, 25, or bus N5, N29 or N52 to Potsdamer Platz. Globus chills with house; Tresor thumps to techno. Cover W DM5, F DM10, Sa DM15-20. Open W and F-Sa 11pm-6am.

Bibo Bar, Lychener Str. 17 (tel. 443 97 98). From U2: Eberswalder Str., walk along Danziger Str. to Lychener Str. DJs change daily, but they're always as crazy and mixed (in every sense) as the bar's clientele. Drinks DM8-12. Open daily 5pm-late.

SO36, Oranienstraße 190 (tel. 61 40 13 06; www.SO36.de), in Kreuzberg. U1, 12, 15: Görlitzer Bahnhof; bus N29: Heinrichplatz; bus N8: Adalbertstr. Berlin's only truly mixed club, with a clientele of hip heteros, gays, and lesbians grooving to a mish-mash of wild genres. Monday trance; Thursday hip-hop/reggae/punk/ska; weekends run the gamut from techno to live concerts. Cover varies. Open daily after 11pm.

HELSINKI, FINLAND

US$1 = 5.61MK (MARKKA, FIM)	**1MK = US$0.18**
CDN$1 = 3.79MK	**1MK = CDN$0.26**
UK£1 = 9.18MK	**1MK = UK£0.11**
IR£1 = 7.55MK	**1MK = IR£0.13**
AUS$1 = 3.67MK	**1MK = AUS$0.27**
NZ$1 = 2.99MK	**1MK = NZ$0.33**
SAR1 = 0.92MK	**1MK = SAR1.08**

PHONE CODES Country code: **358.** International dialing prefix: **00.**

With broad avenues, grand architecture, and well-tended parks, Helsinki is a model of 19th-century city planning. But it looks forward to the next millenium as well; in 2000 it takes its place as an official European City of Culture. The city distinguishes itself with a decidedly multicultural flair: Lutheran and Russian Orthodox cathedrals stand almost face to face, the fruits of the Baltic Sea fill the marketplaces and restaurants, and St. Petersburg and Tallinn are but a short cruise away.

ORIENTATION

Helsinki's main street, **Mannerheimintie,** passes between the bus and train stations as it runs toward the city's center, eventually crossing **Esplanadi.** This tree-lined promenade leads east to **Kauppatori** (Market Square) and the harbor. Both Finnish and Swedish are used on all street signs and maps.

PRACTICAL INFORMATION

Airplanes: Tel. 96 00 81 00. **Buses** 615 (more direct) and 616 run frequently between the **Helsinki-Vantaa airport** and train station square (15mk). A **Finnair bus** shuttles between the airport and the Finnair building at Asemaaukio 3, next to the train station (35min., every 20min. 5am-midnight, 25mk).

Trains: Tel. 707 57 06. To **St. Petersburg** (7hr., 2 per day, 286mk) and **Moscow** (15hr., daily at 5:32pm, 499mk). **Lockers** 10mk per day.

Buses: Tel. 02 00 40 10. The station is between Salomonkatu and Simonkatu; from the train station, turn right and go 2 blocks up Kaivokatu.

Ferries: Silja Line, Mannerheimintie 2 (tel. 980 05 26 82). **Viking Line,** Mannerheimintie 14 (tel. 123 577). **Tallink,** Erottajankatu 19 (tel. 22 82 12 11). Viking Line and **Finnjet** (contact Silja Line) depart from Katajanokka Island, east of Kauppatori (take tram #2 or 4). Silja Line and Tallink sail from South Harbor, south of Kauppatori (take tram #3T).

Local Transportation: Tel. 010 01 11. The Metro, trams, and buses run 5:30am-11pm (some major tram and bus lines, including tram 3T, continue until 1:30am). You can buy single-fare tickets on buses and trams (10mk) or from machines at the Metro station (8mk); 10-trip tickets (75mk) are available at R-kiosks and at the city transport office in the Rautatientori Metro station. Open M-Th 7:30am-6pm, F 7:30am-4pm. Tickets are valid for 1hr. (transfers free); punch your ticket on board. The **Tourist Ticket,** available at city transport and tourist offices, provides unlimited bus, tram, Metro, and local train transit. 1-day 25mk; 3-day 50mk; 5-day 75mk.

Tourist Offices: City Tourist Office, Pohjoisesplanadi 19 (tel. 169 37 57; fax 169 38 39; www.hel.fi). From the train station, walk 2 blocks south on Keskuskatu and turn left on Pohjoisesplanadi. Open May-Sept. M-F 9am-7pm, Sa-Su 9am-3pm; Oct.-Apr. M-F 9am-5pm, Sa 9am-3pm. The **Finnish Tourist Board,** Eteläesplanadi 4 (tel. 41 76 93 00; fax 41 76 93 01; www.mek.fi), has info on special events, transportation routes, and accommodations for all of Finland. Open June-Aug. M-F 8:30am-5pm, Sa 10am-2pm; Sept.-May

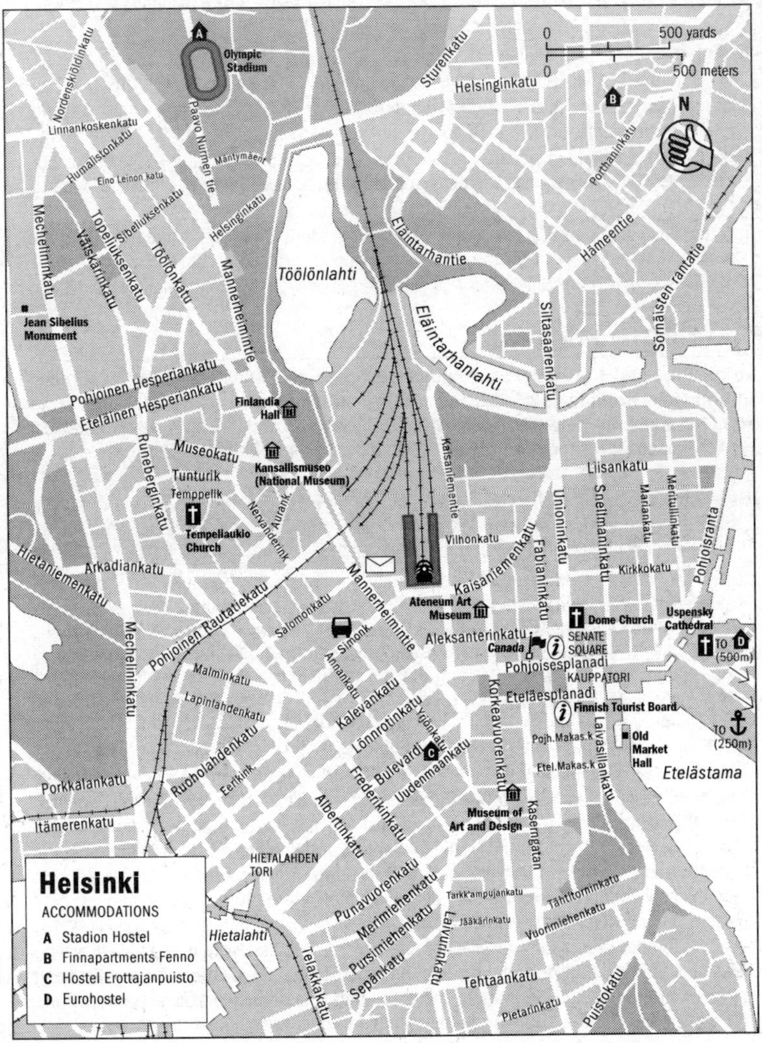

M-F 8:30am-4pm. The **Helsinki Card,** sold at the tourist office, Hotellikeskus, central R-kiosks, and most hotels, provides museum discounts and unlimited local transportation. 1-day pass 120mk; 3-day 180mk.

Budget Travel: Kilroy Travels, Kaivokatu 10 (tel. 680 78 11), sells domestic and international tickets. Open M-F 10am-6pm, Sa 10am-4pm.

Embassies: Canada, Pohjoisesplanadi 25B (tel. 17 11 41). Open M-F 8:30am-4:30pm. **Estonia,** Itäinen Puistotie 10 (tel. 622 02 80). **Ireland,** Erottajankatu 7A (tel. 64 60 06). **Latvia,** Armfeltintie 10 (tel. 476 47 20). **Lithuania,** Rauhankatu 13A (tel. 60 82 10). **Poland,** Armas Lindgrenintie 21 (tel. 684 80 77). **Russia,** Tehtaankatu 1B (tel. 66 18 76). **South Africa,** Rahapajankatu 1A 5 (tel. 65 82 88). **U.K.,** Itäinen Puistotie 17 (tel. 22 86 51 00). Also handles matters for **Australians** and **New Zealanders.** Open M-F 8:30am-5pm. **U.S.,** Itäinen Puistotie 14A (tel. 17 19 31). Open M-F 8:30am-5pm.

Currency Exchange: Exchange, Kaivokatu 6, across from the train station. No fee for cash exchange, but 10mk per traveler's check. Open M-F 8am-8pm, Sa 10am-4pm.

American Express: Area Travel, Mikonkatu 2D, 2nd fl. (tel. 62 87 88). Open M-F 9am-1pm and 2:15-4:30pm. Accepts wired money for members.

Emergencies: Tel. 112. **Police,** tel. 100 22.

24hr. Pharmacy: Yliopiston Apteekki, Mannerheimintie 96 (tel. 41 78 03 00).

Medical Assistance: Aleksin lääkäriasema, Mannerheimintie 8 (tel. 77 50 84 00). Receives and refers foreigners. Open M-F 7:30am-7pm.

Post Office: Mannerheiminaukio 1A (tel. 195 51 17). Address mail to be held: Thomas MCCARTHY, *Poste Restante,* Mannerheiminaukio 1A, **00100** Helsinki, Finland. Open M-F 7am-9pm, Sa 9am-6pm, Su 11am-9pm.

Internet Access: Sonera, Kaivokatu 2, across from the train station, will amaze even the most computer-literate traveler. 15min. free. Open M-F 9am-7pm, Sa 10am-4pm.

Telephones: Shares building with the post office. Open M-F 9am-5pm. **Phone code:** (0)9.

GATEWAY CITIES

ACCOMMODATIONS

During June and July, it's wise to make reservations. Most hostels offer laundry facilities and provide breakfast for a fee. Extra summer hostels are open June through August: try **Hotel Satakunta (HI),** Lapinrinne 1A (tel. 69 58 51; fax 694 22 26), and **Academica (HI),** Hietaniemenkatu 14A (tel. 13 11 43 34; fax 44 12 01).

Hotel Erottanjanpuisto (HI), Uudenmaankatu 9 (tel. 64 21 69; fax 680 27 57). Turn right from the train station, left onto Mannerheimintie, and right onto Erottajankatu; Uudenmaankatu is on the right. Common room with kitchen and a tiny TV . Breakfast 25-35mk. Reserve ahead in summer. Dorms 135mk per HI member. Singles 215, 225mk; doubles 260, 265mk; nonmembers add 15mk each.

Finnapartments Fenno, Franzeninkatu 26 (tel. 773 16 61; fax 701 68 89). From the train station, turn left, follow Kaisaniemenkatu, and bear left onto Unioninkatu (which becomes Siltasaarenkatu); or catch the Metro to Hakaniemi. Then head right on Porthaninkatu, left onto Fleminginkatu, then left again. Basic apartments, some with private kitchens and bathrooms. Sauna. Singles 170-240mk; doubles 320mk.

Eurohostel (HI), Linnankatu 9, Katajanokka (tel. 622 04 70; fax 65 50 44; email euroh@icon.fi; www.eurohostel.fi), 200m from the Viking Line/Finnjet ferry terminal. From the train station, head right to Mannerheimvägen and take tram #2 or 4 (dir: Katajanokka). From Uspensky Cathedral, head down Kanavankatu, turn left on Pikku Satamankatu, and bear right onto Linnankatu. The largest hostel in Finland, with bright rooms, a kitchen and cafe. Sauna. Accepts email reservations. Singles 170mk; doubles 206mk; nonmembers add 15-17mk. Student discounts in off season.

Stadion Hostel (HI), Pohj. Stadiontie 3B (tel. 49 60 71; fax 49 64 66). Take tram #3T, 7A, or 10 from the train station to Olympic Stadium and walk to the opposite side. Kitchen, TV, pool, and nearby sauna. 150 beds. Breakfast 25mk. Paper sheets 15mk. Laundry. Reception June to early Sept. daily 7am-2am; mid-Sept. to May 8-10am and 4pm-2am. Dorms 60mk; doubles 160mk; nonmembers add 15mk each.

FOOD

Even groceries are expensive in Finland, **Alepa supermarket** offers some relief. (Branch under the train station open M-Sa 8am-10pm, Su 10am-10pm.) You can buy fresh veggies, fruit, and fish at **Kauppatori** (Market Square), by the port. (Open June-Aug. M-Sa 7am-2pm and 4-8pm; Sept.-May M-F 7am-2pm).

Zetor, Kaivokatu 10, in Kaivopiha, across from the train station. A bit touristy, but the very essence of Finland: food, drinks, music, dancing, and, of course, a tractor. Entrees 40-100mk. Open M 1pm-1am, Tu-Th 1pm-3am, Su 3pm-1am.

Café Engel, Aleksanterinkatu 26. Light fare for a more serious crowd. Try the variety of coffees (from 11mk) and cakes (from 20mk) while gazing at the cathedral. Open M-Th 7:45am-midnight, F 7:45am-1am, Sa 9:30am-midnight, Su 11am-midnight.

Golden Rax Pizza Buffet, in the Forum, across from the post office. All-you-can-eat pasta and pizza extravaganza (43mk). Open M-Sa 10:30am-10pm, Su 11:30-10pm.

Kasvis, Korkeavuorenkatu 3. Take tram #4 to partake in their elaborate vegetarian buffet. Open M-F 11am-7:30pm, Sa-Su noon-7:30pm.

SIGHTS

Tram #3T offers the city's cheapest tour. Better yet, walk—most sights are packed within 2km of the train station. Pick up a copy of the booklet *See Helsinki on Foot* before you go. The famed architect Alvar Aalto once said of Finland, "Architecture is our form of expression because our language is so impossible," and the bold 20th-century creations amid slick Neoclassical works that suffuse the region prove him right. Much of the layout and architecture of the old center, however, is the brainchild of a German: Carl Engel. After Helsinki became the capital of the Grand Duchy of Finland in 1812, Engel was chosen to design an appropriately grand city. In **Senate Square** (Senaatin Tori), on the corner of Unioninkatu and Aleksanterinkatu, his work is well represented by the **Dome Church** (Tuomiokirkko), completed in 1852. After marveling at the Neoclassical exterior, the austere interior of the Lutheran cathedral comes as quite a contrast. (Open June-Aug. M-Sa 9am-6pm, Su noon-4pm; Sept.-May M-F and Su 10am-4pm, Sa 10am-6pm.) A few blocks to the east, on Katajanokka island, the Byzantine-Slavonic **Uspensky Orthodox Cathedral** (Uspenskinkatedraadi) guards the island with its red and gold cupolas. (Open M and W-F 9:30am-4pm, Tu 9:30am-6pm, Sa 9am-4pm, Su noon-3pm.)

Across from the train station stands Finland's largest art museum, the **Ateneum Taidemuseo,** Kaivokatu 2, with predominantly Finnish art from the 1700s to the 1960s. (Open Tu and F 9am-6pm, W-Th 9am-8pm, Sa-Su 11am-5pm. 15mk, students 10mk; special exhibits 30-35mk.) The controversial new museum of contemporary art, **Kiasma,** Mannerheiminaukio 2, stands next to the statue of Mannerheim. (Open Tu and F 9am-6pm, W-Th 9am-8pm, Sa-Su 11am-5pm. 25mk, students 20mk.) Across the street, **Finlandia Talo,** Mannerheimintie 13E, stands as a testament to **Alvar Aalto,** who designed both the building and the interior and furnishings. (Tel. 402 41. Guided tours 20mk.)

NIGHTLIFE

Sway to afternoon street music in the leafy **Esplanadi** or party on warm nights at **Kaivopuisto park** or **Hietaniemi beach.** Kaivopuisto also hosts open-air concerts on summer Sundays. The free English-language papers *Helsinki This Week*, *Helsinki Happens*, and *City* list popular cafes, bars, nightclubs, and events. Finland is one of a few European countries in which the drinking age—18 for beer and wine, 20 for hard alcohol—is usually enforced; many clubs have a minimum age of 22. Both bouncers and cover charges usually relax on weeknights; speaking English may help you get in. With the exception of licensed restaurants and bars, the state-run liquor store **Alko** holds a monopoly on sales of any alcoholic beverages more potent than lighter beers. (Branches at Mannerheimintie 1 and Salomonkatu 1.

GATEWAY CITIES

Open M-Th 10am-6pm, F 10am-8pm, Sa 9am-4pm.) Starting in the last week of August, the two-week **Helsinki Arts Festival** (tel. 135 45 22; www.helsinkifestival.fi) features everything from ballet to rock concerts to street jugglers.

Fennia, Mikonkatu 17, across from the train station. A Euro-pop disco with a twentysomething crowd. Ages 22+. Cover 30mk. Open M-F 11pm-4am, Sa-Su 8pm-4am.

Storyville, Museokatu 8, near the National Museum. Lives up to promises of "hot jazz to cool blues," with live music nightly after 10pm. No cover. Open daily 8pm-4am.

DTM (Don't Tell Mama), Annankatu 32. Exterior as secretive as its name. A gay and mixed crowd. 20+. Open M-Th and Su 10pm-4am, F-Sa 9pm-4am.

GATEWAY CITIES

VIENNA, AUSTRIA

US$1 = 13.05AS (SCHILLING, OR ATS)	**10AS = US$0.77**
CDN$1 = 8.81AS	**10AS = CDN$1.13**
UK£1 = 21.30AS	**10AS = UK£0.47**
IR£ = 17.47AS	**10AS = IR£0.57**
AUS$1 = 8.51AS	**10AS = AUS$1.18**
NZ$1 = 6.95AS	**10AS = NZ$1.44**
SAR1 = 2.15AS	**10AS = SAR4.65**

PHONE CODES Country code: **43.** International dialing prefix: **900.**

It was not without reason that home-grown satirist Karl Kraus once dubbed Vienna—birthplace of psychoanalysis, atonal music, functionalist architecture, Zionism, and Nazism—a "laboratory for world destruction." Vienna has an important cultural heritage that rivals Paris', thanks to its history of inspired musicians (Mozart, Beethoven, Schubert, Strauss, Brahms), imperial wealth, and impeccable taste in Baroque art and architecture. But Vienna's *fin de siècle* heyday carried the seeds of its own decay—and did so so blatantly that the Viennese in the smoke- and caffeine-permeated days of the great cafe culture analyzed the phenomenon-in-process complacently over coffee. At the height of the city's artistic ferment, the Viennese were already self-mockingly calling it the "merry apocalypse" as they stared down their own dissolution. The smooth veneer of waltz music and whipped cream concealed a darker reality that found expression in Freud's theories, Kafka's writings, and Mahler's music. Today, the city is busy renewing business connections in the former Communist bloc and reestablishing itself as the political, cultural, and economic gateway to Eastern Europe.

GETTING THERE & GETTING AROUND

Airplanes: Wien-Schwechat Flughafen, 18km from Vienna's center, is the home of **Austrian Airlines** (tel. 17 89; open M-F 8am-7pm, Sa-Su 8am-5pm). The S7 connects from the airport (Flughafen/Wolfsthal; on the hr., 38AS) to Wien Mitte/Landstr. on the U3 or U4.

Trains: Tel. 17 17; schedules online at www.bahn.at. There are three main stations. **Westbahnhof,** XV, Mariahilferstr. 132. To: **Budapest** (3-4hr., 9 per day, 436AS) and **Kraków** (6½hr., 2 per day, 492AS). **Südbahnhof,** X, Wiedner Gürtel 1A, mostly sends trains south to: **Bratislava** (1hr., 4 per day, 136AS) and **Prague** (5hr., 3 per day, 524AS). Also to **Poland** and **Russia. Franz-Josefs Bahnhof,** IX, Althamstr. 10, handles commuter rail.

Local Transportation: Excellent **U-Bahn** (subway), **bus, Straßenbahn** (tram), and **S-Bahn** (elevated train) systems cover the city. Single-fare 22AS if puchased on board (19AS from ticket offices, *Tabak,* or U-Bahn stations). The ticket includes transfers; punch it in the machine on the first leg of your journey and don't punch it again if you transfer or it will be invalid (fine 565AS). **24hr. pass** 60AS; **3-day "rover" ticket** 150AS; and **7-day card** 142AS (valid M 9am to following M 9am). The 3-day **Vienna Card** (210AS) includes unlimited transport as well as discounts at museums and sights. Trams and subways stop

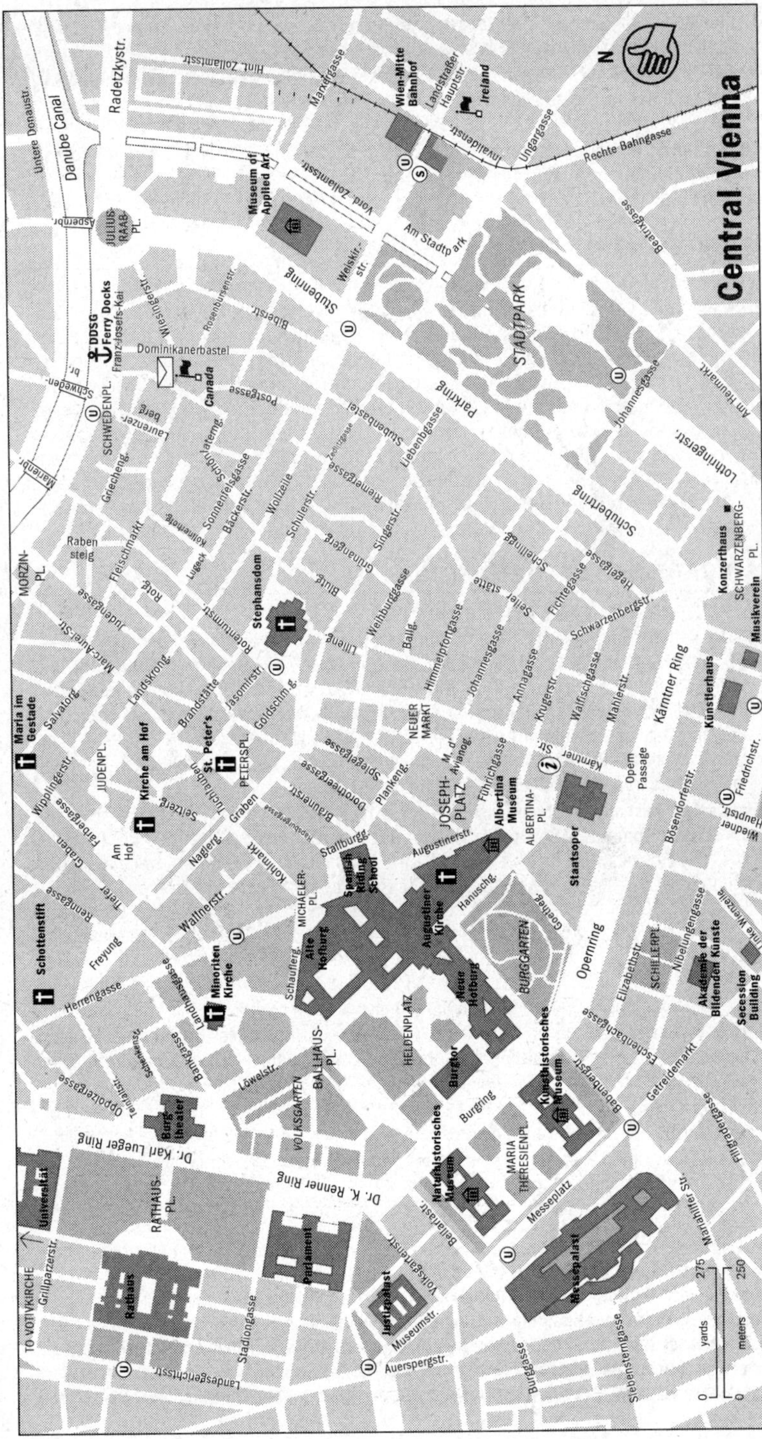
Central Vienna
N
Danube Canal
Untere Donaustr.
Radetzkystr.
Hint. Zollamtsstr.
Marxergasse
Wien-Mitte Bahnhof
Landstraßer Hauptstr.
Ireland
Invalidenstr.
Ungargasse
Rechte Bahngasse
Museum of Applied Art
Vord. Zollamtsstr.
Am Stadtpark
JULIUS-RAAB-PL.
Aspernbr.
Stubenring
Weiskir.-str.
STADTPARK
Beatrixgasse
DDSG Ferry Docks
Franz-Josefs-Kai
Dominikanerbastei
Canada
Wiesingerstr.
Rosenbursenstr.
Biberstr.
Schwedenbr.
SCHWEDENPL.
Laurenzerberg
Postgasse
Parkring
Johannesgasse
Am Heumarkt
Lothringerstr.
Marienbr.
Griecheng.
Schönlaterng.
Sonnenfelsgasse
Stubenbastei
Zedlitzgasse
Riemergasse
Liebenbergasse
Schubertring
Kollnerhofg.
Bäckerstr.
Wollzeile
Schulerstr.
Grünangerg.
Singerstr.
Schellingg.
Fichtegasse
Hegelgasse
Konzerthaus
SCHWARZENBERG-PL.
Raben steig
Fleischmarkt
MORZIN-PL.
Lugeck
Blutg.
Weihburggasse
Seilerstätte
Judengasse
Rotg.
Rotenturmstr.
Stephansdom
Liliengasse
Ballg.
Himmelpfortgasse
Johannesgasse
Annagasse
Schwarzenbergstr.
Musikverein
Marc-Aurel-Str.
Landskrong.
Brandstätte
Jasomirgottstr.
Goldschm.g.
NEUER MARKT
Krugerstr.
Walfischgasse
Mahlerstr.
Kärntner Ring
Künstlerhaus
Salvatorg.
Maria im Gestade
Kirche am Hof
St. Peter's
PETERSPL.
JUDENPL.
Wipplingerstr.
Tuchlauben
Spiegelgasse
Dorotheergasse
Plankeng.
M. d'Avianog.
Führichgasse
Kärntner Str.
Opern Passage
Friedrichstr.
Färbergasse
Seitzerg.
Graben
Bräunerstr.
Habsburgergasse
JOSEPH-PLATZ
Albertina Museum
ALBERTINA-PL.
Staatsoper
Bösendorferstr.
Wiedner Hauptstr.
Am Hof
Naglerg.
Kohlmarkt
Stallburgg.
Augustinerstr.
Spanish Riding School
Augustiner Kirche
Hanuschg.
Goetheg.
Tiefer Graben
Renngasse
Schottenstift
Wallnerstr.
MICHAELER-PL.
Alte Hofburg
BURGGARTEN
Opernring
Elisabethstr.
SCHILLERPL.
Nibelungengasse
Akademie der Bildenden Künste
Linke Wienzeile
Freyung
Herrengasse
Minoriten Kirche
Landhausgasse
Schauflerg.
Neue Hofburg
HELDENPLATZ
BALLHAUS-PL.
Secession Building
Eschenbachgasse
Bankgasse
Schreyvogelg.
Teinfaltstr.
Oppolzergasse
Löwelstr.
Burgtor
Kunsthistorisches Museum
Babenbergerstr.
Getreidemarkt
Burgtheater
VOLKSGARTEN
Burgring
MARIA THERESIENPL.
Dr. Karl Lueger Ring
Naturhistorisches Museum
Messeplatz
Messepalast
Mariahilfer Str.
Fillgradergasse
Universität
RATHAUS-PL.
Dr. K. Renner Ring
Parlament
Bellariastr.
Volksgartenstr.
TO VOTIVKIRCHE
Grillparzerstr.
Rathaus
Stadiongasse
Justizpalast
Museumstr.
Auerspergstr.
Burggasse
Siebensterngasse
Landesgerichtsstr.
0
275
yards
250
meters

running 12:30-5am, but **nightbuses** ("N"; 25AS; passes not valid) run every 30min. along most tram, subway, and bus routes.

Taxis: Tel. 313 00, 401 00, 601 60, 814 00, or 910 11. Stands at Westbahnhof, Südbahnhof, and Karlspl. Rates generally 27AS plus 14AS per km. Surcharges: 27AS Sundays and daily 11pm-6am; 13-26AS for heavy luggage or taxis called by radiophone.

Ride Sharing: Mitfahrzentrale Wien, VIII, Daung. 1A (tel. 408 22 10), off Laudong. To **Prague** 450AS. Open M-F 8am-noon and 2-7pm, Sa-Su 1-3pm.

Bike Rental: At **Wien Nord** and the **Westbahnhof.** 150AS per day, 90AS with train ticket.

ORIENTATION

Vienna is divided into 23 districts *(Bezirke).* The first district is the *innere Stadt,* or Innenstadt (city center), bounded by the name-changing **Ringstraße** (once the site of the old city fortifications) and the Danube. Many of Vienna's major attractions lie along **Opernring, Kärntner Ring,** and **Kärntner Straße** in the south section of the Ring. Districts two through nine radiate clockwise from the center between the Ring and the larger but concentric **Gürtel,** beyond which further districts similarly radiate clockwise. Street signs indicate the district number in Roman or Arabic numerals. *Let's Go* includes district numbers for establishments before the street address. Vienna is a metropolis with crime like any other; be extra careful in Karlspl., and avoid areas of the 5th, 10th, and 14th districts, as well as Landstraßer Hauptstr., Prater Park, and sections of the Gürtel at night.

GATEWAY CITIES

PRACTICAL INFORMATION

TOURIST AND FINANCIAL SERVICES

Tourist Office: Main Office, I, Kärntnerstr. 38, behind the Opera House. Free map. Books 300-400AS rooms for a 40AS fee plus deposit. Open daily 9am-7pm. **Branch** at the **Westbahnhof** open daily Apr.-Oct. 7am-10pm; Nov.-Mar. 7am-9pm. **Jugend-Info Wien** (Vienna Youth Information Service; tel. 17 99; email jiw@blackbox.at), in the underground Bellaria-Passage. Enter from Dr.-Karl-Renner-Ring/Bellaria (tram #1, 2, 46, 49, D, or J) or U2/U3: Volkstheater. Hip staff sells discount youth concert and theater tickets. Get their indispensable *Jugend in Wien.* Open M-Sa noon-7pm.

Embassies: Australia, IV, Mattiellistr. 2-4 (tel. 51 28 58 00), behind Karlskirche. Open M-Th 8:30am-1pm and 2-5:30pm, F 8:30am-1:15pm. **Canada,** I, Laurenzerburg 2, 3rd fl. (tel. 531 38, ext. 3000). Open M-F 8:30am-12:30pm and 1:30-3:30pm. **Ireland,** III, Hilton Center, Landstraßer Hauptstr. 21, 6th fl. (tel. 71 54 24 60; fax 713 60 04). Open M-F 9:30-11:30am and 2-4pm. **New Zealand,** XIX, Springsiedleg. 28 (tel. 318 85 05; fax 318 67 17). **South Africa,** XIX, Sandg. 33 (tel. 320 64 93). Open M-F 8:30am-noon. **U.K.,** III, Jauresg. 10 (tel. 71 61 30; fax 716 13 29 99), near Schloß Belvedere. Open M-F 9:15am-noon. **U.S.,** IX, Boltzmanng. 16 (tel. 313 39), off Währingerstr. Staffed M-F 8:30am-noon and 1-5pm. Open M-F 8:30am-noon.

Currency Exchange: Cirrus/Visa/MC **ATMs** offer excellent rates. **Banks** and **airport exchanges** offer official rates (minimum commission on traveler's checks 65AS, cash 10AS). Most open M-W and F 8am-12:30pm and 1:30-3pm, Th until 5:30pm.

American Express: I, Kärntnerstr. 21-23, P.O. Box 28, A-1015 (tel. 515 40), near Stephanspl. 3% commission. Members' mail held. Open M-F 9am-5:30pm, Sa 9am-noon.

Bisexual, Gay, and Lesbian Services: Rosa Lila Villa, VI, Linke Wienzeile 102 (tel. 586 81 50). Counseling, library, and nightlife info. Open M-F 5-8pm. For gay info, pick up the monthly (German-language) magazine *Connect,* the monthly *Bussi* (free at any gay bar, cafe, or club), or the straight but hip *Falter* newspaper.

EMERGENCY & COMMUNICATIONS

Emergencies: Police, tel. 133. **Ambulance,** tel. 144. **Fire,** tel. 122.

Medical Assistance: Allgemeines Krankenhaus, IX, Währinger Gürtel 18-20 (tel. 404 00). **Emergency care,** tel. 141. Consulates provide lists of English-speaking physicians. For info on **24-hour pharmacies** call 15 50.

Crisis Hotlines: Rape Crisis Hotline, tel. 717 19 (24hr.). **Suicide Hotline,** tel. 713 33 74.

Post Offices: Hauptpostamt, I, Fleischmarkt 19. Address mail to be held: Thomas MANN, *Postlagernde Briefe,* Hauptpostamt, Fleischmarkt 19, **A-1010** Wien, Austria. Open 24hr. **Postal codes** are of the form A-1xx0, where "xx" is the number of the district.

Internet Access: Amadeus Media Cafe, I, Kärntnerstr. 19, on the 5th floor of Steffl department store. Free. Open M-F 9:30am-7pm, Sa 9:30am-5pm. **Café Stein,** IX, Währingerstr. 6 (tel. 319 72 41). 65AS per 30min. Open daily 5-11pm.

Phone code: (0)222

ACCOMMODATIONS

One of the few unpleasant aspects of Vienna is the hunt for cheap rooms from June to September; reserve at least five days ahead, or at the very least call from the train station before 9am. The summer crunch is slightly alleviated in July, when university dorms are converted into makeshift hostels.

Believe It Or Not, VII, Myrtheng. 10, #14 (tel. 526 46 58). From Westbahnhof, take U6 (dir: Heiligenstadt) to Burgg./Stadthalle, then bus #48A (dir: Ring) to Neubaug.; backtrack a block on Burgg. and turn right on Myrtheng. (15min.). From Südbahnhof, take bus #13A (dir: Skodag./Alerstr.) to Kellermanng.; walk left on Neustiftg. and left again on Myrtheng. Sociable hostel in a converted apartment. Two co-ed dorms. The amazing caretaker's personal crash-course on Vienna is a must. Kitchen. Reception 8am-early afternoon. Lockout 10:30am-12:30pm. Reserve ahead. Beds 60AS; Nov.-Easter 110AS.

Hostel Ruthensteiner (HI), XV, Robert-Hamerlingg. 24 (tel. 893 42 02; fax 893 27 96; email hostel.ruthensteiner@telecom.at), 5min. from the Westbahnhof. Turn right as you exit, then go right on Mariahilferstr., left on Haidmannsg., and right on Robert-Hammerlingg. Knowledgeable staff, spotless rooms, and a beautiful courtyard. Breakfast 28AS. Kitchen. Internet. 4-night max. stay. Summer dorm 125AS; 10-bed dorms 145AS; 3- to 5-bed dorms 169AS; singles 245AS; doubles 470AS.

Lauria Apartments, VII, Kaiserstr. 77, #8 (tel. 522 25 55). From Westbahnhof, take tram #5 to Burgg. From Südbahnhof, take tram #18 to Westbahnhof, then tram #5 to Burgg. Modern apartments near the center and the Westbahnhof with TVs and kitchens. Two-night min. for reservations. Credit cards accepted for non-dorm rooms. Dorms 160AS; singles 480AS; doubles 530-700AS; triples 700-800AS; quads 850-940AS.

Hostel Panda, VII, Kaiserstr. 77, 3rd fl. (tel. 522 53 53). From Westbahnhof, take tram #5 to Burgg. From Sudbahnhof, take tram #18 to Westbahnhof first. Fun and eclectic hostel in an old-fashioned Austrian apartment building. 18 mattresses packed into 2 co-ed dorms with huge ceilings and Chinese lanterns. Kitchen and TV. Bring lock for lockers. 160AS; Nov.-Easter 110AS; add 50AS for one-night stay.

Porzellaneum der Wiener Universität, IX, Porzellang. 30 (tel. 31 77 28 20; fax 31 77 28 30), 10min. from the Ring. From Westbahnhof, take tram #5 to Franz-Josefs Bahnhof, then tram D (dir: Südbahnhof) to Fürsteng. From Südbahnhof, take tram D (dir: Nußdorf) to Fürsteng. Singles 190AS; doubles 380AS; quads 760AS.

Wien-West, Hüttelbergstr. 80 (tel. 914 23 14; fax 911 35 94), 8km from the center. From U4: Hütteldorf, take bus #14B or 152 (dir: Campingpl.) to Wien West. Crowded, but grassy and pleasant. Laundry, store, and cooking facilities. Reception 7:30am-9:30pm. Open Mar.-Jan. & July-Aug. 73AS per person, Sept.-June 67AS; 37-42AS per tent, 62-69AS per camper. 2-person cabins 250AS; 4-person 400-440AS.

FOOD

In a world full of uncertainty, the Viennese believe that the least you can do is face things with a full stomach. Food in the city reflects the crazy patchwork empire of the Habsburgs: *Knödeln* (dumplings of Czech origin) and *Ungarische Gulaschsuppe* (Hungarian spicy beef stew) belie Eastern European influences, and even the famed *Wiener Schnitzel* (fried and breaded veal cutlets) probably first appeared in Milan. Vienna is renowned for sublime desserts and chocolates—unbelievably rich, and priced for patrons who are likewise blessed. Most residents, however, maintain that the sumptuous treats are worth every *Groschen.*

GATEWAY CITIES

Gästehäuser, *Imbiße* (food stands), and *Beisln* (pubs) serve inexpensive meals. Cheap meals await in the neighborhood north of the university near the Votivkirche (U2: Schottentor), where **Universitätsstraße** and **Währingerstraße** meet, or the area around the **Rechte** and **Linke Wienzeile** near Naschmarkt (U4: Kettenbrückeg.). The **Naschmarkt** is full of vendors selling aromatic delicacies that you can snack on while shopping at Vienna's premier flea market (weekends only).

Bizi Pizza, I, Rotenturmstr. 4 (tel. 513 37 05), on the corner of Stephanspl. The best deal in the center. Fresh pizza (60-75AS) or pasta (65-75AS) whipped up before your eyes. Also at Franz-Josefs-Kai; Mariahilferstr. 22-24; and X, Favoritenstr. 105. All open daily 11am-11:30pm.

Blue Box, VII, Richterg. 8 (tel. 523 26 82). U3: Neubaug.; turn onto Neubaug. and go right on Richterg. Fresh, flamboyant, and original dishes (Viennese, French, or veggie; 53-116AS). DJs pick music to match the food. Open M 6pm-2am, Tu-Su 10am-2am.

OH Pot, OH Pot, IX, Währingerstr. 22 (tel. 319 42 59). U2: Schottentor. Adorable joint with amazingly good Spanish food at rock-bottom prices. Namesake "pots" (stew-like concoctions) 70-85AS. Open M-F 10:30am-2:30pm and 6-11pm.

Schnitzelwirt Schmidt, VII, Neubaug. 52 (tel. 523 37 71). U2, 3: Volkstheater, then bus #49 to Neubaug. Heaping servings of every kind of *Schnitzel* imaginable (65-115AS). You can ask to wrap up the inevitable leftovers. Open M-Sa 11am-11pm.

Café Hawelka, I, Dorotheerg. 6 (tel. 512 82 30), 3 blocks down Graben from the Stephansdom. With dusty wallpaper, dark wood, and red-striped velvet sofas that haven't been reupholstered in years, this legendary cafe is shabby and glorious. *Buchteln* 35AS. Coffee 30-50AS. Open M and W-Sa 8am-2am, Su 4pm-2am.

Demel, I, Kohlmarkt 14 (tel. 535 17 17), 5min. from the Stephansdom down Graben. Demel's was confectioner to the imperial court until the empire dissolved. Divine confections 40-50AS. Don't miss the *crème du jour.* Open daily 10am-6pm.

SIGHTS

Viennese streets are startling, sketchy, and grandiose. The best way to get to know the city is simply to get lost. Or, ride tram #1 or 2 and gawk to your heart's content.

THE INNER RING. The **First District,** Vienna's social and geographical epicenter, is enclosed on three sides by the massive **Ringstraße** and on the northern end by the **Danube Canal.** If you begin your tour from the main tourist office, the first prominent building in view will be the world-renowned **State Opera House** (Staatsoper). The cheapest way to see its glittering gold, crystal, and red-velvet interior may be to see an opera. *(Tours daily July-Aug. 10, 11am, 1, 2, and 3pm; Sept.-Oct. and May-June 1, 2, and 3pm; Nov.-Apr. 2 and 3pm. 40AS, students 25AS.)* Alfred Hrdlicka's 1988 sculpture **Monument Against War and Fascism** (Monument Gregen Krieg und Faschismus), on Albertinapl., memorializes the suffering of Austrians—especially Austrian Jews—during WWII. From Albertinapl., Tegetthoffstr. leads to the spectacular **New Market** (Neuer Markt), where a graceful fountain and 17th-century church greet visitors. Continue north from here to reach Vienna's most revered landmark, the Gothic **Stephansdom;** the cathedral's smoothly tapering South Tower has become Vienna's emblem; check out the view from the **North Tower** (Nordturm). In the catacombs, the **vault** stores Habsburg innards; their hearts and bodies are scattered in other crypts around town. *(Cathedral tours in English M-Sa 10:30am and 3pm, Su 3pm. 40AS. Spectacular evening tour July-Sept. Sa 7pm. 100AS. South tower open daily 9am-5:30pm. 30AS.)*

IMPERIAL PALACE. The **Imperial Palace** (Hofburg), southeast of the Michaelerpl., was inhabited by the Habsburg emperors until 1918, and now houses the President's office. The enormous complex includes the **Burggarten,** the **Burgkapelle** (where the Vienna Boys' Choir sings Mass on Sunday and religious holidays), and the **Schauräume,** the former private rooms of Emperor Franz Josef. Augustinerstr. leads past the **Albertina,** a palatial wing that now contains a film museum and the celebrated **Collection of Graphic Arts,** with drawings by the likes of Dürer, Michelangelo, da Vinci, Cezanne, and Schiele. *(Tel. 534 83. Open Tu-Sa 10am-5pm. 70AS.)*

Between Josefspl. and Michaelerpl., the Palace Stables (Stallburg) are home to the famous Royal Lipizzaner stallions of the **Spanish Riding School** (Spanische Reitschule). Performances are always sold out and ridiculously expensive; watch them train instead. *(Mid-Feb. to June and Nov. to mid-Dec. Tu-F 10am-noon; Feb. M-Sa 10am-noon, except when the horses tour. Tickets sold at the door at Josefspl., Gate 2, from 8:30am. 100AS.)*

CENTRAL CEMETERY. Music lovers trek out to the **Central Cemetery** (Zentralfriedhof); the second gate leads to the graves of Beethoven, Strauss, and Schönberg, and an honorary monument to Mozart. Gate T or I leads to the **Jewish Cemetery** and Arthur Schnitzler's grave. *(XI, Simmeringer Hauptstr. 234. Tram #71 from Schwarzenbergpl., or tram #72 from Schlachthausg. Trams stop at each of the three main gates; Tor II is the main entrance. You can also take S7 to Zentralfriedhof, which stops along the southwest wall of the cemetery. Open daily May-Aug. 7am-7pm; Mar.-Apr. and Sept.-Oct. 7am-6pm; Nov.-Feb. 8am-5pm. 38AS.)* If you need some cheering up after this experience, visit the **Hundertwasser Haus,** at the corner of Löwenstraße and Kegelgasse in the third district. A wild fantasia of pastel colors, ceramic mosaics, and oblique tile columns make this an eccentric rejection of architectural orthodoxy.

SCHÖNBRUNN AND BELEVEDERE CASTLES. Another must-see is the **Schönbrunn Castle** (Schloß Schönbrunn) and its surrounding gardens, one of the greatest palace complexes in Europe. The six-year-old Mozart played in the **Hall of Mirrors** at the whim of the Empress, and to the profit of the boy's father. Outdoors, the elaborate gardens and hilltop **Gloriette** are ideal for wandering. In summer, many concerts and festivals take place in the palace. *(U4: Schönbrunn. Apartments open daily Apr.-Oct. 8:30am-5pm; Nov.-Mar. 8:30am-4:30pm. Gardens open 6am-dusk. 100AS. Audio tour 90AS, students 80AS. More worthwhile grand tour 120AS, students 105AS; in English 145AS, students 130AS.)* The striking **Belvedere Castle** (Schloß Belvedere), whose sphinx-filled palace gardens begin just behind the Schwarzenbergpl., was once the summer residence of Prince Eugene of Savoy, Austria's greatest military hero. It now houses art by Klimt, Schiele, Kokoschka, and a wing of Baroque and medieval art. *(See **Museums,** below. Take tram D to Schwarzenberg, tram #71 one stop past Schwarzenbergpl., or walk up from Südbahnhof.)*

MUSEUMS

Vienna owes its vast selection of masterpieces both to the acquisitive Habsburgs and the city's own crop of art schools and world-class artists. All museums run by the city of Vienna are free on Friday morning before noon. Individual museum tickets usually cost 20-80AS and are discounted with the **Vienna Card.**

Museum of Art History (Kunsthistorisches Museum; tel. 52 52 40), off the Burgring. The 4th-largest art collection in the world oozes with 15th- to 18th-century Venetian and Flemish paintings, including Bruegels, Rembrandts, and Holbeins. The mural in the lobby is by Klimt. Open Tu-Su 10am-6pm; English tours in summer daily 11am and 3pm. 100AS, students 70AS; tours 30AS.

Austrian Gallery, III, Prinz-Eugen-Str. 27 (tel. 79 55 70), in the Belvedere Palace. Walk from the Südbahnhof or take tram D or #566, 567, 666, 668, or 766 to Prinz-Eugen-Str. The **Upper Belvedere** houses Austrian Art of the 19th-20th centuries, including works by Schiele, Kokoschka, and Klimt. The **Lower Belvedere** contains the **Baroque Museum** and the **Museum of Medieval Austrian Art.** All open Tu-Su 10am-5pm. Combined ticket 60AS, students 30AS; English guided tours 2:30pm.

Secession Building, I, Friedrichstr. 12 (tel. 587 53 07), on the western side of Karlspl. Originally built to give the pioneers of modern art—Klimt, Kokoschka, and Gauguin—space to hang artwork that didn't conform to the *Künstlerhaus*' standards. Open Tu-Sa 10am-6pm, Su and holidays 10am-4pm. 60AS, students 40AS.

Künstlerhaus, Karlspl. 5 (tel. 587 96 63). Once the home of the Viennese artistic establishment, this museum invites temporary exhibits, usually of contemporary and non-E'nsuropean art. The theater hosts numerous film festivals. Open M-W and F-Su 10am-6pm, Th 10am-9pm. 90AS, students 60AS; Monday students 40AS.

ENTERTAINMENT

Vienna's musical history is full of big names: Mozart, Beethoven, and Haydn wrote their greatest masterpieces in Vienna, creating the First Viennese School; a century later, Schönberg, Weber, and Berg teamed up for the Second Viennese School. The **Staatsoper** remains one of the top five companies in the world and performs 300 times from September to June. The world-famous **Wiener Philharmoniker** (Vienna Philharmonic Orchestra) has been directed by the world's finest conductors, including Mahler and Bernstein. Regular performances take place in the **Musikverein,** I, Dumbastr. 3, on the northeast side of Karlspl. (Tel. 505 81 90. Box office open Sept.-June M-F 9am-7:30pm, Sa 9am-5pm. Standing room available.)

NIGHTLIFE

A fact of Viennese nightlife: it starts late. The best nights are Friday and Saturday, beginning around 1am. For the scoop on raves, concerts, and parties, grab the fliers at cafes around town or pick up a copy of the indispensable *Falter* (28AS) for listings of everything from opera to punk concerts to the gay and lesbian scene.

Cato, I, Tiefer Graben 19 (tel. 533 47 90). U3: Herreng. Walk down to Strauchg., turn right, and continue to Tiefer Graben. Laid-back, art-deco bar—you'll be singing songs by the end of the evening. Fab cocktails. Open M-Th and Su 6pm-2am, F-Sa 6pm-4am.

Club Berlin, I, Gonzag. 12 (tel. 533 04 79). Vienna's bold and beautiful wind their way around the downstairs partitions of this simultaneously intimate and expansive wine cellar with great music. Open M-Tu and Su 6pm-2am, F-Sa 6pm-4am.

Alsergrunder Kulturpark, IX, Alserstr. 4 (tel. 407 82 14). A young Viennese crowd flocks to these beautiful grounds for the beer garden, wine and champagne bars, and more. All sorts of people and all sorts of nightlife. Open Apr.-Oct. daily 4pm-2am.

U-4, XII, Schönbrunnerstr. 222 (tel. 85 83 18). U4: Meidling Hauptstr. Keeps the music fresh and the party going. Two dance areas, multiple bars, and rotating theme nights. Thursday gay night. Cover 70-120AS. Open daily 11pm-5am.

İSTANBUL, TURKEY

US$1 = 450,000TL (TURKISH LIRA)	**100,000TL = US$0.22**
CDN$1 = 304,0001TL	**100,000TL = CDN$0.33**
UK£1 = 735,000TL	**100,000TL = UK£0.14**
IR£1 = 605,000TL	**100,000TL = IR£0.17**
AUS$1 = 294,000TL	**100,000TL = AUS$0.34**
NZ$1 = 240,000TL	**100,000TL = NZ$0.42**
SAR1 = 74,000TL	**100,000TL = SAR1.35**

PHONE CODES Country code: **90.** International dialing prefix: **00.**

Straddling two continents and almost three millennia of history, İstanbul exists on an incomprehensible scale. Having withstood innumerable demographic shifts, devastating wars, natural disasters, and foreign occupations, İstanbul is naturally composed of a unique mix of civilizations, a melange evident not only in architecture and religious practice, but also in everyday life. Black-veiled women link arms with their scantily clad daughters on the city's tiny, winding streets, and İstanbul's noveau riche wear Harley Davidson boots to parade through dusty markets filled with street merchants and peddlers selling gold, spices, and aphrodisiacs.

GETTING THERE & GETTING AROUND

Airplanes: Atatürk Havaalanı, 30km from the city. To Sultanahmet take a Havaş **shuttle bus** from either terminal to Aksaray (every 30min., US$6). At Aksaray, walk one block south to Millet Cad. and take an Eminönü-bound tram to the Sultanahmet stop.

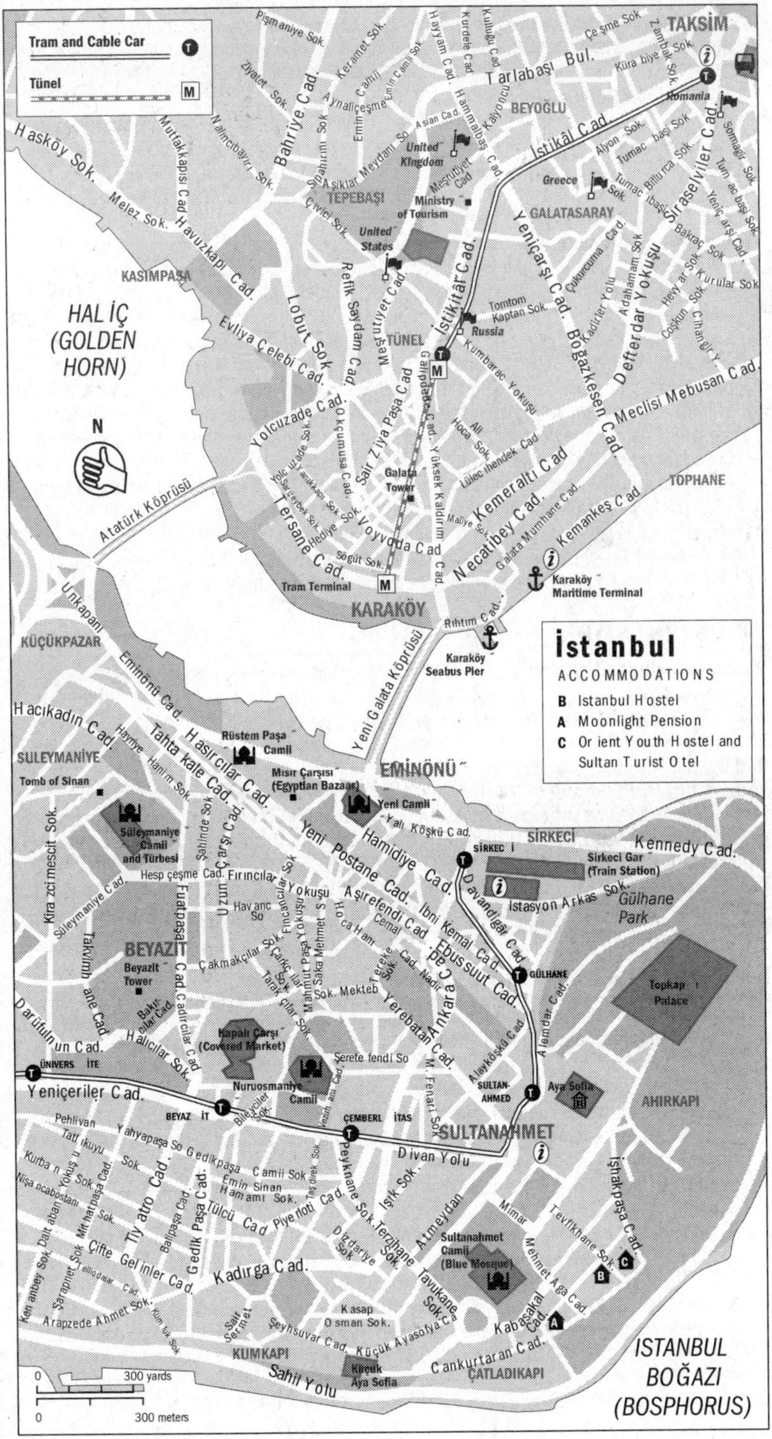
Tram and Cable Car
Tünel
İstanbul
ACCOMMODATIONS
B Istanbul Hostel
A Moonlight Pension
C Orient Youth Hostel and Sultan Turist Otel
HALİÇ (GOLDEN HORN)
ISTANBUL BOĞAZI (BOSPHORUS)
N
TAKSİM
BEYOĞLU
TEPEBAŞI
GALATASARAY
KASIMPAŞA
TÜNEL
TOPHANE
KARAKÖY
KÜÇÜKPAZAR
SULEYMANİYE
EMİNÖNÜ
SIRKECI
BEYAZIT
SULTANAHMET
AHIRKAPI
KUMKAPI
ÇATLADIKAPI
Romania
United Kingdom
Ministry of Tourism
Greece
United States
Russia
Galata Tower
Tram Terminal
Karaköy Maritime Terminal
Karaköy Seabus Pier
Rüstem Paşa Camii
Mısır Çarşısı (Egyptian Bazaar)
Yeni Camii
Tomb of Sinan
Süleymaniye Camii and Türbesi
Sirkeci Gar (Train Station)
Gülhane Park
Topkapı Palace
Beyazıt Tower
Kapalı Çarşı (Covered Market)
Nuruosmaniye Camii
Aya Sofia
Sultanahmet Camii (Blue Mosque)
Küçük Aya Sofia
Atatürk Köprüsü
Yeni Galata Köprüsü
Tarlabaşı Bul.
İstiklâl Cad.
Sıraselviler Cad.
Meclisi Mebusan Cad.
Kennedy Cad.
Yeniçeriler Cad.
Divan Yolu
Kadırga Cad.
Sahil Yolu
Cankurtaran Cad.
Hasköy Sok.
Evliya Çelebi Cad.
Necatibey Cad.
Kemeraltı Cad.
Kemankeş Cad.
Hamidiye Cad.
Ankara Cad.
Yerebatan Cad.
Alemdar Cad.
Ebussuut Cad.
0 300 yards
0 300 meters

Trains: Buses are always quicker and cheaper. **Sirkeci Garı** (tel. (212) 527 00 50), in Eminönü (downhill from Sultanahmet toward the Golden Horn) chugs to Europe. To **Bucharest** (27hr., 1 per day, US$30) and **Budapest** (40hr., 1 per day, US$90).

Buses: Esenler Otobüs Terminal (tel. 658 00 36), Esenler, 3km from the center. Take the tram to Yusufpaşa (1 stop beyond Aksaray; US$.50), walk to the Aksaray Metro station on Adnan Menderes Bul., and take the Metro to the *otogar* (15min., US$0.50). **Parlak Tur** (tel. 658 17 55) heads to **Prague** (2 days, departs Sa at 4pm, US$80). **Ulusoy** (tel. 658 30 00; fax 658 30 10), **Varan** (tel. 658 02 74 or 658 02 77), and **Kamil Koç** (tel. 658 20 00) are also reliable carriers serving Europe.

Local transportation: AKBİL is an electronic ticket system that works on municipal ferries, buses, trams, seabuses, and the subway (but not *dolmuş*). Worthwhile for those staying more than three days; with an initial deposit of US$5 for a plastic tab, you can add money to it in 1,000,000TL increments and save 15-50% on fares. Regular tickets are not interchangeable. Tickets for trams and buses without ticket sellers are available from little white booths, while ferries and seabuses take *jeton* (tokens) available at ferry stops. **Bus** service runs 5am-midnight, dropping off markedly after 10:30pm, arriving every 10min. at most stops. Signs on the front indicate destination, and signs on the right-hand side list the major stops. **Dolmuş** are minibuses that run along a fixed local route. Cheap, and destinations are posted in the front window. Only during daylight hours and early evening. They can be found near most of the major bus hubs, including Aksaray and Eminönü. A **tram** runs from Eminönü to Zeytinburnu.

Taxis: Little yellow Fiats. Be alert if you don't speak Turkish and are catching a cab in Sultanahmet or Taksim. One light on the meter means day rate; 2 lights mean night rate. Check change carefully. Rides within the city shouldn't be more than US$5.

ORIENTATION

Waterways divide İstanbul into three sections. The **Bosphorus Strait** (Boğaz) separates Asia from Europe. Turks call the European side **Avrupa** and the Asian side **Asya.** The **Golden Horn,** a sizeable river originating just outside the city, splits Avrupa into northern and southern parts. Directions in İstanbul are usually further specified by district.Most of the sights and tourist facilities are south of the Golden Horn and toward the eastern end of the peninsula, which is framed by the Horn and the Sea of Marmara. The other half of Avropa is focused on **Taksim Square,** the commercial and social center of the northern bank. Two main arteries radiate from the square: **İstiklâl Caddesi,** the main downtown shopping street, and **Cumhuriyet Caddesi.** The Asian side of İstanbul is primarily residential, but offers plenty of strolling and a more relaxed pace. Sultanahmet, Taksim, and Kadıköy (on the European side) are the districts most relevant for visitors.

PRACTICAL INFORMATION

Tourist Office: In **Sultanahmet,** 3 Divan Yolu (tel./fax 518 87 54), in the white metal kiosk, at the north end of the Hippodrome. Open daily 9am-5pm. **Branches** in the Taksim's Hilton Hotel Arcade on Cumhuriyet Cad, in the Sirkeci train station, in the Atatürk Airport, and the Karaköy Maritime Station.

Travel Agencies: Indigo Tourism and Travel Agency, 24 Akbıyık Cad. (tel. 517 72 66; fax 518 53 33), in Sultanahmet. Sells tickets, books airport shuttle, and holds mail. Open summer daily 8:30am-7:30pm; off-season M-Sa 9:30am-6pm.

Consulates: Australia, 58 Tepecik Yolu, Etiler (tel. 257 70 52). Open M-F 10am-noon. **Canada,** 107/3 Büyükdere Cad., Gayrettepe (tel. 272 51 74; fax 272 34 27). **Ireland** (honorary), 25/A Cumhuriyet Cad., Mobil Altı, Elmadağ (tel. 246 60 25). Open M-F 9:30-11:30am. **New Zealand,** 100-102 Maya Akar Center, Büyükdere Cad., Esentepe (tel. 211 11 14; fax 211 04 73). **South Africa,** 106 Büyükdere Cad., Esentepe (tel. 275 47 93; fax 288 76 42). Open M-F 9am-noon. **U.K.,** 34 Meşrutiyet Cad., Beyoğlu/Tepebaşı (tel. 293 75 40; fax 245 49 89). Open M-F 8:30am-noon. **U.S.,** 104-108 Meşrutiyet Cad., Tepebaşı (tel. 251 36 02; fax 251 32 18). Open M-F 8:30-11am.

Currency exchange: *Bureaux de change* open M-F 8:30am-noon and 1:30-5pm. Most charge no commission. **ATMs** accept most cards and banks exchange traveler's checks.

American Express: Türk Express, 4½ Cumhuriyet Cad., 3rd fl. (tel. 235 95 00), uphill from Taksim Sq. Open M-F 9am-6pm. Their office in the **Hilton Hotel lobby,** Cumhuriyet Cad. (tel. 241 02 48), helps when Türk Express is closed. Open daily 8:30am-8pm.

Tourist Police: In Sultanahmet, at the beginning of Yerebatan Cad. (24hr. hotline 527 45 03 and 528 53 69; fax 512 76 76). **Emergency:** Tel. 155.

Hospitals: American Hospital, Admiral Bristol Hastanesi, 20 Güzelbahçe Sok., Nişantaşı (tel. 231 40 50). The **German Hospital,** 119 Sıraselviler Cad., Taksim (tel. 251 71 00).

Post Office: Most convenient to Sultanahmet is the booth opposite the entrance to Aya Sofia. **Main branch** in Sirkeci, 25 Büyük Postane Sok. Stamp and **currency exchange** services open 8:30am-7pm. 24hr. phones. Address mail to be held: Teddy BEAR, Poste Restante, Merke 3 Posthane, PTT, Sirkeci, 25 Büyük Postane Sok, **5270050** Istanbul.

Phone codes: Avrupa 212; Asya 216.

ACCOMMODATIONS

İstanbul's budget accommodations are concentrated in **Sultanahmet.** Hotels in **Lâleli** are the center of prostitution in İstanbul and should be avoided. Rates sometimes rise by 20% in July and August.

Istanbul Hostel, 35 Kutlugün Sok. (tel. 516 93 80; fax 516 93 84), right down the hill from the Four Seasons Hotel. If you had to choose a hostel floor to eat off, this would be a good choice. Happy Hour 6:30-9:30pm (beer $2). Dorms US$5; singles US$11.

Sultan Hostel, 3 Terbıyık Sok. (tel. 516 92 60; fax 517 16 26), Fez Travel Office at entrance. Around the corner from Orient Hostel. Great views of the Sea of Marmara. The Happy Hour is very happy (5-8pm). Laundry. MC/Visa. Dorms US$5; singles US$9.

Yücelt Hostel/Interyouth Hostel, 6/1 Caferiye Cad. (tel. 513 61 50; fax 512 76 28; email infoşbackpackersturkey.com; www.yucelthostel.com). Free beer until 9pm! More amenities than you could list in 4 lines and (unbelievable but true) three free meals a day. Dorms US$7; singles US$16; doubles US$10. Did we mention free beer?

Moonlight Pension, 87 Akbıyık Cad. (tel. 517 54 29; fax 516 24 80). Away from the madness of the backpacker scene. Rooftop views. Kitchen. Laundry. Internet. Dorms US$5; doubles US$16; triples US$21.

Orient Youth Hostel, 13 Akbıyık Cad. (tel. 517 94 93; fax 518 38 94; email orienthostelşsuperonline.com; www.hostels.com/orienthostel), near Topkapı Palace. It's Happy Hour every day until 10pm. At night the festivities move into the bar to receive Turkey's biggest Australian invasion since Gallipoli. Breakfast included. Internet. Dorms US$5; doubles US$12.50; quads US$5.25.

FOOD

Sultanahmet's heavily-advertised "Turkish" restaurants aren't difficult to find, but much better meals can be found on İstiklâl Cad. and around Taksim. The small Bosphorus towns such as Arnavutköy and Sariyer (on the European side) and Çengelköy (on the Asian side) are the best places for fresh fish. A lamentably overlooked option are street vendors. Good *kebap* shops are everywhere, but quality tends to be better in more residential areas. Ortaköy is the place to go for stuffed baked potatoes. Prices for both are fixed at US$0.20-0.30. There's a **grocery** on every corner. A large and fresh selection of produce can be found in the city's **open-air markets;** the best is the daily one in Beşiktaş, near Barbaros Cad.

Dârüzziyâfe (tel. 511 84 14; fax 526 18 91), behind Sultanahmet Camii on the Hippodrome. *Süleymaniye çorbası* (meat and veggie soup; US$2) is a must. No liquor–sip rosehip nectar instead. Open daily noon-11pm.

Cennet, 90 Divan Yolu (tel. 513 14 16), on the right side of the road as you walk from Sultanahmet toward Aksaray. Divine *gözleme* (cheese pancake; US$1). Live Turkish music nightly. Open daily 10am-midnight. US$1 service charge per person.

Haci Baba, 49 İstiklâl Cad. (tel. 244 18 86 or 245 43 77). Stylish dining room and a terrace overlooking the courtyard of Aya Triada. Entrees US$7. Open daily 10am-10pm.

Afacan, İstiklâl Cad. Two locations, one at the top end by the first movie theater and the second at the other end, past the Galatasaray Lisesi. Seriously good *kebaps* and *dolma.* Bottom open daily 8am-11pm, top open daily 10am-midnight.

SIGHTS

HAGIA SOPHIA (AYA SOFIA). For over 1500 years, the Hagia Sofia has endured as the city's most embattled landmark, having suffered such hardships as the cruelty of gravity, attacks of crusaders, and a second-rate repainting. Intended to cement Justinian's imperial authority and to regain civic control, the church was designed and built by the mathematicians Anthemius of Tralles and Isodorus of Miletus. After five years of construction, the exterior of the church was painted blood red to serve as an unambiguous warning to would-be revolutionaries. Measuring 7570 square meters with a height of 55.6m, it was the grandest building in the world when it opened in 537. Mehmet the Conqueror converted Aya Sofia to a mosque, which it remained until 1932, when it became a museum. *(Museum open Tu-Su 9:30am-4:30pm; gallery open Tu-Su 9:30-11:30am and 1-4pm. US$4.80, students free.)*

BLUE MOSQUE (SULTANAHMET CAMİİ). Located between the Hippodrome and Hagia Sofia, the six-minareted, multi-domed structure is the Blue Mosque (Sultanahmet Camii). Completed in 1617, it was Sultan Ahmet's response to the architectural challenge of Hagia Sofia. *(Open Tu-Sa. Don't visit during prayer times and dress appropriately—no shorts or tank tops and head coverings for women. Donation requested.)*

THE HIPPODROME. Few sites conjure images of the glory of Byzantine Constantinople like the Hippodrome, behind the Blue Mosque. The subterranean bronze stump is all that remains of the **Serpentine Column,** a particularly impressive piece of Imperial plunder. Originally placed at the Oracle of Delphi, the statue consisted of three intertwined snakes whose heads pointed in different directions until Mehmet I conquered the city and decapitated one of them. The southernmost column is the deteriorating **Column of Constantine,** whose original gold-plated bronze tiling was looted by members of the Fourth Crusade during the sack of Constantinople. On the east side of Hippodrome along Atmeydan Sok. is İbrahim Paşa Sarayı, the **Museum of Turkish and Islamic Art.** *(Open Tu-Su 9:30am-4:30pm. US$2, students US$1.20.)*

UNDERGROUND CISTERN (YEREBATAN SARAYI). Sultanahmet's most mysterious, otherworldly attraction is the oft-overlooked Underground Cistern. The underground palace is actually an underground cavern whose shallow water eerily reflects the images of its 336 supporting columns, all illuminated by colored lighting. *(As you stand with your back to Hagia Sofia, the entrance is 175m from the* cami *in the kiosk on the left side of Yerebatan Cad. Open daily 9:30am-5:30pm. US$3, students US$2.50.)*

TOPKAPI PALACE (TOPKAPI SARAYI). Towering over the high ground at the tip of the old city and hidden behind walls up to 12m high stands Topkapı Palace, the nerve center of the Ottoman Empire from the 15th to 19th centuries. The Topkapı was built by Mehmet the Conqueror between 1458 and 1465. The palace morphed into an Imperial residence during the reign of Suleyman the Magnificent. The palace is divided into four courts, all surrounded by the palace walls: the first is a park-like courtyard; the second is the bulk of the palace proper; the third court is the site of the palace school; and the fourth court houses a set of pavilions with amazing views of the Sea of Marmara over the forest canopy of Gülhane. The palace's main entrance is on Babıhümayun Cad., the cobblestone street off Hagia Sofia square.

In the **Palace Treasury,** you'll find the chain mail armor of Murat IV, the legendary Topkapı dagger, and all 86 karats of the **Spoonmaker's Diamond,** so called because it was once traded to a spoonmaker in exchange for three spoons. The **Hall of the Treasury** houses 37 portraits, one for each of the 37 sultans. The **Treasure Dormitory** next door displays a sizeable collection of Islamic Art. On the other side of the courtyard is the **Pavilion of Holy Relics,** housing the booty taken by Selim the Grim. The edifice is lavishly covered from floor to dome in blue İznik tile, with the names of God and Muhammed on calligraphic seals. The room on the left features the staff of Moses, several hairs of Muhammad's beard, and a rather angry letter penned by the Prophet asking a Coptic chieftain to convert to Islam. The **Harem** is the museum's most popular attraction next to the Spoonmaker's Diamond. It served as home of the sultan and his family and breaks down quite nicely into three main areas: the Eunuchs' section, the Women's section, and the Sultan's section. *(Open M and W-Su 9am-4:30pm; mandatory harem tours leave M and W-Su every 30min. 9:30am-3:30pm. Palace US$4, students free; harem US$2.50, students US$1.50.)*

GRAND BAZAAR. Consisting of over 4000 shops, several banks, mosques, police stations, and restaurants, the enormous Grand Bazaar could be a city unto itself. It forms the entrance to the massive mercantile sprawl that starts at Çemberlitaş and covers the hill down to Eminönü, ending at the Egyptian Spice Bazaar (Mısır Çarşısı) and the Golden Horn waterfront. If you plan to bargain, decide on your price beforehand. In order to make sure that your first offer isn't insulting, don't offer less than half of the asking price. Your target price should be somewhere in between your first offer and their stated price. Be wary of buying anything whose value rests on a promise of age or authenticity. *(From Sultanahmet, follow the tram tracks toward Aksaray for 5min. until you see the mosque on your right. Enter the mosque's side gate, and walk with the park on your left to the entrance. Open M-Sa 9am-7pm.)*

ENTERTAINMENT

HAMAMS

Not all *hamams* (baths) have designated female attendants; women should specifically request female washers. Self service is always an option; this wish is best indicated by showing the attendants your bar of soap and wash cloth.

Çemberlitaş Hamamı, 8 Verzirhan Cad. (tel. 522 79 74), just a soap-slide away from the Çemberlitaş tram stop. One of the cleaner places. Built by Sinan in 1584, it's also one of the most beautiful. Both the men's and women's sections have marble interiors under large domes. Vigorous "towel service" after the bath requires a tip of US$1.50-3. Bath US$14, with massage US$18; students US$8, US$12.

Çinli Hamamı, in Fatih, near the butcher shops at the end of Itfaiye Cad. Built for the pirate Barbarossa, this bath is excellent and authentic. It retains a few of its original İznik and Kütahya tiles. Both sections open 9am-8pm. Bath US$4; massage US$4

NIGHTLIFE

Night action is centered around Taksim and İstiklâl Cad. In Sultanahmet all bars are within 100m of another, and have standardized beer prices at US$1-1.25.

Jazz Spot, at the end of Büyük Parmakkapı Sok in Taksim. A mixed group of music lovers sit while live bands lay the funk on thick. Shows nightly at 11pm. Beer US$3. June-Aug. no cover; Sept.-May F-Sa cover US$10. Open daily 11am-4am.

Mordi Cafe Bar, 47 Akbıyık Cad., down the street from the Orient Hostel. Leagues above the other backpacker bars in cleanliness and ambience. Happy Hour until 10pm.

Peyote, İmam Adnan Sok. (tel. 293 32 62), next to Leman Kültür, in Taksim. This humble spot is one of the area's cheapest venues for live music. Shows nightly Tu-Sa 11:30pm. Beer US$1.25. F-Sa cover US$7.50; one drink included. Open M-Sa 6pm-4am.

BEIJING (北京), CHINA

US$1=Y8.278	Y1=US$0.121
CDN$1=Y5.628	Y1=CDN$0.178
UK£1=Y13.149	Y1=UK£0.076
IR£1=Y10.926	Y1=IR£0.092
AUS$1=Y5.454	Y1= AUS$0.183
NZ$1=Y4.439	Y1=NZ$0.225
SAR1=Y3.255	Y1=SAR0.733

PHONE CODES Country code: **86.** international dilaing prefix: 00.

China's forefathers have cultivated the nation's dreams of grandeur for as long as the Chinese have grown rice. Born of these visions of greatness, Beijing's Forbidden City, its Summer Palace, and the nearby Great Wall testify to a long history of imperial ostentation. Today, modern skyscrapers tell of capitalism's encroachment, the latest grand-scale revolution in Beijing's tumultuous history. Life exists for most Beijing residents, however, much as it has for decades. Whether the national capital is your first or last stop on a Trans-Siberian itinerary, take a moment to enjoy Beijing, the enigmatic gateway to the People's Republic of China.

ORIENTATION

Beijing is vast. Sprawling. Immense. Really, really big. Everything in Beijing is far away from everything else, and most of the budget accommodations are littered around the city's perimeters, making them difficult to access. The **Forbidden City** and **Tiananmen Square** form the city center on either side of **Changan Jie** (长安街), the main downtown east-west thoroughfare. **Dazhalan** and **Wangfujing,** southwest and northeast of Tiananmen Square, respectively, have many shopping options.

PRACTICAL INFORMATION

Airplanes: Capital Airport (shôudü jïchâng; 首都机场; tel. 6456 2580) is 1hr. outside the city by taxi (at least Y80; more to book in advance). **Civil Aviation Administration of China (CAAC)** (zhōngguó mínháng; 中国民航), has several offices, but is headquartered in the Aviation Bldg. on 15 Xi Changan Jie (tel. 6601 7755; 24hr. domestic ticket tel. 6256 7811; 24hr. international ticket tel. 6256 6783)

Trains: Foreigners enter and exit Beijing through the **Beijing Main Railway Station** (beïjïng huôchë zhàn; 北京火车站; tel. 6512 8931) or **Beijing West Railway Station** (bêijïng xï zhàn; 北京西站; tel. 6321 6523), located on Lianhuachi Dong Lu near Lianhuachi Park (bus #52).

Travel Agencies: China International Travel Service (CITS; zhōngguó guójì lǚxíngshè; 中国国际旅行社), 9 Jianguomennei Dajie, Beijing International Hotel (tel. 6512 6688, ext. 1751 or 1752), books tickets on the Trans-Siberian. Open M-F 8:30am-noon and 1:30-5pm. The CITS head office is at 1 Jianguomenwai Dajie, World Trade Tower, Unit 100A (tel. 6505 2288, ext. 8110, and 6505 3775; fax 6505 3105). Open M-F 9am-noon and 1-5pm, Sa 9am-noon. CITS also has an English-language information hotline (tel. 6505 2266). **Tianhua International Travel Service** (tiānhuá guójì lǚxíng shè; 天华国际旅行社; tel. 8725 1847; fax 8726 8026), in the back of the hotel, arranges Mongolian, Russian, and Kazakh visas, railway tickets, cheap accommodations in Mongolia, and tours to the Gobi and other tourist spots. Open almost 24hr.

Embassies: Beijing hosts two huge embassy compounds. One is at **Jianguomenwai, near** the Friendship Store, and the other is at Sanlitun, home to dozens of expat bars. **Mongolia,** 2 Xiushui Bei Jie, Jianguomenwai (tel. 6532 1203; fax 6532 5045). Mongolian visas take 2 working days to process (US$16). **Russia,** 4 Dongzhimennei, Beizhong Jie (embassy tel. 6532 2051; visa tel. 6532 1267; fax 6532 4853), is near–but not in–

Sanlitun. For more info on Russian visa requirements, see **Russia Essentials,** p. 551. It is *highly* advisable to obtain a Russian visa before leaving your country of origin.

Currency Exchange: Almost every hotel and hostel can exchange traveler's checks and US$. Any **Bank of China** branch can also exchange money. To cash traveler's checks into US$ (necessary for travel to Russia and Mongolia), head to **China International Trust and Investment Corporation (CITIC)** (zhōngxìn shíyè yínháng; 中信实业银行), 19 Jianguomenwai Dajie, International Bldg. (tel. 6512 2233 and 6500 2255, ext. 3120; fax 6500 4851), next to the Friendship Store.

ATMs: There are over 70 ATMs in Beijing accepting **Visa/Plus** cards. A **Cirrus/MC** ATM is in the SCITECH Tower Shopping Center, 22 Jianguomenwai Dajie. An **AmEx** ATM is located in wing L of the China World Trade Center, 1 Jianguomenwai Dajie.

Emergency: Police: tel. 110. **Fire:** tel. 119 or 6525 0100. **Ambulance:** tel. 120.

Police: Public Security Bureau (gōngān jú; 公安局), 85 Beichizi Dajie (tel. 6524 2063; Foreigners Section tel. 6404 7799, ext 2061; Visa Administrative Dept. tel. 6512 8871 2860), east of the Forbidden City.

Telephones: Almost all accommodations have telephones for international calls. Charges are high. **Directory Assistance:** tel. 114. **International Directory Assistance:** tel. 115.

GATEWAY CITIES

ACCOMMODATIONS

The mid-stretch of **Nansanhuan Lu,** between Yangqiao and Muxiyuan exits, is a backpackers' dream. **Jing Hua, Lihua,** and **Sea Star** are all within 10min. of one another. These outposts provide dirt-cheap dorms, do laundry, rent bikes, serve a spectrum of inexpensive food and drink, and often arrange tours, reserve and confirm tickets, and offer email. What's more, the clientele of these backpackers' havens is fascinating—many have just rolled in off the Trans-Siberian or are perennial itinerants, with stories to tell from the four corners of the globe. Officially, Beijing hotels and hostels do not allow foreigners and Chinese to share rooms—a plot, some say, to keep the capital's foreigners together under supervision—and occasionally prevent unmarried couples from staying together. Unless otherwise stated, check-out is noon, reservations are accepted, and reception is open 24hr.

Jing Hua Youth Hostel (jīnghuá fàndiàn; 京华饭店), Xiluoyuan Nanli, Yongdingmenwai Dajie, Fengtai District (tel. 6722 2211; fax 6721 1455); just tell the taxi driver to go to Yangqiao, or hop on bus #66 from Qianmen to Yangqiao. The huge complex is east of the smelly river from McDonald's. With a pool, a 24hr. bar, co-ed dorms, and an unending flow of travelers, Jing Hua is a cauldron of carousal, arousal, and extra-spousal scandal. More travel tips are exchanged over Y3 beers in the backyard than can be found in any tourist office. The Friendship Bar outside the hotel serves baguettes, muesli, and everything in between. Tourist center arranges everything from trips to Simatai to acrobatic performances. Laundry Y10 per kg. Bike rental Y10 per day with Y400 deposit. Internet Y15 per 30min. Deposit Y50. 30-bed dorm Y25, 4-bed basement dorm Y30, 4-bed new dorm Y35; doubles with bath Y140.

Lihua Hotel (lìhuá fàndiàn; 丽华饭店), 71 Yongdingmenwai, near Yangqiao, Fengtai District (tel. 6721 1144; fax 6721 1367). Take bus #14, 66, or 343 from downtown to Lihua, or bus #324, 368, or 300 to nearby Yangqiao and head south. Nicer than Jing Hua with bright red carpets, two restaurants, and more pleasant room service. Rooms come with A/C. 24hr. hot water. Laundry. Key deposit Y50. 4-bed dorms (single-sex) with communal bath Y30 and Y56; doubles Y132, with bath Y198.

Sea Star Branch (hǎixīng dàjiǔdiàn; 海兴大酒店), 166 Haihutun, Yongwai Mu Xu Yuan, Fengtai District (tel. 6721 8855, ext. 3359 and 3358; fax 6722 7915). A 20min. walk from bus #66's Yangqiao stop; the termini of buses #2 (to Tiananmen), 40, 324, 366 are also nearby. Jing Hua's close cousin, Sea Star is so overrun with loud soldiers and old cigarette butts that only the lost and luckless end up here. Deposit Y50. No reservations. 8- to 10-bed dorms Y25, bunk beds in 4- to 5-bed dorms Y30; doubles Y170.

FOOD

The streets of Beijing burst with food. The *hutongs* overflow with stalls that vary in quality but are consistently low in price; special attention should be paid to the areas around **Qianmen** and **Wangfujing,** and **Tiantan, Ritan,** and **Beihai Parks.** An absolute must-see, the night food market at **Donganmen,** off Wangfujing Dajie, serves treats like fried ice cream and more exotic fare like whole-sparrows-on-a-stick nightly from dusk to 9:30pm. For an easy sit-down meal, head into any restaurant that advertises *jiachangcai* (家常菜). Tasty, filling meals can be had for about Y10-20, but ask to see the prices first, as foreigners are often charged more.

Beijing duck is as intrinsic to the capital's history as *jingiu* and the Forbidden City. Food fit for kings, at prices budget travelers can stomach, is available at **Qianmen Quanjude Roast Duck Restaurant** (qiánmén quánjùdé kǎoyādiàn; 前门全聚德烤鸭店), 32 Qianmen Dajie (tel. 6511 2418 or 6701 1379; fax 6511 2105). Founded in 1864, the third year of Emperor Tongzhi's reign, the restaurant offers myriad gradations of price and poshness. Whether served on styrofoam or china, the duck is the same throughout the restaurant, and Quanjude's duck is the genuine article. A pictorial menu helps to walk tourists through a first-time Beijing duck experience. A plate of duck costs Y25, the pancake wrappers Y2 each, and the extras, like spring rolls and duck heads, priced accordingly. (Open daily 11am-9pm.)

GLOSSARIES

THE CYRILLIC ALPHABET

The Cyrillic alphabet is a script used in Belarus, Bulgaria, Macedonia, Moldova, Serbia, Russia, Ukraine, and throughout the former Soviet Union. On mission in Great Moravia (part of modern-day Czech Republic and Slovakia), two 9th-century monks developed the alphabet's first form in order to translate the Bible into Slavic. The monks, Cyril and Methodius, were Greek (which is why many Cyrillic letters look Greek) and Orthodox, so when Catholic powers gained control of the region that the monks were proselytizing, their disciples fled to the shores of Lake Ohrid (Macedonia), which, at the time, belonged to Bulgaria. There they founded the first Slavic university, and the script spread swiftly to other Slavic lands.

For many centuries, Cyrillic was a source of unity for the Slavic nations who wrote in it, and its use (or non-use) still makes a political statement in some parts of the world. One of the major differences between the otherwise very similar Serb and Croat languages is that Croatian is written in the Latin alphabet, while Serbian is written in Cyrillic. Furthermore, as republics of the former Soviet Union are discovering their roots, they are learning their own scripts instead of Cyrillic, which for decades Moscow had made the empire's *scripta franca*.

The Russian Cyrillic transliteration index is given below. Other languages include some additional letters and pronounce certain letters differently. Each country's language section outlines these distinctions.

CYRILLIC	ENGLISH	PRONOUNCE
А а	a	Garden
Б б	b	Mr. Burns
В в	v	Village People
Г г	g	Galina
Д д	d	David
Е е	ye or e	Yellow
Ё ё	yo	Your
Ж ж	zh	Zhirinovsky
З з	z	Zany
И и	ee	Kathleen
Й й	y	(see * below)
К к	k	Killjoy
Л л	l	Louis
М м	m	Meteor
Н н	n	Nikki
О о	o	Hole
П п	p	Peter the Great
Р р	r	Random
С с	s	Saucy
Т т	t	Tantalize
У у	oo	Doodle
Ф ф	f	Absolutely Fab
Х х	kh	Chutzpah (hkh)
Ц ц	ts	Let's Go
Ч ч	ch	Chinese
Щ ш	sh	Champagne
Ш щ	shch	Khrushchev
ъ	(hard)	(no sound)
ы	y	lit
ь	(soft)	(no sound)
Э э	eh	Alexander
Ю ю	yoo	You
Я я	yah	Yahoo!

* Й creates dipthongs, altering the sounds of the vowels it follows: ОЙ is pronounced "oy" (b*oy*), АЙ is pronounced "aye" (b*ye*), ИЙ is pronounced "ee" (bab*y*), and ЕЙ is pronounced "ehy" (b*ay*).

BULGARIAN (БЪЛГАРСКИ)

Bulgarian pronunciation is much the same as Russian except that "x" is *h*, "щ" is *sht*, and "ъ" is either *a* or *u* (pronounced like the "u" in b*u*g).

PHRASEBOOK

ENGLISH	BULGARIAN	PRONOUNCIATION
Yes/no	Да/Не	dah/neh
Please	Извинете	eez-vi-NEH-teh

ENGLISH	BULGARIAN	PRONOUNCIATION
Thank you	Благодаря	blahg-oh-dahr-YAH
Hello	Добър ден	DOH-bur den
Good-bye	Добиждане	doh-VIZH-dan-eh
Good morning	Добро утро	doh-BROH U-troh
Good night	Лека Нощ	LEH-ka nosht
I beg your pardon?	Моля	MOL-ya
When?	Кога?	ko-GA
Where is...?	Къде е?	kuh-DEH eh
Help	Помощ	PO-mosht
How much does this cost?	Колко Струва?	KOHL-ko STROO-va
Do you have...?	Имате Ли...?	EEH-mah-teh lee
Do you speak English?	Говорите ли Английски?	go-VO-rih-te li an-GLIS-keeh
I don't understand	Не разбирам.	neh rahz-BIH-rahm
I'd like to order...	Искам Да...	EES-kahm da
I'd like a room.	Искам стая	EES-kahm STAH-yah
With shower	с душ/вана	s dush/ VA-na
Will you tell me when to get off?	Извинете, кода тряба да сляза?	eez-vee-NEH-teh ko-GAH TRYAHB-vah dah SLYAH-zah?

GLOSSARY

ENGLISH	BULGARIAN	PRNOUNCE
one	едно	ehd-NO
two	две	dveh
three	три	tree
four	четири	CHEH-tee-ree
five	пет	peht
six	шест	shesht
seven	седем	SEH-dehm
eight	осем	O-sehm
nine	девет	DEH-veht
ten	десет	DEH-seht
twenty	двадесет	DVAH-DEH-seht
fifty	петдесет	peht-deh-SEHT
one hundred	сто	stoh
one thousand	хиляда	hi-LYA-da
left	отляво	ot-LYAH-vo
right	отдясно	ot-DYAHS-no
bus	автобус	ahv-to-BOOS
train	влак	vlahk

ENGLISH	BULGARIAN	PRONOUNCE
arrival	пристигащи	pristigashti
departure	заминаващи	zaminavashti
station	гара	gara
round-trip	отиване и Връщане	o-TEE-van-e ee VRI-shtah-neh
one-way	отиване	o-TEE-vahn-eh
open	отварят	ot-VAR-yaht
closed	затварят	zaht-VAR-yaht
meat	месо	MEH-so
vegetables	зеленчуыи	zelenchuyee
water	вода	vo-DAH
coffee	кафе	kah-FEH
wine	вино	VEE-no
juice	сок	sok
milk	мляко	MLYAH-ko
beer	ьира	BEE-rah
tea	чай	tchai
grocery	бакалия	bah-kah-LIH-ya
bread	хляб	hlyab

CROATIAN

Words are pronounced exactly as they are written; "č" and "ć" are both pronounced "ch," "š" is "sh," and "ž" is "zh." The letter "r" is rolled, except when there's no vowel, then it makes an "er" sound as in "Brrrr!" The letter "j" is equivalent to "y," so *jučer* (yesterday) is pronounced "yuchur."

PHRASEBOOK

ENGLISH	CROATIAN	PRONOUNCIATION
Yes/no	Da/Ne	Da/Neh
Please/You're welcome	Molim	MO-leem

ENGLISH	CROATIAN	PRONOUNCIATION
Thank you	Hvala vam	HVAH-la vahm
Hello/Hi/Good-bye	Zdravo/Bog/Doviđenja	ZDRAH-vo/bog/do-vee-JEHN-ya
Good morning/Good night	Dobro jutro/Laku noć	DO-bro YOO-tro/LA-koo noch
When?	Kada?	KA-da
Where is...?	Gdje je?	GDYE je
Help!	U pomoć!	OO pomoch
Go away	Bježi/Idi odavde	BYEH-zhee/EE-dee
How much does this cost?	Koliko to košta?	KO-li-koh toh KOH-shta
Do you have...?	Imate li...?	EEM-a-teh lee
Do you speak English?	Govorite li engleski?	GO-vor-i-teh lee eng-LEH-ski
I don't understand.	Ne razumijem.	neh ra-ZOO-mi-yem
I'd like to order...	Želio bih naručiti...	Jelim na-ROO-chiti
Check, please.	Račun, molim.	RACH-un mo-leem
I'd like a room.	Želio bih sobu.	ZHEL-i-o bih SO-bu
Will you tell me when to get off?	Hoćete li mi reći kada tebam sići	ho-CHEH-teh lee mee REH-cheh KAH-dah TREH-bahm SEE-chee
I want a ticket to...	Htio bih kartu za...	HTEE-o beeh KAHR-too zah...
When is the next train to...	Kada je slijedenći vlak za...	KAH-dah yeh ZAH-dnyee vlahk za ...
How do I get to...?	Kako mogu doći do ...?	KAH-ko MO-goo DO-chee do...
Where is the bathroom/nearest public phone/center of town?	Gdje je kadom/nalazi najbliža telefonska govornica/centar grada?	gdyeh yeh KAH-dom/NAH-lahzee nahy-BLEE-zhah tehleh-FON-skah govor-NEE-tsah/TSEN-tahr GRAH-dah?

GLOSSARY

ENGLISH	CROATIAN	PRONOUNCE
one	jedan	ehd-NO
two	dva	dveh
three	tri	tree
four	četiri	CHEH-tee-ree
five	pet	peht
six	šest	shesht
seven	sedam	SEH-dahm
eight	osam	O-sehm
nine	devet	DEH-veht
ten	deset	DEH-seht
twenty	dvadeset	DVAH-dehseht
fifty	pedeset	peh-DEH-seht
one hundred	sto	sto
one thousand	tisuća	TEE-soo-chah

ENGLISH	CROATIAN	PRONOUNCE
station	kolodvor	KOL-o-dvor
round-trip	povratna karta	POV-rat-na KAR-ta
one-way	u jednom smjerna	oo YEH-dnom smee-YEH-roo
bread	kruh	krooh
beer	pivo	PEE-voh
tea	čaj	chahy
meat	meso	MEH-so
vegetables	povrče	POH-ver-chay
water	voda	VO-dah
coffee	kava	KAH-vah
wine	vino	VEE-no
juice	sok	sok
left	lijevo	leeyehvo
right	desno	dehtsno

CZECH (ČESKY)

The trick to good pronunciation is to pronouce every letter. Stress is always placed on the first syllable. However, don't confuse stress with elongation. When there is a diacritical over a vowel—such as á, é, í, ó, ú, ů, and ý—this simply means you hold the vowel sound for longer; do not place the emphasis on the vowel. In other words, *dobrý* is pronounced DOH-bree-ee and not doh-BREE. C is prnounced "ts"; g is always hard, as in *g*od; ch, which is considered one letter, is a cross between "h" and "k" and actually comes from the back of your throat (imagine Arabic), but "h" is a comprehensible approximation; j is "y"; r is slightly rolled; and w is "v." The letter ě softens the preceding consonant: dě (also written ď) becomes "dy," as in *děkují* (DYEH-koo-yee-ee, not DEH-koo-yee-ee); mě is "mnye," as in *město* (MNYEH-stoh, not MEH-stoh); ně (also written ň) is "ny," as in *něco* (NYEH-tsoh, not NEH-tso); and tě (also written ť) is "ty," as *tělo* (TYEH-loh, not TEH-loh). All other diacriticals soften the consonant: č is "ch," ř is "rzh" (see "The World's Most Difficult Sound," p. 181), š is "sh," and ž is "zh."

PHRASEBOOK

ENGLISH	CZECH	PRONOUNCIATION
Yes/no	Ano/ne	AH-no/neh
Please/You're welcome	Prosím	PROH-seem
Thank you	Děkuji	DYEH-koo-yih
Hello	Dobrý den	DO-bree den
Good-bye	Na shledanou	NAH sleh-dah-noh-oo
Good morning	Dobré ráno	DO-breh RAH-no
Good night	Dobrou noc	DO-broh NOTS
Sorry/Excuse me	Promiňte	PROH-mihn-teh
Help!	Pomoc!	POH-mots
When?	Kdy?	k-DEE
Where is...?	Kde?	k-DEH
How do I get to...?	Jak se dostanu do...?	YAK seh dohs-TAH-noo doh
How much does this cost?	Kolik stojí?	KOH-lihk STOH-yee
Do you have...?	Máte..?	MAH-teh
Do you speak English?	Mluvíte anglicky?	MLOO-vit-eh ahng-GLIT-ski
I don't understand.	Nerozumím.	NEH-rohz-oo-meem
I don't speak Czech.	Nemluvím český.	NEH-mloo-veem CHESS-kee
Please write it down.	Prosím napište.	PRO-seem nah-PEESH-tye
I'd like to order...	Chtěl bych...	khtyel bikh
I'd like to pay/We'd like to pay.	Zaplatím/zaplatíme.	ZAH-plah-teem/ZAH-plah-tee-meh
Do you have a vacancy?	Máte volný pokoj?	MAH-te VOL-nee PO-koy
I'd like a room.	Želio bih sobu.	ZHEL-i-o bih SO-bu
May I see the room?	Mohl(a) bych se podívat na ten pokoj?	MO-hul (MO-hla) bikh se PO-dyeh-vat na ten PO-koy
Will you tell me when to get off?	Řekněte mi kdy mám vystoupit?	RZHEK-nete mi gdy mahm VI-stohpit
Is this the right train to...?	Je tohle vlak do...?	yeh TOH-leh vlahk DO...
I want a ticket to...	Chtětl a bych jízdenku do...	khytel a bikh YEEZ-denkoo DO...
When is the next train to...	Kdy jede příští vlak do...?	gdi YE-de ... vlak DO-pulznye
Where is the bathroom/nearest telelphone booth/center of town?	Kde je toalety/tady nejbližší telefonní budka/městské centrum?	gde ye TO-aleti/TA-di NE-yblish-nee TE-le-fo-nee BOOT-ka/MNE-HST-skeh TSEN-troom
Would you like to go out with me tonight?	Mohl(a) bych se večer sejít?	MO-hul (MO-hla) bikh se VE-cher SE-yeet
Would you like to dance?	Chtěl(a) byste si zatančit?	khtyehl(a) BI-ste si ZA-tan-chit

GLOSSARY

ENGLISH	CZECH	PRONOUNCE
one	jeden	YEH-den
two	dva	dv-YEH
three	tři	tr-ZHIH
four	čtyři	SHTEER-zhee
five	pět	p-YEHT
six	šest	shest
seven	sedm	SEH-duhm
eight	osm	OSS-uhm

ENGLISH	CZECH	PRONOUNCE
post office	pošta	POSH-ta
stamps	známka	ZNAHM-ka
departure	odjezd	OD-yezd
round-trip	zpáteční	SPAH-tech-nyee
reservation	místenka	mis-TEN-kah
train	vlak	vlahk
airport	letiště	LEH-tish-tyeh
grocery	potraviny	PO-tra-vee-nee

ENGLISH	CZECH	PRONOUNCE
nine	devět	dehv-YEHT
ten	deset	des-SEHT
twenty	dvacet	dvah-TSEHT
thirty	třicet	tr-zhih-TSEHT
forty	čtyřicet	chteer-zhee-TSEHT
fifty	padesát	pah-des-AHT
sixty	šedesát	sheh-des-AHT
seventy	sedmdesát	SE-dum-des-AT
eighty	osmdesát	os-um-des-AHT
ninety	devadesát	deh-vah-des-AT
one hundred	sto	stoh
one thousand	tisíc	TI-seets
Monday	pondělí	PON-dye-lee
Tuesday	úterý	OO-teh-ree
Wednesday	středa	stshreh-dah
Thursday	čtvrtek	CHTV'R-tek
Friday	pátek	PAH-tek
Saturday	sobota	SO-boh-ta
overnight	na jednu noc	NA-yed-noo nots
a few days	několik dnů	NYEH-kolik dnoo
a week	týden	TEE-den
hot	horké	HOR-keh
cold	studené	STU-den-eh
single room	jednolůžkový pokoj	YED-no-loosh-ko-vee PO-koy
double room	dvoulůžkový pokoj	DVOH-loosh-ko-vee PO-koy
reservation	reservaci	mahm RE-zer-va-tsi
with a bath/ shower	s koupelnou/ se sprchnou	SKOH-pel-noh/ SEspur-khoh
pharmacy	lékárna	LEH-kahrna
market	trh	turkh
toilets	toalety	TO-aleti
museum	muzeum	MOO-zeoom
square	náměstí	NAH-mnye-styee
castle	zámek/hrad	ZAH-mek/hrat
church	kostel	KOS-tel
tower	věž	vyesh
wallet	peněženku	PE-nye-zhen-koo
passport	pas	pas
air mail	letecký	LEH-tets-kee

ENGLISH	CZECH	PRONOUNCE
lunch	oběd	OB-yed
menu	listek	LIS-tek
bread	chléb	khleb
vegetables	zelenina	ZE-le-nee-na
beef	hovězí	HO-vye-zee
chicken	kuře	KOO-rzheh
coffee	káva	KAH-va
milk	mléko	MLEH-koh
beer	pivo	PEE-voh
sugar	cukr	TSOO-kur
eggs	vejce	VEY-tse
Sunday	neděle	NEH-dyeh-leh
holiday	prazdniny	PRAHZ-dni-nee
today	dnes	dness
tomorrow	zítra	ZEE-tra
open	otevřeno	O-te-zheno
closed	zavřeno	ZAV-rzhen-o
bank	banka	BAN-ka
exchange	směnárna	smyeh-NAR-na
arrival	příjezd	PREE-yezd
one-way	jen tam	yen tam
ticket	lístek	LIS-tek
station	nádraží	NA-drah-zhee
bus	autobus	OUT-oh-boos
bakery	pekařství	PE-karzh-stvee
breakfast	snídaně	SNEE-dan-ye
dinner	večeře	VE-cher-zhe
left	levé	LEH-vah
right	pravé	PRAH-vah
morning	ráno	RAH-no
afternoon	odpoledne	OT-pol-ed-ne
evening	večer	VE-cher
today	dnes	d-NEHS
tomorrow	zítra	ZEE-trah
spring	jaro	YA-ro
summer	léto	LEH-to
fall	podzim	POD-zim
winter	zima	ZI-ma

GLOSSARIES

ESTONIAN (ESTI KEEL)

PHRASEBOOK

ENGLISH	ESTONIAN	PRONOUNCIATION
Yes/no	Jaa/Ei	yah/rhymes with "hay"
Please	Palun	PAH-luhn
Thank you	Tänan	TÆ-nan
Hello	Tere	TEH-re

ENGLISH	ESTONIAN	PRONOUNCIATION
Good-bye	Head aega	hehaht EYE-kah
Good morning	Tere hommikust	TEH-re ho-mih-KUHST
Good night	Head ööd	hehaht euht
Excuse me	Vabandage	vah-pan-TAGE-euh
When?	Millal?	mih-LAL?
Where is...?	Kus on...?	Kuhs on...
Help!	Appi!	APP-pi
How do I get to...?	Mina soovisin minna...?	MIH-nah soo-VIK-sin MIH-na
How much does this cost?	Kui palju?	Kwee PAL-you?
Do you have...?	Kas teil on ...?	kass tayl on ...?
Do you speak English?	Kas te räägite inglise keelt?	kass teh rah-KIHT-eh ihn-KLIS-eh keelt
I don't understand.	Ma ei saa aru.	mah ay saw AH-rooh
I'd like to order...	Ma sooviksin...	mah SOO-vik-sin
Check, please.	Ma sooviksin maksta	ma soo-vik-sin MAKS-ta
I'd like a room.	Ma sooviksin tuba.	mah SOO-vik-sin TUH-bah
With shower/bath	duššiga/vanniga	DUSH-shi-ga/VAH-ni-ga
Will you tell me when to get off?	Palun öelge kus ma pean väljuma?	PAH-loon EULL-geh koos mah peh-ahn VAHL-yoo-mah?
I want a ticket to...	Ma sooviksin ühte piletit...	mah SOO-veek-seen EWKH-teh PEE-leh-teet...
When is the next train to...?	Millal läheb järgmine rong...?	MEEL-lahl LAA-hehb YAARG-meen-eh rohng...?

GLOSSARY

ENGLISH	ESTONIAN	PRONOUNCE
one	üks	ewks
two	kaks	kaks
three	kolm	kohlm
four	neli	NEH-lee
five	viis	veese
six	kuus	koose
seven	seitse	SEIT-se
eight	kaheksa	KAH-eks-ah
nine	üheksa	EUW-eks-ah
ten	kümme	KEUW-meh
twenty	kakskümmend	KAHKS-kewm-mehnd
fifty	viiskümmend	VEES-kewm-mend
one hundred	sada	SA-da
one thousand	tuhat	TU-hat
left	vasakul	VAH-sah-keul
right	paremal	PAH-reh-mahl

ENGLISH	ESTONIAN	PRONOUNCE
arrival	saabub	SAA-boob
departure	väljub	VAL-yoob
round-trip	edasi-tagasi piletit	E-dasi-TA-gasi PI-let-it
one-way	üheotsa piletit	EW-he-OHT-sah PI-le-tiht
station	jaam	yaam
grocery	toidupood	TOY-du-POOD
bread	leiba	LAY-eeb-a
vegetables	juurvili	YUR-vee-lee
water	vesi	VEH-si
coffee	kohv	kokhv
wine	vein	VAY-een
juice	jamahl	ya-MAXL
milk	piim	peem
beer	ôlu	elu
tea	tee	teee
meat	liha	LI-ha

HUNGARIAN (MAGYAR)

A few starters for pronunciation: "*c*" is pronounced "ts" as in "pots"; "*cs*" is "ch" as in "which"; "*gy*" is "dy" as in "*adieu*"; "*ly*" is "y" as in "yak"; "*s*" is "sh" as in "shard"; "*sz*" is "s" as in "cell-phone"; "*zs*" is "zh" as in "fusion"; and "*a*" is "a" as in "paw." The first syllable is always stressed.

PHRASEBOOK

ENGLISH	MAGYAR	PRONOUNCIATION
Yes/no	Igen/nem	EE-ghen/nem
Please	Kérem	KAY-rem
Thank you	Köszönöm	KUH-suh-num
Hello	Szervusz	SAIR-voose
Good-bye	Viszontlátásra	Vi-sont-lah-tah-shraw
Good morning	Jó reggelt	YOH reh-gehlt
Good night	Jó éjszakát	YOH ay-sokat
Excuse me	Elnézést	EL-nay-zaysht
My name is...	...vagyok	vah-djawk
What is your name?	Hogy hívják	hawdj HEE-vyahk
When?	Mikor?	MI-kor
Where is...?	Hol van...?	hawl von
How do you get to...?	Hogy jutok...?	hawdj YOO-tawk
How much does this cost?	Mennyibe kerül?	MEN-yee-beh KEH-rewl
Do you have...?	Van...?	von
Do you speak English?	Beszél angolul?	BESS-ayl ON-goal-ool
I don't understand.	Nem értem	nem AYR-tem
I don't speak Hungarian.	Nem tudok magyarul.	Nehm TOO-dawk MAH-dyah-rool
Please write it down?	Kérem, írja fel.	KAY-rem, EER-yuh fell.
Speak a little slower, please.	Kérem, beszéljen lassan	KAY-rem, BESS-ayl-yen LUSH-shun
Help!	Ségitség!	she-geet-shayg
I'd like to order...	...kérek.	KAY-rek
Check, please.	A számlát, kérem.	uh SAHM-lot KAY-rem
Do you have a vacancy?	Volna valami?	VAWL-na VO-lom-mee
with shower/bath?	zahanyzós/fürdoszobás?	ZOO-hon-y-aw-yawsh/FEWR-dur-saw-baash
I'd like a room.	Ma sooviksin tuba.	ma SOO-vik-sin TU-ba
May I see the room?	Kas ma saaksin tuba näha?	kas ma SAAAK-sin TU-ba NÆ-ha
No. I don't like it.	Ei. See ei meeldi mulle.	ei. seee ei MEEEL-di muLL-le
That's fine. I'll take it.	See sobib. Ma vôtan selle.	seee SO-bib. ma VEH-tan SEL-le
Will you tell me when to get off?	Palun öelge kus ma pean väljuma?	PA-lun UH-EL-geh kus
I want a ticket to...	Ma sooviksin ühte piletit...	ma SOO-vik-sin ewkh-te PI-le-tit
When is the first/next/last train to...?	Millal läheb esimene/järgmine/viimane rong...?	MI-llal LÆ-heb E-si-mene/YÆRG-mine/VII-mane rong
Where is the nearest (public phone)?	Kus on lähim (avalik telefon)?	kus on LÆ-him (A-va-lik TE-le-fon)
I'm lost.	Ma olen ära eksinud.	ma O-len Æ-ra EK-si-nud
Is this the right train to...?	Kas see rong läheb...?	kas seee rong LÆ-heb RIII-ga
I've lost my...	Ma olen oma...ära kaotanud.	ma O-len O-ma...Æ-ra KAO-ta-nud
Go away!	Távozzék!	TAH-vawz-zayk

GLOSSARIES

GLOSSARY

ENGLISH	MAGYAR	PRONOUNCE	ENGLISH	MAGYAR	PRONOUNCE
one	egy	edge	departure	indulás	IN-dool-ahsh
two	kettő	ket-tuuh	arrival	érkezés	ayr-keh-zaysh
three	három	hah-rom	one-way	csak oda	chok AW-do
four	négy	naydj	round-trip	oda-vissza	AW-do-VEES-so
five	öt	uh-t	ticket	jegyet	YED-et
six	hat	hut	station	pályaudvar	pa-yo-OOT-var
seven	hét	hayte	train	vonat	VAW-not
eight	nyolc	nyoltz	airport	repülőtér	rep-ewlu-TAYR
nine	kilenc	kih-lentz	bus	buss	busss
ten	tíz	tease	single/double	ühelist/kahe-list	EW-hel-ist/KA-hel-ist
twenty	húsz	hoose	with twin beds	kahe voodiga	KA-he VOOO-di-ga
thirty	harminc	har-mintz	with a double bed	kaheinimese voodiga	KA-he-I-ni-mese VOOO-di-ga
forty	negyven	nedj-ven	with a bath/ with a shower	vanniga/ duššiga	VAN-ni-ga/ DUSH-shi-ga
fifty	ötven	ut-ven	post office	posta	pawsh-tuh
sixty	hatvan	hut-von	stamp	bélyeg	BAY-yeg
seventy	hetven	het-ven	airmail	légipostán	LAY-ghee-pawsh-tahn
eighty	nyolcvan	nyoltz-van	bank	bank	bonk
ninety	kilencven	kih-lentz-ven	exchange	valutabeváltó	VO-loo-tob-be-vaal-taw
hundred	száz	saaz	pharmacy	apteek	AP-teeek
thousand	ezer	eh-zehr	market	suur toidukau-plus	suuur TOI-du-KAUP-lus
Monday	hétfő	hayte-phuuh	city center	linnakeskus	LIN-na-KES-kus
Tuesday	kedd	ked	left/right	vasakul/pare-mal	VA-sa-kul/PA-re-mal
Wednesday	szerda	sayr-dah	grocery	élelmiszerbolt	Ay-lel-meser-balt
Thursday	csütörtök	chew-ter-tek	bakery	leivapood	LEI-va-POOOD
Friday	péntek	paine-tek	breakfast	reggeli	REG-gell-ee
Saturday	szombat	SAWM-baht	lunch	ebéd	EB-ayhd
Sunday	vasárnap	VAHSH-ahr-nahp	dinner	vacsora	VOTCH-oh-rah
holiday	ünnepnap	ewn-nap-nop	menu	étlap	ATE-lop
today	ma	mah	milk	tej	tay
tomorrow	holnap	HAWL-nahp	beer	sör	shurr
in the morning	hommikul	HOM-mi-kul	water	víz	veez
during the day	päeval	PÆE-val	juice	gyümölcslé	DYEW-murl-chlay
evening	õhtul	EHKH-tul	coffee	kávé	KAA-vay
spring	kevad	KE-vad	wine	bor	bawr
summer	suvi	SU-vi	bread	kenyér	KEN-yair
fall/winter	sügis/talv	SEW-gis/talv	vegetables	zöldségek	ZULD-segek
rare	kergelt läbiküpsetatud	KER-gelt LÆ-bi-KEWP-se-ta-tud	beef	marhahúst	MOR-ho-hoosht
medium	keskmiselt läbiküpsetatud	KESK-mi-selt LÆ-bi-KEWP-se-ta-tud	pork	sertéshúst	SHER-taysh-hoosht
well-done	hästi läbiküpsetatud	HÆS-ti LÆ-bi-KEWP-se-ta-tud	fish	hal	hull

LATVIAN (LATVISKA)

PHRASEBOOK

ENGLISH	LATVIAN	PRONOUNCIATION
Yes/no	Jā/nē	yah/ney
Please	Lūdzu	LOOD-zuh
Thank you	Paldies	PAHL-dee-yes
Hello	Labdien	LAHB-dyen
Good-bye	Uz redzēšanos	ooz RE-dzeh-shan-was
Good morning	Labrīt	LAHB-reet
Good night	Ar labu nakti	ar LA-boo NA-kti
I beg your pardon?	Atvainojiet	AHT-vye-no-yet
When?	Kad?	KAHD
Where is...?	Kur ir...?	kuhr ihr
Help!	Palīgā!	PAH-lee-gah
How do I get to...?	Kā es varu nokļūt uz...?	kah ess VA-roo NOkly-oot ooz
How much does this cost?	Cik maksā?	sikh MAHK-sah
Do you have...?	Vai jums ir...?	vai yoomss ir
Do you speak English?	Vai jūs runājat angliski?	vai yoos ROO-nah-yat AN-glee-ski
I don't understand.	Es nesaprotu.	ehs NEH-sah-proh-too
I'd like to order...	Es vēlos...	ess VE-lwass
Check, please.	Lūdzu rēķinu.	LOOD-zu RAY-tyi-noo
Do you have any vacancies?	Vai jums ir brīvas istabas?	vai yums ir BREE-vas IS-tab-as
with shower/bath?	zahanyzós/fürdoszobás?	ZOO-hon-y-aw-yawsh/FEWR-dur-saw-baash
May I see the room?	Vai es varu redzēt istabu?	vay ehss VAH-roo REHD-zeht IHS-tah-boo
I want a ticket to...	Es vēlos biļeti uz...	ehss VAAL-wass BIHL-yet-ih ooz
Will you tell me when to get off?	Lūdzu pasakiet, kad jāizkāpj?	LOOD-zoo pah-sah-kee-aht, kahd YAH-IHS-kah-pye

GLOSSARY

ENGLISH	LATVIAN	PRONOUNCE
one	viens	vee-yenz
two	divi	DIH-vih
three	trīs	treese
four	četri	CHEH-trih
five	pieci	PYET-sih
six	seši	SEH-shih
seven	septini	SEHP-tih-nyih
eight	astoņi	AHS-toh-nyih
nine	devini	DEH-vih-nyih
ten	desmit	DEZ-miht
twenty	divdesmit	DIHV-dehs-miht
fifty	piecdesmit	PEE-AHTS-dehs-miht
hundred	simts	sihmts
thousand	tūkstots	TOOKS-twats
juice	sula	SOO-la

ENLIGH	LATVIAN	PRONOUNCE
station	stacija	STAH-tsee-uh
round-trip	turp un atpakaļ	toorp oon AT-pakal
one-way	vienā virzienā	VEEA-nah VIR-zee-an-ah
Please stop here	Lūdzu apstājieties šeit	LOO-dzoo AP-stah-yeea-teeas sheyt
How far?	Cīk talu?	tsik TA-loo
right	pa labi	PAH lah-bih
left	pa kreisi	PAH kreh-ih-sih
grocery	pārtikas veikals	PAHR-tih-kas VEY-kalss
vegetables	dārzeņi	DAR-ze-nyih
bread	maizi	MAI-zi
meat	gaļa	GA-la
water	ūdens	OO-dens
coffee	kafija	KAH-fee-yah
tea	tēja	TAY-yah
beer	alus	AH-lus

LITHUANIAN (LIETUVIŞKAI)

PHRASEBOOK

ENGLISH	LITHUANIAN	PRONOUNCIATION
Yes/no	Taip/ne	TAYE-p/NEH
Please/You're welcome	Prašau	prah-SHAU
Thank you	Ačiū	AH-chyoo
Hello	Labas	LAH-bahss
Good-bye	Viso gero	VEE-soh GEh-roh
Good morning	Labas rytas	LAH-bahss REE-tahss
Good night	Labanaktis	lah-BAH-nahk-tiss
Excuse me/I'm Sorry	Atsiprašau	aHT-sih-prh-SHAU
When?	Kada?	KAH-da
Where is...?	Kur yra...?	Koor ee-RAH
Help!	Gelbėkite!	GYEL-behk-ite
How do I get to...?	Kaip nueti į...?	KYE-p nuh-EH-tih ee
How much does this cost?	Kiek kainuoja?	KEE-yek KYE-new-oh-yah
Do you have...?	Ar turite..?	ahr TU-ryite
Do you speak English?	Ar kalbate angliškai?	AHR KULL-buh-teh AHN-gleesh-kye
I don't understand.	Aš nesuprantu	AHSH neh-soo-PRAHN-too
I'd like to order...	Norėčiau...	nor-RAY-chyow
Check, please.	Sąskaitą, prašau	SAHS-kai-ta, prah-SHAU
Do you have any vacancies?	Ar turite laisvų kambarių?	ahr TU-ryite lai-SVOO KAHM-bah-ryoo
May I see the room?	Ar galiu pamatyti kambarį?	ahr gah-LEE-OO pah-mah-TEE-tih KAHM-bah-ree
I want a ticket to...	Aš norėčiau bilieto į...	ahsh nohr-YEH-chee-ah-oo BYEE-lee-eh-toh ee...

GLOSSARY

ENGLISH	LITHUANIAN	PRONOUNCE
one	vienas	VYEH-nahss
two	du	doo
three	trys	treese
four	keturi	keh-TUH-rih
five	penki	PEHN-kih
six	šeši	SHEH-shih
seven	septyni	sehp-TEE-nih
eight	aštuoni	ahsh-too-OH-ni
nine	devyni	deh-VEE-nih
ten	dešimt	deh-SHIMT
hundred	šimtas	SHIM-tahs
thousand	tukstantis	TOOK-stan-tis
left	kairę	KAH-ihr-aa
right	dešinę	DEHSH-ihn-aa
today	šiandien	SHYEHN-dih-ehn
tomorrow	rytoj	ree-TOY

ENGLISH	LITHUANIAN	PRONOUNCE
arrival	atvyksta	at-VEEK-stah
departure	išvyksta	ish-VEEK-stah
station	stotis	stow-TISS
train station	geležinkelio sto-tis	geh-leh-ZHIN-keh-lio stow-TISS
bus	autobusas	ow-TOH-boo-suhs
train	traukinys	trow-kih-NEES
round-trip	grįžtamasio bili-eto	GREEZH-tah-mah-sio BI-lieto
one-way	i vieną galą	ee VIE-naa GAH-laa
grocery	maisto prekės	MYE-stoh PREH-kays
bread	duona	DWOH-na
vegetables	daržovė	dar-ZHO-ve
water	vanduo	van-DWOH
coffee	kava	KAH-vah
wine	vynas	VEE-nas
juice	sultys	SUL-tyees
beer	alus	AH-lus

GLOSSARIES

POLISH (POLSKI)

The fully phonetic spelling is complicated by some letters not in the Latin alphabet: "*ł*" sounds like a "w"; "*ą*" is a nasal "on"; "*ę*" is a nasal "en." A dash above a consonant softens it: "*ó*" and "*u*" are both equivalent to an "oo." "*Ż*" and "*rz*" are both like the "s" in "pleasure"; "*w*" sounds like "v." The language also has a few consonantal clusters, which are easier to spit out than they seem: "*sz*" is "sh," "*cz*" is "ch," and "*ch*" and "*h*" are equivalent, and sound like the English "h."

PHRASEBOOK

ENGLISH	POLISH	PRONOUNCIATION
Yes/no	Tak/nie	tahk/nyeh
Please/You're welcome	Proszę	PROH-sheh
Thank you	Dziękuję	jen-KOO-yeh
Hello/Good morning	Dzień dobry	jeen DO-brih
Hi (informal)	Cześć	cheshch
Good-bye	Do widzenia	doh veedz-EN-yah
Good night	Dobranoc	doh-BRAH-nots
Bon appetit!	Smacznego	smach-NEG-o
Excuse me/I'm sorry	Przepraszam	psheh-PRAH-shahm
Help!	Na pomoc!	nah POH-mots
My name is...	Nazywam się...	nah-ZIH-vahm sheh...
What is your name?	Jak się pan(i) nazywa?	yak sheh PAN(ee) nah-ZIH-vah
When?	Kiedy?	KYEH-dih
Where is...?	Gdzie jest?	g-JAY yest
How do I get to...?	Którędy do...?	ktoo-REN-dih doh
How much does this cost?	Ile to kosztuje?	EE-leh toh kohsh-TOO-yeh
Do you have...?	Czy są...?	chih sawn
Do you speak English?	Czy pan(i) mówi po angielsku?	chih PAHN(-ee) MOO-vee poh ahn-GYEL-skoo
I don't understand.	Nie rozumiem.	nyeh roh-ZOOM-yem
Please write it down.	Proszę napisać.	PROH-sheh nah-PEE-sahch
Please speak more slowly.	Proszę mówić wolniej.	PROH-sheh MOO-veetch VOHL-nee–eh
Have you a vacancy?	Czy są jakieś wolne pokoje?	chih sawn YAH-kyesh VOHL-neh poh-KOY-eh
Private shower?	z prysznicem	zeh prish-NEE-tsem
I'd like a room.	Chciał(a) bym pokój.	KHTS-HAHW(a) bihm POH-kooy
May I see the room?	Czy mogę zobaczyć pokój?	chi MOH-geh zoh-BAH-chihtsh POH-kooj
No, I don't like it.	Nie podoba mi się.	nyeh poh-DOH-bah mee syeh.
Yes, I'll take it.	Tak, wezmę go.	tahk, VEH-zmeh goh.
Will you tell me when to get off?	Proszę mi powiedzieć kiedy wysiaść?	PROH-sheh mee poh-VYEHD-zhe-htch KYEH-dih VIH-syon-sytch?
I want a ticket to...	Poproszę bilet do...	poh-PROH-sheh BEE-leht do...
When is the first/next/last train to...?	Kiedy jest pierwszy/następny/ostatni pociąg do...?	KYEH-dih yehst PYEHR-fshih/nah-STEH-pnih/oh-STAHT-nyee POHT-shawng do...
Where is the bathroom/nearest public phone/center of town?	Gdzie jest łazienka/budka telefoniczna/centrum miasta?	gd-ZHEH yest wahzh-YEHN-ka/BOO-dkah teh-leh-foh-NEE-chnah/TSEHN-troom MYAH-stah
I'm lost.	Zgubiłem się.	zgoo-BEE-wehm syeh
Is this the right train to...?	Czy to jest pociąg do...?	chih toh yehst POH-chawng doh
I've lost my...	Zgubiłem...	zgoo-BEE-wehm
God is love.	Bóg jest miłoscię.	bohg yehst mee-WOSH-yeh

GLOSSARIES

GLOSSARY

ENGLISH	POLISH	PRONOUNCE
one	jeden	YEH-den
two	dwa	dvah
three	trzy	tshih
four	cztery	ch-TEH-rih
five	pięć	pyench
six	sześć	sheshch
seven	siedem	SHEH-dem
eight	osiem	OH-shem
nine	dziewięć	JYEH-vyench
ten	dziesięć	JYEH-shench
twenty	dwadzieścia	dva-JESH-cha
thirty	trzydzieści	tshi-JESH-chi
forty	czterdzieści	chter-JESH-chih
fifty	pięćdziesiąt	pyench-JESH-awnt
sixty	sześćdziesiąt	sheshch-JESH-awnt
seventy	siedemdziesiąt	shed-em-JESH-awnt
eighty	ośiemdziesiąt	ohsh-em-JEE-shawnt
ninety	dziewięć dziesiąt	JYEH-vyen-JESH-awnt
one hundred	sto	stoh
one thousand	tysiąc	TIH-shawns
Monday	poniedziałek	poh-nyeh-JAH-wehk
Tuesday	wtorek	FTOH-rehk
Wednesday	środa	SHROH-dah
Thursday	czwartek	CHVAHR-tehk
Friday	piątek	PYAWN-tehk
Saturday	sobota	soh-BOH-tah
Sunday	niedziela	nyeh-JEH-lah
holiday	swięto	shvee-EN-toh
today	dzisiaj	JEESH-eye
tomorrow	jutro	YOO-troh
in the morning	rano	RAH-noh
during the day	w ciągu dnia	FTHSOHN-goo dnyah
at night	w nocy	VNOH-tsih
breakfast	śniadanie	shnee-ah-DAHN-yeh
lunch	obiad	OH-byaht
dinner	kolacja	koh-LAH-tsyah

ENGLISH	POLISH	PRONOUNCE
arrivals	przyjazdy	pshi-YAHZ-dih
departures	odjazdy	ohd-YAHZ-dih
ticket	bilet	BEE-leht
round-trip	tam i z pow-rotem	tahm ee spoh-VROH-tehm
one-way	w jedną stronę	VYEHD-nawng STROH-neh
station	dworzec	DVOH-zhets
bus	autobus	OW-toh-boos
reservation	miejscówka	myest-SOOV-ka
train	pociąg	POH-chawnk
airport	lotnisko	laht-NEE-skoh
single room	pokój jednoos-bowy	POH-kooy yehd-noo-soh-BOH-vih
double room	pokój dwuo-sobowy	POH-kooy dvo-hoo-soh-BOH-vih
with a bath	z łazienką	z wah-ZYEHN-kawng
with a shower	z prysznicem	sprih-SHNYEE-tsehm
bank	bank	bahnk
exchange	wymiany walut	vih-MYAH-nih VAH-loot
post office	poczta	POH-chtah
airmail	lotniczą	loht-NYEE-chawng
stamps	znaczki	ZNATCH-kee
bakery	piekarnia	pyeh-KAHR-nee-ah
market	rynok	rih-NOHK
grocery store	sklep spożywczy	sklehp spoh-ZHIV-chih
vegetarian	wegetariański	ve-ge-tahr-YAN-skee
vegetables	jarzyny	yahr-ZHIH-nih
beef	wołowina	vo-wo-VEE-na
pork	wieprzowina	vye-psho-VEE-nah
chicken	kurczę	KOOR-cheh
fish	ryba	RIH-bah
cheese	ser	sehr
bread	chleb	khlehp
water	woda	VOH-dah
coffee	kawa	KAH-vah
tea	herbata	hehr-BAH-tah
milk	mleko	MLEH-koh
wine	wina	VEE-nah
beer	piwo	PEE-voh

GLOSSARIES

ROMANIAN (ROMÂN)

Spoken Romanian is a lot like Italian, but with three additional vowels: "*ă*" (pronounced like "e" in "pet") and the interchangeable "*â*" and "*î*" (like the "i" in "pill"). The other two characters peculiar to the Romanian alphabet are "*ş*" ("sh" in "shiver") and "*ţ*" ("ts" in "tsar"). At the end of a word, "*i*" is essentially dropped. "*Ci*" sounds like the "chea" in "cheat," and "*ce*" sounds like the "che" in "chess." "*Chi*" is pronounced like "kee" in "keen," and "*che*" like "ke" in "kept." "G" before "e" or "i" sounds like "j" as in judge and "gh" before those vowels is like "g" in girl.

PHRASEBOOK

ENGLISH	ROMANIAN	PRONOUNCIATION
Yes/no	Da/nu	dah/noo
Please	Vă rog	vuh rohg
Thank you	Mulţumesc	mool-tsoo-MESK
You're welcome	Cu plăcere	coo pluh-CHEH-reh
Hello	Bună ziua	BOO-nuh zee wah
Good-bye	La revedere	lah reh-veh-DEH-reh
Good morning	Bună dimineaţa	BOO-nuh dee-mee-NYAH-tsa
Good night	Noapte bună	NWAP-teh BOO-ner
Excuse me	Scuzaţi-mă	skoo-ZAH-tz muh
Sorry	Îmi pare rău	im PA-reh rau
My name is...	Mă cheamă...	muh-KYAH-muh
What is your name?	Cum vă numiţi?	koom vuh noo-MEETS
Help!	Ajutor!	AH-zhoot-or
When?	Cind?	kihnd
Where is...?	Unde?	OON-deh
How do I get to...?	Cum se ajunge la...?	koom seh-ZHOON-jeh-la
How much does this cost?	Cît costă?	kiht KOH-stuh
Do you have...?	Aveţi...?	a-VETS
Do you speak English?	Vorbiţi englezeşte?	vor-BEETS ehng-leh-ZESH-te
I don't understand.	Nu înţeleg.	noo-ihn-TZEH-lehg
Please write it down.	Vă rog scrieţi aceasta.	vuh rog SCREE-ets a-CHAS-ta
A little slower, please.	Vorbiţî mai vă rog.	vor-BEETS my vuh rohg
I'd like to order...	Aş vrea nişte...	ash vreh-A NEESH-teh
Check, please.	Plata, vă rog.	PLAH-tah, VUH rohg
Do you have a vacancy?	Aveţi camere libere?	a-VETS KUH-mer-eh LEE-ber-e
With private shower?	cu duş?	koo doosh
I'd like a room.	Aş vreao cameră.	ash vreh-UH KUH-mehr-ahr
May I see the room?	Pot să văd camera, vă rog?	poht sehr vehrd KUH-mehr-uh vehr rohg
No, I don't like it.	Nu-mi place.	noomy PLAH-cheh
It's fine, I'll take it.	E bine, o iau.	yeh BEE-neh oh yah-oo
Will you tell me when to get off?	Puteţi să-mi spuneţi cînd să cobor?	poo-TEHT-sy sermy SPOO-nehtsy kihnd sehr koh-BOHR
I want a ticket to...	Vreau un bilet pentru...	vrah-oo oon bee-LEHT PEHN-troo
When is the first/next/last train to...?	La ce ora pleacă primul/urmatorul/ultimul tren spre...?	lah cheh OH-rehr pleh-UH-kehr PREE-mool/oor-mehr-TOH-rool/OOL-tee-mool trehn spreh...
Where is the bathroom/nearest public phone/center of town?	Unde este cameră de baie/un telefon prin apropiere/centrul oraşului?	OON-deh YEHS-teh KUH-mehr-ahr deh BAH-yeh/oon teh-leh-FOHN preen ah-proh-PYEH-reh
I'm lost.	M-am rătăcit.	mahm rehr-tehr-CHEET

GLOSSARIES

GLOSSARY

ENGLISH	ROMANIAN	PRONOUNCE
one	unu	OO-noo
two	doi	doy
three	trei	tray
four	patru	PAH-tru
five	cinci	CHEEN-ch
six	şase	SHAH-seh
seven	şase	SHAHP-teh
eight	opt	ohpt
nine	nouă	NO-uh
ten	zece	ZEH-cheh
twenty	douăzeci	doh-wah-ZECH
thirty	treizeci	tray-ZECH
forty	patruzeci	pa-TROO-zech
fifty	cincizeci	chin-ZECH
sixty	şaizeci	shay-ZECH
seventy	şaptezeci	shap-teh-ZECH
eighty	optzeci	ohpt-ZECH
ninety	nouăzeci	noah-ZECH
one hundred	o sută	o SOO-tuh
one thousand	o mie	oh MIH-ay
Monday	luni	loon
Tuesday	marţi	marts
Wednesday	miercuri	MEER-kur
Thursday	joi	zhoy
Friday	vineri	VEE-ner
Saturday	sîmbătă	SIM-buh-tuh
Sunday	duminică	duh-MIH-ni-kuh
today	azi	az
tomorrow	mîine	MUH-yih-neh
open	deschis	DESS-kees
closed	închis	un-KEES
in the morning	dimineaţa	dee-mee-NAH-tsa
during the day	după-amiazăş	DOO-pehr-ah-MYAH-sehr
spring	primăvară	PREE-mehr-vahr-ehr
summer	vară	VAH-rehr
autumn	toamnă	TWAM-nehr
winter	iarnă	YAHR-nehr
cheap	ieftin	YEHF-teen
discotheque	discotecă	dees-koh-TEH-kehr
toilets	toaleta	toh-AHL-eh-tah
open	deschideţi	des-KEE-detsy
closed	închideţi	uhn-KEE-detsy
left	stînga	STUHN-guh
right	dreapta	draap-TUH

ENGLISH	ROMANIAN	PRONOUNCE
arrivals	sosiri	so-SEER
departures	plecări	play-CUHR
one-way	dus	doos
round-trip	dus-întors	doos-in-TORS
ticket	bilet	bee-LET
reservation	rezervarea	re-zer-VAR-eh-a
station	gară	GAH-ruh
train	trenul	TRAY-null
bus	autobuz	AHU-toh-booz
airport	aeroportul	air-oh-POR-tull
post office	poşta	POH-shta
stamps	timbru	TEEM-broo
airmail	avion	ahv-ee-OHN
bank	bancă	BAN-cuh
exchange	un birou de de schimb	oon bee-RO deh skeemb
single room	cu un pat	koo oon paht
double with twin beds	cu două paturi	koo doh-wehr PAH-toory
with a double bed	cu pat dublu	koo paht DOO-bloo
with a bath	cu baie	koo BAH-yeh
with a shower	cu duş	koo doosh
passport	paşaportul	pah-shah-POHR-tool
luggage	bagajul	bah-GAHZH-ool
wallet	portofel	pohr-TOH-fehl
hot	cald	kahld
cold	rece	REH-cheh
bakery	o brutărie	o bru-ter-REE-e
grocery	o alimentară	a-lee-men-TA-ra
breakfast	micul dejun	MIK-ul DAY-zhun
lunch	prînz	preunz
dinner	cină	CHEE-nuh
bread	pîine	PUH-yih-nay
beef	carne de vacă	CAR-ne de VA-cuh
pork	carne de porc	CAR-neh deh pork
fish	peşte	PESH-teh
chicken	pui	poo-EE
vegetables	legume	LEH-goom-eh
salad	salate	sah-LAH-teh
salt	sare	SAH-ray
milk	lapte	LAHP-tay
beer	bere	BE-reh
tea	ceai	CHAH-ee
water	apă	AH-puh
coffee	cafea	CAH-fay-ah
wine	vin	VEEN

GLOSSARIES

RUSSIAN (РУССКИЙ)

PHRASEBOOK

ENGLISH	RUSSIAN	PRONOUNCIATION
Yes/no	Да/нет	Dah/N-yet
Please/You're Welcome	Пожалуйста	pa-ZHAL-u-sta
Thank you	Спасибо	spa-SEE-bah
Hello	Добрый день	DOH-brihy DEN
Good-bye	До свидания	das-vee-DAHN-ya
Good Morning	Доброе утро	DOH-broye OO-tra
Excuse me	Извините	eez-vee-NEET-yeh
My name is...	Меня зовут...	men-YA za-VOOT...
What is your name?	Как вас зовут?	kak vas zah-VOOT
Help!	Помогите!	pah-mah-GHEE-te
When?	Когда?	kahg-DAH
Where is...?	Где?	g-dyeh
How much does this cost?	Сколько стоит?	SKOHL'-ka STOW-yeet
Do you have...?	У вас есть...?	oo vas YEST'
Do you speak English?	Вы говорите по-английски?	vy go-vo-REE-te po an-GLEE-ske
I don't understand	Я не понимаю	ya nee pa-nee-MAH-yoo
Please write it down?	Напишите пожалуйста	nah-pee-SHIT'-yeh, pah-ZHAHL-u-stah
A little slower, please.	Медленее, пожалуйста	MYED-lee-nyay-eh
I'd like to order...	Я хотел(а) бы	ya khah-TYEL(ah) bi
Check, please.	Счет, пожалуйста	shchyot, pah-ZHAHL-u-stah
Do you have a vacancy?	У вас есть свободный номер?	oo vahss yehst' svah-BOD-niy NO-mmeer
Private shower?	с душом?	s dushom
I'd like a room.	Я бы хотел(а) номер.	yah khah-TYEHL(ah) NOHM-meer
May I see the room?	Можно посмотреть номер?	MOZH-nah pah-smah-TRYEHTY NOHM-meer
No, I don't like it.	Нет, мне не нравится.	nyeht, mnyeh nee NRAH-veet-sah
Yes, I'll take it.	Да, Это подойдет.	dah, EH-tah pah-dii-DYOHT
Will you tell me when to get off?	Вы мне скажете, когда надо выходить?	vih mnyeh skah-ZHIH-tyeh, kahg-DAH NAH-dah skho-DEE-tyeh
I want a ticket to...	Один билет до...., поиалуйста.	ah-DEEN bee-LYEHT day...., pah-ZHAHLY-stah
How long does the trip take?	Долго ли надо ехать?	DOHL-gah lee NAH-dah YEH-khahty
When is the first/next/last train to...?	Когда первый/следующий/последний поезд на...?	kahg-DAH PYEHR-viy/slyeh-dooy-OOSH-chyeey POH-eezd nah
Where is the bathroom/nearest public phone/center of town?	Где находится туалет/ближайший телефон-автомат/центр города?	gdyeh nah-KHOHD-deets-ah TOO-ah-leht/blee-ZHII-shihy tee-lee-FOHN-ah-tah-MAHT/tsehn-ter GOHR-rah-dah
I'm lost.	Я заблудился.	yah zah-bloo-DEEL-sah.
Is this the right train to...?	Это поезд на...?	EH-tah poh-eezd nah
I've lost my...	Я потерял(а)...	yah pah-teery-AHL(ah)
I think you made a mistake in the bill.	Вы не ошиблись?	vih nee ah-SHIH-bleesy
Go away.	Уходите.	ook-hah-DEE-tee
I don't speak Russian.	Я не говорю по-русски.	yah nyeh gah-vah-RYOO pah ROO-skee

GLOSSARY

ENGLISH	RUSSIAN	PRONOUNCE
one	один	ah-DEEN
two	два	d-VAH
three	три	tree
four	четыре	che-TIH-rih
five	пять	p-YAHT'
six	шесть	SHAY-st'
seven	семь	s-YIM
eight	восемь	VOH-sem
nine	девять	DYEV-yat'
ten	десять	DYES-yat'
twenty	двадцать	d-VAHD-tsat'
thirty	тридцать	TREE-dtsat'
forty	сорок	SOR-ok
fifty	пятьдесят	pya-de-SAHT
sixty	шестьдесят	shays-de-SAHT
seventy	семьдесят	SIM-de-set
eighty	восемьдесят	VO-sim-de-set
ninety	девяносто	de-vya-NO-sta
one hundred	сто	stoh
one thousand	тысяча	TIS-see-cha
Monday	понедельник	pa-ne-DEH-lnik
Tuesday	вторник	FTOR-neek
Wednesday	среда	sreh-DAH
Thursday	четверг	cheht-VERK
Friday	пятница	PYAHT-nit-sah
Saturday	суббота	soo-BOT-tah
Sunday	воскресенье	vahsk-rees-SYEH-nyeh
holiday	день отдыха	dyen OT-di-kha
today	сегодня	se-VOHD-nya
tomorrow	завтра	ZAHV-trah
spring	весна	vees-NAH
summer	лето	LYEH-toh
autumn	осень	OHS-seeny
winter	эима	zee-MAH
closed	закрыт	za-KRIHt
open	открыт	ot-KRIHt
left	налево	nah-LEH-voh
right	направо	nah-PRAH-voh
passport	паспорт	PAHS-pohrt
luggage	багаж	bah-GAHZH
police	милицию	mee-LEE-tsiy-oo

ENGLISH	RUSSIAN	PRONOUNCE
departure	отьезд	ot-JEZD
arrival	приезд	pree-JEZD
one-way	в один конец	v ah-DEEN kah-NYEHTS
round-trip	туда и обратно	too-DAH ee ah-BRAHT-nah
ticket	билет	beel-YET
reservation	предваритель - ный заказ	pred-va-RIT'-el-niy za-KAZ
station	вокзал	vok-ZAL
bus	автобус	av-toh-BOOS
train	поезд	POY-ezd
airport	аэропорт	ayro-PORT
post office	почта	POCH-tah
stamp	марка	MAHR-ka
airmail	авиа	AH-vee-ah
bank	банк	bahnk
exchange	обмен валюты	ob-MEN va-luty
pharmacy	аптека	ahp-TEH-kah
single room	на одного	nah AHD-nah-voh
double room w/twin beds	двоих с двумя кроватями	dvah-EEKH s DVOO-myah krah-VAHTY-ah-mee
double room w/a double bed	двоих с дву-спальной кроватью	dvah-EEKH s DVOO-spahly-nii krah-VAHTY-oo
bakery	булочная	BOO-lahch-nah-yah
grocery	гастроном	GAH-stro-nom
market	рынок	RIHN-nahk
breakfast	завтрак	zav-TRAK
lunch	обед	ob-YED
dinner	ужин	OO-zhin
menu	меню	menu
bread	хлеб	khlyeb
vegetarian	вегетериан	vegh-e-TAH-ree-ahn
vegetables	овощи	oh-VAHSH-chee
beef	говядина	ga-VYA-dee-na
chicken	курица	KOO-ree-tsa
pork	свинина	svee-NEE-na
fish	рыба	RY-ba
cheese	сыр	SYR
milk	молоко	mah-lah-KOH
beer	пиво	PEE-vah
water	вода	vod-DAH
coffee	кофе	KO-fye
juice	сок	sok
wine	вино	vee-NO
tea	чай	chyii

SLOVAK (SLOVENSKY)

When speaking Slovak, the two golden rules are to pronounce every letter—nothing is silent and it's all phonetic—and to emphasize the first syllable. Accents on vowels affect length, not stress. Flick the "r" off the top of your mouth.

PHRASEBOOK

ENGLISH	SLOVAK	PRONOUNCIATION
Yes/no	áno/nie	ah-NOH/NEH
Please	prosím	PROH-seem
Thank you	Ďakujem	DAK-oo-yem
Hello	Dobrý deň	doh-BREE den
Good-bye	Do videnia	doh vee-DEN-eea
Good morning	Dobré ráno	doh-BREH RAH-no
Good night	Dobrú noc	doh-BROO NOTS
Excuse me	Prepáčte mi	PREH-pach-te mee
Sorry	Prepáčte	PREH-pach-te
Help!	Pomoc!	pah-MOTS
When?	Kedy?	keh-DEE
Where is...?	Kde je?	k-DEH yeh
How do I get to...?	Ako sa dostanem...?	AH-koh sa doh-STAN-em
How much does this cost?	Kol'ko to stojí...?	KOHL-ko toh STOH-yee
Do you have...?	Máte..?	MAH-teh
Do you speak English?	Hovoríte po anglicky?	ho-vo-REE-te poh ahng-GLIT-ski
I don't understand.	Nerozumiem	neh-rohz-OOM-ee-em
Please write it down?	Prosím napište to.	PRO-seem nah-PEESH-tye toh
A little slower, please.	Prosím pomalu.	PRO-seem poh-MAH-lo
I'd like to order...	Chtel bych...	khtyel bikh
Check, please.	Prosím, účet.	PRO-seem, OO-chet
Do you have a vacancy?	Máte volnú izbu?	MAH-te VOL-noo iz-BOO

GLOSSARY

ENGLISH	SLOVAK	PRONOUNCE
one	jeden	YED-en
two	dva	dvah
three	tri	tree
four	štyri	sh-TEE-ree
five	pät	peht
six	šest'	shest
seven	sedem	SE-dem
eight	osem	O-sem
nine	devät'	DEH-veht
ten	desat	DEH-saht
twenty	dvadsat'	DVAHD-saht
thirty	tridsat'	TREED-saht
forty	štyridsat'	SHTIH-rihd-saht
fifty	päťdesiat	PEHTY-dehs-ee-aht
sixty	šesťdesiat	SHEST-dehs-yat
seventy	sedmdesiat	SEHDM-dehs-yat

ENGLISH	SLOVAK	PRONOUNCE
arrival	príchod	PREE-khod
departure	odchod	OD-khod
round-trip	zpáteční	SPAH-tech-nee
one-way	jedno směrný	YED-nyo SMER-nye
ticket	lístok	LEE-stok
station	stanica	STAH-nee-tsa
meat	mäso	MEH-so
vegetables	zelenina	ze-LEH-nee-na
water	voda	VO-da
coffee	káva	KAH-va
milk	mlieko	m-LYE-ko
beer	pivo	PEE-vo
eighty	osemdesiat	OH-sehm-dehs-ee-aht
ninety	deväťdesiat	DEH-vehty-dehs-ee-aht
one hundred	sto	stoh
one thousand	tisíc	tih-SEETS

SLOVENIAN (SLOVENSKO)

When speaking Slovene, "*č*" is pronounced "ch," "*š*" is "sh," and "*ž*" is pronounced is "zh." "*R*" is at times a vowel (pronounced "er"), while "*v*" and "*l*" turn silent at the strangest times.

PHRASEBOOK

ENGLISH	SLOVENIAN	PRONOUNCIATION
Yes/no	Ja/Ne	yah/neh
Please	Prosim	PROH-seem
Thank you	Hvala	HVAA-lah
Hello	Zdravo	ze-drah-voh
Good-bye	Na svidenje	nah SVEE-den-yeh
Excuse me	Oprostite	oh-proh-stee-teh
Help!	Na pomoč!	nah poh-MOHCH
How much does this cost?	Koliko to stane?	koh-lee-koh toh stah-neh
Do you have...?	Ali imate...?	AA-li i-MAA-te
Do you speak English?	Govorite angleško?	go-vo-REE-teh ang-LEH-shko
I don't understand	Ne razumem.	neh rah-ZOO-mehm
May I see the room?	Lahko vidim sobo?	lah-KOH VEE-dihm SOH-boh
Will you tell me when to get off?	Mi lahko prosim poveste, kdaj moram izstopiti?	mih lah-KOH PROH-sihm poh-VEH-steh kdaay MOH-rahm EES-toh-pih-tih
I want a ticket to...	Rad(a) bi vozovnico za...	rat (RAA-dah) bih voh-ZOW-nih-tsoh zah
Where is the nearest public phone/center of town?	Kje je najbližja telefonska go vorilnica/center mesta?	kyeh ye nay-BLEEZH-yah teh-leh-FOHN-skah/TSEHN-tehrr MEH-sta

UKRAINIAN

The Ukrainian alphabet resembles Russian (see **The Cyrillic Alphabet**, p. 807), but with a few differences. The most notable additions are the "i" (*ee* sound) and the "ï" (*yee* sound)—the "и" is closest to "s*i*t." The rarely used "є" sounds like "ye" in "yep!" The "ґ" (hard "g") has been reintroduced since independence but is not yet widely used, and the "г," pronounced "g" in Russian, comes out like an "h."

PHRASEBOOK

ENGLISH	UKRAINIAN	PRONOUNCIATION
Yes/no	Так/Ні	tak/nee
Please	Прошу	PRO-shoo
Thank you	Дякую	DYA-kou-yoo
Hello	Добрий день	doh-bree-DEN
Good-bye	До побачення	doh poh-BAH-chen-nya
Excuse me	Вибачте	VIH-bach-te
Where is...?	Де?	deh?
Help!	Поможіт	pah-mah-ZHEET
How much does this cost?	Скільки кошуте?	SKEL-kih kahsh-TOO-ye
Do you have...?	Чи є у вас?	chih yeh oo vahs...
Do you speak English?	Ви говорите по-английски?	Vih-ho-VOR-ihte poh-anh-lih-skih
I don't understand	Я не розумію	Ya ne rah-zoo-mee-yu
Will you tell me when to get off?	Извинете, кога тряба да сляза?	eez-vi-NEH-teh, ko-GAH TRYAB-vah dah SLYAH-zah
I want a ticket to...	Искам един билет до...	EES-kahm eh-DEEN bee-LEHT do

FESTIVALS IN EASTERN EUROPE

COUNTRY	APR. - JUNE	JULY - AUG.	SEPT. - MAR.
BOSNIA	No festivals listed.	No festivals listed.	**Sarajevo Film Festival** Sept., Sarajevo (p. 92)
BULGARIA	**International Jazz Fest.** Aug., Varna (p. 122)	**Madara Music Days** June, Madara (p. 134)	**"Love is Folly" Film Fest.** Sept., Varna (p. 122)
CROATIA	**Animated Film Fest.** June, Zagreb (p. 147) **Eurokaz Theater Fest.** June, Zagreb (p. 147)	**Festival of Sword Dances** July, Korčula (p. 169) **Dubrovnik Summer Fest.** July, Dubrovnik (p. 172)	**International Puppet** Sept., Zagreb (p. 147) **Marco Polo Festival** Sept., Korčula (p. 169)
CZECH REPUBLIC	**Prague Spring** May, Prague (p. 205) **Five-Petal Rose Fest.** June, Č. Krumlov (p. 224)	**Karlovy Vary Film Fest.** July, Karlovy Vary (p. 217) **International Music** Aug.,Č. Krumlov (p. 224)	No festivals listed.
ESTONIA	**Old Town Days** June, Tallinn (p. 245)	**Beersmmer** July, Tallinn (p. 245)	No festivals listed.
HUNGARY	**Sopron Festival Weeks** June, Sopron (p. 303) **Foldvarer Festival** June, B-földvár (p. 313) **Int'l Military Band** June, Debrecen (p. 324) **Szentivánéji Festivities** June, Szombath. (p. 307)	**International Folk Dance** July, Siofok (p. 312) **Béla Bartók Choir Fest.** July, Debrecen (p. 324) **Lipicai (Horse) Festival** July, Szilvásvárad (p. 337) **Baroque Festival** July, Eger (p. 336)	**Haydn Festival** Sept., Fertőd (p. 304) **Hírös Food Festival** Sept., Kecskem. (p. 331) **Eger Vintage Days** Sept., Eger (p. 336) **Budapest Spring** Mar., Budapest (p. 288)
LATVIA	**International Ballooning** May, Sigulda (p. 358)	No festivals listed.	No festivals listed.
LITHUANIA	**Jazz Festival** June, Klaipeda (p. 386)	**Thomas Mann Festival** July, Nida (p. 387).	No festivals listed.
POLAND	**International Short Film** May, Kraków (p. 428) **Probaltica** May, Toruń (p. 471) **Music and Architecture** May, Toruń (p. 471) **Jazz in the Borderlands** May, Zamość (p. 438) **Jazz nad Odrą** May, Wrocław (p. 458) **Fest. of Jewish Culture** June, Kraków (p. 428)	**Outdoor Performances** July, Kraków (p. 428) **Jousting and Medeival** July, Golub (p. 471) **Int'l Street Theater Fest.** July, J. Góra (p. 460) **Country Picnic Fest.** July-Aug., Mrąg. (p. 494) **Highlander Folklore** Aug., Zakopane (p. 445) **Rock and Pop Music** Aug., Sopot (p. 488)	**Jazz Vocalists** Sept., Kraków (p. 428) **Knight's Crossbow** Sept., J. Góra (p. 460) **Antiques and Oddities** Sept., J. Góra (p. 460) **Kraków Jazz Festival** Oct., Kraków (p. 428) **National Blues Music** Nov., Toruń (p. 471)
ROMANIA	**Sibiu Jazz Festival** May-June, Sibiu (p. 528)	**Medieval Festival** July-Aug., Sighiş. (p. 537)	No festivals listed.
RUSSIA	**White Nights Festival** June, St. Pete. (p. 616) **Independent Film Fest.** June, Sochi (p. 654)	No festivals listed.	**Sochi Art Festival** Sept., Sochi (p. 654)
SLOVAKIA	**Ghosts and Spirits** May, Bojnice (p. 684)	No festivals listed.	**Bratislava Music Fest.** Sept.-Oct., Brati. (p. 681)
SLOVENIA	**Slovene Music Days** Apr., Ljubljana (p. 718) **International Jazz Fest.** June, Ljubljana (p. 718)	**Peasants' Wedding Day** July, Lake Bohinj (p. 724) **Int'l Summer Festival** July, Ljubljana (p. 718)	**Cow Ball** Sept., L. Bohinj (p. 724) **International Jazz Fest.** Nov., Ljubljana (p. 718)
UKRAINE	No festivals listed.	**Nuclear Reactor Rave** July, Kazantip (p. 753)	**Kiev Theater Festival** Mar., Kiev (p. 749)

INDEX

INDEX

D

H

I

L

M

INDEX

INDEX

N

O

P

R

INDEX

T

U

V

W

Y

Z

ABOUT LET'S GO

FORTY YEARS OF WISDOM

As a new millennium arrives, *Let's Go: Europe*, now in its 40th edition and translated into seven languages, reigns as the world's bestselling international travel guide. For four decades, travelers criss-crossing the Continent have relied on *Let's Go* for inside information on the hippest backstreet cafes, the most pristine secluded beaches, and the best routes from border to border. In the last 20 years, our rugged researchers have stretched the frontiers of backpacking and expanded our coverage into Asia, Africa, Australia, and the Americas. We're celebrating our 40th birthday with the release of *Let's Go: China*, blazing the traveler's trail from the Forbidden City to the Tibetan frontier; *Let's Go: Perú & Ecuador*, spanning the lands of the ancient Inca Empire; *Let's Go: Middle East*, with coverage from Istanbul to the Persian Gulf; and the maiden edition of *Let's Go: Israel*.

It all started in 1960 when a handful of well-traveled students at Harvard University handed out a 20-page mimeographed pamphlet offering a collection of their tips on budget travel to passengers on student charter flights to Europe. The following year, in response to the instant popularity of the first volume, students traveling to Europe researched the first full-fledged edition of *Let's Go: Europe*, a pocket-sized book featuring honest, practical advice, witty writing, and a decidedly youthful slant on the world. Throughout the 60s and 70s, our guides reflected the times. In 1969 we taught travelers how to get from Paris to Prague on "no dollars a day" by singing in the street. In the 80s and 90s, we looked beyond Europe and North America and set off to all corners of the earth. Meanwhile, we focused in on the world's most exciting urban areas to produce in-depth, fold-out map guides. Our new guides bring the total number of titles to 48, each infused with the spirit of adventure and voice of opinion that travelers around the world have come to count on. But some things never change: our guides are still researched, written, and produced entirely by students who know first-hand how to see the world on the cheap.

HOW WE DO IT

Each guide is completely revised and thoroughly updated every year by a well-traveled set of over 250 students. Every spring, we recruit over 180 researchers and 70 editors to overhaul every book. After several months of training, researcher-writers hit the road for seven weeks of exploration, from Anchorage to Adelaide, Estonia to El Salvador, Iceland to Indonesia. Hired for their rare combination of budget travel sense, writing ability, stamina, and courage, these adventurous travelers know that train strikes, stolen luggage, food poisoning, and marriage proposals are all part of a day's work. Back at our offices, editors work from spring to fall, massaging copy written on Himalayan bus rides into witty, informative prose. A student staff of typesetters, cartographers, publicists, and managers keeps our lively team together. In September, the collected efforts of the summer are delivered to our printer, which turns them into books in record time, so that you have the most up-to-date information available for your vacation. Even as you read this, work on next year's editions is well underway.

WHY WE DO IT

We don't think of budget travel as the last recourse of the destitute; we believe that it's the only way to travel. Living cheaply and simply brings you closer to the people and places you've been saving up to visit. Our books will ease your anxieties and answer your questions about the basics—so you can get off the beaten track and explore. Once you learn the ropes, we encourage you to put *Let's Go* down now and then to strike out on your own. You know as well as we that the best discoveries are often those you make yourself. When you find something worth sharing, please drop us a line. We're Let's Go Publications, 67 Mount Auburn St., Cambridge, MA 02138, USA (email: feedback@letsgo.com). For more info, visit our website, http://www.letsgo.com.

READER QUESTIONNAIRE

Name: ______________________________

Address: ______________________________

City: ______________ **State:** _____ **Country:** ______________

ZIP/Postal Code: __________ **E-mail:** ______________ **How old are you?** ____

And you're...? in high school in college in graduate school employed retired between jobs

Which book(s) have you used? ______________________________

Where have you gone with Let's Go? ______________________________

Have you traveled extensively before? yes no

Had you used Let's Go before? yes no **Would you use it again?** yes no

How did you hear about Let's Go? friend store clerk television review bookstore display ad/promotion internet other: __________

Why did you choose Let's Go? reputation budget focus annual updating wit & incision price other: __________

Which guides have you used? Fodor's Footprint Handbooks Frommer's $-a-day Lonely Planet Moon Guides Rick Steve's Rough Guides UpClose other: __________

Which guide do you prefer? Why? ______________________________

Please rank the following in your Let's Go guide: (1=needs improvement, 5=perfect)

packaging/cover	1 2 3 4 5	food	1 2 3 4 5	maps	1 2 3 4 5
cultural introduction	1 2 3 4 5	sights	1 2 3 4 5	directions	1 2 3 4 5
"Essentials"	1 2 3 4 5	entertainment	1 2 3 4 5	writing style	1 2 3 4 5
practical info	1 2 3 4 5	gay/lesbian info	1 2 3 4 5	budget resources	1 2 3 4 5
accommodations	1 2 3 4 5	up-to-date info	1 2 3 4 5	other: ________	1 2 3 4 5

How long was your trip? one week two wks. three wks. a month 2+ months

Why did you go? sightseeing adventure travel study abroad other: __________

What was your average daily budget, not including flights? ______________

Do you buy a separate map when you visit a foreign city? yes no

Have you used a Let's Go Map Guide? yes no **If you have, which one?** __________

Would you recommend them to others? yes no

Have you visited Let's Go's website? yes no

What would you like to see included on Let's Go's website? ______________

What percentage of your trip planning did you do on the web? ______________

What kind of Let's Go guide would you like to see? recreation (e.g., skiing) phrasebook spring break adventure/trekking first-time travel info Europe altas

Which of the following destinations would you like to see Let's Go cover?

Argentina Brazil Canada Caribbean Chile Costa Rica Cuba Morocco Nepal Russia Scandinavia Southwest USA other: __________

Where did you buy your guidebook? independent bookstore college bookstore travel store Internet chain bookstore gift other: __________

Please fill this out and return it to **Let's Go, St. Martin's Press,** 175 Fifth Ave., New York, NY 10010-7848. All respondents will receive a free subscription to ***The Yellowjacket***, the Let's Go Newsletter. You can find a more extensive version of this survey on the web at http://www.letsgo.com.

Moscow Metro
Rechnoy Vokzal
Vodny Stadion
Voykoskaya
Sokol
Aeroport
Dinamo
Yubileynaya
Likhobori
Seligerskaya
Altufevo
Bibirevo
Otradnoye
Vladykino
Petrovsko-Razumovskaya
Timiryazeskaya
Dmitrovskaya
Sabelovskaya
Ostankino
Marina Roshcha
Dostoevskaya
Chelobitevo
Medvedkovo
Babushkinskaya
Sviblovo
Botanichesky Sad
VDNKh
Alexeevskaya
Rizhskaya
Prospekt Mira
Ulitsa Podbelskovo
Cherkizovskaya
Preobrazhenskaya Ploshchadz
Sokolniki
Krasnoselskaya
Planernaya
Skhodnenskaya
Tushinskaya
Shchukinskaya
Oktyabrskoye Pole
Polezhaevskaya
Begovaya
Ulitsa 1905 goda
Mitino
Volokolamskoye Shosse
Strogino
Krasnopresnenskaya
Krylatskoye
Molodezhnaya
Kuntsevskaya
Pionerskaya
Filoyvsky Park
Bagrationovskaya
Fili
Kutuzovskaya
Studencheskaya
Mendeleevskaya
Ploshchadz Suvorova
Novoslobodskaya
Belorusskaya
Sukharevskaya
Tsvetnoy Bulvar
Barrikadnaya
Krasnoprenenskaya
Turgenevskaya
Chistiye Prudy
Sretensky Bulvar
Komsomolskaya
Krasnye Vorota
Shchoylkovskaya
Pervomayskaya
Izmaylovskaya
Izmaylovskaya Park
Semenovskaya
Elektrozavodskaya
Baumanskaya
Kurskaya
Chkalovskaya
Mayakovskaya
Pushkinskaya
Chekhovskaya
Tverskaya
Lubyanka
Kuznetsky Most
Kievskaya
Park Pobedy
Smolenskaya
Arbatskaya
Okhotny Ryad
Teatralnaya
Ploshchadz Revolyutsii
Kitay-Gorod
Novogireevo
Perevo
Shosse Entuziastov
Aviamotornaya
Ploshchadz Ilicha
Rimskaya
Smolenskaya
Alexsandrovsky Sad
Biblioteka im. Lenina
Arbatskaya
Borovitskaya
Kropotkinskaya
Marxistskaya
Tretyakovskaya
Novokuznetskaya
Taganskaya
Park Kultury
Polyanka
Frunzenskaya
Krestyanskaya Zastava
Proletarskaya
Paveletskaya
Sportivnaya
Leninskiye Gory
Universitet
Prospekt Vernadskovo
Yugo-Zapadnaya
Oktyabrskaya
Dobryninskaya
Serpukhovskaya
Volgogradsky Prospekt
Tekstilshchiki
Kuzminki
Ryazansky Prospekt
Vykhino
Tulskaya
Nagatinskaya
Nagornaya
Nakhimovsky Prospekt
Sevastopolskaya
Kakhovskaya
Varshavskaya
Avtozavodskaya
Kolomenskaya
Kashirskaya
Dubrovka
Kozhukhovkaya
Pechatniki
Shabolovskaya
Leninsky Prospekt
Akademicheskaya
Profsoyuznaya
Noviyc Cheroymushki
Kaluzhskaya
Belyaevo
Konkovo
Toyploy Stan
Yasenevo
Bittsevsky Park
Chertanovskaya
Yuzhnaya
Prazhskaya
Rossoshanskaya
Anino
Kachalovo
Kantemirovskaya
Tsaritsyno
Orekhovo
Domodedovskaya
Krasnogvardeyskaya
Promzona
Volzhskaya
Lyublino
Bratislavskaya
Marino
Brateevo
Borisovo
LEGEND
Sokolnicheskaya
Zamoskvoretskaya
Arbatsko-Pokrovskaya
Filoyvskaya
Koltsevaya
Kaluzhsko-Rizhskaya
Tarasko-Krasnopresnenskaya
Kalininskaya
Timiryazevsko-Serpukhovskaya
Lyublinskaya
Station
Transfer Station

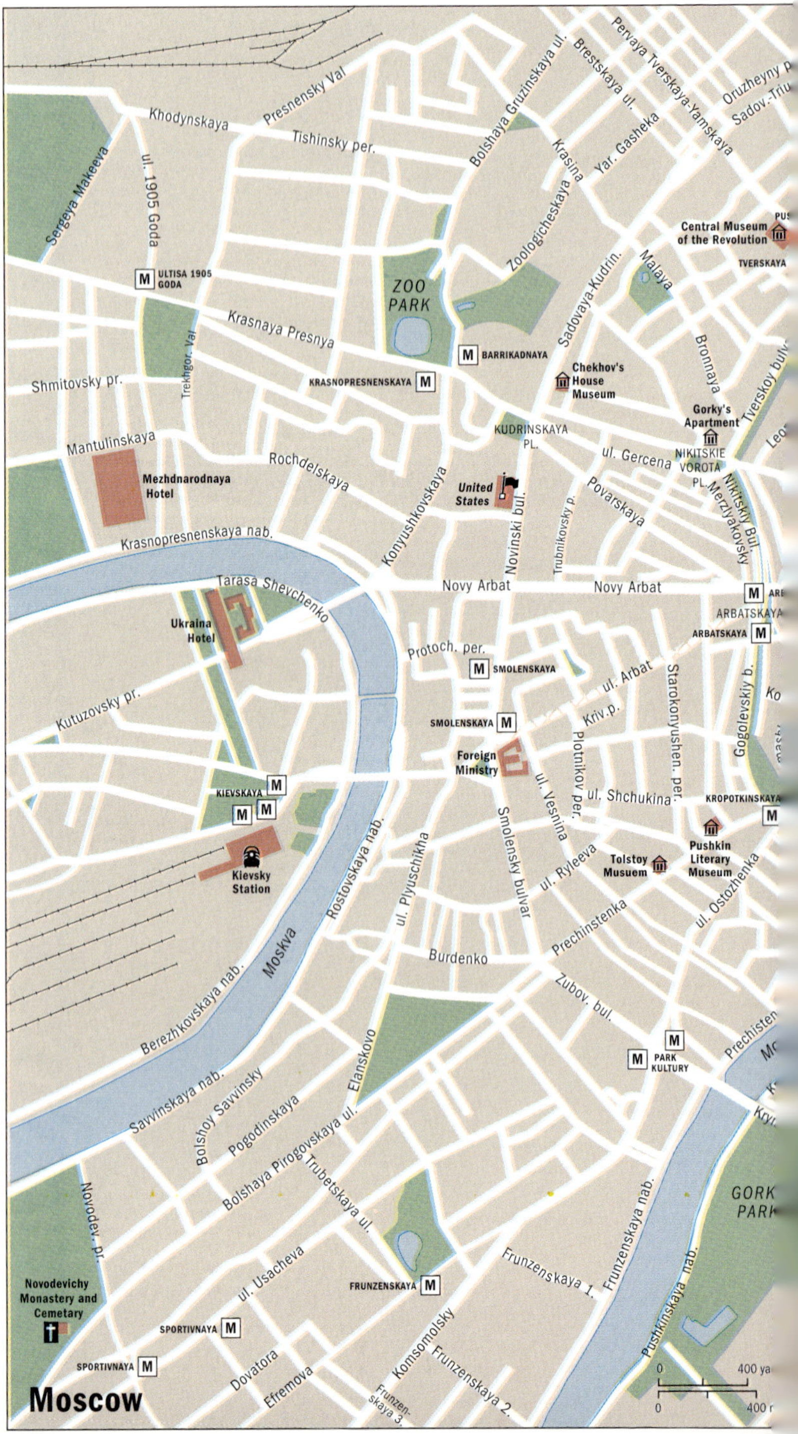
Moscow
Khodynskaya
Presnensky Val
Tishinsky per.
Bolshaya Gruzinskaya ul.
Brestskaya ul.
Pervaya Tverskaya-Yamskaya
Sergeya Makeeva
ul. 1905 Goda
Krasina
Yar. Gasheka
Zoologicheskaya
Central Museum of the Revolution
TVERSKAYA
ULTISA 1905 GODA
ZOO PARK
Sadovaya-Kudrin.
Malaya
Krasnaya Presnya
BARRIKADNAYA
Bronnaya
Shmitovsky pr.
Trekhgor. Val
KRASNOPRESNENSKAYA
Chekhov's House Museum
Gorky's Apartment
Tverskoy
KUDRINSKAYA PL.
Mantulinskaya
ul. Gercena
NIKITSKIE VOROTA PL.
Mezhdnarodnaya Hotel
Rochdelskaya
United States
Povarskaya
Merzlyakovsky
Nikitsky Bul.
Konyushkovskaya
Novinski bul.
Trubnikovsky p.
Krasnopresnenskaya nab.
Tarasa Shevchenko
Novy Arbat
Novy Arbat
ARBATSKAYA
ARBATSKAYA
Ukraina Hotel
Protoch. per.
SMOLENSKAYA
ul. Arbat
Starokonyushen. per.
Gogolevskiy b.
Kutuzovsky pr.
SMOLENSKAYA
Kriv.p.
Plotnikov per.
Foreign Ministry
KIEVSKAYA
ul. Vesnina
ul. Shchukina
KROPOTKINSKAYA
Smolensky bulvar
Pushkin Literary Museum
Kievsky Station
Rostovskaya nab.
ul. Plyushchikha
ul. Ryleeva
Tolstoy Musuem
ul. Ostozhenka
Prechinstenka
Moskva
Burdenko
Zubov. bul.
Berezhkovskaya nab.
PARK KULTURY
Savvinskaya nab.
Bolshoy Savvinsky
Elanskovo
Pogodinskaya
Bolshaya Pirogovskaya ul.
Trubetskaya ul.
Novodev. pr.
Frunzenskaya nab.
Pushkinskaya nab.
Frunzenskaya 1.
ul. Usacheva
FRUNZENSKAYA
Novodevichy Monastery and Cemetary
SPORTIVNAYA
Komsomolsky
Dovatora
Frunzenskaya 2.
SPORTIVNAYA
Efremova
Frunzen-skaya 3.
0
0

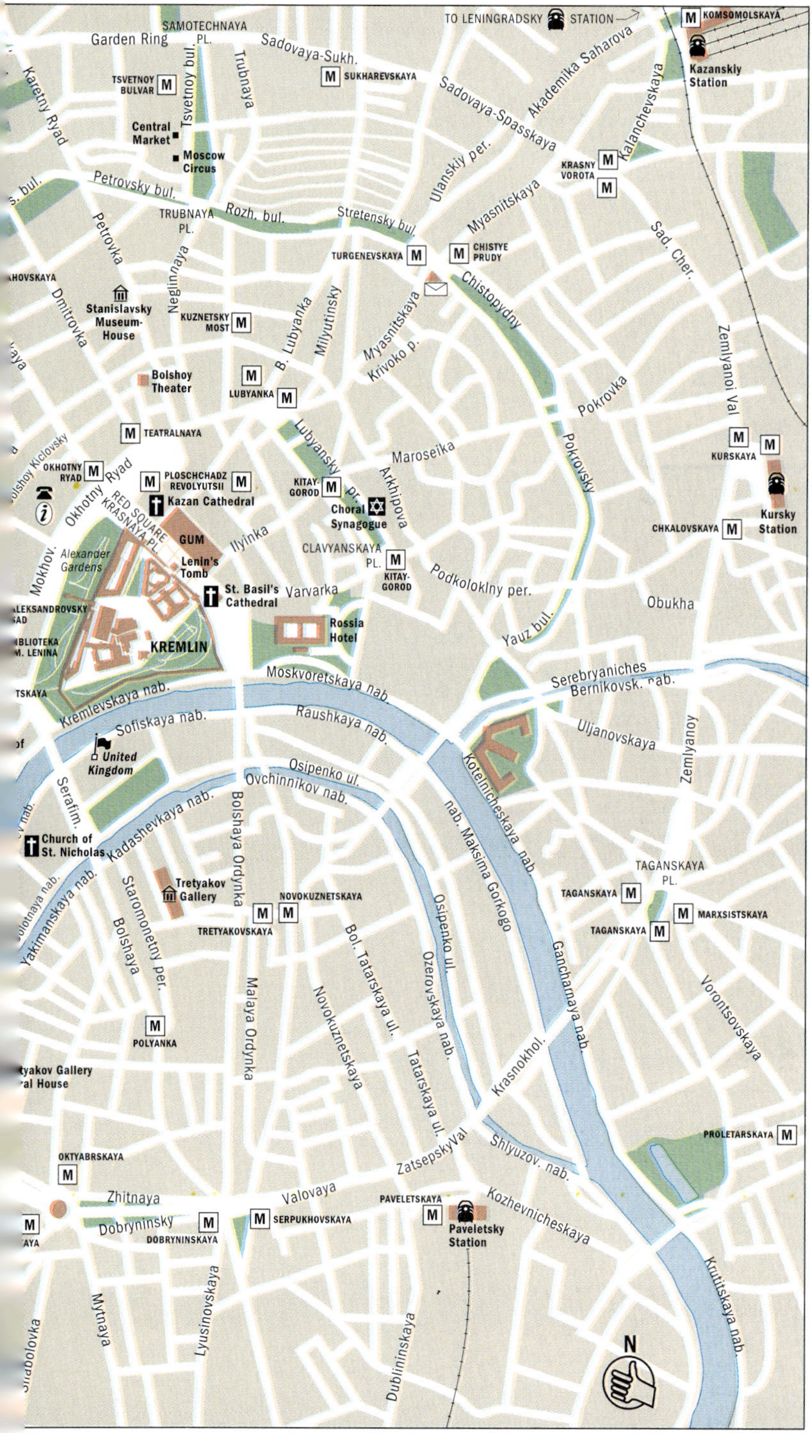
SAMOTECHNAYA PL.
Garden Ring
Sadovaya-Sukh.
TO LENINGRADSKY STATION
KOMSOMOLSKAYA
Kazanskiy Station
Akademika Saharova
Karetny Ryad
TSVETNOY BULVAR
Tsvetnoy bul.
Trubnaya
SUKHAREVSKAYA
Sadovaya-Spasskaya
Central Market
Moscow Circus
Ulanskiy per.
KRASNY VOROTA
Kalanchevskaya
Petrovsky bul.
Rozh. bul.
TRUBNAYA PL.
Stretensky bul.
Myasnitskaya
Petrovka
TURGENEVSKAYA
CHISTYE PRUDY
Sad. Cher.
Chistopydny
Dmitrovka
Stanislavsky Museum-House
Neglinnaya
KUZNETSKY MOST
B. Lubyanka
Milyutinsky
Myasnitskaya
Krivoko p.
Zemlyanoi Val
Bolshoy Theater
LUBYANKA
Pokrovka
TEATRALNAYA
Lubyansky pr.
Maroseika
Pokrovsky
KURSKAYA
OKHOTNY RYAD
Okhotny Ryad
PLOSCHCHADZ REVOLYUTSII
KITAY-GOROD
Arkhipova
Kursky Station
Kazan Cathedral
RED SQUARE
KRASNAYA PL.
Choral Synagogue
CHKALOVSKAYA
GUM
Ilyinka
CLAVYANSKAYA PL.
Alexander Gardens
Lenin's Tomb
KITAY-GOROD
Podkoloklny per.
Mokhov.
St. Basil's Cathedral
Varvarka
Obukha
Rossia Hotel
Yauz bul.
KREMLIN
Moskvoretskaya nab.
Serebryaniches
Bernikovsk. nab.
Kremlevskaya nab.
Sofiskaya nab.
Raushkaya nab.
Uljanovskaya
United Kingdom
Zemlyanoy
Osipenko ul.
Ovchinnikov nab.
Kotelnicheskaya nab.
Serafim.
Kadashevkaya nab.
Bolshaya Ordynka
nab. Maksima Gorkogo
Church of St. Nicholas
TAGANSKAYA PL.
Tretyakov Gallery
Staromonetny per.
NOVOKUZNETSKAYA
TAGANSKAYA
MARXSISTSKAYA
Yakimanskaya nab.
TRETYAKOVSKAYA
Bol. Tatarskaya ul.
Osipenko ul.
Ozerovskaya nab.
Ganchamaya nab.
Bolshaya
Vorontsovskaya
POLYANKA
Malaya Ordynka
Novokuznetskaya
Tatarskaya ul.
Krasnokhol.
PROLETARSKAYA
OKTYABRSKAYA
Zatsepsky Val
Shlyuzov. nab.
Zhitnaya
Valovaya
PAVELETSKAYA
Kozhevnicheskaya
Dobryninsky
SERPUKHOVSKAYA
Paveletsky Station
DOBRYNINSKAYA
Lysinovskaya
Mytnaya
Dubininskaya
Krutitskaya nab.
N

Московское Метро

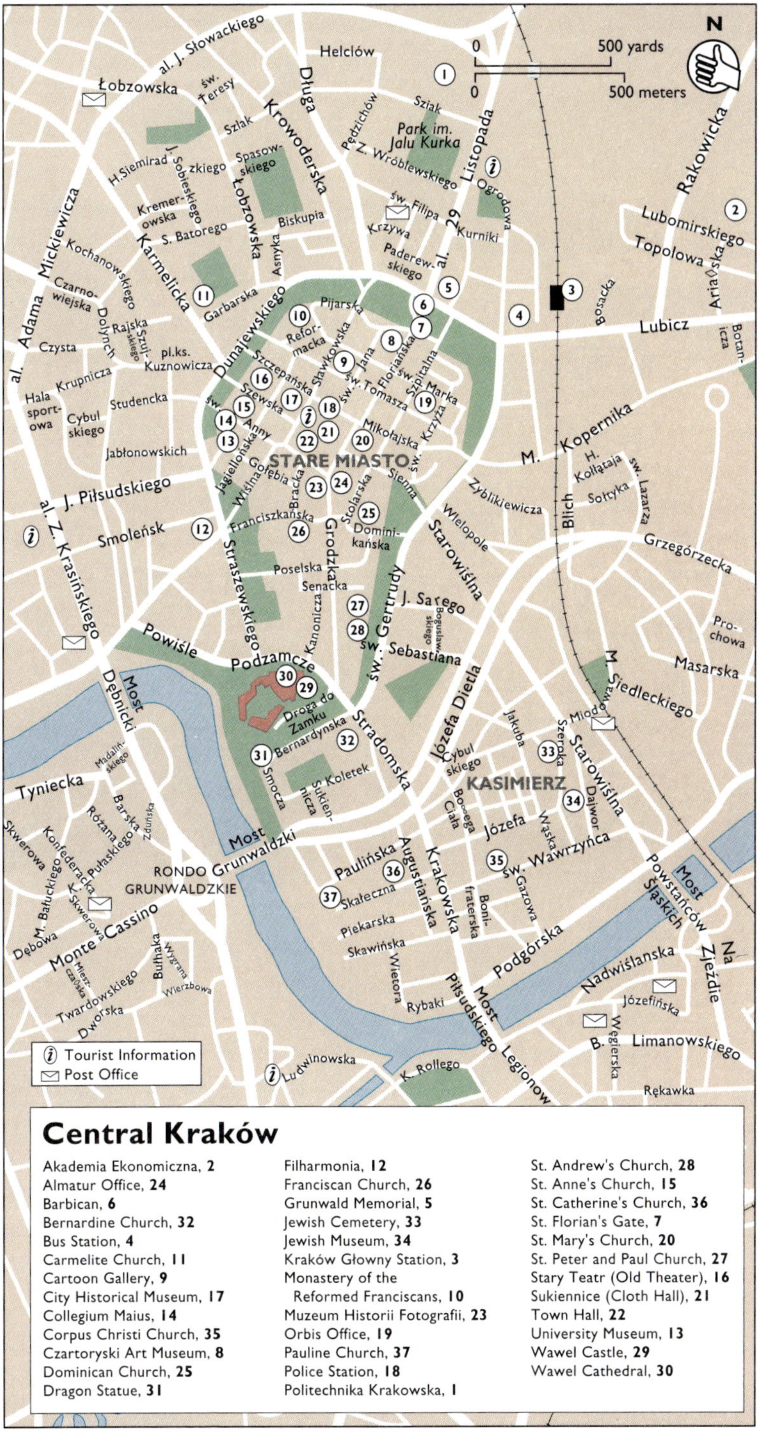

Central Kraków

Prague

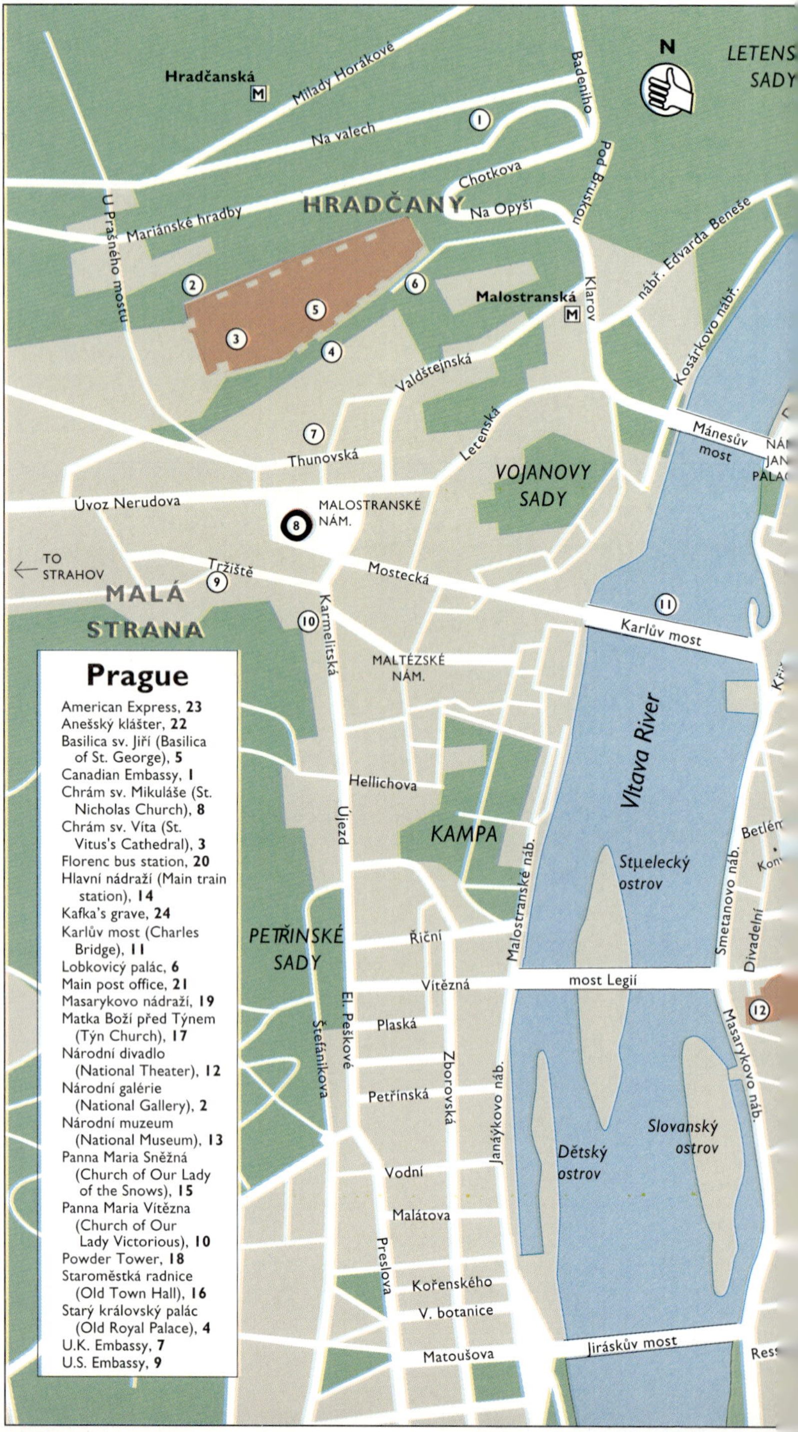
Prague
American Express, 23
Anešský klášter, 22
Basilica sv. Jiří (Basilica of St. George), 5
Canadian Embassy, 1
Chrám sv. Mikuláše (St. Nicholas Church), 8
Chrám sv. Víta (St. Vitus's Cathedral), 3
Florenc bus station, 20
Hlavní nádraží (Main train station), 14
Kafka's grave, 24
Karlův most (Charles Bridge), 11
Lobkovicý palác, 6
Main post office, 21
Masarykovo nádraží, 19
Matka Boží před Týnem (Týn Church), 17
Národní divadlo (National Theater), 12
Národní galérie (National Gallery), 2
Národní muzeum (National Museum), 13
Panna Maria Sněžná (Church of Our Lady of the Snows), 15
Panna Maria Vítězna (Church of Our Lady Victorious), 10
Powder Tower, 18
Staroměstká radnice (Old Town Hall), 16
Starý královský palác (Old Royal Palace), 4
U.K. Embassy, 7
U.S. Embassy, 9
N
Hradčanská
Milady Horákové
Badeniho
Na valech
Chotkova
HRADČANY
Na Opyši
Pod Bruskou
U Prašného mostu
Mariánské hradby
nábř. Edvarda Beneše
Malostranská
Klarov
Kosárkovo nábř.
Valdštejnská
Letenská
Mánesův most
Thunovská
VOJANOVY SADY
Úvoz Nerudova
MALOSTRANSKÉ NÁM.
TO STRAHOV
Tržiště
MALÁ STRANA
Mostecká
Karlův most
Karmelitská
MALTÉZSKÉ NÁM.
Vltava River
Hellichova
Újezd
KAMPA
Malostranské nábř.
Stuelecký ostrov
Smetanovo nábř.
Divadelní
PETŘINSKÉ SADY
Říční
Vítězná
most Legií
Plaská
El. Peškové
Štefánikova
Zborovská
Petřínská
Janáčkovo nábř.
Masarykovo nábř.
Dětský ostrov
Slovanský ostrov
Vodní
Malátova
Preslova
Kořenského
V. botanice
Matoušova
Jiráskův most

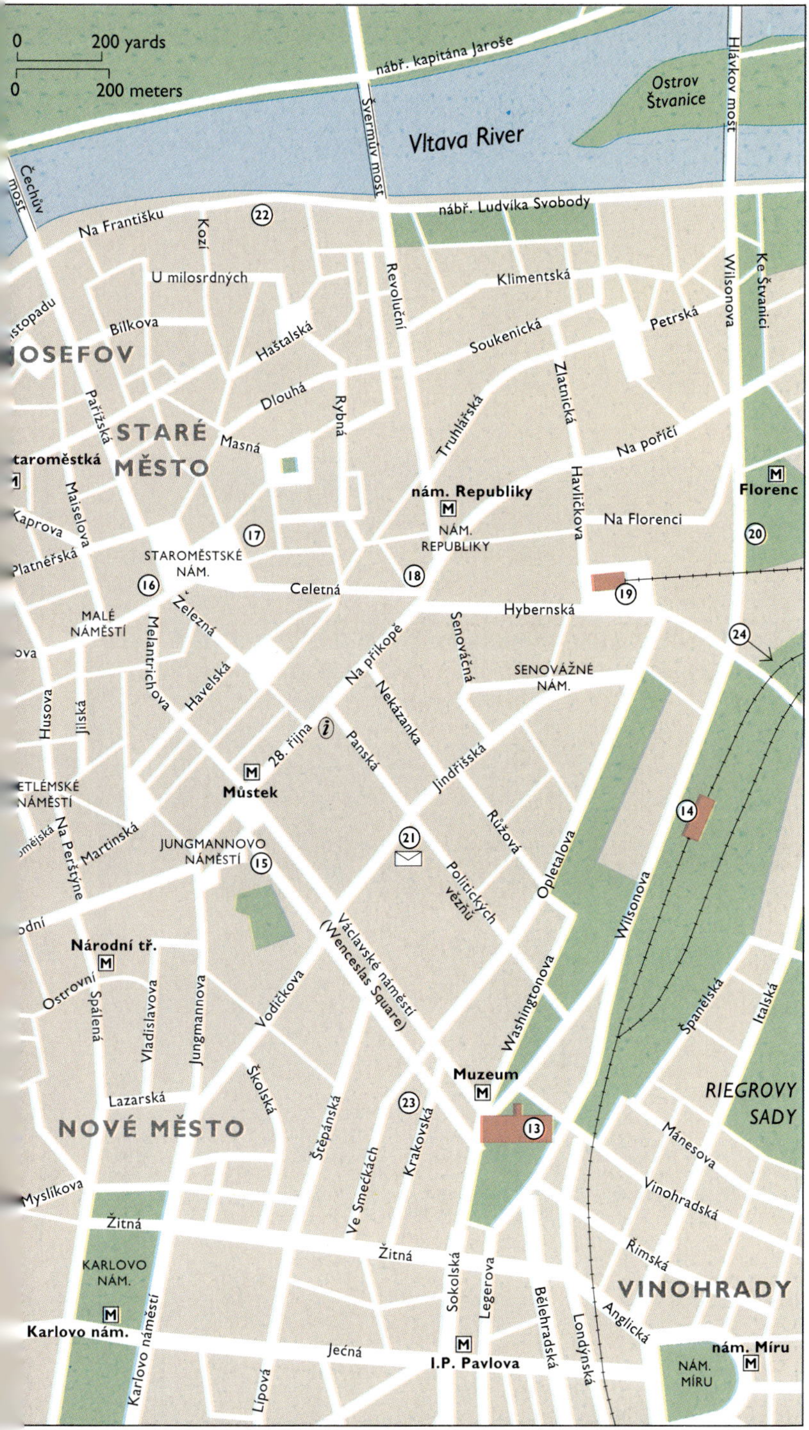
0 200 yards
0 200 meters
nábř. kapitána Jaroše
Ostrov Štvanice
Hlávkov most
Švermův most
Vltava River
Čechův most
nábř. Ludvíka Svobody
Na Františku
Kozí
U milosrdných
Revoluční
Klimentská
Ke Štvanici
Wilsonova
Petrská
Bílkova
Haštalská
Soukenická
JOSEFOV
Pařížská
Dlouhá
Rybná
Truhlářská
Zlatnická
STARÉ MĚSTO
Masná
Na poříčí
Staroměstská
Maiselova
nám. Republiky
NÁM. REPUBLIKY
Havlíčkova
Florenc
Na Florenci
Kaprova
Platnéřská
STAROMĚSTSKÉ NÁM.
Celetná
Hybernská
MALÉ NÁMĚSTÍ
Železná
Melantrichova
Senovážná
SENOVÁŽNÉ NÁM.
Na příkopě
Nekázanka
Havelská
Husova
Jilská
28. října
Panská
Jindřišská
Můstek
BETLÉMSKÉ NÁMĚSTÍ
Na Perštýně
Martinská
JUNGMANNOVO NÁMĚSTÍ
Růžová
Opletalova
Politických vězňů
Wilsonova
Národní tř.
Václavské náměstí (Wenceslas Square)
Washingtonova
Ostrovní
Spálená
Vladislavova
Jungmannova
Vodičkova
Španělská
Italská
Muzeum
RIEGROVY SADY
Školská
Lazarská
NOVÉ MĚSTO
Štěpánská
Ve Smečkách
Krakovská
Mánesova
Vinohradská
Myslíkova
Žitná
Žitná
Římská
KARLOVO NÁM.
Sokolská
Legerova
Bělehradská
VINOHRADY
Anglická
Londýnská
Karlovo nám.
Karlovo náměstí
Ječná
I.P. Pavlova
nám. Míru
NÁM. MÍRU
Lípová
13
14
15
16
17
18
19
20
21
22
23
24

Central Budapest

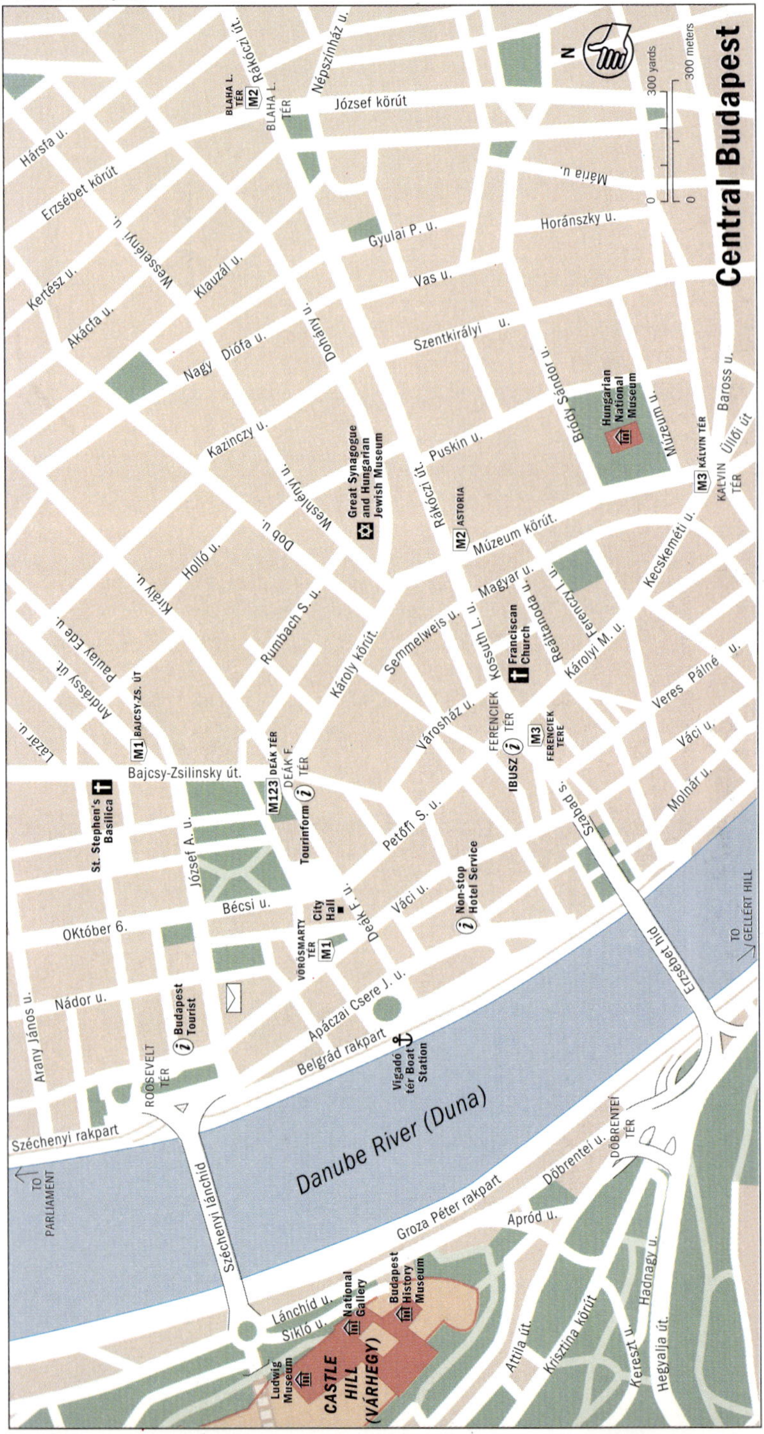